Continuing the tradition of excellence

Racal Marine continues the tradition of excellence established in over 35 years experience in marine electronics. Excellence in an unmatched range of marine products and services with the highest standards of performance, quality and reliability. A range which includes:

● Racal-Decca autopilots and steering controls.
● Racal-Decca engine-room control and surveillance systems.
● Racal-Decca radars for every application — afloat and ashore.
● Racal-Decca radio position-fixing systems.
● Racal-Decca satellite communications systems.
● Hydrographic and oceanographic surveys.

And you know that, if you need help — wherever you are — there's a Racal-Decca depot or service centre to look after you. All part of the same tradition. The tradition of excellence.

Racal Marine

Racal Marine Limited, New Malden, Surrey, KT3 4NW, England. Tel: 01-942 2488 Telex: 22891.

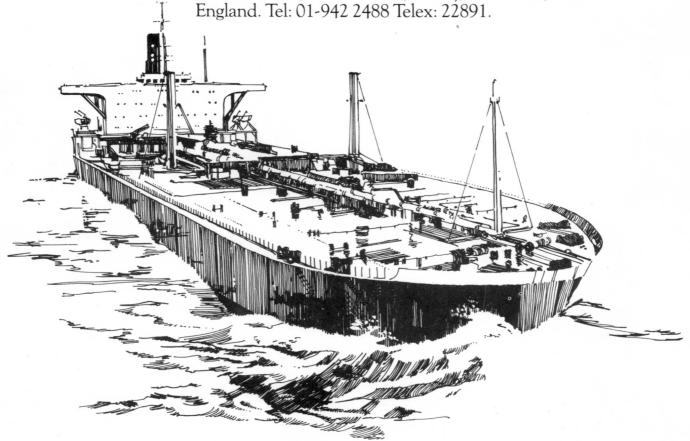

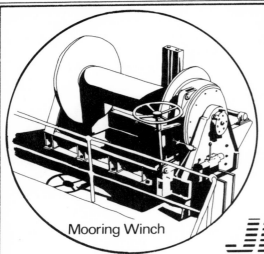
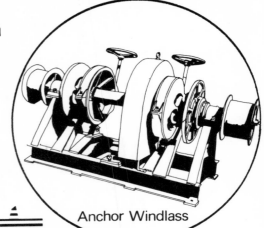

JANE'S MERCHANT SHIPS 1985-86

Jane's Publishing Company Limited, 238 City Road, London EC1V 2PU, England
Jane's Publishing Inc, 13th Floor, 135 West 50th Street, New York, NY 10020, USA

Alphabetical list of advertisers

Classified list of advertisers

JANE'S MERCHANT SHIPS

Merchant ship identification using the Talbot-Booth system

Second Edition

Compiled and edited by
D G Greenman

1985-86

ISBN 0 7106-0807-1

JANE'S YEARBOOKS

"Jane's" is a registered trade mark

In the USA and its dependencies
Jane's Publishing Inc, 13th Floor, 135 West 50th Street, New York, NY 10020, USA

[4]

CONTENTS

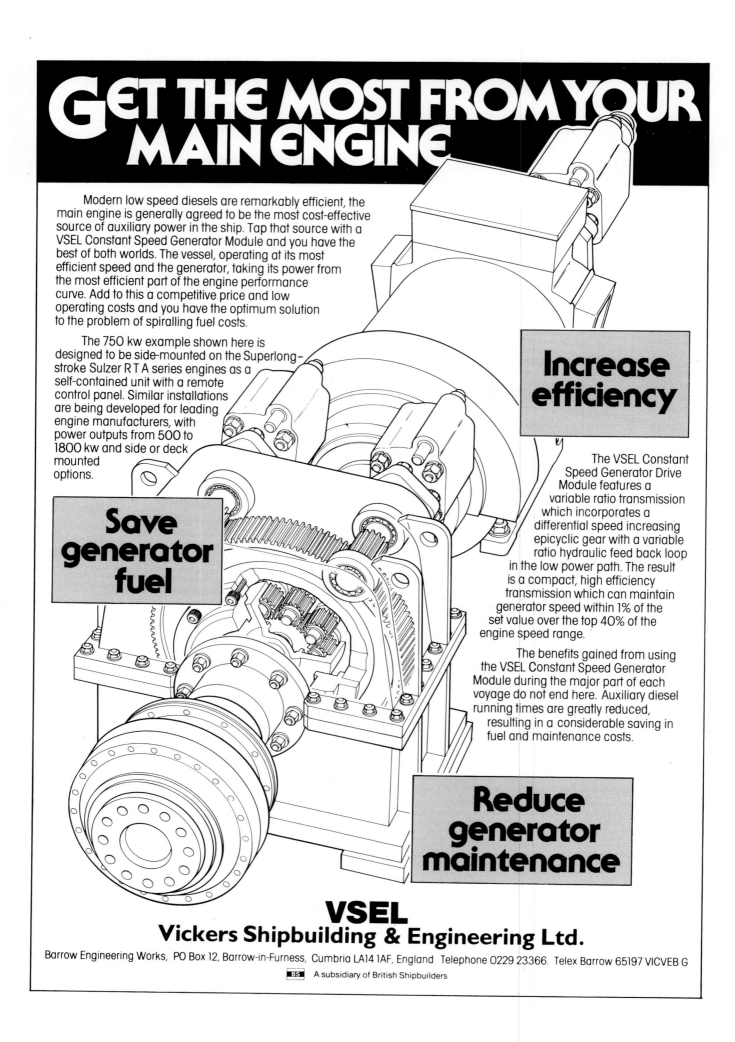

GET THE MOST FROM YOUR MAIN ENGINE

Modern low speed diesels are remarkably efficient, the main engine is generally agreed to be the most cost-effective source of auxiliary power in the ship. Tap that source with a VSEL Constant Speed Generator Module and you have the best of both worlds. The vessel, operating at its most efficient speed and the generator, taking its power from the most efficient part of the engine performance curve. Add to this a competitive price and low operating costs and you have the optimum solution to the problem of spiralling fuel costs.

The 750 kw example shown here is designed to be side-mounted on the Superlong-stroke Sulzer R T A series engines as a self-contained unit with a remote control panel. Similar installations are being developed for leading engine manufacturers, with power outputs from 500 to 1800 kw and side or deck mounted options.

Increase efficiency

The VSEL Constant Speed Generator Drive Module features a variable ratio transmission which incorporates a differential speed increasing epicyclic gear with a variable ratio hydraulic feed back loop in the low power path. The result is a compact, high efficiency transmission which can maintain generator speed within 1% of the set value over the top 40% of the engine speed range.

The benefits gained from using the VSEL Constant Speed Generator Module during the major part of each voyage do not end here. Auxiliary diesel running times are greatly reduced, resulting in a considerable saving in fuel and maintenance costs.

Save generator fuel

Reduce generator maintenance

VSEL
Vickers Shipbuilding & Engineering Ltd.

Barrow Engineering Works, PO Box 12, Barrow-in-Furness, Cumbria LA14 1AF, England Telephone 0229 23366. Telex Barrow 65197 VICVEB G

BS A subsidiary of British Shipbuilders

[6]

INTRODUCTION

This second edition of *Jane's Merchant Ships* has a number of new features, the most obvious and radical being the separation of the drawings from the main text. The advantages of this new format are (1) more drawings on a page giving a larger selection of ships to view at a glance when trying to distinguish similar vessels and (2) each ship name in the text section is on a separate line thus improving clarity and practicability.

The information in the text is much the same but with two major additions: the builder's name and the machinery designer/builder. Shipowners were considered for inclusion but, in these days of "beneficial" owners, managers and agents, the word "shipowner" sounds far too straightforward for the tangled webs which surround the ownership of some vessels. For this reason we consider it impossible to do justice to the subject without including an unreasonable amount of speculation.

In the preliminary sections of the book the main addition is a Guide to Merchant Ship Types. Anyone with a knowledge of merchant ships will know that this subject has become far more involved in these recession-struck days than in the past. Our guide, therefore, is not comprehensive but illustrates most of the major types.

With such a small scale as 1 inch = 200 feet (1:2400) there must be a "cut-off" point and, in the case of *Jane's Merchant Ships*, it is approximately 220 feet (67 metres) in overall length. Having stated that, there are many much shorter vessels illustrated, but only those considered to be of sufficient importance to justify their entry.

We are often asked how comprehensive *Jane's Merchant Ships* is. The simple answer is that, in an industry where so much change is taking place, it is impossible to give an accurate figure. However, we do know that, since the publication of the first edition, more than 8000 pieces of information have been incorporated into this second edition. These include changes of name and flag, vessels broken up or lost, changes of appearance, changes in data etc. In addition, nearly 2000 extra vessels have been included, either added to existing drawings or represented by completely new drawings. There are also many replacement drawings for ships which have substantially altered in appearance.

My use of the plural pronoun throughout this introduction reveals that, rather than having an individual editor, *Jane's Merchant Ships* is produced by an editorial team. Of the many people involved at Jane's I should particularly like to mention Ken Harris, David Moyes, Lesley Dixey and Mark Alderson. Needless to say, Lt Cdr Talbot-Booth has given many hours and much encouragement in the preparation of this "tome" and I am indebted to him. Mention of Lt Cdr Talbot-Booth leads, naturally, to the Ship Recognition Corps, whose extensive records provide the basis of all the material in this book. The Corps always welcomes any information which will help to keep its records, and consequently *Jane's Merchant Ships*, as up-to-date as possible. Please address any correspondence to the Ship Recognition Corps Headquarters, 'Ashburnham', Torrens Drive, Harbledown, Canterbury, Kent CT2 8NF.

Of the many individuals who provided useful material and information I should particularly like to mention the following: Captain E Askew, MN, Mr C Gibby, Mr E Isbister, Mr A Smith, Lieut D F Taylor, RNR and Mr N H Thomson. We would also like to thank the Directorate of Naval Operations and Trade (Ministry of Defence) for their assistance. Philip Neumann of Foto-Flite has, again, given much of his valuable time in selecting photographs for the merchant ship types section and the quality of these prints greatly enhances the book.

David Greenman
November 1984

Kockums AB, Box 832, S-201 80 Malmö, Sweden
Telephone: +46-40-744 00, Telex: 33190 kockum s

A GUIDE TO MERCHANT SHIP TYPES

This brief guide covers most of the major types which appear in the book. It is intended as a guide to identification of a vessel which is at or near sea-level and broadside. It is, therefore, only concerned with certain, significant external features. The size of a vessel has little relevance when it comes to type identification. There has never been a foolproof method of estimating, without the appropriate instruments, a vessel's size, either by tonnage or dimensions, when it is seen at sea with no other ships or suitable objects with which to compare it.

Although there are many more specialised vessels today, the average general cargo ship has become far more versatile both in types of cargo carried and in cargo-handling gear. This creates problems in identification.

The descriptions relating to the photographs are arranged as follows: (1) **Description of type**. Any suitable alternatives appear after it in brackets. (2) **Main features** of the vessel shown in the photograph. (3) **Variations**. Other features which may be seen on this type of vessel and similarities to other types. (4) **Notes**.

The captions to the photographs give the name (flag); gross tonnage (dwt if not available); builder; year of build and other details of the illustrated ship.

All photographs courtesy of FotoFlite.

PASSENGER VESSEL (passenger liner, cruise liner)

Features: large numbers of lifeboats (often with larger landing boats), many decks runing almost the length of the ship, funnel well aft.

Variations: often have small cranes foreward to handle stores etc (usually kingposts in older examples), older vessels have funnel more amidships, decks more stepped in older types and often cut straight off in modern ships (foreward and aft).

ROYAL PRINCESS (Br); 45000; Wartsila; 1984

LARGE PASSENGER FERRY

Features: fewer decks above the upper deck than passenger vessel; fewer lifeboats, which appear larger in relation to the rest of the ship than those of a passenger liner; high freeboard giving a "squat" appearance; absence of cargo handling gear; funnel approximately amidships.

Variations: train ferries are difficult to distinguish from passenger ferries but often have a much lower freeboard aft; "double-ended" ferries where each half of the ship, along its length, is identical.

Notes: practically all modern passenger ferries are ro-ro but the stern ramp is rarely apparent in a broadside view although the stern has a "cut-off" appearance.

CHAMPS ELYSEES (Fr); approx 8500 dwt; Dubigeon-Normandie; 1984; similar to COTES D'AZUR (1981)

GENERAL CARGO — FUNNEL AMIDSHIPS

Features: symmetrical appearance with more than one hatch aft of superstructure; funnel and superstructure just aft of amidships; several masts and kingposts; few lifeboats.

Variations: number of islands can vary (many have a long forecastle); a larger superstructure and extra lifeboats can signify a passenger/cargo vessel, although these are less common now; the occasional deck-crane may be seen; a few containers may be carried as deck cargo.

Notes: a diminishing breed but still many examples in service, mostly from around the early fifties, late sixties. Largely superseded by the ¾-aft and multi-purpose cargo vessels.

STATE OF MADHYA PRADESH (In); 9376; Hindustan; 1965

GENERAL CARGO — FUNNEL ¾-AFT

Features: superstructure well aft of amidships and fairly extensive; extensive array of cargo-handling gear.

Variations: many have a mixture of derricks and cranes and some may have cranes only; a long forecastle is common and many have a long poop beginning at the bridge-front and one hatch only aft of superstructure; the vessel shown has a heavy-lift derrick and these are often seen in this type; containers may be carried as a deck load.

Notes: this type superseded the "funnel-amidships" type but is largely being made redundant by the "multi-purpose" type of cargo vessel represented by the following photograph.

BORUSSIA (FRG); 10898; Boel; 1965; sold 1984

MULTI-PURPOSE CARGO VESSEL

Features: extensive cargo-handling gear consisting of a mixture of different designs; all-aft arrangement of superstructure; prominent forecastle.

Variations: ships of this type often have a ¾-aft configuration; some may also be ro-ro (often quarter ramp) and this would result in a higher freeboard (see drawing number 02724).

Notes: typical of the types of cargo carried by this vessel would be containers, bulk cargo, general cargo, packaged timber, cars and other vehicles.

HOEGH DUKE (Br); 30061; Swan Hunter; 1984; Sisters (Norwegian flag, built by Wartsila): HOEGH DENE, HOEGH DRAKE, HOEGH DYKE

REEFER (refrigerated cargo ship, fruit ship)

Features: large mast houses (containing refrigerating machinery); fairly high freeboard.

Variations: position of superstructure can vary: all-aft (as in the ship illustrated), ¾-aft and amidships (older vessels); older vessels tend to have little cargo gear, just two masts and a long superstructure (see drawings numbers 18270-18380); modern vessels often have several cranes which make them very difficult to distinguish from general cargo ships; for typical examples of modern "funnel-amidships" reefers with cranes, see drawings number 02840 and 02850; for examples of short-sea reefers see numbers 48830 and 52695.

Notes: modern vessels, like the one illustrated, favour palletised cargo and often have several side doors, although these are not normally apparent at a distance; a fairly high freeboard can be a feature.

ANNE B (Ja); 12383; Hashihama; 1984; sister: BETTY B

SHORT-SEA GENERAL CARGO/CONTAINER SHIP

Features: large pedestal cranes on one side only to allow for full deck-load of containers; prominent forecastle and poop and absence of bulwark plating amidships; tall superstructure and funnel.

Notes: this type of vessel is becoming very popular with West German owners and the general design is increasing worldwide; the size of these vessels can vary considerably and a number of smaller ships which could be described as coasters often have large deck cranes (see drawings number 49810 and 49880); the older type of short-sea vessel usually has masts or kingposts (drawing number 81750 is a good example).

WESER GUIDE (FRG); 3784; Brand; 1984

GEARLESS COASTER

Features: forecastle and poop; high hatch combings (usually signifies container capacity); few lifeboats.

Variations: vessels without container capacity will have lower hatch combings; some vessels have no noticeable lifeboats but several liferafts.

Notes: container capacity is a common feature in these vessels.

ECO LUISA (Sp); 1535; Luzuriaga; 1977; sister: ECO MARINA

SEA/RIVER CARGO VESSEL (low air-draught coaster)

Features: low superstructure; very small funnel; significant hatch combings; give an impression of length due to lack of height; bridge stands on a column; heavy islands; light masts.

Variations: some are now appearing with small deck cranes.

Notes: masts hinge, although this is obviously not a recognition feature when seen at sea; the West Germans have specialised in this type over the last few years but Dutch and British owners also have significant numbers.

PATRIA (FRG); 499; H. Peters; 1982; among its sisters (all FRG flag) are: SEA ELBE; OLE JENSEN; HAMMABURG; MERIDIAN II; PAX; POSELDORF; VINETA; ALADIN; BUNGSBERG; PIONIER; SINDBAD; SESAM and ELBSTRAND

FOREWARNED IS FOREARMED

USS Ticonderoga is 'first of class' of 8 guided missile cruisers, in the non-nuclear propelled AEGIS armed vessels programme. A further two ships have been ordered with five more projected. 'Ticonderoga' entered service with the USN fleet in 1983, followed by her sistership 'Yorktown' in 1984.

Jane's Fighting Ships 1984/1985 edition is packed with accurate detailed information, research and photographs of Naval matters worldwide. It is perfectly complemented by Jane's Defence Weekly, where you will find the very latest developments in this field and in defence matters internationally, reported and reviewed in depth the instant they happen.

SHORT-SEA CONTAINER SHIP (container feeder ship)

Features: almost identical to the gearless coaster illustrated previously, although the container ship usually has a higher superstructure as the containers may be stacked two or three high on the hatch covers; heavy forecastle to protect containers; extensions from the hatch covers to the sides of the ship enable more containers to be stacked athwartships.

Variations: cargo handling gear is uncommon in ships of this type but smaller examples of the short-sea cargo/container ship, previously illustrated, may be used in a feeder role.

RHEIN EXPRESS (Be); 25000; Boelwerf; 1984; ex Verhaeren; sister: MAETERLINCK (Be)

GEARLESS BULK CARRIER

Features: superstructure all-aft; large hatch covers but not always so prominent in very large vessels or if seen at a distance.

Variations: many bulk carriers these days also carry containers on the hatch covers; a forecastle is fairly common although many of the largest vessels are flush-decked.

Notes: although similar in general build to a tanker the main distinguishing feature is the absence of large kingposts (or cranes) amidships.

BELL RAIDER (Ih); 1600; Kagoshima; 1977; see drawing no. 73770

GEARED CONTAINER SHIP

Features: large cranes raised above the hatch covers to enable containers to be stowed on deck (gantry forward and pedestal crane aft); prominent hatch combings; heavy forecastle (for container protection); superstructure ¾-aft and very tall.

Variations: most vessels of this type do not have a mixture of cranes such as the vessel illustrated; an all-aft arrangement of superstructure is often seen; some have a large number of cranes (see drawing number 02820); heavy derricks, rather than cranes, are not uncommon (see drawing number 59865).

APPLEBY (Br); 64641; H & W; 1978; launched as Golden Master

GEARED BULK CARRIER

Features: basically the same as the gearless bulk carrier but the geared vessel is usually smaller and almost always has a forecastle and very often a poop as well.

Variations: although cranes are the most popular gear for modern bulk carriers, they can also be seen with kingposts (drawings number 56650-57390 are typical examples) and gantries (drawing number 83030).

Notes: can be easily confused with some modern container ships (particularly with deck cranes or gantries) and general cargo ships. Cranes on tall pedestals, however, will normally help to distinguish the container ship.

NEDLLOYD VAN NECK (Ne); 23930; Giessen-De Noord; 1983; sisters (with two pedestal cranes foreward only): NEDLLOYD VAN DIEMEN; NEDLLOYD VAN NOORT

LARGE CONTAINER SHIP

Features: high freeboard; high forecastle; tall superstructure; absence of cargo handling gear; small cranes on after-end of superstructure (not always easily discerned when in stowed position in the broadside view).

Variations: many of the largest vessels do not have a forecastle but often have a large breakwater screen forward although this is not always apparent in a broadside view; an all-aft design is quite common.

BROOMPARK (Br); 18190; Sunderland; 1982

DEEP-SEA TANKER (oil tanker)

Features: low freeboard when laden but often seen in ballast, when the freeboard will be very high; cranes amidships for hose handling; superstructure all-aft; catwalk from bridge-front to short mast foreward; absence of large hatches on deck.

Variations: the vessel shown here is a ULCC (Ultra Large Crude Carrier) and is larger than the VLCC (Very Large Crude Carrier); the features of these vessels are largely the same as those of smaller types such as the products tanker (for examples see drawings number 66140 and 65730); products tankers usually have a forecastle and a poop and modern examples very often have a crane amidships (see drawings number 51995 and 51996); VLCCs usually have heavy kingposts amidships so the example shown here is not typical in that respect; they are mostly flush-deckers although many have a forecastle; a common feature on VLCCs are small posts along the deck which support floodlights for night operations (see drawing 54800 for example); the older type of tanker with a bridge structure amidships (many examples in the P3 section of drawings) can occasionally be seen but is rapidly disappearing.

Notes: for the purposes of this book, the term tanker refers to an oil tanker to distinguish it from the many other types; it can be very difficult to distinguish an oil tanker from a combination carrier (see later photograph) in a broadside, sea-level view.

BATILLUS (Fr); 275267; L'Atlantique; 1976; until recently the world's largest ship; now superseded by the SEAWISE GIANT (drawing number 54205)

COASTAL TANKER (short-sea tanker)

Features: basically a scaled-down version of the deep-sea oil tanker; kingposts amidships for handling hoses; tall islands creating a deep well between; catwalk between forecastle and poop; prominent vents at break of poop; clutter of pipes, vents etc along upper deck.

Variations: some have crane(s) amidships (see drawing 52070) and others no gear at all (drawing 75020); trunk decks are quite common (drawing number 66480 and 66490); wine tankers can be similar (drawing number 76440) and oil/chemical (drawing number 59020); not all vessels have a catwalk and note that, in the ship illustrated, the catwalk runs, for most of its length, just above the upper deck.

NORTHGATE (Br); 1599; Kanrei; 1980; sisters: IRISHGATE; EASTGATE; WESTGATE

COMBINATION CARRIER (O/O—Ore or Oil; OBO—Ore, Bulk or Oil)

Features: basically those of a tanker at a distance and at sea-level, unless the hatch combings can be distinguished.

Variations: some have been adapted for the carriage of containers on the hatch covers and the vessel illustrated is of this type.

Notes: most of the details given for the oil tanker also apply to the combination carrier; there is no way of distinguishing between an O/O and an OBO.

CAST NARWHAL (Li); 132305; Mitsubishi HI; 1972; now renamed CASTOR (Li)

OIL/CHEMICAL TANKER

Features: similar to oil tanker but without large kingposts amidships in most cases; the vessel featured does have smaller cranes, however.

Variations: some vessels have distinctive clusters of vents (see drawings number 53003 and 53027) which are often a feature of chemical tankers.

OSCO STREAM (No); 21744; Samsung; 1982; sister: OSCO SURF

CHEMICAL TANKER

Features: all-aft design; numerous vents along upper deck; small spherical tank on deck.

Variations: the large clusters of vents referred to in the caption for the oil/chemical tanker photograph are often a feature of chemical tankers (drawings number 53003 and 53027); the crane amidships is typical of the type which can also be seen on products tankers and other types of vessel.

Notes: many of the larger chemical tankers are oil/chemical and it is very difficult to distinguish a pure chemical tanker in most cases.

TRINIDAD AND TOBAGO (Bs); 8823; Sasebo; 1984; sister: HAROLD LA BORDE

LIQUEFIED GAS CARRIER (tanks on deck)

Features: several large spherical tanks, the top halves of which appear above the weather deck; all-aft design; catwalk above tanks.

Variations: most LGCs of this design are large LNG (Liquefied Natural Gas) carriers; one of their outstanding features is a high freeboard (see drawings number 53880, 54070 and 54080 for typical examples); the tanks are sometimes of angular construction.

PRINCE YAMAMOTO (Ja); 6358; Taihei; 1981

LIQUEFIED GAS CARRIER

Features: extensive pipework along weather deck; very prominent, tall vents; superstructure all-aft and tall, high freeboard; large deckhouse ahead of bridge.

Variations: these vessels are usually flush-decked; spherical tanks are sometimes seen on the weather deck (see drawing number 54040); many have a number of large deckhouses often connected by catwalks (see drawing number 54060).

Notes: although it has little bearing on the identification of these vessels, they are split into two types: LPG (Liquefied Petroleum Gas) and LNG (Liquefied Natural Gas); the vessel illustrated is an LPG carrier, as the lettering on the hull reveals.

ISOMERIA (Br); 39932; H & W; 1982; sister: ISOCARDIA

LIQUEFIED GAS CARRIER — SHORT-SEA

Features: weather deck cluttered with piping and vents etc; large deckhouse; all-aft design.

Variations: for other typical examples see the following drawings: 53106, 53108, 53109, 53135, 53610, 80830.

KNUD THOLSTRUP (De); 1999; Nord-Offshore A/S (Norway); 1982; ex Traenafjord; sister: LAURITS THOLSTRUP

RO-RO CONTAINER SHIP

Features: large quarter-ramp on starboard side; high freeboard, often angled-up aft; containers stowed on upper deck.

Variations: a number of vessels have the funnel incorporated into the frame which supports the ramp (see drawing number 52640); for example with slewing ramp see drawing number 80230; drawing number 92910 shows an example with bridge forward; other typical examples are numbers 80180, 80190, 80200 and 80210; note that a number of these vessels have a covered ramp leading from the upper deck to the lower vehicle decks; large numbers of vents along the edge of the upper deck are features although these vary in size, shape and numbers; drawing number 80280 has large, box-like examples of various lengths.

GDANSK II (Pd); 18466; AESA; 1983; sisters: KATOWICE II; POZNAN; WROCLAW

SMALL RO-RO CARGO SHIP

Features: high freeboard, large superstructure (the apparently solid lower part of this vessel's superstructure is, in fact, a tunnel under which trailers can be stowed and driven through); large ramp at stern (giving the impression of being a kingpost when viewed broadside); containers or trailers on deck.

Variations: some vessels have a covered upper-deck so that trailers etc cannot be seen (see drawing number 32340, for example).

Notes: the all-aft design of the vessel illustrated is common in modern vessels but most of the older examples have the superstructure foreward (for examples see drawings number 33240 and 94650); the stern ramp does not always appear above the upper deck and can only be used as a recognition feature if the stern is visible; many ro-ro ships have twin-funnels on the sides of the upper-deck or superstructure to leave space for the vehicle decks.

BALDER VIK (Li); 2462; Galatz; 1983; sisters: BALDER STRAND, BALDER SUND

VEHICLE CARRIER

Features: high freeboard accentuated by the long enclosed decks above the upper-deck, giving a "slab-sided" impression; these upper vehicle decks run from near to the forecastle and sometimes to the stern, although those on the vessel illustrated stop short of the stern; quarter ramp; funnel around ¾-aft.

Notes: some ships have two quarter ramps and others no ramps at all; the side ramps, one of which can be seen lowered in this photograph, are not always evident when stowed.

RABUNION XIX (Le); 1598; Luehring; 1970; converted from general cargo vessel in 1983 (Meyer); ex Beckumersand 1983; for original appearance see former sisters under drawing number 67000

CLOVER ACE (Ja); 17418; Imabari; 1982

SEMI-SUBMERSIBLE HEAVY-LIFT VESSEL

Features: very low freeboard amidships; tall forecastle and poop; bridge foreward.

Variations: drawing number 01010 shows the maximum extent of immersion; drawing number 89684 is an unusual example, being a combined semi-submersible and tanker.

Notes: when seen with a very large deckload, such as the accommodation barge on the vessel shown in the photograph, the very low freeboard may not be immediately apparent.

BARGE CARRIER

Features: very little superstructure and funnels "on deck" giving a long, low appearance; large gantry crane for handling barges; "prongs" at the stern on which the gantry can run out to pick up and drop barges; bridge foreward; barges stowed on deck (could be confused with containers).

Variations: all have the same basic details although the "Seabee" type has a built-in elevator at the stern giving the impression of a tall poop (see drawing number 08860); for other typical examples see drawings number 00010, 00240, 01050, 93030, 93280, 94850; a few of the US flag vessels which had two gantries, one for containers and one for barges, have now been converted to container ships and have one gantry only.

DAN LIFTER (Bs); 18282; Mitsubishi HI; 1982; sister: DAN MOVER

HEAVY-LIFT CARGO SHIP

Features: tall, heavy masts with supports; long, heavy-lift derricks with prominent gear; long, flat upper deck giving ample area for stowage of large, indivisible items.

Variations: among the smaller, specialised vessels there is a large variety of lifting gear; for examples see drawings number 65090, 82080, 82370, 87100, 91170, 90520.

Notes: many general cargo are fitted with heavy-lift derricks (see the photograph of the BORUSSIA earlier in this section) and these are often of the Stuelcken type; in some cases they can be used for handling containers (see drawings number 02811 and 15720 for examples of general cargo vessels with Stuelcken derricks); many smaller heavy-lift ships can carry containers (as the photograph shows) or general cargo.

ACADIA FOREST (Li); 33231; Sumitomo; 1969; sister: ATLANTIC FOREST

LIVESTOCK CARRIER

Features: several tiers of long, distinctive livestock decks.

Variations: practically all the livestock carriers in existence at the moment are conversions from other types of vessel (tankers, passenger ships, bulk carriers etc); in most cases, little has been done to the basic design apart from the addition of livestock decks; for typical examples see the following drawings: 16850, 33040, 41990, 94730, 94890.

JUMBO STELLATWO (NA); 4997; S & B; 1978; ex Internavis II 1982

CABLE-LAYER AND OFFSHORE SUPPORT VESSEL

Features: two large tripods amidships for handling cable; side-mounted cable sheaves (not permanent).

Variations: the vessel illustrated has none of the characteristics of the typical cable layer, which are, principally, bow sheaves and a long, low superstructure similar to a passenger vessel; for typical examples see drawings number 02400, 02410, 02420, 02430, 35170, 35180, 35190.

Notes: the vessel illustrated can be used as a submersible support ship using the large 150-tonne-capacity derrick which can be seen abaft the second tripod.

ITM VENTURER (Br); 9487; Hyundai; 1983

STERN-TRAWLING FISH FACTORY SHIP

Features: not much superstructure; several heavy goalpost masts (the one at the stern often has angled sides); long forecastle.

Variations: although they all have the same basic design, these vessels often vary considerably in size and certain details; for other examples see drawings number 11580-11800 and 12230-12630.

Notes: fisheries research ships will have similar features and be very difficult to distinguish.

LIMB (Ru); 3147; Stralsund; 1981; "Super Atlantik" type

RESEARCH SHIP

Features: large amount of superstructure; 'A' frame aft; long forecastle; many aerials and similar equipment.

Variations: there are many types of research ship (the main ones being hydrographic and oceanographic) and all have the same basic features; types such as survey ships and weather ships can also be classed as research ships for recognition purposes; missile tracking vessels are also research ships but can be distinguished by distinctive domes (see drawing number 94280) or dishes (see drawing number 95025); for typical examples of research ships see drawings number 04220, 04240, 22180, 22300, 34060, 35390.

AKADEMIK BORIS PETROV (Ru); approx. 1700; Hollming; 1984; sister: AKADEMIK M. A. LAVRENTYEV and one further vessel on order

SUBMERSIBLE SUPPORT SHIP (offshore support vessel)

Features: heavy superstructure positioned well foreward; helicopter platform foreward; long forecastle; long, low afterdeck with heavy crane for handling submersibles etc; several large, enclosed lifeboats.

Variations: vessels of this type are often converted trawlers (see drawing number 04245 for example); other typical purpose-built examples are drawings number 09065, 17343 and 01352.

Notes: most vessels involved in the offshore oil and gas industry have a multi-purpose capability, including diving support, standby safety and supply etc; the vessel illustrated is of this type.

SHEARWATER SAPPHIRE (Au); 3936; "De Hoop"; 1982; sister SHEARWATER TOPAZ (Ne)

OIL RIG SUPPLY VESSEL (ORSV)

Features: superstructure, funnels etc foreward on a long forecastle; long afterdeck for stowage of deck cargo; light upright foreward to carry navigation lights etc.

Variations: some earlier vessels have very low, twin funnels at the sides of the deck about ¾-aft.

Notes: only the larger versions of these vessels (which are often pipe carriers) come within the scope of this book, see drawing number 08840, for example; many ORSVs are also tugs, and these are usually referred to as tug/supply vessels; the vessel illustrated is of this type.

IMPERIAL SERVICE (Pa); 670; Drypool; 1971

DREDGER (suction dredger, hopper suction dredger)

Features: very low freeboard, large amount of deck gear, mainly consisting of suction pipes, davits and, very often, a travelling crane; heavy superstructure.

Variations: position of superstructure and funnel can vary considerably; many have the bridge and superstructure well foreward with a separated funnel further aft; for typical examples see drawings number 03980, 37363, 43590, 52280, 76700, 93040 and 95370.

Notes: other types of dredger, such as bucket dredgers and cutter suction, have very distinctive features but do not come within the scope of this book as they are mostly smaller harbour craft; note in the photograph, the davits swung out over the side, supporting the suction pipes; most dredgers have islands because of the very low freeboard.

VOLVOX DELTA (Ne); 5000; IHC Holland; 1984

THE RECOGNITION SYSTEM

The system used in this book is designed to identify either individual ships or a group of very similar or identical ships.

The basis of the system is the noting of three features:

1. The PROFILE, defined as the funnel position (amidships or aft) and the arrangement of the superstructure.

2. The SEQUENCE, defined as the noting of certain prescribed features on the ship in the order in which they occur.

3. The HULL FORM, defined as the arrangment and number of castles, or islands, on the hull.

These features are reported in a simple abbreviated form which is described in the following pages, along with a fuller description of the coding features.

An important fact to remember is that, although many standard nautical terms are used in the system, they are often defined in a very different way. The term hull form is a good example of this. Technically, it refers to the actual shape of the hull, but, in the recognition system, it is the arrangement of islands. All the features used in the system are classified purely by *appearance* and *never by function*. This is one reason why many everyday nautical terms, such as mast or kingpost, have been re-defined for the purposes of the recognition system.

To gain a thorough knowledge of the system it is essential to go through the pages of this manual slowly and in strict order. Learn the definitions and the methods as they are set out and, more importantly, apply them when coding a vessel. Although this may seem unnecessarily pedantic, the appearance of different ships can vary so much that it is left, finally, to the judgement of the observer to decide how a particular vessel should be coded.

The number of elements in the system has deliberately been kept to a mimimum, in order to make it easily memorable. In the sequence, for example, there are only six classifications: kingpost, mast, crane, funnel, gantry and ramp. With the abundance of ships and the increasing diversity in design it is often very difficult to classify these features. By following the prescribed method it should be possible to decide on a classification but, if it is impossible to decide, the solution is to give an *alternative sequence*. Alternative codings can also be applied to the profile and the hull form. Many of the vessels in this book appear under two, or sometimes more, codings.

THE PROFILE

The profile consists of two separate elements: the funnel position (amidships or aft) and the arrangement of the superstructure.

It is very important that the two elements (funnel and superstructure) are considered independently. In other words, after the funnel position has been decided it must be ignored when deciding the superstructure arrangement.

Funnel position

There are two positions: amidships and aft. Note that the ¾-aft position is regarded as funnel amidships if *any part* of the funnel touches the ¾-aft line. Remember that the terms 'amidships' and 'aft' may be defined differently when used in another context.

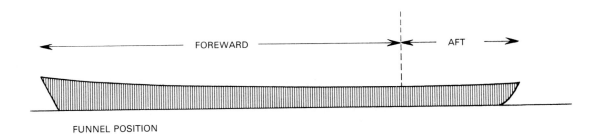

FUNNEL POSITION

Superstructure

For the purposes of classifying a ship's profile, the superstructure is only the main bulk of accommodation, bridge, engineroom casing etc. Smaller structures, such as mast houses, docking bridges and islands, are not considered as superstructure. Although there can be confusion between islands and superstructure (this is also mentioned in the section on hull form), islands appear as integral parts of the hull although they are raised above the upper deck.

Determining the profile

There are *five* profiles in the system.
They are reported as P1, P2, P3, P4 and P5.
The first two profiles, P1 and P2, have the funnel amidships and the other profiles, P3, P4 and P5, have the funnel aft.

Having decided whether the funnel is amidships or aft, the observer then looks at the superstructure to determine the actual profile.
The different arrangements are best shown by drawings.

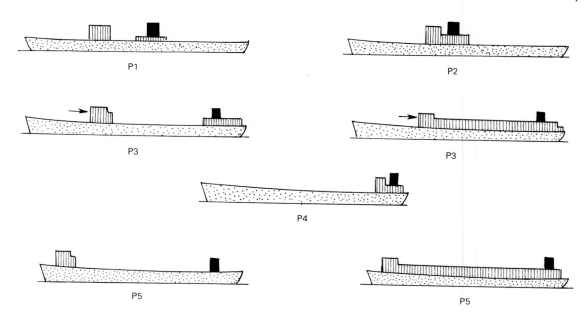

IMPORTANT NOTE. The superstructure is analysed in a different way in the two groups of profiles. In the funnel-amidships group it is the number of blocks of superstructure that determines the profile, regardless of where that superstructure is situated. In the funnel-aft profiles, however, the distinguishing feature is the position of the bridge-front (foreward, amidships or aft) that determines the profile. The number of blocks of superstructure is irrelevant.

Problems in positioning the funnel or superstructure accurately

As the observer normally has to judge by eye where the ¾-aft line falls on a ship, it may be very difficult to decide exactly where the funnel or bridge-front falls. If the observer is undecided the answer is, as stated previously, *give alternative profiles*.

Worked examples

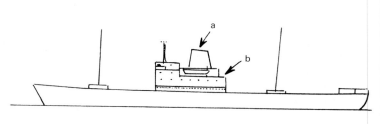

EXAMPLE ONE
1. Where is the funnel positioned?
   The funnel (a) is positioned amidships.
   Therefore, the profile is either P1 or P2.
2. How is the superstructure arranged?
   The superstructure (b) is in one block.
Conclusion: the funnel is amidships; the superstructure is in one block, therefore the profile is P2.

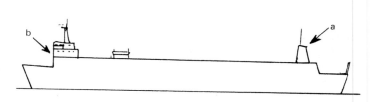

EXAMPLE TWO
1. Where is the funnel positioned?
   The funnel (a) is positioned aft.
   Therefore, the profile is P3, P4 or P5.
2. Where does the bridge-front fall?
   The bridge-front falls foreward.
Conclusion: the funnel is aft; the bridge-front falls foreward, therefore the profile is P5.

THE SEQUENCE

Defined as the noting of certain prescribed features on the ship in the order in which they occur (working foreward to aft).

There are six features which are coded as follows:

Kingpost	K	Funnel	F
Mast	M	Gantry	N
Crane	C	Ramp	R

Apart from the mast and the kingpost, which will be dealt with separately, all these features can be easily identified. It is important to remember that with all cargo gear it is the upright part and not the lifting device, derrick, jib etc, which is considered the principal feature.

The following drawings give the basic shapes of the sequence features. The funnel is normally a prominent and obvious feature, and it has not been illustrated.

Cranes

Although they can be very similar to kingposts, cranes differ principally by the fact that they have a *width* as well as height, whereas the kingpost is merely an upright pole. This is well illustrated in a later section where an upright which is technically a crane has the appearance of a kingpost. Very small cranes, such as those installed to handle small lifeboats or liferafts, are usually too small to code.

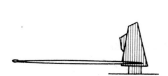  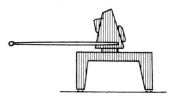 

Gantries

As the drawings show, there are a wide variety of designs although the commonest is the one which gives the appearance of a goalpost from the side. A crane mounted on a gantry is always coded C, as illustrated in the crane drawings.

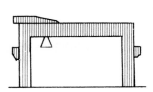 

Ramps

Only the increasingly numerous quarter and stern slewing ramps. The conventional type of stern ramp will simply appear as an upright if it rises above the upper deck or superstructure and may be coded as K or M, according to its height. Codeable ramps can be seen occasionally in the foreward parts of some vessels.

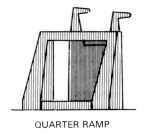

QUARTER RAMP

SLEWING RAMP

Superimposed features

If one coding feature is mounted on another the topmost feature is always coded first; eg a mast from a funnel is coded MF and a mast from a ramp is coded MR.

Masts and Kingposts

Masts and kingposts must be considered together as they are both basically upright poles. They are distinguished by their relative heights. Do not take into account any additions to the upright, such as derricks or a gaff, for example, when deciding upon a classification. The radar mast from the bridge and a mast from the funnel are *always* coded M, if heavy enough to code. As with all the features in the sequence, it is important to forget their technical function and only remember how they are defined within the coding system. In some older vessels, kingposts are often arranged in pairs. These are coded as a *single* K, as a ship is always coded from a complete broadside view, which must be approximated if the vessel is not actually seen broadside. This applies to every aspect of the coding system.

A larger selection of more detailed drawings of masts, kingposts, cranes etc are given in a later section.

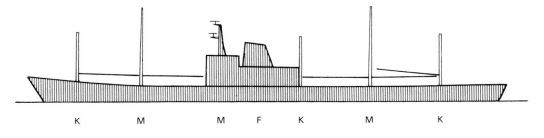

HULL FORM

Defined as the arrangement of castles or islands, on the hull. The reporting method is simple: the castles are numbered 1—forecastle, 2—midcastle, 3—poop and the letter H is placed before the numerals, eg H13, H2. A flush-decked vessel is simply reported as H.

There are a number of possible combinations, the following illustrations show the main ones.

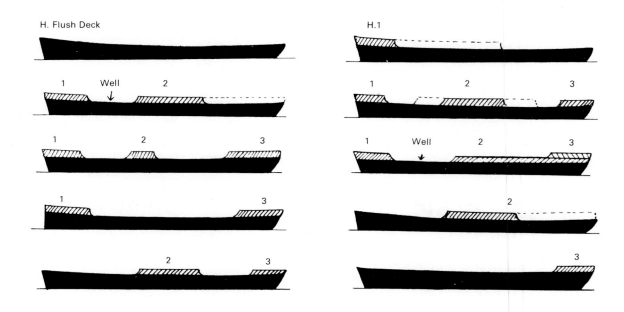

It is sometimes difficult to distinguish islands from superstructure. Islands can be simply defined as structures which stand proud from the upperdeck although incorporated into the hull. They always appear solid although they may have windows. Problems can arise when superstructure is built out practically to the hull sides and can, perhaps, only be identified by openings such as large windows. Passenger ships can be particularly difficult in this respect. The height of an island is normally about the same as one deck of superstructure, about 8 feet. However, there are exceptions. The modern ro-ro ship, for example, often has several decks above the upper-deck which are solidly plated and meet the sides of the hull. They give the appearance of very high islands and should be coded as such.

Other confusions in hull forms

As can be seen from the drawings of hull forms shown previously, the length of island can vary considerably. A forecastle may extend almost to the stern of a vessel but it is still reported as H1 although it may seem to be combined with a midcastle. The same would apply to a midcastle which runs into a poop, it is coded H2. This is only the case, however, if the island begins on, or forward of, the amidships line. If it begins abaft of amidships it is regarded as a poop, H3. If an island begins near the stem but *not at it*, it cannot be regarded as a forecastle but must be a midcastle, H2. Although the islands are called forecastle and midcastle, this does not necessarily indicate their position on the hull. The only definite rules that can be made are that the forecastle must *begin at the stem* and the poop must *end at, or very near, the stern*.

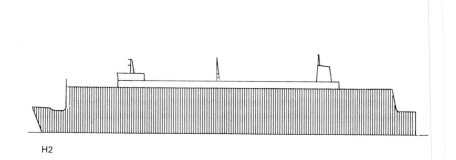

H2

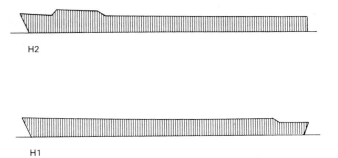

H2

H1

Do not confuse islands with *bulwark plating*. Plating is only about half the height of an average island and should be easily distinguished.

Long hances, see Glossary for definition, often disguise an island and may give the impression of slightly exaggerated sheer. A hull of this type must be regarded as flush-decked, H.

FORECASTLE

H

Another problem is the *trunk-deck*, a common feature on smaller tankers. If a vessel with a trunk-deck is seen silhouetted it may appear to be flush-decked. If the trunk-deck can be seen the islands should be coded, even though the trunk may be the same height as the islands.

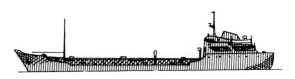

TRUNK DECK TANKER

ADDITIONAL RECOGNITION FEATURES

The next few pages contain features which, although not used in the body of this book, can provide useful recognition information beyond the basic features of profile, sequence and hull form.

Bows (B)

Actually *stems* but coded *bows* (B) to avoid confusion with *sterns* (S)

For recognition purposes bows or sterns are grouped into three classes for coding although there are variations or modifications of most of them.

B1 Straight, Plumb or Vertical. The oldest type which offers resistance to the seas.

B2 Raking or Sloping and Curved and Raking. Angle varies greatly and Clipper or Cable bows come within this group.

B3 Spoon, an outward curve, all rounded and not 'sitting' on the water, and **Icebreaking,** also with an outward curve but angular and straighter. Not always noticeable if ship is laden or in heavy seas.

B1

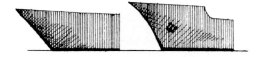

B2

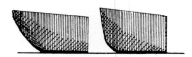

B3

Sterns (S)

Classified and reported in three groups although there are a few variations from the basic types.

S1 Counter or Cut Away. The older type. Second drawing represents a tug or trawler type with deep overhanging counter.

S2 Cruiser. Angle varies. There is a flat Transom stern but silhouetted it appears little different.

S3 Cruiser Spoon. Particularly a feature of German or Russian built ships. The second drawing shows the stern of a typical roll-on/roll-off vessel.

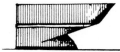

S1

S2

S3

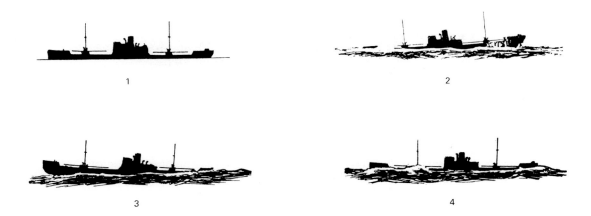

Illusions

A ship in heavy weather may need some watching. The drawings show the same ship pitching heavily when bows and sterns might be wrongly reported—S1 instead of S2 in number 2 and B3 instead of B1 as in number 4.

POSITIONING

The above view shows that ships with varying appearance can have the same basic reporting sequence. This can be overcome by dividing the ship into twelve equal parts and estimating each feature against the scale.

This is a most important step in identification for there are many ships with the same sequence and hull form but the positions and lengths vary considerably. The length of the vessel is divided into twelve equal parts, numbered 0 at the stem and 12 at the stern. Features which fall between dividing lines can be suffixed with a fraction, for example the kingpost on the vessel drawn below falls at 6¾. Any fraction can be used, according to the judgement of the observer. It is important to remember that features such as gantries and some types of cranes can travel fore-and-aft, thus altering the positioning and even the sequence if they pass other features.

The ship shown below is coded:

> P4; KKMFK; H13;
> fo'c'sle length 0 - 1½; aftercastle length 8¾ - 12;
> mast at 9½; kingposts at 2, 6¾ and 10¾;
> superstructure lengths (four decks):
> 9⅓-11, 9⅓-10, 9⅓-10, 9⅓-9¾;
> funnel at 10¼.

Note: the superstructure decks are noted from the lower to the top and the funnel position is for the front of the funnel, at the base.

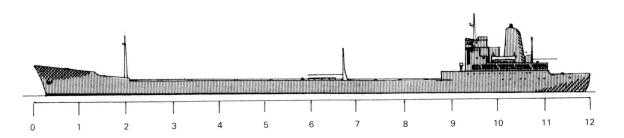

Masts (M)

Parts of a mast

Very tall masts or masts with table tops very high up are common features of many German or Dutch built ships.

Masts are named from foreward: **foremast, mainmast, mizzenmast** (or **aftermast**).

Technically, masts are any poles set along the *centre-line* but for recognition purposes are the *tallest* poles in a ship, either by themselves or by reason of being set on superstructure which *raises them above all other uprights*, such as a signal mast on the bridge.

A *lower mast* with topmast lowered is coded as a kingpost.

Radar masts are only coded if they are sufficiently tall or thick to show in the distant view.

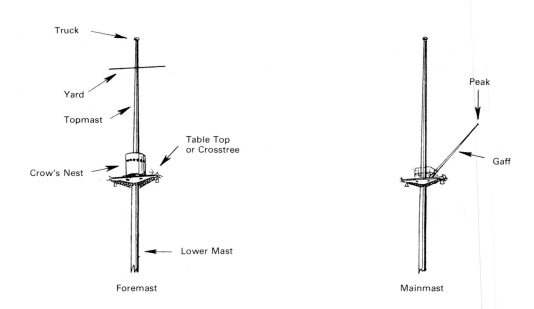

Foremast   Mainmast

Types of mast

There are many types of mast today and whenever possible in the medium view, M should be amplified by more detail, such as M(GP) for a goalpost mast.

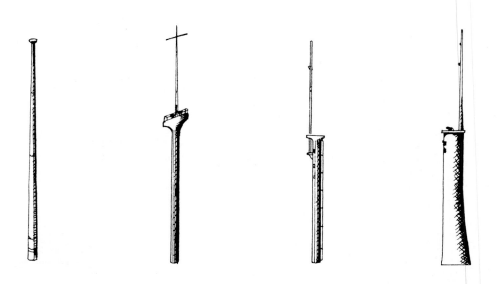

POLE mast   LOWER mast with TOPMAST   FID topmast   HEAVY mast

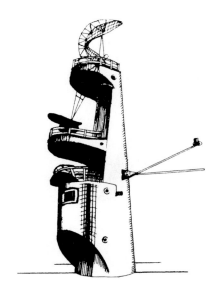

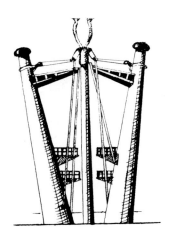

HEAVY 'Military' mast fitted with variations in many ships. Scanners and look-out platforms incorporated in one structure.

FRONT VIEW of STUELCKEN mast for very heavy lifts up to 300 tons or more. When seen broadside looks like a thick lower mast with topmast. Derrick may be stowed vertically or at an angle.

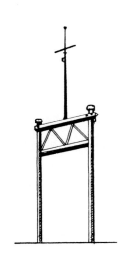

GOALPOST mast. M(GP)

BI-POD mast. M(B)

TRI-POD mast. M(T)

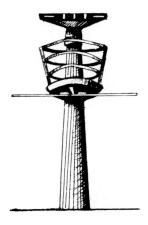

RADAR mast or pole. M(RP)

TOWER or LATTICE mast

'Y' mast

MAST from CRANE. MC   MAST from FUNNEL. MF

Kingposts (K)

Although coded K, kingposts are also known as derrick posts or samson posts.

They are generally similar to the lower portions of masts and indeed may well *be* lower masts with topmasts lowered.

They may be on the centre line (when this should be reported CL) or in pairs, three abreast or even four abreast. If a pair is joined it is coded as goalpost kingpost - K(GP). They are erected near hatchways.

A **kingpost abreast** a mast or funnel is not coded but is reported in the close view.

Hatch gear for working the hatches may look like a kingpost and if so, is reported as K.

Crutches for securing derricks in coasters may, in a small ship, be proportionately large and should be reported as K.

Cranes may sometimes look like kingposts, especially with jibs down and may be coded K, if uncertain.

Kingposts rising from superstructure such as those near funnels on many tankers or bulk carriers are coded K, because although placed high, they are in themselves short and lower than the mast.

Many of the mast types are seen also in kingposts - for example bi-pods, heavy, etc are coded in the same manner: K(B), *Ks against bridge front* are not easy to distinguish.

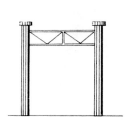
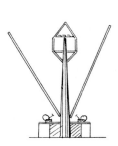

Centre-line LOWER MAST type   GOALPOST type   HALLEN type (variations)   LIEBHERR CRANE coded as K

Cranes (C)

Cranes, while always a feature in a few classes of ships, are now rapidly supplanting masts, kingposts and derricks.

Some are very large indeed but when the jib is stowed it is not always easy to distinguish them from kingposts.

A further difficulty is that many run along the deck on rails and so make the classifying of ships according to the **position** of leading features difficult.

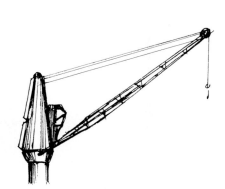
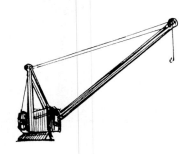

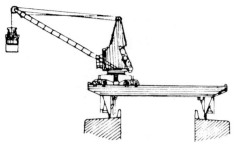

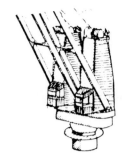

TANDEM CRANE. Each can swing on its individual axis or they can operate as a pair and swing on large base. Usually stowed amidships but may be seen fore and aft. Coded C or CC according to position.

GRAB CRANE on gantry (coded as C not N).

Gantries (N)
Coded N so as not to confuse with goalpost (GP).

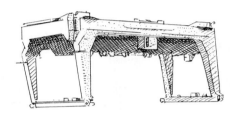

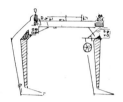

Funnels (F)

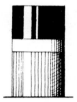

VERTICAL

RAKING TOP

RAKING

CONICAL

COWL TOP

LATTICE WORK

MAST AND FUNNEL COMBINED

NARROW CONICAL

ANGULAR

THORNYCROFT

CLINKER SCREEN

CLINKER SCREEN (small)

WING (US type)

'MOTOR SHIP' type

DOME TOP

PROJECTING PIPE (vary)

BOTTLE type

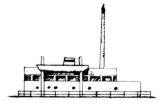

'KINGPOST' type (coded K or F(K))

MATCH-STICK type (common in tankers and usually abreast)

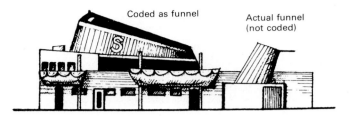

Coded as funnel

Actual funnel (not coded)

FERRY type (one on either side of superstructure)

FUNNEL and BRIDGE merged (a very common type in coasters)

Ventilators (V)

There are many different types and the cowls vary greatly in appearance. Some are characteristic of a particular nationality of build but this is no guide to recognition.

Very conspicuous ventilators and their positions are recorded.

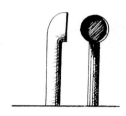

COWL

BONNET (German)

HOUR GLASS or THISTLE (Finnish)

MUSHROOM (British)

RATTLE (German)

Scandinavian

BOX (French)

SQUARE (British)

CANVAS WINDSAIL. In hot weather additional ventilation may be obtained by fixing canvas windsail, secured to the rigging.

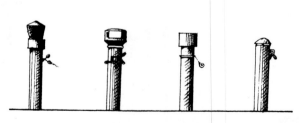

Ventilator tops to kingposts

Deck Houses, Mast Houses or Winch Houses (DH)

These may be quite small, in which case they will be merely recorded as being in a position corresponding to one of the numbers in the 0 to 12 scale. They may, however, be sufficiently large to occupy a full sub-division or even more.

SMALL (common)

LARGE (common)

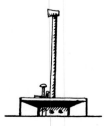

GERMAN type

[30]

Heavy or Jumbo Derrick (HD)

Lashed vertically to mast or kingpost and should be reported. Sometimes mistaken for topmasts but as they stand away from mast quite considerably, the mistake should not be made. Blocks and tackle protected by canvas when not in use. See also Stuelcken derrick.

Lifeboats and Davits

Lifeboats are normally stowed on the boat deck or highest deck. Numbers give an indication of size of ship.

They are stowed under a variety of davit types but the two main ones are (1) those that sit direct on to the deck and (2) those with headroom beneath.

A small **'accident boat'** is usually kept swung outboard in the vicinity of the bridge.

HEAVY derrick

GRAVITY davits

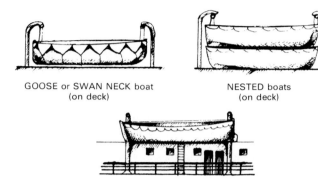

GOOSE or SWAN NECK boat
(on deck)

NESTED boats
(on deck)

GRAVITY davits
(above deck)

TONNAGE AND SIZE

Perhaps the most difficult thing in merchant ship identification is to form an estimation of size, whether it be of tonnage or of length. There is absolutely nothing in external appearance to guarantee either. Ships of almost identical outline may have huge variations and this is particularly so with engines-aft types.

Only experience can help to give a 'feeling' as to whether a ship is large or small and a graph of tonnage to length will only possibly give an approximately 70% accurate result to within 500 or more tons either way.

Merchant ships are shown in registers by **gross tonnage** and **nett tonnage** and these are measurements of **volume** and *not* of **weight**. 100 cubic feet of permanently enclosed space equals 1 gross ton.

Displacement and **deadweight tonnages** *are* a measurement in tons **weight** and the accompanying diagrams will show the differences.

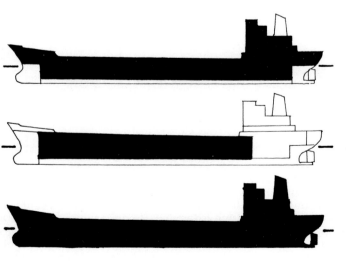

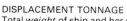

GROSS TONNAGE
Total *volume* of enclosed space. 100 cubic feet = 1 ton.

NETT TONNAGE
The earning capacity. Same as gross less crew quarters, boiler and engine rooms, fuel spaces, etc. dock, canal and harbour dues are paid on this tonnage.

DISPLACEMENT TONNAGE
Total *weight* of ship and her contents which varies in light and loaded state but as registered usually means an average.

DEADWEIGHT TONNAGE
Weight of cargo, fuel, etc required to bring vessel from light to loaded or full displacement. Deadweight tonnage is often expressed in tonnes. This is a metric unit equal to 1000 kilograms, making it practically identical to the imperial ton. (1 tonne = 0.984 imperial tons).

A GUIDE TO AGE AND APPEARANCE

Age

External appearance cannot be accepted as a reliable indication of age. Constructional features still regarded as 'modern' may be seen in ships built twenty or thirty years ago, while those of much more recent date may embody a few which have remained unchanged over the same period.

There has been an acceleration in recent years, largely on account of economic pressure and an urge towards fashion resulting in a somewhat dull uniformity, especially in passenger ships and tankers or bulk carriers.

Again, there are certain types of specialist ships which have been introduced only recently. Others have been rebuilt so that one may see a vessel with a heavily raking stem and modernised superstructure with an older counter stern, and engine aft types have had the bridge removed right aft.

The following generalisations may be of interest and of some little *help* provided that they are not accepted as *proof*.

	Modern	Old
Bows	Very raking or curved	Straight or slightly raking
Bridges	Heavy and enclosed	Open and flat-fronted
Cranes	Large and numerous	Small and scarce
Funnels	Short, fat or 'fancy'	Tall and thin
Hances	Very long and curved	Short and angular
Hull Form	Few islands	Three-island
Masts	Few, single or 'fancy'	More numerous and plain
Profile	Composite	Split
Sterns	Cruiser or spoon	Counter
Superstructures	Streamlines	Open and angular
Ventilators	Few and small	Large and numerous

Speed (bow waves and wakes)

The water displaced by the bow is called the bow wave and is produced more by the hull shape than by the speed.

Older vessels with blunt bows piled up water in front but were generally slow. Often the faster the ship the smaller the wave and as the ship increases speed, the bow wave is formed further back and at high speed may merge with the wake to form one line of white water.

The track left by the ship is called the wake. It is the product of the disturbed water caused by the hull passing through the water, and the water churned up by the screw.

It is more pronounced in modern high-powered vessels with smaller, fast-moving propellers.

Seen from the air the wake caused by a single screw and twin-screwed ships differs.

A deeply laden ship leaves a greater wake as the propeller causes a deeper disturbance of water. A vessel 'light' churns up a great amount of water but only for a short distance.

In addition to the age of vessels, weather conditions naturally affect the appearance.

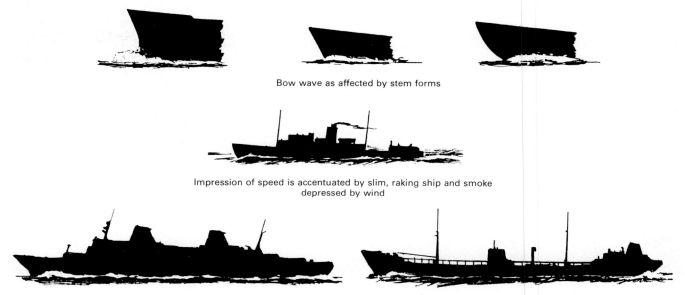

Bow wave as affected by stem forms

Impression of speed is accentuated by slim, raking ship and smoke depressed by wind

A large liner with wash due almost entirely to very high speed

A light ship with half immersed screw creating illusion of speed

Colours

In peace time, colouring adds interest to and helps quite a lot in identification. Most companies have distinctive liveries and this forms a separate study. In addition to main hull colouring, such features as bands on hulls, boot-topping, islands, superstructure, funnels, masts, kingposts, derricks and even larger ventilators, all help to build up a complete picture.

Names

Soviet merchant ships have their names in Cyrillic characters on the bow and on the quarter or round the counter and in Roman characters on the bridge board. This latter may be a little confusing as the transliteration may not always conform to that with which one is familiar. Bulgarian vessels follow a similar procedure.

Greek ships usually have the name in Roman characters on the bow and in Greek characters on the quarter and counter. They do not always have a bridge board. See page 726 for transliterations of Cyrillic and Greek alphabets.

Ships of Moslem countries usually have names on the bow in Arabic but possibly also in Roman characters alongside or below.

Among other countries which also generally follow this custom are: Japan, India, Israel, South Korea, China and Taiwan.

Flags

Merchant ships usually wear certain flags at positions as indicated in the illustration and these may help identification.

(A) Jack—a small ensign, national flag or house flag. Worn in port.

(B) Courtesy or destination flag—ensign of country being visited.

(C) 'Blue Peter'—'P' of international code indicating that vessel is shortly sailing. Blue with white centre.

(D) Pilot flag—vertical, white-red: 'pilot on board'. Vertical, blue and yellow stripes: 'require a pilot'.

(E) Ship's name—a 4-flag hoist from code book.

(F) House or company flag—usually only worn in port.

(G) Ensign worn here usually at sea.

(H) Ensign worn here usually in port.

Contemporary practice of having one mast only means that flags may readily be 'masked' when worn from several halliards from the same yardarm and when combined with radar scanners, etc.

GLOSSARY

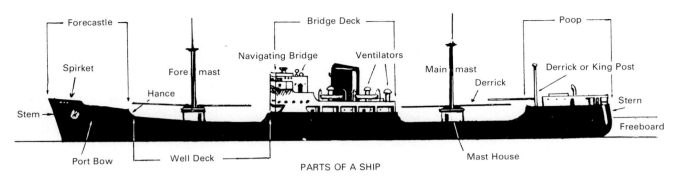

Forecastle — Bridge Deck — Poop

Spirket Fore mast Navigating Bridge Ventilators Main mast Derrick or King Post

Hance Derrick Stern

Stem Freeboard

Port Bow Well Deck Mast House

PARTS OF A SHIP

Parts of a Ship

"A" Frame	A large gantry, with angled sides and often cross-strengthened, which resembles a letter A. Commonly fitted on submersible support vessels for handling submersibles over the stern.
Abaft	Behind an object.
Aft	Towards the stern.
Aftercastle	Raised portion or Island at aft end of a vessel. Also termed the Poop.
Ahead	Directly in advance.
Amidships	Midway between stem and stern.
Angled Ramp	See Quarter Ramp.
Astern	Directly to the rear or behind a vessel.
Athwartships	Across a vessel: at right angles to centre line.
Ballast	Water, sand, etc. to give stability when ship is 'light' or empty of cargo.
Beam	Greatest width of vessel.
Boom	Same as Derrick.
Boot-Topping	Colour of paint along the waterline, between topsides and underwater surface.
Bow Wave	Wave formed under or near the bows when under way.
Bows	Adjacent to the stem: either side near front.
Bridge	Navigating platform running athwartships high up on front part of superstructure.
Bridge Deck	Mid-castle or Island approximately amidships.
Broadside	Complete view of a ship from stem to stern—not foreshortened.
Bulk Cargo	Heavy dry cargo such as ore or coal or bulky like grain or timber.
Bulkhead	Watertight walls which subdivide the hull. Usually transverse.
Bulwark	Plating on deck at side to give shelter or protection in place of railings.
Bunkers	Fuel capacity or space in which fuel is carried.
Cab	Covered portion at outboard ends of bridge wings.
Castle	Raised portion or Island above upper deck.
Catwalk	Raised gangway connecting castles, above the upper deck, especially in tankers.
Centre Line	Imaginary line drawn on deck from stem to stern.
Combination Carrier	A large vessel suitable for the carriage of either bulk or liquid cargoes, but not simultaneously (eg OBO—Ore/Bulk/Oil and OO—Ore/Oil).
Counter	Extreme stern of a ship. Sloping portion of a cutaway stern.
Crosstrees	Platform on top of lower mast or kingpost to which lifting gear is rigged. Also known as Table Tops.
Crow's Nest	Look out platform high up on foremast.

Davits	Curved fittings for supporting and handling boats.
Derrick	Long spar attached to foot of mast or kingpost for cargo handling.
Derrick Post	Vertical post to which derricks are fixed but shorter than a mast. Also known as Kingpost or Samson Post.
Docking Bridge	Athwartships platform aft used when ship is being navigated astern.
Draught	Depth from waterline to keel. Marked in feet or metres at stem and stern.
Ensign	Flag denoting nationality but not always the same as National Flag.
Ensign Staff	Flagstaff right aft from which ensign may be worn.
Flare	Slope outwards of a ship's hull from waterline to upper deck, particularly at bows and stern.
Flush Deck	Uninterrupted top line without castles.
Flying Bridge	Another name for a Catwalk.
Fore and Aft	Along the length of a vessel.
Forecastle	Raised portion or island at foreward end.
Foreward	Towards the fore part—towards the stem.
Freeboard	Depth of hull from waterline to upper deck.
Freeing Ports	Openings in ship's side or bulwarks to allow water to run off. Also known as Scuppers.
Gaff	Light fore and aft spar sometimes fitted to aft mast from which ensigns are worn at sea.
Gallows	Inverted 'U' shaped fitting at sides or stern of a trawler for handling nets.
Geared	A description of a cargo vessel fitted with cargo-handling gear (cranes, derricks etc).
Hance	Curved or sloping portion of side plating at breaks of castles or islands.
Hatch	Opening in deck to give access to cargo holds.
Hatch Covers	Wood or steel coverings to hatch.
Hatch Gear	Short vertical posts between hatches for working covers. If very prominent should be coded as Kingposts.
Hawse Hole	Hole in hull through which anchor cable passes to deck.
Heavy Derrick	Particularly heavy derrick lashed against mast when at sea.
Hold	Compartment for cargo stowage below deck.
Island	Same as Castle. A raised portion of hull above upper deck.
Jack Staff	Small flagstaff in stem at which 'Jack' is worn.
Jumbo Derrick	Very heavy derrick—same as Heavy Derrick.
Kingpost	Same as Derrick Post.
Laden	A vessel with full cargo. Down to her load marks.

[35]

Light	A vessel riding light without cargo. 'In Ballast'.	**Sheer**	Slope upwards of hull at foreward and after ends.
Load Line	Horizontal lines painted on hull amidships to indicate depth to which vessel may be loaded under varying conditions.	**Signal Letters**	A group of 4 letters of International Code allocated to a vessel for identification. The same as her radio call sign.
Lower Mast	Heavily constructed lower portion of a mast if latter is in more than one section.	**Slewing Ramp**	A ramp which can be swung in a horizontal plane (see illustration in Ship Recognition System).
Mast	Vertical or raked pole to support derricks or for signalling purposes. Tallest verticals.	**Spirket Plate**	Raised plating or screen above the upper deck at the stem: varies in length.
Mast House	Large deck house at base of mast or kingpost.	**Starboard Side**	That side of a vessel which is on the right hand when facing foreward. Indicated by GREEN.
Midcastle	Raised portion or island amidships. Same as Bridge Deck.	**Stem**	Extreme foreward part of ship's hull. The cut-water.
Navigating Bridge	A term covering wheel house, chart room and athwartships platform high up on foreward part of superstructure.	**Stern**	Extreme after part of a ship.
Peak	Extreme outward end of Gaff.	**Superstructure**	Upperworks. Deckhouses, etc on upper deck.
Plimsoll Line	Same as Load Line.	**Tonnage**	Size of a ship. As there are various forms of measurement a separate chapter is devoted to it.
Poop	Raised castle at stern; same as Aftercastle.		
Port Side	That side of the vessel which is on the left when facing foreward. Indicated by RED.	**Trunk Deck**	Enclosed structure about two-thirds of the width of a ship joining the islands. Particularly in coastal tankers.
Quarter	Adjacent to stern at either side.		
Quarter Ramp	A large ramp set in the quarter of a vessel's hull (usually starboard) which lowers at an angle enabling its use on a conventional quay when the vessel is alongside. Also known as an Angled Ramp (see illustration in Ship Recognition System).	**Ungeared**	A description of a cargo vessel which has no cargo-handling gear (ie cranes, derricks etc).
		Wake	Disturbed water left astern.
		Washports	Same as Freeing Ports or Scuppers.
		Waterline	Line formed on hull by surface of water.
		Weather Deck	A technical term for a light deck enclosed by plating. Frequently same as upper deck.
Rake	Slope or inclination of mast or funnel.		
Rubbing Strake	Heavy permanent wood, metal or rubber guard along the Hull to protect plating when going alongside. Prominent feature in coasters or small ships.	**Well Deck**	Portion of hull between castles or islands and approximately 7 to 8 feet lower.
		Winch House	Same as Mast or Deckhouse.
Samson Post	Same as Derrick Post or Kingpost.	**Yard**	A light spar rigged athwart a mast for signal purposes.
Scuppers	Same as Freeing Ports.		

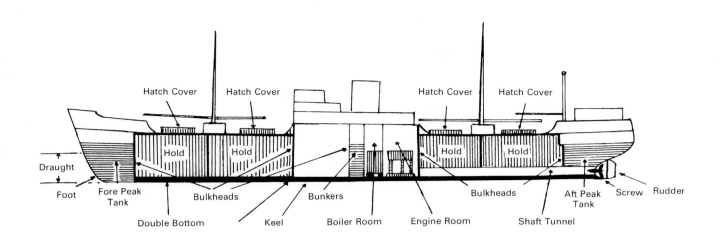

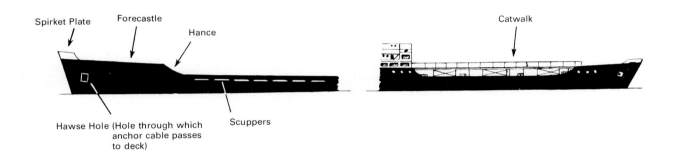

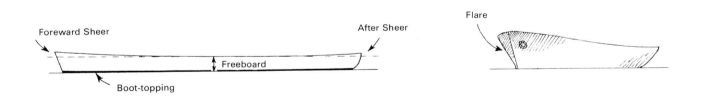

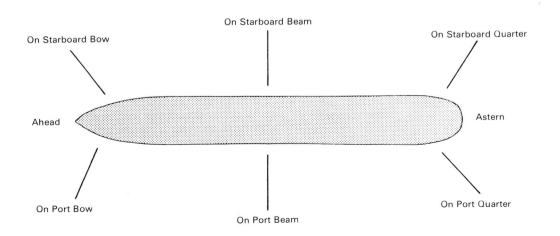

EXPLANATORY NOTES

The book is in two main sections: the **ship drawing section** and the **ship directory and data section**.

1. SHIP DRAWING SECTION

All drawings are to the scale of 1 inch = 200 feet (1:2400)

The drawings are arranged in *five sections*, corresponding to the five profiles, P1-P5.

Within these main sections the drawings are arranged in *alphabetical order of sequence*. This simply means that the sequence is regarded in the same way as words in a dictionary, eg the following sequences are in alphabetical order: C₂F, C₂FK, C₂MF. Vessels with twin funnels, ie funnels side-by-side, are coded as *single funnelled ships*, as only one funnel can be seen in the broadside view. Note that rather than repeat letters in the sequence that fall consecutively, a small number after the letter indicates the number of repetitions, eg KKKMFKK is shown as K₃MFK₂.

Within a particular sequence the drawings are further divided into hull forms. These are arranged in numerical order thus—H, H1, H12, H123, H13, H2, H23, H3.

After having divided and sub-divided the drawings, one may still have several vessels with the same sequence and hull form. These groups are not very large as a rule, so we have made their arrangement conform to general guidelines rather than to strict rules. In most cases we have taken the coded features (masts, kingposts, funnel, etc) and their positioning as the initial distinguishing feature. Explained simply, this means that a vessel with its first coded feature at No 2 on the grid would precede another with its first feature at No 6, and so on. If this system has, however, tended to split up two practically identical vessels which only vary by the positioning of one or two features, we have remained flexible. The type of vessel and size has also been taken into account.

As an aid to identification we have marked certain coded features on the drawings. Masts can be assumed to be on the centre line and kingposts in pairs if they are not marked. If they do not conform to this pattern they are marked (CL for centre line or small silhouettes for goalpost, bi-pod, etc). Most tripods are not indicated as they are obvious from the drawing.

On a vessel which has a line of, for example, centre-line kingposts, the first post only is marked and the remainder simply arrowed (see drawing A below). If there is a combination of features, any that are marked with an arrow only are the same as the last feature foreward that was fully identified (see drawing B below).

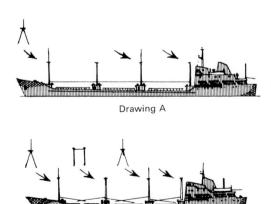

Drawing A

Drawing B

Text beneath drawings. Following the sequence and hull form are the entry number and its corresponding name. If the vessel has sisters or similar ships the final number of the entry is given to indicate how many vessels are covered by the drawing. If the name ship has a communist flag an asterisk appears before the entry number. If, however, the name ship does not have a communist flag but some or all of its sisterships do, no asterisk appears.

A running head on the pages shows the sequence and profile at the start of the left-hand page and the end of the right-hand page.

2. SHIP DIRECTORY AND DATA SECTION

This list follows the same order as the text.

Consecutive number: An asterisk before the number indicates a communist flag vessel. A small disc before an entry number shows that amendments to that entry appear in the addenda, which follows the Ship Directory and Data Section. It will be noticed that the numbers are not always consecutive, this is because the numbers have been retained from the previous edition and the removal of ships or entire entries has resulted in gaps. Use of the existing numbers has also, in some cases, necessitated the use of auxiliary numbers where a gap does not exist: eg a ship entered between 22450 and 22451 will be numbered 22450/1.

Name: Names which have been transliterated, eg Russian and Chinese, use the spellings given in Lloyd's Register. See page 726 for transliterations of Greek and Cyrillic alphabets.

Flag/country of build: Abbreviated form (see following section). Where a vessel has been rebuilt or modified the country/countries where this was carried out are hyphenated after the original builder. A complete entry in this section could therefore appear like this: Li/Ja-Ja (wears the Liberian flag, built in Japan, modified in Japan).

Shipbuilder: Given in brackets after country of build. An abbreviated form is given and the full titles appear in a list. As far as possible, the title given is that which was current at the time when the vessel was built. Where more than one builder is involved, the names are separated by an oblique stroke. In the case of a rebuild or conversion, eg lengthening or change of function, the name of the company responsible is given at the end of the entry where the rebuild details appear. This information has not always been available. The country of rebuild still sometimes appears earlier in the entry after the builder's name, eg Br (Swan Hunter)-Ja indicates a vessel built in the United Kingdom by Swan Hunter and later rebuilt in Japan.

Year of build/major alteration or completion: Example: 1956/65/72 (completed 1956, rebuilt 1965, further rebuilding 1972).

Type of vessel: Abbreviated form (see following section).

Tonnage: GRT to nearest 100-tons. Smaller tonnages are shown exact. Other tonnages shown if the GRT is unavailable are dwt (deadweight) and dspl (full displacement). For open/closed shelterdeck vessels both tonnages are shown.

Dimensions: Length overall x maximum draught. Stated in metres and taken to the nearest centimetre. Imperial measurements (to the nearest hundredth of a foot) follow in brackets. Open/closed shelterdeck vessels have both draughts. Length between perpendiculars (bp) is given if overall length is not available.

Machinery: Abbreviated form (see following section).

Design of main machinery: In most cases this is the designer but, where this is not known, the builder of the machinery is given. The designer and builder are often the same, particularly with older vessels. A list of the abbreviations appears on a later page.

Speed: Service speed in knots.

Ex-names: From the most recent, working back.

Remarks: Special features, details of rebuilding, etc.

Sister ships: Vessels built to the same design as the name ship. Details, such as type of machinery, builder or country of build, can often vary. These are sometimes shown.

Similar ships: Vessels similar enough to the vessel drawn not to warrant a separate drawing. Differences may include—types of mast, kingpost, etc, superstructure, stanchions, funnel, etc.

Flags of sisters/similar ships: The flag of every vessel is shown. However, where there are large groups under the same flag, that flag is shown at the beginning of the group. Occasionally, amongst a group of same-flag ships, a ship of another flag may appear.

ABBREVIATIONS

Flag and Country of Build Abbreviations
These indicate the ensign worn at the time of compilation of the book, and country of build. It is not necessarily the same as nationality of owners.

Vessels may change their flag from time to time without changing ownership. This particularly applies to American or Greek owned tonnage which is frequently registered under Flags of Convenience such as Liberia, Lebanon, Panama.

Ab	Abu Dhabi		Le	Lebanon
Ag	Algeria		Li	Liberia
Al	Albania		Ly	Libya
An	Angola		Ma	Malta
Ar	Argentina		Mb	Mozambique
As	Austria		Me	Mexico
Au	Australia		Mg	Madagascar
Bb	Barbados		Mn	Monaco
Be	Belgium		Mo	Morocco
Bh	Bangladesh		Ms	Mauritius
Bi	Benin		Mt	Mauritania
Bm	Burma		Mv	Maldives
Bn	Bahrain		My	Malaysia
Bo	Bolivia		Na	Nauru
Br	Britain and British Dependencies		NA	Netherlands Antilles
Bs	Bahamas		Ne	Netherlands
Bu	Bulgaria		Ng	Nigeria
Bz	Brazil		Ni	Nicaragua
Ca	Canada		No	Norway
Ch	Chile		NZ	New Zealand
Cm	Comoro Islands		Om	Oman
Cn	Cameroon		Pa	Panama
Co	Colombia		Pd	Poland
CR	Costa Rica		Pe	Peru
Cu	Cuba		Pi	Philippines
CV	Cape Verde		Pk	Pakistan
Cy	Cyprus		Po	Portugal
Cz	Czechoslovakia		Pp	Papua/New Guinea
Db	Dubai		Py	Paraguay
DDR	German Democratic Republic (East)		Qt	Qatar
De	Denmark		RC	People's Republic of China
Do	Dominica		RK	Democratic People's Republic of Korea (North)
Ec	Ecuador		Rm	Romania
Eg	Egypt		Ru	USSR
ES	El Salvador		SA	South Africa
Et	Ethiopia		Sc	Seychelles
Fa	Faroes		Sd	Switzerland
Fi	Finland		Se	Senegal
Fj	Fiji		Sg	Singapore
Fr	France		Sh	Sharjah
FRG	Federal Republic of Germany (West)		Si	Saudi Arabia
Ga	Gabon		SL	Sierra Leone
Ge	Germany—pre 1945		Sn	Surinam
Gh	Ghana		So	Somalia
Gm	Gambia		Sp	Spain
Gn	Guinea		Sr	Sri Lanka (Ceylon)
Gr	Greece		Su	Sudan
Gu	Guatemala		SV	St Vincent and the Grenadines
Gy	Guyana		Sw	Sweden
Ha	Haiti		Sy	Syria
HK	Hong Kong		Ta	Tanzania
Ho	Honduras		Tg	Togo
Hu	Hungary		Th	Thailand
Ia	Indonesia		Tn	Tunisia
Ic	Iceland		To	Tonga
Ih	Ireland		Tr	Trinidad & Tobago
In	India		Tu	Turkey
Iq	Iraq		Tw	Taiwan
Ir	Iran		UAE	United Arab Emirates
Is	Israel		Ug	Uganda
It	Italy		Ur	Uruguay
Iv	Ivory Coast		US	United States of America
Ja	Japan		Va	Vanuatu
Jm	Jamaica		Ve	Venezuela
Jo	Jordan		Vn	Viet-Nam
Ke	Kenya		Ye	Yemen
Kh	Ras al Khaimah		Ys	Yugoslavia
Ko	Republic of Korea (South)		Za	Zambia
Ku	Kuwait		Zr	Zaire

Abbreviations of Ship Types
Vessels of more than one function will have a combination of abbreviations from this list separated by an oblique stroke (e.g. C/HL).

A	Auxiliary		PTF	Passenger/Train Ferry
AT	Asphalt Tanker		R	Cargo Vessel with large Refrigerated capacity
B	Bulk Carrier		Rad	Radio Station
BC	Bulk/Car Carrier		Riv	River Craft
BC/O	Bulk/Car/Ore		Rmt	Replenishment Ship (Naval)
Bg	Barge Carrier		RoC	Ro/Ro Cargo Ship
BO	Bulk/Oil Carrier		RoRo	Roll-on/Roll-off (specific function unknown)
BT	Buoy Tender		RoCF	Ro/Ro Cargo Ferry
BWC	Bulk Carrier—Wood Chip		RoPF	Ro/Ro Passenger Ferry
C	General Dry Cargo Ship		RoPCF	Ro/Ro Passenger Car Ferry
Cbl	Cable Ship		RoVC	Ro/Ro Vehicle Carrier
Cem	Cement Carrier		RS	Research Ship (including hydrographic, oceanographic, etc)
CG	Coast Guard Ship			
Ch	Chemical Tanker		Rst	Replenishment Ship (Naval)
Con	Container Ship		RT	Replenishment Tanker (Naval)
Con R	Container Ship with Refrigerated Capacity		Sal	Salvage Vessel
CP	Cargo Passenger Ship (up to 12 passengers)		SCon	Semi Container Ship
			SDT	Slop Disposal Tanker
CS	Crane Ship		Slu	Sludge Carrier
CTS	Cargo/Training Ship		Sply	Supply Ship
D	Dredger		Spt	Support Ship (Naval)
Dep	Depot Ship		SS	Stern Trawler
Dk	Dock Ship		SSV	Standby Safety Vessel
DS	Drilling Ship		STS	Stern Trawler/Sealer
F	Ferry (probably carrying unberthed passengers)		Sub S	Submersible Support Ship
			TB	Bitumen Tanker
FA	Fleet Auxiliary		TC	Timber Carrier
FC	Fish Carrier		TF	Train Ferry
FF	Fish Factory		Tg	Tug
FFMS	Fishery Mother Ship		Tk	Tanker
FP	Fishery Protection Vessel		TPu	Tanker Pulp
Fru	Fruit Ship		Trlr	Trawler
FT	Stern Trawling Factory Ship		TS	Training Ship
FV	Fishing Vessel		V	Vehicle Carrier (other than Ro/Ro)
HL	Heavy Lift Vessel		Wa	Water Carrier
IB	Ice Breaker		WF	Whale Factory Ship
LC	Landing Craft		Whlr	Whaler
LGC	Liquefied Gas Carrier		WS	Weather Ship
LS	Livestock Carrier		WT	Wine Tanker
LT	Light Tender		Y	Yacht
M	Mining Ship			
MT	Molasses Tanker			
MTV	Missile Tracking Vessel			

Abbreviations of Engine Types

O	Ore Carrier		D-E	Diesel Electric
OBO	Ore/Bulk/Oil		GT	Gas Turbine
OO	Ore/Oil		M	Motor Vessel
ORSV	Oil Rig Supply Vessel		N	Nuclear Power
OSS	Offshore Support Ship		Pdl	Paddle
P	Passenger Ship		R	Reciprocating
Pal	Pallets Carrier		R & LPT	Reciprocating and Low Pressure Turbine
PC	Passenger Cargo Ship (over 12 passengers)		T	Turbine
PCTF	Passenger, Cargo and Train Ferry		T-E	Turbo Electric
PLC	Pipe Laying			
Plt	Pilot Vessel			

All vessels are single screw unless otherwise stated:

Pp	Pipe Carrier		TS	Twin Screw
PR	Passenger Refrigerated Vessel		TrS	Triple Screw
PRiv	Passenger (River)		QS	Quadruple Screw
PtCon	Part Container Ship			

Abbreviations of Shipbuilders Titles

Some companies may have had small changes of title which are not noted.

Aalborg	Aalborg Vaerft A/S	*Denmark*
Aarhus	Aarhus Flydedok (later Dannebrog-qv)	*Denmark*
Abeking	Abeking & Rasmussen, Yacht u Bootswerf	*W Germany*
Adelaide	Adelaide Ship Construction (A division of Adelaide S.S. Industries Pty Ltd)	*Australia*
Adler	Alder Werft, GmbH (later Stephani Werft-qv)	*W Germany*
Admiralteiskiy	Admiralteiskiy Shipyard	*USSR*
Adriatico	Cantieri Riuniti dell'Adriatico (no longer builders) (later Italcantieri-qv)	*Italy*
AESA	Astilleros Espanoles SA (Consortium)	*Spain*
AFNE	Astilleros y Fabricas Navales del Estado SA	*Argentina*
AG "Weser"	Aktien Gesellschaft "Weser" (including AG "Weser" Seebeckwerft) (being reorganised 1984)	*W Germany*
A. Hall	Alexander Hall & Co Ltd (no longer builders)	*Scotland*
Ailsa	Ailsa Shipbuilding Co Ltd (part of British Shipbuilders)	*Scotland*
Akers	Akers Mek Verksted A/S (Aker Group)	*Norway*
Alabama	Alabama Dry Dock and Shipbuilding Co	*USA*
Alberti	Cantiere Navale Alberti	*Italy*
Alexandria	Alexandria Shipyard	*Egypt*
Alfeite	Arsenal do Alfeite	*Portugal*
Alianza	Astilleros Alianza SA	*Argentina*
Allied	Allied Shipbuilders Ltd	*Canada*
Alto Adriatico	Cantieri dell'Alto Adriatico SpA	*Italy*
Amels	Amels BV (formerly C. Amels & Zoon and Scheepswerf & Mfbk "Welgelegen")	*Netherlands*
Amship	The American Ship Building Co (Amship Division)	*USA*
Amsterdamsche D	Amsterdamsche Droogdok Mij NV (no longer builders)	*Netherlands*
Angyalfold	Angyalfold Shipyard, Hungarian Ship & Crane Works	*Hungary*
Ankerlokken	Ankerlokken Group (yards at Floro, Forde and Glommen)	*Norway*
A. Normand	Ch et At Augustin Normand (later part of Havre-qv)	*France*
Ansaldo	Societa per Azioni Ansaldo (later Italcantieri and Muggiano-qv)	*Italy*
A & P	Austin & Pickersgill Ltd (part of British Shipbuilders)	*England*
A. Pahl	Schiffswerft August Pahl	*W Germany*
"Appingedam"	Scheepswerf "Appingedam" NV (see also Gebr Niestern)	*Netherlands*
Appledore	Appledore Shipbuilders Ltd (part of British Shipbuilders)	*England*
Apuania	Nuovi Cantieri Apuania	*Italy*
Ardrossan	Ardrossan Dockyard Ltd (no longer builders)	*Scotland*
Argo	Argo Shipbuilding & Shiprepairing Co	*Greece*
Arnhemsche	Arnhemsche Scheepsbouw Maatschappij NV (no longer builders)	*Netherlands*
Asakawa	Asakawa Zosen KK	*Japan*
"Astano"	Astilleros y Talleres del Noroeste ("ASTANO")	*Spain*
Astarsa	Astilleros Argentinos Rio de la Plata (ASTARSA)	*Argentina*
Astrakhan	Astrakhan Shipyard	*USSR*
Atlantic SB	Atlantic Shipbuilding Co Ltd (later Newport Shipbuilding and Engineering—no longer builders)	*Wales*
Atlantico	Astilleros del Atlantico SA (see Corcho and "Corbasa")	*Spain*
Atlas MaK	Atlas-MaK Maschinenbau GmbH (no longer builders)	*W Germany*
Atlas-Werke	Atlas-Werke AG (later Atlas-MaK-qv)	*W Germany*
Aukra	Aukra Bruk A/S	*Norway*
Austin	S. P. Austin & Son Ltd (later Austin & Pickersgill—see under A & P)	*England*
Australian Commonwealth	Australian Commonwealth Shipping Board (no longer builders)	*Australia*
Avondale	Avondale Shipyards Inc	*USA*
Axpe	Maritima de Axpe SA	*Spain*
Balenciaga	Balenciaga SA	*Spain*
Baltic	Baltic Shipbuilding and Engineering Works	*USSR*
Baltiya	Baltiya Shipyard	*USSR*
Barclay, Curle	Barclay, Curle & Co Ltd (no longer builders)	*Scotland*
Barens	Barens Shipbuilding & Engineering Corp Ltd (later Sandock-Austral Ltd)	*S Africa*
Barkmeijer	Scheepswerf Barkmeijer NV (no longer builders)	*Netherlands*
Barreras	Hijos de J. Barreras SA	*Spain*
Bartram	Bartram & Sons Ltd (no longer builders) (later part of Austin & Pickersgill—see under A & P)	*England*
Bath	Bath Iron Works Corp	*USA*
Batservice	Batservice Verft A/S	*Norway*
Bay	Bay Shipbuilding and Dry Dock Co	*USA*
Bayerische	Bayerische Schiffbau GmbH, Vorm A. Schellenberger	*W Germany*
"Bazan"	Empresa Nacional "Bazan" de Construcciones Navales Militares SA	*Spain*
Beliard, Crichton	Beliard, Crichton & Cie, SA (later Beliard Oostende)	*Belgium*
Beliard-Murdoch	Beliard-Murdoch SA (later Beliard Oostende)	*Belgium*
Beliard Oostende	Scheepswerven Beliard Oostende NV	*Belgium*
Benetti	Cantieri Navali M & B Benetti	*Italy*
Bergens	Bergens Mekaniske Verksteder A/S (part of the Aker Group)	*Norway*
Bethlehem	Bethlehem Shipbuilding Corp (no longer builders)	*USA*
Bethlehem PC	Bethlehem Pacific Coast Steel Corp, Shipbuilding Division (no longer builders)	*USA*
Bethlehem Steel	Bethlehem Steel Corp (previously Bethlehem Steel Co Inc)	*USA*
Beykoz	Denizcilik Anonim Sirketi Beykoz Tersanesi	*Turkey*

Bijlholt	Scheepswerf Bijlholt BV	*Netherlands*
Bijlsma	Scheepswerf G. Bijlsma & Zonen BV	*Netherlands*
Blalids	Blalids Slip & Mek Verksted	*Norway*
Blyth	Blyth Dry Docks & Shipbuilding Co Ltd (no longer builders)	*England*
Blythswood	Blythswood Shipbuilding Co Ltd (no longer builders)	*Scotland*
Bodewes Bergum	Scheepswerf Bodewes Bergum BV (no longer builders)	*Netherlands*
Bodewes BV	Scheepswerven v/h H. H. Bodewes BV	*Netherlands*
Bodewes NV	Scheepswerven Bodewes NV	*Netherlands*
Bodo	Bodo M/V A/S (no longer builders)	*Norway*
Boel	NV Jos Boel & Zonen (J. Boel et Fils) SA (later Boelwerf-qv)	*Belgium*
Boele's Sch	Boele's Scheepswerven & Machinenfabriek BV	*Netherlands*
Boelwerf	NV Boelwerf SA	*Belgium*
Bolson	J. Bolson & Son Ltd (no longer builders)	*England*
Bolsones	Bolsones Verft	*Norway*
Boot	NV Scheepswerf "de Vooruitgang" v/h D. Boot (later Duijvendijk's-qv)	*Netherlands*
Braila	Santierul Naval Braila	*Romania*
Brand	Schiffswerft Heinrich Brand KG	*W Germany*
Brattvag	Brattvag Skipsinnredning A/S	*Norway*
Breda	Cantiere Navale Breda SpA	*Italy*
Bremer V	Bremer Vulkan, Schiffbau und Maschinenfabrik	*W Germany*
Bretagne	Ateliers et Chantiers de Bretagne (no longer builders)	*France*
Broken H	The Broken Hill Proprietary Co Ltd (see Whyalla)	*Australia*
Brooke	Brooke Marine Ltd (part of British Shipbuilders)	*England*
Brown & H	James Brown & Hamer Ltd	*S Africa*
Bruges	Chantiers Navals de Bruges SPRL (later Ch Navals Flandres SA)	*Belgium*
Buesumer	Buesumer Werft GmbH	*W Germany*
Burntisland	Burntisland Shipbuilding Co Ltd (no longer builders)	*Scotland*
Burrard DD	Burrard Dry Dock Co Ltd (later part of Burrard Yarrows Corp)	*Canada*
Burrard Y	Burrard Yarrows Corp	*Canada*
Buschmann	Theodor Buschmann Schiffswerft	*W Germany*
Butler	Walter Butler Shipbuilders Inc (no longer builders)	*USA*
B + V	Blohm + Voss AG	*W Germany*
B & W	B & W Skibsvaerft (formerly Burmeister & Wain's Skibsbyggeri A/S; previously Burmeister & Wain's Maskin-og Skibsbyggeri)	*Denmark*
Cadagua	Astilleros del Cadagua	*Spain*
Cadiz	Astilleros de Cadiz (later part of AESA-qv)	*Spain*
Caen	Chantiers Navals de Caen (no longer builders)	*France*
Caledon	Caledon Shipbuilding & Engineering Co Ltd (later Robb Caledon-qv)	*Scotland*
Cammell Laird	Cammell Laird Shipbuilders Ltd (part of British Shipbuilders)	*England*
Camper & Nicholsons	Camper & Nicholsons Ltd (no longer builders)	*England*
Canadian Vickers	Canadian Vickers Shipyards Ltd (no longer builders)	*Canada*
Caneco	Industrias Reunidas Caneco SA	*Brazil*
Cantabrico	Astilleros Cantabrico y de Riera SA	*Spain*
Cargill	Cargill Inc	*USA*
Carrington	Carrington Slipways Proprietary Ltd	*Australia*
Cassaro	Cantiere Navale Cassaro	*Italy*
Cassens	C. Cassens Schiffswerft (no longer builders)	*W Germany*
CCN	Companhia Comercio e Navegacao. Also CCN Estaleiro Maua (see under Maua)	*Brazil*
C D Tirreno	Cantieri del Tirreno (later part of Riuniti-qv)	*Italy*
Celaya	Astilleros y Talleres Celaya SA	*Spain*
Ch de France	Chantiers de France (no longer builders—later became Dunkerque-Normandie-qv)	*France*
"Chernomorskiy"	"Chernomorskiy" Shipyard	*USSR*
China SB	China Shipbuilding Corp	*Taiwan*
Chongjin	Chongjin Shipyard	*N Korea*
Christy	Christy Corp	*USA*
Chung Hua	Chung Hua, Shanghai Shipyard	*China*
Chung Wah	Chung Wah Shipbuilding & Engineering Co Ltd	*Hong Kong*
Clelands	Clelands Shipbuilders Ltd	*England*
CLEMNA	Societa Cooperativa Responsabilita Limitata Lavaratori Edili, Meccanici, Navali Affini	*Italy*
CNIM	Constructions Navales et Industrielles de la Mediterranee (see also Mediterranee)	*France*
Coaster Const	Coaster Construction Co (1928) Ltd (no longer builders)	*Scotland*
Cochin	Cochin Shipyard Ltd	*India*
Cochrane	Cochrane Shipbuilders Ltd	*England*
Cockatoo	Cockatoo Docks and Engineering Co Pty Ltd (later Vickers Cockatoo Dockyard)	*Australia*
Cockerill	NV Cockerill Yards Hoboken (formerly NV John Cockerill)	*Belgium*
Cockerill-Ougree	NV Cockerill-Ougree (later Cockerill Yards Hoboken)	*Belgium*
Collingwood	Collingwood Shipyards (Div of Canadian Shipbuilding & Engineering Ltd)	*Canada*
"Combiship"	"Combiship" BV	*Netherlands*
Connell	Charles Connell & Co (Shipbuilders) Ltd (no longer builders—became Govan Shipbuilders)	*Scotland*
Consolidated Steel	Consolidated Steel Corp (no longer builders)	*USA*
Constantza	Santierul Naval Constantza	*Romania*
Construcciones SA	Astilleros Construcciones SA	*Spain*
Cook, W & G	Cook, Welton & Gemmell Ltd (no longer builders)	*England*

Coops	Scheepswerf Gebr Coops BV	*Netherlands*
"Corbasa"	Basse Sambre Corcho SA "Corbasa" (later became Atlantico-qv)	*Spain*
Corcho	Corcho Hijos SA (later became "Corbasa"-qv)	*Spain*
Crichton-Vulcan	Wartsila Koncernen AB Crichton-Vulcan Oy (later became Wartsila AB-qv)	*Finland*
Dae Dong	Dae Dong Shipbuilding Co	*S Korea*
Dae Sun	Dae Sun Shipbuilding & Engineering Co Ltd	*S Korea*
Daewoo	Daewoo Shipbuilding & Heavy Machinery Ltd	*S Korea*
Dairen	Dairen Dockyard (later called Dalian Shipyard)	*China*
Dalian	Dalian Shipyard (formerly Dairen Dockyard)	*China*
Dannebrog	Dannebrog Vaerft A/S	*Denmark*
Davie SB	Davie Shipbuilding Ltd	*Canada*
Davie & Sons	G. T. Davie & Sons Ltd (no longer builders)	*Canada*
DCAN	Direction des Constructions et Armes Navales (formerly Arsenal de la Marine National Francaise)	*France*
"De Beer"	Scheepswerf "De Beer" NV	*Netherlands*
"De Biesbosch"	NV Scheepswerf en Machinefabriek "De Biesbosch" NV (later "De Biesbosch"-qv)	*Netherlands*
"De Biesbosch-Dordrecht"	Scheepswerf en Machinenfabriek "De Biesbosch-Dordrecht" BV	*Netherlands*
"De Dollard"	Scheepswerf "De Dollard" (no longer builders)	*Netherlands*
"De Gideon"	Scheepswerf "De Gideon" v/h J. Koster Hzn	*Netherlands*
De Haan & O	Scheepswerf De Haan & Oerlemans (later Verolme Scheepswerf Heusden-qv)	*Netherlands*
"De Hoop"	Scheepswerf "De Hoop" BV	*Netherlands*
"De Klop"	NV Scheepsbouwwerf en Machinefabriek "De Klop" (later IHC Van Rees De Klop)	*Netherlands*
"De Merwede"	BV Scheepswerf & Machinefabriek "De Merwede" v/h Van Vliet & Co	*Netherlands*
Denizcilik	Denizcilik Bankasi TAO	*Turkey*
Denny	William Denny & Bros Ltd (no longer builders)	*Scotland*
"De Noord"	Werf "De Noord" NV (later Giessen-De Noord-qv)	*Netherlands*
"De Schelde"	BV Koninklijke Mij Scheeps & Machinefabriek "De Schelde"	*Netherlands*
Deutsche S und M	Deutsche Schiff und Maschinebau AG Werk Seebeck (later AG "Weser")	*W Germany*
Deutsche Werft	Deutsche Werft Aktiengesellschaft (later Howaldts DW-qv)	*W Germany*
Deutsche Werft Reihers	Deutsche Werft AG Betrieb Reiherstiegwerft (later Howaldts DW-qv)	*W Germany*
"De Waal"	Scheepswerf "De Waal" BV	*Netherlands*
Dong Hae	Dong Hae Shipbuilding Co Ltd	*S Korea*
Dorman Long	Dorman Long Vanderbijl Corp (Dorbyl) Ltd	*S Africa*
Dorman Long SH	Dorman Long Swan Hunter (Pty) Ltd	*S Africa*
Doxford	William Doxford & Sons (Shipbuilders) Ltd (later Doxford & Sunderland-qv)	*England*
Doxford & S	Doxford & Sunderland Ltd (later Sunderland Shipbuilders-qv)	*England*
Drammen	Drammen Slip & Verksted	*Norway*
Drypool	Drypool Engineering & Dry Dock Co Ltd (later Cochrane Shipbuilders-qv)	*England*
Dubigeon	Soc Anon des Anciens Chantiers Dubigeon (later called Dubigeon-Normandie-qv)	*France*
Dubigeon-Normandie	Dubigeon-Normandie SA (see also Loire)	*France*
Duchesne & B	Ateliers de Duchesne & Bossiere SA (later part of Havre-qv)	*France*
Duijvendijk's	T. van Duijvendijk's Scheepswerf BV (no longer builders)	*Netherlands*
Dunkerque-Normandie	Division Constructions Navales de la Societe Metallurgique et Navale Dunkerque-Normandie	*France*
Dunston	Richard Dunston Ltd	*England*
Duro Felguera	Soc Metalurgica Duro Felguera	*Spain*
Earle's	Earle's Shipbuilding & Engineering Co Ltd (no longer builders)	*England*
Ebin/So	Estaleiros Ebin/So SA	*Brazil*
Echevarrrieta y Larrinaga	Echevarrieta y Larrinaga (now part of AESA-qv)	*Spain*
Eides	G. Eides Sonner A/S	*Norway*
E. J. Smit	E. J. Smit & Zoon's Scheepswerven	*Netherlands*
Ekensbergs	Ekensbergs Varv AB (no longer builders)	*Sweden*
Elbewerft	VEB Elbewerft (later Elbewerften-qv)	*E Germany*
Elbewerften	VEB Elbewerften Boizenburg/Rosslau	*E Germany*
"Elcano"	Empresa Nacional "Elcano", Astilleros de Sevilla (now part of AESA-qv)	*Spain*
Eleusis	Eleusis Shipyards SA	*Greece*
Elling	Elling Engineering Co Ltd	*Hong Kong*
Elsflether	Elsflether Werft AG	*W Germany*
Emaq	Emaq-Engenharia e Maquinas SA	*Brazil*
Emden	Nordseewerke Emden GmbH (no longer builders—now Thyssen-qv)	*W Germany*
Equitable	Equitable Shipyards Inc	*USA*
Eriksbergs	Eriksbergs Mekaniska Verkstads AB (no longer builders, now part of Svenska Varv)	*Sweden*
Erste Donau	Erste Donau Dampfschiffahrtsgesellschaft, Schiffswerft Korneuburg (now Korneuberg-qv)	*Austria*
Esercizio	Societa Cantieri Esercizio (no longer builders)	*Italy*
Euskalduna	Compania Euskalduna de Construction y Reparacion de Buques SA (now part of AESA-qv)	*Spain*
Evans Deakin	Evans Deakin Industries Ltd (no longer builders)	*Australia*
Fairfields	Fairfields (Glasgow) Ltd (no longer builders)	*Scotland*
Fairfield SB	Fairfield Shipbuilding & Engineering Co Ltd (later Fairfields (Glasgow) Ltd-qv)	*Scotland*
Falkenbergs	Falkenbergs Varv AB	*Sweden*
Far East-Levingston	Far East-Levingston Shipbuilding Ltd	*Singapore*
Federal SB & DD	Federal Shipbuilding & Dry Dock Co (no longer builders)	*USA*

Fellows & Co	Fellows & Co Ltd (no longer builders)	England
Felszegi	Cantiere Felszegi (later Alto Adriatico-qv)	Italy
Ferguson Bros	Ferguson Bros (Port Glasgow) Ltd (part of British Shipbuilders)	Scotland
Ferguson Indust	Ferguson Industries Ltd	Canada
Ferus Smit	BV Scheepswerf "Ferus Smit"	Netherlands
Finnboda	Finnboda Varf AB (later Gotaverken Finnboda)	Sweden
Flandre	Chantiers Navals de Flandre SA (no longer builders)	Belgium
Fleming & Ferguson	Fleming & Ferguson Ltd (no longer builders)	Scotland
Flender	Flender Werft Aktiengesellschaft (formerly Luebecker Flender-Werke)	W Germany
Flensburger	Flensburger Schiffsbau-Gesellschaft	W Germany
FMC	FMC Corp	USA
Fosen	Fosen Mek Verksteder	Norway
Foundation Mar	Foundation Maritime Ltd (no longer builders)	Canada
"Foxhol"	Scheepswerf "Foxhol" NV (v/h Gebr Muller) (no longer builders)	Netherlands
Framnaes	Framnaes Mek Verksted A/S	Norway
France-Gironde	At et Ch de Dunkerque et Bordeaux (France-Gironde) (later Ch de France)	France
Frederikshavn	Frederikshavn Vaerft A/S	Denmark
Fredriksstad	Fredriksstad Mek Verksted A/S	Norway
"Friesland"	Scheepswerf "Friesland" BV	Netherlands
F. Schichau	F. Schichau GmbH (no longer builders, later became part of Schichau-Unterweser)	Germany
Fujinagata	Fujinagata Zosensho KK (no longer builders, later became part of Mitsui)	Japan
Fukuoka	Fukuoka Zosen (subsidiary of Usuki Tekkosho)	Japan
Fukushima	Fukushima Zosen Tekko KK	Japan
Furness	Furness Shipbuilding Co Ltd (eventually became Smith's Dock Co-qv)	England
Galatz	Santierul Naval Galatz	Romania
Garden Reach	Garden Reach Shipbuilders & Engineers Ltd (formerly Garden Reach Workshops Private Ltd)	India
Gavle	A/B Gavle Varv (no longer builders)	Sweden
Gaye	Gaye Ltd	Turkey
G. Brown	George Brown & Co (Marine) Ltd	Scotland
Gdanska	Stocznia Gdanska im Lenina	Poland
G. Dimitrov	Georgi Dimitrov Shipyard	Bulgaria
Gdynska	Stocznia Gdynska im Komuny Paryskiej	Poland
Gebr Niestern	Scheepswerven Gebroeders Niestern BV (later "Appingedam"-qv)	Netherlands
Geibi	Geibi Zosen Kogyo	Japan
General Dynamics	General Dynamics Corp	USA
"Gheorghiu Dej"	"Gheorghiu Dej" Shipyard (later Angyalfold-qv)	Hungary
Giessen	C. van de Giessen & Zonen's Scheepswerven NV (later Giessen-De Noord)	Netherlands
Giessen-De Noord	van der Giessen-De Noord NV (formed by Giessen & "De Noord"-qv)	Netherlands
Gironde	Forges et Chantiers de la Gironde (later part of Ch de France-qv)	France
Giuliano	Cantiere Navale Giuliano (later Alto Adriatico-qv)	Italy
Gleue	Interessengemeinschaft Gleue Reederei EGS (formerly Renck-qv) (no longer builders)	W Germany
Globe	Globe Engineering Works Ltd (no longer builders)	S Africa
Glommens	A/S Glommens Mek Verksted (later part of Ankerlokken-qv)	Norway
Goole	Goole Shipbuilders Ltd (part of British Shipbuilders)	England
Gotav	Gotaverken Arendal AB (previously AB Gotaverken and other titles. Now incorporated in Svenska Varv)	Sweden
Gotav Solvesborg	Gotaverken Solvesborg AB (formerly Solvesborgs Varvs etc-qv) (no longer builders)	Sweden
Govan	Govan Shipbuilders Ltd (formerly Fairfields-qv) (part of British Shipbuilders)	Scotland
Grangemouth	Grangemouth Dockyard Co Ltd (part of British Shipbuilders)	Scotland
Gravdal	Gravdal Skipsbyggeri (no longer builders)	Norway
Graville	Societe Chantiers de Graville (no longer builders)	France
Gray	William Gray & Co Ltd (no longer builders)	England
Greenock D	Greenock Dockyard Co Ltd (incorporated with Scotts' SB-qv)	Scotland
Groot & VV	Scheepswerf en Machinefabriek De Groot & Van Vliet BV	Netherlands
Gruno	Scheepswerf Bodewes Gruno NV	Netherlands
Gulfport	Gulfport Shipbuilding Corp (subsidiary of Levingston-qv)	USA
Gusto	NV Werf Gusto (later IHC Gusto-qv)	Netherlands
Haarlemsche	Haarlemsche Scheepsbouw Maatschappij NV (no longer builders)	Netherlands
Hagelstein	Alfred Hagelstein Maschinenfabrik-Schiffswerft (no longer builders)	W Germany
Hakata Z	Hakata Zosen KK	Japan
Hakodate	Hakodate Dock Co Ltd	Japan
Halifax	Halifax Shipyards Ltd	Canada
Hall, Russell	Hall, Russell & Co Ltd (part of British Shipbuilders)	Scotland
Halter	Halter Marine Inc	USA
Hamilton	William Hamilton & Co Ltd (no longer builders)	Scotland
Hancocks	Hancocks Shipbuilding Co Ltd (no longer builders)	Wales
Hanseatische	Hanseatische Werft GmbH	W Germany
Hapag-Lloyd	Hapag-Lloyd Werft GmbH	W Germany
Harima	Harima Zosensho KK (later IHI-qv)	Japan
"Harlingen"	Scheepswerf en Reparatiebedrijf "Harlingen" BV	Netherlands
Harms	Norderwerf Ulrich Harms GmbH (later Norderwerft-qv)	W Germany
Harris & Sons	P. K. Harris & Sons Ltd (no longer builders—became Appledore-qv)	England
Hashihama	Hashihama Zosen KK	Japan
Hashimoto	Hashimoto Zosensho	Japan
Hatlo	Hatlo Verksted A/S (later Ulstein Hatlo-qv)	Norway

Haugesund	Haugesund M/V A/S	Norway
Havre	Societe Nouvelle de At et Ch du Havre (incorporates A. Normand & Duchesne & B-qv)	France
Hawthorn, L	Hawthorn, Leslie (Shipbuilders) Ltd (no longer builders—later Swan Hunter)	England
Hayashikane	Hayashikane Shipbuilding & Engineering Co Ltd (Hayashikane Zosen KK)	Japan
Hayes	R. S. Hayes (Pembroke Dock) Ltd (no longer builders)	England
Hegemann	Detlef Hegemann Rolandwerft GmbH	W Germany
Hellenic	Hellenic Shipyards Co	Greece
Helsingborgs	Helsingborgs Varfs Aktiebolag (no longer builders)	Sweden
Helsingor	Helsingor Vaerft A/S (2 previous titles)	Denmark
Higaki Z	Higaki Zosen KK	Japan
Highfield	Highfield Sea-Land Development Ltd	Hong Kong
Hill	Charles Hill & Sons Ltd (no longer builders)	England
Hindustan	Hindustan Shipyard Ltd	India
Hitachi	Hitachi Zosen (Hitachi Shipbuilding & Engineering Co Ltd)	Japan
Hitzler	J. G. Hitzler, Schiffswerft & Maschinenfabrik, Inhaber Franz Hitzler	W Germany
Hjorungavaag	Hjorungavaag Verksted A/S	Norway
"Holland"	BV Scheepswerf en Machinefabriek "Holland" (M. Calje) (no longer builders)	Netherlands
Hollming	Hollming Oy	Finland
Holst	Schiffswerft W. Holst (no longer builders)	W Germany
Honda	Honda Zosen KK	Japan
Hong Kong U	Hong Kong United Dockyards Ltd (merger of Hong Kong & Whampoa and Taikoo-qv) (no longer builders)	Hong Kong
Hong Kong & W	Hong Kong & Whampoa Dock Co Ltd (see Hong Kong United)	Hong Kong
Hong Leong	Hong Leong-Luerssen Shipyard	Malaysia
"Hoogezand" JB	Scheepswerf "Hoogezand" J. Bodewes (later Scheepswerf Hoogezand BV)	Netherlands
Horten	Horten Verft A/S	Norway
Howaldts	Howaldtswerke (later Howaldtswerke Hamburg AG, subsequently Howaldtswerke-Deutsche Werft-qv)	W Germany
Howaldts DW	Howaldtswerke-Deutsche Werft AG (incorporates Deutsche Werft, Howaldtswerke and Kieler Howaldtswerke)	W Germany
H. Peters	Schiffswerft Hugo Peters	W Germany
H. Robb	Henry Robb Ltd (later Robb Caledon-qv)	Scotland
Hudong	Hudong Shipyard (formerly Hu Tung-qv)	China
Huelva	Astilleros de Huelva	Spain
Hung Chi	Hung Chi Shipyard	China
Husumer	Husumer Schiffswerft	W Germany
Hu Tung	Hu Tung Shipyard (later Hudong-qv)	China
H & W	Harland & Wolff Ltd	N Ireland (also formerly Scotland)
Hyundai	Hyundai Heavy Industries (formerly Hyundai Shipbuilding & Heavy Industries Ltd)	S Korea
IHC Gusto	IHC Gusto Staalouw BV (see also Gusto)	Netherlands
IHC Holland	IHC Holland BV (parent of a group of companies)	Netherlands
IHC Smit	IHC Smit BV (previously L. Smit & Smit Kinderdijk-qv)	Netherlands
IHC Verschure	IHC Verschure BV (see Verschure) (no longer builders)	Netherlands
IHI	Ishikawajima Harima Heavy Industries (amalgamation of Ishikiwajima Jukogyo, Harima, Ishikiwajima Zosensho, Harima Zosensho and others. Associated yards in Brazil and Singapore (Jurong))	Japan
Iino	Iino Shipbuilding and Engineering Co (later Maizuru Jukogyo, now part of Hitachi-qv)	Japan
"Ijssel"	Bijker's Aannemingsbedrijf "Ijssel" Werf (no longer builders)	Netherlands
Ijsselwerf	NV Ijsselwerf (later Ysselwerf-qv)	Netherlands
Imabari	Imabari Zosen KK	Japan
Imai S	Imai Seisakusho	Japan
Imai Z	Imai Zosen KK	Japan
Imamura	Imamura Zosensho	Japan
Ingalls	Ingalls Iron Works Co (previously Ingalls SB-qv)	USA
Ingalls SB	Ingalls Shipbuilding Corp (now Litton Systems)	USA
Inglis	A. & J. Inglis Ltd (no longer builders)	Scotland
INMA	Industrie Navali Meccaniche Affini SpA, INMA	Italy
Ish do Brazil	Ishikawajima do Brazil Estaleiros SA ("Ishibras")	Brazil
Ishikiwajima J	Ishikawajima Jukogyo KK (now part of IHI)	Japan
Ishikiwajima S & C	Ishikawajima Ship & Chemical Plant Co Ltd	Japan
Israel Spyds	Israel Shipyards Ltd	Israel
Italcantieri	Italcantieri SpA (incorporates Ansaldo, Adriatico and Navalmeccanica-qv)	Italy
"Ivan Cetenic"	Brodogradiliste "Ivan Cetenic" (later "Inkobrod"—no longer builders)	Yugoslavia
Ivan Dimitrov	Ivan Dimitrov Shipyard	Bulgaria
Jadewerft	Jadewerft Wilhelmshaven GmbH	W Germany
Jan Smit	Werf Jan Smit Czn (later Verolme Scheepswerf-qv)	Netherlands
J. Brown	John Brown & Co (Clydebank) Ltd (no longer builder—became Upper Clyde-qv)	Scotland
Janson BV	Scheepswerf Janson BV	Netherlands
Jeffboat	Jeffboat Inc (formerly Jeffersonville Boat & Machine Co)	USA
Jiangnan	Jiangnan Dockyard & Engineering Works (previously spelt Kiangnan-qv)	China
J & K Smit	J & K Smit's Scheepswerven NV (later IHC Smit-qv)	Netherlands
J. L. Thompson	Joseph L. Thompson & Sons Ltd (later Doxford & Sunderland-qv)	England
Jones	J. A. Jones Construction Co (no longer builders)	USA

Jonker	Scheepswerf en Gashouderbouw v/h Jonker & Stans BV	Netherlands
"Jozo Lozovina-Mosor"	Brodogradiliste "Jozo Lozovina-Mosor"	Yugoslavia
J. S. White	J. Samuel White and Co Ltd (no longer builders)	England
Juliana	SA Juliana Constructora Gijonesa	Spain
Jurong Spyd	Jurong Shipyard Ltd (affiliated with IHI-qv)	Singapore
J. W. Cook	James W. Cook (Wivenhoe) Ltd	England
Kaarbos	Kaarbos Mek Verksted A/S	Norway
Kagoshima	Kagoshima Dock & Iron Works Co Ltd	Japan
Kaiser Co	Kaiser Co Inc (no longer builders)	USA
Kaldnes	Kaldnes Mek Verksted A/S	Norway
Kalmar	Kalmar Varv AB	Sweden
Kama	Kama Shipyard	USSR
Kanasashi	Kanasashi Zosensho (Kanasashi Shipbuilding Co Ltd)	Japan
Kanawa	Kanawa Dock Co Ltd	Japan
Kanda	Kanda Zosensho KK	Japan
Kanrei	Kanrei Zosen KK (Kanrei Shipbuilding Co Ltd)	Japan
Karachi	Karachi Shipyard & Engineering Works	Japan
Karlskrona	Karlskronavarvet AB (incorporated in Svenska Varv. See Orlogs)	Sweden
Karlstads	Karlstads Varv A/B	Sweden
Karmsund	Karmsund Verft & Mek Verksted A/S	Norway
Kasado	Kasado Dockyard Co Ltd	Japan
Kawasaki	Kawasaki Heavy Industries Ltd (previously Kawasaki Dockyard and Kawasaki Jukogyo-qv)	Japan
Kawasaki D	Kawasaki Dockyard Co Ltd (later Kawasaki HI-qv)	Japan
Kawasaki J.	Kawasaki Jukogyo KK (later Kawasaki HI-qv)	Japan
Kegoya	Kegoya Dock KK	Japan
Keppel Shipyard	Keppel Shipyard (Pte) Ltd	Singapore
Khabarovsk	Khabarovsk Shipyard "Osipovskiy Kirov"	USSR
Khalkis	Khalkis Shipyard SA	Greece
Kherson	Kherson Shipyard	USSR
Kiangnan	Kiangnan Dockyard & Engineering Works (later spelt Jiangnan-qv)	China
Kieler H	Kieler Howaldtswerke AG (later Howaldtswerke-Deutsche Werft-qv)	W Germany
Kishigami	Kishigami Zosen KK	Japan
Kishimoto	Kishimoto Zosen KK (formerly Setouchi-qv)	Japan
Kitanihon	Kitanihon Zosen KK	Japan
Kjobenhavns	Kjobenhavns Flydedok & Skibsvaerft (no longer builders)	Denmark
Kleven	M. Kleven M/V	Norway
Kochi Jukogyo	Kochi Jukogyo (Kaisei Zosen) KK (subsidiary of Kurushima-qv)	Japan
Kochiken	Kochiken Zosen KK (no longer builders)	Japan
Kockums	Kockums AB (incorporated in Svenska Varv)	Sweden
Koetter	Schiffswerft Gebrueder Koetter	W Germany
Korea SB	Korea Shipbuilding and Engineering Corp	S Korea
Korneuburg	Schiffswerft Korneuburg AG (incorporated in Osterreichische-qv. originally Erste Donau-qv)	Austria
Koyo	Koyo Dockyard Co Ltd	Japan
Kramer & Booy	Handel & Scheepsbouw Maatschappij Kramer & Booy BV (see Tille)	Netherlands
Krasnoyarsk	Krasnoyarsk Shipyard	USSR
"Krasnoye S"	"Krasnoye Sormovo" Shipyard	USSR
Kremer	D. W. Kremer Sohn GmbH & Co KG (no longer builders)	W Germany
Kristiansands	Kristiansands Mek Verksted A/S	Norway
Kroegerw	Kroegerwerft GmbH	W Germany
Krupp	Friedrich Krupp Germaniawerft AG (no longer builders)	Germany
Kure	Kure Zosensho KK (now part of IHI-qv)	Japan
Kurinoura	Kurinoura Dock KK	Japan
Kurushima	Kurushima Dockyard Co Ltd (see Kochi Jukogyo)	Japan
Kynossura	Kynossura Dockyard Co	Greece
Kyokuyo	Kyokuyo Zosen Tekko KK (Kyokuyo Shipbuilding & Iron Works Co Ltd)	Japan
La Ciotat	Chantiers Navals de la Ciotat	France
Laing	Sir James Laing & Sons Ltd (no longer builders, became part of Doxford & Sunderland)	England
Laiva	Oy Laivateollisuus AB (subsidiary of Valmet-qv)	Finland
Lake Washington	Lake Washington Shipyards (no longer builders)	USA
La Loire	Ateliers et Chantiers de La Loire (subsequently part of Dubigeon-Normandie-qv)	France
La Manche	Ateliers et Chantiers de la Manche	France
La Marina	Servicio Industrial de la Marina	Peru
Lamont	James Lamont & Co Ltd (no longer builders)	England
Langesunds	Langesunds Mek Verksted A/S	Norway
Langvik	Langvik Sarpsborg M/V (no longer builders)	Norway
La Pallice	Chantiers Navals de la Pallice (now part of La Rochelle-Pallice)	France
La Rochelle	Societe Nouvelle des Ateliers et Chantiers de la Rochelle-Pallice (amalgamation of La Rochelle and La Pallice yards)	France
Larvik	Larvik Slip & Verksted A/S (no longer builders)	Norway
La Seine	Ateliers et Chantiers de la Seine Maritime	France
L'Atlantique	Chantiers de L'Atlantique (formerly Saint Nazaire-qv) (a Division of Alsthom-Atlantique)	France
Leninskogo	Leninskogo Komsomola Shipyard	USSR
Levingston	Levingston Shipbuilding Co (see Gulfport)	USA
Lewis	John Lewis & Sons Ltd	Scotland

LF-W	Luebecker Flender-Werke AG (no longer builders—became Flender Werft-qv)	W Germany
Liaaen	A. M. Liaaen A/S	Norway
Liffey	Liffey Dockyard Ltd (no longer builders)	Irish Republic
Liguri	Nuovi Cantieri Liguri SpA (formerly Pietra Ligure-qv)	Italy
Lindenau	Paul Lindenau Schiffswerft	W Germany
Lindholmens	Lindholmens Varv AB (later Eriksbergs—no longer builders)	Sweden
Lisnave	Lisnave Estaleiros Navais de Lisboa SARL (formerly Navalis and Uniao-qv)	Portugal
Lithgows	Lithgows Ltd (no longer builders—later Scott Lithgow-qv)	Scotland
Litton	Litton Systems Inc—see Ingalls SB	USA
Lobnitz	Lobnitz & Co Ltd (later Simons-Lobnitz—no longer builders)	Scotland
Lockheed	Lockheed Shipbuilding & Construction Co (formerly Puget Sound Bridge & Dry Dock-qv)	USA
Lodose	Lodose Varv AB	Sweden
Loire	Ateliers et Chantiers de La Loire—see under La Loire	France
Loire-Normandie	Societe des Chantiers Reunis Loire-Normandie (the two yards in this group were split between Bretagne & Dubigeon-Normandie-qv)	France
Lorenzo	Enrique Lorenzo y Cia SA	Spain
"L. Orlando"	Cantieri Nav "Luigi Orlando"	Italy
"Losinj"	Brodogradiliste "Losinj"	Yugoslavia
Lothe	Brodrene Lothe A/S Flytedokken	Norway
L. Smit	L. Smit & Zoon NV (later IHC Smit-qv)	Netherlands
Luebecker F-W	same as LF-W-qv	W Germany
Luehring	Schiffswerft C. Luehring	W Germany
Luerssen	Fr Luerssen Werft	W Germany
Luzuriaga	Astilleros Luzuriaga SA	Spain
Maizuru	Maizuru Jukogyo KK (now part of Hitachi-qv)	Japan
Mallorca	Astilleros de Mallorca SA (previously Ast de Palma SA)	Spain
Malta DD	Malta Drydocks	Malta
Mandal	Mandal Slip M/V	Norway
Mangalia	Santierul Naval Mangalia	Romania
Manitowoc	Manitowoc Shipbuilding Inc	USA
Marine Indust	Marine Industries Ltd	Canada
Marinens	Marinens Hovedverft (now Horten Verft-qv)	Norway
Marinship	Marinship Corp (no longer builders)	USA
Marmara	Marmara Transport A/S	Turkey
Marstrands	Marstrandsverken FEAB	Sweden
Maryland SB & DD	Maryland Shipbuilding & Drydock Co	USA
Mathias-Thesen	VEB Mathias-Thesen-Werft	E Germany
Mathis	John H. Mathis Co (no longer builders)	USA
Maua	Estaleiro Maua (part of CCN-qv)	Brazil
Mazagon	Mazagon Dock Ltd	India
Mediterranee	Societe des Forges et Chantiers de la Mediterranee (later CNIM-qv)	France
Mediterraneo	Cantieri del Mediterraneo SpA (no longer builders)	Italy
Menzer	Schiffswerft Ernst Menzer	W Germany
Meyer	Jos L. Meyer	W Germany
Middle Docks	Middle Docks & Engineering Co (not shipbuilders)	England
Mie	Mie Zosen KK	Japan
Mihanovich	Cia Argentinos de Nav Mihanovich (no longer builders)	Argentina
Miho	Miho Zosensho KK	Japan
Minami	Minami-Nippon Zosen KK	Japan
Mitchison	T. Mitchison Ltd (no longer builders)	England
Mitsubishi HI	Mitsubishi Heavy Industries Ltd (amalgamation of Shin Mitsubishi HI (formerly Mitsubishi HI Reorganised), Mitsubishi Nippon HI and Mitsubishi Zosen). The abbreviation Mitsubishi HI also covers vessels built by Mitsubishi HI Reorganised	Japan
Mitsubishi J	Mitsubishi Jukogyo (no longer builders—now part of Mitsubishi HI)	Japan
Mitsubishi N	Mitsubishi Nippon Heavy Industries Ltd (no longer builders—now part of Mitsubishi HI)	Japan
Mitsubishi Z	Mitsubishi Zosen KK (formerly Nishi Nippon Jukogyo-qv) (no longer builders—now part of Mitsubishi HI)	Japan
Mitsui	Mitsui Engineering & Shipbuilding Co Ltd (formerly Mitsui Shipbuilding & Engineering) (see Fujinagata & Shikoku)	Japan
Miyoshi	Miyoshi Zosen KK	Japan
M. Jansen	Schiffswerft u Maschinenfabrik Martin Jansen	W Germany
Mjellum & K	Mjellum & Karlsen A/S	Norway
Molde	Molde Verft A/S	Norway
Mondego	Estaleiros Navais do Mondego SARL	Portugal
Morton	Morton Engineering & Dry Dock Co Ltd (no longer builders—later St Lawrence M & M-qv)	Canada
Mort's Dock	Mort's Dock & Engineering Co Ltd (no longer builders)	Australia
Moss R	Moss Rosenberg Verft A/S (incorporates Moss Vaerft and Rosenberg-qv)	Norway
Moss V	Moss Vaerft & Dokk A/S (no longer builders—now part of Moss Rosenberg)	Norway
Muggiano	Cantieri Navale Muggiano SpA (see Ansaldo and Riuniti)	Italy
Murakami	Murakami Hide Zosen KK	Japan
Murueta	Astilleros de Murueta SA	Spain
Musel	Maritima del Musel SA	Spain
Mutzelfeldt	Mutzelfeldtwerft GmbH	W Germany
Nagoya	Nagoya Zosen KK (now part of IHI)	Japan

Naikai	Naikai Shipbuilding & Engineering Co Ltd (an amalgamation of Setoda & Taguma-qv. An affiliate of Hitachi)	Japan
Naka Nippon	Naka Nippon Jukogyo KK (now part of Mitsubishi HI)	Japan
Nakamura	Nakamura Zosen Tekkosho KK	Japan
Nakskov	Nakskov Skibsvaerft A/S	Denmark
Namura	Namura Zosensho KK (Namura Shipbuilding Co Ltd)	Japan
Nantes	Chantiers de Nantes (Bretagne-Loire) (later Bretagne-qv)	France
Narasaki	Narasaki Zosen KK (Narasaki Shipbuilding Co)	Japan
National S & S	National Shipyards & Steel Corp	Philippines
National Steel	National Steel & Shipbuilding Co	USA
Navalis	Navalis Sociedade de Construcao e Reparacao Naval SARL (later Lisnave-qv)	Portugal
"Navalmeccanica"	Cantieri Navali "Navalmeccanica" SA (no longer builders—later Italcantieri-qv)	Italy
Navashinskiy	Navashinskiy Shipyard	USSR
Navire	Oy Navire AB (no longer builders)	Finland
Nederlandsche	Nederalandse Scheepsbouw Maatschappij BV (formerly Nederlandsche Dok en Scheepsbouw)	Netherlands
"Neptun"	VEB Schiffswerft "Neptun" Rostock (formerly Neptunwerft-qv)	E Germany
Neptunwerft	Neptunwerft Rostock GmbH (no longer builders—now "Neptun"-qv)	E Germany
Newport News	Newport News Shipbuilding & Dry Dock Co	USA
Newport SB	Newport Shipbuilding & Engineering Co Ltd (formerly Atlantic Shipbuilding Co-qv) (no longer builders)	Wales
New York SB	The New York Shipbuilding Corporation (no longer builders)	USA
Nichiro	Nichiro Zosen KK (Nichiro Shipbuilding Co Ltd)	Japan
Nieuwe Noord	Nieuwe Noord Nederlandse Scheepswerven BV (previously Noord Nederlandse-qv)	Netherlands
Niigata	Niigata Engineering Co Ltd	Japan
Nipponkai	Nipponkai Heavy Industries Co Ltd	Japan
Nishii	Nishii Dock Co Ltd (no longer builders)	Japan
Nishi Nippon J	Nishi Nippon Jukogyo KK (no longer builders—later Mitsubishi Z-qv)	Japan
Nishi Z	Nishi Zosen KK (Nishi Shipbuilding Co Ltd)	Japan
NKK	Nippon Kokan KK (Tohoku Shipbuilding is an affiliate)	Japan
Nichitsu	Nichitsu Industry KK	Japan
Nobiskrug	Schiffbau Werft Nobiskrug GmbH	W Germany
Noord	Noorde Nederlandse Scheepswerven NV (later Nieuwe Noord Nederlandse-qv)	Netherlands
Norderwerft	KG Norderwerft GmbH & Co (see also Harms. Originally Norderwerft Koser u Meyer)	W Germany
Nordfjord	Nordfjord Verft A/S (formerly Eid Verft)	Norway
Nordso	A/S Nordsovaerftet	Denmark
Norrkopings	Norrkopings Varv & Verksted A/B (later Broderna Ekeroths Metallkonstruktioner—no longer builders)	Sweden
Nosenko	Nosenko Shipyard	USSR
NSW Govt	NSW Government Engineering & Shipbuilding Undertaking, (State Dockyard)	Australia
Nya Solvesborgs	AB Nya Solvesborgs Varvs (previously Solvesborgs; subsequently Gotaverken Solvesborgs—no longer builders)	Sweden
Nya Varv	Nya Varvsaktiebolaget Oresund (later Oresundsvarvet-qv)	Sweden
Nylands	Nylands Verksted (no longer builders) (became part of Aker Group)	Norway
Nymo	A/S Nymo Mek Verksted	Norway
Nystads	Nystads Varv Ab/Uudenkaupungin Telakka Oy (later Rauma-Repola-qv)	Finland
Odense	Odense Staalskibsvaerft A/S	Denmark
Odero	Odero-Terni-Orlando Societa per Azioni, per la Costruzione di Navi, Macchine ed Artiglerie (no longer builders)	Italy
Oderwerke	Oderwerke Maschinenfabrik u Schiffsbauwerft AG (later Stettiner Oderwerke—no longer builders)	Germany
O & K	Orenstein & Koppel Aktiengesellschaft (previously Orenstein-Koppel & Luebecker Maschinenbau AG)	W Germany
Okayama	Okayama Zosen KK (no longer builders)	Japan
Okean	Okean Shipyard (previously Oktyabrskoye Shipyard)	USSR
Oltenitsa	Santierul Naval Oltenitsa	Romania
Omishima	Omishima Dock KK	Japan
Onomichi	Onomichi Zosen (Onomichi Dockyard Co Ltd) (affiliated with Hitachi)	Japan
Orens	Orens M/V (no longer builders)	Norway
Oresunds	Oresundsvarvet AB (later Gotaverken Oresundsvarvet—incorporated in Svenska Varv)	Sweden
Orlogs	Marinverkstaderna Orlogsvarvet (later Karlskronavarvet-qv)	Sweden
Orskovs	Orskovs Staalskibsvaerft I/S	Denmark
Osaka	Osaka Zosensho KK (Osaka Shipbuilding Co Ltd)	Japan
Oshima Dock	Oshima Dock KK	Japan
Oshima Z	Oshima Zosen	Japan
Oskarshamns	Oskarshamns Varv AB	Sweden
Osterreichische	Osterreichische Schiffswerften AG Linz-Korneuburg (see Korneuburg)	Austria
Ottensener	Ottensener Eisenwerk GmbH (no longer builders—later Schlieker-Werft-qv)	W Germany
Palma	Astilleros de Palma SA (later Mallorca-qv)	Spain
Pattje	Scheepswerf "Waterhuizen" NV J. Pattje (later BV Scheepswerf "Waterhuizen" J. Pattje)	Netherlands
Peene	VEB Peene-Werft	E Germany
Pellegrino	Cantieri Navali Pellegrino (later Esercizio-qv)	Italy

Pennsylvania	Pennsylvania Shipyards Inc (no longer builders—later part of Bethlehem Steel)	USA
Perriere	Chantiers et Ateliers de la Perriere	France
Peterson	Peterson Builders Inc	USA
Peter's Schpsbw	Peter's Scheepsbouw BV	Netherlands
Philip	Philip & Son Ltd (no longer builders)	England
Pickersgill	William Pickersgill & Sons Ltd (later Austin & Pickersgill—see under A & P)	England
Pietra Ligure	Cantieri Navali di Pietra Ligure (later Liguri-qv)	Italy
Pollock	James Pollock, Sons & Co Ltd (no longer builders)	England
Polnocna	Stocznia Polnocna im Bohaterow Westerplatte	Poland
Porsgrunds	A/S Porsgrunds M/V (later Porsgrunn-qv)	Norway
Porsgrunn	Porsgrunn Verft A/S (formerly Porsgrunds) (part of Trosvik Group)	Norway
Port Weller	Port Weller Dry Docks Ltd	Canada
Pot	NV Scheepsbouwerf Gebroeders Pot (no longer builders)	Netherlands
Provence	Societe Anonyme des Chantiers et Ateliers de Provence (no longer builders)	France
P. Smit	BV Machinefabriek en Scheepswerven van P. Smit, Jr	Netherlands
Puget Sound	Puget Sound Bridge & Drydock Co (later Lockheed-qv)	USA
Puget Sound ND	Puget Sound Naval Dockyard	USA
Pullman	Pullman Standard Car Manufacturing Co (no longer builders)	USA
Pusey & Jones	The Pusey & Jones Corp (no longer builders)	USA
Pusnaes	Pusnaes Mek Verksted A/S	Norway
Rauma-Repola	Rauma-Repola Oy (see Nystads & Reposaaren)	Finland
Readhead	John Readhead & Sons Ltd (no longer builders—became part of Swan Hunter-qv)	England
Redfern	Redfern Construction Co Ltd (no longer builders)	Canada
Renck	Komm Ges G Renck, Jr (no longer builders—later Gleue-qv)	W Germany
Reposaaren	Reposaaren Konepaja Oy (no longer builders—later part of Rauma-Repola)	Finland
Rhein Nordseew	Rheinstahl Nordseewerke GmbH (later Thyssen Nordseewerke-qv)	W Germany
Rhin	Societe des Chantiers et Ateliers du Rhin (no longer builders)	France
Richards	Richards (Shipbuilders) Ltd	England
Rickmers	Rickmers Werft	W Germany
Rinkai	Rinkai Kogyo KK	Japan
Riuniti	Cantieri Navali Riuniti SpA (formerly Cantieri Navali del Tirreno & Riuniti—see also under CD Tirreno)	Italy
Robb Caledon	Robb Caledon Shipbuilders Ltd (amalgamation of Henry Robb & Caledon) (part of British Shipbuilders)	Scotland
Rolandwerft	Rolandwerft GmbH (no longer builders)	W Germany
Rosenberg	Rosenberg Vaerft A/S (no longer builders—now Moss Rosenberg)	Norway
Rotterdamsche	Rotterdamsche Droogdok Mij BV	Netherlands
Royal Danish Dkyd	Royal Danish Dockyard	Denmark
Ruiz	T. Ruiz de Velasco SA (formerly Astilleros de T. Ruiz de Velasco)	Spain
SABARN	SA Brugeoise d'Arrimage et de Reparations de Navires (SABARN) (no longer builders)	Belgium
Saint John SB	Saint John Shipbuilding & Dry Dock Co Ltd	Canada
Saint Nazaire	Societe Anonyme des Chantiers et Ateliers de Saint Nazaire (Penhoet) (later L'Atlantique-qv)	France
Salamis	Salamis Shipyard Ltd	Greece
Samsung	Samsung Shipbuilding Co Ltd	S Korea
Sander	Scheepsbouw & Reparatiebedrijf Gebroeders Sander BV (no longer builders—now amalgamated with Gebr Niestern-qv)	Netherlands
Sandvikens	Wartsila-Koncernen Ab Sandvikens Skeppsdocka (now part of Wartsila-qv)	Finland
Sanoyasu	Sanoyasu Dockyard Co Ltd	Japan
Santander	Astilleros de Santander SA	Spain
Sarpsborg	Sarpsborg Mek Verksted A/S K/S	Norway
Sasebo	Sasebo Heavy Industries Co Ltd (SSK)	Japan
S & B	Abteilung Werft-und Dockbetrieb Schulte & Bruns (no longer builders)	W Germany
Scarr	Henry Scarr Ltd (later Dunston-qv)	England
Schichau	Same as F. Schichau-qv	W Germany
Schichau-U	Schichau-Unterweser Aktiengesellschaft (amalgamation of F. Schichau and Unterweser-qv)	W Germany
Schiedamsche	Schiedamsche Scheepswerf (no longer builders)	Netherlands
Schlichting	Schlichting Werft, Schlichting & Co	W Germany
Schlieker	Schlieker-Werft, Willy H. Schlieker KG (no longer builders, formerly Ottensener Eisenwerk-qv)	W Germany
Schloemer	Schiffswerft Gebroeder Schloemer	W Germany
Schuerenstedt	Gebrueder Schuerenstedt KG (later Berner Schiffswerft GmbH & Co)	W Germany
Scotstoun	Scotstoun Marine Ltd (part of British Shipbuilders) (no longer builders)	Scotland
Scott Lithgow	Scott Lithgow Ltd (subsidiaries are Lithgows and Scotts' SB-qv)	Scotland
Scott & Sons	Scott & Sons (Bowling) Ltd (part of British Shipbuilders) (no longer builders)	Scotland
Scotts' SB	Scotts' Shipbuilding & Engineering Co (later Scotts' Shipbuilding Co Ltd) (no longer builders—now part of Scott-Lithgow-qv)	Scotland
Seatrain	Seatrain Shipbuilding Corp (no longer builders)	USA
Setoda	Setoda Shipbuilding Co Ltd (Setoda Zosensho) (later Naikai-qv)	Japan
Setouchi	Setouchi Zosen KK (later Kishimoto-qv)	Japan
Seutelvens	Seutelvens Verksted (no longer builders)	Norway
Severney	Severney Shipbuilding Yard (later "Zhdanov"-qv)	USSR
Shikoku	Shikoku Dockyard Co Ltd (now affiliated with Mitsui)	Japan
Shimoda	Shimoda Dockyard Co Ltd	Japan
Shinhama	Shinhama Dockyard Co Ltd	Japan

Shin Naniwa	Shin Naniwa Dock Co Ltd (no longer builders)	*Japan*
Shin Yamamoto	Shin Yamamoto Zosen KK (formerly Yamamoto Zosen)	*Japan*
Shioyama	Shioyama Dockyard Co Ltd (no longer builders)	*Japan*
Shirahama	Shirahama Zosen KK	*Japan*
Short Bros	Short Bros Ltd (no longer builders)	*England*
Sieghold	Schiffswerft u Maschinenfabrik Max Sieghold	*W Germany*
Sietas	J. J. Sietas KG Schiffswerft GmbH & Co	*W Germany*
Simons	William Simons & Co Ltd (later Simons-Lobnitz-qv)	*Scotland*
Simons-Lobnitz	Simons-Lobnitz Ltd (no longer builders. An amalgamation of Lobnitz & Simons-qv)	*Scotland*
Singapore SB	Singapore Shipbuilding & Engineering Ltd	*Singapore*
Singapore Slip	Singapore Slipway & Engineering Co (Pte) Ltd	*Singapore*
Smith's D	Smith's Dock Co Ltd (part of British Shipbuilders)	*England*
Smit K	Smit Kinderdijk VOF (later IHC Smit-qv)	*Netherlands*
Solimano	Cantieri Navali Solimano	*Italy*
Solvesborgs	Solvesborgs Varvs AB (subsequently Gotav Solvesborgs-qv)	*Sweden*
Sonderborg	Sonderborg Skibsvaerft A/S (no longer builders)	*Denmark*
Sorviks	Sorviksvarvet AB (later Udevallavarvet-qv)	*Sweden*
Southeastern	Southeastern Shipbuilding Corp (no longer builders)	*USA*
Soviknes	Soviknes Verft A/S	*Norway*
"Split"	Brodogradiliste i Tvornica Dizel Motora "Split" (later Brodogradiliste "Split")	*Yugoslavia*
Stabilimenti	Stabilimenti Navali SpA (formerly Taranto-qv)	*Italy*
Stami	Scheepsbouw Stami BV	*Netherlands*
Stavanger S & D	Stavanger Stob & Dok (no longer builders)	*Norway*
Steinwerder	Steinwerder Industrie AG (later B + V-qv)	*W Germany*
Stephani	Stephani Werft (no longer builders—later Adler-qv)	*W Germany*
Stephen	Alexander Stephen & Sons Ltd (no longer builders—became part of Upper Clyde Shipbuilders-qv)	*Scotland*
Sterkoder	Sterkoder Mek Verksted A/S	*Norway*
Sterkrade	Gutehoffnungshuette Sterkrade (later Maschinenfabrik Augsburg-Nurnburg)	*W Germany*
St Johns River	St Johns River Shipbuilding Co (no longer builders)	*USA*
St Lawrence M & M	St Lawrence Metal & Marine Works Inc (no longer builders)	*Canada*
Stord	Stord Verft A/S (part of Aker Group)	*Norway*
Storviks	Storviks Mek Verksted A/S	*Norway*
St Pieter	Scheepswerven St Pieter NV (Chantier Naval St Pieter)	*Belgium*
Straits SS	Straits Steamship Co Ltd (no longer builders)	*Malaysia*
Stralsund	VEB Volkswerft Stralsund	*E Germany*
Stroobos	Scheepswerf & Machinefabriek Barkmeijer Stroobos BV (formerly Scheepswerf & Machinefabriek Barkmeijer Fa Tj)	*Netherlands*
Stuelcken	(or Stulcken) H. C. Stuelcken Sohn (no longer builders—now incorporated in Blohm + Voss—see under B + V)	*W Germany*
Suerken	Masch Suerken Stahlbau	*W Germany*
Sumitomo	Sumitomo Heavy Industries Ltd (amalgamation of Sumitomo Mach Co & Uraga HI-qv) (affiliated companies: Nipponkai-qv; Oshima-qv and Malaysia Shipyd & Eng)	*Japan*
Sun SB	Sun Ship Inc Dry Dock Co (formerly Sun Shipbuilding & Dry Dock Co)	*USA*
Sunderland	Sunderland Shipbuilders Ltd (part of British Shipbuilders) (previously Doxford & Sunderland-qv)	*England*
Suurmeyer	Scheepswerf Gebr Suurmeyer BV (no longer builders—previously "Vooruitgang"-qv)	*Netherlands*
Svendborg	Svendborg Skibsvaerft A/S (formerly A/S Svendborg Skibsvaerft og Maskinbyggeri)	*Denmark*
Swan Hunter	Swan Hunter Shipbuilders Ltd (part of British Shipbuilders) (see Swan Hunter & T, Swan Hunter & WR, Readhead, Hawthorn, L and Vickers-Armstrongs etc)	*England*
Swan Hunter & T	Swan Hunter & Tyne Shipbuilders Ltd (formerly Hawthorn, Lesley now part of Swan Hunter)	*England*
Swan Hunter & WR	Swan Hunter & Wigham Richardson Ltd (now part of Swan Hunter)	*England*
Szczecinska	Stocznia Szczecinska im A. Warkskiego	*Poland*
Taguma	Taguma Zosen KK (now amalgamated with Setoda to form Naikai-qv)	*Japan*
Taihei	Taihei Kogyo KK	*Japan*
Taikoo	The Taikoo Dockyard & Engineering Co of Hong Kong Ltd (no longer builders—see under Hong Kong U)	*Hong Kong*
Taiwan SB	Taiwan Shipbuilding Corp (no longer builders—formerly Ingalls-Taiwan SB & DD Co, later part of China SB-qv)	*Taiwan*
Taiyo	Taiyo Zosen KK (Taiyo Shipbuilding Co) (no longer builders—taken over by Hayashikane-qv)	*Japan*
Tampa	Tampa Shipbuilding & Engineering Co (no longer builders)	*USA*
Tangen	Tangen Verft A/S (part of Aker Group)	*Norway*
Taranto	Cantieri Navali di Taranto (later Stabilimenti-qv)	*Italy*
Taskizak	Taskizak Naval Shipyard	*Turkey*
Teraoka	Teraoka Zosensho	*Japan*
Terneuzensche	Terneuzensche Scheepsbouw Maatschappij BV (no longer builders)	*Netherlands*
Thornycroft	John I. Thornycroft & Co Ltd (later Vosper Thornycroft Ltd)	*England*
Thyssen	Thyssen Nordseewerke GmbH (see under Emden & Rhein Nordseew)	*W Germany*
Tille	Tille Scheepsbouw BV (formerly Kramer & Booy-qv)	*Netherlands*
Tirreno	Cantieri Navali del Tirreno e Riuniti (later Riuniti-qv)	*Italy*
"Titovo"	Brodogradiliste "Titovo"	*Yugoslavia*

Todd	Todd Shipyards Corp (various titles)	USA
Todd-Bath	Todd-Bath Iron Shipbuilding Co (later New England SB Corp—no longer builders)	USA
Tohoku	Tohoku Shipbuilding Co Ltd (affiliated to NKK-qv)	Japan
Tokushima ZS	Tokushima Zosen Sangyo	Japan
Ton	Scheepswerf Ton Bodewes BV	Netherlands
Towa	Towa Zosen KK (Towa Shipbuilding Co Ltd)	Japan
Travewerft	Travewerft GmbH (later R. Harmstorf Wasserbau u Travewerft GmbH—no longer builders)	W Germany
Tronder	Tronderverftet A/S	Norway
Trondhjems	Trondhjems Mek Versted A/S (part of Aker Group)	Norway
Trosvik	Trosvik Verksted A/S (Trosvik Group)	Norway
Tsuneishi	Tsuneishi Zosensho	Japan
Turnu-Severin	Santierul Naval Turnu-Severin	Romania
Ube Dock	Ube Dock	Japan
Uddevalla	Uddevallavarvet AB (part of Svenska Varv) (formerly Sorviks-qv)	Sweden
Ujina	Ujina Zosensho KK (no longer builders—affiliated to Kanawa & Hitachi)	Japan
"Uljanik"	Brodogradiliste "Uljanik" (formerly Brodogradiliste i Tvornica Dizel Motora "Uljanik")	Yugoslavia
Ulstein	Ulstein Mek Verksted A/S (see Ulstein H)	Norway
Ulstein H	Ulstein Hatlo A/S (amalgamation of Hatlo (qv) and Ulstein (qv))	Norway
UN de Levante	Union Naval de Levante SA	Spain
Uniao	Companhia Uniao Fabril (later Lisnave-qv)	Portugal
United Spyds	United Shipyards Ltd (no longer builders)	Canada
United SY	United Shipping Yard Co SA	Greece
Unterweser	Schiffbau-Gesellschaft Unterweser AG (later Schichau-Unterweser-qv)	W Germany
Upper Clyde	Upper Clyde Shipbuilders Ltd (consortium of Fairfields, Connell, Stephen and J. Brown-qv. Most of the yards became Govan Shipbuilders-qv)	Scotland
Uraga Dock	Uraga Dock Co Ltd (later Uraga HI-qv)	Japan
Uraga HI	Uraga Heavy Industries Ltd (formerly Uraga Dock-qv. Later Sumitomo-qv)	Japan
US Naval SY	US Naval Shipyards (United States Navy Yards) (The New York yard became Seatrain-qv)	USA
Usuki	Usuki Tekkosho (Usuki Iron Works Ltd) (affiliated to IHI. See also Fukuoka)	Japan
Vaagen	Vaagen Verft A/S (formerly Grotvaagens Verft)	Norway
Valmet	Valmet Oy (see also Laiva)	Finland
Vancouver	Vancouver Shipyards Co Ltd	Canada
van der Werf	Scheepswerf Gebroeders van der Werf BV (later Scheepswerf Ravenstein)	Netherlands
Van Diepen	BV Scheepswerven Gebr van Diepen	Netherlands
Van Lent	Jacht-en Scheepswerf C. van Lent & Zonen BV	Netherlands
Verolme Cork	Verolme Cork Dockyard Ltd (closed in November 1984)	Ireland
Verolme Dok	Verolme Dok-en Scheepsbouw Mij BV (incorporated in Verolme United-qv)	Netherlands
Verolme ER do Brazil	Verolme Estaleiros do Brazil SA	Brazil
Verolme Scheeps	Verolme Scheepswerf Alblasserdam BV (no longer builders—now Giessen-De Noord. Originally Jan Smit-qv)	Netherlands
Verolme SH	Verolme Scheepswerf Heusden BV (incorporated in Verolme United. See De Haan & O)	Netherlands
Verolme U	Verolme United Shipyards (see Verolme Cork, Verolme Dok, Verolme ER do Brazil and Verolme SH)	Netherlands
Verschure	Verschure & Co's Scheepswerf en Machinefabriek NV (later IHC Verschure—no longer builders)	Netherlands
Viana	Estaleiros Navais de Viana do Castelo SARL	Portugal
Vickers-Armstrongs	Vickers-Armstrongs (Shipbuilders) Ltd (previously Vickers-Armstrong Ltd. Now Vickers SB-qv)	England
Vickers Ltd	Vickers Ltd (now Vickers SB-qv)	England
Vickers SB	Vickers Shipbuilding & Engineering Ltd (part of British Shipbuilders) (see Vickers-Armstrongs and Vickers Ltd)	England
Victoria Mach	Victoria Machinery Depot Co Ltd (no longer builders)	Canada
"Visentini"	Cantiere Navale "Visentini" SAS de Visentini Francesco & C	Italy
Volgograd	Volgograd Shipyard	USSR
"Volharding"	Bodewes Scheepswerf "Volharding" BV	Netherlands
Volodarskiy	Volodarskiy Shipyard	USSR
"Vooruitgang"	NV Scheepswerf "Vooruitgang" (Gebr Suurmeyer) (later Suurmeyer-qv)	Netherlands
"Voorwarts"	Scheepswerf "Voorwarts" BV	Netherlands
Vuyk	A. Vuyk & Zonen's Scheepswerven BV (no longer builders)	Netherlands
Vyborg	Vyborg Shipyard	USSR
Wakamatsu	Wakamatsu Zosensho KK	Japan
Walkers Ltd	Walkers Ltd (no longer builders)	Australia
Warnow	VEB Warnowwerft	E Germany
Wartsila	Oy Wartsila AB (and Oy Wartsila AB Helsinki Shipyard. Previously Crichton-Vulcan and Sandvikens-qv)	Finland
Watanabe	Watanabe Zosen KK	Japan
Werftunion	Werftunion GmbH	W Germany
"Westerbroek"	NV Scheepswerf "Westerbroek"	Netherlands
Whyalla	Whyalla Shipbuilding & Engineering Works (no longer builders—previously Broken Hill-qv)	Australia
Wiley	Wiley Manufacturing Co	USA
Willamette	Willamette Iron & Steel Co (no longer builders)	USA
Wilton-Fije	Dok-en Werf Mij Wilton-Fijenoord BV	Netherlands
Wisla	Stocznia Wisla	Poland

Worms	Ateliers et Chantiers de la Seine Maritime (Worms & Cie) (later La Seine-qv)	France
Yamanaka	Yamanaka Zosen	Japan
Yamanishi	Yamanishi Zosen KK (Yamanishi Shipbuilding & Iron Works Inc)	Japan
"Yantar"	"Yantar" Shipyard (formerly Kaliningrad State Shipyard)	USSR
Yarrows & Co	Yarrow & Co Ltd (now Yarrow (Shipbuilders) Ltd) (part of British Shipbuilders)	Scotland
Yarrows Ltd	Yarrows Ltd (later Burrard Yarrows-qv)	Canada
Yorkshire DD	Yorkshire Dry Dock Co Ltd	England
Ysselwerf	Ysselwerf BV (previously Ijsselwerf-qv)	Netherlands
Zaanlandsche	Zaanlandsche Scheepsbouw Maatschappij NV (no longer builders)	Netherlands
Zaliv	Zaliv Shipyard (also known as Kerch Shipyard)	USSR
Zelenodolskiy	Zelenodolskiy Shipyard	USSR
"Zhdanov"	"A. Zhdanov" Shipbuilding Yard (previously Severney-qv)	USSR
"3 Maj"	Brodogradiliste "3 Maj" (formerly Poduzece "3 Maj")	Yugoslavia
"61 Kommunar"	"61 Kommunar" Shipbuilding Yard	USSR

Abbreviations of Engine Builders/Designers

Some of these companies are out of existence now or amalgamated with other companies.

ABO	Associated British Oil Engines	England
Adriatico	Canteiri Riuniti dell'Adriatico (see GMT)	Italy
AEG	Allgemeine Elektricitats-Ges (AEG) (also AEG-Telefunken)	W Germany
AEI	Associated Electric Industries Ltd	England
AG "Weser"	Aktien-Gesellschaft "Weser"	W Germany
Ailsa	Ailsa Shipbuilding Co Ltd	Scotland
Aitchison, Blair	Aitchison, Blair Ltd	Scotland
Ajax Unaflow	Ajax Unaflow Co (see also Unaflow)	USA
Akasaka	Akasaka Tekkosho KK (Akasaka Diesels Ltd)	Japan
Alco	Alco Power Inc	USA
Allgemeine	see AEG	
Alpha	same as Alpha-Diesel qv	
Alpha-Diesel	Alpha-Diesel A/S	Denmark
Alsthom	Alsthom-Atlantique (shipbuilding division is Ch de l'Atlantique)	France
Amos & Smith	Amos & Smith Ltd	England
Ansaldo	Ansaldo SpA (see GMT)	Italy
APE Allen	A. P. E. Allen Ltd (previously W. H. Allen-qv)	England
Appingedammer Brons	see under Brons	
Associated Electric	see under AEI	
Atlas-Diesel	Atlas-Diesel	Sweden
Atlas-MaK	Atlas-MaK Maschinenbau GmbH (see also MaK)	W Germany
Australian Commonwealth	Australian Commonwealth Shipping Board	Australia
Baltic	Baltic Shipbuilding & Engineering Works	USSR
Baudouin	Soc des Moteurs Baudouin	France
Belliss & Morcom	Belliss & Morcom Ltd	England
Bergens	Bergens Mekaniske Verksteder A/S	Norway
Bergius Kelvin	Bergius Kelvin Co Ltd (English Electric group)	Scotland
Bethlehem	Bethlehem Shipbuilding Corp Ltd	USA
Bethlehem Steel	Bethlehem Steel Corp	USA
Blackstone	Blackstone & Co Ltd (see Lister Blackstone and Mirrlees Blackstone)	England
Bofors	A/B Bofors Nohab	Sweden
"Bolnes"	NV Machinefabriek "Bolnes"	Netherlands
Borsig	Borsig GmbH	W Germany
B. Polar	see British Polar	
Bremer V	Schiffbau und Maschinenfabrik Bremer Vulkan	W Germany
Bretagne	Ateliers et Chantiers de Bretagne	France
British Auxiliaries	British Auxiliaries Ltd	Scotland
British Polar	British Polar Engines Ltd (part of Associated British Engineering)	Scotland
Brons	Brons Industrie NV (formerly Appingedammer Brons)	Netherlands
Brown, Boveri	Brown, Boveri & Co Ltd	Switzerland
BTH	B.T.H. Co Ltd	England
B + V	Blohm + Voss AG	W Germany
B & W	Burmeister & Wain's Maskin-og Skibsbyggeri (later B & W Diesel A/S—a subsidiary of MAN-qv)	Denmark
Cammell Laird	Cammell Laird & Co (Shipbuilders & Engineers) Ltd	England
Canadian Allis-Chalmers	Canadian Allis-Chalmers Ltd	Canada
Canadian Iron Foundries	Canada Iron Foundries Ltd	Canada
Canadian GEC	Canadian General Electric Co Ltd (see GEC)	Canada
Canadian Locomotive	Canadian Locomotive Co Ltd	Canada
Caterpillar	Caterpillar Tractor Co	USA
CEM-Parsons	CEM-Parsons (Compagnie Electro-Mécanique)	France
Central Marine	Central Marine Engineering Works	England
Christiansen & Meyer	Christiansen & Meyer	W Germany
CKD Praha	CKD Praha (see Skoda)	Czechoslovakia
Cockerill-Ougree	Société Anonyme Cockerill-Ougree	Belgium
Collingwood	Collingwood Shipyards	Canada
Cooper-Bessemer	Cooper-Bessemer Corp	USA
Crepelle	Crepelle et Compagnie (later Moteurs Crepelle)	France

Creusot	Société des Forges et Atelier du Creusot (later Creusot-Loire)	France
Crichton-Vulcan	Wartsila Concernen A/B Crichton-Vulcan	Finland
Crossley	Crossley Bros Ltd (later Crossley-Premier Engines Ltd)	England
Daihatsu	Daihatsu Diesel Manufacturing Co Ltd	Japan
Darmstadt	Motorenfabrik Darmstadt GmbH (Modag)	W Germany
Davey, Paxman	Davey, Paxman & Co Ltd (later Paxman Diesel-qv)	England
"De Industrie"	D. & J. Boot "De Industrie"	Netherlands
De Laval	De Laval Turbine Inc (later Transamerica De Laval Inc)	USA
Deltic	Deltic diesels built by D. Napier & Son Ltd (subsidiary of English Electric)	England
Denny	William Denny & Bros Ltd	Scotland
"De Schelde"	NV Koninklijke Maatschappij "De Schelde"	Netherlands
Deutz	Deutz design diesels built under licence (see KHD)	
Dieselmotorenwerk Rostock	VEB Dieselmotorenwerk Rostock	E Germany
Dominion	Dominion Bridge Co Ltd	Canada
Doxford	Doxford Engines Ltd	England
Dresdner	Dresdner Masch u Schiffs	Germany
Duncan Stewart	Duncan Stewart & Co Ltd	Scotland
Duvant	Moteurs Duvant	France
Earle's	Earle's Shipbuilding & Engineering Co	England
English Electric	English Electric Co Ltd (later GEC)	England
Enterprise Eng	Enterprise Engine & Machinery Co	USA
Espanola	Soc Espanola de Construccion Naval	Spain
Euskalduna	Cia Euskalduna de Construccion y Reparacion de Buques	Spain
Fairbanks, Morse	Fairbanks, Morse & Co (a division of Colt Industries). Also covers Fairbanks Morse (Canada) Ltd	USA
Fairfield	Fairfield Shipbuilding & Engineering Co Ltd	Scotland
Fairfield-Rowan	see under Fairfield; see under Rowan	
Fiat	Soc per Azioni "Fiat" Sezione Grandi Motori (now GMT-qv)	Italy
Fiat-Borsig	see Borsig	
Fleming & Ferguson	Fleming & Ferguson Ltd	Scotland
France	Ateliers et Chantiers de France (later Dunkerque-Normandie)	France
Franco Tosi	Franco Tosi Industriale SpA	Italy
Frederiksstad	Frederiksstad Mek Verksted A/S	Norway
Frichs	Aktieselskabet Frichs	Denmark
Friedrichshafen	Zahnradfabrik Friedrichshafen AG (later MTU-qv)	W Germany
Ganz	Ganz Hungarian Shipyards & Crane Works (later "Gheorghiu Dej" Shipyard)	Hungary
G. Clark	G. Clark (1938) Ltd (later George Clark & NEM Ltd—part of Richardsons, Westgarth group)	England
GEC	The General Electric Co Ltd (also GEC Diesels, incorporating many diesel engine manufacturing companies)	England
General Metals	General Metals Corp	USA
General Motors	General Motors Corp	USA
GMT	Grandi Motori Trieste SpA (amalgamation of Ansaldo, Fiat and Cantieri Riuniti dell' Adriatico)	Italy
Goerlitzer	Goerlitzer Maschinenbau	E Germany
Gotaverken	AB Gotaverken (later Gotaverken Angteknik AB and Gotaverken Motor AB)	Sweden
Halberstadt	VEB Maschinenbau Halberstadt	E Germany
Hanshin	Hanshin Nainenki Kogyo (Hanshin Diesel Works Ltd)	Japan
Harima	Harima Zosensho KK (later IHI-qv)	Japan
Hawthorn, L	Hawthorn, Leslie (Engineers) Ltd (later Clark Hawthorn Ltd)	England
Hayashikane	Hayashikane Zosen KK	Japan
Hedemora	AB Hedemora Verstader	Sweden
Hendy	Joshua Hendy Iron Works	USA
Henschel	Henschel-Maschb	W Germany
Hitachi	Hitachi Shipbuilding & Engineering Co Ltd (Hitachi Zosen)	Japan
Holeby	Holeby Dieselmotor Fabrik A/S (later B & W Holeby Diesel A/S)	Denmark
Howaldts	Howaldtswerke Hamburg AG (see Howaldts DW)	W Germany
Howaldts DW	Howaldtswerke-Deutsche Werft AG (previously Howaldtswerke Hamburg-qv)	W Germany
Hudong	Hudong Shipyard	China
Humboldt-Deutz	Humboldt-Deutzmotoren (later KHD-qv)	Germany
H & W	Harland & Wolff Ltd	N Ireland & Scotland
IHI	Ishikawajima-Harima Heavy Industries Co Ltd (see also Harima)	Japan
Inglis	The John Inglis Co Ltd	Canada
Ishikawajima J	Ishikawajima Jukogyo KK (later IHI-qv)	Japan
Ito Tekkosho	Ito Tekkosho (Ito Engineering Co Ltd)	Japan
J. Brown	John Brown & Co (Clydebank) Ltd (now John Brown Engineering (Clydebank) Ltd)	Scotland
Jonkopings	Jonkopings Motorfabriek Aktiebolaget. Also Jonkopings Mekaniska Verkstads AB	Sweden
J. S. White	J. Samuel White & Co Ltd	England
Kaldnes	Kaldnes Mek Verksted	Norway
Kawasaki	Kawasaki Heavy Industries Ltd	Japan
KHD	Klockner-Humboldt-Deutz AG (see Deutz and Humboldt-Deutz)	W Germany
Kieler H	Kieler Howaldtswerke AG (later Howaldtswerke-Deutsche Werft-qv)	W Germany
Kincaid	John G. Kincaid & Co Ltd	Scotland
Kirov	Kirov Works	USSR
Kjobenhavns	Kjobenhavns Flydedok & Skibsvaerft	Denmark

Kobe	Kobe Hatsudoki KK (later Kobe Diesel Co Ltd)	*Japan*
Kockums	Kockums Mekaniska Verkstads AB (now Kockums AB)	*Sweden*
Krupp	Fried Krupp Dieselmotoren GmbH. Formerly Fried Krupp Germaniawerft AG (see Krupp-MaK)	*W Germany*
Krupp-MaK	Krupp-MaK Maschinenbau GmbH (formerly MaK-qv)	*W Germany*
Kvaerner	Kvaerner Brug A/S	*Norway*
La Loire	Ateliers et Chantiers de la Loire	*France*
Lang Gepgyar	Lang Gepgyar	*Hungary*
Langesunds	Langesunds Mek Verksted A/S	*Norway*
Larvik	Larvik Slip & Verksted A/S	*Norway*
Lewis	John Lewis & Sons Ltd	*Scotland*
LF-W	Luebecker Flender-Werke	*W Germany*
Liebknecht	VEB Schwermaschinenbau "Karl Liebknecht"	*E Germany*
Lindholmens	A/B Lindholmens Varv	*Sweden*
Lister Blackstone	Lister Blackstone Marine Ltd (later R. A. Lister & Co Ltd. See also Blackstone and Mirrlees Blackstone)	*England*
Lister Blackstone Mirrlees	Lister Blackstone Mirrlees Marine Ltd	*England*
Lobnitz	Lobnitz & Co Ltd (later Simons-Lobnitz Ltd)	*Scotland*
L. Smit	L. Smit & Zoon NV (later IHC Smit)	*Netherlands*
MaK	Maschinenbau Kiel GmbH (formerly Atlas-MaK-qv; now Krupp-MaK-qv)	*W Germany*
Makita	Makita Tekkosho KK	*Japan*
MAN	Maschinenfabrik Augsburg-Nurnberg AG (also own B & W Diesel A/S-qv)	*W Germany*
MAN-Sulzer	see MAN and Sulzer	
Maybach	Maybach Motorenbau GmbH	*W Germany*
Mediterranee	Societe Anonyme des Forges et Chantiers de la Mediterranee	*France*
Mirrlees	Mirrlees National Ltd (now Mirrlees Blackstone-qv)	*England*
Mirrlees, Bickerton & Day	Mirrlees, Bickerton & Day Ltd (later Mirrlees National Ltd, now Mirrlees Blackstone-qv)	*England*
Mirrlees Blackstone	Mirrlees Blackstone Ltd (formerly Mirrlees National-qv)	*England*
Mitsubishi	Mitsubishi Heavy Industries Ltd	*Japan*
Mitsui	Mitsui Engineering & Shipbuilding Co Ltd (B & W design engines)	*Japan*
Moss	Moss Vaerft & Dokk A/S (later Moss Rosenberg Verft)	*Norway*
MTM	La Maquinista Terrestre y Maritima SA	*Spain*
MTU	Motoren-und Turbinen-Union Friedrichshafen GmbH	*W Germany*
MWM	Motorenwerke Mannheim AG	*W Germany*
Nagasaki	Nagasaki Shipbuilding & Engineering Works (Mitsubishi)	*Japan*
National Gas & O	National Gas & Oil Engine Co Ltd	*England*
Nederland	Schps Inst Nederland (later Verolme Machinefabriek Ijsselmonde NV (Verolme United group))	*Netherlands*
Nederlandsche	Nederlandsche Dok en Scheepsbouw Mij vof	*Netherlands*
N.E. Marine	North-Eastern Marine Engineering Co Ltd (see G. Clark)	*England*
Newbury	Newbury Diesel Co Ltd	*England*
Newport News	Newport News Shipbuilding & Dry Dock Co	*USA*
N & H	see under Nydqvist & Holm	*Sweden*
Niigata	Niigata Engineering Co Ltd	*Japan*
Nippon Hatsudoki	Nippon Hatsudoki Co Ltd	*Japan*
Nishi Nippon J	Nishi Nippon Jukogyo KK (later Mitsubishi-qv)	*Japan*
NKK	Nippon Kokan KK (build Pielstick design diesels)	*Japan*
Nordberg	Nordberg Manufacturing Co	*USA*
Normo	Normo Gruppen A/S	*Norway*
Nydqvist & Holm	Nydqvist & Holm Aktiebolag	*Sweden*
Osaka Kiko	Osaka Kiko	*Japan*
Oskarshamns	A/B Oskarshamns Varv	*Sweden*
Ottensener	Ottensener Eisenwerft GmbH (later Schlieker-Werft-qv)	*W Germany*
Pametrada	Parsons & Marine Engineering Turbine Research & Development Association (warship engines)	*Scotland*
Parsons	Parsons Marine Steam Turbine Co	*Scotland*
Paxman	Paxman Diesels Ltd (previously Davey, Paxman-qv)	*England*
Pielstick	SEMT Pielstick (Alsthom-Atlantique group)	*France*
Praha	same as CKD Praha-qv	
Pratt & Whitney	Pratt & Whitney	*USA*
Prescott	Prescott Co	*USA*
Rankin & Blackmore	Rankin & Blackmore Ltd	*Scotland*
Readhead	John Readhead & Sons Ltd	*England*
Rheinmetall-Borsig	Rheinmetall-Borsig	*Germany*
Richardsons, Westgarth	Richardsons, Westgarth & Co Ltd	*England*
Riuniti	Cantieri Navali Riuniti	*Italy*
Rotterdamsche	Rotterdamsche Droogdok Mij NV	*Netherlands*
Rowan	David Rowan & Co Ltd	*Scotland*
Russkiy	Russkiy-Diesel Works	*USSR*
Ruston	Ruston Diesels Ltd (previously Ruston & Hornsby-qv)	*England*
Ruston & Hornsby	Ruston & Hornsby Ltd (English Electric Group—later Ruston Diesels-qv)	*England*
Ruston Paxman	Ruston Paxman Diesels Ltd	*England*
SACM	Société Alsacienne de Constructions Mécaniques	*France*
Scania	A/B Scania Vabis (later Saab-Scania)	*Sweden*
Schlieker	Schlieker-Werft, Willy H. Schliecker KG (formerly Ottensener Eisenwerk-qv)	*W Germany*
Scotts' SB	Scotts' Shipbuilding & Engineering Co Ltd (later Scott Lithgow Ltd)	*Scotland*
SEM	Societe d'Electricité et de Mecanique	*Belgium*
SGCM	Société Generale de Constructions Mecaniques	*France*

SIGMA	Société Industrielle Générale de Mécanique Appliquée "SIGMA"	France
Skoda	Skoda design engines built by CKD Praha-qv	
Smit & Bolnes	Motorenfabriek NV Smit & Bolnes	Netherlands
Smith's D	Smith's Dock Co Ltd	England
Stal-Laval	Stal-Laval Turbin AB	Sweden
Stephen	Alexander Stephen & Sons Ltd	Scotland
Stork	NV Koninklijke Machinefabriek Gebr Stork & Co	Netherlands
Stork-Werkspoor	Stork-Werkspoor Diesel BV (also Spanish subsidiary Naval-Stork-Werkspoor SA)	Netherlands
Sulzer	Sulzer Brothers Ltd (subsidiaries include Compagnie de Construction Mecanique Sulzer (France))	Switzerland
Swan Hunter & WR	Swan Hunter & Wigham Richardson Ltd	England
Swiss Locomotive	Swiss Locomotive & Machine Works Ltd	Switzerland
Thornycroft	John I. Thornycroft & Co Ltd	England
Toyo	Toyo Turbine Manufacturing Co	Japan
Turbinfabrik	Turbinfabrik	E Germany
Uddevalla	Uddevallavarvet AB	Sweden
Unaflow	Unaflow design engines built by Skinner Engine Co and licensees in several countries	USA
Uraga	Uraga Tamashima Diesel Kogyo Works Ltd	Japan
Verschure	NV Verschure & Co's Scheepswerf en Machinefabriek	Netherlands
Vickers-Armstrongs	Vickers-Armstrongs (Engineers) Ltd	England
Volund	A/S Volund	Denmark
Volvo-Penta	Volvo-Penta A/B	Sweden
Vulcan	Vulcan Iron Works	USA
Waggon	Waggon u Maschinenbau	W Germany
Wallsend	Wallsend Slipway & Engineering Co Ltd	England
Wartsila	Oy Wartsila Ab (engines built by Wartsila Vasa factory)	Finland
Werkspoor	NV Werkspoor (now Stork-Werkspoor-qv)	Netherlands
Westinghouse	Westinghouse Electric Corp	USA
W. H. Allen	W. H. Allen Sons & Co Ltd (later APE Allen-qv)	England
White Fuel	White Fuel Oil Eng Co	USA
Wichmann	Wichmann Motorfabrikk A/S	Norway
Wilton-Fije	NV Wilton-Fijenoord dok-en Werf Maatschappij	Netherlands
Yanmar	Yanmar Diesel Engine Co Ltd	Japan
Yarwood	W. J. Yarwood & Sons Ltd	England
"Zgoda"	Zaklady Urzadzen Technicznych "Zgoda" (ZUT "Zgoda")	Poland

Profile 1

CKMKMKFKMK H1
00001 TAE YANG No 11

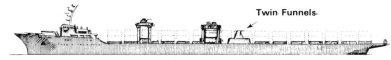

Twin Funnels

CMN₂F/CMNFN/CMFN₂ H1
00010 LASH ATLANTICO → 00019

KC₂MCMCFC₂ H13
00020 PENTA WORLD

KCMKFCK H12
00030 SIRIUS → 00032

KFM H12
00040 RAJAH MAS

CL   CL

K₂CMKF H1
00050 FORT GRANGE → 00051

K₄MKFK H1
00060 ASHLEY LYKES → 00070

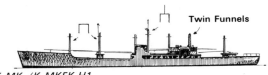

Twin Funnels

K₃MK₃/K₃MKFK H1
00080 ADABELLE LYKES → 00085

K₂MKFK H1
00090 GELA

CL

K₂MKMKFKC H1
00110 KERO

CL   H

K₂M₂KFK₂ H1
00120 ELEFTHERIA

Twin Funnels

KMFK/KMFM H1
★00140 ADMIRAL GOLOVKO → 00149/1

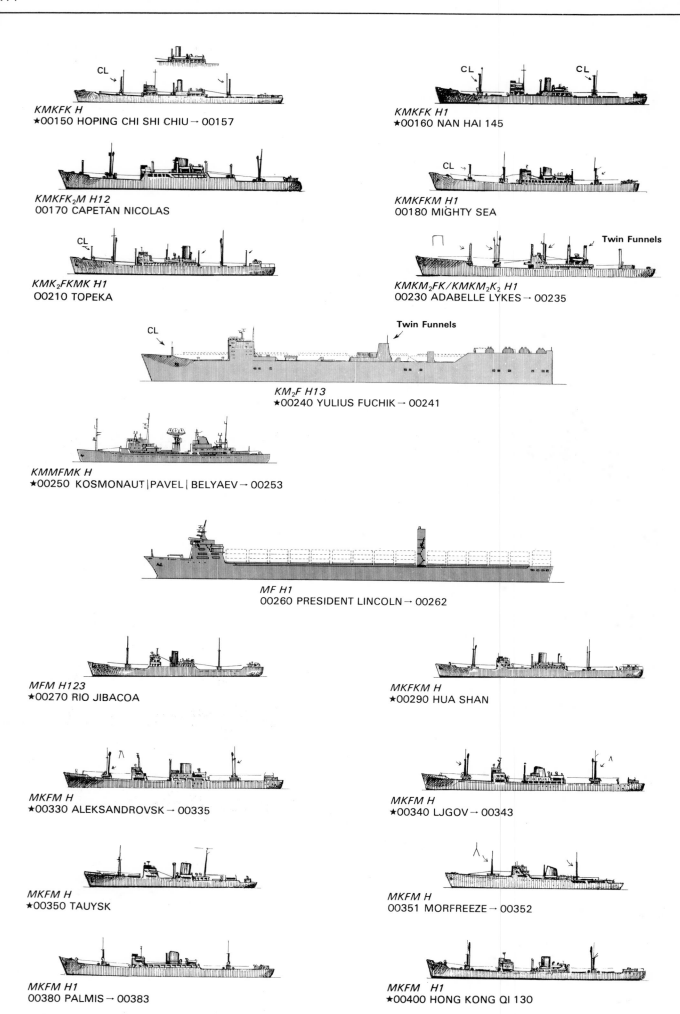

KMKFK H
★00150 HOPING CHI SHI CHIU → 00157

KMKFK H1
★00160 NAN HAI 145

KMKFK₂M H12
00170 CAPETAN NICOLAS

KMKFKM H1
00180 MIGHTY SEA

KMK₂FKMK H1
00210 TOPEKA

KMKM₂FK/KMKM₂K₂ H1
00230 ADABELLE LYKES → 00235

Twin Funnels

KM₂F H13
★00240 YULIUS FUCHIK → 00241

Twin Funnels

KMMFMK H
★00250 KOSMONAUT|PAVEL|BELYAEV → 00253

MF H1
00260 PRESIDENT LINCOLN → 00262

MFM H123
★00270 RIO JIBACOA

MKFKM H
★00290 HUA SHAN

MKFM H
★00330 ALEKSANDROVSK → 00335

MKFM H
★00340 LJGOV → 00343

MKFM H
★00350 TAUYSK

MKFM H
00351 MORFREEZE → 00352

MKFM H1
00380 PALMIS → 00383

MKFM H1
★00400 HONG KONG QI 130

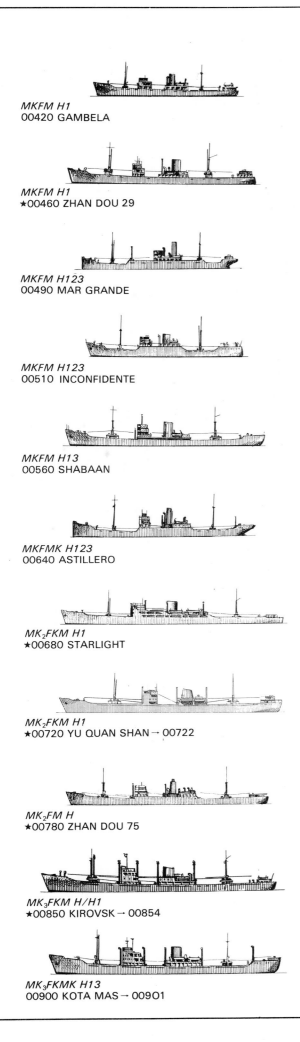
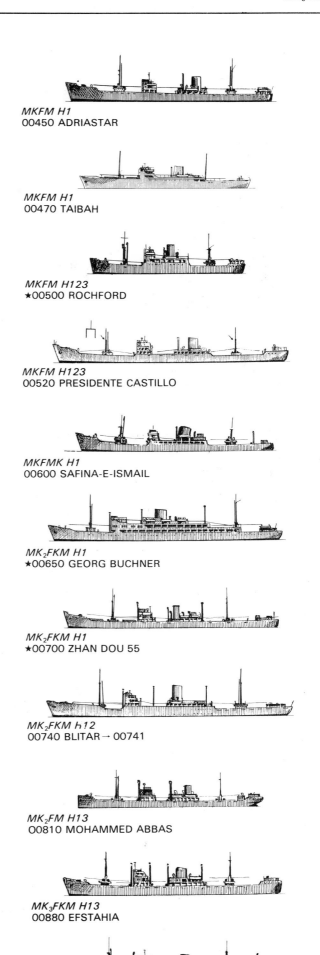

MKFM H1
00420 GAMBELA

MKFM H1
00450 ADRIASTAR

MKFM H1
★00460 ZHAN DOU 29

MKFM H1
00470 TAIBAH

MKFM H123
00490 MAR GRANDE

MKFM H123
★00500 ROCHFORD

MKFM H123
00510 INCONFIDENTE

MKFM H123
00520 PRESIDENTE CASTILLO

MKFM H13
00560 SHABAAN

MKFMK H1
00600 SAFINA-E-ISMAIL

MKFMK H123
00640 ASTILLERO

MK₂FKM H1
★00650 GEORG BUCHNER

MK₂FKM H1
★00680 STARLIGHT

MK₂FKM H1
★00700 ZHAN DOU 55

MK₂FKM H1
★00720 YU QUAN SHAN → 00722

MK₂FKM h12
00740 BLITAR → 00741

MK₂FM H
★00780 ZHAN DOU 75

MK₂FM H13
00810 MOHAMMED ABBAS

MK₃FKM H/H1
★00850 KIROVSK → 00854

MK₃FKM H13
00880 EFSTAHIA

MK₃FKMK H13
00900 KOTA MAS → 00901

MK₃FMK H13
00930 MARGARITA III → 00931

MKMFM H1
★00940 ZHAN DOU 53

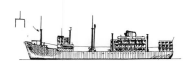

MKMKFK H1
00950 AN-LI

MKMKFKM H
★00960 ZHAN DOU 51 → 00963

M₂F H2
00970 TRANSGERMANIA

M₂F₂KM H12
★00980 GUANGHUA

Twin Funnels

M₂FMF H13
01010 SUPER SERVANT

M₂KFM H
★10120 LJGOV → 01023

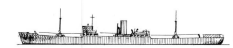

M₂KFM H
★01030 ZHAN DOU 27→01033

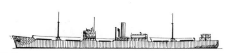

M₂KFM H
★01040 ZHAN DOU 47

Twin Funnels

MNF H1
01050 STONEWALL JACKSON → 01057

4

Profile 2

C_5MFC_2 H13
01060 ZAMBEZE → 01062

C_3MCMFC H1
★01070 BELORETSK → 01075

C_2KC_2KMFK H1
01080 EKA DAYA SAMUDERA

C_2KC_2MFCK H13
01090 GARNET → 01091

C_2KCMFC H13
★01100 PYATIDYESYATILETIYE KOMSOMOLA

C_2KCMFC_3 H1
01110 MARIETTA → 01112

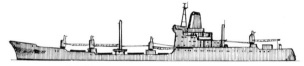

$C_2KCMFKC$ H13
01120 GOLDEN DOLPHIN → 01121

$C_2MC_2MFC_2$ H13
01140 PEMBA

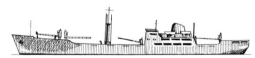

C_2MCFKC H1
01150 TSING YI ISLAND → 01151

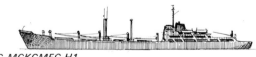

$C_2MCKCMFC$ H1
★01160 KAI HUA

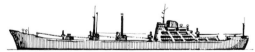

$C_2MCKCMFCK$ H1
★01170 CHANGSHU

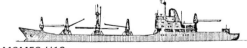

C_2MCMFC H13
★01180 PYATIDYESYATILETIYE KOMSOMOLA

C_2MCMFC H13
01190 OAKWOOD → 01191

C_2MCMFC_2 H13
★01200 ZHEN ZHU QUAN → 01204

C_2MF H
01210 FAIRSTAR

C_2MF H
01220 FAIRWIND→ 01221

C_2MF H
01230 CARLA C

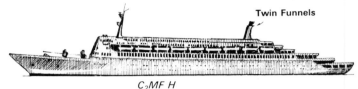

Twin Funnels

C_2MF H
01240 EUGENIO C

C_2MF H
01250 OCEANIC

$C_2MF_2C_2$ H
01260 ORIANA

C_2MFK H
01270 CITTA DI NAPOLI → 01271

C_2MFM H
01290 JUAN MARCH → 01293

C_2MFM H1
01300 NORDLYS → 01302

C_2MFMC H
01310 AL KHAIRAT

C_2M_2F H
01330 VITTORE CARPACCIO

C_2M_2F H
01340 ANTONELLO DA MESSINA

C_2M_2F H
01350 HARALD JARL

C_2M_2FCK H1
01351 POLARSTERN

CFMC₂ H1
01352 STENA CONSTRUCTOR → 01355

CFMC₂K H1
01356 STENA SEASPREAD

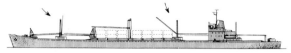

CKC₂KMFK H1
01360 SAINT FRANCOIS → 01361

CKCKMFKC H13
01370 CREST HILL

CKCMFC H13
★01380 'KALININGRAD' type → 01418

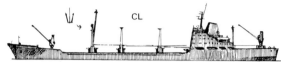

CK³MFKC H13
01430 MONTERREY → 01431

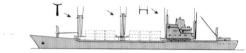

CK₂MFMC H
01435 MARFRIO → 01436

CKMF H
01450 ITALIA

CKMF H1
01460 MUTIARA

CKMFC₂ H1
01470 MONTJOLLY → 01471

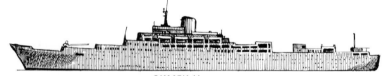

CKMFK H
01480 MARGARITA L.

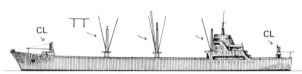

CKMKMFC H
01490 ROVER → 01493

CMC₂FCM H2
01510 KOTA BALI

CMC₂KCMFC H13
01520 J C CRANE → 01522

CMC₂MCFKC H13
01530 DEMON → 01534

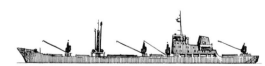

CMC₂MFC H1
★01540 OTRADNOE → 01544

CMC₂MFC₂ H123
01550 HALLAREN → 01551

CMC₂MFC₂MC H13
★01560 METALLURG ANASOV → 01579/1

CMCFCMC H
01580 AKDENIZ → 01581

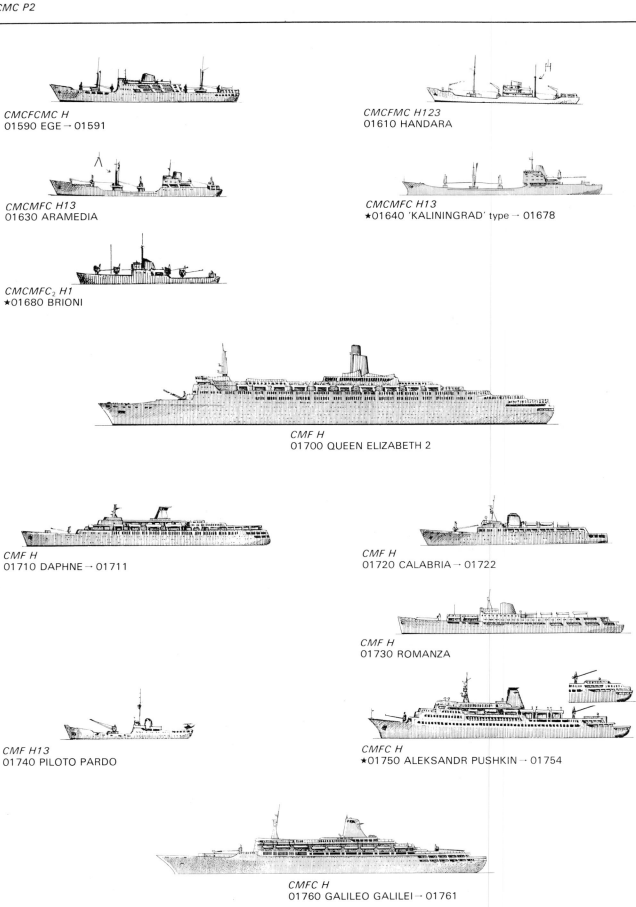

CMCFCMC H
01590 EGE → 01591

CMCFMC H123
01610 HANDARA

CMCMFC H13
01630 ARAMEDIA

CMCMFC H13
★01640 'KALININGRAD' type → 01678

CMCMFC₂ H1
★01680 BRIONI

CMF H
01700 QUEEN ELIZABETH 2

CMF H
01710 DAPHNE → 01711

CMF H
01720 CALABRIA → 01722

CMF H
01730 ROMANZA

CMF H13
01740 PILOTO PARDO

CMFC H
★01750 ALEKSANDR PUSHKIN → 01754

CMFC H
01760 GALILEO GALILEI → 01761

CMFCM H
★01770 DING HU

CMF₂/CMF₂C H1
01780 POLAR STAR → 01781

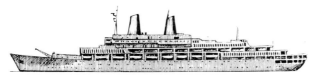

CMF₂K H
01790 ACHILLE LAURO

CMF₂M H
01800 BOREA

CMF₂M H1
01810 PANDELIS

CMFK H
★01820 MINGHUA

CMFK H12
01830 APHRODITE

CMFK₂M H1
01840 LOUIS S. ST. LAURENT

CMFKMC H
01850 HAKUREI MARU

CMFM H
01860 ATLAS

CMFM H
01870 STARWARD → 01871

CMFM H
01890 SAPPHO

CMFM H
01900 AL-QAMAR AL-SAUDI II

CMFM H
01905 DANA CORONA

CMFM H
01910 KONG OLAV V → 01911

CMFM H
01920 ENGLAND

CMFM H
01930 WID → 01931

CMFM H
★01935 ANTONINA   NEZHDANOVA → 01938

CMFM H
01940 KONG OLAV

CMFM H
01950 NORDNORGE

CMFM H
★01960 ABRAU-DYURSO → 01971

CMFM H
★01980 GEORGI DIMITROV → 01981

CMFM H
01990 OLDENBURG

CMFM H
★02000 MIN ZHUI

CMFM H
02020 WAPPEN VON HAMBURG

Twin Funnels

CMFM H
02030 ALTE LIEBE

CMFM H
02040 TSUGARU MARU

CMFM H1
★02060 KAPITAN SOROKIN → 02063

CMFM H1
★02070 MOSKVA → 02074

CMFM H1
★02080 KAPITAN M. IZMAYLOV → 02082

CMFM H12
02090 CAPE DON → 02092

CMFM H12
02100 TAVERNER

CMFM H2
★02110 INGUL → 02111

CMFMC H
★02120 BAYKAL → 02130

CMFMC H
02140 BASHKIRIYA → 02141

CMFMC H
★02150 ADZHARIYA

CMFMC H
★02160 ESTONIYA → 02163

CMFMC H
02170 ESPRESSO CORINTO

CMFMC H
★02180 STEFAN BATORY

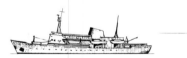

CMFMC H
02190 HUDSON

CMFMC H
02200 JOHN CABOT

CMFMC H
02210 SAUDI ARABIAN

CMFMC H
02220 HAKUREI MARU

CMFMC H1
★02230 KAPITAN SOROKIN → 02233

CMFMC H1
02240 VOIMA

CMFMC₂ H
02250 BUCANERO

CMFMFC H
02260 DANA

CMFMK H12
★02270 MUSSON → 02278

CMFMN H2
★02280 KATYN → 02285

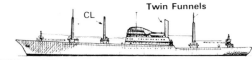

CMKFMC H1
02290 COOLHAVEN → 02293

CMK₂FMK₃ H1
02300 JEFF DAVIS

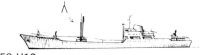

CMKMFC H13
★02310 SCHWARZA

CMKMFKM H1
★02320 FENG BAO → 02328

CM₂ H1
02330 PORTO SANTO → 02331

CM²F H
★02340 MARIYA YERMOLOVA → 02345

CM₂F H
02346 KERINCI → 02348

CM₂F H
★02350 KOLKHIDA → 02359

CM₂F H
02370 LOFOTEN

CM₂F H
02380 FINNMARKEN → 02381

CM₂F H
02390 GENTILE DA FABRIANO → 02391

CM₂F H
02400 LONG LINES

CM₂F H
02410 C.S. MONARCH → 02411

CM₂F H1
★02415 LEONID ILICH BREZHNEV → 02416

CM₂F H2
02420 KUROSHIO MARU

CM₂FC H
02430 KDD MARU

CM₂FC H
02440 BALTIC STAR

CM₂FK H
★02460 AKADEMIK KRYLOV

CM₂FM H1
02470 SAGARDEEP

Twin Funnels

CMN₂F H1
02480 LASH ATLANTICO → 02488

FM H1
02500 CAPE HENLOPEN

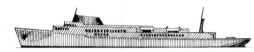

FM H1
02505 AQUARAMA

FMC H1
02510 JEAN CHARCOT

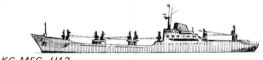

KC₇MFC₂ H13
02515 LUCERO DEL MAR

CL

KC₇MFCK H13
★02520 IRKUTSK → 02530

KC₆MFC₂ H1
02540 PISANG → 02541

KC₆MFK H1
02550 MULTI CARRIER → 02553

KC₅MFC H1
02560 AFRIC STAR → 02565

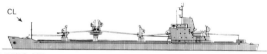

CL

KC₅MFC H1
02567 LLOYD ALEGRETE → 02568

KC₅MFC H13
★02570 HUI QUAN → 02572

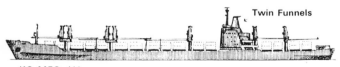

Twin Funnels

KC₅MFC₂ H1
02580 TAMARA → 02582

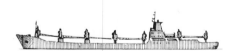

KC⁵MFC² H13
02590 LEENOR → 02591

KC₅MFC₃ H1
02600 SNOW FLAKE → 02607

CL

KC₅MFCK H13
02610 GAIETY → 02611

KC₅MFK H13
02620 POINTE SANS SOUCI → 02622

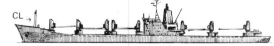

CL

KC₅MFKC₃ H1
02630 SNOW FLAKE → 02637

KC₄KCMFC H1
02640 SEAGULL → 02642

KC₄MFC H1
02650 HILCO SPRINTER → 02652

KC₄MFC H1
02660 AFRIC STAR → 02665

KC₄MFC H13
★02670 SVETLOGORSK → 02682

KC₄MFC H13
★02690 NOVGOROD → 02704

KC₄MFC H13
02710 NEDLLOYD NAGASAKI → 02713

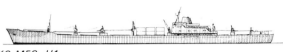

KC₄MFC₂ H1
02720 BRA. → 02723

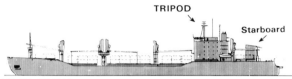

KC₄MFCR H13
★02724 NORILSK → 02728/7

KC₄MFK H1
02729 MONTE ALTO → 02729/4

KC₄MFKC H13
02730 GARIFALIA C

KC₄MFKC H13
02740 TRANSOCEAN REEFER

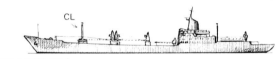

KC₄MFKC H13
02750 SAUDI AL JUBAIL

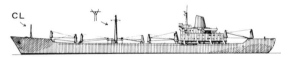

KC³KC³MFC² H13
02760 ANCHAN → 02762

KC₃KMFC₂ H13
02770 BEI SHAN → 02772

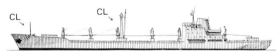

KC₃MC₂MFC H1
02790 ROCADAS → 02806

KC₃MCMFCK H13
02810 CHERRY ORIENT → 02811

KC₃MFC H
02820 NEW ZEALAND CARIBBEAN

KC₃MFC H1
02830 PUNTA STELLA → 02833

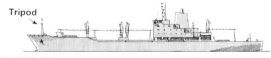

KC₃MFC H1
02840 POCANTICO → 02842

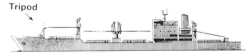

KC₃MFC H1
02844 GLACIAR AMEGHINO → 02846

KC₃ MFC H1
02850 HONOLULU → 02853

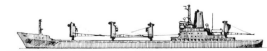

KC₃MFC H1
02860 AL SALAMA → 02861

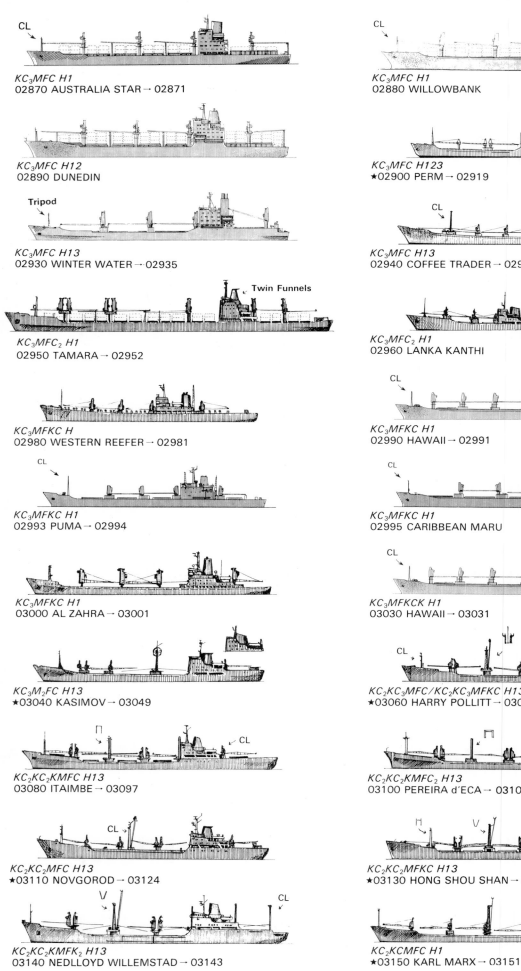
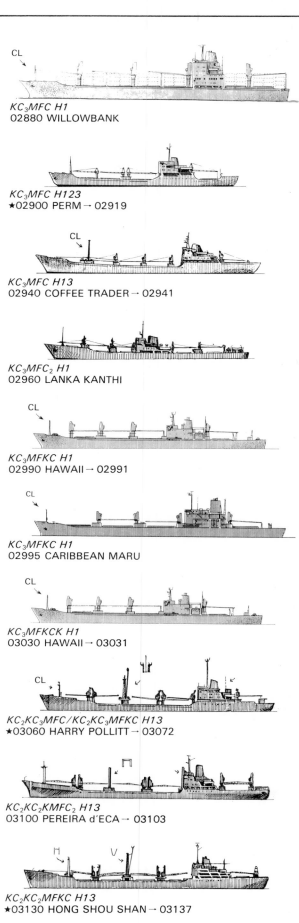

KC₃MFC H1
02870 AUSTRALIA STAR → 02871

KC₃MFC H1
02880 WILLOWBANK

KC₃MFC H12
02890 DUNEDIN

KC₃MFC H123
★02900 PERM → 02919

KC₃MFC H13
02930 WINTER WATER → 02935

KC₃MFC H13
02940 COFFEE TRADER → 02941

KC₃MFC₂ H1
02950 TAMARA → 02952

KC₃MFC₂ H1
02960 LANKA KANTHI

KC₃MFKC H
02980 WESTERN REEFER → 02981

KC₃MFKC H1
02990 HAWAII → 02991

KC₃MFKC H1
02993 PUMA → 02994

KC₃MFKC H1
02995 CARIBBEAN MARU

KC₃MFKC H1
03000 AL ZAHRA → 03001

KC₃MFKCK H1
03030 HAWAII → 03031

KC₃M₂FC H13
★03040 KASIMOV → 03049

KC₂KC₃MFC/KC₂KC₃MFKC H13
★03060 HARRY POLLITT → 03072

KC₂KC₂KMFC H13
03080 ITAIMBE → 03097

KC₂KC₂KMFC₂ H13
03100 PEREIRA d'ECA → 03103

KC₂KC₂MFC H13
★03110 NOVGOROD → 03124

KC₂KC₂MFKC H13
★03130 HONG SHOU SHAN → 03137

KC₂KC₂KMFK₂ H13
03140 NEDLLOYD WILLEMSTAD → 03143

KC₂KCMFC H1
★03150 KARL MARX → 03151

KC₂KCMFC₂ H13
03160 NEDLLOYD AMSTERDAM → 03165

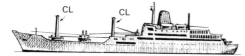

KC₂KCMFK H12
03180 CENTAUR

KC₂K₂MFC₂ H1
03190 MYKONOS → 03191

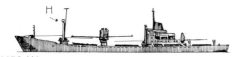

KC₂KMFC H1
03220 RONCESVALLES → 03223

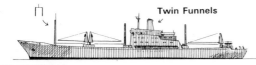

Twin Funnels

KC₂KMFKC H
★03260 KULDIGA → 03263

KC₂MC₃MFC₂ H13
03280 CORTINA

KC₂MC₂KMFKC₂ H1
03300 NEDLLOYD LEUVE → 03302

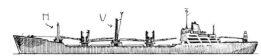

KC₂MC₂MFKC H13
★03340 HONG SHOU SHAN → 03347

CL

KC₂MCMFKC H13
03370 ANDROMEDA

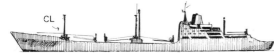

CL

KC₂MCMFKC H13
03390 BELLO

KC₂MFC H1
03420 PUNTA BIANCA

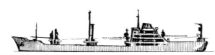

KC²KCMFCK H13
★03170 JIANGCHANG → 03174

KC₂K₂MFC H13
03185 ITAITE → 03189

KC₂K₂MFK H1
03200 BUNGA ORKID → 03201

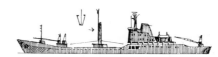

KC₂KMFC H13
★03230 RADZIONKOW → 03253

CL

KC₂MC₃MFC H1
★03270 OMSK → 03272

CL

KC₂MC₂KMFKC H13
03290 HELLENIC PATRIOT

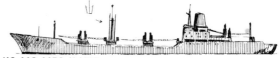

KC₂MC₂MFC₂K H13
03320 RAJAB 1 → 03323

KC₂MCMFKC H13
03360 IDEAL

CL

KC₂MCMFKC H13
03380 REA B

KC₂MFC H
03410 RIO GRANDE → 03412

KC₂MFC H1
03430 IOS 1

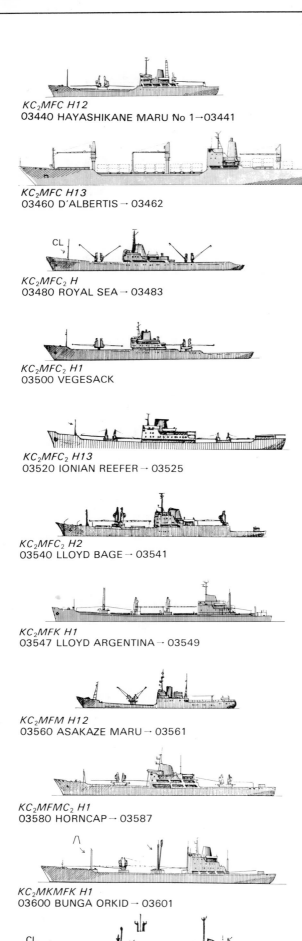
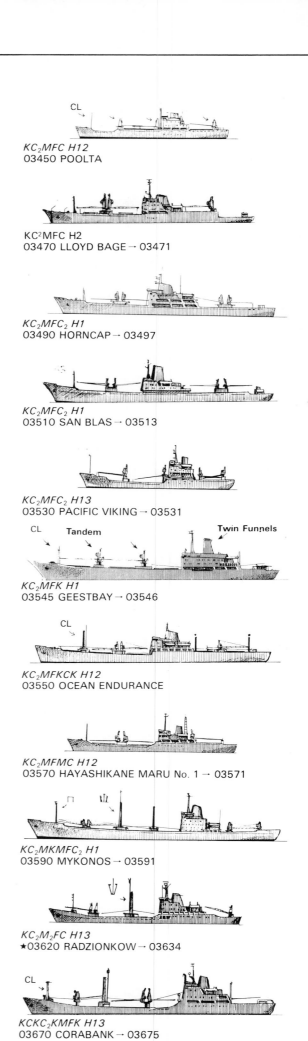

KC₂MFC H12
03440 HAYASHIKANE MARU No 1→03441

KC₂MFC H12
03450 POOLTA

KC₂MFC H13
03460 D'ALBERTIS → 03462

KC²MFC H2
03470 LLOYD BAGE → 03471

KC₂MFC₂ H
03480 ROYAL SEA → 03483

KC₂MFC₂ H1
03490 HORNCAP → 03497

KC₂MFC₂ H1
03500 VEGESACK

KC₂MFC₂ H1
03510 SAN BLAS → 03513

KC₂MFC₂ H13
03520 IONIAN REEFER → 03525

KC₂MFC₂ H13
03530 PACIFIC VIKING → 03531

KC₂MFC₂ H2
03540 LLOYD BAGE → 03541

KC₂MFK H1
03545 GEESTBAY → 03546

KC₂MFK H1
03547 LLOYD ARGENTINA → 03549

KC₂MFKCK H12
03550 OCEAN ENDURANCE

KC₂MFM H12
03560 ASAKAZE MARU → 03561

KC₂MFMC H12
03570 HAYASHIKANE MARU No. 1 → 03571

KC₂MFMC₂ H1
03580 HORNCAP → 03587

KC₂MKMFC₂ H1
03590 MYKONOS → 03591

KC₂MKMFK H1
03600 BUNGA ORKID → 03601

KC₂M₂FC H13
★03620 RADZIONKOW → 03634

KCKC³MFC H13
★03650 HARRY POLLITT → 03663

KCKC₂KMFK H13
03670 CORABANK → 03675

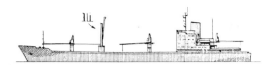

KCKC₂MFC H1
★03690 WARNEMUNDE → 03709

KCKC₂MFC H13
03720 KHALIJ EXPRESS

KCKC₂MFK H13
03730 CORABANK → 03735

KCKCKMFK₂ H1
03740 OCEAN ADVENTURE → 03741

KCKCMFC H1
03750 BOUNTY III → 03751

KCKCMFC H1
03760 MANISTEE → 03763

KCKCMFK H13
★03770 LENINSKAYA GVARDIYA → 03801

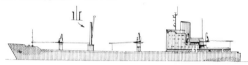

KCKCMFKC H1
03810 WARNEMUNDE → 03829

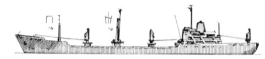

KCKCMFKC H13
03840 MAYON → 03841

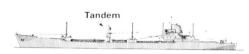

KCK₂MFK H1
03850 BANDA SEA

KCK₂MFK H13
03860 SANTA MAVRA → 03861

KCK²MFM H1
★03870 ALTENBURG → 03885

KCKMFC H1
03890 RONCESVALLES → 03893

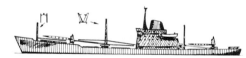

KCKMFKC H1
03900 SPARTAN REEFER → 03901

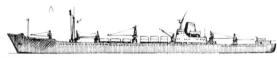

KCMC₄MFC₂ H1
03910 BAHIA BLANCA

KCMC₂MFC H13
03930 KLIN → 03944

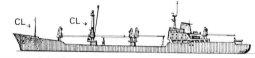

KCMC₂MFC H13
★03950 SOSNOGORSK → 03972

KCMCFC H13
03980 ALPHA BAY

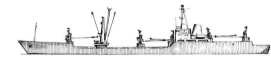

KCMC₂MFC₂ H13
03990 GAZZELLA → 03993

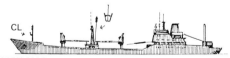

KCMCMFK H13
★04010 LENINSKAYA GVARDIYA → 04041

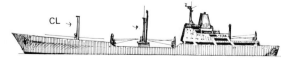

KCMCMFKC H13
★04050 REA B

KCMF H
04060 MONOWAI

KCMF H1
O4070 S. A. AGULHAS

KCMF H1
★04080 STROPTIVYY → 04086

KCMFC H
04090 VEGESACK

KCMFC H1
04100 SAN FRANCISCO → 04103

KCMFC H1
04110 INCOTRANS SPIRIT → 04111

KCMFC₂ H13
04115 SOUTHLAND STAR → 04116

KCMFCR H1
★04120 LEDENICE → 04121

KCMFK H
04130 ANASTASIS

KCMFK H
04140 ISLAS GALAPAGOS → 04143

KCMFM H
04160 SCILLONIAN III

KCMFMC H13
★04180 KIROVSKLES → 04190

KCMFMC H
★04196 XIANG YANG HONG 9

KCMFMFC H1
★O4200 'TOMBA' CLASS

KCMFMN H2
★04210 INGURI

KCM₂FC H1
★04220 NAN HAI 502

KCM₂FC₂ H1
★04230 WILHELM FLORIN → 04233

KCM₂FK H
★04240 ADMIRAL VLADIMIRSKIY → 04241

KCM₂FK H12
04245   BRITISH ENTERPRISE THREE → 04246

KCM₂FKM H1
04250 JALAJAYA

KCM₃F H1
★04253 AKADEMIK SHULEYKIN → 04258

KCM₃FC H1
★04260 NAN HAI 502

KFC H12
04280 GORYO-HO → 04281

KFM H
04300 MARSA

KFM H1
04310 TUI CAKAU II

Tripod   Twin Funnels

KFM H1
04312 SKANDI ALFA

KFMC H1
04320 UGLEN

CL

K₂C₅MFCK H13
04330 GAIETY → 04331

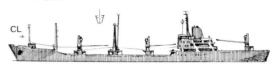

CL

K₂C₂KC₂MFC H13
★04340 HEL → 04344

CL

K₂C₂KCMFCK H1
04350 ALDABI → 04353

K₂C₂KCMFKC H1
04360 MARATHON REEFER → 04361

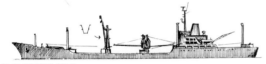

K₂C₂KMFK H13
04370 TACHIRA → 04373

K₂C₂MC₂MFC₂K H13
04380 IRAN EJTEHAD → 04383

CL

K₂CKCKMFK H13
04390 NEDLLOYD KEMBLA → 04394

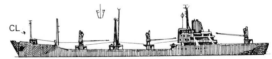

CL

K₂CKCMFC H13
★04400 HEL → 04404

K₂CKCMFKC H1
04410 NILE → 04411

CL

K₂CK₂MFK H13
04420 CHARLOTTENBORG → 04421

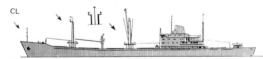

CL

K₂CK₂MFM H1
★04423 ALTENBURG → 04429/1

K₂CKMFK H13
04430 TACHIRA → 04433

CL

K₂CKMFK₂ H13
04440 CIUDAD DE MANIZALES → 04441

CL   CL

K₂CMFCK₂ H13
★04450 DONGSHAN

CL

K₂CMFK₂ H1
04460 CEFALLONIAN WAVES

K₂FK H1
★04470 LIKA → 04474

Λ

K²FK² H1
04480 FELIX S

K₂FKM H13
★04500 LIAZI

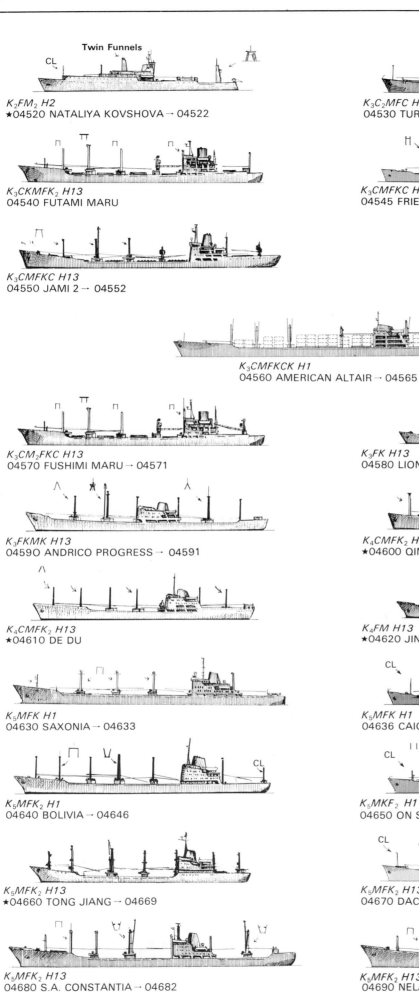
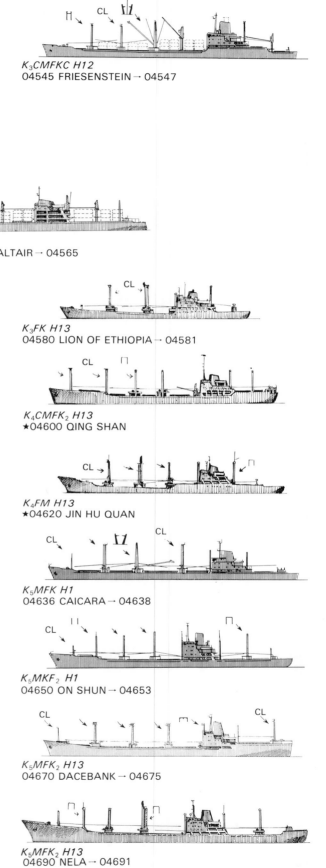

K_2FM_2 $H2$
★04520 NATALIYA KOVSHOVA → 04522

K_3C_2MFC $H13$
04530 TURTLE BAY → 04531

K_3CKMFK_2 $H13$
04540 FUTAMI MARU

K_3CMFKC $H12$
04545 FRIESENSTEIN → 04547

K_3CMFKC $H13$
04550 JAMI 2 → 04552

$K_3CMFKCK$ $H1$
04560 AMERICAN ALTAIR → 04565

K_3CM_2FKC $H13$
04570 FUSHIMI MARU → 04571

K_3FK $H13$
04580 LION OF ETHIOPIA → 04581

K_3FKMK $H13$
04590 ANDRICO PROGRESS → 04591

K_4CMFK_2 $H13$
★04600 QING SHAN

K_4CMFK_2 $H13$
★04610 DE DU

K_4FM $H13$
★04620 JIN HU QUAN

K_5MFK $H1$
04630 SAXONIA → 04633

K_5MFK $H1$
04636 CAICARA → 04638

K_5MFK_2 $H1$
04640 BOLIVIA → 04646

K_5MKF_2 $H1$
04650 ON SHUN → 04653

K_5MFK_2 $H13$
★04660 TONG JIANG → 04669

K_5MFK_2 $H13$
04670 DACEBANK → 04675

K_5MFK_2 $H13$
04680 S.A. CONSTANTIA → 04682

K_5MFK_2 $H13$
04690 NELA → 04691

20

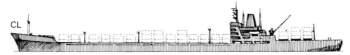

K₄MFCK H13
04700 AUSTRALIA MARU → 04702

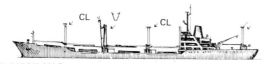

K₄MFCK H13
04710 HELLENIC PRIDE → 04713

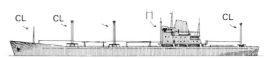

K₄MFK H/H1
04720 BEACON GRANGE → 04722

K₄MFK H1
04730 RIVER ADADA → 04737

K₄MFK H1
04740 TASMAN REX → 04741

K₄MFK H1
04750 MANOLOEVERETT → 04754

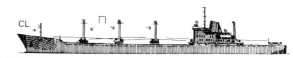

K₄MFK H1
04760 SAXONIA → 04763

K₄MFK H1
04770 CRESTBANK → 04771

K₄MFK H1
04775 VIRGINIA → 04776

K₄MFK H1
04780 HELLENIC CHAMPION → 04788

K₄MFK H1
04800 LLOYD MANDU → 04806

K₄MFK H1
04810 FROTADURBAN → 04815

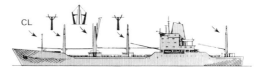

K₄MFK H12
04820 RIVER JIMINI → 04834

K₄MFK H1
04840 DIDO

K₄MFK H1
04850 CIUDAD DE BOGOTA → 04856

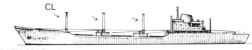

K₄MFK H13
★04860 BAOTING → 04862

K₄MFK H13
★04870 LJUTOMER → 04871

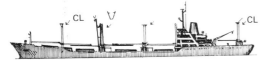

K₄MFK H13
04880 HELLENIC PRIDE → 04883

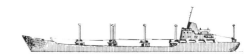

K₄MFK H13
04890 BEATRIZ MONTEIRO → 04891

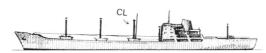

K₄MFK H13
04900 SEA KING

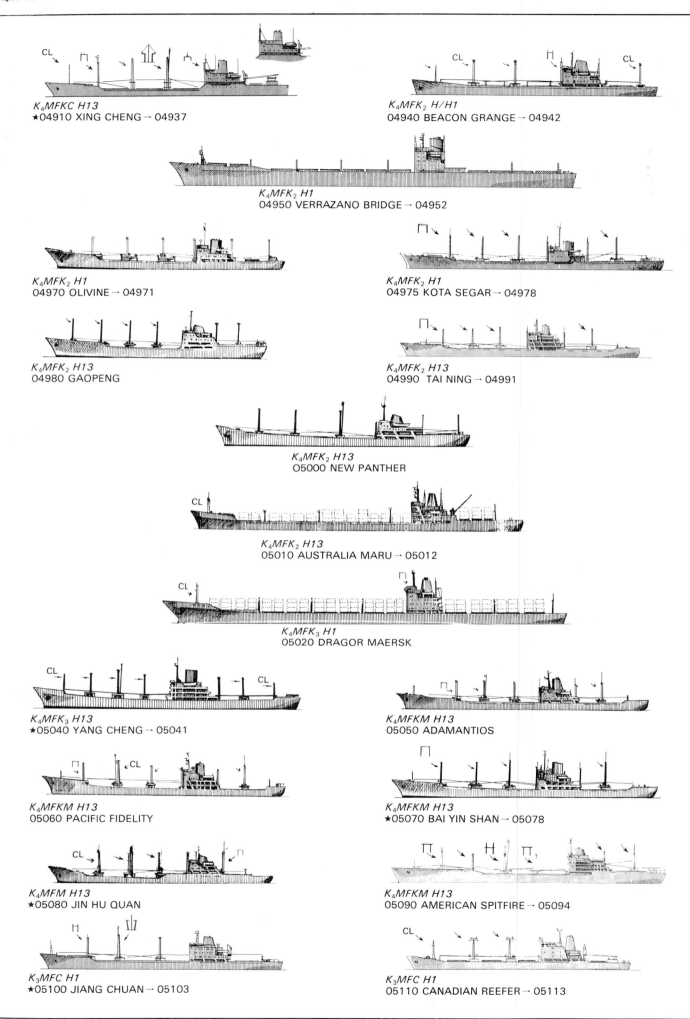

K₄MFKC H13
★04910 XING CHENG → 04937

K₄MFK₂ H/H1
04940 BEACON GRANGE → 04942

K₄MFK₂ H1
04950 VERRAZANO BRIDGE → 04952

K₄MFK₂ H1
04970 OLIVINE → 04971

K₄MFK₂ H1
04975 KOTA SEGAR → 04978

K₄MFK₂ H13
04980 GAOPENG

K₄MFK₂ H13
04990 TAI NING → 04991

K₄MFK₂ H13
05000 NEW PANTHER

K₄MFK₂ H13
05010 AUSTRALIA MARU → 05012

K₄MFK₃ H1
05020 DRAGOR MAERSK

K₄MFK₃ H13
★05040 YANG CHENG → 05041

K₄MFKM H13
05050 ADAMANTIOS

K₄MFKM H13
05060 PACIFIC FIDELITY

K₄MFKM H13
★05070 BAI YIN SHAN → 05078

K₄MFM H13
★05080 JIN HU QUAN

K₄MFKM H13
05090 AMERICAN SPITFIRE → 05094

K₃MFC H1
★05100 JIANG CHUAN → 05103

K₃MFC H1
05110 CANADIAN REEFER → 05113

22

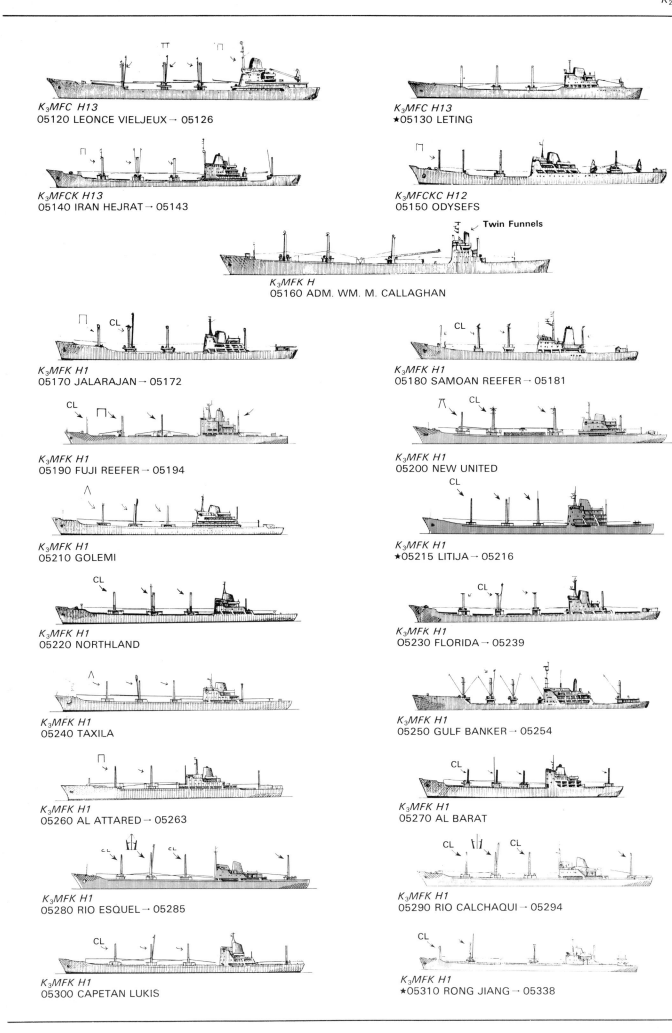

K₃MFC H13
05120 LEONCE VIELJEUX → 05126

K₃MFC H13
★05130 LETING

K₃MFCK H13
05140 IRAN HEJRAT → 05143

K₃MFCKC H12
05150 ODYSEFS

Twin Funnels

K₃MFK H
05160 ADM. WM. M. CALLAGHAN

K₃MFK H1
05170 JALARAJAN → 05172

K₃MFK H1
05180 SAMOAN REEFER → 05181

K₃MFK H1
05190 FUJI REEFER → 05194

K₃MFK H1
05200 NEW UNITED

K₃MFK H1
05210 GOLEMI

K₃MFK H1
★05215 LITIJA → 05216

K₃MFK H1
05220 NORTHLAND

K₃MFK H1
05230 FLORIDA → 05239

K₃MFK H1
05240 TAXILA

K₃MFK H1
05250 GULF BANKER → 05254

K₃MFK H1
05260 AL ATTARED → 05263

K₃MFK H1
05270 AL BARAT

K₃MFK H1
05280 RIO ESQUEL → 05285

K₃MFK H1
05290 RIO CALCHAQUI → 05294

K₃MFK H1
05300 CAPETAN LUKIS

K₃MFK H1
★05310 RONG JIANG → 05338

23

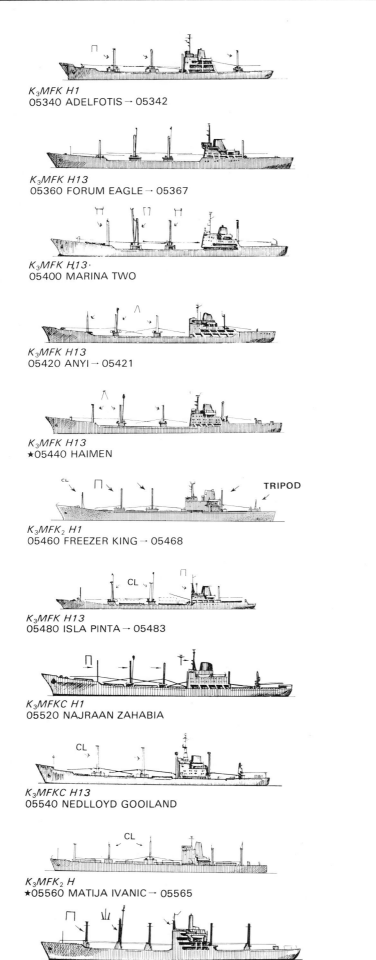
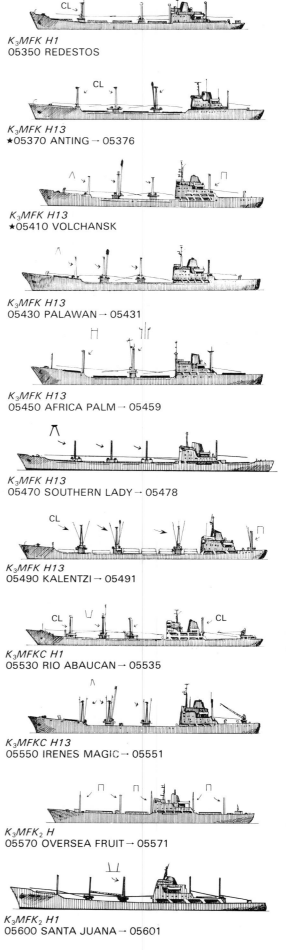

K₃MFK H1
05340 ADELFOTIS → 05342

K₃MFK H1
05350 REDESTOS

K₃MFK H13
05360 FORUM EAGLE → 05367

K₃MFK H13
★05370 ANTING → 05376

K₃MFK H13
05400 MARINA TWO

K₃MFK H13
★05410 VOLCHANSK

K₃MFK H13
05420 ANYI → 05421

K₃MFK H13
05430 PALAWAN → 05431

K₃MFK H13
★05440 HAIMEN

K₃MFK H13
05450 AFRICA PALM → 05459

K₃MFK₂ H1
05460 FREEZER KING → 05468

K₃MFK H13
05470 SOUTHERN LADY → 05478

K₃MFK H13
05480 ISLA PINTA → 05483

K₃MFK H13
05490 KALENTZI → 05491

K₃MFKC H1
05520 NAJRAAN ZAHABIA

K₃MFKC H1
05530 RIO ABAUCAN → 05535

K₃MFKC H13
05540 NEDLLOYD GOOILAND

K₃MFKC H13
05550 IRENES MAGIC → 05551

K₃MFK₂ H
★05560 MATIJA IVANIC → 05565

K₃MFK₂ H
05570 OVERSEA FRUIT → 05571

K₃MFK₂ H1
05580 ELIZABETH LYKES → 05590

K₃MFK₂ H1
05600 SANTA JUANA → 05601

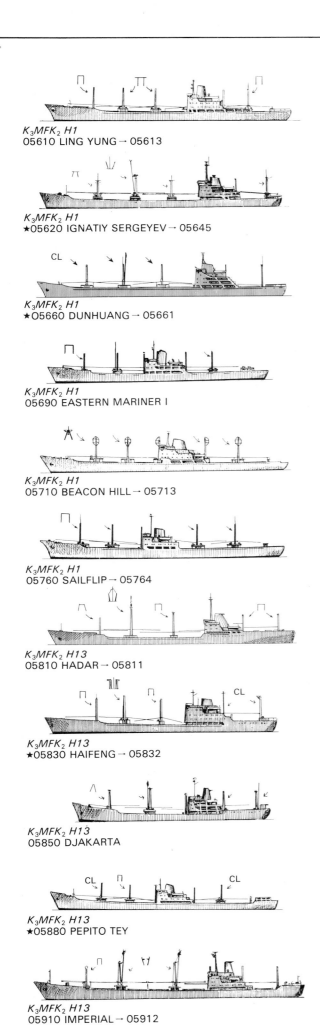
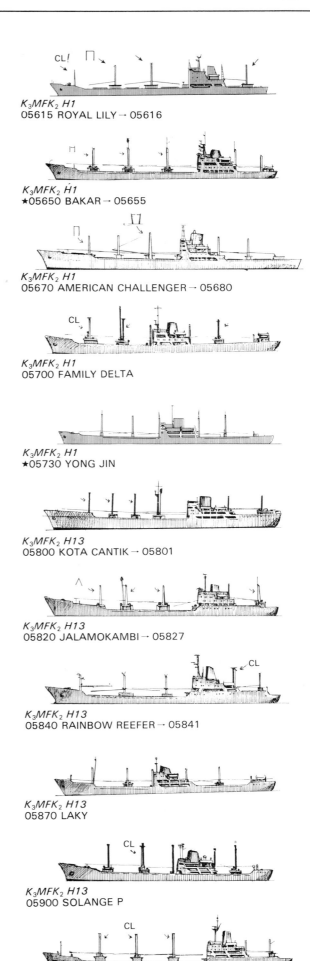

$K_3 MFK_2$ H1
05610 LING YUNG → 05613

$K_3 MFK_2$ H1
05615 ROYAL LILY → 05616

$K_3 MFK_2$ H1
★05620 IGNATIY SERGEYEV → 05645

$K_3 MFK_2$ H1
★05650 BAKAR → 05655

$K_3 MFK_2$ H1
★05660 DUNHUANG → 05661

$K_3 MFK_2$ H1
05670 AMERICAN CHALLENGER → 05680

$K_3 MFK_2$ H1
05690 EASTERN MARINER I

$K_3 MFK_2$ H1
05700 FAMILY DELTA

$K_3 MFK_2$ H1
05710 BEACON HILL → 05713

$K_3 MFK_2$ H1
★05730 YONG JIN

$K_3 MFK_2$ H1
05760 SAILFLIP → 05764

$K_3 MFK_2$ H13
05800 KOTA CANTIK → 05801

$K_3 MFK_2$ H13
05810 HADAR → 05811

$K_3 MFK_2$ H13
05820 JALAMOKAMBI → 05827

$K_3 MFK_2$ H13
★05830 HAIFENG → 05832

$K_3 MFK_2$ H13
05840 RAINBOW REEFER → 05841

$K_3 MFK_2$ H13
05850 DJAKARTA

$K_3 MFK_2$ H13
05870 LAKY

$K_3 MFK_2$ H13
★05880 PEPITO TEY

$K_3 MFK_2$ H13
05900 SOLANGE P

$K_3 MFK_2$ H13
05910 IMPERIAL → 05912

$K_3 MFK_2$ H13
05920 JOHN P

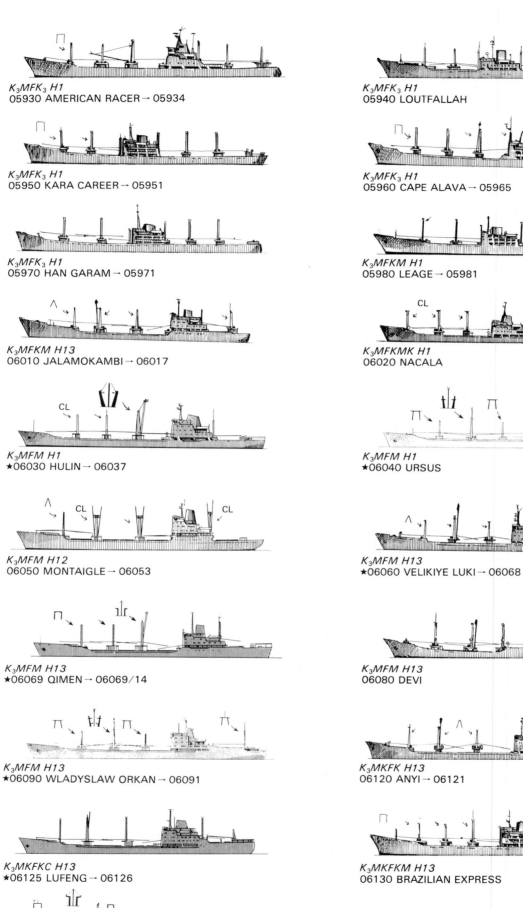

K_3MFK_3 H1
05930 AMERICAN RACER → 05934

K_3MFK_3 H1
05940 LOUTFALLAH

K_3MFK_3 H1
05950 KARA CAREER → 05951

K_3MFK_3 H1
05960 CAPE ALAVA → 05965

K_3MFK_3 H1
05970 HAN GARAM → 05971

K_3MFKM H1
05980 LEAGE → 05981

K_3MFKM H13
06010 JALAMOKAMBI → 06017

K_3MFKMK H1
06020 NACALA

K_3MFM H1
★06030 HULIN → 06037

K_3MFM H1
★06040 URSUS

K_3MFM H12
06050 MONTAIGLE → 06053

K_3MFM H13
★06060 VELIKIYE LUKI → 06068

K_3MFM H13
★06069 QIMEN → 06069/14

K_3MFM H13
06080 DEVI

K_3MFM H13
★06090 WLADYSLAW ORKAN → 06091

K_3MKFK H13
06120 ANYI → 06121

K_3MKFKC H13
★06125 LUFENG → 06126

K_3MKFKM H13
06130 BRAZILIAN EXPRESS

K_3MKFMK H13
★06135 HAIFENG

$K_3M_2FK_2$ H13
★06142 ALBA IULIA → 06143

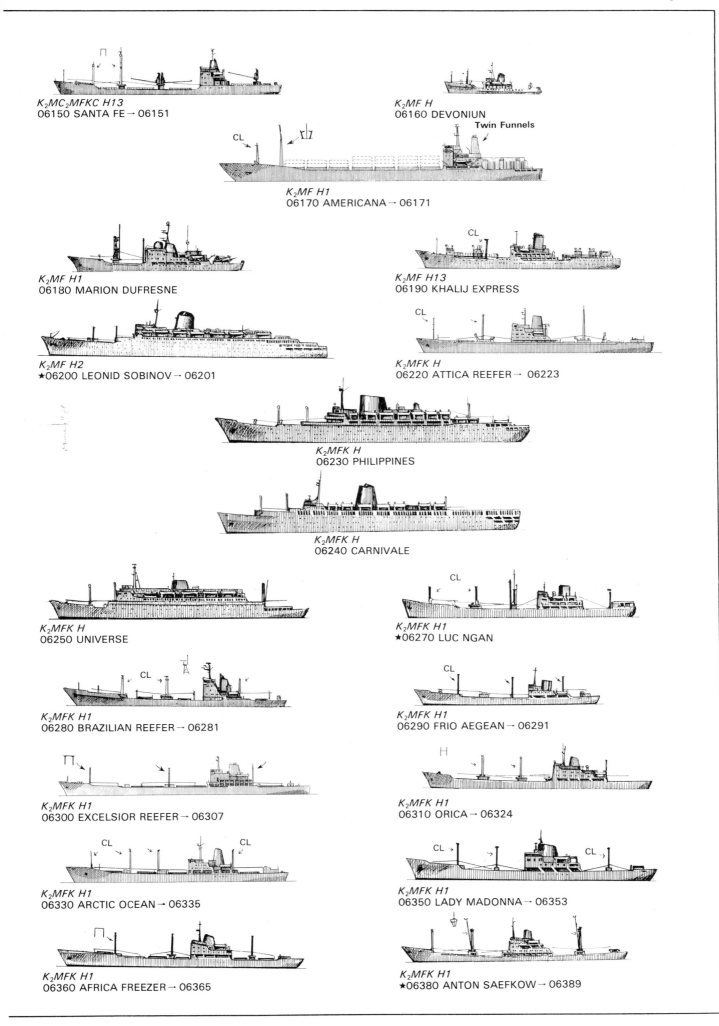

K₂MC₂MFKC H13
06150 SANTA FE → 06151

K₂MF H
06160 DEVONIUN
Twin Funnels

K₂MF H1
06170 AMERICANA → 06171

K₂MF H1
06180 MARION DUFRESNE

K₂MF H13
06190 KHALIJ EXPRESS

K₂MF H2
★06200 LEONID SOBINOV → 06201

K₂MFK H
06220 ATTICA REEFER → 06223

K₂MFK H
06230 PHILIPPINES

K₂MFK H
06240 CARNIVALE

K₂MFK H
06250 UNIVERSE

K₂MFK H1
★06270 LUC NGAN

K₂MFK H1
06280 BRAZILIAN REEFER → 06281

K₂MFK H1
06290 FRIO AEGEAN → 06291

K₂MFK H1
06300 EXCELSIOR REEFER → 06307

K₂MFK H1
06310 ORICA → 06324

K₂MFK H1
06330 ARCTIC OCEAN → 06335

K₂MFK H1
06350 LADY MADONNA → 06353

K₂MFK H1
06360 AFRICA FREEZER → 06365

K₂MFK H1
★06380 ANTON SAEFKOW → 06389

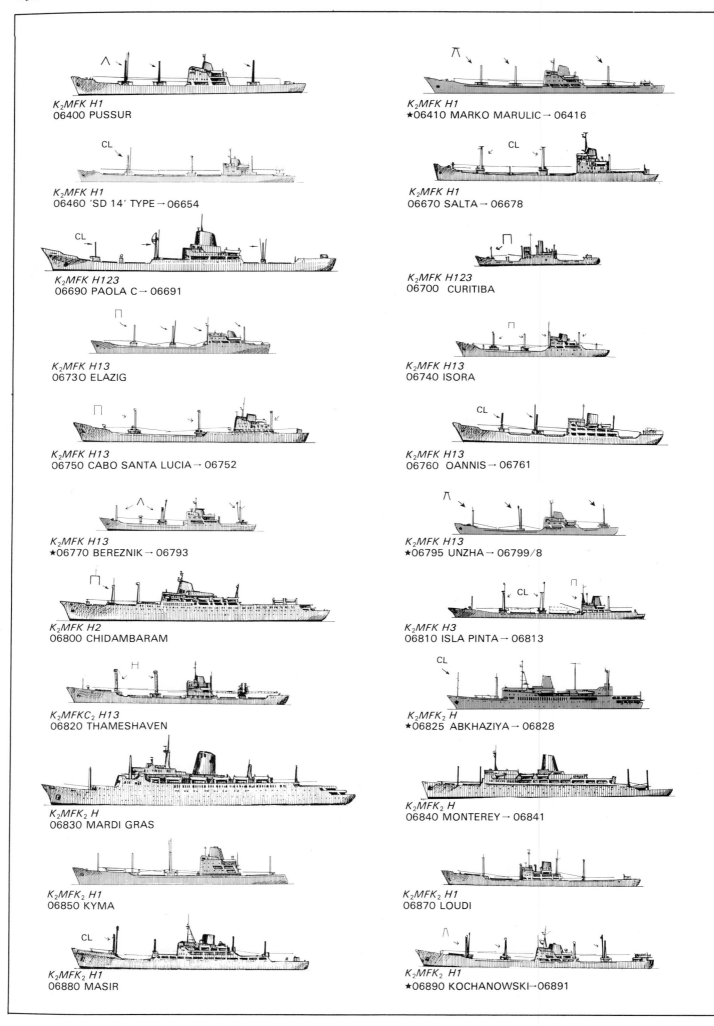

K₂MFK H1
06400 PUSSUR

K₂MFK H1
★06410 MARKO MARULIC → 06416

K₂MFK H1
06460 'SD 14' TYPE → 06654

K₂MFK H1
06670 SALTA → 06678

K₂MFK H123
06690 PAOLA C → 06691

K₂MFK H123
06700 CURITIBA

K₂MFK H13
06730 ELAZIG

K₂MFK H13
06740 ISORA

K₂MFK H13
06750 CABO SANTA LUCIA → 06752

K₂MFK H13
06760 OANNIS → 06761

K₂MFK H13
★06770 BEREZNIK → 06793

K₂MFK H13
★06795 UNZHA → 06799/8

K₂MFK H2
06800 CHIDAMBARAM

K₂MFK H3
06810 ISLA PINTA → 06813

K₂MFKC₂ H13
06820 THAMESHAVEN

K₂MFK₂ H
★06825 ABKHAZIYA → 06828

K₂MFK₂ H
06830 MARDI GRAS

K₂MFK₂ H
06840 MONTEREY → 06841

K₂MFK₂ H1
06850 KYMA

K₂MFK₂ H1
06870 LOUDI

K₂MFK₂ H1
06880 MASIR

K₂MFK₂ H1
★06890 KOCHANOWSKI→06891

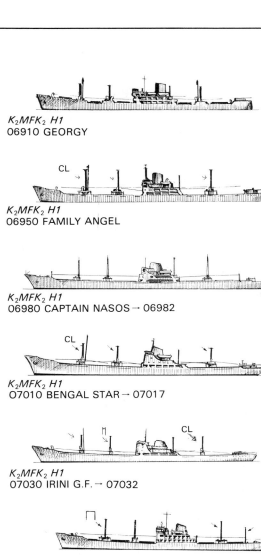

K_2MFK_2 H1
06910 GEORGY

K_2MFK_2 H1
06950 FAMILY ANGEL

K_2MFK_2 H1
06980 CAPTAIN NASOS → 06982

K_2MFK_2 H1
07010 BENGAL STAR → 07017

K_2MFK_2 H1
07030 IRINI G.F. → 07032

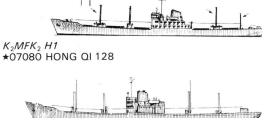

K_2MFK_2 H1
★07080 HONG QI 128

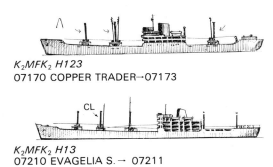

K_2MFK_2 H1
★07100 HYOK SIN

K_2MFK_2 H12
07130 AMAR 1

K_2MFK_2 H123
07170 COPPER TRADER→07173

K_2MFK_2 H13
07210 EVAGELIA S. → 07211

K_2MFK_2 H13
07250 KOTA BERJAYA

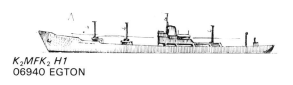

K_2MFK_2 H1
06940 EGTON

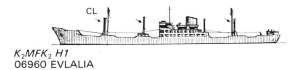

K_2MFK_2 H1
06960 EVLALIA

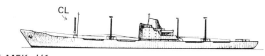

K_2MFK_2 H1
06990 KATRINAMAR → 06992

K_2MFK_2H1
07020 MASTURA ZAHABIA → 07025

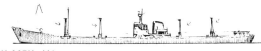

K_2MFK_2 H1
07050 GENIE

K_2MFK_2 H1
07090 SABINE

K_2MFK_2 H1
07120 HWA GEK

K_2MFK_2 H123
07160 SEA ROSE

K_2MFK_2 H123
07180 CITY OF ZUG → 07181

K_2MFK_2 H13
07230 ARGIRO → 07232

K_2MFK_2 H13
07260 AGHIOS GEORGIOS III

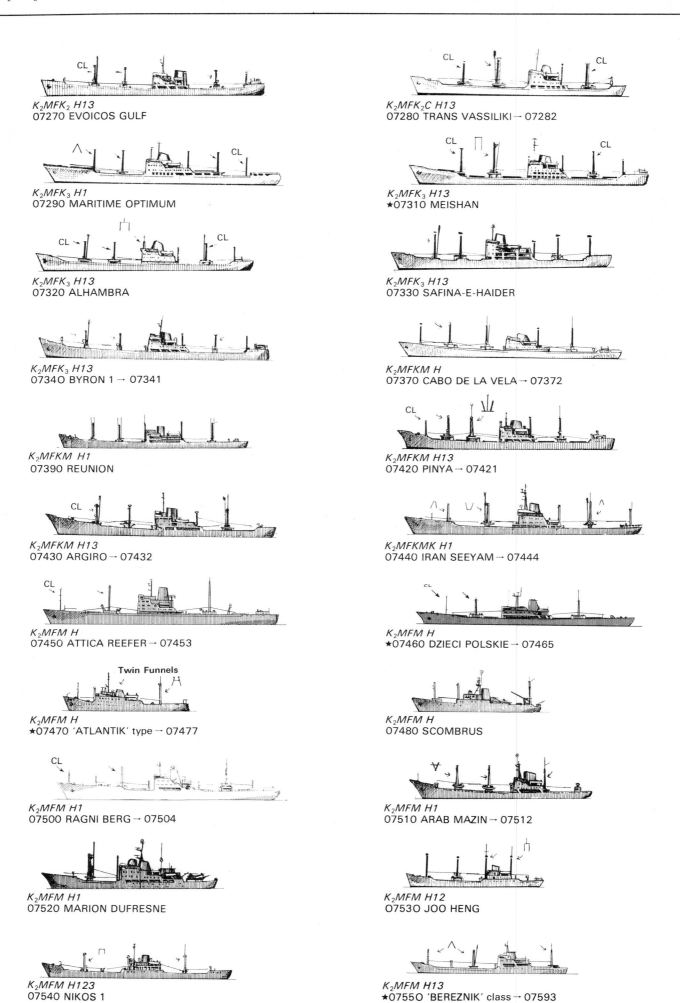

K_2MFK_2 *H13*
07270 EVOICOS GULF

K_2MFK_2C *H13*
07280 TRANS VASSILIKI → 07282

K_2MFK_3 *H1*
07290 MARITIME OPTIMUM

K_2MFK_3 *H13*
★07310 MEISHAN

K_2MFK_3 *H13*
07320 ALHAMBRA

K_2MFK_3 *H13*
07330 SAFINA-E-HAIDER

K_2MFK_3 *H13*
07340 BYRON 1 → 07341

K_2MFKM *H*
07370 CABO DE LA VELA → 07372

K_2MFKM *H1*
07390 REUNION

K_2MFKM *H13*
07420 PINYA → 07421

K_2MFKM *H13*
07430 ARGIRO → 07432

K_2MFKMK *H1*
07440 IRAN SEEYAM → 07444

K_2MFM *H*
07450 ATTICA REEFER → 07453

K_2MFM *H*
★07460 DZIECI POLSKIE → 07465

Twin Funnels

K_2MFM *H*
★07470 'ATLANTIK' type → 07477

K_2MFM *H*
07480 SCOMBRUS

K_2MFM *H1*
07500 RAGNI BERG → 07504

K_2MFM *H1*
07510 ARAB MAZIN → 07512

K_2MFM *H1*
07520 MARION DUFRESNE

K_2MFM *H12*
07530 JOO HENG

K_2MFM *H123*
07540 NIKOS 1

K_2MFM *H13*
★07550 'BEREZNIK' class → 07593

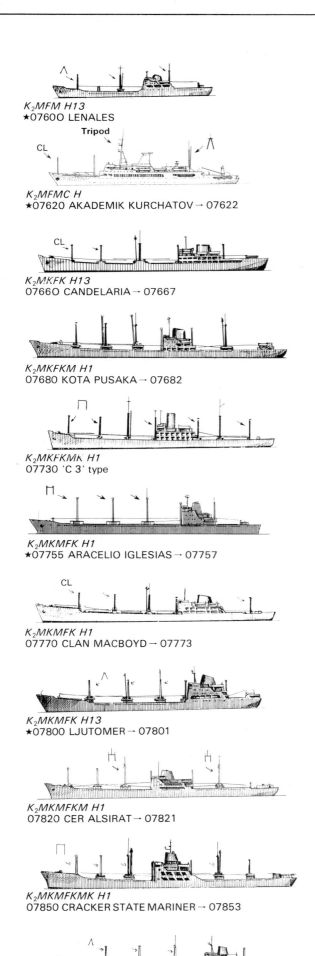

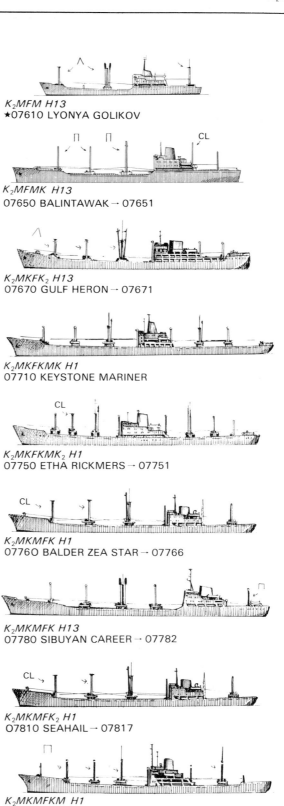

K₂MFM H13
★07600 LENALES

K₂MFM H13
★07610 LYONYA GOLIKOV

Tripod

K₂MFMC H
★07620 AKADEMIK KURCHATOV → 07622

K₂MFMK H13
07650 BALINTAWAK → 07651

K₂MKFK H13
07660 CANDELARIA → 07667

K₂MKFK₂ H13
07670 GULF HERON → 07671

K₂MKFKM H1
07680 KOTA PUSAKA → 07682

K₂MKFKMK H1
07710 KEYSTONE MARINER

K₂MKFKMK H1
07730 'C 3' type

K₂MKFKMK₂ H1
07750 ETHA RICKMERS → 07751

K₂MKMFK H1
★07755 ARACELIO IGLESIAS → 07757

K₂MKMFK H1
07760 BALDER ZEA STAR → 07766

K₂MKMFK H1
07770 CLAN MACBOYD → 07773

K₂MKMFK H13
07780 SIBUYAN CAREER → 07782

K₂MKMFK H13
★07800 LJUTOMER → 07801

K₂MKMFK₂ H1
07810 SEAHAIL → 07817

K₂MKMFKM H1
07820 CER ALSIRAT → 07821

K₂MKMFKM H1
07840 BRAZILIAN EXPRESS → 07842

K₂MKMFKMK H1
07850 CRACKER STATE MARINER → 07853

K₂M₂FC H12
★07860 ANTONI GARNUSZEWSKI → 07863

K₂M₂FK H1
07880 KEBAN → 07885

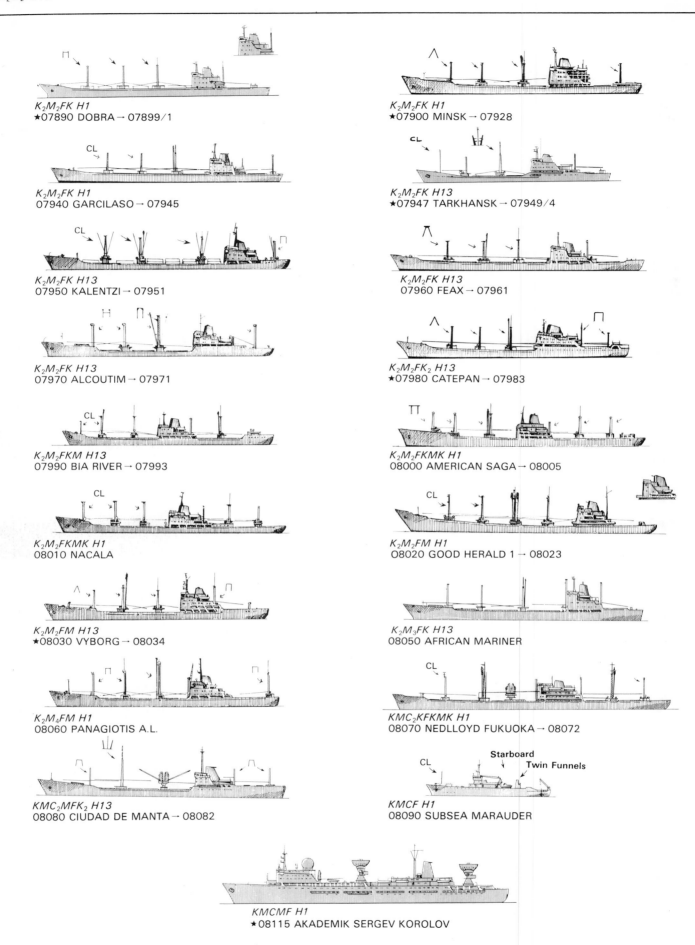

K₂M₂FK H1
★07890 DOBRA → 07899/1

K₂M₂FK H1
★07900 MINSK → 07928

K₂M₂FK H1
07940 GARCILASO → 07945

K₂M₂FK H13
★07947 TARKHANSK → 07949/4

K₂M₂FK H13
07950 KALENTZI → 07951

K₂M₂FK H13
07960 FEAX → 07961

K₂M₂FK H13
07970 ALCOUTIM → 07971

K₂M₂FK₂ H13
★07980 CATEPAN → 07983

K₂M₂FKM H13
07990 BIA RIVER → 07993

K₂M₂FKMK H1
08000 AMERICAN SAGA → 08005

K₂M₂FKMK H1
08010 NACALA

K₂M₂FM H1
08020 GOOD HERALD 1 → 08023

K₂M₂FM H13
★08030 VYBORG → 08034

K₂M₃FK H13
08050 AFRICAN MARINER

K₂M₄FM H1
08060 PANAGIOTIS A.L.

KMC₂KFKMK H1
08070 NEDLLOYD FUKUOKA → 08072

KMC₂MFK₂ H13
08080 CIUDAD DE MANTA → 08082

Starboard
Twin Funnels

KMCF H1
08090 SUBSEA MARAUDER

KMCMF H1
★08115 AKADEMIK SERGEV KOROLOV

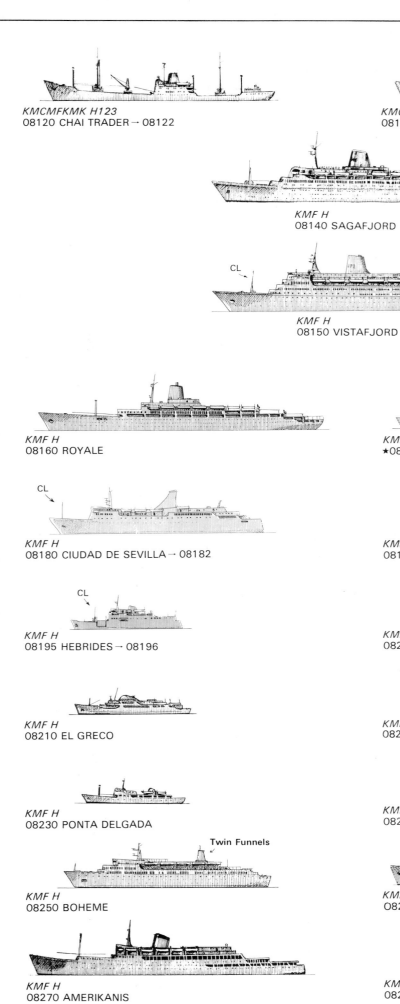
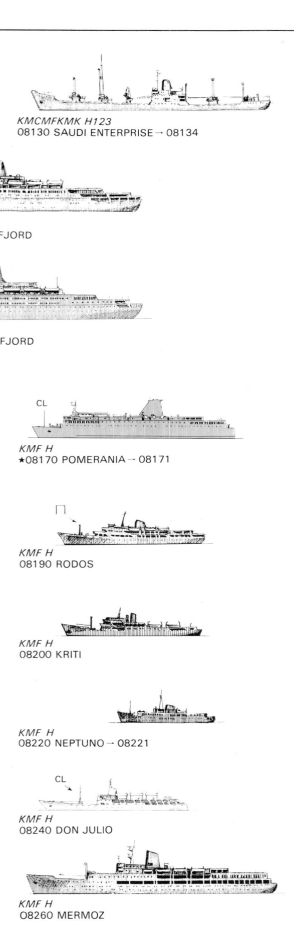

KMCMFKMK H123
08120 CHAI TRADER → 08122

KMCMFKMK H123
08130 SAUDI ENTERPRISE → 08134

KMF H
08140 SAGAFJORD

KMF H
08150 VISTAFJORD

KMF H
08160 ROYALE

KMF H
★08170 POMERANIA → 08171

KMF H
08180 CIUDAD DE SEVILLA → 08182

KMF H
08190 RODOS

KMF H
08195 HEBRIDES → 08196

KMF H
08200 KRITI

KMF H
08210 EL GRECO

KMF H
08220 NEPTUNO → 08221

KMF H
08230 PONTA DELGADA

KMF H
08240 DON JULIO

Twin Funnels

KMF H
08250 BOHEME

KMF H
O8260 MERMOZ

KMF H
08270 AMERIKANIS

KMF H
08280 LA PALMA → 08282

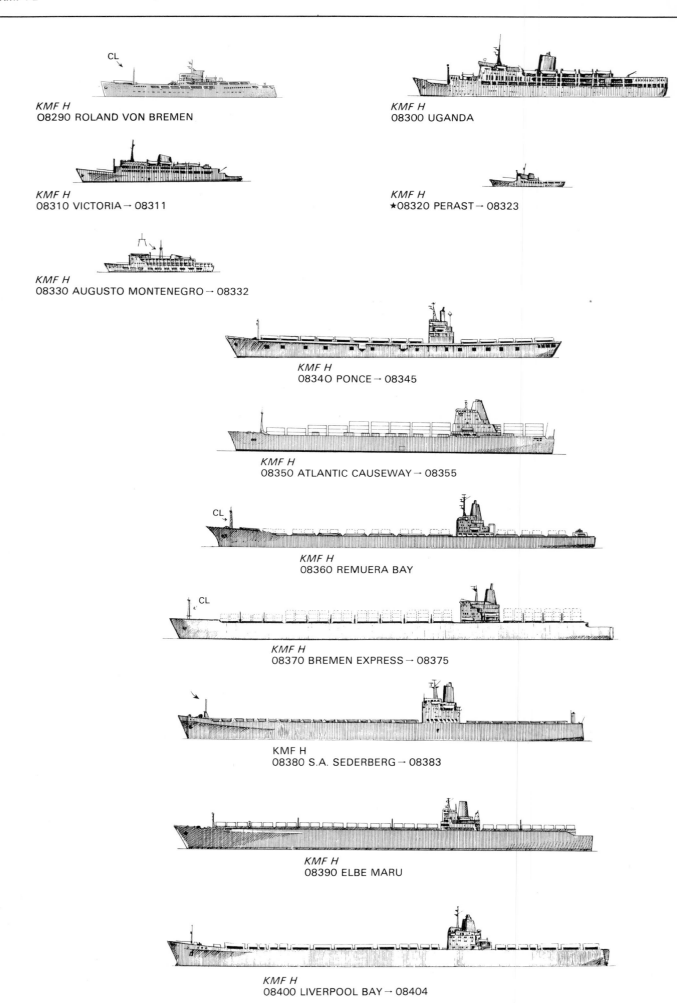

KMF H
08290 ROLAND VON BREMEN

KMF H
08300 UGANDA

KMF H
08310 VICTORIA → 08311

KMF H
★08320 PERAST → 08323

KMF H
08330 AUGUSTO MONTENEGRO → 08332

KMF H
08340 PONCE → 08345

KMF H
08350 ATLANTIC CAUSEWAY → 08355

KMF H
08360 REMUERA BAY

KMF H
08370 BREMEN EXPRESS → 08375

KMF H
08380 S.A. SEDERBERG → 08383

KMF H
08390 ELBE MARU

KMF H
08400 LIVERPOOL BAY → 08404

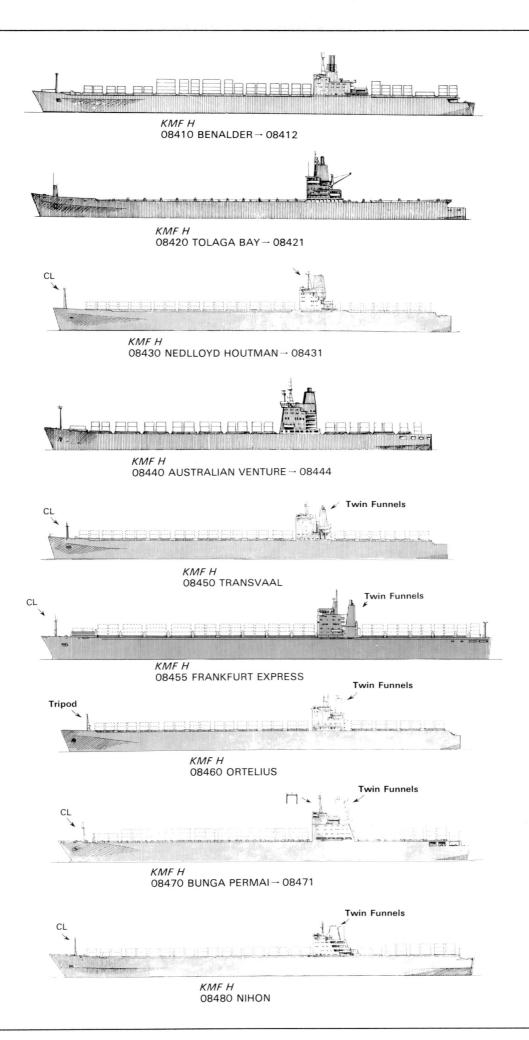

KMF H
08410 BENALDER → 08412

KMF H
08420 TOLAGA BAY → 08421

CL

KMF H
08430 NEDLLOYD HOUTMAN → 08431

KMF H
08440 AUSTRALIAN VENTURE → 08444

CL
Twin Funnels

KMF H
08450 TRANSVAAL

CL
Twin Funnels

KMF H
08455 FRANKFURT EXPRESS

Tripod
Twin Funnels

KMF H
08460 ORTELIUS

CL
Twin Funnels

KMF H
08470 BUNGA PERMAI → 08471

CL
Twin Funnels

KMF H
08480 NIHON

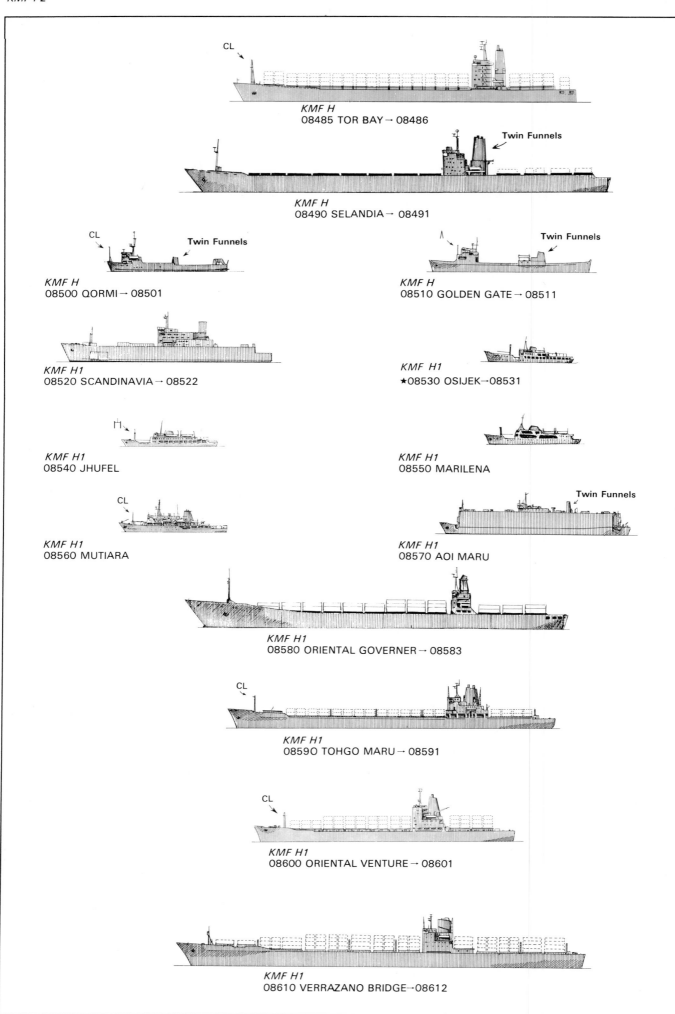

KMF H
08485 TOR BAY → 08486

Twin Funnels

KMF H
08490 SELANDIA → 08491

CL   Twin Funnels

KMF H
08500 QORMI → 08501

Twin Funnels

KMF H
08510 GOLDEN GATE → 08511

KMF H1
08520 SCANDINAVIA → 08522

KMF H1
★08530 OSIJEK → 08531

KMF H1
08540 JHUFEL

KMF H1
08550 MARILENA

CL

KMF H1
08560 MUTIARA

Twin Funnels

KMF H1
08570 AOI MARU

KMF H1
08580 ORIENTAL GOVERNER → 08583

CL

KMF H1
08590 TOHGO MARU → 08591

CL

KMF H1
08600 ORIENTAL VENTURE → 08601

KMF H1
08610 VERRAZANO BRIDGE → 08612

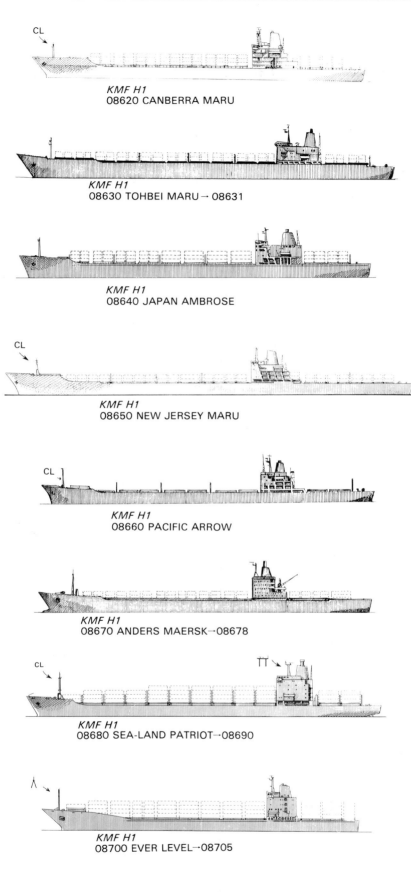

KMF H1
08620 CANBERRA MARU

KMF H1
08630 TOHBEI MARU → 08631

KMF H1
08640 JAPAN AMBROSE

KMF H1
08650 NEW JERSEY MARU

KMF H1
08660 PACIFIC ARROW

KMF H1
08670 ANDERS MAERSK → 08678

KMF H1
08680 SEA-LAND PATRIOT → 08690

KMF H1
08700 EVER LEVEL → 08705

KMF H1
08710 GREAT LAND

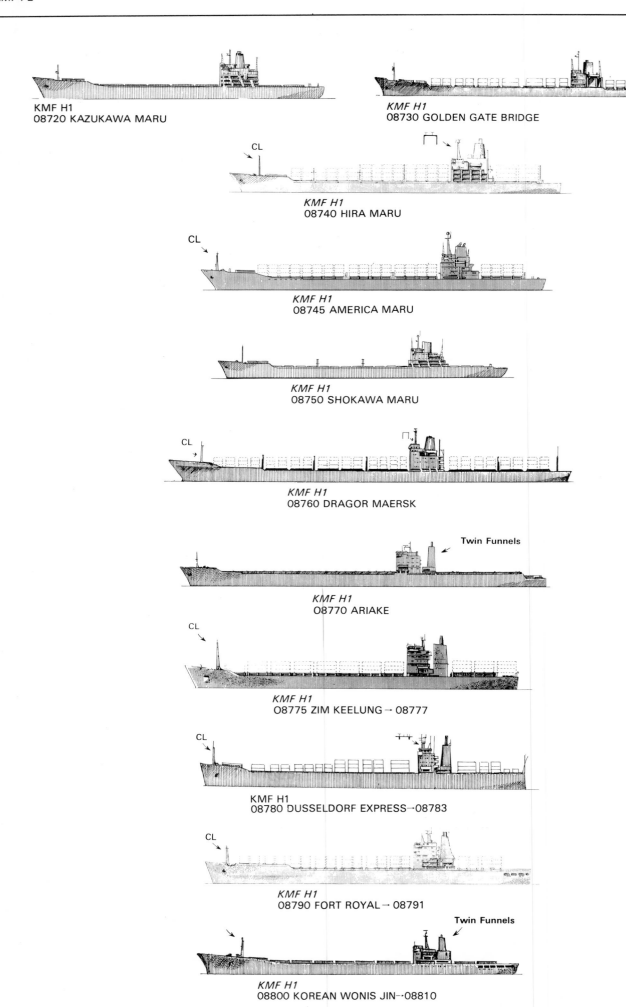

KMF H1
08720 KAZUKAWA MARU

KMF H1
08730 GOLDEN GATE BRIDGE

KMF H1
08740 HIRA MARU

KMF H1
08745 AMERICA MARU

KMF H1
08750 SHOKAWA MARU

KMF H1
08760 DRAGOR MAERSK

Twin Funnels

KMF H1
08770 ARIAKE

KMF H1
08775 ZIM KEELUNG → 08777

KMF H1
08780 DUSSELDORF EXPRESS→08783

KMF H1
08790 FORT ROYAL → 08791

Twin Funnels

KMF H1
08800 KOREAN WONIS JIN→08810

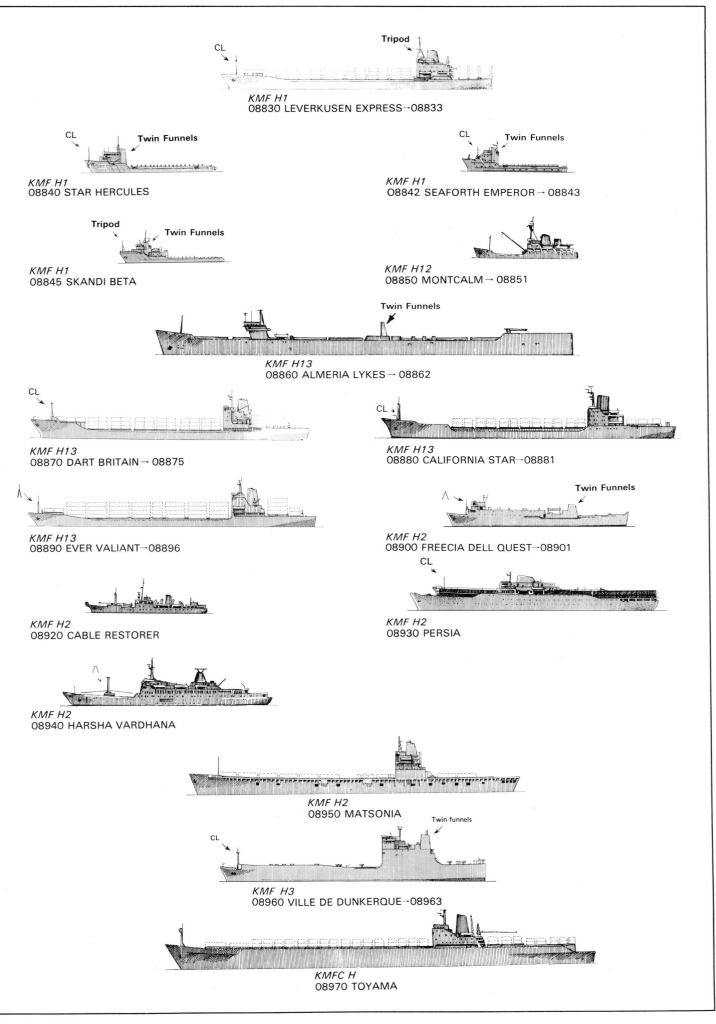

KMF H1
08830 LEVERKUSEN EXPRESS→08833

KMF H1
08840 STAR HERCULES

KMF H1
08842 SEAFORTH EMPEROR → 08843

KMF H1
08845 SKANDI BETA

KMF H12
08850 MONTCALM → 08851

KMF H13
08860 ALMERIA LYKES → 08862

KMF H13
08870 DART BRITAIN → 08875

KMF H13
08880 CALIFORNIA STAR→08881

KMF H13
08890 EVER VALIANT→08896

KMF H2
08900 FREECIA DELL QUEST→08901

KMF H2
08920 CABLE RESTORER

KMF H2
08930 PERSIA

KMF H2
08940 HARSHA VARDHANA

KMF H2
08950 MATSONIA

KMF H3
08960 VILLE DE DUNKERQUE→08963

KMFC H
08970 TOYAMA

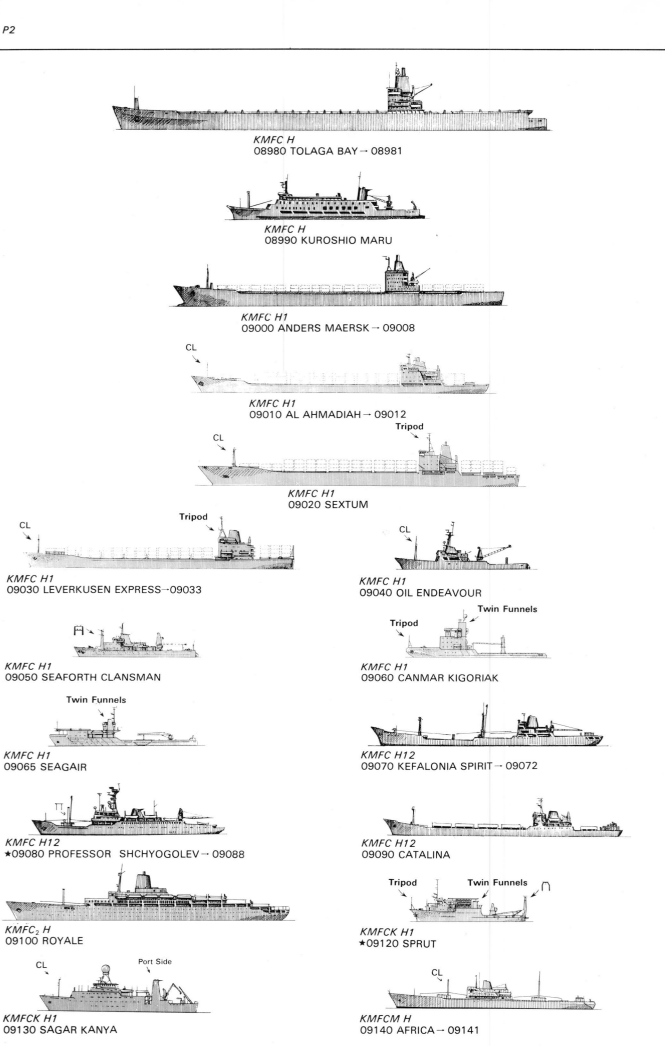

KMFC H
08980 TOLAGA BAY → 08981

KMFC H
08990 KUROSHIO MARU

KMFC H1
09000 ANDERS MAERSK → 09008

CL

KMFC H1
09010 AL AHMADIAH → 09012

CL   Tripod

KMFC H1
09020 SEXTUM

CL   Tripod

KMFC H1
09030 LEVERKUSEN EXPRESS → 09033

CL

KMFC H1
09040 OIL ENDEAVOUR

Twin Funnels
Tripod

KMFC H1
09050 SEAFORTH CLANSMAN

KMFC H1
09060 CANMAR KIGORIAK

Twin Funnels

KMFC H1
09065 SEAGAIR

KMFC H12
09070 KEFALONIA SPIRIT → 09072

KMFC H12
★09080 PROFESSOR SHCHYOGOLEV → 09088

KMFC H12
09090 CATALINA

Tripod   Twin Funnels

KMFC₂ H
09100 ROYALE

KMFCK H1
★09120 SPRUT

CL   Port Side

KMFCK H1
09130 SAGAR KANYA

CL

KMFCM H
09140 AFRICA → 09141

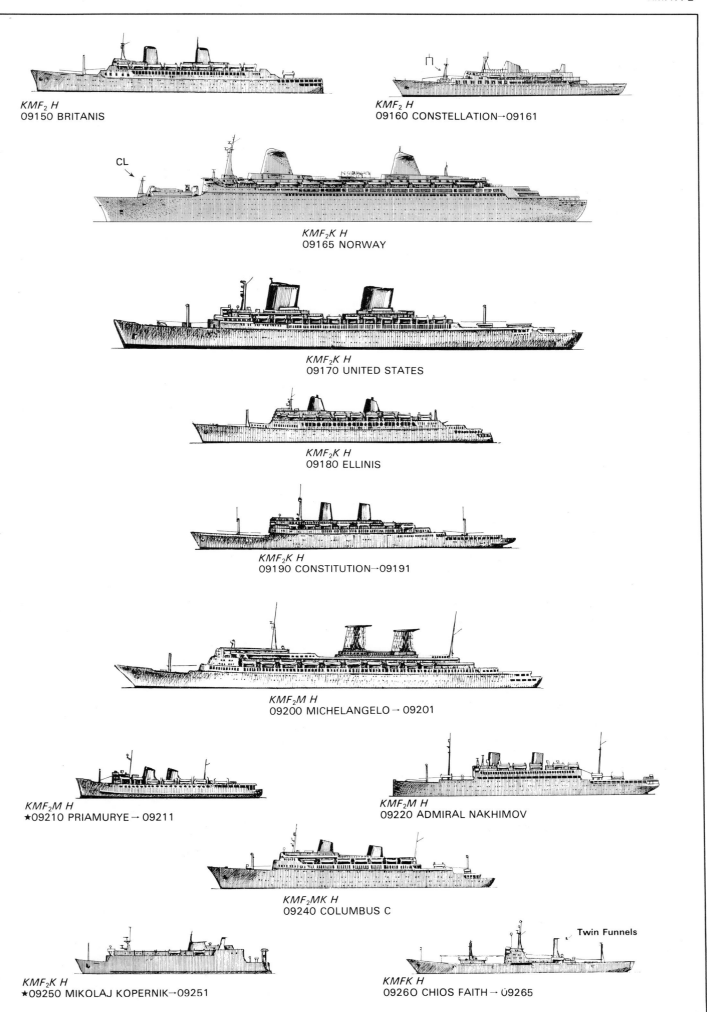

KMF₂ H
09150 BRITANIS

KMF₂ H
09160 CONSTELLATION→09161

CL

KMF₂K H
09165 NORWAY

KMF₂K H
09170 UNITED STATES

KMF₂K H
09180 ELLINIS

KMF₂K H
09190 CONSTITUTION→09191

KMF₂M H
09200 MICHELANGELO→09201

KMF₂M H
★09210 PRIAMURYE→09211

KMF₂M H
09220 ADMIRAL NAKHIMOV

KMF₂MK H
09240 COLUMBUS C

Twin Funnels

KMF₂K H
★09250 MIKOLAJ KOPERNIK→09251

KMFK H
09260 CHIOS FAITH→09265

KMFK H
09270 LIPARI

KMFK H
09280 ST. MARGARETS

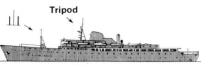

KMFK H
09290 ANG PANGULO

KMFK H
09300 ORION

KMFK H
09310 FLAVIAN

KMFK H
09320 RHAPSODY

KMFK H
09330 VISTAFJORD

KMFK H
09340 VERACRUZ 1

KMFK H
09350 TERAAKA → 09351

KMFK H
★09360 GRUMANT → 09377

KMFK H
★09380 SKRYPLEV → 09387

KMFK H
09390 ACHILLEUS → 09393

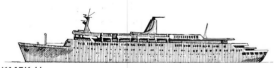

KMFK H
09410 STELLA SOLARIS

KMFK H
09420 MARIANNA VI

KMFK H
09430 NIPPON MARU → 09431

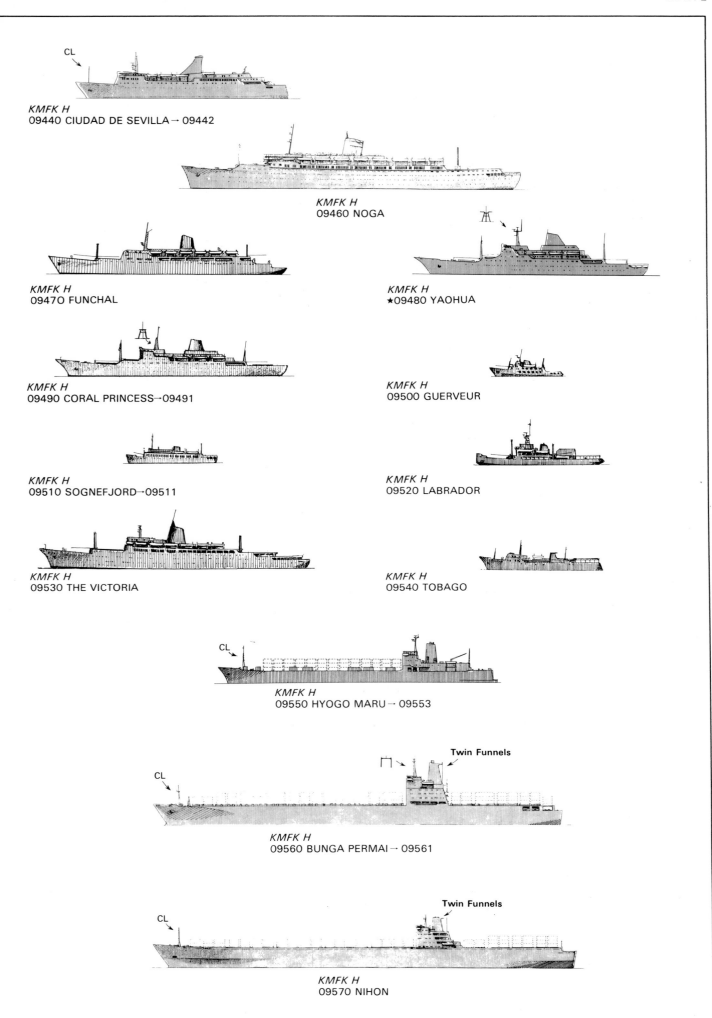

KMFK H
09440 CIUDAD DE SEVILLA → 09442

KMFK H
09460 NOGA

KMFK H
09470 FUNCHAL

KMFK H
★09480 YAOHUA

KMFK H
09490 CORAL PRINCESS→09491

KMFK H
09500 GUERVEUR

KMFK H
09510 SOGNEFJORD→09511

KMFK H
09520 LABRADOR

KMFK H
09530 THE VICTORIA

KMFK H
09540 TOBAGO

KMFK H
09550 HYOGO MARU → 09553

Twin Funnels

KMFK H
09560 BUNGA PERMAI → 09561

Twin Funnels

KMFK H
09570 NIHON

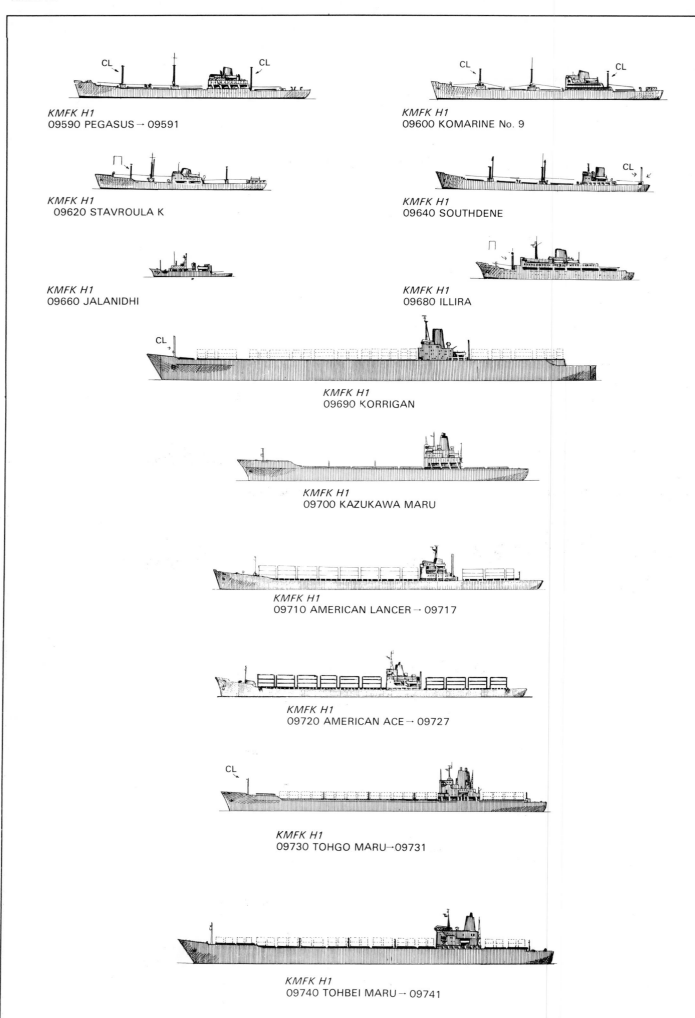

KMFK H1
09590 PEGASUS → 09591

KMFK H1
09600 KOMARINE No. 9

KMFK H1
09620 STAVROULA K

KMFK H1
09640 SOUTHDENE

KMFK H1
09660 JALANIDHI

KMFK H1
09680 ILLIRA

KMFK H1
09690 KORRIGAN

KMFK H1
09700 KAZUKAWA MARU

KMFK H1
09710 AMERICAN LANCER → 09717

KMFK H1
09720 AMERICAN ACE → 09727

KMFK H1
09730 TOHGO MARU → 09731

KMFK H1
09740 TOHBEI MARU → 09741

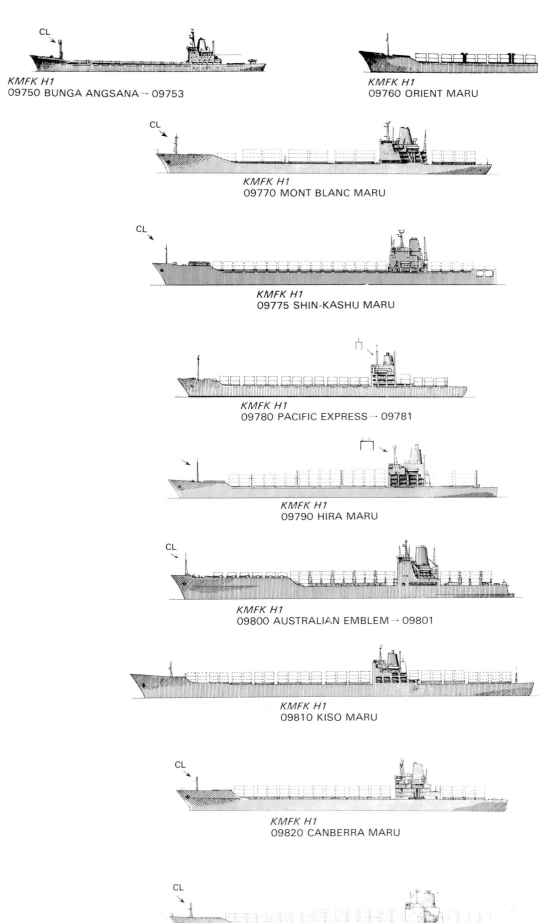

KMFK H1
09750 BUNGA ANGSANA → 09753

KMFK H1
09760 ORIENT MARU

KMFK H1
09770 MONT BLANC MARU

KMFK H1
09775 SHIN-KASHU MARU

KMFK H1
09780 PACIFIC EXPRESS → 09781

KMFK H1
09790 HIRA MARU

KMFK H1
09800 AUSTRALIAN EMBLEM → 09801

KMFK H1
09810 KISO MARU

KMFK H1
09820 CANBERRA MARU

KMFK H1
09830 CHINA CONTAINER → 09842

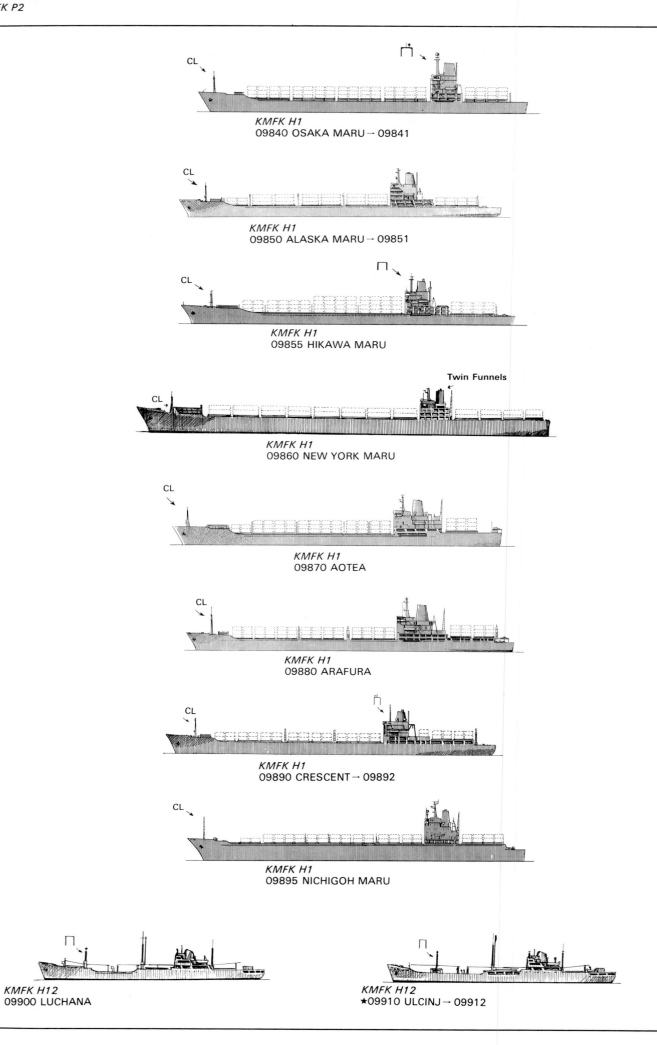

KMFK H1
09840 OSAKA MARU → 09841

KMFK H1
09850 ALASKA MARU → 09851

KMFK H1
09855 HIKAWA MARU

Twin Funnels

KMFK H1
09860 NEW YORK MARU

KMFK H1
09870 AOTEA

KMFK H1
09880 ARAFURA

KMFK H1
09890 CRESCENT → 09892

KMFK H1
09895 NICHIGOH MARU

KMFK H12
09900 LUCHANA

KMFK H12
★09910 ULCINJ → 09912

KMFK H12
09920 CAMSELL

KMFK H12
09925 SANTA MARIA DE LA PAZ → 09926

KMFK H12
09930 MARIAM

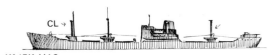

KMFK H13
09940 ALPAC ASIA → 09941

KMFK H13
09950 PENTA-Y → 09951

KMFK H13
09960 CASTLE SPIRIT → 09962

KMFK H13
09980 LAS ARENAS → 09981

KMFK H13
09990 REIYO MARU → 09991

KMFK H13
★09995 GAMZAT TSADASA → 09998

KMFK H13
10000 EVER SHINE → 10003

KMFK H13
10005 PHOLAS

KMFK H2
10010 SALERNUM

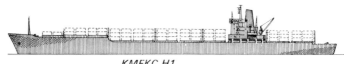

KMFKC H1
10020 ASIA MARU

KMFKC H1
10030 TOYAMA

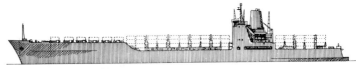

KMFKC H1
10040 AUSTRALIAN EMBLEM → 10041

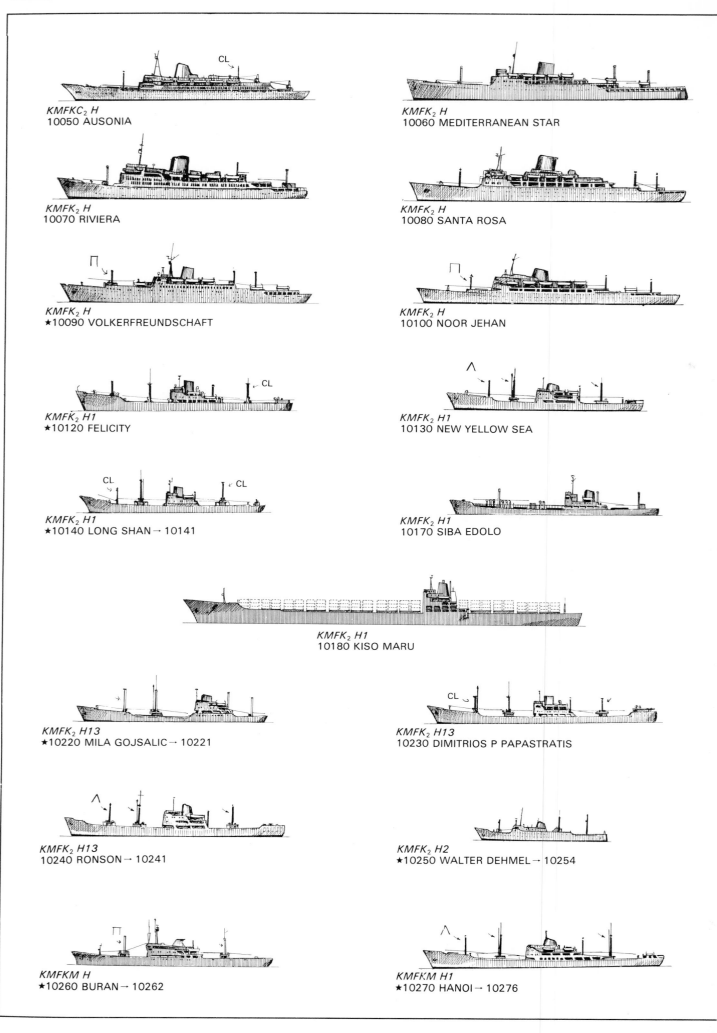

KMFKC₂ H
10050 AUSONIA

KMFK₂ H
10060 MEDITERRANEAN STAR

KMFK₂ H
10070 RIVIERA

KMFK₂ H
10080 SANTA ROSA

KMFK₂ H
★10090 VOLKERFREUNDSCHAFT

KMFK₂ H
10100 NOOR JEHAN

KMFK₂ H1
★10120 FELICITY

KMFK₂ H1
10130 NEW YELLOW SEA

KMFK₂ H1
★10140 LONG SHAN → 10141

KMFK₂ H1
10170 SIBA EDOLO

KMFK₂ H1
10180 KISO MARU

KMFK₂ H13
★10220 MILA GOJSALIC → 10221

KMFK₂ H13
10230 DIMITRIOS P PAPASTRATIS

KMFK₂ H13
10240 RONSON → 10241

KMFK₂ H2
★10250 WALTER DEHMEL → 10254

KMFKM H
★10260 BURAN → 10262

KMFKM H1
★10270 HANOI → 10276

KMFM H
10790 DON EUSEBIO

KMFM H
10800 MANILA CITY

KMFM H
★10810 SEJWAL → 10818

KMFM H
10850 d'IBERVILLE

KMFM H
10860 JOHN A MACDONALD

KMFM H1
★10880 MALAKHOV KURGAN → 10882

KMFM H1
10910 MINOTAURUS

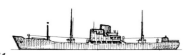

KMFM H1
10920 M. ALEXAND → 10925

KMFM H1
★10930 LINK LOVE

KMFM H1
10940 ABU MISHARI AL KULAIB

KMFM H1
★10990 LIKA → 10994

KMFM H1
★11100 NIKOLA TESLA

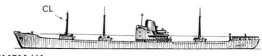

KMFM H1
11110 TAYGETUS → 11114

KMFM H1
11130 LANKA SHANTHI → 11131

KMFM H1
★11140 THEODOR STORM → 11141

KMFM H1
11150 REEFER MANGGIS → 11151

KMFM H1
11160 EMANUEL

KMFM H1
11170 IRISEVERETT → 11173

KMFM H1
11190 INTRA TRANSPORTER

KMFM H1
11210 MISAMIS OCCIDENTAL

KMFM H1
11220 HOKUTO MARU → 11221

KMFM H1
11230 SHINTOKU MARU

KMFM H1
11240 CITY OF HYDRA

KMFM H1
11250 ROYAL ZULU

KMFM H1
11260 EDRA

KMFM H1
11270 AMARYLLIS

KMFM H1
11290 TOULA

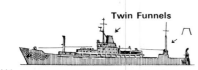

KMFM H1
★11300 KOPET-DAG → 11330

KMFM H1
★11333 BALAKHNA → 11336/3

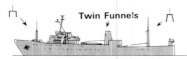

KMFM H1
★11337 AQUILA → 11339

KMFM H1
11340 AMERICAN ENVOY → 11343

KMFM H1
11350 AMERICAN MARKETER → 11355

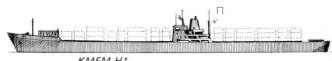

KMFM H1
11360 SANTA PAULA → 11363

KMFM H1
11370 HUDAIBAH

KMFM H12
★11380 BOROVICHI → 11383

KMFM H12
11400 SOZER BIRADERLAR

KMFM H12
11410 DHARINI

KMFM H12
11420 TAISEI MARU

KMFM H123
★11430 CHULYMLES → 11453

KMFM H123
★11460 BASKUNCHAK → 11466

KMFM H123
11470 POSEIDONIA

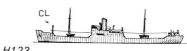

KMFM H123
11480 FARID M

KMFM H13
★11490 INDIGA → 11503

KMFM H13
11520 PANKY

KMFM H13
11530 IONIAN SPIRIT → 11532

KMFM H13
11540 MALDIVE PEARL

KMFM H13
11550 PRESIDENT TAFT → 11553

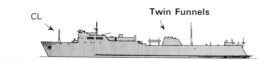

KMFM H2
11560 SIR ROBERT BOND

KMFM H2
11570 RECORDER

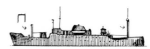

KMFM H2
★11580 KOMETA→ 11608

KMFM H2
★11610 SMOLNYY→ 11636

KMFM H2
★11640 ANDROMEDA→ 11656

KMFM H2
11660 COLUMBA→ 11665

KMFM H2
★11670 VEGA→ 11682

KMFM H2
★11690 PROFESOR SIEDLECKI

KMFM H2
★11695 CARINA

KMFM H2
★11700 RETEZATUL→ 11716

KMFM H2
★11720 TARUSA→ 11789/1

KMFM H2
11790 WLOCZNIK→ 11791

KMFM H2
★11800 'ATLANTIK' class→11980

KMFM H2
11990 BRITISH VOYAGER

KMFM H2
★11995 PRIMORYE

KMFMC H
★12000 AKADEMIK KOROLYOV→ 12003

KMFMK H
★12010 SOVIETSKIY SOYUZ

KMFMK H
12030 ROTTERDAM

KMFMK H
★12035 SHIJIAN

KMFMK H1
★12040 PRIMORJE

KMFMK H1
12070 VISHVA VIVEK

KMFMK H1
★12080 VENICE

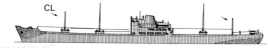

KMFMK H1
12100 SILVER CITY → 12102

KMFMK H1
12110 KUNUNGUAK

KMFMK H123
★12140 CHAPAYEVSK → 12167

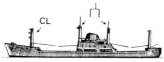

KMFMK H13
12210 SAONA → 12211

KMFMK H2
12220 EMPIRE STATE

KMFMK H2
★12230 KERCH → 12316

KMFMK H2
★12320 'PUSHKIN' class→12327

KMFMK H2
★12340 Modified 'PUSHKIN' class→12353

KMFMK H2
★12360 'MAYAKOVSKIY' class→12373

KMFMK H2
★12380 Modified 'MAYAKOVSKIY' class→12559

KMFMK H2
★12570 AKADEMIK KNIPOVICH → 12580

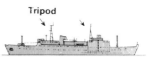

KMFMK H2
★12585 ODISSEY → 12586

KMFMK H2
★12587 ZAKARPATYE → 12589

KMFMK H2
★12590 'LESKOV' class→12599

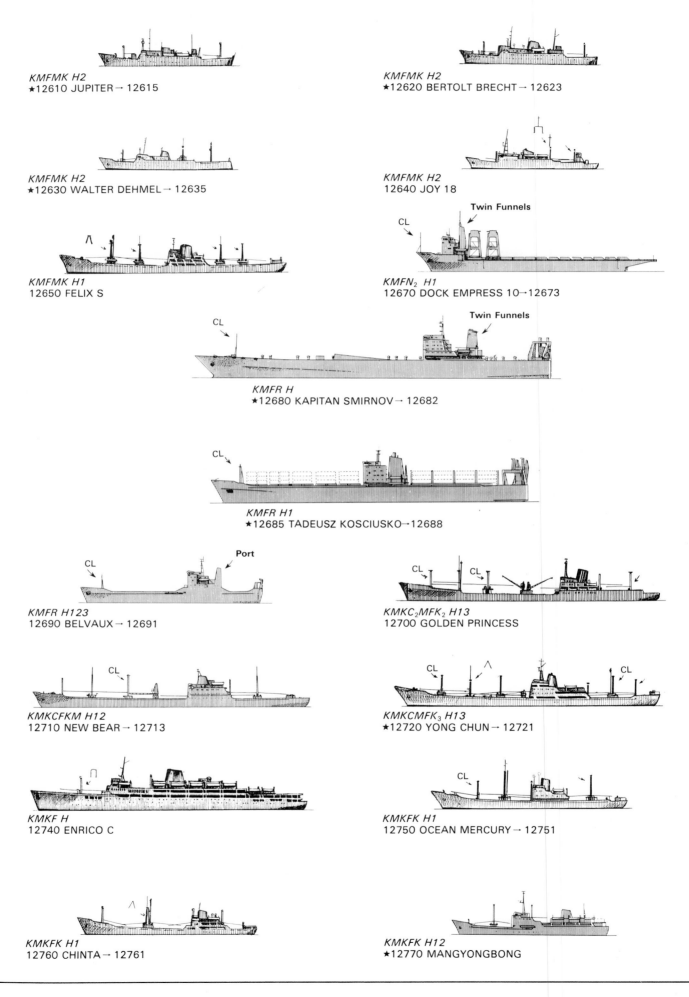

KMFMK H2
★12610 JUPITER → 12615

KMFMK H2
★12620 BERTOLT BRECHT → 12623

KMFMK H2
★12630 WALTER DEHMEL → 12635

KMFMK H2
12640 JOY 18

KMFMK H1
12650 FELIX S

Twin Funnels

CL

KMFN₂ H1
★12670 DOCK EMPRESS 10 → 12673

CL

Twin Funnels

KMFR H
★12680 KAPITAN SMIRNOV → 12682

CL

KMFR H1
★12685 TADEUSZ KOSCIUSKO → 12688

CL

Port

KMFR H123
12690 BELVAUX → 12691

CL   CL

KMKC₂MFK₂ H13
12700 GOLDEN PRINCESS

CL

KMKCFKM H12
12710 NEW BEAR → 12713

CL   CL

KMKCMFK₃ H13
★12720 YONG CHUN → 12721

KMKF H
12740 ENRICO C

CL

KMKFK H1
12750 OCEAN MERCURY → 12751

KMKFK H1
12760 CHINTA → 12761

KMKFK H12
★12770 MANGYONGBONG

Twin Funnels

KMKFK H12
12780 SEAWAY FALCON

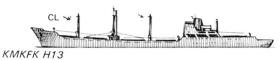

KMKFK H13
★12790 BAIRE → 12794

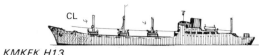

KMKFK H13
12800 TEPIC

KMKFKC H2
12810 AUTOROUTE

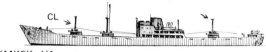

KMKFK₂ H1
12840 MOJAIL-5

KMKFK₂ H1
12850 ANTILLA

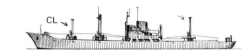

KMKFK₂ H1
12860 OLYMPIAS → 12863

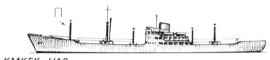

KMKFK₂ H13
12870 NEW DRAGON

KMKFK₂ H13
12880 MAGDALINI K

KMKFK₂ H13
★12900 HUANG JIN SHAN → 12901

KMKFK₂ H13
12910 EURCO R → 12911

KMKFK₃ H1
12940 NATALIA

KMKFK₂ H123
★12960 HONG QI 119→12961

KMKFKM H1
12980 TAIBAH III → 12981

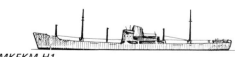

KMKFKM H1
12990 COVADONGA → 12994

KMKFKM H1
★13010 LENINOGORSK → 13016

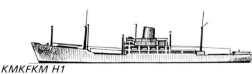

KMKFKM H1
13020 GULF REEFER

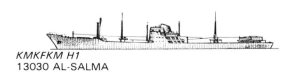

KMKFKM H1
13030 AL-SALMA

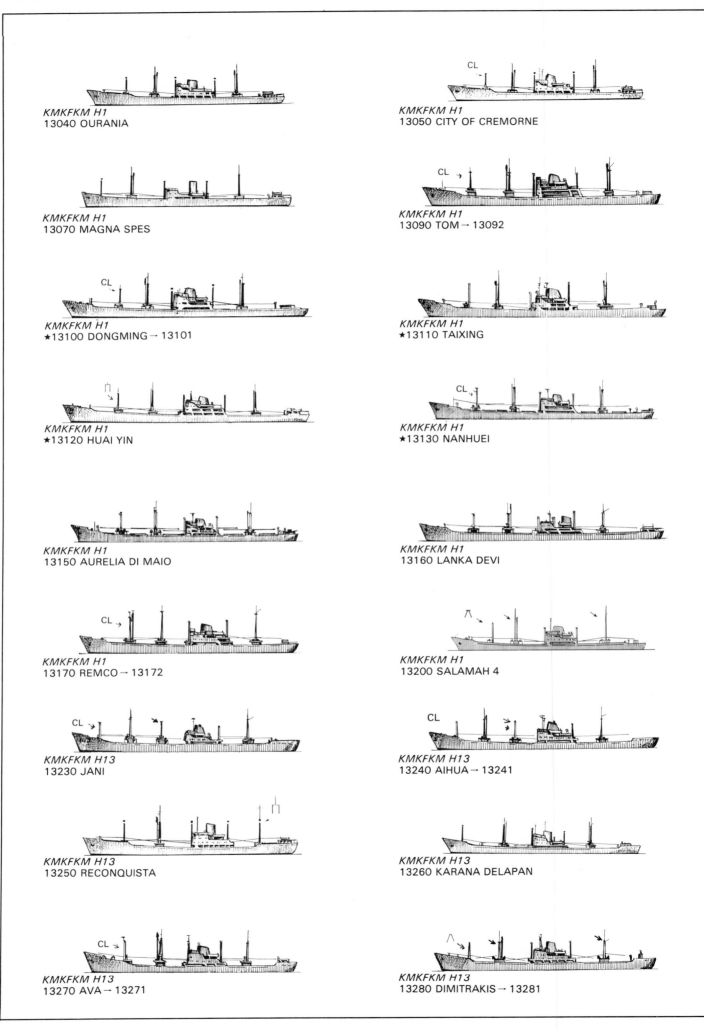

KMKFKM H1
13040 OURANIA

KMKFKM H1
13050 CITY OF CREMORNE

KMKFKM H1
13070 MAGNA SPES

KMKFKM H1
13090 TOM → 13092

KMKFKM H1
★13100 DONGMING → 13101

KMKFKM H1
★13110 TAIXING

KMKFKM H1
★13120 HUAI YIN

KMKFKM H1
★13130 NANHUEI

KMKFKM H1
13150 AURELIA DI MAIO

KMKFKM H1
13160 LANKA DEVI

KMKFKM H1
13170 REMCO → 13172

KMKFKM H1
13200 SALAMAH 4

KMKFKM H13
13230 JANI

KMKFKM H13
13240 AIHUA → 13241

KMKFKM H13
13250 RECONQUISTA

KMKFKM H13
13260 KARANA DELAPAN

KMKFKM H13
13270 AVA → 13271

KMKFKM H13
13280 DIMITRAKIS → 13281

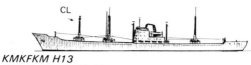

KMKFKM H13
13300 GOLD STREAM → 13301

KMKFKM H13
13310 CHARMYL

KMKFKMK H1
13350 AL SHEHABIA → 13351

KMKFKMK H1
★13370 LINTONG

KMKFKMK H1
13380 LAWANTI → 13393

KMKFKMK H1
13400 BRAVO MARIA

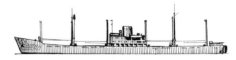

KMKFKMK H1
13410 SAUDI VENTURE

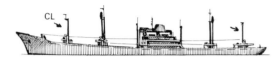

KMKFKMK H1
13430 SAUDI EAGLE → 13431

KMKFKMK H1
13440 GOOD SKIPPER

KMKFKMK H1
13460 BECENA

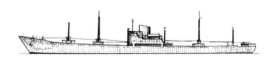

KMKFKMK H1
13470 MEIRU → 13471

KMKFKMK H1
13490 NANHUA → 13493

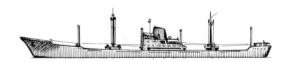

KMKFKMK H13
★13510 N'GOLA → 13514

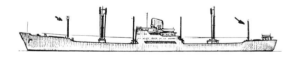

KMKFKMK H13
13520 SAUDI AL MEDINA → 13521

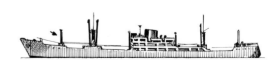

KMKFKMK H13
★13550 XING KONG

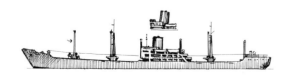

KMKFKMK H13
13560 SUCCESS → 13563

KMKFKMK H13
13580 GOLDEN SAUDIA → 13581

KMKFKMK H13
13590 MILDA A → 13591

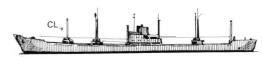

KMKFKMK H13
13610 LELLO DI MAIO

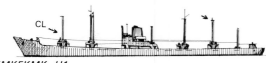

KMKFKMK₂ H1
13630 NANWU

KMKFM H1
★13650 SUPER ATLANTIK type → 13744

KMKFM H1
★13745 PRIZVANIE → 13750

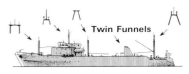

KMKFM H1
★13751 Later 'SUPER ATLANTIK' type → 13777

KMKFM H1
13780 MALDIVE PRIVILEGE

KMKFM H1
13800 RODONAS → 13803

KMKFM H1
13810 GUIRIA → 13813

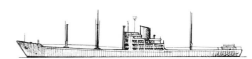

KMKFM H1
13820 SOCRATES

KMKFM H12
★13840 HONG QI 149

KMKFM H123
★13850 MAMAIA

KMKFM H13
13860 MISHA S. AMITY

KMKFMK H1
13890 SILVER CITY → 13892

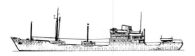

KMKFMK H123
13930 MALDIVE UNITY

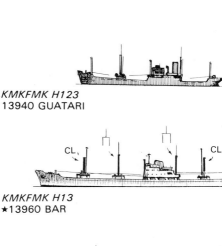

KMKFMK H123
13940 GUATARI

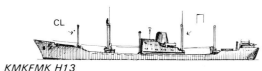

KMKFMK H13
★13950 USKOK

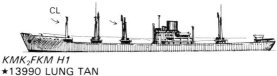

KMKFMK H13
★13960 BAR

KMK₂FK₂ H13
13980 SAUDI ROSE → 13982

KMK₂FKM H1
★13990 LUNG TAN

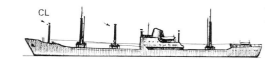

KMK₂FKM H13
14000 DAUNTLESS

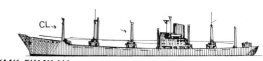

KMK₂FKM H13
14010 LUCKY STAR II

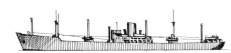

KMK₂FKMK H1
14020 FELICITY

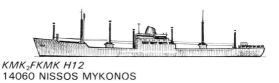

KMK₂FKMK H1
14040 RIEDERSTEIN

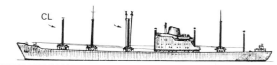

KMK₂FKMK H1
★14050 HONG YIN → 14051

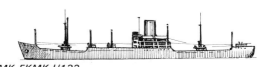

KMK₂FKMK H12
14060 NISSOS MYKONOS

KMK₂FKMK H12
14070 SAFINA-E-ARAB

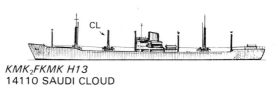

KMK₂FKMK H123
14080 EUROPE II → 14081

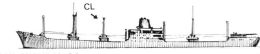

KMK₂FKMK H123
14090 NEW SWAN → 14091

KMK₂FKMK H13
14110 SAUDI CLOUD

KMK₂FM H1
14130 YARA

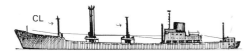

KMK₃MFK H13
14140 GAMA GETAH → 14143

KMK₂MFK H1
14150 CABO SANTA ANA

KMK₂MFK H1
14160 NAKORNTHON

KMK₂MFK H1
14170 MORILLO → 14175

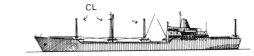

KMK₂MFK H13
14190 PEGASUS → 14192

KMK₂MFK₃ H13
14210 CERAM SEA

KMK₂MFKM H13
14220 SINKAI

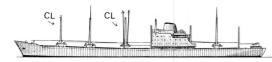

KMK₂MFKMK H1
★14230 HONG YIN → 14231

KMK₂MFKMK H13
14240 JADE

KMKMF H
14260 SAKURA

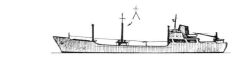

KMKMFC H13
14270 KWANGCHOW

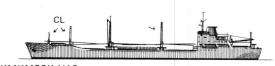

KMKMFCK H13
★14280 FENG NING → 14284

KMKMFK H
14290 BIG ORANGE → 14291

KMKMFK H
★14300 KRUSZWICA → 14306

KMKMFK H
14310 CIDADE DE RIO GRANDE → 14312

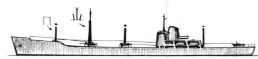

KMKMFK H1
14320 JALARASHMI → 14322

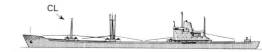

KMKMFK H1
14340 TILLY → 14341

KMKMFK H1
14350 ATLANTICO

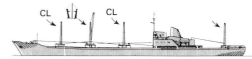

KMKMFK H1
14360 RIO CALCHAQUI → 14364

KMKMFK H13
★14370 PULA → 14395

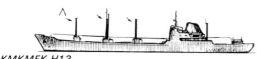

KMKMFK H13
14400 MAZZINI → 14407

Twin Funnels

KMKMFK₂ H1
14420 ELIZABETH LYKES → 14431

KMKMFK₂ H1
★14450 IGNATIY SERGEYEV → 14474

KMKMFK₂ H13
★14480 FRANCISZEK ZUBRZYCKI → 14492

KMKMFK₂ H13
★14500 LU CHENG

KMKMFK₂ H13
14510 SAUDI CROWN

KMKMFK₂ H13
14520 LEONOREVERETT → 14522

KMKMFK₂ H13
14530 SEA CARRIER → 14532

KMKMFK₂ H13
★14540 YU CHUN → 14542

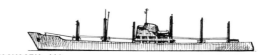

KMKMFK₃ H1
14550 MORMACGLEN → 14557

KMKMFK₂MK H123
★14560 HONG QI 119 → 14561

KMKMFKM H1
14570 ALHANA → 14571

KMKMFKM H1
★14580 EMILIA PLATER → 14584

KMKMFKM H1
14600 CHEVALIER DARBY

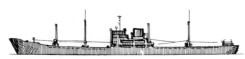

KMKMFKM H1
14610 EASTERN JUPITER

KMKMFKM H1
★14630 FENG QING → 14639/5

KMKMFKM H1
★14640 LIAO YANG

KMKMFKM H13
14660 DIMITRAKIS → 14662

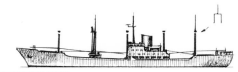

KMKMFKM H13
★14670 QIN HUAI → 14672

KMKMFKMK H1
★14700 DIVNOGORSK → 14701

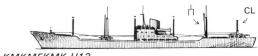

KMKMFKMK H13
14710 TALAVERA

KMKMFKMK H13
14730 KOTA PETANI

KMKMFKMK H13
14740 SAIKYO MARU

KMKMFKMK H13
14750 MALANGE → 14751

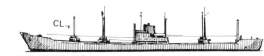

KMKMFKMK H13
14760 LELLO DI MAIO

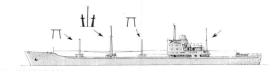

KMKMFM H1
★14770 URSUS

KMKMFM H1
14780 MALDIVE PRIVILEGE

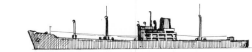

KMKMFM H1
14790 BUNGA ARANDA

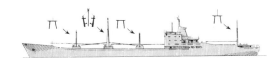

KMKMFM H13
★14800 WLADYSLAW ORKAN → 14801

KMKMFMK H1
14810 PONTALVA → 14814

KMKMFMK H1
14860 DEVON EXPRESS

KMKMFMK H1
14870 THEODOROS

KMKMFMK H13
14880 OHRMAZD

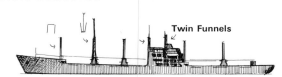

KMKMK₃ H13
14890 ELIZABETH LYKES → 14901

KMKM₂FK₂ H1
★14905 VITYAZ → 14906

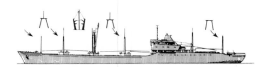

KMKM₂FK₂ H13
14910 VISHVA CHETANA → 14929

KM₂F H
14940 SEA PRINCESS

Tripod

KM₂F H
14950 T.W. NELSON → 14951

CL

KM₂F H1
★14955 AKADEMIK MSTISLAV KELDYSH

Tripod

KM₂F H1
★14960 BIN HAI 511→14961

KM₂F H1
14970 DON VICENTE

Twin Funnels

KM₂F H13
★14975 YULIUS FUCHIK→14975/1

CL   Twin Funnels

KM₂F H2
14976 EUROPEAN CLEARWAY → 14978

CL   Twin Funnels

KM₂F H13
14979 SIGYN

KM₂FC H
14980 DON CLAUDIO

CL

KM₂FC H1
14990 MERCURY

KM₂FC H12
★15000 'PROFESSOR' class

KM₂FCM H13
★15020 DAI YUN SHAN → 15023

KM₂FCR H
15030 KUROSHIO MARU

KM₂FK H
15050 NOGA

KM₂FK H
★15055 HONG WEI 7

KM₂FK H
15060 GOLFO PARADISO → 15061

KM₂FK H1
15070 OLYMPIAN REEFER → 15071

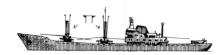

KM₂FK H1
★15080 KRAKOW → 15087

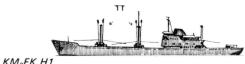

KM₂FK H1
★15090 KRIVAN → 15093

KM₂FK H1
★15095 AKADEMIK MSTISLAV KELDYSH

KM₂FK H13
★15100 FRANZ STENZER → 15102

KM₂FK H13
15110 AGIOS NECTARIOS → 15111

KMMFK H13
★15120 ALEKSANDR DOVZHENKO → 15124

KM₂FKC H13
15130 BANGLAR SWAPNA → 15131

KM₂FK₂ H1
15140 LALAZAR → 15142

KM₂FK₃ H1
★15160 TIRANA

KM₂FKM H
15170 ATRA → 15175

KM₂FKM H1
★15180 HANOI → 15186

KM₂FKM H1
★15190 HEWELIUSZ → 15192

KM₂FKM H1
15200 PRESIDENT HARRISON → 15202

KM₂FKM H1
★15215 CHAO YANG → 15216

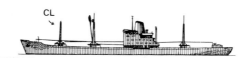

KM₂FKM H1
15220 RIVER → 15223

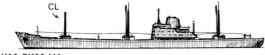

KM₂FKM H1
15230 JALAJYOTI → 15232

KM₂FKM H1
★15240 BASKA → 15243

KM₂FKM H1
15250 BAGH-E-KARACHI → 15252

KM₂FKM H1
15255 GOLDEN TAIF → 15256

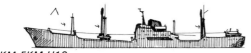

KM₂FKM H13
★15260 SHU YU QUAN → 15261

KM₂FKM H13
15270 BENYA RIVER → 15278

KM₂FKMK H1
★15280 HANKA SAWICKA

KM₂FKMK H1
★15285 BOSNA → 15286

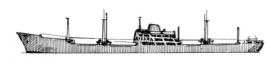

KM₂FKMK H1
★15290 JESENICE → 15291

KM₂FKMK H1
★15300 ANDRZEJ STRUG → 15301

KM₂FKMK H1
15310 IRAN SEEYAM → 15314

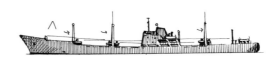

KM₂FKMK H1
★15320 BANAT → 15323

KM₂FKMK H1
15330 NAFEESA → 15333

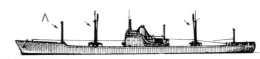

KM₂FKMK H1
★15340 FRANCESCO NULLO → 15353

KM₂FKMK H1
15360 GAY FORTUNE → 15361

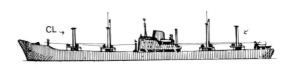

KM₂FKMK H1
15370 PINDAROS → 15375

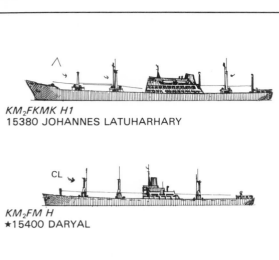

KM₂FKMK H1
15380 JOHANNES LATUHARHARY

KM₂FM H
★15400 DARYAL

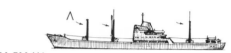

KM₂FM H1
★15420 BUCURESTI → 15421

KM₂FM H1
★15450 OLKUSZ → 15458

KM₂FM H13
★15500 PYARNU → 15502

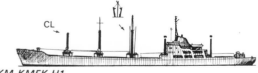

KM₂FMK H1
15550 CYPRUS TRADER

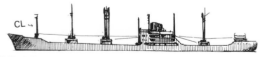

KM₂KMFK H1
★15580 KRASZEWSKI → 15581

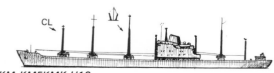

KM₂KMFKM H13
15610 KOTA MURNI → 15612

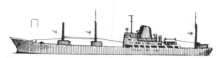

KM₂FM H
15390 LADY JOSEPHINE → 15391

KM₂FM H1
★15410 ANTON SAEFKOW → 15418

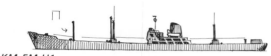

KM₂FM H1
15430 WORLD SHELTER

KM₂FM H13
★15460 SINEGORSK → 15494

KM₂FM H13
★15510 SHURA KOBER → 15540

KM₂FMK H13
15560 AVIAN WREN

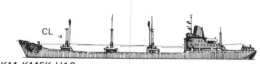

KM₂KMFK H13
15590 VISHVA KARUNA → 15594

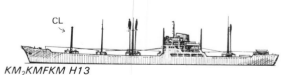

KM₂KMFKM H13
15620 KOTA DEWA → 15621

Left side:
KM₂KMFKMK H13
15630 KOTA WARUNA → 15631

Right side:
KM₃F H12
★15632 RIO AGABAMA → 15639/1

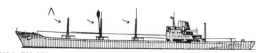

KM₃FK H1
15640 MOENJODARO → 15649

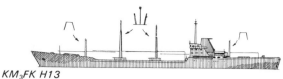

KM₃FK H13
15660 FORUM EAGLE → 15667

KM₃FK H13
15670 MERCHANT PROVIDENCE → 15674

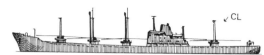

KM₃FK₂ H13
15680 JALAYAMUNA → 15681

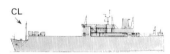

KM₃FMC H2
15690 AUTOROUTE

KM₃FMK₂
15700 AMBASSADOR → 15703

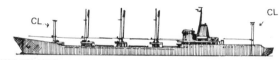

KM₄FK H13
15710 LA GUAIRA → 15711

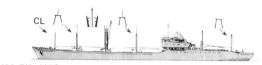

KM₄FK₂ H13
15720 VISHVA BINDU → 15739

KMNF H2
15740 SURREY

KMNMF H1
15750 TACKLER ARABIA → 15752

KMNMFKMK H1
15760 LINCOLN → 15761

KNMF H
15780 KOTKA LILY → 15784

KNMFCR H1
★15790 LEDENICE → 15791

KNMFKN H12
15800 SANTA MAGDALENA → 15803

M H
15810 AYVALIK → 15811

MC₅MFC H1
15820 NISSOS SERIFOS → 15821

MC₄MFC H13
15830 NEDLLOYD WISSEKERK → 15833

MC₄MFKC H1
15840 ESTRELLA DEL MAR

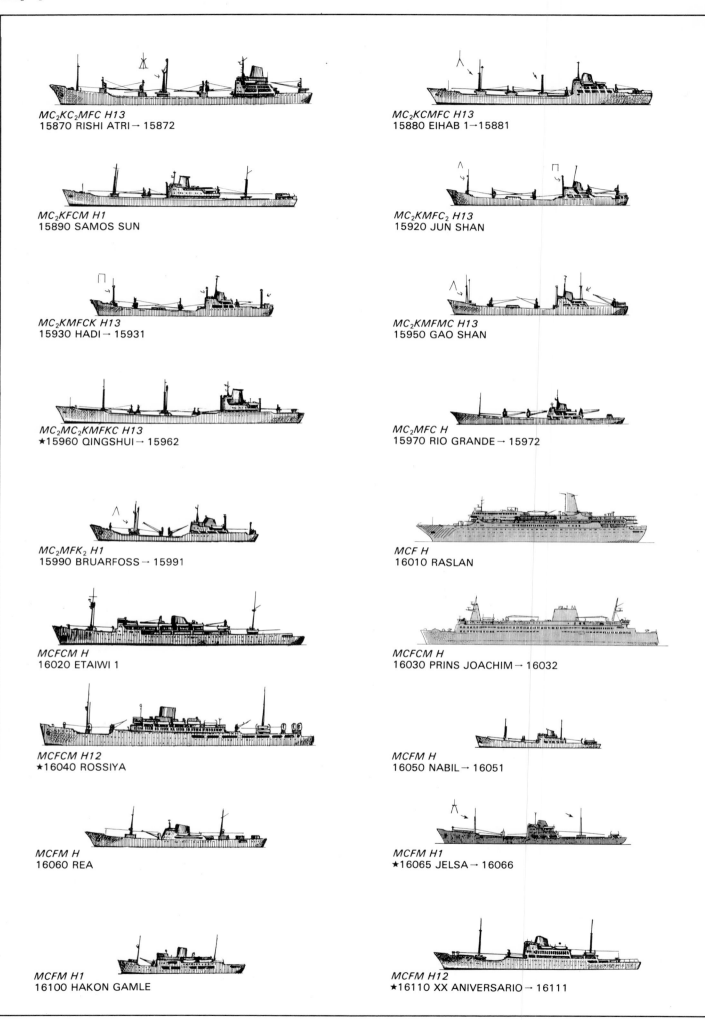

MC₂KC₂MFC H13
15870 RISHI ATRI → 15872

MC₂KCMFC H13
15880 EIHAB 1 → 15881

MC₂KFCM H1
15890 SAMOS SUN

MC₂KMFC₂ H13
15920 JUN SHAN

MC₂KMFCK H13
15930 HADI → 15931

MC₂KMFMC H13
15950 GAO SHAN

MC₂MC₂KMFKC H13
★15960 QINGSHUI → 15962

MC₂MFC H
15970 RIO GRANDE → 15972

MC₂MFK₂ H1
15990 BRUARFOSS → 15991

MCF H
16010 RASLAN

MCFCM H
16020 ETAIWI 1

MCFCM H
16030 PRINS JOACHIM → 16032

MCFCM H12
★16040 ROSSIYA

MCFM H
16050 NABIL → 16051

MCFM H
16060 REA

MCFM H1
★16065 JELSA → 16066

MCFM H1
16100 HAKON GAMLE

MCFM H12
★16110 XX ANIVERSARIO → 16111

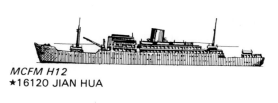

MCFM H12
★16120 JIAN HUA

MCFMC₂ H
★16140 UKRAINA

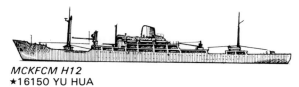

MCKFCM H12
★16150 YU HUA

MCKMFKCK H1
16170 RIO DE JANERIO

MCMCMFC H1
16180 POPI

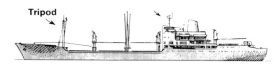

MCMCMFC H13
16190 FABIOLAVILLE → 16191

MCMF H13
16200 SAGAR

MCMFC H
16210 FUJI

MCMFCM H1
16220 ASTERI → 16221

MCMFK H
16230 DISCOVERY

MCMFK H1
16240 BRANSFIELD

MCMFK H1
16250 TOWUTI → 16256

MCMFM H1
16260 EIGAMOIYA

MCMFM H1
★16270 JASLO

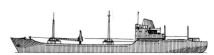

MCM₂FK₂ H13
★16290 SU LONG

MF H
16310 DOULOS

MF H
16320 HELLAS

MF H
★16330 SHAO YAO

MF H
16340 SIRIUS

MF H
16350 BLACK WATCH/JUPITER → 16351

MF H
16370 COLUMBIA

MF H
16380 ST. GEORGE

MF H
16385 KEREN

MF H
16390 DAPHNE → 16391

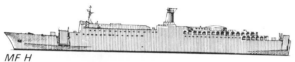

MF H
16400 SUN FLOWER → 16403

MF H
16410 EMPRESS OF AUSTRALIA

MF H
16420 MANUEL SOTO → 16421

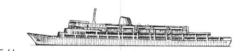

MF H
★16430 GU LANG YU → 16431

MF H
16440 PROVENCE

MF H
16450 PRINCE OF BRITTANY → 16452

MF H
16460 BLUENOSE → 16463

MF H
16470 THE VIKING → 16471

MF H
★16480 VIKING 2

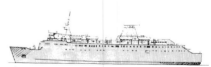

MF H
16490 CONNACHT → 16491

MF H
16500 QUEEN OF THE NORTH

MF H
16510 PRINZ OBERON → 16512

MF H
16520 GOLDEN ODYSSEY

MF H
16530 CIUDAD DE SANTA CRUZ LA PALMA → 16535

MF H
16540 JUPITER

MF H
16550 MELINA → 16551

MF H
16570 GENNARGENTU

MF H
16580 APOLLO III

MF H
16600 GALAXIAS

MF H
16610 ARGONAUT

MF H
16620 KENTAVROS

MF H
16630 ELENA P

MF H
16640 POLIKOS

MF H
16650 EPOMEO PRIMO

MF H
16660 THOR VIKING

MF H
16670 SECHELT QUEEN

MF H
16680 QUEEN OF SIDNEY

MF H
16690 ISLA DE MENORA

MF H
16710 NAUSHON

MF H
★16720 VLADIMIR NAZOR → 16725

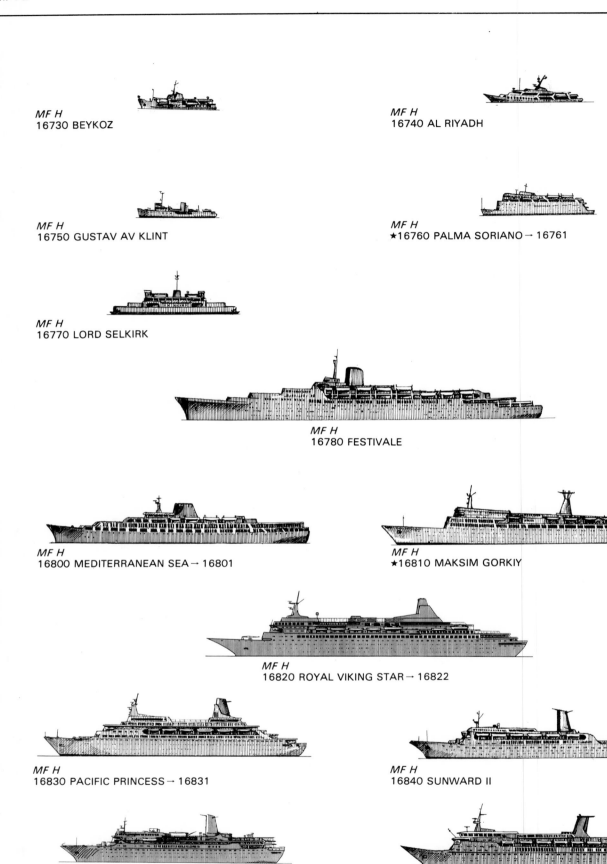

MF H
16730 BEYKOZ

MF H
16740 AL RIYADH

MF H
16750 GUSTAV AV KLINT

MF H
★16760 PALMA SORIANO → 16761

MF H
16770 LORD SELKIRK

MF H
16780 FESTIVALE

MF H
16800 MEDITERRANEAN SEA → 16801

MF H
★16810 MAKSIM GORKIY

MF H
16820 ROYAL VIKING STAR → 16822

MF H
16830 PACIFIC PRINCESS → 16831

MF H
16840 SUNWARD II

MF H
16850 RASLAN

MF H
16860 CUNARD COUNTESS → 16861

MF H
16865 TROPICALE

MF H
16870 SONG OF NORWAY → 16871

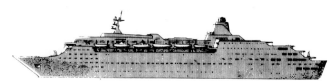

MF H
16875 EUROPA

MF H
16880 VIKING SALLY

MF H
16885 SCANDINAVIA

MF H
16890 TOR BRITANNIA → 16891

MF H
16895 FINLANDIA → 16896

MF H
16900 VISBY → 16901

MF H
16905 TRELLEBORG

MF H
16910 KRONPRINSESSAN VICTORIA → 16911

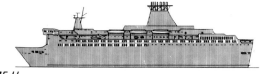

MF H
16913 STENA DANICA → 16914

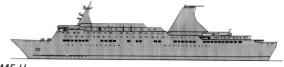

MF H
16915 PRINSESSE RAGNHILD

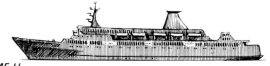

MF H
16920 KRONPRINS HARALD

MF H
16925 ASTOR

MF H
16930 HABIB

MF H
16940 AZUR → 16942

MF H
16945 PRINCESS MAHSURI

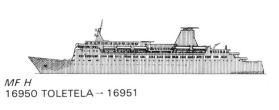

MF H
16950 TOLETELA → 16951

MF H
16955 OLAU HOLLANDIA → 16956

MF H
★16960 ODESSA

MF H
16970 SCANDINAVIAN SUN

MF H
16980 DROTTEN → 16981

MF H
16990 MARINE ATLANTICA → 16993

MF H
17000 SOUTHWARD

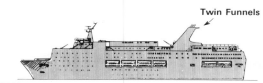

MF H
17010 VIKING SAGA → 17011

MF H
17020 SUN PRINCESS

MF H
17030 CORSICA SERENA II

MF H
17040 QUIBERON

MF H
17050 BOHEME

MF H
17060 NORLAND → 17061

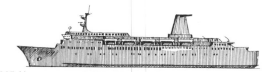

MF H
17070 PETER PAN → 17071

MF H
17080 DANA ANGLIA

MF H
17090 KAMIROS → 17091

MF
17100 PEARL OF SCANDINAVIA

MF H
17120 NORWAVE → 17121

MF H
17130 PIETRO NOVELLI → 17133

MF H
17140 SANTA MARGARITA DOS

MF H
17150 PANAGHIA TINOU

MF H
17160 QUEEN OF VICTORIA → 17166

MF H
17170 CONCEPCION MARINO → 17171

MF H
17190 MERCHANT NAVIGATOR → 17192

MF H1
17200 JERVIS BAY

MF H1
17210 CIUDAD DE TARIFA

MF H1
17220 PRINCE NOVA

MF H1
17230 COHO

MF H1
17240 MONS CALPE

MF H1
17250 SOUND OF ISLAY

MF H13
17260 KIRK EXPRESS

MF H2
17270 ESPRESSO EGITTO → 17273

MF H2
17280 GEDSER

MF H2
17290 FRECCIA DELL'OUEST → 17291

MF H2
17300 COUTANCES → 17301

MF H2
17310 ARGO

MF H2
★17320 ZARNITZA

Tripod　　Twin Funnels

MFC H1
17330 CANMAR KIGORIAK

Twin Funnels

MFC H1
17340 WILDRAKE

Twin Funnels　Port Side

MFC H1
17343 SEABEX ONE

Twin Funnels

MFC H1
17345 SEAWAY CONDOR

Tripod　　Twin Funnels

MFCK　H
★17350 SPRUT

MFCKM H1
17360 DR. FRIDTJOF NANSEN

MFCM H1
17380 SHEARWATER CAPE

MF₂ H
17390 EMERALD SEAS

MF₂ H
17400 SUN FLOWER 11

MF₂M H
17410 TANJUNG PANDAN

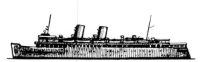

MF₂M H
17420 PRINCESS MARGUERITE → 17421

MF₂M H
17430 CARIDDI

MF₂M H
17440 WAVERLEY

MF₂M H
17450 PILOTA ALSINA → 17451

MF₂M H
17460 SJAELLAND → 17461

Twin Funnels

MF₂M H
17470 OTOME MARU

MF₂M H
★17480 WARNEMUNDE

MF₂M H
★17490 ILYICH

MF₂M H
★17500 DOVATOR → 17529

MF₂M H
★17540 SAVARONA

MF₂M H
17550 N.B. McLEAN

MF₂M H1
★17560 PETR LEBEDEV → 17561

Twin Funnels

MFK H
★17580 EDDA → 17581

MFK H
17590 CIUDAD DE SANTA CRUZ LA PALMA → 17595

MFK H
17600 STELLA SOLARIS

MFK H
17610 GOLDEN ODYSSEY

MFK H
★17620 SHUI HSIEN

MFK H
17630 CIUDAD DE COLONIA

MFK H2
17640 REGENCY

Twin Funnels

MFK₂M H
17650 MALENE OSTERVOLD

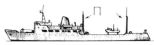

MFKM H
★17660 GALATI → 17661

MFKM H
★17670 ERNST HAECKEL

MFKM H
17680 SOUTHERN RANGER

Twin Funnels

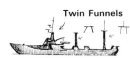

MFKM H
17690 V.U. HAMMERSHAIMB

MFKM H
17700 ARCTIC FREEBOOTER

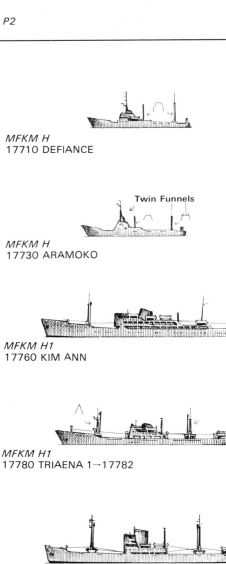

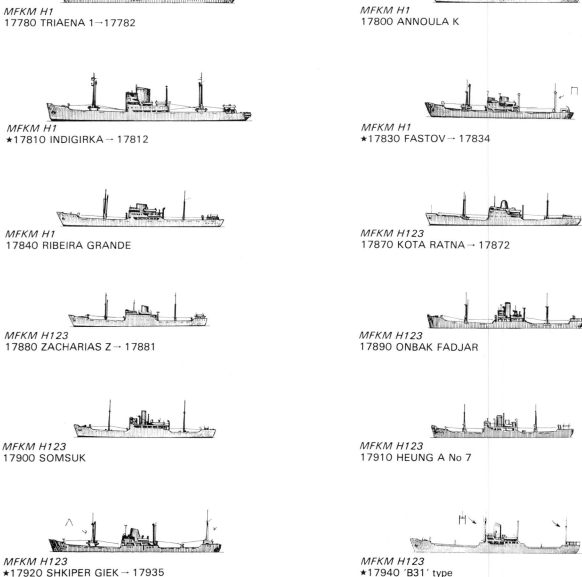

MFKM H
17710 DEFIANCE

MFKM H
17720 SIR FRED PARKES

MFKM H
17730 ARAMOKO

MFKM H
17740 ST. JASON → 17742

MFKM H1
17760 KIM ANN

MFKM H1
17770 MIDNATSOL NORGE→17771

MFKM H1
17780 TRIAENA 1→17782

MFKM H1
17800 ANNOULA K

MFKM H1
★17810 INDIGIRKA → 17812

MFKM H1
★17830 FASTOV→ 17834

MFKM H1
17840 RIBEIRA GRANDE

MFKM H123
17870 KOTA RATNA → 17872

MFKM H123
17880 ZACHARIAS Z→ 17881

MFKM H123
17890 ONBAK FADJAR

MFKM H123
17900 SOMSUK

MFKM H123
17910 HEUNG A No 7

MFKM H123
★17920 SHKIPER GIEK → 17935

MFKM H123
★17940 'B31' type

MFKM H2
★17950 ZVYEROBOY → 17975

MFKM H2
17980 BODO UHSE → 17981

MFKMK H1
★17990 MARTIN ANDERSEN NEXO

MFKMR H2
18000 SERENISSIMA EXPRESS → 18002

MFM H
★18010 BALTIKA

MFM H
★18020 XIN HUA

MFM H
18040 TAMPOMAS

MFM H
18070 APOLLONIA

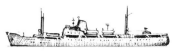

MFM H
★18090 MIKHAIL LOMONOSOV

MFM H
18100 GANN

MFM H
★18110 GONG NONG BING No 10→18111

MFM H
★18120 GONG NONG BING No14→18122

MFM H
18150 TIRTA MULIA → 18158

MFM H
18160 CLANSMAN

MFM H
18170 ORCADIA

MFM H
18180 1-007→18183

MFM H
18190 LEYTE GULF → 18192

MFM H
18200 EL GAUCHO

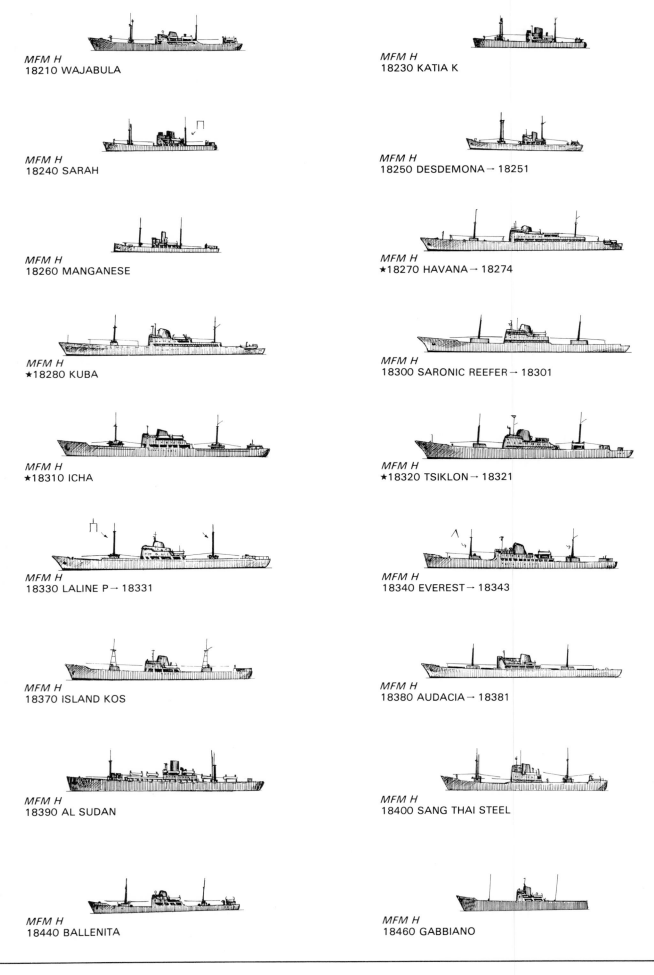

MFM H
18210 WAJABULA

MFM H
18230 KATIA K

MFM H
18240 SARAH

MFM H
18250 DESDEMONA → 18251

MFM H
18260 MANGANESE

MFM H
★18270 HAVANA → 18274

MFM H
★18280 KUBA

MFM H
18300 SARONIC REEFER → 18301

MFM H
★18310 ICHA

MFM H
★18320 TSIKLON → 18321

MFM H
18330 LALINE P → 18331

MFM H
18340 EVEREST → 18343

MFM H
18370 ISLAND KOS

MFM H
18380 AUDACIA → 18381

MFM H
18390 AL SUDAN

MFM H
18400 SANG THAI STEEL

MFM H
18440 BALLENITA

MFM H
18460 GABBIANO

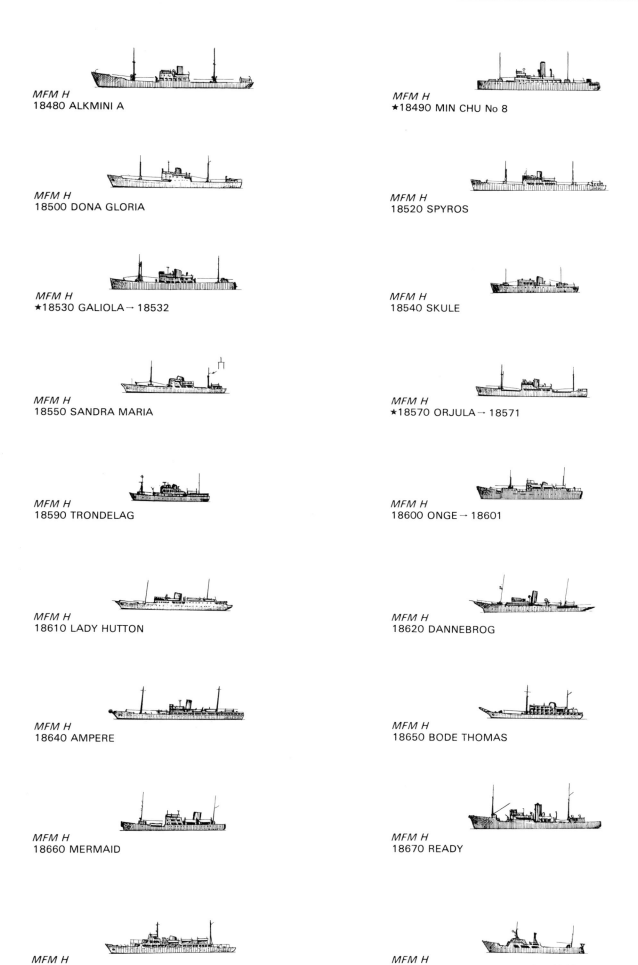

MFM H
18480 ALKMINI A

MFM H
★18490 MIN CHU No 8

MFM H
18500 DONA GLORIA

MFM H
18520 SPYROS

MFM H
★18530 GALIOLA → 18532

MFM H
18540 SKULE

MFM H
18550 SANDRA MARIA

MFM H
★18570 ORJULA → 18571

MFM H
18590 TRONDELAG

MFM H
18600 ONGE → 18601

MFM H
18610 LADY HUTTON

MFM H
18620 DANNEBROG

MFM H
18640 AMPERE

MFM H
18650 BODE THOMAS

MFM H
18660 MERMAID

MFM H
18670 READY

MFM H
18680 SAGAR → 18681

MFM H
18690 VIRGEN DEL CAMINO → 18691

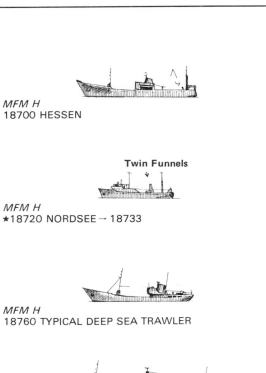

MFM H
18700 HESSEN

MFM H
18710 CORIOLANUS → 18713

Twin Funnels

MFM H
★18720 NORDSEE → 18733

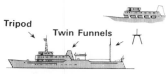

Tripod   Twin Funnels

MFM H
★18740 LASKARA → 18757

MFM H
18760 TYPICAL DEEP SEA TRAWLER

MFM H
18800 KATIPUNAN

MFM H
18810 PRINCESS OF ACADIA

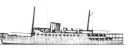

MFM H
18840 MARAKAZ

MFM H
18860 ROANA

MFM H
★18880 MARINA

MFM H
18890 AGOSTINO LAURO

MFM H
18900 BALMORAL

MFM H
18910 SPOKANE → 18911

MFM H
18920 QUEEN OF COQUITLAM → 18921

MFM H
18930 ARVEPRINS KNUD

MFM H
18940 KNUDSHOVED → 18942

Twin Funnels

MFM H
18950 PRINSES CHRISTINA

Twin Funnels

MFM H
18955 MOLENGAT

MFM H
18960 PRINSES MARGRIET → 18962

MFM H
18970 TEXELSTROOM → 18971

MFM H
18980 EVERGREEN STATE → 18982

MFM H
18990 QUEEN OF ALBERNI

MFM H
19000 SECONDO ASPROMONTE → 19001

MFM H
19010 HALSINGBORG → 19011

MFM H
19020 CONFEDERATION

MFM H
19030 BASTO III

MFM H
19040 KIZKULESI → 19041

MFM H
19050 TRANS ST. LAURENT

MFM H
19060 QUEEN OF THE ISLANDS

MFM H
19070 NOORD NEDERLAND

MFM H
19080 BETULA → 19082

MFM H
19090 ECKERO

MFM H
19110 ANGAMOS

MFM H
19120 SARDINIA NOVA

MFM H
19130 ARIADNE

MFM H
19140 GELTING → 19143

MFM H
19150 CHRISTIAN IV

MFM H
19160 YESILADA

MFM H
★19170 SLAVIJA 1

MFM H
★19180 BALKANIJA→ 19184

MFM H
19190 ALDONZA MANRIQUE→ 19191

MFM H
19200 CASAMANCE EXPRESS

MFM H
19210 WILHELMSHAVEN

MFM H
19220 POSEIDON

MFM H
19230 CAVO AZURO→ 19231

MFM H
19240 SKANE

MFM H
19250 FENNIA

MFM H
19260 AGADIR

Twin Funnels

MFM H
19270 VILLA DE AGAETE

MFM H
19280 CIUDAD DE LA LAGUNA

MFM H
19290 BENODET→19297

MFM H
19300 FAIR LADY

MFM H
19310 SEEMOWE II

MFM H
19320 ISLA DE CUBAGUA→ 19321

MFM H
★19330 WAWEL → 19331

MFM H
19350 LUCY MAUD MONTGOMERY

MFM H
19360 DANA SCARLETT → 19361

MFM H
19370 SKOPELOS → 19371

MFM H
19380 GHAWDEX → 19381

MFM H
19390 NEREUS

MFM H
19400 HAMLET → 19401

MFM H
19410 AINOS

MFM H
19420 EARL GODWIN

Twin Funnels

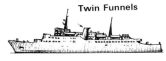

MFM H
19430 SUN BOAT → 19432

Twin Funnels

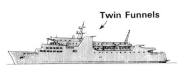

MFM H
19440 QUEEN OF PRINCE RUPERT

Twin Funnels

MFM H
19450 JOHN HAMILTON GRAY

Twin Funnels

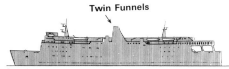

MFM H
19460 ST. ANSELM → 19461

Twin Funnels

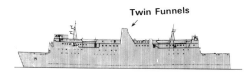

MFM H
19465 ST. DAVID → 19466

Twin Funnels

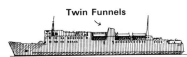

MFM H
19470 LION

Twin Funnels

MFM H
19480 EMSLAND

Twin Funnels   Tripod

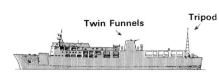

MFM H
19490 VELA → 19491

Twin Funnels

MFM H
19500 TASSILI

MFM H
19510 DONG YANG EXPRESS FERRY No 2

MFM H
19520 HAYATOMO MARU

MFM H
19530 OSADO MARU

MFM H
19540 AMBROSE SHEA

MFM H
19550 THEODOR HEUSS

MFM H
19560 CITY OF MIDLAND → 19562

MFM H
19570 PRINSESSE ANNE-MARIE

MFM H
19580 IKAROS

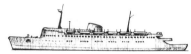

MFM H
19590 KONG FREDERIK IX→19591

MFM H
19600 MARINE CRUISER

MFM H
19610 AGIOS GEORGIOS

MFM H
19620 SCANIA

MFM H
19630 AL ANOUD

MFM H
19640 SAUDI GOLDEN ARROW

MFM H
19650 NORDSCHAU

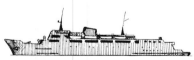

MFM H
19660 SAINT GERMAIN

MFM H
19670 IONIAN GLORY

MFM H
19680 YOTEI MARU → 19686

MFM H
19700 HIYAMA MARU → 19701

MFM H
19710 FERRY HANKYU → 19711

MFM H
19720 PRINCESS OF VANCOUVER

MFM H
19730 HOMERUS

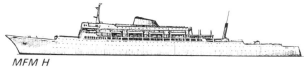

MFM H
19740 VOLENDAM → 19741

MFM H
19750 REGGIO

MFM H
19760 SAN FRANCESCO DI PAOLA

MFM H
19770 NICOLAS MIHANOVICH

MFM H
19780 QUEEN OF TSAWWASSEN

MFM H
19800 GREENPORT

MFM H
19810 LECONTE

MFM H
19860 SOL EXPRESS

MFM H
19890 ST. COLUMBA

MFM H
19900 HENGIST → 19902

MFM H
19910 CHARTRES

MFM H
19920 VORTIGERN

MFM H
19930 PRINS PHILIPPE → 19931

MFM H
19940 PRINCESSE MARIE CHRISTINE → 19942

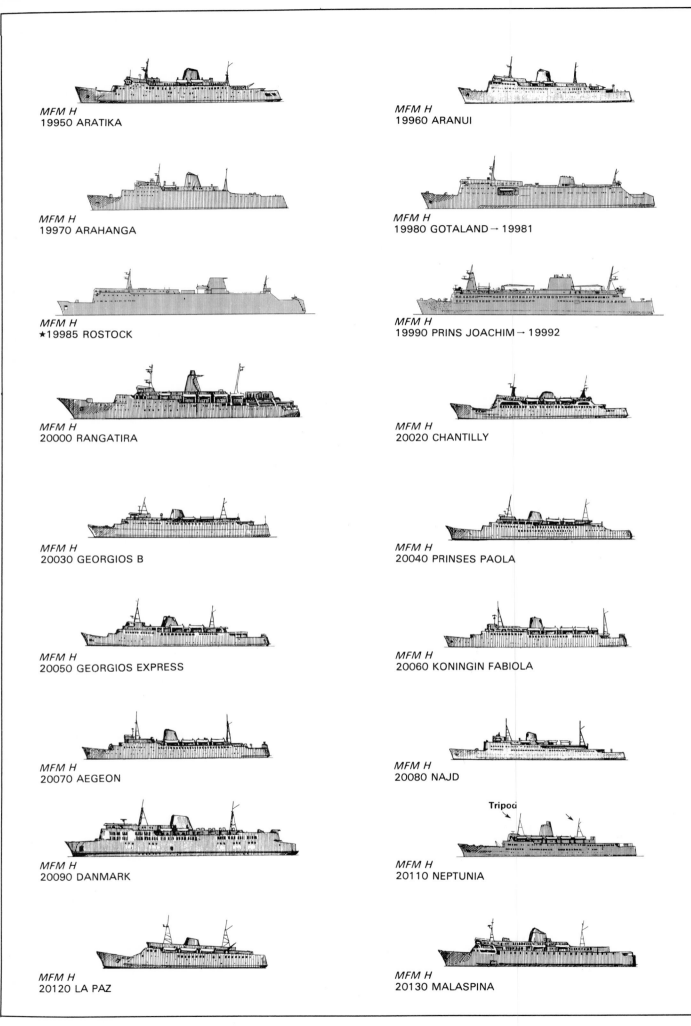

MFM H
19950 ARATIKA

MFM H
19960 ARANUI

MFM H
19970 ARAHANGA

MFM H
19980 GOTALAND → 19981

MFM H
★19985 ROSTOCK

MFM H
19990 PRINS JOACHIM → 19992

MFM H
20000 RANGATIRA

MFM H
20020 CHANTILLY

MFM H
20030 GEORGIOS B

MFM H
20040 PRINSES PAOLA

MFM H
20050 GEORGIOS EXPRESS

MFM H
20060 KONINGIN FABIOLA

MFM H
20070 AEGEON

MFM H
20080 NAJD

MFM H
20090 DANMARK

Tripod

MFM H
20110 NEPTUNIA

MFM H
20120 LA PAZ

MFM H
20130 MALASPINA

MFM H
20140 ALZAHRAA

MFM H
20160 FESTOS

MFM H
20170 HOLGER DANSKE

MFM H
20180 MONA'S QUEEN → 20181

MFM H
20190 FREE ENTERPRISE IV → 20192

MFM H
20200 FREE ENTERPRISE VII → 20201

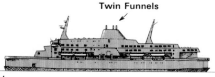

MFM H
20210 SPIRIT OF FREE ENTERPRISE → 20212

MFM H
20220 VIKING VENTURER → 20223

MFM H
20230 FREE ENTERPRISE III

MFM H
20240 MARINE BLUENOSE

MFM H
★20250 SVETI STEFAN

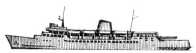

MFM H
20260 EGNATIA

MFM H
20270 TIEPOLO → 20273

MFM H
20280 VILLANDRY → 20281

MFM H
20290 EUROPA FARJAN

MFM H
20300 ILMATAR

MFM H
★20310 SAKHALIN-1 → 20316

MFM H
★20317 CHANG LI → 20319/4

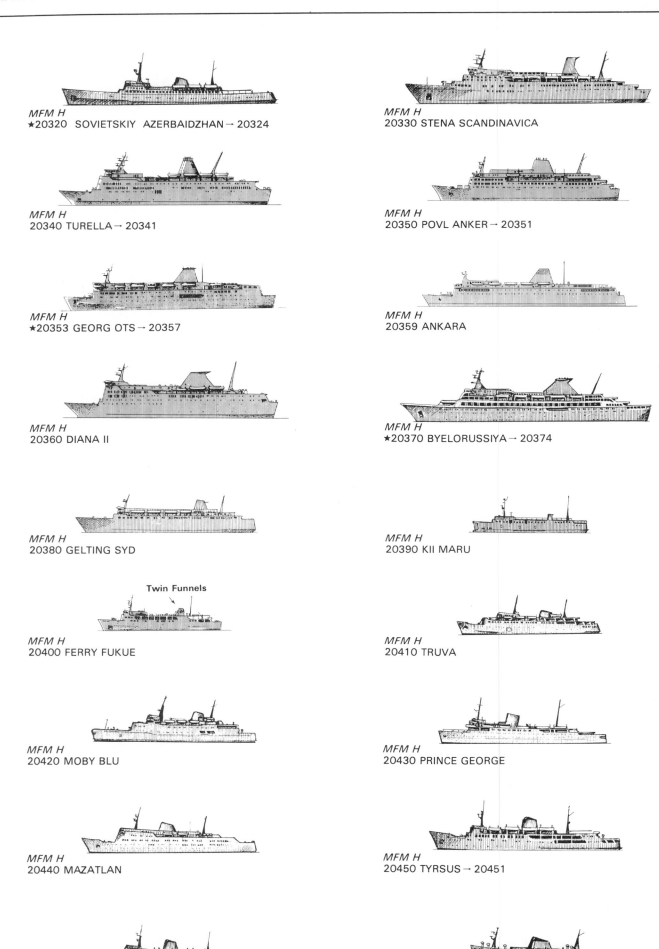

MFM H
★20320 SOVIETSKIY AZERBAIDZHAN → 20324

MFM H
20330 STENA SCANDINAVICA

MFM H
20340 TURELLA → 20341

MFM H
20350 POVL ANKER → 20351

MFM H
★20353 GEORG OTS → 20357

MFM H
20359 ANKARA

MFM H
20360 DIANA II

MFM H
★20370 BYELORUSSIYA → 20374

MFM H
20380 GELTING SYD

MFM H
20390 KII MARU

Twin Funnels

MFM H
20400 FERRY FUKUE

MFM H
20410 TRUVA

MFM H
20420 MOBY BLU

MFM H
20430 PRINCE GEORGE

MFM H
20440 MAZATLAN

MFM H
20450 TYRSUS → 20451

MFM H
20460 JASON

MFM H
20470 KONINGIN JULIANA

MFM H
20480 NORTHERN CRUISER

MFM H
20490 HOLYHEAD

MFM H
20500 MANX MAID → 20501

MFM H
20510 AESAREA → 20511

MFM H
20530 ATHENS EXPRESS

MFM H
★20550 THONG NHAT

MFM H
★20560 JI MEI

MFM H
20570 WINSTON CHURCHILL

MFM H
20580 ORPHEUS

MFM H
20590 STELLA OCEANIS

MFM H
20600 APPIA

MFM H
20610 PRINSESSE ELISABETH

MFM H
20630 SAINT PATRICK II

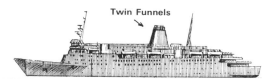

Twin Funnels

MFM H
20640 SILJA STAR → 20643

MFM H
★20650 AYVAZOVSKIY

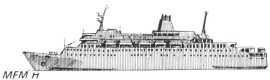

MFM H
20660 NAPOLEON

MFM H
20670 CYRNOS

MFM H
20680 VIKING SALLY

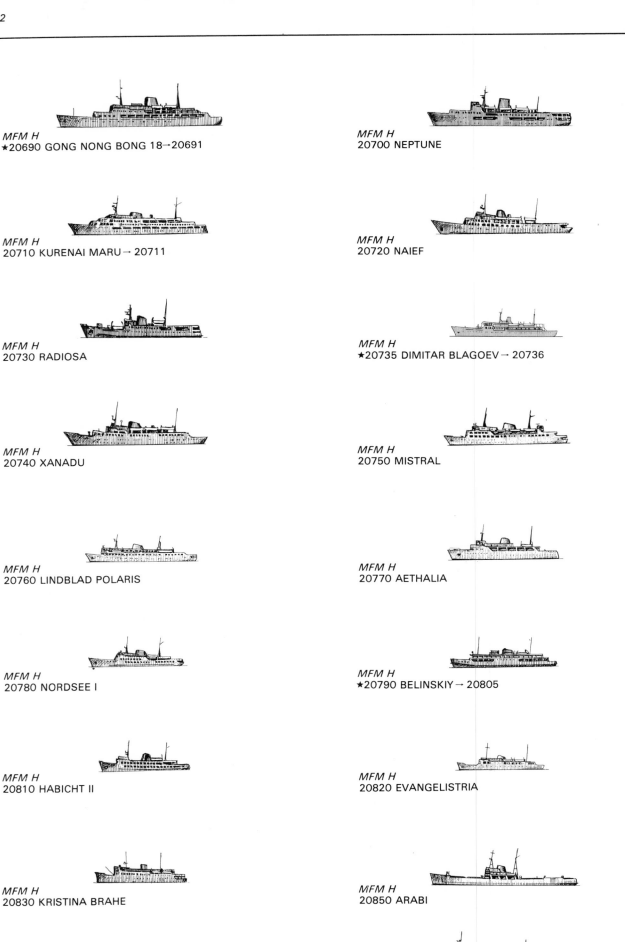

MFM H
★20690 GONG NONG BONG 18→20691

MFM H
20700 NEPTUNE

MFM H
20710 KURENAI MARU→20711

MFM H
20720 NAIEF

MFM H
20730 RADIOSA

MFM H
★20735 DIMITAR BLAGOEV→20736

MFM H
20740 XANADU

MFM H
20750 MISTRAL

MFM H
20760 LINDBLAD POLARIS

MFM H
20770 AETHALIA

MFM H
20780 NORDSEE I

MFM H
★20790 BELINSKIY→20805

MFM H
20810 HABICHT II

MFM H
20820 EVANGELISTRIA

MFM H
20830 KRISTINA BRAHE

MFM H
20850 ARABI

MFM H
20860 ARRAN→20862

MFM H
★20870 YERMAK→20872

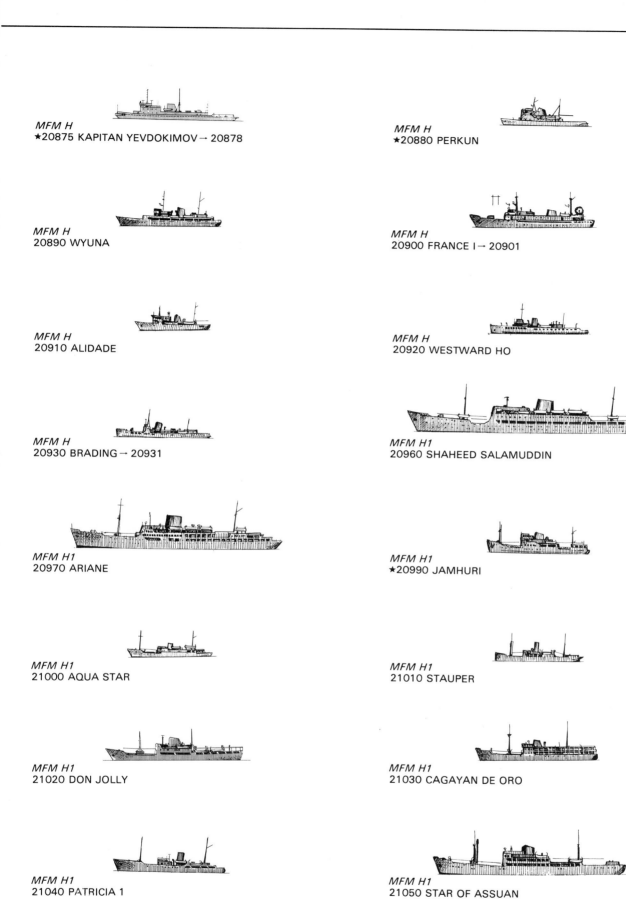

MFM H
★20875 KAPITAN YEVDOKIMOV → 20878

MFM H
★20880 PERKUN

MFM H
20890 WYUNA

MFM H
20900 FRANCE I → 20901

MFM H
20910 ALIDADE

MFM H
20920 WESTWARD HO

MFM H
20930 BRADING → 20931

MFM H1
20960 SHAHEED SALAMUDDIN

MFM H1
20970 ARIANE

MFM H1
★20990 JAMHURI

MFM H1
21000 AQUA STAR

MFM H1
21010 STAUPER

MFM H1
21020 DON JOLLY

MFM H1
21030 CAGAYAN DE ORO

MFM H1
21040 PATRICIA 1

MFM H1
21050 STAR OF ASSUAN

MFM H1
21060 EL HASSAN → 21062

MFM H1
21070 REINA DEL FRIO

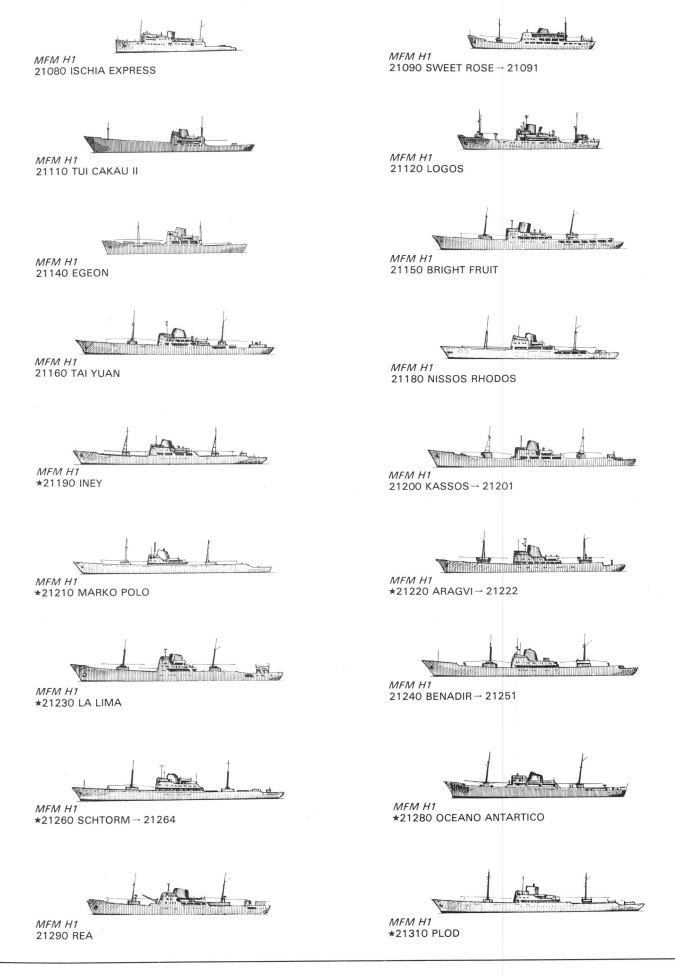

MFM H1
21080 ISCHIA EXPRESS

MFM H1
21090 SWEET ROSE → 21091

MFM H1
21110 TUI CAKAU II

MFM H1
21120 LOGOS

MFM H1
21140 EGEON

MFM H1
21150 BRIGHT FRUIT

MFM H1
21160 TAI YUAN

MFM H1
21180 NISSOS RHODOS

MFM H1
★21190 INEY

MFM H1
21200 KASSOS → 21201

MFM H1
★21210 MARKO POLO

MFM H1
★21220 ARAGVI → 21222

MFM H1
★21230 LA LIMA

MFM H1
21240 BENADIR → 21251

MFM H1
★21260 SCHTORM → 21264

MFM H1
★21280 OCEANO ANTARTICO

MFM H1
21290 REA

MFM H1
★21310 PLOD

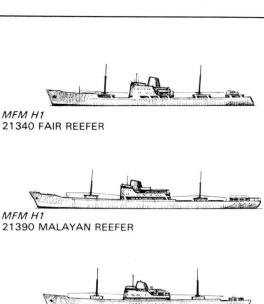

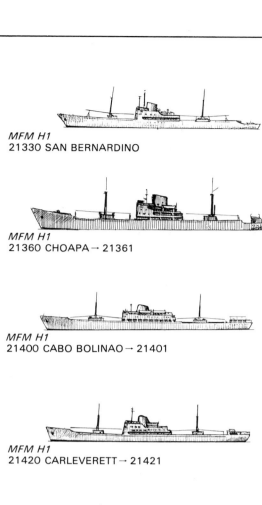

MFM H1
21330 SAN BERNARDINO

MFM H1
21340 FAIR REEFER

MFM H1
21360 CHOAPA → 21361

MFM H1
21390 MALAYAN REEFER

MFM H1
21400 CABO BOLINAO → 21401

MFM H1
21410 JERRYEVERETT → 21412

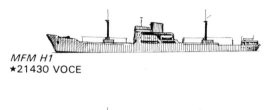

MFM H1
21420 CARLEVERETT → 21421

MFM H1
★21430 VOCE

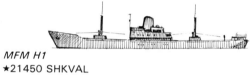

MFM H1
21440 CHALMEVERETT → 21441

MFM H1
★21450 SHKVAL

MFM H1
21460 SAMOS SEA → 21461

MFM H1
21470 CARIBBEAN ARROW → 21472

MFM H1
21480 HEBE 1

MFM H1
21490 GEMA

MFM H1
21500 ESTEBAN S

MFM H1
★21510 VARAZDIN → 21512

MFM H1
21530 RAZZAN 1

MFM H1
★21560 FALESHTY → 21565

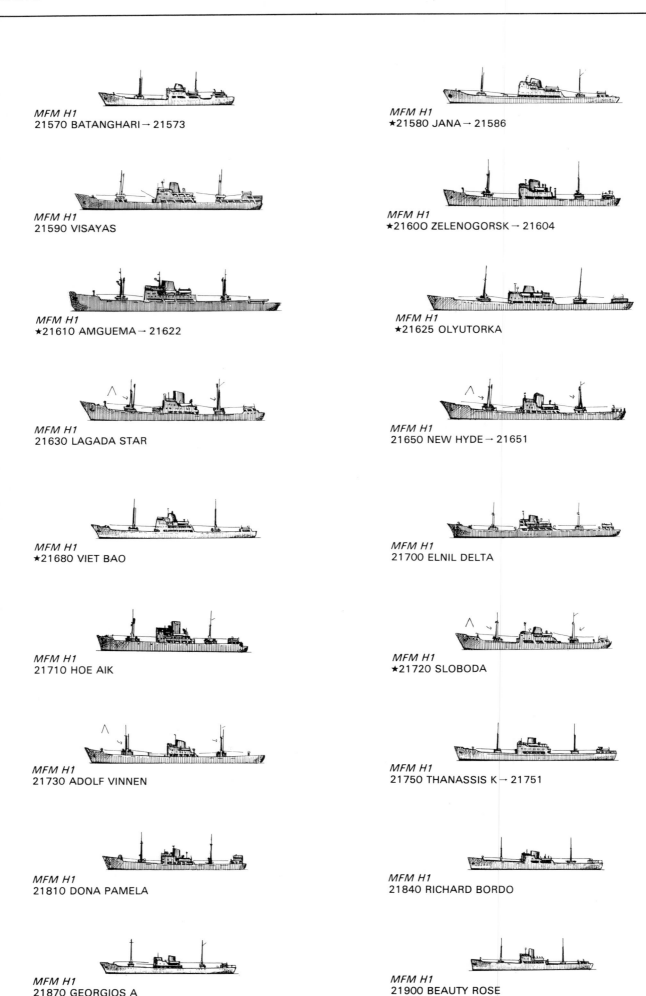

MFM H1
21570 BATANGHARI → 21573

MFM H1
★21580 JANA → 21586

MFM H1
21590 VISAYAS

MFM H1
★21600 ZELENOGORSK → 21604

MFM H1
★21610 AMGUEMA → 21622

MFM H1
★21625 OLYUTORKA

MFM H1
21630 LAGADA STAR

MFM H1
21650 NEW HYDE → 21651

MFM H1
★21680 VIET BAO

MFM H1
21700 ELNIL DELTA

MFM H1
21710 HOE AIK

MFM H1
★21720 SLOBODA

MFM H1
21730 ADOLF VINNEN

MFM H1
21750 THANASSIS K → 21751

MFM H1
21810 DONA PAMELA

MFM H1
21840 RICHARD BORDO

MFM H1
21870 GEORGIOS A

MFM H1
21900 BEAUTY ROSE

MFM H1
21920 KRANTOR→ 21921

MFM H1
21940 KALYMNOS→ 21941

MFM H1
21950 BB 3

MFM H1
21960 ASA-THOR

MFM H1
21970 LADY M→ 21971

MFM H1
22000 NORGE

MFM H1
22010 BONAVISTA

MFM H1
22020 LAURO EXPRESS

MFM H1
22030 JYLLAND

MFM H1
22040 PRINCESS OF NEGROS

MFM H1
22050 PRINSES MARGRIET

MFM H1
22060 CITY OF PIRAEUS→ 22061

MFM H1
22080 BIRD OF PARADISE→ 22081

MFM H1
22110 EVANGELISTRIA

MFM H1
22120 SEIUN MARU

MFM H1
22130 BAFFIN

MFM H1
22140 OCEANIC→ 22141

MFM H1
★22150 MB 18→ 22153

MFM H1
★22160 YAGUAR → 22163

MFM H1
22170 JOHN ROSS → 22171

MFM H1
★22180 NIKOLAI ZUBOV → 22190

MFM H1
★22195 NEVELSKOY

MFM H1
★22200 KAPITAN CHECHKIN → 22205

MFM H1
22210 ALMIRANTE IRIZAR

MFM H1
★22220 DOBRINYA NIKITICH → 22242

MFM H1
★22240 OTTO SCHMIDT

MFM H1
★22250 KAPITAN M. IZMAYLOV → 22252

MFM H1
22260 VOIMA

MFM H1
22270 THULE

MFM H1
22280 CANOPUS → 22281

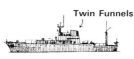

Twin Funnels

MFM H1
22300 CIROLANA

MFM H1
22320 THALASSA

Tripod   Twin Funnels

MFM H1
★22325 SEVER

Twin Funnels

MFM H1
★22330 BELONA → 22340

Twin Funnels

MFM H1
★22350 RYBAK MORSKI → 22351

MFM H1
22360 CLAYMORE

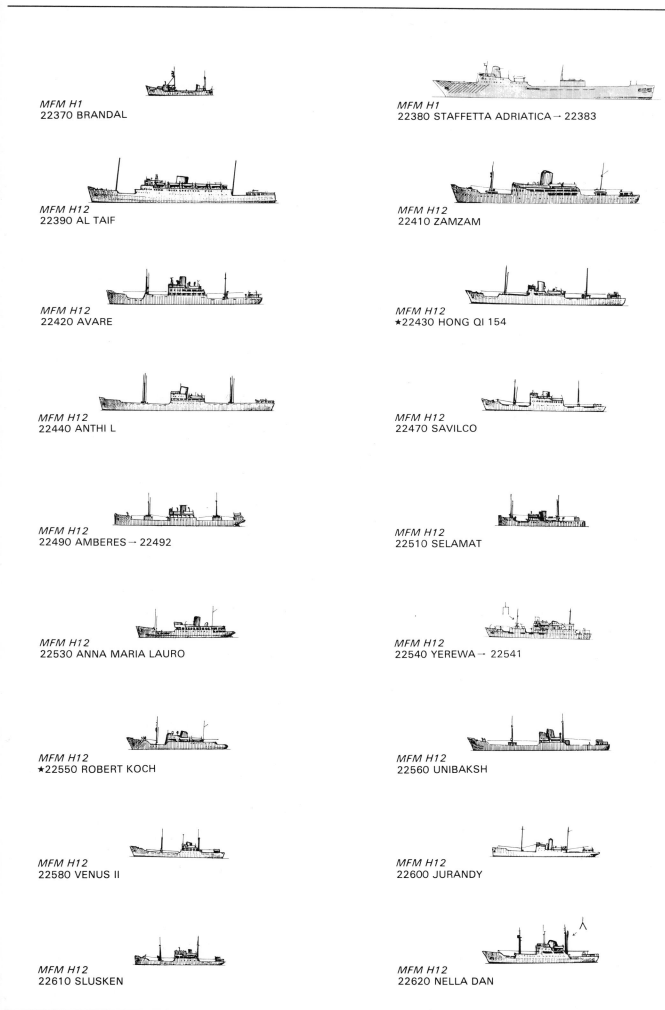

MFM H1
22370 BRANDAL

MFM H1
22380 STAFFETTA ADRIATICA → 22383

MFM H12
22390 AL TAIF

MFM H12
22410 ZAMZAM

MFM H12
22420 AVARE

MFM H12
★22430 HONG QI 154

MFM H12
22440 ANTHI L

MFM H12
22470 SAVILCO

MFM H12
22490 AMBERES → 22492

MFM H12
22510 SELAMAT

MFM H12
22530 ANNA MARIA LAURO

MFM H12
22540 YEREWA → 22541

MFM H12
★22550 ROBERT KOCH

MFM H12
22560 UNIBAKSH

MFM H12
22580 VENUS II

MFM H12
22600 JURANDY

MFM H12
22610 SLUSKEN

MFM H12
22620 NELLA DAN

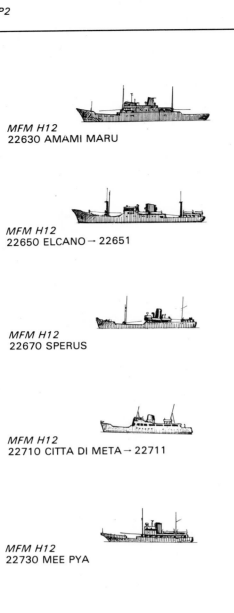

MFM H12
22630 AMAMI MARU

MFM H12
22640 CAPE YORK

MFM H12
22650 ELCANO → 22651

MFM H12
22660 SURAJ

MFM H12
22670 SPERUS

MFM H12
22690 GILBERT J. FOWLER → 22691

MFM H12
22710 CITTA DI META → 22711

MFM H12
★22720 SPASSK → 22723

MFM H12
22730 MEE PYA

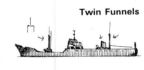

MFM H12
22740 NEPTUNE → 22741

MFM H12
22750 SETANTA

Twin Funnels

MFM H12
22770 JIN YANG No 2 → 22777

MFM H12
22780 SEISELLA

MFM H12
★22790 Modified LEVANT or KOVEL type → 22793

MFM H123
22810 BARBA

MFM H123
22830 THEODOROS II → 22837

MFM H123
★22840 ANDIZHAN → 22885

MFM H123
22930 DEEPA RAYA

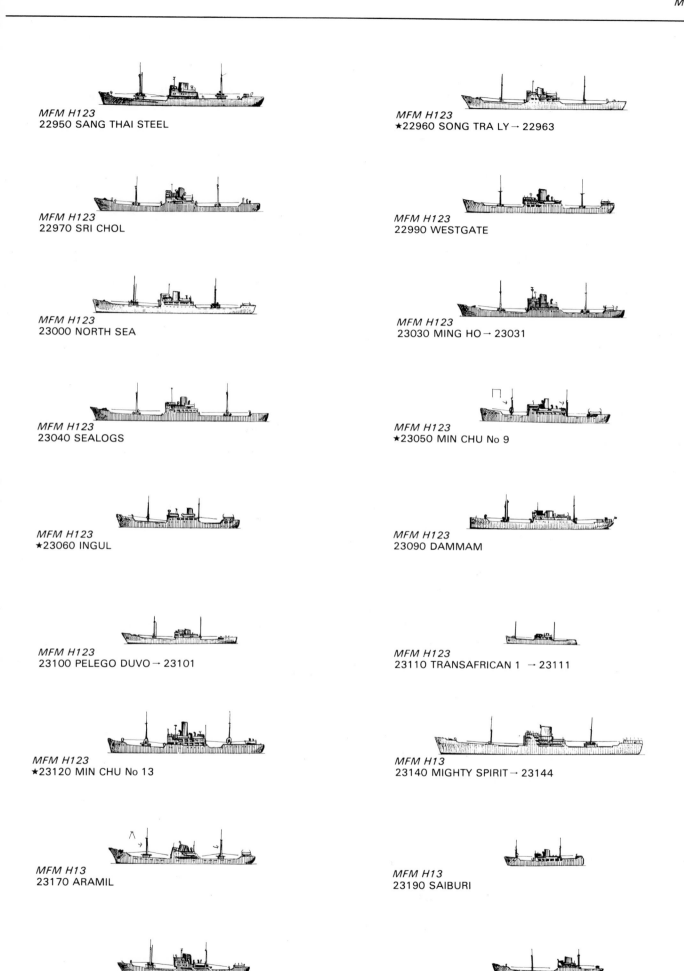

MFM H123
22950 SANG THAI STEEL

MFM H123
★22960 SONG TRA LY → 22963

MFM H123
22970 SRI CHOL

MFM H123
22990 WESTGATE

MFM H123
23000 NORTH SEA

MFM H123
23030 MING HO → 23031

MFM H123
23040 SEALOGS

MFM H123
★23050 MIN CHU No 9

MFM H123
★23060 INGUL

MFM H123
23090 DAMMAM

MFM H123
23100 PELEGO DUVO → 23101

MFM H123
23110 TRANSAFRICAN 1 → 23111

MFM H123
★23120 MIN CHU No 13

MFM H13
23140 MIGHTY SPIRIT → 23144

MFM H13
23170 ARAMIL

MFM H13
23190 SAIBURI

MFM H13
23200 AGIOS NECTARIOS

MFM H13
23210 VENUS II

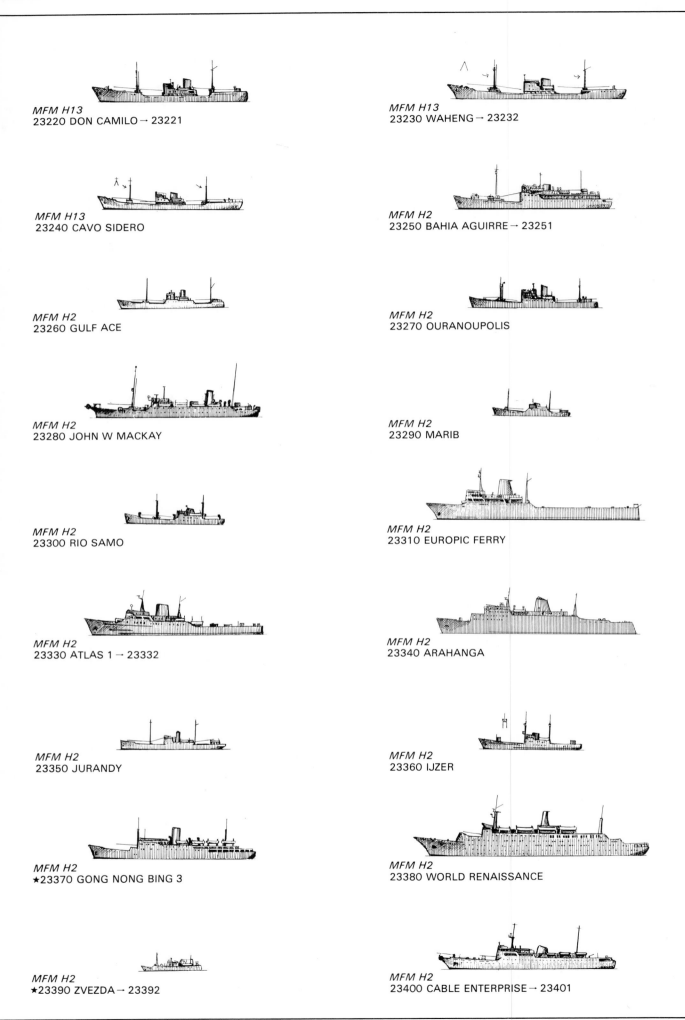

MFM H13
23220 DON CAMILO → 23221

MFM H13
23230 WAHENG → 23232

MFM H13
23240 CAVO SIDERO

MFM H2
23250 BAHIA AGUIRRE → 23251

MFM H2
23260 GULF ACE

MFM H2
23270 OURANOUPOLIS

MFM H2
23280 JOHN W MACKAY

MFM H2
23290 MARIB

MFM H2
23300 RIO SAMO

MFM H2
23310 EUROPIC FERRY

MFM H2
23330 ATLAS 1 → 23332

MFM H2
23340 ARAHANGA

MFM H2
23350 JURANDY

MFM H2
23360 IJZER

MFM H2
★23370 GONG NONG BING 3

MFM H2
23380 WORLD RENAISSANCE

MFM H2
★23390 ZVEZDA → 23392

MFM H2
23400 CABLE ENTERPRISE → 23401

MFM H2
★23410 RYBAK → 23432

Twin Funnels

MFM H2
★23440 AFALA → 23473

MFM H2
★23480 LUCHEGORSK class → 23573

Twin Funnels

MFM H2
23580 WUPPERTAL

MFM H3
23600 CHARRUA → 23601

MFMC H
23610 ALKYON

MFMC H
23620 FEDERAL MAPLE

MFMC H
★23640 VLADIMIR KAVRAYSKIY

MFMC H1
23650 ALMIRANTE IRIZAR

MFMC H1
23660 TOR → 23663

MFMC H1
★23665 MB-29 → 23669

MFMC H1
23670 ALE

MFMCK H13
23680 JOHN BISCOE

MFMF H2
★23690 SASSNITZ

MFMF H
23700 BENODET → 23707

MFMF H
23710 IONIAN STAR → 23711

Twin Funnels

MFMF H
23720 IZU MARU No 3 → 23721

MFMF H
23730 HIDAKA MARU → 23735

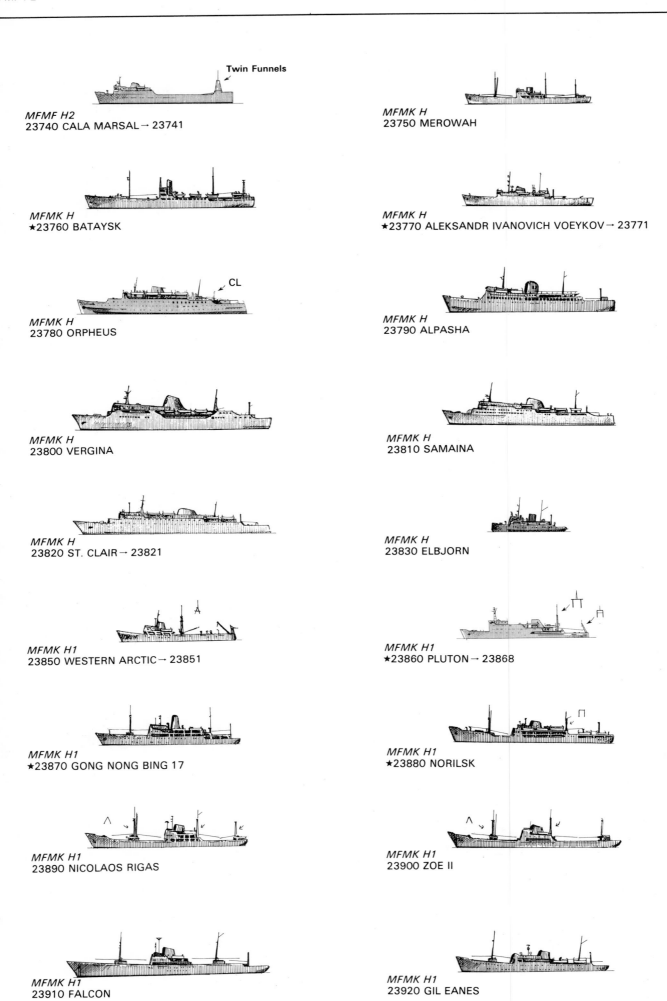

Twin Funnels

MFMF H2
23740 CALA MARSAL → 23741

MFMK H
23750 MEROWAH

MFMK H
★23760 BATAYSK

MFMK H
★23770 ALEKSANDR IVANOVICH VOEYKOV → 23771

CL

MFMK H
23780 ORPHEUS

MFMK H
23790 ALPASHA

MFMK H
23800 VERGINA

MFMK H
23810 SAMAINA

MFMK H
23820 ST. CLAIR → 23821

MFMK H
23830 ELBJORN

MFMK H1
23850 WESTERN ARCTIC → 23851

MFMK H1
★23860 PLUTON → 23868

MFMK H1
★23870 GONG NONG BING 17

MFMK H1
★23880 NORILSK

MFMK H1
23890 NICOLAOS RIGAS

MFMK H1
23900 ZOE II

MFMK H1
23910 FALCON

MFMK H1
23920 GIL EANES

MFMK H1
23930 SIMALI 1 → 23931

MFMK H1
23940 DANBJORN → 23941

MFMK H1
23950 ODEN

MFMK H1
23960 HANSE

MFMK H1
★23970 KAPITAN BELOUSOV → 23972

MFMK H1
23980 MURTAJA → 23982

MFMK H1
23990 ABERTHAW FISHER → 23991

MFMK H12
24010 FAIRFIELD VISCOUNT

MFMK H123
★24030 VOLGOLES → 24111

MFMK H13
24130 WATAMPONE → 24134

MFMK H13
24140 MAURITIUS

MFMK H2
★24145 KAVKAZ → 24146

MFMK H2
24150 ARCTIC TRAWLER → 24151

MFMK₂ H
★24160 JUNGE GARDE → 24161

MFMKM H1
24170 ANTON DOHRN

MFM₂ H
24180 MEROWAH

MFM₂ H
24190 ANITA

MFMR H
24220 TOKYO MARU

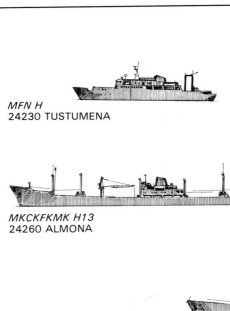

MFN H
24230 TUSTUMENA

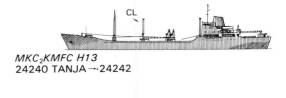

MKC₂KMFC H13
24240 TANJA → 24242

MKCKFKMK H13
24260 ALMONA

MKCKMFKMK H13
24270 APLI CHAU → 24273

MKCMFKM H1
24280 RIO CORRIENTES → 24285

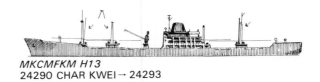

MKCMFKM H13
24290 CHAR KWEI → 24293

MKCMFKMK H13
24300 HAI MENG → 24301

MKF H
★24310 RODINA → 24319

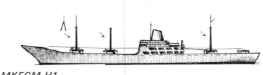

MKFCM H1
24340 PALATINO → 24343

MKFCM H1
24350 ELLITSA → 24351

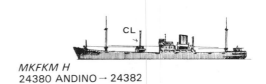

MKFKM H
24380 ANDINO → 24382

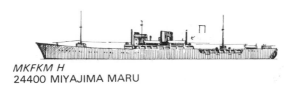

MKFKM H
24400 MIYAJIMA MARU

MKFKM H1
24440 KOTA SINGAPURA → 24441

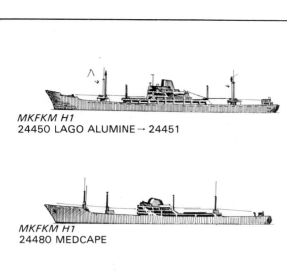

MKFKM H1
24450 LAGO ALUMINE → 24451

MKFKM H1
24470 MARIA SOFIA

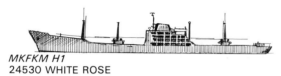

MKFKM H1
24480 MEDCAPE

MKFKM H1
24510 REEFER QUEEN → 24511

MKFKM H1
24530 WHITE ROSE

MKFKM H1
24540 MASTER TONY → 24542

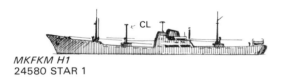

MKFKM H1
★24560 SIENKIEWICZ → 24561

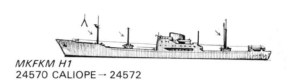

MKFKM H1
24570 CALIOPE → 24572

MKFKM H1
24580 STAR 1

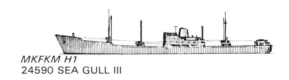

MKFKM H1
24590 SEA GULL III

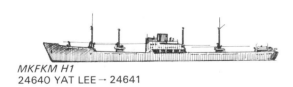

MKFKM H1
24610 POSEIDON C.

MKFKM H1
★24630 PETAR BARON

MKFKM H1
24640 YAT LEE → 24641

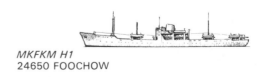

MKFKM H1
24650 FOOCHOW

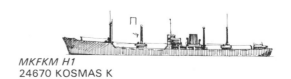

MKFKM H1
24660 MANDARIN

MKFKM H1
24670 KOSMAS K

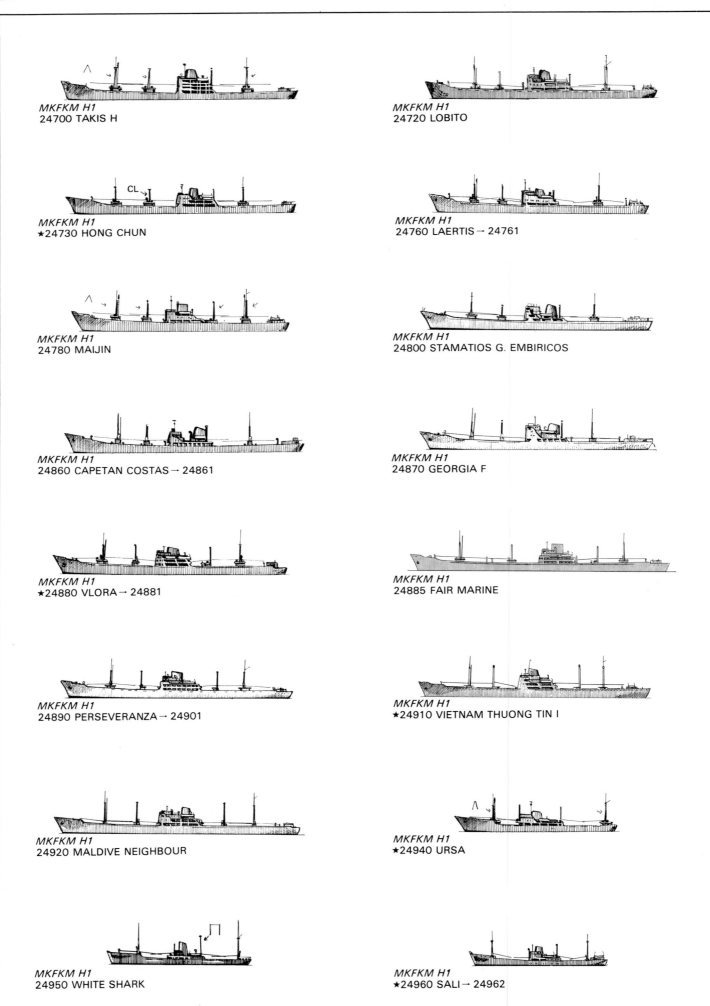

MKFKM H1
24700 TAKIS H

MKFKM H1
24720 LOBITO

MKFKM H1
★24730 HONG CHUN

MKFKM H1
24760 LAERTIS → 24761

MKFKM H1
24780 MAIJIN

MKFKM H1
24800 STAMATIOS G. EMBIRICOS

MKFKM H1
24860 CAPETAN COSTAS → 24861

MKFKM H1
24870 GEORGIA F

MKFKM H1
★24880 VLORA → 24881

MKFKM H1
24885 FAIR MARINE

MKFKM H1
24890 PERSEVERANZA → 24901

MKFKM H1
★24910 VIETNAM THUONG TIN I

MKFKM H1
24920 MALDIVE NEIGHBOUR

MKFKM H1
★24940 URSA

MKFKM H1
24950 WHITE SHARK

MKFKM H1
★24960 SALI → 24962

MKFKM H1
★24970 NADIR

MKFKM H1
★24980 HONG QI 144

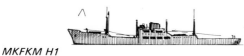

MKFKM H1
24990 CAMPECHE

MKFKM H1
★25000 CHON JIN

MKFKM H1
25010 ATHINAI → 25012

MKFKM H1
★25020 ZHAN DOU No 28

MKFKM H1
★25030 HONG QI 163

MKFKM H1
★25040 ZHAN DOU No 71

MKFKM H1
★25050 ZHAN DOU No 72 → 25051

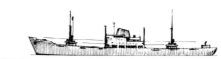

MKFKM H1
25070 JETPUR VICTORY

MKFKM H1
25080 ARIS

MKFKM H1
25100 CONFIDENCE → 25102

MKFKM H1
25140 ARISTO → 25141

MKFKM H1
25170 'HANSA' type → 25174

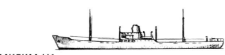

MKFKM H1
25180 LONDINON

MKFKM H1
★25200 PUERTO DE VITA

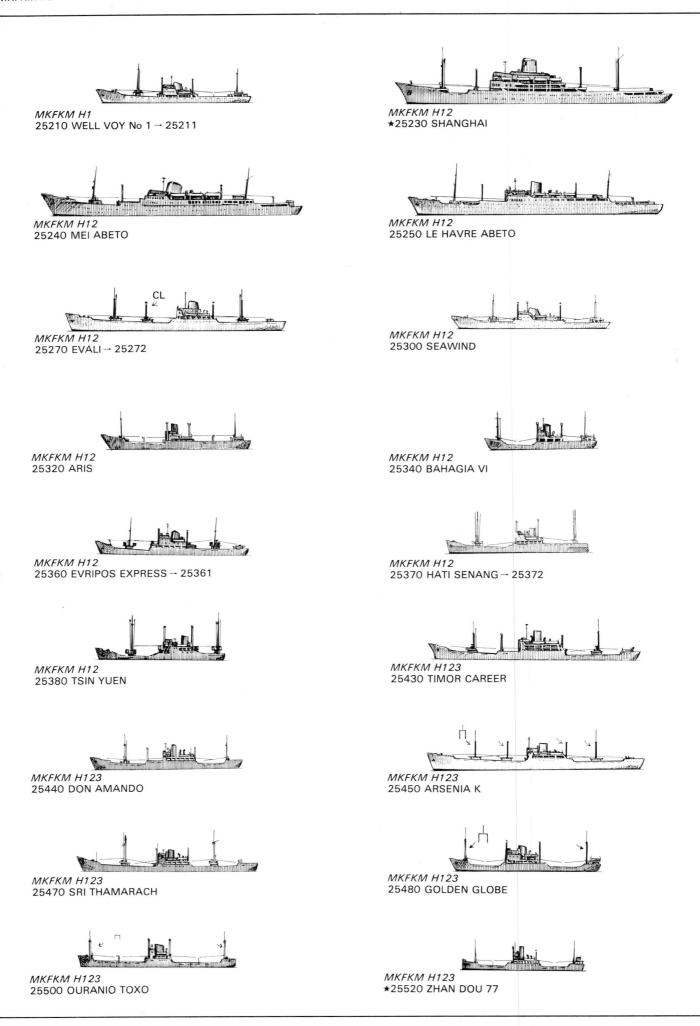

MKFKM H1
25210 WELL VOY No 1 → 25211

MKFKM H12
★25230 SHANGHAI

MKFKM H12
25240 MEI ABETO

MKFKM H12
25250 LE HAVRE ABETO

MKFKM H12
25270 EVALI → 25272

MKFKM H12
25300 SEAWIND

MKFKM H12
25320 ARIS

MKFKM H12
25340 BAHAGIA VI

MKFKM H12
25360 EVRIPOS EXPRESS → 25361

MKFKM H12
25370 HATI SENANG → 25372

MKFKM H12
25380 TSIN YUEN

MKFKM H123
25430 TIMOR CAREER

MKFKM H123
25440 DON AMANDO

MKFKM H123
25450 ARSENIA K

MKFKM H123
25470 SRI THAMARACH

MKFKM H123
25480 GOLDEN GLOBE

MKFKM H123
25500 OURANIO TOXO

MKFKM H123
★25520 ZHAN DOU 77

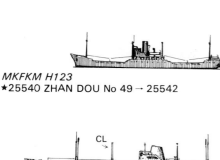

MKFKM H123
★25540 ZHAN DOU No 49 → 25542

MKFKM H123
★25550 'KHASAN' class → 25572

MKFKM H13
25620 VISHVA NIDHI → 25622

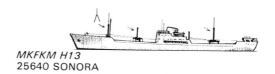

MKFKM H13
25640 SONORA

MKFKM H13
★25650 PEIKIANG

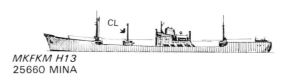

MKFKM H13
25660 MINA

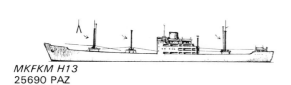

MKFKM H13
25690 PAZ

MKFKM H13
25700 ROSARIO DOS → 25707

MKFKM H13
25710 KOUKOUNARIES K

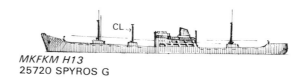

MKFKM H13
25720 SPYROS G

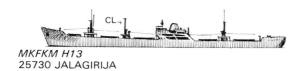

MKFKM H13
25730 JALAGIRIJA

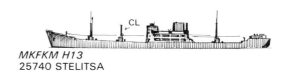

MKFKM H13
25740 STELITSA

MKFKM H13
25750 FORTUNE VICTORY → 25752

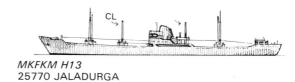

MKFKM H13
25770 JALADURGA

MKFKM H13
25771 VISHVA BHAKTI → 25778

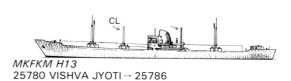

MKFKM H13
25780 VISHVA JYOTI → 25786

MKFKM H13
25790 NELIA

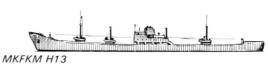

MKFKM H13
25800 PANAGIOTIS XILAS

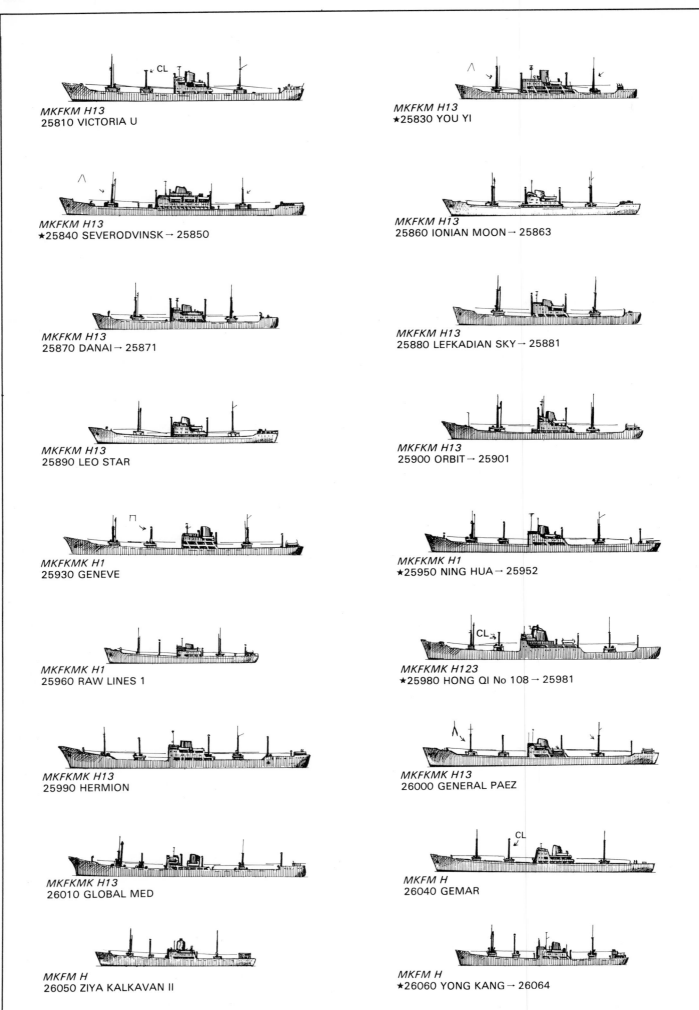

MKFKM H13
25810 VICTORIA U

MKFKM H13
★25830 YOU YI

MKFKM H13
★25840 SEVERODVINSK → 25850

MKFKM H13
25860 IONIAN MOON → 25863

MKFKM H13
25870 DANAI → 25871

MKFKM H13
25880 LEFKADIAN SKY → 25881

MKFKM H13
25890 LEO STAR

MKFKM H13
25900 ORBIT → 25901

MKFKMK H1
25930 GENEVE

MKFKMK H1
★25950 NING HUA → 25952

MKFKMK H1
25960 RAW LINES 1

MKFKMK H123
★25980 HONG QI No 108 → 25981

MKFKMK H13
25990 HERMION

MKFKMK H13
26000 GENERAL PAEZ

MKFKMK H13
26010 GLOBAL MED

MKFM H
26040 GEMAR

MKFM H
26050 ZIYA KALKAVAN II

MKFM H
★26060 YONG KANG → 26064

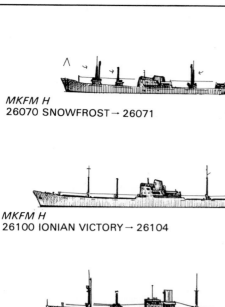

MKFM H
26070 SNOWFROST → 26071

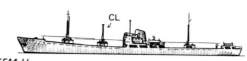

MKFM H
26080 DONG MYUNG → 26082

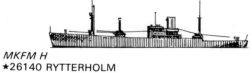

MKFM H
26100 IONIAN VICTORY → 26104

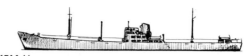

MKFM H
26110 IONIAN SEA → 26113

MKFM H
★26140 RYTTERHOLM

MKFM H
26170 DAVAO CITY

MKFM H
26180 OBA

MKFM H
26200 AL QASEEM

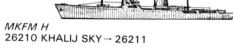

MKFM H
26210 KHALIJ SKY → 26211

MKFM H1
★26220 SOVIETSKAYA ARKTIKA

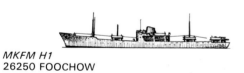

MKFM H1
26250 FOOCHOW

MKFM H1
26270 MANDARIN

MKFM H1
26280 IONIAN GLORY

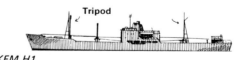

MKFM H1
26300 NAVIKAPOL

MKFM H1
★26320 CIKAT → 26322

MKFM H1
26330 AL FARY

MKFM H1
26350 LI SHAN

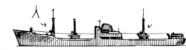

MKFM H1
26370 POSEIDON C

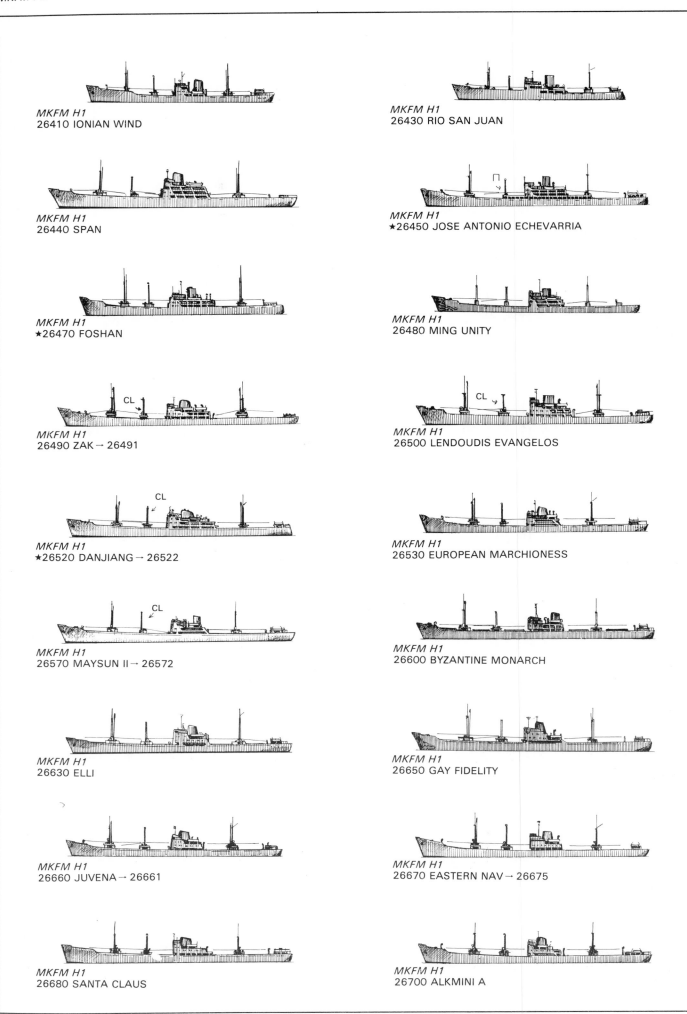

MKFM H1
26410 IONIAN WIND

MKFM H1
26430 RIO SAN JUAN

MKFM H1
26440 SPAN

MKFM H1
★26450 JOSE ANTONIO ECHEVARRIA

MKFM H1
★26470 FOSHAN

MKFM H1
26480 MING UNITY

MKFM H1
26490 ZAK → 26491

MKFM H1
26500 LENDOUDIS EVANGELOS

MKFM H1
★26520 DANJIANG → 26522

MKFM H1
26530 EUROPEAN MARCHIONESS

MKFM H1
26570 MAYSUN II → 26572

MKFM H1
26600 BYZANTINE MONARCH

MKFM H1
26630 ELLI

MKFM H1
26650 GAY FIDELITY

MKFM H1
26660 JUVENA → 26661

MKFM H1
26670 EASTERN NAV → 26675

MKFM H1
26680 SANTA CLAUS

MKFM H1
26700 ALKMINI A

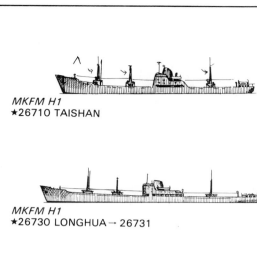

MKFM H1
★26710 TAISHAN

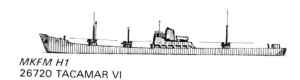

MKFM H1
26720 TACAMAR VI

MKFM H1
★26730 LONGHUA → 26731

MKFM H1
26740 YZONA

MKFM H1
26750 IONIAN SKY → 26753

MKFM H1
26760 UNISON II → 26761

MKFM H1
26770 BARAO DE JACEGUAY → 26771

MKFM H1
★26800 GUANG PING → 26803

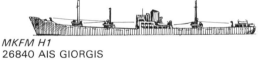

MKFM H1
★26810 HONG QI 138 → 26812

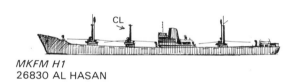

MKFM H1
26830 AL HASAN

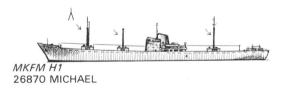

MKFM H1
26840 AIS GIORGIS

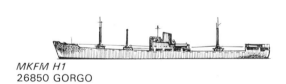

MKFM H1
26850 GORGO

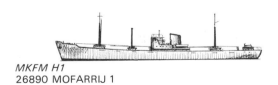

MKFM H1
26870 MICHAEL

MKFM H1
26880 AGIA VARVARA

MKFM H1
26890 MOFARRIJ 1

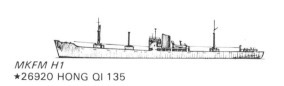

MKFM H1
★26920 HONG QI 135

MKFM H1
26940 PRIMERO DE JUNIO

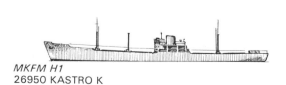

MKFM H1
26950 KASTRO K

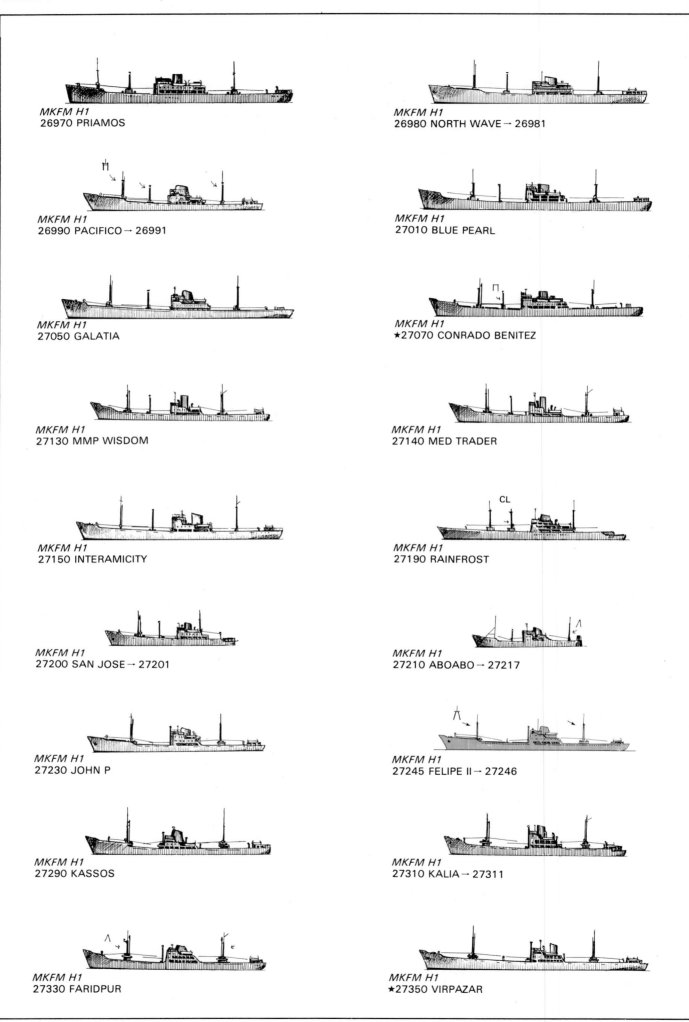

MKFM H1
26970 PRIAMOS

MKFM H1
26980 NORTH WAVE → 26981

MKFM H1
26990 PACIFICO → 26991

MKFM H1
27010 BLUE PEARL

MKFM H1
27050 GALATIA

MKFM H1
★27070 CONRADO BENITEZ

MKFM H1
27130 MMP WISDOM

MKFM H1
27140 MED TRADER

MKFM H1
27150 INTERAMICITY

MKFM H1
27190 RAINFROST

MKFM H1
27200 SAN JOSE → 27201

MKFM H1
27210 ABOABO → 27217

MKFM H1
27230 JOHN P

MKFM H1
27245 FELIPE II → 27246

MKFM H1
27290 KASSOS

MKFM H1
27310 KALIA → 27311

MKFM H1
27330 FARIDPUR

MKFM H1
★27350 VIRPAZAR

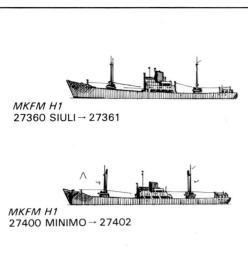

MKFM H1
27360 SIULI → 27361

MKFM H1
27370 OCEAN GLORY

MKFM H1
27400 MINIMO → 27402

MKFM H1
27410 SEA RENOWN

MKFM H1
27430 ASTRONAFTIS

MKFM H1
27440 SCAPLAKE

MKFM H1
★27460 RABA

MKFM H1
27480 WANG No 1

MKFM H1
27490 EASTERN STAR

MKFM H1
★27520 DUNA → 27521

MKFM H1
27540 DONA LOLITA

MKFM H1
27560 NEW HYDE → 27561

MKFM H1
27570 ELEISTRIA V

MKFM H1
27580 FERAX

MKFM H1
27590 LUCY

MKFM H1
27620 PACIFIC MULIA

MKFM H1
27650 SOPHIE

MKFM H1
27690 CEFALLONIAN SUN → 27691

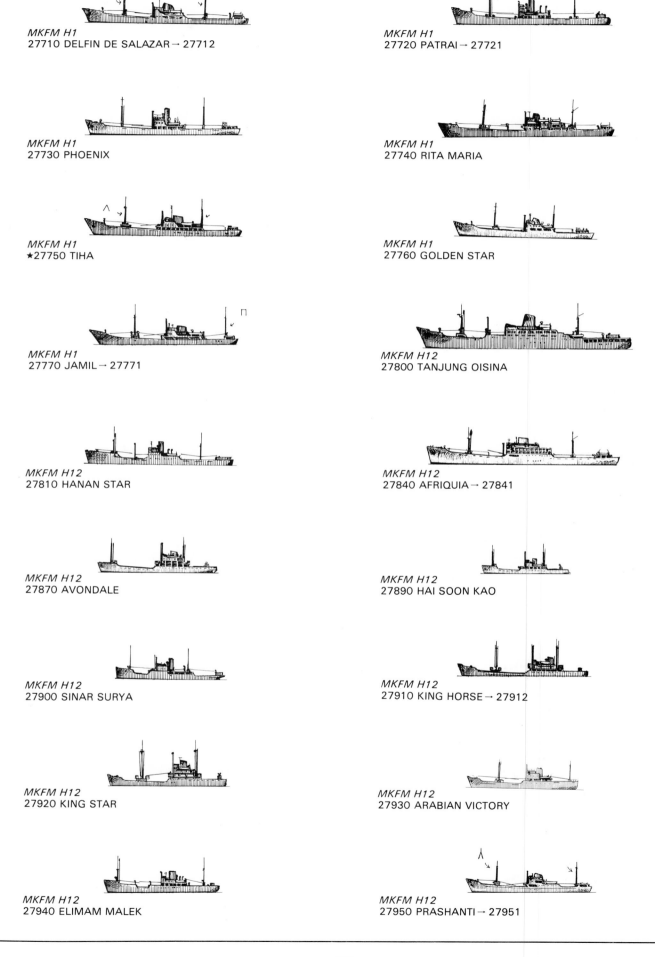

MKFM H1
27710 DELFIN DE SALAZAR → 27712

MKFM H1
27720 PATRAI → 27721

MKFM H1
27730 PHOENIX

MKFM H1
27740 RITA MARIA

MKFM H1
★27750 TIHA

MKFM H1
27760 GOLDEN STAR

MKFM H1
27770 JAMIL → 27771

MKFM H12
27800 TANJUNG OISINA

MKFM H12
27810 HANAN STAR

MKFM H12
27840 AFRIQUIA → 27841

MKFM H12
27870 AVONDALE

MKFM H12
27890 HAI SOON KAO

MKFM H12
27900 SINAR SURYA

MKFM H12
27910 KING HORSE → 27912

MKFM H12
27920 KING STAR

MKFM H12
27930 ARABIAN VICTORY

MKFM H12
27940 ELIMAM MALEK

MKFM H12
27950 PRASHANTI → 27951

MKFM H12
27960 BHOJA MARINER → 27961

MKFM H123
28030 SAREYAH

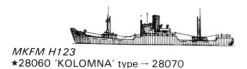

MKFM H123
★28060 'KOLOMNA' type → 28070

MKFM H123
28110 NAKHODA VANANCA

MKFM H13
28150 AKIS S

MKFM H13
28170 LANKA KALYANI

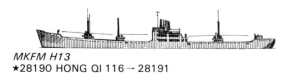

MKFM H13
★28190 HONG QI 116 → 28191

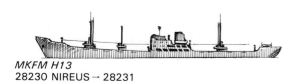

MKFM H13
28210 TURBO P

MKFM H123
28010 MILFORD

MKFM H123
28040 TAI YUNG

MKFM H123
28090 CHIEH SHENG

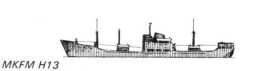

MKFM H123
28120 MUNAWER → 28121

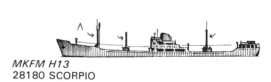

MKFM H13
★28160 LUO DING

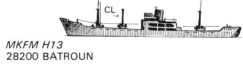

MKFM H13
28180 SCORPIO

MKFM H13
28200 BATROUN

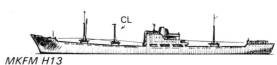

MKFM H13
★28220 HONG MING → 28222

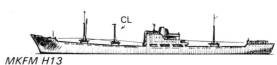

MKFM H13
28230 NIREUS → 28231

MKFM H13
★28250 XING MING

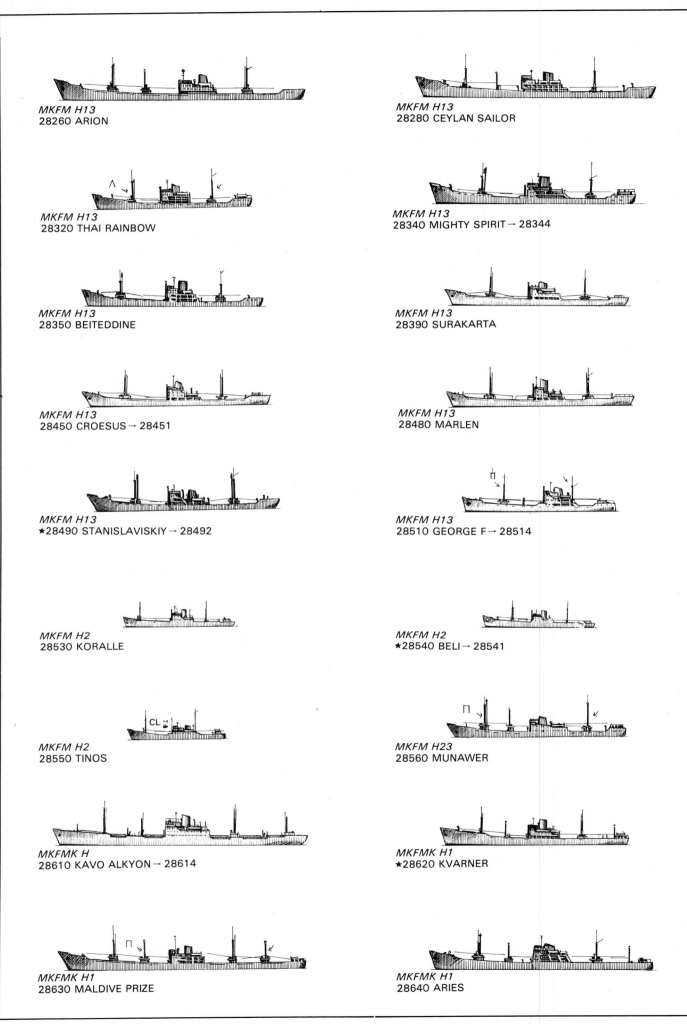

MKFM H13
28260 ARION

MKFM H13
28280 CEYLAN SAILOR

MKFM H13
28320 THAI RAINBOW

MKFM H13
28340 MIGHTY SPIRIT → 28344

MKFM H13
28350 BEITEDDINE

MKFM H13
28390 SURAKARTA

MKFM H13
28450 CROESUS → 28451

MKFM H13
28480 MARLEN

MKFM H13
★28490 STANISLAVISKIY → 28492

MKFM H13
28510 GEORGE F → 28514

MKFM H2
28530 KORALLE

MKFM H2
★28540 BELI → 28541

MKFM H2
28550 TINOS

MKFM H23
28560 MUNAWER

MKFMK H
28610 KAVO ALKYON → 28614

MKFMK H1
★28620 KVARNER

MKFMK H1
28630 MALDIVE PRIZE

MKFMK H1
28640 ARIES

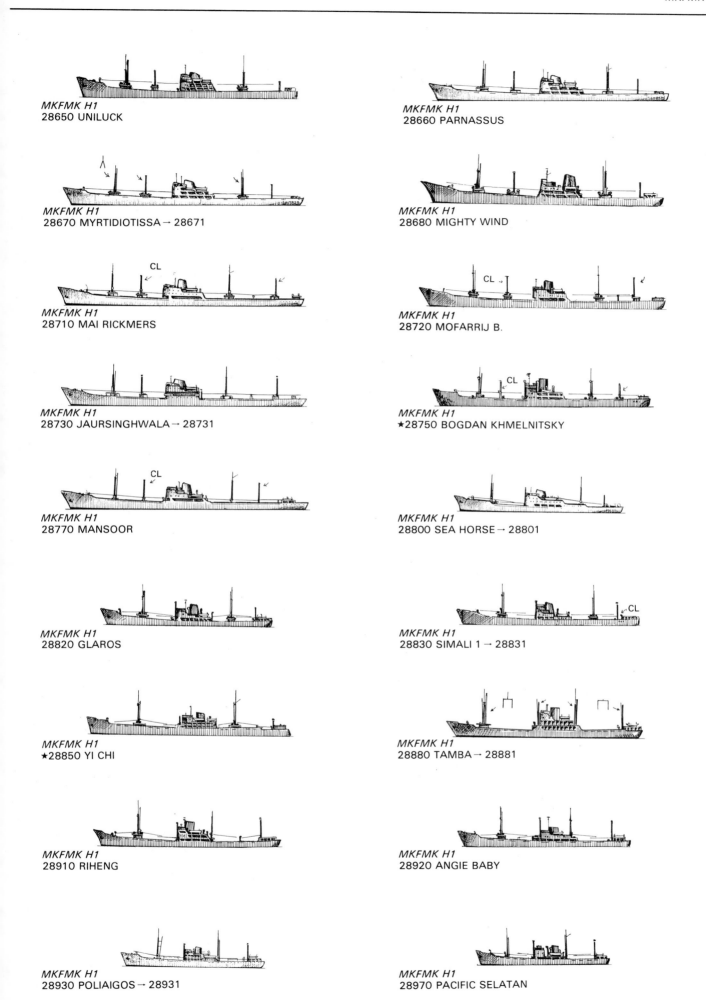

MKFMK H1
28650 UNILUCK

MKFMK H1
28660 PARNASSUS

MKFMK H1
28670 MYRTIDIOTISSA → 28671

MKFMK H1
28680 MIGHTY WIND

MKFMK H1
28710 MAI RICKMERS

MKFMK H1
28720 MOFARRIJ B.

MKFMK H1
28730 JAURSINGHWALA → 28731

MKFMK H1
★28750 BOGDAN KHMELNITSKY

MKFMK H1
28770 MANSOOR

MKFMK H1
28800 SEA HORSE → 28801

MKFMK H1
28820 GLAROS

MKFMK H1
28830 SIMALI 1 → 28831

MKFMK H1
★28850 YI CHI

MKFMK H1
28880 TAMBA → 28881

MKFMK H1
28910 RIHENG

MKFMK H1
28920 ANGIE BABY

MKFMK H1
28930 POLIAIGOS → 28931

MKFMK H1
28970 PACIFIC SELATAN

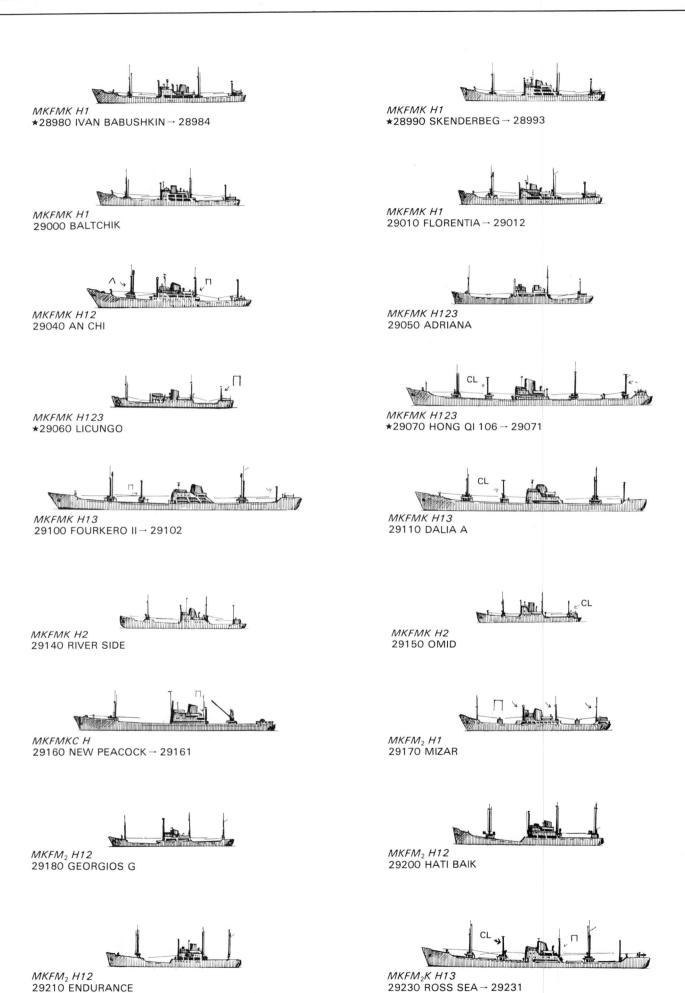

MKFMK H1
★28980 IVAN BABUSHKIN → 28984

MKFMK H1
★28990 SKENDERBEG → 28993

MKFMK H1
29000 BALTCHIK

MKFMK H1
29010 FLORENTIA → 29012

MKFMK H12
29040 AN CHI

MKFMK H123
29050 ADRIANA

MKFMK H123
★29060 LICUNGO

MKFMK H123
★29070 HONG QI 106 → 29071

MKFMK H13
29100 FOURKERO II → 29102

MKFMK H13
29110 DALIA A

MKFMK H2
29140 RIVER SIDE

MKFMK H2
29150 OMID

MKFMKC H
29160 NEW PEACOCK → 29161

MKFM₂ H1
29170 MIZAR

MKFM₂ H12
29180 GEORGIOS G

MKFM₂ H12
29200 HATI BAIK

MKFM₂ H12
29210 ENDURANCE

MKFM₂K H13
29230 ROSS SEA → 29231

MK₂FCM H13
29240 ZUIDER SEA → 29243

MK₂FK H13
29270 LEON PROM

MK₂FK₂ H1
★29280 CHANG HUA

MK₂FK₂M H123
29330 SAUDI SUNRISE → 29331

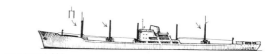

MK₂FKM H1
★29350 TONG HUA

MK₂FKM H1
★29360 NANXIANG → 29364

MK₂FKM H1
29380 HELLENIC DESTINY → 29382

MK₂FKM H1
29410 DIAMANTIS

MK₂FKM H1
29420 TEGAL

MK₂FKM H1
29440 PIURA → 29441

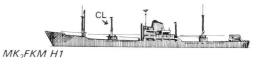

MK₂FKM H1
29450 HERCULUS

MK₂FKM H1
29460 PISTIS → 29461

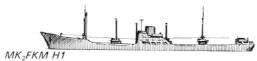

MK₂FKM H1
29470 SURABAYA

MK₂FKM H1
29490 NAVIKAPOL

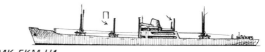

MK₂FKM H1
29500 STATE OF TRAVANCORE-COCHIN

MK₂ FKM H1
29510 KERASOUS

MK₂FKM H1
★29520 CHANG HUA

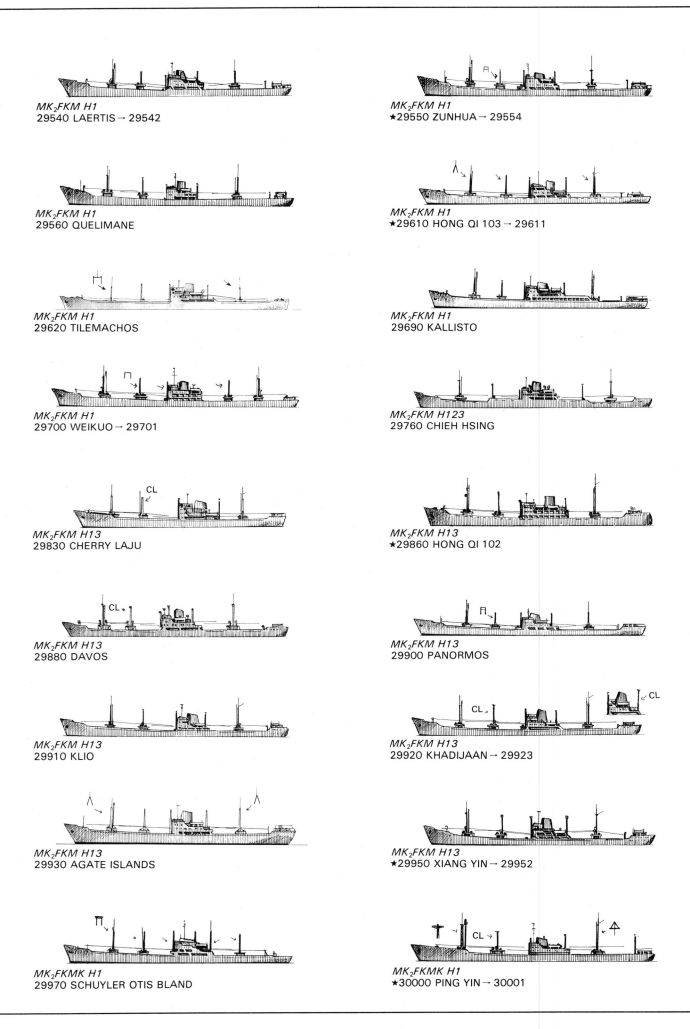

MK₂FKM H1
29540 LAERTIS → 29542

MK₂FKM H1
★29550 ZUNHUA → 29554

MK₂FKM H1
29560 QUELIMANE

MK₂FKM H1
★29610 HONG QI 103 → 29611

MK₂FKM H1
29620 TILEMACHOS

MK₂FKM H1
29690 KALLISTO

MK₂FKM H1
29700 WEIKUO → 29701

MK₂FKM H123
29760 CHIEH HSING

MK₂FKM H13
29830 CHERRY LAJU

MK₂FKM H13
★29860 HONG QI 102

MK₂FKM H13
29880 DAVOS

MK₂FKM H13
29900 PANORMOS

MK₂FKM H13
29910 KLIO

MK₂FKM H13
29920 KHADIJAAN → 29923

MK₂FKM H13
29930 AGATE ISLANDS

MK₂FKM H13
★29950 XIANG YIN → 29952

MK₂FKMK H1
29970 SCHUYLER OTIS BLAND

MK₂FKMK H1
★30000 PING YIN → 30001

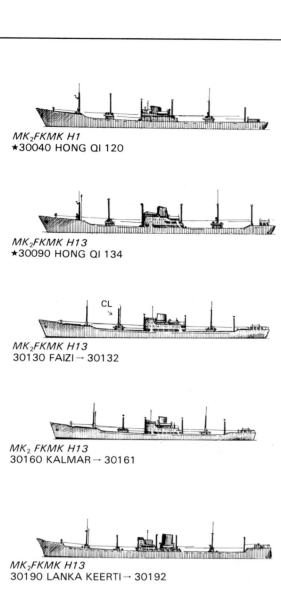

MK₂FKMK H1
★30040 HONG QI 120

MK₂FKMK H13
★30090 HONG QI 134

MK₂FKMK H13
30130 FAIZI → 30132

MK₂ FKMK H13
30160 KALMAR → 30161

MK₂FKMK H13
30190 LANKA KEERTI → 30192

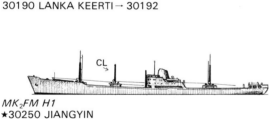

MK₂FM H1
★30250 JIANGYIN

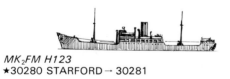

MK₂FM H123
★30280 STARFORD → 30281

MK₂FM H13
30310 VORRAS

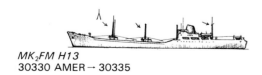

MK₂FM H13
30330 AMER → 30335

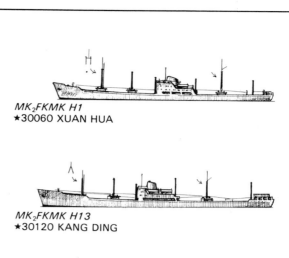

MK₂FKMK H1
★30060 XUAN HUA

MK₂FKMK H13
★30120 KANG DING

MK₂FKMK H13
30150 DELIMA

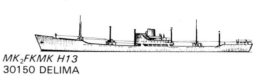

MK₂FKMK H13
30170 RAMONEVERETT → 30172

MK₂FM H1
30230 CHRISTOS K

MK₂FM H1
30270 BANGLAR TARANI

MK₂FM H13
30300 STAR SHIP

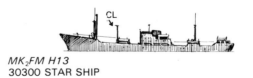

MK₂FM H13
30320 GEORGE F → 30324

MK₂FMC H1
30350 SALAMAH-5

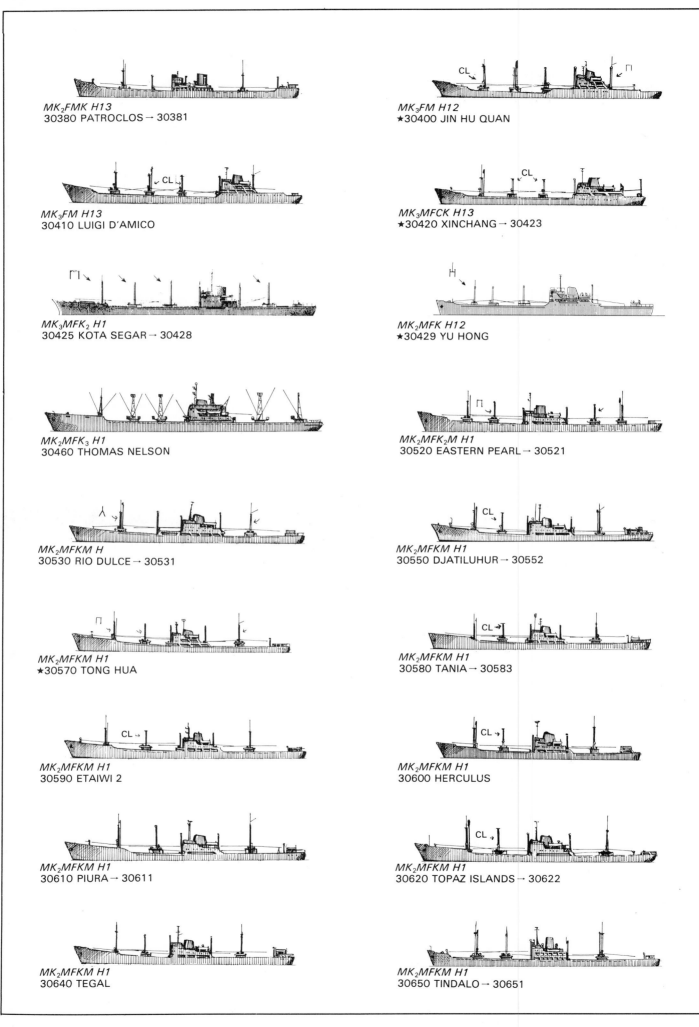

MK₂FMK H13
30380 PATROCLOS → 30381

MK₃FM H12
★30400 JIN HU QUAN

MK₃FM H13
30410 LUIGI D'AMICO

MK₃MFCK H13
★30420 XINCHANG → 30423

MK₃MFK₂ H1
30425 KOTA SEGAR → 30428

MK₂MFK H12
★30429 YU HONG

MK₂MFK₃ H1
30460 THOMAS NELSON

MK₂MFK₂M H1
30520 EASTERN PEARL → 30521

MK₂MFKM H
30530 RIO DULCE → 30531

MK₂MFKM H1
30550 DJATILUHUR → 30552

MK₂MFKM H1
★30570 TONG HUA

MK₂MFKM H1
30580 TANIA → 30583

MK₂MFKM H1
30590 ETAIWI 2

MK₂MFKM H1
30600 HERCULUS

MK₂MFKM H1
30610 PIURA → 30611

MK₂MFKM H1
30620 TOPAZ ISLANDS → 30622

MK₂MFKM H1
30640 TEGAL

MK₂MFKM H1
30650 TINDALO → 30651

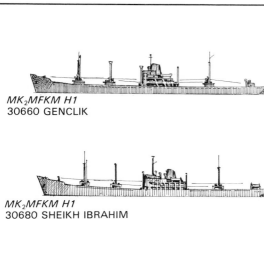

MK₂MFKM H1
30660 GENCLIK

MK₂MFKM H1
30670 SAILFLIP

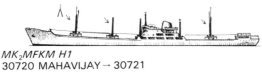

MK₂MFKM H1
30680 SHEIKH IBRAHIM

MK₂MFKM H1
★30690 HOI AN

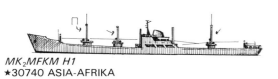

MK₂MFKM H1
30720 MAHAVIJAY → 30721

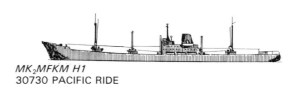

MK₂MFKM H1
30730 PACIFIC RIDE

MK₂MFKM H1
★30740 ASIA-AFRIKA

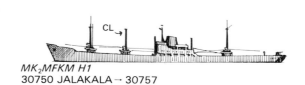

MK₂MFKM H1
30750 JALAKALA → 30757

MK₂MFKM H1
30770 LAERTIS → 30771

MK₂MFKM H1
30800 PHILIPPINE BATAAN → 30801

MK₂MFKM H1
30810 AMIRAL S OKAN → 30811

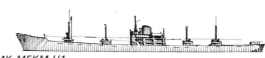

MK₂MFKM H1
★30820 GUANG PING

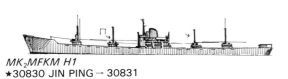

MK₂MFKM H1
★30830 JIN PING → 30831

MK₂MFKM H1
30840 BAIMA → 30843

MK₂MFKM H12
30870 LOK VAIBHAV

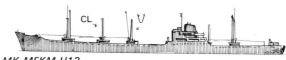

MK₂MFKM H12
30900 CAPITAINE TASMAN → 30902

MK₂MFKM H13
★30930 CHANGDE

MK₂MFKM H13
30940 TAHASIN

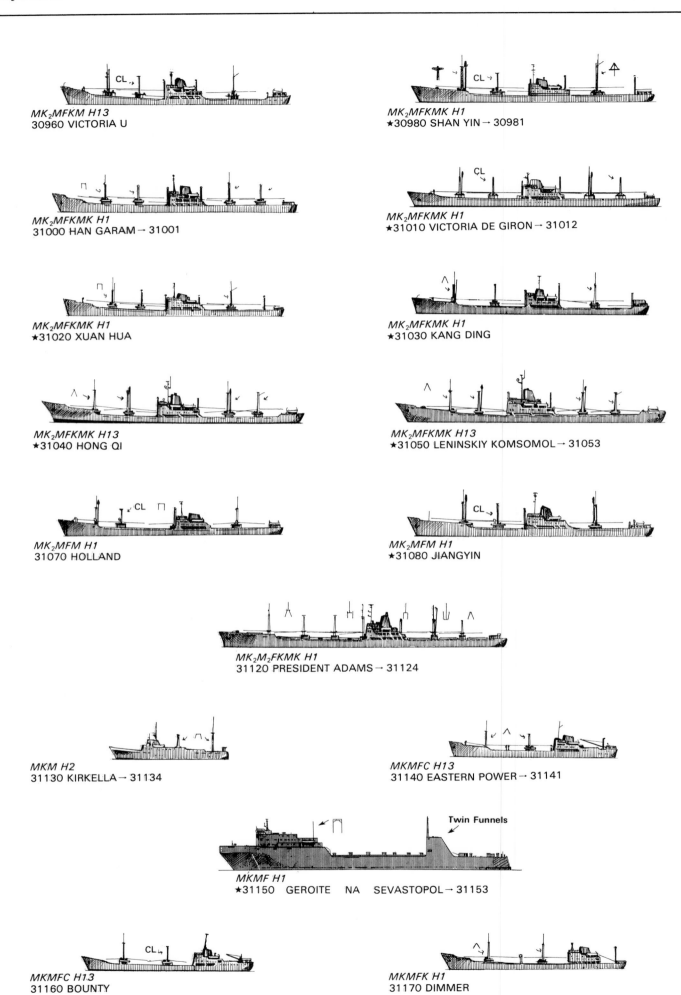

MK₂MFKM H13
30960 VICTORIA U

MK₂MFKMK H1
★30980 SHAN YIN → 30981

MK₂MFKMK H1
31000 HAN GARAM → 31001

MK₂MFKMK H1
★31010 VICTORIA DE GIRON → 31012

MK₂MFKMK H1
★31020 XUAN HUA

MK₂MFKMK H1
★31030 KANG DING

MK₂MFKMK H13
★31040 HONG QI

MK₂MFKMK H13
★31050 LENINSKIY KOMSOMOL → 31053

MK₂MFM H1
31070 HOLLAND

MK₂MFM H1
★31080 JIANGYIN

MK₂M₂FKMK H1
31120 PRESIDENT ADAMS → 31124

MKM H2
31130 KIRKELLA → 31134

MKMFC H13
31140 EASTERN POWER → 31141

Twin Funnels

MKMF H1
★31150 GEROITE   NA   SEVASTOPOL → 31153

MKMFC H13
31160 BOUNTY

MKMFK H1
31170 DIMMER

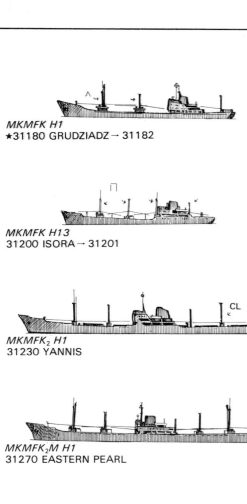

MKMFK H1
★31180 GRUDZIADZ → 31182

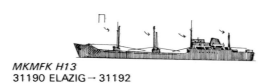

MKMFK H13
31190 ELAZIG → 31192

MKMFK H13
31200 ISORA → 31201

MKMFK₂ H1
31220 MOUNT CARIBBEAN

MKMFK₂ H1
31230 YANNIS

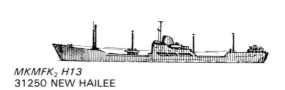

MKMFK₂ H13
31250 NEW HAILEE

MKMFK₂M H1
31270 EASTERN PEARL

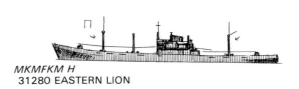

MKMFKM H
31280 EASTERN LION

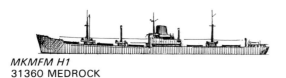

MKMFKM H1
31290 WHITE ROSE

MKMFKM H1
31300 NAGAN → 31305

MKMFKM H1
31320 SILVER EAGLE

MKMFKM H1
31325 LAGO LACAR

MKMFKM H1
★31330 SONG NHUE

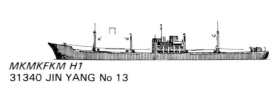

MKMKFKM H1
31340 JIN YANG No 13

MKMFM H1
31360 MEDROCK

MKMFKM H1
31370 IKARIA

MKMFKM H1
31390 JIN YANG No 17 → 31391

MKMFKM H1
31410 BENGAL TOWER

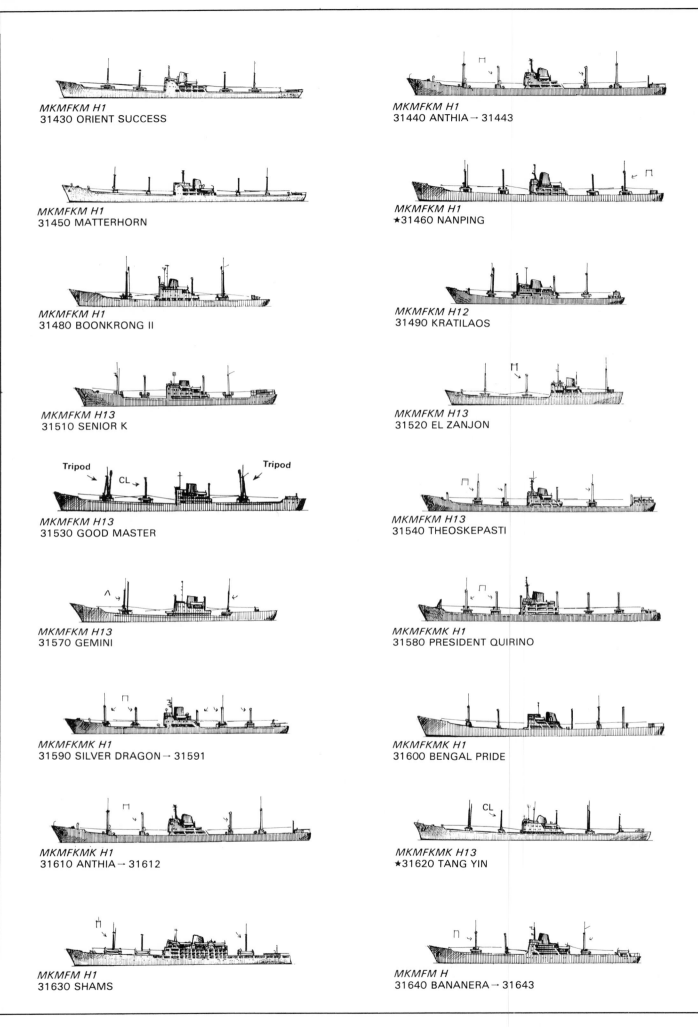

MKMFKM H1
31430 ORIENT SUCCESS

MKMFKM H1
31440 ANTHIA → 31443

MKMFKM H1
31450 MATTERHORN

MKMFKM H1
★31460 NANPING

MKMFKM H1
31480 BOONKRONG II

MKMFKM H12
31490 KRATILAOS

MKMFKM H13
31510 SENIOR K

MKMFKM H13
31520 EL ZANJON

MKMFKM H13
31530 GOOD MASTER

MKMFKM H13
31540 THEOSKEPASTI

MKMFKM H13
31570 GEMINI

MKMFKMK H1
31580 PRESIDENT QUIRINO

MKMFKMK H1
31590 SILVER DRAGON → 31591

MKMFKMK H1
31600 BENGAL PRIDE

MKMFKMK H1
31610 ANTHIA → 31612

MKMFKMK H13
★31620 TANG YIN

MKMFM H1
31630 SHAMS

MKMFM H
31640 BANANERA → 31643

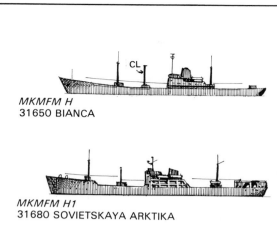

MKMFM H
31650 BIANCA

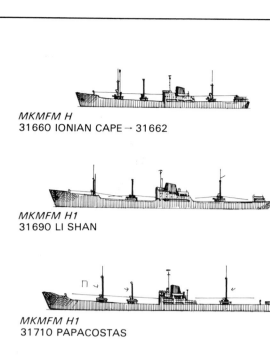

MKMFM H
31660 IONIAN CAPE → 31662

MKMFM H1
31680 SOVIETSKAYA ARKTIKA

MKMFM H1
31690 LI SHAN

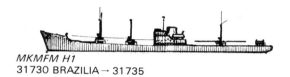

MKMFM H1
31700 LADY KATINA

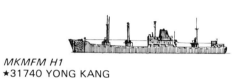

MKMFM H1
31710 PAPACOSTAS

MKMFM H1
31730 BRAZILIA → 31735

MKMFM H1
★31740 YONG KANG

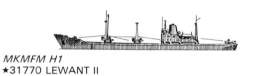

MKMFM H1
31750 DESPINA

MKMFM H1
31760 YUHENG 2

MKMFM H1
★31770 LEWANT II

MKMFM H123
31800 GALAXY II → 31803

MKMFM H123
31810 KARANA ENAM

MKMFM H123
31820 EVER GRACE

MKMFM H123
★31830 ARZAMAS → 31832

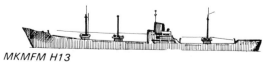

MKMFM H13
★31890 MALAYA VISHERA → 31892

MKMFM H13
31910 AKIS S

MKMFM H13
★31920 HONG MING → 31922

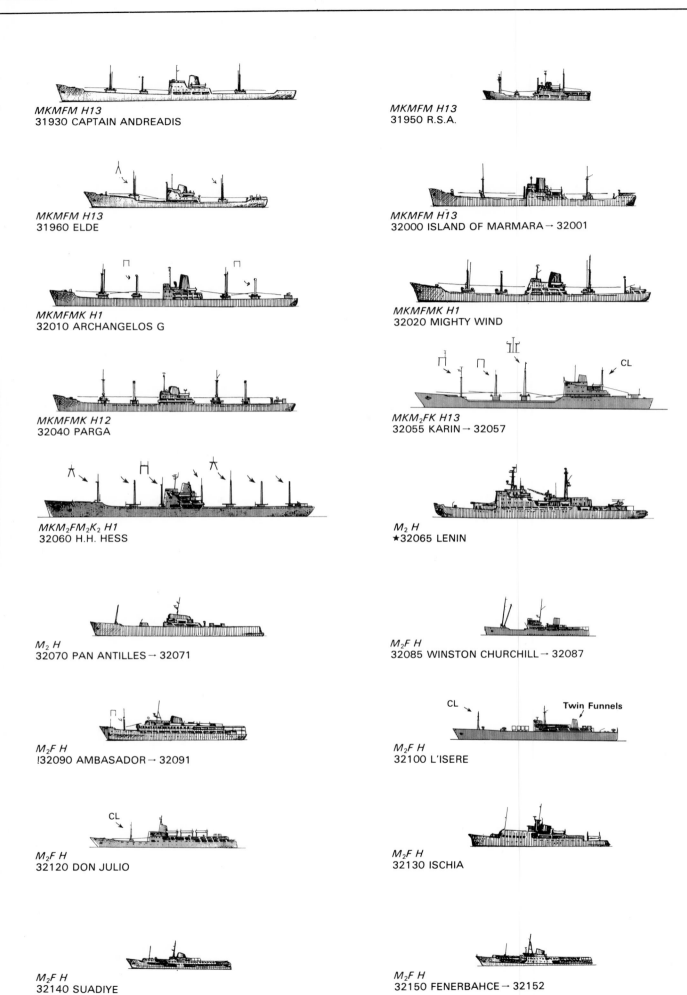

MKMFM H13
31930 CAPTAIN ANDREADIS

MKMFM H13
31950 R.S.A.

MKMFM H13
31960 ELDE

MKMFM H13
32000 ISLAND OF MARMARA → 32001

MKMFMK H1
32010 ARCHANGELOS G

MKMFMK H1
32020 MIGHTY WIND

MKMFMK H12
32040 PARGA

MKM$_2$FK H13
32055 KARIN → 32057

MKM$_2$FM$_2$K$_2$ H1
32060 H.H. HESS

M$_2$ H
★32065 LENIN

M$_2$ H
32070 PAN ANTILLES → 32071

M$_2$F H
32085 WINSTON CHURCHILL → 32087

M$_2$F H
!32090 AMBASADOR → 32091

M$_2$F H
32100 L'ISERE

M$_2$F H
32120 DON JULIO

M$_2$F H
32130 ISCHIA

M$_2$F H
32140 SUADIYE

M$_2$F H
32150 FENERBAHCE → 32152

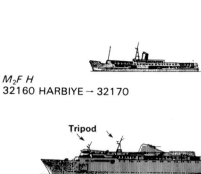

M₂F H
32160 HARBIYE → 32170

M₂F H
32180 GALLURA

M₂F H
32190 MATANUSKA

M₂F H
32200 DANA REGINA

M₂F H
32210 ARMORIQUE

M₂F H
32220 HAMMERSHUS

M₂F H
32230 HANKYU No. 16 → 32231

M₂F H
32240 IZU MARU No. 3 → 32241

M₂F H
32250 PENN AR BED

M₂F H
32260 PRESIDENTE DIAZ ORDAZ

M₂F H
32270 QUEEN OF VICTORIA → 32271

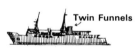

M₂F H
32280 CALEDONIA

M₂F H
★32290 ILIRIJA

M₂F H
32300 POLAR EXPRESS

M₂F H
32310 EOLOS

M₂F H
32320 CONCEPCION MARINO → 32321

M₂F H
★32330 XING HU

M₂F H
32340 STENA SAILER

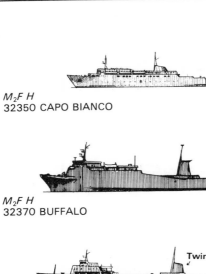

M₂F H
32350 CAPO BIANCO

M₂F H
32360 MERZARIO SYRIA

M₂F H
32370 BUFFALO

M₂F H
32390 MAR CARIBE → 32391

M₂F H
32410 JOLLY BIANCO

M₂F H
32420 STELLA MARIS II

M₂F H
32430 GOLDEN VERGINA → 32431

M₂F H
32440 NORWAVE → 32441

M₂F H
32450 FERRY GOLD → 32452

M₂F H
32460 OZAMIS CITY

M₂F H
32470 COBALT MARU → 32472

M₂F H
32480 IYO MARU → 32481

M₂F H
32490 TROUBRIDGE

M₂F H
32500 DRAGON → 32501

M₂F H
32510 DEUTSCHLAND

M₂F H
32520 PROVENCE

M₂F H
32530 MALTA EXPRESS

M₂F H
32550 DELEDDA → 32557

M₂F H
32560 SAINT ELOI

M₂F H
32570 ISHIKARI → 32571

M₂F H
32580 ARKAS → 32582

M₂F H
32590 GARYOUNIS → 32591

M₂F H
32600 NORLAND → 32601

M₂F H
32610 MIMITSU MARU → 32611

M₂F H
32620 EL ARISH → 32621

M₂F H
32630 SAINT PAULIA → 32634

M₂F H
32640 CASTALIA

M₂FH
32650 AQUARIUS

M₂F H
32660 TAI SHAN → 32662

M₂F H
32670 TIZIANO

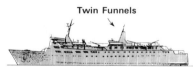

Twin Funnels

M₂F H
32680 LORD SINAI

M₂F H
32690 TINTORETTO

M₂F H
32700 POSEIDON

Twin Funnels

M₂F H
★32710 LIBURNIJA

M₂F H
32720 INNISFALLEN → 32721

M₂F H
32730 FARAH 1

M₂F H
32740 LA VALLETTA

M₂F H
32750 NISSOS CHIOS

M₂F H
32760 PRINSES BEATRIX

M₂F H
32770 ALCAEUS

M₂F H
32780 TIGER → 32781

M₂F H
32790 ANTRIM PRINCESS → 32791

M₂F H
32800 THE VIKING → 32802

M₂F H
32810 STENA NORDICA

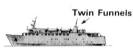

Twin Funnels

M₂F H
32820 SOLIDOR

M₂F H
32830 DISKO

M₂F H
32840 LINDBLAD EXPLORER

M₂F H
32850 WORLD DISCOVERER

M₂F H
32860 LANGELAND II

Twin Funnels

M₂F H
32870 ST. OLA

M₂F H
32880 A. REGINA → 32881

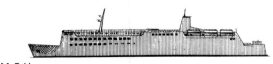

M₂F H
32890 RUGEN

M₂F H
32900 SOL PHRYNE

M₂F H
32910 CANDIA → 32911

M₂F H
★32915 OSETIYA

M₂F H
32920 VENUS

M₂F H
32930 FREDERICK CARTER

M₂F H
32940 C.S. MONARCH → 32941

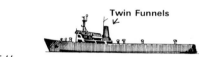

M₂F H
32950 SCHIAFFINO → 32953

M₂F H
32960 MERCHANT NAVIGATOR → 32962

M₂F H
32970 RORO TRADER

M₂F H
32980 ESPRESSO LIGURIA → 32984

M₂F H
32990 KAPTAN SAIT OZEGE → 32991

M₂F H
33000 ATLE → 33001/1

M₂F H
33010 NORTREFF

M₂F H1
33020 FERNANDO ESCANO

M₂F H1
33030 TRADE CONTAINER

M₂F H1
33040 AL-KHALEEJ

M₂F H1
33050 CAPO FALCONARA

M₂F H1
33060 SYDNEY TRADER → 33062

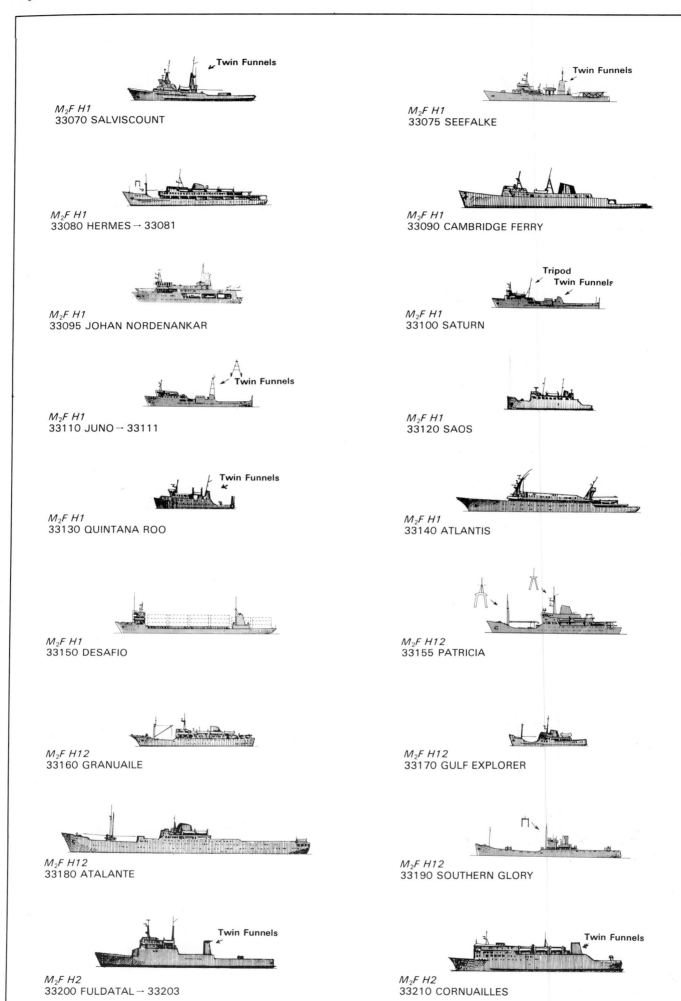

M₂F H1
33070 SALVISCOUNT

M₂F H1
33075 SEEFALKE

M₂F H1
33080 HERMES → 33081

M₂F H1
33090 CAMBRIDGE FERRY

M₂F H1
33095 JOHAN NORDENANKAR

M₂F H1
33100 SATURN

M₂F H1
33110 JUNO → 33111

M₂F H1
33120 SAOS

M₂F H1
33130 QUINTANA ROO

M₂F H1
33140 ATLANTIS

M₂F H1
33150 DESAFIO

M₂F H12
33155 PATRICIA

M₂F H12
33160 GRANUAILE

M₂F H12
33170 GULF EXPLORER

M₂F H12
33180 ATALANTE

M₂F H12
33190 SOUTHERN GLORY

M₂F H2
33200 FULDATAL → 33203

M₂F H2
33210 CORNUAILLES

M_2F H2
33220 BREIZH-IZEL

M_2F H2
33230 HALLEY

M_2F H2
33240 YUSUF ZIYA ONIS

M_2F H2
33250 SVEALAND

M_2F H2
33260 CICERO → 33261

M_2F H2
33270 DORA BALTEA → 33271

M_2F H2
33280 BALTIC EAGLE → 33281

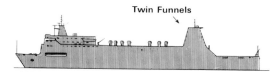

M_2F H2
33285 TRANSFINLANDIA

M_2F H2
33290 ARGO

M_2F H2
33300 FERRY KOGANE MARU → 33301

M_2FC H
33310 AUSTRALIAN ENTERPRISE → 33313

M_2FC H
33320 INIOCHOS EXPRESS II

M_2FC H
★33330 FRITZ HECKERT

M_2FC H1
33340 AL-KHALEEJ

M_2FC H2
33360 LE MANS

M_2FC_2 H
33370 DELEDDA → 33371

M_2F_2K H
★33380 MIKOLAJ KOPERNIK → 33381

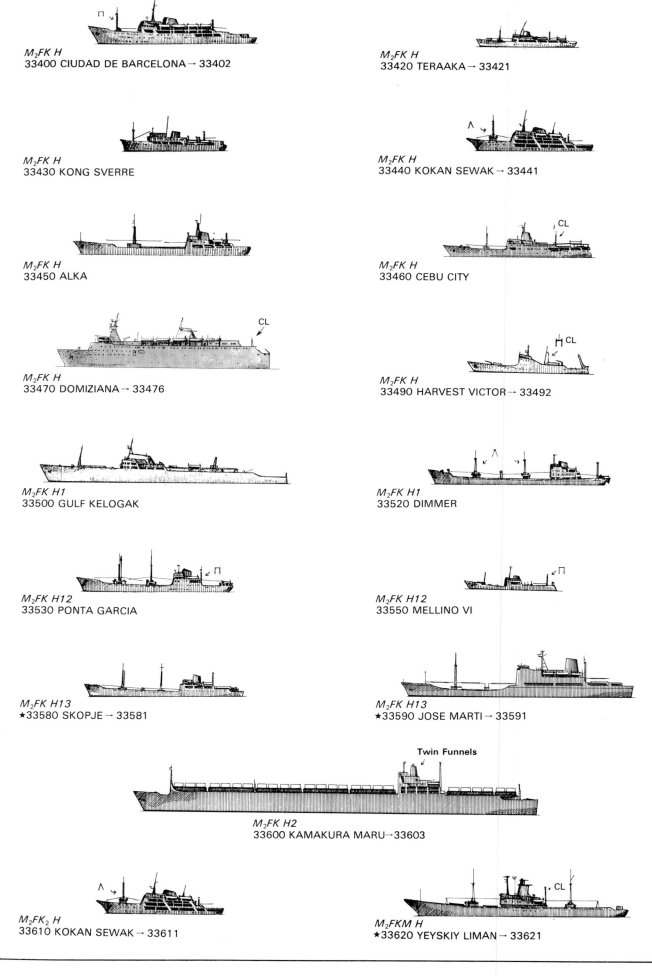

M₂FK H
33400 CIUDAD DE BARCELONA → 33402

M₂FK H
33420 TERAAKA → 33421

M₂FK H
33430 KONG SVERRE

M₂FK H
33440 KOKAN SEWAK → 33441

M₂FK H
33450 ALKA

M₂FK H
33460 CEBU CITY

M₂FK H
33470 DOMIZIANA → 33476

M₂FK H
33490 HARVEST VICTOR → 33492

M₂FK H1
33500 GULF KELOGAK

M₂FK H1
33520 DIMMER

M₂FK H12
33530 PONTA GARCIA

M₂FK H12
33550 MELLINO VI

M₂FK H13
★33580 SKOPJE → 33581

M₂FK H13
★33590 JOSE MARTI → 33591

Twin Funnels

M₂FK H2
33600 KAMAKURA MARU → 33603

M₂FK₂ H
33610 KOKAN SEWAK → 33611

M₂FKM H
★33620 YEYSKIY LIMAN → 33621

M₂FKM H
33630 UNITED REEFER → 33633

M₂FKM H
33640 SAFINA NAJD → 33642

M₂FKM H
33650 NICOLAS → 33651

M₂FKM H1
★33660 WUXI

M₂FKM H1
33670 SALAMAH 1

M₂FKM H123
★33680 CHE HAI No 1 → 33681

M₂FKM H123
★33690 ZHAN DOU 16

M₂FKM H123
★33700 ZHAN DOU 14

M₂FKM H123
★33710 HONG QI 175 → 33711

M₂FKM H123
33720 HAI RYONG

M₂FKM H123
33740 SANTO ANDRE → 33741

MMFKM H13
★33745 TUAN JIE

M₂FM H
33760 ALGAZAYER → 33761

M₂FM H
33770 RAMON ABOITIZ

M₂FM H
33780 DONA MARILYN

M₂FM H
33800 TACLOBAN CITY

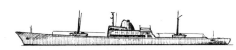

M₂FM H
33810 CHION TRADER → 33811

M₂FM H
33820 HELLAS FREEZER → 33822

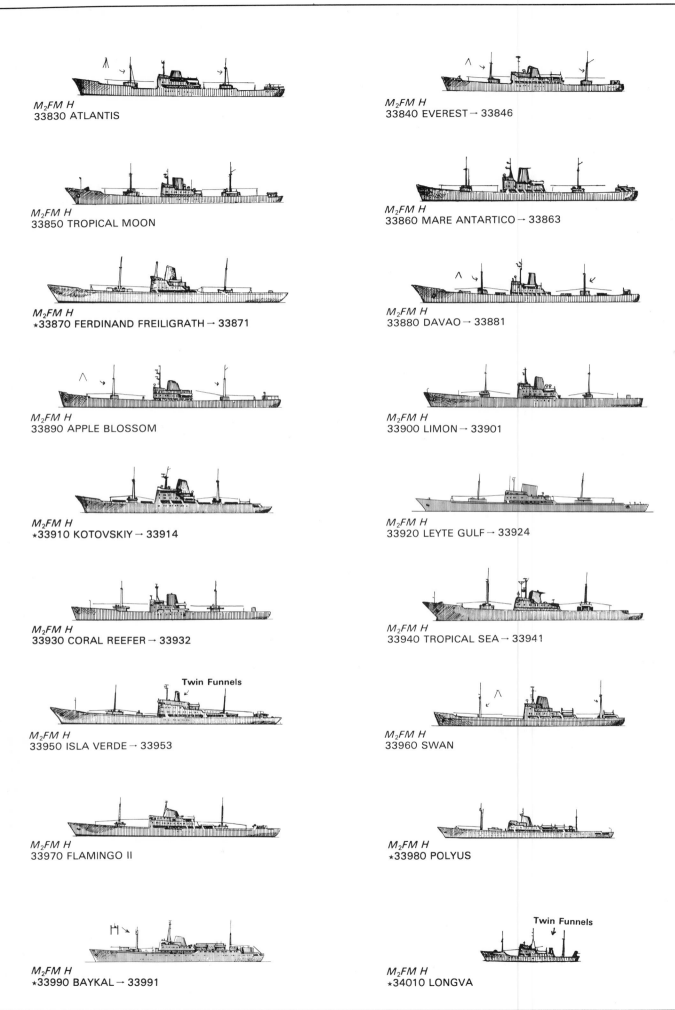

M₂FM H
33830 ATLANTIS

M₂FM H
33840 EVEREST → 33846

M₂FM H
33850 TROPICAL MOON

M₂FM H
33860 MARE ANTARTICO → 33863

M₂FM H
★33870 FERDINAND FREILIGRATH → 33871

M₂FM H
33880 DAVAO → 33881

M₂FM H
33890 APPLE BLOSSOM

M₂FM H
33900 LIMON → 33901

M₂FM H
★33910 KOTOVSKIY → 33914

M₂FM H
33920 LEYTE GULF → 33924

M₂FM H
33930 CORAL REEFER → 33932

M₂FM H
33940 TROPICAL SEA → 33941

Twin Funnels

M₂FM H
33950 ISLA VERDE → 33953

M₂FM H
33960 SWAN

M₂FM H
33970 FLAMINGO II

M₂FM H
★33980 POLYUS

Twin Funnels

M₂FM H
★33990 BAYKAL → 33991

M₂FM H
★34010 LONGVA

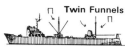

M₂FM H
34020 TAIYO MARU No 68 → 34024

M₂FM H
★34025 ISLA DE LA JUVENTUD

M₂FM H
34030 HARENGUS

M₂FM H
34040 MARIA PAOLINA G.

M₂FM H
34050 CAGAYAN DE ORO CITY

M₂FM H
34060 FRITHJOF

M₂FM H
34070 CUMULUS

M₂FM H
34080 FIORITA

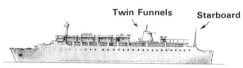

M₂FM H
34090 EL DJAZAIR

M₂FM H1
★34100 AMGUEMA → 34111

M₂FM H1
34120 MACHITIS

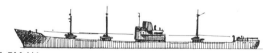

M₂FM H1
34140 GREENVILLE → 34143

M₂FM H1
★34150 LIKA → 34154

M₂FM H1
34180 MALDIVE FAITH

M₂FM H1
34190 PATRIS

M₂FM H1
34200 BONITA → 34225

M₂FM H1
★34240 ILYA METCHNIKOV → 34245

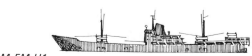

M₂FM H1
34250 FILIPINAS

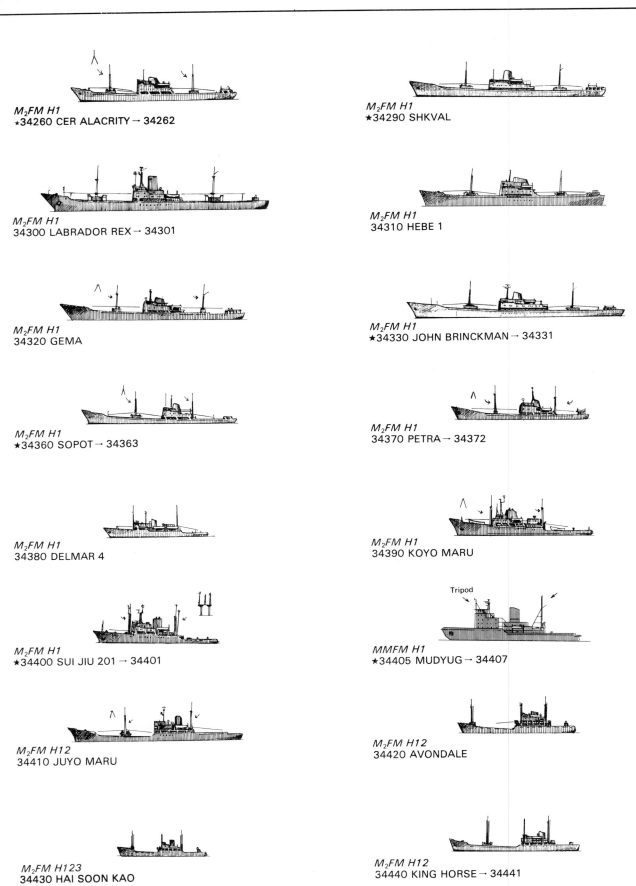

M₂FM H1
★34260 CER ALACRITY → 34262

M₂FM H1
★34290 SHKVAL

M₂FM H1
34300 LABRADOR REX → 34301

M₂FM H1
34310 HEBE 1

M₂FM H1
34320 GEMA

M₂FM H1
★34330 JOHN BRINCKMAN → 34331

M₂FM H1
★34360 SOPOT → 34363

M₂FM H1
34370 PETRA → 34372

M₂FM H1
34380 DELMAR 4

M₂FM H1
34390 KOYO MARU

M₂FM H1
★34400 SUI JIU 201 → 34401

Tripod

MMFM H1
★34405 MUDYUG → 34407

M₂FM H12
34410 JUYO MARU

M₂FM H12
34420 AVONDALE

M₂FM H123
34430 HAI SOON KAO

M₂FM H12
34440 KING HORSE → 34441

M₂FM H12
34450 OKINAWA MARU

Twin Funnels

M₂FM H12
★34460 LONGVA

M₂FM H123
★34470 ANDIZHAN → 34515

M₂FM H123
34530 TWILIGHT

M₂FM H123
★34540 ANGARSK

M₂FM H13
34570 MIMAR SINAN

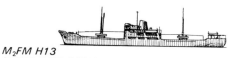

M₂FM H13
34580 GAZI OSMAN PASA → 34582

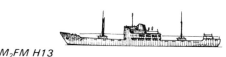

M₂FM H13
34590 DENIZLI

M₂FM H13
34600 REIYO MARU

M₂FM H2
★34610 TARUSA → 34677

M₂FM H2
34700 BAHIA AGUIRRE → 34701

M₂FMC H
★34710 ZENIT → 34712

M₂FMC H
34720 HAKUHO MARU

M₂FMK H1
34740 G.O. SARS

M₂FM₂ H1
34750 ANNOULA TSIRIS

M₂FM₂ H12
34770 HATI SENANG → 34771

M₂FN H2
34780 STAFFORD

M₂K H/H1
34790 METEOR

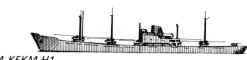

M₂KFKM H1
34800 REMCO → 34802

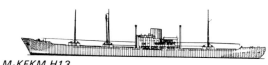

M₂KFKM H13
34820 SAUDI AL TAIF

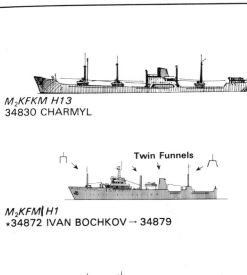

M₂KFKM H13
34830 CHARMYL

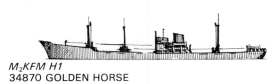

M₂KFM H1
34870 GOLDEN HORSE

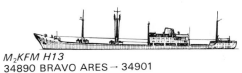

Twin Funnels

M₂KFM H1
★34872 IVAN BOCHKOV → 34879

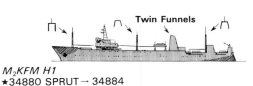

Twin Funnels

M₂KFM H1
★34880 SPRUT → 34884

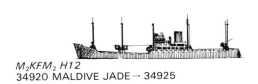

M₂KFM H13
34890 BRAVO ARES → 34901

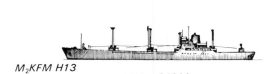

M₂KFM H13
34910 LION OF ETHIOPIA → 34911

M₂KFM₂ H12
34920 MALDIVE JADE → 34925

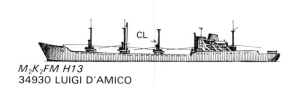

CL

M₂K₂FM H13
34930 LUIGI D'AMICO

M₂KMFKC H1
34940 GOOILAND

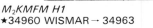

M₂KMFM H1
★34960 WISMAR → 34963

M₃ H
34970 BHANURANGSI

M₃F H
34980 MARIMO

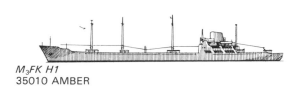

M₃F H2
34990 FERRY KOGANE MARU → 34991

M₃FC H
★35000 PRESIDENTE MACIAS NGUEMA

M₃FK H1
35010 AMBER

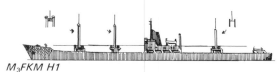

M₃FKM H1
★35030 ZHENJIANG → 35031

M₃FKM H13
35040 SAKUMO LAGOON → 35043

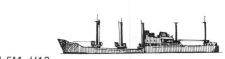

M₃FM₂ H12
35070 MARINA

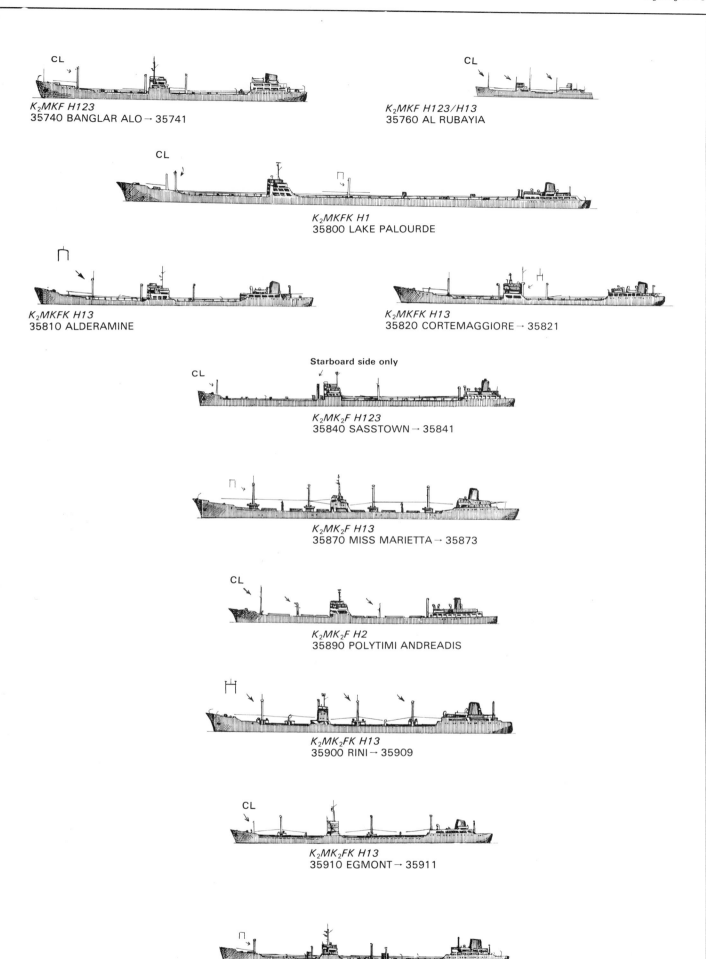

CL
K₂MKF H123
35740 BANGLAR ALO → 35741

CL
K₂MKF H123/H13
35760 AL RUBAYIA

CL
K₂MKFK H1
35800 LAKE PALOURDE

K₂MKFK H13
35810 ALDERAMINE

K₂MKFK H13
35820 CORTEMAGGIORE → 35821

Starboard side only

CL
K₂MK₂F H123
35840 SASSTOWN → 35841

K₂MK₂F H13
35870 MISS MARIETTA → 35873

CL
K₂MK₂F H2
35890 POLYTIMI ANDREADIS

K₂MK₂FK H13
35900 RINI → 35909

CL
K₂MK₂FK H13
35910 EGMONT → 35911

K₂MK₃FK H123
★35920 CUU LONG I → 35921

K₂MK₃FK H123
35940 BANGLAR KHEYA

K₂MK₃FK H123
35950 RODOSTO

K₂MK₄F H1
35960 ASHTABULA → 35962

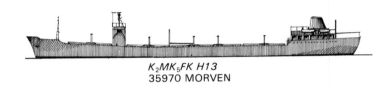

K₂MK₅FK H13
35970 MORVEN

K₂MK₂MF H
★35980 HONG QI 112

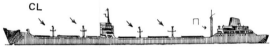

K₂MK₂MF H13
★35990 HONG QI 112 → 35991

K₂MK₂MFK H
36000 SHIKISHIMA MARU

K₂MKMFK H
36010 POSSIDONIA

K₂MKMFK H13
36020 GREEK FRIENDSHIP → 36021

K₂MKMKFKC H1
36040 KERO

K₂M₂KFK₂ H13
36050 ELEFTHERIA

KM H12
36060 TARRY → 36062

KM H12
36070 BLACKWELL POINT → 36076

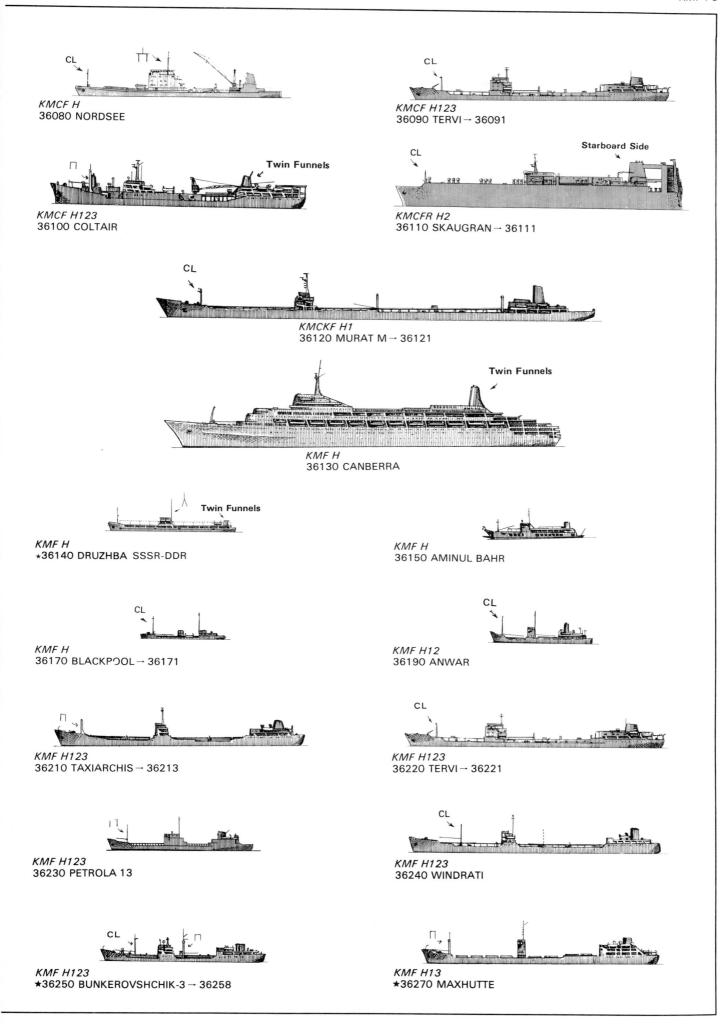

KMCF H
36080 NORDSEE

KMCF H123
36090 TERVI → 36091

KMCF H123
36100 COLTAIR

Twin Funnels

KMCFR H2
36110 SKAUGRAN → 36111

Starboard Side

KMCKF H1
36120 MURAT M → 36121

Twin Funnels

KMF H
36130 CANBERRA

Twin Funnels

KMF H
★36140 DRUZHBA SSSR-DDR

KMF H
36150 AMINUL BAHR

KMF H
36170 BLACKPOOL → 36171

KMF H12
36190 ANWAR

KMF H123
36210 TAXIARCHIS → 36213

KMF H123
36220 TERVI → 36221

KMF H123
36230 PETROLA 13

KMF H123
36240 WINDRATI

KMF H123
★36250 BUNKEROVSHCHIK-3 → 36258

KMF H13
★36270 MAXHUTTE

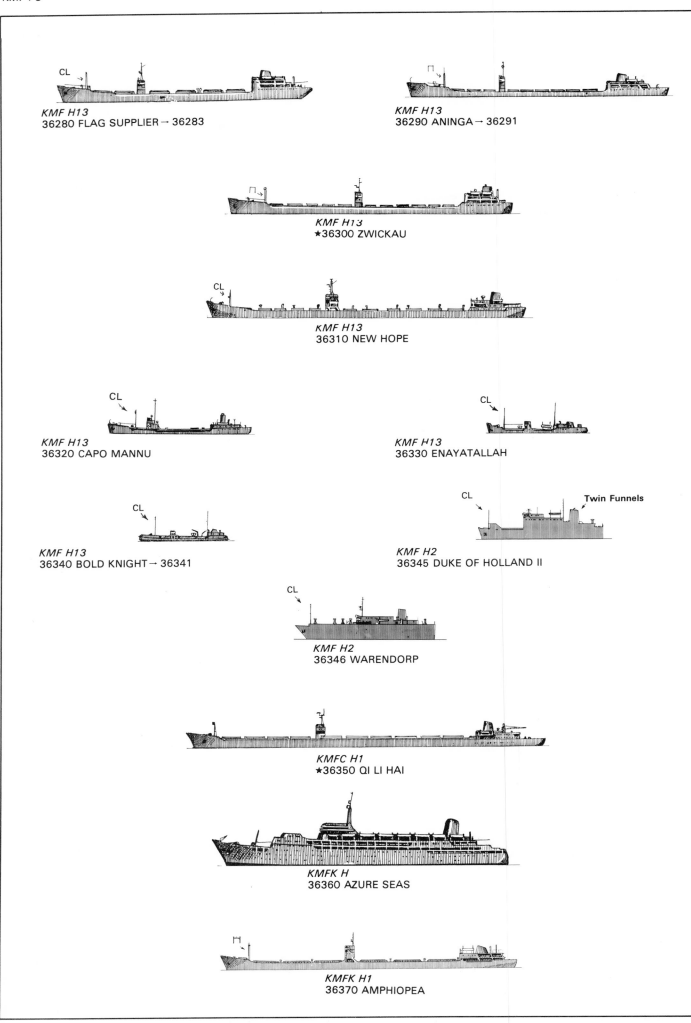

KMF H13
36280 FLAG SUPPLIER → 36283

KMF H13
36290 ANINGA → 36291

KMF H13
★36300 ZWICKAU

KMF H13
36310 NEW HOPE

KMF H13
36320 CAPO MANNU

KMF H13
36330 ENAYATALLAH

Twin Funnels

KMF H13
36340 BOLD KNIGHT → 36341

KMF H2
36345 DUKE OF HOLLAND II

KMF H2
36346 WARENDORP

KMFC H1
★36350 QI LI HAI

KMFK H
36360 AZURE SEAS

KMFK H1
36370 AMPHIOPEA

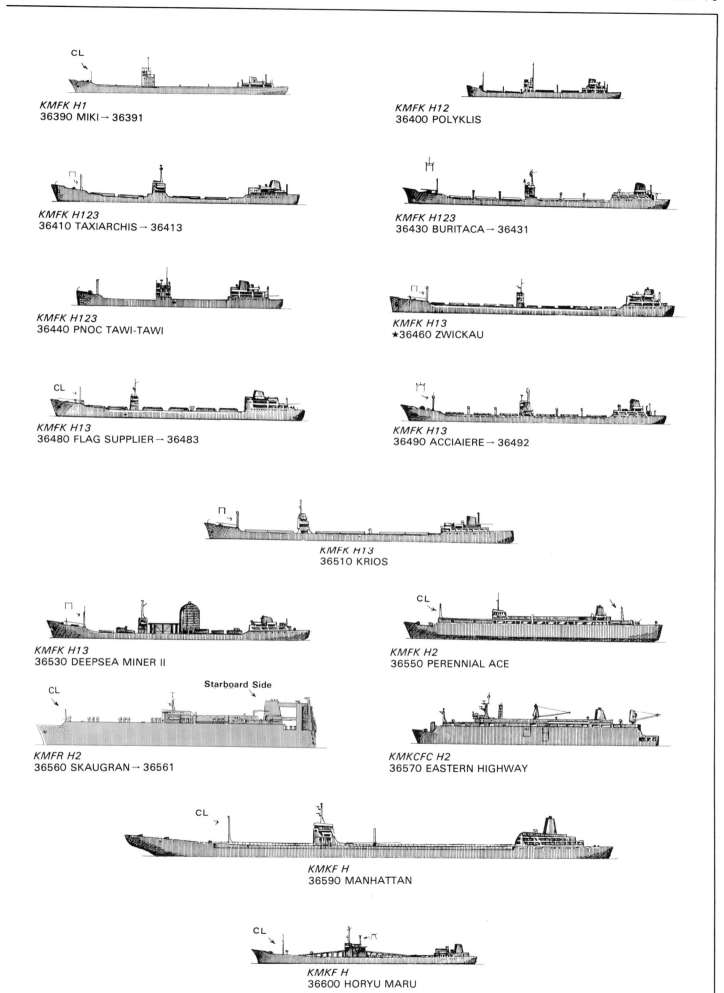

KMFK H1
36390 MIKI → 36391

KMFK H12
36400 POLYKLIS

KMFK H123
36410 TAXIARCHIS → 36413

KMFK H123
36430 BURITACA → 36431

KMFK H123
36440 PNOC TAWI-TAWI

KMFK H13
★36460 ZWICKAU

KMFK H13
36480 FLAG SUPPLIER → 36483

KMFK H13
36490 ACCIAIERE → 36492

KMFK H13
36510 KRIOS

KMFK H13
36530 DEEPSEA MINER II

KMFK H2
36550 PERENNIAL ACE

Starboard Side

KMFR H2
36560 SKAUGRAN → 36561

KMKCFC H2
36570 EASTERN HIGHWAY

KMKF H
36590 MANHATTAN

KMKF H
36600 HORYU MARU

KMKF H1
36610 OVERSEAS NATALIE

KMKF H123
36630 PRIMERO

KMKF H123
36640 ST. EMILION

KMKF H123
36650 MONTPELIER VICTORY → 36655

KMKF H123
36670 TEXACO GEORGIA → 36674

KMKF H123
36680 TEXACO SKANDINAVIA → 36683

KMKF H123
36690 INDIANO

KMKF H123
★36700 DA QING No 37

KMKF H123
36710 NIDO OIL

KMKF H123
★36720 QI LIN HU

KMKF H123
36730 OASIS

KMKF H123
36740 PUNTA ANGELES → 36742

KMKF H123
36770 TEXACO MAINE

KMKF H123
36780 PYRROS V

KMKF H123
36790 TZINA M

KMKF H123
36800 AMERICAN EXPLORER

KMKF H123
★36820 TOUNDYA

KMKF H123
36830 AGAMEL

KMKF H123
★36840 PEKIN → 36846

KMKF H123
36850 BEAUJOLAIS

KMKF H123
★36860 SOFIYA → 36882

KMKF H123
★36890 ARGON → 36921

KMKF H123
★36940 GIUSEPPE GARIBALDI

KMKF H123
★36950 DA QING No 35

KMKF H123
36960 AHMED AL-BAKRY II

KMKF H123
36970 ALSAD ALAALY

KMKF H123
36990 TEXACO OSLO

KMKF H123
★37000 MIR

KMKF H123
37010 ABIDA → 37014

KMKF H123
37020 PERMINA SAMUDRA V

KMKF H123
37050 CAMPOLLANO

KMKF H123
37100 PETROLA 33 → 37101

KMKF H123
37170 NIKITAS

KMKF H13
37180 KYMO → 37181

KMKF H13
★37253 DA QING No 232 → 37259

KMKF H13
37260 METON → 37262

KMKF H13
37270 ONDINA

KMKF H13
37290 EIFEL

KMKF H13
★37300 PLOVDIV

KMKF H13
★37310 PLISKA → 37211

KMKF H13
37320 BINTANG SAMUDRA III

KMKF H13
37330 BERRY

KMKF H13
37340 KAMELA

KMKF H13
37363 GEOPOTES 12 → 37368

KMKFK H
37380 SAN TOMAS SECONDO → 37381

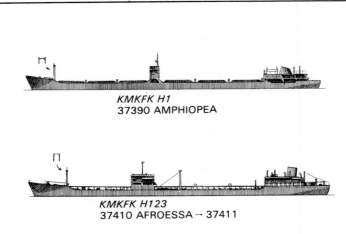

KMKFK H1
37390 AMPHIOPEA

KMKFK H123
37410 AFROESSA → 37411

KMKFK H123
37420 FEOSO STAR

KMKFK H123
37450 PETROMAR ROSARIO

KMKFK H123
37480 ALSAD ALAALY

KMKFK H123
37500 WHITE BEACH

KMKFK H123
37510 ACAVUS → 37514

KMKFK H123
37530 HATTAN

KMKFK H123
37540 HIPPO

KMKFK H123
37550 DEA BROVIG

KMKFK H123
37570 GEORGIOS V → 37571

KMKFK H123
37600 WASHINGTON TRADER → 37602

KMKFK H123
37610 TRANSUD II

KMKFK H123
37620 KAPETAN MARKOS N. L.

KMKFK H123
37630 MARIPRIMA

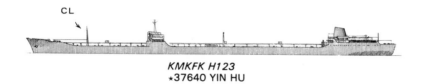

KMKFK H123
★37640 YIN HU

KMKFK H123
37650 SOUTHERN CONQUEST

KMKFK H123
37680 CABO GUARDIAN → 37681

KMKFK H123
37700 VERDI → 37701

KMKFK H123
37720 LUJAN DE CUYO

KMKFK H123
37740 AL HUSSEIN B

KMKFK H13
★37780 TRUD

KMKFK H13
37790 FLORENCE → 37797

KMKFK H13
37810 PETROLA 36

KMKFK H13
37830 MARIE MAERSK

KMKFK H13
37850 LUSSIN

KMKFK H13
37860 SANTISIMA TRINIDAD → 37861

KMKFK H13
37870 ANINGA → 37871

KMKFK H2
37880 JINYU MARU

KMKFM H1
37890 ESTADO DA GUANABARA

KMK₂F H1
37900 MURAT M. → 37901

KMK₂F H1
37910 PRESIDENTE DEODORO → 37911

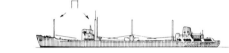

KMK₂F H1
37920 PANAGIS K

KMK₂F H1
37930 ABOITIZ CONCARRIER III

KMK₂F H12
37950 MATCO AVON

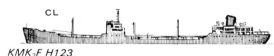

KMK₂F H123
37970 THERMOPYLAI

KMK₂F H123
37980 ARAUCANO

KMK₂F H123
37990 AGAMEL

KMK₂F H123
38010 EXXON BOSTON → 38011

KMK₂F H123
38020 GULFCREST → 38024

KMK₂F H123
38030 COVE SAILOR

KMK₂F H123
38040 PENNSYLVANIA SUN → 38041

KMK₂F H123
38070 ESSO WARWICKSHIRE

KMK₂F H123
38090 MERSIN

KMK₂F H123
38100 MOBIL FUEL → 38102

KMK₂F H123
38120 MOBILOIL → 38121

KMK₂F H123
38130 VIGIL

KMK₂F H123
38140 NICOLE SEA → 38141

KMK₂F H123
38160 KOREA EDINBURGH

KMK₂F H123
38170 KEYSTONER

KMK₂F H123
38180 STATHEROS

KMK₂F H123
38190 AL SABAH IV → 38191

KMK₂F H123
38200 RALLYTIME III

KMK₂F H123
38210 PAVLOS V → 38212

KMK₂F H123
38230 GEORGIOS

KMK₂F H123
38270 FEOSO AMBASSADOR

KMK₂F H123
38320 CHAPARAL II

KMK₂F H123
★38330 DA QING 235 → 38341

KMK₂F H13
★38361 DA QING No. 29 → 38362

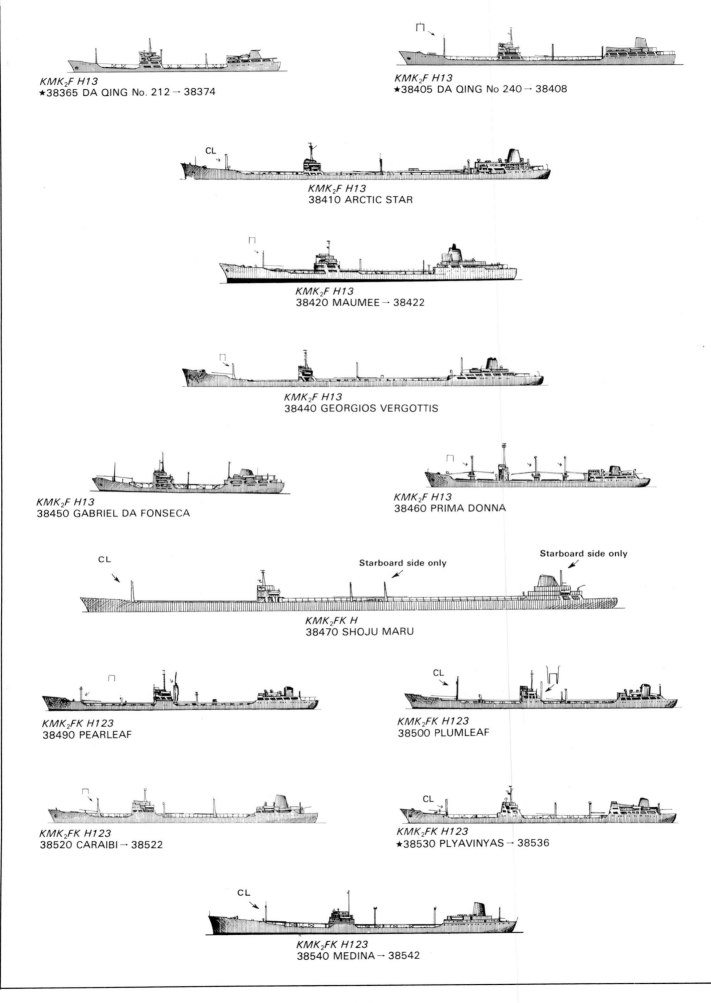

KMK₂F H13
★38365 DA QING No. 212 → 38374

KMK₂F H13
★38405 DA QING No 240 → 38408

KMK₂F H13
38410 ARCTIC STAR

KMK₂F H13
38420 MAUMEE → 38422

KMK₂F H13
38440 GEORGIOS VERGOTTIS

KMK₂F H13
38450 GABRIEL DA FONSECA

KMK₂F H13
38460 PRIMA DONNA

KMK₂FK H
38470 SHOJU MARU

KMK₂FK H123
38490 PEARLEAF

KMK₂FK H123
38500 PLUMLEAF

KMK₂FK H123
38520 CARAIBI → 38522

KMK₂FK H123
★38530 PLYAVINYAS → 38536

KMK₂FK H123
38540 MEDINA → 38542

KMK₂FK H123
38560 LAGOVEN MARACAIBO → 38561

KMK₂FK H123
38570 EXXON GETTYSBURG → 38573

KMK₂FK H123
★38580 GIORDANO BRUNO → 38582

KMK₂FK H123
38600 AMAZONA

KMK₂FK H123
★38610 BAUSKA → 38614

KMK₂FK H123
★38620 DA QING 230

KMK₂FK H123
38630 SICILMOTOR

KMK₂FK H123
38650 CATHERINE Y

KMK₂FK H123
38660 HONESTAS

KMK₂FK H123
38670 CAMPORROJO → 38674

KMK₂FK H123
★38690 DA QING No 253

KMK₂FK H123
★38700 DA QING No 251

KMK₂FK H123
38720 MARGARITIS → 38721

KMK₂FK H123
38730 SCAPMOUNT → 38732

KMK₂FK H123
38740 AL SABAH IV

KMK₂FK H123
38750 RODOSTO

KMK₂FK H123
38760 PAVLOS V → 38762

KMK₂FK H123
38780 ADRIATIKI

KMK₂FK H123
38790 SAN MARCO → 38792

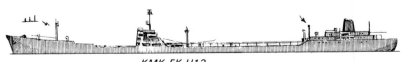

KMK₂FK H13
38820 COVE LEADER

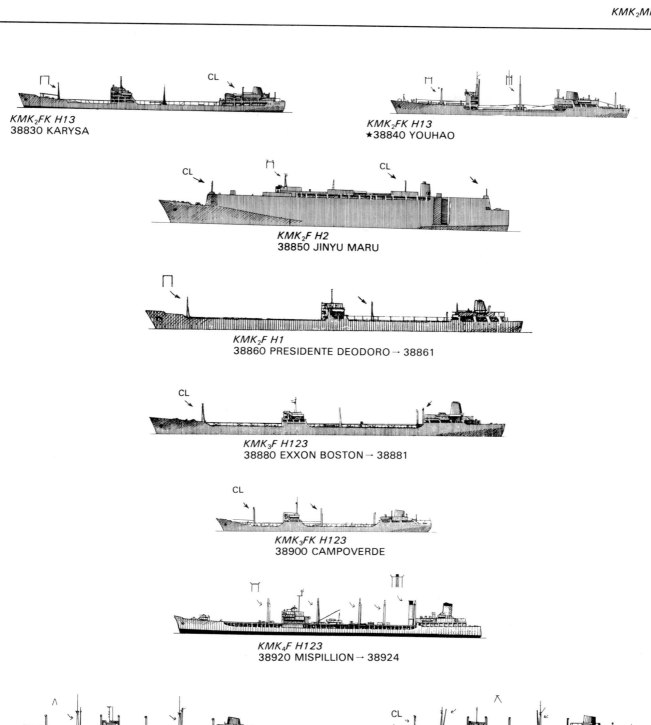

KMK₂FK H13
38830 KARYSA

KMK₂FK H13
★38840 YOUHAO

KMK₂F H2
38850 JINYU MARU

KMK₂F H1
38860 PRESIDENTE DEODORO → 38861

KMK₃F H123
38880 EXXON BOSTON → 38881

KMK₃FK H123
38900 CAMPOVERDE

KMK₄F H123
38920 MISPILLION → 38924

KMK₃MKF H13
38930 ASPASIA M → 38932

KMK₃MKFK H1
38940 ASAHAN → 38941

KMK₂MF H123
★38950 DESNA

KMK₂MF H123
38960 PROVIDER

KMK₂MFK H12
38980 KOYO MARU

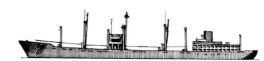

KMK₂MKFK H1
★38990 QUE LIN → 38992

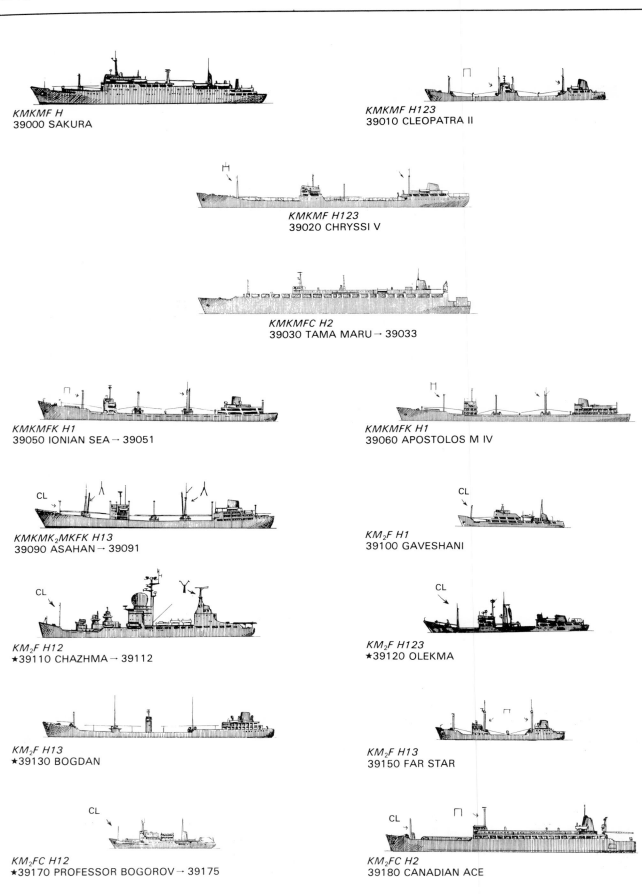

KMKMF H
39000 SAKURA

KMKMF H123
39010 CLEOPATRA II

KMKMF H123
39020 CHRYSSI V

KMKMFC H2
39030 TAMA MARU → 39033

KMKMFK H1
39050 IONIAN SEA → 39051

KMKMFK H1
39060 APOSTOLOS M IV

KMKMK₂MKFK H13
39090 ASAHAN → 39091

KM₂F H1
39100 GAVESHANI

KM₂F H12
★39110 CHAZHMA → 39112

KM₂F H123
★39120 OLEKMA

KM₂F H13
★39130 BOGDAN

KM₂F H13
39150 FAR STAR

KM₂FC H12
★39170 PROFESSOR BOGOROV → 39175

KM₂FC H2
39180 CANADIAN ACE

KM₂FK H123
39200 PAN VIGOR

KM₂KF H
39220 CAVACO

KM₂KF H1
39230 SARFARAZ RAFIQI → 39231

KM₂KF H1
39240 KAPETAN ANDREAS

KM₂KF H12
39250 CIRO SECONDO → 39251

CL

KM₂KMKFK H
39260 LEDEA → 39261

KM₃KF H12
39270 LAGO IZABAL → 39271

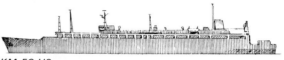

KM₄FC H2
39280 LOTUS ACE → 39282

MC₂MF H3
★39290 STARITSA

MCF H123
★39300 POEL → 39302

MCMC₂F H13
39320 STO. NINO

MCMF H1
39330 TSUGARU

MF H
39340 CHRYSANTHY H

MF H123
39360 VITTORIO GARDELLA

MF H13
39370 SUNSHINE ISLAND

MF H13
39380 BERESFORD → 39381

Twin Funnels

MF H2
39390 INCAN SUPERIOR → 39391

MFM H
39400 BHAGIRATHI

MFM H2
★39410 VSEVOLOD BERYEZKIN → 39419

MFM H2
39420 CANABAL → 39421

MKF H
★39450 RODINA → 39459

MKF H1
39460 ANTARES → 39461

MKFM H1
39490 SHIELDHALL

MK₂C₂K₂FK H1
39500 UHENBELS

MK₃MF H13
39530 SANTO ANTONIO DO TRIUNFO → 39532

MK₃MK₅FK H123
39560 FLORA

MK₂MF H
39580 SERIFOS

MK₂MF H
39590 FLORIAN

MK₂MF H
39600 ABILITY → 39601

MK₂MF H
39610 UNISON I → 39612

MK₂MF H
39620 NIKOS

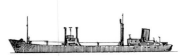

MK₂MF H
39630 ELEISTRIA IV

MK₂MF H
39650 CEMENTO PUERTO RICO → 39651

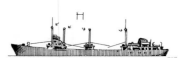

MK₂MF H
★39660 BAIA MARE → 39662

MK₂MF H
★39670 GALATI → 39674

MK₂MF H1
39700 EVER

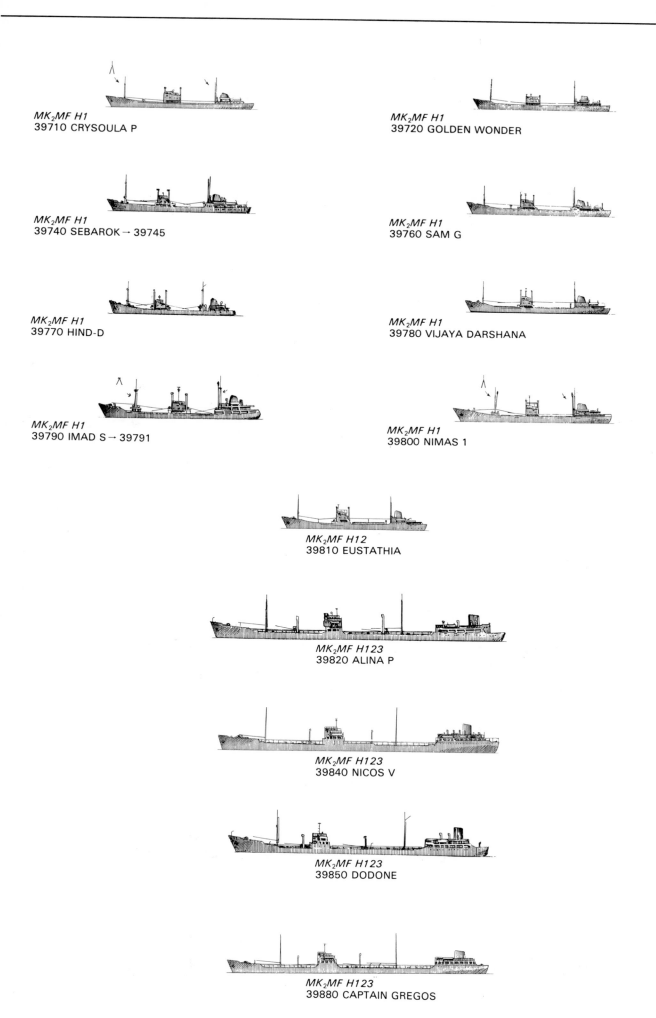

MK₂MF H1
39710 CRYSOULA P

MK₂MF H1
39720 GOLDEN WONDER

MK₂MF H1
39740 SEBAROK → 39745

MK₂MF H1
39760 SAM G

MK₂MF H1
39770 HIND-D

MK₂MF H1
39780 VIJAYA DARSHANA

MK₂MF H1
39790 IMAD S → 39791

MK₂MF H1
39800 NIMAS 1

MK₂MF H12
39810 EUSTATHIA

MK₂MF H123
39820 ALINA P

MK₂MF H123
39840 NICOS V

MK₂MF H123
39850 DODONE

MK₂MF H123
39880 CAPTAIN GREGOS

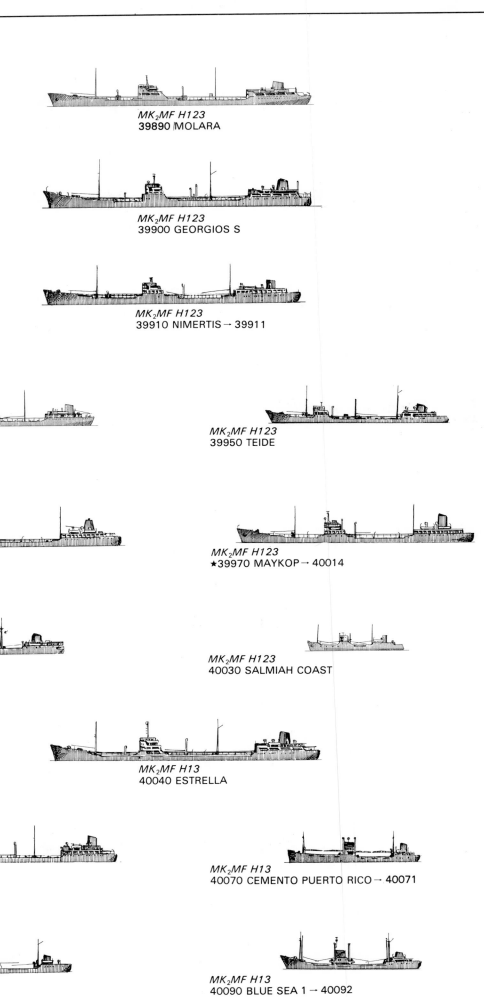

MK₂MF H123
39890 MOLARA

MK₂MF H123
39900 GEORGIOS S

MK₂MF H123
39910 NIMERTIS → 39911

MK₂MF H123
★39930 DA QING No 410

MK₂MF H123
39950 TEIDE

MK₂MF H123
★39960 KLAIPEDA → 39961

MK₂MF H123
★39970 MAYKOP → 40014

MK₂MF H123
40020 TAT LEE No 3

MK₂MF H123
40030 SALMIAH COAST

MK₂MF H13
40040 ESTRELLA

MK₂MF H13
★40060 DA QING No 15

MK₂MF H13
40070 CEMENTO PUERTO RICO → 40071

MK₂MF H13
40080 NICOLAS V

MK₂MF H13
40090 BLUE SEA 1 → 40092

MK₂MF H13
40100 ABU SIMBEL → 40102

MK₂MF H13
40110 PHILIPPOS

MK₂MF H13
40120 CHERRY CHEPAT

CL

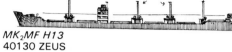

MK₂MF H13
40130 ZEUS

MK₂MF H3
40140 SANTA MARIA III

MK₂MF H3
40160 FAHAD

Twin Funnels

MK₂MFC H
40170 PRESERVER → 40171

MK₂MFK H123
40200 LAPU LAPU → 40202

MK₂MFK H123
40220 GEORGIOS S

MK₂MFK H13
★40230 DRZIC

MK₂MFK H13
★40240 PLITVICE → 40241

MK₂MFK H13
40250 GELIGA → 40251

MK₂MKF H123
40260 CAPO MADRE

MK₂MKF H123
40290 THEOUPOLIS

CL

MKMCF H
40320 BEXLEY → 40323

MKMF H
40350 ROSA

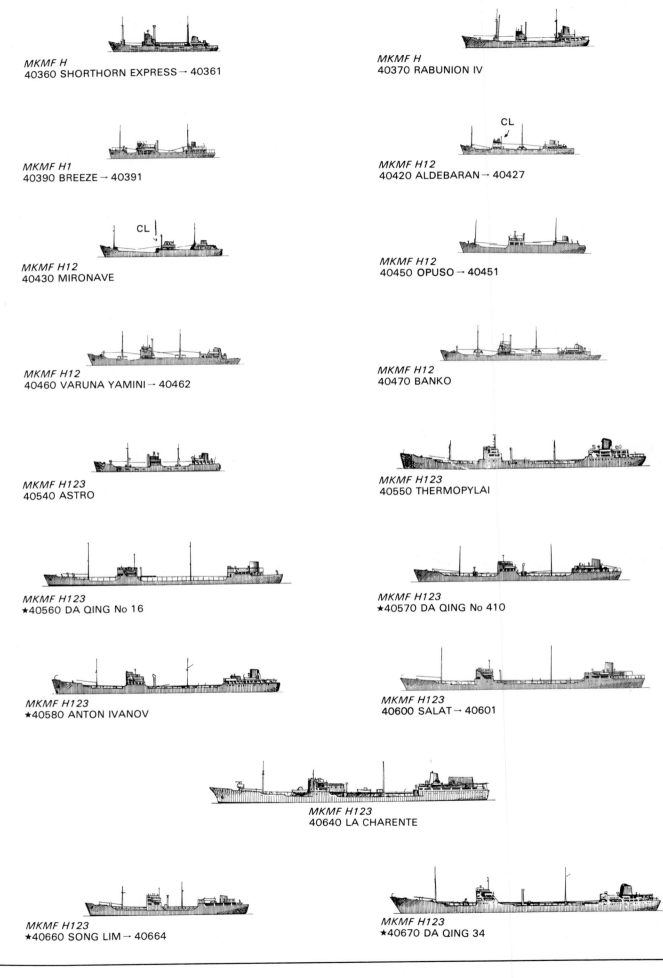

MKMF H
40360 SHORTHORN EXPRESS → 40361

MKMF H
40370 RABUNION IV

MKMF H1
40390 BREEZE → 40391

MKMF H12
40420 ALDEBARAN → 40427

MKMF H12
40430 MIRONAVE

MKMF H12
40450 OPUSO → 40451

MKMF H12
40460 VARUNA YAMINI → 40462

MKMF H12
40470 BANKO

MKMF H123
40540 ASTRO

MKMF H123
40550 THERMOPYLAI

MKMF H123
★40560 DA QING No 16

MKMF H123
★40570 DA QING No 410

MKMF H123
★40580 ANTON IVANOV

MKMF H123
40600 SALAT → 40601

MKMF H123
40640 LA CHARENTE

MKMF H123
★40660 SONG LIM → 40664

MKMF H123
★40670 DA QING 34

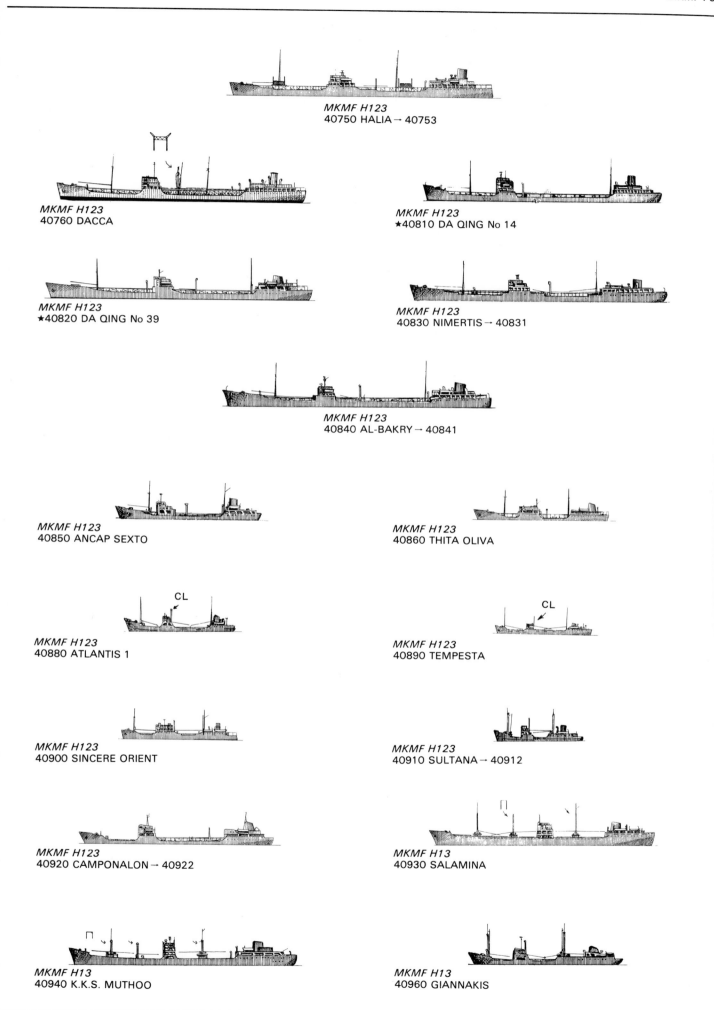

MKMF H123
40750 HALIA → 40753

MKMF H123
40760 DACCA

MKMF H123
★40810 DA QING No 14

MKMF H123
★40820 DA QING No 39

MKMF H123
40830 NIMERTIS → 40831

MKMF H123
40840 AL-BAKRY → 40841

MKMF H123
40850 ANCAP SEXTO

MKMF H123
40860 THITA OLIVA

MKMF H123
40880 ATLANTIS 1

MKMF H123
40890 TEMPESTA

MKMF H123
40900 SINCERE ORIENT

MKMF H123
40910 SULTANA → 40912

MKMF H123
40920 CAMPONALON → 40922

MKMF H13
40930 SALAMINA

MKMF H13
40940 K.K.S. MUTHOO

MKMF H13
40960 GIANNAKIS

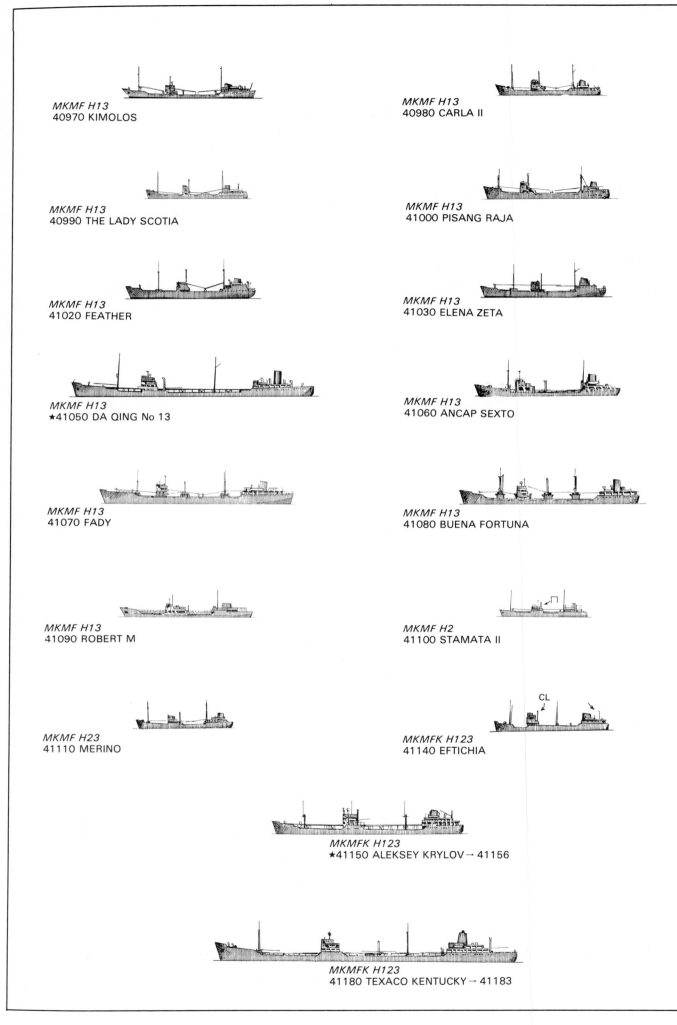

MKMF H13
40970 KIMOLOS

MKMF H13
40980 CARLA II

MKMF H13
40990 THE LADY SCOTIA

MKMF H13
41000 PISANG RAJA

MKMF H13
41020 FEATHER

MKMF H13
41030 ELENA ZETA

MKMF H13
★41050 DA QING No 13

MKMF H13
41060 ANCAP SEXTO

MKMF H13
41070 FADY

MKMF H13
41080 BUENA FORTUNA

MKMF H13
41090 ROBERT M

MKMF H2
41100 STAMATA II

MKMF H23
41110 MERINO

MKMFK H123
41140 EFTICHIA

MKMFK H123
★41150 ALEKSEY KRYLOV → 41156

MKMFK H123
41180 TEXACO KENTUCKY → 41183

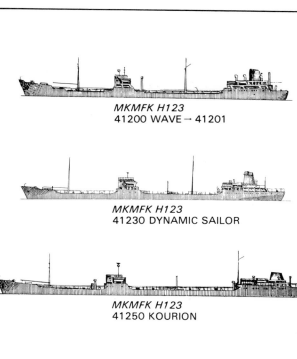

MKMFK H123
41200 WAVE → 41201

MKMFK H123
41230 DYNAMIC SAILOR

MKMFK H123
41250 KOURION

MKMFK H13
41280 ELEISTRIA VIII

MKMKF H
41300 MAGED → 41303

MKMKF H
★41310 ORADEA → 41329

MKMKF H1
41340 KATERINA K

MKMKF H1
41360 MAYA I → 41361

MKMKF H1
41370 FODELE II

MKMKF H12
41380 GEORGIOS A

MKMKF H123
41390 INDIANO

MKMKF H123
★41410 HONG QI 105

MKMKF H123
41420 VOLUNTAS → 41423

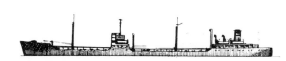

MKMKF H123
41460 TALLULAH → 41463

MKMKF H123
41480 HALIA → 41483

MKMKF H123
41490 CAPO MADRE

MKMKF H123
41500 SAN DENIS

MKMKF H13
41530 MAYA I → 41531

MKMKFK H1
41550 GEOPOTES VI

MKMKFK H123
41570 STAR

MKMKFK H13
41580 ALDERAMINE

MKMKFK H13
41590 RINI → 41599

MKMKFK H13
★41610 XUE CHENG → 41611

MKMK₂F H123
41620 LSCO PIONEER → 41621

MKMK₂F H123
★41630 PRAHOVA

MKMK₂F H2
41670 POLYTIMI ANDREADIS

MKMKMKFK H13
41720 KRITON

MKMKMK₂F H13
41740 REGENT → 41741

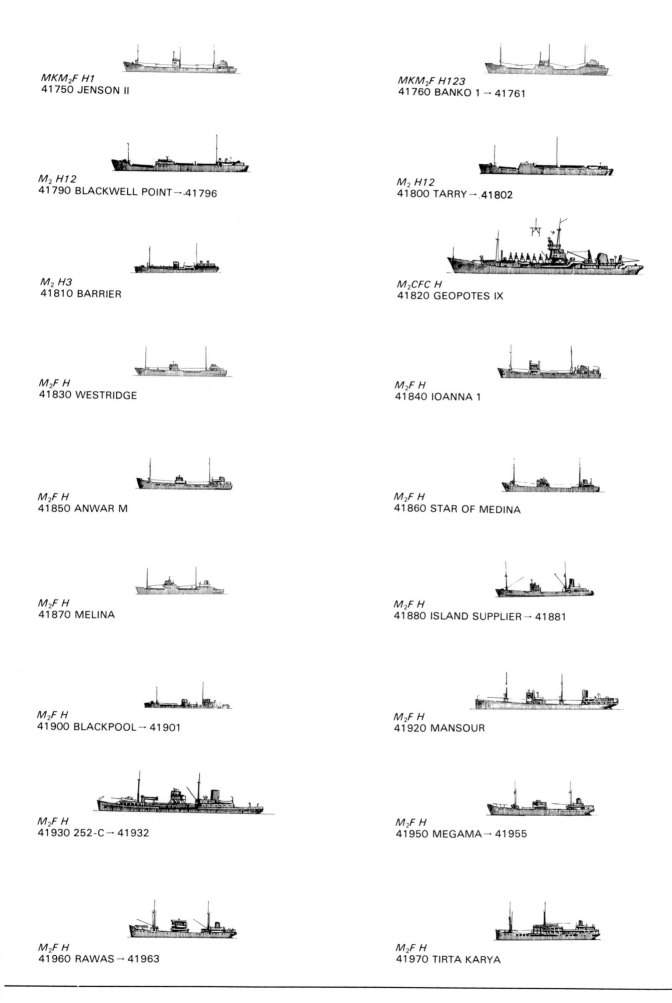

MKM₂F H1
41750 JENSON II

MKM₂F H123
41760 BANKO 1 → 41761

M₂ H12
41790 BLACKWELL POINT → 41796

M₂ H12
41800 TARRY → 41802

M₂ H3
41810 BARRIER

M₂CFC H
41820 GEOPOTES IX

M₂F H
41830 WESTRIDGE

M₂F H
41840 IOANNA 1

M₂F H
41850 ANWAR M

M₂F H
41860 STAR OF MEDINA

M₂F H
41870 MELINA

M₂F H
41880 ISLAND SUPPLIER → 41881

M₂F H
41900 BLACKPOOL → 41901

M₂F H
41920 MANSOUR

M₂F H
41930 252-C → 41932

M₂F H
41950 MEGAMA → 41955

M₂F H
41960 RAWAS → 41963

M₂F H
41970 TIRTA KARYA

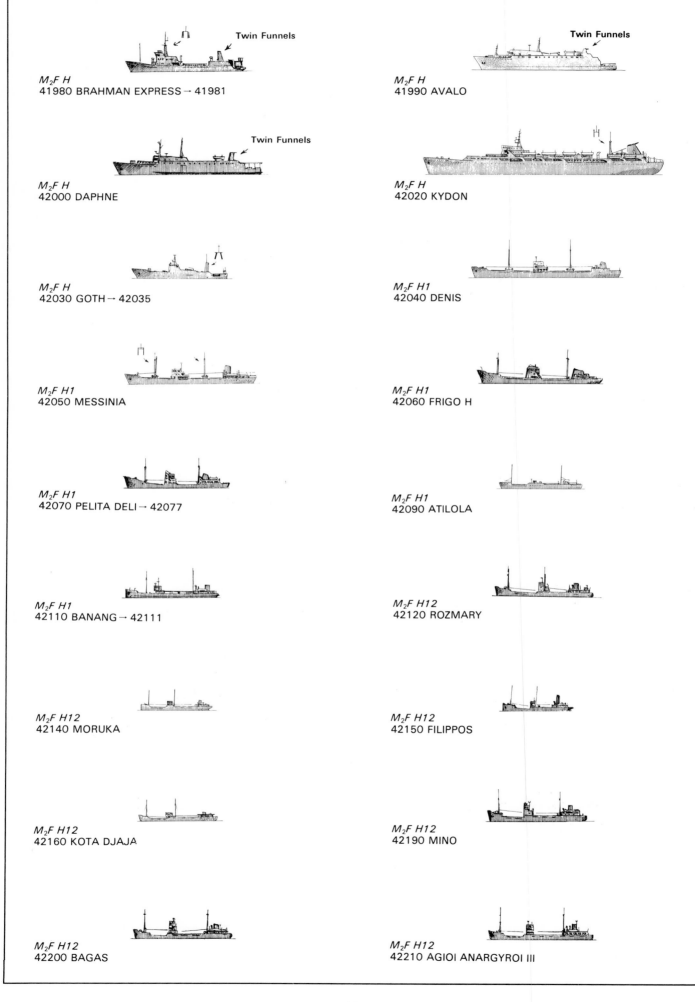

Twin Funnels

M₂F H
41980 BRAHMAN EXPRESS → 41981

Twin Funnels

M₂F H
41990 AVALO

Twin Funnels

M₂F H
42000 DAPHNE

M₂F H
42020 KYDON

M₂F H
42030 GOTH → 42035

M₂F H1
42040 DENIS

M₂F H1
42050 MESSINIA

M₂F H1
42060 FRIGO H

M₂F H1
42070 PELITA DELI → 42077

M₂F H1
42090 ATILOLA

M₂F H1
42110 BANANG → 42111

M₂F H12
42120 ROZMARY

M₂F H12
42140 MORUKA

M₂F H12
42150 FILIPPOS

M₂F H12
42160 KOTA DJAJA

M₂F H12
42190 MINO

M₂F H12
42200 BAGAS

M₂F H12
42210 AGIOI ANARGYROI III

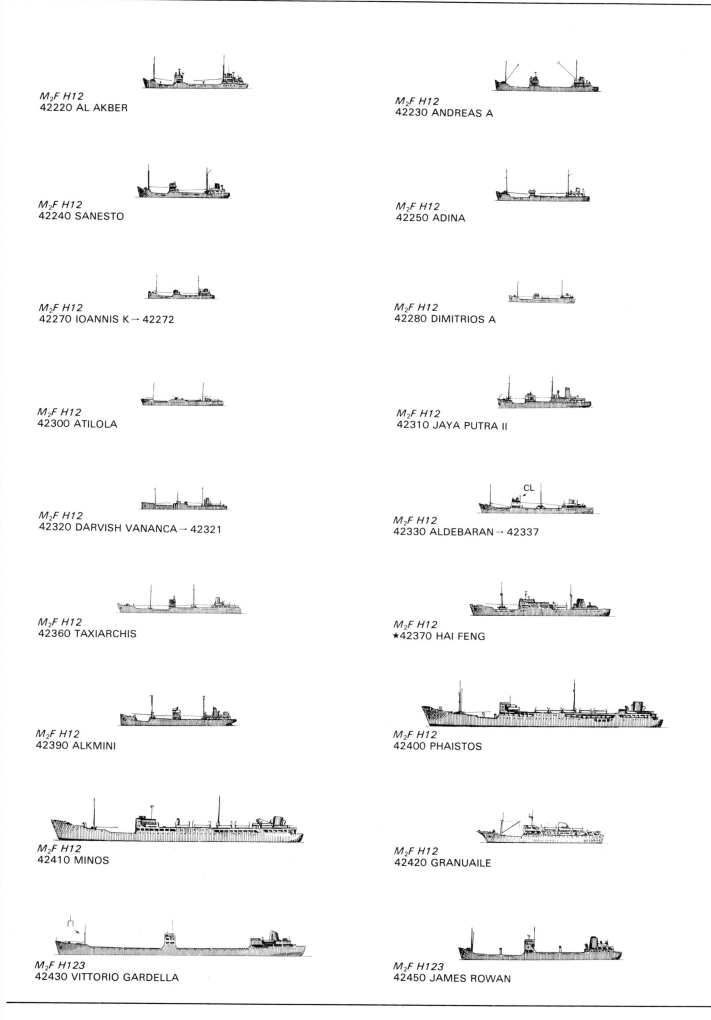

M_2F H12
42220 AL AKBER

M_2F H12
42230 ANDREAS A

M_2F H12
42240 SANESTO

M_2F H12
42250 ADINA

M_2F H12
42270 IOANNIS K → 42272

M_2F H12
42280 DIMITRIOS A

M_2F H12
42300 ATILOLA

M_2F H12
42310 JAYA PUTRA II

M_2F H12
42320 DARVISH VANANCA → 42321

M_2F H12
42330 ALDEBARAN → 42337

M_2F H12
42360 TAXIARCHIS

M_2F H12
★42370 HAI FENG

M_2F H12
42390 ALKMINI

M_2F H12
42400 PHAISTOS

M_2F H12
42410 MINOS

M_2F H12
42420 GRANUAILE

M_2F H123
42430 VITTORIO GARDELLA

M_2F H123
42450 JAMES ROWAN

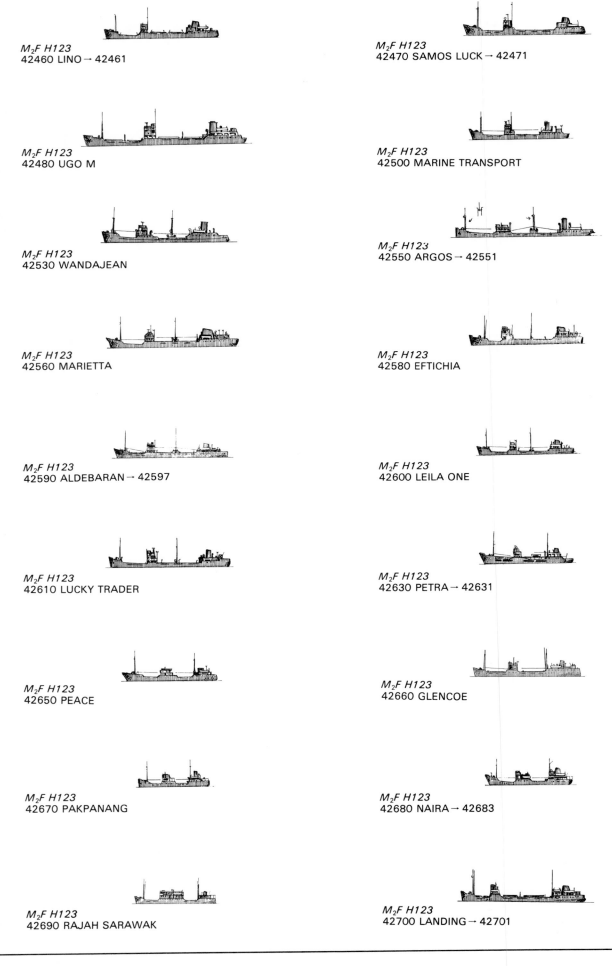

M₂F H123
42460 LINO → 42461

M₂F H123
42470 SAMOS LUCK → 42471

M₂F H123
42480 UGO M

M₂F H123
42500 MARINE TRANSPORT

M₂F H123
42530 WANDAJEAN

M₂F H123
42550 ARGOS → 42551

M₂F H123
42560 MARIETTA

M₂F H123
42580 EFTICHIA

M₂F H123
42590 ALDEBARAN → 42597

M₂F H123
42600 LEILA ONE

M₂F H123
42610 LUCKY TRADER

M₂F H123
42630 PETRA → 42631

M₂F H123
42650 PEACE

M₂F H123
42660 GLENCOE

M₂F H123
42670 PAKPANANG

M₂F H123
42680 NAIRA → 42683

M₂F H123
42690 RAJAH SARAWAK

M₂F H123
42700 LANDING → 42701

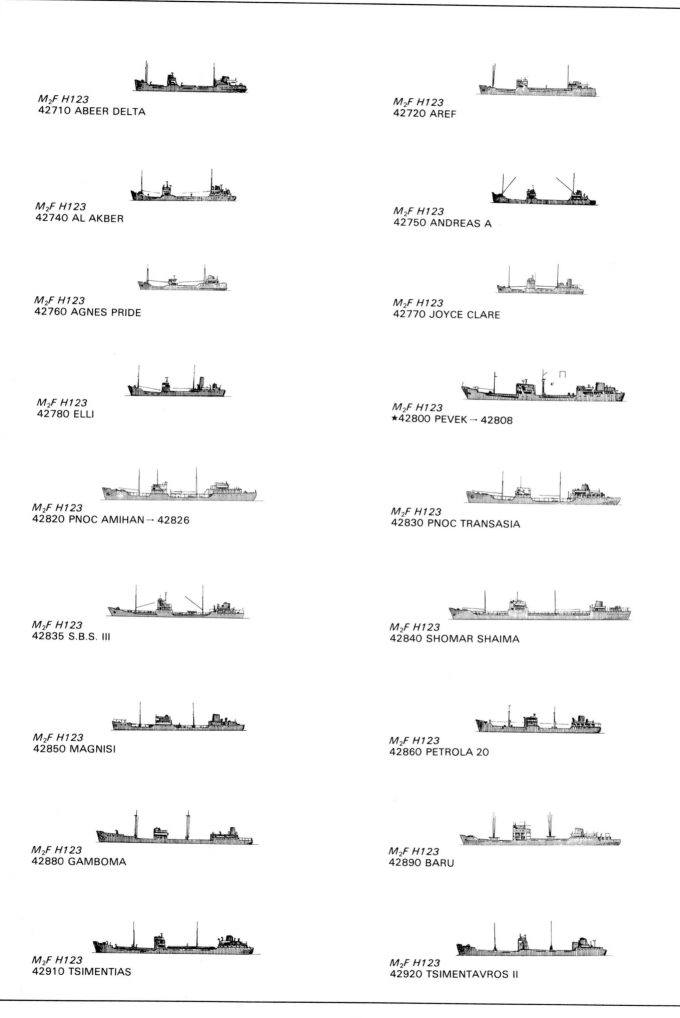

M₂F H123
42710 ABEER DELTA

M₂F H123
42720 AREF

M₂F H123
42740 AL AKBER

M₂F H123
42750 ANDREAS A

M₂F H123
42760 AGNES PRIDE

M₂F H123
42770 JOYCE CLARE

M₂F H123
42780 ELLI

M₂F H123
★42800 PEVEK → 42808

M₂F H123
42820 PNOC AMIHAN → 42826

M₂F H123
42830 PNOC TRANSASIA

M₂F H123
42835 S.B.S. III

M₂F H123
42840 SHOMAR SHAIMA

M₂F H123
42850 MAGNISI

M₂F H123
42860 PETROLA 20

M₂F H123
42880 GAMBOMA

M₂F H123
42890 BARU

M₂F H123
42910 TSIMENTIAS

M₂F H123
42920 TSIMENTAVROS II

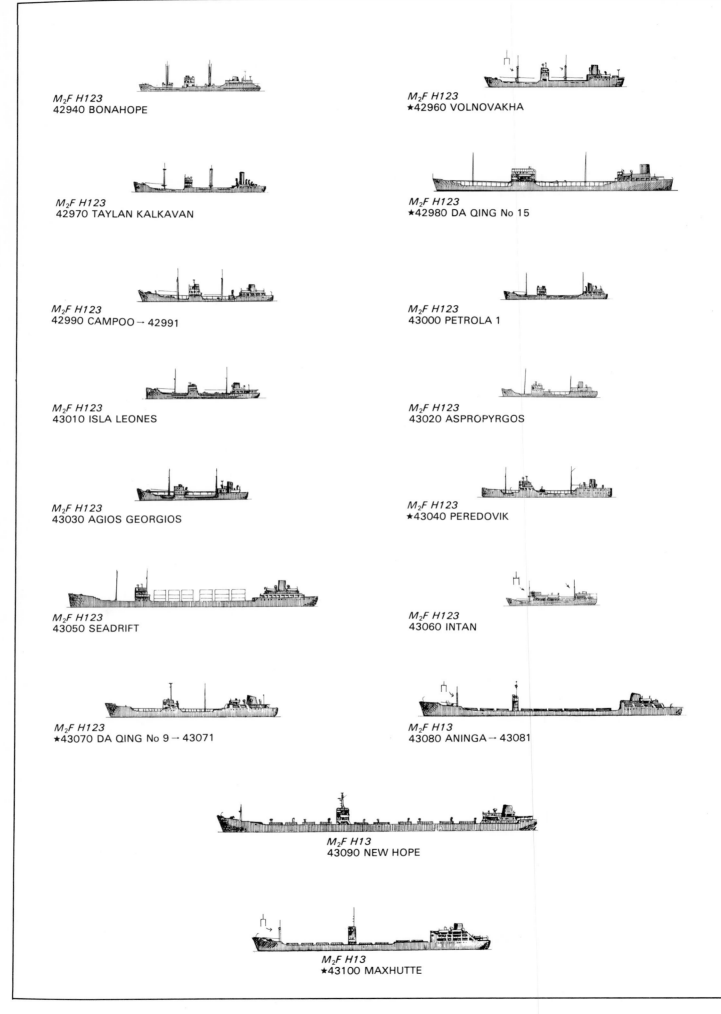

M₂F H123
42940 BONAHOPE

M₂F H123
★42960 VOLNOVAKHA

M₂F H123
42970 TAYLAN KALKAVAN

M₂F H123
★42980 DA QING No 15

M₂F H123
42990 CAMPOO → 42991

M₂F H123
43000 PETROLA 1

M₂F H123
43010 ISLA LEONES

M₂F H123
43020 ASPROPYRGOS

M₂F H123
43030 AGIOS GEORGIOS

M₂F H123
★43040 PEREDOVIK

M₂F H123
43050 SEADRIFT

M₂F H123
43060 INTAN

M₂F H123
★43070 DA QING No 9 → 43071

M₂F H13
43080 ANINGA → 43081

M₂F H13
43090 NEW HOPE

M₂F H13
★43100 MAXHUTTE

M₂F H13
★43110 ZWICKAU

M₂F H13
43120 DONA HELENA → 43125

M₂F H13
43140 PADJONGE → 43149

M₂F H13
43160 ANTONELLO → 43162

M₂F H13
43180 SANTA → 43181

M₂F H13
43190 LALANG → 43198

M₂F H13
43220 IMPERIAL SARNIA

M₂F H13
43230 GUNGA DIN II

M₂F H13
43250 ROSARITO

M₂F H13
43260 BERING TRADER

M₂F H13
43270 PERMINA IX

M₂F H13
43280 ANTONELLOESSE

M₂F H13
43290 MURASAKI MARU

M₂F H13
★43300 LAMUT → 43301

M₂F H13
43310 ACRE → 43314

M₂F H2
43320 OSHEA EXPRESS

M₂F H3
43330 EVDOXIA K

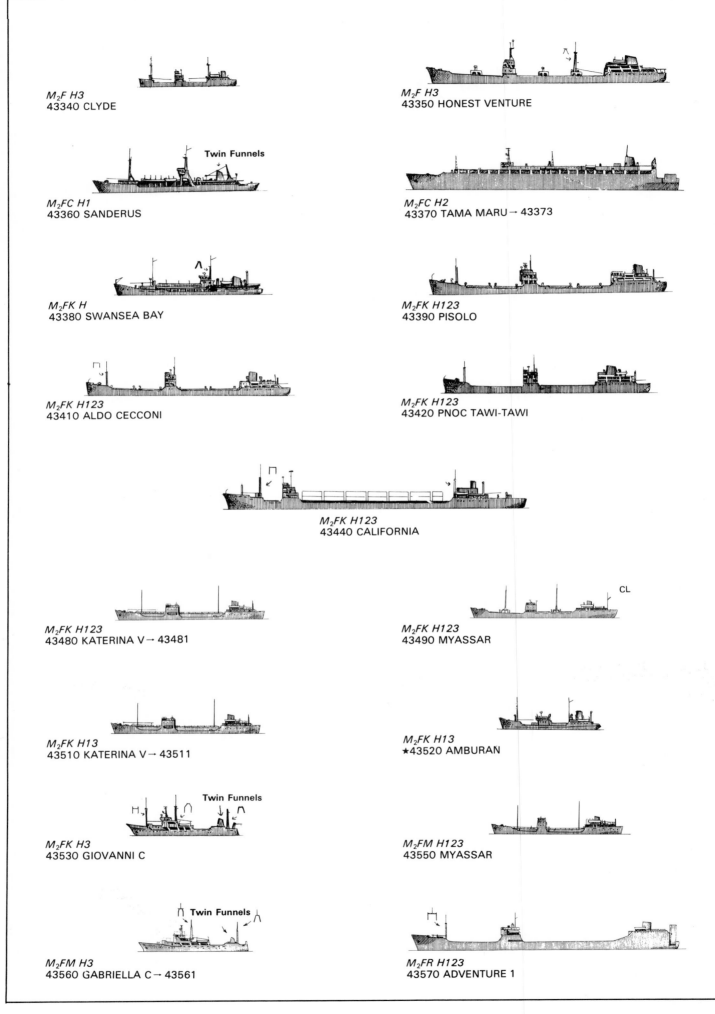

M₂F H3
43340 CLYDE

M₂F H3
43350 HONEST VENTURE

M₂FC H1
43360 SANDERUS

Twin Funnels

M₂FC H2
43370 TAMA MARU → 43373

M₂FK H
43380 SWANSEA BAY

M₂FK H123
43390 PISOLO

M₂FK H123
43410 ALDO CECCONI

M₂FK H123
43420 PNOC TAWI-TAWI

M₂FK H123
43440 CALIFORNIA

M₂FK H123
43480 KATERINA V → 43481

M₂FK H123
43490 MYASSAR

CL

M₂FK H13
43510 KATERINA V → 43511

M₂FK H13
★43520 AMBURAN

M₂FK H3
43530 GIOVANNI C

Twin Funnels

M₂FM H123
43550 MYASSAR

M₂FM H3
43560 GABRIELLA C → 43561

Twin Funnels

M₂FR H123
43570 ADVENTURE 1

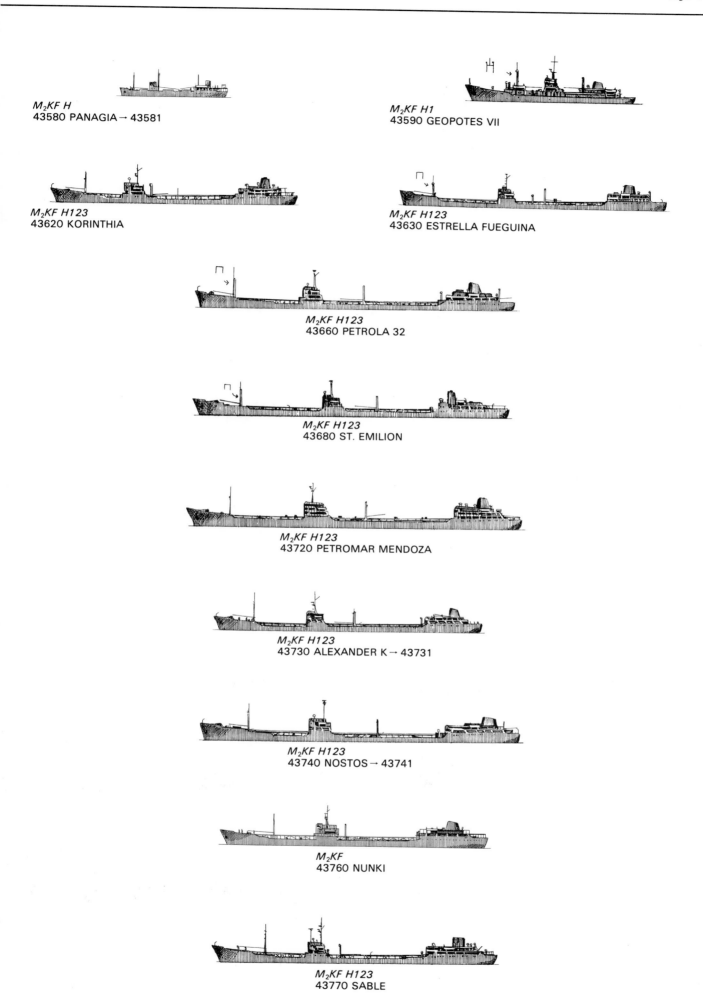

M₂KF H
43580 PANAGIA → 43581

M₂KF H1
43590 GEOPOTES VII

M₂KF H123
43620 KORINTHIA

M₂KF H123
43630 ESTRELLA FUEGUINA

M₂KF H123
43660 PETROLA 32

M₂KF H123
43680 ST. EMILION

M₂KF H123
43720 PETROMAR MENDOZA

M₂KF H123
43730 ALEXANDER K → 43731

M₂KF H123
43740 NOSTOS → 43741

M₂KF
43760 NUNKI

M₂KF H123
43770 SABLE

M₂KF H123
★43790 ARGON → 43821

M₂KF H123
43840 AELLO

M₂KF H123
43850 PERMINA SAMUDRA V

M₂KF H123
43860 GEORGIOS M II

M₂KF H123
43870 EMOULI

M₂KF H123
43880 PALMIRA ZETA

M₂KF H123
43900 AHMED AL-BAKRY II

M₂KF H123
43930 HAMEN

M₂KF H123
43940 MAGDUS

M₂KF H123
43960 NIKITAS

M₂KF H13
44000 TEXACO ALASKA

M₂KF H13
44010 NEFELI → 44011

M₂KF H13
44040 GOLDEN EASTERN → 44041

M₂KF H13
44080 MALDIVE NATION → 44081

M₂KF H13
★44100 BOLSHEVIK KARAYEV → 44127

M₂KFK H123
★44140 BATUMI

M₂KFK H123
44160 MARIPRIMA

M₂KFK H123
44180 PETROSTAR IV

M₂KFK H123
44190 IONIO

M₂KFK H123
44200 SHOMAR HANAN

M₂KFK H123
44210 AMASTRA → 44216

M₂KFK H123
44220 PETROMAR ROSARIO

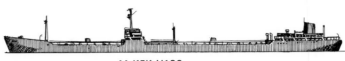

M₂KFK H123
44250 VERDI → 44251

M₂KFK H123
44260 EVA P → 44261

M₂KFK H123
44270 LEFKAS

M₂KFK H123
44280 ANDREA MANTEGNA

M₂KFK H123
44290 TOXOTIS

M₂KFK H123
44310 WASHINGTON TRADER → 44312

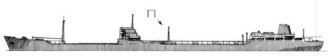

M₂KFK H123
44340 WHITE BEACH

M₂KFK H123
44360 DEMOSTHENES V

M₂KFK H123
★44370 ELGAVA → 44371

M₂KFK H123
44390 MALDIVE NATION → 44391

M₂KFK H13
★44410 → DRUZHBA

M₂KFK H13
44420 MARIE MAERSK

M₂KFK H13
44430 LUSSIN

M₂KFK H13
44440 SORONG

M₂KFK H13
44460 ANINGA → 44461

M₂KFK H13
44480 BLUE SKY

M₂KFK H13
44490 STRONG SKIPPER

M₂KFK H13
★44510 PADEREWSKI → 44514

M₂KFK H13
44520 LEFTERIS II

M₂K₂F H12
44540 OBSERVER

M₂K₂F H123
44550 SAO GABRIEL

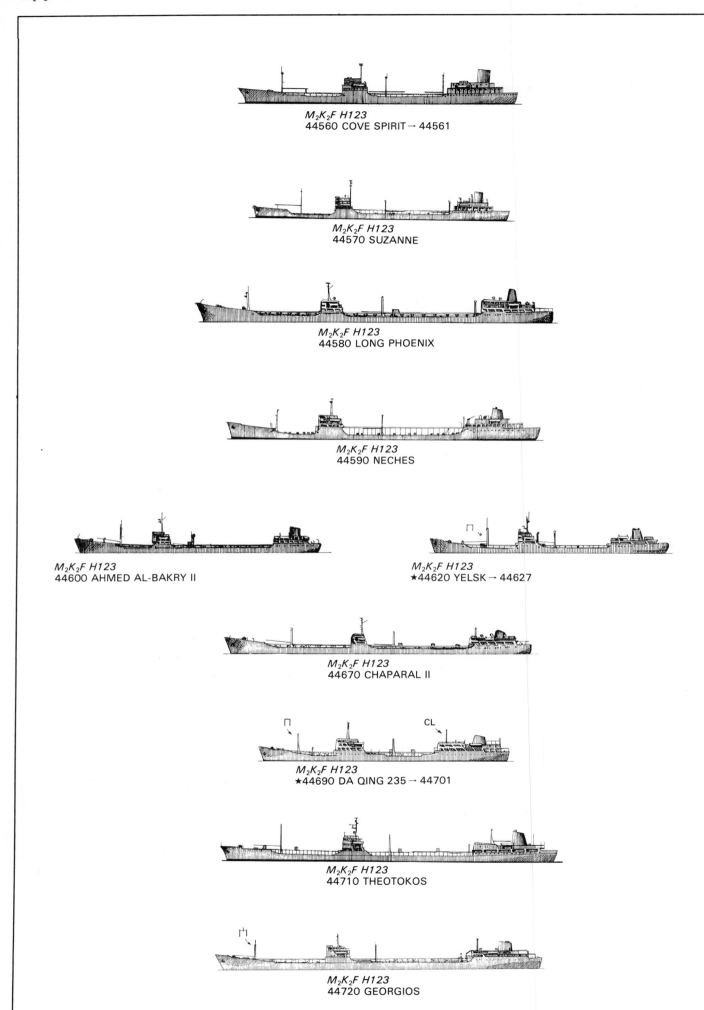

M₂K₂F H123
44560 COVE SPIRIT → 44561

M₂K₂F H123
44570 SUZANNE

M₂K₂F H123
44580 LONG PHOENIX

M₂K₂F H123
44590 NECHES

M₂K₂F H123
44600 AHMED AL-BAKRY II

M₂K₂F H123
★44620 YELSK → 44627

M₂K₂F H123
44670 CHAPARAL II

M₂K₂F H123
★44690 DA QING 235 → 44701

M₂K₂F H123
44710 THEOTOKOS

M₂K₂F H123
44720 GEORGIOS

M₂K₂FK H123
44760 CAMPOGRIS → 44761

M₂K₂FK H123
44780 ESTRELLA FUEGUINA

M₂K₂FK H123
44790 RHINO

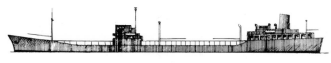

M₂K₂FK H123
44800 COVE NAVIGATOR

M₂K₂FK H123
44810 MEDINA → 44812

M₂K₂FK H123
44840 CAMPORROJO → 44844

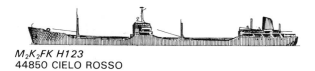

M₂K₂FK H123
44850 CIELO ROSSO

M₂K₂FK H123
44870 SCAPMOUNT → 44872

M₂K₂FK H123
44880 CAMPORRASO → 44882

M₂K₂MF H123
★44890 RAVA RUSSKAYA

M₂KMF H12
44900 VARUNA YAMINI → 44902

M₂KMF H123
44910 CHERRY JET

M₂KMF H123
44930 CHRYSSI V

M₂KMFK H123
★44950 ALEKSEY KRYLOV → 44956

M₂KMFK H13
44960 NELY P → 44961

M₂KMFK H13
44970 TOLMIROS

M₂KMFK H13
44990 ELEISTRIA VIII

M₂KMKF H13
45010 TAFELBERG

M₂KMKFK H123
45020 LITTLE NIKOS

M₂KMKFK H13
★45030 WU XING → 45031

M₂KMK₂F H123
45040 MARIAS → 45041

M₂KMK₂F H13
45050 NEOSHO → 45055

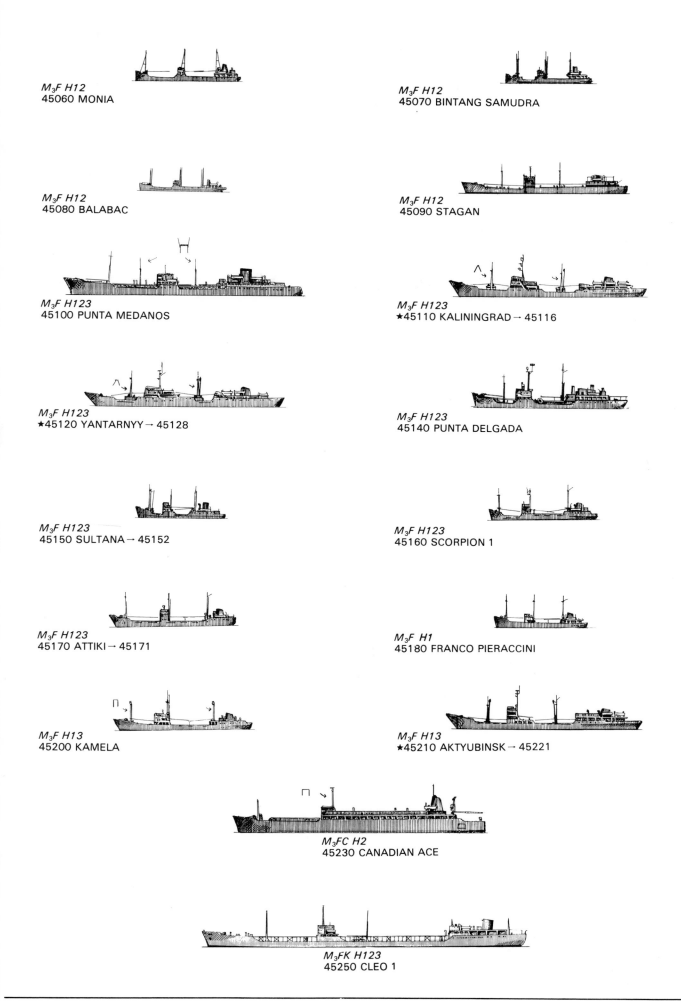

M₃F H12
45060 MONIA

M₃F H12
45070 BINTANG SAMUDRA

M₃F H12
45080 BALABAC

M₃F H12
45090 STAGAN

M₃F H123
45100 PUNTA MEDANOS

M₃F H123
★45110 KALININGRAD → 45116

M₃F H123
★45120 YANTARNYY → 45128

M₃F H123
45140 PUNTA DELGADA

M₃F H123
45150 SULTANA → 45152

M₃F H123
45160 SCORPION 1

M₃F H123
45170 ATTIKI → 45171

M₃F H1
45180 FRANCO PIERACCINI

M₃F H13
45200 KAMELA

M₃F H13
★45210 AKTYUBINSK → 45221

M₃FC H2
45230 CANADIAN ACE

M₃FK H123
45250 CLEO 1

M₃KMF H1
★45270 KONSTITUTSIYA SSSR → 45275

M₄F H123
45280 SAO GABRIEL

M₄FK H1
★45290 PYATIDYESYATILYETIYE SSSR → 45292

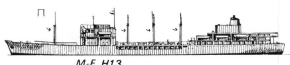

M₅F H13
45310 MONTT → 45311

M₅FK H123
45320 SUPPLY

M₆F H13
45330 OLMEDA → 45332

Profile 4

C_3MC_3MFC H13
★45350 POLTAVA → 45409

C_3MF H1
45420 HELLA

C_3MF H1
45430 RIJNBORG → 45431

C_3MF H1
45440 → AGELIKI II

C_3MF H1
45450 KEMAL II → 45452

C_3MF H123
45460 MIRAMAR PRIMA → 45461

C_3MFK H3
45470 SUNLUCK

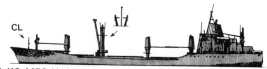

CL

C_2KC_2MFC H13
45480 JUMPA → 45483

$C_2MCKCMFC$ H1
★45490 KAI HUA

C_2MF H
45500 AGENOR

C_2MF H
45510 TYRO

C_2MF H13
45520 SEA STRUGGLER

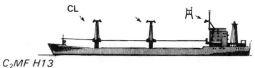

CL

C_2MF H13
45530 SLOMAN NEREUS → 45533

C_2MF H13
★45540 OSKOL

CL

CKC_2KMFK H1
45550 SAINT FRANCOIS → 45551

CL

CK_4MF H13
45560 HIGHSEA PROMISE

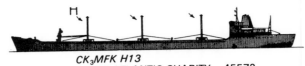

CK₃MFK H13
45570 ATLANTIC CHARITY → 45572

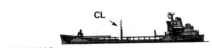

CKMF H13
45580 IMPERIAL SKEENA

CKMF H13
★45590 MANYCH → 45591

CKMK H
45600 ODIN → 45601

CMC₂KCMFC H13
45610 ATHINAI → 45611

CMC₂MF H1
45620 SHEARWATER BAY

CMC₂MFC H1
★45630 OLA → 45634

CMCMF H1
45640 SUNFLOWER

CMCMF H1
45650 BILBARAKAH → 45651

CMCMF H1
45670 LAUTAN ENAM

CMCMF H13
★45680 IZHMALES → 45691

CMF H
★45700 OSKOL III type

CMF H1
★45710 DORNBUSCH

CMF H3
★45720 ALLIGATOR III class

CMFK H13
★45730 AMGA

CMFK H13
45740 CHALLENGER I

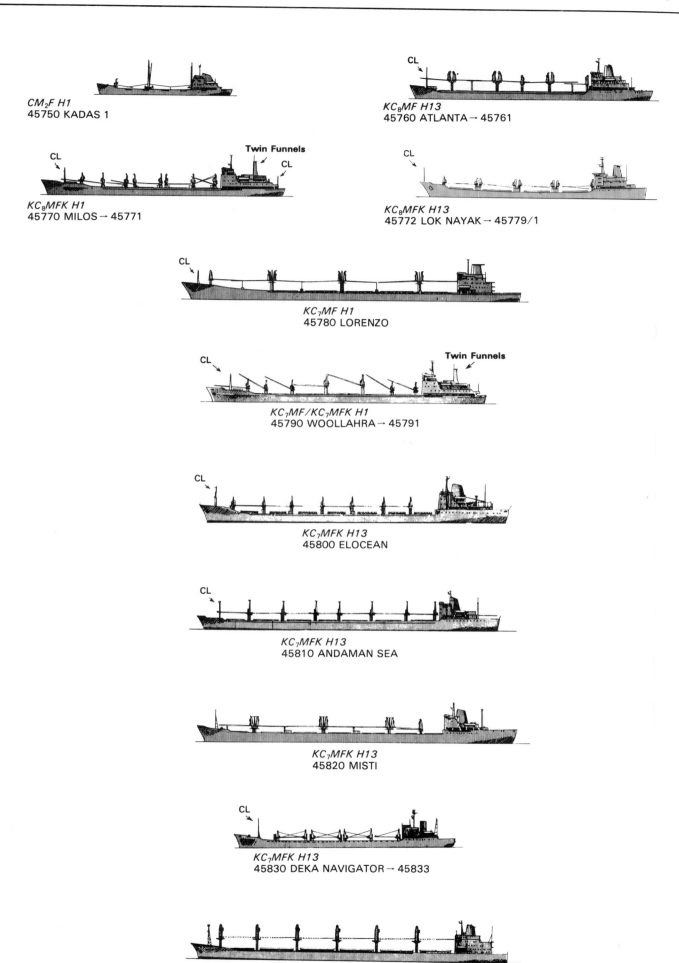

CM₂F H1
45750 KADAS 1

KC₈MF H13
45760 ATLANTA → 45761

KC₈MFK H1
45770 MILOS → 45771

KC₈MFK H13
45772 LOK NAYAK → 45779/1

KC₇MF H1
45780 LORENZO

KC₇MF/KC₇MFK H1
45790 WOOLLAHRA → 45791

KC₇MFK H13
45800 ELOCEAN

KC₇MFK H13
45810 ANDAMAN SEA

KC₇MFK H13
45820 MISTI

KC₇MFK H13
45830 DEKA NAVIGATOR → 45833

KC₆MF H1
45840 WARSCHAU → 45843

KC₆MF H1
45845 OAK SUN

KC₆MF H1
45850 BUDAPEST → 45851

KC₆MF H13
45860 DESPINA GIAVRIDIS → 45862

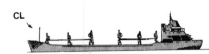

KC₆MF H13
45880 NGAPARA → 45883

KC₆MF H13
★45890 KUANG HAI

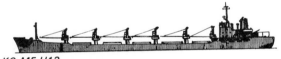

KC₆MF H13
45900 ABBY

KC₆MF H13
45910 ARIEL → 45912

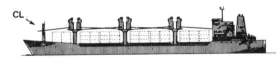

KC₆MF H13
45920 UNIDO → 45921

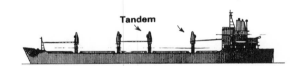

KC₆MF H13
45930 SAMOA → 45936

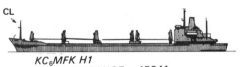

KC₆MFK H1
45940 MESANGE → 45941

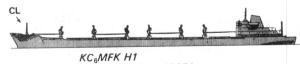

KC₆MFK H1
45950 VITINA → 45951

KC₆MFK H1
45960 CHENNAI JAYAM → 45964

KC₆MFK H1
★45967 GU HAI

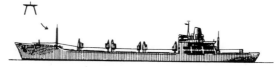

KC₆MFK H1
45970 MULTI CARRIER → 45973

KC₆MFK H13
★45980 QINGHAI → 45981

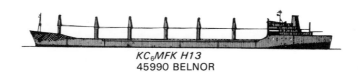

KC₆MFK H13
45990 BELNOR

KC₆MFK H13
46000 BELSTAR → 46010

KC₆MFK H13
46020 DESPINA GIAVRIDIS → 46022

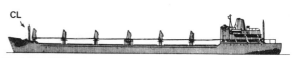

KC₆MFK H13
46030 GINA JULIANO

KC₆MFK H13
46040 HACI SEFER KALKAVAN → 46041

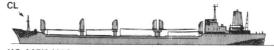

KC₆MFK H13
46050 ASTRA PEAK → 46052

KC₆MFK H13
46060 AL TAJDAR

KC₆MFK H13
46070 MARITSA P LEMOS → 46074

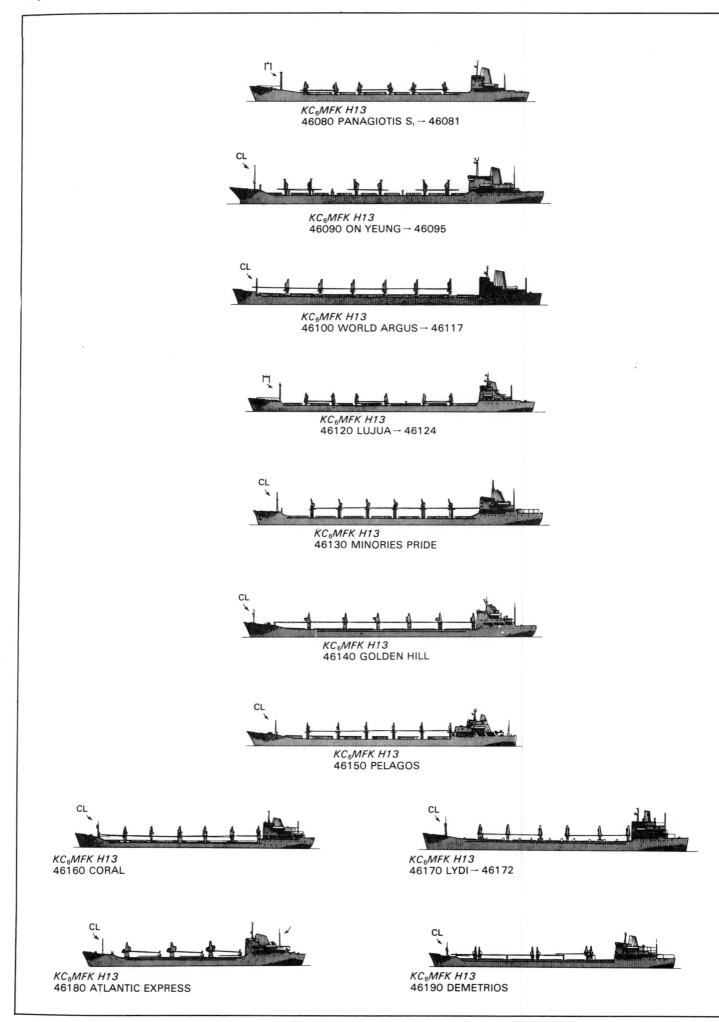

KC₆MFK H13
46080 PANAGIOTIS S, → 46081

KC₆MFK H13
46090 ON YEUNG → 46095

KC₆MFK H13
46100 WORLD ARGUS → 46117

KC₆MFK H13
46120 LUJUA → 46124

KC₆MFK H13
46130 MINORIES PRIDE

KC₆MFK H13
46140 GOLDEN HILL

KC₆MFK H13
46150 PELAGOS

KC₆MFK H13
46160 CORAL

KC₆MFK H13
46170 LYDI → 46172

KC₆MFK H13
46180 ATLANTIC EXPRESS

KC₆MFK H13
46190 DEMETRIOS

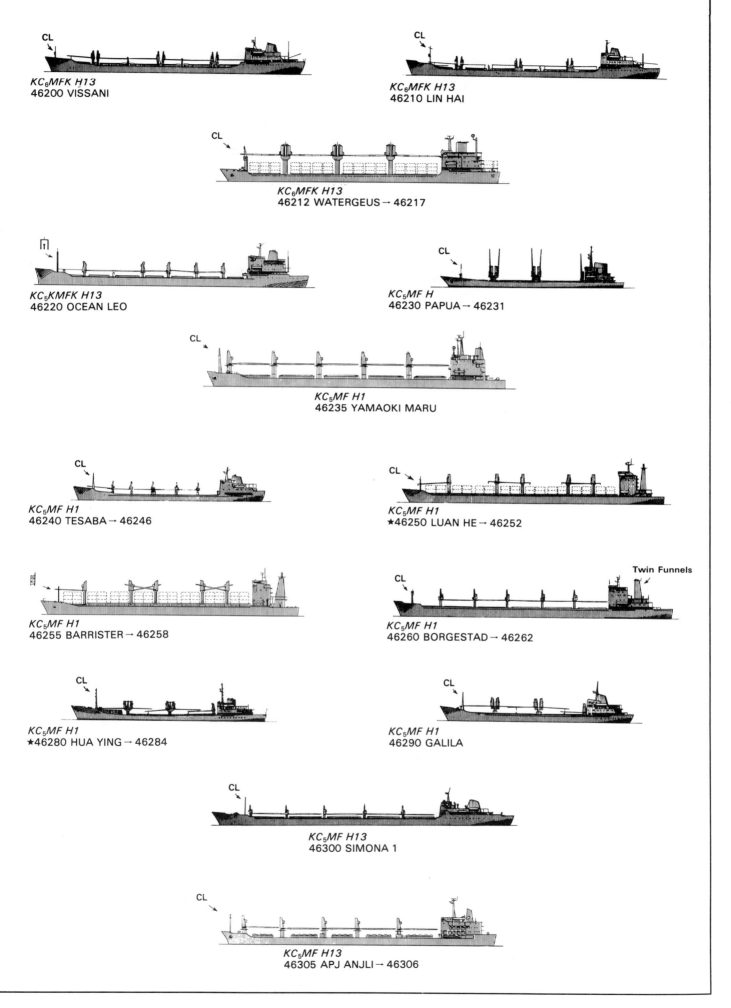

KC₆MFK H13
46200 VISSANI

KC₆MFK H13
46210 LIN HAI

KC₆MFK H13
46212 WATERGEUS → 46217

KC₅KMFK H13
46220 OCEAN LEO

KC₅MF H
46230 PAPUA → 46231

KC₅MF H1
46235 YAMAOKI MARU

KC₅MF H1
46240 TESABA → 46246

KC₅MF H1
★46250 LUAN HE → 46252

KC₅MF H1
46255 BARRISTER → 46258

Twin Funnels

KC₅MF H1
46260 BORGESTAD → 46262

KC₅MF H1
★46280 HUA YING → 46284

KC₅MF H1
46290 GALILA

KC₅MF H13
46300 SIMONA 1

KC₅MF H13
46305 APJ ANJLI → 46306

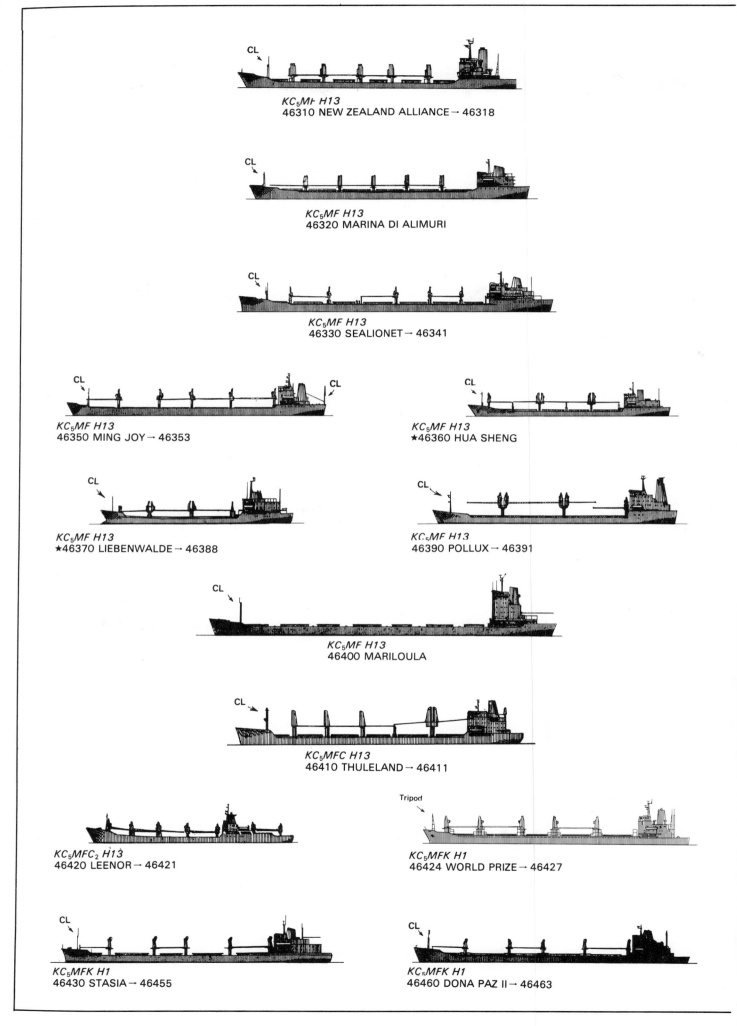

KC₅MF H13
46310 NEW ZEALAND ALLIANCE → 46318

KC₅MF H13
46320 MARINA DI ALIMURI

KC₅MF H13
46330 SEALIONET → 46341

KC₅MF H13
46350 MING JOY → 46353

KC₅MF H13
★46360 HUA SHENG

KC₅MF H13
★46370 LIEBENWALDE → 46388

KC₅MF H13
46390 POLLUX → 46391

KC₅MF H13
46400 MARILOULA

KC₅MFC H13
46410 THULELAND → 46411

KC₅MFC₂ H13
46420 LEENOR → 46421

KC₅MFK H1
46424 WORLD PRIZE → 46427

KC₅MFK H1
46430 STASIA → 46455

KC₅MFK H1
46460 DONA PAZ II → 46463

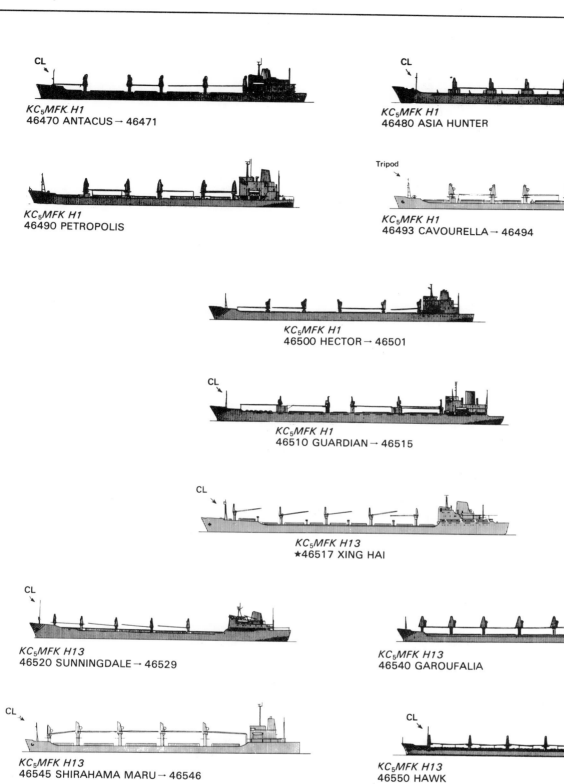

KC₅MFK H1
46470 ANTACUS → 46471

KC₅MFK H1
46480 ASIA HUNTER

KC₅MFK H1
46490 PETROPOLIS

KC₅MFK H1
46493 CAVOURELLA → 46494

KC₅MFK H1
46500 HECTOR → 46501

KC₅MFK H1
46510 GUARDIAN → 46515

KC₅MFK H13
★46517 XING HAI

KC₅MFK H13
46520 SUNNINGDALE → 46529

KC₅MFK H13
46540 GAROUFALIA

KC₅MFK H13
46545 SHIRAHAMA MARU → 46546

KC₅MFK H13
46550 HAWK

KC₅MFK H13
46555 NEPTUNE DOLPHIN → 46556

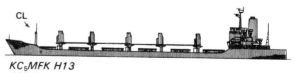

KC₅MFK H13
46560 NEW ZEALAND ALLIANCE → 46568

KC₅MFK H13
46580 ACHILLES → 46590

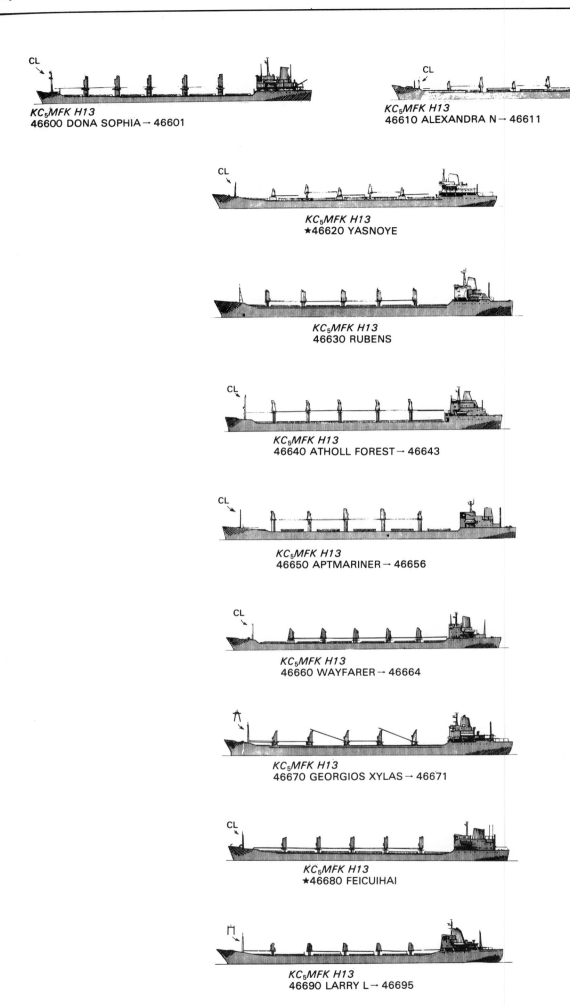

CL
KC₅MFK H13
46600 DONA SOPHIA → 46601

CL
KC₅MFK H13
46610 ALEXANDRA N → 46611

CL
KC₅MFK H13
★46620 YASNOYE

KC₅MFK H13
46630 RUBENS

CL
KC₅MFK H13
46640 ATHOLL FOREST → 46643

CL
KC₅MFK H13
46650 APTMARINER → 46656

CL
KC₅MFK H13
46660 WAYFARER → 46664

KC₅MFK H13
46670 GEORGIOS XYLAS → 46671

CL
KC₅MFK H13
★46680 FEICUIHAI

KC₅MFK H13
46690 LARRY L → 46695

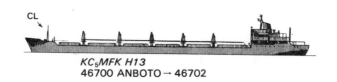

CL

KC5MFK H13
46700 ANBOTO → 46702

KC5MFK H13
46710 CAPE STROVILI → 46712

CL

KC5MFK H13
46720 NAN TA → 46722

CL

KC5MFK H13
46730 TRAMCO AMITY → 46731

KC5MFK H13
46740 P S PALIOS → 46741

CL

KC5MFK H13
★46750 BIN HAI

KC5MFK H13
46760 OCEAN LEO

CL

KC5MFK H13
46770 IBN ABDOUN → 46780

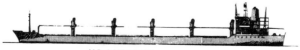

KC5MFK H13
46790 FORT YALE → 46792

KC₅MFK H13
46800 FORT NELSON → 46802

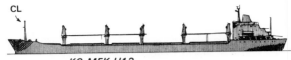

KC₅MFK H13
46810 IRISH CEDAR → 46811

KC₅MFK H13
46820 WILLIAM R ADAMS

KC₅MFK H13
46830 SONID → 46831

KC₅MFK H13
46840 EASTERN BRIDE

KC₅MFK H13
46850 HERUVIUM

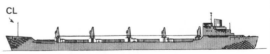

KC₅MFK H13
46860 AMSTELDIEP → 46861

KC₅MFK H13
46870 EASTERN VALLEY → 46875

KC₅MFK H13
46880 MARIA G L → 46895

KC₅MFK H13
46900 ARPAD → 46905

KC₅MFK H13
46910 GEORGIS A GEORGILIS → 46915

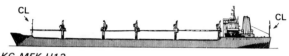

KC₅MFK H13
46920 MING JOY → 46923

KC₅MFK H13
46924 ZENO → 46929/3

KC₅MFK H13
46930 NEDROMA → 46931

KC₅MFK H13
46940 CELERINA → 46944

KC₅MFK H13
46950 CELTIC SKY

KC₅MFK H13
46951 WORLD FRATERNITY → 46957

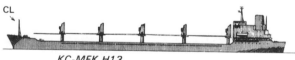

KC₅MFK H13
46960 RIMBA MERANTI → 46961

KC₅MFK H13
46970 BAHAMASTARS

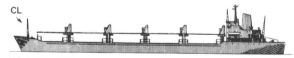

KC₅MFK H13
46980 MICHEL DELMAS

KC₅MFK H13
46990 JAVARA → 46993

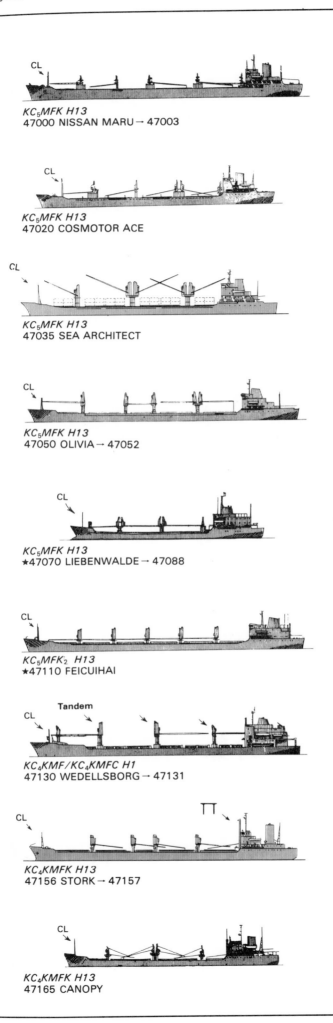
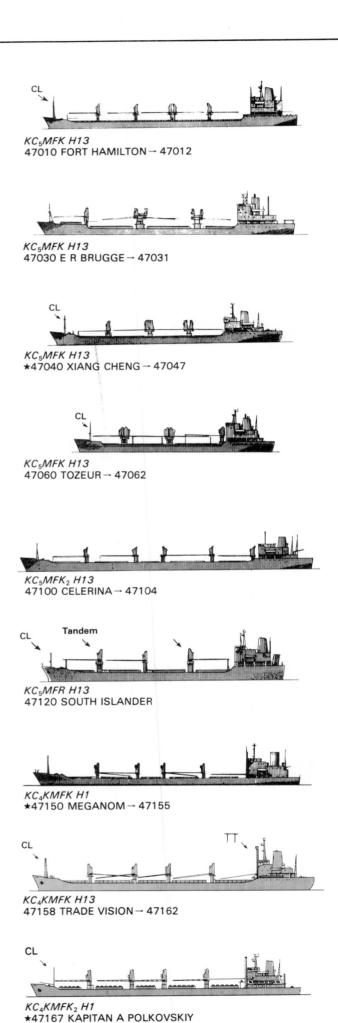

KC₅MFK H13
47000 NISSAN MARU → 47003

KC₅MFK H13
47010 FORT HAMILTON → 47012

KC₅MFK H13
47020 COSMOTOR ACE

KC₅MFK H13
47030 E R BRUGGE → 47031

KC₅MFK H13
47035 SEA ARCHITECT

KC₅MFK H13
★47040 XIANG CHENG → 47047

KC₅MFK H13
47050 OLIVIA → 47052

KC₅MFK H13
47060 TOZEUR → 47062

KC₅MFK H13
★47070 LIEBENWALDE → 47088

KC₅MFK₂ H13
47100 CELERINA → 47104

KC₅MFK₂ H13
★47110 FEICUIHAI

KC₅MFR H13
47120 SOUTH ISLANDER

KC₄KMF/KC₄KMFC H1
47130 WEDELLSBORG → 47131

KC₄KMFK H1
★47150 MEGANOM → 47155

KC₄KMFK H13
47156 STORK → 47157

KC₄KMFK H13
47158 TRADE VISION → 47162

KC₄KMFK H13
47165 CANOPY

KC₄KMFK₂ H1
★47167 KAPITAN A POLKOVSKIY

KC₄MF H
★47170 MIN YUN HAI

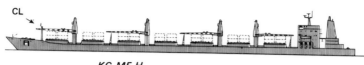

KC₄MF H
47180 RANGELOCK → 47181

KC₄MF H1
47185 CO-OP EXPRESS 1 → 47186

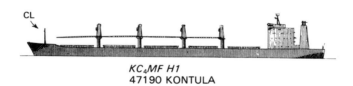

KC₄MF H1
47190 KONTULA

KC₄MF| H1
47195 NORASIA REBECCA → 47199

KC₄MF H1
47200 RADIANT VENTURE → 47211

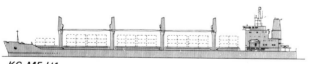

KC₄MF H1
47213 WAARDRECHT → 47215

KC₄MF H1
47216 NATHALIE DELMAS → 47219

KC₄MF H1
47220 MEERDRECHT → 47226

KC₄MF H1
47230 WINDRAIDER → 47232

KC₄MF H1
★47240 LING JIANG → 47241

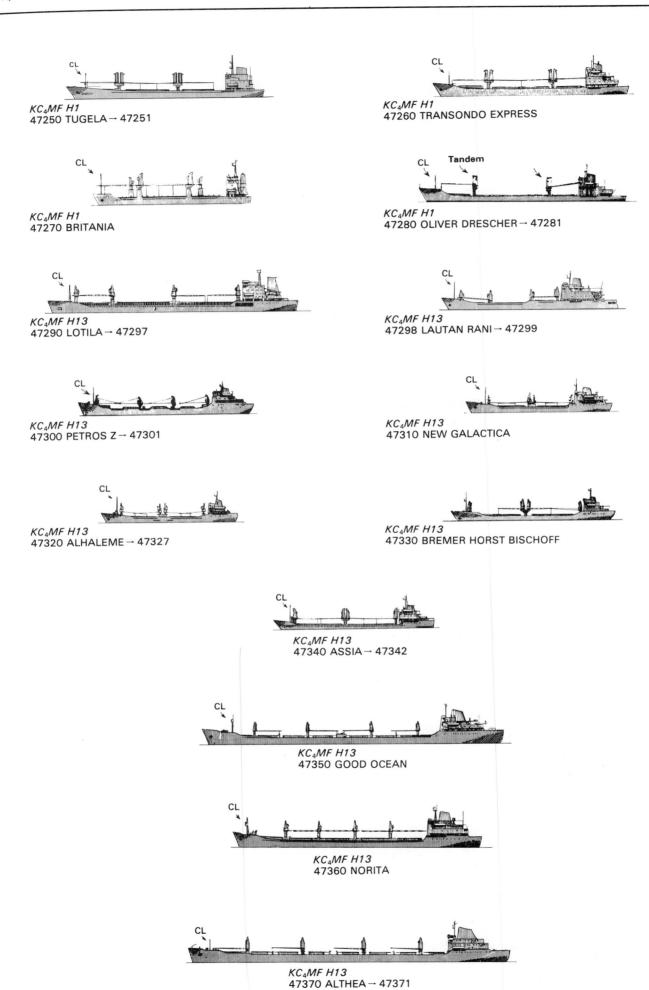

KC₄MF H1
47250 TUGELA → 47251

KC₄MF H1
47260 TRANSONDO EXPRESS

KC₄MF H1
47270 BRITANIA

KC₄MF H1
47280 OLIVER DRESCHER → 47281

KC₄MF H13
47290 LOTILA → 47297

KC₄MF H13
47298 LAUTAN RANI → 47299

KC₄MF H13
47300 PETROS Z → 47301

KC₄MF H13
47310 NEW GALACTICA

KC₄MF H13
47320 ALHALEME → 47327

KC₄MF H13
47330 BREMER HORST BISCHOFF

KC₄MF H13
47340 ASSIA → 47342

KC₄MF H13
47350 GOOD OCEAN

KC₄MF H13
47360 NORITA

KC₄MF H13
47370 ALTHEA → 47371

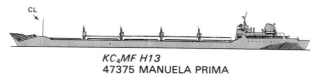

KC₄MF H13
47375 MANUELA PRIMA

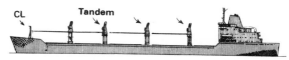

KC₄MF H13
47380 MARCHEN MAERSK → 47383

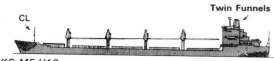

KC₄MF H13
47390 HAE YUNG EASTERN → 47399

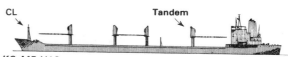

KC₄MF H13
47410 MING SPRING → 47415

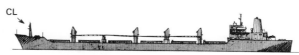

KC₄MF H13
47420 KIELDRECHT → 47421

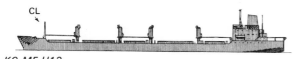

KC₄MF H13
47430 PAGNET → 47431

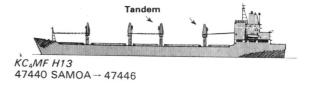

KC₄MF H13
47440 SAMOA → 47446

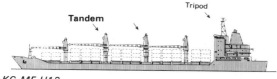

KC₄MF H13
47447 OVE SKOU

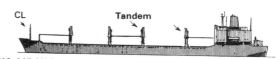

KC₄MF H13
47450 SONGKHLA → 47451

KC₄MF H13
47460 ANGELIKI H → 47461

KC₄MF H13
47470 KYRIAKOULA D, LEMOS

KC₄MF H13
47480 AL TAMMAR

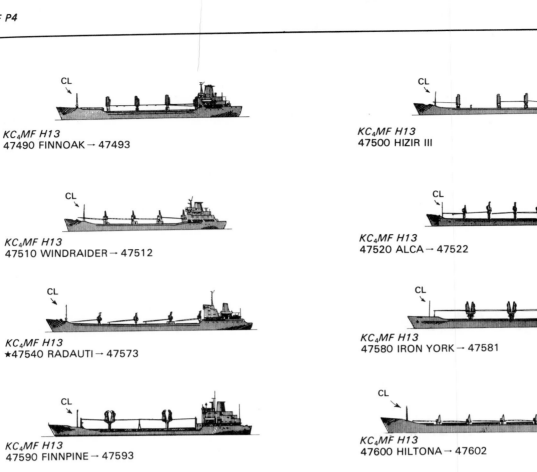

KC₄MF H13
47490 FINNOAK → 47493

KC₄MF H13
47500 HIZIR III

KC₄MF H13
47510 WINDRAIDER → 47512

KC₄MF H13
47520 ALCA → 47522

KC₄MF H13
★47540 RADAUTI → 47573

KC₄MF H13
47580 IRON YORK → 47581

KC₄MF H13
47590 FINNPINE → 47593

KC₄MF H13
47600 HILTONA → 47602

KC₄MF H13
★47610 TRANSPORTOWIEC → 47613

KC₄MF H13
47615 KARIN → 47616

KC₄MF H3
47620 SHAYMA THREE

KC₄MFC H1
47630 TAMARITA → 47631

KC₄MFC H13
47635 NEDLLOYD MARSEILLE → 47637

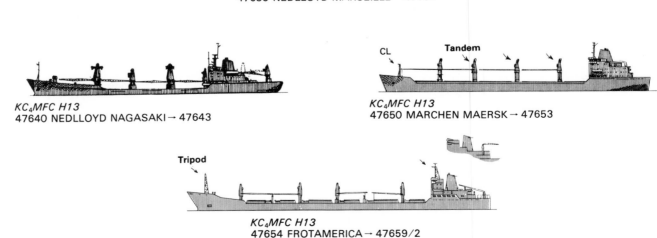

KC₄MFC H13
47640 NEDLLOYD NAGASAKI → 47643

KC₄MFC H13
47650 MARCHEN MAERSK → 47653

KC₄MFC H13
47654 FROTAMERICA → 47659/2

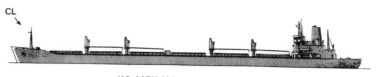

CL

KC₄MFK H1
47660 ALKYONIS → 47661

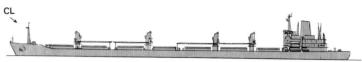

CL

KC₄MFK H1
47665 GENERAL AGUINALDO → 47666

CL

KC₄MFK H1
47670 FAIR WIND

CL

KC₄MFK H1
47671 MAERSK SERANGOON → 47672

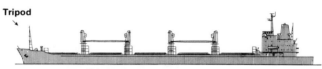

Tripod

KC₄MFK H1
47674 MARITIME VICTOR → 47677

CL

KC₄MFK H1
47680 MARGARITA → 47681

CL

KC₄MFK H1
47690 OLYMPIC PHOENIX → 47693

CL

KC₄MFK H1
47700 DAMODAR TANABE → 47701

CL

KC₄MFK H1
★47710 DUBROVNIK → 47711

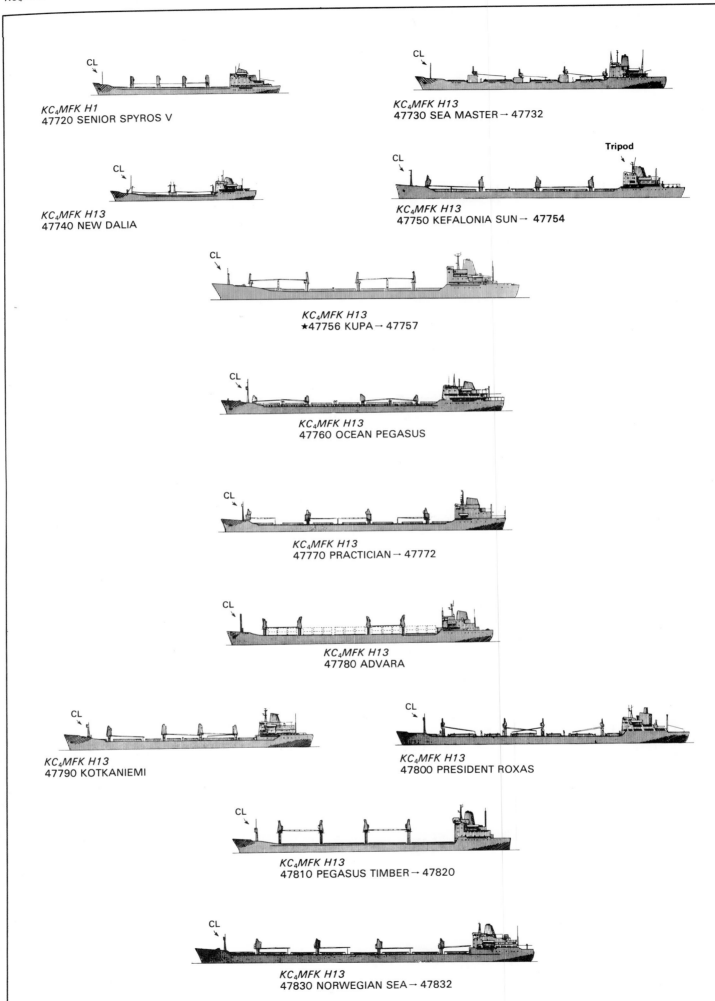

CL

KC₄MFK H1
47720 SENIOR SPYROS V

CL

KC₄MFK H13
47730 SEA MASTER → 47732

CL

KC₄MFK H13
47740 NEW DALIA

CL

Tripod

KC₄MFK H13
47750 KEFALONIA SUN → 47754

CL

KC₄MFK H13
★47756 KUPA → 47757

CL

KC₄MFK H13
47760 OCEAN PEGASUS

CL

KC₄MFK H13
47770 PRACTICIAN → 47772

CL

KC₄MFK H13
47780 ADVARA

CL

KC₄MFK H13
47790 KOTKANIEMI

CL

KC₄MFK H13
47800 PRESIDENT ROXAS

CL

KC₄MFK H13
47810 PEGASUS TIMBER → 47820

CL

KC₄MFK H13
47830 NORWEGIAN SEA → 47832

KC₄MFK H13
47840 SEA WIND

KC₄MFK H13
47850 MARE ITALICO

KC₄MFK H13
47860 ALKYON

KC₄MFK H13
47870 KILMUN → 47873

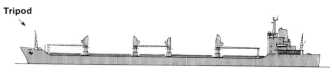

KC₄MFK H13
47874 HOLCK-LARSEN → 47879

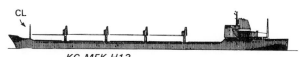

KC₄MFK H13
47880 STAR CAPELLA → 47885

KC₄MFK H13
47890 NORITA

KC₄MFK H13
47900 PAGNET → 47901

KC₄MFK H13
47910 CHIARA S → 47911

KC₄MFK H13
47920 RIO PLATA → 47922

KC₄MFK H13
47925 PEPE LE MOKO → 47926

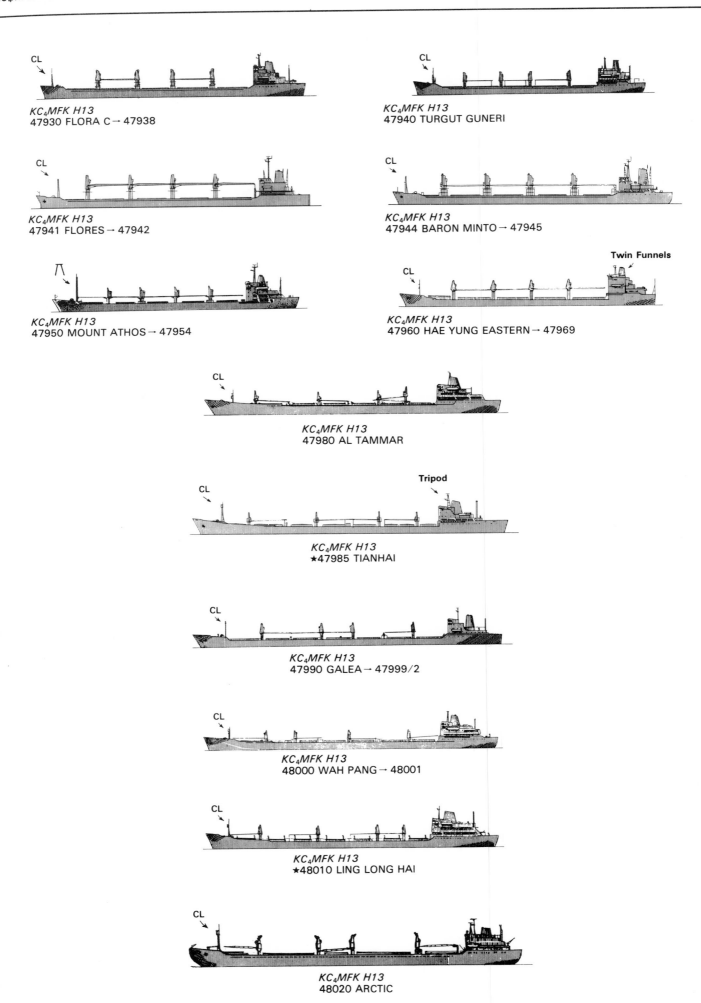

CL

KC₄MFK H13
47930 FLORA C → 47938

CL

KC₄MFK H13
47940 TURGUT GUNERI

CL

KC₄MFK H13
47941 FLORES → 47942

CL

KC₄MFK H13
47944 BARON MINTO → 47945

KC₄MFK H13
47950 MOUNT ATHOS → 47954

Twin Funnels

CL

KC₄MFK H13
47960 HAE YUNG EASTERN → 47969

CL

KC₄MFK H13
47980 AL TAMMAR

Tripod

CL

KC₄MFK H13
★47985 TIANHAI

CL

KC₄MFK H13
47990 GALEA → 47999/2

CL

KC₄MFK H13
48000 WAH PANG → 48001

CL

KC₄MFK H13
★48010 LING LONG HAI

CL

KC₄MFK H13
48020 ARCTIC

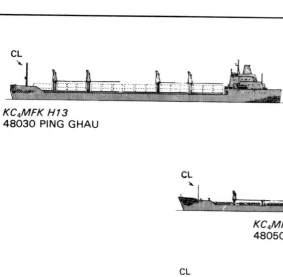

KC₄MFK H13
48030 PING GHAU

KC₄MFK H13
48040 IRAN DAHR → 48043

KC₄MFK H13
48050 JAG SHAKTI → 48061

KC₄MFK H13
★48062 DINARA → 48066

KC₄MFK H13
48070 BANDERAS → 48071

KC₄MFK H13
48072 REGINA FERRAZ → 48079/2

KC₄MFK H13
48080 VENI II → 48084

KC₄MFK H13
48100 CORDIALITY → 48102

KC₄MFK H13
48110 POSEIDON → 48111

KC₄MFK H13
48120 GLYFADA SUN

KC₄MFK H13
48140 CAPTAIN NICOLAS → 48141

KC₄MFK H13
48150 ARIETTA GREGOS → 48158

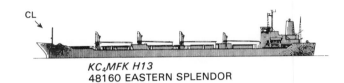

KC₄MFK H13
48160 EASTERN SPLENDOR

KC₄MFK H13
48170 AQUACHARM → 48178

KC₄MFK H13
48180 AEGIS MAJESTIC → 48197

KC₄MFK H13
48200 KAVO MATAPAS → 48201

KC₄MFK H13
★48210 PINO DEL AGUA → 48215

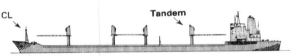

KC₄MFK H13
48220 MING SPRING → 48225

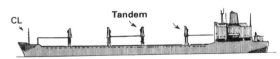

KC₄MFK H13
48230 SONGKHLA → 48231

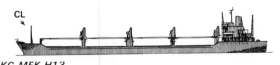

KC₄MFK H13
48250 SEIYEI MARU

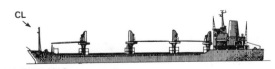

KC₄MFK H13
48260 ANDRE DELMAS → 48261

KC₄MFK H13
48270 KOREAN PEARL

KC₄MFK H13
48280 JAMAICAN STARS → 48283

KC₄MFK H13
48290 ATLANTIS EXPRESS

KC₄MFK H13
48300 WELLPARK → 48302

KC₄MFK H13
48310 BLUEBIRD → 48311

KC₄MFK H13
48340 KASSANDRA → 48342

KC₄MFK H13
48350 SIAM VENTURE

KC₄MFK H13
48360 JAMAICA FAREWELL → 48361

KC₄MFK H13
48362 VISHVA PANKAJ → 48367

KC₄MFK H13
48370 CORRIENTES II → 48379

KC₄MFKC H13
48380 TRANSOCEAN REEFER

KC₄MFKC H13
48383 ANWAR → 48385/8

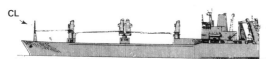

KC₄MFKR H3
48390 SEKI ROKAKO → 48391

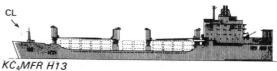

KC₄MFR H13
48400 ILE DE LA REUNION → 48405

KC₃KC₅MFK H1
48410 MILOS → 48411

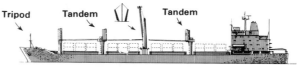

KC₃KC₂MF H1
48420 NARA → 48423

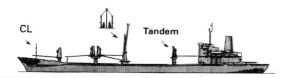

KC₃KCMF H1
★48430 IVAN ZAGUBANSKI → 48466

KC₃KCMF H13
48470 HALLA PILOT → 48471

KC₃KCMFK H13
★48480 PREDEAL

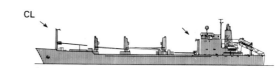

KC₃KMF H1
48485 BLUMENTHAL → 48486

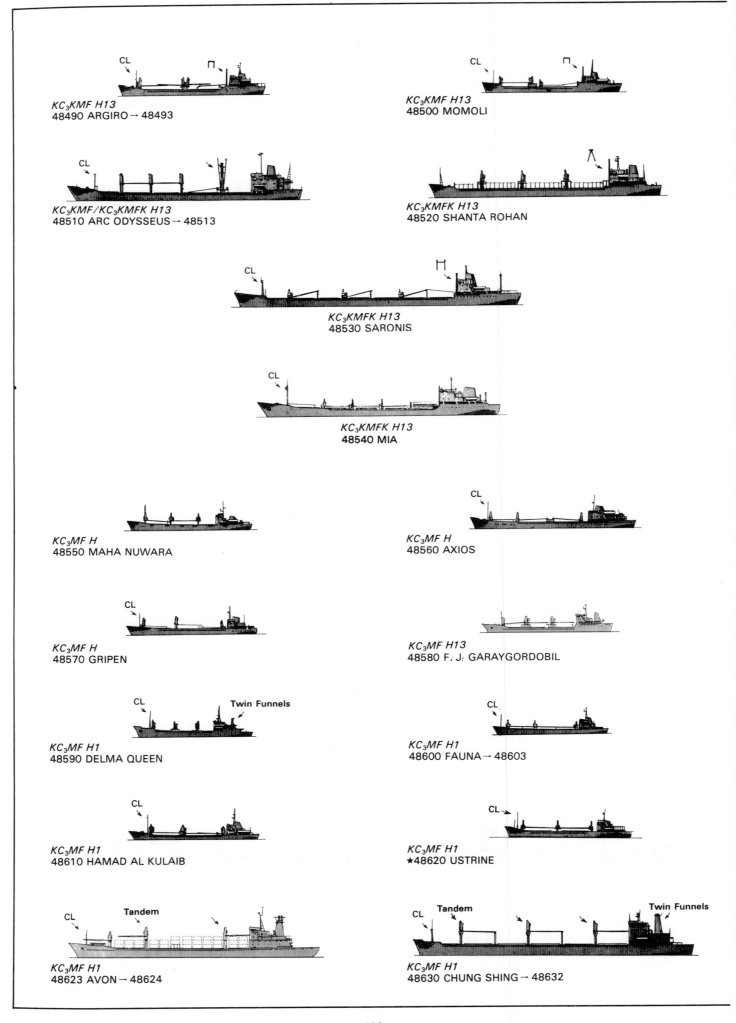

KC₃KMF H13
48490 ARGIRO → 48493

KC₃KMF H13
48500 MOMOLI

KC₃KMF/KC₃KMFK H13
48510 ARC ODYSSEUS → 48513

KC₃KMFK H13
48520 SHANTA ROHAN

KC₃KMFK H13
48530 SARONIS

KC₃KMFK H13
48540 MIA

KC₃MF H
48550 MAHA NUWARA

KC₃MF H
48560 AXIOS

KC₃MF H
48570 GRIPEN

KC₃MF H13
48580 F. J. GARAYGORDOBIL

KC₃MF H1
48590 DELMA QUEEN

KC₃MF H1
48600 FAUNA → 48603

KC₃MF H1
48610 HAMAD AL KULAIB

KC₃MF H1
★48620 USTRINE

KC₃MF H1
48623 AVON → 48624

KC₃MF H1
48630 CHUNG SHING → 48632

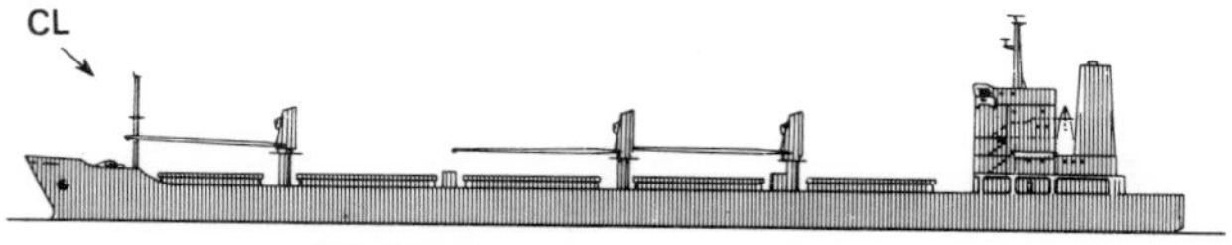

KC_3MF H1
★48635 GOSPIC → 48637

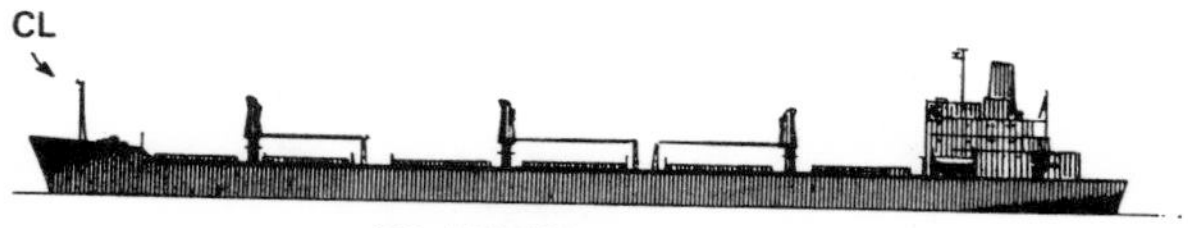

KC_3MF H1
48640 DASHAKI

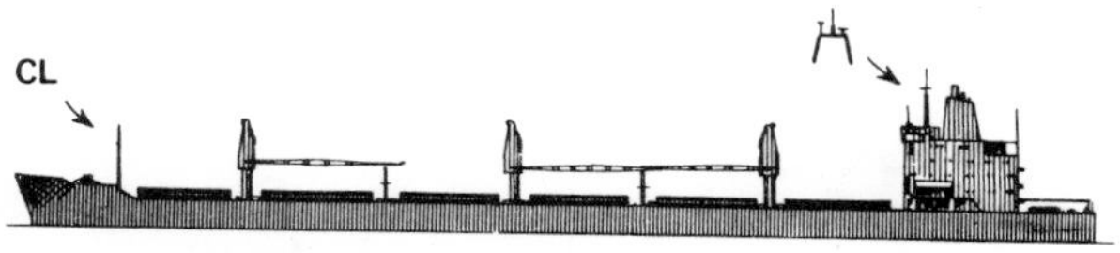

KC_3MF H1
48650 TORM HERDIS → 48653

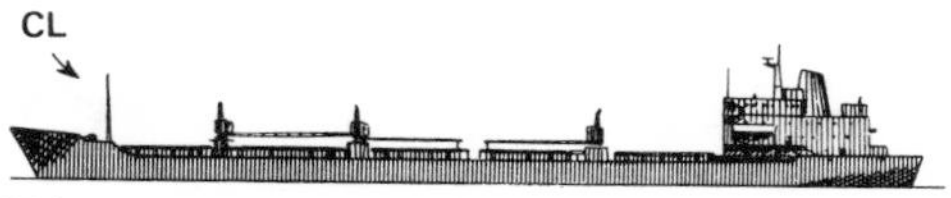

KC_3MF H1
★48660 KOPALNIA GRZYBOW → 48661

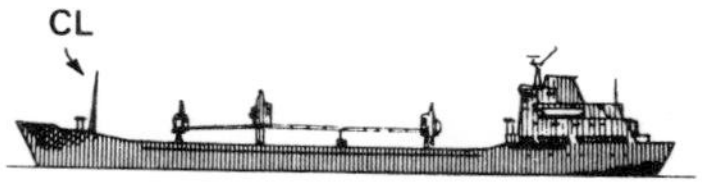

KC_3MF H1
48670 HOELIEN → 48671

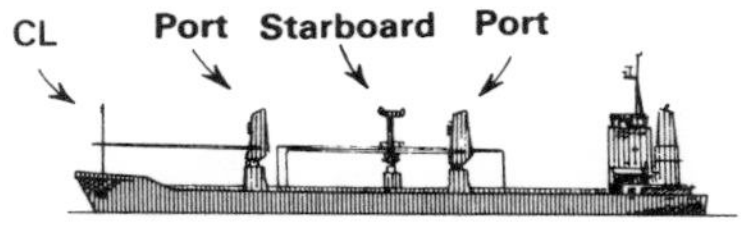

KC_3MF H1
48680 CONTI BELGICA

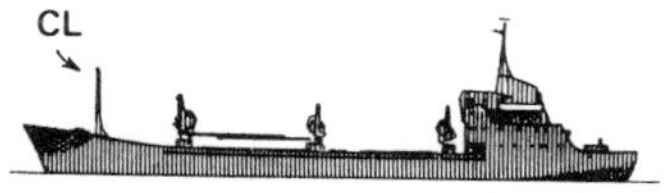

KC_3MF H1
48690 GULF VENTURE

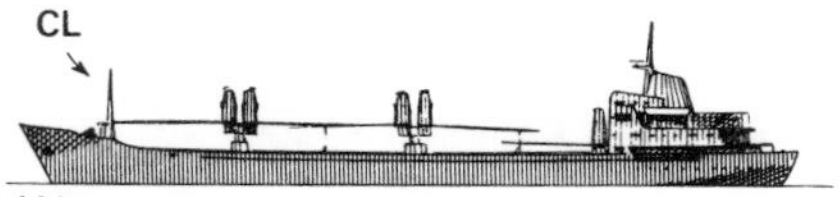

KC_3MF H1
48700 GALILA

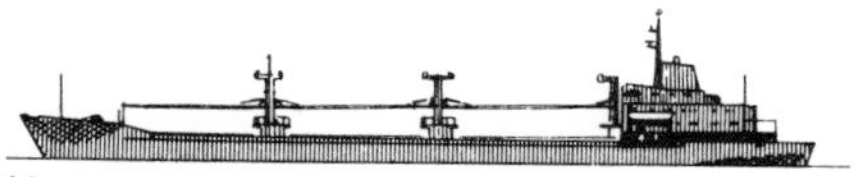

KC_3MF H1
48710 KEMAL II → 48712

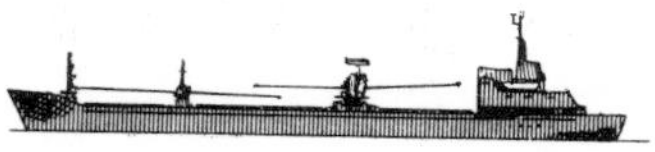

KC_3MF H123
48720 MIRAMAR PRIMA → 48721

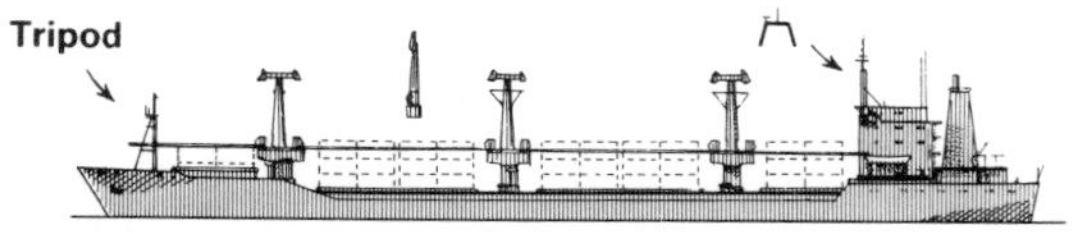

KC_3MF H13
48730 SLOMAN MERCUR → 48731

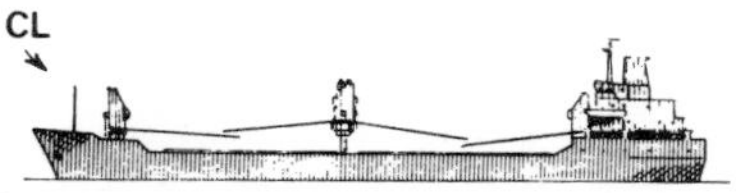

KC_3MF H13
48740 CORONA

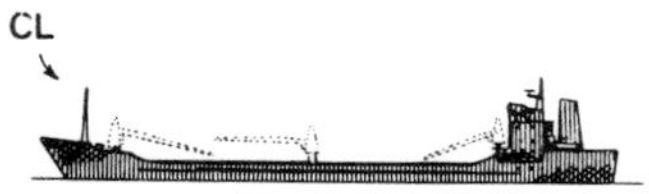

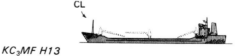

KC_3MF H13
48750 LESLIE GAULT → 48753

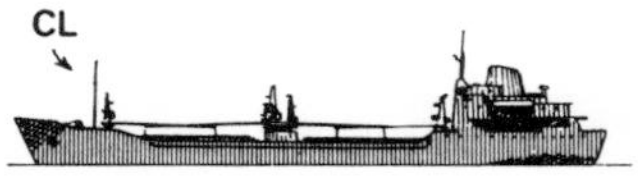

KC_3MF H13
48760 NEW GALACTICA

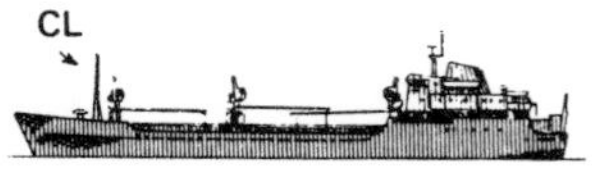

KC_3MF H13
★48770 RISNJAK → 48771

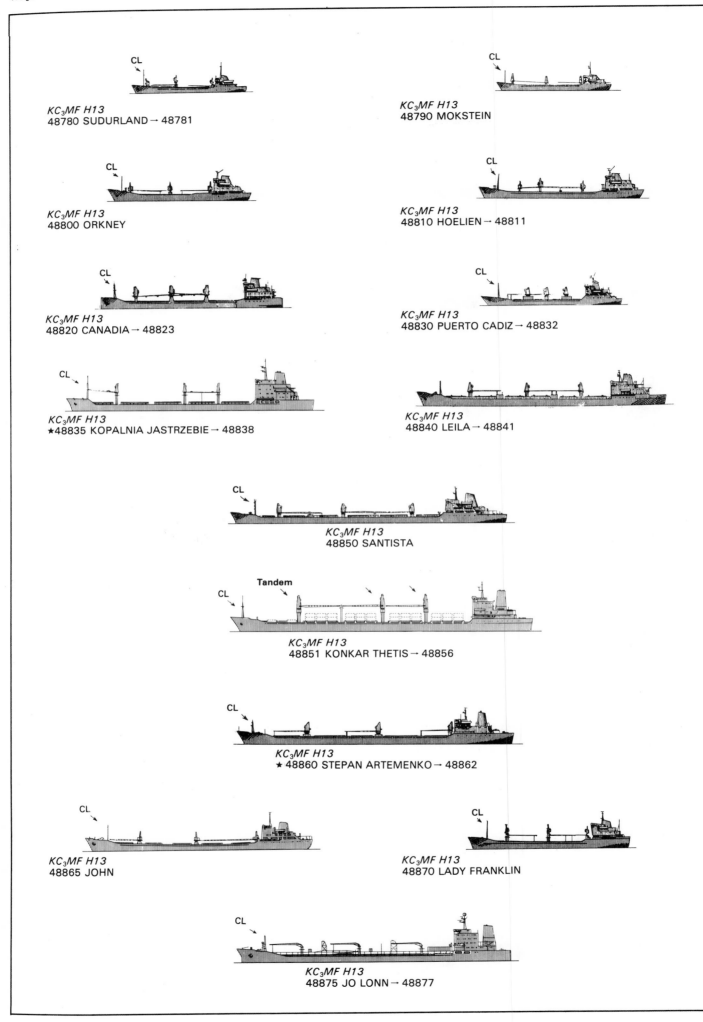

KC₃MF H13
48780 SUDURLAND → 48781

KC₃MF H13
48790 MOKSTEIN

KC₃MF H13
48800 ORKNEY

KC₃MF H13
48810 HOELIEN → 48811

KC₃MF H13
48820 CANADIA → 48823

KC₃MF H13
48830 PUERTO CADIZ → 48832

KC₃MF H13
★48835 KOPALNIA JASTRZEBIE → 48838

KC₃MF H13
48840 LEILA → 48841

KC₃MF H13
48850 SANTISTA

Tandem

KC₃MF H13
48851 KONKAR THETIS → 48856

KC₃MF H13
★ 48860 STEPAN ARTEMENKO → 48862

KC₃MF H13
48865 JOHN

KC₃MF H13
48870 LADY FRANKLIN

KC₃MF H13
48875 JO LONN → 48877

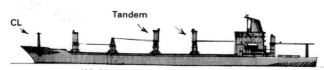

KC₃MFC H1
48880.HELENE DELMAS → 48883

KC₃MFC H1
48890 VAN DYCK → 48891

KC₃MFC H13
48900 LA PALLICE → 48910

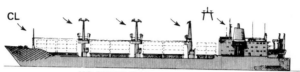

KC₃MFCR H13
48920 ELISABETH MAERSK

KC₃MFK H
48930 BUNGA SETAWAR → 48933

KC₃MFK H
48940 TOHOKU MARU → 48951

KC₃MFK H
48960 WORLD WOOD → 48962

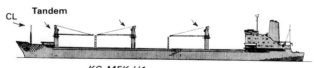

KC₃MFK H1
48970 ARCTIC TROLL → 48973

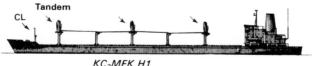

KC₃MFK H1
48980 WILLINE TARO

KC₃MFK H1
48990 WORLD FINANCE → 48996

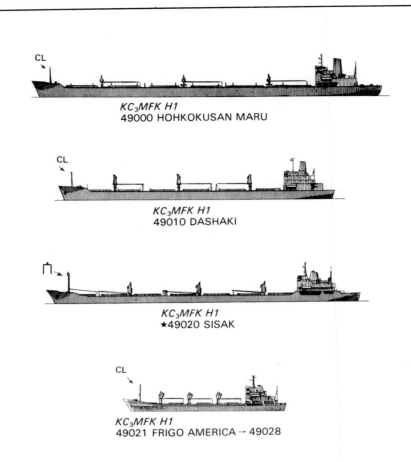

CL
KC₃MFK H1
49000 HOHKOKUSAN MARU

CL
KC₃MFK H1
49010 DASHAKI

KC₃MFK H1
★49020 SISAK

CL
KC₃MFK H1
49021 FRIGO AMERICA → 49028

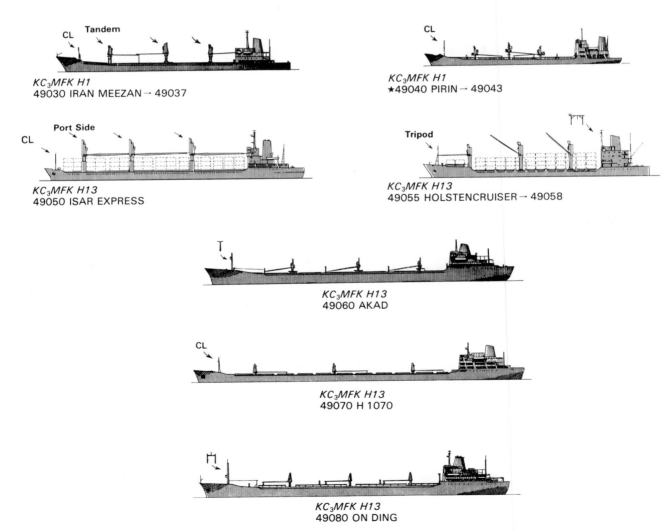

Tandem
CL
KC₃MFK H1
49030 IRAN MEEZAN → 49037

CL
KC₃MFK H1
★49040 PIRIN → 49043

Port Side
CL
KC₃MFK H13
49050 ISAR EXPRESS

Tripod
KC₃MFK H13
49055 HOLSTENCRUISER → 49058

KC₃MFK H13
49060 AKAD

CL
KC₃MFK H13
49070 H 1070

KC₃MFK H13
49080 ON DING

KC₃MFK H13
49090 TASMAN SEA

KC₃MFK H13
★49100 YASENYEVO → 49101

KC₃MFK H13
49110 ALEXANDROS G TSAVLIRIS → 49111

KC₃MFK H13
49120 AZTECA

KC₃MFK H13
★49130 YING GE HAI → 49131

KC₃MFK H13
49140 THALASSOPOROS

KC₃MFK H13
49150 HADJANNA → 49152

KC₃MFK H13
★49160 BUZLUDJA → 49163

KC₃MFK H13
49170 NORDKAP → 49174

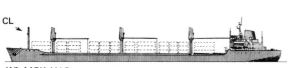

KC₃MFK H13
49180 SHARK BAY → 49181

KC₃MFK H13
49190 GEORGIAN GLORY → 49191

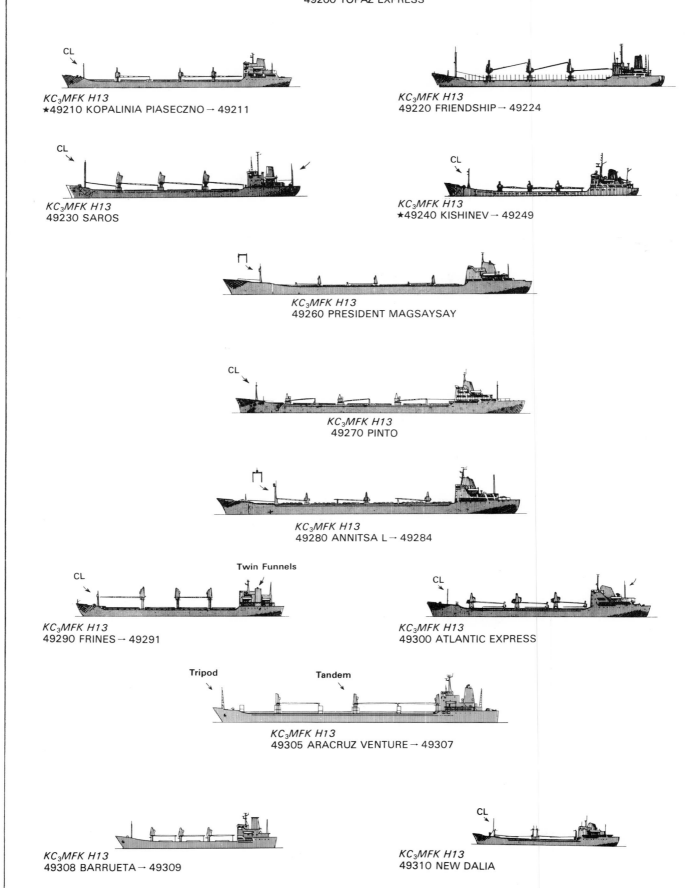

KC₃MFK H13
49200 TOPAZ EXPRESS

KC₃MFK H13
★49210 KOPALINIA PIASECZNO → 49211

KC₃MFK H13
49220 FRIENDSHIP → 49224

KC₃MFK H13
49230 SAROS

KC₃MFK H13
★49240 KISHINEV → 49249

KC₃MFK H13
49260 PRESIDENT MAGSAYSAY

KC₃MFK H13
49270 PINTO

KC₃MFK H13
49280 ANNITSA L → 49284

Twin Funnels

KC₃MFK H13
49290 FRINES → 49291

KC₃MFK H13
49300 ATLANTIC EXPRESS

Tripod   Tandem

KC₃MFK H13
49305 ARACRUZ VENTURE → 49307

KC₃MFK H13
49308 BARRUETA → 49309

KC₃MFK H13
49310 NEW DALIA

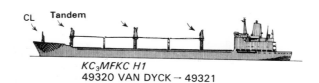

KC₃MFKC H1
49320 VAN DYCK → 49321

KC₃MFKR H13
49330 MEIHOU → 49331

KC₃MFM H13
49340 PARMENION

KC₃MFMC H13
★49342 VIKTOR TKACHYOV → 49349

KC₃MFR H13
49350 WHITE NILE → 49354

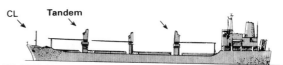

KC₃MFR H13
49360 SOUTH ISLANDER

KC₃MKFK H13
49370 RAINBOW 1

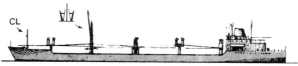

KC₂KC₄MFK H13
49380 IBN SHUHAID → 49414

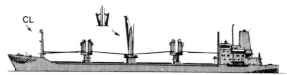

KC₂KC₂KMF H1
49420 NEDLLOYD BAHRAIN → 49423

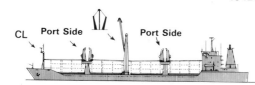

KC₂KC₂MF H13
49425 SANDRA WESCH → 49428

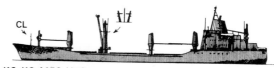

KC₂KC₂MFC H13
49430 JUMPA → 49433

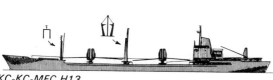

KC₂KC₂MFC H13
49440 KIEL → 49441

KC₂KC₂MFK H13
49450 KSAR ETTIR → 49452

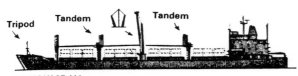

KC₂KCKMF H1
49460 NARA → 49463

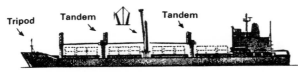

KC₂KCMF H1
49510 NARA → 49513

KC₂KCMF H13
49530 ANJOU → 49532

KC₂KCMFK H1
49550 EIFFEL → 49553

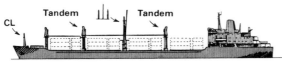

KC₂KCMFKC H13
49580 THALASSINI MANA → 49581

KC₂KMF H
49600 AMERICA → 49602

KC₂KMF H1
49620 EAST RAINBOW → 49621

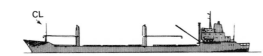

KC₂KMF H13
49640 TRISTAN → 49642

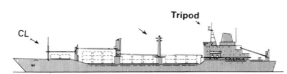

KC₂KMFC H13
★49655 JACEK MALCZEWSKI → 49658

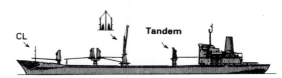

KC₂KCMF H1
★49470 IVAN ZAGUBANSKI → 49506

KC₂KCMF H13
49520 HALLA PILOT → 49521

KC₂KCMFC H13
49540 YDRA

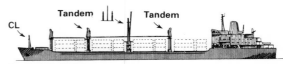

KC₂KCMFK H13
49560 THALASSINI MANA → 49561

KC₂KMF H
49590 VILLABLANCA → 49593

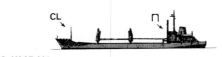

KC₂KMF H1
49610 KRIS MELELA → 49612

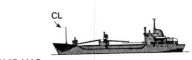

KC₂KMF H13
49630 VILLABLANCA → 49633

KC₂KMF H13
49650 ELISABETH

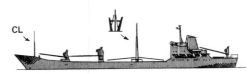

KC₂KMFC H13
49660 EGE YILDIZI → 49664

KC₂KMFK H1
49670 TAIWO→49672

KC₂KMFK H13
49680 ABUQIR → 49683

KC₂KMFK H13
49690 SANTA MONICA 1

KC₂KMFK H13
49700 RATNA MANORAMA → 49705

KC₂MC₄MF H1
49710 BANGLAR MITA → 49713

KC₂MC₃MFC H1
★49720 OMSK → 49722

KC₂MC₂MFK H13
49730 PICHIT SAMUT

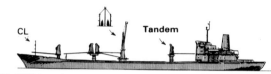

KC₂MCMF H1
49740 IVAN ZAGUBANSKI → 49777

KC₂MCMF H13
49775 HALLA PILOT → 49776

KC₂MF H
49790 AGENOR

KC₂MF H
49800 CARIBE → 49802

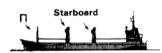

KC₂MF H
49810 LELIEGRACHT → 49829/2

KC₂MF H
49830 LEE SHARON → 49831

KC₂MF H
49840 ATLANTIC SEA

KC₂MF H1
49850 SENTOSA → 49853

KC₂MF H1
49860 LABORE → 49862

KC₂MF H1
49865 ISLAND → 49867

KC₂MF H1
49870 WESTERMOOR

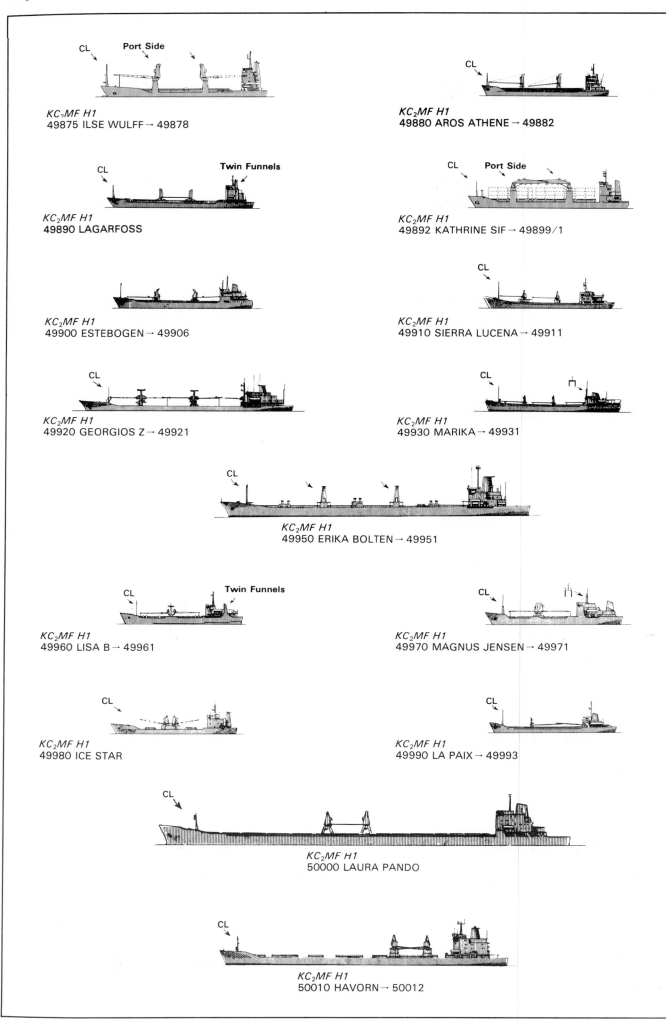

KC₂MF H1
49875 ILSE WULFF → 49878

KC₂MF H1
49880 AROS ATHENE → 49882

KC₂MF H1
49890 LAGARFOSS

KC₂MF H1
49892 KATHRINE SIF → 49899/1

KC₂MF H1
49900 ESTEBOGEN → 49906

KC₂MF H1
49910 SIERRA LUCENA → 49911

KC₂MF H1
49920 GEORGIOS Z → 49921

KC₂MF H1
49930 MARIKA → 49931

KC₂MF H1
49950 ERIKA BOLTEN → 49951

KC₂MF H1
49960 LISA B → 49961

KC₂MF H1
49970 MAGNUS JENSEN → 49971

KC₂MF H1
49980 ICE STAR

KC₂MF H1
49990 LA PAIX → 49993

KC₂MF H1
50000 LAURA PANDO

KC₂MF H1
50010 HAVORN → 50012

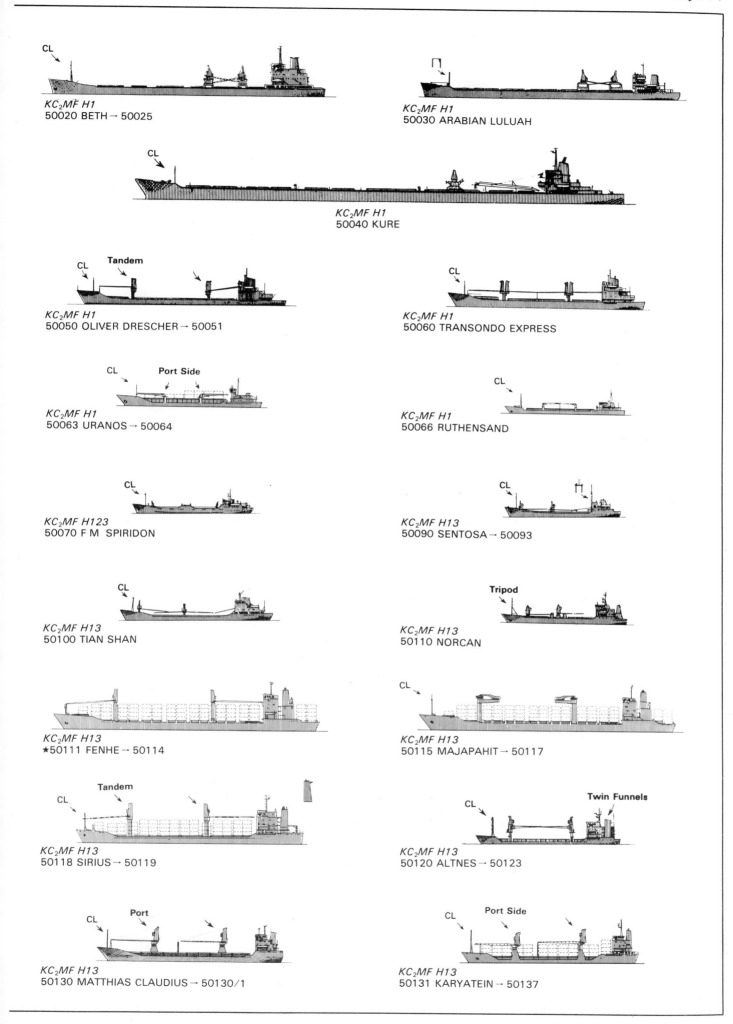

KC₂MF H1
50020 BETH → 50025

KC₂MF H1
50030 ARABIAN LULUAH

KC₂MF H1
50040 KURE

KC₂MF H1
50050 OLIVER DRESCHER → 50051

KC₂MF H1
50060 TRANSONDO EXPRESS

KC₂MF H1
50063 URANOS → 50064

KC₂MF H1
50066 RUTHENSAND

KC₂MF H123
50070 F M SPIRIDON

KC₂MF H13
50090 SENTOSA → 50093

KC₂MF H13
50100 TIAN SHAN

KC₂MF H13
50110 NORCAN

KC₂MF H13
★50111 FENHE → 50114

KC₂MF H13
50115 MAJAPAHIT → 50117

KC₂MF H13
50118 SIRIUS → 50119

KC₂MF H13
50120 ALTNES → 50123

KC₂MF H13
50130 MATTHIAS CLAUDIUS → 50130/1

KC₂MF H13
50131 KARYATEIN → 50137

KC₂MF H13
50140 HANSETOR → 50143

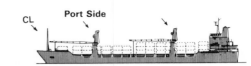

KC₂MF H13
50145 WESTERLAND → 50152

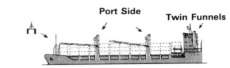

KC₂MF H13
50155 VILLE DE GABES → 50157

KC₂MF H13
50160 LEMAR → 50161

KC₂MF H13
50180 ANEMOS → 50181

KC₂MF H13
50190 MARGARETHA SMITS → 50194

KC₂MF H13
50200 URRIDAFOSS → 50205

KC₂MF H13
50210 RIO BESAYA → 50212

KC₂MF H13
50220 HANIA T → 50221

KC₂MF H13
50230 FRISIAN LINER

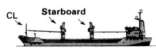

KC₂MF H13
50240 DELFBORG

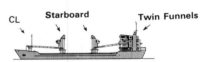

KC₂MF H13
50243 CLAUDIA SMITS → 50245

KC₂MF H13
50250 VISTEN

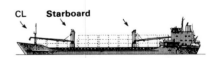

KC₂MF H13
50260 BERNHARD S → 50262

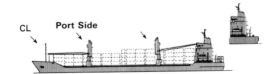

KC₂MF H13
50263 AUSTRALIAN EAGLE → 50269/6

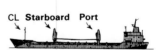

KC₂MF H13
50270 JUNIOR LILIAN

KC₂MF H13
★50280 SOVIETSKIY VOIN → 50299

KC₂MF H13
50310 PEP STAR → 50313

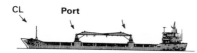

KC₂MF H13
50320 PUNTA ARENAS

KC₂MF H13
50330 CARIB DAWN → 50333

KC₂MF H13
50340 ESTEBOGEN → 50344

KC₂MF H13
50350 BUNGA PENAGA → 50351

KC₂MF H13
50370 ALTAIR → 50371

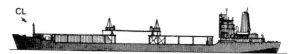

KC₂MF H13
50380 PUERTO RICO → 50385

KC₂MF H13
50390 SIR BEDIVERE → 50395

KC₂MF H13
50400 CAPO MELE → 50401

KC₂MF H13
50410 BIAKH → 50417

KC₂MF H13
50420 MALOJA → 50421

KC₂MF H13
★50430 LE DU → 50431

KC₂MF H13
★50440 MARLOW → 50450

KC₂MF H13
★50460 BOLESLAWIEC → 50470

KC₂MF H13
50480 BOXY → 50481

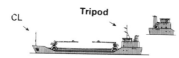

KC₂MF H13
50485 NORBRIT FAITH → 50486

KC₂MF H13
50490 ATLANTIC FISHER → 50492

KC₂MF H13
50510 FARNES → 50511

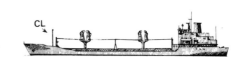

KC₂MF H13
50520 FINNPINE → 50523

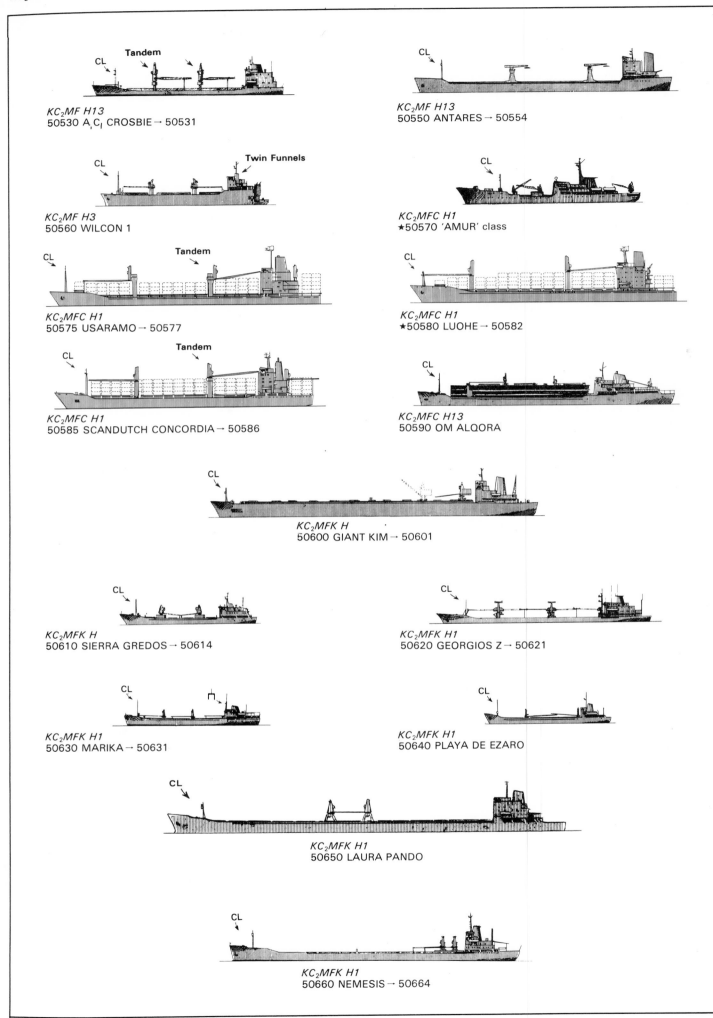

KC₂MF H13
50530 A,C, CROSBIE → 50531

KC₂MF H13
50550 ANTARES → 50554

KC₂MF H3
50560 WILCON 1

KC₂MFC H1
★50570 'AMUR' class

KC₂MFC H1
50575 USARAMO → 50577

KC₂MFC H1
★50580 LUOHE → 50582

KC₂MFC H1
50585 SCANDUTCH CONCORDIA → 50586

KC₂MFC H13
50590 OM ALQORA

KC₂MFK H
50600 GIANT KIM → 50601

KC₂MFK H
50610 SIERRA GREDOS → 50614

KC₂MFK H1
50620 GEORGIOS Z → 50621

KC₂MFK H1
50630 MARIKA → 50631

KC₂MFK H1
50640 PLAYA DE EZARO

KC₂MFK H1
50650 LAURA PANDO

KC₂MFK H1
50660 NEMESIS → 50664

KC₂MFK H1
★50670 GRIGORIY ALEKSEYEV → 50671

KC₂MFK H1
50680 BAHIA PORTETE → 50693

KC₂MFK H1
50700 RASELTIN → 50703

KC₂MFK H13
50704 AFRICAN GARDENIA → 50709/1

KC₂MFK H13
50710 LEMAR → 50711

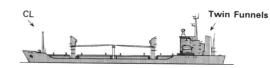

KC₂MFK H13
50720 FJELLNES → 50721

KC₂MFK H13
★50730 SOVIETSKAYA YAKUTIYA → 50762

KC₂MFK H13
★50763 VASILIY SHUKSHIN → 50769

KC₂MFK H13
★50770 BAKU → 50788

KC₂MFK H13
50800 HVASSAFELL → 50801

KC₂MFK H13
50810 MEONIA

KC₂MFK H13
50820 BIAKH → 50827

KC₂MFK H13
50830 CAPO MELE → 50831

KC₂MFK H13
50840 DOLLART → 50843

KC₂MFK H13
50850 PUNTA ARENAS

KC₂MFK H13
50860 MIRAMAR → 50861

KC₂MFK H13
50870 JAMAICA FAREWELL → 50871

KC₂MFK H13
50880 CLARA CLAUSEN

KC₂MFK H13
50890 JAPAN TUNA No 2

KC₂MFM H13
★50900 DOLMATOVO

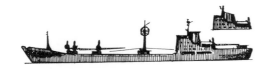

KC₂M₂FC H13
★50910 KASIMOV → 50918

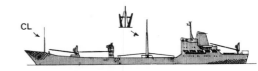

KC₂M₂FC H13
50930 EGE YILDIZI → 50934

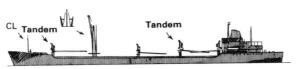

KCKC₃MFK H13
50940 IBN SHUHAID → 50974

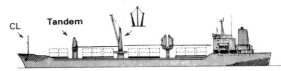

KCKC₂MF H13
50980 TABORA → 50981

KCKC₂MF H13
50990 DIJEY → 50991

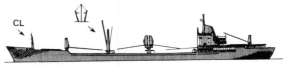

KCKC₂MFC H13
51000 VILLE DE MARSEILLE → 51002

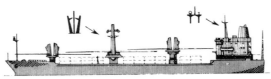

KCKC₂MFK H13
51010 WAKANAMI MARU → 51013

KCKCKCKMFK H1
51020 BUNKO MARU

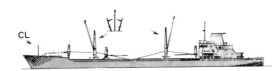

KCKCKCMF H1
51030 VALERIA → 51036

KCKCKCMF H1
51040 IBERIA

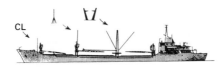

KCKCKCMF H13
51050 BOA ESPERANCA → 51052

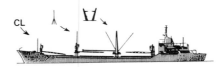

KCKCKCMFK H13
51060 MARCOS SOUZA DANTAS

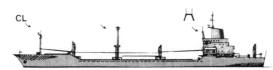

KCKCKMFC H13
51070 CREUSE → 51076

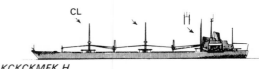

KCKCKMFK H
51080 KOTA MUTIARA → 51085

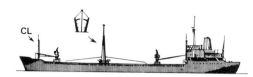

KCKCKMFK H13
51090 BOIN → 51091

KCKCKMFK H13
51100 YOUNG SPORTSMAN → 51101

KCKCKCMFK H13
51110 JESBON → 51113

KCKCKMFK₂ H1
51120 OCEAN ADVENTURE → 51121

KCKCMF H1
51130 WOLWOL → 51131

KCKCMF H13
51140 KANGUK → 51141

KCKCMF H13
51150 CITY OF TEMA → 51151

KCKCMF H13
51160 IRAN MEEAD → 51164

KCKCMF H13
51170 FRANKY → 51171

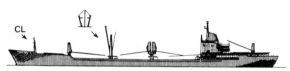

KCKCMFC H13
51180 VILLE DE MARSEILLE → 51182

KCKCMFK H1
51190 LOS TEQUES → 51191

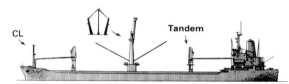

KCKCMFK H13
51210 ALTAI MARU → 51211

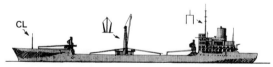

KCKCMFK H13
51220 WAKAUME MARU

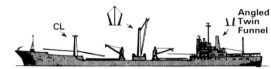

KCKCMFK H13
51230 IRAN NAHAD

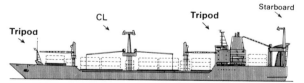

KCKCMFMR H13
51235 COSTA ARABICA → 51236

KCK₂CMFCK H13
51240 FORUM CRAFTSMAN

KCK₁₂MFC H13
51250 IRON CARPENTARIA → 51251

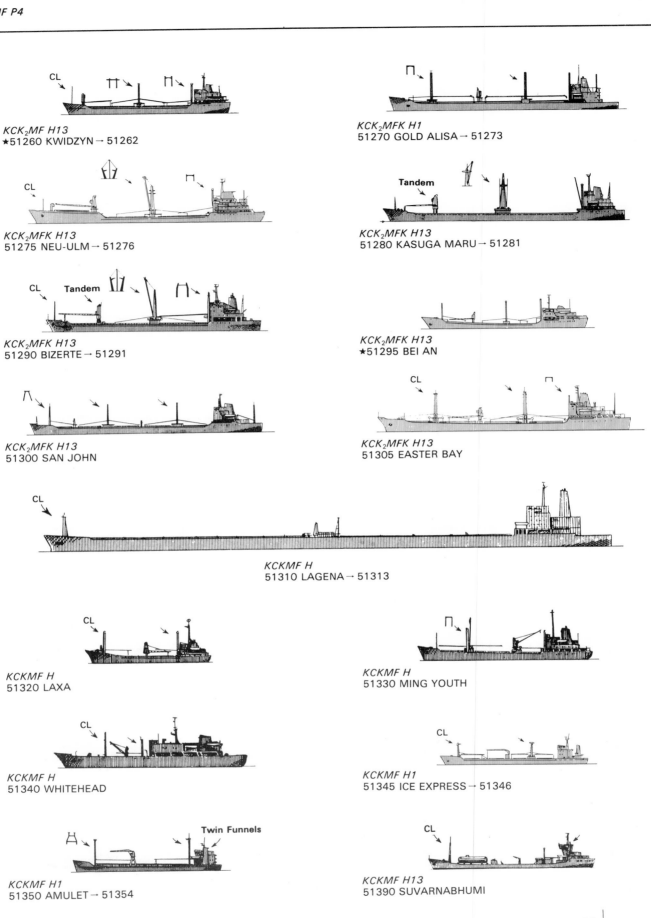

KCK₂MF H13
★51260 KWIDZYN → 51262

KCK₂MFK H1
51270 GOLD ALISA → 51273

KCK₂MFK H13
51275 NEU-ULM → 51276

KCK₂MFK H13
51280 KASUGA MARU → 51281

KCK₂MFK H13
51290 BIZERTE → 51291

KCK₂MFK H13
★51295 BEI AN

KCK₂MFK H13
51300 SAN JOHN

KCK₂MFK H13
51305 EASTER BAY

KCKMF H
51310 LAGENA → 51313

KCKMF H
51320 LAXA

KCKMF H
51330 MING YOUTH

KCKMF H
51340 WHITEHEAD

KCKMF H1
51345 ICE EXPRESS → 51346

KCKMF H1
51350 AMULET → 51354

Twin Funnels

KCKMF H13
51390 SUVARNABHUMI

KCKMF H13
51400 STROMBOLI → 51401

KCKMFK H1
51420 MALACCA MARU

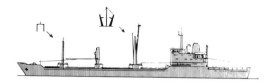

KCKMFK H13
51423 EL OBEID → 51427

KCKMFK H13
★51430 HONG GU CHENG

KCM H3
51440 INSTALLER I

KCMC₃MFK H1
51450 SANTA CRUZ → 51451

KCMC₂MF H13
51460 DIJEY → 51461

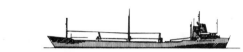

KCMCKMFK H13
51470 NILE CARRIER

KCMCKMFK H13
51480 BOIN → 51481

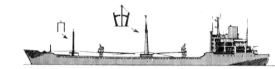

KCMCKMFK H13
51490 JESBON → 51493

KCMCMF H1
51500 WOLWOL → 51501

KCMCMF H1
51510 ARCTIC VIKING

KCMCMF H123
51520 GIAMAICA

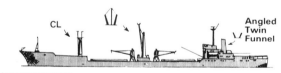

KCMCMF H13
51530 IRAN MEEAD → 51534

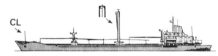

KCMCMFK H1
★51540 JIN RUN → 51543

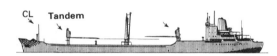

KCMCMFK H13
51550 GOLDEN ABIDJAN → 51551

KCMCMFK H13
51560 ATLAS MARU → 51561

KCMCM₂F H1
51580 SUNFLOWER

KCMF H
51590 NAI LUISA

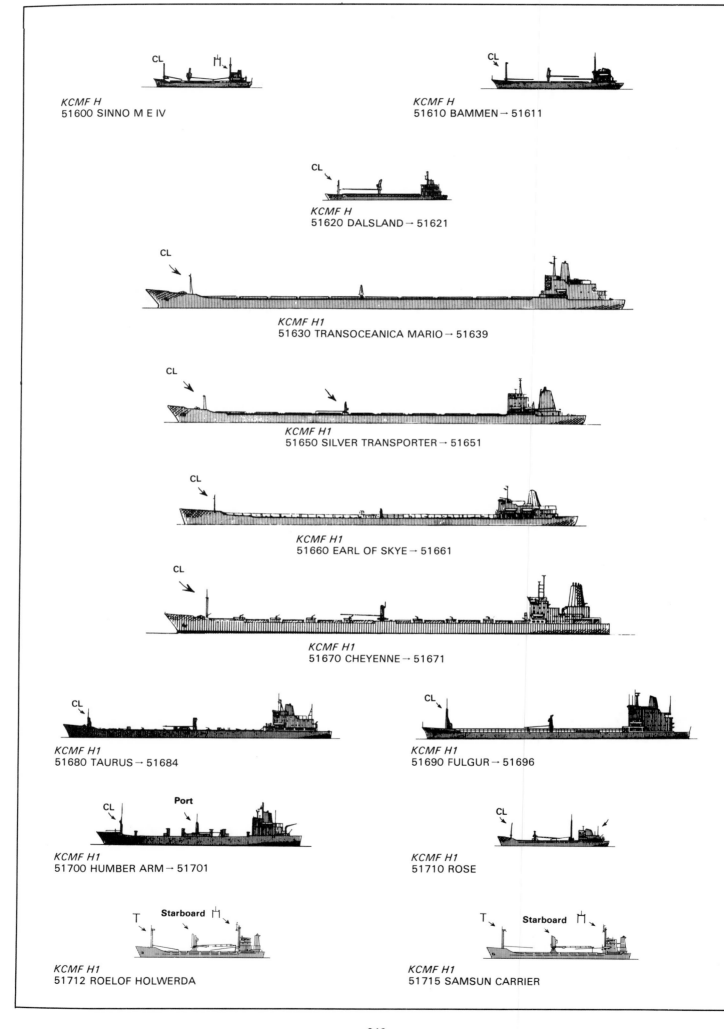

KCMF H
51600 SINNO M E IV

KCMF H
51610 BAMMEN → 51611

KCMF H
51620 DALSLAND → 51621

KCMF H1
51630 TRANSOCEANICA MARIO → 51639

KCMF H1
51650 SILVER TRANSPORTER → 51651

KCMF H1
51660 EARL OF SKYE → 51661

KCMF H1
51670 CHEYENNE → 51671

KCMF H1
51680 TAURUS → 51684

KCMF H1
51690 FULGUR → 51696

KCMF H1
51700 HUMBER ARM → 51701

KCMF H1
51710 ROSE

KCMF H1
51712 ROELOF HOLWERDA

KCMF H1
51715 SAMSUN CARRIER

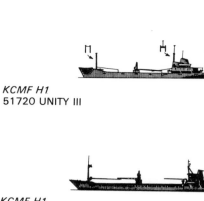

KCMF H1
51720 UNITY III

KCMF H1
51730 SEVEN → 51731

KCMF H1
51740 PEP REGULUS → 51744

KCMF H1
51745 UNION NELSON → 51747

KCMF H1
51750 BELGICA

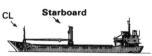

KCMF H1
51760 CHRISTA THIELEMANN → 51762

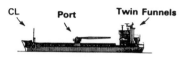

KCMF H1
51780 GERMA TARA → 51788

KCMF H1
51800 STAPAFELL

KCMF H1
51810 VILLIERS → 51812

KCMF H1
51820 LISA B → 51821

KCMF H1
51830 ALNEGMA ALKHADRA

KCMF H1
51840 NORRLAND

KCMF H1
51850 ASD HEKTOR → 51852

KCMF H1
51860 HELEN → 51865

KCMF H1
51870 CARIBE MARINER → 51872

KCMF H1
51880 KURE

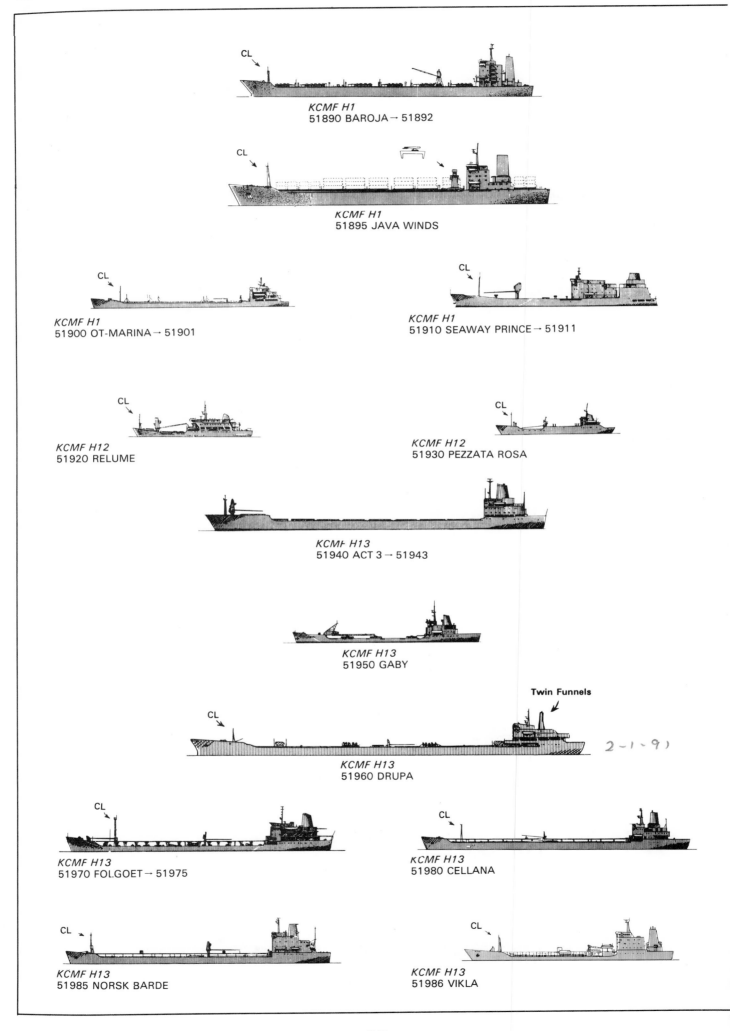

KCMF H1
51890 BAROJA → 51892

KCMF H1
51895 JAVA WINDS

KCMF H1
51900 OT-MARINA → 51901

KCMF H1
51910 SEAWAY PRINCE → 51911

KCMF H12
51920 RELUME

KCMF H12
51930 PEZZATA ROSA

KCMF H13
51940 ACT 3 → 51943

KCMF H13
51950 GABY

Twin Funnels

KCMF H13
51960 DRUPA

2-1-91

KCMF H13
51970 FOLGOET → 51975

KCMF H13
51980 CELLANA

KCMF H13
51985 NORSK BARDE

KCMF H13
51986 VIKLA

CL

KCMF H13
51987 EMDEN

Tripod

KCMF H13
★51988 VENTSPILS → 51989/3

CL

KCMF H13
51990 LUNNI → 51993

CL

KCMF H13
51995 PARITA

CL   **Tripod**

KCMF H13
51996 TEBO OLYMPIA → 51999

CL

KCMF H13
★52000 MARLOW → 52011

CL

KCMF H13
★52020 BALKHASH → 52022

CL

KCMF H13
52030 NOORDLAND

CL

KCMF H13
52040 NOVA → 52041

CL   **Tandem**   **Twin Funnels**

KCMF H13
52043 ALIDA SMITS → 52048

CL

KCMF H13
52050 AL SULTANA

CL

KCMF H13
52060 GOLIATH

CL

KCMF H13
★52070 BUNA → 52071

CL   **Twin Funnels**

KCMF H13
52074 ESSO FINLANDIA

CL

KCMF H13
52080 STAPAFELL

CL

KCMF H13
52090 BALDER B → 52093

Tripod

KCMF H13
52100 BINTANG BOLONG

CL

KCMF H13
52110 CARICOM EXPRESS → 52111

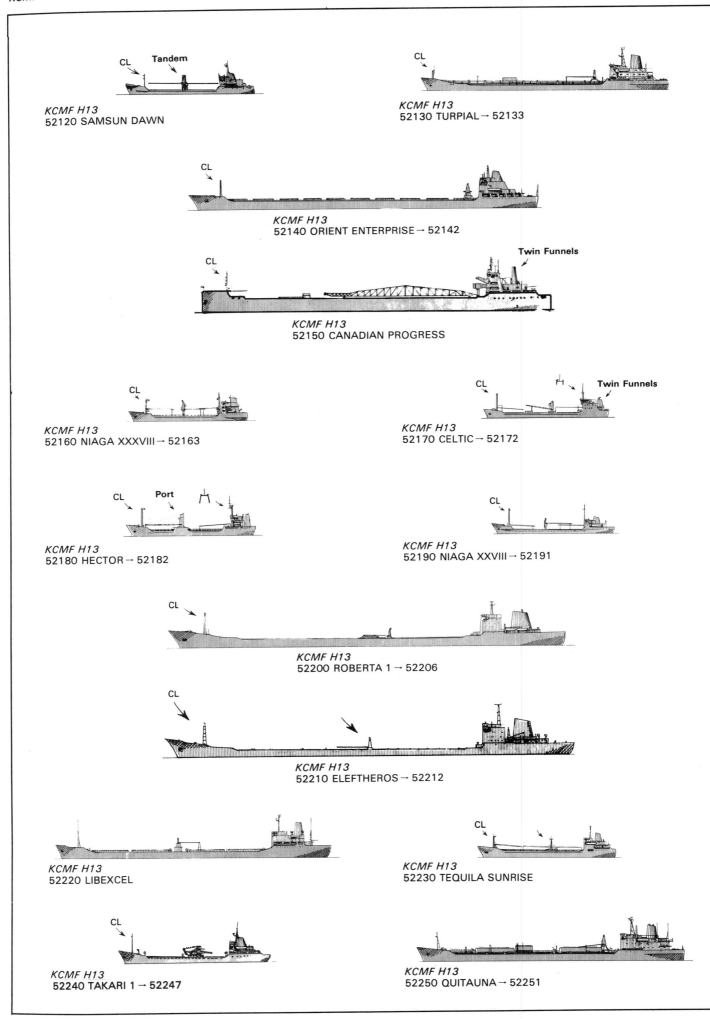

KCMF H13
52120 SAMSUN DAWN

KCMF H13
52130 TURPIAL → 52133

KCMF H13
52140 ORIENT ENTERPRISE → 52142

KCMF H13
52150 CANADIAN PROGRESS

KCMF H13
52160 NIAGA XXXVIII → 52163

KCMF H13
52170 CELTIC → 52172

KCMF H13
52180 HECTOR → 52182

KCMF H13
52190 NIAGA XXVIII → 52191

KCMF H13
52200 ROBERTA 1 → 52206

KCMF H13
52210 ELEFTHEROS → 52212

KCMF H13
52220 LIBEXCEL

KCMF H13
52230 TEQUILA SUNRISE

KCMF H13
52240 TAKARI 1 → 52247

KCMF H13
52250 QUITAUNA → 52251

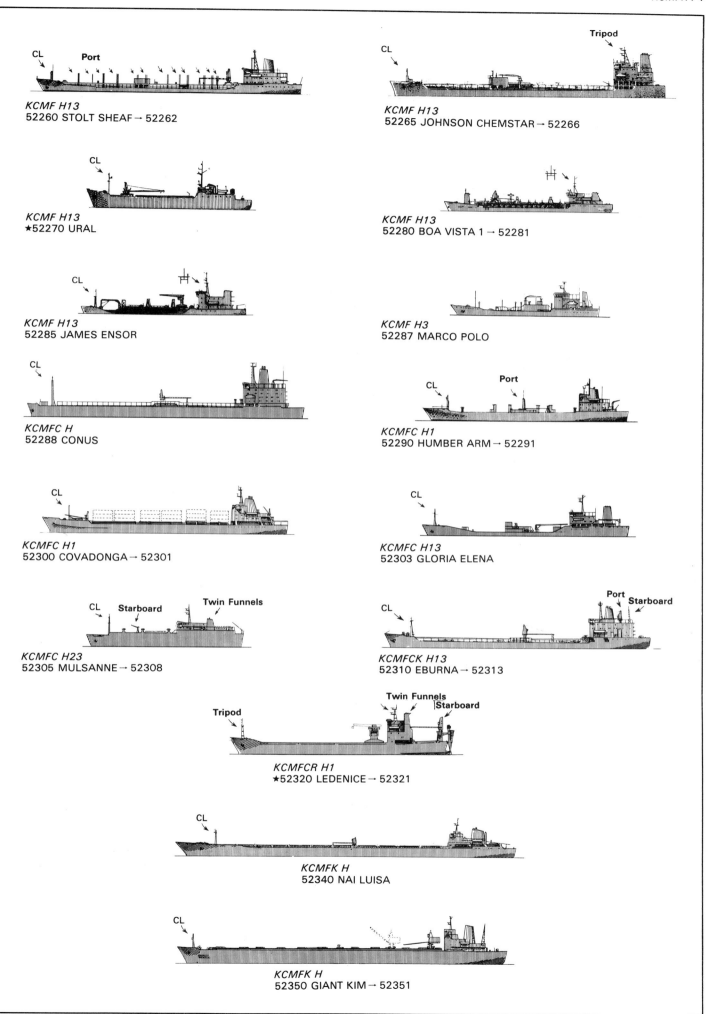

KCMF H13
52260 STOLT SHEAF → 52262

KCMF H13
52265 JOHNSON CHEMSTAR → 52266

KCMF H13
★52270 URAL

KCMF H13
52280 BOA VISTA 1 → 52281

KCMF H13
52285 JAMES ENSOR

KCMF H3
52287 MARCO POLO

KCMFC H
52288 CONUS

KCMFC H1
52290 HUMBER ARM → 52291

KCMFC H1
52300 COVADONGA → 52301

KCMFC H13
52303 GLORIA ELENA

KCMFC H23
52305 MULSANNE → 52308

KCMFCK H13
52310 EBURNA → 52313

KCMFCR H1
★52320 LEDENICE → 52321

KCMFK H
52340 NAI LUISA

KCMFK H
52350 GIANT KIM → 52351

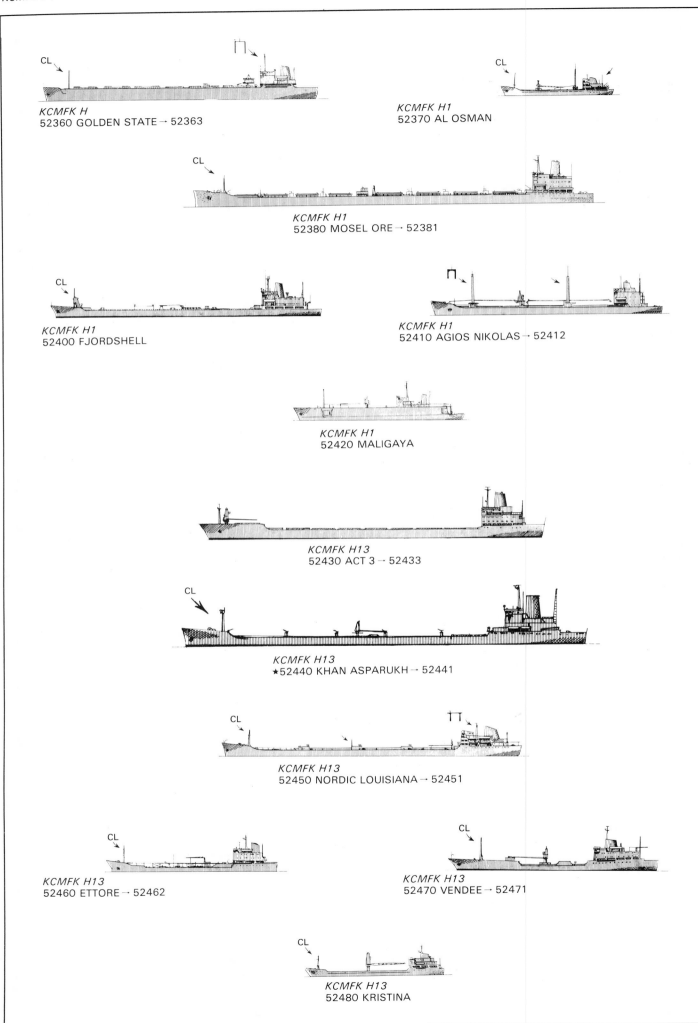

KCMFK H
52360 GOLDEN STATE → 52363

KCMFK H1
52370 AL OSMAN

KCMFK H1
52380 MOSEL ORE → 52381

KCMFK H1
52400 FJORDSHELL

KCMFK H1
52410 AGIOS NIKOLAS → 52412

KCMFK H1
52420 MALIGAYA

KCMFK H13
52430 ACT 3 → 52433

KCMFK H13
★52440 KHAN ASPARUKH → 52441

KCMFK H13
52450 NORDIC LOUISIANA → 52451

KCMFK H13
52460 ETTORE → 52462

KCMFK H13
52470 VENDEE → 52471

KCMFK H13
52480 KRISTINA

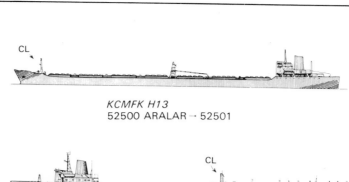

KCMFK H13
52500 ARALAR → 52501

KCMFK H13
52510 TURPIAL → 52513

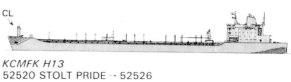

KCMFK H13
52520 STOLT PRIDE → 52526

KCMFK H13
52530 ORIENT ENTERPRISE → 52532

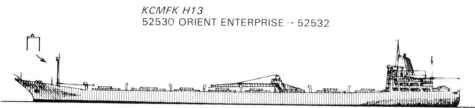

KCMFK H13
52540 MARCONA CONVEYOR

KCMFK H13
52550 DAVID P REYNOLDS

KCMFK H13
52560 SAUNIERE

KCMFK H13
52570 HAUKUR

KCMFK H2
52590 BLUE SHINYO

Twin Funnels

KCMFK H3
52600 ASTREA

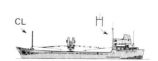

KCMFK H3
52610 HVASSAFELL → 52611

KCMFKC H13
52613 HELVETIA → 52614

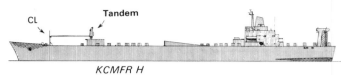

KCMFR H
52620 TYSON LYKES → 52623

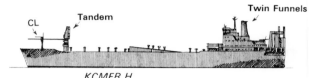

KCMFR H
52630 PARALLA → 52632

KCMFR H3
52640 BARBER TONSBERG → 52645

KCMKF H13
52650 LIBERTADOR SAN MARTIN → 52652

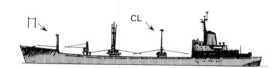

KCMKMF H13
52660 ILO → 52661

KCMKMF H13
52670 AL-SAYESTHA → 52671

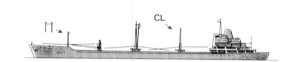

KCMKMFK H1
52680 TARBELA → 52682

KCMKMFK H13
52690 KASUGA MARU → 52691

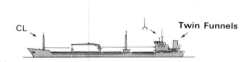

KCM₂F H1
52695 ICELANDIC → 52678

KCM₂F H1
52700 AMULET → 52704

KCM₂F H1
52710 UNITY III

KCM₂F H13
52720 COMBI TRADER → 52721

KCM₂FK H
52730 THORLINA

KCM₂FK H13
★52735 BAO AN → 52737

KCNMF H/H1
52740 FRANK H. BROWN

KFM H
★52745 ALI AMIROV

KFM H1
52750 MERINO EXPRESS

KFM H1
52760 CLAN ROSE → 52761

KFM H13
52770 SERIUS → 52773

K₂C₅MFK H13
52780 ALEXANDRA N → 52781

K₂C₃MFK H13
52790 GEORGIAN GLORY → 52791

K₂C₃MFK H13
52800 SALLY D → 52801

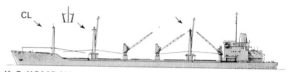

K₂C₂KCMF H1
52810 BERTRAM RICKMERS → 52811

K₂C₂KCMFCK H1
52820 ALDABI → 52823

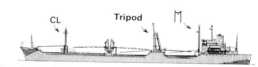

K₂C₂KMFK H13
★52830 YAN SHAN

K₂C₂KMFK H13
52840 TRIBELS

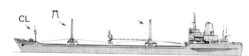

K₂C₂KMFK H13
52850 HAE WOO No. 3 → 52851

K₂C₂KMFK H13
52860 RATNA MANORAMA → 52865

K₂C₂MFK H1
52863 BOLAN → 52868

K₂CKC₂KMFK H1
52870 TOYOTA MARU No 16 → 52871

K₂CKCKCKMFK H1
52880 BUNKO MARU

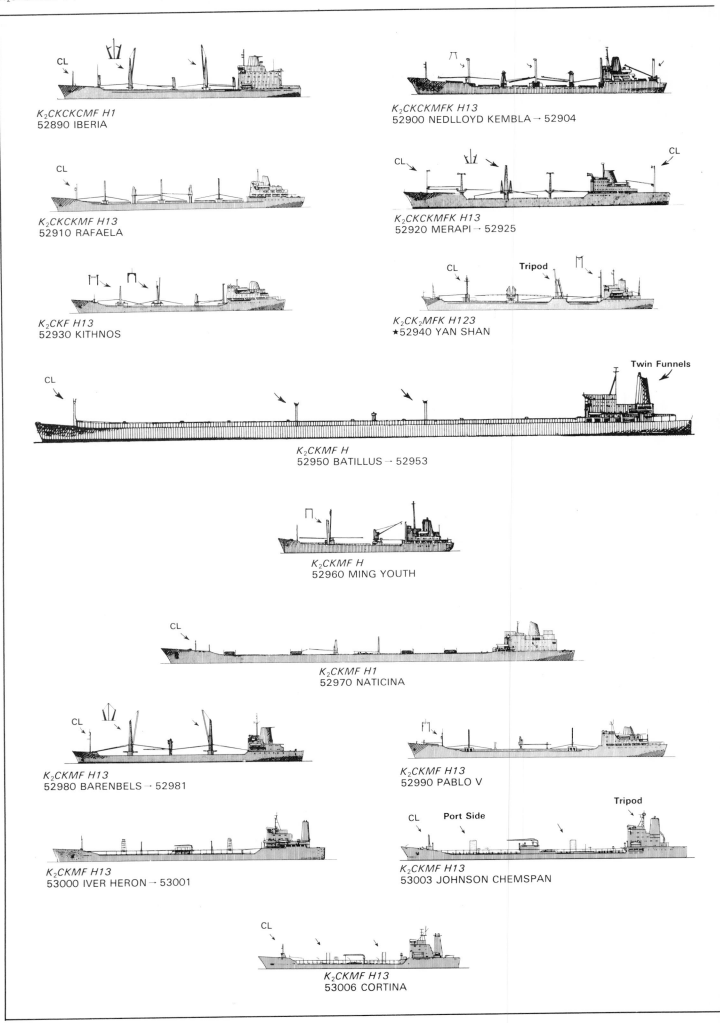

K₂CKCKCMF H1
52890 IBERIA

K₂CKCKMFK H13
52900 NEDLLOYD KEMBLA → 52904

K₂CKCKMF H13
52910 RAFAELA

K₂CKCKMFK H13
52920 MERAPI → 52925

K₂CKF H13
52930 KITHNOS

K₂CK₂MFK H123
★52940 YAN SHAN

K₂CKMF H
52950 BATILLUS → 52953

K₂CKMF H
52960 MING YOUTH

K₂CKMF H1
52970 NATICINA

K₂CKMF H13
52980 BARENBELS → 52981

K₂CKMF H13
52990 PABLO V

K₂CKMF H13
53000 IVER HERON → 53001

K₂CKMF H13
53003 JOHNSON CHEMSPAN

K₂CKMF H13
53006 CORTINA

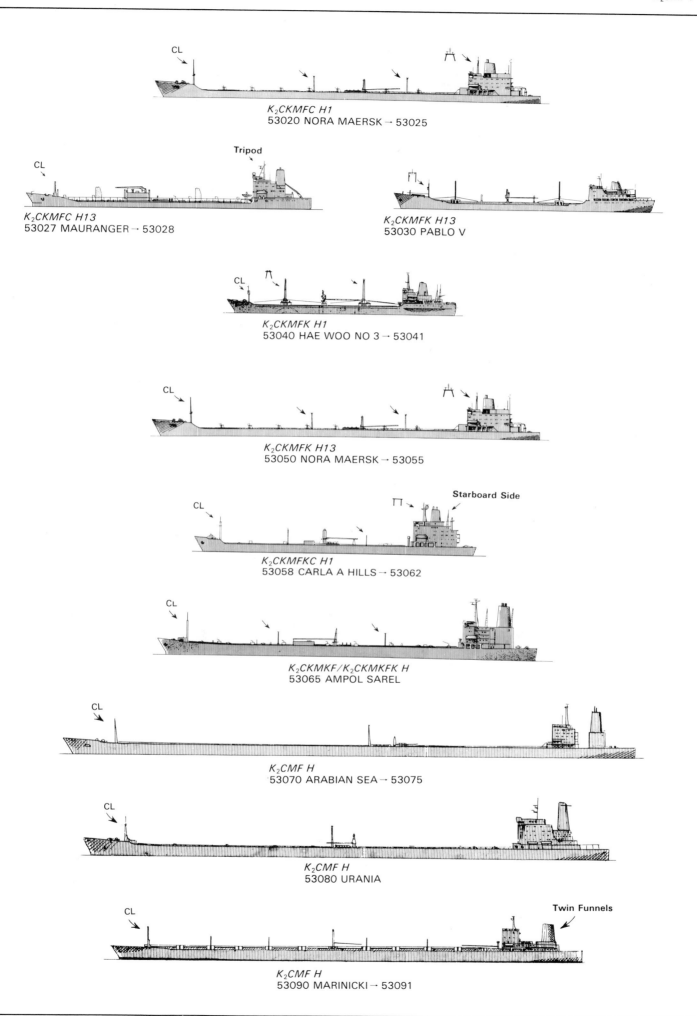

K₂CKMFC H1
53020 NORA MAERSK → 53025

Tripod

K₂CKMFC H13
53027 MAURANGER → 53028

K₂CKMFK H13
53030 PABLO V

K₂CKMFK H1
53040 HAE WOO NO 3 → 53041

K₂CKMFK H13
53050 NORA MAERSK → 53055

Starboard Side

K₂CKMFKC H1
53058 CARLA A HILLS → 53062

K₂CKMKF/K₂CKMKFK H
53065 AMPOL SAREL

K₂CMF H
53070 ARABIAN SEA → 53075

K₂CMF H
53080 URANIA

Twin Funnels

K₂CMF H
53090 MARINICKI → 53091

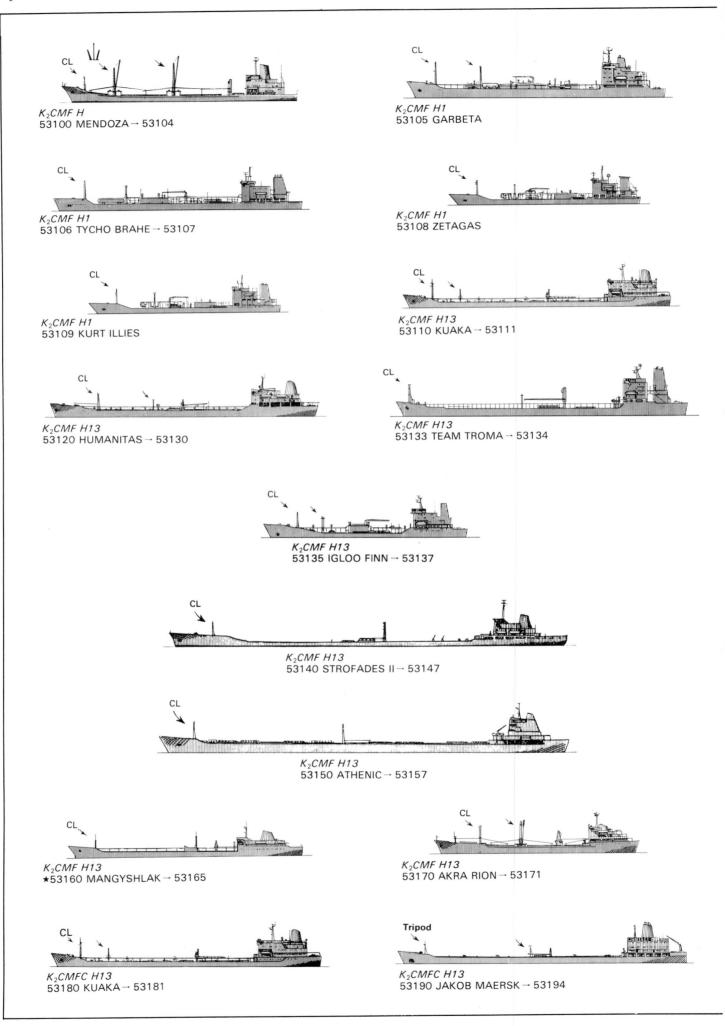

K₂CMF H
53100 MENDOZA → 53104

K₂CMF H1
53105 GARBETA

K₂CMF H1
53106 TYCHO BRAHE → 53107

K₂CMF H1
53108 ZETAGAS

K₂CMF H1
53109 KURT ILLIES

K₂CMF H13
53110 KUAKA → 53111

K₂CMF H13
53120 HUMANITAS → 53130

K₂CMF H13
53133 TEAM TROMA → 53134

K₂CMF H13
53135 IGLOO FINN → 53137

K₂CMF H13
53140 STROFADES II → 53147

K₂CMF H13
53150 ATHENIC → 53157

K₂CMF H13
★53160 MANGYSHLAK → 53165

K₂CMF H13
53170 AKRA RION → 53171

K₂CMFC H13
53180 KUAKA → 53181

K₂CMFC H13
53190 JAKOB MAERSK → 53194

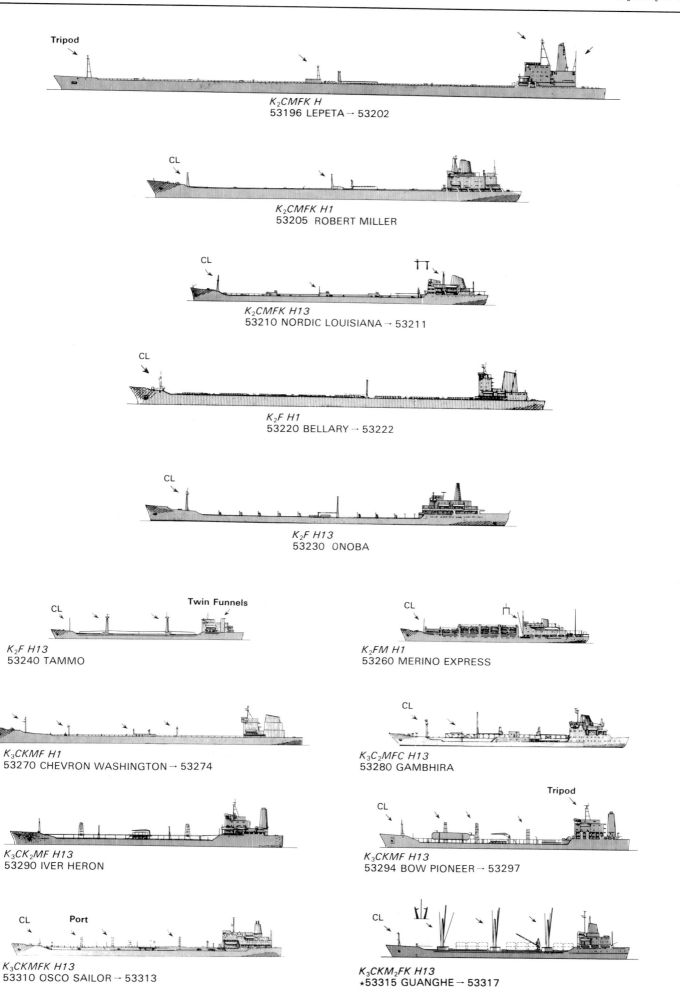

Tripod

K_2CMFK H
53196 LEPETA → 53202

CL

K_2CMFK H1
53205 ROBERT MILLER

CL

K_2CMFK H13
53210 NORDIC LOUISIANA → 53211

CL

K_2F H1
53220 BELLARY → 53222

CL

K_2F H13
53230 ONOBA

CL   **Twin Funnels**

K_2F H13
53240 TAMMO

CL

K_2FM H1
53260 MERINO EXPRESS

K_3CKMF H1
53270 CHEVRON WASHINGTON → 53274

CL

K_3C_2MFC H13
53280 GAMBHIRA

K_3CK_2MF H13
53290 IVER HERON

Tripod

CL

K_3CKMF H13
53294 BOW PIONEER → 53297

CL   **Port**

K_3CKMFK H13
53310 OSCO SAILOR → 53313

CL

K_3CKM_2FK H13
★53315 GUANGHE → 53317

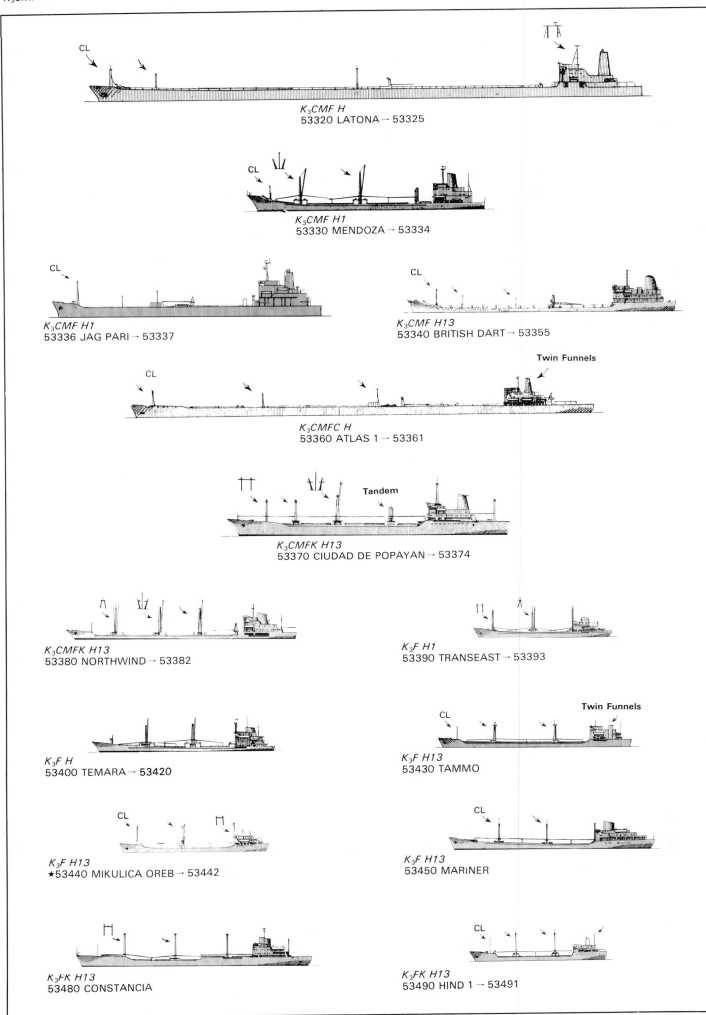

K₃CMF H
53320 LATONA → 53325

K₃CMF H1
53330 MENDOZA → 53334

K₃CMF H1
53336 JAG PARI → 53337

K₃CMF H13
53340 BRITISH DART → 53355

Twin Funnels

K₃CMFC H
53360 ATLAS 1 → 53361

Tandem

K₃CMFK H13
53370 CIUDAD DE POPAYAN → 53374

K₃CMFK H13
53380 NORTHWIND → 53382

K₃F H1
53390 TRANSEAST → 53393

K₃F H
53400 TEMARA → **53420**

Twin Funnels

K₃F H13
53430 TAMMO

K₃F H13
★53440 MIKULICA OREB → 53442

K₃F H13
53450 MARINER

K₃FK H13
53480 CONSTANCIA

K₃FK H13
53490 HIND 1 → 53491

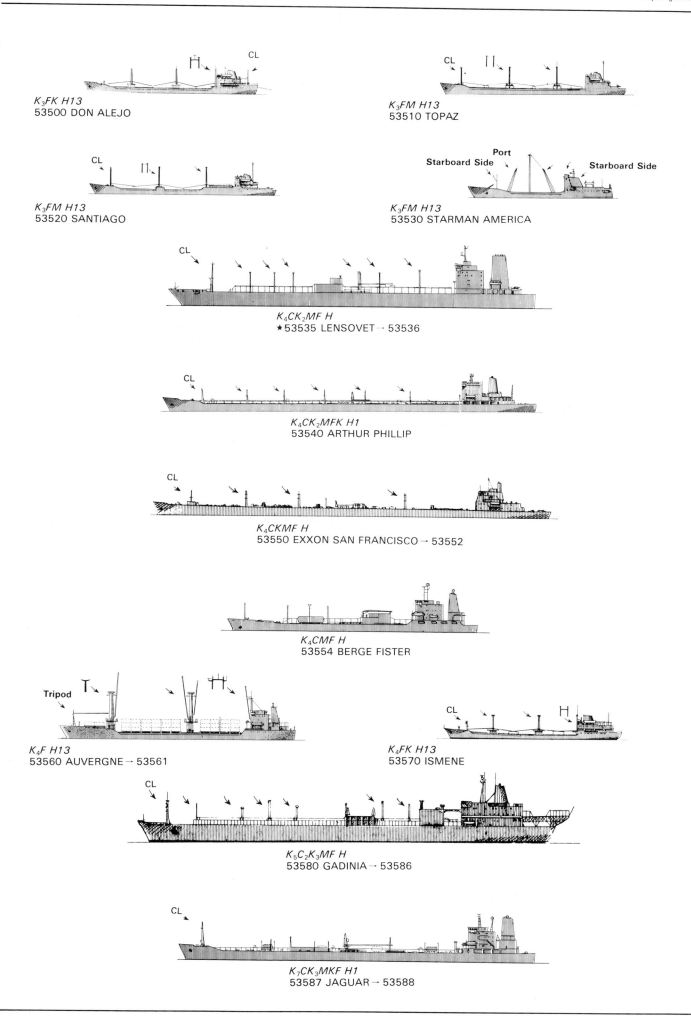

K_3FK H13
53500 DON ALEJO

K_3FM H13
53510 TOPAZ

K_3FM H13
53520 SANTIAGO

K_3FM H13
53530 STARMAN AMERICA

K_4CK_2MF H
★53535 LENSOVET ·· 53536

K_4CK_2MFK H1
53540 ARTHUR PHILLIP

K_4CKMF H
53550 EXXON SAN FRANCISCO → 53552

K_4CMF H
53554 BERGE FISTER

K_4F H13
53560 AUVERGNE → 53561

K_4FK H13
53570 ISMENE

$K_5C_2K_3MF$ H
53580 GADINIA → 53586

K_7CK_3MKF H1
53587 JAGUAR → 53588

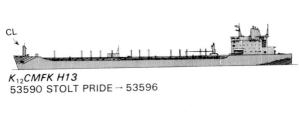

K₁₂CMFK H13
53590 STOLT PRIDE → 53596

K₁₃CMF H13
53600 STOLT SHEAF → 53602

K₁₃MF H13
53610 HAPPY FALCON → 53611

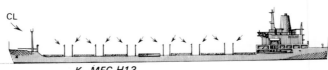

K₁₃MFC H13
53620 IRON CARPENTARIA → 53621

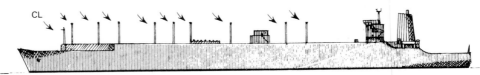

K₁₀MF H1/H2
53640 EL PASO PAUL KAYSER → 53642

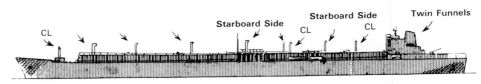

K₉MF H
53650 BEN FRANKLIN → 53651

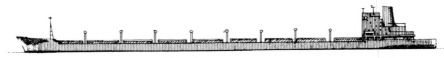

K₉MF H1
53660 ITALMARE → 53669

K₉MFK H1
53680 DONAU MARU → 53687

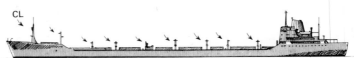

K₉MFK H13
53700 ARCHANGELOS III → 53702

K₉MFK H13
53710 LABRADOR CURRENT → 53712

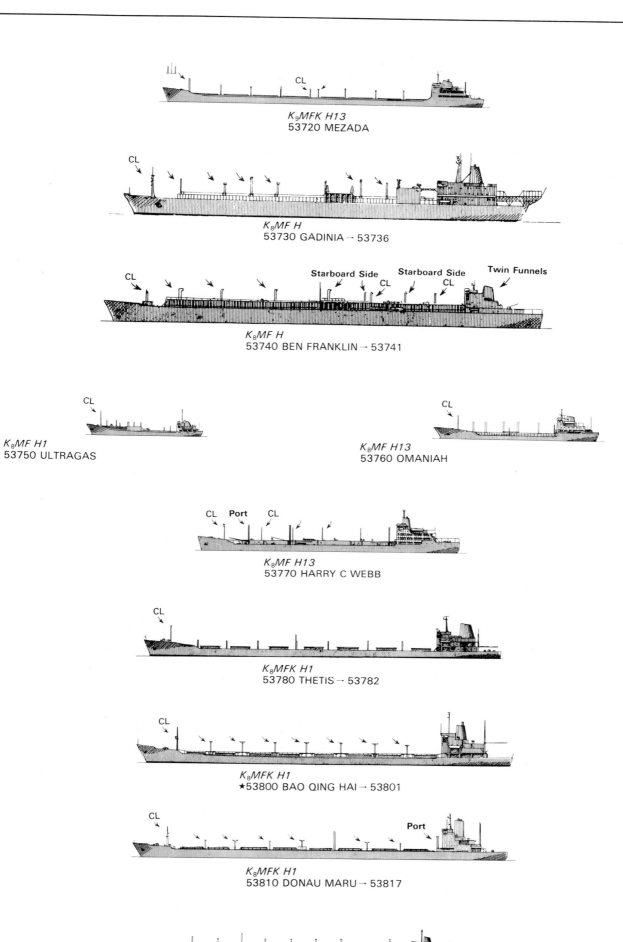

K₉MFK H13
53720 MEZADA

K₈MF H
53730 GADINIA → 53736

K₈MF H
53740 BEN FRANKLIN → 53741

K₈MF H1
53750 ULTRAGAS

K₈MF H13
53760 OMANIAH

K₈MF H13
53770 HARRY C WEBB

K₈MFK H1
53780 THETIS → 53782

K₈MFK H1
★53800 BAO QING HAI → 53801

K₈MFK H1
53810 DONAU MARU → 53817

K₈MFK H13
53820 JAGAT NETA → 53821

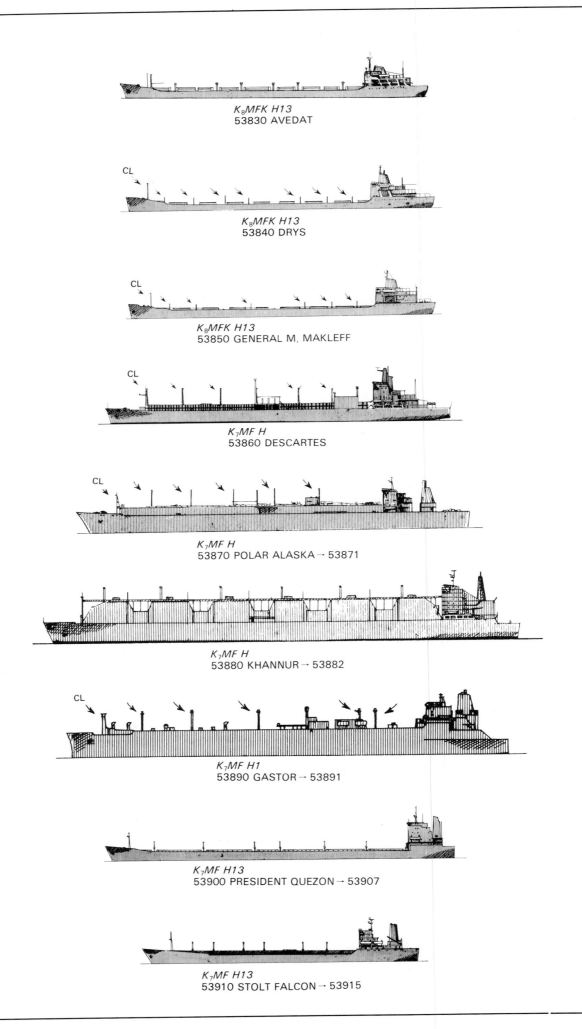

K₈MFK H13
53830 AVEDAT

CL

K₈MFK H13
53840 DRYS

CL

K₈MFK H13
53850 GENERAL M, MAKLEFF

CL

K₇MF H
53860 DESCARTES

CL

K₇MF H
53870 POLAR ALASKA → 53871

K₇MF H
53880 KHANNUR → 53882

CL

K₇MF H1
53890 GASTOR → 53891

K₇MF H13
53900 PRESIDENT QUEZON → 53907

K₇MF H13
53910 STOLT FALCON → 53915

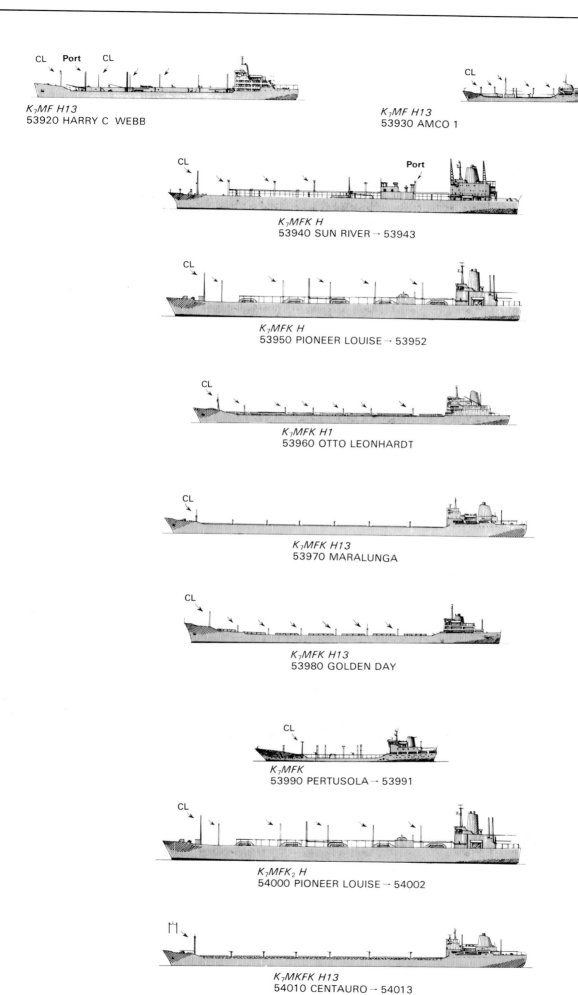

K₇MF H13
53930 AMCO 1

K₇MFK H
53940 SUN RIVER → 53943

K₇MFK H
53950 PIONEER LOUISE → 53952

K₇MFK H1
53960 OTTO LEONHARDT

K₇MFK H13
53970 MARALUNGA

K₇MFK H13
53980 GOLDEN DAY

K₇MFK
53990 PERTUSOLA → 53991

K₇MFK₂ H
54000 PIONEER LOUISE → 54002

K₇MKFK H13
54010 CENTAURO → 54013

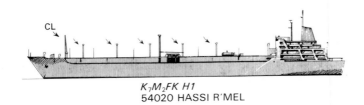

K₇M₂FK H1
54020 HASSI R'MEL

K₆MF H
54030 WORLD BRIGADIER → **54037**

K₆MF H
54040 MONGE → 54045

K₆MF H
54047 NYHAMMER

K₆MF H
54050 METHANIA

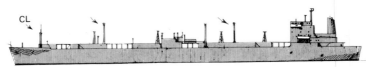

K₆MF H
54060 STAFFORDSHIRE

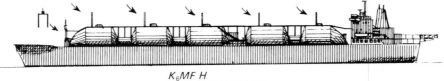

K₆MF H
54070 POLLENGER

K₆MF H
54080 HOEGH GANDRIA → 54081

K₆MF H1
54090 GOLFO DI PALERMO

K₆MF H1
54100 ANANGEL HARMONY

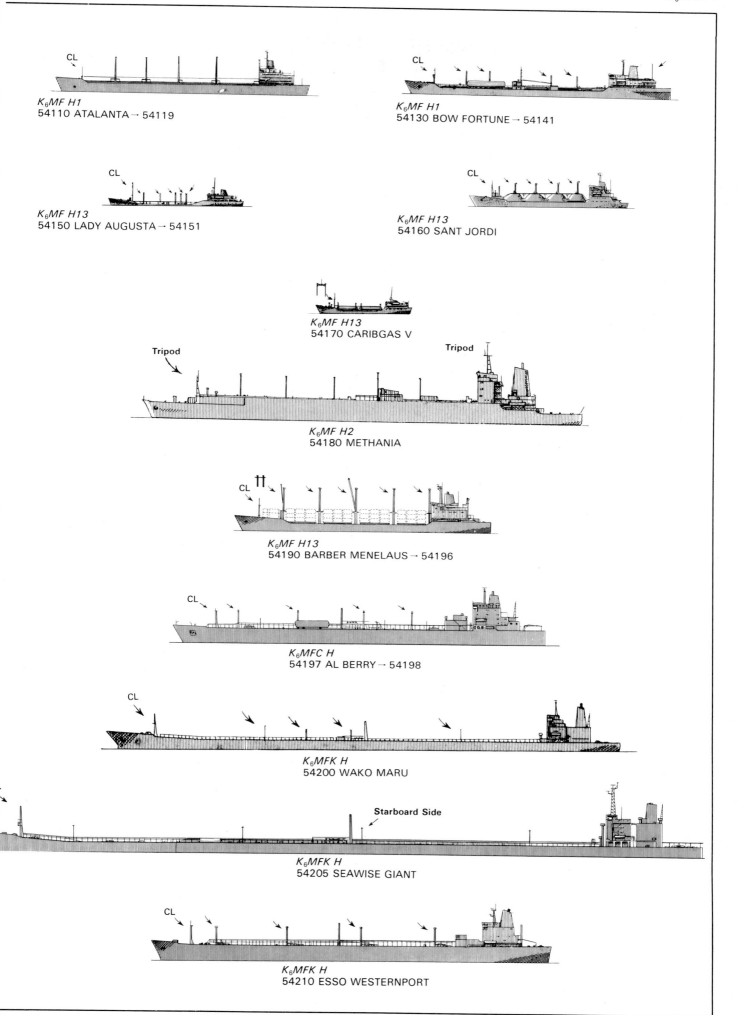

K₆MF H1
54110 ATALANTA → 54119

K₆MF H1
54130 BOW FORTUNE → 54141

K₆MF H13
54150 LADY AUGUSTA → 54151

K₆MF H13
54160 SANT JORDI

K₆MF H13
54170 CARIBGAS V

Tripod   Tripod

K₆MF H2
54180 METHANIA

K₆MF H13
54190 BARBER MENELAUS → 54196

K₆MFC H
54197 AL BERRY → 54198

K₆MFK H
54200 WAKO MARU

Starboard Side

K₆MFK H
54205 SEAWISE GIANT

K₆MFK H
54210 ESSO WESTERNPORT

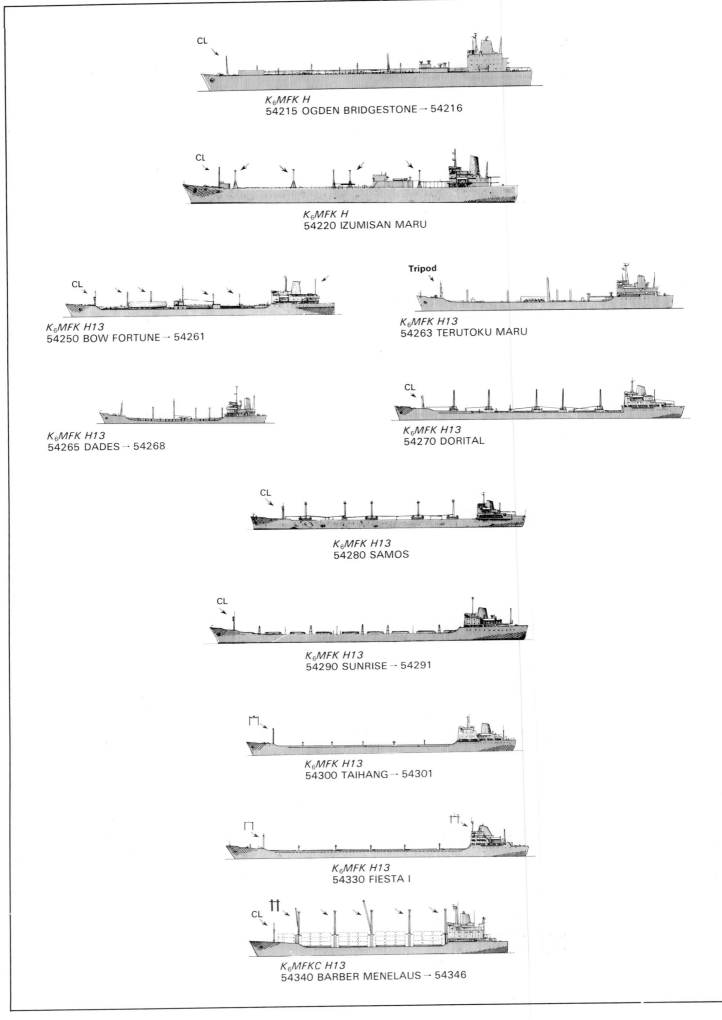

CL

K₆MFK H
54215 OGDEN BRIDGESTONE → 54216

CL

K₆MFK H
54220 IZUMISAN MARU

CL

K₆MFK H13
54250 BOW FORTUNE → 54261

Tripod

K₆MFK H13
54263 TERUTOKU MARU

K₆MFK H13
54265 DADES → 54268

CL

K₆MFK H13
54270 DORITAL

CL

K₆MFK H13
54280 SAMOS

CL

K₆MFK H13
54290 SUNRISE → 54291

K₆MFK H13
54300 TAIHANG → 54301

K₆MFK H13
54330 FIESTA I

CL

K₆MFKC H13
54340 BARBER MENELAUS → 54346

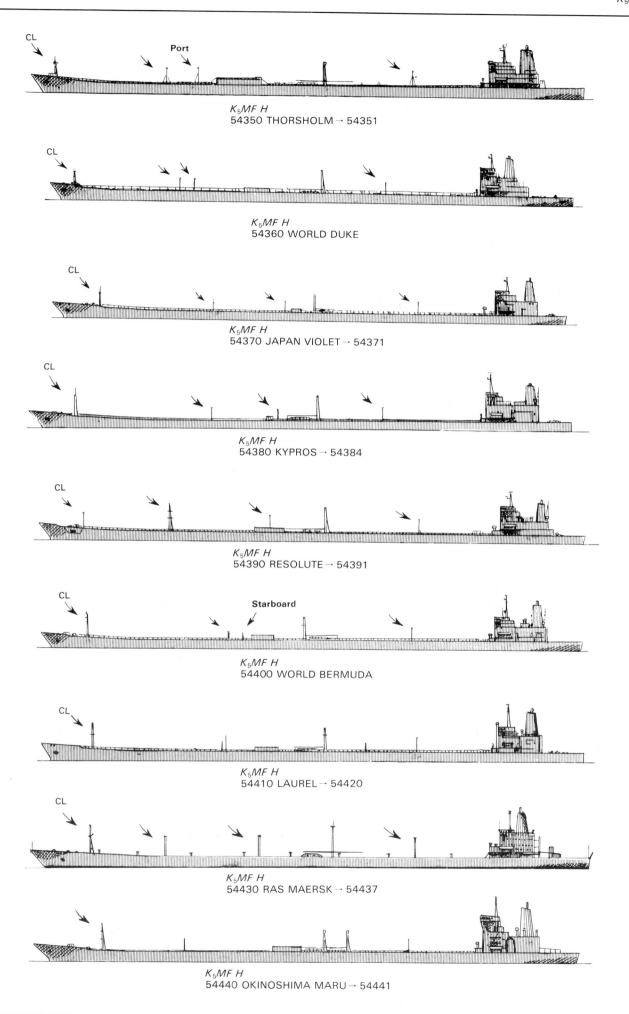

K_5MF H
54350 THORSHOLM → 54351

K_5MF H
54360 WORLD DUKE

K_5MF H
54370 JAPAN VIOLET → 54371

K_5MF H
54380 KYPROS → 54384

K_5MF H
54390 RESOLUTE → 54391

K_5MF H
54400 WORLD BERMUDA

K_5MF H
54410 LAUREL → 54420

K_5MF H
54430 RAS MAERSK → 54437

K_5MF H
54440 OKINOSHIMA MARU → 54441

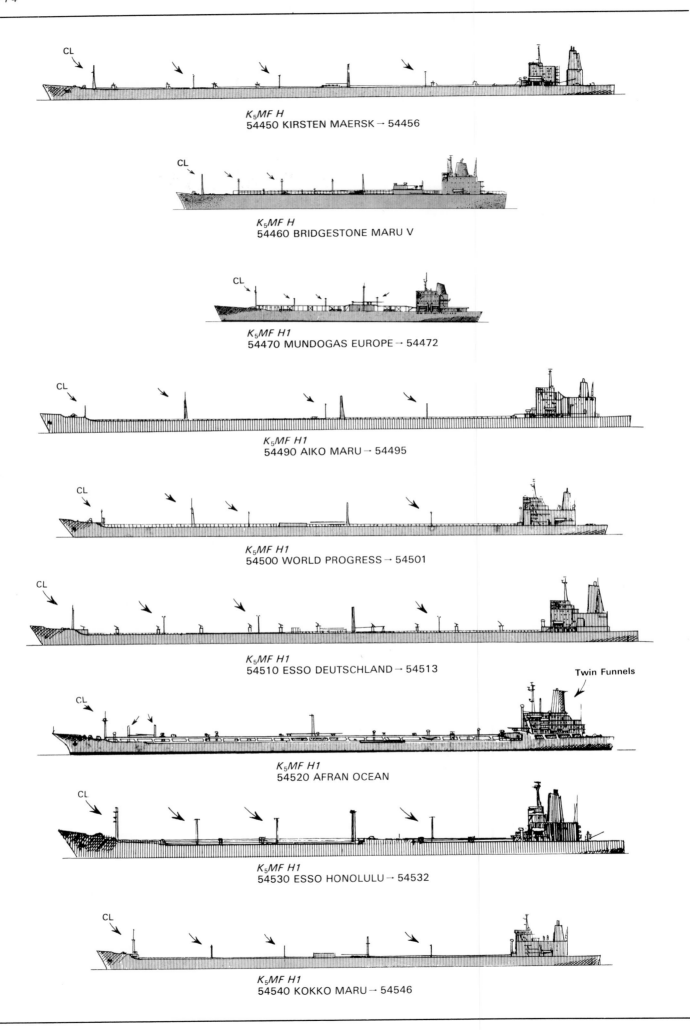

CL
K_5MF H
54450 KIRSTEN MAERSK → 54456

CL
K_5MF H
54460 BRIDGESTONE MARU V

CL
K_5MF H1
54470 MUNDOGAS EUROPE → 54472

CL
K_5MF H1
54490 AIKO MARU → 54495

CL
K_5MF H1
54500 WORLD PROGRESS → 54501

CL
K_5MF H1
54510 ESSO DEUTSCHLAND → 54513

Twin Funnels

CL
K_5MF H1
54520 AFRAN OCEAN

CL
K_5MF H1
54530 ESSO HONOLULU → 54532

CL
K_5MF H1
54540 KOKKO MARU → 54546

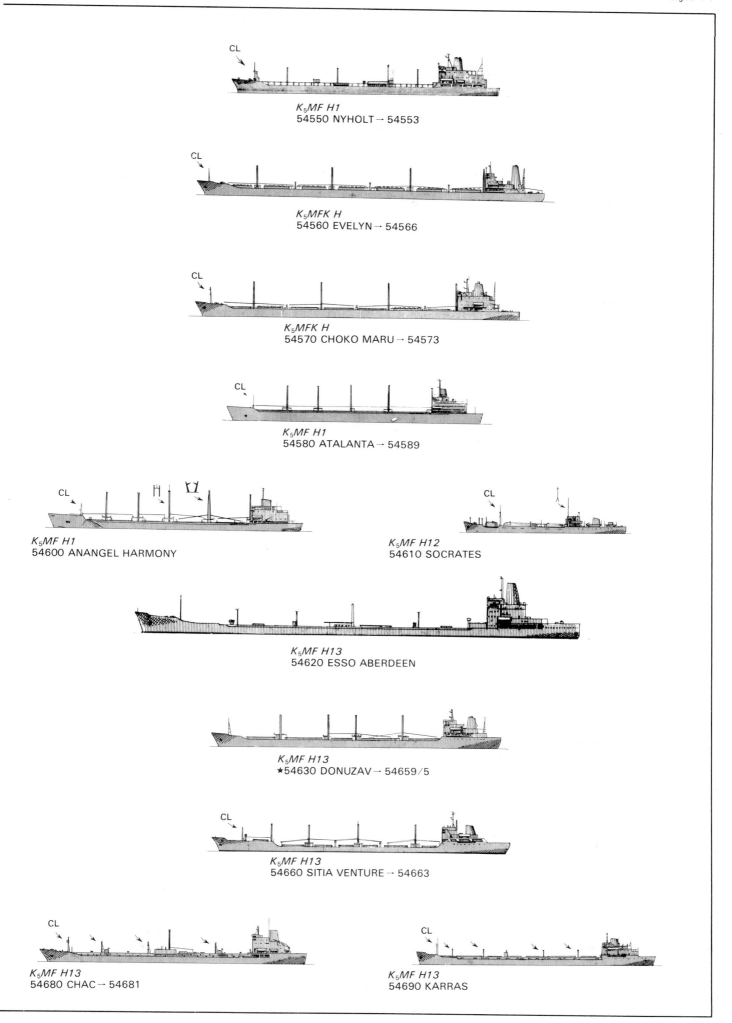

K_5MF H1
54550 NYHOLT → 54553

K_5MFK H
54560 EVELYN → 54566

K_5MFK H
54570 CHOKO MARU → 54573

K_5MF H1
54580 ATALANTA → 54589

K_5MF H1
54600 ANANGEL HARMONY

K_5MF H12
54610 SOCRATES

K_5MF H13
54620 ESSO ABERDEEN

K_5MF H13
★54630 DONUZAV → 54659/5

K_5MF H13
54660 SITIA VENTURE → 54663

K_5MF H13
54680 CHAC → 54681

K_5MF H13
54690 KARRAS

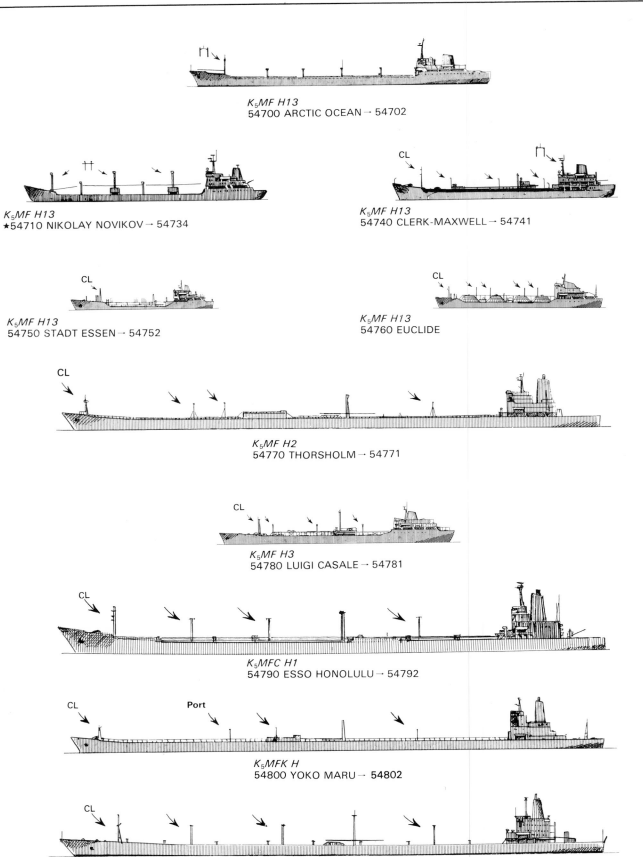

K₅MF H13
54700 ARCTIC OCEAN → 54702

K₅MF H13
★54710 NIKOLAY NOVIKOV → 54734

K₅MF H13
54740 CLERK-MAXWELL → 54741

K₅MF H13
54750 STADT ESSEN → 54752

K₅MF H13
54760 EUCLIDE

K₅MF H2
54770 THORSHOLM → 54771

K₅MF H3
54780 LUIGI CASALE → 54781

K₅MFC H1
54790 ESSO HONOLULU → 54792

K₅MFK H
54800 YOKO MARU → **54802**

K₅MFK H
54810 RAS MAERSK → 54817

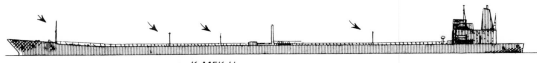

K₅MFK H
54820 ENERGY GROWTH

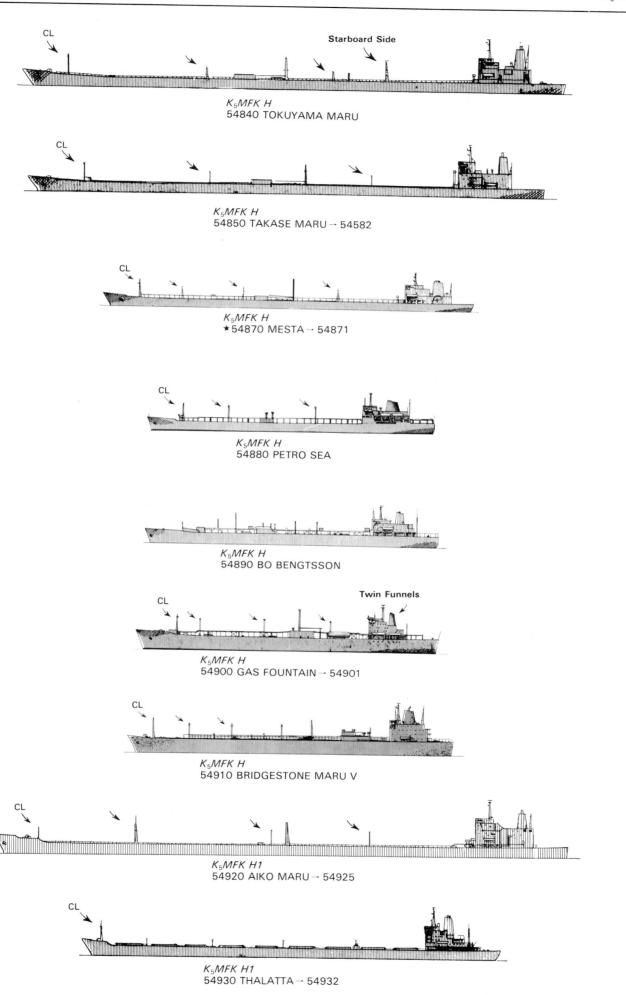

CL

Starboard Side

K₅MFK H
54840 TOKUYAMA MARU

CL

K₅MFK H
54850 TAKASE MARU → 54582

CL

K₅MFK H
★ 54870 MESTA → 54871

CL

K₅MFK H
54880 PETRO SEA

K₅MFK H
54890 BO BENGTSSON

Twin Funnels

CL

K₅MFK H
54900 GAS FOUNTAIN → 54901

CL

K₅MFK H
54910 BRIDGESTONE MARU V

CL

K₅MFK H1
54920 AIKO MARU → 54925

CL

K₅MFK H1
54930 THALATTA → 54932

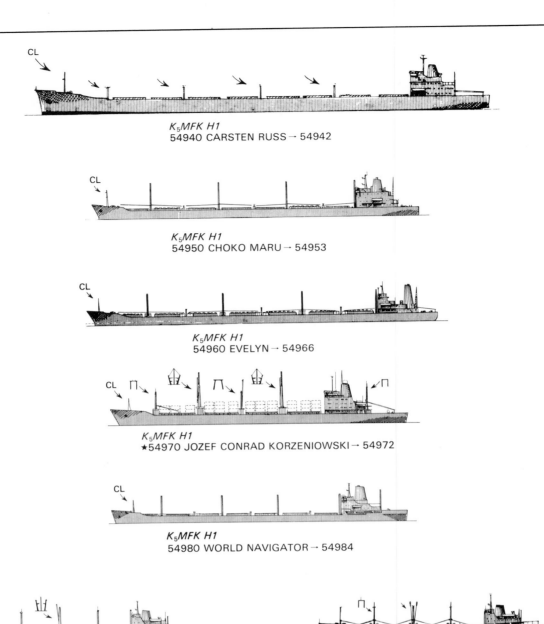

K_5MFK H1
54940 CARSTEN RUSS → 54942

K_5MFK H1
54950 CHOKO MARU → 54953

K_5MFK H1
54960 EVELYN → 54966

K_5MFK H1
★54970 JOZEF CONRAD KORZENIOWSKI → 54972

K_5MFK H1
54980 WORLD NAVIGATOR → 54984

K_5MFK H1
55000 DIANA → 55001

K_5MFK H1
55010 PRESIDENTE KENNEDY → 55015

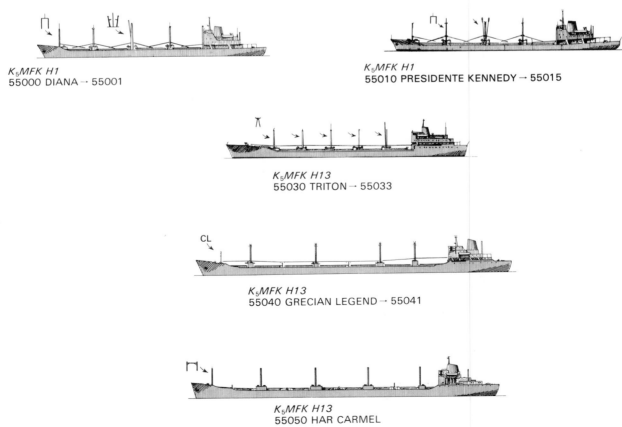

K_5MFK H13
55030 TRITON → 55033

K_5MFK H13
55040 GRECIAN LEGEND → 55041

K_5MFK H13
55050 HAR CARMEL

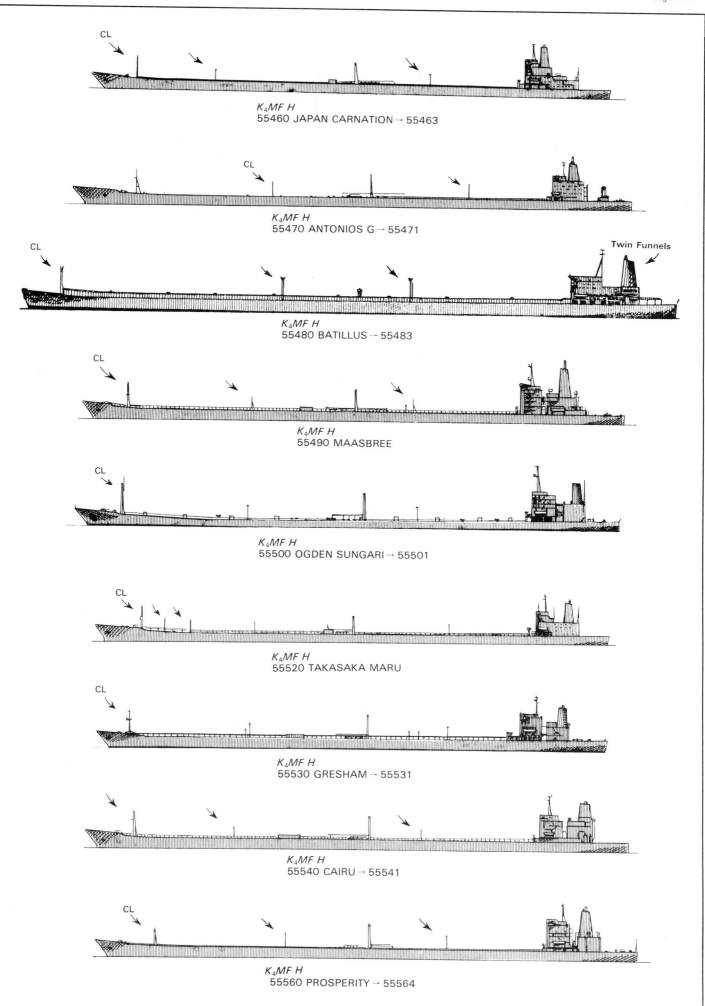

CL

K₄MF H
55460 JAPAN CARNATION → 55463

CL

K₄MF H
55470 ANTONIOS G → 55471

CL

Twin Funnels

K₄MF H
55480 BATILLUS → 55483

CL

K₄MF H
55490 MAASBREE

CL

K₄MF H
55500 OGDEN SUNGARI → 55501

CL

K₄MF H
55520 TAKASAKA MARU

CL

K₄MF H
55530 GRESHAM → 55531

K₄MF H
55540 CAIRU → 55541

CL

K₄MF H
55560 PROSPERITY → 55564

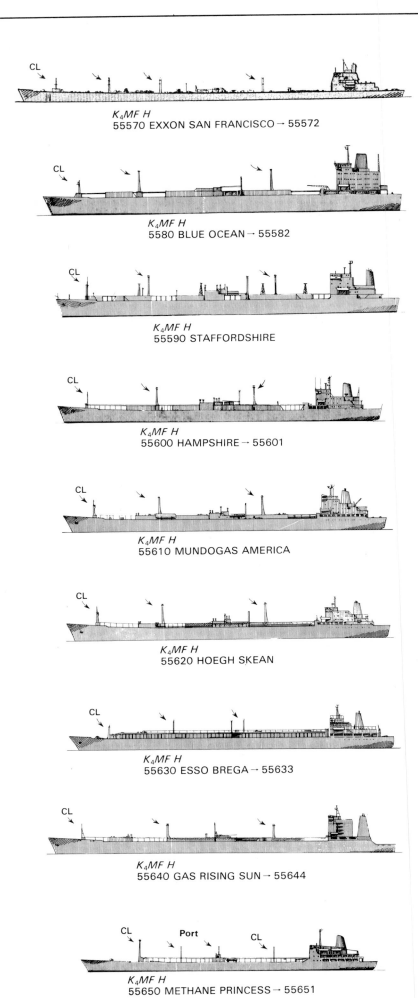

K$_4$MF H
55570 EXXON SAN FRANCISCO → 55572

K$_4$MF H
5580 BLUE OCEAN → 55582

K$_4$MF H
55590 STAFFORDSHIRE

K$_4$MF H
55600 HAMPSHIRE → 55601

K$_4$MF H
55610 MUNDOGAS AMERICA

K$_4$MF H
55620 HOEGH SKEAN

K$_4$MF H
55630 ESSO BREGA → 55633

K$_4$MF H
55640 GAS RISING SUN → 55644

K$_4$MF H
55650 METHANE PRINCESS → 55651

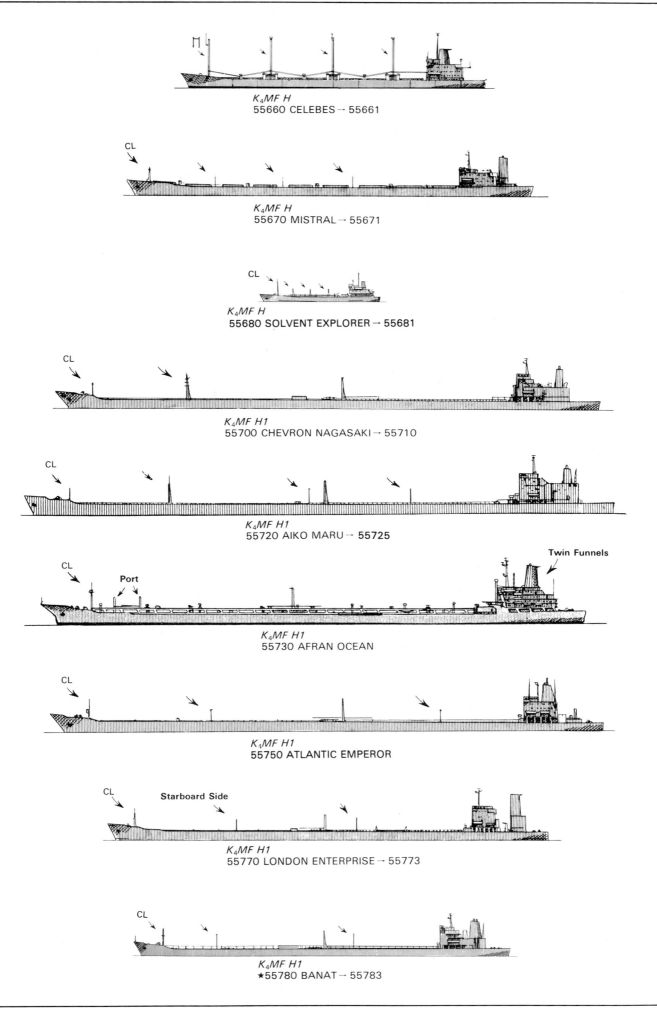

K_4MF H
55660 CELEBES → 55661

CL

K_4MF H
55670 MISTRAL → 55671

CL

K_4MF H
55680 SOLVENT EXPLORER → 55681

CL

K_4MF H1
55700 CHEVRON NAGASAKI → 55710

CL

K_4MF H1
55720 AIKO MARU → 55725

CL   Port   Twin Funnels

K_4MF H1
55730 AFRAN OCEAN

CL

K_4MF H1
55750 ATLANTIC EMPEROR

CL   Starboard Side

K_4MF H1
55770 LONDON ENTERPRISE → 55773

CL

K_4MF H1
★55780 BANAT → 55783

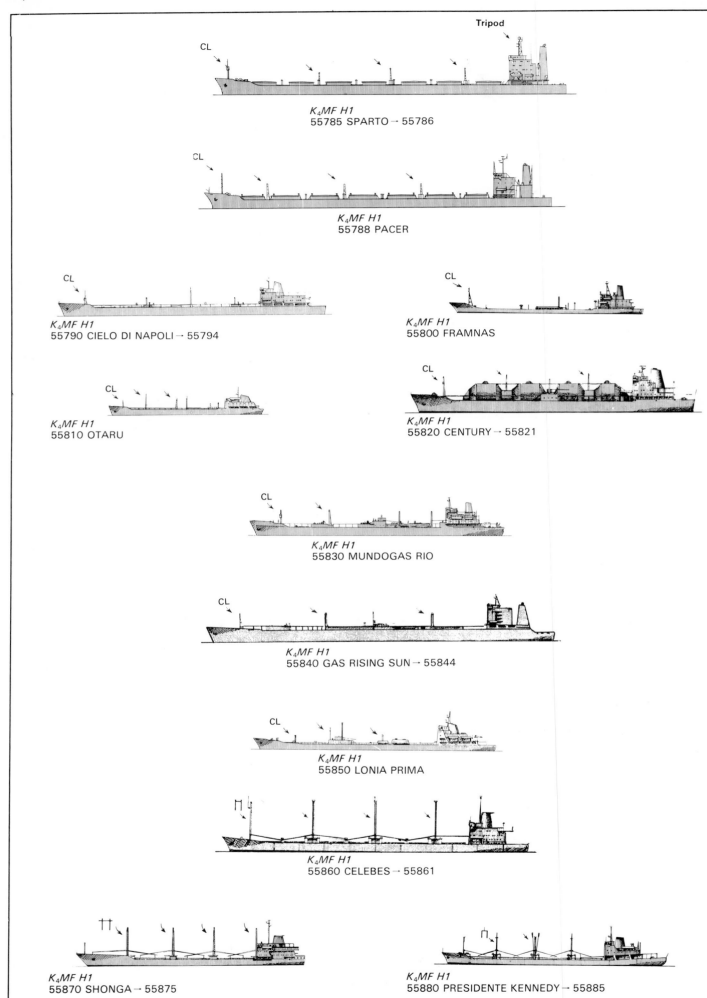

K₄MF H1
55785 SPARTO → 55786

K₄MF H1
55788 PACER

K₄MF H1
55790 CIELO DI NAPOLI → 55794

K₄MF H1
55800 FRAMNAS

K₄MF H1
55810 OTARU

K₄MF H1
55820 CENTURY → 55821

K₄MF H1
55830 MUNDOGAS RIO

K₄MF H1
55840 GAS RISING SUN → 55844

K₄MF H1
55850 LONIA PRIMA

K₄MF H1
55860 CELEBES → 55861

K₄MF H1
55870 SHONGA → 55875

K₄MF H1
55880 PRESIDENTE KENNEDY → 55885

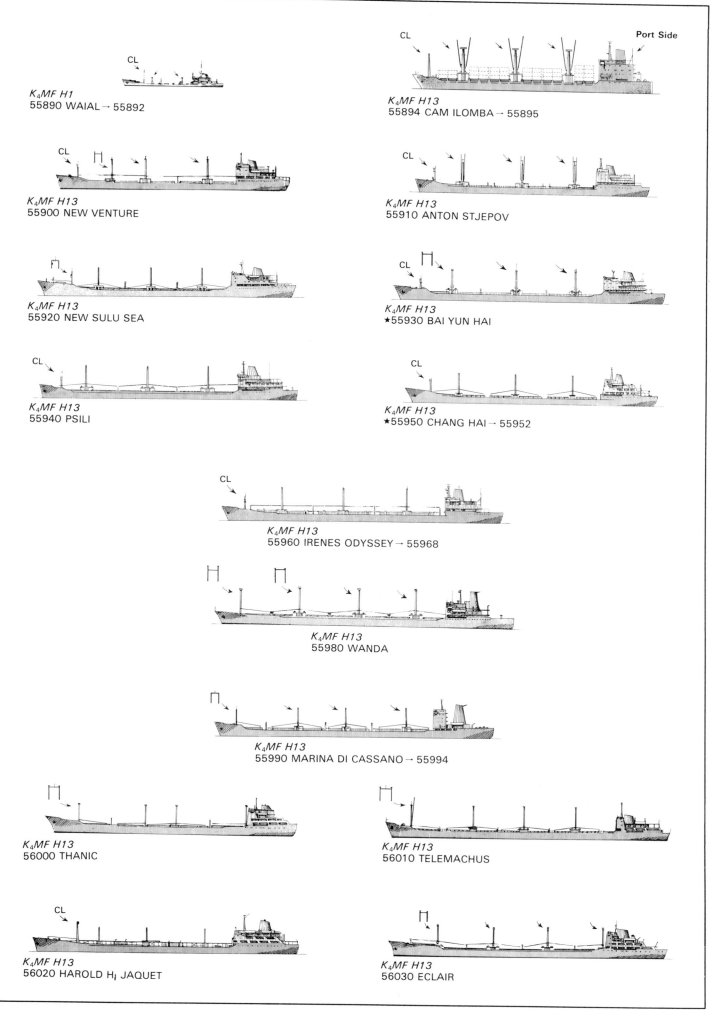

K₄MF H1
55890 WAIAL → 55892

K₄MF H13
55894 CAM ILOMBA → 55895

K₄MF H13
55900 NEW VENTURE

K₄MF H13
55910 ANTON STJEPOV

K₄MF H13
55920 NEW SULU SEA

K₄MF H13
★55930 BAI YUN HAI

K₄MF H13
55940 PSILI

K₄MF H13
★55950 CHANG HAI → 55952

K₄MF H13
55960 IRENES ODYSSEY → 55968

K₄MF H13
55980 WANDA

K₄MF H13
55990 MARINA DI CASSANO → 55994

K₄MF H13
56000 THANIC

K₄MF H13
56010 TELEMACHUS

K₄MF H13
56020 HAROLD Hᵢ JAQUET

K₄MF H13
56030 ECLAIR

K₄MF H13
56040 BANDAK

K₄MF H13
56050 ELIZA → 56051

K₄MF H13
56060 ARETHUSA

K₄MF H13
56090 SLOMAN MERCUR → 56091

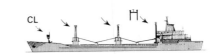

K₄MF H13
56100 LAGO PETEN ITZA

K₄MF H13
56110 MILAS → 56113

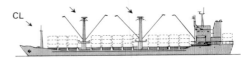

K₄MF H13
56115 ANDROMEDA STAR → 56118

K₄MF H13
56120 EDITA → 56122

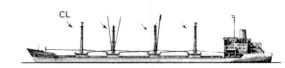

K₄MF H13
56130 FLAVIA

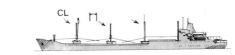

K₄MF H13
56140 KASSIAN GLORY

K₄MF H13
56150 HAVIS

K₄MF H13
56160 ADELIA → 56161

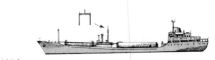

K₄MF H13
56170 GAZ PIONEER → 56172

K₄MF H13
56180 PRESIDENT DELCOURT

K₄MF H13
56185 SILVERHAWK

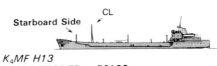

K₄MF H13
56190 TRADER → 56192

K₄MF H13
56200 ODET → 56201

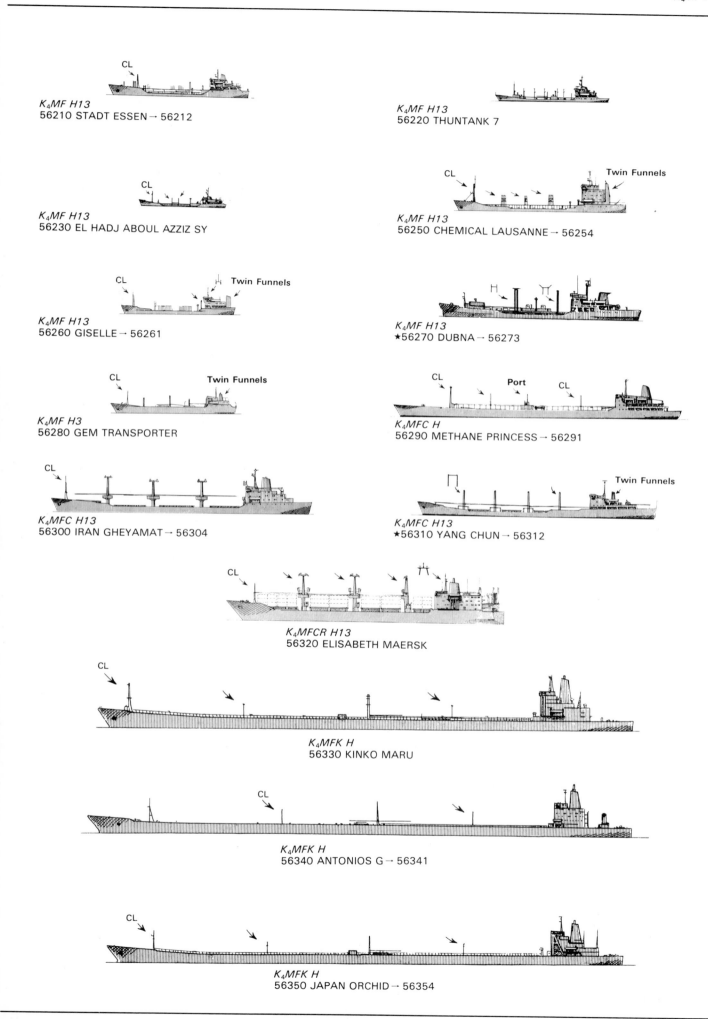

K₄MF H13
56210 STADT ESSEN → 56212

K₄MF H13
56220 THUNTANK 7

K₄MF H13
56230 EL HADJ ABOUL AZZIZ SY

K₄MF H13
56250 CHEMICAL LAUSANNE → 56254

K₄MF H13
56260 GISELLE → 56261

K₄MF H13
★56270 DUBNA → 56273

K₄MF H3
56280 GEM TRANSPORTER

K₄MFC H
56290 METHANE PRINCESS → 56291

K₄MFC H13
56300 IRAN GHEYAMAT → 56304

K₄MFC H13
★56310 YANG CHUN → 56312

K₄MFCR H13
56320 ELISABETH MAERSK

K₄MFK H
56330 KINKO MARU

K₄MFK H
56340 ANTONIOS G → 56341

K₄MFK H
56350 JAPAN ORCHID → 56354

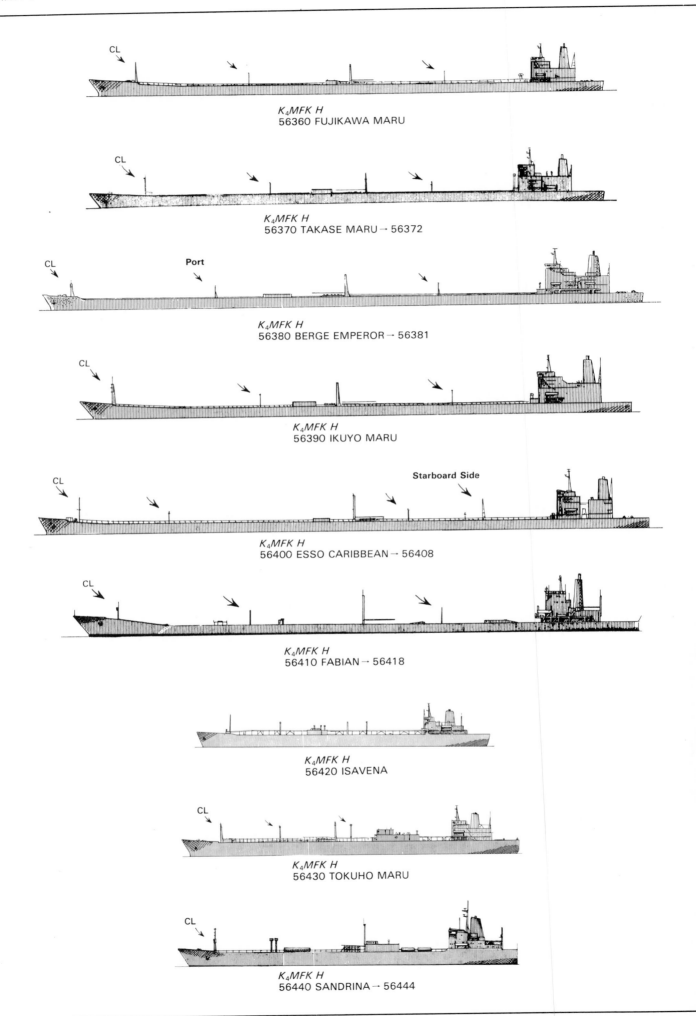

K₄MFK H
56360 FUJIKAWA MARU

K₄MFK H
56370 TAKASE MARU → 56372

K₄MFK H
56380 BERGE EMPEROR → 56381

K₄MFK H
56390 IKUYO MARU

K₄MFK H
56400 ESSO CARIBBEAN → 56408

K₄MFK H
56410 FABIAN → 56418

K₄MFK H
56420 ISAVENA

K₄MFK H
56430 TOKUHO MARU

K₄MFK H
56440 SANDRINA → 56444

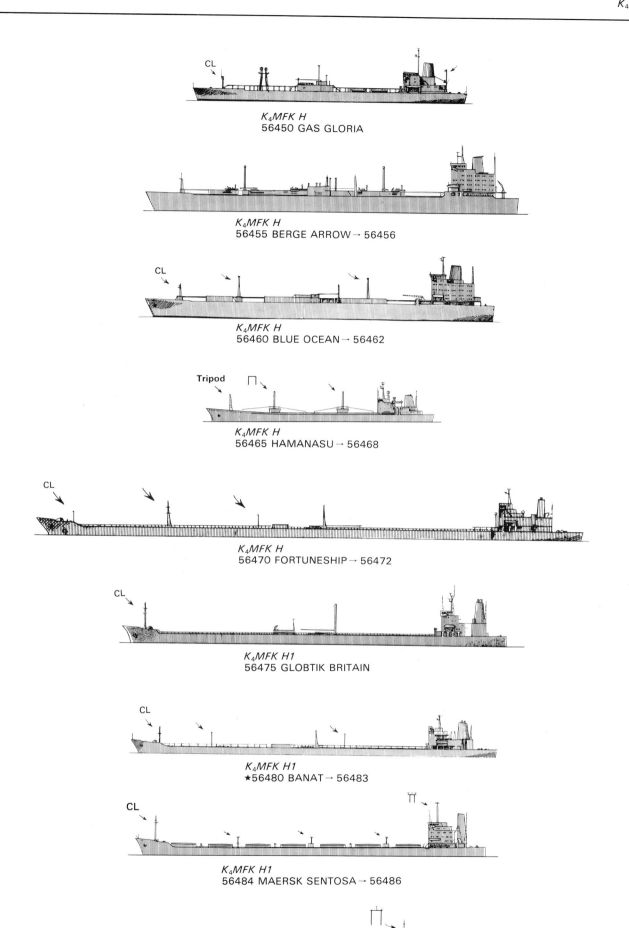

K₄MFK H
56450 GAS GLORIA

K₄MFK H
56455 BERGE ARROW → 56456

K₄MFK H
56460 BLUE OCEAN → 56462

K₄MFK H
56465 HAMANASU → 56468

K₄MFK H
56470 FORTUNESHIP → 56472

K₄MFK H1
56475 GLOBTIK BRITAIN

K₄MFK H1
★56480 BANAT → 56483

K₄MFK H1
56484 MAERSK SENTOSA → 56486

K₄MFK H1
56490 STELLA

K₄MFK H1
56500 SEAKITTIE → 56504

K₄MFK H1
56510 NESTOR

K₄MFK H1
56520 ERITHIANI → 56524

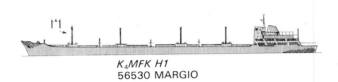

K₄MFK H1
56530 MARGIO

K₄MFK H1
56540 EASTERN WISEMAN

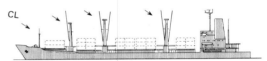

K₄MFK H1
56545 INDIAN HIGHSEA SUCCESS → 56546

K₄MFK H1
56550 PRESIDENTE KENNEDY → 56555

K₄MFK H1
56560 PALM TRADER → 56561

K₄MFK H1
56570 MARLY

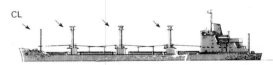

K₄MFK H1
56575 MURREE → 56577

K₄MFK H1
56580 OROYA → 56581

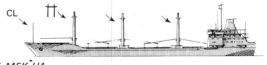

K₄MFK H1
56590 SOKOTO → 56595

K₄MFK H1
56600 SHONGA → 56605

K₄MFK H1
56610 LITSA → 56611

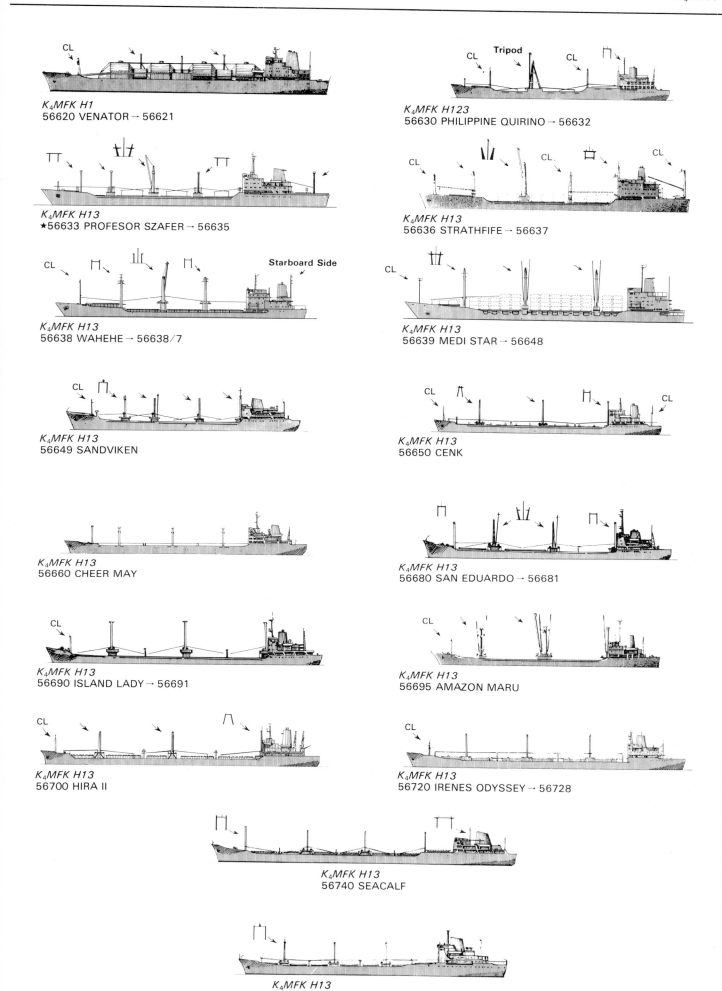

K₄MFK H1
56620 VENATOR → 56621

K₄MFK H123
56630 PHILIPPINE QUIRINO → 56632

K₄MFK H13
★56633 PROFESOR SZAFER → 56635

K₄MFK H13
56636 STRATHFIFE → 56637

K₄MFK H13
56638 WAHEHE → 56638/7

K₄MFK H13
56639 MEDI STAR → 56648

K₄MFK H13
56649 SANDVIKEN

K₄MFK H13
56650 CENK

K₄MFK H13
56660 CHEER MAY

K₄MFK H13
56680 SAN EDUARDO → 56681

K₄MFK H13
56690 ISLAND LADY → 56691

K₄MFK H13
56695 AMAZON MARU

K₄MFK H13
56700 HIRA II

K₄MFK H13
56720 IRENES ODYSSEY → 56728

K₄MFK H13
56740 SEACALF

K₄MFK H13
56750 ATLAS CHALLENGER → 56754

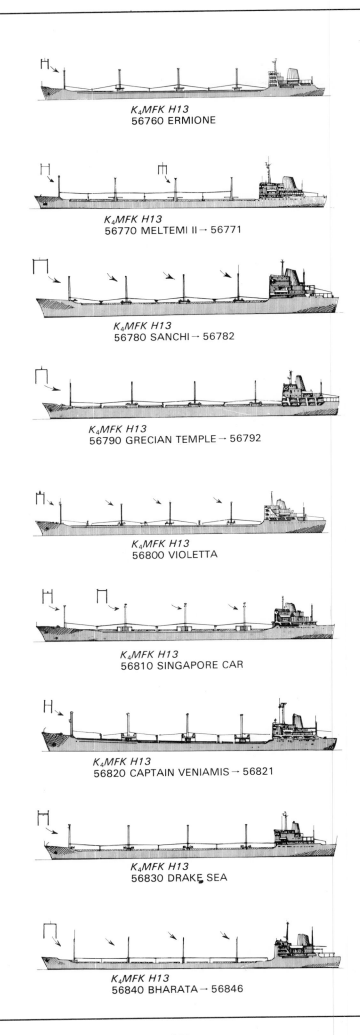

K₄MFK H13
56760 ERMIONE

K₄MFK H13
56770 MELTEMI II → 56771

K₄MFK H13
56780 SANCHI → 56782

K₄MFK H13
56790 GRECIAN TEMPLE → 56792

K₄MFK H13
56800 VIOLETTA

K₄MFK H13
56810 SINGAPORE CAR

K₄MFK H13
56820 CAPTAIN VENIAMIS → 56821

K₄MFK H13
56830 DRAKE SEA

K₄MFK H13
56840 BHARATA → 56846

K₄MFK H13
★56850 HUA HAI

K₄MFK H13
56860 MOUNT OTHRYS → 56863

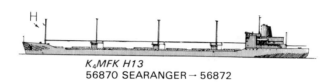

K₄MFK H13
56870 SEARANGER → 56872

K₄MFK H13
★56880 BEI HAI → 56881

K₄MFK H13
56900 MOFARRIJ C

K₄MFK H13
56920 FLORES

K₄MFK H13
56930 DOBROTA → 56931

K₄MFK H13
56940 JOANA → 56942

K₄MFK H13
56950 JILL CORD

K₄MFK H13
56960 SPLENDID HOPE

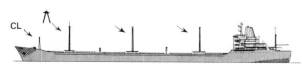

K₄MFK H13
56970 IRENES FANTASY → 56973

K₄MFK H13
56980 AGIA ERINI II → 56991

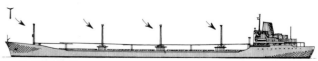

K₄MFK H13
★57000 ZHIHAI → 57009/2

K₄MFK H13
★57010 YUN HAI → 57011

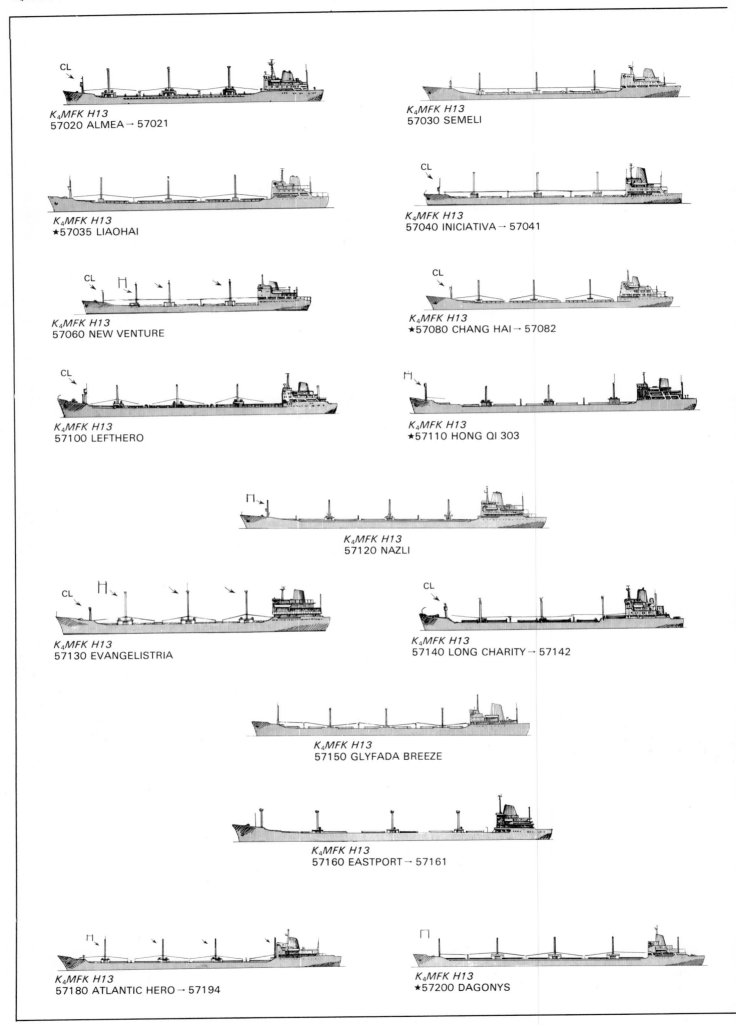

K₄MFK H13
57020 ALMEA → 57021

K₄MFK H13
57030 SEMELI

K₄MFK H13
★57035 LIAOHAI

K₄MFK H13
57040 INICIATIVA → 57041

K₄MFK H13
57060 NEW VENTURE

K₄MFK H13
★57080 CHANG HAI → 57082

K₄MFK H13
57100 LEFTHERO

K₄MFK H13
★57110 HONG QI 303

K₄MFK H13
57120 NAZLI

K₄MFK H13
57130 EVANGELISTRIA

K₄MFK H13
57140 LONG CHARITY → 57142

K₄MFK H13
57150 GLYFADA BREEZE

K₄MFK H13
57160 EASTPORT → 57161

K₄MFK H13
57180 ATLANTIC HERO → 57194

K₄MFK H13
★57200 DAGONYS

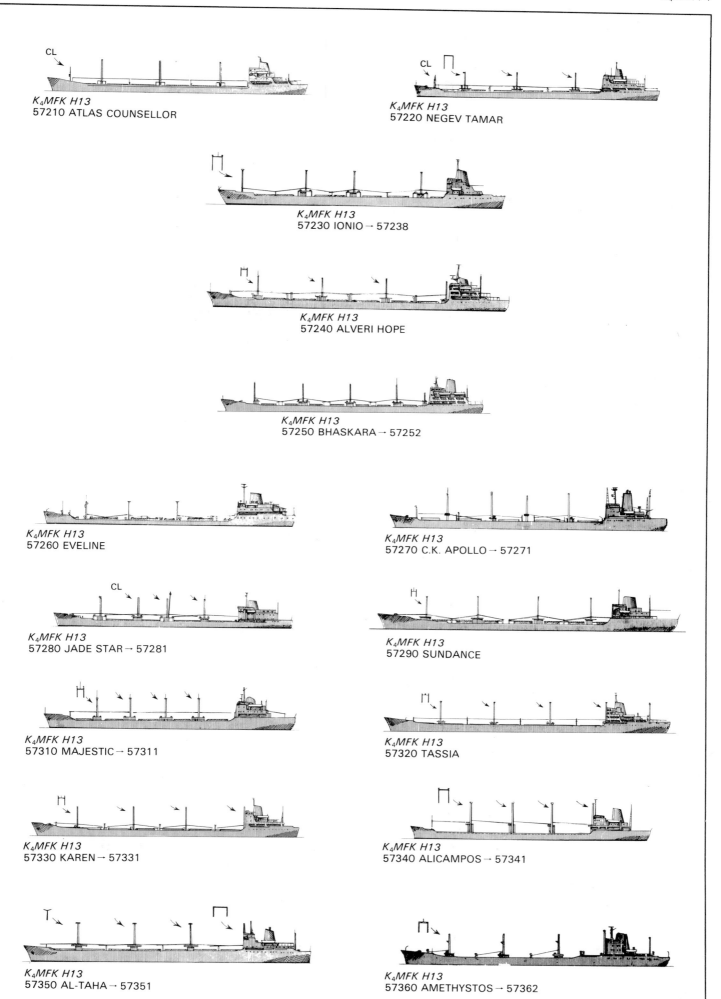

K₄MFK H13
57210 ATLAS COUNSELLOR

K₄MFK H13
57220 NEGEV TAMAR

K₄MFK H13
57230 IONIO → 57238

K₄MFK H13
57240 ALVERI HOPE

K₄MFK H13
57250 BHASKARA → 57252

K₄MFK H13
57260 EVELINE

K₄MFK H13
57270 C.K. APOLLO → 57271

K₄MFK H13
57280 JADE STAR → 57281

K₄MFK H13
57290 SUNDANCE

K₄MFK H13
57310 MAJESTIC → 57311

K₄MFK H13
57320 TASSIA

K₄MFK H13
57330 KAREN → 57331

K₄MFK H13
57340 ALICAMPOS → 57341

K₄MFK H13
57350 AL-TAHA → 57351

K₄MFK H13
57360 AMETHYSTOS → 57362

K₄MFK H13
★57370 LONG HAI → 57371

K₄MFK H13
57380 KEFALONIA LIGHT → 57383

K₄MFK H13
★57390 DONG HAI

K₄MFK H13
57400 TAI LIENG

K₄MFK H13
57410 FIVE STAR

K₄MFK H13
57420 TEL-AVIV → 57421

K₄MFK H13
★57440 VELENJE → 57444

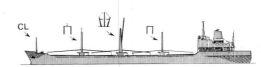

K₄MFK H13
★57450 LONG CHUAN JIANG → 57451

K₄MFK H13
57460 INDIAN PRESTIGE → 57463

K₄MFK H13
57470 IRENES EMERALD → 57471

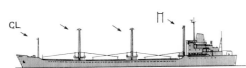

K₄MFK H13
57475 BRAVE THEMIS → 57476

K₄MFK H13
57480 ALPINA → 57481

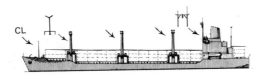

K₄MFK H13
57490 HOLSTENSAILOR → 57492

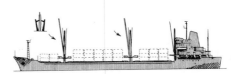

K₄MFK H13
★57500 KARIPANDE → 57501

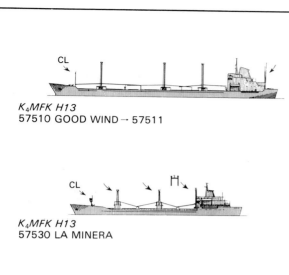

K₄MFK H13
57510 GOOD WIND → 57511

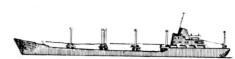

K₄MFK H13
57520 BEATRIZ MONTEIRO → 57524

K₄MFK H13
57530 LA MINERA

K₄MFK H13
57540 BLUE SHINE → 57543

K₄MFK H13
57550 POLWIND → 57562

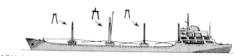

K₄MFK H13
57570 IRENE

K₄MFK H13
57580 AL KAHERAH

K₄MFK H13
57590 ALBION → 57594

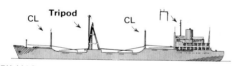

K₄MFK H13
57600 ANITA 1 → 57613/2

K₄MFK H13
57614 YUE RIVER → 57619/11

K₄MFK H13
57620 PHILIPPINE QUIRINO → 57622

K₄MFK H13
57623 NIGERIA VENTURE → 57624

K₄MFK H13
57625 GLORY OCEAN → 57627

K₄MFK H13
★57628 TONGGON AE GUK

K₄MFK H13
★57630 LIVNY → 57636

K₄MFK H13
57660 STOLT SEA → 57664

K₄MFK H13
57670 WILTSHIRE

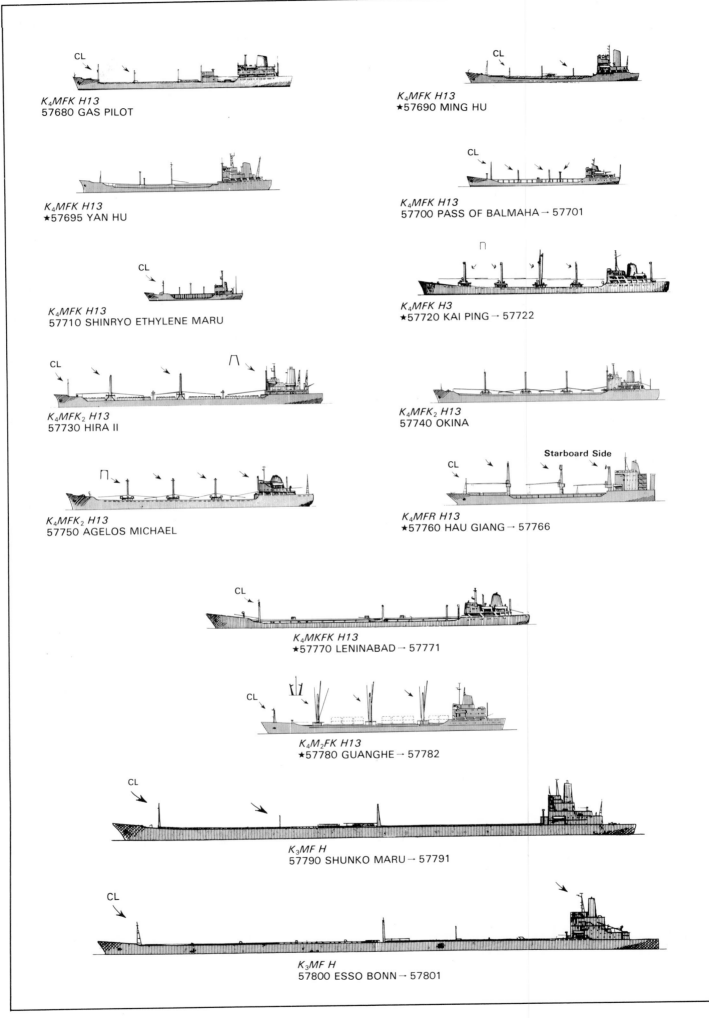

K₄MFK H13
57680 GAS PILOT

K₄MFK H13
★57690 MING HU

K₄MFK H13
★57695 YAN HU

K₄MFK H13
57700 PASS OF BALMAHA → 57701

K₄MFK H13
57710 SHINRYO ETHYLENE MARU

K₄MFK H3
★57720 KAI PING → 57722

K₄MFK₂ H13
57730 HIRA II

K₄MFK₂ H13
57740 OKINA

K₄MFK₂ H13
57750 AGELOS MICHAEL

K₄MFR H13
★57760 HAU GIANG → 57766

K₄MKFK H13
★57770 LENINABAD → 57771

K₄M₂FK H13
★57780 GUANGHE → 57782

K₃MF H
57790 SHUNKO MARU → 57791

K₃MF H
57800 ESSO BONN → 57801

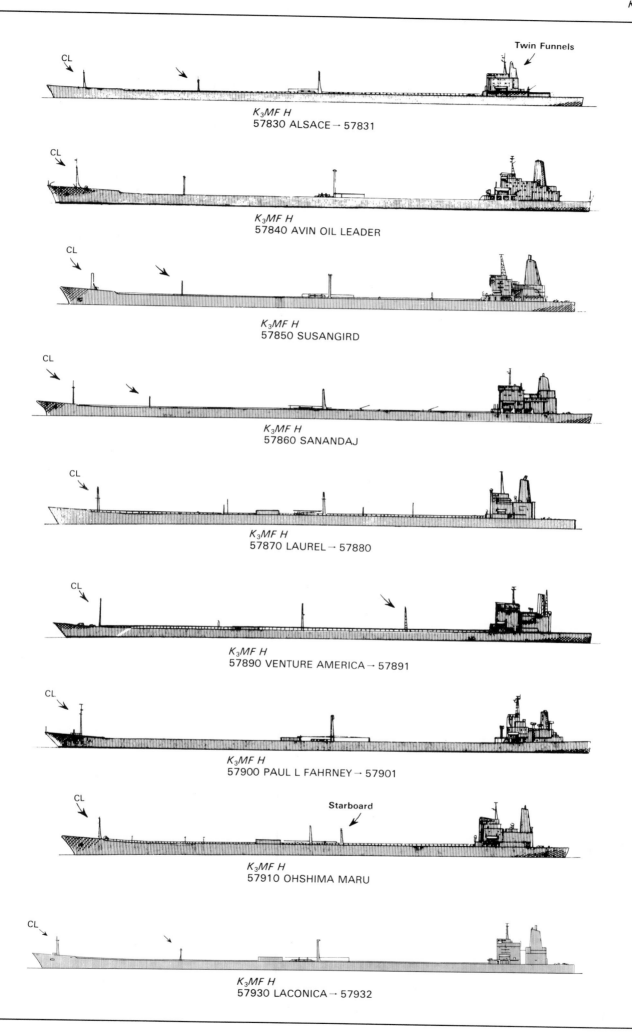

CL

Twin Funnels

K₃MF H
57830 ALSACE → 57831

CL

K₃MF H
57840 AVIN OIL LEADER

CL

K₃MF H
57850 SUSANGIRD

CL

K₃MF H
57860 SANANDAJ

CL

K₃MF H
57870 LAUREL → 57880

CL

K₃MF H
57890 VENTURE AMERICA → 57891

CL

K₃MF H
57900 PAUL L FAHRNEY → 57901

CL

Starboard

K₃MF H
57910 OHSHIMA MARU

CL

K₃MF H
57930 LACONICA → 57932

295

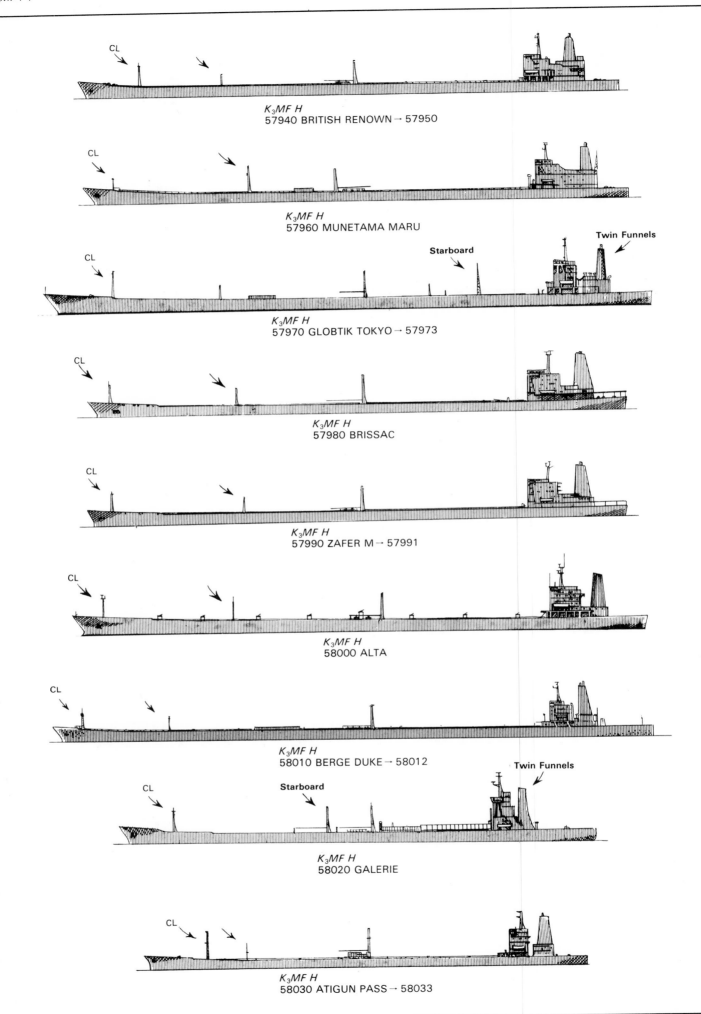

K₃MF H
57940 BRITISH RENOWN → 57950

K₃MF H
57960 MUNETAMA MARU

K₃MF H
57970 GLOBTIK TOKYO → 57973

K₃MF H
57980 BRISSAC

K₃MF H
57990 ZAFER M → 57991

K₃MF H
58000 ALTA

K₃MF H
58010 BERGE DUKE → 58012

K₃MF H
58020 GALERIE

K₃MF H
58030 ATIGUN PASS → 58033

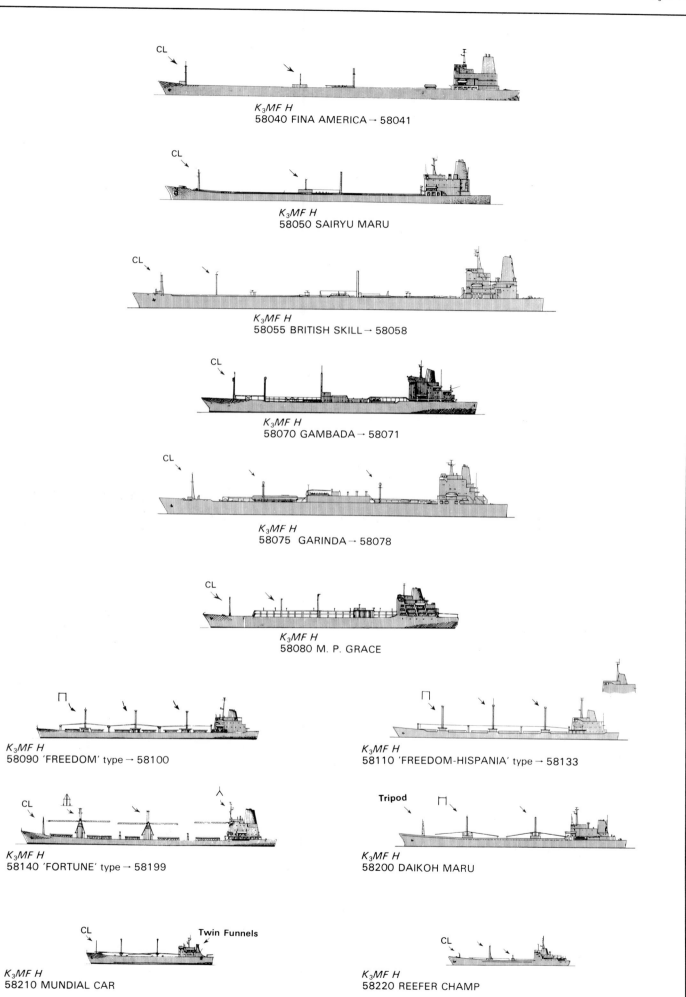

K₃MF H
58040 FINA AMERICA → 58041

K₃MF H
58050 SAIRYU MARU

K₃MF H
58055 BRITISH SKILL → 58058

K₃MF H
58070 GAMBADA → 58071

K₃MF H
58075 GARINDA → 58078

K₃MF H
58080 M. P. GRACE

K₃MF H
58090 'FREEDOM' type → 58100

K₃MF H
58110 'FREEDOM-HISPANIA' type → 58133

K₃MF H
58140 'FORTUNE' type → 58199

K₃MF H
58200 DAIKOH MARU

K₃MF H
58210 MUNDIAL CAR

K₃MF H
58220 REEFER CHAMP

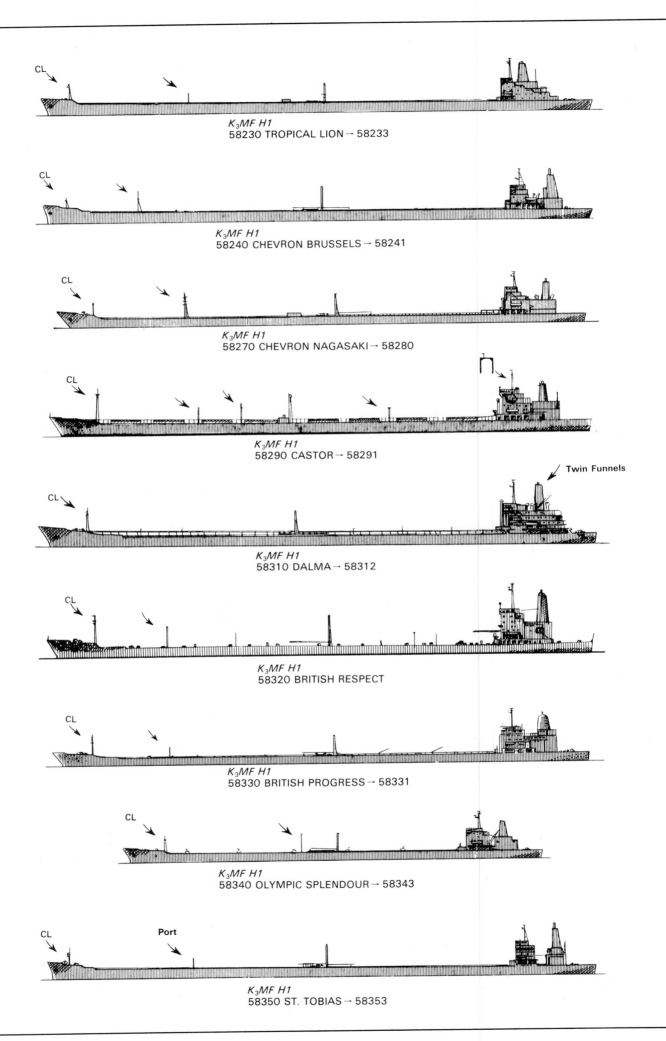

K₃MF H1
58230 TROPICAL LION → 58233

K₃MF H1
58240 CHEVRON BRUSSELS → 58241

K₃MF H1
58270 CHEVRON NAGASAKI → 58280

K₃MF H1
58290 CASTOR → 58291

Twin Funnels

K₃MF H1
58310 DALMA → 58312

K₃MF H1
58320 BRITISH RESPECT

K₃MF H1
58330 BRITISH PROGRESS → 58331

K₃MF H1
58340 OLYMPIC SPLENDOUR → 58343

Port

K₃MF H1
58350 ST. TOBIAS → 58353

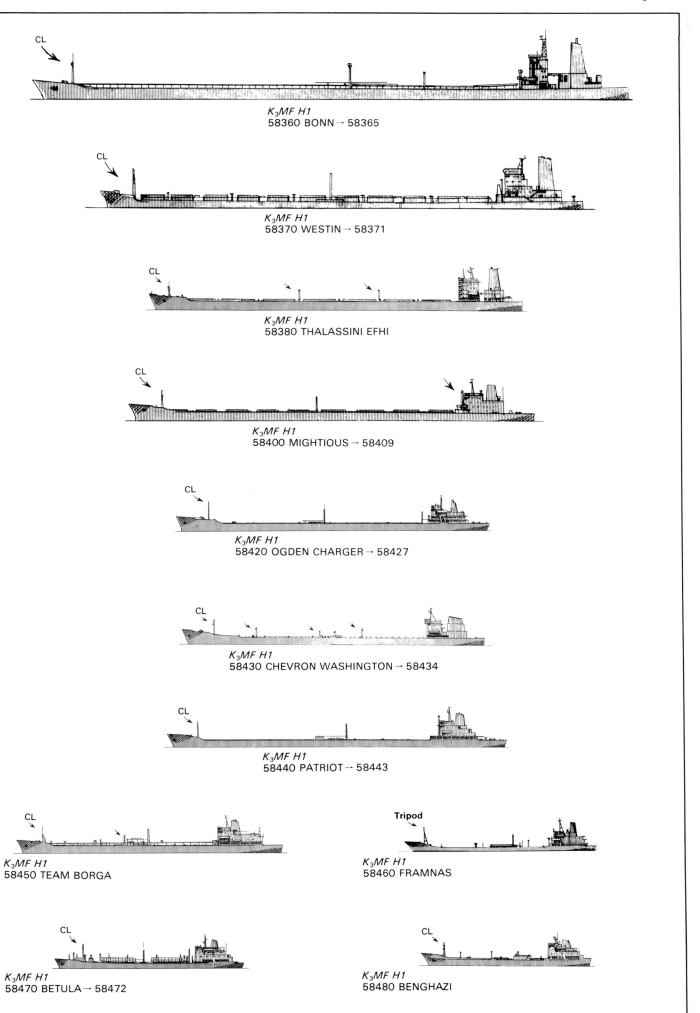

K₃MF H1
58360 BONN → 58365

K₃MF H1
58370 WESTIN → 58371

K₃MF H1
58380 THALASSINI EFHI

K₃MF H1
58400 MIGHTIOUS → 58409

K₃MF H1
58420 OGDEN CHARGER → 58427

K₃MF H1
58430 CHEVRON WASHINGTON → 58434

K₃MF H1
58440 PATRIOT → 58443

K₃MF H1
58450 TEAM BORGA

K₃MF H1
58460 FRAMNAS

K₃MF H1
58470 BETULA → 58472

K₃MF H1
58480 BENGHAZI

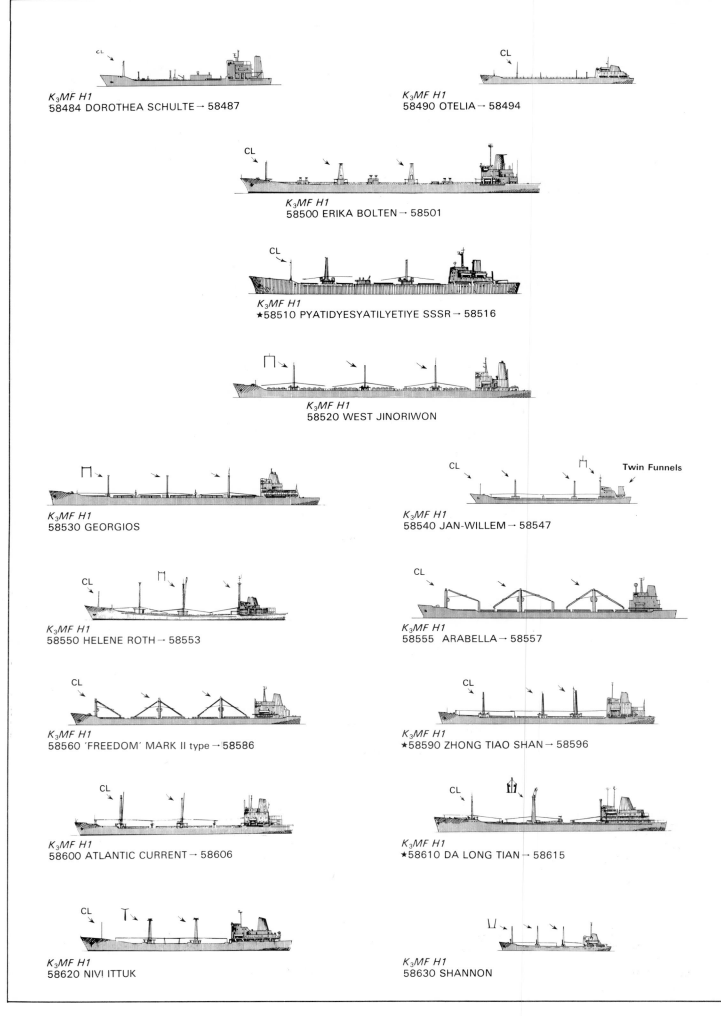

K₃MF H1
58484 DOROTHEA SCHULTE→ 58487

K₃MF H1
58490 OTELIA → 58494

K₃MF H1
58500 ERIKA BOLTEN → 58501

K₃MF H1
★58510 PYATIDYESYATILYETIYE SSSR → 58516

K₃MF H1
58520 WEST JINORIWON

K₃MF H1
58530 GEORGIOS

K₃MF H1
58540 JAN-WILLEM → 58547

Twin Funnels

K₃MF H1
58550 HELENE ROTH → 58553

K₃MF H1
58555 ARABELLA → 58557

K₃MF H1
58560 'FREEDOM' MARK II type → 58586

K₃MF H1
★58590 ZHONG TIAO SHAN → 58596

K₃MF H1
58600 ATLANTIC CURRENT → 58606

K₃MF H1
★58610 DA LONG TIAN → 58615

K₃MF H1
58620 NIVI ITTUK

K₃MF H1
58630 SHANNON

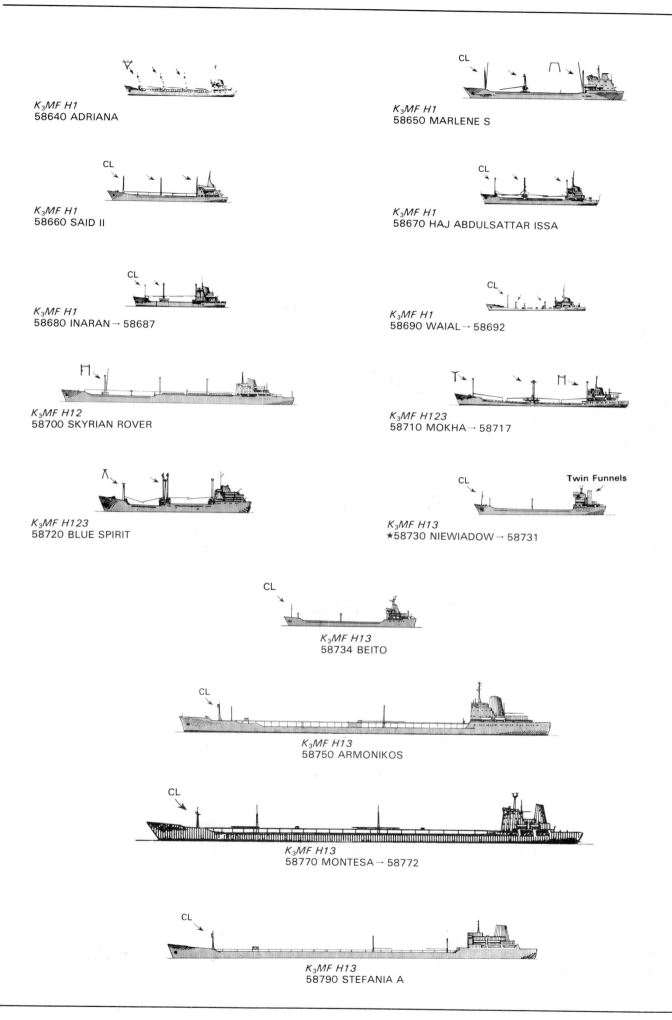

K₃MF H1
58640 ADRIANA

K₃MF H1
58650 MARLENE S

K₃MF H1
58660 SAID II

K₃MF H1
58670 HAJ ABDULSATTAR ISSA

K₃MF H1
58680 INARAN → 58687

K₃MF H1
58690 WAIAL → 58692

K₃MF H12
58700 SKYRIAN ROVER

K₃MF H123
58710 MOKHA → 58717

K₃MF H123
58720 BLUE SPIRIT

K₃MF H13
★58730 NIEWIADOW → 58731

K₃MF H13
58734 BEITO

K₃MF H13
58750 ARMONIKOS

K₃MF H13
58770 MONTESA → 58772

K₃MF H13
58790 STEFANIA A

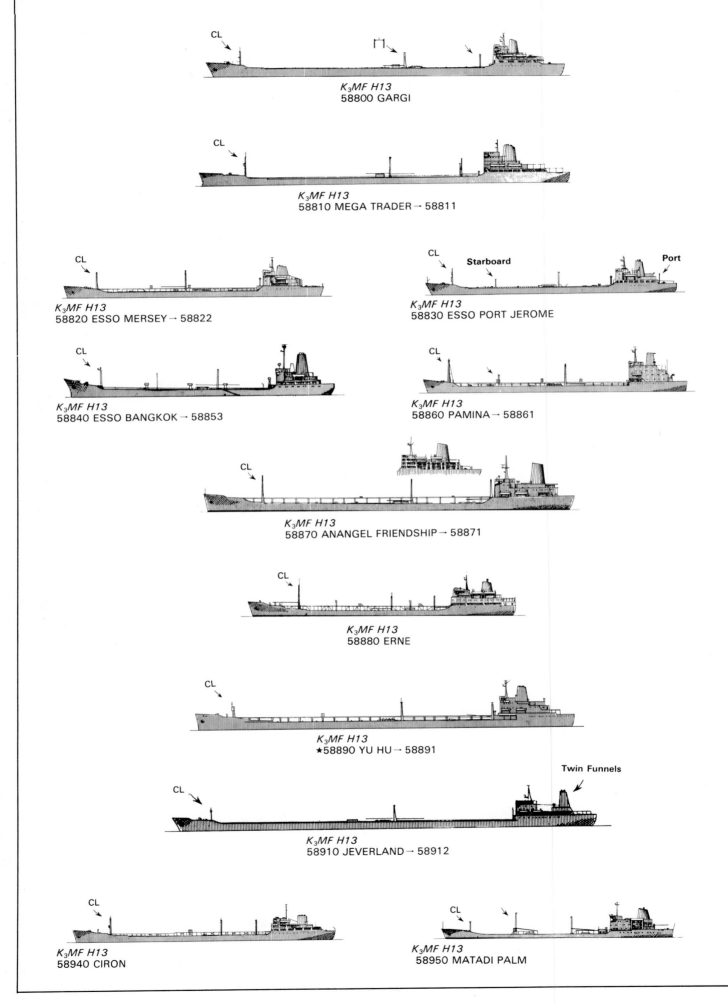

K₃MF H13
58800 GARGI

K₃MF H13
58810 MEGA TRADER → 58811

K₃MF H13
58820 ESSO MERSEY → 58822

K₃MF H13
58830 ESSO PORT JEROME

K₃MF H13
58840 ESSO BANGKOK → 58853

K₃MF H13
58860 PAMINA → 58861

K₃MF H13
58870 ANANGEL FRIENDSHIP → 58871

K₃MF H13
58880 ERNE

K₃MF H13
★58890 YU HU → 58891

K₃MF H13
58910 JEVERLAND → 58912

K₃MF H13
58940 CIRON

K₃MF H13
58950 MATADI PALM

K₃MF H13
58960 MARINE CHEMIST

K₃MF H13
58970 IBN ROCHD → 58973

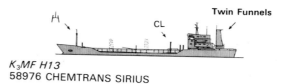

K₃MF H13
58976 CHEMTRANS SIRIUS

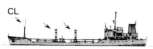

K₃MF H13
58980 PRESIDENT DELCOURT

K₃MF H13
58990 STELLAMAN → 58991

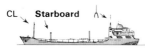

K₃MF H13
59000 CENTAURMAN → 59001

K₃MF H13
59010 LA BAHIA → 59011

K₃MF H13
59020 ISLAND JESTER

K₃MF H13
59030 DEVON CURLEW → 59032

K₃MF H13
59050 ALCHIMIST LUBECK → 59051

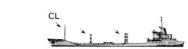

K₃MF H13
59060 ASTRAMAN → 59061

K₃MF H13
59070 ALCHIMIST ROTTERDAM → 59074

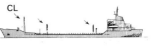

K₃MF H13
59080 CAPT. F. GAIGNEROT → 59081

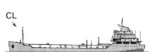

K₃MF H13
59090 ODET → 59091

K₃MF H13
59100 MARE NOVUM → 59102

K₃MF H13
59110 THUNTANK I

K₃MF H13
59120 LUDWIG

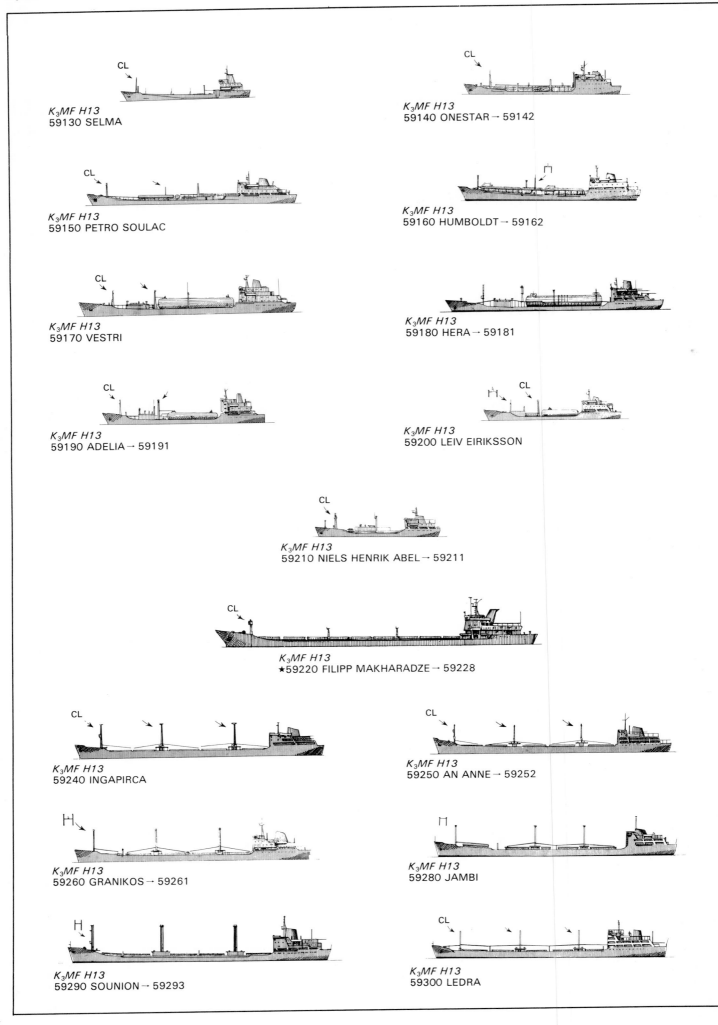

K₃MF H13
59130 SELMA

K₃MF H13
59140 ONESTAR → 59142

K₃MF H13
59150 PETRO SOULAC

K₃MF H13
59160 HUMBOLDT → 59162

K₃MF H13
59170 VESTRI

K₃MF H13
59180 HERA → 59181

K₃MF H13
59190 ADELIA → 59191

K₃MF H13
59200 LEIV EIRIKSSON

K₃MF H13
59210 NIELS HENRIK ABEL → 59211

K₃MF H13
★59220 FILIPP MAKHARADZE → 59228

K₃MF H13
59240 INGAPIRCA

K₃MF H13
59250 AN ANNE → 59252

K₃MF H13
59260 GRANIKOS → 59261

K₃MF H13
59280 JAMBI

K₃MF H13
59290 SOUNION → 59293

K₃MF H13
59300 LEDRA

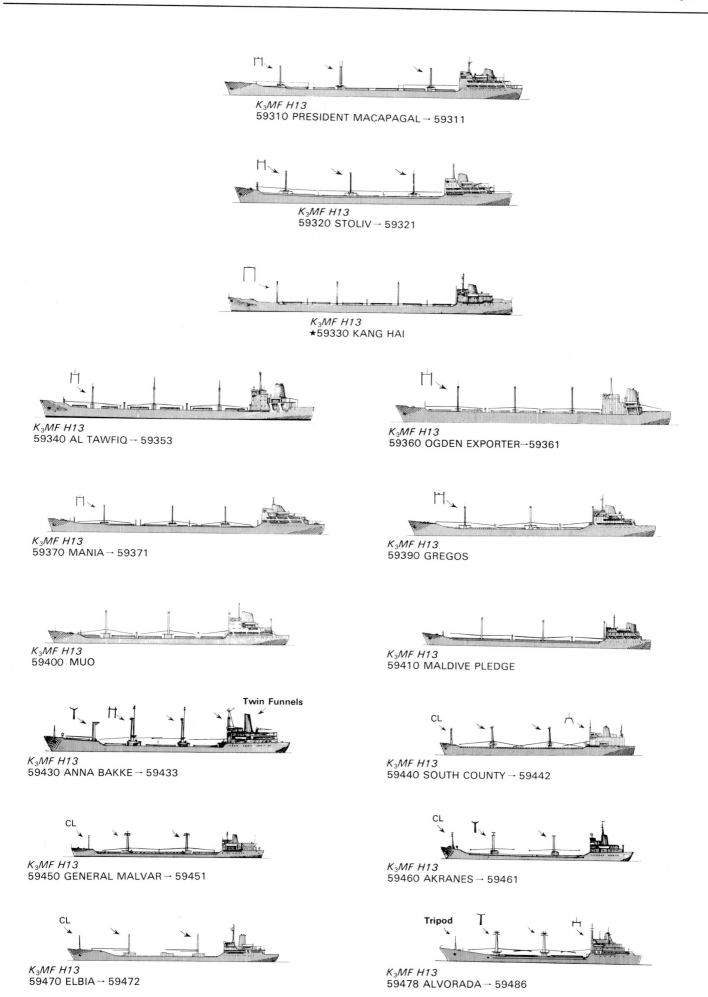

K₃MF H13
59310 PRESIDENT MACAPAGAL → 59311

K₃MF H13
59320 STOLIV → 59321

K₃MF H13
★59330 KANG HAI

K₃MF H13
59340 AL TAWFIQ → 59353

K₃MF H13
59360 OGDEN EXPORTER → 59361

K₃MF H13
59370 MANIA → 59371

K₃MF H13
59390 GREGOS

K₃MF H13
59400 MUO

K₃MF H13
59410 MALDIVE PLEDGE

Twin Funnels

K₃MF H13
59430 ANNA BAKKE → 59433

CL

K₃MF H13
59440 SOUTH COUNTY → 59442

CL

K₃MF H13
59450 GENERAL MALVAR → 59451

CL

K₃MF H13
59460 AKRANES → 59461

CL

K₃MF H13
59470 ELBIA → 59472

Tripod

K₃MF H13
59478 ALVORADA → 59486

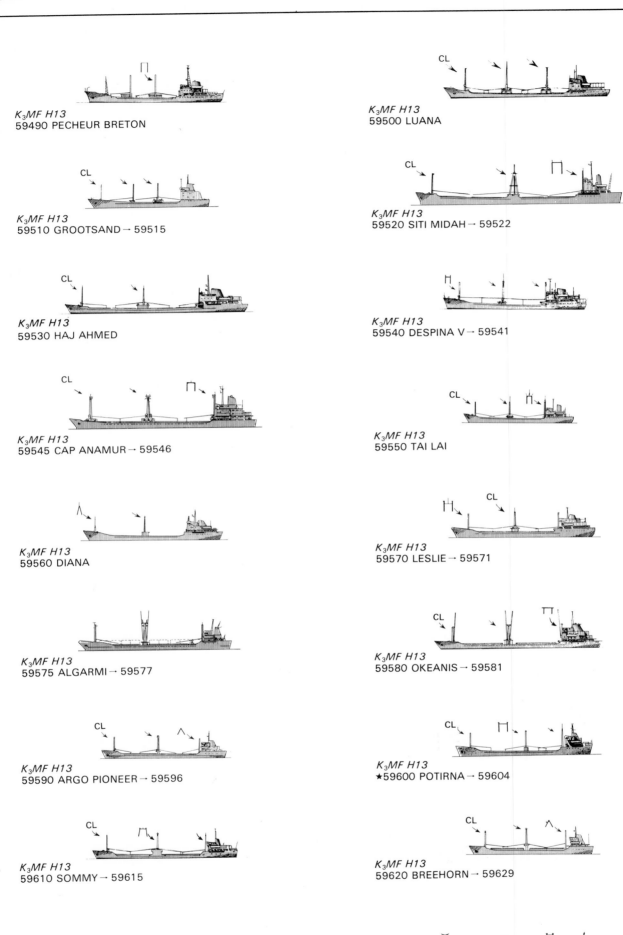

K₃MF H13
59490 PECHEUR BRETON

K₃MF H13
59500 LUANA

K₃MF H13
59510 GROOTSAND → 59515

K₃MF H13
59520 SITI MIDAH → 59522

K₃MF H13
59530 HAJ AHMED

K₃MF H13
59540 DESPINA V → 59541

K₃MF H13
59545 CAP ANAMUR → 59546

K₃MF H13
59550 TAI LAI

K₃MF H13
59560 DIANA

K₃MF H13
59570 LESLIE → 59571

K₃MF H13
59575 ALGARMI → 59577

K₃MF H13
59580 OKEANIS → 59581

K₃MF H13
59590 ARGO PIONEER → 59596

K₃MF H13
★59600 POTIRNA → 59604

K₃MF H13
59610 SOMMY → 59615

K₃MF H13
59620 BREEHORN → 59629

K₃MF H13
59630 LAURA

K₃MF H13
59640 MOKHA → 59647

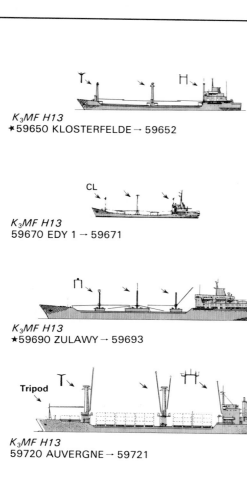

K₃MF H13
★59650 KLOSTERFELDE → 59652

K₃MF H13
59660 BLUE SPIRIT

K₃MF H13
59670 EDY 1 → 59671

K₃MF H13
59680 ALAMAK

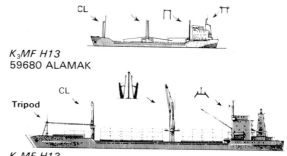

K₃MF H13
★59690 ZULAWY → 59693

K₃MF H13
59710 MOSEL → 59711

K₃MF H13
59720 AUVERGNE → 59721

K₃MF H13
59730 KOWIE → 59735

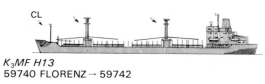

K₃MF H13
59740 FLORENZ → 59742

K₃MF H13
59750 LINERA → 59758

K₃MF H13
59770 EDITA → 59772

K₃MF H13
59780 SARI BUDI → 59782

K₃MF H13
★59790 PRVIC

K₃MF H13
59800 MILAS → 59803

K₃MF H2
59810 BERGE DUKE → 59812

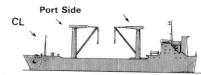

K₃MF H3
59815 MONT VENTOUX

K₃MF H3
59820 GROOTSAND → 59825

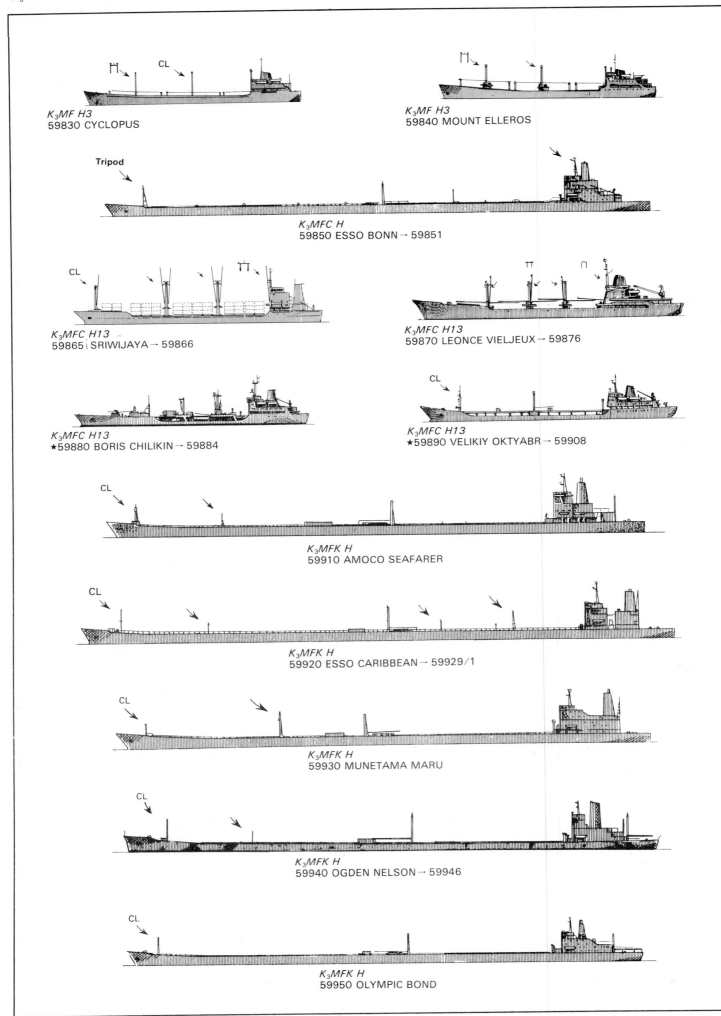

K₃MF H3
59830 CYCLOPUS

K₃MF H3
59840 MOUNT ELLEROS

Tripod

K₃MFC H
59850 ESSO BONN → 59851

K₃MFC H13
59865 SRIWIJAYA → 59866

K₃MFC H13
59870 LEONCE VIELJEUX → 59876

K₃MFC H13
★59880 BORIS CHILIKIN → 59884

K₃MFC H13
★59890 VELIKIY OKTYABR → 59908

K₃MFK H
59910 AMOCO SEAFARER

K₃MFK H
59920 ESSO CARIBBEAN → 59929/1

K₃MFK H
59930 MUNETAMA MARU

K₃MFK H
59940 OGDEN NELSON → 59946

K₃MFK H
59950 OLYMPIC BOND

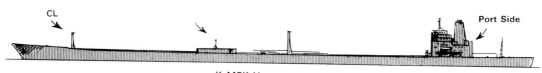

K₃MFK H
59960 MEITAI MARU

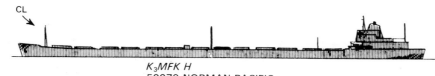

K₃MFK H
59970 NORMAN PACIFIC

K₃MFK H
59980 TRADE ENDEAVOR

K₃MFK H
59990 ESSO FUJI

K₃MFK H
59995 → YUHO MARU

K₃MFK H
59997 COLUMBIA LIBERTY → 59998

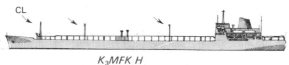

K₃MFK H
60000 PETRO SEA

K₃MFK H
60010 GAS GLORIA

K₃MFK H
60020 WAITAKI → 60022

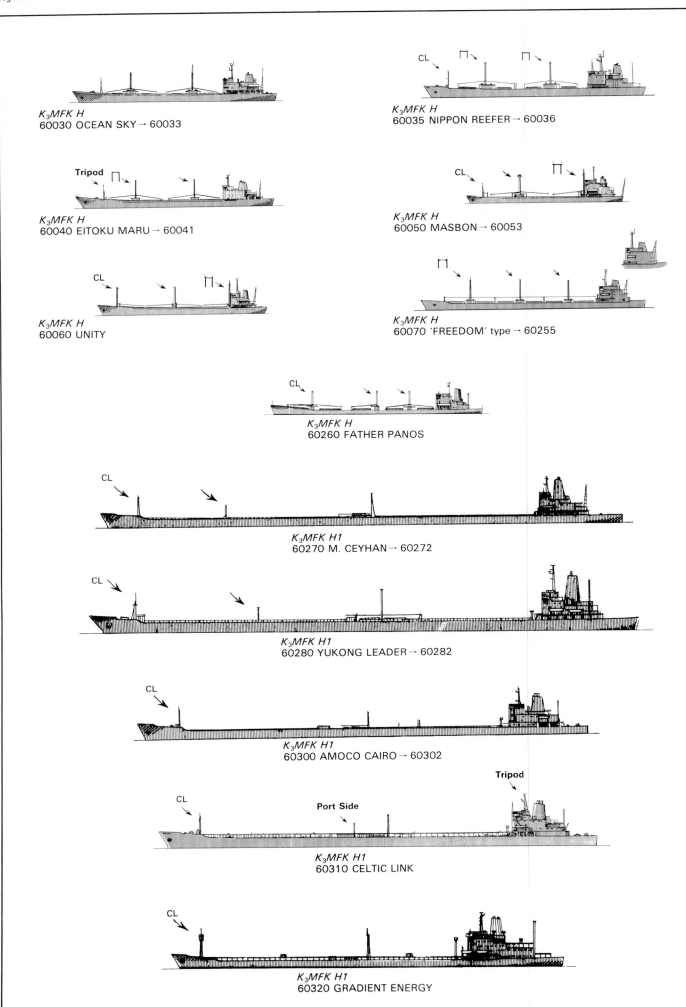

K₃MFK H
60030 OCEAN SKY → 60033

K₃MFK H
60035 NIPPON REEFER → 60036

K₃MFK H
60040 EITOKU MARU → 60041

K₃MFK H
60050 MASBON → 60053

K₃MFK H
60060 UNITY

K₃MFK H
60070 'FREEDOM' type → 60255

K₃MFK H
60260 FATHER PANOS

K₃MFK H1
60270 M. CEYHAN → 60272

K₃MFK H1
60280 YUKONG LEADER → 60282

K₃MFK H1
60300 AMOCO CAIRO → 60302

K₃MFK H1
60310 CELTIC LINK

K₃MFK H1
60320 GRADIENT ENERGY

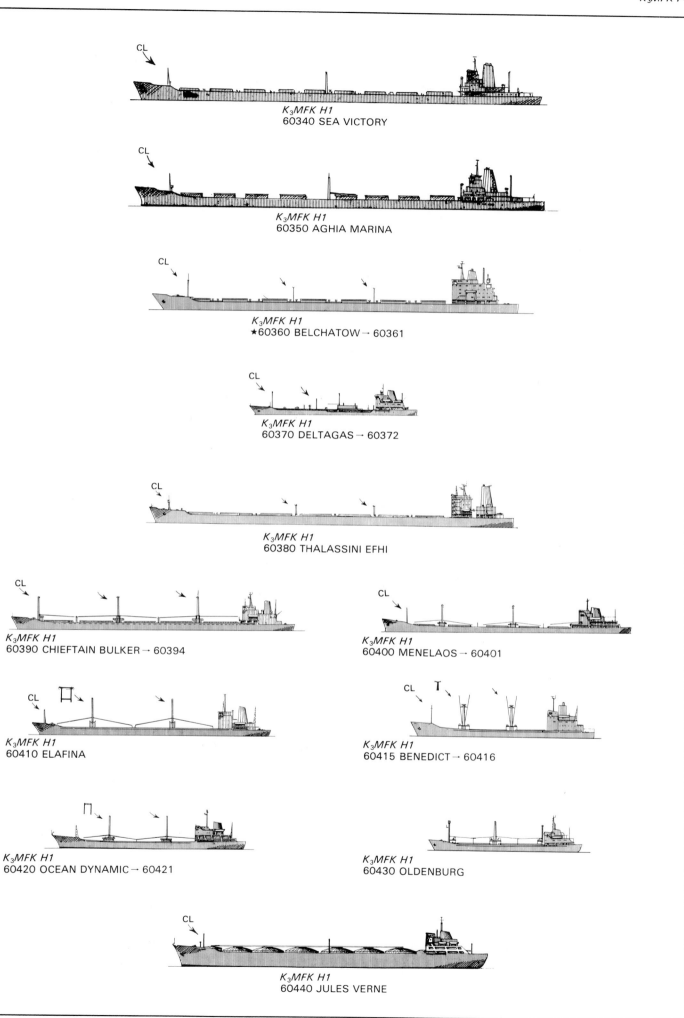

K₃MFK H1
60340 SEA VICTORY

K₃MFK H1
60350 AGHIA MARINA

K₃MFK H1
★60360 BELCHATOW → 60361

K₃MFK H1
60370 DELTAGAS → 60372

K₃MFK H1
60380 THALASSINI EFHI

K₃MFK H1
60390 CHIEFTAIN BULKER → 60394

K₃MFK H1
60400 MENELAOS → 60401

K₃MFK H1
60410 ELAFINA

K₃MFK H1
60415 BENEDICT → 60416

K₃MFK H1
60420 OCEAN DYNAMIC → 60421

K₃MFK H1
60430 OLDENBURG

K₃MFK H1
60440 JULES VERNE

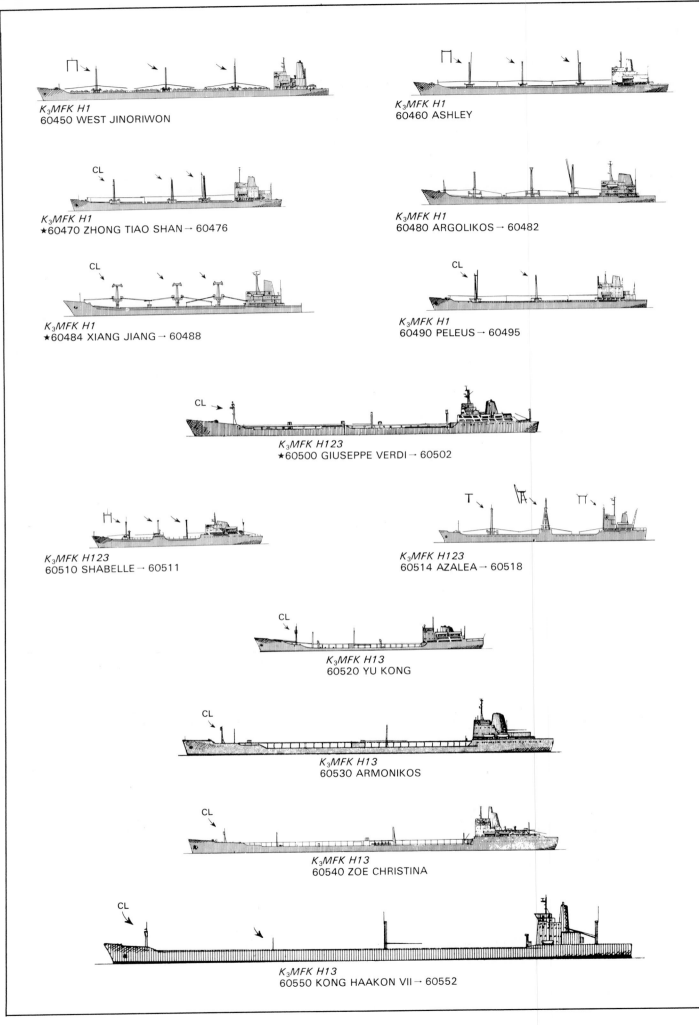

K₃MFK H1
60450 WEST JINORIWON

K₃MFK H1
60460 ASHLEY

K₃MFK H1
★60470 ZHONG TIAO SHAN → 60476

K₃MFK H1
60480 ARGOLIKOS → 60482

K₃MFK H1
★60484 XIANG JIANG → 60488

K₃MFK H1
60490 PELEUS → 60495

K₃MFK H123
★60500 GIUSEPPE VERDI → 60502

K₃MFK H123
60510 SHABELLE → 60511

K₃MFK H123
60514 AZALEA → 60518

K₃MFK H13
60520 YU KONG

K₃MFK H13
60530 ARMONIKOS

K₃MFK H13
60540 ZOE CHRISTINA

K₃MFK H13
60550 KONG HAAKON VII → 60552

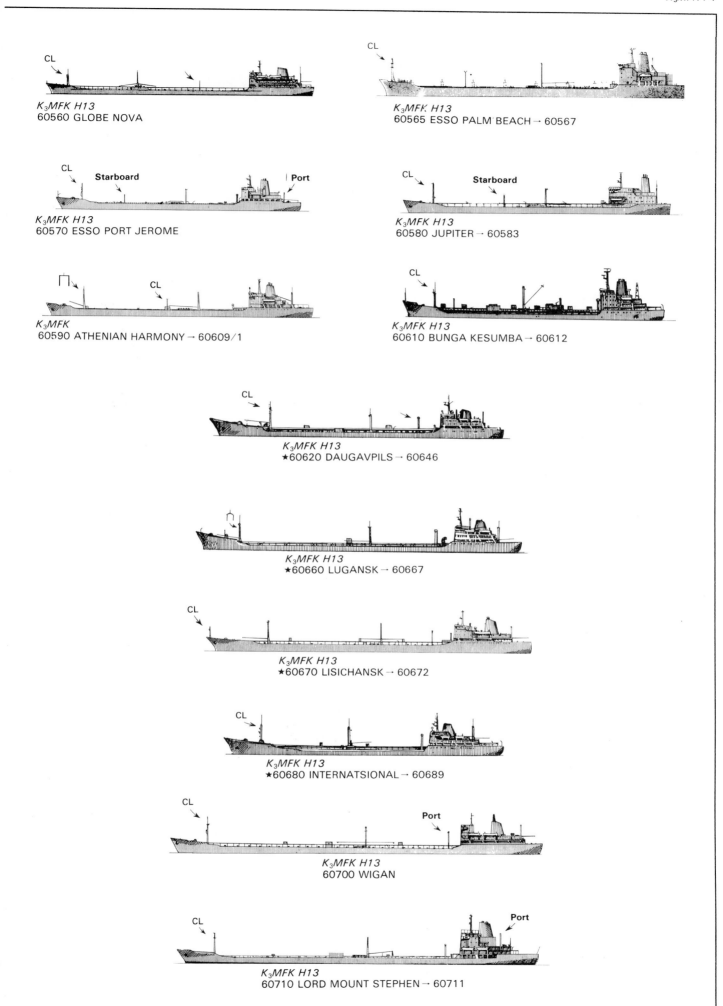

K₃MFK H13
60560 GLOBE NOVA

K₃MFK H13
60565 ESSO PALM BEACH → 60567

K₃MFK H13
60570 ESSO PORT JEROME

K₃MFK H13
60580 JUPITER → 60583

K₃MFK
60590 ATHENIAN HARMONY → 60609/1

K₃MFK H13
60610 BUNGA KESUMBA → 60612

K₃MFK H13
★60620 DAUGAVPILS → 60646

K₃MFK H13
★60660 LUGANSK → 60667

K₃MFK H13
★60670 LISICHANSK → 60672

K₃MFK H13
★60680 INTERNATSIONAL → 60689

K₃MFK H13
60700 WIGAN

K₃MFK H13
60710 LORD MOUNT STEPHEN → 60711

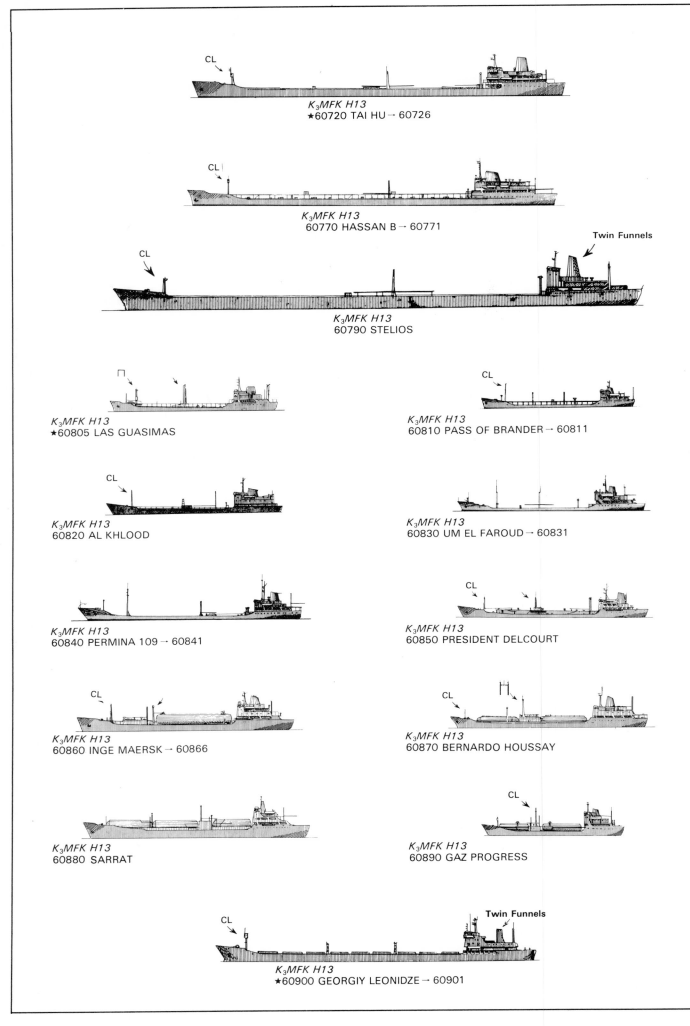

K₃MFK H13
★60720 TAI HU → 60726

K₃MFK H13
60770 HASSAN B → 60771

K₃MFK H13
60790 STELIOS

Twin Funnels

K₃MFK H13
★60805 LAS GUASIMAS

K₃MFK H13
60810 PASS OF BRANDER → 60811

K₃MFK H13
60820 AL KHLOOD

K₃MFK H13
60830 UM EL FAROUD → 60831

K₃MFK H13
60840 PERMINA 109 → 60841

K₃MFK H13
60850 PRESIDENT DELCOURT

K₃MFK H13
60860 INGE MAERSK → 60866

K₃MFK H13
60870 BERNARDO HOUSSAY

K₃MFK H13
60880 SARRAT

K₃MFK H13
60890 GAZ PROGRESS

Twin Funnels

K₃MFK H13
★60900 GEORGIY LEONIDZE → 60901

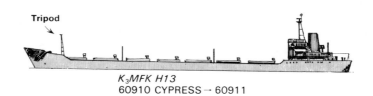

K₃MFK H13
60910 CYPRESS → 60911

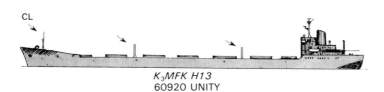

K₃MFK H13
60920 UNITY

K₃MFK H13
60940 SOUTH COUNTY → 60942

K₃MFK H13
60950 GHADAMES → 60956

K₃MFK H13
60960 AKBAR

K₃MFK H13
60970 TAISEI MARU No 98

K₃MFK H13
60980 URANUS 1

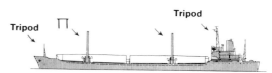

K₃MFK H13
60990 JOHNNY → 60994

K₃MFK H13
61000 ROSANA → 61002

K₃MFK H13
61005 HELMUT HERMANN

K₃MFK H13
61010 SANAGA → 61036

K₃MFK H13
61040 ARCHIMEDES → 61044/1

K₃MFK H13
61045 GLORY OCEAN → 61047

K₃MFK H13
61050 MAR TRANSPORTER → 61054/1

K₃MFK H13
61055 YUE RIVER → 61059/11

K₃MFK H13
61060 GOMASA → 61062

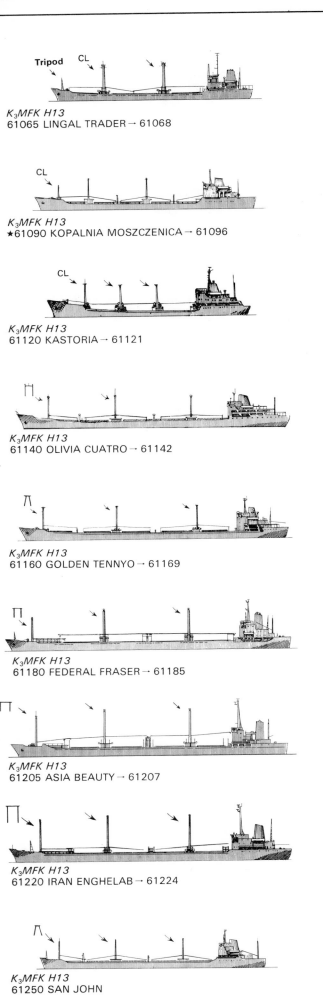
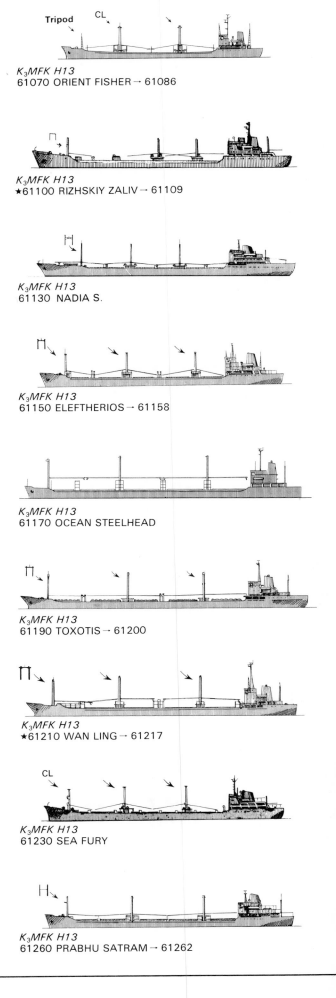

K₃MFK H13
61065 LINGAL TRADER → 61068

K₃MFK H13
61070 ORIENT FISHER → 61086

K₃MFK H13
★61090 KOPALNIA MOSZCZENICA → 61096

K₃MFK H13
★61100 RIZHSKIY ZALIV → 61109

K₃MFK H13
61120 KASTORIA → 61121

K₃MFK H13
61130 NADIA S.

K₃MFK H13
61140 OLIVIA CUATRO → 61142

K₃MFK H13
61150 ELEFTHERIOS → 61158

K₃MFK H13
61160 GOLDEN TENNYO → 61169

K₃MFK H13
61170 OCEAN STEELHEAD

K₃MFK H13
61180 FEDERAL FRASER → 61185

K₃MFK H13
61190 TOXOTIS → 61200

K₃MFK H13
61205 ASIA BEAUTY → 61207

K₃MFK H13
★61210 WAN LING → 61217

K₃MFK H13
61220 IRAN ENGHELAB → 61224

K₃MFK H13
61230 SEA FURY

K₃MFK H13
61250 SAN JOHN

K₃MFK H13
61260 PRABHU SATRAM → 61262

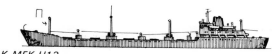

K₃MFK H13
★61270 PRIBOY → 61275

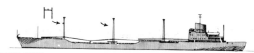

K₃MFK H13
61280 CONSTANCIA

K₃MFK H13
61290 TIARET → 61292

K₃MFK H13
★61310 JING HAI → 61313

K₃MFK H13
61320 GENERAL CAPINPIN → 61325

K₃MFK H13
61330 SOUNION → 61333

K₃MFK H13
61340 SALAMIS → 61341

K₃MFK H13
61350 SPERANZA

K₃MFK H13
61360 SAN GEORGE

K₃MFK H13
61380 EKTON

K₃MFK H13
61390 TRANSCOLUMBIA → 61391

K₃MFK H13
61400 DOUCE FRANCE III → 61409/16

K₃MFK H13
61410 AMBIKA → 61412

K₃MFK H13
61420 CAMPHOR → 61421

K₃MFK H13
61430 SEA LINDEN

K₃MFK H13
61440 SITI NOVA → 61444

K₃MFK H13
61450 QUEEN VASSILIKI II → 61451

K₃MFK H13
61460 ARCADIAN SUN → 61467

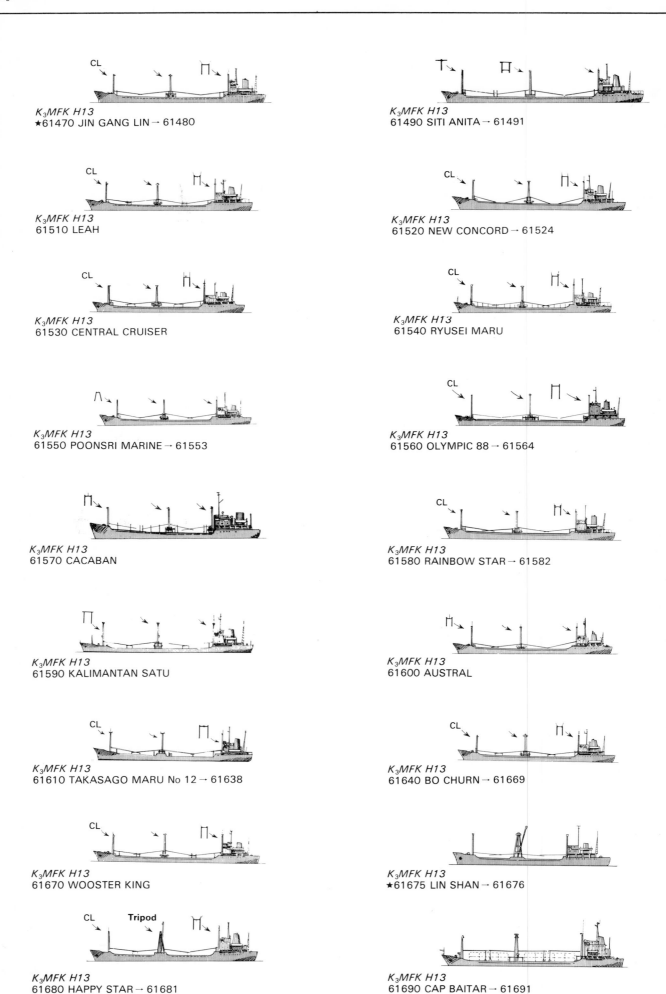

K₃MFK H13
★61470 JIN GANG LIN → 61480

K₃MFK H13
61490 SITI ANITA → 61491

K₃MFK H13
61510 LEAH

K₃MFK H13
61520 NEW CONCORD → 61524

K₃MFK H13
61530 CENTRAL CRUISER

K₃MFK H13
61540 RYUSEI MARU

K₃MFK H13
61550 POONSRI MARINE → 61553

K₃MFK H13
61560 OLYMPIC 88 → 61564

K₃MFK H13
61570 CACABAN

K₃MFK H13
61580 RAINBOW STAR → 61582

K₃MFK H13
61590 KALIMANTAN SATU

K₃MFK H13
61600 AUSTRAL

K₃MFK H13
61610 TAKASAGO MARU No 12 → 61638

K₃MFK H13
61640 BO CHURN → 61669

K₃MFK H13
61670 WOOSTER KING

K₃MFK H13
★61675 LIN SHAN → 61676

K₃MFK H13
61680 HAPPY STAR → 61681

K₃MFK H13
61690 CAP BAITAR → 61691

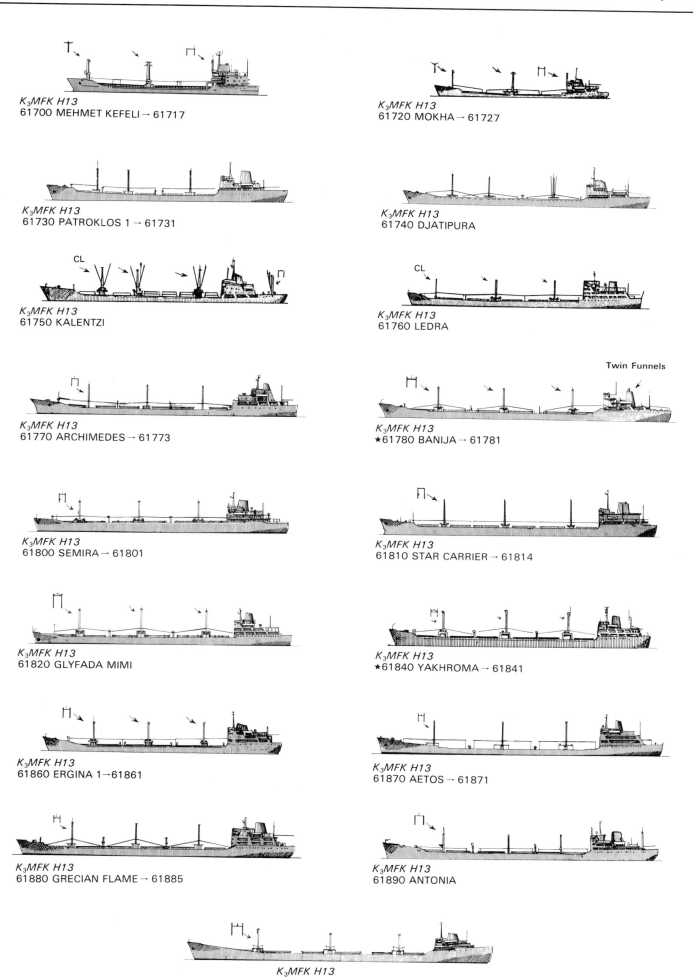

K₃MFK H13
61700 MEHMET KEFELI → 61717

K₃MFK H13
61720 MOKHA → 61727

K₃MFK H13
61730 PATROKLOS 1 → 61731

K₃MFK H13
61740 DJATIPURA

K₃MFK H13
61750 KALENTZI

K₃MFK H13
61760 LEDRA

K₃MFK H13
61770 ARCHIMEDES → 61773

Twin Funnels

K₃MFK H13
★61780 BANIJA → 61781

K₃MFK H13
61800 SEMIRA → 61801

K₃MFK H13
61810 STAR CARRIER → 61814

K₃MFK H13
61820 GLYFADA MIMI

K₃MFK H13
★61840 YAKHROMA → 61841

K₃MFK H13
61860 ERGINA 1 → 61861

K₃MFK H13
61870 AETOS → 61871

K₃MFK H13
61880 GRECIAN FLAME → 61885

K₃MFK H13
61890 ANTONIA

K₃MFK H13
61900 MARINA → 61901

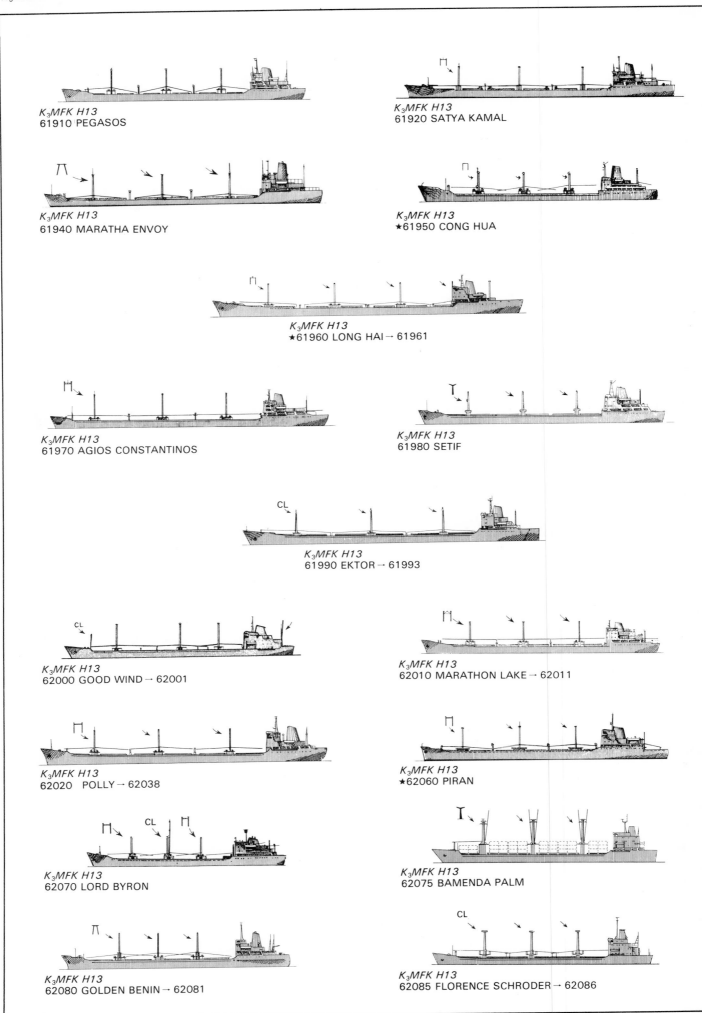

K₃MFK H13
61910 PEGASOS

K₃MFK H13
61920 SATYA KAMAL

K₃MFK H13
61940 MARATHA ENVOY

K₃MFK H13
★61950 CONG HUA

K₃MFK H13
★61960 LONG HAI → 61961

K₃MFK H13
61970 AGIOS CONSTANTINOS

K₃MFK H13
61980 SETIF

K₃MFK H13
61990 EKTOR → 61993

K₃MFK H13
62000 GOOD WIND → 62001

K₃MFK H13
62010 MARATHON LAKE → 62011

K₃MFK H13
62020 POLLY → 62038

K₃MFK H13
★62060 PIRAN

K₃MFK H13
62070 LORD BYRON

K₃MFK H13
62075 BAMENDA PALM

K₃MFK H13
62080 GOLDEN BENIN → 62081

K₃MFK H13
62085 FLORENCE SCHRODER → 62086

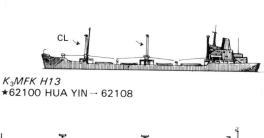

K₃MFK H13
★62100 HUA YIN → 62108

K₃MFK H13
62110   LEIDENSCHAFT → 62111

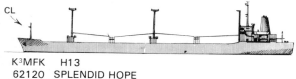

K³MFK   H13
62120   SPLENDID HOPE

K₃MFK H13
62130 FRANK DELMAS

K₃MFK H13
62140 ELEFTHERIOS → 62143

K₃MFK H13
62150 VASILAKIS

K₃MFK H13
62160 MUO

K₃MFK H13
62170 ARCADIAN SKY → 62171

K₃MFK H13
★62180 KOPER → 62181

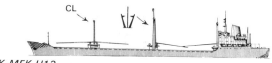

K₃MFK H13
★62190 DACHENG → 62191

K₃MFK H13
62200 OKPO PEARL

K₃MFK H13
62210 CENK

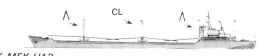

K₃MFK H13
62220 PACIFIC FAIR → 62226

K₃MFK H13
62230 ATAIR → 62235

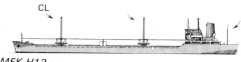

K₃MFK H13
62240 ANITA 1 → 62254

K₃MFK H13
62270 HSIEH YUNG → 62272

K₃MFK H13
62280 CAPIRA

K₃MFK H13
62290 AGIOS LOUKAS

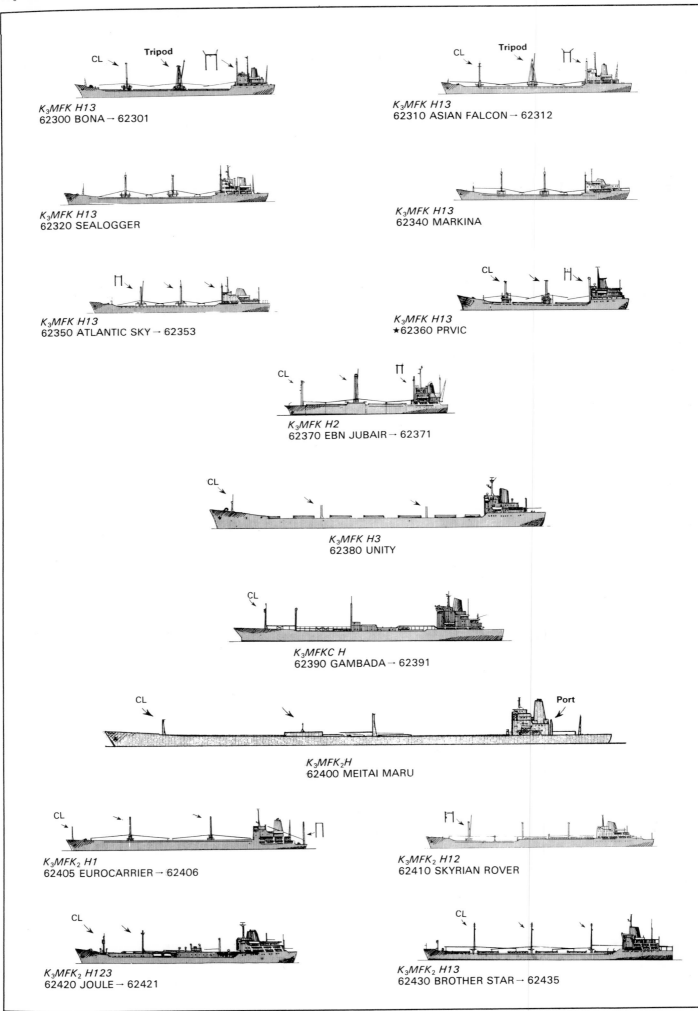

K₃MFK H13
62300 BONA → 62301

K₃MFK H13
62310 ASIAN FALCON → 62312

K₃MFK H13
62320 SEALOGGER

K₃MFK H13
62340 MARKINA

K₃MFK H13
62350 ATLANTIC SKY → 62353

K₃MFK H13
★62360 PRVIC

K₃MFK H2
62370 EBN JUBAIR → 62371

K₃MFK H3
62380 UNITY

K₃MFKC H
62390 GAMBADA → 62391

K₃MFK₂H
62400 MEITAI MARU

K₃MFK₂ H1
62405 EUROCARRIER → 62406

K₃MFK₂ H12
62410 SKYRIAN ROVER

K₃MFK₂ H123
62420 JOULE → 62421

K₃MFK₂ H13
62430 BROTHER STAR → 62435

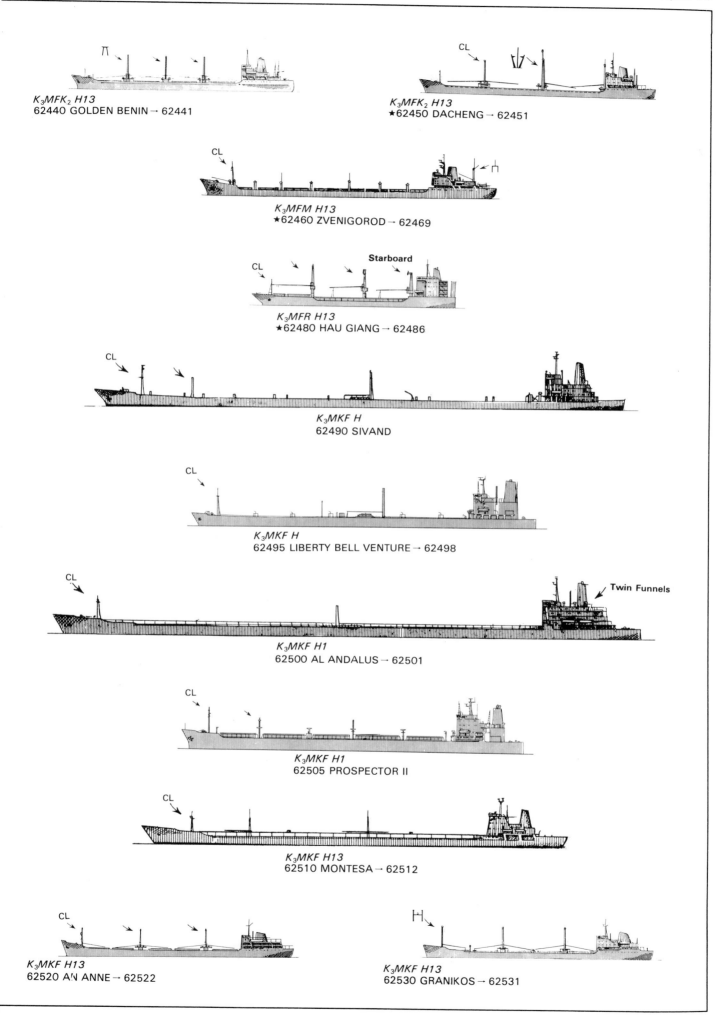

K₃MFK₂ H13
62440 GOLDEN BENIN → 62441

K₃MFK₂ H13
★62450 DACHENG → 62451

K₃MFM H13
★62460 ZVENIGOROD → 62469

K₃MFR H13
★62480 HAU GIANG → 62486

K₃MKF H
62490 SIVAND

K₃MKF H
62495 LIBERTY BELL VENTURE → 62498

K₃MKF H1
62500 AL ANDALUS → 62501

K₃MKF H1
62505 PROSPECTOR II

K₃MKF H13
62510 MONTESA → 62512

K₃MKF H13
62520 AN ANNE → 62522

K₃MKF H13
62530 GRANIKOS → 62531

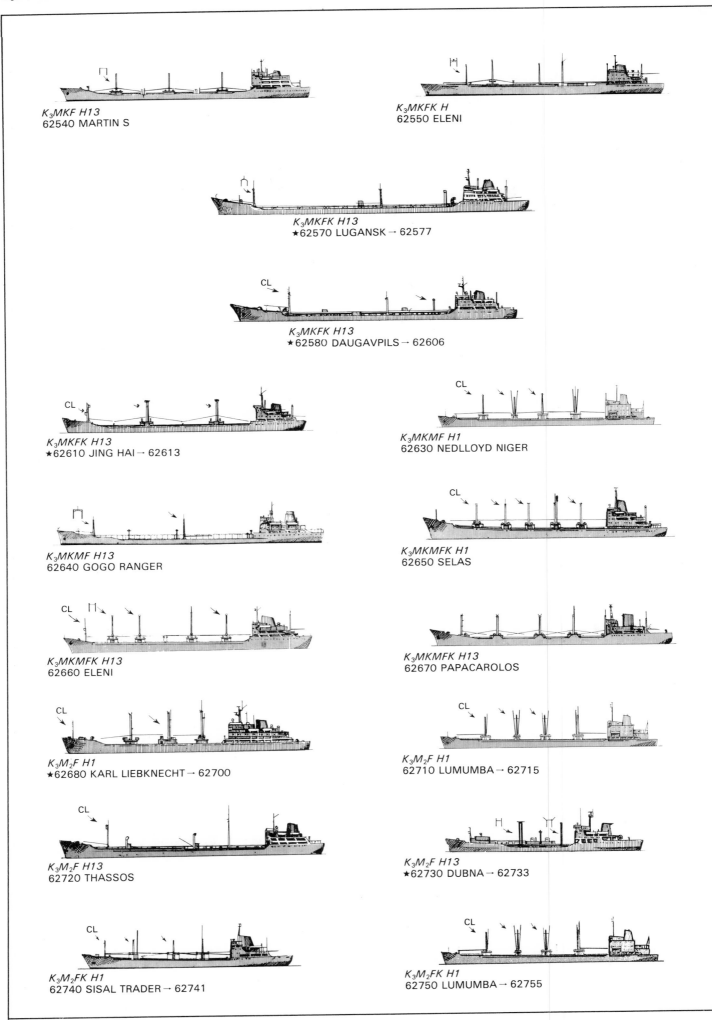

K₃MKF H13
62540 MARTIN S

K₃MKFK H
62550 ELENI

K₃MKFK H13
★62570 LUGANSK → 62577

K₃MKFK H13
★62580 DAUGAVPILS → 62606

K₃MKFK H13
★62610 JING HAI → 62613

K₃MKMF H1
62630 NEDLLOYD NIGER

K₃MKMF H13
62640 GOGO RANGER

K₃MKMFK H1
62650 SELAS

K₃MKMFK H13
62660 ELENI

K₃MKMFK H13
62670 PAPACAROLOS

K₃M₂F H1
★62680 KARL LIEBKNECHT → 62700

K₃M₂F H1
62710 LUMUMBA → 62715

K₃M₂F H13
62720 THASSOS

K₃M₂F H13
★62730 DUBNA → 62733

K₃M₂FK H1
62740 SISAL TRADER → 62741

K₃M₂FK H1
62750 LUMUMBA → 62755

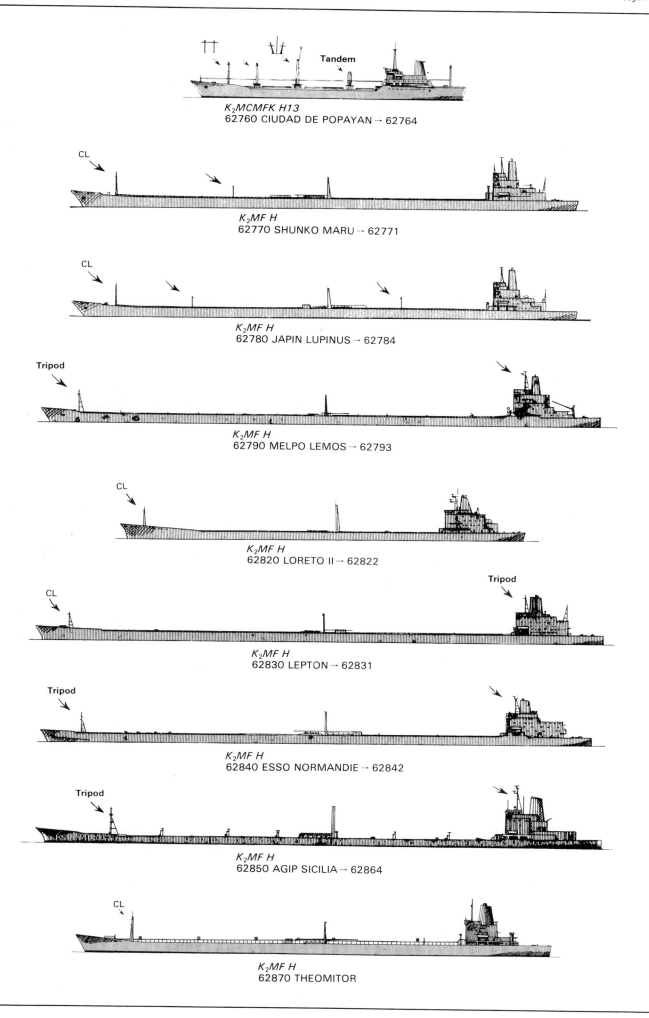

Tandem

K₂MCMFK H13
62760 CIUDAD DE POPAYAN → 62764

CL
K₂MF H
62770 SHUNKO MARU → 62771

CL
K₂MF H
62780 JAPIN LUPINUS → 62784

Tripod
K₂MF H
62790 MELPO LEMOS → 62793

CL
K₂MF H
62820 LORETO II → 62822

CL Tripod
K₂MF H
62830 LEPTON → 62831

Tripod
K₂MF H
62840 ESSO NORMANDIE → 62842

Tripod
K₂MF H
62850 AGIP SICILIA → 62864

CL
K₂MF H
62870 THEOMITOR

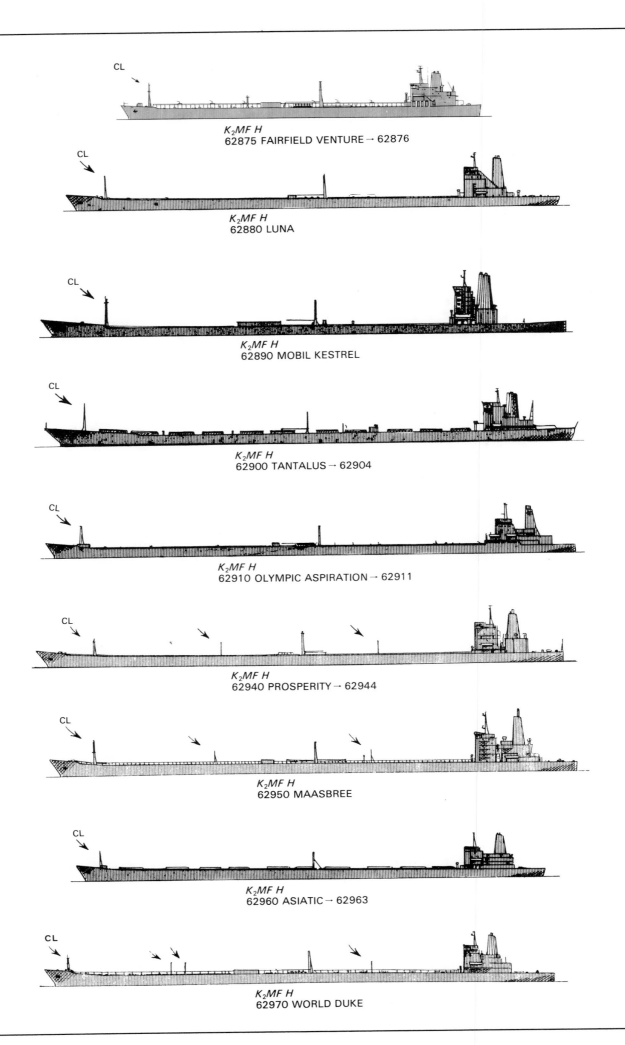

K₂MF H
62875 FAIRFIELD VENTURE → 62876

K₂MF H
62880 LUNA

K₂MF H
62890 MOBIL KESTREL

K₂MF H
62900 TANTALUS → 62904

K₂MF H
62910 OLYMPIC ASPIRATION → 62911

K₂MF H
62940 PROSPERITY → 62944

K₂MF H
62950 MAASBREE

K₂MF H
62960 ASIATIC → 62963

K₂MF H
62970 WORLD DUKE

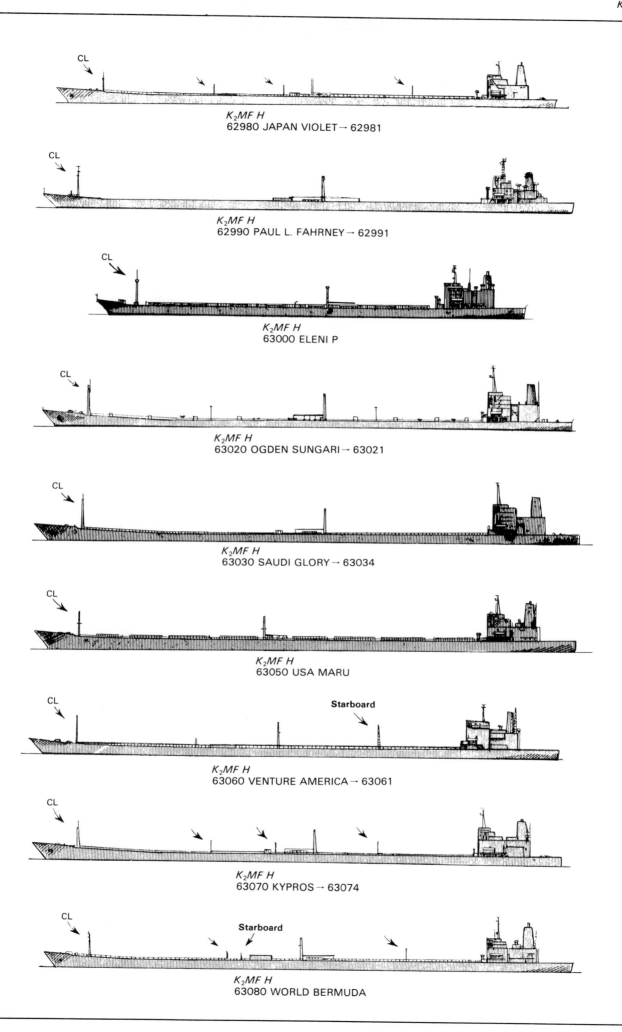

K₂MF H
62980 JAPAN VIOLET → 62981

K₂MF H
62990 PAUL L. FAHRNEY → 62991

K₂MF H
63000 ELENI P

K₂MF H
63020 OGDEN SUNGARI → 63021

K₂MF H
63030 SAUDI GLORY → 63034

K₂MF H
63050 USA MARU

K₂MF H
63060 VENTURE AMERICA → 63061

K₂MF H
63070 KYPROS → 63074

K₂MF H
63080 WORLD BERMUDA

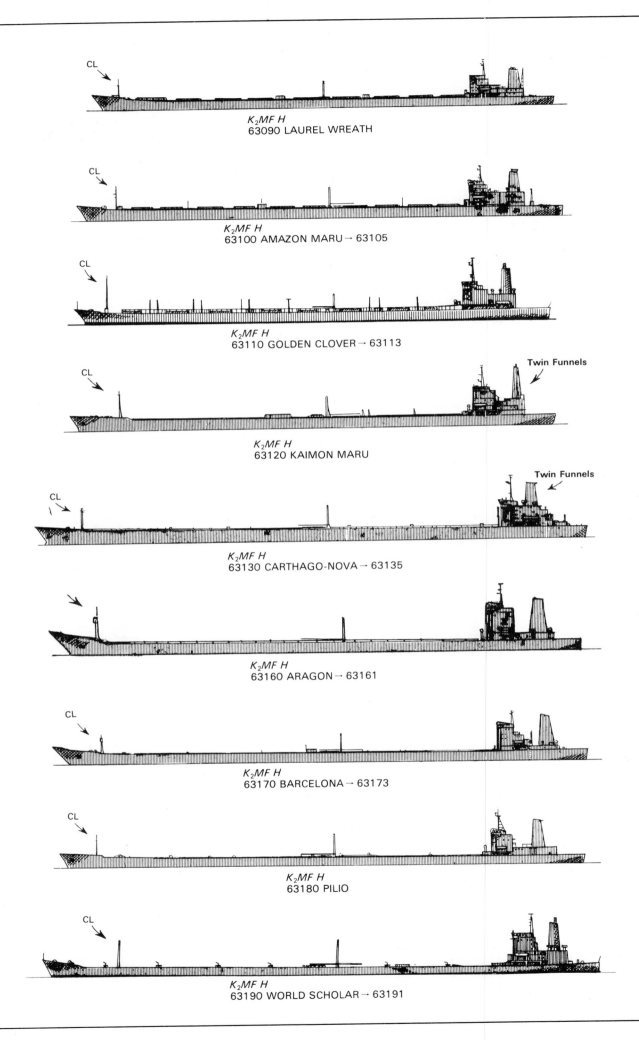

K₂MF H
63090 LAUREL WREATH

K₂MF H
63100 AMAZON MARU → 63105

K₂MF H
63110 GOLDEN CLOVER → 63113

K₂MF H
63120 KAIMON MARU

K₂MF H
63130 CARTHAGO-NOVA → 63135

K₂MF H
63160 ARAGON → 63161

K₂MF H
63170 BARCELONA → 63173

K₂MF H
63180 PILIO

K₂MF H
63190 WORLD SCHOLAR → 63191

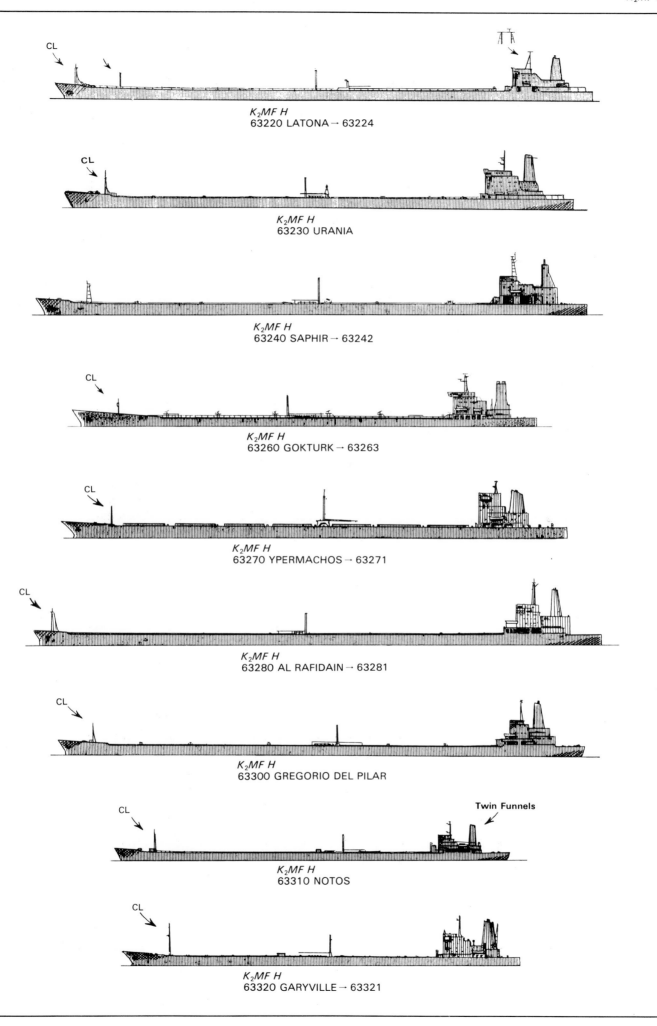

CL

K₂MF H
63220 LATONA → 63224

CL

K₂MF H
63230 URANIA

K₂MF H
63240 SAPHIR → 63242

CL

K₂MF H
63260 GOKTURK → 63263

CL

K₂MF H
63270 YPERMACHOS → 63271

CL

K₂MF H
63280 AL RAFIDAIN → 63281

CL

K₂MF H
63300 GREGORIO DEL PILAR

CL

Twin Funnels

K₂MF H
63310 NOTOS

CL

K₂MF H
63320 GARYVILLE → 63321

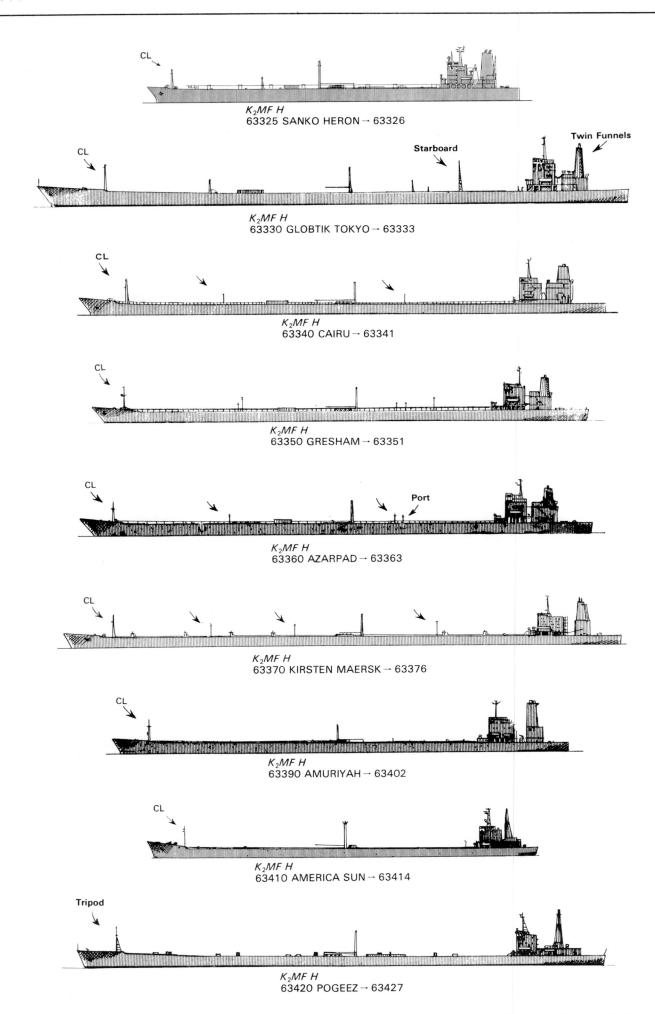

K₂MF H
63325 SANKO HERON → 63326

K₂MF H
63330 GLOBTIK TOKYO → 63333

K₂MF H
63340 CAIRU → 63341

K₂MF H
63350 GRESHAM → 63351

K₂MF H
63360 AZARPAD → 63363

K₂MF H
63370 KIRSTEN MAERSK → 63376

K₂MF H
63390 AMURIYAH → 63402

K₂MF H
63410 AMERICA SUN → 63414

K₂MF H
63420 POGEEZ → 63427

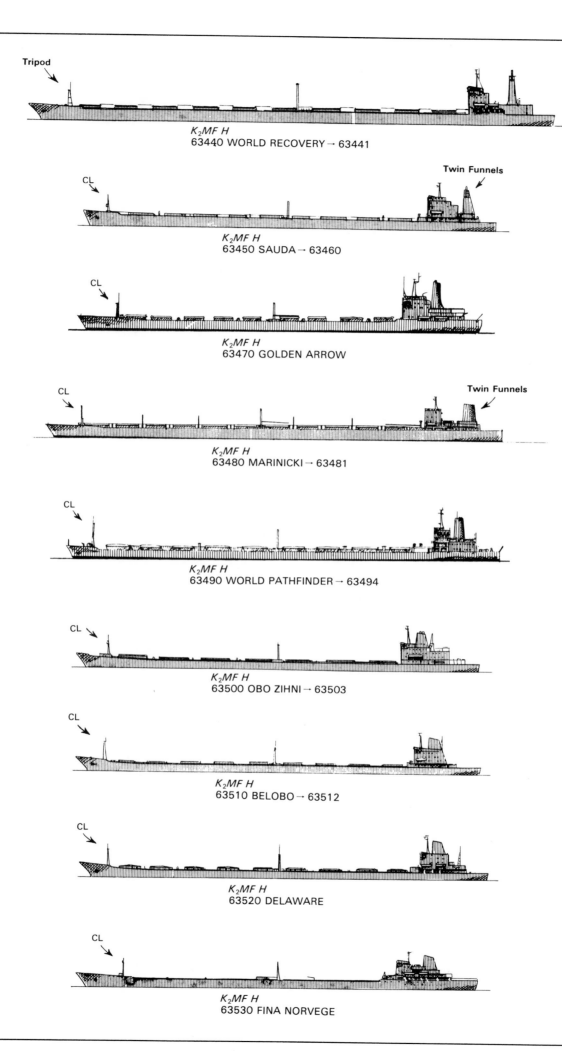

Tripod

K₂MF H
63440 WORLD RECOVERY → 63441

CL — **Twin Funnels**

K₂MF H
63450 SAUDA → 63460

CL

K₂MF H
63470 GOLDEN ARROW

CL — **Twin Funnels**

K₂MF H
63480 MARINICKI → 63481

CL

K₂MF H
63490 WORLD PATHFINDER → 63494

CL

K₂MF H
63500 OBO ZIHNI → 63503

CL

K₂MF H
63510 BELOBO → 63512

CL

K₂MF H
63520 DELAWARE

CL

K₂MF H
63530 FINA NORVEGE

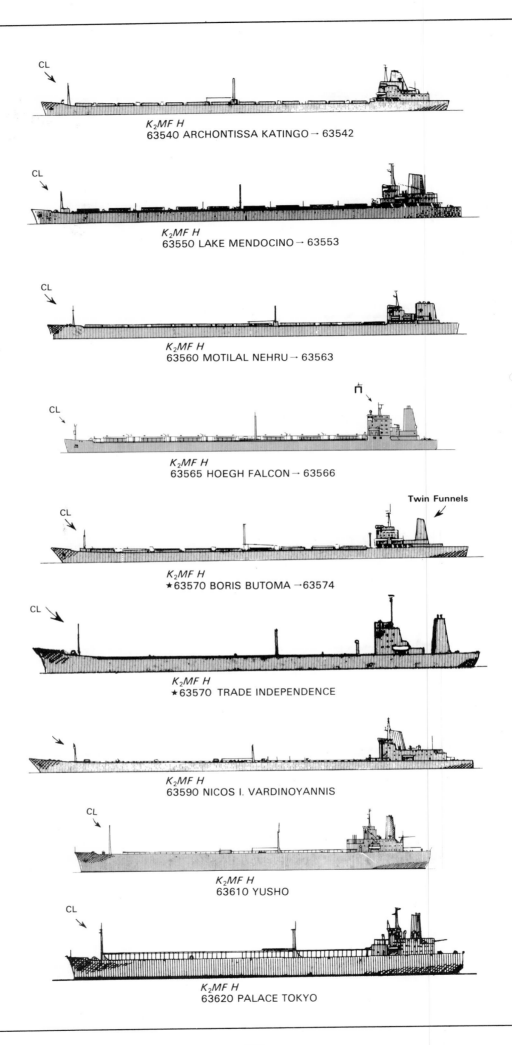

CL

K₂MF H
63540 ARCHONTISSA KATINGO → 63542

CL

K₂MF H
63550 LAKE MENDOCINO → 63553

CL

K₂MF H
63560 MOTILAL NEHRU → 63563

CL

K₂MF H
63565 HOEGH FALCON → 63566

Twin Funnels

CL

K₂MF H
★63570 BORIS BUTOMA → 63574

CL

K₂MF H
★63570 TRADE INDEPENDENCE

K₂MF H
63590 NICOS I. VARDINOYANNIS

CL

K₂MF H
63610 YUSHO

CL

K₂MF H
63620 PALACE TOKYO

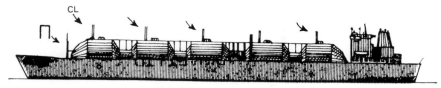

K₂MF H
63630 NORMAN LADY

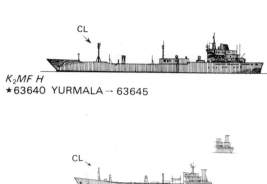

K₂MF H
★63640 YURMALA → 63645

K₂MF H
63650 CHEMTRANS WEGA

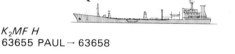

K₂MF H
63655 PAUL → 63658

K₂MF H
63660 AFRICAN HYACINTH → 63661

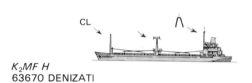

K₂MF H
63670 DENIZATI

K₂MF H
63680 ALEDREESI → 63690

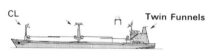

K₂MF H
63700 GULF DUCHESS → 63701

K₂MF H
63710 ABIRIBA → 63714

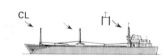

K₂MF H
63720 BRAGA → 63721

K₂MF H
★63730 GAN QUAN → 63731

K₂MF H
63740 MINOGAZ 1

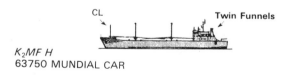

K₂MF H
63750 MUNDIAL CAR

K₂MF H
63760 NIKI AGUSTINA

K₂MF H
63770 NEWTON

K₂MF H1
63780 FORT FRASER

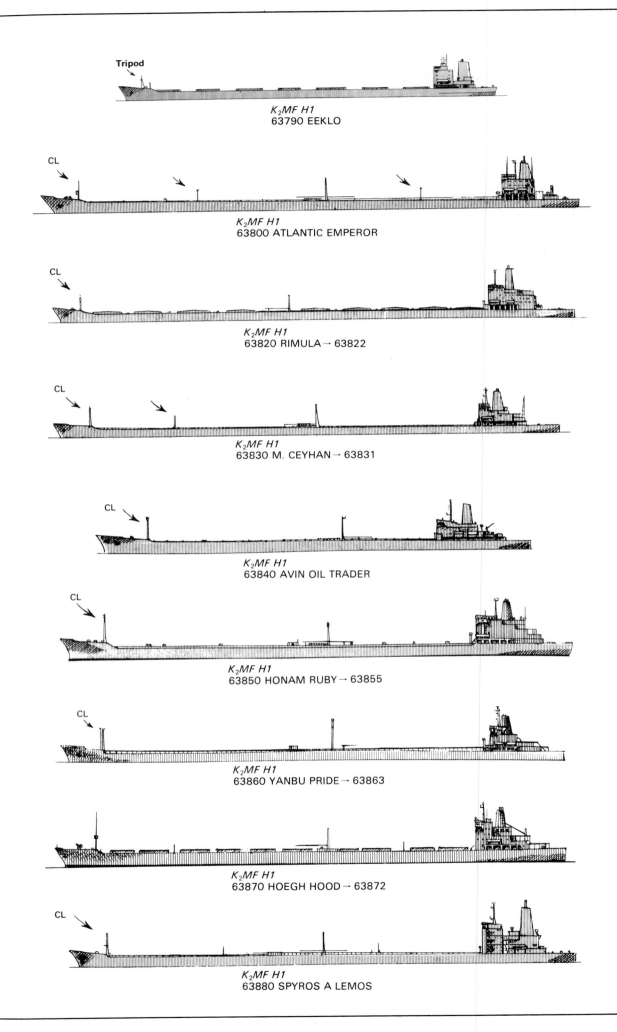

K₂MF H1
63790 EEKLO

K₂MF H1
63800 ATLANTIC EMPEROR

K₂MF H1
63820 RIMULA → 63822

K₂MF H1
63830 M. CEYHAN → 63831

K₂MF H1
63840 AVIN OIL TRADER

K₂MF H1
63850 HONAM RUBY → 63855

K₂MF H1
63860 YANBU PRIDE → 63863

K₂MF H1
63870 HOEGH HOOD → 63872

K₂MF H1
63880 SPYROS A LEMOS

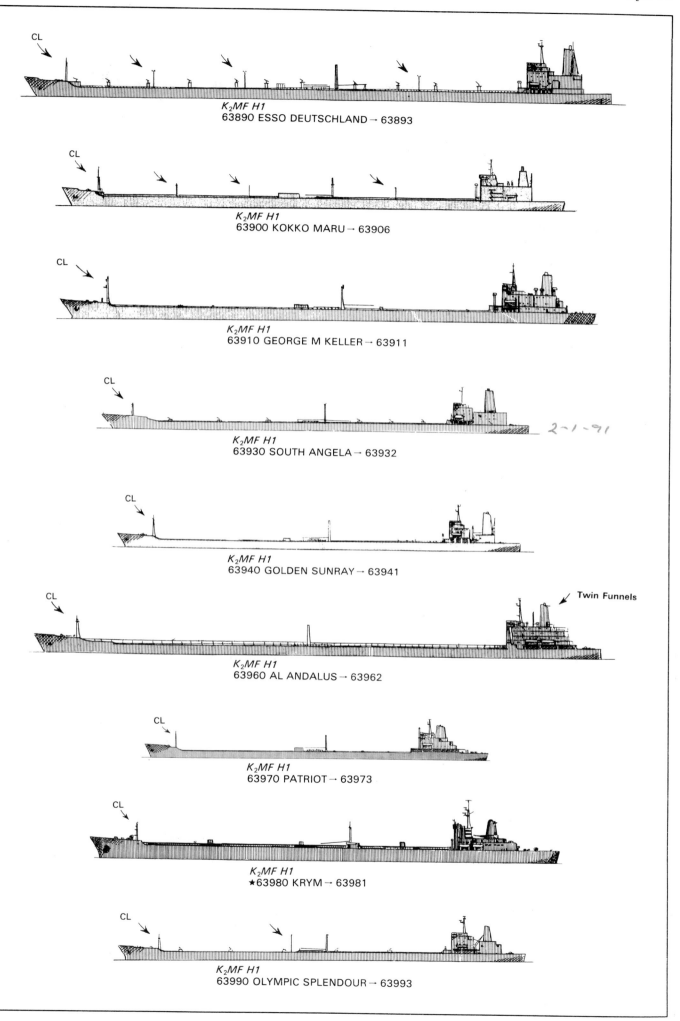

CL

K₂MF H1
63890 ESSO DEUTSCHLAND → 63893

CL

K₂MF H1
63900 KOKKO MARU → 63906

CL

K₂MF H1
63910 GEORGE M KELLER → 63911

CL

K₂MF H1
63930 SOUTH ANGELA → 63932

2-1-91

CL

K₂MF H1
63940 GOLDEN SUNRAY → 63941

CL

Twin Funnels

K₂MF H1
63960 AL ANDALUS → 63962

CL

K₂MF H1
63970 PATRIOT → 63973

CL

K₂MF H1
★63980 KRYM → 63981

CL

K₂MF H1
63990 OLYMPIC SPLENDOUR → 63993

335

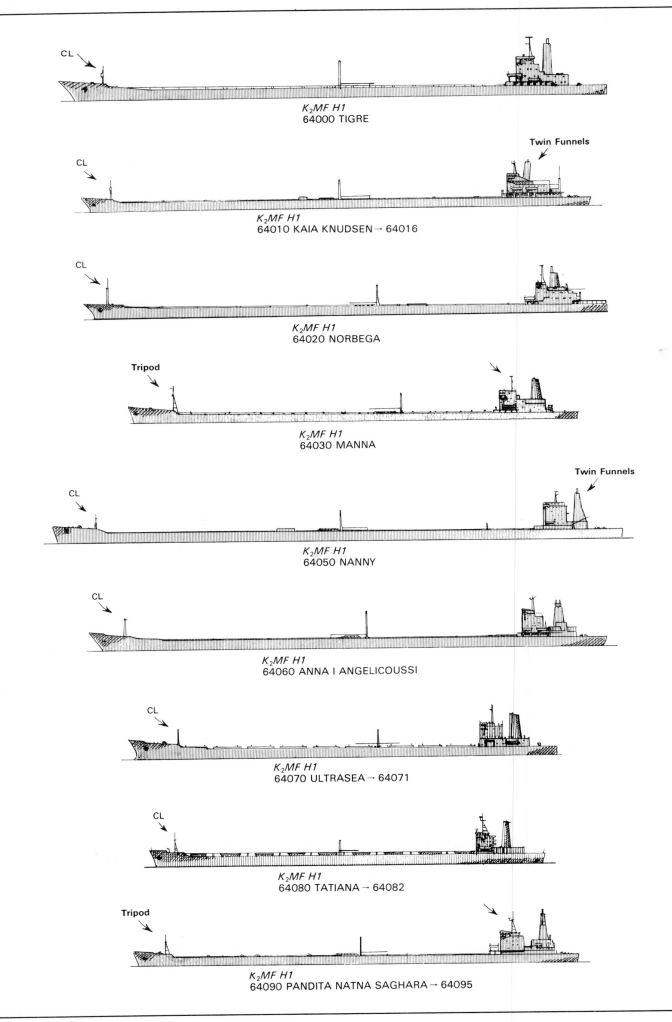

CL

K₂MF H1
64000 TIGRE

CL

Twin Funnels

K₂MF H1
64010 KAIA KNUDSEN → 64016

CL

K₂MF H1
64020 NORBEGA

Tripod

K₂MF H1
64030 MANNA

CL

Twin Funnels

K₂MF H1
64050 NANNY

CL

K₂MF H1
64060 ANNA I ANGELICOUSSI

CL

K₂MF H1
64070 ULTRASEA → 64071

CL

K₂MF H1
64080 TATIANA → 64082

Tripod

K₂MF H1
64090 PANDITA NATNA SAGHARA → 64095

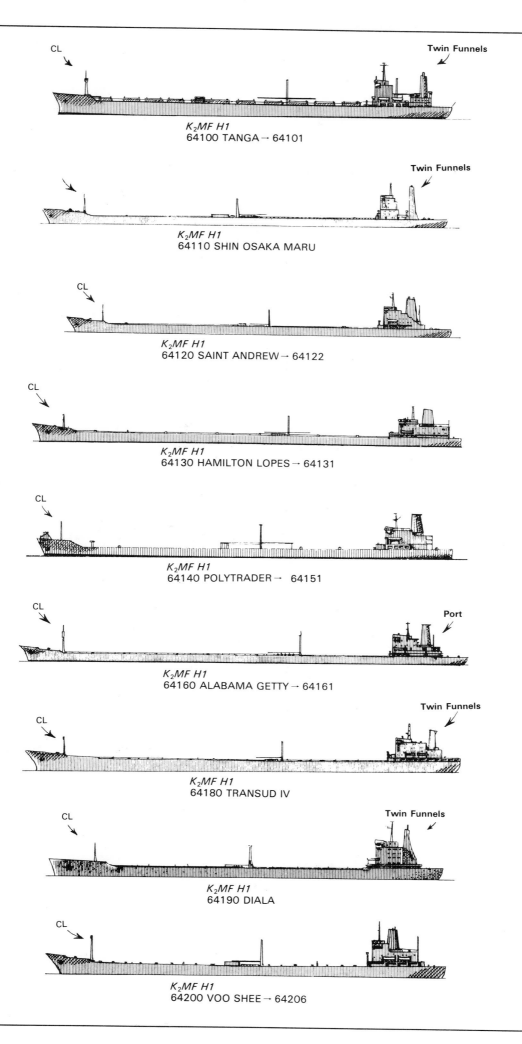

K₂MF H1
64100 TANGA → 64101

K₂MF H1
64110 SHIN OSAKA MARU

K₂MF H1
64120 SAINT ANDREW → 64122

K₂MF H1
64130 HAMILTON LOPES → 64131

K₂MF H1
64140 POLYTRADER → 64151

K₂MF H1
64160 ALABAMA GETTY → 64161

K₂MF H1
64180 TRANSUD IV

K₂MF H1
64190 DIALA

K₂MF H1
64200 VOO SHEE → 64206

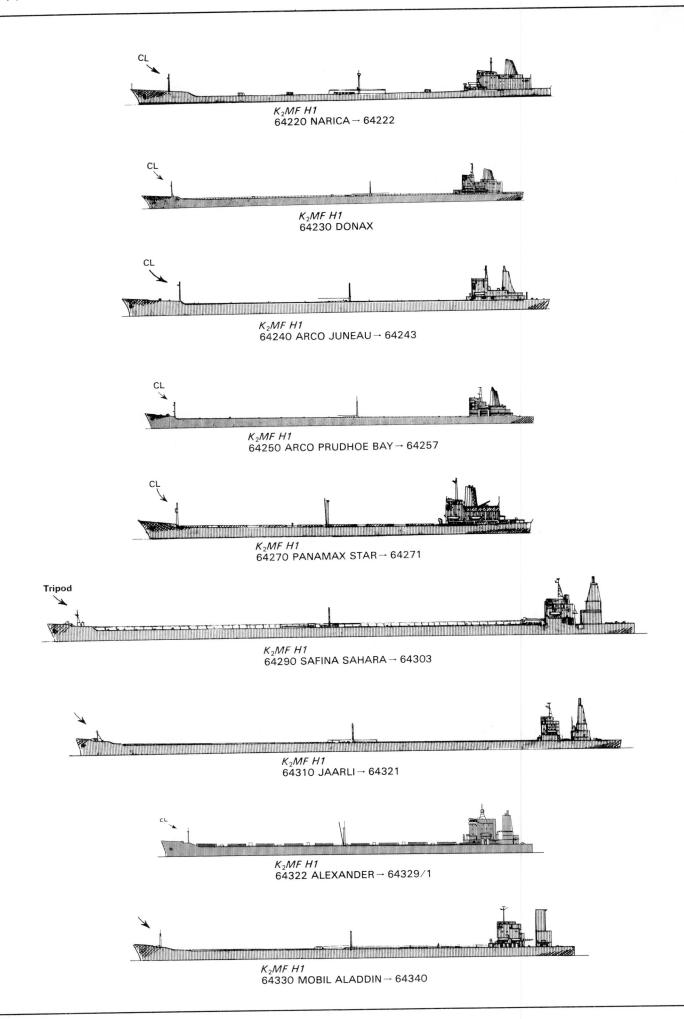

K₂MF H1
64220 NARICA → 64222

K₂MF H1
64230 DONAX

K₂MF H1
64240 ARCO JUNEAU → 64243

K₂MF H1
64250 ARCO PRUDHOE BAY → 64257

K₂MF H1
64270 PANAMAX STAR → 64271

K₂MF H1
64290 SAFINA SAHARA → 64303

K₂MF H1
64310 JAARLI → 64321

K₂MF H1
64322 ALEXANDER → 64329/1

K₂MF H1
64330 MOBIL ALADDIN → 64340

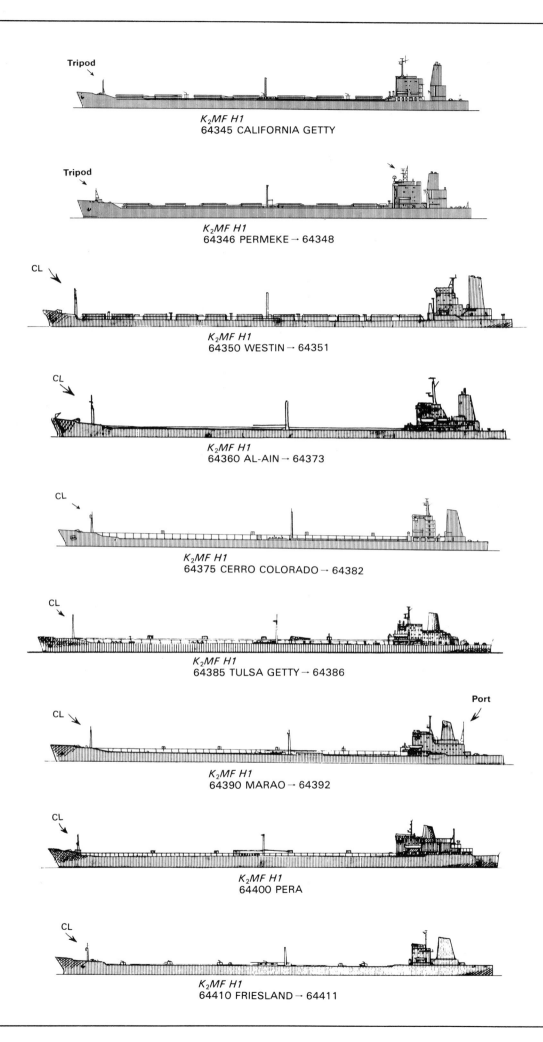

K₂MF H1
64345 CALIFORNIA GETTY

K₂MF H1
64346 PERMEKE → 64348

K₂MF H1
64350 WESTIN → 64351

K₂MF H1
64360 AL-AIN → 64373

K₂MF H1
64375 CERRO COLORADO → 64382

K₂MF H1
64385 TULSA GETTY → 64386

K₂MF H1
64390 MARAO → 64392

K₂MF H1
64400 PERA

K₂MF H1
64410 FRIESLAND → 64411

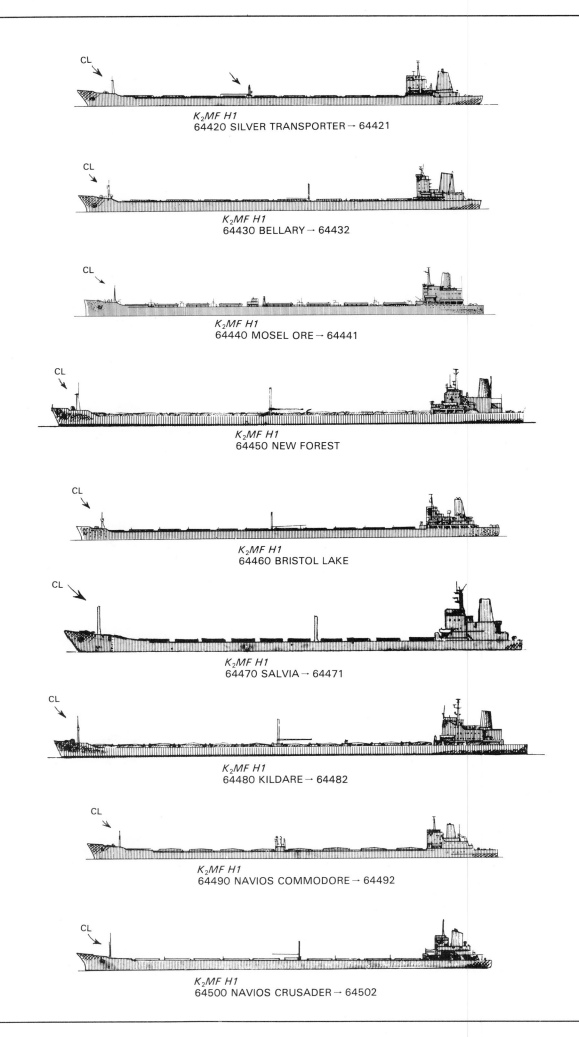

K₂MF H1
64420 SILVER TRANSPORTER → 64421

K₂MF H1
64430 BELLARY → 64432

K₂MF H1
64440 MOSEL ORE → 64441

K₂MF H1
64450 NEW FOREST

K₂MF H1
64460 BRISTOL LAKE

K₂MF H1
64470 SALVIA → 64471

K₂MF H1
64480 KILDARE → 64482

K₂MF H1
64490 NAVIOS COMMODORE → 64492

K₂MF H1
64500 NAVIOS CRUSADER → 64502

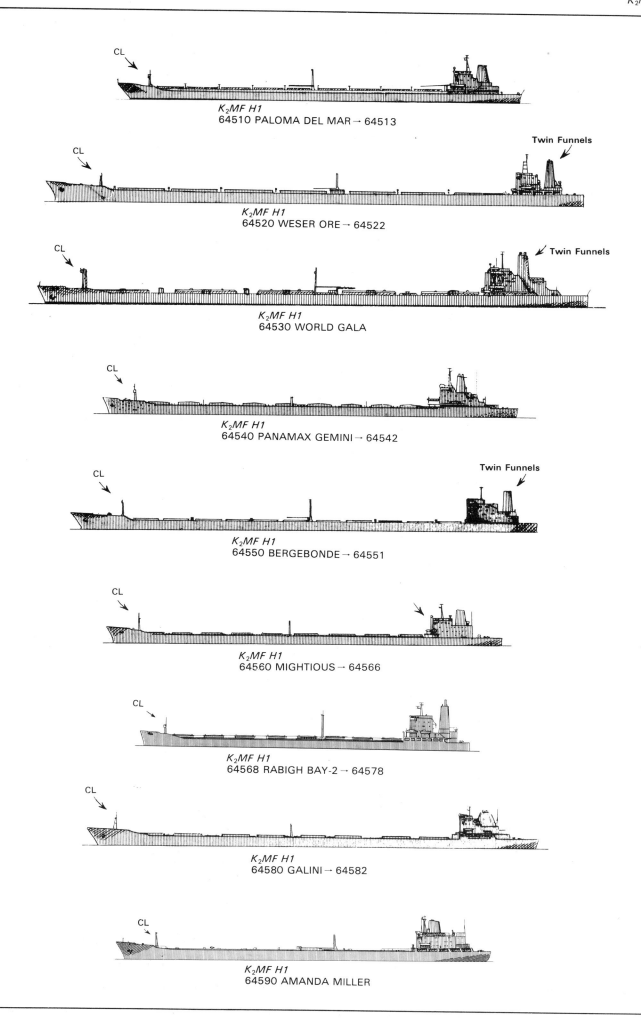

CL
K₂MF H1
64510 PALOMA DEL MAR → 64513

CL
Twin Funnels
K₂MF H1
64520 WESER ORE → 64522

CL
Twin Funnels
K₂MF H1
64530 WORLD GALA

CL
K₂MF H1
64540 PANAMAX GEMINI → 64542

CL
Twin Funnels
K₂MF H1
64550 BERGEBONDE → 64551

CL
K₂MF H1
64560 MIGHTIOUS → 64566

CL
K₂MF H1
64568 RABIGH BAY-2 → 64578

CL
K₂MF H1
64580 GALINI → 64582

CL
K₂MF H1
64590 AMANDA MILLER

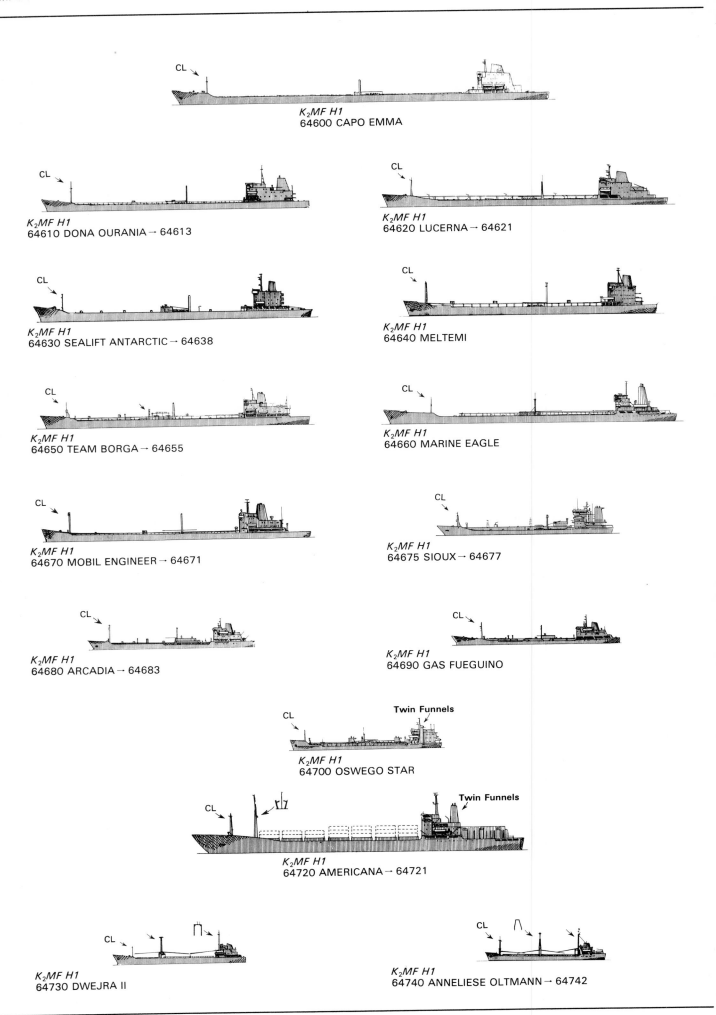

CL

K₂MF H1
64600 CAPO EMMA

CL

K₂MF H1
64610 DONA OURANIA → 64613

CL

K₂MF H1
64620 LUCERNA → 64621

CL

K₂MF H1
64630 SEALIFT ANTARCTIC → 64638

CL

K₂MF H1
64640 MELTEMI

CL

K₂MF H1
64650 TEAM BORGA → 64655

CL

K₂MF H1
64660 MARINE EAGLE

CL

K₂MF H1
64670 MOBIL ENGINEER → 64671

CL

K₂MF H1
64675 SIOUX → 64677

CL

K₂MF H1
64680 ARCADIA → 64683

CL

K₂MF H1
64690 GAS FUEGUINO

CL   **Twin Funnels**

K₂MF H1
64700 OSWEGO STAR

CL   **Twin Funnels**

K₂MF H1
64720 AMERICANA → 64721

CL

K₂MF H1
64730 DWEJRA II

CL

K₂MF H1
64740 ANNELIESE OLTMANN → 64742

342

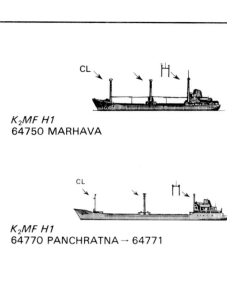

K₂MF H1
64750 MARHAVA

K₂MF H1
64760 FADEL

K₂MF H1
64770 PANCHRATNA → 64771

K₂MF H1
★64780 QU JIANG

K₂MF H1
64790 RECOMONE → 64794

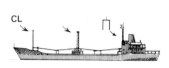

K₂MF H1
64800 PELOR

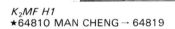

K₂MF H1
★64810 MAN CHENG → 64819

K₂MF H1
64830 EIDER → 64831

K₂MF H1
64840 CELAL CESUR → 64841

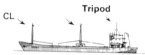

K₂MF H1
64850 NIAGA XLI → 64867

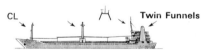

K₂MF H1
64890 KAREN WINTHER

K₂MF H1
64900 NAJA ITTUK → 64901

K₂MF H1
64910 HELEN → 64915

K₂MF H1
64920 ZUHAL K → 64921

K₂MF H1
64930 TEMARA → 64950

K₂MF H1
64960 IBN ROCHD → 64970

K₂MF H1
64980 FLENSAU → 64981

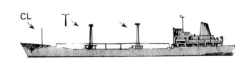

K₂MF H1
64990 NIVI ITTUK

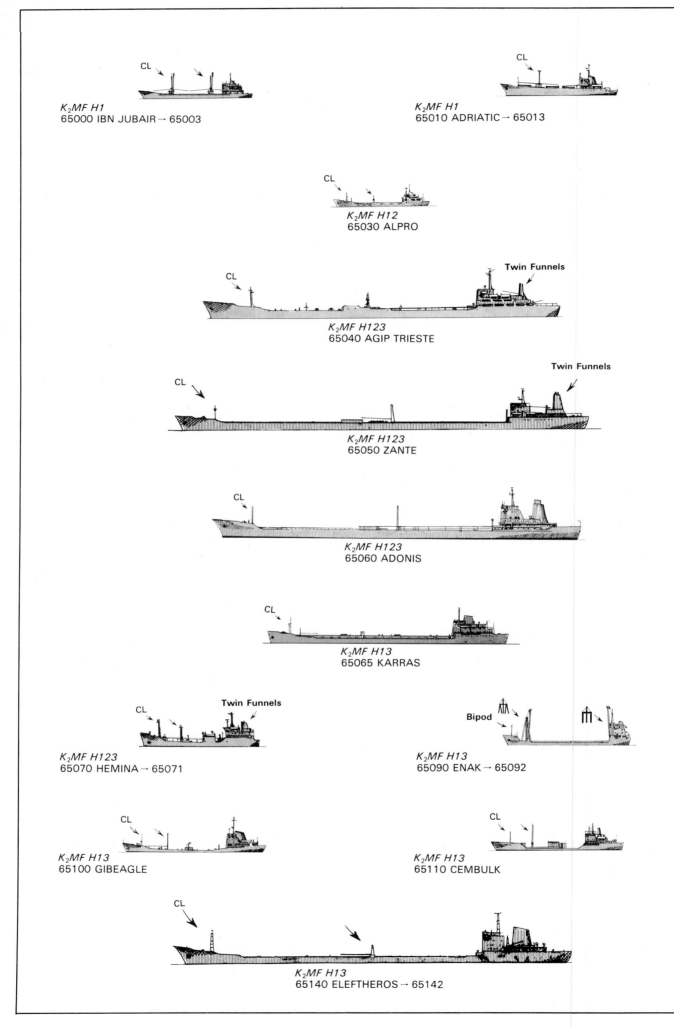

K₂MF H1
65000 IBN JUBAIR → 65003

K₂MF H1
65010 ADRIATIC → 65013

K₂MF H12
65030 ALPRO

K₂MF H123
65040 AGIP TRIESTE

K₂MF H123
65050 ZANTE

K₂MF H123
65060 ADONIS

K₂MF H13
65065 KARRAS

K₂MF H123
65070 HEMINA → 65071

K₂MF H13
65090 ENAK → 65092

K₂MF H13
65100 GIBEAGLE

K₂MF H13
65110 CEMBULK

K₂MF H13
65140 ELEFTHEROS → 65142

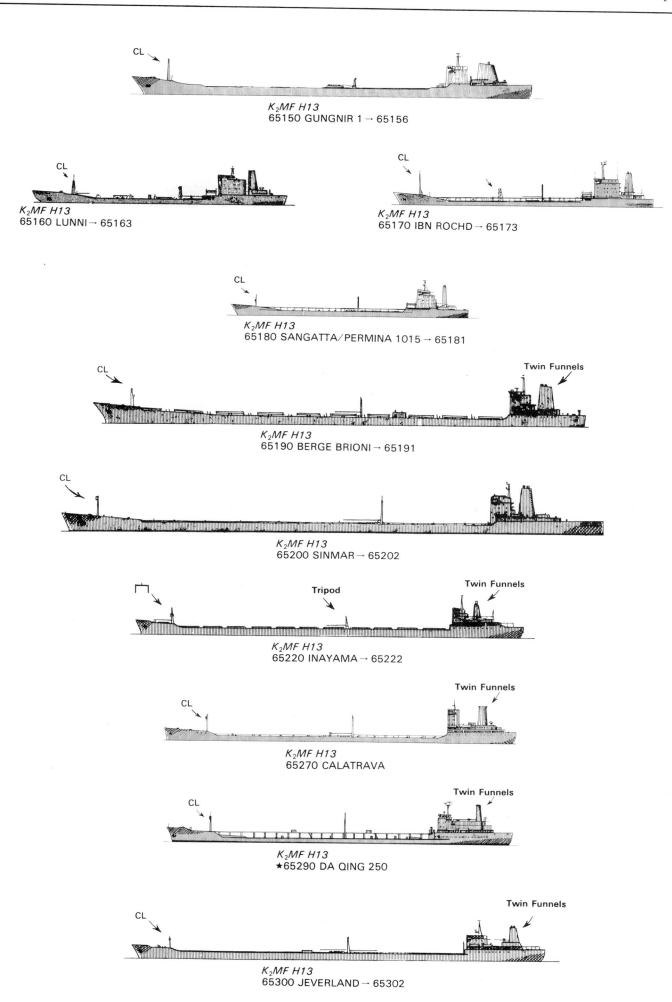

CL

K₂MF H13
65150 GUNGNIR 1 → 65156

CL

K₂MF H13
65160 LUNNI → 65163

CL

K₂MF H13
65170 IBN ROCHD → 65173

CL

K₂MF H13
65180 SANGATTA/PERMINA 1015 → 65181

CL   Twin Funnels

K₂MF H13
65190 BERGE BRIONI → 65191

CL

K₂MF H13
65200 SINMAR → 65202

Tripod   Twin Funnels

K₂MF H13
65220 INAYAMA → 65222

CL   Twin Funnels

K₂MF H13
65270 CALATRAVA

CL   Twin Funnels

K₂MF H13
★65290 DA QING 250

Twin Funnels

CL

K₂MF H13
65300 JEVERLAND → 65302

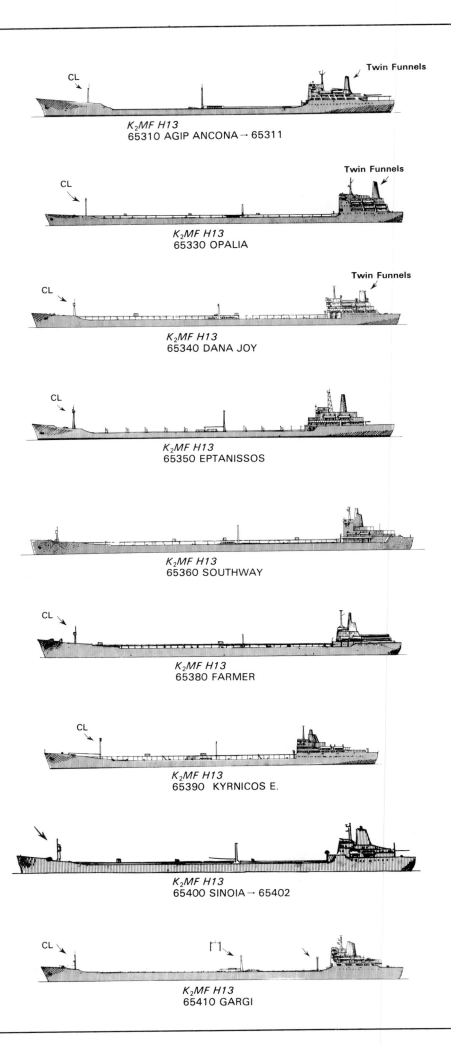

K₂MF H13
65310 AGIP ANCONA → 65311

K₂MF H13
65330 OPALIA

K₂MF H13
65340 DANA JOY

K₂MF H13
65350 EPTANISSOS

K₂MF H13
65360 SOUTHWAY

K₂MF H13
65380 FARMER

K₂MF H13
65390 KYRNICOS E.

K₂MF H13
65400 SINOIA → 65402

K₂MF H13
65410 GARGI

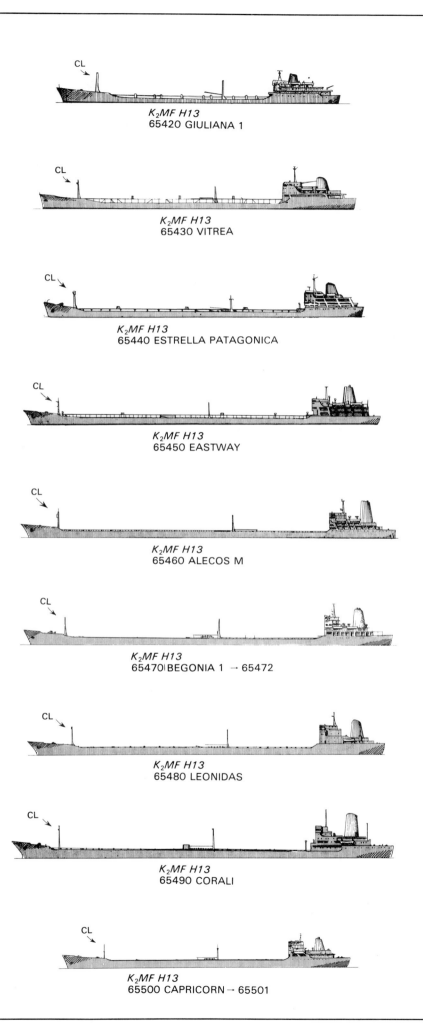

CL

K₂MF H13
65420 GIULIANA 1

CL

K₂MF H13
65430 VITREA

CL

K₂MF H13
65440 ESTRELLA PATAGONICA

CL

K₂MF H13
65450 EASTWAY

CL

K₂MF H13
65460 ALECOS M

CL

K₂MF H13
65470 BEGONIA 1 → 65472

CL

K₂MF H13
65480 LEONIDAS

CL

K₂MF H13
65490 CORALI

CL

K₂MF H13
65500 CAPRICORN → 65501

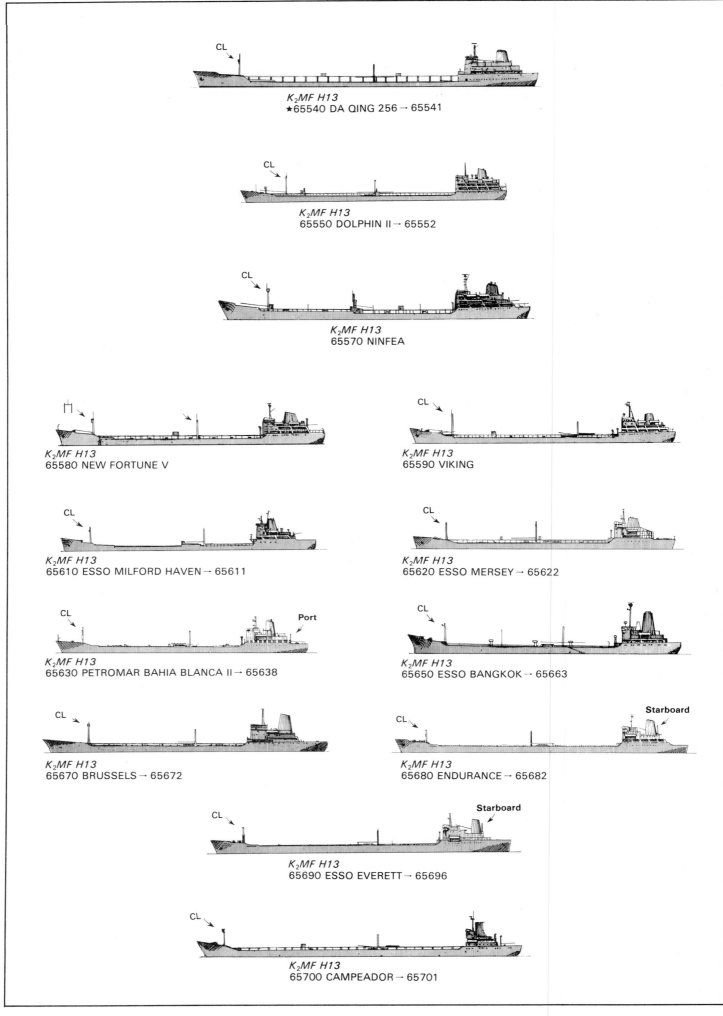

K₂MF H13
★65540 DA QING 256 → 65541

K₂MF H13
65550 DOLPHIN II → 65552

K₂MF H13
65570 NINFEA

K₂MF H13
65580 NEW FORTUNE V

K₂MF H13
65590 VIKING

K₂MF H13
65610 ESSO MILFORD HAVEN → 65611

K₂MF H13
65620 ESSO MERSEY → 65622

K₂MF H13
65630 PETROMAR BAHIA BLANCA II → 65638

K₂MF H13
65650 ESSO BANGKOK → 65663

K₂MF H13
65670 BRUSSELS → 65672

K₂MF H13
65680 ENDURANCE → 65682

K₂MF H13
65690 ESSO EVERETT → 65696

K₂MF H13
65700 CAMPEADOR → 65701

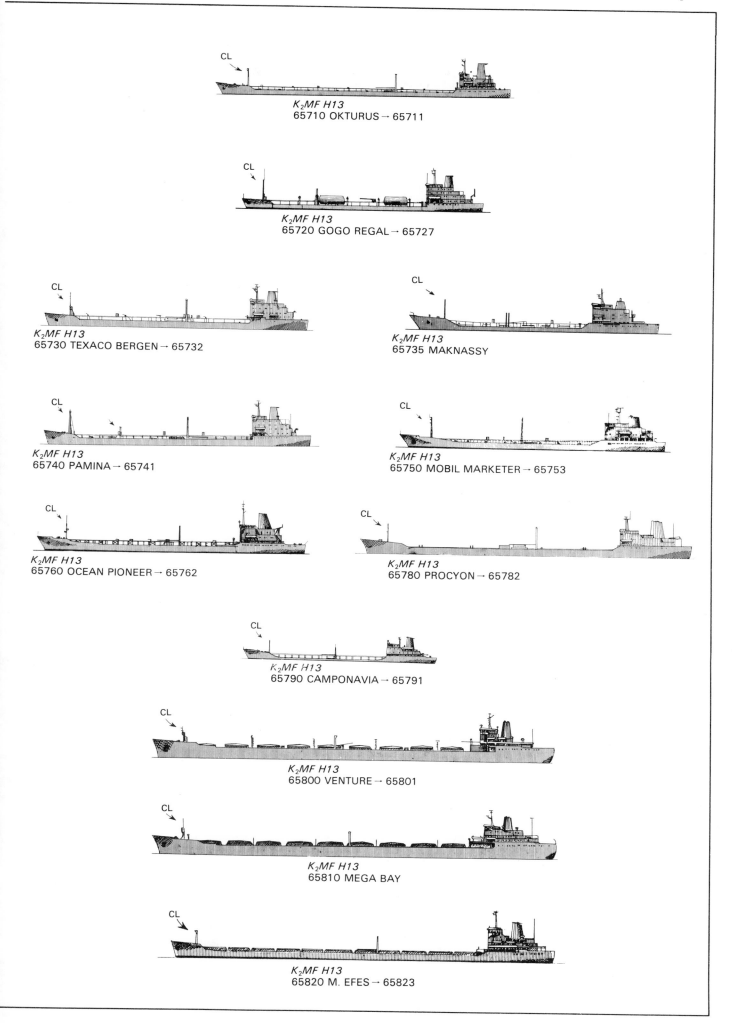

CL
K₂MF H13
65710 OKTURUS → 65711

CL
K₂MF H13
65720 GOGO REGAL → 65727

CL
K₂MF H13
65730 TEXACO BERGEN → 65732

CL
K₂MF H13
65735 MAKNASSY

CL
K₂MF H13
65740 PAMINA → 65741

CL
K₂MF H13
65750 MOBIL MARKETER → 65753

CL
K₂MF H13
65760 OCEAN PIONEER → 65762

CL
K₂MF H13
65780 PROCYON → 65782

CL
K₂MF H13
65790 CAMPONAVIA → 65791

CL
K₂MF H13
65800 VENTURE → 65801

CL
K₂MF H13
65810 MEGA BAY

CL
K₂MF H13
65820 M. EFES → 65823

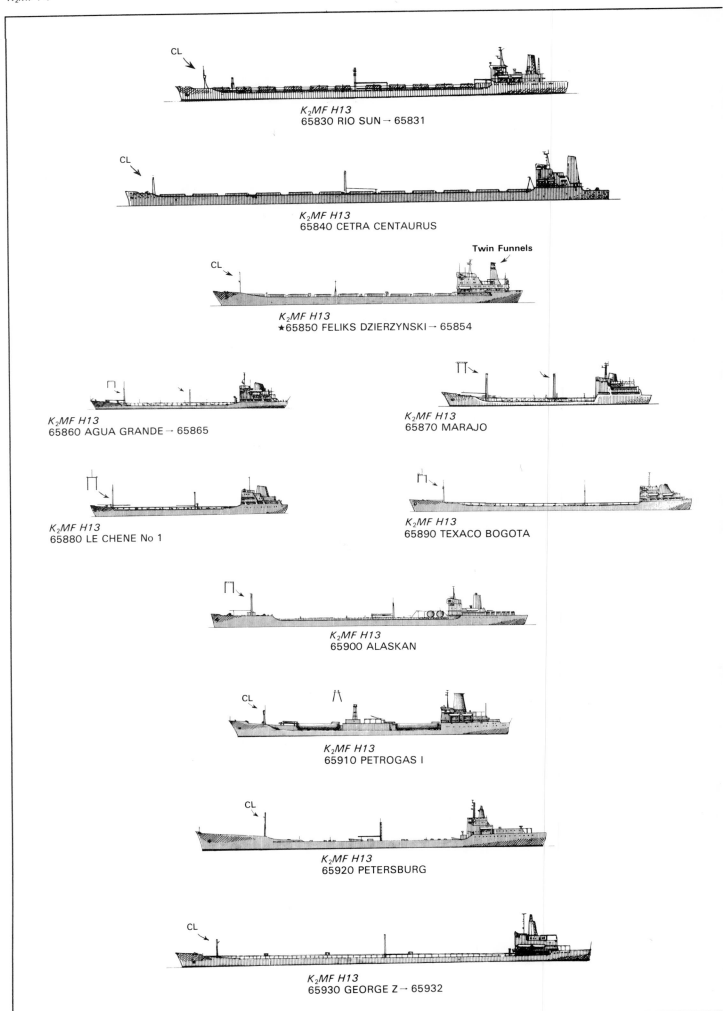

K₂MF H13
65830 RIO SUN → 65831

K₂MF H13
65840 CETRA CENTAURUS

Twin Funnels

K₂MF H13
★65850 FELIKS DZIERZYNSKI → 65854

K₂MF H13
65860 AGUA GRANDE → 65865

K₂MF H13
65870 MARAJO

K₂MF H13
65880 LE CHENE No 1

K₂MF H13
65890 TEXACO BOGOTA

K₂MF H13
65900 ALASKAN

K₂MF H13
65910 PETROGAS I

K₂MF H13
65920 PETERSBURG

K₂MF H13
65930 GEORGE Z → 65932

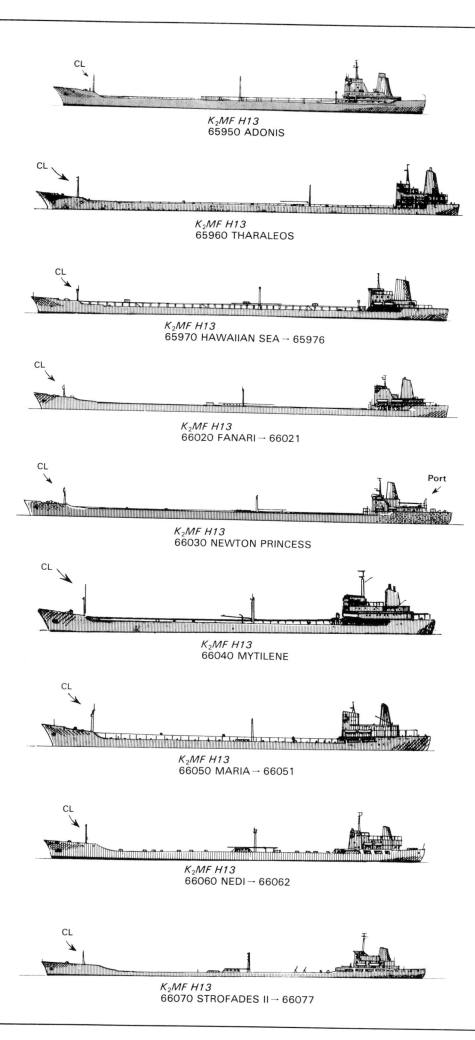

K₂MF H13
65950 ADONIS

K₂MF H13
65960 THARALEOS

K₂MF H13
65970 HAWAIIAN SEA → 65976

K₂MF H13
66020 FANARI → 66021

K₂MF H13
66030 NEWTON PRINCESS

K₂MF H13
66040 MYTILENE

K₂MF H13
66050 MARIA → 66051

K₂MF H13
66060 NEDI → 66062

K₂MF H13
66070 STROFADES II → 66077

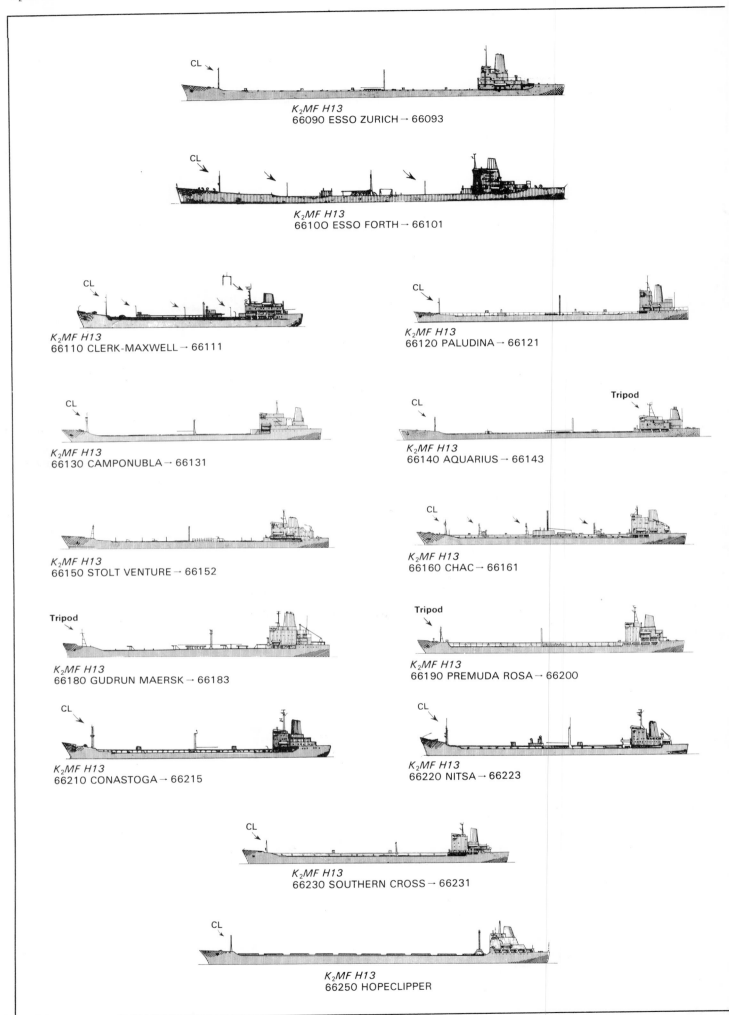

K₂MF H13
66090 ESSO ZURICH → 66093

K₂MF H13
66100 ESSO FORTH → 66101

K₂MF H13
66110 CLERK-MAXWELL → 66111

K₂MF H13
66120 PALUDINA → 66121

K₂MF H13
66130 CAMPONUBLA → 66131

K₂MF H13
66140 AQUARIUS → 66143

K₂MF H13
66150 STOLT VENTURE → 66152

K₂MF H13
66160 CHAC → 66161

K₂MF H13
66180 GUDRUN MAERSK → 66183

K₂MF H13
66190 PREMUDA ROSA → 66200

K₂MF H13
66210 CONASTOGA → 66215

K₂MF H13
66220 NITSA → 66223

K₂MF H13
66230 SOUTHERN CROSS → 66231

K₂MF H13
66250 HOPECLIPPER

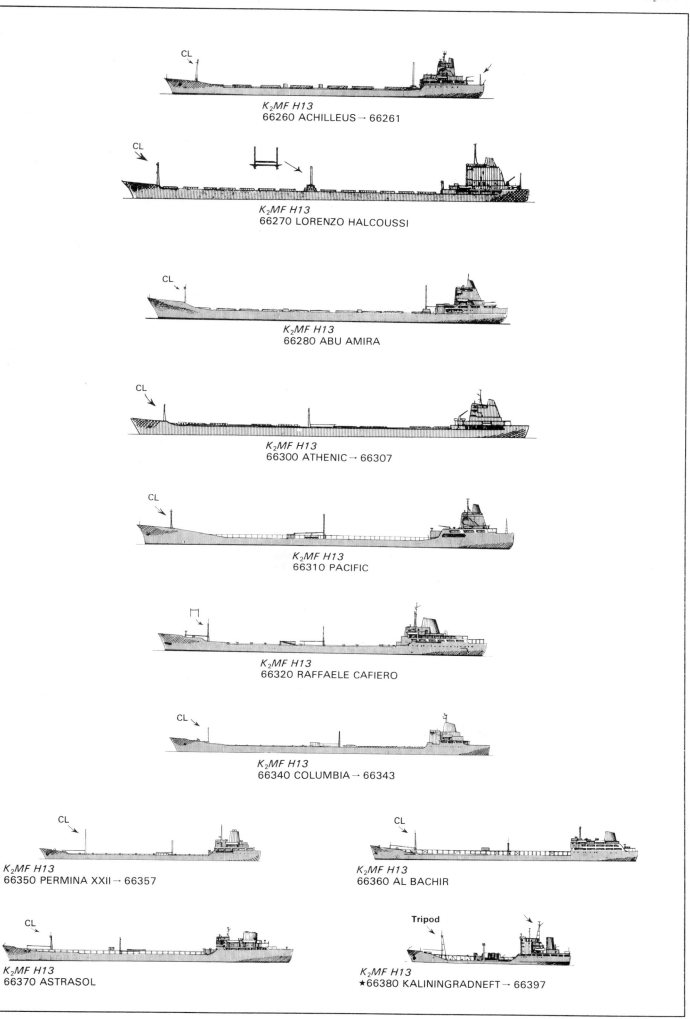

K₂MF H13
66260 ACHILLEUS → 66261

K₂MF H13
66270 LORENZO HALCOUSSI

K₂MF H13
66280 ABU AMIRA

K₂MF H13
66300 ATHENIC → 66307

K₂MF H13
66310 PACIFIC

K₂MF H13
66320 RAFFAELE CAFIERO

K₂MF H13
66340 COLUMBIA → 66343

K₂MF H13
66350 PERMINA XXII → 66357

K₂MF H13
66360 AL BACHIR

K₂MF H13
66370 ASTRASOL

K₂MF H13
★66380 KALININGRADNEFT → 66397

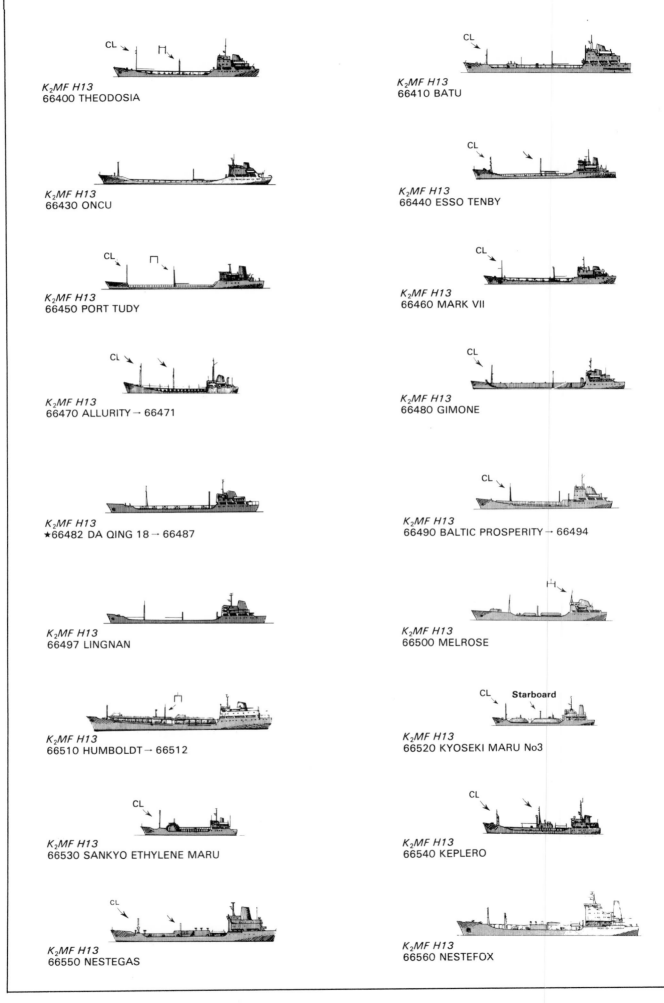

K₂MF H13
66400 THEODOSIA

K₂MF H13
66410 BATU

K₂MF H13
66430 ONCU

K₂MF H13
66440 ESSO TENBY

K₂MF H13
66450 PORT TUDY

K₂MF H13
66460 MARK VII

K₂MF H13
66470 ALLURITY → 66471

K₂MF H13
66480 GIMONE

K₂MF H13
★66482 DA QING 18 → 66487

K₂MF H13
66490 BALTIC PROSPERITY → 66494

K₂MF H13
66497 LINGNAN

K₂MF H13
66500 MELROSE

K₂MF H13
66510 HUMBOLDT → 66512

K₂MF H13
66520 KYOSEKI MARU No3

K₂MF H13
66530 SANKYO ETHYLENE MARU

K₂MF H13
66540 KEPLERO

K₂MF H13
66550 NESTEGAS

K₂MF H13
66560 NESTEFOX

K₂MF H13
66570 ALCHEMIST BREMEN → 66575

K₂MF H13
66577 CABLEMAN → 66579

K₂MF H13
66580 AL GHASSANI

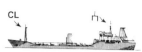

K₂MF H13
66590 ANNA BROERE

K₂MF H13
66600 DUTCH GLORY → 66602

K₂MF H13
66610 BENVENUE → 66612

K₂MF H13
66620 ISMARA → 66622

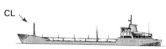

K₂MF H13
66630 MOBIL LUBCHEM

K₂MF H13
66635 SILVERHAWK

K₂MF H13
66640 PICCOLA → 66641

K₂MF H13
66650 GUN → 66652

K₂MF H13
66660 PETROSTAR V → 66661

K₂MF H13
66670 BRAENNAREN

K₂MF H13
66680 THORAIIA

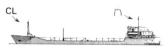

K₂MF H13
66690 VINGASJO

K₂MF H13
66700 PYTHEAS → 66701

K₂MF H13
66710 SENKAKU MARU → 66712

K₂MF H13
66720 KINGSABBEY

K₂MF H13
66730 HAPPY FALCON → 66731

K₂MF H13
66740 NIELS HENRIK ABEL → 66741

K₂MF H13
66750 FORT POINT → 66751

K₂MF H13
66760 SCANCARRIER

K₂MF H13
66770 RECOMONE → 66774

K₂MF H13
66790 ANTARES

K₂MF H13
66800 ARUNTO → 66813

K₂MF H13
66830 NIAGA XXIV → 66831

K₂MF H13
66840 DONA PETRA M.R. → 66842

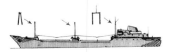

K₂MF H13
66850 GAVILAN → 66851

K₂MF H13
66860 STRAITS VENTURE

K₂MF H13
66870 COLOMBO MARU → 66871

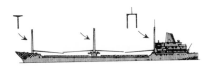

K₂MF H13
66880 AL HODEIDAH → 66886

K₂MF H13
66890 FAITH → 66891

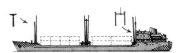

K₂MF H13
66900 ILHA DE SAO MIGUEL → 66901

K₂MF H13
66905 NORDFJORD → 66907

K₂MF H13
66910 HIRMA

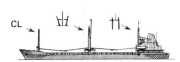

K₂MF H13
66920 NORTHRIDGE

K₂MF H13
66930 ZEIDA → 66933

K₂MF H13
66940 AMALI

K₂MF H13
★66950 BOSUT → 66958

K₂MF H13
66970 BREEKANT → 66974

K₂MF H13
★66980 JAROSLAW

K₂MF H13
66990 MARIANN → 66991

K₂MF H13
67000 AMIR → 67004

K₂MF H13
★67010 ANTON GUBARYEV → 67032

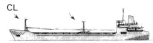

K₂MF H13
67040 TEQUILA SUNRISE

K₂MF H13
★67050 RUCIANE

K₂MF H13
67060 CARICOM EXPRESS → 67061

K₂MF H13
67070 FRISIAN TRADER

K₂MF H13
67080 HOOP

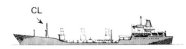

K₂MF H13
67090 LA BAHIA → 67091

K₂MF H13
67100 ZOR → 67101

K₂MF H13
67110 MANITOU → 67112

K₂MF H13
67120 THUNTANK 1

K₂MF H13
67130 CORNELIA

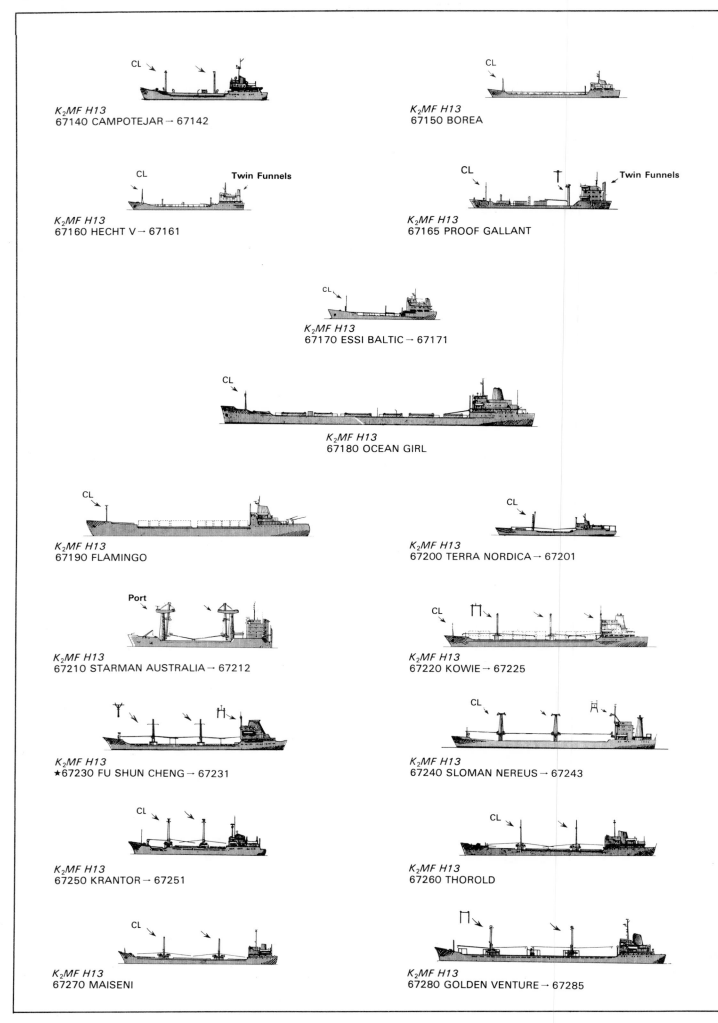

K₂MF H13
67140 CAMPOTEJAR → 67142

K₂MF H13
67150 BOREA

K₂MF H13
67160 HECHT V → 67161

K₂MF H13
67165 PROOF GALLANT

K₂MF H13
67170 ESSI BALTIC → 67171

K₂MF H13
67180 OCEAN GIRL

K₂MF H13
67190 FLAMINGO

K₂MF H13
67200 TERRA NORDICA → 67201

K₂MF H13
67210 STARMAN AUSTRALIA → 67212

K₂MF H13
67220 KOWIE → 67225

K₂MF H13
★67230 FU SHUN CHENG → 67231

K₂MF H13
67240 SLOMAN NEREUS → 67243

K₂MF H13
67250 KRANTOR → 67251

K₂MF H13
67260 THOROLD

K₂MF H13
67270 MAISENI

K₂MF H13
67280 GOLDEN VENTURE → 67285

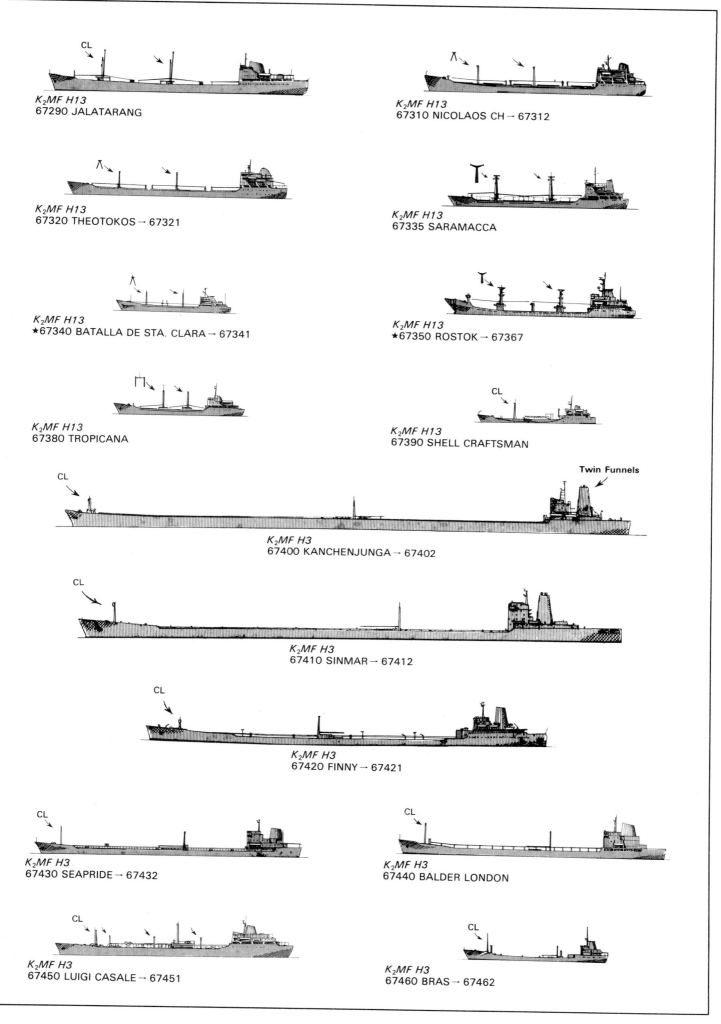

K₂MF H13
67290 JALATARANG

K₂MF H13
67310 NICOLAOS CH → 67312

K₂MF H13
67320 THEOTOKOS → 67321

K₂MF H13
67335 SARAMACCA

K₂MF H13
★67340 BATALLA DE STA. CLARA → 67341

K₂MF H13
★67350 ROSTOK → 67367

K₂MF H13
67380 TROPICANA

K₂MF H13
67390 SHELL CRAFTSMAN

K₂MF H3
67400 KANCHENJUNGA → 67402

K₂MF H3
67410 SINMAR → 67412

K₂MF H3
67420 FINNY → 67421

K₂MF H3
67430 SEAPRIDE → 67432

K₂MF H3
67440 BALDER LONDON

K₂MF H3
67450 LUIGI CASALE → 67451

K₂MF H3
67460 BRAS → 67462

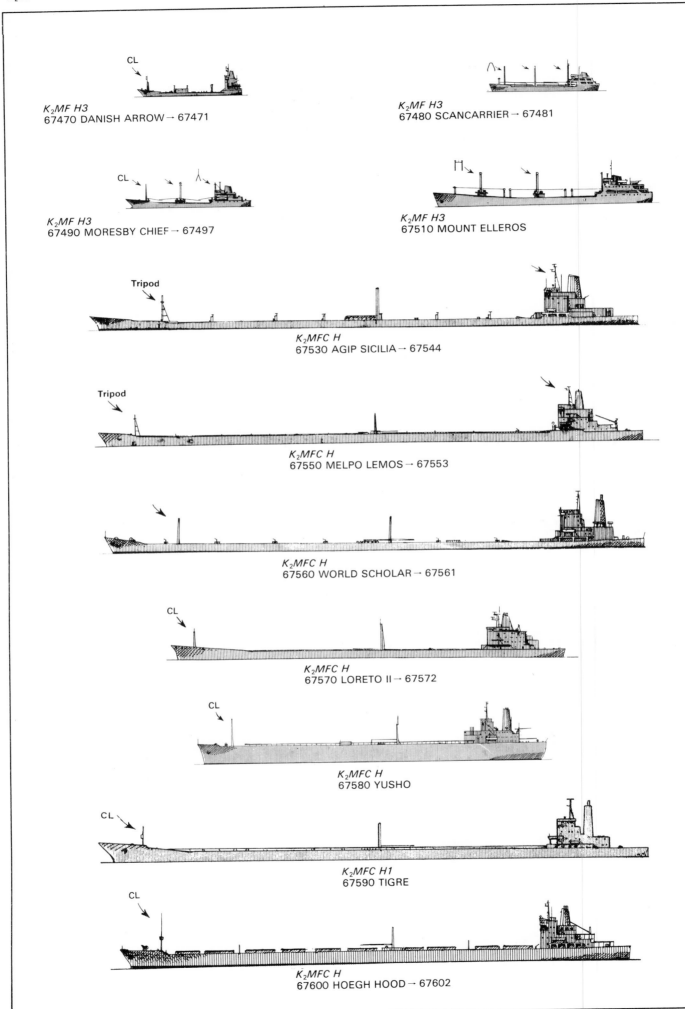

K₂MF H3
67470 DANISH ARROW → 67471

K₂MF H3
67480 SCANCARRIER → 67481

K₂MF H3
67490 MORESBY CHIEF → 67497

K₂MF H3
67510 MOUNT ELLEROS

K₂MFC H
67530 AGIP SICILIA → 67544

K₂MFC H
67550 MELPO LEMOS → 67553

K₂MFC H
67560 WORLD SCHOLAR → 67561

K₂MFC H
67570 LORETO II → 67572

K₂MFC H
67580 YUSHO

K₂MFC H1
67590 TIGRE

K₂MFC H
67600 HOEGH HOOD → 67602

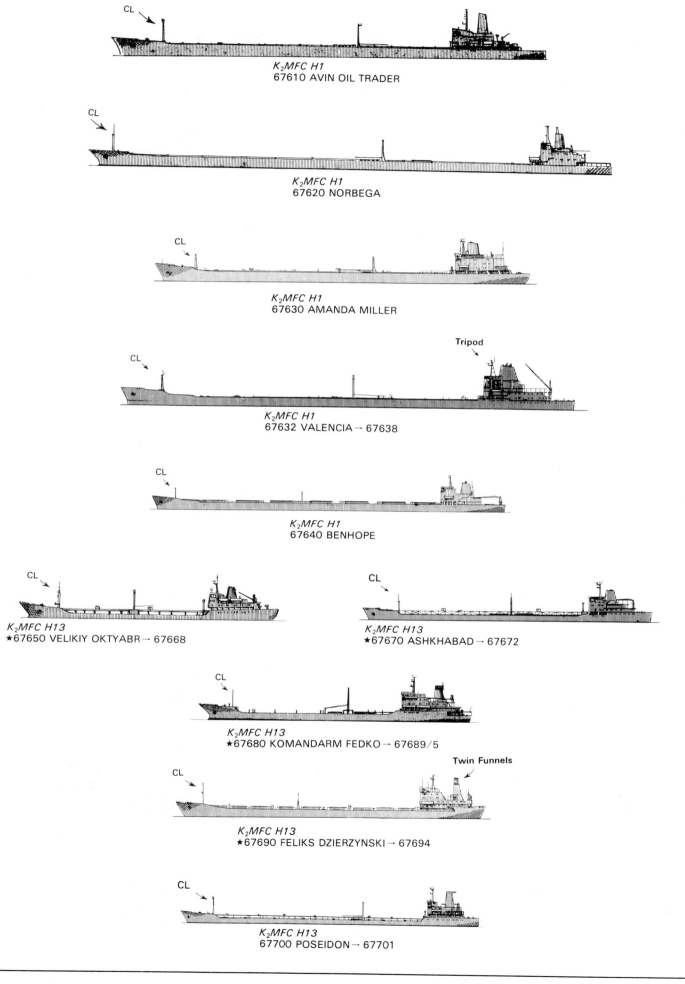

CL

K₂MFC H1
67610 AVIN OIL TRADER

CL

K₂MFC H1
67620 NORBEGA

CL

K₂MFC H1
67630 AMANDA MILLER

CL Tripod

K₂MFC H1
67632 VALENCIA → 67638

CL

K₂MFC H1
67640 BENHOPE

CL

K₂MFC H13
★67650 VELIKIY OKTYABR → 67668

CL

K₂MFC H13
★67670 ASHKHABAD → 67672

CL

K₂MFC H13
★67680 KOMANDARM FEDKO → 67689/5

CL Twin Funnels

K₂MFC H13
★67690 FELIKS DZIERZYNSKI → 67694

CL

K₂MFC H13
67700 POSEIDON → 67701

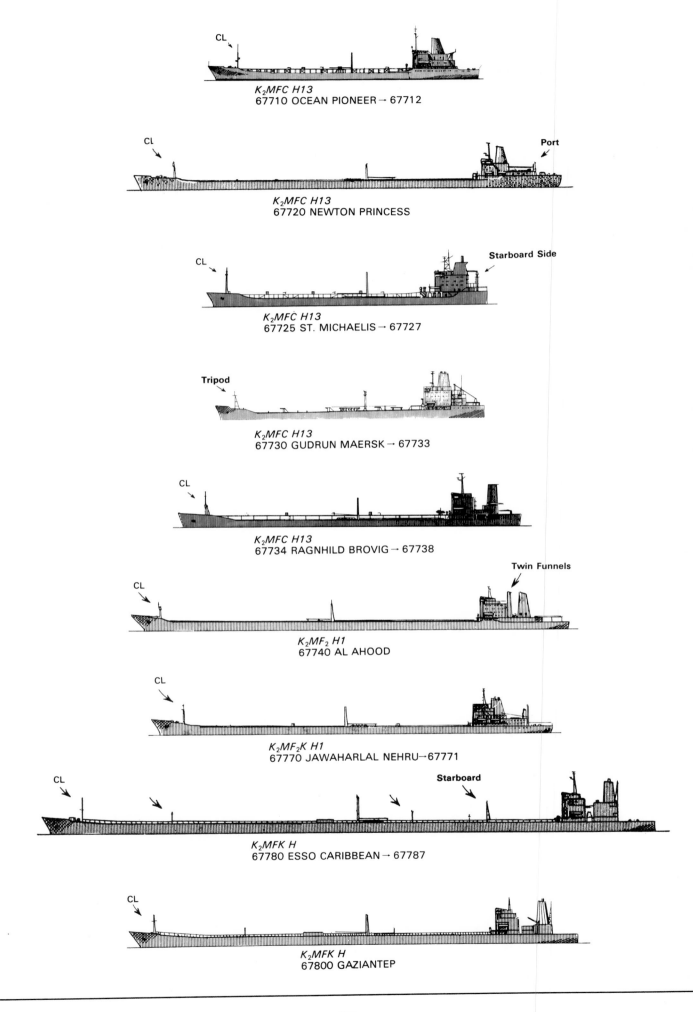

CL

K₂MFC H13
67710 OCEAN PIONEER → 67712

CL

Port

K₂MFC H13
67720 NEWTON PRINCESS

CL

Starboard Side

K₂MFC H13
67725 ST. MICHAELIS → 67727

Tripod

K₂MFC H13
67730 GUDRUN MAERSK → 67733

CL

K₂MFC H13
67734 RAGNHILD BROVIG → 67738

Twin Funnels

CL

K₂MF₂ H1
67740 AL AHOOD

CL

K₂MF₂K H1
67770 JAWAHARLAL NEHRU → 67771

CL

Starboard

K₂MFK H
67780 ESSO CARIBBEAN → 67787

CL

K₂MFK H
67800 GAZIANTEP

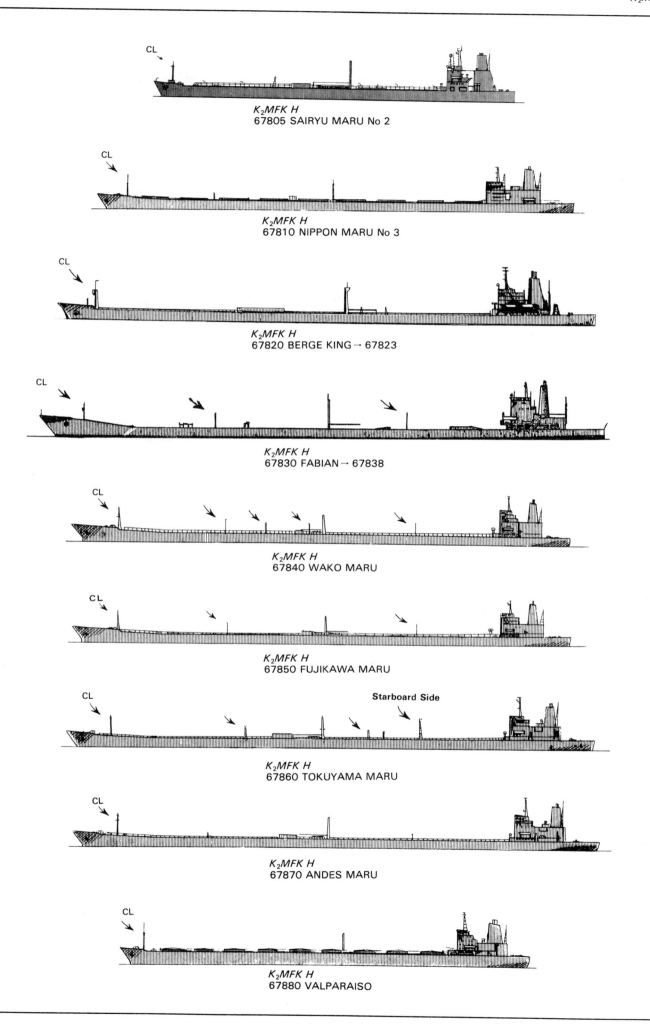

K₂MFK H
67805 SAIRYU MARU No 2

K₂MFK H
67810 NIPPON MARU No 3

K₂MFK H
67820 BERGE KING → 67823

K₂MFK H
67830 FABIAN → 67838

K₂MFK H
67840 WAKO MARU

K₂MFK H
67850 FUJIKAWA MARU

Starboard Side

K₂MFK H
67860 TOKUYAMA MARU

K₂MFK H
67870 ANDES MARU

K₂MFK H
67880 VALPARAISO

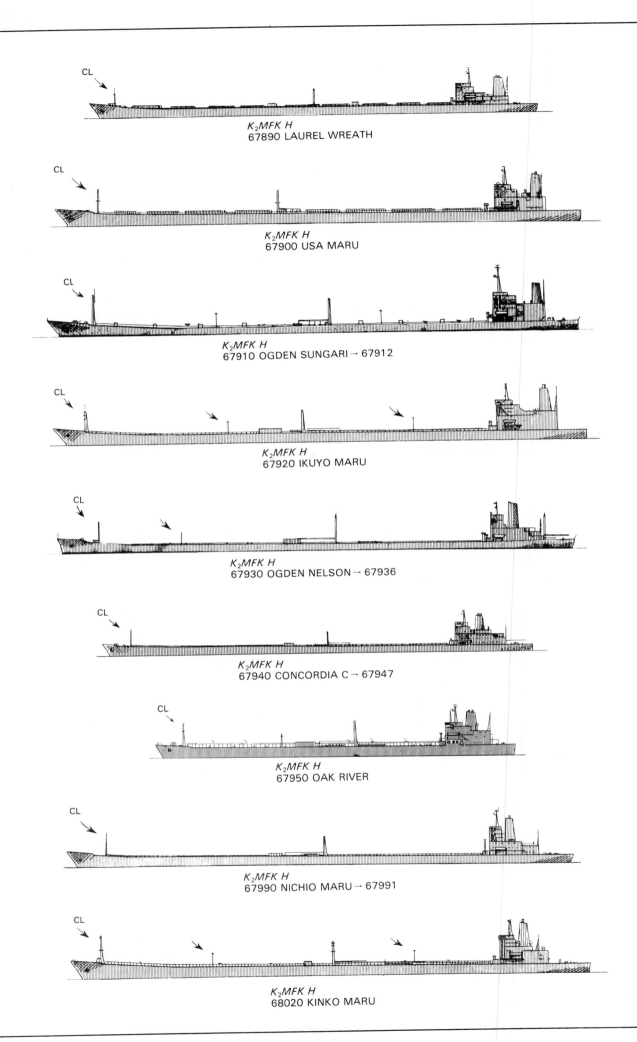

CL

K₂MFK H
67890 LAUREL WREATH

CL

K₂MFK H
67900 USA MARU

CL

K₂MFK H
67910 OGDEN SUNGARI → 67912

CL

K₂MFK H
67920 IKUYO MARU

CL

K₂MFK H
67930 OGDEN NELSON → 67936

CL

K₂MFK H
67940 CONCORDIA C → 67947

CL

K₂MFK H
67950 OAK RIVER

CL

K₂MFK H
67990 NICHIO MARU → 67991

CL

K₂MFK H
68020 KINKO MARU

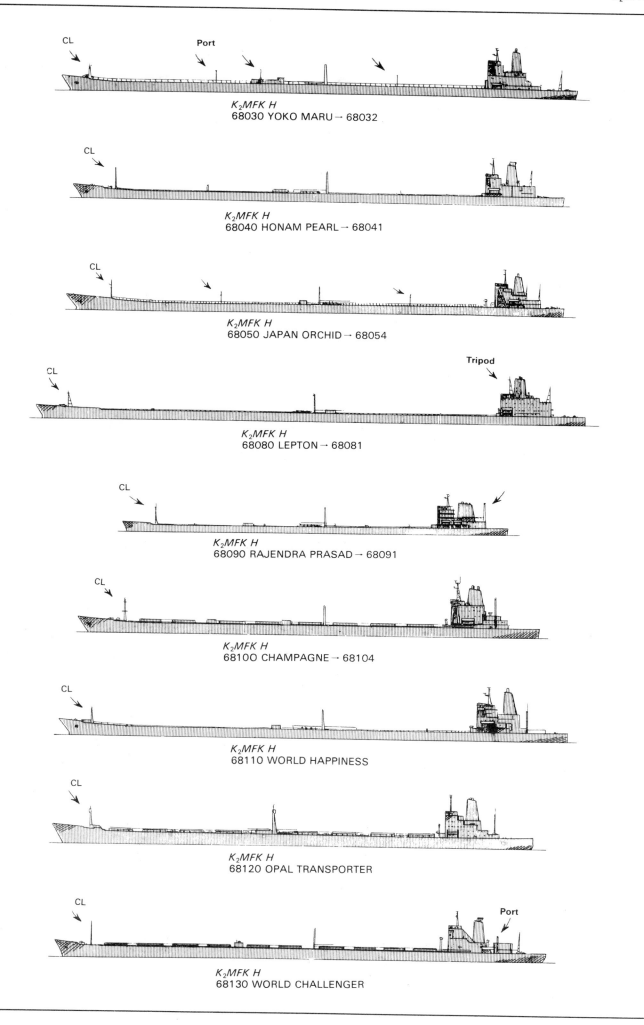

K₂MFK H
68030 YOKO MARU → 68032

K₂MFK H
68040 HONAM PEARL → 68041

K₂MFK H
68050 JAPAN ORCHID → 68054

K₂MFK H
68080 LEPTON → 68081

K₂MFK H
68090 RAJENDRA PRASAD → 68091

K₂MFK H
68100 CHAMPAGNE → 68104

K₂MFK H
68110 WORLD HAPPINESS

K₂MFK H
68120 OPAL TRANSPORTER

K₂MFK H
68130 WORLD CHALLENGER

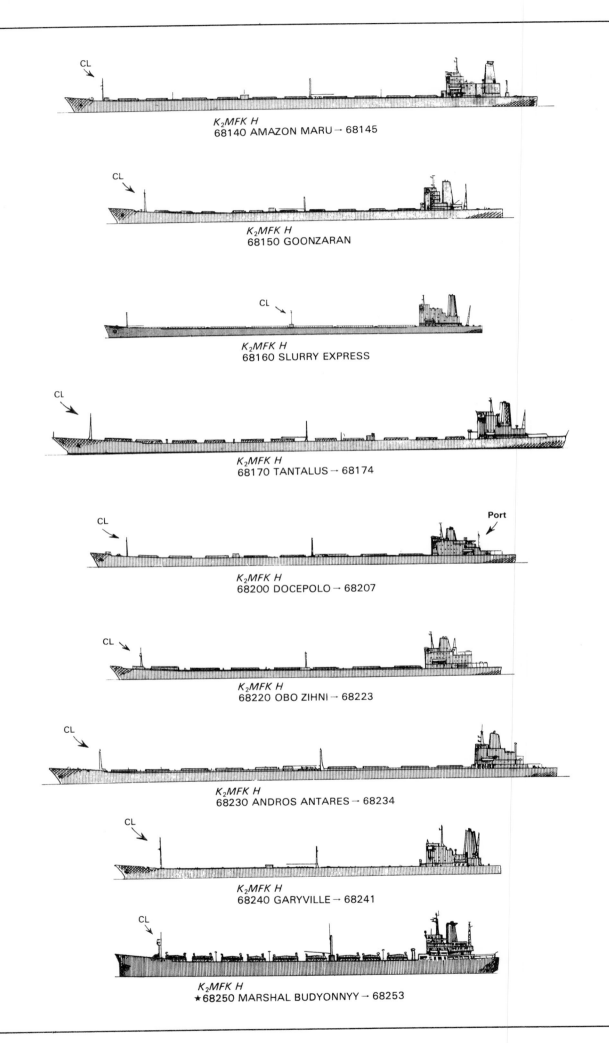

CL

K₂MFK H
68140 AMAZON MARU → 68145

CL

K₂MFK H
68150 GOONZARAN

CL

K₂MFK H
68160 SLURRY EXPRESS

CL

K₂MFK H
68170 TANTALUS → 68174

CL

Port

K₂MFK H
68200 DOCEPOLO → 68207

CL

K₂MFK H
68220 OBO ZIHNI → 68223

CL

K₂MFK H
68230 ANDROS ANTARES → 68234

CL

K₂MFK H
68240 GARYVILLE → 68241

CL

K₂MFK H
★68250 MARSHAL BUDYONNYY → 68253

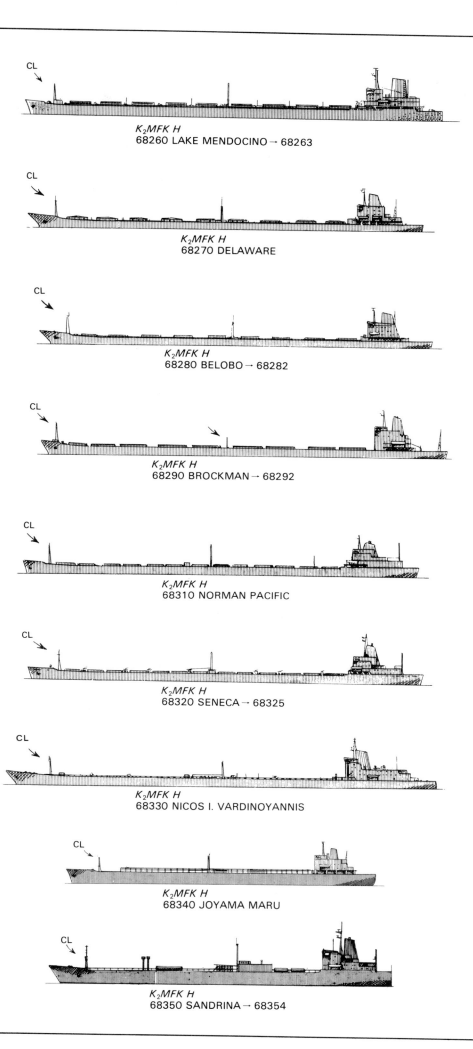

K₂MFK H
68260 LAKE MENDOCINO → 68263

K₂MFK H
68270 DELAWARE

K₂MFK H
68280 BELOBO → 68282

K₂MFK H
68290 BROCKMAN → 68292

K₂MFK H
68310 NORMAN PACIFIC

K₂MFK H
68320 SENECA → 68325

K₂MFK H
68330 NICOS I. VARDINOYANNIS

K₂MFK H
68340 JOYAMA MARU

K₂MFK H
68350 SANDRINA → 68354

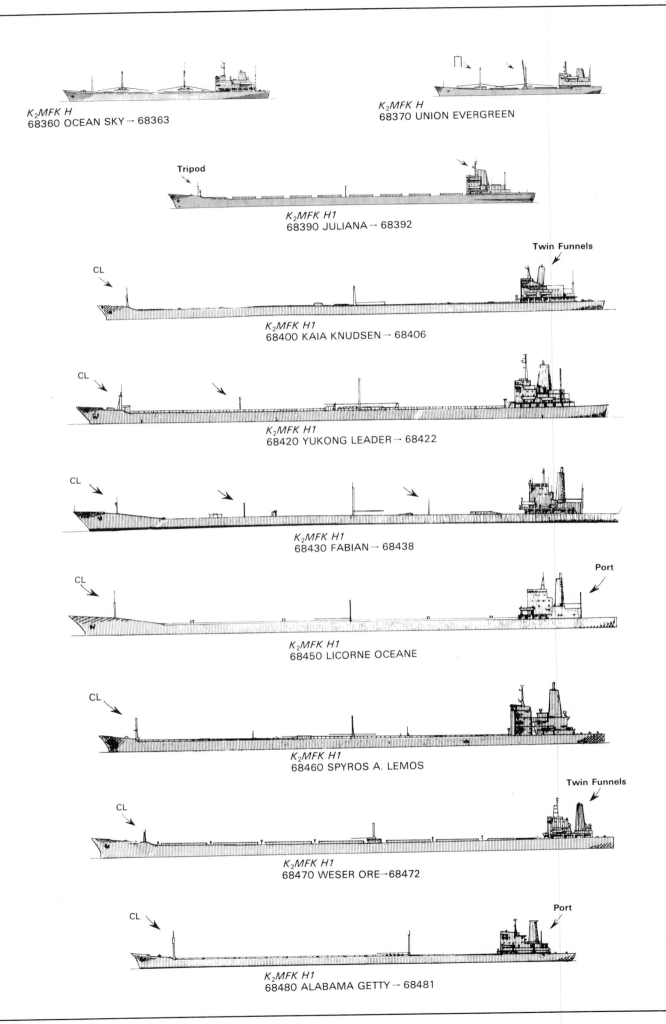

$K_2MFK\ H$
68360 OCEAN SKY → 68363

$K_2MFK\ H$
68370 UNION EVERGREEN

Tripod

$K_2MFK\ H1$
68390 JULIANA → 68392

Twin Funnels

CL

$K_2MFK\ H1$
68400 KAIA KNUDSEN → 68406

CL

$K_2MFK\ H1$
68420 YUKONG LEADER → 68422

CL

$K_2MFK\ H1$
68430 FABIAN → 68438

Port

CL

$K_2MFK\ H1$
68450 LICORNE OCEANE

CL

$K_2MFK\ H1$
68460 SPYROS A. LEMOS

Twin Funnels

CL

$K_2MFK\ H1$
68470 WESER ORE → 68472

Port

CL

$K_2MFK\ H1$
68480 ALABAMA GETTY → 68481

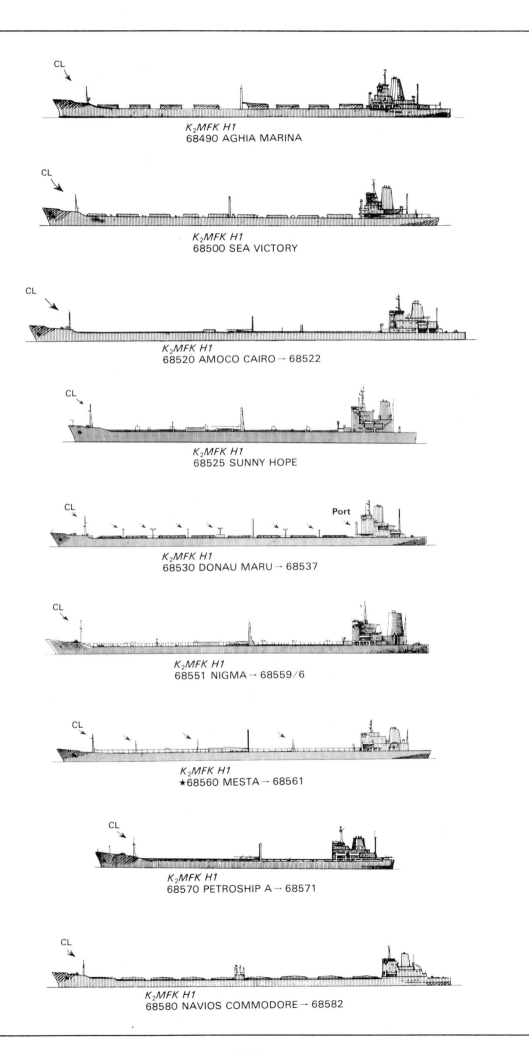

CL

K₂MFK H1
68490 AGHIA MARINA

CL

K₂MFK H1
68500 SEA VICTORY

CL

K₂MFK H1
68520 AMOCO CAIRO → 68522

CL

K₂MFK H1
68525 SUNNY HOPE

CL   **Port**

K₂MFK H1
68530 DONAU MARU → 68537

CL

K₂MFK H1
68551 NIGMA → 68559/6

CL

K₂MFK H1
★68560 MESTA → 68561

CL

K₂MFK H1
68570 PETROSHIP A → 68571

CL

K₂MFK H1
68580 NAVIOS COMMODORE → 68582

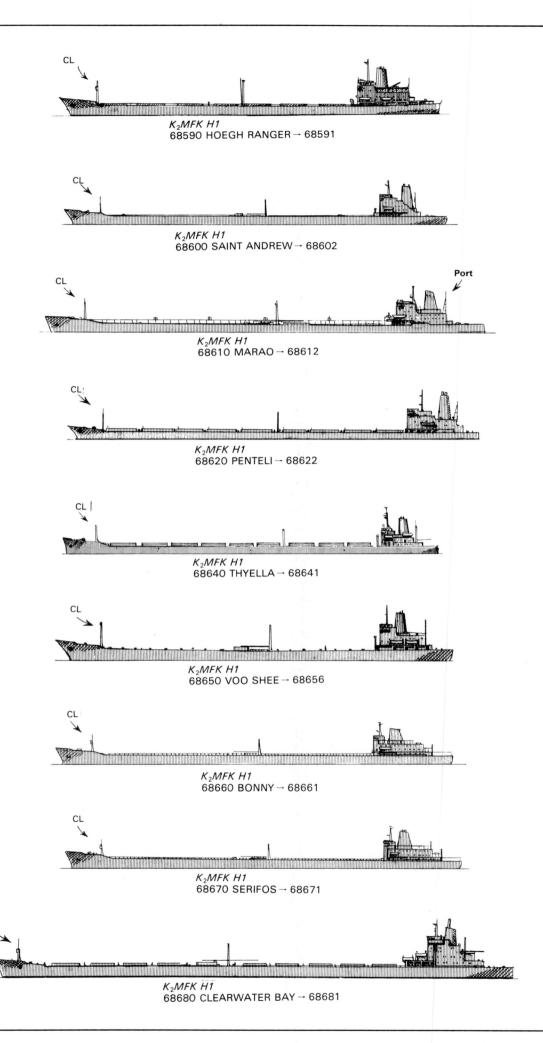

CL

K₂MFK H1
68590 HOEGH RANGER → 68591

CL

K₂MFK H1
68600 SAINT ANDREW → 68602

CL   Port

K₂MFK H1
68610 MARAO → 68612

CL

K₂MFK H1
68620 PENTELI → 68622

CL

K₂MFK H1
68640 THYELLA → 68641

CL

K₂MFK H1
68650 VOO SHEE → 68656

CL

K₂MFK H1
68660 BONNY → 68661

CL

K₂MFK H1
68670 SERIFOS → 68671

CL

K₂MFK H1
68680 CLEARWATER BAY → 68681

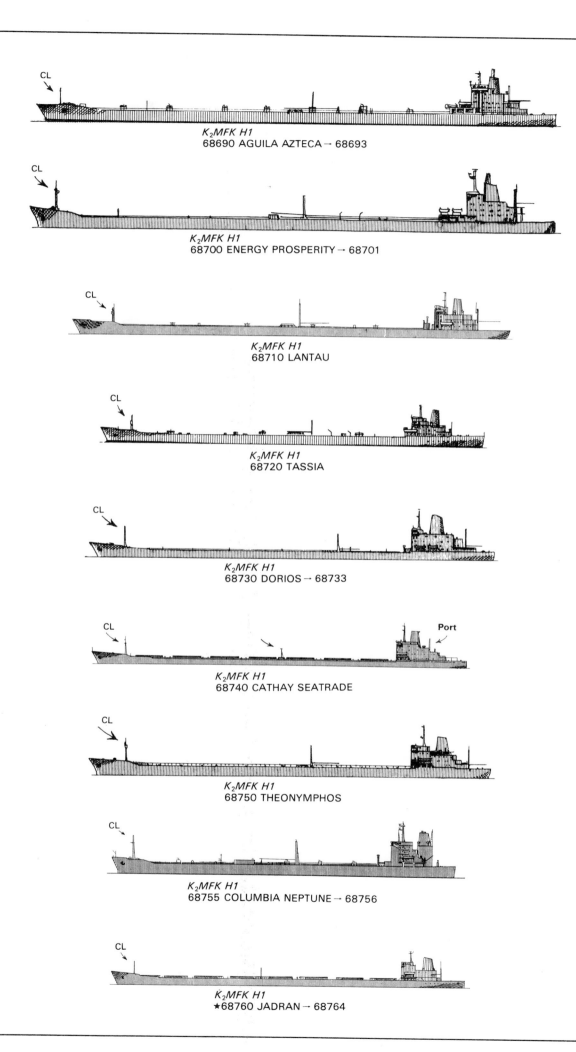

K₂MFK H1
68690 AGUILA AZTECA → 68693

K₂MFK H1
68700 ENERGY PROSPERITY → 68701

K₂MFK H1
68710 LANTAU

K₂MFK H1
68720 TASSIA

K₂MFK H1
68730 DORIOS → 68733

K₂MFK H1
68740 CATHAY SEATRADE

K₂MFK H1
68750 THEONYMPHOS

K₂MFK H1
68755 COLUMBIA NEPTUNE → 68756

K₂MFK H1
★68760 JADRAN → 68764

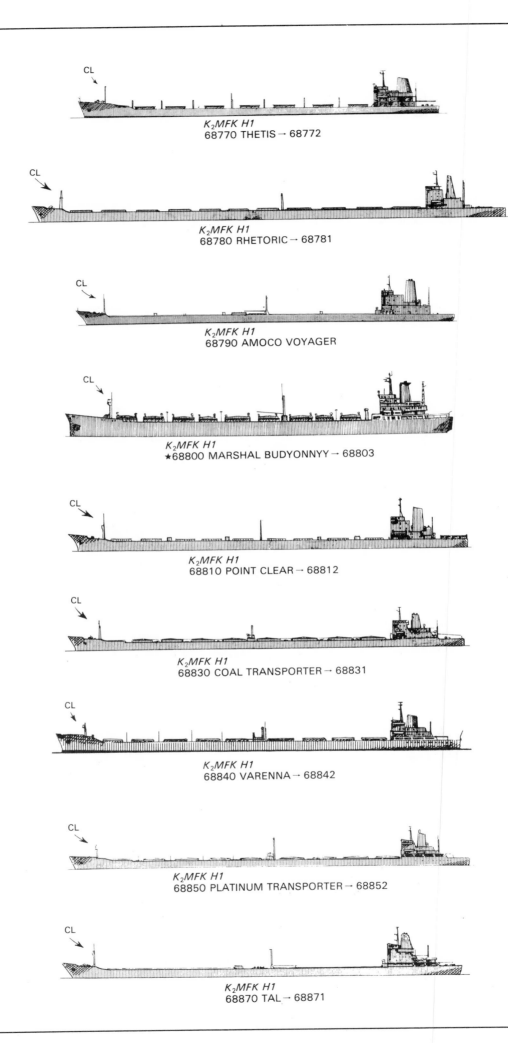

CL
K₂MFK H1
68770 THETIS → 68772

CL
K₂MFK H1
68780 RHETORIC → 68781

CL
K₂MFK H1
68790 AMOCO VOYAGER

CL
K₂MFK H1
★68800 MARSHAL BUDYONNYY → 68803

CL
K₂MFK H1
68810 POINT CLEAR → 68812

CL
K₂MFK H1
68830 COAL TRANSPORTER → 68831

CL
K₂MFK H1
68840 VARENNA → 68842

CL
K₂MFK H1
68850 PLATINUM TRANSPORTER → 68852

CL
K₂MFK H1
68870 TAL → 68871

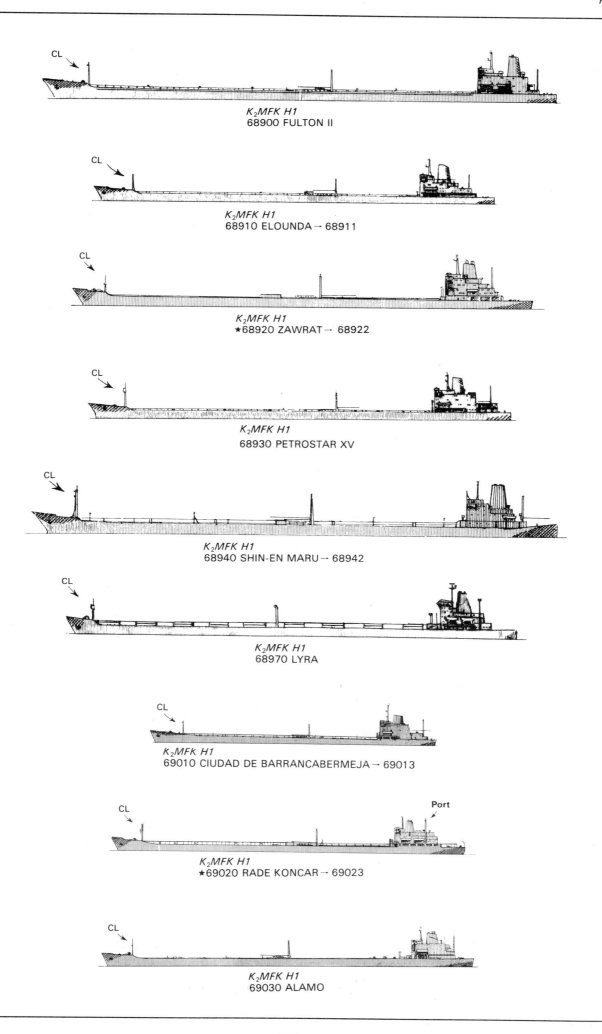

CL

K₂MFK H1
68900 FULTON II

CL

K₂MFK H1
68910 ELOUNDA → 68911

CL

K₂MFK H1
★68920 ZAWRAT → 68922

CL

K₂MFK H1
68930 PETROSTAR XV

CL

K₂MFK H1
68940 SHIN-EN MARU → 68942

CL

K₂MFK H1
68970 LYRA

CL

K₂MFK H1
69010 CIUDAD DE BARRANCABERMEJA → 69013

CL   Port

K₂MFK H1
★69020 RADE KONCAR → 69023

CL

K₂MFK H1
69030 ALAMO

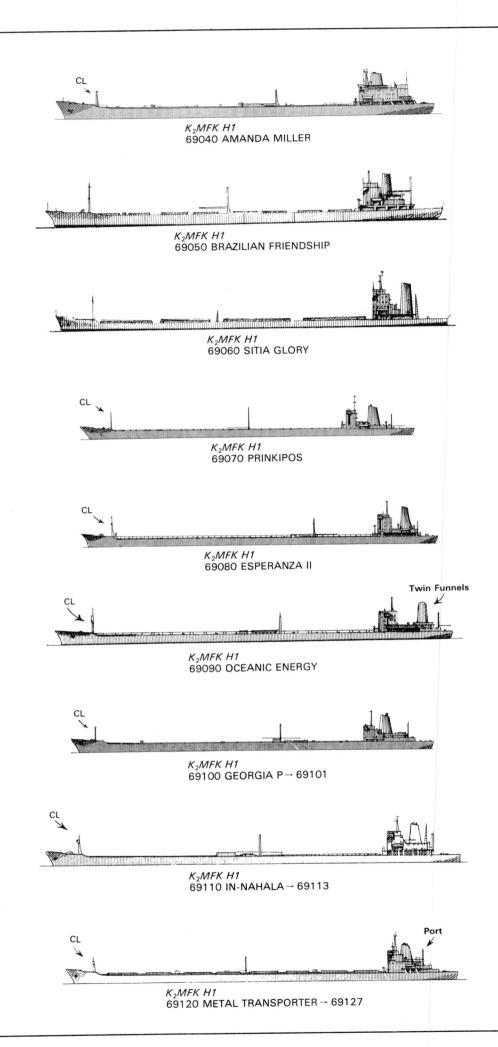

K₂MFK H1
69040 AMANDA MILLER

K₂MFK H1
69050 BRAZILIAN FRIENDSHIP

K₂MFK H1
69060 SITIA GLORY

K₂MFK H1
69070 PRINKIPOS

K₂MFK H1
69080 ESPERANZA II

Twin Funnels

K₂MFK H1
69090 OCEANIC ENERGY

K₂MFK H1
69100 GEORGIA P → 69101

K₂MFK H1
69110 IN-NAHALA → 69113

Port

K₂MFK H1
69120 METAL TRANSPORTER → 69127

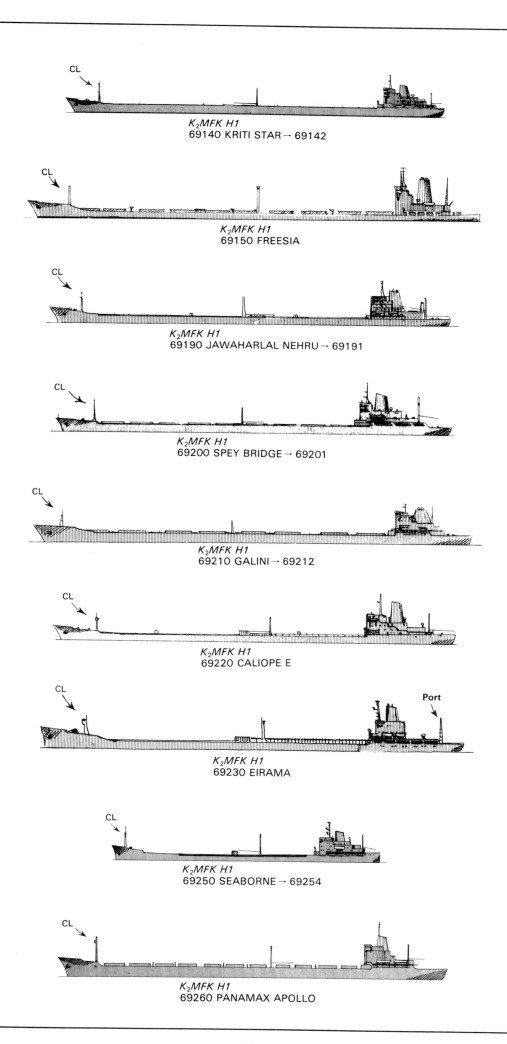

K₂MFK H1
69140 KRITI STAR → 69142

K₂MFK H1
69150 FREESIA

K₂MFK H1
69190 JAWAHARLAL NEHRU → 69191

K₂MFK H1
69200 SPEY BRIDGE → 69201

K₂MFK H1
69210 GALINI → 69212

K₂MFK H1
69220 CALIOPE E

K₂MFK H1
69230 EIRAMA

K₂MFK H1
69250 SEABORNE → 69254

K₂MFK H1
69260 PANAMAX APOLLO

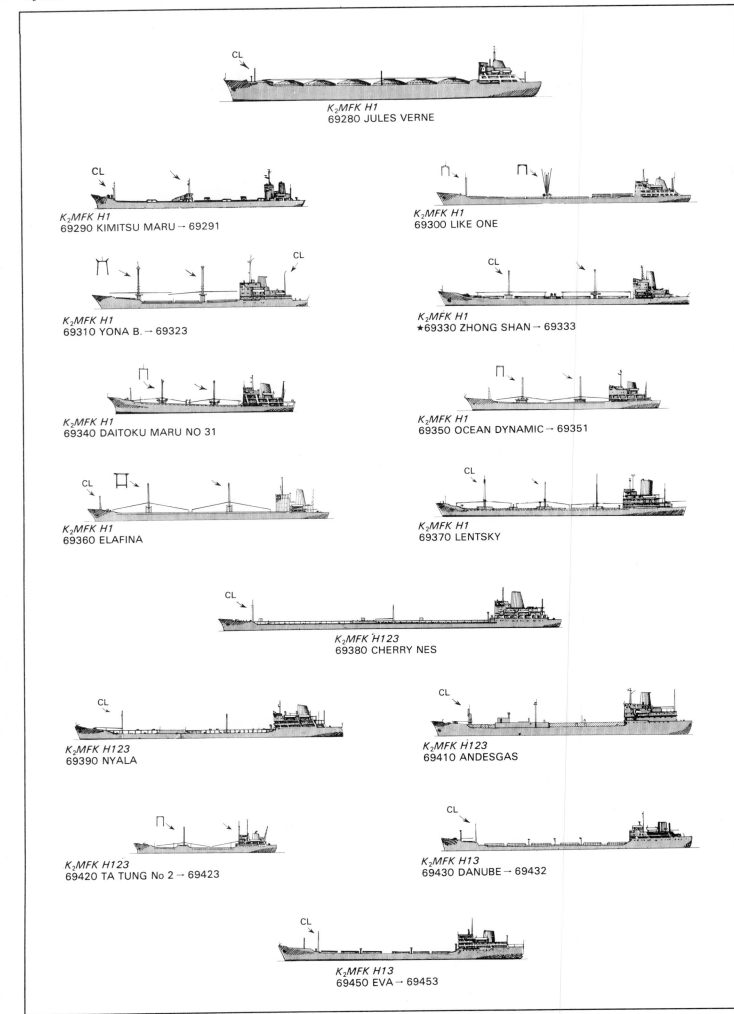

K₂MFK H1
69280 JULES VERNE

K₂MFK H1
69290 KIMITSU MARU → 69291

K₂MFK H1
69300 LIKE ONE

K₂MFK H1
69310 YONA B. → 69323

K₂MFK H1
★69330 ZHONG SHAN → 69333

K₂MFK H1
69340 DAITOKU MARU NO 31

K₂MFK H1
69350 OCEAN DYNAMIC → 69351

K₂MFK H1
69360 ELAFINA

K₂MFK H1
69370 LENTSKY

K₂MFK H123
69380 CHERRY NES

K₂MFK H123
69390 NYALA

K₂MFK H123
69410 ANDESGAS

K₂MFK H123
69420 TA TUNG No 2 → 69423

K₂MFK H13
69430 DANUBE → 69432

K₂MFK H13
69450 EVA → 69453

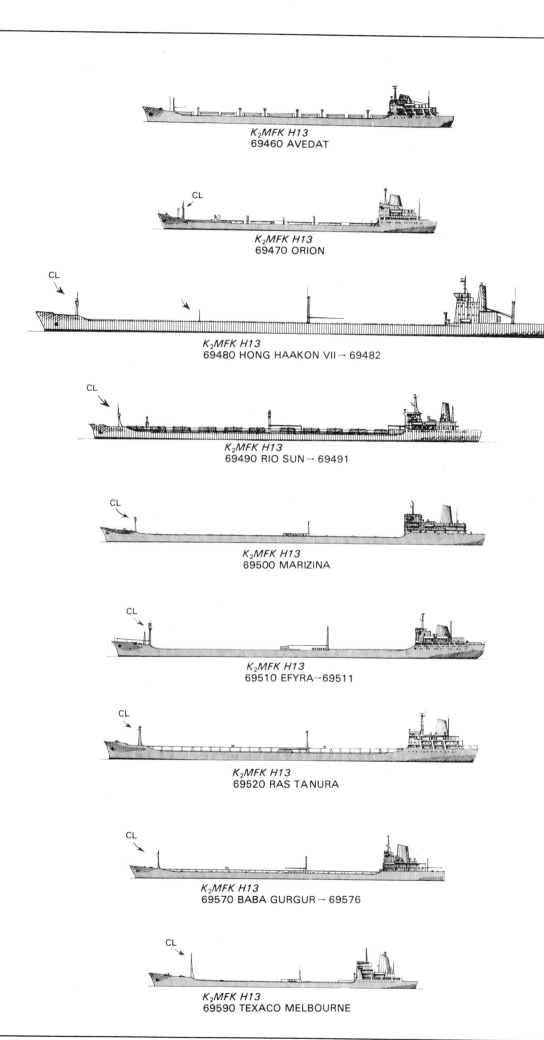

K₂MFK H13
69460 AVEDAT

CL

K₂MFK H13
69470 ORION

CL

K₂MFK H13
69480 HONG HAAKON VII → 69482

CL

K₂MFK H13
69490 RIO SUN → 69491

CL

K₂MFK H13
69500 MARIZINA

CL

K₂MFK H13
69510 EFYRA → 69511

CL

K₂MFK H13
69520 RAS TANURA

CL

K₂MFK H13
69570 BABA GURGUR → 69576

CL

K₂MFK H13
69590 TEXACO MELBOURNE

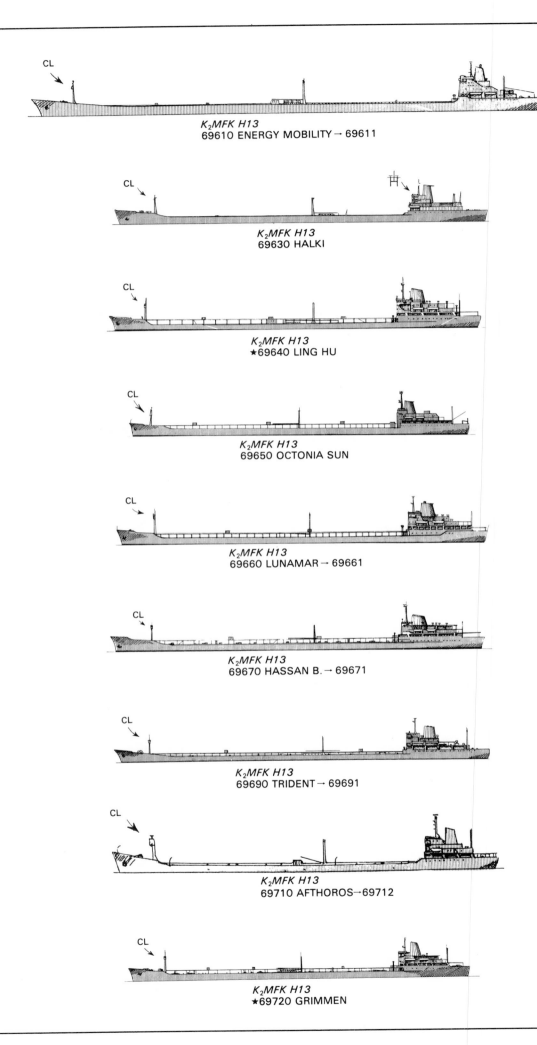

K₂MFK H13
69610 ENERGY MOBILITY → 69611

K₂MFK H13
69630 HALKI

K₂MFK H13
★69640 LING HU

K₂MFK H13
69650 OCTONIA SUN

K₂MFK H13
69660 LUNAMAR → 69661

K₂MFK H13
69670 HASSAN B. → 69671

K₂MFK H13
69690 TRIDENT → 69691

K₂MFK H13
69710 AFTHOROS → 69712

K₂MFK H13
★69720 GRIMMEN

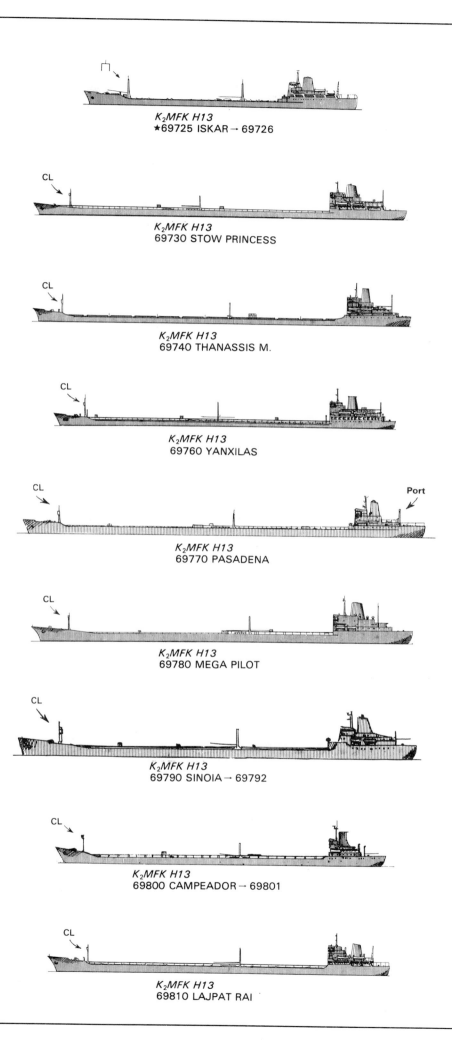

K₂MFK H13
★69725 ISKAR → 69726

K₂MFK H13
69730 STOW PRINCESS

K₂MFK H13
69740 THANASSIS M.

K₂MFK H13
69760 YANXILAS

K₂MFK H13
69770 PASADENA

K₂MFK H13
69780 MEGA PILOT

K₂MFK H13
69790 SINOIA → 69792

K₂MFK H13
69800 CAMPEADOR → 69801

K₂MFK H13
69810 LAJPAT RAI

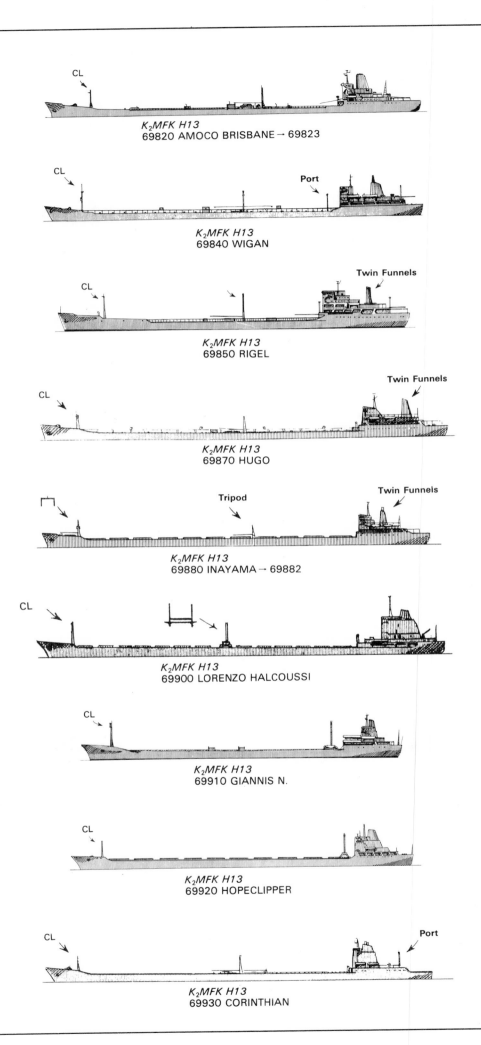

CL

K₂MFK H13
69820 AMOCO BRISBANE → 69823

CL · Port

K₂MFK H13
69840 WIGAN

CL · Twin Funnels

K₂MFK H13
69850 RIGEL

CL · Twin Funnels

K₂MFK H13
69870 HUGO

Tripod · Twin Funnels

K₂MFK H13
69880 INAYAMA → 69882

CL

K₂MFK H13
69900 LORENZO HALCOUSSI

CL

K₂MFK H13
69910 GIANNIS N.

CL

K₂MFK H13
69920 HOPECLIPPER

CL · Port

K₂MFK H13
69930 CORINTHIAN

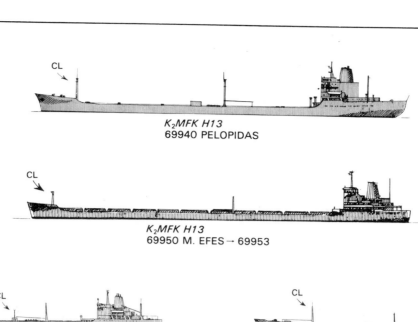

K₂MFK H13
69940 PELOPIDAS

K₂MFK H13
69950 M. EFES → 69953

K₂MFK H13
69960 ATHENIAN HARMONY → 69980

K₂MFK H13
69990 BENITO JUAREZ → 69998

K₂MFK H13
70000 PETROMAR BAHIA BLANCA II → 70008

K₂MFK H13
70010 MATSUKAZE

K₂MFK H13
★70020 SAMOTLOR → 70033

K₂MFK H13
70040 MANUEL AVILA COMACHO → 70045

K₂MFK H13
70050 MAGIC MERCURY → 70058

K₂MFK H13
70060 BEJAIA → 70067

K₂MFK H13
70070 BUNGA KESUMBA → 70072

K₂MFK H13
70080 POMELLA → 70081

K₂MFK H13
70090 GLOBE EMPRESS → 70095

K₂MFK H13
70100 TAURUS ERRE → 70102

K₂MFK H13
70110 ENDURANCE → 70112

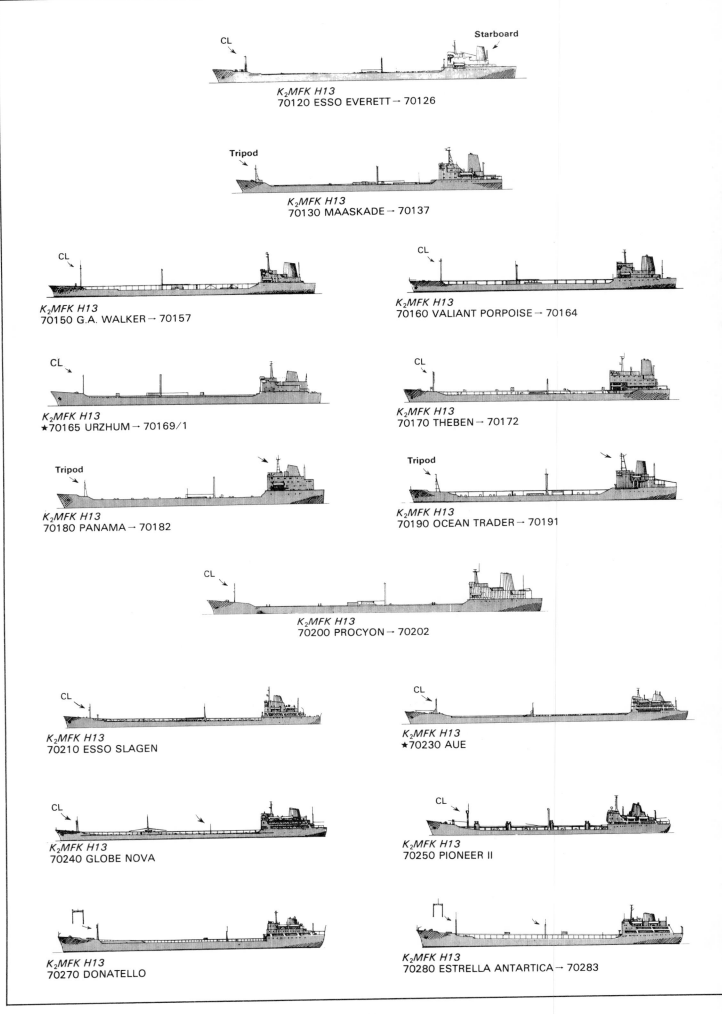

CL → Starboard

K₂MFK H13
70120 ESSO EVERETT → 70126

Tripod

K₂MFK H13
70130 MAASKADE → 70137

CL

K₂MFK H13
70150 G.A. WALKER → 70157

CL

K₂MFK H13
70160 VALIANT PORPOISE → 70164

CL

K₂MFK H13
★70165 URZHUM → 70169/1

CL

K₂MFK H13
70170 THEBEN → 70172

Tripod

K₂MFK H13
70180 PANAMA → 70182

Tripod

K₂MFK H13
70190 OCEAN TRADER → 70191

CL

K₂MFK H13
70200 PROCYON → 70202

CL

K₂MFK H13
70210 ESSO SLAGEN

CL

K₂MFK H13
★70230 AUE

CL

K₂MFK H13
70240 GLOBE NOVA

CL

K₂MFK H13
70250 PIONEER II

K₂MFK H13
70270 DONATELLO

K₂MFK H13
70280 ESTRELLA ANTARTICA → 70283

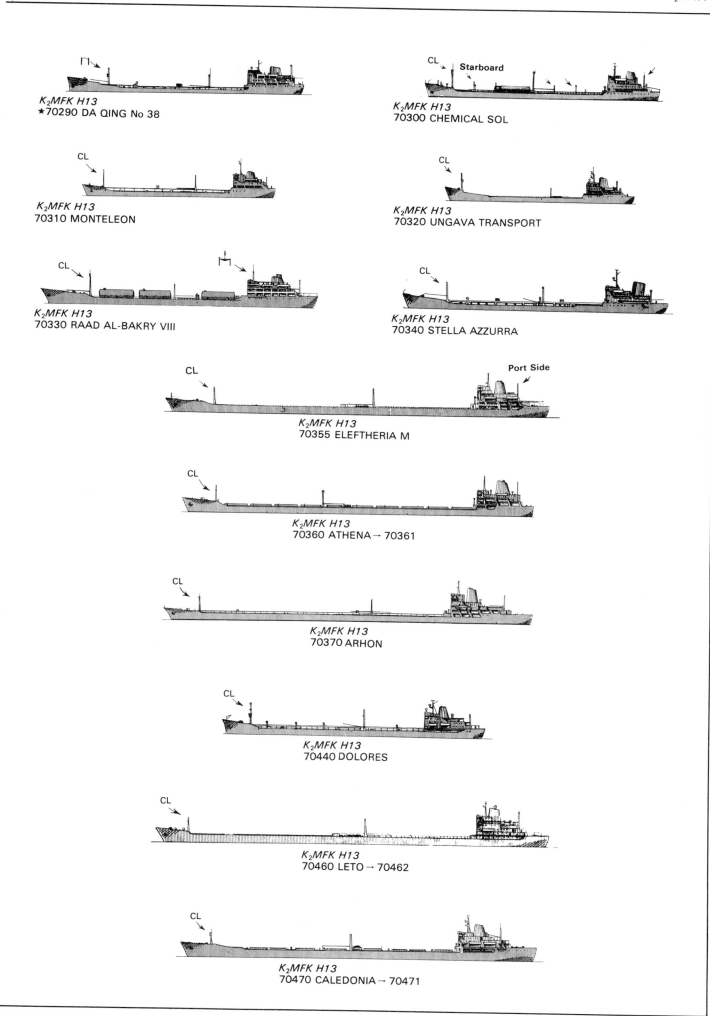

K₂MFK H13
★70290 DA QING No 38

K₂MFK H13
70300 CHEMICAL SOL

K₂MFK H13
70310 MONTELEON

K₂MFK H13
70320 UNGAVA TRANSPORT

K₂MFK H13
70330 RAAD AL-BAKRY VIII

K₂MFK H13
70340 STELLA AZZURRA

K₂MFK H13
70355 ELEFTHERIA M

K₂MFK H13
70360 ATHENA → 70361

K₂MFK H13
70370 ARHON

K₂MFK H13
70440 DOLORES

K₂MFK H13
70460 LETO → 70462

K₂MFK H13
70470 CALEDONIA → 70471

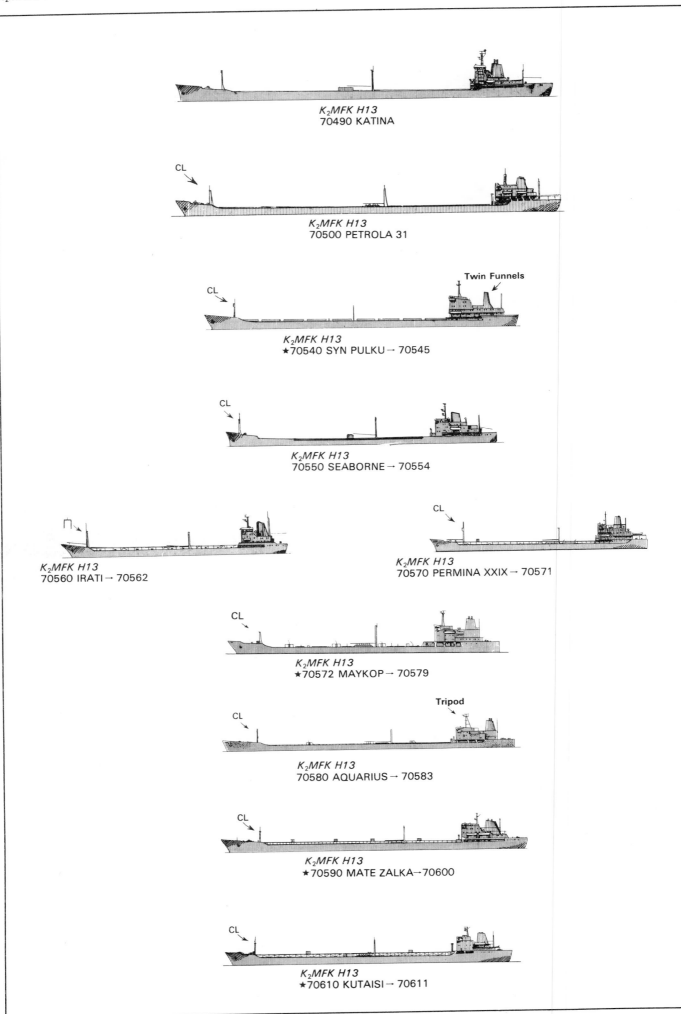

K₂MFK H13
70490 KATINA

K₂MFK H13
70500 PETROLA 31

Twin Funnels

K₂MFK H13
★70540 SYN PULKU → 70545

K₂MFK H13
70550 SEABORNE → 70554

K₂MFK H13
70560 IRATI → 70562

K₂MFK H13
70570 PERMINA XXIX → 70571

K₂MFK H13
★70572 MAYKOP → 70579

Tripod

K₂MFK H13
70580 AQUARIUS → 70583

K₂MFK H13
★70590 MATE ZALKA → 70600

K₂MFK H13
★70610 KUTAISI → 70611

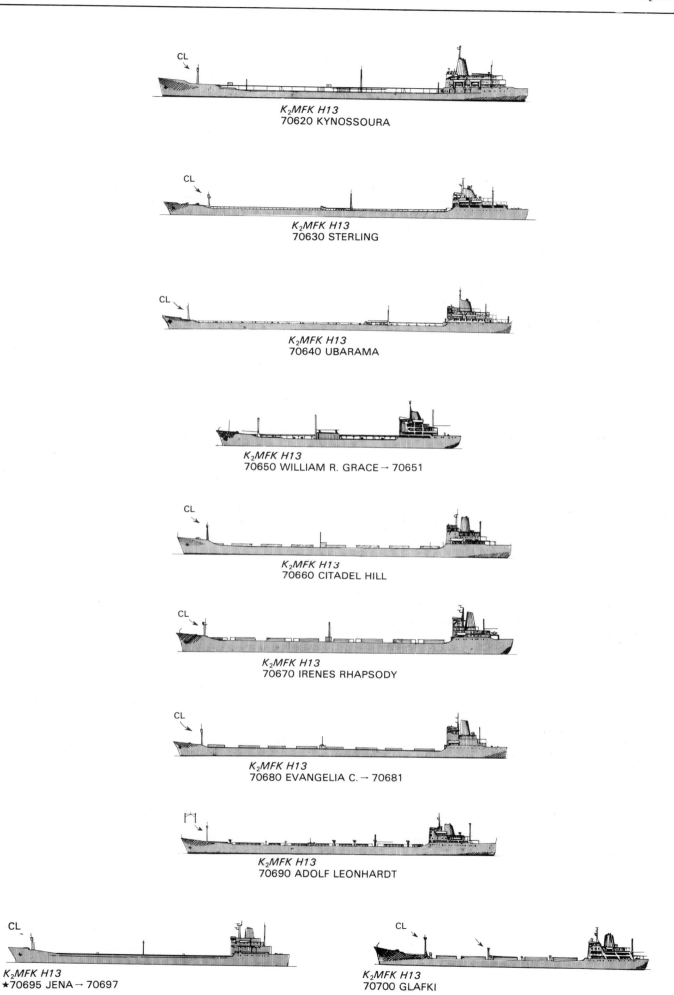

CL

K₂MFK H13
70620 KYNOSSOURA

CL

K₂MFK H13
70630 STERLING

CL

K₂MFK H13
70640 UBARAMA

K₂MFK H13
70650 WILLIAM R. GRACE → 70651

CL

K₂MFK H13
70660 CITADEL HILL

CL

K₂MFK H13
70670 IRENES RHAPSODY

CL

K₂MFK H13
70680 EVANGELIA C. → 70681

K₂MFK H13
70690 ADOLF LEONHARDT

CL

K₂MFK H13
★70695 JENA → 70697

CL

K₂MFK H13
70700 GLAFKI

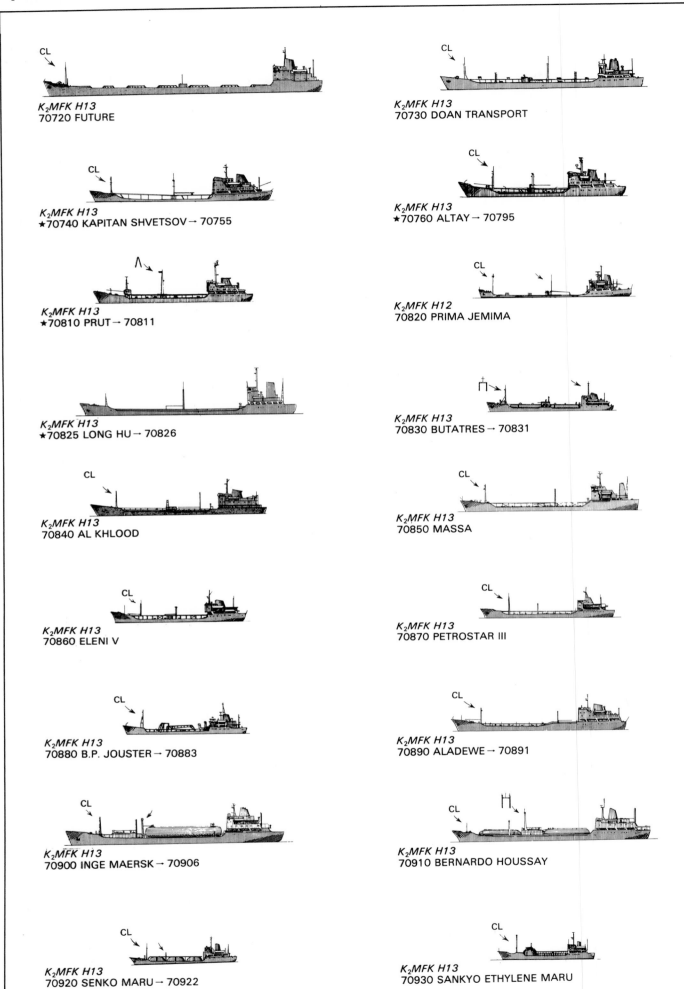

K₂MFK H13
70720 FUTURE

K₂MFK H13
70730 DOAN TRANSPORT

K₂MFK H13
★70740 KAPITAN SHVETSOV → 70755

K₂MFK H13
★70760 ALTAY → 70795

K₂MFK H13
★70810 PRUT → 70811

K₂MFK H12
70820 PRIMA JEMIMA

K₂MFK H13
★70825 LONG HU → 70826

K₂MFK H13
70830 BUTATRES → 70831

K₂MFK H13
70840 AL KHLOOD

K₂MFK H13
70850 MASSA

K₂MFK H13
70860 ELENI V

K₂MFK H13
70870 PETROSTAR III

K₂MFK H13
70880 B.P. JOUSTER → 70883

K₂MFK H13
70890 ALADEWE → 70891

K₂MFK H13
70900 INGE MAERSK → 70906

K₂MFK H13
70910 BERNARDO HOUSSAY

K₂MFK H13
70920 SENKO MARU → 70922

K₂MFK H13
70930 SANKYO ETHYLENE MARU

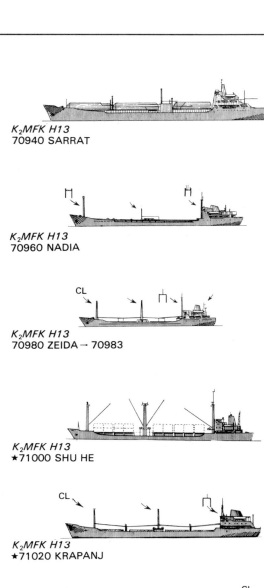

K₂MFK H13
70940 SARRAT

K₂MFK H13
70960 NADIA

K₂MFK H13
70980 ZEIDA → 70983

K₂MFK H13
★71000 SHU HE

K₂MFK H13
★71020 KRAPANJ

K₂MFK H13
★71040 PIONER MOSKVY→71061

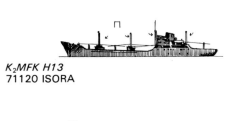

K₂MFK H13
71100 DON ALEJO

K₂MFK H13
71120 ISORA

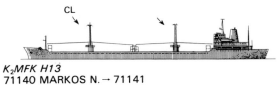

K₂MFK H13
71140 MARKOS N. → 71141

K₂MFK H13
70950 JAVELIN → 70953

K₂MFK H13
70970 ETHEL EVERARD

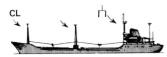

K₂MFK H13
★70990 BOSUT → 70998

K₂MFK H13
★71010 KORCULA

K₂MFK H13
71030 LEO SHARPY → 71034

K₂MFK H13
71090 VISHVA PREM → 71093

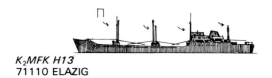

K₂MFK H13
71110 ELAZIG

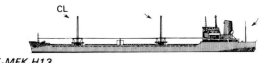

K₂MFK H13
71130 PACIFIC FAIR → 71136

K₂MFK H13
71150 PACIFIC QUEEN → 71159

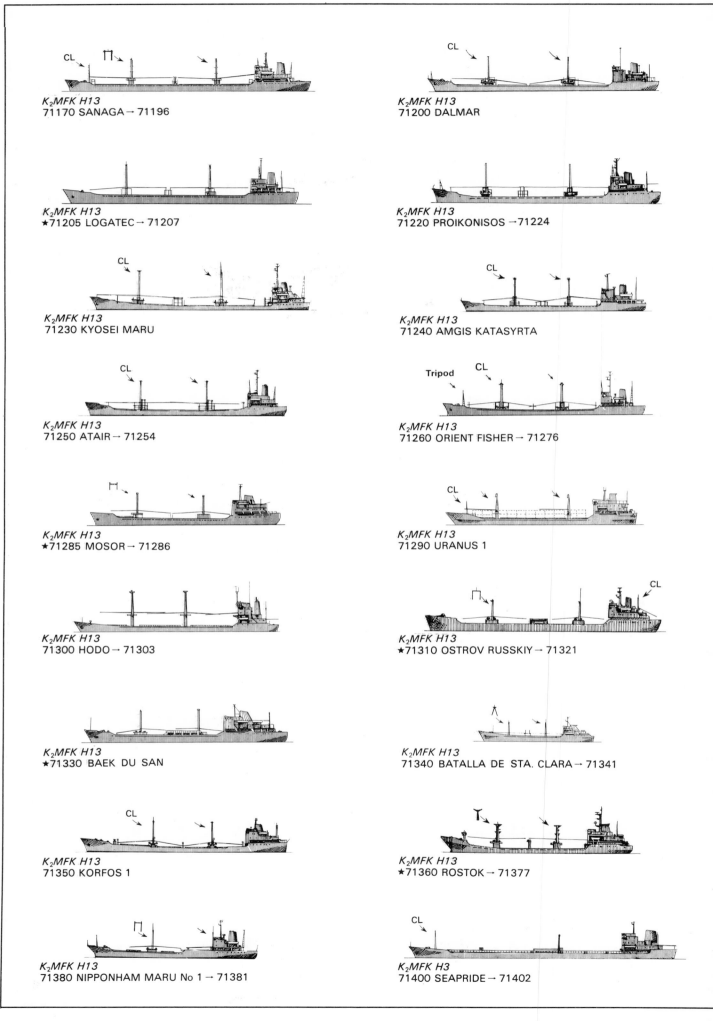

K₂MFK H13
71170 SANAGA → 71196

K₂MFK H13
71200 DALMAR

K₂MFK H13
★71205 LOGATEC → 71207

K₂MFK H13
71220 PROIKONISOS → 71224

K₂MFK H13
71230 KYOSEI MARU

K₂MFK H13
71240 AMGIS KATASYRTA

K₂MFK H13
71250 ATAIR → 71254

K₂MFK H13
71260 ORIENT FISHER → 71276

K₂MFK H13
★71285 MOSOR → 71286

K₂MFK H13
71290 URANUS 1

K₂MFK H13
71300 HODO → 71303

K₂MFK H13
★71310 OSTROV RUSSKIY → 71321

K₂MFK H13
★71330 BAEK DU SAN

K₂MFK H13
71340 BATALLA DE STA. CLARA → 71341

K₂MFK H13
71350 KORFOS 1

K₂MFK H13
★71360 ROSTOK → 71377

K₂MFK H13
71380 NIPPONHAM MARU No 1 → 71381

K₂MFK H3
71400 SEAPRIDE → 71402

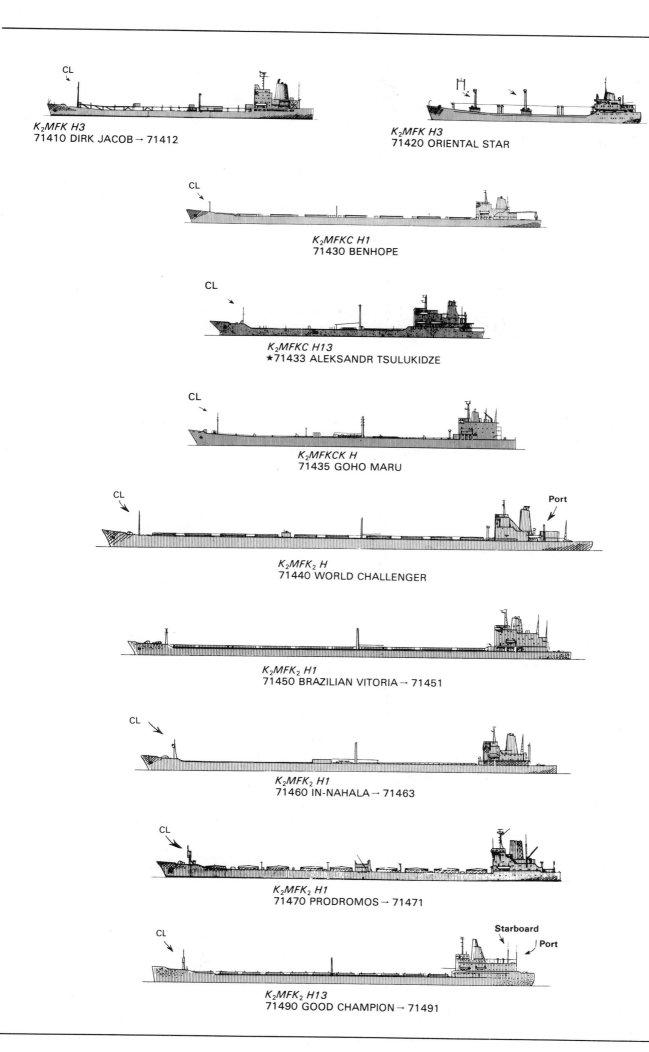

CL

K₂MFK H3
71410 DIRK JACOB → 71412

K₂MFK H3
71420 ORIENTAL STAR

CL

K₂MFKC H1
71430 BENHOPE

CL

K₂MFKC H13
★71433 ALEKSANDR TSULUKIDZE

CL

K₂MFKCK H
71435 GOHO MARU

CL   Port

K₂MFK₂ H
71440 WORLD CHALLENGER

K₂MFK₂ H1
71450 BRAZILIAN VITORIA → 71451

CL

K₂MFK₂ H1
71460 IN-NAHALA → 71463

CL

K₂MFK₂ H1
71470 PRODROMOS → 71471

CL   Starboard
                               Port

K₂MFK₂ H13
71490 GOOD CHAMPION → 71491

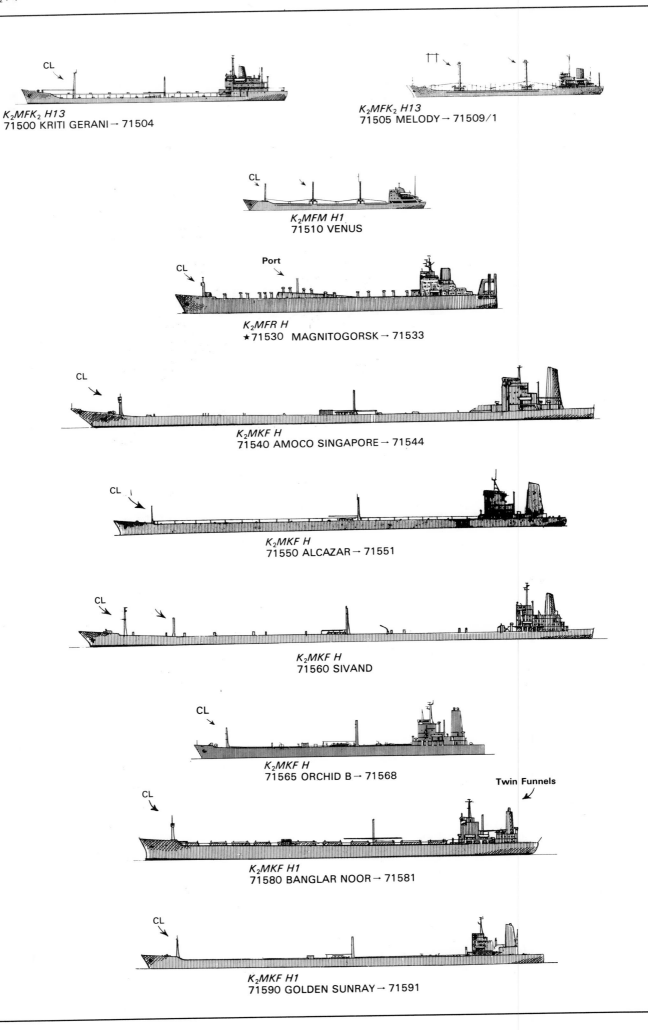

CL
K₂MFK₂ H13
71500 KRITI GERANI→ 71504

K₂MFK₂ H13
71505 MELODY→ 71509/1

CL
K₂MFM H1
71510 VENUS

CL   Port
K₂MFR H
★71530 MAGNITOGORSK→ 71533

CL
K₂MKF H
71540 AMOCO SINGAPORE→ 71544

CL
K₂MKF H
71550 ALCAZAR→ 71551

CL
K₂MKF H
71560 SIVAND

CL
K₂MKF H
71565 ORCHID B→ 71568

Twin Funnels

CL
K₂MKF H1
71580 BANGLAR NOOR→ 71581

CL
K₂MKF H1
71590 GOLDEN SUNRAY→ 71591

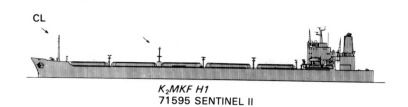

K₂MKF H1
71595 SENTINEL II

K₂MKF H13
71600 LIBERTADOR SAN MARTIN → 71602

K₂MKFK H1
★71610 HONG HU

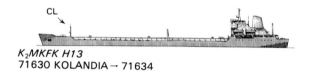

K₂MKFK H13
71630 KOLANDIA → 71634

K₂MKFK H13
71640 VISHVA KAUSHAL → 71643

K₂MKFM H13
71650 STARMAN AMERICA

K₂MK₄MF H13
71660 AMCO 1

K₂MK₃MFK H13
★71670 LENINSKIY LUCH → 71674

K₂MK₂MF H13
★71680 PRIGNITZ → 71682

K₂MK₂MFK H1
71690 DIANA → 71691

K₂MKMF H13
71710 ANNITA

K₂MKMF H13
71720 KASSIAN GLORY

K₂MKMF H13
71730 ARETHUSA

K₂MKMFCK H13
71740 FERNANDOEVERETT → 71744

K₂MKMFK H1
71750 RASSEM

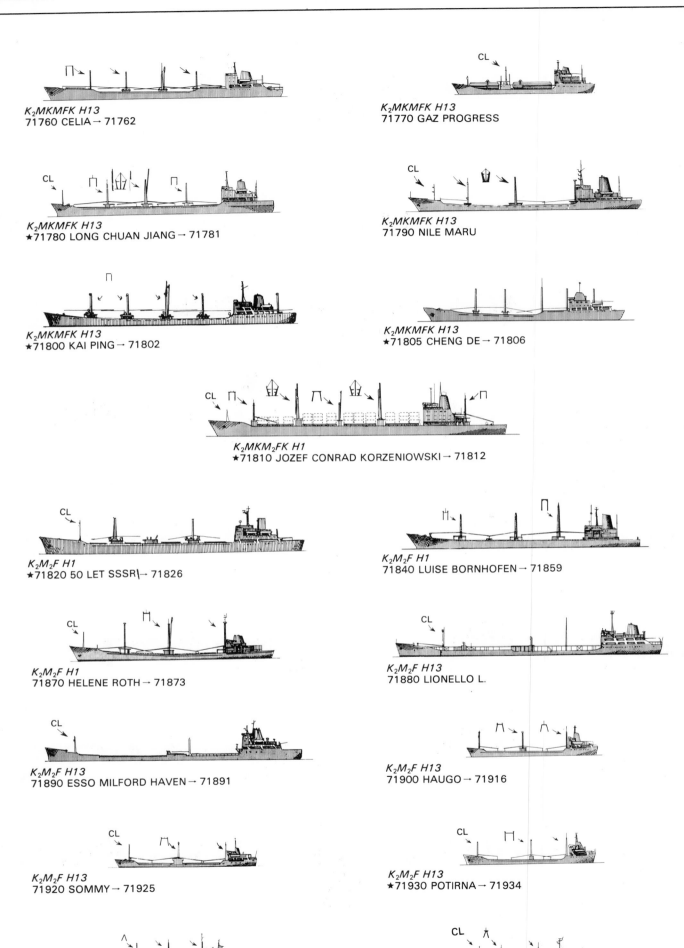

K₂MKMFK H13
71760 CELIA → 71762

K₂MKMFK H13
71770 GAZ PROGRESS

K₂MKMFK H13
★71780 LONG CHUAN JIANG → 71781

K₂MKMFK H13
71790 NILE MARU

K₂MKMFK H13
★71800 KAI PING → 71802

K₂MKMFK H13
★71805 CHENG DE → 71806

K₂MKM₂FK H1
★71810 JOZEF CONRAD KORZENIOWSKI → 71812

K₂M₂F H1
★71820 50 LET SSSR\ → 71826

K₂M₂F H1
71840 LUISE BORNHOFEN → 71859

K₂M₂F H1
71870 HELENE ROTH → 71873

K₂M₂F H13
71880 LIONELLO L.

K₂M₂F H13
71890 ESSO MILFORD HAVEN → 71891

K₂M₂F H13
71900 HAUGO → 71916

K₂M₂F H13
71920 SOMMY → 71925

K₂M₂F H13
★71930 POTIRNA → 71934

K₂M₂F H13
71940 NIAGA XXVI → 71942

K₂M₂F H13
71945 ASKO → 71947

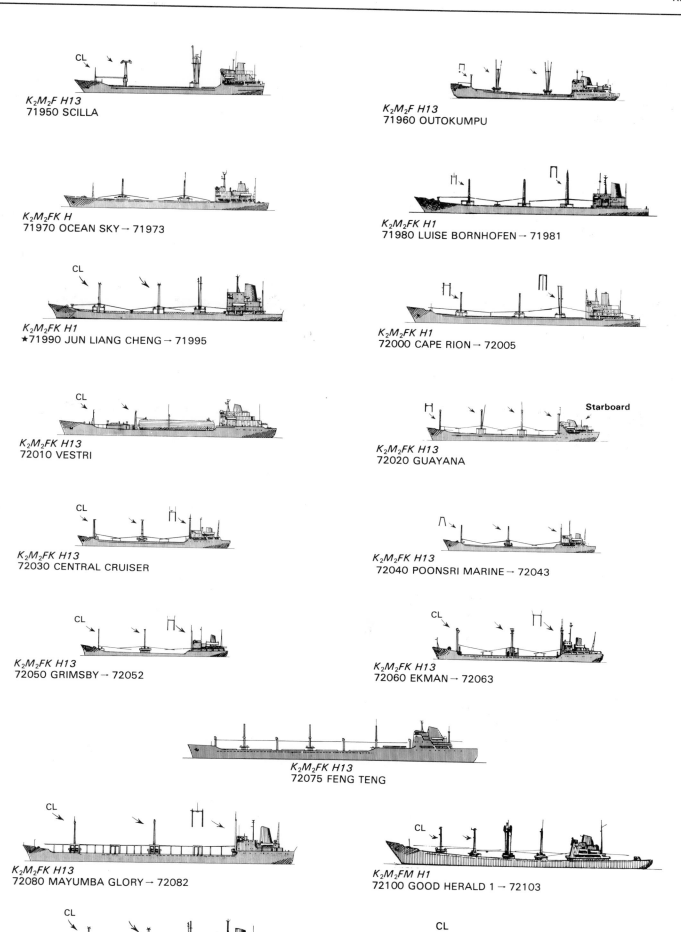

K₂M₂F H13
71950 SCILLA

K₂M₂F H13
71960 OUTOKUMPU

K₂M₂FK H
71970 OCEAN SKY → 71973

K₂M₂FK H1
71980 LUISE BORNHOFEN → 71981

K₂M₂FK H1
★71990 JUN LIANG CHENG → 71995

K₂M₂FK H1
72000 CAPE RION → 72005

K₂M₂FK H13
72010 VESTRI

K₂M₂FK H13
72020 GUAYANA

K₂M₂FK H13
72030 CENTRAL CRUISER

K₂M₂FK H13
72040 POONSRI MARINE → 72043

K₂M₂FK H13
72050 GRIMSBY → 72052

K₂M₂FK H13
72060 EKMAN → 72063

K₂M₂FK H13
72075 FENG TENG

K₂M₂FK H13
72080 MAYUMBA GLORY → 72082

K₂M₂FM H1
72100 GOOD HERALD 1 → 72103

K₂M₂FM H1
★72110 JUN LIANG CHENG → 72115

KM H1
72117 GOLF

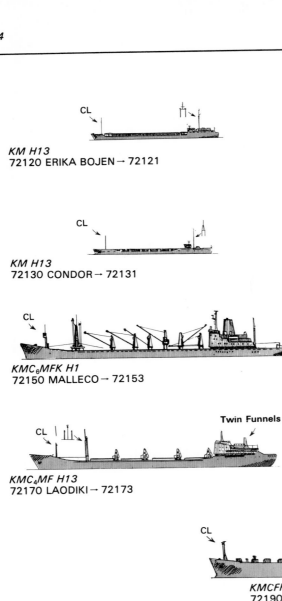

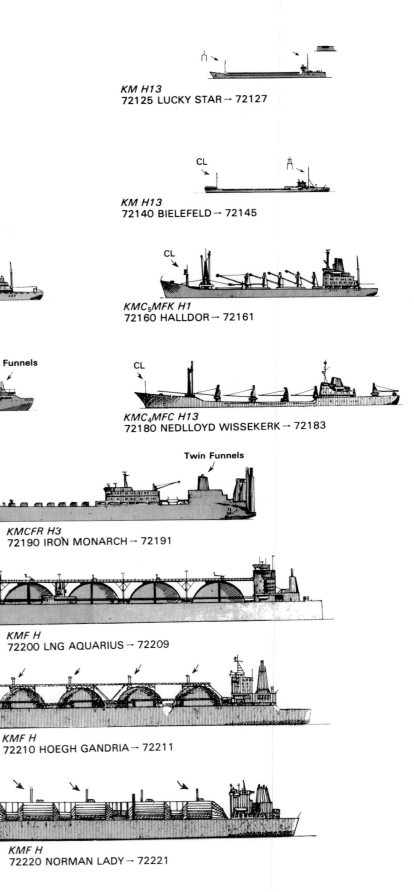

KM H13
72120 ERIKA BOJEN → 72121

KM H13
72125 LUCKY STAR → 72127

KM H13
72130 CONDOR → 72131

KM H13
72140 BIELEFELD → 72145

KMC₆MFK H1
72150 MALLECO → 72153

KMC₅MFK H1
72160 HALLDOR → 72161

Twin Funnels

KMC₄MF H13
72170 LAODIKI → 72173

KMC₄MFC H13
72180 NEDLLOYD WISSEKERK → 72183

Twin Funnels

KMCFR H3
72190 IRON MONARCH → 72191

KMF H
72200 LNG AQUARIUS → 72209

KMF H
72210 HOEGH GANDRIA → 72211

KMF H
72220 NORMAN LADY → 72221

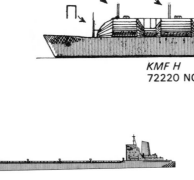

KMF H
72230 FORUM PRIDE → 72231

KMF H
72240 NACIONAL AVEIRO → 72241

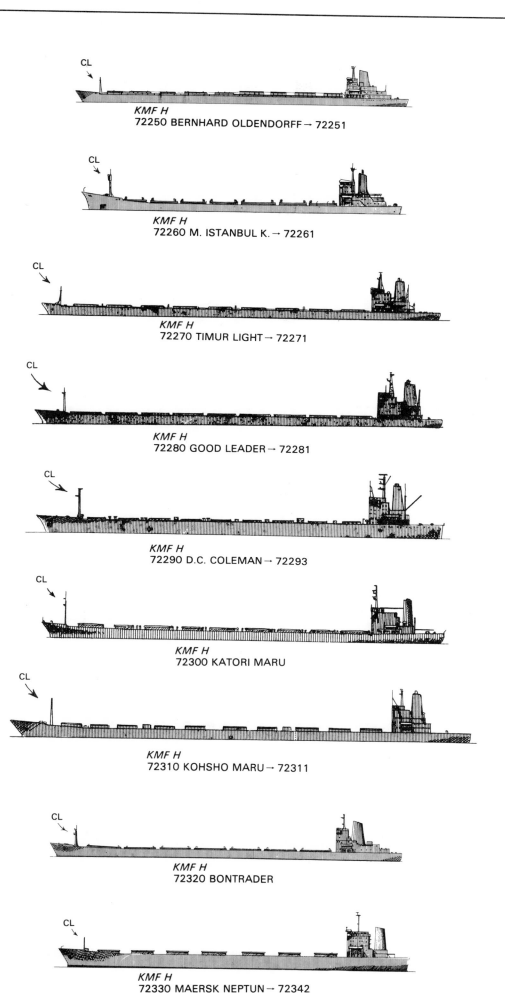

KMF H
72250 BERNHARD OLDENDORFF → 72251

KMF H
72260 M. ISTANBUL K. → 72261

KMF H
72270 TIMUR LIGHT → 72271

KMF H
72280 GOOD LEADER → 72281

KMF H
72290 D.C. COLEMAN → 72293

KMF H
72300 KATORI MARU

KMF H
72310 KOHSHO MARU → 72311

KMF H
72320 BONTRADER

KMF H
72330 MAERSK NEPTUN → 72342

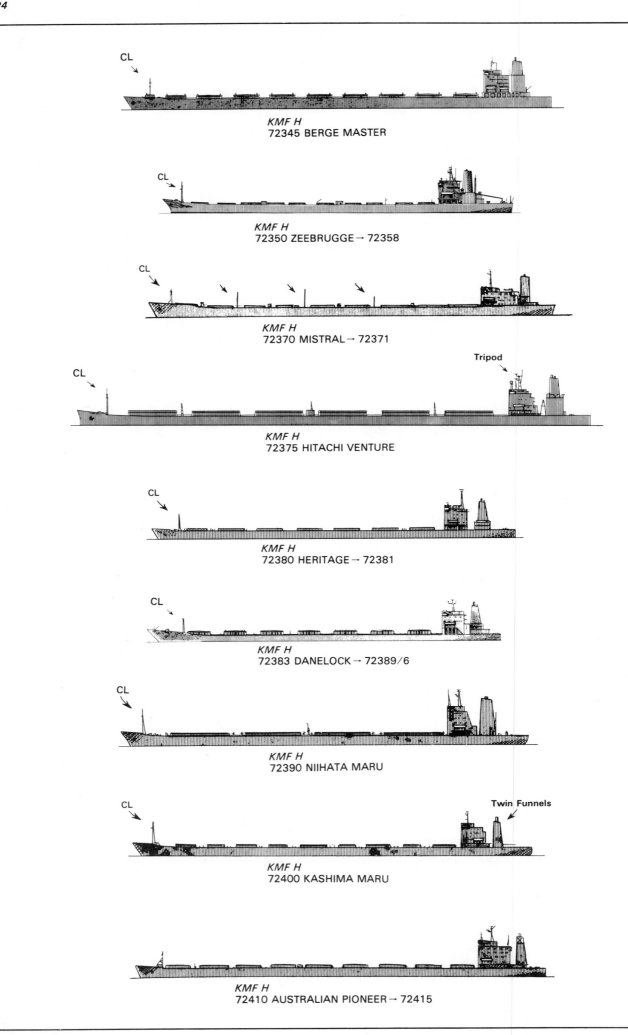

CL
KMF H
72345 BERGE MASTER

CL
KMF H
72350 ZEEBRUGGE → 72358

CL
KMF H
72370 MISTRAL → 72371

CL
Tripod
KMF H
72375 HITACHI VENTURE

CL
KMF H
72380 HERITAGE → 72381

CL
KMF H
72383 DANELOCK → 72389/6

CL
KMF H
72390 NIIHATA MARU

CL
Twin Funnels
KMF H
72400 KASHIMA MARU

KMF H
72410 AUSTRALIAN PIONEER → 72415

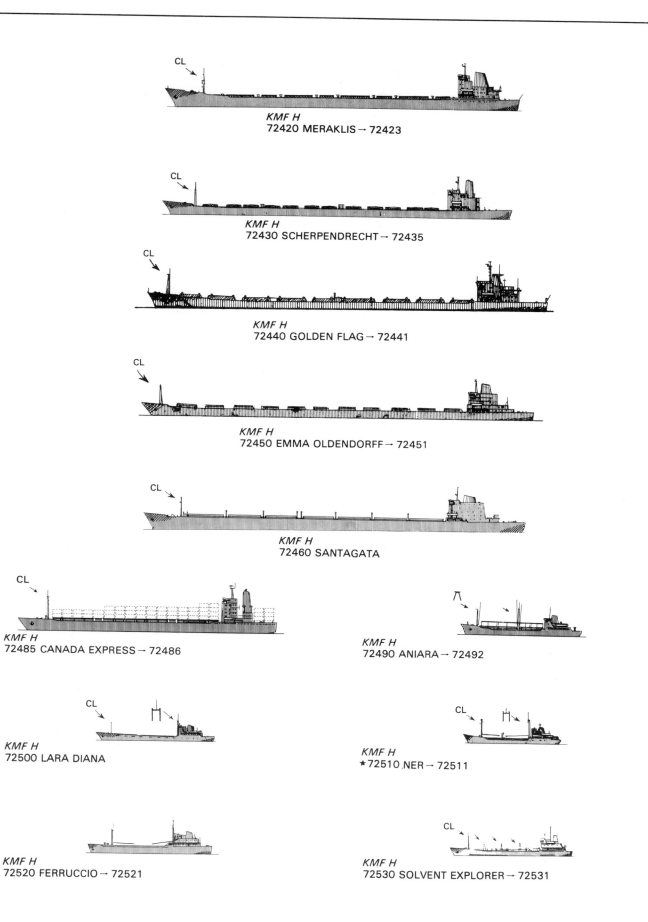

KMF H
72420 MERAKLIS → 72423

KMF H
72430 SCHERPENDRECHT → 72435

KMF H
72440 GOLDEN FLAG → 72441

KMF H
72450 EMMA OLDENDORFF → 72451

KMF H
72460 SANTAGATA

KMF H
72485 CANADA EXPRESS → 72486

KMF H
72490 ANIARA → 72492

KMF H
72500 LARA DIANA

KMF H
★72510 NER → 72511

KMF H
72520 FERRUCCIO → 72521

KMF H
72530 SOLVENT EXPLORER → 72531

KMF H
72535 RODENBEK → 72540

KMF H
72550 OT-MARINA → 72551

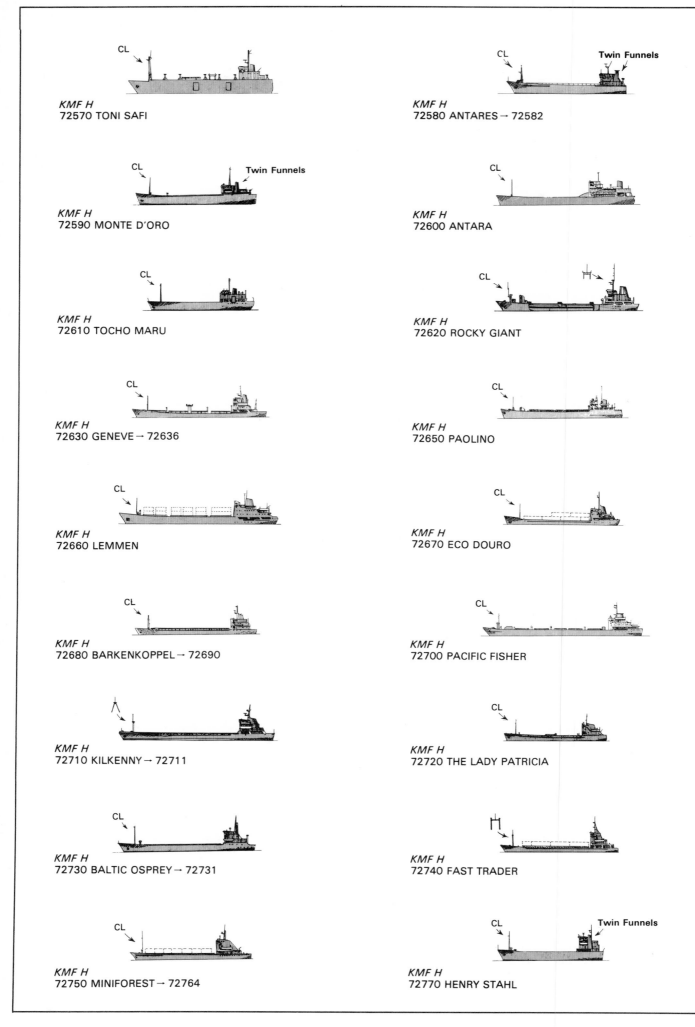

KMF H
72570 TONI SAFI

KMF H
72580 ANTARES → 72582

KMF H
72590 MONTE D'ORO

KMF H
72600 ANTARA

KMF H
72610 TOCHO MARU

KMF H
72620 ROCKY GIANT

KMF H
72630 GENEVE → 72636

KMF H
72650 PAOLINO

KMF H
72660 LEMMEN

KMF H
72670 ECO DOURO

KMF H
72680 BARKENKOPPEL → 72690

KMF H
72700 PACIFIC FISHER

KMF H
72710 KILKENNY → 72711

KMF H
72720 THE LADY PATRICIA

KMF H
72730 BALTIC OSPREY → 72731

KMF H
72740 FAST TRADER

KMF H
72750 MINIFOREST → 72764

KMF H
72770 HENRY STAHL

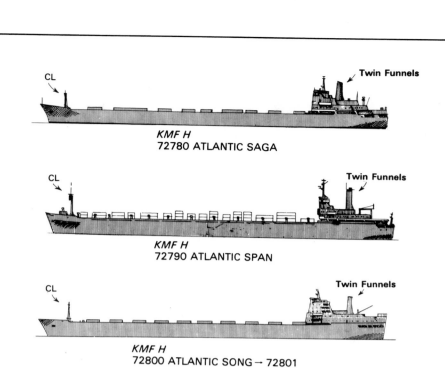

KMF H
72780 ATLANTIC SAGA

KMF H
72790 ATLANTIC SPAN

KMF H
72800 ATLANTIC SONG → 72801

KMF H
72810 LYSAGHT ENTERPRISE → 72811

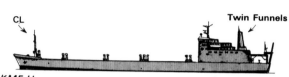

KMF H
72820 KAPRIFOL → 72822

KMF H
72830 CORA → 72832

KMF H
72840 TUULIA → 72843

KMF H
72850 TRANSCONTAINER 1

KMF H
72860 FREDENHAGEN

KMF H
72870 MARY HOLYMAN

KMF H
72880 RAAD

KMF H
72890 FRIGO MURAT → 72891

KMF H
★72900 GAN QUAN → 72901

KMF H
72910 ATLANTIC

KMF H
72930 REEFER CHAMP

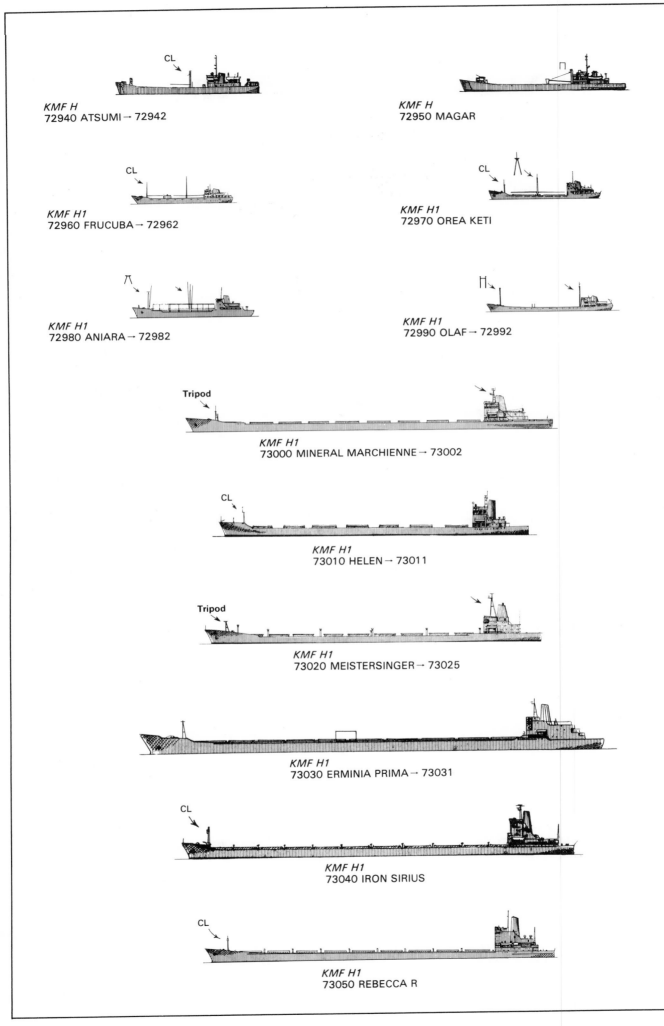

KMF H
72940 ATSUMI → 72942

KMF H
72950 MAGAR

KMF H1
72960 FRUCUBA → 72962

KMF H1
72970 OREA KETI

KMF H1
72980 ANIARA → 72982

KMF H1
72990 OLAF → 72992

Tripod

KMF H1
73000 MINERAL MARCHIENNE → 73002

KMF H1
73010 HELEN → 73011

Tripod

KMF H1
73020 MEISTERSINGER → 73025

KMF H1
73030 ERMINIA PRIMA → 73031

KMF H1
73040 IRON SIRIUS

KMF H1
73050 REBECCA R

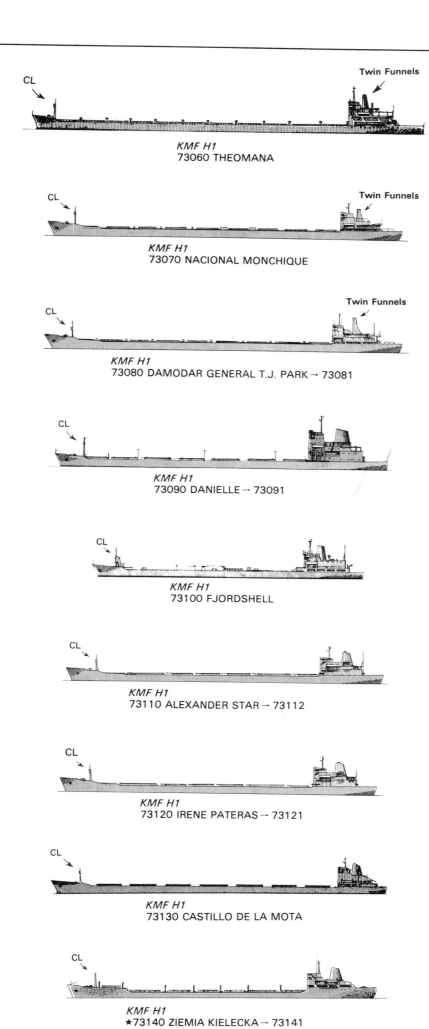

KMF H1
73060 THEOMANA

KMF H1
73070 NACIONAL MONCHIQUE

KMF H1
73080 DAMODAR GENERAL T.J. PARK → 73081

KMF H1
73090 DANIELLE → 73091

KMF H1
73100 FJORDSHELL

KMF H1
73110 ALEXANDER STAR → 73112

KMF H1
73120 IRENE PATERAS → 73121

KMF H1
73130 CASTILLO DE LA MOTA

KMF H1
★73140 ZIEMIA KIELECKA → 73141

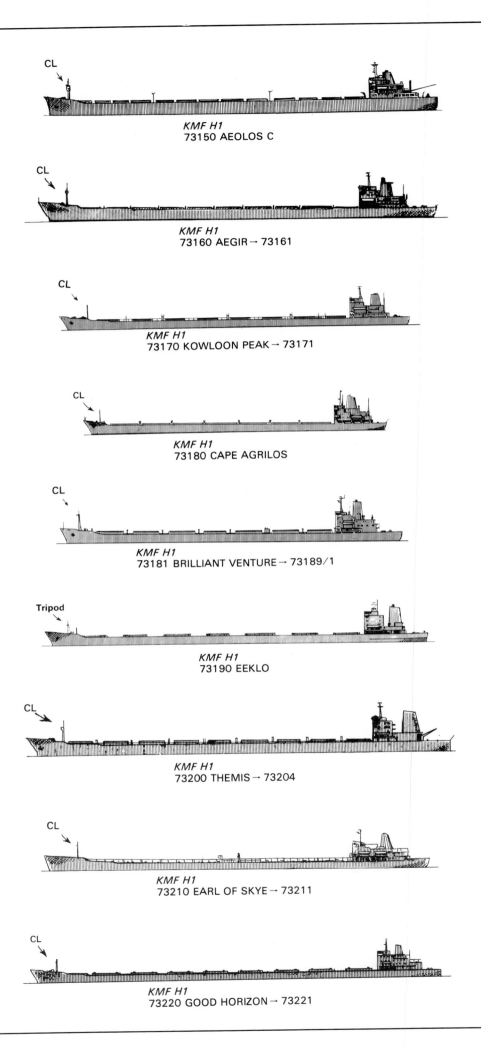

KMF H1
73150 AEOLOS C

KMF H1
73160 AEGIR → 73161

KMF H1
73170 KOWLOON PEAK → 73171

KMF H1
73180 CAPE AGRILOS

KMF H1
73181 BRILLIANT VENTURE → 73189/1

KMF H1
73190 EEKLO

KMF H1
73200 THEMIS → 73204

KMF H1
73210 EARL OF SKYE → 73211

KMF H1
73220 GOOD HORIZON → 73221

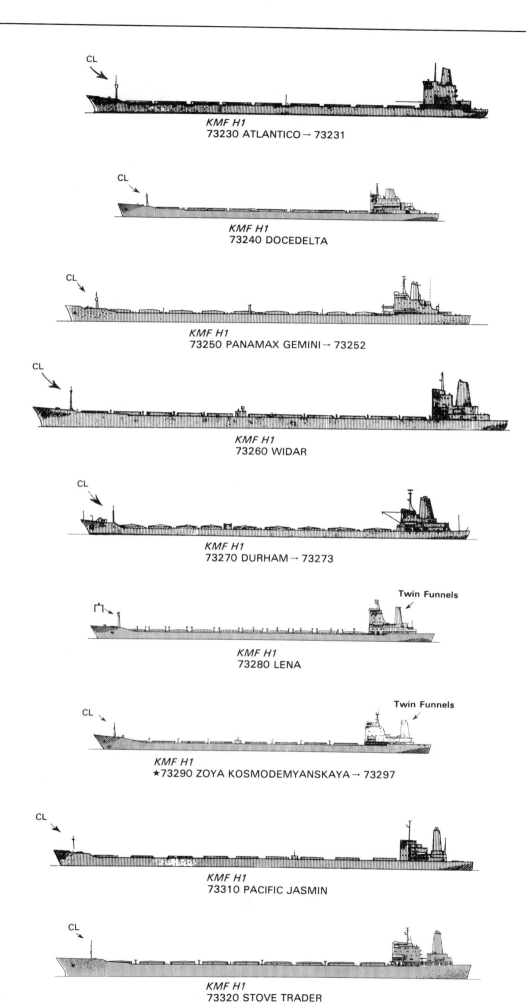

CL

KMF H1
73230 ATLANTICO → 73231

CL

KMF H1
73240 DOCEDELTA

CL

KMF H1
73250 PANAMAX GEMINI → 73252

CL

KMF H1
73260 WIDAR

CL

KMF H1
73270 DURHAM → 73273

Twin Funnels

KMF H1
73280 LENA

Twin Funnels

CL

KMF H1
★73290 ZOYA KOSMODEMYANSKAYA → 73297

CL

KMF H1
73310 PACIFIC JASMIN

CL

KMF H1
73320 STOVE TRADER

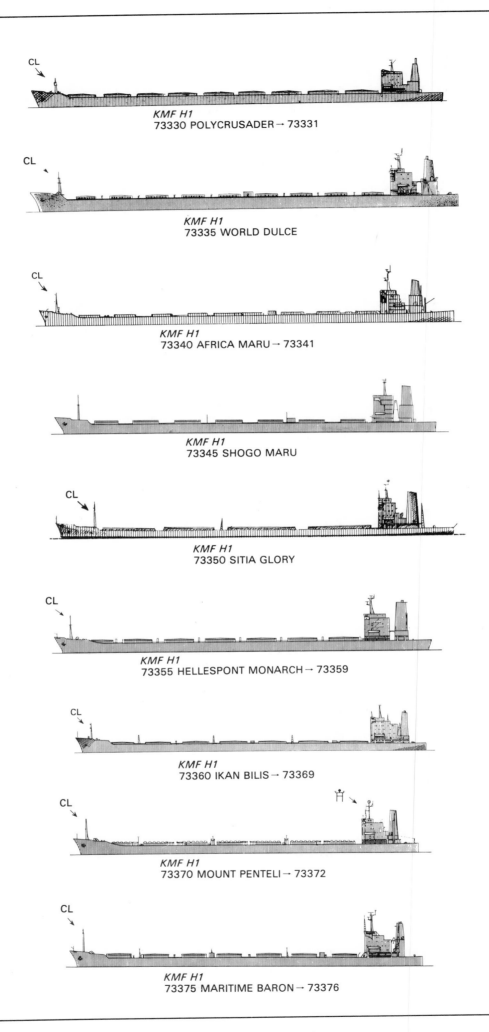

KMF H1
73330 POLYCRUSADER → 73331

KMF H1
73335 WORLD DULCE

KMF H1
73340 AFRICA MARU → 73341

KMF H1
73345 SHOGO MARU

KMF H1
73350 SITIA GLORY

KMF H1
73355 HELLESPONT MONARCH → 73359

KMF H1
73360 IKAN BILIS → 73369

KMF H1
73370 MOUNT PENTELI → 73372

KMF H1
73375 MARITIME BARON → 73376

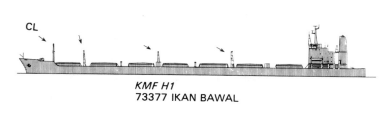

KMF H1
73377 IKAN BAWAL

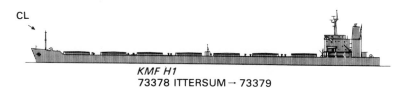

KMF H1
73378 ITTERSUM → 73379

KMF H1
73380 ITALMARE → 73389

KMF H1
73400 CARIBIA EXPRESS → 73409

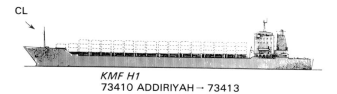

KMF H1
73410 ADDIRIYAH → 73413

KMF H1
73420 BALTIMORE

KMF H1
73430 ACADIA → 73431

KMF H1
73433 HANJIN BUSAN → 73436

KMF H1
73437 KOREAN JACEWON → 73439

KMF H1
73440 KOREAN WONIS SUN → 73450

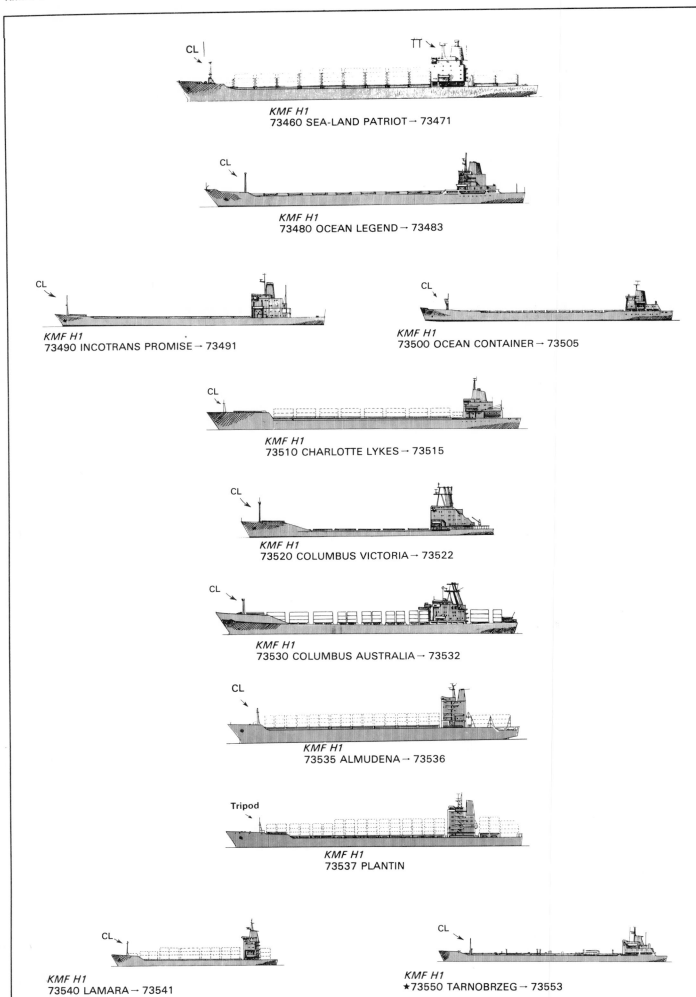

KMF H1
73460 SEA-LAND PATRIOT → 73471

KMF H1
73480 OCEAN LEGEND → 73483

KMF H1
73490 INCOTRANS PROMISE → 73491

KMF H1
73500 OCEAN CONTAINER → 73505

KMF H1
73510 CHARLOTTE LYKES → 73515

KMF H1
73520 COLUMBUS VICTORIA → 73522

KMF H1
73530 COLUMBUS AUSTRALIA → 73532

KMF H1
73535 ALMUDENA → 73536

KMF H1
73537 PLANTIN

KMF H1
73540 LAMARA → 73541

KMF H1
★73550 TARNOBRZEG → 73553

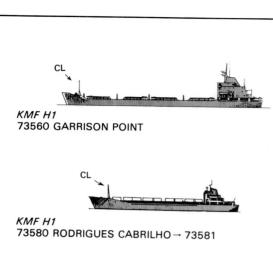

KMF H1
73560 GARRISON POINT

KMF H1
73570 ZIM MANILA II → 73571

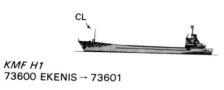

KMF H1
73580 RODRIGUES CABRILHO → 73581

KMF H1
73590 MARGARITA II

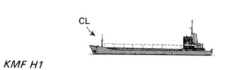

KMF H1
73600 EKENIS → 73601

KMF H1
73610 COMMODORE ENTERPRISE

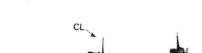

KMF H1
73620 EL GUAIQUERI

KMF H1
73630 DOLPHIN POINT

KMF H1
73640 ISABEL → 73642

KMF H1
★73650 SKRZAT → 73653

KMF H1
73660 FRAT 1 → 73361

KMF H1
73670 LADY ULRIKA → 73653

KMF H1
73680 SPECIALITY → 73682

KMF H1
73690 PIONEER CONTAINER

KMF H1
73700 FAST TRADER

Twin Funnels

KMF H1
73710 HENRY STAHL

Twin Funnels

KMF H1
73720 REGINE → 73726

KMF H1
73730 BONAVENTURE II → 73735

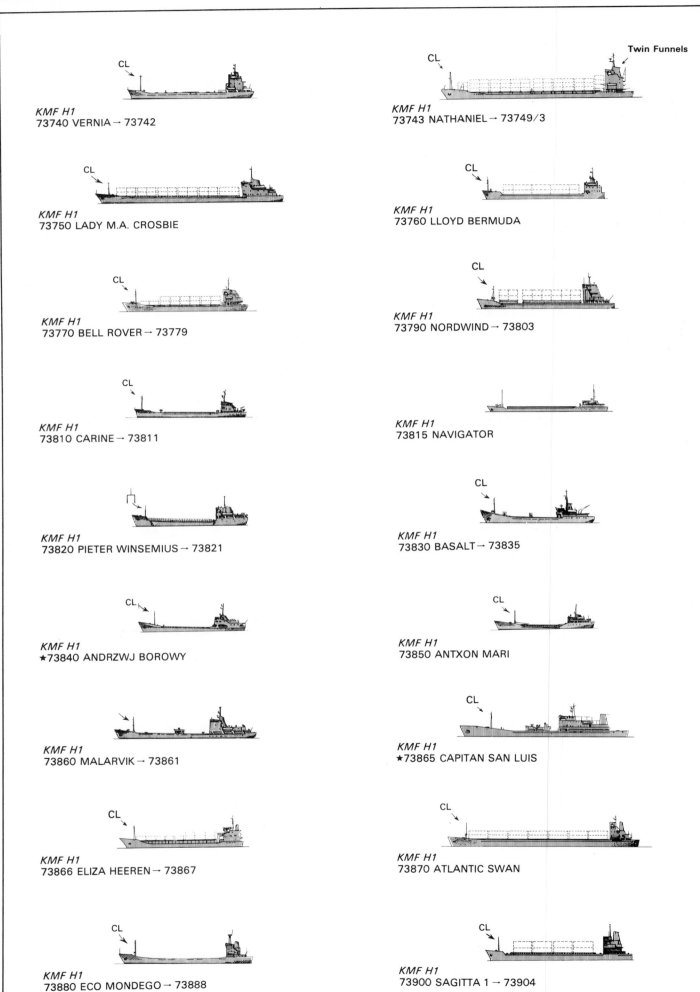

KMF H1
73740 VERNIA → 73742

Twin Funnels

KMF H1
73743 NATHANIEL → 73749/3

KMF H1
73750 LADY M.A. CROSBIE

KMF H1
73760 LLOYD BERMUDA

KMF H1
73770 BELL ROVER → 73779

KMF H1
73790 NORDWIND → 73803

KMF H1
73810 CARINE → 73811

KMF H1
73815 NAVIGATOR

KMF H1
73820 PIETER WINSEMIUS → 73821

KMF H1
73830 BASALT → 73835

KMF H1
★73840 ANDRZWJ BOROWY

KMF H1
73850 ANTXON MARI

KMF H1
73860 MALARVIK → 73861

KMF H1
★73865 CAPITAN SAN LUIS

KMF H1
73866 ELIZA HEEREN → 73867

KMF H1
73870 ATLANTIC SWAN

KMF H1
73880 ECO MONDEGO → 73888

KMF H1
73900 SAGITTA 1 → 73904

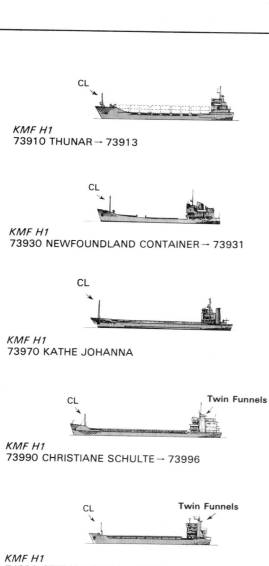

KMF H1
73910 THUNAR → 73913

KMF H1
73920 OUEZZANE → 73924

KMF H1
73930 NEWFOUNDLAND CONTAINER → 73931

KMF H1
73940 VANTAGE → 73965

KMF H1
73970 KATHE JOHANNA

KMF H1
73980 SERTAN → 73981

KMF H1
73990 CHRISTIANE SCHULTE → 73996

KMF H1
★73997 SIBIRSKIY 2101 → 73999/7

KMF H1
74000 GERMA KARMA → 74002

KMF H1
74005 VELA

KMF H1
74010 DELTA

KMF H1
74015 YMIR → 74017

KMF H1
74020 DONAR → 74024

KMF H1
74030 ANNIKA

KMF H1
74040 ALFA

KMF H1
74050 ARISTEOS → 74051

KMF H1
74060 ATLANTIC PREMIER → 74061

KMF H1
74070 MONT LOUIS

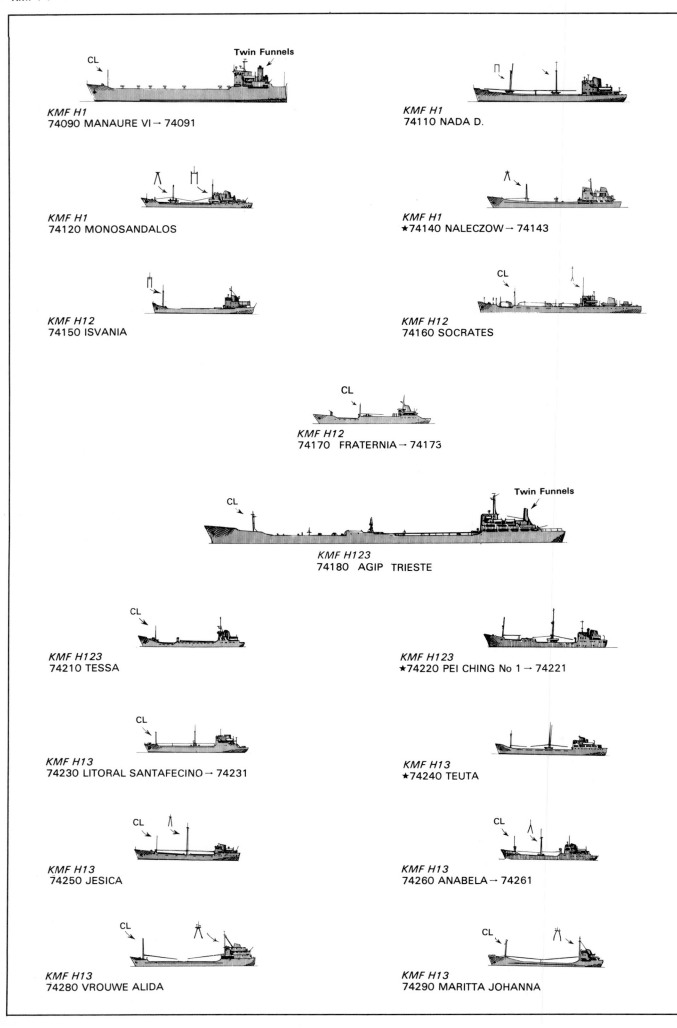

KMF H1
74090 MANAURE VI → 74091

KMF H1
74110 NADA D.

KMF H1
74120 MONOSANDALOS

KMF H1
★74140 NALECZOW → 74143

KMF H12
74150 ISVANIA

KMF H12
74160 SOCRATES

KMF H12
74170 FRATERNIA → 74173

KMF H123
74180 AGIP TRIESTE

KMF H123
74210 TESSA

KMF H123
★74220 PEI CHING No 1 → 74221

KMF H13
74230 LITORAL SANTAFECINO → 74231

KMF H13
★74240 TEUTA

KMF H13
74250 JESICA

KMF H13
74260 ANABELA → 74261

KMF H13
74280 VROUWE ALIDA

KMF H13
74290 MARITTA JOHANNA

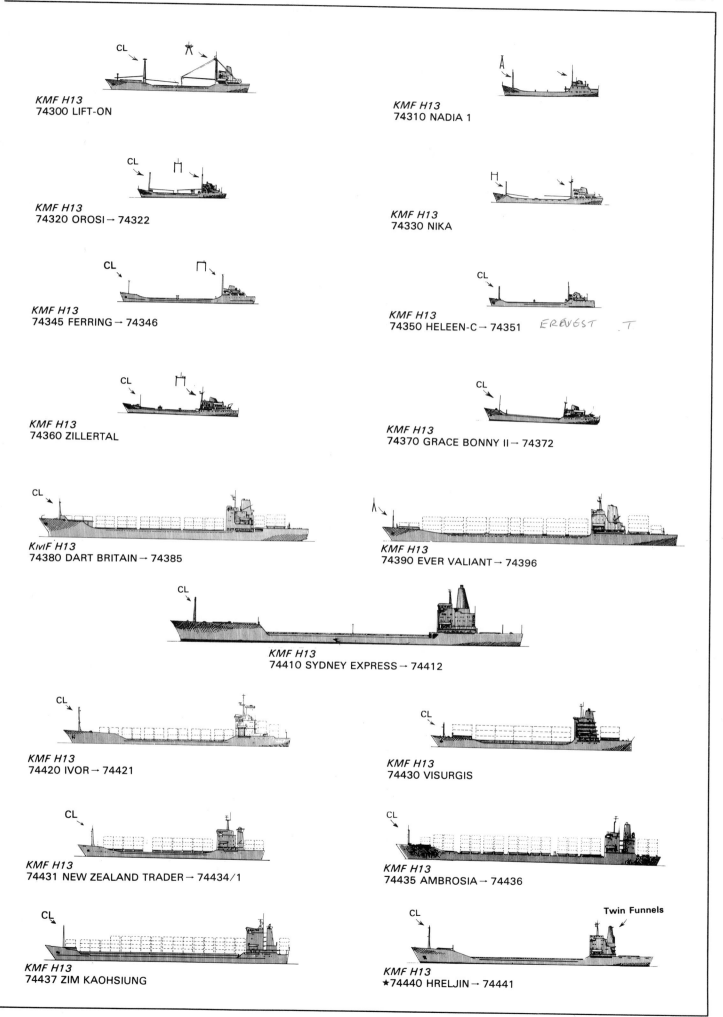

KMF H13
74300 LIFT-ON

KMF H13
74310 NADIA 1

KMF H13
74320 OROSI → 74322

KMF H13
74330 NIKA

KMF H13
74345 FERRING → 74346

KMF H13
74350 HELEEN-C → 74351   *EREVEST   T*

KMF H13
74360 ZILLERTAL

KMF H13
74370 GRACE BONNY II → 74372

KMF H13
74380 DART BRITAIN → 74385

KMF H13
74390 EVER VALIANT → 74396

KMF H13
74410 SYDNEY EXPRESS → 74412

KMF H13
74420 IVOR → 74421

KMF H13
74430 VISURGIS

KMF H13
74431 NEW ZEALAND TRADER → 74434/1

KMF H13
74435 AMBROSIA → 74436

KMF H13
74437 ZIM KAOHSIUNG

KMF H13
★74440 HRELJIN → 74441

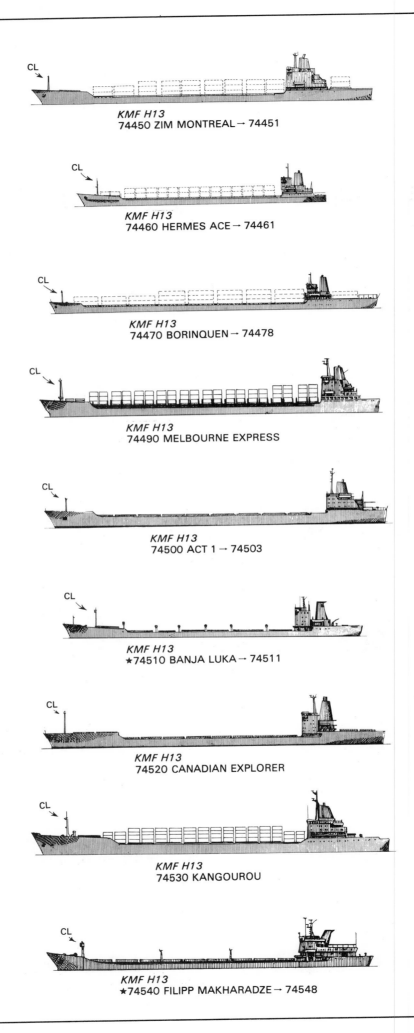

KMF H13
74450 ZIM MONTREAL → 74451

KMF H13
74460 HERMES ACE → 74461

KMF H13
74470 BORINQUEN → 74478

KMF H13
74490 MELBOURNE EXPRESS

KMF H13
74500 ACT 1 → 74503

KMF H13
★74510 BANJA LUKA → 74511

KMF H13
74520 CANADIAN EXPLORER

KMF H13
74530 KANGOUROU

KMF H13
★74540 FILIPP MAKHARADZE → 74548

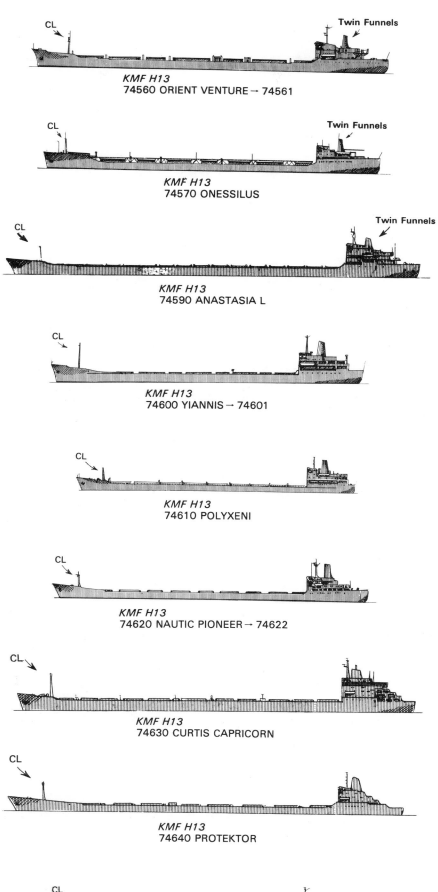

CL — Twin Funnels

KMF H13
74560 ORIENT VENTURE → 74561

CL — Twin Funnels

KMF H13
74570 ONESSILUS

CL — Twin Funnels

KMF H13
74590 ANASTASIA L

CL

KMF H13
74600 YIANNIS → 74601

CL

KMF H13
74610 POLYXENI

CL

KMF H13
74620 NAUTIC PIONEER → 74622

CL

KMF H13
74630 CURTIS CAPRICORN

CL

KMF H13
74640 PROTEKTOR

CL

KMF H13
74650 TRUE ENDEAVOUR → 74651

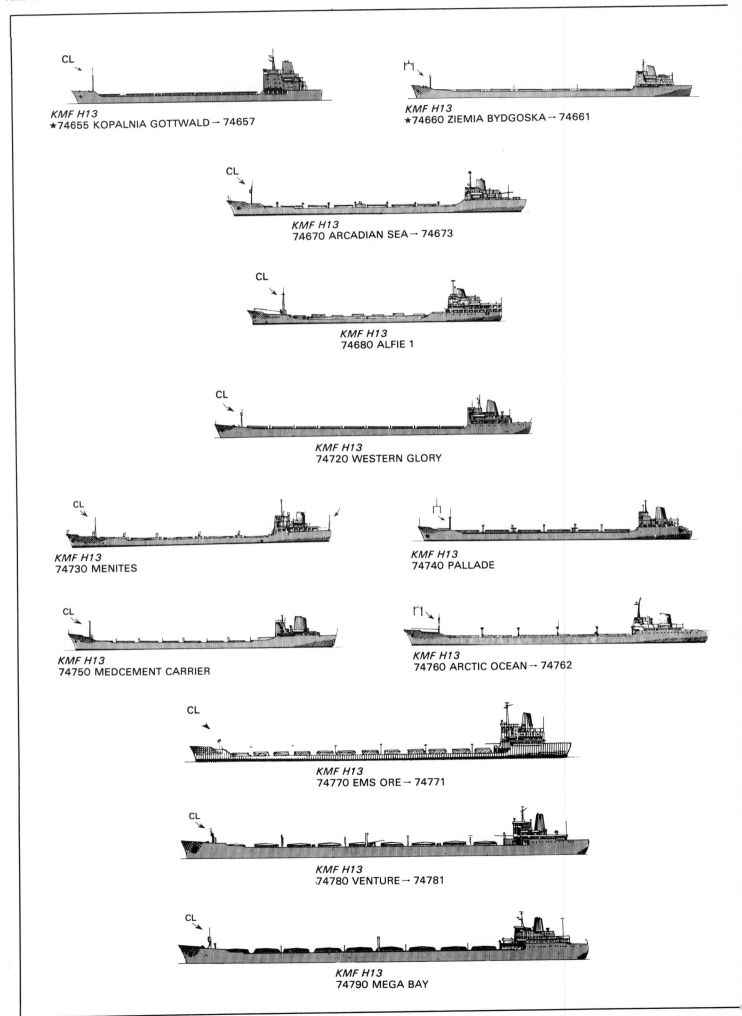

KMF H13
★74655 KOPALNIA GOTTWALD→74657

KMF H13
★74660 ZIEMIA BYDGOSKA→74661

KMF H13
74670 ARCADIAN SEA→74673

KMF H13
74680 ALFIE 1

KMF H13
74720 WESTERN GLORY

KMF H13
74730 MENITES

KMF H13
74740 PALLADE

KMF H13
74750 MEDCEMENT CARRIER

KMF H13
74760 ARCTIC OCEAN→74762

KMF H13
74770 EMS ORE→74771

KMF H13
74780 VENTURE→74781

KMF H13
74790 MEGA BAY

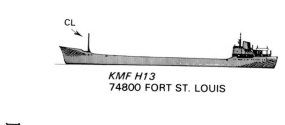

KMF H13
74800 FORT ST. LOUIS

KMF H13
74810 OCEAN LADY

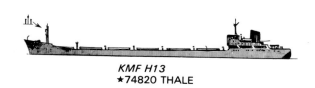

KMF H13
★74820 THALE

KMF H13
74830 CASTLE POINT

KMF H13
74840 ISLAND CONTAINER

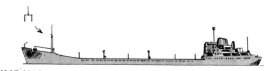

KMF H13
74850 DELTA FLAG

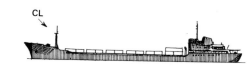

KMF H13
74860 FRANKFURT EXPRESS

KMF H13
★74870 HUAI HAI → 74871

KMF H13
74880 ALIKI

KMF H13
74890 ROSYTH

KMF H13
74900 RAUTARUUKKI → 74902

KMF H13
74910 BERGON

KMF H13
74920 ALBRIGHT PIONEER → 74921

KMF H13
74930 CAPE RACE → 74931

KMF H13
74940 PAXO → 74946

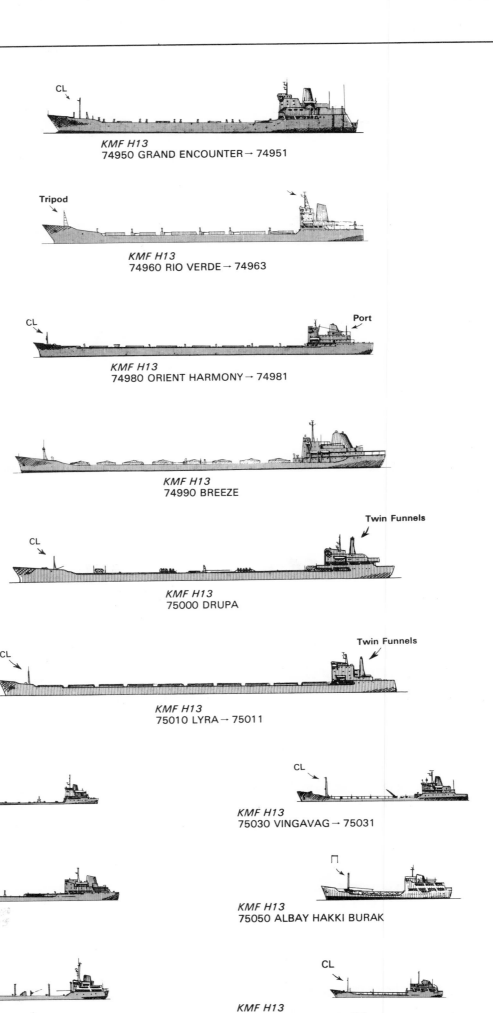

KMF H13
74950 GRAND ENCOUNTER → 74951

KMF H13
74960 RIO VERDE → 74963

KMF H13
74980 ORIENT HARMONY → 74981

KMF H13
74990 BREEZE

KMF H13
75000 DRUPA

KMF H13
75010 LYRA → 75011

KMF H13
75020 RUDDERMAN

KMF H13
75030 VINGAVAG → 75031

KMF H13
75040 SAVE

KMF H13
75050 ALBAY HAKKI BURAK

KMF H13
75060 BILLESBORG → 75061

KMF H13
75070 ASPERITY → 75071

KMF H13
75080 ROCHE'S POINT

KMF H13
75085 ESSO PLYMOUTH — *Guidsman*

KMF H13
75090 ESSO INVERNESS → 75091

KMF H13
75100 SAND SAPPHIRE

KMF H13
75110 DEVON CURLEW → 75112

KMF H13
75130 BENVENUE → 75132

KMF H13
75140 UNICORN DANIEL → 75141

KMF H13
75150 DUTCH GLORY → 75152

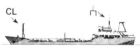

KMF H13
75160 ANNA BROERE

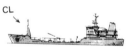

KMF H13
★75170 BUNA → 75171

KMF H13
75172 MULTITANK ADRIA → 75175

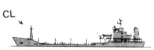

KMF H13
75177 HANNE LUPE

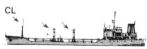

KMF H13
75180 CENTAURMAN → 75181

KMF H13
75190 STELLAMAN → 75191

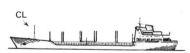

KMF H13
75200 OMANIAH

KMF H13
75210 LA COLINA → 75212

KMF H13
75220 KIISLA

KMF H13
75221 SHELL MARKETER → 75223

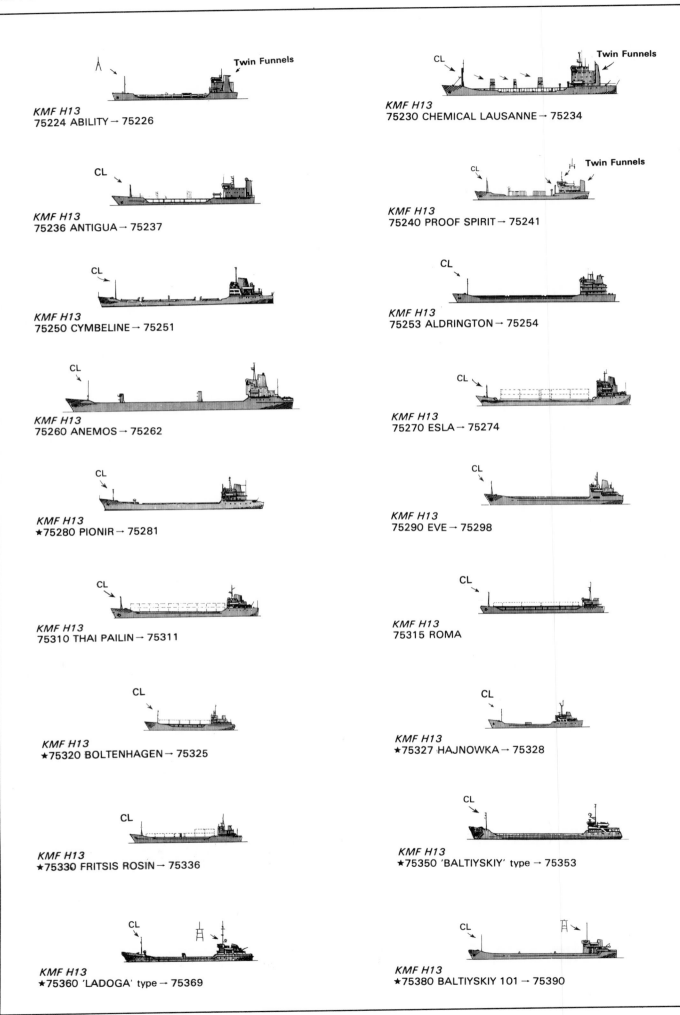

KMF H13
75224 ABILITY → 75226

KMF H13
75230 CHEMICAL LAUSANNE → 75234

KMF H13
75236 ANTIGUA → 75237

KMF H13
75240 PROOF SPIRIT → 75241

KMF H13
75250 CYMBELINE → 75251

KMF H13
75253 ALDRINGTON → 75254

KMF H13
75260 ANEMOS → 75262

KMF H13
75270 ESLA → 75274

KMF H13
★75280 PIONIR → 75281

KMF H13
75290 EVE → 75298

KMF H13
75310 THAI PAILIN → 75311

KMF H13
75315 ROMA

KMF H13
★75320 BOLTENHAGEN → 75325

KMF H13
★75327 HAJNOWKA → 75328

KMF H13
★75330 FRITSIS ROSIN → 75336

KMF H13
★75350 'BALTIYSKIY' type → 75353

KMF H13
★75360 'LADOGA' type → 75369

KMF H13
★75380 BALTIYSKIY 101 → 75390

KMF H13
★75400 SAYMENSKIY KANAL → 75410

KMF H13
★75412 MIELEC → 75415

KMF H13
75420 STERN

KMF H13
75430 ORAN

KMF H13
75440 EMINENCE → 75441

KMF H13
75450 FRED EVERARD → 75459

KMF H13
75470 SECURITY → 75471

KMF H13
75480 FAIRMEAD → 75484

KMF H13
75490 STEVEN K

KMF H13
75500 PAULINA BRINKMAN → 75510

KMF H13
75520 GEZIENA

KMF H13
75530 IJSSELMEER → 75532

KMF H13
75533 ARKLOW CASTLE → 75539

KMF H13
75540 SYLVIA ALPHA → 75545

KMF H13
75550 MATHILDE → 75552

KMF H13
75560 ALTAPPEN → 75562

KMF H13
75565 PEACOCK VENTURE

KMF H13
75570 LESLIE GAULT → 75573

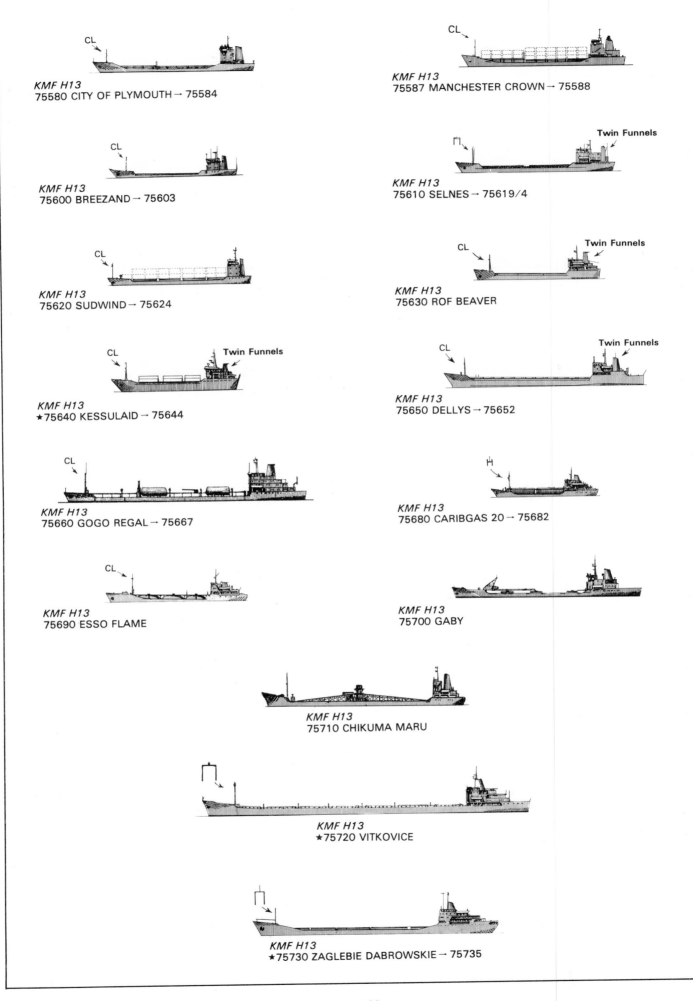

KMF H13
75580 CITY OF PLYMOUTH → 75584

KMF H13
75587 MANCHESTER CROWN → 75588

KMF H13
75600 BREEZAND → 75603

KMF H13
75610 SELNES → 75619/4

KMF H13
75620 SUDWIND → 75624

KMF H13
75630 ROF BEAVER

KMF H13
★75640 KESSULAID → 75644

KMF H13
75650 DELLYS → 75652

KMF H13
75660 GOGO REGAL → 75667

KMF H13
75680 CARIBGAS 20 → 75682

KMF H13
75690 ESSO FLAME

KMF H13
75700 GABY

KMF H13
75710 CHIKUMA MARU

KMF H13
★75720 VITKOVICE

KMF H13
★75730 ZAGLEBIE DABROWSKIE → 75735

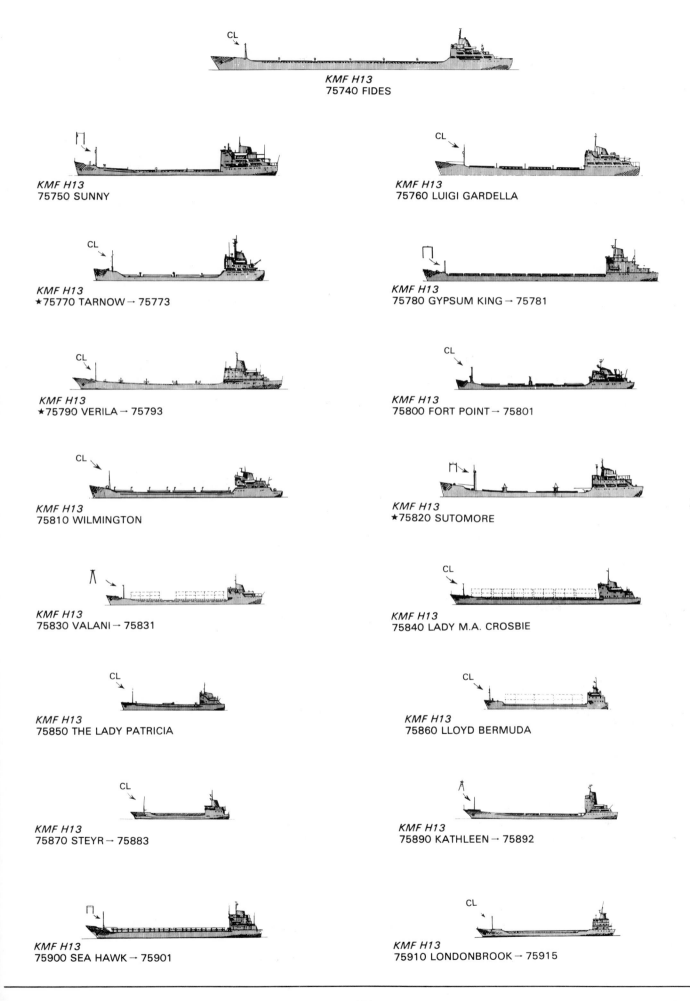

KMF H13
75740 FIDES

KMF H13
75750 SUNNY

KMF H13
75760 LUIGI GARDELLA

KMF H13
★75770 TARNOW → 75773

KMF H13
75780 GYPSUM KING → 75781

KMF H13
★75790 VERILA → 75793

KMF H13
75800 FORT POINT → 75801

KMF H13
75810 WILMINGTON

KMF H13
★75820 SUTOMORE

KMF H13
75830 VALANI → 75831

KMF H13
75840 LADY M.A. CROSBIE

KMF H13
75850 THE LADY PATRICIA

KMF H13
75860 LLOYD BERMUDA

KMF H13
75870 STEYR → 75883

KMF H13
75890 KATHLEEN → 75892

KMF H13
75900 SEA HAWK → 75901

KMF H13
75910 LONDONBROOK → 75915

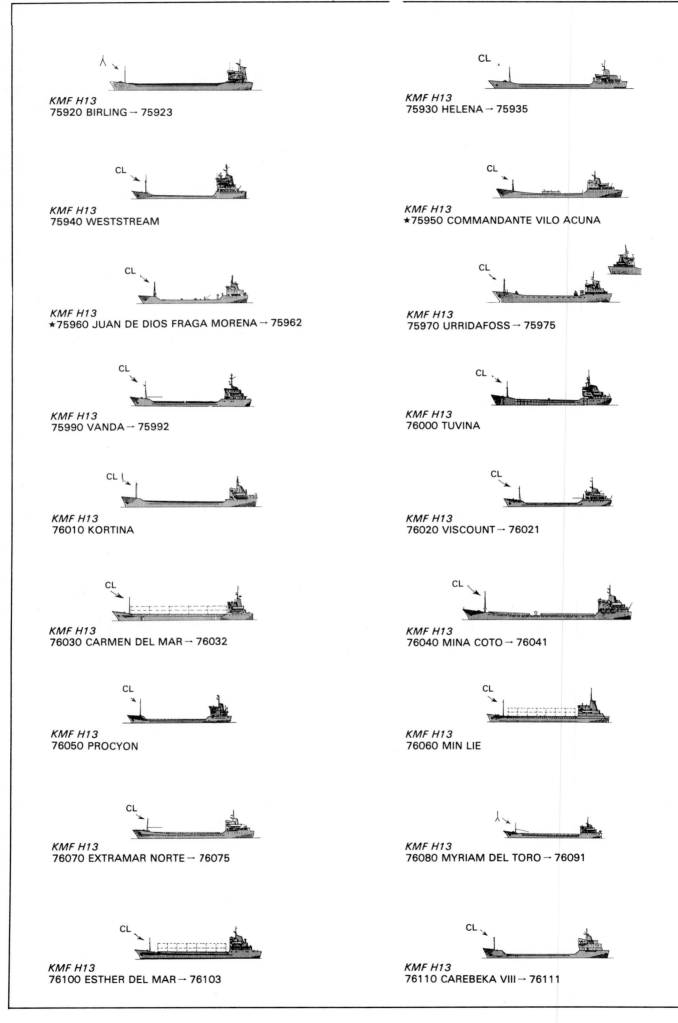

KMF H13
75920 BIRLING → 75923

KMF H13
75930 HELENA → 75935

KMF H13
75940 WESTSTREAM

KMF H13
★75950 COMMANDANTE VILO ACUNA

KMF H13
★75960 JUAN DE DIOS FRAGA MORENA → 75962

KMF H13
75970 URRIDAFOSS → 75975

KMF H13
75990 VANDA → 75992

KMF H13
76000 TUVINA

KMF H13
76010 KORTINA

KMF H13
76020 VISCOUNT → 76021

KMF H13
76030 CARMEN DEL MAR → 76032

KMF H13
76040 MINA COTO → 76041

KMF H13
76050 PROCYON

KMF H13
76060 MIN LIE

KMF H13
76070 EXTRAMAR NORTE → 76075

KMF H13
76080 MYRIAM DEL TORO → 76091

KMF H13
76100 ESTHER DEL MAR → 76103

KMF H13
76110 CAREBEKA VIII → 76111

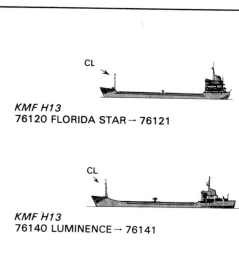

KMF H13
76120 FLORIDA STAR → 76121

KMF H13
76130 BEEDING

KMF H13
76140 LUMINENCE → 76141

KMF H13
76150 DAUNT ROCK → 76153

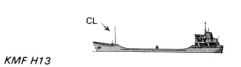

KMF H13
76160 HAJE NAIME

KMF H13
76170 FORMOSA CONTAINER → 76172

KMF H13
76180 NAUTILUS → 76182

KMF H13
76190 FENJA

KMF H13
76191 SELENA → 76193

KMF H13
76195 JOHANNA V → 76197

KMF H13
76200 ALICIA

KMF H13
76210 TAKARI I → 76217

Twin Funnels

KMF H13
★76220 STAROGARD GDANSKI → 76221

KMF H13
76230 ODET → 76231

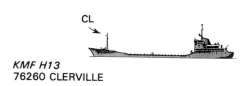

KMF H13
76240 ISMARA → 76242

KMF H13
★76250 DA QING No 216 → 76252

KMF H13
76260 CLERVILLE

KMF H13
76270 LEMAN

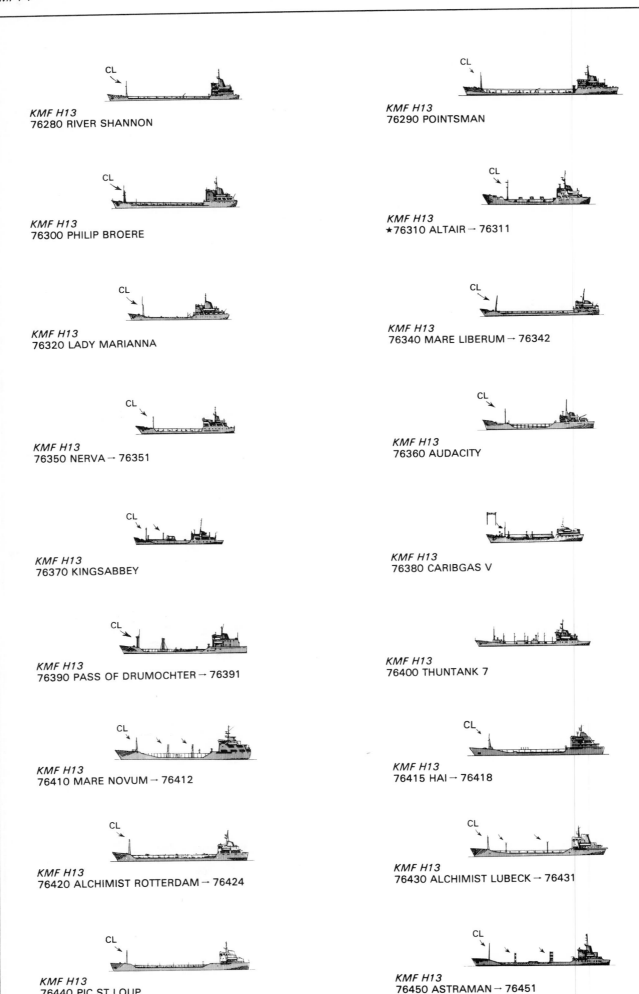

KMF H13
76280 RIVER SHANNON

KMF H13
76290 POINTSMAN

KMF H13
76300 PHILIP BROERE

KMF H13
★76310 ALTAIR → 76311

KMF H13
76320 LADY MARIANNA

KMF H13
76340 MARE LIBERUM → 76342

KMF H13
76350 NERVA → 76351

KMF H13
76360 AUDACITY

KMF H13
76370 KINGSABBEY

KMF H13
76380 CARIBGAS V

KMF H13
76390 PASS OF DRUMOCHTER → 76391

KMF H13
76400 THUNTANK 7

KMF H13
76410 MARE NOVUM → 76412

KMF H13
76415 HAI → 76418

KMF H13
76420 ALCHIMIST ROTTERDAM → 76424

KMF H13
76430 ALCHIMIST LUBECK → 76431

KMF H13
76440 PIC ST LOUP

KMF H13
76450 ASTRAMAN → 76451

KMF H13
76460 ERIKA BOJEN →76461

KMF H13
76470 CONDOR → 76471

KMF H13
76472 DEIKE → 76479/6

KMF H13
76480 BIELEFELD → 76485

KMF H13
★76490 IVAN AIVAZOVSKIY → 76537

KMF H13
76560 GIANNIS DIMAKIS III

KMF H13
★76570 COMBATE DE PALMAMOCHA

KMF H13
★76580 ABRAM ARKHIPOV → 76591

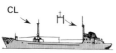

KMF H13
76600 GEVISA → 76605

KMF H13
76610 ISELTAL → 76612

KMF H13
★76630 CHEMIK → 76631

KMF H13
★76640 RUCIANE

KMF H13
76650 PIAVE

KMF H13
76660 NADIA 2

KMF H13
76680 DUTCH SAILOR → 76681

KMF H13
76700 PACIFIQUE

KMF H13
76710 SAINT MITRE

KMF H13
76720 UNYO MARU → 76722

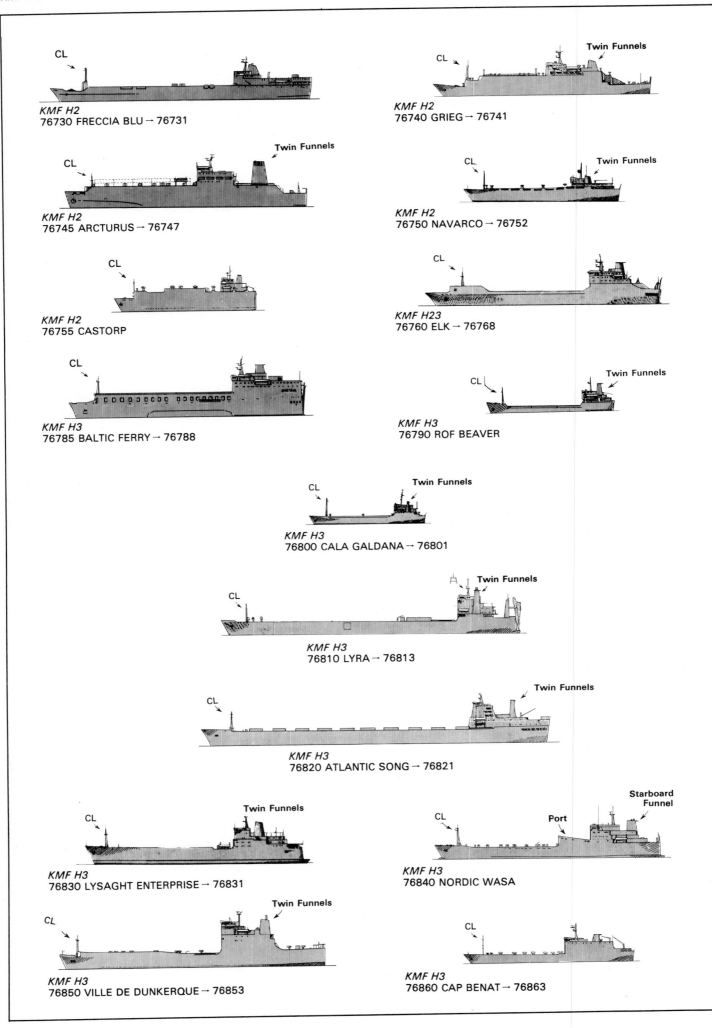

CL
KMF H2
76730 FRECCIA BLU → 76731

CL — Twin Funnels
KMF H2
76740 GRIEG → 76741

CL — Twin Funnels
KMF H2
76745 ARCTURUS → 76747

CL — Twin Funnels
KMF H2
76750 NAVARCO → 76752

CL
KMF H2
76755 CASTORP

CL
KMF H23
76760 ELK → 76768

CL
KMF H3
76785 BALTIC FERRY → 76788

CL — Twin Funnels
KMF H3
76790 ROF BEAVER

CL — Twin Funnels
KMF H3
76800 CALA GALDANA → 76801

CL — Twin Funnels
KMF H3
76810 LYRA → 76813

CL — Twin Funnels
KMF H3
76820 ATLANTIC SONG → 76821

CL — Twin Funnels
KMF H3
76830 LYSAGHT ENTERPRISE → 76831

CL — Port — Starboard Funnel
KMF H3
76840 NORDIC WASA

CL — Twin Funnels
KMF H3
76850 VILLE DE DUNKERQUE → 76853

CL
KMF H3
76860 CAP BENAT → 76863

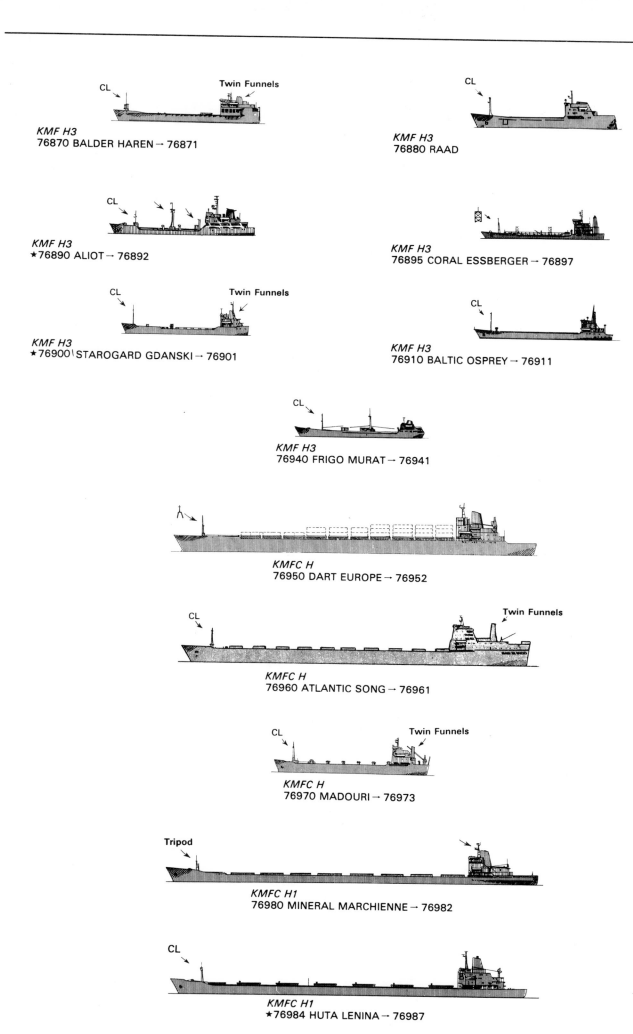

CL   Twin Funnels

KMF H3
76870 BALDER HAREN → 76871

CL

KMF H3
76880 RAAD

CL

KMF H3
★76890 ALIOT → 76892

KMF H3
76895 CORAL ESSBERGER → 76897

CL   Twin Funnels

KMF H3
★76900 STAROGARD GDANSKI → 76901

CL

KMF H3
76910 BALTIC OSPREY → 76911

CL

KMF H3
76940 FRIGO MURAT → 76941

KMFC H
76950 DART EUROPE → 76952

CL   Twin Funnels

KMFC H
76960 ATLANTIC SONG → 76961

CL   Twin Funnels

KMFC H
76970 MADOURI → 76973

Tripod

KMFC H1
76980 MINERAL MARCHIENNE → 76982

CL

KMFC H1
★76984 HUTA LENINA → 76987

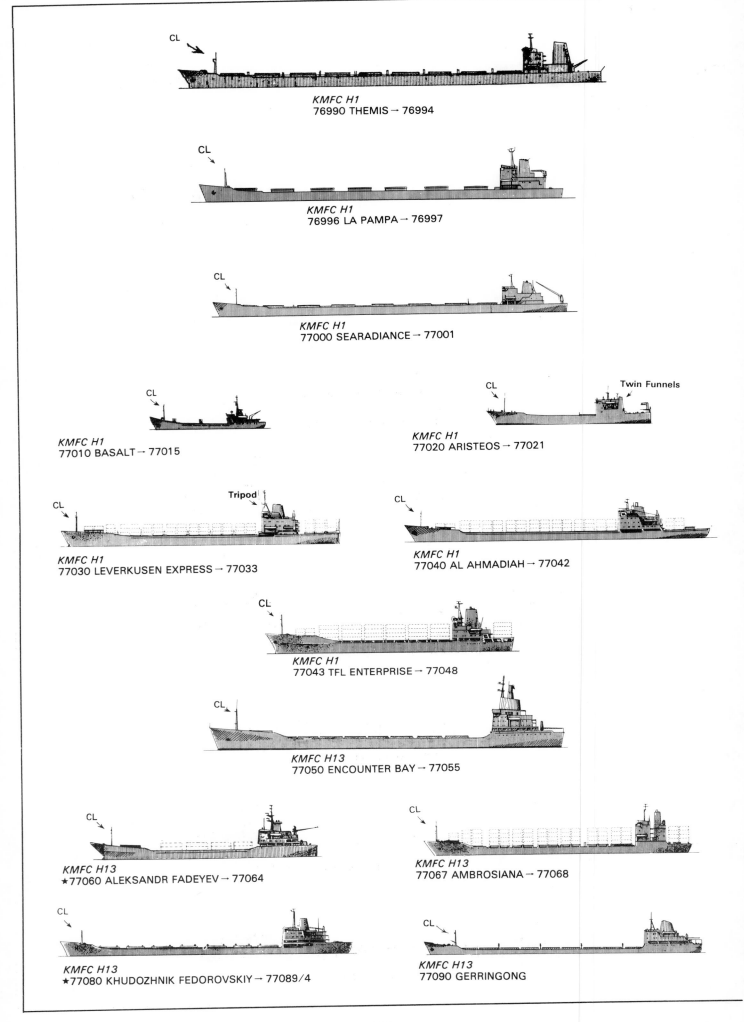

KMFC H1
76990 THEMIS → 76994

KMFC H1
76996 LA PAMPA → 76997

KMFC H1
77000 SEARADIANCE → 77001

KMFC H1
77010 BASALT → 77015

KMFC H1
77020 ARISTEOS → 77021

KMFC H1
77030 LEVERKUSEN EXPRESS → 77033

KMFC H1
77040 AL AHMADIAH → 77042

KMFC H1
77043 TFL ENTERPRISE → 77048

KMFC H13
77050 ENCOUNTER BAY → 77055

KMFC H13
★77060 ALEKSANDR FADEYEV → 77064

KMFC H13
77067 AMBROSIANA → 77068

KMFC H13
★77080 KHUDOZHNIK FEDOROVSKIY → 77089/4

KMFC H13
77090 GERRINGONG

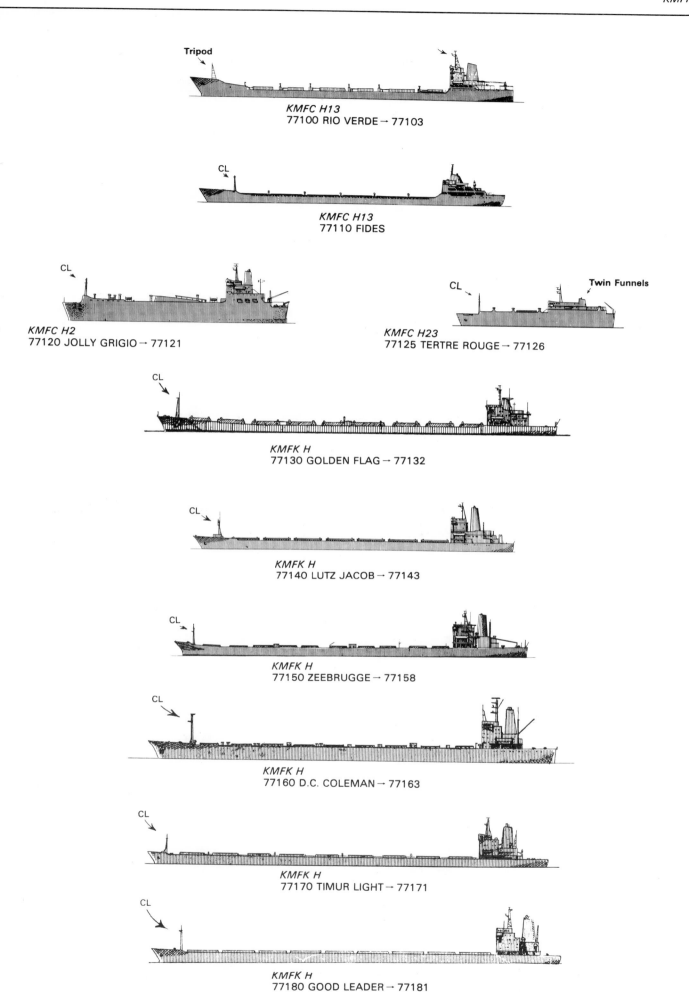

Tripod

KMFC H13
77100 RIO VERDE → 77103

CL

KMFC H13
77110 FIDES

CL

KMFC H2
77120 JOLLY GRIGIO → 77121

CL   **Twin Funnels**

KMFC H23
77125 TERTRE ROUGE → 77126

CL

KMFK H
77130 GOLDEN FLAG → 77132

CL

KMFK H
77140 LUTZ JACOB → 77143

CL

KMFK H
77150 ZEEBRUGGE → 77158

CL

KMFK H
77160 D.C. COLEMAN → 77163

CL

KMFK H
77170 TIMUR LIGHT → 77171

CL

KMFK H
77180 GOOD LEADER → 77181

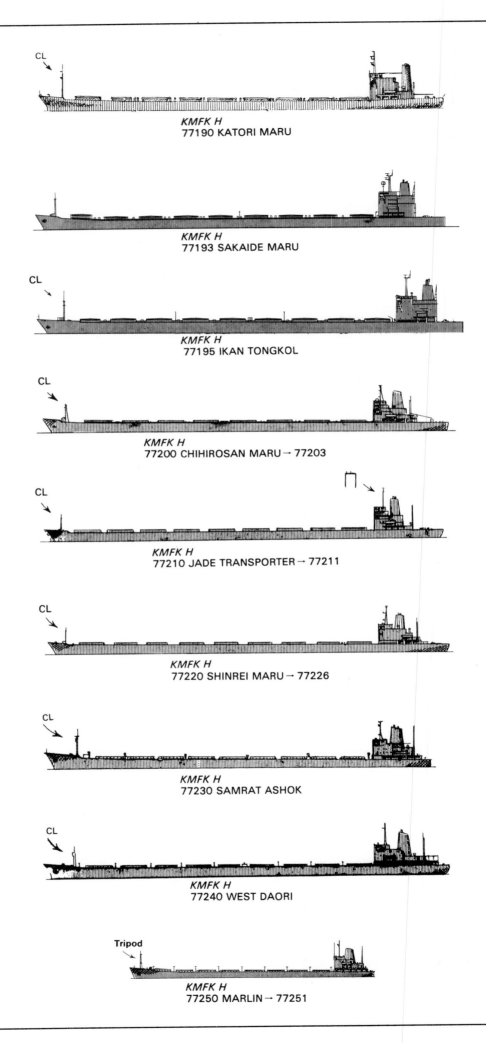

CL

KMFK H
77190 KATORI MARU

KMFK H
77193 SAKAIDE MARU

CL

KMFK H
77195 IKAN TONGKOL

CL

KMFK H
77200 CHIHIROSAN MARU → 77203

CL

KMFK H
77210 JADE TRANSPORTER → 77211

CL

KMFK H
77220 SHINREI MARU → 77226

CL

KMFK H
77230 SAMRAT ASHOK

CL

KMFK H
77240 WEST DAORI

Tripod

KMFK H
77250 MARLIN → 77251

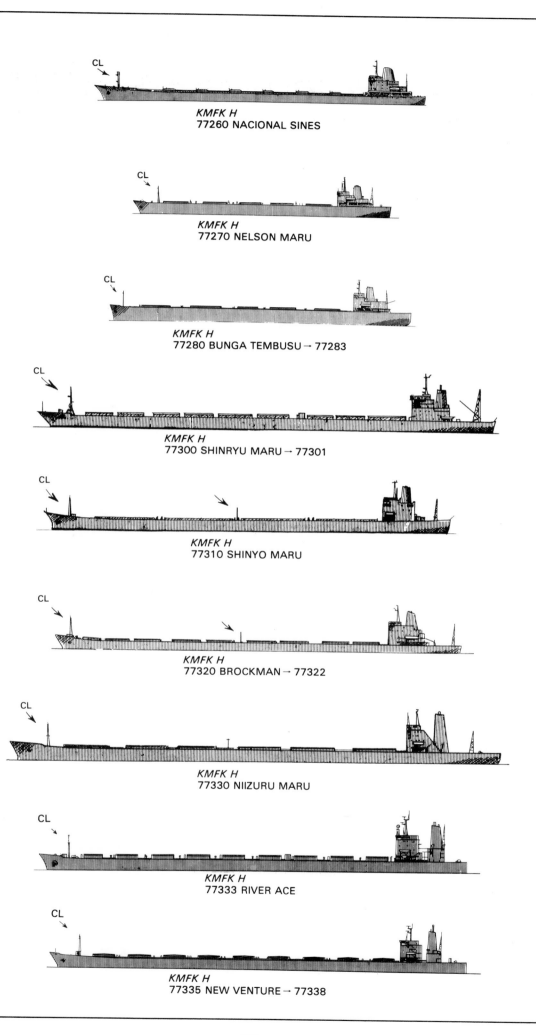

CL
KMFK H
77260 NACIONAL SINES

CL
KMFK H
77270 NELSON MARU

CL
KMFK H
77280 BUNGA TEMBUSU → 77283

CL
KMFK H
77300 SHINRYU MARU → 77301

CL
KMFK H
77310 SHINYO MARU

CL
KMFK H
77320 BROCKMAN → 77322

CL
KMFK H
77330 NIIZURU MARU

CL
KMFK H
77333 RIVER ACE

CL
KMFK H
77335 NEW VENTURE → 77338

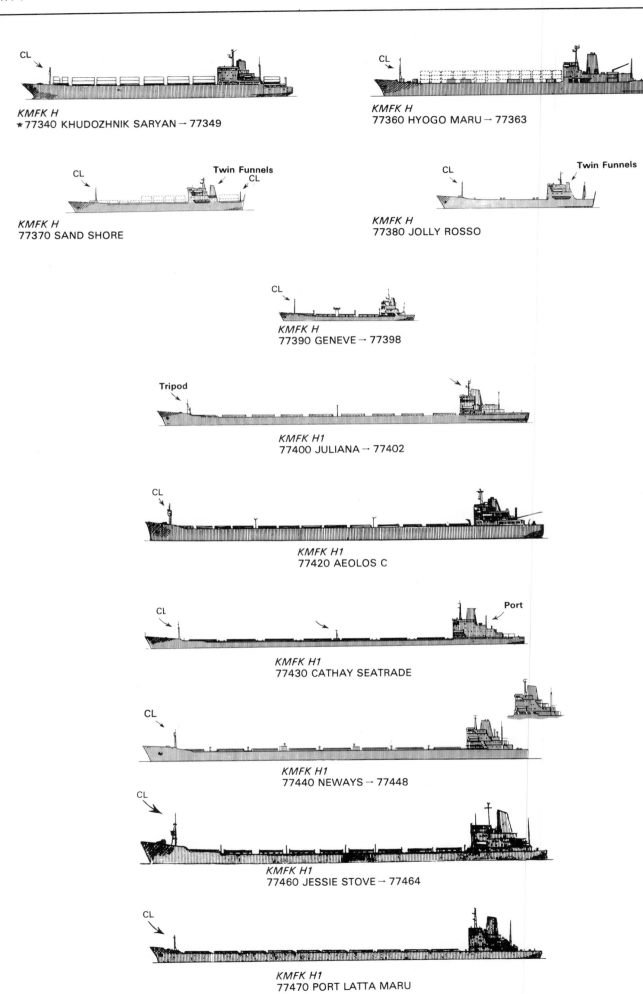

KMFK H
★77340 KHUDOZHNIK SARYAN → 77349

KMFK H
77360 HYOGO MARU → 77363

KMFK H
77370 SAND SHORE

KMFK H
77380 JOLLY ROSSO

KMFK H
77390 GENEVE → 77398

KMFK H1
77400 JULIANA → 77402

KMFK H1
77420 AEOLOS C

KMFK H1
77430 CATHAY SEATRADE

KMFK H1
77440 NEWAYS → 77448

KMFK H1
77460 JESSIE STOVE → 77464

KMFK H1
77470 PORT LATTA MARU

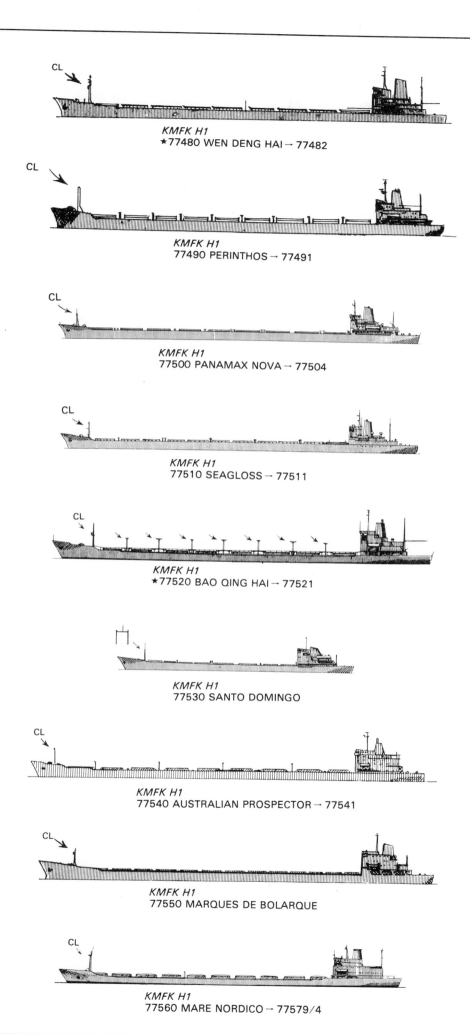

KMFK H1
★77480 WEN DENG HAI → 77482

KMFK H1
77490 PERINTHOS → 77491

KMFK H1
77500 PANAMAX NOVA → 77504

KMFK H1
77510 SEAGLOSS → 77511

KMFK H1
★77520 BAO QING HAI → 77521

KMFK H1
77530 SANTO DOMINGO

KMFK H1
77540 AUSTRALIAN PROSPECTOR → 77541

KMFK H1
77550 MARQUES DE BOLARQUE

KMFK H1
77560 MARE NORDICO → 77579/4

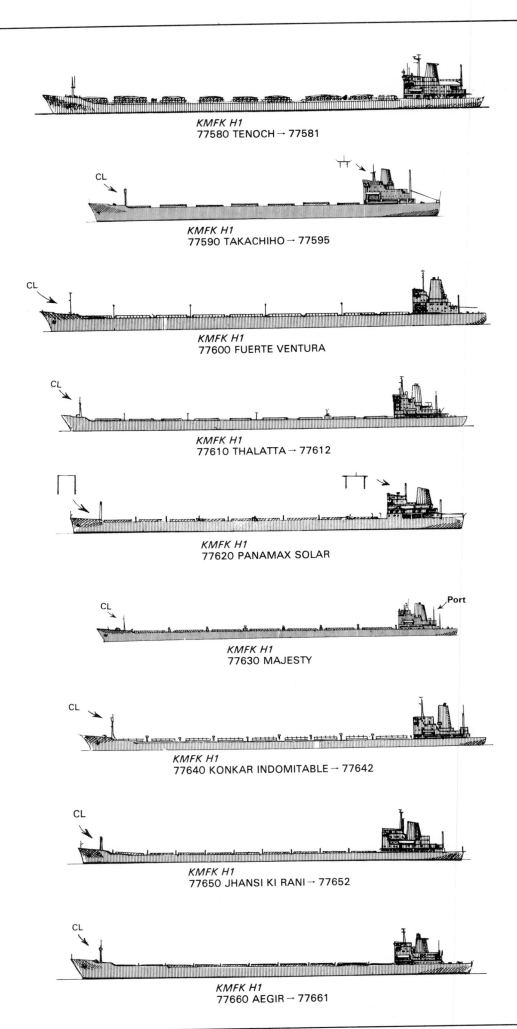

KMFK H1
77580 TENOCH → 77581

KMFK H1
77590 TAKACHIHO → 77595

KMFK H1
77600 FUERTE VENTURA

KMFK H1
77610 THALATTA → 77612

KMFK H1
77620 PANAMAX SOLAR

KMFK H1
77630 MAJESTY

KMFK H1
77640 KONKAR INDOMITABLE → 77642

KMFK H1
77650 JHANSI KI RANI → 77652

KMFK H1
77660 AEGIR → 77661

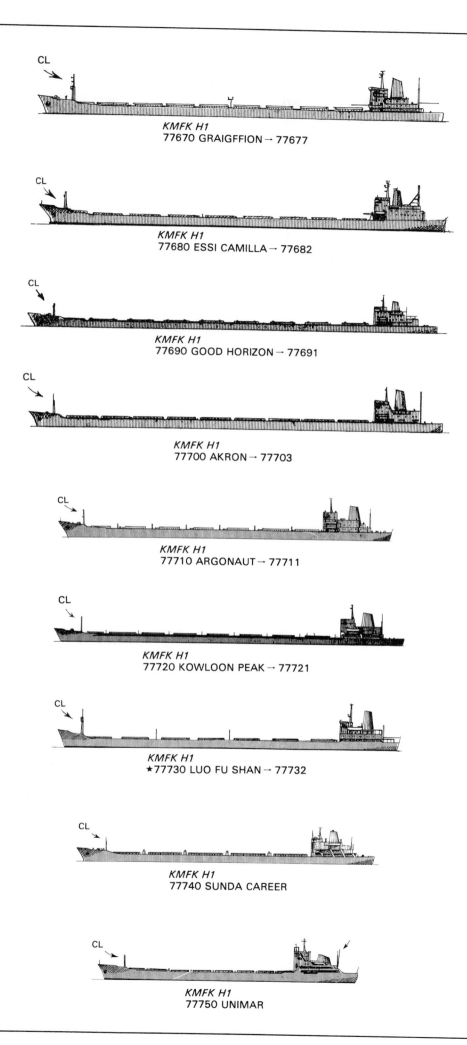

KMFK H1
77670 GRAIGFFION → 77677

KMFK H1
77680 ESSI CAMILLA → 77682

KMFK H1
77690 GOOD HORIZON → 77691

KMFK H1
77700 AKRON → 77703

KMFK H1
77710 ARGONAUT → 77711

KMFK H1
77720 KOWLOON PEAK → 77721

KMFK H1
★77730 LUO FU SHAN → 77732

KMFK H1
77740 SUNDA CAREER

KMFK H1
77750 UNIMAR

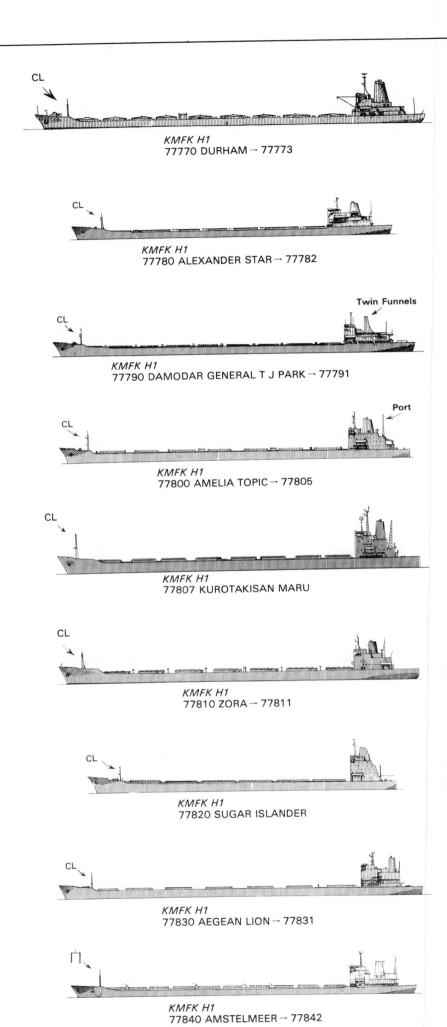

CL

KMFK H1
77770 DURHAM → 77773

CL

KMFK H1
77780 ALEXANDER STAR → 77782

Twin Funnels

CL

KMFK H1
77790 DAMODAR GENERAL T J PARK → 77791

Port

CL

KMFK H1
77800 AMELIA TOPIC → 77805

CL

KMFK H1
77807 KUROTAKISAN MARU

CL

KMFK H1
77810 ZORA → 77811

CL

KMFK H1
77820 SUGAR ISLANDER

CL

KMFK H1
77830 AEGEAN LION → 77831

KMFK H1
77840 AMSTELMEER → 77842

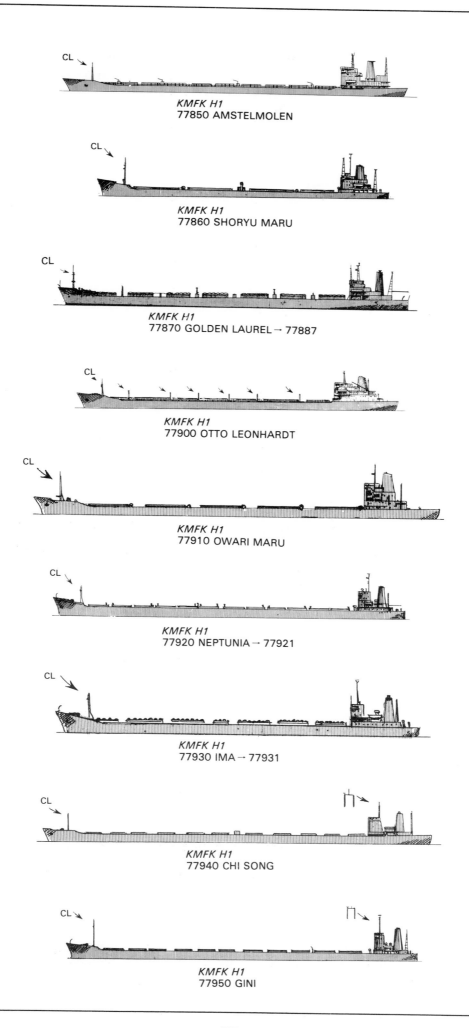

KMFK H1
77850 AMSTELMOLEN

KMFK H1
77860 SHORYU MARU

KMFK H1
77870 GOLDEN LAUREL → 77887

KMFK H1
77900 OTTO LEONHARDT

KMFK H1
77910 OWARI MARU

KMFK H1
77920 NEPTUNIA → 77921

KMFK H1
77930 IMA → 77931

KMFK H1
77940 CHI SONG

KMFK H1
77950 GINI

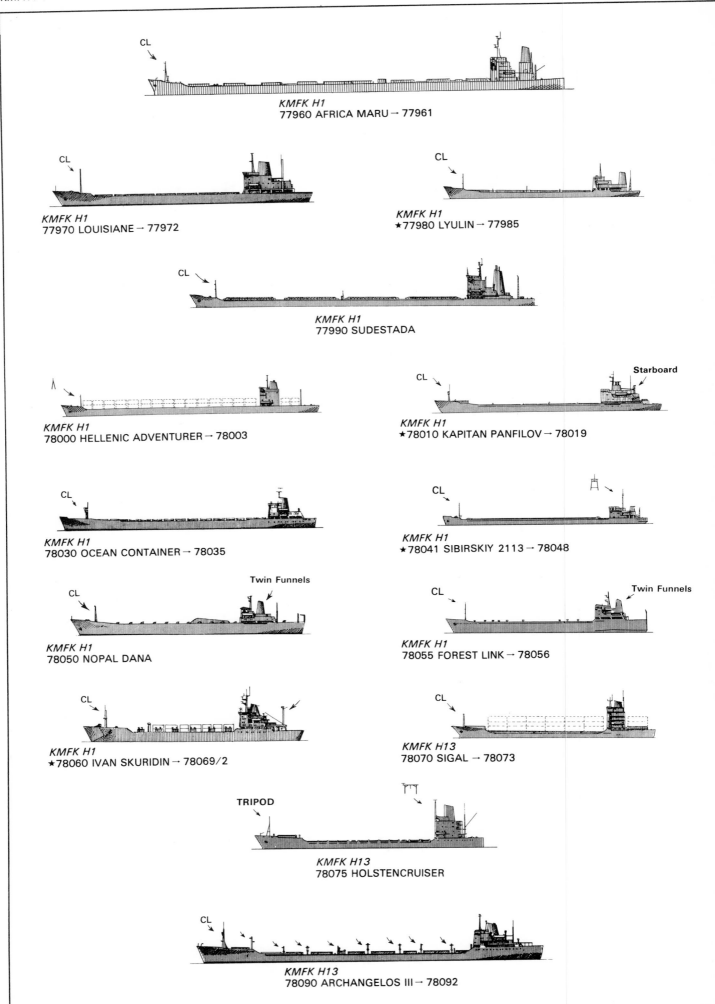

KMFK H1
77960 AFRICA MARU → 77961

KMFK H1
77970 LOUISIANE → 77972

KMFK H1
★77980 LYULIN → 77985

KMFK H1
77990 SUDESTADA

KMFK H1
78000 HELLENIC ADVENTURER → 78003

KMFK H1
★78010 KAPITAN PANFILOV → 78019

KMFK H1
78030 OCEAN CONTAINER → 78035

KMFK H1
★78041 SIBIRSKIY 2113 → 78048

KMFK H1
78050 NOPAL DANA

KMFK H1
78055 FOREST LINK → 78056

KMFK H1
★78060 IVAN SKURIDIN → 78069/2

KMFK H13
78070 SIGAL → 78073

KMFK H13
78075 HOLSTENCRUISER

KMFK H13
78090 ARCHANGELOS III → 78092

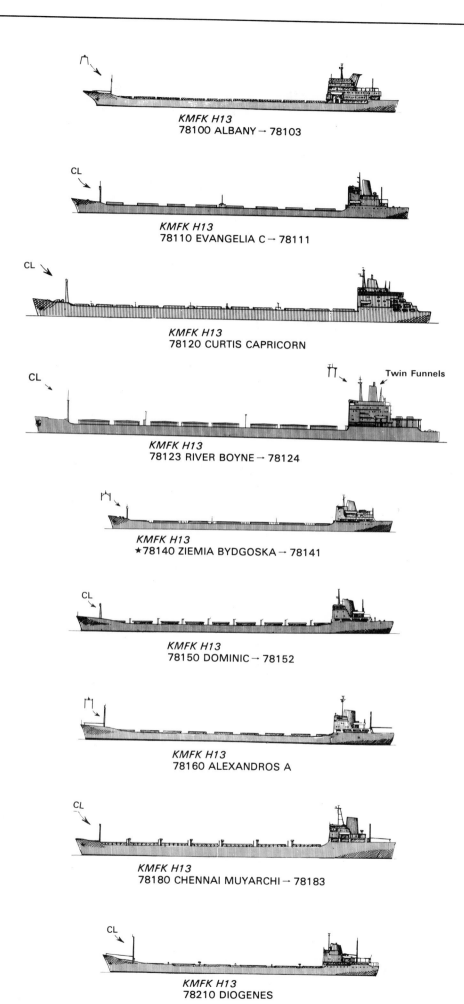

KMFK H13
78100 ALBANY → 78103

KMFK H13
78110 EVANGELIA C → 78111

KMFK H13
78120 CURTIS CAPRICORN

Twin Funnels

KMFK H13
78123 RIVER BOYNE → 78124

KMFK H13
★78140 ZIEMIA BYDGOSKA → 78141

KMFK H13
78150 DOMINIC → 78152

KMFK H13
78160 ALEXANDROS A

KMFK H13
78180 CHENNAI MUYARCHI → 78183

KMFK H13
78210 DIOGENES

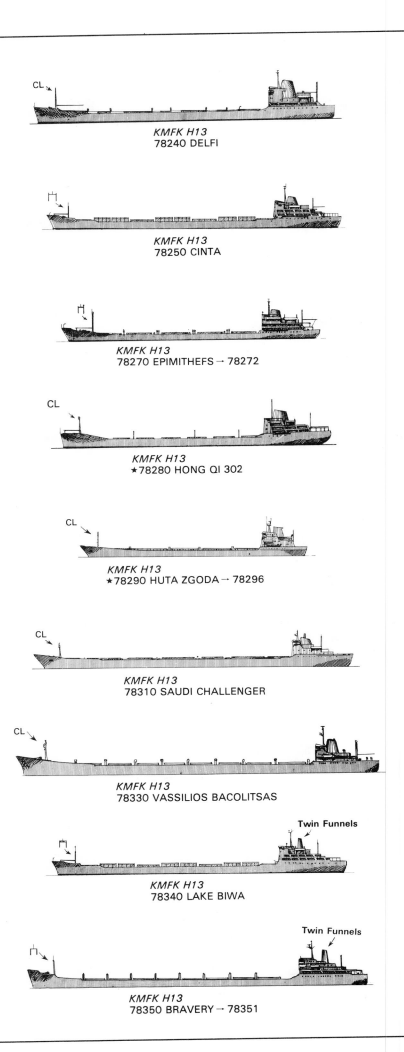

KMFK H13
78240 DELFI

KMFK H13
78250 CINTA

KMFK H13
78270 EPIMITHEFS → 78272

KMFK H13
★78280 HONG QI 302

KMFK H13
★78290 HUTA ZGODA → 78296

KMFK H13
78310 SAUDI CHALLENGER

KMFK H13
78330 VASSILIOS BACOLITSAS

Twin Funnels

KMFK H13
78340 LAKE BIWA

Twin Funnels

KMFK H13
78350 BRAVERY → 78351

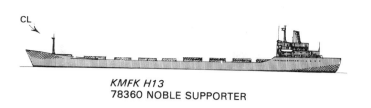

KMFK H13
78360 NOBLE SUPPORTER

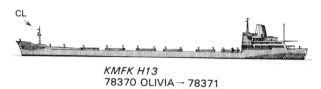

KMFK H13
78370 OLIVIA → 78371

KMFK H13
78380 ARCADIAN SEA → 78383

KMFK H13
78390 NAROTTAM MORARJEE → 78392

KMFK H13
78400 MARION → 78402

KMFK H13
78410 SEAGLOSS → 78411

KMFK H13
78420 PAN UNION → 78426

KMFK H13
78430 ST.PAUL → 78432

Twin Funnels

KMFK H13
78450 ANASTASIA L

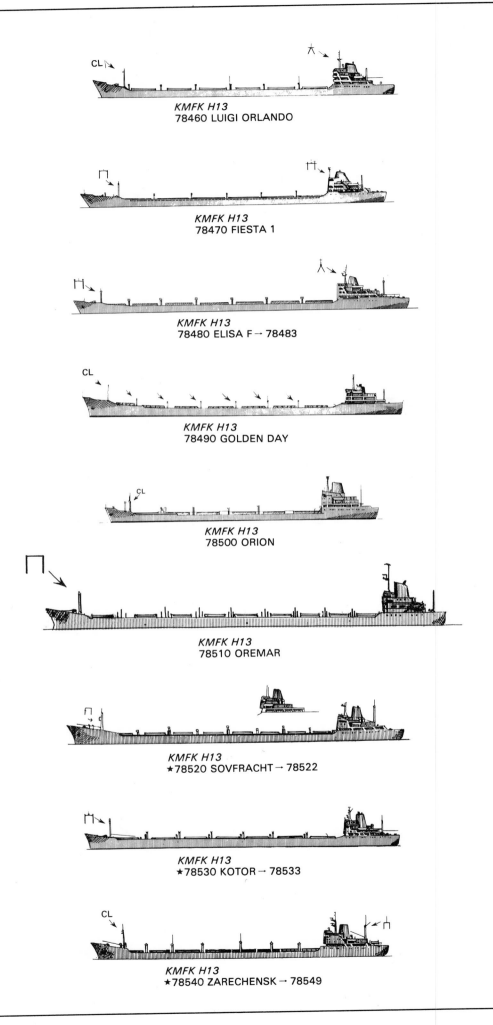

KMFK H13
78460 LUIGI ORLANDO

KMFK H13
78470 FIESTA 1

KMFK H13
78480 ELISA F → 78483

KMFK H13
78490 GOLDEN DAY

KMFK H13
78500 ORION

KMFK H13
78510 OREMAR

KMFK H13
★78520 SOVFRACHT → 78522

KMFK H13
★78530 KOTOR → 78533

KMFK H13
★78540 ZARECHENSK → 78549

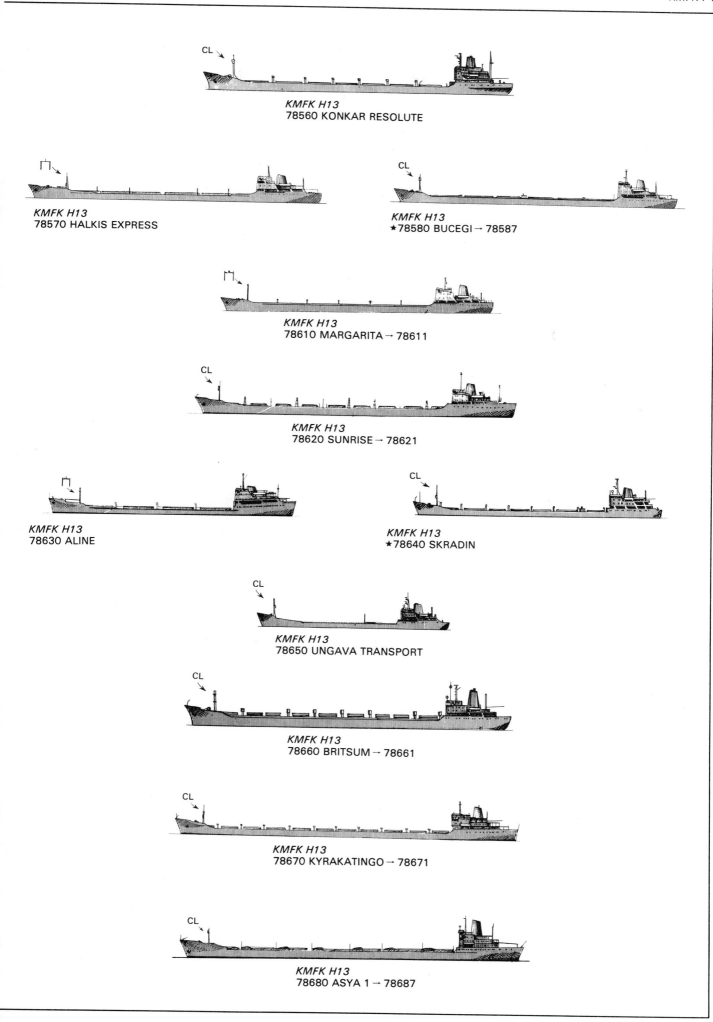

KMFK H13
78560 KONKAR RESOLUTE

KMFK H13
78570 HALKIS EXPRESS

KMFK H13
★78580 BUCEGI → 78587

KMFK H13
78610 MARGARITA → 78611

KMFK H13
78620 SUNRISE → 78621

KMFK H13
78630 ALINE

KMFK H13
★78640 SKRADIN

KMFK H13
78650 UNGAVA TRANSPORT

KMFK H13
78660 BRITSUM → 78661

KMFK H13
78670 KYRAKATINGO → 78671

KMFK H13
78680 ASYA 1 → 78687

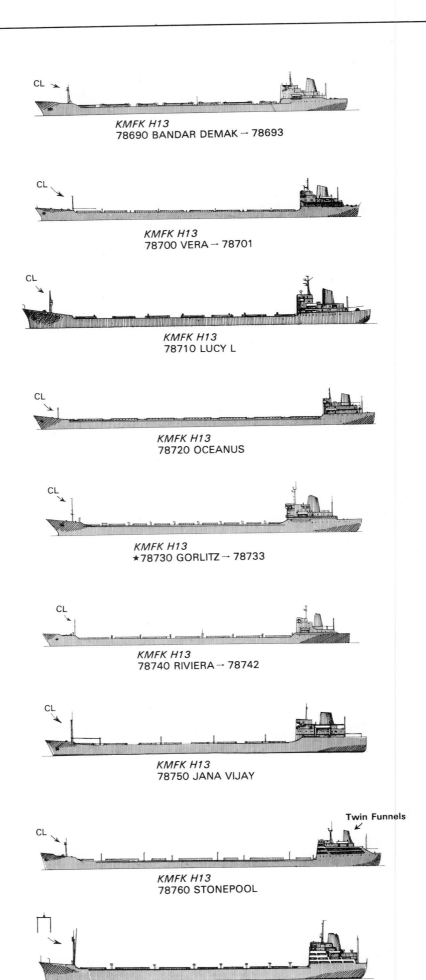

CL

KMFK H13
78690 BANDAR DEMAK → 78693

CL

KMFK H13
78700 VERA → 78701

CL

KMFK H13
78710 LUCY L

CL

KMFK H13
78720 OCEANUS

CL

KMFK H13
★78730 GORLITZ → 78733

CL

KMFK H13
78740 RIVIERA → 78742

CL

KMFK H13
78750 JANA VIJAY

Twin Funnels

CL

KMFK H13
78760 STONEPOOL

KMFK H13
78770 MATILDE R. → 78773

KMFK H13
78780 FALSTRIA → 78781

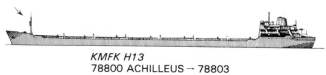

KMFK H13
78800 ACHILLEUS → 78803

KMFK H13
78830 LUIS PEREDA

KMFK H13
★78841 PIONIERUL → 78848

KMFK   H13
78850 MUSALA → 78852

KMFK H13
78860 VITABULK

KMFK H13
78880 TONY → 78881

KMFK H13
★78890 PODGORICA

KMFK H13
★78991 VLADIMIR LENORSKIY → 78897

KMFK H13
78900 ALPHA

KMFK H13
78910 DALLINGTON → 78913

KMFK H13
78914 WASHINGTON

KMFK H13
78915 SUMBURGH HEAD → 78917

KMFK H13
★78920 HUAI HAI → 78921

KMFK H13
78930 CARIBBEAN CARRIER → 78931

KMFK H13
★78940 KOSICE

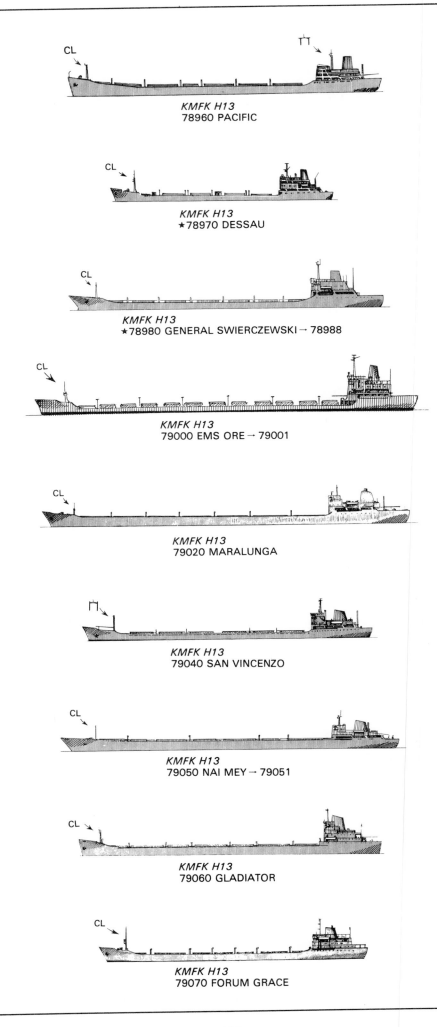

KMFK H13
78960 PACIFIC

KMFK H13
★78970 DESSAU

KMFK H13
★78980 GENERAL SWIERCZEWSKI → 78988

KMFK H13
79000 EMS ORE → 79001

KMFK H13
79020 MARALUNGA

KMFK H13
79040 SAN VINCENZO

KMFK H13
79050 NAI MEY → 79051

KMFK H13
79060 GLADIATOR

KMFK H13
79070 FORUM GRACE

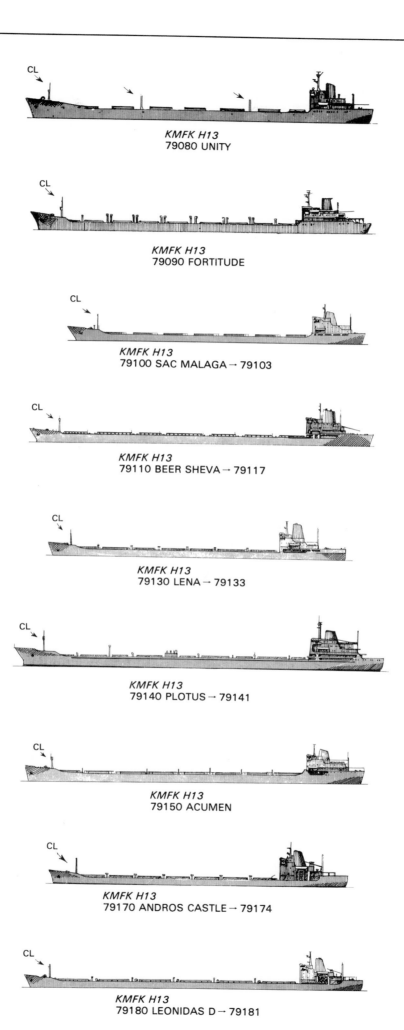

KMFK H13
79080 UNITY

KMFK H13
79090 FORTITUDE

KMFK H13
79100 SAC MALAGA → 79103

KMFK H13
79110 BEER SHEVA → 79117

KMFK H13
79130 LENA → 79133

KMFK H13
79140 PLOTUS → 79141

KMFK H13
79150 ACUMEN

KMFK H13
79170 ANDROS CASTLE → 79174

KMFK H13
79180 LEONIDAS D → 79181

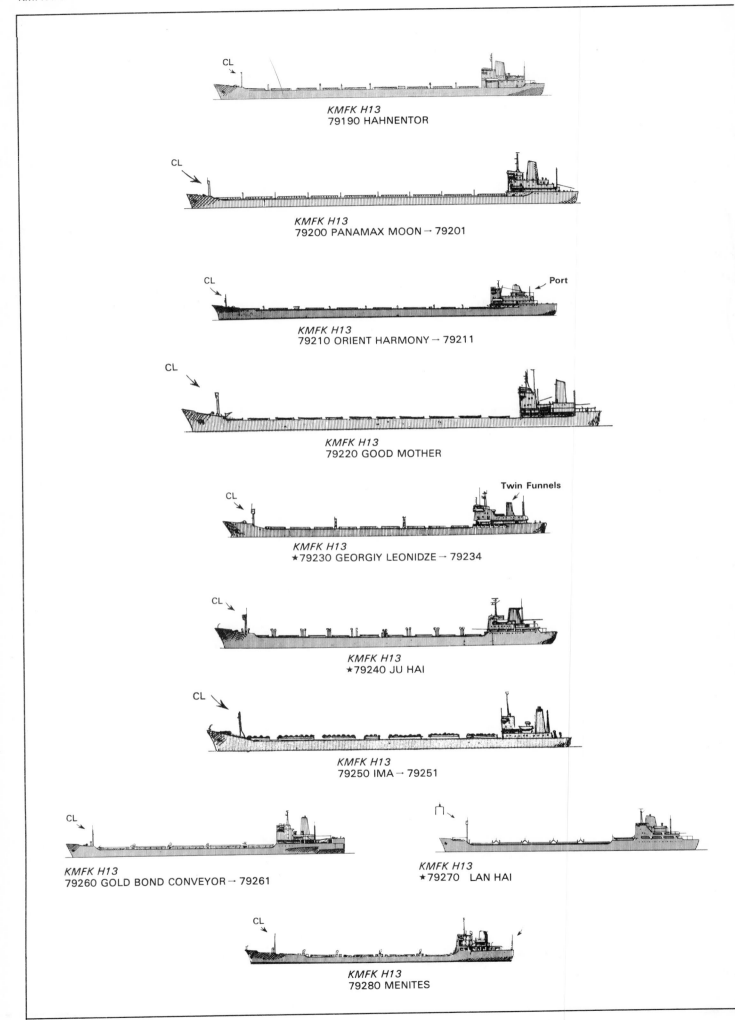

CL
KMFK H13
79190 HAHNENTOR

CL
KMFK H13
79200 PANAMAX MOON → 79201

CL
Port
KMFK H13
79210 ORIENT HARMONY → 79211

CL
KMFK H13
79220 GOOD MOTHER

CL
Twin Funnels
KMFK H13
★79230 GEORGIY LEONIDZE → 79234

CL
KMFK H13
★79240 JU HAI

CL
KMFK H13
79250 IMA → 79251

CL
KMFK H13
79260 GOLD BOND CONVEYOR → 79261

KMFK H13
★79270   LAN HAI

CL
KMFK H13
79280 MENITES

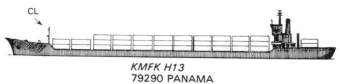

KMFK H13
79290 PANAMA

KMFK H13
79300 WERRA EXPRESS → 79302

KMFK H13
79310 HERMES ACE → 79311

KMFK H13
79320 BREEZAND → 79323

KMFK H13
★79340 'SORMOVSKIY'type → 79444

KMFK H13
★79450 NEFTERUDOVOZ

KMFK H13
★79500 'BALTIYSKIY'type

KMFK H13
★79550 PIONER NAKHODKI → 79555

KMFK H13
79560 TUDELA

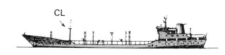

KMFK H13
79570 PERTUSOLA → 79571

KMFK H13
79580 COMMANDANT HENRY → 79581

KMFK H13
79590 BP JOUSTER → 79593

KMFK H13
79600 SENKO MARU → 79602

KMFK H13
79610 GREEN SEA

KMFK H13
79620 KOKUSHU MARU No. 2

KMFK H13
79630 BUTAUNO → 79631

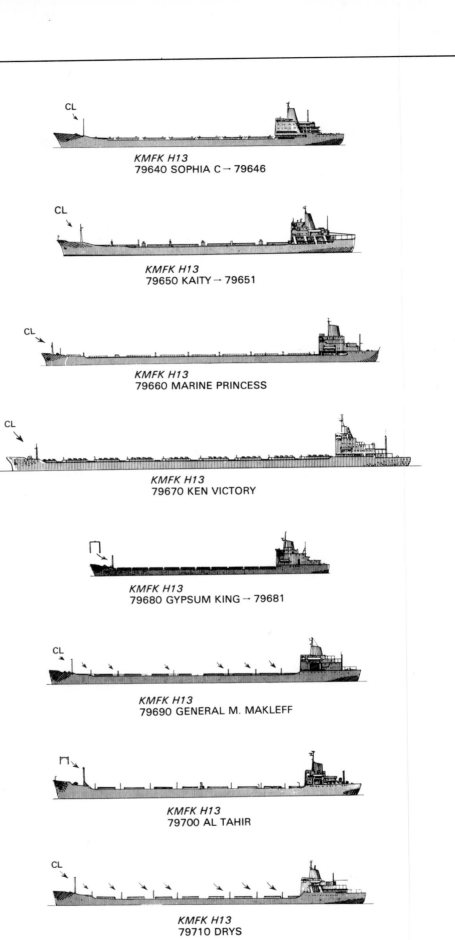

KMFK H13
79640 SOPHIA C → 79646

KMFK H13
79650 KAITY → 79651

KMFK H13
79660 MARINE PRINCESS

KMFK H13
79670 KEN VICTORY

KMFK H13
79680 GYPSUM KING → 79681

KMFK H13
79690 GENERAL M. MAKLEFF

KMFK H13
79700 AL TAHIR

KMFK H13
79710 DRYS

KMFK H13
79720 FUTURE

KMFK H13
★79730 LUBBENAU → 79735

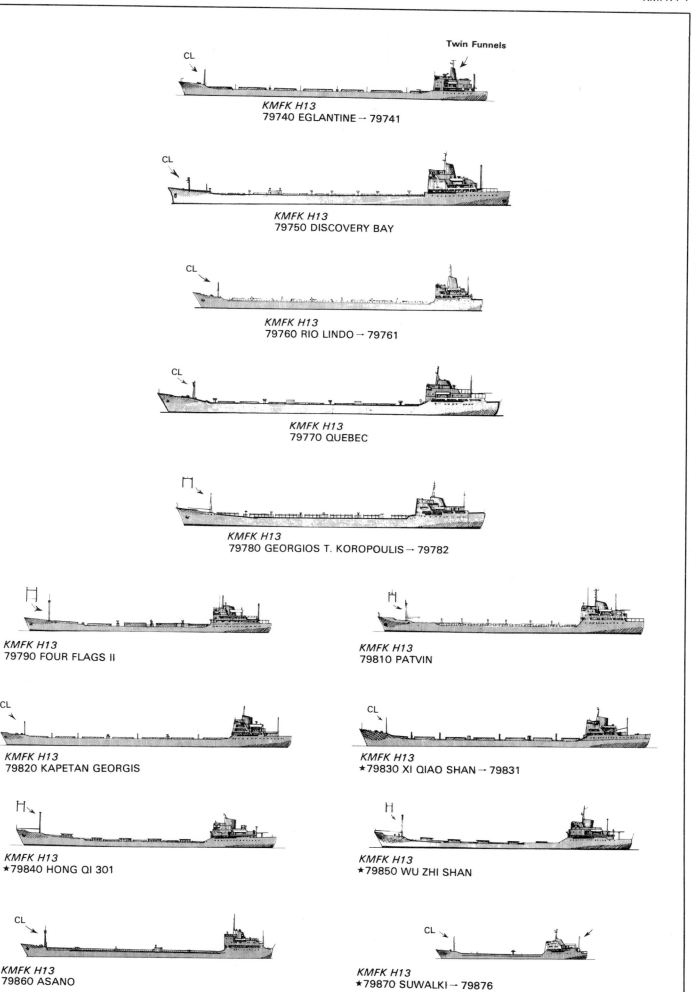

KMFK H13
79740 EGLANTINE → 79741

KMFK H13
79750 DISCOVERY BAY

KMFK H13
79760 RIO LINDO → 79761

KMFK H13
79770 QUEBEC

KMFK H13
79780 GEORGIOS T. KOROPOULIS → 79782

KMFK H13
79790 FOUR FLAGS II

KMFK H13
79810 PATVIN

KMFK H13
79820 KAPETAN GEORGIS

KMFK H13
★79830 XI QIAO SHAN → 79831

KMFK H13
★79840 HONG QI 301

KMFK H13
★79850 WU ZHI SHAN

KMFK H13
79860 ASANO

KMFK H13
★79870 SUWALKI → 79876

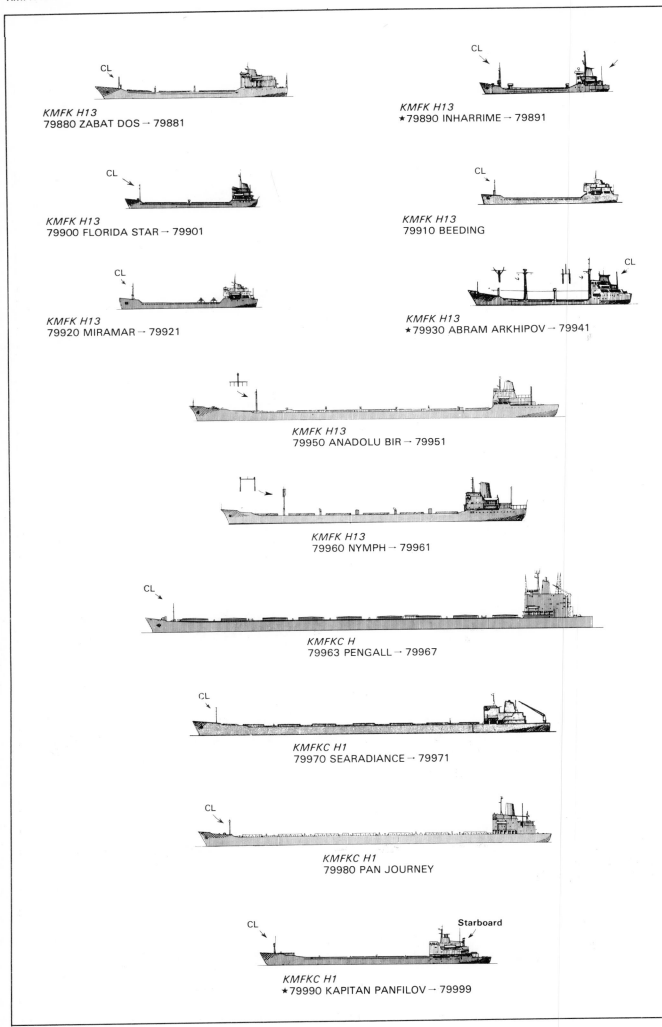

KMFK H13
79880 ZABAT DOS → 79881

KMFK H13
★79890 INHARRIME → 79891

KMFK H13
79900 FLORIDA STAR → 79901

KMFK H13
79910 BEEDING

KMFK H13
79920 MIRAMAR → 79921

KMFK H13
★79930 ABRAM ARKHIPOV → 79941

KMFK H13
79950 ANADOLU BIR → 79951

KMFK H13
79960 NYMPH → 79961

KMFKC H
79963 PENGALL → 79967

KMFKC H1
79970 SEARADIANCE → 79971

KMFKC H1
79980 PAN JOURNEY

KMFKC H1
★79990 KAPITAN PANFILOV → 79999

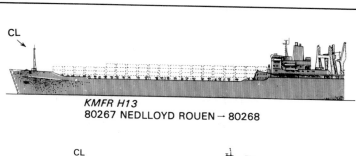

KMFR H13
80267 NEDLLOYD ROUEN → 80268

KMFR H23
80270 ELK → 80278

KMFR H3
80280 SAUDI ABHA → 80283

KMFR H3
80290 BOOGABILLA → 80293

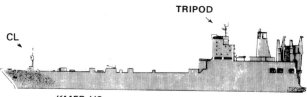

KMFR H3
80294 BULLAREN

KMFR H3
80296 ANDREA MERZARIO → 80297

KMKF H
80300 KUSHIRO MARU

KMKF H1
80320 GOLD CLOUD

KMKF H1
80330 SOFIA

KMKF H1
80340 TRANSEAST → 80343

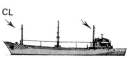

KMKF H1
80350 PREVEZE → 80357

KMKF H1
80370 KOREAN WONIS-SUN → 80380

KMKF H1
80385 PACIFIC PROMINENCE → 80386

KMKF H12
80390 GOLD CLOUD

KMKF H12 & H123
80400 MONTONE → 80403

KMKF H123
80410 CIRO TERZO

KMKF H123
80420 PLAYA → 80422

KMKF H123
80430 MARE AMICO

KMKF H13
80460 CONDE DEL CADAGUA

KMKF H13
80490 MASTROGIORGIS

KMKF H13
80500 QUICKTHORN

KMKF H13
★80520 KORNAT → 80521

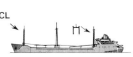

KMKF H13
80530 ANTHOULA I → 80531

KMKF H13
80540 VANGELI

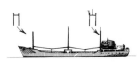

KMKF H13
80550 RAMSLI

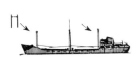

KMKF H13
80570 CHARTA

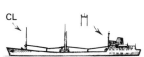

KMKF H13
80590 LAGO FORTUNE

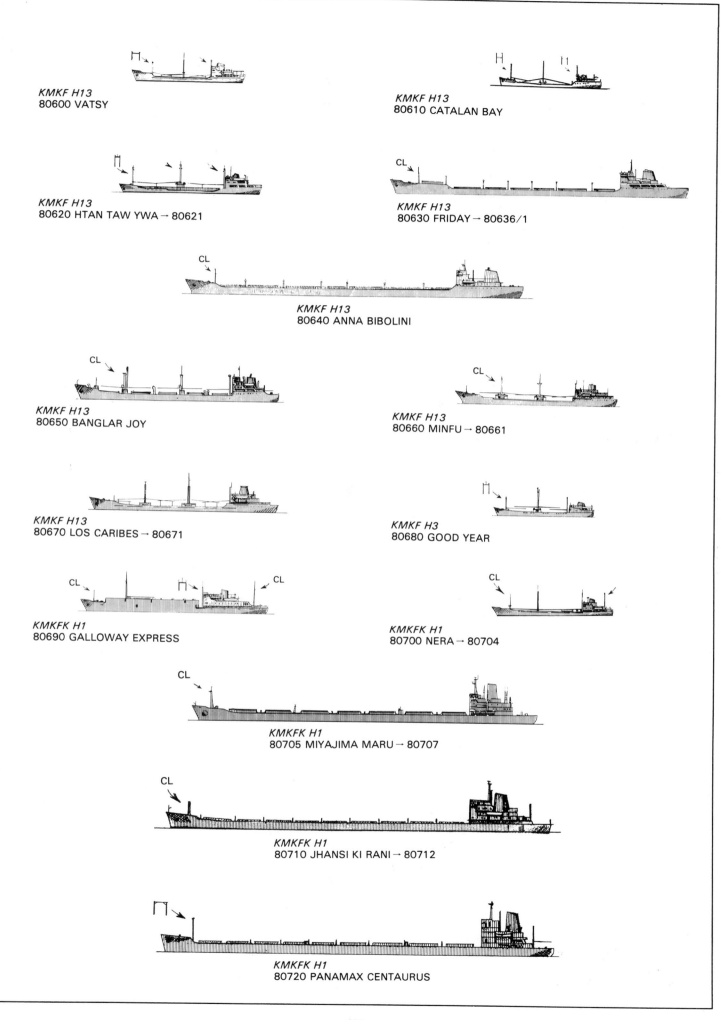

KMKF H13
80600 VATSY

KMKF H13
80610 CATALAN BAY

KMKF H13
80620 HTAN TAW YWA → 80621

KMKF H13
80630 FRIDAY → 80636/1

KMKF H13
80640 ANNA BIBOLINI

KMKF H13
80650 BANGLAR JOY

KMKF H13
80660 MINFU → 80661

KMKF H13
80670 LOS CARIBES → 80671

KMKF H3
80680 GOOD YEAR

KMKFK H1
80690 GALLOWAY EXPRESS

KMKFK H1
80700 NERA → 80704

KMKFK H1
80705 MIYAJIMA MARU → 80707

KMKFK H1
80710 JHANSI KI RANI → 80712

KMKFK H1
80720 PANAMAX CENTAURUS

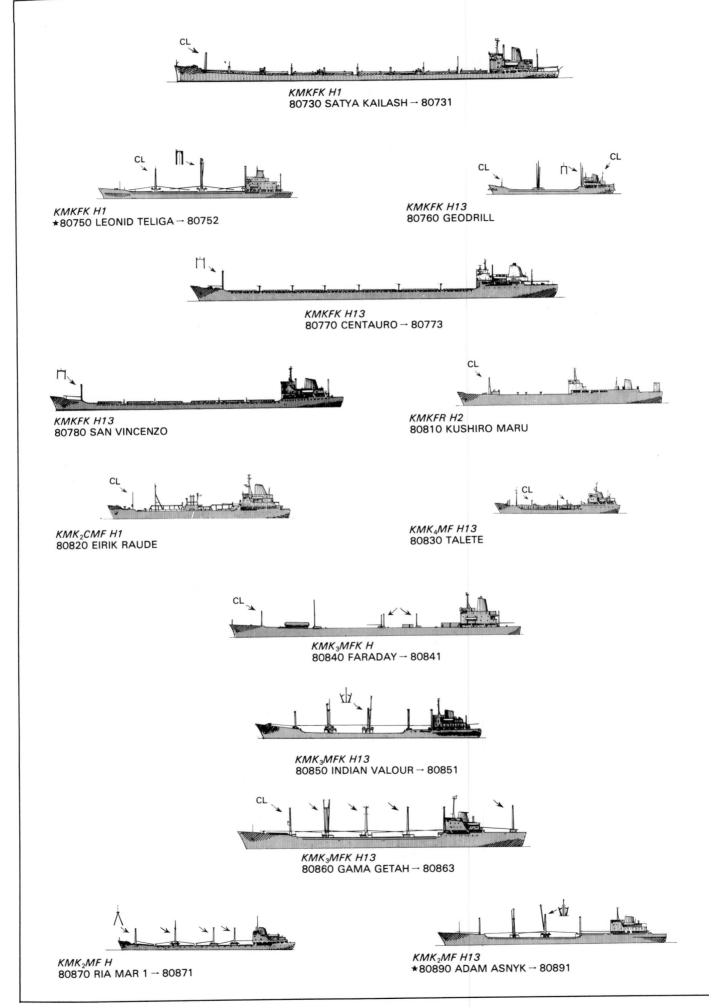

KMKFK H1
80730 SATYA KAILASH → 80731

KMKFK H1
★80750 LEONID TELIGA → 80752

KMKFK H13
80760 GEODRILL

KMKFK H13
80770 CENTAURO → 80773

KMKFK H13
80780 SAN VINCENZO

KMKFR H2
80810 KUSHIRO MARU

KMK₂CMF H1
80820 EIRIK RAUDE

KMK₄MF H13
80830 TALETE

KMK₃MFK H
80840 FARADAY → 80841

KMK₃MFK H13
80850 INDIAN VALOUR → 80851

KMK₃MFK H13
80860 GAMA GETAH → 80863

KMK₂MF H
80870 RIA MAR 1 → 80871

KMK₂MF H13
★80890 ADAM ASNYK → 80891

KMK₂MF H13
★80900 PETKO R. SLAVEJNOV → 80902

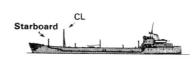

KMK₂MF H13
80910 TRADER → 80912

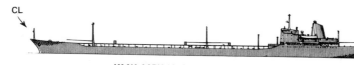

KMK₂MFK H13
★80920 LISICHANSK → 80922

KMK₂MFK H13
80930 DOBROTA → 80931

KMK₂MFK H13
80940 IRENE

KMKMF H
80970 FREO ZUTA

KMKMF H
80980 FREEZER LEVA → 80983

KMKMF H
80990 ABOITIZ CONCARRIER IX

KMKMF H
★81000 NOVY BUG → 81004

KMKMF H1
★81010 DA LONG TIAN → 81015

KMKMF H1
81020 MATINA

KMKMF H1
81030 MUMTAZ

KMKMF H1
81040 MARIA K

KMKMF H1
81050 HAJ ABDUL RAHMAN → 81502

KMKMF H1
81060 WILCON III

KMKMF H1
★81070 KRUSEVO → 81071

KMKMF H1
81080 MUSING

459

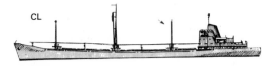

KMKMF H1
81090 HIMALAYA

KMKMF H1
81100 BODRUM → 81103

KMKMF H1
81110 GOLDEN WAVE → 81111

KMKMF H12
81120 PETROLA 30 → 81121

KMKMF H123
81130 LEEGAS → 81133

KMKMF H123
81140 AVLIS EXPRESS → 81142

KMKMF H13
81150 NEAPOLI

KMKMF H13
81160 PERMINA VIII

KMKMF H13
81170 BETINA THOLSTRUP

KMKMF H13
81180 MATADI PALM

KMKMF H13
81190 LUANA

KMKMF H13
★81195 TATARSTAN → 81197

KMKMF H13
81200 SITI MIDAH → 81202

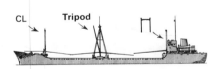

KMKMF H13
81220 BUNGA VANDA

KMKMF H13
81230 DESPINA V → 81231

KMKMF H13
81240 LAGADA BAY

KMKMF H13
81250 NAVI STAR

KMKMF H13
81260 DIMACHK

KMKMF H13
81270 MARANAR

KMKMF H13
81280 STORM

KMKMF H13
81290 NICOS A → 81291

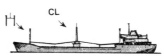

KMKMF H13
81300 LESLIE → 81301

KMKMF H13
★81310 CAMAGUEY

KMKMF H13
81320 ARIEL 1

KMKMF H13
81330 CARIGULF PIONEER

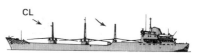

KMKMF H13
81340 TACAMAR VII

KMKMF H13
★81350 ZULAWY → 81353

KMKMF H13
81370 UNION BALTIMORE

KMKMF H13
★81380 YONG CHENG → 81381

KMKMF H13
81390 ASTRID SCHULTE → 81391

KMKMF H13
★81400 ALIOT → 81402

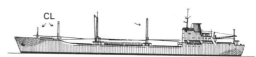

KMKMFCK H13
81410 FERNANDOEVERETT → 81414

KMKMFK H
81420 EBN JUBAIR → 81421

KMKMFK H1
81430 AL REAFA 1

KMKMFK H1
81440 RASSEM

KMKMFK H1
★81450 LEONID TELIGA → 81453

KMKMFK H13
81460 PERMINA 109 → 81461

KMKMFK H13
81470 ELISABETTA MONTANARI → 81473

KMKMFK H13
81480 OLIVIA CUATRO → 81482

KMKMFK H13
★81490 PRIBOY → 81495

KMKMFK H13
81500 YACU WASI

KMKMFK H13
81510 MICHALIS K

KMKMFK H13
81520 SKIPPER

KMKMFK H13
81530 AEGEAN SEA → 81531

KMKMFK H13
81540 PATROKLOS 1 → 81541

KMKMFK H13
81550 IOTA → 81551

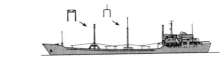

KMKMFK H13
★81555 SLATINA → 81562

KMKMFK₂ H13
81580 BRADEVERETT → 81582

KMKMKMFK H1
81590 SELAS

KMKMKMFK H13
81600 SHENG LI

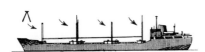

KMKM₂F H13
81610 GULF TRADER

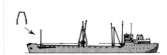

KMKM₂F H3
81620 BAHARI

KMKM₂FK H13
81630 SEMELI

KMKM₂FK H13
★81640 ZAKOPANE → 81647

KMKM₃F H13
81660 BAILUNDO → 81661

KM₂F H
81670 WIHAR 1

KM₂F H
81680 MINOGAZ 1

KM₂F H
81690 ALBAFRIGO → 81692

KM₂F H
81700 FREEZER LEVA → 81703

KM₂F H1
81710 AGOIS ELEFTHERIOS → 81711

KM₂F H1
81720 DWEJRA II

KM₂F H1
81730 P. KROL

KM₂F H1
81740 NORMAND EXPRESS

KM₂F H1
81750 JARASH → 81751

KM₂F H1
81760 FRANCISKA SCHULTE

KM₂F H1
81770 ANNELIESE OLTMANN → 81771

KM₂F H1
81780 RASHIDAH → 81783

KM₂F H1
81790 LAVINIA COPPOLA

KM₂F H1
★81800 LISKI

KM₂F H1
81810 MAMBDOUN

KM₂F H1
81820 ADI VITI → 81825

KM₂F H1
81830 SUN EAGLE 1

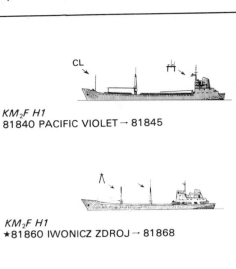

KM₂F H1
81840 PACIFIC VIOLET → 81845

KM₂F H1
★81850 DIKA → 81851

KM₂F H1
★81860 IWONICZ ZDROJ → 81868

KM₂F H12
81880 GABRIELE

KM₂F H13
81900 CEMBULK

KM₂F H13
81910 MALDEA

KM₂F H13
81920 POLAR GAS → 81921

KM₂F H13
81930 ARMENISTIS 1

KM₂F H13
81940 ARANUI → 81942

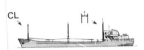

KM₂F H13
81950 TRIOS → 81957

KM₂F H13
81970 HTAN TAW YWA → 81971

KM₂F H13
81980 IRO

KM₂F H13
81990 SKIATHOS

KM₂F H13
82000 SADAROZA → 82001

KM₂F H13
82010 MARA

KM₂F H13
82020 CAPAL

KM₂F H13
82030 FAITH → 82031

KM₂F H13
82040 WESER BROKER

KM₂F H13
82050 VICTORIA → 82054

KM₂F H13
82060 TRIANTAFILOS M.→82062

KM₂F H13
82070 ADI VITI → 82075

KM₂F H13
82080 GIANT

KM₂F H13
82100 ALTA MAR

KM₂F H13
★82110 BRAD → 82141

KM₂F H13
82150 CEMENTIA → 82151

KM₂F H13
82155 MARYLANDER → 82156

KM₂F H13
82160 MENELAOS TH → 82161

KM₂F H13
82170 FRISIAN TRADER

KM₂F H13
82180 CORAL MAEANDRA

KM₂F H13
82190 GLARIOS

KM₂F H13
82200 GOGO RANGER

KM₂F H13
82210 FRED H BILLUPS

KM₂F H13
★82220 URICANI → 82229

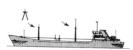

KM₂F H13
82240 FISKO → 82241

KM₂F H13
82250 GIANNIS DIMAKIS III

KM₂F H13
★82260 WARNA → 82268

KM₂F H13
82280 CEMENT KING

KM₂F H3
82310 DEEPA JUWITA

KM₂FK H1
82330 NIKKO MARU No. 53 → 82332

KM₂FK H13
★82350 TU MEN JIANG → 82353

KM₂FK H13
82370 STELLAPRIMA

KM₂FK H13
★82390 BRAD → 82421

KM₂FK H13
★82435 VRHNIKA

KM₂FK H13
82450 STEVE GLORY → 82454

KM₂FK H13
82480 NAM SAN

KM₂F H3
82300 ACQUAVIVA

KM₂FK H1
82320 NYMIT

KM₂FK H1
82340 GEBE OLDENDORFF

KM₂EK H13
82360 HIND 1 → 82361

KM₂FK H13
82380 SHOHO MARU

KM₂FK H13
82430 KYOSEI MARU

KM₂FK H13
82440 DAYAKA

KM₂FK H13
★82460 OSTROV RUSSKIY → 82470

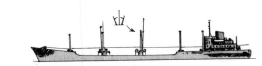

KM₂K₂MFK H13
82490 INDIAN VALOUR → 82491

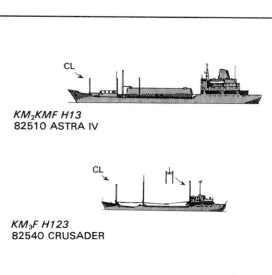

KM₂KMF H13
82510 ASTRA IV

KM₃F H1
82530 TORM AMERICA

KM₃F H123
82540 CRUSADER

KM₃F H123
★82550 PAN SHAN

KM₃F H13
82560 NAM IL → 82561

KM₃F H13
82570 SRI PHEN SINN

KM₃F H13
82580 TAI LAI

KM₃F H13
82590 KING LEAR

KM₃F H13
82600 ALTA MAR

KM₃FK H13
82610 BARENTS SEA

KM₃FK H13
★82620 TU MEN JIANG → 82623

KM₃FK H13
82630 SAUDI TAJ

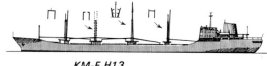

KM₃FK H13
82640 MAR TRANSPORTER → 82645

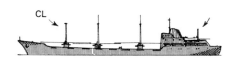

KM₃FK H13
82650 VILLE DE MAHEBOURG

KM₅F H13
82660 BAILUNDO → 82661

KNCMFK H13
82670 THEOGENNITOR

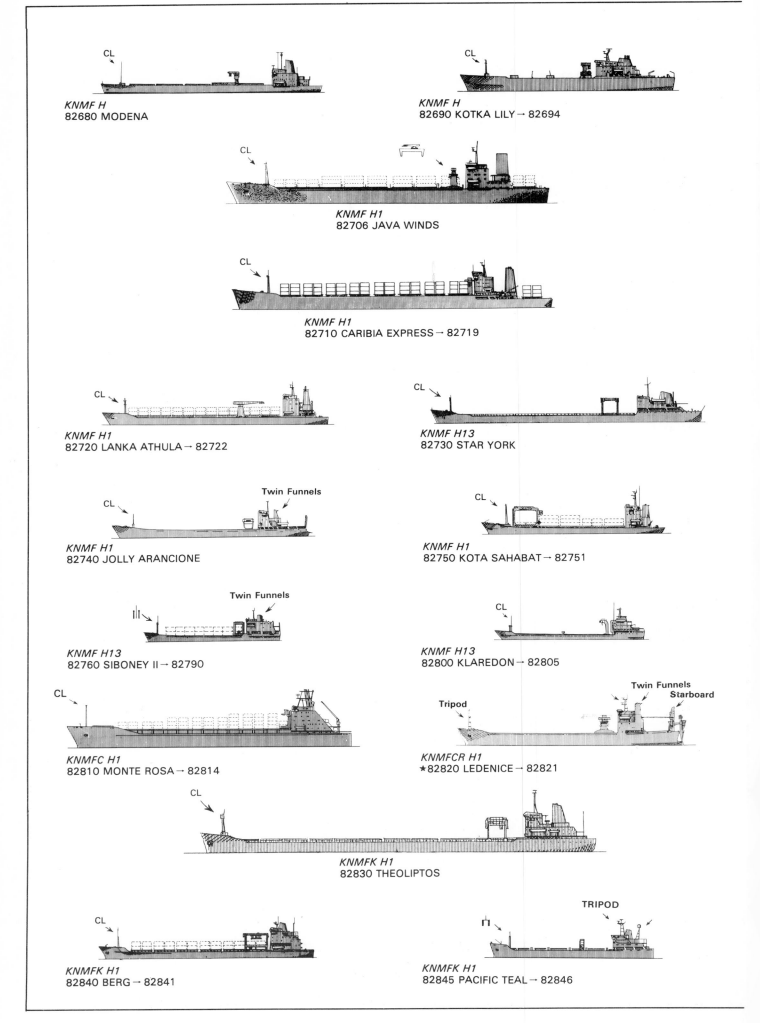

KNMF H
82680 MODENA

KNMF H
82690 KOTKA LILY → 82694

KNMF H1
82706 JAVA WINDS

KNMF H1
82710 CARIBIA EXPRESS → 82719

KNMF H1
82720 LANKA ATHULA → 82722

KNMF H13
82730 STAR YORK

Twin Funnels

KNMF H1
82740 JOLLY ARANCIONE

KNMF H1
82750 KOTA SAHABAT → 82751

Twin Funnels

KNMF H13
82760 SIBONEY II → 82790

KNMF H13
82800 KLAREDON → 82805

KNMFC H1
82810 MONTE ROSA → 82814

Twin Funnels
Starboard

Tripod

KNMFCR H1
★82820 LEDENICE → 82821

KNMFK H1
82830 THEOLIPTOS

TRIPOD

KNMFK H1
82840 BERG → 82841

KNMFK H1
82845 PACIFIC TEAL → 82846

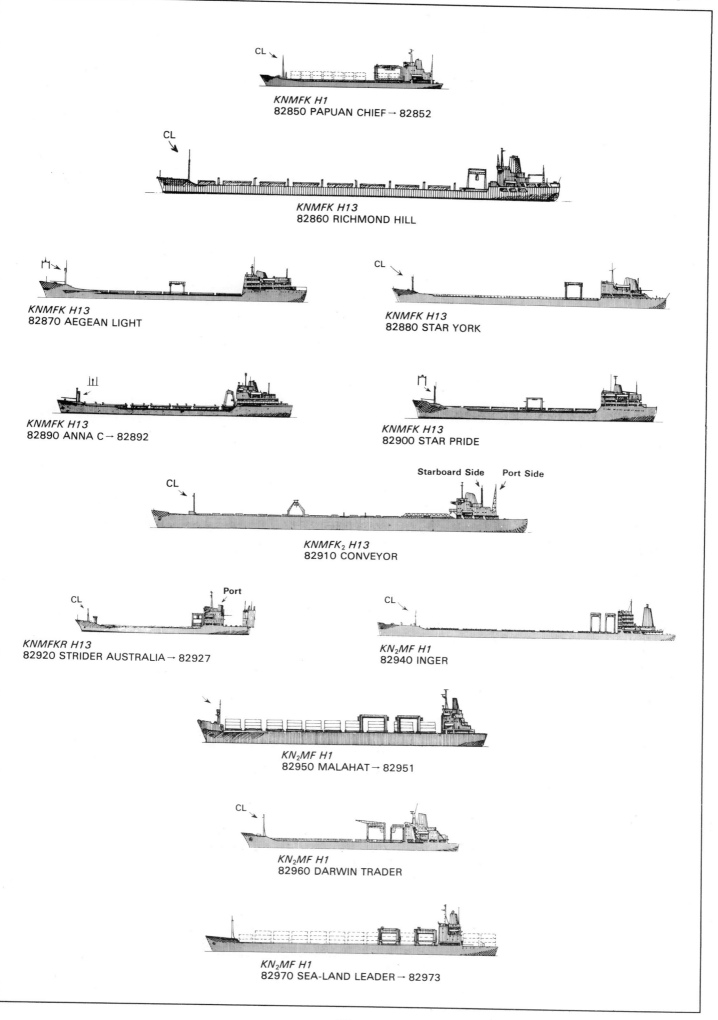

KNMFK H1
82850 PAPUAN CHIEF → 82852

KNMFK H13
82860 RICHMOND HILL

KNMFK H13
82870 AEGEAN LIGHT

KNMFK H13
82880 STAR YORK

KNMFK H13
82890 ANNA C → 82892

KNMFK H13
82900 STAR PRIDE

KNMFK₂ H13
82910 CONVEYOR

KNMFKR H13
82920 STRIDER AUSTRALIA → 82927

KN₂MF H1
82940 INGER

KN₂MF H1
82950 MALAHAT → 82951

KN₂MF H1
82960 DARWIN TRADER

KN₂MF H1
82970 SEA-LAND LEADER → 82973

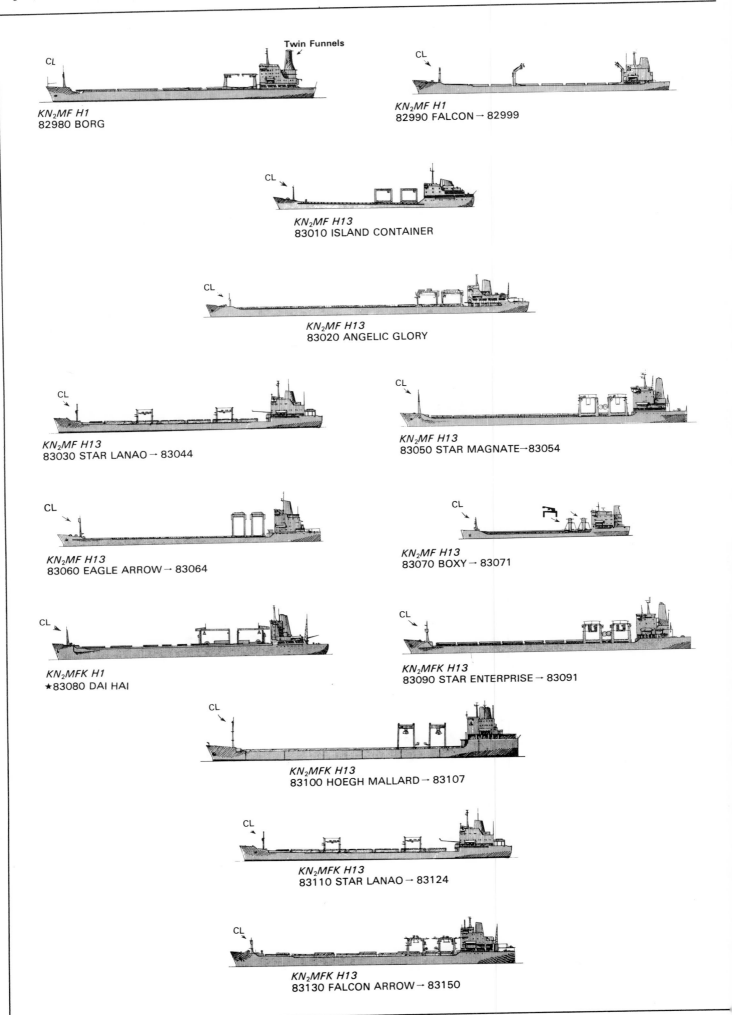

KN₂MF H1
82980 BORG

KN₂MF H1
82990 FALCON → 82999

KN₂MF H13
83010 ISLAND CONTAINER

KN₂MF H13
83020 ANGELIC GLORY

KN₂MF H13
83030 STAR LANAO → 83044

KN₂MF H13
83050 STAR MAGNATE→83054

KN₂MF H13
83060 EAGLE ARROW → 83064

KN₂MF H13
83070 BOXY → 83071

KN₂MFK H1
★83080 DAI HAI

KN₂MFK H13
83090 STAR ENTERPRISE → 83091

KN₂MFK H13
83100 HOEGH MALLARD → 83107

KN₂MFK H13
83110 STAR LANAO → 83124

KN₂MFK H13
83130 FALCON ARROW → 83150

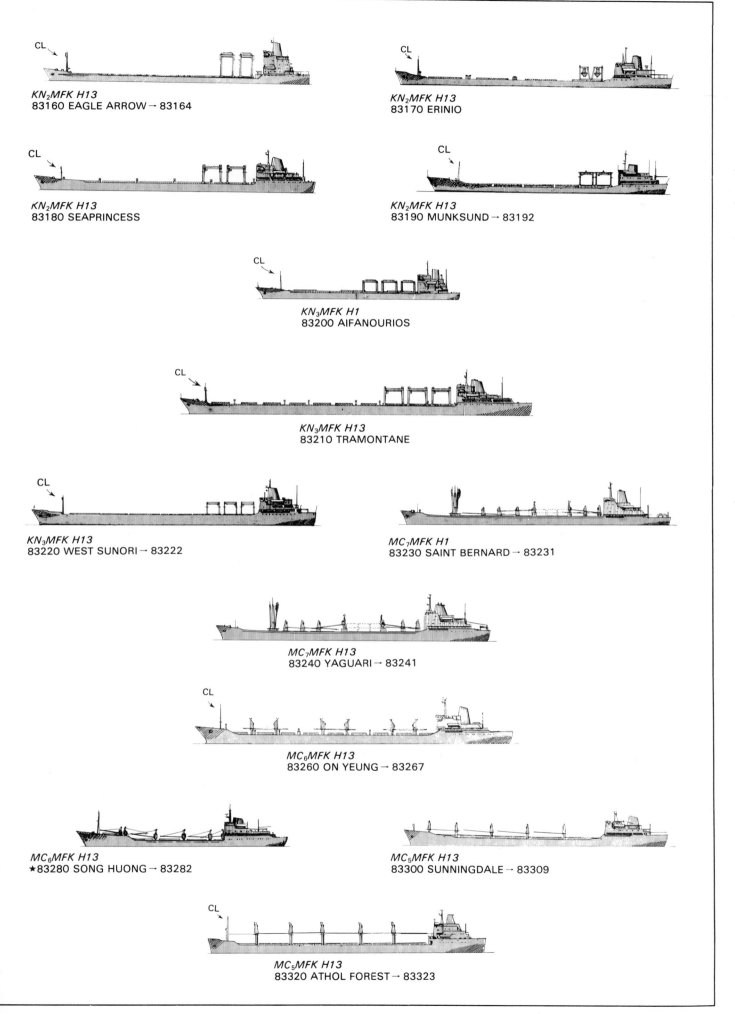

KN₂MFK H13
83160 EAGLE ARROW → 83164

KN₂MFK H13
83170 ERINIO

KN₂MFK H13
83180 SEAPRINCESS

KN₂MFK H13
83190 MUNKSUND → 83192

KN₃MFK H1
83200 AIFANOURIOS

KN₃MFK H13
83210 TRAMONTANE

KN₃MFK H13
83220 WEST SUNORI → 83222

MC₇MFK H1
83230 SAINT BERNARD → 83231

MC₇MFK H13
83240 YAGUARI → 83241

MC₆MFK H13
83260 ON YEUNG → 83267

MC₆MFK H13
★83280 SONG HUONG → 83282

MC₅MFK H13
83300 SUNNINGDALE → 83309

MC₅MFK H13
83320 ATHOL FOREST → 83323

MC₅MFK H13
83330 JAVARA → 83333

MC₅MFK H13
83340 CEBU → 83343

MC₄MF H1
83360 SUNRISE → 83367

MC₄MF H13
83380 ALHALEMI → 83387

MC₄MFC H13
83400 NEDLLOYD WISSEKERK → 83403

MC₄MFK H13
83410 PING CHAU

MC₄MFK H13
83420 PANDORA

MC₄MFM H13
★83430 DEBALTSEVO → 83443

MC₃MF H1
83450 SUNRISE → 83457

MC₃MF H1
83470 PHA SHWE GYAW YWA

MC₃MF H13
83480 CARIBIC

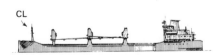

MC₃MF H13
83490 CANADIA → 83493

MC₃MF H13
83510 DETTIFOSS → 83512

MC₃MF H3
83520 PINGUINO

MC₃MFK H
83530 DIANA

MC₃MFK H1
83540 PLAYA DEL MEDANO

MC₃MFK H13
83550 HADJANNA → 83552

MC₂KC₂MFC H13
83570 RISHI ATRI→83572

MC₂KMF H13
★83575 DING HAI

MC₂MC₂KMFK H13
83580 KOTA MAKMUR → 83582

MC₂MF H
83590 ATHANASIOS-S

MC₂MF H
83600 AFEDULA M → 83619

MC₂MF H1
83630 MADELEINE

MC₂MF H12
83640 SIGURD JARL → 83641

MC₂MF H13
83660 DON NICKY

MC₂MF H13
83670 CARIB DAWN → 83673

MC₂MF H13
★83680 CHEREPOVETS → 83694

MC₂MF H13
83700 LUCKY LADY → 83715

MC₂MF H13
★83720 BATAK → ₁83734

MC₂MF H13
83740 EVITA II

MC₂MF H13
83750 CABO FRIO

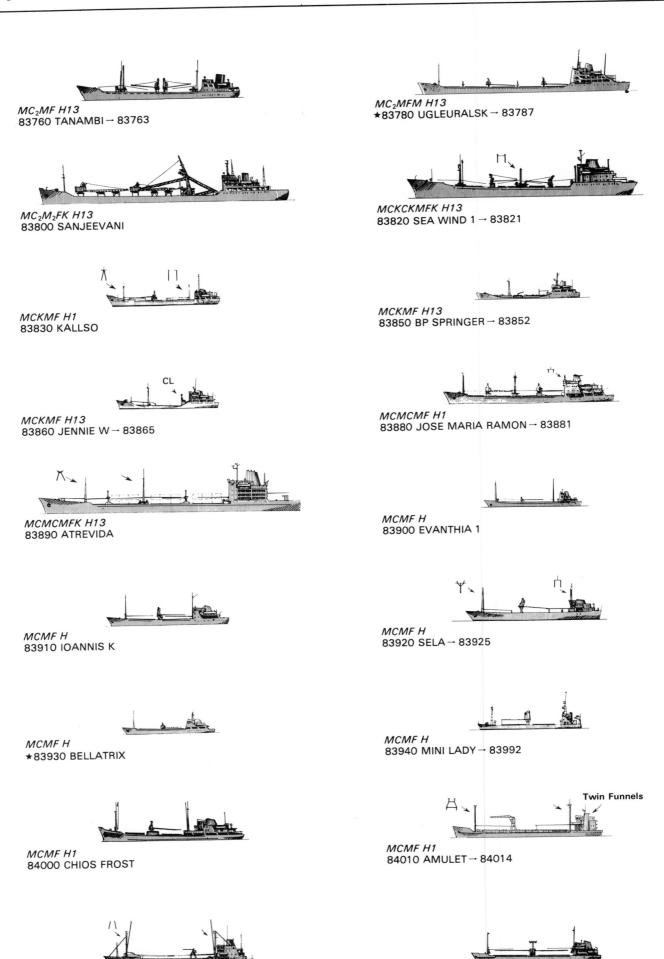

MC₂MF H13
83760 TANAMBI → 83763

MC₂MFM H13
★83780 UGLEURALSK → 83787

MC₂M₂FK H13
83800 SANJEEVANI

MCKCKMFK H13
83820 SEA WIND 1 → 83821

MCKMF H1
83830 KALLSO

MCKMF H13
83850 BP SPRINGER → 83852

MCKMF H13
83860 JENNIE W → 83865

MCMCMF H1
83880 JOSE MARIA RAMON → 83881

MCMCMFK H13
83890 ATREVIDA

MCMF H
83900 EVANTHIA 1

MCMF H
83910 IOANNIS K

MCMF H
83920 SELA → 83925

MCMF H
★83930 BELLATRIX

MCMF H
83940 MINI LADY → 83992

MCMF H1
84000 CHIOS FROST

MCMF H1
84010 AMULET → 84014

MCMF H1
84020 SAMSON SCAN → 84021

MCMF H1
84030 CELTIC CRUSADER

MCMF H1
84040 SEVEN → 84041

Tripod

MCMF H1
84050 MARINE PACKER

MCMF H1
84060 PEP REGULUS → 84064

Twin Funnels

MCMF H1
84070 ARNAFELL → 84080

MCMF H1
84090 SINGULARITY

MCMF H1
84100 NAWAF → 84101

MCMF H1
84110 LUN SHAN → 84113

MCMF H1
84120 MARINA

CL

MCMF H13
84130 NIAGA XXVIII → 84131

MCMF H13
84140 DON NICKY

CL

MCMF H13
★84150 BALKHASH → 84152

MCMF H13
84160 LIBEXCEL

MCMF H13
84170 LUN SHAN → 84173

CL

MCMF H13
84180 FOLGOET → 84185

MCMF H13
84190 MARIVERDA IV → 84194

MCMF H13
84200 IVORY

CL

MCMF H13
★84210 GALATA → 84213

Twin Funnels

MCM₂F H3
84220 CARIB SUN

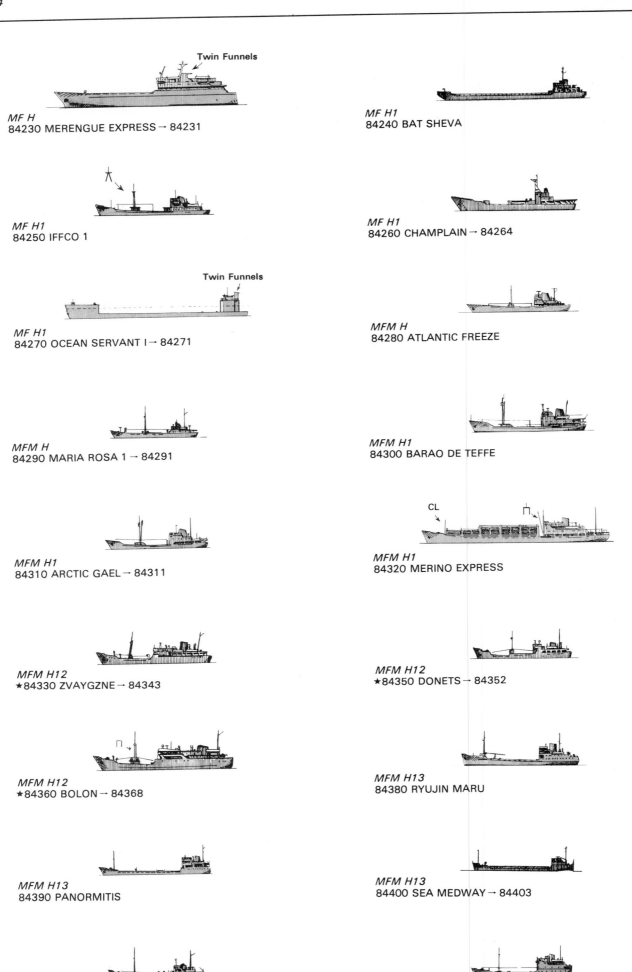

MF H
84230 MERENGUE EXPRESS → 84231

MF H1
84240 BAT SHEVA

MF H1
84250 IFFCO 1

MF H1
84260 CHAMPLAIN → 84264

MF H1
84270 OCEAN SERVANT I → 84271

MFM H
84280 ATLANTIC FREEZE

MFM H
84290 MARIA ROSA 1 → 84291

MFM H1
84300 BARAO DE TEFFE

MFM H1
84310 ARCTIC GAEL → 84311

MFM H1
84320 MERINO EXPRESS

MFM H12
★84330 ZVAYGZNE → 84343

MFM H12
★84350 DONETS → 84352

MFM H12
★84360 BOLON → 84368

MFM H13
84380 RYUJIN MARU

MFM H13
84390 PANORMITIS

MFM H13
84400 SEA MEDWAY → 84403

MFM H13
84410 PALMAIOLA

MFM H13
84420 ALKYON

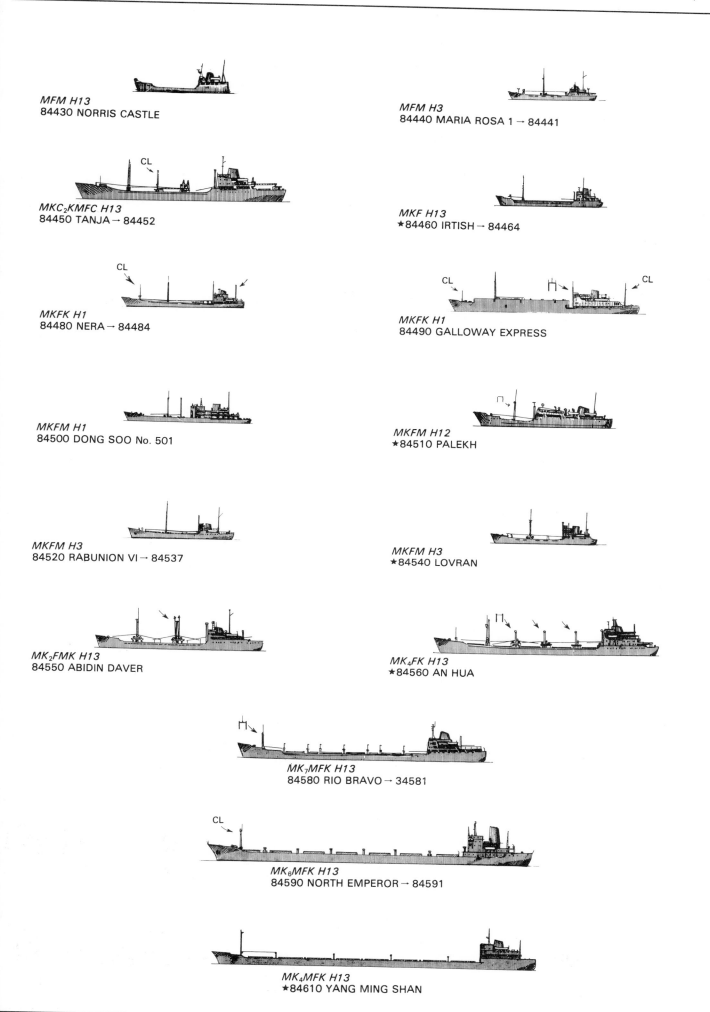

MFM H13
84430 NORRIS CASTLE

MFM H3
84440 MARIA ROSA 1 → 84441

MKC₂KMFC H13
84450 TANJA → 84452

MKF H13
★84460 IRTISH → 84464

MKFK H1
84480 NERA → 84484

MKFK H1
84490 GALLOWAY EXPRESS

MKFM H1
84500 DONG SOO No. 501

MKFM H12
★84510 PALEKH

MKFM H3
84520 RABUNION VI → 84537

MKFM H3
★84540 LOVRAN

MK₂FMK H13
84550 ABIDIN DAVER

MK₄FK H13
★84560 AN HUA

MK₇MFK H13
84580 RIO BRAVO → 34581

MK₆MFK H13
84590 NORTH EMPEROR → 84591

MK₄MFK H13
★84610 YANG MING SHAN

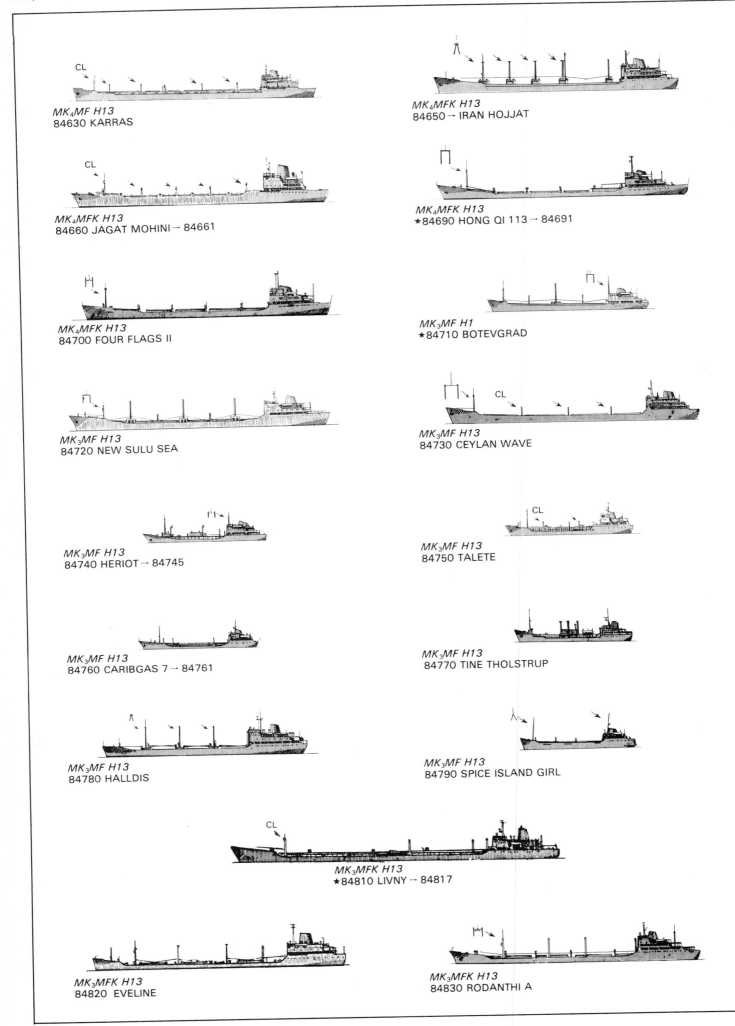

MK₄MF H13
84630 KARRAS

MK₄MFK H13
84650 → IRAN HOJJAT

MK₄MFK H13
84660 JAGAT MOHINI → 84661

MK₄MFK H13
★84690 HONG QI 113 → 84691

MK₄MFK H13
84700 FOUR FLAGS II

MK₃MF H1
★84710 BOTEVGRAD

MK₃MF H13
84720 NEW SULU SEA

MK₃MF H13
84730 CEYLAN WAVE

MK₃MF H13
84740 HERIOT → 84745

MK₃MF H13
84750 TALETE

MK₃MF H13
84760 CARIBGAS 7 → 84761

MK₃MF H13
84770 TINE THOLSTRUP

MK₃MF H13
84780 HALLDIS

MK₃MF H13
84790 SPICE ISLAND GIRL

MK₃MFK H13
★84810 LIVNY → 84817

MK₃MFK H13
84820 EVELINE

MK₃MFK H13
84830 RODANTHI A

MK₃MFK H13
84840 HADIOTIS

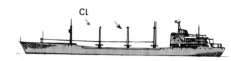

MK₃MFK H13
84850 DAVID SALMAN

MK₃MFK H13
84860 AL KAHERAH

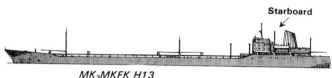

MK₃MKFK H13
★84870 LENINABAD → 84871

MK₂MF H
★84880 CAPITAN OLO PANTOJA→84881

MK₂MF H1
84900 STUDLAFOSS

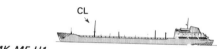

MK₂MF H1
84910 OTELIA → 84914

MK₂MF H13
84920 CANAIMA → 84921

MK₂MF H13
84930 ZINGARA → 84935

MK₂MF H13
★84940 OELSA → 84944

MK₂MF H13
84950 HERIOT → 84955

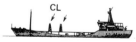

MK₂MF H13
84960 SULFURICO → 84963

MK₂MF H13
84970 SILVERMERLIN → 84971

MK₂MF H13
84980 PASS OF CAIRNWELL → 84981

MK₂MF H13
84990 CAP FALCONE → 84991

MK₂MF H13
85000 KIRSTEN THOLSTRUP → 85002

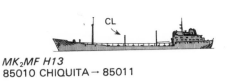

MK₂MF H13
85010 CHIQUITA → 85011

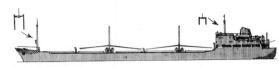

MK₂MFK H13
85030 PALMEA

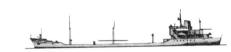

MK₂MFK H13
85050 PATROKLOS 1 → 85051

MK₂MFK H13
85060 FENG SHENG

MK₂MFK H13
85070 UM EL FAROUD → 85072

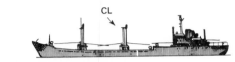

MK₂MFK H13
85080 KHADER WALI → 85081

MKMF H
85100 SETE CIDADES → 85101

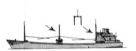

MKMF H
85110 VILI

MKMF H
85130 LONE TERKOL

MKMF H
85150 SELAT MAKASSAR → 85151

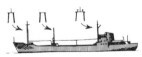

MKMF H1
★85170 BOTEVGRAD → 85171

MKMF H1
85180 SETE CIDADES → 85181

MKMF H1
85190 FIVE FLOWERS → 85191

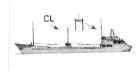

MKMF H1
85200 JVONNE

MKMF H1
85210 JUMBO JOIST

MKMF H1
85220 ALEXANDER → 85221

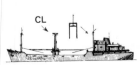

MKMF H1
85230 IBN JUBAIR → 85233

MKMF H1
85240 SALEH 2 → 85241

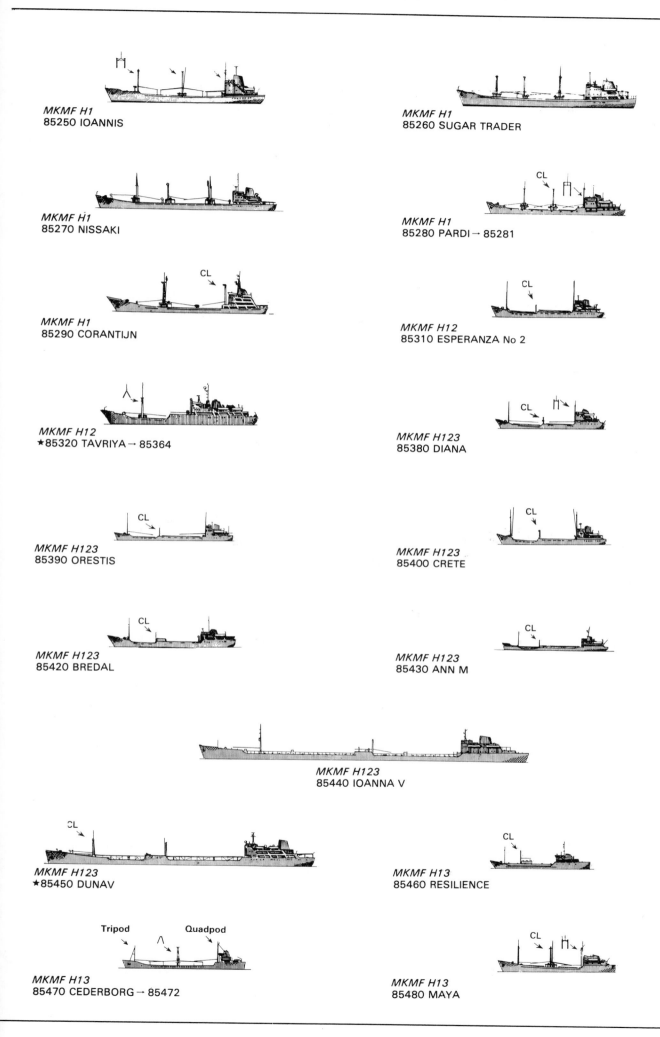

MKMF H1
85250 IOANNIS

MKMF H1
85260 SUGAR TRADER

MKMF H1
85270 NISSAKI

MKMF H1
85280 PARDI → 85281

MKMF H1
85290 CORANTIJN

MKMF H12
85310 ESPERANZA No 2

MKMF H12
★85320 TAVRIYA → 85364

MKMF H123
85380 DIANA

MKMF H123
85390 ORESTIS

MKMF H123
85400 CRETE

MKMF H123
85420 BREDAL

MKMF H123
85430 ANN M

MKMF H123
85440 IOANNA V

MKMF H123
★85450 DUNAV

MKMF H13
85460 RESILIENCE

Tripod Quadpod

MKMF H13
85470 CEDERBORG → 85472

MKMF H13
85480 MAYA

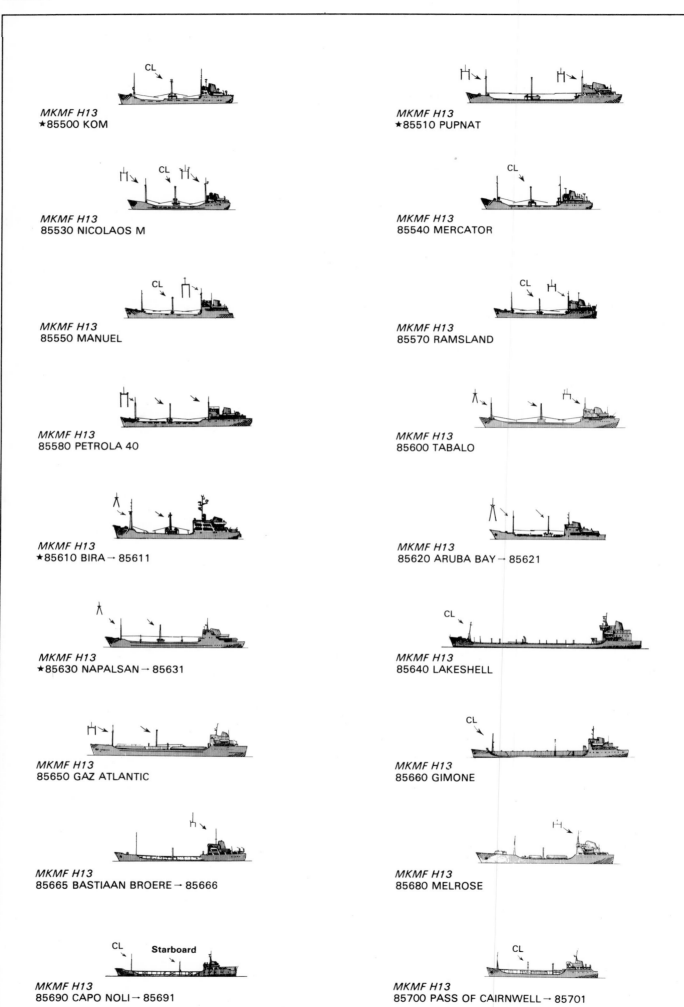

MKMF H13
★85500 KOM

MKMF H13
★85510 PUPNAT

MKMF H13
85530 NICOLAOS M

MKMF H13
85540 MERCATOR

MKMF H13
85550 MANUEL

MKMF H13
85570 RAMSLAND

MKMF H13
85580 PETROLA 40

MKMF H13
85600 TABALO

MKMF H13
★85610 BIRA → 85611

MKMF H13
85620 ARUBA BAY → 85621

MKMF H13
★85630 NAPALSAN → 85631

MKMF H13
85640 LAKESHELL

MKMF H13
85650 GAZ ATLANTIC

MKMF H13
85660 GIMONE

MKMF H13
85665 BASTIAAN BROERE → 85666

MKMF H13
85680 MELROSE

MKMF H13
85690 CAPO NOLI → 85691

MKMF H13
85700 PASS OF CAIRNWELL → 85701

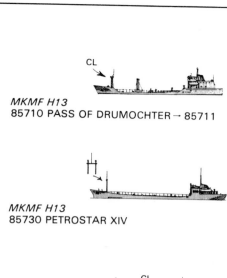

MKMF H13
85710 PASS OF DRUMOCHTER → 85711

MKMF H13
85720 JOHN WILSON

MKMF H13
85730 PETROSTAR XIV

MKMF H13
85740 DALAVIK

MKMF H13
85750 HALLIBURTON 602

MKMF H13
85760 REDO

MKMF H13
85770 AL BACHIR

MKMF H13
85780 DOLPHIN II → 85782

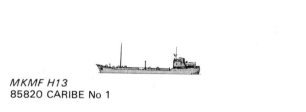

MKMF H13
85790 ORYX → 85791

MKMF H13
85810 RIO GRANDE

MKMF H13
85820 CARIBE No 1

MKMF H13
85840 HAR7

MKMF H13
85850 IVO DORMIO

MKMF H13
85860 BETTY THERESA

MKMF H13
85870 JENNIE W → 85875

MKMF H13
★85880 KLYAZMA → 85890

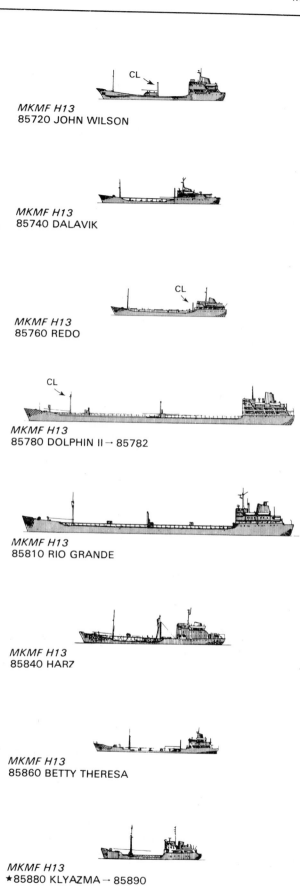
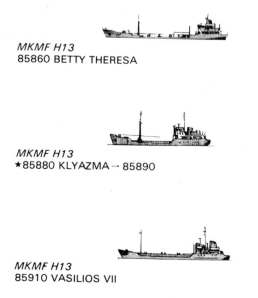

MKMF H13
85900 ROCAS

MKMF H13
85910 VASILIOS VII

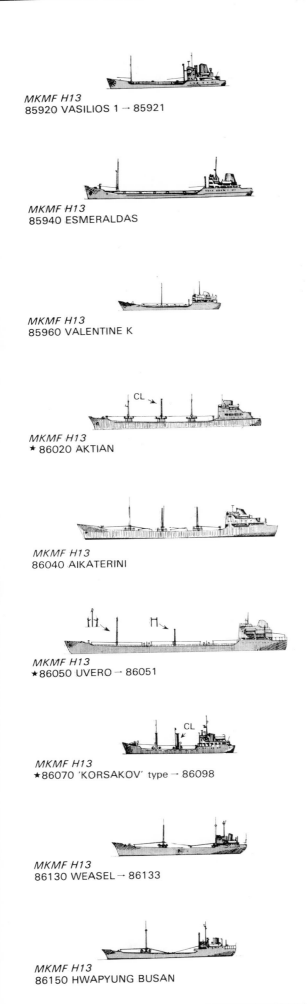

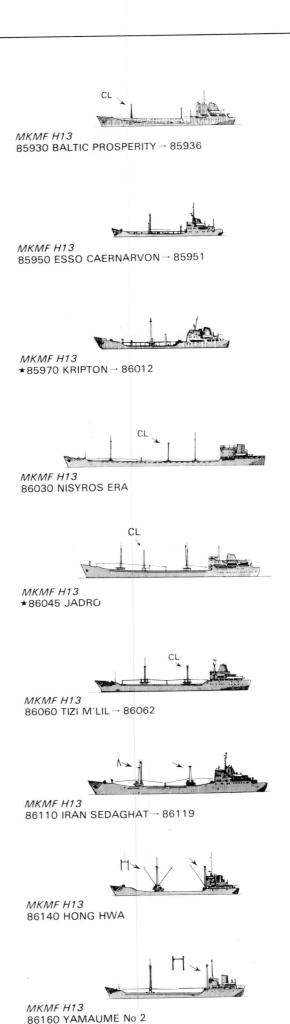

MKMF H13
85920 VASILIOS 1 → 85921

MKMF H13
85930 BALTIC PROSPERITY → 85936

MKMF H13
85940 ESMERALDAS

MKMF H13
85950 ESSO CAERNARVON → 85951

MKMF H13
85960 VALENTINE K

MKMF H13
★85970 KRIPTON → 86012

MKMF H13
★ 86020 AKTIAN

MKMF H13
86030 NISYROS ERA

MKMF H13
86040 AIKATERINI

MKMF H13
★86045 JADRO

MKMF H13
★86050 UVERO → 86051

MKMF H13
86060 TIZI M'LIL → 86062

MKMF H13
★86070 'KORSAKOV' type → 86098

MKMF H13
86110 IRAN SEDAGHAT → 86119

MKMF H13
86130 WEASEL → 86133

MKMF H13
86140 HONG HWA

MKMF H13
86150 HWAPYUNG BUSAN

MKMF H13
86160 YAMAUME No 2

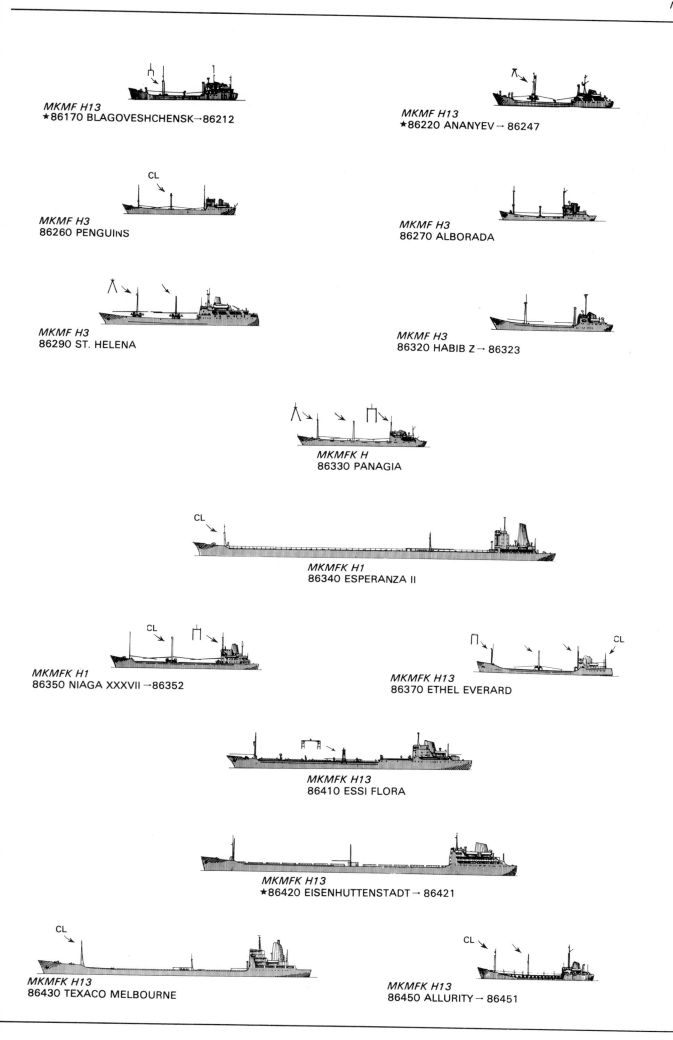

MKMF H13
★86170 BLAGOVESHCHENSK→86212

MKMF H13
★86220 ANANYEV → 86247

MKMF H3
86260 PENGUINS

MKMF H3
86270 ALBORADA

MKMF H3
86290 ST. HELENA

MKMF H3
86320 HABIB Z → 86323

MKMFK H
86330 PANAGIA

MKMFK H1
86340 ESPERANZA II

MKMFK H1
86350 NIAGA XXXVII →86352

MKMFK H13
86370 ETHEL EVERARD

MKMFK H13
86410 ESSI FLORA

MKMFK H13
★86420 EISENHUTTENSTADT → 86421

MKMFK H13
86430 TEXACO MELBOURNE

MKMFK H13
86450 ALLURITY → 86451

MKMFK H13
86460 ALICIA 1 → 86461

MKMFK H13
★86470 KEGUMS → 86471

MKMFK H13
86480 BENITO JUAREZ → 86488

MKMFK H13
86500 PETROSTAR XVI

MKMFK H13
86510 PETROSTAR III

MKMFK H13
★86520 POMORAVLJE → 86523

MKMFK H13
86530 TSIMISARAKA

MKMFK H13
★86540 OZERNOYE → 86544

MKMFK H13
86550 IONIAN PRINCESS

MKMFK H13
86560 ISORA

MKMFK H13
86570 KORFOS 1

MKMFK H13
86590 ESSO CAERNARVON → 86591

MKMFK H13
86600 DOUGGA → 86601

MKMFK H13
86610 O DAE YANG No 106 → 86612

MKMFK H13
86620 HAI MING

MKMFK H13
86630 NIPPONHAM MARU No 1 → 86631

MKMKF H13
★86640 LU DING

MKMKF H13
86650 RIO GRANDE

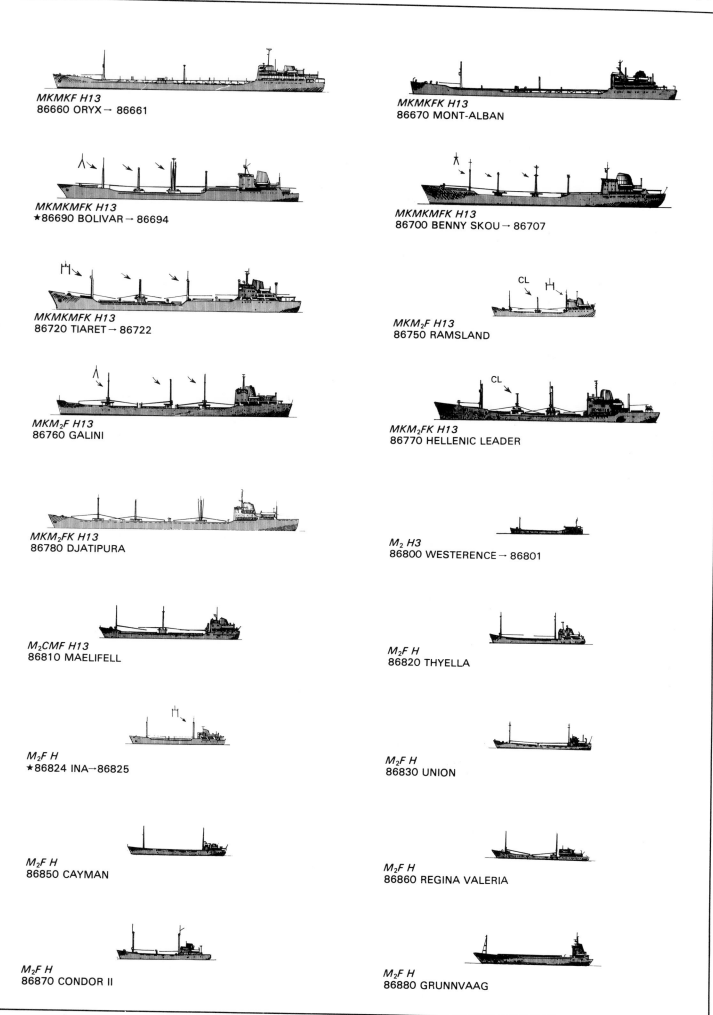

MKMKF H13
86660 ORYX → 86661

MKMKFK H13
86670 MONT-ALBAN

MKMKMFK H13
★86690 BOLIVAR → 86694

MKMKMFK H13
86700 BENNY SKOU → 86707

MKMKMFK H13
86720 TIARET → 86722

MKM₂F H13
86750 RAMSLAND

MKM₂F H13
86760 GALINI

MKM₂FK H13
86770 HELLENIC LEADER

MKM₂FK H13
86780 DJATIPURA

M₂ H3
86800 WESTERENCE → 86801

M₂CMF H13
86810 MAELIFELL

M₂F H
86820 THYELLA

M₂F H
★86824 INA → 86825

M₂F H
86830 UNION

M₂F H
86850 CAYMAN

M₂F H
86860 REGINA VALERIA

M₂F H
86870 CONDOR II

M₂F H
86880 GRUNNVAAG

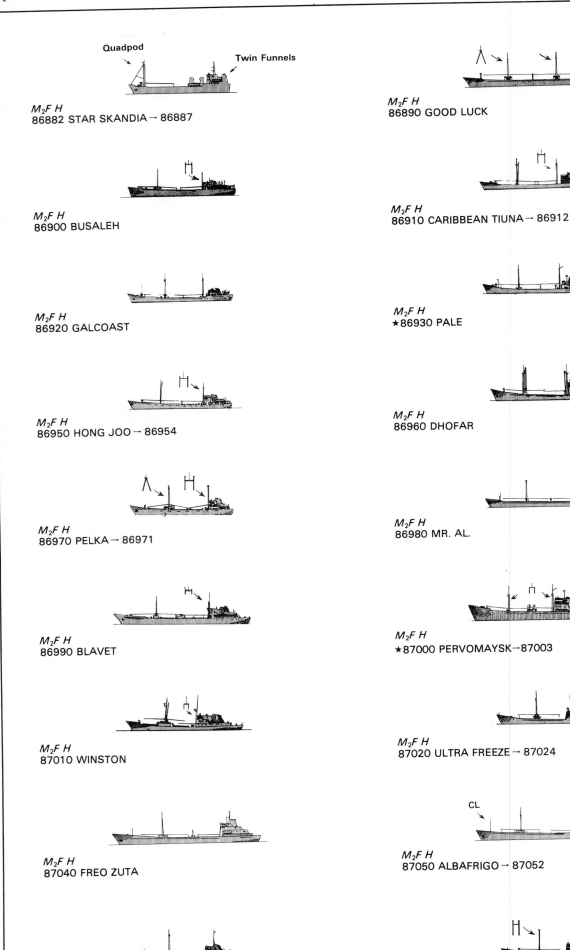

Quadpod

Twin Funnels

M₂F H
86882 STAR SKANDIA → 86887

M₂F H
86890 GOOD LUCK

M₂F H
86900 BUSALEH

M₂F H
86910 CARIBBEAN TIUNA → 86912

M₂F H
86920 GALCOAST

M₂F H
★86930 PALE

M₂F H
86950 HONG JOO → 86954

M₂F H
86960 DHOFAR

M₂F H
86970 PELKA → 86971

M₂F H
86980 MR. AL.

M₂F H
86990 BLAVET

M₂F H
★87000 PERVOMAYSK → 87003

M₂F H
87010 WINSTON

M₂F H
87020 ULTRA FREEZE → 87024

CL

M₂F H
87040 FREO ZUTA

M₂F H
87050 ALBAFRIGO → 87052

M₂F H
87060 AGIOS NEKTARIOS

M₂F H
87070 BLUE MOON → 87071

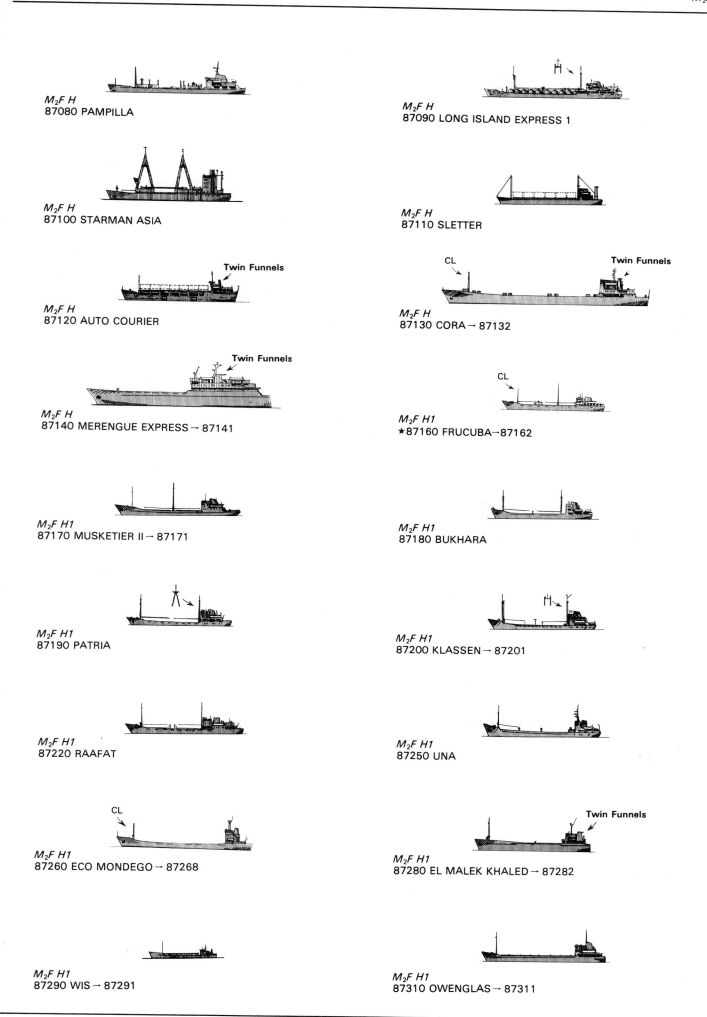

M₂F H
87080 PAMPILLA

M₂F H
87090 LONG ISLAND EXPRESS 1

M₂F H
87100 STARMAN ASIA

M₂F H
87110 SLETTER

M₂F H
87120 AUTO COURIER

Twin Funnels

CL   Twin Funnels

M₂F H
87130 CORA → 87132

Twin Funnels

M₂F H
87140 MERENGUE EXPRESS → 87141

CL

M₂F H1
★87160 FRUCUBA→87162

M₂F H1
87170 MUSKETIER II → 87171

M₂F H1
87180 BUKHARA

M₂F H1
87190 PATRIA

M₂F H1
87200 KLASSEN → 87201

M₂F H1
87220 RAAFAT

M₂F H1
87250 UNA

CL

M₂F H1
87260 ECO MONDEGO → 87268

Twin Funnels

M₂F H1
87280 EL MALEK KHALED → 87282

M₂F H1
87290 WIS → 87291

M₂F H1
87310 OWENGLAS → 87311

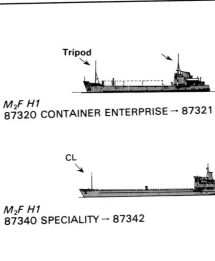

M₂F H1
87320 CONTAINER ENTERPRISE → 87321

M₂F H1
87330 LINDE → 87331

M₂F H1
87340 SPECIALITY → 87342

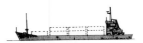

M₂F H1
87350 MIRAMAR → 87353

M₂F H1
87360 SEA FREIGHTLINER I → 87361

M₂F H1
87370 KUWAIT → 87371

M₂F H1
87380 SIN HOCK CHEW

M₂F H1
87390 PANTANASSA → 87391

M₂F H1
87400 FRIO DOLPHIN

M₂F H1
87410 ANGSA MAS

M₂F H1
87420 AMAZON TRADER → 87426

M₂F H1
87450 NAGINA

M₂F H1
★87470 ZHAN DOU 59 → 87471

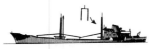

M₂F H1
87480 M.A. ULUSOY → 87485

M₂F H1
87500 FRIGO ISABEL

M₂F H1
★87505 LAS MERCEDES

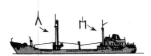

M₂F H1
87510 CAMARGO

M₂F H1
87520 ALEJANDRA G

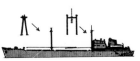

M₂F H1
87530 OCEAN FREEZE

M₂F H1
87450 ZENITH

M₂F H1
87550 MALIANO → 87553

M₂F H1
87560 AGROTAI

M₂F H1
87570 PUERTO DE CHACABUCO → 87572

M₂F H1
87580 MARIMAR

M₂F H1
87590 BATIK

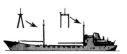

M₂F H1
87600 PELIKI

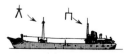

M₂F H1
87610 AGIOS NIKOLAOS → 87611

M₂F H1
★87620 FUNDADOR

M₂F H1
87630 SELE

M₂F H1
★87640 BEGA → 87643

M₂F H1
87650 CIVRA

M₂F H1
87660 PLAYA DE MASPALOMAS → 87661

M₂F H1
87670 URSULA → 87674

M₂F H1
87680 JACARANDA

M₂F H1
87690 FIVE RIVERS → 87694

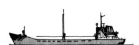

M₂F H1
87700 SCHILDMEER → 87705

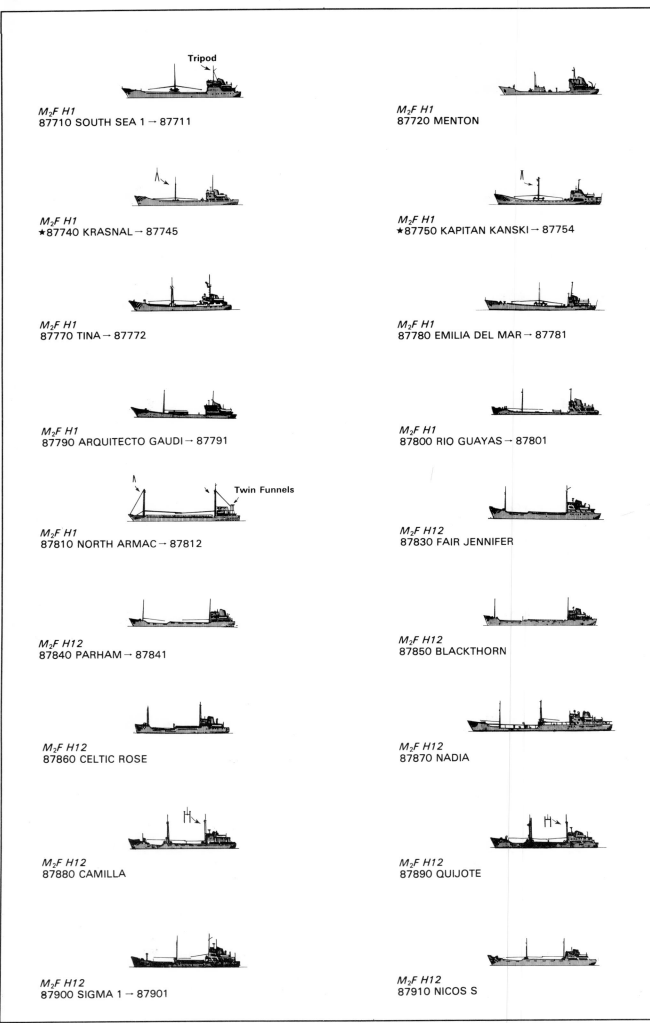

M₂F H1
87710 SOUTH SEA 1 → 87711

M₂F H1
87720 MENTON

M₂F H1
★87740 KRASNAL → 87745

M₂F H1
★87750 KAPITAN KANSKI → 87754

M₂F H1
87770 TINA → 87772

M₂F H1
87780 EMILIA DEL MAR → 87781

M₂F H1
87790 ARQUITECTO GAUDI → 87791

M₂F H1
87800 RIO GUAYAS → 87801

M₂F H1
87810 NORTH ARMAC → 87812

M₂F H12
87830 FAIR JENNIFER

M₂F H12
87840 PARHAM → 87841

M₂F H12
87850 BLACKTHORN

M₂F H12
87860 CELTIC ROSE

M₂F H12
87870 NADIA

M₂F H12
87880 CAMILLA

M₂F H12
87890 QUIJOTE

M₂F H12
87900 SIGMA 1 → 87901

M₂F H12
87910 NICOS S

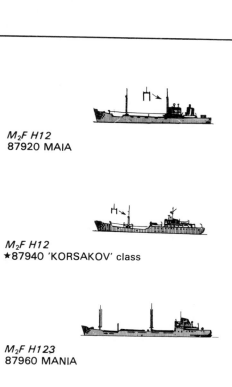

M₂F H12
87920 MAIA

M₂F H12
87930 DE HOOP

M₂F H12
★87940 'KORSAKOV' class

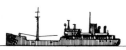

M₂F H12
★87950 ZVAYGZNE

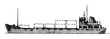

M₂F H123
87960 MANIA

M₂F H123
87980 FYLRIX

M₂F H123
87990 PARHAM → 87991

M₂F H123
88000 BRENDONIA → 88003

M₂F H123
88010 DENTON VENTURE

M₂F H123
88020 CHIOS AEINAFTIS

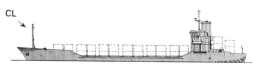

M₂F H123
88030 NIKE → 88031

M₂F H123
88040 ORPENA

M₂F H123
88050 SAINT AIDAN

M₂F H123
88080 SULTANA 1

M₂F H13
88090 IVOR → 88091

M₂F H13
88100 EVE → 88109

M₂F H13
88110 JENNY → 88115

M₂F H13
88120 KARIN

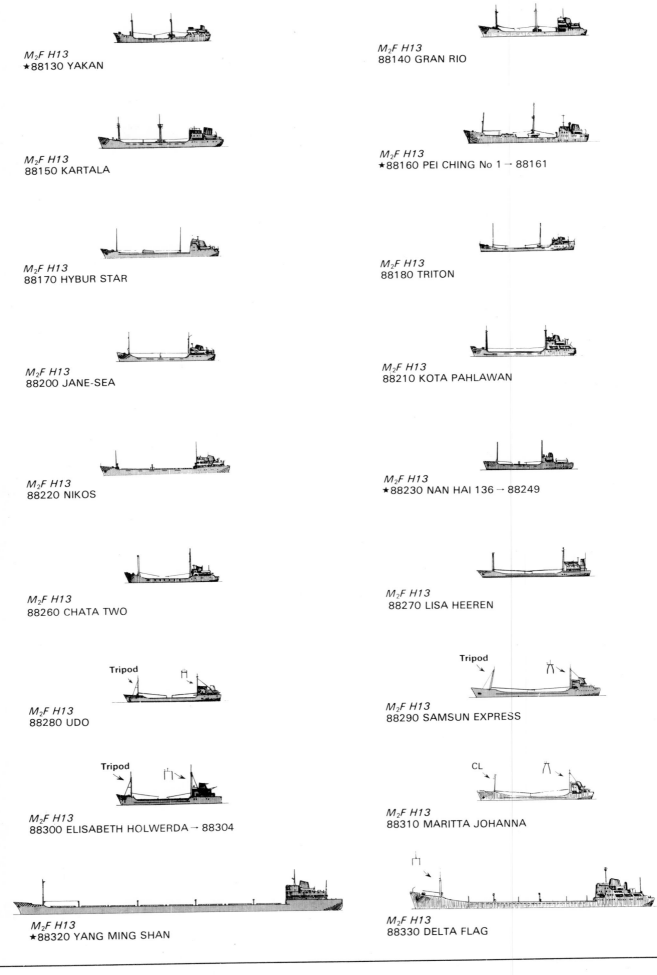

M₂F H13
★88130 YAKAN

M₂F H13
88140 GRAN RIO

M₂F H13
88150 KARTALA

M₂F H13
★88160 PEI CHING No 1 → 88161

M₂F H13
88170 HYBUR STAR

M₂F H13
88180 TRITON

M₂F H13
88200 JANE-SEA

M₂F H13
88210 KOTA PAHLAWAN

M₂F H13
88220 NIKOS

M₂F H13
★88230 NAN HAI 136 → 88249

M₂F H13
88260 CHATA TWO

M₂F H13
88270 LISA HEEREN

M₂F H13
88280 UDO

Tripod

M₂F H13
88290 SAMSUN EXPRESS

Tripod

M₂F H13
88300 ELISABETH HOLWERDA → 88304

Tripod

M₂F H13
88310 MARITTA JOHANNA

CL

M₂F H13
★88320 YANG MING SHAN

M₂F H13
88330 DELTA FLAG

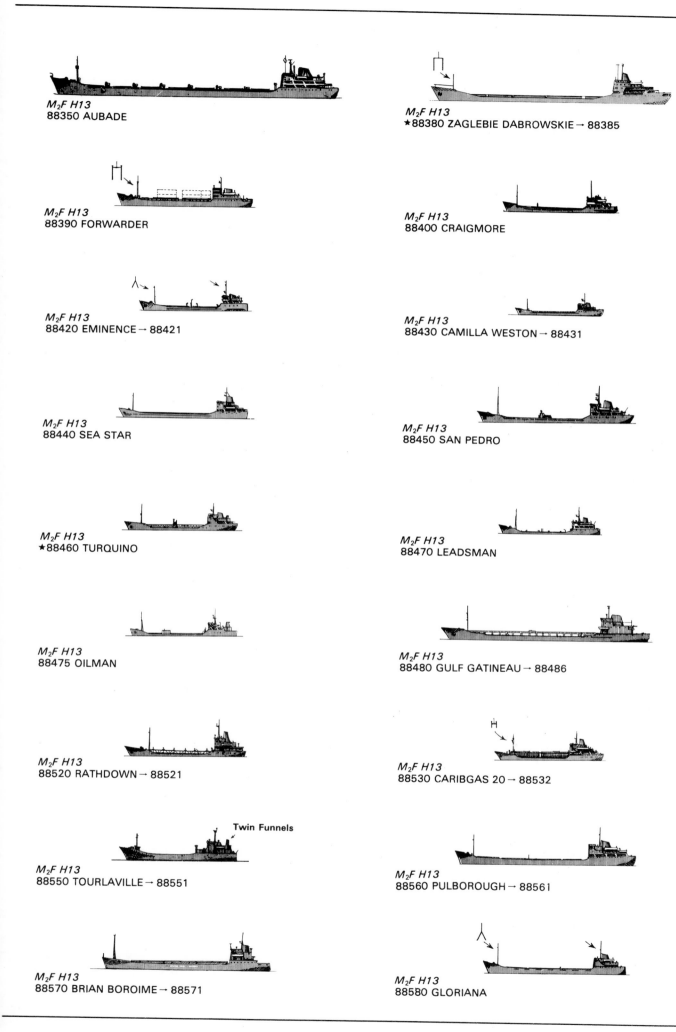

M₂F H13
88350 AUBADE

M₂F H13
★88380 ZAGLEBIE DABROWSKIE → 88385

M₂F H13
88390 FORWARDER

M₂F H13
88400 CRAIGMORE

M₂F H13
88420 EMINENCE → 88421

M₂F H13
88430 CAMILLA WESTON → 88431

M₂F H13
88440 SEA STAR

M₂F H13
88450 SAN PEDRO

M₂F H13
★88460 TURQUINO

M₂F H13
88470 LEADSMAN

M₂F H13
88475 OILMAN

M₂F H13
88480 GULF GATINEAU → 88486

M₂F H13
88520 RATHDOWN → 88521

M₂F H13
88530 CARIBGAS 20 → 88532

Twin Funnels

M₂F H13
88550 TOURLAVILLE → 88551

M₂F H13
88560 PULBOROUGH → 88561

M₂F H13
88570 BRIAN BOROIME → 88571

M₂F H13
88580 GLORIANA

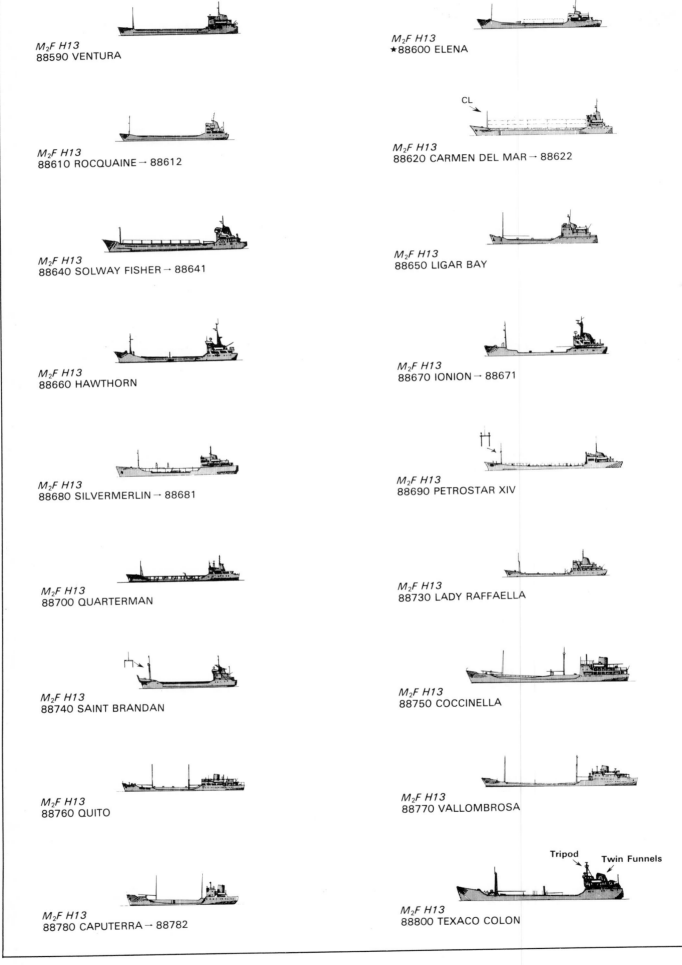

M₂F H13
88590 VENTURA

M₂F H13
★88600 ELENA

M₂F H13
88610 ROCQUAINE → 88612

CL

M₂F H13
88620 CARMEN DEL MAR → 88622

M₂F H13
88640 SOLWAY FISHER → 88641

M₂F H13
88650 LIGAR BAY

M₂F H13
88660 HAWTHORN

M₂F H13
88670 IONION → 88671

M₂F H13
88680 SILVERMERLIN → 88681

M₂F H13
88690 PETROSTAR XIV

M₂F H13
88700 QUARTERMAN

M₂F H13
88730 LADY RAFFAELLA

M₂F H13
88740 SAINT BRANDAN

M₂F H13
88750 COCCINELLA

M₂F H13
88760 QUITO

M₂F H13
88770 VALLOMBROSA

Tripod   Twin Funnels

M₂F H13
88780 CAPUTERRA → 88782

M₂F H13
88800 TEXACO COLON

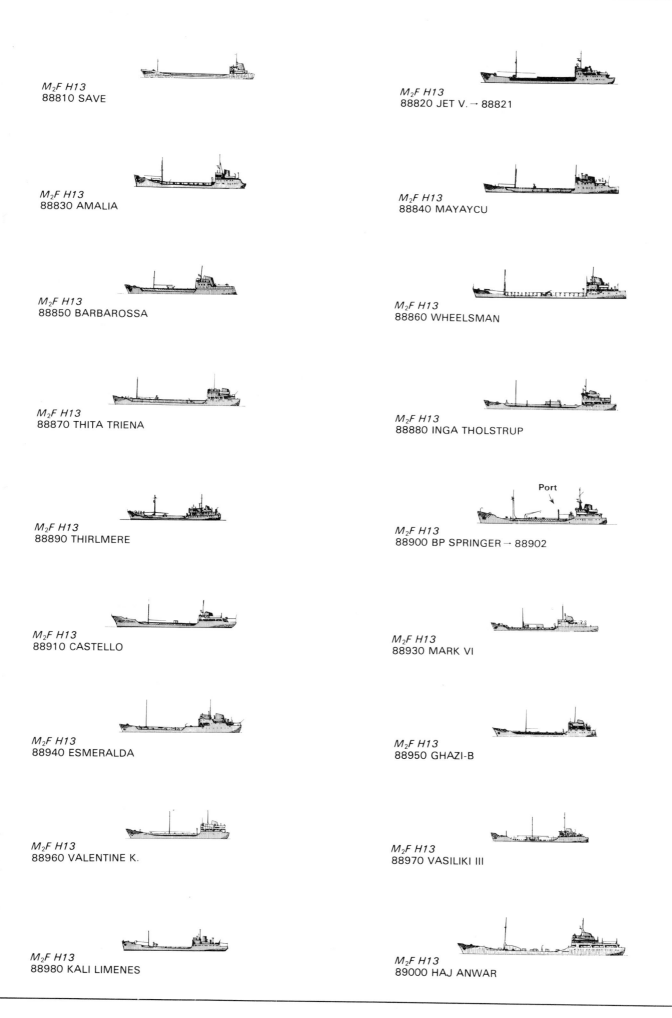

M₂F H13
88810 SAVE

M₂F H13
88820 JET V. → 88821

M₂F H13
88830 AMALIA

M₂F H13
88840 MAYAYCU

M₂F H13
88850 BARBAROSSA

M₂F H13
88860 WHEELSMAN

M₂F H13
88870 THITA TRIENA

M₂F H13
88880 INGA THOLSTRUP

M₂F H13
88890 THIRLMERE

M₂F H13
88900 BP SPRINGER → 88902

M₂F H13
88910 CASTELLO

M₂F H13
88930 MARK VI

M₂F H13
88940 ESMERALDA

M₂F H13
88950 GHAZI-B

M₂F H13
88960 VALENTINE K.

M₂F H13
88970 VASILIKI III

M₂F H13
88980 KALI LIMENES

M₂F H13
89000 HAJ ANWAR

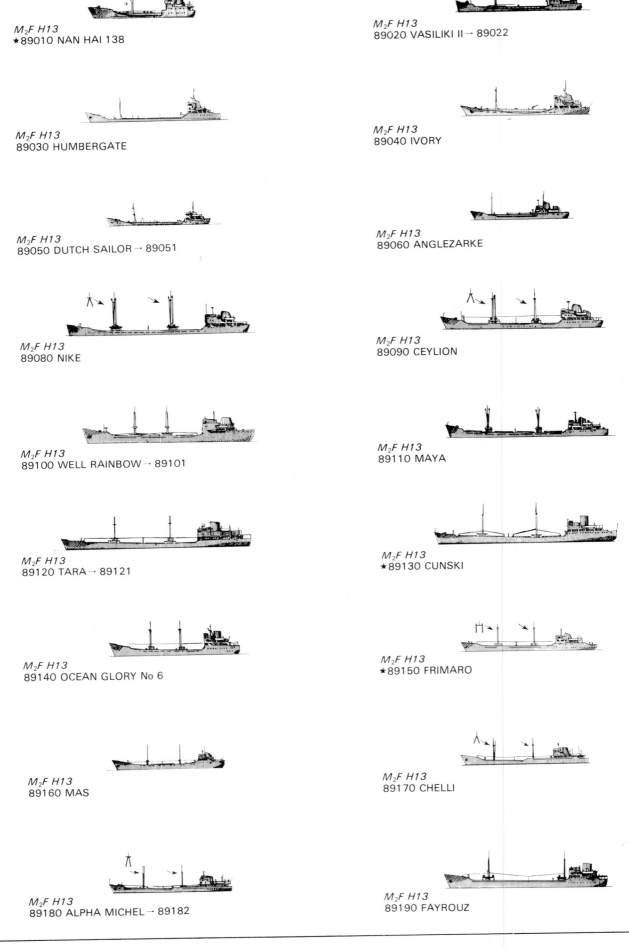

M₂F H13
★89010 NAN HAI 138

M₂F H13
89020 VASILIKI II → 89022

M₂F H13
89030 HUMBERGATE

M₂F H13
89040 IVORY

M₂F H13
89050 DUTCH SAILOR → 89051

M₂F H13
89060 ANGLEZARKE

M₂F H13
89080 NIKE

M₂F H13
89090 CEYLION

M₂F H13
89100 WELL RAINBOW → 89101

M₂F H13
89110 MAYA

M₂F H13
89120 TARA → 89121

M₂F H13
★89130 CUNSKI

M₂F H13
89140 OCEAN GLORY No 6

M₂F H13
★89150 FRIMARO

M₂F H13
89160 MAS

M₂F H13
89170 CHELLI

M₂F H13
89180 ALPHA MICHEL → 89182

M₂F H13
89190 FAYROUZ

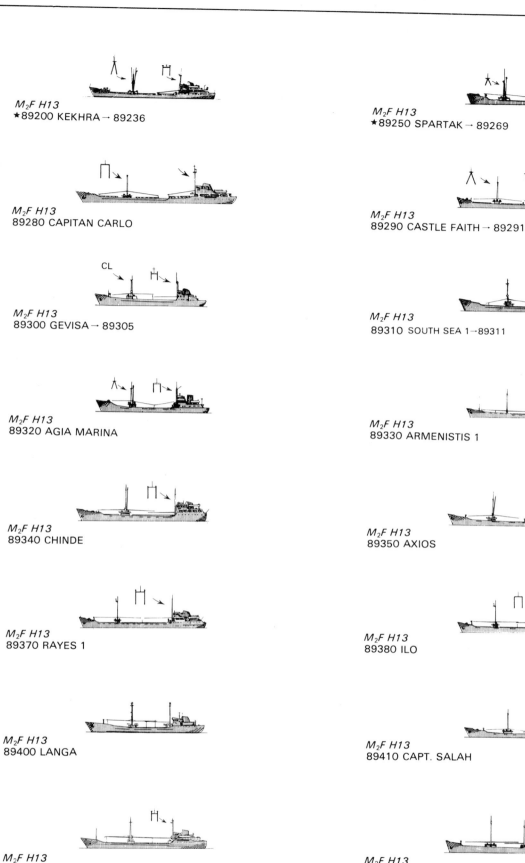

M₂F H13
★89200 KEKHRA → 89236

M₂F H13
★89250 SPARTAK → 89269

M₂F H13
89280 CAPITAN CARLO

M₂F H13
89290 CASTLE FAITH → 89291

M₂F H13
89300 GEVISA → 89305

M₂F H13
89310 SOUTH SEA 1→89311

M₂F H13
89320 AGIA MARINA

M₂F H13
89330 ARMENISTIS 1

M₂F H13
89340 CHINDE

M₂F H13
89350 AXIOS

M₂F H13
89370 RAYES 1

M₂F H13
89380 ILO

M₂F H13
89400 LANGA

M₂F H13
89410 CAPT. SALAH

M₂F H13
89420 ARANUI → 89422

M₂F H13
89430 CHERRY BAGUS

M₂F H13
89440 MAWAR

M₂F H13
89450 APOLLONIA VII

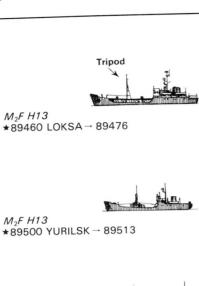

M₂F H13
★89460 LOKSA → 89476

M₂F H13
89490 ARAGONITE

M₂F H13
★89500 YURILSK → 89513

M₂F H13
89520 YUZBASI TOLUNAY

M₂F H13
89530 CARIBGAS DOS

M₂F H13
89550 UCANCA

M₂F H13
89560 BLUE MOON → 89561

M₂F H13
89570 NORTHERN

M₂F H13
89580 SAINT MITRE

M₂F H13
89590 FAIRLANE → 89591

M₂F H13
89600 GABRIELLA → 89602

M₂F H13
89610 DANIELLA

M₂F H13
89620 FAIRLIFT

M₂F H13
★89630 MOLUNAT

M₂F H13
89650 TROPIC STAR

M₂F H13
★89660 IVAN AIVAZOVSKIY

M₂F H13
89670 CHIKUMA MARU

M₂F H13
★89680 SEVERODVINSKIY · 89682

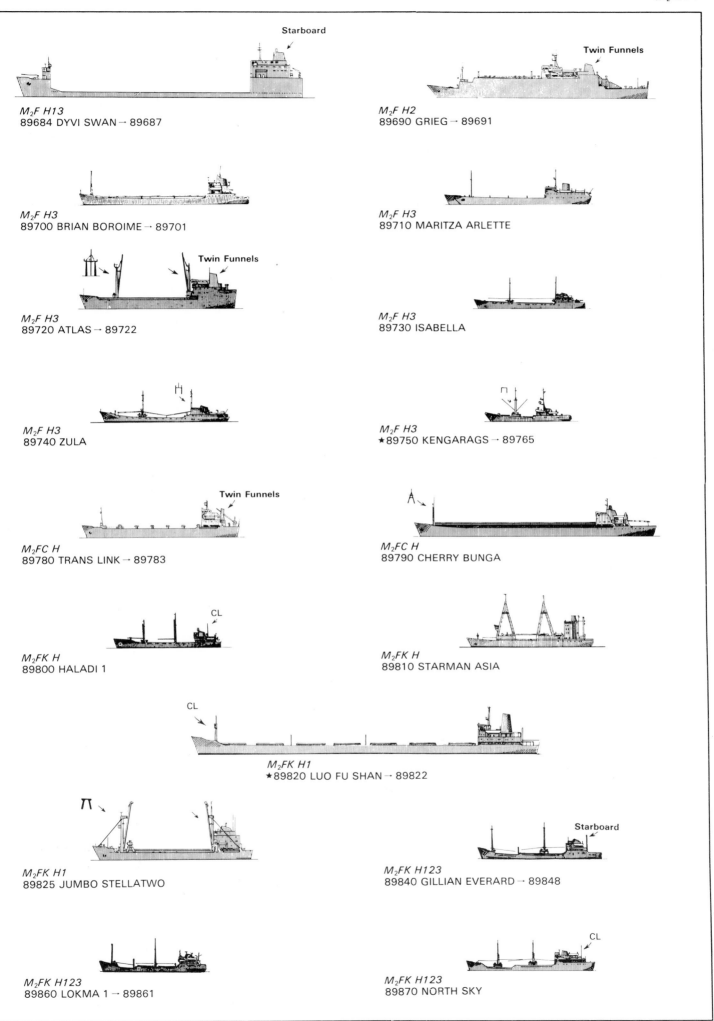

M₂F H13
89684 DYVI SWAN → 89687

M₂F H2
89690 GRIEG → 89691

M₂F H3
89700 BRIAN BOROIME → 89701

M₂F H3
89710 MARITZA ARLETTE

M₂F H3
89720 ATLAS → 89722

M₂F H3
89730 ISABELLA

M₂F H3
89740 ZULA

M₂F H3
★89750 KENGARAGS → 89765

M₂FC H
89780 TRANS LINK → 89783

M₂FC H
89790 CHERRY BUNGA

M₂FK H
89800 HALADI 1

M₂FK H
89810 STARMAN ASIA

M₂FK H1
★89820 LUO FU SHAN → 89822

M₂FK H1
89825 JUMBO STELLATWO

M₂FK H123
89840 GILLIAN EVERARD → 89848

M₂FK H123
89860 LOKMA 1 → 89861

M₂FK H123
89870 NORTH SKY

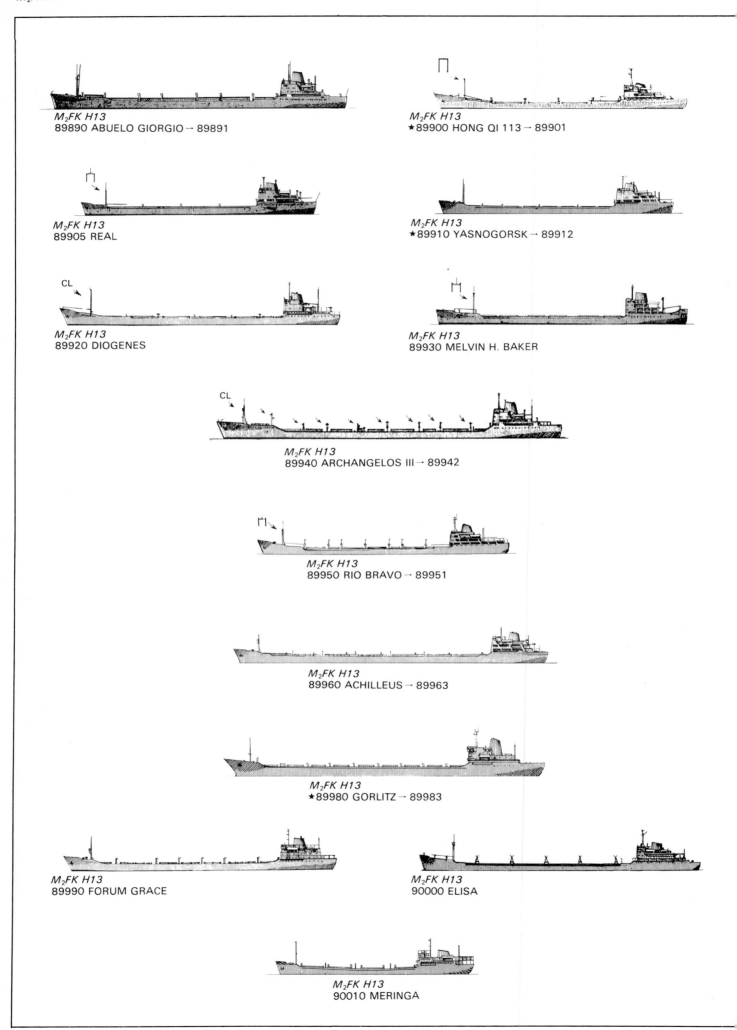

M₂FK H13
89890 ABUELO GIORGIO → 89891

M₂FK H13
★89900 HONG QI 113 → 89901

M₂FK H13
89905 REAL

M₂FK H13
★89910 YASNOGORSK → 89912

M₂FK H13
89920 DIOGENES

M₂FK H13
89930 MELVIN H. BAKER

M₂FK H13
89940 ARCHANGELOS III → 89942

M₂FK H13
89950 RIO BRAVO → 89951

M₂FK H13
89960 ACHILLEUS → 89963

M₂FK H13
★89980 GORLITZ → 89983

M₂FK H13
89990 FORUM GRACE

M₂FK H13
90000 ELISA

M₂FK H13
90010 MERINGA

M₂FK H13
90020 NORTH EMPEROR → 90021

M₂FK H13
★90030 'BALTIYSKIY' type

M₂FK H13
90060 CECILE ERICKSON

M₂FK H13
90070 ROCQUAINE → 90072

M₂FK H13
90080 BRIDGEMAN → 90081

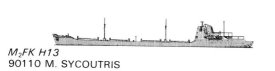

M₂FK H13
90090 VASILIKI V

M₂FK H13
90100 KOSMOS

M₂FK H13
90110 M. SYCOUTRIS

M₂FK H13
90120 JOHN M

Twin Funnels

M₂FK H13
90130 FRANK M → 90131

M₂FK H13
90140 ALACRITY

M₂FK H13
★90150 KUSTANAY → 90154

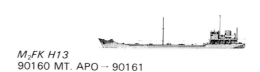

M₂FK H13
90160 MT. APO → 90161

M₂FK H13
90170 KEMAL KOLOTOGLU → 90171

M₂FK H13
★90175 SONG DO HO

Tripod

M₂FK H13
90180 MULTI SERVICE 125

M₂FK H13
★90190 YANA → 90101

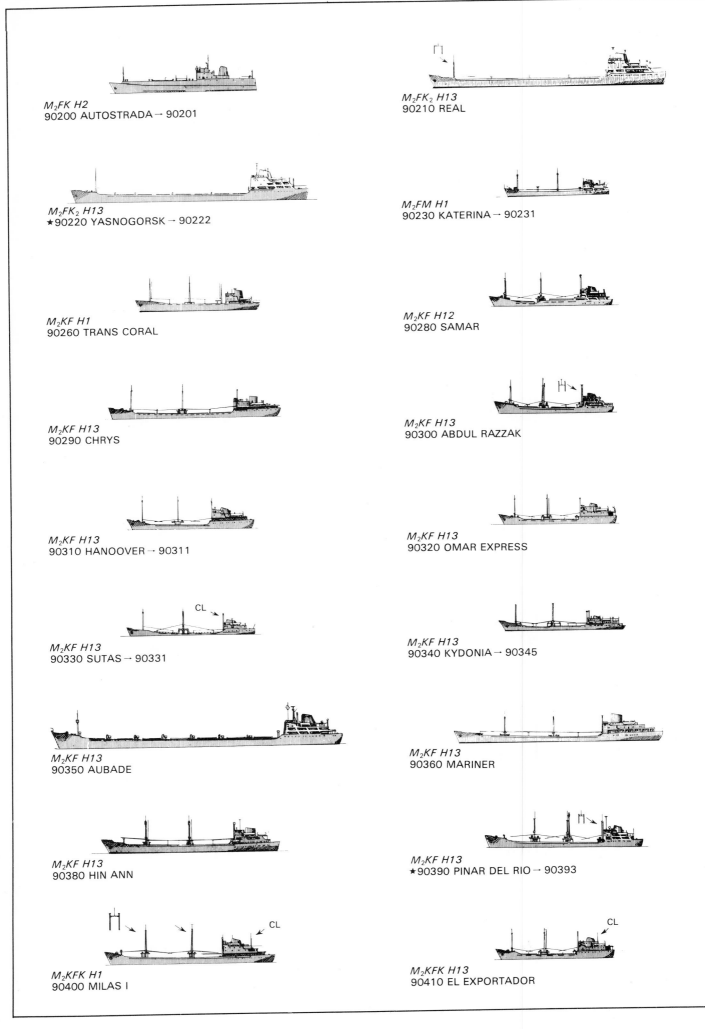

M₂FK H2
90200 AUTOSTRADA → 90201

M₂FK₂ H13
90210 REAL

M₂FK₂ H13
★90220 YASNOGORSK → 90222

M₂FM H1
90230 KATERINA → 90231

M₂KF H1
90260 TRANS CORAL

M₂KF H12
90280 SAMAR

M₂KF H13
90290 CHRYS

M₂KF H13
90300 ABDUL RAZZAK

M₂KF H13
90310 HANOOVER → 90311

M₂KF H13
90320 OMAR EXPRESS

M₂KF H13
90330 SUTAS → 90331

M₂KF H13
90340 KYDONIA → 90345

M₂KF H13
90350 AUBADE

M₂KF H13
90360 MARINER

M₂KF H13
90380 HIN ANN

M₂KF H13
★90390 PINAR DEL RIO → 90393

M₂KFK H1
90400 MILAS I

M₂KFK H13
90410 EL EXPORTADOR

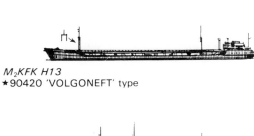

M₂KFK H13
★90420 'VOLGONEFT' type

M₂KFM H1
90450 MARATHON → 90454

M₂KFM H1
90470 KOTA BAHAGIA → 90472

M₂KFM H13
90480 KETTY

M₂KFM H13
90490 ARISTOTELIS → 90491

M₂K₂MFK H13
90500 ALPINA → 90501

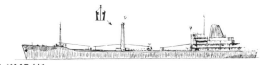

M₂KMF H1
★90510 DA LONG TIAN → 90515

M₂KMF H1
90520 MOTHI

M₂KMF H1
90530 ZSA ZSA → 90536

M₂KMF H1
90550 GOLDEN WAVE → 90551

M₂KMF H13
★90560 MEZENLES → 90564

M₂KMF H13
90570 AL JAMAL

M₂KMF H13
★90580 LIDIA DOCE

M₂KMF H13
90590 CARIGULF PIONEER

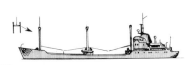

M₂KMF H13
★90600 OELSA → 90604

M₂KMF H13
90610 SEAJAY → 90614

M₂KMF H13
90620 GUARDIAN → 90621

M₂KMF H13
90630 ANASTASIA Y → 90631

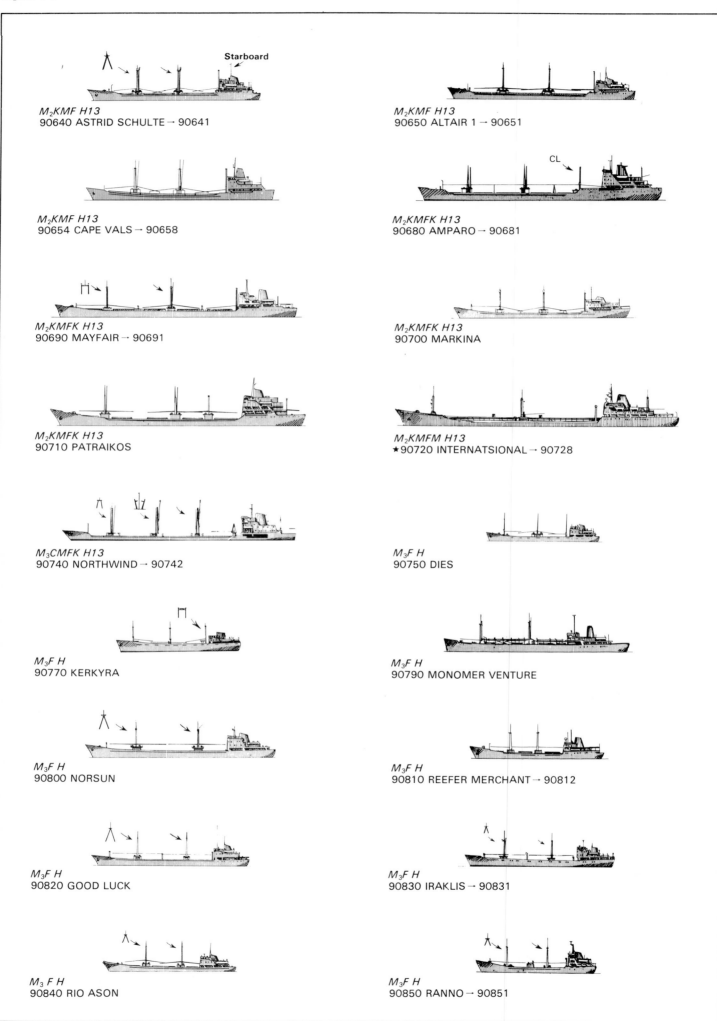

Starboard

M_2KMF H13
90640 ASTRID SCHULTE → 90641

M_2KMF H13
90650 ALTAIR 1 → 90651

M_2KMF H13
90654 CAPE VALS → 90658

CL

M_2KMFK H13
90680 AMPARO → 90681

M_2KMFK H13
90690 MAYFAIR → 90691

M_2KMFK H13
90700 MARKINA

M_2KMFK H13
90710 PATRAIKOS

M_2KMFM H13
★90720 INTERNATSIONAL → 90728

M_3CMFK H13
90740 NORTHWIND → 90742

M_3F H
90750 DIES

M_3F H
90770 KERKYRA

M_3F H
90790 MONOMER VENTURE

M_3F H
90800 NORSUN

M_3F H
90810 REEFER MERCHANT → 90812

M_3F H
90820 GOOD LUCK

M_3F H
90830 IRAKLIS → 90831

$M_3 F$ H
90840 RIO ASON

M_3F H
90850 RANNO → 90851

M₃F H
90860 ATLANTIC ISLE → 90862

M₃F H1
90870 TUKWILA CHIEF → 90872

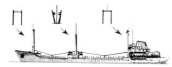

M₃F H1
★90880 SECIL BRASIL

M₃F H1
★90890 KURILA → 90896

M₃F H1
90910 KATERINA

M₃F H1
90930 SALLY ANN

M₃F H1
90940 OCEANIA → 90944

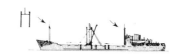

M₃F H1
90950 JUMBO JOIST

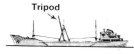

M₃F H1
90960 VALKENBURG

M₃F H1
90970 PIA DANIELSEN → 90973

M₃F H1
90980 MINNESOTA → 90982

M₃F H1
90990 DIBI HAMID → 90992

M₃F H1
91000 LADY SYLVIA

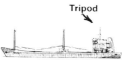

M₃F H1
91010 ANTARCTIC → 91011

M₃F H1
91020 PACIFIC COUNTESS → 91021

M₃F H1
91030 NIAGA XLI → 91051

M₃F H1
91070 ZSA ZSA → 91076

M₃F H1
91090 MARIA IRENE

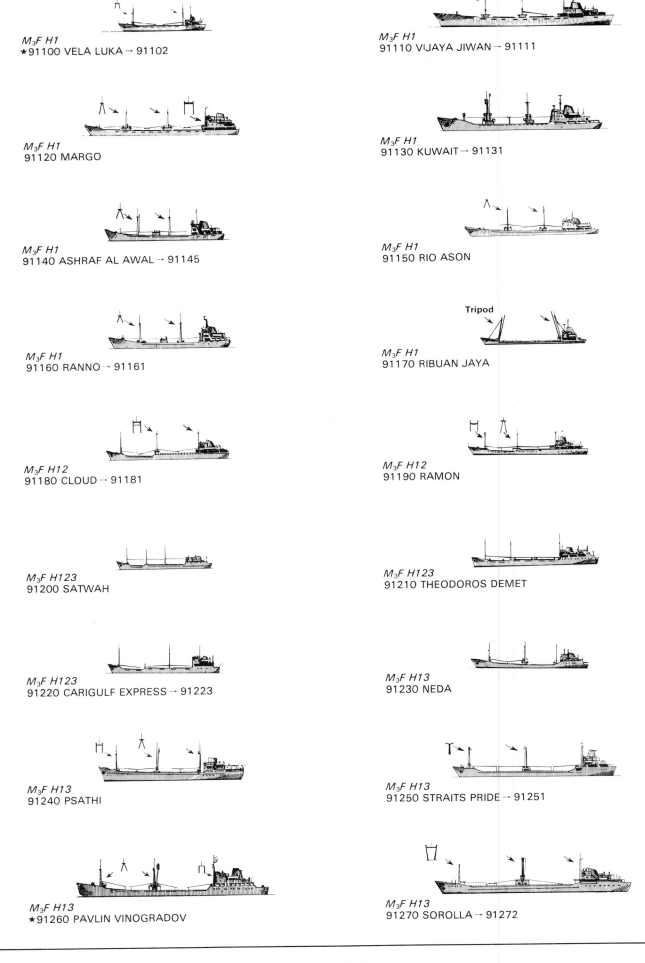

M₃F H1
★91100 VELA LUKA → 91102

M₃F H1
91110 VIJAYA JIWAN → 91111

M₃F H1
91120 MARGO

M₃F H1
91130 KUWAIT → 91131

M₃F H1
91140 ASHRAF AL AWAL → 91145

M₃F H1
91150 RIO ASON

M₃F H1
91160 RANNO → 91161

Tripod

M₃F H1
91170 RIBUAN JAYA

M₃F H12
91180 CLOUD → 91181

M₃F H12
91190 RAMON

M₃F H123
91200 SATWAH

M₃F H123
91210 THEODOROS DEMET

M₃F H123
91220 CARIGULF EXPRESS → 91223

M₃F H13
91230 NEDA

M₃F H13
91240 PSATHI

M₃F H13
91250 STRAITS PRIDE → 91251

M₃F H13
★91260 PAVLIN VINOGRADOV

M₃F H13
91270 SOROLLA → 91272

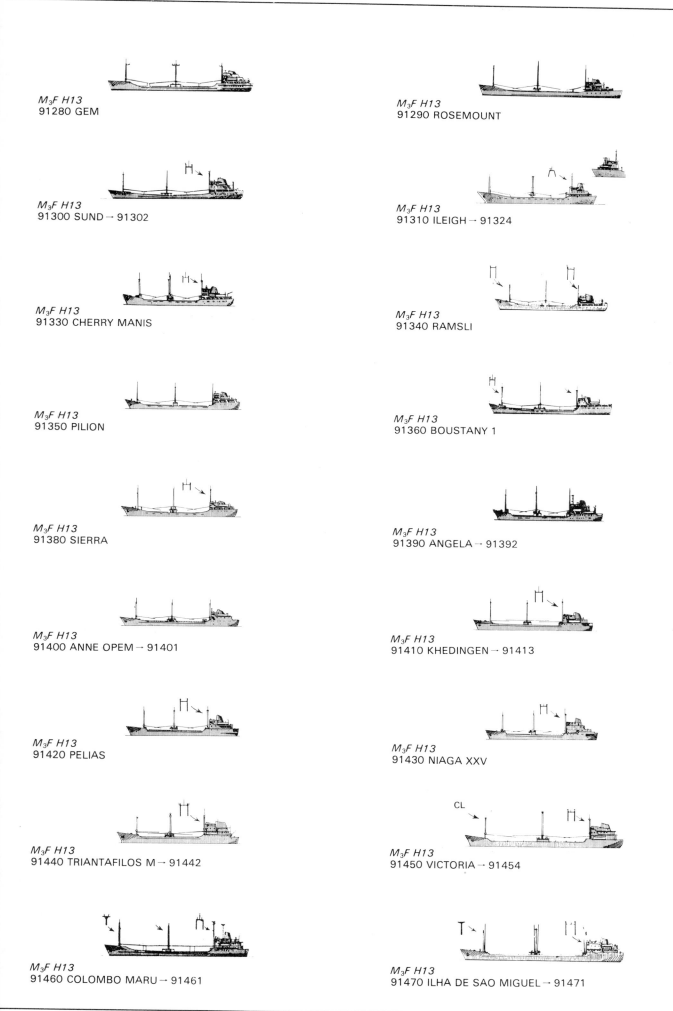

M₃F H13
91280 GEM

M₃F H13
91290 ROSEMOUNT

M₃F H13
91300 SUND → 91302

M₃F H13
91310 ILEIGH → 91324

M₃F H13
91330 CHERRY MANIS

M₃F H13
91340 RAMSLI

M₃F H13
91350 PILION

M₃F H13
91360 BOUSTANY 1

M₃F H13
91380 SIERRA

M₃F H13
91390 ANGELA → 91392

M₃F H13
91400 ANNE OPEM → 91401

M₃F H13
91410 KHEDINGEN → 91413

M₃F H13
91420 PELIAS

M₃F H13
91430 NIAGA XXV

M₃F H13
91440 TRIANTAFILOS M → 91442

M₃F H13
91450 VICTORIA → 91454

M₃F H13
91460 COLOMBO MARU → 91461

M₃F H13
91470 ILHA DE SAO MIGUEL → 91471

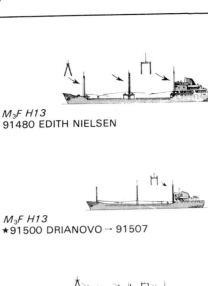

M₃F H13
91480 EDITH NIELSEN

M₃F H13
91490 NIAGA XXIV → 91491

M₃F H13
★91500 DRIANOVO → 91507

M₃F H13
91510 NAVI STAR

M₃F H13
★91520 SUSAK → 91522

M₃F H13
91530 CEDERBORG → 91532

M₃F H13
91540 ASTOR

M₃F H13
91550 BREEKANT → 91554

M₃F H13
91560 KRIS

M₃F H13
★91570 MIKULIC OREB → 91572

M₃F H13
91580 FAITH

M₃F H13
91600 TEXACO BOGOTA

M₃F H13
91610 STELLA PROCYON

M₃F H13
91630 FIRETHORN

M₃F H13
91640 LILIAN S → 91641

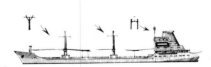

M₃F H13
★91650 FU SHUN CHENG → 91651

M₃F H13
91660 THOROLD

M₃F H13
91670 KRANTOR → 91671

M₃F H13
★91680 FRIMARO

M₃F H13
91690 OCEAN GLORY No 6

M₃F H13
★91700 SOFIA → 91702

M₃F H13
91710 IRAN SEDAGHAT → 91719

M₃F H13
91730 TARABLOS

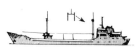

M₃F H13
91740 FALCON REEFER

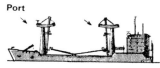

M₃F H13
91750 STARMAN AUSTRALIA → 91752

M₃F H3
91760 DEBORAH I

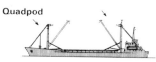

M₃F H3
★91765 JAHORINA

M₃F H3
91770 REEFER MERCHANT → 91772

M₃F H3
91780 ATLANTIC ISLE → 91782

M₃FC H
★91790 PRESIDENTE MACIAS NGUEMA

M₃FK H1
91800 NYMIT

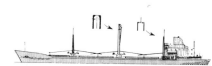

M₃FK H1
91810 PALLAS → 91811

M₃FK H123
91820 CARIGULF EXPRESS → 91823

M₃FK H13
91830 MUHIEDDINE → 91850

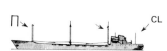

M₃FK H13
91860 SPYROS G II

M₃FK H13
91870 DON ALEJO

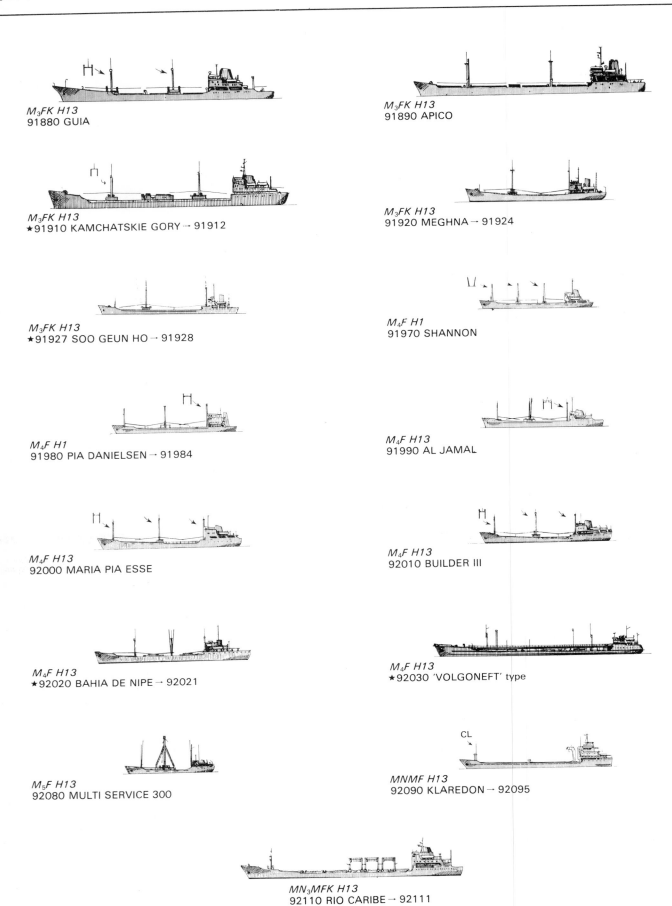

M₃FK H13
91880 GUIA

M₃FK H13
91890 APICO

M₃FK H13
★91910 KAMCHATSKIE GORY → 91912

M₃FK H13
91920 MEGHNA → 91924

M₃FK H13
★91927 SOO GEUN HO → 91928

M₄F H1
91970 SHANNON

M₄F H1
91980 PIA DANIELSEN → 91984

M₄F H13
91990 AL JAMAL

M₄F H13
92000 MARIA PIA ESSE

M₄F H13
92010 BUILDER III

M₄F H13
★92020 BAHIA DE NIPE → 92021

M₄F H13
★92030 'VOLGONEFT' type

M₅F H13
92080 MULTI SERVICE 300

MNMF H13
92090 KLAREDON → 92095

MN₃MFK H13
92110 RIO CARIBE → 92111

Profile 5

CMC₂KMF H1
★92150 VOSTOCK

CMC_2KMF H1
★92150 VOSTOCK

CMFM H2
★92160 EMBA → 92162

$CMKC_3MC_2FC$ H1
92170 DEL MUNDO → 92174

CMN_2FK_2 H1
92180 HAPPY MAMMOTH

$KCMCM_2F$ H1
92190 TREUENBELS

$K_2CKCMF/K_3C_2MF/K_3MF$ H1
★92200 DADE → 92204

K_2MC_2KF H1
92210 J.W. BATES

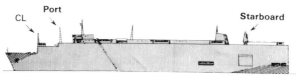

K_2MKMFC H2
92220 PRESIDENT → 92222

K₂M₂CMF H
★ 92230 DATONG → 92233

K₂M₂F H1
★ 92240 DADE → 92244

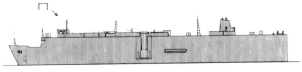

K₂M₃F H2
92247 CHIJIN MARU → 92249

CL

KM H1
92260 KILDARE

CL

KM H3
92270 CONDOCK I → 92271

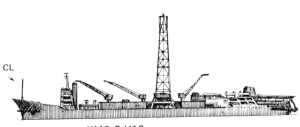

CL

KMC₃F H13
92280 DANWOOD ICE

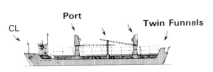

CL   Port   Twin Funnels

KMC₂F H1
92290 SLOMAN RANGER → 92303

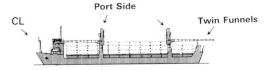

CL   Port Side   Twin Funnels

KMC₂F H13
92305 NORLANDIA → 92306

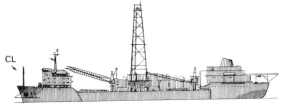

CL

KMC₂F H13
92310 NEDDRILL I → 92311

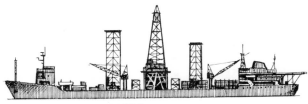

KMC₂MF H13
92320 GLOMAR EXPLORER

KMCF H
92330 PORSOY → 92332

Twin Funnels

KMCF H1
92350 SASSARI 1

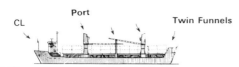

KMCKCF H1
92360 SLOMAN RANGER → 92367

KMCKMKF H13
★92380 VLADIVOSTOK → 92381

KMF H
92400 IRIS → 92401

KMF H1
92410 INAGUA LIGHT → 92414

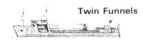

KMF H1
92420 SASSARI 1

KMF H1
92430 KILDARE

KMF H13
★92435 KOSMONAUT YURIY GAGARIN

KMF H3
92440 CONDOCK 1 → 92441

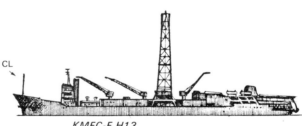

KMFC₃F H13
92450 DANWOOD ICE

KMF₂ H13
92455 SUPER SERVANT 3 → 92456

KMFK H13
92460 DANSBORG

KMFR H
92470 UNION ROTORUA → 92471

KMKF H13
92490 VESTA

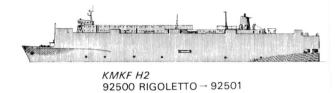

KMKF H2
92500 RIGOLETTO → 92501

KMKFK H13
92510 DANSBORG

KMKFM H
92520 PIA ANGELA → 92523

KMKFR H
92530 UNION ROTORUA → 92531

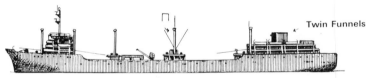

KMK₂CMKF H13
92540 GAE CHEOG

KMK₂F H1
92550 PELTO SEAHORSE

KMK₂F H13
92560 HAMANA

KMK₂F H2
92570 PRINCE MARU No 7

KMK₃FK H13
92590 PETER RICKMERS

KMK₃MK₂F H13
92600 WICHITA → 92606

KMKMF H
92620 KOYO MARU No 2 → 92623

KMKMF H13
92630 CHALLWA V

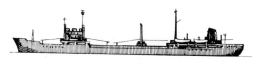

KMKMF H13
★ 92640 LIAO YING

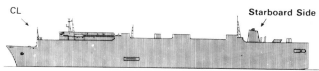

KMKMF H2
92645 TOYOFUJI No 7

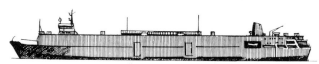

KMKMFC H
92650 DYVI SKAGERAK → 92654

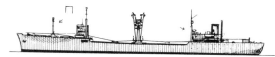

KMKMFK H13
92660 PVT. LEONARD C. BROSTROM

KM₂F H
92690 TRUCK TRADER

KM₂F H1
92700 STARMAN AFRICA → 92701

KM₂F H13
92710 BEAGLE → 92716

KM₂F H2
92730 DON CARLOS → 92731

KM₂FK H2
92740 MARI-LIFT

KM₂FM H1
92750 DONG BANK No 71

KM₃F H
★ 92780 CHIL BO SAN → 92781

KM₃F H12
★ 92782 MAR OCEANO → 92789/1

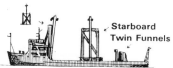

KM₂NF H1
92790 GOLIATH

KMNF H1
92800 HAPPY RIDER → 92801

KMNKF H1
92810 ACADIA FOREST → 92811

MC H13
92820 OCEAN BUILDER 1

MC₂ H13
92830 ORCA

MC₃F H13
92840 SEDCO 445 → 92842

MC₃MC₂F H1
92850 DEL MUNDO → 92854

MC₃MC₂FK H1
92860 DEL ORO → 92862

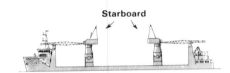

MC₂F H1
92870 HAIA BRAVE

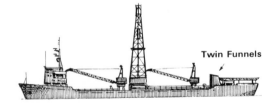

MC₂F H13
92880 BEN OCEAN LANCER → 92888

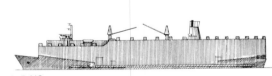

MC₂F H2
92890 NOPAL VERDE → 92891

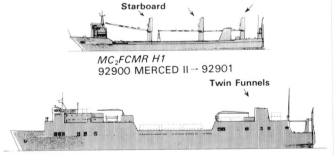

MC₂FCMR H1
92900 MERCED II → 92901

MC₂FMR H23
92910 FINNROSE → 92911

MC₂MF H1
92920 ASPEN

MC₂MF H13
92930 EMERALD

MC₂MF H23
92932 AMERICAN EAGLE → 92934

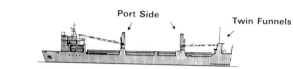

MC₂MF H3
92936 RAGNA GORTHON → 92938

MCF H1
92940 SAIPEM DUE

MCF H1
92950 ARABELLA → 92957

MCF H1
92970 LILLIAN XXII → 92974

MCFC H1
92980 HIRYU → 92981

MCFC H2
92990 PACIFIC HIGHWAY → 92991

MCMF H
93000 KARMSUND → 93002

MCMF H
93010 NORDKYN → 93012

MCMF H1
93030 BACO-LINER 1 → 93032

MCMF H1
93040 SCHELDE II

MCMF H1
93050 CIUDAD DE BARRANQUILLA

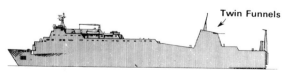

MCMFK H2
★93060 TRAPEZITZA → 93061

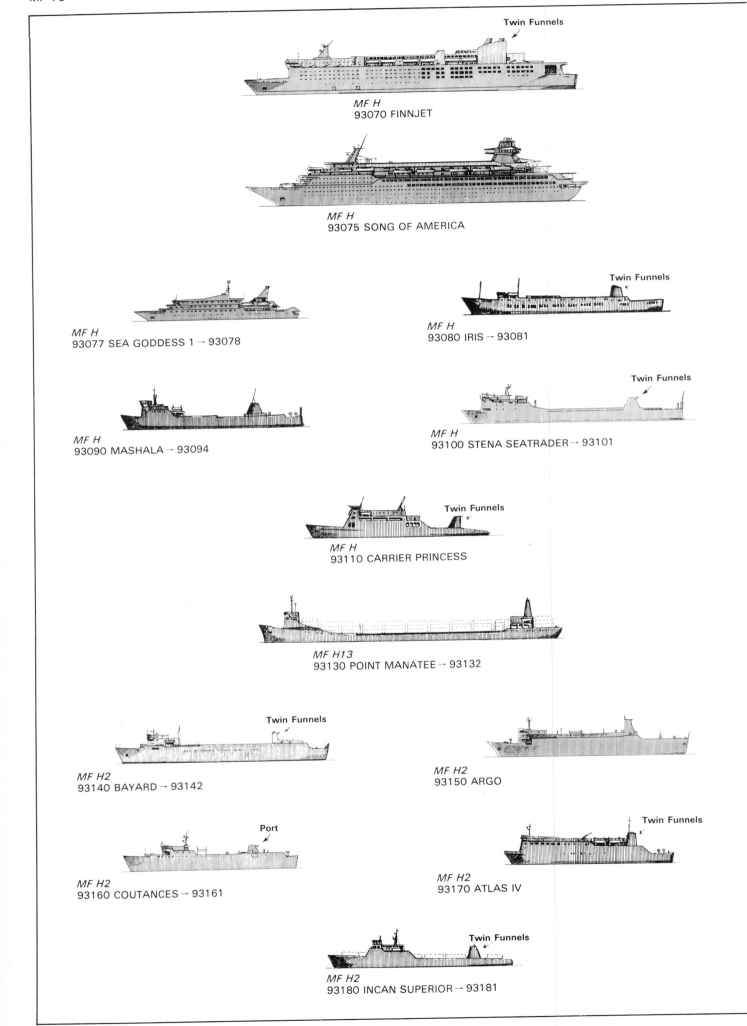

Twin Funnels

MF H
93070 FINNJET

MF H
93075 SONG OF AMERICA

MF H
93077 SEA GODDESS 1 → 93078

Twin Funnels

MF H
93080 IRIS → 93081

MF H
93090 MASHALA → 93094

Twin Funnels

MF H
93100 STENA SEATRADER → 93101

Twin Funnels

MF H
93110 CARRIER PRINCESS

MF H13
93130 POINT MANATEE → 93132

Twin Funnels

MF H2
93140 BAYARD → 93142

MF H2
93150 ARGO

Port

MF H2
93160 COUTANCES → 93161

Twin Funnels

MF H2
93170 ATLAS IV

Twin Funnels

MF H2
93180 INCAN SUPERIOR → 93181

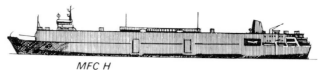

MFC H
93190 DYVI SKAGERAK → 93194

MFK H1
93200 ARCTIC SALVOR

MFM H
93210 KIRK CHALLENGER

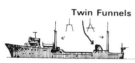

MFM H13
93240 USURBIL → 93241

MFM H2
93250 TOR CALEDONIA → 93252

MFM H2
93255 NORDIC LINK → 93257

MFM H2
93260 SAINT REMY → 93262

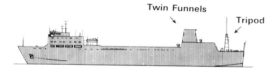

MFM H2
93265 BORE QUEEN → 93266

MFM H23
93270 UNION DUNEDIN → 93271

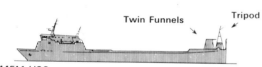

MFM H23
93272 MERCANDIAN PRESIDENT → 93279/1

MFMF H
93280 BACAT 1

MFMF H2
93290 CALA MARSAL → 93291

MFMR H1
93300 LARIMAR → 93301

MFMR H2
★93310 NAN KOU → 93315

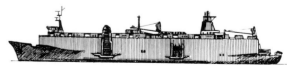

MKCFC H
93330 ARGUS CARRIER

MKCFMR H13
93340 THEBELAND → 93347

MKCMF H
93360 DANA AMERICA → 93363

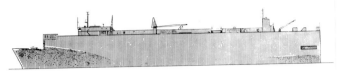

MKCMF/MKCMFC H2
93370 SCANDINAVIAN HIGHWAY

MKF H
✸ 93380 VLADIMIR ILYCH → 93385

MKF H13
93390 POINT MANATEE → 93392

MKFM H
93400 TAIYO MARU No 71 → 93401

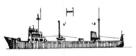

MKFM H
93410 TAIYO MARU No 65 → 93413

MKFM H23
93420 UNION DUNEDIN → 93421

MKFMK H
93430 SWELLMASTER

MKFMR H3
93440 SHINSEI MARU

MK₂F H13
93450 KAZUSHIMA MARU

MK₅FM H
93460 ESSAYONS

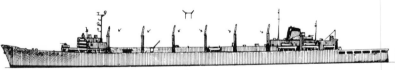

MK₆MFK H
93470 SACRAMENTO → 93473

MK₃MF H13
93480 TOPIRA

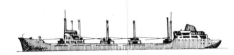

MK₃MF H13
93490 SAN ANTONIO DO TRIUNFO → 93492

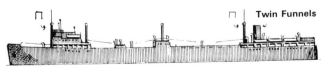

MK₂MF H
93500 NISSHIN MARU No 2

MK₂MF H
93510 AUTO TRADER → 93512

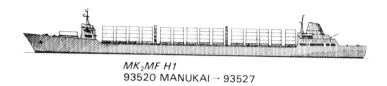

MK₂MF H1
93520 MANUKAI → 93527

MK₂MF H13
93540 NISSHIN MARU No 3

MK₂MF H13
93550 L'INTERPECHE

MK₂MF H13
93560 ARAUCA

MK₂MF H13
93570 HILLAH

MK₂MF H2
93580 SILVER HOPE

MK₂MKF H1
93590 KYOKUSEI MARU

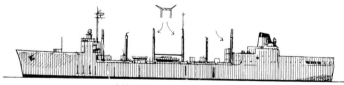

MK₂MK₂F H13
93610 WICHITA → 93616

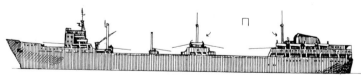

MK₂M₂F H
★ 93630 SOVIETSKAYA ROSSIYA

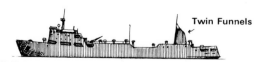

MKMF H
93640 MARAMA

MKMF H
93650 AKORA → 93653

MKMF H1
★93660 VOSTOCK

MKMF H1
★93670 GEROITE NA SEVASTOPOL → 93673

MKMF H13
★93680 ANDREY ZAKHAROV → 93693

MKMF H2
93720 RIGOLETTO → 93721

MKMKF H1
★93730 PROFESSOR BARANOV → 93764

MKMKF H13
★93770 NISSHIN MARU

MKMKF H13
★93780 VILIS LACIS → 93787

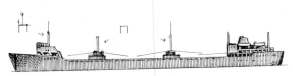

MKMKFK H13
★93800 SEVEROURALSK → 93807

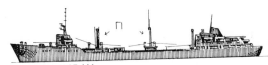

MKMKMF H1
★93820 POGRANICHNIK LEONOV → 93854

MKM₂F H1
★93860 SOVIETSKAYA UKRAINA

MKM$_2$F H1
★ 93870 PIONERSK → 93883

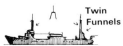

M$_2$ H2
93885 UCHI

M$_2$F H
93890 SIR CARADOC → 93892

M$_2$F H
93900 BEGONIA

M$_2$F H
93910 GEORGIA → 93911

M$_2$F H
93920 AUTO TRADER → 93922

M$_2$F H
93930 PEVERIL → 93936

M$_2$F H
93950 MARINE EVANGELINE

M$_2$F H
93960 CARRIER PRINCESS

M$_2$F H
93970 CIUDAD DE CEUTA → 93971

M$_2$F H
93975 MANX VIKING

M$_2$F H
93980 AICHI MARU

M$_2$F H
93990 KIRSTEN BRAVO → 93991

M$_2$F H
94000 HERTHA

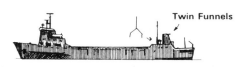

M$_2$F H
94010 AETOS → 94013

M$_2$F H
94020 BUENAVISTA → 94021

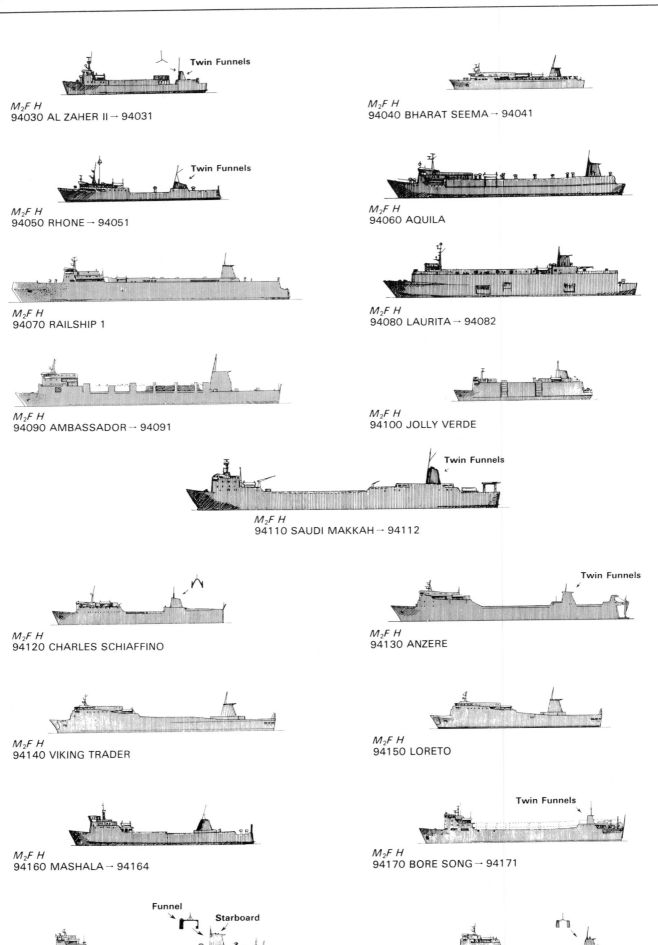

M_2F H
94030 AL ZAHER II → 94031

Twin Funnels

M_2F H
94040 BHARAT SEEMA → 94041

M_2F H
94050 RHONE → 94051

Twin Funnels

M_2F H
94060 AQUILA

M_2F H
94070 RAILSHIP 1

M_2F H
94080 LAURITA → 94082

M_2F H
94090 AMBASSADOR → 94091

M_2F H
94100 JOLLY VERDE

Twin Funnels

M_2F H
94110 SAUDI MAKKAH → 94112

M_2F H
94120 CHARLES SCHIAFFINO

Twin Funnels

M_2F H
94130 ANZERE

M_2F H
94140 VIKING TRADER

M_2F H
94150 LORETO

M_2F H
94160 MASHALA → 94164

Twin Funnels

M_2F H
94170 BORE SONG → 94171

Funnel   Starboard

M_2F H
94180. BRITTA ODEN → 94182

M_2F H
94190 CORAL GABLES

M₂F H
94200 BACAT I

M₂F H
94210 IVA → 94211

M₂F H
94220 SEADRAKE

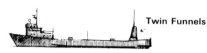

M₂F H
94230 SOL GEORGIOS

M₂F H
94240 VOLCAN DE YAIZA → 94243

M₂F H
94250 TUI CAKAU III

M₂F H
94260 MAUNALEI → 94261

M₂F H
94270 C. V. LIGHTNING → 94277

M₂F H
★ 94280 KOSMONAUT VLADIMIR KOMAROV

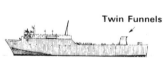

M₂F H1
94290 MATHILDA → 94295

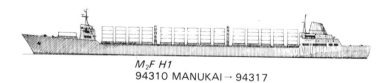

M₂F H1
94310 MANUKAI → 94317

M₂F H1
94330 CAST SALMON

M₂F H1
94340 DESAFIO

M₂F H1
94350 KAIRYU MARU

M₂F H1
94360 BALI

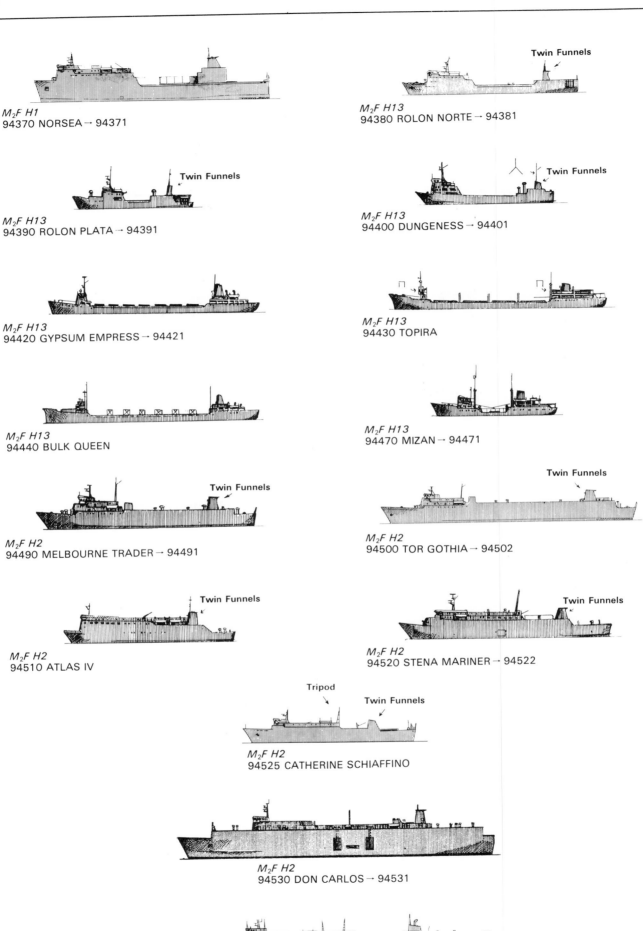

M₂F H1
94370 NORSEA → 94371

M₂F H13
94380 ROLON NORTE → 94381

Twin Funnels

M₂F H13
94390 ROLON PLATA → 94391

Twin Funnels

M₂F H13
94400 DUNGENESS → 94401

Twin Funnels

M₂F H13
94420 GYPSUM EMPRESS → 94421

M₂F H13
94430 TOPIRA

M₂F H13
94440 BULK QUEEN

M₂F H13
94470 MIZAN → 94471

M₂F H2
94490 MELBOURNE TRADER → 94491

Twin Funnels

M₂F H2
94500 TOR GOTHIA → 94502

Twin Funnels

M₂F H2
94510 ATLAS IV

Twin Funnels

M₂F H2
94520 STENA MARINER → 94522

Twin Funnels

Tripod

Twin Funnels

M₂F H2
94525 CATHERINE SCHIAFFINO

M₂F H2
94530 DON CARLOS → 94531

M₂F H2
94535 GLORIOUS ACE → 94537

M₂F H2
94540 ARGO

M₂F H2
94550 BALTIC EAGLE → 94551

M₂F H2
94560 BORE SKY → 94562

M₂F H2
94570 DORA BALTEA → 94572

M₂F H2
94580 ATLAS III

M₂F H2
94590 TRANSGERMANIA

M₂F H2
94600 BUFFALO

M₂F H2
94605 DARNIA

M₂F H2
94610 PUMA → 94611

M₂F H2
94613 ROLL GALICIA → 94616

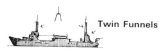

M₂F H2
94620 ANZERE

M₂F H2
94630 CORAL GABLES

M₂F H2
94640 UCHI

M₂F H23
94650 MERCANDIAN TRANSPORTER II → 94658

M₂F H3
94660 HONG LEE → 94661

M₂F H3
94670 AL ZAHER IV → 94671

M₂F H3
94680 ANTONIO SUARDIAZ

M₂F H3
94690 ROSE SCHIAFFINO → 94691

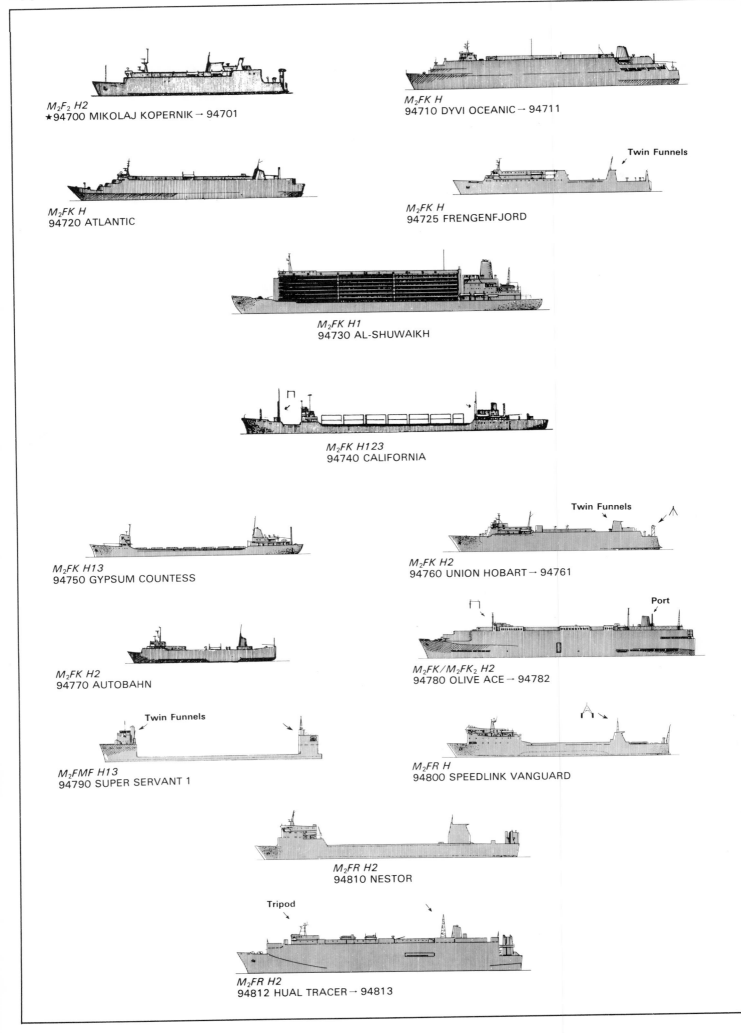

M_2F_2 H2
★94700 MIKOLAJ KOPERNIK → 94701

M_2FK H
94710 DYVI OCEANIC → 94711

M_2FK H
94720 ATLANTIC

M_2FK H
94725 FRENGENFJORD

Twin Funnels

M_2FK H1
94730 AL-SHUWAIKH

M_2FK H123
94740 CALIFORNIA

M_2FK H13
94750 GYPSUM COUNTESS

Twin Funnels

M_2FK H2
94760 UNION HOBART → 94761

Port

M_2FK H2
94770 AUTOBAHN

M_2FK/M_2FK_2 H2
94780 OLIVE ACE → 94782

Twin Funnels

M_2FMF H13
94790 SUPER SERVANT 1

M_2FR H
94800 SPEEDLINK VANGUARD

M_2FR H2
94810 NESTOR

Tripod

M_2FR H2
94812 HUAL TRACER → 94813

M₂FR H2
94815 MADAME BUTTERFLY → 94818

M₂FR H2
94820 NOPAL MASCOT

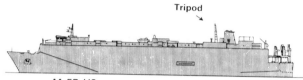

M₂FR H2
94824 HUAL ANGELITA → 94827

M₂FR H23
94830 NORDIC STREAM → 94832

M₂KFK H2
★94850 HONG HE KOU → 94851

M₂KFM H
94860 DAISHIN MARU No 11

M₂KFM H
94870 KAI YANG → 94873

M₂K₂F H
94880 CHIKUBU MARU

M₂K₂FK₂ H13
94890 ROSBORG

M₂K₂FM H
94900 TAIYO MARU No 83 → 94902

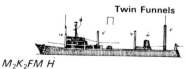

M₂K₂FM H
94910 DAISHIN MARU No 12 → 94911

M₂KMF H
94920 SHIRANE MARU → 94921

Twin Funnels

M₂KMF H
94930 KISO MARU

M₃CMFMC H2
94940 TOYOTA MARU No 10 → 94942

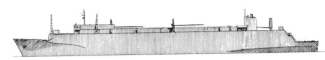

M₃C₂MFC H2
94950 PACIFIC HIGHWAY → 94951

M₃C₂MFC H2
94960 EUROPEAN HIGHWAY → 94964

M₃F H
94970 PERLIS → 94972

M₃F H
94980 AUBY

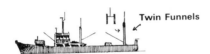

Twin Funnels

M₃F H
94990 AKORA → 94993

Twin Funnels

M₃F H
95000 GOLDEN DRAGON No 1

Twin Funnels

M₃F H
95010 WEYMOUTH → 95011

Starboard

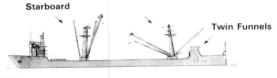

Twin Funnels

M₃F H13
95020 PROJECT AMERICAS → 95022

M₃F H2
★95025 YUAN WANG 1 → 95026

M₃F H2
95030 MERMAID ACE

M₃F H2
95040 RIGOLETTO → 95041

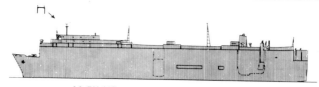

M₃FK H2
95045 ASTRO COACH → 95046

M₃FM H
95050 DAISHIN MARU No 23

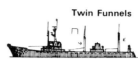

M₃FM H
95060 DAISHIN MARU No 16

M₃KFM H
95070 TAIYO MARU No 83 → 95072

M₄F H
95080 FUJI → 95085

M₄F H1
95100 TSUDA MARU

M₄F H1
95110 YAMATO MARU → 95111

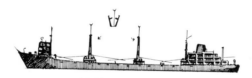

M₄FK H1
95120 SILVER GLORY

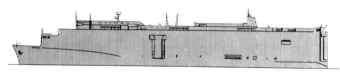

M₆F H2
95125 EUROPEAN VENTURE

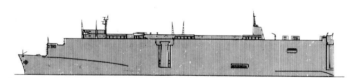

M₆F H2
95126 YOKOHAMA MARU → 95127

M₂N₂F H1
95130 LEVANTE EXPRESS → 95132

MN H1
95140 MAUNA KEA

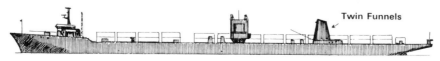

MNF H1
95150 BILDERDYK → 95152

MNF H1
95160 ARABELLA → 95167

MNF H2
95180 DANA FUTURA → 95181

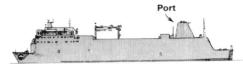

MNFM H2
95190 DANA MAXIMA

MNMF H1
95200 BACO-LINER 1 → 95202

MNMNF H
95210 CIUDAD DE CEUTA → 95211

MNMNF/MN₂F H
95220 MONTE BANDERAS → 95222

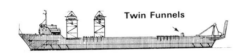

MN₂F/MN₂FK₂ H1
95230 HAPPY MAMMOTH

MN₂FM H1
95240 HAPPY MARINER

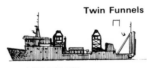

MN₂FM H1
★95250 BROCKEN

Ship Directory and Data Section

00001 **TAE YANG No 11** Ko/No (Akers) 1947; FF; 7100; 155 × 5 (509 × 16); TM (B&W); 17; ex *Shin Hung* 1970; ex *Bataan* 1967; Converted from cargo ship 1967

● 00010 **LASH ATLANTICO** US/US (Avondale) 1972; Bg/Con; 26400; 250 × 10.7 (820 × 35.5); T (De Laval); 21; Both Gantries (N) can move right aft thus altering sequence. Could also be P5. 'LASH' type Sisters (US flag) (overall lengths vary):
00011 **LASH ITALIA**
00012 **LASH PACIFICO**
00013 **AUSTRAL LIGHTNING** ex *Lash Espana* 1976; ex *Australia Bear* 1975; ex *Philippine Bear* 1975
00015 **DELTA MAR**
00016 **DELTA SUD**
00017 **DELTA NORTE**
00018 **DELTA CARIBE** ex *Lash Turkiye*
00019 **AUSTRAL MOON** ex *Australia Bear* 1975; ex *Philippine Bear* 1975

00020 **PENTA WORLD** Sg/Br (Connell) 1964; C/HL; 6100/8800; 150.37 × 7.67/9.04 (493.34 × 25. 17/29.69); M(Sulzer); —; ex *Inventor* 1981

00030 **SIRIUS** US (Navy)/Br (Swan, Hunter) 1966; Spt; 12300; 159.7 × 25.4 (524 × 25.5); M (Sulzer); 20; ex *Lyness* 1981; Helicopter platform aft. Hull could be H
Sisters:
00031 **STROMNESS** (Br)
00032 **SPICA** US (Navy) ex *Tarbatness* 1981

00040 **RAJAH MAS** My/Br (Straits SS) 1955; P; 600; 51.1 × 2.6 (168 × 8.5); M (Ruston & Hornsby); 10; ex *Rejang* 1969

00050 **FORT GRANGE** Br/Br (Scotts' SB) 1978; Rst/FA; 16000; 183.78 × 9 (602.95 × 29.53); M (Sulzer): 20; Operated by the RFA; Helicopter platform
Sister:
00051 **FORT AUSTIN** (Br)

00060 **ASHLEY LYKES** US/US (Bethlehem Steel) 1962; P Con; 11800; 179 × 10.3 (588 × 24.5); T (GEC); 18; Lengthened 'Pacer' or 'Gulf Pride' class;
Sisters (US flag):
00061 **BRINTON LYKES**
00062 **JAMES LYKES**
00063 **JEAN LYKES**
00064 **JOHN LYKES**
00065 **JOSEPH LYKES**
00066 **NANCY LYKES**
00067 **SOLON TURMAN**
00068 **MARJORIE LYKES**
00069 **THOMPSON LYKES**
00070 **ZOELLA LYKES**

00080 **ADABELLE LYKES** US/US (Bethlehem Steel) 1963; Pt. Con; 9900; 150.8 × 10.3 (495 × 35.5); T (GEC); 18; Some ships have sequence KMKM₂FK
Sisters (US flag):
00081 **AIMEE LYKES**
00082 **ALLISON LYKES**
00083 **CHARLOTTE LYKES**
00084 **CHRISTOPHER LYKES**
00085 **SHELDON LYKES**

00090 **GELA** Gr/Br (Bartram) 1962; C; 9600; 152 × 9.2 (499 × 30.5); M (B & W); 15; ex *Southgate* 1970; ex *Arlington Court* 1963

00110 **KERO** Pe/Br (Doxford) 1961; C/HL; 6000/8700; 149 × 9 (488 × 30); M (Doxford); 16; ex *Sea Luck* 1979; ex *Tactician* 1979

00120 **ELEFTHERIA** Gr/Br (Doxford) 1960; C/HL; 6400/8400; 150 × 9 (490 × 30); M (Doxford); 15; ex *Adventurer* 1979

★ 00140 **ADMIRAL GOLOVKO** Ru/Ru (—) 1975; FT; 4500; 112.81 × 6.52 (370.11 × 21.39); M (CKD Praha); 17
Sisters (Ru flag):
★ 00141 **ADMIRAL KOLYSHKIN**
★ 00142 **ALEKSANDR TORTSYEV**
★ 00143 **IVAN SIVKO**
★ 00144 **KAPITAN TELOV**
★ 00145 **MARSHAL YAKUBOVSKIY**
★ 00146 **PYOTR SGIBNEV (or PETR SGIBNEV)**
★ 00147 **ALEKSEY GENERALOV**
★ 00148 **GENERAL RODIMTSYEV**
★ 00149 **KAPITAN MAKLAKOV**
★ 00149/1 **KONSTANTIN DUSHENOV**

★ 00150 **HOPING CHI SHI CHIU** RC/Ca (Burrard DD) 1943; C; 7000; 134 × 8.2 (422 × 27); R (Inglis); 10; ex *Aegean Sea*; ex *Taygetos*; ex *Laurentian Seas*; ex *Fort Brandon*
Sisters (RC flag):
★ 00151 **HOPING CHI SHI LIU** ex *Athens*, ex *Akko*; ex *Vancouver City*; ex *Fort Wallace*
★ 00152 **HOPING CHI SHI WU** ex *Kasert*, ex *Ternate*; ex *Govert Fiinck*; ex *Ocean Athlete*
★ 00153 **HOPING ER SHI CHI** ex *Nord Sky*; ex *Temple Bar*; ex *Fort St James*
★ 00154 **HOPING SAN SHI** ex *Gunn*, ex *Yamaska*; ex *Yamaska Park*
★ 00155 **HOPING SHI SAN** ex *Nueva Gloria*; ex *Lake Okanagan*; ex *Rupert Park*
★ 00156 **HOPING WU SHI** ex *Longford*; ex *Marika*; ex *Tarsian*; ex *Fort St Paul*
★ 00157 **HOPING WU SHI I** ex *Hereford*; ex *Novor Isobel*; ex *Fort Ticonderoga*
All these ships were built as WWII standard types

★ 00160 **NAN HAI 145** RC/Br (Pickersgill) 1943; C; 6000; 126.4 × 8 (415 × 26); R (G Clark); 10; ex *Norwind* 1967; ex *Graiglwyd* 1959; ex *Kingsborough* 1951; ex *Chertsey* 1947

00170 **CAPETAN NICOLAS** Cy/Br (Vickers Armstrongs) 1957; C/R; 11100; 156 × 9.3 (512 × 31); TSM; (H & W) 18.5; ex *Canopic* 1975; KP also abreast funnel

00180 **MIGHTY SEA** Pa/Br (Blyth) 1958; C; 5400/9100; 140 × 7.8 (460 × 26); M (Doxford); 14; ex *Silver Shark* 1983; ex *Vassiliakis* 1983; ex *Elena M* 1978; ex *Caxton* 1968

00210 **TOPEKA** Pa/Ge (Bremer V) 1938; C; 5100; 133.8 × 7.3 (438 × 24); M (Bremer V); 15; ex *Lacasielle* 1976; ex *Togo* 1968; ex *Stella Marina* 1956; ex *Tilthorn* 1954; ex *Svalbard* 1954; ex *Togo* 1947; Converted from passenger ship

00230 **ADABELLE LYKES** US/US (Bethlehem) 1963; S. Con; 9900; 150 × 10.3 (495 × 34.5); T; (GEC); 18
Sisters (US flag):
00231 **AIMEE LYKES**
00232 **ALLISON LYKES**
00233 **CHARLOTTE LYKES**
00234 **CHRISTOPHER LYKES**
Some ships K₃MK₃

★ 00240 **YULIUS FUCHIK** Ru/Fi (Valmet) 1978; Bg/Con; 22800/35900; 266.45 × —/11 (874.18 × —/36.09); TSM (Pielstick); 20; May be spelt JULIUS FUCIK
Sister (Ru flag):
★ 00241 **TIBOR SZAMUELY**

★ 00250 **KOSMONAUT PAVEL BELYAEV** Ru/Ru (Zhdanov) 1963/77; RS; 5500; 123.15 × 6.71 (404 × 22.01); M (B & W); 14.75; ex *Vytegrales* 1974; Converted from cargo ship 1977
Sisters (Ru flag):
★ 00251 **KOSMONAUT GEORGIY DOBROVOLSKIY** ex *Nazar Gubin* 1978
★ 00252 **KOSMONAUT VIKTOR PATSAYEV** ex *Semyon Kosinov* 1978
★ 00253 **KOSMONAUT VLADISLAV VOLKOV** ex *Yeniseyles* 1974

★ 00260 **PRESIDENT LINCOLN** US/US (Avondale) 1982; Con; 40600; 262.14 × 10.68 (860 × 35.04); M (Sulzer); 23.25;
Sisters (US flag):
00261 **PRESIDENT MONROE**
00262 **PRESIDENT WASHINGTON**

★ 00270 **RIO JIBACOA** Cu/Br (Lithgows) 1946; C; 3700; 112 × 6.6 (368 × 22); R (Rankin & Blackmore); 10; ex *Dundrennan* 1957; ex *Coulbreck* 1954; KP abreast the funnel

★ 00290 **HUA SHAN** RC/Br (Doxford) 1949; C; 5400; 135 × 7.9 (443 × 26); M (Doxford); 12.5; ex *Yunglutation*; ex *Trelyon* 1963

★ 00330 **ALEKSANDROVSK** Ru/Fi (Crichton-Vulcan) 1960; C; 5400; 139 × 7.9 (457 × 28); M (Sulzer); 14.5
Sisters (Ru flag):
★ 00331 **ATKARSK**
★ 00332 **BERDYANSK**
★ 00333 **KISLOVODSK**

★ 00334 **SRETENSK**
★ 00335 **DOLINSK** (on naval service as a survey ship)

★ 00340 **LJGOV** Ru/Fi (Crichton-Vulcan) 1961; C; 5400; 139 × 7.9 (457 × 26); M (Sulzer); 16
Sisters (Ru flag):
★ 00341 **ALAPAYEVSK**
★ 00342 **ALMETYEVSK**
★ 00343 **CHERNYAKHOVSK**

★ 00350 **TAUYSK** Ru/FRG (Bremer V) 1956; R; 3800; 110.6 × 7 (363 × 23); M (MAN); 15; ex *Amalienburg* 1964; ex *Bonita* 1963

00351 **MORFREEZE** Pa/Fr (Nantes) 1962; R; 4700; 115.27 × 6.1 (378.18 × 20.01) M (Pielstick); 17; ex *Opaline Bay* 1982; ex *Lethe* 1979; ex *Espadon* 1977
Sister:
00352 **KHALIJ SKY** (Pa) ex *Tarpon* 1978

● 00380 **PALMIS** Gr/Br (A & P) 1958; C; 5400/7800; 141.76 × —/8.70 (465 × —/28.54); M (Doxford); 13.5; ex *Artiba* 1976; ex *Baron Kinnaird* 1968
Sisters:
00381 **AGHIOS NICOLAOS** (Ma) ex *Baron Pentland* 1968
00382 **FILIO AVGERIS** (Gr) ex *Dirphys 11* 1980; ex *Baron Minto* 1967
00383 **SEA GLORY** (Gr) Ex *Bordabarri* 1978; ex *Baron Wemyss* 1968

★ 00400 **HONG Q1 130** RC/Br (Readhead) 1955; C; 8000; 140.5 × 8.4 (461 × 28); R & LPT (Readhead); 12.5; ex *Xing Huo*; ex *Hoping Wu Shi Ssu*; ex *Kyvernitis* 1959; ex *Diamantis Pateras* 1957

★ 00420 **GAMBELA** My/Sw (Lindholmens) 1943/45; C; 1600; 90.35 × 5.86 (296 × 19.23); M (B & W); 13; ex *Hongkong Line* 1975; ex *Paragon* 1974; ex *Slinde* 1965; ex *Industria* 1962

00450 **ADRIASTAR** Cy/De (Nakskov) 1949; C; 4800; 132 × 7.8 (433 × 25.8); M (B & W); 14; ex *Gina Juliano* 1976; ex *Northwild* 1970; ex *Nordhval* 1969

★ 00460 **ZHAN DOU 29** RC/De (B & W) 1935; C; 4600; 121.6 × 7.4 (399 × 24.6); TM; (B & W); 12; ex *Ho Ping 29* 1967; ex *Asbjorn* 1958

00470 **TAIBAH** Cy/Sw (Oresunds) 1953; R; 3600; 110.47 × 7.01 (362.43 23); M (Gotaverken); ex *Fresca* 1978; ex *Soyokaze* 1977; ex *Penja* 1972

00490 **MAR GRANDE** Ar/De (B & W) 1928; C; 3200; 103.6 × -(340 × -); M; (B & W); 10; ex *Rio Grande* 1971; ex *Rio Iguazu* 1967; ex *Bretagne* 1942

★ 00500 **ROCHFORD** RC/Br (Short Bros) 1946; CP; 3400; 100 × 6.3 (328 × 20.7); R (G Clark); 12; ex *Taksang* 1962

00510 **INCONFIDENTE** Bz/Ne (Boele's Sch) 1937; C; 2900; 102.4 × 6.3 (336 × 20.5); TM (Stork) 10

00520 **PRESIDENTE CASTILLO** Ar/Fr (La Loire) 1948; C; 6500/8700; 153 × 7.7 (502 × 25.7); M (Sulzer); 14; ex *Tara* 1961; ex *Charles L D* 1959

● 00560 **SHABAAN** Pa/Br (J L Thompson) 1960; C; 7900; 137.8 × 8.8 (452 × 26.11); M (Doxford); 13.5; ex *Panetolikon* 1981; ex *Ingleton* 1970; ex *Thistleroy* 1966; KP abreast the funnel

00600 **SAFINA-E-ISMAIL** Pk/Br (A&P) 1958; C; 8500; 141.74 × 8.72 (465 × 28.61); M (Doxford); 13.5; ex *Essex Trader* 1963

00640 **ASTILLERO** Sp/Sp (Echevarrieta y Larrinaga) 1920; C; 3500; 104 × 6.6 (341 × 21.1); R (Kincaid); —; ex *Gayarre* 1967; ex *Arichachu* 1939

★ 00650 **GEORG BUCHNER** DDR/Be (Cockerill) 1951; PC; 11100; 153.6 × 8.4 (504 × 27.6); M (B&W); 16; ex *Charlesville* 1967; May be slightly altered in appearance

★ 00680 **STARLIGHT** RC/Br (Denny) 1944; C; 7400; 136.7 × 8.4 (449 × 27.1); M (B&W); 12.5; ex *Parnon* 1979; ex *La Cumbre* 1959; ex *Empire Macdermott* 1948

★ 00700 **ZHAN DOU 55** RC/Br (Caledon) 1943; C; 7000; 136.2 × 7.9 (447 × 26); R (Fairfield); 10; ex *Ho Ping 55* 1967; ex *Wishford* 1959; ex *Demetrius D.S.* 1958; ex *Scottish Monarch* 1957

★ 00720 **YU QUAN SHAN** RC/No (Framnaes) 1959; C; 5800; 146.06 × 8.09 (479.2 × 26.54); M (Sulzer);

17; ex *Thorsriver* 1977
Sister:
★00722 **LU LIANG SHAN** (RC) ex *Thorstream* 1978

●00740 **BLITAR** Ia/Ne (Wilton-Fije) 1949; PC; 9400; 157 × 9.6 (515 21.3); TM (Sulzer); 16
Sister:
00741 **LANGKOES** (Ia)

★00780 **ZHAN DOU 75** RC/US (Todd-Bath) 1942; C; 7100; 134.7 × 8.2 (442 × 27); R (Dominion); 11; ex *Ho Ping 75* 1967; ex *Kasert* 1960; ex *Ternate* 1959; ex *Govert Fiinck* 1947; ex *Ocean Athlete* 1943

00810 **MOHAMMED ABBAS** Db/De (B&W) 1929; C; 4300; 116 × 7.4 (381 × 24.9), TSM (MAN); 10.5; ex *Dukegat* 1969; ex *Ursula Schulte* 1966; ex *Sachsenwald* 1953; ex *Somerville* 1950

★00850 **KIROVSK** Ru/Fi (Crichton-Vulcan) 1957; C; 5500; 139.40 × 7.86 (457 × 25.90); M (Sulzer); 16
Sisters:
★00851 **IZHEVSK** (Ru)
★00852 **XUCHANG** (RC) ex *Lidice* 1967
Similar (bi-pod masts):
00853 **ABULWAFA** (Eg) ex *Aconcagua* 1976
00854 **ABULFEDA** (Eg) ex *Araguaya* 1976

00880 **EFSTATHIA** Gr/Ne (Vuyk) 1957; C; 7200; 140.90 × 7.65 (462.2 × 25.1); M (MAN); 16; ex *Athinai II* 1980; ex *Sporades* 1978; ex *Asynja* 1972

00900 **KOTA MAS** Sg/Sw (Eriksbergs) 1953; C; 7000; 155.5 × 8.4 (510 × 27.6); M (B & W); 17.5; ex *Theben* 1978
Similar:
00901 **TOYA** (Sg) ex *Themis* 1975

●00930 **MARGARITA III** Cy/Sw (Gotav) 1949; C; 4700; 130.7 × 8 (429 × 25.7); M (Gotavarken); 15; ex *Maximinus* 1981; ex *Kassiopi* 1970; ex *Tennessee* 1968
Similar (Raking-topped funnel):
00931 **AGILITY** (Gr) ex *Ion* 1970; ex *Texas* 1968

★00940 **ZHAN DOU 53** RC/Br (Bartram) 1945; C; 7100; 134.4 × 8.2 (441 × 27); R (Duncan Stewart); 11; ex *Hoping 53*; ex *Yangtze Breeze* 1959; ex *Jan Jeronimo* 1958; ex *Matador* 1958; ex *Markab* 1956; ex *Empire Mauritius* 1947

00950 **AN-LI** Ho/Br (Caledon) 1951; PC; 3200; 96 × 5.6 (314 × 18.9); TSM (British Polar); 12.5; ex *Kimanis* 1982

★00960 **ZHAN DOU 51** RC/Ca (United Spyds) 1943; C; 7100; 134.4 × 8.2 (411 × 27); R (Dominion); 11; ex *Hoping 51*
Similar (RC flag):
★00962 **ZHAN DOU 76** ex *Hoping 76*
★00963 **ZHAN DOU 79** ex *Hoping 79*

00970 **TRANSGERMANIA** FRG/FRG (Sietas) 1976; RoC; 5600; 135.45 × 6.05 (444.39 × 19.85); TSM (MAN); 19; Stern ramp

★00980 **GUANGHUA** RC/Br (H&W) 1930; PC; 14200; 166 × 8.7 (545 × 29); TSM (B&W); 15; ex *Slapy* 1960; ex *Marianna* 1960; ex *Highland Princess* 1959

01010 **SUPER SERVANT 1** Ne/Ja (Oshima Z) 1979; RoC/HL; 10200; 139 × 6.18 (456 × 20.28); TSM (Stork-Werkspoor); 13; Submersible; broken-line shows extent of maximum immersion

★01020 **LJGOV** Ru/Fi (Crichton-Vulcan) 1961; C; 5400; 139.2 × 7.9 (457 × 25.8) M (Sulzer); 14.5
Sisters (Ru flag):
★01021 **ALAPAYEVSK**
★01022 **ALMATYEVSK**
★01023 **CHERNYAKHOVSK**

★01030 **ZHAN DOU 27** RC/Ca (Burrard DD) 1944; C; 7000; 134.1 × 8.5 (440 × 27.75); R (Dominion); 10; ex *Hoping 27*
Similar (RC Flag):
★01031 **ZHAN DOU 30** ex *Hoping 30*
★01032 **ZHAN DOU 50** ex *Hoping 50*
★01033 **ZHAN DOU 52** ex *Hoping 52*

★01040 **ZHAN DOU 47** RC/Br (Burntisland) 1941; C; 7200; 132.9 × 7.9 (436 × 26); R (Rowan); 11; ex *Ho Ping 47* 1967; ex *Mastro Stelios* 1960; ex *Norton* 1956

●01050 **STONEWALL JACKSON** US/US (Avondale) 1974; Bg; 32270; 272.55 × 11.62 (894.19 × 28.12); T (De Laval); 22 'LASH' type
Sisters (US flag):
01051 **ROBERT E. LEE**
01052 **SAM HOUSTON**
01053 **BUTTON GWINNETT** ex *Green Valley* 1980
01054 **GEORGE WYTHE** ex *Green Island* 1980
01055 **WILLIAM HOOPER** ex *Green Harbour* 1980
Probable Sisters:
01056 **BENJAMIN HARRISON**
01057 **EDWARD RUTLEDGE**

01060 **ZAMBEZE** Fr/Fr (France-Gironde) 1971; C; 13200; 167 × 10.8 (548 × 35.75); M (B&W); 23
Sisters:
01061 **ZEEBRUGGE** (Fr)
01062 **TOULON** (Fr) ex *Zelande* 1983

★01070 **BELORETSK** Ru/De (Nakskov) 1962; C; 10500; 160.3 × 9.6 (526 × 31.7); M (B&W); 18.5
Sisters (Ru flag):
★01071 **BELITSK**
★01072 **BELOVODSK**
★01073 **KOSMONAUT**
Similar (Ru flag):
★01074 **BEREZNIKI**
★01075 **BIYSK**

●01080 **EKA DAYA SAMUDERA** Ia/Br (H&W) 1966; C; 7100/10300; 155 × 9.3 (509 × 30.6); M (B&W); —; ex *Orcoma* 1979

01090 **GARNET** Pa/Sw (Lindholmens) 1968; C; 5900/9400; 153.9 × 8.6 (505 × 28.25); M (Pielstick); 18.5; ex *Maihar* 1978
Sister:
01091 **TURQUOISE** (Pa) ex *Mahsud* 1978

★01100 **PYATIDYESYATILETIYE KOMSOMOLA** Ru/Ru ('Zhdanov') 1968; C; 3900/5600; 129.9 × 7.8 (426 × 25.7); M (B & W); 16.5; 'Kaliningrad' type. Also known as **50 LETIYE KOMSOMOLA**

01110 **MARIETTA** Gr/Br (Caledon) 1965; R; 6100/8300; 149 × 9.3 (489 × 30.65); M (Sulzer); 19; ex *Port Albany* 1972
Sister:
01111 **JULIETTA** (Gr) ex *Port Huon* 1972
Similar (Conical funnel):
01112 **ANGELIKI** (Gr) ex *Port Burnie* 1972

01120 **GOLDEN DOLPHIN** Gr/Br (Upper Clyde) 1968; R; 12400/16300; 186.5 × 10.8 (612 × 35.5); TSM (Sulzer); 21.5; ex *Matra* 1983; ex *Port Caroline* 1981
Sister:
01121 **GOLDEN GLORY** (Gr) ex *Manaar* 1983; ex *Port Chalmers* 1981

★01140 **PEMBA** Mb/Ja (Mitsui) 1960; CP; 5100; 138 × 7.7 (454 × 25.2); M (B&W); 17; ex *Porto Amelia* 1976; ex *Tenos* 1970

01150 **TSING YI ISLAND** Pa/Br (Readhead) 1966; C; 6300/8800; 153.3 × 8.4 (503 × 27.56); M (Doxford); 17; ex *Strathanna* 1978; ex *Registan* 1975
Sister:
01151 **GOLDEN BEAR** (Pa) ex *Kellett Island* 1983; ex *Strathangus* 1978; ex *Serbistan* 1975

★01160 **KAI HUA** RC/Sw (Gotav.) 1958; C; 6400/10100; 149.3 × 9.8 (490 × 32.1); M (Gotavarken); 15.5; ex *Gaoyan* 1976; ex *Aristanax* 1973; ex *W R Lundgren* 1976

★01170 **CHANGSHU** RC/Sw (Gotav) 1958; C/TS; 6900/10500; 149.3 × 9 (490 × 29.55); M (Gotavarken); 15; ex *Chiang Kiang* 1970; ex *G D Kennedy* 1967

★01180 **PYATIDYESYATILETIYE KOMSOMOLA** Ru/Ru ('Zhdanov') 1968; C; 3900/5600; 129.9 × 7.8 (426 × 25.7); M (B&W); 16.5; 'Kaliningrad' type. Also known as **50 LETIYE KOMSOMOLA**

01190 **OAKWOOD** Pa/De (Helsingor) 1964; C; 2600/4600; 121.01 × /7.01 (397 × /22. 9); M (B&W); 16; ex *Neptune Beryl* 1980; ex *Olau Jarl* 1970; ex *Cap Egmont* 1970; ex *Cap Flinders* 1967; ex *Olau Jarl* 1966; ex *Sardinia* 1966; ex *Olau Jarl* 1964
Sister:
01191 **TEAKWOOD** (Pa) ex *Neptune Jasper* 1980; ex *Cap Nelson* 1970; ex *Olau Knud* 1966

★01200 **ZHEN ZHU QUAN** RC/Br (H&W) 1961; C; 6700; 129.88 × 7.79 (426 × 25.56); M (B&W) 16; ex *Supachai Bulakul* 1980; ex *Shendi* 1980; ex *Bombala* 1971
Sisters:
01202 **SEASPRITE** (Li) ex *Bunga Kenanga* 1978; ex *Bulimba* 1971
01203 **SPIJKENISSE** (Pa) ex *Maridi* 1980; ex *Barpeta* 1971
★01204 **YANG ZI JIANG 3** (RC) ex *Dina* 1982; ex *Mahabhakti* 1980; ex *Trikora Djaya* 1973; ex *Sumatra Breeze* 1971; ex *Bamora* 1971

01210 **FAIRSTAR** Li/Br (Fairfields) 1957; P; 21500; 185.6 × 8.4 (609 × 27.7); TST (Fairfield); 20; ex *Oxfordshire* 1964

01220 **FAIRWIND** Li/Br (J Brown) 1957; P; 16700; 185.3 × 8.9 (608 × 29.4); TST (J Brown); 20; ex *Sylvania* 1968
Sister:
01221 **FAIRSEA** (Li) ex *Fairland* 1971; ex *Carinthia* 1968

01230 **CARLA C** It/Fr (Ch de France) 1952; P;

20000; 182.9 × 8.6 (600 × 28.2); TST (Stork-Werkspoor); 23; ex *Flandre* 1968

01240 **EUGENIO C** It/It (Adriatico) 1966; P; 30600; 217 × 8.6 (773 × 28.4); TST (De Laval); 27

01250 **OCEANIC** Pa/It (Adriatico) 1965; P; 27600; 238 × 8.6 (782 × 28.4); TST (Adriatico); 26.5

01260 **ORIANA** Br/Br (Vickers-Armstrongs) 1960; P; 41900; 245 × 9.75 (804 × 32); TST (Vickers-Armstrongs); 27.5

01270 **CITTA DI NAPOLI** It/It ('Navalmeccanica') 1962; P; 5700; 120.4 × 5.4 (395 × 17.9); TSM (Fiat); 19.5
Sister:
01271 **CITTA DI NUORO** (It)

01290 **JUAN MARCH** Sp/Sp (UN de Levante) 1966; RoPCF; 6900; 130.8 × 5.4 (429 × 17.9); TSM (B&W); 21
Sisters (Sp flag):
01291 **CIUDAD DE COMPOSTELA**
01292 **LAS PALMAS DE GRAN CANARIA**
01293 **SANTA CRUZ DE TENERIFFE**

01300 **NORDLYS** No/De (Aalborg) 1951; P; 2200; 80.2 × 4.5 (263 × 14.9); M (B&W); 15.5
Sisters (No Flag):
01301 **NORDSTJERNEN**
01302 **POLARLYS**

01310 **AL KHAIRAT** Ku/Br (Ailsa) 1960; P; 2900; 90.2 × 4.6 (296 × 15.2); M (Sulzer); 16; ex *St. Clair II* 1977; ex *Saint Clair* 1977

01330 **VITTORE CARPACCIO** It/It (Apuania) 1963; P; 1200; 72.24 × 3.68 (237 × 12.07); M (Fiat); 12.25; May be rebuilt—see **ANTONELLO DA MESSINA**

01340 **ANTONELLO DA MESSINA** It/It (Apuania) 1963; RoC/F; 1200; 72.27 × 3.66 (237.10 × 12); M (Fiat); Bow & stern doors/ramp. Converted from passenger; original sister *Vittore Carpaccio* may be similarly converted-which see

★01350 **HARALD JARL** No/No (Trondhjems) 1960; P; 2600; 87.4 × 4.6 (287 × 15.2); M (B&W); 16

01351 **POLARSTERN** FRG/FRG (Howaldts DW) 1982; RS/IB/Sply.; 10900; 117.56 × 10.5 (385.7 × 34.45); TSM (KHD); 12

01352 **STENA CONSTRUCTOR** Sw/Sw (Oresunds) 1980; OSS; 5800; 111.50 × 6.70 (366 × 21.98); TrS D-E (Polar); 15.5; May now have an 'A-frame' aft—see **STENA SEASPREAD**
Similar:
01353 **STENA SEASPREAD** (Sw)
01354 **BAR PROTECTOR** (Bs) ex *Stena Protector*;
01355 **DILIGENCE** (Br) ex *Stena Inspector* (operated by RFA)
01356 **STENA SEASPREAD** Br/Sw (Oresunds) 1980; OSS; 6100; 112. × 6.84 (367.5 × 22.4); TrS D-E (Polar); 16; Other sisters may now also have 'A-frame' aft—see **STENA CONSTRUCTOR** etc

●01360 **SAINT FRANCOIS** Fr/Br (Bartram)—Po 1970/78; C/Con; 12400; 174.53 × 8.49 (573 × 27.85); M (Sulzer); 16; Modified 'SD 14' type. Lengthened and converted 1978 (Lisnave)
Sister:
01361 **SAINT PAUL** (Fr)

01370 **CREST HILL** Br/Br (Bartram) 1967; R; 6000/8400; 151.5 × 9 (497 × 29.6); M (Sulzer); —; ex *Timaru Star* 1983

★01380 **'KALININGRAD'** type; —/Ru ('Zhdanov') 1969; C; 3900/5600; 129 × 6.55/7.83 (426 × 21.9/25.69); M (B&W); 16; There are 2 types-the earlier ones having cranes by the foremast
Sisters (Ru flag):
★01381 **DONETSKIY KOMSOMOLETS**
★01382 **DONETSKIY KHIMIK**
★01383 **DONETSKIY METALLURG**
★01384 **DONETSKIY SHAKHTER**
★01385 **KOMSOMOLETS**
★01386 **BRYANSKIY MASHINOSTROITEL**
★01387 **LENINSKIYE ISKRY**
★01388 **KRASNOYARSKI KOMSOMOLETS**
★01389 **KOMSOMOLETS ARMENII**
★01390 **KOMSOMOLETS AZERBAYDZHANA**
★01391 **KOMSOMOLETS GRUZII**
★01392 **KOMSOMOLETS MOLDAVII**
★01394 **KOMSOMOLETS SPASSKA**
★01395 **KOMSOMOLETS USSURIYSKA**
★01396 **KOMSOMOLETS VLADIVOSTOKA**
★01397 **KOMSOMOLETS ROSSII**
★01398 **KOMSOMOLETS KAZAKHSTANA**
★01399 **KOMSOMOLETS ADZHARII**
★01400 **KOMSOMOLETS BYELORUSSII**
★01401 **KOMSOMOLETS TURKMENII**
★01402 **KOMSOMOLETS PRAVDA**

★01403 **MOSKOVSKIY KOMSOMOLETS**
★01404 **ZHDANOVSKIY KOMSOMOLETS**
★01405 **30-LETIYE POBEDY** (or TRIDTSATILE-TIYE POBEDY)
★01406 **RABOCHAYA SMENA**
★01407 **SMENA**
★01408 **STARYY BOLSHEVIK**
(Rm flag):
★01409 **SALAJ**
★01410 **NASAUD**
(Eg flag, Eg built-Alexandria):
01411 **RAMSES II**
01412 **NEFERTITI**
01413 **ISIS**
01414 **AMOUN**
01415 **THUTMOSE**
01416 **AHMOS**
01417 **IKHNATON**
01418 **MEMPHIS**

01430 **MONTERREY** Me/Ys ('Split') 1971; Pt. Con; 12600; 173.1 × 10.1 (568 × 32.11); M (Sulzer); —
Sister:
01431 **TOLUCA** (Me)

01435 **MARFRIO** Ar/De (Helsingor) 1970; C/Con/R; 6100/8200; 136.61 × 6.92/9.32 (448 × 22.70/30.58); M (B&W); 19.25; ex Lindfield 1980; ex Limpsfield 1976; ex Olau Rolf 1973; ex Cap Melville 1973
Sister:
01436 **SEAFROST** (Li) ex Mayfield 1980; ex Olau Pil 1973; ex Cap Colville 1972; launched as Olau Pil

01450 **ITALIA** It/It (Felszegi) 1967; P; 12200; 149 × 6.4 (489 × 21.1); TSM (MTU); 19

01460 **MUTIARA** My/My (Hong Leong) 1977; SS; 1900 dst; 71 × 4(232.94 × 13.12); M (Deutz); 16; Operated by Malaysian Navy. Helicopter deck aft

●01470 **MONTJOLLY II** Pa/Be (Bruges) 1957; C; 1400; 87.94 × 5.30 (286 × 17.39); M (KHD); 13; ex Gloria L 1983; ex Belgia 1967
Sister:
★01471 **ZLARIN** (Ys) ex Reine Astrid 1965

01480 **MARGARITA L** Pa/Br (Cammell Laird) 1960; P; 34200; 238.6 × 9.8 (783 × 32.1); TST (Cammell Laird); 23.5; ex Windsor Castle 1978

01490 **ROVER** US/US (Ingalls SB) 1969; RoVC-/Con; 11800; 183.2 × 10.4 (603 × 34.1); T (GEC); 23.5; ex American Rover 1983; ex Defiance 1982; ex Mormacsea 1970
Sisters (US flag):
01491 **GREAT REPUBLIC** ex Mormacsky 1970
01492 **RAPID** ex American Rapid 1983; ex Red Jacket 1981; ex Mormacstar 1970
01493 **YOUNG AMERICA** ex Mormacsun 1970

●01510 **KOTA BALI** My/Ne (Giessen) 1950; CP; 9000; 146 × 7.2 (479 × 23.7); TSM (Werkspoor); 16.5; ex Tjiwani 1974

●01520 **J C CRANE** Pa/Sw (Gotav.) 1961; C; 8100/11300; 156 × 8.73/9.4 (513 × 28.64/30.8); M (Gotaverken); 17; ex Mirrabooka 1982. At least one of this class (possibly all) has had the mast and kingpost in the well replaced by sets of tandem cranes
Sisters:
01521 **VENUS DEL MAR** (Ur) ex Temnaren 1979
01522 **ATHINAI** (Gr) ex Popi 1980

01530 **DEMON** Br/Ne ('De Noord') 1960; CP 6700; 151 × 8 (496 × 26.2); M (Stork); 16; ex Fedon 1983; ex Ifestos 1980; ex Algorab 1978
Sisters: (RC flag):
★01531 **LI SHUI** ex Texas 1973; ex Aludra 1969
★01532 **GUANGSHUI** ex Tortugas 1973; ex Alchiba 1969
★01533 **JIANSHUI** ex Tennesee 1973; ex Alnitak 1969
★01534 **WENSHUI** ex Tampa 1973; ex Alamak 1969

★01540 **OTRADNOE** Ru/Ja (Hitachi) 1964; C; 11100; 157 × 9.4 (518 × 30.9); M (B&W); 18; Cranes abreast foremast
Sisters (Ru flag):
★01541 **OLA**
★01542 **OREKHOV**
★01543 **ORSHA**
★01544 **OSTROGOZHSK**

01550 **HALLAREN** Gr/Sw (Gotav.) 1960; R; 6700; 142.6 × 7.2 (468 × 23.9); M (Gotaverken); 17
Sister:
01551 **VINGAREN** (Gr)

★01560 **METALLURG ANASOV** Ru/Ru (Kherson) 1962; C; 8300/11200; 170 × 8.25/9.75 (558 × 27.07/32); T (Kirov); 18; Ships vary slightly. Some have lighter masts or masts from funnel
Sisters (Ru flag):
★01561 **AKADEMIK SHIMANSKIY**

★01562 **BRATSTVO**
★01563 **FREDERIK ZHOLIO-KYURI**
★01564 **KHIRURG VISHNEVSKIY**
★01565 **KRASNAYA PRESNYA**
★01566 **KRASNOE ZNAMYA**
★01567 **KRASNYY-OKTYABAR**
★01568 **KREML**
★01569 **LENINSKIY PIONER**
★01570 **METALLURG BARDIN**
★01571 **METALLURG KURAKO**
★01572 **PARIZHSKAYA KOMMUNA** (gas turbines)
★01573 **RAVENSTVO**
★01574 **SVOBODA**
★01575 **TRANSBALT**
★01576 **VALENTINA TERESHKOVA**
★01577 **YUNYY LENINETS**
★01578 **YURIY GAGARIN**
★01579 **FIZIK KURCHATOV**
★01579A **KHIMIK ZELINSKIY**

01580 **AKDENIZ** Tu/FRG (A G 'Weser') 1955; P; 8800; 144.7 × 6.1 (474 × 20.3); TSM (MAN); 18.5
Sister:
01581 **KARADENIZ** (Tu)

01590 **EGE** Tu/FRG (A G 'Weser'); P; 6000; 122 × 5.8 (402 × 19); M (MAN); 14
Sister:
01591 **IZMIR** (Tu)

01610 **HANDARA** Sg/Ne (Boele's Sch.) 1954; C; 2700; 96.93 × 5.78 (318 × 18.96); M (Stork); 12.25; ex Van Noort 1969

●01630 **ARAMEDIA** Pa/Sw (Helsingborgs) 1960; C; 2200/3500; 110.22 × —/7.29 (362 × —/23.92); M (B&W); 14.5; ex Weida 1981; ex Olau Drot 1968; ex Adviser 1967; ex Olau Drot 1962; ex Olav Drot 1961; launched as Hibata

★01640 **'KALININGRAD'** type; —/Ru ('Zhdanov') 1969; C; 3900/5600; 129 × 6.55/7.85 (426 × 21.49/25.69); M (B&W); 16; There are 2 types—the earlier ones having cranes by the foremast
Sisters (Ru flag):
★01641 **DONETSKIY KOMSOMOLETS**
★01642 **DONETSKIY KHIMIK**
★01643 **DONETSKIY METALLURG**
★01644 **DONETSKIY SHAKHTER**
★01645 **KOMSOMOLETS**
★01646 **BRYANSKIY MASHINOSTROITEL**
★01647 **LENINSKIYE ISKRY**
★01648 **KRASNOYARSKI KOMSOMOLETS**
★01649 **KOMSOMOLETS ARMENII**
★01650 **KOMSOMOLETS AZERBAYDZHANA**
★01651 **KOMSOMOLETS GRUZII**
★01652 **KOMSOMOLETS MOLDAVII**
★01654 **KOMSOMOLETS SPASSKA**
★01655 **KOMSOMOLETS USSURIYSKA**
★01656 **KOMSOMOLETS VLADIVOSTOKA**
★01657 **KOMSOMOLETS ROSSII**
★01658 **KOMSOMOLETS KAZAKHSTANA**
★01659 **KOMSOMOLETS ADZHARII**
★01660 **KOMSOMOLETS BYELORUSSII**
★01661 **KOMSOMOLETS TURKMENII**
★01662 **KOMSOMOLETS PRAVDA**
★01663 **MOSKOVSKIY KOMSOMOLETS**
★01664 **ZHDANOVSKIY KOMSOMOLETS**
★01665 **30-LETIYE POBEDY** (or TRIDTSATILE-TIYE POBEDY)
★01666 **RABOCHAYA SMENA**
★01667 **SMENA**
★01668 **STARYY BOLSHEVIK**
(Rm flag):
★01669 **SALAJ**
★01670 **NASAUD**
(Eg flag):
01671 **RAMSES II**
01672 **NEFERTITI**
01673 **ISIS**
01674 **AMOUN**
01675 **THUTMOSE**
01676 **AHMOS**
01677 **IKHNATON**
01678 **MEMPHIS**

★01680 **BRIONI** Ys/Br (Connell) 1962; C; 1600; 90 × 5.2 (295 × 17.1); M (Polar); 13; ex Tuskar 1968

01700 **QUEEN ELIZABETH 2** Br/Br (Upper Clyde) 1969; P; 67000; 293 × 10 (963 × 32.8); TST (J Brown); 28.5

01710 **DAPHNE** Gr/Br (Swan Hunter)—Gr 1959/75; P; 11700; 162 × 10 (533 × 32.1); TSM (Doxford); 17; ex Akrotiri Express 1974; ex Port Sydney 1972; Rebuilt from a cargo ship 1975 (Khalkis)
Sister:
01711 **DANAE** (Gr); ex Therissos' Express 1974; ex Port Melbourne 1972

01720 **CALABRIA** It/It (Riuniti) 1952; RoPF; 4800; 116.7 × 5.8 (383 × 19); TSM (Fiat); 16.5

Sisters:
01721 **SANT ANDREA** (Gr) ex Lazio 1980
01722 **SICILIA** (It)

01730 **ROMANZA** Pa/Ge (B+V) 1939; P; 7500; 148 × 6.7 (488 × 22); D-E (MAN); 16; ex Aurelia 1970; ex Beaverbrae 1954; ex Huascaran 1947

01740 **PILOTO PARDO** Ch/Ne (Haarlemsche) 1959; SS; 200 Dspl; 82.3 × 4.6 (269 × 15); D—E (—); 14; Antarctic patrol ship; Helicopter platform

★01750 **ALEKSANDR PUSHKIN** Ru/DDR (Mathias-Thesen) 1965; P; 19900; 176 × 8 (577 × 26.1); TM (Sulzer); 20.5
Similar (Ru flag):
★01751 **IVAN FRANKO**
★01752 **SHOTA RUSTAVELI**
★01753 **TARAS SHEVCHENKO**
★01754 **MIKHAIL LERMONTOV**

●01760 **GALILEO GALILEI** It/It (Adriatico) 1963; P; 27900; 213.65 × 8.65 (700.95 × 28.38); TSM (De Laval); 25.5
Sister:
01761 **GUGLIELMO MARCONI** '(It)

★01770 **DING HU** RC/De (B&W) 1952; P; 2800; 93 × 4.4 (305 × 14.5); M (B&W); 15; ex Bao Feng 1980; ex Kongedybet 1979

01780 **POLAR STAR** US/US (Lockheed) 1976; IB; 12100 displ; 121.6 × 9.5 (399 × 31); Trs GT & D—E (Pratt & Whitney/Alco); 18; Helicopter platform and hangar
Sister:
01781 **POLAR SEA** (US)

01790 **ACHILLE LAURO** It/Ne ('De Schelde') 1947/65; P; 23600; 191 × 8.5 (627 × 28); TSM (Sulzer); 22; ex Willem Ruys 1965

●01800 **BOREA** Fi/Sw (Oskarshamns) 1960; PF; 3900; 100 × 4.9 (330 × 16); R & T (Oskarshamns); 15; ex Bore 1978

01810 **PANDELIS** Gr/US (US Naval SY) 1944; P; 1160; 67 × 2.8 (220 × 9); TSM (GEC); 18; ex B-A-M-29; ex Jasper

★01820 **MINGHUA** RC/Fr (L'Atlantique) 1962; P; 14200; 168 × 6.6 (551 × 21.9); TM (B&W); 22.5; ex Ancerville 1973

01830 **APHRODITE** Cy/Br (H&W) 1948; P; 4800; 111.82 × 4.6 (366.86 × 15.09); TSM (H&W); 17.5; ex Leinster 1 1969; ex Leinster 1968; Converted from ferry

01840 **LOUIS S. ST. LAURENT** Ca/Ca (Canadian Vickers) 1967; 1B; 13000 Dspl; 111 × 9.4 (367 × 31); Trs D-E (Canadian GEC); —; Helicopter hangar and deck

01850 **HAKUREI MARU** Ja/Ja (Mitsubishi HI) 1975; RS/SS; 1800; 87 × 5 (286 × 16.5); M (Akasaka); 15

01860 **ATLAS** Gr/Ne (Wilton-Fije) 1951/72; P; 9100; 153.3 × 8.6 (503 × 28.9); T (GEC); 17; ex Ryndam 1972; ex Waterman 1968; ex Ryndam 1968; Rebuilt 1972

01870 **STARWARD** No/FRG (AG 'Weser') 1968; P; 12900; 160 × 6.3 (525 × 20.5); TSM (MAN); 21; Side Doors
Similar:
01871 **SKYWARD** (No)

01890 **SAPPHO** Gr/Br (Cammell Laird) 1966; RoPF; 6500; 140 × 54 (460 × 17.6); TSM (Mirrlees); 18; ex Spero 1973

01900 **AL-QAMAR AL-SAUDI II** Si/It (Tirreno) 1970; RoPF; 6700; 125 × 5.2 (410 × 17.1), TSM (B&W); 21; ex Dana Sirena 1983; ex Dana Corona 1980; ex Trekroner 1971

01905 **DANA CORONA** De/It (Tirreno) 1969/80; RoPF; 8000; 124.85 × 5.21 (410 × 17.09); TSM (B&W); 21; ex Robin Hood 1979; ex Dana Sirena 1979; ex Robin Hood 1978; ex Dana Sirena 1978; ex Robin Hood 1977; ex Olau Dana 1977; ex Dana Sirena 1975; ex Aalborghus 1971. Bow, stern & side doors; Rebuilt 1980 (Aalborg)

01910 **KONG OLAV V** De/It (Tirreno) 1968; RoPF; 8000; 125 × 5.2 (411 × 17); TSM; 21
Sister:
01911 **PRINCESSE MARGARETHE** (De)

01920 **ENGLAND** Br/De (Helsingor) 1964; RoPF; 8100; 140 × 5.5 (459 × 18.1); TSM (B&W); 21

●01930 **WID** Si/De (Helsingor) 1957; P; 4300; 121 × 5.2 (397 × 17.2); TSM (B&W); 20.5; ex Prinsen 1978; ex Prinsessan 1978; ex Prinsessen 1971; ex Princesse Margrethe 1968

Sister:
★ 01931 JI MEI (RC) ex *Minfung* 1981; ex *Baronessan* 1980; ex *Taiwan* 1972; ex *Olav* 1969; ex *Kong Olav V* 1968

★ 01935 ANTONINA NEZHDANOVA Ru/Ys (Titovo) 1978; P; 3900; 100.01 × 4.65 (328 × 15.26); TSM (B&W); 17.25
Sisters (Ru flag):
★ 01936 OLGA SADOVSKAYA
★ 01937 KLAVDIYA YELANSKAYA
Possible sister (may be CMMF—see Mariya Yermolova etc):
★ 01938 OLGA ANDROVSKAYA (Ru)

01940 KONG OLAV No/No (Bergens) 1964; P; 2600; 87.5 × 4.6 (287 × 15.2); M (B&W); 16.5

01950 NORDNORGE No/No (Akers) 1964; P; 2600; 87.5 × 4.6 (287 × 15.2); M (B&W); 16.5

★ 01960 ABRAU-DYURSO Ru/Bu (G Dimitrov) 1964; P; 1000; 64 × 3 (211 × 10); M (Liebknecht); 13
Sisters (Ru flag):
★ 01963 ALUSHTA
★ 01964 AY-PETRI
★ 01965 PROFESSOR KOLESNIKOV ex *Aytodor* 1983
★ 01966 GURIEV
★ 01967 ADMIRAL LUNIN ex *Vanemuyne* 1968; ex *Artek* 1966
★ 01971 VASIL KOLAROV

★ 01980 GEORGI DIMITROV Bu/Bu (G Dimitrov) 1957; P; 900; 62.7 × 3 (206 × 10); M (Liebknecht); 12
Sister:
★ 01981 VASIL KOLAROV

01990 OLDENBURG FRG/FRG (Rolandwerft) 1958; F; 300; 43.6 × 1.5 (143 × 5); TSM (MWM); 11.5

★ 02000 MIN ZHUI RC/De (B&W) 1961; P; 5000; 98 × 4.8 (322 × 14.11); M (B&W); 16; ex *Bornholm* 1980

02020 WAPPEN VON HAMBURG FRG/FRG (Howaldts) 1965; P; 4400; 109.7 × 4.2 (360 × 13.7); TSM (MAN); 21.5; ex *Lucaya* 1966; ex *Wappen Von Hamburg* 1965

02030 ALTE LIEBE FRG/FRG (B+V) 1962; P; 3800; 104 × 4 (341 × 13.2); TSM (Ottensener); 21; ex *Wappen* 1966; ex *Wappen Von Hamburg* 1964

02040 TSUGARU MARU Ja/Ja (Mitsubishi HI) 1969; Cbl; 1700; 84.5 × 4.6 (278 × 15.1); M (Kobe); 13.5

★ 02060 KAPITAN SOROKIN Ru/Fi (Wartsila) 1977; IB; 10600; 131.88 × 8.5 (432.68 × 27.89); Trs D-E (Sulzer); 19; Helicopter deck
Sister:
★ 02061 KAPITAN NIKOLAYEV (Ru)
Similar (sloping funnel, bridge front stepped):
★ 02062 KAPITAN DRANITSYN (Ru)
★ 02063 KAPITAN KLEBNIKOV (Ru)

★ 02070 MOSKVA Ru/Fi (Sandvikens) 1960; IB; 9400; 122 × 10.7 (401 × 35.6); Trs D-E (Sulzer); 18; Helicopter Deck and 2 Helicopters
Sisters (Ru flag):
★ 02071 KIEV
★ 02072 LENINGRAD
★ 02073 MURMANSK
★ 02074 VLADIVOSTOK

★ 02080 KAPITAN M IZMAYLOV Ru/Fi (Wartsila) 1976; IB/Sal; 1400; 56.3 × 42 (184 × 14); TSD-E (Wartsila) 14 Sisters:
★ 02081 KAPITAN A RADZHABOV (Ru)
★ 02082 KAPITAN KOSOLAPOV (Ru)

02090 CAPE DON Au/Au (NSW Govt.) 1963; LT; 2100; 74 × 4.3 (243 × 14.4); M (Polar); —
Sisters (Au flag):
02091 CAPE MORETON
02092 CAPE PILAR

02100 TAVERNER Ca/Ca (Collingwood) 1962; PC; 1100; 57.41 × 3.83 (188.4 × 12.57); TSM (Fairbanks, Morse); 13

★ 02110 INGUL Ru/Fi (Sandvikens) 1962; Cbl; 5600; 130.41 × 5.21 (427.85 × 17.09); TS D-E (Sulzer); 14; 'KLASMA' Class
Sister:
★ 02111 JANA (may be spelt YANA) (Ru)

★ 02120 BAYKAL Ru/DDR (Mathias-Thesen) 1964; P; 5200; 122.1 × 5.2 (401 × 17); TSM; 17 (MAN)
Similar—vary in details (Ru flag):
★ 02122 GRIGORIY ORDZHONIKDZE
★ 02123 KHABAROVSK
★ 02125 MARIYA ULYANOVA
★ 02126 M URITSKIY
★ 02127 NIKOLAYEVSK
★ 02128 PETROPAVLOVSK
★ 02130 VATSLAV VOROVSKIY

Some of these may be rebuilt like ESTONIA (which see)

★ 02140 BASHKIRIYA Ru/DDR (Mathias-Thesen) 1964; P; 5300; 122.15 × 5.27 (400.75 × 17.29); TSM (MAN); 17; May be modified like ESTONIA—which see
Sister:
★ 02141 KUBAN (Ru) ex *Nadezhda Krupskaya*; (Naval troopship)

★ 02150 ADZHARIYA Ru/DDR (Mathias-Thesen) 1964; P; 5300; 122 × 5.2 (401 × 17); TSM (MAN); 17; May be modified like ESTONIYA—which see

★ 02160 ESTONIYA Ru/DDR (Mathias-Thesen) 1960; P; 4900; 122 × 5.2 (401 × 17); TSM (MAN); 17
Sisters (Ru flag):
★ 02161 LATVIYA
★ 02162 MIKHAIL KALININ (larger pipes from funnel and different type of crane—see inset)
★ 02162A FELIKS DZERZHINSKIY
★ 02162B LITVA
★ 02162C PRIAMURYE ex *Vladivostock* 1968
★ 02162D TURKMENIYA

02170 ESPRESSO CORINTO It/Fr (CNIM) 1967; RoPF; 6900; 130 × 5.3 (427 × 17.5); TSM (Fiat); 21.5; ex *Avenir* 1976

★ 02180 STEFAN BATORY Pd/Ne (Wilton-Fije) 1952; P; 15000; 153.3 × 8.7 (503 × 18.9); T (GEC); 16.5; ex *Maasdam* 1965

02190 HUDSON Ca/Ca (Saint John SB) 1963; IB/SS; 3700; 90.5 × 6.3 (297 × 20.7); TSD-E (Dominion); —; Helicopter

02200 JOHN CABOT Ca/Ca (Canadian Vickers) 1965; IB/Cbl; 5100; 95.4 × 6.7 (313 × 22); TS D-E (Fairbanks Morse); —; Helicopter

● 02210 SAUDI ARABIAN Si/No (Bergens) 1966; RoPF; 8500; 140 × 5.3 (458 × 17.4); TSM (B&W); 20; ex *Grand Flotel* 1980; ex *Ile De Beaute* 1976; ex *Sunward* 1973

02220 HAKUREI MARU Ja/Ja (Mitsubishi HI) 1974; RS/SS; 1800; 87 × 5 (286 × 16.5); M (Akasaka); 15

★ 02230 KAPITAN SOROKIN Ru/Fi (Wartsila) 1977; IB; 10600; 131.88 × 8.5 (432.68 × 27.89); TrS D-E (Sulzer); 19; Helicopter deck
Sister (Ru flag):
★ 02231 KAPITAN NIKOLAYEV
Similar (sloping funnel top, bridge front stepped):
★ 02232 KAPITAN DRANITSYN
★ 02233 KAPITAN KLEBNIKOV

02240 VOIMA Fi/Fi (Sandvikens) Fi 1954/79; IB; —; 83.52 × —(274 × —); TSD-E (Wartsila)—; Rebuilt 1978-79 (Wartsila)

02250 BUCANERO Ec/Br (Caledon) 1950; PC; 2000; 87.2 × 4.5 (286 × 14.9); TSM (British Polar); 14; ex *St. Ninian* 1976

02260 DANA De/De (Dannebrog) 1981; RS/SS; 2500; 78.44 × 5.93 (257 × 19.46); M (B&W); 12

★ 02270 MUSSON Ru/Pd (Szczecinska) 1967; RS; 3300; 97 × 5.2 (319 × 17.1); TSM (Sulzer)—; 'B88' type
Sisters (Ru flag):
★ 02271 ERNST KRENKEL
★ 02272 GEORGIY USHAKOV
★ 02273 OKEAN
★ 02274 PASSAT
★ 02275 PRIBOY
★ 02276 PRILIV
★ 02277 VICTOR BUGAEV ex *Poryv*
★ 02278 VOLNA

★ 02280 KATYN Ru/Fi (Wartsila) 1973; Cbl; 6000; 130.41 × 5.75 (427.8 × 18.86); TS D-E (Wartsila); 14; 'KLASMA' class also known as KATUNJ
Sisters (Ru flag):
★ 02281 DONETS
★ 02282 ZNA (or TSNA)
Possible sisters (may be KCMFMN—see INGUR):
★ 02283 ZEYA
★ 02284 TAVDA
★ 02285 KALAR

● 02290 COOLHAVEN Ne/FRG (Kieler H) 1961; C; 7600/10000; 159.42 × 7.54/8.46 (523 × 24.74/27.76); M (MAN); 19; ex *Cap San Augustin* 1982
Sisters:
02291 SAN DIEGO (Pa) ex *Cap San Diego* 1982
02292 CAP SAN MARCO (FRG)
02293 SAN ANTONIO (Pa) ex *Cap San Antonio* 1982

02300 JEFF DAVIS US/US (Bethlehem Steel) 1962;

C; 8500/12800; 172 × —/9.63 (565 × —/31.59); T (Westinghouse)—; ex *Canada Bear* 1975; ex *China Bear* 1974

★ 02310 SCHWARZA DDR/De (Helsingborgs) 1962; C; 2300/3500; 110 × 6/7.16 (362 × 19.69/23.49); M (B&W); 15; ex *Olau Ege* 1968; ex *Benefactor* 1967; Launched as *Olau Ege*

● 02320 FENG BAO RC/RC (—) 1975; C; 10300; 161.5 × 9 (530 × 30); M (—); —; Cranes abreast mainmast
Sisters (RC flag):
★ 02321 FENG LANG
★ 02322 FENG GUANG
★ 02324 FENG YUN ex *Feng Jin*
★ 02325 FENG MAO
★ 02326 FENG MING
★ 02327 FENGYUN
★ 02328 FENGZHAN
Note: some of these may have a crane aft

02330 PORTO SANTO Pa/Fr (Nantes) 1962; ST; 1800; 78 × 5.6 (256 × 18.5); M (Nantes); 14.5; ex *Colonel Pleven II* 1982
02331 AUSTRAL (Fr) ex *Pierre Pleven* 1980

★ 02340 MARIYA YERMOLOVA Ru/Ys ('Titovo') 1974; P; 3900; 100 × 4.5 (328 × 14.1); TSM (B&W); 17
Sisters (Ru flag):
★ 02341 ALLA TARASOVA
★ 02343 LYUBOV ORLOVA
★ 02344 MARIYA SAVINA
★ 02345 OLGA ANDROVSKAYA (may have mainmast aft—see ANTONINA NEZHDANOVA)

02346 KERINCI Ia/FRG (Meyer) 1983; F; 14000; 144.02 × 5.90 (473 × 19.36); TSM (Krupp-Mak); 20.
Sisters (Ia flag):
02347 KAMBUNA
02348 RINJANI
One further sister on order

★ 02350 KOLKHIDA Ru/Ru ('Zhdanov') 1961; P; 3200; 101.5 × 4 (333 × 13); TSM (CKD Praha); 14.5; Some ships have taller funnel; Some ships may not have crane
Sisters (Ru flag):
★ 02351 BUKOVINA
★ 02352 KIRGHIZSTAN
★ 02353 MOLDAVIA
★ 02355 TADZHAKISTAN
★ 02356 TALLINN ex *Svanetiya*
★ 02357 TATARIYA
★ 02358 UZBEKISTAN
Possible sister (Ru flag):
★ 02359 AFGHANISTAN

02370 LOFOTEN No/No (Akers) 1964; P; 2600; 87.4 × 4.6 (287 × 15.2); M (B&W); 16.5

02380 FINNMARKEN No/FRG (B+V) 1956; P; 2200; 81.3 × 4.5 (267 × 14.9); M (MAN); 16
Sister:
02381 RAGNVALD JARL (No)

● 02390 GENTILE DA FABRIANO It/It (Apuania) 1962; P; 2200; 95 × 3.7 (312 × 12.4); TSM (Fiat); 19.5
Sister:
02391 MARAM (Fi); ex *Kalakukko* 1981; ex *Andrea Mantegna*

02400 LONG LINES US/FRG (Schlieker) 1963; Cbl; 11300; 156 × 8.2 (512 × 26.9); TST-E (GEC); 15

02410 C S MONARCH Br/Br (Robb Caledon) 1975; Cbl; 3500; 95.4 × 4.8 (313 × 15.9); M (British Polar); 15
Sister:
02411 C S IRIS (Br)

★ 02415 LEONID ILICH BREZHNEV Ru/Ru (Baltic) 1974; IB; 18200; 148.00 × 11.00 (485.6 × 36.09); Trs T-E (Nuclear); —; ex *Arktika* 1982
Sister (Ru flag):
★ 02416 SIBIR

02420 KUROSHIO MARU Ja/Ja (Mitsubishi HI) 1975; Cbl; 3300; 119.3 × 5.6 (392 × 18.5); M (MAN); 16.5

02430 KDD MARU Ja/Ja (Mitsubishi HI) 1967; Cbl; 4300; 114 × 6 (374 × 19.6); TSM (Kobe); 16

02440 BALTIC STAR FRG/FRG (Howaldts.) 1963; P; 2800; 91.4 × 3.8 (300 × 12.1); TSM (KHD); 19.5; ex *Stena Finlandica* 1975; ex *Helgoland* 1972

★ 02460 AKADEMIK KRYLOV Ru/DDR (—) —; RS; 9100 Dsp; 147 × —(483 × —); M (—); 15

02470 SAGARDEEP In/Ys ('Titovo') 1964; LT; 2800; 100 × — (327 × —); TSM (Pielstick); 19.75

● 02480 LASH ATLANTICO US/US (Avondale) 1972; Bg/Con; 26400; 250 × 10.7 (820 × 35.5); T (De

Laval); 21: Both gantries (N) can be moved right aft, thus altering sequence. Also coded P5; 'LASH' type Sisters (overall lengths vary) (US flag):
02481 **LASH ITALIA**
02482 **LASH PACIFICO**
02483 **AUSTRAL LIGHTNING** ex *LASH Espana* 1976
02484 **AUSTRAL MOON** ex *Australia Bear* 1975; ex *Philippine Bear* 1975
02485 **DELTA MAR**
02486 **DELTA SUD**
02487 **DELTA NORTE**
02488 **DELTA CARIBE** ex *Lash Turkiye*

02500 **CAPE HENLOPEN** US/US (Jeffboat) 1944; PF; 1500; 96.3 × 3.1 (316 × 10.2); TSM (General Motors); —; ex *Virginia Beach* 1964

02505 **AQUARAMA** US/US (Sun SB) 1945; RoPF; 12800; 150.9 × 5.2 (495 × 17.3); T (GEC); 19; ex *Marine Star* 1955; Converted from cargo ship 1956

02510 **JEAN CHARCOT** Fr/Fr (CNIM) 1965; RS; 2100; 74.5 × 5 (244 × 16.5); TS D-E (MAN); 15

02515 **LUCERO DEL MAR** Ur/De (Helsingor) 1963; C/R; 5900; 143 × 7.6 (469 × 25); M (B&W); 17; ex *Tijuca* 1980; ex *Norma* 1980

★02520 **IRKUTSK** Ru/DDR (Warnow) 1968; C; 4800/8500; 151 × 8.8 (497 × 29.9); M (MAN); 17
Sisters (Ru flag):
★02521 **IZHORA**
★02522 **IZMAIL**
★02523 **KARAGANDA**
★02524 **TULA**
★02525 **SANTIAGO DE CUBA** ex *Ilovaysk* 1976
★02526 **AKADEMIK FILATOV**
★02527 **AKADEMIK IOSIF ORBELI**
★02528 **AKADEMIK RYKACHEV**
★02529 **AKADEMIK SHUKHOV**
★02530 **AKADEMIK YURYEV**

02540 **PISANG** Sg/Fi (Wartsila) 1968; R; 9600; 154 × 8.5 (506 × 28); M (Pielstick); 21; ex *Aconcagua Valley* 1981
Sister:
02541 **DURIAN** (Sg) ex *San Joaquin Valley* 1981

02550 **MULTI CARRIER** Pa/Ja (Mitsubishi HI) 1967; C; 6700; 156 × 8.6 (511 × 28.4); M (Sulzer); 18.5; ex *Sacramento Maru*
Sisters:
02551 **CHOHU CAREER** (Pa) ex *San Francisco Maru*
02552 **TRANS KOSTAS** (Gr) ex *Bilquis* 1982; ex *Savannah Maru* 1982
02553 **ELENA** (Ma) ex *Helen* 1981; ex *St. Louis Maru* 1981

02560 **AFRIC STAR** Br/Br (Smith's D) 1975; R; 7600/8900; 155.8 × 9.2 (511 × 30.05); M (B&W); 24
Sisters (Br flag):
02561 **ALMEDA STAR**
02562 **ANDALUCIA STAR**
02563 **AVELONA STAR**
02564 **ALMERIA STAR**
(No flag):
02565 **HIDLEFJORD** ex *Avila Star* 1980

02567 **LLOYD ALEGRETE** Bz/Bz (CCN) 1981; C; 8600/11400; 160.03 × —/9.22 (525 × —/30.25); M (MAN); 17.75; 'Pri—121' type
Sister:
02568 **LLOYD BAHIA** (Bz)

★02570 **HUI QUAN** RC/Fr (CNIM) 1969; R; 6700; 140 × 8.2 (459 × 26.9); M (Pielstick); 20.5; ex *Pointe Allegre* 1979
Sisters:
02571 **MONTEGO BAY II** (Pa) ex *Callao* 1982; ex *Pointe Des Colibris* 1979
★02572 **YANG QUAN** (RC); ex *Pointe Marlin* 1979

02580 **TAMARA** Sw/Fi (Wartsila) 1974; Con; 22300; 209 × 9.5 (686 × 31); TSM (Wartsila); 23
Sisters:
02581 **MALMROS MONSOON** (Br)
02582 **NAGARA** (Sw)

02590 **LEENOR** Is/Fi (Rauma-Repola) 1963; C; 3000/5000; 130.7 × 7.3 (430 × 24.1); M (Sulzer); 16; Lengthened 1970; ex *Argo* 1981
Sister:
02591 **SASSA** (Pa) ex *Leeor* 1982; ex *Virgo* 1981

●02600 **SNOW FLAKE** Sw/Fr (La Ciotat) 1972; R; 11400; 173 × 9.3 (569 × 30.5); M (Sulzer); 22.5; Side Doors
Sisters:
02601 **MALAYAN QUEEN** (Pi) ex *Snow Ball* 1981
02602 **SNOW CRYSTAL** (Sw)
02603 **SNOW DRIFT** (Sw)
02604 **MALAYAN EMPRESS** (Pi) ex *Snow Flower* 1983

02605 **MALAYAN KING** (Pi) ex *Snow Land* 1981
02606 **SNOW STORM** (Br)
02607 **SNOW HILL** (Br)

02610 **GAIETY** Br/Br (Burntisland) 1964; C; 6700; 130.7 × 7.8 (429 × 25.6); M (B&W); 16.5; ex *Cufic* 1977; ex *Newfoundland* 1976; ex *Cufic* 1974; ex *Newfoundland* 1973
Sister:
02611 **ARAB DABBOR** (Si) ex *Booker Valiant* 1979; ex *Tropic* 1978; ex *Nova Scotia* 1976; ex *Tropic* 1974; ex *Nova Scotia* 1973

02620 **POINTE SANS SOUCI** Fr/Fr (Dubigeon-Normandie) 1973; RoC/Con; 6500; 155.4 × 8.2 (510 × 26.9); M (Pielstick); 20; Stern ramp/door—side door
Sisters (Fr flag):
02621 **POINTE LA ROSE**
02622 **POINTE MADAME**

●02630 **SNOW FLAKE** Sw/Fr (La Ciotat) 1972; R; 11400; 173 × 9.3 (569 × 30.5); M (Sulzer); 22.5, Side Doors
Sisters:
02631 **MALAYAN QUEEN** (Pi) ex *Snow Ball* 1981
02632 **SNOW CRYSTAL** (Sw)
02633 **SNOW DRIFT** (Sw)
02634 **MALAYAN EMPRESS** (Pi) ex *Snow Flower* 1983
02635 **MALAYAN KING** (Pi) ex *Snow Land* 1981
02636 **SNOW STORM** (Br)
02637 **SNOW HILL** (Br)

02640 **SEAGULL** Gr/Br (Robb Caledon) 1971; C; 7100/9800; 153 × 9.1 (502 × 30.9); M (Doxford); 18; ex *St. John* 1982; ex *City of Hull* 1980
Sisters (Gr flag):
02641 **SEA LORD** ex *City of London* 1980
02642 **MARIANTHE** ex *City of Liverpool* 1980

02650 **HILCO SPRINTER** No/No (Framnaes) 1979; R; 6800/9100; 155.7 × 7.5/9.8 (510.9 × 24.6/32.1); M (Sulzer); 22 (trials)
Sisters:
02651 **SCAMPER UNIVERSAL** (Pa) ex *Hilco Scamper*
02652 **STIRLING UNIVERSAL** (Br) ex *Hilco Speedster*

02660 **AFRIC STAR** Br/Br (Smith's D) 1975; R; 7600/9800; 155.8 × 9.2 (511 × 30.1); M (B&W); 24
Sisters:
02661 **ALMEDA STAR** (Br)
02662 **ANDALUCIA STAR** (Br)
02663 **AVELONA STAR** (Br)
02664 **ALMERIA STAR** (Br)
02665 **HIDLEFJORD** (No) ex *Avila Star* 1980

★02670 **SVETLOGORSK** Ru/Ru (Kherson) 1970; C; 6300/8900; 152.7 × 9.3 (501 × 30.85); M (B&W) 17
Sisters (Ru flag):
★02671 **AKADEMIK EVGENIY PATON**
★02672 **ILYA KULIK**
★02673 **SEREBRYANSK**
★02674 **SEVAN**
★02675 **SYZRAN**
Similar (smaller cranes arranged in pairs) (Ru flag):
★02676 **SARNY**
★02677 **SEROV**
★02678 **SEVERODONETSK**
★02679 **SLAVYANSK**
★02680 **SVANETIYA**
★02681 **KOMSOMOLSKAYA SLAVA**
★02682 **SOCHI**

★02690 **NOVGOROD** Ru/Fi (Wartsila) 1967; C; 5800/8800; 150.9 × 9 (495 × 29.6); M (Sulzer); 18
Sisters (Ru flag):
★02691 **NOVOSIBIRSK**
★02692 **NOVOKUZNETSK**
★02693 **NOVOKUIBYSHEVSK**
★02694 **NOVOMOSKOVSK**
★02695 **NOVOTROITSK**
★02696 **NOVOVYATSK**
★02697 **NOVOALTAISK**
★02698 **NOVOMIRGOROD**
★02699 **NOVOPOLOTSK**
★02700 **NOVODRUZHESK**
★02701 **NOVOLVOVSK**
★02702 **NOVZYBKOV**
★02703 **NOVOGRUDOK**
★02704 **NOVOVOLYNSK**
Some later ships vary in superstructure. Some can be fitted with a heavy-lift derrick. See drawing under KC₂KC₂MFC

02710 **NEDLLOYD NAGASAKI** Ne/Ne ('De Schelde') 1972; C; 12100; 165 × 9.7 (543 × 32); M (Sulzer); 21; ex *Straat Nagasaki* 1978
Sisters (Ne flag):
92711 **NEDLLOYD NAGOYA** ex *Straat Nagoya* 1978;
02712 **NEDLLOYD NAPIER** ex *Straat Napier* 1978;

02713 **NEDLLOYD NASSAU** ex *Straat Nassau* 1978

●02720 **BRA** Br/Sw (Lindholmens) 1968; Con; 10300; 173.3 × 8.7 (568 × 28.4); TSM (Lindholmens); 18.5; ex *Brasilia* 1983; Converted from cargo ship
Sister:
02722 **SANTOS III** (Pa) ex *Santos* 1983
Similar (shorter funnel):
02723 **ROCK** (Pa) ex *Montevideo* 1981

★02724 **NORILSK** Ru/Fi (Wartsila) 1982; C/Con/RoC; 18600; 174.02 × 10.52 (570.9 × 34.51); M (Sulzer); Side ramp
Sisters (Ru flag):
★02725 **NIZHNEYANSK**
★02726 **MONCHEGORSK**
★02727 **OKHA**
★02728 **TIKSI**
★02728/1 **IGARKA**
★02728/2 **BRATSK**
★02728/3 **KOLA**
★02728/4 **ARKHANGELSK**
★02728/5 **AMDERMA**
★02728/6 **KANDALAKSHA**
★02728/7 **KEMEROVO**

02729 **MONTE ALTO** Bz/Bz (CCN) 1979; C; 9100; 140.95 × 8.92 (462 × 29.27); M (MAN); 15; 'SD14' type
Sisters:
02729/1 **MONTE CRISTO** (Bz)
02729/2 **MONTE PASCOAL** (Bz)
Similar (radar mast just foreward of funnel):
02729/3 **ANA LUISA** (Bz)
Probably similar:
02729/4 **ALESSANDRA** (Bz)

02730 **GARIFALIA C** Gr/Br (Swan Hunter) 1970; C; 6400/9800; 155.7 × 9.2 (511 × 30.25); M (Doxford); 17; ex *Strathaird* 1979; ex *Nigaristan* 1975

02740 **TRANSOCEAN REEFER** Pi/Ja (Shikoku) 1969; R; 4700; 135 × 7.1 (443 × 23.2); M (B&W); 17; ex *Penta* 1980; ex *Aotearoa* 1972

●02750 **SAUDI AL JUBAIL** Si/Ja (NKK) 1967; C; 7300/10200; 161.8 × 10 (531 × 33.1); M (B&W); 20; ex *Nedlloyd Holland* 1983; ex *Straat Holland* 1978

●02760 **ANCHAN** Th/Ja (Mitsui) 1967; C; 9900; 171 × 9.1 (563 × 30.1); M (B&W); 21; ex *Strathardle* 1979
Sisters:
02761 **BANJAMAS** (Th) ex *Strathbrora* 1979
02762 **TZELEPI** (Gr) ex *Chuanchom* 1980; ex *Strathconon* 1979

02770 **BEI SHAN** Pa/Sw (Oresunds) 1958; C; 3700; 106 × 7 (349 × 22.35); M (Gotaverken); 15; ex *Bonnard* 1975
Sisters:
02771 **NAN SHANG** (Pa) ex *Braque* 1975
02772 **JULIE A** (Pa) ex *Beaver Spirit* 1983; ex *Carmen A* 1981; ex *Botticelli* 1975

●02790 **ROCADAS** Po/Ru ('Chernomorskiy') 1971; C; 12100; 169.86 × 10.06 (557.28 × 33.01); M (B&W); 18; ex *Tropico* 1971; 'FEODOSIYA' type
Similar:
02791 **SERPA PINTO** (Po) ex *Tropicalia* 1971
02792 **SEA HERON** (Pa) ex *Monarch* 1982
02793 **KALOMIRA V** (Gr) ex *Monsoon* 1982
02794 **DIMITRIS** (Gr) ex *Ikaros* 1980.
(Ru flag):
★02795 **KAPITAN ALEKSEYEV**
★02796 **KAPITAN CHIRKOV**
★02797 **KAPITAN DZHURASHEVICH**
★02798 **KAPITAN KADETSKIY**
★02799 **KAPITAN KAMINSKIY**
★02800 **KAPITAN KUSHNARENKO**
★02801 **KAPITAN ANISTRATYENKO**
★02802 **KAPITAN GEORGIY BAGLAY**
★02803 **KAPITAN LEONTIY BORISENKO**
★02804 **KAPITAN LEV SOLOVYEV**
★02805 **KAPITAN MODEST IVANOV**
★02806 **KAPITAN SLIPKO**

02810 **CHERRY ORIENT** Sg/Br (Doxford & S) 1968; C; 5600/8500; 150.6 × 8.9 (494 × 29.3); M (Sulzer); 18; ex *Historian* 1981;
Sister:
02811 **CHERRY CRYSTAL** (Sg) ex *Magician* 1981

02820 **NEW ZEALAND CARIBBEAN** Br/FRG (Bremer V) 1980; Con; 19600; 169.4 × 10.02 (555.77 × 32.87); M (MAN); 19

02830 **PUNTA STELLA** It/It (Muggiano) 1976; R; 7200/9400; 152.8 × 9.2 (503 × 30); M (GMT); 23
Sisters:
02831 **PUNTA VERDE** (It)
02832 **RIO JUBONES** (Ec) ex *Punta Sole* 1978
02833 **PUNTA BIANCA** (It) (see KC₂MFC) may also have this sequence

539

● 02840 **POCANTICO** Be/Be (Boelwerf) 1979; R; 7000; 151.26 × 8.7 (496.26 × 28.54); M (MAN); 21
Sisters (Be flag):
02841 **POCAHONTAS**
02842 **POTOMAC**

02844 **GLACIAR AMEGHINO** Ar/Ar (Alianza) 1981; R; 9000; 146.51 × 9.23 (480.7 × 30.28); M (Sulzer); 20; Side doors
Sisters (Ar flag):
02845 **GLACIAR PERITO MORENO**
02846 **GLACIAR VIEDMA**

● 02850 **HONOLULU** Ne/Ne (Giessen-de Noord) 1979; R; 8000; 155 × 8.8 (508.53 × 28.87); M (Sulzer); 21.6
Sisters (Ne flag):
02851 **CHRISTINA**
02852 **LANAI**
02853 **RIO FRIO**

02860 **AL SALAMA** Sh/Br (Scotstoun) 1975; R; 8000/10400; 157.3 × 9.3 (516 × 30); M (B&W); 20.5; ex *Loch Maree* 1981
Sister:
02861 **AL ZAHRA** (Sh) ex *Loch Lomond* 1981

02870 **AUSTRALIA STAR** Br/Br (Smith's D) 1978; Con; 17100; 168.87 × 9.37 (554.04 × 39.74); M (Sulzer); 18
Sister:
02871 **NEW ZEALAND STAR** (Br)

02880 **WILLOWBANK** Br/Br (Smith's D) 1980; Con; 18200; 171.13 × 9.35 (561.45 × 30.68); M (B&W); 19

02890 **DUNEDIN** Br/Br (Swan Hunter) 1980; Con; 18140; 171.1 × 9.37 (561.35 × 30.74); M (B&W); 19

★ 02900 **PERM** Ru/Ru (Vyborg) 1969; C; 4800; 122 × 7.2 (400 × 23.5); M (B&W); 14.5
Sisters (Ru flag):
★ 02901 **PALANGA**
★ 02902 **PAMIR**
★ 02903 **PARAMUSHIR**
★ 02904 **PAROMAY**
★ 02905 **PARGOLOVO**
★ 02906 **PAVLOVO**
★ 02907 **PECHENGA**
★ 02908 **PERTOMINSK**
★ 02909 **PETROKREPOST**
★ 02910 **PETROVSKIY**
★ 02911 **PETROZAVODSK**
★ 02912 **PLESETSK**
★ 02913 **POMORYE**
★ 02914 **PONOY**
★ 02915 **PROKOPYEVSK**
★ 02916 **PREZHEVALSK**
★ 02917 **PULKOVO**
★ 02918 **PUSHLAKHTA**
★ 02919 **PUSTOZERSK**

02930 **WINTER WATER** Sw/Sw (Gotav) 1979; R; 11800; 169 × 10.1 (554.46 × 33.14); M (B&W); 21.9
Sisters (Sw flag):
02931 **WINTER MOON**
02932 **WINTER SEA**
02933 **WINTER STAR**
02934 **WINTER SUN**
02935 **WINTER WAVE**

02940 **COFFEE TRADER** Gr/Ne (Pot) 1968; CP; 5200; 155 × 8.5 (477 × 28); M (Stork); 18; ex *Mercurius* 1980
Sister:
02941 **ALEXANDER'S POWER** (Gr) ex *Agios Giannis* 1981; ex *Elena Altomare* 1980; ex *Neptunus* 1979

02950 **TAMARA** Sw/Fi (Wartsila) 1974; Con; 22300; 209 × 9.5 (686 × 31); M (Wartsila); 23
Sisters:
02951 **MALMROS MONSOON** (Br)
02952 **NAGARA** (Sw)

02960 **LANKA KANTHI** Sr/Sw (Lindholmens) 1962; CP; 5700; 129 × 7.1 (424 × 23.4); M (Lindholmens); 14.5; ex *Huangyan* 1973; ex *Dawning* 1970; ex *Convallaria* 1970

02980 **WESTERN REEFER** Pa/Ja (Kochi Jukogyo) 1973; R; 7400; 141.1 × 8.1 (463 × 26); M (MAN); 21; ex *Toei Maru* 1980
Sister:
02981 **EASTERN REEFER** (Pa) ex *Toyu Maru* 1980

02990 **HAWAII** Ja/Ja (Kochi Jukogyo) 1979; R; 6500; 151.11 × 8.62 (495.77 × 28.28); M (Pielstick);
—
Sister:
02991 **BARRIOS** (Ja)

02993 **PUMA** Ja/Ja (Kurushima) 1978; R; 7200; 143.52 × 8.52 (471 × 27.95); M (Pielstick); 20

Sister:
02994 **PANTHER** (Ja)

● 02995 **CARIBBEAN MARU** Ja/Ja (Kurushima) 1979; R; 10500; 160.51 × 8.67 (526.61 × 28.44); M (MAN); 19.5; 8 side doors; Can carry vehicles

03000 **AL ZAHRA** Sh/Br (Scotstoun) 1975; R; 8000/10400; 157.3 × 9.3 (516 × 30); M (B&W); 20.5; ex *Loch Maree* 1981
Sister:
03001 **AL SALAMA** (Sh) ex *Loch Lomond* 1981

03030 **HAWAII** Ja/Ja (Kochi Jukogyo) 1979; R; 6500; 151.11 × 8.62 (495.77 × 28.28); M (Pielstick);
—
Sister:
03031 **BARRIOS** (Ja)

★ 03040 **KASIMOV** Ru/Fi (Wartsila) 1962; C; 9300; 147 × 9.1 (482 × 30); M (Sulzer); 15.25
Sisters (Ru flag):
★ 03041 **KALININABAD**
★ 03042 **KANEV**
★ 03043 **KARACHAJEVO-CHERKESSIJA**
★ 03045 **KASPIJSK**
★ 03046 **KIMOVSK**
★ 03047 **KOVROV**
★ 03048 **KRASNOUFIMSK**
Similar:
★ 03049 **KRASNOGRAD** (Ru)

★ 03060 **HARRY POLLITT** Ru/DDR (Warnow) 1971; C; 9300; 151.5 × 9 (497 × 29.5); M (MAN); 17; Some sisters vary in details; Some have small kingpost abaft funnel as indicated in drawing
Sisters (Ru flag):
★ 03061 **VALERIAN KUIBYSHEV**
★ 03062 **WILLIAM FOSTER**
★ 03063 **ANATOLIY LUNACHARSKIY**
★ 03064 **ANNA ULYANOVA**
★ 03065 **ALEKSANDR ULYANOV**
★ 03066 **DMITRIY ULYANOV**
★ 03067 **ILYA ULYANOV**
★ 03068 **NIKOLAY KRYLENKO**
★ 03069 **NIKOLAY POGODIN**
★ 03070 **OLGA ULYANOVA**
★ 03071 **VLADIMIR ILYCH**
★ 03072 **BORIS ZHEMCHUZIN**

● 03080 **ITAIMBE** Bz/Bz (Ish. do Brazil) 1970; C; 10800; 161 × 9.7 (528 × 31.9) M (Sulzer); 20.5
Sisters (Bz flag):
03083 **ITAPUI**
03084 **ITAQUICE**
03085 **ITAGIBA**
03087 **ITAPUCA**
03089 **ITAPURA**
03090 **ITASSUCE**
03091 **COPACABANA**
03092 **FLAMENGO**
03093 **FROTARIO**
03094 **FROTASANTOS**
03095 **MARINGA**
03096 **OLINDA**
(Po flag):
03097 **CARVALHO ARAUJO**

● 03100 **PEREIRA d'ECA** Po/Bz (Verolme E R do Brazil) 1972; C; 7800/11200; 161 × 9.6 (528 × 31.5); M (B&W); 20.5; Launched as *Juno*
Probable sisters (Bz flag):
03101 **MINERVA**
03102 **ZEUS**
03103 **NETUNO**

★ 03110 **NOVGOROD** Ru/Fi (Wartsila) 1967; C; 5800/8800; 150.9 × 9 (495 × 29.5); M (Sulzer); 18; Heavy lift derrick is not normally fitted; See alternative entry under KC₄MFC;
Sisters (Ru flag):
★ 03111 **NOVOSIBIRSK**
★ 03112 **NOVOKUZNETSK**
★ 03113 **NOVOKUIBYSHEVSK**
★ 03114 **NOVOMOSKOVSK**
★ 03115 **NOVOTROITSK**
★ 03116 **NOVOVYATSK**
★ 03117 **NOVOALTAISK**
★ 03118 **NOVOMIRGOROD**
★ 03119 **NOVOPOLOTSK**
★ 03120 **NOVODRUZHESK**
★ 03121 **NOVOLVOVSK**
★ 03122 **NOVOZYBKOV**
★ 03123 **NOVOGRUDOK**
★ 03124 **NOVOVOLYNSK**

★ 03130 **HONG SHOU SHAN** RC/Fr (La Ciotat) 1966; C; 10400; 158 × 9.5 (516 × 32); M (Sulzer); 19; ex *Ango* 1978
Sisters:
★ 03031 **LIAN YUN SHAN** (RC) ex *Dupleix* 1978
★ 03132 **WU TAI SHAN** (RC) ex *Forbin* 1978
03133 **JOHN PERO** (Pa) ex *Bougainville* 1982

03134 **LENDWORLD** (Gr) ex *Surcouf* 1983;
03135 **LENDATLANTIC** (Gr) ex *Tourville* 1983
03136 **TUYUTI** (Ur) ex *Kerguelen* 1981
03137 **GENERAL DE MIRANDA** (Ve) ex *Joinville* 1982

03140 **NEDLLOYD WILLEMSTAD** Ne/Ne (P Smit) 1970; CP; 7200; 169 × 8.3 (555 × 27.1); M (B&W); 21; ex *Willemstad* 1982; ex *Amsterdam* 1981; ex *Trident Amsterdam* 1980; Side doors
Sisters:
03141 **NEDLLOYD ORANJESTAD** (NA) ex *Oranjestad* 1982; ex *Rotterdam* 1981; ex *Trident Rotterdam* 1980;
03142 **CARACAS** (Ve)
03143 **VENEZUELA** (Ve)

★ 03150 **KARL MARX** DDR/DDR (Warnow) 1971; C; 11000; 166.4 × 9.5 (546 × 31.35); M (Sulzer); 21.5
Sister:
★ 03151 **FRIEDRICH ENGELS** (DDR)

● 03160 **NEDLLOYD AMSTERDAM** Ne/Ne (Verolme Scheeps) 1968; C; 7300/10500; 161 × 10.3 (528 × 33.7); M (Stork); 20; ex *Straat Amsterdam* 1978; ex *Safocean Amsterdam* 1976; ex *Straat Amsterdam* 1970
Sisters:
03161 **NEDLLOYD ADELAIDE** (Ne) ex *Safocean Adelaide* 1978; ex *Straat Adelaide* 1970
03162 **NEDLLOYD AUCKLAND** (Ne) ex *Safocean Auckland* 1980; ex *Straat Auckland* 1970
Possible sisters:
03163 **VICTORIA 1** (Pa) ex *Nedlloyd Agulhas* 1983; ex *Victoria 1* 1982; ex *Nedlloyd Agulhas* 1980; ex *Straat Agulhas* 1978
03164 **ACONCAGUA** (Ar) ex *Nedlloyd Algoa* 1980; ex *Straat Algoa* 1978;
03165 **NEDLLOYD ALBANY** (Ne) ex *Safocean Albany* 1980; ex *Straat Accra* 1970

★ 03170 **JIANGCHANG** RC/Sw (Lindholmens) 1964; C; 3600/5600; 124 × 8.2 (407 × 26.9); M (Gotaverken); 17; ex *Jianchang* 1983; ex *Statesman* 1977
Sisters (RC flag):
★ 03171 **JINCHANG** ex *Discoverer* 1977
★ 03172 **YICHANG** ex *Naturalist* 1977
★ 03173 **WU CHANG** ex *Novelist* 1977
★ 03174 **YONGCHANG** ex *Philosopher* 1977

03180 **CENTAUR** Sg/Br (J Brown) 1963; P/LS; 8000; 146 × 8 (481 × 26.4); TSM (B&W); 20

03185 **ITAITE** Bz/Bz (Ish. do Brazil) 1971/1981; C/Con; 11800; 176.94 × 9.6 (581 × 31.50); M (Sulzer); 20; Converted from cargo and lengthened 1981 (Thyssen)
Sisters (Bz flag):
03186 **ITANAGE**
03187 **ITAPE**
03188 **ITAPAGE**
03189 **ITAQUATIA**

03190 **MYKONOS** Gr/Br (Stephen) 1967; R; 9000/12300; 166 × 9.8 (546 × 32.4); M (Sulzer); 19; ex *NZ Aorangi* 1979; ex *Majestic* 1974
Similar:
03191 **SERIFOS** (Gr) ex *NZ Waitangi* 1980; ex *Britannic* 1974

03200 **BUNGA ORKID** My/Ja (Mitsubishi HI) 1971; C; 10700; 153 × 9.7 (502 × 31.9); M (Sulzer); 23
Sister:
03201 **BUNGA TANJONG** (My)

03220 **RONCESVALLES** Sp/Sp ('Bazan') 1972; C; 5500; 140 × 7.5 (460 × 24.6); M (Sulzer); 18
Sisters (Sp flag):
03221 **BELEN**
03222 **GALEONA**
03223 **VALVANUZ**

★ 03230 **RADZIONKOW** Pd/Pd (Szczecinska) 1973; C; 3500/5500; 124 × 7.3 (407 × 24.1); M (Sulzer); 15.5; 'B432' type
Sisters (Pd flag):
★ 03231 **BOCHNIA**
★ 03232 **CHELM**
★ 03233 **GARWOLIN**
★ 03234 **HENRYK LEMBERG**
★ 03235 **OSTROLEKA**
★ 03236 **WIELICZKA**
★ 03237 **SKOCZOW**
★ 03238 **SIEMIATYCZE**
(Sy flag):
03249 **AL YARMOUK**
03250 **BARADA**
(Eg flag):
03251 **AL ESRAA**
03252 **AL HAMRAA**
03253 **ASMAA**

03260 **KULDIGA** Ru/Br (Scotts' SB) 1971; R; 5900;

149.3 × 8.5 (490 × 27.9); M (Sulzer); 21; ex *Geest Tide* 1981
Sisters:
★03261 **KANDAVA** (Ru) ex *Geestcrest* 1981;
03262 **GEESTLAND** (Br)
03263 **GEESTSTAR** (Br)

★03270 **OMSK** Ru/Ja (Hitachi) 1961; C; 7500/10900; 155 × 9.6 (509 × 31.5); M (B&W); 17
Sisters (Ru flag):
★03271 **OKHOTSK**
★03272 **ORENBURG**

03280 **CORTINA** It/Br (A&P) 1965; C; 8500; 160.3 × 0.3 (526 × 31.6); M (Sulzer); 19; ex *Concordia Gulf* 1974; ex *Australia Star* 1972

● 03290 **HELLENIC PATRIOT** Gr/Ne (Nederlandsche) 1962; C; 6800/9700; 159 × 8.6 (521 × 28.5); M (Gotaverken); 17.5; ex *Marit* 1975; ex *Nippon* 1974

03300 **NEDLLOYD LEUVE** Ne/Ja (NKK) 1966; C; 12900; 162 × 9.4 (532 × 29.9); M (Stork); 20; ex *Leuve Lloyd* 1978
Sisters (Ne flag):
03301 **NEDLLOYD LOIRE** ex *Loire Lloyd* 1978
03302 **NEDLLOYD LINGE** ex *Nederlinge* 1978

● 03320 **RAJAB 1** Si/Ja (Mitsubishi HI) 1966; C; 9600/12300; 172 × 10.2 (564 × 33.5); M (Sulzer); 21; ex *Patroclus* 1983; ex *Glenalmond* 1973
Sisters:
03321 **SAUDI KAWTHER** (Si) ex *Kweichow* 1982; ex *Phemius* 1978; ex *Glenfinlas* 1972
03322 **IRAN EJTEHAD** (Ir)ex *Gulf Osprey* 1983; ex *Phrontis* 1982; ex *Pembrokeshire* 1972
03323 **SAUDI ZAMZAH** (Si) ex *Kwangsi* 1982; ex *Perseus* 1978; ex *Radnorshire* 1972

★03340 **HONG SHOU SHAN** RC/Fr (La Ciotat) 1966; C; 10400; 158 × 9.5 (516 × 32); M (Sulzer); 19; ex *Ango* 1978
Sisters:
★03341 **LIAN YUN SHAN** (RC) ex *Dupleix* 1978
★03342 **WU TAI SHAN** (RC) ex *Forbin* 1978
03343 **JOHN PERO** (Pa) ex *Bougainville* 1982
03344 **LENDATLANTIC** (Gr) ex *Tourville* 1983
03345 **LENDWORLD** (Gr) ex *Surcouf* 1983
03346 **TUYUTI** (Ur) ex *Kerguelen* 1981;
03347 **GENERAL DE MIRANDA** (Ve) ex *Joinville* 1982

03360 **IDEAL** Ma/Br (Readhead)1965; C; 7000/9300; 153.3 × 8.6 (503 × 28.2); M (Doxford); 17; ex *Irenes Ideal* 1982; ex *Strathappin* 1979; ex *Shahristan* 1975

03370 **ANDROMEDA** Gr/Br (Swan Hunter) 1969; C; 6400/9600; 155.7 × 9.1 (511 × 30.2); M (Doxford); 17.5; ex *Aeolian Star* 1981; ex *Stratharlick* 1980; ex *Tabaristan* 1975

● 03380 **REA B** Pa /Br (Connell) 1967; C; 9400/11500; 171.6 × 10.1 (562 × 33.4); M (Sulzer); 21; ex *Da Verrazano* 1980; ex *Benalbanach* 1962

03390 **BELLO** Br/Br (Connell) 1965; C; 8800/11800; 171.6 × 10.2 (563 × 33.8); M (Sulzer); 21.5; ex *Tina B* 1982; ex *Da Noli* 1980; ex *Benledi* 1972

03410 **RIO GRANDE** Ar/Sp (AESA) 1967; R; 2600; 110 × 6.5 (361 × 21.2); M (B&W); 19; ex *Playa De Las Nieves* 1978
Sisters:
03411 **ALBACORA FRIGO** (Sp) ex *Playa Blanca* 1983
03412 **USHUAIA** (Ar) ex *Playa De Naos* 1979; ex *Playa Naos* 1969

03420 **PUNTA BIANCA** It/It (Muggiano) 1975; R; 9400; 152.8 × 9.1 (501 × 30); M (GMT); 23; May be KC₃MFC—See 'PUNTA STELLA'

03430 **IOS 1** Pa/Ar (AFNE) 1970; C; 4000; 106.3 × 6.8 (348 × 22.4); M (Fiat); 18; ex *Cipolleti* 1980

03440 **HAYASHIKANE MARU NO 1** Ja/Ja (Hayashikane) 1967; C; 3700; 111 × 6.8 (364 × 22.6); M (Kobe); 16
Sister:
03441 **HAYASHIKANE MARU NO 2** (Ja)

03450 **POOLTA** Br/Br (H Robb) 1959; C; 2900; 100 × 4.9 (329 × 16.4); M (Sulzer); 11; lengthened 1968

03460 **D'ALBERTIS** It/It (Italcantieri) 1978; C/Con; 17800; 186.44 × 10.02 (611.68 × 32.87); M (GMT); 23
Sisters (It flag):
03461 **DA MOSTO**
03462 **PANCALDO**

03470 **LLOYD BAGE** Bz/Bz (Caneco) 1973; R; 6700; 140 × 8.3 (459 × 27.3); M (Sulzer); 21
Sister:
03471 **LLOYD SANTOS** (Bz)

● 03480 **ROYAL SEA** Gr/Bz (Maua) 1968; R; 4200; 126.2 × 7 (414 × 23); M (MAN); 18.5; ex *Inga Polaris* 1980; ex *Alberto Cocozza* 1978
03482 **ADRIATIC FREEZER** (Gr) ex *Frigo Tiete* 1981
03483 **NISSOS KYTHERA** (Ma) ex *Rafael Lotito* 1983

● 03490 **HORNCAP** Li/Fr (France-Gironde) 1968; R; 4400/8600; 144.1 × 7.5 (473 24.8); M (B&W); 21.5; ex *Aquilon* 1981
Sisters:
03491 **HORNBAY** (Li) ex *Fort Sainte Marie* 1981
03492 **MARYBETH** (Li) ex *Fribourg* 1979
03493 **ORQUE** (Fr) ex *Ivondro* 1974
03494 **NARVAL** (Fr)
03495 **ONO** (Iv) ex *Favorita* 1983
03496 **CAYENNE** (Li) ex *Belouga* 1980
03497 **JUNIPER** (Li) ex *Marsouin* 1980

● 03500 **VEGESACK** Pa/FRG (Bremer V) 1959; R; 3100; 134.7 × 6.1 (442 × 20); M (MAN); 18

03510 **SAN BLAS** Pi/Sw (Eriksbergs)1967; R; 6400; 149 × 8.7 (489 × 28.9); M (B&W); 20.25
Sisters:
03511 **SAN BRUNO** (Pi)
03512 **SAN BENITO** (Fi)
03513 **MALAYAN PRINCESS** (Pi) ex *Coriander* 1981; ex *Oregano* 1980; ex *Regan* 1979; ex *Tasmanic* 1979

● 03520 **IONIAN REEFER** Gr/Sw (Eriksbergs) 1965; R; 6500/8000; 150 × 8.4 (490 × 27.6); M (B&W); 19; ex *Australic* 1978
Sisters:
03521 **ANTIPOLIS** (Gr) ex *Antilope* 1981
03522 **ALTCAR** (Br) ex *Arawak* 1979
03523 **CROWN PEAK** (Gr) ex *Island Peak* 1984; ex *Argonaftis* 1982; ex *Argonaut II* 1981; ex *Argonaut* 1978
03524 **ATHOS 1** (Gr) ex *Ariel 1* 1981; ex *Ariel* 1978
03525 **AEGEAN REEFER** (Gr) ex *Albany* 1978

03530 **PACIFIC VIKING** Sg/Hong Kong (Taikoo) 1964; C; 3200; 99.3 × 5.7 (326 × 18.7); M (British Polar); 13; ex *Atlantic Viking* 1979; ex *Karepo* 1978
Sister:
03531 **PACIFIC OCEAN** (Sg) ex *Karetu* 1980

03540 **LLOYD BAGE** Bz/Bz (Caneco)1973; R; 6700; 140 × 8.3 (459 × 27.3); M (Sulzer); 21
Sister:
03541 **LLOYD SANTOS** (Bz)

03545 **GEESTBAY** Br/Br (Smith's D) 1981; R/CP; 7700; 159.07 × 8.82 (521.8 × 28.94); M (B&W); 19.5
Sister:
03546 **GEESTPORT** (Br)

03547 **LLOYD ARGENTINA** Bz/Bz (CCN) 1981; C; 5800/9100; 141 × —/8.82 (463 × —/28.94); M (MAN); 15; 'SD14' (modified)
Sisters:
03548 **LLOYD MEXICO** (Bz)
03549 **LLOYD HOUSTON** (Bz)

03550 **OCEAN ENDURANCE** Pk/Br (Bartram) 1966; PC; 7500/10300; 153 × 9.2 (502 × 30.4); M (Sulzer); 17.5

03560 **ASAKAZE MARU** Ja/Ja (Miho) 1967; R; 2800; 104 × 6.3 (342 × 20); M (IHI); 15.75
Sister:
03561 **HARUKAZE MARU** (Ja)

03570 **HAYASHIKANE MARU NO 1** Ja/Ja (Hayashikane) 1967; C; 3700; 111.11 × 6.87 (365 × 22.54); M (Kobe); 16
Sister:
03571 **HAYASHIKANE MARU NO 2** (Ja)

● 03580 **HORNCAP** Li/Fr (France-Gironde) 1968; R; 4400/8600; 144.1 × 7.5 (473 × 24.8); M (B&W); 21.5; ex *Aquilon* 1981
Sisters:
03581 **HORNBAY** (Li) ex *Fort Sainte Marie* 1981;
03582 **MARYBETH** (Li) ex *Fribourg* 1979;
03583 **ORQUE** (Fr) ex *Ivondro* 1974
03584 **NARVAL** (Fr)
03585 **ONO** (Iv) ex *Favorita* 1983
03586 **CAYENNE** (Li) ex *Belouga* 1980
03587 **JUNIPER** (Li) ex *Marsouin* 1980

03590 **MYKONOS** Gr/Br (Stephen) 1967; R; 9000/12300; 166 × 9.8 (546 × 32.4); M (Sulzer); 19; ex *NZ Aorangi* 1979; ex *Majestic* 1974
Similar:
03591 **SERIFOS** (Gr) ex *NZ Waitangi* 1980; ex *Britannic* 1974

03600 **BUNGA ORKID** My/Ja (Mitsubishi HI)1971; C; 10700; 153 × 9.7 (502 × 31.9); M (Sulzer); 23
Sister:
03601 **BUNGA TANJONG** (My)

★03620 **RADZIONKOW** Pd/Pd (Szczecinska) 1973; C; 3500/5500; 124 × 7.3 (407 × 24.1); M (Sulzer); 15.5; 'B432' type
Sisters (Pd flag):
★03621 **BOCHNIA**
★03622 **CHELM**
★03623 **GARWOLIN**
★03624 **HENRYK LEMBERG**
★03625 **OSTROLEKA**
★03627 **SKOCZOW**
★03628 **SIEMIATYCZE**
★03629 **WIELICZKA**
(Eg flag):
03630 **AL ESRAA**
03631 **AL HAMRAA**
03632 **ASMAA**
(Sy flag):
03633 **AL YARMOUK**
03634 **BARADA**

★03650 **HARRY POLLITT** Ru/DDR (Warnow)1971; C; 9300; 151.5 × 9 (497 × 29.5); M (MAN); 17
Sisters (Ru flag):
★03651 **VALERIAN KUIBYSHEV**
★03652 **BORIS ZHEMCHUZIN**
★03653 **WILLIAM FOSTER**
★03654 **ANATOLIY LUNACHARSKIY**
★03656 **ANNA ULYANOVA**
★03657 **ALEXSANDR ULYNOV**
★03658 **DIMITRIY ULYANOV**
★03659 **ILYA ULYANOV**
★03660 **NIKOLAY KRYLENKO**
★03661 **NIKOLAY POGODIN**
★03662 **OLGA ULYANOVA**
★03663 **VLADIMIR ILYCH**

● 03670 **CORABANK** Br/Br (Swan Hunter) 1972; C; 7900/11400; 148.5 × 9.6 (520 × 31.7); M (Doxford); 18.75
Sisters (Br flag):
03671 **CLYDEBANK**
03672 **FORTHBANK**
03673 **IVYBANK**
03674 **MEADOWBANK**
03675 **MORAYBANK**

★03690 **WARNEMUNDE** Ru/DDR (Warnow) 1972; C; 11000; 150.2 × 8.9 (493 × 29); M (MAN); 19.25; 'Mercator' type. Ships may vary slightly
Sisters (Ru flag):
★03691 **PALEKH**
★93692 **PAVLODAR**
★03693 **PAVLOGRAD**
★03694 **PESTOVO**
★03695 **PETRODVORETS**
★03696 **POLESSK**
★03697 **PRAVDINSK**
★03698 **PRIMORSK**
★03699 **PSKOV**
★03700 **PUTIVL**
★03701 **PERVOMAYSK**
★03702 **SALVADOR ALLENDE**
★03703 **WALTER ULBRICHT**
★03704 **DEKABRIST**
★03705 **NADEZHDA KRUPSKAYA**
Similar (DDR flag):
★03706 **MUHLHAUSEN**
★03707 **NORDHAUSEN**
★03708 **SANGERHAUSEN**
★03709 **SONDERHAUSEN**

03720 **KHALIJ EXPRESS** (Pa) Fr/Fr (L'Atlantique) 1967; CP; 6000/9800; 149.3 × 7.4 (490 × 24.7); M (Pielstick); 17; ex *Dione* 1983; ex *Suffren* 1978

● 03730 **CORABANK** Br/Br (Swan Hunter) 1972; C; 7900/11400; 148.5 × 9.6 (520 × 31.7); M (Doxford); 18.75
Sisters (Br flag):
03731 **CLYDEBANK**
03732 **FORTHBANK**
03733 **IVYBANK**
03734 **MEADOWBANK**
03735 **MORAYBANK**

03740 **OCEAN ADVENTURE** Li/Ja (Nipponkai) 1970; C; 8500; 148.7 × 8.7 (488 × 28.8); M (Sulzer); 15.75; ex *Japan Caobo* 1983
Sister:
03741 **JAPAN CANELA** (Li)—number of cranes may vary

03750 **BOUNTY III** Fr/Br (Doxford & S) 1966; C; 5500/7500; 141.7 × 9.7 (465 × 28.1); M (Fairfield-Rowan); —; ex *Javron* 1981; ex *Ilkon Dalio* 1976; ex *Coventry City* 1974;
Sister:
03751 **PANORMOS HORIZON** (Pa) ex *Free Spirit* 1982; ex *Ilkon Polly* 1980; ex *Toronto City* 1974

● 03760 **MANISTEE** Br/Ja (Kawasaki) 1972; R; 6500; 144.5 × 7.4 (474 × 24.5); M (MAN); 20.5
Sisters (Br flag):

03761 **MAGDALENA**
03762 **MANZANARES**
03763 **MAZATEC**

★03770 **LENINSKAYA GVARDIYA** Ru/Pd (Szcecinska) 1972; C; 6600; 135 × 7.5 (443 × 24.5); M (Sulzer); 15.5; 'B 46' type
Sisters (Ru flag):
★03771 **ALEKSANDR VINOKUROV**
★03772 **ALEKSANDRA ARTYUKHINA**
★03773 **ANDREY ANDREYEV**
★03774 **FEDOR PETROV**
★03775 **GLEB KRZHIZHANOVSKIY**
★03776 **IOSIF DUBROVINSKIY**
★03777 **IVAN BYELOSTOTSKIY**
★03778 **IVAN POKROVSKIY**
★03779 **IOHANNES LAURISTIN**
★03780 **LEON POPOV**
★03781 **LYUDMILA STAL**
★03782 **MATVEY MURANOV**
★03783 **MAXIM LITVINOV**
★03784 **MIKHAIL VLADIMIRSKIY**
★03785 **MIKHAIL OLMINSKIY**
★03786 **NIKOLAY SEMASHKA**
★03787 **NIKOLAY SHVERNIK**
★03788 **OLGA VARENTSOVA**
★03789 **OSIP PYATNITSKIY**
★03790 **PANTELEYMON LEPESHINSKIY**
★03791 **PETR KRASIKOV**
★03792 **SERGEY GUSEV**
★03793 **SUREN SPANDARYAN**
★03794 **VERA LEBEDEVA**
★03795 **VIKTOR KURNATOVSKIY**
★03796 **VASILY SHELGUNOV**
★03797 **YAAN ANVELT**
★03799 **PAVEL DAUGE**
★03800 **SVORTSOV-STEPANOV**
★03801 **YEMELYAN YAROSLAVSKIY**

03840 **MAYON** Pi/Fr (La Ciotat) 1970; C; 7500/10700; 157 × 9.7 (515 × 32); M (Sulzer); 18; ex Ville De Hambourg 1979
Sister:
03841 **PUERTO PRINCESA** (Pi) ex Ville de Rotterdam

03850 **BANDA SEA** Sg/Bz (Maua) 1976; C; 9200; 140.98 × 8.82 (462.53 × 28.94); M (MAN); 15; ex Banda Sea; 'SD 14' type (Modified)

03860 **SANTA MAVRA** Gr/Ja (Fujinagata) 1967; C; 6200; 157 × 7.5 (515 × 24.4); M (B&W); 17.25; ex Skodsborg 1983; ex Banana 1979
Sister:
03861 **BROTHERS UNION** (Gr) ex Stjerneborg 1983; ex Kinshasa 1979

★03870 **ALTENBURG** DDR/DDR (Warnow) 1967; C; 5400/8500; 150.2 × 8.2 (493 × 26.11); M (MAN); 17; 'XD' type
Sisters (DDR flag):
★03871 **BERNBURG**
★03872 **BLANKENBURG**
★03873 **BOIZENBURG**
★03874 **EILENBURG**
★03875 **FREYBURG**
★03876 **MAGDEBURG**
★03877 **MEYENBURG**
★03878 **NAUMBURG**
★03879 **NIENBURG**
★03880 **ORANIENBURG**
★03881 **QUEDLINBURG**
★03882 **ROSTOCK**
★03883 **NEUBRANDENBURG**
★03884 **RONNEBURG**
★03885 **SCHWARZBURG**

03890 **RONCESVALLES** Sp/Sp ('Bazan') 1972; C; 5500; 140 × 7.5 (460 × 24.6); M (Sulzer); 18
Sisters (Sp flag):
03891 **BELEN**
03892 **GALEONA**
03893 **VALVANUZ**

● 03900 **SPARTAN REEFER** Gr/Br (Vickers Ltd) 1964; R6400/7800; 147 × 8.8 (481 × 29.2); M (Sulzer); 18 ex Laurentic 1980
Sister:
03901 **KHALIJ CRYSTAL** (Li) ex Port Launay 1981; ex Zealandic 1980

03910 **BAHIA BLANCA** Sw/Sw (Lindholmens) 1965/68; Pt Con; 10400; 173 × 8.7 (569 × 28.7); M (Pielstick); 19; converted from general cargo & lengthened 1968

03930 **KLIN** Ru/Fi (Wartsila) 1964; C; 6600/9400; 147 × 9.1 (482 × 30); M (Sulzer); 17.5
Sisters (Ru flag):
★03931 **KOMSOMOLETS ESTONII**
★03932 **KOMSOMOLETS KIRGIZII**
★03933 **KOMSOMOLETS LATVII**
★03934 **KOMSOMOLETS LITVY**
★03935 **KOMSOMOLETS TADZHIKISTANA**

★03936 **KOMSOMOLETS UZBEKISTANA**
★03937 **KOMMUNARSK**
★03938 **KRASNOGVARDEYSK**
★03939 **KRASNOKAMSK**
★03940 **KRASNODON**
★03941 **KRASNOUFIMSK**
★03942 **KRASNOURALSK**
★03943 **KRASNOZAVODSK**
★03944 **KRASNOE SELO**

★03950 **SOSNOGORSK** Ru/Ru (Kherson) 1969; C; 6800/8900; 153 × 9.1 (501 × 29.8); M (B&W); 17; Cranes abreast mast
Sisters (Ru flag):
★03951 **SIDOR KOVPAK**
★03952 **SOKOL**
★03953 **SUZDAL**
★03955 **KAPITAN PLAUSHEVSKIY**
★03956 **STOLETIYE PARIZHOSKOY KOMMUNY**
★03957 **IVAN KOROBTSOV**
★03958 **GENERAL VLADIMIR ZAIMOV**
Some of the following may be KC₄MFC—like Svetlogorsk:
★03959 **VALERIY MEZHLAUK**
★03960 **VALENTIN KHUTORSKOY**
★03961 **KAPITAN LUKHMANOV**
★03962 **ALEKSANDR TSYURUPA**
★03963 **ANDREY LAVROV**
★03964 **KAPITAN SHANTSBERG**
★03965 **KLIM VOROSHILOV**
★03966 **KOMANDARM MATVEYEV**
★03967 **PROFESSOR BUZNIK**
★03968 **AKADEMIK YANGEL**
Sisters (Cranes ahead of bridge may be abreast) (Eg flag):
03969 **ISMAILIYA**
03970 **PORT SAID**
03971 **SUEZ**
03972 **ALEXANDRIA**

03980 **ALPHA BAY** Br/Ne (IHC Smit) 1980; D; 5700; 112 × 6.35 (367.45 × 20.83); M (Stork—Werkspoor); 13.7

03990 **GAZZELLA** It/It (Italcantieri) 1969; Pt Con; 12400; 152.8 × 9.6 (534 × 31.10); M (Fiat); 20
Sisters (It flag):
03991 **CAPRIOLO**
03992 **CERVO**
03993 **TIGRE**

★04010 **LENINSKAYA GVARDIYA** Ru/Pd (Szcecinska) 1972; C; 6600; 135 × 7.5 (443 × 24.5); M (Sulzer); 15.5; 'B 46' type
Sisters (Ru flag):
★04011 **ALEKSANDR VINOKUROV**
★04012 **ALEKSANDRA ARTYUKHINA**
★04013 **ANDREY ANDREYEV**
★04014 **FEDOR PETROV**
★04015 **GLEB KRZHIZHANOVSKIY**
★04016 **IOSIF DUBROVINSKIY**
★04017 **IVAN BYELOSTOTSKIY**
★04018 **IVAN POKROVSKIY**
★04019 **IOHANNES LAURISTIN**
★04020 **LEON POPOV**
★04021 **LYUDMILA STAL**
★04022 **MATVEY MURANOV**
★04023 **MAXIM LITVINOV**
★04024 **MIKHAIL VLADIMIRSKIY**
★04025 **MIKHAIL OLMINSKIY**
★04026 **NIKOLAY SEMASHKO**
★04027 **NIKOLAY SHVERNIK**
★04028 **OLGA VARENTSOVA**
★04029 **OSIP PYATNITSKIY**
★04030 **PANTELEYMON LEPESHINSKIY**
★04031 **PETR KRASIKOV**
★04032 **SERGEY GUSEV**
★04033 **SUREN SPANDARYAN**
★04034 **VERA LEBEDEVA**
★04035 **VIKTOR KURNATOVSKIY**
★04036 **VASILY SHELGUNOV**
★04037 **YAAN ANVELT**
★04038 **YELENE STASOVA**
★04039 **PAVEL DAUGE**
★04040 **SVORTSOV—STEPANOV**
★04041 **YEMELYAN YAROSLAVSKIY**

● 04050 **REA B** Pa/Br (Connell) 1967; C; 9400/11500; 171.6 × 10.1 (562 × 33.4); M (Sulzer); 21; ex Da Verrazano 1980; ex Benbanach 1972

04060 **MONOWAI** NZ/Br (Grangemouth) 1960/77; SS; —; 90.34 × 5.21 (296.36 17.09); TSM (Sulzer); —; Operated by New Zealand Navy; Converted from cargo/passenger 1976/77 (Scott Lithgow); Helicopter deck

04070 **S A AGULHAS** SA/Ja (Mitsubishi HI) 1978; RS/SS; 5400; 109.45 × 6.06 (359.09 19.88); M (Mirrlees); 14.5; helicopter deck; Travelling crane in Forward well

★04080 **STROPTIVYY** Ru/Fi (Wartsila) 1979;

Sal/Tg; 4200 displ; 69.8 × 6.5 (229 × 21.33); M (Pielstick); 15
Sisters (Ru flag):
★04081 **SPRAVEDLIVYY**
★04082 **STAKHANOVETS**
★04083 **SIBIRKIJ**
★04084 **SUVOROVETS**
Similar:
★04085 **FOBOS** (Ru)
★04086 **DEIMOS** (Ru)

● 04090 **VEGESACK** Pa/FRG (Bremer V) 1959; R; 3100; 134.7 × 6.1 (442 × 20); M (MAN); 18

04100 **SAN FRANCISCO** Sw/Fi (Wartsila) 1970; Con; 16100; 174.25 × 10.08 (571.69 × 33.07); TSM (Pielstick); 23
Sisters:
04101 **ANTONIA JOHNSON** (Sw)
04101/1 **MARGARET JOHNSON** (Sw)
Similar (superstructure varies):
04102 **AXEL JOHNSON** (Sw)
04103 **ANNIE JOHNSON** (Sw)

04110 **INCOTRANS SPIRIT** Ne/Ne (Nederlandsche) 1979; Con; 29400; 202 × 10.5 (662.73 × 34.45); M (Sulzer); 21
Sister:
04111 **CHINA WINDS** (Ne) ex Incotrans Speed 1983

04115 **SOUTHLAND STAR** Br/FRG (Bremer V) 1967/78; C/Con; 7800/11400; 168.40 × 8.94/9.97 (552 × 29.33/32.71); M (MAN); 21.5; Converted from reefer and lengthened 1978 (Bremer V)
Sister:
04116 **WELLINGTON STAR** (Br) ex New Zealand Star 1977

★04120 **LEDENICE** Ys/Ys ('3 Maj') 1979; RoC/Con/C; 5600; 144.4 × 6.5 (473.75 × 21.33); M (Pielstick); 17.9; stern slewing ramp; travelling crane in forward well
Sister:
★04121 **BRIBIR** (Ys)

04130 **ANASTASIS** Ma/It (Adriatico) 1953; PC; 11700; 159.09 × 7.19 (522 × 23.59); TSM (Fiat); 19.75; ex Victoria 1978

04140 **ISLAS GALAPAGOS** Ec/It (Apuania) 1968; R; 6600; 139 × 7.6 (457 × 25); M (Fiat); —
Sisters:
04141 **RIO AMAZONAS** (Ec)
★04142 **OCEANO PACIFICO** (Cu)
★04143 **OCEANO INDIO** (Cu)

★04160 **SCILLONIAN III** Br/Br (Appledore) 1977; P; 1200; 68 × 2.9 (224 × 9.5); M (Mirrlees); 15.5

★04180 **KIROVSKLES** Ru/Fi (Nystads) 1962; TC/C; 2900; 102 × 5.7 (335 × 18.9); M (B&W); 12.25
Sisters (Ru flag):
★04181 **BAYKALLES**
★04183 **KAMCHATSKLES**
★04184 **KARELYALES**
★04185 **KOLYMALES**
★04186 **KOTLASLES**
★04187 **KRASNOGORSKLES**
★04188 **KUNGURLES**
★04189 **KOVDALES**
★04190 **VOLOGDALES**

★04196 **XIANG YANG HONG 9** RC/RC (—) 1978; RS; 3000; 122 × 7.24 (400 × 23.75); M (—); 18

★04200 **'TOMBA' CLASS** Ru/Ru (—) 1975; Repair/FA; 5200 displ; 107 × 6 (351 × 20); M (—); —; Class of at least 3 ships operated by the Soviet Navy

★04210 **INGURI** Ru/Fi (Wartsila) 1978; Cbl; 6000; 130.41 × 5.75 (427.8 × 18.8); TS D—E (Wartsila); 14; Modified 'KLASMA' type; Others in this class may also have this sequence—see DONETS

★04220 **NAN HAI 502** RC/Ja (Mitsubishi HI) 1979; SS/RS; 900; 65.7 × — (215.55 × —); M (Yanmar); 13

★04230 **WILHELM FLORIN** DDR/DDR (Warnow) 1964; C; 5000/7700; 142.3 × 7.2 (467 × 23.7); M (MAN); 14.5;
Sisters (DDR flag):
★04231 **EDGAR ANDRE**
★04232 **ERNST SCHNELLER**
★04233 **WERNER SEELENBINDER**

★04240 **ADMIRAL VLADIMIRSKIY** Ru/— 1975; RS; —; 147 × — (483 × —); —; 20
Sister:
★04241 **IVAN KRUZHENSTERN** (Ru)

04245 **BRITISH ENTERPRISE THREE** Br/FRG (Rickmers) 1965/77; Sub S; 1600; 75.90 × 4.79 (249 × 15.72); M (MAN); 14; ex Intersub Three 1981; ex Othmarschen 1976; Converted from stern trawler 1977 (Rickmers); 'A' Frame may be removed
Sister:

04246 BRITISH ENTERPRISE FOUR (Br) ex *Intersub Four* 1981; ex *Altona* 1976

04250 JALAJAYA In/FRG (Rhein Nordseew) 1966; C; 8300/10900; 158.43 × 8.53/9.66 (519.78 × 27.99/31.69); M (MAN); 16; Three original sisters (JALAJYOTI etc) may also have this sequence now—which see

★04253 AKADEMIK SHULEYKIN Ru/Fi (Laiva) 1982; RS; 1800; 71.61 × 4.75 (235 × 15.58); M (Russkiy); 12
Sisters (Ru flag):
★04254 AKADEMIK SHOKALSKIY
★04255 PROFESSOR KHROMOV
★04256 PROFESSOR MULTANOVSKIY
★04257 PROFESSOR PAVEL MOLCHANOV
★04258 PROFESSOR BAYKONOVSKIY

★04260 NAN HAI 502 RC/Ja (Mitsubishi HI) 1979; SS/RS; 900; 65.7 × —(215.55 × —); M (Yanmar); 13

04280 GORYO-HO Ko/Br (Upper Clyde) 1971; D; 8000; 132 × 10.3 (434 × 34); M (Mirrlees); 13.5; ex *Delta Bay* 1978
Similar:
04281 HUMBER RIVER (Br)

04300 MARSA Ma/Br (Swan Hunter & WR) 1947; CP; 1800; 90.5 × 5.2 (297 × 17.3); R & LPT (Swan Hunter & WR); 13.5; ex *Oleos* 1974; ex *Malcolm Page* 1970; ex *Leo* 1967

●04310 TUI CAKAU II Fiji/Fr (Mediterranee) 1961/71; RoC; 1800; 107 × 5.1 (360 × 17); M (Sulzer); 15.75; ex *Capitaine Scott* 1979; ex *Blida* 1978; Converted from cargo ship 1971, and lengthened, Bow and side doors

04312 SKANDI ALFA No/FRG (Suerken) 1981; ORSV; 500/1400; 67.72 × 4.99 (222.2 × 16.37); TSM (Wichmann); 16

04320 UGLEN No/No (Nymo) 1978; Crane ship; 1600; 78.57 × 3.25 (257.76 × 10.66); TS D-E; (Normo); 10; Drawing shows sheerlegs in stowed position. Twin funnels

04330 GAIETY Br/Br (Burntisland) 1964; C; 6700; 130.7 × 78 (429 × 25.6); M (B&W); 16.5; ex *Cufic* 1977; ex *Newfoundland* 1976; ex *Cufic* 1974; ex *Newfoundland* 1973
Sister:
04331 ARAB DABBOR (Si); ex *Booker Valiant* 1979; ex *Tropic* 1978; ex *Nova Scotia* 1976; ex *Tropic* 1974; ex *Nova Scotia* 1973

★04340 HEL Pd/De (Nakskov) 1970; C; 7700/11000; 166.7 × 9.7 (547 × 31.9); M (B&W) 20.75
Sisters (Pd flag):
★04341 JASTARNIA-BOR
★04342 JURATA
★04343 WLADYSLAWOWO
★04344 KUZNICA

04350 ALDABI Ne/Ne (Giessen-De Noord) 1977; Pt.Con; 9800; 142 × 9.5 (466 × 31); M (Stork-Werkspoor); approx. 16.25
Sisters (Ne flag):
04351 ALHENA
04352 ALNATI
04353 ALPHACCA

04360 MARATHON REEFER Gr/Ja (Mitsui) 1968; R; 9500; 164 × 9.2 (540 × 30.2); M (Mitsui) 21; ex *Wild Marlin* 1981; ex *Manapouri* 1977
Sister:
04361 MACEDONIAN REEFER (Gr) ex *Wild Mallard* 1981; ex *Mataura* 1977

04370 TACHIRA Ve/Fi (Navire) 1976; C; 10300; 159 × 9.8 (522 × 32); M (Sulzer); 18.25
Sisters (Ve flag):
04371 TRUJILLO
04372 ARAGUA
04373 FALCON

●04380 IRAN EJTEHAD Ir/Ja (Mitsubishi HI) 1966; C; 9600/12300; 172 × 10.2 (564 × 33.5); M (Sulzer); 21; ex *Gulf Osprey* 1983; ex *Phrontis* 1982; ex *Pembrokeshire* 1972
Sisters:
04381 RAJAB 1 (Si) ex *Patroclus* 1983; ex *Glenalmond* 1973
04382 SAUDI KAWTHER (Si) ex *Kweichow* 1982; ex *Phemius* 1978; ex *Glenfinlas* 1972
04383 SAUDI ZAMZAH (Si) ex *Kwangsi* 1982; ex *Perseus* 1978; ex *Radnorshire* 1972

04390 NEDLLOYD KEMBLA Ne/Ja (Mitsubishi HI) 1971; C; 7900/12400; 162 × 10.4 (533 × 34); M (Sulzer); 17
Sisters (Ne flag) (Superstructure may vary slightly):
04391 NEDLLOYD KIMBERLEY
04392 NEDLLOYD KINGSTON

04393 NEDLLOYD KYOTO
04394 NEDLLOYD KATWIJK

04400 HEL Pd/De (Nakskov) 1970; C; 7700/11000; 166.7 × 9.7 (547 × 31.9); M (B&W); 20.75
Sisters (Pd flag):
★04401 JASTARNIA-BOR
★04402 JURATA
★04403 KUZNICA
★04404 WLADYSLAWOWO

04410 NILE Eg/Ja (Mitsui) 1970; C; 7300; 155.7 × 9.1 (511 × 20.6); M (B&W); 18.5; ex *Corinto Maru* 1983
Sister:
04411 CURACAO MARU (Ja)

04420 CHARLOTTENBORG De/De (Nakskov) 1972; C; 6700/9700; 153.6 × 9.4 (504 × 30.9); M (B&W); 18; ex *Afrika* 1979
Sister:
04421 CHRISTIANSBORG (De); ex *Bretagne* 1979

★04423 ALTENBURG DDR/DDR (Warnow) 1967, C; 5400/8500; 150.2 × 7.26/8.20 (493 × 23.82/26.90); M (MAN) 18.5; 'XD' type
Sisters (DDR flag):
★04424 BERNBURG
★04424/1 BLANKENBURG
★04424/2 BOIZENBURG
★04425 EILENBURG
★04425/1 FREYBURG
★04425/2 MAGDEBURG
★04426 MEYENBURG
★04426/1 NAUMBURG
★04426/2 NIENBURG
★04427 ORANIENBURG
★04427/1 QUEDLINBURG
★04428 ROSTOCK
★04428/1 NEUBRANDENBURG
★04429 RONNEBURG
★04429/1 SCHWARZBURG

04430 TACHIRA Ve/Fi (Navire) 1976; C; 10300; 159 × 9.8 (522 × 32); M (Sulzer); 18.25
Sisters (Ve flag):
04431 TRUJILLO
04432 ARAGUA
004433 FALCON

04440 CIUDAD DE MANIZALES Co/Sp (AESA) 1971; Pt.Con; 7300; 166 × 9.4 (545 × 30.9); M (Sulzer); 21
Sister:
04441 CIUDAD DE MEDELLIN (Co)

★04450 DONGSHAN RC/FRG (Luebecker F-W) 1961; CP; 9900; 154 × 8.8 (505 × 29.1); M (MAN); 17; ex *Havlom* 1972

04460 CEFALLONIAN WAVES Gr/Fr(Loire) 1952; C; 6000; 149.3 × 7.8 (490 × 25.5); M (Sulzer); 14.5; ex *Bellerive* 1981; ex *Nigerian Explorer* 1980; ex *Austrian Explorer* 1980; ex *Sauzon* 1976; ex *Leopold L D* 1964

★04470 LIKA Ys/Ys ('3 Maj') 1957; C; 6000/8800; 146.01 × 7.86/— (479 × 25.79/—); M (Sulzer); 14
Sisters:
★04471 DEBRALINA 1 (Ys) ex *Petka* 1983
★04472 SLAVONIJA (Ys)
★04473 TREPCA (Ys)
★04474 ZETA (Ys)

04480 FELIX S. Pa/It (Felszegi) 1959; C; 8900; 148.7 × 9.1 (488 × 29.8); M (Sulzer); 15.5; ex *San Felice* 1982

★04500 LIAZI Mb/Po (Mondego) 1957; CP; 1300; 78.6 × 4.3 (258 × 14); TSM (Werkspoor); 11.25

★04520 NATALIYA KOVSHOVA Ru/Fr (Nantes) 1965; FT; 6300; 129 × 7 (423 × 23.1); D-E (Pielstick); 13.5
Sisters (Ru flag):
★04521 ANATOLIY KHALIN
★04522 MARIYA POLIVANOVA

04530 TURTLE BAY Sg/FRG (Luebecker F-W)1972; C; 6900/9800; 149 × 9.4 (488 × 30.7) M (B+V); 19; ex *Santa Cruz* 1982; ex *Lloyd Melbourne* 1980; ex *Santa Cruz* 1979
Sister:
04531 SANTA FE (Sg)

04540 FUTAMI MARU Ja/Ja (Hitachi) 1971; Pt. Con; 11000; 159 × 9.4 (522 × 30.8); M (B&W); 18.25

04545 FRIESENSTEIN FRG/FRG (Luebecker F-W) 1967/80; C/Con; 12700; 176.54 × 10.10 (579 × 33.14); M (Bremer V); 20.5; Converted from cargo, lengthened and widened 1980 (Thyssen). Pipe from funnel is telescopic
Sisters (FRG flag):
04546 HOLSTENSTEIN
04547 SCHWABENSTEIN

04550 JAMI 2 Ir/Ja (Mitsui) 1966; C; 10400; 166 × 9.1 (545 × 29.6); M (B&W); 22.75; ex *Bremen Maru* 1983
Sisters:
04551 MOWLAVI (Ir) ex *Barcelona Maru* 1983
04552 IRAN RESHADAT (Ir) ex *Bergen Maru* 1983

04560 AMERICAN ALTAIR US/US (Ingalls SB) 1965/76 C/Con; 14000; 203 × 9.5 (666 × 31.17); T (GEC); 21; ex *Mormacaltair* 1983; Converted from cargo ship and lengthened 1976 (Todd)
Sister:
04561 AMERICAN DRACO (US) ex *Mormacdraco* 1983
Probable sisters (US flag):
04562 AMERICAN ARGO ex *Mormacargo* 1983
04563 AMERICAN RIGEL ex *Mormacrigel* 1983
04564 AMERICAN RESERVIST ex *Mormaclynx* 1983
04565 AMERICAN VEGA ex *Mormacvega* 1983

04570 FUSHIMI MARU Ja/Ja (Mitsubishi HI) 1970; C; 10900; 158 × 9.8 (519 × 30.8); M (Sulzer); 18.25
Sister:
04571 FUSO MARU (Ja)

04580 LION OF ETHIOPIA Et/Ne (Verolme Dok) 1966; C; 5200; 121 × 8 (397 × 26); M (MAN); ex *Lion of Judah* 1975
Sister:
04581 QUEEN OF SHEEBA (Et)

●04590 ANDRICO PROGRESS Pa/Fr (France-Gironde) 1963; CP; 7200/10700; 157 9.4 (515 × 30.7); M (B&W); 15.5; ex *Gorron* 1983; ex *Union Norfolk* 1983; ex *Gabus* 1982; ex *Hoegh Elan* 1979
Sister:
04591 ANDRICO UNITY (Pa) ex *Soppero* 1983; ex *Union Auckland* 1983; ex *Gurami* 1981; ex *Hoegh Elite* 1979

★04600 QING SHAN RC/FRG (Rickmers) 1960; CP; 9300; 154 × 8.9 (505 × 29); M (MAN); 17.25; ex *Havskar* 1972; Side doors

★04610 DE DU RC/Sw (Oresunds) 1962; CP; 9600; 143 × 9 7 (469 × 31.9); M (Gotaverken); 17; ex *Gaoyu* 1973; ex *Havtjeld* 1972; Side doors

★04620 JIN HU QUAN RC/Sp (AESA) 1967; C; 8300; 143 × 9.3 (468 × 30.6); M (Sulzer); 15; ex *Mar Cantabrico* 1982

04630 SAXONIA Br/De (Aalborg) 1972; R; 8500/12000; 175 × 9.1 (575 × 30.1); M (B&W); 23.5; ex *Gladiola* 1976
Sisters (Br flag):
04631 SAMARIA ex *Chrysantema* 1976
04632 SCYTHIA ex *Iris Queen* 1976
04633 SERVIA ex *Orchidea* 1976

04636 CAICARA Bz/Bz (Maua) 1975; C; 6900/10300; 160.05 × 8.22/9.22 (525 × 26.97/30.25); M (MAN); 17; 'Prinasa 121' type
Probable sisters:
04637 AMALIA (Bz)
04638 JOANA (Bz)

04640 BOLIVIA Bo/FRG (B+V) 1965; CP; 8100/10900; 165 × 9.7 (540 × 32); M (MAN); 21; ex *Alemannia* 1979
Sisters (FRG flag):
04641 BAVARIA
04642 BORUSSIA
04643 HAMMONIA
04644 HOLSATIA
04655 THURINGA
04646 SAUDI JAMAL (Si) ex *Westfalia* 1982

04650 ON SHUN Pa/Ja (Kasado) 1968; C; 9800; 155.8 × 9.4 (511 × 30.84); M (MAN); 21.5; ex *Korean Frontier* 1978
Sisters (Pa flag):
04651 ON TAT ex *Korean Exporter* 1978
04652 ON WO ex *Korean Pioneer* 1978
04653 ON PING ex *Korean Trader* 1978

●★04660 TONG JIANG RC/FRG (B+V) 1967; C; 5600/7300; 135.80 × 7.42/8.60 (446 × 24.0/28.0); M (B+V); 18.75; ex *Trier* 1978
Sisters (third kingpost is a Stulcken in some ships):
★04661 HUANG LONG SHAN (RC) ex *Hagen* 1978
★04662 TAI HANG SHAN (RC) ex *Hamburg* 1978
★04663 PU JIANG (RC) ex *Speyer* 1978
★04664 MIAO FENG SHAN (RC) ex *Hattingen* 1979
04665 HEIDELBERG (FRG)
04666 CORAIN I (Pa) ex *Hanau* 1979
04667 CORAIN II (Pa) ex *Heilbronn* 1979
04668 CONSTELLATION FAROS (Gr) ex *Hannover* 1982
04669 CONSTELLATION GALAXY (Gr) ex *Goslar* 1982; ex *Frankfurt* 1980

04670 DACEBANK Br/Br (Sunderland) 1979; C/Con; 12200; 161.82 × 9.95 (530.9 × 32.64); M

(Doxford); 16.6
Sisters (Br flag):
04671 **PIKEBANK**
04672 **ROACHBANK**
04673 **ROMNEY** ex *Ruddbank* 1983
04674 **TENCHBANK**
04675 **TROUTBANK**

04680 **S A CONSTANTIA** SA/Ja (Mitsui) 1968; Pt.
Con; 8900/12200; 182 × 9.3/9.6 (598 × 30.5/32);
M (Sulzer); 21; Lengthened 1975
Sisters (SA flag):
04681 **S A MORGENSTER**
04682 **S A VERGELEGEN**

● 04690 **NELA** Ma/Ja (Fujinagata) 1966; Pt. Con;
8900/12300; 181.8 × 8.4/9.6 (596 × 27.3/32); M
(Sulzer); 21; Lengthened 1974; ex *S A Huguenot*
1982
Sister:
04691 **S A ALPHEN** (SA)

04700 **AUSTRALIA MARU** Ja/Ja (Mitsui) 1969;
Con; 24000; 213 × 10.4 (699 × 34.5); M (B&W); 22.5
Similar:
04701 **ASIA MARU** (Ja)
04702 **BEISHU MARU** (Ja)

● 04710 **HELLENIC PRIDE** Gr/Fi (Wartsila) 1971; CP;
6800/10300; 159 × 8.2/9.8 (523 × 23/32); M
(Sulzer); 18
Sister (Gr flag):
04713 **HELLENIC STAR**

● 04720 **BEACON GRANGE** Br/Br (Cammell Laird)
1973; Pt. Con; 8400/12300; 162 × 8.6/9.8 (530 ×
28/32.4); M (B&W); 18; ex *Orduna* 1982
Sisters:
04721 **OCEANHAVEN** (Br) ex *Andes* 1982; ex *Orte-
ga* 1980
04722 **RUBENS** (Li) ex *Morning Sun* 1980; ex *Orbeta*
1980

04730 **RIVER ADADA** Ng/Ys ('Split') 1979; C/Con;
13200; 173 × 9.15 (567.59 × 30.02); M (Sulzer); 19
Sisters (Ng flag):
04731 **RIVER OJI**
04732 **RIVER MAJIDUN**
04733 **RIVER OLI**
04734 **RIVER GURARA**
04735 **RIVER OSHUN**
04736 **RIVER OGBESE**
04737 **RIVER MAJE**

04740 **TASMAN REX** Ja/Ja (Koyo) 1979; R; 10200;
168.05 × 8.65 (551.35 × 28.38); M (Sulzer); 21
Probable sister:
04741 **HUMBOLDT REX** (Ja)

04750 **MANOLOEVERETT** Li/Ja (Sasebo) 1965; C;
5900; 140 × 8.6 (458 × 24.11); M (Sulzer); 17
Sisters (Li flag):
04751 **JOHNEVERETT**
04752 **HUGHEVERETT**
04753 **MURRAYEVERETT**
04754 **THOMASEVERETT**

04760 **SAXONIA** Br/De (Aalborg) 1972; R;
8500/12000; 175 × 9.1/—(575 × 30.1/—); M
(B&W); 23.5; ex *Gladiola* 1976
Sisters (Br flag):
04761 **SAMARIA** ex *Chrysantema* 1976;
04762 **SCYTHIA** ex *Iris Queen* 1976
04763 **SERVIA** ex *Orchidea* 1976

04770 **CRESTBANK** Br/Br (Sunderland) 1978; C;
12200; 161.5 × 9.7 (529.86 × 31.82); M (Doxford) 16
Sister:
04771 **FENBANK** (Br)

04775 **VIRGINIA** Li/Br (Doxford & S) 1972; C;
7100/11000; 161.45 × 9.76 (530 × 32.02); M (Doxford); 16.5; ex *Lancashire* 1982
Sister:
04776 **TEXAS** (Li) ex *Herefordshire* 1982

● 04780 **HELLENIC CHAMPION** Gr/Gr (Hellenic)
1971; CP; 5900/9000; 143 × 8.8/8.8 (470 × 26/29);
M (MAN); 16.5; 'SD 14' Liner type
Sisters (Gr flag):
04782 **HELLENIC CHALLENGER**
04783 **HELLENIC IDEAL**
04784 **HELLENIC NAVIGATOR**
04785 **GRIGORIOS C IV**
Similar ('SD 14' type)
04786 **BELLE** (Pa) ex *Belle Isle* 1983;
04787 **BELLE ROSE** (Br)
04788 **PAMIT C** (Cy) ex *Westland* 1983; ex *Nedlloyd
Westland* 1982; ex *Westland* 1982

04800 **LLOYD MANDU** Bz/Bz (CCN) 1979; C;
11400; 160.02 × 9.21 (525 × 30.22); M (MAN); 17;
'PRINASA 121' type
Sister (Bz flag):
04806 **LLOYD TUPIARA**

04810 **FROTADURBAN** Bz/Bz (CCN) 1980; C;
8600/11400; 160.03 × —/9.21 (525 × —/30.22); M
(MAN); 17; 'Prinasa 121' type
Sister:
04811 **FROTASINGAPORE** (Bz)
Probable sisters (Bz flag):
04812 **FROTAKOBE**
04813 **FROTAMANILA**
04814 **CELINA TORREALBA**
Possible sister (Bz flag):
04815 **NICIA**

04820 **RIVER JIMINI** Ng/Ko (Hyundai) 1979;
C/Con; 7200/11000; 147.26 × 8.56/— (483.14 ×
28.08/—); M (B&W); 16.1
Sisters (Ng flag):
04821 **RIVER ABOINE**
04822 **RIVER ASAB**
04823 **RIVER OSSE**
04824 **RIVER RIMA**
04825 **RIVER MADA**
04826 **RIVER ANDONI**
04827 **RIVER GUMA**
04828 **RIVER KERAWA**
04829 **RIVER NGADA**
04830 **RIVER IKPAN**
Similar (Gh flag) without Stulcken derrick:
04831 **TANO RIVER**
04832 **VOLTA RIVER**
04833 **SISSILI RIVER**
04834 **KETA LAGOON** ex *Tynebank* 1982; ex *Keta
Lagoon* 1981

04840 **DIDO** Gr/Br (A&P) 1970; C; 7200/10300;
160 × 8.2/9.2 (525 × 27/30.3); M (Doxford); 16.5; ex
Armadale 1981; 'SD 15' type

04850 **CIUDAD DE BOGOTA** Co/FRG (Stuelcken)
1964; CP; 11700; 166 × 9.1 (545 × 30.1); M (Sulzer);
19
Sisters (Co flag):
04851 **CIUDAD DE BUCARAMANGA**
04852 **CIUDAD DE BUENAVENTURA**
04853 **CIUDAD DE CUCUTA**
04854 **RIO CAUCA** ex *Republica de Colombia* 1982
04855 **RIO MAGDALENA**
04856 **REPUBLICA DEL ECUADOR**

★ 04860 **BAOTING** RC/Fi (Rauma-Repola) 1965; C;
7300/9800; 151 × 8.6/9.7 (496 × 28/32); M (Gotaverken); 18; ex *Datuho* 1972; ex *Wihuri* 1971
Sisters (Pd flag):
★ 04861 **MIKOLAJ REJ** ex *Wirta* 1973
★ 04862 **FRYCZ MODRZEWSKI** ex *Wilma* 1972

★ 04870 **LJUTOMER** Ys/Ys ('Uljanik') 1965; CP;
6200/8100; 146.4 × 8.2 (480 × 2.7); M (B&W); 17.5
Sister:
★ 04871 **LJUBLJANA** (Ys)

● 04880 **HELLENIC PRIDE** Gr/Fi (Wartsila) 1971; CP;
6800/10300; 159 × 8.2/9.8 (528 × 27/32); M
(Sulzer); 18
Sister (Gr flag):
04883 **HELLENIC STAR**

04890 **BEATRIZ MONTEIRO** Bz/Bz 1964; C;
6200/8300; 142 × 8.2/— (466 × 27/—); M; 18.5; ex
Julio Regis 1982
Sister:
04891 **CELESTINO** (Bz)

04900 **SEA KING** Li/Br (Connell) 1964; C;
7800/10800; 157 × 8.5/9.6 (516 × 28/31.5); M
(B&W); 16; ex *Bordatxoa* 1982; ex *Scotstoun* 1972

★ 04910 **XING CHENG** RC/DDR (Warnow) 1973; C;
6300/9400; 144.99 × 7.3/— (492 × 23.95/—); M
(MAN); —; ex *Golden Harvest* 1978; ex *Union Aotearoa* 1978; 'Meridian' type
Sisters:
★ 04911 **DRESDEN** (DDR) ex *Hawk* 1979
★ 04912 **HALLE** (DDR) ex *Merlin I* 1979
★ 04913 **SUHL** (DDR) ex *Phenix I* 1979
★ 04914 **KARL MARX STADT** (DDR) ex *Crop* 1980;
ex *Condor* 1980
★ 04915 **KRASICA** (Ys)
★ 04916 **KRK** (Ys)
★ 04917 **MOSCENICE** (Ys)
★ 04918 **MOTOVUN** (Ys)
04919 **CYNTHIA G** (Li) ex *Falcon* 1979
04920 **MARCIA** (Li) ex *Eagle* 1979
Similar (superstructure differs—see inset):
★ 04921 **COTTBUS** (DDR)
★ 04922 **FRANKFURT/ODER** (DDR)
★ 04923 **ERFURT** (DDR)
★ 04924 **BERLIN-HAUPSTADT DER DDR** (DDR)
★ 04925 **LEIPZIG** (DDR)
★ 04926 **POTSDAM** (DDR)
★ 04927 **HERCEGNOVI** (Ys)
★ 04928 **SLOVENIJA** (Ys)
★ 04929 **VOJVODINA** (Ys)
★ 04930 **TIVAT** (Ys)
★ 04931 **RISAN** (Ys)

04932 **VISHVA MOHINI** (In)
04933 **VISHVA NANDINI** (In)
04934 **JALAMURUGAN** (In)
04935 **JALAMUDRA** (In)
04936 **VISHVA PRAYAS** (In)
04937 **VISHVA KAUMUDI** (In)

● 04940 **BEACON GRANGE** Br/Br (Cammell Laird)
1973; Pt. Con; 8400/12300; 162 × 8.6/9.8 (530 ×
28/32.4); M (B&W); 18; ex *Orduna* 1982
Sisters:
04941 **OCEANHAVEN** (Br) ex *Andes* 1982; ex *Orte-
ga* 1980
04942 **RUBENS** (Li) ex *Morning Sun* 1980; ex *Orbita*
1980

04950 **VERRAZANO BRIDGE** Ja/Ja (Kawasaki)
1973; Con; 39500; 265 × 11.9 (868 × 39); TSM
(MAN); 26.5
Similar:
04951 **SEVEN SEAS BRIDGE** (Ja)
04952 **HONG KONG CONTAINER** (Li)

04970 **OLIVINE** Pa/Ja (Kawasaki D) 1965; C; 880;
151 × 8.8 (496 × 29.2); M (MAN); 17.5; ex *Denmark
Maru* 1979
Sister:
04971 **HOLLAND MARU** (Ja)

● 04975 **KOTA SEGAR** Sg/Ja (Kawasaki D) 1967; C;
10800; 167.01 × 9.58 (547.93 × 31.43); M (MAN);
20; ex *France Maru* 1983
Sisters:
04976 **C C ORIENT** (Pa) ex *Union Victoria* 1983; ex
Italy Maru 1982
04977 **C C RED SEA** (Pa) ex *Union Bahama* 1983; ex
Portugal Maru 1982
04978 **KOTA SALAM** (Sg) ex *Spain Maru* 1982

04980 **GAOPENG** Pa/Sw (Oresunds) 1956; CP;
5400; 143 × 8.1 (469 × 26.4); M (Gotaverken); 17; ex
Havjo 1972

04990 **TAI NING** Tw/Ja (Mitsubishi HI) 1968; C;
10000; 155.4 × 9.45 (509.84 × 31); M (MAN); 18.25
Sister:
04991 **TAI SUN** (Tw)

05000 **NEW PANTHER** Sg/Br (Connell) 1964; C;
8200/11900; 162 × 8.6/— (533 × 28.3); M (Sulzer);
19; ex *Bendearg* 1981

05010 **AUSTRALIA MARU** Ja/Ja (Mitsui) 1969;
Con; 2400; 213 × 10.4 (699 × 34.5); M (B&W); 22.5
Similar:
05011 **ASIA MARU** (Ja)
05012 **BEISHU MARU** (Ja)

05020 **DRAGOR MAERSK** De/Ja (IHI) 1974; Con;
38500; 260 × 11.8 (851 × 38.6); TSM (Sulzer); 26.5;
ex *Svendborg Maersk* 1981; ex *TFL Charleston* 1980;
ex *Seatrain Charleston* 1980; ex *Svendborg Maersk*
1979

★ 05040 **YANG CHENG** RC/Br (Fairfield SB) 1962;
R; 9600/11500; 166 × 9.1/9.5 (544 × 30.1/31.5); M
(Sulzer); 20; ex *Harvest* 1979; ex *Glenogle* 1978
Sister:
★ 05041 **QING HE CHENG** (RC) ex *Glenfalloch* 1978

05050 **ADAMANTIOS** Li/Ja (Hitachi) 1971; C;
7300; 157 × 9.4 (515 × 30.8); M (B&W); 18.75; ex
President Kasavubu 1983

05060 **PACIFIC FIDELITY** Li/Ja (IHI) 1969; C;
10500; 159 × 9.7 (523 × 32.2); M (Sulzer); 19; ex
Union Sunrise 1983

★ 05070 **BAI YIN SHAN** RC/Ja (Hitachi) 1966; C;
10100; 157.03 × 9.45 (517 × 31); M (B&W); 18.5; ex
Izumo Maru 1982
Sisters:
05071 **SELMA** (Si) ex *Char Ho* 1983; ex *Ibaraki Maru*
1978
05072 **FAMILY ARROW** (Gr) ex *Isumi Maru* 1981;
05073 **ZINC TRADER** (Pa) ex *Iwashiro Maru* 1982
05074 **AFRICAN EXPRESS** (Pa) ex *Yamagata Maru*
1979;
05075 **NAJAT** (Si) ex *Char An* 1982; ex *Ise Maru*
1978;
05076 **SOMALI NAVIGATOR** (So) ex *Iyo* 1982; ex
Iyo Maru 1979
05077 **GUNONG MAS** (Pa) ex *Royal Ruby* 1983; ex
Iwaki Maru 1975;
05078 **BRAZILIAN EXPRESS** (Pa) ex *Yamaguchi
Maru* 1980

★ 05080 **JIN HU QUAN** RC/Sp (AESA) 1967; C;
8300; 143 × 9.3 (468 × 30.6); M (Sulzer); 15; ex *Mar
Cantabrico* 1982

05090 **AMERICAN SPITFIRE** US/US (Avondale)
1969; C/Con; 9500; 176.49 × 9.4 (579.04 × 30.84);
T (GEC); 23; ex *Idaho* 1981
Sisters (US flag):
05091 **AMERICAN TITAN** ex *Colorado* 1981

05093 **AMERICAN TROJAN** ex *Montana* 1981
05094 **AMERICAN MONARCH** ex *Wyoming* 1981

★05100 **JIANG CHUAN** RC/Ys ('3 Maj') 1973; C; 7500/10700; 157 × —/9.2 (519 × —/30.5); M (Sulzer); 18
Sisters (RC flag):
★05101 **HAN CHUAN**
★05102 **YIN CHUAN**
★05103 **TONG CHUAN**

05110 **CANADIAN REEFER** De/De (Aalborg) 1979; R; 8800; 144.35 × 10.14 (473.59 × 33.27); M (B&W); 22
Sister:
05111 **ECUADORIAN REEFER** (De)
Sisters (Japanese built):
05112 **ASIAN REEFER** (De)
05113 **BALKAN REEFER** (De)

05120 **LEONCE VIELJEUX** Fr/Fr (La Ciotat) 1970; C; 7900/12500; 171 × 7.7/9.7 (561 × 25.6/32); M (Sulzer); 19
Sisters:
05121 **SANTA RITA** (Pe) ex *Christian Vieljeux* 1981 (Fr flag):
05122 **THONON** ex *Eric Vieljeux* 1979
05123 **GEORGES VIELJEUX**
05124 **PIERRE VIELJEUX**
Possibly similar:
05125 **CUZCO II** (Pe) ex *Patrick Vieljeux* 1981
05126 **LIMA II** (Pe) ex *Stephane Vieljeux* 1981; ex *Taj* 1979; ex *Stephane Vieljeux* 1979

★05130 **LETING** RC/Fi (Rauma-Repola) 1966; C; 7400/9900; 151 × 8.6/9.7 (496 × 28/31.7); M (Gotaverken); 18; ex *Wisa* 1971

05140 **IRAN HEJRAT** Ir/Fr (La Ciotat) 1967; C; 10200; 161 × 9.1 (529 × 29.8); M (Sulzer); 17.5; ex *Arya Sara* 1980; ex *Lucie Delmas* 1973
Sisters (Ir flag):
05141 **IRAN NEHZAT** ex *Arya Omid* 1980; ex *Helene Delmas* 1973
05142 **IRAN SHAD** ex *Arya Shad* ex *Irma Delmas*
05143 **IRAN BESAT** ex *Iran Pake* 1980; ex *Arya Pake* 1980; ex *Marie Delmas* 1973

05150 **ODYSEFS** Ma/Br (Swan Hunter & WR) 1963; R; 11100; 165 × 9.8 (538 × 32.3); TSM (H&W); 18; ex *Medic* 1979

05160 **ADM WM M CALLAGHAN** US/US (Sun SB) 1967; C/RoC; 24500; 211 × 8.9 (604 × 29); TSGT (GEC/Pratt & Whitney); 26; stern door

05170 **JALARAJAN** In/Br (Lithgows) 1966; C; 11300; 160 × 9.4 (535 × 31); M (B&W); 16
Sisters (In flag) with Stulcken derrick on second kingpost:
05171 **JALARATNA**
05172 **JALARASHMI**

05180 **SAMOAN REEFER** De/De (Aalborg) 1973; R; 5900; 145 × 8.8 (477 × 28.10); M (B&W); 22.5; side doors
Sister:
05181 **TUNISIAN REEFER** (De)

05190 **FUJI REEFER** Ja/Ja (Hitachi) 1979; R; 7200; 144.95 × 8.07 (475.56 × 26.48); M (B&W); 20
Sisters (Ja flag):
05191 **SAKURA REEFER**
05192 **ARIAKE REEFER**
05193 **AKEBONO REEFER**
05194 **TOKYO REEFER**

05200 **NEW UNITED** Pa/Ne (Giessen) 1961/76; C/Con; 9400; 162.54 × — (533.27 × —); M (Stork); 17; ex *Sun Opal* 1982; ex *Hupeh* 1981; ex *Sidonia* 1967; Lengthened and converted from cargo 1976 (Hong Kong U)

05210 **GOLEMI** Gr/Br (Bartram) 1965; C; 5800; 143.31 × 7.85 (470 × 25.75); M (Stork); 16.75; ex *Gold Star* 1981; ex *Anat* 1974; ex *Sicilia* 1968

★05215 **LITIJA** Ys/Sp ('Bazan') 1969; C/Con; 5500/8500; 148.57 × —/8.42 (487 —/27.62); M (Sulzer); 18
Sister:
★05216 **PAG** (Ys)

05220 **NORTHLAND** Pa/Br (Bartram) 1967; C; 7900/10500; 156 × 8.8/9.6 (512 × 29/31.5); M (Sulzer); 16; ex *John* 1982; ex *Lutetian* 1979

05230 **FLORIDA** Li/Br (Doxford & S) 1972; C; 7600/11500; 161.45 × —/9.75 (530 × —/32); M (Doxford); 17; ex *Fleetbank* 1981
Sisters:
05231 **SANJOHN BAY** (Pa) ex *Beaverbank* 1981
05232 **CALIFORNIA** (Li) ex *Birchbank* 1981
05233 **ELLY** (Gr) ex *Cedarbank* 1983
05234 **INDIANA** (Li) ex *Riverbank* 1982
05235 **ARGONAFTIS** (Gr) ex *Streambank* 1983

05236 **COLORADO** (Li) ex *Cloverbank* 1981
05237 **MARAKI** (Gr) ex *Firbank* 1983
05238 **ALKAIOS** (Gr) ex *Nessbank* 1981
05239 **AMPHION** (Gr) ex *Laganbank* 1981

05240 **TAXILA** Pk/Ys ('Split') 1968; 1968; C; 5900/8900; 155 —/9.3 (507 × —/30.8); M (Sulzer); 18.15

● 05250 **GULF BANKER** US/US (Avondale) 1964; CP; 9500; 151 × 9.8 495 ×32); T (GEC); | GULF ANDES class
Sisters (US flag):
05251 **GULF FARMER**
05252 **GULF MERCHANT**
05253 **GULF SHIPPER**
05254 **GULF TRADER**

05260 **AL ATTARED** Si/Ja (Kawasaki) 1969; R; 6400 145 × 7.4 (474 × 24.4); M (MAN); 20.5; ex *Matina* 1983
Sisters:
05261 **AL ZOHAL** (Si) ex *Morant* 1983
05262 **AL MOSHTAREE** (Si) ex *Motagua* 1983
05263 **AL ZAHRAH** (Si) ex *Musa* 1983

● 05270 **AL BARAT** Si/Br (Burntisland) 1965; C; 8100; 141 × 8.8 (452 × 28.11); M (Sulzer); —; ex *Tenbury* 1974

05280 **RIO ESQUEL** Ar/Ar (Astarsa) 1976; C; 9100; 147.63 × 8.26 (484.35 × 27.1); M (GMT); 18
Sisters (Ar flag):
05281 **RIO CINCEL**
05282 **RIO DESEADO**
05283 **RIO LIMAY**
05284 **RIO OLIVIA**
05285 **TIO TEUCO**

05290 **RIO CALCHAQUI** Ar/Ar (AFNE) 1970; C; 10400; 152.71 × 8.68 (501.02 × 28.48); M (GMT); 17.5
Sisters (Ar flag):
05292 **RIO IGUAZU**
05293 **PARANA**
05294 **RIO GUALEGUAY**

05300 **CAPETAN LUKIS** Gr/Br (Doxford & S) 1969; C; 10800; 159 × 9.7 (523 × 31.8); M (B&W); 17; ex *Marigo R* 1979

● ★05310 **RONG JIANG** RC/Br (A&P) 1978; C; 9100; 141 × 8.86 (462 × 29.07); M (Sulzer); 14.75; ex *Morviken* 1981; 'SD 14' type
Sisters:
★05311 **MAXIMO GOMEZ** (Cu) ex *Australind* 1980
★05312 **KIFANGONDO** (An) ex *Sea Hawk* 1979
★05313 **LUNDOGE** (An) ex *Aegira* 1979
★05314 **THAI-BINH** (Vn)
★05315 **LUCNAM** (Vn)
★05316 **TO-LICH** (Vn)
★05317 **SONG DUONG** (Vn) ex *Dalworth* 1979
05318 **YUANJIANG** (RC)
★05319 **HUNJIANG** (RC)
Similar (Series IV):
★05320 **PING JIANG** (RC) ex *Funing* 1982
05321 **MOUNTAIN AZALEA** (Pa) ex *Derwent* 1982
05322 **PIVA** (Pa) ex *Belloc* 1982
★05323 **SHUN YI** (RC) ex *Boswell*
★05324 **AN DONG JIANG** (RC) ex *Bronte* 1983
★05325 **AN FU JIANG** (RC) ex *Browning* 1983
05326 **AFRICAN EXPRESS** (Ne)
05327 **EUROPEAN EXPRESS** (Ne)
05328 **EMPROS** (Gr)
05329 **GRAND FAITH** (Li)
05330 **JADE II** (Gr)
05331 **JADE III** (Gr)
05323 **UNITED DRIVE** (Br)
05333 **UNITED EFFORT** (Br)
05334 **UNITED ENTERPRISE** (Br)
05335 **UNITED SPIRIT** (Br)
05336 **LILAC ISLANDS** (Pa) ex *Carrianna Lilac* 1983
05337 **LOTUS ISLANDS** (Pa) ex *Carrianna Lotus* 1983
05338 **SUNDERLAND VENTURE** (Br)

05340 **ADELFOTIS** Gr/Ja (IHI) 1967; C; 7000; 138× 8.7 (458 × 28.8); M (Sulzer); 16.25; ex *Japan Kauri* 1977
Sisters (Gr flag):
05341 **KRONOS** ex *Japan Totara* 1977
05342 **NAFTILOS** ex *Japan Rimu* 1977

05350 **REDESTOS** Cy/Br (A&P) 1974; C; 9000; 141 × 8.9 (463 × 29); M (Sulzer); 15; 'SD 14' type. ex *Nedlloyd Waterland* 1983; ex *Waterland* 1982

05360 **FORUM EAGLE** Gr/Pd (Gdanska) 1970; C; 6900/10200; 161 × 19.7 (528 × —/31.1); M (Sulzer); 20.5; ex *Amaralina* 1983; 'B 444' type
Similar (Bz flag):
05361 **ITABERA**
05362 **ITATINGA**
05363 **FORUM HOPE** (Gr) ex *Botafogo* 1983

05364 **BERNARDINO CORREA**
05365 **FORUM PROGRESS** (Gr) ex *Arpoador* 1983 (lengthened)
05366 **PRETORIANO** (Ar) ex *Frotabeira* 1983
05367 **MARIA DA PENHA** ex *Frotatokyo* 1978

★05370 **ANTING** RC/Fi (Rauma-Repola) 1970; C; 7000/9800; 151.8 × 8.7/9.8 (498 × 28.5/32); M (Gotaverken) 18; ex *Kunlungshan* 1971
Sisters (RC flag):
★05371 **CHANGTING** ex *Wutaishan* 1972
★05372 **HUATING** ex *Liupanshan* 1973
★05373 **JIANGTING** ex *Dahsueshan* 1972
★05374 **WANGTING** ex *Taihanshan* 1971
Possible sisters (RC flag):
★05375 **YANGTING**
★05376 **YUTING**

★05400 **MARINA TWO** Ma/DDR (Warnow) 1969; C; 9000; 151 × 9 (495 × 29.8); M (MAN); 17.5; ex *African Beryl* 1982; ex *Saint Michel* 1980; 'OZEAN' type

★05410 **VOLCHANSK** Ru/DDR (Warnow) 1968; C; 9500; 150.8 × 8.9 (494 × 29.3); M (MAN); 16.5

05420 **ANYI** Pa/DDR (Warnow) 1969; C; 5600; 151.2 × 9 (496 × 29.8); M (MAN); 20; ex *Neptune Amethyst* 1974; 'OZEAN' type;
Sister:
05421 **IRENES LOGIC** (Gr) ex *Clisson* 1980; ex *Velocity* 1977; ex *Andu* 1974; ex *Neptune Aquamarine* 1974

● 05430 **PALAWAN** Li/DDR (Warnow) 1969; C; 8800; 150.5 × 9 (495 × 29.8); M (MAN); 18.5; ex *Ville De Reims* 1976
Sister:
05431 **NASIPIT BAY** (Pi) ex *Corregidor* 1980; ex *Ville De Sete* 1978

★05440 **HAIMEN** RC/DDR (Warnow) 1968; C; 9500; 151 × 8.8 (494 × 29.3) M (MAN); —

● 05450 **AFRICA PALM** Br/DDR (Warnow) 1972; C; 6200/10000; 152.86 × 7.59/9.40 (501 × 25.0/31.0); M (MAN); 18.5; ex *Santa Barbara Pacific* 1982; ex *Africa Palm* 1983; ex *Joruna* 1974; 'OZEAN' type
Sisters:
05452 **AUBRAC** (Fr) ex *Anne Reed* 1975
05453 **POLNORD** (No) ex *Karen Reed* .1980; ex *Nortrans Karen* 1980; ex *Karen Reed* 1975
05454 **FLEVOLAND** (Ne) ex *Nedlloyd Flevoland* 1983; ex *Flevoland* 1982; ex *Jomara*
05455 **SALLAND** (Ne) ex *Nedlloyd Salland* 1983; ex *Salland*
Probable sisters:
05456 **STATE OF HIMACHAL PRADESH** (In) ex *Jolandia* 1974
05457 **ACHILLEUS** (Le) ex *Aludra* 1983
05458 **POLSUND** (Li) ex *Ambon* 1983; ex *Hornsund* 1981; ex *Torasund* 1978; ex *Nortrans Tora* 1977; ex *Torasund* 1977
05459 **POLFJORD** (Li) ex *Torafjord*

● 05460 **FREEZER KING** UAE/Ja (Kochi Jukogyo) 1978; R; 7700; 140.67 × 8.32 (461.52 × 27.3); M (IHI); 20
Sisters:
05461 **WHITE BILLOW** (Br) ex *Freezer Prince* 1983
05462 **WHITE CASCADE** (Br) ex *Freezer Queen* 1982;
05463 **KHALIJ REEFER** (Ja)
Possible sisters:
05465 **KHALIJ FREEZER** (Ja)
05466 **KHALIJ FROST** (Ja)
05467 **KHALIJ COOLER** (Ja)
05468 **FREEZER ACE** (Pa)

05470 **SOUTHERN LADY** Pa/Br (Doxford & S) 1971; C; 7800/11300; 163× —/9.7 (540× —/31.9) M (Sulzer); 18; ex *Benefactor* 1982; ex *Ion*
Sisters:
05472 **FINIX** (Gr)
05473 **IASON** (Gr)
05474 **IKTINOS** (Gr)
05475 **ION** (Gr)
05476 **ATALANTI** (Li)
Similar:
05477 **FEAX** (Gr)
05478 **FAETHON** (Gr)

05480 **ISLA PINTA** Pa/FRG (Schlichting) 1972; C; 3700/7200; 131 × 7/8.2 (431 × 23/27); M (MAN); 18; ex *Baron* 1979; ex *Wilhelm Bornhofen* 1973
Sisters:
05481 **ISLA FERNANDINA** (Pa) ex *Bate Bridge* 1981; ex *Adviser* 1975; ex *Hans Bornhofen* 1973
05482 **ISLA GENOVESA** (Pa) ex *Max Bornhofen* 1980; ex *Rapid Bridge* 1976; ex *Specialist* 1974; ex *Max Bornhofen* 1973;
★05483 **XIONG YUE CHENG** (RC) ex *Opulence*

1982; ex *Xiong Yue Cheng* 1981; ex *Elisabeth Born-hofen* 1978; ex *Citos* 1975; ex *Elisabeth Bornhofen* 1973

05490 **KALENTZI** Gr/Fr (Nantes) 1964/71; C; 4600/7600; 159.19 × 6.68/7.92 (522 × 22/30.1); M (Pielstick); —; ex *Giant Pilot* 1981; ex *Gold Pilot* 1978; ex *Hadar* 1977; lengthened 1971
Sisters:
05491 **ROGET** (Pa) ex *Yafo* 1980; ex *Dolly* 1979; ex *Yafo* 1979

05520 **NAJRAAN ZAHABIA** Si/Ja (Uraga HI)1966; C; 11100; 160 × 9.3 (523 × 30.1); M (Sulzer); 19.5; ex *Oriental Queen* 1982

05530 **RIO ABAUCAN** Ar/Sp ('Bazan') 1973; C; 8600/10200; 150.9 × 7.6/8.2 (495 × 25/27.1); M (Sulzer); 18
Sisters (Ar flag):
05531 **RIO LOS SAUCES**
05533 **RIO CALINGASTA**
05534 **RIO MARAPA**
05535 **RIO NEUQUEN**

05540 **NEDLLOYD GOOILAND** Ne/Ne (P. Smit) 1969; C; 4800; 148 × 7 (484 × 23.4); M (Sulzer); 15.5 ex *Gooiland* 1982

05550 **IRENES MAGIC** Gr/DDR (Warnow.) 1968; C; 8700; 151 × 8.8 (495 × 29); M (MAN); 16.5; ex *Anjou* 1979.
Possible sister:
05551 **PANAGHIA P** (Gr) ex *Auvergne* 1979

★05560 **MATIJA IVANIC** Ys/Be (Cockerill) 1969; C; 6100/9300; 141 × 19.3 (461 × 131); M (Stork); 14; 'UNITY' type
Sisters (Ys flag):
★05561 **MATIJA GUBEC**
★05562 **MARKO ORESKOVIC**
★05563 **MOSA PIJADE**
★05564 **PROMINA**
★05565 **SIBENIK**

05570 **OVERSEA FRUIT** Pa/Ja (Hayashikane) 1971; C; 6500; 134 × 7.5 (440 × 24.8); M (Sulzer); 21.75
Sister:
05571 **PHILIPPINES FRUIT** (Pa) ex *Comfort* 1977

05580 **ELIZABETH LYKES** US/US (Avondale) 1964; CP; 7400/11000; 165 × 8.5/9.9 (540 28/31.8); T (Westinghouse); 20
Sisters (US flag):
05581 **FREDERICK LYKES**
05582 **GENEVIEVE LYKES**
05583 **HOWELL LYKES**
05584 **LETITIA LYKES**
05585 **LOUISE LYKES**
05586 **MALLORY LYKES**
05587 **MASON LYKES**
05588 **RUTH LYKES**
05589 **STELLA LYKES**
05590 **VELMA LYKES**

05600 **SANTA JUANA** US/US (Bethlehem Steel) 1966; C; 7200/11000; 165 × —/9.5 (554 —/31.8); T (GEC); 21; ex *Delta America* 1980; ex *Prudential Seajet* 1979
Sister:
05601 **SANTA ADELA** (US); ex *Delta Africa* 1980; ex *Prudential Oceanjet* 1979

05610 **LING YUNG** Tw/Ja (Uraga HI) 1968; C; 11200; 159 × 9.2 (522 × 30.5); M (Sulzer); 19.5
Sisters:
05611 **YEH YUNG** (Tw)
05612 **CAYAMBE** (Li) ex *Eidanger* 1983; ex *Singapore Pride* 1976
05613 **COTOPAXI** (Ec) ex *Villanger* 1983; ex *Singapore Triumph* 1976

05615 **ROYAL LILY** Pa/Ja (Hayashikane) 1979; R; 7200; 140.52 × 8.82 (461 × 28.94); M (Sulzer); 20; Four side doors
Possibly similar:
05616 **SEKI REX** (Ja)

★05620 **IGNATIY SERGEYEV** Ru/Pd (Gdanska) 1968; C; 10200; 154.5 × 9.5 (507 × 29.6); M (Sulzer); 16.5; 'B40/B401' type 'KOMMUNIST' class
Sisters (Ru flag):
★05621 **GEORGIY CHICHERIN**
★05622 **GEORGIY DIMITROV**
★05623 **ERNST THALMANN**
★05624 **GIUSEPPE DI VITTORIO**
★05625 **50 LET SOVIET SOVIETSKOY**
★05626 **UKRAINY**
★05627 **HO CHIN MIN**
★05628 **INESSA ARMAND**
★05629 **IONA YAKIR**
★05630 **JEANNE LABOURBE**
★05631 **KARL LIEBKNECHT**
★05632 **KOMMUNIST**

★05633 **KOMMUNISTICHESKOYE ZNAMYA**
★05634 **BELA KHUN**
★05635 **DMITRY POLUYAN**
★05636 **NIKOLAY KREMLYANSKIY**
★05637 **FRIEDRICH ENGELS**
★05638 **ROSA LUXEMBURG**
★05639 **FRANTS BOGUSH**
★05640 **TOYVO ANTIKAYNEN**
(Tu flag) B442 type:
05641 **GENERAL A. F. CEBESOY**
05642 **GENERAL K. ORBAY**
05643 **GENERAL R. GUMUSBALA**
05644 **GENERAL Z. DOGAN**
(Pd flag)
★05645 **KONIN**

★05650 **BAKAR** Ys/It (Italcantieri) 1969; C; 6200; 152.3 × — (500 × —); M (Fiat); 18
Sisters (Ys flag):
★05651 **KRALJEVICA**
★05652 **PAZIN**
★05653 **KASTAV**
Very similar:
★05654 **KRANJCEVIC**
★05655 **GORAN KOVACIC**

★05660 **DUNHUANG** RC/Br (Doxford & S) 1967; C; 8300/11400; 159 × 8.5/9.4 (523 × 27.3/31); M (Sulzer); —
Sister:
★05661 **JINSHA** (RC)

05670 **AMERICAN CHALLENGER** US/US (Newport News) 1962; C; 8200/11100; 171 × —/9.6 (561 —/31.7); T (Westinghouse); 21
Sisters (US) flag):
05671 **AMERICAN CHAMPION**
05672 **AMERICAN CHARGER**
05673 **AMERICAN CHIEFTAIN**
05674 **AMERICAN CORSAIR**
05675 **COURIER** ex *American Courier*
05676 **PIONEER COMMANDER** ex *American Commander* 1967
05677 **PIONEER CONTENDER** ex *American Contender* 1966
05678 **PIONEER CONTRACTOR** ex *American Contractor* 1966
05679 **PIONEER CRUSADER** ex *American Crusader* 1966
05680 **PIONEER MOON** ex *American Moon* 1962

05690 **EASTERN MARINER I** Pa/Br (Connell) 1959; C; 8000; 142.6 × 9.1 (468 × 30); M (Doxford); 13; ex *Anastasia* 1980; ex *Broompark* 1969

05700 **FAMILY DELTA** Gr/Br (Connell) 1962; C; 7100/9900; 154.9 × 8.3/9.4 (508 × 27/31); M (Sulzer); 16; ex *Delta* 1980; ex *Singapore Progress* 1979; ex *Strathnaver* 1978; ex *Jumna* 1975

● 05710 **BEACON HILL** Br/Br (Lithgows) 1966; R; 8200; 161 × 8.6 (528 × 29.5); M (Sulzer); 19.5; ex *Fares Reefer* 1981; ex *Westmorland* 1980
Sisters:
05711 **CAPETAN LEONIDAS** (Gr) ex *Reefer Princess* 1981; ex *Tongariro* 1979
05713 **MANDAMA** (Sg) ex *Taupo* 1980

★05730 **YONG JIN** RK/Ja (Nipponkai) 1958; C; 7400; 137.27 × 8.57 (433.9 × 28.12); M (Sulzer); 13.75; ex *Jong Dzin* 1979; ex *Chuoh Maru* 1972

● 05760 **SAILFLIP** Cy/Ja (Kawasaki D) 1961; C; 9000; 156 × 8.7 (513 × 28.6); M (MAN); 16.5; ex *Christos St Arapakis* 1981; ex *Man Hing* 1979; ex *Andino* 1979; ex *Florida Maru* 1973
Sisters:
05763 **ROSS CAREER** (Pa) ex *Tennessee Maru* 1979
05764 **UNION KINGSTON** (Pa) ex *Sanshin Victory* 1980; ex *Texas Maru* 1973

05800 **KOTA CANTIK** Sg/Br (Vickers-Armstrongs) 1962; CP; 7300/9700; 154 × 8.4/9 (527.5/29); M (Sulzer); 18; ex *City of Toronto* 1978; ex *City of Eastbourne* 1971
Sister:
05801 **KOTA CAHAYA** (Sg) ex *City of Ottawa* 1978; ex *City of Glasgow* 1971

05810 **HADAR** Is/Pd (Gdanska) 1972; Pt.Con; 7000/11700; 161 × —/9.7 (518 × —/31.11); M (Sulzer); 21; ex *Sao Tome* 1982; 'B 434' type
Sister:
05811 **TAPUZ** (Is) ex *Sofala* 1982

● 05820 **JALAMOKAMBI** In/DDR (Warnow) 1972; C; 9600; 153 × 9.3 (500 × 30.9); M (MAN); 18.25; 'OZEAN' type
Sisters (In flag):
05823 **JALAMOHAN**
05824 **JALAMAYUR**
05825 **JALAMANGALA**
05826 **JALAMATSYA**
05827 **JALAMOTI**

★05830 **HAIFENG** RC/DDR (Warnow.) 1969; C; 8900; 150.5 × 8.8 (494 × 29.3); M (MAN); 17; 'OZEAN' type
Sisters:
★05831 **LUFENG** (RC)
★05832 **XINFENG** (RC)

05840 **RAINBOW REEFER** Pa/Fr (CNIM) 1969; R; 9600; 148.4 × 8.5 (487 × 28); M (Pielstick); 20.5; ex *Flamar Pride* 1982; ex *Fort La Reine* 1980
Sister:
05841 **RAINBOW FREEZER** (Pa) ex *Flamar Progress* 1982; ex *Fort Pontchartrain* 1980

05850 **DJAKARTA** Pa/Ja (IHI) 1961; CP; 6000; 130 × 8.2 (426 × 27); M (Sulzer); 14.75; ex *Djakarta Maru* 1976

05870 **LAKY** Gr/Sw (Uddevalla) 1956; C; 6100/8700; 142.4 × 8/9 (466 × 26/30; M (Gotaverken); 14; ex *Kimberley* 1979; ex *Cretan Harmony* 1976; ex *Harmony* 1974; ex *Truth* 1971

★05880 **PEPITO TEY** Cu/Sw (Oskarshamns) 1961; C; 6000/8800; 148.4 × 8.2/9.1 (487 × 27/30); M (Gotaverken); 15; ex *Marble Islands* 1975; ex *Hansa* 1972

● 05900 **SOLANGE P** Pa/FRG (Bremer V) 1960; C; 8300; 144.18 × 8.50 (473 × 27.89); M (MAN); 15; ex *Lemania* 1982; ex *Aliakmon Prosperity* 1982; ex *Silver* 1974; ex *Silver Land* 1974; ex *Gedera* 1973

05910 **IMPERIAL** Li/FRG (Rhein Nordseew) 1971; RoC/Pt. Con; 7800/17000; 174 × 7.9/9.1 (572 × 26/30); M (Sulzer); 20; ex *Finn-Amer* 1981; ex *Concordia Amer* 1978; ex *Finn-Amer* 1977; stern and side doors
Sisters:
05911 **COPIAPO** (Li) ex *Northern Sapphire* 1981; ex *Finnbuilder* 1981; ex *Concordia Builder* 1978; ex *Finnbuilder* 1977
05912 **ACONCAGUA** (Ch) ex *Finnsailor* 1981; ex *Concordia Sailor* 1978; ex *Finnsailor* 1976

05920 **JOHN P** Gr/Br (Connell) 1968; C; 8300/12000; 162 × 8.6/10 (532 × 28/33); M (Sulzer); 22; ex *Benstac* 1982

05930 **AMERICAN RACER** US/US (Sun SB) 1964; Pt. Con; 7500/11200; 166 × —/9.74 (542 × —/31.96); T (GEC); 21
Sisters (US flag):
05931 **AMERICAN RANGER**
05932 **AMERICAN RELIANCE**
05933 **MORMACDAWN** ex *Austral Patriot* 1980; ex *American Resolute* 1969
05934 **MORMACMOON** ex *Austral Pilot* 1980; ex *American Rover* 1969

05940 **LOUTFALLAH** Si/Ja (Mitsubishi HI) 1959; C; 9100; 162.2 × 9.2 (532 × 30.1); M (Sulzer); 17.5; ex *Union Yenbo* 1983; ex *Union Bangkok* 1979; ex *Yenbo* 1979; ex *Royal Fortune* 1978; ex *Seattle Maru* 1975

● 05950 **KARA CAREER** Pa/Ja (Mitsubishi Z) 1960; C; 9500; 160 × 9.3 (524 × 30.5); M (Mitsubishi); 18.5; ex *Brooklyn Maru* 1975
Sister:
05951 **PRESIDENT GARCIA** (Pi) ex *Rio Tuxpan* 1979; ex *Manhattan Maru* 1975

05960 **CAPE ALAVA** US/US (Ingalls SB) 1962; C; 11300; 174.3 × 9.4 (572 × 30.1); T (GEC); 20; ex *Comet* 1980; ex *African Comet* 1980
Sisters (US flag):
05961 **DAWN** ex *African Dawn* 1980
05962 **CAPE ALEXANDER** ex *Mercury* 1980; ex *African Mercury* 1980
05963 **CAPE ANN** ex *Meteor* 1980; ex *African Meteor* 1980
05964 **CAPE ARCHWAY** ex *Neptune* 1980; ex *African Neptune* 1980
05965 **CAPE AVINOF** ex *Sun* 1980; ex *African Sun* 1980

05970 **HAN GARAM** Ko/Ja (Mitsui) 1959; C; 9400; 156.57 × 8.80 (514 × 28.87); M (B&W); 18; ex *Sea Brave* 1978; ex *Momijisan Maru* 1973
Sister:
05971 **HAN NURI** (Ko) ex *Sea Discoverer* 1978; ex *Matsudosan Maru* 1974

● 05980 **LEAGE** Gr/Ja (Hitachi) 1961; C; 8800; 154 × 9.2 (505 × 30.4); M (B&W); 18.5; ex *Tasaharu Maru* 1975
Similar:
05981 **SMINARCHOS FRANGISTAS** (Gr) ex *Yamatoshima Maru* 1977

● 06010 **JALAMOKAMBI** In/DDR (Warnow.) 1972; C; 9600; 153 × 9.3 (500 × 30.9) M (MAN); 18.25; 'OZEAN' type
Sisters (In flag):

06012 **JALAMANGALA**
06014 **JALAMATSYA**
06015 **JALAMOHAN**
06016 **JALAMOTI**
06017 **JALAMAYOR**

06020 **NACALA** Po/Hong Kong (Taikoo) 1966; C; 9100; 149 × 9.1 (489 × 29.10); M (Sulzer); 18; ex *Hunan* 1968

★06030 **HULIN** RC/Ys ('Split') 1974; C; 6300/9700; 160 × —/9.4 (525 × —/30.10); M (MAN); 19.25
Sisters (RC flag):
★06031 **CHUNGLIN**
★06032 **SONGLIN**
★06033 **TIANLIN**
★06034 **YANGLIN**
★06035 **YULIN'**
★06036 **TAOLIN**
Possible sister:
★06037 **LONGLIN**

★06040 **URSUS** Pd/Pd (Gdanska) 1972; C; 6400/10100; 154.7 × —/8.97 (507.55 × —/29.43); M (Sulzer); 17.75; 'B442' type

06050 **MONTAIGLE** Be/Be (Cockerill) 1968; CP; 7100/11500; 161 × 7.9/9.9 (528 × 26/32.6); M (B&W); 19
Sisters (Be flag):
06051 **MONTENAKEN**
06052 **MONTFORT**
06053 **MONTSALVA**

★06060 **VELIKIYE LUKI** Ru/DDR (Warnow) 1964; C; 9400; 150.6 × 8.8 (494 × 29.3); M (MAN); 16.5
Sisters:
★06061 **VEREYA** (Ru)
★06062 **VELIZH** (Ru)
★06063 **CHAMWINO** (Ta) ex *Changcheng* 1972; ex *Al Mubarakiah* 1972; ex *Jolanda* 1966
Similar:
★06064 **JIANGMIN** (RC)
★06065 **YUMEN** (RC)
06067 **ANTONIS** (Gr) ex *African Amber* 1982; ex *Cariba* 1979
06068 **BARU TRUST** (Gr) ex *African Coral* 1982; ex *Cassarate* 1980

★06069 **QIMEN** RC/DDR (Warnow) 1973; C; 9700; 151.72 × 9.30 (498 × 30.51); M (MAN); 17; 'OZEAN' type
Sisters (RC flag):
★06069/1 **DOUMEN**
★06069/2 **HONGMEN**
★06069/3 **LONGMEN**
★06069/4 **TIANMEN**
★06069/5 **WUMEN**
★06069/6 **XIAMEN**
★06069/7 **YANMEN**
★06069/8 **YIMEN**
★06069/9 **YONGMEN**
(Cz flag)
★06069/10 **MIR**
(Rm flag)
★06069/11 **COTNARI**
★06069/12 **DRAGASANI**
★06069/13 **FOCSANI**

06080 **DEVI** Sr/Sp (AESA) 1963; C; 6200/9400; 156.8 × 8/9.3 (515 × 26/30.3); M (Sulzer); 16 ex *Eternal Peace* 1982; ex *Mighty* 1981; ex *Sincerity* 1977; ex *Moheli* 1977; ex *Chatwood* 1969

★06090 **WLAYDYSLAW ORKAN** Pd/Pd (Gdanska) 1971; C; 6400/10100; 153.74 × —/8.97 (504.4 × —/29.43); M (Sulzer); 18; Modified 'B442' type
Sister:
★06091 **LUCJAN SZENWALD** (Pd)

06120 **ANYI** Pa/DDR (Warnow) 1969; C; 8700; 151.7 × 9.9 (496 × 29.7); M (MAN); 20 ex *Neptune Amethyst* 1974; 'OZEAN' type
Sister:
06121 **IRENES LOGIC** (Gr) ex *Clisson* 1980; ex *Velocity* 1977; ex *Andu* 1974; ex *Neptune Aquamarine* 1974

★06125 **LUFENG** RC/DDR (Warnow) 1970; C; 9100; 150.68 × 8.92 (494 × 29.27); M (MAN); —
Sister:
★06126 **XINFENG** (RC)

06130 **BRAZILIAN EXPRESS** Pi/Ja (Mitsubishi HI) 1965; C; 10000; 161 × 9.3 (528 × 30.6); M (Mitsubishi); 19.5; ex *Yamaguchi Maru* 1980

★06135 **HAIFENG** RC/DDR (Warnow) 1969; C; 8900; 150.68 × 8.92 (494 × 29.27); M (MAN); 17

★06142 **ALBA IULIA** Rm/Pd (Szczecinska) 1976; C; 5300/8100; 145.07 × 7.46/9.08 (476 × 24.47/29.79); M (Sulzer); 18.5 'B478' type
Sister:
★06143 **CURTEA DE ARGES** (Rm)

06150 **SANTA FE** Sg/FRG (LF-W) 1972; C; 6900/9800; 148.6 × 7.9/9.4 (488 × 26/30.7); M (Pielstick); 19
Sister:
06151 **TURTLE BAY** (Sg) ex *Santa Cruz* 1982; ex *Lloyd Melbourne* 1980; ex *Santa Cruz* 1979

06160 **DEVONIUN** Br/Br (Thornycroft) 1956; P; 900; 64 × 3 (210 × 9.7); TSM (Ruston & Hornsby); 15.5 ex *Devonia* 1982; ex *Scillonian* 1977

06170 **AMERICANA** It/It (Italcantieri) 1974; Con/V; 22200; 208 × 10.3 (683 × 34.1); T (GEC); 23.5; Side door on port side
Sister:
06171 **ITALICA** (It)

06180 **MARION DUFRESNE** Fr/Fr (Havre) 1973; RS/C/P; 6600; 112.1 × 6.3 (368 × 20.8); M (Pielstick); 15

06190 **KHALIJ EXPRESS** Si/Br (Cammell Laird) 1955/75; LS; 8100; 134 × 7.7 (440 × 25.3); T (Cammell Laird); 15; ex *United Challenger* 1976; ex *Malaysia* 1976; ex *Hubert* 1964; Converted from cargo ship 1976

★06200 **LEONID SOBINOV** Ru/Br (J Brown) 1954; P; 21400; 185 × 8.7 (608 × 28.7); TST (J Brown); 20; ex *Carmania* 1973; ex *Saxonia* 1962
Sister:
★06201 **FEDOR SHALYAPIN** (Ru) ex *Franconia* 1973; ex *Ivernia* 1962

06220 **ATTICA REEFER** Gr/FRG (LF-W) 1973; R; 7600; 155 × 8.8 (507 × 28.7); M (MAN); 22.5; ex *Wild Cormorant* 1981
Sisters:
06221 **ATHENIAN REEFER** (Gr) ex *Wild Curlew* 1981
06222 **CARIBBEAN UNIVERSAL** (Br) ex *Polar Costa Rica* 1980
06223 **EDINBURGH UNIVERSAL** (Br) ex *Polar Honduras* 1980

06230 **PHILIPPINES** Pi/It (Adriatico) 1952; P; 27100; 207 × 8.5 (680 × 28); TSM (Fiat); 21; ex *Ocean King* 1983; ex *Great Sea* 1980; ex *Augustus* 1976

06240 **CARNIVALE** Pa/Br (Fairfield SB) 1956; P; 19000; 195 × 8.8 (640 × 29); TST (Fairfield); 21; ex *Queen Anna Maria* 1975; ex *Empress of Britain* 1964

06250 **UNIVERSE** Li/US (Sun SB) 1953; P; 14000; 172 × 8.6 (564 × 28.7); T (GEC); 20; ex *Universe Campus* 1976; ex *Atlantic* 1971; ex *Badger Mariner* 1957

★06270 **LUC NGAN** Vn/Br (Readhead) 1963; C; 6800/9300; 153 × 7.8/8.8 (503 × 26/29); M (Doxford); 17; ex *Amber Star* 1980; ex *Strathassynt* 1978; ex *Turkistan* 1975

06280 **BRAZILIAN REEFER** Bs/No (Drammen) 1975; R; 6300/8400; 143.4 × 9.4 (470 × 31); M (Pielstick); 23.5; ex *Bremerhaven* 1981
Sister (with tripod mast):
06281 **BELGIAN REEFER** (Bs) ex *Blumenthal* 1981

●06290 **FRIO AEGEAN** Pa/Br (Stephen) 1960; R; 3600; 120 × 6.1 (393 × 20.1); M (Sulzer); 18; ex *Calavittoria* 1979; ex *Mendoza Star* 1967; ex *Chatham* 1962; Lengthened 1964
Sister:
06291 **GAFREDO** (Pa) ex *Calagaribaldi* 1981; ex *Santos Star* 1966; ex *Constable* 1962

06300 **EXCELSIOR REEFER** Pa/Ja (Kanda) 1973; R; 10300; 163.02 × 8.99 (534.84 × 29.49); M (B&W); 20; ex *Ryutu Reefer* 1981
Sisters:
06301 **PACIFIC REEFER** (Pa)
06302 **UNITY REEFER** (Pa) ex *Sonoda Reefer* 1976
(Cu flag):
★06303 **GOLFO DE BATABANO**
★06304 **GOLFO DE GUACANAYBO**
★06305 **GOLFO DE GUANAHACABIBES**
★06306 **OCEANO ATLANTICO** Launched as *Ocean Reefer*
★06307 **OCEANO ARTICO**

●06310 **ORICA** Ho/No (Akers) 1965; R; 6000/8200; 148 × 8.5/9.1 (485 × 28/30); M (B&W); 20; ex *Avocadocore* 1976
Sisters:
06311 **CHAITEN** (Li) ex *Bananacore* 1976
06312 **OMOA** (Ch) ex *Lemoncore* 1976
06313 **OLANCHO** (Ch) ex *Mangocore* 1976
06314 **CONDORA** (Li) ex *Persimmoncore* 1977
06315 **CONDATA** (Li) ex *Tangarinecore* 1974
06316 **ROSEMARY** (Pa) ex *Guava* 1980; ex *Guavacore* 1974
06317 **ANONA** (FRG) ex *Anonacore* 1974
06317 **CLEMENTINE** (FRG)
06318 **PECAN** (FRG)

06319 **NECTARINE** (FRG) ex *Nectarinecore* 1975
06321 **CHILLAN** (Ch) ex *Ceiba* 1980; ex *Mandarincore* 1976
06322 **ARIANE I** (Li) ex *Sultana* 1976
06323 **SATSUMA** (FRG) ex *Satsumacore* 1975
06324 **CHOLGUAN** (Ch) ex *Corinto* 1980; ex *Sabracore* 1976

06330 **ARCTIC OCEAN** Li/De (Aalborg) 1968; R; 6000; 145.3 × 8.8 (477 × 28.11); M (B&W); 22.5; ex *Italian Reefer* 1978
Sisters:
06331 **INDIAN OCEAN** (Li) ex *Nippon Reefer* 1978
06332 **PERUVIAN REEFER** (Bs) ex *Persian Reefer* 1982
06333 **ROMAN REEFER** (Bs)
Similar:
06334 **SAMOAN REEFER** (De)
06335 **TUNISIAN REEFER** (De)

06350 **LADY MADONNA** Gr/Br (Greenock D) 1965; R; 8000; 161.2 × 8.5 (529 × 28.3); M (B&W); 17.5; ex *Winchester Universal* 1980; ex *Winchester Castle* 1980; ex *Clan Ramsay* 1977
Sisters:
06351 **PSARA REEFER** (Gr) ex *Balmoral Universal* 1982; ex *Balmoral Castle* 1980; ex *Clan Robertson* 1976
06352 **SYROS REEFER** (Gr) ex *Kinpurnie Universal* 1982; ex *Kinpurnie Castle* 1980; ex *Clan Ross* 1976
06353 **GOLDEN SEA** (Gr) ex *Dover Universal* 1981; ex *Dover Castle* 1979; ex *Clan Ranald* 1977

06360 **AFRICA FREEZER** Pa/Br (Greenock D) 1963; R; 6800; 158.4 × 7.6 (520 × 25); M (B&W); 17; ex *Passat Universal* 1982; ex *Letaba* 1979; ex *S A Letaba* 1977; ex *Letaba* 1966
Sisters:
06361 **AEGEAN WAVE** (Gr) ex *Pampero Universal* 1981; ex *Drakenstein* 1980; ex *S A Drakenstein* 1977; ex *Drakenstein* 1966
06362 **KAWKAB 1** (Si) ex *Mistral Universal* 1982; ex *Hexrivier* 1979; ex *S A Hexrivier* 1978
06363 **ASIA FREEZER** (Pa) ex *Papagayo Universal* 1982; ex *Tzaneen* 1979; ex *S A Tzaneen* 1977; ex *Tzaneen* 1966
06364 **AEGEAN PRIDE** (Gr) ex *Monsone Universal* 1982; ex *Langkloof* 1979; ex *S A Langkloof* 1977; ex *Langkloof* 1966
06365 **AL MAREEKH** (Si) ex *Meltem Universal* 1982; ex *Zebediela* 1980; ex *S A Zebediela* 1977

★06380 **ANTON SAEFKOW** DDR/DDR (Warnow) 1965; C; 5000/7700; 142 × 7.2/8.5 (466 × 23.6/28); M (MAN); 14.5
Similar (DDR flag):
★06381 **HEINZ KAPELLE**
★06382 **LIESELOTTE HERRMANN**
★06383 **RUDOLF BREITSCHIED**
★06384 **ALBIN KOBIS**
★06385 **BERNHARD BASTLEIN**
★06386 **MAX REICHPIETSCH**
Possible sisters (DDR flag):
★06387 **JOHN SCHEHR**
★06388 **GEORG SCHUMANN**
★06389 **MATHIAS THESEN**

06400 **PUSSUR** Pk/Br (Bartram) 1965; C; 6200/8800; 152 × —/8.7 (498 × —/28.6); M (Sulzer); ex *Teesta*

●★06410 **MARKO MARULIC** Ys/Ys ('Split') 1959; C; 6200/8900; 154 × —/9 (504 × —/29.7); M (Fiat) 16
Sisters:
★06411 **NATKO NODILO** (Ys)
★06412 **LUKA BOTIC** (Ys)
★06413 **SUBICEVAC** (Ys) ex *Gundulic* 1966
06414 **AGIOS CONSTANTINOS** (Gr) ex *Murter* 1980; ex *Ruder Boskovic* 1972
★06415 **MAO LIN** (RC) ex *Mindanao Sea* 1976; ex *Castasegna* 1973; ex *Cruzeiro do Sul* 1965
06416 **MOLUCCA SEA** (Pa) ex *Corviglia* 1973

●06460 **'SD 14' TYPE** —/Br etc 1968 onwards; C; approx 9000; 141 × 8 (463 × 29); M (Sulzer; MAN; Doxford); 14; Standard British 'Liberty' replacement design. Built in Br (A&P; Bartram) and under licence in Bz (CCN; Maua) and Gr (Hellenic). Ships vary slightly in appearance (mast houses; taller superstructure; heavy derricks etc.)
(Br flag)
06462 **CARLOW HILL** ex *Lindenhall* 1982
06463 **SEA MOON**
Gr flag:
06480 **AEGIS FAME**
06481 **AEGIS BANNER**
06482 **AEGIS TRADE**
06483 **LOYALTY**
06484 **ANNA DRACOPOULOS**
06487 **ATHANASSIA**
06488 **MARI**
06490 **GIANNIS XILAS** ex *Colin*
06491 **DESPINA**

06492 **DORA PAPALIOS**
06493 **FROSSO K.**
06495 **JADE BAY** ex *Ramon De Larrinaga* 1972
06496 **JOHN MICHALOS**
06498 **KONSTANTIS YEMELOS** ex *Hellenic Renaissance*
06499 **MARIA K**
06501 **EPIMENIDIS** ex *Cape Pride* 1980; ex *Togo* 1976
06503 **IO** ex *Alioussa* 1980; ex *Carina* 1980
06504 **GOOD DOLPHIN** ex *Aegis Venture* 1980; ex *Venturer* 1977
06505 **GOOD SUN** ex *Mimis N Papalios* 1980
06506 **GOOD LORD** ex *George N Papalios* 1980
06507 **GOOD PATRIOT** ex *Aegis Island* 1980; ex *Degedo*
06508 **ALEXION HOPE** ex *Konstantis Yemelos* 1981
06590 **GIANNIS M** ex *Nefos II*
06511 **AEGIS FREEDOM** ex *Nea Hellas* 1976
06512 **NEOTIS**
06513 **IRINI II** ex *Durban Carrier* 1981; ex *Cosmokrat* 1980
06514 **PANAGHIS VERGOTTIS**
06515 **REA**
06517 **ROSARIO**
06518 **SAN GEORGE**
06521 **SCAPWIND**
06522 **SEA TRADER**
06523 **SILVER CLOUD**
06524 **SKLERION**
06525 **STEPHANOS VERGOTTIS**
06526 **JUVENTUS** ex *Tanganyika* 1977
06528 **TOXOTIS**
06532 **MAKRA** ex *Patricia M* 1980; ex *Patricia* 1979
06533 **GIORGIS** ex *Porto Alegre* 1980; ex *Vermelha*; ex *Babitonga* 1974
06534 **AKARNANIA** ex *London Bombardier*
06535 **KAPTAMICHALIS** ex *Nicolaos D.D.* 1979
06537 **AGIA SKEPI** ex *Capetan Giannis*
06538 **FEDORA** ex *Rodrigo Torrealba* 1981
06539 **ANANGEL CHAMPION** ex *Tortugas* 1981; ex *Cape Rion* 1981; ex *Erewan*
06539A **ATHERAS** ex *Vergray* 1979; ex *Rupert de Larrinaga* 1975
06539B **FREEDOM A S** ex *Ceresio* 1983
06539C **VARDIANI** ex *Vergstar* 1978; ex *Miguel de Larrinaga* 1975
06539D **RIO** ex *L L Antuerpia* 1983
Possible sister (Gr flag):
06540 **KATERINA DRACOPOULOS**
(Bz flag):
06550 **L.L. PERU**
06551 **L L CHILE**
06552 **L L EQUADOR**
06553 **L L COLOMBIA**
06555 **LLOYD HAMBURGO**
06556 **LLOYD LIVERPOOL**
06558 **LLOYD BRAS**
06559 **LLOYD GENOVA**
06560 **LLOYD MARSELHA**
06561 **REGINA CELI**
06562 **SEMIRAMIS**
06563 **SERRA AZUL**
06564 **SERRA BRANCA**
06565 **SERRA DOURADA**
06566 **SERRA VERDE**
(Sg flag):
06581 **SPLENDID FORTUNE** ex *Catharina Oldendorff* 1981
06582 **DORTHE OLDENDORFF**
06583 **FAIR SPIRIT** ex *Eibe Oldendorff* 1981
06584 **HILLE OLDENDORFF**
06585 **HAPPY CHANCE** ex *Hinrich Oldendorff* 1981
06586 **IMME OLDENDORFF**
06587 **ARAFURA SEA** ex *Santa Ines* 1982
06589 **TIBATI** ex *Jocasta* 1978; ex *Natal* 1977
06590 **NEW WHALE** ex *London Fusilier*
(Li flag):
06600 **LEIRIA** ex *Santa Ursula* 1982
06601 **MARSHA**
06604 **FUTURE HOPE**
06605 **GOOD FAITH**
06606 **GLOBE TRADER**
(Cu flag):
★06610 **1 CONGRESO DEL PARTIDO** ex *Maisi*
★06611 **MONCADA** ex *Belic*
★06612 **CARLOS MANUEL DE CESPEDES**
★06613 **IGNACIO AGRAMONTE**
★06614 **CALIXTO CARCIA** ex *Ajanna* 1980;
★06615 **BARTOLOME MOSA** ex *Strathdirk* 1982
★06616 **DONATO MARMOL** ex *Strathdevon* 1982
(Pa flag):
06620 **LADY ISABEL** ex *Cosmonaut* 1980
06621 **COLOSSUS** ex *Merlion* 1980; ex *Transvaal* 1977; ex *Cluden*
06622 **CLAUDIA KOGEL** ex *Santa Maja* 1976; ex *Santa Maya* 1971; ex *Santa Maja*
06623 **JOSEF ROTH** ex *Santa Vassiliki* 1976
06624 **STAR I** ex *Star*; ex *Cosmostar* 1974
06625 **THOMAS ROTH** ex *Santa Katerina* 1975

06626 **AGATE** ex *Welsh Trident* 1978
06627 **QUARTZ** ex *Welsh Endeavour* 1978
06628 **SILAGA** ex *Asian Liner* 1980; ex *London Cavalier* 1979
06629 **NEW PANDA** ex *Dunelmia* 1980;
06630 **ATROPOS** ex *Taxiarchis* 1982
06631 **CALY** ex *Capetan Markos* 1981;
06632 **CONCORDIA I** ex *Integrity II* 1983; ex *Niger Basin* 1982; ex *Juventus* 1983
06633 **DANIELLA** ex *Ithaki* 1981
06634 **EMERALD ISLANDS** ex *Strathdoon* 1982
06635 **WORLD OCEANIC** ex *Fortune King* 1983; ex *Samos Progress* 1981; ex *Santa Amalia* 1976
06636 **HONESTY II** ex *Niger Valley* 1981; ex *Carrel* 1976
06637 **LORI R** ex *Ermioni* 1982; ex *Sacha*
06638 **MICHELLE C** ex *Ariadne* 1981
06639 **MOOLCHAND** ex *Ardenhall* 1981; ex *Dunelmia* 1976
06639/1 **NACIONAL SETUBAL** ex *Santa Isabella* 1982
06639/2 **PILARMAST** ex *Niki II* 1983; ex *Niki* 1983
06639/3 **POMONA** ex *Virtus* 1981
06639/4 **RECALADA LIGHT** ex *Juanita Halkias* 1983; ex *Ioannis S* 1974; ex *Prodromos* 1971
06639/5 **RUBY ISLANDS** ex *Strathduns* 1982
06639/6 **TOROS BAY** ex *Tiger Bay* 1982; ex *Holstenbek* 1979; ex *Santa Clio* 1976
06639/7 **UNITY I** ex *Unity* 1982; ex *Rinoula* 1981
06639/8 **WELSH JAY** ex *Welsh Troubador* 1979
06639/9 **CAPTAIN GEORGE L** ex *L.L. Rotterdam* 1983
06639/10 **MAR COURRIER** ex *Maria* 1983
06639/11 **NACIONAL SAGRES** ex *Aracaju* 1983
(Various flags):
06640 **VARUNA KACHHAPI** (In) ex *Capetan Manolis* 1979
06641 **JALAPUTRA** (In) ex *Moldova* 1976
06642 **BANGLAR BAANI** (Bh) ex *Industria* 1979
★06643 **HOJI YA HENDA** (An) ex *Anax* 1978
★06644 **EBO** (An) ex *Rio Conquista* 1979
06646 **MARINER** (Cy) ex *Anavissos* 1983; ex *Argolis* 1980; ex *Janey* 1980
06647 **PARANA STAR** (Cy) ex *Heinrich Arnold Schulte* 1977
06648 **FIRST JAY** (Cy) ex *Cosmopolitan*; ex *London Grenadier*
06649 **GLASGOW** (Cy) ex *Avalaki* 1980; ex *Nicola* 1979
06650 **OCEAN ENVOY** (Pk)
06650A **SAFINA-E-BARKAT** (Pk) ex *Phoevos* 1982; ex *City of Exeter* 1979; ex *Strathdare* 1974
★06651 **RUMIJA** (Ys) ex *Arrino* 1978
★06652 **MEI JIANG** (RC) ex *Ormos* 1978
★06652A **NAN JIANG** (RC) ex *Sea Lion* 1982
06653 **ANGOL** (Ch)
06654 **ANAKENA** (Ch)
See also under K3MFK—MORVIKEN etc. Some of these vessels may have this sequence

06670 **SALTA** Ar/Br (Robb Caledon) 1976; C; 9100; 141 × 8.9 (463 × 29); M (Doxford); 15.5; Modified 'SD 14' type
Sisters (Ar flag):
06671 **JUJUY II**
06672 **TUCUMAN**
06672/1 **ALMIRANTE STORNI**
Probable sisters (Ar built-AFNE):
06673 **LIBERTADOR GENERAL JOSE DE SAN MARTIN**
06674 **PRESIDENTE RAMON CASTILLO**
06675 **NEUQUEN II**
06677 **DR ATILIO MALVAGNI**
06678 **GENERAL MANUEL BELGRANO**

●06690 **PAOLA C** It/Br (Swan Hunter & WR) 1965; R; 10500; 181 × 9.5 (593 × 3.1); TSM (Sulzer); 22.5; ex *Good Hope Castle* 1978
Sister:
06691 **FRANCA** (Ma) ex *Franca C* 1983; ex *Southampton Castle* 1978

06700 **CURITIBA** Bz/Br (Ailsa) 1943; C; 1900; 80.1 × 5.4 (263 × 18); R (Ailsa); 10; ex *Shetland* 1959; ex *Zealand* 1954

06730 **ELAZIG** Tu/No (Drammen) 1960; C; 3000/4800; 116.3 × 6.5/7.9 (382 × 21.5/26); M (Sulzer); 8; ex *Marosa* 1960

06740 **ISORA** Sp/Sp ('Astano') 1967; C; 1600; 96.7 × 5.7 (317 × 18.5); M (B&W); —; ex *Lago San Mauricio* 1975

●06750 **CABO SANTA LUCIA** Sp/Sp ('Astano') 1968; C; 9400; 154.5 × 8.9 (507 × 29); M (B&W); 18; ex *Garcia Munte* 1983
Sister:
06751 **FRATERNITY** (Gr) ex *Tenacity* 1977; ex *Joaquin Ponte Naya* 1975
06752 **NINETA** (Pa) ex *Alexander's Ismini* 1983; ex *Cabo Santa Clara* 1980; ex *Ragar* 1974

●06760 **IOANNIS** Gr/Ne (Nederlandsche) 1961; C; 4900/7000; 134 × 7.3/8.6 (440 × 24/28.5); M (Sulzer); 15.5; ex *Adrianos* 1979; ex *Dalesman* 1978
Sister:
06761 **BARU SPIRIT** (Gr) ex *Link Trust* 1981; ex *Explorer* 1978

★06770 **BEREZNIK** Ru/Fi (Valmet) 1968; C/TC; 2700; 102 × 6.2 (335 × 20.2); M (B&W); 13.5; Ships vary in appearance
Sisters:
★06771 **GUS-KHRUSTNYY**
★06772 **KAPSUKAS**
★06773 **KASHINO**
★06774 **KARA**
★06775 **KALININGRAD**
★06776 **KAPITAN GASTELLO**
★06777 **KEDAYNYAY**
★06778 **KINGISEPP**
★06779 **KOPORYE**
★06780 **KRASNOBORSK**
★06781 **KOSTINO**
★06782 **KUZMINKI**
★06783 **KUPISHKIS**
★06784 **KUNTSEVO**
★06785 **LYUBAN**
★06786 **JOSE DIAS**
★06787 **TURKU**
★06788 **VORONEZH**
★06789 **SOFIA PEROVSKAYA**
★06790 **TSIGLOMEN**
★06791 **VELIKIYE USTYUG**
★06792 **KIKCHIK**
★06793 **KAMCHADAL**

★06795 **UNZHA** Ru/Ru (Navashinsky) 1968; C/TC; 3000; 104.50 × 6.05 (343 × 19.85); M (B&W); 13.5; Some sisters have goalpost on forecastle and poop
Sisters (Ru flag—Ru built):
★06795/1 **ALDAN**
★06795/2 **AYAN** (or AJAN)
★06795/3 **EGVEKINOT**
★06795/4 **JANA** (or YANA)
★06795/5 **KEM**
★06795/6 **KONDOPOGA**
★06796 **KORSAKOV**
★06796/1 **LAKHTA**
★06796/2 **OMOLON**
★06796/3 **PROKOPIY GALUSHIN**
★06796/4 **SELENGA**
★06796/5 **SIBIRLES**
★06796/6 **SIBIRTSYEVO** ex *Manzovka*
★06796/7 **TERNEY**
★06796/8 **VERKHOYANSKLES**
★06796/9 **VYATKALES**
★06797 **VZMORYE**
★06797/1 **YAKUTSKLES**
Sisters (Ru flag—Rm built (Galatz)):
★06797 **ANTON BUYUKLY**
★06797/2 **BORIS NIKOLAICHUK**
★06797/3 **CHERNIGOV**
★06797/5 **KARAGA**
★06798 **KATANGLI**
★06798/1 **KAVALEROVO**
★06798/2 **KAZATIN**
★06798/3 **KILIYA**
★06798/4 **KIRENSK**
★06798/5 **KOREIZ**
★06798/6 **KRASNOARMEYSK**
★06798/7 **KRASNOPOLYE**
★06798/8 **KRASNOTURINSK**
★06799 **KRYMSK**
★06799/1 **KULUNDA**
★06799/2 **KUSTANAY**
★06799/3 **KUZNETSK**
★06799/4 **LEONID SMIRNYKH**
★06799/5 **STEPAN SAVUSHKIN**
★06799/6 **TUSHINO**
★06799/7 **TYMOVSK**
★06799/8 **YEVGENIY CHAPLANOV** or EVGENIY CHAPLANOV)

06800 **CHIDAMBARAM** In/Fr (France-Gironde) 1966; PC; 17200; 174 × 8 (571 × 26.3); TSM (Sulzer); 10; ex *Pasteur* 1973

06810 **ISLA PINTA** Pa/FRG (Schlichting) 1972; C; 4000/6300; 131.2 × 7/8.2 (431 × 23/27); M (MAN); 18; ex *Baron* 1979; ex *Wilhelm Bornhofen* 1973
Sisters:
06811 **OPULENCE** (Pa) ex *Xiong Yue Cheng* 1981; ex *Elisabeth Bornhofen* 1978; ex *Citos* 1975; ex *Elisabeth Bornhofen* 1972
06812 **ISLA FERNANDINA** (Pa) ex *Bate Bridge* 1981; ex *Adviser* 1975; ex *Hans Bornhofen* 1973
06813 **ISLA GENOVESA** (Pa) ex *Max Bornhofen* 1980; ex *Rapidbridge* 1976; ex *Specialist* 1974; ex *Max Bornhofen* 1973

●06820 **THAMESHAVEN** Ne/Br (Hall, Russell) 1971; C; 9000; 143 × 8.5 (469 × 28); M (B&W); —

★06825 **ABKHAZIYA** Ru/DDR (Mathias-Thesen) 1972; RS; 4800; 123.86 × 6.54 (406 × 21.46); TS VI (MAN); 17.5
Sisters (Ru flag):
★06826 **ADZHARIYA**
★06827 **BASHKIRIYA**
★06828 **MOLDAVIYA**

06830 **MARDI GRAS** Pa/Br (Vickers-Armstrongs) 1961; P; 18300; 198 × 8.8 (650 × 29); TST (Vickers-Armstrongs); 20; ex *Empress of Canada*

06840 **MONTEREY** US/US (Bethlehem Steel) 1952/56; P; 14800; 172 × 9 (564 × 29.6); T (Bethlehem Steel); 20; ex *Free State Mariner* 1956; converted from cargo ship 1956
Sister:
★06841 **JING JIANG** (RC) ex *Mariposa* 1983; ex *Pine Tree Mariner* 1956

06850 **KYMA** Gr/FRG (Bremer V) 1960; R; 7800; 139.5 × 8.8 (458 × 28.9) M (MAN); 17; ex *Amalric* 1977

06870 **LOUDI** Ma/Ja (Fujinagata) 1961; C; 4100/5700; 128 × —/8 (420 × —/26.6); M (B&W); 15.25; ex *Nafsika III* 1982; ex *Rio Branco* 1981; ex *Kappa Champion* 1979; ex *New Guinea Trader*; ex *Wellington Maru* 1971; ex *Shoan Maru* 1967

06880 **MASIR** Br/Br (H&W) 1961; R; 8300/10500; 152.3 × 8.7/9.5 (500 × 28.3/31.3); M (H&W); 17; ex *Masirah* 1982; ex *Port Alfred* 1978

★06890 **KOCHANOWSKI** Pd/Ys ('3 Maj') 1962; CP; 5700/8200; 148.4 × 7.6/8.6 (487 × 25.1/28); M (Sulzer); 15.25
Sister:
★06891 **WYSPIANSKI** (Pd)

06910 **GEORGY** Cy/Br (Doxford) 1954; C; 6000/8100; 141 × 7.8/8.5 (464 × 25.6/28); M (Doxford); 13 ex *George* 1976; ex *Barrister* 1974

06940 **EGTON** Br/Br (Bartram) 1962; C; 7200/10000; 155 × 8.3/9.3 (508 × 27.3/30); M (Doxford); —

● 06950 **FAMILY ANGEL** Gr/Br (Hamilton); C; 700/9900; 154 × 8.3/9.4 (505 × 27.3/31); M (Sulzer); 15; ex *Siam Bay* 1980; ex *Strathtruim* 1977; ex *Treneglos* 1974

06960 **EVLALIA** Gr/Br (Doxford) 1959; C; 6800/8600; 149.0 × —/9.30 (488.8 × —/30.51); M (Doxford); —; ex *Plainsman* 1979

06980 **CAPTAIN NASOS** Gr/Ne ('De Schelde') 1962; C; 10400; 158 × 9.7 (517 × 31.6); M (Sulzer); 14.25 ex *Vasilis* 1983; ex *Waardrecht* 1976
Sisters:
06981 **PANAGIA ELEOUSSA** (Gr) ex *Mariana 1* 1979; ex *Wieldrecht* 1977
06982 **RATAN** (Pa) ex *Khoobchand* 1981; ex *Andriana II* 1979; ex *Woensdrecht* 1976

06990 **KATRINAMAR** Pa/Br (Doxford) 1965; C; 7200/9800; 154.62 × 8.31/9.44 (507.28 × 27.26/30.97); M (Sulzer); ex *Bordagain* 1982; ex *Worcestershire* 1976
Sister:
06992 **FURAMA** (Pa) ex *Warwickshire*

07010 **BENGAL STAR** Bh/Br (Doxford) 1965; C; 7600/10100; 155 × 8.4/9.5 (507 × 27.4/31); M (Doxford); 15; ex *Family Unity* 1982; ex *Ernebank* 1980
Sisters:
07011 **AL BASEER** (Li) ex *Shirrabank* 1981
07012 **SHINIAS** (Gr) ex *Beechbank* 1979
Similar:
07013 **NIKITAS F** (Gr) ex *Hollybank* 1979
07014 **DEPPY** (Pa) ex *Bristol* 1983; ex *Sprucebank* 1979
07015 **GOOD LION** (Gr) ex *Tweedbank* 1979
07016 **GOOD BREEZE** (Gr) ex *Taybank* 1979
07017 **TEVIOTBAN** (Br) ex *Teviotbank* 1979

07020 **MASTURA ZAHABIA** Si/Br (H&W) 1964; C; 7600/10400; 156 × 8.5/9 (512 × 28/31); M (B&W); 14.5; ex *Argonaut* 1982; ex *Hazelbank* 1979
Sisters:
07021 **KAVO GROSSOS** (Gr) ex *Gowanbank* 1979
07022 **KAVO YOSSONAS** (Gr) ex *Maplebank* 1979
07023 **GULF HAWK** (Br) ex *Nairnbank* 1979
07024 **LENDOUDIS KIKI** (Gr) ex *Rowanbank* 1979
★07025 **KANG DONG** (RK) ex *Oceanaut* 1980; ex *Irisbank* 1979

● 07030 **IRINI G.F.** Gr/Br (Doxford) 1962; C; 6200/8400; 148 × 8/8.8 (487 × 26/29); M (Doxford); 14; ex *Inverbank* 1978
Sisters (Gr flag):
07031 **VALI PERO** ex *Laurelbank* 1979
07032 **GOOD SPIRIT** ex *Oakbank* 1978

07050 **GENIE** Gr/Br (Doxford) 1959; C; 7300/9600; 155 × —/9.2 (509 × —/30.4); M (Doxford); 15; ex *Miss Chandris* 1969

★07080 **HONG QI 128** RC/Br (Bartram) 1955; 6300; 145 × 8.2 (476 × 26.11); M (B&W); 13.5; ex *Huangshi*; ex *Salina* 1966; ex *La Orilla* 1961

● 07090 **SABINE** Pa/Ja (Fujinagata) 1959; C; 6200/8700; 147 × —/8.8 (483 × —/29); M (B&W); 14; ex *Fortune Y* 1983; ex *Ioannis A* 1980; ex *Towa Maru* 1971

★07100 **HYOK SIN** RK/Ja (Hakodate) 1958; C; 8400; 149.59 × 8.79 (490.78 × 28.84); M (MAN); 13.5; ex *Kyokuyo Maru* 1974

07120 **HWA GEK** Sg/Br (Bartram) 1961; CP; 7000/9200; 152 × —/19 (499 × —/29.7); M (Sulzer); 15; ex *Londoner* 1971

07130 **AMAR 1** Pa/Br (Burntisland) 1960; CP; 4700; 113.4 × 7.3 (501 × 28/30.3); M (Doxford); 14.5; ex *Amar* 1982; ex *Tamara* 1980; ex *Lancastrian Prince* 1971

07160 **SEA ROSE** Pa/Ja (NKK) 1956; C; 6300; 137.6 × 8.2 (451 × 26.10); M (Mitsubishi); 14; ex *Madras Maru* 1975

07170 **COPPER TRADER** Gr/Br (Lithgows) 1963; C; 7700; 141.74 × 7.75 (465 × 25.43); M (Sulzer); 16; ex *Cam Ayous* 1981; ex *Forcados* 1976
Sister:
07173 **COTTON TRADER** (Gr) ex *Cam Azobe* 1981; ex *Fulani* 1976

● 07180 **CITY OF ZUG** Cy/Br (Scotts' SB) 1962; C; 7700; 141.7 × 7.8 (465 × 15.5); M (Sulzer); 16; ex *Alexanders Trust* 1983; ex *Leonor Maria* 1980; ex *Falaba* 1978
Sister:
07181 **LEMINA** (Cy) ex *Alexanders Faith* 1983; ex *Magda Josefina* 1980; ex *Fourah Bay* 1978

07210 **EVAGELIA S** Gr/Br (Stephen) 1963; C; 6200/9200; 146.6 × 7.6/8.6 (481 × 25/28); M (Sulzer); 16; ex *Aglaos* 1980; ex *Mahout* 1978
Sister:
07211 **KARA UNICORN** (Pa) ex *Markhor* 1982

● 07230 **ARGIRO** Gr/Br (Fairfield SB) 1959; C; 7100/8800; 149.6 × 8.3/9.2 (491 × 27.3/30.3); M (Doxford); 15.5; ex *Shropshire* 1972
Sisters:
07231 **KOTA MEWAH** (Sg) ex *Mozambique* 1976; ex *Cheshire* 1968
07232 **SEA RELIANCE** (Pa) ex *Bordabekoa* 1981; ex *Yorkshire* 1971; ex *Eastern Princess* 1964; ex *Yorkshire* 1963

07250 **KOTA BERJAYA** Sg/Hong Kong (Taikoo) 1962; CP; 5800; 128.7 × 7.5 (422 × 24.6); M (Doxford); 11.5; ex *Rogers Trader* 1982; ex *Kweilin* 1974

07260 **AGHIOS GEORGIOS III** Gr/Br (Scotts' SB) 1961; C; 5900/8300; 140.21 × 8.03/8.21 (460 × 26.35/26.94); M (Doxford); 14; ex *San Georgio III* 1980; ex *Deido* 1979

07270 **EVOICOS GULF** Gr/Br (H&W) 1963; C; 6300/8500; 147.3 × 8/8.9 (483 × 26/29); M (H&W); 15; ex *Lossiebank* 1979; KP abreast funnel

● 07280 **TRANS VASSILIKI** Gr/Fr (Mediterranee) 1964; C; 4800/7100; 138.6 × 7.4/8.6 (455 × 24.4/28); M (Sulzer); 17.5; ex *Gold Bridge* 1981; ex *Mazal* 1974
Sister (Li flag):
07282 **GOLD BEETLE** ex *Nogah* 1974

07290 **MARITIME OPTIMUM** Th/Pd (Gdanska) 1961; C; 6100; 153.7 × 8.34 (504.27 × 27.36); M (Sulzer); 14.5; ex *Ablon* 1979; ex *Rhone* 1967; ex *Francois L D* 1961; launched as *Charles L D*; 'B54' type

★07310 **MEISHAN** RC/FRG (LF-W) 1959; CP; 9800; 154 × 8.8 (505 × 29.1) M (MAN); 17; ex *Havsul* 1972

07320 **ALHAMBRA** Gr/Fr (Provence) 1964; C; 7900; 141.10 × 8.67 (463 × 28.44); M (Sulzer); 16; ex *Henri Delmas* 1974

07330 **SAFINA-E-HAIDER** Pk/Br (Fairfield SB) 1963; CP; 6700/8900; 142 × 8.4/9.4 (465 × 27/30.5); M (Sulzer); —; ex *Lancashire* 1970

● 07340 **BYRON 1** Pa/Br (H&W) 1963; C; 6400/8700; 147 × 8/8.9 (483 × 26/29); M (B&W); 15; ex *Castor* 1983; ex *Roybank* 1979
Sister:
07341 **GOLDEN NIGERIA** (Pa) ex *Weybank* 1979

07370 **CABO DE LA VELA** Co/FRG (Stuelcken) 1957; C; 5200; 144.79 × 7.19 (475 × 23.59); M (MAN); —; ex *Ciudad de Tunja* 1983

Sisters (Gr flag):
07371 **CEFALLONIAN CHARIS** ex *Ciudad de Barranquilla* 1981
07372 **CEFALLONIAN PROSPERITY** ex *Manuel Mejia* 1981

07390 **REUNION** Sg/Au (Mort's Dock) 1953; C; 3700; 123.6 × 6.9 (406 × 22.8); M (Doxford); 12; ex *Colin Four* 1976; ex *Boonaroo* 1970

07420 **PINYA** Bm/Ja (Hitachi) 1963; C; 5200/7400; 137.9 × 7.3/8.4 (452 × 23.6/27.5); M (B&W); 15
Sister:
07421 **MERGUI** (Bm)

● 07430 **ARGIRO** Gr/Br (Fairfield SB) 1959; C; 7100/8800; 149.6 × 8.3/9.2 (491 × 27.3/30.3); M (Doxford); 15.5; ex *Shropshire* 1972
Sisters:
07431 **KOTA MEWAH** (Sg) ex *Mozambique* 1976; ex *Cheshire* 1968
07432 **SEA RELIANCE** (Pa) ex *Bordabekoa* 1981; ex *Yorkshire* 1971; ex *Eastern Princess* 1964; ex *Yorkshire* 1963

07440 **IRAN SEEYAM** Ir/Po (Viana) 1974; C; 9200; 153 × 9.1 (501 × 30); M (Sulzer); 18; ex *Arya Sun* 1980
Sisters:
★07441 **MAJOR SUCHARSKI** (Pd)
★07442 **MARIAN BUCZEK** (Pd)
07443 **IRAN SALAM** (Ir) ex *Iran Zar* 1980; ex *Arya Zar* 1980
07444 **IRAN KALAM** (Ir) ex *Iran Seem* 1980; ex *Arya Seem* 1980

07450 **ATTICA REEFER** Gr/FRG (LF-W) 1973; R; 7600; 154.5 × 8.7 (507 × 28.7); M (MAN); 22.5; ex *Wild Cormorant* 1981
Sisters:
07451 **ATHENIAN REEFER** (Gr) ex *Wild Curlew* 1981
07452 **EDINBURGH UNIVERSAL** (Br) ex *Polar Honduras* 1980
07453 **CARIBBEAN UNIVERSAL** (Br) ex *Polar Costa Rica* 1980

★07460 **DZIECI POLSKIE** Pd/Po (Alfeite) 1978; R; 3300/6400; 139.63 × 6.62/7.78 (458 × 21.72/25.52); M (Sulzer); 22.5; 8 side doors. 'B437' type. Completed in Poland (Gdanska). Some vessels under entry number 10740 may also be like this
Sisters (Po built):
★07461 **GDYNSKI KOSYNIER** (Pd) (builder-Lisnave):
★07462 **ZYRARDOW** (Pd)
Sisters (Pd built-Gdanska):
07463 **RIO CUYAMEL** (Ho)
07464 **RIO SIXAOLA** (Pa)
07465 **RIO SULACO** (Ho)

★07470 **'ATLANTIK'** type Ru/DDR (Stralsund) —; FT; 2200 approx; 82 × 5.3; (269 × 17.6); M (Liebknecht); 14.25; Many 'Atlantik' type ships may have this appearance (see others under KMFM)
Sisters:
★07471 **BAROGRAF**
★07472 **DIPLOT**
★07473 **GEROI ADZHIMUSHKAYA**
★07474 **KURSOGRAF**
★07475 **MAKELIS BUKA**
★07476 **RODONIT**
★07477 **SERDOLIK**

07480 **SCOMBRUS** FRG/FRG (Rickmers) 1975; FT; 2000; 81 × 5.8 (266 × 19); M (Atlas-MaK); 16

07500 **RAGNI BERG** No/No (Drammen) 1978; R; 7000; 144.45 × 9.01 (473.92 × 29.56); M (Sulzer); 21.9; 'Drammen' type
Sister:
07501 **ZAIN AL-QAWS** (Iq) ex *Elisabeth Berg* 1981
07501/1 **PAQUISHA** (Ec) ex *Rio Palora* 1981
Similar:
07502 **RIO CHONE** (Ec)
07503 **RIO ESMERALDAS** (Ec)
07504 **RIO BABAHOYA** (Ec)

07510 **ARAB MAZIN** Si/Br (Hall, Russell) 1967; C; 2600/4400; 114 × 6.5/7.4 (374 × 21.4/24.3); M (MAN); 15.25; ex *Christl Hermann* 1982; ex *Duburg* 1974
Sisters:
07511 **SAMAR SEA** (Pi) ex *Topaz* 1981; ex *Troyburg* 1973
07512 **SULU BAY** (Pi) ex *Tourmalin* 1981; ex *Glucksburg* 1973

07520 **MARION DUFRESNE** Fr/Fr (Havre) 1973; RS/C/P; 6600; 112.1 × 6.3 (368 × 20.8); M (Pielstick); 15

07530 **JOO HENG** Pa/Ne (Boele's Sch) 1950; C; 1800; 85.45 × 4.03 (280.4 × 13.22); M (Polar); 10.75; ex *Eastern Fortune* 1979; ex *Sea Unity* 1972; ex

Eastern Unity 1970; ex Sambas 1968

07540 NIKOS 1 Gr/Ja (Mitsubishi Z) 1960; C; 4800; 119.36 × 7.52 (391.6 × 24.67); M (Sulzer); 14; ex Pema 1982; ex Dragon 1 1975; ex Anakan Maru 1973

★ 07550 'BEREZNIK' class. Ru/Fi (Valmet) 1968; C/TC; 2700; 102 × 6.2 (334 × 20.4); M (B&W); 13.5; Ships vary. Radar mast often from bridge top.
Similar (Ru flag):
★ 07551 CHAZHMA
★ 07552 BLAGOVESHCHENSK
★ 07553 ILYINSK
★ 07554 ILICHOVO
★ 07555 KAMCHADAL
★ 07556 TOBOL
★ 07557 YANTARNYY
★ 07558 KRETINGA
★ 07559 KOZYREVSK
★ 07560 LOMONOSOVO
★ 07561 PRAVDA
★ 07562 MIRNYY
★ 07563 PALANA
★ 07564 VAGA
★ 07565 KHARLOV
★ 07566 KRASNOYARSK
★ 07567 LIGOVO
★ 07568 KAMCHATSKIY
★ 07569 KOMSOMOLETS
★ 07570 TURKU
★ 07571 LYUBAN
★ 07572 KINGISEPP
★ 07573 KRASNOBORSK
★ 07574 VELIKIY USTYUG
★ 07575 TSIGLOMEN
★ 07576 KUPISHKIS
★ 07577 KALININGRAD
★ 07578 KUZMINKI
★ 07579 KOSTINO
★ 07580 KARA
★ 07581 GUSKHRUSTALNYY
★ 07582 KOPORYE
★ 07583 KASHINO
★ 07584 KIKHCHIK
★ 07585 KAPITAN GASTELLO
★ 07586 SOFIYA PEROVSKAYA
★ 07587 JOSE DIAS
★ 07588 VORONEZH
★ 07589 KUNTSEVO
★ 07590 KIMRY
★ 07591 KEDAYNYAY
★ 07592 KAPSUKAS
★ 07592 TAMPERE
★ 07593 SHUSENSKOYE

★ 07600 LENALES Ru/Fi (Nystads) 1964; C/TC; 2900; 102 × 6.2 (334 × 20.4); M (B&W); 13.75; May be other vessels of the 'BEREZNIK' class with this appearance—see previous entry

★ 07610 LYONYA GOLIKOV Ru/DDR ('Neptun') 1968; C; 3600; 105.7 × 6.8 (347 × 22.4); M (MAN); 13.75; May be other ships of this class with this sequence. See 'SHURA KOBER' class under KM₂FM

★ 07620 AKADEMIK KURCHATOV Ru/DDR (Mathias-Thesen) 1966; RS; 5500; 123.88 × 6.06 (406.43 × 19.88); TSM (MAN); 18.25
Sister:
★ 07621 AKADEMIK VERNADSKIY (Ru)
Similar (funnel top differs):
★ 07622 DMITRIY MENDELEYEV (Ru) (may be spelt DMITRIY MENDELEEV)

● 07650 BALINTAWAK Pa/FRG (LF-W) 1969; C; 6200/10200; 148.6 × 8/9.4 (488 × 26.3/31); M (MAN); 19; ex Oder 1978
Sister:
07651 ANTIPOLO (Li) ex Saar 1978

● 07660 CANDELARIA Pa/Br (Greenock D) 1962; C; 6100/9000; 151.4 × 8.6 (497 × 28.2); M (Sulzer); 16; ex Marianne 1983; ex Clan Graham 1981
Sisters:
07661 IRAN HEMMET (Ir) ex Arya Man 1980; ex Clan Forbes 1968
07662 IRAN OKHUVAT (Ir) ex Arya Sep 1980; ex Clan Farquharson 1968
★ 07664 LU CHUN (RC) ex Atlantic Ocean 1975; ex Arya Far 1971; ex Clan Finlay 1968
07665 NEW EAGLE (Pa) ex Clan Macnab 1980
07666 LICHIANG (Sg) ex Clan Macnair 1980
07667 ENRIQUETA (Pa) ex Clan Grant 1980

07670 GULF HERON Br/Br (J Brown) 1959; C; 7000/9000; 150.58 × —/8.86 (494 × —/29.07); M (Doxford); 15; ex Clan Macindoe 1979
Sister:
07671 GOLDEN CITY (Sg) ex Clan Macilwraith 1978

● 07680 KOTA PUSAKA Sg/Ne (Rotterdamsche) 1962; C; 6900/9600; 161.04 × 6.97/8.87 (528 ×

22.87/29.10); M (Stork); —; ex Nedlloyd Main 1982; ex Main Lloyd 1977
Sisters:
07681 SAUDI MOHAMED REZA (Si) ex Nedlloyd Schie 1982; ex Schie Lloyd 1978
07682 SAUDI JEDDAH (Si) ex Nedlloyd Madison 1982; ex Madison Lloyd 1978

07710 KEYSTONE MARINER US/US (Sun SB) 1952; C; 9100/12500; 160.51 × —/9.56 (527 × —/31.69); T (GEC); 20; ex Iberville 1978; ex Hongkong Bear 1972; ex Keystone Mariner 1960; 'MARINER' class

07730 'C 3' type —/US 1943; CP; 7900; 150 × 9.1 (492 × 29.5); T; 16.5; May still be some vessels of this type in service or in reserve

07750 ETHA RICKMERS Pa/FRG (A. G. 'Weser') 1958; C; 9200/12700; 166.6 × 8.6/9.7 (547 × 28.2/32); M (Krupp); 18; ex Etha 1975; ex Munchen 1970
Sister:
07751 SOPHIE RICKMERS (Sg) ex Dresden 1970

★ 07755 ARACELIO IGLESIAS Cu/Ys ('3 Maj') 1977; C; 10100; 148.01 × 8.99 (486 × 29.49); M (Sulzer); 16
Sisters:
★ 07756 JESUS MENENDEZ (Cu)
★ 07757 LAZARO PENA (Cu)

07760 BALDER ZEA STAR Gr/Ja (Hitachi) 1966; CP; 8900; 141 × 8.6 (463 × 28.2); M (B&W); 15.75; ex Zea Star 1981; ex Bismark Career 1980; ex Guatemala Maru 1978
Similar (some may have cranes):
07761 BALDER CHUANCHOW (Pa) ex Halmahera Career 1981; ex Honduras Maru 1978
07762 BALDER ZEA DAWN (Gr) ex Ionian Career 1980; ex El Salvador Maru 1979
07763 SEAHAIL (Cy) ex Bahama Maru 1983
07764 SPHINX (Eg) ex Sea Link 1982; ex Colombia Maru 1981
07765 EVPO KETTY (Pa) ex Treasure Island 1982; ex Dominica Maru 1980
07766 PYRAMIDS (Eg) ex Haiti Maru 1982
07767 MY KATERINA (Cy) ex Venezuela Maru 1983

● 07770 CLAN MACBOYD Br/Br (Greenock D) 1962; C; 5900/8800; 154.8 × 7.4/8.7 (508 × 24.3/28.6); M (Sulzer); 16.5; ex Clan Macgillivray 1981
Sisters:
07772 INDIAN TRIBUNE (In) ex Clan Macgowan 1970
Similar (1 boat aside and larger mast houses):
07773 PACIFIC AMBER (Li) ex African Diamond 1982; ex Clan Alpine 1981

07780 SIBUYAN CAREER Pa/De (B&W) 1963; C; 12300; 170.7 × 8.9 (560 × 29.3); M (B&W); —; ex Tobias Maersk 1981
Sister:
07782 NEW STALLION (Pa) ex Trein Maersk 1981

★ 07800 LJUTOMER Ys/Ys ('Uljanik') 1964; CP; 6200/8100; 146.4 × —/8.2 (481 × —/27); M (B&W); 17.5
Sister:
★ 07801 LJUBLJANA (Ys)

07810 SEAHAIL Cy/Ja (Hitachi) 1970; CP; 8900; 141 × 8.6 (463 × 28.2); M (B&W); 15.75; ex Bahama Maru 1983
Possibly similar:
07811 BALDER CHUANCHOW (Pa) ex Halmahera Career 1981; ex Honduras Maru 1978
07812 BALDER ZEA DAWN (Gr) ex Ionian Career 1980; ex El Salvador Maru 1979
07813 MY KATERINA (Cy) ex Venezuela Maru 1983
07814 PYRAMIDS (Eg) ex Haiti Maru 1982
07815 EVPO KETTY (Pa) ex Treasure Island 1982; ex Dominica Maru 1980
07816 BALDER ZEA STAR (Gr) ex Zea Star 1981; ex Bismark Career 1980; ex Guatemala Maru 1978
07817 SPHINX (Eg) ex Sea Link 1982; ex Colombia Maru 1981

● 07820 CER ALSIRAT Pa/It (Ansaldo) 1959; C; 7000; 152.58 × 8.21 (500.6 × 26.94); M (Fiat); 16; ex Filomena Lembo 1981; ex Carlin Fassio 1971
Sisters:
07821 AL HAIDER (Qt) ex Bao Shan 1983; ex Zinal 1980; ex Giuanin Fassio 1971

07840 BRAZILIAN EXPRESS Pi/Ja (Mitsubishi HI) 1965; CP; 10000; 161 × 9.3 (528 × 30.6); M (Mitsubishi); 19.5; ex Yamaguchi Maru 1980
Sister:
07842 GUNONG MAS (Pa) ex Royal Ruby 1983; ex Iwaki Maru 1975

07850 CRACKER STATE MARINER US/US (Newport News) 1954; C; 9100; 171.8 × 9.4 (564 × 31); T (GEC); 20; ex Export Defender 1978; ex President

Coolidge 1974; ex Cracker State Mariner 1956; Modified 'MARINER' type
Sisters (US flag):
07851 OLD DOMINION STATE ex Export Diplomat 1978; ex President Hayes 1974; ex Old Dominion Mariner 1956
07852 LONE STAR MARINER ex Export Democracy 1978; ex President Arthur 1974; ex Lone Star Mariner 1956
07853 HOOSIER MARINER ex Carter Braxton 1980; ex President Buchanan 1974; ex Hoosier Mariner 1959

★ 07860 ANTONI GARNUSZEWSKI Pd/Pd (Szczecinska) 1974; C/TS; 6000; 122.2 × 7.4 (401 × 24.3); M (Sulzer); 15.75; 'B.80' type
Sisters:
★ 07861 KAPITAN LEDOCHOWSKI (Pd)
★ 07862 NEPTUN (Rm)
★ 07863 NICOLA VAPTZAROV (Bu)

★ 07880 KEBAN Tu/Ys ('Jozo Lozovina-Mosor') 1971; C; 9000; 154.3 × 9.3 (506 30.6); M (MAN); —
Sisters (Tu flag) (sequence may vary):
07881 ARAS
07882 DICLE
07883 FIRAT
07884 GEDIZ
07885 MERIC

★ 07890 DOBRA Ys/Ys ('3 Maj') 1969; C; 6100/9400; 145 × —/9.1 (476 × 29.10); M (Sulzer); 15.5; ex Betelgeuse 1983; 'Zagreb' type
Sisters (Ys flag):
★ 07891 RJECINA ex Arcturus 1983
★ 07892 KORANA ex Bellatrix 1983
★ 07893 MREZNICA ex Denebola 1983
Similar (five deck superstructure (see inset) and centre-line kingposts):
★ 07894 CRIKVENICA (Ys)
★ 07895 LOSINJ (Ys)
★ 07896 OPATIJA (Ys)
★ 07897 RAB (Ys)
Similar (kingposts against bridgefront and five-deck superstructure):
★ 07898 ARACELIO IGLESIAS (Cu)
★ 07899 JESUS MENENDEZ (Cu)
★ 07899A LAZARO PENA

★ 07900 MINSK Ru/Pd (Gdanska) 1964; C; 7400/9700; 155 × 7.4/9 (508 × 24.3/29.10); M (Sulzer); 17.25; 'B 44' type
Sisters (Ru flag):
★ 07901 MATSESTA
★ 07902 MARGELAN
★ 07903 MARIINSK
★ 07904 MARNEULI
★ 07905 MTSENSK
★ 07906 MEDYN
★ 07907 MEZHDURECHENSK
★ 07908 MEZHGORYE
★ 07909 MICHURIN
★ 07910 MILLEROVO
★ 07911 MOZHAISK
★ 07912 MOLOCHANSK
★ 07913 MORSHANSK
★ 07914 MUKACHEVO
★ 07915 MOLODOGVARDEYSK
★ 07916 MOZYR
★ 07917 MUROM
★ 07918 MYTISHCHI
★ 07919 ALEKSEY TOLSTOY
★ 07920 BORIS GORBATOV
★ 07921 DMITRIY FURMANOV
★ 07922 IVAN GONCHAROV
★ 07923 NIKOLAY NEKRASOV
★ 07924 SAMUIL MARSHAK
★ 07925 ANTON MAKARENKO
★ 07926 BORIS LAVRENEV
★ 07927 FEDOR GADKOV
★ 07928 ROMAN ROLLAN

07940 GARCILASO Pe/Fi 1969; C; 5800/9500; 150.5 × —/9.4 (494 × —/30.8); M —
Sisters (Pe flag):
07941 CHOCANO
07942 PALMA
07943 SABOGAL
07944 TELLO
07945 VALLEJO

★ 07947 TARKHANSK Ru/Pd (Szczecinska) 1978; C/FC; 3500/5500; 123.93 × —/7.32 (406 × —/24.02); M (Sulzer); 15.75; 'B432' type
Sisters (Ru flag):
★ 07947/1 KASHIRSKOYE
★ 07947/2 KULIKOVO
★ 07948 SARATOVSK
★ 07948/1 TALNIKI
★ 07948/2 TARASOVSK
★ 07948/3 TEREKHOVSK
★ 07948/4 TERNOVSK
★ 07949 TIMOFEYEVSK

★07949/1 TITOVSK
★07949/2 TOKARYEVSK
★07949/3 TRUNOVSK
★07949/4 TULSK

●07950 KALENTZI Gr/Fr (Nantes 1964/71; C; 4600/7600; 159.19 × 6.68/7.92 (522 × 22/30.1); M (Pielstick); — ex Giant Pilot 1981; ex Gold Pilot 1978; ex Hadar 1977; lengthened 1971
Sister:
07951 ROGET (Pa) ex Yafo 1980; ex Dolly 1979; ex Yafo 1979

07960 FEAX Gr/Br (Doxford & S) 1970; C; 11500; 164.5 × 9.7 (544 × 32); M (Sulzer); 17
Sister:
07961 FAETHON (Gr)

07970 ALCOUTIM Po/FRG (L F-W) 1968; C; 10500; 148.1 × 9.7 (487 × 31); M (MAN); 19; ex Castorp 1972
Sister:
07971 AMARANTE (Po) ex Lubeck 1972

07980 CATEPAN Pa/Ys ('3 Maj') 1965; CP; 6800; 149 × 7.2 (489 × 23.8); M (Sulzer); 18; ex Abu Rashid 1983; ex Tuhobic 1981
Sisters:
07981 SALEM A (Eg) ex Abu Alia 1984; ex Klek 1981
07982 SALEM N (Eg) ex Abu Hosna 1984; ex Visevica 1981
07983 SALEM S (Eg) ex Abu Yussuf 1 1983; ex Zvir 1981

●07990 BIA RIVER Gh/Ja (Uraga HI) 1965; C; 4900/7500; 138.7 × —/8.5 (455 × —/28); M (Sulzer); —
Sister (Gh flag):
07991 OTI RIVER
Similar (Gh flag):
07992 SUBIN RIVER
07993 KLORTE LAGOON (Funnel heights vary)

08000 AMERICAN SAGA US/US (National Steel) 1961; PtCon; 9300/12700; 172 × —/9.7 (565 × —/31.7); T (GEC); 20; ex Mormacsaga 1983; ex M M Dant
Sisters (US flag):
08001 SANTA ANNA ex C E Dant
08002 AMERICAN SEA ex Mormacsea 1983
08003 AMERICAN TIDE ex Mormactide 1983
08004 MORMACWAVE
08005 CALIFORNIA ex Santa Rita 1980; ex California

08010 NACALA Po/Hong Kong (Taikoo) 1966; CP; 9100; 149 × 9.1 (489 × 29.10); M (Sulzer); 18; ex Hunan 1968

08020 GOOD HERALD 1 Pa/Ne (Rotterdamsche) 1960; C; 7200; 163 × 8.2 (534 × 26.11); M (Stork); 17; ex Good Herald 1982; ex Gaasterdyk 1978
Sister:
08021 HELLENIC SKY (Gr) ex Grebbedyk 1974
Similar (see inset):
08022 HELLENIC GRACE (Gr) ex Gorredyk 1974
08023 H. CAPELO (Po) ex Moerdyk 1973

★08030 VYBORG Ru/DDR (Warnow) 1964; C; 5500/8500; 151 × 7.2/8.9 (494 × 23.6/29); M (MAN); 16.5
Sisters (Ru flag):
★08032 VATUTINO
★08032 VYAZMA
★08033 VOLZHSK
Similar:
★08034 JIANG MEN (RC)

08050 AFRICAN MARINER Li/FRG (A G Weser) 1971; C; 6300/9200; 155.23 × 7.93/9.20 (509.28 × 26.02/30.18); M (MAN); 20; ex Covadonga 1 1980; ex Covadonga 1980; ex Rhodos 1978; ex Peter Bornhofen 1973

08060 PANAGIOTIS A L Gr/Ja (Hayashikane) 1970; C; 4900/7700; 147 × 8.9 (482 × 29); M (Sulzer); 15; ex Saint Matthieu 1981; ex Hoegh Bonny 1975; ex Central Mariner

●08070 NEDLLOYD FUKUOKA Ne/Ne (P Smit) 1961/70; C/Con; 8300; 180.22 × 8.07 (591 × 26.48); M (Stork); 17.5; ex Straat Fukuoka 1977; ex Sloterkerk 1973; Lengthened 1970
Sisters:
08071 NEW HORSE (Pa) ex Nedlloyd Forcados 1983; ex Straat Forcados 1978; ex Servaaskerk 1973
08072 KOTA WISATA (Sr) ex Nedlloyd Fresco 1982; ex Straat Fresco 1978; ex Schiekerk 1973

08080 CIUDAD DE MANTA Ec/Pd (Gdanska) 1972; C/Con; 7300/9700; 161 × 8.9/9.7 (528 × 29/3); M (Sulzer); 20.5; 'B434' type
Sisters:
08081 ARCTIC OCEAN (Li) ex Ciudad de Cali 1984
08082 CIUDAD DE IBAGUE (Co)

08090 SUBSEA MARAUDER Br/No (Trondhjems) 1967; Sub S; 1500; 80.2 × 5.6 (263 × 18.6); M (Wartsila); 14; ex Star Pisces 1980; ex Gadus 1976; Converted from trawler 1976 (Boele's); Also reported as SUBSEA BUCCANEER

★08115 AKADEMIK SERGEY KOROLOV Ru/Ru ('Chernomorskiy') 1970; RS; 17100; 181.90 × 7.95 (597 × 26.08); M (B&W); 17.5; Space tracking

08120 CHAI TRADER Gr/Ne ('Ijssel') 1958; CP; 4800/6900; 146 × 6.5/7.4 (480 × 21.3/24); M (Stork); 14.5; ex Straat Lagos 1978; ex Van Der Hagen 1967
Sister (Sg flag)
08122 KOTA RAJA ex Straat Luzon 1978; ex Van Spilbergen

●08130 SAUDI ENTERPRISE Si/Ne ('De Merwede') 1960; CP; 6200/8900; 158 × 7.3/8.3 (519 × 24/27.2); M (B&W); 16; ex Nedlloyd Cumberland 1978; ex Straat Cumberland 1977
Sisters:
08131 KOTA CEMPAKA (Sg) ex Nedlloyd Clarence 1979; ex Straat Clarence 1978
08132 CAPITAINE COOK (Fr) ex Nedlloyd Clement 1979; ex Straat Clement 1978; ex Asia Express 1974; ex Straat Clement 1973
08133 MERCURY LAKE (Pa) ex Nedlloyd Colombo 1980; ex Straat Colombo 1977; ex Asian Explorer 1974; ex Straat Colombo 1973
08134 CAPITAINE LA PEROUSE (Fr) ex Nedlloyd Chatham 1979; ex Straat Chatham 1978

08140 SAGAFJORD Bs/Fr (Mediterranee) 1965; P; 24000; 189 × 8.2 (620 × 27.1); TSM (Sulzer); 20

08150 VISTAFJORD Bs/Br (Swan Hunter) 1973; P; 24900; 191 × 8.2 (627 × 27); TSM (Sulzer); 20

08160 ROYALE Pa/It (Ansaldo) 1958; P; 20400; 185 × 8.6 (606 × 28.5); TST (Ansaldo); 21; ex Federico C 1983

★08170 POMERANIA Pd/Pd (Szczecinska) 1978; RoPCF; 7400; 127.25 × 5.42 (417.49 × 17.78); M (Sulzer); 20.4; 'B490' type
Sister (May be MFM-see ANKARA (Tu)):
★08171 SILESIA (Pd)

08180 CIUDAD DE SEVILLA Sp/Sp (UN de Levante) 1980; RoPCF; 7400; 138.5 × 5.5 (454 × 18.04); TSM (MAN); 21; stern door
Sisters (Sp flag):
08181 CIUDAD DE SALAMANCA
08182 CIUDAD DE CACERES

08190 RODOS Gr/US (Lake Washington) 1946; P; 2500; 95 × 4.2 (310 × 14); TSM (Fairbanks, Morse); 18

08195 HEBRIDES Br/Br (Hall, Russell) 1964; RoPCF; 1400; 71.63 × 2.74 (235 × 8.99); TSM (Crossley); 14.5
Sister:
08196 COLUMBA (Br)

08200 KRITI Gr/Br (Earle's) 1929; P; 2100; 89 × 4.7 (293 × 15.5); R (Earle's); 13; ex Melrose Abbey II 1959; ex Melrose Abbey 1958

08210 EL GRECO Gr/Br (Fairfield SB) 1936; P; 1200; 75 × 2.7 (245 × 9); TSM (MAN); 15; ex Galaxias 1966; ex Nea Hellas 1964; ex Ellas 1963; ex Marchioness of Graham 1959

●08220 NEPTUNO Gr/Ys ('Uljanik') 1954; P; 600; 58 × 2.7 (189 × 8.10); TSM (MAN); 14.5; ex Meltemi 1 1978; ex Maribor 1966
Sister:
08221 APOLLO 1 (Gr) ex Meltemi II 1983; ex Mostar 1966

08230 PONTA DELGADA Po/Po (Navalis) 1962; P; 1100; 67 × 3.6 (220 × 11.6 M (Sulzer); 15

08240 DON JULIO Pi/Ja (Maizuru) 1967; PC; 2100; 95.66 × 5.16 (313.85 × 16.93); M (B&W); 17.5

08250 BOHEME FRG/Fi (Wartsila) 1968; P; 10300; 134 × 5.5 (441 × 18.1); TSM (Sulzer); 20

08260 MERMOZ Fr/Fr (L'Atlantique) 1957; P; 13800; 162 × 6.4 (532 × 21); TSM (B&W); 17; ex Jean Mermoz 1970

08270 AMERIKANIS Gr/Br (H&W) 1952; P; 16500; 176 × 7.8 (577 × 25.7); TST (Parsons); 19.5; ex Kenya Castle; Rebuilt 1962

8280 LA PALMA Cy/Fr (Gironde) 1952; P; 10900; 150 × 7.4 (493 × 24.5); TSM (B&W); 17; ex La Perla 1980; ex Delphi 1977; ex Ferdinand De Lesseps 1969
Possibly similar:
08281 EROS (Gr) ex Chrysovalandou II 1980; ex Patra 1978; ex Olympia 1972; ex Pierre Loti 1970
08282 OCEANOS (Gr) ex Eastern Princess 1976; ex Ancona 1974; ex Mykinai 1971; ex Jean Laborde 1970

08290 ROLAND VON BREMEN FRG/De (Helsingor) — It 1939/66; F; 4400; 114 × 5.91 (374 × 19.39); TSM (B&W); 19 ex Indian Reefer 1966; ex Rio Gallegos 1946; ex Indian Reefer 1942; converted from reefer 1966

08300 UGANDA Br/Br (Barclay, Curle) 1952; P; 16900; 165 × 7.7 (540 × 25.3); TST (Wallsend); 16

08310 VICTORIA Sp/Sp (UN de Levante) 1952; RoPF; 104 × 5 (340 × 16.9); TSM (B&W); 17; ex 5 De Agosto 1952; stern door
Sister:
08311 VIRGEN DE AFRICA (Sp)

★08320 PERAST Ys/Ys ('Losinj') 1962; PF; 335; 445 × 3 (146 × 9.10); TSM (Alpha); 13
Sisters (Ys flag):
★08321 POROZINA
★08322 POSTIRA
★08323 PUNAT

08330 AUGUSTO MONTENEGRO Bz/Ne (Amsterdamsche D) 1955; P/C/F (Riv) 1400; 7.40 × 2.41 (234.25 × 7.91); TSM (Sulzer); 11
Sisters:
08331 LAURO SODRE (Bz)
08332 LOBO D'ALMADA (Bz)

08340 PONCE US/US (Sun SB) 1968/81; RoC-/Con; 17600; 241.03 × 9.02 (790.78 × 29.59); T (GEC); 25.5; ex Ponce de Leon 1977; Lengthened 1981 (note—vessel is drawn to original length and there is now an extra deck level foreward of bridge)
Similar:
08341 BAYAMON (US) ex Eric K Holzer 1977; ex Bayamon; ex Eric K Holzer 1975;
08342 FORTALEZA (US)
08343 GULF BEAR (US) (lengthened to 241m (1976) and now has extra deck level foreward of bridge) ex El Taino
08344 PUERTO RICO (US)
08345 WESTWARD VENTURE (US) (also has extra deck foreward of bridge)

08350 ATLANTIC CAUSEWAY Br/Br (Swan Hunter) 1969; RoC/Con; 14900; 212 × 9.3 (696 × 30.6); TST (AEI); 23; stern doors
Sisters:
08352 ATLANTIC CINDERELLA (Sw)
08353 ATLANTIC COGNAC (Fr)
08354 ATLANTIC CHAMPAGNE (Fr)
08355 ATLANTIC CROWN (Ne)

08360 REMUERA BAY Br/Br (Swan Hunter) 1973; Con; 42000; 252 × 11 (827 × 32.6); M (Sulzer); 21; ex Remuera 1977

●08370 BREMEN EXPRESS FRG/FRG (Bremer V) 1972; Con; 57500; 187 × 12 (942 × 39.6); T (Stal-Laval); 23
Sisters:
08371 HAMBURG EXPRESS (FRG)
08372 HONGKONG EXPRESS (FRG)
08373 TOKIO EXPRESS (FRG)
08374 NEDLLOYD DEJIMA (Ne)
08375 NEDLLOYD DELFT (Ne)

08380 S A SEDERBERG SA/Fr (France-Gironde) 1978; Con; 53000; 258.53 × 13 (841.48 × 42.65); TSM (Sulzer); 21
Sisters (SA flag):
08381 S A HELDERBERG
08382 S A WATERBERG
08383 S A WINTERBERG

08390 ELBE MARU Ja/Ja (Mitsui) 1972; Con; 51600; 269 × 11.9 (883 × 39.4); TrSM (B&W); 27.5

08400 LIVERPOOL BAY Br/FRG (Howaldts DW) 1972; Con; 58900; 290 × 13 (950 × 42.9); TSM (Sulzer); —
Sisters (Br flag):
08401 CARDIGAN BAY
08402 KOWLOON BAY
08403 OSAKA BAY
08404 TOKYO BAY

08410 BENALDER Br/FRG (Howaldts DW) 1972; Con; 58400; 290 × 13 (950 × 42.7); TSM (MAN); —
Sisters (Br flag):
08411 BENAVON
08412 CITY OF EDINBURGH

08420 TOLAGA BAY Br/FRG (A G 'Weser') 1977; Con; 53800; 258.55 × 13.02 (848.26 × 42.72); TSM (MAN); 21.5; ex Table Bay 1982; ex Barcelona 1981; ex Table Bay 1979
Sister:
08421 CITY OF DURBAN (Br) ex Portland Bay 1983; ex City of Durban 1982

08430 NEDLLOYD HOUTMAN Ne/Ne (Verolme

Dok (aft section); Nederlandsche (fwd section) 1977;
Con; 52600; 258.5 × 13.03 (848.1 × 42.75); TSM
(Sulzer); 21.5; ex *Largs Bay* 1982; ex *Nedlloyd Hout-
man* 1981
Sister:
08431 **NEDLLOYD HOORN** (Ne)

08440 **AUSTRALIAN VENTURE** Au/FRG (Bremer
V) 1977; Con; 44000; 249 × 11 (820 × 37); M (MAN);
24
Sisters:
08441 **ACT 7** (Br)
08442 **RESOLUTION BAY** (Br)
08443 **MAIRANGI BAY** (Br)
08444 **NEW ZEALAND PACIFIC** (NZ)

08450 **TRANSVAAL** FRG/FRG (Howaldts DW)
1978; Con; 52600; 258.53 × 13.02 (848.2 × 42.72);
TSM (MAN); 23

08455 **FRANKFURT EXPRESS** FRG/FRG (Howaldts DW) 1981; Con; 58400; 287.71 × 13.03 (944
× 42.75); TSM (MAN); 23

08460 **ORTELIUS** Be/Be (Boelwerf) 1978; Con;
52400; 258.53 × 13 (848.2 × 42.65); TSM (Sulzer);
22.75

08470 **BUNGA PERMAI** My/Ja (Sumitomo) 1979;
Con; 43500; 267 × 13 (875.98 × 42.65); M (Sulzer);
26
Sister:
08471 **BUNGA SURIA** (My)

08480 **NIHON** Sw/Sw (Oresunds) 1972; Con;
50800; 275.22 × 11.58 (902.95 × 37.99); TSM
(Gotaverken); 26; Lengthened by 15m 1984; Drawing
shows vessel prior to this

08485 **TOR BAY** Br/FRG (Thyssen) 1982; Con;
34000; 216.08 × 11.02 (709 × 36.15); M (B&W);
17.5
Sister:
08486 **PROVIDENCE BAY** (Br)

08490 **SELANDIA** De/De (B&W) 1972; Con; 50000;
274.3 × 12 (900 × 38); TrSM (B&W); 26; Lengthened
by 15m 1984; Drawing shows vessel prior to this;
Sistership also lengthened
Sister:
08491 **JUTLANDIA** (De)

08500 **QORMI** Ma/Fr (Dubigeon-Normandie) 1973;
RoC; 1000; 74.99 × 3.2 (262.43 × 10.5); TSM (Alpha); 13; ex *Poole Antelope* 1976
Sister:
★08501 **BIN HAI 504** (RC) ex *Dauphin de Cherbourg*
1983

08510 **GOLDEN GATE** Pa/It ('L Orlando') 1969;
RoC; 1600; 105.5 × 5 (346 × 16.9); TSM (Fiat); —; ex
Tango Express 1983; ex *Corriere Dell'est* 1978; ex
Espresso Campania 1971
Sister:
08511 **FALCON EXPRESS** (Pa) ex *Guatemala* 1982;
ex *Corriere del Sud* 1981; ex *Espresso Calabria* 1971

08520 **SCANDINAVIA** Sw/Fi (Wartsila) 1969; RoC;
6200; 137.4 × 5.7 (451 × 18.9); TSM (Pielstick); 18;
ex *Polaris* 1984; ex *Finncarrier* 1975; Stern doors;
Now fitted with additional deckhouse
Sisters (Fi flag):
08521 **FINNFELLOW**
08522 **CAPELLA** ex *Hans Gutzeit* 1982

★08530 **OSIJEK** Ys/Ys ('Uljanik') 1954; PC; 600;
57.71 × 2.89 (189 × 9.48); TSM (Waggon); 15.5
Sister:
08531 **PATRIZIA** (It) ex *Novi Sad* 1972

08540 **JHUFEL** Pi/Ja (Niigata) 1956; F; 780; 62.36 ×
3 (204.59 × 9.84); M (Niigata); 15; ex *Yumeji Maru*
1979

08550 **MARILENA** Gr/Gr (Thornycroft—lengthened
and completed by Camper & Nicholsons) 1911; C;
1200; 71 × 5.5 (233 × 18.3); TSM (MAN); 16; ex
Costakis Toyals 1960; ex *Marie* 1946; ex *Patris*; ex
Conqueror; ex *Emerald*; ex *Marynthea*; converted
yacht

08560 **MUTIARA** My/My (Hong Leong) 1977; SS;
1900 dst; 71 × 4 (232.94 × 13.12); M (Deutz); 16;
Operated by Malaysian Navy. Helicopter deck aft

08570 **AOI MARU** Ja/Ja (Mitsui) 1968; RoVC; 2600;
124 × 5 (407 × 18.5); TSM (B&W); 20

08580 **ORIENTAL GOVERNER** Pa/FRG (Rhein
Nordseew) 1971; Con; 30900; 243 × 10.7 (799 ×
35.2); M (Stork-Werkspoor); 20; ex *Seapac Trenton*
1981; ex *Euroliner* 1981
Sisters:
08581 **ORIENTAL KNIGHT** (Pa) ex *Seapac Valley
Forge* 1981; ex *Eurofreighter* 1981
08582 **ORIENTAL MINISTER** (Pa) ex *Seapac Bunker Hill* 1982; ex *Asialiner* 1981

08583 **ORIENTAL DIPLOMAT** (Pa) ex *Seapac Concord* 1982; ex *Asiafreighter* 1981

08590 **TOHGO MARU** Ja/Ja (Hitachi) 1970; Con;
23300; 212 × 9.5 (696 × 31.4); M (B&W); 23
Similar:
08591 **YAMASHIN MARU** (Ja)

08600 **ORIENTAL VENTURE** Br/Br (Smith's D)
1980; Con; 17400; 168.89 × 9.15 (554.1 × 30.02); M
(Sulzer); 20; ex *Rhein Express* 1982; ex *Oriental
Venture* 1981; ex *Manchester Venture* 1980; ex
Marseille 1980; ex *Manchester Venture* 1979; ex
Seatrain Bennington 1979; ex *Manchester Venture*
1977.
Sister:
08601 **ORIENTAL EXPERT** (Br) ex *Ibn Majid* 1983;
ex *Manchester Vanguard* 1982; ex *Oriental Vanguard* 1981; ex *Manchester Vanguard* 1980; ex *Keelung* 1980; ex *Manchester Vanguard* 1979; ex *Seatrain Trenton* 1978; ex *Manchester Vanguard* 1977

08610 **VERRAZANO BRIDGE** Ja/Ja (Kawasaki)
1973; Con; 39500; 165 × 12 (868 × 39.4); TSM
(MAN); 26.5
Sister:
08611 **HONGKONG CONTAINER** (Li)
Similar:
08612 **SEVEN SEAS BRIDGE** (Ja)

08620 **CANBERRA MARU** Ja/Ja (Mitsui) 1979;
Con; 32200; 216.3 × 11.52 (709.64 × 37.8); M
(B&W); 22.3

08630 **TOHBEI MARU** Ja/Ja (Hitachi) 1972; Con;
35500; 246 × 10.5 (807 × 34.7); M(—); —
Sister:
08631 **YASHIMA MARU** (Ja)

08640 **JAPAN AMBROSE** Ja/Ja (IHI) 1972; Con;
33300; 228 × 11; (748 × 30.6); T (IHI); 25

08650 **NEW JERSEY MARU** Ja/Ja (Mitsui) 1973;
Con; 37800; 263.28 × 11.5 (863.78 × 37.73); TSM
(B&W); 26

08660 **PACIFIC ARROW** Ja/Ja (IHI) 1973; Con;
30000; 219 × 11 (719 × 36.10); M (Sulzer); 22

● 08670 **ANDERS MAERSK** De/FRG (B+V) 1976;
Con; 29900; 224.95 × 11.52 (737 × 37.6); M(—);
24.75; Lengthened 1978
Sisters (De flag):
08671 **ADRIAN MAERSK**
08672 **ALBERT MAERSK**
08673 **ANNA MAERSK**
08674 **ARTHUR MAERSK**
08675 **AXEL MAERSK**
08676 **ARILD MAERSK**
08677 **ALVA MAERSK**
Similar (longer forecastle):
08678 **ARNOLD MAERSK**

08680 **SEA-LAND PATRIOT** US/Ja (Mitsubishi HI)
1980; Con; 24900; 226.96 × 10 (744.42 × 32.8); M
(Sulzer); 22; 'D-9' class
Sisters (US flag):
08681 **SEA-LAND DEFENDER**
08682 **SEA-LAND EXPLORER**
08683 **SEA-LAND DEVELOPER**
08684 **SEA-LAND EXPRESS**
08685 **SEA-LAND FREEDOM**
08686 **SEA-LAND INDEPENDENCE**
08687 **SEA-LAND MARINER**
08688 **SEA-LAND VOYAGER**
The following sisters were built in Ko (Hyundai):
08689 **SEA-LAND ENDURANCE**
08690 **SEA-LAND INNOVATOR**

08700 **EVER LEVEL** Tw/Ja (Onomichi) 1980; Con;
23300; 202.6 × 11.23 (665 × 36.84); M (Sulzer); 21;
ex *Ever Light* 1983
Sisters:
08701 **EVER LAUREL** (Pa) ex *Ever Large* 1983
08702 **EVER LIVING** (Pa) ex *Ever Lucky* 1983
08703 **EVER LYRIC** (Pa) ex *Ever Loyal* 1983
08704 **EVER LINKING** (Pa)
08705 **EVER LOADING** (Pa)

08710 **GREAT LAND** US/US (Sun SB) 1975; RoC;
17600; 241 × — (791 × —); T (GEC); 25

08720 **KAZUKAWA MARU** Ja/Ja (IHI) 1970; Con;
20500; 188.02 × 10.72 (61'7 × 35.17); M (Sulzer);
21.5; ex *Golden Arrow* 1980

08730 **GOLDEN GATE BRIDGE** Ja/Ja (Kawasaki
D) 1968; Con; 16900; 189 × 9.9 (620 × 33.6); M
(MAN); 22.25

08740 **HIRA MARU** Ja/Ja (Mitsubishi HI) 1978;
Con; 24800; 214.61 × 10.5 (704 × 34.45); M (Sulzer);
23

08745 **AMERICA MARU** Ja/Ja (Mitsui) 1982; Con;
31900; 222.51 × 11.62 (730 × 38.12); M (B&W);
22.25

08750 **SHOKAWA MARU** Ja/Ja (Hitachi) 1968;
Con; 16600; 188 × 9.4 (617 × 30.11); M (B&W); 22.5;
ex *Kashu Maru* 1981

08760 **DRAGOR MAERSK** De/Ja (IHI) 1974; Con;
38500; 261 × 11.7 (853 × 38.6); TSM (Sulzer); 26.5;
ex *Svendborg Maersk* 1980; ex *TFL Charleston* 1980;
ex *Seatrain Charleston* 1980; ex *Svendborg Maersk*
1979

08770 **ARIAKE** Br/FRG (Flender) 1976; Con; 37500;
238 × 11.6 (781 × 38); TSM (MAN); 26

08775 **ZIM KEELUNG** Is/Ne (Giessen-De Noord)
1981; Con; 29400; 210.22 × 11.5 (689.7 × 37.73); M
(Sulzer); 22.5
Sisters (Is flag):
08776 **ZIM SAVANNAH**
08777 **ZIM BARCELONA**

08780 **DUSSELDORF EXPRESS** FRG/FRG (Flender) 1977; Con; 32900; 209.94 × 11.02 (688.78 ×
36.15); M (MAN); 22
Sisters (FRG flag):
08781 **KOLN EXPRESS**
08782 **NURNBERG EXPRESS**
08783 **STUTTGART EXPRESS**

08790 **FORT ROYAL** Fr/Fr (Dunkerque-Normandie)
1979; Con; 32200; 210 × 11.02 (688.98 × 36.15);
TSM (Pielstick); 22
Sister:
08791 **FORT FLEUR d'EPEE** (Fr)

08800 **KOREAN WONIS JIN** Ko/It (Italcantieri)
1971; Con; 25800; 208 × 10.4 (683 × 34.1); T
(Westinghouse); 23.5; ex *Korean Commander* 1980;
ex *Taeping* 1977
Sisters:
08801 **ZIM CALIFORNIA** (Li) ex *Taeho* 1976
08802 **ZIM GENOVA** (Is)
08803 **ZIM HAIFA** (Is)
08804 **ZIM NEW YORK** (Is)
08805 **ZIM TOKYO** (Is)
Similar:
08806 **MEDITERRANEA** (It)
08807 **NIPPONICA** (It)
Similar (with garage abaft superstructure):
08808 **AFRICA** (It)
08809 **EUROPA** (It)
08810 **S A LANGEBERG** (SA)

08830 **LEVERKUSEN EXPRESS** FRG/FRG (Howaldts DW) — FRG 1970/78; Con; 16700; 176.49 ×
10.59 (579 × 34.74); M (MAN); —; ex *Leverkusen*
1978; converted from general cargo, lengthened and
widened 1978 (Bremer V)
Sisters (FRG flag):
08831 **ERLANGEN EXPRESS** ex *Incotrans Progress* 1982; ex *Erlangen Express* 1981; ex *Erlangen*
1979
08832 **HOECHST EXPRESS** ex *Incotrans Promise*
1982; ex *Hoecht Express* 1981; ex *Hoechst* 1979
08833 **LUDWIGSHAFEN EXPRESS** ex *Ludwigshafen* 1979

08840 **STAR HERCULES** Br/Br (Appledore) 1980;
Sply/Spt; 1600; 82.56 × 4.47 (270.87 × 14.67); TSM
(Ruston); 13

08842 **SEAFORTH EMPEROR** Br/Sg (Singapore
Slip) 1982; ORSV; 1600; 67.47 × 6.10 (221.4 20.01);
TSD-E (Wartsila); 12.5
Sister:
08843 **SEAFORTH MONARCH** (Br)

08845 **SKANDI BETA** No/FRG (Suerken) 1982;
ORSV; 500/1400; 67.87 × 5.00 (222.7 × 16.4); TSM
(Wichmann); —

08850 **MONTCALM** Ca/Ca (Davie SB) 1957; IB/LT;
2000; 67 × 4.9 (220 × 16.4); TSM (Unaflow); 13
Similar (Ca flag):
08851 **WOLFE**

08860 **ALMERIA LYKES** US/US (General Dynamics) 1972; Bg; 21700; 267 × 11.9 (876 × 38.2); T
(GEC); 19.5; 'Seabee' type; stern elevator
Sisters (US flag):
08861 **DOCTOR LYKES**
08862 **TILLIE LYKES**

08870 **DART BRITAIN** Br/Ja (Namura) 1979; Con;
15600; 177.03 × 10.13 (583.96 × 33.12); M (Sulzer);
19; ex *Seapac Oriskany* 1981; ex *Seatrain Oriskany*
1981
Sisters:
08871 **TFL FRANKLIN** (FRG) ex *Seatrain Bennington* 1981
08872 **DART ATLANTICA** (Br) ex *Seapac Chesapeake* 1981; ex *Seatrain Chesapeake* 1981
08873 **DART CONTINENT** (Be) ex *Seapac Yorktown*
1981; ex *Seatrain Yorktown* 1981
08874 **DART AMERICANA** (Br) ex *Seapac Independence* 1981; ex *Seatrain Independence* 1981

08875 **TFL JEFFERSON** (Br) ex *Seatrain Saratoga* 1980

08880 **CALIFORNIA STAR** Br/FRG (Bremer V) 1971; Con; 19100; 189 × 10 (616 × 33); M (MAN); 21.5
Sister:
08881 **COLUMBIA STAR** (Br)

08890 **EVER VALIANT** Pa/Ja (Hayashikane) 1977; Con; 14400; 186.75 × 10.02 (612.7 × 32.87); M (Sulzer); 22
Similar:
08891 **HANJIN KWANG YANG** (Pa) ex *Ever Victory* 1983
08892 **HANJIN CHEJU** (Pa) ex *Ever Voyager* 1983
08893 **EVER VIGOR** (Tw)
08894 **EVER VITAL** (Tw)
Probably similar:
08895 **EVER VALOR** (Pa)
08896 **EVER VALUE** (Pa)

08900 **FRECCIA DELL'OUEST** It/It ('L Orlando') 1975; RoCF; 2600; 117.51 × 5.066 (385.5 × 16.62); TSM (GMT); 20; ex *Corriere Dell'Ouest* 1979
Sister:
08901 **FRECCIA DEL NORD** (It) ex *Corriere Del Nord* 1979

08920 **CABLE RESTORER** SA/Br (Swan Hunter & WR) 1944; Cbl; 1500; 77 × 5 (255 × 17); TSR (Swan Hunter & WR); 1O; ex *Retriever III* 1961; ex *Retriever* 1960

08930 **PERSIA** Le/It (Adriatico) 1953/77; LS; 8800; 159.09 × 8.35 (521.85 × 27.4); TSM (Adriatico); 19; ex *Asia* 1975; Converted from passenger 1977

08940 **HARSHA VARDHANA** In/In (Mazagon) 1974; PC; 8900; 132.6 × 7 (435 × 23); M (Sulzer); 17

08950 **MATSONIA** US/US (Sun SB) 1973; RoC-/Con; 15300; 213.37 × 8.56 (700 × 28.08); T (GEC); 25; Side doors

08960 **VILLE DE DUNKERQUE** Fr/Fr (Dunkerque-Normandie) 1978; RoC; 8700; 169.25 × 7.74 (555.2 × 25.3); M (CCM); ex *Foss Dunkerque* 1981; ex *Ville De Dunkerque* 1979; Stern door/ramp. Side doors.
Sisters (Fr flag):
08961 **VILLE DU HAVRE** ex *Foss Havre* 1981; ex *Ville Du Havre* 1979
08962 **RO-RO MANHATTAN**
08963 **RO-RO GENOVA** ex *Qatar Express* 1981; ex *Ro-Ro Genova* 1979

08970 **TOYAMA** No/Ja (Mitsui) 1972; Con; 52200; 275 × 11 (903 × 36.4); TrSM (B&W); 26.25; Lengthened by 15m 1984. Drawing shows vessel prior to this conversion

08980 **TOLAGA BAY** Br/FRG (A G 'Weser') 1977; Con; 53800; 258.55 × 13.02 (848.26 × 42.72); TSM (MAN); 21.5; ex *Table Bay* 1982; ex *Barcelona* 1981; ex *Table Bay* 1979
Sister: 08981 **CITY OF DURBAN** (Br) ex *Portland Bay* 1983; ex *City of Durban* 1982

08990 **KUROSHIO MARU** Ja/Ja (Hayashikane) 1971; F; 4900; 124 × 5.5 (407 × 17.10); TSM (NKK); 23

● 09000 **ANDERS MAERSK** De/FRG (B+V) 1976; Con; 29900; 224.95 × 11.52 (737 × 37.6); M (—); 24.75; Lengthened 1978
Sisters (De flag):
09001 **ADRIAN MAERSK**
09002 **ALBERT MAERSK**
09003 **ANNA MAERSK**
09004 **ARTHUR MAERSK**
09005 **AXEL MAERSK**
09006 **ARILD MAERSK**
09007 **ALVA MAERSK**
Similar (longer forecastle):
09008 **ARNOLD MAERSK**

09010 **AL AHMADIAH** Si/Ru (Nosenko) 1969/80; Con; 14400; 194.33 × 9.5 (637.57 × 31.17); M (B&W); 18.5; Converted from cargoship of 'Feodosiya' type 1980 (AESA)
Sisters:
09011 **AL RUMAITHIAH** (Iq)
09012 **AL SHAMIAH** (Ku)

09020 **SEXTUM** It/It (Italcantieri) 1980; Con; 26800; 208.12 × 10.66 (682.81 × 34.97); M (GMT); 22; ex *Ercole Lauro* 1982

09030 **LEVERKUSEN EXPRESS** FRG/FRG (Howaldts DW) 1970/78; Con; 16700; 176.49 × 10.59 (579 × 34.74); M (MAN); 21; ex *Leverkusen* 1978; Converted from general cargo, lengthened and widened 1978 (Bremer V)
Sisters (FRG flag):
09031 **ERLANGEN EXPRESS** ex *Incotrans Progress* 1982; ex *Erlangen Express* 1981; ex *Erlangen* 1979

09032 **HOECHST EXPRESS** ex *Incotrans Promise* 1982; ex *Hoechst Express* 1981; ex *Hoechst* 1979
09033 **LUDWIGSHAFEN EXPRESS** ex *Ludwigshafen* 1979

09040 **OIL ENDEAVOUR** Br/Fr (La Ciotat) 1967/77; Diving support; 1900; 84.82 × 5.64 (278.28 × 18.5); D-E (MAN); 14.5; ex *Marie De Grace* 1976; Converted from stern trawler (Swan Hunter)

09050 **SEAFORTH CLANSMAN** Br/Br (Cochrane) 1977; OSS; 2000; 78.62 × 5 (257.9 × 16.4); TSM (Mirrlees Blackstone); 13; Diving support ship—stern ramp

09060 **CANMAR KIGORIAK** Ca/Ca (Saint John SB) 1980; IB/Tg/Sply; 3600; 91.06 × 8.54 (298.75 × 28.02); M (Sulzer); 18.6 (max)

09065 **SEAGAIR** Br/Br (Richards) 1982; OSS; 2800; 94.32 × 4.67 (309 × 15.32); TSD-E (B Polar); 13.5

09070 **KEFALONIA SPIRIT** Cy/Sp (Euskalduna) 1965; C; 6000/8300; 146 × —/— (480 × —/—); M (MAN); 16; ex *Monte Saja* 1974
Sister:
09071 **BANGLAR UPOHAR** (Bh) ex *Monte Sollube* 1973
Similar:
09072 **BANGLAR ASHA** (Bh) ex *Mosor* 1973; ex *Garciani* 1970

★ 09080 **PROFESSOR SHCHYOGOLEV** Ru/Pd (Szczecinska) 1970; C/TS; 6000; 122 × 7.3 (402 × 24.2); M (Sulzer); 15.5; 'B 80' type
Sisters (Ru flag):
★ 09081 **PROFESSOR KUDREVICH**
★ 09082 **PROFESSOR ANICHKOV**
★ 09083 **PROFESSOR PAVLENKO**
★ 09084 **PROFESSOR RYBALTOVSKIY**
★ 09085 **PROFESSOR KLYUSTIN**
★ 09086 **PROFESSOR YUSHENKO**
Similar (light mast from funnel):
★ 09087 **PROFESSOR UKHOV**
★ 09088 **PROFESSOR MINYAYEV**

★ 09090 **CATALINA** Ca/Br (A&P) 1965; Con; 9100; 151 × 8.1 (495 × 28.1); M (Sulzer); 17; ex *Sunhermine*; ex *Inishowen Head* 1979; ex *Cast Beaver* 1977; ex *Inishowen Head* 1973; Converted from cargo ship (H&W)

★ 09100 **ROYALE** Pa/It (Ansaldo) 1958; P; 20400; 185 × 8.6 (606 × 28.5); TST (Ansaldo); 21; ex *Federico C* 1983

★ 09120 **SPRUT** Ru/Fi (Wartsila) 1979; Spt; 730 dwt; 77. × 5.35 (262.62 × 17.55); TSM (Wartsila); 14; ex *Swan Ocean* 1982; Helicopter deck. Radar mast and 'A' frame are hinged

09130 **SAGAR KANYA** In/FRG (Schlichting) 1983; RS; 4200; 100.51 × 5.60 (330 × 18.37); TSD-E (Krupp Mak); —; Superstructure differs on starboard side; extra boat beneath bridge deck (boat deck extended foreward)

09140 **AFRICA** Gr/Be (Boel) 1965; R; 5100; 135 × 6.5 (440 × 21.9); M (MAN); 20; ex *Frubel America* 1980
Sister:
09141 **ORIENTAL FRUIT** (Pa) ex *Frubel Europa* 1979

09150 **BRITANIS** Gr/US (Bethlehem) 1932; P; 18300; 192 × 8.6 (630 × 28); TST (Bethlehem); 21.5; ex *Lurline* 1970; ex *Matsonia* 1963; ex *Monterey* 1956

09160 **CONSTELLATION** Gr/Ys ('Uljanik') 1962; P; 12400; 150 × 5.5 (492 × 18.5); TSM (B&W); 18.5; ex *Danaos* 1978; ex *Anna Nery* 1978
Sister:
09161 **NIPPON MARU** (Ja) ex *P S Seven Seas* 1978; ex *Rosa Da Fonseca* 1975

09165 **NORWAY** No/Fr (L'Atlantique) FRG 1961/80; P; 70200; 315 × 10.3 (1034 × 34); TST (CEM-Parsons); 17; ex *France;* Modernised and rebuilt 1979/80 (Hapag-Lloyd)

09170 **UNITED STATES** US/US (Newport News) 1952; P; 38200; 3O1 × 10 (988 × 33); QST (Westinghouse); 30

09180 **ELLINIS** Gr/US (Bethlehem) 1932; P; 18600; 193 × 8.6 (634 × 28); TST (Bethlehem); 21; ex *Lurline* 1963

09190 **CONSTITUTION** US/US (Bethlehem Steel) 1951; P; 20300; 208 × 9 (683 × 30); TST (Bethlehem Steel); 22.5; ex *Oceanic Constitution* 1982; ex *Constitution* 1974
Sister:
09191 **INDEPENDENCE** (US) ex *Oceanic Independence* 1982; ex *Independence* 1974

09200 **MICHELANGELO** Ir/It (Ansaldo) 1965; P; 49500; 276 × 9.3 (906 × 30); TST (Ansaldo); 26.5; Used as accommodation ships by the Iranian Navy. May be renamed
Sister:
09201 **RAFFAELLO** (Ir)

★ 09210 **PRIAMURYE** Ru/Ru (—) 1957; P; 5800; 119 × 6.7 (391 × 19); D-E (—); 16
Sister:
★ 09211 **ZABAYKALYE**

★ 09220 **ADMIRAL NAKHIMOV** Ru/Ge (Bremer V) 1925; P; 17100; 174.33 × 11.81 (572 × 38.75); TSR (Bremer V); 16; ex *Berlin* 1947

09240 **COLUMBUS C** Pa/Ne ('De Schelde') 1953; P; 16300; 182 × 8.2 (598 × 2.7); 19; ex *Europa* 1981; ex *Kungsholm* 1965; Satellite Navigation dome has now been fitted to foreward funnel

★ 09250 **MIKOLAJ KOPERNIK** Pd/No (Trosvik) 1973; TF; 2600; 126 × 4.6 (412 × 150); TSM (Sulzer); 16
Sister:
★ 09251 **JAN HEWELIUSZ** (Pd)

09260 **CHIOS FAITH** Gr/FRG (B+V) 1968; R; 3800/5600; 148 × 6.6/8.2 (485 × 18.6/27); M (Ottensener); 23; ex *Polar Argentina* 1982
Sisters:
09261 **POLAR BRASIL** (Gr)
09262 **POLAR COLOMBIA** (Li)
09263 **CHIOS SPIRIT** (Gr) ex *Polar Ecuador* 1982
09264 **POLAR PARAGUAY** (Gr)
09265 **POLAR URUGUAY** (Li)

09270 **LIPARI** It/It (Cassaro) 1956; PC; 1600; 86 × 3.8 (282 × 12.6); TSM (Ansaldo); —

09280 **ST MARGARETS** Br/Br (Swan Hunter & WR) 1944; Cbl; 1500; 76 × 4.8 (252 × 16.3); TSR (—); 12; Owned by Ministry of Defence

09290 **ANG PANGULO** Pi/Ja (ishikawajima J) 1959; Y; 2200; 83 × 4.9 (275 × 17); TSM (—); 16.5; ex *The President;* ex *Roxas;* ex *Lapu-Lapu;* Presidential Yacht

09300 **ORION** Gr/It (Ansaldo) 1953; P; 6100; 127 × 5.4 (416 × 17.5); TST (Nordberg); 17; ex *Achilleus* 1968

09310 **FLAVIAN** Pa/Br (J Brown) 1947; P; 15500; 169 × 8 (556 × 27); TST (J Brown); 18; ex *Flavia* 1982; ex *Media* 1961; Converted from passenger/cargo

09320 **RHAPSODY** Bs/Ne (Wilton-Fije) 1957; P; 24400; 196 × 8 (643 × 26.1); TST (Wilton-Fije); 19; ex *Statendam* 1982

09330 **VISTAFJORD** Bs/Br (Swan Hunter) 1973; P; 24900; 191 × 8.2 (627 × 27); TSM (Sulzer); 20

09340 **VERACRUZ I** Pa/FRG (Deutsche Werft) 1957; P; 9900; 149 × 6.6 (488 × 21.5); TST (Allgemeine); 20; ex *Freeport* 1976; ex *Carnivale* 1974; ex *Theodor Herzl* 1969; May be spelt **VERACRUZ PRIMERO**

09350 **TERAAKA** Br/Ys ('Titovo') 1959; C; 1000; 64.3 × 3.9 (211 × 12.11); M (Sulzer); 15; ex *Ninikoria* 1975; ex *Opatija* 1968
Sister:
09351 **FRANCISCO DE MIRANDA** (Ve) ex *Orebic* 1967

★ 09360 **GRUMANT** Ru/De (B&W) 1964; FT; 4700; 103 × 5.5 (337 × 18.3); M (B&W); 14; Differs from SKRYPLEV by having both KP's on houses)
Sisters (Ru flag):
★ 09361 **GEIZER**
★ 09362 **GLETCHER**
★ 09363 **KAPITAN SKORNYAKOV** ex *Golfstrim*
★ 09364 **KURS**
★ 09365 **NAVIGATOR**
★ 09366 **SKAZOCHNIK ANDERSEN**
Similar (Ru flag):
★ 09368 **PAVLOVO**
★ 09369 **PELENGATOR**
★ 09370 **PEREMYSHLJ**
★ 09371 **PRILUKI**
★ 09372 **PROKOPYEVSK**
★ 09373 **ZELENOBORSK**
★ 09374 **MAGNIT**
★ 09375 **BUSSOL**
★ 09376 **EKHOLOT**
★ 09377 **LOKATOR**

● ★ 09380 **SKRYPLEV** Ru/De (B&W) 1962; FT; 4700; 103×5.5 (337×18.3); M(B&W); 14
Sisters (Ru flag):
★ 09381 **DAVYDOV**
★ 09382 **SOVIETSK**
★ 09383 **VITUS BERING**

Possible sisters:
★09384 **APETIT**
★09385 **KOMPAS**
★09386 **KONDOR**
★09387 **ZAPOLYARNYY**

09390 **ACHILLEUS** Gr/It (Taranto) 1952; PC; 1700; 82 × 4.6 (269 × 13.1); TSM (Fiat); 14; ex *Kolokotronis* 1971
Sisters (Gr flag):
09391 **ALEXANDROS** ex *Karaiskakis*
09392 **KANARIS**
09393 **MIAOULIS**

09410 **STELLA SOLARIS** Gr/Fr (Ch de France) 1953; P; 10600; 166 × 7.9 (545 × 26); TST (La Loire); 21; ex *Stella V.* 1970; ex *Cambodge* 1970

09420 **MARIANNA VI** Pa/Br (Stephen) 1951; P; 14100; 164 × 7.7 (537 × 25.1); TSM (Stephen); 16; ex *Aureol* 1974; Being used as an accommodation ship. Probably has a helicopter platform aft

09430 **NIPPON MARU** Ja/Ys ('Split') 1962; P; 9700; 150 × 5 (493 × 17); TSM (B&W) ex *P/S Seven Seas* 1977; ex *Rosa Da Fonseca* 1975
Sister:
09431 **CONSTELLATION** (Gr) ex *Danaos* 1978; ex *Anna Nery* 1978

09440 **CIUDAD DE SEVILLA** Sp/Sp (UN de Levante) 1980; RoPCF; 7400; 138.5 × 5.5 (454.4 × 18.04); TSM (MAN); 21; Stern door
Sisters:
09441 **CIUDAD DE SALAMANCA** (Sp)
09442 **CIUDAD DE CACERES** (Sp)

09460 **NOGA** Pa/US (Newport News) 1940/79; P; 26400; 220.38 × 9.98 (723 × 32.74); TST (Newport News); 22.5; ex *Italis* 1980; ex *America* 1979; ex *Australis* 1978; ex *America* 1964; ex *West Point* 1946; ex *America* 1942; Modernised 1979. Converted to floating hotel 1980; Probably altered in appearance

09470 **FUNCHAL** Po/De (Helsingor) 1961; P; 9800; 153 × 6.2 (501 × 20.3); TST (Stork-Werkspoor); 20

●★09480 **YAOHUA** RC/Fr (L'Atlantique) 1967; P; 10200; 149 × 6.6 (489 × 21.8); TSM (CCM); 21

09490 **CORAL PRINCESS** Br/Sp (Euskalduna) 1962; P; 9600; 146 × 5.5 (478 × 18); TSM (B&W); 17; ex *Princesa Leopoldina* 1970
Sister:
09491 **AQUAMARINE** (Gr) ex *Marco Polo* 1978; ex *Princesa Isabel* 1969

09500 **GUERVEUR** Fr/Fr (Perriere) 1966; RoPF; 500; 45.1 × 2.3 (148 × 7.8); TSM (Crepelle); 12.5

09510 **SOGNEFJORD** No/US (Pullman) 1943; PC; 9600; 146 × 5.5 (478 × 18); TSM (General Motors); 15
Sister:
09511 **KILWICK** (No) ex *Sunnfjord II* 1983; ex *Sunnfjord* 1978

09520 **LABRADOR** Ca/Ca (Marine Indust) 1953; IB; 3800; 82 × 9.1 (269 × 30.1); TSD-E (Fairbanks, Morse); 16; Helicopter deck and hangar; Operated by Canadian Coast Guard

09530 **THE VICTORIA** Gr/Br (H&W) 1936; P; 11900; 173.4 × 8 (573 × 26.2); TSM (Fiat); 16; ex *Victoria* 1977; ex *Dunnottar Castle* 1958

09540 **TOBAGO** Br/Ne ('De Hoop') 1970; RoPF; 1500; 76 × 3.3 (250 × 11); TSM (Alco); —; ex *Santa Margarita* 1976; Bow and stern doors

09550 **HYOGO MARU** Ja/Ja (Kawasaki) 1973; RoC/Con; 9100; 181 × 8.9 (594 × 29); M (MAN); 21
Similar (Au flag):
09551 **AUSTRALIAN SEAROADER**
Similar (lengthened by 29 metres):
09552 **AUSTRALIAN ENTERPRISE** (Au)
09552 **AUSTRALIAN EXPLORER** (Au) ex *Matthew Flinders* 1975

09560 **BUNGA PERMAI** My/Ja (Sumitomo) 1979; Con; 43500; 267 × 13 (875.98 × 42.65); M (Sulzer); 26
Sister:
09561 **BUNGA SURIA** (My)

09570 **NIHON** Sw/Sw (Oresunds) 1972; Con; 50800; 275.22 × 11.58 (902.95 × 37.99); TrS M (Gotaverken); 26; Lengthened by 15m 1984; Drawings show vessel prior to this

09590 **PEGASUS** Gr/Br (Barclay, Curle) 1963; C; 6900/9700; 153 × —/9.6 (501 × —/30.7); M (Sulzer); 16; ex *Natale* 1981; ex *Hopepeak* 1969
Sisters:
09591 **BLUE BAY** (Gr) ex *Lord Hastings* 1980; ex *Eleni E F* 1974; ex *Hopecrag* 1971

09600 **KOMARINE NO 9** Ko/Br (Short Bros) 1963; C; 9800; 148 × 9.1 (484 × 30); M (Sulzer); —; ex *Chrysovalandou Tria* 1981; ex *Marika Venizelos* 1973; ex *Radley* 1968

09620 **STAVROULA K** Gr/De (Helsingborgs) 1952; C; 2400; 110 × 6.1 (362 × 19.9); M (B&W); 15; ex *Pinelopi A* 1981; ex *Elster* 1979; ex *Erik Banck* 1964

09640 **SOUTHDENE** Pa/Br (Bartram) 1962; C; 7800; 141 × 8.7 (461 × 28.7); M (Gotaverken); 14.5; ex *Sea Victory* 1981; ex *Egidia* 1981; ex *Alexandros B* 1977; ex *Avisfaith* 1971

09660 **JALANIDHI** Ia/Ja (Sasebo) 1963; RS; 750; 54 × 3.4 (177 × 11.2); M (MAN); 12

09680 **ILLIRIA** Gr/It (Pellegrino) 1962; P; 3900; 101 × 5 (333 × 17); M (Fiat); 18

09690 **KORRIGAN** Fr/FRG (Howaldts DW) 1973; Con; 57200; 289 × 13 (947 × 42.7); TSM (—); 22.5

09700 **KAZUKAWA MARU** Ja/Ja (IHI) 1970; Con; 16600; 188 × 10.7 (617 × 35); M (Sulzer); 21.5; ex *Golden Arrow* 1980

09710 **AMERICAN LANCER** US/US (Sun SB) 1969; Con; 18900; 214 × 9.8 (701 × 32.2); T(GEC); 22
Sisters (US flag):
09711 **AMERICAN LEGION**
09712 **AMERICAN LIBERTY**
09713 **AMERICAN LARK**
09714 **AMERICAN LYNX**
09715 **AMERICAN ASTRONAUT**
09716 **AMERICAN APOLLO**
09717 **AMERICAN AQUARIUS**

09720 **AMERICAN ACE** US/US (Bethlehem Steel) 1953/70; Con; 15800; 202 × 9.1 (661 × 29.6); T (Bethlehem Steel); 20; ex *Pioneer Moon* 1970; ex *Mountain Mariner* 1956; Lengthened and converted from cargo ship 1970
Sisters (US flag):
09721 **AMERICAN ALLIANCE** ex *Pioneer Mill* 1970; ex *Show Me Mariner* 1956
09722 **AMERICAN ARGOSY** ex *Pioneer Main* 1970; ex *Cotton Mariner* 1956
09723 **AMERICAN ARCHER** ex *Pioneer Mist* 1970; ex *Peninsular Mariner* 1956
09724 **AMERICAN ACCORD** ex *Pioneer Mart* 1971; ex *Sunflower Mariner* 1956
09725 **AMERICAN LEADER** ex *Pioneer Minx* 1970; ex *Gopher Mariner* 1956
09726 **AMERICAN LEGACY** ex *Pioneer Ming* 1971; ex *Silver Mariner* 1956
09727 **AMERICAN LEGEND** ex *Pioneer Myth* 1971; ex *Pelican Mariner* 1956

09730 **TOHGO MARU** Ja/Ja (Hitachi) 1970; Con; 23300; 212 × 9.4 (696 × 31.2); M (B&W); 23
Similar:
09731 **YAMASHIN MARU** (Ja)

09740 **TOHBEI MARU** Ja/Ja (Hitachi) 1972; Con; 35500; 246 × 10.6 (808 × 35); M (—); —
Sister:
09741 **YASHIMA MARU** (Ja)

09750 **BUNGA ANGSANA** My/Ja (Mitsubishi HI) 1972/77; Con; 11500; 155.96×8.68 (511.35× 28.48); M (Sulzer); 17; Converted from general cargo 1977 (Malaysian Spyd)
Sisters (My flag):
09751 **BUNGA TERATAI**
09752 **BUNGA MELATI**
09753 **BUNGA SEROJA**

09760 **ORIENT MARU** Ja/Ja (Mitsubishi HI) 1968; Con; 16400; 187 × 9.5 (614 × 31); M (Sulzer); 22.5; ex *American Maru* 1981

09770 **MONT BLANC MARU** Ja/Ja (Mitsui) 1974; Con; 30000; 217 × 11.71 (711.94 × 38.42); M (B&W); 23

09775 **SHIN-KASHU MARU** Ja/Ja (Hitachi) 1981; Con; 31000; 221.5 × 11.03 (727 × 36.19); M (B&W); 22.75; May be spelt **SHINKASHU MARU**

09780 **PACIFIC EXPRESS** Ko/Ja (Mitsubishi HI) 1968; Con; 16200; 187 × 10.5 (614 × 34.3); M (MAN); 22.5; ex *Hakone Maru* 1978
Sister:
09781 **HARUNA MARU** (Ja)

09790 **HIRA MARU** Ja/Ja (Mitsubishi HI) 1978; Con; 24800; 214.61 ×10.5 (704 × 34.45); M (Sulzer); 23

09800 **AUSTRALIAN EMBLEM** Au/Ja (Kawasaki) 1975; RoC/Con; 23200; 222.3 × 10.5 (731 × 35); M (MAN); 22.75; Stern door
Sister:
09801 **AUSTRALIAN ESCORT** (Au) ex *James Cook* 1976

09810 **KISO MARU** Ja/Ja (IHI) 1973; Con; 38500; 261 × 11.8 (857 × 38.6); M (Sulzer); —

09820 **CANBERRA MARU** Ja/Ja (Mitsui) 1979; Con; 32200; 216.3 × 11.53 (709.65 × 37.83); M (B&W); 22.3

●09830 **CHINA CONTAINER** Tw/Tw (China SB) 1979; Con; 32500; 221.7×11.5 (727.36× 37.73); M (Sulzer); 23
Sisters:
09830/1 **KAWANA** (Sg) ex *Ace Concord* 1982
09830/2 **ORIENTAL PATRIOT** (Tw)
09830/3 **NEPTUNE PEARL** (Sg)
09830/4 **NEPTUNE CORAL** (Sg) (may be modified)
Similar—shorter (Tw flag):
09831 **MING GALAXY**
09832 **MING GLORY**
09833 **MING MOON**
09834 **MING OCEAN**
09835 **MING STAR**
09836 **MING SUN**
09837 **MING UNIVERSE**
09837/1 **MING COMFORT**
09837/2 **MING ENERGY**
09837/3 **MING FORTUNE**
09837/4 **MING LONGEVITY**
Similar (231 metres):
09838 **NEPTUNE AMBER** (Sg)
09839 **NEPTUNE CRYSTAL** (Sg)
09839/1 **NEPTUNE DIAMOND** (Sg)
Similar (260 metres):
09839/2 **NEPTUNE GARNET** (Sg)
09839/3 **NEPTUNE JADE** (Sg)

09840 **OSAKA MARU** Ja/Ja (Mitsubishi HI) 1981; Con; 31400; 211 × 11.62 (692 × 38.12); M (Sulzer); 18
Possible sister:
09841 **HAYAKAWA MARU** (Ja)

09850 **ALASKA MARU** Ja/Ja (Mitsubishi HI) 1973; Con; 23600; 209 × 10.6 (686 × 35); M (Sulzer); 22.5
Possible sister:
09851 **HAKUSAN MARU** (Ja)

09855 **HIKAWA MARU** Ja/Ja (NKK) 1974; Con; 24800; 213 × 10.52 (700 × 34.51); M (Sulzer); 23

09860 **NEW YORK MARU** Ja/Ja (Mitsubishi HI) 1972; Con; 38800; 263 × 11.5 (863 × 37.9); TSM (Sulzer); 24.75

09870 **AOTEA** Br/Ja (Mitsui) 1970; Con; 24400; 213 × 10.5 (700 × 34.5); M (B&W); 23; ex *Ariake* 1977

09880 **ARAFURA** Br/Ja (Mitsubishi HI) 1970; Con; 25200; 211.49 × 10.53 (693.86 × 34.55); M (B&W); 23

09890 **CRESCENT** Pa/Ja (Mitsubishi HI) 1969; Con; 23700; 212 × 9.4 (697 × 31.3); M (Sulzer); 23; ex *Hakozaki Maru* 1981
Similar:
09891 **HIEI MARU** (Ja)
Similar (pole radar mast):
09892 **BEISHU MARU** (Ja)

09895 **NICHIGOH MARU** Ja/Ja (Hitachi) 1980; Con; 37000; 217.18 × 11.53 (712 × 37.83); M (B&W); 21

09900 **LUCHANA** Sp/Sp (Euskalduna) 1964; C; 5900/8300; 145 × 7.9/9.7 (475 × 26/32); M (Euskalduna); 15.25

●★09910 **ULCINJ** Ys/Sp (Euskalduna) 1961; C; 5700/8200; 145 × —/9.1 (475 × —/29.9); M (B&W); 12.5; ex *Martin Zubizarreta* 1969
Sister:
09912 **FLORIANA** (Ma) ex *Demarg* 1983; ex *Bermeo* 1975

09920 **CAMSELL** Ca/Ca (Burrard DD, lengthened and completed by Yarrows) 1959; IB/LT; 2000; 68.2 × 6.4 (224 × 21); TSD-E (Fairbanks, Morse); 13; Operated by Canadian Coast Guard

09925 **SANTA MARIA DE LA PAZ** Sp/Sp (UN de Levante) 1967; P/C; 1200; 66.93 × 3.73 (220 × 12.24); M (MTM); 15
Sister:
09926 **SANTA MARIA DE LA CARIDAD** (Sp)

09930 **MARIAM** Le/No (Larvik) 1919; C; 840; 63 × 4.2 (206 × 13.11); R (Larvik); 9.5; ex *Sirius* 1963

●09940 **ALPAC ASIA** Br/Br (Doxford) 1962; C; 7500/10100; 153 × 9.4 (500 × 31); M (Doxford); 15.5; ex *Sara Lupe* 1980; ex *Cardiff City* 1972; KP abreast funnel
Sister:
09941 **ALPAC AFRICA** (Br) ex *Maria Elisa* 1980; ex *Houston City* 1972

●09950 **PENTA-Y** Sg/Br (Doxford) 1960; C; 10300;

155 × 9.2 (510 × 30.7); M (Doxford); 15; ex *Tong Beng* 1978; ex *Executive Venture* 1974; ex *Devon City*; KP abreast funnel
Sister:
09951 **MALDIVE PROMOTER** (Mv) ex *Tong Jit* 1980; ex *Alexander A S* 1973; ex *Orient City* 1972

09960 **CASTLE SPIRIT** Gr/Sp (Corcho) 1958; C; 2700; 96 × 6.1 (314 × 19.11); M (B&W); 13; ex *Picoblanco* 1981
Sisters:
09961 **CASTLE DIGNITY** (Ma) ex *Picoverde* 1982
09962 **INTER II** (Pa)—may be INTERDOS; ex *Picoazul* 1980

09980 **LAS ARENAS** Sp/Sp (AESA) 1960; C; 6400/8700; 145 × 7.9/8.9 (475 × 26/29); M (B&W); 13
Sister:
09981 **VALENTINA FRIAS** (Sp)

09990 **REIYO MARU** Ja/Ja (Hayashikane) 1967; C; 3400; 111 × 6.9 (365 × 23); M (Kobe); 16
Possibly similar:
09991 **JUYO MARU** (Ja)

★09995 **GAMZAT TSADASA** Ru/Ys ('Uljanik') 1971/80; Con; 12300; 176.23 × 9.80 (578 × 32.15); M (B&W); 17.75; Converted to container and lengthened 1980 (Jurong Spyd)
Sisters (Ru flag):
★09996 **IVAN KOTLYAREVSKIY**
★09997 **KONSTANTIN PAULOVSKIY**
★09998 **NOVIKOV PRIBOY**

10000 **EVER SHINE** Pa/Ja (Hayashikane) 1976; Con; 10200; 160.8 × 9.4 (528 × 31); M (B&W); 20
Sisters (Pa flag):
10001 **EVER SPRING**
10002 **EVER SUMMIT**
10003 **EVER SUPERB**

10005 **PHOLAS** Br/Br (Caledon) 1958/74; DS; 3800; 99.12 × 7 (325.2 × 22.97); M (Sulzer); 10; ex *Wimpey Sealab* 1980; ex *Elizabeth Bowater* 1972; Converted from general cargo 1974 (Middle Docks); Helicopter platform aft

10010 **SALERNUM** It/It ('Navalmeccanica') 1956; Cbl; 2800; 104 × 5.7 (342 × 19); TSM (Fiat); 15

10020 **ASIA MARU** Ja/Ja (Hitachi) 1971; Con; 24300; 212 × 10.6 (699 × 35); M (B&W); 22.5

10030 **TOYAMA** No/Ja (Mitsui) 1972; Con; 52200; 275 × 11.1 (903 × 36.5); TrSM (B&W); 26.25; Lengthened by 15 m 1984. Drawing shows vessel prior to this

10040 **AUSTRALIAN EMBLEM** Au/Ja (Kawasaki) 1975; RoC/Con; 23200; 222.3 × 10.5 (731 × 35); M (MAN); 22.75; Stern doors
Sister:
10041 **AUSTRALIAN ESCORT** (Au) ex *James Cook* 1976

● 10050 **AUSONIA** It/It (Adriatico) 1957; PC; 11900; 159.3 × 6.5 (523 × 21.4); TST (Adriatico); 20.75

10060 **MEDITERRANEAN STAR** Gr/Br (H&W) 1950; P; 16300; 181.2 × 8.9 (595 × 29.2); TSM (B&W); 18.5; ex *Mediterranean Island* 1981; ex *Patris* 1980; ex *Bloemfontein Castle* 1959

10070 **RIVIERA** (Gr/Br (Vickers-Armstrongs) 1951; P; 13600; 157.3 × 7.3 (517 × 24); TST (Vickers-Armstrongs); 18; ex *Venus* 1978; ex *Varna* 1977; ex *Ocean Monarch* 1967

10080 **SANTA ROSA** US/US (Newport News) 1958; PC; 11400; 177.9 × 8.3 (584 × 27.3); TST (GEC); 20

★10090 **VOLKERFREUNDSCHAFT** DDR/Sw (Gotaverken) 1948; PC; 12100; 160.1 × 7.5 (525 × 24.8); TSM (Gotaverken); 19; ex *Stockholm* 1960

10100 **NOOR JEHAN** In/Sp (AESA) 1959; PC; 14200; 169.58 × 8.30 (556 × 27.23); TSM (Sulzer); 20; ex *Cabo San Vicente* 1975

★10120 **FELICITY** RC/Br (Readhead) 1956; CP; 5600; 137 × 7.6/8.9 (450 × 25/29.3); T (Readhead); 13.5; ex *Avis Ornis* 1970; ex *New York City* 1968

10130 **NEW YELLOW SEA** Pa/Ja (Mitsui) 1956; C; 4400; (27.11 × 7.44 (417 × 24.41); M (B&W); 17; ex *Yellow Sea* 1976; ex *Hallborg* 1975; ex *Milos* 1966

★10140 **LONG SHAN** RC/FRG (Bremer V) 1959; C; 3000/4900; 126.1 × 6.5/7.6 (414 × 21.6/25); M (Bremer V); 14.5; ex *Minshan* 1978; ex *Illstein* 1972
Sister:
10141 **MINTSUNG** (Pa) ex *Wiedstein* 1972

10170 **SIBA EDOLO** It/Br (Doxford) 1960; C; 5000; 134 × 8.4 (440 × 27.3); M (Doxford); —; ex *Capo San Marco* 1983; ex *Montcalm* 1971

10180 **KISO MARU** Ja/Ja (IHI) 1973; Con; 38500;

261 × 11.8 (857 × 38.6); M (—); —

★10220 **MILA GOJSALIC** Ys/FRG (Rhein Nordseew) 1960; CP; 4500/6600; 139 × 7.2/8.8 (455 × 23/28.9); M (MAN); 16.5; ex *Barberbrook* 1975; ex *Fernbrook* 1973
Sister:
10221 **RAS DEDGEN** (Et) ex *Barbergate* 1975; ex *Ferngate* 1973

10230 **DIMITRIOS P PAPASTRATIS** Gr/Br (Lithgows) 1959; C; 6000/8400; 147 × 7.9/9 (482 × 26/29); M (B&W); 14; ex *Ioannis* 1982; ex *Strathnevis* 1978; ex *Nurjehan* 1975; ex *Advocate* 1973; ex *Nurjehan* 1971

10240 **RONSON** Gr/Br (Swan Hunter & WR) 1963; C; 6100; 142 × 8 (465 × 26.1); M (Sulzer); 15.5; ex *Ahmadu Bello* 1981
Sister:
10241 **RONHILL** (Gr) ex *Nnamdi Azikiwe* 1981

★10250 **WALTER DEHMEL** DDR/DDR (Mathias-Thesen) 1963; FT; 2900; 85.3 × 5.3 (280 × 17.6); M (Dieselmotorenwerk Rostock); 13.5
Sisters (DDR flag):
★10251 **BERNHARD KELLERMANN**
★10252 **PETER KAST**
★10253 **PETER NELL**
★10254 **RUDOLF LEONHARD**

★10260 **BURAN** Pd/Pd (Gdanska) 1972; FC; 2900/5100; 120 × —/7.3 (92 × —/24); M (B&W); 18; **'B 433'** type
Sisters (Pd flag):
★10261 **HALNIAK**
★10262 **LEWANTER**

★10270 **HANOI** Pd/Pd (Gdanska) 1960; CP; 6900; 154 × 8.3 (505 × 27.4); M (Sulzer); 15.5; **'B 54'** type
Sisters:
★10271 **PEKIN** (Pd)
★10272 **PHENIAN** (Pd)
Similar:
★10273 **ZHEN XING** (RC) ex *Yi Xing* 1982; ex *Konopnicka* 1979
★10274 **CHI CHENG** (RC) ex *Internacional* 1979; ex *Guo Ji* 1963
★10275 **GONZALEZ LINES** (Cu)
★10276 **COMMANDANTE CAMILO CIENFUEGOS** (Cu)

★10280 **ROMER** Pd/Pd (Szczecinska) 1964; CP; 5600; 146 × 7.6 (479 × 25.1); M (Sulzer); 16.25; **'B 516'** type
Similar (goalpost abaft superstructure):
★10281 **HENRYK JENDZHA** (Pd)

● ★10290 **VISHVA VIBHUTI** In/Pd (Gdynska) 1966; C; 6100/9000; 153 × 7.7/8.9 (500 × 25.4/29); M (Sulzer); —; **'B 42'** type
Sisters (In flag):
10291 **VISHVA MAHIMA**
10292 **VISHVA KALYAN**
10293 **VISHVA RAKSHA**

● ★10310 **KOROTAN** Ys/Ys ('Uljanik') 1960; CP; 5800/8600; 149 × —/9.2 (488 × —/29.1); M (B&W); 14.5; ex *Trbovlje* 1960
Sisters:
★10311 **GORANKA** (Ys)
10313 **SAMUDRA JYOTI** (In) ex *Ratna Usha* 1980; ex *Jala Ratna Usha* 1964; ex *Ratna Usha* 1963; ex *Zrennanin* 1961

10320 **NEW YELLOW SEA** Pa/Ja (Mitsui) 1956; C; 4400; 127.11 × 7.44 (417 × 24.41); M (B&W); 17; ex *Yellow Sea* 1976; ex *Hallborg* 1975; ex *Milos* 1966

★10350 **STEFAN CZARNIECKI** Pd/De (Nakskov) 1967; CP; 6900/10200; 154 × 7.9/8.5 (504 × 26/28); M (Sulzer); 16
Sisters (Pd flag):
★10351 **GRUNWALD**
★10352 **WESTERPLATTE**

● 10360 **ANNA A** Gr/Ne ('De Schelde') 1957; C; 10400; 157 × 9.6 (516 × 31.5); M (Sulzer); 16; ex *Artemidi IV* 1982; ex *Limnos* 1976; ex *Argo Ollandia* 1975; ex *Santa Alexandra* 1973; ex *Argo Ollandia* 1968
Sisters:
10361 **LANKA RATNA** (Sr) ex *Argo Chios* 1975; ex *Santa Fotini* 1973; ex *Argo Chios* 1969
10362 **AZOV SEA** (Pa) ex *Island Mariner* 1973
10363 **KOTA ABADI** (Sg) ex *Argo Ellas* 1975; ex *Santa Anna* 1973; ex *Argo Ellas* 1969
Similar:
10365 **KATIE** (Gr) ex *Katwijk* 1979
★10366 **CHANGMING** (RC) ex *Island Skipper* 1976
10367 **ALEXANDROS** (Gr) ex *Atlas*; ex *Argo Afaia*
10368 **AL KULSUM** (Pk) ex *Dorthe Oldendorff* 1970

10370 **LANKA RANI** Sr/Ne ('De Schelde') 1961; C; 7100/10400; 157 × 8.4/9.6 (517 × 27.6/31.3); M

(Sulzer); 16 ex *Finnamore Valley* 1971

● 10410 **ARABIAN MERCHANT** Ma/Br (Bartram) 1961; C; 6300/8500; 145 × 8.3/9.1 (477 × 27.6/30); M (Gotaverken); 14.5; ex *Johanna U.* 1983; ex *Australind* 1975

★10430 **ANADYR** Ru/Pd (Gdanska) 1952; TC/C; 3600; 108 × 6.7 (355 × 22); R & LPT ('Zgoda'); 11.5; **'B 31'** type
Sisters (Ru flag):
★10431 **ADAM MITSKEVICH**
★10432 **ALEKSEY CHIRIKOV**
★10433 **BELORUSSIYA**
★10434 **CHEREMKHOVO**
★10435 **JAN ANVELT**
★10436 **YULIYA ZHEMAYTE**
★10437 **KEMEROVO**
★10438 **KHUDOZHNIK V KRAYNEV**
★10439 **KUZBASS**
★10441 **MIKHAIL LAZAREV**
★10443 **NOVAYA ZEMLYA**
★10444 **PETROPAVLOVSK-KAMCHATSKIY**
★10445 **PRIMORSK**
★10449 **SARATOV**
★10451 **SEVEROMORSK**
★10452 **SHAKHTY**
★10453 **STEPAN KRASHENNINNIKOV**
★10454 **ULYANOVSK**
★10455 **VASILIY GOLOVNIN**
★10457 **VORKUTA**
★10458 **VYACHESLAV SHISHKOV**
★10459 **KADIEVKA**
(RC flag):
★10460 **HE PING 23** ex *Zhan Dou 23*; ex *Hoping 23* 1967; ex *Radom* 1956
★10461 **HE PING 24** ex *Zhan Dou 24*; ex *Hoping 24* 1967; ex *Lodz* 1956
★10462 **HOPING SAN SHI CHI** ex *Ostroda* 1957
★10463 **HOPING SAN SHI CHIU** ex *Rozewie* 1957
★10464 **HOPING SAN SHI ER** ex *Kalisz* 1956
★10465 **HOPING SAN SHI PA** ex *Karwia* 1957

10490 **NEW HAINING** Pa/FRG (Kieler H) 1960; CP; 5100/7200; 138 × 7.2/8.6 (453 × 23.6/28.1); M (MAN); 16.5; ex *Desanmar* 1982; ex *Ebel* 1980; ex *Birgitte Skou* 1980
Sister:
★10491 **SHU YU QUAN** (RC) ex *Cherry Crystal* 1980; ex *Maren Skou* 1980

10510 **PANCHDEEP** In/In (Hindustan) 1959; C; 5400; 118 × 7.5 (387 × 24.7); M (MAN) 13; ex *Indian Industry* 1981

★10520 **SONG GIANH** Vn/Hong Kong (Taikoo) 1955; C; 3900/5700; 128.66 × —/7.34 (422 × —/24.08); M (Doxford); 14.5; ex *Kim Seng* 1977; ex *Fortune Glory* 1971; ex *Chungking* 1965

10530 **PRESIDENT TAFT** US/US (Ingalls SB) 1967; Con; 17300; 202.4 × 9.4 (664 × 30.10); T (GEC); 23; Lengthened and converted from cargo 1972
Sisters (US flag):
10531 **PRESIDENT VAN BUREN**
10532 **PRESIDENT FILLMORE**
10533 **PRESIDENT McKINLEY**

★10535 **DELTA DUNARII** Rm/Pd (Gdanska) 1968; FT; 2700; 88.02 × 5.60 (289 × 18.37); M (Fiat); 13.5; **'B 22'** type
Sister:
★10536 **MAREA NEAGRA** (Rm)

★10540 **REGULUS** Pd/Pd (Gdanska) 1976; FT; 2600; 89.06 × 5.6 (292.19 × 18.37); M (Sulzer); 17.75; **'B414'** type
Sisters (Pd flag):
★10542 **SAGITTA**
★10543 **ANTARES**
★10544 **ARCTURUS**
★10545 **INDUS**

★10560 **QIANJIN** RC/Pd (Szczecinska) 1965; C; 6900; 154 × 8.3 (505 × 27.4); M (Sulzer); 15; ex *Henryk Jendza*; **'B454'** type

★10570 **FRANCESCO NULLO** Pd/Pd (Gdynska) 1964; C; 5700/8600; 152.6 × 7.7/8.8 (501 × 25.4/29); M (Sulzer); 15.5; **'B41'** type
Sister (Pd flag):
★10571 **LENINO**
Similar (larger funnel) (Pd flag):
★10572 **ALEKSANDER ZAWADSKI**
★10573 **GWARDIA LUDOWA**
★10574 **LENINGRAD**
★10575 **JOZEF WYBICKI** ex *Sebastian Klonowicz*
★10576 **PIOTR DUNIN**
★10577 **SMOLNY**
★10578 **STANISLAW DUBOIS**
(RC flag) (some may have small funnels):
★10580 **HAINING**
★10581 **JINING**

★10582 **XINGNING**
★10583 **YONGNING**

★10590 **BAO SHAN** RC/FRG (Howaldts) 1959; CP; 6500/8300; 155 × 8/9 (510 × 26/30); M (Howaldts); 17.5; ex *Minglang* 1975; ex *Worms* 1972
Sisters:
★10591 **XIUSHAN** (RC) ex *Minglao* 1975; ex *Wiesbaden* 1972
★10592 **YUSHAN** (RC) ex *Mingwei* 1975; ex *Wein* 1972; One of these ships may have been renamed **A SHAN**

10600 **ANGELIKI S** Gr/Br (A&P) 1962; C; 10700; 160 × 9.9 (526 × 32.3); M (Sulzer); 16.5; ex *Ilios* 1983; ex *Vasilios R* 1977

★10610 **SIMFEROPOL** Ru/Pd (Gdanska) 1962; C; 6600/9200; 155 × 7.8/8.9 (508 × 26/29.3); M (Sulzer); 15; 'B43' type
Sisters (Ru flag):
★10611 **SALAVAT**
★10612 **SEMIPALATINSK**
★10613 **SLAVSK**
★10614 **SLUTSK**
★10615 **SOVIETSK**

●10620 **PINDAROS** Gr/Sw (Uddevalla) 1963; C; 7900/10700; 162 × 8.7/9.5 (531 × 28.3/31); M (Gotaverken); 16.5; ex *London Craftsman* 1976
Sisters:
10621 **PLOTINOS** (Gr) ex *London Citizen* 1977
10622 **SKAROS** (Cy) ex *Olympiakos* 1983; ex *Agia Marina* 1981; ex *London Statesman* 1979
Similar:
10623 **RIVA** (Gr) ex *London Banker* 1973
10624 **SINGAPORE FORTUNE** (Sg) ex *London Advocate* 1973
★10625 **LIMING** (RC) ex *London Tradesman* 1964

10630 **MUKAIRISH ALTHALETH** Si/De (B&W) 1947/70; LS; 8000; 165.03 × 9.23 (541.44 × 30.28); TSM (B&W); —; ex *Al Messilah* 1981; ex *Linda Clausen* 1974; ex *Kambodia* 1969; ex *Brandenburg* 1946; Converted from general cargo. Side doors

10640 **JUDITH P** Pa/Pd (Szczecinska) 1958; C/TC; 2600; 95 × 5.5 (311 × 18.1); R ('Zgoda'); 12; ex *Homer* 1981; ex *Kalliopi* 1979; ex *Opole* 1977; 'B 32' type. Others of this type may also have this sequence see **BIELSKO** under KMFMK

10660 **MIMOSA TRADER** Gr/Ne (Boele's Sch.) 1957; CP; 5300; 138 × 7.4 (455 × 24.6); M (B&W); 16; ex *Straat Johore* 1978

●10670 **MANICA** Po/FRG (Deutsche Werft) 1961; CP; 9200; 157 × 9.2 (516 × 30.7); M (MAN); 18; ex *Kulmerland* 1971
Sisters (some may have a tall mast from bridge):
10671 **MUNSTERLANDES** (Gr) ex *Munsterland* 1979
10672 **CONGO** (Po) ex *Nurnberg* 1971
10673 **MUXIMA** (Po) ex *Wolfsburg* 1971
★10674 **N'GOLA** (An) ex *Blumenthal* 1971

10680 **SAUDI YENBO** UAE/Ne (Giessen-de Noord) 1964; C; 7300/9900; 165 × 8/9 (541 × 26/29.8); M(Stork); 19; ex *Nedlloyd Korea* 1983; ex *Straat Korea* 1977; ex *Kloosterkerk* 1971
Sister:
10681 **SAUDI AL GHASIM** (Si) ex *Nedlloyd Kobe* 1983; ex *Straat Kobe* 1977; ex *Kouderkerk* 1971

●10700 **MECIS FLAG** Le/Ys ('Uljanik') 1966; CP; 3300/5200; 120 × 7.2/— (395 × 23/—); M (B&W) 15.5; ex *Kordofan* 1980
Sisters:
10701 **MECIS PIONEER** (Le) ex *El Gezira* 1980
10702 **MECIS LEADER** (Le) ex *Sennar* 1980

10710 **AFRICA** Gr/Be (Boel) 1965; Fru; 5100; 134 × 6.6 (441 × 21.6); M (MAN); 20; ex *Frubel America* 1980
Sister:
10711 **ORIENTAL FRUIT** (Pa) ex *Frubel Europa* 1979

★10720 **YANIS RAYNIS** Ru/Pd (Gdanska) 1971; R; 5200; 119.4 × 7.3 (393 × 23.11); M (B&W); 19; 'B 443' Type
Sisters (Ru flag):
★10721 **ALEKSANDRA KOLLONTAY**
★10722 **HENRI BARBUSSE**
★10723 **LARISA REYSNER**
★10724 **KARLIS ZIEDINS**
★10725 **KLARA ZETKIN**
★10726 **MARINA RASKOVA**
★10727 **OTOMAR OSHKALIN**
★10728 **POLINA OSIPENKO**
★10729 **YANIS LENTSMANIS**
★10730 **JAKOV ALKSNIS**
★10731 **ZENTA OZOLA**

★10740 **NIKOLAY KOPERNIK** Ru/Pd (Gdanska)

1974; R; 6400; 140 × 7.7 (460 × 25.6); M (Sulzer); 21.75; 'B 437' type
Sisters (Ru flag) (Some have a light pole foreward):
★10741 **ARISTARKH BELOPOLSKIY**
★10742 **FEDOR BREDIKHIN**
★10743 **MIKHAIL LOMONOSOV**
★10744 **PAVEL PARENAGO**
★10745 **PAVEL SHTERNBERG**
★10746 **VASILIY FESENKOV**
★10747 **VASILIY STRUVE**
★10748 **IVAN POLZUNOV**
★10749 **IVAN KULIBIN**
★10750 **PROFESSOR POPOV**
★10751 **ILYA METCHNIKOV**
★10752 **AKADEMIK ARTOBOLEVSKIY**
★10753 **AKADEMIK KHOKHLOV**
10754 **RIO SIXAOLA** (Pa) ex *Rio Ulua* 1980
10755 **RIO CUYAMEL** (Ho)
10756 **RIO SULACO** (Ho)
(Pd flag):
★10757 **GDYNSKI KOSYNIER**
★10758 **DZIECI POLSKIE**
★10759 **ZYRARDOW**

★10760 **BURAN** Pd/Pd (Gdanska) 1972; FC; 2900/5100; 120 × —/7.3 (392 × —/24); M (B&W); 18; 'B 433' type
Sisters (Pd flag):
★10761 **HALNIAK**
★10762 **LEWANTER**

10770 **DOLPHIN IV** Gr/FRG (Deutsche Werft) 1956; P; 8900; 153 × 8 (501 × 26.7); T (Allgemeine); 19; ex *Ithaca* 1979; ex *Amelia de Mello* 1972; ex *Zion* 1966

★10780 **OKAH** Ru/— 1959; P; 800; 61 × — (200 × —); M; 12

10790 **DON EUSEBIO** Pi/Ja (Onomichi) 1969; PC; 3600; 111.2 × 5.5 (365 × 18); M (Sulzer); 18.5; ex *Tokyo Maru* 1978

10800 **MANILA CITY** Pi/Ja (Mitsubishi HI) 1970; P; 3000; 106 × 4.6 (349 × 15.3); TSM (Mitsubishi); 20.5; ex *Nihon Maru* 1976

★10810 **SEJWAL** Pd/Pd (Gdynska) 1968; FT; 2500; 87 × 5.3 (286 × 17.7); M (Sulzer); 13.5; 'B 18' type
Sisters (Pd flag):
★10811 **FOKA**
★10812 **KASZALOT**
★10813 **NARWAL**
★10814 **HOMAR**
★10815 **ORKA**
★10816 **FINWAL**
★10817 **LANGUSTA**
★10818 **PLETWAL**

●10850 **d'IBERVILLE** Ca/Ca (Davie SB) 1953; IB; 5700; 94.8 × 9.2 (311 × 30.5); TSR (Unaflow); 16

10860 **JOHN A MACDONALD** Ca/Ca (Davie SB) 1960; IB/P; 6200; 96 × 8.5 (315 × 28.2); TrSD-E (Fairbanks, Morse); 15.5; Helicopter deck; Canadian Coast Guard

★10880 **MALAKHOV KURGAN** Ru/De (Aalborg) 1953; FC; 3700/5500; 124 × 5.9/7.4 (407 × 19.6/24.5); M (B&W); 17.5; ex *Dolores* 1964; ex *Brazilian Reefer* 1963
Sisters (Ru flag):
★10881 **MATROS KOSHKA** ex *Domingo* 1964; ex *Mexican Reefer* 1964
★10882 **SLAVA SEVASTOPOLYA** ex *Darien* 1964; ex *Peruvian Reefer* 1963

●10910 **MINOTAURUS** Gr/Sp ('Bazan') 1957; C; 4800; 132 × 7.5 (437 × 24.8); TSM (Sulzer); 16.5; ex *Cefallonian Wave* 1980; ex *Cabo Santa Marta* 1979; ex *Pedro de Valdivia*

10920 **M ALEXAND** Pa/Ne (Rotterdamsche) 1951; CP; 2100/3400; 107.5 × 6/— (353 × 19.7/—); M (MAN); 13; ex *Lady Salla* 1977; ex *Nausika* 1974; ex *Kastor* 1970; ex *Rimon* 1965
Sister:
10921 **ATHENA** (Gr) ex *Kronios* 1970; ex *Tamar* 1965
Similar:
10922 **SEA LORD** (Pa) ex *Giannoula K* 1983; ex *Cefallonian Sea* 1981; ex *Degero* 1977
10923 **CEFALLONIAN SKY** (Gr) ex *Eckero* 1977
Similar (larger):
★10924 **PULA** (Ys)
★10925 **ZADAR** (Ys)

●10930 **LINK LOVE** Gr/Br (Burntisland) 1962; C; 9000; 147.22 × 8.90 (483 × 29.2); M (Gotaverken); 15; ex *Margo* 1980

●10940 **ABU MISHARI AL KULAIB** Ku/Sp (Euskalduna) 1961; C; 3100; 105.72 × 5.9 (346.8 × 19.36); M (MAN); 15; ex *Arga* 1979

★10990 **LIKA** Ys/Ys ('3 Maj') 1957; C; 6000/8800; 146.01 × 7.86/— (479 × 25.79/—); M (Sulzer); 14

Sisters (Ys flag):
★10991 **DEBRALINA 1** ex *Petka* 1983
★10992 **SLAVONIJA**
★10993 **TREPCA**
★10994 **ZETA**

★11100 **NIKOLA TESLA** Ys/Ys ('Split') 1957; C; 5900/8600; 146 × 7.8/9 (479 × 25.8/29.5); M (B&W); 14

11110 **TAYGETUS** Ma/Ne (Boele's Sch) 1962; C; 7200/9600; 152.6 × 8.4/9.2 (508 × 27.6/30.3); M (B&W); 13; ex *Patagonia Argentina* 1983; ex *Hollands Dreef* 1972
Sisters:
11111 **AISHAH** (Pa) ex *Santiago* 1983; ex *Pampa Argentina* 1980; ex *Hollands Diep* 1970
11112 **AL FAHD** (Si) ex *Greenville* 1982; ex *Amstelhoek* 1973
11113 **SAKINA** (Pa) ex *Najma* 1982; ex *Harlandsville* 1982; ex *Hollands Duin* 1973
11114 **KHATIJAH** (My) ex *Bayville* 1983; ex *Amstelstad* 1977

●11130 **LANKA SHANTHI** Sr/Be (Boel) 1964; C; 6500/9500; 146.9 × 8/9.2 (482 × 25.1/30.2); M (Sulzer); 14.5; ex *Heering Elsie* 1973; ex *Loucas N* 1970
Sister:
11131 **IRENE D** (Gr) ex *Master Nicos* 1980

★11140 **THEODOR STORM** DDR/Be (Boel) 1966; R; 5000; 135 × 6.8 (443 × 22.3); M (MAN); 21
Sister:
★11141 **THEODOR FONTANE** (DDR)

11150 **REEFER MANGGIS** Sg/No (Drammen) 1977; R; 5000/6900; 144.5 × 9 (474 × 29.8); M (Sulzer); 22.75; ex *Wild Gannet* 1983; 'DRAMMEN' type
Sister:
11151 **REEFER NANGKA** (Sg) ex *Wild Grebe* 1982

11160 **EMANUEL** Sg/No (Drammen) 1976; R; 5100/7000; 144.2 × 8.99 (473.1 × 29.49); M (Sulzer); 22.75; 'DRAMMEN' type

11170 **IRISEVERETT** Li/Be (Boel) 1967; R; 5200; 135.1 × 6.8 (443 × 22.4); M (MAN) 21; ex *Coyoles* 1982; ex *Frubel Asia* 1977
Sisters (Li flag):
11171 **MALLOWEVERETT** ex *Estrella* 1982; ex *Frubel Africa*
11172 **LAURELEVERETT** ex *Guayaquil* 1981; ex *Frubel Oceania*
11173 **COENTROEVERETT** ex *Santa Marta* 1982; ex *Frubel Prinses Paola*

●11190 **INTRA TRANSPORTER** Pa/FRG (A G 'Weser') 1953; C; 5600/8500; 143.1 × 8/9 (470 × 26.5/30); M (MAN); 13.75; ex *Dynamikos* 1981; ex *Freienfels* 1972

11210 **MISAMIS OCCIDENTAL** Pi/Ja (Hayashikane) 1970; PC; 1900; 88.9 × 4.9 (292 × 16.1); M (B&W); 18

11220 **HOKUTO MARU** Ja/Ja (NKK) 1976; TS; 5900; 125 × 5.8 (411 × 19); T (Kawasaki); 18
Similar (centre-line kingpost forward):
1121 **TAISEI MARU** (Ja)

11230 **SHINTOKU MARU** Ja/Ja (NKK) 1962; TS; 3500; 100.8 × 5.1 (331 × 16.1); M (Kobe); 13

●11240 **CITY OF HYDRA** Gr/Br (Denny) 1955; F; 1000; 58.6 × 2.8 (192 × 9.2); TSM (Denny); 12.5; ex *Claymore* 1976

11250 **ROYAL ZULU** SA/Sp (U N de Levante) 1964; PC; 1200; 67.06 × 3.18 (220 × 10.43); TSM (MTM); 15.25; ex *Santa Maria de las Nieves* 1982

11260 **EDRA** It/It (Felszegi) 1962; F; 500; 64 × 2.7 (210 × 9); TSM (Fiat); —

11270 **AMARYLLIS** Ja/Ja (Kurushima) 1967; Sal/Tg; 1800; 73 × 6 (240 × 19.8); TSM (Mitsui); 13

11290 **TOULA** Sp/Sp (Barreras) 1963; FT; 1600; 73.9 × — (246 × —); M (Werkspoor); 12

★11300 **KOPET-DAG** Ru/Ru (Okean) 1970; FT; 3300; 107.5 × 6.2 (353 × 20.4); D-E (—); 13
Sisters (Ru flag):
★11301 **ALTAY**
★11302 **AMBARCHIK**
★11303 **ASKANIYA**
★11304 **BELOMORY**
★11305 **ELBRUS**
★11306 **GOLFSTRIM**
★11307 **KHOLMOGORY**
★11308 **KIVACH**
★11309 **PAMIR**
★11310 **PEVEK**
★11311 **PODMOSKOVYE**
★11312 **POLESYE**

★11313 **KARPATY**
★11314 **BEREZNIKI**
★11315 **NOKUYEV**
★11316 **KARAKUMY**
★11317 **VOLGOBALT**
★11318 **ANDREY ANDREYEV**
★11319 **RZHEV**
★11320 **KHIBINY**
★11321 **DIKSON**
★11322 **PRIKARPATYE**
★11323 **ZAKAVKAZYE**
★11324 **KOTELNICH**
★11325 **POVOLZHYE**
★11326 **KARPOGORY**
★11327 **PRIONEZHYE**
★11328 **VERKHOYANY**
★11329 **ZAVOLZHYE**
★11330 **VALDAY**

★11333 **BALAKHNA** Ru/Ru (—) 1981; FT; 3400; 103.71 × 5.80 (340 × 19.03); M (CKD Praha); 14
Sisters (Ru flag—some have more rake on stem):
★11334 **BAKLANOVO**
★11334/1 **ALEKSANDR TYURIN**
★11334/2 **ALEKSEY STAKHANOV**
★11334/3 **BABAYEVSK**
★11335 **BABYKINO**
★11335/1 **BAGANOVO**
★11335/2 **BAGAREVO**
★11335/3 **BAYEVO**
★11335/4 **KAPITAN REDKOKASHA**
★11336 **MYS ZOLOTOY**
★11336/1 **PULKOVSKIY MERIDIAN**
★11336/2 **NOVOURALSK**
★11336/3 **SLAVYANSKIY**

★11337 **AQUILA** Pd/Pd (Polnocna) 1981; FT; 3700; 102.6 × 5.97 (337 × 19.59); M (Sulzer); 16.25; **'B407'** type
Sisters (Pd flag):
★11338 **CASSJOPEJA**
★11339 **AQUARIUS**

11340 **AMERICAN ENVOY** US/US (Ingalls SB) 1972/77; Con; 31000; 247.81 × 10.08 (813.02 × 33.07); T (Westinghouse); 23; ex Austral Envoy 1983; Lengthened 1977; This vessel was lengthened again in 1983. The drawing shows it before this. Sisters also lengthened
Sisters (US flag):
11341 **AMERICAN ENTENTE** ex Austral Entente 1984
11342 **AMERICAN PIONEER** ex Austral Pioneer 1984
11343 **AMERICAN PURITAN** ex Austral Puritan 1984

11350 **AMERICAN MARKETER** US/US (Ingalls SB) 1973; Con; 21200; 203.7 × 9.6 (669 × 31.5); T (Westinghouse); 23; ex Austral Ensign 1981
Sister (US flag):
11352 **AMERICAN MERCHANT** ex Austral Endurance 1981
Similar (US flag):
11352 **PRESIDENT JEFFERSON**
11354 **PRESIDENT PIERCE**
11355 **PRESIDENT JOHNSON**

11360 **SANTA PAULA** US/US (Todd) 1962; Con; 16500; 203.6 × 19.2 (668 × 33.4); T (GEC); 20; ex President Eisenhower 1983; ex Philippine Mail 1975; Lengthened and converted from a 'C.6' type cargo vessel 1972
Sisters (US flag):
11361 **PRESIDENT KENNEDY** ex Oregon Mail 1975
11363 **PRESIDENT TRUMAN** ex Japan Mail 1975

11370 **HUDAIBAH** Pa/FRG (Flensburger) 1952; C; 8800; 143.5 × 8.5 (471 × 27.1); M (MAN); 13; ex Alexa IV 1982; ex Alexa 1981; ex Democritos 1973; ex Julia 1967

★11380 **BOROVICHI** Ru/Ru ('Zhdanov') 1965; RS; 5300; 122 × 4.7 (400 × 15.3); M (B&W); 15; Missile tracking vessel. Converted from cargo ship 1967
Sisters (Ru flag):
★11381 **KEGOSTROV**
★11382 **MORZHOVETS**
★11383 **NEVEL**

11400 **SOZER BIRADERLAR** Tu/Sw (Oskarshamns) 1946; CP; 3700; 104.5 × 6.3 (343 × 20.8); R & LPT (Rhein Metall-Borsig); 10; ex Odemis 1976; ex Heimdal 1946

11410 **DHARINI** In/Ca (Foundation Mar) 1944; FA; 2900; 100 × 5.8 (324 × 19); R (—); 9; ex La Petite Hermine; ex Ketowna Park 1953; Converted 1960 from cargo ship. Indian Navy

11420 **TAISEI MARU** Ja/Ja (Mitsubishi J) 1948; TS; 2500; 95.2 × 4.5 (309 × 14.1); T (Nippon Hatsudoki); 10.5; ex Otaru Maru 1953

★11430 **CHULYMLES** Ru/Ru ('Zhdanov') 1963; C; 4500; 122 × 6.78 (400 × 22.24); M (B&W); 14.5
Sisters (Ru flag):
★11432 **ISAKOGORKA**
★11433 **IVAN CHERNYKH**
★11434 **KILDIN**
★11436 **KRASNAYA GORKA**
★11438 **NISHNIJ TAGIL**
★11439 **NOVAYA LADOGA**
★11440 **NOVAYA ZEMLYA**
★11441 **OKA**
★11442 **PORKHOV**
★11443 **SANGARLES**
★11445 **TAYMYR**
★11446 **VASYA ALEKSEEV**
★11447 **VOSKHOD**
★11448 **VOSTOK 2**
★11449 **VOSTOK 5**
★11450 **VOSTOK 6**
★11451 **VYTEGRA**
★11452 **YAMAL**
★11453 **ZOLOTITZA**

★11460 **BASKUNCHAK** Ru/Ru ('Zhdanov') 1964; RS; 4900; 122.1 × 4.3 (400.3 × 14); M (B&W); 15, ex Vostok 4; Modified cargo vessels. Helicopter deck
Sisters (Ru flag):
★11461 **APSHERON** ex Tosnoles
★11462 **DAURIYA** ex Suzdal
★11463 **DIKSON** ex Vagales
★11464 **DONBASS** ex Kirishi
★11465 **SEVAN** ex Vyborgles
★11466 **TAMAN** ex Vostok 3

11470 **POSEIDONIA** Cy/Br (Denny) 1948; P; 3800; 193.6 × 4.4 (340 × 14.8); TSM (Sulzer); 17; ex Innisfallen I 1969; ex Innisfallen 1969; After-superstructure modified and docking bridge removed c. 1980

11480 **FARID M** Le/Sw (Oskarshamns) 1954; C; 2000; 90.5 × 5.3 (297 × 17.5); R (Oskarshamns); 11; ex Afami Star 1980; ex Elenitsa S 1978; ex Vaigu 1973; ex Malla 1966; ex Sinikka 1959; ex Gundel 1958; ex Nordanvik 1958

★11490 **INDIGA** Ru/Fi (Valmet) 1965; C/TC; 2900; 102 × 6 (334 × 19.6); M (B&W); 13.75
Sisters (Ru flag):
★11491 **JANALES**
★11492 **KHATANGALES**
★11493 **KOSTROMALES**
★11494 **KODINO**
★11495 **NEVALES**
★11496 **OLYUTORKA**
★11497 **DIKSON**
★11498 **KOLGUYEV**
★11499 **PERVOURALSK**
★11500 **SALDUS**
★11501 **SHEKSNALES**
★11502 **ZEYALES**
★11503 **KAMALES**

11520 **PANKY** Pa/FRG (Kroegerw) 1958; C; 2300; 86.8 × 5.5 (285 × 18.4); M (MWM); 11.25; ex Noren 1971

●11530 **IONIAN SPIRIT** Ma/FRG (O&K) 1958; C; 2400/4000; 113 × 6.1/7.3 (370 × 20/24); M (MAN) 12.5; ex Cefallonian Spirit 1982; ex Rugen; ex Marivia 1963
Sisters:
11531 **LAMBROS** (Cy) ex Transword Sailor 1983; ex Varild 1977
11532 **SING TAO** (Sg); ex Lobiva 1972; ex Georgia 1961

●11540 **MALDIVE PEARL** Mv/Br (H Robb) 1956; C; 3100; 107 × 6.2 (351 × 20.3); M (Sulzer); 13.5 ex Climax Pearl 1981; ex City of Izmir 1975; ex Flaminian 1974

11550 **PRESIDENT TAFT** US/US (Ingalls SB) 1967; Con; 17300; 202 × 9.3 (664 × 30.8); T (GEC); converted from cargo ship and lengthened 1972
Sisters:
11551 **PRESIDENT VAN BUREN** (US)
11552 **PRESIDENT FILLMORE** (US)
11553 **PRESIDENT MCKINLEY** (US)

11560 **SIR ROBERT BOND** Ca/Ca (Port Weller) 1975; RoC/TF; 10400; 135.34 × 5.11 (444.03 × 16.77); TSM (Ruston Paxman); 17; stern door had some conversion work around 1978 which may have altered appearance

11570 **RECORDER** Br/Br (Swan Hunter & WR) 1954; Cbl; 3300; 103.6 × 5.5 (340 × 18.6); TrS (Swan Hunter & WR); 11

★11580 **KOMETA** Ru/Pd (Gdanska) 1962; FT; 2900; 83. × 5.5 (273 × 18); **'B.26' type** (early version)
Sisters (Ru flag):
★11581 **GRIGORIY POLUYANOV**
★11582 **ILYA KATUNIN**

★11583 **KILDIN**
★11584 **KOSMOS**
★11585 **KOLSKIY**
★11586 **MIKHAIL IVCHENKO**
★11587 **OLENEGORSK**
★11588 **PLANETA**
★11589 **PLUTONIY**
★11590 **PERLAMUTR**
★11591 **POLYARNYY**
★11592 **REVOLYUTSIYA**
★11593 **RYBACHIY**
★11594 **TRALFLOT**
★11595 **VOSKHOD**
★11596 **VSPOLOKH**
★11597 **ZARNITSA**
★11598 **BISON**
★11599 **LUNJ**
★11600 **MUROMSK**
★11601 **PARALLAKS**
★11602 **KIROVSK** ex Tur
★11603 **OLENTUY**
★11604 **ONEKOTAN**
★11605 **SIYANIE**
The following are converted to Fishery Research Trawlers (Ru flag):
★11606 **PROGRESS**
★11607 **NIKOLAY KONONOV**
★11608 **POLYARNOYE SIYANIE**

★11610 **SMOLNYY** Ru/Pd (Gdanska) 1969; FT; 2900; 8.32 × 5.5 (273 × 18); M (Sulzer); 11.75; 'B.26' type (later version)
Sisters (Ru flag):
★11611 **POLOTSK**
★11612 **SELIGER**
★11613 **KAPITAN DEMIDOV**
★11614 **KRASNOPUTILOVETS**
★11615 **LAZURNYY**
★11616 **NOVOKUIBYSHEVSK**
★11617 **PINAGORIY**
★11618 **VASILIY KOSENKHOV**
★11619 **VAYGACH**
★11620 **SLAVGOROD**
★11621 **VYBORGSKAYA STORONA**
★11622 **VYMPEL**
★11623 **BOLSHEVIK**
★11624 **SEVERYANIN**
★11625 **ANATOLIY BREDOV**
★11626 **NIKYEL**
★11627 **TIMOFEY KHRYUKIN** ex Kapitan Demidov
★11628 **SULOY**
★11629 **ANTON LOPATIN**
★11630 **TOROS**
★11631 **SALYUT**
★11632 **NARVSKAYA ZASTAVA**
★11633 **ZODCHIY**
★11634 **LENINGRAD**
★11635 **ZELENETS**
Similar (pole foremast) (Ru flag):
★11636 **YURIY KOSTIKOV** (others may also have this feature)

★11640 **ANDROMEDA** Pd/Pd (Gdanska) 1964; FT; 2800; 85 × 5.5 (279 × 18); M ('Zgoda'); 12.5; **'B 15'** type
Sisters (Pd flag):
★11644 **MERKURY**
★11646 **JOWISZ**
★11649 **GENERAL RACHIMOW**
Sisters (Pe flag):
11650 **ANTLIA**
11652 **ARIES**
11653 **AURIGA**
11654 **FENIKS**
11655 **VIRGO**
Possible sister (Pe flag):
11656 **APUS**

11660 **COLUMBA** Pe/Pd (Gdanska) 1967; FT; 2300; 83 × 5.5 (270 × 18.1); M (Sulzer); 12.5; **'B 15'** type
Sisters:
11661 **CRATER** (Pe)
11662 **CYGNUS** (Pd)
★11663 **CENTAURUS** (Pd)
Probable sisters:
★11664 **CETUS** (Pd)
11665 **APUS** (Pe)

★11670 **VEGA** Pd/Pd (Gdanska) 1973; FT; 2700; 88 × 5.6 (289 × 18.8); M (Sulzer); 15; **'B 419'** type
Sisters (Pd flag):
★11672 **DENEBOLA**
★11673 **PERSEUS**
★11674 **GEMINI**
★11675 **SIRIUS**
(Rm flag):
★11676 **HARGHITA**
★11677 **IEZER**
★11678 **SEMENIC**
★11679 **CLABUCET**
★11681 **INAU**
★11682 **MINDRA**

★11690 **PROFESOR SIEDLECKI** Pd/Pd (Gdanska) 1971; ST/RS; 2800; 89.3 × 5.5 (293 × 18); D-E (Fiat); 14; **'B424'** type

★11695 **CARINA** Pd/Pd (Gdanska) 1967; FT; 2600; 87.97 × 5.60 (289 × 18.37); M (Fiat); 13; **'B22'** type

★11700 **RETEZATUL** Rm/Pd (Gdanska) 1972; FT; 2700; 88 × 5.6 (289 × 18.4); M (Fiat); 13.75; **'B 22'** type
Sisters (Rm flag):
★11702 **MOLDOVEANU**
★11703 **NEGOIU**
★11704 **SINOE** ex *Leo*
★11706 **CARAIMAN**
★11707 **CEAHLEAUL** launched as *Saturn*
★11708 **RAZELM** launched as *Lepus*
(Pd flag):
★11709 **TUCANA**
★11710 **LEPUS**
★11711 **LACERTA**
★11712 **SATURN**
★11713 **LYRA**
★11714 **TAURUS**
★11716 **LIBRA**

★11720 **TARUSA** Ru/Ru ('Chernomorskiy') 1974; FT; 2300; 83.27 × — (273 × —); M (Skoda); —
Sisters (Ru flag):
★11721 **BYKOVO**
★11722 **BYELOMORSK**
★11723 **LOVOZYERO**
★11724 **MYS GROTOVYY**
★11725 **MYS KURILSKIY**
★11726 **MYS LOPATKA**
★11727 **MYS PROKOFYEVA**
★11728 **MYS RATMANOVA**
★11729 **MYS TAYMYR**
★11730 **MYS VAYGACH**
★11731 **MYS VORONINA**
★11732 **NAROCH**
★11733 **NEVYANSK**
★11734 **BORISPOL**
★11735 **DOMODYEDOVO**
★11736 **KRONSHTADT**
★11737 **MYS ARKTICHESKIY**
★11738 **TORZHOK**
★11739 **SOLOVIETSKIY**
★11740 **SHEREMTYEVO**
★11741 **GEROI ZAPOLYARYA**
★11742 **BIRYUSINSK**
★11743 **VNUKOVO**
★11744 **NOVYY MIR**
★11745 **ZELEZNOGORSK**
★11746 **ZNAMYA POBEDY**
★11747 **30-LETIYE POBEDY**
★11748 **MYS BUDYONNOGO**
★11749 **MYS CHELYUSKIN**
★11750 **MYS FRUNZE**
★11751 **MYS KRONOTSKIY**
★11752 **MYS OTRADNYY**
★11753 **MYS VODOPADNYY**
★11754 **URGAL**
★11757 **KHAROVSK**
★11758 **TIKHOOKEANSKIY**
★11759 **TYNDA**
★11760 **MYS ILMOVYY**
★11761 **MYS KUZNETSOVA**
★11762 **MYS SILINA**
★11763 **MYS CHASOVOY**
★11764 **MYS CHAYKOVSKOGO**
★11765 **MYS GROZNYY**
★11766 **MYS SKALISTYY**
★11767 **MURMANSELD**
★11769 **VERKHOVINA**
★11770 **MYS SVOBODNYY**
★11772 **SOVGANSKIY KOMSOMOLETS**
★11773 **GANGUT**
★11774 **TSIMLYANSK**
★11775 **VYSOVSK**
★11776 **VYSHOGOROD**
★11777 **MYS TIKHIY**
★11778 **MYS DALNIY**
★11779 **NIKOLAYEVSKIY KORABEL**
★11780 **ANDREY MARKIN**
★11781 **ILYA VOLYNKIN**
★11782 **IYUN KORAN**
★11783 **TANTAL**
★11784 **XVI SYEZD PROFSOYUZOV**
★11785 **XVIII SYEZD VLKSM**
★11786 **MYS BABUSHKIN**
★11787 **MYS OSTROVSKOGO**
★11788 **MYS YUNONY**
Sisters (Iq flag):
11788/1 **FOREL** ex *Seversk* 1981
11788/2 **GATTAN** ex *Linakhamari* 1981
11789 **KEFAL** ex *Zashchitnik Zapolyarya* 1980
11789/1 **SHABOOT** ex *Desyataya Pyatiletka* 1977

★11790 **WLOCZNIK** Cy/Pd (Gdanska) 1975; FT; 2600; 88.5 × 5.6 (291 × 18.4); M (Sulzer); 17.75; **'B 414'** type

Sister:
★11791 **POLLUKS** (Pd)

★11800 **'ATLANTIK'** class Ru/DDR (Stralsund) 1966; FT; 2200; 82.1 × 5.1 (270 × 17); M (Liebknecht); 13.5; Built 1966-1977
Similar (Ru flag):
★11801 **AYU-DAG**
★11802 **AKHILLES**
★11803 **AKHTUBA**
★11804 **AKHUN**
★11805 **AKMOLINSK**
★11806 **AKUSTIK**
★11807 **ALKA**
★11808 **ALEKSANDROVSK**
★11809 **ALEKSEY BORDUNOV**
★11810 **ALMA**
★11811 **ALSU**
★11812 **AMDERMA**
★11813 **AMGA**
★11814 **ASPHERON**
★11815 **ARDATOV**
★11816 **ARGUN**
★11817 **ARMENIYA**
★11818 **ARTEK**
★11819 **ARZAMAS**
★11820 **ASTRONOM**
★11821 **ATOLL**
★11822 **AVIATOR**
★11823 **AY-PETRI**
★11824 **AZURIT**
★11825 **BALTA**
★11826 **BATUMI** ex *Askaniya*
★11827 **BAZALT**
★11828 **BEREZEN**
★11829 **BUREVESTNIK**
★11830 **BYELOVO** ex *Mongugay*
★11831 **DARYAL**
★11832 **DNEPRODZERZHINSK**
★11833 **DRUZHBA SSSR-GDR** ex *Krustalnyy*
★11834 **YEYSK** (or EYSK)
★11835 **FEDOR GLADKOV**
★11836 **GELIOGRAF**
★11837 **GEROI ADZHIMUSHKAYA**
★11838 **ILMEN**
★11839 **ILYICHYOVSK**
★11840 **IMERITI**
★11841 **IZMAIL**
★11842 **KAKHETI**
★11843 **KAZANTIP**
★11844 **KIROVOGRAD**
★11845 **KOBULETI** ex *Zaporozhye*
★11846 **KORUND**
★11847 **KVADRANT**
★11848 **LENINOGORSK**
★11849 **LIMAN**
★11850 **LVOV**
★11851 **M BORISOV** ex *Marksist*
★11852 **MEGANOM**
★11853 **MELITOPOL**
★11854 **METEORIT**
★11855 **MIKHAIL VIDOV** ex *Initsiator*
★11856 **MITRIDAT**
★11857 **NADEZHDA**
★11858 **NIKOLAY BROVTSYEV**
★11859 **NIKOLAYEV**
★11860 **OKTANT**
★11861 **OKTYABRSKOYE**
★11862 **OREL**
★11863 **ORLETS**
★11864 **ORLINOYE**
★11865 **PEREDOVIK**
★11866 **PETR LIZYUKOV**
★11867 **PISATEL**
★11868 **PITSUNDA**
★11869 **PLANERIST**
★11870 **PLUTON**
★11871 **POLEVOD**
★11872 **POLTAVA** ex *Kondor* 1979
★11873 **PRAVOVYED**
★11874 **PRILIV**
★11875 **PROLIV**
★11876 **PROMYSLOVIK**
★11877 **PROPAGANDIST**
★11878 **PROSVETITEL**
★11879 **PUBLIKIST**
★11880 **PYATIGORSK**
★11881 **POET**
★11882 **SADKO**
★11883 **SAKARTVELO**
★11884 **SALKHINO**
★11885 **SAPUN GORA**
★11886 **SERGEY KANDACHIK** ex *Alatau*
★11887 **SHVENTOY**
★11888 **SIVASH**
★11889 **SKALISTYY**
★11890 **SOKOLINOYE**
★11891 **SOINTSEDAR**
★11892 **SOPKA GEROYEV**
★11893 **SOYUZ**
★11894 **MIKHAIL KORNITSKIY** ex *Sozidatel*

★11895 **SUMY**
★11896 **TAGANROG**
★11897 **TAVRIDA**
★11898 **TIKHORETSK**
★11899 **TIMOFEY GORNOV**
★11900 **TSKHALTUBO**
★11901 **TULEN KABILOV**
★11902 **UGOLNYY**
★11903 **VASILY GOLOVKIN**
★11904 **VENERA IV**
★11905 **VOLKHOVSTROY**
★11906 **VOLNOMER**
★11907 **VZMORYE**
★11908 **YUKHAN SMUUL**
★11909 **YULIMISTE**
★11910 **YURIY MALAKHOV**
★11911 **YUTNIEKS**
★11912 **YUZHNOMORSK** ex *Tafuin*
★11914 **ZHEMAYTIYA**
★11915 **ZOLOTOY KOLOS**
The following are from a different yard (Mathias-Thesen) (Ru flag):
★11916 **AGATOVYY**
★11917 **ARAGONIT**
★11918 **BARIT**
★11919 **BOKSIT**
★11920 **DIONIS**
★11921 **DOLOMIT**
★11922 **IZUMRUDNYY**
★11923 **KALINOVO**
★11924 **KALTAN**
★11925 **KARAGACH**
★11926 **KAVRAY**
★11927 **KHRUSTALNYY**
★11928 **KREMEN**
★11929 **KLIMOVO**
★11930 **MAKELIS BUKA**
★11931 **MRAMORNY**
★11932 **PIRIT**
★11933 **RODONIT**
★11934 **RUBINOVYY**
★11935 **SEDA**
★11936 **TESEY**
★11937 **ZYEMCHUSNYY**
★11938 **SERDOLIK**
The following are Fishery Research Ships (some have alterations— extended boat deck etc) (Ru flag):
★11939 **ALBA**
★11940 **ASTEROID**
★11941 **ARTEMIDA**
★11942 **BAKHCHISARAY**
★11943 **CHATYR-DAG**
★11944 **EVRIKA**
★11945 **FIOLENT**
★11946 **GERAKL**
★11947 **KAMENSKOYE**
★11948 **KARA-DAG**
★11949 **KHRONOMETR**
★11950 **MILOGRADOVO**
★11951 **PROFESSOR**
★11952 **PROFESSOR MESYATSYEV**
★11953 **SHANTAR**
★11954 **ZUND**
★11955 **ZVEZDA KRIMA**
(Bu flag):
★11956 **ALKA**
★11957 **BEKAS**
★11958 **FLAMINGO**
★11959 **GLARUS**
★11960 **KONDOR**
★11961 **LIMOZA**
★11962 **LORNA**
★11963 **MELANITA**
★11964 **OLUSHA**
★11965 **PINGVIN**
★11966 **RALIDA**
★11967 **ZIKONIYA**
(Cu flag):
★11968 **PLAYA COLORADO**
★11969 **PLAYA DUABA**
★11970 **PLAYA GIRON**
★11971 **PLAYITAS** ex *Playa Larga* 1980
★11972 **PLAYA VARADERO** ex *Playa de Varadero* 1980
(Rm flag):
★11973 **IALOMITA**
★11974 **JIUL**
★11975 **MILCOV**
★11976 **MURES**
★11977 **NEAJLOV**
★11978 **SIRET**
★11979 **SOMES**
★11980 **TROTUS**

11990 **BRITISH VOYAGER** Br/Br (Simons) 1959; Submersible support ship; 3000; 83.8 × 7.3 (275 × 23.5); D-E (Ruston & Hornsby); —; ex *Vickers Voyager* 1980; ex *Fairtry II* 1972; Converted from trawler 1973

★11995 **PRIMORYE** Ru/Ru (—) —; RS; 3400 (displacement); 83.6 × 6.00 (275 × 19.69); M (—); 13;

Based on hull of 'Mayakovskiy' class trawler

★12000 **AKADEMIK KOROLYOV** Ru/DDR (Mathias-Thesen) 1967; RS; 5500; 124.3×6 (408×19.11); TSM (MAN); 18.15
Sisters (Ru flag) (These may vary slightly):
★12001 **AKADEMIK SHIRSHOV**
★12002 **PROFESSOR VISE**
★12003 **PROFESSOR ZUBOV**

★12010 **SOVIETSKIY SOYUZ** Ru/Ge (B+V) 1923; P; 23000; 205 × 9.6 (673×31.6); TST (B+V); 19.25; ex *Hansa* 1950; ex *Albert Ballin* 1935; Lengthened 1934

12030 **ROTTERDAM** NA/Ne (Rotterdamsche) 1959; P; 37800; 228 × 9 (749 × 29.8); TST ('De Schelde'); 21.5

★12035 **SHIJIAN** RC/RC (—) 1968; RS; 3000; 94.73 × 4.75 (311 × 15.58); M (—); 16

★12040 **PRIMORJE** Ys/Ys ('3 Maj') 1961; C; 7000/9400; 155 × 8.2 (509 × 26.11); M (Sulzer); 18.5

12070 **VISHVA VIVEK** In/FRG (A G 'Weser') 1959; C; 10800; 159×9.2 (522×30.4); M (MAN); 14.5; ex *Figaro* 1968

★12080 **VENICE** RC/Br (Gray) 1958; C; 6800/8500; 145.7 × —/9.1 (478 × —/30); M (B&W); 14.5; ex *Cleveland* 1964

12100 **SILVER CITY** Gr/FRG (A G 'Weser') 1960; C; 10600; 159.01 × 9.55 (521.7 × 31.33); M (MAN); 14.5; ex *Aristoklis* 1976; ex *Numerian* 1970
Similar:
12101 **PANAGHIA LOURION** (Gr) ex *Hadjitsakos* 1972
12102 **LAERTIS** (Gr) ex *Chios*

12110 **KUNUNGUAK** De/De (Frederikshavn) 1964; PC; 2300; 74.5 × 4 (244 × 13.1); M (B&W); 13

★12140 **CHAPAYEVSK** Ru/Pd (Szczecinska) 1957; C; 2500; 94.7 × 5.5 (308 × 18) R ('Zgoda'); 11.5; '**B 32**' type
Similar (Ru flag):
★12142 **CHERNOGORSK**
★12143 **CHERVONOGRAD**
★12144 **CHUGUYEV**
★12145 **CHIGIRIN**
★12146 **INGUL**
★12147 **KONSTANTINOVKA** ex *Christiakovo* 1965;
★12148 **PROLETARSK**
★12149 **SHAKHTERSK** ex *Terek;*
★12150 **TOM**
★12151 **UKRAINE**
(Al flag):
★12152 **LIRIJA**
★12153 **PARTIZANI**
(RC flag):
★12154 **HOPING SAN SHI WU** ex *Wicko* 1956
★12155 **ZHAN DOU 41** ex *Ho Ping 41* 1967; ex *Mamry* 1957
★12156 **HOPING SSU SHI** ex *Sniardwy* 1957
★12157 **HOPING SSU SHI ER** ex *Gardno* 1956
★12158 **NAN HAI 158** ex *Jamno* 1956
★12159 **HONG QI 159** ex *Nan Hai 159;* ex *Lebsko* 1957
(Pd flag):
★12161 **OPOLE**
(Eg flag):
12162 **SALEM B** ex *Benha* 1981
(Cy flag):
12166 **SUMMER BREEZE** ex *Malbork* 1976
(Br flag):
12167 **TULUM** ex *Gniezno*

12210 **SAONA** Pa/Fr (Bretagne) 1961; C; 3100; 99.2 × 5.7 (325 × 19); M (Pielstick); 19; ex *Demetris* 1981; ex *Reefer Princess* 1979; ex *Fontsy* 1979; ex *Boree* 1976
Sister:
12211 **AMALTHEA** (Pa) ex *Amalthee*

12220 **EMPIRE STATE** US/US (New York SB) 1952; PC/TS; 13300; 162.7 × 8. 4 (534 × 27. 6); T (GEC); 19.5 ex *Upshur* 1973; ex *President Hayes* 1952; Converted troopship

★12230 **KERCH** Ru/DDR (Stralsund) 1961; FT; 1900; 79.8 × 5.2 (262 × 17); M (Liebknecht); 12.5; 'TROPIK' class—1961-1966
Similar ('Ru flag):
★12231 **ABRANTSEVO**
★12232 **ALDERAMIN**
★12233 **ALIOT**
★12234 **ALMAK**
★12235 **ALUPKA**
★12236 **ALUSHTA**
★12237 **ANDROMEDA**
★12238 **ANTARES**
★12239 **ARGO**

★12240 **BALAKLAVA**
★12241 **BOLSHEVO**
★12242 **DENEB**
★12243 **DOBROVOLSK**
★12244 **ERIDAN**
★12245 **FEODOSIYA**
★12246 **GORECHJE**
★12247 **GURIYA**
★12248 **GURJEVSK**
★12249 **GURZUF**
★12250 **HERKULES**
★12251 **IVAN GOLUBETS**
★12252 **KAIRA**
★12253 **KALJMAR**
★12254 **KANOPUS**
★12255 **KARTLI**
★12256 **KASSIOPEYA**
★12257 **KLYAZMA**
★12258 **KOLKHIDA**
★12259 **KRASNODAR** ex *Morskaya Zvezda*
★12260 **KOREIZ**
★12261 **LANGUST**
★12262 **LEONID SEVRYUKOV** ex *Sarich*
★12263 **LIVADIYA**
★12264 **MTSKHETSA**
★12265 **MISKHOR**
★12266 **MIZAR**
★12267 **NADIR**
★12268 **N FILCHENKOV** —may be **NIKOLAY FILCHENKOV**
★12269 **NIKOLSK**
★12270 **OREANDRA**
★12271 **ORION**
★12272 **OZERSK**
★12273 **PALLADA**
★12274 **PERSEY**
★12275 **PORECHIE**
★12276 **POTI** ex *Lebedj*
★12277 **REPINO**
★12278 **ROSLAVL**
★12279 **RUSLAN**
★12280 **RUSTAVI**
★12281 **RUZA**
★12282 **SALGIR**
★12283 **SATURN**
★12284 **SEMYON EMELYANOV**
★12285 **SHOTA RUSTAVELI'**
★12286 **SIMEIZ**
★12287 **SIRIUS**
★12288 **SLAVSK**
★12289 **STRELETS**
★12290 **TBILISI**
★12291 **TSEFEY**
★12292 **TSENTAUR**
★12293 **VEGA**
★12295 **YALTA**
★12296 **YEVPATORIYE**
★12297 **YUZHNYY KREST**
★12298 **ZARAYSK**
The following have been converted to Research Ships (Ru flag):
★12299 **BELOGORSK**
★12300 **FLAMINGO**
★12301 **KALLISTO**
★12302 **KERCHENSKIY**
★12303 **KOMSOMOLETS** ex *Yuznyy Krest*
★12304 **KOZEROG**
★12305 **LESNOY**
★12306 **LIRA**
★12307 **NAUKA**
★12308 **PEGAS**
★12309 **RADUGA**
★12310 **SHEDAR**
(Bu flag):
★12311 **ALBATROS**
★12312 **BUREVESTNIK**
★12313 **FENIX**
★12314 **PELIKAN**
★12315 **TCHAIKA**
(Gh flag):
12316 **TROPIK**

★12320 '**PUSHKIN**' class. Ru/FRG (Kieler H) 1955/57; FT; 2500-3000; 84.5 × 5.5 (278 × 18); M (MAN); 12.5
Similar (Ru flag):
★12321 **DOSTOYEVSKIY**
★12324 **NOVIKOV-PRIBOY**
★12325 **SALTIKOV SHCHEDRIN**
★12326 **SERAFIMOVICH**
★12327 **YAROSLAVL**

★12340 Modified '**PUSHKIN**' class. Ru/FRG (Kieler H) 1955/57; FT; 2500/3000; 84.5 5.5 (278 × 18); M (MAN); 12.5
Similar (Ru flag):
★12341 **ASHKHABAD**
★12342 **CHEKHOV**
★12343 **DUSHANBE** ex *Stalinbad*
★12344 **IZHEVSK**
★12345 **KHABAROVSK**

★12346 **MURMANSK** ex *Voroshilovgrad*
★12347 **NIKOLAY OSTROVSKIY**
★12348 **SEVERNOYE SIYANIE**
★12349 **SVERDLOVSK**
★12350 **ULYANOVSK**
★12351 **ZAVOLZHSK**
★12352 **ZLATOUST**
★12353 **ZHIGULEVSK**

★12360 '**MAYAKOVSKIY**' class. Ru/Ru (—) 1958/59; FT; 3200; 84.7 × 5.6 (278 × 18.4); M (Skoda); 13.75; Distinguished from 'Modified Mayakovskiy class' by having a pole foremast
Similar (Ru flag):
★12361 **BELINSKIY**
★12362 **CHERNYSHEVSKIY**
★12363 **GLEB USPENSKIY**
★12364 **GRIBOYEDOV**
★12365 **KOLTSOV**
★12366 **KOROLENKO**
★12367 **KRISHYANS VOLDEMARS**
★12369 **LEV TOLSTOY**
★12370 **MAYAKOVSKIY**
★12371 **RADISHEV**
★12372 **ZHUKOVSKIY**
(Gr flag):
12373 **ANASTASIOS** ex *Rea* 1979; ex *Krylov* 1965

★12380 Modified '**MAYAKOVSKIY**' class. Ru/Ru ('Chernomorskiy'/Baltiya/Nosenko) 1959/68; FT; 3200; 78 × 5.5 (256 × 18); M (Skoda); 12
Similar (Ru flag):
★12382 **AFANASAY NIKITIN**
★12383 **AGAT**
★12384 **ALFONSAS CHEPONIS**
★12385 **ALEKSANDR MAKSUTOV**
★12386 **ALEKSEY GMYREV**
★12387 **AIEKSEY MAKHALIN**
★12388 **ALMAZ**
★12389 **AMETIST**
★12390 **AMURSK**
★12391 **ANISIMOVKA** ex *Kangauz*
★12392 **ANTCHAR**
★12393 **ANTON TAMMSAARE**
★12394 **ANTS LAYKMAA**
★12395 **ARALSK** ex *Arsenyev*
★12396 **ARKOVO**
★12397 **ARSENEYEV**
★12398 **ASKOLD**
★12399 **ASTRA**
★12400 **AUGUST ALLE**
★12401 **BAKAYEVO** ex *Sidimi*
★12402 **BAYKAL**
★12403 **BARABASH**
★12404 **BARABINSK**
★12405 **BASARGIN**
★12406 **BERILL**
★12407 **BIKIN**
★12409 **BIRSHTONAS**
★12410 **BIRYUZA**
★12411 **BRASLAV**
★12412 **BRILLIANT**
★12413 **BOSFOR**
★12414 **BYELKINO** ex *Suyfun*
★12415 **DANKO**
★12416 **DIOMID**
★12417 **DMITRY FURMANOV**
★12418 **DRUSKININKAY**
★12419 **DZINTARYURA**
★12420 **EDUARD SYRMUS**
★12421 **EDUARD VEYDENBAUM**
★12422 **ELEKRENAY**
★12423 **ESTAFETA OKTYABRYA** ex *Uzbekistan*
★12424 **EVALD TAMMLAAN**
★12425 **FEDOR KRAYNOV**
★12426 **50 LET VLKSM**
★12427 **15 SYEZD VLKSM**
★12428 **GALIFAN BATARSHIN**
★12429 **GRANAT**
★12430 **GRIGORIY SHELIKOV**
★12431 **GUBERTAS BORISA**
★12432 **HANS LIEBERECHT**
★12433 **IMANT SUDMALIS**
★12434 **IOKHAN KYOLER**
★12435 **IONAS BILYUNAS**
★12436 **IOZAS VITAS**
★12437 **ITELMAN**
★12438 **IVAN DVORSKIY**
★12439 **IVAN CHERNOPYATKO**
★12440 **IVAN PANOV**
★12441 **IZUMRUD**
★12442 **JAAN KOORT**
★12443 **JAKHONT**
★12444 **JAKOV SMUSHKEVICH**
★12445 **JAN BERZIN**
★12446 **JAN FABRITSIUS**
★12447 **JAN RUDZUTAK**
★12448 **JOHANNES RUVEN**
★12449 **JUHAN SIUTISTE**
★12450 **JUOZAS VAREYKIS**
★12451 **JUOZAS GREYFENBERGIS**

★12452 KAAREL LIYMAND
★12453 KAPITAN ANDREI TARAN
★12454 KAROLIS POZHELA
★12455 KASKAD
★12456 KAZAKHSTAN
★12457 KHERMAN ARBON
★12458 KINGAN
★12459 KHRUSTAL
★12460 KOMMUNIST
★12461 KOMMUNIST UKRAINY
★12462 KOMSOMOL UKRAINI
★12463 KORALL
★12464 KRAYEV
★12465 KRISTALL
★12466 KRISTIONAS DONELAYTIS
★12467 KRISTYAN RAUD
★12468 KUBA
★12469 LAGUNA
★12470 LAZURIT
★12471 LEON PAEGLE
★12472 LESOGORSK
★12473 LINARD LAYTSEN
★12474 LYUDAS GIRA
★12475 MALAKHIT
★12476 MAMIN SIBIRYAK
★12477 MARK RESHETNIKOV
★12478 MART SAAR
★12479 MATIS PLUDON
★12480 MESKUPAS ADOMAS
★12481 MGACHI
★12482 MIKOLOYUS CHYURLYONIS
★12483 MONGOLIYA
★12484 MRAMOR
★12485 NADEZHDINSK
★12486 NAKHODKA
★12487 NIKOLAY OSTROVSKIY
★12488 NOVAYA ERA
★12489 OPALA
★12490 OSKAR LUTS
★12491 OTROG
★12492 OZYORNYE KLYUCHI
★12493 PAKHACHA
★12494 PASIONARIYA
★12495 PECHENGA
★12496 PEREKAT
★12497 PETR STUCHKA
★12498 PETRODVORETS
★12499 PIONER UKRAINY
★12500 PIONER ZAPOLYARYA
★12501 POSYET
★12502 PRIAMURYE ex Glafki 1969
★12503 PRIOZERSK ex Meliti 1969
★12504 PRANAS EYDUKYAVICHUS
★12505 PULKOVO
★12506 PUTIVL ex Thetis 1969
★12507 PYOTR OVCHINNIKOV
★12508 RAPOLAS CHARNAS
★12509 ROBERT EYDEMAN
★12510 RUBIN
★12511 RUDOLF BLAUMANIS
★12512 SAKHALIN
★12513 SAMARGA
★12514 SAPFIR
★12515 SEMYON DEZHNEV
★12516 SERGEY YESENIN
★12517 SEROGLAZKA
★12518 SEVERNAYA PALMIRA
★12520 TARAS SHEVCHENKO ex Shevchenko
★12521 SHTURMAN YELAGIN
★12522 SHYAULYAY
★12523 SIBIRYAK
★12524 SNABZHENETS PERVYY
★12525 SOVGAVAN
★12526 SOVIETSKIE PROFSOYUZY
★12527 STANYUKOVICH
★12528 STAR
★12529 TADZHIKISTAN
★12530 TAYSHET
★12531 TAMAN
★12532 TEODOR NETTE
★12533 TERNEY
★12534 TIKHVIN
★12535 TOPAZ
★12536 TRETYAKOVO
★12537 TRUDOVYE RESERVY
★12538 TURGENEV
★12539 TURMALIN
★12540 VALENTIN KOTELNIKOV
★12541 VALERIY BYKOVSKIY
★12542 VASILY VINEVITIN
★12543 VITALIY BONIVUR
★12544 VITAUTAS MONTVILA
★12545 VITAUTAS PUTNA
★12546 VLADAS REKASHYUS
★12547 VLADIMIR ATLASOV
★12548 VOSKHOD
★12549 YANTAR
★12550 YARONIMAS UBORYAVICHUS ex Persey 1966
★12551 YASHMA
★12551 YUBILEY OKTYABRYA

★12552 YUNOST
★12553 YUOZAS GARYALIS
★12554 YUOZAS VAREYKIS
★12555 ZIGMAS ANGARETIS
(Bu flag):
★12556 BAKLAN
★12557 FREGATA
★12558 LEBED
(Gh flag):
12559 MANKOADZE

★12570 AKADEMIK KNIPOVICH Ru/Ru (Nosenko) 1964; RS; 2300; 84.7 × 5.8 (278 × 19); M (Praha); 13; 'MAYAKOVSKIY' class; both masts tripod
Similar (Ru flag):
★12571 PERSEY III
★12573 PROFESSOR DERYUGIN
★12573 AKADEMIK BERG
★12574 ATLANT
★12575 ANDRUS YOKHANI
★12576 ARGUS
★12577 EKVATOR
★12578 GIZHIGA
★12579 NEPTUN
★12580 POSEYDON

★12585 ODISSEY Ru/Ru (—) 1970; Sub S; 2800; 84.66 × 5.80 (278 × 19.03); M (CKD Praha); 12.5; Converted from 'MAYAKOVSKIY' class trawler. May be spelt ODISSEJ. Shell doors in hull move apart laterally to reveal a large hold where the submersible is housed
Similar:
★12586 IKHTIANDR (Ru)

★12587 ZAKARPATYE Ru/Ru (—) —; RS; 3400 (displacement); 83.6 × 6.00 (274.3 × 19.69); M (—); 13; Based on hull of 'MAYAKOVSKIY' class trawler
Sisters (Ru flag):
★12588 ZABAYKALYE
★12589 ZAPOROZHYE

★12590 'LESKOV' class Ru/Pd (Gdanska) 1960/63; FT; 2800; 84.6 × 5.3 (277 × 17.6); M (Sulzer); 12.5; 'B 15' type
Similar (Ru flag):
★12591 DRUZHBA
★12592 GONCHAROV
★12593 KUPRIN
★12594 LESKOV ex Chernyshevski
★12595 LUNNIK
★12596 MIR
★12597 MAMIN SIBIRYAK
★12598 ORBITA
★12599 SPUTNIK

★12610 JUPITER Pd/Pd (Gdanska) 1963; FT; 2300; 83 × 5.5 (272 × 18); M (Sulzer); 12.5; 'B 15' type
Sisters (Ru flag):
★12611 KASTOR
★12612 NEPTUN
★12614 URAN
★12615 DALMOR

★12620 BERTOLT BRECHT DDR/DDR (Mathias-Thesen) 1959; FT; 3000; 86 × 5.3 (281 × 17.4); M (Halberstadt); 12.5
Similar (DDR flag):
★12621 ERIK WEINERT
★12622 F C WEISKOPF
★12623 JOHANNES R. BECKER

★12630 WALTER DEHMEL DDR/DDR (Mathias-Thesen) 1963; FT: 3000; 85.6 × 5.3 (281 × 17.5); M (Dieselmotorenwerk Rostock); 13.5
Sisters (DDR flag):
★12631 BERNHARD KELLERMANN
★12632 FRIEDRICH WOLF
★12633 PETER KAST
★12634 PETER NELL
★12635 RUDOLF LEONHARD

12640 JOY 18 Pa/Br (Lewis) 1954; FT: 2600; 85.6 × 7 (281 × 22.9); M (Lewis); 12; ex Fairtry 1 1969; ex Fairtry 1959

12650 FELIX S Pa/It (Felszegi) 1959; C; 8900; 148.7 × 9.1 (488 × 29.8); M (Sulzer); 15.5; ex San Felice 1982

12670 DOCK EXPRESS 10 Ne/Ne (Verolme S H) 1979; Dk/RoC/HL; 5500; 153.76 × 8.9 (504.46 × 29.2); M (Stork-Werkspoor); 16; Stern door
Sisters (Ne flag):
12671 DOCK EXPRESS 11
12672 DOCK EXPRESS 12
Similar (longer):
12673 DOCK EXPRESS 20 (Ne)

★12680 KAPITAN SMIRNOV Ru/Ru ('Chernomorskiy') 1979; RoC/Con; 14300; 227.3 × 9.87 (745.74 × 32.38); TS GT/M (—); 25; Quarter ramp
Sisters:
★12681 KAPITAN MEZENTSEV (Ru) different type of ramp;

★12682 INZHENER YERMOSHKIN (Ru)

★12685 TADEUSZ KOSCIUSKO Pd/Fr (La Ciotat) 1981; RoC/Con; 30100; 200.26 × 9.52 (657 × 31.23); M (Sulzer); 20.75; Starboard quarter ramp
Sisters (Pd flag):
★12686 KAZIMIERZ PULASKI
★12687 STEFAN STARZYNSKI
★12688 WLADYSLAW SIKORSKI

12690 BELVAUX Be/Be (Cockerill) 1979; RoC; 3500; 116.7 × 6.2 (382.87 × 20.34); M (Mirrlees Blackstone); 15; Stern slewing ramp
Sister:
12691 CLERVAUX (Be)

● 12700 GOLDEN PRINCESS Pa/Br (Bartram) 1964; R; 7000/9300; 165 × 8.2/8.8 (541 × 17/29); M (Sulzer); —; ex America Star 1982; Lengthened 1973

12710 NEW BEAR Pa/Ne (P Smit) 1964; CP; 8200/10900; 177 × 8.1/9.4 (581 × 27/30.11); M (Sulzer); 20; ex Nedlloyd Fremantle 1983; ex Straat Fremantle 1977; ex Asian Enterprise 1975; ex Straat Fremantle 1973
Sisters:
12711 KOTA WIRAWAN (Sr) ex Nedlloyd Franklin 1983; ex Straat Franklin
12712 KOTA WIJAYA (Sr) ex Nedlloyd Freetown 1983; ex Straat Freetown; ex Asian Ensign 1975; ex Straat Freetown 1973
12713 KOTA WANGSA (Sr) ex Nedlloyd Frazer 1983; ex Straat Frazer 1977; ex Asian Endeavour 1975; ex Straat Frazer 1973

★12720 YONG CHUN RC/Br (Connell) 1963; CP; 8100/10900; 168 × 9/10.2 (550 × 30/33.6); M (Sulzer); 20; ex Benarmin 1972
Sister:
★12721 YICHUN (RC) ex Benvalla 1972

12740 ENRICO C It/Br (Swan Hunter & WR) 1951; P; 13600; 176.7 × 7.5 (579 × 24.8); TST (Parsons); 18.5; ex Provence 1965

12750 OCEAN MERCURY Pa/FRG (Bremer V) 1957; CP; 4900; 126 × 7.5 (414 × 26.8); M (Bremer V); 14.5; ex Xiang Shan 1981; ex Minai 1976; ex Siegstein 1972
Sister:
★12751 WAN PING (RC) ex Ocean Jupiter 1983; ex Lei Shan 1981; ex Minhao 1977; ex Spreestein 1972

12760 CHINTA Gr/Sp (AESA) 1959; C; 3200; 113 × 6.5 (371 × 21.6); M (B&W); 15; ex Stefanoemme 1980; ex Comillas; ex Benizar 1967
Sister:
12761 IKAN (Gr) ex Federicaemme 1980; ex Ruisenada; ex Beniel 1967

★12770 MANGYONGBONG RK/RK (Chongjin) 1971; PC; 3600; 99.98 × 5.00 (328 × 16.40); M (—); 13.5

12780 SEAWAY FALCON No/FRG (M Jansen) 1975; Offshore Support Vessel; 1600; 80.1 × 4.4 (263 × 14.6); M (MWM); 14

★12790 BAIRE Cu/Sp ('Astano') 1966; C; 7000/9400; 157 × 8/9 (515 × 27/29.9); M (Sulzer);
Sisters (Cu flag):
★12791 CERRO PELADO
★12792 EL JIGUE
★12793 MAFFO
★12794 13 DE MARZO

12800 TEPIC Me/Br (Hall, Russell) 1961; CP; 4500; 127 × 7.2 (416 × 23.7); M (Sulzer); 15; ex Bibi 1977; ex Letitia 1967

12810 AUTOROUTE Br/Ja (Mitsui) 1979; RoVC; 2500; 100.01 × 4.21 (328.12 × 13.81); M (B&W); 15.25; Stern door/ramp

12840 MOJAIL-5 Ho/Br (Readhead) 1958; C; 9700; 152.18 × 9.17 (499 × 30.09); M (Sulzer); 16; ex Kapetan Xilas 1979; ex Atlas 1973; may be spelt MOAJIL-5

12850 ANTILLA Sg/Br (Connell) 1963; C; 7100/9900; 155 × 8.3/9.4 (508 × 27.4/30.1); M (Sulzer); —; ex Silver Gate 1979; ex Strathnairn; ex Kohinur 1975

12860 OLYMPIAS Gr/FRG (Rickmers) 1958; C; 5400; 131.4 × 6.6 (431 × 21.8); M (Fiat-Borsig); 14.75; ex Birk 1973; ex Lutjenburg 1968; ex Flavia 1964
Sisters:
12861 AMALINDA (Gr) ex Holstendeich; ex Lechstein 1972
12862 SHEIKH ALI (Si) ex Christoforos T 1982; ex Syros 1981; ex Holstenfleet; ex Nabstein 1972
12863 SEA RELIANCE 1 (Pa) ex Gaudeamus 1976; ex Holstenbank 1976; ex Bella 1972; ex Bellavia

12870 **NEW DRAGON** Sg/Br (Swan Hunter) 1957; C; 6000/8500; 152.36 × 7.25/8.45 (500 × 23.79/27.72); M (Doxford); —; ex *Katsina Palm* 1978

12880 **MAGDALINI K** Gr/Br (Bremer V) 1958; C; 5500/8100; 144.18 × 7.18/— (473 × 23.56/—); M (MAN); 14; ex *Ionian Sky* 1981; ex *Elenma* 1977; ex *Akassa Palm* 1972

★12900 **HUANG JIN SHAN** RC/FRG (Bremer V) 1961; C; 5600/8000; 144 × 7.2/8.5 (473 × 23.6/28); M (MAN); 14; ex *European Express*; ex *Ebony* 1980; ex *Jasper*—; ex *Opal*—; ex *Beer Sheva* 1976
Sister:
12901 **LIA PERO** (Gr) ex *Petromare Star* 1980; ex *Teverya* 1979; ex *Gold Moon* 1977; ex *Teverya* 1976

●12910 **EURCO R** Br/Br (Swan Hunter & WR) 1960; C; 5500/7800; 144.33 × 7.65 (473.5 × 25.10); M (Doxford); 16; ex *Richmond* 1984; ex *Peruvian Trader* 1981; ex *Minoa* 1980; ex *Lobito Pal* 1980; ex *Lobito Palm* 1979;
Sister:
12911 **DAPHNEMAR** (Pa) ex *Ilesha Palm* 1979

●12940 **NATALIA** Pa/Br (J Brown) 1953; R; 10900; 160.3 × 9.3 (526 × 30.8); M (Sulzer); 16; ex *Mahmout* 1979; ex *Otaki* 1976

★12960 **HONG QI 119** RC/Br (H&W) 1956; C; 5900/7600; 150.09 × 7.12/8.66 (492.4 × 23.36/28.41); M (H&W); —; ex *Hungmien* 1977; ex *Dolius* 1972; ex *Glenfruin* 1972; ex *Dolius* 1970
Sister:
★12961 **HONG QI 137** (RC) ex *Hungsia* 1979; ex *Demodocus* 1973; ex *Glenroy* 1972; ex *Demodocus* 1970

12980 **TAIBAH III** Si/FRG (Howaldts) 1956; C; 6400/9000; 153.02 × 7.72/9.71 (502 × 25.33/31.86); M (Howaldts); ex *Korinthos* 1982; ex *Cap Ortegal* 1971
Sister:
12981 **PENELOPE II** (Gr) ex *Cap Finisterre* 1971

12990 **COVADONGA** Co/Br (Fairfield SB) 1951; CP; 4200; 129 × 7 (424 × 22.9); M (Doxford); 14; ex *Ciudad De Medellin* 1969
Sisters:
12991 **LIBERTADOR BOLIVAR** (Bo-Navy) ex *Ciudad De Barquisimento* 1978
Similar:
12992 **MARACAIBO** (Ve Navy) ex *Ciudad de Maracaibo* 1982
12993 **PICHINCHA** (Ec) ex *Rio Guayas* 1979; ex *Ciudad De Quito* 1977
12994 **DARIEN** (Co) ex *Maitama* 1974; ex *Ciudad De Manizales* 1970

★13010 **LENINOGORSK** Ru/Pd (Gdanska) 1958; C; 9900; 154 × 8.7 (505 × 28.8); M (Fiat); 16; 'B 54' type
Sisters (Ru flag):
★13011 **BOLSHEVIK SUKHANOV**
★13012 **DEPUTAT LUTSKIY**
★13013 **LABINSK**
★13014 **LESOZAVODSK**
★13015 **PARTIZAN BONNIVUR**
★13016 **SOLNECHNOGORSK**

13020 **GULF REEFER** Gr/Br (Bartram) 1960; C; 7700; 139 × 8.8 (455 × 28.1); M (Sulzer); 17; ex *Patricia U* 1982; ex *Turakina* 1977; May have mainmast removed

13030 **AL-SALMA** Bh/In (Hindustan) 1958; C; 5100/7200; 144.96 × 6.48/7.33 (475.6 × 21.26/24.05); M (MAN); 12; ex *Jalaveera* 1980

13040 **OURANIA** Gr/FRG (Kieler H) 1953; CP; 4200; 127 × 7.3 (415 × 23.1); M (MAN); 15; ex *Schauenburg* 1970

●13050 **CITY OF CREMORNE** Cy/FRG (Kieler H) 1959; CP; 3700/5700; 126 × 7.2/8.3 (414 × 23.6/27.3); M (Kieler H); 15.75; ex *Medi Sun* 1981; ex *Quiche* 1980; ex *Medi-Sun* 1979; ex *Volta Virtue* 1973; ex *Medi-Sun* 1972; ex *Breitenburg* 1971; ex *Syllum* 1970

13070 **MAGNA SPES** Cy/De (B&W) 1947; CP; 4800/7000; 134 × 8.08/— (440 × 26.6/—); M (B&W); 14; ex *Spalmatori Islands* 1972; ex *Eva Christensen* 1967; ex *Colombia* 1966

13090 **TOM** Gr/Ne (Gusto) 1959; C; 6600/8000; 146.08 × 8/8.81 (479.27 × 26.25/28.9); M (Stork); 15; ex *Sea Glory* 1979; ex *Leiderkerk* 1978
Similar:
13092 **KOTA JAYA** (Sg) ex *Nedlloyd Bovenkerk*; ex *Bovenkerk* 1977

★13100 **DONGMING** RC/Ne ('De Schelde') 1964; C; 10400; 157 × 9.6 (516 × 31.6); M (Sulzer); 15; ex *Sea Amber* 1973

Sister:
★13101 **KUNMING** (RC) ex *Sea Coral* 1973

★13110 **TAIXING** RC/Ne (Sulzer) 1960; C; 7300/10400; 158 × 8.4/— (517 × 27.3/—); M (Sulzer); 16; ex *Beniowski* 1971; ex *Argo Altis*

★13120 **HUAI YIN** RC/FRG (Schlieker) 1959; CP; 6700/1000; 158 × 8.2/9.3 (518 × 27/30.6); M (MAN); 16; ex *Yellow Sea* 1970; ex *Jag Jiwan* 1964; ex *Jala Jag Jiwan* 1963; ex *Jag Jiwan* 1959

★13130 **NANHUEI** RC/Fi (Crichton-Vulcan) 1961; C; 6400/9100; 146 × 8.5/9.1 (479 × 28/30); M (Sulzer); 15.5; ex *Brilliance* 1970; ex *Wiiri* 1979

●13150 **AURELIA DI MAIO** It/Fi (Crichton-Vulcan) 1961; C; 9000; 146 × 9.1 (479 × 29.1); M (Sulzer); 15.25; ex *Andrea Gritti* 1979; ex *Wilke* 1969

13160 **LANKA DEVI** Sr/Br (Short Bros) 1962; C; 7000/9900; 155.8 × 8.3/9.2 (511 × 27.3/30.2); M (B&W) 14.75; ex *Aramis* 1972

13170 **REMCO** Gh/FRG (L F-W) 1959; C; 5000; 140.16 × 7.65 (459.8 × 25.10); M (Sulzer); 16; ex *Adom* 1980; ex *Volta Peace* 1977; ex *Kamperdyk* 1972
Sisters:
13171 **FERIAL** (Gh) ex *Odupon* 1980; ex *Volta Wisdom* 1977; ex *Korendyk* 1972
13172 **UTILA PRINCESS** (Ho) ex *Mazoa VII* 1982; ex *Brezice* 1982; ex *Kloosterdyk* 1970

13200 **SALAMAH 4** UAE/FRG (Rickmers) 1956; C; 3000/5300; 130 × 5.39/7.38 (426 × 20.96/24.21); M (Borsig); 14.5; ex *Gulf Pride* 1982; ex *Naxos* 1981; ex *Holstendamm* 1978; ex *Goslar* 1973; ex *Franz* 1959; ex *Franz Ohlrogge* 1958

13230 **JANI** Ng/FRG (Weser') 1954; CP; 8800; 146 × 8 (479 × 26.2); M; 13; ex *Ahmadu Tijani* 1980; ex *Santa Rita* 1972

13240 **AIHUA** Pa/FRG (Howaldts) 1955; CP; 6800; 154.4 × 7.7 (507 × 25.4); M (Howaldts); 16; ex *Cap Norte* 1973
Sister:
13241 **AIMIN** (Pa) ex *Cap Vilano* 1974

13250 **RECONQUISTA** Ur/FRG (Kieler H) 1956; CP; 4700/7000; 137.5 × 7.2/8.5 (451 × 23.6/28); M (MAN); 16; ex *Punta Atalaya* 1978; ex *Nopal Progress* 1974

13260 **KARANA DELAPAN** Li/FRG (Stuelcken) 1961; CP; 3300/5300; 127 × 6.8/7.7 (418 × 22.4/25.6); M (MAN); 14.5; ex *Mera* 1977; ex *Mitra* 1977; ex *Leora* 1976; ex *Leada* 1971

13270 **AVA** Bm/FRG (A G 'Weser') 1963; C; 4900/7400; 135 × 7.2/— (455 × 23.6/—); M (B&W); 15.5
Sister:
13271 **BASSEIN** (Bm)

13280 **DIMITRAKIS** Ma/Be (Boel) 1961; CP; 5200/7800; 141.2 × 7.8/8.8 (464 × 25.6/29); M (MAN); 16; ex *Marina P* 1983; ex *Manaure III* 1980; ex *Good Luck* 1977; ex *Anvers* 1973
Sister:
13281 **HELENA C** (Gr) ex *Good Hope* 1975; ex *Gand* 1973

13300 **GOLD STREAM** Li/Ja (Uraga HI) 1963; C; 4700/7100; 137.5 × 7.5/8.7 (451 × 24.6/28.6); M (Sulzer); 16.25; ex *Sahar* 1974
Sister:
13301 **GOLD MOUNTAIN** (Li) ex *Tsedek* 1974

13310 **CHARMYL** Cy/Ne ('De Schelde') 1963; C; 4900/7400; 140.49 × —/8.52 (461 × —/27.85); M (Sulzer); —; ex *Lake Bosomtwe* 1981

13350 **AL SHEHABIA** Sr/Sw (Eriksbergs) 1963; CP; 4900/7300; 137.7 × 8/8.8 (452 × 26.3/28.1); M (B&W); 16.5; ex *Ellen* 1980; ex *Neva* 1979; ex *Nopal Neva*; ex *Nopal Alkimos* 1975; ex *Nopal Rex* 1973; ex *Earlville* 1964
Sister:
13351 **JUNIOR K** (Le) ex *Roseville* 1974

★13370 **LINTONG** RC/Pd (Gdanska) 1957; C; 6800; 153.90 × 8.33 (505 × 27.33); M (Fiat); —; ex *Orlik* 1967; ex *Hoping Wu Shi* 1960; ex *Fryderyk Chopin* 1959; 'B 54' type

13380 **LAWANTI** Pa/FRG (Howaldts) 1956; CP; 6300; 155.5 × 8 (510 × 26.2); M (Howaldts); 17; ex *Erlangen* 1969
Sisters:
★13383 **YING SHAN** (RC) ex *Min Chiang*; ex *Weimar* 1972
Similar (funnel and superstructure variations, twin KP foreward, etc.):
13387 **JUTHA KARNCHANA** (Th) ex *Rheinland*
13388 **JUTHA RAJATA** (Th) ex *Vogtland* 1977

13390 **MAN PO** (Pa) ex *Zea Beach* 1980; ex *Zircon* 1980; ex *Kalahari*

★13391 **BAO SHAN** (RC) ex *Minglang* 1975; ex *Worms* 1972

★13392 **XIUSHAN** (RC) ex *Mingyao* 1975; ex *Wiesbaden* 1972

★13393 **BA SHAN** (RC) ex *Yushan* 1980; ex *Mingwei*; ex *Wien*

13400 **BRAVO MARIA** Gr/Ne (Giessen) 1953; CP; 4500; 131.6 × 6.8 (432 × 22.5); M (Sulzer); 14; ex *Eemland* 1975

13410 **SAUDI VENTURE** Si/Ne (Amsterdamsche D) 1957; CP; 5000; 131.7 × 7.2 (432 × 23.8); M (Sulzer); 14.5; ex *Kennemerland* 1981

13430 **SAUDI EAGLE** Si/Ne (P Smit) 1960; CP; 7300/9700; 161 × —/9 (528 × —/29.6); M (B&W); 17.5 ex *Nedlloyd Serooskerk* 1981; ex *Serooskerk* 1977
Sister:
13431 **SAUDI FALCON** (Si) ex *Nedlloyd Simonskerk* 1981; ex *Simonskerk* 1977

●13440 **GOOD SKIPPER** Pa/Ne (Giessen) 1957; C; 7000/9100; 154.64 × 8.02/8.9 (507.35 × 26.31/29.2); M (B&W); 17; ex *Zonnekerk* 1977

13460 **BECENA** Pa/FRG (Bremer V) 1953; C; 5600; 151.80 × 7.60 (498 × 24.93); M (Bremer V); 16.5; ex *Koln* 1973

13470 **MEIRU** Pa/FRG (Bremer V) 1955; CP; 5600; 152 × 7.6 (498 × 26.1); M (Howaldts); 14.5; ex *Tannstein* 1972
Sister:
13471 **MEIKI** (Pa) ex *Torstein* 1973

13490 **NANHUA** Pa/FRG (L F-W) 1954; CP; 7000; 167 × 8 (542 × 26.2); M (Bremer V); 17.5; ex *Travestein* 1973
Sisters (Pa flag):
13491 **NANTAO** ex *Westerstein* 1973
Similar (taller KPs abaft funnel):
13492 **NANKUO** ex *Havelstein* 1973
13493 **NANCHENG** ex *Werrastein* 1973

●★13510 **N'GOLA** An/FRG (Howaldts) 1961; C; 6800/9400; 159 × 8/9.2 (520 × 26/30.4); M (MAN); 18.5; ex *Blumenthal* 1971
Sisters:
13511 **CONGO** (Po) ex *Nurnberg* 1971
13512 **MANICA** (Po) ex *Kulmerland* 1971
13513 **MUXIMA** (Po) ex *Wolfsburg* 1971
13514 **MUNSTERLANDES** (Gr) ex *Munsterland*

●13520 **SAUDI AL MEDINA** Si/FRG (Howaldts) 1962; C; 7200/10000; 164 × 8.3/9.1 (537 × 27.6/29. 11); M (Sulzer); 20; ex *Saudi Al Madirah* 1982; ex *Nedlloyd Rhone* 1982; ex *Neder Rhone*
Sister:
13521 **SAUDI AMBASSADOR** (Si) ex *Nedlloyd Rijn* 1981; ex *Neder Rijn*

★13550 **XING KONG** RC/Br (Greenock D) 1958; C; 7300; 153.24 × 8.3 (502.76 × 27.23); M (Doxford); 16.25; ex *Trinity Splendour* 1980; ex *Clan Menzies* 1979

13560 **SUCCESS** Pa/FRG (Howaldts) 1958; C; 7200/9400; 154.87 × 8.03/8.96 (508.1 × 26.35/29.4); M (MAN) 17.5; ex *Faulad Sardar* 1981; ex *Indian Strength* 1979
Sisters (In flag):
13561 **INDIAN TRIUMPH**
13562 **INDIAN TRUST**
Similar (see inset):
13563 **INDIAN SECURITY** (In)

●13580 **GOLDEN SAUDIA** Si/FRG (Kieler H) 1962; CP; 6800/9800; 157 × 8/9 (515 × 26/29); M (MAN); 16.5; ex *Pulau Bali* 1981; ex *Hoegh Dyke* 1979
Similar:
13581 **EASTERN HUNTER** (Sg) ex *Nopal Vega* 1978; ex *Concordia Vega* 1969; ex *Hoegh Drake* 1969

●13590 **MILDA A** Ma/Ne (Nederlandsche) 1956; C; 7000/9000; 150.35 × —/9.31 (493.3 × —/30.54); M (Stork); 17; ex *Giovanna C* 1982; ex *Ommenkerk* 1974
Sister:
13591 **DAMENHAN** (Pa) ex *Anna C* 1981; ex *Oldenkerk* 1974

13610 **LELLO DI MAIO** It/FRG (L F-W) 1961; CP; 6900/9200; 152 × 8.2/9.2 (497 × 27/30.4); M (MAN); 16.25; ex *Tanga* 1972; ex *Novia* 1963

13630 **NANWU** Pa/FRG (Howaldts) 1953; C; 6700; 167.29 × 8.01 (548.6 × 26.28); M (Bremer V); —; ex *Neckarstein* 1973; Lengthened and re-engined 1964

★13650 **SUPER ATLANTIK** type Ru/DDR (Stralsund) 1972 onwards; FT; 4000; 102 × 5.2 (335 × 17); M (MAN); 15

Sisters (Ru flag):
★13652 AKHILLEON
★13653 AUKSHAYTIKA
★13654 APOGEY
★13655 ARABAT
★13657 BATILMAN
★13658 BERKUT
★13659 BAGRATIONOVSK
★13660 BIOSFERA
★13664 FOROS
★13668 GRANIT
★13669 GEFEST
★13670 GARPUNNER PROKOPYENKO
★13671 GENERAL OSTRYAKOV
★13672 GRIGORIY OVODOVSKIY
★13673 IOSIF LAPUSHKIN
★13674 JAN RAINBERG
★13675 JOAKIM VACIETIS
★13676 KURSHAYA DUGA
★13678 KOMMUNAR
★13679 LYUDMILA PAVLICHENKO
★13680 LEMBIT PERN
★13681 MAMAYEV KURGAN
★13682 MUSTYARV
★13683 MALAYA ZEMLYA
★13684 MYS CHAKO
★13686 MEZOSFERA
★13687 MIKHAIL ORLOV
★13688 NIKOLAY BERAZIN
★13689 NIKIFOR PAVLOV
★13690 NIKOLAY TSYGANOV
★13690/1 ORFEY
★13694 PATROKL
★13695 PRESIDENT PIK (May be spelt PREZIDENT PIECK)
★13696 PERIGEY
★13697 PEYPSI
★13699 PETROGRĄDSKAYA STORONA
★13700 RETAVAS
★13701 SALANTI
★13702 SERGEY LYULIN
★13703 SCHILUTE
★13705 SAADYARV
★13706 STRATOSFERA
★13710 TRIPOSFERA
★13711 TRITON
★13712 TRUSEVIK MORYA
★13713 TEMRYUCHANIN
★13714 TAURAGE
★13715 TURAYDA
★13716 TSEMESSKAYA BUKHTA
★13717 TAMULA
★13720 VAGULA
★13721 VASILIY FOMIN
★13722 VOROSHILOVGRAD
★13723 VASILIY REVYAKIN
★13724 YURMALA
★13725 YURBARKAS
★13726 YONAVA
★13727 ZVEZDA
★13728 ZNAMYA KERCHIL
★13729 ZEFIR
(Rm flag):
★13732 BISTRITA
★13734 CERNA
★13735 CINDRELUL
★13736 DORNA
★13738 PUTNA
★13739 TIRNAVA
(DDR flag):
★13740 LUDWIG TUREK
Similar (bridge configuration differs, see inset):
★13741 AZOV (Ru)
★13742 PROMETEY (Ru)
★13743 SUVALKIYA (Ru)
★13744 GENERAL CHERNYAKHOVSKIY (Ru)

★13745 PRIZVANIE Ru/DDR (Stralsund) 1979; FT/TS; 3300; 101.83×5.60 (334×18.37); M (MAN); 14.75; Modified 'Super Atlantik' type. Differs from standard design by centre kingpost foreward, position of boats etc.
Sisters (Ru flag):
★13746 GLOBUS
★13747 PROFESSOR KLENOVA
★13748 PROFESSOR KOZHIN
★13749 PROFESSOR NIKOLSKIY
★13750 PROFESSOR VOYEVODIN

● ★13751 Later 'SUPER ATLANTIK' type Ru/DDR (Stralsund) 1977 onwards; FT; 3100; 101.45×5.70 (333 18.70); M (MAN); 14.75; Differs from earlier 'Super Atlantik' principally by filled-in well abaft superstructure. Some may have boats ahead of funnels (LUDWIG RENN has this feature)
Sisters (Ru flag):
13751/1 ADAYKHOKH
★13751/2 AKHMETA
★13751/3 BALTISKAYA KOSA
★13751/4 BORIS TSINDELIS
★13751/5 DARVIN

★13751/6 DONISAR
★13751/7 GALDOR
★13751/8 ILYA KULIN
★13751/9 GEYA
★13751/10 GRIGORIY TERENTYEV
★13751/11 GEROYEVKA
★13751/12 GARPUNER ZARVA
★13752 KALPER
★13752/1 IVAN KORZUNOV
★13752/2 KONSTANTIN ALEKSEYEV
★13752/3 KULIKOVO POLYE
★13752/4 NARODNYY OPOLCHENETS
★13752/5 NIKOLAY GRIBANOV
★13752/6 NOVOANGARSK
★13752/7 NOVOARKHANGELSK
★13753 NOVASBEST
★13753/1 NOVOBATAYSK
★13753/2 NOVOBIRYUSINSKIY
★13753/3 NOVOBOBRUYSK
★13753/4 NOVODRUTSK
★13753/5 NOVOKACHALINSK
★13753/6 NOVOKAZALINSK
★13753/7 NOVOKIYEVKA
★13753/8 NOVOKOTORSK
★13753/9 NOVOLADOZHSKIY
★13753/10 NOVOMALTINSK
★13753/11 NOVONIKOLSK
★13753/12 NOVOORSK
★13753/13 NOVOORENBURG
★13753/14 NOVOPSKOV
★13753/15 NOVOSOKOLNIKI
★13753/16 NOVOYELNYA
★13753/17 NOVOYENISEYSK
★13754 NOVOZLATOPOL
★13754/1 SELENA
★13754/2 SOKRAT
★13754/3 SUGAN
★13754/4 STRALSUNDSKIY KORABEL
★13754/5 URANIYA
★13754/6 VIYTNA
★13754/7 VOZROZHDENIYE
★13754/8 ASTAN KESAYEV
★13754/9 ELVA
★13754/10 BORIS ALEKSEYEV
★13754/11 GROM
★13754/12 FYODOR YEROZIDI
★13754/13 PELAGIAL
★13754/14 NEVSKAYA DUBROVSKA
★13754/15 MISA
★113754/16 NIKOLAY PUSTOVOYTENKO
★13754/17 KAUGURI
★13755 NOVOROSSIYSKIY RABOCHIY
★13755/1 KHARKU
★13755/2 TSVETKOVO
★13755/3 NIKOLAY AFANASYEV
★13755/4 MAKSIM KHOMYAKOV
★13755/5 CHERCHESK
★13755/6 ARKADIY CHERNYSHEV
★13755/7 GAZGAN
★13755/8 BORODINSKOYE POLYE
★13755/9 GISSAR
★13755/10 GNEVNYY
★13756 INZHENER YUDINTSYEV
★13757 LIMB
★13758 MECHISLOVAS GEDVILAS
★13759 MLECHNYY PUT
★13760 PATRIOT
★13761 RUSSOYE POLYE
★13761/1 SEKSTAN
★13762 SHAPOSHNIKOVO
★13762/1 SHAKOPOVO
★13763 SHEPETOVKA
★13763/1 TELSHYAY
★13764 VASILIY GRECHISNIKOV
★13764/1 YASTREBOVO
★13765 VOLNYY VETER
★13766 ZVYEZDA ASOVA
★13766/1 YEVGENIY POLYAKOV
★13767 ZVYEZDA CHERNOMORYA
★13767/1 ZVYEZDA SEVASTOPOLYA
★13768 KAPITAN PURGIN
(DDR flag):
★13768/1 A EDUARD CLAUDIUS
★13769 ARNOLD ZWEIG
★13769/1 LUDWIG RENN (boats ahead of funnels)

(Rm flag):
★13770 BAHLUI
★13771 CRISUL ALB
★13772 DIMBOVITA
★13773 JIJIA
★13774 OLTET
★13774/1 OZANIA
(Rm flag—Rm built (Braila):
★13774/2 PARING
★13774/3 RODNA
The following Ru flag vessels are Fishery Research but are probably similar:
★13775 NOVOCHEBOKSARSK
★13776 NOVOUKRAINA
★13777 NOVOLYANOVSK

● 13780 MALDIVE PRIVILEGE Mv/Br (Scotts' SB) 1959; C; 11300; 161.2×9.5 (530×3.1); M (Doxford); 15; ex Styliani 1981; ex Capetan Costis 1981; ex Constantinos T 1978; ex N Zografia 1975; ex Lord Gladstone 1969

13800 RODONAS Gr/De (Helsingor) 1952; CP; 1600; 92.3×6.1 (303×19.5); M (B&W); 13; ex Elvira M; ex Bangsbo 1968
Similar:
13802 ABUSABAA 1 (Cy) ex Guardian 1979; ex Cyprian Producer 1976; ex Borreby 1967
13803 COURAGE (Cy) ex Cyprian Trader 1976; ex Bygholm 1967

13810 GUIRIA Ve/Ne (Vuyk) 1955; CP; 3500; 116×6.3 (381.4×20.6); M (Nordberg); 14.75; ex Anzoategui
Sisters (Ve flag):
13811 RENATA B ex Merida 1979
13812 LAS MOROCHAS ex Sucre 1979
13813 YARACUY

13820 SOCRATES Gr/FRG (A G 'Weser') 1958; CP; 5700/8600; 143×8/9 (470×26/29); M (MAN); ex Sternal Trader 1981; ex Axenfels; ex Narendra Laxmi 1972; ex Axenfels 1972; ex Schelde 1969

★13840 HONG QI 149 RC/US (Tampa SB) 1940; C; 6000; 140×8.4 (459×27.8); M (Nordberg); 14; ex Laodong; ex Warszawa 1963; ex Bastasen 1951; ex Axel Salen 1951; ex Sea Witch 1947; 'C 2' type

★13850 MAMAIA Rm/Ru (Severney) 1930; C; 4000; 112×7.3 (366×24); M (Sulzer); 11; ex Friedrich Engels 1962

13860 MISHA S AMITY Pa/FRG (Lindenau) 1961; CP; 4000; 108×7.5 (354×24.4); M (MAN); 15; ex Tara 1982; ex Varykino Adventurer 1970; ex Prins Maurits 1969

13890 SILVER CITY Gr/FRG (A G 'Weser') 1960; C; 10600; 159.01 × 9.55 (521.7 × 31.33); M (MAN); 14.5; ex Aristoklis 1976; ex Numerian 1970
Similar:
13891 PANAGHIA LOURION (Gr) ex Hadjitsakos 1972;
13892 LAERTIS (Gr) ex Chios

● 13930 MALDIVE UNITY Mv/Ne (Giessen) 1954; PC; 4100; 110×6.7 (360×22.1); M (B&W); 14.5; ex Houtman 1972

13940 GUATARI Ho/Br (Stephen) 1936; C; 2300; 102×6.8 (335×22.5); M (Sulzer); ex Gambali 1979; ex Golden Dragon 1969; ex Primal Prosperity 1968; ex Miranda 1968; ex Carolina 1967; ex Kauri 1963

★13950 USKOK Ys/FRG (Howaldts) 1961; C; 7400; 139.3×8.8 (457×29.6); M (MAN); 14.5; ex Siletta 1968

★13960 BAR Ys/Fr (Mediterranee) 1956; CP; 6300/8700; 145×—/9.3 (475×—/30.6); M (Sulzer); 14; ex Roald Amundsen 1968

13980 SAUDI ROSE Si/FRG (Bremer V) 1958; CP; 6200/8500; 147×7.8/9 (482×25.6/29.4); M (Bremer V); 17.5; ex Buchenstein 1981
Sisters:
13981 SAUDI PALM (Si) ex Burgenstein 1981
13982 SANDRA S (Pa) ex Buntenstein 1980

★13990 LUNG TAN RC/Ne (Wilton-Fije) 1958; C; 6800/9600; 161.12 × 8.00/8.87 529 × 26.25/29.10); M (Sulzer); 18 ex Galungan 1982 ex Nedlloyd Mississippi 1979 ex Mississippi Lloyd 1977

14000 DAUNTLESS Pa/Sw (Oskarshamns) 1960; CP; 6900; 150.8×8.8 (495×28.11); M (Gotaverken); 17; ex Concordia Venus 1981; ex Concordia Viking 1980

14010 LUCKY STAR II Pa/It (Odera) 1948; C; 2400; 93.2 × 5.6 (306 × 18.5); M (Fiat); 12; ex Vounitso 1978; ex Karterado 1976; ex Nordheide 1973; ex Garnes 1966

● 14020 FELICITY Gr/De (B&W) 1950; CP; 5300; 136 × 7.9 (446 × 25.10); M (B&W); 15; ex Ioanna 1971 ex Leoville 1967

● 14040 RIEDERSTEIN Sg/FRG (Howaldts) 1960; C; 9700; 161 × 9.3 (527 × 30.6); M (MAN); 17.5

★14050 HONG YIN RC/FRG (Howaldts) 1960; CP; 7000/9000; 162×8/9 (533×26/30); M (Fiat); 18.5; ex Ostfriesland 1979; ex Neuharlingersiel 1970
Sister:
★14051 DE YIN (RC) ex Elbeland 1979

14060 NISSOS MYKONOS Gr/Sw (Kockums) 1961; CP; 5700; 148×8.2 (484×26.8); M (MAN); 17.5; ex Black Swan 1976

14070 SAFINA—E—ARAB Pk/Sp (AESA) 1962;

CP; 8500; 141 × 7 (461 × 23.1); M (Sulzer); 15

14080 **EUROPE II** Gr/Br (Caledon) 1960; C; 6000/8200; 150.8 × 7.1/8.8 (495 × 23.3/28.10); M (B&W); 16.5 ex *Opobo* 1979; ex *Rhexenor* 1977; ex *Maron* 1975
Sister (Gr flag):
14081 **EUROPE** ex *Owerri* 1979; ex *Stentor* 1977; ex *Memnon* 1975

14090 **NEW SWAN** Sg/Ne (P-Smit) 1960; C; 7000/9200; 154.16 × 8.05/9.43 (505.77 × 26.41/30.94); M (B&W); 17.5 ex *Nedlloyd Rio* 1979; ex *Straat Rio* 1977
14091 **NEW DOVE** (Pa) ex *Win Dove* 1979; ex *Nedlloyd Van Diemen* 1979; ex *Straat Van Diemen* 1977

●14110 **SAUDI CLOUD** Si/De (Odense) 1957; C; 6400; 151.54 × 8.36 (497.18 × 27.43); M (B&W); 17.5; ex *Leda Maersk* 1981

14130 **YARA** Si/Au (Evans Deakin) 1962; PC; 4100; 98.7 × 5.5 (334 × 18.2); M (British Polar); 13; ex *Hong Kong Fir* 1974; ex *Kangaroo* 1973

14140 **GAMA GETAH** Pa/Fi (Wartsila) 1967/75; C; 8200/12100; 182.61 × 8.05/9.4 (599.11 × 26.41 /30.84); M (Sulzer); 17; ex *Hoegh Opal* 1982; Lengthened 1975 (Kawasaki)
Sisters:
14141 **GAMA KASIA** (Pa) ex *Hoegh Orchid* 1982
14142 **GAMA PALA** (Pa) ex *Hoegh Orris* 1982
Similar (taller funnel, etc):
14143 **GAMA ROBUSTA** (Pa) ex *Hoegh Pilot* 1982

14150 **CABO SANTA ANA** Sp/Ne (Wilton-Fije) 1961; C; 6200/8500; 144.2 × 8.1/8.8 (473 × 26.9/29); M (MAN); 16; ex *Katendrecht* 1974

14160 **NAKORNTHON** Th/Br (Burntisland) 1964; CP; 4400/6500; 134.1 × 7.2 (440 × 23.8/26.7); M (Sulzer); 16; ex *Thonburi* 1973; ex *Halifax City* 1972

●14170 **MORILLO** FRG/No (Bergens) 1971; R; 6900/9700; 155.8 × 8.6/9.2 (511 × 28.2/33); M (B&W); 22
Sisters:
14171 **ATLANTIC OCEAN** (Li) ex *Tangelo* 1976
14172 **TROPICAL LAND** (Ec) ex *Brunsland* 1978; ex *Maranga* 1976
14173 **CARINTHIA** (Br) ex *Cantaloup* 1976
14174 **CARMANIA** (Br) ex *Orange* 1976
14175 **CHERRY** (FRG)

14190 **PEGASUS** Gr/FRG (Howaldts DW) 1969; C; 4500; 133.4 × 7.4 (438 × 24.4); M (MAN); 17.5; ex *Louisiane* 1980; ex *Hornmeer* 1975
Sisters:
★14191 **YU CAI** (RC) ex *Horngolf* 1981
14192 **YACU WAYO** (Pe) ex *Andromeda* 1982; ex *Hattingen* 1981; ex *Hornwind*

14210 **CERAM SEA** Pa/Br (Connell) 1958; CP; 5600/9900; 155.8 × 8.3/9.2 (511 × 27.3/30.3); M (Doxford); 17; ex *Fernstate* 1976

14220 **SINKAI** Pa/Ne (Rotterdamsche) 1953; C; 8000/10500; 161.8 × 8.39/9.14 (530.84 × 27.53/29.99); M (Sulzer); 16.5; ex *Karimun* 1972

★14230 **HONG YIN** RC/FRG (Howaldts) 1960; CP; 7000/9900; 162 × 8/9 (533 × 26/30); M (Fiat); 18.5; ex *Ostriesland* 1979
Sister:
★14231 **DE YIN** (RC) ex *Elbeland* 1979

14240 **JADE** Cy/De (Nakskov) 1956; C; 6500; 149.69 × 8.4 (491.12 × 27.56); M (B&W); 17.25; ex *Star Antares* 1980; ex *Solholt* 1963; ex *Ivaran* 1962

●14260 **SAKURA** Ja/Ja (Mitsubishi HI) 1962; PC; 12500; 157 × 8.6 (516 × 28.3); M (Mitsubishi); 17; ex *Sakura Maru* 1972

14270 **KWANGCHOW** Pa/De (Helsingborgs) 1963; CP; 2300; 110 × 4.7 (362 × 15.6); M (B&W); 15; ex *Frontier* 1980; ex *Crusader* 1969

★14280 **FENG NING** RC/Fi (Crichton-Vulcan) 1964; CP; 8700; 152 × 8.6 (500 × 28.7); M (Sulzer); 16; ex *Hue Lu* 1983; ex *Poyang* 1981; ex *Asian Exporter* 1975; ex *Finnboston* 1973; ex *Finnenso* 1974
Similar:
14281 **CORDILLERA** (Ch) ex *Finnarrow* 1980; ex *Visaholm* 1976; ex *Finnarrow* 1971
14282 **CORRAL** (Pa) ex *Mah* 1980; ex *Finnenso* 1980
14283 **FERNANDOEVERETT** (Li) ex *Finnhawk* 1980; ex *Maltesholm* 1976; ex *Finnhawk* 1971
14284 **CONDOR** (Ch) ex *Palladia* 1980; ex *Finnmaid* 1979

●14290 **BIG ORANGE** Sg/Pd (Szczecinska) 1958; CP; 3400; 124 × 6.5 (407 × 21.4); M (MAN); 14.5; ex *Krystina* 1981; ex *Krynica* 1979; **'B55'** type

Sister:
14291 **MICHALIS** (Gr) ex *Olesnica* 1981

●★14300 **KRUSZWICA** Pd/Pd (Szczecinska) 1961; CP; 3400; 124 × 6.5 (407 × 21.4); M (B&W); 15.5; **'B55'** type
Sisters:
14302 **JAN FOUR** (Sr) ex *Jan Zizka* 1983
14304 **KOSTIS** (Ma) ex *Swidnica* 1981
14305 **GRAZKA** (Gr) ex *Szczawnica* 1984
★14306 **WISLICA** (Pd)

14310 **CIDADE DE RIO GRANDE** Bz/Pd (Szczecinska) 1959; C; 3200/4600; 124×6.5/— (407×21.4/—); M (MAN); 15; ex *Cabo De Sao Roque* 1981; **'B 55'** type
Sisters (Bz flag):
14311 **CABO DE SANTA MARTA**
14312 **CABO FRIO**

14320 **JALARASHMI** In/Br (Lithgows) 1966; C; 11300; 160 × 9.4 (525 × 31); M (B&W); 16
Similar (Stulcken masts):
14321 **JALARAJAN** (In)
14322 **JALARATNA** (In)

14340 **TILLY** Pa/FRG (Deutsche Werft) 1967/74; C; 5200; 151.47 × 7.27/8.03 (496.95 × 23.85/26.35); M (MAN); 17.75; ex *Tilly Russ*; Lengthened 1974
Sister:
14341 **PAUL** (Pa) ex *Pampana* 1981; ex *Paul Lorenz Russ* 1979

14350 **ATLANTICO** Gr/Br (Caledon) 1967; C; 4400/6400; 131 × 7.3/8.5 (430 × 23.6/28); M (MAN); 17.5; ex *GME. Atlantico* 1983; ex *Atlantico* 1982; ex *Luise* 1975; ex *Luise Bornhofen* 1973

14360 **RIO CALCHAQUI** Ar/Ar (AFNE) 1970; C; 10400; 152.71 × 8.68 (501.02 × 28.48); M (GMT); 17.5
Sisters (Ar flag):
14362 **RIO IGUAZU**
14363 **RIO PARANA**
14364 **RIO GUALEGUAY**

★14370 **PULA** Ru/Ys ('Uljanik') 1964; C; 8000/10100; 160 × 9.7 (525 × 26/32); M (B&W) 18
Sisters (Ru flag):
★14371 **ALEKSANDR BLOK**
★14372 **ALEKSANDR GERTSEN**
★14373 **ALEKSANDR GRIN**
★14374 **ALEKSANDR SERAFIMOVIC**
★14375 **ALEKSANDR VERMISHEV**
★14376 **ALISHER NAVOI**
★14377 **ANTON CHEKOV**
★14378 **ARKADY GAYDAR**
★14379 **DEMYAN BEDNYY**
★14380 **DMITRIY GULIA**
★14381 **DUBROVNIK**
★14382 **GAVRIIL DERZHAVIN**
★14383 **MAKHTUM-KULI**
★14384 **MUSA DZHALIL**
★14385 **NAZIM KHIKMET**
★14386 **NIKOLAY DUBROLYUBOV**
★14387 **NIKOLAY GOGOL**
★14388 **NIKOLAY KARAMZIM**
★14389 **NIKOLAY OGARYEV**
★14390 **OVANES TUMANYAN**
★14391 **SERGEY YESENIN**
★14392 **SULEYMAN STALSKIY**
★14393 **VISSARION BELINSKIY**
★14394 **VLADIMIR KOROLENKO**
★14395 **VLADIMIR MAYAKOVSKIY**

14400 **MAZZINI** It/No (Bergens) 1966; C; 4500; 141 × 7.4 (463 × 24.5); M (B&W); 19; ex *Alberta* 1972
Sisters:
14401 **ZANET** (Gr) ex *Michigan* 1980
14403 **MARHABA** (In) ex *Ontario* 1979
14404 **CRISPI** (It) ex *Wisconsin* 1972
14405 **D'AZEGLIO** (It) ex *Nebraska* 1972
14406 **ERMIONI** (Gr) ex *Missouri* 1980
14407 **TAIBAH IV** (Si) ex *Nour* 1983; ex *Manitoba* 1980

14420 **ELIZABETH LYKES** US/US (Avondale) 1966; CP; 7400/11000; 165 × 8.5/10 (542 ×28/33); T (Westinghouse); 20
Sisters (US flag):
14421 **DOLLY TURMAN**
14422 **FREDERICK LYKES**
14423 **GENEVIEVE LYKES**
14424 **HOWELL LYKES**
14425 **LETITIA LYKES**
14426 **LOUISE LYKES**
14427 **MALLORY LYKES**
14428 **MASON LYKES**
14429 **RUTH LYKES**
14430 **STELLA LYKES**
14431 **VELMA LYKES**

★14450 **IGNATIY SERGEYEV** Ru/Pd (Gdanska) 1968; C; 10200; 154.5×9.5 (507×29.6); M (Sulzer);

16.5; **'B40/B401** 'type 'KOMMUNIST' class
Similar (Ru flag):
★14451 **GEORGIY CHICHERIN**
★14452 **GEORGIY DMITROV**
★14453 **ERNST THALMANN**
★14454 **GIUSEPPE DI VITTORIO**
★14455 **50 LET SOVIETSKOY UKRAINY**
★14456 **HO CHI MIN**
★14457 **INESSA ARMAND**
★14458 **IONA YAKIR**
★14459 **JEANNE LABOURBE**
★14460 **KARL LIEBKNECHT**
★14461 **KOMMUNIST**
★14462 **KOMMUNISTICHESKOYE-ZNAMYA**
★14463 **BELA KHUN**
★14464 **DMITRY POLUYAN**
★14465 **NIKOLAY KREMLYANSKIY**
★14466 **FRIEDRICH ENGELS**
★14467 **ROSA LUXEMBURG**
★14468 **FRANTS BOGUSH**
★14469 **TOYVO ANTIKAYNEN**
(Tu flag) (**B442** type):
14470 **GENERAL A.F. CEBESOY**
14471 **GENERAL K. ORBAY**
14472 **GENERAL R. GUMUSBALA**
14473 **GENERAL Z. DOGAN**
(Pd flag):
★14474 **KONIN**

★14480 **FRANCISZEK ZUBRZYCKI** Pd/Pd (Gdanska) 1973; Con; 7200/10100; 161 × —/9.7 (529 × — /32); M (Sulzer); 21; **'B438'** type
Sisters (Pd flag):
★14482 **BRONISLAW LACHOWICZ**
★14483 **EUGENIUSZ KWIATKOWSKI**
★14484 **MIECZYSLAW KALINOWSKI**
★14485 **ROMAN PAZINSKI**
★14486 **TADEUSZ OCIOSZYNSKI**
★14487 **GENERAL STANISLAW POPLAWSKI**
(Ec flag):
14488 **ISLA SANTAY** launched as *Aleksandr Rylke*
14489 **ISLA BALTRA**
(Bz flag):
14491 **CANTUARIA**
14492 **CALANDRINI**

★14500 **LU CHENG** RC/FRG (Deutsche Werft) 1966; CP; 10500; 156 × 9.2 (509 × 30.6); M (MAN); 19; ex *SA. Tugela-land* 1980; ex *Tugelaland* 1974; ex *Concordia Land* 1973; ex *Tugelnd* 1972

14510 **SAUDI CROWN** Si/Sw (Oresunds) 1962; C; 5300/7900; 141 × 7.8/8.8 (462 × 25.9/29); M (Gotaverken); 16.5; ex *Kariba* 1979; ex *Lena Christina Brodin* 1965

14520 **LEONOREVERETT** Li/FRG (Rhein Nordseew) 1962; Con; 6500/8800; 150 × 7/8.5 (493 × 23/28); M (B&W); 16; ex *Finnclipper* 1978; Converted from cargo ships and lengthened 1968
Sisters:
14521 **BRADEVERETT** (Li) ex *Finnforest* 1979
14522 **ROSSEVERETT** (Li) ex *Finneagle* 1979; ex *Trolleholm* 1976; ex *Finneagle* 1971

●14530 **SEA CARRIER** Pa/FRG (Kieler H) 1962; C; 2700; 108 × 7.5 (355 × 24.6); M (MAN) 15; ex *Dexter* 1982; ex *Lama* 1979; ex *Lara Viking* 1973; ex *Concordia Lara* 1971; ex *Lara Viking* 1970; ex *Svanefjell* 1969
Sisters (Po flag):
14531 **CABO BOJADOR** ex *Haukefjell* 1971
14532 **CABO VERDE** ex *Sirefjell* 1971

★14540 **YU CHUN** RC/Br (Lithgows) 1962; C; 7500/9700; 159 × 8.4/9.4 (502 × 27.6/31); M (B&W); —; ex *Norwegian Sea* 1976; ex *Salimiah* 1973; ex *Clarkforth* 1965
Similar:
14542 **OLYMPUS** (Gr) ex *Arteaga* 1981; ex *Elysia* 1969; ex *Highland* 1968

14550 **MORMACGLEN** US/US (Todd) 1961; C; 6600/9300; 147.3 × —/9.58 (483 × —/31.4); T (GEC); 19
similar (operated by US Navy (Military Sealift Command) as Cargo Ships):
14551 **NORTHERN LIGHT** ex *Cove* 1980; ex *Mormaccove* 1977
14552 **SOUTHERN CROSS** ex *Trade* 1980; ex *Mormactrade* 1977
14553 **VEGA** ex *Bay* 1980; ex *Mormacbay* 1977
The following will be acquired by the US Navy over the next few years:
14554 **LAKE** (US) ex *Mormaclake* 1977
14555 **PRIDE** (US) ex *Mormacpride* 1977
14556 **SCAN** (US) ex *Mormacscan* 1977
14557 **CAPE** (US) ex *Mormaccape* 1983

★14560 **HONG QI 119** RC/Br (H&W) 1956; C; 5900/7600; 150.09 × 7.12/8.66 (492.4 × 23.36/28.4); M (H&W); —; ex *Hungmien* 1977; ex

Dolius 1972; ex *Glenfruin* 1972; ex *Dolius* 1970
Sister:
★14561 **HONG QI 137** (RC) ex *Hungsia* 1979; ex *Demodocus* 1973; ex *Glenroy* 1972; ex *Demodocus* 1970

● 14570 **ALHANA** Ku/FRG (Flensburger) 1960; CP; 7000/9800; 167 × —/9.1 (548 × —/30); M (MAN); 17.5; ex *Express* 1981; ex *Hamburg Express* 1980; ex *Kaapland*; ex *SA. Kaapland*; ex *Kaapland* 1973; Lengthened 1970
Sister:
14571 **SARIA** (Si) ex *Rini* 1982; ex *SA. Krugerland*; ex *Krugerland* 1974

● ★14580 **EMILIA PLATER** Pd/Pd (Gdanska) 1959; CP; 6700; 154 × 8.3 (506 × 27.6); M (Sulzer); 15.5; '**B54**' type
Sisters (Pd flag):
★14582 **JAN MATEJKO**
★14583 **JANEK KRASICKI**
★14585 **LUDWIK SOLSKI**

14600 **CHEVALIER DARBY** Pa/Ja (Harima) 1957; C; 7100; 136.63 × 8.37 (448.26 × 27.46); M (Harima); 13.25; ex *Mediterranean Darby* 1975; ex *Hikone Maru* 1973

14610 **EASTERN JUPITER** Pa/Ja (Fujinagata) 1957; C; 8700; 147 × 8.8 (483 × 29); M (B&W); 13.5; ex *Kensho Maru* 1974

★14630 **FENG QING** RC/RC (—) 1974; C; 10300; 161.6 × 9.1 (530 × 30); M(—); —; Probable sisters (some may have radar mast from bridge—see LIAO YANG) (RC flag):
★14631 **FENG CAI**
★14632 **FENG GE**
★14633 **FENGLEI**
★14634 **FENGTAI**
★14635 **FENGTAO**
★14636 **FENGXIANG**
★14637 **FENGYAN**
★14638 **FENGYANG**
★14639 **FENGYI**
★14639/1 **FENGYING**
★14639/2 **HUI YANG**
★14639/3 **JIEYANG**
★14639/4 **XINYANG**
★14639/5 **YUEYANG**

★14640 **LIAO YANG** RC/RC (—) 1974; C; 9900; 161.55 × 9.15 (530 × 30.02); M (—); —; Differs from **FENG QING** (which see) only by radar mast being separated from funnel; Other vessels of this type may have this feature

14660 **DIMITRAKIS** Ma/Be (Boel) 1961; CP; 5200/7800; 141.2 × 7.8/8.8 (464 × 25.6/29); M (MAN); 16; ex *Marina P* 1983; ex *Manaure III* 1980; ex *Good Luck* 1977; ex *Anvers* 1973
Sisters:
14661 **HELENA C** (Gr) ex *Good Hope* 1975; ex *Gand* 1973
14662 **SHABNAM** (Li) ex *Scherazade* 1976; ex *Uniolympia* 1973; ex *Escaut* 1973

★14670 **QIN HUAI** RC/FRG (Kieler H) 1960; CP; 7500; 143.2 × 8.5 (470 × 27.1); M (MAN); 17; *Pateverett* 1982; ex *Nopal Express* 1977
Similar (lighter mast from bridge):
14672 **PUNTA ATALAYA** (Li) ex *Nopal Express* 1974

14690 **ONE WEST NO 7** Ko/Ja (Mitsubishi Z) 1960; CP; 9300; 156.3 × 9 (513 × 30); M (Mitsubishi); 18; ex *Korean Runner* 1978; ex *Crystal Laurel* 1977; ex *Seta Maru* 1971

★14700 **DIVNOGORSK** Ru/Pd (Szczecinska) 1961; C; 6400; 164 × 8.8 (505 × 29); M (Sulzer); 16; '**B 54**' type
Sister:
★14701 **MEDNOGORSK** (Ru)

14710 **TALAVERA** Br/FRG (Kieler H) 1961; CP; 5100/7400; 143 × 7.7/8.5 (471 × 25.6/28); M (MAN); 17; ex *Nopal Star* 1977

14730 **KOTA PETANI** Br/Br (Caledon) 1963; C; 7300/10200; 155 × 8.5/9.2 (509 × 28/30.2); M (Sulzer); 16; ex *Benarty* 1981

14740 **SAIKYO MARU** Ja/Ja (Mitsubishi Z) 1961; CP; 9200; 156.4 × 9 (513 × 29.7); M (Mitsubishi); 18.25

14750 **MALANGE** Po/Po (Viana) 1971; C; 12200; 171.6 × 9.2 (563 × 30.2); M (Sulzer); 18
Sister:
14751 **PORTO** (Po)

14760 **LELLO DI MAIO** It/FRG (LF-W) 1961; CP; 6400/8900; 151.6 × 8.2/9.2 (497 × 27/30); M (MAN); 16.25; ex *Tanga*; ex *Novia* 1963

★14770 **URSUS** Pd/Pd (Gdanska) 1972; C;

6400/10100; 154.7 × —/8.97 (507.55 × —/29.43); M (Sulzer); 17.75; '**B442**' type

● 14780 **MALDIVE PRIVILEGE** Mv/Br (Scotts' SB) 1959; C; 11300; 161.2 × 9.5 (530 × 31); M (Doxford); 15; ex *Styliani* 1981; ex *Capetan Costis* 1981; ex *Constantinos T* 1978; ex *N Zografia* 1975; ex *Lord Gladstone* 1969

14790 **BUNGA ARANDA** Sg/Ja (IHI) 1958; C; 7700; 139.91 × 8.81 (459 × 28.9); M (MAN); 14.5; ex *New Castle* 1981; ex *Yamato* 1976; ex *Kyozui Maru* 1972

★14800 **WLADYSLAW ORKAN** Pd/Pd (Gdanska) 1971; C; 6400/10100; 154.74 × —/8.97 (504.4 ×—/29.43); M (Sulzer); 18; Modified '**B442**' type
Sister:
★14801 **LUCJAN SZENWALD** (Pd)

14810 **PONTALVA** Pa/Ja (Kure) 1960; C; 10000; 155.51 × 9.02 (510.2 × 29.59); M (Sulzer); 18.25; ex *Galleon Ruby* 1980; ex *Philippines* 1978
Sister:
14811 **GALLEON CORAL** (Pi) ex *Philippine President Garcia* 1978
Similar:
14812 **BADJAO** (Pi) ex *Philippine Rizal* 1982
14813 **MARANAO** (Pi) ex *Philippine Antonio Luna* 1982
14814 **PHILIPPINE BATAAN** (Pi)

● 14860 **DEVON EXPRESS** Li/Br (Ardrossan) 1954; LS; 1500; 90.1 × 5.2 (297 × 17); TSM (G Clark); 14; ex *Lairdsglen* 1974; Converted from a cargo ship

● 14870 **THEODOROS** Gr/Fr (Provence) 1961; C/WT; 4500/6600; 130 × 7/8.1 (427 ×23/26.3); M (Doxford); 15; ex *Alexander Emmous* 1982; ex *Apostolos K* 1981; ex *Jacques Bingen* 1972

14880 **OHRMAZD** Pk/Br (Burntisland) 1968; C; 8000/11000; 156.83 × —/9 (515 × —/29.2); M (Sulzer); 19

14890 **ELIZABETH LYKES** US/US (Avondale) 1966; CP; 7400/11000; 165 × 8.5/10 (542 × 28/33); T (Westinghouse); 20
Sisters (US flag):
14891 **DOLLY TURMAN**
14892 **FREDERICK LYKES**
14893 **GENEVIEVE LYKES**
14894 **HOWELL LYKES**
14895 **LETITIA LYKES**
14896 **LOUISE LYKES**
14897 **MALLORY LYKES**
14898 **MASON LYKES**
14899 **RUTH LYKES**
14900 **STELLA LYKES**
14901 **VELMA LYKES**

★14905 **VITYAZ** Ru/Pd (Szczecinska) 1981; RS; 4800; 110.93× 5.70 (364× 18.70); TSM (Sulzer); 16; '**B86**' type
Sister:
★14906 **AKADEMIK ALEKSANDR NESMEYANOV** (Ru)

14910 **VISHVA CHETANA** In/Pd (Szczecinska) 1969; C; 5400/8100; 145.37× 7.36/9.09 (476.94× 24.15/29.82); M (Sulzer); 17.5; ex *Vishva Chetna* 1969; launched as *Zygmunt August*; '**B445**' type
Sisters (In flag):
14911 **VISHVA BINDU**
14912 **VISHVA SANDESH** launched as *Zygmunt Stary*
14913 **VISHVA VIKAS** launched as *Wladyslaw Jagiello*
(Pd flag):
★14914 **WLADYSLAW JAGIELLO**
★14915 **WLADYSLAW LOKIETEK**
★14916 **ZYGMUNT AUGUST**
★14917 **ZYGMUNT STARY**
★14918 **ZYGMUNT III WAZA**
★14919 **MIESZKO 1**
★14920 **BOLESLAW CHOBRY**
★14921 **BOLESLAW SMIALY**
★14922 **BOLESLAW KRZYWOUSTY**
(Ir flag):
14923 **IRAN EKRAM** ex *Arya Rokh* 1980
14924 **IRAN ELHAM** ex *Arya Kish* 1980
14925 **IRAN GHEYAM** ex *Arya Rooz* 1980
(Fr flag):
14926 **COURSON** ex *Arya Dad* 1971; ex *Boleslaw Krzywousty* (RC flag):
★14927 **JIANG CHENG** ex *Wladyslaw IV*
Sisters ('**B474**' type):
★14928 **CSOKONAI** (Hu)
★14929 **RADNOTI** (Hu)

14940 **SEA PRINCESS** Br/Br (J Brown) 1966/79; P; 26700; 201.23 × 8.56 (approx) (660.2 ×28.08); TSM (Gotaverken); 21; ex *Kungsholm* 1978; rebuilt 1978/79 (Bremer V)

14950 **T W NELSON** US/Ja (Mitsubishi HI) 1978;

RS; 2600; 86.64 × 4.82 (284.25 × 15.81); M (Daihatsu); 15.25; helicopter deck
Similar (taller funnel etc):
14951 **MOBIL SEARCH** (US)

★14955 **AKADEMIK MSTISLAV KELDYSH** Ru/Fi (Hollming) 1981; RS; 5500; 122.21 × 5.9 (400.95 × 19.36); TSM (Wartsila); 16; Inset drawing shows detail of starboard side superstructure

★14960 **BIN HAI 511** RC/Ja (Mitsui) 1978; RS; 1300; 79.00 × 4.60 (259.2 × 15.09); TSM (Daihatsu); 15.75
Sister:
★14961 **BIN HAI 512** (RC)

14970 **DON VICENTE** Pi/Ja (Niigata) 1969; F; 1100; 77.35 × 3.77 (253.77 × 12.37); TSM (Niigata); 17

★14975 **YULIUS FUCHIK** Ru/Fi (Valmet) 1978; Bg/Con; 22800/35900; 266.45 × —/11 (874.18 × —/36.09); TSM (Pielstick); 20; may be spelt **JULIUS FUCIK**; Deck stowage of barges indicated by dotted lines
Sister:
★14975A **TIBOR SZAMUELY** (Ru)

14976 **EUROPEAN CLEARWAY** Br/FRG (Schichau-U) 1976; RoC; 3300; 118.32 × 5.82 (388.2 × 19.09); TSM (Stork-Werkspoor); 18.5; Bow door-/ramp and stern door/ramp
Sister:
14977 **EUROPEAN TRADER** (Br)
Similar (funnel shape differs-see inset):
14978 **EUROPEAN ENTERPRISE** (Br)

14979 **SIGYN** Fr/Fr (Havre) 1982; RoC; 3900; 90.02 × 3.99 (295 × 13.09); TSM (B&W); 11; Stern door; Bow thrusters; Irradiated nuclear fuel carrier

14980 **DON CLAUDIO** Pi/Ja (Sanoyasu) 1965; F; 2700; 93 × 5.4 (306 × 17.6); M (B&W); 18.5; ex *Okinoshima Maru*

14990 **MERCURY** Br/Br (Cammell Laird) 1962; Cbl; 9000; 144.1 × 7.5 (473 × 24.7); TSD-E (English Electric); 16

★15000 '**PROFESSOR**' class Ru/Pd (Szczecinska) 1970; CTS; 6000; 122 × 7.3 (401 × 24.2); M (Sulzer); '**B-80**' class; Several vessels of this class may have this sequence; Superstructure varies; Full list under KMFC-H12 (Professor Shchyogolev)—which see

★15020 **DAI YUN SHAN** RC/De (Nakskov) 1965; CP; 4800/7500; 137.5 × 7.1/8.7 (451 × 23/28.6); M (B&W); 17.5; ex *Jytte Skou*
Sisters:
★15021 **BAI YUN SHAN** (RC) ex *Susanne Skou* 1980
★15022 **HUANG PU JIANG** (RC) ex *Lotte Skou* 1980
★15023 **FU CHUNG JIANG** (RC) ex *Benny Skou* 1980

15030 **KUROSHIO MARU** Ja/Ja (Hayashikane) 1971; F; 4900; 124 × 5.5 (407 × 17.1); TSM (NKK); 23

15050 **NOGA** Pa/US (Newport News) 1940/79; P; 26400; 220.38 × 9.98 (723 × 32.74); TST (Newport News); 22.5; ex *Italis* 1980; ex *America* 1979; ex *Australis* 1978; ex *America* 1964; ex *West Point* 1946; ex *America* 1942; Modernised c.1979; converted to a floating hotel in 1980; probably altered in appearance

★15055 **HONG WEI 7** RC/RC (—) 1969; PC; 2000; 73 × — (239.5 × —); —; 17

15060 **GOLFO PARADISO** It/FRG (Sietas) 1968; RoC; 1500; 95 × — (312 × —); TSM (KHD); 16; stern door
Sister:
★15061 **RAPOCA** (Ys) ex *Caribbean Enterprise* 1975

15070 **OLYMPIAN REEFER** Gr/No (Bergens) 1971; R; 7300/9700; 156 × 8.4/9.1 (511 × 27.6/30.1); M (B&W); 21; ex *Wild Auk*
Sister:
15071 **DELPHIC REEFER** (Gr) ex *Wild Avocet* 1980

● ★15080 **KRAKOW** Pd/Pd (Szczecinska) 1965; P; 3400/5500; 124 × 6.5/6.9 (407 × 21.6/23); M (Cegielski); 16; '**B455**' type
Sisters (Pd flag):
★15081 **CZESTOCHOWA**
★15082 **GDYNIA II**
★15084 **LUBLIN**
★15085 **RADOM**
★15086 **RZESZOW**
★15087 **WARSZAWA**

★15090 **KRIVAN** Cz/Pd (Szczecinska) 1970; CP; 3400/5500; 124 × 6.5/6.9 (407 × 21.6/23); M (Sulzer); 16; '**B455**' type
Sisters (Cz flag):

★15091 **RADHOST**
★15092 **SITNO**
★15093 **BLANIK**

★15095 **AKADEMIK MSTISLAV KELDYSH** Ru/Fi 1981; RS; 5500; 122.21 × 5.9 (400.95 × 19.36); TSM; 16; Inset drawing shows detail of starboard side superstructure

★15100 **FRANZ STENZER** DDR/Ja (Mitsui) 1965; C; 6000/6400; 131 × 6.8/7.9 (430 × 22/26); M (B&W); 17; ex LLoyd Helsinki; ex Transatlantic 1972
Sisters:
★15101 **YU YING** (RC) ex Nyanda 1981; ex Transontario 1972;
★15102 **YU QING** (RC) ex Boogalla 1981; ex Transmichigan 1972

★15110 **AGIOS NECTARIOS** Gr/FRG (Stuelcken) 1955; C; 5000; 116.7 × 7.8 (383 × 25.6); M (MAN); 12.5; ex Iris 1979; ex United Victory 1976; ex Mariel 1973; ex Naguilan 1965; ex Commerz 1961;
Sister:
15111 **SEA HAWK** (Pa) ex Allipen 1976; ex Continent 1961

★15120 **ALEKSANDR DOVZHENKO** Ru/Rm (Galatz) 1965; C/TC; 2700; 100.67 × 6.00 (330 × 19.69); M (Fiat); 13.75
Sisters (Ru Flag):
★15121 **GEORGIY VASILIEV**
★15122 **SERGEY EYZENSHTEYN**
★15123 **SERGEY VASILIEV**
★15124 **VSEVOLOD PUDOVKIN**

★15130 **BANGLAR SWAPNA** Bh/FRG (AG 'Weser') 1971; C; 6900; 131 × 8.4 (429 × 27); M (MAN); 17.5; ex Transcanada 1964
Sister:
15131 **BANGLAR PROGOTI** (Bh) ex Transamerica 1974

15140 **LALAZAR** Pk/Pk (Karachi) 1973; C; 6000/9000; 154.7 × 9.2 (508 × 30.6); M (MAN); 17
Sister:
15141 **SHALAMAR** (Pk)
Possible sister:
★15142 **BAYNUNAH** (Sh)

★15160 **TIRANA** Al/Pd (Gdynska) 1970; CP; 5800/8700; 153 × —/9 (502 × /29.9); M (Sulzer); 16.25; 'B41' type

★15170 **ATRA** Pa/Sp ('Elcano') 1960; CP; 5300; 145 7.3 (475 × 24); M (Sulzer); 17; ex Rio Atrato 1980; ex Ciudad De Armenia 1977
Sisters:
15172 **ADHEMAR** (Co) ex Ciudad de Pereira 1982
15173 **CEFALLONIAN AMBITION** (Gr) ex Ciudad De Guayaquil 1980
Similar:
15174 **CEFALLONIAN CHARIS** (Gr) ex Ciudad de Barranquila 1981
15175 **CABO DE LA VELA** (Co) ex Ciudad de Tunja 1983

★15180 **HANOI** Pd/Pd (Gdanska) 1960; CP; 6900; 154 × 8.3 (505 × 27.4); M (Sulzer); 15.5; 'B-54' type
Sisters (Pd flag):
★15181 **FEKIN**
★15182 **PHENIAN**
Similar:
★15183 **ZHEN XING** (RC) ex Yi Xing 1982; ex Konopnicka
★15184 **CHI CHENG** (RC) ex Internacional 1979; ex Guo Ji 1963
★15185 **GONZALEZ LINES** (Cu)
★15186 **COMMANDANTE CAMILO CIENFUEGOS** (Cu)

★15190 **HEWELIUSZ** Pd/Pd (Szczecinska) 1962; C; 5700; 145.78 × 7.70 (478.2 × 25.26); M (CCM); 16.5; 'B516' type
Sisters (Pd flag):
★15191 **SNIADECKI**
★15192 **STASZIC**

15200 **PRESIDENT HARRISON** US/US (National Steel) 1966; Con; 16800; 204 × 10.2 (669 × 33.6); T (GEC); Converted from a cargo ship and lengthened 1963
Sisters (US flag):
15201 **PRESIDENT MONROE**
15202 **PRESIDENT POLK**

★15215 **CHAO YANG** RC/RC (Jiangnan) 1968; C; 9900; 161.50 × 9.50 (530 × 31.17); M (Sulzer); 15.5
Sister:
★15216 **XIANG YANG** (RC)

15220 **RIVER** Cy/FRG (Rhein Nordseew) 1968; C; 5400/7800; 137 × 7.6/8.7 (448 × 25/28.8); M (B&W); 16.5; ex River Niger 1983
Sisters:
15221 **DYNASTY** (Cy) ex River Benue 1983

15222 **RIVER ETHIOPE** (Ng)
15223 **SHOGUN** (Cy) ex River Ogun 1984

15230 **JALAJYOTI** In/FRG (Rhein Nordseew) 1966; C; 8300/10900; 158.43 × 8.5/9.66 (519.78 × 27.89/31.69); M (MAN); 16 ex Apj Ambar 1966; may now be KCM₂FKM—see Jalajaya
Sister:
15232 **APJ PRIYA** (In)

★15240 **BASKA** Ys/Ys ('Split') 1960; C; 4400/6700; 136 × 7.1/7.5 (447 × 23.6/24.9); M (Fiat); 17.25
Sisters (Ys flag):
★15242 **GROBNIK**
★15243 **NOVI VINODOLSKI**

15250 **BAGH-E-KARACHI** Pk/Ys ('Split') 1964; C; 6100/9000; 155 × 8.2/9 (509 × 27/29.9); M (Sulzer); 17.5
Sisters (Pk flag):
15251 **BAGH-E-DACCA**
15252 **CHENAB**

15255 **GOLDEN TAIF** Si/Br (Doxford & S) 1968; C; 7800/11000; 164.42 × —/9.53 (539 × —/31.27); M (Doxford); 16.5; ex Golden Bahrain 1982; ex Tarpon Springs 1981; ex Nicholas Livanos 1969
Sister:
15256 **CONSTANTINOS MALTEZOS** (Cy) ex N G Livanos 1983

★15260 **SHU YU QUAN** RC/FRG (Kieler H) 1961; CP; 5200/7200; 138 × 7.2/8.6 (454 × 23.6/28.3); M (MAN) 16.5; ex Cherry Crystal 1980; ex Maren Skou 1980
Sister:
15261 **NEW HAINING** (Pa) ex Desanmar 1982; ex Ebel 1980; ex Birgitte Skou

15270 **BENYA RIVER** Gh/Br (Swan Hunter & WR) 1965; CP; 4900/7300; 139 × —/8.5 (455 × —/27.8); M (Sulzer); 17
Sisters (Gh flag):
15271 **NAKWA RIVER**
15272 **KORLE LAGOON**
15273 **SAKUMO LAGOON**
Similar: (Gh flag)
15275 **BIA RIVER**
15276 **OTI RIVER**
15277 **SUBIN RIVER**
15278 **KLORTE LAGOON**

★15280 **HANKA SAWICKA** Pd/Pd (Szczecinska) 1962; CP; 6900; 154.1 × 8.3 (506 × 27.4); M (Sulzer); 15.5; 'B-54' type

★15285 **BOSNA** Ys/Ys ('3 Maj') 1969; C; 7000/9500; 155.02 × 8.16/— (509 × 26.77/—); M (Stork); 18; ex Pleiades 1969
Sister:
★15286 **HRVATSKA** (Ys) ex Cassiopeia 1969

★15290 **JESENICE** Ys/Ys ('3 Maj') 1960; C; 7000/9500; 155 × 8.2/9.5 (509 × 27/31.3); M (Sulzer); 18.5
Sister:
★15291 **KOSTRENA** (Ys)

★15300 **ANDRZEJ STRUG** Pd/Pd (Szczecinska) 1963; CP; 6900; 153 × 8.3 (502 × 27.2); M (Sulzer); 17; 'B-54' type
Sister:
★15301 **WLADYSLAW BRONIEWSKI** (Pd)

15310 **IRAN SEEYAM** Ir/Po (Viana) 1974; C; 9200; 153 × 9.1 (502 × 30); M (Sulzer); 18; ex Arya Sun 1980
Sisters (Ir flag):
15311 **IRAN KALAM** ex Iran Seem 1980; ex Arya Seem
15312 **IRAN SALAM** ex Iran Zar 1980; ex Arya Zar
(Pd flag):
★15313 **MAJOR SUCHARSKI**
★15314 **MARIAN BUCZEK**

★15320 **BANAT** Ys/Ys ('3 Maj') 1963; C; 6300/9000; 152 × —/9 (498 × —/29.5); M (Sulzer); 15
Sisters (Ys flag):
★15321 **METOHIJA**
★15322 **SUMADIJA**
★15323 **MOSLAVINA**

15330 **NAFEESA** Si/Be (Cockerill-Ougree) 1963; CP; 7300/10300; 158 × 8.3/9.2 (517 × 27.3/30.4); M (Sulzer); 16.5; ex Char Ning 1982; ex Jordaens 1980
Sisters:
15331 **TREASURY ALPHA** (Pa) ex Breughel 1982
15332 **CHRISTINA** (Gr) ex Memling 1983; ex Rubens 1972
15333 **SANTA CLARA** (Pa) ex Teniers 1982

★15340 **FRANCESCO NULLO** Pd/Pd (Gdynska) 1964; C; 5700/8600; 152.6 × 7.7/8.8 (501 × 25.4/29); M (Sulzer); 15.5; 'B-41' type

Sister (Pd flag):
★15341 **LENINO**
Similar (larger funnels): (Pd flag):
★15342 **ALEKSANDER ZAWADSKI**
★15343 **GWARDIA LUDOWA**
★15344 **LENINGRAD**
★15345 **JOZEF WYBICKI** ex Sebastian Klonowicz
★15346 **PIOTR DUNIN**
★15347 **SNOLNY**
★15348 **STANISLAW DUBOIS**
Similar (some may have small funnel) (RC flag):
★15349 **CHANGNING**
★15350 **HAINING**
★15351 **JINING**
★15352 **XINGNING**
★15353 **YONGNING**

15360 **GAY FORTUNE** Gr/Pd (Gdynska) 1971; CP; 5800/8700 153 × 7.7/9.1 (502 × 25.3/30); M (Sulzer); 16.25; ex Pontevedra 1981; ex Moroni; ex Langon 1971; 'B-41' type
Probable sister:
★15361 **PULKOWNIK DABEK** (Pd)

15370 **PINDAROS** Gr/Sw (Uddevalla) 1963; C; 7900/10700; 162 × 8.7/9.5 (531 × 28.3/31); M (Gotaverken); 16.5; ex London Craftsman 1976
Sisters:
15371 **PLOTINOS** (Gr); ex London Citizen 1977;
15372 **SKAROS** (Cy) ex Olympiakos 1983; ex Agia Marina 1981; ex London Statesman 1979
Similar:
15373 **RIVA** (Gr) ex London banker 1973
15374 **SINGAPORE FORTUNE** (Sg) ex London Advocate 1973
★15375 **LIMING** (RC) ex London Tradesman 1964

15380 **JOHANNES LATUHARHARY** Ia/Pd (Szczecinska) 1964; C; 6900; 153.93 × 8.29 (505 × 27.20); M (Sulzer); 15

15390 **LADY JOSEPHINE** Pa/Fr (Provence) 1964; R; 4200; 125 × 7.6 (410 × 25); M (Doxford); 20.75; ex Fort Josephine 1977
Sister:
15391 **LORD TRINITE** (Pa) ex Fort Trinite 1977

★15400 **DARYAL** Ru/US (Southeastern) 1943; C; 7200; 134.58 × 8.46 (442 × 27.76); R (Vulcan); 10; ex Orata 1963; ex Wilford 1957; ex George Whitefield 1947; 'Liberty' type

★15410 **ANTON SAEFKOW** DDR/DDR (Warnow) 1965; C; 5000/7700; 142 × 7.2 /8.5 (466 × 23.6/28); M (MAN); —
Similar (DDR flag):
★15411 **HEINZ KAPELLE**
★15412 **LIESELOTTE HERRMANN**
★15413 **RUDOLF BREITSCHEID**
★15414 **ALBIN KOBIS**
★15415 **MAX REICHPIETSCH**
Possible sisters:(DDR flag):
★15416 **JOHN SCHEHR**
★15417 **GEORG SCHUMANN**
★15418 **MATHIAS THESEN**

★15420 **BUCURESTI** Rm/Ys ('3 Maj') 1962; C; 6700/9200; 152 × 8.1/9 (500 × 26.4/29.8); M (Sulzer); 14
Similar (lower superstructure):
★15421 **DOBROGEA** (Rm)

15430 **WORLD SHELTER** Pa/Br (Blyth) 1957; C; 9200; 150.2 × 8.9 (493 × 29.3); M (Doxford); 14; ex Theotokos 1982; ex King Theseus

★15450 **OLKUSZ** Pd/Pd (Szczecinska) 1960; CP; 3000; 114.3 × 6.3 (375 × 20.6); M (MAN); 15; 'B-59' type
Sisters (Pd flag):
★15451 **OJCOW**
15452 **ZAHI** (Le) ex Oliwa 1980;
★15453 **ORLOWO**
★15454 **ORNETA**
Similar (Ia flag):
15455 **SAPUDI**
15456 **SANGIHE**
15457 **SALAJAR**
15458 **SAWU**

★15460 **SINEGORSK** Ru/DDR ('Neptun') 1963; C; 3200; 106 × 6.6 (347 × 21.3); M (MAN); 12.5; ex Gzhatsk 1974; 'Povonets' type
Sisters (Ru flag):
★15461 **BARGUZIN**
★15462 **BIRYUZA**
★15463 **BUKHTARMA**
★15464 **DALNEGORSK** ex Tetyukhe
★15465 **GORNO-ALTAYSK**
★15466 **GRISHA AKOPIAN** ex Sula
★15467 **GRUMANT**
★15468 **GULBENE**
★15469 **HELTERMAA**

★15470 **KAMCHATKA**
★15471 **KOKHTLA**
★15472 **KOVDOR**
★15473 **KYPU**
★15474 **MANYCH**
★15475 **MURMAN**
★15476 **NEVER**
★15477 **NIZHNEUDINSK**
★15478 **OLENEGORSK**
★15479 **PAYDE**
★15480 **PERESLAVL-ZALESSIK**
★15481 **SEGEZHA**
★15482 **SELEMDZHA**
★15483 **SEVORODVINSK**
★15484 **SHILKA**
★15485 **SPASSK-DALNIY**
★15486 **STEPAN KHALTURIN**
★15487 **SVIRSK**
★15488 **SYKTYVKAR**
★15489 **TUNGUSKA**
★15490 **USSURI**
★15491 **VILYANY**
★15492 **VYRU**
★15493 **ZAPOLYARNYY**
Similar (Space Monitoring Ship):
★15494 **RISTNA** (Ru)

★15500 **PYARNU** Ru/DDR ('Neptun') 1963; C; 3200; 106 × 6.7 (347 × 21.6); M (MAN); 13.75; 'Povonets' type
Sisters (Ru flag):
★15501 **NOVOVORONEZH**
★15502 **POVONETS**

★15510 **SHURA KOBER** Ru/DDR ('Neptun') 1971; C; 3600; 105.7 × 6.7 (347 × 21.6); M (MAN); 13.75; 'Pioner' type
Sisters (Ru flag):
★15511 **ARKADIY KAMANIN**
★15512 **BORIYA TSARIKOV**
★15513 **GALYA KOMLEVA**
★15514 **KOLYA MYGATIN**
★15515 **LARA MIKHEYENKO**
★15516 **LYONYA GOLYKOV**
★15517 **MARAT KOZEY**
★15518 **NINA KUKOVEROVA**
★15520 **PAVLIK LARISHKIN**
★15521 **PIONER**
★15522 **PIONERSKAYA PRAVDA**
★15523 **PIONERSKAYA ZORKA**
★15524 **SASHA BORODULIN**
★15525 **SASHA KONDRATYEV**
★15526 **SASHA KOTOV**
★15527 **SASHA KOVALYOV**
★15528 **TOLYA KOMAR**
★15529 **TOLYA SHUMOV**
★15530 **TONYA BONDARCHUK**
★15531 **VALYA KOTIK**
★15532 **VALERIY VOLKOV**
★15533 **VASYA KOROBKO**
★15534 **VASYA SHISHKOVSKIY**
★15535 **VITYA CHALENKO**
★15536 **VITYA KHONENKO**
★15537 **VITYA SITNITSA**
★15538 **VOLODYA SCHERBATSEVICH**
★15539 **YUTA BONDAROVSKAYA**
★15540 **ZINA PORTNOVA**

15550 **CYPRUS TRADER** Cy/Br (A&P) 1965; C; 7200/10600; 157.2 × 8.3/9.1 (516 × 27.6/30); M (Sulzer); 16; ex Maritsa III 1983; ex Maritsa 1974; ex Exning 1973

15560 **AVIAN WREN** Pa/Ne (Giessen-De Nord) 1963; CP; 5900/8300; 151.2 × 8.1/8.2 (496 × 26.3/26.8); M (Stork); —ex Eemhaven 1982

★15580 **KRASZEWSKI** Pd/De (Odense) 1963; CP; 7200/10400; 153.3 × 8.3/9.1 (503 × 27.6/30); M (B&W); 16
Sister:
★15581 **JIAXING** (RC) ex Dlugosz 1970

15590 **VISHVA KARUNA** In/In (Hindustan) 1973; C; 7000/10000; 154 × 9.2 (506 × 30.6); M (Sulzer); 17.5
Sisters (In flag):
15591 **VISHVA MADHURI**
15592 **VISHVA MAMTA**
15593 **VISHVA BANDHAN**
15594 **VISHVA YASH**

15610 **KOTA MURNI** Sg/FRG (Howaldts) 1960; CP; 7300/10000; 159 × 8.3/9.3 (522 × 27.6/30.6); M (Stork); 17.5; ex Nedlloyd Ebro 1981; ex Neder Ebro 1977
Sister:
15612 **KOTA MAJU** (Sg) ex Nedlloyd Elbe; ex Neder Elbe

15620 **KOTA DEWA** Sg/Ne (Giessen) 1958; CP; 8000; 163.4 × 8.8 (536 × 29); M (Stork); 17; ex Nedlloyd Karakorum 1978; ex Karakorum 1977

Sister:
15621 **SAUDI AL DAMMAM** (Si) ex Nedlloyd Weser 1982; ex Weser 1977

● 15630 **KOTA WARUNA** Sr/FRG (Rhein Nordseew) 1966; CP; 7000/10200; 163 × 8/9 (534 26/30); M (Sulzer); 18; ex Hannoverland 1983
Sister:
15631 **WESERLAND** (FRG) ex Lloyd Sydney 1982; ex Weserland

★15632 **RIO AGABAMA** Cu/Sp (Construcciones SA) 1975; FT; 3900; 106.86×5.63 (351×18.47); M (Deutz);—
Sisters (Cu flag):
★15632/1 **RIO ALMENDARES**
★15632/2 **RIO ARIMAO**
★15632/3 **RIO BAYAMO**
★15633 **RIO CANIMAR**
★15633/1 **RIO CAONAO**
★15633/2 **RIO CAUTO**
★15633/3 **RIO CONTRAMAESTRE**
★15633/4 **RIO CUYAGUATEJE**
★15633/5 **RIO DAMUJI**
★15634 **RIO HANABANA**
★15634/1 **RIO JATIBONICO**
★15634/2 **RIO JIBACOA**
★15634/3 **RIO JOBABO**
★15634/4 **RIO LA PALMA**
★15634/5 **RIO LAS CASAS**
★15635 **RIO LOS PALACIOS**
★15635/1 **RIO MAYABEQUE**
★15636 **RIO MAYARI**
★15636/1 **RIO MOA**
★15637 **RIO NAJASA**
★15637/1 **RIO SAGUA**
★15638 **RIO SALADO**
★15638/1 **RIO TOA**
★15639 **RIO YATERAS**
★15639/1 **RIO ZAZA**

15640 **MOENJODARO** Pk/Ys ('Split') 1968; C; 5900/8900; 154.5 × —/9.1 (507 × —/30); M (Sulzer); —
Sisters (Pk flag):
15641 **RANGAMATI**
15642 **SUNDERBANS**
15643 **TAXILA**
(Tu flag):
15644 **ARAS**
15645 **DICLE**
15646 **FIRAT**
15647 **GEDIZ**
15648 **KEBAN**
15649 **MERIC**

15660 **FORUM EAGLE** Gr/Pd (Gdanska) 1970; C; 6900/10200; 161 × —/9.7 (528 × —/31.11); M (Sulzer); 20.5; ex Amaralina 1983; 'B-444' type
Sisters:
15661 **ITABERA** (Bz)
15662 **ITATINGA** (Bz)
15663 **FORUM HOPE** (Gr) ex Botafogo 1983
15664 **BERNARDINO CORREA** (Po)
15665 **FORUM PROGRESS** (Gr) ex Arpoader 1983
Similar (lengthened):
15666 **PRETORIANO** (Ar) ex Frotabeira 1983
15667 **MARIA DA PENHA** (Bz) ex Frotatokyo

15670 **MERCHANT PROVIDENCE** Br/FRG (Deutsche Werft) 1965; CP; 6400/9300; 156 × —/9 (511 × —/30); M (MAN); 18.25; ex Artico 1983; ex Tabora 1974
Sisters:
15671 **NIKOS** (Gr) ex Taveta 1975
15672 **KOTA SEJATI** (Sg) ex Tsavo 1983; ex Stellenbosch
15673 **BALDER JIANGCHOW** (Pa) ex Lloyd Brisbane 1981; ex Tanga 1981; ex Lloyd Brisbane 1980; ex Swellendam 1979
★15674 **GEORG HANDKE** (DDR) ex Talana 1977

15680 **JALAYAMUNA** In/FRG (Rhein Nordseew) 1972; Pt Con; 7800/10900; 158.4 × 8.5/9.6 (520 × 28/31.7); M (MAN); 16.25
Sister:
15681 **JALAYAMINI** (In)

15690 **AUTOROUTE** Br/Ja (Mitsui) 1979; Ro VC; 2500; 100.01 × 4.21 (328.12 × 13.81); M (B&W); 15.25; Stern door/ramp

15700 **AMBASSADOR** US/US (New York SB) 1960; C; 7800; 150.1 × 8.5 (493 × 28.1); T (GEC); 18.5; ex Export Ambassador 1980
Sisters (US flag):
15701 **ADVENTURER** ex Export Adventurer 1980
15702 **AIDE** ex Export Aide 1980
15703 **AGENT** ex Export Agent 1980; Vessels transferred to US Reserve Fleet

15710 **LA GUAIRA** Ve/FRG (Howaldts DW) 1970; C; 8400/11500; 165 × 9/9.8 (541 × 30/32.3); M (Fiat); 22; ex Coralstone 1972

Sisters:
15711 **MARACAIBO** (Ve) ex Rubystone 1972

15720 **VISHVA BINDU** In/Pd (Szczecinska) 1969; C; 5400/8100; 145.3 × 7.5/9 (477 × 24.6/29.11); M (Sulzer); 17.5; 'B-445' type
Sisters (In flag):
15721 **VISHVA CHETANA** ex Vishva Chetna 1969; ex Zygmunt August
15722 **VISHVA SANDESH** ex Zygmunt Stary
15723 **VISHVA VIKAS** ex Wladyslaw Jagiello
(Pd flag):
★15724 **WLADYSLAW JAGIELLO**
★15725 **WLADYSLAW LOKIETEK**
★15726 **ZYGMUNT AUGUST**
★15727 **ZYGMUNT STARY**
★15728 **ZYGMUNT III WAZA**
★15729 **MIESZKO I**
★15730 **BOLESLAW CHOBRY**
★15731 **BOLESLAW SMIALY**
★15732 **BOLESLAW KRZYWOUSTY**
(Ir flag):
15733 **IRAN ELHAM** ex Arya Kish
15734 **IRAN EKRAM** ex Arya Rokh
15735 **IRAN GHEYAM** ex Arya Rooz
(RC flag)
★15736 **JIANG CHENG** launched as Wladyslaw IV
(Fr flag):
15737 **COURSON** ex Arya Dad 1971; ex Boleslaw Krzywousty
Sisters ('B474' type):
★15738 **CSOKONAI** (Hu);
★15739 **RADNOTI** (Hu)

15740 **SURREY** Br/De (Helsingor) 1969/75; RoC; 4100; 132.7 × 5.8 (435 × 19); TSM (B&W); 17.75; Stern door; Lengthened 1975 (Amsterdamsche D)

15750 **TACKLER ARABIA** Br/Ja (Kasado) 1978; RoC/Con; 2800; 114.8 × 5.25 (376.6 × 17.22); M (MaK); 15.5; ex Maersk Rando 1982; ex Tackler Arabia 1981; 'Tackler' type
Sisters:
15751 **TACKLER DOSINIA** (Br) ex Totara 1983; ex Tackler Dosinia 1981
15752 **TAJIN** (Me)

15760 **LINCOLN** US/US (Bethlehem PC) 1962; Pt.Con; 13300; 172 × 9.6 (564 × 31.8); T (Bethlehem Steel); 20; ex President Lincoln 1980
Sister:
15761 **TYLER** (US) ex President Tyler 1979; Both vessels transferred to US Reserve fleet

15780 **KOTKA LILY** Fi/Fi (Rauma-Repola) 1972; RoC; 4300; 138 × 6.7 (451 × 21.1); TSM (Stork-Werkspoor); 18; ex Nedlloyd Rockanje 1983; ex Rheinfels 1976; ex Antares 1975; Stern door
Sisters:
15781 **ORION** (Fi)
15782 **SIRIUS** (Fi)
15783 **LIPA** (Pa) ex Baltic Enterprise 1983
15784 **BALTIC PROGRESS** (Br)

★15790 **LEDENICE** Ys/Ys ('3 Maj') 1979; RoC/Con/C; 5600; 144.4 × 6.5 (473.75 × 21.33); M (Pielstick); 17.9; Travelling gantry with deck crane; Stern slewing ramp
Probable sister:
★15791 **BRIBIR** (Ys)

15800 **SANTA MAGDALENA** US/US (Bethlehem Steel) 1963; PC/Con; 11200; 166 × 8.8 (545 × 29.1); T (GEC); 20
Sisters (US flag):
15801 **SANTA MARIA**
15802 **SANTA MARIANA**
15803 **SANTA MERCEDES**

15810 **AYVALIK** Tu/Ne (P Smit) 1952; PC; 1900; 86 × 3.8 (285 × 12.6); TSM (B&W); 16
Sister:
15811 **GEMLIK** (Tu)

15820 **NISSOS SERIFOS** Ma/Sw (Lindholmens) 1964; R; 5800; 138.5 × 7.6 (454 × 25); M (Lindholmens); 19.25; ex Bamenda 1982; ex Rio Negro Valley 1970
Sister:
15821 **NISSOS SPETSES** (Ma) ex Manoka 1982; ex Yakima Valley 1970

● 15830 **NEDLLOYD WISSEKERK** Ne/Ne (P Smit) 1967; C; 7400/10700; 166.6 × 7.8/9.6 (546 × 25.6/31.6); M (Stork); 20
Sisters (Ne flag):
15831 **NEDLLOYD WAALEKERK** ex Waalerkerk 1977
15832 **NEDLLOYD WILLEMSKERK** ex Willemskerk 1977
15833 **NEDLLOYD WESTERKERK** ex Westerkerk 1977

15840 **ESTRELLA DEL MAR** Ur/Sw (Eriksbergs)

1961; CP; 5700/7500; 142.6 × 7.8/8.7 (46.8 × 25.6/28.6); M (B&W) 17; ex *Estrella*

15870 RISHI ATRI In/De (Nakskov) 1966; CP; 7700; 164 × 8.6 (540 × 28.2); M (B&W); 20.75; ex *Aranya*
Sisters:
15871 RISHI AGASTI (In) ex *Arosia*
15872 AZUMA (Gr)

15880 EIHAB 1 Eg/Sw (Lindholmens) 1962; CP; 6000/8500; 143.7 × 8/8.5 (471 × 26/28.3); M (Gotaverken); 17.5; ex *Alabama* 1977
Sister:
15881 ELAMIR FAHD (Eg) ex *Arizona* 1977

15890 SAMOS SUN Gr/Sw (Eriksbergs) 1961; 6700; 149 × 8.5 (490 × 28); M (B&W); 18.5; ex *Lake Eyre* 1975

15920 JUN SHAN Pa/No (Akers) 1957; CP; 4500; 115.3 × 6.8 (378 × 22.6); M (B&W); 15.25; ex *Briseis* 1975

● **15930 HADI** Sh/Sw (Oresunds) 1955; CP; 3800; 114 × 6.8 (375 × 22.6); M (Gotaverken); 15.25; ex *Telaura* 1980; ex *Balkis* 1975
Similar (foremast bipod):
15931 RUSHDI (UAE) ex *Taipan Pride* 1982; ex *Telanca* 1980; ex *Baghdad* 1975

15950 GAO SHAN Pa/No (Stord) 1956; CP; 4500; 115.3 × 6.8 (378 × 22.6); M (B&W); 15.25; ex *Bosphorus* 1975

★ **15960 QINGSHUI** RC/Ne (Nederlandsche) 1964; C; 6300/9400; 158.6 × 7.7/8.5 ×521 (25.4/28); M (Gotaverken) 17.5; ex *Nara*
Sister: (RC) flag:
★ **15961 TIANSHUI** ex *Nicobar* 1972
Similar:(RC' flag):
★ **15962 HENGSHUI** ex *Nagasaki* 1972

15970 RIO GRANDE Ar/Sp 1967; CP; 2600; 110 × 6.4 (361 × 21); M; 19; ex *Playa De Las Nieves* 1978
Sisters:
15971 ALBACORA FRIGO (Sp) ex *Playa Blanca* 1983
15972 USHUAIA (Ar) ex *Playa De Naos*

● **15990 BRUARFOSS** Pa/De (Aalborg) 1960; C; 2300/3100; 102 × 6.3/6.8 (336 × 20.6/22.4); M (B&W); 15
Sister:
15991 ELFO (Pa) ex *Selfoss* 1982

16010 RASLAN Qt/Ne (P Smit)-Sw 1972/75; LS; 5600; 148.11 × 6.83 (485.93 × 22.41); TSM (Stork-Werkspoor); 14.75; ex *Procyon* 1982; ex *Linda Clausen* 1980; ex *Cunard Ambassador* 1975; Side doors. Converted from passenger ship 1975 (Oresunds)

16020 ETAIWI 1 Si/Ne ('De Schelde') 1951-69; LS; 7200; 159.39 × — (523 × —); TSM ('De Schelde'); 18; ex *Cormoran* 1980; ex *Alberto Dodero* 1969; Converted from passenger/cargo 1969

16030 PRINS JOACHIM De/De (Nakskov) 1980; TF/RoPCF; 10600; 152 × 5.6 (498.69 × 18.37); TSM (Alpha-Diesel); 18; Bow and stern doors
Sisters: (De flag):
16031 DRONNING INGRID
16032 KRONPRINS FREDERIK

★ **16040 ROSSIYA** Ru/Ge (Deutsche Werft Reihers) 1938; PC; 17900; 182 × 7.1 (589 × 25); TSD-E (MAN); 15; ex *Empire Welland* 1946; ex *Patria* 1945

16050 NABIL Le/Sw (Eriksbergs) 1946; C; 1600; 80.42 × 5.07 (263.85 × 16.63); M (B&W); 12; ex *Alexis* 1973; ex *Fay* 1971; ex *Vela* 1968
Sister:
16051 WILLY (Ho) ex *Sami* 1982; ex *Capitaine Cook* 1978; ex *Jacques del Mar II* 1969; ex *Sletbay* 1967; ex *Diana* 1967

16060 REA Gr/Sw (Helsingor) 1956; R; 3300/4300; 116.8 × 6.4/— (383 × 20.8/—); M (B&W); 17.5 ex *Lastrigoni* 1973; ex *Coolgardie* 1969

★ **16065 JELSA** Ys/Ys ('Jozo Lozovina-Mosor') 1962; C; 2500; 121.01 × 5.57 (397 × 18.27); M (B&W); 15.5; Lengthened 1968
Sister:
★ **16066 OMIS** (Ys)

★ **16100 HAKON GAMLE** No/De (Aalborg) 1952; P; 2200; 80.8 × 4.5 (265 × 15.2); M (Atlas-Diesel); 15; ex *Hakon Jarl* 1983

★ **16110 XX ANIVERSARIO** Cu/Ne (Pot) 1957; PC; 7500; 131.6 × 7 (432 × 23.8); M (Stork); 15.5; ex *Oranje Nassau* 1973
Sister:
★ **16111 VIETNAM HEROICO** (Cu) ex *Prins Der Nederlanden* 1973

★ **16120 JIAN HUA** RC/Fr (Saint Nazaire) 1951; PC;

9500; 150 × 6.9 (479 × 22.9); M (B&W); 16; ex *Foch* 1967

★ **16140 UKRAINA** Ru/De (B&W) 1938; PC; 6400; 132 × 5.7 (432× 15.9); TSM (B&W); 21; ex *Basarabia* 1948

★ **16150 YU HUA** RC/Ne (Wilton-Fije) 1958; PC; 11900/13600; 178 × 8.1/9 (584× 26.8/29.5); TSM (MAN); 18.5; ex *Nieuw Holland* 1974; ex *Randfontein* 1971

16170 RIO DE JANERIO Gr/No (Tangen) 1957; CP; 3100/4900; 121 × 6.6/7.3 (397 × 21.8/24); M (Gotaverken); 15.5

16180 POPI Gr/De (Nakskov) 1967; CP; 10900; 166 × 9.6 (545 × 31.7); M (B&W); 20.75; ex *Tinos* 1980; ex *Alameda*

16190 FABIOLAVILLE Be/Be (Cockerill) 1972; PC; 9300/13500; 161.14 × 7.93/9.89 (528.67 × 26.05/32.48); M (B&W) 20
Sister:
16191 KANANGA (Zr)

16200 SAGAR Pa/Br (Scott & Sons) 1965; C; 1300; 68 × 4.2 (224 × 13.9); M (British Polar); 12; ex *Voorspeler* 1981

16210 FUJI Ja/Ja (NKK) 1965; RS/IB; 5300 Disp; 100 × 8.8 (328 × 29); TSM (—); 17; Hangar and three helicopters

16220 ASTERI Gr/FRG(B+V)1965; R; 6200; 137 × 7.9 (450 × 25.5); M(B+V) 20; ex *Hood River Valley* 1971
Sister:
16221 ATALANTI (Gr) ex *Okanagan Valley* 1971

16230 DISCOVERY Br/Br (Hall, Russell) 1962; RS; 2700; 79.5 × 4.7 (261 × 15.6); D-E (Ruston & Hornsby); —

16240 BRANSFIELD Br/Br (Robb Caledon) 1970; RS; 4800; 99 × 6.7 (325 × 22); D-E (Mirrlees Blackstone); —

16250 TOWUTI Ia/Pd (Szczecinska) 1962; C; 3400; 96 × 4.5 (316 × 14.8); M (Sulzer); 12; 'B 450' type
Sisters (Ia flag):
16251 TOBELO
16252 TOGARAN
16253 TOKALA
16254 TOLANDO
16255 TOMAKO
16256 TOMBATU

16260 EIGAMOIYA Na/Br (Robb Caledon) 1969; CP; 4400; 112 × 7.6 (367 × 25); M (Mirrlees); 15

★ **16270 JASLO** Pd/De (Aalborg) 1967; C; 2300; 101.5 × 6 (335 × 19.8); M (Sulzer); 15

★ **16290 SU LONG** RC/FRG (A Pahl) 1964; CP; 3400/5300; 125.9 × 6.7/7.8 (413 × 22/25.6); M (B&W); 16.5; ex *Mikelden* 1982; ex *River Gongola*; ex *Poeldyk* 1974

16310 DOULOS Ma/US (Newport News) 1914; PC; 6800; 130.3 × 5.6 (428 × 18.2); M (Fiat); 15; ex *Franca C*; ex *Roma* 1952; ex *Medina* 1949; Converted to a floating book exhibition ship. Re-engined 1952

16320 HELLAS Gr/Br (Stephen) 1935; CP; 4300; 108 × 4.6 (355 × 15.1); T (Stephen); 16; ex *Taroona* 1959

★ **16330 SHAO YAO** RC/China (—) 1947; P; 1600; 76.2 × 4.5 (250 × 15); R (—); 10; River service

16340 SIRIUS Gr/Br (Fairfield SB) 1948; RoPF; 8900; 151.8 × 8.4 (498 × 27.6); T (Fairfield); 15.5; ex *Chania* 1971; ex *Warwickshire* 1965

16350 BLACK WATCH/JUPITER No/FRG (L F-W) 1966; RoPF; 9500; 141.6 × 6.5 (466 × 22); TSM (Pielstick); 22; Serves as Black Watch in winter and as Jupiter in summer.
Sister:
16351 BLACK PRINCE/VENUS (No)

16370 COLUMBIA US/US (Lockheed) 1974; F; 3900; 127.4 × 5.3 (418× 17.5); TSM (De Laval); 21

16380 ST. GEORGE Br/Br (Swan Hunter & T) 1968; RoPF; 7400; 128 × 5 (420 × 16.5) TSM (Ruston & Hornsby); 21; Bow and stern doors

16385 KEREN Br/Br (Cammell Laird) 1974; RoPF; 9000; 130.08 × 5.19 (427 × 17.03); TSM (Stork Werkspoor); 21; ex *St. Edmund* 1983; Bow & stern doors. Used by the Royal Navy as a troopship

16390 DAPHNE Gr/Br (Swan Hunter & WR) 1959; P; 11700; 162 × 10 (533 × 32.1); TSM (Swan Hunter); 17; ex *Akrotiri Express* 1974; ex *Port Sydney* 1972; Rebuilt from a cargo ship (Khalkis)
Sister:

16391 DANAE (Gr) ex *Therissos Express* 1974; ex *Port Melbourne* 1972

16400 SUN FLOWER Ja/Ja (Kawasaki) 1972; RoPF; 11300; 185 × 6.4 (607 × 21); TSM (MAN); 24.75
Sisters (Ja flag):
16401 SUN FLOWER 2
16402 SUN FLOWER 5
16403 SUN FLOWER 8

16410 EMPRESS OF AUSTRALIA Br/Au (Cockatoo) 1965; RoPF; 8200; 135.6 × 6.1 (445 × 20.1); TSM (MAN); 17

16420 MANUEL SOTO Sp/Sp (U N de Levante) 1976; RoPF; 9100; 140.8 × 6.4 (462 × 21); TSM (MAN); 23.5
Sister:
16421 J.J. SISTER (Sp)

★ **16430 GU LANG YU** RC/Sp (AESA) 1964; F; 6400; 130.3 × 4.2 (428 × 14); TSM (B&W); 18; ex *Ming Yi* 1979; ex *Ciudad de Buenos Aires*; Side doors
Sister:
16431 CITY OF RHODOS (Gr) ex *33 Orientales* 1980

16440 PROVENCE Fr/It (Pietra Ligure) 1974; RoPF; 7800; 142.32 × 5.79 (467 × 19); TSM (Pielstick); 23; Bow and stern doors

16450 PRINCE OF BRITTANY Fr/FRG (Unterweser) 1970; RoPF; 5500; 118.5 × 5 (389 × 16.5); TSM (Pielstick); —; ex *Prince of Fundy*; Bow stern & side doors
Sister:
16451 SAINT COLUM-1 (Br) ex *Saint Patrick* 1982
Similar:
16452 ZEELAND (No) ex *Peter Wessel* 1983

● **16460 BLUENOSE** Ca/Ys ('Jozo Lozovina-Mosor') 1973; RoPF; 6300; 124.9 × 5.3 (410 × 17.6); TSM (Pielstick); 22; Bow and stern doors; deepened & widened 1977; ex *Jutlandica* 1982; ex *Stena Jutlandica* 1982
Sister:
16462 STENA NORDICA (Be) ex *Stena Danica* 1981; launched as *Stena Nordica*
Similar:
16463 SCOTIA PRIDE (Pa) ex *Stena Olympica* 1982

16470 THE VIKING Fi/FRG (Unterweser) 1974; RoPF; 4400; 118 × 5 (388× 16.5); TSM (MAN); 21; ex *Kalle III* 1983; ex *Kattegat II*
Sister:
16471 DJURSLAND (De) ex *Djursland II* 1980

★ **16480 VIKING 2** Ys/FRG (Unterweser) 1971; RoP; 4000; 118 × 5 (387 × 16.5); TSM (MAN); 21; ex *Njegos* 1984; ex *Travemunde* 1980; Bow, stern & side doors

16490 CONNACHT Ih/Ih (Verolme Cork) 1978; RoPCF; 6000; 122.03 × 4.82 (400.36 × 15.81); TSM (Atlas-Mak); 20; Bow & stern doors/ramps
Sister:
16491 LEINSTER (Ih)

16500 QUEEN OF THE NORTH Ca/FRG (A. G. 'Weser') 1969; RoPF; 8800; 125 × 4.87 (410.1 × 15.98); TSM (MAN); 22.5; ex *Queen of Surrey* 1980; ex *Stena Danica* 1974; Bow & stern doors

16510 PRINZ OBERON FRG/FRG (Nobiskrug) 1970; RoPF; 7900; 134 × 4.9 (440 × 16.3); TSM (Pielstick); 22; ex *Prins Oberon*; Stern & side doors
Similar:
16511 PRINZ HAMLET (FRG)
16512 NORRONA (Fa) ex *Gustav Vasa* 1983

16520 GOLDEN ODYSSEY Gr/De (Helsingor) 1974; P; 6800; 130.2 × 5.2 (427 × 17.2); TSM (MaK); 21

16530 CIUDAD DE SANTA CRUZ LA PALMA Sp/Sp (UN de Levante) 1972; RoPF; 7500; 137.8 × 5.7 (452 × 18.1); TSM (MAN); 22.5; ex *Ciudad de Palma* 1982; ex *Canguro Cabo San Sebastian* 1980; Stern door
Sisters (Sp flag):
16531 CIUDAD DE PALMA (Sp) ex *Ciudad de Santa Cruz la Palma*; ex *Canguro Cabo San Jorge*
16532 CIUDAD DE BADAJOZ
16533 CIUDAD DE SEVILLA
16534 CIUDAD DE CACERES
16535 CIUDAD DE SALAMANCA

16450 JUPITER Gr/Fr (Bretagne) 1961; PC; 6300; 126.6 × 6.4 (415 × 21); M (Pielstick); 16; ex *Alexandros* 1970; ex *Moledet* 1970; Also known as **ZEUS**

16550 MELINA Gr/Fr (Bretagne) 1949; P; 5100; 113.6 × 6.91 (373 × 22.8); T (Bretagne) 15; ex *Azrou* 1968
Similar:
16551 KHALID 1 (UAE) ex *Bella Maria* 1983; ex

Delos 1980; ex *Azemmour* 1969

16570 **GENNARGENTU** It/It (Riuniti) 1965; RoPF; 4900; 122 × 5.5 (411 × 16.3); TSM (Fiat); 16

16580 **APOLLO III** Sw/Sw (Finnboda) 1962; RoPF; 4300; 101.4 × 4.8 (333 × 15.7); M (Unaflow); 16.5; ex *Svea Jarl* 1976; Side doors

16600 **GALAXIAS** Gr/Br (H&W) 1957; P; 4900; 104.32 × 4.81 (342.26 × 15.78); TSM (H&W); 17.5; ex *Scottish Coast* 1969; Converted from ferry

16610 **ARGONAUT** Gr/Ge (Krupp) 1929; P; 4000; 93.2 × 5.6 (306 × 16); TSM (Krupp); 13; ex *Orion* 1964; ex *Vixen* 1950; ex *Orion* 1947; Converted from a yacht 1947; Also known as **ARGONAFTIS**

16620 **KENTAVROS** Gr/US (US Naval SY) 1941; P; 2500; 94.9 × 4.6 (312 × 15); TSM (General Motors); 15.5; ex *Barnegat* 1963; Former USN seaplane tender

16630 **ELENA P** Gr/Ge (Neptunwerft) 1944; F; 1100; 68.3 × 2.7 (224 × 9); TSM (MaK); 14; ex *Lilli Scarlett* 1964; ex *Harald Ivers* 1954; ex *M608* (German Minesweeper)

16640 **POLIKOS** Gr/Ca (Redfern) 1943; C; —; 68.6 × 5 (225 × 16.5); TSM (Henschel); 18; ex *Athina* 1961; ex *Adrias* 1961; ex *Cyclades* 1958; Built as HMS *Persian*

16650 **EPOMEO PRIMO** It/Ys ('Uljanik') 1953; P; 630; 54.1 × 2.9 (178 × 9.8); TSM (Fiat); 14.5; ex *Aleksa Santic* 1971

16660 **THOR VIKING** Ma/Sw (Falkenbergs) 1958; F; 500; 45.6 × — (150 × —); M (Volvo-Penta); 12; ex *Duc De Normandie* 1981; ex *Thor Viking* 1973

16670 **SECHELT QUEEN** Ca/US (Todd) 1947; RoPF; 5000; 96.9 × 4 (321 × 13.2); TSD-E (General Motors); 16.5; ex *Chinook II* 1963; ex *Chinook* 1955

16680 **QUEEN OF SIDNEY** Ca/Ca (Victoria Mach) 1960; RoPF; 3100; 102.4 × 3.8 (336 × 12.6); TSM (Mirrlees, Bickerton & Day); 8; ex *Sidney* 1963

16690 **ISLA DE MENORA** Sp/Ne (Schiedamsche) 1961; RoPF; 1600; 78.9 × 2.9 (251 × 9.8); TSM (KHD); 15; ex *Linda Scarlett* 1971

16710 **NAUSHON** US/US (Mathis) 1957; RoPF; 2700; 70 × 3.1 (230 × 10.3); TSR (Unaflow); 17; ex *Nantucket* 1975

★16720 **VLADIMIR NAZOR** Ys/Ys ('Uljanik') 1952; C; 430; 54.2 × 2.9 (178 × 9.8); TSM (Sulzer); 14
Sisters (Ys flag):
★16721 **VUK KARADZIC**
★16723 **NJEGOS'**
Similar (passenger ships):
16724 **CASAICCIOLA EXPRESS** (It) ex *Campania Prima* 1980; ex *Ivan Cankar* 1973
16725 **CAMPANIA SECONDA** (It) ex *Kosta Racin* 1973

16730 **BEYKOZ** Tu/Tu (Denizcilik) 1959; F; 500; 47.1 × 2.4 (153 × 8); TSM (Fiat); —

16740 **AL RIYADH** Si/Ne (Van Lent) 1978; Y; —; 64.64 × 3 (212 × 9.84); M (MTU); 21; Helicopter deck. Also known as **ALRIYAD**

16750 **GUSTAV AV KLINT** Sw/Sw (Finnboda) 1941; RS; 500; 52 × 4.7 (170 × 15.7); M (Atlas-Diesel); 10; Rebuilt 1963

★16760 **PALMA SORIANO** Cu/Sp ('Bazan') 1967; RoPF; 2000; 72.9 × 3.2 (239 × 10.7); TSM (MAN); —
Sister:
★16761 **JIBACOA** (Cu)

16770 **LORD SELKIRK** Ca/Ca (Ferguson Indust) 1958; RoPF; 1800; 79 × 3.7 (259 × 12.1); TSM (Werkspoor); —

16780 **FESTIVALE** Pa/Br (J Brown)- Ja 1961/78; P; 26600; 231.71 × 9.75 (760.2 × 31.99); TST (J Brown); 23.5; ex *S.A. Vaal* 1977; ex *Transvaal Castle* 1966; rebuilt 1978 (Kawasaki)

16800 **MEDITERRANEAN SEA** Cy/Br (Vickers-Armstrongs) 1953; RoPF; 16400; 164.9 × 6.4 (541 × 21); TSM (Doxford); —; ex *City of Exeter* 1972; converted from a Passenger Cargo Ship 1972
Sister:
16801 **MEDITERRANEAN SKY** (Gr) ex *City of York* 1971

★16810 **MAKSIM GORKIY** Ru/FRG (Howaldts DW) 1969; P; 25000; 194.6 × 8.3 (627 × 27); TST (Allgemeine); 23; ex *Hanseatic* 1974; ex *Hamburg* 1973

16820 **ROYAL VIKING STAR** No/Fi (Wartsila)— FRG 1972/81; P; 21800; 205.47 × 7.55 (674 × 24.77); TSM (Wartsila); 21.5; lengthened 1981 (A. G. 'Weser')

Sisters (no flag):
16821 **ROYAL VIKING SEA**
16822 **ROYAL VIKING SKY**

16830 **PACIFIC PRINCESS** Br/FRG (Rhein Nordseew) 1971; P; 19900; 168.7 × 7.7 (553.6 × 25.3); TSM (Fiat); 21.5; ex *Sea Venture* 1975
Sister:
16831 **ISLAND PRINCESS** (Br) ex *Island Venture* 1972

16840 **SUNWARD II** No/Ne (Rotterdamsche) 1971; P; 14200; 148.1 × 5.9 (486 × 19.6); TSM (Stork-Werkspoor); 21.5; ex *Cunard Adventurer* 1977

16850 **RASLAN** Qt/Ne (P Smit) 1972/75; LS; 5600; 148.11 × 6.83 (485.93 × 22.41); TSM (Stork-Werkspoor); 14.75; ex *Procyon* 1982 ex *Linda Clausen* 1980 ex *Cunard Ambassador* 1975; side doors; converted from Passenger 1975 (Oresunds)

16860 **CUNARD COUNTESS** Br/De (B&W) 1976; P; 17500; 164 × 5.8 (538 × 19); TSM (B&W); 21.5
Sister:
16861 **CUNARD PRINCESS** (Bs) ex *Cunard Conquest* 1977

16865 **TROPICALE** Li/De (Aalborg) 1981; P; 22900; 204.76 × 7.12 (672 × 23.36); TSM (Sulzer); 19.5

16870 **SONG OF NORWAY** No/Fi (Wartsila) 1969/78; P; 23000; 194.32 × — (637.47 × —); TSM (Sulzer); 20.5; lengthened 1978 (Wartsila)
Sister:
16871 **NORDIC PRINCE** (No)
Similar (unlengthened sister):
16872 **SUN VIKING** (No)

16875 **EUROPA** FRG/FRG (Bremer V) 1981; P; 35000; 196 × 8.35 (643 × 27.4); TSM (MAN); 18

16880 **VIKING SALLY** Fi/FRG (Meyer) 1980; RoPCF; 15600; 155.43 × 5.55 (509.94 × 18.21); TSM (MAN); 21.2; stern ramp

16885 **SCANDINAVIA** Bs/Fr (Dubigeon-Normandie) 1982; P/RoC; 26700; 185.25 × 6.85 (608 × 22.47); TSM (B&W); 18; 2 stern doors

16890 **TOR BRITANNIA** De/FRG (Flender) 1975; RoPCF; 15700; 182.4 × 6.3 (598.6 × 20.9); TSM (Pielstick); 26; ex *Scandinavian Star* 1982; ex *Tor Britannia* 1981
Sister:
16891 **TOR SCANDINAVIA** (De) ex *World-Wide Expo* 1982; ex *Tor Scandinavia* 1982

16895 **FINLANDIA** Fi/Fi (Wartsila) 1981; RoPF; 25700; 166.02 × 6.72 (544.69 × 22.05); TSM (Pielstick); 22; Bow door/ramp and 2 stern door/ramps
Sister (Sw flag):
16896 **SILVIA REGINA**

16900 **VISBY** Sw/Sw (Oresunds) 1980; RoPCF; 14900; 142.33 × 5.5 (466.96 × 18.04); TSM (B&W); 21; three stern door/ramps. Bow door/ramp
Sister:
16901 **WASA STAR** (Sw)

16905 **TRELLEBORG** Sw/Sw (Oresunds) 1982; TF; 10900; 170.19 × 5.82 (558 × 19.09); TSM (MAN); 18.25; Side door/stern door

16910 **KRONPRINSESSAN VICTORIA** Sw/Sw (Gotav) 1981; RoPCF; 15000; 150 × 6 (492.13 × 19.69); TSM (Wartsila); —; three stern ramps. Bow door/ramp. Helicopter pad aft
Sister:
16911 **ST. NICHOLAS** (Br) ex *Prinsessan Birgitta* 1983

16913 **STENA DANICA** Sw/Fr (Dunkerque-Normandie) 1983; RoPCF; 16500; 152.23 × 6.32 (499 × 20.73); TSM (Sulzer); 21; Bow door/2 stern doors/2 side doors
Sister:
16914 **STENA JUTLANDICA** (Sw)

16915 **PRINSESSE RAGNHILD** No/FRG (Howaldts DW) 1981; RoPCF; 16300; 170.47 × 5.82 (559 × 19.09); TSM (Stork-Werkspoor); 21.75; Bow door/2 stern doors

16920 **KRONPRINS HARALD** No/FRG (Nobiskrug) 1976; RoPCF; 12800; 156.4 × 5.4 (513.6 × 5.18); TSM (Stork-Werkspoor); 22

16925 **ASTOR** SA/FRG (Howaldts DW) 1981; P; 18800; 164.34 × 6.10 (539 × 20.01); TSM (MAN); 18

16930 **HABIB** Tn/FRG (Nobiskrug) 1978; P/RoC; 11200; 143.31 × 5.97 (470.18 × 19.59); TSM (Atlas-Mak); 22; Bow door/ramp, stern ramp

16940 **AZUR** Fr/Fr (Dubigeon Normandie) 1971; RoPCF; 11600; 142.1 × 5.45 (466 × 18); TSM (Pielstick); 23; ex *Eagle* 1975; stern door
Similar:

16941 **BOLERO** (No) ex *Scandinavica* 1982; ex *Bolero* (top superstructure deck now extended towards funnels and side ramps fitted foreward and aft)
16942 **MASSALIA** (Fr)

16945 **PRINCESS MAHSURI** FRG/FRG (Howaldts DW) 1980; P; 7800; 122.51 × 5.01 (402 × 16.44); TSM (MaK); 17; ex *Berlin* 1982

16950 **TOLETELA** Ly/Sp (UN de Levante) 1974; RoPCF; 10800; 151.5 × 6.5 (500.6 × 21.6); TSM (MAN); 22; ex *Monte Toledo* 1977; Stern & side doors
Sister:
16951 **GARNATA** (Ly) ex *Monte Granada* 1977

16955 **OLAU HOLLANDIA** FRG/FRG (A. G. 'Weser') 1981; RoPCF; 15200; 153.4 × 5.82 (503 × 19.09); TSM (Pielstick); 21; Bow & 2 stern doors
Sister:
16956 **OLAU BRITANNIA** (FRG)

★16960 **ODESSA** Ru/Br (Vickers SB) 1974; P; 13800; 136.3 × 5.8 (447.6 × 19); TSM (Pielstick); 19; ex *Copenhagen* 1975

16970 **SCANDINAVIAN SUN** Bs/FRG (O & K) 1968; RoPCF; 10000; 134.5 × 5.5 (441.6 × 18); TSM (Pielstick); —; ex *Caribe* 1981; ex *Svea Star* 1976; ex *Freeport* 1974; ex *Freeport 1* 1974; ex *Freeport*

16980 **DROTTEN** Sw/Ys ('Jozo Lozovina-Mosor') 1972; RoPF; 6700; 123.9 × (406.3 × 16.9); TSM (Polar); 20; ex *Visby* 1980
Similar:
16981 **GOTLAND** (Sw)

16990 **MARINE ATLANTICA** Ca/FRG (Rickmers) 1975; RoPF; 5400; 120 × 5.9 (394 × 19.3); TSM (Atlas-MaK); 20.25
Sisters:
16991 **MARINE NAUTICA** (Ca) ex *Stena Nautica* 1974
16992 **REINE ASTRID** (Be) ex *Stena Nautica* 1983; ex *Stena Nordica* 1981; ex *Hellas* 1980; ex *Stena Nordica* 1980; ex *Hellas* 1979; ex *Stena Nordica* 1978
16993 **STENA NORMANDICA** (Sw) ex *Normandica*; ex *Stena Normandica*

17000 **SOUTHWARD** No/It (Tirreno) 1971; P; 16600; 163.4 × 6.5 (536.6 × 21.6); TSM (Fiat); 21.5

17010 **VIKING SAGA** Fi/Fi (Wartsila) 1980; RoPCF; 13900; 145.01 × 5.5 (475.75 × 18.04); TSM (Pielstick); 21; Bow door/ramp. Stern ramp
Sister:
17011 **VIKING SONG** (Fi)

17020 **SUN PRINCESS** Br/It (Tirreno) 1972; P; 17400; 163.3 × 6.5 (536 × 21.6); TSM (Fiat); 15.5; ex *Spirit of London* 1974

17030 **CORSICA SERENA II** Pa/FRG (Nobiskrug) 1974; RoPF; 4800; 118.7 × 5 (390 × 17); TSM (Atlas-MaK); 20.75; ex *Europafarjan III* 1983

17040 **QUIBERON** Sw/FRG (Nobiskrug) 1975; RoPF; 7900; 129 × 4.9 (424 × 16.5); TSM (Stork-Werkspoor); 22; ex *Nils Dacke* 1981; Stern doors

17050 **BOHEME** FRG/Fi (Wartsila) 1968; P; 10300; 134.3 × 5.5 (440 × 18); TSM (Sulzer); —

17060 **NORLAND** Br/FRG (A. G. 'Weser') 1974; RoPF; 13000; 153 × 6.2 (502 × 20.3); TSM (Stork-Werkspoor); 19
Sister:
17061 **NORSTAR** (Ne)

17070 **PETER PAN** FRG/FRG (Nobiskrug) 1974; RoPCF; 12500; 148.9 × 5.5 (488 × 18); TSM (Pielstick); 22; Bow & stern doors
Sister:
17071 **NILS HOLGERSSON** (FRG)

17080 **DANA ANGLIA** De/De (Aalborg) 1978; RoPCF; 14400; 152.91 × 5.71 (501.67 × 18.73); TSM (Pielstick); 21; Bow & stern doors

17090 **KAMIROS** Gr/Fi (Wartsila) 1966; RoPCF; 7500; 134.32 × 5.72 (440.7 × 18.77); TSM (Sulzer); 20; ex *Roussillon* 1980; ex *Prinz Hamlet* 1970; ex *Prins Hamlet* 1969
Similar:
17091 **PRINSESSAN** (Fi) ex *Finnhansa* 1977

17120 **NORWAVE** Br/FRG (A. G. 'Weser') 1965; RoC; 3500; 108.8 × 5 (357 × 16.4); TSM (Smit & Bolnes); 15; Bow & stern doors
Sister:
17121 **NORWIND** (Ne)

17130 **PIETRO NOVELLI** It/It (Riuniti) 1979; RoPCF; 1600; 91 × 4 (298.56 × 13.12); TSM (GMT); 18; Bow & stern doors
Sisters:
17131 **PIERRA DELLA FRANCESCA** (It) (may be **PIERO DELLA FRANCESCA**)

17132 **MARMORICA** (It)
Possible sister:
17133 **OGLASA** (It)

17140 **SANTA MARGARITA DOS** Ve/De (Aalborg) 1960; RoPF; 2200; 86.5 × 4.4 (284 × 13.9); TSM (Polar); 17; ex *General Jose Artigas;* ex *Botnia Express* 1975; ex *Prinsessan Christina* 1967

17150 **PANAGHIA TINOU** Gr/Ne ('De Merwede') 1960; RoPCF; 6200; 120 × 4.9 (394 × 16); TSM (MAN); 21; ex *Captain Constantinos;* ex *Koningin Wilhelmina*

17160 **QUEEN OF VICTORIA** Ca/Ca (Victoria Mach) 1962; RoPF; 4900; 130 × 3.8 (427 × 12.6); TSM (Atlas-MaK); 18; ex *City of Victoria* 1963; Bow & stern doors; Lengthened 1970; deepened by 3 metres 1981. Drawing shows vessel before this modification
Sisters (Ca flag):
17161 **QUEEN OF VANCOUVER** ex *City of Vancouver* 1963
17162 **QUEEN OF SAANICH**
17163 **QUEEN OF ESQUIMALT**
Similar (not deepened) (Ca flag):
17164 **QUEEN OF BURNABY**
17165 **QUEEN OF NANAIMO**
17166 **QUEEN OF NEW WESTMINSTER**

17170 **CONCEPCION MARINO** Ve/No (Trondhjems) 1979; RoPCF; 6200; 105 × 3.8 (344.48 × 12.47); TSM (KHD); 17; Bow door/ramp & stern ramp
Sister:
17171 **CACICA ISABEL** (Ve)

17190 **MERCHANT NAVIGATOR** Br/No (Ankerlokken) 1972; RoC; 1600; 108.64 × 4.95 (356 × 16.24); TSM (Pielstick); 18; ex *Lady Tone* 1982; ex *Lagan Bridge;* ex *Ilka* 1979
Sister:
17191 **LUCIE** (De) ex *Lady Lucienne* 1982; ex *Star Express* 1980; ex *Lalli* 1980
Similar:
17192 **SIR LAMORAK** (Br) ex *Lakespan Ontario* 1983; ex *Lady Catherine* 1981; ex *Lune Bridge* 1981; ex *Anu* 1980; (chartered by RFA)

17200 **JERVIS BAY** Au/Au (NSW Govt) 1969; TS; 6800; 135.7 × 6.1 (445 × 20); TSM (Pielstick); 17.5; ex *Australian Trader;* Stern door. Operated by Australian Navy

17210 **CIUDAD DE TARIFA** Sp/Sp (UN de Levante) 1961; F; 3400; 103.2 × 5.1 (338 × 16.9); TSM (B&W); 17

17220 **PRINCE NOVA** Ca/Ca (Ferguson Indust) 1964; RoPF; 1800; 75.8 × 3.8 (249 × 12.4); TSM (Fairbanks, Morse); —

17230 **COHO** US/US (Puget Sound) 1959; F; 5300; 104.1 × 3.8 (342 × 12.6); TSM (Cooper-Bessemer);
—

17240 **MONS CALPE** Br/Br (Ailsa) 1954; RoPF; 2000; 86.3 × 3.2 (283 × 10.6); TSM (British Polar); —

17250 **SOUND OF ISLAY** Br/Br (Ferguson Bros) 1969; RoPF; 280; 43.4 × 1.6 (142 × 5.3); TSM (Bergius Kelvin); 10.75

17260 **KIRK EXPRESS** Br/FRG (Sietas) 1968; RoC; 1600; 91.5 × 4.5 (300 × 14.1); TSM (KHD); 16; ex *Jamaican Provider*

17270 **ESPRESSO EGITTO** It/It ('L. Orlando') 1973; RoC; 4700; 125.5 × 5.5 (412 × 18.2); TSM (GMT); 21; ex *Espresso Cagliari* 1980;
Sisters (It flag):
17271 **ESPRESSO GRECIA** ex *Espresso Livorno* 1980
17272 **ESPRESSO VENEZIA**
17273 **ESPRESSO RAVENNA**

17280 **GEDSER** De/FRG (Schichau-U) 1976; RoPCF; 5300; 123.02 × 5.82 (403.61 × 19.09); TSM (Stork-Werkspoor); 18.5; Bow & side doors. Stern door/ramp

17290 **FRECCIA DELL'OUEST** It/It ('L. Orlando') 1975; RoC; 2600; 117.5 × 4.9 (385 × 16.1); TSM (GMT); 20; ex *Corriere Dell'Ouest*
Sister:
17291 **FRECCIA DEL NORD** (It) ex *Corriere Del Nord*

17300 **COUTANCES** Fr/Fr (Havre) 1978; RoC; 2600; 110 × 4.5 (360.89 × 14.7); M (Atlas-MaK); 17.5; Bow & stern door
Sister:
17301 **PURBECK** (Fr)

17310 **ARGO** FRG/FRG (Kroegerw) 1976; RoC; 3900; 127 × 5.4/6.6 (417 × 17.1/21.8); TSM (KHD); 19.5; ex *Argo-Hellas* 1980; ex *Brabant* 1978; ex *Argo* 1977; Stern door

★17320 **ZARNITZA** Ru/DDR (Stralsund) 1957; F; 350; 39 × 2.9 (128 × 9.7); M (Liebknecht); 10.5

17330 **CANMAR KIGORIAK** Ca/Ca (Saint John SB) 1980; IB/Tg/Sply; 3600; 91.06 × 8.54 (298.75 × 28 02); M (Sulzer); 18.6 (max)

17340 **WILDRAKE** No/No (Stord) 1979; OSS; 1800; 77.8 × 4.6 (255.25 × 15.09); M (Bergens); 14; Helicopter deck foreward

● 17343 **SEABEX ONE** FRG/FRG (Nobiskrug) 1981; OSS; 5000; 106.81 × 5.52 (350 × 18.11); TSD-E (Krupp MaK); 12

17345 **SEAWAY CONDOR** No/FRG (Nobiskrug) 1982; OSS; 4500; 101.94 × 5.52 (334 × 18.11); TSD-E (Krupp MaK); 11.75

★17350 **SPRUT** Ru/Fi (Wartsila) 1979; OSS; —; 77 × 5.35 (252.62 × 17.55); M (Wartsila); 14; Helicopter deck. Stern gantry

17360 **DR. FRIDTJOF NANSEN** No/No (Mjellum & K) 1974; RS/ST; 500; 46.4 × 4.1 (152 × 13.5); M (Bergens); 13.5

17380 **SHEARWATER CAPE** Br/FRG (A. G. 'Weser') 1967; Submersible Support Ship; 1300; 79.7 × 4.7 (262 × 15.6); TSD-E (KHD); 10; ex *Seaforth Cape* 1983; ex *Tiko I* 1976; Converted Fish Factory/Stern Trawler. Stern ramp

17390 **EMERALD SEAS** Pa/US (Federal SB & DD) 1944; P; 18900; 184 × 8 (604 × 27); TST (De Laval); 19; ex *Atlantis* 1972; ex *President Roosevelt* 1970; ex *Leilani* 1961; ex *Laguardia* 1956; ex *General W. P. Richardson* 1949

17400 **SUN FLOWER 11** Ja/Ja (Kurushima) 1974; P/RoPF; 13600; 196 × 6.6 (643 × 21); TM (MAN); 25

17410 **TANJUNG PANDAN** Ia/Ge¹(B+V) 1936; P; 17900; 176 × 8 (578 × 27); TSM (MAN); 17; ex *Gunung Djati* 1979; ex *Empire Orwell* 1959; ex *Empire Doon* 1949; ex *Pretoria* 1945

17420 **PRINCESS MARGUERITE** Ca/Br (Fairfield SB) 1949; P; 5900; 114 × 4.6 (375 × 15); TSD-E (BTH); 23.5; Now used as a museum ship
Sister:
17421 **PRINCESS PATRICIA** (Ca)

17430 **CARIDDI** It/It (Adriatico) 1931/53; P/TF; 3100; 124 × 4 (407 × 13); TrS,D-E (Franco Tosi) 13.5

17440 **WAVERLEY** Br/Br (Inglis) 1947; P; 700; 73 × 1.9 (240 × 6); R (Rankin & Blackmore); 14; Paddle steamer

17450 **PILOTA ALSINA** Ar (Navy)/Sp (UN de Levante) 1963; P/Riv; 4000; 105 × 2.4 (345 × 8); TrS M (MTM); 14; ex *Ciudad De Formosa* 1981
Sister:
17451 **CIUDAD DE MAR DEL PLATA II** (Ar) ex *Ciudad de la Plata* 1980

17460 **SJAELLAND** De/De (Helsingor) 1951; P/TF; 3000; 110 × 4 (363 × 13.5); TSM (B&W); —; ex *Dronning Ingrid* 1979
Sister:
17461 **FYN** (De)

17470 **OTOME MARU** Ja/Ja (Kanda) 1972; RoPF 3500; 100.03 × 3.47; (328 × 11.38); M (Niigata); 19.5

★17480 **WARNEMUNDE** DDR/DDR ('Neptun') 1962; P/TF; 6100; 136 × 4.7 (449 × 16); TSM (Halberstadt); 18

★17490 **ILYICH** Ru/Fi (Wartsila) 1973; RoPF; 8500; 128 × 5.7 (420 × 19.5); TSM (Sulzer); 22; ex *Stena Baltica* 1983; ex *Skandia* 1983; ex *Bore I* 1980

★17500 **DOVATOR** Ru/DDR (Mathias-Thesen) 1955; P/Riv; 1400; 96 × 2.7 (316 × 9); M (—); 12
Sisters (Ru flag):
★17501 **ALEKSANDR NEVSKII**
★17502 **ALIOSHA POPOVICH**
★17503 **ALTAI**
★17504 **BAGRATION**
★17505 **CHKALOV**
★17506 **DMITRI POZHARSKII**
★17507 **DMITRI DONSKOI**
★17508 **DOBRYNA NIKITCH**
★17509 **ERNST TELMAN**
★17510 **FRIDRICH ENGELS**
★17511 **G.V. PLEKHANOV**
★17512 **GENERAL CHERNIAKOVSKI**
★17513 **GOGOL**
★17514 **ILITCH**
★17515 **ILYA MUROMETS**
★17516 **KARL LIEBKNECHT**
★17517 **KARL MARX**
★17518 **KAVRAZ**
★17519 **KRUPSKAYA**
★17520 **KRYLOV**

★17521 **MATROSOV**
★17522 **MIKHAIL KUTUZOV**
★17523 **N. GASTELLO**
★17524 **RODINA**
★17525 **RYLYEV**
★17526 **TARAS SHEVCHENKO**
★17527 **TIMIRYAZEV**
★17528 **URAL**
★17529 **VYSHINSKII**

★17540 **SAVARONA** Tu/Ge¹(B+V) 1931; TS; 4700 Dst; 125 × 6.3 (409 × 20.5); TST¹(B+V) 18

17550 **N.B. McLEAN** Ca/Ca (Halifax) 1930; IB; 3300; 79 × 6 (260 × 19.5); TSR (Collingwood); 13; KP's abreast both masts

★17560 **PETR LEBEDEV** Ru/Fi (Wartsila) 1957; RS; 3600; 94 × 5.8 (309 × 19); M (Sulzer); 13.5 ex *Chapayev* 1960; May be spelt **PYOTR LEBEDEV**
Sister:
★17561 **SERGEI VAVILOV** (Ru) ex *Furmanov* 1960

● 17580 **EDDA** Pd/Fr (Dubigeon-Normandie) 1972; RoPF; 7800; 126.9 × 5.2 (416 × 17.1); TSM (Pielstick); ex *Rogalin* 1983; ex *Aallotar;* Bow & stern doors
Sister:
17581 **ODYSSEAS ELYTIS** (Gr) ex *Mediterranean Sun* 1982; ex *Regina;* ex *Svea Regina*

17590 **CIUDAD DE SANTA CRUZ LA PALMA** Sp/Sp (UN de Levante) 1972; RoPF; 7500; 137.8 × 5.7 (452 × 18.1); TSM (MAN); 22.5 ex *Ciudad de Palma* 1982; ex *Canguro Cabo San Sebastian* 1981; Stern door
Sisters (Sp flag):
17591 **CIUDAD DE PALMA** ex *Ciudad de Santa Cruz la Palma* 1982; ex *Canguro Cabo San Jorge* 1981;
17592 **CIUDAD DE BADAJOZ**
17593 **CIUDAD DE SEVILLA**
17594 **CIUDAD DE CACERES**
17595 **CIUDAD DE SALAMANCA**

17600 **STELLA SOLARIS** Gr/Fr (Ch. de France) 1953; P; 10600; 166 × 7.9 (545 × 26); TST (La Loire)-; ex *Stella V* 1970; ex *Cambodge* 1970

17610 **GOLDEN ODYSSEY** Gr/De (Helsingor) 1974; P; 6800; 130.2 × 5.2 (427 × 17.2); TSM (MaK); 21

★17620 **SHUI HSIEN** RC/Ca (—) 1948; F; 3100; 86.6 × 3.7 (284 × 12); T (—); 14

17630 **CIUDAD DE COLONIA** Ar/Ar (Mihanovich) 1939; F; 1300; 66.5 × 2.6 (218 × 8.6); TSD-E (Atlas Diesel); 21.

17640 **REGENCY** Pa/Br (H&W) 1952; P; 4800; 103.5 × 4.8 (340 × 15.1); TSM (H&W); 16; ex *Apollon II* 1981; ex *Achilleus* 1969; ex *Semiramis II* 1969; ex *Orpheus* 1969; ex *Irish Coast* 1968

17650 **MALENE OSTERVOLD** No/Br (Cochrane) 1965; ST; 800; 63 × — (207 × —); D-E (MaK); ex *Ross Intrepid* 1976; ex *Ross Kennedy* 1966; ex *Cape Kennedy* 1966

★17660 **GALATI** Rm/Ja (Hitachi) 1964; FT; 3600; 93.1 × 5 (305 × 16.3); M (B&W); 13
Sister:
★17661 **CONSTANTA** (Rm)

★17670 **ERNST HAECKEL** DDR/DDR (Mathias-Thesen) 1962; RS/ST; 1600; 67.7 × 4.9 (222 × 16.1); M (Goerlitzer); 11.5

17680 **SOUTHERN RANGER** SA/Br (Hall, Russell) 1962; ST; 1400; 67.3 × — (240 × —); D-E (English Electric); —; ex *Bluefin;* ex *Junella* 1973

17690 **V. U. HAMMERSHAIMB** Fa/Br (Cochrane) 1964; ST; 800; 63 × — (207 × —); D-E (KHD); —; ex *Ross Valiant* 1975

17700 **ARCTIC FREEBOOTER** Br/Br (Goole) 1966; ST; 1200; 67.84 × — (221 × —); M (Mirrlees); —

17710 **DEFIANCE** Br/Br (Lewis) 1966; ST; 1100; 66.4 × 4.7 (218 × 15.6); M (Mirrlees); 14.5

17720 **SIR FRED PARKES** Br/Br (Hall, Russell) 1966/83; SSV; 1000; 67.82 × 4.57 (223 × 14.99); M (Mirrlees); 13.5; Converted from stern trawler 1983

17730 **ARAMOKO** Ng/Br (Cochrane) 1966; ST; 1100; 65.7 × — (215 × —); M (Ruston); —; ex *Ross Vanguard* 1982

17740 **ST. JASON** Br/Br (Ferguson Bros) 1967; ST; 1300; 66.2 × — (217 × —); M (British Polar); 14
Sisters (Br flag):
17741 **ST. JASPER**
17742 **ST. JEROME**

17760 **KIM ANN** Sg/Br (Bartram) 1951; PC; 7700;

131.6 × 7.6 (432 × 25.8); TSM (Doxford); 14.5; ex *Timor* 1974

17770 **MIDNATSOL NORGE** No/It (Riuniti) 1949; PC; 2100; 81.56 × 4.50 (267.6 × 14.76); M (Fiat); 15.5; ex *Midnatsol II* 1983; ex *Midnatsol* 1982
Sister:
17771 **RALEN** (No) ex *Vesteralen II* 1983; ex *Vesteralen* 1983

17780 **TRIAENA 1** Cy/De (Helsingor) 1956; C; 2700/3900; 108.4 × —/6.9 (356 ×—/22.8); M (B&W); 14; ex *Aspaki* 1977; ex *Varres* 1976; ex *Barma* 1974; ex *Eurodawn* 1972; ex *Oklahoma* 1970
Similar (Le flag):
17781 **BAABDA** ex *Athos* 1973
17782 **BERYTE** ex *Skyros* 1973

17800 **ANNOULA K** Pa/Ne (Jan Smit) 1953; C; 2200; 96 × 6 (315 × 19.7); M (Nederland); 13; ex *Anna III*; ex *Annita* 1973; ex *Pallas* 1968

★17810 **INDIGIRKA** Ru/Ne ('De Schelde') 1957; C; 6000/7500; 130.2 × 7.9/8.2 (427 × 26/27); D-E ('De Schelde'); 15
Sisters (Ru flag):
★17811 **ANGARA**
★17812 **BAYKAL**

★17830 **FASTOV** Ru/Fi (Crichton-Vulcan) 1958; C; 1700; 94.2 × 5.7 (309 × 18.7); M (Sulzer); 13.5
Sisters (Ru flag):
★17831 **FATEZH**
★17832 **FLORESHTY**
★17833 **FROLOVO**
★17834 **FRYAZINO**

17840 **RIBEIRA GRANDE** Po/Ne (Vuyk) 1948; C; 2400; 106.6 × 5.9 (350 × 19.4); M (Sulzer); 14

★17870 **KOTA RATNA** Sg/Ne ('De Waal') 1959; CP; 2300/3300; 99.5 × 5.4/6.8 (326 × 17.11/22.4); M (Werkspoor); 13.75; ex *Mercury Gulf* 1975; ex *Tjiliwong* 1972
Sisters (Sg flag):
17871 **KOTA RIA** ex *Tjitarum* 1975
17872 **KOTA RUKUN** ex *Mercury Cove* 1975; ex *Tjimanuk* 1972

17880 **ZACHARIAS Z** Cy/Be (Boel) 1949; C; 1600; 88.3 × 5.5 (310 × 18.1); M (MWM); 12; ex *Marguerite* 1966
Similar (Gr flag):
17881 **PANTANASSA** ex *Fulmar Wish* 1975; ex *Nissos Serifos* 1973; ex *Aleppo* 1964; ex *Alegritta* 1958; ex *Escaut* 1958

17890 **ONBAK FADJAR** Ia/Ca (Saint John SB) 1945; C; 3100; 100 × 6.4 (329 × 21); R (Canada Iron Foundries); 9.5; ex *Ocean Fortune* 1968; ex *Curran* 1957; ex *Sugar Producer* 1956; ex *Makena II* 1950; ex *Oakmount* 1948; ex *Oakmount Park* 1947; 'SCANDINAVIAN' type

17900 **SOMSUK** Th/Ja (Mitsubishi J) 1948; CP; 2100; 90.3 × 5.8 (296 × 18.11); M (Kobe); 10.5; ex *Wing Peng*; ex *Kwok Wah*; ex *Fortune Light*; ex *Kafar*; ex *Yamasho Maru* 1972; ex *Hosho Maru* 1967

17910 **HEUNG A No 7** Ko/Ja (Mitsubishi J) 1949; C; 2100; 90.4 × 6 (297 × 19.8); M (Hanshin); 9.5; ex *Fukiharu Maru* 1967

★17920 **SHKIPER GIEK** Ru/Pd (Gdanska) 1959; C; 3700; 108.3 × 6.6 (355 × 21.8); R (Zgoda); 12.25; 'B-31' type
Sisters (Ru flag):
★17921 **ADMIRAL SARYCHEV**
★17922 **ALEKSANDR BARANOV**
★17923 **ALEKSANDR POPOV**
★17924 **ALEKSANDR TEREKHIN**
★17925 **BOSHNYAKOVO**
★17927 **GORODETSKIY**
★17928 **KAPITAN GRITSUK** ex *Shantar*
★17929 **NIKOLAY BOSHNYAK**
★17930 **VELSK**
★17931 **ELETS**
★17932 **MOREKHOD**
★17933 **KUSKOV**
Similar:
★17934 **DURRESI** (Al)
Similar (converted to fish carrier):
★17935 **ARKHANGELSK** (Ru)

★17940 **'B 31'** type. Ru/Pd (Gdanska) —; C/B; approx 3800; 108.26 × 6.66 (355.8 × 21.85); R & LPT ('Zgoda'); approx. 11.5; Several vessels in this class may be modified like this—see no 10430 (Anadyr etc)

★17950 **ZVYEROBOY** Ru/Pd (Polnocna) 1973; ST/S; 2000; 72.8 × 4.9 (239 × 16.2); D-E (Sulzer) 13; 'B-422' type
Sisters (Ru flag):
★17951 **LAPLANDIYA**
★17952 **SEREBRYANKA**

★17953 **BYELOKAMENKA**
★17954 **BYEREZINA**
★17955 **ZALESOVO**
★17956 **LIMENDA**
★17957 **ZAGORIANA**
★17958 **ZASLONOVO**
★17959 **ZYKOVO**
★17960 **ZVYAGIHO**
★17961 **TAYBOLA**
★17962 **GREMIKHA**
★17963 **ZAKHAROVO**
★17964 **ZVYERYEVO**
★17965 **ZUBOVO**
★17966 **VARSHUGA**
★17967 **TIERIBERKA**
★17968 **PROFESSOR SERGEY DOROFEYEV**
★17969 **PROFESSOR NESTOR SMYERNOV**
★17970 **TITOVKA**
★17971 **ZADORIE**
★17972 **ZAGORSKIY**
★17973 **ZUBARYEVO**
★17974 **MEZEN**
★17975 **KHARLOVKA**

★17980 **BODO UHSE** DDR/DDR (Mathias-Thesen) 1965; FT; 3200; 87.7 × 5.7 (288 × 18.9); M (Dieselmotorenwerk Rostock) 14
Sister:
★17981 **WILLI BREDEL** (DDR)

★17990 **MARTIN ANDERSEN NEXO** DDR/FRG (Howaldts) 1951; FF; 4800; 120.4 × 6 (395 × 19.7); M (MAN); 16.5; ex *Pegasus* 1960; Converted from a cargo ship 1960

18000 **SERENISSIMA EXPRESS** It/Ja (Hayashikane) 1976; RoC; 6800; 147.6 × 6.6 (484 × 21.8); M (MAN); 19.5; Stern and quarter doors
Sisters:
18001 **ANGLIA EXPRESS** (It)
18002 **ALLEMAGNA EXPRESS** (It)

★18010 **BALTIKA** Ru/Ne (Nederlandsche) 1940; PC; 7500; 135.7 × 6.3 (445 × 20.1); TST-E (Stork); 15; ex *Vyacheslav Molotov* 1957

★18020 **XIN HUA** RC/No (Fredriksstad) 1942; C; 2500; 88.2 × 4.6 (290 × 15.2); R (Fredriksstad); 13.5; ex *Sigurd Jarl* 1960

18040 **TAMPOMAS** Ia/Ne ('De Schelde') 1956; PC; 7200; 128.6 × 6.3 (422 × 20.8); M (MAN); 15

18070 **APOLLONIA** Gr/Br (Swan Hunter & WR) 1948; P; 5300; 122.6 × 6 (402 × 19.7); TST (Parsons); 19.5; ex *Sidi Bel Abbes* 1963

★18090 **MIKHAIL LOMONOSOV** Ru/DDR ('Neptun') 1957; RS; 3900; 102.4 × 6 (335 × 19.7); R (Liebknecht); 13

18100 **GANN** No/No (Nylands) 1950; F; 1500; 67.6 × 4.8 (222 × 15.9); M (Atlas-Diesel); 16; ex *Vikingfjord* ex *Sandes* 1974

★18110 **GONG NONG BING No 10** RC/RC (—) 1955; PC; 2700; 79.9 × 4.3 (262 × 14); R (—); 10; ex *Min Chu No 10*
Sister:
★18111 **GONG NONG BING No 11** (RC) ex *Min Chu No 11*

★18120 **GONG NONG BING No 14** RC/RC (—) 1958; PC; 2500; 90.5 × — (297 × —); R (—); 12; ex *Min Chu No 14*
Sisters (RC flag):
★18121 **GONG NONG BING No 15** ex *Min Chu No 15*
★18122 **GONG NONG BING No 16** ex *Min Chu No 16*

18150 **TIRTA MULIA** Pa /Ne (P Smit) 1935; C; 2100; 84.2 × 4.5 (276 × 14.9); M (Sulzer); 11; ex *Ban Ho Hin* 1973; ex *Janssens* 1958;
Similar (Ia Flag):
18151 **DUMAS PERDANA** ex *Bian* 1983; ex *Carino* 1962; ex *Kalianda* 1960
18152 **KEBON AGUNG** ex *Kaloekoe* 1973
18153 **KAROSSA**
18154 **KAHAGIA IV** ex *Kedawung* 1974; ex *Kasimbar* 1973
18155 **KOMERING** ex *Gana* 1962; ex *Kaimana* 1960
18156 **LEMATANG** ex *Viso* 1962; ex *Kalabahi* 1960;
18157 **MUSI** ex *Merito* 1962; ex *Karaton* 1960
18158 **OGAN** ex *Fama* 1962; ex *Kalianget* 1960

18160 **CLANSMAN** Br/Br (Hall, Russell) 1964; RoPF; 1700; 81 × 2.7 (266 × 9); TSM (Crossley); 14.5; Bow & stern doors. Lengthened 1973 (Ailsa)

18170 **ORCADIA** Br/Br (Hall, Russell) 1962; F/LS; 900; 50 × 2.9 (164 × 9.7); M (British Polar); 12

18180 **1-007** Bh/FRG (Meyer) 1964; F; 1000; 55.5 × 2.3 (182 × 7.6); TSM (KHD); 10.5; ex *Monirul Haque*

1975; ex *EPSC Zakia* 1967
Sisters (Bh Flag):
18181 **1-001** ex *Alauddin Ahmed* 1975
18182 **1-002** ex *Abdul Matin* 1975; ex *EPSC Zubeida* 1967
18183 **C5-214** ex *Tajul Islam* 1975

● 18190 **LEYTE GULF** Pi/Fr (Loire-Normandie) 1957; R; 3700; 113.4 × 7.1 (372 × 23.3); M (B&W); 17.5; ex *Foulaya* 1969
Sister (Gr flag):
18192 **ANASTASIA** ex *Stork* 1980; ex *Sougueta* 1978

18200 **EL GAUCHO** Pa/FRG (Hanseatische) 1960; C; 2100; 108.06 × 6.1 (354.53 20.01); M (Pielstick); 18; ex *Ellaki* 1977; ex *Algor* 1972; ex *Bodetal* 1968

18210 **WAJABULA** La/Fi (Valmet) 1959; C/F; 2500; 96.9 × 4.2 (318 × 13.11); M (MAN); 11; ex *Halmahera* 1963

18230 **KATIA K.** Pa/Br (H.Robb) 1957; C; 1300; 70.9 × — (233 × —); M (British Polar); 11.5; ex *Alinda* 1982; ex *Ile de Saint Pierre* 1981; ex *Sandpiper* 1967

18240 **SARAH** Ca/Br (Grangemouth) 1956; C; 900; 70.8 × 3.9 (232 × 12.11); M (British Polar); 11.5; ex *Gannet* 1968

18250 **DESDEMONA** Ar/FRG (Stuelcken) 1952; C; 2100; 77.7 × 5.9 (255 × 19.6); M (Waggon); 11
Sister:
18251 **CLEOPATRA** (Ar)

18260 **MANGANESE** Eg/Ge (Norderwerft) 1925; C; 960; 67.4 × 5.5 (221 × 18.2); R (Dresdner); —; ex *Laconia* 1965; ex *Herakleion* 1948; ex *Empire Contract* 1945; ex *Wiedau* 1945

★18270 **HAVANA** Ru/FRG (Kieler H) 1955; FC; 3100; 128.8 × 6.1 (423 × 20); M (Kieler H); 17; ex *Brunshausen* 1963; Could be called **GAVANA**
Sisters (Ru flag):
★18271 **BORA** ex *Brunsholm* 1964
★18272 **MUSSON** ex *Brunsdeich* 1964
★18273 **PASSAT** ex *Brunseck* 1964
★18274 **PLAYA HIRON** ex *Brunsbuttel*; May be called **PLAIYA KHIRON**

★18280 **KUBA** Ru/FRG (LF-W) 1955; FC; 3200; 130.5 × 6.1 (431 × 20); M (MAN); 16; ex *Quartett* 1963

18300 **SARONIC REEFER** Gr/Sp (Euskalduna) 1967; R; 3200/4300; 134.3 × —/17.1 (441 × 23.3); M (Sulzer); 20; ex *Sevillan Reefer* 1979; ex *Portugalete* 1972
Sister:
18301 **IKARIAN REEFER** (Gr) ex *Iberian Reefer*; ex *Plencia* 1972

★18310 **ICHA** Ru/Be (Boel) 1953; R; 6100; 132 × 7 (433 × 23.1); M (Gotaverken); 18.5; ex *Carib* 1964

★18320 **TSIKLON** Ru/FRG (B V) 1963; FC; 4700; 135.2 × 7.2 (444 × 23.7); M (MAN); 21; ex *Brunshausen* 1966; Converted general cargo ship 1966
Sister:
18321 **URAGAN** ex *Brunsbuttel* 1967

18330 **LALINE P.** Pa/Be (Flandre) 1960; R; 6200; 139.2 × 7.2 (457 × 23.7); M (MAN); —; ex *Baltic Freezer* 1982; ex *Ondine*
Sister:
18331 **NICOLAS P.** (Pa) ex *Med Freezer* 1983; ex *Orpheus*

18340 **EVEREST** Pa/Fr (Provence) 1956; R; 5000; 114.9 × 6.5 (377 × 21.5); M (B&W); 16.5; ex *Transfruco* 1983; ex *Fruco* 1983; ex *Cuzco* 1973; ex *Fort Caroline* 1969
Similar (Pa flag):
18341 **LORD CREVECOEUR** ex *Fort Crevecoeur* 1976
18342 **LORD DE FRANCE** ex *Fort de France* 1973
18343 **LORD FLEUR D'EPEE** ex *Fort Fleur d'Epee* 1975

● 18370 **ISLAND KOS** Gr/Sw (Uddevalla) 1956; R; 3400; 123.8 × 6.4 (406 × 21); M (Uddevalla); 18; ex *Kos* 1981; ex *Frubel Maria* 1966; ex *Karin Thorden* 1958

18380 **AUDACIA** Ur/No (Framnaes) 1964; R; 4200; 128.1 × 7.8 (420 × 25.6); M (Sulzer); 19; ex *Para*; ex *Vikfrost* 1977; ex *Thorsdrott* 1972
Sister:
18381 **ISADORE HECHT** (Pa) ex *Clydefirth* 1980; ex *Vikfrio* 1974; ex *Thorsoy* 1972

18390 **AL SUDAN** Eg/US (Consolidated Steel) 1944; PC; 7400; 127.11 × 8.15 (418 × 26.9); T (Hendy); 14.5; ex *Empire Arquebus* 1947; ex *Cicero* 1946; ex *Empire Arquebus* 1945; launched as *Cape St Vincent*; converted 'C1' type

18400 **SANG THAI STEEL** Th/FRG (Stuelcken) 1958; CP; 2300/3500; 106.2 × 7.4 (438 × 23.6); M (Ottensener); 14; ex*Dexena* 1981; ex*Ulsnis* 1976; ex *Volumnia* 1969; ex*Lealott* 1966; ex *Volumnia* 1963

18440 **BALLENITA** Pa/No (Norrkopings) 1957; CP; 2200/2700; 95 × 5.4/6.4 (310 ×18/21); M (Sulzer); 15

18460 **GABBIANO** It/Hong Kong (Hong Kong & W) 1967; RoC; 1100; 81.2 × 3.1 (267 × 10.6); M (British Polar); 12.5; ex*Annarita Seconda* 1978; ex*Holmlea* 1975; ex *Seaway Princess* 1970; Stern door

● 18480 **ALKMINI A.** Gr/Sw (Lindholmens) 1937; C; 2500; 100.97 × 5.69 (331.27 ×18.67); M (Atlas-Diesel); 12; ex*Mercia* 1974; ex*Mylle* 1969; ex*Frigg* 1961; ex*Pan* 1957; ex*Astri* 1952; May be broken up

★18490 **MIN CHU No 8** RC/China (—) 1924; C; 1900; 79.2 × 4.9 (260 × 16); R (—); 10

18500 **DONA GLORIA** Pi/Sw (Ekensbergs) 1947; C; 1800; 86 × 5.9 (282 × 19.6); M (Atlas-Diesel); 13; ex *Don Sulpicio* 1969; ex *Colombia* 1964

18520 **SPYROS** Cy/Sw (Finnboda) 1939; C; 1500; 87.58 × 5.44 (287 × 17.85); M (Atlas-Diesel); 12; ex *Gianvittorioemme* 1973; ex *Fidra* 1966

★18530 **GALIOLA** Ys/Br (Austin) 1954; C; 1100/1800; 79 × —/5.5 (260 × —/18); M (Sulzer) 13; ex*Adjutant* 1966
Sisters (Ys flag):
★18531 **OTOK** ex *Horizont* 1973; ex*Ringdove* 1967
★18532 **ORUDA** ex *Whitewing* 1967

18540 **SKULE** No/No (Trosvik) 1949; TS; 700; 48 × 5.4 (167 × 17.6); M (Atlas- Diesel); 12; ex*Soroy* 1966

18550 **SANDRA MARIA** Ia/It (Felszegi) 1952; C; 800; 67.2 × 4.6 (221 × 15.2); M (MaK); 11.5; ex *Alessandra*

★18570 **ORJULA** Ys/Br (Grangemouth) 1948; C; 1000; 71.5 × 4.2 (235 × 13.11); M (British Polar); 12; ex *Woodcock* 1964;
Sister:
★18571 **RABAC** (Ys) ex *Labin* 1967; ex *Ptarmigan* 1963

18590 **TRONDELAG** No/No (Stord) 1950; TS; 600; 49.2 × 3.5 (161 × 11.6); M (Atlas-MaK); 12; ex*Aure* 1964

18600 **ONGE** In/In (Mazagon) 1969; F/LS; 1300; 68.3 × 2.9 (224 × 9.6); M (Liebknecht); 12
Sister:
18601 **YEREWA** (In)

18610 **LADY HUTTON** Sw/Ge (Krupp) 1924; TS; 1600; 75 × 4.8 (246 × 15.9); TSM (Krupp); 13; ex *Vikingfjord* 1981; ex*Gann* 1978; ex*Marina* 1960; ex *Brand VI* 1960; ex *Court Adeler* 1956; ex*King* 1950; ex *Troubadour* 1948; ex *Warrior*; ex *Vanadis*; Converted yacht

18620 **DANNEBROG** De/De (Royal Danish Dkyd) 1931; Royal Yacht; 1100; 75 × 3.4 (246× 11.2); TSM (—); 14; Modified 1980 (Helsingor)

18640 **AMPERE** Fr/Fr (Saint Nazaire) 1951; Cbl; 2200; 85. 3 × 5.1 (289 × 16.1); TST (Parsons); 15

18650 **BODE THOMAS** Ng/Br (Brooke) 1960; BT; 1200; 62.8 × 3.5 (206 × 11.7); TSM (Mirrlees Blackstone); —

18660 **MERMAID** Br/Br (J.S. White) 1959; LT; 1400; 67.4 × 4 (221 × 13); TSD-E (English Electric);

18670 **READY** Br/Br (Blyth) 1947; —; 1900; 81.41 × 4.20 (267 × 13.9); TSR (G.Clark); 12

18680 **SAGAR** In/Br (Blyth) 1964; Plt; 2000; 83.6 × 4.7 (274 × 15.7); TSM (MAN); —
Sister:
18681 **SAMUDRA** (In)

18690 **VIRGEN DEL CAMINO** Sp/Sp (Construcciones SA) 1963; ST; 930; 61 × 5 (200 × 16.6); M (MWM); 14; ex *Mar Austral* 1967;
Similar:
★18691 **ISLA DE LA JUVENTUD** (Cu) ex *Arminza* 1967

18700 **HESSEN** FRG/FRG (Rickmers) 1960; FT; 1000; 73 × 4.4 (239 × 14.3); D-E (KHD); —

18710 **CORIOLANUS** Br/Br (Yarrow & Co.) 1967; ST; 1100; 63.4 × 4.6 (208 × 15); M (Mirrlees); 15.5
Sisters (Br flag):
18711 **CASSIO**
18712 **OTHELLO**
18713 **ORSINO**

★18720 **NORDSEE** DDR/DDR (Elbewerft) 1966; FT; 640; 48.9 × 3.5 (160.3 × 11.4); M (Liebknecht); 12

Sisters (DDR flag):
★18721 **ATLANTIK**
★18722 **BARENTSEE**
★18723 **GROSSER BELT**
★18724 **JAN MAYEN**
★18725 **KATTEGAT**
★18726 **LOFOTEN**
★18727 **MALANGEN**
★18728 **NORDMEER**
★18729 **ORKNEY**
★18730 **SILVER PIT**
★18731 **SUND**
★18732 **SVINOY**
★18733 **SKAGERRAK**

★18740 **LASKARA** Pd/Pd (Gdynska) 1968; FT; 1500; 75.6 × 5 (248 × 17); M (Fiat); 14.5; '**B-29**' type Sisters (Pd flag): (later vessels have stanchions in open superstructure and more pronounced sheer foreward etc—see inset)
★18741 **KABRYL**
★18742 **KANARYJKA**
★18743 **KANTAR**
★18744 **KNIAZIK**
★18745 **KOLEN**
★18746 **KORWIN**
★18747 **KULBAK**
★18748 **KULBIN**
★18749 **KUNATKA**
★18750 **LATERNA**
★18751 **LIKODYN**
★18752 **LIKOMUR**
★18753 **LIKOSAR**
★18754 **LIKOWAL**
★18755 **LODOWIK**
★18756 **LUTJAN**
★18757 **LUZYTANKA**

18760 **TYPICAL DEEP SEA TRAWLER** Approx 700-900; 64 to 70 × 5.1 to 5.5 (210 to 230 × 17 to 18); M; 15 approx

18800 **KATIPUNAN** Pi/Ja (Mitsui) 1947; F; 1100; 65.00 × 3.45 (213 × 11.32); TSM (Kobe); 14; ex*Hikari Maru* 1974

18810 **PRINCESS OF ACADIA** Ca/Ca (Saint John SB) 1971; RoPF; 10100; 146.3 × 4.6 (480 × 15.3); TSM (General Motors); 15.5; ex *Princess of Nova*

18840 **MARAKAZ** Tu/Ge (Krupp) 1938; PC; 1400; 80 × 3.4 (263 × 11.1); TST (Krupp); 15

18860 **ROANA** Cy/De (Svendborg) 1954; RoPF; 1300; 60.1 × 3.6 (197 × 11.8); M (B&W); 12.75; ex *Ostersoen* 1973

★18880 **MARINA** Ys/De (Frederikshavn) 1936; RoPF; 1000; 71.8 × 3.4 (236 × 11.2); TSM (Atlas-Diesel); 14; ex *Christofer Polhem* 1964; ex*Kronprinsessan Ingrid* 1935; Stern door. Lengthened 1950

18890 **AGOSTINO LAURO** It/De (Aalborg) 1935; F; 500; 60 × 3.6 (197 × 11.9); TSM (B&W); 14; ex *Isefjord* 1966

18900 **BALMORAL** Br/Br (Thornycroft) 1949; F; 700; 62 × 2 (204 × 6.7); TSM (Newbury); 14.5

18910 **SPOKANE** US/US (Todd) 1972; RoPF; 3200; 134.1 × 5.2 (440 × 17.2); D-E (General Motors); 20
Sister:
18911 **WALLA-WALLA** (US)

18920 **QUEEN OF COQUITLAM** Ca/Ca (Burrard DD) 1976; RoPF; 6600; 139.3 × 5.3 (457 × 17.8); M (MaK); 20
Sister:
18921 **QUEEN OF COWICHAN** (Ca)

18930 **ARVEPRINS KNUD** De/De (Helsingor) 1963; RoPF; 4800; 129.9 × 4.6 (426 × 15.1); TSM (B&W); 19; Bow and stern doors

18940 **KNUDSHOVED** De/De (Helsingor) 1961; RoC; 3900; 109.2 × 4.6 (358 × 15.1); TSM (B&W); 16
Sister (De flag):
18941 **SPROGO**
Similar (De flag):
18942 **HALSSKOV**

18950 **PRINSES CHRISTINA** Ne/Ne ('De Merwede') 1968; RoPF; 3100; 113.6 × 4.6 (373 × 15.2); D-E (MAN); 18.5; Bow and stern doors

18955 **MOLENGAT** Ne/Ne (Verolme SH) 1980; RoPF; 3300; 88.42 × 3.80 (291 × 12.47); TD-E (MaK); 13.5

18960 **PRINSES MARGRIET** Ne/Ne (Giessen-De Noord) 1963; RoPF; 2300; 102 × 4.8 (345 ×15.1); D-E (MAN); 16
Sisters (Ne flag):
18961 **PRINSES BEATRIX**
18962 **PRINSES IRENE**

18970 **TEXELSTROOM** Ne/Ne (P Smit) 1966; RoPF; 2700; 68 × — (223 × —); D-E (Lister Blackstone); —
Sister:
18971 **MARSDIEP** (Ne)

18980 **EVERGREEN STATE** US/US (—) 1954; RoPF; 1500; 94.5 × 4.6 (310 × 15); TSD-E (—); 15
Sisters (US flag):
18981 **KLAHOWYA**
18982 **TILLIKUM**

● 18990 **QUEEN OF ALBERNI** Ca/Ca (Vancouver) 1976; RoPF/TF; 5300; 139.3 × 5.49 (457.02 ×18.01); TSM (MaK); 22

19000 **SECONDO ASPROMONTE** It/It (Tirreno) 1948; RoC/TF; 1600; 97.7 × 3.8 (321 × 12.5); TSM (Franco Tosi); 12.5; ex*Aspromonte* 1949
Sister:
19001 **MONGIBELLO** (It)

● 19010 **HALSINBORG** De/De (Svendborg) 1960; RoPF/TF; 1050; 80.9 × 3.6 (265 × 11.1); D-E (Frichs); 11
Similar (raised boats):
19011 **HELSINGOR** (De)

19020 **CONFEDERATION** Ca/Ca (Halifax) 1962; RoPF; 2400; 86.5 × 4.2 (284 × 13.9); TSD-E (Davey, Paxman); —

19030 **BASTO III** No/No (Ankerlokken) 1968; RoPF; 1200; 65.6 × 3.4 (215 × 11.2); M (Sulzer); —; Bow and stern doors

19040 **KIZKULESI** Tu/Fr (Dubigeon) 1951; RoPF; 1000; 60 × 3 (197 × 9.10); M (Sulzer); —
Sister:
19041 **KASIMPASA** (Tu)

19050 **TRANS ST. LAURENT** Ca/Ca (Davie & Sons) 1963; RoPF; 2200; 79.8 × — (262 × —); TSM (Alpha-Diesel); —

19060 **QUEEN OF THE ISLANDS** Ca/Ca (Burrard DD) 1963; RoPF; 1700; 71.9 × — (263 × —); TSM (Fairbanks, Morse); —; Bow & stern doors

19070 **NOORD NEDERLAND** Ne/Sw (Finnboda) 1960; RoPF; 1100; 48 × 3.7 (158 × 11.6); TSM (Ruston & Hornsby); —; ex *Primula* 1976

19080 **BETULA** Sw/FRG (Meyer) 1968; RoPF; 2300; 71.3 × 4 (234 × 13.1); TSM (KHD); 14.5; Bow & stern doors
Similar (Sw flag):
19081 **REGULA**
19082 **URSULA**

19090 **ECKERO** Fi/FRG (Meyer) 1971; RoF; 3000; 86.3 × 4 (283 × 13.1); TSM (Ruston Paxman); 17; ex *Svea Scarlett* 1982

19110 **ANGAMOS** Ch/FRG (O&K) 1966; Spt; 3600; 93.9 × 4.3 (308 × 14.2); TSM (Pielstick); —; ex*Puerto Montt;* ex *Presidente Aguirre Cerda* 1974; ex*Kobenhavn* 1973; Operated by Chilean Navy. Now has large pipes from rear of funnel

19120 **SARDINIA NOVA** It/FRG (LF-W) 1966; RoPF; 7300; 138 × 5.5 (453 × 18); TSM (Pielstick); 23; ex *Espresso Olbia* 1982; ex *Tor Anglia;* Bow & stern doors

19130 **ARIADNE** Gr/FRG (LF-W) 1967; RoPF; 10700; 138 × 5.5 (453 × 18); TSM (Pielstick); 23; ex *Tor Hollandia* 1975; Bow & stern doors

19140 **GELTING** De/FRG (O&K) 1963; RoPF; 2500; 93.2 × 4 (306 × 13.2); TSM (MWM); 19; ex *Mille* 1976; ex*Falster* 1968; ex *Gedster* 1968; Bow & stern doors
Sister:
19141 **CORSICA NOVA** (Pa) ex *Corsika Nova* 1979; ex *Europafarjan II* 1976; ex *Travemunde* 1970
Similar:
19142 **THJELVAR** (Sw) ex *Gotland*
★19143 **TIAN HU** (RC) ex *Skandynawia* 1981; ex *Visby* 1970

19150 **CHRISTIAN IV** No/De (Aalborg) 1968; RoC/TF; 2700; 87.3 × 4.1 (286 × 13.6); TSM (Holeby); 19; Stern and side doors

19160 **YESILADA** Tu/De (Aalborg) 1968; RoPF; 3100; 87.2 × 4.2 (186 × 13.9); TSM (B&W); 19.5; ex *Peter Wessel* 1971

★19170 **SLAVIJA 1** Ys/Br (Bartram) 1963; RoPF; 3000; 88.3 × 4.2 (290 × 13.9); TSM (MAN); —; ex *Slavija;* ex *Skipper Clement* 1976; ex *Jens Kofoed* 1965

★19180 **BALKANIJA** Ys/De (Aalborg) 1966; RoPF; 2400; 92.7 × 4.2 (304 × 13.9); TSM (B&W); 19.5; ex *Dania Gloria* 1981; ex*Mette Mo;* ex*Mette Mols* 1974
Sisters:
19181 **CARAVAGGIO** (It) ex *Maren Mo* 1975; ex

Maren Mols 1975
19182 **SMYRIL** (Fa) ex *Morten Mols* 1975
19183 **TEISTIN** (Fa) ex *Mikkel Mols* 1980
Similar:
19184 **ALMIRANTE LUIS BIRON** (Ve) ex *Lasse* 1973

19190 **ALDONZA MANRIQUE** Ve/FRG (Unterweser) 1964; RoPF; 3100; 98.4 × 4.3 (323 × 14.2); TSM (MAN); 19; ex *Olau East* 1975; ex *Julle* 1975; ex *Hundested* 1972; Bow & stern doors
Sister:
19191 **CORSICA MARINA** (Pa) ex *Olau West;* ex *Kalle* 1975; ex *Grenaa* 1971

19200 **CASAMANCE EXPRESS** Se/FRG (Rolandwerft) 1965; F; 1900; 77.6 × 3.4 (255 × 11.2); TSM (MAN); 18; ex *Espresso Brindisi* 1982; ex *Chrysanthemum;* ex *Marianna* 1975; ex *Holiday Princess* 1971; ex *Stella Marina* 1970; Side doors

● 19210 **WILHEMSHAVEN** FRG/FRG (Rolandwerft) 1963; F; 1600; 75 × 3.4 (246 × 11.2); TSM (MAN); 17.5

19220 **POSEIDON** FRG/No (Ulstein) 1964; F; 1100; 65.5 × 2.9 (215 × 9.1); TSM (KHD); —

19230 **CAVO AZURO** Gr/FRG (Sietas) 1959; F; 900; 61.8 × 3.2 (203 × 10.6); TSM (MWM); 14.5; ex *Portokalis Ilios* 1980; ex *Orange Sun* 1967
Sister:
19231 **HARLEKIN** (FRG) ex *Tom Kyle* 1977; ex *Orange Moon* 1961

19240 **SKANE** Sw/Sw (Uddevalla) 1966; RoPF/TF; 6500; 147.7 × 5.5 (484 × 17.5); TSM (Pielstick); —

19250 **FENNIA** Fi/Sw (Oresunds) 1966; RoPF; 6400; 128.3 × 5 (421 × 16.5); TSM (Atlas-MaK); 18.5; Bow & stern doors

19260 **AGADIR** Mo/FRG (Meyer) 1969; RoPF; 3800; 108.1 × 4.6 (355 × 15.1); TSM (MAN); 20; ex *Prinz Hamlet II* 1974; ex *Vikingfjord* 1970; Bow, stern & side doors

19270 **VILLA DE AGAETE** Sp/Fi (Wartsila) 1970; RoPF; 4100; 101.6 × 5 (334 × 16.6); TSM (Wartsila); 13; ex *Floria* 1975; Bow and stern doors

19280 **CIUDAD DE LA LAGUNA** Sp/Fi (Wartsila) 1967; RoF; 3500; 101.6 × 4.9 (334 × 16.2); TSM (Wartsila); 19; ex *Botnia* 1975

● 19290 **BENODET** De/FRG (Meyer) 1970; RoPCF; 4200; 109 × 4.6 (357 × 15); TSM (KHD); 18.5; ex *Gelting Nord* 1984; ex *Olau Kent* 1980; ex *Apollo* 1976
Similar:
19291 **VIKING EXPRESS** (Fi) ex *Viking 1* 1983
19292 **EARL GRANVILLE** (Br) ex *Viking 4*
19293 **VIKING 3** (Fi) ex *Wasa Express* 1982; ex *Viking 3* 1976
19294 **BOTNIA EXPRESS** (Fi) ex *Diana* 1979
19295 **COROMUEL** (Me)
19296 **PUERTO VALLARTA** (Me)
19297 **AZTECA** (Me)

19300 **FAIR LADY** FRG/FRG (Mutzelfeldt) 1970; F; 900; 68.6 × 2.2 (225 × 7); TSM (MWM); 18

19310 **SEEMOWE II** FRG/FRG (Husumer) 1969; F; 1000; 58.9 × 2.9 (193 × 9.8); TSM (Atlas-MaK); 15; ex *Malmo* 1976

19320 **ISLA DE CUBAGUA** Ve/Fi (Sandvikens) 1961; RoPF; 3700; 101.6 × 4.6 (334 × 15.2); TSM (Wartsila); 18; ex *Skandia* 1974; Bow and stern doors
Sister:
19321 **ISLA DE COCHE** (Ve) ex *Nordica* 1974

★ 19330 **WAWEL** Pd/FRG (Nobiskrug) 1965; RoPF; 3800; 110.2 × 4.4 (362 × 14.4); TSM (MAN); 20; ex *Gustav Vasa* 1973; Bow and stern doors
Similar:
19331 **IONIAN STAR** (Gr) ex *Leif Eriksson* 1976; ex *Prins Bertil* 1966

19350 **LUCY MAUD MONTGOMERY** Ca/Fr (La Seine) 1965; RoPF; 4200; 86 × 3.9 (262 × 12.8); TSM (KHD); 17.5; ex *Stena Danica* 1970; Bow and stern doors

19360 **DANA SCARLETT** Sw/Sw (Oresunds) 1964; RoCF; 1700; 65.3 × 3.2 (214 × 10.6); TSM (KHD); 14.75; Bow and stern doors
Similar (shorter top deck):
19361 **CAROLA** (Sw)

19370 **SKOPELOS** Gr/Sw (Langesunds) 1965; RoPF; 1400; 71 × 3.8 (233 × 12.6); TSM (MWM); —; ex *Viking 2* 1979; ex *Gotlandia* 1978; Bow and stern doors
Sister:
19371 **BENITO JUAREZ** (Me) ex *Olanningen* 1972

19380 **GHAWDEX** Ma/FRG (Adler) 1962; RoPF;

2300; 88 × 4 (289 × 13.2); TSM (MAN); 16.5; ex *Rotna* 1979; ex *Kalle* 1971
Sister:
19381 **GIOTTO** (It) ex *Corsica Serena* 1980; ex *Tanger* 1975; ex *Julle*

19390 **NEREUS** Gr/Sw (Uddevalla) 1964; RoPF; 2500; 78.5 × 3.9 (258 × 12.8); TSM (KHD); —; ex *Polhem* 1981; ex *Scania Express* 1976; ex *Scania* 1971

19400 **HAMLET** Sw/FRG (Luerssen) 1968; RoPF; 2100; 73.5 × 3.8 (241 × 12.6); TSM (Atlas-MaK); 14.5; Bow and stern doors
Sister:
19401 **OFELIA** (Sw)

19410 **AINOS** Gr/Sw (Solvesborgs) 1964; F; 2400; 71.9 × — (236 × —); TSM (KHD); 17; ex *Manic;* ex *Apollo* 1968

19420 **EARL GODWIN** Br/Sw (Oresunds) 1966; RoPF; 4000; 99.2 × 4.4 (325 × 14.6); TSM (KHD); 20.25; ex *Svea Drott* 1975; Bow & stern doors

19430 **SUN BOAT** Cy/No (Kaldnes) 1964; RoPF; 3700; 99.5 × 4.4 (326 × 14.6); TSM (Pielstick); 20; ex *Viking Victory* 1982; ex *Viking I* 1976; ex *Carferry Viking I;* Bow & stern doors
Sisters:
19431 **TERJE VIGEN** (No) ex *Viking III* 1982
19432 **EARL WILLIAM** (Br) ex *Carferry Viking II* 1977; ex *Viking II* 1964

19440 **QUEEN OF PRINCE RUPERT** Ca/Ca (Victoria Mach) 1966; RoPF; 5900; 101.12 × 4.64 (331.76 × 15.22); TSM (Mirrlees); —; Bow & stern doors

19450 **JOHN HAMILTON GRAY** Ca/Ca (Marine Indust) 1968; RoC/IB; 11300; 122.1 × 6.2 (401 × 20.3); TD-E (Fairbanks, Morse); 18; Stern doors

19460 **ST. ANSELM** Br/Br (H&W) 1980; RoPCF; 8200; 129.4 × 4.72 (424.54 × 15.49); TSM (Pielstick); 19.5; Bow and stern doors; Modified 1982/83
Sister (Br flag):
19461 **ST. CHRISTOPHER**

19465 **ST. DAVID** Br/Br (H&W) 1981; RoPCF; 7100; 129.65 × 4.84 (425 × 15.88); TSM (Pielstick); 19.5; Bow and stern doors
Similar:
19466 **GALLOWAY PRINCESS** (Br)

19470 **LION** Br/Br (Cammell Laird) 1967; RoPF; 3900; 111 × 4.3 (365 × 14); TSM (Pielstick); 20.25; Bow and stern doors

19480 **EMSLAND** FRG/Ja (Usuki) 1977; RoPF; 1600; 78.52 × 3.35 (257.61 × 10.99); TSM (Niigata); 16; Bow door/ramp; Stern door/ramp

19490 **VELA** Ja/Ja (Naikai) 1979; RoPF; 3700; 120.58 × 5.3 (395.6 × 17.39); TSM (NKK); 20; Bow door/ramp; Stern door/ramp; Side doors/ramps
Sister:
19491 **VESTA** (Ja)

19500 **TASSILI** Ag/Ja (Mitsubishi HI) 1971; RoPF; 10200; 130.38 × 5.62 (427.76 × 18.44); TSM (Mitsubishi); —; ex *Central No 1* 1973; Bow, stern and side doors

19510 **DONG YANG EXPRESS FERRY NO 2** Ko/Ja (Naikai) 1975; RoPF; 2700; 90.5 × 4 (297 × 13.2); TSM (Niigata); —; ex *Kamome* 1979

19520 **HAYATOMO MARU** Ja/Ja (Shikoku) 1971; RoPF; 3400; 105 × 4.4 (344 × 14.6); TSM (Mitsubishi); 18.25; ex *Tosa* 1977

19530 **DONA CONCHITA** Pa/Ja (Ishikawajima S&C) 1969; RoPF; 1900; 82 × 3.45 (269.03 × 11.32); TSM (Niigata); 16.5; ex *Osado Maru* 1983

19540 **AMBROSE SHEA** Ca/Ca (Marine Indust) 1967; RoPF; 9500; 120.6 × 6.3 (396 × 20); TD-E (Cooper-Bessemer); 16.5; Stern door

19550 **THEODOR HEUSS** FRG/FRG (Kieler H) 1957; TF; 5600; 136 × 4.9 (446 × 16); TD-E (Maybach); —

19560 **CITY OF MIDLAND** US/US (Manitowoc) 1941; RoPF/TF; 4000; 124 × 5.7 (407 × 18.7); TSM (Unaflow); 18; ex *City of Midland 41* 1983
Sisters (US flag):
19561 **BADGER**
19562 **SPARTAN**

19570 **PRINSESSE ANNE-MARIE** De/De (Aalborg) 1960; RoPF; 3500; 103.4 × 4.6 (339 × 15); TSM (B&W); 18

19580 **IKAROS** Gr/No (Marinens) 1961; F; 2400; 87.4 × 4.4 (287 × 14.6); TSM (B&W); 17; ex *Corsica Star* 1979; ex *Nordek* 1973; ex *Kattegat* 1969

19590 **KONG FREDERIK IX** De/De (Helsingor)

1954; RoPF; 4100; 114.3 × 4.5 (375 × 14.1); TSM (B&W); 18
Similar:
19591 **PRINSESSE BENEDIKTE** (De)

● 19600 **MARINE CRUISER** Br/Au (NSW Govt) 1959; RoPF; 4100; 113.3 × 4.7 (372 × 15.7); TSM (Nydqvist & Holm); 17.75; ex *Princess of Tasmania* 1975; Stern door

19610 **AGIOS GEORGIOS** Gr/De (Aalborg) 1956; RoPF; 2000; 70.9 × 3.7 (232 × 12.1); TSM (B&W); 15; ex *Mastrogiorgis* 1976; ex *Absalon* 1975

19620 **SCANIA** Sw/De (Aalborg) 1972; RoPF; 2200; 74.2 × 3.8 (243 × 12.6); TSM (Nydqvist & Holm); 14.5; Bow, stern and side doors

19630 **AL ANOUD** Eg/Fi (Helsingor) 1955; RoPF; 2200; 84.4 × 4.5 (277 × 15); TSM (Polar); 17; ex *Wasa Express* 1975; ex *Thjelvar* 1964; ex *Prinsessan Margaretha* 1962; Side and stern doors

19640 **SAUDI GOLDEN ARROW** Si/No (Marinens) 1960; RoCF; 2200; 87.5 × 4.4 (287 × 14.6); TSM (B&W); —; ex *Europafergen*

19650 **NORDSCHAU** FRG/De (Aalborg) 1956; RoPF; 2000; 70.9 × 3.7 (233 × 12.6); TSM (Nydqvist & Holm); 14.75; ex *Gripen* 1976

19660 **SAINT GERMAIN** Fr/De (Helsingor) 1951; RoCF/TF; 3100; 115.8 × 4.1 (380 × 13.6); TSM (B&W); 16.5

19670 **IONIAN GLORY** Gr/Fr (Loire-Normandie) 1958; RoPF; 3500; 115 × 4 (377 × 13.1); TSM (Pielstick); 20; Stern door ex *Compiegne* 1982

19680 **YOTEI MARU** Ja/Ja (Hitachi) 1965; RoCF/TF; 5400; 140 × 5.2 (433 × 17.1); TSM (B&W); 18; Stern door
Sisters (Ja flag):
19681 **TAISETU MARU**
19682 **HAKKODA MARU**
19683 **MASHU MARU**
19684 **MATSUMAE MARU**
19685 **TSUGARU MARU**
19686 **TOWADA MARU**

19700 **HIYAMA MARU** Ja/Ja (Mitsubishi HI) 1955; TF; 3400; 119.2 × 4.7 (393 × 15.6); TSM (Mitsubishi); 15
Sister:
19701 **SORACHI MARU** (Ja)

19710 **FERRY HANKYU** Ja/Ja (Hayashikane) 1968; RoCF; 5000; 127 × 4.5 (416 × 15); TSM (MAN); 18
Sister:
19711 **FERRY KANPU** (Ja) ex *Hankyu Maru No 6*

19720 **PRINCESS OF VANCOUVER** Ca/Br (Stephen) 1955/82; RoPF/TF; 5600; 126.8 × 4.5 (416 × 15); TSM (General Motors); 15.5; Modified 1982 — bow door and new stern door fitted (Burrard Y)

19730 **HOMERUS** Gr/De (Helsingor) 1958; RoC; 6500; 137.7 × 5.4 (452 × 17.9); TSM (B&W); 18 ex *Trelleborg;* Stern door

● 19740 **VOLENDAM** NA/US (Ingalls SB) 1958; P; 15300; 188.2 × 8.4 (617.6 × 28); TST (GEC); 23; ex *Monarch Sun;* ex *Volendam* 1975; ex *Brasil* 1972
Sister:
19741 **VEENDAM** (NA) ex *Monarch Star* ex *Veendam* 1976; ex *Brasil* 1975; ex *Veendam* 1974; ex *Argentina* 1972

19750 **REGGIO** It/It (CD Tirreno) 1960; RoPF/TF; 3700; 126.8 × 4.3 (416 × 14); TSM (B&W); 15; Bow and stern doors

19760 **SAN FRANCESCO DI PAOLA** It/It (CD Tirreno) 1964; RoPF/TF; 4000; 128.5 × 4.3 (422 × 14.7); TSM (B&W); 15; Bow and side doors

19770 **NICOLAS MIHANOVICH** Ar/Ar (Astarsa) 1962; F; 1800; 89.6 × 2.6 (294 × 8.7); TrS D-E (KHD); 16

19780 **QUEEN OF TSAWWASSEN** Ca/Ca (Burrard DD) 1960; RoPF; 3100; 102.4 × 3.8 (336 × 12.6); TSM (Mirrlees, Bickerton & Day); —; ex *Tsawwassen* 1962

19800 **GREENPORT** US/US (Sun SB) 1936; F; 2400; 106.7 × 3.2 (350 × 10.6); TSR (Unaflow); 13; ex *New Jersey;* ex *Princess Anne* 1964

19810 **LECONTE** US/US (Peterson) 1974; RoPF; 1300; 71.9 × 3.9 (236 × 13); TSM (General Motors); 15.5

19860 **SOL EXPRESS** Cy/Br (Swan Hunter & WR) 1965; RoPF; 3600; 112.5 × 3.9 (369 × 12.9); TST (Wallsend); 19.5; ex *Earl Siward* 1981; ex *Dover* 1977; Stern door

19890 **ST COLUMBA** Br/De (Aalborg) 1977; RoPF;

7800; 128.6 × 4.7 (425 × 16); TSM (Stork-Werkspoor); 19.5

19900 **HENGIST** Br/Fr (DCAN) 1972; RoPF; 5600; 118.1 × 4.1 (387 × 13.6); TSM (Pielstick); 19.5; Bow & stern doors
Sisters (Br flag):
19901 **HORSA**
19902 **SENLAC**

19910 **CHARTRES** Fr/Fr (Dubigeon-Normandie) 1974; RoPF/TF; 4600; 115.4 × 4.2 (379 × 13.8); TSM (Pielstick); 20.5; Bow and stern doors

19920 **VORTIGERN** Br/Br (Swan Hunter) 1969; RoPF; 4400; 114.6 × 4.1 (376 × 13.4); TSM (Pielstick); 19.5; Bow and stern doors

19930 **PRINS PHILIPPE** Be/Be (Boelwerf) 1973; RoPF; 5100; 118 × 4.2 (387 × 13.8); TSM (Pielstick); 22; Bow and stern doors
Sister:
19931 **PRINCE LAURENT** (Be)

19940 **PRINCESSE MARIE CHRISTINE** Be/Be (Cockerill) 1975; RoPF; 5500; 118.4 × 4.5 (387 × 15); TSM (Pielstick); 22; Bow and stern doors
Sisters (Be flag):
19941 **PRINSES MARIA ESMERALDA**
19942 **PRINS ALBERT**

19950 **ARATIKA** NZ/Fr (Dubigeon-Normandie) 1974; RoPF/TF; 3900; 127.7 × 4.9 (419 × 16.2); TSM (Pielstick); 17.5; Stern door; Converted 1977 (Hong Kong U)

19960 **ARANUI** NZ/Br (Vickers Ltd) 1966; RoPF/TF; 4500; 112.2 × 4.8 (368 × 15.8); TSD-E (English Electric); 17

19970 **ARAHANGA** NZ/Br (Upper Clyde) 1972; RoPF/TF; 39'; 127.5 × 4.9 (418 × 16); TSM (Pielstick); 17; Stern door

19980 **GOTALAND** Sw/De (Nakskov) 1973; RoPF/TF; 5200; 148 × 5.6 (486 × 18.6); TSM (Pielstick); 18.5; Stern and side doors
Similar (lengthened by 33.6 metres (110 feet)):
19981 **SVEALAND AV MALMO** (Sw) ex *Svealand* 1982

★19985 **ROSTOCK** DDR/No (Bergens) 1977; RoPF/TF; 6100; 158.35 × 5.55 (520 × 18.21); TSM (MAN); 20.5; Stern door and 2 side doors (starboard)

19990 **PRINS JOACHIM** De/De (Nakskov) 1980; RoPF/TF; 10600; 152 × 5.6 (498.69 × 18.37); TSM (Alpha-Diesel); 18; bow and stern ramps
Sisters (De flag):
19991 **DRONNING INGRID**
19992 **KRONPRINS FREDERIK**

20000 **RANGATIRA** Br/Br (Swan Hunter) 1972; RoPF; 9400; 152.6 × 5.3 (500 × 17.6); TS T-E (Associated Electric); 21; Stern door; Used as floating hotel; Now has helicopter pad aft (not shown on drawing)

20020 **CHANTILLY** Fr/Fr (Dubigeon-Normandie) 1965; RoPF; 3400; 109.9 × 4 (361 × 13); TSM (Pielstick)

20030 **GEORGIOS B** Cy/Be (Boelwerf) 1968; RoPF; 3200; 118 × 3.8 (387.4 × 12.8); TSM (Sulzer); 22; stern door; ex *Princesse Astrid* 1983

20040 **PRINSES PAOLA** Be/Be (Cockerill) 1966; F; 3400/3800; 117.1 × —/3.8 (385 × —/12.8); TSM (Sulzer); 24

20050 **GEORGIOS EXPRESS** Gr/Be (Cockerill) 1965; RoPF; 3200; 117.8 × 3.8 (387 × 12.5); TSM (Sulzer); 21; ex *Georgios B* 1983; ex *Roi Baudouin* 1983; Stern door

20060 **KONINGIN FABIOLA** Be/Be (Boel) 1962; RoPF; 3100; 117.3 × 3.8 (385 × 12.6); TSM (Sulzer); 20; Stern door

20070 **AEGEON** Gr/Be (Cockerill-Ougree) 1958; RoPF; 2800; 116.9 × 3.9 (383 × 12.9); TSM (Sulzer); 21; ex *Artevelde* 1976; Bow and stern doors

20080 **NAJD** Pa/Be (Cockerill-Ougree) 1956; F; 3400/3800; 144 × —/4 (374 × —/13); TSM (Sulzer); 22; ex *Roi Leopold III*

20090 **DANMARK** De/De (Helsingor) 1968; RoPF/TF; 6400; 144.5 × 5.5 (474 × 18); TSM (B&W); 17; Bow and stern doors

20110 **NEPTUNIA** Cy/Br (H&W) 1956; P/RoC; 4400; 114.64 × 4.52 (376 × 14.83); TST (H&W); —; ex *Duke of Argyll* 1975; Rebuilt. Further modernised. Aft superstructure extended and docking bridge removed

20120 **LA PAZ** Me/Ja (Kure) 1964; RoPF; 2500; 109 × 4.3 (358 × 14.2); TSM (B&W); —; Bow door

20130 **MALASPINA** US/US (Puget Sound) 1963;

RoPF; 2900; 124.2 × 4.9 (407.8 × 16); TSM (General Metals); —; Lengthened 1972. Stern door

20140 **ALZAHRAA** Eg/Sw (Uddevalla) 1968; RoPF/TF; 5600; 115.7 × 4.9 (379.8 × 16); TSM (Pielstick); —; ex *Drottningen;* Bow and stern doors

20160 **FESTOS** Gr/Sw (Lindholmens) 1966; RoPF; 8000; 141.2 × 5.5 (463 × 18); TSM (Lindholmens); 18; ex *Folkliner;* ex *Olau Finn* 1982; ex *Finnpartner* 1976; ex *Stena Atlantica* 1973; ex *Saga* 1971; Stern door

20170 **HOLGER DANSKE** No/FRG (Hanseatische) 1961; RoPF; 3700; 109.8 × 4.2 (360 × 13.1); TSM (Pielstick); —

20180 **MONA'S QUEEN** Br/Br (Ailsa) 1972; RoPF; 3000; 104.5 × 3.6 (343 × 12); TSM (Pielstick); 21
Sister:
20181 **LADY OF MANN** (Br)

20190 **FREE ENTERPRISE IV** Br/Ne (Gusto) 1969; RoPF; 5000; 117.5 × 4.3 (385.6 × 14.3); TrSM (MAN); 20.75; Bow and stern doors
Sisters:
20191 **FREE ENTERPRISE V** (Br)
20192 **FREE ENTERPRISE VI** (Br)

20200 **FREE ENTERPRISE VII** Br/Ne (IHC Gusto) 1973; RoPF; 5000; 117.51 × 4.38 (385.53 × 14.37); TrSM (Stork-Werkspoor); 21; Bow and stern doors. Mainmast further aft than on 'FREE ENTERPRISE IV'—which see
Similar (Longer):
20201 **FREE ENTERPRISE VIII** (Br)

20210 **SPIRIT OF FREE ENTERPRISE** Br/FRG (Schichau-U) 1979; RoPF; 8000; 131.96 × 5.71 (432.94 × 18.73); TrSM (Sulzer); 22; Bow and stern doors
Sisters (Br flag)
20211 **HERALD OF FREE ENTERPRISE**
20212 **PRIDE OF FREE ENTERPRISE**

20220 **VIKING VENTURER** Br/De (Aalborg) 1975; RoPF; 6400; 128.8 × 4.5 (422.3 × 15); TrSM (Stork-Werkspoor); 20.75; Bow and stern doors
Sisters (Br flag):
20221 **VIKING VALIANT**
20222 **VIKING VISCOUNT**
20223 **VIKING VOYAGER**

20230 **FREE ENTERPRISE III** Br/Ne (Gusto) 1966; RoPF; 4700; 117.5 × 4 (385 × 13); TSM (MAN); 20; Bow and stern doors

20240 **MARINE BLUENOSE** Ca/Ca (Davie SB) 1955; RoPF; 6400; 105.4 × 5 (346 × 16.7); TSM (Fairbanks Morse); 18.5; ex *Bluenose*

★20250 **SVETI STEFAN** Ys/De (Aalborg) 1958; RoPF; 1600; 85.5 × 4 (281 × 13); TSM (B&W); 15; ex *Djursland* 1965; Bow and stern doors

20260 **EGNATIA** Gr/Fr (Loire-Normandie) 1960; RoPF; 6200; 115.4 × 4.1 (379 × 13.6); TSM (Sulzer); 18; Bow and stern doors

20270 **TIEPOLO** It/It (Italcantieri) 1968; RoPF; 5300; 126.3 × 5.47 (414.4 × 17.95); TSM (Fiat); 18.5; ex *Canguro Bianco* 1983
Sisters (Si flag):
20271 **YUM** ex *Canguro Bruno* 1982
20272 **DURR** ex *Canguro Verde* 1981
20273 **SINDIBAD** ex *Espresso Rosso* 1982; ex *Canguro Rosso*

20280 **VILLANDRY** Fr/Fr (Dubigeon-Normandie) 1964; RoPF; 3400; 104.9 × 4 (344 × 13); TSM (Pielstick); 21; Bow and stern doors
Sister:
20281 **VALENCAY** (Fr)

20290 **EUROPAFARJAN** Sw/De (Aalborg) 1971; RoPF; 5800; 123.4 × 5.2 (405 × 17.6); TSM (Polar); 21.5; ex *Prinsessan Desiree;* Bow and stern doors

20300 **ILMATAR** Fi/Fi (Sandvikens) 1964; P; 7200; 128.3 × 4.4 (421 × 14.6); TrSM (Sulzer); 20; Side doors; Lengthened 1973 (Howaldts DW). Extensively modified in 1978/79 (Wartsila)

★20310 **SAKHALIN-1** Ru/Ru ('Yantar') 1963; RoPF/TF; 5000; 127 × 6.2 (417 × 20.3); D-E (—); 18; Stern door
Sisters (Ru flag):
★20311 **SAKHALIN-2**
★20312 **SAKHALIN-3**
★20313 **SAKHALIN-4**
★20314 **SAKHALIN-5**
★20315 **SAKHALIN-6**
★20316 **SAKHALIN-7**

★20317 **CHANG LI** RC/RC (—) 1976; P; 5900; 138.0 × 7.00 (453 × 22.97); TSM (—); 18
Sisters (RC flag):

★20318 **CHANG ZHENG**
★20319 **CHANG SHAN**
Possible sisters (RC flag):
★20319/1 **CHANG XIU**
★20319/2 **CHANG JIN**
★20319/3 **CHANG KEN**
★20319/4 **CHANG SHEN**

★20320 **SOVIETSKIY AZERBAIDZHAN** Ru/Ru ('Krasnoye S') 1963; RoPF/TF; 8800; 133.6 × 4.5 (438 × 15.1); Tr SD-E (—); 14; Stern door
Sisters (Ru flag):
★20321 **SOVIETSKIY TURKMENISTAN**
★20322 **SOVIETSKIY KAZAKHSTAN**
★20323 **SOVIETSKIY UZBEKISTAN**
★20324 **GAMID SULTANOV**

20330 **STENA SCANDINAVICA** Sw/Fi (Wartsila) 1974; RoPF; 8800; 152.4 × 5.6 (500 × 20); TSM (Pielstick); 24; ex *Prinsessan Birgitta* 1982; Bow and stern doors

20340 **TURELLA** Fi/Fi (Wartsila) 1979; RoPF; 10500; 136.11 × 5.5 (446.56 × 18.04); TSM (Wartsila); 21.3; Bow ramp and two stern ramps. Side door (extra superstructure fwd of funnel):
Sister:
20341 **ROSELLA** (Fi)

20350 **POVL ANKER** De/De (Aalborg) 1978; RoPF; 8200; 121.19 × 5.15 (397.6 × 16.9); TSM (Alpha-Diesel); 20; Bow door/ramp. Two stern doors/ramps. Side doors
Sister:
20351 **JENS KOFOED** (De)

★20353 **GEORG OTS** Ru/Pd (Szczecinska) 1980; RoPF; 11496; 134 × 5.46 (439.6 × 17.91); TSM (Sulzer); 19;
'B493' type
Sisters (Ru flag) (some are 'B492' type):
★20354 **DMITRIY SHOSTAKOVICH**
★20355 **LEV TOLSTOY**
★20356 **KONSTANTIN SIMONOV**
★20357 **MIKHAIL SUSLOV** ex *Vasiliy Solovyev Sedoy*

20359 **ANKARA** Tu/Pd (Szczecinska) 1983; RoPCF; 7400; 127.44 × 5.42 (418 × 17.78); TSM (Sulzer); 20.25; ex *Mazowia;* Bow and stern doors

20360 **DIANA II** Sw/FRG (Meyer) 1979; RoPF; 11700; 137.2 × 5.65 (450.13 × 18.54); TSM (MAN); 21.5; Bow door/ramp. Two stern ramps

★20370 **BYELORUSSIYA** Ru/Fi (Wartsila) 1975; RoPF/P; 16600; 157 × 6.2 (516 × 20.4); TSM (Pielstick); 21.25; Bow, stern and side doors
Sisters (Ru flag):
★20371 **GRUZIYA**
★20372 **AZERBAYDZHAN**
★20373 **LEONID BREZHNEV** ex *Kareliya* 1982
★20374 **KAZAKHSTAN** Now converted to cruise liner—bow door permanently closed. Excursion boats fitted etc

20380 **GELTING SYD** De/FRG (Meyer) 1974; RoPF; 4200; 115.2 × 4.5 (378 × 15); TSM (Ruston Paxman); 19.25; ex *Stella Scarlett* 1981; Bow and stern doors

20390 **KII MARU** Ja/Ja (Hitachi) 1964; F; 1600; 73.7 × 3.6 (242 × 12); TSM (Daihatsu); 14

20400 **FERRY FUKUE** Ja/Ja (Naikai) 1978; RoPF; 1900; 79.6 × 3.7 (261.35 × 12.14); TSM (Daihatsu); 17.25; Bow and stern ramp/doors

20410 **TRUVA** Tu/Fr (Dubigeon-Normandie) 1967; RoPF; 3400; 91.6 × 4.2 (300.6 × 14); TSM (MWM); 19

20420 **MOBY BLU** It/Ne (Gusto) 1965; RoPF; 4000; 108.1 × 4 (355 × 13.3); TSM (MAN); 19; ex *Free Enterprise II* 1982; Bow and stern doors

20430 **PRINCE GEORGE** Ca/Ca (Yarrows Ltd) 1948; P; 5800; 106.7 × 5.4 (350 × 7.7); TSR (Unaflow); 15.5

20440 **MAZATLAN** Me/De (Helsingor) 1965; RoPF; 5000; 108.9 × 4.6 (357 × 15.3); TSM (B&W); 17.5; ex *Akershus* 1973; Bow door, ramp and side doors

20450 **TYRSUS** It/It (Riuniti) 1961; RoPF/TF; 4300; 119.9 × 5.3 (393 × 15.1); TSM (Fiat); 16
Sister:
20451 **HERMAEA** (It)

20460 **JASON** Gr/It (Adriatico) 1965; P; 3700; 97.16 × 4.51 (318.8 × 14.8); TSM (Sulzer); 15; ex *Eros* 1966; Converted from Roro Ferry 1967

20470 **KONINGIN JULIANA** Ne/Br (Cammell Laird) 1968; RoPF; 6700; 131 × 5 (430 × 16.9); TSM (MAN); 21; Bow and stern doors

20480 **NORTHERN CRUISER** Ca/Br (G Brown) 1962; RoPF; 1400; 57.7 × 2.8 (189.6 × 9.6); M

(British Polar); —; ex N.A. Comeau 1977

20490 **HOLYHEAD** Gr/Br (Cammell Laird) 1947; P; 3700; 97.95 × 4.19 (321.36 × 13.75); TST (Cammell Laird); 15; ex St David 1970

20500 **MANX MAID** Br/Br (Cammell Laird) 1962; RoPF; 2700; 104.8 × 3.8 (344 × 12.3); TST (Cammell Laird); 21; Side doors
Sister:
20501 **BEN-MY-CHREE** (Br)

20510 **AESAREA** Pa/Br (JS White) 1960; F; 4000; 98.2 × 4.1 (322 × 13.7); TSM (JS White); 19.5; ex Caesarea 1981
Sister:
20511 **SAUDI GOLDEN STAR** (Si) ex Golden Star 1981; ex Aquamart 1978; ex Sarnia 1978

20530 **ATHENS EXPRESS** Gr/Be (Cockerill) 1949; RoPF; 2600; 114.3 × 3.8 (372 × 12.5); TSM (Sulzer); 20; ex Leto 1976; ex Prinses Josephine Charlotte 1976; ex Car Ferry 1952; Stern door

★20550 **THONG NHAT** Vn/FRG (Kieler H) 1961; RoPF; 7000; 138.3 × 5.5 (454 × 18); TSM (MAN); 19.5; ex Ha Long 1978; ex Kronprins Harald 1975; Side doors

★20560 **JI MEI** RC/FRG (Kieler H) 1966; RoPF; 7700; 140.8 × 5.8 (463 × 18.1); TSM (MAN); 21.5; ex Jin Tiang 1983; ex Amatista 1983; ex Janina 1981; ex Prinsesse Ragnhild 1980; Side doors

20570 **WINSTON CHURCHILL** De/It (Tirreno) 1967; RoPF; 8700; 140.7 × 5.5 (460 × 18.1); TSM (B&W); 23; Bow door and ramp; Stern door and ramp

20580 **ORPHEUS** Gr/Br (H&W) 1948/70; P; 5100; 111.82 × 4.88 (366.86 × 16.01); TSM (H&W); 15; ex Theseus 1969; ex Munster I 1968; ex Munster 1968; Converted from ferry 1970

20590 **STELLA OCEANIS** Gr/It (Adriatico) 1965; P; 4000; 105.1 × 4.5 (365 × 13.11); TSM (Sulzer); 17; ex Aphrodite 1966

20600 **APPIA** It/It (Breda) 1961; F; 6100; 122.5 × 5.5 (402 × 16.3); TSM (Adriatico); 17

20610 **PRINSESSE ELISABETH** De/De (Aalborg) 1964; RoPF; 3600; 103.4 × 4.6 (339 × 15.1); TSM (B&W); 18

20630 **SAINT PATRICK II** Ih/FRG (Sietas) 1973; RoPF; 7200; 125.6 × 5.3 (412 × 17.5); TSM (Stork-Werkspoor); 23; ex Aurella 1982; Bow and stern doors

20640 **SILJA STAR** Fi/Fr (Dubigeon-Normandie) 1975; RoPF; 12300; 153.1 × 5.1 (500.6 × 17); TSM (Pielstick); 22; ex Bore Star 1971; Bow door and ramp; Stern door and ramp
Sisters:
20641 **SUNDANCER** (Bs) ex Svea Corona 1984
20643 **SVEA CORONA** (Sw) ex Dana Gloria; ex Wellamo 1981

★20650 **AYVAZOVSKIY** Ru/Fr (Dubigeon-Normandie) 1977; P; 7100; 121.49 × 4.4 (398.59 × 14.44); TSM (Pielstick); 18.25

20660 **NAPOLEON** Fr/Fr (Dubigeon-Normandie) 1976; RoPF; 14900; 155 × 6.4 (509 × 21); TSM (Pielstick); 23.5

20670 **CYRNOS** Fr/Fr (Dubigeon-Normandie) 1979; RoPF; approx 12000; 138.65 × 6.16 (454.89 × 20.21); TSM (Pielstick); 22; Bow and stern ramp/doors

20680 **VIKING SALLY** Fi/FRG (Meyer) 1980; RoPF; 15600; 155.43 × 5.55 (509.94 × 18.21); TSM (MAN); 21.2; Bow door/ramp; Two stern ramps

★20690 **GONG NONG BONG 18** RC/RC (—) 1960; P; 2500; 107 × — (350 × —); TSM (—); 16; ex Min Chu No 18
Sister:
★20691 **GONG NONG BONG 19** (RC) ex Min Chu No 19

20700 **NEPTUNE** Gr/De (Aalborg) 1955; P; 2400; 90.2 × 5.4 (296 × 18); M (B&W); 18; ex Meteor 1971

20710 **KURENAI MARU** Ja/Ja (Mitsubishi HI) 1960; F; 3000; 86.7 × 3.9 (285 × 12.9); TSM (Sulzer); 18
Sister:
20711 **MURASAKI MARU** (Ja)

20720 **NAIEF** Qt/FRG (Norderwerft) 1957; Y; 2800; 90.2 × 3.7 (296 × 12.1); TSD-E (Maybach); 19.5; ex Stella Solaris 1971; ex Bunte Kuh; Converted from a passenger ship

20730 **RADIOSA** Gr/Br (Denny) 1947/72; P; 1600; 76.66 × 3.72 (251.51 × 12.2); TSM (Sulzer); 12; ex

Exeter 1972; ex Winchester 1971; Converted from cargo ship

★20735 **DIMITAR BLAGOEV** Bu/Bu (G Dimitrov) 1969; P; 1100; 68.00 × 5.46 (223 × 17.91); M (Russkiy); —
Sister:
★20736 **GEORGI KIRKOV** (Bu)

20740 **XANADU** US/FRG (Steinwerder) 1955; P; 2600; 89.5 × 3.8 (293 × 12.6); TSD-E (Maybach); 18; ex Pacific Star 1972; ex Polar Star 1970; ex Delos 1967; ex Wappen Von Hamburg 1960

20750 **MISTRAL** Gr/De (Aalborg) 1962; RoPF; 1900; 78.8 × 4 (259 × 13.2); TSM (B&W); 15; ex Saronic Sun 1982; ex Ornen 1981; Side doors

20760 **LINDBLAD POLARIS** Sw/Sw (Solvesborgs) 1960; RoF; 2000; 72.1 × 4.1 (236 × 13.4); TSM (Nydqvist & Holm); 16.5; ex Oresund 1981

20770 **AETHALIA** It/It (C D Tirreno) 1956; RoPF; 1300; 72.3 × 3.5 (237 × 11.7); TSM (Fiat); 14

20780 **NORDSEE I** FRG/FRG (Sietas) 1961; F; 981; 59.7 × 2.8 (196 × 9.3); TSM (MaK); 15.5; ex Kobenhavn 1975; ex Hein Godenwind 1969

★20790 **BELINSKIY** Ru/DDR (—) 1955; P/Riv; 1100; 65.2 × 2.4 (214 × 8); M (—); 12
Sisters (Ru flag):
★20791 **BALKHASH**
★20792 **BAYKAL**
★20793 **CHERNISHEVSKIY**
★20794 **ISYK KOL**
★20795 **KOROLENKO**
★20796 **KOTOVSKIY**
★20797 **LADOGA**
★20798 **LENINSKIY**
★20799 **MAMIN SIBIRYAK**
★20800 **MEKHANIK KALUSHNIKOV**
★20801 **MEKHANIK KULUBIN**
★20802 **ONEGA**
★20803 **RADISHEV**
★20804 **SERGEI TSENSKAY**
★20805 **SEVAN**

20810 **HABICHT II** FRG/FRG (Schlichting) 1959; F; 900; 54.3 × 3.1 (178 × 10.3); TSM (Darmstadt); 15; ex Baltica I; ex Orestad 1973; ex Alte Liebe 1962

20820 **EVANGELISTRIA** Gr/US (Pullman) 1943; F; 1000; 54.9 × — (184 × —); TSM (General Motors); —; ex Despina 1969; Converted warship

20830 **KRISTINA BRAHE** Fi/US (Pullman) 1943; P; 1000; 56.5 × 2.6 (185 × 8.6); TSM (General Motors); 15; ex Sunnhordland 1974

20850 **ARABI** Si/Br (Ailsa) 1960; LS; 2700; 94.6 × 4 (310 × 13.1); TSM (British Polar); 13.5; ex Slieve Donard 1976

20860 **ARRAN** Br/Br (Denny) 1953; RoF; 540; 56.7 × 2.3 (186 × 7.5); TSM (British Polar); 15.5; Side doors
Sisters:
20861 **MEDITERRANEAN SUN** (Gr) ex Bute 1980
20862 **MEDITERRANEAN STAR** (Gr) ex Cowal 1981

★20870 **YERMAK** Ru/Fi (Wartsila) 1973; IB; 12200; 135 × 11 (445 × 37); Trs D-E (Sulzer); 19
Sisters (Ru flag):
★20871 **ADMIRAL MAKAROV**
★20872 **KRASIN**

●★20875 **KAPITAN YEVDOKIMOV** Ru/Fi (Wartsila) 1983; IB; 76.5 × 2.50 (251 × 8.20); TrSD-E (Wartsila); 13.5; River service. May be spelt **KAPITAN EVDO-KIMOV**
Sisters (Ru flag):
★20876 **KAPITAN BABICHEV**
★20877 **KAPITAN CHUDINOV**
★20878 **KAPITAN BORODKIN**
Plus 3 more on order

★20880 **PERKUN** Pd/Br (Harris & Sons) 1963; IB-/Sal; 1200; 56.5 × 5 (185 × 16.3); TSD-E (Ruston & Hornsby); 10

20890 **WYUNA** Br/Br (Ferguson Bros) 1953; TS; 1300; 63.6 × 4.8 (209 × 15); TSD-E (English Electric); —

20900 **FRANCE I** Fr/Fr (Mediterranee) 1959; RS; 1900; 76.4 × — (251 × —); TSD-E (Davey, Paxman); 14.75
Sister:
20901 **FRANCE II** (Fr)

20910 **ALIDADE** Fr/Fr (La Manche) 1964; TS; 640; 45.8 × 2.9 (150 × 9.3); M (Duvant); 13.5

20920 **WESTWARD HO** Br/Br (Thornycroft) 1938; F; 600; 60.9 × 1.8 (200 × 6); TSM (English Electric);

15; ex Vecta 1966

20930 **BRADING** Br/Br (Denny) 1948; F; 1000; 61 × 2.1 (200 × 7); TSM (Sulzer); 14
Sister (Br flag):
20931 **SOUTHSEA**

20960 **SHAHEED SALAMUDDIN** Bh/Fr (Saint Nazaire) 1953; PC; 11700; 162 × 6.9 (532 × 20); TSM (B&W); 16; ex Hizb-Ul-Bahr 1981; ex Eastern Queen 1977; ex President 1972; ex General Mangin 1969

20970 **ARIANE** Pa/Br (Swan Hunter & WR) 1951; P; 6700; 138.4 × 5.8 (454 × 19); T (Parsons); 19; ex Bon Vivant 1979; ex Freeport II 1974; ex Ariadne 1973; ex Patricia 1957

★20990 **JAMHURI** Ta/Br (Philip) 1956; F; 1500; 66.6 × 4 (219 × 13.1); TSM (British Polar); 13; ex Seyyd Khalifa 1963

21000 **AQUA STAR** Br/Br (A Hall) 1951; RS; 650; 54.3 × 3.8 (178 × 12.6); M (British Polar); 11; ex St. Ola 1975

21010 **STAUPER** No/No (Stavanger S&D) 1929; Repair Ship; 850; 57.4 × 5 (188 × 16.6); M (General Motors); 12; ex Tungenes 1965; ex Rogaland 1964; Converted Passenger Cargo Ship

21020 **DON JOLLY** Pi/FRG (A G 'Weser') 1968; PC/F; 1500; 88.02 × 4.82 (288.78 × 15.81); M (Atlas-MaK); 15.75; ex Sweet Grace 1983

21030 **CAGAYAN DE ORO** Pi/Ja (Hitachi) 1955; P; 1500; 77.2 × 4.7 (253 × 15.6); TSM (B&W); —; ex Cagayan 1956

21040 **PATRICIA 1** Br/Br (Smith's D) 1938; —; 1100; 70.7 × 3.9 (232 × 13); TSD-E (English Electric); 10; ex Patricia 1982

21050 **STAR OF ASSUAN** Eg/Br (Caledon) 1948; PC; 5500; 119.9 × 7.2 (398 × 23.7); M (Doxford); 13.5

21060 **EL HASSAN** Eg/It (Ansaldo) 1959; PC; 4400; 109.2 × 5.9; (358 × 19.3); TSM (Adriatico); 15.75; ex Brennero
Sisters:
21061 **ABU EL KASSEM** (Eg) ex Bernina
21062 **STELVIO** (It)

21070 **REINA DEL FRIO** Ar/De (Kjobenhavns) 1927; R; 1600; 84.8 × 5.5 (278 × 18); R (Kjobenhavns); 11; ex Freezer Queen 1960; ex Bruarfoss 1957

21080 **ISCHIA EXPRESS** It/De (Aalborg) 1936; RoPF; 1000; 78 × 4 (257 × 13); M (B&W); 15; ex Freia VI 1977; ex Freia 1975; Side doors

21090 **SWEET ROSE** Pi/Pi (National S&S) 1960; F; 1800; 84.8 × 4.8 (278 × 15.6); M (Sulzer); 13.75; ex General Roxas 1965
Similar:
21091 **DONA ANITA** (Pi) ex Dona Ana 1976; ex Governor B. Lopez 1966

●21110 **TUI CAKAU II** Fiji/Fr (Mediterranee) 1961; RoPF; 1800; 107 × 5.1 (360 × 17); M (Sulzer); 15.75; ex Capitaine Scott; ex Blida; Converted from Cargo 1971; Lengthened 1971; Bow and side doors

21120 **LOGOS** Sg/De (Helsingor) 1949; PC; 2300; 82 × 5.6 (269 × 18.5); M (B&W); 13; ex Umanak 1971; At present being used as a missionary ship

21140 **EGEON** Pa/Fr (Mediterranee) 1959; C/WT; 1600/2400; 93 × 5.3/7 (306 × 17.6/23); M (Sulzer); 15; ex Ainikolas 1983; ex Elly V 1980; ex Relizane 1975

21150 **BRIGHT FRUIT** Pa/FRG (Kieler H) 1955; R; 3000; 126 × 5.8 (413 × 20); M (Kieler H); 17; ex Blue Fruit 1977; ex Chen Cheng 1973; ex Ahrensburg 1968

21160 **TAI YUAN** Tw/FRG (Deutsche Werft) 1955; R; 2800; 120.1 × 6.2 (424 × 20.1); M (MAN); 16.5; ex Tai Yun 1967; ex Horncap 1967

●21180 **NISSOS RHODOS** Pa/It (Tirreno) 1957; R; 3200; 114.7 × 6.3 (376 × 20.8); M (Fiat); 16; ex Annette 1976; ex Marcia 1975; ex Marzia Tomellini Fassio 1970

★21190 **INEY** Ru/Fi (Valmet) 1957; R; 3400; 123.8 × 6.4 (406 × 21); M (Gotaverken); 18; ex Trubadur 1964; ex Brita Thorden 1963

●21200 **KASSOS** Gr/Sw (Uddevalla) 1956; R; 3400; 123.8 × 6.4 (406 × 21); M (Gotaverken); 18; ex Frubel Julia 1966; ex Aase Thorden 1958
Sister:
21201 **ISLAND KOS** (Gr) ex Kos 1981; ex Frubel Maria 1966; ex Karin Thorden 1958

★21210 **MARKO POLO** Ys/FRG (Kieler H) 1958; R; 3000/4000; 126.12 × 6.10/7.02 (414

×20.01/23.03); M (MAN); 17; ex *Crux* 1973; ex *Cap Domingo* 1970

21220 **ARAGVI** Ru/FRG (Kieler H) 1960; R; 3600; 120.6 × 7.1 (396 × 23.3); M (MAN); 18.5
Sisters (Ru flag):
★21221 **INGUR**
★21222 **KURA**

★21230 **LA LIMA** Cu/De (Helsingor) 1959; R; 3400/4800; 132.5 × 6.2/8 (435 × 20.4/26.3); M (B&W); 19; ex *Realengo 18* 1966; ex *Algeneb* 1966; ex *Yugala* 1966

21240 **BENADIR** So/FRG (B+V) 1964; R; 4800; 136 × 6.6 (444 × 21.3); M (MAN); 21; ex *Brunsland* 1971
Sisters:
21241 **TROPICAL SUN** (Li) ex *Brunshausen* 1978
21242 **TROPICAL QUEEN** (Li) ex *Brunsbuttel* 1978
21243 **COMFORT** (Tw) ex *Pacific Fruit* 1981; ex *Ronirel* 1978; ex *Brunsholm* 1972
21244 **AEGEAN SPIRIT** (Gr) ex *Playas* 1981; ex *Aspassia* 1977; ex *Brunskappel* 1972
21247 **ROYAL STAR** (Gr) ex *Vera U* 1980; ex *Katingaki* 1976; ex *Brunsgard* 1971
(Ru flag):
★21248 **TSIKLON** ex *Brunshausen* 1966
★21249 **URAGAN** ex *Brunsbuttel* 1967
★21250 **DNEPROVSKIY LIMAN** ex *Brunstor* 1975
★21251 **DNESTROVSKIY LIMAN** ex *Brunshoeft* 1975

★21280 **OCEANO ANTARTICO** Cu/De (Helsingor) 1949; R; 2700; 110.8 × 6.3 (364 × 20.8); M (B&W); 16; ex *Coolady* 1969; ex *Coolangatta* 1969; ex *Fruit Queen*

21290 **REA** Gr/De (Helsingor) 1956; R; 4300; 116.8 × 6.4 (383 × 20.8); M (B&W); 17.5; ex *Lastrigoni* 1974; ex *Coolgardie* 1969

★21310 **PLOD** Ys/FRG (Deutsche Werft) 1960; R; 3400/4700; 134.6 × 6.1/6.5 (442 × 20.1/21.5); M (MAN); 18.5; ex *Pentelikon* 1974

21330 **SAN BERNARDINO** Pi/FRG (B+V) 1959; R; 3100; 129 × 6.1 (424 × 20.2); M (MAN); 18.5; ex *Hirson* 1972; ex *Alsterblick* 1970

21340 **FAIR REEFER** Pa/De (Aalborg) 1962; R; 4700; 132.82 × 7.88 (435.8 × 25.85); TSM (B&W); —; ex *Ecuadorian Reefer* 1978

●21360 **CHOAPA** Li/De (Odense) 1964; R; 7900; 148.1 × 8.6 (486 × 26.4); M (B&W); 20.5; ex *Thuro Maersk* 1975
Sister:
21361 **PACIFIC OCEAN** (Li) ex *Magleby Maersk* 1975

21390 **MALAYAN REEFER** Pi/Sw (Eriksbergs) 1960; R; 8100; 148 × 8.4 (488 × 27.6); M (B&W); 18.5; ex *Atitlan* 1977

21400 **CABO BOLINAO** Pi/Sw (Eriksbergs) 1956; R; 4800/6000; 135.39 × —/7.80 (444.2 × —/25.59); M (B&W); —; ex *Cayman* 1971
Sister:
★21401 **ICHA** (Ru) ex *Carib* 1964

21410 **JERRYEVERETT** Li/Sw (Kockums) 1960; R; 4900; 133.4 × 7.6 (438 × 25.1); M (MAN); 18; ex *Coral Sea* 1969
Sisters (Li flag):
21411 **EWALDEVERETT** ex *Pearl Sea* 1972
21412 **WADEEVERETT** ex *Crystal Sea* 1972

21420 **CARLEVERETT** Li/Sw (Gotav.) 1962; R; 4900; 131.1 × 7.1 (430 × 23.2); M (Gotaverken); 18; ex *Northland*
Sister:
21421 **KELLYEVERETT** (Li) ex *North Isle*

★21430 **VOCE** Ys/De (Odense) 1961; R; 4700; 132.6 × 7.8 (435 × 25.3); M (B&W); 19.5; ex *Dragor Maersk* 1974

21440 **CHALMEVERETT** Li/Sw (Eriksbergs) 1960; R; 5000; 134.1 × 7.6 (440 × 25.1); M (B&W); 17.75; ex *Baltic Sea* 1969
Sister:
21441 **FLORA II** (Li) ex *North Sea* 1970

★21450 **SHKVAL** Ru/Sw (Oresunds) 1963; R; 4200; 126.4 × 7.3 (415 × 24); M (Gotaverken); 17; ex *Bakke Reefer* 1975

21460 **SAMOS SEA** Gr/No (Framnaes) 1965; R; 5700; 128.1 × 7.8 (420 × 25.6); M (Sulzer); 19; ex *Golar Fruit* 1977
Sister:
21461 **SAMOS STORM** (Gr) ex *Golar Tryg* 1977

21470 **CARIBBEAN ARROW** Pa/FRG (Stuelcken) 1952; C; 3700; 106.4 × 6.8 (349 × 22.4); M (MAN); 13; ex *Martha S* 1975; ex *Ria M* 1974; ex *Armonia* 1973; ex *Freattys* 1972; ex *Diana* 1970; ex *Ciudad De*

Bucaramanga 1965; ex *Brunshausen* 1953
Sister:
21471 **ALMA M** (Pa) ex *Nedon* 1980; ex *Ciudad De Santa Marta*
Similar:
21472 **KHENGIS** (Co) ex *Zamira* 1980; ex *Ciudad De Popayan*

●21480 **HEBE 1** Pa/Fr (Bretagne) 1960; C/WT; 5200; 118.2 × 7.1 (388 × 23.6); M (Pielstick); 19; ex *Hebe* 1982

21490 **GEMA** Pa/Ne (Verschure) 1959; R; 2700/3800; 115 × 6.1/6.8 (377 × 22/22.10); M (MAN); 17; ex *Salta* 1977; ex *Brunstal* 1970; ex *Baleares* 1966

21500 **ESTEBAN S** Me/Ne (Haarlemsche) 1952; C; 1100; 82.00 × 4.24 (269 × 13.91); M (MAN); 12.5; ex *Loreto* 1975; ex *Mogador* 1964

●★21510 **VARAZDIN** Ys/Ys ('3 Maj') 1958; C; 1000; 83.4 × 4.3 (274 × 14.3); M (Sulzer); 13.25; ex *Vodice* 1976; ex *Varazdin* 1969
Sisters (Ys flag):
★21511 **PIROT**
★21512 **ZEMUN** ex *Kaprije* 1976; ex *Zemun* 1969

21530 **RAZZAN 1** Le/Sw (Lindholmens) 1955; C; 2700; 100.26 × 6.80 (329 × 22.31); M (Gotaverken); 14.25; ex *Victoria K* 1982; ex *Kotronas Village* 1980; ex *Darling* 1977; ex *Dimitrakis* 1973; ex *Ragunda* 1971; ex *Almeria* 1967

★21560 **FALESHTY** Ru/Fi (Crichton-Vulcan) 1959; C; 1700; 94.5 × 5.7 (309 × 18.7); M (Sulzer); 13.5
Sisters (Ru flag):
★21561 **FARAB**
★21562 **FAYZABAD**
★21563 **FIRYUZA** ex *Firoza*
★21564 **FRYANOVO**
★21565 **SEINE** ex *Firovo* 1960

21570 **BATANGHARI** la/Ne (van der Werf) 1957; C; 2600; 87 × 3.9 (285 × 12.11); M (MAN); 11.5
Sisters (la flag):
21571 **BENGAWAN**
21572 **BOGOWONTO**
21573 **BRANTAS**

★21580 **JANA** Ru/FRG (O&K) 1955; FC; 3800; 111.2 × 6.2 (365 × 21); M (MAN); 14
Sisters (Ru flag):
★21581 **INDIGIRKA**
★21582 **KONDA**
★21583 **KULOY**
★21584 **NEMAN**
★21585 **TULOMA**
★21586 **UMANJ**

21590 **VISAYAS** Pi/FRG (Bremer V) 1963; C; 4300; 117 × 7.6 (384 × 25); M (Bremer V); —

★21600 **ZELENOGORSK** Ru/Ne ('De Klop') 1955; C/FC; 3600; 114.7 × 6.5 (377 × 18); M (Sulzer); 13
Sisters (Ru flag):
★21601 **BALTIYSK**
★21602 **CHERNYAKHOVSK**
★21603 **GVARDEYSK**
★21604 **SVETLOGORSK**

★21610 **AMGUEMA** Ru/Ru (Leninskogo) 1962; C; 8100; 133 × 8.9 (436 × 30); D-E (—); 15; Polar service
Sister (Ru flag):
★21611 **PENZHINA**
Similar (some have helicopter deck) (Ru flag):
★21612 **GIZHIGA**
★21613 **KAPITAN BONDARENKO**
★21614 **KAPITAN GOTSKIY**
★21615 **KAPITAN KONDRATYEV**
★21616 **KAPITAN MARKOV**
★21617 **KAPITAN MYSHEVSKIY**
★21618 **NAVARIN**
★21619 **PAVEL PONOMARYEV**
★21620 **VANKAREM**
★21621 **VASILIY FEDOSEYEV**
★21622 **MIKHAIL SOMOV** (research ship)

★21625 **OLYUTORKA** Ru/Sw (Ekensbergs) 1955; R; 5900; 132 × 7.6 (433 × 25); M (Gotaverken); 18; ex *San Blas* 1964

21630 **LAGADA STAR** Gr/FRG (Nobiskrug) 1954; CP; 2700/4200; 114.8 × 5.7/6 (377 × 21.5/25); M (MaK); 14; ex *Nahost Transporter* 1977; ex *Christel Vinnen* 1977; ex *Troyburg* 1966

21650 **NEW HYDE** Pa/FRG (Nobiskrug) 1958; CP; 2600/4100; 115 × 6.5/7.6 (377 × 21.5/24.11); M (MAN); 14.5; ex *Sun Kwong* 1979; ex *Edwin Reith* 1973
Sister:
21651 **NEW HERO** (Pa) ex *Sun Sang* 1980; ex *Magdalena Reith* 1972

★21680 **VIET BAO** Vn/DDR ('Neptun') 1956; C;

2700; 106 × 6.3 (345 × 20.9); R (Lentz); 13; ex *Christo Botev* 1969

21700 **ELNIL DELTA** Eg/It (Adriatico) 1953; C; 2700; 111 × 6 (365 × 19.8); M (Sulzer); 14.5; ex *El Nil* 1983

21710 **HOE AIK** Sg/De (B&W) 1949; C; 2900; 94.67 × 6.48 (310.6 × 21.26); M (B&W); 17; ex *East Cape* 1980; ex *Lagarfoss*

★21720 **SLOBODA** Ys/Ys ('3 Maj') 1958; C; 1600; 94.47 × 5.50 (310 × 18.04); M (Sulzer); 14.75

21730 **ADOLF VINNEN** FRG/FRG (Rickmers) 1955; C; 3000/4900; 124.3 × 6.6/7.5 (408 × 21.8 /24.7); M (Waggon); 13.5

21750 **THANASSIS K** Pa/Sw (Eriksbergs) 1953; C; 2300; 104.2 × 6.1 (342 × 20); M (B&W); 16; ex *Fortuna Reefer* 1982; ex *Bonzo* 1975; ex *Bajamar* 1968; ex *Leeward Islands* 1964
Sister:
21751 **NATHALIE D** (Pa) ex *Hamdan* 1976; ex *Nathalie D* 1974; ex *Bambi* 1974; ex *Mardina Reefer* 1972; ex *Bambi* 1971; ex *Banaderos* 1968; ex *Windward Islands* 1964

21810 **DONA PAMELA** Pi/Sw (Solvesbergs) 1950; C; 1400/2300; 88.8 × 5.2/— (291 × 17.2/—); M (Atlas-Diesel); 14; ex *Gothong*; ex *Cap Spartel* 1963; ex *Cap Gris Nez* 1956

21840 **RICHARD BORDO** SV/Sw (Helsingborgs) 1950; C; 1500; 87 × 4.9 (285 × 16.2); M (B&W); 11.5; ex *Mystras* 1978; ex *Navarino Bay* 1972; ex *Immen* 1969

21870 **GEORGIOS A** Gr/FRG (O&K) 1952; C; 1700; 93.7 × 5.7 (307 × 18.9); M (MAN); 14; ex *Giannis K* 1979; ex *Melilla* 1977

21900 **BEAUTY ROSE** Pa/No (Langesunds) 1951; C; 1400; 78.6 × 5.3 (258 × 17.3); R (Langesunds); 10.5; ex *Hwa Hang* 1973; ex *Chichow Frog* 1970; ex *Kristina* 1968; ex *Kollbryn* 1958

21920 **KRANTOR** Gr/Ne ('De Merwede') 1947; C; 1500; 78.6 × 5.5 (258 × 18); M (Stork); 12; ex *Citta Di Atene*; ex *Prins Frederik Hendrik* 1966
Sister:
21921 **MICHELE GAROFANO** (It) ex *Prins Frederik Willem* 1966

21940 **KALYMNOS** Gr/De (Aalborg) 1948; PC; 1500; 72.8 × 3.8 (239 × 12.6); TSM (Atlas-Diesel); —; ex *Arcadia* 1969; ex *Kalymnos* 1968; ex *Hekla* 1966
Similar:
21941 **NWAKUSO** (Ng) ex *Ventura Beach*; ex *Lucaya* 1973; ex *Esja* 1969

21950 **BB 3** No/Br (J Brown) 1951; RoC/TF; 3200; 121.88 × 3.68 (400 × 12.07); TSM (Sulzer); 12.25; ex *Norfolk Ferry* 1984

21960 **ASA-THOR** De/De (Nakskov) 1965; RoC/TF; 3500; 131.7 × 4.5 (452 × 15); TSM (B&W); —

21970 **LADY M** Cy/Br (H&W) 1967; RoPF; 4300; 115 × 4.1 (378 × 13.6); TSM (Pielstick); 17; ex *Ulster Prince* 1982; Stern door
Sister:
21971 **MED SEA** (Cy) ex *Ulster Queen* 1982

22000 **NORGE** No/Br (Camper & Nicholsons) 1937; Royal Yacht; 1700 (TYM); 80.1 × 4.6 (263 × 15.2); TSM (Bergens); 17; ex *Philante*

22010 **BONAVISTA** Ca/Br (Hall, Russell) 1956; PC; 1200; 66.5 × 5.2 (215 × 17.2); M (Fairbanks, Morse); 12

22020 **LAURO EXPRESS** It/US (Pullman) 1943; RoCF; 500; 57.8 × 2.7 (190 × 8); TSM (General Motors); 15; ex *Haugesund* 1973; ex *HMS Kilburnie*

22030 **JYLLAND** Ma/US (Pullman) 1943; PC; 800; 57.3 × 2.6 (185 × 8.4); TSM (Pullman); 15; ex *HMS Kilbride*

22040 **PRINCESS OF NEGROS** Pi/Hong Kong (Hong Kong & W) 1962; F; 500; 61.7 × 3.2 (203 × 10.7); TSM (Alpha-Diesel); —

22050 **PRINSES MARGRIET** Ne/Ne (Vuyk) 1966; TS; 1600; 69 × 4.5 (226 × 15); M (Stork); —

●22060 **CITY OF PIRAEUS** Gr/Br (Inglis) 1953; F; 500; 50.3 × 1.7 (165 × 5.8); TSM (British Polar); 14; ex *Maid of Argyll* 1975
Sister:
22061 **ALA** (Pa) ex *Maid of Skelmorlie* 1972

22080 **BIRD OF PARADISE** Tr/Br (Ferguson Bros) 1960; F; 1300; 60.6 × 3 (199 × 10); TSM (Crossley); 13
Sister:
22081 **SCARLET IBIS** (Tr)

22110 **EVANGELISTRIA** Gr/Br (Lewis) 1943; Trlr;

500; 49.9 × 4.4 (164 × 14.6); M (Werkspoor); 10; ex *Grassholm* 1956

22120 **SEIUN MARU** Ja/Ja (NKK) 1968; TS; 5000; 114.6 × 5.8 (376 × 19); M (B&W); 16.5

22130 **BAFFIN** Ca/Ca (Canadian Vickers) 1957; IB/RS; 3500; 87 × 5.7 (286 × 18.1); TSM (Fairbanks, Morse); 15.5

22140 **OCEANIC** FRG/FRG (Schichau) 1968; Tg/Sal; 2000; 87.2 × 6 (286 × 19); M (KHD); 22
Sister:
22141 **ARCTIC** (FRG)

★22150 **MB 18** Ru/Fi (Rauma-Repola) 1977; Tg; 1500; 63.51 × 5.2 (208.37 × 17.06); M (Russkiy); 13
Sisters (Ru flag):
★22151 **MB 15**
★22152 **MB 105**
★22153 **MB 119**

★22160 **YAGUAR** Ru/Ru (Admiralteiskiy) 1976; Tg/Sal; 2800; 92.79 × 5.8 (304.43 × 19.03); M (—); 18.5
Sister (Ru flag):
★22161 **BARS**
Similar (USSR Naval Service) INGUL class:
★22162 **MASHUK**
★22163 **PAMIR** (possibly renamed **INGUL**)

22170 **JOHN ROSS** Br/SA (Brown & H) 1976; Tg/Sal; 2800; 94.6 × 9 (311 × 30); M (Mirrlees Blackstone); 20; ex *S A John Ross* 1977
Sister:
22171 **WOLRAAD WOLTEMADE** (Br) ex *S A Wolraad Woltemade*

★22180 **NIKOLAI ZUBOV** Ru/Pd (Szczecinska) 1964; RS/SS; 2700 Dspl; 90 × 4.6 (295 × 15); TSM (—); 16.5
Sisters (Ru flag):
★22181 **ALEKSEY CHIRIKOV**
★22182 **ANDREY VILKITSKIY**
★22183 **BORIS DAVIDOV**
★22184 **FEDOR LITKE**
★22185 **SEMYON CHELYUSKIN**
★22186 **SEMYON DEZHNEV**
★22187 **T BELLINGSGAUSEN**
★22188 **VASILIY GOLOVNIN**
The following are Intelligence Collectors (Ru flag):
★22189 **GAVRIL SARITCHEV**
★22190 **KHARITON LAPTEV**

★22195 **NEVELSKOY** Ru/— (—); —; RS; 2600 (displacement); 83.0 × 3.50 (272 × 11.48); M (—); 17; Probably built around 1960

★22200 **KAPITAN CHECHKIN** Ru/Fi (Wartsila) 1977; IB; 1700; 77.6 × 3.25 (254.59 × 10.66); TrS D-E (Wartsila); 14; River Service
Sisters (Ru flag):
★22201 **KAPITAN CHADAYEV**
★22202 **KAPITAN PLAHIN**
★22203 **KAPITAN ZARUBIN**
★22204 **KAPITAN BUKAYEV**
★22205 **KAPITAN KRUTOV**

22210 **ALMIRANTE IRIZAR** Ar/Fi (Wartsila) 1978; IB/P; 10100; 119.31 × 9.5 (391.44 × 31.17); TSM (Pielstick); 16.5; Helicopter deck

★22220 **DOBRINYA NIKITICH** Ru/Ru (Admiralteiskiy) 1961; IB; Approx 2300; 68 × 5.5 (223 × 18.9); TrS D-E (—); 13.75; May be spelt **DOBRINYA NIKITCH**
Sisters (Ru flag)—Some are Naval manned:
★22221 **AFANASIY NIKITIN** ex *Ledokol 2*
★22222 **BURAN**
★22223 **YEROFEY KHABAROV** ex *Ledokol 5*
★22224 **FEDOR LITKE**
★22226 **ILYA MUROMETS**
★22227 **IVAN MOSKVITIN**
★22228 **IVAN KRUZENSHTERN** ex *Ledokol 6*
★22230 **PERESVET**
★22231 **PLUG**
★22232 **SADKO**
★22233 **SEMYON DEZHNEV**
★22234 **SEMEN CHELYUSKIN** ex *Ledokol 8*
★22235 **VASILIY POYARKHOV** ex *Ledokol 1*
★22236 **VASILIY PRONCHISHCHEV** ex *Ledokol 1*
★22237 **VLADIMIR RUSANOV** ex *Ledokol 7*
★22238 **YURIY LISYANSKIY** ex *Ledokol 9*
★22239 **VYUGA**
★22240 **STEPHAN JANTZEN** (DDR)
The following are sometimes used for polar research:
★22241 **GEORGIY SEDOV** (Ru)
★22242 **PYOTR PAKHTUSOV** (Ru) ex *Mendeleyev* 1982; ex *Pyotr Pakhtusov*; ex *Ledokol 10* (may be spelt **PETR PAKHTUSOV**)

★22240 **OTTO SCHMIDT** Ru/Ru (Admiralteiskiy) 1979; RS/IB; 2800; 73.00 × 6.62 (240 × 21.72); TSD-E (—); 15

★22250 **KAPITAN M IZMAYLOV** Ru/Fi (Wartsila) 1976; IB/Sal; 1400; 56.3 × 4.2 (184 × 14); TSD-E (Wartsila); 14
Sisters (Ru flag):
★22251 **KAPITAN A RADZHABOV**
★22252 **KAPITAN KOSOLAPOV**

22260 **VOIMA** Fi/Fi (Sandvikens) Fi 1954/79; IB; —; 83.52 × — (274 × —); TS D-E (Wartsila); —; Rebuilt 1978/79 (Wartsila)

22270 **THULE** Sw/Sw (Orlogs) 1953; IB; 1900; 62.2 × 4.9 (204 × 15.11); TrS D-E (Nydqvist & Holm); 13

22280 **CANOPUS** Bz/Ja (Ishikawajima J) 1958; SS; 1500 Dspl; 78 × 3.7 (256 × 12.2); TSM (Sulzer); 15
Sister:
22281 **SIRIUS** (Bz)

22300 **CIROLANA** Br/Br (Ferguson Bros) 1970; ST/RS; 1700; 72.5 × 5 (238 × 17); D-E (W H Allen); 14

22320 **THALASSA** Fr/Fr (A Normand) 1960; ST/RS; 1200; 66.1 × 4.6 (217 × 15.1); M (Duvant); 12

★22325 **SEVER** Ru/Ru ('Chernomorskiy') 1967; RS; 1900; 71.02 × 5.02 (233 × 16.47); D-E (—); 13.25; Converted from stern trawler

★22330 **BELONA** Pd/Pd (Gdynska) 1964; FT; 1000, 69.3 × 5 (228 × 16.7); M (Mirrlees); 13.5; 'B-23' type
Sisters (Pd flag):
★22331 **ALBAKORA**
★22332 **BARAKUDA**
★22333 **BARBATA**
★22334 **BARWENA**
★22335 **DORADA**
★22336 **GRANIK**
★22337 **KONGER**
★22338 **RAMADA**
★22339 **TARPOL**
★22340 **TASERGAL**

★22350 **RYBAK MORSKI** Pd/Pd (Gdynska) 1976; FT; 2600; 89 × 5.2 (292 × 17); M (Sulzer); 15.25; 'B-89' type
Sister:
★22351 **ADMIRAL ARCISZEWSKI** (Pd)

22360 **CLAYMORE** Br/Br (Robb Caledon) 1978; RoPF; 450 dwt; 76.9 × 2.72 (252.3 × 8.92); TSM (Mirrlees Blackstone); 15.5; Stern ramp and side ramps

22370 **BRANDAL** Ca/Ca (Halifax) 1965; RS; 500; 41.6 × — (136 × —); M (Appingedammer Brons); —; Converted stern trawler

22380 **STAFFETTA ADRIATICA** It/It (Apuania) 1969; RoC; 4700; 141.03 × 5.88 (462.7 × 19.29); TSD-E (Fiat); 19; ex *Canguro Giallo* 1973; Stern door
Sisters (It flag):
22381 **CANGURO GRIGIO** ex *Staffetta Jonica* 1978; ex *Canguro Grigio* 1973
22382 **STAFFETTA TIRRENICA** ex *Canguro Biondo* 1973
22383 **CANGURO FULVO**

22390 **AL TAIF** Si/Br (H&W) 1949; F; 5300; 121 × 4.52 (397 × 14); M (B&W); 15; ex *Cambria*; May be known as **ALTAIF**

22410 **ZAMZAM** Cy/It (Taranto) 1952; PC; 5200; 116.9 × 5.8 (383 × 19.1); TSM (Fiat); 18; ex *Messapia* 1975

22420 **AVARE** Bz/Br (Gray) 1949; C; 2700; 99.4 × 5.8 (326 × 19); R (Central Marine); 12.5; ex *Sao Miguel* 1972; ex *Valborg Nielsen* 1960

★22430 **HONG QI 154** RC/Br (Blyth) 1950; C; 2500; 101.8 × 5.8 (334 × 18.11); R (N E Marine); —; ex *Sunny Boy* 1961; ex *Nepos* 1960; ex *Fana* 1959

22440 **ANTHI L** Gr/Fr (Caen) 1954; C; 3700; 112.3 × 6.8 (368 × 21.4); R (France); 11.5; ex *Araya* 1973; ex *Antee* 1969

22470 **SAVILCO** Gr/Ge (Luebecker) 1938; C; 1800; 79.3 × 5.4 (260 × 17.7); M (MAN); 13; ex *Nissos Thassos* 1970; ex *Wickenburgh* 1963; ex *Margeca* 1947; ex *Empire Coningsby* 1946; ex *Adler* 1945

22490 **AMBERES** Ar/Br (Inglis) 1930; C; 1500; 87.7 × 3.7 (288 × 11.2); TSM (H&W); 11; Converted to a barge
Similar (Ar flag):
22491 **CARDIFF**
22492 **GENOVA**

22510 **SELAMAT** Pa/Hong Kong (Hong Kong & W) 1937; C; 690; 52.8 × 4.1 (173 × 13.5); M (H&W); 19; ex *Soon Huat* 1961; ex *La Paloma* 1958; ex *Paloma* 1958; ex *Muliama* 1957

22530 **ANNA MARIA LAURO** It/Ge (Oderwerke) 1913; F; 900; 67.9 × 2.8 (214 × 9.6); TSM (MWM); —

ex *Isola Del Sole* 1965; ex *Kehrwieder* 1963; ex *Gluckauf* 1960; ex *Bubendey*

22540 **YEREWA** In/In (Mazagon) 1965; PC; 1600; 68.3 × 2.9 (224 × 9.7); TSM (MAN); 12
Sister:
22541 **ONGE** (In)

★22550 **ROBERT KOCH** DDR/DDR ('Neptun') 1955; Hospital Ship; 1100; 66.1 × 4.8 (217 × 15.7); M (Goerlitzer); 14

22560 **UNIBAKSH** In/FRG (LF-W) 1956; C; 2700; 92 × 5.9 (302 × 19.5); M (MAN); 12; ex *Rosanna* 1977; ex *Jalatapi* 1974

22580 **VENUS II** Do/It (Adriatico) 1947; C; 900; 67.2 × 4.1 (199 × 13.11); M (Fiat); 10.5; Lengthened 1960; ex *Andy*; ex *Greta H* 1959; ex *Bakke Boy* 1952; ex *Vagan* 1951

★22600 **JURANDY** Bz/US (Todd) 1920; C; 1400; 69.2 × 4.1 (227 × 16.9); R (White Fuel); —; ex *Rio Bravo* 1955; ex *Lloyd Cuarto* 1952; ex *Taku* 1946; ex *Ormes* 1939

22610 **SLUSKEN** Pa/No (Kaldnes) 1919; C; 650; 53.8 × 4.1 (176 × 13.6); R (Kaldnes); —; ex *Magnhild* 1959; ex *Bras* 1956; ex *Raftsund* 1946; ex *Bras*

22620 **NELLA DAN** De/De (Aalborg) 1961; PC; 2200; 75.2 × 6.6 (245 × 21.7); M (B&W); 13

22630 **AMAMI MARU** Ja/Ja (Mitsubishi HI) 1968; F; 1500; 83.1 × 4.1 (273 × 13.3); M (Mitsubishi); 17

22640 **CAPE YORK** Tw/Au (Australian Commonwealth) 1925; LT; 1500; 71.8 × 4.5 (235 × 14.8); R (Australian Commonwealth); 10

22650 **ELCANO** Pi/Ja (Hitachi) 1955; PC; 2000; 87.3 × 5 (288 × 16.7); M (Hitachi); —
Sister:
22651 **LEGAZPI** (Pi) ex *Legaspi* 1980

22660 **SURAJ** UAE/Br (Burntisland) 1956; C; 2500; 102 × 5.9 (335 × 19.4); M (Doxford); 12; ex *Omar* 1983; ex *Rodania* 1975; ex *Eleftherotria* 1972; ex *Northumbrian Prince* 1968

22670 **SPERUS** Br/Br (Caledon) 1939; RS; 900; 64.3 × 4 (211 × 13); TSM (British Auxiliaries); 12; ex *Hesperus*; Converted from Cargo; converted from lighthouse tender

22690 **GILBERT J FOWLER** Br/Br (Ferguson Bros) 1971; Sludge Carrier; 2500; 91 × 5.4 (299 × 17.6); TSM (Lister Blackstone Mirrlees); 12.75
Sister:
22691 **CONSORTIUM 1** (Br)

22710 **CITTA DI META** It/Br (Thornycroft) 1959; RoPF; 670; 58.3 × 1.8 (191 × 6); TSM (Crossley); 14; ex *Carisbrooke Castle* 1974; Bow door and ramp
Sister:
22711 **LE GOBELET D'ARGENT** (Ca) ex *Osborne Castle* 1980

★22720 **SPASSK** Ru/Pd (—); —; MTV; 3800; 144.8 × 6.1 (475 × 20); TSR (—); 15; ex *Suchan*; Converted from 'B31' type cargo vessel c 1958 (in Russia)
Similar (Ru flag):
★22721 **CHUKOTKA**
★22722 **SAKHALIN**
★22723 **SIBIR**

22730 **MEE PYA** Bm/Br (Fleming & Ferguson) 1954; LT; 900; 61 × 3.8 (200 × 12.6); R (Fleming & Ferguson); 11

22740 **NEPTUNE** US/US (Pusey & Jones) 1946; Cbl; 4000; 112.8 × 5.8 (370 × 18); TSR (General Electric); 14; ex *William H G Bullard*; Helicopter deck
Sister:
22741 **ALBERT J MEYER** (US)

22750 **SETANTA** Ih/Ih (Liffey) 1953; Patrol Craft; 1200; 71 × 4 (233 × 12.11); TSR (—); 12.5; ex *Isolda* 1976; Irish Navy. Former lighthouse tender

22770 **JIN YANG No 2** Ch/Ja (Hayashikane) 1960; FT; 900; 75 × 5.3 (245 × 17.4); M (Hayashikane); 12.5; ex *Taiyo Maru No 62* 1977
Sisters:
22771 **CHALLWA No 2** (Pe) ex *Taiyo Maru No 73* 1976
22771/1 **JIN YANG No 1** (Ch) ex *Tayo Maru No 63* 1977
22772 **SAM WON No 27** (Pa) ex *Taiyo Maru No 61* 1974
(Ja flag):
22774 **TAIYO MARU No 67**
22775 **TAIYO MARU No 68**
22776 **TAIYO MARU No 71**
22777 **TAIYO MARU No 72**

22780 **SEISELLA** Br/Br (Hall, Russell) 1969; RS/OSS; 1500; 69.6 × 4.6 (229 × 15); M (Mirrlees);

—; ex *Southella* 1980; Converted from trawler 1981

● ★22790 Modified **LEVANT** or **KOVEL** type Ru/DDR ('Neptun') c 1958; —; 3400; 103.97 × 6.58 (341.1 × 21.6); M (—); 12.5; Modified from cargo vessel. Naval Auxiliary
Possible names (Ru flag):
★22791 **LAKHTA**
★22792 **VENUTA**
★22793 **VILYUY**

22810 **BARBA** Pa/De (Helsingor) 1954; C; 2800; 101.2 × 6 (332 × 19.7); M (B&W); 13; ex *Eurabia Wave* 1979; ex *Sperber* 1975; ex *Abelone Vendila* 1962

● 22830 **THEODOROS II** Cy/Pd (Gdanska) 1960; C; 3800; 108.2 × 6.6 (355 × 21.1); M (B&W); 14; ex *Desanmar* 1980; ex *Torres* 'B-31' type
Sisters:
22831 **CIDADE DE IMPERATRIZ** (Bz) ex *Mosqueiro* 1981
22832 **GUARUJA** (Cy)
22833 **LEBLON** (Cy)
22834 **VAL-DE-CAES** (Bz) ex *Dom Ambrogio* 1967; ex *Tambau* 1961
22835 **MERITIA** (Cy) ex *Lina* 1980; ex *Itapua* 1980
22836 **IOANNIS III** (Cy) ex *Anna L;* ex *Iracema* 1981
22837 **CIDADE DE ALCANTARA** (Bz) ex *Waldemar Pinheiro* 1980; ex *Dom Alexandre* 1967; ex *Boa Viagem* 1961

● 22840 **ANDIZHAN** Ru/DDR ('Neptun') 1958; C; 3200; 104.2 × 6.6 (341 × 22); M (Goerlitzer); 12.5; 'LEVANT' or 'KOVEL' type
Sisters (Ru flag):
★22841 **BARABINSK**
★22842 **BIKIN**
★22843 **BOTSMAN ZOTOV** ex *Mongugay*
★22844 **CHELYABINSK**
★22845 **DALNERECHENSK** ex *Iman* 1973
★22846 **DALNIY**
★22847 **DAUGAVA**
★22848 **EMETSK**
★22849 **EYSK**
★22850 **HOROL**
★22851 **IZHMA**
★22852 **KHOLMOGORY**
★22853 **JASNOMORSK**
★22855 **KOVEL**
★22856 **KYARDLA**
★22857 **LAZAREV**
★22858 **LOKSA**
★22859 **LUDZA**
★22860 **MAHTRA**
★22861 **MGA**
★22862 **MURMASH**
★22863 **NAGAEVO**
★22864 **NAMANGAN**
★22865 **POLYARNYY**
★22866 **POSYET**
★22867 **RAKVERE**
★22868 **RAZDOLNOYE**
★22869 **REVDA**
★22870 **RAZLIV**
★22871 **RENI**
★22872 **REPINO**
★22873 **SALSK**
★22874 **SARANSK**
★22875 **SHENKURSK**
★22876 **SOBOLEVO**
★22877 **SIGULDA**
★22878 **SYRVE**
★22879 **SINEGORSK**
★22880 **TURUKHANSK**
★22881 **VANINO**
Ships vary slightly. Some have large radar mast from bridge.
(Vn flag):
★22882 **HONG HA** ex *Zaisan*
★22883 **SONGDA** ex *Sinegorsk* 1974
★22884 **SONG KHAN** ex *Turkestan* 1975
(An flag):
★22885 **LENIN** ex *Kapitan Voolens* 1978; ex *Amata* 1967

22930 **DEEPA RAYA** Ia/Ja (Mitsui) 1948; PC; 2000; 89.6 × 5.6 (294 × 18.5); M (Mitsui); 11.5; ex *Bachtera Kita;* ex *Tokachisan Maru No 2* 1962; ex *Tokatisan Maru* 1960

22950 **SANG THAI STEEL** Th/FRG (Stuelcken) 1958; C; 2300/3600 106.20 × —/7.34 (348.4 × —/24.08); M (Ottensener); 14; ex *Dexena* 1981; ex *Ulsnis* 1976; ex *Volumnia* 1969; ex *Lealott* 1966; ex *Volumnia* 1963

★22960 **SONG TRA LY** Vn/Ja (Hitachi) 1958; C; 3200; 106.2 × 6.4 (348 × 21.1); M (Ito Tekkosho); 12; ex *Pioneer Star;* ex *Golden Star;* ex *Mineshima Maru* 1973
Similar:
22961 **KWEI YING** (Pa) ex *Dynamic Enterprise* 1974;

ex *Kyoto Maru* 1970; ex *Taisei Maru* 1967
22963 **MING PING** (Pa) ex *Quarry Bay* 1977; ex *An Kang* 1976; ex *United Endeavour* 1974; ex *Foremost* 1974; ex *Confidence* 1973; ex *Sanmei Maru* 1970; ex *Kowa Maru* 1969; ex *Shoho Maru* 1967

22970 **SRI CHOL** Th/Ja (Hitachi) 1958; C; 3400; 106.2 × 6.4 (348 × 21.1); M (Sulzer); 12; ex *Hirashima Maru* 1969

22990 **WESTGATE** Pa/Sw (Gotav) 1938; C; 1800; 97.5 × — (320 × —); TSM (B&W); 15; ex *Safco I* 1958; ex *Duala* 1951

23000 **NORTH SEA** Pa/Ja (Kure) 1957; C; 3200; 104.6 × 6.2 (343 × 20.5); M (Mitsubishi); 13; ex *Florida* 1979; ex *Aetios* 1979; ex *Mary K* 1978; ex *Carmenzita* 1975; ex *Vanessa* 1974; ex *Tosei Maru* 1970

23030 **MING HO** Pa/Ja (Sasebo) 1957; C; 3300; 105.7 × 6.4 (347 × 21); M (Niigata); 12; ex *Mount Davis;* ex *An Shun;* ex *Yunan* 1973; ex *Yunan Maru* 1971; ex *Nisshin Maru* 1967
Sister:
23031 **NAGARAT** (Th) ex *Eastern Comet* 1980; ex *Chozan Maru* 1957

● 23040 **SEALOGS** Pa/Ja (Mitsubishi Z) 1957; CP; 4500; 113.9 × 7.5 (374 × 24.6); M (Mitsubishi); 12; ex *Lucky Willing* 1982; ex *Krung Siam* 1979; ex *Enoura Maru* 1970

★23050 **MIN CHU No 9** RC/RC (—) 1954; C; 2200; 82.6 × 5.2 (271 × 17); R (—); 11

★23060 **INGUL** Ru/Ru (—) 1959; FC; 1600; 73.1 × 4.5 (262 × 17); M (Russkiy); 9.5

23090 **DAMMAM** Si/Br (H&W) 1927; C; 1300; 86 × 5.4 (282 × 17.7); M (B&W); 12; ex *Palacio* 1958

23100 **PELEGO DUVO** My/Ca (St Lawrence M&M) 1948; C; 1200; 74 × 4.3 (242 × 14); M (Fairbanks, Morse); 12; ex *Lautan Lima* 1981; ex *Falisa* 1976; ex *Cartaxo* 1972
Sister:
23101 **GULF FRIO** (Gr) ex *Porto Pylos* 1981; ex *Porto Frio* 1980; ex *Transfrio* 1978; ex *Colares* 1966

23110 **TRANSAFRICAN I** Pa/Ne ('De Gideon') 1937; C; 200; 46 × 2.6 (152 × 8.5); M ('Bolnes'); 8.5; ex *Casana* 1968; ex *Hada* 1948
Sister:
23111 **OMAR** (Le) ex *Lassi* 1970; ex *Saad* 1968; ex *Zero* 1966; ex *Santoni* 1958; ex *Gladan* 1957; ex *Inland* 1944; ex *Karanan* 1939

★23120 **MIN CHU No 13** RC/Ja (—) —; CP; 2200; 98.1 × — (322 × —); R (—); 11

● 23140 **MIGHTY SPIRIT** Pa/Br (Swan Hunter & WR) 1957; C; 4900; 32.3 × 7.5 (434 × 24.7); M (Sulzer); 14.75; ex *Eurydice* 1981; ex *City of Guildford*
Sisters:
23142 **SUERTE** (Gr) ex *City of Gloucester*
23144 **ISLAND OF MARMARA** (Gr) ex *City of St Albans*

23170 **ARAMIL** Sp/Sp (Duro Felguera) 1963; C; 2500; 92.3 × 6.4 (303 × 21); M (Sulzer); 12.5

23190 **SAIBURI** Th/Hong Kong (Hong Kong & W) 1937; C; 600; 49.2 × 3.6 (161 × 11.8); M (H&W); 9; ex *Hung Hai* 1948; ex *Moamoa* 1946

23200 **AGIOS NECTARIOS** Cy/FRG (Rickmers) 1955; C; 1600; 84 × 4.5 (277 × 15); M (KHD); 12; ex *Antofagasta* 1977

23210 **VENUS II** Do/It (Adriatico) 1947; C; 900; 67 × 4.2 (221 × 13.7); M (Fiat); 10.5; ex *Andy;* ex *Greta H* 1959; ex *Bakke Boy* 1952; ex *Vagan* 1951; Lengthened 1960

23220 **DON CAMILO** Pi/FRG (Bremer V) 1951; CP; 2400; 105 × 6.2 (345 × 20.3); M (Bremer V); 16; ex *Lichtenstein* 1968
Sister:
23221 **DONA JULIETA** (Pi) ex *Don Lorenzo;* ex *Liebenstein* 1968

23230 **WAHENG** Pa/FRG (Nobiskrug) 1959; C; 4200; 114.9 × 7.7 (377 × 25.4); M (MAN); 14.5; ex *Kaethe Jebsen* 1977
Sister:
23232 **WAH FAI** (Pa) ex *Clara Jebsen*

23240 **CAVO SIDERO** Gr/FRG (O&K) 1954; CP; 2700; 93.6 × 7.1 (307 × 18.7); M (MAN); 14; ex *Piraeusburg* 1973; ex *Casablanca* 1973

● 23250 **BAHIA AGUIRRE** Ar/Ca (Halifax) 1950; Transport; 3800; 95 × 7.9 (335 × 13.8); TSM (Nordberg); 16; Argentine Navy
Sister:
23251 **BAHIA BUEN SUCESO** (Ar)

23260 **GULF ACE** Pa/Br (Ailsa) 1937; C; 800; 68 ×

4.9 (223 × 16.1); M (Polar); 9; ex *Al Madani* 1980; ex *Toula* 1975; ex *Nissos Sifnos* 1969; ex *Crane* 1964

23270 **OURANOUPOLIS** Gr/Br (Austin) 1949; C; 1200/1600; 79 × 4.6/5.7 (259 × 15.2/17.5); TSM (British Polar); 12; ex *Auk* 1965

23280 **JOHN W MACKAY** Br/Br (Swan Hunter & WR) 1922; Cbl; 4100; 110.2 × 7.7 (361.6 × 25.6); TSR (Swan Hunter & WR); 11.5

23290 **MARIB** Ye/Ne ('De Gideon') 1938; C; 460; 47.9 × 2.8 (157 × 9.3); M (Humboldt-Deutz); —; ex *Frontier* 1952

23300 **RIO SAMO** Sp/Ca (Morton) 1941; C; 800; 62.6 × 5.3 (205 × 17.6); M (Polar); 14.5; ex *La Ceiba* 1947; ex *Arvida*

23310 **EUROPIC FERRY** Br/Br (Swan Hunter) 1968; RoC; 4200; 137.6 × 4.6 (451 × 15.2); TSM (Pielstick); 19.25; Stern door

23330 **ATLAS 1.** Gr/Br (Ailsa) 1961; RoC; 2500; 110.2 × 3.9 (361 × 12.1); TSM (Davey Paxman); 14; ex *Cerdic Ferry* 1981; Stern door/ramp
Sister:
23331 **ATLAS II** (Gr) ex *Doric Ferry* 1981
Similar (lengthened):
23332 **GAELIC FERRY** (Br)

23340 **ARAHANGA** NZ/Br (Upper Clyde) 1972; RoC/TF; 3900; 127.5 × 4.9 (418 × 16.1); TSM (Pielstick); 17; Stern door

23350 **JURANDY** Bz/US (Todd) 1920; C; 1400; 69.2 × 5.1 (227 × 17.1); R (White Fuel); —; ex *Rio Bravo* 1955; ex *Lloyd Cuarto* 1952; ex *Taku* 1946; ex *Ormes* 1939

23360 **IJZER** Be/Be (Beliard, Crichton) 1954; LS; 1200; 66.9 × 3.6 (220 × 11.1); M (SEM); 15

★23370 **GONG NONG BING 3** RC/Ja (—) 1940; CP; 3200; 103.9 × 4.3 (431 × 14); R & LPT (—); 13.5; ex *Min Chu No 3*

23380 **WORLD RENAISSANCE** Gr/Fr (L'Atlantique) 1966; P; 11700; 150 × 6.2 (492 × 20.5); TSM (B&W); 18.5; ex *Homeric;* ex *Renaissance*

★23390 **ZVEZDA** Ru/DDR (—) 1957; F; 350; 39.3 × 3.5 (129 × 11.4); M (—); 10
Sisters (Ru flag):
★23391 **ZARNITSA**
★23392 **YUG**

23400 **CABLE ENTERPRISE** Br/Br (Cammell Laird) 1964; Cbl; 4400; 113.2 × 5 (371 × 19.1); TSD-E (English Electric); 15
Similar:
23401 **RETRIEVER** (Br)

★23410 **RYBAK** Ru/DDR (Peene) 1968; ST; 1000; 63.1 × 4.8 (207 × 15.6); M (Dieselmotorenwerk Rostock); —; 'JUNGE WELT' class
Sisters:
★23411 **RYBACHKA** (Ru)
(DDR flag):
★23412 **ARTHUR BECKER**
★23413 **BRUNO TESCH**
★23414 **CARLO SCHONHAAR**
★23415 **ELVIRA EISENSCHNEIDER**
★23416 **ERICH STEINFURTH**
★23417 **EUGEN SCHONHAAR**
★23418 **GRETE WALTER**
★23419 **HANNO GUNTHER**
★23420 **HEINZ KAPELLE**
★23421 **HEINZ PRIESS**
★23422 **HERBERT BAUM**
★23423 **HERBERT TSCHAPE**
★23424 **HERTA LINDER**
★23425 **KARL WOLF**
★23426 **MAGNUS POSER**
★23427 **PETER GORING**
★23428 **PHILIPP MULLER**
★23429 **RUDI ARNT**
★23430 **RUDOLF SCHWARZ**
★23431 **WALTER BARTH**
★23432 **WERNER KUBE**

★23440 **AFALA** Bu/Pd (Gdynska) 1974; FT; 2500; 89 × 5.2 (292 × 17.3); M (Sulzer); 15.5; 'B-418' type
Sisters (Some have lifeboat between funnel & bridge)
(Bu flag):
★23441 **AKTINJA**
★23442 **ALFEUS**
★23443 **ARGONAUT**
★23444 **FIZALIA**
★23445 **KAPRELA**
★23446 **OFELIA**
★23447 **ROTALIA**
★23448 **SAGITA**
(Pd flag):
★23449 **AMAREL**
★23450 **BONITO**

★23451 DELFIN
★23452 GARNELA
★23453 GRINWAL
★23454 HAJDUK
★23455 HUMBAK
★23456 KALMAR
★23457 MORS
★23458 PARMA
★23459 REKIN
★23460 WALEN
The following are identical but 'B-417' type (Pd flag):
★23461 KOLIAS
★23462 MANTA
★23463 MARLIN
★23464 ORCYN
★23465 ORLEN
★23466 OTOL
★23467 PROFESSOR BOGUCKI
★23468 TAZAR
★23469 TUNEK
(Iq flag):
23470 AL AHWAR
23471 AL KAHLA
23472 AL RAZAZA
23473 SAWA (Launched as Saira)

★23480 LUCHEGORSK class; Ru/Ru (Baltiya/'Chernomorskiy') 1969; FT; 3000; 83.9 × 5.7 (275 × 19); M (CKD Praha); 12
Sisters (Ru flag):
★23481 MATEMATIK
★23482 MYS SINYAVINA
★23483 MYS YEGOROVA
★23484 MYS YELAGINA
★23485 RUSNE
★23486 LUNOKHOD I
★23487 SIMYAVINO
★23488 VIKTOR KHUDYAKOV
★23489 MYS BELKINA
★23490 LUCHEGORSK
★23491 MYS BOBROVA
★23492 MYS GAMOVA
★23493 MYS KRYLOVA
★23494 MYS LAZARYEVA
★23495 MYS OBRUCHYEVA
★23496 MYS BARANOVA
★23497 MYS GRINA
★23498 MYS MALTSYEVA
★23499 MYS NADEZHDY
★23500 MYS OREKHOVA
★23501 MYS OSIPOVA
★23502 MYS YERMAK
★23503 MYS YUDINA
★23504 RUDOLF SIRGE
★23505 RUDOLF VAKMAN
★23506 SAMSHIT
★23507 SUDUVA
★23508 TRAKAY
★23509 TURKUL
★23510 TYMLAT
★23511 VOLDEMAR AZIN
★23512 BURAN
★23513 IVAN GREN
★23514 KVARTS
★23515 OTTO RYASTAS
★23516 TIRASPOL
★23517 VULKAN
★23518 ALEKSANDR BOGOLYUBOV
★23519 KUULUNDA
★23520 GDOV
★23522 XV SYEZD PROFSOYUZOV
★23523 DZUKIYA
★23524 DZINTERKRASTS
★23525 VALKA
★23526 TRUSKAVETS
★23527 PSKOV
★23528 ALEKSANDRIT
★23529 TIGIL
★23530 PETROZAVODSK
★23531 KORCHAGINETS ex Kargopol 1981 (now converted to fish carrier—may be altered in appearance)
★23532 NIKOLAYEVSKIY KOMSOMOLETS
★23533 PAUDZHA
★23534 FEODOR OKK
★23535 IOKHANNES SEMPER
★23536 KARAGAT
★23537 MIKHAIL BARSUKOV
★23538 MYS SHELIKHOVA
★23539 KAZALINSK
★23540 PETROKREPOST
★23541 SAMARA
★23542 KAZATIN
★23543 KOMSOMOL
★23544 LATVII
★23545 TOLBACHIK
★23546 TUMAN-2
★23547 DAYNAVA
★23548 DZINTARZEME
★23549 AKVAMARIN
★23550 GRAD

★23551 KALAR
★23552 KALITVA
★23553 KANDALAKSHA
★23554 KHAYRYUZOVO
★23555 KIRIR
★23556 KLYUCHEYSKOY
★23557 KOTAYKA
★23558 KORENGA
★23559 KRASNOGVARDEYETS
★23560 KUSHKA
★23561 LABRADOR
★23562 MALKI
★23563 MEDIK
★23564 METEOROLOG
★23565 MARS-2
★23566 NIDA
★23567 NIKOLAY PAPIVIN
★23568 PASSAT-2
★23569 RIKHARD MIRRING
The following are Fishery Research Vessels (Ru flag):
★23571 PROGRESS
★23572 SALEKHARD
★23573 VOLZHANIN

23580 WUPPERTAL FRG/FRG (Rickmers) 1977; RoC; 1600; 116.31 × 5.3 (381.59 × 17.39); TSM (Atlas-MaK); 16; ex Canaima 1979; ex Wuppertal 1978; Stern ramp

23600 CHARRUA Bz/Sw (Ekensbergs) 1951; C; 1900; 95.4 × 5.8 (313 × 19); M (B&W); 15; ex Carlsham 1953
Sister:
23601 SAO JOSE (Bz) ex Minuano 1977

23610 ALKYON Gr/De (Helsingor) 1949; P; 4200; 114.5 × 5.6 (375 × 18.3); TSM (B&W); 20; ex Mimika L 1979; ex Copenhagen 1969; ex Kronprinsesse Ingrid 1969

23620 FEDERAL MAPLE Br/Ca (Canadian Vickers) 1961; PC; 3200; 90.8 × 4.7 (298 × 15.7); M (Fairbanks, Morse); 15

★23640 VLADIMIR KAVRAYSKIY Ru/Ru (Admiralteiskiy) 1962; RS; 2500 Dspl; 68 × 5.5 (223 × 18.1); TrSM (—); 13.75; Converted from 'Dobrynya Nikitch' class (IB); Helicopter platform aft

23650 ALMIRANTE IRIZAR Ar/Fi (Wartsila) 1978; IB/P; 10100; 119.31 × 9.5 (391.44 × 31.17); TSM (Pielstick); 16.5; Helicopter deck

23660 TOR Sw/Fi (Wartsila) 1964; IB: 4200; 84.5 × 6.2 (277 × 20.4); TSD-E (Sulzer); 18
Similar:
23661 TARMO (Fi)
23662 VARMA (Fi)
23663 NJORD (Sw)

★23665 MB-29 Ru/Fi (Rauma Repola) 1982; Tg/Sal; 1400; 63.51 × 5.10 (208 × 16.73); TSM (Russkiy); 14
Sisters (Ru flag):
★23665/1 MB-32
★23666/1 MB-35
★23666/1 MB-36
★23667 MB-38
★23667/1 MB-61
★23668 MB-62
★23669 MB-64

23670 ALE Sw/Fi (Wartsila) 1973; IB; 488 Dspl; 46 × 5 (151 × 16.3); TSM (—); 14

23680 JOHN BISCOE Br/Br (Fleming & Ferguson) 1956; RS; 1600; 67.06 × 5.01 (220 × 16.44); D-E (Mirrlees Blackstone); 11; Antarctic research

★23690 SASSNITZ DDR/FRG ('Neptun') 1959; P/RoVC; 6200; 137 × 5.8 (450 × 19); TSM (Halberstadt); 18

● 23700 BENODET De/FRG (Meyer) 1970; RoPCF; 4200; 109 × 4.6 (357 × 15); TSM (KHD); 18.5; ex Gelting Nord 1984; ex Olau Kent 1980; ex Apollo 1976
Similar:
23701 VIKING EXPRESS (Fi) ex Viking 1 1983
23702 VIKING 3 ex Wasa Express 1982; ex Viking III 1976
23703 COROMUEL (Me)
23704 PUERTO VALLARTA (Me)
23705 BOTNIA EXPRESS (Fi) ex Diana 1979
23706 EARL GRANVILLE (Br) ex Viking 4 1980
23707 AZTECA (Me)

23710 IONIAN STAR Gr/FRG (Nobiskrug) 1964; RoPCF; 6100; 115 × 4.7 (378 × 15); TSM (MAN); 20; ex Lief Eriksson 1976; ex Prins Bertil 1966
Similar:
★23711 WAWEL (Pd) ex Gustav Vasa 1973

23720 IZU MARU No 3 Ja/Ja (Hashihama) 1972; RoPCF; 7500; 137.85 × 5.61 (452.26 × 18.41); TSM (Pielstick); 21.5; ex Cassiopeia; Bow and stern ramps
Sister:

23721 IZU MARU No 11 (Ja) ex Albatross

23730 HIDAKA MARU Ja/Ja (Mitsubishi HI) 1969; RoC/TF; 4100; 144.5 × 5.2 (474 × 17); M (MAN); 18
Sisters (Ja flag):
23731 HIYAMA MARU
23732 ISHIKARI MARU
23733 OSHIMA MARU
23734 SORACHI MARU
23735 TOKACHI MARU

23740 CALA MARSAL Sp/Sp (Mallorca) 1971; RoC; 900; 88.91 × 4.18 (291.69 × 13.71); M (B&W); 17
Sister:
23741 CALA LLONGA (Sp)

23750 MEROWAH My/Br (G Brown) 1949; CP; 1200; 80.2 × 5.1 (236 × 16.8); M (Nydqvist & Holm); 12; ex Oribi 1971; ex Kong Dag 1958

★23760 BATAYSK Ru/Pd (Gdanska) 1955; TS; 4900; 108.3 × 6.1 (355 × 21); R ('Zgoda'); 11.5; Converted from 'B-31' type cargo vessel

★23770 ALEKSANDR IVANOVICH VOEYKOV Ru/Ru (Nosenko) 1959; RS; 3200; 84.7 × 5.5 (278 × 18); M (Russkiy); 13; Also known as A I VOEYKOV; Converted 'MAYAKOYSKIY' class trawler
Sister:
★23771 YU M SHOKALSKIY (Ru)

23780 ORPHEUS Gr/Br (H&W) 1948/70; P; 5100; 111.82 × 4.88 (366.86 × 16.01); TSM (H&W); 15; ex Theseus 1969; ex Munster I 1968; ex Munster 1968; Converted from ferry 1970

23790 ALPASHA Si/Fr (Mediterranee) 1969; P; 5300; 108.7 × 4.8 (357 × 16.8); TSM (Pielstick); 18; ex Napoleon 1974; Side doors

23800 VERGINA Gr/Be (Cockerill-Ougree) 1964; RoPF; 6400; 127.8 × 5.1 (419 × 16.1); TSM (Fiat); 18; ex Golden Sky 1980; ex Saudi Moon; ex El Greco 1976; ex Dan 1976; ex Bilu 1967

23810 SAMAINA Gr/FRG (Hanseatische) 1962; RoPF; 3800; 110 × 4.5 (361 × 14.8); TSM (Pielstick); 18; ex Mary Poppins 1976; ex Gosta Berling 1975; ex Escapade 1967; ex Gosta Berling 1967; ex Nils Holgersson 1967

23820 ST CLAIR Br/FRG (LF-W) 1965; RoPF; 4500; 123.3 × 4.8 (404 × 15.7); TSM (Pielstick); —; ex Terje Vigen 1977; ex S F Panther 1975; ex Peter Pan 1973
Sister:
23821 EUROPAFARJAN IV (FRG) ex Oliver Twist 1978

23830 ELBJORN De/De (Frederikshavn) 1954; IB; 900; 47 × 4.4 (157 × 14.5); D-E (Frichs); 14

23850 WESTERN ARCTIC Pa/It (Apuania) 1965; RS; 1600; 74.4 × 4.9 (244 × 16); D-E (KHD); —; ex Aspa Terzo 1979; Converted from trawler 1980
Sister:
23851 ASPA QUARTO (It)

● ★23860 PLUTON Ru/Pd (Gdanska) 1978; RS; approx 2000 Dspl; 82 × 4 (268.9 × 13.1); M (Sulzer); 18
Sisters (Ru flag):
★23861 GIDROLOG
★23862 PEGAS
★23863 PERSEY
★23864 SENEZH
★23865 STRELETS
★23866 TAYGA
★23867 YUG
★23868 ZODIAC

★23870 GONG NONG BING 17 RC/RC (—) 1959; PC; 2500; 90.5 × — (297 × —); M (—); 12.5 ex Min Chu No 17

★23880 NORILSK Ru/It (Mediterraneo) 1951; PC; 3500; 101.9 × 5.5 (334 × 17.11); TSM (Fiat); 13

23890 NICOLAOS RIGAS Gr/It (Felszegi) 1958; C; 3600; 103.4 × 7.5 (339 × 24.8); M (Fiat); 12.5; ex Australe 1976; ex Ut Prosperatis 1969; ex San Sebastiano 1962

23900 ZOE II Gr/It (Felszegi) 1956; C; 2700; 111 × 7.2 (365 × 23.8); M (Sulzer); 15; ex Theseus 1980; ex Tassos Tsiris 1979; ex Indiana 1975

● 23910 FALCON Gr/FRG (Kieler H) 1959; R; 4100; 126 × 7 (413 × 23); M (MAN); 17.75; ex Northern Ice 1982; ex Cacique Yanquetruz 1973; ex Cap Valiente 1970

23920 GIL EANES Po/Po (Viana) 1955; Hospital and depot ship; 3500; 98.6 × 5.5 (324 × 18); TSM (Fairbanks, Morse); —

23930 SIMALI 1. Th/FRG (Flensburger) 1951; CP; 2700/4300; 116.3 × —/7.3 (382 × —/24); M (MAN); 13; ex Siam Queen 1976; ex Nikitas II 1974; ex Nordhaff 1971; ex Naguilan 1969; ex Atlas 1959

Sister:
23931 **DIMITRIS** (Pa) ex *Apostolos M II* 1980; ex *Diana* 1978; ex *Nordmark* 1974; ex *Don Pedro* 1967; ex *Levante* 1966

23940 **DANBJORN** De/De (Odense) 1965; IB; 3000; 75.4 × 6 (247 × 19.8); TSD-E (B&W); —
Sister:
23941 **ISBJORN** (De)

23950 **ODEN** Sw/Fi (Sandvikens) 1957; IB; 3400; 83.5 × 7 (274 × 23); TSD-E (Nydqvist & Holm); —

23960 **HANSE** FRG/Fi (Sandvikens) 1965; IB; 2800; 74.7 × 5.9 (245 × 19.2); TSD-E (Wartsila); —

★23970 **KAPITAN BELOUSOV** Ru/Fi (Sandvikens) 1955; IB; 3700; 83.2 × 7 (273 × 23); TSD-E (Wartsila); 15
Sisters (Ru flag):
★23971 **KAPITAN MELEKHOV**
★23972 **KAPITAN VORONIN**

23980 **MURTAJA** Fi/Fi (Sandvikens) 1959; IB; 2700; 74.2 × 5.8 (243 × 19); TSD-E (Sulzer); —
Sister:
23981 **KARHU** (Fi)
Similar (heavy foremast)
23982 **SAMPO** (Fi)

23990 **ABERTHAW FISHER** Br/Br (Ailsa) 1966; RoC; 2400; 86.6 × 4.6 (284 × 15.1); TSD-E (WH Allen); 11
Sister:
23991 **KINGSNORTH FISHER** (Br)

24010 **FAIRFIELD VISCOUNT** Br/Ih (Liffey) 1960; Submersible Support Ship; 1600; 88 × 5.1 (280 × 16.1); M (Sulzer); ex *British Viscount* 1981; ex *Vickers Viscount* 1980; ex *Meath*; Converted Livestock Carrier

● ★24030 **VOLGOLES** Ru/Pd (Gdanska) 1960; C/TC; 4600; 123.9 × 6.9 (406 × 22.8); M (Sulzer); 14.75; '**B-514**' type
Similar (Ru flag):
★24031 **ABAGURLES**
★24032 **ABAKANLES**
★24033 **ALAPAYEVSKLES**
★24034 **ALATYRLES**
★24035 **ALDANLES**
★24036 **ANADYRLES**
★24037 **ANDOMALES**
★24038 **ANGARSKLES**
★24039 **ARKHANGELSKLES**
★24041 **DVINOLES**
★24042 **KAPITAN BELOSHAPKIN** ex *Adimiles*
★24043 **KOMILES**
★24044 **PRIMORLES**
★24045 **SEVERLES**
The following are of the later '**B-45**' type (Ru flag):
★24047 **BELOMORSKLES**
★24048 **ALTAYLES**
★24049 **ARGUN**
★24050 **AMURSKLES**
★24051 **ANGARLES**
★24052 **BALAKHNALES**
★24053 **BUREYALES**
★24054 **BRATSKLES**
★24055 **BUKHARA**
★24056 **BARNAUL**
★24057 **BELOZERSKLES**
★24058 **BEREZINALES**
★24059 **BAYKONUR**
★24060 **BOBRUYSKLES**
★24061 **BRASLAVLES**
★24062 **BODAYBO**
★24063 **DARASUN**
★24064 **DZHURMA**
★24065 **GRODEKOVO**
★24066 **ELEKTROSTAL**
★24067 **KRASKINO**
★24068 **KUNGUR**
★24069 **KANDALAKSHALES**
★24070 **KRANSK**
★24071 **KHATANGA**
★24072 **KHOLMSK**
★24073 **KOVDA**
★24074 **MIRONYCH**
★24075 **MEKHANIK RYBASHUK**
★24076 **NORDVIK**
★24077 **NARYAN—MAR**
★24078 **NIKOLAY MIRONOV**
★24079 **OREKHOVO—ZUYEVO**
★24080 **PORONIN**
★24081 **KAPITAN ABAKUMOV** ex *Tulomales*
★24082 **PRIDYATLES**
★24083 **PUTYATIN**
★24084 **POBYEDINO**
★14085 **RUZA**
★24086 **RUBTSOVSK**
★24087 **SAKHALINLES**
★24088 **SHADRINSK**

★24089 **SAYANLES**
★24090 **SEGEZHALES**
★24091 **SALEKHARD**
★24092 **SHATURA**
★24093 **RAYCHIKHINSK**
★24094 **SELENGALES**
★24095 **SUNGARI**
★24096 **TOBOLLES**
★24097 **TAYGONOS**
★24098 **TULOMA**
★24099 **TYUMEN**
★24100 **TAYGA**
★24101 **TAYSHEN**
★24102 **ULANUDE**
★24103 **URALLES**
★24104 **VETUGALES**
★24105 **VYCHEGDALES**
★24106 **VILYUYLES**
★24107 **VOSRESENSK**
★24108 **VALDAYLES**
★24109 **VOLGA** ex *Konoshales*
★24110 **VORKUTA**
★24111 **ZABAYKALSK**

24130 **WATAMPONE** Ia/FRG (Meyer) 1959; C; 2200; 85 × 5.2 (279 × 17.1); M (MAN); 12
Sisters (Ia flag):
24131 **WAKOLO**
24132 **WANDEBORI**
24133 **WARISANO**
24134 **WATUDAMBO**

24140 **MAURITIUS** Br/FRG (Meyer) 1955; PC; 2100; 84.8 × 5.2 (278 × 17.1); M (KHD); 11.5

★24145 **KAVKAZ** Ru/Ru (—) —; RS; 3400 (displacement); 83.6 × 6.00 (274 × 19.69); M (—); 13; Based on hull of 'MAYAKOVSKIY' class trawler
Sister:
★24146 **KRYM** (Ru)

24150 **ARCTIC TRAWLER** US/US (Maryland SB & DD) 1969; FT; 1600; 90 × 5.7 (314 × 18.6); D-E (General Motors); —; ex *Seafreeze Atlantic* 1980
Sister:
24151 **ROYAL SEA** (US) ex *Seafreeze Pacific* 1973

★24160 **JUNGE GARDE** DDR/DDR (Mathias-Thesen) 1967; FT; 10200; 141.4 × 7.8 (464 × 25.9); D-E (Dieselmotorenwerk Rostock); 14
Sister:
★24161 **JUNGE WELT** (DDR)

24170 **ANTON DOHRN** FRG/FRG (A G 'Weser') 1963; RS/ST; 1900; 83.3 × 5.2 (230 × 17.1); D-E (Maybach); —; ex *Walther Herwig* 1972

24180 **MEROWAH** My/Br (G Brown) 1949; CP; 1200; 80.2 × 5.1 (263 × 16.8); M (Nydqvist & Holm); 12; ex *Oribi* 1971; ex *Kong Dag* 1958

★24190 **ANITA** Vn/No (Akers) 1928; C; 1200; 77 × 5 (253 × 16.5); R (Akers); 12.5; ex *Bonn* 1961

24220 **TOKYO MARU** Ja/Ja (Hayashikane) 1976; RoC; 6700; 147.5 × 6.6 (484 × 21.7); M (MAN); 19

24230 **TUSTUMENA** US/US (Christy) 1964; F; 2200; 90 × 4.4 (295 × 14.6); TSM (Fairbanks, Morse); —; Lengthened 1969 (Bethlehem Steel)

24240 **TANJA** Pa/Fi (Crichton-Vulcan) 1961; C; 4200; 135 × 8.6 (443 × 28); M (Gotaverken); 16; ex *Schloss Tarasp* 1983; ex *Tatrina* 1980; ex *Thebeland* 1976; Lengthened 1963
Sisters:
★24241 **RUI CHANG** (RC) ex *Tyrusland*
24242 **BRIGHTNESS** (Pa) ex *Trojaland*

24260 **ALMONA** Pa/Br (Connell) 1957; Pt Con; 7700/10100; 171.7 × 8.1/9.1 (564 × 26.8/30); M (MAN); 18; ex *Warri Express* 1980; ex *Temeraire* 1978; Lengthened and converted from cargo vessel 1970

● 24270 **APLI CHAU** Pa/FRG (Deutsche Werft) 1958; Pt Con; 8600/11700; 188.7 × 7.9/8.6 (619 × 26/28.3); M (B&W); 18; ex *Tagaytay*; Lengthened & converted from a cargo ship 1970
Sisters (Pa flag):
24271 **GINA** ex *Tai Ping* 1980
24272 **LAMTONG CHAU** ex *Sunshine Island* 1982; ex *Tema*; ex *Traviata* 1977
Similar (first KP is centre line):
24273 **REGINA S** ex *Tarantel* (Pa)

24280 **RIO CORRIENTES** Ar/Ys ('3 Maj') 1962; C; 8500; 157.3 × 8.3 (516 × 27.3); Cranes before bridge may be removed (see **LAGO LACAR**); M (Fiat); —
Sisters (Ar flag):
24281 **RIO CARCARANA**
24285 **LAGO TRAFUL**

● 24290 **CHAR KWEI** Pa/Fr (La Ciotat) 1965; C; 7800; 175.3 × 8 (575 × 26.4); M (Sulzer); 18; ex *Vaucluse*

1981; Lengthened 1972
Sisters:
24291 **FAWZIA** (Si) ex *Char Yeung* 1982; ex *Var* 1980
24292 **WAHEED** (Si) ex *Char Kang* 1982; ex *Vienne*
Probable sister:
24293 **SAMIRA** (Si) ex *Char Hang* 1982; ex *Velay* 1979

24300 **HAI MENG** Pa/Sw (Gotav) 1962/71; C/Con; 8200; 170.62 × 7.91 (560 × 25.95); M (Gotaverken); 16.5; ex *Emma Bakke* 1981; Lengthened and converted from cargo vessel 1971
Probably similar:
24301 **SANTOS** (Pa) ex *Gudrun Bakke* 1981

★24310 **RODINA** Ru/Pd (Polnocna) 1979; FF; 1700/2600; 85 × 6 (moulded) (278.87 × 16.96); M (Sulzer); 16; Tuna Seiner; Helicopter deck forward; **B 406** type
Sisters (Ru flag):
24311 **TIORA**
24312 **TROCHUS**
24313 **UVAROVSK**
24314 **IVAN BORZOV**
24315 **UZGORSK**
24316 **ZEMLYANSK**
24317 **GORYACHEGORSK**
24318 **YEVGENIY PREOBRAZENSKIY**
24319 **TRYDAKNA**

24340 **PALATINO** It/It (Adriatico) 1963; CP; 7000; 153.5 × 7.8 (504 × 25.9); M (Fiat); —
Sisters (It flag):
24341 **ESQUILINO**
24342 **QUIRINALE**
24343 **VIMINALE**

24350 **ELLITSA** Ma/It (Adriatico) 1956; C; 5000; 130.4 × 7.3 (428 × 24); M (Sulzer); 15; ex *Rosandra* 1982
Similar (bi-pod KP's):
24351 **ISONZO** (It)

24380 **ANDINO** Pa/Ne (Duijvendijk's) 1956; CP; 1800; 109 × 5.3 (358 × 17.6); M (Sulzer); 14.5; ex *Ana* 1980; ex *Crispin* 1974; Lengthened 1964
Sisters:
24381 **WEST POINT** (Pa) ex *Amalia* 1981; ex *Angie* 1980; ex *Cyril* 1978; ex *Sheridan* 1967
24382 **AN HING** (Va) ex *Barouk* 1982; ex *Cuthbert* 1977; ex *Spenser* 1967

24400 **MIYAJIMA MARU** Ja/Ja (Hitachi) 1953; C; 8300; 151.3 × 8.3 (496 × 27.4); M (B&W); 14.5; May be a Whale Factory Ship

24440 **KOTA SINGAPURA** Sg/Sp (UN de Levante) 1964; PC; 7700; 133.1 × 7.6 (437 × 25); M (B&W); 16; ex *Ciudad De Pamplona* 1981
Sister:
★24441 **TONG AN** (RC) ex *New Phoenix* 1983; ex *Villa de Bilbao* 1981

24450 **LAGO ALUMINE** Ar/Ar (AFNE) 1965; C; 6100; 145 × 7.5 (476 × 14.6); M (MAN); 16
Sister:
24451 **LAGO ARGENTINO** (Ar)

24470 **MARIA SOFIA** Gr/Br (J L Thompson) 1961; C; 9100; 144 × 8.6 (472 × 27.9); M (Doxford); 15; ex *Hermione* 1979; ex *Hermiston* 1970; ex *St Rosario* 1963

24480 **MEDCAPE** Gr/Br (Laing) 1962; C; 6200/8800; 144 × 8.1/9.2 (473 × 26.3/30.2); M (B&W); 15; ex *Alikrator* 1976; ex *Teakwood* 1970

24510 **REEFER QUEEN** Gr/Br (Stephen) 1962; C; 7600; 148.8 × 8.6 (488 × 28.2); M (Sulzer); 16.5; ex *Piako*
Sister:
24511 **AEGEAN SKY** (Gr) ex *Somerset*

24530 **WHITE ROSE** Gr/Be (Cockerill-Ougree) 1960; C; 6900; 156.01 × 8.05 (512 × 26.41); M (B&W); 18; ex *Vivarais* 1978

● 24540 **MASTER TONY K.** Le/De (Helsingor) 1959; C; 4100/6100; 126.9 × 7.31/8.41 (416 × 24/27.6); M (B&W); 16.5; ex *Grete Skou* 1974
Sisters:
24541 **DELFINI V** (Pa) ex *Flora V* 1980; ex *Victoria U* 1979; ex *Maria U* 1978; ex *Hanne Skou* 1974
★24542 **XIN LE** (RC) ex *Melantho C* 1981; ex *Mette Skou* 1979

★24560 **SIENKIEWICZ** Pd/De (Helsingor) 1959; CP; 5300/7700; 138.7 × 7.8/8.7 (455 × 25.7/28.7); M (B&W); 16.25
Sister:
★24561 **ZEROMSKI** (Pd)

● 24570 **CALIOPE** Pa/De (Helsingor) 1960; C; 5300/7500; 137.42 × 7.88/8.77 (451 ×

25.85/28.77); M (B&W); 15; ex *Filia* 1981; ex *Enrico Dandolo* 1977; ex *Arizona* 1967
Sisters:
24571 **AL MEDINA** (Si) ex *Kitmeer* 1981; ex *Uganda* 1980; ex *Colorado* 1968
24572 **TENACITY** (Cy) ex *Ujamaa* 1979; ex *Pennsylvania* 1969

24580 **STAR 1** Gr/De (Nakskov) 1958; CP; 4900/7100; 137.6 × 7.5/8 (452 × 24.7/26.1); M (B&W); 16; ex *El Quetzal* 1980; ex *Torm Alice*; ex *Alice Torm* 1974

24590 **SEA GULL III** Pa/No (Bergens) 1954; CP; 7000; 134.7 × 8.4 (442 × 27.7); M (B&W); 15; ex *Punta Lara* 1980; ex *Antartico* 1976; ex *Hardanger* 1969

24610 **POSEIDON C** Pa/Sw (Finnboda) 1956; C; 3600; 108.8 × 5.9 (357 × 19.5); M (Fiat); 15; ex *Riodon* 1979; ex *Drucilla U* 1975; ex *Farida* 1972

★24630 **PETAR BARON** Bu/Br (J L Thompson) 1949; C; 7400; 139.3 × 8.4 (457 × 27.7); M (Doxford); 15; ex *Alkaid* 1971; ex *Brandanger* 1965

24640 **YAT LEE** Pa/Sw (Kockums) 1950; CP; 8100; 147.7 × 8.7 (485 × 28.7); M (MAN); 17; ex *Shansi* 1977; ex *Berganger* 1969
Sister:
24641 **YAT SHING** (Pa) ex *Soochow* 1977; ex *Moldanger* 1970

24650 **FOOCHOW** Pa/Sw (Helsingborgs) 1955; PC; 2700/3900; 109 × 6/7.6 (357 × 19.8/25); M (B&W); 15; ex *Hoi Ying*

24660 **MANDARIN** Pa/Sw (Helsingborgs) 1949; PC; 2200; 104 × 5.8 (341 × 18.1); M (B&W); 14; ex *Kam Fai* 1979; ex *Affluent Country* 1976; ex *Hoi Houw* 1974

24670 **KOSMAS K** Cy/Ja (Mitsui) 1951; C; 7100; 137.95 × 8.47 (453 × 27.9); M (B&W); 12.5; ex *Magnolia* 1976; ex *Meitoku Maru* 1970

24700 **TAKIS H** Gr/Fr (La Ciotat) 1957; C; 6500; 148.95 × 7.93 (488.7 × 26.02); M (B&W); 16; ex *Si-Kiang* 1978

24720 **LOBITO** Po/Po (Viana) 1959; C; 6000; 145 × 8 (475 × 26 6); M (Doxford); 14

★24730 **HONG CHUN** RC/Br (Blythswood) 1957; C; 6900/9600; 153.6 × —/9.7 (504 × —/32); M (Doxford); 15.5; ex *Crete Sea* 1977; ex *Grecian Emblem* 1974

24760 **LAERTIS** Gr/Sw (Ekensbergs) 1959; C; 6100/9000; 147.8 × 8.2/9.1 (485 × 26.1/29.11); M (B&W); —; ex *Star Altair* 1979; ex *Vimeira* 1965; ex *Port Denison* 1965; ex *Vimeira* 1960; ex *Fair Lady*
Probable sister:
24761 **PINELOPI** (Gr) ex *Star Aldebaran*; ex *Kensington*

24780 **MAIJIN** Pa/FRG (Rickmers) 1957; C; 5200/7700; 151.19 × 7.56/8.66 (496 × 24.8/28.44); M (MAN); 15; ex *R C Rickmers* 1973

24800 **STAMATIOS G EMBIRICOS** Gr/Br (Doxford) 1956; C; 8900; 148.1 × 9.2 (486 × 29.7); M (Doxford); —
Similar:
24861 **GOLDEN SEASON** (Sg) ex *Riverbank* 1974

24870 **GEORGIA F** Gr/Br (Doxford) 1961; C; 6200/8400; 148.47 × 7.98/8.81 (487 × 26.18/28.90); M (Doxford); 14; ex *Bessie* 1980; ex *Testbank* 1978

★24880 **VLORA** Al/It (Riuniti) 1960; C; 8600; 147.7 × 9 (485 × 29.6); M (B&W); —; ex *Ilice* 1961
Sister:
★24881 **SHKODRA** (Al)

24885 **FAIR MARINE** Pa/It (Riuniti) 1955; C; 10200; 166.07 × 8.91 (544 × 29.23); M (B&W); 15; ex *Cosmos Success* 1981; ex *Tong Sing* 1978; ex *Tideo* 1976; Lengthened 1962

24890 **PERSEVERANZA** Pa/It (Riuniti) 1957; C; 8700; 147.6 × 9.1 (484 × 29); M (B&W); 15; ex *Atreo* 1979
Sister:
★24891 **VAMPO** (Al) ex *Fineo* 1969
Similar:
24892 **MOSCHA D** (Gr) ex *Argolis* 1975; ex *Azotea* 1964
★24895 **HONG QI 118** (RC) ex *Jollity* 1977; ex *Sunetna* 1964
★24896 **JIANDE** (RC) ex *Mirto* 1973
Similar (conical funnel):

24898 **SAFINA-E-REHMAT** (Pk) ex *Federico Parodi* 1965
24899 **BELLE P** (Pa) ex *Elviuba* 1981; ex *Lattuga* 1977; ex *Giorgio Parodi* 1965
Similar (bi-pod masts and 1st kingpost):
★24901 **HONG QI 132** (RC) ex *Nebulae*; ex *Nebula* 1977; ex *Albatros* 1964

★24910 **VIETNAM THUONG TIN 1.** Vn/It (Taranto) 1956; C; 6300; 148.6 × 8.1 (488 × 26.4); M (Fiat); 14.25; ex *Sonia* 1969; ex *Ville de Diego Suarez* 1965; ex *Pietro Canale* 1962

24920 **MALDIVE NEIGHBOUR** Mv/Ja (Hitachi) 1958; C; 6600/9900; 158.05 × —/9.51 (519 × —/31.20); M (B&W); 16; ex *Angeliki* 1980; ex *Jurko Topic* 1978; ex *Olga Topic* 1973

★24940 **URSA** Ys/FRG (Kroegerw) 1958; R; 1800/2900; 101.7 × —/6.8 (334 × —/22.4); M (MAN); 15.5; ex *Verdaguer* 1971

24950 **WHITE SHARK** Gr/FRG (A G 'Weser') 1952; C; 1600; 93.6 × 5.4 (307 × 17.9); M (MAN); 12; ex *Arcturus* 1976

★24960 **SALI** Ys/FRG (Flensburger) 1950; C; 2500; 88.7 × 6.3 (291 × 21); M (Krupp); 12; ex *Hector* 1960
Similar:
24961 **ALEXANDROS K** (Cy) ex *Darnley* 1976; ex *Myriam Fidelity* 1974; ex *Manolis L* 1972; ex *Nin* 1972; ex *Hercules* 1960
24962 **NEW FORMULA II** (Pa) ex *Tailiat* 1981; ex *Cheng Hsing*; ex *Ta Hung* 1976; ex *Agia Marina* 1973; ex *Hestia* 1970

★24970 **NADIR** Ys/FRG (Ottensener) 1957; C; 2900; 101.9 × 6.8 (334 × 18.1); M (MAN); —; ex *Zenit* 1973; ex *Sailor Prince* 1970; ex *Velarde* 1969

★24980 **HONG QI 144** RC/It (Ansaldo) 1941; CP; 8400; 144 × 8.2 (472 × 26.1); M (Fiat); 14; ex *Chongming* 1977; ex *Malgorzata Fornalska* 1965; ex *Guiseppe Canepa* 1955; ex *Luciano Manara* 1953

24990 **CAMPECHE** Me/Sw (Oresunds) 1954; C; 2300; 107.6 × 5.9 (353 × 19.4); M (Gotaverken); 14.75; ex *Gunvor Brovig* 1963

★25000 **CHON JIN** RC/De (B&W) 1943/47; CP; 4300; 132 × 7.8 (433 × 25.2); M (B&W); 14.5; ex *Mickiewicz* 1979; ex *Gladys Dan* 1950; ex *Helga Dan* 1947; ex *Frankenland*

25010 **ATHINAI** Gr/Ja (Iino) 1956; CP; 2900; 111.6 × 6.4 (366 × 21.2); M (MAN); 16
Sister (Gr flag):
25012 **TURKIA**

★25020 **ZHAN DOU No 28** RC/RC (Kiangnan) 1958; C; 4700; 115.5 × 6.7 (379 × 22); R (—); 12; ex *Hoping No 28*; KP abreast funnel

★25030 **HONG QI 163** RC/RC (—) 1958; C; 5000; 115.5 × 6.7 (379 × 22); R (—); 12; ex *Heping*

★25040 **ZHAN DOU No 71** RC/RC (—) 1961; C; 4700; 115.5 × 6.7 (379 × 22); R (—); 12; ex *Hoping No 71*

★25050 **ZHAN DOU No 72** RC/RC (—) 1960; C; 4700; 115.5 × 6.7 (379 × 22); R (—); 12; ex *Hoping No 72*
Sister:
★25051 **LIAO YUAN** (RC)

25070 **JETPUR VICTORY** Sg/Br (Hall, Russell) 1959; R; 5400; 117.7 × 8 (386 × 25.1); M (B&W); 13.5; ex *Maria* 1981; ex *Mimi M* 1974; ex *Eleuthera* 1971

25080 **ARIS** Cy/FRG (O&K) 1959; CP; 4500; 115.6 × 7.4 (379 × 24.1); M (Stork); 13.5; e *Vivi* 1983; ex *Antonia* 1980; ex *Annleea U* 1977; ex *Dahomeykust* 1972

25100 **CONFIDENCE** Pa/FRG (Luebecker F-W) 1957; C; 3000; 118.95 × 6.81 (390.3 × 22.34); M (Sulzer); 14.75; ex *Freiburg* 1972
Similar:
★25101 **CANG SHAN** (RC) ex *Siehting* 1977; ex *Silver Cloud* 1973; ex *Remscheid* 1971
★25102 **LAN SHAN** (RC) ex *Siehmin* 1976; ex *Omega* 1973; ex *Solingen*

25140 **ARISTO** Pa/Sp ('Elcano') 1957; CP; 2300; 105.7 × 6.1 (347 × 20.1); M (Sulzer); 16.2; ex *Ramiro Perez* 1982; ex *Torres de Cuarte* 1969
Sister:
25141 **COTTY** (Pa) ex *Juan Claudio* 1982; ex *Torres de Serranos* 1969

25170 **'HANSA'** type c1947; C; 2700; 109.6 × 6.3 (360 × 20.8); R & LPT; 11; Standard WW2 design built in occupied countries
Sisters:
25171 **PESQUERA** (Cy) ex *Messala*; ex *Leader Two*

1970; ex *P Xilas* 1969; ex *Mira* 1963; ex *Danholm* 1955; ex *Stensnaes*
25172 **KR AVINASH** (In) ex *Saint Bertrand* 1963; ex *Jacques Duroux* 1957; ex *Spiekeroog* 1947
25173 **KINGFORD** (So) ex *Henri Story* 1960
★25174 **SERPUKOV** (Ru) ex *Mekhanik Afanasiev*

25180 **LONDINON** Gr/FRG (Bremer V) 1950; C; 2700; 109.4 × 6.4 (359 × 20.1); R & LPT (Ottensener); 12; ex *Antares* 1966

★25200 **PUERTO DE VITA** Cu/Ne ('De Hoop') 1951; C; 3400; 126.1 × 7.1 (410 × 23.5); M (Sulzer); 15; ex *Equus*; ex *Pygmalion Jupiter* 1976; ex *Sovereign Sapphire* 1975; ex *Triton Ambassador* 1973; ex *Finntrader* 1970

25210 **WELL VOY No 1** Pa/FRG (Nobiskrug) 1953; C; 1600; 99.1 × 5.6 (325 × 18.2); M (MaK); 15.5; ex *Ritapoint*; ex *Wah Po*; ex *Glory Star*; ex *Shintoko Maru* 1975; ex *Expert Maru*; ex *Southern Dragon* 1973; ex *Silver Swan* 1970; ex *Baltic Importer* 1969
Sister:
25211 **MONCALVO** (It) ex *Medov Italia* 1973; ex *Baltic Trader* 1971

★25230 **SHANGHAI** RC/Be (Cockerill-Ougree) 1957; PC; 12800/13500; 170 × 8.2/8.6 (558 × 27/28.2); T (Cockerill-Ougree); 16.5; ex *Cathay*; ex *Baudouinville* 1961; May be known as **KENGH SIN**

●25240 **MEI ABETO** Pa/Fr (Saint Nazaire) 1952; PC; 12700; 163.6 × 8.5 (537 × 27.1); TSM (Sulzer); 16; ex *Louis Lumiere* 1967

25250 **LE HAVRE ABETO** Pa/Fr (La Loire) 1952; PC; 12000; 163.6 × 8.5 (537 × 27.1); TSM (Sulzer); 16; ex *Charles Tellier* 1967

25270 **EVALI** Gr/Fr (Loire Normandie) 1959; C; 7100; 140.5 × 7.93 (460.9 × 26.02); M (Sulzer); 15; ex *Tatiana* 1976
Sisters:
25271 **GEORGIOS M** (Gr) ex *Kossou* 1978; ex *Tayga* 1968
25272 **PACTOLOS** (Gr) ex *Ariadni Pa* 1980; ex *Akrou* 1977; ex *Tidra* 1973; Launched as *Timia*

●25300 **SEAWIND** Gr/FRG (Ottensener) 1957; CP; 1800/2900; 101.9 × 5.5/7.1 (334 × 18/23.3); M (MAN); 15.75; ex *Moska* 1980; ex *Baltic Express*

25320 **ARIS** Gr/FRG (LF-W) 1951; C; 2500; 92.7 × 6.1 (304 × 21); R (LF-W); 12; ex *Kormoranos*; ex *Challenger S*; ex *Ilsabe Oldendorf* 1969; ex *Herman Sauber* 1960

25340 **BAHAGIA VI** Ia/No (Moss V) 1950; C; 1100; 70 × 4.6 (230 × 15.2); R (Moss); 11.5; ex *Daya Kurnia* 1975; ex *Slidre Barat* 1973; ex *Berby* 1965

25360 **EVRIPOS EXPRESS** Gr/Br (Burntisland) 1956; Cem; 2700; 94.5 × 5.8 (310 × 18.1); M (British Polar); 11; ex *Faros* 1978; ex *Burwah*
Similar:
25361 **MACEDON** (Br)

25370 **HATI SENANG** My/Br (H Robb) 1950; C; 2500; 93.1 × 5.3 (306 × 17.5); TSM (British Polar); 9.75; ex *Kawati* 1980; ex *Kawatiri* 1972
Sisters:
25371 **BERJAYA** (My) ex *Tung Lee*; ex *Bonatrade* 1974; ex *Konui* 1969
25372 **TUNG PAO** (Pa) ex *Karana III* 1974; ex *Paladin* 1969; ex *Kaitangata* 1968

25380 **TSIN YUEN** Sg/Br (H Robb) 1953; C; 2000; 81 × 5 (266 × 16.6); M (Sulzer); 11; ex *King Luck* 1980; ex *Karamu* 1972

25430 **TIMOR CAREER** Pa/Ja (Hitachi) 1951; CP; 6800; 136.2 × 8.4 (447 × 27.7); M (Mitsubishi); 13; ex *Lucky Kingwah* 1977; ex *Green Bank* 1977; ex *Fiji Maru* 1974; ex *Gekko Maru No 2* 1964; ex *Gekko Maru* 1963

25440 **DON AMANDO** Pi/Ja (Kawasaki J) 1949; C; 3200; 98.6 × 6.4 (324 × 21); M (Ito Tekkosho); 11.5; ex *J R One* 1983; ex *Dona Paz* 1974; ex *Dona Hortencia* 1969; ex *Tomokawa Maru* 1966

25450 **ARSENIA K.** Gr/Ja (Hakodate) 1952; C; 6900; 141.5 × 7.9 (450 × 26); M (Sulzer); 14; ex *Despina A. II* 1981; ex *Goodluck* 1973; ex *Achaika Harmony* 1970; ex *Hokkai Maru* 1970

25470 **SRI THAMARACH** Th/Ja (Usuki) 1958; C; 4100; 116 × 6.9 (381 × 22.8); M (Ito Tekkosho); 11.5; ex *Kashima Maru* 1970

25480 **GOLDEN GLOBE** Pa/Br (Hall, Russell) 1957; C; 1600; 93.6 × 5.8 (307 × 19.4); M (Sulzer); 12.5; ex *Abel Tasman* 1975

25500 **OURANIO TOXO** Gr/Ne (Pot) 1953; C; 2600; 99.2 × 5.6 (326 × 18.5); M (Stork); 12.5; ex *Nikolaos G.* 1981; ex *Sofia*; ex *Margareta* 1977

★25520 **ZHAN DOU 77** RC/US (Butler) 1943; C; 1900; 78.9 × 5.5 (259 × 18); R (Prescott); 10; ex *Ho Ping 77* 1967; ex *Hansford* 1960; ex *Inchulva* 1959; ex *Elkanah Crowell* 1951; 'JEEP' type

★25540 **ZHAN DOU No 49** RC/RC (Kiangnan) 1959; C; 2400; 93.3 × 5.8 (306 × 19); R (—); 10; ex *Hoping No 49*
Similar (RC flag):
★25541 **ZHAN DOU No 65** ex *Hoping No 65*
★25542 **ZHAN DOU No 66** ex *Hoping No 66*

★25550 'KHASAN' class Ru/Fi (Crichton-Vulcan) 1954; C; 2600; 90.5 × 5.6 (295 × 18); R (Crichton-Vulcan); 10
Sisters (Ru flag):
★25551 **AMDERMA**
★25552 **ALCHEVSK**
★25553 **ARMAVIR**
★25554 **DNESTR**
★25555 **DONETS**
★25556 **DONETSK** ex *Stalino*
★25557 **IMANDRA**
★25558 **MIRGOROD**
★25559 **MOGILEV**
★25560 **PINSK**
★25561 **PRIKUMSK**
★25562 **PYATIGORSK**
★25563 **RYAZHSK** ex *Budjonnovsk*
★25564 **SLAVYANKA** ex *Voroshilovgrad*
★25565 **YENISEYSK**
★25566 **ZAPADNAYA DVINA**
(RC flag):
★25567 **HOPING ER SHI ER** ex *Runa* 1956
★25568 **HOPING ER SHI I** ex *Rita* 1955
★25569 **HOPING SAN SHI SAN** ex *Ragni* 1956
★25570 **HOPING SAN SHI I** ex *Rosita* 1956
★25571 **HOPING SHI PA** ex *Rosa* 1955
★25572 **HOPING SHI CHIU** ex *Renata* 1955

25620 **VISHVA NIDHI** In/In (Hindustan) 1961; CP; 6200; 155.2 × 7.8 (509 × 25.9); M (MAN); 17
Similar (In flag):
25621 **STATE OF RAJASTHAN**
25622 **STATE OF UTTAR PRADESH**

25640 **SONORA** Me/De (Helsingor) 1955; CP; 3300; 121.3 × 6.4 (398 × 21.1); M (B&W); 16; ex *Gina Maria* 1977; ex *Corneville* 1971

●★25650 **PEIKIANG** RC/De (Helsingor) 1958; C; 3200/5200; 122.7 × 6.6/7.4 (403 × 21.1/24.4); M (B&W); 16; ex *Titania* 1971; ex *Crestville* 1961

25660 **MINA** Si/FRG (Rhein Nordseew) 1959; C; 6800/9400; 154.9×8/9 (508 26.3/29.9); M (MAN); 15.5; ex *Almina* 1982; ex *New Sea Pioneer* 1982; ex *Sea Pioneer* 1976; ex *Ariel* 1972; ex *Ariana* 1966

25690 **PAZ** Pa/Be (Cockerill-Ougree) 1960; CP; 6400/9200; 147.1 × 6.4/9.3 (483 × 21/29.1); M (Sulzer); 14; ex *Montalto*

●25700 **ROSARIO DOS** Pa/Be (Cockerill-Ougree) 1958; C; 6200/8900; 147.12 × 8.28/9.27 (483 × 27/32); M (Sulzer); 13; ex *Mobeka*
Sisters:
25703 **LORETO** (Pa) ex *Mokoto*
25704 **GOOD WARRIOR** (Gr) ex *Swazi Warrior* 1980; ex *Moliro* 1978
★25705 **HYANG SAN** (RK) ex *Good Fighter* 1980; ex *Mokambo*
25706 **ASIA PALHO** (Ko) ex *Okito* 1980; ex *Joseph Okito* 1975; ex *Congo Moko* 1967
25707 **SAMBOW CHAMPION** (Ko) ex *Asia Guho* 1981; ex *Mpolo*; ex *Maurice Mpolo* 1976; ex *Congo Zolo* 1967

25710 **KOUKOUNARIES K** Gr/FRG (Kieler H) 1958; C; 9900; 157.2 × 9.1 (516 × 29.9); M (MAN); 15.75; ex *Aliakmon Breeze* 1981; ex *Belinda* 1969

25720 **SPYROS G** Gr/Br (J L Thompson) 1963; C; 7700/10700; 155.6 × 8/8.9 (510 26.1/29.4); M (Doxford); —; ex *Pleias* 1981; ex *Silverleaf* 1968

25730 **JALAGIRIJA** In/Br (Laing) 1963; C; 10700; 155.6 × 9.2 (510 × 30); M (B&W); 15.5; ex *Rosewood* 1968

25740 **STELITSA** Gr/Br (Doxford) 1955; C; 8000; 141.5 × 8.4 (464 × 26.11); M (Doxford); 15; ex *Osia Irini Chrysovalandou* 1979; ex *Georgetta* 1975; ex *Ellispontos* 1967

25750 **FORTUNE VICTORY** Pa/Hong Kong (Taikoo) 1959; C; 4000/5700; 128.7 × 6.9/7.5 (422 × 22.8/24.8); M (Doxford); —; ex *Orient Victory* 1976; ex *Kweichow* 1974; ex *Norman* 1968; ex *Kweichow* 1966
Similar:
25751 **WAYFUL** (Pa) ex *California* 1983; ex *Kwangtung* 1978; ex *Norman* 1966; ex *Kwangtung* 1965
25752 **STRAITS STAR** (Sg) ex *Bangkok Star*; ex *New*

Guinea Chief 1977; ex *Kwangsi* 1971

25770 **JALADURGA** In/FRG (LF-W) 1960; C; 6300/9200; 154 × 7.8/9.2 (505 × 25.7/30); M (MAN); 17

25771 **VISHVA BHAKTI** In/In (Hindustan) 1968; C; 6400/9300; 154.13 × 7.77/9.22 (506 × 25.49/30.25); M (Sulzer); 14
Sisters:
25772 **VISHVA SHOBHA** (In)
25773 **VISHVA SHAKTI** (In)
25774 **VISHVA SIDDHI** (In)
25775 **VISHVA DHARMA** (In)
25776 **VISHVA VIKRAM** (In)
25777 **BANGLAR SAMPAD** (Bh) ex *Vishva Darshan* 1973
Possible sister (may have kingpost forward):
25778 **VISHVA NAYAK** (In)

25780 **VISHVA JYOTI** In/FRG (LF-W) 1959; C; 6200/9200; 154 × 7.8/9.2 (505 × 25.7/30); M (MAN); 17; ex *Jala Vishva Jyoti* 1961; ex *Vishva Jyoti* 1961
Sisters (In flag):
25782 **VISHVA MANGAL**
25783 **VISHVA MAYA**
25784 **STATE OF PUNJAB**
(Bh flag):
25785 **BANGLAR DOOT** ex *Vishva Prem* 1972
(Rm flag):
★25786 **VRANCEA** ex *Vishva Shanti* 1972

25790 **NELIA** Pa/Sw (Oresunds) 1955; CP; 5100; 140.5 × 7.8 (461 × 25.7); M (Gotaverken); 15.5; ex *Santa Lucia II* 1978; ex *Lars Meling*; ex *Hoegh Meling* 1977; ex *Lars Meling* 1969

25800 **PANAGIOTIS XILAS** Gr/FRG (Howaldts) 1958; C; 6200/8800; 151.31 × —/9.07 (496 × —/29.75); M (MAN); 15; ex *Isapostoloi* 1973; ex *Diamantis Pateras* 1972

25810 **VICTORIA U** Li/FRG (Howaldts) 1960; C; 6000/8900; 149.41 × —/9.15 (490× —/30.02); M (MAN); 15; ex *Pishtaz Iran* 1979; ex *Rotte* 1975

★25830 **YOU YI** RC/RC (—) 1959; C; 4900; 116.4 × 6.7 (382 × 22); R (—); 12

★25840 **SEVERODVINSK** Ru/Pd (Gdanska) 1958; FF; 10000; 155 × 8.2 (510 × 26.11); TSR & LPT ('Zgoda'); 14.5; 'B-62' type
Sisters (Ru flag):
★25841 **ARMAN**
★25842 **CHUKOTKO**
★25843 **IVAN FEDEROV**
★25844 **JOHANNES VARES**
★25845 **PECHENGA**
★25846 **RIGA**
★25847 **SOVIETSKAYA KAMCHATKA**
★25848 **SOVIETSKAYA SAKHALIN**
★25849 **SOVIETSKAYA LITVA**
★25850 **SVIATOGOR**

25860 **IONIAN MOON** Ma/FRG (B+V) 1961; CP; 3400/5400; 126.3 × 6.8/7.8 (414 × 22.3/25.9); M (MAN); 16.5; ex *Ionian Beach* 1983; ex *Omega Kassos* 1983; ex *Viktoria Roth*; ex *Mailand* 1973
Sisters:
25861 **MAH II** (Th) ex *Poros Island* 1980; ex *Tunis* 1974
25862 **MAHARASHMI** (In) ex *Madrid* 1974; ex *Sloman Madrid*
Similar:
25863 **EMIRATES EXPRESS** (UAE) ex *Skipper* 1983; ex *Gazia D* 1982; ex *Helena*; ex *Acapulco* 1970

25870 **DANAI** Th/Ne (Jan Smit) 1954; CP; 3400; 118.4 × 6.4 (388 × 21); M (Stork); 13.5; ex *Pichit Samut* 1982; ex *Beninkust*
Sister:
25871 **YACU TAITO** (Pe) ex *Universe* 1974; ex *Camerounkust* 1969

●25880 **LEFKADIAN SKY** Gr/Ne (Arnhemsche) 1960; CP; 4500; 113.9 × 7.1 (390 × 22.1); M (Werkspoor); 14; ex *Sounion* 1980; ex *Akra Sounion* 1979; ex *Liberiakust* 1971
Sister:
25881 **CEYOCEAN** (Sr) ex *Datsun* 1981; ex *Rion* 1981; ex *Akra Rion* 1979; ex *Togokust* 1971

25890 **LEO STAR** Sg/FRG (O&K) 1958; C; 3100/5200; 120.91 × 6.63/7.90 (397 × 21.75/25.92); M (MAN); 14; ex *Marburg* 1974

25900 **ORBIT** Pa/FRG (B+V) 1961; C; 3100/4800; 121.2 × 6.8/7.8 (380 × 22.3/25.9); M (MAN); 16; ex *Dalia D* 1983; ex *Najade* 1981
Sister:
25901 **ATHENS SEA** (Cy) ex *Nereus* 1976

25930 **GENEVE** Sd/Ys ('3 Maj') 1960; C; 6400/9300; 152.9 × 8.1/9 (502 × 26.7/29.8); M (Sulzer); —

★25950 **NING HUA** RC/Sw (Gotav) 1958; C; 6300/9400; 149 × 9 (449 × 29.6); M (Gotaverken); 15; ex *New East Sea* 1976; ex *East Sea* 1972; ex *Vingrom* 1967
Sister:
25951 **SAI JONG** (Ko) ex *Longta* 1965; ex *Vinni* 1964
Similar:
★25952 **TANGSHAN** (RC) ex *Varda* 1966

25960 **RAW LINES 1** Le/Sw (Kockums) 1952; C; 1900; 98.1 × 5.9 (322 × 19.3); M (MAN); 14; ex *Eurabia Wind* 1980; ex *Kap Arkona* 1975; ex *Ingrid Gorthon* 1966

★25980 **HONG QI No 108** RC/Br (Hamilton) 1960; C; 7000/8700; 150×8.2/9 (490×26.9/29.6); T (Rowan); 17.5; ex *Yungming* 1975; ex *Humi Nasita* 1973; ex *Malancha* 1971; ex *Alaunia* 1969
Sister:
★25981 **HONG QI No 107** (RC) ex *Yungjian* 1975; ex *Humi Mahis* 1973; ex *Macharda* 1971; ex *Andania* 1969

25990 **HERMION** No/Ne (Neder;andsche) 1959; CP; 9500; 155.9 × 8.8 (511 × 28.9); M (Stork); 17.5; ex *Hoyanger* 1974; Side doors

26000 **GENERAL PAEZ** Ve/Sw (Kockums) 1958; C; 9700; 151.6 × 9.3 (497 × 30.7); M (MAN); 15; ex *Hosanger* 1976

26010 **GLOBAL MED** Li/Br (H&W) 1962; C; 6300/8600; 147.33 $ 7.98/8.91 (483 × 26.18/29.23); M (H&W); 15; ex *Terrie U* 1980; ex *Global Med* 1978; ex *Springbank* 1978

●26040 **GEMAR** Ia/FRG (Emden) 1955; C; 5300; 143.7 × 7.6 (471 × 24.11); M (MAN); 13.25; ex *Geert Howaldt* 1972

26050 **ZIYA KALKAVAN II** Tu/No (Moss V) 1951; C; 3700; 102.8 × 7.41 (337.3 × 24.31); R (Moss); 12; ex *S. Manioglu* 1979; ex *Kirsehir* 1977; ex *Bonita* 1953

★26060 **YONG KANG** RC/No (Moss V) 1960; C; 2500/3800; 102.1 × 6.06/7.46 (335 × 19.88/24.48); M (B&W); 14; ex *Hengshan* 1977; ex *Beaverelm* 1971; ex *Roga* 1962
Similar:
★26062 **YUHAI** (RC) ex *Mounthwa*; ex *Snefjeld* 1967
★26064 **MULDE** (DDR) ex *Sunima* 1965

26070 **SNOWFROST** Gr/De (Aalborg) 1963; R; 2400; 106.9 × 5.8 (351 × 18.2); M (B&W); 15.5; ex *Frio Dolphin* 1979; ex *Kalimantan Fortune*; ex *C. Joyce* 1976; ex *Petunia* 1974
Sister:
26071 **ALGILANI** (In) ex *C. Ranee* 1976; ex *Magnolia* 1974

26080 **DONG MYUNG** Ko/FRG (Flensburger) 1955; CP; 8700; 143.5 × 8.6 (471 × 28.2); M (MAN); 13; ex *Nordstern* 1965
Similar:
26081 **NORDWIND** (FRG)
26082 **BREMEN** (Pa) ex *Nordland* 1970

●26100 **IONIAN VICTORY** Ma/FRG (Emden) 1954; C; 8200; 144.3 × 8.8 (473 × 29); M (MAN); 13; ex *Agios Gerassimos* 1982; ex *River Rose* 1976; ex *Progressus* 1974; ex *President* 1974; ex *Probitas* 1972; ex *Nefeli* 1970; ex *Widar* 1967
Similar:
26101 **CAMELIA** (Cy) ex *Bello F.* 1969; ex *Baldur* 1965
26102 **THREE OCEAN** (Ko) ex *Namyang Dragon* 1980; ex *Aegir* 1965
Similar (bi-pod masts):
26104 **BRAVO LUIS** (Gr) ex *Luis* 1977; ex *Hodur* 1971

●26110 **IONIAN SEA** Ma/FRG (Emden) 1952; C; 7300; 143.7 × 7.6 (471 × 24.1); M (MAN); 12.5; ex *Nikolaos A.* 1982; ex *Annrose* 1975; ex *Breeze* 1973; ex *Wildrose* 1973; ex *Francisca Hendrik Fisser* 1968
Similar (with mast houses):
26113 **AIS GIORGIS** (Gr) ex *Aghios Nectarios* 1980; ex *Splendor* 1976; ex *Primrose* 1973; ex *Karen Reed* 1968

★26140 **RYTTERHOLM** RC/US (Pennsylvania) 1943; C; 5200; 125.69 × 7.56 (412 × 24.80); M (Nordberg); 13.5; ex *Strom Forest* 1970; ex *Sunrose* 1970; ex *Alf Lindeberg* 1954; ex *Cape North* 1943; 'C 1' type

26170 **DAVAO CITY** Pi/De (Frederikshavn) 1956; PC; 1500; 89.3 × 5.7 (293 × 18.8); M (B&W); 12; ex *Tagbilaran City* 1972; ex *Bellona* 1972; Probably has more superstructure decks

26180 **OBA** Pa/No (Trondhjems) 1951; CP; 3000; 98.7 × 6.9 (324 × 17.7); M (Sulzer); 13; ex *Elloba* 1981; ex *Blue Sky* 1980; ex *Nia* 1977; ex *Rita V* 1970; ex *Masuna V* 1966; ex *Geffen* 1965; ex *Mim* 1952

26200 **AL QASEEM** Si/Fr (Loire-Normandie) 1957; R; 2800; 115.5 × 5.8 (379 × 19.1); M (B&W); 16; ex *Bambara* 1973

26210 **KHALIJ SKY** Pa/Fr (Loire-Normandie) 1960; C; 4900; 114.94 × 6 (377.1 × 19.69); M (Pielstick); 18; ex *Tarpon* 1978
Sister:
26211 **MORFREEZE** (Pa) ex *Opaline Bay* 1982; ex *Lethe* 1980; ex *Espadon* 1977

★26220 **SOVIETSKAYA ARKTIKA** Ru/Br (Short Bros) 1951; R; 9000; 140.6 × 7 (461 × 26); M (Doxford); 12; ex *Stanhope* 1954

26250 **FOOCHOW** Pa/Sw (Helsingborgs) 1955; PC; 2700/3900; 108.9×6/7 (357×19.8/22.11); M (B&W); 15; ex *Hoi Ying* 1981

26270 **MANDARIN** Pa/Sw (Helsingborgs) 1949; PC; 2200; 104 × 5.7 (341 × 18.1); M (B&W); 14; ex *Kam Fai* 1979; ex *Affluent Country* 1976; ex *Hoi Houw* 1974

26280 **IONIAN GLORY** Ma/De (B&W) 1955; CP; 5700; 120.1 × 7.4 (394 × 24.5); M (B&W); 14.25; ex *Cefallonian Glory* 1982; ex *Uckermark*; ex *Lotte Skou* 1964

26300 **NAVIKAPOL** Pa/Sw (Uddevalla) 1954; CP; 4200; 132.2 × 7.7 (434 × 25.7); M (Uddevalla); 18; ex *Lindenstein* 1976; ex *Clary Thorden* 1965

★26320 **CIKAT** Ys/Ys ('3 Maj') 1954; C; 3100; 119.4 × 6.7 (392 × 22); M (Sulzer); 16; ex *Triglav* 1980
Sisters (Ys flag):
★26321 **SELCE** ex *Lovcen* 1982
★26322 **DOLFIN** ex *Velebit* 1980

26330 **AL FARY** UAE/Sw (Oresunds) 1947; C; 2200; 106.7 × 5.9 (350 × 19.3); M (Gotaverken); 14.5; ex *Dynamic 1* 1982; ex *Olympios Apollon* 1979; ex *Ambelos*; ex *Bengazi* 1968

26350 **LI SHAN** Pa/FRG (Deutsche Werft) 1958; C; 3900; 143.19 × 6.58 (470 × 21.59); M (MAN); 16.5; ex *Hornstern* 1975

26370 **POSEIDON C** Pa/Sw (Finnboda) 1956; C; 3600; 108.82 × 5.92 (357 × 19.5); M (Fiat); 15; ex *Riodon* 1979; ex *Drucilla U* 1975; ex *Farida* 1972

26410 **IONIAN WIND** Ma/De (B&W) 1943; CP; 3800; 117.7 × 7.4 (386 × 24); M (B&W); 13.5; ex *Eleni A* 1982; ex *Hugo Kollataj* 1975; ex *Benny Skou*

26430 **RIO SAN JUAN** Ar/De (Nakskov) 1936; R; 2300; 108 × 5.8 (354 × 18.11); M (B&W); 12; ex *American Reefer* 1942

● 26440 **SPAN** Ma/Br (Blythswood) 1958; C; 10700; 159.1 × 9.5 (522 × 31.1); M (Doxford); —; ex *Athina* 1983; ex *North Countess* 1979

★26450 **JOSE ANTONIO ECHEVARRIA** Cu/Fr (Worms) 1949; CP; 9100; 142.4 × 8.9 (480 × 29.1); M (Sulzer); 17; ex *Ville* 1970; ex *Ville de Tamatave* 1970

★26470 **FOSHAN** RC/Fr (Mediterranee) 1949; C; 5100; 129.5 × 7.3 (425 × 23.11); T (Mediterranee); 13.5; ex *Julius Fucik* 1965; ex *Volta* 1954

26480 **MING UNITY** Tw/Ja (Nipponkai) 1957; C; 7300; 132.2 × 8.6 (434 × 28.3); M (Sulzer); 14.5; ex *Yunn Ming* 1977; ex *Hai Min* 1963

26490 **ZAK** Pa/Br (Readhead) 1962; C; 7300/10000; 154.9 × 8.3/9.3 (508 × 27.3/30.6); M (Sulzer); 15; ex *Strathtay*; ex *Trebartha* 1975
Sister:
26491 **EVIA** (Gr) ex *Strathteviot*; ex *Trefusis* 1975

26500 **LENDOUDIS EVANGELOS** Gr/Br (Hamilton) 1961; C; 6300/8600; 148.7 × 8.2/8.9 (488 × 26.5/29.4); M (Sulzer); —; ex *Trevalgan* 1978

★26520 **DANJIANG** RC/Fr (La Seine) 1957; CP; 5800/8000; 145.4 × 7.9/8.7 (477 × 26/28.5); M (B&W); 16; ex *Ville De Dunkerque* 1976
Sister:
★26521 **LIU KIANG** (RC) ex *Ville De Rouen* 1976
Similar:
26522 **PROFITIS ELIAS** (Gr) ex *Guyane* 1976; ex *Ville De Djibouti* 1965

26530 **EUROPEAN MARCHIONESS** Ma/Ne (Vuyk) 1959; C; 8600; 145.60 × 8.71 (478 × 28.58); M (Sulzer); —; ex *North Marchioness* 1979

● 26570 **MAYSUN II** Gr/FRG (LF-W) 1958; C; 5700; 151.7 × 7.6 (498 × 25.1); M (MAN); 12.75; ex *Bonita 1* 1981; ex *Emar* 1980; ex *Efor* 1977; ex *Providentia* 1974; ex *Karpfanger* 1970
Sister:
26571 **MIGHTY BREEZE** (Pa) ex *Palmyra* 1980; ex *Kersten Miles* 1971
Similar:
26572 **PEARL CITY** (Pa) ex *Calypso N.* 1980; ex

Simon Von Utrecht 1971

26600 **BYZANTINE MONARCH** Gr/Br (Bartram) 1959; C; 9400; 152.2 × 9.5 (500 × 31.2); M (B&W); 13.75; ex *Scottish Monarch* 1968

26630 **ELLI** Gr/FRG (Rhein Nordseew) 1958; CP; 6400; 144.3 × 7.9 (473 × 25.11); M (MAN); 12.5; ex *Machiavelli* 1980; ex *Alfred Theodor* 1979

26650 **GAY FIDELITY** Gr/FRG (LF-W) 1956; C; 5600/8200; 149.4 × 8.2/9 (490 × 26.1/29.6); M (Howaldts); 15; ex *Catharina Oldendorff* 1974

26660 **JUVENA** Gr/FRG (Deutsche Werft) 1956; CP; 4900; 138.9 × 7.6 (456 × 25); M (MAN); 15.25; ex *Ubena* 1977
Sister:
26661 **SAPLA** (Bh) ex *Blue Tiger* 1980; ex *Doctor Lello* 1976; ex *Usaramo* 1974

26670 **EASTERN NAV** Pa/Ja (Mitsubishi HI) 1957; C; 6500/9400; 148.5 × — (487 × —); M (Sulzer); 14; ex *Eastar* 1979; ex *Skarva* 1973; ex *Edda* 1964
Sisters:
26672 **KUSU ISLAND** (Sg) ex *Bolmaren*; ex *Artemedi III* 1975; ex *Sefra* 1975; ex *Cape of Good Hope* 1961
26673 **AMAR** (Gr) ex *E.D. Papalios*
26674 **PROMETHEUS** (Gr) ex *Ocean Prosper* 1968; ex *Surna* 1965; ex *Cape Agulhas* 1961; ex *Sira* 1975
26675 **NELSON** (Ma) ex *Theanto A S* 1984; ex *Polaris* 1970

● 26680 **SANTA CLAUS** Pa/Sw (Eriksbergs) 1957; CP; 9000; 145 × 9.3 (476 × 29.3); M (B&W); 15.25; ex *San Nicolaos* 1984; ex *Capto* 1968

● 26700 **ALKMINI A** Gr/Sw (Eriksbergs) 1957; C; 6400/8900; 144.99 × 8.03/9.35 (475.69 × 26.35/30.68); M (B&W); 14.5; ex *Stella* 1982; ex *Sunpolynesia* 1971

★26710 **TAISHAN** RC/Sw (Oresunds) 1957; CP; 2700/4400; 112.5 × 6.4/7.5 (369 × 20.9/24.7); M (Gotaverken); 13; ex *Nordica* 1968

● 26720 **TACAMAR VI** Pa/Fr (France-Gironde) 1961; C; 11000; 158 × 9.6 (518 × 30.9); M (B&W); 15.5; ex *Tepuy* 1980; ex *Antonios Coulouthros*

★26730 **LONGHUA** RC/Sw (Eriksbergs) 1959; C; 8800; 145 × 9.4 (476 × 30.1); M (B&W); 14; ex *Bibo* 1975; ex *Aristokratis* 1974; ex *Kollbjorg* 1969
Sister:
26731 **VITASEA** (Gr) ex *Aristovoulos* 1975; ex *Kollgrim* 1970

26740 **YZONA** Cy/Sw (Oresunds) 1952; C; 3300; 103.7 × 6.5 (340 × 21.4); M (Gotaverken); 13; ex *Seabreeze* 1973; ex *Norma* 1968; ex *Norinda* 1963

26750 **IONIAN SKY** Ma/FRG (Deutsche Werft) 1951; CP; 3800; 131.6 × 6.6 (432 × 21.7); M (MAN); 13.5; ex *Agia Efimia* 1982; ex *Euna* 1976; ex *Anita* 1972
Similar:
26751 **BENGUELA CURRENT** (Li) ex *Balkan*
26753 **LONGTIME** (Pa) ex *Lucedy* 1976; ex *Natal D* 1972; ex *Natal* 1969

26760 **UNISON II** Sg/Ne ('De Merwede') 1955/60; C; 2000; 92.97 × 5.44 (305 × 17.1); M (Werkspoor); 12.5; ex *Hong Eng* 1981; ex *Atlantic Klif* 1974; ex *Prins Casimir* 1967; Lengthened 1960
Sister:
26761 **ARAXOS** (Gr) ex *Marinos* 1973; ex *Mina* 1971; ex *Gaelic Prince* 1970; ex *Mina* 1969; ex *Prins Willem V* 1967

● 26770 **BARAO DE JACEGUAY** Bz/Bz (Maua) 1963; C; 3600/5000; 116.7 × —/7.1 (383 × —/23.3); M (MAN); 12.5
Sister (Bz flag):
26771 **BARAO DO RIO BRANCO**

★26800 **GUANG PING** RC/FRG (A G 'Weser') 1958; C; 9300; 153.7 × 9.3 (504 × 30.5); M (MAN); —; ex *Mirtoan Sea* 1976; ex *Dimitra* 1973; ex *Continental Merchant* 1969; ex *Otterburn* 1966; ex *Continental Carrier* 1962
Sisters:
26801 **AGRILIA** (Pa) ex *Santiago* 1981; ex *Continental Pioneer* 1968
26803 **STATE OF MAHARASHTRA** (In) ex *Oregon Leader* 1960; ex *Continental Leader*

★26810 **HONG QI 138** RC/FRG (A G 'Weser') 1957; C; 9500; 153.7 × 9 (504 × 29.7); M (MAN); 15; ex *New Sapphire* 1980; ex *Sapphire* 1976; ex *Sparto* 1970; ex *Captantonis* 1963
Similar:
26811 **ZEENA** (Pa) ex *Kyrakatingo* 1973
26812 **VARUNA ADHAR** (In) ex *Lok Adhar* 1979; ex *Hooghly*; ex *Dimitris*

26830 **AL HASAN** Pk/FRG (A G 'Weser') 1958; C; 9200; 153.7 × 9.3 (504 × 30.2); M (MAN); 15; ex

Helga Schroder 1965

● 26840 **AIS GIORGIS** Gr/FRG (Emden) 1955; C; 5800; 143.7 × 7.60 (471.5 × 24.93); M (MAN); 13; ex *Aghios Nectarios* 1980; ex *Splendor* 1976; ex *Primrose* 1973; ex *Karen Reed* 1973

26850 **GORGO** Gr/De (Nakskov) 1958; C; 5000/7100; 140 × 7.9/8.3 (459 × 26/27.4); M (B&W); 16.5; ex *Nordholm* 1974

26870 **MICHAEL** Ma/FRG (Flensburger) 1956; C; 6100; 147.9 × 8.02 (485 × 26.31); M (MAN); 13.75; ex *Otira* 1982; ex *Aliartos* 1982; ex *Hinrich Oldendorff* 1974

26880 **AGIA VARVARA** Gr/Br (Scotts' SB) 1958; C; 9400; 152.79 × 9.39 (501 × 30.81); M (Doxford); 14.5; ex *Arma* 1976; ex *Lord Codrington* 1968

● 26890 **MOFARRIJ 1** Si/FRG (Deutsche Werft) 1953; CP; 3600; 131.8 × 6.6 (432 × 21.6); M (MAN); 13; ex *Interharmony* 1982; ex *Blue Albacore* 1980; ex *Hornberg* 1971

★26920 **HONG QI 135** RC/De (B&W) 1945; C; 5000; 134.3 × 7.8 (442 × 25.7); M (B&W); 13; ex *Song Jiang*; ex *Pokoj* 1966; ex *Dansborg* 1951

26940 **PRIMERO DE JUNIO** Me/Sp (Euskalduna) 1959; P/TS (Troopship); 6800; 130.8 × 6.9 (429 × 22.6); M (Sulzer); 17; ex *Monte Anaga* 1974; Mexican Navy

26950 **KASTRO K** Gr/Br (Cammell Laird) 1954; C; 6000; 143.1 × 8.2 (470 × 27.1); M (Sulzer); 13; ex *Iris* 1981; ex *Doris* 1973

26970 **PRIAMOS** Cy/Sw (Gotaverken) 1945; C; 5800; 144.6 × 7.8 (474 × 25.8); M (B&W); 16.75; ex *Amphitrite* 1972; ex *Wangaratta* 1967

● 26980 **NORTH WAVE** Gr/Br (Lithgows) 1954; C; 7800; 138.64 × 8.29 (454.8 × 27.2); M (Doxford); 11; ex *Aegean Navigator* 1977; ex *Laurice Fidelity* 1974; ex *Humanity* 1973; ex *Deuterornis* 1971; ex *Dunster* 1969; ex *Temple Lane* 1968
Sister:
26981 **IRINI** (Gr) ex *Temple Main* 1969

● 26990 **PACIFICO** Ec/Pd (Gdanska) 1950/53; C; 2700; 114.08 × 6.20 (374.3 × 20.34); M (Sulzer); 14; ex *Kopernik* 1977; ex *Lodz* 1953
'B50' type
Sister:
26991 **VASSILIKI** (Gr) ex *Nova Huta* 1976; Launched as *Warszawa*

27010 **BLUE PEARL** Pa/Br (Short Bros) 1952; C; 6000; 144.1 × 7.9 (473 × 25.9); M (B&W); 12; ex *Yannis* 1974; ex *Ashoka Jayanti* 1970; ex *Barrington Court* 1963

27050 **GALATIA** Li/Ja (Mitsubishi HI) 1956; C; 6400/9500; 148.5 × —/9.5 (487 × —/30.6); M (Sulzer); 13.5

★27070 **CONRADO BENITEZ** Cu/Ca (Burrard DD) 1947; C; 6700; 133.1 × 8.6 (437 × 28.3); M (Doxford); 15; ex *Ciudad de Montreal* 1962; ex *Canadian Constructor* 1962

27130 **MMP WISDOM** In/FRG (O&K) 1958; C; 3900; 109.1 × 6.9 (358 × 22.1); R & LPT (Christiansen & Meyer); 12.5; ex *Starlight Splendour* 1982; ex *Lasbek* 1971

27140 **MED TRADER** Cy/FRG (O&K) 1956; C; 2500/3900. 109.3 × —/6.29 (358 × —/22.1); M (Christiansen & Meyer); 12.5; ex *Margo Transoceanic* 1978; ex *Christiana* 1974; ex *Eilbek* 1971

27150 **INTERAMICITY** Gr/FRG (Deutsche Werft) 1951; CP; 3600; 131.7 × 6.6 (432 × 21.6); M (MAN); 13; ex *Blue Marlin* 1979; ex *Hornsund* 1969

27190 **RAINFROST** Gr/Ne (Nederlandsche) 1960; R; 4800; 120.4 × 7.2 (395 × 23.6); M (Gotaverken); 18.25; ex *Victor* 1980; ex *Mungo* 1977

27200 **SAN JOSE** Pi/No (Bergens) 1948; CP; 1300; 84.7 × 4.8 (278 × 15.8); M (Sulzer); 12; ex *Fanafjord* 1971; ex *Delfinus* 1970; Lengthened 1962
Similar:
27201 **CORAL** (Cy) ex *Citta Di Marsiglia*; ex *Canopus* 1965

27210 **ABOABO** Gh/No (Tangen) 1965; ST; 1500; 70.6 × 4.8 (232 × 15.9); M (B&W); —
Sisters (Gh flag):
27211 **AGYIMFRA**
27212 **ADA**
27213 **ASUBONE**
27214 **CHECHEKU**
27215 **FANOMA**
27216 **SHAMA**
(Is flag):
27217 **AZGAD III**

27230 JOHN P Gr/Ne ('De Biesbosch') 1953; C; 2500; 112.50 × 6.66 (369 × 21.85); M (MAN); 13.5; ex Panorea 1976; ex Finnbirch 1973; ex Martti Ragnar 1959

27245 FELIPE II Pa/Ys ('Jozo Lozovina-Mosor') 1966; C; 2300; 121.16 × 6.27 (398 × 20.57); M (B&W); 15; ex Francisca; ex Guania 1975; ex Francisco Miguel 1974; ex Bol 1970; Lengthened 1968
Sister:
27246 NIARCHOS (Ho) ex Alanje 1984; ex Castilla 1983; ex Mitu 1975; ex Felipe 1974; ex Solin 1970

27290 KASSOS Cy/FRG (A G 'Weser') 1953; C; 2600; 115.6 × 6.35 (379 × 20.83); 14; ex Algenib 1962

27310 KALIA Cy/FRG (Luebecker F-W) 1952; C; 2800; 115.6 × 6.32 (379 × 20.73); M (Waggon); 13; ex Medsky 1979; ex Roland Russ 1976
Sister:
27311 SANTA KATERINA (Pa) ex Cairo 1967

27330 FARIDPUR Bh/Ne ('De Beer') 1959; C; 3200/4700; 117.5 × —/7.7 (385 × —/25.1); M (MAN); 14; ex Madhumati 1973; ex Mary Nubel 1968

★**27350 VIRPAZAR** Ys/FRG (LF-W) 1951; C; 5300; 146.92 × 7.68 (482 × 25.2); M (MAN); 12; ex Captain Ottavio 1974; ex Klaus Schoke 1971

27360 SIULI Bh/FRG (O&K) 1953; CP; 2800; 110.4 × 6.5 (362 × 21.4); M (Sulzer); 14; ex Cordillera; ex Naumberg 1969
Sister:
27361 NAGINA TRADER (UAE) ex Albadr 1982; ex Bulsook 1980; ex Jane Phoenix 1973; ex Weissenburg 1971

27370 OCEAN GLORY Cy/FRG (Howaldts) 1951; C; 2500/4000; 100 × —/7.1 (328 × —/23.4); M (MAN); 12.5; ex Dennis B 1978; ex Rigoleto 1978; ex Dennis B 1976; ex Mirya 1974; ex Merak 1973; ex Beate Bolten 1967; ex Bochum 1960; ex Ernst Blumenfeld 1959

27400 MINIMO Pa/FRG (Kieler H) 1961; CP; 2600/3700; 108.4 × 6.3/7.4 (356 × 20.67/24.1); M (MAN); 14; ex Byblos; ex Ratzeburg 1972
Similar (taller funnel):
★**27401 PAN LONG** (RC) ex Fresenburg 1982
Similar (boats on deck):
27401 YACA RUNA (Pe) ex Vesta 1972; ex Armin Russ 1967; ex Stubbenhuk 1964

27410 SEA RENOWN Pa/FRG (Emden) 1953; C; 3400/4800; 121.5 × 6.4/7.4 (399 × 21.1/24.2); M (KHD); 12.5; ex Aspassia M 1980; ex Ernst Mittmann 1972; ex Bornheim 1965

27430 ASTRONAFTIS Gr/No (Pusnaes) 1960; C; 2500/3900; 108.2 × 6.3/7.5 (355 × 20.8/24.8); M (Gotaverken); 14.5; ex Sundove 1969; ex Spurt 1965; ex Mabella 1963

27440 SCAPLAKE Gr/Ne (Jan Smit) 1953; C; 3900; 126 × 7.1 (413 × 23.4); M (Sulzer); 15; ex Gina 1971; ex Finnpulp 1968

★**27460 RABA** Hu/FRG (O&K) 1951; C; 2700; 110.39 × 6.42 (362 × 21.2); M (MAN); 14; ex Duisburg 1971

27480 WANG No. 1 Th/FRG (Ottensener) 1958; CP; 5800; 129.1 × 8.1 (424 × 26.5); M (Ottensener); 14.5; ex Happy Willing 1983; ex Kitsa S 1980; ex Leanna 1972; ex Danholm 1965

27490 EASTERN STAR Sg/Sw (Svendborg) 1958; CP; 3200; 104.8 × 6.8 (344 × 22.6); M (B&W); —; ex Joo Chuan 1980; ex Crystal 1979; ex Aase Nielsen 1972

★**27520 DUNA** Hu/FRG (Howaldts) 1951; CP; 2400; 102.2 × 6.3 (312 × 20.8); M (MAN); 12.5; ex Elisabeth Bornhofen 1970
Sister:
27521 FLAMINGO (Gr) ex Nordlander 1974; ex Karl Grammerstorf 1968

27540 DONA LOLITA Ho/FRG (Deutsche Werft) 1952; CP; 2700; 111 × 6.7 (365 × 22); M (MAN); 14; ex Arizona 1975; ex El Gavilan 1973; ex El Cafetero 1970

27560 NEW HYDE Pa/FRG (Nobiskrug) 1958; CP; 2600/4100; 115 × 6.5/7.6 (377 × 21.5/24.11); M (MAN); 14.5; ex Sun Kwong 1979; ex Edwin Reith 1973
Sister:
27561 NEW HERO (Pa) ex Sun Sang 1980; ex Magdalena Reith 1972

27570 ELEISTRIA V Cy/Sw (Lindholmens) 1955; C; 2500/4000; 110.7 × 6.2/7.4 (363 × 20.3/24.3); M (Gotaverken); 13; ex Olympias 1973; ex I W Winck 1969

27580 FERAX Pa/FRG (Howaldts) 1950; C; 1700; 100.2 × 5.4 (328 × 17.8); R & LPT (Lentz); 10.5; ex Saba 1973; ex Ferax 1972; ex Duburg 1963

27590 LUCY Pa/Sw (Finnboda) 1954; C; 2600; 109.02 × 5.92 (358 × 19.42); M (Fiat); 15; ex El Centroamericano 1973; ex Gudmundra 1971

27620 PACIFIC MULIA My/FRG (Howaldts) 1955/59; C; 1900; 90.63 × 5.60 (297.3 × 18.37); M (Howaldts); 12; ex Arta 1980; ex Ravnefjell 1967; Lengthened 1959

27650 SOPHIE Cy/Ne ('De Hoop') 1953; CP; 1800; 93 × 5.4 (305 × 17.8); M (Swiss Locomotive); 13; ex Joliette 1972; Lengthened 1959

27690 CEFALLONIAN SUN Gr/FRG (O&K) 1952; C; 2500; 106.5 × 6.17 (349.4 × 20.24); M (MAN); 13.5; ex Colibri 1 1981; ex Nigerian Importer 1981; ex Austrian Importer 1980; ex Michele Maglione 1977; ex Capitano Vito 1973; ex Ludolf Oldendorff 1970
Similar:
27691 AETOPETRA (Pa) ex Constantinos 1979; ex Flottbek 1968

27710 DELFIN DE SALAZAR Sp/Sp ('Bazan') 1958; CP; 2500; 105.6 × 6.1 (347 × 20.1); M (Sulzer); 16.5; ex El Salazar 1972
Sisters (Sp flag):
27711 DELFIN ADRIATICO ex El Priorato 1972
27712 DELFIN DEL CANTABRICO ex El Baztan 1972

27720 PATRAI Gr/FRG (Flensburger) 1947; CP; 2800; 109.6 × 6.3 (359.3 × 20.6); R & LPT (Verschure); 10; ex Empire Patrai 1953; ex Empire Towy 1950
Similar:
27721 ULISSE I (Gr)

27730 PHOENIX Gr/Br (Smith's D) 1948; CP; 2100/3300; 99.5 × 5.8/6.4 (327 × 18.11/21); R (Smith's D); 11.5; ex Aristidis S 1976; ex Irini M; ex Voco 1963; ex Lovland 1960

27740 RITA MARIA Po/Po (Uniao) 1953; C; 3700; 112.4 × 5.8 (369 × 19); M (Sulzer); 14

★**27750 TIHA** Ys/FRG (Kroegerw) 1959; C/WT; 1800/3000; 101.7 × 5.5/6.7 (334 × 19/22); M (MAN); —; ex Vargas 1971

27760 GOLDEN STAR Ma/No (Norrkopings) 1955; R; 1600; 90.2 × 5.4 (296 × 17); M (Sulzer); 15; ex Captain Saeed 1982; ex Rafig II 1981; ex Betty Mae 1975; ex Armasal I 1974; ex Mardina Cooler 1973; ex Vikfrost 1972; ex Vera 1966

27770 JAMIL Le/Ne (De Haan & O) 1956; C; 1500/2300; 93.7 × 5.2/6.2 (307 × 17.6/20.3); M (MAN); 14; ex Speedmedit 1975; ex Polaris 1973
Sister:
27771 ZENA (Le) ex Speedafric 1975; ex Astrea 1973

27800 TANJUNG OISINA Ia (Navy)/Ne ('De Merwede') 1959; PC; 8500; 138.9 × 8.6 (456 × 28.3); M (MAN); 16.5; ex Tjut Njak Dhien 1982; ex Prinses Irene 1965

27810 HANAN STAR Sy/Br (Burntisland) 1946; C; 2000; 93.9 × 5.9 (308 × 19.3); R (Rowan); 12; ex Hanan 1981; ex Germania 1977; ex Kittiwake 1955

27840 AFRIQUIA Eg/It (Adriatico) 1948; PC; 6400; 124.36 × 7.27 (408 × 23.1); M (Adriatico); 14; ex Star of Luxor II 1982; ex Star of Luxor 1981
Sister:
27841 PORT SAID (Eg)

27870 AVONDALE Pa/Br (H Robb) 1956; C; 1900; 76.9 × 4.3 (252 × 14); M (British Polar); 10; ex Bismarck Sea 1981; ex Cobargo 1978; ex Kumalla 1973

27890 HAI SOON KAO Th/Br (H Robb) 1949; C; 930; 56.9 × 3.7 (187 × 12.3); TSM (British Polar); 10; ex Mamani 1982; ex Mamatu 1973; ex Mamaku 1973

27900 SINAR SURYA My/De (B&W) 1934; C; 1100; 68.6 × 3.9 (225 × 12.8); M (B&W); 10.5; ex Sri Makhota; ex Ocean Life 1973; ex Union Pacific 1972; ex Wyrallah 1969; ex Colorado Del Mar 1967; ex Tamata 1966; ex Colorado Del Mar 1964; ex Wyrallah 1961

27910 KING HORSE Sg/Br 1955; C; 2000; 81.6 × 4.9 (268 × 15.11); M; 11; ex Navau 1971; ex Navua 1971
Sisters:
27911 KING TOWER (Sg) ex Konni 1971;
27912 KITA (My) ex Meladji 1980; ex Kaimai 1972

27920 KING STAR Sg/Br (H Robb) 1957; C; 1900; 76.9 × 4.5 (252 × 14.1); M (British Polar); 11; ex Koonya 1971

27930 ARABIAN VICTORY Pa/Br (Ardrossan) 1955; C; 1400; 71.07 × 4.47 (233.17 × 14.67); M (British Polar); —; ex Asian Queen 1980; ex John Monash 1976; ex Marra 1966

27940 ELIMAM MALEK Pa/Br (Lamont) 1950; CP; 1000; 72.1 × 4.9 (237 × 16.2); M (Nydqvist & Holm); 12; ex Krefan 1979; ex Oscar 1978; ex Panagia Tourliani 1972; ex Eystein Jarl 1968

27950 PRASHANTI In/Be (Bruges) 1958; CP; 1200; 80.6 × 4.8 (264 × 15.6); M (MAN); 12.5; ex Sai Nanak 1982; ex Janaki 1980
Sister:
27951 VIJAYA VASANT (In) ex Jahnavi 1977

27960 BHOJA MARINER Pa/FRG (Unterweser) 1952; CP; 1200; 80.1 × 4.3 (263 × 14.2); M (KHD); 12; ex Irini P 1980; ex Sloman Algier 1976; ex Castor 1969
Sisters:
27961 CHRISTOS M (Cy) ex Minos 1977; ex Jason 1976

28010 MILFORD Pa/Ja (Uraga Dock) 1951; C; 6200; 136.6 × 8 (447 × 26.1); M (Sulzer); 14; ex Michaelson Pearl 1974; ex Gemini Pioneer 1973; ex Samoa Maru 1972; ex Usa Maru 1967

28030 SAREYAH Db/Ja (Ishikawajima J) 1951; C; 4600; 121.21 × 7.31 (399 × 24.2); M (B&W); 12; ex A-Trader 1980; ex Sea King 1979; ex Golden Venture 1980; ex Nachisan 1976; ex Nachisan Maru 1971

28040 TAI YUNG Pa/It (Felszegi) 1963; CP; 4000; 114.9 × 7 (377 × 23); M (Fiat); 13.5

★**28060 'KOLOMNA' type** —/DDR ('Neptun') 1956; C; 3300; 102.4 × 6.6 (335 × 21.8); R & LPT (Liebknecht); 12.5
Sisters (Ru flag):
★**28061 NEZHIN**
★**28062 SMELA**
★**28063 BALASHOV**
★**28064 KOTLAS** Some others are probably Naval Depot Ships
(RC flag):
★**28065 ZHAN DOU 44** ex Hoping No44
★**28066 ZHAN DOU 45** ex Hoping No45
★**28067 ZHAN DOU 155** ex Ho Ping 155 1967;
★**28068 ZHAN DOU 156** ex Ho Ping 156 1967
(Gr flag):
28069 LION OF CHAERONEA ex Smaragdi 1968; ex Rostock 1965
Similar:
★**28070 ANGARSK** (Ru) —KP ahead of Bridge much lower. Also drawn as MMFM—other Russian vessels may also be like this

28090 CHIEH SHENG Pa/Ja (Hitachi) 1951; C; 5000; 120.7 × 7.4 (396 × 24.2); T (Ishikawajima J); 12.75; ex Burma Maru 1971; ex Ginko Maru 1956

28110 NAKHODA VANANCA Ir/Ne ('De Gideon') 1939; C; 370; 53.5 × 3.1 (175 × 10.1); M (Alpha); 8.5; ex Arvi 1968; ex Costis 1964; ex Sigyn 1961; ex Aegir 1939

28120 MUNAWER UAE/Gr/It (Apuania) 1958; C; 4200; 113.6 × 7.7 (373 × 25.7); M (Sulzer); 14.75; ex Proodos 1982; ex Diakan Progress 1976; ex Golden Condor 1970; ex Lucky Dragon 1969; ex Piek 1968
Sister:
28121 ARIES (Pa) ex Nimas II 1981; ex Ketty 1981; ex Zea Sky 1980; ex Designer 1975; ex Seamerchant 1971; ex Happy Bird 1969; ex Green Dragon 1969; ex Pan 1968

28150 AKIS S Gr/Sw (Oresunds) 1957; C; 4000/6200; 130.7 × 7.1/8.2 (429 × 23.4/27.1); M (Gotaverken); 14.5; ex Mireille 1974; ex Dalhem 1970

★**28160 LUO DING** RC/No (Moss V) 1964; PC; 3200/4500; 110.6 × 6.5/7.6 (363 × 21.4/24.11); M (B&W); 14; ex Hoi Kung

28170 LANKA KALYANI Sr/De (Helsingor) 1960; C; 5200; 122.7 × 7.4 (403 × 24.8); M (B&W); 16; ex Hankiang 1973; ex Tema 1971; ex Brookville 1963

28180 SCORPIO Pa/Sw (Oresunds) 1958; C; 6400; 130.7 × 8.2 (429 × 27.1); M (Gotaverken); 15.5; ex ZB-Owl No 7 1983; ex Arcadia 1982; ex Skeldervik 1972

★**28190 HONG QI 116** RC/It (Taranto) 1957; C; 6400/8600; 151 × 8.9 (495 × 29.2); M (Fiat); 14; ex Feita 1977; ex Nara 1972; ex Calliope 1961
Sister:
★**28191 HONG QI 115** (RC) ex Feihang 1977; ex Nausicaa 1972; ex Mary Sophia 1961

28200 BATROUN Le/Br (H Robb) 1960; C; 3400; 111.8 × 6.4 (367 × 21); M (Sulzer); —; ex City of Famagusta 1977; ex Arcadian 1974

583

● 28210 **TURBO P.** Pa/FRG (Howaldts) 1956; C; 8800; 149.4 × 9 (490 × 29.5); M (Sulzer); 13.5; ex *Freeway* 1981; ex *Georgios Lentoudis* 1980; ex *Aegean Dolphin* 1973

● ★28220 **HONG MING** RC/Ne ('De Biesbosch-Dordrecht') 1959; C; 6300/8600; 150.1 × 8.2/8.8 (492 × 26.11/29); M (Sulzer); 13; ex *Banda Sea* 1976; ex *Amstelmolen* 1972
Sisters (RC flag):
★28221 **YONG MING** ex *Java Sea* 1976; ex *Amstelsuis* 1972
★28222 **SAN MING** ex *Bali Sea* 1976; ex *Amstelveld* 1972

28230 **NIREUS** Gr/FRG (Kieler H) 1956; C; 9900; 155.2 × 9.3 (509 × 30.6); M (Sulzer); 15.75; ex *Orpheus* 1977
Similar:
★28231 **GUIYIN** (RC) ex *Siungfei* 1976; ex *Phoevos* 1974

★28250 **XING MING** RC/Ne ('De Hoop') 1961; CP; 9100; 154.7 × 8.8 (508 × 29); M (Stork); —; ex *Fuchunkiang* 1976; ex *Elin Hope* 1970

● 28260 **ARION** Gr/FRG (Kieler H) 1960; C; 7300/10000; 157.8 × 9.3 (518 × 30.7); M (Sulzer); —; ex *Kallixenos* 1981; ex *Ermis* 1974; ex *Alkman* 1974

● 28280 **CEYLAN SAILOR** Sr/Br (Bartram) 1960; C; 9600; 152.2 × 9.3 (499 × 30.7); M (Doxford); 12.5; ex *Aspyr* 1982; ex *Durmitor*; ex *Silverbeck* 1965

28320 **THAI RAINBOW** Th/FRG (Flensburger) 1955; C; 3400; 99.1 × 7.1 (325 × 23.1); M (MAN); 13.5; ex *Michael Jebsen*

● 28340 **MIGHTY SPIRIT** Pa/Br (Swan Hunter & WR) 1957; C; 4900; 132.3 × 7.5 (434 × 24.7); M (Sulzer); 14.75; ex *Eurydice* 1981; ex *City of Guildford*
Sisters:
28342 **SUERTE** (Gr) ex *City of Gloucester*
28344 **ISLAND OF MARMARA** (Gr) ex *City of St Albans*

28350 **BEITEDDINE** Le/Br (H Robb) 1960; C; 3400; 111.5 × 6.4 (366 × 21); M (Sulzer); 13.5; ex *City of Limassol* 1977; ex *Rapallo* 1975

28390 **SURAKARTA** Ia/Ja (Kawasaki D) 1955; C; 3500; 117.2 × 6.6 (385 × 21.6); M (MAN); 11; ex *East Breeze* 1974; ex *Eastern Muse* 1970; ex *East Breeze*

● 28450 **CROESUS** Le/FRG (Elsflether) 1959; CP; 5000; 119.8 × 7.9 (393 × 26); M (Fiat); 14.5; ex *Great Maurice* 1979; ex *Bintang Pagi* 1977; ex *Apeliotis* 1973; ex *Zosma* 1971; ex *Wahehe* 1965
Sister:
28451 **CADMUS** (Gr) ex *Rima Tsiris* 1981; ex *Bintang Lima* 1977; ex *Aparktias* 1973; ex *Gemma* 1971; ex *Wadai* 1965

28480 **MARLEN** Gr/FRG (Elsflether) 1957; C; 3400/5100; 119.8 × 7/7.9 (393 × 22.1/26.1); M (Atlas-MaK); 14; ex *Magdalene Vinnen* 1979

★28490 **STANISLAVSKIY** Ru/Be (Boel) 1956; C; 3100; 120.4 × 6.7 (395 × 22.1); M (Sulzer); 14
Sisters (Ru flag):
★28491 **IVAN MOSKVIN**
★28492 **LEONID LEONIDOV**

28510 **GEORGE F.** Gr/Br (Cammell Laird) 1959; CP; 3800; 99.1 × 7.3 (325 × 24.1); M (Sulzer); 12; ex *Quebec* 1976; ex *Alice Bowater* 1969
Similar:
28511 **KRETAN SPIRIT** (Gr) ex *Constance Bowater*
28512 **PROMETHEUS V** (Pa) ex *Kretan Glory* 1982; ex *Nina Bowater* 1977
28513 **ALEXANDRA** (Gr) ex *Aginor*; ex *Gigi* 1976; ex *Gladys Bowater* 1972
28514 **NAZ K** (Tu) ex *Malero M. 1* 1983; ex *Tassos K*; ex *Charlotte*; ex *Phyllis Bowater* 1973

28530 **KORALLE** Ca/Sw (Oresunds) 1937; CP; 800; 70.6 × 4.6 (232 × 15.2); M (Atlas-Diesel); 12; ex *Wiros* 1959

★28540 **BELI** Ys/Sw (Oresunds) 1938; C; 900; 71.9 × 4.6 (236 × 15.2); M (Atlas-Diesel); 12; ex *Platak* 1967; ex *Wiril* 1961
Similar:
★28541 **RASA** (Ys) ex *Plavnik* 1967; ex *Waria* 1961

28550 **TINOS** Cy/Ne ('De Gideon') 1938; C; 530; 58.8 × 4.6 (193 × 15.1); M (Humboldt-Deutz); 10.5; ex *Demetra 1* 1980; ex *Christos II* 1977; ex *Drake* 1966

28560 **MUNAWER** UAE/It (Apuania) 1958; C; 4200; 113.6 × 7.7 (373 × 25.7); M (Sulzer); 14.75; ex *Proodos* 1982; ex *Diakan Progress* 1976; ex *Golden Condor* 1970; ex *Lucky Dragon* 1969; ex *Piek* 1968

28610 **KAVO ALKYON** Gr/FRG (Flensburger) 1961; C; 10900; 162.9 × 9.4 (534 × 30.9); M (MAN); 14; ex *Stad Kampen* 1968
Similar:
28611 **KAVO DELFINI** (Gr) ex *Stad Maastricht* 1968
28612 **ANGELIKI** (Gr) ex *Port Antonio* 1973; ex *Stad Den Haag* 1972
28613 **OCEANIA** (Pa) ex *Ocean* 1982; ex *Ocean Intrepid* 1980; ex *Port Royal* 1973; ex *Stad Zwolle* 1972
28614 **AVAX** (Gr) ex *Port Maria* 1973; ex *Stad Vlaardingen* 1972

★28620 **KVARNER** Ys/Sw (Kockums) 1946; C; 3200; 121.4 × 6.9 (398 × 22.9); M (MAN); 15; ex *Alida Gorthon* 1961

● 28630 **MALDIVE PRIZE** Mv/Ja (Hitachi) 1956; C; 9800; 158.1 × 9.5 (519 × 30.7); M (B&W); 14.5; ex *Yinka Folawiyo* 1980; ex *Ocean Seigneur* 1975; ex *Capetan Yemelos* 1959

28640 **ARIES** Gr/Br (A&P) 1960; C; 5400/7800; 142.9 × 8/8.7 (469 × 26.3/28.6); M (Doxford); —; ex *Alekos K*; ex *Inchona* 1975; ex *Glanely* 1969

● 28650 **UNILUCK** Gr/Br (Bartram) 1961; C; 5500/7600; 140.4 × —/8.7 (461 × —/28.6); M (Doxford); —; ex *Swede Tonia* 1982; ex *Marytonia* 1976; ex *Landwade* 1972

● 28660 **PARNASSUS** Ma/FRG (A G 'Weser') 1962; C; 9500; 153.7 × 9 (504 × 29.6); M (Sulzer); 15; ex *Thracian Nana* 1981; ex *Morias* 1979; ex *Maria* 1978

28670 **MYRTIDIOTISSA** Gr/FRG (A G 'Weser') 1957; C; 9300; 153.7 × 9 (504 × 29.6); M (Sulzer); 14; ex *Ioannis* 1958
Sister:
28671 **OTHON** (Gr)

28680 **MIGHTY WIND** Pa/Ys ('3 Maj') 1959; C; 6000/8900; 152.3 × 8.3/9.2 (500 × 27.4/30.3); M (Sulzer); 15; ex *Avra* 1981; ex *Agios Fanourios* 1976; ex *Platon* 1974; ex *Kyvernitis* 1972

28710 **MAI RICKMERS** Sg/FRG (Emden) 1957; C; 8000/10500; 157.41 × —/9.36 (516.4 × —/30.71); M (MAN); 14; ex *Erik Blumenfeld* 1965

● 28720 **MOFARRIJ B** Si/FRG (Rhein Nordseew) 1957; C; 10200; 157.9 × 9.1 (518 × 30); M (MAN); 14; ex *Interactivity* 1982; ex *Drastirios* 1979; ex *Madison Friendship* 1973

28730 **JAURSINGHWALA** Pa/FRG (Deutsche Werft) 1957; C; 7000/10200; 157 × —/9.23 (515 × —/30.28); M (MAN); 14.5; ex *Vassilis Katsikis* 1980; ex *Adelfotis* 1973; ex *Har Canaan* 1972
Sister:
★28731 **RENATO GUITART** (Cu) ex *Jade Islands*; ex *Johannes Russ* 1972

★28750 **BOGDAN KHMELNITSKY** Ru/Br (Gray) 1954; C; 7300; 136 × 8.2 (446 × 27); R & LPT (Central Marine); 11.75; ex *Stanpool*

28770 **MANSOOR** Pk/FRG (Rhein Nordseew) 1958; C; 8600/10600; 157.9 × 8.4/9.2 (518 × 27.7/30.3); M (MAN); 14; ex *Mujahid* 1967; ex *Thor* 1966; ex *Fritz Thyssen* 1965

28800 **SEA HORSE** Le/Sw (Oresunds) 1951; C; 2300; 107.55 × 5.87 (353 × 19.26); M (Gotaverken); 14; ex *Tollense* 1978; ex *Itajai* 1965
Sister:
28801 **LOULLIA** (Pa) ex *Zschopau*

● 28820 **GLAROS** Ma/FRG (Emden) 1952; PC; 2700; 110 × 6.4 (361 × 21); M (MAN); 11; ex *Ionian Star* 1983; ex *Cefallonian Star* 1982; ex *Spree*; ex *Else* 1962

28830 **SIMALI 1** Th/FRG (Flensburger) 1951; CP; 2700; 116.3 × 7.3 (382 × 24); M (MAN); 13; ex *Siam Queen* 1976; ex *Nikitas II* 1974; ex *Nordhaff* 1971; ex *Naguilan* 1969; ex *Atlas* 1959
Sister:
28831 **DIMITRIS** (Gr) ex *Apostolos M II* 1980; ex *Diana* 1978; ex *Nordmark* 1974; ex *Don Pedro* 1967; ex *Levante* 1966

★28850 **YI CHI** RC/Br (H&W) 1947; C; 4000; 128.05 × 6.78 (420 × 22.24); M (B&W); 15.5; ex *Seasage* 1977; ex *Morbihan* 1964

● 28880 **TAMBA** Se/Fr (La Seine) 1956; C/WT; 5000; 119.4 × 7.3 (394 × 24); M (CCM); 14; ex *Laurent Schiaffino*
Sister:
28881 **ILE DE LA MARTINIQUE** (Fr) ex *Rose Schiaffino*

28910 **RIHENG** Pa/FRG (Emden) 1955; C; 2900; 119.5 × 6.5 (392 × 21.4); M (MAN); 14; ex *Liheng* 1976; ex *Cadiz* 1972; ex *Falkental* 1961

28920 **ANGIE BABY** Pa/FRG (A G 'Weser') 1954; C; 2400/3700; 108.2 × 6.1/7.2 (355 × 20.6/23.9); M (Borsig); 13; ex *Antony* 1978; ex *Elisabeth Berger* 1971

28930 **POLIAIGOS** Cy/Ne ('De Schelde') 1949; C; 2900; 91.8 × 5.6 (301 × 18.5); M (Stork); 12; ex *Odigitria B* 1983; ex *Nissos Paros* 1973; ex *Pacaya* 1964; ex *Ijssel* 1961
Sister:
28931 **AGIOS FANOURIOS VI** (Gr) ex *Panagoula D* 1977; ex *Agios Fanourios* 1977; ex *Panagoula D*; ex *Nissos Skyros* 1974; ex *Takana* 1964; ex *Maas* 1961

28970 **PACIFIC SELATAN** My/Be (Boel) 1954; C; 1600; 92.03 × 5.63 (302 × 18.47); M (Werkspoor); 10; ex *Sumber Tunas 103* 1978; ex *Beau Eagle* 1975; ex *Tandjung Sopi* 1973; ex *Alexander Herzen* 1958

★28980 **IVAN BABUSHKIN** Ru/Be (Boel) 1956; C; 1800; 101.1 × 5.8 (333 × 18.1); M (Sulzer); 13
Sisters (Ru flag):
★28981 **NIKOLAY CHERNYSHEVSKIY**
★28982 **NIKOLAY OSTROVSKIY**
★28983 **VASILIY DOKUCHAEV**
★28984 **YAKOV SVERDLOV**

★28990 **SKENDERBEG** Al/Bu (G Dimitrov) 1959; C; 1900; 92.5 × 4.7 (304 × 15.8); M (Liebknecht); 13;
Also known as **GJERGJ KASTRIOTI**
Sisters:
★28991 **BURGAS** (Bu)
★28992 **PKHEN HOA** (RK)
★28993 **PYONG HWA** (RK) ex *Mir*

29000 **BALTCHIK** Pa/Be (Boel) 1949; C; 1800; 92.1 × 5.6 (302 × 18.6); M (Werkspoor); 12; ex *Maria S* 1982; ex *Eagle* 1979; ex *Baltchik* 1979; ex *Nikola Vaptzarov* 1976; Modified 'HANSA' type

29010 **FLORENTIA** Ho/Bu (G Dimitrov) 1962; C; 1700; 92.4 × 5.6 (303 × 18.6); M (CKD Praha); 13; ex *Pierros* 1983; ex *Jiskra* 1980
Sisters:
★29011 **SLIVEN** (Bu)
★29012 **GABROVO** (Bu)

29040 **AN CHI** Pa/FRG (Nobiskrug) 1955; CP; 2200; 101.9 × 5.4 (334 × 17.9); M (MAN); 16; ex *Sumber Tunas III* 1983; ex *Ocean Cheer* 1969; ex *Valdes* 1968

29050 **ADRIANA** Pa/Ja (Mitsui) 1948; C; 2200; 90.5 × 5.6 (297 × 18.6); M (Niigata); 10.5; ex *Wan Khim* 1974; ex *Glory No 3* 1972; ex *Turtle No 5* 1969; ex *Poti No 1* 1967; ex *Teshiosan Maru* 1965

★29060 **LICUNGO** Mb/Br (Grangemouth) 1948; CP; 1000; 77.9 × 3.9 (256 × 12.11); TSM (Mirrlees, Bickerton & Day); 11

★29070 **HONG QI 106** RC/FRG (LF-W) 1957; C; 7200/10100; 156.1 × 8.1/9 (512 × 26.8/29.7); M (MAN); 14; ex *Irish Sea* 1975; ex *Henriette Wilhelmine Schulte* 1973
Sisters:
29071 **ARCADIAN STAR** (Gr) ex *Maddalena* 1977; ex *Ilse Schulte* 1971

29100 **FOURKERO II** Gr/Ys ('3 Maj') 1963; C; 7300/10200; 162.49 × 8.2/9.4 (533 × 26.11/30) M (Sulzer); 15; ex *Filadelphos* 1981; ex *Arya Sam* 1977; ex *Filadelphus* 1975; ex *Leandros* 1974
Sisters:
29101 **DIMITRIOS** (Gr)
★29102 **PODGORA** (Ys) ex *Mitera Kallipi* 1971

29110 **DALIA A.** Ma/FRG (Luebecker F-W) 1957; C; 9100; 148.01 × 9.30 (485.6 × 30.51); M (MAN); 14.75; ex *Enterprise* 1982; ex *Grecian Valour* 1980

29140 **RIVER SIDE** Pa/Sw (Nya Varv) 1935; C; 1000; 78.3 × 4.6 (257 × 15.2); M (Kockums); 10; ex *Aristides* 1979; ex *Margit* 1965; ex *Warun* 1957; Lengthened 1957

29150 **OMID** Ir/Sw (Oresunds) 1945; C; 600; 63.4 × 3.6 (208 × 11.1); M (Atlas-Diesel); 11; ex *Rabeha* 1975; ex *Hooda* 1972; ex *Bella* 1970; ex *Tento* 1964; ex *Ronnskar*

29160 **NEW PEACOCK** Sg/Sw (Lindholmens) 1960/76; Con; 3500/5500; 129.1 × 7.1/8.1 (424 × 24.4/26.6); M (Gotaverken); 15.5; ex *Idefjord* 1981; Converted from cargo ship 1976 (Aalborg)
Sister:
★29161 **JIN XIAN QUAN** (RC) ex *Boonkrong*; ex *Topdalsfjord*

29170 **MIZAR** It/Fr (Dubigeon) 1957; C/WT; 1600; 95.6 × 5.3 (314 × 17.4); M (Fiat); 13.75; ex *Attilio Ievoli* 1980; ex *Cap Tainaron* 1974; ex *Cap Sim* 1968

29180 **GEORGIOS** Cy/Sw (Stuelcken) 1956; C; 1600; 84.2 × 4.8 (265 × 15.9); M (MaK); 11.75; ex *Olympios Zeus* 1980; ex *Martha Peters*; ex *Tetuan* 1963

29200 **HATI BAIK** My/Br (H Robb) 1956; C; 2600; 93.9 × 5.3 (308 × 17.5); TSM (British Polar) 11; ex

Katoa 1980; ex *Kaitoa* 1972

29210 **ENDURANCE** Pa/Au (NSW Govt) 1954; C; 3400; 97.1 × 5.7 (288 × 18.7); TSM (Mirrlees); 10; ex *Dongara* 1972; ex *Wangara* 1966; Lengthened 1967

29230 **ROSS SEA** Pa/FRG (LF-W) 1956; C; 5900/8700; 145.9 × 8.2/9.1 (497 × 26.1/30); M (MAN); 15; ex *Senator Possehl* 1971
Sister:
29231 **PALIZZI** (It) ex *Lubeck* 1969

29240 **ZUIDER SEA** Pa/De (Nakskov) 1954; C; 5900/8400; 149.7 × 7.75/— (491 × 25.43/—); M (B&W); 16.75; ex *Sumbawa* 1972
Sister:
29241 **OFFSHORE PROVIDER** (Pa) ex *Paclog Sealink* 1982; ex *Songkhla* 1974
Similar (Pole masts):
★29242 **HONG QI 102** (RC) ex *Celebes Sea* 1975; ex *Panama* 1972
★29243 **KARA SEA** (RC) ex *Magdala* 1972

●29270 **LEON PROM** Fr/Sw (Helsingborgs) 1958; C; 3700; 106.6 × 6.9 (350 × 22.7); M (B&W); 15; ex *Cordova* 1967

★29280 **CHANG HUA** RC/Sw (Oskarshamns) 1957; C; 8700; 147.8 × 8.1 (485 × 29.11); M (B&W); —; ex *Hemisphere*; ex *Dagrun* 1963

●29330 **SAUDI SUNRISE** Si/Ne (Giessen) 1954; C; 7800/10200; 157.99 × 8.52/9.91 (518 × 28/31.9); M (B&W); 16.5; ex *Mercury Gulf* 1981; ex *Straat Mozambique* 1977
Sister:
29331 **SAUDI LUCK** (Si) ex *Saudi Sun* 1982; ex *Mercury Bay* 1980; ex *Straat Bali* 1977

★29350 **TONG HUA** RC/Sw (Uddevalla) 1958; C; 6300/8600; 142.5 × 8.3/9.1 (467 × 27.4/29.1); M (Gotaverken); 15; ex *Arafura Sea* 1976; ex *Tysla* 1972; ex *Bay Master* 1965; ex *Golden Master* 1960

●★29360 **NANXIANG** RC/Sw (Uddevalla) 1959; C; 6200/8700; 142.4 × 8.28/9.04 (467 × 27.17/29.66); M (Gotaverken); 15; ex *Antarctica* 1971; ex *Older* 1964
Sisters:
★29361 **DUNGHUA** (RC) ex *Dunhua* 1982; ex *East Fortune* 1970; ex *Sollen* 1963
29362 **TANIA** (Sg) ex *Hoegh Augvald* 1978; ex *Augvald* 1969
29364 **BARAKATALLAH** (Si) ex *Marcana 1* 1981; ex *Maracana* 1980; ex *Arquero* 1977; ex *Trude* 1974; ex *Gruno Trude* 1973; ex *Hoegh Trude* 1973; ex *Gruno Trude* 1971; ex *Porthos* 1970

●29380 **HELLENIC DESTINY** Gr/FRG (Rhein Nordseew) 1960; CP; 7300; 154.6 × 8 (507 × 26.2); M (MAN); 17
Sisters (Gr flag):
29381 **HELLENIC LAUREL**
29382 **HELLENIC SPLENDOUR**

29410 **DIAMANTIS** Gr/Sw (Uddevalla) 1956; CP; 6100/8200; 142.5 × 8.1/9 (467 × 26.5/29.8); M (Gotaverken); 14.75; ex *Capetan Lazaros*; ex *Polydora* 1975; ex *Mont Blanc* 1972; ex *Sunoak* 1961

●29420 **TEGAL** Ia/No (Akers) 1955; CP; 5700; 142.3 × 7.9 (467 × 26); M (B&W); 16; ex *Horda* 1974

29440 **PIURA** Pe/FRG (Deutsche Werft) 1959; CP; 6400/9000; 150.9 × 7.7/8.9 (495 × 25.3/29.4); M (MAN); 16.5; ex *Monte Cristo* 1979; ex *Hornbelt* 1977
Sister:
29441 **TACNA** (Pe) ex *Hornsee* 1972

29450 **HERCULUS** Gr/De (Helsingor) 1953; C; 4000/5700; 129.2 × 7.4/7.7 (424 × 24.5/25.6); M (B&W); 16; ex *Cefallonian Ambition* 1980; ex *Vogtland*; ex *Freya Torm* 1965

29460 **PISTIS** Gr/Sw (Lindholmens) 1955; CP; 3800; 129.1 × 7.1 (423 × 23.4); M (Gotaverken); 14; ex *Drammensfjord* 1974
Sister:
29461 **ELPIS** (Gr) ex *Tanafjord* 1974

29470 **SURABAYA** Ia/No (Fredrikstad) 1952; CP; 4100/6300; 132.6 × 7.22/7.94 (435 × 23.69/26.05); M (Gotaverken); 14.5; ex *Curling* 1975; ex *Byklefjell* 1970; ex *Puerto Somoza* 1958; ex *Byklefjell* 1956

29490 **NAVIKAPOL** Pa/Sw (Uddevalla) 1954; CP; 4200; 132.2 × 7.7 (434 × 25.1); M (Uddevalla); 18; ex *Lindenstein* 1976; ex *Clary Thorden* 1965

29500 **STATE OF TRAVANCORE-COCHIN** In/FRG (LF-W) 1954; CP; 6200; 146.9 × 7.6 (482 × 25); M (MAN); 13.5

29510 **KERASOUS II** Pa/It (Breda) 1959; C; 8600; 145.5 × 8.8 (477 × 29); M (Fiat); —; ex *Pistis* 1982; ex *Cervinia II* 1981; ex *Cervinia* 1980; ex *Lorenzo Mar-*

cello 1964

●★29520 **CHANG HUA** RC/Sw (Oskarshamns) 1957; C; 8700; 147.83 × 9.12 (485 × 29.92); M (B&W); —; ex *Hemisphere* 1975; ex *Dagrun* 1963

29540 **LAERTIS** Gr/Sw (Ekensbergs) 1959; CP; 6100/9000; 147.8 × 8.2/9.1 (485 × 26.1/29.11); M (B&W); —; ex *Star Altair* 1979; ex *Vimeira* 1965; ex *Port Denison* 1965; ex *Vimeira* 1960; ex *Fair Lady* Probable sister:
29542 **PINELOPI** (Gr) ex *Star Aldebaran*; ex *Kensington*

★29550 **ZUNHUA** RC/Sw (Oskarshamns) 1961; C; 5900/8900; 147.8 × 8.3/9.3 (485 × 26.9/29.11); M (Gotaverken); —; ex *Weddell Sea* 1975; ex *Salvada* 1971
Sisters:
★29551 **XING HUA** (RC) ex *Changpaishan* 1970; ex *Saldura* 1967
★29552 **YONG DING** (RC) ex *Patrice* 1977; ex *Patricia* 1976; ex *Salambria* 1973
★29553 **DE HUA** (RC) ex *Eastglory* 1975; ex *Saldanha* 1967; ex *Sunny Queen*
29554 **DIAKLIS** (Gr) ex *Despina R*; ex *Dawn Grandeur* 1976; ex *Salvina* 1972

29560 **QUELIMANE** Po/Sw (Oskarshamns) 1963; CP; 6100/8700; 147.8 × 8.2/9.1 (485 × 26.2/29.9); M (Gotaverken); 15; ex *Evina* 1968

★29610 **HONG QI 103** RC/FRG (Flensburger) 1958; CP; 6000/10600; 147.9 × 7.8/8.5 (485 × 25.9/27.9); M (MAN); 14; ex *Black Sea* 1975; ex *Indus* 1972; ex *Arya Indus* 1970; ex *Indus* 1968
Sister:
★29611 **LINYIN** (RC) ex *Baltic Sea* 1977; ex *Maas* 1973

29620 **TILEMACHOS** Gr/Br (Burntisland) 1958; C; 6500; 146.01 × 8.51 (479.04 × 27.92); M (B&W); —; ex *Star Bellatrix* 1978; ex *Capetan Cardamilitis* 1959

●29690 **KALLISTO** Gr/Sw (Eriksbergs) 1956; CP; 5400; 139.9 × 7.7 (459 × 25.5); M (B&W); 17.5; ex *Karpo* 1976; ex *Indiana* 1976

●29700 **WEIKUO** Pa/Ja (Hitachi) 1958; C; 9300; 156.6 × 9.3 (514 × 30.6); M (B&W); 18; ex *Yamawaka Maru* 1973
Sisters:
29701 **WEILI** (Pa) ex *Yamataka Maru* 1973

29760 **CHIEH HSING** Pa/Ja (Nishi Nippon J) 1952; C; 7600; 151 × 8.4 (495 × 27.7); TSM (Nishi Nippon J); 15.5; ex *Tomishima Maru* 1972

●29830 **CHERRY LAJU** Sg/De (B&W) 1957/60; C; 3800/5900; 135.52 × —/6.74 (445 × —/22.11); M (B&W); 14.75; ex *Jens Maersk* 1979; Lengthened 1960 (Mitsui)

★29860 **HONG QI 102** RC/Ja (Naka Nippon) 1950; C; 6600/8800; 146.7 × 8.1/— (481 × 27.8/—); M (B&W); 16; ex *Celebes Sea* 1975; ex *Panama* 1972

29880 **DAVOS** Sd/FRG (Howaldts) 1961; C; 8900; 149.4 × 9.1 (487 × 29.1); M (Howaldts); 15; ex *Yemelos* 1973; ex *Steintor* 1971

29900 **PANORMOS** Cy/Sw (Oskarshamns) 1961; C; 6000/8800; 148.4 × —/9.3 (487 × —/30.5); M (Gotaverken); 15; ex *Salmela* 1972

29910 **KLIO** Gr/FRG (Deutsche Werft) 1958; C; 6200/8800; 146.31 × 8.14/9.13 (480 × 26.71/29.95); M (MAN); 14; ex *Lisianne*; ex *Gimletun* 1969; ex *Mostum* 1965

29920 **KHADIJAAN** Pa/FRG (LF-W) 1956; C; 6100/8900; 146 × 8.2/9.1 (479 × 26.11/29.1); M (MAN); 15; ex *Roman Emperor* 1976; ex *Svolder* 1974; ex *Hoegh Svolder* 1972; ex *Svolder* 1970
Similar (inset):
29921 **BANGLAR MAITRI** (Bh) ex *Bangla Rego* 1974; ex *Rego* 1973
29922 **MACCA** (Si) ex *Sophia II* 1982; ex *Sophia Minerva* 1978; ex *Hoegh Fram* 1977; ex *Minerva* 1974
29923 **INNAREN** (Gr) ex *Eptanissos* 1977; ex *Bogatyr* 1973; ex *Leiv Eriksson* 1965

29930 **AGATE ISLANDS** Pa/Sw (Oskarshamns) 1959; CP; 5900/8700; 148.3 × 8.2/9.1 (487 × 26.11/29.1); M (Gotaverken); 15.5; ex *Brott* 1973

●★29950 **XIANG YIN** RC/FRG (Deutsche Werft) 1956; C; 8700; 145.3 × 9.1 (480 × 29.1); M (MAN); 15; ex *Arctic Ocean* 1976; ex *Blue Master* 1964
Similar:
29952 **SHAHZAD** (Ho) ex *Pardesi* 1983; ex *Rajaan* 1981; ex *Hopewell* 1976; ex *St Lawrence* 1973; ex *Kostantis M* 1971; ex *Somerville* 1969

29970 **SCHUYLER OTIS BLAND** US/US (Ingalls SB) 1951; C; 8900; 145.7 × 9.1 (478 × 30); T (—);

18.5; Operated by Military Sealift Command; Sold 1979. May be broken up

★30000 **PING YIN** RC/FRG (Deutsche Werft) 1962; CP; 6300/10000; 155.9 $ 7.7/9.1 (511 × 25.6/30); M (MAN); 17.5; ex *Pacific Ocean* 1974; ex *Transvaal* 1972
Sister:
★30001 **SHAN YIN** (RC) ex *Indian Ocean* 1974; ex *Tanganyika* 1971

★30040 **HONG QI 120** RC/Ne (Jan Smit) 1956; CP; 6000; 147.5 × 8.1 (484 × 26.4); M (MAN); 15; ex *Minfung* 1976; ex *Witmarsum* 1972

★30060 **XUAN HUA** RC/Sw (Oresunds) 1956; CP; 6000/9000; 141.08 × 8.19/9.21 (463 × 26.9/30.1); M (Gotaverken); 14; ex *Steed* 1976; ex *Broland* 1970; ex *O A Brodin* 1961

★30090 **HONG QI 134** RC/FRG (Deutsche Werft) 1956; C; 6200/9000; 151.14 × 7.74/8.10 (496 × 25.39/26.57); M (B&W); 17.25; ex *Bihua* 1979; ex *Eastern Cliff* 1972; ex *Hoegh Cliff* 1967

★30120 **KANG DING** RC/Sw (Kockums) 1956; CP; 10400; 151.6 × 9.3 (497 × 30.7); M (Kockums); 14.75; ex *Ocean Travel* 1970; ex *Northern Clipper* 1963

30130 **FAIZI** Ir/Sw (Eriksbergs) 1955; C; 6100/8300; 147.05 × 7.86/8.23 (482 × 25.9/27); M (B&W); 17; ex *Iran Shahr* 1977; ex *Minikoi* 1972
Similar:
★30132 **NINGDU** (RC) ex *Bining* 1976; ex *Koto* 1973

30150 **DELIMA** Pa/Sw (Eriksbergs) 1950; C; 4900/7900; 138.5 × 7.7/8.6 (454 × 25.2/28.1); M (B&W); 14; ex *Beryl* 1972; ex *Prodromos Vita* 1970; ex *Brotrade* 1968; ex *Kungadland* 1966

30160 **KALMAR** Gr/Sw (Eriksbergs) 1951; CP; 4000; 131.3 × 8.4 (431 × 27.7); M (B&W); 16.5; ex *Myson* 1976; ex *Concordia Myson* 1972; ex *Myson* 1971; ex *Vibyholm* 1969
Sister:
30161 **NEW HYSAN** (Pa) ex *Sea Challenger* 1973; ex *Braheholm* 1967

30170 **RAMONEVERETT** Li/Fi (Crichton-Vulcan) 1960; CP; 5800/8000; 147.1 × 7.9/9.1 (482 × 25.9/29.9); M (Gotaverken); 17; ex *Mandalay*
Sister (Goalpost kingposts at either end of superstructure):
30171 **OHIO** (Le) ex *Dafnos* 1980; ex *Sameland* 1978; ex *Svaneholm* 1973

●30190 **LANKA KEERTI** Sr/Br (H&W) 1958; C; 6300/8600; 147.3 × 7.80/8.70 (483 × 25.59/28.54); M (H&W); 15; ex *Dartbank* 1975
Similar:
30191 **FORTUNE STAR** (Pa) ex *Avonbank* 1977
30192 **BLUE WAVE** (Gr) ex *Elmbank* 1976

30230 **CHRISTOS K.** Sg/Sw (Oskarshamns) 1957; C; 4000/6200; 130.9 × 7.2/8.3 (428 × 23.5/27.6); M (Gotaverkens); 14.25; ex *Nopal Sun*; ex *Martin Thore* 1966

★30250 **JIANGYIN** RC/FRG (Rhein Nordseew) 1958; C; 6800/9500; 153.1 × 8.1/9.1 (502 × 26.3/29.8); M (MAN); 15.5; ex *Hwang Ho* 1970; ex *Henri G* 1968

30270 **BANGLAR TARANI** Bh/De (Nakskov) 1962; C; 4700/6700; 133.5 × 7.8/8.6 (438 × 25.8/28.3); M (B&W); 14.5; ex *Gautatyr* 1973

★30280 **STARFORD** RC/Br (Gray) 1950; CP; 3500; 101.1 × 6.3 (332 × 20.7); R (Central Marine); 11.5; ex *Funing* 1964
Similar:
★30281 **WISHFORD** (RC)

30300 **STAR SHIP** Gr/No (Moss V) 1962; CP; 4600; 110.5 × 7.6 (363 × 25); M (B&W); 15.5; ex *Taipoosek* 1981

30310 **VORRAS** Gr/No (Moss V) 1955; C; 3700; 125.71 × 7.12 (412 × 23.36); M (B&W); 14.5; ex *Arpa* 1978; ex *Palma* 1973

30320 **GEORGE F.** Gr/Br (Cammell Laird) 1959; CP; 3800; 99.1 × 7.3 (325 × 24.1); M (Sulzer); 12; ex *Quebec* 1976; ex *Alice Bowater* 1969
Similar:
30321 **KRETAN SPIRIT** (Gr) ex *Constance Bowater*
30322 **AGINOR** (Gr) ex *Gigi* 1976; ex *Gladys Bowater* 1972
30323 **PROMETHEUS V** (Pa) ex *Kretan Glory* 1982; ex *Nina Bowater* 1977
30324 **NAZ K** (Tu) ex *Malero M.1* 1983; ex *Tassos K.* 1982; ex *Charlotte*; ex *Phyllis Bowater* 1973

30330 **AMER** UAE/Sw (Finnboda) 1957; C; 2900; 114.5 × 6.2 (376 × 20.6); M (B&W); 15; ex *Gran Canaria* 1983; ex *Frederica* 1965

Sister:
30331 **ACORES** (Po)
Similar:
★30332 **HONG QI 165** (RC) ex *Baodi*; ex *Svensksund* 1973
★30333 **HU JIU LAO 5** (RC) ex *Yuguan* 1983 ex *Stock*
30335 **MALDIVE VISION** (Mv) ex *Aegis* 1982; ex *Verna* 1982; ex *Marion* 1966; ex *Maronia* 1963; ex *Marion*

30350 **SALAMAH-5** UAE/Sw (Lindholmens) 1958; C; 3600; 129.11 × 7.12 (423.59 × 23.36); M (Gotaverken); 14.5; ex *Jebel Ali 2* 1983; ex *Diamant* 1980; ex *Skiensfjord* 1977

30380 **PATROCLOS** Cy/Br (H&W) 1955; C; 7700; 138.69 × — (455.02 × —); M (H&W); 14; ex *Foylebank* 1973; KP abreast the funnel
Sisters:
30381 **EASTERN SATURN** (Pa) ex *Golden Sea* 1974; ex *Pola Anna* 1973; ex *Laganbank*

★30400 **JIN HU QUAN** RC/Sp (AESA) 1967; C; 8300; 142.5 × 9.4 (468 × 30 6); M (Sulzer); —; ex *Mar Cantabrico* 1982

30410 **LUIGI D'AMICO** It/Sp (AESA) 1964; C; 9100; 156.9 × 9.1 (515 × 29.9); M (Sulzer); —; ex *Orient Mariner* 1969

★30420 **XINGHANG** RC/Fi (Crichton-Vulcan) 1963; CP; 4200/6400; 134.7 × 7.3/8.2 (445 × 23.1/26.1); M (Gotaverken); 16; ex *Sunnanland* 1977; ex *Sagaholm* 1972
Sisters (RC flag):
★30421 **YIDU** ex *Odensholm* 1971
★30422 **JIANGDU** ex *Vretaholm* 1971
★30423 **CHANGDU** ex *Blankaholm* 1971

● 30425 **KOTA SEGAR** Sg/Ja (Kawasaki) 1967; C; 10800; 167.01 × 9.58 (547.93 × 31.43); M (MAN); 20; ex *France Maru* 1983
Sisters:
30426 **C.C. ORIENT** (Pa) ex *Union Victoria* 1983; ex *Italy Maru* 1982
30427 **C.C. RED SEA** (Pa) ex *Union Bahama* 1983; ex *Portugal Maru* 1982
30428 **KOTA SALAM** (Sg) ex *Spain Maru* 1982

★30429 **YU HONG** RC/Br (A&P) 1961; C; 5600/8000; 138.94 × 8.078/8.084 (456 × 26.5/26.52); M (Sulzer); 15.5; ex *Shengli* 1974; ex *Torr Head* 1972

30460 **THOMAS NELSON** US/US (Bethlehem Steel) 1962; C; 8700/12500; 172.2 × —/9.6 (565 × —/31.8); T (Westinghouse); 20; ex *Nathanael Greene* 1977; ex *Philippine Bear* 1975

● 30520 **EASTERN PEARL** Pa/Ja (Mitsubishi HI) 1962; C; 9200; 156.14 × 9.21 (512 × 30.22); M (Sulzer); 18.25; ex *Tacoma Maru* 1981
Sister:
30521 **EASTERN LEADER** (Pa) ex *Norfolk Maru* 1980

30530 **RIO DULCE** Ar/Sp (Cadiz) 1964; C; 5900; 149.6 × 7.2 (491 × 23.9); M (Sulzer); 19.5
Sister:
30531 **RIO SALADO** (Ar)

● 30550 **DJATILUHUR** Ia/No (Mariners) 1961; CP; 7100/9300; 153.2 × —/9.1 (503 × —/29.11); M (Gotaverken); 15; ex *Anne Reed* 1968
Similar:
30552 **MAYFLOWER** (Pa) ex *Lima* 1981; ex *Kenosha* 1976; ex *Haldor Virik*; ex *Neptun* 1958

★30570 **TONG HUA** RC/Sw (Uddevalla) 1958; C; 6300/8600; 142.5 × 8.3/9.1 (467 × 27.2/29.11); M (Gotaverken); 15; ex *Arafura Sea*; ex *Tysla* 1972; ex *Bay Master* 1965; ex *Golden Master* 1960

● 30580 **TANIA** Si/Sw (Uddevalla) 1958; C; 6200/8600; 142.42 × 8.05/9.21 (467.26 × 26.41/30.22); M (Gotaverken); 15; ex *Hoegh Augvald*; ex *Augvald*
Similar:
★30582 **DUNGHUA** (RC) ex *Dunhua* 1983; ex *Eastfortune* 1970; ex *Sollen* 1963
★30583 **NANXIANG** (RC) ex *Antarctica* 1971; ex *Older* 1964

30590 **ETAIWI 2** Si/FRG (Rhein Nordseew) 1961; CP; 7000/9500; 153 × 8.1/9 (502 ×26.5/29.8); M (MAN); 15; ex *Golden Jeddah* 1983; ex *Longavi*; ex *Hiram* 1968

30600 **HERCULUS** Le/De (Helsingor) 1953; C; 4000/5700; 129.2 × 7.4/7.7 (424 × 24.6/25.6); M (B&W); 16; ex *Cefallonian Ambition* 1980; ex *Vogtland*; ex *Freya Torm* 1965

30610 **PIURA** Pe/FRG (Deutsche Werft) 1959; CP; 6400/9000; 150.9 × 7.7/8.9 (495 × 25.3/29.4); M (MAN); 16.5; ex *Monte Cristo* 1979; ex *Hornbelt* 1977

Sister:
30611 **TACNA** (Pe) ex *Hornsee* 1972

30620 **TOPAZ ISLANDS** Pa/Ne (Giessen-De Noord) 1963; C; 6300/9000; 152.3 × 8.1/9 (526 × 26.5/29.7); M (MAN); —; ex *Pendrecht* 1973; ex *Hurley Beacon* 1967
Sisters:
30621 **OPAL ISLANDS** (Pa) ex *Pooldrecht* 1973; ex *Brecon Beacon* 1968
30622 **AMBER ISLANDS** (Pa) ex *Papendrecht* 1973; ex *Holsworthy Beacon* 1968

● 30640 **TEGAL** Ia/No (Akers) 1955; CP; 5700; 142.3 × 8 (467 × 26); M (B&W); 15; ex *Horda* 1974

30650 **TINDALO** Pi/Ja (Iino) 1960; C; 6600; 147.8 × 8.9 (485 × 29.3); M (Sulzer); —
Sister:
30651 **NATIONAL STEEL TWO** (Pi) ex *Philippine Admiral* 1974; ex *Dagohoy* 1964

30660 **GENCLIK** Tu/It (Taranto) 1961; CP; 9000; 150.8 × 8.9 (495 × 29.3); M (Fiat); 16.5

30670 **SAILFLIP** Cy/Ja (Kawasaki D) 1961; C; 9000; 156.3 × 8.7 (513 × 28.6); M (MAN); 16.5; ex *Christos St Arapakis* 1981; ex *Man Hing* 1981; ex *Andino* 1979; ex *Florida Maru* 1973

30680 **SHEIKH IBRAHIM** Si/Ja (Hitachi) 1959; C; 6000/8400; 149.3 × —/9.1 (490 ×—/29.2); M (B&W); 14; ex *Elhawi Shams* 1983; ex *Nazakat* 1982; ex *Apostolos A* 1981; ex *Kladno* 1973

★30690 **HOI AN** Vn/Ja (Uraga Dock) 1960; CP; 9000; 144 × 8.9 (475 × 29.3); M (Sulzer); 14.5; ex *Universe Star*; ex *General Lim*

● 30720 **MAHAVIJAY** In/Ja (Hitachi) 1962; C; 6500/9100; 149.3 × 8/9.1 (490 × 26.3/29. 4); M (B&W); 14; ex *Maha Jag Vijay* 1976; ex *Jag Vijay* 1975
Sister:
30721 **SAMUDRA DAYA** (In) ex *Mahabir* 1977; ex *Jag Shanti* 1973

● 30730 **PACIFIC RIDE** Cy/Ja (Hitachi) 1960; CP; 9500; 149.2 × 9.1 (490 × 30); M (B&W); 18; ex *Pacific Pride* 1980; ex *Transocean Merchant* 1977

★30740 **ASIA-AFRIKA** RC/FRG (Oskarshamns) 1960; CP; 6200/9000; 147.9 × 8.2/9.1 (485 × 26.9/29.11); M (Gotaverken); 15; ex *Yafel* 1967; ex *Gyda* 1967

30750 **JALAKALA** In/In (Hindustan) 1964; C; 6500/9400; 153.0 × 7.72/8.92 (502 × 25.33/29.27); M (MAN); 16.5
Sisters (In flag):
30751 **JALAKANTA**
30752 **JALAKENDRA**
30753 **STATE OF MADHYA PRADESH**
30754 **STATE OF MYSORE**
30755 **STATE OF WEST BENGAL**
30756 **VISHVA SEVA**
30757 **VISHVA TIRTH**

30770 **LAERTIS** Ma/Sw (Ekensbergs) 1959; C; 6100/9000; 147.83 × 8.18/9.12 (485 × 26.84/29.92); M (B&W); —; ex *Star Altair* 1978; ex *Vimeira* 1965; ex *Port Denison* 1965; ex *Vimeira* 1960; Launched as Fair Lady
Sister:
30771 **PINELOPI** (Gr) ex *Star Aldebaran* 1978; ex *Kensington* 1963

30800 **PHILIPPINE BATAAN** Pi/Ja (Mitsubishi N) 1960; CP; 9900; 156.1 × 9.2 (512 × 30.1); M (Sulzer); 18.25
Sister:
30801 **MARANAO** (Pi) ex *Philippine Antonio Luna* 1982; ex *Philippine Leyte*

30810 **AMIRAL S OKAN** Tu/Tu (Denizcilik) 1970; C; 9800; 155.5 × 9 (509 × 29.1); M (B&W); 18
Sister:
30811 **AMIRAL S ALTINCAN** (Tu)

★30820 **GUANG PING** RC/Ja (Hitachi) 1959; C; 9200; 156.52 × 9.31 (513.5 × 30.54); M (B&W); 18; ex *Weili* 1976; ex *Yamataka Maru* 1973

★30830 **JIN PING** RC/Ja (Hitachi) 1958; C; 9200; 156.6 × 9.3 (514 × 30.6); M (B&W); 18; ex *Weimin* 1976; ex *Yamakimi Maru* 1973
Sister:
30831 **WEIKUO** (Pa) ex *Yamawaka Maru* 1973

30840 **BAIMA** Pa/Ja (Hitachi) 1958; C; 9100; 157.05 ×9.28 (515.26 ×30.45); M (B&W); 18; ex *Kamoharu Maru* 1972
Sisters:
30841 **BAIPAO** (Pa) ex *Shigaharu Maru* 1973★
★30842 **DONGPING** (RC) ex *Baisiung* 1977; ex *Tagaharu Maru* 1973
30843 **CAPTAIN JOHN** (Gr) ex *Captain George*; ex

Maru 1974

30870 **LOK VAIBHAV** In/Ja (Kurushima) 1966; CP; 4600; 114 × 7.1 (375 × 23.6); M (MAN); 16.5; ex *Rich Trader* 1975

30900 **CAPITAINE TASMAN** Fr/Fr (La Ciotat) 1963; C; 7800; 172.4 × 8.4 (566 × 27.3); M (B&W); 16.5; ex *Concordia Ion* 1981; ex *Ion* 1980; ex *Circea* 1977; Lengthened 1971
Sisters:
30901 **CAPITAINE WALLIS** (Fr) ex *Polydora* 1981; ex *Cypria* 1977
30902 **DIEGO** (Pa) ex *Danaos* 1983; ex *Concordia Danaos* 1981; ex *Danaos* 1980; ex *Capraia* 1977

★30930 **CHANGDE** RC/Sw (Oskarshamns) 1964; CP; 9000; 148.4 × 9.1 (487 × 30); M (Gotaverken); —; ex *Peony* 1970; ex *Bonde*

30940 **TAHASIN** Bh/Ja (Osaka) 1960; C; 8700; 148.42 × 9.09 (486.9 × 29.82); M (B&W); 14.5; ex *Caledonia* 1982; ex *Man Sing* 1981; ex *Pacific Glory* 1979; ex *Maria Rosello* 1977

30960 **VICTORIA U.** Li/FRG (Howaldts) 1960; C; 6000/8900; 149.41 × —/9.15 (490 ×—/30.02); M (MAN); 15; ex *Pishtaz Iran* 1979; ex *Rotte* 1975

★30980 **SHAN YIN** RC/FRG (Deutsche Werft) 1961; C; 6300/9600; 155.9 × 7.7/9.1 (511 × 25.5/29.11); M (MAN); 17.5; ex *Indian Ocean* 1974; ex *Tanganyika* 1971;
Sister:
★30981 **PING YIN** (RC) ex *Pacific Ocean* 1974; ex *Transvaal* 1972

31000 **HAN GARAM** Ko/Ja (Mitsui) 1959; C; 9500; 156.57 × 8.8; (514 ×28.87); M (B&W); 18; ex *Sea Brave* 1978; ex *Momijisan Maru* 1974
Sisters:
31001 **HAN NURI** (Ko) ex *Sea Discoverer* 1978; ex *Matsudosan Maru* 1974

★31010 **VICTORIA DE GIRON** Cu/Sw (Uddevalla) 1969; C; 11000; 161.9 × 9.8 (531 × 32.6); M (B&W); —
Sisters (Cu flag):
★31011 **PLAYA LARGA**
★31012 **BAHIA DE COCHINOS**

★31020 **XUAN HUA** RC/Sw (Oresunds) 1956; C; 6000/9000; 141.08 × 8.19/9.21 (462.86 × 26.87/30.22); M (Gotaverken); 14; ex *Steed* 1976; ex *Broland* 1970; ex *O.A. Brodin* 1961

★31030 **KANG DING** RC/Sw (Kockums) 1956; CP; 10400; 151.6 × 9.3 (498 × 30.6); M (Kockums); 14.75; ex *Oceantravel* 1970; ex *Northern Clipper* 1963

★31040 **HONG QI** RC/RC (Dariren) 1964; C; 11500; 171 × — (560 × —); T (—); —

★31050 **LENINSKIY KOMSOMOL** Ru/Ru (Kherson) 1960; C; 12000; 170 × 9.7 (558 × 32); T (Kirov); 19
Sisters (Ru flag):
★31051 **FIZIK LEBEDYEV**
★31052 **FIZIK VAVILOV**
★31053 **METALLURG BAYKOV**

● 31070 **HOLLAND** Gr/Ja (Mitsui) 1961; CP; 4900; 145.7 × 7.2 (478 × 23.6); M (B&W); 16.5; Lengthened 1969; ex *Armada Clipper* 1980; ex *Holland* 1979

★31080 **JIANGYIN** RC/FRG (Rhein Nordseew) 1958; C; 6800/9500; 153.1 × 8.1/9 (502 × 26.3/30); M (MAN); 15.5; ex *Hwang Ho* 1970; ex *Henri G* 1968

31120 **PRESIDENT ADAMS** US/US (Newport News) 1968; Pt Con; 11600/15900; 184.4 ×9.5/10.7 (605 × 31.3/35); T (GEC); 21; ex *Alaskan Mail*
Sisters (US flag):
31121 **PRESIDENT CLEVELAND** ex *American Mail* 1978
31122 **PRESIDENT JACKSON** ex *Indian Mail* 1978
31123 **PRESIDENT WILSON** ex *Hong Kong Mail* 1978
31124 **PRESIDENT TAYLOR** ex *Korean Mail* 1978

31130 **KIRKELLA** Br/Br (Hall, Russell) 1965; ST; 1200; 69.4 × — (228 × —); D-E (English Electric); —
Similar:
31132 **ARCHIMEDES** (No) ex *Swanella* 1981
3133 **NORTHERN HORIZON** (Br) (converted to survey ship); ex *Marbella* 1980
31134 **SOUTHERN FIGHTER** (SA) ex *Yellowfin* 1977; ex *Northella* 1973

31140 **EASTERN POWER** Pa/De (B&W) 1956; CP; 2400/3300; 105.2 × 5.8/— (345 × 19.2/—); M (B&W); 14; ex *Eastern Progress* 1976; ex *Salamaua* 1974; ex *Iberia* 1969

Sister:
31141 GEM CARRIERS (UAE) ex *Klitos* 1982; ex *Alexandros* 1980; ex*Basel*; ex *Veneranda M* 1973; ex *Massilia* 1970

★**31150 GEROITE NA SEVASTOPOL** Bu/No (Framnaes) 1978; RoC/TF; 9600; 185.45 × 7.42 (608.43 × 24.34); TSM (B&W); 19; Stern door
Sister (builder—Fredriksstad):
★**31151 GEROITE NA ODESSA** (Bu)
Similar (Ys built—'Uljanik'):
★**31152 GEROI PLEVNY** (Ru)
★**31153 GEROI SHIPKI** (Ru)

31160 BOUNTY Fr/Sw (Helsingborgs) 1951; CP; 2400; 105.5 × 5.7 (346 × 18.11); M (Gotaverken); 15.5; ex *Capitaine La Perouse* 1981; ex *Capitaine La Perouse* 1975; ex *Negosky* 1973; ex *Bayard* 1972

31170 DIMMER Pa/Sw (Lindholmens) **1961**; C; 4500; 115.1 × 7.5 (378 × 24.7); M (Gotaverken); 15; ex *Tevega* 1981; ex *Nordia* 1974; ex *Nordic*

★**31180 GRUDZIADZ** Pd/Pd (Szczecinska) **1963**; C; 2900; 113.5 × 6.4 (373 × 20.2); M (B&W); 15.5; '**B-49**' type
Sisters (Pd flag):
★**31181 GLOGOW**
★**31182 GORLICE**

31190 ELAZIG Tu/No (Drammen) 1960; C; 3000/4800; 116.29 × 6.45/7.92 (382 × 21.16/25.98); M (Sulzer); 13; ex *Marosa* 1960
Sisters:
31191 HELMAR (Pa) ex *Horizon* 1980; ex *Concordia Lord* 1970; ex *Lord Viking* 1969
31192 NUEVA ESPARTA (Venezuelan Navy) ex*Lise* 1960

31200 ISORA Sp/Sp ('Astano') 1967; R; 1600; 96.7 × 5.7 (317 × 18.6); M (B&W); —; ex *Lago San Mauricio* 1975
Sister:
31201 ARONA (Sp) ex *Carmen M Pinillos* 1975

⬤ **31220 MOUNT CARIBBEAN** Pa/Ja (Fujinagata) 1962; C; 6500; 133 × 8.2 (437 × 20.7); M; 14.75; ex *Meihohsan Maru*

31230 YANNIS Gr/Br (Doxford) 1963; C; 11200; 164.4 × 9.5 (539 × 31.3); M (Doxford); 16

31250 NEW HAILEE Pa/FRG (Kieler H) 1959; CP; 4900/7200; 138.1 × 7.2/8.6 (453 × 23.6/28); M (MAN); 16; ex *Hai Lee* 1981; ex *Makefjell* 1972

⬤ **31270 EASTERN PEARL** Pa/Ja (Mitsubishi HI) 1962; C; 9200; 156.1 × 9.2 (512 × 30); M (Sulzer); 18.25; ex *Tacoma Maru* 1981

★**31280 EASTERN LION** RC/Br (Barclay Curle) 1952; C; 5500/7500; 141.8 × 7.9/8.3 (465 × 26/27); M (Doxford); 13.5; ex *Jag Ketu* 1967; ex *Windsor* 1963

31290 WHITE ROSE Gr/Be (Cockerill-Ougree) 1960; C; 6900; 156 × 8 (512 × 26.5); M (B&W); 18; ex *Vivarais* 1978

31300 NAGAN Le/De (Helsingor) 1962; CP; 4200; 126.9 × 7.3 (416.4 × 24); M (B&W); 17; ex*Helle Skou*
Sisters:
31301 NEW HAIHUNG (Pa) ex *Damian* 1982; ex *Inger Skou*
31302 KIRSTEN SKOU (De)
31303 ANTZELA (Gr) ex *Carenero* 1981; ex *Mads Skou*
★**31305 XIN LE** (RC) ex*Melantho C* 1982; ex*Mette Skou*

31320 SILVER EAGLE Tw/Ja (Kawasaki D) 1959; C; 8300; 143 × 8.1 (469 × 26.5); M (MAN); 14.75; ex *Victory Goddess* 1980; ex*Chieh Hwang* 1979; ex*Goh Shu Maru* 1974

31325 LAGO LACAR Ar/Ys ('Split') 1962; C; 8500; 157.23 × 8.23 (516 × 27.00); M (Fiat); —; Others of this class probably have this sequence now (see **RIO CORRIENTES** etc)

★**31330 SONG NHUE** Vn/Ja (Harima) 1960; CP; 7200; 136.6 × 8.4 (448 × 26.9); M (Sulzer); 14.75; ex *Unique Star* 1980; ex *Beaufort Career* 1976; ex *Caribbean Star* 1975; ex *Soei Maru* 1974

31340 JIN YANG No 13 Ko/Ja (Namura) 1957; C; 7600; 138 × 8.7 (453 × 28.6); M (MAN); 14.25; ex *Papeete* 1976; ex *Tokelau Maru* 1972; ex *Eishun Maru* 1971

31360 MEDROCK Gr/Sw (Uddevalla) 1965; C; 9000; 145 × 8.9 (476 × 29.3); M (B&W); 15; ex *Fauskanger* 1980

31370 IKARIA Gr/Be (Boel) 1964; CP; 7200/10900; 159.3 × 8.1/9.5 (523 × 26.8/30.3); M (MAN); 15; ex

Mokaria 1983

31390 JIN YANG No 17 Ko/Ja (Ishikawajima) 1957; CP; 5800; 126 × 8 (414 × 26.3); M (MAN); 12.25; ex *Peace Rose* 1978; ex *Mikumo Maru* 1975
Similar:
31391 MUNAKATA MARU (Ja)

31410 BENGAL TOWER Bh/It (Taranto) 1958; C; 6300/8600; 148.65 × 8.11/9.27 (482 × 26.61/30.41); M (Fiat); 16; ex*Islami Jhanda* 1980; ex *Goldstone* 1979; Launched as *Moonstone*

31430 ORIENT SUCCESS Pa/Ja (Iino) 1958; C; 7700; 139.6 × 8.6 (458 × 28.1); M (Sulzer); 13.5; ex *Sakishima Maru* 1974

31440 ANTHIA Cy/Br (Doxford) 1964; C; 7600/11000; 164.4 × 9.6 (539 × 31.6); M (Doxford); —; ex *Nephele* 1975; ex *Katherine* 1973
Sisters:
31441 ABHA ZAHABIA (Si) ex *Golden Singapore* 1982; ex *Pearl Island* 1982
Probably similar:
31443 GOLDEN YENBO (Pa) ex*Tarpon Silver* 1981; ex *Aliki Livanos* 1969

31450 MATTERHORN Gr/Ja (Hitachi) 1962; C; 6600/9700; 156.9 × 8.4/9.5 (515 × 27.6/31.5); M (B&W); —; ex *Maliakos* 1983; ex *Athenian*; ex *Van Star* 1969; ex *Dona Nancy* 1968

★**31460 NANPING** RC/Ja (Mitsubishi HI) 1964; CP; 9100; 156.5 × 9.3 (513 × 30.6); M (Mitsubishi); 18.25; ex *Flores Sea* 1974; ex *Don Antonio* 1972

31480 BOONKRONG II Th/FRG (Rickmers) 1963; C; 3400/5300; 126.6 × 6.5/7.6 (415 × 21.5/25); M (Sulzer); —; ex*Captain Glyptis* 1982; ex*Carola* 1980; ex *Calanda* 1979

31490 KRATILAOS Pa/FRG (O&K) 1960; C; 2700/4000; 111.61 × 6.30/7.44 (366 × 20.67/24.41); M (MAN); 14; ex *Kronos* 1980; ex *Dimo* 1980; ex *Liberty* 1978; ex *Naharija* 1976

31510 SENIOR K Le/Ne (Nederlandsche) 1958; CP; 5200/7200; 128.8 × —/8.5 (422 × —/28); M (Stork); 16; ex *Porsanger* 1972

31520 EL ZANJON Pa/Ja (Osaka) 1959; C; 3800; 113.6 × 6.8 (373 × 22.4); M (Kawasaki); 12; ex *Caribbean Pearl*; ex *Zipounas* 1976; ex *Yubari Maru* 1970

31530 GOOD MASTER Gr/Ne ('De Schelde') 1962; CP; 6200/8900; 147.2 × 8.3/9 (483 × 27.3/29.8); M (Sulzer); 15; ex *Mol*

31540 THEOSKEPASTI Gr/Sw (Oskarshamns) 1961; CP; 8900; 148.4 × 9.1 (487 × 30); M (Gotaverken); 15; ex *Laja*; ex *Holthill* 1969

31570 GEMINI Gr/FRG (Rickmers) 1966; CP; 5500; 127.4 × 7.6 (415 × 25.1); M (MAN); 15.5; ex *Carl Offersen*

31580 PRESIDENT QUIRINO Pi/Ja (IHI) 1962; C; 9200; 156 × 9 (512 × 29.8); M (Sulzer); 17.25; ex *Daiwa Maru* 1983

31590 SILVER DRAGON Tw/Ja (Kawasaki D) 1957; C; 8400; 143.11 × 8.1 (469.52 × 26.58); M (MAN); 14.5; ex *Victory Gleam* 1981; ex *Chile Maru* 1974
Sister:
31591 GOLDEN DRAGON (Tw) ex *Victory Glory* 1980; ex *Peru Maru* 1974

31600 BENGAL PRIDE Bh/Br (Doxford) 1962; C; 7000/9900; 155.2 × —/9.3 (509 × —/30.6); M (Doxford); 14.5; ex *Trader* 1981; ex *Pearl Trader*

31610 ANTHIA Cy/Br (Doxford) 1964; C; 7600/11000; 164.4 × 9.6 (539 × 31.6); M (Doxford); —; ex *Nephele* 1975, ex *Katherine* 1973
Sisters:
31611 ABHA ZAHABIA (Si) ex *Golden Singapore* 1982; ex *Pearl Island* 1982
Probably similar:
31612 GOLDEN YENBO (Pa) ex*Tarpon Silver* 1981; ex *Aliki Livanos* 1969

★**31620 TANG YIN** RC/FRG (LF-W) 1960; C; 7800/9200; 151.4 × 8.3/9.3 (497 × 27/30.4); M (MAN); 16; ex *Arabian Sea* 1974; ex *Hanse* 1971

31630 SHAMS Pk/Ja (Hitachi) 1960; PC; 8900; 143.3 × 6.7 (470 × 22.1); TSM (B&W); 17

31640 BANANERA Pa/It (Ansaldo) 1964; R; 5100; 132.9 × 6.4 (436 × 21); M (B&W); 18.5; ex *Mare Arabico* 1981
Sisters:
31641 MARE CARIBICO (It)
31642 BANANA EXPRESS (Ec) ex *Mare Somalo* 1978
31643 JUBA (So) ex *Mare Italico* 1974

31650 BIANCA Bs/FRG (B+V) 1965; R; 5700; 131.4× — (431 × —); M (MAN); 20.5; ex*Biafra* 1981

31660 IONIAN CAPE Ma/No (Moss V) 1958; CP; 2400/3800; 108.2 × 6.3/7.4 (355 × 20.1/24.3); M (Werkspoor); ex *Alexandros A* 1982; ex *Unstrut*; ex *Arctic Tern* 1965
Similar (more conical funnel)
31661 IONIAN GRACE (Ma) ex *Cefallonian Grace* 1982; ex *Mulde*; ex *Sunima* 1965
31662 IONIAN DESTINY (Ma) ex *Cefallonian Destiny* 1982; ex *Bode*; ex *Arctic Gull* 1965

★**31680 SOVIETSKAYA ARKTIKA** Ru/Br (Short Bros) 1951; FC; 9000; 140.6 × 7 (461 × 26); M (Doxford); 12; ex *Stanhope* 1954; Converted from general cargo

31690 LI SHAN Pa/FRG (Deutsche Werft) 1958; C; 3300; 143.19 × 6.56 (468.7 × 21.52); M (MAN); 16; ex *Hornstern* 1975

⬤ **31700 LADY KATINA** Gr/Ne ('De Noord') 1959; C; 2900; 116.6 × 6.4 (383 × 21); M (Stord); 14; ex*Katina* 1983; ex *Sommaro* 1975

31710 PAPACOSTAS Gr/Ja (Mitsubishi HI) 1958; C; 9600; 148.52 × 9.52 (487 × 31.23); M (Sulzer); 14; ex *Artemidi II* 1974; ex *Pleiades* 1970

⬤ **31730 BRAZILIA** Pa/Ja (Mitsubishi HI) 1957; C; 6500/9400; 148.52 × —/9.53 (487.27 ×—731.27); M (Sulzer); 14; ex *Eastern Nav* 1983; ex*Eastar* 1979; ex *Skarva* 1973; ex *Edda* 1964
Sisters:
31732 KUSU ISLAND (Sg) ex *Bolmaren* 1978; ex *Artemedi III* 1976; ex *Sefra* 1975; ex *Cape of Good Hope* 1961
31733 PROMETHEUS (Gr) ex *Ocean Prosper* 1968; ex *Surna* 1965; ex *Cape Agulhas* 1961; ex *Sira Polaris* 1970
31734 NELSON (Ma) ex *Theanto A S* 1984; ex *Polaris* 1970
31735 AMAR (Gr) ex *E D Papalios* 1979; ex *Fenix* 1966

⬤ **31750 DESPINA** Gr/Ne (Amsterdamsche D) 1958; CP; 2300; 105.4 × 6.1 (346 × 19.10); M (Werkspoor); 15; ex *Werra* ex *Fravizo* 1964

31760 YUHENG 2 Pa/No (Moss V) 1962; C; 2400/3800; 108.2 × 6.3/7.4 (355 × 20.9/24.1); M (B&W); 15; ex *Rosenort* 1983 ex *Nyco* 1963

★**31770 LEWANT II** Pd/De (Aalborg) 1967; C; 3000; 114.5 × 6.3 (375 × 20.6); M (B&W); —

31800 GALAXY II Gr/Ja (Sanoyasu) 1956; C; 5000; 122.8 × 7.6 (403 × 25); M (B&W); 13; ex*Silk* 1981; ex *Silver Fir*; ex *Ceylon Maru* 1974
Sisters:
31801 EXPRESS CARRIER (Ma) ex *Apostolos M.1* 1982; ex *Silver Sun* 1979; ex *Canberra Maru* 1972
31802 ADAMANTIOS S (Gr) ex *Silver Dolphin* 1974; ex *Colombo Maru* 1972
31803 JIANG LOONG (Pa) ex*Dragon Express* 1981; ex *Ta Peng No 3* 1979; ex *Celebes Maru* 1970

31810 KARANA ENAM Ia/Ja (Hitachi) 1960; C; 4800; 120.8 × 7.4 (396 × 24.6); M (Sulzer); 13; ex *Oceanic* 1977; ex *Shigeshima Maru* 1969

31820 EVER GRACE Pa/Ja (Hitachi) 1957; CP; 4900; 120.8 × 7.3 (396 × 24); M (B&W); 12.5; ex *Dewi* 1980; ex*Asano No 1* 1977; ex*Nikko Maru* 1973

★**31830 ARZAMAS** Ru/DDR ('Neptun') 1955; C; 3300; 102.4 × 6.6 (329 × 21.6); R & LPT (Liebknecht); 12.5
Similar:
★**31831 ZHAN DOU 155** (RC) ex*Ho Ping 155* 1967
★**31832 ZHAN DOU 156** (RC) ex *Ho Ping No 156* 1967

★**31890 MALAYA VISHERA** Ru/Ru (—) 1964; C/TC; 2900; 100.84 × 6.00 (331 × 19.69); M (CKD Praha); 13
Sisters (Ru flag):
★**31891 MALOYAROSLAVETS**
★**31892 SUKHONALES**

31910 AKIS S Gr/Sw (Oresunds) 1957; C; 3900/6200; 130.7 × 7.1/8.2 (428 × 23.4/27.1); M (Gotaverken); 14.5; ex *Mireille* 1974; ex *Dalhem* 1970

⬤ ★**31920 HONG MING** RC/Ne ('De Biesbosch-Dordrecht') 1959; C; 6300/8600; 150 × 8.2/8.8 (492 × 26.3/29); M (Sulzer); 13; ex *Banda Sea* 1976; ex *Amstelmolen* 1972
Sisters (RC flag):
★**31921 SAN MING** ex *Bali* 1976; ex *Amstelveld* 1972
★**31922 YONG MING** ex *Java Sea* 1976; ex *Amstelsluis* 1972

⬤ **31930 CAPTAIN ANDREADIS** Gr/Ys ('3 Maj')

1960; C; 9300; 153.2 × 9.3 (503 × 29.9); M (Sulzer); 14; ex *Charalarıbos N Pateras* 1980; ex *Capetan Nicolas* 1961

31950 R.S.A. SA/Ja (Fujinagata) 1961; RS; 1600; 68.9 × — (227 × —); M (Sulzer); 11.5

31960 ELDE Gr/FRG (Stuelcken) 1958; C; 5000; 118 × 8 (387 × 26); M (B&W); —; ex *Kasem Samut;* ex *Tumlaren* 1970

● **32000 ISLAND OF MARMARA** Gr/Br (Denny) 1960; C; 4800/7000; 132.1 × 7.6/8.1 (434 × 24.7/26.2); M (Sulzer); 14.75; ex *City of St Albans*
Sister:
32001 SUERTE (Pa) ex *City of Gloucester*

32010 ARCHANGELOS G. Gr/Ja (Hitachi) 1960; C; 10100; 158 × 9.5 (519 × 31); M (B&W); —

● **32020 MIGHTY WIND** Pa/Ys ('3 Maj') 1959; C; 6000/8900; 152.3 × 8.3/9.2 (500 × 27.6/30.3); M (Sulzer); 15; ex *Avra* 1981; ex *Agios Fanourios* 1976; ex *Platon* 1974; ex *Kyvernitis* 1972

32040 PARGA Gr/FRG (Deutsche Werft) 1959; C; 6800/10100; 157 × —/9.24 (515 × —/30.31); M (MAN); 14.5; ex *Simoa* 1976

32055 KARIN Pa/DDR (Warnow) 1971; C; 6200/9100; 152.76 × 7.56/9.30 (501 × 24.80/30.51); M (MAN); 18; ex *Holstental* 1981; ex *Concordia Foam* 1979; ex *Holstental* 1979; ex *Armatan* 1975; 'Ozean' type
Similar:
32056 TAMATAVE (Mg)
32057 DELFINI (Li) ex *Aliakmon River;* ex *Aunis* 1980

32060 H. H. HESS US/US (National Steel) 1965; RS; 9400/12400; 171.8 × —/9.6 (564 × —/31.6); T (GEC); 20; ex *Canada Mail;* U S Military Sealift Command

★ **32065 LENIN** Ru/Ru (Baltic) 1959; IB; 14100; 134 × 16 (440 × 34.6); TrS N T-E (—); 18; New reactors fitted c. 1971

● **32070 PAN ANTILLES** Li/US (Maryland SB & DD) 1960; Con; 4700; 110.3 × 4.8 (361 × 15.11); TSM (Enterprise Eng); 16; ex *Floridian* 1974
Sister:
32071 ALEUTIAN DEVELOPER (Li) ex *New Yorker* 1976

32085 WINSTON CHURCHILL Br/Br (J S White) 1963; LT; 1500; 67.72 × 3.98 (222 × 13.06); TSD-E (English Electric); 13.5; helicopter platform
Sisters:
32086 STELLA (Br)
32087 SIREN (Br)

★ **32090 AMBASADOR** Ys/Ys ('Split') 1958; PC; 2600; 90 × 4.7 (296 × 15.6); TSM (Sulzer); 17.5; ex *Jedinstvo* 1979
Similar:
32091 HERMES (Gr) ex *Messager* 1976; ex *Jugoslavija* 1971

32100 L'ISERE Fr/No (Ankerlokken) 1970; RoC; 1100; 105.34 × 3.80 (346 × 12.47); TSM (N&H); 15.5; ex *Jolly Giallo* 1976; ex *Trailer Express* 1974; Stern door and 2 side doors

32120 DON JULIO Pi/Ja (Maizuru) 1967; PC; 2100; 95.66 × 5.16 (313.85 × 16.93); M (B&W); 17.5

32130 ISCHIA It/Br (Denny) 1948; RoPCF; 1500; 87.9 × 2.6 (288 × 8.6); TSM (Sulzer); 19; ex *Autocarrier* 1973; ex *Royal Sovereign* 1967; Converted from passenger ship

32140 SUADIYE Tu/Tu (Denizcilik) 1964; F; 600; 67 × 2.6 (220 × 8.6); TSM (Fiat); —

32150 FENERBAHCE Tu/Br (Denny) 1952; F; 1000; 73.1 × 3.4 (240 × 11.2); TSM (Sulzer); —
Sisters (Tu flag)
32151 DOLMABAHCE
32152 PASABAHCE

32160 HARBIYE Tu/Br (Fairfield SB) 1961; F; 800; 69.7 × 2.7 (229 × 8.8); TSR (Christiansen & Meyer); 15
Sisters (Tu flag):
32161 A KAVAGI
32162 ATAKOY ex *Genclik* 1961
32161 TEGMEN ALI IHSAN KALMAZ ex *Ihsan Kalmaz* 1982
32165 INKILAP
32166 KANLIKA
32167 PENDIK
32168 TURAN
32169 EMEKSIZ
32170 KUZGUNCUK

32180 GALLURA It/It (Tirreno) 1968; F; 4900; 123 ×

5.5 (404 × 18); TSM (Fiat); —

32190 MATANUSKA US/US (Puget Sound) 1963/78; RoPF; 3000; 124.36 × 4.98 (408 × 16.34); TSM (General Metals); 18; Lengthened 1978 (Willamette)

32200 DANA REGINA De/De (Aalborg) 1974; RoPCF; 12200; 153.7 × 6 (504 × 20); TSM (B&W); 21.5; Bow stern & port side doors

32210 ARMORIQUE Fr/Fr (Havre) 1972; RoPCF; 5700; 116.6 × 4.3 (382 × 14); TSM (Pielstick); 18; ex *Terje Vigen* 1975; Bow & stern doors

32220 HAMMERSHUS De/FRG (Meyer) 1967; RoPCF; 2900; 86.4 × 3.8 (283 × 12.6); TSM (KHD); 18; Side door; Rebuilt 1981 but may not be altered externally

● **32230 HANKYU No 16** Ja/Ja (Kanda) 1972; RoC/F; 5700; 135.49 × 5.23 (444.52 × 17.16); TSM (IHI); 21; ex *Tsukushi*
Sister:
32231 HANKYU No. 17 (Ja) ex *Hakata*

32240 IZU MARU No 3 Ja/Ja (Hashihama) 1972; RoPF; 7500; 137.85 × 5.61 (452.26 × 18.41); TSM (Pielstick); 21.5; ex *Cassiopeia;* Bow and stern ramps
Sister:
32241 IZU MARU No 11 (Ja) ex *Albatross*

32250 PENN AR BED Fr/Fr (La Rochelle) 1974; RoPCF; 2900; 109.5 × 5.5 (359 × 18); TSM (Pielstick); 19

32260 PRESIDENTE DIAZ ORDAZ Me/No (Trondhjems) 1961; RoPCF; 2900; 90.3 × 4.1 (296 × 13.6); TSM (Nydqvist & Holm); 18; ex *Cort Adeler* 1970; Bow and stern doors

32270 QUEEN OF VICTORIA Ca/Ca (Victoria Mach) 1962; RoPCF; 4900; 130 × 3.8 (427 × 12.6); TSM (Atlas-MaK); 18; ex *City of Victoria* 1963; Lengthened 1970; Bow & stern doors; Heightened by 3 metres and modified 1982 (Burrard Y); Drawing shows vessel before this modification
Sister:
32271 QUEEN OF VANCOUVER (Ca) ex *City of Victoria* 1963

32280 CALEDONIA Br/No (Langesunds) 1966; RoPCF; 1200; 61.8 × 3.2 (203 × 10.4); TSM (MAN); 15; ex *Stena Baltica* 1970

★ **32290 ILIRIJA** Ys/FRG (Meyer) 1963; RoPCF; 2000; 80.5 × 4.1 (264 × 14.6); TSM (KHD); 16.5; ex *Bornholmerpilen* 1971

● **32300 POLAR EXPRESS** Fi/De (Aalborg) 1963; RoPCF; 2900; 91.3 × 4.2 (299 × 13.78); TSM (Nydqvist & Holm); 18; ex *Prinsessan Margaretha* 1970; Bow door

32310 EOLOS Gr/FRG (Hanseatische) 1962; RoPCF; 3000; 96 × 4.7 (315 × 14); TSM (Nohab); 16; ex *Gryf* 1981; ex *Finndana* 1967; ex *Hansa Express* 1966; Bow and stern doors

32320 CONCEPCION MARINO Ve/No (Trondhjems) 1978; RoPF; 6200; 105.01 × 3.9 (344.52 × 12.8); TSM (KHD); 17; Bow and stern doors
Sister:
32321 CACICA ISABEL (Ve)

★ **32330 XING HU** RC/Sp (AESA) 1967; PC; 4400; 104.9 × 4.3 (344 × 13.5); TSM (B&W); 19.5; ex *Dona Montserrat* 1980; ex *West Star* 1975; ex *Cabo Izarra* 1970

★ **32340 STENA SAILER** Ih/Ih (Verolme Cork) 1975; RoC; 2400; 119 × 4.6 (391 × 15); TSM (British Polar); 18; ex *Dundalk* 1980; Bow and stern ramps and doors

32350 CAPO BIANCO It/De (Aarhus) 1960; RoPCF; 2300; 88.5 × 4.6 (290 × 15); TSM (Polar); 17.5; ex *Flaminia Nova* 1974; ex *Holmia* 1971; ex *Calmar Nyckel* 1965; ex *Prins Bertil* 1964; Bow and stern doors

32360 MERZARIO SYRIA Sw/Sw (Kalmar) 1968; RoC; 1100; 89.3 × 4.1 (293 × 14); M (Nydqvist & Holm); 18; ex *Scandic* 1977; Stern door

32370 BUFFALO Br/FRG (Sietas) 1974; RoC; 3500; 125 × 3.8 (410 × 13); TSM (KHD); 19.5

32390 MAR CARIBE Br/FRG (O&K) 1967; RoC; 2600; 104 × 5.4 (342 × 18); M (Atlas-MaK); 18; Stern door
Similar:
32391 RHONE (Fr) ex *Rhonebal;* ex *Norcape;* ex *Rhonetal*

32410 JOLLY BIANCO It/FRG (Meyer) 1969; RoC; 2900; 129.3 × 5 (424 × 17); TSM (KHD); 17; ex *Servus;* Stern door and ramp; Lengthened 1971 (Amsterdamsche D)

32420 STELLA MARIS II. Gr/FRG (Adler) 1960; P; 2700; 88.2 × 4.4 (289 × 11.6); TSM (KHD); 18.5; ex *Bremerhaven* 1965

32430 GOLDEN VERGINA Gr/Fr (L'Atlantique) 1966; RoPCF; 4600; 115 × 4.4 (378 × 14.6); TSM (Pielstick); 21; ex *Corse* 1982; Bow and stern doors
Sister:
32431 NAIAS II (Gr) ex *Comte de Nice* 1983; ex *Provence* 1966

32440 NORWAVE Br/FRG (AG 'Weser') 1965; RoPCF; 3500; 108.8 × 4.9 (356 × 16); TSM (Smith & Bolnes); 15; Bow and stern doors
Sister:
32441 NORWIND (Ne)

32450 FERRY GOLD Ja/Ja (Hayashikane) 1970; F; 4100; 117.5 × 4.4 (385 × 14.6); TSM (Kawasaki); 18
Sisters:
32451 FERRY PEARL (Ja)
32452 SWEET RORO (Pa) ex *Ferry Ruby* 1982

32460 OZAMIS CITY Pi/Ja (Mitsubishi HI) 1965; C/F; 2900; 91.7 × 4.2 (301 × 13.6); M (MAN); 18.5 ex *Iligan City* 1980; ex *Fuji*

32470 COBALT MARU Ja/Ja (Mitsubishi HI) 1967; F; 3200; 89.3 × 3.9 (293 × 13); TSM (Kobe); 13.5
Possible sister:
32471 IVORY MARU (Ja)
Similar (smaller):
32472 SUMIRE MARU (Ja)

32480 IYO MARU Ja/Ja (Hitachi) 1966; RoPCF; 3100; 89.4 × 3.7 (276 × 12.2); TSM (B&W); 15.25
Sister:
32481 TOSA MARU (Ja)

32490 TROUBRIDGE Br/Au (Evans Deakin) 1961; RoPCF; 2000; 91.4 × 3.7 (300 × 12.1); TSM (British Polar); 14.5

32500 DRAGON Br/Fr (Dubigeon-Normandie/Bretagne) 1967; RoPCF; 6100; 134.6 × 4.8 (440 × 15.9); TSM (Pielstick); 19
Sister:
32501 LEOPARD (Fr)

32510 DEUTSCHLAND FRG/FRG (Nobiskrug) 1972; RoPCF; 6100; 144.1 × 5.9 (473 × 19.3); TS D-E (Friedrichshafen); 19.5; Bow and stern doors

32520 PROVENCE Fr/It (Pietra Ligure) 1974; RoPCF; 7800; 142.3 × 5.8 (467 × 19); TSM (Pielstick); 23; Bow, side & stern doors

32530 MALTA EXPRESS It/FRG (Unterweser) 1968; RoPCF; 3900; 115 × 4.8 (377 × 15.6); TSM (MAN); —; ex *Gedser* 1976

32550 DELEDDA It/It (Italcantieri) 1978; RoPCF; 6500; 131.02 × 5.62 (429.86 × 18.44); TSM (GMT); 20.5; Stern and side doors
Sisters (It flag):
32551 VERGA
32552 BOCCACCIO
32553 CARDUCCI
32554 LEOPARDI
32555 MANZONI
32556 PASCOLI
32557 PETRARCA

32560 SAINT ELOI Fr/It (Pietra Ligure) 1972; RoPCF; 4600; 114.6 × 4.1 (376 × 13); TSM (Pielstick); 19.5

32570 ISHIKARI Ja/Ja (Naikai) 1974; RoPCF; 12900; 188.4 × — (618.11 × —); TSM (MAN); 21.5; Lengthened 1980
Sister:
32571 DAISETSU (Ja)

32580 ARKAS Ja/Ja (Setoda) 1972; RoPCF; 9700; 167.2 × 6.3 (548 × 20.6); TSM (B&W); 21
Sister:
32581 ALBIREO (Ja)
Similar:
32582 MARIMO (Ja)

32590 GARYOUNIS Ly/Ja (Naikai) 1973; P/RoC; 9600; 166.53 × 6.47 (546.36 × 21.23); TSM (Pielstick); 20.5; ex *Mashu* 1977
Similar (may not have lifeboats, or fewer lifeboats):
32591 SAROMA (Ja)

32600 NORLAND Br/FRG (A G 'Weser') 1974; RoPCF; 13000; 153 × 6.2 (502 × 20.3); TSM (Stork-Werkspoor); 19; Stern door and ramp and side door
Sister:
32601 NORSTAR (Ne)

32610 MIMITSU MARU Ja/Ja (Naikai) 1973; RoPCF; 9600; 160 × — (525 × —); TSM (MAN); 27
Similar:
32611 TAKACHIHO MARU (Ja)

32620 EL ARISH Eg/No (Bergens) 1980; RoPCF;

4600; 105 × 4.13 (344.5 × 13.55); TSM (Normo); 19; Stern door/ramp
Sister:
32621 EL TOR (Eg)

32630 SAINT PAULIA Ja/Ja (NKK) 1971; RoPCF; 6000; 118 × 5.7 (387 × 19); TSM (Pielstick); 16
Sister:
32631 ZERALDA (Ag) ex Bougainvillea 1976
Similar:
32632 HOGGAR (Ag) ex Hibiscus 1976
32633 TIPAZA (Ag) ex Phenix 1976
32634 HAMAYU (Ja)

32640 CASTALIA Gr/Gr (Kynossura) 1974; RoPCF; 5300; 132 × 5.3 (433 × 17.6); TSM (MaK); 18

32650 AQUARIUS Gr/Gr (United SY) 1972; P; 4600; 103.7 × 4.7 (340 × 15.6); TSM (Pielstick); 19.5

32660 TAI SHAN Br/Ja (Niigata) 1972; F; 2100; 78.64 × 3.18 (258 × 10.43); TSM (Niigata); 17.5
Sister (Br flag):
32661 LO SHAN
32662 NAM SHAN

32670 TIZIANO It/It (Apuania) 1970; RoPCF; 3500; 101.2 × 4.3 (332 × 14); TSM (Fiat); 18

32680 LORD SINAI Eg/Fr (Mediterranee) 1966; RoPCF; 4800; 114.99 × 4.92 (377.26 × 16.14); TSM (Pielstick); 19.5; ex Nuits St George 1982; ex Fred Scamaroni 1980; Bow and stern doors; Side doors

32690 TINTORETTO It/It (Apuania) 1966; RoC/F; 2700; 100 × 4.3 (328 × 14.3); TSM (Fiat); 18; ex Jacopo Tintoretto 1983

32700 POSEIDON FRG/No (Ulstein) 1964; F; 1100; 65.5 × 2.9 (215 × 9.6); TSM (KHD); —

★32710 LIBURNIJA Ys/Ne ('De Merwede') 1965; RoPCF; 3000; 89.2 × 4.2 (292 × 14); TSM (Sulzer); 15; Bow and stern doors

32720 INNISFALLEN Ih/Ih (Verolme Cork) 1969; RoPCF; 4800; 118.3 × 4.5 (388 × 13.6); TSM (MAN); 20; ex Leinster 1980; Bow and stern doors
Sister:
32721 CORSICA VIVA (Pa) ex Innisfallen 1980

32730 FARAH 1 Pa/FRG (Nobiskrug) 1968; RoPCF; 4100; 110.2 × 4.5 (362 × 14.6); TSM (MAN); 21.5; ex Munster 1983

32740 LA VALLETTA It/It (Pellegrino) 1971; RoPCF; 2100; 89.5 × 4.3 (297 × 14); TSM (Ansaldo); 16; Bow and stern doors

32750 NISSOS CHIOS Gr/Ys ('Titovo') 1967; RoPCF; 3200; 97.5 × 4.8 (320 × 15.9); TSM (Sulzer); 18; ex Kapella; Bow and stern doors

32760 PRINSES BEATRIX Ne/Ne (Verolme SH) 1978; RoPCF; 9400; 131.02 × 5.17 (429.86 × 16.96); TSM (Stork-Werkspoor); 21; Bow and stern doors/ramps

32770 ALCAEUS Gr/Ys ('Titovo') 1970; RoPCF; 3900; 99.2 × 4.8 (325 × 16); TSM (Sulzer); 18; ex Marella 1981; Bow and stern doors

32780 TIGER Br/De (Helsingor) 1972; RoPCF; 4000; 104.04 × 4.37 (341.34 × 14.38); TSM (B&W); 20.25; ex Kattegat 1978; Bow & stern doors; Also known as 'n.f. TIGER'
Sister:
32781 PANTHER (Br) ex Lasse II; ex Djursland 1974; also known as n.f. PANTHER

32790 ANTRIM PRINCESS Br/Br (Hawthorn, L) 1967; RoPCF; 3600; 112.6 × 3.7 (369 × 12.3); TSM (Pielstick); 19.5
Similar:
32791 AILSA PRINCESS (Br)

32800 THE VIKING Fi/FRG (Unterweser) 1974; RoPCF; 4400; 118 × 5 (388 × 16.9); TSM (MAN); 21; ex Kalle III 1983; Bow and stern doors
Sister:
32801 DJURSLAND (De) ex Djursland II 1980
Similar:
★32802 VIKING 2 (Ys) ex Njegos 1984; ex Travemunde 1980

32810 STENA NORDICA Sw/De (Aalborg) 1969; RoPCF; 5700; 123.5 × 5.2 (405 × 17); TSM (Nydqvist & Holm); 20.5; ex Prinsessan Christina 1983; ex Safe Christina 1982; ex Prinsessan Christina 1981; Bow and stern doors

32820 SOLIDOR Fr/FRG (Meyer) 1965; RoC/F; 900; 63.61 × 3.48 (208.7 × 11.42); TSM (MaK); 15; ex Langeland 1977; Bow door

32830 DISKO De/De (Svendborg) 1968; PC; 2200; 70.5 × 4 (230 × 13); M (MAN); 14

● 32840 LINDBLAD EXPLORER Pa/Fi (Nystads)

1969; P; 2300; 72.9 × 4.2 (239 × 14); M (Atlas—MaK); 15; Side door

32850 WORLD DISCOVERER Sg/FRG (Schichau-U) 1973; P; 3400; 71.4 × 4.2 (234 × 14); M (Atlas-MaK); 16.5; ex Bewa Discoverer 1973

32860 LANGELAND II De/Ne ('Combiship') 1977; RoPCF; 1600; 70.01 × 3.81 (229.69) × 12.5); TSM (Atlas-MaK) 15.5; Bow and stern doors; Also known as LANGELAND TO

32870 ST. OLA Br/Br (Hall, Russell) 1974; RoPCF; 1300; 70.2 × 4 (230 × 13); TSM (British Polar); 15; Bow and stern doors

32880 A REGINA Pa/Sw (Langesunds) 1967; RoPCF; 5200; 111 × 4.8 (361 × 16); TSM (MAN) 23.5; ex Stena Germanica; Bow and stern doors
Sister:
32881 SOL OLYMPIA (Cy) ex Viking 6 1983; ex Goelo 1982; ex Viking 6 1980; ex Wickersham 1974; ex Stena Britannica 1968

★32890 RUGEN DDR/DDR ('Neptun') 1972; RoPCF/F; 6500; 152 × 5.6 (500 × 18.3); TSM (MAN) 20.9; Stern and side doors

32900 SOL PHRYNE Cy/Ja (Mitsubishi J) 1948; RoC/F; 5900; 118.67 × — (389.34 × —); TSM (Werkspoor); 17; ex Aeolis 1977; ex Taisetsu Maru 1967

32910 CANDIA Gr/Ja (Sumitomo) 1971; RoPCF; 5800; 130 × 5.5 (427 × 18); TSM (MAN); 19.5; ex Central No2 1972
Possible sister:
32911 RETHIMNON (Gr) ex Central No5 1972

● ★32915 OSETIYA Ru/Ru (Zhdanov) 1963; P; 3200; 101.50 × 3.85 (333 × 12.63); TSM (CKD Praha); 14.5; Rebuilt as cruise ship

32920 VENUS Ja/Ja (Naikai) 1975; RoPCF; 3500; 120 × 4.9 (395 × 16); TSM (Pielstick); 20

32930 FREDERICK CARTER Ca/Ca (Davie SB) 1968; RoC/TF; 1200; 148.1 × 6.4 (486 × 21); TSM (Crossley); 18; Stern doors

32940 C.S. MONARCH Br/Br (Robb Caledon) 1975; Cbl; 3900; 95.4 × 4.8 (313 × 15.6); M (British Polar); 15
Sister:
32941 C.S. IRIS (Br)

32950 SCHIAFFINO Fr/FRG (Kroegerw) 1970; RoC; 1000; 97 × 4.1 (319 × 13.6); TSM (Atlas-MaK); 16; ex Neckartal 1974; Stern door
Sisters:
32951 MIRANDA 1 (Pa) ex Cotentin 1981; ex Saaletal 1974; ex Thule 1971
32952 ST. MAGNUS (Br) ex Dorset; ex Ulster Sportsman 1976; ex Donautal 1974
32953 POINTER (Br) ex Preseli 1977; ex Antwerpen 1974

32960 MERCHANT NAVIGATOR Br/No (Ankerlokken) 1972; RoC; 1600; 108.64 × 4.95 (356 × 16.24); TSM (Pielstick); 18; ex Lady Tone 1982; ex Lagan Bridge 1981; ex Ilka 1979
Sister:
32961 LUCIE (De) ex Lady Lucienne 1982; ex Star Express 1980; ex Lalli 1980
Similar:
32962 SIR LAMORAK (Br) ex Lakespan Ontario 1983; ex Lady Catherine 1981; ex Lune Bridge 1981; ex Anu 1980; (chartered to RFA)

32970 RORO TRADER Gr/No (Langvik) 1971; RoC; 1600; 109.81 × 4.95 (360 × 16.24); TSM (MAN); 17.5; ex Starmark 1981; Stern door

32980 ESPRESSO LIGURIA It/It ('L Orlando') 1967; RoC; 2000; 104.7 × 5.1 (343 × 16.1); TSM (Sulzer); 19; Stern doors
Sister (It flag):
32984 BERBERA II (Gr) ex Atlantic Princess 1981; ex Espresso Lombardia 1981

32990 KAPTAN SAIT OZEGE Tu/FRG (Schichau-U) 1977; RoC; 2200; 110.52 × 4.98 (362.6 × 16.34); TSM (MAN-Sulzer); 17; Bow & stern door/ramp
Sister:
32991 KAPTAN NECDET OR (Tu)

33000 ATLE Sw/Fi (Wartsila) 1974; IB; 6900; 104.6 × 8.3 (343 × 27.3); TSD-E (Pielstick); 18.5
Sisters:
33001 FREJ (Sw)
33001/1 YMER (Sw)
33002 URHO (Fi)
33003 SISU (Fi)

33010 NORTREFF No/No (Pusnaes) 1955; Trlr; 960; 65.9 × 4.9 (216 × 16.4); M (Liebknecht); 14; Converted Whaler

33020 FERNANDO ESCANO Pi/FRG (M Jansen) 1968; CP; 1800; 89.4 × 4.1 (293 × 13.3); M (KHD); —; ex Fernando Escano II 1980

33030 TRADE CONTAINER Pa/Br (Burntisland) 1962; Con; 4700; 113.1 × 7.2 (371 × 23.1); M (Sulzer); 14; ex Moira 1981; ex C.P. Explorer 1973; ex Beaverpine 1971; Converted cargo ship (Boele's Sch)

33040 AL-KHALEEJ Ku/Sw (Oresunds)-Hong Kong 1965/75/78; LS; 7700/10100; 160 — (524.9 × —); M (Gotaverken); 19.5; ex White Ocean 1975; Converted from reefer 1975 (Taikoo); Lengthened 1978 (Hong Kong U)

33050 CAPO FALCONARA It/De (Helsingor) 1937; F; 2000; 100 × 4.9 (328 × 16.1); TSM (B&W); 19; ex Express Ferry Angelina Lauro; ex Corsica Express 1975; ex Konprins Olav 1967

33060 SYDNEY TRADER Br/Au (Evans Deakin) 1969; RoC; 6300; 136.7 × 6.4 (449 × 21.1); TSM (MAN); 17.5; Stern door
Sisters (Br flag):
33061 BRISBANE TRADER
33062 TOWNSVILLE TRADER

33070 SALVISCOUNT Sg/Br (Robb Caledon) 1971; Tg; 2000; 80.7 × 7.4 (265 × 24.3); M (Pielstick); 18; ex Lloydsman 1980

33075 SEEFALKE FRG/FRG (O&K) 1981; FP; 1800; 83.7 × 4.72 (273 × 15.49); TSM (MWM); 17; Helicopter platform

33080 HERMES Gr/Ys ('Split') 1956; P; 2600; 90.1 × 4.5 (296 × 15.3); TSM (Sulzer); 18; ex Messenger 1976; ex Jugoslavija 1971
Similar:
★33081 AMBASADOR (Ys) ex Jedinstvo 1979

33090 CAMBRIDGE FERRY Br/Br (Hawthorn, L) 1963; RoC/TF; 3300; 122.8 × 3.7 (440 × 12.2); TSM (Mirrlees); 13.5

33095 JOHAN NORDENANKAR Sw/Sw (Falkenbergs) 1980; RS; 1800; 73 × 3.8 (239.5 × 12.47); M (Hedemora); 13; Helicopter deck aft

33100 SATURN Br/Br (Ailsa) 1977; RoC/F; 900; 69.53 × 2.44 (228.12 × 8.01); TSM (Mirrlees Blackstone); 14; Stern ramp; Port and starboard side ramps

33110 JUNO Br/Br (Lamont) 1974; RoC/F; 900; 69.17 × 2.41 (226.94 × 7.91); TSM (Mirrlees Blackstone); 14; Stern door and side doors
Sister:
33111 JUPITER (Br)

33120 SAOS Gr/De (Aalborg) 1964; RoC/F; 700; 54.9 × 3 (180 × 9.1); TSM (Jonkopings); 11; ex Drogden

33130 QUINTANA ROO Me/No (Hatlo) 1969; RoC/F; 550; 49.4 × 2.5 (162 × 8.3); TSM (Lister Blackstone); 14; ex Sound of Jura 1976; Bow door and stern ramp

33140 ATLANTIS Gr/Gr (Hellenic) 1973; Y; 2600; 115.8 × 4.3 (380 × 14); TSM (Pielstick); 22

33150 DESAFIO Sp/Sp (Lorenzo) 1979; Con; 2000; 103.45 × 6.43 (339.4 × 21.1); M (Deutz); 15

33155 PATRICIA Br/Br (H Robb) 1982; BT/LT; 2500; 86.34 × 4.41 (283 × 14.47); TSD-E (Ruston); 14; Helicopter platform

33160 GRANUAILE Ih/Br (Ferguson Bros) 1970; BT/LT; 2000; 80.7 × 4 (265 × 13.1); TSM (W H Allen); 13.5

33170 GULF EXPLORER NZ/Br (Hill) 1965; F; 500; 47.8 × 2.9 (157 × 9.6); TSM (Ruston & Hornsby); 13; ex Olovaha 1982; ex Queen of the Isles 1971

33180 ATALANTE Gr/Fr (DCAN) 1953; P; 13100; 167.3 × 7.9 (549. × 25.9); TSM (Creusot); 17; ex Tahitien 1972

33190 SOUTHERN GLORY My/Au (NSW Govt) 1951; C/B; 2400; 93.07 × 5.34 (305.35 × 17.52); TSM (British Polar); 10; ex Southern Cross; ex Lisa Miller 1979; ex Karoon 1968

● 33200 FULDATAL FRG/FRG (Rickmers) 1971; RoC; 1600; 114.9 × 5.7 (377 × 18.1); TSM (Atlas-MaK); 17; ex Norcove 1975; ex Falcon 1972; ex Fuldatal
Sisters:
33201 CARIARI (Pa) ex Cantoclaro 1982; ex Travetal 1978
33202 WESERTAL (FRG) ex Meyer Express 1973; ex Wesertal 1972
Similar:
33203 WUPPERTAL (FRG) ex Canaima 1977

33210 CORNOUILLES Fr/No (Bergens) 1977; RoPCF; 3000; 109.7 × — (360 × —); TSM (Pielstick);

19; Bow and stern doors

33220 BREIZH-IZEL Fr/Hong Kong (Taikoo) 1970; RoC; 2700; 111.66 × 4.97 (366.34 × 16.31); TSM (Pielstick); 17.5; ex *Inichios Express* 1980; ex *Rata Hills* 1978; ex *Wanaka* 1976; Stern door. Iniochos Express No 2 (See under MMFC) may now be similar

33230 HALLEY Pa/Au (NSW Govt.) 1961; RoC; 1700; 98.3 × 4.6 (323 × 15.1); TSM (Deltic); 14.5; ex *Bass Trader* 1975; Stern door

33240 YUSUF ZIYA ONIS Tu/No (Ankerlokken) 1979; RoC; 2400; 113.4 × 5.51 (372 × 18.08); M (Normo); 15; ex *Dr. Adnan Biren* 1982; Stern door-/ramp

33250 SVEALAND Sw/De (Helsingor) 1971; RoF; 4000; 118 × 5 (387 × 16.9); TSM (MaK); 18; Stern and side doors; Lengthened by 36.4m in 1984 (Fosen); Drawing shows vessel before this modification

● **33260 CICERO** Br/Br (Smith's D) 1978; RoC; 5100; 147.12 × 6.88 (482.68 × 22.57); TSM (Pielstick); 18; Stern door/ramp
Sister:
33261 CAVALLO (Ca)

33270 DORA BALTEA It/It (Apuania) 1975; RoC; 3500; 135.52 × 6 (444.62 × 19.67); TSM (Fiat); 18.5; Stern door/ramp; side doors/ramps
Similar (Larger):
33271 DORA RIPARIA (It)

33280 BALTIC EAGLE Br/Fi (Rauma-Repola) 1979; RoC; 6400; 137.12 × 8.21 (449.87 × 26.94); TSM (Stork-Werkspoor); 18. Two stern doors/ramps
Sister:
★ **33281 INOWROCLAW** (Pd)

33285 TRANSFINLANDIA FRG/FRG (Flender) 1981; RoC; 8100; 157.82 × 8.24 (518 × 27.03); TSM (B&W); 14.5; Stern door

33290 ARGO FRG/FRG (Kroegerw) 1976; RoC; 3900; 127 × 5.4/6.6 (417 × 17.1/21.8); TSM (KHD); 19.5; ex *Argo-Hellas* 1980; ex *Brabant* 1978; ex *Argo* 1977; Stern door

33300 FERRY KOGANE MARU Ja/Ja (Nipponkai) 1973; RoPF; 7000; 132 × 5.5 (434 × 18.2); TSM (Pielstick); 19.5; ex *Argo* 1980
Sister:
33301 ALNASL (Ja)

33310 AUSTRALIAN ENTERPRISE Au/Ja (Kawasaki) 1969; RoC; 9300; 181.8 × 9 (596 × 29.5); M (MAN); 21; Lengthened 1978; Stern door
Sisters:
33311 AUSTRALIAN EXPLORER (Au) ex *Matthew Flinders* 1975
Sister (unlengthened):
33312 AUSTRALIAN SEAROADER (Au)
Similar: (unlengthened)
33313 HYOGO MARU (Ja)

33320 INIOCHOS EXPRESS II Gr/Hong Kong (Taikoo) 1967; RoC; 2900; 111.7 × 5 (366 × 16.9); TSM (British Polar); 16.5; ex *Coastal Ranger* 1979; ex *Hawea* 1976; Stern door; Crane may be removed; See BREIZH-IZEL under MMF

★ **33330 FRITZ HECKERT** DDR/DDR (Mathias-Thesen) 1961; P; 7400; 141.3 × 5.5 (463 × 18.3); TS GT/M (Turbinfabrik/Dieselmotorenwerk Rostock); 17

33340 AL-KHALEEJ Ku/Sw (Oresunds) - Hong Kong 1965/75/78; LS; 7700/10100; 160 × — (524.93 × —); M (Gotaverken); 19.5; ex *White Ocean* 1975; Converted from reefer 1975 (Taikoo); Lengthened 1978 (Hong Kong U)

★ **33360 LE MANS** Fr/Fr (Dubigeon-Normandie) 1978; RoC; 4200; 120.33 × 5.9 (394.78 × 19.36); TSM (Atlas-MaK); 16; Stern door/ramp. Side doors

33370 DELEDDA It/It (Italcantieri) 1978; RoPCF; 6500; 131.02 × 5.61 (429.86 × 18.41); TSM (GMT); 20.5; Stern and side doors
Sister:
33371 VERGA (It)

★ **33380 MIKOLAJ KOPERNIK** Pd/No (Trosvik) 1973; TF 2600; 126 × 4.6 (412 × 150); TSM (Sulzer); 16
Similar:
★ **33381 JAN HEWELIUSZ** (Pd)

33400 CIUDAD DE BARCELONA Sp/Sp (U N de Levante) 1955; PC; 5200; 106.4 × 5 (348 × 16.5); TSM (B&W); 17.5; ex *Playa De Formentor* 1956
Similar:
33402 CIUDAD DE GRANADA (Sp)

33420 TERAAKA Br/Ys ('Titovo') 1959; PC; 1000; 64.4 × 4 (211 × 13); M (Sulzer); 15; ex *Ninikoria*; ex *Opatija* 1968
Sister:
33421 FRANCISCO DE MIRANDA (Ve) ex *Orebic* 1967

33430 KONG SVERRE Ms/US (Pullman) 1943; F; 1300; 65.5 × — (215 × —); TSM (General Motors); 15; ex *Stavanger* 1973; ex *Kilchattan*

33440 KOKAN SEWAK In/Ys ('Titovo') 1964; PC; 1900; 76.9 × 4.3 (252 × 14.2); TSM (Sulzer); 15
Sister:
33441 KONKAN SHAKTI (In) ex *Sarita* 1977

33450 ALKA Pa/Fr (La Ciotat) 1966; R; 4300; 111.8 × 6.5 (367 × 21.4); M (Sulzer); 19.75; ex *Laric* 1982; ex *Polar B.V.* 1982; ex *Remjay* 1981; ex *Aegean Destiny* 1980; ex *Matupi* 1980; ex *Harvest Gold*; ex *Frigomar* 1975; ex *Oyonnax* 1971

33460 CEBU CITY Pi/Ja (Niigata) 1972; PC/F; 2500; 98.76 × 5.21; (324 × 17.09); M (B&W); 18

33470 DOMIZIANA It/It (Italcantieri) 1979; RoPCF; 10500; 136 × 5.9 (446.19 × 19.36); TSM (GMT); 20; Stern ramp. Side doors
Sisters (It flag):
33471 CLODIA
33472 NOMENTANA
33473 EMILIA
33474 AURELIA
33475 TIBURTINA
Possible sister:
33476 FLAMINIA

33490 HARVEST VICTOR SA/Fr (La Rochelle) 1966; ST; 1100; 77 × — (253 × —); M (MAN); 14.5; ex *Southern Victor* 1980; ex *Pierre Vidal* 1977
Similar:
33491 JOSEPH DUHAMEL (Fr)
33492 GRAND PECHE

33500 GULF KELOGAK Ca/Ja (Kure) 1959; RoC/TF; 5600; 157.9 × 5.6 (518 × 18.4); TST (GEC); 16.5; ex *Alaska* 1982; ex *City of New Orleans* 1964; Bow door

33520 DIMMER Pa/Sw (Lindholmens) 1961; C; 4500; 115.1 × 7.5 (378 × 24.5); M (Gotaverken); 15; ex *Tevega* 1981; ex *Nordia* 1974; ex *Nordic*

33530 PONTA GARCIA Po/Po (Viana) 1960; CP; 1800; 97.4 × 5.2 (320 × 17.2); M (Sulzer); 12

33550 MELLINO VI Ar/FRG (Rickmers) 1957; ST; 680; 58.8 × — (193 × —); M (KHD); 14; ex *Carl Kampf* 1978

★ **33580 SKOPJE** Ys/Ys ('3 Maj') 1949; C; 3100; 101.9 × 6.60 (334 × 21.65); M (Fiat); 14
Sister:
★ **33581 TITOGRAD** (Ys)

★ **33590 JOSE MARTI** Cu/De (Helsingor) 1977; C/TS; 10000; 149.1 × 9 (489 × 30); M (B&W); 16.5
Sister:
33591 IBN KHALDOON (Iq)

33600 KAMAKURA MARU Ja/Ja (Mitsubishi HI) 1971; Con; 51100; 261 × 12 (856 × 39.1); TSM (—); —;
Sisters (Ja flag):
33601 KITANO MARU
33601 KURAMA MARU
33603 RHINE MARU

33610 KOKAN SEWAK In/Ys ('Titovo') 1964; PC; 1900; 76.9 × 4.3 (252 × 14.2); TSM (Sulzer); 15
Sister:
33611 KONKAN SHAKTI (In) ex *Sarita* 1977

★ **33620 YEYSKIY LIMAN** Ru/FRG (Howaldts DW) 1968; R; 3400; 139 × 6.5/7.6 (456 × 21 /25.2); M (MAN); 22.75; ex *Sloman Alsterpark* 1975
Sister:
★ **33621 AKHTARSKIY LIMAN** (Ru) ex *Sloman Alstertor*

33630 UNITED REEFER Pa/FRG (Deutsche Werft) 1966; R; 3400/4900; 139 × 6.4/7.6 (456 × 21.1/24.1); M (MAN); 22; ex *Pekari*
Sisters (Pa flag):
33631 GRAND UNITED ex *Persimmon*
33632 GRAND UNION ex *Pica*
33633 GRAND FAIR ex *Pirol*

33640 SAFINA NAJD Si/FRG (Deutsche Werf) 1964; R; 3800/5300; 141.8 × 6.3/7.3 (465 × 20.6/23.1); M (MAN); 21; ex *Ice Pilot* 1981; ex *Frostfjord*; ex *Pisang* 1971
Sisters:
33641 SAFINA RIYADH (Si) ex *Ice Merchant* 1981; ex *Snefjord*; ex *Puna* 1972
33642 SYROS (Gr) ex *Pongal* 1974

33650 NICOLAS P Pa/Be (Flandre) 1961; R; 6100; 139.2 × 7.2 (457 × 23.7); M (Fiat); —; ex *Med Freezer* 1983; ex *Orpheus*
Sister:
33651 LALINE P (Pa) ex *Baltic Freezer* 1982; ex *Ondine*

★ **33660 WUXI** RC/Ys ('Uljanik') 1958; C; 9300; 149.3 × 8.9 (490 × 29.2); M (B&W); ex *Mir* 1967; ex *Polet*

33670 SALAMAH 1 UAE/Ne (Diujvendijk's) 1953; C; 1500; 89.9 × 5.2 (295 × 17); M (Fiat); 14; ex *Salamah* 1983; ex *Dagus* 1982; ex *Christos* 1980; ex *Irene Star* 1977; ex *Cap Krios* 1970; ex *Cap Blanc* 1969

★ **33680 CHE HAI No 1** RC/RC (—) 1960; C; 2400; 93.3 × 5.8 (306 × 19); R (—); 10
Sister:
★ **33681 CHE HAI No 2** (RC)

★ **33690 ZHAN DOU 16** RC/US (—) 1945; C; 1900; 78.9 × 5.5 (259 × 18); R (—); 11; ex *Hoping 16*

33700 ZHAN DOU 14 RC/US (—) 1943; C; 1900; 78.9 × 5.5 (259 × 18); R (—); 11; ex *Hoping 14*

★ **33710 HONG QI 175** RC/US (Avondale) 1944; C; 1900; 78.9 × 5.5 (259 × 18); R (Ajax Uniflow); 10.5; ex *Nan Hai* 1975; ex *Lin Shen* 1958; ex *Hai Lien* 1946; ex *E.C. Gardner* 1946
Sister:
★ **33711 BAHIA SANTIAGO DE CUBA** (Cu) ex *Pebane* 1956; ex *Phinas Winsor* 1948

33720 HAI RYONG Ko/Ja (Hitachi) 1949; C; 2700; 96.6 × 6.3 (317 × 20.1); M (Hanshin); 10.5; ex *Tai Jin Maru* 1966

33740 SANTO ANDRE Bz/Pd (Gdanska) 1958; C; 3600; 108.26 × 6.65 (355.18 × 21.82); M (Holeby); —; 'B-31' type
Sister:
33741 SANTO AMARO (Bz)

★ **33745 TUAN JIE** RC/RC (Dalian) 1964; C; 4900; 121.01 × — (397 × —); —; —; May be spelt **TUAN CHIEH**

33760 ALGAZAYER Eg/FRG (Deutsche Werft) 1962; PC; 4400; 108 × 4.4 (354 × 14.7); M (MAN); 15.5
Sister:
33761 SYRIA (Eg)

33770 RAMON ABOITIZ Pi/Ja (Mitsubishi Z) 1955; P; 1100; 68.9 × 3.9 (226 × 13); M (Mitsubishi); 14; ex *Aklan* 1974; ex *Takachiho Maru* 1971

33780 DONA MARILYN Pi/Ja (Onomichi) 1966; PC; 3000; 97.6 × 4.5 (320 × 15); M (Niigata); 19.5; ex *Dona Ana* 1980; ex *Otohime Maru* 1976

33800 TACLOBAN CITY Pi/Ja (Sanoyasu) 1962; C; 2000; 91 × 4.5 (299 × 14.6); M (Kobe); 18.5; ex *Naminoue Maru* 1976

● **33810 CHION TRADER** Gr/FRG (B+V) 1964; R; 3400/4900; 137.6 × 6.4/7.8 (451 × 20.11/25.9); M (B+V); 20; ex *Davao* 1981; ex *Polarlight* 1974
Similar:
33811 KHUMBU 1 (Pa) ex *Chion Carrier* 1983; ex *Darien* 1981; ex *Polarstein* 1974

33820 HELLAS FREEZER Gr/Be (Flandres) 1962; C; 4600; 139.1 × 7.2 (457 × 23.7); M (Borsig); 18; ex *Elsfleth* 1982
Similar:
33821 THUNDERFROST (Gr) ex *Minden* 1982
33822 AVRAFROST (Gr) ex *Nienburg* 1982

33830 ATLANTIS Gr/No (Akers) 1960; R; 5800; 133.3 × 7.2 (437 × 23.5); M (B&W); 18; ex *Hidleifjord*

33840 EVEREST Pa/Fr (Provence) 1956; R; 5000; 114.9 × 6.5 (377 × 21.5); M (B&W); 16.5; ex *Transfruco* 1983; ex *Fruco* 1983; ex *Cuzco* 1973; ex *Fort Caroline* 1969
Sisters (Pa flag):
33841 LORD DE FRANCE ex *Fort De France* 1973
33842 LORD CREVECOEUR ex *Fort Crevecoeur* 1973
33843 LORD FLEUR D'EPEE ex *Fort Fleur D'Epee* 1973
33844 LORD D'ORLEANS ex *Fort D'Orleans* 1973
33846 HONEST SPRING ex *Harokaze* 1976; ex *Ta Shun* 1973; ex *Ica* 1972; ex *Fort Royal* 1969

33850 TROPICAL MOON Li/FRG (Howaldts) 1965; R; 3400/4700; 136 × 6.2/6.6 (446 × 20.4/24.6); M (MAN); 21; ex *Brunskamp* 1978; ex *Blexen* 1975; ex *Augustenburg* 1972

33860 MARE ANTARTICO It/It (Ansaldo) 1966; R; 7000; 142.4 × 7.5 (466 × 24.7); M (B&W); 20
Sisters:
33861 BANANA CARRIER (Pa) ex *Mare Artico*

1982
33862 **MARE AUSTRALE** (It)
33863 **BANANA TRADER** (Pa) ex *Mare Boreale* 1982

★33870 **FERDINAND FREILIGRATH** DDR/Br (Scotts' SB) 1967; R; 5600; 152.7 × 7.6 (501 × 25); M (B&W); 21; ex *Parma II* 1974; ex *Parma* 1973; Also known as F. FREILIGRATH
Sister:
★33871 **GEORG WEERTH** (DDR) ex *Padua* 1974

33880 **DAVAO** Pi/Ja (Kawasaki D) 1964; R; 5000; 142.1 × 7.3 (466 × 23.22); M (MAN) 20; ex *Ecuador Maru* 1964
Sister:
33881 **MINDANAO** (Li) ex *Captain Cook*; ex *Costa Rica Maru* 1975

33890 **APPLE BLOSSOM** Li/Ja (Kawasaki D) 1969; R; 7000; 141 × 8.1 (463 × 27); M (MAN); —; ex *Banagrande* 1977

33900 **LIMON** Li/No (Mariners) 1968; R; 6700; 139.4 × 7.9 (457 × 26); M (Sulzer); 22.5; ex *Golar Freeze* 1976
Sister (used as a fish carrier):
★33901 **BRESTSKAYA KREPOST** (Ru) ex *Golar Nel* 1975

★33910 **KOTOVSKIY** Ru/It (Breda) 1968; R; 4100; 121.7 × 7.5 (401 × 24); M (Fiat); 18
Sisters (Ru flag):
★33911 **NIKOLAY SHCHORS**
★33912 **PARKHOMENKO**
★33913 **SERGEI LAZO**
★33914 **CHAPAEV**

33920 **LEYTE GULF** Pi/FRG (Kieler H) 1966; R; 5500; 148 × 8 (486 × 26); M (MAN); 23; ex *Orpheus* 1983; ex *Ahrensburg*
Sister:
33921 **PANAY GULF** (Pi) ex *Ondine* 1983; ex *Angelburg* 1978
Similar:
33922 **DAVAO GULF** (Pa) ex *Olympos* 1982; ex *Aldenburg* 1979
33923 **ARTLENBURG** (FRG)
33924 **ODYSSEUS** (Li) ex *Asseburg*

33930 **CORAL REEFER** Pa/No (Framnaes) 1968; R; 4200; 128 × 7.8 (420 × 26.6); M (Sulzer); 19; ex *Corinthian Reefer* 1981; ex *Vikfreezer*
Similar:
33931 **AUDACIA** (Ur) ex *Para*; ex *Vikfrost* 1977
33932 **ISADORE HECHT** (Pa) ex *Clydefirth* 1980; ex *Vikfrio* 1974; ex *Thorsoy* 1972

33940 **TROPICAL SEA** Li/FRG (LF-W) 1968; R; 3300; 135.9 × 6.5 (446 × 21.6); M (B+V); 22; ex *Brunsrode* 1978
Sister:
33941 **TROPICAL GOLD** (Li) ex *Brunswick* 1978

33950 **ISLA VERDE** Li/Ne (Nederlandsche) 1964; R; 4300; 148.8 × 8.8 (488 × 21.11); M (Sulzer); 21; ex *North Star* 1975; ex *Geestbay* 1973
Sisters:
33951 **KIMOLOS** (Gr) ex *Geestport* 1973
33953 **TURTLE** (Bs) ex *Nyombe* 1981; ex *Geestcape* 1975

33960 **SWAN** Gr/Fr (Nantes) 1963; R; 5400; 120.7 × 7.2 (396 × 23.6); M (B&W); 18.25; ex *Karukera* 1978

33970 **FLAMINGO II.** Pa/Sp ('Elcano') 1963; R; 4700; 137.3 × — (450.6 × —); M (Sulzer); 18; ex *Flamingo* 1982; ex *Assouba* 1980; ex *Har Bashan* 1973; ex *Atlantic Arrow* 1967; ex *Northpole* 1966

★33980 **POLYUS** Ru/DDR ('Neptun') 1962; RS; 3900; 112 × 6 (368 × 20); D-E (Dieselmotorenwerk Rostock); 13.5

33990 **BAYKAL** Ru/DDR ('Neptun') 1964; RS; 3900; 111.56 × 6 (366 × 19.69); D-E (Dieselmotorenwerk Rostock); 13.5
Sister:
★33991 **BALKHASH** (Ru)

★34010 **LONGVA** Ru/No (Liaaen) 1962; RS; 800; 63 × 4.9 (206 × 16); M (KHD); 13

34020 **TAIYO MARU No 68** Ja/Ja (Hayashikane) 1961; ST; 1500; 75.5 × 5.5 (248 × 18); M (Hayashikane); 14.25
Sisters (Ja flag):
34021 **TAIYO MARU No 67**
34022 **TAIYO MARU No 71**
34023 **TAIYO MARU No 72**
34024 **TAIYO MARU No 73**

★34025 **ISLA DE LA JUVENTUD** Cu/Sp (AESA) 1967; SS; 1600; 70.31 × 5.47 (231 × 17.95); M (MWM); 13; ex *Arminza* 1967

34030 **HARENGUS** FRG/FRG (Harms) 1972; ST; 1700; 81 × 5.3 (263 × 17.6); M (Atlas-MaK); 16

34040 **MARIA PAOLINA G** It/It (Giuliano) 1956; RS; 1900; 78.21 × 4.47 (257 × 14.9); M (Fiat); 13; ex *Noli* 1962; ex *Capo Faro* 1961

● 34050 **CAGAYAN DE ORO CITY** Pi/Ja (Mitsubishi HI) 1970; F/C; 2100; 89.16 × 4.41 (293 × 14.47); TSM (Niigata); 18.5; ex *Hibiscus* 1977

34060 **FRITHJOF** FRG/FRG (Schlichting) 1968; RS; 1600; 76 × 5.2 (250 × 17); D-E (Maybach); 16

34070 **CUMULUS** Ne/Ne (van der Werf) 1963; RS/WS; 2000; 71.1 × 4.6 (233 × 15.1); M (Werkspoor); 12.75

34080 **FIORITA** Pa/Br (J Brown) 1950; P; 3500; 114.9 × 4.6 (377 × 15); TST (J Brown); 17; ex *Amsterdam* 1970

34090 **EL DJAZAIR** Ag/Ja (Kanasashi) 1972; RoPCF; 12100; 130.38 × 5.62 (427.76 × 18.44); TSM (MAN); 19.5; ex *Central No 3* 1973; Bow door; Side door; Stern door

---

★34100 **AMGUEMA** Ru/Ru (Leninskogo) 1962; C; 8100; 133 × 8.9 (437 × 29); D-E (—); 15
Sisters (ships vary slightly—Ru flag):
★34101 **GIZHIGA**
★34102 **KAPITAN BONDARENKO**
★34103 **KAPITAN MARKOV**
★34104 **KAPITAN GOTSKIY**
★34105 **KAPITAN KONDRATYEV**
★34106 **KAPITAN MYSHEVSKIY**
★34107 **NAVARIN**
★34108 **PENZHINA**
★34109 **VANKAREM**
★34110 **VASILIY FEDOSEYEV**
★34111 **PAVEL PONOMARYEV**

34120 **MACHITIS** Gr/Ys ('3 Maj') 1957; C; 8900; 152.51 × 9.31 (500.4 × 30.51); M (Sulzer); 14

34140 **GREENVILLE** Li/Ne (Giessen) 1960; C; 6900/9500; 155.1 × 8.3/9.1 (509 × 27.6/30); M (Sulzer); 13; ex *Amstelhoek* 1973
Sisters:
34141 **SAKINA** (Pa) ex *Najma* 1982; ex *Harlandsville* 1982; ex *Hollands Duin* 1973
34142 **AISHAH** (Pa) ex *Santiago* 1983; ex *Pampa Argentina* 1981; ex *Hollands Diep* 1970
34143 **TAYGETUS** (Ma) ex *Patagonia Argentina* 1983; ex *Hollands Dreef* 1972

★34150 **LIKA** Ys/Ys ('3 Maj') 1957; C; 6000/8800; 146.01 × 7.86/— (479 × 25.79/—); M (Sulzer) 14
Sisters:
★34151 **DEBRALINA 1** (Ys) ex *Petka* 1983
★34152 **SLAVONIJA** (Ys)
★34153 **TREPCA** (Ys)
★34154 **ZETA** (Ys)

● 34180 **MALDIVE FAITH** Mv/Br (H Robb) 1960; C; 2500; 100.1 × 5.9 (330 × 19.4); M (Sulzer); 13.5; ex *Islami* 1983; ex *Maldive Trust* 1981; ex *Aaro* 1972

34190 **PATRIS** Gr/Fr (Bretagne) 1962; O; 10400; 152.0 × 9.34 (498 × 30.64); M (Pielstick); 14.5; ex *Ile Saint Louis* 1972; ex *Halonia* 1968

● 34200 **BONITA** Ec/No (Drammen) 1970; R; 4900/6700; 140.7 × 8.3/9 (462 × 27/30); M (Sulzer); 22.5; ex *Bering* 1975; ex *Beringcore* 1975; 'DRAMMEN' type
Sisters:
34201 **ALASKA I** (FRG) ex *Alaska*; ex *Alaskacore* 1975; ex *Slevik* 1969
34202 **ANTARCTIC** (FRG) ex *Antarcticore* 1975
34203 **SMARA** (Mo) ex *Cayman* 1976; ex *Greenland* 1975
34204 **FRIGOANTARTICO** (Pa)
34205 **CAP FRIO** (Pa) ex *Frigoartico* 1982
34206 **NORDLAND V** (Pa) ex *Nordland* 1980
34207 **ICELAND** (FRG)
34208 **CHIOS PRIDE** (Gr) ex *Tuscan Star*; ex *Labrador Clipper* 1975
34209 **EUROPA FREEZER** (Gr) ex *Andania* 1981; ex *Glasgow Clipper* 1976
34210 **BOLIVAR** (Li) ex *Golar Frost* 1976
34211 **LUCKY** (Gr) ex *Timur Girl* 1983; ex *Hilco Girl* 1981; ex *Golar Girl*
34212 **SIERRA NEVADA** (Ve) ex *Ragni Berg* 1977; ex *Golar Ragni* 1976; ex *Kongsfjell*
34213 **REEFER DUKU** (Sg) ex *Wild Fulmar* 1982
34213/1 **REEFER CIKU** (Sg) ex *Wild Flamingo* 1983
★34214 **GERHART HAUPTMANN** (DDR) ex *King Egbert* 1978; ex *Liverpool Clipper* 1976
★34215 **ERNST MORITZ ARNDT** (DDR) ex *King Edmund*; ex *Bristol Clipper* 1976
34216 **OCEAN FREEZER** (Gr) ex *Alaunia* 1981; ex *Cardiff Clipper* 1977
34217 **IFNI** (Mo)

34218 **IMILCHIL** (Mo)
34219 **IMOUZZER** (Mo)
★34220 **THEODOR KORNER** (DDR)
34221 **SALINAS** (Br) ex *London Clipper* 1976
34222 **AMERICA FREEZER** (Gr) ex *Alsatia* 1981; ex *Edinburgh Clipper* 1977
34223 **AUSTRALIA FREEZER** (Gr) ex *Andria* 1981; ex *Teeside Clipper* 1977
34224 **SIJILMASSA** (Mo) ex *Kungshamn*; ex *Lapland* 1976
34225 **CHIOS CLIPPER** (Gr) ex *Trojan Star* 1980; ex *Newcastle Clipper* 1976

★34240 **ILYA METCHNIKOV** Ru/Fr (Loire) 1956; C; 4100/5600; 129.7 × 6.8/7.5 (426 × 22.5/24.8); T (Bretagne); 14
Sisters (Ru flag):
★34241 **IVAN PAVLOV**
★34242 **IVAN SECHENOV**
★34243 **NIKOLAY BURDYENKO**
★34244 **NIKOLAY PIROGOV**
★34245 **SERGEY BOTKIN**

34250 **FILIPINAS** Pi/FRG (Bremer V) 1968; C; 5000; 121 × 7.7 (397 × 25.3); M (MAN); —

● 34260 **CER ALACTRITY** Li/Ys ('Titovo') 1961; C; 2000/3100; 106.2 × —/5.9 (348 × —/19.6); M (Sulzer); 14; ex *Frano Supilo* 1981
Sisters (Ys flag):
34261 **CER AMITY** (Pa) ex *Matko Laginja* 1981
34262 **CER AGILITY** (Pa) ex *Ivan Mazuranic* 1981

★34290 **SHKVAL** Ru/Sw (Oresunds) 1963; R; 4200; 126.4 × 7.3 (415 × 24); M (Gotaverken); 17; ex *Bakke Reefer* 1975

● 34300 **LABRADOR REX** Li/Be (Boelwerf) 1969; R; 3900/5800; 149.2 × 6.2/7.8 (489 × 20.7/25.8); M (MAN); 22; ex *Pontos* 1982
Sister:
34301 **KUROSHIO REX** (Li) ex *Pomona* 1982

● 34310 **HEBE 1** Pa/Fr (Bretagne) 1960; R/WT; 5200; 118.2 × 7.1 (388 × 23.6); M (Pielstick); 19; ex *Hebe* 1982

34320 **GEMA** Pa/Ne (Verschure) 1959; R; 2700/3800; 114.97 × 6.12/6.82 (377 × 20.2/22.38); M (MAN); 17; ex *Salta* 1977; ex *Brunstal* 1970; ex *Baleares* 1966

★34330 **JOHN BRINCKMAN** DDR/Sw (Oresunds) 1964; R; 4600/6300; 138.8 × —/7.9 (455 × —/25.11); M (Gotaverken); 19; ex *Belnippon* 1973
Sister:
★34331 **FRITZ REUTER** (DDR) ex *Pacific Express* 1973

★34360 **SOPOT** Pd/De (Aalborg) 1966; C; 2000/3000; 99.6 × 5.7/6.3 (327 × 19/22.3); M (B&W); 14.25
Sisters (Pd flag):
★34361 **SANDOMIERZ**
★34362 **SANOK**
★34363 **SLUPSK**

● 34370 **PETRA** Jo/Pd (Gdynska) 1961; C; 1300; 86.4 × 4.6 (284 × 15.2); M (Sulzer); 14.5; ex *Deblin* 1982; 'B-513' type
Sisters:
★34371 **KOSZALIN** (Pd)
34372 **MAHMOUDY** (Eg) ex *Wolin* 1981

34380 **DELMAR 4** Br/Ja (Mitsubishi Z) 1960; Sal; 1200; 66.8 × 4.5 (219 × 14.9); M (Sulzer); 13.5; ex *Asian Star*; ex *Hayashio Maru*

34390 **KOYO MARU** Ja /Ja (Mitsubishi HI) 1967; Sal/Tg; 2100; 85.5 × 6 (280.6 × 19.9); M (MAN); 17.25

★34400 **SUI JIU 201** RC/Ja (Hitachi) 1975; Sal/Tg; 2200; 87.03 × 6.1 (285.5 × 20); M (B&W); 18.75
Sister:
★34401 **HUI JIU 101** (RC)

★34405 **MUDYUG** Ru/Fi (Wartsila) 1982; IB/Tg; 5300; 92.00 × 6.50 (302 × 21.33); TSM (Wartsila); 16.5
Sisters (Ru flag):
★34406 **MAGADAN**
★34407 **DIKSON**

34410 **JUYO MARU** Ja/Ja (Hayashikane) 1968; R. 3400; 111.1 × 6.9 (365 × 22.6); M (Kobe); 16

34420 **AVONDALE** Pa/Br (H Robb) 1956; C; 1900; 76.9 × 4.3 (252 × 14); M (British Polar); 10; ex *Bismarck Sea* 1981; ex *Cobargo* 1978; ex *Kumalla* 1973

34430 **HAI SOON KAO** Th/Br (H Robb) 1949; C; 900; 56.9 × 3.7 (187 × 12.3); TSM (British Polar); 10; ex *Mamani* 1982; ex *Mamatu* 1973; ex *Mamaku* 1973

34440 KING HORSE Sg/Br (H Robb) 1955; C; 1900; 81.6 × 4.9 (268 × 15.11); M (Sulzer); 11; ex *Navua* 1971
Sister:
34441 KING TOWER (Sg) ex *Konini* 1971

34450 OKINAWA MARU Ja/Ja (Onomichi) 1956; C; 1600; 82.1 × 5 (269 × 16.5); M (Uraga); 16.5

★**34460 LONGVA** Ru/No (Liaaen) 1962; RS; 800; 63 × 4.9 (206 × 16); M (KHD); 13

● ★**34470 ANDIZHAN** Ru/DDR ('Neptun') 1958; C; 3200; 104.2 × 6.6 (341 × 22); M (Goerlitzer); 12.5; 'LEVANT' or 'KOVEL' type. Some ships may vary slightly. Some have large radar mast from bridge
Similar (Ru flag):
★**34471 BARABINSK**
★**34472 BIKIN**
★**34473 BOTSMAN ZOTOV** ex *Mongugay*
★**34474 CHELYABINSK**
★**34475 DALNERECHENSK** ex *Iman* 1973
★**34476 DALNIY**
★**34477 DAUGAVA**
★**34478 EMETSK**
★**34479 EYSK**
★**34480 HOROL**
★**34481 IZHMA**
★**34482 KHOLMOGORY**
★**34483 JASNORMORSK**
★**34485 KOVEL**
★**34486 KYARDLA**
★**34487 LAZAREV**
★**34488 LOKSA**
★**34489 LUDZA**
★**34490 MAHTRA**
★**34491 MGA**
★**34492 MURMASHI**
★**34493 NAGAEVO**
★**34494 NAMANGAN**
★**34495 POLYARNYY**
★**34496 POSYET**
★**34497 RAKVERE**
★**34498 RAZDOLNOYE**
★**34499 REVDA**
★**34500 RAZLIV**
★**34501 RENI**
★**34501 REPINO**
★**34501 SALSK**
★**34504 SARANSK**
★**34505 SHENKURSK**
★**34506 SOBOLEVO**
★**34507 SIGULDA**
★**34508 SYRVE**
★**34509 SINEGORSK**
★**34510 TURUKHANSK**
★**34511 VANINO**
★**34512 ZAISAN**
★**34513 SONGDA** (Vn) ex *Sinegorsk* 1974
★**34514 SONG KHAN** (Vn) ex *Turkestan* 1975
★**34515 LENIN** (An) ex *Kapitan Voðlens* 1978; ex *Amata* 1967

34530 TWILIGHT Pa/Ja (Mitsubishi Z) 1956; C; 4000; 113.5 × 6.8 (372 × 22.2); M (Mitsubishi); 11; ex *Ever Grace* 1980; ex *Twilight* 1979; ex *Greenlake* 1977; ex *Nasipit Maru* 1972

★**34540 ANGARSK** Ru/DDR ('Neptun') 1956; C; 3300; 1O2.42 × 6.65 (335 × 23.8); T (Liebknecht); 12.5

34570 MIMAR SINAN Tu/Ja (Nipponkai) 1961; CP; 5400; 124.5 × 7.8 (4O9 × 25.8); M (Sulzer); 14.5

34580 GAZI OSMAN PASA Tu/Ja (Mitsubishi Z) 1961; CP; 37OO; 106.6 × 6.7 (350 × 21.11); M (Sulzer); 13
Sisters (Tu flag):
★**34581 MITHAT PASA**
34582 27 MAYIS

34590 DENIZLI Tu/Ja (Sanoyasu) 1955; C; 3000; 102.4 × 6.2 (336 × 204); M (Uraga); 14

34600 REIYO MARU Ja/Ja (Hayashikane) 1967; R; 3400; 111.1 × 6.9 (364 × 22.6); M (Kobe); 16

★**34610 TARUSA** Ru/Ru ('Chernomorskiy') 1974; FT; 2300; 83.27 × — (273 × —); M (Skoda); —
Sisters (Ru flag):
★**34611 BYKOVO**
★**34612 BYELOMORSK**
★**34613 LOVOZYERO**
★**34614 MYS GROTOVYY**
★**34615 MYS KURILSKIY**
★**34616 MYS LOPATKA**
★**34617 MYS PROKOFYEVA**
★**34618 MYS RATMANOVA**
★**34619 MYS TAYMYR**
★**34620 MYS VAYGACH**
★**34621 MYS VORONINA**
★**34622 NAROCH**
★**34623 NEVYANSK**

★**34624 BORISPOL**
★**36245 DOMODYEDOVO**
★**34626 KRONSHTADT**
★**34627 MYS ARKTICHESKIY**
★**34628 TORZHOK**
★**34629 SOLOVIETSKIY**
★**34630 SHEREMTYEVO**
★**34631 GEROI ZAPOLYARYA**
★**34632 BIRYUSINSK**
★**34633 VNUKOVO**
★**34634 NOVYY MIR**
★**34635 ZELEZNOGORSK**
★**34636 ZNAMYA POBEDY**
★**34637 30-LET POBEDY**
★**34638 MYS BUDYONNOGO**
★**34639 MYS CHELYUSKIN**
★**34640 MYS FRUNZE**
★**34641 MYS KRONOTSKIY**
★**34642 MYS OTRADNYY**
★**34643 MYS VODOPADNYY**
★**34644 URGAL**
★**34648 KHAROVSK**
★**34649 TIKHOOKEANSKIY**
★**34650 TYNDA**
★**34651 MYS ILMOVYY**
★**34652 MYS KUZNETSOVA**
★**34653 MYS SILINA**
★**34654 MYS CHASOVOY**
★**34655 MYS CHAYKOVSKOGO**
★**34656 MYS GROZNYY**
★**34657 MYS SKALISTYY**
★**34658 MURMANSELD**
★**34660 VERKHOVINA**
★**34661 MYS SVOBODNYY**
★**34663 SOVGANSKIY KOMSOMOLETS**
★**34664 GANGUT**
★**34665 TSIMLYANSK**
★**34666 VYOVSK**
★**34667 VYSHOGOROD**
★**34668 MYS TIKHIY**
★**34669 MYS DALNIY**
★**34670 NIKOLAYEVSKIY KORABEL**
★**34671 MYS BABUSKIN**
★**34672 MYS OSTROVSKOGO**
★**34673 MYS YUNONY**
(Iq flag):
34674 FOREL ex *Seversk* 1981
34675 GATTAN ex *Linakhamari* 1981
34676 KEFAL ex *Zashchitnik Zapolyarya* 1980
34677 SHABOOT ex *Desyataya Pyatiletka* 1977

● **34700 BAHIA AGUIRRE** Ar/Ca (Halifax) 1950; Transport; 3800; 95 × 7.9 (335 × 13.8); TSM (Nordberg); 16; Argentine Navy
34701 BAHIA BUEN SUCESO (Ar)

★**34710 ZENIT** Ru/DDR ('Neptun') 1961; TS; 4400; 104.9 × 6.2 (344 × 20); M (Goerlitzer); 13.75
Sisters (Ru flag):
★**34711 GORIZONT**
★**34712 MERIDIAN**

34720 HAKUHO MARU Ja/Ja (Mitsubishi HI) 1966; RS; 3200; 94.9 × 5.5 (311 × 18); TSD-E (MAN); 12.5

34740 G. O. SARS No/No (Mjellum & K) 1970; RS/ST; 1400; 70 × 5 (230 × 16); M (Bergens); 15

34750 ANNOULA TSIRIS Cy/Fr (Dubigeon) 1958; C; 2900; 98.91 × 6.90 (324.5 × 22.64); M (Pielstick); 17; ex *Circe* 1978

34770 HATI SENANG My/Br (H Robb) 1950; C; 2500; 93.07 × 5.33 (305 × 17.49); TSM (British Polar); 9.75; ex *Kawati* 1979; ex *Kawatiri* 1972
Sister:
34771 BERJAYA (My) ex *Tung Lee* 1977; ex *Bonatrade* 1974; ex *Konui* 1969

34780 STAFFORD De/De 1967; RoC; 26OO; 124.2 × 5 (407 × 16.6); TSM; 19.5; Stern door; Lengthened 1973

34790 METEOR FRG/FRG (A G 'Weser') 1964; RS/ST; 2600; 82.1 × 5.1 (269 × 16.11); D-E (Maybach); —

34800 REMCO Gh/FRG (LF-W) 1959; C; 5000; 140.16 × 7.65 (459.8 × 25.1O); M (Sulzer); 16; ex *Adom* 198O; ex *Volta Peace* 1977; ex *Kamperdyk* 1972
Sisters:
34801 FERIAL (Gh) ex *Odupon* 1980; ex *Volta Wisdom* 1977; ex *Korendyk* 1972
34802 UTILA PRINCESS (Ho) ex *Mazoa VII* 1983; ex *Brezice* 1982; ex *Kloosterdyk* 1970

34820 SAUDI AL TAIF Si/Ne (Verolme Scheeps) 1962; CP; 68OO; 157.8 × 8 (518 × 26.9); M (Sulzer); 17.5; ex *Nedlloyd Amstelland* 1982; ex *Amstelland* 1981

34830 CHARMYL Cy/Ne ('De Schelde') 1963; C; 4900/7400; 140.49 × —/8.52 (461 × —/27.95); M

(Sulzer); —; ex *Lake Bosomtwe* 1981

● **34870 GOLDEN HORSE** Sg/Ne ('De Noord') 1956; C; 7800; 143.62 × 7.86 (471 × 25.79); M (Werkspoor); 14.5; ex *Parkhaven* 1973

● ★**34872 IVAN BOCHKOV** Ru/Pd (Gdanska) 1978; FT; 2900; 94.01 × 5.67 (308 × 18.60); M ('Zgoda'); 15.75; 'B408' type
Sisters (Ru flag):
★**34873 ALEKSANDR BORISOV**
★**34873/1 ALEKSANDR GRIAZNOV**
★**34873/2 NIKOLAY ZAKORKIN**
★**34873/3 IVAN ZIMAKOV**
★**34874 MIKHAIL KVASHNIKOV**
★**34874/1 PAVEL KAYKOV**
★**34874/2 KAZAN** (or **KASAN**)
★**34874/3 LEONID YELKIN**
★**34875 MIKHAIL BORONIN**
★**34875/1 SEMYON LAPSHENKOV**
★**34875/2 VIKTOR STRELTSOV**
★**34875/3 LEONID IVANOV**
★**34875/4 MIKHAIL VERBITSKIY**
★**34876 YEOFIM KRIVOSEYEV**
★**34876/1 KONSTANTIN FOMTSHENKO**
★**34876/2 KAPITAN ANDREYEV**
★**34877 SERGEY MAKAREVICH**
★**34877/1 LEONID NOVOSPASSKIY**
★**34878 PAVEL PANIN**
★**34879 DMITRIY POKROVICH**

★**34880 SPRUT** Ru/Pd (Polnocna) 1978; FT; 4800; 119 × 6.5 (390.42 × 21.33); M (Sulzer); 15; 'B-400' type
Sisters (Ru flag):
★**34881 ARKHIMED**
★**34882 PLUNGE**
★**34883 PRUZANIY**
★**34884 PASVALIS**

● **34890 BRAVO ARES** Gr/Ne (Amsterdamsche D) 1959; CP; 4200/6100; 129.2 × 6.5/7.3 (424 × 21.6/24); M (Stork); 16.25; ex *Ares* 1977; lengthened 1966
Sisters:
34891 DENIS M. (Gr) ex *Achilles*
34892 GRIGOROUSA (Cy) ex *Marika T* 1983; ex *Archimedes* 1977
34893 ARABIAN KARIMAN (Ma) ex *Celestial* 1983; ex *Aristoteles* 1978
34894 BRAVO CERES (Gr) ex *Ceres* 1977
34895 ASTEROID (Gr) ex *Diogenes* 1978
34896 COSMOS (Ho) ex *Ganymedes*
34897 YACU CASPI (Pe) ex *Hercules*
34898 SIRICHAL BULAKUL (Th) ex *Alkyon* 1981; ex *Ulysees*
34899 NIKI R (Gr) ex *Hermes*
34900 BRAVO KATERINA (Gr) ex *Palamedes*
34901 PERICLES (Gr)

34910 LION OF ETHIOPIA Et/Ne (Verolme Dok) 1966; C; 5200; 121 × 7.9 (397 × 26); M (MAN); —; ex *Lion of Judah* 1975
Sister:
34911 QUEEN OF SHEEBA (Et)

● **34920 MALDIVE JADE** Mv/Br (Stephen) 1956; C; 3700; 105.3 × 6.8 (345 × 22.4); M (Sulzer); 12.5; ex *Climax Jade* 1981; ex *Kaituna* 1975
Sisters:
34921 MALDIVE TOPAZ (Mv) ex *Climax Topaz* 1981; ex *Kaimiro* 1975
34922 SANTA URSULA (Pa) ex *Katea* 1976
34923 IMPERIAL STAR (Pa) ex *Coral Sea* 1977; ex *Kawerau* 1975
34924 MALDIVE AMBASSADOR (Mv) ex *Koraki* 1975
34925 SOUTH PACIFIC (Mv) ex *Koranui* 1975

34930 LUIGI D'AMICO It/Sp (AESA) 1964; C; 9100; 156.9 × 7.9 (519 × 29.9); M (Sulzer); —; ex *Orient Mariner* 1969

34940 GOOILAND Ne/Ne (P Smit) 1969; C; 4900; 147.5 × 7.1 (484 × 23); M (Sulzer); 15.5

★**34960 WISMAR** DDR/DDR (Mathias-Thesen) 1968; CP; 3700/5700; 129.4 × 6.7/7.6 (424 × 22/25); M (MAN); 16; 'AFRIKA' type
Sisters (DDR flag):
★**34961 FREDERIC JOLIOT CURIE**
★**34962 STOLLBERG**
★**34963 WITTENBERG**

34970 BHANURANGSI Th/De (Nakskov) 1927; C; 700; 64 × 2.9 (210 × 9.9); TSM (B&W); 10

34980 MARIMO Ja/Ja (Setoda) 1971; RoPCF; 9200; 166 × 6.3 (545 × 20.6); TSM (B&W); 20.75; Stern door and ramp; 2 side doors & ramps

34990 FERRY KOGANE MARU Ja/Ja (Nipponkai) 1973; RoPCF; 6900; 132 × 5.5 (433 × 18); TSM (Pielstick); 19.5; ex *Argo* 1980
Sister:

34991 **ALNASL** (Ja)

★35000 **PRESIDENTE MACIAS NGUEMA** Gn/Ja (Shikoku) 1973; PC; 3300; 100.51 × 5.68 (329.76 × 18.64); M (B&W); 14; ex *Hai Ou*

35010 **AMBER** Cy/Ne (J & K Smit) 1962; C; 10600; 157.4 × 9.7 (516 × 32); M (Stork); 16.5; ex *Centaurus* 1973

★35030 **ZHENJIANG** RC/Fr (France-Gironde) 1966; C; 7800/10900; 158 × 8.5/9.4 (520 × 28/31); M (B&W); —
Sister:
★35031 **JIUJIANG** (RC)

● 35040 **SAKUMO LAGOON** Gh/Br (Swan Hunter & WR) 1964; CP; 4800/7300; 138.5 × 7.3/8.4 (454 × 23.11/27.8); M (Sulzer); 17
Sisters (Gh flag):
35041 **BENYA RIVER**
35042 **NAKWA RIVER**
35043 **KORLE LAGOON**

35070 **MARINA** Pa/Au (Evans Deakin) 1960; C; 4100; 103.6 × 7 (341 × 22.1); M (Doxford); 12.5; ex *Mundoora* 1977

35080 **CELESTINO** Bz/Bz (Verolme ER do Brazil) 1968; C; 6200/8300; 142.3 × 8.2/9.2 (467 × 27/30); M (MAN)

35090 **FUJI** Ch/Ja (Mitsui) 1968; ST/FF; 3900; 102.3 × 5.9 (336 × 19.6); M (B&W); 13.75; ex *Fuji Maru* 1979
Similar (Ja flag):
35091 **HARUNA MARU**
35092 **KONGO MARU**
35093 **NIITAKA MARU**
35094 **TSUDA MARU**

35100 **ACADIA FOREST** Li/Ja (Sumitomo) 1969; Bg; 38900; 261.4 × 12.1 (857 × 40); M (Sulzer); 19; 'LASH' type
Sister:
35101 **ATLANTIC FOREST** (Li)
Similar:
35102 **BILDERDYK** (Ne)

35110 **DANA FUTURA** De/De (Helsingor) 1975; RoC; 6000; 144 × 7 (474 × 23); TSM (B&W); 22.5; ex *Drosselfels*; ex *Damman Express* 1976; ex *Dana Futura* 1976
Sister:
35111 **DANIA HAFNIA** (De) ex *Drachenfels*; ex *Dana Gloria* 1976

35120 **BAYANO** Br/Sp (Barreras) 1972; Con; 4100; 104.3 × 5.8 (344 × 19); TSM (Deutz); 17.5
Sister:
35121 **BARRANCA** (Br)

● 35130 **LASH ATLANTICO** US/US (Avondale) 1972; Bg/Con; 26400; 250 × 10.7 (820 × 35.5); T (De Laval); 21; Both gantries (N) can move-thus altering sequence. Could also be P5. 'LASH' type
Sisters (US flag) (overall lengths vary):
35131 **LASH ITALIA**
35132 **LASH PACIFICO**
35133 **AUSTRAL LIGHTNING** ex *Lash Espana* 1976; ex *Austral Bear* 1975; ex *Philippine Bear* 1975
35134 **DELTA MAR**
35135 **DELTA SUD**
35136 **DELTA NORTE**
35137 **DELTA CARIBE** ex *Lash Turkiye*
35138 **AUSTRAL MOON** ex *Australia Bear* 1975; ex *Philippine Bear* 1975

35140 **CONTENDER ARGENT** Br/It (Breda) 1981; RoC/Con; 11400; 173.01 × 8.19 (568 × 26.87); TSM (Pielstick); 19; Door on starboard bow and starboard side
Sister:
35141 **CONTENDER BEZANT** (Br) (to be converted to a mini aircraft carrier; to be manned by the RFA)

★35150 **STAKHANOVETS KOTOV** Ru/Fi (Hollming) 1978; RoC/Dk; 4300; 135.53 × 6.2 (444.65 × 20.34); TSM (Pielstick); 14.25; Stern door
Sisters (Ru flag):
★35151 **STAKHANOVETS PETRASH**
★35152 **STAKHANOVETS YERMOLENKO**

35160 **HAPPY MARINER** Ne/Ne (Verolme U) 1972; Dk; 2400; 105.7 × 5 (347 × 17); TSM (Caterpillar); 12.75; ex *Docklift 1* 1982; Stern ramp

★35170 **INGUL** Ru/Fi (Sandvikens) 1962; Cbl; 5600; 130.41 × 5.2 (427.85 × 17.06); TSD-E (Sulzer); 14; 'KLASMA' class
Sister:
★35171 **JANA** (Ru) (may be spelt **YANA**)

★35180 **KATUNJ** Ru/Fi (Wartsila) 1973; Cbl; 6000; 130.41 × 5.75 (427.85 × 18.86); TSD-E (Wartsila); 14; May be spelt **KATYN**; 'KLASMA' class

Sisters:
★35181 **DONETS** (Ru)
★35182 **TSNA** (Ru) (may be spelt **ZNA**)

★35190 **INGURI** Ru/Fi (Wartsila) 1978; Cbl; 6000; 130.41 × 5.75 (427.85 × 18.86); TSD-E (Wartsila); 14; 'KLASMA' class.

35220 **OCEANIC** Pa/It (Adriatico) 1965; P; 27600; 238.44 × 8.63 (782.28 × 28.31); TST (Adriatico); 26.5

35230 **EUGENIO C.** It/It (Adriatico) 1966; PC; 30600; 217.5 × 8.6 (713.5 × 28.2); TST (De Laval); 27

35240 **ZUIDERKRUIS** Ne/Ne (Verolme Scheeps) 1975; Spt/FA; 16900 Dspl; 169.6 × 8.2 (566 × 27); M (Werkspoor); 21; 'POOLSTER' class. 5 helicopters

35250 **POOLSTER** Ne/Ne (Rotterdamsche) 1964; Spt/FA; 16800 Dspl; 169.6 × 8.2 (556 × 27); T (Pametrada); 21; 5 helicopters

35260 **ITALIA** It/It (Felszegi) 1967; PC; 12200; 149 × 6.4 (489 × 21.01); M (MTU); 19

★35270 **HANGZHOU** RC/DDR (Warnow) 1958; C; 6500; 157.44 × 8.38 (517 × 27.49); TSM (Halberstadt); 14.5; ex *Dukla* 1965; Launched as *Solidaritat*
Sisters:
★35271 **LANZHOU** (RC) ex *Orava* 1965; ex *Zeromski* 1959; ex *Volkerfreundschaft* 1957
★35272 **SIERRA MAESTRA** (Cu)

35280 **TAINARON** Li/Sw (Eriksbergs) 1955/75; DS; 9900; 177.65 × 9.12 (582 × 29.92); M (B&W); 15; ex *Bolivar* 1969; ex *Cerro Bolivar* 1968; Converted from Ore Carrier 1975 (Hong Kong U)

35290 **LAKE LOTHING** Br/Br (H. Robb) 1955; D; 660; 50.42 × 4.11 (165.42 × 13.48); M (Ruston & Hornsby); 9
Similar (Br flag):
35291 **GRASSENDALE**
35292 **HEDON SAND** ex *Kenfig* 1981

★35310 **KASPIY** Ru/DDR (Mathias-Thesen) 1968; FV; 1100; 65.51 × 3.61 (214.93 × 11.83); M (Liebknecht); 10.75
Sisters (Ru flag):
★35311 **NEVEZHIS**
★35312 **NEVKA**
★35313 **OKA**
★35314 **LENA**
Probable sisters (Ru flag):
★35315 **AKHTUBA**
★35316 **AMU-DARYA**
★35317 **FONTANKA**
★35318 **GORKY**
★35319 **INDIGIRKA** (fish carrier)
★35320 **KAMA**
★35321 **KAPITAN EVSEYEV** ex *Syr-Darya* 1971
★35322 **KURA**
★35323 **KOLYMA**
★35324 **LENINGRADETS**
★35325 **OB**
★35326 **PSKOVITYANKA**
★35327 **RAZLIV**
★35328 **RADVILISKIS**
★35329 **ROKISHKIS**
★35330 **SUKHONA**
★35331 **SVIR**
★35332 **TAMAN**
★35333 **VYCHEGDA**
★35334 **50 LET VLKSM**
★35335 **ANADYR**
Similar (Ru flag):
★35336 **RAND-1**
★35337 **RAND-2**
★35338 **RAND-3**
★35339 **RAND-4**

35350 **FINNMARKEN** No/FRG (B+V) 1956; PC; 2200; 81.31 × 4.51 (266.8 × 14.8); M (MAN); 16
Sister:
35351 **RAGNVALD JARL** (No)

35360 **LOFOTEN** No/No (Akers) 1964; PC; 2600; 87.43 × 4.62 (286.8 × 15.17); M (B&W); 16.75

● ★35370 **KOLKHIDA** Ru/Ru ('Zhdanov') 1961; P; 3200; 101.5 × 4 (333 × 13); TSM (CKD Praha) 14.5
Sisters—Some ships have taller funnel. Some may not have crane. (Ru flag):
★35371 **BUKOVINA**
★35372 **KIRGHIZSTAN**
★35373 **MOLDAVIA**
★35374 **TADZHAKISTAN**
★35375 **TALLINN** ex *Svanetiya*
★35376 **TATARIYA**
★35377 **UZBEKISTAN**
Possible sister (Ru flag):
★35378 **AFGHANISTAN**

★35390 **IZUMRUD** Ru/Ru (—) 1970; RS; 3900; 99.37 × 5.4 (326 × 17.75); D-E (—); 13.75

35400 **MUTSU** Ja/Ja (IHI) 1969; RS/C; 8200; 130.46 × 6.9 (428 × 22.67); NT (IHI); 16.5

35410 **KUROSHIO MARU** Ja/Ja (Mitsubishi HI) 1975; Cbl; 3300; 119.31 × 5.59 (391.44 × 18.34); M (MAN); 16.5

★35420 **DMITRY OVTSYN** Ru/Fi (Laiva) 1970; RS; 1100; 66.83 × 4.12 (219.26 × 13.52); M (KHD); 13.75
Possible sisters (Ru flag) (Some may be like Sergey Kravkov—H1—next entry):
★35421 **DMITRY LAPTEV**
★35422 **DMITRY STERLEGOV**
★35423 **EDUARD TOLL**
★35424 **NIKOLAY YEVGENOV**
★35425 **NIKOLAY KOLOMEYTSYEV**
★35426 **STEPAN MALYGIN**
★35427 **VALERIAN ALBANOV**
★35428 **VLADIMIR SUKHOTSKIY**

★35440 **SERGEY KRAVKOV** Ru/Fi (Laiva) 1974; RS; 1100; 68.23 × 4.15 (223.85 × 13.62); M(KHD); 13.5; Some units of **Dmitry Ovtsyn** type—previous entry—may have this appearance

35450 **KDD MARU** Ja/Ja (Mitsubishi HI) 1967; Cbl; 4200; 114 × 6.32 (374 × 20.73); TSM (Kobe); 16

35460 **AQUARIUS** It/It (Ansaldo) 1960; B; 12800; 174.83 × 9.98 (573.6 × 32.74); M (Fiat); 14; launched as *Gorallina*
Possibly similar (It flag):
35461 **CORONA AUSTRALE**
35462 **AURIGA**
May be other ships of this class with this appearance. See **PIVIERE**

35470 **PENTA WORLD** Sg/Br (Connell) 1964; C/HL; 6100/8800; 150.37 × 7.67/9.04 (493.34 × 25.17/29.69); M (Sulzer); —; ex *Inventor* 1981

● ★35480 **BOJNICE** Cz/Hu (Angyafold) 1966; C; 1400; 81.39 × 3.1 (267.03 × 10.16); TSM (Lang Gepgyar); 12
Sisters:
★35481 **LEDNICE** (Cz)
★35482 **CEGLED** (Hu)
★35483 **SZEKESFEHERVAR** (Hu)
★35484 **UJPEST** (Hu)

35490 **PADANG** Ia/De (Nakskov) 1964; C; 7600; 159.5 × 8.1 (523.3 × 26.6); M (B&W); 18.25; ex *Andorra*

35500 **PETER L** Gr/Ja (NKK) 1961; B; 13400; 178.98 × 9.55 (587.2 × 31.33); M (B&W); 16.5
Probable sister:
35501 **CAPTAIN JOHN L** (Gr)

35510 **JERKO TOMASIC** Ys/Ys ('Titovo') 1958; C; 1000; 77.15 × 3 (253.12 × 9.84); TSM (MWM); 12; ex *Privala* 1978; ex *Tamnava* 1971
Similar (now converted to fishing craft—probably altered in appearance):
★35512 **MARKO MILAT** (Ys) ex *Plitvine* 1975

35520 **ALPHA BAY** Br/Ne (IHC Smit) 1980; D; 5700; 112 × 6.25 (367.45 × 25); TSM (Werkspoor); 13.7; Split hopper suction dredger

35530 **SKAUBORD** No/No (Fredriksstad) 1979; RoC; 31100; 182.51 × 12.02 (598.79 × 39.44); M (B&W); 14.8; Stern quarter ramp/door

35535 **MONTLHERY** Fr/Fr (La Rochelle) 1982; RoC; 1600; 116.52 × 5.25 (382 × 17.22); TSM (Pielstick); 15.5
Sister:
35536 **LE CASTELLET** (Fr)

35540 **MUTSU** Ja/Ja (IHI) 1969; RS/C; 8200; 130.46 × 6.9 (428 × 22.67); NT (IHI); 16.5

35570 **ELVINA** Cy/Br (Ardrossan) 1942; C; 500; 61.47 × 3.26 (201.68 × 10.7); M (Polar); 10.5; ex *Hamid* 1980; ex *Alamin* 1972; ex *Ulster Spinner* 1968; ex *Guernsey Coast* 1955; ex *Ulster Duke* 1947

35580 **BURITACA** Co/It (Ansaldo) 1956; B; 11300; 165.5 × 9.31 (543 × 30.54); M (Fiat); 14; ex *Giovanni Ansaldo* 1982
Similar (goalpost forward):
35581 **ORSA MINORE** (It)

35590 **ACCIAIERE** It/It (Ansaldo) 1957; B; 11300; 165.46 × 9.3 (542.85 × 30.51); M (Fiat); 13
Sisters:
35591 **CORONA BOREALE** (It)
35592 **LAMINATORE** (It)
Similar (Pole mast forward):
35594 **AUCTORITAS** (It)

35600 **BAY** US/US (National Steel) 1961; C; 7900/10700; 150.27 × —/9.32 (493 × —/30.58); T (GEC); 18.5; ex *Export Bay* 1980
Sisters (US flag):
35601 **BUILDER** ex *Export Builder* 1980

35602 **BUYER** ex *Export Buyer* 1980
35603 **BANNER** ex *Export Banner* 1982
Sisters (May have cranes removed):
35604 **COURIER** (US) ex *Export Courier* 1981
35605 **EXPORT CHALLENGER** (US)
35606 **EXPORT CHAMPION** (US)
35607 **EXPORT COMMERCE** (US)

35610 **ODELIA** Ho/Hu ('Gheorghiu Dej') 1958; C; 1200; 80.4 × 3.1 (263.8 × 10.7); TSM (Lang Gepgyar); 12; ex *Leros II* 1977; ex *Krateros* 1976; ex *Theofanis L* 1975; ex *Tina* 1973; ex *Hazam* 1970

35620 **IRVINGWOOD** Br/Ca (Davie & Sons) 1952/57; Tk; 2500; 79.23 × 5.81 (259.94 × 19.06); M (General Motors); 10; Converted from general cargo 1957

35640 **MAGED** Le /Hu ('Gheorghiu Dej') 1960; C; 1200; 81.92 × 3.09 (268.77 × 10.14); TSM (Lang Gepgyar); 11; ex *Christina* 1975; ex *Badacsony* 1970
Sisters:
35641 **CARIBI** (Le) ex *Hala* 1982; ex *Aref* 1980; ex *Vittoria* 1975; ex *Csepel* 1970
35642 **SUNNY L** (Pa) ex *Annamina K* 1980; ex *Carpenter* 1977; ex *Ningpo Violet* 1975; ex *Dunaujvaros* 1974
35643 **BUILDER** (Sg) ex *Ningpo Lilac* 1975; ex *Borsod* 1974

35650 **BALTIMORE TRADER** US/US (Bethlehem Steel) 1955/71; Tk; 31100; 243.85 × 12.16 (800 × 39.9); T (Bethlehem Steel); 17.5; ex *P W Thirtle* 1971; Aft sections built 1955; Forward and cargo sections built 1971 (Newport News)

35660 **ARISTON** It/Fi (Valmet) 1960/70; C; 1500/2500; 100.44 × 4.92/5.64 (329.53 × 16.15/18.5); M (Sulzer); 13.5; ex *Span Quarta* 1980; ex *Inha*; Lengthened 1970
Sisters:
35661 **KATERINA A** (Ma) ex *Inio*
★35662 **TAI WU SHAN** (RC) ex *Chengpa Shan* 1980; ex *Tellus* 1970
★35663 **TAI YANG SHAN** (RC) ex *Tabi Shan* 1980; ex *Titania*
35664 **JORDAN** (Eg) ex *Triton* 1976

★35670 **LUN** Ys/Fi (Valmet) 1958; C; 1400; 89.03 × 4.88 (292.1 × 16.01); M (Sulzer); 13; ex *Inari* 1974
Sister:
★35671 **RAD** (Ys) ex *Ivalo* 1974
Similar:
35672 **HERO** (Pa) ex *Skopelos Sea* 1982; ex *Heros* 1974
35673 **NICOLAKIS** (Cy) ex *Poseidon* 1974
35674 **HEROIC SAILOR** (Gr) ex *Salla*
35675 **NATHALIE** (Cy) ex *Ettore* 1978; ex *Mira* 1974

35680 **SERAFIM II** Pa/FRG (Luerssen) 1956; C; 1800; 95 × 5.64 (311.7 × 18.5); M (MAN); 12.5; ex *Kreon* 1979; ex *Alcyone* 1979
Sisters:
35681 **MUNZUR** (Pa) ex *Rigel* 1981; ex *Alcor* 1980
35682 **KHALIL III** (Cy) ex *Kyros* 1982; ex *Attikon* 1978; ex *Alioth* 1975

● 35690 **PETROLA 33** Gr/Br (H&W) 1951; Tk; 16500; 190 × 10.29 (623.36 × 33.75); M (H&W); 14; ex *Petrola XXXIII* 1976; ex *Marianna II* 1975; ex *Bolette* 1964
Sister:
35691 **PETROLA 34** (Gr) ex *Petrola XXXIV* 1976; ex *Margarita II* 1975; ex *Dalfonn* 1966

35710 **VOLUNTAS** It/Sw (Uddevalla) 1957; Tk; 12400; 170.72 × 9.63 (560.11 × 31.59); M (Gotaverken); 14; ex *Pepita* 1977
Similar:
35711 **MARGARETA** (Gr) ex *Stolt Margareta* 1981; ex *Anniken* 1974; ex *Margareta* 1961
35712 **EASTERN MARINER** (Tw)
35713 **ALEXANDROS** (Cy) ex *Wilana* 1969

★35720 **DA QING No 36** RC/No (Akers) 1957; Tk; 10200; 162.29 × 9.32 (532.45 × 30.56); M (B&W); 14.5; ex *Ta Ching No 36*; ex *Vivi* 1970

35740 **BANGLAR ALO** Bh/De (Nakskov) 1960; Tk; 12300; 170.64 × 9.41 (559.84 × 30.88); M (B&W); 16; ex *Stolt Vidar* 1976; ex *Stolt Sveve* 1974; ex *Sveve* 1971; ex *Nakskov* 1970
Sister:
35741 **GARZAN** (Bh) ex *Asia* 1960

35760 **AL RUBAYIA** Pa/Br (Ardrossan) 1943; C; 900; 74.07 × 4.26 (243.01 × 14); M (British Auxiliaries); 11; ex *Eleistra*; ex *Southern Coast* 1967; ex *Forth* 1962; ex *Colebrooke* 1959; ex *Southern Coast* 1955

● 35800 **LAKE PALOURDE** Li/US (Newport News) 1959; Tk; 61300; 297.01 × 15.69 (974.44 × 51.48); T (Newport News); —; Lengthened 1965 (Kure)

35810 **ALDERAMINE** It/It (Adriatico) 1954; Tk; 12600; 172.24 × 9.6 (565.1 × 31.5); M (Adriatico); 15

● 35820 **CORTEMAGGIORE** It/It ('Navalmeccanica') 1955; Tk; 12600; 172.24 × 9.6 (565.1 × 31.5); M (Adriatico); 15
Sister:
35821 **PIBIDUE** (It) ex *Giuseppina Napoleone* 1973; ex *Cassiopea* 1968

35840 **SASSTOWN** Li/US (Sun SB)—Ja 1943/64; Tk; 17500; 199.68 × 10.47 (655.12 × 34.33); T-E (GEC); 14; ex *Hess Fuel* 1963; ex *Conastoga* 1953; Aft section launched as *Hobkirks Hill;* Forward and cargo sections built Ja 1963 (Mitsubishi N); Aft section built US 1943; Lengthened 1969
Sister:
35841 **TIMBO** (Li) ex *Hess Voyager* 1963; ex *Red Canyon* 1956

35870 **MISS MARIETTA** Gr/FRG (Rhein Nordseew) 1966; C; 22200; 204.96 × 11.37 (672.44 × 37.3); M (Sulzer); —
Sisters (Gr flag):
35871 **MICHALAKIS**
35872 **MARY**
35873 **MASTER PETROS**

35890 **POLYTIMI ANDREADIS** Gr/US (Sun SB) — Gr 1943/63; B; 14400; 172.37 × 10.1 (565.52 × 33.14); T-E (Westinghouse); —; ex *Fort Niagara* 1948; Converted from a T-2 tanker and lengthened (Hellenic)

35900 **RINI** Gr/Ys ('Split') 1963; B; 15900; 191.47 × 10.86 (628.18 × 35.63); M (Sulzer); 16; ex *Lenio Ch* 1983; ex *Archangelos* 1981; ex *Archangel* 1968; ex *Archangelos* 1963
Sisters:
35901 **ALFITO** (Gr) ex *Meandros* 1980
35902 **MARELIA** (Pa) ex *Calliroy* 1983; ex *Theofano Livanos* 1980
Similar:
★35903 **HUA TAI** (RC) ex *Atlantic Champion* 1978
★35904 **HUA YANG** (RC) ex *Atlantic Eagle* 1979;
★35905 **HUA HONG** (RC) ex *Atlantic Star* 1979
35906 **MOFARRIJ G** (Si) ex *Interfelicity* 1983; ex *Iamatikos* 1980; ex *Southern Breeze* 1973; ex *Atlantic Breeze* 1972
35907 **CAPTAIN YANNIS** (Gr) ex *Evros* 1981
35908 **MATHILDE** (Pa) ex *Thermopylai;* ex *Kapetanissa* 1976; ex *Kalliopi Pateras* 1972
35909 **NESTOS** (Li)

★35920 **CUU LONG I** Vn/Sw (Eriksbergs) 1964; Tk; 12900; 170.67 × 9.74 (559.94 × 31.56); M (B&W); 15; ex *Grenanger* 1975
Sister:
★35921 **CUU LONG II** (Vn) ex *Austanger* 1975

35940 **BANGLAR KHEYA** Bh/Sw (Uddevalla) 1961; Tk; 12400; 170.72 × 9.63 (560.1 × 31.6); M (Gotaverken); 15; ex *Anja* 1976; ex *Wilchief* 1972

35950 **RODOSTO** Gr/No (Rosenberg) 1960; Tk; 20400; 200.95 × 10.9 (629.28 × 35.76); M (B&W); 15.75; ex *Hallanger* 1973

35960 **ASHTABULA** US/US (Bethlehem Steel) 1943; RT/FA; 34000 Dspl; 196 × 10.7 (644 × 35); TST (Bethlehem Steel); 18; Jumboised 'T-3' type
Sisters:
35961 **CALOOSAHATCHEE** (US)
35962 **CANISTEO** (US)

● 35970 **MORVEN** Li/It (Felszegi) 1961; OO; 17500; 212.15 × 10.78 (696 × 35.37); M (B&W); 14; Launched as *Olin Mathieson*

★35980 **HONG QI 112; & ALAMAR;** May now have this appearance. See next entry

★35990 **HONG QI 112** RC/FRG (AG 'Weser') 1957; C; 11900; 166.5 × 9.05 (546.26 × 29.69); M (MAN); 14; ex *New Red Sea* 1976; ex *Red Sea* 1976; ex *Praunheim* 1972
Sister:
35991 **ALAMAR** (Cy) ex *Berkersheim* 1972
These two ships may now be like previous drawing

36000 **SHIKISHIMA MARU** Ja/Ja (Hitachi) 1961; FF; 9200; 145.9 × 7.85 (478.67 × 25.75); M (B&W); 14.75

36010 **POSSIDONIA** Gr/Ja (Hitachi) 1955; C; 5100; 113.14 × 7.98 (371.19 × 26.18); M (Hitachi); 12.5; ex *Itsukishima Maru* 1977

36020 **GREEK FRIENDSHIP** Gr/Ja (NKK) 1963; B; 13500; 177.83 × 9.55 (583.43 × 31.33); M (B&W); 16.5; ex *Ionian Skipper* 1980
Sister:
36021 **IONIAN MARINER** (Li)

36040 **KERO** Pe/Br (Doxford) 1961; C/HL; 6000/8700; 148.8 × 7.93/9.11 (488.19 × 26/92); M (Doxford); —; ex *Sea Luck* 1980; ex *Tactician* 1979

36050 **ELEFTHERIA** Gr/Br (Doxford) 1960; C/HL; 6400/8400; 149.43 × —/9 (490.26 × —/29.53); M (Doxford); 15; ex *Adventurer* 1979

36060 **TARRY** Pa/Br (Hall, Russell) 1958; C; 1900; 83.88 × 5.2 (275.2 × 17.09); M (British Polar); —; ex *Arring* 1982; ex *Tarring* 1981; ex *Lambeth* 1970
Sisters:
36062 **VASILIS IV** (Gr) ex *Maro;* ex *Chris* 1974; ex *Acyro* 1972; ex *Croydon* 1971

36070 **BLACKWELL POINT** Pa/Br (Austin) 1951; C; 1800; 82.45 × 5.2 (270.5 × 17.06); M (Sulzer); 11; ex *Blackwall Point*
Sisters:
36072 **CHRISTOFOROS** (Gr) ex *Epic* 1976; ex *Birling* 1975; ex *Thomas Hardie* 1968
36073 **GRANITT** (No) ex *Horsham* 1973; ex *Murdoch* 1966
36074 **LINERA** (Br) ex *La Molinera* 1972; ex *Sanderstead* 1967; ex *Samuel Clegg* 1967
36075 **FABIO SAVERIO** (It) (deepened 1970) ex *Captain Alberto* 1975; ex *Brightling* 1970; ex *Falconer Birks* 1970
36076 **TITIKA** (Gr) ex *Keynes* 1975; ex *Accum* 1967

36080 **NORDSEE** FRG/FRG (O&K) 1978; D; 8700; 131.76 × 6.9 (432.28 × 22.64); TSM (Atlas-MaK); 11.25

36090 **TERVI** Fi/Fi (Rauma-Repola) 1963; Tk; 11100; 164.83 × 9.2 (540.78 × 30.18); M (Gotaverken); 14.5
Sister:
36091 **PALVA** (Fi)

36100 **COLTAIR** Br/Br (Smith's D) 1960/76; OSS; 11000; 160.1 × 9.18 (525.26 × 30.12); M (Doxford); 14.5; ex *Forties Kiwi* 1982; ex *British Kiwi* 1976; Converted from a tanker (Boele's Sch)

36110 **SKAUGRAN** No/No (Fredriksstad) 1979; RoC; 31100; 182.5 × 11.99 (598.75 × 39.34); M (B&W); 14.8; Stern quarter ramp/door
Similar:
36111 **SKEENA** (Br)

36120 **MURAT M** Tu/FRG (Rhein Nordseew) 1970; Tk; 62400; 274.3 × 15.43 (899.93 × 50.62); M (Sulzer); 17 ex *Enskeri* 1982
Sister:
36121 **TIISKERI** (Fi)

36130 **CANBERRA** Br/Br (H&W) 1961; P; 44000/44800; 149.49 × 8.54/9.99 (818.54 × 28.01/32.78); TST-E (Associated Electric); 27.5

★36140 **DRUZHBA** SSSR-DDR (Elbewerften) 1977; Riv/C/Con; —; 82 × 2.5 (269.2 × 8.57); TSM (—); 20.75

36150 **AMINUL BAHR** Bh/Ne (Verschure) 1953; D; 900; 78.95 × — (259.02 × —); TSR (Verschure); —

36170 **BLACKPOOL** Br/Br (H.Robb) 1962; Tk; 530; 52.2 × 2.91 (171.26 × 9.55); M (KHD); —; ex *Uno* 1972
Sister:
36171 **BRADFORD** (Br) ex *Toro* 1972

36190 **ANWAR** Le/Br (Scott & Sons) 1941; C; 900; 64.32 × 4.1 (211.02 × 13.45); M (British Auxiliaries); 10; ex *Aghios Spyridon* 1970; ex *Lochee* 1966; ex *Gowrie* 1948; ex *Empire Cape* 1945

● 36210 **TAXIARCHIS** Gr/Br (Blyth) 1961; O; 10600; 155.66 × 8.54 (510.7 × 28.02); M (Doxford); 13; ex *Michalis* 1980; ex *Dukesgarth* 1976
Sister:
36213 **THEOSKEPASTI** (Pa) ex *Knightsgarth* 1975

36220 **TERVI** Fi/Fi (Rauma-Repola) 1963; Tk; 11100; 164.83 × 9.2 (540.78 × 30.18); M (Gotaverken); 14.5
Sister:
36221 **PALVA** (Fi)

36230 **PETROLA 13** Gr/Ne (van der Werf) 1952; AT; 2300; 92.74 × 5.74 (304.27 × 18.83); M (Werkspoor); 10.5; ex *Petrola XIII* 1976; ex *Petro Asphalt II;* ex *Esso Calor* 1973; ex *Esso Le Caroubier* 1968

36240 **WINDRATI** Pa/Br (Furness) 1952; Tk; 10500; 159.42 × 8.87 (523.03 × 29.1); M (Doxford); 13; ex *Sea Jasper* 1966; ex *Wheatfield* 1964

★36250 **BUNKEROVSCHCHIK-3** Ru/Fi (Rauma-Repola) 1958; Tk; 3100; 105.11 × 6.13 (344.85 × 10.1); M (B&W); 13.5; ex *Pevek* 1978
Sisters (Ru flag):
★36251 **ARTYOM**
★36252 **BALTA**
★36253 **MOZYR**
★36254 **PIRYATIN**
★36255 **VENTSPILS**
★36256 **VILYUYSK**

★36257 **ZOLOTOY ROG**
★36258 **KOKAND**

★36270 **MAXHUTTE** DDR/Sw (Gotav) 1955; OO; 8500; 149 × 8.48 (488.85 × 27.83); M (Gotaverken); 13.5; ex *Ledaro* 1975; ex *Vindafjord* 1974

36280 **FLAG SUPPLIER** Pa/Sw (Kockums) 1956; O; 13400; 163.35 × 9.65 (536.91 × 31.66); M (MAN); 15; ex *Riesa;* ex *Cassiopeia* 1965
Sister:
36281 **TELLHOLM** (Fi) ex *Danwood Snow* 1975; ex *Silver City* 1974; ex *Nortrans Enterprise* 1973; ex *Bulk Enterprise* 1970
Similar:
36282 **TAKA** (Gr) ex *World Skill* 1971
36283 **POSEIDON 8** (Gr) ex *Forum Plessot* 1982; ex *Jihad* 1981; ex *Tommy II* 1981; ex *Argo Leader* 1976; ex *World Seafarer* 1972

36290 **ANINGA** It/FRG (Schlieker) 1960; O; 12200; 166.43 × 9.42 (546.03 × 30.91); M (B&W); 15.5; ex *Rigote* 1975; ex *Tyne Ore* 1975
Sister:
36291 **SEQUOIA** (It) ex *Quijote;* ex *Tees Ore* 1975

★36300 **ZWICKAU** DDR/Sw (Kockums) 1958; OO; 15600; 181.60 × 10.04 (596 × 32.94); M (MAN); 14.5; ex *Vitafors* 1969

36310 **NEW HOPE** Ma/Ja (NKK) 1962; B; 21100; 204.12 × 11.14 (670 × 36.55); M (B&W); 16; ex *Kikkos I* 1984; ex *Sotir* 1983; ex *Marchen* 1973; ex *Jesper Maersk* 1965

36320 **CAPO MANNU** It/Br (Grangemouth) 1944; Tk; 2400; 92 × 5.49 (301.84 × 18.01); R (Rowan); 9; ex *Janson* 1966; ex *Mobilsud* 1964; ex *Cassian* 1954; ex *Refast* 1953; ex *Empire Pym* 1946

36330 **ENAYATALLAH** Si/Br (Scarr) 1959; Tk; 900; 64.17 × 3.47 (210.53 × 11.38); M (B Polar); 9.5; ex *Maldive Adventure* 1977; ex *Friston* 1975

36340 **BOLD KNIGHT** Br/FRG (Bayerische) 1960; Tk; 464; 51.72 × 2.44 (169.69 × 8); M (KHD); 9.5
Probable sister:
36341 **PORTFIELD** (Br) ex *Black Knight* 1980

36345 **DUKE OF HOLLAND II.** Ne/Ne (Amels) 1981; RoC; 1600; 79.43 × 4.40 (261 × 14.44); TSM (KHD); 14.5; Stern door

36346 **WARENDORP** FRG/FRG (S&B) 1974; RoVC; 900; 89.87 × 4.59 (295 × 15.06); M (KHD); 14.5; Stern door/2 side doors

★36350 **QI LI HAI** RC/Be (Cockerill) 1965; O; 33000; 229.67 × 12.4 (753.51 × 40.68); M (Sulzer); —; ex *Mineral Seraing*

36360 **AZURE SEAS** Pa/Br (H&W) 1955; P; 16500; 184.06 × 7.98 (603.87 × 26.18); TST (H&W); 20; ex *Calypso* 1980; ex *Southern Cross* 1973

36370 **AMPHIOPEA** Gr/Fr (Loire-Normandie) 1962; O; 19400; 188.6 × 10.3 (618.77 × 33.79); M (B&W); —; ex *Amphiope* 1980

36390 **MIKI** Pa/Ne ('De Hoop') 1958; B; 7300; 139.07 × 9.23 (456.27 × 30.29); M (MAN); 13.5; ex *Eubal* 1983; ex *Miki* 1982; ex *Afovos* 1981; ex *Nicolas Maris;* ex *Kreeft* 1965
Sister:
★36391 **PERELIK** (Bu) ex *Alioth* 1970; ex *Rhone* 1968; ex *Alioth* 1967; ex *Tweelingen* 1965

36400 **POLYKLIS** Gr/Br (A&P) 1958; C; 3100; 97.54 × 6.27 (320 × 20.57); M (British Polar); 11; ex *Capitan Carlo* 1980; ex *Mathios* 1976; ex *Saint Andreas* 1975; ex *Southwark* 1968

36410 **TAXIARCHIS** Gr/Br (Blyth) 1961; O; 10600; 155.66 × 8.54 (510.7 × 28.02); M (Doxford); 13; ex *Michalos* 1980; ex *Dukesgarth* 1976
Sister:
36413 **THEOSKEPASTI** (Pa) ex *Knightsgarth* 1975

36430 **BURITACA** Co/It (Ansaldo) 1956; B; 11300; 165.5 × 9.31 (543 × 30.54); M (Fiat); 14; ex *Giovanni Ansaldo* 1982
Similar (goalpost foreward):
36431 **ORSA MINORE** (It)

36440 **PNOC TAWI-TAWI** Pi/Br (Connell) 1960; OO; 5300; 130.23 × 7.79 (427.26 × 25.56); M (Doxford); 11; ex *LSCO Tawi-Tawi* 1980; ex *Klar* 1976; ex *Crinan* 1974; Converted from ore carrier 1977; Dwg shows vessel before conversion

★36460 **ZWICKAU** DDR/Sw (Kockums) 1958; OO; 15600; 181.60 × 10.04 (596 × 32.94); M (MAN); 14.5; ex *Vitafors* 1969

36480 **FLAG SUPPLIER** Pa/Sw (Kockums) 1956; O; 13400; 163.35 × 9.65 (536.91 × 31.66); M (MAN);

15; ex *Riesa;* ex *Cassiopeia* 1965
Sister:
36481 **TELLHOLM** (Fi) ex *Danwood Snow* 1975; ex *Silver City* 1974; ex *Nortrans Enterprise* 1973; ex *Bulk Enterprise* 1970
Similar:
36482 **TAKA** (Gr) ex *World Skill* 1971
36483 **POSEIDON 8** (Gr) ex *Forum Plessot* 1982; ex *Jihad* 1981; ex *Tommy II* 1981; ex *Argo Leader* 1976; ex *World Seafarer* 1972

36490 **ACCIAIERE** It/It (Ansaldo) 1957; B; 11300; 165.46 × 9.3 (542.85 × 30.51); M (Fiat); 13
Sisters:
36491 **CORONA BOREALE** (It)
36492 **LAMINATORE** (It)
Similar (Pole mast forward):
36494 **AUCTORITAS** (It)

36510 **KRIOS** Gr/FRG (B+V) 1959; B; 17000; 195.79 × 10.63 (642.36 × 34.88); M (MAN); 15; ex *Fiona* 1971

36530 **DEEPSEA MINER II** Li/FRG (Schlieker) 1959; M; 8200; 166.43 × 9.41 (546.03 × 30.87); M (B&W); 15; ex *Weser Ore* 1976; Converted ore carrier (Todd)

36550 **PERENNIAL ACE** Pa/Ja (Mitsui) 1974; RoVC; 10900; 161.68 × 6.71 (530.45 × 22.01); M (B&W); 18.5

36560 **SKAUGRAN** No/No (Fredriksstad) 1979; RoC; 31100; 182.5 × 11.99 (598.75 × 39.34); M (B&W); 14.8; Stern quarter ramp/door
Similar:
36561 **SKEENA** (Br)

36570 **EASTERN HIGHWAY** Ja/Ja (Tsuneishi) 1977; RoVC; 11400; 152.3 × 7.62 (499.67 × 25); M (B&W); 18.5

36590 **MANHATTAN** US/US (Bethlehem Steel) 1962/69; Tk/IB; 62400; 306.48 × 16.09 (1005.51 × 52.79); TST (Bethlehem Steel); 17.5; Converted from tanker, lengthened and widened

36600 **HORYU MARU** Ja/Ja (NKK) 1964; Cem; 7700; 140.01 × 7.42 (459.35 × 24.34); M (MAN); 13

36610 **OVERSEAS NATALIE** US/US (Bethlehem Steel) 1961; Tk; 41000; 262.14 × 14.05 (860.04 × 46.1); T (Bethlehem Steel); 17; ex *Western Hunter;* ex *Orion Hunter* 1964

36630 **PRIMERO** Fi/De (Nakskov) 1959; Tk; 13600; 175.17 × 9.46 (574.71 × 31.04); M (B&W); 15.25

36640 **ST. EMILION** US/US (Bethlehem Steel) 1956; Tk; 19500; 201.48 × 10.87 (661 × 35.6); T (Bethlehem Steel); 16.5; ex *Banner* 1983; ex *Cities Service Miami* 1976

36650 **MONTPELIER VICTORY** US/US (Bethlehem Steel) 1961; Tk; 28000; 222.44 × 12.14 (736.35 × 39.81); T (Bethlehem Steel); 18.25
Similar (US flag):
36652 **MOUNT WASHINGTON**
36653 **MOUNT VERNON VICTORY**
36654 **OVERSEAS JOYCE** ex *Mayflower* 1966
36655 **COVE TRADE** ex *Transeastern* 1977

36670 **TEXACO GEORGIA** US/US (Bethlehem Steel) 1964; Tk; 16500; 184.31 × 10.64 (604.69 × 34.9); T (Bethlehem Steel); 17.5
Sisters (US flag):
36671 **TEXACO MARYLAND**
36672 **TEXACO MASSACHUSETTS**
36673 **TEXACO MONTANA**
36674 **TEXACO RHODE ISLAND**

36680 **TEXACO SKANDINAVIA** No/No (Fredriksstad) 1962; Tk; 13200; 176.33 × 9.64 (578.51 × 31.63); M (Gotaverken); 15
Sister:
36681 **TEXACO NORGE** (No)
Similar:
36682 **TEXACO OSLO** (No)
36683 **FIVE LAKES** (Pa) ex *Texaco Gloucester* 1981; ex *Regent Eagle* 1969

36690 **INDIANO** It/No (Bergens) 1960; Tk; 12200; 169.73 × 9.67 (556.86 × 31.73); M (Stork); 14; ex *Serenitas* 1983; ex *Stolt Filia* 1981; ex *Folia* 1980; ex *Stolt Filia* 1980; ex *Stolt Argobay;* ex *Stolt Hawk* 1973; ex *Osthav* 1968

36700 **DA QING No 37** RC/No (Akers) 1958; Tk; 11100; 167.65 × 9.48 (550.03 × 31.1); M (B&W); 14.5; ex *Pet* 1970; ex *Norsk Viking* 1969; ex *Farmand* 1963

36710 **NIDO OIL** Pa/Sw (Eriksbergs) 1963; Tk; 26400; 215.22 × 11.95 (706.1 × 39.2); M (B&W); 16; ex *Wah Fu* 1982; ex *Jin Hu* 1981; ex *Wanyi* 1973; ex *Antilla* 1973; ex *Tigre* 1969

★36720 **QI LIN HU** RC/De (Odense) 1960; Tk; 16200; 194.24 × 10.67 (637.27 × 35.01); M (B&W); —; ex *Chinshakiang* 1977; ex *Gjertrud Maersk* 1971

36730 **OASIS** Pa/Sw (Eriksbergs) 1962; Tk; 22400; 208.03 × 11.56 (682.51 × 37.93); M (B&W); —; ex *Gota River* 1981

36740 **PUNTA ANGELES** Pa/Ja (Hitachi) 1965; Tk; 12500; 170.69 × 9.34 (560 × 30.64); M (B&W); 15; ex *Sonap II* 1975; ex *Tuborg* 1975
Sister:
★36741 **CHUN HU** (RC) ex *Binjiang* 1976; ex *Viborg* 1975
Similar:
36742 **MOLLENDO** (Pe-Navy) ex *Amalienborg* 1967

36770 **TEXACO MAINE** Pa/US (Bethlehem Steel) 1959; Tk; 28700; 224.44 × 12.0 (736.4 × 39.60); T (Bethlehem Steel); 16; ex *Maine* 1960

36780 **PYRROS V** Gr/Ja (Mitsui) 1957; Tk; 12900; 170.67 × 9.83 (560 × 32.25); M (B&W); —; ex *Palaemon* 1977; ex *Charles P* 1970; ex *Anders Maersk* 1965

36790 **TZINA M** Gr/Sw (Oresunds) 1963; Tk; 28000; 220.73 × 11.83 (724.18 × 38.81); M (Gotaverken); 16; ex *Eric K Fernstrom* 1970; ex *Eric Fernstrom*

36800 **AMERICAN EXPLORER** US/US (Ingalls SB) 1959; Tk; 22500 Dwt; 187.5 × 9.8 (615 × 32); T (De Laval); 20; Operated by Military Sealift Command

★36820 **TOUNDYA** Bu/No (Stord) 1963; Tk; 26800; 213.62 × 11.76 (700.85 × 38.58); M (B&W); 15.5; ex *Buganda* 1969

36830 **AGAMEL** Pa/Sw (Uddevalla) 1962; Tk; 22300; 212.86 × 11.24 (698.36 × 36.88); TSM (Gotaverken); 16.25; ex *Tulip B* 1983; ex *Overseas Ambassador* 1976

★36840 **PEKIN** Ru/Ru (Baltic) 1959; Tk; 20300; 202.8 × 11.98 (665.35 × 39.32); T (Kirov); 17.5
Sisters (Ru flag):
★36841 **BUCHAREST**
★36842 **BUDAPEST**
★36843 **PHENIAN**
★36844 **PRAGA**
★36845 **VARSHAVA**
★36846 **ULAN-BATOR**

36850 **BEAUJOLAIS** US/US (Newport News) 1954; Tk; 17100; 191.42 × 10.25 (628 × 33.63); T (Newport News); 16.5; ex *New York Getty* 1982; ex *Flying A-New York* 1968

★36860 **SOFIYA** Ru/Ru (Admiralteiskiy) 1963; Tk; 31800; 230.51 × 11.81 (756.27 × 38.89); T (Kirov); 16.5
Sisters (Ru flag):
★36861 **AKHTUBA** ex *Hanoi* 1969
★36862 **BELGRAD**
★36863 **BRATISLAVA**
★36864 **GDYNIA**
★36865 **HAVANA**
★36866 **VARNA**
★36867 **DRESDEN**
★36868 **GDANSK**
★36869 **MAURICE THOREZ**
★36870 **OTTO GROTEVOHL**
★36871 **PALMIRO TOGLIATTI**
★36872 **GEORGE GEORGIU-DEZH**
★36873 **KOMSOMOLETS KUBANI**
★36874 **BURGAS**
★36875 **GEROI BRESTA**
★36876 **KHULIO ANTONIO MELYA**
★36877 **RICHARD SORGE**
★36878 **PYATIDYESYATILYETIYE OKTYABRYA** (also known as **50 LETIYE OKTYABRYA**)
★36879 **KOMSOMOLETS LENINGRADA**
★36880 **MEKHANIK AFANASYEV**
★36881 **BORODINO**
(Gr flag):
36882 **VORRAS** ex *Hassi Messaoud* 1980

★36890 **ARGON** Ru/Fi (Rauma-Repola) 1963; Tk; 3400; 105.39 × 6.22 (345.77 × 20.42); M (B&W); 14.25
Sisters (Ru flag):
★36891 **ALUKSNE**
★36892 **APE**
★36893 **AKTASH**
★36894 **AKSAY**
★36895 **ABRENE**
★36896 **AMURSK**
★36897 **APSHERONSK**
★36898 **ARAKS**
★36899 **ANAPKA**
★36900 **LYUBERTSY**
★36901 **SINEGORSK**
★36902 **ALEKSEYEVKA**
★36903 **ALEKSEYEVSK**
★36904 **ANIVA**

★36905 **ALAGIR**
★36906 **ALEYSK**
★36907 **ALEKSIN**
★36908 **ANAPA**
★36909 **EVENSK**
★36910 **ABAGUR**
★36911 **ARDATOV**
★36912 **DARNITZA**
★36913 **EREBUS**
★36914 **INKERMAN**
★36915 **VOLFRAM**
★36916 **IMAN**
★36917 **RADIY**
★36918 **ABAKAN**
★36919 **TYUMENNEFT**
★36920 **YUGLA**
(Cu flag):
★36921 **CUBA** ex *Artsyz* 1962

★36940 **GIUSEPPE GARIBALDI** Ru/It (Ansaldo) 1959/61; Tk; 20700; 203.08 × 10.43 (666.27 × 34.22); T (Ansaldo); 15.5; launched as *Maria Adelaide*; also known as **DZHUZEPPE GARIBALDI**

★36950 **DA QING No 35** RC/No (Fredriksstad) 1958; Tk; 10200; 165.13 × 9.3 (541.77 × 30.51); M (Gotaverken); 15; ex *Anne* 1970; ex *Belstar* 1964

36960 **AHMED AL-BAKRY II** Si/De (Tangen) 1955; Tk; 8900; 154.84 × 8.66 (508 × 28.41); M (Werkspoor); 13; ex *Pibimare Prima* 1981; ex *Stolt Freddy* 1969; ex *Stolt Niagara* 1967; ex *Freddy* 1964

36970 **ALSAD ALAALY** Eg/FRG (Deutsche Werft) 1960; Tk; 13200; 170.69 × 9.4 (560 × 30.84); M (MAN); 15

36990 **TEXACO OSLO** No/Br (Blythswood) 1960; Tk; 12900; 174.9 × 9.64 (574 × 31.63); M (Doxford); 14.5

●★37000 **MIR** Ru/Ja (Harima) 1960; Tk; 25000; 214.03 × 11.38 (702.2 × 37.32); T (Ishikawajima J); 16.25; Launched as *Kate N L*

37010 **ABIDA** Ne/Ne (P Smit) 1958; Tk; 12200; 170.42 × 9.08 (559.12 × 29.79); M (B&W); 14.5
Sisters (Ne flag):
37011 **ACILA**
37012 **ACMAEA**
314 **ACTEON**

37020 **PERMINA SAMUDRA V** Li/FRG (Kieler H) 1958; Tk; 16000; 189.14 × 10.91 (620.53 × 35.79); M (B&W); —; ex *Lindos* 1971; ex *Benstream* 1967; ex *Ring Chief* 1964

37050 **CAMPOLLANO** Sp/Sp (UN de Levante) 1960; Tk; 3800; 109.4 × 5.89 (358.92 × 19.29); M (B&W); 13

●37100 **PETROLA 33** Gr/Br (H&W) 1951; Tk; 16500; 190 × 10.28 (623.36 × 33.73); M (H&W); 14; ex *Petrola XXXIII*; ex *Marianna III*
Similar:
37101 **PETROLA 34** (Gr) ex *Petrola XXXIV* 1976; ex *Margarita II* 1975; ex *Dalfonn* 1966

37170 **NIKITAS** Cy/Fi (Crichton-Vulcan) 1942/51; C; 2300; 88.5 × 5.18 (290.35 × 16.99); M (MWM); 10; ex *Santa Paola* 1972; ex *Emil Berger* 1969; ex *Genoa*

37180 **KYMO** Li/Ja (Mitsubishi N) 1956; Tk; 24200; 211.72 × 11.31 (694.62 × 37.2); T (Hitachi); 16.5
Sister:
37181 **NEFELI** (Li)

★37253 **DA QING No 232** RC/RC (—) 1974; Tk; 10000; 163 × 9.4 (535 × 30.84); M (—); —
Sister (RC flag):
★37253/1 **DA QING 231**
Possible sisters (RC flag):
★37254 **DA QING 45**
★37254/1 **DA QING 46**
★37255 **DA QING 47**
★37255/1 **DA QING 48**
★37256 **DA QING 49**
★37256/1 **DA QING 50**
★37257 **DA QING 52**
★37257/1 **DA QING 53**
★37258 **DA QING 233**
★37259 **DA QING 234**

●37260 **METON** US/US (Ingalls) 1959; Tk; 18300; 202.90 × 11.10 (665.7 × 36.42); T (Westinghouse); 17.5; ex *Eagle Voyager* 1977
Sisters:
37261 **BALDBUTTE** (US) ex *Barbara Jane* 1973
37262 **SAROULA** (US) ex *Exxon Seattle* 1979; ex *Esso Seattle* 1973; ex *Saroula* 1964

37270 **ONDINA** Ne/Ne (Rotterdamsche) 1961; Tk; 31000; 228.61 × 12.19 (250.03 × 39.99); T (Rotterdamsche); 16.75

37290 **EIFEL** FRG/FRG (Norderwerft) 1963; RT/FA;

4700 Dspl; 102 × 7.1 (334 × 23.3); M (—); 13; ex *Friedrich Jung* 1963

★37300 **PLOVDIV** Bu/Sw (Norrkopings) 1960; C; 4900; 106.76 × 7.51 (350.26 × 24.46); M (MaK); 14.5; ex *Faust* 1966.

★37310 **PLISKA** Bu/Sw (Norrkopings) 1959; C; 4500; 106.41 × 7.53 (349.11 × 24.7); M (MaK); 13.5; ex *Fidelio* 1966
Sister:
★37211 **RUSSE** (Bu) ex *Falstaff* 1966

37320 **BINTANG SAMUDRA III** Ia/FRG (Adler) 1954; C; 690/1100; 68.89 × 371/4.37 (226.02 × 12.17/14.34); M (Waggon); 12; ex *Cherry Laju* 1972; ex *Habicht* 1969

37330 **BERRY** Fr/FRG (Rolandwerft) 1958; RS/FA; 2700 Dspl; 86.7 × 4.6 (285 × 15); M (MWM); 15; ex *Medoc* 1964; Converted cargo ship

37340 **KAMELA** UAE/FRG (Kroeger) 1955; C; 1600; 86.72 × 6.08 (285 × 19.95); M (MWM); 14; ex *Ive* 1983; ex *Nives* 1980; ex *Vives* 1970

37363 **GEOPOTES 12**. Pa/Br (Cammell Laird) 1969; D; 3000; 95.00 × 5.00 (312 × 16.40); TrSM (English Electric); 10; ex *Transmundum II* 1974
Sisters:
37364 **TRANSMUNDUM 1** (FRG)
★37365 **LONG CHAU** (Vn) ex *Transmundum IV* 1974
Probable sister:
37366 **BEACHWAY** (NA) ex *Transmundum III* 1974
37367 **VOLVOX FRISIA** (Ne) ex *Transmundum VI* 1973
37368 **VOLVOX ZELANDIA** (Ne) ex *Transmundum V* 1973

37380 **SAN TOMAS SECONDO** It/Ne (Verschure) 1966; D; 3100; 95.64 × 5.94 (313.78 × 19.49); TSM (Smit & Bolnes); —; ex *San Tomas* 1979; ex *Maria Luisa I* 1977; ex *Willemstad* 1977; ex *Luisa*
Sister:
37381 **ORANJESTAD** (NA) ex *Yolanda* 1970

37390 **AMPHIOPEA** Gr/Fr (Loire-Normandie) 1962; O; 19400; 188.6 × 10.3 (618.77 × 33.79); M (B&W); —; ex *Amphiope* 1979

37410 **AFROESSA** Gr/Ne (Giessen) 1956; Tk; 17300; 191.42 × 10.26 (628 × 33.66); T (Stork); 17; ex *Alexandros* 1979; ex *Petrola 23* 1979; ex *Petrola XXIII* 1976; ex *Esso Gothenburg* 1975; ex *Esso Nederland* 1962
Similar (builder—Cammell Laird):
37411 **GOLDEN FALCON** (Br) ex *Elaine* 1966; ex *Mobil Light* 1964; ex *Stanvac India* 1962

37420 **FEOSO STAR** Pa/Ja (Nagoya) 1958; Tk; 12800; 170.59 × 9.48 (559.68 × 31.1); M (Sulzer); 15.5; ex *Stella* 1976; ex *Aiva* 1974; ex *Eiwa Maru* 1968

37450 **PETROMAR ROSARIO** Ar/FRG (Deutsche Werft) 1960; Tk; 22400; 211.23 × 11.33 (693 × 37); T ('De Schelde'); 17; ex *Esso Nurnberg* 1978

37480 **ALSAD ALAALY** Eg/FRG (Deutsche Werft) 1960; Tk; 13200; 170.69 × 9.4 (560 × 30.84); M (MAN); 15

37500 **WHITE BEACH** Pa/Ja (Mitsubishi Z) 1956; Tk; 19800; 203.18 × 10.07 (666.6 × 33.04); T (Mitsubishi); 16; ex *Athenian Runner* 1975; ex *Marietta* 1972

●37510 **ACAVUS** Br/FRG (Bremer V) 1958; Tk; 12300; 170.34 × 9.35 (559 × 30.68); T (Brown, Boveri); 14.5
Sisters:
37510 **ACHATINA** (Br)
37511 **AMASTRA** (Br)
37512 **AULICA** (Br)
37513 **SUNNY** (Cy) ex *Stonegate* 1982
37514 **UJE** (Pa) ex *Amoria*

37530 **HATTAN** Gr/Br (Blyth) 1958; Tk; 12400; 170.69 × 9.44 (560 × 30.97); M (Doxford); 14.5; ex *Yannis P. V.*; ex *Marionga* 1976; ex *Corhaven* 1965

37540 **HIPPO** Gr/FRG (Deutsche Werft) 1960; Tk; 13100; 170.69 × 9.69 (560 × 31.79); M (MAN); —; ex *Stolt Hippo* 1980; ex *Darien* 1974; ex *Fabio* 1964

37550 **DEA BROVIG** Li/No (Marinens) 1962; Tk; 12900; 170.69 × 9.6 (560 × 31.5); M (Doxford); 14; ex *Gylfe* 1976; ex *Nina Borthen* 1968

37570 **GEORGIOS V** Gr/Br (H&W) 1961; Tk; 18800; 196.07 × 10.86 (643.29 × 35.63); M (H&W); 15.75; ex *George Peacock* 1969
Similar:
37571 **CHAPARAL II** (Pa) ex *Midas Touch* 1981; ex *Galaxias*; ex *Norsk Drott* 1968

37600 **WASHINGTON TRADER** US/US (Newport News) 1959; Tk; 24500; 217.08 × 11.53 (712.2 ×

37.83); T (De Laval); 17; ex *Thetis* 1975
Sister:
37601 **ACHILLES** (US)
Possibly similar:
37602 **SOUTHWEST CAPE** (Li) ex *G.S. Livanos* 1973

37610 **TRANSUD II** Li/FRG (Deutsche Werft) 1960; Tk; 16000; 187.2 × 10.18 (614.17 × 33.4); M (MAN); 15.25; ex *San Juan* 1977; ex *Nebo* 1974; ex *Topaz* 1960

37620 **KAPETAN MARKOS N L** Gr/Ja (Kure) 1962; Tk; 39200; 236.23 × 13.74 (775.03 × 45.08); M (Sulzer); 15.75; ex *Ise Maru* 1972

37630 **MARIPRIMA** Li/Sw (Kockums) 1961; Tk; 30200; 227.34 × 12.01 (745.87 × 39.4); T (De Laval); 16.75; ex *Esso Stockholm* 1977

★37640 **YIN HU** RC/Sw (Uddevalla) 1964; Tk; 35000; 235.87 × 12.21 (773.85 × 40.06); M (MAN); 15.5; ex *Harwi* 1974; May be spelt **YINHU**

37650 **SOUTHERN CONQUEST** Li/Be (Cockerill-Ougree) 1959; Tk; 18200; 201.51 × 10.64 (661.12 × 34.91); T (De Laval); 16; ex *Conquest* 1977; ex *Northern Conquest* 1975; ex *Atlantic Conquest* 1963

S7680 **CABO GUARDIAN** Ar/Sw (Eriksbergs) 1964; Tk; 26600; 215.22 × 11.95 (706.1 × 39.21); M (B&W); 15.5; ex *Polykarp* 1982
Similar:
37681 **EVA P** (Cy) ex *Saga* 1983; ex *Rion* 1982; ex *Polycastle* 1980

●37700 **VERDI** Pa/De (Odense) 1964; Tk; 21600; 209.15 × 11.27 (686.19 × 36.98); M (B&W); 15.5; ex *Athina* 1982; ex *Oluf Maersk* 1980; ex *Karen Maersk* 1978
Sister:
37701 **HENNING MAERSK** (De)

37720 **LUJAN DE CUYO** Ar/De (Odense) 1962; Tk; 23600; 215.75 × 11.77 (708 × 38.62); T (GEC); 15.5; ex *Kristine Maersk* 1972

37740 **AL HUSSEIN B** Pa/Ja (Mitsubishi Z) 1962; Tk; 28200; 224.34 × 11.53 (736.02 × 37.83); M (Mitsubishi); 15.5; ex *Pacific Century*; ex *Seiwa Maru* 1973

★37780 **TRUD** Ru/Ys ('3 Maj') 1960; Tk; 17900; 192.36 × 10.24 (631.1 × 33.59); T (De Laval); 16; ex *Fraternity*

●37790 **FLORENCE** US/US (Newport News) 1954; Tk; 17400; 191.42 × 10.23 (628.02 × 33.56); T (Newport News); 16; ex *Exxon Florence* 1982; ex *Esso Florence* 1973
Possible sisters (US flag):
37791 **EXXON CHESTER** ex *Esso Chester* 1973
37792 **EXXON HUNTINGTON** ex *Esso Huntington* 1973
37793 **EXXON NEWARK** ex *Esso Newark* 1973
37794 **EXXON BANGOR** ex *Esso Bangor* 1973
37796 **SAN MARCOS** ex *Transpanama* 1976; ex *Ocean Pioneer* 1968; ex *Esso Jacksonville* 1964; ex *Esso Suez* 1962
Similar (Be built—Ar flag):
37797 **PETROMAR CAMPANA** ex *Esso Antwerp* 1961

37810 **PETROLA 36** Gr/Sw (Kockums) 1960; Tk; 26500; 213.21 × 11.59 (699.51 × 38.02); T (De Laval); 17.25. ex *Petrola XXXVI* 1976; ex *Spiro* 1975; ex *Petrola XVII*; ex *Esso Brussels* 1973

●37830 **MARIE MAERSK** De/De (Odense) 1962; Tk; 21600; 209.15 × 10.75 (686.19 × 35.27); M (B&W); 15

37850 **LUSSIN** It/FRG (Deutsche Werft) 1959; Tk; 12600; 170.7 × 9.43 (560 × 30.94); T (Allgemeine); 14.5; ex *Partula* 1981

37860 **SANTISIMA TRINIDAD** Ar/Fr (Mediterranee) 1963; O; 14700; 199.02 × 10.97 (652.95 × 33.99); M (Gotaverken); 14; ex *Skamandros* 1977; ex *Gerald L D* 1973
Sister:
★37861 **SUN CHON** (RK) ex *Cosmos Faith*; ex *Pierre L D* 1977

37870 **ANINGA** It/FRG (Schlieker) 1961; O; 9100; 166.43 × 9.42 (546.03 × 30.91); M (B&W); 15.5; ex *Tyne Ore* 1975
Sister:
37871 **SEQUOIA** (It) ex *Tees Ore* 1975

37880 **JINYU MARU** Ja/Ja (Mitsubishi HI) 1974; RoVC; 16100; 224.98 × 9.32 (738.12 × 30.58); M (Sulzer); 20.5; Side doors

37890 **ESTADO DA GUANABARA** Bz/Br (Upper Clyde) 1973; D; 5000; 104.02 bp × 8.39 (341.27 × 27.53); TSM (MAN); 13; ex *Guanabara* 1977

37900 **MURAT M**. Tu/FRG (Rhein Nordseew) 1970; Tk; 62400; 274.3 × 15.43 (899.93 × 50.62); M (Sulzer); 17; ex *Enskeri* 1982
Sister:
37901 **TIISKERI** (Fi)

37910 **PRESIDENTE DEODORO** Bz/Ja (NKK) 1960/67; Tk; 29900; 241.05 × 12.26 (790.85 × 40.22); T (Ishikawajima J); —; Lengthened and deepened 1967 (Mitsubishi HI)
Sister:
37911 **PRESIDENTE FLORIANO** (Bz)

37920 **PANAGIS K** Pa/Br (A&P) 1959; C; 3000/4400; 115.27 × 6.55/7.47 (378 × 21.49/24.51); M (Sulzer); 14.5; ex *Efi* 1980; ex *Ilkon Niki* 1979; ex *Manchester Fame* 1970; ex *Cairnglen* 1966; ex *Manchester Fame* 1965

37930 **ABOITIZ CONCARRIER III**. Pi/Sw (Norrkopings) 1957; CP; 1300; 89.08 × 4.88 (292.26 × 16.01); M (MAN); 13; ex *Martina* 1979; ex *Vega* 1973; Converted from cargo ship

37950 **MATCO AVON** Br/FRG (Bremer V) —Ja 1964/68/76; Tk; 43700; 266.68 × 14.11 (874.93 × 46.29); T (Bremer V); 16.25; Lengthened and deepened 1968 (Mitsubishi HI); Converted tanker 1976; Used for offshore loading

37970 **THERMOPYLAI**. Gr/No (Fredriksstad) 1955; Tk; 9000; 156.62 × 8.72 (513.85 × 28.61); M (Fredriksstad); 13.5; ex *Anina* 1978; ex *Fossland* 1963; ex *Slemdal* 1961

37980 **ARAUCANO** Ch/De (B&W) 1967; RT/FA; 17300 Dspl; 151.8 × 8.8 (498 × 29); M (B&W), 15.5

37990 **AGAMEL** Pa/Sw (Uddevalla) 1962; Tk; 22300; 212.86 × 11.24 (698.36 × 36.88); TSM (Gotaverken); 16.25; ex *Tulip B* 1983; ex *Overseas Ambassador* 1976

38010 **EXXON BOSTON** US/US (Newport News) 1960; Tk; 30700; 225.56 × 12.02 (740.03 × 39.42); T (Newport News); 16.5; ex *Esso Boston* 1973
Sister:
38011 **EXXON BALTIMORE** (US) ex *Esso Baltimore* 1973

38020 **GULFCREST** US/US (Bethlehem Steel) 1959; Tk; 18000; 196.55 × 10.56 (644.85 × 34.64); T (Bethlehem Steel); 17
Sisters (US flag):
38021 **GULFPRIDE**
38022 **GULFSOLAR**
38023 **GULFSUPREME**
38024 **GULFSPRAY**

38030 **COVE SAILOR** US/US (Bethlehem PC) 1959; Tk; 20600; 201.48 × 10.86 (661.02 × 35.63); T (Bethlehem Steel); 16.5; ex *Erna Elizabeth* 1979

38040 **PENNSYLVANIA SUN** US/US (Sun SB) 1959; Tk; 26300; 227.08 × 11.96 (745 × 39.25); T (Westinghouse); 17
Sister:
38041 **TEXAS SUN** (US)

38070 **ESSO WARWICKSHIRE** Br/FRG (A.G. 'Weser') 1962; Tk; 48000; 262.54 × 14.99 (862 × 49.18); T (A.G. 'Weser'); 17; Converted for offshore loading 1976

38090 **MERSIN** Tu/FRG (Bremer V) 1955; Tk; 11300; 165.18 × 9.17 (541.93 × 30.09); M (Bremer V); 14.5; ex *Faust* 1962

38100 **MOBIL FUEL** US/US (Bethlehem Steel) 1957; Tk; 18700; 196.5 × 10.55 (644.68 × 34.61); T (Parsons); 16.5
Sister (US flag):
38102 **NAECO** ex *Mobil Power*

38120 **MOBILOIL** US/US (Sun SB) 1959; Tk; 18600; 195.38 × 10.84 (641.01 × 35.55); T (GEC); 17.25
Sister:
38121 **MOBIL AERO** (US)

● 38130 **VIGIL** Li/FRG (Bremer V) 1964; Tk; 31300; 224.04 × 10.98 (735.04 × 36.02); T (Bremer V); 16.75; ex *Mobil Vigilant* 1982

● 38140 **NICOLE SEA** Pa/Sw (Eriksbergs) 1960; Tk; 22400; 208.03 × 11.58 (682.51 × 37.98); M (Eriksbergs); —; ex *Omar B* 1982; ex *Finale* 1980; ex *Bergemaster* 1968
Similar:
38141 **AL MORGAN** (Eg) ex *Bergesund* 1967

38160 **KOREA EDINBURGH** Ko/Br (Scotts' SB) 1956; Tk; 11800; 170.39 × 9.62 (559.1 × 31.7); T (Scotts' SB); 15; ex *Texaco Edinburgh* 1971; ex *Caltex Edinburgh* 1968

38170 **KEYSTONER** US/US (Bethlehem Steel) 1953; Tk; 11400; 168 × 9.35 (551.18 × 30.67); T

(Bethlehem Steel); 15

38180 **STATHEROS** Gr/No (Tangen) 1964; Tk; 41400; 253.02 × 13.65 (830.1 × 45); M (B&W); 17; ex *Cardo* 1975

38190 **AL SABAH IV** Si/Sw (Gotav) 1961; Tk; 26400; 213.65 × 11.74 (701 × 38.52); TSM (Gotaverken); 16; ex *Dagny* 1972; ex *O.T. Tonnevold* 1967
Similar (kingposts on after superstructure nearer funnel):
38191 **CABO CORRIENTES 1** (Ar) ex *Sven Salen* 1977

● 38200 **RALLYTIME III** Pa/De (B&W) 1962; Tk; 25500; 208.59 × 11.61 (684.35 × 38.09); M (B&W); 16.5; ex *Zeitz* 1982; ex *Daghild* 1969

38210 **PAVLOS V** Gr/De (Odense) 1958; Tk; 18300; 200.13 × 10.36 (656.59 × 33.99); M (B&W); 16.5; ex *Rainbow*; ex *Global Leader*; ex *Thomas G Chimples* 1977; ex *Matheos* 1972; ex *Floreal* 1968
Sisters:
38211 **TAMMANNA** (Sr) ex *Monaco* 1975; ex *Mauritius* 1974; ex *Monseau* 1971
38212 **SWAN LAKE** (Gr) ex *Calvados* 1976; ex *Svenord* 1972; ex *Passy* 1971

38230 **GEORGIOS** Gr/Sw (Eriksbergs) 1960; Tk; 23500; 208.03 × 11.56 (682.51 × 37.93); M (B&W); 15; ex *Hoegh Fulmar* 1968

38270 **FEOSO AMBASSADOR** Pa/Sw (Oresunds) 1961; Tk. 24800; 213.42 × 11.81 (700.2 × 37.57); M (Gotaverken); 17; ex *Schwedt* 1979; ex *Sea Serpent* 1969

38320 **CHAPARAL II** Pa/Br (H&W) 1961; Tk; 18600; 196.22 × 10.52 (643.77 × 34.51); M (B&W); 15; ex *Midas Touch* 1981; ex *Galaxias*; ex *Norsk Drott* 1968

● ★ 38330 **DA QING 235** RC/Br (Lithgows) 1959; Tk; 10700; 160.17 × 9.14 (525.5 × 30); M (B&W); 14.5; ex *Tingjiang*; ex *British Trust* 1976
Similar:
★ 38331 **DA QING 136** (RC) ex *Zhujiang*; ex *British Fulmar* 1976
38332 **ORIENTAL UNITY** (Li) ex *British Cygnet* 1977; ex *B P Explorer* 1969; ex *B P Endeavour* 1967; ex *British Cygnet* 1964
38335 **NEWHAVEN** (Pa) ex *Hanjiang* 1981; ex *British Gannet* 1976
38337 **WENJIANG** (Br) ex *British Curlew* 1976
38338 **NOAH VI** (Ir) ex *British Swift* 1977
38339 **FAL XI** (UAE) ex *Lot* 1983; ex *British Robin* 1977
38341 **PENHORS** (Fr) ex *British Mallard* 1978

★ 38361 **DA QING No 29** RC/RC (Hung Chi) 1971; Tk; 10000; 160.03 × 9.4 (525 × 30.84); M (—); —
Sister:
★ 38362 **DA QING 30** (RC)

★ 38365 **DA QING No 212** RC/Rm (Turnu-Severin) 1974; Tk; 4900; 128.89 × 4.20 (423 × 13.78); TSM (Liebknecht); 10.5
Sisters (RC flag):
★ 38366 **DA QING 213**
★ 38367 **DA QING 214**
★ 38368 **DA QING 215**
★ 38369 **DA QING 412**
★ 38370 **DA QING 413**
★ 38371 **DA QING 414**
★ 38372 **DA QING 415**
★ 38373 **DA QING 416**
★ 38374 **DA QING 417**

★ 38405 **DA QING No 240** RC/RC (Hung Chi) 1975; Tk; 18000; 178 × — (584 × —); M (—); 15.5
Sisters:
★ 38406 **DA QING No 241** (RC)
★ 38407 **DA QING No 42** (RC)
★ 38408 **DA QING No 44** (RC)

38410 **ARCTIC STAR** Li/Sw (Gotav) 1964; Tk; 30200; 236.23 × 12.39 (775 × 40.65); M (Gotaverken); 15; ex *Palma* 1976

38420 **MAUMEE** US/US (Ingalls SB) 1956; Tk; 25000 Dwt; 189 × 9.8 (620 × 32); T (Westinghouse); 18; Operated by Military Sealift Command
Sisters (US flag):
38421 **SHOSHONE**
38422 **YUKON**

38440 **GEORGIOS VERGOTTIS** Gr/Ja (Mitsubishi HI) 1966; Tk; 30600; 236.23 × 12.38 (775.03 × 40.61); M (Sulzer); —

38450 **GABRIEL DA FONSECA** Bz/FRG (Ottensener) 1959; Tk; 4700; 122.87 × 7.28 (403.12 × 23.88); M (MAN); 14

38460 **PRIMA DONNA** Pa/FRG 1955; C; 8700; 144.66 × 8.43 (474.61 × 27.67); M (MAN); 12.5; ex *Prima King* 1982; ex *Nidar* 1968; ex *Estello* 1962

38470 **SHOJU MARU** Ja/Ja (IHI) 1969; Tk; 109100; 315.37 × 18.85 (1034.68 × 61.83); T (IHI); 16

38490 **PEARLEAF** Br/Br (Blythswood) 1960; RT/FA; 12400; 173.2 × 9.2 (568 × 30); M (Doxford); 16

38500 **PLUMLEAF** Br/Br (Blyth) 1960; RT/FA; 26500 Dspl; 163 × 9.2 (560 × 30); M (Doxford); 15.5

38520 **CARAIBI** It/Sp ('Bazan') 1957; Tk; 12700; 170.62 × 9.51 (559.78 × 31.2); M (Gotaverken); 14; ex *Valmaseda* 1975
Similar:
38521 **CAMPANAR** (Sp) ex *Compostilla* 1974
38522 **CAMPAZAS** (Sp) ex *Ribagorzana* 1974

★ 38530 **PLYAVINYAS** Ru/Pd (Gdynska) 1967; Tk; 12600; 176.89 × 9.5 (580.35 × 31.17); M (Sulzer); 16.25; 'B-70' type
Sisters (Ru flag):
★ 38531 **LIMBAZHI**
★ 38532 **PREYLI**
★ 38533 **RIGA**
★ 38534 **VALMIERA**
★ 38535 **TALSY**
★ 38536 **TSESIS**

38540 **MEDINA** US/US (Sun SB) 1953; Tk; 18800; 195.38 × 10.81 (641 × 35.46); T (Westinghouse); 16.5; ex *Delaware Sun* 1982
Sisters (US flag):
38541 **COVE MARINER** ex *Eastern Sun* 1982
38542 **WESTERN SUN**

38560 **LAGOVEN MARACAIBO** Ve/Ja (Hitachi) 1959/64; Tk; 24100; 212.15 × 10.95; (696.03 × 35.92); T (Hitachi); 15; ex *Esso Maracaibo* 1976; Lengthened 1964
Sister:
38561 **LAGOVEN CARACAS** (Ve) ex *Esso Caracas* 1976

38570 **EXXON GETTYSBURG** US/US (Newport News) 1957; Tk; 23700; 217.94 × 11.84 (715.03 × 38.85); T (Newport News); 18.25; ex *Esso Gettysberg* 1973
Sisters (US flag):
38571 **EXXON JAMESTOWN** ex *Esso Jamestown* 1973
38572 **EXXON LEXINGTON** ex *Esso Lexington* 1973
38573 **EXXON WASHINGTON** ex *Washington* 1973

★ 38580 **GIORDANO BRUNO** Ru/It (Ansaldo) 1964; Tk; 31300; 227.01 × 12.14 (744.78 × 39.83); M (Fiat); 15.75; Also known as **DZHORDANO BRUNO**
Sisters (Ru flag):
★ 38581 **FEDOR POLETAEV**
★ 38582 **LEONARDO DA VINCI**

38600 **AMAZONA** Pa/Sw (Gotav) 1962; Tk; 21500; 208.92 × 10.88 (685.43 × 35.71); M (Gotaverken); 15.25; ex *Gothic Lady* 1981; ex *Holma* 1974

★ 38610 **BAUSKA** Ru/Pd (Gdanska) 1962; Tk. 12600; 176.94 × 9.55 (580.51 × 31.33); M (Sulzer); 15.25; ex *Profesor Huber* 'B-70' type
Sisters:
★ 38611 **BALAKLAVA** (Ru) (Shorter funnel and forepart of superstructure more open)
★ 38612 **BALDONE** (Ru)
★ 38613 **BALVY** (Ru)
★ 38614 **DA QING No 17** (RC) ex *Prof. M.T. Huber* 1964

★ 38620 **DA QING 230** RC/Ys ('Uljanik') 1959; Tk; 13300; 170.69 × 9.5 (560 × 31.17); M (B&W); —; ex *Hong Hu*; ex *Ostrava* 1965; ex *Istina* 1959

● 38630 **SICILMOTOR** It/It (Ansaldo) 1958; Tk; 20600; 204.81 × 10.89 (671.95 × 35.73); M (Fiat); 16.5

38650 **CATHERINE Y** Pa/Ys ('Uljanik') 1960; Tk; 13000; 170.69 × 9.77 (560 × 32.04); M (B&W); 15; ex *Catherine* 1982; ex *Stolt Catherine* 1980; ex *Stolt Aegean* 1978; ex *Stolt Gemini* 1973; ex *Dioskurol* 1969

● 38660 **HONESTAS** It/Ys ('Uljanik') 1961; Tk; 13700; 170.67 × 9.45 (559.94 × 31); M (B&W); 15; ex *Beskidy* 1977; Ice strengthened

38670 **CAMPORROJO** Sp/Sp (UN de Levante) 1963; Tk; 7000; 141.79 × 7.76 (465.2 × 25.46); M (B&W); 13.7
Sister (Sp flag):
38671 **CAMPOGULES**
Possible sisters (Sp flag):
38672 **CAMPOCERRADO**
38673 **CAMPOAZUR**
38674 **CAMPORRUBIO**

★ 38690 **DA QING No 253** RC/De (B&W) 1974; Tk;

33800; 236.23 × 12.42 (775.03 × 40.73); M (B&W); 16.5; ex *Jian Hu* 1977; ex *Vesthav* 1974

★38700 **DA QING No 251** RC/Sw (Eriksbergs) 1964; Tk; 26600; 215.22 × 11.94 (706.1 × 39.17); M (B&W); 15.25; ex *Pinghu* 1974; ex *Guldregn* 1974; ex *Regina* 1973; ex *Nova* 1967

38720 **MARGARITIS** Cy/Fr (L'Atlantique) 1963; Tk; 36700; 242.91 × 12.85 (767.93 × 42.15); M (B&W); —; ex *Citta di Savona* 1983; ex *Berge Charles* 1968
Sister:
38721 **GERMIK** (Tu) ex *Berge Racine* 1967

● 38730 **SCAPMOUNT** Gr/Sw (Eriksbergs) 1961; Tk; 22000; 208.03 × 11.56 (682.51 × 37.94); M (B&W); 16.5; ex *Mirfak* 1973; ex *Toscana* 1972
Similar:
38731 **TRINITE** (Gr) ex *Theoskepasti* 1983; ex *Despina Mihalinou* 1982; ex *Eugenia II* 1979; ex *Dana* 1974; ex *Noto* 1974; ex *Torino* 1969
★38732 **WOLFEN** (DDR) ex *Tarim* 1968

38740 **AL SABAH IV** Si/Sw (Gotav) 1961; Tk; 26400; 213.65 × 11.74 (701 × 38.52); TSM (Gotaverken); 16; ex *Dagny* 1972; ex *O.T. Tonnevold* 1967

38750 **RODOSTO** Gr/No (Rosenberg) 1960; Tk; 20400; 200.95 × 10.90 (659 × 35.76); M (B&W); 15.75; ex *Hallanger* 1973

38760 **PAVLOS V** Gr/De (Odense) 1958; Tk; 18300; 200.13 × 10.36 (656.59 × 33.99); M (B&W); 16.5; ex *Rainbow*; ex *Global Leader*; ex *Thomas G. Chimples* 1977; ex *Matheos* 1972; ex *Floreal* 1968
Sisters:
38761 **TAMMANNA** (Sr) ex *Monaco* 1975; ex *Mauritius* 1974; ex *Monseau* 1971
38762 **SWAN LAKE** (Gr) ex *Calvados* 1976; ex *Svenord* 1972; ex *Passy* 1971

38780 **ADRIATIKI** Gr/No (Fredriksstad) 1963; Tk; 30600; 228.58 × 12.62 (749.93 × 40.23); TSM (Gotaverken); 16.5; ex *Sverre Rex*; ex *Tank Rex* 1978

● 38790 **SAN MARCO** Pa/It (Breda) 1960; B; 10700; 166.48 × 9.35 (547.83 × 30.68); M (Fiat); 15.75; ex *Gungnir III* 1980; ex *Saint Etienne* 1979; ex *San Martin* 1970; ex *Portovado* 1968
Similar (Li flag):
38791 **DEVONSHIRE** ex *Saint Raphael* 1981; ex *Portovenere* 1968
38792 **EGMONT** ex *Saint Marcel* 1982; ex *Portofino* 1968

38820 **COVE LEADER** US/US (Newport News) 1959; Tk; 40500; 246.9 × 14.33 (810.04 × 46.71); T (Newport News); 17.25; ex *Vantage Defender*; ex *National Defender* 1973

38830 **KARYSA** Pa/Sw (Kockums) 1963; Tk; 22600; 202.83 × 11.55 (665.45 × 37.89); M (MAN); 15.75; ex *Montebello* 1982; ex *Tank Princess* 1977

★38840 **YOUHAO** RC/FRG (Rickmers) 1959; C/HL; 8400; 153.88 × 9.03 (504.86 × 29.63); M (MAN); —; ex *Etha Rickmers* 1964

38850 **JINYU MARU** Ja/Ja (Mitsubishi HI) 1974; RoVC; 16100; 224.98 × 9.32 (738.12 × 30.58); M (Sulzer); 20.5

38860 **PRESIDENTE DEODORO** Bz/Ja (NKK) 1960/67; Tk (Ishikawajima J); 29900; 241.05 × 12.26 (791 × 37); T; —; Lengthened and deepened 1967 (Mitsubishi HI)
Sister:
38861 **PRESIDENTE FLORIANO** (Bz)

38880 **EXXON BOSTON** US/US (Newport News) 1960; Tk; 30700; 225.56 × 12.02 (740 × 39.47); T (Newport News) 16.5; ex *Esso Boston* 1973
Sister:
38881 **EXXON BALTIMORE** (US) ex *Esso Baltimore* 1973

38900 **CAMPOVERDE** Sp/Sp (AESA) 1958; Tk; 6600; 138.99 × 7.76 (456 × 25.46); M (B&W) 13.5

38920 **MISPILLION** US/US (Sun SB) 1945; RT/FA; 34200 Dspl; 197 × 10.8 (648 × 35.5); TST (Westinghouse); 16; Jumboised 'T-3' type
Sisters (US flag):
38921 **NAVASOTA**
38922 **PAWCATUCK**
38923 **WACCAMAW**
Similar:
38924 **PASSUMPSIC**

38930 **ASPASIA M** Gr/No (Nakskov) 1961; C; 9900; 159.72 × 8.1 (524 × 26.57); M (B&W); 18; ex *Man Fung* 1980; ex *Asmara* 1978
Sister:
38932 **POMALAA** (Ia) ex *Boribana* 1977;

● 38940 **ASAHAN** Ia/De (B&W) 1959; C; 8700; 151.82 × 8.41 (498.1 × 27.56); M (B&W); 17.5; ex

Basra 1977
Sister:
★38941 **NORB** (Br) ex *Ifewara* 1981; ex *Beira* 1975

★38950 **DESNA** Ru/Ru (—) —; RT/FA; 8200; 136.5 × 7 (448.49 × 22.97); M; (Russkiy); —; Converted from 'KAZBEK' class tanker

38960 **PROVIDER** Ca/Ca (Davie SB) 1963; Rst/FA; 20000; 169.2 × 9.8 (555 × 32); T (—); 30; 3 helicopters, hangar and flight deck

38980 **KOYO MARU** Ja/Ja (Mitsubishi Z) 1955; C; 7500; 139.66 × 8.08 (458.2 × 26.51); M (Mitsubishi); 14.5

★38990 **QUE LIN** RC/FRG (A.G. 'Weser') 1954; C; 6900; 155.78 × 8.27 (511.09 × 27.13); M (Sulzer); 17.25; ex *Goldenfels* 1968
Sister:
★38991 **HONG QI 126** (RC) ex *Jilin*; ex *Gutenfels*
Similar:
38992 **ATHENS STAR** (Gr) ex *Silver Coast* 1980; ex *Kandelfels* 1977

● 39000 **SAKURA** Ja/Ja (Mitsubishi HI) 1962; PC; 12500; 157.03 × 8.8 (515.19 × 28.25); M (Mitsubishi); 17; ex *Sakura Maru* 1971

● 39010 **CLEOPATRA II** Gr/Fr (Provence) 1957; C; 4300; 115.93 × 6.2 (380.35 × 20.33); M (Doxford); 13.5; ex *Alfa* 1980; ex *Mostaganem* 1980; ex *Cap Sideros* 1970; ex *S.N.A.5* 1969

39020 **CHRYSSI V** Gr/Fr (Gironde) 1961; Tk; 13400; 175.34 × 9.5 (575.26 × 31); M (B&W); 15; ex *Euterpe* 1978; ex *Thale* 1976; ex *Lacon* 1972; ex *Athen* 1968; ex *Athene* 1966.

39030 **TAMA MARU** Ja/Ja (Hitachi) 1972; RoVC; 7000; 174.5 × 7.21 (572.5 × 23.67); M (B&W); 18
Sisters (Ja flag):
39031 **SAGAMI MARU**
39032 **SURUGA MARU**
39033 **TSURUMI MARU**

● 39050 **IONIAN SEA** Pa/FRG (Kieler H) 1956; C; 9100; 151.42 × 9.09 (496.78 × 29.81); M (MAN) 14.5; ex *Ocean Regina* 1973; ex *Lancelot* 1963
Sister:
39051 **SARONICOS GULF** (Gr) ex *Minoan Trader* 1973; ex *Aquila* 1972; ex *Heering Christel* 1967; ex *Polarvind* 1964

39060 **APOSTOLOS M IV** Gr/FRG (Kieler H) 1956; C; 9200; 151.39 × 9.09 (496.69 × 29.82); M (MAN); 14; ex *Hadji Dimitar* 1980; ex *Avior* 1970; ex *Bronnoy* 1966

● 39090 **ASAHAN** Ia/De (B&W) 1959; C; 8700; 151.82 × 8.41 (498.1 × 27.56); M (B&W); 17.5; ex *Basra* 1977
Sister:
39091 **NORB** (Br) ex *Ifewara* 1981; ex *Beira* 1975

39100 **GAVESHANI** In/Br (Simons Lobnitz) 1964/75; RS; 1600; 67.98 × 3.57 (223.03 × 11.71); TSM (MAN); 10; ex *Hopper Barge No. 2* 1975; Converted from dredger 1975 (Garden Reach)

★39110 **CHAZHMA** Ru/— 1963; Missile Tracking; 5300 Dspl; 132.8 × 6.1 (437 × 20); M(—); 18; ex *Dangara*; Carries 1 helicopter
Similar (Ru flag):
★39111 **CHUMIKAN** ex *Dolgeschtschelje*
★39112 **DESNA**

★39120 **OLEKMA** Ru/Fi (Rauma-Repola) 1964; RT; 3400; 105.11 × 6.22 (344.85 × 20.41); M (B&W); 13.5; Converted from tanker. May be others in this class similarly converted

★39130 **BOGDAN** Bu/Sw (Gotav) 1946; O; 8800; 149 × 8.46 (488.85 × 27.76); M (Gotaverken); 13; ex *Atlas* 1970; ex *Raunala* 1963; Converted from ore/oil

39150 **FAR STAR** Ho/Ne (Gusto) 1953; C; 1000; 78.87 × 4.32 (258.76 × 14.17); M ('De Industrie'); 13.5; ex *Don Emilio* 1979; ex *Coban*; ex *Sea Saga* 1974; ex *Trito* 1968

★39170 **PROFESSOR BOGOROV** Ru/Fi (Laiva) 1976; RS; 1200; 68.76 × 4.21 (225.6 × 13.81); M (KHD); 13.5
Sisters (Ru flag):
★39171 **PROFESSOR KURENTSOV**
★39172 **PROFESSOR VODYANITSKIY**
★39173 **FEDOR MATISEN**
Possible sister:
★39174 **GEORGIY MAKSIMOV** (Ru)
Similar (different crane & no gantry aft):
★39175 **IVAN KIREYEV** (Ru)

39180 **CANADIAN ACE** Pa/Ja (Mitsui) 1971; RoVC; 11500; 161.65 × 6.68 (530.35 × 21.91); M (B&W); 18.5; ex *Canada Maru* 1980

39200 **PAN VIGOR** Ko/Ja (Mitsubishi HI) 1962; O;

29400; 221.04 × 11.43 (725.2 × 37.5); M (Sulzer); 17.25; ex *Chestnut Heroine* 1980; ex *Singapura Pertama* 1977; ex *Yuho Maru* 1973

39220 **CAVACO** Gr/FRG (Stuelcken) 1953; C; 5300; 132.14 × 7.67 (433.53 × 25.17); D-E (MaK); 15; ex *Hawkstone* 1972; ex *Falkenstein* 1971

39230 **SARFARAZ RAFIQI** Pk/FRG (A.G. 'Weser') 1966; C; 700/9400; 152.18 × —/9.27 (499.28 × —/30.4); M (MAN); 18.5; Launched as *Sarfraz Rafiqi*
Sister:
39231 **AZIZ BHATTI** (Pk)

39240 **KAPETAN ANDREAS** Pa/FRG (Luerssen) 1957; C; 3800; 108.01 × 7.06 (354.36 × 23.16); M (MAN); 13.5; ex *Alphard* 1980

39250 **CIRO SECONDO** It/De (Aalborg) 1956; C; 2900; 101.78 × 5.99 (333.92 × 19.48); M (B&W); 14; ex *Alppila* 1971; ex *Lena Mariane* 1968; ex *Bretland* 1964
Similar:
39251 **LAGO IZABAL** (Gu) ex *Skaga Sif* 1976; ex *Skaga* 1973; ex *Concordia* 1969

● 39260 **LEDEA** Gr/FRG (A G 'Weser') 1963; BC/O; 17900; 182.79 × 10.55 (599.7 × 34.61); ; (MAN); 16; ex *Medea* 1977
Sister:
39261 **SAPHO** (Gr) ex *Carmen* 1977

39270 **LAGO IZABAL** Gu/De (Aalborg) 1964; C; 3400; 110.50 × 6.27 (363 × 20.57); M (B&W); 14.5; ex *Skaga Sif* 1976; ex *Skaga* 1973; ex *Concordia* 1969
Similar:
39271 **CIRO SECONDO** (It) ex *Alppila* 1971; ex *Lena Marianne* 1968; ex *Bretland* 1964

39280 **LOTUS ACE** Pa/Ja (Naikai) 1976; C; 6100; 174.5 × 7.2 (572.5 × 23.63); M (B&W); 18; ex *Laurel* 1983
Sisters:
39281 **QUEEN OPAL** (Pa) ex *Violet* 1983
39282 **UNITED SPIRIT** (Li)

★39290 **STARITSA** Ru/—; No further details available

★39300 **POEL** DDR/DDR (Peene) 1960; Tk/FA; 600 Dwt; 59.5 × 3.8 (195 × 12.5); M (—); 14; ex *Riems*; Type 600
Similar:
★39301 **HIDDENSEE** (DDR)
★39302 **RIEMS** (DDR)

39320 **STO NINO** Pi/Br (Grangemouth) 1954; C; 1700; 85.68 × 4.32 (281.1 × 14.17); M (B&W); 11.5; ex *Connie* 1981; ex *Helma Taylor* 1973; ex *Marielisa* 1970; ex *Galle* 1968; ex *El Nasser* 1961

39330 **TSUGARU** Ja/Ja (Mitsubishi Z) 1955; Cbl/FA; 2150 Dspl; 103 × 4.9 (337.8 × 16); TSM (MAN); 13

39340 **CHRYSANTHY H** Gr/Br (Pollock) 1955; Tk; 315; 45.12 × — (148.03 × —); M (Blackstone); —; ex *B.P. Haulier* 1976

39360 **VITTORIO GARDELLA** It/Br (Lithgows) 1959; O; 10300; 159.87 × 8.55 (524.5 × 28.06); M (B&W); 12.5; ex *Cape Franklin* 1974

39370 **SUNSHINE ISLAND** Gy/Br (Cammell Laird) 1950; MT; 800; 55.89 × 3.6 (183.37 × 11.92); R (Yarwood); 8.5; ex *Athelbrook* 1972

39380 **BERESFORD** Br/Ne (Bodewes N.V.) 1959; Tk; 300; 42.22 × 2.11 (138.52 × 6.92); M (Lister Blackstone); 7.5
Sister:
39381 **BACCARAT** (Br)

39390 **INCAN SUPERIOR** Ca/Ca (Burrard DD) 1974; RoC/F; 3800; 116.41 × 20.22 (381.92 × 66.34); TSM (General Motors); 14
Similar:
39391 **INCAN ST LAURENT** (Ca)

39400 **BHAGIRATHI** In/Br 1957; D; 4700; 113.39 × 5.5 (372.01 × 18.04); TSR; —;

★39410 **VSEVOLOD BERYEZKIN** Ru/Ru (Khabarovsk) 1975; RS; 700; 54.87 × 3.66 (180.02 × 12.01); M (Liebknecht); 11.75
Sisters (Ru flag):
★39411 **VALERIAN URYVAYEV**
★39412 **YAKOV GAKKEL**
★39413 **DALNIYE ZELYENTSK**
★39414 **ISKATEL**
★39415 **ISSLEDOVATEL**
★39416 **LEV TITO**
★39417 **MORSKOY GEOFIZIK**
★39418 **RUDOLF SAMOYLOVICH**
★39419 **VULKANLOG**

39420 **CANABAL** Sp/Sp (Construcciones SA) 1976;

V; 1300; 88.02 × 5.18 (288.78 × 16.99); M (Deutz); 14; Side doors
Sister:
39421 COBRES (Sp)

★39450 RODINA Ru/Pd (Polnocna) 1978; FF 1800 Dwt; 85 × 6 (moulded) (278.87 × 19.69); M (Sulzer); 16; Tuna Seiner; Helicopter deck foreward
Sisters (Ru flag):
★39451 TIORA
★39452 UVAROVSK
★39453 UZGORSK
★39454 GORYACHEGORSK
★39455 TROCHUS
★39456 IVAN BORZOV
★39457 ZEMLYANSK
★39458 YEVGENIY PREOBRAZENSKIY
★39459 TRYDAKNA

39460 ANTARES Pa/Ca (Victoria Mach) 1946; C; 1400; 68.33 × 5.04 (224.18 × 16.54); R (Canadian Allis-Chalmers); 9; ex Ta Chung 1970; ex Hwa Lien; ex Hai Ping 1950; ex Haiyu 1946; Launched as Ottawa Pandora
Similar:
★39461 NAN HAI 169 (RC)

39490 SHIELDHALL Br/Br (Lobnitz) 1955; Slu; 1800; 81.69 × 4.06 (268.01 × 13.32); TSR (Lobnitz);
—

39500 UHENBELS Gr/FRG (A G 'Weser') 1959/68; C/HL; 10400; 156.65 × 9.02 (513.94 × 29.59); M (MAN); 14.5; ex Uhenfels 1980; Rebuilt 1968

39530 SANTO ANTONIO DO TRIUNFO Bz/Fi (Valmet) 1960; C; 4000/6400; 126.8 × 6.78/— (416.01 × 22.24/—); M (B&W); —; ex Todos Os Santos 1980
Sisters (Bz flag):
39531 ALBERTO MONTEIRO ex Guanabara 1980
39532 VITORIA DA CONQUISTA ex Turiacu

39560 FLORA US/US (Bethlehem Steel) 1948; O; 10900; 177.65 × 10.46 (582.84 × 34.32); T (Bethlehem Steel); 16.25; ex Flor; ex Bethflor 1975; ex Baltore 1960; 'C.5-S-AXI' type

39580 SERIFOS Cy/FRG (Nobiskrug) 1951; C; 800; 69.78 × 5.06 (228.94 × 16.60); M (MaK); 12; ex Milos 1 1978; ex Lothar 1976; ex Heimo Reckmann 1965

39590 FLORIAN Pa/FRG (Howaldts) 1951; C; 900; 78.59 × 4.37 (257.84 × 14.37); M (B+V); 11; ex Konsul I 1977; ex Konsul Sartori 1962

39600 ABILITY Cy/FRG (Nobiskrug) 1951; C; 1000; 82.1 × 4.2 (269.36 × 13.78); M (MaK); 12; ex Faethon 1980; ex Parthenon 1976; ex Nautic 1970; ex Baumwall 1967; ex Steinhoft 1957
Sister:
39601 VENEZIA (Cy) ex Pounta.1977; ex Antonios B 1976; ex Odigitria Ventouri 1973; ex Alexia 1966; ex Atlanta 1963

39610 UNISON 1 Sg/FRG (Nobiskrug) 1955; C; 1600; 76.54 × .8 (251.12 × 19.03); M (MaK); 12; ex Botilla 1973; ex Botilla Russ 1970
Similar:
39611 GEORGIOS G II (Pa) ex Lancaster Trader 1975; ex Noorbeek 1973; ex Ness 1970
39612 MAGIDA (UAE) ex El Wodad 1983; ex Dena 1982; ex El Widad; ex Ehrenfeld 1970

39620 NIKOS Br/FRG (Nobiskrug) 1954; C; 1100/1800; 85.55 × 5.16 (280.68 16.93); M (MaK); 12; ex Costamar 1980; ex Doric Merchant 1980; ex Fadi 1977; ex Obrestad 1973; ex Mira 1961

39630 ELEISTRIA IV Cy/FRG (A G 'Weser') 1952; C; 2500; 104.98 × 6.2 (344.42 × 20.34); M (MaK); 13; ex Almaflora 1973; ex Alstertal 1966

39650 CEMENTO PUERTO RICO Pa/Sw (Ekensbergs) 1944; Cem; 1400; 73.39 × 4.54 (240.78 × 14.9); M (Nydqvist & Holm); 11.5; ex Cementiere 1973; ex Sunnanvik 1961; ex Vika I 1959; ex Helga Cords 1946
Sister:
39651 LAS MINAS (Cy) ex Pyliastron 1974; ex Paola 1971; ex Ceti 1969; ex Altair III 1964; ex Diana 1961

★39660 BAIA MARE Rm/Rm (Galatz) 1965; C; 2100/3100; 100.62 × 5.5/6.58 (330.12 × 18.04/21.59); M (Sulzer); 12.5
Sisters (Rm flag):
★39661 CLUJ
★39662 VICTORIA

★39670 GALATI Rm/Rm (Galatz) 1960; C; 2100/3100; 100.62 × 5.5/6.59 (330.12 × 18.04/21.62); M (Sulzer); 12.5; Heavy derrick amidships
Sisters:
★39671 SUCEAVA (Rm)
★39672 BRAILA (Rm)

39673 ANEMOS (Gr) ex Nikolaos Kontaras 1973; Launched as Nanji
39674 IVI (Gr) ex Magdalini 1973

39700 EVER Sg/FRG (Lindenau) 1955; C; 1200/1900; 78.64 × 5.13/6.22 (258 × 16.83/20.41); M (KHD); 12; ex Gisela Vennamann 1974; ex Don Roberto 1965; ex Burkhard Brohan 1963

39710 CRYSOULA P Gr/FRG (Norderwerft) 1957; C; 2400; 95.41 × 6.03 (313.02 × 19.78); M (MaK); 12.5; ex Transworld Navigator 1979; ex Anastasia E 1975; ex Insco Jem 1971

39720 GOLDEN WONDER Sg/FRG (Norderwerft) 1952; C; 1500; 87.89 × 5.34 (288.35 × 17.52); M(MaK); 12.5; ex Ville De Morondava 1973; ex Chateau Yquem 1967; ex Jutta Schroder 1958

39740 SEBAROK My/FRG (Nobiskrug) 1953; C; 1300; 90.12 × 4.69 (295.67 × 15.39); M (MaK); 12; ex Doris Taylor 1977; ex Gisela Russ 1970
Similar:
39741 BONA TIDE (Sg) ex Dijksgracht 1974; ex West March 1970; ex Nanni Russ 1969
39743 CANALGRANDE (Pa) ex Bleichen 1970
39744 ARIS V (Gr) ex Sea Avon 1976; ex Cornish Chieftain 1975; ex Realengracht 1974; ex Burstah 1970
39745 MARIFLIP (Gr) ex Annet 1981; ex Rio d'Oro 1980; ex Borgesch 1970

39760 SAM G Pa/FRG (Nobiskrug) 1961; C; 1400; 93.4 × 4.67 (306.43 × 15.32); M (Schlieker); 13.5; ex Tynemouth 1979; ex Manaure 1978; ex Helene Russ 1972

39770 HIND-D Le/FRG (Travewerft) 1957; C; 1100; 79.56 × 5.59 (261.02 × 18.34); M (MaK); 12.5; ex Meldin 1979; ex G. Pappas 1977; ex Georgios P.A. 1975; ex Soultana 1975; ex Pride of Candia 1974; ex Eduard Schupp 1971; ex Maja 1967

39780 VIJAYA DARSHANA In/FRG (Nobiskrug)1957; C; 1400/2300; 93.4 × 4.67/6.07 (306.43 × 15.32/19.91); M (KHD); 12; ex Erato 1971; ex Erika Bischoff 1962

39790 IMAD S Fr/FRG (Norderwerft) 1958; C/WT; 2400/3400; 192.01 × 6.1/7.18 (334.68 × 20.01/23.56); M (MaK); 14.5; ex Ville De Port Louis 1979; ex Chateau Lafite 1969; ex Linda Scarlett 1961
Sister:
39791 DIEGO SUAREZ (Mg) ex Chateau Margaux 1970; ex Fanny Scarlett 1960

39800 NIMAS 1 Pa/FRG (Norderwerft) 1956; C; 2100/3300; 101.96 × 6.09/— (334.5 × 19.98/—); M (MaK); 14.5; ex Symmetria 1981; ex Ernst Schroder

39810 EUSTATHIA Gr/FRG (Nobiskrug) 1958; C; 1300/2200; 93.38 × 4.67/6.1 (306.36 × 15.32/20.01); M (KHD); 12; ex Sabine Howaldt 1971

39820 ALINA P Pa/Br (Vickers-Armstrongs) 1958; Tk; 16700; 187.61 × 9.88 (615.52 × 32.41); M (Doxford); 13; ex Sirocco 1982; ex Canto 1968

39840 NICOS V Gr/Br (Furness) 1949; Tk; 16000; 179.48 × 10.16 (588.85 × 33.33); M (Doxford); 14; ex Bjorntangen 1966; ex Ferncastle 1964

39850 DODONE Gr/FRG (Bremer V) 1954; Tk; 11300; 165.18 × 8.87 (541.93 × 29.1); M (MAN); 14; ex Vinga 1970

39880 CAPTAIN GREGOS Pa/Sw (Gotav) 1954; Tk; 10900; 167.57 × 9.2 (549.77 × 30.18); M (Gotaverken); 14; ex Ariege 1980; ex Valais 1972; ex Aghios Haralampos 1970; ex Justus Waller 1966

39890 MOLARA It/Ne (Bergens) 1958; Tk; 12900; 172.78 × 9.72 (566.86 × 31.9); M (Stork); 15; ex Cielo Azzurro 1974; ex Tobruk 1968; ex Nordhav 1966

39900 GEORGIOS S Pa/Br (Blyth) 1959; Tk; 12300; 170.69 × 9.43 (560 × 30.94); M (Sulzer); 14.5; ex Daniel-1 1983; ex Daniel 1983; ex Ithaki Sailor 1981; ex Elpetroil 1973; ex Hamilton Trader 1973

39910 NIMERTIS Li/Br (Scotts' SB) 1952; Tk; 11200; 168.87 × 9.21 (554.04 × 30.22); M (Doxford); 13.5
Sister:
39911 LADY DOROTHY (Li)

★39930 DA QING No 410 RC/Sw (Gotav) 1950; Tk; 5500; 132.62 × 7.9 (435.1 × 25.92); M (Gotaverken); —; ex Taipieng 1978; ex Anco Sailor 1966; ex Sandefjord 1964

39950 TEIDE Sp/Sp ('Bazan') 1956; RT/FA; 2700 Dspl; 117.5 × 6.2 (385.5 × 20.3); M (—); 12

★39960 KLAIPEDA Ru/Ru (Admiralteiskiy) 1954; Tk; 7700; 145.5 × 8.52 (477.36 × 27.95); M (Skoda); 12.25; 'KAZBEK' class
Sister:
★39961 ZHDANOV (Ru)

★39970 MAYKOP Ru/Ru (Admiralteiskiy) 1953; Tk; 7700; 145.5 × 8.71 (477.36 × 28.58); M (Skoda); 12.25; 'KAZBEK' class
Sisters (Ru flag):
★39971 MAYKOP
★39972 VOLGODON
★39973 ASHKHABAD
★39975 KAZBEK
★39976 KERCH
★39977 POTI
★39980 FRUNZE
★39981 GRIGORIY VAKULENCHUK
★39982 TENDRA ex Ochakov 1980
★39983 CHKALOV
★39985 IVANOVO
★39986 SLAVGOROD
★39987 CHEBOKSARY ex Andrey Vishinsky 1962
★39988 VINNITSA
★39989 ZHITOMIR
★39990 BUGURUSLAN
★39993 ELBRUS
★39994 KOMSOMOLETS UKRAINY
★39997 KREMENCHUG
★39998 ROVNO
★39999 SUMY
★40000 MOSKALVO
★40001 MAKHACKHALA
★40002 SVERDLOVSK
★40003 KOSTROMA
★40006 MOLODECHNO
★40007 KOMSOMOL
★40008 KURSK
★40009 GELENDZHIK ex Stanislav 1974
★40010 VLADIMIR
★40011 SAMARKAND
The following are operated by the Soviet Navy and others from the list above may be naval manned from time to time
★40013 ALATYR
★40014 VOLKHOV

40020 TAT LEE No 3 My/Br (Grangemouth) 1955; C; 2700; 88.32 × 5.34 (289.76 × 17.52); M (B&W); 12; ex Kagowa 1982; ex Jacques Del Mar 1971; ex Tulagi 1970

40030 SALMIAH COAST Ku/Br (Ardrossan) 1946; C; 500; 61.42 × 3.28 (201.51 × 10.76); M (British Polar); 11; ex Kentish Coast 1968; ex Ulster Weaver 1964; ex Jersey Coast 1954; ex Ulster Duchess 1946

40040 ESTRELLA Fi/Sw (Gotav) 1956; Tk; 12600; 169.81 × 9.54 (557.12 × 31.3); M (Gotaverken); 15.25; ex Synia 1969

★40060 DA QING No 15 RC/Br (J.L. Thompson) 1952; Tk; 10100; 154.11 × 6.86 (505.61 × 22.51); M (Doxford); 12; ex Santa Fortuna 1974; ex Sandalwood 1962

40070 CEMENTO PUERTO RICO Pa/Sw (Ekensbergs) 1944; Cem; 1400; 73.39 × 4.54 (240.78 × 14.9); M (Nydqvist & Holm); 11.5; ex Cementiere 1973; ex Sunnanvik 1961; ex Vika I 1959; ex Helga Cords 1946
Sister:
40071 LAS MINAS (Cy) ex Pyliastron 1974; ex Paola 1971; ex Ceti 1969; ex Altair III 1964; ex Diana 1961

40080 NICOLAS V Pa/FRG (Sterkrade) 1954; C; 1200; 87.33 × 4.6 (286.52 × 15.09); M (MAN); 14; ex Themar T 1983; ex Poseidon 1982; ex Karina 1981; ex Felice 1980; ex Regina 1976; ex Belem 1968; ex Radbod 1957

●40090 BLUE SEA 1 Pa/DDR ('Neptun') 1961; C; 1900; 90.1 × 5.69 (295.6 × 18.67); M (KHD); 12.5; ex Blue Sea 1982; ex Heinrich Wesch 1972; ex Mari 1965
Sister:
40091 BLUE SKY (Cy) ex Kirsten Wesch 1972; ex Bari 1964
Similar:
40092 BLUE CRYSTAL (Pa) ex Niuvakai 1982; ex Wilri 1963

40100 ABU SIMBEL Eg/DDR ('Neptun') 1960; C; 1900; 85.2 × 5.72 (279.53 × 18.77); M (KHD); —; ex Mari 1961
Sister (Eg flag):
40101 BLOUDAN ex Ilri
40102 HELWAN

40110 PHILIPPOS Cy/FRG (Sterkrade) 1954; C; 1200/1900; 86.77 × 4.6/5.7 (284.68 × 15.09/18.7); M (MAN); 11.5; ex Gerasimos K 1981; ex Maria Froso 1975; ex Iddan 1974; ex Mercator 1965

40120 CHERRY CHEPAT My/Br (H. Robb) 1938; C; 700; 61.22 × 4.17 (200.85 × 13.68); TSM (British

Auxiliaries); 12; ex *Sarang* 1970; ex *Kopara* 1966

40130 ZEUS Gr/Br (Caledon) 1960; B; 11700; 170.39 × 8.95 (559.02 × 29.36); M (Doxford); 14.5; ex *Sugar Exporter* 1976; ex *Athelprincess* 1966; Lengthened 1965

40140 SANTA MARIA III Pa/FRG (Sterkrade) 1953; C; 1100/1900; 82.3 × 4.45/5.94 (270.01 × 14.6/19.5); TSM (MAN); 12.5; ex *San Nicolas* 1983; ex *Homberg* 1968

40160 FAHAD Si/FRG (Nobiskrug) 1953; C; 1300; 74.22 × 5.41 (243.5 × 17.75); M (MaK); 12; ex *Grace Sailor* 1978; ex *Gilette* 1976; ex *Golfstraum* 1966; ex *Eric Reckmann* 1964

40170 PRESERVER Ca/Ca (Saint John SB) 1970; Rst/FA; 24700 Dspl; 172 × 9.1 (564 × 30); T (—); —; Helicopters; Operated by Royal Canadian Navy
Sister:
40171 PROTECTEUR (Ca)

● **40200 LAPU LAPU** Pi/Ne (Giessen) 1955; Tk; 9100; 152.74 × 8.33 (501.12 × 27.33); M (B&W); 13; ex *Camitia* 1975
Sisters (Ne flag):
40201 CINULIA
40202 CRANIA

40220 GEORGIOS S Pa/Br (Blyth) 1959; Tk; 12300; 170.69 × 9.43 (560 × 30.94); M (Sulzer); 14.5; ex *Daniel I* 1983; ex *Daniel* 1983; ex *Ithaki Sailor* 1981; ex *Elpetroil* 1973; ex *Hamilton Trader* 1973

★**40230 DRZIC** Ys/Ys ('Split') 1961; C; 7400/10200; 161.6 × —/9.39 (530.18 × —/30.81); M (Sulzer); 16

★**40240 PLITVICE** Ys/Ys ('Split') 1964; C; 7500/10500; 166.2 × 8.12/9.11 (545.28 × 26.64/29.89); M (Sulzer); 16
Sister:
★**40241 KRAGUJEVAC** (Ys)

● **40250 GELIGA** Ia/FRG (B+V) 1958; C; 7600/10300; 160.53 × —/9.09 (527 × —/29.82); M (MAN); 14.5; ex *Rhenania* 1973
Sister:
40251 VISHVA SUDHA (In) ex *Westfalia* 1962

40260 CAPO MADRE It/Sw (Uddevalla) 1953; Tk; 11900; 173.01 × 9.65 (567.62 × 31.66); M (Uddevalla); 14.5; ex *Norse Lion* 1968

40290 THEOUPOLIS Cy/Fr (Gironde) 1958; C; 9000/11800; 169.02 × 8.41/9.55 (554.53 × 27.59/31.33); M (B&W); 16; ex *Keharitomeni* 1982; ex *Christina 1*; ex *Louis Delmas* 1976; ex *Rocroi* 1966

40320 BEXLEY Br/Br (Caledon) 1966; Slu; 2200; 89.87 × 4.06 (294.85 × 13.32); TSM (Ruston & Hornsby); 12
Sisters (Br flag):
40321 HOUNSLOW
40322 NEWHAM
40323 SIR JOSEPH BAZALGETTE

40350 ROSA Pe/Br (Goole) 1950; C/WT; 800; 69.45 × 4.29 (227.2 × 14.07); M (British Polar); 12; ex *Christine* 1960

40360 SHORTHORN EXPRESS Ne/Ne (Arnhemsche) 1957; LS; 500; 68.56 × 3.57 (224.93 × 11.77); M (Werkspoor); 12.5; ex *Hontestroom* 1969; Converted from cargo ship
Sister:
40361 FRISIAN EXPRESS (Ne) ex *Vliestroom* 1969

40370 RABUNION IV Le/Br (Hall, Russell) 1950; LS; 800; 78.47 × 5.29 (257.48 × 17.36); M (British Polar); 12; ex *Lamaya* 1976; ex *Agrocorp 1* 1974; ex *Sofia* 1973; ex *Barok* 1971; Side doors

40390 BREEZE Pi/Br (Grangemouth) 1946; C; 2100; 67.02 × 4.9 (222.51 × 16.08); M (Kincaid); 9; ex *Bentong* 1966
Sister:
40391 BRUAS (My)

40420 ALDEBARAN Ho/Br (Grangemouth) 1957; C; 1500; 73.44 × 4.79 (290.94 × 19.72); M (Newbury); —; ex *Marys Ketch* 1982; ex *Alfred Everard* 1978
Similar:
40421 AGHIA MARINA (Gr) ex *Serenity* 1967
40422 ROBERT KOCH (Ca) ex *Guardian Carrier* 1977; ex *Ethel Everard* 1963
40423 RAMONA (Pa) ex *Sanguity* 1978
40424 IOANNIS (Cy) ex *Selectivity* 1976
40425 CRYSTAL ISLAND (Pa) ex *Despina T* 1980; ex *Simularity* 1975
40426 VANDARATANA (Ia) ex *Prajogo 1* 1983; ex *King On* 1983; ex *Stability*
40427 KALKAVANLAR (Tu) ex *Marianne K* 1982; ex *Safanourios* 1972; ex *Singularity* 1971

40430 MIRONAVE Bz/Ge (Unterweser) 1939; C;

1200; 76.15 × 4.26 (249.84 × 13.98); TSM (MAN); 8; ex *Sao Leopoldo* 1965; ex *Ila* 1952; ex *Galtnes* 1947; ex *Empire Conclave* 1946; ex *Luna* 1945

40450 OPUSO Ng/Sw (Solvesborgs) 1946; C; 1600; 81.74 × 4.56 (268.18 × 14.96); TSM (Atlas-Diesel); 9; ex *Warigi* 1968; ex *Mexico* 1962; ex *Tachira* 1955; ex *Consul Sartori*
Sister:
40451 BUENO (Pa) ex *San Salvador* 1973; ex *Yucatan* 1970; ex *Anzoategui* 1955; ex *Maya*

40460 VARUNA YAMINI In/FRG (Meyer) 1962; C; 3200; 97.92 × 6.98 (321.26 × 22.9); M (MAN); 14.25; ex *Fiepko Ten Doornkaat* 1972
Sisters:
40461 VARUNA YAN (In) ex *Ellen Klautschke* 1972
40462 MARIA A (Gr) ex *Caroline Schulte* 1978; ex *Gertrud Ten Doornkaat* 1973

40470 BANKO Pa/FRG (Meyer) 1962; C; 2100/3300; 103 × —/6.91 (337.93 × —/22.67); M (Borsig); 15; ex *Sabine II* 1983; ex *Sabine I* 1980; ex *City of Bochum*; ex *Annemarie Kruger* 1976

40540 ASTRO Cy/No (Porsgrunds) 1952; C; 1600; 78.64 × 5.39 (258.01 × 17.68); M (MAN); 10; ex *Heroic Junior* 1980; ex *Diala* 1973

40550 THERMOPYLAI Gr/No (Fredriksstad) 1955; Tk; 9000; 156.62 × 8.72 (513.85 × 28.61); M (Fredriksstad); 13.5; ex *Anina* 1978; ex *Fossland* 1963; ex *Slemdal* 1961

★**40560 DA QING No 16** RC/Sw (Eriksbergs) 1952; Tk; 11600; 170.54 × 9.27 (559.51 × 30.41); M (B&W); 14; ex *Barbro* 1964

★**40570 DA QING No 410** RC/Sw (Gotav) 1959; Tk; 5500; 132.62 × 7.9 (435.1 × 25.92); M (Gotaverken); —; ex *Taipieng* 1978; ex *Anco Sailor* 1966; ex *Sandefjord* 1964

★**40580 ANTON IVANOV** Bu/Sw (Gotav) 1945; Tk; 8500; 147.38 × 8.51 (483.53 × 27.92); M (Gotaverken); 13; ex *Margit Reuter* 1960; ex *Kratos* 1958

40600 SALAT Fr/No (Fredriksstad) 1952; Tk; 8900; 156.37 × 8.74 (513.02 × 28.67); M (Gotaverken); 11.5; ex *Noema II* 1969; ex *Viva* 1964
Sister:
40601 SELINTI (It) ex *Hornfighter* 1968

40640 LA CHARENTE Fr/No (Kaldnes) 1957; RT/FA; 2600 Dspl; 179 × 9.3 (587.2 × 30.3); T (GEC); 17.5; ex *Beaufort* 1964; Converted from a tanker; Helicopter platform and hangar

★**40660 SONG LIM** RK/Fi (Rauma-Repola) 1955; Tk; 3100; 105.06 × 6.13 (344.69 × 20.11); M (Nydqvist & Holm); 15; ex *Progress*; ex *Bunju* 1968; ex *Drogobitz* 1958
Sisters:
★**40662 DA QING No 10** (RC) ex *Chien She 10*; ex *Beskidy* 1958
★**40663 DA QING No 11** (RC) ex *Chien She 11*; ex *Tatry* 1958
★**40664 LOKBATAN** (Ru)

★**40670 DA QING 34** RC/No (Fredriksstad) 1958; Tk; 10200; 165.16 × 9.3 (541.86 × 30.51); M (Gotaverken); 15; ex *Norclipper* 1970; ex *Horn Clipper* 1968

● **40750 HALIA** Br/Br (Hawthorn, L) 1958; Tk; 11900; 169.4 × 9.35 (555.77 × 30.68); T (Hawthorn, L); 14.5; Fenders on deck for lightening operations
Similar:
40751 PETROLA 11 (Gr) ex *Petrola XI* 1976; ex *Kenia* 1973
40752 PETROLA 17 (Gr) ex *Petrola XVII* 1976; ex *Petrola X* 1975; ex *Krebsia* 1973
40753 KYLIX (Ne)

40760 DACCA Pk/US (—) 1942/44; RT/FA; 22380 Dspl; 159.7 × 9.4 (523.5 × 30.9); T-E (—); 15; ex *Mission Santa Cruz* 1963; Modified T.2 type

40830 NIMERTIS Li/Br (Scotts' SB) 1952; Tk; 11200; 168.87 × 9.21 (554.04 × 30.22); M (Doxford); 13.5
Sister:
40831 LADY DOROTHY (Li)

● **40840 AL-BAKRY** Si/Ja (Mitsui) 1957; Tk; 12600; 170.69 × 9.95 (560.01 × 32.64); M (B&W); 14.5; ex *Lina Christensen* 1977; ex *Mostank* 1973
Sister:

40841 MARANO (It) ex *Angela Scinicariello*; ex *Francesco Crispi* 1974; ex *Skotland* 1962

40850 ANCAP SEXTO Ur/FRG (A G 'Weser') 1956; Tk; 2100; 91.57 × 4.52 (300.43 × 14.83); TSR & LPT (A G 'Weser'); 12

40860 THITA OLIVA Gr/Fr (La Pallice) 1954; Tk; 2000; 87.53 × 5.2 (287.17 × 17.06); M (Bretagne); 13; ex *Aghia Irini* 1980; ex *Anna Fanny* 1971; ex *Marcel Mounier* 1970

40880 ATLANTIS 1 Cy/Br (Lamont) 1956; C; 67.59 × 4.2 (220.44 × 13.78); M (British Polar); 10.5; ex *Elpis N* 1980; ex *Elias G II*; ex *Yewmount* 1974

40890 TEMPESTA Cy/Br (Goole) 1956; C; 770; 62.18 × 3.62 (204 × 11.88); M (Newbury); —; ex *Centuriy* 1976

40900 SINCERE ORIENT Pa/Br (H Robb) 1937; C; 1000; 74.58 × 4.24 (244.69 × 13.91); TSM (British Auxiliaries); 12; ex *Voorloper* 1968; ex *Sofala* 1955

40910 SULTANA Pi/Au (Walkers Ltd) 1948; C; 700; 55.73 × 3.40 (182.84 × 11.15); M (Mirrlees); 9.5; ex *Helen J* 1967; ex *Enfield* 1965
Sisters:
40911 MALUKA (Pp) ex *Euroa* 1965
40912 DONA LILY (Pi) ex *Nukumanu* 1975; ex *Waiben* 1966; ex *Elmore*

40920 CAMPONALON Sp/Sp (Juliana) 1969; Tk; 4600; 123.68 × 6.04 (405.77 × 19.82); M (Espanola); 16
Sisters (Sp flag):
40921 CAMPODARRO
40922 CAMPOGENIL

40930 SALAMINA Pa/FRG (Flensburger) 1953; C; 5800/8400; 144.48 × 7.88/8.56 (474.02 × 25.85/28.08); M (MAN); 12; ex *Apus* 1981; ex *Kosmos* 1980; ex *Dobrota*; ex *Marie* 1972; ex *Schwanheim* 1971

40940 K.K.S MUTHOO Sg/Fr (Gironde) 1957; C; 6500/9000; 146.01 × 8.25/9.17 (479.04 × 27.07/30.09); M (B&W); 14.5; ex *Captain D Gregos* 1980; ex *Elias Xilas* 1973; ex *Roland* 1964

40960 GIANNAKIS Gr/FRG (Ottensener) 1958; C; 2600; 97.77 × 6.87 (324.05 × 22.54); M (Ottensener); 12; ex *Kalliope* 1971; ex *Karl Leonhardt* 1965

40970 KIMOLOS Gr/Ne ('De Merwede') 1955; Cem; 1600; 85.37 × 4.92 (280.09 × 16.14); M (Werkspoor); 11; ex *Hektor*; ex *Pargasport* 1975

40980 CARLA II Pa/FRG (Sterkrade) 1952; C; 1000; 67.01 × 4.83 (219.85 × 15.85); M (KHD); 11; ex *Junhouriya* 1981; ex *Erika Hendrik Fisser* 1975; ex *Concordia* 1972; ex *I.C. Ertel* 1971; ex *Hochmeister* 1970; ex *Erika Hendrik Fisser* 1958

40990 THE LADY SCOTIA Me/Br (Ailsa) 1952; C; 1200; 65.03 × 3.82 (213.35 × 12.53); M (British Polar); 11; ex *The Lady Grania* 1974

41000 PISANG RAJA Ia/Ne (Duijvendijk's) 1955; C; 1100/1700; 78.57 × 4.22 (257.78 × 13.85); M (KHD); 12; ex *Sea Express* 1969; ex *Svanefjell* 1962

41020 FEATHER Cy/Fr (Bretagne) 1953; C; 1300; 83.01 × 4.55 (272.34 × 14.93); M (Bretagne); 13; ex *Taxiarchis* 1980; ex *African Express* 1976; ex *Aliki* 1974; ex *Evora* 1970; ex *Agdal* 1968; ex *Pont-Aven* 1965

41030 ELENA ZETA It/Ne ('De Biesbosch') 1952; C/WT; 1300; 81.49 × 4.42 (267.36 × 14.5); M (SGCM); 13; ex *Orsola* 1978; ex *Oujda*

★**41050 DA QING No 13** RC/Ge (Bremer V) 1937; Tk; 9900; 155.66 × 8.64 (510.7 × 28.35); M (Bremer V); 11.5; ex *Chien She No 13*; ex *Bramora* 1961; ex *Erling Brovig* 1946

41060 ANCAP SEXTO Ur/FRG (A G 'Weser') 1956; Tk; 2100; 81.57 × 4.52 (300.43 × 14.83); TSR & LPT (A G 'Weser'); 12

41070 FADY Eg/Br (Hall, Russell) 1949; C; 6800; 123.94 × 7.27 (406.69 × 23.85); M (Doxford); 12.5; ex *Raffaella* 1982; ex *Philippopoulis* 1979; ex *Dobri Voinikov* 1970; ex *Aldebaran* 1970; ex *Nordpol* 1964

41080 BUENA FORTUNA Pa/No (Rosenberg) 1948; C; 2100/3300; 100.26 × —/5.54 (328.94 × —/18.19); T (Fredriksstad); 12; ex *Mitera Assimina* 1971; ex *Perseus* 1969; ex *Bemar* 1959; ex *Frameggen* 1956

41090 ROBERT M Br/Hong Kong (Hong Kong & W) 1970; Tk/TB; 1600; 85.04 × 4.44 (279 × 14.75); M (MAN); 11.75; ex *Cree* 1977

41100 STAMATA II Gr/Br (Caledon) 1937; C; 450; 56.95 × 3.34 (186.84 × 10.96); M (British Auxiliaries); 9.5; ex *Theodoros* 1976; ex *Allen Commodore*

1966; ex *Goldfinch* 1962

41110 MERINO Au/Br (Scott & Sons) 1949/69; FF; 550; 56 × 3.33 (187.01 × 10.93); M (British Polar); 10; Converted from cargo 1969; May be altered in appearance

41140 EFTICHIA Gr/Br (Grangemouth) 1952; C; 1500; 73.41 × 4.92 (240.85 × 16.14); M (British Polar); 11.5; ex *Agios Fanourios V* 1981; ex *Ivy* 1976; ex *Astroland* 1975; ex *Totland* 1975

★**41150 ALEKSEY KRYLOV** Ru/Ru (—) 1955; Tk; 3700; 123.5 × 4.31 (406.5 × 15.46); TSM (Russkiy); 10.75; Caspian Sea Service
Sisters (Ru flag):
★**41152 IVAN ZEMNUKHOV**
★**41153 LYUBOV SHEVTSOVA**
★**41154 LIZA CHAYKINA**
★**41155 SERGEY TYULENIN**
★**41156 ULYANA GROMOVA**

41180 TEXACO KENTUCKY Pa/US (Bethlehem Steel) 1949; Tk; 17900; 190.38 × 10.55 (624.61 × 34.61); T (Bethlehem Steel); 15.75; ex *Kentucky* 1960
Sisters (Pa flag):
41181 TEXACO OHIO ex *Ohio* 1961
41182 TEXACO PENNSYLVANIA ex *Pennsylvania* 1960
41183 TEXACO TEXAS ex *Texas* 1960

41200 WAVE Li/Sp (AESA) 1958; Tk; 12700; 172.5 × 9.48 (568.94 × 31.1); M (B&W); 14; ex *Alinta* 1976; ex *Escombreras* 1973
Possible sister:
41201 GOGO RAHN (Pa) ex *Albuera*

● **41230 DYNAMIC SAILOR** Gr/Br (Furness) 1958; Tk; 11500; 169.6 × 9.55 (556.43 × 31.33); T (Richardsons Westgarth); 14.5; ex *Humilaria* 1973

41250 KOURION Cy/No (Rosenberg) 1959; Tk; 20500; 200.95 × 10.9 (659.28 × 35.76); M (B&W); 16.5; ex *Savvas* 1983; ex *Kongsvang* 1974

41280 ELEISTRIA VIII Gr/Ys ('Split') 1959; C; 9200; 153.14 × 9.11 (502.43 × 29.89); M (Fiat); 13; ex *Tariq* 1977; ex *Shuguang* 1965; ex *Matang* 1964

41300 MAGED Le/Hu ('Gheorghiu Dej') 1960; C; 1200; 81.92 × 3.09 (268.88 × 10.14); TSM (Lang Gepgyar); 11; ex *Christina* 1975; ex *Badacsony* 1970
Sisters:
41301 CARIBI (Le) ex *Hala* 1982; ex *Aref* 1980; ex *Vittoria* 1975; ex *Csepel* 1970
41302 SUNNY L (Pa) ex *Annamina K* 1980; ex *Carpenter* 1977; ex *Ningpo Violet* 1975; ex *Dunaujvaros* 1974
41303 BUILDER (Sg) ex *Ningpo Lilac* 1975; ex *Borsod* 1974

● ★**41310 ORADEA** Rm/Rm (Galatz) 1963; C; 2100/3100; 100.62 × 5.5/6.59 (330.12 × 18.04/21.62); M (Sulzer); 12.5.
Sisters (Rm flag):
★**41311 CRAIOVA**
★**41312 TIMISOARA**
★**41313 BRASOV**
★**41314 DEVA**
★**41315 IASI**
★**41317 SIBIU**
★**41318 BACAU**
★**41319 TIRGOVISTE**
★**41320 TIRGU MURES**
(RC flag):
★**41321 CHANG AN**
★**41322 HONG QI 150**
★**41323 HONG QI 151**
★**41324 HONG QI 152**
★**41325 HONG QI 153**
★**41326 HUAI AN**
★**41327 ILIA**
★**41328 XIN AN**
(Cy flag):
41329 VASSILOS ex *Vaslui* 1982

41340 KATERINA K Cy/Sw (Norrkopings) 1953; C; 1100; 83.01 × 5.77 (272.34 × 18.93); M (Nydqvist & Holm); 11.5; ex *Mar Del Sud* 1974; ex *Medov Morocco* 1974; ex *Morocco* 1970; ex *Kong Inge* 1967

41360 MAYA 1 Gu/FRG (Nobiskrug) 1958; C; 2600/4000; 114.81 × 6.71/7.69 (376.67 × 22.01/25.23); D-E (MWM); 14.5; ex *Medi Sea* 1978; ex *Tipu* 1978; ex *Medi Sea* 1977; ex *Mildburg* 1971; ex *Archsum* 1970
Sister:
41361 COBAN (Gu) ex *Norburg*; ex *Medi Star* 1976; ex *Norburg* 1971; ex *Tinnum* 1970

41370 FODELE II Cy/Br (Readhead) 1957; B; 7700; 144.89 × 7.89 (475.36 × 25.89); M (Doxford); 13; ex *San Roberto* 1974; ex *East Breeze* 1967; ex *Hudson Point* 1966

41380 GEORGIOS A Gr/Br (Austin) 1947; C; 1000;

68.59 × 4.55 (225.03 × 14.93); M (British Polar); 10.5; ex *Ciciliana* 1972; ex *Seaford* 1971

41390 INDIANO It/No (Bergens) 1960; Tk; 12200; 169.73 × 9.67 (557 × 31.73); M (Stork); 14; ex *Serenitas* 1983; ex *Stolt Filia* 1981; ex *Folia* 1981; ex *Stolt Filia* 1980; ex *Stolt Argobay* 1978; ex *Stolt Hawk* 1973; ex *Osthav* 1968

★**41410 HONG QI 105** RC/Sw (Kockums) 1953/61; C; 10400; 162.57 × 8.9 (533.37 × 59.2); M (MAN); 14.5; ex *New North Sea* 1975; ex *Calypso* 1972; ex *Bannervale* 1970; ex *Ocean Clipper* 1960; Converted from tanker 1960

41420 VOLUNTAS It/Sw (Uddevalla) 1957; Tk; 12400; 170.72 × 9.63 (560.11 × 31.59); M (Gotaverken); 14; ex *Pepita* 1977
Similar:
41421 MARGARETA (Gr) ex *Stolt Margareta* 1981; ex *Anniken* 1974; ex *Margarita* 1961
41422 EASTERN MARINER (Tw)
41423 ALEXANDROS (Cy) ex *Wilana* 1969

41460 TALLULAH US/US (Sun SB) 1943; Tk/FA; 22400 Dspl; 159.6 × 9.2 (523.5 × 30); T-E (—); 15; ex *Valley Forge*; 'T-2' type; 'SUAMICO' class
Sisters (US flag):
41461 MILLICOMA ex *Conastoga*; ex *Kings Mountain*
41462 SAUGATUCK ex *Newton*
41463 SCHUYLKILL ex *Louisberg*

● **41480 HALIA** Br/Br (Hawthorn, L) 1958; Tk; 11900; 169.4 × 9.35 (555.77 × 30.68); T (Hawthorn, L); 14.5; Fenders on deck for lightening operations
Similar:
41481 PETROLA 11 (Gr) ex *Petrola XI* 1976; ex *Kenia* 1973
41482 PETROLA 17 (Gr) ex *Petrola XVII* 1976; ex *Petrola X* 1975; ex *Krebsia* 1973
41483 KYLIX (Ne)

41490 CAPO MADRE It/Sw (Uddevalla) 1953; Tk; 11900; 173.01 × 9.65 (567.62 × 31.66); M (Uddevalla); 14.5; ex *Norse Lion* 1968

41500 SAN DENIS Gr/Br (H Robb) 1952; C; 1700; 80.78 × 5.23 (265.03 × 17.16); M (British Polar); 10; ex *Marwick Head* 1969

41530 MAYA 1 Gu/FRG (Nobiskrug) 1958; C; 2600/4000; 114.81 × 671/7.69 (376.67 × 22.01/25/23); D-E (MWM); 14.5; ex *Medi Sea* 1978; ex *Tipu* 1978; ex *Medi Sea* 1977; ex *Mildburg* 1971; ex *Archsum* 1970
Sister:
41531 COBAN (Gu) ex *Norburg*; ex *Medi Star* 1976; ex *Norburg* 1971; ex *Tinnum* 1970

41550 GEOPOTES VI Ne/Ne (L Smit) 1963; D; 5100; 101.72 × 7.54 (333.73 × 24.74); TSM (Smit & Bolnes); 12.5

41570 STAR Gr/No (Framnaes) 1956; Tk; 10300; 161.47 × 9.27 (529.76 × 30.41); M (Gotaverken); 15; ex *Akti* 1976; ex *Texaco Europe* 1969; ex *Europe* 1959

41580 ALDERAMINE It/It (Adriatico) 1954; Tk; 12600; 172.24 × 9.6 (565.1 × 31.5); M (Adriatico); 15

41590 RINI Gr/Ys ('Split') 1963; B; 15900; 191.47 × 10.86 (621.18 × 35.63); M (Sulzer); 16; ex *Lenio Ch* 1983; ex *Archangelos* 1981; ex *Archangel* 1968; ex *Archangelos* 1963
Sisters:
41591 ALFITO (Gr) ex *Meandros* 1980
41592 MARELIA (Pa) ex *Calliroy* 1983; ex *Theofano Livanos* 1980
Similar:
★**41593 HUA TAI** (RC) ex *Atlantic Champion* 1978
★**41594 HUA YANG** (RC) ex *Atlantic Eagle* 1979
★**41595 HUA HONG** (RC) ex *Atlantic Star* 1979
41596 MOFARRIJ G (Si) ex *Interfelicity* 1983; ex *Iamatikos* 1980; ex *Southern Breeze* 1973; ex *Atlantic Breeze* 1972
41597 CAPTAIN YANNIS (Gr) ex *Evros* 1981
41598 NESTOS (Li)
41599 MATHILDE (Pa) ex *Thermopylai*; ex *Kapetanissa* 1976; ex *Kalliopi Pateras* 1972

★**41610 XUE CHENG** RC/Ys ('Split') 1959; C; 7000/9200; 153.09 × 8.19/9.01 (502.26 × 26.87/29.56); M (Fiat); 15; ex *Wu Xing* 1981; ex *Chopin* 1979
Sister:
★**41611 YU CHENG** (RC) ex *Zamenhof* 1982

41620 LSCO PIONEER Pi/Ja (Hitachi) 1955; Tk; 2400; 85.35 × 5.18 (280.02 × 16.99); TSM (General Motors); 8; ex *Caltex Luzon* 1969; ex *Caltex Medan* 1959
Similar:
41621 ZIWAY HAIQ (Et) ex *Chevron Gorinchem* 1969; ex *Caltex Gorinchem* 1968; ex *Caltex Padang*

1959

★**41630 PRAHOVA** Rm/Sw (Uddevalla) 1957; Tk; 12400; 173.41 × 9.35 (569 × 30.68); M (Gotaverken); 13.5; ex *Pace* 1964; ex *Dorothea Basse* 1962; ex *Stanvale* 1957

41670 POLYTIMI ANDREADIS Gr/US (Sun SB) — Gr 1943/63; B; 14400; 172.37 × 10.1 (565.52 × 33.14); T-E (Westinghouse); —; ex *Fort Niagara* 1948; Lengthened and converted from T-2 tanker 1963 (Hellenic)

41720 KRITON Gr/It (Mediterraneo) 1959; C; 5700/7400; 134.25 × 7.08/8.5 (440.25 × 23.23/27.89); M (Fiat); 14.5; ex *Tabou* 1978; ex *Saint Marc* 1973

41740 REGENT Br/Br (H&W) 1967; Rst/FA; 18000; 195.1 × 8 (640 × 26.1); T (AEI); —
Sister:
41741 RESOURCE (Br)

41750 JENSON II My/Ne (Gebr. Niestern) 1953; C; 500/1000; 73.49 × 3.58/4.32 (241.71 × 11.75/14.17); M ('De Industrie'); 12.5; ex *Tanja Holwerda* 1981; ex *Kroonborg* 1973

● **41760 BANKO 1** Pa/Ne (Amels) 1957; C; 1600; 79.43 × 5 (260.6 × 16.4); M (Werkspoor); 11; ex *Mukairish Al Rabee* 1983; ex *Christine 1*; ex *Balticborg*
Sister:
41761 ARGYRO M (Gr) ex *Bothniaborg* 1980

41790 BLACKWELL POINT Pa/Br (Austin) 1951; C; 1800; 82.45 × 5.2 (270.5 × 17.06); M (Sulzer); 11; ex *Blackwall Point*
Sisters:
41792 CHRISTOFOROS (Gr) ex *Epic* 1976; ex *Birling* 1975; ex *Thomas Hardie* 1968
41793 GRANITT (No) ex *Horsham* 1973; ex *Murdoch* 1966
41794 LINERA (Br) ex *La Molinera* 1972; ex *Sanderstead* 1967; ex *Samuel Clegg* 1967
41795 FABIO SAVERIO (It) (deepened 1970); ex *Capitan Alberto* 1975; ex *Brightling* 1970; ex *Falconer Birks* 1970
41796 TITIKA (Gr) ex *Keynes* 1975; ex *Accum* 1967

41800 TARRY Pa/Br (Hall, Russell) 1958; C; 1900; 83.88 × 5.2 (275.2 × 17.09); M (British Polar); —; ex *Arring* 1982; ex *Tarring* 1981; ex *Lambeth* 1970
Sisters:
41802 VASILIS IV (Gr) ex *Maro*; ex *Chris* 1974; ex *Acyro* 1972; ex *Croydon* 1971

41810 BARRIER Br/Br (Pollock) 1958; Tk; 500; 52.35 × 2.68 (171.75 × 8.79); M (KHD); 9.5; ex *Ulco* 1972

41820 GEOPOTES IX Ne/Ne (Gusto) 1966; D; 7800; 126.02 × 6.8 (513.45 × 22.31); TSM (Smit & Bolnes); 12.5

41830 WESTRIDGE Br/Ne (Pattje) 1951; C; 450; 60.13 × 3.08 (197.28 × 10.1); M (KHD); 10; ex *Arnoudspolder* 1965

41840 IOANNA 1 Pa/FRG (Unterweser) 1952; C; 600; 65.46 × 3.55 (214.76 × 11.64); M (MaK); 12; ex *Ekaterini Str* 1980; ex *Agia Irini* 1980; ex *Agia Irene*; ex *Lure* 1974; ex *Frances M* 1971; ex *Lure* 1970; ex *Kanavelic* 1969; ex *Anglia* 1964; ex *Joachim Hendrik Fisser* 1959

41850 ANWAR M Le/Ne (E.J. Smit) 1948; C; 450; 56.6 × 3.32 (185.7 × 10.9); M (Werkspoor); 10; ex *Anis III* 1981; ex *Seabreeze*; ex *Dita Smits* 1962; ex *Wester-Eems* 1959

41860 STAR OF MEDINA Si/Ne (Van Diepen) 1940; C; 400; 57.3 × 2.82 (188.02 × 9.25); M (KHD); 8; ex *Moira* 1966; ex *Greenfinch* 1966; ex *Empire Daffodil* 1946; ex *Caribe II* 1940

41870 MELINA Gr/Br (Hall, Russell) 1946; LS; 450; 57.28 × 3.66 (187.93 × 12); M (British Polar); 11.5; ex *Grigoris* 1980; ex *St Clement* 1976

41880 ISLAND SUPPLIER Br/Br (Furness) 1935; C; 650; 54.87 (Bp) × — (180 × —); TSM (British Auxiliaries); 10; ex *Southern Star* 1969; ex *Fauvette* 1963
Sister:
41881 TWILLINGATE (Ca) ex *Corncrake* 1967

41900 BLACKPOOL Br/Br (H Robb) 1962; Tk; 530; 52.2 × 2.91 (171.26 × 9.55); M (KHD); —; ex *Uno* 1972
Sister:
41901 BRADFORD (Br) ex *Toro* 1972

41920 MANSOUR Si/Ne (J & K Smit) 1920; C; 2400; 90.84 × 5.94 (298.03 × 19.5); M (Werkspoor); 10; ex *Ras Tanura* 1961; ex *San Miguel* 1958

41930 252-C Ar/Br (Fleming & Ferguson) 1950; D;

3400; 105.21 × — (345.18 × —); TSD-E (English Electric); —; ex *Eva Peron* 252-C; ex *La Plata* 1953; ex *M.O.P.* 225C 1951
Sisters:
41931 253-C (Ar) ex *253-C-La Trabajadora*; ex *M.O.P.* 226-C 1952;
41932 254-C (Ar) ex *254-C-Lealtad*; ex *M.O.P.* 227-C 1952

41950 MEGAMA Pa/Ne (Boele's Sch) 1947; C; 1300; 68.59 × 4.83 (225 × 15.9); M (Atlas-Diesel); 10; ex *Balisa* 1967; ex *Andong* 1965; ex *Anata* 1965; ex *Selat Madura* 1964; ex *Bagan* 1959
Similar:
41951 HI-CALIBRE (My) ex *Mulia* 1982; ex *Mesinga* 1979; ex *Messina* 1976; ex *Batina* 1967; ex *Annam* 1965; ex *Anna* 1965; ex *Selat Makassar* 1964; ex *Balanipa* 1960
41952 LAUTAN TIGA (My) ex *Mesolo* 1979; ex *Merinda* 1977; ex *Baboma* 1967; ex *Angas* 1965; ex *Angora* 1965; ex *Selat Bangka* 1964; ex *Banggaal* 1959
41953 MELITA (Pa) ex *Balanda* 1967; ex *Selat Bali* 1964; ex *Hock Hai* 1961; ex *Hock Heng* 1951; ex *Brattheim* 1950
41954 MESAWA (Pa) ex *Medduno* 1969; ex *Basongo* 1967; ex *Anban* 1965; ex *Molopo* 1964; ex *Selat Singkep* 1964; ex *Nyora* 1963; ex *Empire Conifer* 1947; ex *Adrian* 1945
41955 KING LION (Sg) ex *San Blas* 1966; ex *Bona* 1966; ex *San Blas* 1965; ex *Kali Mas* 1964; ex *Bakongan* 1960

41960 RAWAS Ia/Ne (Rotterdamsche) 1950; C; 2100; 69.3 × 4.9 (227.36 × 16.09); M (Nydqvist & Holm); 10; ex *Ancon* 1965; ex *Barumun* 1959
Similar (Ia flag):
41961 RUPIT ex *Teluk Wap* 1968; ex *Bravo* 1965; ex *Banjoewangi* 1959
41962 ENIM ex *Teluk Korio* 1968; ex *Celestial* 1965; ex *Barito* 1959
41963 KELEKAR ex *Teluk Kamrau* 1968; ex *Pollera* 1965; ex *Batoebahra* 1959

41970 TIRTA KARYA Pa/Ne (Giessen) 1930; C; 1000; 64.67 × 3.07 (212.17 × 10.08); M (Sulzer); 8; ex *Ban Ho Liong* 1973; ex *Toba* 1958

41980 BRAHMAN EXPRESS Va/Ne (Arnhemsche) 1966; RoVC/C/LS; 500; 80.75 × — (264.9 × —); M (MAN); 14; ex *Car Express* 1981; ex *Rijnstroom* 1976
Sister:
41981 MEDITERRANEAN EXPRESS (Ne) ex *Amstelstroom* 1975

41990 AVALO Pa/No (Trosvik) 1968; LS; 1200; 92 × 4.74 (301.84 × 15.55); TSM (Atlas-MaK); 15; ex *Federal Avalon* 1980; ex *Seaspeed Trailer* 1974; ex *Skyway* 1973; ex *Mandeville* 1970; Converted from Ro/Ro cargo 1980 (Meyer)

42000 DAPHNE Pa/Fr (Havre) 1968; RoVC/C; 1200; 92.03 × 4.76 (301.94 × 15.63); TSM (Atlas-MaK); 15; ex *Irish Shamrock* 1982; ex *Daphne* 1982; ex *Bravo Contender* 1974; ex *Sealord Contender* 1969

42020 KYDON Gr/Ne (P Smit) 1953/69; RoPCF; 10700; 153.93 × 8.64 (505.02 × 28.34); M (B&W); 14.25; ex *Wirakel* 1968; Converted from tanker 1969

● **42030 GOTH** Br/Br (Ferguson Bros) 1974; ST; 1400; 59.75 × 5.34 (196.03 × 17.52); M (Mirrlees Blackstone); —
Sisters (Br flag):
42031 NORSE
42032 ROMAN
Similar:
42033 DANE (Br)
42034 PICT (Br)
42035 SIKU (De) ex *Junella* 1983

42040 DENIS Ma/FRG (A G 'Weser') 1942/50; C; 2300; 95.64 × 6.1 (313.68 × 21.55); M (MAN); 9; ex *Cleopatra* 1976; ex *Heddernheim* 1971; Launched 1942, completed 1950

·**42050 MESSINIA** Cy/No (Akers) 1948; LS; 1400; 84.46 × 5.65 (277.1 × 18.5); M (B&W); 10.75; ex *Balblom* 1971; Converted from cargo

42060 FRIGO H Cy/Ne (Nieuwe Noord) 1963; R; 500/1100; 78.36 × 3.71 (257.09 × 12.17); T (MAN); 16; ex *Frigo Queen* 1982; ex *Meres* 1976; ex *Sonja* 1973

42070 PELITA DELI Ia/Pd (Gdynska) 1960; C; 700; 65.82 × 3.72 (215.94 × 12.2); M (Alpha-Diesel); —; ex *Mangga* 1974; 'B-471' type
Sisters (Ia flag):
42071 NANGKA
42072 DUKUH
42073 DUREN
42074 DJERUK
42075 DEEPA SAKTI ex *Lengkeng* 1974

42076 RAMBUTAN
(Pa flag):
42077 BUILDER II ex *Equator* 1977; ex *Duwet* 1976

42090 ATILOLA Ng/Ne ('De Dollard') 1958; C; 500; 53.7 × 3.02 (176.18 × 9.94); M (Werkspoor); 10; ex *Anjou* 1970; ex *President E Chalas* 1963

42110 BANANG Ia/Br (H Robb) 1946; C; 900; 68.28 × 4.26 (224 × 13.97); M (B&W); 9; ex *Cindee* 1974; ex *Katul* 1967
Similar:
★**42111 MIN CHU No 7** (RC) ex *Haiyun* 1951; ex *Ottawa Palat*; Also known as **MIN CHU CHI**

42120 ROZMARY Gr/Br (Inglis) 1941; C; 900; 64.32 × 4.11 (211 × 13.48); M (British Auxiliaries); 10; ex *Libya* 1971; ex *Peregrine* 1965; ex *Empire Spinney* 1946

42140 MORUKA Pa/Br (Scott & Sons) 1936; C; 370; 43.35 × 4.12 (142.22 × 13.52); M (Volund); 8; ex *Henrik* 1970; ex *Karin Bahnsen* 1965; ex *Putte Pan* 1962; ex *Granita* 1959; ex *Bamboo* 1953

42150 FILIPPOS Gr/Br (Scott & Sons) 1947; C; 420; 45.14 × 3.81 (148.1 × 12.5); M (KHD); 12; ex *Sinergasia* 1970; ex *George Callitsis* 1969; ex *Monksville* 1964; ex *Ebony* 1953

42160 KOTA DJAJA Ia/Ne ('De Waal') 1952; C; 450; 49.64 × 3.26 (162.86 × 10.7); M (MaK); 10; ex *Fem* 1973; ex *Myfem* 1969

42190 MINO Gr/Br (Burntisland) 1946; C; 860; 58.63 × 4.17 (192.36 × 13.68); M (British Polar); 10; ex *Domino Run*; ex *Dromineer* 1964; ex *Knebworth* 1960

42200 BAGAS Ia/Br (Goole) 1946; C; 960; 63.81 × 4.15 (209.35 × 13.62); M (British Polar); 10; ex *Sandy* 1964; ex *Maltara* 1967; ex *Ino* 1954

42210 AGIOI ANARGYROI III Gr/Br (Goole) 1950; C; 980; 66.93 × 4.15 (219.59 × 13.62); M (KHD); 10.5; ex *Firth Fisher* 1971; ex *Turkis* 1954

42220 AL AKBER Pa/Br (Goole) 1952; C; 1100; 66.12 × 4.23 (216.93 × 13.88); M (British Polar); 11; ex *Howth Trader* 1975; ex *Hawthorn* 1974; ex *Harglen* 1968; ex *Irish Heather* 1964

42230 ANDREAS A Cy/Ih (Liffey) 1954; C; 1000; 66.45 × 4.33 (218.01 × 14.21); M (British Polar); 10; ex *Al-Hassan* 1976; ex *Yewtree* 1974; ex *Irish Fern* 1964

42240 SANESTO Cy/Br (Grangemouth) 1947; C; 500; 55.96 × 3.51 (183.6 × 11.5); M (Newbury); 10.5; ex *Kapetan Kostantis* 1977; ex *Austerity* 1967

42250 ADINA Br/Br (Fellows & Co) 1954; C; 600; 55.94 × 3.52 (183.53 × 11.55); M (Newbury); —; ex *Severity* 1975

42270 IOANNIS K Gr/Br (G. Brown) 1931; C; 350; 41.21 × 3.05 (135.2 × 10); M (Newbury); 8.5; ex *Giankaros* 1971; ex *Activity* 1966
Similar:
42271 SKORPIOS (Gr) ex *Apricity* 1965
42272 STAR I (Cy) ex *Soula* 1976; ex *Aridity* 1966

42280 DIMITRIOS A. Gr/Br (G. Brown) 1935; C; 410; 43.56 × 2.98 (142.91 × 9.78); M (Newbury); 10.5; ex *Aseity* 1966

42300 ATILOLA Ng/Ne ('De Dollard') 1958; C; 480; 53.7 × 3.02 (176.18 × 9.94); M (Werkspoor); 10; ex *Anjou* 1970; ex *President E. Chalas* 1963

42310 JAYA PUTRA II. Ia/Br (Coaster Const.) 1926; C; 950; 62.62 × 3.81 (205.45 × 12.5); M (Sulzer); 10; ex *Floreta* 1973; ex *Kybra* 1958

42320 DARVISH VANANCA Ir/Fr (Caen) 1949; C; 380; 51.69 × 3.13 (169.59 × 10.27); M (Werkspoor); 10.5; ex *Seine* 1967; ex *Dijonnais* 1964
Sister:
42321 SHIRDEL VANANCA (Ir) ex *Normandy* 1967; ex *Gatinals* 1954

42330 ALDEBARAN Ho/Br (Grangemouth) 1957; C; 1500; 73.44 × 4.79 (290.94 × 19.72); M (Newbury); —; ex *Marys Ketch* 1982; ex *Alfred Everard* 1978
Similar:
42331 AGHIA MARINA (Gr) ex *Serenity* 1967
42332 ROBERT KOCH (Ca) ex *Guardian Carrier* 1977; ex *Ethel Everard* 1963
42333 RAMONA (Pa) ex *Sanguity* 1978
42334 IOANNIS (Cy) ex *Selectivity* 1975
42335 CRYSTAL ISLAND (Pa) ex *Despina T* 1980; ex *Simularity* 1975
42336 VANDARATANA (Ia) ex *Prajogo 1* 1983; ex *King On* 1983; ex *Stability*
42337 KALKAVANLAR (Tu) ex *Marianne K* 1982; ex *Safanourios* 1972; ex *Singularity* 1971

42360 TAXIARCHIS Gr/Br (Grangemouth) 1938; C;

1500; 79.71 × 4.67 (261.52 × 15.32); M (Polar); 8; ex *Paskalis* 1968; ex *Eildon* 1966

★**42370 HAI FENG** RC/RC (—) 1960; FFMS; 2500; 86.86 × — (285 × —); M (—)

42390 ALKMINI Gr/Pd (Oderwerke) 1923; C; 1200; 73.94 × 4.4 (242.59 × 14.44); M (Krupp); 9; ex *Constantinos* 1969; ex *Rask* 1967; ex *Hesnes* 1953; ex *Paul L-M Russ* 1947

42400 PHAISTOS Gr/Sw (Kockums) 1951/65; RoPF; 8100; 151.29 × 4.6 (496.36 × 15.09); M (MAN); 13.5; ex *Maria Gorthon* 1963; Converted from tanker 1965

● **42410 MINOS** Gr/Sw (Kockums) 1952/66; RoPF; 9500; 162.57 × 4.9 (533.37 × 16.08); M (MAN); 14.75; ex *Soya-Margareta* 1964; Converted from tanker 1966

42420 GRANUAILE Ih/Br (Ferguson Bros) 1970; LT; 2000; 80.68 × 4.01 (264.7 × 13.16); TSM (W.H Allen); 13.5

42430 VITTORIO GARDELLA It/Br (Lithgows) 1959; O; 10300; 159.87 × 8.55 (524.51 × 28.05); M (B&W); 12.5; ex *Cape Franklin* 1974

42450 JAMES ROWAN Br/Br (Hall, Russell) 1955; B; 2900; 103.64 × 5.51 (340 × 18.08); R (N E Marine); 11.25

● **42460 LINO** Ho/Br (A Hall) 1958; C; 1300; 76.21 × 4.25 (250.03 × 13.94); M (British Polar); 11; ex *Ballylesson* 1982
Sister:
42461 SIMONE (Pa) ex *Alla El Deen* 1982; ex *Ballyloran* 1981

42470 SAMOS LUCK Cy/Br (Hall, Russell), 1963; C; 1600; 78.03 × 4.62 (256 × 15.16); M (Polar); 11.5; ex *Ballyrory* 1983
Sister:
42471 BALLYRUSH (Br)

42480 UGO M It/Br (A&P) 1955. C; 3000; 104.86 × 6.06 (344.03 × 19.88); R (N.E. Marine); 10.25; ex *Giovanni Trento* 1977; ex *Bearwood* 1968

42500 MARINE TRANSPORT Ca/Br (Grangemouth) 1946; C; 870; 64.17 × 4.12 (210.53 × 13.52); M (Caterpillar); 14; ex *C. Omer* 1972; ex *C. Omer Marie* 1967; ex *Vauquelin* 1966; ex *Crichtoun* 1965

42530 WANDAJEAN Pa/Br (H. Robb) 1938; C; 1500; 81.36 × 4.09 (266.93 × 13.42); TSM (British Auxiliaries); 13; ex *Cubahama* 1982; ex *Kaula* 1982; ex *Cubahama* 1982

42550 ARGOS Ar/Br (H. Robb) 1935; C; 2200; 87.48 × 3.2 (287 × 10.5); TSM (Atlas-Diesel); 10
Similar:
42551 AGUILA II (Ar)

42560 MARIETTA Cy/Br (Lewis) 1952; C; 1600; 83.22 × 5.15 (273.03 × 16.9); M (Doxford); 11.5; ex *Dimitrios G* 1972; ex *Cardiffbrook* 1969

42580 EFTICHIA Gr/Br (Grangemouth) 1952; C; 1500; 73.41 × 4.92 (240.85 × 16.14); M (British Polar); 11.5; ex *Agios Fanourios V* 1981; ex *Ivy* 1976; ex *Astroland* 1975; ex *Totland* 1975

42590 ALDEBARAN Ho/Br (Grangemouth) 1957; C; 1500; 73.44 × 4.79 (290.94 × 19.72); M (Newbury); —; ex *Marys Ketch* 1982; ex *Alfred Everard* 1978
Similar:
42591 AGHIA MARINA (Gr) ex *Serenity* 1967
42592 ROBERT KOCH (Ca) ex *Guardian Carrier* 1977; ex *Ethel Everard* 1963
42593 RAMONA (Pa) ex *Sanguity* 1978
42594 IOANNIS (Cy) ex *Selectivity* 1975
42595 CRYSTAL ISLAND (Pa) ex *Despina T* 1980; ex *Simularity* 1975
42596 VANDARATANA (Ia) ex *Prajogo 1* 1983; ex *King On* 1983; ex *Stability*
42597 KALKAVANLAR (Tu) ex *Marianne K* 1982; ex *Safanourios* 1972; ex *Singularity* 1971

42600 LEILA ONE Le/Br (A. Hall) 1957; C; 1000; 64.93 × 4.3 (213.02 × 14.11); M (British Polar); 10.5; ex *Frances B* 1974; ex *Blisworth* 1971

42610 LUCKY TRADER Cy/Br (Austin) 1951; C; 1500; 77.25 × 4.79 (253.45 × 15.72); M (Sulzer); 10.5; ex *Ballyrobert* 1977; ex *Ardingly* 1971

42630 PETRA It/Fr (Caen) 1954; Tk; 700; 59.8 × 4.01 (196.19 × 13.16); M (CCM); 11; ex *S Biagio* 1969; ex *John-M* 1965
Similar:
42631 PETRO BOUSCAT (Se) ex *Jupiter* 1968; ex *Konny-M* 1965

42650 PEACE Pa/Ne (Van Diepen) 1940/73; Rad; 350; 57.31 × 2.84 (188.02 × 9.32); M (KHD); 9; ex *Cito* 1969; ex *Westpolder* 1960; ex *Rolf* 1950; Con-

verted cargo ship 1973

42660 **GLENCOE** Ca/Br (Goole) 1947; C; 1100; 69.04 × 4.29 (226.51 × 14.07); M (British Polar); 10.5; ex Teal 1963

42670 **PAKPANANG** Th/De (Nakskov) 1935; C; 300; 45.73 × 2.31 (150.03 × 7.58); TSM (B&W); 11

42680 **NAIRA** Ia/It (Adriatico)1953; C; 500; 55.33 × 2.93 (181.53 × 9.61); M (General Metals); 10
Sisters (Ia flag):
42681 **NURAGE**
42682 **PANTAI**
42683 **NAULI** ex Nukaha 1959

42690 **RAJAH SARAWAK** Pa/Ne (Vuyk) 1936; C; 450; 50.36 × 3.07 (165.22 × 10.07); M (Ruston & Hornsby); —; ex Kerandji 1967; ex Kian Tiong 1960; ex Rokan 1958; ex Lorentz 1954; ex Comorien 1953; ex Koningin Emma 1951

42700 **LANDING** Pa/Br (A&P) 1957; C; 1800; 79.86 × 4.72 (262 × 15.49); M (Sulzer); 10.5; ex Lancing 1978; Lengthened 1969
Sister:
42701 **TRANS COMMERCE** (Pa) ex Agia Anna 1982; ex Sassa 1980; ex Portslade 1977

42710 **ABEER DELTA** Eg/Br (A&P) 1955; C; 1600; 73.77 × 4.81 (242.03 × 15.78); M (Sulzer); 10.5; ex Sallywalter 1980; ex Ballywalter; ex Steyning 1971

42720 **AREF** Le/Br (Grangemouth) 1959; C; 1600; 74.73 × 4.86 (245.18 × 15.95); M (British Polar); 11; ex Ballycastle 1981; ex Cowdray 1976

42740 **AL AKBER** Pa/Br (Goole) 1952; C; 1100; 66.12 × 4.23 (216.93 × 13.88); M (British Polar); 11; ex Howth Trader 1975; ex Hawthorn 1974; ex Harglen 1968; ex Irish Heather 1964

42750 **ANDREAS A** Cy/Ih (Liffey) 1954; C; 1000; 66.45 × 4.33 (218.01 × 14.21); M (British Polar); 10; ex Al-Hassan 1976; ex Yewtree 1974; ex Irish Fern 1964

42760 **AGNES PRIDE** Pa/Ne (Pattje) 1956; C; 650; 57.36 × 3.47 (188.19 × 11.38); M (Werkspoor); —; ex Singapore Ramin 1982; ex Cherry Molek 1973; ex Alugori I 1968; ex St. Abbs Head 1967

● 42770 **JOYCE CLARE** Cy/Br (Scott & Sons) 1952; C; 620; 55.61 × 3.87 (182.45 × 12.7); M (British Polar); 10.5; ex Elvina 1980; ex Lissa 1979; ex Lady McGowan 1977

42780 **ELLI** Gr/Br (Lewis) 1946; C; 1000; 66.6 × 4.24 (218.5 × 13.91); R (Lewis); 10; ex Saint Nicholas 1969; ex Rudry 1966; ex Londonbrook 1963

★ 42800 **PEVEK** Ru/Fi (Rauma-Repola) 1958; Tk; 3100; 105.11 × 6.13 (344.85 × 20.1); M (B&W); 13.5
Sisters (Ru flag):
★ 42801 **ARTYOM**
★ 42802 **BALTA**
★ 42803 **MOZYR**
★ 42804 **PIRYATIN**
★ 42805 **VENTSPILS**
★ 42806 **VILYUYSK**
★ 42807 **ZOLOTOY ROG**
★ 42808 **KOKAND**

42820 **PNOC AMIHAN** Pi/US (Jones) 1945; Tk; 3200; 99.68 × 5.89 (327.03 × 19.32); M (Nordberg); 13; ex LSCO Amihan 1982; ex Amihan 1968; ex Deneb 1967; ex Stanvac Sunda 1963; ex Tankhaven II 1959; ex Tantallon 1948; 'T-1' type
Similar:
42821 **PNOC CANTHO** (Pi) ex LSCO Cantho 1982; ex Mobil Bataan 1969; ex Stanvac Bataan 1962; ex Stanvac Alcor 1961; ex Tankhaven I 1959; ex Tannadice 1948
42822 **LSCO CAMRANH** (Pi) ex Mobil Micronesia 1969; ex Capella 1967; ex Stanvac Sumba 1963; ex Tankhaven III 1959; ex Senith 1948; ex Tannagull 1948
42823 **PNOC PETROPARCEL** (Pi) ex LSCO Petroparcel 1982; ex Sea Transport 1971; ex Sea Transporter 1959; ex Transea 1956; ex Tellico 1951;
The following are US Navy and are known as 'Peconic' class
42824 **RINCON** ex Tarland
42825 **NODAWAY** ex Beldridge
42826 **PETALUMA** ex Racoon Bend

42830 **PNOC TRANSASIA** Pi/US (Todd) 1945; Tk; 3100; 99.12 × 5.9 (325.2 × 19.36); M (Nordberg); 10.5; ex LSCO Transasia 1982; ex Chevron 1970; ex Brea Olinda 1946; ex Taverton 1945

42835 **S.B.S. III** Sg/Ja (Shioyama) 1958; Tk; 2000; 86.70 × 5.94 (284 × 19.49); M (Akasaka); 12.5; ex Shodai Maru 1973

42840 **SHOMAR SHAIMA** Si/Br (Smith's D) 1954; Ch; 3700; 115.25 × 6.85 (378.12 × 22.47); M (Sulzer); 13; ex Gertrude Wiener II 1980; ex Sylphiden

1975; ex Norvest 1974; Lengthened 1966; Converted Chemical Tanker 1975

42850 **MAGNISI** It/It (Riuniti) 1943/48; Tk; 1800; 84.61 × 5.13 (277.59 × 16.83); M (Fiat); 11; ex Yann Roullet 1960; ex Satellite 1949; Launched 1943. Completed 1948

42860 **PETROLA 20** Gr/No (Porsgrunds) 1949; C; 1600; 78.64 × 5.39 (258 × 17.68); M (MWM); 10; ex Petrola XX 1976; ex Michael S 1976; ex Divina 1975

42880 **GAMBOMA** Pa/Br (Smith's D) 1938; C; 2600; 97.95 × 6.44 (321.36 × 21.13); M (Werkspoor); 10.5; ex Padola 1966; ex Galula 1965; ex Tong Poh 1964; ex Cerion 1956

42890 **BARU** Cy/Br (Hall, Russell) 1960; C; 3100; 103.33 × 5.94 (339.01 × 19.49); M (British Polar); 10; ex Venturer 1977; ex Tafawa Belewa 1966

42910 **TSIMENTIAS** Pa/Br (Hall, Russell) 1957; C; 3400; 103.33 × 6.17 (339.01 × 20.24); M (Sulzer); —; ex Panagia 1977; ex Brenzett 1976; ex Astro Venture 1975; ex Kappa Progress 1974; ex Corsea 1972

42920 **TSIMENTAVROS II** Gr/Br (Burntisland) 1950; C; 2700; 95.71 × 6.07 (314 × 19.91); M (B&W); 11; ex Anastassios 1977; ex Waterland 1971

42940 **BONAHOPE** Sg/Br (H Robb) 1952; C; 1400; 77.42 × 4.61 (254 × 15.12); M (British Polar); 11; ex Wareatea 1971

★ 42960 **VOLNOVAKHA** Ru/Pd (Gdanska) 1953; O; 2000; 87.00 × 5.36 (285.43 × 17.59); R ('Zgoda'); 9.5; 'B-30' type

42970 **TAYLAN KALKAVAN** Tu/Br (Grangemouth) 1945; C; 2000; 85.81 × 5.43 (281.53 × 17.82); R (N.E. Marine); 9.5; ex Abdullah 1976; ex Braywood 1959; ex Empire Vauxhall 1946

★ 42980 **DA QING No. 15** RC/Br (J.L. Thompson) 1952; Tk; 10100; 154.11 × 8.86 (505.61 × 29.07); M (Doxford); 12; ex Santa Fortuna 1964; ex Sandalwood 1962

42990 **CAMPOO** Sp/Sp (Corcho) 1955; Tk; 1900; 83.39 × 5.14 (273.59 × 16.86); M (Espanola); 9.5
Sister:
42991 **CAMPROVIN** (Sp)

43000 **PETROLA 1** Gr/Br (Goole) 1947; Tk; 1000; 67.49 × 3.96 (221.42 × 12.99); R (Amos & Smith); 9; ex Petrola I 1976; ex Authenticity 1966; ex Anis 1954; ex Empire Harp 1948; Lengthened 1956

43010 **ISLA LEONES** Ar/De (Nakskov) 1934; Tk; 1800; 84.23 × 5.03 (276.35 × 16.5); M (B&W); 10; ex El Rioplatense 1952

43020 **ASPROPYRGOS** Gr/Br (Short Bros.) 1946; Tk; 950; 61.42 × 4.1 (201.51 × 13.45); M (British Polar); 9.5; ex Pireaus IV 1971; ex Austility 1969; ex Forreria 1951; ex Empire Tedlora 1947

43030 **AGIOS GEORGIOS** Gr/Br (G. Brown) 1950; Tk; 1200; 70.54 × 4.22 (231.43 × 13.85); M (Thornycroft); —; ex Athena 1975; ex Atonality 1967

★ 43040 **PEREDOVIK** Ru/Ru (—) 1940; Tk; 1900; 83.01 × 5.56 (272.34 × 18.24); M (—); —

43050 **SEADRIFT** US/US (Sun SB) 1942/61 Con/Ch; 9100; 159.57 × 9 (523.52 × 29.53); T-E (GEC); 14.5; ex Carbide Seadrift 1980; ex Michigan Sun 1960; ex White Plains 1948; Converted from T-2 tanker 1961. May be broken up

43060 **INTAN** Ia/Ne (Ferus Smit) 1954; C; 700; 58.53 × 2.93 (192.03 × 9.61); M (Werkspoor); 9

★ 43070 **DA QING No 9** RC/RC (—) 1960; Tk; 3300; 111.24 × — (361 × —), M (—); 12.2; ex Chien She No. 9
Sister:
★ 43071 **DA QING No 12** (RC) ex Chien She No. 12

43080 **ANINGA** It/FRG (Schlieker) 1960; O; 9100; 166.43 × 9.42 (546.03 × 30.91); M (B&W); 15.5; ex Rigote 1975; ex Tyne Ore 1975
Sister:
43081 **SEQUOIA** (It) ex Quijote; ex Tees Ore 1975

43090 **NEW HOPE** Ma/Ja (NKK) 1962; B; 21100; 204.12 × 11.14 (670 × 36.55); M (B&W); 16; ex Kikkos 1 1984; ex Sotir 1983; ex Marchen 1973; ex Jesper Maersk 1965

★ 43100 **MAXHUTTE** DDR/Sw (Gotav) 1955; OO; 8500; 149 × 8.58 (488.85 × 27.82) M (Gotaverken); 13.5; ex Ledaro 1975; ex Vindafjord 1974

★ 43110 **ZWICKAU** DDR/Sw (Kockums) 1958; OO; 15600; 181.82 × 10.04 (595.87 × 32.91); M (MAN); 14; ex Vitafors 1969

43120 **DONA HELENA** Pi/Fr (Provence) 1949; C; 2000; 95.41 × 5.88 (313.02 × 19.29); M (Sulzer); 13;

ex Don Alberto 1977; ex Atlas 1968
Similar:
43121 **KOSTAKIS** (Gr) ex Annoula 1973; ex Tadia 1968; ex Vaccares 1957; ex Cap Couronne 1955
43122 **DONA RITA** (Pi) ex Marania 1967; ex Tafna 1964; ex Cheik
43123 **DONA ANGELINA** (Pi) ex Valdor 1972; ex Tougourt 1969
43124 **TARTOUS STAR** (Sy) ex Lamia Star 1978; ex Panagiotis V 1976; ex Concorde 1971; ex Phryne 1969; ex Dunkerque 1962; ex Kroumir 1960
The following is converted to a Fish Factory Mother Ship:
43125 **ROSS KELETCHEKIS** (Pa) ex Tell 1966

43140 **PADJONGE** Ia/Be (Boel) 1953; C; 550; 57.31 × 3.18 (188.02 × 10.43); M (Enterprise Eng); 9
Sisters (Ia flag):
43141 **PAJANGAN**
43142 **PANEHAN**
43143 **PAPADO**
43144 **PASIGI**
43145 **PALIAT**
43146 **PAHEPA**
43147 **PASOSO**
43148 **SABANG** ex Pasudu 1980
43149 **KOTA SILAT XII** ex Pailowa

43160 **ANTONELLO** Pa/Br (Scarr) 1949; C; 450; 48.77 × 3.48 (160.01 × 11.42); M (British Polar); 10; ex St. Patrick 1966; ex Asopi 1975; ex Eliva 1971; ex Doxa 1970; ex Somme 1967
Sisters:
43161 **RANIA B** (Cy) ex Lelia 1976; ex Anna Maria 1974; ex Panagiotis 1974; ex Anna 1 1972; ex Natasa 1972; ex Maltese Trader 1971; ex Rachel Pace 1969; ex Grouville 1969; ex Escaut 1965
★ 43162 **PERNAT** (Ys) ex Silver Trader 1974; ex Brookbank Trader 1973; ex Meuse 1971

43180 **SANTA** Br/Ne (Ijsselwerf) 1955; Tk; 430; 48.24 × 2.3 (158.27 × 7.55); M (MAN); 8.5; ex B.G. 1 1983; ex Blackfriars; ex Mobil Fuel 1970
Similar (larger):
43181 **CASTOR** (Gr) ex Buckingham 1983; ex Banco 1972

43190 **LALANG** Ia/FRG (Rolandwerft) 1953; C; 520; 57.87 × 3.38 (189.86 × 11.09); M (Enterprise Eng); 10; ex Lagong 1973
Sisters (Ia flag):
43191 **LAIRAN**
43192 **LAKOR**
43193 **LAKOTA**
43194 **LANDU**
43195 **LAPONDA**
43196 **LAWAK**
43197 **LAWANDRA**
43198 **BIMA** ex Lawin

43220 **IMPERIAL SARNIA** Ca/Br (Collingwood) 1948/54; Tk; 4900; 124.54 × 6.67 (408.6 × 21.88); T (Inglis); 12.5

43230 **GUNGA DIN II** Pa/It (Pellegrino) 1951; Tk; 1100; 66.32 × 5.39 (217.59 × 17.68); M (Fiat); 10.5; ex Punta Gaudio 1980; ex Domenico Ievoli 1980; ex Grazia Pellegrino 1973

43250 **ROSARITO** Ec/Sw (Eriksbergs) 1940; Tk; 1300; 78.01 × 4.56 (255.94 × 14.96); M (Nydqvist & Holm); 12; ex Nordica 1973; ex Svea Reuter 1969; ex Soya VI 1943

43260 **BERING TRADER** US/US (Manitowoc) 1938; Tk; 2000; 88.4 × 5.14 (290.03 × 16.86); TSM (Nordberg); 10.5; ex Raymond J Bushey 1982; ex Traverse City Socony 1962

43270 **PERMINA IX** Ia/Ja (Setoda) 1957; Tk; 1600; 72.64 × 5.3 (238.32 × 17.39); M (Niigata); 12.5; ex Kakushin Maru 1966

43280 **ANTONELLOESSE** It/No (Glommens) 1949; Tk; 1100; 73.21 × 4.64 (240.19 × 15.22); M (Atlas-Diesel); 12; ex Luigia Montanari 1975; ex Luigia N. 1960; ex Saphir 1956

43290 **MURASAKI MARU** Ja/Ja (Harima) 1954; Tk; 800; 63.51 × 4.8 (208.37 × 15.75); M (Osaka Kiko); 10.5; ex Kyoei Maru No. 3 1961; ex Fukuyo Maru 1955

★ 43300 **LAMUT** Ru/Ja (Hitachi) 1959; FF; 5000; 110.27 × 5.9 (361.78 × 19.36); M (B&W); 12.5
Sister:
★ 43301 **NIKOLAY ISAYENKO** (Ru)

43310 **ACRE** Bz/Ja (Uraga Dock) 1951; Tk; 1800; 85.35 × 4.27 (280.02 × 14.01); M (Kawasaki); 10; ex FNP Sao Paulo 1954; ex Salte 58 1953
Sisters (Bz flag):
43311 **PARANA** ex FNP Parana 1954; ex Salte 51 1953
43312 **PERNAMBUCO** ex FNP Pernambuco 1954;

ex *Salte 52* 1953

43313 RIO GRANDE DO NORTE ex *FNP Rio Grande Do Norte* 1954; ex *Salte 54* 1953

43314 RIO GRANDE DO SUL ex *FNP Rio Grande Do Sul* 1954; ex *Salte 55* 1953

● **43320 OSHEA EXPRESS** Br/Br (Robb Caledon) 1970; V; 1200; 91.5 × 3.93 (300.2 × 12.89); M (MaK); —; ex *Clearway*; ex *Speedway* 1970

43330 EVDOXIA K Cy/Br (Grangemouth) 1949; C; 1000/1550; 78.77 × —/5.21 (258.43 × —/17.09); M (Polar); 12.5; ex *Las Minas* 1973; ex *Salamis* 1972; ex *Argostoli II* 1970; ex *Melrose* 1966

43340 CLYDE Ca/Br (H. Robb) 1950; C; 750; 63.66 × 3.75 (208.86 × 12.3); M (British Polar); 11.5; ex *Hirondelle* 1966

43350 HONEST VENTURE Pa/Br (Bartram) 1958; C; 9600; 150.81 × 9.48 (494.78 × 31.1); M (Doxford); 12; ex *Dona Mira* 1981; ex *Charlton Mira* 1969

43360 SANDERUS Be/Ne ('De Klop') 1968; D; 5000; 103 × — (337.93 × —); TSM (MAN); —

43370 TAMA MARU Ja/Ja (Hitachi) 1972; RoVC; 7000; 174.5 × 7.21 (572.51 × 23.65); M (B&W); 18
Sisters (Ja flag):
43371 SURUGA MARU
43372 SAGAMI MARU
43373 TSURUMI MARU

43380 SWANSEA BAY Br/Ne (Vuyk) 1966; D; 2900; 94.49 × 5.67 (310.01 × 18.6); TSM (Smit & Bolnes); 12; ex *Tees Bay* 1979; ex *Cap D'Antifer* 1972; ex *Tees Bay* 1970

43390 PISOLO It/Br (Smith's D) 1958; O; 10000; 153.93 × 8.81 (505 × 28.90); M (Doxford); 11.75; ex *Newlands* 1975; ex *Kappa Unity* 1974; ex *Pennyworth* 1973

43410 ALDO CECCONI It/Br (Lithgows) 1953; O; 6600; 130.16 × 7.95 (427.03 × 26.08); R (Rankin & Blackmore); 11; ex *Gleddoch* 1970

43420 PNOC TAWI-TAWI Pi/Br (Connell) 1960; OO; 5300; 130.23 × 7.79 (427.26 × 5.56); M (Doxford); 11; ex *LSCO Tawi-Tawi* 1980; ex *Klar* 1976; ex *Crinan* 1974

43440 CALIFORNIA US/US (Kaiser Co.) 1946/54/60; C/Con; 13600; 193 × 10.06 (633.2 × 33.01); T (Hendy); 16.75; ex *Californian* 1980; ex *Mount Greylock* 1951; Lengthened 1954; Converted from 'C4' cargo to Ore/Oil 1954; Converted from Ore/Oil to Cargo/Container 1960

43480 KATERINA V Gr/Br (Goole) 1958; Tk; 2600; 94.52 × 5.75 (310.1 × 18.86); M (Newbury); 10; ex *Eleni* 1973; ex *Grit* 1968; At Jeddah May 1978. Being used as an oil storage vessel
Similar:
43481 TAMIM II (Pa) ex *Petroclis* 1982; ex *Assurity* 1969

43490 MYASSAR Le/Br (Goole) 1954; C; 2500; 93.38 × 5.47 (306.36 × 17.95); M (Newbury); 10; ex *Myassa* 1980; ex *Georgina V. Everard* 1978

43510 KATERINA V Gr/Br (Goole) 1958; Tk; 2600; 94.52 × 5.75 (310.1 × 18.86); M (Newbury); 10; ex *Eleni* 1973; ex *Grit* 1968; At Jeddah May 1978, being used as an oil storage vessel
Similar:
43511 TAMIM II (Pa) ex *Petroclis* 1982; ex *Assurity* 1969

★ **43520 AMBURAN** Ru/Ge (F Schichau) 1939; Tk; 640; 64.01 × 3.13 (210.01 × 10.27); TSM (—); 13; ex *Berta* 1946

43530 GIOVANNI C It/It (Benetti) 1967; ST; 1200; 67.01 × 3.05 (219.85 × 10.01); M (MAN); 14; ex *Giovanni Cefalu* 1978; ex *Storione* 1971

43560 GABRIELLA C It/It (Benetti) 1971; ST; 1300; 70.01 × 4.2 (229.69 × 13.78); M (MAN); 15.5
Sister:
43561 MARIA C. (It)

43570 ADVENTURE 1 Gr/Sw (Eriksbergs) 1954/76; RoC; 5400; 170.52 × 6.03 (559.45 × 19.78); M (Eriksbergs); 16.25; ex *Elena* 1980; ex *Dolphin Elena* 1980; ex *Tabriz* 1976; ex *Damianos* 1975; ex *Tabriz* 1967; Converted from a tanker 1976

43580 PANAGIA Gr/No (Moss V) 1939; C; 870; 68.41 × 4.81 (224.44 × 15.78); M (MAN); 11; ex *Faneromini* 1975; ex *Pelops* 1972; ex *Andenes* 1964
Sister:
43581 SOFIA A (Gr) ex *Sophia A* 1979; ex *Pellini* 1973; ex *Stamsund* 1966

43590 GEOPOTES VII Ne/Ne (P. Smit) 1963; D; 4300; 107.63 × 8.04 (353.12 × 26.38); TSM (Smit & Bolnes); 12

43620 KORINTHIA Gr/No (Fredriksstad) 1955; Tk; 9000; 156.62 × 8.72 (513.85 × 28.61); M (Fredriksstad); 13.5; ex *Korenthia* 1982; ex *Thermopylae II* 1981; ex *Anette* 1978; ex *Robert Stove* 1963

43630 ESTRELLA FUEGUINA Ar/Sw (Eriksbergs) 1962; Tk; 12800; 170.67 × 9.74 (559.94 × 31.96); M (B&W); 14.5; ex *Polystar* 1978

43660 PETROLA 32 Gr/FRG (Deutsche Werft) 1957; Tk; 22000; 201.17 × 10.93 (660.01 × 35.86); T (Allgemeine); —; ex *Petrola XXXII* 1976; ex *Apollo XI* 1975; ex *Caroline Oetker* 1969

43680 ST. EMILION US/US (Bethlehem Steel) 1956; Tk; 19500; 201.48 × 10.87 (661 × 35.66); T (Bethlehem Steel); 16.5; ex *Banner* 1983; ex *Cities Service Miami* 1976

43720 PETROMAR MENDOZA Ar/Ne (Giessen) 1960; Tk; 23600; 211.31 × 11.32 (693.27 × 37.14); T (Werkspoor); 17; ex *Esso Amsterdam* 1970

43730 ALEXANDER K Le/Sw (Kockums) 1960; Tk; 12700; 170.01 × 9.73 (557.78 × 31.92); M (MAN); 15.5; ex *Paros* 1982; ex *Peter*; ex *Kef Hawk* 1977; ex *Aspo* 1974; ex *Agneta Billner* 1972
Sister:
★ **43731 NANJIANG** (RC) ex *Gunilla Billner* 1975

43740 NOSTOS Gr/No (Stord) 1960; Tk; 21600; 202.7 × 11.15 (665.03 × 36.58); M (B&W); 16; ex *Sunny Lady* 1977; ex *Polarsol* 1972
Sister:
43741 PAYAS (Tu) ex *Thorstrand* 1967

43760 NUNKI It/It (Breda) 1959; Tk; 13000; 169.93 × 9.65 (558 × 31.66); M (Fiat); 15.5; ex *Marinella d'Amico* 1981

43770 SABLE Pa/FRG (Bremer V) 1957; Tk; 13700; 180.14 × 9.82 (591.01 × 32.22); M (MAN); 14.5; ex *Cherry Bay*; ex *Herulv* 1978; ex *Johs Stove* 1967

★ **43790 ARGON** Ru/Fi (Rauma-Repola) 1963; Tk; 3400; 105.39 × 6.22 (345.77 × 20.42); M (B&W) 14.25
Sisters (Ru flag):
★ **43791 ALUKSNE**
★ **43792 APE**
★ **43793 AKTASH**
★ **43794 AKSAY**
★ **43795 ABRENE**
★ **43796 AMURSK**
★ **43797 APSHERONSK**
★ **43798 ARAKS**
★ **43799 ANAPKA**
★ **43800 LYUBERTSY**
★ **43801 SINEGORSK**
★ **43802 ALEKSEYEVKA**
★ **43803 ALEKSEYEVSK**
★ **43804 ANIVA**
★ **43805 ALAGIR**
★ **43806 ALEYSK**
★ **43807 ALEKSIN**
★ **43808 ANAPA**
★ **43809 EVENSK**
★ **43810 ABAGUR**
★ **43811 ARDATOV**
★ **43812 DARNITZA**
★ **43813 EREBUS**
★ **43814 INKERMAN**
★ **43815 VOLFRAM**
★ **43816 IMAN**
★ **43817 RADIY**
★ **43818 ABAKAN**
★ **43819 TYUMENNEFT**
★ **43820 YUGLA**
(Cu flag):
★ **43821 CUBA** ex *Artsyz* 1962

43840 AELLO Li/Ja (Hitachi) 1957; Tk; 20700; 206.97 × 11.62 (679.04 × 38.12); T (Hitachi); 16

43850 PERMINA SAMUDRA V Li/FRG (Kieler H) 1958; Tk; 16000; 189.14 × 10.91 (620.53 × 35.79); M (B&W); —; ex *Lindos* 1971; ex *Benstream* 1967; ex *Ring Chief* 1964

● **43860 GEORGIOS M II** Gr/Sw (Eriksbergs) 1958; Tk; 16600; 187.76 × 10.5 (616.01 × 34.38); M (B&W); 16; ex *Kronoholm* 1967

43870 EMOULI Gr/Br (Swan Hunter & WR) 1958; Tk; 20700; 202.67 × 10.99 (664.93 × 36.06); T (Wallsend); 16.25; ex *Petrola 19* 1980; ex *Petrola XIX* 1976; ex *Llanishen* 1974

43880 PALMIRA ZETA It/Be (Boel) 1958; Tk; 12500; 170.69 × 9.65 (560.01 × 31.66); M (B&W); 15; ex *Ocean Tanker* 1977; ex *Fina Allemagne* 1975; ex *Purfina Allemagne* 1960

43900 AHMED AL-BAKRY II Si/No (Tangen) 1955; Tk; 8900; 154.84 × 8.66 (508 × 28.41); M (Werkspoor); 13; ex *Pibimare Prima* 1981; ex *Stolt Freddy*

1969; ex *Stolt Niagara* 1969; ex *Freddy* 1964

43930 HAMEN No/Br (Austin) 1949; C; 1400; 76.79 × 4.77 (251.94 × 15.65); M (Wichmann); 10; ex *Tandik* 1963; ex *Pompey Power* 1960

43940 MAGDUS Cy/Br (Grangemouth) 1949; C; 1000; 65.11 × 4.34 (213.62 × 14.24); M (British Polar); 10.5; ex *Babi* 1980; ex *Ioulia K* 1973; ex *Mayfair Sapphire* 1973; ex *Sapphire* 1958

43960 NIKITAS Cy/Fi (Crichton-Vulcan) 1951; C; 2300; 88.5 × 5.18 (290.35 × 16.99); M (MWM); 10; ex *Santa Paola* 1972; ex *Emil Berger* 1969; ex *Genoa*

44000 TEXACO ALASKA Pa/Sw (Kockums) 1960; Tk; 24100; 213.21 × 11.16 (699.51 × 36.61); T (Kockums); 16.5

44010 NEFELI Li/Ja (Mitsubishi N) 1958; Tk; 24300; 211.72 × 10.89 (694.62 × 35.73); T (Hitachi); —
Sister:
44011 KYMO (Li)

44040 GOLDEN EASTERN Sg/Hong Kong (Taikoo) 1953; C; 1700; 84.49 × 4.86 (277.2 × 15.94); M (Sulzer); 12; ex *Sletholm* 1972; ex *Hendrik* 1964
Sister:
44041 GOLDEN SOURCE (Sg) ex *Sletfjord* 1972; ex *Hervar* 1964

● **44080 MALDIVE NATION** Mv/Fr (Mediterranee) 1957; B; 10000; 149.38 × 9.14 (490.09 × 30.02); M (Mediterranee); 14; ex *Sealord 1* 1980; ex *Utvik* 1973; ex *Africa* 1962
Sister:
44081 NIKY (Gr) ex *Vestland* 1970

★ **44100 BOLSHEVIK KARAYEV** Ru/Bu (G Dimitrov) 1959; Tk; 3800; 123.5 × 4.4 (405.18 × 14.44); TSM (Russkiy); 10.5; Caspian Sea Service
Sisters (Ru flag):
★ **44101 FEDYA GUBANOV**
★ **44102 PAMYAT 26 KOMISSAROV**
★ **44103 ALMA-ATA**
★ **44104 GYURGYAN**
★ **44104 NEFTECHALA**
★ **44106 DZHEBRAIL**
★ **44107 UDZHARY**
★ **44108 AY-PETRI**
★ **44109 NEBIT DAG**
★ **44110 NUREK**
★ **44111 SURAKHANY**
★ **44112 ORDZHONIKIDZENNEFT**
★ **44113 SABUNCHI**
★ **44114 SHIRVANNEFT**
★ **44115 BUZOVNY**
★ **44116 DZHORAT**
★ **44117 MARDAKYANY**
★ **44118 MASHITAGI**
★ **44119 KARAKUM KANAL**
★ **44120 MANGYSHLAK**
★ **44121 KIROVABAD**
★ **44122 EMBA**
★ **44123 NAKHICHEVAN** (wine tanker)
★ **44124 PORT ILYICH**
★ **44125 VOLGONEFTGAROZ**
★ **44126 ZHIGANSK**
(RC flag):
★ **44127 ERMA**

★ **44140 BATUMI** Ru/De (Odense) 1932; Tk; 6600; 129.27 × 8.27 (424.11 × 27.13); M (B&W); 11.5; ex *Batum* 1939; ex *Batumsky Soviet* 1934

44160 MARIPRIMA Li/Sw (Kockums) 1961; Tk; 30200; 227.34 × 12.01 (745.87 × 39.4); T (De Laval); 16.75; ex *Esso Stockholm* 1977

44180 PETROSTAR IV Si/Sw (Kockums) 1959; Tk; 12600; 170.03 × 9.7 (557.84 × 31.82); M (Kockums); 14; ex *Lidfold* 1975; ex *Lidvard* 1967

44190 IONIO It/Sw (Kockums) 1958; Tk; 12700; 170.03 × 9.44 (557.78 × 30.97); M (Kockums); 15.5; ex *Bitterfield*; ex *Southern Clipper* 1963

● **44200 SHOMAR HANAN** Si/Sw (Kockums) 1959; Tk; 15600; 184.87 × 10.19 (606.53 × 33.43); M (MAN); —; ex *Angela F*; ex *Sirius* 1967; in use as a bunkering vessel at Jeddah

44210 AMASTRA Br/Br (Smith's D) 1958; Tk; 12300; 170.39 × 9.36 (559.02 × 30.71); M (Doxford); 14.5
Similar:
44211 UJE (Pa) ex *Amoria*
44214 AULICA (Br)
44215 ACHATINA (Br)
44216 SUNNY (Cy) ex *Stonegate* 1982

44220 PETROMAR ROSARIO Ar/FRG (Deutsche Werft) 1960; Tk; 22400; 211.23 × 11.33 (693.01 × 37.17); T ('De Schelde'); 17; ex *Esso Nurnberg*

● **44250 VERDI** Pa/De (Odense) 1964; Tk; 21600;

209.15 × 11.27 (686.19 × 36.98); M(B&W); 15.5; ex *Athina* 1982; ex *Oluf Maersk* 1980; ex *Karen Maersk* 1978
Sister:
44251 HENNING MAERSK (De)

44260 EVA P Cy/Sw (Eriksbergs) 1963; Tk; 26400; 215.22 × 11.94 (706.1 × 39.17); M (B&W); 15.25; ex *Saga* 1983; ex *Rion* 1982; ex *Polycastle* 1980
Similar:
44261 CABO GUARDIAN (Ar) ex *Polykarp* 1982

●**44270 LEFKAS** Gr/Ne (Nederlandsche) 1962; Tk; 16400; 188.83 × 10.35 (619.52 × 33.96); M (Stork); 15.75; ex *Delian Apollon* 1978

44280 ANDREA MANTEGNA Pa/Gr (Hellenic) 1961; Tk; 16000; 187.36 × 10.34 (614.7 × 33.92); M (Stork); 15; ex *Port Renard* 1982; ex *Yalton* 1974; ex *World Hope* 1973

44290 TOXOTIS Cy/Be (Boel) 1960; Tk; 12900; 170.75 × 9.65 (560.2 × 31.66); M (B&W); 15; ex *Jaguar* 1981; ex *Toxotis* 1980; ex *Stolt Athenian* 1976; ex *Stolt Progress* 1972; ex *Olga Nielsen* 1966

44310 WASHINGTON TRADER US/US (Newport News) 1959; Tk; 24500; 217.08 × 11.53 (712.2 × 37.83); T (De Laval); 17; ex *Thetis* 1975
Sister:
44311 ACHILLES (US)
Possibly similar:
44312 SOUTHWEST CAPE (Li) ex *G.S. Livanos* 1973

44340 WHITE BEACH Pa/Ja (Mitsubishi Z) 1956; Tk; 19800; 203.18 × 10.07 (666.6 × 33.04); T (Mitsubishi); 16; ex *Athenian Runner* 1975; ex *Marietta* 1972

44360 DEMOSTHENES V Gr/Ne (Nederlandsche) 1958; Tk; 16300; 187.36 × 10.31 (614.7 × 33.83); M (Nederlandsche); 15; ex *Naess Lion* 1969

★**44370 ELGAVA** Ru/Sw (Gavle) 1961; Tk; 2900; 104.88 × 6.1 (344.09 × 20.01); M(B&W); 14; May be spelt **YELGAVA**
Sister:
★**44371 TUKUMS** (Ru)

●**44390 MALDIVE NATION** Mv/Fr (Mediterranee) 1957; B; 10000; 149.38 × 9.14 (490.09 × 30.02); M (Mediterranee); 14; ex *Sealord 1* 1980; ex *Utvik* 1973; ex *Africa* 1962
Sister:
44391 NIKY (Gr) ex *Vestland* 1970

●★**44410 DRUZHBA** Ru/Ja (Iino) 1960; Tk; 25700; 214.89 × 11.43 (705.02 × 37.5); T (Hitachi); 16.75; launched as the *Golden Arrow*

●**44420 MARIE MAERSK** De/De (Odense) 1962; Tk; 21600; 209.15 × 10.75 (686.19 × 35.27); M (B&W); 15

44430 LUSSIN It/FRG (Deutsche Werft) 1959; Tk; 13000; 170.69 × 9.43 (560.01 × 30.94); T (Allgemeine); 14.5; ex *Partula* 1981

44440 SORONG Ia/Ys (—) 1965; RT/FA; 5100 Dwt; 112 × 6.6 (367.4 × 21.6); —; 15

44460 ANINGA It/FRG (Schlieker) 1960; O; 9100; 166.43 × 9.42 (546.03 × 30.91); M (B&W); 15.5; ex *Rigote* 1975; ex *Tyne Ore*
Sister:
44461 SEQUOIA (It) ex *Quijote*; ex *Tees Ore* 1975

44480 BLUE SKY Si/Br (Ardrossan) 1940; C; 700; 63.89 × 4.15 (209.61 × 13.62); M (British Auxiliaries); 11; ex *Star of Ibrahim* 1973; ex *Jersey Coast* 1967; ex *Moray Coast* 1954

●**44490 STRONG SKIPPER** Gr/Fr (Mediterranee) 1956; C; 8800; 144.76 × 9.45 (474.03 × 31); M (Sulzer); 14.25; ex *John Leo* 1982; ex *Andriotis* 1978; ex *George M Embiricos* 1970; ex *Wavecrest* 1962

★**44510 PADEREWSKI** Pd/Ys ('Split') 1960; C; 7200/9300; 152.81 × 8.05/9.01 (501.35 × 26.41/29.56); M (Fiat); 15.5
Sisters:
★**44511 HUA XING** (RC) ex *Moniuszko* 1982
★**44512 FANG XING** (RC) ex *Szymanowski* 1983
★**44513 NOWOWIEJSKI** (Pd)
★**44514 BAO XING** (RC) ex *Wieniawski* 1977

44520 LEFTERIS II Gr/Ys ('Split') 1958; C; 6500/9100; 153.17 × 8.08/9.02 (503 × 26.51/29.59); M (Fiat); 14.5; ex *Kerman* 1976; ex *Gertrud Therese* 1969; ex *Wasaborg* 1965

44540 OBSERVER US/US (Sun SB) 1943/53; Tk; 17600; 181.03 b.p. × 10.19 (593.93 × 33.43); T-E (Westinghouse); 13; forward & cargo sections ex *Santa Helena* 1966; ex *Wapello* 1964; aft section ex *Trustco* 1966; ex *Esso Shreveport* 1962; ex *Front Royal* 1948; Joined 1966

44550 SAO GABRIEL Po/Po (Viana) 1963; RT/FA; 9900; 146 × 8 (479 × 26.2); T (Pametrada); 17

44560 COVE SPIRIT US/US (Sun SB) 1954; Tk; 16200; 179.08 × 10.45 (587.53 × 34.28); T (De Laval); 16.75; ex *Eclipse*
Similar (US flag):
44561 CHEYENNE ex *Mobilgas* 1983

●**44570 SUZANNE** US/US (Sun SB) 1945/58; Tk; 12300; 174.35 × 9.48 (572 × 31.10); T-E (Westinghouse); 14.5; ex *Gulftiger* 1981; ex *Gulfhorn* 1958; ex *Roxbury Hill* 1947; Lengthened 1958 (Ingalls SB)

44580 LONG PHOENIX Pa/FRG (Howaldts) 1961; Tk; 29700; 225.74 × 12.03 (740.62 × 39.48); M (Sulzer); 16.5; ex *Esso Norway* 1970; ex *Norway* 1970; ex *Esso Norway* 1968

44590 NECHES US/US (Bethlehem PC) 1958; Tk; 20100; 201.48 × 10.87 (690.55 × 36.66); T (Bethlehem Steel); 16.5; ex *Santa Paula* 1982; ex *Hans Isbrandtsen* 1971

44600 AHMED AL-BAKRY II Si/No (Tangen) 1955; Tk; 8900; 154.84 × 8.66 (508 × 28.41); M (Werkspoor); 13; ex *Pibimare Prima* 1981; ex *Stolt Freddy* 1959; ex *Stolt Niagara* 1969; ex *Freddy* 1964

★**44620 YELSK** Ru/Ru (Admiralteiskiy) 1960; Tk; 7900; 145.5 × 8.69 (477.36 × 28.51); M (Skoda); —
Sisters (Ru flag):
★**44621 EGORYEVSK**
★**44622 LIEPAYA**
★**44623 YELNYA**
★**44624 YESSENTUKI**
(Gr flag)
44626 ALEXIA ex *Leuna 1* 1981
(Pa flag)
44627 MATE 1 ex *Aris* 1981; ex *Port Maria* 1980; ex *Zeitz* 1968

44670 CHAPARAL II Pa/Br (H&W) 1961; Tk; 18600; 196.22 × 10.52 (643.77 × 34.91); M (B&W); 15; ex *Midas Touch* 1981; ex *Galaxias*; ex *Norsk Drott* 1968

●★**44690 DA QING 235** RC/Br (Lithgows) 1959; Tk; 10700; 160.18 × 9.16 (525.52 × 30.05); M (B&W); 14.5; ex *Tingjiang*; ex *British Trust* 1976
Similar:
★**44691 DA QING 136** (RC) ex *Zhujiang*; ex *British Fulmar* 1976
44692 ORIENTAL UNITY (Li) ex *British Cygnet* 1977; ex *BP Explorer* 1969; ex *BP Endeavour* 1967; ex *British Cygnet* 1964
44697 WENJIANG (Br) ex *British Curlew* 1976
44698 NOAH VI (Ir) ex *British Swift* 1977
44699 FAL XI (UAE) ex *Lot* 1983; ex *British Robin* 1977
44701 PENHORS (Fr) ex *British Mallard* 1980

44710 THEOTOKOS Gr/De (Odense) 1962; Tk; 24700; 212.12 × 11.74 (695.93 × 38.52); M (B&W); 16; ex *Water Prince*; ex *Vincenzia* 1973; ex *Jetta Dan* 1969

●**44720 GEORGIOS** Gr/Sw (Eriksbergs) 1960; Tk; 23500; 208.03 × 11.56 (682.51 × 37.93); M (B&W); 15; ex *Hoegh Fulmar* 1968

44760 CAMPOGRIS Sp/Sp (UN de Levante) 1959; Tk; 7100; 139.05 × 7.76 (456.2 × 25.46); M (Espanola); 13.75
Sister:
44761 CAMPONEGRO (Sp)

44780 ESTRELLA FUEGUINA Ar/Sw (Eriksbergs) 1962; Tk; 12800; 170.67 × 9.74 (559.94 × 31.96); M (B&W); 14.5; ex *Polystar* 1978

44790 RHINO Gr/FRG (Deutsche Werft) 1959; Tk. 12500; 170.69 × 9.68 (560.01 × 31.76); M (MAN); 15; ex *Stolt Rhino*; ex *Sunrana* 1973; ex *John Augustus Essberger* 1970

44800 COVE NAVIGATOR US/US (New York SB) 1951; Tk; 19500; 201.02 × 10.58 (659.5 × 34.71); T (Westinghouse); 15.5; ex *Mount Navigator* 1978; ex *Atlantic Navigator* 1974

44810 MEDINA US/US (Sun SB) 1953; Tk; 18800; 195.38 × 10.81 (641.01 × 35.47); T (Westinghouse); 16.5; ex *Delaware Sun* 1981
Sisters (US flag):
44811 COVE MARINER ex *Eastern Sun* 1982
44812 WESTERN SUN

44840 CAMPORROJO Sp/Sp (UN de Levante) 1963; Tk; 7000; 141.79 × 7.76 (465.2 × 25.46); M (B&W); 13.7
Sister (Sp flag):
44841 CAMPOGULES
Possible sisters (Sp flag):
44842 CAMPOCERRADO
44843 CAMPOAZUR
44844 CAMPORRUBIO

44850 CIELO ROSSO It/Ne (Nederlandsche) 1959; Tk; 13300; 170.69 × 9.67 (560.01 × 31.73); M (Stork); 14.5; ex *Eidsfoss* 1968

●**44870 SCAPMOUNT** Gr/Sw (Eriksbergs) 1961; Tk; 22000; 208.03 × 11.56 (682.51 × 37.93); M (B&W); 16.5; ex *Mirfak* 1973; ex *Toscana* 1972
Similar:
★**44871 WOLFEN** (DDR) ex *Tarim* 1968
44872 TRINITE (Gr) ex *Theoskepasti* 1983; ex *Despina Mihalinou* 1982; ex *Eugenia II* 1979; ex *Dana* 1974; ex *Noto* 1974; ex *Torino* 1969

44880 CAMPORRASO Sp/Sp (AESA) 1962; Tk; 6600; 139.05 × 7.76 (456.2 × 25.46); M (B&W); 14
Sister:
44881 CAMPORRUBIO (Sp)
Possible sister:
44882 CAMPOCERRADO (Sp)

★**44890 RAVA RUSSKAYA** Ru/Ru (Kherson) 1960; Tk; 7700; 145.5 × 8.67 (477.36 × 28.44); M (Skoda); 12.25; 'KAZBEK' class. May be others of this class with similar appearance

44900 VARUNA YAMINI In/FRG (Meyer) 1962; C; 3200; 97.92 × 6.98 (321.26 × 22.9); M (MAN); 14.25; ex *Fiepko Ten Doornkaat* 1972
Sisters:
44901 VARUNA YAN (In) ex *Ellen Klautschke* 1972
44902 MARIA A (Gr) ex *Caroline Schulte* 1978; ex *Gertrud Ten Doornkaat* 1973

44910 CHERRY JET Sg/Ja (Uraga Dock) 1956; Tk; 12800; 171.74 × 9.73 (563.45 × 31.92); M (Sulzer); 14.5; ex *Conoco Jet*; ex *Continental Jet* 1967; ex *Mercantile Trader* 1967; ex *Uraga* 1966

44930 CHRYSSI V Gr/Fr (Gironde) 1961; Tk; 13400; 175.34 × 9.5 (575.26 × 31); M (B&W); 15; ex *Euterpe* 1978; ex *Thale* 1976; ex *Lacon* 1972; ex *Athen* 1968; ex *Athene* 1966

★**44950 ALEKSEY KRYLOV** Ru/Ru (—) 1955; Tk; 3700; 123.5 × 4.31 (405.18 × 14.14); TSM (Russkiy); 10.75; Caspian Sea Service
Sisters (Ru flag):
★**44952 IVAN ZEMNUKHOV**
★**44953 LYUBOV SHEVTSOVA**
★**44954 SERGEY TYULENIN**
★**44955 ULYANA GROMOVA**
★**44956 LIZA CHAYKINA**

44960 NELY P Gr/Sw (Gotav) 1957; Tk; 12500; 169.81 × 9.56 (557.12 × 31.36); M (Gotaverken); 14.5; ex *Saija* 1974; ex *Berit* 1969
Similar:
44961 ESTRELLA (Fi) ex *Synia* 1969

●**44970 TOLMIROS** Gr/Br (Lithgows) 1963; Tk; 31600; 233.48 × 12.34 (766.01 × 40.49); M (Sulzer); 16.25; ex *Theodora* 1975; ex *Thorshammer* 1969

44990 ELEISTRIA VIII Gr/Ys ('Split') 1959; C; 9200; 153.14 × 9.11 (502.43 × 29.89); M (Fiat); 13; ex *Tariq* 1977; ex *Shuguang* 1965; ex *Matang* 1964

45010 TAFELBERG SA/De (Nakskov) 1959; RT/FA; 12500; 170.6 × — (559.9 × —); M (B&W); 15.5; ex *Annam* 1965; Converted from tanker (Barens/Brown & H). Now has a helicopter deck (not shown)

45020 LITTLE NIKOS Gr/Sw (Gotav) 1961; Tk; 21900; 209.1 × 11.12 (686.02 × 36.48); M (Gotaverken); 16; ex *Theodoti* 1977; ex *Radny* 1970; May be spelt **LITTLE NICOS**

★**45030 WU XING** Rc/Ys ('Split') 1959; C; 7000/9200; 153.09 × 19/9.01 (502.26 × 26.87/29.56); M (Fiat); 15; ex *Chopin* 1979
Sister:
★**45031 XUE CHENG** (RC) ex *Yu Cheng* 1981; ex *Zamenhof* 1981

45040 MARIAS US/US (Bethlehem Steel) 1944; RT/FA; 25500 Dspl; 168.6 × 10.1 (553 × 33); TST (Bethlehem Steel); 18; 'CIMARRON' class type
Sister:
45041 TALUGA (US)

45050 NEOSHO US/US (Bethlehem Steel) 1954; RT/FA; 38000 Dspl; 199.6 × 10.7 (655.35 × 35.1); TST (—); 20
Sisters (US flag):
45051 MISSISSINEWA
45052 HASSAYAMPA
45053 KAWISHIWI
45054 TRUCKEE
45055 PONCHATOULA

45060 MONIA Pa/Br (Austin) 1938; C; 1000; 67.21 × 4.45 (220.51 × 14.6); M (Wichmann); 11; ex *Anne Opem* 1974; ex *Siravik* 1973; ex *Stokkvik* 1970; ex *Svelgen* 1964; ex *Eleanor Brooke* 1957

45070 BINTANG SAMUDRA IV Ia/Br (Scott &

Sons) 1936; C; 660; 55.2 × 3.78 (181.1 × 12.4); M (Polar); 9.5; ex *Babinda*

45080 **BALABAC** Pi/Br (Scott & Sons) 1933; C; 630; 54.72 × 3.78 (179.53 × 12.4); M (British Auxiliaries); 10; ex *Breeze* 1966

● 45090 **STAGAN** Cy/Br (Burntisland) 1959; C; 3800; 105.16 × 6.27 (345.01 × 20.57); M (B&W); 11; ex *Milos II* 1983; ex *Storrington* 1979

45100 **PUNTA MEDANOS** Ar/Br (Swan Hunter & WR) 1950; RT/FA; 16300 Dspl; 153.1 × 8.7 (502 × 28.5); TST (Wallsend); 18

★45110 **KALININGRAD** Ru/Ru (Baltic) 1959; FC; 5500; 130.79 × 6.72 (429.1 × 22.05); D-E (—); 16.5
Sisters (Ru flag):
★45111 **SEVASTOPOL**
★45112 **SIMFEROPOL**
★45113 **ARSENYEV**
★45114 **EGERSHELD**
★45115 **CHURKIN**
★45116 **IRKUTSK**

★45120 **YANTARNYY** Ru/Ru (Baltic) 1964; FC; 5500; 130.92 × 6.72 (429.53 × 22.05); D-E (—); 16.25
Sisters (Ru flag):
★45121 **BASHKIR**
★45122 **AUGUST JAKOBSON**
★45123 **NIKOLAY ZYSTSTAR**
Possible sisters (Ru flag):
★45124 **VOLCHANSK**
★45125 **VOLOGDA**
★45126 **KOMISSAR POLUKHIN** ex *Karel* 1971
★45127 **KOSMONAUT KOMAROV**
★45128 **ZABAYKALYE**

45140 **PUNTA DELGADA** Ar/US (St. Johns River) 1945; Tk/FA; 6100 Dspl; 99.1 × 6.1 (325 × 20); M Westinghouse); 11.5; ex *Sugarland*; ex *Nanticoke*; 'T-1' type

45150 **SULTANA** Pi/Au (Walkers Ltd) 1948; C; 700; 55.73 × 3.40 (182.84 × 11.15); M (Mirrlees); 9.5; ex *Helen J.* 1967; ex *Enfield* 1965
Sisters:
45151 **MALUKA** (Pp) ex *Euroa* 1965
45152 **DONA LILY** (Pi) ex *Nukumanu* 1975; ex *Waiben* 1966; ex *Elmore*

45160 **SCORPION 1** Pa/Br (Hall, Russell) 1946; C; 1000; 60.04 × 4.34 (226.51 × 14.24); M (British Polar); 11; ex *J.B. Banville* 1978; ex *Maridan C*; ex *Lunan* 1969

45170 **ATTIKI** Gr/Ne (Amels) 1961; C; 1400; 81.79 × 4.31 (268.34 × 14.14); M ('De Industrie'); 13; ex *Nassauborg* 1980; Lengthened 1969
Sister:
45171 **KATINA C** (Gr) ex *Prinsenborg* 1980

45180 **FRANCO PIERACCINI** It/Ne (Terneuzensche) 1950; C; 500; 64.22 × 3.25 (210.7 × 10.66); M (Sulzer); —; ex *Egbert Wagenborg* 1966

45200 **KAMELA** UAE/FRG (Kroeger) 1955; C; 1600; 86.72 × 6.08 (285 × 19.95); M (MWM); 14; ex *Ive* 1983; ex *Nives* 1980; ex *Vives* 1970

★45210 **AKTYUBINSK** Ru/Ru (Baltic) 1956; FC; 5200; 130.92 × 7.49 (429.53 × 24.57); D-E (—); 17.5
Sisters (Ru flag):
★45211 **KURGAN**
★45212 **TITANIYA** ex *Zelenogradsk* 1971
★45213 **TSELINOGRAD** ex *Akmolinsk*
★45214 **IVAN STEPANOV**
★45215 **KAMENOGORSK**
★45217 **VOLOCHAYEVSK**
★45218 **KRAMATORSK**
★45219 **PRIVOLZHSK**
★45220 **YAROSLAVL**
Similar (cargo ship):
★45221 **KUYBYSHEVGES** (Ru)

45230 **CANADIAN ACE** Pa/Ja (Mitsui) 1971; RoVC; 11500; 161.65 × 6.68 (530.35 × 21.92); M (B&W); 18.5; ex *Canada Maru* 1980

45250 **CLEO 1** Pa/Ja (Hitachi) 1957; Tk; 20900; 206.99 × 10.64 (679.1 × 34.91); M (B&W); 15.5; ex *Cleo* 1982; ex *Yuyo Maru No 8* 1973

★45270 **KONSTITUTSIYA SSSR** Ru/Pd (Gdanska) 1979; FF; 15800; 178.3 × 7.2 (584.97 × 23.62); M (B&W); 14.5; 'B-670' type. Helicopter deck aft.
Sisters (Ru flag):
★45271 **RYBAK KAMCHATSKIY**
★45272 **RYBAK PRIMORIYA**
★45273 **RYBAK CHUKOTKI**
★45274 **PISHCHEVAYA INDUSTRIYA**
★45275 **RYBAK VLADIVOSTOKA**

45280 **SAO GABRIEL** Po/Po (Viana) 1963; RT/FA; 9900; 146 × 8 (479 × 26.2); T (Pametrada); 17

★45290 **PYATIDYESYATILYETIYE SSSR** Ru/Ru (Admiralteiskiy) 1973; FF; 18500; 197.31 × 8.1 (647.34 × 26.57); M (B&W); 14.5; ex *Posyet*; Also known as **50 LET SSSR**
Sisters (Ru flag):
★45291 **VASILIY CHERNYSHYEV**
★45292 **YEVGENIY LEBEDYEV**

45310 **MONTT** Ch-(Navy)/Br (Hawthorn, L) 1963; RT; 14100; 177.91 × 10.28 (583.69 × 33.73); T (Hawthorn, L); 17; ex *Tidepool* 1982; Helicopter deck and hangar
Sister:
45311 **TIDESPRING** (Br) RFA operated

45320 **SUPPLY** Au/Br (H&W) 1955; RT/FA; 11200; 177.8 × 9.8 (583 × 32); T (—); 17.25; ex *Tide Austral* 1962

45330 **OLMEDA** Br/Br (Swan Hunter & WR) 1965; RT/FA; 18600; 197.52 × 10.36 (648.03 × 33.99); T (Wallsend); 19; ex *Oleander* 1967; Helicopter deck and hangar
Sisters (Br flag):
45331 **OLNA**
45332 **OLWEN** ex *Olynthus* 1967

● ★45350 **POLTAVA** Ru/Ru (Nosenko) 1962; C; 9800; 155.68 × 9.09 (510.76 × 29.82); M (B&W); 15
Sisters (Ru flag):
★45351 **PEREKOP**
★45352 **POLOTSK**
★45353 **NIKOLAYEV**
★45354 **PAVLOVSK**
★45355 **PRIDNEPROVSK**
★45356 **BABUSHKIN**
★45357 **BAKURIANI**
★45358 **BERISLAV**
★45359 **PARTIZANSKAYA ISKRA**
★45360 **KAPITAN VISLOBOKOV**
★45361 **PARTIZANSKAYA SLAVA**
★45362 **BRYANSKIY RABOCHIY**
★45363 **BALASHIKHA**
★45364 **BAYMAK**
★45365 **BELGOROD DNESTROVSKIY**
★45366 **BEREZOVKA**
★45367 **OKTYABRSKAYA**
★45368 **REVOLYUTSIYA**
Similar (Hu flag):
★45369 **ADY**
★45370 **PETOFI**
(Ku flag):
45381 **AL SHIDADIAH**
45382 **AL SOLAIBIAH**
45383 **AL SALEHIAH**
(Iq flag):
45384 **BAGHDAD**
45385 **BABYLON**
45386 **BASRAH**
45387 **SINDBAD**
(Sg flag):
45389 **ALBANY** ex *Pangani* 1980; ex *Brunshagen* 1969
45390 **WESTGATE** ex *Palabora*; ex *Brunswick* 1968
(Gr flag):
45391 **MELPO K** ex *Al Jabiriah* 1981
45392 **EFTYHIA**
45393 **POLYXENI** ex *Al Farwaniah* 1984
45394 **PEBANE** ex *Brunshain* 1971
(In flag):
45395 **VISHVA UMANG**
45396 **VISHVA TARANG**
45397 **VISHVA ASHA**
45398 **VISHVA ABHA**
(Li flag):
45400 **ARMONIA** ex *Pelindaba* 1983; ex *Brunshost* 1971
(Tg flag):
45402 **PAYIME** ex *Paranga* 1980; ex *Brunsbrock* 1971
(Cy flag):
45402/1 **ANESTO D** ex *Al Omariah* 1983
45402/2 **NEW FAITH** ex *Pongala* 1983
45403 **GREGORIOS D** ex *Al Mansouriah* 1983
45404 **PROSPERITAS** ex *Al Aridhiah* 1983
(Jo flag):
45405 **BADRE** ex *Al Gurainiah* 1982
45406 **MO'TAH** ex *Al Khalidiah* 1982
(Pa flag):
45407 **DOLLY II** ex *Evgenia* 1982
45408 **ALEXA II** ex *Al Kadisiah* 1981
45409 **ROSA S** ex *Al Odailiah* 1981

45420 **HELLA** Be/FRG (Norderwerft) 1970; C; 2900; 97.24 × 5.2 (319.02 × 17.06); M (KHD); 14.5; ex *Ilse Russ* 1977

45430 **RIJNBORG** Ne/Ne (Amels) 1970; C; 1800; 81.79 × 5.18 (268 × 16.99); M (MWM); 13
Sister:
45431 **SCHELDEBORG** (Ne)

45440 **AGELIKI II** Gr/Sw (Lodose) 1957; C; 500;

71.43 × 3.85 (234.35 × 12.63); M (Alpha-Diesel); 12; ex *Marie-Aude* 1978; ex *Staffan* 1969; Launched as *Palma*

45450 **KEMAL II** Tu/FRG (Nobiskrug) 1971; C; 2800/5000; 125.02 × 6.56/7.65 (410.17 × 21.52/25.1); M (B+V); 17; ex *Arion* 1982; ex *Tolmi* 1981; ex *Mette Bewa* 1976; ex *Cap Matapan* 1974
Sisters:
45451 **AZUR MED** (Li) ex *Happy Med* 1982; ex *Timi* 1981; ex *Rikke Bewa* 1976; ex *Cap Carmel* 1974
45452 **CAPE ITEA** (Gr) ex *Samos Island*; ex *Cap Anamur* 1973

● 45460 **MIRAMAR PRIMA** It/FRG (Elsflether) 1966; C; 1600; 85.81 × 5.12 (281.53 × 16.79); M (MaK) 12.5; ex *Tony's Luck* 1980; ex *Atreus*; ex *Ingrid Retzlaff* 1974
Sister:
45461 **ROSARITA** (Pa) ex *New Hope*; ex *Erich Retzlaff* 1974

45470 **SUNLUCK** Cy/No (Sarpsborg) 1966; C; 3300; 105.36 × 6.42 (346 × 21.06); M (B&W); 14; ex *Rudolf* 1976

45480 **JUMPA** Th/Br (Swan Hunter) 1970; C; 8000/11200; 156.98 × 8.2/9.62 (515.02 × 26.9/31.56); M (Sulzer); 19; ex *Strathmay* 1982; ex *Manora* 1975
Sisters:
45481 **KANNIKAR** (Th) ex *Strathmeigle* 1982; ex *Merkara* 1975
45482 **INTANIN** (Th) ex *Strathmore* 1982; ex *Morvada* 1975
45483 **SONIA M** (Br) ex *Strathmuir* 1982; ex *Mulbera* 1975

★45490 **KAI HUA** RC/Sw (Gotav) 1958; C; 6400/10100; 149.36 × —/9.81 (490.03 × —/32.19); M (Gotaverken); 15.75; ex *Gaoyan* 1976; ex *Aristanax* 1973; ex *W R Lundgren* 1967

45500 **AGENOR** FRG/FRG (S&B) 1964; C; 500; 73 × 3.6 (239.5 × 11.81); M (KHD); 13

45510 **TYRO** Ne/Ne (Giessen-De Noord) 1967; C; 1300; 84.23 × 4.49 (276.34 × 14.73); M (MWM); 14

45520 **SEA STRUGGLER** Gr/FRG (LF-W) 1964; C; 1200/1900; 81.23 × 4.83/5.87 (266.5 × 15.85/19.26); M (MAN); 13; ex *Elpirea* 1978; ex *Zebras Success* 1978; ex *Fredenhagen* 1974

45530 **SLOMAN NEREUS** FRG/FRG (Howaldts DW) 1977; C; 4400/7400; 129.52 × 6.87/8.06 (424.93 × 11.53/26.44); M (Atlas-MaK); 17; ex *Tabuco* 1980; ex *Sloman Nereus* 1980; ex *Carol Nereus* 1980; ex *Sloman Nereus* 1978; 'CL-10' type
Sisters (FRG flag):
45531 **SLOMAN NAJADE**
45532 **STUBBENHUK**
45533 **STEINHOFT** ex *E.L.M.A. Seis* 1982; ex *Steinhoft* 1981; ex *Gongola Hope* 1979; ex *Steinhoft* 1978

★45540 **OSKOL** class Ru/Pd (—) 1963/70; FA; 2500 Dspl; 90 × 4.5 (295.28 × 14.8); TSM (—); 16

● 45550 **SAINT FRANCOIS** Fr/Br (Bartram)—Po 1970/78; C/Con; 12400; 174.53 × 8.48 (572.6 × 27.82); M (Sulzer); 16; Modified 'SD 14' type. Lengthened and converted from general cargo (Lisnave)
Sister:
45551 **ST. PAUL** (Fr)

45560 **HIGHSEA PROMISE** Sg/FRG (B+V) 1970; C; 6700/10100; 162.8 × 7.5/8.94 (534.12 × 24.6/29.33); M (Pielstick); 18; ex *Dalmatia* 1980; ex *Concord Dalmatia* 1978; ex *Dalmatia* 1977; 'Pioneer' type

45570 **ATLANTIC CHARITY** Li/Ja (Hakodate) 1970; B; 16000; 180.32 × 10.64 (591.6 × 34.9); M (Sulzer); 15.25
Possible sisters:
45571 **ANGEBALTIC** (Gr) ex *Atlantic Challenge* 1981
45572 **BUDI** (Li) ex *Teno* 1981; ex *Mina L. Cambanis* 1975; ex *East Breeze* 1969 (May now have a gantry crane)

45580 **IMPERIAL SKEENA** Ca/Ca (Burrard DD) 1970; Tk; 3000; 91.45 × 5.56 (300.03 × 18.24); TS (British Polar); 12.5

★45590 **MANYCH** Ru/Ru (—) 1972; A/Rmt; 7500 Dspl; 115 × 6 (377 × 20); M (—); —
Sister:
★45591 **TAGIL** (Ru)

45600 **ODIN** FRG/US (—) —; FA/Repair Ship; 3500 Dspl; 100 × 2.8 (328 × 9.2); TSM (General Motors); 11.5; ex *U.S.S. Ulysses*
Sister:
45601 **WOTAN** (FRG) ex *U.S.S. Diomedes*

45610 **ATHINAI** Gr/Sw (Lindholmens) 1962; C;

7800/11100; 156.32 × 8.74/9.47 (513 × 28.67/31.07); M (Gotaverken); 17.75; ex *Popi* 1980; ex *Klipparen* 1979; ex *Cortina* 1974; ex *Goonawarra* 1971; At least one of this class, maybe both, has had the mast and kingpost in the well replaced by sets of tandem cranes
Sister (builder-Gotav):

45611 VENUS DEL MAR (Ur) ex *Temnaren* 1979; ex *Sestriere* 1975; ex *Parrakoola* 1971

45620 SHEARWATER BAY SA/FRG (Luerssen) 1964; C; 800/2000; 83.19 × 3.6/5.39 (272.93 × 11.81/17.68); M (KHD); 13.5; ex *Zwartkops* 1980; ex *Lohengrin* 1969

★**45630 OLA** Ru/Ja (Hitachi) 1964; C; 11100; 154.77 × 9.59 (507.78 × 31.46); M (B&W); 17.25
Sisters (Ru flag):
★**45631 OTRADNOE**
★**45632 OREKHOV**
★**45633 ORSHA**
★**45634 OSTRAGOZHSK**

45640 SUNFLOWER Ma/FRG (A Pahl) 1959; C; 2800/4000; 105.92 × 6.72/7.6 (347 × 22.05/24.93); M (KHD); 15; ex *Santa Pola* 1982; ex *Holstenland*; ex *Lindaunis* 1974; ex *Cap Bonavista* 1970

45650 BILBARAKAH Pa/Be (Beliard-Murdoch) 1963; C; 1200/1900; 83.19 × 5.02/6.12 (272.93 × 16.47/20.08); M(MAN); 14; ex *Southern Isles* 1979; ex *Helmi* 1973
Similar:
45651 ARIS EPTA (Cy) ex *Aris VII* 1982; ex *Armando Reveron* 1981; ex *Alefani* 1976; ex *Alhena* 1974

45670 LAUTAN ENAM My/FRG (Luerssen) 1953; C; 1600; 76.79 × 5.44 (251.93 × 17.85); M (MaK); 8; ex *Menado* 1980; ex *Ingane* 1977; ex *Skagenhorn* 1964; ex *Colonia* 1961

★**45680 IZHMALES** Ru/Fi (Valmet) 1962; C; 2900; 102.32 × 5.91 (335.7 × 19.39); M (B&W); 13
Sisters (Ru flag):
★**45681 IRKUTSKLES**
★**45682 IGARKALES**
★**45683 INKURLES**
★**45684 IRBITLES**
★**45685 IRSHALES**
★**45686 IZHEVSKLES**
★**45687 ILMENLES**
★**45688 IRTYSHLES**
★**45689 IZHORALES**
★**45690 ISTRA**
★**45691 PERMLES**

★**45700 OSKOL III** type. Ru/Pd (—) 1963/70; FA; 2500 Dspl; 90 × 4.5 (295.28 × 14.8); TSM (—); 16

★**45710 DORNBUSCH** DDR/DDR (Peene) 1965; Cbl/BT; 750; 64 × 3.35 (210 × 11); D-E (Johannisthal); 13.5

★**45720 ALLIGATOR III** class. Ru/Ru (—) 1968; A/LC; 4100 Dspl; 113 × 4.4 (371 × 12); TSM (—); 18

●★**45730 AMGA** Ru/Ru (—) —; A/Missile Support Ship; 6400 Dspl; 102 × 5.8 (361 × 19); M (—); 18

45740 CHALLENGER 1 Li/Ne (Jan Smit) 1956; CS; 10900; 193.2 × 10.25 (633.86 × 33.63); T (Stork); 16; ex *Challenger* 1970; ex *P G Thulin*; Widened 1970; Converted Ore/Oil Carrier 1970 (Boele's Sch)

45750 KADAS 1 Gh/FRG (Adler) 1960; C; 1400/2200; 86.39 × 5.02/6.02 (238.43 × 16.47/19.75); M (Borsig); 13; ex *Gulf Anglia* 1977; ex *Alkes* 1975; ex *Alk*; Lengthened 1967

45760 ATLANTA Fi/Br (Smith's D) 1972; C; 8900; 154.9 × 9.17 (508.2 × 30.08); M (Sulzer); 19
Sister:
45761 AURORA (Fi)

●**45770 MILOS** Li/Sw (Eriksbergs) 1966; C; 7300/10700; 156.17 × 8.36/9.52 (512.37 × 27.42/31.23); M (B&W); 19; ex *Pulawy* 1982; ex *Waitara* 1973; 'Scandia' type
Sister:
45771 HELLENIC SEAMAN (Gr) ex *Killara* 1975

45772 LOK NAYAK In/Rm (Galatz) 1974; B; 10900; (145.12 × 10.15 (476 × 33.30); M (Sulzer); 16
Sisters (In flag):
45773 LOK PALAK
45774 LOK MANYA
45775 LOK SAHAYAK
45776 LOK VIHAR
45777 ANUPAMA
45778 ANNAPURNA
45779 ARCHANA
45779/1 ARADHANA

45780 LORENZO Pa/FRG (LF-W) 1969; B; 26100; 216.14 × 11.87 (709.12 × 38.94); M (MAN); 16; ex

Cast Porpoise 1982; ex *E R Montreal* 1978; ex *Reinhart Lorenz Russ* 1975; Used as a container ship; May have cranes removed

●**45790 WOOLLAHRA** Sw/Sw (Eriksbergs) - Br 1967/71; C/Con; 9400/13100; 178.54 × 8.47/9.51 (585.76 × 27.79/31.2); M (B&W); 17.5; ex *Saint Jacques* 1981; ex *Woolahra* 1978; Lengthened and converted from general cargo 1971 (Swan Hunter)
Sister:
45791 SAINT LUC (Fr) ex *Talarah* 1980

45800 ELOCEAN Gr/FRG (Bremer V) 1965; B; 20500; 196.63 × 11.03 (645.11 × 36.19); M(MAN); 15.25; ex *Stove Vulcan* 1973

45810 ANDAMAN SEA Pa/Br (Upper Clyde) 1969; B; 22200; 193.1 × 11.25 (633.53 × 36.91); M (Sulzer); 15.5; ex *Northamptonshire*; ex *Volnay*

45820 MISTI Pe/Be (Boelwerf) 1969; B; 22400; 203.77 × 11.37 (668.53 × 37.3); M (MAN); 15.5; ex *Asean Objective* 1981; ex *E.R. Scaldia*; Now converted to bulk/container, may be altered in appearance

45830 DEKA NAVIGATOR Gr/Ja (Namura) 1965; C; 7700; 139.93 × 8.7 (459.08 × 28.54); M (Sulzer); 15.5; ex *Rio De Janeiro Maru*
Sisters:
45831 MATHILDA (Gr) ex *Rosario Maru* 1980
45832 AL-KHAMES (Si) ex *Char Loong* 1982; ex *Cheer Cetus* 1980; ex *Recife Maru*
45833 AL-KHAMES 2 (Si) ex *Char Hoong* 1982; ex *Cape Cetus*; ex *Rio Grande Maru*

45840 WARSCHAU FRG/FRG (Flensburger) 1976; B; 30300; 213.39 × 12.17 (700.09 × 39.93); M (MAN); 16
Sisters:
45841 EMMA JOHANNA (FRG)
45842 DRESDEN (FRG)
45843 THAMESFIELD (Br)

45845 OAK SUN Li/Ja (Koyo) 1982; B; 29500; 223.15 × 13.02 (732 × 42.72); M (B&W); 14.75

●**45850 BUDAPEST** Sg/FRG (Bremer V) 1971; B; 24600; 203.18 × 11.6 (666.6 × 38.06); M (MAN); 16
Probably similar:
45851 PRAG (Sg)

●**45860 DESPINA GIAVRIDIS** Gr/No (Fredriksstad) 1967; B; 11700; 165.64 × 9.31 (543.44 × 30.54); (Gotaverken); 14.5; ex *Bulk Pioneer* 1977
Sisters:
45861 THEODOROS GIAVRIDIS (Gr) ex *Bulk Explorer* 1975
45862 ATLANTIC MARINER (Li) ex *Sunward* 1980; ex *Rea* 1978; ex *Ringar* 1972

45880 NGAPARA NZ/Br (Caledon) 1966; C; 4500; 111.89 × 7.16 (367 × 23.49); M (British Polar); 12.5
Sisters:
45881 NGAHERE (NZ)
45882 GIANT TREASURE (Pa) ex *Ngakuta* 1983
45883 FADEL G (Le) ex *Anthony P.* 1981; ex *Kapetan Antonis* 1981; ex *Florentia* 1977; ex *Ngatoro* 1976

★**45890 KUANG HAI** RC/No (Fredriksstad) 1965; B; 21900; 193.35 × 11.15 (634.35 × 36.58); M (Gotaverken); 14.5; ex *Roald Jarl* 1974

45900 ABBY Pa/Ja (IHI) 1965; C; 12500; 165.31 × 8.99 (542.36 × 29.49); M (Sulzer); 14; ex *Philippi* 1982; ex *Wako Maru* 1975

45910 ARIEL Fi/De (Helsingor) 1970; C; 4900/7600; 147.02 × 6.79/7.7 (482.34 × 22.28/25.26); M (B&W); 17.5; Lengthened 1974
Sisters (Fi flag):
45911 RHEA
45912 PALLAS

45920 UNIDO FRG/Ko (Korea SB) 1979; C/Con; 13000; 155 × 8.7 (508.5 × 28.54); M (Sulzer); 17
Sister:
45921 AMADO (FRG)

●**45930 SAMOA** De/De (Nakskov) 1978; C; 16200; 159.42 × 10.59 (523.03 × 34.74); M (B&W); 16
Sisters (De flag):
45931 SARGODHA
45933 TARASCO ex *Siena* 1983
45934 SINALOA
(Pk flag):
45935 MAKRAN
(Ir Flag):
45936 IRAN TEYFOURI ex *Simba* 1984

45940 MESANGE Ca/Sw (Eriksbergs) 1969; C; 6000/9600; 140.04 × 7.89/9.52 (459.45 × 25.89/31.23); M (Pielstick); 16.75; ex *Sunemerillon* 1982; ex *Boreland* 1979; 'Scandia' type
Sister:
★**45941 YU JIANG** (RC) ex *Birkaland*

45950 VITINA Gr/Br (A&P) 1975; B; 15000; 183.04

× 10.47 (600.52 × 34.35); M (Sulzer); 15; ex *Anna M* 1978; 'B-26' type
Sister:
45951 KASSOS (Gr) ex *Camilla M* 1980

45960 CHENNAI JAYAM In/FRG (Bremer V) 1965; B; 24400; 203.16 × 11.6 (666.54 × 38.05); M (MAN); 14
Sisters (In flag):
45961 CHENNAI OOKKAM
45962 CHENNAI PERUMAI
45963 CHENNAI SADHANAI
45964 CHENNAI SELVAM

★**45967 GU HAI** RC/Sw (Uddevalla) 1968; B; 26500; 217.61 × 12.81 (714 × 42.03); M (B&W); 15.5; ex *Spyros A. Lemos* 1974

45970 MULTI CARRIER Pa/Ja (Mitsubishi HI) 1967; C; 6700; 155.73 × 8.64 (510.92 × 28.34); M (Sulzer); 18.5; ex *Sacramento Maru*
Sisters:
45971 ELENA (Ma) ex *Helen* 1981; ex *St. Louis Maru* 1980
45972 CHAOHU CAREER (Pa) ex *San Francisco Maru*
45973 TRANS KOSTAS (Gr) ex *Bilquis* 1982; ex *Savannah Maru* 1982

★**45980 QINGHAI** RC/Br (Blyth) 1962; B; 14500; 188.63 × 9.78 (618.86 × 32.08); M (Sulzer); 15; ex *Ipanema* 1973; ex *Corcovado* 1973; ex *Chapel River* 1970
Similar:
45981 SAINT NEKTARIOS (Li) ex *Artadi* 1982; ex *Canopus* 1973; ex *Pacific Princess* 1970

45990 BELNOR No/No (Fredriksstad) 1977; B; 23000; 193.45 × 11.77 (634.67 × 38.61); M (Sulzer); —; ex *Norbulk* 1984; ex *Melsomvik* 1979

46000 BELSTAR No/No (Fredriksstad) 1972; B; 22500; 193.45 × 11.76 (634.68 × 38.58); M (Gotaverken); 15
Similar:
46001 ALEPPO (Sw)
46002 PAN DYNASTY (Ko) ex *Belita* 1977; ex *Viator* 1974
46003 SKYPTRON (Gr) ex *Dolores De Plandolit* 1981; ex *Sandvaag* 1978
46004 STOVE CAMPBELL (No)
46005 STOVE TRANSPORT (Sw)
(RC flag):
★**46006 AN HAI** ex *Sandar* 1977
★**46007 HU PO HAI** ex *Bulk Promoter* 1977
★**46008 JIN HAI** ex *Ringstad* 1977
★**46009 LIULINHAI** ex *Belnor* 1977
★**46010 MEI GUI HAI** ex *Bulk Prospector* 1977

●**46020 DESPINA GIAVRIDIS** Gr/No (Fredriksstad) 1967; B; 11700; 165.64 × 9.31 (543.44 × 30.54); M (Gotaverken); 14.5; ex *Bulk Pioneer* 1977
Sisters:
46021 THEODOROS GIAVRIDIS (Gr) ex *Bulk Explorer* 1975
46022 ATLANTIC MARINER (Li) ex *Sunward* 1980; ex *Rea* 1978; ex *Ringar* 1972

46030 GINA JULIANO It/Ja (Namura) 1967; B; 15700; 174.83 × 10.22 (572.11 × 33.53); M (B&W); 15.5; ex *Ross Sea* 1978

●**46040 HACI SEFER KALKAVAN** Tu/No (Haugesund) 1973; B; 11200; 161.55 × 9.7 (530.02 × 31.82); M (Gotaverken); 15.5; ex *Kiki Yemelos* 1982; ex *Cape Clear* 1973
Sister:
46041 SATYA SOHAN (In) ex *Baron Forbes* 1973

46050 ASTRA PEAK Pa/Ja (NKK) 1976; C; 12800; 161.02 × 10.37 (528.28 × 34.02); M (Sulzer); 17
Sisters (Pa flag):
46051 GLORIA PEAK
46052 PRIMERA PEAK

46060 AL TAJDAR Li/FRG (Bremer V) 1965; B; 20500; 196.55 × 11.03 (644.85 × 36.18); M (MAN); 15; ex *Germa*; ex *Claro* 1974; ex *Olav Ringdal* 1970

46070 MARITSA P LEMOS Gr/Ys ('3 Maj') 1972; B; 17500; 196.6 × 10.86 (645.01 × 35.63); M (Sulzer); 15.5
Sister:
★**46071 WU SHENG HAI** (RC) ex *Nicolaos Pateras* 1980
Similar:
★**46073 ZHAO YANG HAI** (RC) ex *Mericunda*
★**46074 HERCEGOVINA** (Ys)

46080 PANAGIOTIS S Gr/Sp (Juliana/Euskalduna) 1966; C; 13000; 173.31 × 10.26 (568.6 × 33.66); M (Sulzer); 14.5; ex *Emilia Loverdos* 1975; ex *Vizcaya* 1973
Similar:
46081 MONTE ZALAMA (Sp) lengthened and may

have an extra crane

46090 **ON YEUNG** Pa/Ru (Baltic) 1972; B; 23200; 199.9 × 11.23 (655.84 × 36.84); M (B&W) 16; ex *Figaro* 1978; 'Baltika' type
Sister:
46091 **BEDFORD** (Li) ex *Saint Etienne* 1982; ex *Ravenna*; ex *Nopal Ravenna* 1976; ex *Star Ravenna* 1975
Similar:
46092 **ON LEE** (Pa) ex *Madame Butterfly* 1978
46093 **AKBAR** (Br) ex *Traviata* 1977
46094 **WILLIAM** (Sg) ex *August Bolten* 1977; Launched as *Renate*
Possibly similar:
46095 **LUIS BANCHERO** (Pe)

46100 **WORLD ARGUS** Gr/Gr (Hellenic) 1973; B; 19500; 193.43 × 11.35 (634.61 × 37.23); M (Sulzer); 15
Similar (Gr flag):
46101 **WORLD APOLLO**
46102 **WORLD ARES**
46103 **WORLD AJAX**
46104 **WORLD AGAMEMNON**
46105 **WORLD ARETUS**
46106 **WORLD MARINE**
46107 **DAPHNE**
46108 **FOTINI**
46109 **JOANNA**
46110 **APHRODITE**
46111 **TARPON SEALANE**
46112 **MILLY GREGOS** ex *Scapwill*
46113 **WORLD AMPHION**
46114 **ANITA DAN** (Bs) ex *Asian Adventuress* 1981; ex *Aldgate* 1979; ex *Scapdale* 1979
46115 **IRON CUMBERLAND** (Br) ex *World Achilles* (Li flag)
46116 **WORLD ACHILLES II**
Possible sister:
46117 **WORLD AEGEUS** (Gr)

46120 **LUJUA** Sp/Sp (Euskalduna) 1968; B; 15500; 183.12 × 10.52 (600.78 × 34.51); M (MAN); 15
Sisters (Sp flag):
46121 **MONTE ZAPOLA**
46122 **MONTE ZAMBURU**
46123 **MONTE ZARAYA**
46124 **SERANTES**

46130 **MINORIES PRIDE** Pa/Ne (Verolme Scheeps) 1964; B; 18300; 183.9 × 11.17 (603.35 × 36.64); M (MAN); —; ex *Liberian Statesman* 1981; ex *President William V S. Tubman* 1973

46140 **GOLDEN HILL** Pa/Ne (Verolme Scheeps) 1965; B; 16600; 196.42 × 10.91 (611.61 × 35.79); M (Stork); 14.5; ex *Amstelburcht* 1982; ex *Hollands Burcht* 1977

46150 **PELAGOS** Gr/Ja (Osaka) 1967; B; 16000; 171.58 × 10.23 (562.93 × 33.56); M (Sulzer); 15; ex *Neptune* 1976; ex *Jean* 1969

46160 **CORAL** Ko/De (B&W) 1965; B; 10300; 152.43 × 9.06 (500.09 × 29.72); M (B&W); 14.75; ex *Belita* 1974

46170 **LYDI** Gr/Sw (Uddevalla) 1970; B; 13000; 168.99 × 10.27 (554.43 × 33.69); M (B&W); 16; ex *Norse Captain* 1982; ex *Norse Viking* 1980
Sisters:
46171 **PATRICIA** (Gr) ex *Norse Captain*
46172 **EIRA** (Fi) ex *Norse River* 1982

46180 **ATLANTIC EXPRESS** LI/De (B&W) 1960; C; 5800; 141.54 × 7.87 (464.37 × 25.82); M (B&W); 16; ex *Domino Crystal* 1973

46190 **DEMETRIOS** Gr/Sw (Oresunds) 1967; B; 10800; 156.85 × 9.32 (514.6 × 30.57); M (Gotaverken); 15; ex *Eleftherotria*; ex *Bertil Karlbom* 1972

46200 **VISSANI** Pa/No (Fredriksstad) 1966; B; 11300; 165.67 × 9.29 (543.53 × 30.48); M (Gotaverken); 15; ex *Universe Clipper* 1983; ex *Tradition* 1980; ex *Lamant* 1975; ex *Belcargo* 1973

★46210 **LIN HAI** RC/FRG (Bremer V) 1966; B; 10700; 161.6 × 9.36 (530.18 × 30.7); M (MAN); 14.5; ex *Atenalia* 1976; ex *Aleppo* 1973

●46212 **WATERGEUS** Ne/DDR (Mathias-Thesen) 1980; C/Con; 15800; 178.52 × 10.11 (586 × 33.17); M (MAN); 15; ex *Papagena* 1981; 'MBC' type
Sisters:
46213 **IRENE GREENWOOD** (Au) ex *Stephan Reeckmann* 1984
46214 **KWEILIN** (Br) ex *Palapur* 1982
46215 **MIRA** (Sg) ex *Finnsailor* 1983; ex *Paloma* 1983
46216 **VEGA** (Sg) ex *Pamina* 1982; ex *CP Hunter* 1981; ex *Pamina* 1980
46217 **NORASIA DAGMAR** (Li) ex *Dagmar Reeckmann* 1983

46220 **OCEAN LEO** Pa/Sw (Oresunds) 1968; B; 17000; 175.27 × 10.24 (575.03 × 33.59); M (Gotaverken); 15; ex *Valetta* 1982

46230 **PAPUA** Sg/FRG (O&K) 1971; C; 5100; 117.2 × 7.53 (384.51 × 24.7); M (Atlas-MaK); 16.5; ex *Waigani Express* 1981; ex *Ballatrix* 1978
Sister:
46231 **LANKA MAHAPOLA** (Sg) ex *Niugini* 1982; ex *Niugini Express* 1982; ex *Beteigueze* 1978

46235 **YAMAOKI MARU** Ja/Ja (Kasado) 1981; B; 30000; 190.03 × 12.12 (623 × 39.76); M (Mitsubishi); 14

●46240 **TESABA** Cy/Sp (Cadiz) 1964; C; 2700/4300; 121.37 × 6.09/6.95 (398.19 × 19.98/22.8); M (Gotaverken); 15; ex *Valencia* 1977; ex *Hispania* 1968; Lengthened 1968
Sisters:
46241 **TELINDA** (Cy) ex *Hangving* 1977; ex *Gallia* 1974
46242 **TEMURA** (Cy) ex *Industria* 1977
46243 **EDDAR EL BEIDA** (Sy) ex *Bonne Bay* 1984; ex *Scania* 1973
46244 **GADA** (Eg) ex *Ikaria* 1974; ex *Italia* 1974
46245 **SCOL RESIDENT** (Sw) ex *Sagoland* 1978
★46246 **XINDU** (RC) ex *Dalmatia* 1976

●★46250 **LUAN HE** RC/FRG (Howaldts DW) 1978; C/Con; 169.02 × 9.95 (554.53 × 32.64); M (Pielstick); 15; ex *Victoria Bay* 1983; ex *Columbia* 1981; ex *Arabian Strength* 1979; Launched as *Columbia*
Sisters:
★46251 **TUO HE** (RC) ex *California* 1983; ex *Arabian Endeavour* 1981; Launched as *California*
★46252 **WEI HE** (RC) ex *Nedlloyd Caledonia* 1983; ex *Caledonia* 1981

●46255 **BARRISTER** FRG/FRG (Howaldts DW) 1981; B/Con; 18600; 169.04 × 9.96 (555 × 32.68); M (Sulzer); 16.5; ex *Carmen* 1981
Sisters:
46256 **CITY OF LIVERPOOL** (FRG)
46257 **CONSCIENCE** (FRG)
46258 **CRANACH** (FRG)

46260 **BORGESTAD** No/Ys ('Uljanik') 1969; B; 18500; 163.02 × 11.09 (534.84 × 36.38); M (B&W); 15.5
Sisters:
46261 **MILENA** (No)
46262 **SHIROGANE** (Br) ex *Silvermain* 1982

●★46280 **HUA YING** RC/FRG (Unterweser) 1969; C; 3100/5600; 124.49 × 6.3/7.55 (408.43 × 20.67/24.77); M (KHD); 17; ex *Wah Ying* 1984; ex *Cathrin* 1983; ex *Franziska Drescher* 1978; ex *Wahele* 1977; ex *Ede Sottorf* 1975
Sisters:
★46281 **NAN KUN** (RC) ex *Tandoc* 1983; ex *Terzia* 1981; ex *Wille 1* 1980; ex *Columbus Noumea* 1978; ex *Willi Reith* 1977
46282 **BARBARA LEONHARDT** (Pa) ex *Wille II* 1980; ex *Columbus Tahiti* 1978; ex *Meta Reith* 1977
Similar:
46283 **PARTEM** (Pa) ex *Maco* 1982; ex *Freestar* 1982; ex *Albega* 1980; ex *Matten 1* 1980; ex *Matthias Reith* 1978;
46284 **JOLO** (Pa) ex *Mega* 1983; ex *Tama* 1982; ex *Matten II* 1980; ex *Grethe Reith* 1978

46290 **GALILA** Is/FRG (O&K) 1967; C; 3000/4900; 123.4 × 6.45/7.59 (405 × 21.16/24.9); M (MAN); —; launched as *Cinnamon Bay*

46300 **SIMONA 1** Pa/It ('Navalmeccanica') 1963; B; 17300; 192.01 × 10.59 (629.95 × 39.74); M (Fiat); —; ex *Simonetta* 1981

46305 **APJ ANJLI** In/Ja (Kanasashi) 1982; B; 16900; 176.00 × 10.40 (577 × 34.12); M (Sulzer); 14.8
Sister:
46306 **APJ SUSHMA** (In)

●46310 **NEW ZEALAND ALLIANCE** Br/Ja (NKK) 1976; B; 20100; 177.02 × 11.16 (580.77 × 36.61); M (Sulzer); 15.5; ex *Eastern Alliance* 1982; ex *Bolnes* 1981
Sisters:
★46311 **VLADIMIR GAVRILOV** (Ru) ex *Borgnes* 1983;
46312 **BRAVENES** (Li)
★46313 **PYOTR SMORODIN** (Ru) ex *Becknes* 1983
46314 **BELLNES** (Li)
46315 **BEDOUIN BIRKNES** (Li) ex *Birknes* 1977
46316 **BROOKNES** (FRG)
46317 **GENERAL MASCARDO** (Pi) ex *Brisknes* 1983
46318 **IRON CAPRICORN** (Br) launched as *Bergnes*

46320 **MARINA DI ALIMURI** It/Br (Lithgows) 1972; B; 22900; 178.31 × 10.36 (585 × 33.99); M (B&W); 15; ex *Bernes* 1980

46330 **SEALIONET** Pa/Sw (Gotav) 1965; B; 22100; 200.31 × 11.1 (657.19 × 36.42); M (Gotaverken); —; ex *Robert Stove* 1978; ex *Vesteroy* 1973
Similar:
46331 **GOULIAS** (Gr) ex *Norbega* 1977; ex *Stormqueen* 1971
46332 **OSMAN AKSOY** (Tu) ex *Union Spirit* 1981; ex *Dagland* 1973
46333 **GLYFADA FAITH** (Gr) ex *Norbrott*
46334 **CHI STAR** (Pa) ex *Aegis Storm*; ex *Vinni* 1974
46335 **STALO 2** (Gr) ex *Athos* 1974
★46336 **BAI YUN HAI** (RC) ex *Aegis Thunder*; ex *Vigan* 1974
46337 **IRENES SUCCESS** (Gr) ex *Petingo* 1974; ex *Vanessa* 1970
★46338 **MING HAI** (RC) ex *Rudolph Olsen* 1974
★46339 **JIA HAI** (RC) ex *Pytheas* 1977
★46340 **ZHEN RONG HAI** (RC) ex *Amax McGregor* 1980
★46341 **HENNIGSDORF** (DDR) ex *Pontos* 1972

★46350 **MING JOY** Tw/Ja (Sanoyasu) 1971; B; 16100; 165.56 × 10.42 (543.17 × 34.18); M (Sulzer); 14.5; ex *Ji Ming* 1977; ex *Hai Jung* 1973; '26-BC-5' type
Sisters (Tw flag):
46351 **MING LEADER** ex *Li Ming* 1977; ex *Hai Lo* 1973
46352 **MING SHINE** ex *Shin Ming* 1977; ex *Hai Chuan* 1973
Possible sister (Ko flag):
46353 **GLOBAL STAR** ex *Manna* 1980; ex *Thai Yung* 1973

★46360 **HUA SHENG** RC/Fi (Valmet) 1971; C; 3700/6200; 129.09 × 6.62/7.97 (423.52 × 21.72/26.15); M (B&W); ex *Yan He*; ex *Herakles* 1980

★46370 **LIEBENWALDE** DDR/DDR ('Neptun') 1977; C; 3500/5700; 120.61 × —/7.83 (395.7 × —/25.69); M (MAN); 16.75
Sisters (DDR flag):
★46371 **CUNEWALDE**
★46372 **LUCKENWALDE**
★46373 **SCHONWALDE**
★46374 **GERINGSWALDE**
★46375 **MITTENWALDE**
★46376 **FURSTENWALDE**
★46377 **EICHWALDE**
★46378 **RUDOLF DIESEL**
★46379 **ARENDSEE**
★46380 **BLANKENSEE**
★46381 **FLESSENSEE**
★46382 **MUGGELSEE**
★46383 **WERBELLINSEE**
★46384 **KOLPINSEE**
★46385 **INSELSEE**
★46386 **RHINSEE**
★46387 **SCHWIELOSEE**
★46388 **TRENNTSEE**

46390 **POLLUX** Fi/No (Haugesund) 1977; C; 7400/14700; 154.97 × 7.48/9.2 (508.43 × 24.54/30.18); M (Sulzer); 17
Sister:
46391 **PATRIA** (Fi)

46400 **MARILOULA** Cy/De (B&W) 1974; B; 30300; 221.75 × 12.09 (727.52 × 39.66); M (B&W) 16; ex *Milross* 1982; ex *Rodin* 1976; Cranes not shown on drawing as exact positions are not known

46410 **THULELAND** Sw/Sw (Eriksbergs) 1977; B; 21100; 185.86 × 11.28 (609.77 × 37); M (B&W); 16
Sister:
46411 **COLUMBIALAND** (Sw) ex *Seatrain London* 1979; ex *Columbialand* 1979

46420 **LEENOR** Is/Fi (Rauma-Repola) 1963; C; 3000/5000; 130.97 × 6.21/7.34 (429.69 × 20.37/24); M (Sulzer); 16; ex *Argo* 1981; Lengthened 1970
Sister:
46421 **SASSA** (Pa) ex *Leeor* 1982; ex *Virgo* 1981

46424 **WORLD PRIZE** Pa/Ja (Osaka) 1980; B; 14400; 170.52 × 10.06 (559 × 33.01); M (B&W); 14.75
Sisters:
46425 **WORLD CHEER** (Pa)
46426 **WORLD GLEN** (Pa)
★46427 **KAPITAN TRUBKIN** (Ru) ex *Manila Spirit* 1983; ex *Jaylock* 1981

●46430 **STASIA** Gr/Br (Upper Clyde) 1970; B; 16600; 173.59 × 9.96 (569.52 × 32.67); M (B&W); 15.25; ex *Vancouver City*; 'CARDIFF' class
Sisters:
46431 **PORT ALBERNI CITY** (Br)
46432 **YAQUI** (Pa) ex *Prince Rupert City* 1982
46433 **LACANDON** (Sg) ex *Victoria City* 1983

46434 **OLMECA** (Pa) ex *Fresno City* 1982
46435 **TACOMA CITY** (Br)
46436 **KASSIA** (Gr) ex *New Westminster City* 1983
Similar:
46437 **HOMERIC DAWN** (Gr) ex *Norse Pilot* 1984
46438 **NORSE MARSHAL** (Br)
(Ih flag):
46443 **IRISH MAPLE**
(RC flag):
★46446 **AN DA HAI** ex *Norse Trader* 1977
(Gr flag):
46448 **ANASTASIOS** ex *Cinchona* 1981
46449 **SIGANTO A S** ex *Irish Pine* 1983
46450 **ELPIDOFOROS** ex *Camara* 1981
(Li flag):
46451 **ALEV** ex *Irish Oak* 1982
(Pa flag):
46452 **CONSTANTIA** ex *Irish Larch* 1983
46453 **KEFALONIA HOPE** ex *Norse Carrier* 1982; ex
Norse Herald 1981
(Tu flag):
46454 **NAZLI K** ex *Star Oriole* 1982; ex *Golden
Oriole* 1981
46455 **ZEYNEP K** ex *Golden Anne* 1982

46460 **DONA PAZ II** Pi/Br (Govan) 1977; B; 16200;
175.14 × 9.96 (574.6 × 32.67); M (B&W); 15; ex
Dona Paz 1981; 'Cardiff' class
Sisters (Pi flag):
46461 **DONA MAGDALENA**
46462 **DONA HORTENCIA II**
46463 **DON SALVADOR III**

46470 **ANTACUS** Li/Br (Scotstoun) 1973; B; 16700;
175.11 × 9.98 (574.5 × 32.74); M (B&W); 15.5; ex
Atlas 1981; ex *Chi Grace*; ex *Harfleet*; 'Cardiff' class
Sister:
46471 **ARION** (Li) ex *Andromeda* 1981; ex *Chi Trust*
1980; ex *Harfleur* 1979

● 46480 **ASIA HUNTER** Li/Ja (Sumitomo) 1971; B;
17600; 171.25 × 11.02 (561.84 × 36.15); M (Sulzer);
15

46490 **PETROPOLIS** Gr/Ja (Osaka) 1977; B; 15600;
169.63 × 9.62 (556.53 × 31.56); M (Sulzer); 15; ex
Triton 1982

46493 **CAVOURELLA** Li/Ja (Osaka) 1982; B;
15600; 169.60 × 9.62 (556 × 31.56); M (Sulzer); 15
Probable sister:
46494 **MIA** (Li)

46500 **HECTOR** Gr/Ja (Osaka) 1975; B; 14500;
169.63 × 9.57 (556.52 × 31.39); M (Sulzer); 15.5; ex
Marina Grande 1982; ex *Astros* 1980
Sister:
46501 **DESERT WIND** (Li)

46510 **GUARDIAN** Cy/Ja (Namura) 1971; B;
19400; 187 × 10.79 (613.52 × 35.4); M (Sulzer);
14.5; ex *Toyota Maru No 14* 1982
Sister:
46511 **VANGUARD** (Cy) ex *Vanguard Alpha* 1983;
ex *Soyo Maru* 1978
46512 **ELENI M** (Ma) ex *Toyota Maru No 7* 1981
46513 **SEASONG** (Cy) ex *Antonelli* 1983; ex *Toyota
Maru No 8* 1981
Similar:
46514 **TOYOTA MARU No 19** (Ja)
46515 **HAN RIVER** (Ko) ex *Chiba* 1982

★46517 **XING HAI** RC/FRG (Flensburger) 1961; B;
19300; 196.37 × 11.00 (644 × 36.09); M (MAN);
15.5; ex *Solomon Sea* 1974; ex *Pina* 1973; ex *Naess
Favorita* 1968

● 46520 **SUNNINGDALE** Sg/No (Fredriksstad) 1969;
B; 11300; 165.67 × 9.31 (543.53 × 30.54); M (Gotaverken); 15.5; ex *Stove Tradition*
Similar:
46521 **ELJIANNI** (Gr) ex *Melsomvik* 1973
46522 **NEGEV ORON** (Li) ex *Agioi Victores* 1981; ex
Expectation 1976
46523 **MARIA X** (Gr) ex *Stove Ocean* 1977; ex
Belocean 1975
46524 **UNION AUCKLAND** (Br) ex *Columbia*
46526 **GEORGIOS F** (Gr) ex *Frixos D* 1980; ex *James
Stove* 1973
46527 **CAROLINE** (Pa) ex *Eastwind* 1980; ex *Stove
Scotia* 1973
46528 **TELFAIR TRADER** (Li) ex *Santa Pola* 1981; ex
Ringvard 1973
★46529 **AN JI HAI** (RC) ex *Stove Friend* 1977

46540 **GAROUFALIA** Gr/Ja (Kasado) 1968; B;
12300; 158.5 × 9.18 (520 × 30.12); M (Sulzer); 15; ex
Pacific Defender 1982

46545 **SHIRAHAMA MARU** Ja/Ja (NKK) 1980; B;
17800; 175.01 × 10.45 (574 × 34.28); M (Pielstick);
14.25; ex *Sea Virgo* 1982; ex *Virgo Ace* 1982; ex
Universal Beauty 1982
Sister:

46546 **NOJIMA MARU** (Ja) ex *Cadmus Star* 1982;
ex *Sea Anemone* 1982; ex *Universal Benefit* 1982

46550 **HAWK** Cy/Ja (NKK) 1964; C; 10300; 150.68
× 9.02 (494.35 × 29.59); M (Sulzer); 14.5; ex *Atlantic
Ocean* 1982; ex *Atlantica* 1981; ex *Ashby Maru* 1976

46555 **NEPTUNE DOLPHIN** FRG/FRG (A G 'Weser') 1980; C/Con; 9200; 145.01 × 8.21 (476 ×
26.94); M (MaK); 17.75; ex *Sofati Canada* 1982; ex
Holstencarrier 1982; ex *E.L.M.A. Dos* 1982; ex *Holstencarrier* 1980; 'Key 12' type
Sister:
46556 **HOLSTENRACER** (FRG)

● 46560 **NEW ZEALAND ALLIANCE** Br/Ja (NKK)
1976; B; 20100; 177.02 × 11.16 (580.77 × 36.61); M
(Sulzer); 15.5; ex *Eastern Alliance* 1982; ex *Bolnes*
1981
Sisters:
★46561 **VLADIMIR GAVRILOV** (Ru) ex *Borgnes*
1983
46562 **BRAVENES** (Li)
★46563 **PYOTR SMORODIN** (Ru) ex *Becknes* 1983
46564 **BELLNES** (Li)
46565 **BEDOUIN BIRKNES** (Li) ex *Birknes* 1977
46566 **BROOKNES** (FRG)
46567 **GENER   MASCARDO** (Pi) ex *Brisknes*
1983
46568 **IRON CAPRICORN** (Br) Launched as
Bergnes

46580 **ACHILLES** Sg/Ja (Mitsui) 1972; B; 16400;
176.77 × 10.66 (579.95 × 34.97); M (B&W); 15.25
Sisters:
46581 **AJAX** (Br)
★46582 **AYTODOR** (Ru) ex *Anchises* 1983
46583 **ALICIA** (Gr) ex *Protoporos* 1983; ex *Agamemnon* 1978
46584 **SIDERIS** (Li) ex *Antenor* 1978
Similar:
46585 **CHLOE** (Gr) ex *Ocean Rentis* 1976; Launched
as *Ocean Retla*
46586 **SHENANDOAH** (Gr)
46587 **KENTUCKY HOME** (Gr)
46588 **SABIE** (Pa) ex *S A Sabie*
★46589 **PRESIDENTE ALLENDE** (Cu)
46589/1 **MARILY** (Gr) ex *Paget* 1980; ex *Endeavor*
1977
Possibly similar
46590 **S A SKUKUZA** (SA) ex *Skukuza* 1975

46600 **DONA SOPHIA** Gr/Ja (Kasado) 1978; B;
15200; 172.02 × 10.63 (564.37 × 34.88); M (Sulzer);
17
Similar:
46601 **GEORGIS GERONTAS** (Gr)

46610 **ALEXANDRA N** In/Sw (Kockums) 1965; B;
16700; 175.88 × 10.43 (577.03 × 34.22); M (MAN);
15; ex *Falkanger* 1974
Sister:
46611 **CHARISMA N** (In) ex *Fossanger* 1974

★46620 **YASMOYE** Ru/No (Kaldnes) 1967; B;
15800; 180.3 × 10.21 (591.54 × 33.5); M (Gotaverk-
en); 15; ex *Cornas*; ex *Torm Gyda* 1977; ex *Gyda* 1974

46630 **RUBENS** Br/Be (Boelwerf) 1976; B; 18000;
190.02 × 10.79 (623.42 × 35.4); M (MAN); 15.75

46640 **ATHOLL FOREST** Gr/Sw (Oresunds) 1967;
B; 17400; 175.22 × 9.88 (574.86 × 32.41); M (Gotaverken); 15.5; ex *Columbialand* 1976
Sister:
46641 **OCEAN VENUS** (Pa) ex *Karamu Forest* 1981;
ex *Victoria* 1977
Similar:
46642 **KANUKA FOREST** (Sg) ex *Gimleland* 1977
46643 **ASIAN FOREST** (Gr) ex *Caledonian Forest*
1978; ex *Virginia* 1976; ex *Gimleskog* 1972

46650 **APTMARINER** Br/Br (Sunderland) 1979; B;
18000; 188.75 × 10.66 (619.3 × 34.97); M (Doxford);
15; ex *Devonbrook* 1980
Sisters:
46651 **HANDYMARINER** (Br) ex *Durhambrook*
1980
46652 **NOSIRA LIN** (Br)
46653 **NOSIRA SHARON** (Br)
46654 **NOSIRA MADELEINE** (Br)
46655 **DARYA KAMAL** (Br)
46656 **DARYA MA** (Br)

● 46660 **WAYFARER** Br/Ja (NKK) 1973; B; 16300;
174.1 × 10.97 (571.19 × 35.99); M (Sulzer); 15.5
Sisters:
46661 **WANDERER** (Br)
46662 **WARRIOR** (Br)
Probably similar:
46663 **PENMARCH** (Fr)
46664 **ROSELINE** (Fr)

46670 **GEORGIOS XYLAS** Gr/Ja (Mitsui) 1970; B;

18600; 182.61 × 10.69 (599.11 × 35.07); M (Sulzer);
16
Sister:
46671 **ANDRIOTIS** (Gr) ex *Master Stefanos* 1981

★46680 **FEICUIHAI** RC/Br (Lithgows) 1973; B;
22900; 178.31 × 10.38 (585.01 × 34.05); M (B&W);
15; ex *Silverdon* 1978; ex *Bravenes* 1973

● 46690 **LARRY L** Gr/Ja (Hakodate) 1970; B; 16300;
182 × 10.64 (597.11 × 34.9); M (Sulzer); 14.5
Sisters (Gr flag):
46691 **CATHERINE L**
46692 **GRACE L**
46693 **PATRICIA L**
Similar:
46694 **EVY L**
46695 **MARILYN L**

46700 **ANBOTO** Li/No (Kaldnes) 1971; B; 15800;
180.3 × 10.19 (591.53 × 33.43); M (B&W); 16; ex
Penerf 1981
Sisters:
46701 **MENHIR** (Li) ex *Penhir*
46702 **NOBLE EVELYN** (Li) ex *Magic Sun* 1984; ex
Ondine

● 46710 **CAPE STROVILI** Gr/Ja (Hitachi) 1958; B;
13700; 173.64 × 10.41 (569.68 × 34.15); M (B&W);
15; ex *Delphic Eagle* 1973; ex *Paphos* 1971
Sister:
46711 **BAHIA MAGDALENA** (Pa) ex *Chavez* 1980;
ex *Pacific Carrier* 1979; ex *Delphic Oracle* 1969
Similar:
46712 **MYLOI** (Gr) ex *Agatha F* 1983; ex *Delphic
Miracle* 1981

46720 **NAN TA** Sg/Br (Upper Clyde) 1969; B; 16800;
176.79 × 10.6 (580 × 34.77); M (B&W); 15.25; ex
Scotspark 1981
Sisters:
46721 **HALLA CARAVAN** (Ko) ex *Ga Chau* 1983; ex
Glenpark 1982
★46722 **YIN SHAN HAI** (RC) ex *Vancouver Island*
1978

46730 **TRAMCO AMITY** Br/De (B&W) 1969; B;
29800; 218.85 × 12.1 (718.01 × 39.69); M (B&W);
15.5; ex *Cast Seal* 1982; ex *Bianca* 1977; Used as
container ship; Cranes may have been removed
Sister:
46731 **TRAMCO GLORY** (Br) ex *Cast Dolphin* 1982

46740 **P.S. PALIOS** Gr/FRG (Rhein Nordseew)
1963; B; 20300; 192.34 × 10.71 (631.03 × 35.13); M
(B&W); 15; ex *Holthorn* 1977
Sister:
46741 **SEA WALRUS** (Pa) ex *Mabu* 1978; ex *Fernwind* 1974

★46750 **BIN HAI** RC/Sw (Lindholmens) 1963; B;
20400; 195.13 × 11.02 (640.19 × 36.15); M (Gotaverken); 14.75; ex *Mai Bente* 1973

46760 **OCEAN LEO** Pa/No (Oresunds) 1968; B;
17000; 175.27 × 10.24 (575.03 × 33.59); M (Gotaverkens); 15; ex *Valetta* 1982

46770 **IBN ABDOUN** Ku/Br (Scotstoun) 1976; C;
15500; 175.32 × 10.42 (575.19 × 34.18); M (B&W);
16; 'KUWAIT' Class
Sisters (Ku flag):
46772 **IBN BAJJAH**
46773 **IBN HAZM**
46774 **IBN SINA**
46775 **IBN ZUHR**
46776 **IBN JUBAYR**
Similar (Ko flag) (Ko built-Hyundai):
46777 **OCEAN ACE**
46778 **OCEAN BEAUTY**
46779 **OCEAN CROWN**
46780 **OCEAN DUKE**

46790 **FORT YALE** Br/Ja (Sanoyasu) 1977; B;
17300; 172.85 × 10.40 (567.09 × 34.12); M (B&W);
15.75
Sisters:
46791 **FORT KAMLOOPS** (Br)
46792 **FORT VICTORIA** (Br)

46800 **FORT NELSON** Br/Ja (Sanoyasu) 1975; B;
21900; 184 × 11.06 (603.67 × 36.28); M (B&W); 15
Sisters:
46801 **FORT CALGARY** (Br)
46802 **FORT NANAIMO** (Br) ex *Leda* 1980

46810 **IRISH CEDAR** Ih/Ja (Hayashikane) 1977; B;
17300; 176.82 × 10.35 (580.12 × 33.95); M (B&W);
15
Sister:
46811 **IRISH ROWAN** (Ih)

46820 **WILLIAM R ADAMS** Li/Ja (Namura) 1968;
B; 10700; 147.02 × 8.49 (482.34 × 27.85); M (B&W);
14

46830 **SONID** Gr/Ja (Osaka) 1968; B; 11700; 156.45 × 9.79 (513.29 × 32.12); M (B&W); 14.75; ex *Rachel* 1980
Sister:
46831 **ANNIKA N** (Gr) ex *World Virtue* 1980

46840 **EASTERN BRIDE** Pa/Ja (Hayashikane) 1977; B; 16000; 176.89 × 10.34 (580.34 × 33.92); M (B&W); 15

46850 **HERUVIUM** Pa/Ja (Namura) 1978; B; 16000; 177.04 × 10.41 (580.84 × 34.16); M (Sulzer); 15.5; ex *Toxon* 1983

46860 **AMSTELDIEP** Ne/Ne (Giessen-De Noord) 1970; B; 12600; 160.1 × 9.93 (526.26 × 32.58); M (Sulzer); 14.5; ex *Putten* 1977
Sister:
46861 **AMSTELDREEF** (Ne) ex *Voorne* 1977

46870 **EASTERN VALLEY** Br/Ja (Hayashikane) 1975; B; 17200; 176.94 × 10.31 (580.51 × 33.82); M (Sulzer); 14.75; ex *Cardiff City* 1983; ex *Jade City* 1975
Sisters:
46871 **WESTERN VALLEY** (Br) ex *Devon City* 1983; launched as *Pearl City*
46872 **OPAL CITY** (Li) ex *Star Opal* 1982; ex *Opal City* 1979
46873 **STAR PROTOMACHOS** (Gr) ex *Protomachos* 1982; ex *Star Emerald* 1981; ex *Emerald City* 1979
46874 **HAE BARAKI** (Ko) ex *Asian Assurance* 1981
Probable sister:
46875 **EUROASIA CONCORDE** (Li)

46880 **MARIA G L** Gr/Ja (Namura) 1974; B; 15900; 178.49 × 10.42 (585.6 × 34.19); M (Sulzer); 14.75
Sister:
46881 **ODYSSEY 10** (Gr)
Possible sister:
46882 **KALLIOPI L** (Gr)
Similar:
46883 **EVER HONOR** (Tw)
46884 **SILVER ZEPHYR** (Li)
46885 **PACBARON** (Li)
46886 **CONTINENTAL CARRIER** (Li) ex *Packing* 1980
46887 **PACDUCHESS** (Li)
46888 **ORIENT UNION** (Pa) ex *Grand Enterprise* 1981
46889 **SEA TRANSPORT** (Li)
46890 **ISPARTA** (Tu)
46891 **URFA** (Tu)
46892 **ISLAND MARINER** (Gr)
46893 **LUCY** (Gr)
Possibly similar:
46894 **PACBARONESS** (Li)
46895 **PACDUKE** (Li)

● 46900 **ARPAD** Tu/Ru (Baltic) 1969; B; 23400; 199.83 × 11.24 (655.61 × 36.87); M (B&W); 15.75; ex *Rigoletto* 1976; 'Baltika' type
Similar:
46901 **CEBU** (Sg) ex *Care* 1980; ex *Carola P* 1979; ex *Carola Reith* 1978
Probably similar:
46902 **NADIA** (Cy) ex *Nortrans Vision* 1983
46903 **ON TUNG** (Pa) ex *Nortrans Kathe* 1979
46904 **CRESCO** (No)
46904/1 **ALCOR** (Li) ex *Ataman* 1984; ex *Tento* 1979
Probable sister:
46905 **LABO** (Sg) ex *Mare* 1980; ex *Magdalena* 1979; ex *Magdalena Reith* 1978

46910 **GEORGIS A GEORGILIS** Gr/Ja (Namura) 1976; B; 16000; 176.99 × 10.4 (580.67 × 34.12); M (Sulzer); 15.5
Sisters:
46911 **ANTONIS P LEMOS** (Gr)
46912 **ADITYA KIRAN** (In) ex *Ilena* 1982
Possibly similar:
46913 **AEGEON** (Gr) ex *Ioannis Martinos* 1982
46914 **EUROSEA** (Gr)
46915 **EUROUNITY** (Gr)

46920 **MING JOY** Tw/Ja (Sanoyasu) 1971; B; 16100; 165.5 × 10.42 (543.17 × 34.18); M (Sulzer); 14.5; ex *Ji Ming* 1977; ex *Hai Jung* 1973; '26-BC-5' type
Sisters:
46921 **MING LEADER** (Tw) ex *Li Ming* 1977; ex *Hi Lo* 1973
46922 **MING SHINE** (Tw) ex *Shin Ming* 1977; ex *Hai Chuan* 1973
Possible sister:
46923 **GLOBAL STAR** (Ko) ex *Manna* 1980; ex *Thai Yung* 1973

46924 **ZENO** Gr/Ja (Sanoyasu) 1982; B; 22700; 182.68 × 12.12 (599 × 39.76); M (Sulzer); 15.25
Probable sisters:
46925 **ARTEMIS** (Gr)

46926 **ALMI SKY** (Gr) ex *Alameda* 1983; ex *Holylight* 1981

46927 **ALEXANDRIA** (Gr) ex *Alexander Venture* 1979

46928 **ARBELA** (Gr) ex *Belladona Venture* 1980

46929 **PETRA** (Gr)
46929/1 **ANTIGONE** (Gr)
46929/2 **BUNGA SRIPAGI** (Mv):
46929/3 **FILIA WAVE** (Gr) ex *Maritime Investor* 1983

46930 **NEDROMA** Ag/Ja (Hitachi) 1978; B; 15900; 172.27 × 10.25 (565.19 × 33.63); M (B&W); 16.25
Sister:
46931 **NEMEMCHA** (Ag)

46940 **CELERINA** Sd/Ja (Osaka) 1975; B; 20600; 185.5 × 10.9 (608.59 × 35.76); M (Sulzer); 15.25; ex *Cruzeiro Do Sol* 1983
Sisters:
46941 **NORDLAND** (Sd) ex *Diavolezza* 1982
46942 **ROMANDIE** (Sd)
Similar:
46943 **NIKEA** (Gr) ex *Federal Katsura* 1979
46944 **MONTANA** (Gr) ex *Federal Hudson* 1979

46950 **CELTIC SKY** Pa/Ja (Kanasashi) 1976; B; 15900; 176.03 × 10.1 (577.53 × 33.14); M (B&W); 15; ex *Splendid Albatross* 1980

● 46951 **WORLD FRATERNITY** Pa/RC (Hudong) 1983; B; 22000; 186 × 11.25 (610.23 × 36.91); M (B&W); —
Possible sisters:
46952 **IRAN AFZAL** (Ir) ex *Manila Faith* 1984; launched as *Primelock*
46953 **STAR ORIENT** (Pa)
Sisters (Ja built-Osaka):
46954 **WORLD AMITY** (Pa)
46955 **WORLD ASPIRATION** (Pa)
46956 **WORLD HARVEST** (Pa)
46957 **WORLD OAK** (Br)

46960 **RIMBA MERANTI** My/Ja (Namura) 1976; B; 15500; 177.43 × 9.87 (582.12 × 32.38); M (Sulzer); 15
Possible sister:
46961 **RIMBA RAMIN** (My)

46970 **BAHAMASTARS** Pa/Ja (Sanoyasu) 1977; B; 16600; 169.58 × 10.3 (556.36 × 33.99); M (Sulzer); 14.75; ex *Kako Maru* 1982

46980 **MICHEL DELMAS** Fr/Ja (Usuki) 1976; B; 16300; 172.5 × 10.35 (565.94 × 33.95); M (Sulzer); 13

46990 **JAVARA** Li/De (B&W) 1970; B; 25200; 192.06 × 10.12 (630.12 × 33.2); M (B&W); 15.5; ex *Skogstad* 1976
Sisters:
46991 **TROLL VIKING** (Li) ex *Mannheim* 1981; ex *Roland Bremen* 1974
46992 **TROLL MAPLE** (Li) ex *Kelkheim* 1981; ex *Roland Kelkheim* 1971; Launched as *Kelkheim*
Similar:
46993 **JANEGA**

● 47000 **NISSAN MARU** Ja/Ja (Maizuru) 1970; B; 17400; 175.52 × 10.91 (575.85 × 35.79); M (B&W); 14.5
Sisters:
47001 **SILVER EXPRESS** (Pa) ex *Kanagawa Maru* 1980
47002 **HIRATSUKA MARU** (Ja);
Possible sister:
47003 **TOCHIGI MARU** (Ja)

47010 **FORT HAMILTON** Br/Ja (Sanoyasu) 1978; B; 14100; 169.9 × 9.79 (527.95 × 32.12); M (B&W); 14
Sisters (Br flag):
47011 **FORT CARLETON**
47012 **FORT WALSH**

● 47020 **COSMOTOR ACE** Pa/Ja (Hitachi) 1968; B; 11200; 152.25 × 8.99 (499.5 × 29.49); M (B&W); 14; ex *Honmoku Maru*

● 47030 **E R BRUGGE** Be/Be (Boelwerf) 1978; C; 13400; 163.5 × 10.25 (536.5 × 27.5); M (MAN); 17
Sister:
47031 **HODEIDAH CROWN** (Be) ex *Hapag Lloyd Kiel* 1983; ex *E.R. Brussel* 1983; ex *Cast Walrus* 1982; ex *E.R. Brussel* 1981; ex *C.P. Hunter* 1980; ex *E.R. Brussel* 1980

47035 **SEA ARCHITECT** Pa/RC (Chung Hua) 1981; C/Con; 7500/12200; 164.32 × —/9.74 (539 × —/31.96); M (B&W); 16

★ 47040 **XIANG CHENG** RC/Ja (Mitsui) 1976; C; 7000/11400; 147.71 × —/9.63 (484.61 × —/31.59); M (B&W); 15; ex *Star Procyon*; ex *Aristeidis* 1977; 'Mitsui-Concord 18' type
Sister:

★ 47041 **RONG CHENG** (RC) ex *Aristoxenos* 1979
Possible sisters:
47042 **JALABALA** (In) ex *Aristonofos* 1976
47043 **MIXORAM** (In) launched as *Aristofon*
★ 47044 **YUN CHENG** (RC) ex *Aristodikos*
★ 47045 **TONG CHENG** (RC) ex *Aristonidas* 1979
47046 **ARUNACHAL PRADESH** (In) launched as *Aristolaos*
47047 **STAR ALCYONE** (Pa) ex *Aristomachos* 1976

47050 **OLIVIA** Bz/Bz (CCN) 1977; B; 17300; 173.18 × 9.72 (568.17 × 31.89); M (MAN); 15.5; 'Prinasa 26/15' type
Possible sisters:
47051 **ATACAMA** (Ch)
47052 **ARAUCO** (Ch)

47060 **TOZEUR** Tn/Ja (Naikai) 1977; C; 6500; 127.29 × 7.9 (417.62 × 25.92); M (B&W); 18
Possible sisters:
47061 **EL JEM** (Tn)
Possibly similar:
47062 **TOYOFUJI No 2** (Ja)

★ 47070 **LIEBENWALDE** DDR/DDR ('Neptun') 1977; C; 3500/5700; 120.61 × —/7.83 (395.7 × —/25.69); M (MAN); 16.75
Sisters (DDR flag):
★ 47071 **CUNEWALDE**
★ 47072 **LUCKENWALDE**
★ 47073 **SCHONWALDE**
★ 47074 **GERINGSWALDE**
★ 47075 **MITTENWALDE**
★ 47076 **FURSTENWALDE**
★ 47077 **EICHWALDE**
★ 47078 **RUDOLF DIESEL**
★ 47079 **ARENDSEE**
★ 47080 **BLANKENSEE**
★ 47081 **FLEESENSEE**
★ 47082 **MUGGELSEE**
★ 47083 **WERBELLINSEE**
★ 47084 **KOLPINSEE**
★ 47085 **INSELSEE**
★ 47086 **RHINSEE**
★ 47087 **SCHWIELOSEE**
★ 47088 **TRENNTSEE**

47100 **CELERINA** Sd/Ja (Osaka) 1975; B; 20600; 185.5 × 10.9 (608.59 × 35.76); M (Sulzer); 15.25; ex *Cruzeiro Do Sol* 1983
Sisters:
47101 **NORDLAND** (Sd) ex *Diavolezza* 1982
47102 **ROMANDIE** (Sd)
Similar:
47103 **NIKEA** (Gr) ex *Federal Katsura* 1979
47104 **MONTANA** (Gr) ex *Federal Hudson* 1979

★ 47110 **FEICUIHAI** RC/Br (Lithgows) 1973; B; 22900; 178.31 × 10.38 (585.01 × 34.05); M (B&W); 15; ex *Silverdon* 1978; ex *Bravenes* 1973

47120 **SOUTH ISLANDER** Pa/Ja (Namura) 1977; C/RoC; 8400; 155.53 × 8.92 (510.27 × 29.27); M (MAN); 16.25; ex *Fiji Maru* 1981

47130 **WEDELLSBORG** De/Ja (Kawasaki) 1978; C/Con 16400; 174.02 × 10.15 (570.93 × 33.3); M (MAN); 18.25; ex *Hoegh Borg* 1983; ex *Hoegh John* 1982; ex *John Bakke* 1982
Sister:
47131 **FRIJSENBORG** (De) ex *Marie Bakke* 1982

★ 47150 **MEGANOM** Ru/Ja (Osaka) 1970; B; 15900; 170.52 × 10.06 (559.45 × 33); M (B&W); 15; ex *Maritime Brilliance* 1983
Sisters:
★ 47151 **TARKHANKUT** (Ru) ex *Maritime Dominion* 1983
47152 **GOLDEN LOTUS** (Li)
47153 **GOLDEN ORCHID** (Li)
47154 **FIVE ISLANDS** (Li) ex *Fedsteel* 1983; ex *Aiko Maru* 1974
47155 **KARYATIS** (Gr) ex *Fedtrade* 1983; ex *Zenko Maru* 1975
47156 **STORK** Gr/Ja (Hakodate) 1970; B; 15300; 171.71 × 10.09 (563 × 33.10); M (B&W); 15; ex *Spray Cap* 1983
Sister:
47157 **GULL** (Gr) ex *Spray Stan* 1983

47158 **TRADE VISION** Li/Ja (Sumitomo) 1971; B; 18700; 180.02 × 10.87 (591 × 35.66); M (Sulzer); 15.25; ex *Bluesky* 1981
★ 47159 **NOVO MESTO** (Ys) ex *Geiko Maru* 1974;
Probable sisters:
47160 **GRACE BOEING** (Li)
47161 **MOZART FESTIVAL** (Li)
Similar:
47162 **ASIA FALCON** (Li)

47165 **CANOPY** Pa/Ja (Sanoyasu) 1967; O; 7400; 135.03 × 7.93 (443 × 26.01); M (MAN); 14.5; ex *Spencer Maru* 1977

★47167 **KAPITAN A POLKOVSKIY** Ru/Ja (Hitachi) 1978; B; 15600; 172.88 × 9.73 (567 × 31.92); M (Sulzer); 15; ex *Kopelia* 1983

★47170 **MIN YUN HAI** RC/Ih (Verolme Cork) 1968; B; 22200; 192.67 × 11.38 (632.12 × 37.33); M (MAN); 15.5; ex *Pelopidas* 1981; ex *Irish Elm*

47180 **RANGELOCK** Br/De (B&W) 1982; B/Con; 36200; 225.03 × 13.08 (738 × 42.91); M (B&W); 15
Sister:
47181 **SEALOCK** (Br)

47185 **CO-OP EXPRESS 1** Pa/Ja (Hitachi) 1982; B/V; 32100; 210.01 × 12.42 (689 × 40.75); M (B&W); 14; Side doors (port & starboard)
Sister:
47186 **CO-OP EXPRESS II** (Pa)

47190 **KONTULA** Fi/Fi (Wartsila) 1980; B/IB; 19900; 179(BP) × 10.5 (587.27 × 4.92); M (Sulzer); 15

●47195 **NORASIA REBECCA** FRG/FRG (Howaldts DW) 1982; B/Con; 18500; 169.15 × 9.96 (555 × 32.68); M (Sulzer); 16.5; ex *Rebecca Wesch* 1983
Sisters:
47196 **NORASIA GABRIELE** (FRG) ex *Victoria Bay* 1983; ex *Gabriele Wesch* 1983
47197 **NORASIA KARSTEN** (FRG) ex *Karsten Wesch*
47198 **CASTOR** (FRG)
47199 **NORASIA CARTHAGO** (FRG) ex *Carthago* 1984

●47200 **RADIANT VENTURE** Li/Ja (IHI) 1977; B; 19400; 187.74 × 10.76 (613.51 × 35.3); M (Sulzer); 15.5; 'Future 32' type
Sisters (number of cranes may vary):
47201 **ROSINA TOPIC** (Li)
47202 **SOVEREIGN VENTURE** (Li)
47203 **PAN EXPRESS** (Ko) ex *Primula* 1981
47204 **PAN QUEEN** (Ko) ex *Primavera 1* 1981; ex *Primavera* 1980
47205 **BISCHOFSTOR** (FRG)
47206 **CARLO M** (Li)
47207 **ANDROS OCEANIA** (Gr)
47209 **FAIRNESS** (Li)
47210 **MARIA TOPIC** (Li)
47211 **JUNO** (Li)

●47213 **WAARDRECHT** Ne/Sw (Oresunds) 1982; B/Con; 26200; 186.54 × 11.90 (612 × 39.04); M (B&W); 16; ex *Ibn Al Kadi* 1983; Launched as *Waardrecht*
Sisters:
47214 **WIELDRECHT** (Ne)
47215 **WOENSDRECHT** (Ne)

47216 **NATHALIE DELMAS** Fr/Fr (L'Atlantique) 1982; C/Con; 20400; 177.00 × 11.42 (581 × 37.47); M (Pielstick); 18
Sisters:
47217 **PATRICIA DELMAS** (Fr)
47218 **RENEE DELMAS** (Fr)
47219 **SUZANNE DELMAS** (Fr)

47220 **MEERDRECHT** Ne/Sw (Gotav) 1978; B/Con; 26700; 191.4 × 11.33 (627.95 × 37.17); M (B&W); —; ex *Ibn Atik* 1982; ex *Meerdrecht* 1980; ex *Seatrain Rotterdam* 1980; ex *Meerdrecht* 1978; 'Columbus 44' type
Sisters:
47221 **MIJDRECHT** (Ne) ex *Seatrain Amsterdam* 1980; ex *Mijdrecht* 1978
47222 **ARLBERG** (As) ex *Star Abadan*; ex *Arlberg* 1979
47223 **DEVOTION** (Pa)
47224 **FRUITION** (Pa)
47225 **UNISON** (Pa)
47226 **MOORDRECHT** (Ne)

47230 **WINDRAIDER** Sw/Fi (Warsila) 1966; C; 4100; 102.11 × 7.58 (335 × 24.86); M (Sulzer); 15; ex *Staros* 1983; ex *Hangete* 1981; ex *Nils Gorthon* 1976
Sisters:
47231 **RED STONE** (Sw) ex *Arctic* 1984; ex *Margit Gorthon* 1976
47232 **HISPANIOLA** (Pa) ex *Gregerso* 1983

★47240 **LING JIANG** RC/Fi (Rauma-Repola) 1960; C; 2000; 96.91 × 5.81 (317.94 × 19.06); M (MAN); 13; ex *Ai Shan* 1982; ex *Lisa* 1975; ex *Simpele* 1973
Sister:
★47241 **KAO JIANG** (RC) ex *Po Sea* 1980; ex *Svano* 1975; ex *Varjakka* 1974; ex *Kaipola* 1969

47250 **TUGELA** Pa/FRG (O&K) 1971; C; 3400/5800; 126.83 × 6.51/7.36 (416.1 × 21.35/24.14); M (Atlas-MaK); 16.5; ex *Katjana* 1981
Sister:
47251 **TROPIC DAWN** (Sg) ex *Steindamm* 1981; ex *Mesurado* 1975; ex *Samos Sky* 1974; ex *Steindamm* 1973

47260 **TRANSONDO EXPRESS** Pa/FRG (Unterweser) 1972; C; 3400/6000; 124.52 × 6.59/8.12 (408.53 × 21.62/26.64); M (KHD); 17; ex *Stefan Drescher* 1982; ex *Wadai* 1975; ex *Ede Foldenfjord* 1974; ex *Ede Wittorf* 1973

47270 **BRITANIA** FRG/FRG (Sietas) 1979; C/Con; 1600/3800; 99.98 × 5.53/— (328 × 18.14/—); M (Atlas-MaK); 15; ex *Conti Britania* 1980; Smaller cranes are on starboard side and larger ones on port

47280 **OLIVER DRESCHER** FRG/FRG (Schichau-U) 1973; C; 3500/6200; 132.52 × 6.5/8 (434.77 × 21.32/26.24); M (KHD); 17; ex *Lloyd Philadelphia* 1980; ex *Oliver Drescher* 1978; ex *Ede Sinstorf* 1975
Similar:
47281 **LLOYD NEW YORK** (FRG) ex *Macaela Drescher* 1978

47290 **LOTILA** Fi/Sp (Juliana) 1977; B; 6800/12400; 159.21 × 6.87/9.15 (522.34 × 22.53/30.02); M (Sulzer); 16
Sisters (Fi flag):
47291 **FINNFIGHTER** ex *Kaipola* 1980
47292 **FINNOCEANIS** ex *Walki* 1980
47293 **SALLA** ex *Walki Paper* 1980
47294 **FINNARCTIS**
47295 **VARJAKKA**
47296 **POKKINEN**
47297 **FINNPOLARIS**

47298 **LAUTAN RANI** My/Au (Broken H) 1964; C/RoC; 3000; 113.67 × 5.72 (373 × 18.77); TSM (Mirrlees); 17; ex *Seaway Queen* 1980; Stern door
Sister:
47299 **PONTENEGRO** (Gr) ex *Lucky Trader* 1980; ex *Sentosa Trader* 1978; ex *Seaway King* 1977

●47300 **PETROS Z** Ma/Sw (Solvesborgs) 1966; C; 1900; 110.09 × 4.82 (361.19 × 15.81); M (Gotaverken); 14.5; ex *Tatai Queen* 1984; ex *Andrew* 1980; ex *Andrew Salman* 1976; Side door; Lengthened 1971
Sister:
47301 **TATAI SEA** (Gr) ex *Michael* 1980; ex *Michael Salman* 1976

47310 **NEW GALACTICA** Sg/Sw (Finnboda) 1962; C; 1600/2800; 93.81 × 5.07/5.76 (308 × 16.63/18.90); M (Fiat); 13; ex *Atlas* 1982; ex *Grim* 1969

47320 **ALHALEME** Eg/Sp (Juliana) 1971; C; 1200; 87 × 4.87 (285.43 × 15.97); M (Stork-Werkspoor); 13.5; ex *Benimusa* 1980
Sisters:
47321 **INTER IV** (Pa) ex *Benimamet* 1981
47322 **NIAGA XXXVI** (Ia) ex *Benisalem* 1981
47323 **ALHAKEM** (Eg) ex *Beniajan*
47324 **NIAGA XXXV** (Ia) ex *Benifaraig* 1981
Similar (shorter):
47325 **MARIA ZAKELINA S** (Gr) ex *Benimar* 1977
47326 **ALHAMBRA** (Eg) ex *Benisa* 1978
47327 **BENIALI** (Sp)

47330 **BREMER HORST BISCHOFF** FRG/FRG (Rolandwerft) 1971; C; 1400; 104.63 × 5.04 (343.27 × 16.53); M (KHD); 17

47340 **ASSIA** It/DDR ('Neptun') 1971; C; 3200; 104.12 × 5.79 (341.6 × 19); M (Dieselmotorenwerk Rostock); 14; ex *Brigitte* 1983; ex *Phaedra* 1983; ex *Hanseatic*
Possible sister (may have a gantry):
47341 **ADA** (Pa) ex *Varde* 1981; ex *Brunvard* 1977
Probably similar:
47342 **IDA 1** (Pa) ex *Hilde* 1981; ex *Brunhild* 1977

47350 **GOOD OCEAN** Gr/FRG (Rhein Nordseew) 1966; B; 21400; 191.55 × 11.32 (628.45 × 37.14); M (B&W); 15.75; ex *Solholt* 1979

47360 **NORITA** No/Br (Scotts' SB) 1970; B; 12600; 158.53 × 9.51 (520.11 × 31.2); M (Sulzer); 15; ex *Ingeren* 1979

47370 **ALTHEA** Gr/Gr (Eleusis) 1973; B; 22400; 205.01 × 11.74 (672.6 × 38.51); M (Sulzer); 15.5
Sister:
47371 **AKTEA** (Gr)

●47375 **MANUELA PRIMA** It/It ('Navalmeccanica') 1965; B; 17300; 192 × 10.59 (629.92 × 34.74); M (Ansaldo); —

47380 **MARCHEN MAERSK** De/De (Nakskov) 1974; C/Con; 10400/15900; 170.69 × 9.35/10.27 (560.01 × 30.68/33.69); M (B&W); 20.5
Sisters (De flag):
47381 **MARGRETHE MAERSK**
47382 **McKINNEY MAERSK**
47383 **MATHILDE MAERSK**

47390 **HAE YUNG EASTERN** Ko/No (Haugesund) 1970; B; 14500; 162.87 × 10.42 (534.35 × 34.18); M (Stork-Werkspoor); —; ex *Baron Ardrossan* 1981
Sisters:

47391 **RENA** (Gr) ex *Kilchrenan* 1983; ex *Tanjong Pasir* 1983; ex *Baron Wemyss* 1981
47392 **CAPE HAWK** (Br)
47393 **HAE YUNG GOLD** (Ko) ex *Cape Grafton* 1980
47394 **CAPE GRENVILLE** (Br)
47395 **KILLIN** (Br) ex *Tanjong Tokong* 1983; ex *Cape Horn* 1981
47396 **CAPE ANTIBES** (Gr) ex *Temple Inn* 1979
47397 **ANADOLU GUNEY** (Tu) ex *Island* 1983; ex *Sneland* 1983; ex *Southland* 1983; ex *Sneland* 1982
47398 **KATERINA E** (Gr) ex *Westocean* 1980; ex *Vestland*
Similar (lengthened to 188m and may have an extra crane):
47399 **TRANSOCEAN PEARL** (Pi) ex *Federal St Clair* 1981 ex *Baron Inchcape* 1977

47410 **MING SPRING** Tw/Tw (China SB) 1978; C; 18600; 172.02 × 10.6 (564.37 × 34.78); M (Sulzer); 17
Sisters (Tw flag):
47411 **MING SUMMER**
47412 **MING AUTUMN**
47413 **MING WINTER**
Probable sisters:
47414 **TAO YUAN** (Tw) ex *Tai Hsiung* 1982
47415 **YE LAN** (Tw) ex *Tai Lung* 1982

47420 **KIELDRECHT** Ne/Ja (NKK) 1977; B; 16200; 178.11 × 10.9 (584.35 × 35.76); M (Sulzer); 15.5
Sister:
47421 **KATENDRECHT** (NA)

47430 **PAGNET** Li/FRG (A G 'Weser') 1976; C; 14600; 171.41 × 10.45 (562.37 × 34.28); M (Sulzer); 16.25; ex *Pagnol* 1980; 'Key 26' type
Sister:
47431 **RAIMOL** (Li) ex *Raimu* 1980

●47440 **SAMOA** De/De (Nakskov) 1978; C; 16200; 159.42 × 10.59 (523.03 × 34.74); M (B&W); 16
Sisters (De flag):
47441 **SARGODHA**
47443 **TARASCO** ex *Siena* 1983
47444 **SINALOA**
(Pk flag):
47445 **MAKRAN**
(Ir flag):
47446 **IRAN TEYFOURI** ex *Simba* 1984

●47447 **OVE SKOU** De/De (Aalborg) 1982; C/Con; 11000/16500; 159.57 × 7.69/10.35 (524 × 25.23/33.96); M (B&W); 16.5

47450 **SONGKHLA** De/Ja (Mitsui) 1977; B/Con; 16100; 158.02 × 10.59 (518.44 × 34.74); M (B&W); 16.25
Sister:
47451 **SUMBAWA** (Bs)

47460 **ANGELIKI H** Gr/No (Horten) 1971; B; 13400; 159.21 × 9.76 (522.34 × 32.02); M (Sulzer); 15; ex *Kilmarnock* 1983; ex *Baron MaClay*
Sister:
47461 **KILDRUMMY** (Br) ex *Tanjong Utara* 1983; ex *Cape Leeuwin* 1982

47470 **KYRIAKOULA D LEMOS** Gr/Ja (Hitachi) 1966; B; 20500; 194.01 × 11.89 (636.52 × 39.01); M (B&W); —

47480 **AL TAMMAR** Li/No (Kaldnes) 1964; B; 17200; 186.82 × 11.22 (612.93 × 36.81); M (Gotaverken); 14; ex *Westbulk* 1980

47490 **FINNOAK** Fi/Fi (Wartsila) 1971; C; 3100/5700; 118.32 × 6.41/7.44 (388.2 × 21.03/24.5); M (Sulzer); 14.75; ex *Kaipola* 1975
Sisters (Fi flag):
47491 **CLIO** ex *Finnkraft* 1982; ex *Valkeokoski* 1977
47492 **KOITELI**
47493 **TUIRA**

47500 **HIZIR III** Tu/Fi (Wartsila) 1969; C; 4500; 116.01 × 7.41 (380.61 × 24.31); M (Sulzer); 15; ex *Germundo* 1983

47510 **WINDRAIDER** Sw/Fi (Wartsila) 1966; C; 4100; 102.11 × 7.58 (335 × 24.86); M (Sulzer); 15; ex *Staros* 1983; ex *Hangete* 1981; ex *Nils Gorthon* 1976
Sisters:
47511 **RED STONE** (Sw) ex *Arctic* 1984; ex *Margit Gorthon* 1976
47512 **HISPANIOLA** (Pa) ex *Gregerso* 1983

47520 **ALCA** Fi/Sw (Finnboda) 1967; C; 1600/2900; 93.81 × 5.08/6.6 (307.77 × 16.66/21.65); M (Atlas-MaK); 14
Sisters (Fi flag):
47521 **DORIS**
47522 **HAMNO**

●★47540 **RADAUTI** Rm/Rm (Galatz) 1974; C; 4400/6300; 130.77 × 6.6/8.1 (429.04 × 21.65/26.57); M (Sulzer); 15.75
Sisters (Rm flag):

★47541 FAGET
★47542 FIERBINTI
★47543 FILIDARA
★47544 CALIMANESTI
★47545 FAUREI
★47546 FAGARAS
★47547 BUSTENI
★47548 TELEORMAN
★47549 FIRIZA
★47550 BIHOR
★47551 OLANESTI
★47552 FILIASI
★47553 SATU MARE
★47554 ODORHEI
★47555 SIMERIA
★47556 GORJ
★47557 FRUNZANESTI
★47558 FRASINET
★47559 FELIX
★47560 DOLJ
★47561 CACIULATA
★47562 FIENI
★47563 RUPEA
★47564 HATEG
★47565 ORAVITA
★47566 GOVORA
★47567 FUNDULEA
★47568 GIURGU
★47569 HIRSOVA
★47570 HUSI
★47571 GRIVITA
(Bu flag):
★47572 STEFAN KARADJA
★47573 ZAHARI STOIANOV

47590 FINNPINE Fi/Fi (Valmet) 1971; C; 3900/6600; 129.39 × 6.43 /8.07 (424.51 × 21.1/24.48); M (B&W); 17.25
Sisters:
47591 IRVING FOREST (Br) ex Finnalpino 1983
47592 CASTOR (Fi) ex Finntrader 1982
47593 CARELIA (Fi) ex Finnwood 1982

47600 HILTONA Pa/Pd (Szczecinska) 1966; C; 7500/10700; 156.34 × 8.13/8.89 (512.93 × 26.67/29.17); M (Sulzer); 15.5; ex Wlokniarz 1980; 'B-512' type
Sister:
47601 MAK (Pa) ex Gornik 1983
Possible sister:
47602 ELEISTRIA (Gr) ex Metalowiec 1980; (may have cranes removed)

●★47610 TRANSPORTOWIEC Pd/Pd (Szczecinska) 1964; C; 7500/10600; 155.76 × 8.13/8.9 (511.02 × 26.67/29.2); M (Sulzer); 14.25; 'B512' type
Possibly similar:
★47612 CHEMIK (Pd)
47613 KARUNA (Sr) ex Energetyk 1983; (may not have cranes)

47615 KARIN FRG/FRG (Brand) 1981; C/Con; 1600/4200; 112.86 × 5.10/7.59 (370 × 16.73/24.90); M (Krupp MaK); 16
Sister:
47616 DORIS (FRG)

●47620 SHAYMA THREE UAE/Sw (Helsingborgs) 1957; C; 2500/4000; 105.29 × 5.87/6.48 (345.44 × 19.26/21.26); M (Gotaverken); 12.75; ex Viki-Lam 1982; ex Neva 1971

47630 TAMARITA No/Ja (Sumitomo) 1976; B; 17900; 169.98 × 10.26 (557.68 × 33.66); M (Sulzer); 15; ex Mosriver 1982
Sister:
47631 FERMITA (No) ex Moslake 1982

●47635 NEDLLOYD MARSEILLE Ne/Ca (Marine Indust) 1978/80; C/Con; 10000/13500; 187.15 × 8.37/9.69 (614 × 27.46/31.79); M (MAN); 17.25; ex Amstelslot 1980; ex Marindus Rimouski 1979; lengthened 1980 (NKK)
Sisters (Ne flag):
47636 NEDLLOYD MADRAS ex Amstelstad 1980; ex Marindus Quebec 1979
47637 MANILA ex Nedlloyd Manila 1984; ex Manila 1983; ex Nedlloyd Manila 1982; ex Amstelsluis 1980; ex Marindus Trois Rivieres 1979

47640 NEDLLOYD NAGASAKI Ne/Ne ('De Schelde') 1972; C; 12100; 165 × 9.65 (543 × 32); M (Sulzer); 21; ex Straat Nagasaki 1977
Sisters (Ne flag):
47641 NEDLLOYD NAGOYA ex Straat Nagoya
47642 NEDLLOYD NAPIER ex Straat Napier
47643 NEDLLOYD NASSAU ex Straat Nassau

47650 MARCHEN MAERSK De/De (Nakskov) 1974; C/Con; 10400/15900; 170.69 × 9.34/10.27 (560.01 × 30.68/33.69); M (B&W); 20.5
Sisters (De flag):
47651 MARGRETHE MAERSK
47652 McKINNEY MAERSK

47653 MATHILDE MAERSK

●47654 FROTAMERICA Bz/Bz (Emaq) 1979; B; 21700; 193.81 × 10.91 (636 × 35.79); M (Sulzer); 15
Sisters (Bz flag) (some may be gearless):
47655 FROTABRASIL
47656 FROTACHILE
47657 FROTARGENTINA
47658 FROTAURUGUAY
47659 ALMIRANTE ANICETO
Similar (after crane in different position—see inset):
47659/1 MULHEIM (Pa)
47659/2 GOLDEN RIO (Li) launched as Weinheim

47660 ALKYONIS Gr/Ja (Koyo) 1976; B; 30300; 222.99 × 12.32 (731.59 × 40.42); M (B&W); 14.5; ex Pacific Master 1982
Possible sister:
47661 NEW APOLLO (Li)

47665 GENERAL AGUINALDO Pi/Ja (Koyo) 1982; B; 29800; 223.15 × 12.45 (732 × 40.85); M (B&W); 14.5; ex Limelock 1982
Possible sister:
★47666 JIAO ZHOU HAI (RC) ex Koyo Venture 1980

47670 FAIR WIND Gr/Br (A&P) 1964; B; 17600; 188.07 × 10.57 (617.03 × 34.68); M (Sulzer); 14.5; ex Alexandra; ex Benhiant 1978; ex Cramond 1977; ex Benhiant 1975; ex Wearfield 1973

47671 MAERSK SERANGOON Sg/Ja (Hitachi) 1983; B; 30700; 224.5 × 12.96 (737 × 42.52); M (B&W); 17.5
Probable sister:
47672 MAERSK SEMBAWANG (Sg)

47674 MARITIME VICTOR Pa/Ja (Osaka) 1981; B; 21500; 188.58 × 11.00 (619 × 36.09); M (Sulzer); 17.75
Sisters (Pa flag):
47675 MARITIME LEADER
47676 MARITIME PRIDE
Probable sister:
47677 MARITIME QUEEN (Pa)

47680 MARGARITA Gr/Br (A&P) 1966; B; 18100; 188.07 × 11.02 (617.03 × 36.15); M (Sulzer); 15; ex Margarita Chandris 1977
Probable sister:
47681 MARI CHANDRIS (Gr)

47690 OLYMPIC PHOENIX Pa/Br (A&P) 1977; B; 15800; 183.04 × 10.71 (600.5 × 35.14); M (Sulzer); 15; ex London Baron 1983; 'B-26' type
Sisters (Pa flag):
47691 OLYMPIC LIBERTY ex London Earl 1983
47692 OLYMPIC PROMISE ex London Viscount 1983
47693 OLYMPIC LEADER ex London Voyager 1983; ex Welsh Voyager 1982

47700 DAMODAR TANABE In/Ys ('Split') 1969; B; 24573; 193.11 × 11.88 (635.51 × 38.97); M (MAN); 15.75; Cranes travel athwartships
Sister:
47701 DAMODAR TASAKA (In)

●★47710 DUBROVNIK Ys/Sp (AESA) 1971; B; 14700; 164.85 × 10.17 (540.85 × 33.37); M(Sulzer); 13.5; launched as Magdalena Del Mar
Sister:
47711 MAGDALENA DEL MAR (Sp)

47720 SENIOR SPYROS V Cy/Sp ('Astano') 1964; C; 3200/5000; 119.26 × 6.4/7.32 (391.27 × 21/24.02); M (Gotaverken); —; ex Spyros 1982; ex Hesperus 1980; ex Akera 1964; Lengthened 1971

●47730 SEA MASTER Ma/Ja (Kawasaki D) 1968; B/Vehicles; 12400; 159.04 × 9.55 (521.78 × 31.33); M (MAN); 14.5; ex Pioneer No 1 1982; ex Toyota Maru No 1 1979
Sisters:
47731 SEA STAR (Ma) ex Pioneer No 2 1982; ex Toyota Maru No 2 1973
47732 PIONEER No 3 (Ja) ex Toyota Maru No 3

47740 NEW DALIA Eg/De (Langesunds) 1969; C; 1600/2700; 93.88 × 5.07/6.37 (307.68 × 16.63/20.9); M (Sulzer); 13.5; ex Nanoula 1983; ex Tamaris; ex Finnrover 1973; ex Nina 1971

●47750 KEFALONIA SUN Gr/Ih (Verolme Cork) 1966; B; 18800; 183.93 × 11.17 (603.45 × 36.65); M (MAN); 15.5; ex Sea Crest 1980; ex New Adventure 1973
Similar:
47751 AMSTELPARK (Ne)
47752 AMSTELLAAN (NA)
Similar (mast from funnel):
47754 ELKA (Gr) ex Elias K 1981; ex Samos Glory; ex James Benedict 1972

★47756 KUPA Ys/Ys ('3 Maj') 1973; B; 18300; 196.6 × 10.82 (645 × 35.50); M (Sulzer); 15.75; ex Adriatik

1983
Sister:
★47757 SAVA (Ys)

47760 OCEAN PEGASUS Gr/Ne (Verolme Scheeps) 1961; B; 16600; 180.6 × 10.8 (592.52 × 35.43); M (MAN); 14.5; ex Skauvann 1965

47770 PRACTICIAN Br/Br (Cammell Laird) 1972; B; 20100; 180.96 × 11.23 (593.7 × 36.84); M (Doxford); 15; ex Letchworth 1978
Sisters (Br flag):
47771 HUMANIST ex Naworth 1978
47772 PROGRESSIST ex Oakworth 1978

●47780 ADVARA Sg/Br (Upper Clyde) 1970; C/Con; 17600; 175.27 × 9.88 (575.03 × 32.41); M (Sulzer); 15.25; ex Kyoto Forest 1975; converted from bulk carrier and shortened 1975

47790 KOTKANIEMI Fi/Fi (Wartsila) 1968; B; 12100; 158.32 × 9.59 (519.42 × 31.46); M (Sulzer); 14.5

47800 PRESIDENT ROXAS Pi/FRG (Flensburger) 1963; B; 17500; 186.16 × 9.71 (610.76 × 31.86); M (MAN); 15; ex Alaric 1982; ex Menkar 1979; ex Tosca 1977; ex Donau 1968

●47810 PEGASUS TIMBER Ko/DDR (Mathias-Thesen) 1972; B/Con; 16200; 176.16 × 10.11 (579.59 × 33.17); M (MAN); 15.5; ex Foochow 1980; ex Bella Coola 1977
Sisters:
47811 LIONS ROCK (Li) ex Arctic Wasa 1983
47812 KUNG HEI (Li) ex Galapagos 1984; ex Baltic Wasa
47813 ORKNEY (Li) ex Celtic Wasa 1979
47814 TASMANIA (Li) ex Delphic Wasa 1980
47815 SALAMIS (Li) ex Gothic Wasa 1980
47816 FINNTIMBER (Fi)
47817 SYLVO (No)
Possible sisters:
47819 ARIA (Gr)
47820 ARIADNE (Gr)

47830 NORWEGIAN SEA Li/No (Haugesund) 1969; B; 19300; 216.14 × 10.99 (709.12 × 36.06); M (Sulzer); 16; ex Benfri 1978; ex Andwi 1974
Similar:
47831 BERING SEA (Pa) ex Nanfri 1978
47832 CASPIAN SEA (Pa) ex Lorfri 1978; ex Doberg 1975; ex Rolwi 1974

47840 SEA WIND Ma/Ja (Mitsubishi HI) 1968; B; 34600; 235.52 × 13.74 (772.7 × 45.08); M (Sulzer); —; ex Proso 1984

47850 MARE ITALICO It/Ja (Usuki) 1974; B; 17200; 178.39 × 10.65 (585.27 × 34.94); M (Sulzer); 15.5; ex Acedrelas 1980; ex Cedrela 1980

47860 ALKYON Gr/Sw (Oresunds) 1968; B; 17400; 185.12 × 10.22 (607.35 × 33.53); M (Gotaverken); 16; ex Jarl R Trapp

47870 KILMUN Br/Br (Govan) 1976; B; 16600; 175.11 × 10.14 (574.51 × 33.27); M (B&W); 15; ex Cape Ortegal 1982; 'CARDIFF' class
Sister (Br flag):
47871 CAPE RODNEY
Similar:
47872 ANTHIPPE L (Gr) ex Baron Napier 1983
47873 EVANGELOS L (Gr) ex Baron Pentland 1983

47874 HOLCK-LARSEN In/Ja (Rinkai/Nipponkai) 1980/81; B; 16100; 191.29 × 9.50 (628 × 31.17); M (B&W); —; ex Eggarlock 1982; Foreward section built Rinkai 1980; After section built Nipponkai 1981
Sisters:
47875 SOREN TOUBRO (In) ex Oak Star 1982
47876 PROTECTOR (Gr) ex El General 1983
47877 REGENT PALM (Pa)
Possibly similar (shorter):
47878 LINDEN (Pa)
47879 LUPIN (Pa)

47880 STAR CAPELLA Gr/Ja (Hakodate) 1973; B; 14700; 177.96 × 10.69 (583.86 × 35.07); M (Sulzer); 15
Sister:
47880/1 IRON KIRBY (Br) ex Iron Kerry 1983; ex Star Kerry 1975
Possible sisters:
47881 STAR CASTOR (Gr)
47882 STAR UNITED (Pa) ex Star Nestor 1980
47883 RATNA VANDANA (In) ex Star Lily 1977
47885 IRON KESTREL (Br) ex Star Kestrel 1975

47890 NORITA No/Br (Scotts' SB) 1970; B; 12600; 158.53 × 9.51 (520.11 × 31.2); M (Sulzer); 15; ex Ingeren 1979

47900 PAGNET Li/FRG (A G 'Weser') 1976; C; 14600; 171.41 × 10.45 (562.37 × 34.28); M (Sulzer); 16.25; ex Pagnol 1980; 'Key 26' type

Sister:
47901 **RAIMOL** (Li) ex *Raimu* 1980

47910 **CHIARA S.** Pa/It (Breda) 1963; B; 17200;
192.03 × 10.59 (630 × 34.74); M (Fiat); 15.5; ex
Nai Carolina 1982. ex *Carolina Lolli-Ghetti* 1974, ex
Lerici Seconda 1969
Similar:
★47911 **GUI HAI** (RC) ex *Adriatic Sea* 1976; ex
Angelo Scinicariello 1973

● 47920 **RIO PLATA** Gr/Ja (Osaka) 1970; B; 13900;
174.5 × 9.92 (572.5 × 32.54); M (Sulzer); 14.75; ex
Ocean Navigator; ex Cosmos Fomalhaut 1979
Sisters (Li flag):
47921 **ASIA ANVIL** ex *Asia Hawk* 1981
47922 **ASIA SWALLOW**

47925 **PEPE LE MOKO** Li/Ja (Mitsubishi HI) 1982;
B; 19300; 178.00 × 10.74 (584 × 35.24); M (Mitsubishi); 14.7
Sister:
47926 **SKY HAWK** (Li)

● 47930 **FLORA C** Gr/Ja (Koyo) 1978; B; 15400; 169
× 9.72 (556.43 × 31.89); M (Sulzer); 16
Sisters (Gr flag):
47931 **JOHN C**
47932 **SOPHIE C**
Possible sisters (Gr flag):
47933 **DESERT PRINCE**
47934 **DESERT QUEEN**
Similar:
47935 **CHRISTINA C** (Gr)
47936 **EUGENIE C** (Gr)
47937 **BUENA FORTUNA** (Gr)
47938 **DESERT FALCON** (Gr)

47940 **TURGUT GUNERI** Tu/Sw (Uddevalla) 1969;
B; 9900; 147.55 × 8.94 (484.09 × 29.33); M (Gotaverken); 15; ex *Garden Sun* 1977; ex *Gervalla* 1973

47941 **FLORES** Pa/Ja (NKK) 1982; B; 16000;
175.00 × 10.45 (574 × 34.28); M (Sulzer); 15.2
Sister:
47942 **FARISI** (Pa)

47944 **BARON MINTO** Ja/Ja (Tsuneishi) 1982; B;
18800; 179.00 × 11.53 (587 × 37.83); M (B&W);
14.5
Sister:
47945 **FELICIA** (Pa)

47950 **MOUNT ATHOS** Gr/Ja (NKK) 1977; B;
12500; 155.71 × 9.9 (510.86 × 32.48); M (Sulzer);
17.5; ex *Sachsenhausen* 1978
Sisters (Gr flag):
47951 **GOLDEN TRADER**
47952 **GOLDEN CHALLENGER**
47953 **GOLDEN POLYDINAMOS**
47954 **ALKMAN** ex *Golden Polykleitos*

47960 **HAE YUNG EASTERN** Ko/No (Haugesund)
1970; B; 14500; 162.87 × 10.42 (534.35 × 34.18); M
(Stork-Werkspoor); —; ex *Baron Ardossan* 1981
Sisters:
47961 **RENA** (Gr) ex *Kilchrenan* 1983; ex *Tanjong
Pasir* 1983; ex *Baron Wemyss* 1981
47962 **CAPE HAWK** (Br)
47963 **HAE YUNG GOLD** (Ko) ex *Cape Grafton* 1980
47964 **CAPE GRENVILLE** (Br)
47965 **KILLIN** (Br) ex *Tanjong Tokong* 1983; ex *Cape
Horn* 1981
47966 **CAPE ANTIBES** (Gr) ex *Temple Inn* 1979
47967 **ANADOLU GUNEY** (Tu) ex *Island* 1983; ex
Sneland 1983; ex *Southland* 1983; ex *Sneland* 1982
47968 **KATERINA E** (Gr) ex *Westocean* 1980; ex
Vestland
Similar (lengthened to 188m and may have an extra
crane):
47969 **TRANSOCEAN PEARL** (Pi) ex *Federal St
Clair* 1981; ex *Baron Inchcape* 1977

47980 **AL TAMMAR** Li/No (Kaldnes) 1964; B;
17200; 186.82 × 11.22 (612.93 × 36.81); M (Gotaverken); 14; ex *Westbulk* 1980

★47985 **TIANHAI** RC/Be (Boel) 1965; B; 20500;
203.77 × 11.25 (669 × 36.91); M (MAN); —; ex
Priamos 1975

47990 **GALEA** Sp/Sp (AESA) 1974; B; 19900;
196.02 × 11.15 (643.1 × 36.58); M (Sulzer); 15
Possible sister (may be gearless):
47991 **RIVIERA** (Li) ex *Fadura*
Sisters:
47992 **FINNBEAVER** (Fi) ex *Passad* 1978; ex *Matai*
1978
47993 **FINNFURY** (Fi) ex *Monsun* 1978; ex *Forano*
1978
47994 **LITA** (Fi)
47995 **NAN FUNG** (Fi)
47996 **PAMPERO** (Fi)
47997 **ADIB** (Ir) ex *Patricia* 1982
47998 **AMIN** (Ir) ex *Caldereta* 1982

47999 **AMIS** (Ir) ex *Altano* 1982
47999/2 **VITALITY** (Pa) ex *Levante*

48000 **WAH PANG** Pa/No (Haugesund) 1966; B;
18200; 187.03 × 11.26 (613.62 × 36.9); M (Sulzer);
16.5; ex *Wah Shun* 1981; ex *Itel Volans* 1980; ex
Amax Trader 1976; ex *Skausund* 1974
Sister (may have 7 cranes):
★48001 **WEI HAI** (RC) ex *Fruen* 1973; ex *Lysland*
1970

★48010 **LING LONG HAI** RC/No (Bergens) 1963; B;
18800; 185.66 × 11.2 (609.12 × 36.75); M (Gotaverken); 14.5; ex *Norbu*

48020 **ARCTIC** Ca/Ca (Port Weller) 1978; B/IB;
19400; 209.51 × 10.97 (687.37 × 35.99); M (MAN);
15.5

48030 **PING CHAU** Pa/Sw (Oresunds) 1968;
C/Con; 17400; 172.22 × 9.9 (565.03 × 32.48); M
(Gotaverken); 16; ex *Asia Pacific* 1984; ex *Andros*
1983; ex *Fermland* 1975; Converted from bulk carrier
1975

48040 **IRAN DAHR** Ir/Ja (NKK) 1971; B; 10400;
155.48 × 9.9 (510.1 × 32.48); M (Sulzer); 15.25; ex
Asia Morality 1983
Sisters (Ir flag):
48041 **IRAN NASR** ex *Asia Flamingo* 1983
48042 **SAADI** ex *Asia Gold* 1983
48043 **IRAN SABR** ex *Asia Loyalty* 1983

48050 **JAG SHAKTI** In/Sp (AESA) 1972; B; 15500;
182.84 × 10.55 (599.88 × 34.61); M (Sulzer); 15.5;
ex *Cunard Caravel* 1974; 'Euskalduna 27' type
Sisters:
48051 **JAG SHANTI** (In) ex *Cunard Campaigner*
1974
48052 **AENEAS** (Sg) ex *Cunard Carrier* 1978
48053 **GREAT CITY** (Pa) ex *Chieftain* 1981; ex
Cunard Chieftain 1978
48054 **EL CHAMPION** (Pi) ex *Cunard Champion*
1978
48055 **IONIAN CARRIER** (Gr) ex *Cunard Calaman-
da* 1978
48056 **OLYMPIC HISTORY** (Gr) ex *Cunard Carron-
ade* 1978
48057 **OLYMPIC HARMONY** (Li) ex *Cunard Cavalier* 1978
Similar:
48058 **COBETAS** (Sp)
48059 **DEUSTO** (Sp)
Possibly similar:
48060 **LAURENTINE** (Fr)
48061 **PENMEN** (Fr)

★48062 **DINARA** Ys/Sp (AESA) 1974; B; 15400;
182.71 × 10.53 (599 × 34.55); M (Sulzer); 16
Sisters:
★48063 **CVIJETA ZUZORIC** (Ys)
★48064 **RUDER BOSKOVIC** (Ys)
Similar (see inset):
★48065 **BEOGRAD** (Ys)
★48066 **DANILOVGRAD** (Ys)

48070 **BANDERAS** Sp/Sp (AESA) 1970; B; 15600;
183.12 × 10.51 (600.79 × 34.48); M (MAN) 14
Sister:
48071 **LEKEITIO** (Sp)

● 48072 **REGINA FERRAZ** Bz/Bz (CCN) 1980; B;
17900; 173.18 × 9.72 (568 × 31.89); M (MAN); 15;
'Prinasa 26/15' type
48073 **GRAZIELLA FERRAZ** (Bz)
48074 **ALCYON** (Bz)
48075 **ALMARIS** (Bz)
48076 **TAQUY** (Bz)
48077 **FELICIDADE FERRAZ** (Bz)
Similar (smaller funnel separated from radar mast):
48078 **CAPE ARNHEM** (Br)
48079 **CAPE FINISTERRE** (Br)
48079/1 **CAPE TRAFALGAR** (Br)
48079/2 **BARON KINNAIRD** (Br)

48080 **VENI II** Gr/Sp (AESA) 1977; B; 17000;
181.11 × 10.65 (594.19 × 34.94); M (Sulzer); 15; ex
Kara 1984
Sisters:
48081 **SUCCESSOR III** (Gr) ex *Kelo* 1984
48082 **MELA** (Pa) ex *Pamela* 1983
48083 **PHILIPPE L.D.** (Fr) ex *Peter* 1982
48084 **PUHOS** (Fi)

48100 **CORDIALITY** Pa/Sp (AESA) 1979; B; 19800;
197.6 × 11.11 (648.3 × 36.45); M (Sulzer); 15.1; ex
Angela Pando 1980
Sisters:
48101 **IRAN MOTHARAI** (Ir) ex *Marcoplata* 1983
48102 **ROG** (Li) ex *Sokorri* 1981

48110 **POSEIDON** Gr/Ja (Sanoyasu) 1968; B;
10700; 147.5 × 9.09 (483.93 × 29.82); M (Pielstick);
16.5; 'Sanoyasu 16BC5' type
Sister:

48111 **PROTEUS** (Gr) ex *Petraia* 1982

48120 **GLYFADA SUN** Gr/Ja (IHI) 1965; C; 16400;
175.98 × 10.31 (577.36 × 33.83); M (Sulzer); 16.75;
ex *Star Taro* 1980

48140 **CAPTAIN NICOLAS** Gr/No (Horten) 1968; B;
13600; 160.86 × 9.78 (527.76 × 32.09); M (Sulzer);
16; ex *Cape Sable* 1978;
Sister:
48141 **CHANDA** (In) ex *Cape Wrath* 1976

● 48150 **ARIETTA GREGOS** Gr/Bu (G Dimitrov)
1973; B; 23700; 201.3 × 11.23 (660.43 × 36.84); M
(B&W); 15; ex *Tropwind*
Sister:
48151 **KARIN VATIS** (Gr) ex *Tropwave*
Similar (different type of cranes):
48152 **AMSTELVLIET** (Ne)
48153 **AMSTELVAART** (Ne)
48154 **AMSTELVOORN** (Ne)
48155 **FALCON SEA** (Pa)
48156 **PROSPERITY SEA** (Pa)
48157 **ROC SEA** (Pa)
Similar (may not have deck cranes):
★48158 **MEKHANIK P KILIMENCHUK** (Ru) ex *Kamar* 1983

48160 **EASTERN SPLENDOR** Pa/Ja (Kurushima)
1976; BC; 20200; 178.87 × 11.12 (586.84 × 36.48);
M (MAN); 15.5; ex *Toshu Maru* 1983

48170 **AQUACHARM** Li/Ja (IHI) 1968; B; 25200;
202.72 × 12.27 (665.09 × 49.26); M (Sulzer); 15.5
Similar:
48171 **AQUAFAITH** (Li)
48172 **AQUAGLORY** (Li)
48173 **AQUAGRACE** (Li)
48174 **AQUAJOY** (Li)
48175 **AQUABELLE** (Gr) ex *Carras* 1983
48176 **M.G. TSANGARIS** (Gr)
Possibly similar (may not have cranes):
48177 **AQUAGEM** (Li)
48178 **LUCENDRO** (Li) ex *Aquabelle*

● 48180 **AEGIS MAJESTIC** Gr/Sp (AESA) 1974; C;
12500; 159.01 × 9.77 (521.68 × 32.05); M (Sulzer);
—; 'SANTA FE 77' type
Sisters (Gr flag):
48181 **AEGIS ATHENIC**
48182 **AEGIS ATOMIC**
48183 **AEGIS BALTIC**
48184 **AEGIS BRITANNIC**
48185 **AEGIS COSMIC**
48186 **AEGIS DORIC**
48187 **AEGIS DYNAMIC**
48188 **AEGIS HARMONIC**
48188/1 **AEGIS HELLENIC**
48189 **AEGIS HISPANIC**
48190 **AEGIS IONIC**
48191 **AEGIS LOGIC**
48192 **AEGIS LYRIC**
48193 **AEGIS MAGIC**
48194 **AEGIS MYSTIC**
48195 **AEGIS PRACTIC**
48196 **AEGIS SONIC**
48197 **AEGIS TOPIC**

48200 **KAVO MATAPAS** Gr/Sp (U N De Levante)
1977; C; 8700/12700; 159.01 × —/9.77 (521.68 ×
—/32.05); M (Sulzer); 15.5; ex *Mishref*; 'SANTA FE
77' type
Sister:
48201 **KAVO PEIRATIS** (Gr) ex *Jumairah* 1978

★48210 **PINO DEL AGUA** Cu/Sp ('Bazan') 1977; C;
9500 approx.; 148.06 × 8.96 (485.76 × 29.4); M
(MAN); 15.5; ex *Angel Perez*; 'CARTAGO' class
Probable sisters:
48211 **JURINA** (Sp) ex *Elena Perez* 1981
★48212 **LAS COLORADAS** (Cu) ex *Alvaro Perez*
1979
★48213 **PALMA MOCHA** (Cu) ex *Ramon Perez* 1980
★48214 **ALEGRIA DE PIO** (Cu) ex *Gabriel Perez*
1980
48215 **ALCA** (Sp)

48220 **MING SPRING** Tw/Tw (China SB) 1978; C;
18600; 172.02 × 10.6 (564.37 × 34.78); M (Sulzer);
17
Sisters (Tw flag):
48221 **MING SUMMER**
48222 **MING AUTUMN**
48223 **MING WINTER**
Probable sisters (Tw flag):
48224 **TAO YUAN** ex *Tai Hsiung* 1982
48225 **YE LAN** ex *Tai Lung* 1982

48320 **SONGKHLA** De/Ja (Mitsui) 1977; B/Con;
16100; 158.02 × 10.59 (518.44 × 34.74); M (B&W);
16.25
Sister:
48231 **SUMBAWA** (Bs)

48250 **SEIYEI MARU** Ja/Ja (Usuki) 1977; B; 14300;

160.03 × 9.92 (525.03 × 32.55); M (Pielstick); 14.5

48260 ANDRE DELMAS Fr/Ja (Usuki) 1976; B; 14600; 156.01 × 10.35 (511.84 × 33.96); M (Sulzer); 15.5
Probable sister (may have kingposts):
48261 **LUCIEN DELMAS** (Fr)

48270 KOREAN PEARL Pa/Ja (Mitsui) 1970; B; 11800; 155.05 × 9.14 (508.7 × 29.99); M(B&W); 14.75; ex *Woko Maru* 1975

●**48280 JAMAICAN STARS** Pa/Ja (Kanasashi) 1970; B; 12300; 155.1 × 9.19 (508.86 × 30.15); M (Mitsui); 14.75; ex *Kinko Maru* 1982
Probable Sisters:
48281 **EUROFREEDOM** (Cy) ex *Kanezhizu Maru* 1983
48282 **CARIBBEAN STARS** (Pa) ex *Kikuko Maru* 1982
48283 **ELEUROPA** (Gr) ex *Kanekiyo Maru* 1973

48290 ATLANTIS EXPRESS Cy/Ja (Namura) 1972; B; 11000; 150.12 × 9.73 (492.52 × 31.92); M (Sulzer); 14.5; ex *South Express* 1983; ex *Inachus Star* 1979; ex *Amazon Maru* 1975

48300 WELLPARK Br/Ja (Mitsubishi HI) 1977; B; 18622; 170.01 × 10.21 (557.77 × 33.5); M (Sulzer); 15.5
Sisters:
48301 **LAMMA FOREST** (Br) ex *Clarkspey* 1981; ex *Star Bay* 1981; ex *Clarkspey* 1978
48302 **MARIA SITINAS** (Gr) ex *Trongate* 1983

48310 BLUEBIRD Li/Ja (Hitachi) 1968; B; 11200; 150 × 8.99 (492 × 29.49); M (B&W); 14.25; ex *Hoyu Star* 1983; ex *Bluebird* 1981
Similar:
48311 **SEABLUE** (Ma) ex *Eurotransport* 1983; ex *Ho Shin* 1977; ex *Zama Maru* 1975

48340 KASSANDRA Pa/FRG (Rhein Nordseew) 1969; B; 14300; 163.56 × 10.03 (536.61 × 32.91); M (Fiat); 16; ex *Tellus* 1980; ex *Evamo* 1978
Sisters (No flag):
48341 **DICTO**
48342 **SPERO**

48350 SIAM VENTURE Li/Ja (Shikoku) 1972; B; 7300; 130 × 8.3 (426.51 × 27.23); M (Sulzer); 14

48360 JAMAICA FAREWELL Li/Ja (Hitachi) 1975; C; 13500; 161.6 × 9.93 (530.18 × 32.58); M (B&W); 15.5; 'Hitachi UT-20' type
Sister:
48361 **MARI BOEING** (Li)

48362 VISHVA PANKAJ In/Br (Sunderland) 1980; C/Con; 8900/12800; 152.03 × —/9.52 (499 × —/31.23); (Sulzer); 15.75
Sisters (In flag):
48363 **VISHVA PALLAV**
48364 **VISHVA PARIMAL**
48365 **VISHVA PARIJAT**
48366 **VISHVA PARAG**
48367 **VISHVA PRAFULLA**

48370 CORRIENTES II Ar/Sp (AESA) 1977; C; 12600; 159.01 × 9.76 (521.69 × 32.02); M (Sulzer); 16; 'Santa Fe' 77' type
Sisters (Ar flag):
48371 **CHACO**
48372 **ENTRE RIOS II**
48373 **FORMOSA**
48374 **RIO NEGRO II**
48375 **SANTA CRUZ II**
48376 **TIERRA DEL FUEGO II**
48377 **MISIONES II**
48378 **SANTA FE II**
48379 **CHUBUT**

48380 TRANSOCEAN REEFER Pi/Ja (Shikoku) 1969; R; 5000; 135 × 7.1 (443 × 23.2); M (B&W); 17; ex *Penta* 1980; ex *Aotearoa* 1972

48383 ANWAR Mo/Bu (G Dimitrov) 1975; B; 16200; 185.43 × 10.25 (608.37 × 33.63); M (Sulzer); 15
Sister:
48384 **BOUJNIBA** (Mo)
Similar:
★48385 **ROJEN** (Bu)
48385/1 **EL CARRIER** (Pi)
48385/2 **EL COMMODORE** (Pa)
48385/3 **EL CRUSADER** (Pi)
48385/4 **KITHAIRONAS** (Gr)
48385/5 **OCEAN SEAGULL** (Gr)
48385/6 **TARPON STAR** (Gr)
48385/7 **TARPON SUN** (Gr)
Similar (may be converted to a cement carrier—see Helvetia):
48385/8 **JUVENITA** (Pa)
Probably similar (Cu flag):
48386 **26 DE JULIO**
48387 **ANTONIO MACEO**

●**48390 SEKI ROKAKO** Ja/Ja (Tsuneishi) 1979; Con/RoC; 17400; 152 × 9.08 (498.7 × 29.79); M (Pielstick) 17; Quarter ramp
Sister:
48391 **SEKI ROKEL** (Ja)

48400 ILE DE LA REUNION Fr/Fr (L'Atlantique) 1977; RoC/Con; 13900; 163.79 × 10.74 (537.36 × 35.23); M (Pielstick); 20.75; ex *Degas* 1983; Stern door/ramp
Sisters (Fr flag)
48401 **ILE MAURICE** ex *Cezanne* 1983
48402 **RENOIR**
48403 **MONET**
48404 **GAUGUIN**
48405 **UTRILLO**

●**48410 MILOS** Li/Sw (Eriksbergs) 1966; C; 7300/10700; 156.17 × 8.36/9.52 (512.37 × 27.43/31.23); M (B&W); 19; ex *Pulawy* 1982; ex *Waitara* 1973; 'Scandia' type; Sheerlegs are not permanent
Sister:
48411 **HELLENIC SEAMAN** (Gr) ex *Killara* 1975

●**48420 NARA** Fr/No (Kaldnes) 1977; C; 10100/17000; 171.41 × —/10.55 (562.4 × —/34.61); M (B&W); 18.25
Sisters:
48421 **NAUSICAA** (Fr)
48422 **HOEGH STAR** (No) ex *Concordia Star* 1983; ex *Costa Atlantica* 1983; ex *Concordia Star* 1982
48423 **HOEGH SUN** (No) ex *Concordia Sun* 1983; ex *Costa Mediterranea* 1983; ex *Concordia Sun* 1982

●★48430 **IVAN ZAGUBANSKI** Bu/Ru (Kherson) 1975; C; 11800; 162.31 × 9.17 (532.51 × 30.09); M (B&W); 18; 'Dnepr' type
Sisters (Bu flag):
★48431 **CHRISTO BOTEV**
★48432 **GOTZE DELCHEV**
★48433 **LUBEN KARAVELOV**
★48434 **KAPITAN PETKO VOIVODA**
★48435 **VASIL LEVSKY**
(Ru flag):
★48436 **GRIGORIY PETRENKO**
★48437 **NIKITA MITCHENKO**
★48438 **PETR DUTOV**
★48439 **IVAN SHEPETKOV**
★48440 **IVAN MOSKALENKO**
★48441 **GEROI PANFILOVTSY**
★48442 **VASILY KLOCHKOV**
★48443 **NIKOLAY ANANYEV**
★48444 **NIKOLAY MAKSIMOV**
★48445 **PETR YEMTSOV**
★48446 **YAKOV BONDARENKO**
★48447 **SOVIETSKIYE PROFSOYUZY**
(Ys flag):
★48448 **ADMIRAL PURISIC**
★48449 **HEROJ PAIC**
★48450 **HEROJ KOSTA STAMENKOVIC**
★48451 **HEROJ SENJANOVIC**
(Rm flag):
★48452 **ZALAU**
(Cu flag):
★48453 **JOSE ANTONIO ECHEVERRIA**
★48454 **JULIO ANTONIO MELLA**
★48455 **30 DE NOVIEMBRE**
★48456 **XI FESTIVAL**
(Br flag):
48457 **LYCAON**
(Hu flag):
★48460 **VOROSMARTY**
(Gr flag):
48461 **ATHINA K**
48462 **FAMILY FOTINI**
48463 **FAMILY ANTHONY**
48464 **TAUFAU** ex *Santa Elena* 1983;
(Li flag):
48465 **ACDIR II** ex *Jugoagent* 1983;
(Pa flag):
48466 **EVIA LUCK** ex *Laertes* 1982

48470 HALLA PILOT Ko/Br (Swan Hunter) 1970; C; 6700/10000; 154.13 × 8.17/9.62 (505.68 × 26.8/31.56); M (B&W); 17; ex *Strathcarrol*; ex *Aska* 1975
Sister:
48471 **HALLA PRIDE** (Ko) ex *Strathcarron*; ex *Amra* 1976

★48480 **PREDEAL** Rm/Br (Doxford & S) 1966; C; 10800; 162.46 × 9.38 (533 × 30.77); M (B&W); 18.25

48485 BLUMENTHAL FRG/FRG (Flender) 1984; R; 9500; 145.60 × 9.45 (478 × 31.00); M (MAN); 21.7; ex *Helene Jacob*; Free-Fall lifeboat system aft, on port side, obscures a crane on the starboard side. Four side doors
48486 BREMERHAVEN (FRG) ex *Walter Jacob*

48490 ARGIRO Cy/Br (H Robb) 1967; C; 1500; 93.88 × 5.08 (308 × 16.66); M (Mirrlees); 13; ex *Aldebaran II* 1980; ex *City of Athens* 1977; ex *Salmo* 1974
Sisters:
48491 **WAYBRIDGE** (Br) ex *Gracechurch* 1983; ex *City of Sparta* 1977; ex *Sorrento* 1974
48492 **PAXI** (Cy) ex *Pyrgos Star* 1981; ex *City of Corinth* 1978; ex *Salerno* 1975
Similar:
48493 **KOTA JADE** (Sg) ex *City of Valetta*; ex *Athenian*

48500 MOMOLI Pa/No (Akers) 1956; C; 2100; 88.40 × 5.81 (290 × 19.06); M (B&W); 14.5; ex *Ray* 1979; ex *Perama* 1976; ex *Vatnasund* 1972; ex *Brabant* 1972

48510 ARC ODYSSEUS Gr/FRG (Bremer V) 1976; C; 7700/10800; 150.65 × 8.03/9.35 (494.26 × 26.35/30.68); M (MAN); 16; ex *City of Winchester* 1981; 'Bremen Progress' type (Series A)
Sisters:
48512 **ARC AEOLOS** (Gr) ex *City of Canterbury* 1981
48513 **CITY OF YORK** (Br)

48520 SHANTA ROHAN In/Ja (Sanoyasu) 1969; B; 10300; 148.37 × 8.98 (486.79 × 29.46); M (Sulzer); 15; ex *Fort St John* 1980; ex *Pacific Logger* 1977

48530 SARONIS Gr/Be (Boel) 1962; B; 13700; 182.96 × 10.08 (600.26 × 33.07); M (B&W); 15.5; ex *Georgios A* 1981; ex *Patignies* 1974

48540 MIA Pa/FRG (Rickmers) 1961; B; 9900; 153.8 × 9.40 (504.6 × 30.84); M (MAN); 14; ex *Ocean Gold* 1980; ex *Balto* 1974

48550 MAHA NUWARA Sr/No (Sarpsborg) 1964; C; 800; 79.18 × 4.11 (259.78 × 13.48); M (Werkspoor); 12.5; ex *San George* 1980; ex *Potos Beach* 1977; ex *Doctor George* 1976; ex *Spaarnestroom* 1975

48560 AXIOS Gr/Sw (Helsingborgs) 1958; C; 2400/3900; 105.29 × 5.87/6.48 (345.44 × 19.26/21.26); M (Gotaverken); 12.5; ex *Inga* 1982

48570 GRIPEN Sg/Sw (Falkenbergs) 1964; C; 600; 83.55 × 3.67 (274.11 × 12.04); M (MWM); 12; ex *Aspen* 1970

●**48580 F J GARAYGORDOBIL** Sp/Sp (Cadagua) 1981; R; 1600; 83.70 × 5.31 (275 × 17.42); M (Deutz); 13.4

48590 DELMA QUEEN UAE/No (Ulstein) 1967; C; 1400; 75.85 × 6.05 (248.85 × 19.85); 14; ex *Chantala Fortune*; ex *Lorena* 1981; ex *Lorena Horn* 1970

48600 FAUNA Gr/FRG (Unterweser) 1966; C; 800/1400; 73.34 × 4.01/5.38 (240.62 × 13.16/17.65); M (KHD); 12.5
Sister:
48601 **FORTUNA 1** (Gr) ex *Fortuna* 1978;
Similar:
48602 **ASTARTE** (It)
48603 **REWI** (FRG) ex *Achilles* 1978

48610 HAMAD AL KULAIB Ku/Sp ('Corbasa') 1967; C; 1000/1600; 82.53 × 5.98/7.04 (270.76 × 19.62/23.09); M (Stork-Werkspoor); 16.25; ex *San Remo* 1982

★48620 **USTRINE** Ys/FRG (Kroegerw) 1960; C; 900/1600; 80.17 × —/5.64 (263.02 × —/18.5); M (MAN); 13; ex *Baltic Sprite* 1974

48623 AVON FRG/Ru (Kherson) 1976/79; Con; 12200; 162.52 × 10.12 (533 × 33.20); M (B&W); 16.5; ex *Monte Sarmiento* 1983; ex *Columbus Tasmania* 1980; ex *Santa Rosa* 1979; Converted from 'DNEPR' class cargo vessel 1979 (Flender)
Sister:
48624 **SAXON STAR** (FRG) ex *Columbus California* 1983; ex *Monte Olivia* 1982; ex *Columbus Taranaki* 1980; ex *Santa Rita* 1979

●**48630 CHUNG SHING** Br/Ys ('Uljanik') 1971; B; 20700; 179 × 11.09 (587.27 × 36.38); M (B&W) 16; ex *Silverfjord* 1982
Sisters:
48631 **BLUE MASTER** (No)
48632 **ARICA** (Pa) ex *Taurus* 1981; ex *Norbeth* 1978
★48635 **GOSPIC** Ys/Ja (IHI) 1977; B; 22100; 187.74 × 10.76 (616 × 35.30); M (Sulzer); 14.5; 'Future 32' type
★48636 **MOLAT** (Ys)
★48637 **RUDO** (Ys)

48640 DASHAKI Li/Ne (Verolme SH) 1972; B; 14300; 175.67 × 10.25 (576 × 33.63); M (MAN); 15.5; ex *Ocean Coracle* 1980; ex *Andromed* 1977; ex *Andromeda* 1976

48650 TORM HERDIS De/De (Odense) 1977; B;

25600; 182.99 × 11 (600.4 × 36.1); M (Sulzer); 15
Sisters:
★48651 **PROFESSOR KOSTIUKOV** (Ru) ex *Torn Helvig* 1983
48652 **TORM HILDE** (De)
★48653 **INZHENIER PARKHONTUK** (Ru) ex *Torm Helene* 1983

★48660 **KOPALNIA GRZYBOW** Pd/Sp (AESA) 1972; B; 9200; 145.01 × 8.36 (475.75 × 27.43); M (Sulzer); 16
Sister:
★48661 **KOPALNIA MACHOW** (Pd)

48670 **HOELIEN** Sg/Fi (Crichton-Vulcan) 1965; C; 2100/3300; 105.29 × 5.51/6.54 (345 × 18.08/21.46); M (Sulzer); 14.5; ex *Clio* 1980; ex *Nefertari* 1979; ex *Clio* 1978; Side doors; Lengthened 1970 (Valmet)
Sister:
48671 **YAEL** (Is) ex *Fennia* 1979; ex *Semiramis* 1979; ex *Fennia* 1978

48680 **CONTI BELGICA** FRG/FRG (Sietas) 1978; C; 1600/4000; 101.01 × 5.53 (328.12 × 18.14); M (Atlas-MaK); 15; ex *Ville d'Aurore* 1982; ex *Martinique* 1981; ex *Conti Belgica* 1980

48690 **GULF VENTURE** Cy/Br (Doxford) 1965; C/V; 1800; 97.9 × 5.5 (321.2 × 18.05); M (MAN); 14; ex *Melville Venture* 1981; ex *Baltic Venture* 1980

48700 **GALILA** Is/FRG (O&K) 1967; C; 3000/4900; 123.4 × 6.45/7.59 (405 × 21.16/24.9); M (MAN); —; Launched as *Cinnamon Bay*

48710 **KEMAL II** Tu/FRG (Nobiskrug) 1971; C; 2800/5000; 125.02 × 6.5/7.65 (410.17 × 21.52/25.1); M (B+V); 17; ex *Tolmi* 1981; ex *Mette Bewa* 1976; ex *Cap Matapan* 1974
Sisters:
48711 **AZUR MED** (Li) ex *Happy Med* 1982; ex *Timi* 1981; ex *Rikke Bewa* 1976; ex *Cap Carmel* 1974
48712 **CAPE ITEA** (Gr) ex *Samos Island;* ex *Cap Anamur* 1973

●48720 **MIRAMAR PRIMA** It/FRG (Elsflether) 1966; C; 1600; 85.81 × 5.12 (281.53 × 16.79); M (MaK); 12.5; ex *Tony's Luck* 1980; ex *Atreus* 1980; ex *Ingrid Retzlaff* 1974
Sister:
48721 **ROSARITA** (Pa) ex *New Hope;* ex *Erich Retzlaff* 1974

●48730 **SLOMAN MERCUR** FRG/FRG (Howaldts DW) 1979; C/Con; 5800/9500; 154.05 × 8.14/7.16 (505.41 × 26.7/23.49); M (Atlas-MaK); 17.5; ex *Carol Mercur* 1980; ex *Sloman Mercur* 1979; Cranes can rotate and are probably stowed in the position shown in the inset
Sister:
48731 **SLOMAN MIRA** (FRG)

48740 **CORONA** Fi/No (Kleven) 1972; C; 2100/4000; 106.61 × 5.47/7.08 (349.77 × 17.95/23.23); M (Stork-Werkspoor); —; ex *Finnmaster* 1982

48750 **LESLIE GAULT** Br/Br (Appledore) 1977; C; 1600; 91.52 × 5.16 (300.26 × 16.93); M (Mirrlees Blackstone); 12.5; Deck cranes may be removed
Sisters (Br flag):
48751 **CERINTHUS**
48752 **GALLIC FJORD**
48753 **MARKINCH**

48760 **NEW GALACTICA** Sg/Sw (Finnboda) 1962; C; 1600/2800; 93.81 × 5.07/5.76 (308 × 16.63/18.90); M (Fiat); 13; ex *Atlas* 1982; ex *Grim* 1969

★48770 **RISNJAK** Ys/Fi (Rauma-Repola) 1967; RoC; 1800/3300; 100.01 × 5.56/6.22 (328.11 × 18.24/20.41); M (MWM); 15; ex *Bore VI* 1974; Stern door
Sister:
48771 **AFROS** (Gr) ex *Bore V* 1977

48780 **SUDURLAND** Ic/Fi (Laiva) 1964; C; 500/1100; 73.21 × 3.65/4.99 (240.19 × 11.97/16.39); M (MAN); 12; ex *Tavi* 1974
Probable sister:
48781 **LOKKY** (It) ex *Elkas* 1979; ex *Normannbay* 1977; ex *Lokki* 1973

48790 **MOKSTEIN** No/FRG (Schuerenstedt) 1966; C; 500/1200; 73.61 × 3.6/5.25 (241.5 × 11.81/17.22); M (Atlas-MaK); 12.5; ex *Henriette R* 1974

48800 **ORKNEY** Pa/Fi (Wartsila) 1967; C; 2800; 91.55 × 5.42/6.52 (300.36 × 17.78/21.39); M (Sulzer); 13.5; ex *Auriga* 1982

48810 **HOELIEN** Sg/Fi (Crichton-Vulcan) 1965; C; 2100/3300; 105.29 × 5.51/6.54 (345.44 ×

18.08/21.46); M (Sulzer); 14.5; ex *Clio* 1980; ex *Nefertari* 1979; ex *Clio* 1978; Lengthened 1970 (Valmet); Side doors
Sister:
48811 **YAEL** (Is) ex *Fennia* 1979; ex *Semiramis* 1979; ex *Fennia* 1978

48820 **CANADIA** Sw/Fi (Hollming) 1970; C; 3000/5600; 144.31 × 5.79/8.08 (375 × 18.99/28.47); M (B&W); 15; ex *Maria Gorthon* 1981; Lengthened 1975
Sisters:
48821 **TEVERA** (Cy) ex *Ada Gorthon* 1983
48822 **FEDERAL PIONEER** (Ca) ex *Carl Gorthon* 1980
48823 **AGIOS MATTHEOS** (Gr) ex *Ivan Gorthon* 1981

48830 **PUERTO CADIZ** Sp/Sp (Cadagua) 1979; R; 1400; 90.4 × 5.11 (296.6 × 16.77); M (Deutz); 14
Sisters (Sp flag):
48831 **FERO CADIZ**
48832 **MAR CADIZ**

★48835 **KOPALNIA JASTRZEBIE** Pd/Br (Govan) 1979; B; 11000; 158.53 × 8.38 (520 × 27.49); M (B&W); 15
Sisters:
★48836 **KOPALNIA MYSLOWICE** (Pd)
★48837 **KOPALNIA SIEMIANOWICE** (Pd)
★48838 **KOPALNIA SZOMBIERKI** (Pd)

48840 **LEILA** Cy/No (Horten) 1969; B; 13500; 160.86 × 9.97 (527.76 × 32.71); M (Stork-Werkspoor); 15; ex *Solitaire* 1978; ex *Temple Arch* 1977
Sister:
48841 **BOTOGAN** (Pi) ex *Baybridge* 1983; ex *Freedom A S* 1980; ex *Cape York* 1979

48850 **SANTISTA** Bz/Bz (Ish do Brazil) 1973; B; 13000; 176.41 × 10.08 (578.77 × 33.07); M (Sulzer); 14.5

48851 **KONKAR THETIS** Gr/Ys ('Uljanik') 1981; C/Con; 16400; 193.17 × 10.20 (634 × 33.46); M (B&W); 16.75
Sister:
48852 **KONKAR TRIAINA** (Gr)
Probable sisters:
48853 **KONKAR DORIS** (Gr)
48854 **KONKAR NEREUS** (Gr)
48855 **KONKAR POSEIDON** (Gr)
48856 **KONKAR TRITON** (Gr)

★48860 **STEPAN ARTEMENKO** Ru/Ja (NKK) 1977; B; 15900; 178.21 × 10.92 (584.68 × 35.83); M (Sulzer); 15.5; ex *Lavinia V* 1983
Sisters:
★48861 **KAPITAN MEDVEDEV** (Ru) ex *Felicia V* 1983
★48862 **MEKHANIK DREN** (Ru) ex *Patricia V* 1983

48865 **JOHN** SV/Ja (Mitsui) 1956; B; 8900; 144.63 × 8.61 (475 × 28.25); M (B&W); 12; ex *Someri* 1984; ex *John Wilson* 1973

48870 **LADY FRANKLIN** Ca/FRG (Kroegerw) 1970; RoC; 2100; 103.43 × 5.94 (339.33 × 19.49); M (MAN); —; ex *Baltic Valiant* 1981; Stern door

48875 **JO LONN** No/No (Bergens) 1982; Tk/Ch; 21600; 175.01 × 10.74 (574 × 35.24); M (B&W); 15.5
Sisters:
48876 **JO BIRK** (No)
48877 **JO OAK** (Ne)

48880 **HELENE DELMAS** Fr/Fr (L'Atlantique) 1978; Con; 18900; 188.63 × 11.42 (618.86 × 37.47); M (Pielstick); 20
Sisters (Fr flag):
48881 **IRMA DELMAS**
48882 **LUCIE DELMAS**
48883 **MARIE DELMAS**

48890 **VAN DYCK** Be/Ja (Sasebo) 1977; B/Con; 15000; 164.12 × 10.01 (538.45 × 32.84); M (Sulzer); 16.5
Sister:
48891 **QUELLIN** (Be)

48900 **LA PALLICE** Fr/Ca (Marine Indust) 1975; C; 6600/11500; 160.15 × 10.05 (525.43 × 32.97); M (MAN); 18; 'MARINDUS' class
Sisters:
48901 **LA ROCHELLE** (Bs) ex *Namrata;* ex *La Rochelle* 1982; ex *Franco Express;* ex *Namrata* 1982; ex *La Rochelle* 1982
48902 **NATHALIE** (Pa) ex *Jalapoitiers* 1982; ex *Poitiers* 1981
48903 **MARIS OTTER** (Pa) ex *Rochefort* 1983
48904 **MARIS SPORTSMAN** (Pa) ex *Ile de France 1* 1983; ex *Royan* 1982
48905 **CELYA** (Pa) ex *Tours* 1982

(Ag flag):
48906 **BABOR**
48907 **BIBAN**
(Ia flag):
48908 **SUHADIWARNO PANANG** ex *Amstelstroom* 1980; ex *Marindus Montreal* 1979; ex *Aristandros*
48909 **L JALABERT BONTANG** ex *Amstelstraat* 1980; ex *Marindus Sorel* 1979; ex *Aristeides*
48910 **PALEMBANG** ex *Amstelstrand* 1980; ex *Marindus Tracy* 1979; ex *Aristarchos*

48920 **ELISABETH MAERSK** De/De (Odense) 1980; RoC/Con/C; 13700/22000; 182.28 × 9.76/11.85 (598 × 32.02/38.88); M (Sulzer); 18.5; quarter ramp (starboard); 'Carolina' type

48930 **BUNGA SETAWAR** My/Ja (Miho) 1976; C; 1800/3000; 86.01 × 6.06/6.39 (282.18 × 19.88/20.96); M (Hanshin); 12.5
Sisters (My flag):
48931 **BUNGA MAS**
48932 **BUNGA BINDANG**
Probable sister:
48933 **BUNGA GELANG** (My)

48940 **TOHOKU MARU** Ja/Ja (Hitachi) 1971; BWC; 34800; 197.01 × 10.99 (646.35 × 36.08); M (B&W); 13.5
Similar:
48941 **TAIKAI MARU** (Ja)
48942 **KASUGAI MARU** (Ja)
48943 **SENDAI** (Pa)
48944 **NEW INDEPENDENCE** (Li)
48945 **PACIFIC VENTURE** (Li)
48946 **SUNNY STATE** (Li)
48947 **SCANSILVA** (Li)
48948 **OJI MARU No 1** (Ja)
48949 **SCANSPRUCE** (Li)
48949/1 **ALPINE ROSE** (Pa) ex *Tonami Maru* 1981
48949/2 **BRAZILIAN SKY** (Li) ex *Gohyo* 1983
48949/3 **DAIHO MARU** (Ja)
48949/4 **GOIDEN GRAMPUS** (Li) ex *Silvana* 1977
Similar:
48950 **EHIME MARU** (Ja)—cranes on travelling gantries
48951 **PRINCE OF TOKYO** (Li)—large bins by hatches 2, 4 & 6

48960 **WORLD WOOD** Li/Ja (Hayashikane) 1974; BWC; 37000; 205.44 × 11.3 (674.02 × 37.07); M (Sulzer); 13.5
Possibly similar (Li flag):
48961 **ORIENTAL TAIO**
48962 **UNIVERSAL TAIO**

48970 **ARCTIC TROLL** Br/Ys ('3 Maj') 1971; B; 22200; 183.32 × 11.37 (601.44 × 37.3); M (Sulzer); 15.75
Sisters:
48971 **TROLL LAKE** (Br)
48972 **TROLL PARK** (Br)
48973 **CIELO DI GENOVA** (It) ex *Troll River* 1980 (Converted to container ship 1977)

48980 **WILLINE TARO** Sg/No (Kaldnes) 1970; Con; 20200; 187.43 × 10.76 (614.93 × 35.3); M (Sulzer); 15.75; ex *Troll Forest* 1980. Converted from bulk carrier 1977

48990 **WORLD FINANCE** Li/Ja (Osaka) 1974; B; 20500; 184.97 × 11.34 (606.85 × 37.2); M (Sulzer); 14.75
Sisters (Li flag):
48991 **STREAM BOLLARD**
48992 **STREAM DOLPHIN**
48993 **STREAM HAWSER**
48994 **STREAM RUDDER**
Similar (Li flag):
48995 **ASIA HERON**
48996 **ASIA INDUSTRY**

49000 **HOHKOKUSAN MARU** Ja/Ja (Mitsui) 1969; B; 34100; 222.99 × 11.84 (731.59 × 38.84); M (B&W); 14.5

49010 **DASHAKI** Li/Ne (Verolme SH) 1972; B; 14300; 175.67 × 10.25 (576 × 33.63); M (MAN); 15.5; ex *Ocean Coracle* 1980; ex *Andromed* 1977; ex *Andromeda* 1976

★49020 **SISAK** Ys/Ys ('Split') 1967; B; 23700; 201.02 × 11.5 (659.51 × 37.73); M (Fiat); 15

49021 **FRIGO AMERICA** Sp/Sp (AESA) 1980; R; 3600; 103.74 × 6.3 (340.35 × 20.67); M (B&W); —
Sisters (Sp flag):
49022 **FRIGO AFRICA**
49023 **FRIGO ASIA**
49024 **FRIGO ESPANA**
49025 **FRIGO EUROPA**
49026 **FRIGO OCEANIA**
49027 **FRIGO LAS PALMAS** launched as *Polo Sur*
49028 **FRIGO TENERIFE**

49030 **IRAN MEEZAN** It/FRG (A G 'Weser') 1975; C; 10200; 149.79 × 9.26 (488.85 × 30.38); M (MAN); 16.5; ex *Arya Soroosh* 1980; '36-L' type
Sisters (Ir flag):
49032 **IRAN SOKAN** ex *Iran Navid* 1980; ex *Arya Navid* 1980
49033 **IRAN BORHAN** ex *Arya Gohar* 1980
49034 **IRAN EHSAN** ex *Arya Akhtar* 1980; ex *Aristaios* 1975
49035 **IRAN VOJDAN** ex *Iran Kay* 1980; ex *Arya Kay* 1980; launched as *Aristonidas*
49037 **IRAN BAYAN** ex *Arya Sepand* 1980; ex *Aristonimos* 1975

★49040 **PIRIN** Bu/Ja (Hakodate) 1965; B; 6100; 126.02 × 7.6 (413.45 × 24.93); M (B&W); 13
Sisters (Bu flag):
★49041 **SREDNA GORA**
★49042 **STARA PLANINA**
★49043 **STRADJA**

49050 **ISAR EXPRESS** Sg/Ja (Nipponkai) 1973/79; Con; 14200; 170.77 × 9.36 (560 × 30.71); M (B&W); 16; ex *Ibn Al Suwaidi* 1982; ex *Frauenfels* 1980; ex *Aristipos* 1974; Converted from 'Mitsui-Concord' type cargo vessel and lengthened 1979. Others of this class may also have deck cranes now—see 'WERRA EXPRESS' etc

49055 **HOLSTENCRUISER** Pa/FRG (A.G. 'Weser') 1980; C/Con; 8800; 145.01 × 8.21 (476 × 26.94); M (MaK); 17.75; 'Key 12' type
Similar (2nd and 3rd cranes are tandem):
49056 **NEPTUNE DOLPHIN** (FRG) ex *Sofati Canada* 1982; ex *Holstencarrier* 1982; ex *E,L.M.A. Dos* 1982; ex *Holstencarrier* 1980;
49057 **HOLSTENRACER** (FRG)
Similar (slightly larger):
49058 **SAVANNAH** (FRG)

49060 **AKAD** Tu/Sw (Uddevalla) 1966; B; 21600; 196.91 × 11.33 (646 × 37.17); M (B&W); 15.5; ex *Sangstad* 1975

49070 **H 1070** Br/Ca (Saint John SB) 1966; OO; 21200; 210.47×10.95 (690.52×35.93); T (Canadian GEC); 15.5

49080 **ON DING** Pa/Sw (Uddevalla) 1966; B; 20700; 196.32×10.88 (644.09×35.69); M (B&W); 16.25; ex *Orania*

49090 **TASMAN SEA** Pa/Sw (Gotav) 1962; B; 16400; 178.09 × 10.48 (584.28 × 34.38); M (Gotaverken); 15; ex *Theresie* 1973; Cranes may be on travelling gantries

★49100 **YASENYEVO** Ru/No (Kaldnes) 1967; B; 15800; 180.3 × 10.21 (591.54 × 33.5); M (Gotaverken); 15.5; ex *Gigondas* 1980; ex *Torm Ragnhild* 1977; ex *Ragnhild* 1974
Similar:
★49101 **YAGOTIN** (Ru) ex *Julienas* 1980

49110 **ALEXANDROS G. TSAVLIRIS** Gr/Bz 1978; B; 15700; 173.18 × 9.72 (568.17 × 31.89); M; 15.5; 'Prinasa 26/15' type
Sister:
49111 **CLAIRE A. TSAVLIRIS** (Gr)

49120 **AZTECA** Me/Pd (Szczecinska) 1969; B; 16000; 186.01 × 10.57 (610.27 × 34.68); M (Sulzer); 'B-449' type

★49130 **YING GE HAI** RC/Ja (Fujinagata) 1967; B; 15600; 178.01 × 10.17 (584.02 × 33.37); M (B&W); 15; ex *Normandiet* 1977
Similar:
49131 **TURKIYE** (Tu) ex *Himmerland* 1977

49140 **THALASSOPOROS** Gr/No (Haugesund) 1968; B; 12700; 161.55 × 9.7 (530 × 31.82); M (Sulzer); 16; ex *Kreon* 1984; ex *Bennevis* 1981; ex *Baron Dunmore* 1977

49150 **HADJANNA** Gr/FRG (Bremer V) 1965; B; 18000; 196.63 × 11.04 (645.11 × 36.22); M (MAN); —; ex *Amica* 1974
Similar (RC flag):
★49151 **GUANG HAI** ex *Angelic Protector* 1975; ex *Aino* 1968
★49152 **QIONG HAI** ex *Arica* 1974

★49160 **BUZLUDJA** Bu/Ja (Setoda) 1968; B; 9100; 139.83 × 9.26 (458.75 × 30.38); M (B&W); 15
Sisters (Bu flag):
★49161 **MURGASH**
★49162 **LUDOGORETZ**
★49163 **OBORISHTE**

49170 **NORDKAP** De/Ja (Mitsui) 1975; B/Con; 19600; 179.03 × 10.97 (587.37 × 35.99); M (B&W); 15
Sisters (De flag):
49171 **NORDPOL**
49172 **NORDTRAMP**

49173 **NORDKYN**
49174 **NORDHVAL**

●49180 **SHARK BAY** Sg/Br (Upper Clyde) 1969/77; Con; 17700; 175.27×9.91 (575.3×32.51); M (Sulzer); 15.5; ex *Vancouver Forest* 1981; Converted from Bulk Carrier 1977
Sister:
49181 **WILLINE TOYO** (Sg) ex *Havrais* 1980; ex *Conon Forest*

49190 **GEORGIAN GLORY** Gr/Sw (Kockums) 1962; B; 16600; 175.88 × 11 (577.03 × 36.06); M (MAN); 14.5; ex *Sighaug* 1966
Sister:
49191 **EUROPEAN MASTER** (Gr) ex *Cestos Bay* 1980; ex *Pantokrator* 1979; ex *Pan* 1972; ex *Theologos* 1970; ex *Siganka* 1966

49200 **TOPAZ EXPRESS** Pa/Ja (Mitsubishi HI) 1960; B- 14300; 177.02×9.59 (580.77×31.46); M (Sulzer); 16.25; ex *Zoodohos* 1983; ex *Rio Zaire* 1982; ex *Nikitas Roussos* 1970

★49210 **KOPALNIA PIASECZNO** Pd/Sp (AESA) 1971; B; 9100; 146.72 × 8.27 (481.36 × 27.13); M (Sulzer); 15.5
Sister:
★49211 **KOPALNIA JEZIORKO** (Pd)

●49220 **FRIENDSHIP** Cy/Ja (Fujinagata) 1965; C; 8900; 147.02 × 8.61 (482.34 × 28.25); M (B&W); 15; ex *Irenes Friendship* 1983; ex *Wakamiyasan Maru* 1977
Sisters:
49221 **ORIENT TRUST** (Pa) ex *Wakaosan Maru* 1978
49222 **ORIENT PINE** (Pa) ex *Wakatakesan Maru* 1974
49223 **IOANNIS** (Gr) ex *Wakanesan Maru* 1979
49224 **MARESOL** (Li) ex *Wakasugisan Maru* 1979

49230 **SAROS** Cy/Ja (Kanasashi) 1969; C; 10000; 148.93 × 8.89 (488.62 × 29.17); M (B&W); 14; ex *Kaneyoshi Maru* 1983

★49240 **KISHINEV** Ru/Ru (Navashinskiy) 1968; C (sea/river); 3600; 123.53 × 4.5 (405.28 × 14.76); TSM (Russkiy); 11.75
Sisters (Ru flag):
★49241 **ALEKSANDR POKALCHUK**
★49242 **GORKOVSKAYA KOMSOMOLIYA**
★49243 **NIKOLAY SHCHETININ** ex *Buor-Khaya* 1980
★49244 **PETR GUTCHENKO**
★49245 **SHURA BURLACHENKO**
★49246 **GORNYAK**
★49247 **HELME**
★49248 **MUOSTAKH**
★49249 **SERGEY BURYACHEK**

49260 **PRESIDENT MAGSAYSAY** Pi/Ys ('3 Maj') 1963; B; 17700; 196.5 × 10.86 (644.68 × 35.63); M (Sulzer); 16; ex *Dimitris L F* 1983; ex *Alida Gorthon* 1974

49270 **PINTO** Gr/Be (Boel) 1963; B; 14200; 183.22 × 10.42 (601.12 × 34.19); M (MAN); 15; ex *Mairoula* 1983; ex *Irene S Lemos* 1973

●49280 **ANNITSA L** Gr/Ja (Uraga HI) 1965; B; 19500; 193.02 × 11.17 (633.26 × 36.64); M (Sulzer); —
Sisters:
49281 **CAPTAIN GEORGE L** (Gr)
Similar:
49282 **DIMITRIS P** (Cy) ex *Wah Hing* 1983; ex *Itel Carina* 1980; ex *Christina II* 1973
49283 **ALADIN** (Pa) ex *Wah Long* 1984; ex *Wah Fat* 1982; ex *Itel Pegasus* 1980; ex *Genie* 1973
49284 **WAH LOK** (Pa) ex *Wah Lee* 1981; ex *Itel Taurus* 1980; ex *Marina* 1973

49290 **FRINES** Li/Ja (NKK) 1978; C; 8100; 134.52 × 8.67 (441.34 × 28.44); M (Pielstick); 14.75
Sister:
49291 **FINNSNES** (Li)

49300 **ATLANTIC EXPRESS** Li/De (B&W) 1960; C; 5800; 141.54 × 7.87 (464.37 × 25.82); M (B&W); 16; ex *Domino Crystal* 1973

49305 **ARACRUZ VENTURE** Li/Ja (Kanda) 1980; B; 18600; 183 × 10.88 (600 × 35.70); M (Sulzer); —
Sister:
49306 **BRAZIL VENTURE** (Li)
Probable sister:
49307 **MOSMAN STAR** (Li)

49308 **BARRUETA** Sp/Sp (Juliana) 1982; R; 3500; 103.73 × 6.67 (340 × 21.88); M (B&W); 15.7
Sister:
49309 **GUIARD** (Sp)

49310 **NEW DALIA** Eg/De (Langesunds) 1963; C; 1600/2700; 93.78 × 5.07/6.37 (307.68 × 16.63/20.9); M (Sulzer); 13.5; ex *Nanoula* 1983; ex

Tamaris; ex *Finnrover* 1973; ex *Nina* 1971

49320 **VAN DYCK** Be/Ja (Sasebo) 1977; B/Con; 15000; 164.12 × 10.01 (538.45 × 32.84); M (Sulzer); 16.5
Sister:
49321 **QUELLIN** (Be)

49330 **MEIHOU** Pa/Ja (Sanoyasu) 1978; B/RoVC; 26200; 184.72 × 12 (606.04 × 39.37); M (MAN); 15; ex *Meihou Maru* 1982; Stern quarter ramp
Sister:
49331 **NIPPOU MARU** (Ja)

49340 **PARMENION** Gr/Sp (AESA) 1973; C; 7800/11400; 147.02 × —/9.9 (482.35 × —/32.48); M (MAN); 15.5; ex *Med Victory* 1983; ex *Irene* 1981; 'Santa Fe' type

●★49342 **VIKTOR TKACHYOV** Ru/DDR (Warnow) 1981; B/Con; 13500; 162.11 × 9.88 (532 × 32.41); M (MAN); 14.75; Ice strengthened; 'UL-ESC' type
Sisters (Ru flag):
★49343 **KAPITAN BOCHEK**
★49344 **KAPITAN CHUKHCHIN**
★49345 **KAPITAN SVIRIDOV**
★49346 **KAPITAN V TSIRUL**
★49347 **KAPITAN VODENKO**
Probable sisters (Ru flag):
★49348 **KAPITAN KUDLAY**
★49349 **KAPITAN VAKULA**

49350 **WHITE NILE** Su/De (B&W) 1979; RoC-/Con/C/HL; 9100; 132.9 × 9.4 (436 × 30.84); M (B&W); 16; Slewing stern ramp; 'Hamlet-Multiflex' type
Sister:
49351 **BLUE NILE** (Su)
Similar:
49352 **ABUEGILA** (Eg)
49353 **ABURDEES** (Eg)
49354 **ABUZENIMA** (Eg)

49360 **SOUTH ISLANDER** Pa/Ja (Namura) 1977; C/RoC; 8400; 155.53 × 8.92 (510.27 × 29.27); M (MAN); 16.25; ex *Fiji Maru* 1981

49370 **RAINBOW 1** Pa/It (Ansaldo) 1963; B; 16000; 185.25 × 9.84 (607.78 × 32.28); M (Fiat); 16.25; ex *South Wind* 1982; ex *Transoceanica Elena* 1980

49380 **IBN SHUHAID** Ku/Ko (Hyundai) 1977; C; 11100/15400; 175.32 × —/10.4 (575.2 × —/34.12); M (B&W); 16; 'KUWAIT' class
Sisters (Ku flag) (some Br built (Govan)):
49381 **IBN AL-ATHEER**
49383 **IBN AL-MOATAZ**
49384 **IBN ALBEITAR**
49385 **IBN ASAKIR**
49386 **IBN BASSAM**
49387 **IBN BATTOTAH**
49388 **IBN DURAID**
49389 **IBN HAYYAN**
49390 **IBN KHALDOON**
49391 **IBN KHALLIKAN**
49392 **IBN MALIK**
49393 **IBN QUTAIBAH**
49394 **IBN RUSHD**
49395 **IBN TUFAIL**
49396 **IBN YOUNUS**
49397 **AL SALIMIAH**
49398 **AL MUBARAKIAH**
49399 **AL YAMAMAH**
49400 **AL FUJAIRAH**
49401 **AL MUHARRAQ**
49402 **AL RAYYAN**
49403 **AHMAD AL-FATEH**
49404 **ARAFAT**
49405 **DANAH**
49406 **FATHULKHAIR**
49407 **HIJAZ**
49408 **JILFAR**
49409 **QAROUH**
49410 **KUBBAR**
49411 **SALAH ALDEEN**
49412 **THEEKAR**
49413 **TABUK**
(Qt flag):
49414 **IBN AL-NAFEES**

49420 **NEDLLOYD BAHRAIN** Ne/Ne (Giessen-De Noord) 1978; C; 13200; 173.03 × 10 (567.68 × 32.81); M (Sulzer); 17
Sisters (Ne flag):
49421 **NEDLLOYD BALTIMORE**
49422 **NEDLLOYD BANGKOK**
49423 **NEDLLOYD BARCELONA**

49425 **SANDRA WESCH** FRG/FRG (Howaldts DW) 1979; C/Con; 8200; 141.69 × 7.85 (465 × 25.75); M (MAN); 15.75; ex *Ville de Sandra*; ex *Sandra Wesch* 1981; ex *Tynebank* 1980; ex *Sandra Wesch* 1979
Sisters:
49426 **CHRISTIAN WESCH** (FRG)

49427 **JONNY WESCH** (FRG) ex *Bretagne* 1983
49428 **MAGDALENE WESCH** (FRG)

49430 **JUMPA** Th/Br (Swan Hunter) 1970; C; 8000/11200; 156.98 × 8.2/9.62 (515.02 × 26.9/31.56); M (Sulzer); 19; ex *Strathmay* 1982; ex *Manora* 1975
Sisters:
49431 **KANNIKAR** (Th) ex *Strathmeigle* 1982; ex *Merkara* 1975
49432 **INTANIN** (Th) ex *Strathmore* 1982; ex *Morvada* 1975
49433 **SONIA M** (Br) ex *Strathmuir* 1982; ex *Mulbera* 1975

49440 **KIEL** Ms/Fr (La Ciotat) 1972; C; 8100/12600; 171.2 × 8.43/9.71 (561.68 × 27.66/31.86); M (Sulzer); 20; ex *Valence* 1984; ex *Ville de Valence* 1983
Sister:
49441 **VILLE DE GENES** (Fr)

49450 **KSAR ETTIR** Ag/Ja (Kanasashi) 1977; C; 12800; 156.11 × 9.9 (512.77 × 32.48); M (B&W) 15
Sisters (Ag flag):
49451 **KSAR CHELLALA**
49452 **KSAR EL BOUKHARI**

● 49460 **NARA** Fr/No (Kaldnes) 1977; C; 10100/17000; 171.41 × —/10.55 (562.3 × —/34.61); M (B&W); 18.25
Sisters:
49461 **NAUSICAA** (Fr)
49462 **HOEGH STAR** (No) ex *Concordia Star* 1983; ex *Costa Atlantica* 1983; ex *Concordia Star* 1982
49463 **HOEGH SUN** (No) ex *Concordia Sun* 1983; ex *Costa Mediterranea* 1983; ex *Concordia Sun* 1982

● ★49470 **IVAN ZAGUBANSKI** Bu/Ru (Kherson) 1975; C; 11800; 162.31 × 9.17 (532.51 × 30.09); M (B&W); 18; 'Dnepr' type
Sisters (Bu flag):
★49471 **CHRISTO BOTEV**
★49472 **GOTZE DELCHEV**
★49473 **LUBEN KARAVELOV**
★49474 **KAPITAN PETKO VOIVODA**
★49475 **VASIL LEVSKY**
(Ru flag):
★49476 **GRIGORIY PETRENKO**
★49477 **NIKITA MITCHENKO**
★49478 **PETR DUTOV**
★49479 **IVAN SHEPETKOV**
★49480 **IVAN MUSKALENKO**
★49481 **GEROI PANFILOVTSY**
★49482 **VASILY KLOCHKOV**
★49483 **NIKOLAY ANANYEV**
★49484 **NIKOLAY MAKSIMOV**
★49485 **PETR YEMTSOV**
★49486 **YAKOV BONDARENKO**
★49487 **SOVIETSKIYE PROFSOYUZY**
(Ys flag):
★49488 **ADMIRAL PURISIC**
★49489 **HEROJ PAIC**
★49490 **HEROJ KOSTA STAMENKOVIC**
★49491 **HEROJ SENJANOVIC**
(Rm flag):
★49492 **ZALAU**
(Cu flag):
★49493 **JOSE ANTONIO ECHEVERRIA**
★49494 **JULIO ANTONIO MELLA**
★49495 **30 DE NOVIEMBRE**
★49496 **XI FESTIVAL**
(Br flag):
49497 **LYCAON**
(Hu flag):
★49500 **VOROSMARTY**
(Li flag):
49501 **ACDIR II** ex *Jugoagent* 1983
(Pa flag):
49502 **EVIA LUCK** ex *Laertes* 1982
(Gr flag):
49503 **TAUFAU** ex *Santa Elena* 1983
49504 **ATHINA K**
49505 **FAMILY FOTINI**
49506 **FAMILY ANTHONY**

● 49510 **NARA** Fr/No (Kaldnes) 1977; C; 10100/17000; 171.41 × —/10.55 (562.3 × —/34.61); M (B&W); 18.25
Sisters:
49511 **NAUSICAA** (Fr)
49512 **HOEGH STAR** (No) ex *Concordia Star* 1983; ex *Costa Atlantica* 1983; ex *Concordia Star* 1982
49513 **HOEGH SUN** (No) ex *Concordia Sun* 1983; ex *Costa Mediterranea* 1983; ex *Concordia Sun* 1982

49520 **HALLA PILOT** Ko/Br (Swan Hunter) 1970; C; 6700/10000; 154.13 × 8.17/9.62 (505.68 × 26.8/31.56); M (B&W); 17; ex *Strathcarrol*; ex *Aska* 1975
Sister:
49521 **HALLA PRIDE** (Ko) ex *Strathcarron*; ex *Amra* 1976

49530 **ANJOU** Fr/Sp (AESA) 1978; C/Con; 16500;

173.01 × 10.5 (567.62 × 34.45); M (Pielstick); 17.5; ex *Ville de Brest* 1983; Stulcken derrick amidships
Sisters (Fr flag):
49531 **ARTOIS** ex *Ville de Reims* 1983
49532 **VILLE DE ROUEN**

49540 **YDRA** Gr/Br (Smith's D) 1966; C; 8300; 153.04 × 8.78 (502.1 × 28.81); M (Pielstick); 17.5; ex *Biokovo* 1980; ex *Manchester Port* 1971

49550 **EIFFEL** Fr/Ja (Mitsubishi HI) 1977; C/Con; 16600; 163.02 × 10 (534.84 × 32.81); M (Sulzer); 18
Sisters (Fr flag):
49551 **HAUSSMANN**
49552 **MANSART** ex *Hapag Lloyd Trier* 1982; ex *Mansart* 1982
49553 **SOUFFLOT**

49560 **THALASSINI MANA** Gr/Ja (Mitsui) 1977; C/Con; 14500; 165 × 10.48 (451.34 × 34.38); M (B&W); 18.5; ex *Amerika*; ex *Arabian Leader*; ex *Amerika* 1978
Sister:
49561 **THALASSINI KYRA** (Gr) ex *Nigeria*; ex *Arabian Progress*; ex *Nigeria* 1978

49580 **THALASSINI MANA** Gr/Ja (Mitsui) 1977; C/Con; 14500; 165 × 10.48 (451.34 × 34.38); M (B&W); 18.5; ex *Amerika*; ex *Arabian Leader*; ex *Amerika* 1978
Sister:
49581 **THALASSINI KYRA** (Gr) ex *Nigeria*; ex *Arabian Progress*; ex *Nigeria* 1978

49590 **VILLABLANCA** Sp/Sp ('Elcano') 1965; C; 2300; 83.67 × 5.42 (274.51 × 17.78); M (Gotaverken); 13; ex *Astene 94* 1967; Launched as *Bretagne*
Sisters (Sp flag):
49591 **VILLAFRANCA** ex *Astene 97* 1968
49592 **VILLAFRIA** ex *Astene 96* 1968
49593 **VILLAVERDE** ex *Astene 95* 1968

49600 **AMERICA** US/US (Equitable) 1979; Con/C/R; 1000; 90.07 × 4.5 (295.5 × 14.76); M (Fairbanks, Morse); 13.75
Sisters (US flag):
49601 **RAINBOW HOPE** ex *Amazonia*
49602 **ANTILLIA**

49610 **KRIS MELELA** My/SA (Barens) 1969; C; 2100/3100; 95.71 × 5.67/6.55 (314.01 × 18.6/21.49); M (Sulzer); 13.5; ex *Tugela* 1980
Sister:
49611 **KRIS MADURA** (My) ex *Pongola* 1980
Probable sister:
49612 **KRIS MERUBI** (My) ex *Sezela* 1983

49620 **EAST RAINBOW** Pa/Sw (Ekensbergs) 1961; C; 4500; 114 × 7.34 (374.02 × 24.08); M (B&W); 15; ex *Tesira*; ex *Maj Ragne* 1973
Possible sister:
49621 **FADULALLAH** (Si) ex *Nobel* 1983; ex *Sigri* 1982; ex *Akra Sigri* 1979; ex *Birgit Ragne* 1976

49630 **VILLABLANCA** Sp/Sp ('Elcano') 1965; C; 2300; 83.67 × 5.42 (274.51 × 17.78); M (Gotaverken); 13; ex *Astene 94* 1967; Launched as *Bretagne*
Sisters (Sp flag):
49631 **VILLAFRANCA** ex *Astene 97* 1968
49632 **VILLAFRIA** ex *Astene 96* 1968
49633 **VILLAVERDE** ex *Astene 95* 1968

● 49640 **TRISTAN** FRG/FRG (O & K) 1974; C; 8400; 143.85 × 8.31 (471.99 × 27.26); M (Pielstick); 18; ex *Hodeidah Crown* 1983; ex *Tristan* 1981; ex *Columbus Caribic* 1980; Launched as *Tristan*
Sisters (FRG flag):
49641 **RIENZI** ex *Agaba Crown* 1983; ex *Rienzi* 1981; ex *Bavaria Singapore* 1980; ex *Columbus Capricorn* 1980; Launched as *Rienzi*
49642 **MUSCAT BAY** ex *Monte Pascoal* 1981; ex *Senta* 1981; ex *Columbus Coromandel* 1980; Launched as *Senta*

● 49650 **ELISABETH** Gr/Sw (Lindholmens) 1963; B; 11300; 152.56 × 9.16 (500.52 × 30.05); M (Gotaverken); 14.5; ex *Alimar* 1981; ex *Karmalu* 1979; ex *Santa Claus* 1976; ex *Kanangoora* 1973

★49655 **JACEK MALCZEWSKI** Pd/Ca (Marine Indust) 1979; C/Con; 13000; 168.36 × 10.50 (552 × 34.45); M (Sulzer); 21.25
Sisters:
★49656 **ARTUR GROTTGER** (Pd)
★49657 **BOLESLAW RUMINSKI** (Pd)
★49658 **JOZEF CHELMONSKI** (Pd)

● 49660 **EGE YILDIZI** Tu/Bz (Emaq) 1976; C; 5600/7700; 142.02 × 7.67 (465.95 × 25.16); M (Sulzer); 18; ex *Lloyd Humaita* 1983
Sisters (Bz flag):
49661 **LLOYD CUIABA**
49662 **LLOYD MARABA**
49663 **LLOYD ALTAMIRA**
49664 **LLOYD SANTAREM**

49670 **TAIWO** Li/Ja (Uraga HI) 1968; B; 15700; 162.01 × 10.61 (531.53 × 34.81); M (Sulzer); 15; ex *Princess Aurora* 1981
Sisters:
49671 **MARITIME ALLIANCE** (Pa)
49672 **TAIHO** (Li) ex *Snow White* 1980

49680 **ABUQIR** Eg/Ja (Kurushima) 1976; C; 4700; 114.33 × 7.25 (375.1 × 23.79); M (Mitsubishi); 16.75
Sisters (Eg flag):
49681 **ALMANDARAH**
49682 **ALMOUNTAZAH 1**
49683 **MARYUT**

● 49690 **SANTA MONICA 1** Pa/Ja (Maizuru) 1969; C; 12100; 158.6 × 8.99 (520.34 × 29.49); M (Sulzer); 14; ex *Saganoseki Maru* 1974

49700 **RATNA MANORAMA** In/Sp (AESA) 1973; C; 11200; 147.02 × 9.81 (482.35 × 32.19); M (MAN); 15.5; 'Santa Fe' type
Sister:
49701 **RATNA KIRTI** (In)
Similar:
49702 **AEGIS BLAZE** (Gr)
Probably similar:
49703 **AEGIS HARVEST** (Gr)
49704 **AEGIS STOIC** (Gr)
49705 **AEGIS WISDOM** (Gr)

49710 **BANGLAR MITA** Bh/Sw (Eriksbergs) 1966; C; 7300/10700; 156.14 × 8.4/9.51 (512.27 × 27.56/31.2); M (B&W); 19; ex *Hokkaido* 1977
Sisters:
49711 **BANGLAR MAAN** (Bh) ex *Hirado* 1977
49712 **HALLBORG** (Li) ex *Hakone*
49713 **SIFNOS** (Gr) ex *Hondo*

★49720 **OMSK** Ru/Ja (Hitachi); 1961; C; 7500/10900; 155 × 9.6 (509 × 31.5); M (B&W); 17
Sisters (Ru flag):
★49721 **OKHOTSK**
★49722 **ORENBURG**

49730 **PICHIT SAMUT** Th/Sw (Lindholmens) 1966; C; 3500/5800; 127.4 × 8.2 (418 × 26.9); M (Pielstick); 16; ex *Bangpra-In* 1983; ex *Trader*

● 49740 **IVAN ZAGUBANSKI** Bu/Ru (Kherson) 1975; C; 11800; 162.31 × 9.17 (532.51 × 30.09); M (B&W); 18; 'Dnepr' type
Sisters (Bu flag):
★49741 **CHRISTO BOTEV**
★49742 **GOTZE DELCHEV**
★49743 **LUBEN KARAVELOV**
★49744 **KAPITAN PETKO VOIVODA**
★49745 **VASIL LEVSKY**
(Ru flag):
★49746 **GRIGORIY PETRENKO**
★49747 **NIKITA MITCHENKO**
★49748 **PETR DUTOV**
★49749 **IVAN SHEPETKOV**
★49750 **IVAN MOSKALENKO**
★49751 **GEROI PANFILOVTSY**
★49752 **VASILY KLOCHKOV**
★49753 **NIKOLAY ANANYEV**
★49754 **NIKOLAY MAKSIMOV**
★49755 **PETR YEMTSOV**
★49756 **YAKOV BONDARENKO**
★49757 **SOVIETSKIYE PROFSOYUZY**
(Ys flag):
★49758 **ADMIRAL PURISIC**
★49759 **HEROJ PAIC**
★49760 **HEROJ KOSTA STAMENKOVIC**
★49761 **HEROJ SENJANOVIC**
(Rm flag):
★49762 **ZALAU**
(Cu flag):
★49763 **JOSE ANTONIO ECHEVERRIA**
★49764 **JULIO ANTONIO MELLA**
★49765 **30 DE NOVIEMBRE**
★49766 **XI FESTIVAL**
(Br flag):
49767 **LYCAON**
(Hu flag):
★49770 **VOROSMARTY**
(Li flag):
49772 **ACDIR II** ex *Jugoagent* 1983
(Pa flag):
49773 **EVIA LUCK** ex *Laertes* 1982
(Gr flag):
49774 **TAUFAU** ex *Santa Elena* 1983
49775 **ATHINA K**
49776 **FAMILY FOTINI**
49777 **FAMILY ANTHONY**

49790 **AGENOR** FRG/FRG (S&B) 1964; C; 500; 73 × 3.6 (239.5 × 11.81); M (KHD); 13

49800 **CARIBE** Co/Sp (Ruiz) 1971; C; 2400; 96.93 × 3.86 (318.01 × 12.66); TSM (MAN) 12; ex *Planta De Betania* 1982
Sisters (Co flag):
49801 **PLANTA DE MAMONAL**

49802 SALINA DE MANAURE

49810 LELIEGRACHT Ne/Ja (Miho) 1976; C; 1600; 80.22 × 5.98 (263.19 × 19.62); M (Hanshin); 13.5
Sisters (Ne Flag):
49811 LEIDSEGRACHT
49812 LIJNBAANSGRACHT
49813 LINDENGRACHT
49814 LAURIERGRACHT
49815 LOOIESGRACHT
49816 RAAMGRACHT
49817 REALENGRACHT
49818 REGULIERSGRACHT
49819 RIJPGRACHT
49820 RINGGRACHT
49821 ROZENGRACHT
49822 SCHIPPERSGRACHT
49823 SINGELGRACHT
49824 SPIEGELGRACHT
49825 STADIONGRACHT ex Seliba 1978
49826 BEKENGRACHT
49827 BARENTZGRACHT
49828 BEURSGRACHT
49829 BONTEGRACHT
49829/1 BICKERSGRACHT
49829/2 BATAAFGRACHT

49830 LEE SHARON Is/No (Kaldnes) 1966; C; 1300; 83.47 × 4.64 (273.85 × 15.22); M (Werkspoor); 14.5; ex Brilliant 1976
Similar:
49831 CYRUS (Le) ex Bretagne 1976 (converted to livestock carrier)

49840 ATLANTIC SEA Ne/FRG (Kroegerw) 1965; C; 500; 72.07 × 3.71 (236.45 × 12.17); M (KHD); 12; ex Okdine 1978; ex Nordfeld 1974; ex Fryken 1971

● **49850 SENTOSA** My/Fi (Laiva) 1961; C; 500/1100; 73.21 × 3.65/5 (240.19 × 11.97/16.4), M (Crossley); 11.5; ex Melina 1982; ex Melina 1 1981; ex Pelina 1980; ex Vikla 1972
Sisters:
49851 TRANSAFE STAR (Pa) ex Arab Alriyad 1980; ex Gulf Oman 1974; ex Kurki 1971
49852 SAFETY UNION (Pa) ex Arab Najad 1981; ex Gulf Mazoon 1974; ex Sotka 1971
49853 NADAZ (Sy) ex Elissar 1982; ex Baltic Sea 1977; ex Morso 1974; ex Ancylus II 1972; ex Tiira 1971

49860 LABORE Pa/Sw (Oskarshamns) 1965; C; 500/1300; 72.14 × 3.54/5.46 (236.68 × 11.61/17.91); M (KHD); 12.5; ex Bore XI 1972
Sisters:
49861 KARE (Fi) ex Bore IV 1972
49862 EASTERN GOLD (Sg) ex Medway 1982; ex Obrestad 1978; ex Bore VIII 1973

● **49865 ISLAND** Sg/Sg (Singapore SB) 1982; Con; 5200; 120.61 × 6.49 (396 × 21.29); M (Pielstick); 15; ex Hellenic Island 1983
49866 CAPE (Sg) ex Hellenic Cape 1983
49867 DAWN (Sg) ex Hellenic Dawn 1983

49870 WESTERMOOR FRG/FRG (Sietas) 1977; Con; 1600; 97.54×|5.39 (320.01×|17.68); M (Atlas-MaK); 14

● **49875 ILSE WULFF** FRG/FRG (Sietas) 1982; C/Con; 3900; 106.48 × 7.71 (349 ×|25.30); M (Krupp MaK); 15
49876 HELIOS (FRG)
49877 ORIOLUS (FRG)
49878 VILLE DU PONANT (FRG); Launched as Marjon

● **49880 AROS ATHENE** FRG/FRG (Sietas) 1976; C/Con; 1000; 81.41 × 5.04 (267.09 × 16.54); M (Atlas-MaK);¡—; ex Elbstrom 1983; ex Aros Athene 1982; ex Elbstrom 1979; Travelling cranes
Sister:
49881 HOVE (FRG)
Similar:
49882 JACOB BECKER (FRG)

49890 LAGARFOSS Ic/FRG (Sietas) 1977; C; 1600; 93.53 × 6.06 (306.86 × 19.88); M (Atlas-MaK); 14.5; ex John Wulff 1983; Travelling cranes
Sister:
49891 HILDEGARD WULFF (FRG)

● **49892 KATHRINE SIF** De/De (Orskovs) 1981; C/Con; 1600; 101.3 × 5.54 (332 × 18.18); M (MaK); 13.5; ex Frellsen Annette 1982; ex Jugo Carrier 1982; ex Frellsen Annette 1981
Sisters:
49893 ANNE SIF (De) ex Frellsen Birgitte 1982
49894 LOTTE SCHEEL (De)
49895 METTE SIF (De)
49896 SCANDUTCH ORIENT (De) ex Susanne Sif 1983; ex Frellsen Eva 1982; ex Jugo Express 1982; ex Frellsen Eva 1981
49897 PETER SIF

Probable sisters:
49898 BRAVO SIF (De)
49899 EDEL SIF (De)
49899/1 MAJ SANDVED (De)

● **49900 ESTEBOGEN** Pa/FRG (Sietas) 1972; C/Con; 1000; 88.50 × 5.27 (290.35 × 17.32); M (Atlas MaK); 14; ex Scol Unit 1978; ex Estebogen 1975
Sisters:
49901 RODANO (It) ex Progress Link 1982; ex Scol Progress 1981
49902 SUDURLAND (Ic) ex Kristina V 1982; ex Scol Spirit 1980
49903 BALTICA (Pa) ex Scol Hunter 1977; ex Baltica 1976
49904 INGEBORG II (FRG) ex Norrsundet 1982; ex Ursa 1977
49905 PATRICIA (FRG) ex Scol Action 1977; ex Patricia 1976
Similar:
49906 JORK (Pa) ex Scol Valiant 1977; ex Jork 1975

49910 SIERRA LUCENA Sp/Sp ('Corbasa') 1967; R; 1600; 83.47 × 5.01; (273.85 × 16.44); M (Sterk-Werkspoor); 16
Sister:
49911 SIERRA LUNA (Sp)

49920 GEORGIOS Z Pa/FRG (Lindenau) 1970; C; 3500/5900; 136.81 × 6.47/7.51 (448.85 × 21.23/24.64); M (Atlas-MaK); 15.5; ex Nadina 1982; ex Barbarella 1978
Possible sister:
49921 MAREN 1 (Tu) ex Stintfang 1982; ex Bianca 1973; Launched as Stintfang

49930 MARIKA Gr/No (Solvesborgs) 1962; C; 1500; 86.01 × 4.69 (282.19 × 15.39); M (KHD); 14.5; ex Arneb 1969; Launched as Albertina
Sister:
49931 PIREAS (Gr) ex Deneb 1969; Launched as Fredrika

49950 ERIKA BOLTEN FRG/FRG (LF-W) 1973; BC; 20300- 196.32×10.9 (644.09×35.76); M (GMT) 18
Sister:
49951 NATALIE BOLTEN (FRG)

49960 LISA B Tu/FRG (Sietas) 1967; RoC; 1000; 78.03 × 4.29 (256 × 14.07); M (Atlas-MaK); —; ex Taos 1974; ex Wasa 1973; Bow and stern doors
Sister:
49961 DENA 1 (Tu) ex Alpilles 1983; ex Hansa 1972

49970 MAGNUS JENSEN De/De (Dannebrog) 1979; C; 2400; 95.51 × 5.3 (313.35 × 17.39); M (Alpha-Diesel); 14.5
Sister:
49971 JOHAN PETERSEN (De)

49980 ICE STAR De/De (Orskovs) 1979; R; 1000; 80.20 × 4.71 (263.12 × 15.45); M (Atlas-MaK); 14.7; Side door

49990 LA PAIX Le/Ne (Arnhemsche) 1963; C; 600; 81.03 × 3.83 (265.85 × 12.57); M (KHD); 12; ex Edda 1980; Lengthened 1969
Sister:
49991 PLAYA DE EZARO (Sp) ex Cedar Glory 1980; ex Vega 1978
Similar (unlengthened):
49992 JAMAL B (Cy) ex Athlos III 1983; ex Stavros H 1980; ex Ask 1977
49993 AL SALAM 1 (Le) ex La Paix 1978; ex Embla 1977

50000 LAURA PANDO Sp/Sp (AESA) 1971; B; 45000; 254.03 × 14.39 (833.43 × 47.21); M (B&W); 15.75; ex Soledad Maria 1982; Travelling cranes

50010 HAVORN No/FRG (Howaldts DW) 1977; O; 23500; 182.91 × 11.89 (600.1 × 39.01); M (MAN); 14.75; Travelling cranes
Sisters (No flag):
50011 HAVFALK
50012 HAVJO

50020 BETH No/Pd (Gdynska) 1978; B; 22100; 176.59 × 11.51 (579.36 × 37.76); M (Sulzer); 16; 'B515' type; Travelling cranes
Sisters (No flag):
50021 BARDU
50022 BARRY
50023 BAUCHI
50024 BAVANG
50025 BERGO

50030 ARABIAN LULUAH Pa/Sw (Kockums)-FRG 1954/62; B; 13600; 166 × 10.35 (544.62 × 33.96); M (MAN); 14; ex Havjarl 1974; Aft section 1954; Forward & cargo section 1962 (LF-W); Converted from tanker; Travelling cranes

50040 KURE Li/Ja (IHI) 1971; B; 76000; 303.82 × 17.45 (996.78 × 57.25); T (IHI); 15.5; ex Universe Kure 1980; Launched as Cedros Pacific; Travelling cranes

50050 OLIVER DRESCHER FRG/FRG (Schichau-U) 1973; C; 3500/6200; 132.52 × 6.5/8 (434.77 × 21.32/26.24); M (KHD); 17; ex Lloyd Philadelphia 1980; ex Oliver Drescher 1978; ex Ede Sinstorf 1975
Similar:
50051 MACAELA DRESCHER (FRG) ex Lloyd New York 1980; ex Macaela Drescher 1978

50060 TRANSONDO EXPRESS Pa/FRG (Unterweser) 1972; C; 3400/6000; 124.52 × 6.59/8.12 (408.53 × 21.62/26.64); M (KHD); 17; ex Stefan Drescher 1982; ex Wadai 1975; ex Ede Foldenfjord 1974; ex Ede Wittorf 1973

50063 URANOS FRG/FRG (H Peters) 1982; C/Con; 1000; 93.63 × 4.41 (307 × 14.47); M (Deutz); 10.6
Sister:
50064 HAMMONIA (FRG)

50066 RUTHENSAND FRG/FRG (Luehring) 1981; C/Con; 1000; 78.59 × 4.60 (258 × 15.09); M (Krupp-MaK); 10.25

50070 F M SPIRIDON Le/Ne ('Vooruitgang') 1960; R; 800; 77.32 × 4.02 (253.67 × 13.19); M (Werkspoor); 11.5; ex Costas II 1982; ex Costas 1980; ex Markab II 1979; ex Markab 1969

● **50090 SENTOSA** My/Fi (Laiva) 1961; C; 500/1100; 73.21 × 3.65/5 (240.19 × 11.97/16.4), M (Crossley); 11.5; ex Melina 1982; ex Melina 1 1981; ex Pelina 1980; ex Vikla 1972
Sisters:
50091 TRANSAFE STAR (Pa) ex Arab Alriyadh 1980; ex Gulf Oman 1974; ex Kurki 1971
50092 SAFETY UNION (Pa) ex Arab Najad 1981; ex Gulf Mazoon 1974; ex Sotka 1971
50093 NADAZ (Sy) ex Elissar 1982; ex Baltic Sea 1977; ex Morso 1974; ex Ancylus 1972; ex Tiira 1971

50100 TIAN SHAN Pa/Fi (Crichton-Vulcan) 1965; C; 1800/3000; 96.91 × 5.4/6.57 (317.95 × 17.72/21.56); M (Sulzer); 13; ex Finnreel 1977; ex Annika 1971

50110 NORCAN No/No (Ulstein H) 1979; FC; 1200; 79.44 × 5.12 (260.63 × 16.8); M (Atlas-MaK); 14

● ★ **50111 FENHE** RC/FRG (Schlichting) 1982; Con; 16100; 170.21 × 9.66 (558 × 31.69); M (MAN); 18.75
Sisters (RC flag):
★ **50112 QINGHE**
★ **50113 TANGHE**
Similar (builder—Flensburger):
50114 COPACABANA (Bz) (plus one other on order for Bz)

50115 MAJAPAHIT Ia/FRG (Flensburger) 1982; Con; 15500; 170.21 × 9.68 (558 × 31.76); M (MAN); 18.5
Sisters (Ia flag):
50116 GOWA
50117 JAYAKARTA

50118 SIRIUS FRG/FRG (Flender) 1981; C/Con; 9100; 147.40 × 8.16 (484 × 26.77); M (Krupp MaK); 16
Similar (funnel differs—see inset):
50119 KATJANA (FRG) ex Contship Asia 1983; ex Katjana 1982

50120 ALTNES No/No (Kleven) 1978; C; 3000; 92.03 × 6.4 (301.94 × 21); M (Stork-Werkspoor); 13.5
Probable sisters (No flag):
50121 GARNES
50122 KORSNES
50123 VIGNES

● **50130 MATTHIAS CLAUDIUS** FRG/FRG (Husumer) 1979; C; 1600/3200; 104.5 × 5.45/6.65 (343.85 × 17.88/21.82); M (KHD); 14.25; ex Lakmuthu 1984; ex Matthias Claudius 1983; ex Karthago 1983; ex Matthias Claudius 1979
Sister:
50130/1 KALKARA (FRG)

● **50131 KARYATEIN** FRG/FRG (Sietas) 1980; C/Con; 3300; 113.16 × 6.49 (371 × 21.29); M (MaK); 15
Similar:
50132 NEPTUNE MARLIN (FRG) ex Westerhamn 1983; ex Sofati Canada 1983; ex Eastmed Princess 1983; ex Westerhamn 1982
50133 KASTAMONU (FRG) launched as Alcyone
Similar (Be built-St Pieter):
50134 AHLERS BREEZE (Be)
50135 AHLERS BRIDGE (Be)
Similar (may not have extended poop):
50136 KARTHAGO (FRG) ex Esteclipper 1983; ex Mediterranean Eagle 1982; ex Esteclipper 1982

50137 **KAHIRA** (FRG) ex *Estetrader* 1983; ex *Auvergne*; ex *Estetrader*

50140 **HANSETOR** FRG/FRG (Sietas) 1978; C/Con; 1600/3200; 104.76 × 5.58/— (343.7 × 18.31/—); M (Atlas-MaK); 15; ex *Kahira* 1983; Launched as *Hansetor*
Sisters (FRG flag):
50141 **OSTEBAY** ex *Kalymnos* 1981; ex *Ostebay* 1979
50142 **KARAMAN** ex *Hansadam* 1979
50143 **REGULUS**

● 50145 **WESTERLAND** FRG/FRG (Sietas) 1981; C/Con; 7900; 133.31 × 8.67 (437 × 28.44); M (Hitachi); 16.5; 'Type 114'
Sisters:
50146 **AMARANTA** (FRG)
50147 **TUXPAN** (Me)
50148 **TUMILCO** (Me)
50149 **DHAULAGIRI** (FRG) ex *Ville de Lumiere* 1983; ex *Pacific* 1982
50150 **ALEXANDER SCHRODER** (FRG)
50151 **AQABA CROWN** (FRG) ex *Ursus* 1983
50152 **ANNAPURNA** (FRG) ex *Ville d'Aurore* 1983; launched as *David Bluhm*

● 50155 **VILLE DE GABES** FRG/FRG (Cassens) 1982; RoC/Con; 1600/4000; 99.95 × 4.91/6.08 (328 × 16.11/19.95); M (MaK); 13; ex *Maris* 1984; Stern door/ramp
Sisters (FRG flag):
50156 **STEPHAN-J**
50157 **MARIA-J** ex *Ville de Syrte II* 1984; ex *Maria-J* 1984

50160 **LEMAR** Li/FRG (Nobiskrug) 1972; C; 3400/6000; 142.73 × 6.5/7.68 (468.27 × 21.32/25.2); M (Atlas-MaK); 16.5; ex *Cape Freels* 1982; ex *Fleethorn* 1974
Sister:
50161 **ROSA ROTH** (Cy) ex *Cape Breton* 1978; ex *Sandhorn* 1973

50180 **ANEMOS** Gr/FRG (O&K) 1976; Con; 8400; 143.82 × 8.32 (471.85 × 27.3); M (Pielstick); 18.25
Sister:
50181 **PELAGOS** (Gr)

50190 **MARGARETHA SMITS** Ne/Ne (Groot & VV) 1976; C; 1600; 84.21 × 6.32 (276.8 × 20.73); M (Smit & Bolnes); 13; Travelling cranes
Sister:
50191 **MARIJKE** (Cy) ex *Marijke Smits* 1983
Probable sisters:
50192 **MAKIRI SMITS** (Ne)
50193 **MARIA GREEN** (Cy) ex *Maria Smits* 1983
50194 **CARICOM VENTURER** (Bb) ex *Marinus Smits* 1983

50200 **URRIDAFOSS** Ic/De (Frederikshavn) 1971; C; 500; 76.61 × 3.47 (251.35 × 11.38); M (Alpha-Diesel); 12; ex *Merc Europa* 1974; Travelling cranes; Starboard side of superstructure differs (see inset)
Sisters:
50201 **ASMAA** (Mo) ex *Merc Phoenecia* 1977
50202 **MERIEM** (Mo) ex *Eco Sado* 1981; ex *Merc Asia* 1973
50203 **ECO TEJO** (Po) ex *Merc Continental* 1973
50204 **GRUNDARFOSS** (Ic) ex *Merc Australia* 1974
50205 **NEXUS** (Pa) ex *Albert S* 1978; ex *Nordsee* 1977; ex *Merc Groenlandia* 1974

50210 **RIO BESAYA** Sp/Sp ('Astano') 1967; C; 1000/1700; 86.24 × —/5.02 (282.94 × —/16.47); M (B&W); 13.5
Sister:
50211 **BAIA DE SAO BRAS** (Pa) ex *Rio Nansa* 1971
Probably similar:
50212 **TREVINCA** (Sp)

50220 **HANIA T** Pa/Fi (Laiva) 1965; C; 500/1700; 75.42 × 3.56/5.41 (247.44 × 11.68/17.75); M (Wartsila); 13.75; ex *Capella* 1980; Side doors
Sister:
50221 **ATHLOS IV** (Cy) ex *Nordgard* 1981; ex *Canopus* 1980

50230 **FRISIAN LINER** Ne/Ne (Amels) 1977; C; 1600; 82.71 × 5.99 (271.36 × 19.65); M (Atlas-MaK); 13; ex *Jan Tavenier* 1981

50240 **DELFBORG** Ne/Ne (Amels) 1978; C; 3700; 83.06 × 7.8 (272.5 × 25.59); M (Bofors); 13

● 50243 **CLAUDIA SMITS** Ne/Ne (Groot & VV) 1981; C; 1700/3600; 84.21 × 5.73/8.38 (276 × 18.8/27.49); M (Stork-Werkspoor); 12
Sisters (Ne flag):
50244 **CAROLA SMITS**
50245 **CECILIA SMITS** (plus 3 more on order)

50250 **VISTEN** Ne/Ne (Amels) 1977; C; 3200; 83.88 × 7.62 (275.2 × 34.99); M (Atlas-MaK); 13

50260 **BERNHARD S** FRG/FRG (Brand) 1978;

C/Con; 2700/5200; 117.2 × 7.7/— (384.5 × 25.26/—); M (MaK); 16; ex *Ville de Lumiere* 1982; ex *Bernhard S* 1980
Sisters (FRG flag):
50261 **KARIN**
50262 **DORIS**

● 50263 **AUSTRALIAN EAGLE** FRG/FRG (Rickmers) 1981; C/Con; 5200; 126.29 × 6.57 (414 × 21.56); M (Akasaka); 15.5; ex *Champion* 1982
Sisters (FRG flag) (Superstructure differs on some—see inset)
50264 **E.L.M.A. CINCO** ex *Esteturm* 1981
50265 **TAURIA** ex *Arabian Eagle* 1983; ex *Tauria* 1982
50266 **WEJADIA** ex *E.L.M.A. Siete* 1983; ex *Wejadia*
50267 **SINGAPORE EAGLE** ex *Premier* 1983
50268 **GOTHIA** ex *European Eagle* 1983; ex *Gothia* 1982
50269 **EUROPEAN EAGLE** ex *Marivia* 1983
50269/1 **LEERORT**
50269/2 **LILIENTHAL**
50269/3 **MEDITERRANEAN EAGLE** ex *Estebrugge* 1982
Probable sisters (FRG flag):
50269/4 **CONTSHIP EUROPE** ex *Husum* 1983
50269/5 **HEIDE**
50269/6 **ASIAN EAGLE** ex *Dorte* 1983

50270 **JUNIOR LILIAN** De/Ne (Tille) 1976; C; 1600; 93 × 5.59 (305.12 × 18.34); M (B&W); 13

★ 50280 **SOVIETSKIY VOIN** Ru/Ru (Vyborg) 1968; C; 1700; 82 × 5.43 (269.03 × 17.82); M (CKD Praha); 12.75
Sisters (Ru flag):
★ 50281 **KONSTANTIN SHESTAKOV**
★ 50282 **ALEKSANDR PANKRATOV**
★ 50283 **ARSENIY MOSKVIN**
★ 50284 **EVGENIY NIKONOV**
★ 50285 **KONSTANTIN SAVELYEV**
★ 50286 **ANDREY IVANOV**
★ 50287 **EVGENIY ONUFRIEV**
★ 50288 **JAKOV KUNDER**
★ 50289 **KONSTANTIN KORSHUNOV**
★ 50290 **NARVSKAYA ZASTAVA**
★ 50291 **VYBORGSKAYA STORONA**
★ 50292 **LENINGRADSKIY OPOLCHENETS**
★ 50293 **LENINGRADSKIY PARTIZAN**
★ 50294 **SOVETSKIY POGRANICHNIK**
★ 50295 **ALEKSANDR MIROSHNIKOV**
★ 50296 **NIKOLAY EMELYANOV**
★ 50297 **SOVIETSKIY MORYAK**
★ 50298 **VYACHESLAV DENISOV**
★ 50299 **YAKOV REZNICHENKO**

● 50310 **PEP STAR** De/De (Orskovs) 1977; C; 500/1400; 71.91×3.76/5.67 (235.93×12.34); M (Atlas-MaK); 13
Sisters (De flag):
50311 **PEP SUN**
50312 **PEP SPICA**
50313 **PEP SIRIUS**

50320 **PUNTA ARENAS** De/Ne (Kramer & Booy)-De 1974/79; Con/HL; 2000; 106.43 × 5.45; (349.18 × 17.88); M (B&W); approx 13.5; ex *Junior Longo* 1982; ex *Junior Lilo* 1979; Converted from cargo 1979 (Helsingor)

● 50330 **CARIB DAWN** Br/De (Sonderborg) 1975; C; 1400; 78.77 × 5.06 (258.43 × 16.6); M (Alpha-Diesel); 12.5; ex *Birdie* 1980; ex *Esther Silvana* 1980; ex *Esther Bech* 1978; Travelling cranes
Sister:
50331 **CARIB EVE** (Br) ex *Louise Bravo* 1981
Similar (Sg flag) (Converted to research ships and may be altered in appearance):
50332 **SOFIE BRAVO**
50333 **OLGA BRAVO**

● 50340 **ESTEBOGEN** Pa/FRG (Sietas) 1972; C/Con; 1000; 88.5 × 5.28 (290.35 × 17.32); M (Atlas-MaK); 14; ex *Scol Unit*; ex *Estebogen* 1975
Sisters:
50341 **RODANO** (It) ex *Progress Link* 1982; ex *Scol Progress* 1981
50342 **SUDURLAND** (Ic) ex *Kristina V* 1982; ex *Scol Spirit* 1980
50343 **BALTICA** (Pa) ex *Scol Hunter* 1977; ex *Baltica* 1976
50343/1 **INGEBORG II** (FRG) ex *Norrsundet* 1982; ex *Ursa* 1977
50343/2 **PATRICIA** (FRG) ex *Scol Action* 1977; ex *Patricia* 1976
Similar:
50344 **JORK** (Pa) ex *Scol Valiant* 1977; ex *Jork* 1975

50350 **BUNGA PENAGA** My/Ja (Osaka) 1979; Con; 3900; 102.4 × 6.2; (335.96 × 20.34); M (Pielstick); 14.6
Sister:
50351 **BUNGA DAHLIA** (My)

50370 **ALTAIR** Pa/Fi (Wartsila) 1966; C; 1600/2800; 91.55 × 5.41/6.52 (300.36 × 17.75/21.4); M (Crichton-Vulcan); 14
Sister:
50371 **SHETLAND** (Cy) ex *Algenib* 1982

50380 **PUERTO RICO** US/US (Marinship) 1944/67; RoC; 8000; 170.67 × 8.25 (559.94 × 27.07); T-E (GEC); 16; ex *Seatrain Puerto Rico* 1977; ex *Fruitvale Hills* 1967; ex *Mission San Luis Obispo* 1966; Converted from T-2 tankers
Sisters (US flag):
50381 **CAROLINA** ex *Seatrain Carolina* 1978; ex *Mission Santa Barbara* 1966
50382 **FLORIDA** ex *Seatrain Florida* 1978; ex *Pamanset* 1968
50383 **MAINE** ex *Seatraine Maine* 1978; ex *Ohio* 1967; ex *Mission San Jose* 1966; ex *Mercury* 1967; ex *Mission San Juan* 1966; ex *Maine* 1967; ex *Tomahawk* 1966
50384 **MARYLAND** ex *Seatrain Maryland* 1978; ex *San Jacinto* 1965; ex *Mission San Carlos* 1966
50385 **OHIO** ex *Seatrain Ohio* 1978; ex *Mission San Diego* 1967; ex *Maine* 1967; ex *Tomahawk* 1966; ex *Ohio* 1967; ex *Mission San Jose* 1966

★ 50390 **SIR BEDIVERE** Br/Br (Hawthorn, L) 1967; P/RoC/FA; 4500; 126.02 × 3.98 (413.45 × 13.06); TSM (Mirrlees); 17.25
Sisters (Br flag):
50391 **SIR LANCELOT**
50303 **SIR GERAINT**
50394 **SIR PERCIVAL**
50395 **SIR TRISTRAM**

50400 **CAPO MELE** It/Fr (La Ciotat) 1969; O; 12500; 151.97 × 9.9 (498.59 × 32.48); M (Pielstick); 16; ex *La Cordillera* 1974; ex *Alain L.D.* 1973; Travelling cranes
Sister:
50401 **DORIC CARRIER** (Gr) ex *Robert L D*

50410 **BIAKH** Pa/Ja (IHI) 1967; B; 11700; 153.93 × 10.25 (505.02 × 33.63); M (Sulzer); 15.5; Travelling cranes
Sisters:
50413 **ABU BASMA** (Si) ex *Bani* 1983
★ 50415 **JI HAI 10** (RC) ex *Havfru* 1983
50416 **UCO XVII** (Bn) ex *Havmann* 1983
Similar (aft KP alongside funnel on port side):
50417 **P STAR II** (Li) ex *Mombaka* 1982; ex *Finna* 1980

50420 **MALOJA** Sd/FRG (Schuerenstedt) 1975; C/Con; 7700; 143.82 × 7.54 (471.85 × 24.74); M (MAN); 15.5; ex *Petra Crown* 1983; ex *Maloja* 1979; ex *Ida* 1979; ex *Vinland* 1979; ex *Maersk Tempo* 1978; ex *Vinland* 1977; Travelling cranes
Sister:
50421 **CALANDA** (Sd) ex *Sofati Continent* 1983; ex *Calanda* 1982; ex *Iren* 1979; ex *Skotland* 1979

★ 50430 **LE DU** RC/Sw (Oskarshamns) 1961; C; 4500/6700; 125.02 × 6.75/8.53 (410.17 × 22.15/27.99); M (Gotaverken); 15; ex *Husaro* 1976
Sister:
50431 **RIO NEVERI** (Ve) ex *Tiuna* 1982; ex *Segero* 1976

★ 50440 **MARLOW** DDR/DDR (Elbewerften) 1971; C/Con; 300; 57.87 × 3.68 (189.96 × 12.07); M (Liebknecht); 12; 'Boizenburg' type
Sisters (DDR flag):
★ 50441 **HAGENOW**
★ 50442 **MILTZOW**
★ 50443 **MIROW**
★ 50444 **NEUBOKOW**
★ 50445 **RAKOW**
★ 50446 **SATOW**
★ 50447 **SEMLOW**
★ 50448 **TORGELOW**
★ 50449 **ZUROW**
★ 50450 **ZUSSOW**

★ 50460 **BOLESLAWIEC** Pd/Br (Govan) 1979; B; 3000; 95 × 6.08 (311.68 × 19.95); M (Sulzer); 12.25; Travelling cranes
Sisters (Pd flag):
★ 50461 **CHORZOW**
★ 50462 **WYSZKOW**
★ 50463 **MLAWA**
★ 50464 **GNIEZNO II**
★ 50465 **SIERADZ**
★ 50466 **BYTOM**
★ 50467 **ZGORZELEC**
★ 50468 **KOSCIERZYNA**
★ 50469 **LOMZA**
★ 50470 **WIELUN**
Some of these vessels may not have cranes

50480 **BOXY** Sw/Sw (Kalmar) 1978; B/TC 6200; 121 × 7.62 (396.98 × 25); M (B&W); 14.6; Travelling

---

619

cranes. The jibs are normally stowed athwartships as shown
Sister:
50481 **DONNY** (Sw) ex *Dania* 1983

50485 **NORBRIT FAITH** Br/Br (Cochrane) 1982; B; 1600; 70.13 × 4.96 (230 × 16.27); M (APE Allen); 11; Travelling cranes
Sister:
50486 **NORBRIT HOPE** (Br)

● 50490 **ATLANTIC FISHER** Br/Br (Appledore) 1976; C; 3700; 102.04 × 6.93 (334.78 × 22.74); M (Mirrlees Blackstone); 14; ex *Sandgate* 1982; Travelling cranes
Sisters:
50491 **SOUTHERN STAR** (Li) ex *Feray* 1983; ex *Southgate* 1983
50492 **HERMENIA** (Br) ex *Saltersgate* 1982; ex *Green Park* 1977

50510 **FARNES** Li/Ja (NKK) 1978; C; 8100; 134.52 × 8.67 (441.34 × 28.44); M (Pielstick); 14.75
Probable sister:
50511 **FIRMNES** (Li)

50520 **FINNPINE** Fi/Fi (Valmet) 1971; C; 3900/6600; 129.39 × 6.43/8.07 (424.51 × 21.1/24.48); M (B&W); 17.25
Sisters:
50521 **IRVING FOREST** (Br) ex *Finnalpino* 1983
50522 **CASTOR** (Fi) ex *Finntrader* 1982
50523 **CARELIA** (Fi) ex *Finnwood* 1982

50530 **A C CROSBIE** Ca/Br (Robb Caledon) 1972; C/Con; 7100; 122.81 × 8.1 (402.92 × 26.57); M (Pielstick); 15; ex *Ida Lundrigan* 1976
Sister:
50531 **OCEAN CHALLENGE** (Pa) ex *Gomba Challenge* 1980; ex *Simonburn* 1979; ex *City of Pretoria* 1977; ex *Ria Jean McMurtry* 1976

50550 **ANTARES** Fi/Ko (Hyundai) 1978; B; 13000; 163.96 × 8.65 (537.93 × 28.38); M (MAN); 15.75; ex *Chase One* 1979; ex*Antares* 1978; Travelling cranes; 'HD16F' type
Sisters (Fi flag):
50551 **ALDEBARAN** ex *Khalij Enterprise* 1978
50552 **ATALAYA** ex *Chase Two* 1979; ex *Atalaya* 1978
50553 **ASTREA** ex *Chase Four* 1979; ex*Astrea* 1978
50554 **ANDERSO** ex *Chase Three* 1979; ex*Anderso* 1978

50560 **WILCON 1** Pi/Ja (Ujina) 1970; RoC/C; 2200; 107.42 × 5.38 (352.43 × 17.65); M (Pielstick); 14.75; ex *Hokuto Maru* 1978; Port and starboard quarter ramps

★ 50570 **'AMUR'** class; Ru/Pd (—) 1969; A/Repairs; 6400 Dspl; 115 × 5.5 (377 × 18); TSM (—); 18; 24 ships in class

● 50575 **USARAMO** FRG/FRG (A G 'Weser') 1982; Con; 20400; 173.98 × 11.22 (571 × 36.81); M (B&W); 18.7
Sisters:
50576 **UBENA** (FRG)
50577 **USAMBARA** (FRG)

★ 50580 **LUOHE** RC/FRG (A G 'Weser') 1983; Con; 19900; 170.21 × 10.73 (558 × 35.20); M (MAN); 17.75
Sisters:
★ 50581 **SHAHE** (RC)
★ 50582 **LIAOHE** (RC)

● 50585 **SCANDUTCH CONCORDIA** FRG/FRG (Thyssen) 1983; Con; 17800; 166.07 × 11.61 (545 × 38.09); M (B&W); —; ex *Concordia* 1983
Sister:
50586 **SCANDUTCH CORONA** (FRG) ex *Corona* 1983

50590 **OM ALQORA** Si/No (Nakskov) 1965; LS; 8000; 164.45 × 8.15 (539.53 × 26.74); M (B&W); 20.75; ex *Dorrit Clausen* 1981; ex *Ancona* 1976; Converted from cargo ship 1977 (Gotav)

50600 **GIANT KIM** Li/Ja (IHI) 1971; B; 32100; 209.02 × 10.99 (685.76 × 36.05); M (Sulzer); 15.75; ex *Triabunna* 1982; ex*Nego Triabunna* 1980; Travelling cranes
Sister:
50601 **SILVICULTURE** (Li)

50610 **SIERRA GREDOS** Sp/Sp (Musel) 1979; R; 1200; 85.9 × 4.9 (281.82 × 16.08); M (Deutz); 14.4
Probable sisters (Sp flag):
50611 **SIERRA GRANA**
50612 **SIERRA GRANERA**
50613 **SIERRA GUADELUPE**
50614 **SIERRA GUARDARRAMA**

50620 **GEORGIOS Z** Pa/FRG (Lindenau) 1970; C; 3500/5900; 136.81 × 6.47/7.51 (448.85 ×

21.23/24.64); M (Atlas-MaK); 15.5; ex *Nadina* 1982; ex *Barbarella* 1970
Possible sister:
50621 **MAREN 1** (Tu) ex *Stintfang* 1982; ex *Bianca* 1973; Launched as *Stintfang*

50630 **MARIKA** Gr/Sw (Solvesborgs) 1962; C; 1500; 86.01 × 4.69 (282.19 × 15.39); M (KHD); 14.5; ex *Arneb* 1969; Launched as *Albertina*
Sister:
50631 **PIREAS** (Gr) ex *Deneb* 1969; Launched as *Fredrika*

50640 **PLAYA DE EZARO** Sp/Ne (Arnhemsche) 1963; C; 600; 81.03 × 3.83 (265.85 × 12.57); M (KHD); 12; ex *Cedar Glory* 1980; ex *Vega* 1978; Lengthened 1969

50650 **LAURA PANDO** Sp/Sp (AESA) 1971; B; 45000; 254.03 × 14.39 (833.43 × 47.21); M (B&W); 15.75; ex *Soledad Maria* 1982; Travelling cranes

● 50660 **NEMESIS** Gr/Sw (Oresunds) 1966; B/V; 18800; 185.66 × 10.71 (609.12 × 35.13); M (Gotaverken); 15; ex*Fidelio* 1981; ex*Citadel* 1976; Travelling cranes
Sisters:
50661 **JILL** (Ma) ex *Avro International* 1984; ex *Philippine Orchid* 1983; ex *Hual Orchid* 1980; ex *Andreas U* 1979
50662 **POSIDON** (Gr) ex *Falstaff* 1981; ex *Daphne* 1977
50663 **PHILIPPINE JASMINE** (Pi) ex *Hual Jasmine* 1980; ex *Johan U* 1979
50664 **PHILIPPINE ROSAL** (Pi) ex*Hual Rosal* 1980; ex *Axel U* 1979

★ 50670 **GRIGORIY ALEKSEYEV** Ru/Ja (Hitachi) 1974; BWC; 18400; 169.45 × 9.88 (555.94 × 32.41); M (B&W); 14.5; Travelling cranes
Sister:
★ 50671 **PAVEL RYBIN** (Ru)

50680 **BAHIA PORTETE** Co/Pd (Gdynska) 1971; B; 18000; 163.2 × 10.99 (535.43 × 36.05); M (Sulzer); 15; ex*Havbjorn* 1982; Travelling cranes; 'B-523' type
Sisters (No flag):
50681 **HAVKATT**
50682 **HAVTROLL**
50683 **BAJKA**
50684 **BAKAR**
50685 **BALAO**
50686 **BANTA**
50688 **BARWA**
50689 **BERGLJOT**
50690 **BLIX**
50691 **STAVERN**
50692 **TRYM**
(Co flag):
50693 **LA GUAJIRA** ex *Baro* 1981

50700 **RASELTIN** Eg/Ja (Setouchi) 1976; C; 5800; 119.06 × 7.45 (390.61 × 24.44); M (B&W); 14.5
Sisters (Eg flag):
50701 **ALANFUSHI**
50702 **ALCHATBY**
50703 **ALIBRAHIMIYA**

50704 **AFRICAN GARDENIA** Li/Ja (Shimoda) 1981; B; 5200; 135.52 × 6.32 (447 × 20.73); M (Akasaka); 15
Probable sisters:
50705 **AFRICAN CAMELLIA** (Li)
50706 **AFRICAN DAHLIA** (Li)
50707 **AFRICAN EVERGREEN** (Li)
50708 **AFRICAN FERN** (Li)
Possible sisters:
50709 **AFRICAN AZALEA** (Li)
50709/1 **AFRICAN BEGONIA** (Li)

50710 **LEMAR** Li/FRG (Nobiskrug) 1972; C; 3400/6000; 142.73 × 6.5/7.68 (468.27 × 21.32/25.2); M (Atlas-MaK); 16; ex *Cape Freels* 1982; ex *Fleethorn* 1974
Sister:
50711 **ROSA ROTH** (Cy) ex *Cape Breton* 1978; ex *Sandhorn* 1973

50720 **FJELLNES** Pa/Ja (Miho) 1982; B; 7400; 129.04 × 8.42 (423 × 27.62); M (Pielstick); 14.5
Sister:
50721 **FOSSNES** (Li)

★ 50730 **SOVIETSKAYA YAKUTIYA** Ru/Ru (Navashinskiy) 1972; C(Sea/River); 3600; 123.53 × 4.5 (405.28 × 14.76); TSM (Russkiy); 11.75
Sisters (Ru flag):
★ 50731 **AFANASIY BOGATYREV**
★ 50732 **FYODOR POPOV**
★ 50733 **YAKUB KOLAS**
★ 50734 **IVAN STROD**
★ 50735 **KONSTANTIN ZASLONOV**
★ 50736 **KOZELSK**
★ 50737 **KHUDOZHNIK KUINDZHA**
★ 50738 **YANKA KUPALA**

★ 50739 **FIZULI**
★ 50740 **VAGIF**
★ 50741 **VASILIY YAN**
★ 50742 **AVETIK ISAAKYAN**
★ 50743 **BERDY KERBABAYEV**
★ 50744 **BULUNKHAN**
★ 50745 **KIGILYAKH**
★ 50746 **ANDREY KIZHEVATOV**
★ 50747 **DMITRIY KANTEMIR**
★ 50748 **KHUDOZHNIK PLASTOV**
★ 50749 **SERGEY GRITSEVETS**
★ 50750 **FYODOR OKHLOPOV**
★ 50751 **MIKAIL MUSHFIK**
★ 50752 **KOMANDARM GAY**
★ 50753 **ISIDOR BARAKHOV**
★ 50754 **ILYA SELVINSKIY**
★ 50755 **MAKSIM AMMOSOV**
★ 50756 **NIKOLAY ZAZOLOTSKIY**
★ 50757 **NIZAMI**
★ 50758 **PLATON OYUNSKIY**
★ 50759 **OGNYAN NAYDOV**
★ 50760 **ASHUG ALEKSER**
★ 50761 **DZHAFER DZHABARLY**
★ 50762 **KOSTA KHETAGUROV**

★ 50763 **VASILIY SHUKSHIN** Ru/Ru (Navashinskiy) 1978; C(Sea/River); 4400; 124.39 × 5.50 (408 × 18.04); TSM (—); 13; Has four deck cranes
Sisters (Ru flag):
★ 50764 **MAKSIM RYLSKIY**
★ 50765 **MIKHAIL LUKONIN**
★ 50766 **SADRIDDIN AYNI**
★ 50767 **SERGEY SMIRNOV**
★ 50768 **VIKTOR KHARA**
★ 50769 **YURIY KRINOV**

★ 50770 **BAKU** Ru/Ru (Navashinskiy) 1959; C; 3400; 120.02 × 4.4 (393.77 × 14.44); TSM (Russkiy); 11.5; 'Caspian-Volgo-Balt' type
Sisters (Ru flag):
★ 50771 **INZHENIER BELOV**
★ 50772 **AGDAM**
★ 50773 **AKSTAFA**
★ 50774 **GEOKCHAY**
★ 50775 **MURGAB**
★ 50776 **SHAMKHOR**
★ 50777 **ASTARA**
★ 50778 **SALYANY**
★ 50779 **YANGI-YUL**
★ 50780 **KASPIY**
★ 50781 **HIMKI**
★ 50782 **SABIRABAD**
★ 50783 **HOROL**
★ 50784 **KUBATLY**
★ 50785 **NAVASHINO**
★ 50786 **SAATLY**
★ 50787 **ZANGELAN**
★ 50788 **KHASAVYURT** ex *Sangar* 1983; ex*Hasavjurt*

50800 **HVASSAFELL** Ic/FRG (Buesumer) 1971; C; 900/1800; 80.17 × 4.07/5.87 (263.02 × 13.36/19.25); M (KHD); 14
Similar:
50801 **SKAFTAFELL** (Ic)

50810 **MEONIA** Br/Sw (Falkenbergs) 1972; C; 1600/2500; 87.03 × 5.89/6.83 (285.53 × 19.32/22.4); M (Nydqvist & Holm); 12.5; ex*Eos* 1982

50820 **BIAKH** Pa/Ja (IHI) 1967; B; 11700; 153.93 × 10.25 (505.02 × 33.63); M (Sulzer); 15.5; Travelling cranes
Sisters:
50823 **ABU BASMA** (Si) ex *Bani* 1983
★ 50825 **JI HAI 10** (RC) ex *Havfru* 1983
50826 **UCO XVII** (Br) ex *Havmann* 1983
Similar (aft KP alongside funnel on Port Side):
50827 **P STAR II** (Li) ex *Mombaka* 1982; ex *Finna* 1980

50830 **CAPO MELE** It/Fr (La Ciotat) 1969; O; 12500; 151.97 × 9.9 (498.59 × 32.48); M (Pielstick); 16; ex *La Cordillera* 1974; ex *Alain L D* 1973; Travelling cranes
Sister:
50831 **DORIC CARRIER** (Gr) ex *Robert L D*

50840 **DOLLART** FRG/FRG (S&B) 1976; C; 1000/2900; 91.09 × 4.8/6.91 (298.85 × 15.75/22.67); M (KHD); 14.5; Travelling cranes
Sisters (FRG flag):
50841 **JAN WILHELM**
50842 **OSTEREMS**
50843 **LUHE**

50850 **PUNTA ARENAS** De/Ne (Kramer & Booy) De 1974/79; Con/HL; 2000; 106.43 × 5.45 (349.18 × 17.88); M (B&W); approx 13.5; ex*Junior Longo* 1982; ex *Junior Lilo* 1979; Converted from cargo 1979 (Helsingor)

50860 **MIRAMAR** Sw/Sw (Falkenbergs) 1971; C; 1600; 87.03 × 4.96 (285.53 × 16.27); M (Appinge-

dammer Brons); 12; Cranes may have been removed;
ex *Anders* 1983
Sister:
50861 **FALKENBERG** (FRG) ex *Pontos* 1976; ex
Falkenberg 1973; Launched as *Isotat*

50870 **JAMAICA FAREWELL** Li/Ja (Hitachi) 1975;
C; 13500; 161.6 × 9.93 (530.18 × 32.58); M (B&W);
15.5; 'Hitachi UT-20' type
Sister:
50871 **MARI BOEING** (Li)

50880 **CLARA CLAUSEN** De/No (Tangen) 1966;
LS; 5900; 154.59 × 6.74 (507.19 × 22.11); M (B&W);
15; ex *Maple* 1976; ex *Sunmaple* 1969; Converted
bulk carrier (Gotaverken)

50890 **JAPAN TUNA No. 2** Ja/Ja (Hitachi) 1979;
Sply/Hospital; 6500; 128.38 × 8.2 (421.19 × 26.9);
M (Mitsubishi); 15.7

★50900 **DOLMATOVO** Ru/DDR (Warnow) 1960; B;
6800; 139.5 × 8 (457.68 × 26.25); M (MAN); 14.25

★50910 **KASIMOV** Ru/Fi (Crichton-Vulcan) 1962;
C; 9300; 147 × 9.1 (482 × 30); M (Sulzer); 15.35
Sisters (Ru flag):
★50911 **KALININABAD**
★50912 **KANEV**
★50913 **KARACHAJEVO-CHERKESSIJA**
★50914 **KASPIJSK**
★50915 **KIMOVSK**
★50916 **KOVROV**
★50917 **KRASNOUFIMSK**
Similar:
★50918 **KRASNOGRAD**

●50930 **EGE YILDIZI** Tu/Bz (Emaq) 1976; C;
5600/7700; 142.02 × 7.67 (465.95 × 25.16); M
(Sulzer); 18; ex *Lloyd Humaita* 1983
Sisters (Bz flag):
50931 **LLOYD CUIABA**
50932 **LLOYD MARABA**
50933 **LLOYD ALTAMIRA**
50934 **LLOYD SANTAREM**

50940 **IBN SHUHAID** Ku/Ko (Hyundai) 1977; C;
11100/15400; 175.32 × —/10.4 (575.2 × —
/34.12); M (B&W); 16; 'Kuwait' class
Sisters (Ku flag) (Some Br built-Govan):
50941 **IBN AL-ATHEER**
50943 **IBN AL-MOATHAZ**
50944 **IBN ALBEITAR**
50945 **IBN ASAKIR**
50946 **IBN BASSAM**
50947 **IBN BATTOTAH**
50948 **IBN DURAID**
50949 **IBN HAYYAN**
50950 **IBN KHALDOON**
50951 **IBN KHALLIKAN**
50952 **IBN MALIK**
50953 **IBN QUTAIBAH**
50954 **IBN RUSHD**
50955 **IBN TUFAIL**
50956 **IBN YOUNUS**
50957 **AL SALIMIAH**
50958 **AL MUBARAKIAH**
50959 **AL YAMAMAH**
50960 **AL FUJAIRAH**
50961 **AL MUHARRAQ**
50962 **AL RAYYAN**
50963 **AHMAD AL-FATEH**
50964 **ARAFAT**
50965 **DANAH**
50966 **FATHULKHAIR**
50967 **HIJAZ**
50968 **JILFAR**
50969 **QAROUH**
50970 **KUBBAR**
50971 **SALAH ALDEEN**
50972 **THEEKAR**
50973 **TABUK**
(Qt flag):
50974 **IBN AL-NAFEES**

●50980 **TABORA** FRG/Ja (Hitachi) 1977; C; 13700;
161.53 × 19 (529.95 × 32.8); M (B&W); 16.25; 'UC-
20' type
Sister:
50981 **TAGAMA** (Sg) ex *Talana* 1978; Launched as
Transkei

50990 **DIJEY** Cy/FRG (Meyer) 1968; C; 3100/5100;
119.97 × 6.45/7.6 (393.6 × 21.16/24.93); M (KHD);
16.5; ex *Katie* 1983; ex *Marianne* 1980; ex *Tenos*
1975; ex *Marianne* 1971
Sister:
★50991 **QIAN TANG JIANG** (RC) ex *Madeleine*
1977

51000 **VILLE DE MARSEILLE** Fr/Fr (La Ciotat)
1974; C; 12600; 171.02 × 9.7 (561.08 × 31.82); M
(Sulzer); 20
Sisters (Fr flag):

51001 **VILLE DE NANTES**
51002 **VILLE DE STRASBOURG**

51010 **WAKANAMI MARU** Ja/Ja (Mitsubishi HI)
1978; C/Con/HL; 14500; 162.52 × 10.45 (533.2 ×
34.28); M (MAN); 18
Sister:
51011 **WAKAMIZU MARU** (Ja)
Similar (second pair of cranes on travelling gantry,
heavier KP foreward):
51012 **WAKAGIKU MARU** (Ja)
51013 **WAKATAKE MARU** (Ja)

51020 **BUNKO MARU** Ja/Ja (Hitachi) 1976; C;
30700; 215.02 × 12.4 (705.45 × 40.68); M (Sulzer);
14.75; 'Hi-bulk 50' type

●51030 **VALERIA** Li/FRG (LF-W) 1970; C/HL;
7500/10600; 153.27 × 9.06/10.12 (502.85 ×
29.72/33.2); M (MAN); 20; ex *Lone Star* 1981; ex
Steinfels 1980
Sisters:
51031 **EMILIA S** (Pa) ex *Sternenfels* 1980
51032 **FRANCESCA** (Pa) ex *Stockenfels* 1980
51033 **MANILA** (Pi) ex *Stolzenfels* 1980
51034 **ZAMBOANGA** (Li) ex *Strahlenfels* 1980
51035 **TORM AMERICA** (Sg) ex *Godenfels* 1980;
ex *Atlantica Montreal* 1976; ex *Goldenfels* 1972
51036 **SANTA MONICA** (FRG) ex *Torm Africa* 1983;
ex *Deneb* 1981; ex *Gutenfels*; ex *Atlantica New York*
1973; ex *Gutenfels*

51040 **IBERIA** FRG/FRG (LF-W) 1972; C/HL/TS;
8000/11200; 153.24 × 9.06/10.07 (502.75 ×
29.72/33.2); M (MAN); 20; ex *Sturmfels* 1980

51050 **BOA ESPERANCA** Bz/Bz (Verolme ER do
Brazil) 1969; C; 4300/5400; 121.04 × —/7.7;
(397.11 × —/25.26); M (MAN); 16
Probable sister (may have kingpost aft):
51052 **PEDRO TEIXEIRA** (Bz)

51060 **MARCOS SOUZA DANTAS** Bz/Bz (Verolme
ER do Brazil) 1969; C; 4300/5400; 121.04 × —/7.7;
(397.11 × —/25.26); M (MAN); 16

51070 **CREUSE** Fr/Ca (Marine Indust) 1973; C;
11800; 159.01 × 8.18 (521.68 × 26.83); M (Pielstick); 18.5; 'Marindus' type
Sisters (Fr flag):
51071 **COTES DU NORD**
51072 **CORREZE**
51071 **CANTAL**
51074 **MUNGO** ex *Calvados* 1983
(Ar flag):
51075 **PUNTA MALVINAS**.ex *Frontenac*
51076 **PUNTA BRAVA** ex *Joliette*

51080 **KOTA MUTIARA** Sg/Ja (Mitsubishi HI)
1967; C; 9300; 137.78 × 9.05 (452.03 × 29.69); M
(Mitsubishi); 14.5; ex *Nedlloyd Talbot* 1982; ex *Straat
Talbot* 1977; ex *Ocean Prima* 1970
Sisters:
51081 **KOTA MULIA** (Sg) ex *Nedlloyd Tauranga*
1982; ex *Straat Tauranga* 1977; ex *Pipat Samut*
1970; Launched as *Ocean Unity*
51082 **JAG RAKSHAK** (In) ex *Makakiran* 1983; ex
Jag Ravi 1980; ex *Green Walrus* 1971
51083 **JAG RATNA** (In) ex *Mahakirti* 1982; ex *Jag
Rekha* 1982; ex *Purple Dolphin* 1971
51084 **SIGI SIGI** (Ia) ex *Ocean Unity* 1977; (this
vessel may have the sequence KC₆KMFK)
51085 **MUHUTI** (Ia) ex *Sea Dolphin* 1977; ex *Pichai
Samut* 1971

51090 **BOIN** Ko/Ja (Hitachi) 1970; C; 8400; 140.06
× 8.99 (459.51 × 29.49); M (B&W); 15.5; ex *Clintona*
1980; ex *Yamashige Maru* 1980
Sister:
51091 **YANNIS** (Gr) ex *Niishige Maru*

51100 **YOUNG SPORTSMAN** Pa/Ja (Onomichi)
1979; C; 11500; 156.53 × 9.1 (513.55 × 29.86); M
(Sulzer); 15.4; ex *Van Ocean* 1980
Sister:
51101 **VAN ENTERPRISE** (Pa)

51110 **JESBON** Ko/Ja (Hayashikane) 1971; C;
9500; 155.56 × 9.3 (510.36 × 30.51); M (Sulzer);
16.75; ex *Nichiwa Maru*
Sisters:
51111 **MONISBON** (Ko) ex *Pacific* 1982; ex *Nichibu
Maru* 1980
51112 **MONIMBO** (Ni) ex *Palm Islands* 1980
Probable sister:
51113 **SHINKAWA MARU** (Ja)

51120 **OCEAN ADVENTURE** Li/Ja (Nipponkai)
1970; C; 8500; 148.75 × 8.73 (488.02 × 28.64); M
(Sulzer); 15.75; ex *Japan Caobo* 1983
Sister:
51121 **JAPAN CANELA** (Li)

51130 **WOLWOL** Et/De (Orskovs) 1977; C; 1600;
98.96 × 5.73 (324.67 × 18.79); M (Alpha-Diesel); 13;

ex *Pep Coral* 1982
Sister:
51131 **KEIY KOKEB** (Et) ex *Pep Comet* 1982

51140 **KANGUK** Ca/Sw (Finnboda) 1964; C;
1600/2800; 93.81 × 5.07/5.76 (307.77 ×
16.63/18.9); M (Fiat); ex *Hudson Venture* 1982; ex
Silva 1980; ex *Gondul* 1971
Similar:
51141 **PALM BEACH** (Pa) ex *Asta* 1983

51150 **CITY OF TEMA** Gh/Br (H.Robb) 1968; C;
1500; 93.88 × 5.08 (308 × 16.67); M (Mirrlees); 13;
ex *City of Patras* 1978; ex *Silvio* 1974
Sister:
51151 **REZEKI** (Ia) ex *City of Ankara* 1978; ex *Sangro*
1974

51160 **IRAN MEEAD** Ir/Be (Cockerill) 1970; C;
12000; 160.51 × 9.79 (526.6 × 32.12) M (B&W);
16.5; ex *Arya Gam* 1980; Travelling cranes
Sisters (Ir flag):
51161 **IRAN MEELAD** ex *Arya Nur*
51162 **IRAN ABAD** ex *Arya Taj*
51163 **IRAN ERSHAD** ex *Arya Tab*
51164 **IRAN JAHAD** ex *Arya Pas*

51170 **FRANKY** Gr/Br (Burntisland) 1963; C; 5400;
122.84 × 7.3 (403.02 × 23.95); M (Sulzer); 15.25; ex
Katy 1981; ex *Booker Vanguard*
Sister:
51171 **AL AMIRAH** (Qt) ex *Booker Viking* 1980

51180 **VILLE DE MARSEILLE** Fr/Fr (La Ciotat)
1974; C; 12600; 171.02 × 9.7 (561.08 × 31.82); M
(Sulzer); 20
Sisters (Fr flag):
51181 **VILLE DE NANTES**
51182 **VILLE DE STRASBOURG**

51190 **LOS TEQUES** Pa/Br (Hall, Russell) 1972; C;
2700; 105.16 × 6.26 (345.01 × 20.54); M (Piestick);
15.5; ex *Makaria*
Sister:
51191 **SIBONEY** (Pa) ex *Melita*

51210 **ALTAI MARU** Ja/Ja (Sanoyasu) 1979; C/HL;
16000; 166.12 × 10.39 (545 × 34.09); M (Sulzer); 16
Sister:
51211 **HIMALAYA MARU** (Ja)

51220 **WAKAUME MARU** Ja/Ja (Namura) 1970;
C/HL; 9900; 156.55 × 9.02 (513.61 × 29.59); M
(B&W); 16.75

51230 **IRAN NAHAD** Ir/Be (Cockerill) 1970; C;
12100; 160.51 × 9.79 (526.6 × 32.12); M (B&W); 19;
ex *Arya Naz* 1980; Travelling cranes

51235 **COSTA ARABICA** It/It (Italcantieri) 1981;
C/RoC/Con; 13000/20100; 177.37 × 9.07/11.55
(582 × 29.76/37.89); M (GMT); 18; Starboard quarter ramp
Sister:
51236 **COSTA LIGURE** (It)

51240 **FORUM CRAFTSMAN** Gr/Br (Doxford & S)
1972; C/HL; 6700/10200; 162.01 × 8.01/9.36
(531.52 × 26.28/30.7); M (Sulzer); 17; ex *Craftsman*
1981

51250 **IRON CARPENTARIA** Au/Au (Whyalla)
1977; B; 25900; 202.72 × 12.52 (665.09 × 41.07); M
(Wartsila); 15
Sister:
51251 **IRON CURTIS** (Au)

★51260 **KWIDZYN** Pd/Pd (Gdanska) 1974; C; 2800;
106.38 × 5.68 (349.02 × 18.64); M (Sulzer); 14; 'B-
472' type
Sisters (Pd flag):
★51261 **LEBORK**
★51262 **WEJHEROWO**

51270 **GOLD ALISA** Br/Br (Upper Clyde) 1973; C;
7800/11900; 147.2 × 8.59/10.02 (482.93 ×
28.18/32.87); M (Sulzer); —; ex *Alisa* 1980; 'CLYDE'
class
Sisters (Br flag):
51271 **GOLD HILLA** ex *Hilla*
51272 **GOLD ORLI** ex *Orli*
51273 **GOLD VARDA** ex *Varda*

51275 **NEU-ULM** Pa/DDR ('Neptun') 1974; C/HL;
5700/9500; 150.37 × 7.69/9.05 (493 ×
25.23/29.69); M (MAN); 17; ex *Bari* 1979; ex *Petra*
1976; Launched as *Bari*
Sister:
51276 **DENEB** (Sg) ex *Roland Oceanic* 1982; ex
Neuenburg 1980

51280 **KASUGA MARU** Ja/Ja (Onomichi) 1976;
C/HL; 11800; 145.00 × 9.58 (478.70 × 31.43); M
(Pielstick); 15
Similar (larger):
51281 **KATORI MARU** (Ja)

51290 BIZERTE Tn/Ja (Naikai) 1979; C/B; 7800; 137.31 × 7 (450.49 × 22.97); M (B&W); approx 15; Designed for the transportation of phosphate rock
Sister:
51291 KAIROUAN (Tn)

★**51295 BEI AN** RC/Rm (Galatz) 1974; C; 1900/3300; 106.13 × 5.64/7.04 (348 × 18.50/23.10); M (Sulzer); 14

51300 SAN JOHN Gr/Ja (Sanoyasu) 1967; B; 10300; 147.53 × 9.07 (484.02 × 29.76); M (Sulzer); 15; ex Grand Justice 1980

51305 EASTER BAY Li/Ja (Mitsubishi HI) 1975; C; 9200/13000; 162.10 × 8.79/10.60 (532 × 28.84/34.78); M (Sulzer); 15; ex Maritime Carrier 1983

●**51310 LAGENA** FRG/FRG (Bremer V) 1974; Tk; 162000; 351.49 × 22.38 (1153.18 × 73.43); T (Stal-Laval); —
Sisters (FRG flag):
51311 LIOTINA
51312 LOTTIA
Similar:
51313 AJDABYA (Ly)

51320 LAXA Ic/FRG (Jadewerft) 1967; C; 1000; 79.51 × 4.42 (260.85 × 14.5); M (KHD); 13; ex Simone 1975; ex Rolandseck 1973

51330 MING YOUTH Tw/Tw (Taiwan SB) 1969; C; 3700; 107.04 × 7.08 (351.18 × 23.23); M (MAN); 14.5; ex Yu Ming 1977; ex Hai Li 1973

51340 WHITEHEAD Br/Br (Scotts' SB) 1971; A/Trials ship; 3000 Dspl; 88.8 × 5.2 (291.34 × 17); M (Paxman); 15.5

51345 ICE EXPRESS Ne/Ne (Ysselwerf) 1979/83; R; 2700; 94.49 × — (310 × —); M (KHD); 14.5; Lengthened 1983 (Ysselwerf)
Sister:
51346 COLD EXPRESS (Ne)

51350 AMULET De/De (Svendborg) 1975; C; 1600; 94.39 × 5.77 (309.67 × 18.93); M (Alpha-Diesel); 13; Travelling cranes
Sisters:
51351 TALISMAN (De)
51352 KEFLAVIK (Ic) ex Charm 1982
51353 FETISH (De)
51354 MEDALLION (De)

51390 SUVARNABHUMI Th/Br (Robb Caledon) 1969; Ch/LPG/Tk; 3100; 106.13 × 4.65 (348.19 × 15.26); TSM (English Electric); 11

51400 STROMBOLI It/It (Riuniti) 1975; A/Rmt; 8700 Dspl; 123 × 6.5 (403.54 × 21.32); M (Fiat); 20
Sister:
51401 VESUVIO (It)

51420 MALACCA MARU Ja/Ja (Kawasaki) 1978; C/HL; 15900; 157.03 × 9.5 (515.19 × 31.17); M (MAN); 15.5

51423 EL OBEID Su/Ys ('3 Maj') 1979; C; 6300/9700; 149.41 × 8.50/8.77 (490 × 27.89/28.77); M (B&W); 16.5
Sisters (Su flag):
51424 GEDAREF
51425 DONGOLA
51426 MERAWI
51427 DARFUR

★**51430 HONG GU CHENG** RC/Ja (Mitsubishi HI) 1970; C; 10600; 151.16 × 9.17 (496 × 30.09); M (Sulzer); 15; ex Ocean Sailor 1977; ex Nils Amelon 1975; 'MM-14' type

51440 INSTALLER 1 Li/Ne (Duijvendijk's) 1960; BT; 1800; 81.9 × 5.32 (268.7 × 17.45); M ('Bolnes'); 13; ex Skadi 1979; Converted from general cargo and shortened 1969 (IHC Holland); Helicopter platform aft

51450 SANTA CRUZ Li/Sw (Eriksbergs) 1969; C; 6200/9600; 140.04 × 7.89/9.53 (459.45 × 25.88/31.26); M (Pielstick); 16.5; ex Seafalcon 1983; ex Isfahan; 'Scandia' type
Sister:
★**51451 TONG BAI SHAN** (RC) ex Turtle Bay; ex Indus 1979

51460 DIJEY Cy/FRG (Meyer) 1968; C; 3100/5100; 119.97 × 6.45/7.6 (393.6 × 21.16/24.93); M (KHD); 16.5; ex Katie 1983; ex Marianne 1980; ex Tenos 1975; ex Marianne 1971
Sister:
★**51461 QIAN TANG JIANG** (RC) ex Madeleine 1977

51470 NILE CARRIER Eg/Pd (Gdanska) 1968; C; 2200/4100; 116.52 × 5.73/— (382.28 × 18.79/—); M (Mirrlees Blackstone); 14; ex Fouad K 1983; ex Booker Vulcan 1983; ex Seahawk 1974; ex Concordia

Star 1970; ex Sea Viking 1969; ex Seahawk 1968; 'B-448' type

51480 BOIN Ko/Ja (Hitachi) 1970; C; 8400; 140.06 × 8.99 (459.51 × 29.49); M (B&W); 15.5; ex Clintona 1980; ex Yamashige Maru 1980
Sister:
51481 YANNIS (Gr) ex Nishige Maru

51490 JESBON Ko/Ja (Hayashikane) 1971; C; 9500; 155.56 × 9.3 (510.36 × 30.51); M (Sulzer); 16.75; ex Nichiwa Maru
Sisters:
51491 MONISBON (Ko) ex Pacific 1982; ex Nichibu Maru 1980
51492 MONIMBO (Ni) ex Palm Islands 1980
Probable sister:
51493 SHINKAWA MARU (Ja)

51500 WOLWOL Et/De (Orskovs) 1977; C; 1600; 98.96 × 5.73 (324.67 × 18.79); M (Alpha-Diesel); 13; ex Pep Coral 1982
Sister:
51501 KEIY KOKEB (Et) ex Pep Comet 1982

51510 ARCTIC VIKING Br/FRG (Kroegerw) 1967; C; 700/1600; 74.53 × 4.09/5.17 (244.52 × 13.41/16.96); M (MWM); 14; ex Baltic Viking 1981

51520 GIAMAICA It/FRG (Kroegerw) 1960; C; 1600; 87.08 × 4.98 (285.7 × 16.34); M (MaK); 12.5; ex Captain Gigetto 1975; ex Indal Retzlaff 1972; ex Indal 1965

51530 IRAN MEEAD Ir/Be (Cockerill) 1970; C; 12000; 149.79 × 9.26 (491.44 × 30.38); M (B&W); 16.5; ex Arya Gam 1980
Sisters (Ir flag):
51531 IRAN ABAD ex Arya Taj 1980
51532 IRAN MEELAD ex Arya Nur 1980
51533 IRAN ERSHAD ex Arya Tab 1980
51534 IRAN JAHAD ex Arya Pas

●★**51540 JIN RUN** RC/FRG (Nobiskrug) 1970; C; 2800/5000; 125.02 × 6.56/7.64 (410.17 × 21.52/25.06); M (Atlas-MaK); 17; ex Industria 1984; ex Cap Serrat 1983
Sisters:
51541 TESINA (Cy) ex Andra 1984; ex Marheike; ex Eastern River 1975; ex Cap Sunion 1974
51542 AMAZONIA (Pe) ex Mistral Del Norte 1981; ex Cap Sidero 1976
51543 MAHONIA (Sg) ex Nordbay 1980; ex Cap Saray 1976

51550 GOLDEN ABIDJAN Pa/No (Framnaes) 1970; C; 11500; 155.53 × 9.4 (510.26 × 30.84); M (B&W); 17; ex Golden Togo 1982; ex Ariadne 1980; ex Norlanda 1978
Sister:
★**51551 GAN JIANG** (RC) ex Norbella

51560 ATLAS MARU Ja/Ja (Mitsubishi HI) 1978; C/HL; 15100; 161.02 × 9.5 (528.28 × 31.16); M (Sulzer); 15.25
Sister:
51561 ANDES MARU (Ja)

51580 SUNFLOWER Ma/FRG (A Pahl) 1959; C; 2800/4000; 105.92 × 6.72/7.6 (347 × 22.05/24.93); M (KHD); 15; ex Santa Pola 1982; ex Holstenland; ex Lindaunis 1974; ex Cap Bonavista 1970

51590 NAI LUISA It/It (Breda) 1969; OBO; 26200; 216.42 × 12.45 (710 × 40.85); M (Fiat); 15.5; ex Luisa Lolli Ghetti 1974

51600 SINNO M E IV Le/No (Kristiansands) 1965; C; 500/1500; 72.73 × 3.55/4.61 (238.62 × 11.65/15.12); M (Caterpillar); 13.25; ex Scandinavian Express 1981; ex Bastant 1979

51610 BAMMEN Sw/FRG (Luehring) 1968; C; 700/1600; 83.9 × 3.71/4.61 (275.26 × 12.17/15.12); M (Atlas-MaK); 12.5; ex Sommen 1980; Lengthened 1973
Sister:
51611 SKAGERN (Sw)

●**51620 DALSLAND** FRG/Ja (Nishi Z) 1977; C; 1000; 75.47 × 4.77 (247.6 × 15.65); M (Yanmar); 12.5
Sister:
51621 GOTALAND (FRG)

51630 TRANSOCEANICA MARIO It/It (Italcantieri) 1973; OO; 72400; 297.21 × 16.18 (975.1 × 53.08); T (Ansaldo); 16.5
Possibly similar:
51635 NAI MARIA AMELIA (It) ex Maria Amelia Lolli Ghetti 1974
51636 ELIOS (It)
51637 BRASILIA (It)
51638 ARETUSA (It)
51639 WEST WONORI (Pa) ex Ocean Dolphin 1979; ex Ernesto Fassio

51650 SILVER TRANSPORTER Tw/It (Italcantieri) 1968; 00; 48500; 260.1 × 15.2 (853.35 × 49.87); M (Fiat); —; ex Marcona Transporter 1982; ex Ross Sound 1973; ex Rivalta 1971
Possible sister:
51651 ASTAKOS (Li) ex Hastings 1977; ex Ross Point 1975; ex Vittorio Valletta 1971

51660 EARL OF SKYE Br/Br (H&W) 1966; Tk; 37800; 248.65 × 12.90 (816 × 42.32); M (B&W); 15.5; ex British Centaur 1983
Sister:
51661 HALCYON MED (Gr) ex British Captain 1976

51670 CHEYENNE Li/FRG (Thyssen) 1977; BO; 62300; 273.26 × 16.38 (896.52 × 53.74); M (B&W); 15.75; ex Saggat 1978
Sister:
51671 CAYUGA (Li) ex Suorva 1978

51680 TAURUS Gr/Fi (Wartsila) 1977; Tk; 18700; 171.35 × 11.38 (562.17 × 37.34); M (Sulzer); 16.25; ex Messiniaki Akti
Sisters:
51681 GERD MAERSK (De) ex Messiniaki Anatoli
51682 VEGA (Gr) ex Messiniaki Avgi
51683 CARUAO (Ve) Launched as Messiniaki Avra
51684 PARIATA (Ve) launched as Messiniaki Aktida

51690 FULGUR Li/No (Haugesund) 1974; Tk; 19300; 170.69 × 11.37 (560 × 37.3); M (MAN); 15.5
Sisters (Li flag):
51691 FELANIA
51692 FELIPES
51693 FICUS
51694 FLAMMULINA
51695 FOSSARUS
51696 FUSUS

51700 HUMBER ARM Li/FRG (Schichau-U) 1976; RoC; 3700; 130.03 × 6.68 (426.6 × 21.92); M (Pielstick) 16; Side door
Sister:
51701 CORNER BROOK (Li)

51710 ROSE Le/Ne (EJ Smit) 1965; C; 500; 71.99 × 3.82 (236.18 × 12.53); M (MAN); 12.75; ex Al Osman 1982; ex Zeeburgh 1979

51712 ROELOF HOLWERDA Ne/Ne (Stroobos) 1982; C/Con; 1600/3300; 82.70 × 6.42/8.35 (271 × 21.06/27.40); M (Stork-Werkspoor); 12

51715 SAMSUN CARRIER Ne/Ne (Stroobos) 1982; C/Con; 1900/3900; 92.44 × 6.30/8.11 (303 × 20.67/26.61); M (Stork-Werkspoor); 12

51720 UNITY III Pa/FRG (Luerssen) 1965; C; 1100/1900; 83.04 × 4.77/6.14 (272.44 × 15.65/20.14); M (KHD); 14; ex Tatai 1983; ex Neptune Hercules; ex Anglian 1975; ex Neptune Hercules 1974; ex Hercules 1972

51730 SEVEN It/Ne ('Friesland') 1969; C; 600/1500; 77.65 × 4.14/5.83 (254.75 × 13.58/19.12); M (Atlas-MaK); 12; ex Mangen 1982
Sister:
51731 WADDENZEE (Ne) ex Unden

●**51740 PEP REGULUS** De/De (Frederikshavn) 1977; C; 1600; 96.53 × 5.64 (316.69 × 18.51); M (Atlas-MaK); 12.25; 'COMMANDER' class
Sisters:
51741 POLYDORUS (Ne) ex Mercandian Admiral
51742 CASABLANCA (FRG) ex Mercandian Ambassador 1980
51743 SEVILLA (FRG) ex Mercandian Commander 1980
51744 PEP RIGEL (De) ex Mercandian Queen 1981

51745 UNION NELSON NZ/Ko (Dong Hae) 1980; C/Con; 1700/3100; 96.37 × 5.75/6.60 (316 × 18.86/21.65); M (MWM); 14.5; ex Sunny Karina 1981
51746 SUNNY CHRISTINA (Li);
51747 AMPURIA (Cy) ex Sunny Bettina 1983

51750 BELGICA FRG/FRG (Nobiskrug) 1980; C/Con; 1000; 89 × 4.59; (291.99 × 15.06); M (KHD); 13.2; ex Heidkamp 1980

51760 CHRISTA THIELEMANN FRG/FRG (Brand) 1979; C/Con; 1000; 86.2 × 4.87 (283 × 15.98); M (Atlas-MaK); approx. 13.7
Sisters:
51761 NICOLE (FRG)
51762 STENHOLM (FRG)

●**51780 GERMA TARA** Sg/Sg (Singapore Slip) 1978; C/B/Con; 1600/3300; 81 × 5.75/— (265.75 × 18.86/—); M (MaK); 13.5; The crane may not be fitted. This could also apply to any, or all, of the sisters. The deck crane may be obscured when containers are carried. See GERMA KARMA under KMF
Sisters:
51781 GERMA FONDAL (No)

51782 **GERMA FOREST** (Ma)
51783 **GERMA FRAM** (Sg)
51784 **MARE GARANT** (Pa) ex *Germa Garant* 1982;
ex *Germa Lina* 1980; ex *Lina* 1980
51785 **GERMA LIONEL** (No) ex *Lionel* 1979
51786 **UNIT LINK** (Sw) ex *Germa Pride* 1982
51787 **SIRT** (Tu) ex *Germa Lady* 1982
Probable sister:
51788 **KATAWA** (Sg)

51800 **STAPAFELL** Ic/FRG (Hitzler) 1979; Tk; 1400;
75.74 × 4.79 (248.49 × 15.72); M (KHD); 13.5

51810 — — (Viana) 1972; C/Con; 3900;
46.6 × — (316.93 × —); 13; ex
Elisabeth Fisser 1979; Travelling cranes
Sisters:
51811 **BAUCIS** (Cy) ex *Alice Bolten* 1973
51812 **TABLA** (Cy) ex *Boca Tabla* 1982; ex *Imela
Fisser* 1973

51820 **LISA B** Tu/FRG (Sietas) 1967; RoC; 1000;
78.03 × 4.29 (256 × 14.07); M (Atlas-MaK); —; ex
Dena 1 1982; ex *Zejtun* 1982; ex *Taos* 1974; ex *Wasa*
1973; Bow and stern doors
Sister:
51821 **DENA 1** (Tu) ex *Alpilles* 1983; ex *Hansa* 1972

51830 **ALNEGMA ALKHADRA** Si/Br (Cochrane)
1969; Pal; 700; 75.32 × 3.4 (247.11 × 11.15); TSM
(Mirrlees Blackstone); 13.75; ex *Al-Majja 1* 1982; ex
Redsea Express 1981; ex *Dangeld* 1977; 2 side doors

51840 **NORRLAND** FRG/FRG (Werftunion) 1977;
C; 1000; 80.7 × — (264.76 × —); M (Atlas-MaK); 13.5

51850 **ASD HEKTOR** Sg/Gr (Salamis) 1977;
C/Con; 2000; 106.2 × 5.02 (348.43 × 16.47); TSM
(KHD); 16
Sisters (may be gearless):
51851 **LAMARA** (Sg) ex *Meteor II* 1982
51852 **METEOR 1** (Sg)

51860 **HELEN** Pa/Sg (Singapore Slip) 1975; C;
1600; 69.07 × 4.23 (226.6 × 13.87); TSM (MWM); 9;
ex *Ocean Pioneer* 1983; ex *Asean Pioneer* 1981
Sisters (Pa flag):
51861 **ANGELA** ex *Ocean Property* 1983; ex *Asean
Prosperity* 1981
51864 **OCEAN PROGRESS** ex *Asean Progress*
1980
51865 **YVONNE C** ex *Ocean Promoter* 1983; ex
Asean Promoter 1980

● 51870 **CARIBE MARINER** Pa/Ja (Yamanishi)
1976; Con; 1600/4200; 117.46 × 4.93/6.49
(385.36 × 16.17/21.29); M (MAN); 16.25; ex *Contract Mariner* 1982; ex *Zepatlantic* 1978; ex *Gulf
Pioneer* 1978; Launched as *Zepatlantic;* Travelling
cranes
★51871 **WEN HE** (RC) ex *Contract Carrier* 1982; ex
Zepbaltic 1978; ex *Dafra Northsea*
51872 **ZEPPACIFIC** (Sg) ex *Contract Trader* 1983; ex
Zeppacific 1978; ex *Dafra Red Sea* 1978; ex *Gulf
Trader* 1977; Launched as *Zeppacific*

51880 **KURE** Li/Ja (IHI) 1971; B; 76000; 303.82 ×
17.45 (996.78 × 57.25); T (IHI) 15.5; ex *Universe
Kure* 1980; launched as *Cedros Pacific;* Travelling
cranes

51890 **BAROJA** Sp/Sp (AESA) 1979; B/Cem;
22500; 186.65 × 9.75 (612.37 × 31.99); M (Sulzer);
approx. 15; Travelling crane
Sister:
51891 **UNAMUNO** (Sp)
51892 **GURIDI** (Sp)

51895 **JAVA WINDS** Ne/Ne (Giessen-De Noord)
1980; Con; 28400; 204.02 × 10.21 (669.36 × 33.5);
M (Sulzer) —; ex *Nedlloyd Zeelandia* 1983; ex *Benattow* 1982

● 51900 **OT-MARINA** Sw/Sw (Oskarshamns) 1972;
Tk/Ch; 5800; 126.12 × 7.2 (413.78 × 23.6); M
(Ruston Paxman); 14.25; ex *Marina* 1982
Sister (Sw flag):
51901 **CARIA** (Br) ex *Maria* 1981

51910 **SEAWAY PRINCE** Au/Au (Whyalla) 1975;
RoC; 4200; 132.44 × 6.42 (434.51 × 21.06); TSGT (J
Brown); 18; Stern door/ramp
Sister:
51911 **SEAWAY PRINCESS** (Au)

51920 **RELUME** Br/Br (Ailsa) 1979; BT; 1600; 75.94
× 3.75 (249.15 × 12.3); TSM (A P E Allen); —; Bow
thruster

51930 **PEZZATA ROSA** It/No (Hatlo) 1964; C; 500;
75.8 × 3.77 (248.68 × 12.37); M (MaK); 12.25; ex
Pirholm 1979; ex *Neerlandia* 1976

51940 **ACT 3** Br/FRG (Bremer V) 1971; Con; 23800;

217.25 × 10.52 (712.76 × 34.51); T (Stal-Laval); 22.5
Sisters (Br flag):
51941 **ACT 4**
51942 **ACT 5**
51943 **AUSTRALIAN EXPORTER**

51950 **GABY** Pa/Sp (Cadiz) 1969; Cem; 5300;
120.12 × 7.03 (394.09 × 23.06); TSM (Sulzer); —; ex
Anahuac II 1981

51960 **DRUPA** Br/FRG (Deutsche Werft) 1966; Tk;
39800; 243.8 × 13.25 (799.87 × 43.47); T (Stal-
Laval); 14; Fenders on upper deck are on port side

51970 **FOLGOET** Fr/Sw (Eriksbergs) 1968; Tk;
15100; 169.63 × 9.55 (556.52 × 31.33); M (B&W);
16; ex *British Liberty* 1981
Similar:
51971 **PETER KIRK** (Pa) ex *Hala* 1981; ex *British
Loyalty* 1981
51972 **BRITISH SECURITY** (Br)
51973 **BRITISH TENACITY** (Br)
51974 **SEBASTIANO** (Pa) ex *British Unity* 1981
51975 **BRITISH FIDELITY** (Br)

51980 **CELLANA** Au/Au (Whyalla) 1968; Tk; 16000;
171.02 × 9.78 (561.09 × 32.08); M (Sulzer); 14.5

51985 **NORSK BARDE** No/No (Horten) 1976; Tk;
18000; 168.76 × 10.9 (553.67 × 35.76); M (Sulzer);
16

51986 **VIKLA** Fi/Fi (Valmet) 1982; Ch; 6300; 133.31
× 7.22 (437 × 23.69); M (Pielstick); 15

51987 **EMDEN** FRG/FRG (Husumer) 1980; Ch;
4000; 112.40 × 7.00 (369 × 22.97); M (KHD); 15; ex
Bomin Emden 1983

★51988 **VENTSPILS** Ru/Fi (Rauma-Repola) 1983;
Tk; 4810; 115.80 × 7.00 (380 × 22.97); M (B&W); 14;
Ice strengthened
Sisters (Ru flag):
★51989 **ALEYSK**
★51989/1 **KASHIRA**
Possible sisters (Ru flag):
★51989/2 **RASDOLNOYE**
★51989/3 **TAGANROG**

51990 **LUNNI** Fi/FRG (Nobiskrug) 1976; Tk/IB;
11000; 162.01 × 9.5 (531.52 × 31.16); M (Atlas-
MaK); 14.5
Sisters (Fi flag):
51991 **SOTKA**
51992 **TIIRA**
51993 **UIKKU**

51995 **PARITA** Fi/Fi (Wartsila) 1982; Tk; 25600;
187.64 × 11.62 (616 × 38.12); M (Sulzer); 15

51996 **TEBO OLYMPIA** Fi/Fi (Valmet) 1980; Tk;
8900; 140.93 × 7.30 (462 × 23.95); M (Wartsila); 15
Sisters:
51997 **SHELLTRANS** (Fi)
51998 **MELKKI** (Fi) ex *Polar Scan* 1983
51999 **RANKKI** (Fi) ex *Arctic Scan* 1983

★52000 **MARLOW** DDR/DDR (Elbewerften) 1971;
C/Con; 300; 57.87 × 3.68 (189.86 × 12.07); M
(Liebknecht); 12; **'Boizenburg'** type
Sisters (DDR flag):
★52001 **HAGENOW**
★52002 **MILTZOW**
★52003 **MIROW**
★52004 **NEUBOKOW**
★52006 **RAKOW**
★52007 **SATOW**
★52008 **SEMLOW**
★52009 **TORGELOW**
★52010 **ZUROW**
★52011 **ZUSSOW**

★52020 **BALKHASH** Ru/Ru (Krasnoyarsk) 1969; C;
1100; 72.12 × 4.63 (236.61 × 15.19); M (Russkiy); 11
Sisters (Ru flag):
★52021 **BAKHCHISARAY**
★52022 **BELOMORYE**

52030 **NOORDLAND** Ne/Ne (Bijlsma) 1977; C;
1600; 81.44 × 4.78 (267.2 × 15.68); M (Atlas-MaK);
11.5

52040 **NOVA** Sw/Ne (Kramer & Booy) 1975; C;
1600; 93 × 5.58 (305.12 × 18.31); M (Alpha-Diesel);
13; ex *Junior Lotte* 1983; Travelling crane
Sister:
52041 **MARIE** (Sw) ex *Junior Lone* 1983

52043 **ALIDA SMITS** Ne/Ne (Groot & VV) 1978; C;
1600/3500; 83.70 × 5.74/8.38 (275 ×
18.83/27.49); M (Atlas-MaK); 12
Sisters:
52044 **ALSYTA SMITS** (Ne)
52045 **ANDREA SMITS** (Ne)
Similar (longer sisters):
52046 **AMANDA SMITS** (Ne)

52047 **ANGELA SMITS** (Ne)
52048 **ANITA SMITS** (Ne)

52050 **AL SULTANA** O/Ne (Bijlsma) 1975; FA/Spt;
900; 65.4 × 4.2 (214.56 × 13.77); M (Mirrlees Blackstone); 11

52060 **GOLIATH** Au/Au (Carrington) 1978; Cem;
3400; 95.03 × 5.8 (311.78 × 19.03); M (Mitsubishi);
14

★52070 **BUNA** DDR/Ne (Vuyk) 1979; Ch; 1800;
73.46 × 4.91 (241 × 16.11); M (Atlas-MaK); 13
Sister:
★52071 **SCHKOPAU** (DDR) (may be spelt **ZSCHJO-
PAU**)

52074 **ESSO FINLANDIA** Fi/Fi (Navire) 1981; Ch;
4400; 107.02 × 7.30 (351 × 23.95); TSM (Wartsila);
13.5

52080 **STAPAFELL** Ic/FRG (Hitzler) 1979; Tk; 1400;
75.74 × 4.79 (248.49 × 15.72); M (KHD); 13.5

52090 **BALDER B** De/De (Orskovs) 1974; C;
500/1400; 71.48 × 3.76/5.68 (234.51 ×
12.34/18.63); M (Alpha-Diesel); 12; ex *Lykke Bewa*
1978
Sisters:
52091 **ARTIS** (Cy) ex *Gibtwo* 1983; ex *Kantara K*
1982; ex *Koerier* 1980; ex *Lita Bewa* 1978
52092 **HAVSO** (Sw) ex *Karin Bewa* 1976
Possible sister:
52093 **NIAGA XX** (Ia) ex *Nina Bewa* 1978

52100 **BINTANG BOLONG** Gm/No (Hjorungavaag)
1976; C; 1600; 63.71 × 6.59 (209.02 × 21.62); M
(Normo); 12; ex *Janada* 1978; Travelling crane

52110 **CARICOM EXPRESS** Bb/Ne (Groot & VV)
1976; C; 1600; 84.31 × 6.32 (276.6 × 20.73); M (Smit
& Bolnes); 13; ex *Kirsten Smits* 1983; Travelling
crane
Probable sister:
52111 **CARICOM VENTURE** (Bb) ex *Marinus Smits*
1983

52120 **SAMSUN DAWN** Ne/Ne ('Friesland') 1976;
C; 1600; 81.92 × 6.05 (268.77 × 19.85); M (KHD); 12;
ex *Annette* 1983

52130 **TURPIAL** Ve/Be (Boelwerf) 1970; Tk; 11100;
158.58 × 9.47 (520.27 × 31.67); M (MAN); 15.5; ex
Stolt Norness 1982; Travelling crane
Sisters (Li flag):
52131 **STOLT CROWN**
52132 **STOLT CASTLE**
52133 **STOLT SYDNESS**

52140 **ORIENT ENTERPRISE** Li/Ja (Kure) 1968; B;
35500; 223.96 × 13.7 (734.78 × 44.94); M (Sulzer);
15; ex *Prometheus;* Travelling crane
Possible sisters (Gr flag):
52141 **AFOVOS**
52142 **THEOGENNITOR** ex *Agamemnon*

52150 **CANADIAN PROGRESS** Ca/Ca (Port Weller) 1968; B; 21400; 222.51 × 8.73 (730 × 28.64); M
(Ruston & Hornsby); 14.5

52160 **NIAGA XXXVIII** Ia/Ne ('Vooruitgang') 1973;
C; 1600; 77.09 × 5.81 (252.92 × 19.06); M (Atlas-
MaK); 12.5; ex *Westwal* 1981; ex *Schoonebeek*
1981; ex *Aerdenhout* 1975
Sister:
52161 **LORIA** (It) ex *Azores Star* 1981; ex *Groesbeek*
1980
Probable sisters:
52162 **NIAGA XXXIX** (Ia) ex *Wiidswal* 1982; ex
Sambeek 1980
52163 **SCHOUWENBANK** (Ne) ex *Wedlooper* 1980

52170 **CELTIC** Ne/Ne ('Friesland') 1979/82; R;
1200; approx 80.5 × — (approx 264 × —); M (KHD); —;
Lengthened 1982
Sisters (Ne flag):
52171 **ATLANTIC**
52172 **BALTIC**

52180 **HECTOR** Ne/Ne (Amels) 1979; C/Con;
1600/3000; 82.78 × 5.93/7.39 (271.59 ×
19.46/24.25); M (Stork-Werkspoor); approx. 12.5; ex
Nestor 1981
Sisters (Ne flag):
52181 **MENTOR**
52182 **STENTOR**

52190 **NIAGA XXVIII** Ia/Ne ('Vooruitgang') 1970; C;
1500; 78.75 × 5.84 (258.37 × 19.16); M (Werkspoor);
12; ex *Peter H* 1980; ex *Holland;* ex *Heerengracht*
1979; ex *Hilverenbeek* 1973
Sister:
52191 **NIAGA XXXII** (Ia) ex *Noordwal* 1980

● 52200 **ROBERTA 1** Pa/It (Adriatico) 1966; Tk;
45000; 253.6 × 13.32 (832.02 × 43.7); M (Adriatico);

16.25; ex *Elizabeth II* 1981; ex *Margaret Simone* 1980; ex *Petra* 1973; ex *Warwick Fort* 1971
Similar:
52202 DRASTIRIOS (Gr) ex *Sarissola* 1981; ex *Claudio R* 1979
52203 FILIKOS (Gr) ex *Ombrina* 1981; ex *Monica R* 1979
52204 IRINIKOS (Gr) ex *Scrivia* 1981; ex *Andrea Leopoldo*
Similar (Bulk/Oil):
52206 SHINWA (In) ex *Daya Parvati;* ex *Ross Head* 1977

52210 ELEFTHEROS Gr/It (Adriatico) 1966; Tk; 48700; 253.6×13.29 (832.02×43.6); M (Fiat); —; ex *Santa Cristina Prima* 1981
Sisters (Gr flag):
52211 POLYMICHANOS ex *Santa Anna Prima* 1982
52212 DYNAMIKOS ex *Santa Augusta* 1982

52220 LIBEXCEL Pa/Ja (Sumitomo) 1969; O; 17900; 175.04 × 11 (574.28 × 36.09); M (Sulzer); 14.25; ex *Nikkei Maru No 3* 1983

52230 TEQUILA SUNRISE FRG/FRG (Sietas) 1970; C; 1000; 87.61 × 5.29 (287.43 × 17.35); M (KHD); 14.5; ex *Svealand* 1981; ex *Conti Syria* 1980; ex *Svealand* 1979; ex *Helga Russ* 1979; ex *Svealand* 1977; ex *Royal Enterprise* 1975; Launched as *Svealand*

52240 TAKARI 1 Ia/FRG (O&K) 1966; C; 2300; 94.9 × 5.26 (311.35 × 17.26); M (MAN); 12.5
Sisters (Ia flag):
52241 TAKARI II
52242 TAKARI III
52243 TAKARI IV
52244 TAKARI V
52245 TAKARI VI
52246 TAKARI VII
52247 TAKARI VIII

52250 QUITAUNA Bz/Be (Boelwerf) 1975; Ch; 14300; 170.72 × 10.21 (560.1 × 33.49); M (MAN); 16; Travelling crane
Sister:
52251 QUIXADA (Bz)

52260 STOLT SHEAF Li/Be (Boelwerf) 1972; Tk/Ch; 14600; 170.72 × 10.54 (560.1 × 34.58); M (MAN); 13.75; Travelling crane
Sisters:
52261 STOLT BOEL (Li)
52262 STOLT LLANDAFF (Pa)

52265 JOHNSON CHEMSTAR Sw/Sw (Kockums) 1980; Ch; 22200; 175.01 × 10.7 (574.18 × 35.1); TSM (Pielstick); 16.3 (Trials)
Sister:
52266 JOHNSON CHEMSUN (Sw)

★**52270 URAL** Ru/Ru (—) —; A/Spt. Nuclear; 4000 Dspl; 103 × 6 (337.92 × 19.68); M (—)

52280 BOA VISTA 1 Bz/Ne (IHC Smit) 1977; D; 5500; 107.52 × 7.49; (352.76 × 24.57); TSM (Sulzer); 12
Sister:
52281 MACAPA (Bz)

52285 JAMES ENSOR Be/Be (St Pieter) 1980; D; 4200; 105.21 × 6 (345.18 × 19.69); TSM (KHD); 12.5; Trailing suction hopper dredger

52287 MARCO POLO No/No (Kristiansands) 1982; LGC; 4200; 95.66 × 7.12 (314 × 23.36); M (Wichmann); 13

52288 CONUS Au/Ja (Mitsubishi HI) 19S1; Tk/Ch; 26300; 177.71 × 12.02 (583 × 39.44); M (Sulzer); 14.5

52290 HUMBER ARM Li/FRG (Schichau-U) 1976; RoC; 3700; 130.03 × 6.68 (426.6 × 21.92); M (Pielstick); 16; Side door
Sister:
52291 CORNER BROOK (Li)

52300 COVADONGA Sp/Au (Whyalla) 1969; Con; 12800; 156.67 × 9.17 (514 × 30.08); M (Sulzer); 17.5; ex *CP Hunter* 1981; ex *Seatrain Galveston* 1980; ex *Trans Europa* 1979; ex *Trans Europa* 1978; ex *Kanimbla* 1976
Sisters:
52301 GUADALUPE 1 (Sp) ex *Seatrain Texas* 1979; ex *Trans America* 1979; ex *Cheshire Endeavour* 1979; ex *Trans America* 1978; ex *Manoora* 1976

52303 GLORIA ELENA Pa/FRG (Sietas) 1981; Cem; 7900; 136.00 × 8.11 (446 × 26.61); M (B&W); 15

52305 MULSANNE Fr/Fr (Havre) 1974; RoC; 1600; 100.46 × 4.38 (330 × 14.37); TSM (Atlas-MaK); 15
Sister:
52306 ARNAGE (Fr)

Similar (no crane foreward):
52307 TERTRE ROUGE (Fr)
Probably similar:
52308 HUNAUDIERES (Fr)

52310 EBURNA Br/Ja (Mitsui) 1979; Tk; 19800; 170 × 11.04 (557.74 × 36.22); M (B&W); 14.1
Sisters (Br flag):
52311 ERVILIA
52312 EUPLECTA
52313 EBALINA

★**52320 LEDENICE** Ys/Ys ('3 Maj') 1979; RoC-/Con/C; 5600; 144.4 × 6.5 (473.75 × 21.33); M (Pielstick) 17.9; Travelling gantry (with slewing deck crane). Stern slewing ramp
Probable sister:
★**52321 BRIBIR** (Ys)

52340 NAI LUISA It/It (Breda) 1970; OBO; 28700; 216.42 × 12.45 (710 × 40.85); M (Fiat); 15.5; ex *Luisa Lolli Ghetti* 1974

52350 GIANT KIM Li/Ja (IHI) 1971; B; 32100; 209.02 × 10.99 (685.76 × 36.05); M (Sulzer); 15.75; ex *Triabunna* 1982; ex *Nego Triabunna* 1980; Travelling cranes
Sister:
52351 SILVICULTURE (Li)

52360 GOLDEN STATE Li/Ja (NKK) 1964; B; 17400; 174.02 × 9.92 (570.93 × 32.55); M (MAN); 13.5; ex *Kure Maru* 1976; Travelling crane
Similar:
52361 BLUE STAR (Ko) ex *Honshu Maru* 1978
52362 VICTORY STAR (Pa) ex *Orient Pegasus* 1983; ex *Sunway* 1980; ex *Marusumi Maru* 1978;
52363 GLORY STAR (Pa) ex *Hiro Maru* 1982

52370 AL OSMAN Le/Ne (E J Smit) 1965; C; 5OO; 71.99 × 3.82 (236.18 × 12.53); M (MAN); 12.75; ex *Zeeburgh* 1979

52380 MOSEL ORE Li/Sw (Gotav) 1969; OO; 58800; 253.02 × 15.13 (830.12 × 49.64); M (Gotaverken); 15; ex *Baron Venture* 1980; ex *Pajala* 1978
Sister
52381 SAAR ORE (Li) ex *United Venture;* ex *Porjus* 1978; ex *Flowergate* 1974

52400 FJORDSHELL No/No (Haugesund) 1973; Tk; 18600; 170.69 × 11.37 (560 × 37.3); M (Sulzer); 16

52410 AGIOS NIKOLAS Gr/Br (Upper Clyde) 1971; C; 7500/11900; 147.2 × 6.76/10 (482.93 × 22.18/32.81); M (Sulzer); 18.75; ex *Sig Ragne;* 'CLYDE' class
Sisters (Li flag):
52411 SAMJOHN GOVERNOR
52412 SAMJOHN PIONEER

52420 MALIGAYA Pi/Ja (Hayashikane) 1969; RoC; 2400; 107.7 × 4.49 (353.34 × 14.73); TSM (Niigata); 14.75; ex *Hokuo Maru* 1981

52430 ACT 3 Br/FRG (Bremer V) 1971; Con; 23800; 217.25 × 10.52 (712.76 × 34.51); T (Stal-Laval); 22.5
Sisters (Br flag):
52431 ACT 4
52432 ACT 5
52433 AUSTRALIAN EXPORTER

★**52440 KHAN ASPARUKH** Bu/Bu (G Dimitrov) 1976; Tk; 59900; 244.48 × 15.5 (802.1 × 50.85); M (Sulzer); 14.5
Probable sister:
52441 OLYMPIC STAR (Li) ex *Khan Krun*

52450 NORDIC LOUISIANA Br/Br (Furness) 1964; Sulphur Carrier; 18600; 188.98 × 10.35 (620.01 × 33.96); M (Sulzer); 16; ex *Naess Louisiana* 1973
Sister:
52451 NORDIC TEXAS (Br) ex *Naess Texas*

52460 ETTORE It/No (Ankerlokken) 1974; Tk; 4500; 107.93 × 8.08 (354.1 × 26.51); M (B&W); 14; ex *Joarctic* 1978
Sisters:
52461 HUMBOLT (No) ex *Joalaska* 1978
52462 TANIT (Gr) ex *Essi Atlantic;* ex *Joatlantic* 1978

52470 VENDEE Br/Br (Swan Hunter) 1972; C; 6100; 132.29 × 7.34 (434.02 × 24.08); M (Doxford); 18; ex *Zaida* 1975
Sister:
52471 VOSGES (Br) ex *Zaira* 1975

52480 KRISTINA Sw/Sw (Falkenbergs) 1970; C/Con; 1600; 87.03 × 4.96; (285.53 × 16.27); M (Appingedammer Brons); 12; ex *Alice* 1973

52500 ARALAR Sp/Sp (AESA) 1971; B; 29300; 206.86 × 13.35 (678.67 × 43.79); M (Sulzer); 16; Travelling crane
Similar:

52501 SPRY CARRIER (Pa) ex *Angela Pando* 1982; ex *Pilar Maria* 1981

52510 TURPIAL Ve/Be (Boelwerf) 1970; Tk; 11100; 158.58 × 9.47 (520.27 × 31.67); M (MAN); 15.5; ex *Stolt Norness* 1982; Travelling crane
Sisters (Li flag):
52511 STOLT CROWN
52512 STOLT CASTLE
52513 STOLT SYDNESS

52520 STOLT PRIDE Li/Fr (Dubigeon-Normandie) 1976; Tk; 12500; 170.69 × 9.68 (560 × 31.76); M (Sulzer); 15; Travelling crane
Sisters (Li flag):
52521 STOLT SPIRIT
52522 STOLT SINCERITY
52523 STOLT INTEGRITY
52524 STOLT TENACITY
51525 STOLT LOYALTY
52526 STOLT EXCELLENCE

52530 ORIENT ENTERPRISE Li/Ja (Kure) 1968; B; 35500; 223.96 × 13.7 (734.78 × 44.94); M (Sulzer); 15; ex *Prometheus;* Travelling crane
Possible sisters:
52531 THEOGENNITOR (Gr) ex *Agamemnon*
52532 AFOVOS (Gr)

52540 MARCONA CONVEYOR Li/Ja (Hakodate) 1967; B; 32600; 259.75 × 13.58 (852.19 × 44.55); M (Sulzer); 16.25; ex *Aragonite Islander* 1973; ex *Fotini L* 1971

52550 DAVID P REYNOLDS Li/FRG (Howaldts DW) 1970; B; 28600; 226.7 × 12.79 (743.76 × 41.96); T (Allgemeine); 16

52560 SAUNIERE Ca/Br (Lithgows) 1970; B; 13100; 195.94 × 9.54 (642.85 × 31.29); M (B&W); 15; ex *Algosea* 1982; ex *Brooknes* 1976. Lengthened 1976 (Swan Hunter)

52570 HAUKUR Ic/No (Aukra) 1966; Cem; 1000; 65.03 × 4 (213.35 × 13.12); M (KHD); 12; ex *Freyfaxi* 1983; Launched as *Faxi;* Travelling crane

52590 BLUE SHINYO Ja/Ja (Geibi) 1970; RoC; 1700; 92 × 4.91 (301.84 × 16.11); M (Hanshin); 14; ex *Rio Borde* 1980; ex *Koyo Maru* 1979

52600 ASTREA No/No (Fosen) 1979; RoC/Con; 1600; 109 × 4.79 (357.61 × 15.72); M (Wichmann); 17; Stern ramp. Side door on starboard side

52610 HVASSAFELL Ic/FRG (Buesumer) 1971; C; 900/1800; 80.17 × 4.07/5.87 (263.02 × 13.36/19.25); M (KHD); 14.
Possible sister :
52611 SKAFTAFELL (Ic)

52613 HELVETIA Pa/Bu (G Dimitrov) 1980/81; B/Cem; 15300; 184.61 × 10.31 (606 × 33.83); M (Sulzer); —; Converted from bulk carrier 1981 (Sietas)
Possible sister (may not be converted-also under KC₄MFKC)
52614 JUVENTIA (Pa)

52620 TYSON LYKES US/US (Bath) 1976; RoC; 13200; 208.72 × 9.8 (684.77 × 32.15); T (GEC); 23; ex *Maine* 1979; Quarter door/ramp
Sisters (US flag):
52621 CHARLES LYKES ex *Nevada* 1979
52622 MERCURY (US Navy) ex *Illinois* 1980
52623 JUPITER (US Navy) ex *Lipscomb Lykes* 1980; ex *Arizona*

52630 PARALLA Sw/Sw (Eriksbergs) 1971; RoC; 13400; 199.02 × 9.59 (652.95 × 31.46); M (Pielstick); 21; Stern doors
Sisters:
52631 ALLUNGA (Au)
52632 DILKARA (Br)

52640 BARBER TONSBERG No/No (Kaldnes) 1979; RoC/Con; 22100; 228.5 × 10.8 (749.67 × 35.43); M (B&W); 22; Starboard quarter ramp
Sister:
52641 BARBER TAIF (No)
Similar (Ja built—Mitsubishi HI; Differences include funnel shape, design of crane etc):
52642 BARBER NARA (Sw)
52643 BARBER PRIAM (Br)
52644 BARBER PERSEUS (Br)
52645 BARBER TOBA (No)

52650 LIBERTADOR SAN MARTIN Ar/Ar (Alianza) 1979; Tk; 10000; 153 × 8.24 (501.97 × 27.03); M (Sulzer); 15
Sisters (Ar flag):
52651 INGENIERO VILLA
52652 MINISTRO EXCURRA (also reported as **MINISTRO EZCURRA**)

52660 ILO Pe/Pe (La Marina) 1972; C; 8600; 153.88 × 9.39 (504.86 × 30.81); M (B&W); 19.5; Naval

service
Sister:
52661 **RIMAC** (Pe)

52670 **AL-SAYESTHA** Bh/FRG (A G 'Weser') 1962; C/HL; 5500; 127.11 × 7.78 (417.03 × 25.52); M (B&W); 15.75; ex *Arco Iris* 1982; ex *Amara* 1981; ex *Astir II*; ex *Naxos Trader* 1978; ex *Evia* 1977; ex *Pacific* 1972; ex *Tripoli* 1969; ex *Axenfels* 1965; Travelling crane
Sister:
52671 **MYOMA YWA** (Bm) ex *Altenfels* 1969

52680 **TARBELA** Pk/FRG (A G 'Weser') 1968; C; 7000/9000; 153.88× —/9.27 (504.86×—/30.41); M (MAN); —
Sisters (Pk flag):
52681 **KAPTAI**
52682 **WARSAK**

52690 **KASUGA MARU** Ja/Ja (Onomichi) 1976; C/HL; 11800; 145.9 × 9.5 (478.67 × 31.16); M (Pielstick); 15
Similar (larger):
52691 **KATORI MARU** (Ja)

52695 **ICELANDIC** Ne/Ne-Ne (Van Diepen) 1979/83; R; 3600 (DWT); 101.26 × 5.28 (332 × 17.32); M (KHD); —; lengthened 1983 (Boele's Sch)
Sisters:
52696 **ARCTIC** (Ne)
52697 **INDIANIC** (Ne)
52678 **TEMPO** (Ne)

52700 **AMULET** De/De (Svendborg) 1975; C; 1600; 94.39 × 5.77 (309.67 × 18.93); M (Alpha-Diesel); 13; Travelling cranes
Sisters:
52701 **TALISMAN** (De)
52702 **KEFLAVIK** (Ic) ex *Charm* 1982
52703 **FETISH** (De)
52704 **MEDALLION** (De)

52710 **UNITY III** Pa/FRG (Luerssen) 1965; C; 1100/1900; 83.04 × 4.77/6.14 (272.44 × 15.66/20.14); M (KHD); 14; ex *Tatai* 1983; ex *Neptun Hercules*; ex *Anglian* 1975; ex *Neptun Hercules* 1974; ex *Hercules* 1972

● 52720 **COMBI TRADER** Ne/De (Orskovs) 1975; C; 1400; 71.48× 5.74 (234.51×18.83); M (Atlas-MaK); 12; ex *Ocean Coast* 1975
Sister:
52720/1 **TRIVIA** (NA) ex *Pacific Trader* 1981; ex *Pacific Coast* 1978
Similar:
52721 **ADRIANA** (It) ex *Rijnhaven* 1982; Launched as *Janne*

52730 **THORLINA** Cy/Ja (Miho) 1966; RoC/LC; 3600; 78.49 × 4.37 (257.51 × 14.33); TSM (Daihatsu); 10.5; ex *Navesa Norma* 1982; ex *Maritime Resource* 1980; ex *Oman Venture* 1978; ex *Cosmos* 1975; Bow doors

★ 52735 **BAO AN** RC/Rm (Galatz) 1975; C; 2500/3600; 106.13 × 5.64/7.10 (348 × 18.50/23.29); M (Sulzer); 14.5
Sisters:
★ 52736 **DONG AN** (RC)
★ 52737 **JIANG AN** (RC)

52740 **FRANK H BROWN** Ca/Ca (Canadian Vickers) 1965; Con; 8000; 120.12 × 6.12 (394.09 × 20.08); TSM (Polar); —; May be converted to a barge

★ 52745 **ALI AMIROV** Ru/Fr (Dubigeon-Normandie) 1977; DS; 1700; 72.80 × 3.20 (239 × 10.50); TSD-E (Crepelle); 10; ex *Specsudno 1*

52750 **MERINO EXPRESS** Li/Ne (Vuyk) 1960; LS; 2400/3400; 119.49 × 5.68/6.41 (392.03 × 18.64/21.03); M (Stork); 16; ex *Cap Farina* 1976; ex *Caribbean Express* 1974; ex *Kreon* 1973; Converted from cargo ship 1976 (Meyer)

● 52760 **CLAN ROSE** Pa/Br (Hill) 1954/68; C; 1300; 84.82 × 4.17 (278.28 × 13.68); M (British Polar); 10.5; ex *Apollo* 1982; Lengthened 1968
Sister:
52761 **KATERINA M** (Ma) ex *Ageliki III* 1982; ex *Echo* 1980

52770 **SERIUS** Ho/Br (Inglis) 1959; C; 1100; 74.48 × 4.03 (244.36 × 13.22); M (Ruston & Hornsby); 12; ex *Sirius* 1982; ex *Star* 1977; ex *Orwell Quay* 1976; ex *Gulf Sea* 1975; ex *Leeds* 1972
Sister:
52771 **GULF COAST** (Cy) ex *Wakefield*
Similar:
52773 **AGIOS NIKOLAOS** (Gr) ex *Victory* 1982; ex *Jean R* 1980; ex *Raven* 1977; ex *Selby* 1973

52780 **ALEXANDRA N** In/Sw (Kockums) 1965; B; 16700; 175.88 × 10.43 (577.03 × 34.22); M (MAN); 15; ex *Falkanger* 1974

52781 **CHARISMA N** (In) ex *Fossanger* 1974

52790 **GEORGIAN GLORY** Gr/Sw (Kockums) 1962; B; 16600; 175.88 × 11 (577.03 × 36.09); M (MAN); 14.5; ex *Sighaug* 1966
Sister:
52791 **EUROPEAN MASTER** (Gr) ex *Cestos Bay* 1980; ex *Pantokrator* 1979; ex *Pan* 1972; ex *Theologos* 1970; ex *Siganka* 1966

52800 **SALLY D** Li/Ja (Mitsui) 1968; B; 15500; 178.14 × 10.27 (584.45 × 33.69); M (Sulzer); 15.5; ex *Continental Shipper* 1983
Sister:
52801 **ATHANASIOS K** (Gr) ex *Continental Pioneer* 1983

52810 **BERTRAM RICKMERS** FRG/FRG (Bremer V/Rickmers)-FRG 1970/79; C/Con; 10000/14400; 170.7 × 10.68/9.87 (560.04 × 35.04/32.38); M (MAN); 17.5; ex *Leverkusen* (Forebody). Hull is made up using forebody of Leverkusen (Howaldts DW)
Sister:
52811 **RENEE RICKMERS** (FRG) ex *Ludwigshafen* (Forebody)

52820 **ALDABI** Ne/Ne (Giessen-De Noord) 1977; C/Con; 9800; 143.06 × 4.49 (469.36 × 14.73); M (Stork-Werkspoor); 16.25
Sisters (Ne flag):
52821 **ALHENA**
52822 **ALNATI**
52823 **ALPHACCA**

★ 52830 **YAN SHAN** RC/Ja (Kanawa) 1976; C; 11300; 148.01 × 9.5 (485.6 × 31.17); M (B&W); 15; ex *Aloha* 1980

52840 **TRIBELS** Gr/Ja (Nipponkai) 1974; C/HL; 6900/11600; 147.71 × 8.08/9.63 (484.61 × 26.51/31.59); M (B&W); 18.5; ex *Trifels* 1980; ex *Aristogenis* 1975. Converted from 'Mitsui-Concord' type cargo vessel

52850 **HAE WOO No 3** Ko/Ja (Mitsui) 1971; C; 6500/10100; 145.7 × 8.01/9.27 (478.02 × 26.28/30.41); M (B&W); 16; ex *Ranenfjord* 1981; 'Concord' type
Sister:
52851 **HAE WOO No 2** (Ko) ex *Lyngenfjord* 1982

52860 **RATNA MANORAMA** In/Sp (AESA) 1973; C; 11200; 147.02 × 9.81 (482.35 × 32.19); M (MAN); 15.5; 'Santa Fe' type
Sister:
52861 **RATNA KIRTI** (In) launched as *Aegis Grace*
Similar:
52862 **AEGIS BLAZE** (Gr)
Probably similar (Gr flag):
56862/1 **AEGIS HARVEST**
56862/2 **AEGIS STOIC**
56862/3 **AEGIS WISDOM**

● 52863 **BOLAN** Pk/Ja (Kawasaki) 1980; C/Con; 8100/12500; 153.02 × 8.25/9.75 (502 × 27.07/31.99); M (MAN); —
Sisters (Pk flag):
52864 **CHITRAL**
52865 **SARGODHA**
52866 **HYDERABAD**
52867 **MULTAN**
52868 **MALAKAND**

52870 **TOYOTA MARU No 16** Ja/Ja (Kurushima) 1971; BC; 23200; 187.51 × 12.12 (615.19 × 39.76); M (MAN); 14.5
Probable sister:
52871 **PACIFIC ROAD** (Ja) ex *Toyota Maru No 17* 1982; (May now be converted to a ro/ro ship)

52880 **BUNKO MARU** Ja/Ja (Hitachi) 1976; B; 30700; 215.02 × 12.4 (705.45 × 40.68); M (Sulzer); 14.75; 'Hi-Bulk-50' type

52890 **IBERIA** FRG/FRG (LF-W) 1972; C/HL/TS; 8000/11200; 153.24 × 9.06/10.07 (502.75 × 29.72/33.2); M (MAN); 20; ex *Sturmfels* 1980

52900 **NEDLLOYD KEMBLA** Ne/Ja (Mitsubishi HI) 1971; C; 7900/12400; 162 × 10.4 (533 × 34); M (Sulzer); 17
Sisters (superstructure may vary slightly) (Ne flag):
52901 **NEDLLOYD KIMBERLEY**
52902 **NEDLLOYD KINGSTON**
52903 **NEDLLOYD KYOTO**
52904 **NEDLLOYD KATWIJK**

52910 **RAFAELA** Pa/No (Haugesund) 1963; B; 12800; 162.16 × 9.7 (532.02 × 31.82); (Sulzer); 15; ex *Gungnir V* 1982; ex *Sunray*; ex *Tonto* 1964

● 52920 **MERAPI** Gr/Pd (Gdanska) 1977; C/HL; 12600; 169.83 × 9.76 (557.18 × 32.02); M (Sulzer); 18; ex *Stratheden* 1982; 'B-466' type
Sisters:

52921 **MERBABU** (Gr) ex *Rheinbels* 1983; ex *Strathelgin* 1982
52922 **TANNENBELS** (Gr) ex *Stratherrol* 1982
52923 **ALTENBELS** (Gr) ex *Strathesk* 1982
52924 **STRATHETTRICK** (Br)
52925 **LINDENBELS** (Gr) ex *Strathewe* 1982

52930 **KITHNOS** Pa/No (Fredriksstad) 1962; C; 4800/7400; 137.14 × 7.3/8.69 (449.93 × 23.95/28.51); M (Gotaverken); 15.5; ex *Vingaholm* 1975; ex *Felis* 1967

★ 52940 **YAN SHAN** RC/Ja (Kanawa) 1976; C; 11300; 148.01 × 9.5 (485.6 × 31.17); M (B&W); 15; ex *Aloha* 1980

52950 **BATILLUS** Fr/Fr (L'Atlantique) 1976; Tk; 273600; 414.21 × 28.5 (1358.96 × 93.5); TST (Stal-Laval); 16
Sisters (Fr flag):
52951 **BELLAMYA**
52953 **PRAIRIAL**

52960 **MING YOUTH** Tw/Tw (Taiwan SB) 1969; C; 3700; 107.04 × 7.08 (351.18 × 23.23); (MAN); 14.5; ex *Yu Ming* 1977; ex *Hai Li* 1973

52970 **NATICINA** Br/De (Odense) 1967; Tk; 60700; 265.18 × 14.95 (870 × 49.05); M (Sulzer); 15; Used for lightening

52980 **BARENBELS** Gr/FRG (Flender) 1976; C/HL; 7400/11800; 149.16 × 8.1/9.6 (489.37 × 26.57/31.5); M (MAN); 16; ex *Barenbels* 1980
Sister:
52981 **ATLAS** (Gr) ex *Hispania* 1981; ex *Brauenfels* 1980

52990 **PABLO V** Ag/No (Fredriksstad) 1962; C; 12600; 166.48 × 10.19 (546.19 × 33.43) M (Gotaverken); 13.5; ex *Venabu* 1974

53000 **IVER HERON** No/No (Sarpsborg) 1979; Ch; 19800; 173.7 × 10.5 (569.88 × 34.45); M (B&W); approx. 14.5
Similar:
53001 **BOW FIGHTER** (No)

53003 **JOHNSON CHEMSPAN** Sg/No (Ankerlokken) 1983; Tk/Ch; 18700; 182.71 × 10.06 (599 × 33.01); M (B&W); 15.5

53006 **CORTINA** Sw/FRG (Schichau-U) 1981; Tk/Ch; 6500; 131.53 × 8.40 (432 × 27.56); M (Krupp MaK); 14.75

53020 **NORA MAERSK** De/De (Odense) 1977; Tk; 39200; 247.25 × 13.17 (811.2 × 43.21); M (Sulzer); 16.5
Sisters (De flag):
53021 **NELE MAERSK**
53022 **NELLY MAERSK**
53023 **NICOLAI MAERSK**
53024 **NICOLINE MAERSK**
53025 **NIELS MAERSK**

53027 **MAURANGER** No/No (Ankerlokken) 1981; Tk/Ch 18700; 182.79 × 10.07 (600 × 33.04); M (B&W); 16; Launched as *Kaupanger*
Sister:
53028 **JO CLIPPER** (No) launched as *Polux*

53030 **PABLO V** Ag/No (Fredriksstad) 1962; C; 12600; 166.48 × 10.19 (546.19 × 33.43); M (Gotaverken); 13.5; ex *Venabu* 1974

53040 **HAE WOO No 3** Ko/Ja (Mitsui) 1971; C; 6500/10100; 145.7 × 8.01/9.27 (478.02 × 26.28/30.41); M (B&W); 16; ex *Ranenfjord* 1981; 'Concord' type
Sister:
53041 **HAE WOO No 2** (Ko) ex *Lyngenfjord* 1982

53050 **NORA MAERSK** De/De (Odense) 1977; Tk; 39200; 247.25 × 13.17 (811.2 × 43.21); M (Sulzer); 16.5
Sisters (De flag):
53051 **NELE MAERSK**
53052 **NELLY MAERSK**
53053 **NICOLAI MAERSK**
53054 **NICOLINE MAERSK**
53055 **NIELS MAERSK**

53058 **CARLA A HILLS** Li/Ja (Mitsubishi HI) 1981; Tk; 21600; 179.20 × 10.95 (588 × 35.93); M (Sulzer); 14.9
Sisters:
53059 **ALDEN W. CLAUSEN** (Li)
53060 **GEORGE H. WEYERHAUSER** (Li)
53061 **KENNETH T. DERR** (Bs)
Probable sister:
53062 **CHEVRON PACIFIC** (Li)

53065 **AMPOL SAREL** Au/Ja (Mitsubishi HI) 1979; Tk; 65100; 243 × 13.74 (797.24 × 45.08); M (Sulzer); 15.6

... Carolina; Modified *GL-73* type
Sister:
53561 **CHARLOTTA** (FRG) ex *Testbank* 1981; ex *Charlotta*

53570 **ISMENE** Gr/DDR ('Neptun') 1968; C; 4200; 114.74 × 6.48 (376.44 × 21.26); M (MAN); 14; ex

Similar:
53702 **TRADE LIGHT** (Gr) ex *Baldur* 1978

● 53710 **LABRADOR CURRENT** Li/FRG (LF-W) 1962; B; 17700; 200.01 × 9.81 (656.2 × 32.19); M (MAN); 16; ex *Vulkan* 1972
Similar (Li flag):

Sister:
53891 **NESTOR** (Pa)

53900 **PRESIDENT QUEZON** Pi/Ko (Hyundai) 1978; B; 22000; 222.51 × 9.7 (730 × 31.82); M (B&W); 14; ex *Federal Clyde* 1981

● 53070 **ARABIAN SEA** Si/De (Odense) 1975; Tk; 160400; 354.57 × 23.83 (1163.29 × 78.18); T (Stal-Laval); 15.75; ex *Linga* 1981
53071 **ALSAMA ALARABIA** (Si) ex *Arabian Sky* 1981; ex *Limatula* 1981
53072 **PARADISE** (Pa) ex *Liparus* 1984
53073 **ORPHEUM** (Pa) ex *Limnea* 1983

★ 53160 **MANGYSHLAK** Ru/Ru (Astrakhan) 1969; Tk; 8400; 150.02 × 8 (492 × 26.25); M (Skoda); 13.5
Sisters (Ru flag):
★ 53161 **GENERAL ASLANOV**
★ 53162 **GENERAL BABAYAN**
★ 53163 **KAFUR MAMEDOV**
★ 53164 **NIKIFOR ROGOV**

53311 **OSCO SPIRIT** (No)
53312 **OSCO SIERRA** (Li) ex *Carbo Sierra* 1976
53313 **OSCO STRIPE** (Li) ex *Carbo Stripe* 1975

★ 53315 **GUANGHE** RC/FRG (Flensburger) 1972; C/Con; 7200/11100; 154.87 × 8.31/9.80 (508 × 27.26/32.15); M (MAN); 18.5; ex *Lutz Jacob* 1973;

Sisters (Li flag):
53901 **FEDERAL CALUMET**
53902 **FEDERAL RHINE**
53903 **FEDERAL SCHELDE**
Similar (smaller funnel, lower superstructure etc. Be built (Cockerill):
53904 **FEDERAL DANUBE** (Be)
53905 **FEDERAL MAAS** (Be)
53906 **FEDERAL OTTAWA** (Be)
53907 **FEDERAL THAMES** (Be)

53910 **STOLT FALCON** Li/Ko (Korea SB) 1978; Ch; 21000; 173.64 × 11.58 (569.69 × 37.99); M (Sulzer); 15.5; ex *Stolt Seoul*
Probable sisters (Li flag):
53911 **STOLT OSPREY** ex *Stolt Busan*
53912 **STOLT HAWK** ex *Stolt Inchon*
53913 **STOLT HERON** ex *Stolt Yosu*
53914 **STOLT CONDOR** ex *Stolt Okpo* 1979
53915 **STOLT EAGLE** ex *Stolt Ulsan* 1979

53920 **HARRY C WEBB** Li/Ne (Verolme Dok) 1965; Tk/Ch; 11900; 167.65 × 9.52 (550 × 31.24); T (GEC); 16.5

53930 **AMCO 1** Pa/Fr (Havre) 1965; LGC; 1800; 80.88 × 3.61 (265.35 × 11.84); M (MAN); 14.25; ex *Sorine Tholstrup* 1980; ex *Niels Henrik Abel* 1970

53940 **SUN RIVER** Ja/Ja (Kawasaki) 1974; LGC; 45600; 224.01 × 11.89 (734.94 × 39.01); M (MAN); 16
Similar (Li flag):
53941 **WORLD CONCORD**
53942 **WORLD CREATION**
53943 **WORLD VIGOUR**

53950 **PIONEER LOUISE** Li/Ja (Mitsubishi HI) 1976; LGC; 42300; 228.02 × 12.05 (748.1 × 39.53); M (MAN); 15.75
Possible sisters:
53951 **GAS DIANA** (Li)
53952 **GAS GEMINI** (Li)

53960 **OTTO LEONHARDT** FRG/FRG (Kieler H) 1967; B; 23400; 202.34 × 11.27 (663.85 × 36.98); M (MAN); 16

53970 **MARALUNGA** It/It (Ansaldo) 1962; B; 26400; 229.74 × 11.7 (753.74 × 38.39); M (Fiat); 16; ex *Maria Amelia Lolli Ghetti* 1966; Lengthened 1968

53980 **GOLDEN DAY** Pa/Br (Fairfield SB) 1965; B; 21500; 201.78 × 11.18 (662.01 × 36.68); M (Sulzer); 15; ex *Suzanne H.* 1983; ex *Suzanne* 1980; ex *Garthnewydd* 1972; ex *Cluden* 1972

53990 **PERTUSOLA** It/It (Benetti) 1975; Tk; 4000; 117.66 × 7.32 (386.02 × 24.02); M (GMT); 15.5
Sister:
53991 **PUGIOLA** (It)

54000 **PIONEER LOUISE** Li/Ja (Mitsubishi HI) 1976; LGC; 42300; 228.02 × 12.05 (748.1 × 39.53); M (MAN); 15.75
Possible sisters:
54001 **GAS DIANA** (Li)
54002 **GAS GEMINI** (Li)

54010 **CENTAURO** It/It (Ansaldo) 1962; B; 26400; 229.75 × 11.73 (753.77 × 38.48); 15; Lengthened 1967
Sister (It flag):
54011 **POSEIDON**
Possibly similar:
54013 **GALASSIA** (It)

54020 **HASSI R'MEL** Ag/Fr (CNIM) 1971; LGC; 31400; 200.01 × 8.5 (656.2 × 27.89); T (Stal Laval); 16

54030 **WORLD BRIGADIER** Pa/Ja (Kawasaki) 1974; Tk; 105200; 319.31 × 19.53 (1047.6 × 64.07); T (Kawasaki); 16.5
Similar:
54031 **WORLD AZALEA** (Pa)
54032 **WORLD COMET** (Pa)
54034 **TACTIC** (Gr)
54035 **ZUIKO MARU** (Ja) ex *Manhattan King* 1981
Possible sisters:
54036 **EASTERN LAUREL** (Pa) ex *World Philippines* 1980
54037 **WORLD SOVEREIGN** (Pa)

54040 **MONGE** Fr/Fr (La Ciotat) 1977; LGC; 43700; 231.12 × 13.55 (758.27 × 44.46); M (Pielstick); 20
Probable sister:
54041 **GAS ENTERPRISE** (Br) ex *Razi* 1980
Similar (Ku flag):
54042 **GAS AL-AHMADI**
54043 **GAS AL-BURGAN**
54044 **GAS AL-KUWAIT**
54045 **GAS AL-MINAGISH**

54047 **NYHAMMER** No/Fr (La Ciotat) 1975; LGC; 40400; 230.89 × 12.62 (758 × 21.40); M (Sulzer); 18

54050 **METHANIA** Be/Be (Boelwerf) 1978; LGC; 78100; 280.02 × 11.23 (918.7 × 36.84); T (Deutz); 19

54060 **STAFFORDSHIRE** Li/Fr (France-Gironde) 1977; LGC; 41700; 226.32 × 13.03 (742.52 × 42.75); M (Sulzer); 17

54070 **POLLENGER** Br/No (Moss R) 1974; LGC; 76500; 261.4 × 10.5 (857.6 × 34.45); T (Kvaerner); 19.5; ex *LNG Challenger* 1979

54080 **HOEGH GANDRIA** No/FRG (Howaldts DW) 1977; LGC; 95700; 287.54 × 11.52 (943.37 × 37.8); T (A G 'Weser'); 20
Sister:
54081 **GOLAR FREEZE** (No)

54090 **GOLFO DI PALERMO** It/It (Ansaldo) 1960; B; 12900; 174.91 × 9.99 (573.85 × 32.78); M (Fiat);

54100 **ANANGEL HARMONY** Gr/FRG (B+V) 1968; B; 12300; 162.19 × 10.36 (532.12 × 33.99); M (Ottensener); 16.5; ex *Normannia* 1980. 'Pioneer' type

54110 **ATALANTA** Gr/FRG (B+V) 1969; C; 13300; 162.21 × 10.38 (532.19 × 34.06); M (Pielstick); 16.5; ex *Jag Darshan* 1983; 'Pioneer' type
Sisters (In flag):
54111 **JAG DEESH**
54112 **JAG DHARMA**
54113 **JAG DHIR**
54114 **JAG DOOT**
54115 **JAGAT PRIYA**
54116 **DAMODOR GANGA**
54117 **INDIAN GLORY**
54118 **INDIAN GRACE**
54119 **VEER VARUNA** ex *Jag Dev* 1978

54130 **BOW FORTUNE** No/Pd (Szczecinska) 1975; Ch; 17100; 170.52 × 11.08 (559.45 × 36.35); M (Sulzer); 17; 'B-76' type
Sisters (No flag):
54131 **BOW SEA**
54132 **BOW SKY**
54133 **BOW SPRING**
54134 **BOW STAR**
54135 **BOW SUN**
54136 **BRIMANGER**
54137 **NORDANGER**
54138 **PORSANGER**
54139 **RISANGER**
54140 **SPINANGER**
54141 **TORVANGER**

54150 **LADY AUGUSTA** It/Br (Richards) 1970; Tk/Ch; 1800; 86.87 × 5.44 (285 × 17.85); M (Atlas-MaK); 13; ex *Stainless Warrior* 1976
Sister:
54151 **INGER WONSILD** (De) ex *Silwon* 1981; ex *Stainless Duke* 1978; (First vent has been repositioned nearer the second; This may also apply to **LADY AUGUSTA**)

54160 **SANT JORDI** Sp/Sp (Ruiz) 1973/76; LGC; 5500; 109.86 × 5.75 (360.43 × 18.86); M (B&W); 15; Launched 1973; Completed 1976

54170 **CARIBGAS V** Pa/Fr (Duchesne & B) 1963; LGC; 1200; 62.03 × 4.27 (203.51 × 14.01); M (MAN); 12; ex *Celia* 1979; ex *Celsius* 1976

54180 **METHANIA** Be/Be (Boelwerf) 1978; LGC; 78100; 280.02 × 11.23 (918.7 × 36.84); T (Deutz); 19

● 54190 **BARBER MENELAUS** Pa/Ja (Mitsubishi HI) 1977; C/Con; 10400/16000; 164.52 × 8.74/10.62 (540 × 28.67/34.84); M (Sulzer); 18; ex *Menelaus* 1980; 'MP-20' type
Sisters:
54191 **BARBER MEMNON** (Pa) ex *Memnon* 1980
54192 **MENESTHEUS** (Pa) ex *Barber Menestheus* 1983; ex *Menestheus* 1980
54193 **MELAMPUS** (Br)
Sisters (Br-built: Scotts' SB):
54194 **MARON** (Br) ex *Studland Bay* 1982; ex *Maron* 1981
54195 **MENTOR** (Br) ex *City of London* 1983; ex *Mentor* 1981
54196 **MYRMIDON** (Br)

54197 **AL BERRY** Si/Fr (L'Atlantique) 1979; LGC; 48900; 222.10 × 13.52 (729 × 44.36); M (Pielstick); 19.5
Sister:
54198 **AL BIDA** (Ku)

54200 **WAKO MARU** Ja/Ja (Kawasaki) 1975; Tk; 116400; 319.92 × 19.66 (1049.61 × 64.5); T (Kawasaki); 16.5

54205 **SEAWISE GIANT** Li/Ja (Sumitomo) 1976/79/80; Tk; 239000; 458.45 × 24.61 (1504 ×

80.74); T (Stal-Laval); 15.5; Launched as *Oppama*; Lengthened 1980 (NKK)

54210 **ESSO WESTERNPORT** Bs/Fr (La Ciotat) 1977; LGC; 54100; 255.13 × 12.6 (837.04 × 41.34); M (Sulzer); 16.75

54215 **OGDEN BRIDGESTONE** Pa/Ja (Kawasaki) 1973; LGC; 36100; 210.50 × 12.53 (691 × 41.11); M (MAN); 15.5
Sister:
54216 **WORLD BRIDGESTONE** (Pa)

54220 **IZUMISAN MARU** Ja/Ja (Mitsui) 1970; LGC; 38900; 215.09 × 11.01 (705.67 × 36.12); M (B&W); 16

54250 **BOW FORTUNE** No/Pd (Szczecinska) 1975; Ch; 17100; 170.52 × 11.08 (559.45 × 36.35); M (Sulzer); 17; 'B-76' type
Sisters (No flag):
54251 **BOW SEA**
54232 **BOW SKY**
54253 **BOW SPRING**
54254 **BOW STAR**
54255 **BOW SUN**
54256 **BRIMANGER**
54257 **NORDANGER**
54258 **PORSANGER**
54259 **RISANGER**
54260 **SPINANGER**
54261 **TORVANGER**

54263 **TERUTOKU MARU** Ja/Ja (Koyo) 1978; Tk/Ch; 14900; 163.00 × 9.22 (535 × 30.25); M (B&W); 14.75

54265 **DADES** Mo/Ja (Miyoshi) 1977; Tk; 3700; 106.03 × 6.80 (348 × 22.31); M (Akasaka); 13.5; ex *Fujiaki Maru* 1977
Possibly similar:
54266 **DAE WON** (Ko)
54267 **SAPEN 1** (Tu) ex *Blue Sky* 1977
★ 54268 **TIEN GIANG** (Vn) ex *Fujiaki Maru* 1976

● 54270 **DORITAL** Pa/Sw (Oresunds) 1964; B; 15600; 185.25 × 9.82 (607.78 × 32.22); M (Gotaverken); 15; ex *Kingsnorth* 1981; ex *Grimland* 1973

54280 **SAMOS** Gr/Sw (Oresunds) 1966; B; 17200; 185.25 × 9.82 (607.78 × 32.22); M (Gotaverken); —; ex *Despina C* 1968

54290 **SUNRISE** Li/FRG (Bremer V) 1963; B; 23000; 214.18 × 11.66 (702.69 × 38.26); M (MAN); 15; ex *Skyline* 1980; ex *Leros* 1978; ex *Splendid Honour* 1977; ex *Delphina* 1974
Sister:
★ 54291 **TIAN SHUI HAI** (RC) ex *Dorado* 1979

54300 **TAIHANG** Pa/Be (Boel)-Be 1958/69; B; 11700; 172.27 × 9.07 (565 × 29.76); M (MAN); 13.5; ex *Tonje* 1982; ex *Calbe* 1981; ex *Marly 1* 1965; Lengthened 1969 (Cockerill)
Sister:
54301 **MARGARITA** (Gr) ex *Georgios C* 1980; ex *Tielrode* 1974; ex *Tamise* 1966

54330 **FIESTA 1** Pa/It (Adriatico) 1962; B; 16000; 193.66 × 10.39 (635.37 × 34.09); M (Fiat); —; ex *Fenice* 1977

● 54340 **BARBER MENELAUS** Pa/Ja (Mitsubishi HI) 1977; C/Con; 10400/16000; 164.52 × 8.74/10.62 (540 × 28.67/34.84); M (Sulzer); 18; ex *Menelaus* 1980; 'MP-20' type
Sisters:
54341 **BARBER MEMNON** (Pa) ex *Memnon* 1980
54342 **MENESTHEUS** (Pa) ex *Barber Menestheus* 1983; ex *Menestheus* 1980
54343 **MELAMPUS** (Br)
Sisters (Br-built: Scotts' SB):
54344 **MARON** (Br) ex *Studland Bay* 1982; ex *Maron* 1981
54345 **MENTOR** (Br) ex *City of London* 1983; ex *Mentor* 1981
54346 **MYRMIDON** (Br)

54350 **THORSHOLM** No/Ja (Mitsui) 1973; Tk; 140000; 342.91 × 21.78 (1125.03 × 71.46); M (B&W); 14.75
Sister:
54351 **THORSAGA** (No)

54360 **WORLD DUKE** Pa/Ja (Mitsui) 1975; Tk; 111400; 324.01 × 20.03 (1063.03 × 65.68); T (Stal-Laval); 16.5

54370 **JAPAN VIOLET** Ja/Ja (Kawasaki) 1974; Tk; 116300; 319.95 × 19.66 (1049.7 × 64.5); T (Kawasaki); 16.25; Launched as *World Consul*
Similar:
54371 **ENERGY GROWTH** (Li)

54380 **KYPROS** Cy/Ja (Sumitomo) 1974; Tk; 122900; 340.8 × 21.07 (1118.11 × 69.13); T (Stal-

Laval); 15.5; ex *Saint Marcet* 1983
Sisters (Li flag):
54381 PRIMROSE
54382 VENTURE EUROPE ex *Conoco Europe* 1978
Probable sister:
54383 VENTURE CANADA (Li) ex *Conoco Canada*
Possible sister:
54384 WORLD CANADA (Li)

● **54390 RESOLUTE** Li/Ja (Mitsubishi HI) 1973; Tk; 152300; 340.01 × 24.68 (1115.52 × 80.97); T (Mitsubishi); 15.5; ex *Venoil* 1980
Sister:
54391 ALEXANDER THE GREAT (Gr) ex *Venpet* 1980

54400 WORLD BERMUDA Li/Ja (IHI) 1974; Tk; 117800; 336.99 × 21.05 (1105.61 × 69.06); T (IHI); 16; Launched as *World Monarch*

54410 LAUREL Li/Ja (IHI) 1972; Tk; 117200; 336.36 × 20.29 (1103.54 × 66.57); T (IHI); 16.75; ex *Universe Pioneer* 1980
Similar (Li flag):
54411 UNIVERSE BURMAH
54412 UNIVERSE EXPLORER
54413 ARCADIA ex *Universe Guardian* 1980
54414 PECONIC ex *Universe Mariner* 1980
54415 MOSELLE ex *Universe Monitor* 1980
54416 MENANTIC ex *Universe Ranger* 1980
54417 HAMLET ex *Universe Sentinel* 1980
54418 ARISTOTLE S ONASSIS ex *Universe Frontier* 1977
(Pa flag):
54419 TEXACO CARIBBEAN
54420 TEXACO VERAGUAS

54430 RAS MAERSK De/De (Odense) 1973; Tk; 143100; 347.18 × 22.22 (1139.04 × 72.9); T (Stal-Laval); 15
Sisters:
54431 MATTERHORN (Li) ex *Robert Maersk* 1983
54432 ROMO MAERSK (De)
54435 TEXACO IRELAND (Pa) ex *Roy Maersk* 1976
54436 TEXACO NEDERLAND (Pa) ex *Rosa Maersk* 1975
54437 TEXACO BRASIL (Pa) ex *Richard Maersk* 1975

54440 OKINOSHIMA MARU Ja/Ja (Mitsubishi HI) 1970; Tk; 130900; 337.5 × 19.74 (1107.28 × 64.76); T (Mitsubishi); 15.5
Possibly similar:
54441 TAKAMIYA MARU (Ja)

54450 KIRSTEN MAERSK De/De (Odense) 1975; Tk; 167200; 370.47 × 22.46 (1215.45 × 73.69); T (Stal-Laval); 15.75
Similar (De flag):
54451 KARAMA MAERSK
54452 KAREN MAERSK
54453 KAROLINE MAERSK
54454 KATE MAERSK
54455 KATRINE MAERSK
54456 KRISTINE MAERSK

54460 BRIDGESTONE MARU V Ja/Ja (Kawasaki) 1969; LGC; 40900; 210.52 × 12.2 (690.68 × 40.03); M (MAN); 14.75

54470 MUNDOGAS EUROPE No/Fr (La Ciotat) 1968; LGC; 16500; 171.1 × 9.03 (561.35 × 29.63); M (Fiat); 17; ex *Fernwind* 1979; ex *Kristian Birkland* 1975
Sisters:
54471 DISCARIA (Li) ex *Fernvalley* 1979; ex *Cypress* 1973
54472 MUNDOGAS PACIFIC (No) ex *Fernwood* 1979; ex *Gas Master* 1974

54490 AIKO MARU Ja/Ja (Mitsubishi) 1976; Tk; 209800; 365.87 × 22.9 (1200.36 × 75.13); T (Mitsubishi); 15.75
Sisters:
54491 JINKO MARU (Ja)
54492 AL REKKAH (Ku)
54493 CHEVRON SOUTH AMERICA (Li)
54494 CHEVRON NORTH AMERICA (Li)
54495 DAVID PACKARD (Li)

54500 WORLD PROGRESS Li/Ja (Mitsubishi HI) 1973; Tk; 105800; 320.90 × 19.85 (1053 × 65.12); T (Mitsubishi); 15.75
Possibly similar:
54501 WESTERN CITY (Li) ex *World City* 1979

54510 ESSO DEUTSCHLAND FRG/Ja (Kawasaki) 1976; Tk; 203900; 378.01 × 22.98 (1240.19 × 75.39); T (Kawasaki); 15.75
Probable sister:
54511 HILDA KNUDSEN (No)
Possibly similar:
54512 CORAGGIO (It)
54513 ROBINSON (Li) ex *Golar Patricia*

54520 AFRAN OCEAN Li/Sp ('Astano') 1974; Tk; 171300; 347.94 × 24.83 (1141 × 81.43); TST (Kawásaki); 14.5; ex *Ocean Park* 1982

54530 ESSO HONOLULU Bs/Ja (Hitachi) 1974; Tk; 133000; 343.01 × 22.05 (1125.36 × 72.34); T (Hitachi); 16.25
Sisters (Bs flag):
54531 ESSO BILBAO
54532 ESSO OSAKA

● **54540 KOKKO MARU** Ja/Ja (Mitsubishi HI) 1973; Tk; 117600; 321.83 × 19.89 (1056 × 64.99); T (Mitsubishi); 15.75
Similar (Ja flag):
54541 AMUR MARU
54542 JAPAN ADONIS
54543 JAPAN ASTER
54544 HOEN MARU
54545 TOKIWA MARU
54546 TOTTORI MARU

54550 NYHOLT No/Fi (Wartsila) 1975; Ch; 17900; 170.72 × 11.37 (560.1 × 37.3); M (Sulzer); 16.25
Sisters (No flag):
54551 NYHORN
54552 BOW FAGUS
54553 BOW FLOWER

54560 EVELYN Li/Ja (Hitachi) 1971; C; 30300; 225 × 12.46 (738.19 × 40.88); M (Sulzer); 14.75
Sisters:
54561 PAN ZENITH (Ko) ex *Ivory* 1981
54562 GLOBAL PEACE (Ko) ex *Peace Venture* 1981
54563 K. CHALLENGER (Pa) ex *World Vanguard* 1983
54564 VELA (Li)
54565 STAMY (Gr)
54566 TOPAZ (Cy) ex *Norman Venture* 1982; ex *Jaguar*

54570 CHOKO MARU Ja/Ja (IHI) 1970; B; 32000; 208.01 × 11.73 (682.45 × 38.48); M (Sulzer); 14.75
Similar:
54571 MEXICAN GULF (Li)
54572 EUTHALIA (Gr) ex *Spray Derrick* 1983
54573 STAR CLIPPER (Ko) ex *Uniona* 1983; ex *Y.S. Venture*

54580 ATALANTA Gr/FRG (B+V) 1969; C; 13300; 162.21 × 10.38 (532.19 × 34.06); M (Pielstick); 16.5; ex *Jag Darshan* 1983; 'Pioneer' type
Sisters (In flag):
54581 JAG DEESH
54582 JAG DHARMA
54583 JAG DHIR
54584 JAG DOOT
54585 JAGAT PRIYA
54586 DAMODAR GANGA
54587 INDIAN GLORY
54588 INDIAN GRACE
54589 VEER VARUNA ex *Jag Dev* 1978

54600 ANANGEL HARMONY Gr/FRG (B+V) 1968; B; 12300; 162.19 × 10.36 (532.12 × 33.99); M (Ottensener); 16.5; ex *Normannia* 1980; 'Pioneer' type

54610 SOCRATES Pa/Fr (A Normand) 1954/61; LGC; 1100; 73.11 × 4.17 (239.86 × 13.68); M (Pielstick); 10; ex *Marcelin Berthelot* 1978; ex *Cantenac* 1961; Converted from cargo 1961

54620 ESSO ABERDEEN Br/Ja (Kawasaki D) 1967; Tk; 59300; 276.51 × 14.87 (907.19 × 48.79); T (Kawasaki); 17; ex *Imperial Ottawa* 1978

★ **54630 DONUZAV** Ru/Ja (Osaka) 1971; B; 19700; 185.5 × 11.15 (608.6 × 36.58); M (Sulzer); 14.75; ex *Maritime Ace* 1983
Sisters (Pa flag):
54634 MARITIME TRADER
(Li flag):
54637 WINEDROP ex *Eastern Hornet* 1982
54639 EASTERN LILAC
54650 GOLDEN DAISY
54652 WORLD RUBY
(My flag):
54653 BUNGA CHEMPAKA
Similar:
54654 ARETHOUSA II (Gr) ex *Erradale* 1983
(Ko flag):
54656 HAI KEUM ex *Samick Atlantic* 1982; ex *Eastern Jade* 1981; ex *Marquee* 1980; ex *Eastern Jade* 1979
(Si flag):
54657 ABU SALAMA ex *Golden Dolphin* 1981
54659 SAQR AL DAMMAM ex *Maritime Unity* 1982
54659/2 SAQR JEDDAH ex *Maritime Challenge* 1982
54659/3 SAQR JIZAN ex *Maritime Justice* 1982
54659/4 SAQR JUBAIL ex *Maritime Harmony* 1982
54659/5 SAQR YANBU ex *Maritime Fortune* 1982

● **54660 SITIA VENTURE** Pa/It ('Navalmeccanica') 1966; B; 16000; 190.48 × 10.61 (624.93 × 34.81); M (Fiat); —; ex *Mare Felice* 1982
Sisters:
54661 ARTHUR (Pa) ex *Marlindo* 1982; ex *Mare Placido* 1981
54662 SAUDI GIZAN (Si) ex *Marbella* 1984; ex *Mare Sereno* 1981
54663 DELJES (Me) ex *Sitia Spirit* 1983; ex *Mare Tranquillo* 1982

54680 CHAC Me/No (Ankerlokken) 1976; Ch; 17600; 170.72 × 10.01 (560.1 × 32.84); M (B&W); 15.5; ex *Fossanger* 1977
Sister:
54681 BACAB (Me) ex *Bow Clipper* 1977

54690 KARRAS Pa/Sw (Lindholmens) 1962; B; 10800; 152.56 × 9.16 (500.52 × 30.05); M (Lindholmens); 14.25; ex *Kimoliaki Aigli* 1983; ex *Oinoussian Captain* 1981; ex *Falster* 1972

54700 ARCTIC OCEAN Cy/It (Breda) 1962; B; 17300; 192.03 × 10.61 (630.02 × 34.81); M (Fiat); 16; ex *Polinnia* 1981
Sisters:
54701 MINORIES PROGRESS (Pa) ex *Massimo Primo* 1981
54702 TRADE WIND (Gr) ex *Umberto d'Amato* 1980; ex *Peppina d'Amato* 1978; ex *Donatella* 1978

★ **54710 NIKOLAY NOVIKOV** Ru/Pd (Gdanska) 1973; B/TC; 10200; 150.27 × 8.69 (493.01 × 28.51); M (Sulzer); 15; 'B-436' type
Sisters (Ru flag):
★ **54711 IVAN SYRYKH**
★ **54712 VLADIMIR MORDVINOV**
★ **54713 VLADIMIR TIMOFEYEV**
The following are 'B 540' type (Ru flag):
★ **54714 KAPITAN MOCHALOV**
★ **54715 KAPITAN BAKANOV**
★ **54716 KAPITAN KIRIY**
★ **54717 KONSTANTIN PETROVSKIY**
★ **54718 MEKHANIK GORDYENKO**
★ **54719 VLAS NICHKOV**
★ **54720 KAPITAN DUBLITSKIY**
★ **54721 KAPITAN MILOVZOROV**
★ **54722 KAPITAN SAMOYLENKO**
★ **54723 PETR SMIDOVICH**
★ **54724 VASILIY MUSINSKIY**
★ **54725 KAPITAN BURMAKIN**
★ **54726 KAPITAN GLAZACHYEV**
★ **54727 KAPITAN VASILYEVSKIY**
★ **54728 KAPITAN ZAMYATIN**
★ **54729 YURIY SAVINOV**
★ **54730 BOTSMAN MOSHKOV**
★ **54731 FEDOR VARAKSIN**
★ **54732 KAPITAN SHEVCHENKO**
★ **54733 KAPITAN LYUBCHENKO**
★ **54734 PETR STRELKOV**

54740 CLERK-MAXWELL Br/Br (Hawthorn, L) 1966; LGC; 8300; 140.67 × 8.25 (461.52 × 27.07); M (Sulzer); 17
Similar:
54741 MARIANO ESCOBEDO (Me)

54750 STADT ESSEN Pa/No (Batservice) 1971; Tk; 1600; 91.22 × 5.53 (299.28 × 18.14); M (English Electric); 13; ex *Multitank Badenia* 1981; ex *Mark* 1974
Sisters:
54751 MULTITANK HAMMONIA (Cy) ex *Multitank Rhenania*
54752 MULTITANK WESTFALIA (Pa) ex *Seamark* 1974

54760 EUCLIDE It/Fr (Havre) 1971; LGC; 5100; 107.02 × 6.09 (351.12 × 19.98); M (Sulzer); 15.5; ex *Euclides* 1976

54770 THORSHOLM No/Ja (Mitsui) 1973; Tk; 140000; 342.91 × 21.78 (1125.03 × 71.46); M (B&W); 14.75
Sister:
54771 THORSAGA (No)

54780 LUIGI CASALE It/It (La Ciotat) 1966; LGC; 10900; 150.48 × 8.86 (493.7 × 29.06); M (Sulzer); 16; ex *Capella* 1973; ex *Franklin* 1967; ex *Capella* 1967; Launched as *Benjamin Franklin*
Sister:
54781 PYTHAGORE (Pa) ex *Arquimedes* 1975

54790 ESSO HONOLULU Bs/Ja (Hitachi) 1974; Tk; 133000; 343.01 × 22.05 (1125.36 × 72.34); T (Hitachi); 16.25
Sisters (Bs flag):
54791 ESSO BILBAO
54792 ESSO OSAKA

54800 YOKO MARU Ja/Ja (Mitsui) 1975; Tk; 135100; 331.5 × 20.55 (1087.6 × 67.42); T (Stal-Laval); 16.25; ex *Barbara T Shaheen* 1976

Similar:
54801 **JAPAN COSMOS** (Ja)
54802 **MOBIL SWIFT** (Li) ex *Takakurasan Maru* 1978

54810 **RAS MAERSK** De/De (Odense) 1973; Tk; 143100; 347.18 × 22.22 (1139.04 × 72.9); T (Stal-Laval); 15
Sisters:
54811 **MATTERHORN** (Li) ex *Robert Maersk* 1983
54812 **ROMO MAERSK** (De)
54815 **TEXACO IRELAND** (Pa) ex *Roy Maersk* 1976
54816 **TEXACO NEDERLAND** (Pa) ex *Rosa Maersk* 1975
54817 **TEXACO BRASIL** (Pa) ex *Richard Maersk* 1975

54820 **ENERGY GROWTH** Li/Ja (Kawasaki) 1974; Tk; 105700; 319.92 × 19.66 (1049.61 × 64.5); T (Kawasaki); 16

54840 **TOKUYAMA MARU** Ja/Ja (IHI) 1975; Tk; 136100; 337.07 × 19.94 (1105.87 × 65.42); T (IHI); 16.25

● 54850 **TAKASE MARU** Ja/Ja (Mitsubishi HI) 1970; Tk; 111700; 319.74 × 74.19 (1049.02 × 62.34); T (Mitsubishi); 16
Similar:
54851 **WORLD MITSUBISHI** (Li)
54852 **TAKAOKA MARU** (Ja)

★54870 **MESTA** Bu/Ja (Kasado) 1974; Tk; 46800; 237.01 × 12.92 (777.59 × 42.39); M (Sulzer); 16.5
Sister:
★54871 **OSAM** (Bu)

54880 **PETRO SEA** Th/Ja (Mitsubishi N) 1962; LGC; 17800; 183.72 × 10.54 (602.76 × 34.58); M (MAN); 18.5; ex *Sea Petro* 1983; ex *Petron Gasul* 1982; ex *Contank Bridgestone* 1980; ex *Bridgestone Multina* 1978; ex *Bridgestone Maru* 1971; In use as a storage vessel

54890 **BO BENGTSSON** Pa/Ja (Mitsubishi HI) 1966; LGC; 24500; 187.48 × 10.52 (615.1 × 34.51); M (MAN); 15; ex *Yamahide Maru* 1982

54900 **GAS FOUNTAIN** Pa/Fr (La Ciotat) 1969; LGC; 23800; 197.52 × 9.91 (648.03 × 32.51); M (Fiat); 16.5; ex *Gay Lussac* 1981
Sister:
54901 **CAVENDISH** (Br)

54910 **BRIDGESTONE MARU V** Ja/Ja (Kawasaki) 1969; LGC; 41000; 210.52 × 12.2 (690.68 × 40.03); M (MAN); 14.75

54920 **AIKO MARU** Ja/Ja (Mitsubishi HI) 1976; Tk; 209800; 365.87 × 22.9 (1200.36 × 75.13); T (Mitsubishi); 15.75
Sisters:
54921 **JINKO MARU** (Ja)
54922 **AL REKKAH** (Ku)
54923 **CHEVRON SOUTH AMERICA** (Li)
54924 **CHEVRON NORTH AMERICA** (Li)
54925 **DAVID PACKARD** (Li)

54930 **THALATTA** No/Ja (Mitsubishi HI) 1973; B; 65900; 261.02 × 16.5 (856.36 × 54.13); M (Sulzer); 15; ex *Yu Sing* 1983; ex *Erskine Bridge* 1982
Sister:
54931 **POHANG** (Ko) ex *Lake Almanor* 1983; ex *Severn Bridge* 1976
Similar:
54932 **TAGELUS** (Ne) ex *Stirling Bridge* 1979

54940 **CARSTEN RUSS** FRG/FRG (A G 'Weser') 1971; B; 74500; 282.23 × 16.42 (925.95 × 53.87); M (B&W); 15.75
Sister:
54941 **JACOB RUSS** (FRG)
Similar:
54942 **FUERTE VENTURA** (FRG) ex *Stadt Bremen* 1979

54950 **CHOKO MARU** Ja/Ja (IHI) 1970; B; 32000; 208.01 × 11.73 (682.45 × 38.48); M (Sulzer); 14.75
Similar:
54951 **MEXICAN GULF** (Li)
54952 **EUTHALIA** (Gr) ex *Spray Derrick* 1983
54953 **STAR CLIPPER** (Ko) ex *Uniona* 1983; ex *Y S Venture*

54960 **EVELYN** Li/Ja (Hitachi) 1971; C; 30300; 225 × 12.46 (738.19 × 40.88); M (Sulzer); 14.75
Sisters:
54961 **PAN ZENITH** (Ko) ex *Ivory* 1981
54962 **GLOBAL PEACE** (Ko) ex *Peace Venture* 1981
54963 **K. CHALLENGER** (Pa) ex *World Challenger* 1983
54964 **VELA** (Li)
54965 **STAMY** (Gr)
54966 **TOPAZ** (Cy) ex *Norman Venture* 1982; ex *Jaguar*

★54970 **JOZEF CONRAD KORZENIOWSKI** Pd/Pd (Szczecinska) 1978; C/Con; 17600; 190.28 × 9.55 (624.28 × 31.33); M (Pielstick); 25; 'B-467' type
Sisters (Pd flag):
54971 **ADAM MICKIEWICZ**
54972 **GENERAL FR KLEEBERG**

54980 **WORLD NAVIGATOR** Li/Ja (Mitsui) 1967; B; 22800; 190.02 × 12.27 (623.43 × 40.26); M (B&W); 15
Sisters (Li flag):
54981 **WORLD NEGOTIATOR**
54982 **WORLD NEWS**
54983 **WORLD NOBILITY**
54984 **WORLD NOMAD** Some may not be fitted with cargo gear; See **WORLD NEIGHBOUR**

55000 **DIANA** Bz/Bz (Ish do Brazil) 1968; C; 6900; 145.52 × 8.75 (477.43 × 28.71); M (Sulzer); 17; ex *Bage* 1968
Probable sister:
55001 **CORINA** (Bz) ex *Curvelo* 1968

55010 **PRESIDENTE KENNEDY** Bz/Bz (Ish do Brazil) 1965; C; 6900/9100; 145.5 × 7.94/8.75 (477.36 × 26.05/28.7); M (Sulzer); 15.5
Sisters:
55011 **ALMIRANTE GRACA ARNHA** (Bz)
55012 **EL MEXICANO** (Me)
55013 **PUEBLA** (Me)
Similar:
55014 **BUARQUE** (Bz)
55015 **BRAVO GEORGE** (Gr) ex *Romeo Braga* 1981

55030 **TRITON** Gr/Sw (Gotav) 1963; C; 11100; 154.84 × 9.48 (508 × 31.1); M (Gotaverken); —; ex *Swazi Maiden* 1979; ex *Triton* 1978; ex *Jag Anand* 1976; ex *Cedar* 1968
Similar:
55032 **LEDA** (Gr) ex *Geira* 1978; ex *Sungeira* 1972; ex *Geira* 1969
55033 **IRAN HOJJAT** (Ir) ex *Arya Far* 1980; ex *Arya Pey* 1973; ex *Vinstra* 1969

55040 **GRECIAN LEGEND** Li/Br (Scotts' SB) 1969; B; 23000; 201.78 × 11.61 (662 × 38.09); M (Sulzer); 15
Sister:
55041 **GRECIAN SPIRIT** (Gr)

● 55050 **HAR CARMEL** Is/Br (J L Thompson) 1965; B; 22000; 196.76 × 11.73 (645.54 × 38.48); M (Sulzer); 14; ex *Har Carmel I* 1973; ex *Sheaf Mount* 1972

★55060 **DONUZLAV** Ru/Ja (Osaka) 1971; B; 19700; 185.5 × 11.15 (608.6 × 36.58); M (Sulzer); 14.75; ex *Maritime Ace* 1983
Sisters (Pa flag):
55064 **MARITIME TRADER**
(Li flag):
55067 **WINEDROP** ex *Eastern Hornet* 1982
55069 **EASTERN LILAC**
55071 **GOLDEN DAISY**
55073 **WORLD RUBY**
(My flag):
55074 **BUNGA CHEMPAKA**
Similar:
55075 **ARETHOUSA II** (Gr) ex *Erradale* 1983
(Ko flag):
55076 **HAI KEUM** ex *Samick Atlantic* 1982; ex *Eastern Jade* 1981; ex *Marquee* 1980; ex *Eastern Jade* 1979
(Si flag):
55077 **ABU SALAMA** ex *Golden Dolphin* 1981
55079 **SAQR AL DAMMAM** ex *Maritime Unity* 1982
55079/1 **SAQR JEDDAH** ex *Maritime Challenge* 1982
55079/2 **SAQR JIZAN** ex *Maritime Justice* 1982
55079/3 **SAQR JUBAIL** ex *Maritime Harmony* 1982
55079/4 **SAQR YANBU** ex *Maritime Fortune* 1982

55080 **ALICAMPOS** Gr/Ja (Hitachi) 1968; B; 11400; 156.17 × 9.53 (512.37 × 31.27); M (B&W); 15; ex *Maritime Queen* 1980; 'Hitachi Standard 18' type
Sister:
55081 **MARITIME PIONEER** (Pa)

55090 **AIGEORGIS** Gr/Ja (Hitachi) 1964; C; 8100; 137.52 × 8.31 (451.18 × 27.26); M (B&W); 14.5; ex *Solomon Career* 1980; ex *Yamatada Maru* 1976

● 55100 **ALBION** Sr/Ja (Sanoyasu) 1968; B; 9400; 143.68 × 8.99 (472 × 29.5); M (MAN); 14.5; ex *Lisana* 1983
Similar:
55101 **ENATON** (Gr) ex *Maritime Leader* 1979
55102 **MARIA XILAS** (Gr) ex *Eastern Union* 1971

55110 **LUISE LEONHARDT** FRG/FRG (Flensburger) 1971; C; 7600/10900; 154.87 × 8.66/9.79 (508.1 × 28.41/32.12); M (MAN); 18.5; ex *Maersk Pinto* 1981; ex *Maersk Mango* 1978; ex *Luise Leon-

hardt* 1975

55120 **NORSE TRANSPORTER** Tu/No (Fredriksstad) 1966; B; 16900; 190.79 × 10.12 (625.95 × 33.2); M (Gotaverken); 17.5

★55130 **KARSKOYE MORE** Ru/Fr (CNIM) 1972; FC; 18300; 186.8 × 7.75 (612.86 × 25.43); M (Pielstick); 19
Sister:
★55131 **OKHOTSKOYE MORE** (Ru)

55140 **WORLD NAVIGATOR** Li/Ja (Mitsui) 1967; B; 22800; 190.02 × 12.27 (623.43 × 40.26); M (B&W); 15
Sisters:
55141 **WORLD NEGOTIATOR** (Li)
55142 **WORLD NEWS** (Li)
55143 **WORLD NOBILITY** (Li)
55144 **WORLD NOMAD** (Li); Some may not be fitted with cargo gear. See **WORLD NEIGHBOUR**

55150 **MARATHA PROGRESS** In/FRG (Howaldts) 1964; B; 22200; 197.97 × 11.29 (649.51 × 37.04); M (MAN); 15

55160 **PAPACAROLOS** Gr/Ja (Mitsubishi N) 1959; O; 10200; 156.11 × 8.54 (512.17 × 28.02); M (MAN); 13; ex *Tomiura Maru* 1975

● 55170 **IAPETOS** Sg/No (Fredriksstad) 1963; B; 16300; 186.52 × 10.78 (611.94 × 35.37); M (Gotaverken); 17; ex *Turicum*; ex *Ivory Star* 1975; ex *Jarosa* 1972

55200 **LILLIAN** Pa/Br (Scotts' SB) 1964; B; 16300; 186.09 × 10.85 (610.53 × 35.6); M (Sulzer); —; ex *Epta Dafnes* 1983; ex *Anthony* 1981; ex *Graigwerdd* 1974
Sister:
55201 **GLOBAL SUN** (Ko) ex *Graigffion*

55210 **NEDLLOYD EVEREST** Li/Ne (Verolme Scheeps) 1973; B/Con; 18100; 181.67 × 11.24 (596.03 × 36.88); M (MAN); 16; ex *Capetan Manolis Hazimanolis* 1981; ex *Seatrain Baltimore* 1980; ex *Capetan Manolis Hazimanolis*; ex *Hamburger Wappen* 1977; Converted from bulk carrier 1978 (B+V)
Sister:
55211 **NALO EXPRESS** (Sg) ex *Hapag Lloyd Express*; ex *Ocean Trader* 1982; ex *Barendrecht* 1980; ex *Arabian Unity*; ex *Barendrecht* 1978; ex *Hamburger Flagge* 1978

55220 **BHASKARA** In/Ja (Mitsubishi HI) 1965; OO; 15500; 169.02 × 9.63 (554.53 × 31.6); M (Sulzer); 14.5; ex *Bhaskara Jayanti* 1973
Sisters:
55221 **CHANAKYA** (In) ex *Chanakya Jayanti* 1974
55222 **LEELAVATI** (In) ex *Leelavati Jayanti* 1974

55230 **TAI TUNG** Tw/Ja (Oskarshamns) 1964; C; 10700/11100; 155.25 × 8.92/9.45 (509.35 × 29.27/31); M (Gotaverken); 15; ex *Ocean Endurance* 1973; ex *Steel Engineer* 1971; ex *Blue Master* 1969

● 55250 **KOREAN CEMENT II** Pa/Ja (Hitachi) 1962; O; 15600; 176.84 × 9.83 (580.18 × 32.25); M (B&W); 13.25; ex *Sunny Trader* 1982; ex *Kotoura Maru* 1971

★55270 **KRAS** Ys/Ys ('Uljanik') 1968; B; 8600; 138.46 × 9 (454.27 × 29.53); M (B&W); 13

★55280 **NIKOLAY NOVIKOV** Ru/Pd (Gdanska) 1973; B/TC; 10200; 150.27 × 8.69 (493.01 × 28.51); M (Sulzer); 15; 'B-436' type
Sisters:
★55281 **IVAN SYRYKH**
★55282 **VLADIMIR MORDVINOV**
★55283 **VLADIMIR TIMOFEYEV**
The following are 'B-540' type (Ru flag):
★55284 **KAPITAN MOCHALOV**
★55285 **KAPITAN BAKANOV**
★55286 **KAPITAN KIRIY**
★55287 **KONSTANTIN PETROVSKIY**
★55288 **MEKHANIK GORDYENKO**
★55289 **VLAS NICHKOV**
★55290 **KAPITAN DUBLITSKIY**
★55291 **KAPITAN MILOVZOROV**
★55292 **KAPITAN SAMOYLENKO**
★55293 **PETR SMIDOVICH**
★55294 **VASILIY MUSINSKIY**
★55295 **KAPITAN BURMAKIN**
★55296 **KAPITAN GLAZACHYEV**
★55297 **KAPITAN VASILYEVSKIY**
★55298 **KAPITAN ZAMYATIN**
★55299 **YURIY SAVINOV**
★55300 **BOTSMAN MOSHKOV**
★55301 **FEDOR VARAKSIN**
★55302 **KAPITAN SHEVCHENKO**
★55303 **KAPITAN LYUBCHENKO**
★55304 **PETR STRELKOV**

55310 **SOFIE** Sw/Sw (Oskarshamns) 1974; Tk; 18300; 170.77 × 10.97 (560.27 × 35.99); M (Gotaverken); 15.5

Sisters:
55311 **SONJA** (Sw)
55312 **RABIGH BAY 1** (Gr) ex *Susanne* 1980
Similar:
★55313 **TATRY** (Pd)
55314 **ATHENIAN VENTURE** (Cy) ex *Karkonosze* 1983
★55315 **PIENINY II** (Pd)
55316 **BEJAIA** (Ag); Launched as *Messiniaki Proodos*
55317 **BETHIOUA** (Ag); Launched as *Messiniaki Doxa*

55320 **PAVAN DOOT** In/Br (Swan Hunter) 1971; Tk/Ch; 16500; 170.82 × 9.91 (560.43 × 32.51); M (B&W); 14.75; ex *Mercator* 1981; ex *Stolt Lion* 1981

55330 **CHEMICAL SOL** Li/No (Akers) 1967; Tk/Ch; 9400; 149.41 × 9.02 (490.19 × 29.59); M (B&W); 16; ex *Canso Transport* 1981; ex *Lonn*

55340 **WILTSHIRE** Br/Br (Swan Hunter & T) 1968; LGC; 10000; 151.7 × 8.23 (497.7 × 27); M (Doxford); 16

55350 **DAVID GAS** Li/Sw (Kockums) 1969; LGC; 18000; 184.74 × 9.7 (606.1 × 31.82); M (MAN); 17; ex *Danian Gas* 1983; ex *Reliance Gas* 1977; ex *Amy Multina* 1977; ex *Phillips Arkansas* 1971

55360 **SHELDON GAS** Li/Fr (La Ciotat) 1967; LGC; 15000; 177.2 × 7.72 (581.36 × 25.33); M (Sulzer); 16; ex *Isfonn* 1983

●55380 **SIRENA** Li/No (Nakskov) 1963; O; 18800; 184.16 × 10.55 (604.2 × 34.61); M (B&W); 13; ex *Vivita* 1977
Sister:
55381 **VIDA** (Li) ex *Livanita* 1978
Similar:
55382 **BEATRICE** (Li) ex *Senorita* 1977
55383 **HERA** (Li) ex *Angelita* 1978

55390 **REGAL SKY** Gr/FRG (Kieler H) 1963; B; 14700; 179.38 × 10.93 (588.52 × 35.86); M (MAN); 14; ex *Lancing* 1973

55400 **JAGAT MOHINI** In/FRG (Rhein Nordseew) 1958; B; 12200; 160.97 × 9.39 (528.12 × 30.8); M (MAN); 13; ex *Rheinstahl* 1969
Sister:
55401 **JAGAT SWAMINI** (In) ex *Otto Springorum* 1971

★55410 **MUSALA** Bu/Ja (Hitachi) 1967; B; 9100; 139.83 × 9.26 (458.76 × 30.38); M (B&W); 14
Sisters:
★55411 **RUEN** (Bu)
★55412 **VEJEN** (Bu)

55420 **TONY** Gr/FRG (A G 'Weser') 1962; B; 6200; 121.34 × 8.51 (398.1 × 27.92); M (MAN); 13; ex *Atlas* 1979; ex *Eckenheim* 1974
Sister:
55421 **ATLANTIS** (Gr) ex *Langelsheim* 1974

55430 **CAPITAN ALBERTO** It/Br (Blythswood) 1957; O; 9900; 153.96 × 8.84 (505 × 29.03); M (Doxford); 12; ex *Sagamore* 1975

55440 **AFRAN OCEAN** Li/Sp ('Astano') 1974; Tk; 171300; 347.94 × 24.83 (1141 × 81.43); TST (Kawasaki); 14.5; ex *Ocean Park* 1982

55460 **JAPAN CARNATION** Ja/Ja (Hitachi) 1972; Tk; 120500; 325.03 × 19.45 (1066 × 63.81); T (Hitachi); 15.5
Similar:
55461 **WORLD ADMIRAL** (Li)
55462 **WORLD AMBASSADOR** (Li)
55463 **KHARK** (Ir)

55470 **ANTONIOS G** Li/De (Odense) 1973; Tk; 129700; 347.23 × 22.22 (1139.21 × 72.9); T (Stal-Laval); 16; ex *Rania Chandris* 1976
Similar:
55471 **TORILL KNUDSEN** (Li)

55480 **BATILLUS** Fr/Fr (L'Atlantique) 1976; Tk; 273600; 414.21 × 28.5 (1358.96 × 93.5); TST (Stal-Laval); 16
Sisters (Fr flag):
55481 **BELLAMYA**
55483 **PRAIRIAL**

55490 **MAASBREE** Ne/Ja (IHI) 1973; Tk; 135400; 337.07 × 21.05 (1105.87 × 69.06); T (IHI); 16; ex *Sinde* 1973

●55500 **OGDEN SUNGARI** Li/Ja (Sumitomo) 1975; Tk; 124100; 338.87 × 21.01 (1111.78 × 68.93); T (Toyo); 16
Similar:
55501 **MOSCLIFF** (No) (now converted to a motor ship)

55520 **TAKASAKA MARU** Ja/Ja (Kawasaki) 1976;

Tk; 116500; 319.95 × 19.74 (1049.7 × 64.76); T (Kawasaki); 15.25

55530 **GRESHAM** Li/Ja (IHI) 1975; Tk; 104400; 317 × 20.79 (1040.03 × 68.21); T (IHI); 16
Probable sister:
55531 **LOMBARD** (Li)

55540 **CAIRU** Bz/Ja (IHI) 1974; Tk; 129400; 337.09 × 21.62 (1105.94 × 70.93); T (IHI) 15.75
Sister:
55541 **VIDAL DE NEGREIROS** (Bz)

55560 **PROSPERITY** Li/Ko (Hyundai) 1974; Tk; 124700; 344.43 × 20.77 (1130.02 × 68.14); T (Stal-Laval); 16; ex *Atlantic Baron* 1977
Sister:
55561 **KOREA SUN** (Ko) launched as *Atlantic Baroness*
Possible sisters:
55562 **KOREA STAR** (Ko)
55563 **KOREA BANNER** (Ko)
55564 **CATTLEYA** (Li)

55570 **EXXON SAN FRANCISCO** US/US (Avondale) 1969; Tk; 381000; 246.84 × 12.6 (809.84 × 41.34) T (GEC); 17.5; ex *Esso San Francisco* 1973
Sisters:
55571 **EXXON BATON ROUGE** (US) ex *Esso Baton Rouge* 1973
55572 **EXXON PHILADELPHIA** (US) ex *Esso Philadelphia* 1973

55580 **BLUE OCEAN** Li/Pd (Gdynska) 1976; LGC; 48500; 229.32 × 12.7 (752.36 × 41.67); M (Sulzer); 17.25; ex *Hoegh Swallow*; 'B-550' type
Sisters:
55581 **PETROLAGAS-2** (Gr) ex *Hoegh Swift* 1981
55582 **HOEGH SWORD** (No)

●55590 **STAFFORDSHIRE** Li/Fr (France-Gironde) 1977; LGC; 41700; 226.32 × 13.03 (742.52 × 42.75); M (Sulzer); 17

55600 **HAMPSHIRE** Br/Fr (France-Gironde) 1974; LGC; 32100; 207.08 × 11.28 (679.43×37.01); M (Sulzer); 17.5
Sister:
55601 **DEVONSHIRE** (Br)

55610 **MUNDOGAS AMERICA** US/No (Moss R) 1972; LGC; 32200; 207.07 × 11.32 (679.36 × 37.14); M (Sulzer); 17.5; ex *Garmula*

55620 **HOEGH SKEAN** No/No (Moss R) 1971; LGC/Tk; 31900; 207.07 × 11.32 (679.36 × 37.14); M (Sulzer); 18; ex *Hoegh Multina* 1977

●55630 **ESSO BREGA** It/It (Italcantieri) 1969; LGC; 30400; 207.73 × 9.17 (681.53 × 30.09); T (De Laval);
—
Sisters:
55631 **ESSO LIGURIA** (It)
55632 **ESSO PORTOVENERE** (It)
55633 **LAIETA** (Sp) (builder—'Astano')

55640 **GAS RISING SUN** Ja/Fi (Wartsila) 1978; LGC; 45000; 223 × 13 (731.63 × 42.65); M (Sulzer); 16.7
Sisters (No flag):
55641 **BERGE SISU**
55642 **BERGE SISAR**
55643 **BERGE SAGA**
55643/1 **BERGE STRAND**
55643/2 **BERGE SUND**
(Li flag)
55644 **GOLAR FROST**

55650 **METHANE PRINCESS** Br/Br (Vickers Armstrong) 1964; LGC; 21900; 189.31 × 10.7 (621.1 × 35.1); T (Vickers Armstrong); 17.25
Sister:
55651 **METHANE PROGRESS** (Br)

55660 **CELEBES** Pa/FRG (LF-W) 1970; B; 18600; 196.32 × 10.95 (644 × 35.76); M (Borsig); 16.5; ex *Evelyn Bolten* 1979
Sister:
55661 **MARIANNE BOLTEN** (Pa) ex *Hermann Schulte* 1978

55670 **MISTRAL** Li/FRG (Flender) 1974; B; 44700; 260.79 × 14.2 (855.61 × 46.59); M (B&W); 16.5; ex *Golden Cameo* 1982; ex *Malmland* 1978
Sister:
★55671 **MIAN ZHU HAI** (RC) ex *Thalassini Avra* 1980; ex *Ferroland* 1978

55680 **SOLVENT EXPLORER** Br/FRG (Hitzler) 1974; Ch; 1500; 77.12 × 4.78 (253.02 × 15.68); M (Atlas-MaK); 12; ex *Essberger Pilot* 1977
Sister:
55681 **ELLEN ESSBERGER** (FRG) ex *Solvent Venturer* 1981; ex *Essberger Pioneer* 1977

55700 **CHEVRON NAGASAKI** Li/Ja (Mitsubishi HI)

1974; Tk; 118100; 338.64 × 20.56 (1111.1 × 67.4); T (Mitsubishi); 15.25
Sisters (Li flag):
55701 **CHEVRON PERTH**
55702 **CHEVRON FELUY**
55703 **CHARLES PIGOTT**
Possible sisters:
55704 **CHEVRON COPENHAGEN** (Li)
55705 **AL-FALAH** (Si) ex *Chevron Edinburgh* 1982
55706 **OTTO N MILLER** (Li)
55707 **L W FUNKHAUSER** (Li)
55708 **C W KITTO** (Li)
Similar:
55709 **ASIR** (Si) ex *Texaco Italia* 1983
55710 **TEXACO JAPAN** (Pa)

55720 **AIKO MARU** Ja/Ja (Mitsubishi HI) 1976; Tk; 209800; 365.87 × 22.9 (1200.36 × 75.13); T (Mitsubishi); 15.75
Sisters:
55721 **JINKO MARU** (Ja)
55722 **AL REKKAH** (Ku)
55723 **CHEVRON SOUTH AMERICA** (Li)
55724 **CHEVRON NORTH AMERICA** (Li)
55725 **DAVID PACKARD** (Li)

55730 **AFRAN OCEAN** Li/Sp ('Astano') 1974; Tk; 171300; 347.94 × 24.83 (1141 × 81.43); TST (Kawasaki); 14.5; ex *Ocean Park* 1982

55750 **ATLANTIC EMPEROR** Li/De (Odense) 1974; Tk; 128400; 347.23 × 22.32 (1139.21 × 73.23); T (Stal-Laval); 15.5

55770 **LONDON ENTERPRISE** Br/Sw (Gotav) 1974; Tk; 74400; 270.01 × 17.07 (885.86 × 56); M (B&W); 16.25
Sisters:
55771 **LONDON GLORY** (Br)
55772 **OVERSEAS ARGONAUT** (Br)
55773 **N'TCHENGUE** (Ga)

★55780 **BANAT** Rm/Ja (IHI) 1975; Tk; 46900; 242.12 × 13.61 (794.36 × 44.65); M (Sulzer); 15.75
Sisters (Rm flag):
★55781 **CRISANA**
★55782 **DACIA**
★55783 **MUNTENIA**

55785 **SPARTO** Li/Ja (Hitachi) 1981; B; 36000; 224.52 × 12.40 (737 × 40.68); M (Sulzer); 15; ex *Jaraconda* 1983
Sister:
55786 **GORTYS** (Li) ex *Jasaka* 1982

55788 **PACER** Li/Ja (Hitachi) 1982; B; 31800; 225.00×12.40 (738×40.68); M (B&W); 15; 'Hitachi Panamax Mk II' type

55790 **CIELO DI NAPOLI** It/No (Horten) 1970; Ch; 18700; 170.67 × 11.37 (559.94 × 37.3); M (Sulzer); 15.5; ex *Team Astwi* 1979; Launched as *Astwi*
Sisters:
55791 **TEAM HADA** (No) ex *Hada* 1982; ex *Team Castor*
55792 **TEAM SOLVIKEN** (No) ex *Solviken* 1982; ex *Team Pollux*
55793 **MYKONOS** (Li) ex *Team Augwi* 1979
55794 **MYRTEA** (Li) ex *Team Hilwi* 1979

55800 **FRAMNAS** Sw/Sw (Nya Solvesborgs) 1972/73; Bitumen/Oil Carrier; 4300; 122.84 × 5.74 (403.02 × 18.83); M (Pielstick); 14.25; Launched 1972; Lengthened and completed 1973 (Nya Solvesborgs)

55810 **OTARU** Sw/Sw (Lodose) 1969; Tk/Ch; 2700; 99.01 × 9.36 (324.84 × 30.71); M (MWM); 12.5

55820 **CENTURY** No/No (Moss R) 1975; 27100; 181.54 × 9.42 (595.6 × 30.91); M (Sulzer); 19; ex *Lucian* 1980; Converted from Gas Turbine 1980
Similar:
55821 **VENATOR** (No)

55830 **MUNDOGAS RIO** No/No (Moss V) 1967; LGC; 13200; 162.57 × 9.52 (533.37 × 31.23); M (Sulzer); 17

55840 **GAS RISING SUN** Ja/Fi (Wartsila) 1978; LGC; 45000; 223 × 13 (732.63 × 42.65); M (Sulzer); 16.7
Sisters (No flag):
55841 **BERGE SISU**
55842 **BERGE SISAR**
55843 **BERGE SAGA**
55843/1 **BERGE STRAND**
55843/2 **BERGE SUND**
(Li flag)
55844 **GOLAR FROST**

55850 **LONIA PRIMA** It/Fr (CNIM) 1967; LGC; 10800; 154.51 × 7.7 (506.92 × 25.26); M (Sulzer); 16; ex *Capo Ovest* 1982; ex *Mariotte* 1976; ex *Aeolos* 1968

55860 **CELEBES** Pa/FRG (LF-W) 1970; B; 18600;

196.32 × 10.95 (644 × 35.76); M (Borsig); 16.5; ex *Evelyn Bolten* 1979
Sister:
55861 MARIANNE BOLTEN (Pa) ex *Hermann Schulte* 1978

55870 SHONGA Br/Pd (Szczecinska) 1973; C/Con; 5700/9200; 145.73 × 7.04/8.4 (478.12 × 23.1/27.56); M (Sulzer); 16.5. 'B-430' type
Sisters:
55871 SHERRY (Li) ex *Sherbro* 1984
55872 APAPA PALM (Br) ex *Schauenburg* 1977
55873 MEXICO 1 (Pi) ex *Mexico* 1982; ex *Hasselburg* 1980; ex *Hoegh Apapa* 1979; ex *Apapa Palm* 1977; ex *Hasselburg* 1976
55874 MONSUN (FRG) ex *Sapele* 1979; ex *Monsun* 1976
55875 RIVER HADEJIA (Ng)

55880 PRESIDENTE KENNEDY Bz/Bz (Ish do Brazil) 1965; C; 6900/9100; 145.5 × 7.94/8.75 (477.36 × 26.05/28.7); M (Sulzer); 15.5
Sisters:
55881 ALMIRANTE GRACA ARANHA (Bz)
55882 EL MEXICANO (Me)
55883 PUEBLA (Me)
Similar:
55884 BUARQUE (Bz)
55885 BRAVO GEORGE (Gr) ex *Romeo Braga* 1981

55890 WAIAL Si/FRG (Rolandwerft) 1968; Tk; 500; 64.9 × 3.75 (212.93 × 12.3); M (Atlas-MaK); 12; ex *Bill Roberts* 1981
Sisters:
55891 MAGID (Si) ex *Harry Lewis* 1981 (being used as bunkering vessel)
55892 SUSANNA (Fa) ex *Peder Lysgaard* 1981

●**55894 CAM ILOMBA** Cn/FRG (A.G. 'Weser') 1979; C/Con; 7500; 152.20 × 8.02 (499 × 26.31); M (MAN); 15.5
Sister:
55895 CAM IROKO (Cn)

55900 NEW VENTURE Cy/Sw (Kockums) 1962; B; 9000; 149.76 × 8.97 (491.34 × 29.43); M (MAN); 13.5; ex *Strofades* 1982; ex *Delfin* 1972; ex *Sonata* 1968

55910 ANTON STJEPOV SV/Sw (Kockums) 1962; B; 10900; 149.99 × 9.55 (492.09 × 31.33); M (MAN); 14; ex *Bellami* 1976

55920 NEW SULU SEA Pa/No (Fredriksstad) 1961; C; 12200; 166.48 × 10.20 (546 × 33.46); M (Gotaverken); 15; ex *Sulu Sea* 1976; ex *Gjendefjell* 1972; ex *Angeline* 1968

★**55930 BAI YUN HAI** RC/Ys ('Uljanik') 1967; B; 13800; 174.05 × 9.02 (571.03 × 29.59); M (B&W); —; ex *Sunima* 1977

55940 PSILI Gr/No (Bergens) 1965; B; 12400; 165.08 × 10.42 (541.6 × 34.19); M (Gotaverken); 16; ex *Wilfred* 1977

★**55950 CHANG HAI** RC/No (Haugesund) 1964; B; 12800; 162.16 × 9.7 (532 × 31.8); M (B&W); 14.5; ex *Bris* 1974
Sisters:
55951 TRAKYA 1 (Tu) ex *Iscelu* 1981; ex *Polarland* 1977
55952 VALHALL (No)

55960 IRENES ODYSSEY Pa/No (Kaldnes) 1969; B; 13800; 180.32 × 10.21 (591.6 × 33.5); M (B&W); —; ex *Bella Maersk* 1982
Sister:
55961 IRENES GALAXY (Pa) ex *Brigit Maersk* 1982
Similar:
55962 SUNWARD II (Br) ex *Maersk Commander* 1981
55963 CAR STAR (Li) ex *Maersk Cadet* 1983
55964 JAY BHAVANI (In) ex *Jay Gouri* 1982; ex *Danila* 1981; ex *Maersk Captain*
55965 IRENES ZEST (Li) ex *Golden Mistral* 1980; ex *Hoegh Mistral* 1978
55966 GLYFADA (Gr) ex *Golden Minerva* 1980; ex *Hoegh Minerva* 1978
55967 A G FANOURIOS (Gr) ex *Golden Miranda* 1983; ex *Hoegh Miranda* 1978
55968 IRENES ZEAL (Gr) ex *Leal* 1980; ex *Belhudson* 1976; Launched as *Belveni*

55980 WANDA Gr/FRG (LF-W) 1966; B; 15600; 189.92 × 9.89 (623.1 × 32.45); M (MAN); 17; ex *Weser* 1980

55990 MARINA DI CASSANO It/It (Ansaldo) 1968; B; 14800; 178.44 × 10.12 (585.43 × 33.2); M (Ansaldo); 15.5; ex *Kyungju* 1978
Sister:
55991 HANYANG (Ko)
Similar (Ys flag):
★**55992 DRAVA**

★**55993 KIDRIC B**
★**55994 KRAIGHER B**

56000 THANIC Gr/Br (A&P) 1961/66; B; 9500; 161.47 × 7.89 (529.76 × 25.89); M (Sulzer); 12.5; ex *Caribbean Memories* 1980; ex *Thanic* 1980; ex *Caribbean Memories* 1980; ex *Booker Venture* 1978; Lengthened 1966

56010 TELEMACHUS Le/Br (A&P) 1964; B; 15900; 181.36 × 10.52 (595.01 × 34.51); M (Sulzer); 14.5; ex *Ixia* 1981

56020 HAROLD H JAQUET Li/Sw (Gotav) 1958; Ch; 9800; 170.69 × 9.45 (560 × 31); T (De Laval); 15.25; ex *Arctic* 1964; ex *Meline* 1963; Converted oil tanker

56030 ECLAIR Gr/Sp ('Elcano') 1964; B; 13800; 173.72 × 9.86 (570 × 32.35); M (B&W); —; ex *Santa Alicia* 1979

56040 BANDAK No/De (B&W) 1974; B; 30300; 221.75 × 12.09 (727.53 × 39.67); M (B&W); 16; ex *Milles* 1976

56050 ELIZA Sg/No (Porsgrunds) 1969; C; 6200; 128.28 × 8.48 (420.87 × 27.82); M (MAN); 13; ex *Dimona* 1978
Sister:
56051 ALEXANDRA T (Gr) ex *Alexandros T*; ex *Diagara*

56060 ARETHUSA Gr/Ja (Mitsubishi HI) 1963; B; 9800; 153.52 × 9.18 (503.67 × 30.12); M (Sulzer); 14.5; ex *Maritime Star* 1978; ex *Dona Viviana* 1969

●**56090 SLOMAN MERCUR** FRG/FRG (Howaldts DW) 1979; C/Con; 9600; 154.05 × 7.16/8.14 (505.41 × 23.49/26.7); M (Atlas-MaK); 17.75; ex *Carol Mercur*; ex *Sloman Mercur* 1979; Cranes can rotate and are probably stowed in the position shown in the inset
Sister:
56091 SLOMAN MIRA (FRG)

56100 LAGO PETEN ITZA Gu/FRG (Lindenau) 1969; C; 4200; 112.83 × 6.9 (370.18 × 22.64); M (Sulzer); 13.75; ex *La Minera* 1983; ex *Fossheim* 1978

56110 MILAS Tu/FRG (Lindenau) 1970; C; 4000; 117 × 6.61 (383.86 × 21.69); M (Atlas-MaK); 15; ex *John M* 1983; ex *John M Rehder* 1983
Similar:
56112 ADELAIDE (Cy) ex *Leo Schroder* 1983
56113 LUTZ SCHRODER (FRG)

56115 ANDROMEDA STAR Sg/Ko (Dong Hae) 1982; B/Con; 7900; 135.30 × 7.70 (444 × 25.26); M (Mitsubishi); 15.46
Sisters:
56116 BENGAL PROGRESS (Sg) ex *Andromache* 1983
56117 MOANA PACIFIC (Cy) ex *Esther Schulte* 1983
56118 MARIANNE SCHULTE (Cy)

●**56120 EDITA** Pa/FRG (O&K) 1972; C; 5000/8300; 143.8 × 7.07/8.33 (471.78 × 23.19/27.33); M (Pielstick); 18; ex *Edith Howaldt Russ* 1980; ex *Cambridge* 1976; ex *Edith Howaldt Russ* 1975; Launched as *Edith Howaldt*
Sisters:
56121 ALBION STAR (FRG) ex *Rheingold* 1982; ex *Columbus California* 1979; ex *Rheingold* 1973
56122 DEVON (FRG) ex *Walkure* 1982; ex *Bavaria Trieste* 1980; ex *Columbus Canada* 1980; Launched as *Walkure*

56130 FLAVIA FRG/FRG (Bremer V) 1977; C; 7600/11000; 157.38 × 8.07/9.28 (516.34 × 26.48/30.45); M (MAN); 16; **BREMEN PROGRESS** 'B' type

56140 KASSIAN GLORY Gr/Fi (Valmet) 1959; C; 2700/4600; 121.52 × 6.1/7.67 (398.69 × 20.01/25.16); M (Akers); —; ex *Altmark* 1981; ex *Inge Toft* 1964

56150 HAVIS No/No (Moss V) 1970; LGC; 11200; 146.77 × 10.61 (481.53 × 34.81); M (MAN); 17

56160 ADELIA Pa/No (Moss R) 1971; LGC/Ch; 3500; 106.05 × 6.45 (347.93 × 21.16); M (Stork-Werkspoor); 15; ex *Tordenskiold* 1983
Similar:
56161 ROALD AMUNDSEN (No)

56170 GAZ PIONEER Pa/Fr (La Ciotat) 1965; LGC; 4200; 110.85 × 6.67 (363.68 × 21.88); M (B&W); 13.5 ex *Frostfonn* 1978
Sisters:
56171 GAZ UNITY (Pa) ex *Nordfonn*
56172 GAZ MED (Gr) ex *Gerolamo Gardano* 1980; ex *Sydfonn* 1972

56180 PRESIDENT DELCOURT Fr/It (Pietra Ligure) 1972; Ch; 6000; 125.46 × 7.75 (411.61 × 25.43); M (Fiat); 17

56185 SILVERHAWK Br/Br (Cammell Laird) 1969; Tk/Ch; 6800; 130.21 × 7.53 (427.2 × 24.7); M (Pielstick); 14.5

56190 TRADER Cy/Br (Clelands) 1970; Tk; 3300; 98.3 × 6.55 (322.51 × 21.49); M (English Electric); 12.75; ex *Texaco Warrior* 1984; ex *Anteriority* 1975; ex *Thuntank 6* 1972
Sister:
56191 EKFJORD (Sw) ex *Amity* 1977; ex *Pointe De Toulinguet* 1976; ex *Amity* 1975; ex *Thuntank 5* 1972
Similar:
56192 UNICORN JONI (Li) ex *Rathmore* 1982; ex *Alk* 1977

56200 ODET Fr/FRG (Buesumer) 1975; WT; 1600; 90.1 × 5.72 (295.6 × 18.77); M (Atlas-MaK) 13.5
Sister:
56201 RHONE (Sd)

56210 STADT ESSEN Pa/No (Batservice) 1971; Tk; 1600; 91.22 × 5.53 (299.28 × 18.14); M (English Electric); 13; ex *Multitank Badenia* 1981; ex *Mark* 1974
Sisters:
56211 MULTITANK HAMMONIA (Cy) ex *Multitank Rhenania*
56212 MULTITANK WESTFALIA (Pa) ex *Seamark* 1974

56220 THUNTANK 7 Sw/Sw (Falkenbergs) 1967; Ch; 1200; 72.95 × 5.17 (239.34 × 16.96); M (KHD); 12.5; ex *Thungas* 1975; ex *Thungas 1* 1974; ex *Porsgrunn* 1974

56230 EL HADJ ABOUL AZZIZ SY Se/Fr (Duchesne & B) 1964; C; 500; 57.71 × 3.51 (189.34 × 11.52); M (Baudouin); 11; ex *Pythagore* 1975; Drawing is before conversion from LGC. Coding and appearance may have altered

56250 CHEMICAL LAUSANNE Li/FRG (O&K) 1974; Ch; 3900; 109 × 8.54 (357.61 × 28.02); M (Atlas-MaK); 14.5; ex *Alchimist Lausanne* 1980
Sisters:
56251 CHEMIST LUTETIA (Li)
56252 QUIMICO LISBOA (Pa)
56253 QUIMICO LEIXOES (Po)
56254 CHIMISTE SAYID (Mo)

56260 GISELLE Pi/Ne (Groot & VV) 1975; Ch; 1500; 73.46 × 6.15 (241.01 × 20.18); M ('Bolnes'); 12.5; ex *Proof Spirit* 1983
Sister:
56261 PROOF TRADER (Li)

★**56270 DUBNA** Ru/Fi (Rauma-Repola) 1974; RT; 6000; 130 × 7.19 (426.51 × 23.59); M (B&W); 16
Sisters (Ru flag):
★**56271 IRKUT**
★**56272 PECHENGA**
★**56273 SVENTA**

56280 GEM TRANSPORTER Sh/FRG (S&B) 1968; RoC; 1000; 81.01 × 5.06 (265.78 × 16.6); M (KHD); 14.5; ex *Bifrost* 1981; ex *Niolon* 1977; ex *Arktos* 1974

56290 METHANE PRINCESS Br/Br (Vickers-Armstrongs) 1964; LGC; 21900; 189.31 × 10.7 (621.1 × 35.1); T (Vickers-Armstrongs); 17.25
Sister:
56291 METHANE PROGRESS (Br)

56300 IRAN GHEYAMAT Ir/Ja (Sumitomo) 1978; C/Con; 14400; 166.61 × 10.52 (546.62 × 34.51); M (B&W); 18; ex *Arya Shams* 1980
Sisters (Ir flag):
56301 IRAN EMAMAT ex *Arya Jahan* 1980
56302 IRAN KEYHAN ex *Arya Keyhan* 1980
56303 IRAN SEPEHR ex *Arya Sepehr* 1980
56304 IRAN SHAHAB ex *Arya Shahab* 1980

★**56310 YANG CHUN** RC/Br (Smith's D) 1963; C; 5500/8200; 153.07× —/8.83 (502.2× —/28.97); M (Sulzer); 17; ex *Ber Sea* 1974; ex *Manchester Commerce* 1970
Sister:
56312 ONE WEST No 8 (Ko) ex *Korean Winner* 1978; ex *Manchester City* 1971

56320 ELIZABETH MAERSK De/De (Odense) 1980; RoC/Con/C; 13700/22000; 182.28 × 9.76/11.85 (598 × 32.02/38.88); M (Sulzer); 18.5; Quarter ramp (starboard) 'Caroliner' type

56330 KINKO MARU Ja/Ja (NKK) 1971; Tk; 129200; 331.53 × 20.53 (1087.7 × 67.36); T (IHI); 15.75

56340 ANTONIOS G Li/De (Odense) 1973; Tk; 129700; 347.23 × 22.22 (1139.21 × 72.9); T (Stal-Laval); 16; ex *Rania Chandris* 1976

Similar:
56341 TORILL KNUDSEN (No)

56350 JAPAN ORCHID Ja/Ja (Kawasaki) 1971; Tk; 116100; 318.83 × 19.51 (1046.03 × 64.01); T (Kawasaki); 16.25
Similar:
56351 HARMONY VENTURE (Li)
56352 TIVOLI (Ja)
56354 WORLD SAGA (Li) ex *Ujigawa Maru* 1977

56360 FUJIKAWA MARU Ja/Ja (Kawasaki) 1975; Tk; 116800; 319.95 × 19.66 (1049.7 × 64.5); T (Kawasaki); 16.75

56370 TAKASE MARU Ja/Ja (Mitsubishi HI) 1970; Tk; 111700; 319.74 × 74.19 (1049.02 × 62.34); T (Mitsubishi); 16
Similar:
56371 WORLD MITSUBISHI (Li)
56372 TAKOAKA MARU (Ja)

56380 BERGE EMPEROR No/Ja (Mitsui) 1975; Tk; 211400; 391.83 × 22.63 (1285.5 × 74.25); T (Stal-Laval); 15.5
Sister:
56381 BERGE EMPRESS (No)

56390 IKUYO MARU Ja/Ja (Sasebo) 1972; Tk; 128700; 341.13 × 20.04 (1119.19 × 65.75); T (IHI) 15.5

56400 ESSO CARIBBEAN Li/Ja (IHI) 1976; Tk; 208100; 378.39 × 22.27 (1241.44 × 73.06); T (IHI); 15.25; ex *Andros Petros* 1977
Sisters:
56401 BURMAH ENDEAVOUR (Br)
56402 BURMAH ENTERPRISE (Br)
56403 ESSO MEDITERRANEAN (Li) ex *Homeric* 1977
Similar:
56404 ANDROS CHRYSSI (Li)
56405 AKAMA MARU (Ja)
56406 ISE MARU (Ja)
56407 SETAGAWA MARU (Ja)
56408 SHUHO MARU (Ja)

56410 FABIAN No/No (Stord) 1972; Tk; 140500; 347.84 × 22.14 (1114.21 × 72.64); T (Kvaerner); 15.5
Sisters:
56411 BERGE BORG (No) ex *Julian* 1982
56412 OCEAN TRADER (No) ex *Vespasian* 1982
Possibly similar (no short uprights on deck):
56413 BERGE CHIEF (No) ex *Berge Beaumont* 1982; ex *Beaumont* 1981
56414 BERGE PILOT (No) ex *Berge Beaurivage* 1982; ex *Beaurivage* 1981
Similar:
56415 BERGE BIG (No) ex *Cyprian* 1982
56416 SIR CHARLES HAMBRO (No)
56417 SEABORN (Cy) ex *Norborn* 1983; ex *Songa* 1971
56418 COUGAR (Cy) ex *Norbright* 1983; ex *Radny* 1977

56420 ISAVENA Pa/Ja (Mitsubishi HI) 1984; LGC; 21500; 187.51 × 10.49 (615.19 × 34.42); M (MAN); 15; ex *Grand Rextar* 1981; ex *Bridgestone Maru II* 1974

56430 TOKUHO MARU Ja/Ja (Mitsui) 1973; LGC; 39100; 215.07×11.14 (705.61×36.55); M (B&W); 16

56440 SANDRINA Pa/Fr (CNIM) 1973; LGC; 34300; 216.47 × 11.02 (710.2 × 36.15); M (Sulzer); 17.5; ex *Atlante* 1980; ex *Providence Multina; ex Dorsetown* 1973
Sisters:
56441 STENA OCEANICA (Br) ex *Mandrill* 1980; ex *Malmros Multina* 1979; ex *Dovertown* 1974
56442 ANTILLA BAY (NA)
Similar:
56443 REYNOSA (Me)
56444 MONTERREY (Me)

56450 GAS GLORIA Ko/FRG (A G 'Weser') 1968; LGC; 19700; 173.84 × 10.26 (570.34 × 33.66); M (Sulzer); 17.5; ex *Antilla Cape* 1983

56455 BERGE ARROW Li/Pd (Gdynska) 1977; LGC; 42700; 229.32 × 12.90 (752 × 42.32); M (Sulzer); 17.5; ex *Northern Arrow* 1983; 'B-551' type
Sister:
56456 BERGE EAGLE (No) ex *Northern Eagle 1* 1983

56460 BLUE OCEAN Li/Pd (Gdynska) 1976; LGC; 48500; 229.32 × 12.7 (752.36 × 41.67); M (Sulzer); 17.25; ex *Hoegh Swallow*; 'B-550' type
Sisters:
56461 PETROLAGAS-2 (Gr) ex *Hoegh Swift* 1981
56462 HOEGH SWORD (No)

56465 HAMANASU Ja/Ja (Shikoku) 1982; R; 5900;

145.52 × 6.77 (477 × 22.21); M (B&W); —
Sisters:
56466 SUZURAN (Ja)
56467 ASUKA REEFER (Ja)
Probable sister:
56468 REEFER PENGUIN (Ja)

56470 FORTUNESHIP L Li/Ja (Mitsubishi HI) 1975; Tk; 118200; 338.62 × 20.4 (1110.96 × 67.25); T (Mitsubishi); 15; ex *Grand Brilliance* 1982
Sister:
56471 FELLOWSHIP L (Li) ex *Grand Alliance* 1982
Possible sister:
56472 FRIENDSHIP L (Li) ex *Grand Concordance* 1982

56475 GLOBTIK BRITAIN Bs/Ja (Hitachi) 1980; Tk; 55300; 243.52 × 12.68 (799 × 41.60); M (B&W); 14.75

★**56480 BANAT** Rm/Ja (IHI) 1975; Tk; 46900; 242.12 × 13.61 (794.36 × 44.65); M (Sulzer); 15.75
Sisters (Rm flag):
★**56481 CRISANA**
★**56482 DACIA**
★**56483 MUNTENIA**

56484 MAERSK SENTOSA Sg/Ja (Hitachi) 1981; B; 30700; 224.52 × 12.96 (737 × 42.52); M (B&W); 17.5
Sisters:
56485 MAERSK SEBAROK (Sg)
56486 MAERSK SELETAR (Sg)

56490 STELLA Gr/Ja (IHI) 1969; B; 23500; 193.5 × 11.4 (634.97 × 37.4); M (Sulzer); 14.25; ex *Eagle Glory* 1982

56500 SEAKITTIE Br/Br (A&P) 1975; B; 15900; 183.04 × 10.47 (600.53 × 34.35); M (Sulzer); 15.5; ex *Cairnsmore* 1978; 'B-26' type
Sisters:
56501 NORTHERN CHERRY (Pa) ex *Lynton Grange* 1982
56502 LILY VILLAGE (Pa) ex *Upwey Grange* 1982
56503 LEON (Gr)
Possible sister:
56504 RIGHTEOUS (Li)

56510 NESTOR Gr/Ys ('Split') 1968; B; 25800; 205.8 × 11.93 (675.2 × 39.14); M (Fiat); —; ex *Archontas* 1973

56520 ERITHIANI Gr/Ja (NKK) 1968; B; 19700; 184.36 × 11.17 (604.86 × 36.65); M (Sulzer); 15.25; ex *South Glory* 1981; ex *Janova* 1978
Sister:
56521 ELAFI (Gr); ex *Sandefjord* 1974
Similar (mast from funnel):
56522 ARIETTA (Gr) ex *Japana* 1978; ex *Nopal Japana* 1976; ex *Japana* 1974
56523 JONNI (Gr) ex *Janita* 1978
56524 HAUNDOY (Pe) ex *Kate N.L* 1980; Launched as *World Centenary*

56530 MARGIO Li/Br (A&P) 1965; B; 17200; 188.07 × 10.86 (617.03 × 35.63); M (Sulzer); 14; ex *Baron Inverforth* 1969

56540 EASTERN WISEMAN Li/Ja (Sumitomo) 1972; B; 15500; 162.01 × 10.64 (531.53 × 34.91); M (Sulzer); 14.5

56545 INDIAN HIGHSEA SUCCESS Sg/FRG (A G 'Weser') 1982; C/Con; 7100/11200; 147.40 × 8.31/9.78 (484 × 27.26/32.09); M (MaK); 16.6; ex *Highsea Success* 1983; 'Key 17' type
Sister:
56546 INDIAN HIGHSEA SPLENDOUR (Sg) ex *Highsea Splendour* 1983

56550 PRESIDENTE KENNEDY Bz/Bz (Ish do Brazil) 1965; C; 6900/9100; 145.5 × 7.94/8.75 (477.36 × 26.05/28.7); M (Sulzer); 15.5
Sisters:
56551 ALMIRANTE GRACA ARANHA (Bz)
56552 EL MEXICANO (Me)
56553 PUEBLA (Me)
Similar:
56554 BUARQUE Bz)
56555 BRAVO GEORGE (Gr) ex *Romeo Braga* 1981

56560 PALM TRADER Gr/Br (Readhead) 1963; C; 5100; 133.13 × 7.49 (436.78 × 24.57); M (Sulzer); 16.5; ex *Beroona* 1978; ex *Media* 1971
Sister:
56561 RICE TRADER (Gr) ex *Wambiri; ex Staship 1* 1973; ex *Parthia* 1971

56570 MARLY Li/FRG (Rickmers) 1976; C; 9500; 139.58 × 9.17 (457.94 × 30.09); M (MAN); 16; ex *Susanne* 1979; 'German Liberty' type

56575 MURREE Pk/Br (A&P) 1981; C; 7900/11900; 152.03 × 9.49/— (498.79 × 31.14/—); M (Sulzer); —; 'SD 18' type
Sisters (Pk flag):
56576 AYUBIA

56577 KAGHAN

●**56580 OROYA** Br/Br (Lithgows) 1978; C; 9000/14100; 163.15 × 9.68 (535.27 × 31.76); M (Sulzer); 16.5
Sister:
56581 OROPESA (Br)

56590 SOKOTO Br/Pd (Szczecinska) 1979; C/Con; 9100; 145.85 × 7.65 (478.5 × 25.1); M (Sulzer); 16.8; ex *Bello Folawiyo* 1984; ex *Sokoto* 1983; 'B-430' type
Sisters:
56591 SEKONDI (Br)
56592 SAPELE (Br)
56593 GUATEMALA (Li)
56594 HONDURAS (Li) ex *Hoegh Apapa* 1981; ex *Honduras* 1980
56595 COSTA RICA (Li)

56600 SHONGA Br/Pd (Szczecinska) 1973; C/Con; 5700/9200; 145.73 × 7.04/8.4 (478.12 × 23.1/27.56); M (Sulzer); 16.5; 'B-430' type
Sisters:
56601 SHERRY (Li) ex *Sherbro* 1984
56602 APAPA PALM (Br) ex *Schauenburg* 1977
56603 MEXICO 1 (Pi) ex *Mexico* 1982; ex *Hasselburg* 1980; ex *Hoegh Apapa* 1979; ex *Apapa Palm* 1977; ex *Hasselburg* 1976
56604 MONSUN (FRG) ex *Sapele* 1979; ex *Monsun* 1976
56605 RIVER HADEJIA (Ng)

56610 LITSA Li/Ja (Setouchi) 1977; C; 6200; 119.41 × 7.41 (391.77 × 24.31); M (B&W); 16; ex *Laurie U* 1982
Sister:
56611 ANGELIKI (Li) ex *Maria U* 1982

56620 VENATOR No/No (Moss V) 1973; LGC; 27300; 181.54 × 9.42 (595.6 × 30.9); M (Sulzer); 20; Converted from gas turbine 1980
Sister:
56621 CENTURY (No) ex *Lucian* 1980

●**56630 PHILIPPINE QUIRINO** Pi/Ja (Mitsubishi HI) 1967; C/HL; 7800; 138.51 × 8.48 (454.43 × 27.82); M (Mitsubishi); 15.25; ex *Wakamatsu* 1983; ex *Wakamatsu Maru* 1982
Similar:
★**56631 RONG HUA SHAN** (RC) ex *Wakaura Maru* 1983
56632 WAKAKUSA MARU (Ja)

★**56633 PROFESOR SZAFER** Pd/Ys ('Uljanik') 1978; C/Con; 10800/16400; 180.42 × —/9.65 (592 × —/31.66); M (Sulzer); 22
Sisters:
★**56634 PROFESOR MIERZEJEWSKI** (Pd)
★**56635 PROFESOR RYLKE** (Pd)

56636 STRATHFIFE Br/Ja (Mitsui) 1978; C/Con/HL; 7900/13400; 169 × —/9.75 (554.46 × —/31.99); M (B&W); 18.75
Sister:
56637 STRATHFYNE (Br)

56638 WAHEHE Pa/DDR (Warnow) 1982; C/Con; 7200/11900; 158.05 × —/10.18 (519 × —/33.40); M(MAN); 13; 'Monsun' type
Sisters:
56638/1 PRESIDENTE IBANEZ (Pa) ex *Wangoni* 1983
56638/2 PRESIDENTE GONZALEZ VIDELA (Pa) ex *Wadai* 1983
Similar (bulwark plating in well and poop, taller funnel etc):
56638/3 FANEOS (Gr)
56638/4 FILON (Gr)
Probably similar:
56638/5 ATHENIAN SPIRIT (Cy)
56638/6 WOERMANN WADAI (Tg) ex *Wadai*
56638/7 RAHIM (Sg) ex *Eastern Moon*

●**56639 MEDI STAR** Li/Pd (Szczecinska) 1981; C/Con; 9500/14100; 175.57 × —/10.01 (576 × —/32.84); M (Sulzer); 18; 'B-181' type
Sisters:
56640 MEDI SEA (Li)
56641 LAGOS PALM (Br)
56642 LLOYD AUSTRALIA (Br) ex *Lokoja Palm* 1984; ex *Wameru* 1983; ex *Lokoja Palm* 1983
Possible sisters:
56643 RIJEKA EXPRESS (Sg); Launched as *Medi Express*
56644 TOLEDO (Li)
56645 LAREDO (Li)
56646 EURO SEA (FRG)
56647 EURO STAR (FRG)
56648 EURO SUN (FRG)

●**56649 SANDVIKEN** Pa/Sw (Oskarshamns) 1962; C; 7200/9300; 148.47 × 8.21/9.25 (487.1 × 26.9/30.3); M (Gotaverken); —

56650 **CENK** Tu/Ja (Sanoyasu) 1971; B; 9400; 147.53 × 9.27 (484 × 30.41); M (MAN); 14.75; ex *Eastern Mariner* 1983; '16 BC 5' type

56660 **CHEER MAY** Pa/Ja (NKK) 1959; O; 9900; 154.11 × 8.54 (505.61 × 28.02); M (MAN); 13; ex *Tien Shin* 1977; ex *Nittei Maru* 1975

56680 **SAN EDUARDO** Li/Ja (Hakodate) 1971; B; 15100; 160.99 × 10.79 (528.2 × 35.4); M (Sulzer); 14.5; ex *Pacific Era* 1981
Sister:
56681 **SAN ANTONIO** (Li) ex *Pacific Saga* 1982

56690 **ISLAND LADY** Gr/Ja (Hitachi) 1971; B; 15700; 174.71 × 10.31 (573.2 × 33.8); M (B&W); 15.5; ex *Island Archon* 1982
Sister:
★56691 **YI NING HAI** (RC) ex *Island Sun* 1978

56695 **AMAZON MARU** Ja/Ja (Tohoku) 1974; C/HL; 8300; 143.52 × 8.36 (470.87 × 27.43); M (Akasaka); 15

●56700 **HIRA II** Tu/Ja (Sasebo) 1971; B; 15700; 174.53 × 10.19 (572.6 × 33.43); M (Sulzer); 15; ex *Asia Fidelity* 1983

56720 **IRENES ODYSSEY** Pa/No (Kaldnes) 1969; B; 15900; 180.32 × 10.21 (591.6 × 33.5); M (B&W); —; ex *Bella Maersk* 1982
Sister:
56721 **IRENES GALAXY** (Pa) ex *Brigit Maersk* 1982
Similar:
56722 **SUNWARD II** (Br) ex *Maersk Commander* 1981
56723 **CAR STAR** (Li) ex *Maersk Cadet* 1983
56724 **JAY BHAVANI** (In) ex *Jay Gouri* 1982; ex *Danila* 1981; ex *Maersk Captain*
56725 **IRENES ZEST** (Li) ex *Golden Mistral* 1980; ex *Hoegh Mistral* 1978
56726 **GLYFADA** (Gr) ex *Golden Minerva* 1980; ex *Hoegh Minerva* 1978
56727 **A G FANOURIOS** (Gr) ex *Golden Miranda* 1983; ex *Hoegh Miranda* 1977
56728 **IRENES ZEAL** (Gr) ex *Leal* 1980; ex *Belhudson* 1976; Launched as *Belveni*

56740 **SEACALF** Pa/Br (Furness) 1965; B; 21400; 192.03 × 10.75 (630 × 35.3); M (Sulzer); 15.5; ex *Prodromos* 1978; ex *Simonburn* 1972

56750 **ATLAS CHALLENGER** Ko/Sw (Uddevalla) 1962; B; 12200; 169.17 × 9.7 (555.02 × 31.82); M (Gotaverken); 15.75; ex *Ronacastle* 1972; ex *Cap Rona* 1972; ex *Ronacastle* 1965
Sisters:
56751 **FORUM SUN** (Gr) ex *Ariel* 1982; ex *Thorsodd* 1970
56752 **BARBARY** (Mv) ex *Aristides* 1981; ex *Hafnia* 1975
56753 **WELL RUNNER** (Pa) ex *United Sky* 1982; ex *Eastern Rose* 1980; ex *Aegis Fury* 1979; ex *Ariel* 1970
56754 **MARAZUL 1** (Pa) ex *Glyfada Summer;* ex *Norse Lady* 1973

56760 **ERMIONE** Gr/Br (Readhead) 1968; B; 16100; 182.2 × 10.64 (597.77 × 34.91); M (Sulzer); 14.5; ex *Timur Swift* 1983; ex *Zinnia* 1983

56770 **MELTEMI II** Pa/FRG (Howaldts DW) 1968; B; 15800; 186.93 × 10.59 (613.3 × 34.7); M (MAN); 17; ex *Pacific Skou* 1983
Sister:
56771 **LENA II** (Pa) ex *Atlantic Skou* 1983

56780 **SANCHI** In/Ys ('3 Maj') 1968; B; 23400; 193.5 × 11.58 (635.1 × 38); M (Sulzer); 14.25
Sisters (In flag):
56781 **AJANTA**
56782 **NALANDA**

56790 **GRECIAN TEMPLE** Li/Ja (IHI) 1966; B; 23600; 191.01 × 11.7 (626.67 × 38.4); M (Sulzer); ·15; ex *Resplendent* 1970
Sisters (Gr flag):
56791 **CAPETAN TASSOS**
56792 **ANASTASSIA**

56800 **VIOLETTA** Gr/Ja (Mitsui) 1965; B; 15700; 186.01 × 10.68 (610.3 × 35); M (B&W); 17; ex *Leonidas Z Cambanis* 1983

56810 **SINGAPORE CAR** Sg/FRG (LF-W) 1963; B; 15300; 189.9 × 9.88 (623.03 × 32.41); M (Fiat); 17.25; ex *Captain Juan Fonseca* 1980; ex *Friendly Islands* 1979; ex *Johann Schulte* 1974

56820 **CAPTAIN VENIAMIS** Gr/FRG (Kieler H) 1967; B; 15700; 186.9 × 10.55 (613.2 × 34.6); M (MAN); 17; ex *Georg Russ* 1980; ex *Nordstern* 1975
Sister:
56821 **AZURRA** (Pa) ex *Maryland 1* 1983; ex *Lutetian* 1983; ex *Margarethe Bolten* 1979; ex *Stadt Wolfsburg* 1978

56830 **DRAKE SEA** Pa/FRG (Kieler H) 1968; B; 15000; 186.9 × 9.89 (613.19 × 32.45); M (Kieler H); 17; ex *Belgrano* 1978

56840 **BHARATA** In/Ja (Mitsubishi Z) 1963; B; 21300; 191.12 × 10.97 (627.03 × 35.99); M (Sulzer); 12.5; ex *Bharata Jayanti* 1974
Sisters (In flag):
56841 **DEVARAYA** ex *Devaraya Jayanti* 1974
56842 **KANISHKA** ex *Kanishka Jayanti* 1974
56843 **LAXMI** ex *Akbar Jayanti* 1974
56844 **PARVATI** ex *Gotama Jayanti* 1975
56845 **SAMUDRAGUPTA** ex *Samudragupta Jayanti* 1975
56846 **SHAHJEHAN** ex *Shahjehan Jayanti* 1974

★56850 **HUA HAI** RC/Br (J.L. Thompson) 1964; B; 16400; 182.43 × 9.93 (598.52 × 32.58); M (Doxford); 15.5; ex *China Sea* 1976; ex *Silksworth* 1972

56860 **MOUNT OTHRYS** Gr/Ys ('3 Maj') 1968; B; 18800; 199.63 × 10.85 (655 × 35.6); M (Sulzer); 15.5; ex *Welsh Minstrel* 1978
Sisters:
★56861 **JIN ZHOU HAI** (RC) ex *Doric Arrow* 1980
56862 **HELLAS IN ETERNITY** (Gr)
56863 **APOLLON** (Gr)

56870 **SEARANGER** Cy/Br (Doxford & S) 1970; B; 19100; 182.58 × 10.67 (599.01 × 35.01); M (Doxford); 16; ex *Berkshire* 1983
Sisters:
56871 **MARIA** (Gr) ex *Cheshire* 1983
56872 **GEORGIOS TSAKIROGLOU** (Gr) ex *Oxfordshire* 1978

★56880 **BEI HAI** RC/FRG (LF-W) 1963; B; 15500; 190.13 × 9.88 (623.8 × 32.4); M (Fiat); 17.5; ex *Margarethe Bolten* 1974
Sister:
★56881 **FU JIN HAI** (RC) ex *Marie Luise Bolten* 1978

●56900 **MOFARRIJ C.** Si/It (Ansaldo) 1962; C; 10900; 166.45 × 9.519 (546.1 × 31.2); M (Ansaldo); 14; ex *West River* 1983

●56920 **FLORES** Li/Sw (Oresunds) 1968; B; 17300; 185.17 × 10.23 (607.5 × 33.6); M (Gotaverken); 16; ex *Irish Wasa* 1981; ex *Nordic Wasa* 1977; ex *Lisa Brodin* 1971

56930 **DOBROTA** Ma/Ja (Nagoya) 1960; B; 11100; 161.96 × 9.21 (531.4 × 30.21); M (B&W); 14.75; ex *Rosina Topic*
Sister:
56931 **LJUTA** (Ma) ex *Serafin Topic* 1979

56940 **JOANA** Gr/Ja (Mitsui) 1969; B; 15900; 178.01 × 10.57 (584 × 34.7); M (Sulzer); 16
Sisters (goalpost kingposts):
56941 **ANASTASIA Y** (Gr)
★56942 **JIA YU HAI** (RC) ex *Lorina* 1978

●56950 **JILL CORD** De/Ja (Mitsui) 1973; B; 19600; 179.03 × 10.96 (587.4 × 36); M (B&W); 15.25

56960 **SPLENDID HOPE** Pa/Ja (Shin Yamamoto) 1974; B; 16800; 181.52 × 10.06 (592.26 × 34.74); M (Sulzer); 15; ex *Seiho Maru* 1978

56970 **IRENES FANTASY** Gr/No (Kaldnes) 1968; B; 13400; 165.03 × 9.82 (541.44 × 32.22); M (Gotaverken); 16; ex *Aventicum;* ex *Ivory Neptune* 1976; ex *Jannetta* 1974
Similar:
56971 **ASTRAL** (Li) ex *Austral* 1983; ex *Jawaga* 1977
56972 **FLAG FORTUNE** (Gr) ex *Cara* 1982; ex *Jacara* 1976
56973 **DESPINA Z** (Gr) ex *Semi* 1981; ex *Jalanta* 1977

56980 **AGIA ERINI II** Gr/Ja (Mitsui) 1970; B; 18600; 182.61 × 10.63 (599.11 × 34.88); M (Sulzer) 16
Sisters:
56981 **FOSO** (Gr)
56982 **HALLA CHAMPION** (Ko) ex *Puffin Pride* 1981; ex *Cindy* 1980
56983 **SILVAPLANA** (Li)
Similar:
56985 **MARGARITE 1** (Gr) ex *Margarite* 1982
56986 **CAPETAN COSTIS 1** (Gr)
56987 **SOUTH WIND** (Gr) ex *Kika* 1983; ex *Karen* 1980
56988 **CHARALAMBOS F** (Gr) ex *Mary S* 1980
56989 **BONANZA** (Gr) ex *Efploia* 1981; ex *Bonanza* 1975
56990 **KATERINA** (Li) ex *Scotstoun* 1980; ex *Forestland* 1975; ex *Ruby* 1969
56991 **JAY DURGA** (In) ex *Rio Ell* 1980; ex *Ruby* 1975

★57000 **ZHIHAI** RC/Ja (Mitsui) 1968; B; 15400; 176.61 × 10.06 (579.43 × 33.01); M (Sulzer); 17; ex *Aurora II* 1976
Similar:
57001 **AGIOS NIKOLAOS III** (Gr)
57002 **GEORGE S. EMBIRICOS** (Gr)
57003 **MAISTROS** (Li)
57004 **DORYFOROS** (Gr)
57005 **NICOLAOS S. EMBIRICOS** (Gr)
★57006 **YONG FENG HAI** (RC) ex *Costas Frangos* 1978
57008 **GEORGIS PROIS** (Gr)
57009 **ANNAMINA** (Pa) ex *Kostis Prois* 1983
57009/1 **ANDREAS LEMOS** (Gr) ex *Sophia* 1976
57009/2 **RODOSI** (Gr) ex *Koronda* 1980; ex *Angelica* 1976

★57010 **YUN HAI** RC/Sw (Uddevalla) 1963; B; 20100; 196.32 × 10.88 (644.09 × 35.7); M (Gotaverken); —; ex *Andaman Sea* 1974; ex *Robert Stove* 1973
Sister:
57011 **SEA CONQUEROR** (Pa) ex *Dona Elvira* 1983; ex *Gausdal* 1978

57020 **ALMEA** Cy/No (Fredrikstad) 1967; B; 13600; 166.12 × 10.36 (545 × 34); M (Gotaverken); 15; ex *Mitera Irene* 1983; ex *Sparto* 1980; ex *Vingnes* 1977
Sister:
57021 **SUNRIVER** (Li) ex *Dagrun* 1976

57030 **SEMELI** Gr/No (Fredrikstad) 1963; B; 11200; 164.83 × 9.18 (540.78 × 30.12); M (Gotaverken); 14; ex *Mareva A S;* ex *Mesna* 1973; ex *Axel B Lorentzen* 1969

★57035 **LIAOHAI** RC/Ja (Mitsubishi Z) 1961; B; 15700; 176.79 × 10.66 (580 × 34.97); M (MAN); 15.25; ex *Mosdale* 1974

57040 **INICIATIVA** Pa/No (Kaldnes) 1965; B; 13000; 164.9 × 10.02 (541 × 32.9); M (Fiat); 15.5; ex *Aalsum* 1978; ex *Fernleaf* 1973
Similar:
57041 **BASTION** (Cy) ex *Bastion Alpha* 1982; ex *Bussum* 1980; ex *Ferngulf* 1974

57060 **NEW VENTURE** Cy/Sw (Kockums) 1962; B; 9000; 149.76 × 8.97 (491.34 × 29.43); M (MAN); 13.5; ex *Strofades* 1982; ex *Delfin* 1972; ex *Sonata* 1968

★57080 **CHANG HAI** RC/No (Haugesund) 1964; B; 12800; 162.16 × 9.7 (532 × 31.8); M (B&W); 14.5; ex *Bris* 1974
Sisters:
57081 **TRAKYA** (Tu) ex *Iscelu* 1981; ex *Polarland* 1977
57082 **VALHALL** (No)

●57100 **LEFTHERO** Pa/Sw (Kockums) 1962; B; 14000; 175.98 × 10.83 (577 × 35.53); M (MAN); 14; ex *Cretan Liberty* 1977; ex *Conwell* 1974; ex *Erling H Samuelsen* 1971

★57110 **HONG QI 303** RC/Br (J L Thompson) 1963; B; 16500; 182.43 × 10.52 (598.52 × 34.51); M (Gotaverken); 15; ex *Dan Hai* 1980; ex *Kollfinn* 1974

57120 **NAZLI** Tu/Sw (Uddevalla) 1966; B; 20500; 196.32 × 10.89 (644.09 × 35.73); M (B&W); 15.75; ex *Aegnoussiotis* 1982; ex *Kollgeir* 1975

57130 **EVANGELISTRIA** Gr/Ys ('Uljanik') 1967; B; 12800; 174.05 × 9.14 (571.03 × 29.99); M (B&W); 15.5; ex *Avonfield* 1981; Launched as *Bjorn Stange*

57140 **LONG CHARITY** No/FRG (Rhein Nordseew) 1969; B; 14100; 169.02 × 10.12 (554.5 × 33.2); M (Fiat); 16
Sisters:
57141 **DAYSPRING** (Pa) ex *Fernfield* 1978
57142 **OINOUSSAI** (Cy) ex *Oinoussai Alpha* 1982; ex *Ferndale* 1978
57142 **NEFELI** (Gr) ex *Winsum* 1982; ex *Fernside* 1977

●57150 **GLYFADA BREEZE** Gr/Ja (Osaka) 1965; B; 17400; 176.71 × 10.71 (579.76 × 35.14); M (B&W); 14; ex *Oriental Merchant;* ex *Rosello* 1977

57160 **EASTPORT** Gr/Br (Fairfields) 1967; B; 27000; 203.66 × 12.04 (668.18 × 39.5); M (Sulzer); 15.25; ex *Indian City* 1977
Sister:
57161 **ORIENT CORAL** (Li) ex *Olmeca* 1980; ex *Atlantic* 1979; ex *Atlantic City* 1976

57180 **ATLANTIC HERO** Gr/Ja (Hakodate) 1969; B; 16200; 180.8 × 10.69 (593.18 × 35.07); M (Sulzer); 15
Sisters (Gr flag):
57181 **ATLANTIC HAWK**
57182 **ATLANTIC HELMSMAN**
57183 **ATLANTIC HERITAGE**
57184 **ATLANTIC HORIZON**
57185 **ALIAKMON**

57186 **NAFTILOS** ex *Chrysanthi G L* 1983
57187 **GLAFKOS**
57188 **ATHINA ZAFIRAKIS**
57189 **VOMAR** ex *Maria Voyazides* 1976
57190 **IOANNIS ZAFIRAKIS**
57191 **ANTAIOS**
57192 **DIAS**
(RC flag):
★57193 **HENG CHUN HAI** ex *Golden River;* ex *Venthisikimi* 1978
(Pa flag):
57194 **IRISH SEA** ex *Dimitros Criticos* 1980

★57200 **DAGONYS** Ru/Br (Scotts' SB) 1971; B; 18600; 186.11 × 10.83 (610.6 × 35.53); M (Sulzer); 14; ex *Cumbria* 1980

57210 **ATLAS COUNSELLOR** Ko/No (Kaldnes) 1963; B; 12800; 168.43 × 9.44 (552.59 × 30.97); M (MAN); 14.5; ex *Jarabella* 1972

57220 **NEGEV TAMAR** Pa/Sw (Oresunds) 1964; B; 11000; 155.45 × 9.2 (510 × 30.2); M (Gotaverken); 15; ex *Negev Zin* 1982; ex *Moira V* 1981; ex *Lady Victoria* 1980; ex *Nego Victoria* 1975

57230 **IONIO** Gr/Sp (AESA) 1970; B; 15400; 183.12 × 10.58 (600.79 × 34.71); M (MAN); 14; ex *Aegis Destiny*
Sisters:
57231 **AEGIS BRAVERY** (Gr)
57232 **AEGIS PROGRESS** (Gr)
57233 **SHANTA SHIBANI** (In) ex *Aegis Kingdom*
57234 **BOKA** (SV) ex *Betis* 1982; ex *Arenal* 1975
★57235 **SKADARLIJA** (Ys) ex *Macarena* 1982; ex *Triana* 1975
57236 **ERZURUM** (Tu)
57237 **ERDEMIR** (Tu)
57238 **OLYMPIC HOPE** (Gr) ex *Graigaur* 1978; ex *Torre Del Oro* 1975

57240 **ALVERI HOPE** Li/Fr (Mediterranee) 1965; B; 18400; 193.5 × 10.94 (634.84 × 35.9); M (Sulzer); 15; ex *Atlantic Hope* 1982

57250 **BHASKARA** In/Ja (Mitsubishi HI) 1965; OO; 15500; 169.02 × 9.63 (554.53 × 31.6); M (Sulzer); 14.5; ex *Bhaskara Jayanti* 1973
Sisters (In flag):
57251 **CHANAKYA** ex *Chanakya Jayanti* 1974
57252 **LEELAVATI** ex *Leelavati Jayanti* 1974

57260 **EVELINE** Gr/Sw (Eriksbergs) 1963; B; 11900; 163.23 × 9.38 (535.53 × 30.77); M (B&W); 15.5; ex *Ocean Triton* 1981; ex *Troja* 1970

57270 **C K APOLLO** Li/Ja (Mitsubishi HI) 1967; B; 14800; 175.32 × 10.1 (575.2 × 33.14); M (Sulzer); 15; ex *Golar Arrow* 1975
Sister:
57271 **DEKA FRATERNITY** (Gr) ex *Adelfotis* 1981; ex *Golar Bow* 1975

57280 **JADE STAR** Pa/Br (Upper Clyde) 1968; C; 10600; 152.25 × 9.11 (499.5 × 29.9); M (Ruston & Hornsby); 16; ex *Welsh City* 1977
Sister:
57281 **NEPTUNE STAR** (Pa) ex *Cornish City* 1977

57290 **SUNDANCE** Li/FRG (Rhein Nordseew) 1965; B; 19000; 191.32 × 11.3 (627.69 × 37.7); M (MAN); 14; ex *Captain Demosthenes* 1982

57310 **MAJESTIC** Gr/Ja (Hakodate) 1965; B; 10600; 156.72 × 9.29 (514.1 × 30.5); M (Sulzer); —; ex *Maxim* 1976
Possibly similar:
57311 **SILVER SHELTON** (Li)

57320 **TASSIA** Gr/Be (Boel) 1962; B; 14200; 182.25 × 10.4 (597.9 × 34.1); M (Sulzer); 15; ex *Konstantia;* ex *Ntina J Patera* 1973

57330 **KAREN** Pa/Ja (Hakodate) 1966; B; 16300; 174.76 × 10.95 (573.36 × 35.93); M (Sulzer); 14.5; ex *Epta Veli* 1983; ex *Corona* 1980; ex *Coropuna* 1979; ex *North Breeze* 1974
Sister:
57331 **FANNYAN** (Li) ex *Newhaven* 1982; ex *Glyntaf* 1971; Launched as *East Breeze*

●57340 **ALICAMPOS** Gr/Ja (Hitachi) 1968; B; 14400; 156.17 × 9.53 (512.37 × 31.27); M (B&W); 15; ex *Maritime Queen* 1980; 'Hitachi Standard 18' type
Sister:
57341 **MARITIME PIONEER** (Pa)

●57350 **AL-TAHA** Li/Br (A&P) 1970; B; 14700; 182.89 × 10.15 (600.03 × 33.3); M (Sulzer); —; ex *County Clare* 1974; 'B-25' type
Sister:
57351 **YERUPAJA** (Pe) ex *Star Helene* 1974; ex *Helene* 1973

●57360 **AMETHYSTOS** Li/Bz (CCN) 1968; B; 13100;

169.2 × 9.68 (555.12 × 31.76); M (MAN); 15; ex *Docelago;* ex *Antonio Ferraz* 1970
Sisters:
57361 **LYNX** (Gr) ex *Docepraia* 1982; ex *Jayme Maia* 1970;
57362 **CYPRIOT MARINER** (Cy) ex *Rhodian River* 1983; ex *Sonia* 1983; ex *Docegolfo* 1977; ex *Amannoon Camara* 1970; These vessels may be K₂MFK

★57370 **LONG HAI** RC/Be (Boelwerf) 1968; B; 25000; 203.77 × 11.48 (668.54 × 37.66); M (MAN); —; ex *Agioi Victores* 1974
Sister:
★57371 **PING HAI** (RC) ex *Ioannis N Pateras* 1974

57380 **KEFALONIA LIGHT** Cy/Ja (IHI) 1967; B; 23100; 185.02 × 11.78 (607.02 × 38.65); M (Sulzer); 15; ex *Eastern Freedom* 1980
Sisters:
57381 **NIOBE** (Ma) ex *Eastern Merit* 1980
57382 **TARPON SENTINEL** (Gr) ex *Eredine* 1974
57383 **SAM SOO** (Pa) ex *Grinda* 1980; ex *World Gemini*

★57390 **DONG HAI** RC/Br (Smith's D) 1965; B; 17000; 184.59 × 10.22 (605.61 × 33.53); M (Sulzer); —; ex *Theomana* 1973; ex *Riley* 1968

57400 **TAI LIENG** Tw/Br (Connell) 1965; B; 21350; 192.03 × 11.09 (630 × 36.4); M (B&W); 14.75; ex *Tai Lien* 1976; ex *Ocean Skipper* 1974; ex *Mountpark* 1974

57410 **FIVE STAR** Li/Br (Scotts' SB) 1967; B; 24000; 201.78 × 11.62 (662 × 38.12); M (MAN); 15; ex *Gulf Kestrel* 1983; ex *Dunster Grange* 1982; ex *Clyde Bridge* 1977

57420 **TEL-AVIV** Is/FRG (Deutsche Werft) 1963; B; 20300; 200.18 × 10.36 (656.76 × 34); M (MAN); 15.5
Sister:
57421 **ARAD** (Is)

★57440 **VELENJE** Ys/Ja (Mitsui) 1976; C/HL; 7400/11900; 147.71 × 9.63 (484.61 × 31.59); M (B&W); 16; 'Mitsui-Concord 18' type
Sisters (Ys flag):
★57441 **MARIBOR**
★57442 **KRANJ**
★57443 **CELJE**
★57444 **KAMNIK**

★57450 **LONG CHUAN JIANG** RC/Ja (Mitsui) 1971; C; 6600/10200; 147.7 × 8.02/9.1 (478 × 26.31/29.8); M (B&W); 17; ex *Heelsum* 1978; 'Mitsui-Concord 15'type
Sister:
★57451 **JIN CHENG JIANG** (RC) ex *Leersum* 1977

57460 **INDIAN PRESTIGE** In/Ja (Mitsui) 1971; C; 12000; 147.71 × 9.63 (484.61 × 31.59); M (B&W); 15; ex *Aristagoras* 1974; 'Mitsui-Concord 18' type
Sisters (In flag):
57461 **INDIAN PROGRESS** ex *Aristodimos* 1974
57462 **INDIAN PROSPERITY** ex *Ioanna* 1975
Similar (heavy lift, fitted with Stulcken derricks):
57463 **TRAUTENBELS** (Gr) ex *Trautenfels* 1980; ex *Ehrenfels* 1975; ex *Aristokleidis* 1975

57470 **IRENES EMERALD** Gr/Ja (Tsuneishi) 1977; B; 10200; 144 × 8.87 (472.4 × 29.1); M (B&W); 14.25; ex *Pacific Emerald* 1980; ex *Montmartre* 1980
Sister:
57471 **IRENES SAPPHIRE** (Gr) ex *Atlantic Emerald* 1980; ex *Montparnasse* 1980

57475 **BRAVE THEMIS** Cy/Ja (Tohoku) 1973; C; 9300; 138.99 × 8.92 (456 × 29.27); M (Hitachi); 13; ex *Basel* 1983; ex *Ocean Angin* 1973
Sister:
★57476 **UELEN** (Ru) ex *Windford* 1976

57480 **ALPINA** Sd/FRG (Flensburger) 1970; C; 6900/9600; 139.76 × 8.22/9.19 (458.53 × 26.97/30.15); M (Bremer V); 16; 'German Liberty' type
Possible sister:
57481 **ASCONA** (Sd)

57490 **HOLSTENSAILOR** FRG/FRG (A G 'Weser') 1978; C; 8700; 146.01 × 8.16 (479.04 × 26.77); M (Atlas-MaK); 18; 'Key 12' type
Sisters:
★57491 **BUZET** (Ys) ex *Holstenclipper* 1982; ex *Seaway Clipper* 1980; ex *Holstenclipper*
57492 **HOLSTENTRADER** (FRG)

★57500 **KARIPANDE** An/Ja (Ujina) 1977; C; 8500; 133.2 × 8.83 (437.01 × 28.97); M (B&W); 16.75; ex *Bianka Leonhardt* 1981
Sister:
★57501 **KASSAMBA** (An) ex *Britta Leonhardt* 1981; ex *Britta* 1980; ex *Britta Leonhardt* 1977

57510 **GOOD WIND** Pa/Sp (AESA) 1970; C; 11300;

147.02 × 9.87 (482.34 × 32.4); M (MAN); 16; ex *Good Helmsman* 1978; ex *David, Marquess of Milford Haven* 1973; 'Santa-Fe' type
Sister:
57511 **PAPHOS** (Cy) ex *Panagia Myrtidiotissa* 1984; ex *Jocelyne* 1980

57520 **BEATRIZ MONTEIRO** Bz/Bz (Verolme E R do Brazil) 1964; C; 6200/8300; 142 × 8.2/— (466 × 27/—); M (MAN); 18.5; ex *Julio Regis* 1982
Possibly similar (some have Stulcken derricks):
57521 **CELESTINO** (Bz)
57522 **KOTA RAKYAT** (Sg) ex *Petropolis* 1983; ex *Lajes* 1968
57523 **CARLOS BORGES** (Bz) ex *Navem Piratini* 1971; Launched as *Midosi*
57524 **GONCALO** (Bz) ex *Campos* 1968

57530 **LAGO PETEN ITZA** Gu/FRG (Lindenau) 1969; C; 4200; 112.83 × 6.9 (370.18 × 22.64); M (Sulzer); 13.75; ex *La Minera* 1983; ex *Fossheim* 1978

57540 **BLUE SHINE** Pa/DDR ('Neptun') 1968; C; 4200; 114.71 × 6.48 (376.35 × 21.26); M (MAN); 14.5; ex *Hesperia* 1983; ex *Joruna* 1969
Sisters:
★57541 **BOLGRAD** (Ru) ex *McDermott;* ex *Bolina* 1979; ex *Jotina* 1977; Launched as *Sigyn*
★57542 **BORISLAV** (Ru) ex *Jane Austen* 1980; ex *Roselina* 1978; ex *Joselin* 1977
57543 **ARK** (Tu) ex *Loretta* 1983; ex *Attu;* ex *Joulla* 1975

57550 **POLWIND** Li/DDR ('Neptun') 1970; C/Con; 5100/7900; 146.23 × 8.89 (479.76 × 29.17); M (MAN); —; ex *Helene Presthus* 1982; ex *Brittenburg* 1981; ex *Eastern Street* 1977; ex *Lloyd New York* 1975; ex *Hamburger Damm* 1973; ex *Tasco* 1971; Launched as *Hamburger Damm* 'Neptun' type
Similar:
57551 **JOWAKI** (Pa) ex *Spetses Island* 1982; ex *Dafra Trader* 1978; ex *Lloyd Philadelphia* 1975; ex *Hamburger Wall* 1973; ex *Sparreholm* 1971; ex *Hamburger Wall* 1970
57552 **EIGIGU** (Na) ex *Booker Challenge* 1983; ex *Sol Michel;* ex *Lloyd Copenhague* 1976; ex *Sol Michel* 1972
57553 **CIELO DI TRIESTE** (It) ex *Booker Crusade* 1983; ex *Sol Neptun;* ex *Wolfgang Russ* 1977; ex *Sol Neptun* 1976
57554 **POLSTAR** (Li) ex *Anna Presthus* 1983; ex *Swedru* 1978; ex *Anna Presthus* 1976
57555 **ZEBA** (Cy) ex *Roland Atlantic* 1983; ex *Freedeburg* 1979; ex *Lloyd Estocolmo* 1978; Launched as *Freedeburg*
57556 **NEPTUNE** (Cy) ex *Pacific* 1983; ex *Roland Pacific* 1983; ex *Muggenburg;* ex *Lloyd Jacksonville* 1979; ex *Muggenburg* 1975
57557 **CIELO DI LIVORNO** (It) ex *Booker Courage* 1983; ex *Brageland* 1980
57558 **ARAWA BAY** (Sg) ex *Balticland* 1982
57559 **BARDALAND** (Sw)
57562 **ISLA PINZON** (Sg) ex *Wilhelm Wesch* 1983; ex *Lloyd Maryland* 1981; ex *Wilhelm Wesch* 1980; ex *Ilri* 1979; ex *Newfoundland* 1975; ex *Ana Luisa* 1974; ex *Ilri* 1972

57570 **IRENE** Pi/Ja (Hayashikane) 1966; C; 7100; 131.93 × 7.6 (432.8 × 24.9); M (Hitachi); 15

57580 **AL KAHERAH** Eg/Sw (Uddevalla) 1961; C; 4100/5900; 126.93 × 6.81/8.14 (416.44 × 22.34/26.71); M (Gotaverken); 16.25; ex *Seahorse* 1975; ex *Concordia Seahorse* 1975; ex *Seahorse* 1972; ex *Sunseahorse* 1972; ex *Seahorse* 1963

●57590 **ALBION** Sr/Ja (Sanoyasu) 1968; B; 10200; 143.68 × 8.99 (472 × 29.5); M (MAN); 14.5; ex *Lisana* 1983
Similar:
57591 **ENATON** (Gr) ex *Maritime Leader* 1979
57592 **MARIA XILAS** (Gr) ex *Eastern Union* 1971
57593 **PAN BLESS** (Ko) ex *Pan Star* 1979; ex *Banario* 1974
57594 **DESPINA G K** (Gr) ex *New Venture* 1975

57600 **ANITA 1** Cy/Ja (Watanabe) 1976; C; 5000; 117.61 × 7.3 (385.8 × 23.9); M (Mitsubishi); 16; ex *Anita* 1981
Sisters (Sg flag):
57601 **NORDHEIM**
57602 **NORDFELS**
57603 **NORDHOLM**
57604 **NORDMARK**
57606 **RHOMBUS** (As) ex *Wachau* 1984; ex *Bayu* 1983; ex *Rhombus* 1979
57607 **KIRSTEN WESCH**
(Cy flag):
57608 **HELEN SCHULTE**
57609 **JOHANNA SCHULTE**
57609/1 **RAUTE** ex *Singapura* 1983; ex *Raute* 1979
(Gr flag):

57610 KAREN
(Li flag):
57611 CORAL VOLANS
(Pa flag):
57613 NEPTUNE VOLANS
57613/1| RAINBOW VOLANS
(Tu flag):
57613/2 TOROS ALIZE ex *Rio Explorer* 1983

57614 YUE RIVER Ja/Ja (Kochiken) 1975; C/TC; 6200; 129.98 × 7.75 (426.4 × 25.43); M (Mitsubishi); 13.25; ex *Kong Hoi* 1976
Sisters:
57615 YUE MAN (Pa)
57616 BRIGHT MELBOURNE (Pa)
Possible sisters:
57617 AGATHA (Gr) ex *Pearl Lotus* 1979
57618 EXTRACO 1 (Pi) ex *Pearl River* 1979
57619 EXTRACO II (Pi) ex *Ocean Explotar* 1978
57619/1 GREAT HONOR (Pa) ex *Great Success* 1976
57619/2 SALVIA STAR (Pi) ex *Caribbean Hope* 1982; ex *Ruby Lotus* 1979
57619/3 SEIBUN MARU (Ja) ex *Ho Chung* 1981
57619/4 MARIA MARIOS H (Gr) ex *Sunny Sydney* 1979
57619/6 SUN ALKES (Ja) ex *Matsufukujin Maru* 1979
57619/7 BETTY No 2 (Ia) ex *Timber Leader* 1981
57619/8 TYCHE (Pa)
57619/10 HIRA-1 (Tu) ex *Virgo* 1982; ex *Sun Antares* 1979
57619/11 WONJIN (Ko) ex *Namyang Crown* 1980; ex *Nanpo Maru* 1976

● **57620 PHILIPPINE QUIRINO** Pi/Ja (Mitsubishi HI) 1967; C/HL; 7800; 138.51 × 8.48 (454.43 × 27.82); M (Mitsubishi); 15.25; ex *Wakamatsu* 1983; ex *Wakamatsu Maru* 1982
Similar:
★ **57621 RONG HUA SHAN** (RC) ex *Wakaura Maru* 1983
57622 WAKAKUSA MARU (Ja)

57623 NIGERIA VENTURE Li/Ja (Narasaki) 1977; C/RoC/HL; 11900; 156.22 × 10.17 (513 × 33.37); M (MAN); 14.75; Quarter ramps (port and starboard)
Sister:
57624 LAGOS VENTURE (Li)

● **57625 GLORY OCEAN** Ja/Ja (Yamanishi) 1977; C/TC; 10700; 146.08 × 9.31 (479.27 × 30.54); M (Akasaka); 14
Sister:
57625/1 SWEET SULTAN (Pa)
Similar:
57626 COBALT ISLANDS (Li) ex *Pacific Charger* 1981
57627 BALDER HOPE (Pa)

★ **57628 TONGGON AE GUK** RK/Ja (Imai Z) 1976; C; 5400; 117.48 × 7.64 (385 × 25.07); M (Hanshin); 13.5; ex *Ae Guk* 1977; May be called **TONGGON AE GUK HO**

★ **57630 LIVNY** Ru/Ja (IHI) 1963; Tk; 22500; 207.04 × 11.11 (679.27 × 36.45); M (Sulzer); 17.25
Sisters (Ru flag):
★ **57631 LOZOVAYA**
★ **57632 LENINAKAN**
★ **57633 LYUDINOVO**
Possible sisters (Ru flag):
★ **57634 LENKORAN**
★ **57635 LISICHANSK**
★ **57636 LYUBOTIN**

57660 STOLT SEA (Eriksbergs) 1970; Tk; 14600; 169.6 × 9.56 (556.4 × 31.4); M (B&W); 16.25; ex *Anco Sea* 1973
Sisters:
57661 STOLT SPAN (Li) ex *Anco Span* 1973
57662 STOLT SPUR (Li) ex *Anco Spur* 1973
57663 STOLT SURF (Li) ex *Anco Ville* 1973
57664 IVER SWAN (No) ex *Anco Swan* 1976

57670 WILTSHIRE Br/Br (Swan Hunter & T) 1968; LGC; 10000; 151.7 × 8.23 (497.7 × 27); M (Doxford); 16

57680 GAS PILOT Li/Br (Scotts' SB) 1968; LGC; 8200; 140.49 × 8.17 (461 × 26.8); M (Sulzer); 16.5; ex *Gas Lion*

★ **57690 MING HU** RC/Ja (Taihei) 1974; Tk; 5100; 110.24 × 7.88 (361.68 × 25.85); M (Mitsubishi); 13.5; ex *Pointe De Tallagrip* 1976; ex *Olau Thor* 1975

★ **57695 YAN HU** RC/Ja (Imai Z) 1972; Tk; 5200; 122.36 × 7.95 (401 × 26.08); M (Mitsubishi); 15; ex *Ocean Trader* 1974

57700 PASS OF BALMAHA Br/Br (Dunston) 1975; Ch; 2500; 97.52 × 6.2 (319.95 × 20.35); M (Mirrlees Blackstone); 15
Similar:
57701 PASS OF BRANDER (Br)

57710 SHINRYO ETHYLENE MARU Ja/Ja (Miho) 1971; LGC; 980; 63.1 × 3.7 (207 × 12.1); M (Akasaka); 11

★ **57720 KAI PING** RC/Ja (Iino) 1961; C; 8300/10700; 156.19 × —/9.48 (512.43 × —/31.1); M (Sulzer); 15; ex *Oceanic* 1973
Similar:
57722 TROVATORE (Br) ex *Athina B* 1977; ex *Fay* 1976; ex *Leonidas Voyazides* 1976; ex *World Japonica* 1965

● **57730 HIRA II** Tu/Ja (Sasebo) 1971; B; 15700; 174.53 × 10.19 (572.6 × 33.43); M (Sulzer); 15; ex *Asia Fidelity* 1983

57740 OKINA Pa/Ja (Sanoyasu) 1964; C; 9000; 144.63 × 8.76 (474.51 × 28.74); M (Sulzer); 14.5; ex *Midas Apollo* 1983; ex *Kyokko Maru* 1972

57750 AGELOS MICHAEL Li/Ja (Hakodate) 1964; B; 9800; 152.51 × 9.58 (500.4 × 31.4); M (Sulzer); 14.5; ex *World Yuri* 1973

★ **57760 HAU GIANG** Vn/De (B&W) 1977; RoC; 9700; 132.92 × 9.4 (436.09 × 30.84); M (Alpha-Diesel); 15; Launched as *Hamlet Alice;* '**Hamlet-Multiflex**' type
Sisters:
57761 PILBARA (Au) ex *Hamlet Arabia* 1981
57762 KOOLINDA (Au) ex *Hamlet Saudia* 1981
★ **57763 NEN JIANG** (RC) ex *Nopal Audrey* 1978
★ **57764 IZVESTIYA** (Ru)
57765 KIMBERLEY (Au)
★ **57766 KNUD JESPERSEN** (Ru) ex *Aleksey Stakhanov*

★ **57770 LENINABAD** Ru/Ja (IHI) 1964; Tk; 23100; 207.04 × 11.11 (679.27 × 36.45); M (Sulzer); 16.5
Sister:
★ **57771 LUTSK** (Ru)

★ **57780 GUANGHE** RC/FRG (Flensburger) 1972; C/Con; 7200/11100; 154.87 × 8.31/9.80 (508 × 27.26/32.15); M(MAN); 18.5; ex *Lutz Jacob* 1973; May be fitted with a travelling crane
Sisters:
★ **57781 ABEL SANTAMARIA** (Cu) ex *Sula* 1975; ex *Ursula Jacob* 1974
★ **57782 FRANK PAIS** (Cu) ex *Nate* 1975; ex *Renate Jacob* 1974

57790 SHUNKO MARU Ja/Ja (Hitachi) 1974; Tk; 120500; 324.01 × 19.43 (1063.02 × 63.75); T (Kawasaki); 15.75
Similar:
57791 HOKO MARU (Ja)

57800 ESSO BONN FRG/FRG (A G 'Weser') 1974; Tk; 126200; 347.81 × 20.05 (1141 × 65.78); T(GEC); 15.5; Launched as *Esso Bilbao*
Similar:
57801 ESSO SABA (NA)

57830 ALSACE Fr/Fr (La Ciotat) 1975; Tk; 118700; 334.12 × 20.34 (1096.19 × 66.73); T (Stal-Laval); 15.5
Possibly similar:
57831 AQUITANE (Fr)

● **57840 AVIN OIL LEADER** Gr/FRG (Howaldts DW) 1969; Tk; 104610; 325.33 × 18.98 (1067.4 × 62.3); T (Allgemeine); 15.5; ex *Sipca Jubail;* ex *Sipca II* 1978; ex *Texaco Hamburg* 1978

57850 SUSANGIRD Ir/Fr (L'Atlantique) 1973; Tk; 111980; 329.62 × 19.41 (1081.4 × 63.66); T (Stal-Laval); 15.5; ex *British Pride* 1982

57860 SANANDAJ Ir/Ne (Verolme Dok) 1974; Tk; 131400; 344.41 × 19.95 (1129.95 × 65.45); T(GEC); 16; ex *British Promise* 1982

57870 LAUREL Li/Ja (IHI) 1972; Tk; 117200; 336.36 × 20.29 (1103.54 × 66.57); T (IHI); 16.75; ex *Universe Pioneer* 1980
Similar (Li flag):
57871 UNIVERSE BURMAH
57872 UNIVERSE EXPLORER
57873 ARCADIA ex *Universe Guardian* 1980
57874 PECONIC ex *Universe Mariner* 1980
57875 MOSELLE ex *Universe Monitor* 1980
57876 MENANTIC ex *Universe Ranger* 1980
57877 HAMLET ex *Universe Sentinel* 1980
57878 ARISTOTLE S ONASSIS ex *Universe Frontier* 1977
(Pa flag):
57879 TEXACO CARIBBEAN
57880 TEXACO VERAGUAS

57890 VENTURE AMERICA Li/Ja (IHI) 1973; Tk; 119700; 337.12 × 21.01 (1106.04 × 68.93); T (IHI); 16; ex *Conoco America* 1978
Possibly similar:
57891 VENTURE INDEPENDENCE (Li) ex *Conoco*

Independence 1978

57900 PAUL L FAHRNEY Li/Ja (Mitsubish HI) 1971; Tk; 119960; 337.5 × 20.49 (1107.03 × 67.2); T (Nagasaki); 15.5
Sister:
57901 J R GREY (Li)

57910 OHSHIMA MARU Ja/Ja (IHI) 1971; Tk; 116830; 317.03 × 20.04 (1040.1 × 65.7); T (IHI); 16.5

57930 LACONICA NA/Ja (Mitsui) 1975; Tk; 159600; 343.62 × 22.37 (1127.36 × 73.39); T (Kawasaki); 15.25
Sisters:
57931 LANISTES (Br)
57932 LITIOPA (Br)

57940 BRITISH RENOWN Br/Ja (Mitsubishi HI) 1974; Tk; 133000; 338.64 × 20.66 (1111.02 × 67.78); T (Nagasaki); 14.5
Possible sisters (Br flag):
57941 BRITISH NORNESS
57942 BRITISH RANGER
57943 BRITISH RELIANCE
57944 BRITISH RESOLUTION
57945 BRITISH RESOURCE (motor ship)
57946 BRITISH TRIDENT
Similar (Fr flag):
57947 CHAMBORD
57948 CHAUMONT
57949 CHENONCEAUX
57950 CHINON

57960 MUNETAMA MARU Ja/Ja (Sasebo) 1973; Tk; 128800; 341.11 × 20.04 (1119.13 × 65.75); (Mitsubishi); 15.25

57970 GLOBTIK TOKYO Br/Ja (IHI) 1973; Tk; 238230; 378.88 × 28.2 (1243 × 92.5); T (IHI); 15
Sisters:
57971 GLOBTIK LONDON (Br)
57972 NISSEI MARU (Ja)
Similar:
57973 NISSEKI MARU (Ja)

57980 BRISSAC Fr/Fr (La Ciotat) 1976; Tk; 117900; 334.12 × 20.34 (1096.19 × 66.73); T (Stal-Laval); 15.5

57990 ZAFER M Tu/Fr (La Ciotat) 1970; Tk; 118400; 334.02 × 20.34 (1095.9 × 66.7); T (Stal-Laval); 15.5; ex *Blois* 1981
Sister:
57991 POLYS (Cy) ex *Beaugency* 1982

58000 ALTA Cy/Fr 1976; Tk; 162200; 352.76 × 22.5 (1157.3 × 73.8); T (Stal-Laval); 15.5; ex *Al Rawdatain* 1983

58010 BERGE DUKE No/Ja (Mitsui) 1973; Tk; 139800; 342.91 × 21.78 (1125.03 × 71.8); M (B&W); 15.5
Sisters (No flag):
58011 BERGE SEPTIMUS
58012 BERGE LORD

58020 GALERIE Pa/Ja (Mitsui) 1968; Tk; 81700; 293.02 × 16.1 (961.35 × 52.82); M (B&W); 16; ex *Lania* 1982; ex *Badr* 1981; ex *Tohkohsan Maru* 1975

58030 ATIGUN PASS US/US (Avondale) 1977; Tk; 74300; 276.16 × 17.47 (906.04 × 57.32); T (GEC); 14
Sisters (US flag):
58031 BROOKS RANGE
58032 KEYSTONE CANYON
58033 THOMPSON PASS

58040 FINA AMERICA Be/Ja (Mitsubishi HI) 1978; Tk; 55500; 231 × 12.11 (757.87 × 39.73); M (Sulzer); 16.5; ex *Nordic Faith* 1982
Sister:
58041 EASTERN ENTERPRISE (Br) ex *Nordic Spirit* 1981

58050 SAIRYU MARU Ja/Ja (Hitachi) 1978; Tk; 34900; 209.51 × 12.08 (687.37 × 39.63); M (Pielstick); 15

58055 BRITISH SKILL Br/Br (H&W) 1983; Tk; 66000; 261.32 × 17.33 (857 × 56.86); M (B&W); 13.5
Sisters:
58056 BRITISH SUCCESS (Br)
58057 BRITISH SPIRIT (Br) (builder Scott Lithgow)
58058 BP ACHIEVER (Au) (builder Swan Hunter)

58070 GAMBADA Br/Br (Cammell Laird) 1973; LGC; 21360; 177.86 × 10.02 (583.5 × 32.9); M (B&W); 16.25
Sister:
58071 GAZANA (Br)

58075 GARINDA Br/FRG (Thyssen) 1977; LGC; 34900; 219.51 × 11.80 (720 × 38.71); M (MAN); 16.75

Sisters:
58076 GALCONDA (Br)
58077 GALPARA (Br);
58078 GARALA (Br)

58080 M. P. GRACE Li/Ja (IHI) 1967; LGC; 13500; 162.8 × 8.4 (534.12 × 27.56); M (Sulzer); 16

58090 'FREEDOM' type Gr/Ja (IHI) 1967; C; 11000; 141.76 × 8.77 (465.1 × 28.8); M (Pielstick); 14.5; Later ships are K₃MFK. Some of the following have taller funnels
(Gr flag):
58091 KHIAN CAPTAIN
58092 KHIAN ENGINEER
58093 KHIAN HILL
58094 KHIAN ISLAND
58095 KHIAN SAILOR
58096 KHIAN SEA
58097 KHIAN STAR
58098 KHIAN SUN
58099 KHIAN WAVE
58100 KHIAN ZEPHYR

58110 'FREEDOM-HISPANIA' type —/Sp (AESA-/Cadiz/UN de Levante) and Ar (Alianza) 1968 onw-onto,wards; 9900; 143.69×9.29 (471.42×30.48); M (Sulzer); 15.5
Sisters (Ar flag):
58111 MARBONITA
58112 MARLINDA
(Ch flag):
58117 LAGO MAIHUE
(Gr flag):
58119 MARIA GLYPTIS ex *Lago Puyehue* 1981
58120 GOOD FRIEND ex *Virpazar* 1973
58121 ADONIS T ex *Theoharis* 1980; ex *Tivano* 1975
(Li flag):
58122 EASTERN PIONEER ex *Cigoitia* 1980
58123 ALTAJ ex *Aiboa* 1975
(Sg flag):
58124 GREZ ex *Elianne* 1979
(Pa flag):
58125 MUTAN CAREER ex *Ancud* 1980
58126 FAJAR ex *Lago Rinihue* 1980
58126/1 LAMBORN ex *Lago Hualaihue* 1982
58126/2 NARISSA ex *Nadilla* 1982; ex *Nonna Raffaella* 1981
58126/3 NOMADA ex *Lago Lanalhue* 1983
58126/4 POYANG CAREER ex *Aysen* 1981
(Ys flag):
★**58128 GETALDIC**
★**58129 GUNDULIC**
★**58130 IVO VOJNOVIC**
★**58131 KOLASIN**
★**58132 MAVRO VETRANIC**
(Cy flag):
58133 FAVORITA ex *Lago Llanquihue* 1983

58140 'FORTUNE' type —/Ja (IHI) 1971 onwards; B; 13160; 164.34 × 9.87 (539.2 × 32.4); M (Pielstick); 14.5
Sisters (Gr flag):
58141 ACROPOLIS
58142 AKRITAS
58143 ALKYONIS
58144 AMILLA
58145 ANANGEL GLORY
58146 ANANGEL HONOUR
58147 ANANGEL HOPE
58148 ANANGEL LIBERTY
58149 ANANGEL PROSPERITY
58150 ANANGEL TRIUMPH
58151 ANANGEL WISDOM
58152 ANDROS MENTOR
58153 ARETI
58154 ASTERION
58155 ASTIR
58155/1 ATREUS
58157 CHERRY FLOWER
58158 EVIMERIA
58159 LOUCAS N
58160 MARIA N
58161 PISTIS
58162 SANTORINI
58163 SEA TIGER
58164 TUAREG ex *Theano*
58164/1 PILOS
58164/2 ATREUS
Possible sisters (Gr flag):
58165 ANANGEL FORTUNE
58166 ANANGEL HAPPINESS
58167 ANANGEL PEACE
58168 ARION
58170 CHERRY
Sisters (Li flag):
58171 AKADEMOS
58172 AL SADIQ ex *Zuiho*
58173 AL SALAAM
58174 AL SAMAD
58175 AL SAMIE

58176 ANDROS TRANSPORT
58176/1 AUSTRALIAN GRAIN
58177 CAROLINE P ex *Vera Venture*
58178 FORTUNE LEADER
58179 PACGLORY
58180 UNILUCK
Probable sisters (Li flag):
58181 OHTORI
58182 SHUN OH
58183 UNIQUE FORTUNE
58184 YULSAN POSEIDON ex *Ryuho*
Sisters (Pa flag):
58184/1 ARMERIA ex *Maple 2* 1983 ex *Jasper* 1983
58185 BENIGNITY
58186 HONESTY
58186/1 LADYLIKE ex *Attica* 1983
Probable sisters¦ (Pa flag):
58187 JOLLITY ex *Everjust* 1980
58187/1 LADY FORTUNE ex *Unique Fortune* 1983
Sisters (Pi flag):
58188 TRANSOCEAN TRANSPORT II ex *Tradewind West* 1977
58189 VALOR
58190 ORONMONTE ex *Everray* 1980
58191 RIA LUNA ex *Tradewind East*
(Tu flag):
58192 KOCAELI 1
(Ja flag):
58193 ATHOL
(Cu flag):
★**58194 XIII CONGRESO** ex *Uniasia*
(Ys flag):
★**58195 DUGI OTOK**
★**58196 NIN**
★**58197 NOVIGRAD**
★**58198 RAVNI KOTARI**
(No flag):
58199 CHIMO

58200 DAIKOH MARU Ja/Ja (Shikoku) 1982; R; 6000; 145.5 × 6.80 (477 × 22.31); M (B&W); —

58210 MUNDIAL CAR Le/FRG (Sietas) 1965; C; 1000; 81.84 × 5.1 (268.5 × 16.7); M (KHD); 11; ex *Passat* 1982

58220 REEFER CHAMP Br/FRG (Schlichting) 1966; R; 500/1200; 75.57 × 3.81/5.02 (247.93 × 12.5/16.47); M (MaK); 15; ex *Visko Reefer* 1983; ex *Keppo* 1975

58230 TROPICAL LION Li/Br (Swan Hunter); 1972; Tk; 125300; 345.5 × 20.07 (1133.5 × 65.85); T (AEI); 15.5; ex *London Lion* 1978
Sisters:
58231 MERIDIAN SKY (Li) ex *Windsor Lion* 1982
58232 THERMIDOR (Fr) ex *Opportunity;* Launched as *Tyne Pride*
58233 AGIOS NIKOLAOS THALASSOPOROS (Pa) ex *Everett F. Wells* 1982

58240 CHEVRON BRUSSELS Li/Sw (Kockums) 1972; Tk; 122800; 340.52 × 20.07 (1117.19 × 65.85); T (Stal-Laval); 16; Now shortened to approx 278m (914). 150000 DWT. Draught 16m (53'). Drawn to original length
Sister:
58241 CHEVRON LONDON (Li)

58270 CHEVRON NAGASAKI Li/Ja (Mitsubishi HI) 1974; Tk; 118100; 338.64 × 20.56 (1111.1 × 67.4); T (Mitsubishi); 15.25
Sisters (Li flag):
58271 CHEVRON PERTH
58272 CHEVRON FELUY
58273 CHARLES PIGOTT
Possible sisters: (Li flag):
58274 CHEVRON COPENHAGEN
58275 CHEVRON EDINBURGH
58276 OTTO N. MILLER
58277 L W FUNKHAUSER
58278 C W KITTO
Similar:
58279 ASIR (Si) ex *Texaco Italia* 1983
58280 TEXACO JAPAN (Li)

58290 CASTOR Li/Ja (Mitsubishi HI) 1972; OO; 132300; 335.67 × 20.62 (1101.28 × 67.65); T (Mitsubishi); 15.75; ex *Cast Narwhal* 1983; ex *Nordic Conqueror* 1980; ex *Naess Ambassador* 1974
Sister:
58291 ALKISMA ALARABIA (Si) ex *Lauderdale* 1982

58310 DALMA Li/Sp ('Astano') 1975; Tk; 124200; 349.82 × 20.19 (1147.7 × 66.24); TSM (Sulzer); 16.5; Launched as *Afran Odyssey*
Similar:
58311 AL ANDALAS (Ku)
Possibly similar:
58312 SANTA MARIA (Sp) launched as *La Santa Maria*

58320 BRITISH RESPECT Br/Ja (Kawasaki) 1974; Tk; 136600; 336.03 × 21.21 (1102.5 × 69.6); T (Kawasaki); 17

58330 BRITISH PROGRESS Br/Ne (Nederlandsche) 1973; Tk; 117500; 330.01 × 19.9 (1082.71 × 65.29); T (GEC); 16
Sister:
58331 BRITISH PURPOSE (Br)

58340 OLYMPIC SPLENDOUR Gr/Br (Swan Hunter) 1976; Tk; 66300; 260.33 × 15.18 (854.1 × 49.8); M (Sulzer); 16; ex *Geroi Sevastopolya;* Launched as *Kyra Lynn*
Sisters:
58341 ARTEMIS GAROFALIDIS (Gr) ex *Geroi Novorossiyska;* Launched as *Interoceanic I*
58342 AFRAN EQUATOR (Li) ex *Geroi Kerchi;* ex *Interoceanic II;* Launched as *Robcap VI*
Similar:
58343 YORKSHIRE (Br)

58350 ST. TOBIAS Li/Sw (Kockums) 1971; Tk; 125400; 340.06 × 20.07 (1115.68 × 65.85); T (Kockums); 15.75; ex *Jatuli* 1982; ex *Gordian;* ex *Hudson Friendship* 1976
Similar:
58352 SEA SCOUT (Sw)
58353 SAFINA SWIFT (Si) ex *Sea Swift* 1980

58360 BONN FRG/FRG (A G 'Weser') 1976; Tk; 188700; 370.24 × 22.59 (1214.7 × 74.1); T (GEC); 16; 'Europa' type
Sisters:
58361 KLELIA (Cy) ex *Bremen* 1983; ex *Vassiliki Colocotronis* 1976
58362 BERLIN (Li) ex *Ioannis Colocotronis* 1976
58363 BRAZILIAN HOPE (Li) launched as *World Giant*
58364 MINOTAUR (Cy) ex *Shat-Alarab* 1984
58365 WAHRAN (Ag)

58370 WESTIN Ko/Fr (Grance-Gironde) 1974; OBO; 76400; 299.25 × 17.6 (981.79 × 57.74); M (Sulzer); 16; ex *Recife* 1982
Sister:
58371 GULF BEAUFORT (Ca) ex *Yemanja* 1983

58380 THALASSINI EFHI Gr/Ja (Mitsui) 1976; B; 42300; 239.05 × 14 (784.28 × 45.93); M (B&W); 15.2; ex *Ikan Bawal* 1980; ex *Thorsdrake* 1979

58400 MIGHTIOUS Pa/Sw (Gotaverken) 1972; OBO; 56300; 256.04 × 15.08 (840.03 × 49.48); M (B&W); 15.75; ex *Cast Shearwater* 1983; ex *Cast Osprey* 1981; ex *Anglia Team*
Sisters (Br flag):
58403 LONDON TEAM
58404 SCANDIA TEAM
(In flag):
58406 WALCHAND
(Li flag):
58407 BOUKADOURA ex *Navios Conqueror* 1983; ex *Sevonia Team* 1981
(Pa flag):
58408 OSTIA ex *Cast Gannet* 1982; ex *Suecia Team*
58409 OSWAYO ex *Cast Skua* 1982; ex *Norvegia Team*

58420 OGDEN CHARGER US/US (Bethlehem Steel) 1969; Tk; 20900; 201.23 × 11.17 (660.2 × 36.65); T (GEC); 16; ex *Eagle Charger*
Sisters (US flag):
58421 OGDEN LEADER ex *Eagle Leader*
58422 OVERSEAS ALICE
58423 OVERSEAS VALDEZ ex *Overseas Audrey* 1971
58424 OVERSEAS VIVIAN
58425 OGDEN CHAMPION ex *Penn Champion* 1974
58426 OGDEN WABASH
58427 OGDEN WILLAMETTE

58430 CHEVRON WASHINGTON US/US (FMC) 1976; Tk; 16900; 198.13 × 11.35 (650.03 × 37.24); GT (GEC); 15
Sisters (US flag):
58431 CHEVRON COLORADO
58432 CHEVRON LOUISIANA
58433 CHEVRON OREGON
58434 CHEVRON ARIZONA

58440 PATRIOT US/US (Todd) 1975; Tk; 21600; 216.8 × 10.52 (711.29 × 34.51); M (Pielstick); 16; ex *Zapata Patriot* 1981
Sisters (US flag):
58441 COURIER ex *Zapata Courier* 1981
58442 RANGER ex *Zapata Ranger* 1981
58443 ROVER ex *Zapata Rover* 1981

58450 TEAM BORGA No/No (Horten) 1973; Ch; 18700; 170.62 × 11.37 (559.78 × 37.3); M (Sulzer); 16; ex *Borga* 1981; ex *Team Vesta*

58460 FRAMNAS Sw/Sw (Nya Solvesborgs)

1972/73; Bitumen/Oil carrier; 4300; 122.84 × 5.74 (403.02 × 18.83); M (Pielstick); 14.25; Launched 1972, lengthened and completed 1973

58470 BETULA Li/No (Moss V) 1970; Ck; 5500/6700; 120.83 × 8.55/9.06 (396.42 × 28.05/29.72); M (B&W); 14.5; ex *Jo Rogn* 1983; ex *Bow Rogn* 1980
Similar:
58471 AURITA (Li) ex *Jo Gran* 1983; ex *Bow Gran* 1980
58472 JO LIND (No) ex *Bow Lind* 1980

58480 BENGHAZI Ag/FRG (Meyer) 1978; LGC; 4600; 108.8 × 7.5 (356.96 × 24.61); M (KHD); 16.6

58484 DOROTHEA SCHULTE FRG/FRG (Meyer) 1981; LGC/Ch; 4900; 111.03 × 7.51 (364 × 24.64); M (B&W); 14.25
Sisters (FRG flag):
58485 HERMANN SCHULTE
58486 GAZ NORDSEE
58487 GAZ PACIFIC

● **58490 OTELIA** Sw/Sw (Lodose) 1969; Tk; 2700; 98.94 × 6.43 (324.61 × 21.1); M (MWM); 12
Similar:
58491 OTTAWA (Sw)
58492 KHALIJIAH (Ku) ex *Otello* 1978
58493 OTARU (Sw)
58494 WOTONI (Ma) ex *Otoni* 1977

58500 ERIKA BOLTEN FRG/FRG (LF-W) 1973; BC; 20300; 196.32 × 10.9 (644.1 × 35.8); M (GMT); 18
Sister:
58501 NATALIE BOLTEN

★ **58510 PYATIDYESYATILYETIYE SSSR** Ru/Ru ('61 Kommunar) 1973; FC; 13100; 172.12 × 8.1 (564.7 × 26.57); M (B&W); 19; Also known as **50 Let SSSR**
Sisters (Ru flag):
★ **58511 BERINGOV PROLIV**
★ **58512 IRBENSKIY PROLIV**
★ **58513 PROLIV LAPERUZA**
★ **58514 PROLIV SANNIKOVO**
★ **58515 PROLIV VILKITSKOGO**
★ **58516 XXV SYEZD KPSS**

58520 WEST JINORIWON Pa/Ja (Sumitomo) 1972; B; 24600; 194.01 × 11.44 (636.52 × 37.53); M (Sulzer); 14.75; ex *Inveralmond* 1980

58530 GEORGIOS Gr/Ja (Uraga HI) 1966; B; 15800; 173.51 × 10.11 (569.26 × 33.17); M (Sulzer); 14.5; ex *Finnish Wasa*; ex *General Aguinaldo* 1973

58540 JAN-WILLEM Ne/Ne (Nieuwe Noord) 1977/83; R; 3000; 101.94 × — (334 × —); M (KHD); —; Lengthened 1983 (Nederlandse)
Sisters (Ne flag):
58541 CALAFIA
58542 CASABLANCA
58543 INCA
58544 LAURA CHRISTINA
58545 MAGDALENA
58546 MATHILDA
58547 MAYA

58550 HELENE ROTH Cy/FRG (Unterweser) 1969; C; 3310/5560; 124.49 × 6.4/8 (408.4 × 21/26.2); M (KHD); 17
Sisters:
58551 ERIKA NABER (FRG) ex *Erika Schulte* 1978
58552 BANGKOK (Th) ex *Carbet* 1982; ex *Gunther Schulte* 1976; ex *Wameru* 1976; ex *Gunther Schulte* 1975
58553 EL GRECO (Gr) ex *Carimare* 1983; ex *Wangoni* 1976; ex *Auguste Schulte* 1975

58555 ARABELLA Gr/Ja (IHI) 1983; B/Con; 13600; 164.34 × 9.85 (539 × 32.32); M (Pielstick); 14.5; 'Friendship' type
Sisters:
58556 AMARYLLIS (Gr)
58557 AGAMEMNON (Gr)

● **58560 'FREEDOM' MARK II** type. —/Ja (IHI) 1977 onwards; C; 11000; 137 (bp) × 9.45 (449.48 × 31); M (Pielstick); 13.5; Also licensed to be built in Brazil
Sisters (Gr flag):
58561 ANANGEL ARES launched as *Al Ahad;*
58565 ANTIOPI
58567 ALTIS
58568 ANTHOS
58569 ATHLON
58570 AVLIS
58571 ALKMINI
58572 AMAZON
58573 ARAN
58574 EFDIM HOPE
58575 EFDIM JUNIOR ex *Al Awal* 1979
58576 GHIKAS
58577 MILOS ISLAND
58578 NEMEA

58579 PELLA
58580 ANANGEL SKY ex *Suncaribe* 1982; ex *Anangel Sky* 1979
58581 SUNGUAJIRA ex *Anangel Victory*
58582 SUNARAWAK ex *Anangel Apollo* 1979
58583 AMARANTOS
58584 NAXOS ISLAND
58585 SUNTAIRONA ex *Poros Island* 1982
(Bs flag):
58586 YORKTOWN ex *Al Aleem*

★ **58590 ZHONG TIAO SHAN** RC/FRG (Bremer V) 1970; C; 6600/9300; 139.58× —/9.19 (457.94×—/30.15); M (MAN); 16; ex *Atlantis* 1978; 'German Liberty' type
Sisters:
★ **58591 HAN YIN** (RC) ex *Okeanis* 1974
★ **58592 XIN AN JIANG** (RC) ex *Octavia* 1977
★ **58593 FENG HUANG SHAN** (RC) ex *Ia* 1978; ex *Niriis* 1974;
58594 ALTAVIA (FRG)
58595 NOVIA (FRG)
58596 LONTUE (Li) ex *Megalopolis* 1976

● **58600 ATLANTIC CURRENT** Li/FRG (Flensburger) 1968; C; 6350/9000; 139.73 × —/9.02 (458.4 × —/29.6); M (Borsig); —; ex *Dirk Mittman* 1971; ex *Sundirk* 1971; ex *Dirk Mittman* 1969; 'German Liberty' type
Similar:
58601 THEOCHARIS (Pa) ex *Josef Stewing* 1981; ex *Fjord Liner*; ex *Josef Stewing*; ex *Vigrafjord* 1977; ex *Josef Stewing* 1976; ex *Rheinfels* 1970; Launched as *Josef Stewing*
58602 GOLDEN GHANA (Pa) ex *Sloman Senior*
★ **58603 SHI JING SHAN** (RC) ex *Saxonia* 1977; ex *Sunsaxonia* 1971
58604 PETRADI (Gr) ex *Pitria* 1980
Possibly similar:
58605 GOLDEN CAMEROON (Pa) ex *Minerva* 1980
58606 ATTIKA HOPE (Gr) ex *Sunhope* 1976; ex *Attika Hope* 1973

★ **58610 DA LONG TIAN** RC/Ja (A G 'Weser') 1966; C/HL; 7010/9450; 152.25 × 8.31/9.48 (499.5 × 27.2/31.1); M (MAN); 19; ex *Crostafels* 1978
Sisters:
★ **58611 DA HONG QIAO** (RC) ex *Kybfels* 1979
★ **58612 WU YI SHAN** (RC) ex *Birkenfels* 1978
★ **58613 DA QING SHAN** (RC) ex *Schonfels*
58614 AIAS (Gr) ex *Falkenfels* 1981
58615 HOHENBELS (Gr) ex *Hohenfels*

58620 NIVI ITTUK De/De (Aalborg) 1973; R; 5000; 135.11 × 7.62 (443.3 × 25); M (B&W); 17; ex *Bamsa Dan* 1983

● **58630 SHANNON** Cy/FRG (Hitzler) 1966; C; 1000; 71.61 × 4.98 (234.94 × 16.34); M (Atlas-MaK); 11.5; ex *Bulk Navigator* 1983; ex *Stockhorn* 1981; ex *Uthoern* 1976; ex *Uthorn* 1972

58640 ADRIANA Ne/Sw (Finnboda) 1965; C; 800/1500; 72.47 × 3.6/5.02 (237.8 × 11.8/16.5); M (KHD); 11.5; ex *Klarenbeek* 1976; ex *Silva* 1971

58650 MARLENE S. FRG/FRG (Brand) 1977; C; 1600/3800; 102.88 × 5.11/7.29 (337.53 × 16.76/23.92); M (Atlas-MaK); 15

58660 SAID II Cy/FRG (Brand) 1966; C; 1600; 74.76 × 5.99 (245.3 × 19.6); M (KHD); 13.5; ex *Conti Misr* 1981; ex *Trojan Prince* 1974; ex *Daneriver* 1973; ex *Per Basse* 1972; ex *Lockflethersand* 1972

58670 HAJ ABDULSATTAR ISSA Le/Ne ('De Hoop') 1967; Wine carrier; 500; 76.38 × 4.29 (250.59 × 14.07); M (MAN); 14; ex *Notre Dame d'Afrique* 1982; ex *Kharsis* 1976

58680 INARAN Ia/No (Sterkoder) 1977; C; 650; 59.92 × 3.65 (196.6 × 12); M (Stork-Werkspoor); —;
Sisters (Ia flag):
58681 INABUKWA
58682 IKAGURI
58683 ISABELA
58684 ILOSANGI
58685 ILOLUTA
58686 IRIMAWA
58687 IWERI

58690 WAIAL Si/FRG (Rolandwerft) 1968; Tk; 500; 64.9 × 3.75 (212.93 × 12.3); M (Atlas-MaK); 12; ex *Bill Roberts* 1981
Sisters:
58691 MAGID (Si) ex *Harry Lewis* 1981 (being used as bunkering vessel)
58692 SUSANNA (Fa) ex *Peder Lysgaard* 1981

● **58700 SKYRIAN ROVER** Gr/Sw (Uddevalla) 1958; 8600; 148.7 × 8.81 (487.86 × 28.9); M (Gotaverken); 15.25; ex *Skyrian Spirit* 1980; ex *Lefteris* 1980; ex *Sunriver* 1974

58710 MOKHA Si/DDR ('Neptun') 1967; C; 2600/4000; 112.1 × 7.17 (367.78 × 23.52); M (Werkspoor); 13.5; ex *Eurabia Spring* 1978; ex *Clari* 1975; ex *Karlsburg* 1970; ex *Claudia Maria* 1967
Sister:
58711 LE ROVE (Fr) ex *Scol Independent* 1975; ex *Germanic* 1975; ex *Wilri* 1974; ex *Atlanta* 1973
Similar:
58712 TRITON (Gr) ex *Irenes Sun* 1980; ex *Blockland* 1977; ex *Jiri* 1969; ex *Hoegh Jiri* 1968; ex *Jiri* 1966
58713 ORION (Gr) ex *Irenes Sea* 1981; ex *Werderland* 1977; ex *Wilri* 1969; ex *Hoegh Wilri* 1969; ex *Wilri* 1967
58714 CAPTAIN COSMAS M (Pa) ex *Conti Almania* 1982; ex *Grimsnis* 1975; ex *Hein Jenevelt* 1970; ex *Bari* 1968
58715 SANAA (Si) ex *Eurabia Progress*; ex *Claudia Maria* 1975
58716 BILSTEIN (FRG) ex *Duburg* 1980; ex *Bilstein* 1978; ex *Conti Syria* 1978; ex *Antony* 1977; ex *Bilstein* 1975; ex *Hoegh Susann* 1968; Launched as *Susan Von Bargen*
58717 LIDES (Pa) ex *Cavally* 1983; ex *Rinkenis* 1975; ex *Dirk van Minder* 1970; ex *Mari* 1968; ex *Hoegh Mari* 1968; ex *Mari* 1967

58720 BLUE SPIRIT Cy/DDR ('Neptun') 1964; C; 2800; 97.57×6.63 (320×21.75); M(MAN); 13; ex *Egon Wesch* 1973; ex *Jiri* 1965

★ **58730 NIEWIADOW** Pd/Pd (Gdanska) 1978; C; 1600; 84.18 × 5.73 (276.18 × 18.8); M (Fiat); 14; Launched as *Ran*; 'B-431' type
Sister:
★ **58731 LIPSK N/BIEBRZA** (Pd)

58734 BEITO No/Pd (Gdanska) 1976; C; 1600; 84.13 × 5.32 (276 × 17.45); M (GMT); —; ex *Ask* 1982; 'B-431' type

● **58750 ARMONIKOS** Gr/Sw (Kockums) 1963; Tk; 36800; 236.33 × 12.63 (775.36 × 41.44); M (MAN); 17.25; ex *Vestalis* 1975

58770 MONTESA Sp/Sp (Cadiz) 1969; Tk; 58800; 269.35 × 14.17 (884 × 46.14); M (Sulzer); —
Similar:
58771 MUNATONES (Sp)
Similar (converted to storage vessel 1982):
58772 AFRAN ZENITH (Li) ex *La Nina* 1979

58790 STEFANIA A. Gr/No (Stord) 1964; Tk; 34800; 236.23 × 12.84 (775.03 × 42.13); M (B&W); 16; ex *Yeo* 1983; ex *Yeota E* 1982; ex *Woodburn* 1979; ex *Halcyon Loch* 1974; ex *Sibeau* 1973; ex *Beau* 1972

58800 GARGI In/Ja (Mitsubishi Z) 1964; Tk; 34700; 229.95 × 12.03 (754.43 × 39.47); M (Sulzer); 16.5; ex *Vikram Jayanti* 1974

● **58810 MEGA TRADER** Li/Ja (Mitsubishi HI) 1965; Tk; 34900; 236.2 × 12.85 (774.93 × 42.16); M (Sulzer); 16; ex *Frances Hammer* 1981; ex *Samuel B. Mosher* 1969
Sister:
58811 MEGA TRAVELLER (Li) ex *Julius Hammer* 1981; ex *Russell H. Green* 1977

58820 ESSO MERSEY Br/Br (Cammell Laird) 1972; Tk; 12300; 166.5 × 9.21 (546.26 × 30.22); M (Pielstick); 15.5
Sisters (Br flag):
58821 ESSO CLYDE
58822 ESSO SEVERN

58830 ESSO PORT JEROME Fr/Ja (Hitachi) 1972; Tk; 12800; 161.02 × 9.76 (528.28 × 32.02); (B&W); 15; ex *Esso Kumamoto* 1980; '22 Type'; Some others in this class may have this sequence

● **58840 ESSO BANGKOK** Pa/Ja (IHI) 1968; Tk; 13000; 170.08× 9.40 (558× 30.87); M (Sulzer); 14.5
Sisters:
58841 ESSO BOMBAY (Pa)
58842 ALEXIA V (Pa) ex *Esso Interamerica* 1982
58843 TESUBU II (Pa) ex *Esso Kure* 1982
58844 TESUBU III (Pa) ex *Esso Karachi* 1983
58845 TESUBI IV (Pa) ex *Esso Nagasaki* 1983
58846 ESSO PORT DICKSON (Sg)
58847 ESSO YOKOHAMA (Sg)
58848 ESSO HUMBER (Br) ex *Esso Penang* 1978
58849 ESSO TEES (Br) ex *Esso Bataan* 1983
58850 ESSO TYNE (Br) ex *Esso Kobe* 1982
58851 LACONIA II (Cy) ex *Esso Malacca* 1983
58852 ESSO VENEZIA (It) ex *Esso Chittagong* 1981
58853 ESRAM (Tu) ex *Tesubu* 1983; ex *Esso Goa* 1982

58860 PAMINA Fi/No (Horten) 1975; Tk; 168.76 × 10.9 (553.67 × 36.76); M (Sulzer); 16; ex *Pandora C* 1983; ex *Ardmay*

Sister:
58861 **IDA HELENE** (Li) ex *Ardmore* 1983

● 58870 **ANANGEL FRIENDSHIP** Gr/Br (Barclay, Curle) 1965; Tk; 35300; 236.46 × 13.22 (775.79 × 43.37); M (B&W); 16.25; ex *Opawa* 1974
Similar (see inset):
58871 **ANANGEL PRUDENCE** (Gr) ex *Orissa* 1974

● 58880 **ERNE** Br/Br (Connell) 1962; Tk; 13700; 170.62 × 9.47 (559.78 × 31.07); T (Barclay, Curle); 14.5

★ 58890 **YU HU** RC/Sw (Gotav) 1966; Tk; 40900; 239.28 × 12.74 (785 × 41.8); M (Gotaverken); 16.75; ex *Vanja* 1972
58891 **AURELIA** (Pa) ex *Velma* 1972

58910 **JEVERLAND** FRG/Ja (Hitachi) 1967; Tk; 49200; 263.51 × 14.63 (864.53 × 47.99); M (B&W); 16; ex *Mobil Weser* 1983; ex *Al Bilad*; ex *Berge Sigval* 1975
Similar:
58911 **CIS BROVIG** (Li)
58912 **ZANTE** (Gr) ex *Vivita* 1983; ex *Bergevik* 1978

58940 **CIRON** Fr/Br (Stephen) 1960; Tk; 12500; 167.47 × 9.54 (549.44 × 31.3); M (Sulzer); 15; ex *Red Sea Venture* 1980; ex *Pollo* 1977; ex *Mobil Apex* 1969

58950 **MATADI PALM** Br/Br (Swan Hunter) 1970; Tk; 8900; 147.83 × 8.55 (485 × 28.05); M (Doxford); 15

58960 **MARINE CHEMIST** US/US (Ingalls) 1970; Tk/Ch; 20200; 204.93 × 11.05 (672.34 × 36.25); T (GEC); 16.5

58970 **IBN ROCHD** Mo/Ne ('De Hoop') 1977; Ch; 13500; 172.29 × 10.5   × 34.45); M (Pielstick); 17
Sister:
58971 **IBN ALBANNA** (Mo)
Sisters (Norwegian built):
58972 **IBN OTMAN** (Mo)
58973 **IBN SINA** (Mo)

58976 **CHEMTRANS SIRIUS** FRG/FRG (Kroegerw) 1976; Ch; 4100; 114.03 × 7.34 (374 × 24.08); M (MaK); 15.75

58980 **PRESIDENT DELCOURT** Fr/It (Pietra Ligure) 1972; Ch; 6000; 125.46 × 7.75 (411.61 × 25.43); M (Fiat); 17

58990 **STELLAMAN** Br/Br (Cochrane) 1976; Ch; 1500; 79.51 × 5.27 (260.86 × 17.29); M (W.H. Allen); 13.75
Sister:
58991 **MARSMAN** (Br)

59000 **CENTAURMAN** Br/Br (Hall, Russell) 1976; Ch; 2500; 89.18 × 5.9 (292.59 × 19.36); M (Mirrlees Blackstone); 13.5; ex *Essex Trophy* 1983; ex *Centaurman* 1983
Sister:
59001 **VEGAMAN** (Br) ex *Essex Triumph* 1983; ex *Vegaman* 1983

59010 **LA BAHIA** Br/No (Ankerlokken) 1972; Ch; 1600; 100.72 × 5.89 (330.45 × 19.32); M (Nydqvist & Holm); 16; ex *Wavemark* 1974
Sister:
59011 **LA FALDA** (Br) ex *Sunmark* 1974

59020 **ISLAND JESTER** Pa/No (Moss V) 1964; Tk/Ch; 1200; 76.03 × 4.6 (249.44 × 15.09); M (MaK); 11.5; ex *Winblow* 1978; ex *Sireglen* 1970; ex *Rubicon* 1968

59030 **DEVON CURLEW** Br/Sp (Ruiz) 1969; Ch; 800; 68.18 × 3.96 (223.69 × 12.99); M (Stork Werkspoor) 12.5; ex *Fenol*
Sisters:
59031 **HIAWATHA** (Pa) ex *Dorset Fulmar* 1982; ex *Formol* 1979
59032 **THITA STAINLESS** (Gr) ex *Metanol* 1974

59050 **ALCHIMIST LUBECK** Cy/FRG (Menzer) 1970; Ch; 1600; 87.03 × 5.1 (285.53 × 16.73); M (Atlas-MaK); 12.5
Possible sister:
59051 **ALCHIMIST FLENSBURG** (Cy) ex *Chemathene* 1980; ex *Alchimist Flensburg* 1979

59060 **ASTRAMAN** Br/Br (Cochrane) 1973; Ch; 1600; 87.41 × 5.5 (286.78 × 18.04); M (Ruston Paxman); 14
Sister:
59061 **POLARISMAN** (Br)

59070 **ALCHIMIST ROTTERDAM** Cy/Sw (Kalmar) 1973; Ch; 1600; 85.86 × 5.4 (281.69 × 17.72); M (Alpha-Diesel); 13.5; ex *Chemaphrodite* 1980; ex *Alchimist Marathon* 1979; ex *Alchimist Rotterdam* 1978; ex *Chimiste Nantes* 1977

Sisters (Sg flag):
59071 **MULTITANK FRISIA** ex *Ofrisia* 1974; ex *Frisia* 1973; ex *Monsun* 1972
59072 **MULTITANK HOLSATIA** ex *Holsatia* 1974
Similar (Fr flag):
59073 **POINTE DU ROC**
59074 **POINTE DU VAN** ex *Pointe De Penharn*

59080 **CAPT F GAIGNEROT** Pa/Ne (Groot & VV) 1974; Ch; 1600; 90.76 × 5.49 (297.77 × 18.01); M (Atlas-MaK); 14
Sister:
59081 **RHIN** (Sd)—type WT/Ch

59090 **ODET** Fr/FRG (Buesumer) 1975; WT; 1600; 90.1 × 5.72 (295.6 × 18.77); M (Atlas-MaK); 13.5
Sister:
59091 **RHONE** (Sd)

59100 **MARE NOVUM** Ne/No (Karmsund) 1977; Ch; 1600; 83.01 × 5.91 (272.34 × 19.4); M (Smit & Bolnes); 13
Sisters (Ne flag):
59101 **MARE BONUM**
59102 **MARE MAGNUM**

59110 **THUNTANK 1** Sw/Sw (Falkenbergs) 1973; Ch; 3700; 107.19 × 6.7 (351.67 × 21.98); M (Polar); 12

59120 **LUDWIG** FRG/FRG (Kroegerw) 1969; Tk; 1200; 81.11 × 4.97 (266.11 × 16.3); M (MWM); 12

59130 **SELMA** Mo/No (Vaagen) 1972; Ch; 1600; 82.71 × 6.37 (271.36 × 20.9); M (Atlas-MaK); 12.5; ex *Pointe de Lervily* 1944; ex *Bras* 1974

59140 **ONESTAR** Sg/No (Akers) 1965; Tk; 3000; 100.87 × 6.1 (330.94 × 19.95); M (B&W); 12.5; ex *One Star* 1980; ex *Lotos* 1974
Sisters:
59141 **JENNY** (Va) ex *Canaima* 1982; ex *Onesky* 1982; ex *Liana* 1975
59142 **BETACRUX** (It) ex *Haensel* 1977; ex *Hassel* 1975

59150 **PETRO SOULAC** Pa/Sw (Ekensbergs) 1963; LGC/Tk; 6200; 134.73 × 6.97 (442.03 × 22.87); M (B&W); 14; ex *Sulfo* 1975; ex *Selje* 1973

59160 **HUMBOLDT** Br/Fr (La Ciotat) 1968; LGC; 5200; 116.9 × 6.5 (383.53 × 21.33); M (MAN); 17
Similar:
59161 **BERGA** (Ag) ex *Pascal* 1970
59162 **LAVOISIER** (Ar)

59170 **VESTRI** No/No (Moss V) 1971; LGC; 9000; 138.72 × 9.23 (455.12 × 30.28); M (Sulzer); 17

59180 **HERA** No/No (Moss R) 1977; LGC; 9100; 138.72 × 11.04 (455.12 × 36.22); M (Sulzer); 17.75
Sister:
59181 **HEROS** (No)

59190 **ADELIA** Pa/No (Moss R) 1971; LGC/Ch; 3500; 106.05 × 6.45 (347.93 × 21.16); M (Stork-Werkspoor); 15; ex *Tordenskiold* 1983
Similar:
59191 **ROALD ADMUNDSEN** (No)

59200 **LEIV EIRIKSSON** No/No (Seutelvens) 197·; LGC; 2500; 88.14 × 6.38 (289.17 × 20.93); M (Sulzer); 13

59210 **NIELS HENRIK ABEL** No/Ne (Pattje) 1973; LGC; 1600; 79.48 × 6.04 (260.76 × 19.82); M (Atlas-MaK); 13.5; launched as *Anita*
Sister:
59211 **SIGURD JORSALFAR** (No)

★ 59220 **FILIPP MAKHARADZE** Ru/Pd (Szczecinska) 1972; B; 20300; 198.71 × 10.68 (651.93 × 35.03); M (Sulzer); 15; 'B-447' type
Sisters (Ru flag):
★ 59221 **NIKO NIKOLADZE**
★ 59222 **MIKHA TSKHAKAYA**
(Pd flag):
★ 59224 **OBRONCY POCZTY**
★ 59225 **POWSTANIEC SLASKI**
★ 59226 **SIEKIERKI**
★ 59227 **TOBRUK**
(Cy flag):
59228 **AGAPI** ex *Czwartacy Al* 1983

59240 **INGAPIRCA** Pa/Br (Scotts' SB) 1966; B; 11100; 158.5 × 8.99 (520.01 × 29.49); M (Sulzer); 14; ex *Ocean Sovereign* 1983; ex *Bolnes* 1972

59250 **AN ANNE** Li/Br (Lithgows) 1962; B; 9900; 152.56 × 8.66 (500.52 × 28.41); M (B&W); 14.75; ex *Kian An* 1982; ex *Bernes* 1972
Sister:
59251 **APILIOTIS** (Li) ex *Brimnes* 1970
Similar:
59252 **ELPIDA** (Gr) ex *Granton* 1978; ex *Binsnes* 1970

● 59260 **GRANIKOS** Gr/FRG (Kieler H) 1961; B; 9400; 151.19 × 9.21 (496.03 × 30.22); M (Kieler H); 14.75; ex *Captain Pappis* 1980; ex *Ogooue* 1976; ex *Dracula* 1973; ex *Ringulv* 1969
Sister:
59261 **SILVERCORN** (Li) ex *Jagona* 1973.

59280 **JAMBI** Pa/Br (A&P) 1962; B; 10700; 154.67 × 9.02 (507.48 × 29.59); M (Doxford); 14; ex *Giuca* 1982; ex *Rozelbay* 1982; ex *Federal Salso* 1978; ex *Federal Tyne* 1971; ex *Scottish Trader* 1968

59290 **SOUNION** Gr/Br (Lithgows) 1968; B; 13900; 167.65 × 9.58 (550.03 × 31.43); M (B&W); 15.5; ex *Sugar Crystal*
Sister:
59291 **CAPE AVANTI DUE** (Gr) ex *Sugar Producer*
Similar (centre line kingposts):
59292 **SEA TRANSPORTER** (Gr) ex *Kefalonia Wind* 1984; ex *Sugar Transporter*
59293 **KEFALONIA STAR** (Gr) ex *Sugar Refiner*

● 59300 **LEDRA** Ma/Br (Bartram) 1959; B; 10100; 158.05 × 9.68 (518.54 × 31.76); M (Doxford); 14.25; ex *Sea Ranger* 1984; ex *Wandby* 1972

59310 **PRESIDENT MACAPAGAL** Pi/No (Bergens) 1959; B; 15300; 190.66 × 10.87 (625.52 × 35.66); M (Sulzer); 14.5; ex *Caspiana* 1982; ex *Theomitor III* 1976; ex *Gaucho Cruz* 1970; ex *Hilwi* 1969; Lengthened 1965 (Gotaverken)
Sister:
59311 **MOFARRIJ D** (Si) ex *Interspirit* 1983; ex *Anna* 1981; ex *Gerwi* 1972

● 59320 **STOLIV** SV/Br (H&W) 1963; B; 9900; 163.53 × 9.2 (536.5 × 30.18); M (B&W); 14; ex *Tivat* 1983; ex *Jean*; ex *Eleoussa* 1976; ex *Athenoula* 1972; ex *Belisland* 1970
Sister:
59321 **CEYLAN SKIPPER** (Sr) ex *Mercur* 1982; ex *Agni*; ex *Grigoroussa* 1976; ex *Keharitomeni* 1972; ex *Ringwood* 1969

★ 59330 **KANG HAI** RC/Br (Smith's D) 1956; B; 18100; 182.81 × 10.95 (599.77 × 32.93); M (Sulzer); 15; ex *Benvorlich* 1976; ex *Ribera* 1973

59340 **AL TAWFIQ** Li/Ja (NKK) 1965; B; 15600; 175.6 × 10.88 (576.12 × 35.7); M (Sulzer); 16.25; ex *Olympic Palm* 1982
Sisters:
59341 **AL TAHSEEN** (Li) ex *Olympic Pearl* 1982
59342 **OLYMPIC PEGASUS** (Li)
59343 **FLORISSANT** (Pa) ex *Olympic Phaethon* 1983
59344 **OLYMPIC PIONEER** (Li)
Similar (Longer poop):
59345 **OLYMPIC PEACE** (Li)
59346 **OLYMPIC POWER** (Li)
59347 **OLYMPIC PRESTIGE** (Li)
59348 **AL KARIM** (Li) ex *Olympic Pride* 1983
59349 **OLYMPIC PROGRESS** (Gr)
59350 **ALBION 1** (Pa) ex *Albion* 1983; ex *North Atlantic Valour* 1975; ex *Albion* 1973
59351 **MARYLISA** (Gr)
59352 **WINSTON** (Gr) ex *Zita* 1977
59353 **MAR PACIFICO** (Pe) ex *Amstelbrink* 1983; ex *Hollands Brink* 1977

59360 **OGDEN EXPORTER** Li/Ja (NKK) 1966; B; 15600; 175.6 × 10.78 (576.12 × 35.37); M (Sulzer); 15; ex *Oriental Exporter* 1970
Sister:
59361 **AL MALIK** (Li) ex *Ogden Importer* 1983; ex *Oriental Importer* 1970

59370 **MANIA** Gr/Br (A&P) 1963; B; 13500; 177.71 × 9.6 (583.04 × 31.5); M (Gotaverken); 14.5; ex *Pollux* 1980; ex *Assios* 1978; ex *Homer* 1970; ex *Middlesex Trader* 1969
Similar:
59371 **CORAJE** (Ur) ex *Saturn;* ex *Surrey Trader* 1970

59390 **GREGOS** Gr/FRG (Bremer V) 1959; B; 9200; 157.82 × 9.68 (517.78 × 31.76); M (MAN); 14.25; ex *Ostria* 1975; ex *Bulk Trader* 1972

59400 **MUO** Pa/FRG (Flensburger) 1963; B; 9500; 153.98 × 9.13 (503.18 × 29.95); M (MAN); 13.5; ex *Bijela* 1983; ex *Rigel* 1977; ex *Splendid Breeze* 1977; ex *Executive Trader* 1974; ex *Bernhard* 1973

● 59410 **MALDIVE PLEDGE** Mv/Br (Bartram) 1960; C; 9100; 145.62 × 9.35 (477.76 × 30.68); M (Doxford); 13.5; ex *Valiant* 1981; ex *Santa Cruz* 1972; ex *La Laguna* 1965

59430 **ANNA BAKKE** Pi/Sp (AESA) 1972; C; 11600; 154.64 × 10.37 (507.35 × 34.02); M (B&W); 18; ex *Seaborne* 1983; ex *Ria Sol* 1982; ex *Kudu* 1981; ex *Aquamarin* 1972
Sisters:

59431 ELIZABETH BAKKE (Pi) ex *Steadfast* 1983; ex *Ria Mar* 1982; ex *Gherenuk* 1981; Launched as *Topas*;

59432 GIOACCHINO LAURO (It) launched as *Turkis*

59433 ANIELLO (Pa) ex *Jogoo* 1980; ex *Turmalin* 1978

59440 SOUTH COUNTY Li/Ko (Dae Sun) 1976; B; 6800; 125 × 7.56 (410.1 × 24.8); M (Mitsubishi); 14.25; ex *Roebuck* 1982
Sisters:
59441 SOUTH FAITH (Li) ex *Ravenswood* 1982
59442 FALKON (Sw) ex *Riverina* 1982

59450 GENERAL MALVAR Pi/FRG (Luerssen) 1972; C; 4900; 123.32 × 6.85 (404.59 × 22.47); M (Bergens); 13.25; ex *Fiducia* 1983; ex *Furunes* 1980
Sister:
59451 GENERAL LUNA (Pi) ex *Fjordnes* 1981

59460 AKRANES Ic/FRG (Luerssen) 1970; C; 4800; 123.25 × 6.99 (404.36 × 22.93); M (Bergens); 13.5; ex *Fossnes* 1981; ex *Midiboy* 1977; ex *Brinknes* 1973; Lengthened 1974 (Swan Hunter)
Sister:
59461 GENERAL LIM (Pi) ex *Fjellnes* 1980; ex *Jennes* 1977; ex *Midigirl* 1976; ex *Jennes* 1974

59470 ELBIA Pa/FRG (Sietas); 1978; Cem; 7000; 135.01 × 8.02 (442.95 × 26.31); M (KHD); —
Similar (Pa flag):
59471 ASPIA
59472 FLORIA

59478 ALVORADA Gr/Ba (Ebin/So) 1977; C; 3400/5900; 127.39 × —/8.06 (418 × —/26.44); M (Pielstick); 15
Sisters:
59479 SILVER MED (Li) launched as *Lis Bewa*
59480 GOLDEN MED (Li) launched as *Kirsten Bewa*
59481 ATLANTIC JOY (Gr) ex *Aurora* 1978
Probable sisters:
59482 MARIANNA (Gr)
59483 SARONIC (Gr)
59484 REA SILVIA (It) launched as *Syros Island*
59485 GEHAN AL SADAT (Eg) launched as *Naxos Island*
59486 GEHAN AL SADAT II (Eg) launched as *Nicolas Condaras*

59490 PECHEUR BRETON Fr/Ne ('De Hoop') 1961; FC; 1000; 88.4 × 4.1 (290.03 × 13.45); M (Werkspoor); 15; ex *Ljosafoss* 1972; ex *Echo* 1969; Converted from cargo 1972

59500 LUANA Pa/FRG (Nobiskrug) 1965; C; 3200; 106.63 × 6.99 (349.84 × 22.93); M (MAN); 13.5; ex *Maxi Porr* 1980

59510 GROOTSAND Cy/FRG (Buesumer) 1978; R; 1600; 78.11 × 5.75 (256.27 × 18.86); M (MaK); 14
Sisters (Cy flag):
59511 WITTSAND
59512 REEFER KNIGHT ex *Yorksand* 1980
59513 KNIEPSAND
(Sd flag):
59514 BASILEA
59515 TURICIA

● **59520 SITI MIDAH** Pa/Ja (Kurushima) 1971; C/HL; 7000; 131.81 × 8.23 (432.5 × 26); M (Kobe); 14; ex *Sri Hamida* 1983; ex *Sun Eternal* 1983; ex *Seiyo Maru* 1982
Sisters:
59521 IPPOLITOS (Gr) ex *Sakura Maru* 1980
59522 FORUM STAR (Gr) ex *Tachibana Maru*

59530 HAJ AHMED Sy/Sw (Ekensbergs) 1958; C; 5000; 117.63 × 7.57 (385.93 × 24.84); M (B&W); 13; ex *Ingerseks* 1982

● **59540 DESPINA V** Pa/Ne ('Ijssel') 1971; C; 3000; 91.45 × 7.18 (300.03 × 23.56); M (MAN); 13.5; ex *Belemar* 1983; ex *Reem 1* 1982; ex *Raha* 1980; ex *Nelly Maersk* 1976
Sister:
59541 MARIANNA (Gr) ex *Atlas River* 1980; ex *Niels Maersk* 1976

59545 CAP ANAMUR Pa/Ja (Watanabe) 1977; C; 5300; 118.70 × 7.10 (389 × 23.29); M (Mitsubishi); 17.5
Similar:
59546 AGONISTIS (Gr) launched as *Cap Andreas*

59550 TAI LAI Tw/Ja (Setoda) 1962; C; 1000; 69.73 × 4.59 (228.76 × 15.06); M (Hanshin); 11; ex *Yamatsune Maru* 1969

● **59560 DIANA** Le/Fi (Valmet) 1962; C; 1900; 85.81 × 5.39 (281.53 × 17.68); M (KHD); 13; ex *Elefsis* 1982; ex *Lady Sabina* 1979; ex *Ceclona* 1974; ex *Pirjo* 1970

59570 LESLIE Gr/FRG (Lindenau) 1965; C; 2400; 92.06 × 5.6 (302.03 × 18.37); M (Sulzer); 13; ex *Anna Rehder* 1973

★ **59571 KRKA** (Ys) ex *Matthias Rehder* 1974

59575 ALGARMI Sp/Sp (Barreras) 1979; C/Con; 1800/2800; 97.36 × —/6.24 (319 × —/20.47); M (Deutz); 15
Sisters:
59576 ALALMA (Sp)
59577 ALYOLEX (Sp)

59580 OKEANIS Gr/Gr (Eleusis) 1973; C; 3700; 107.52 × 6.69 (352.76 × 21.95); M (MAN); 14.5
Sister:
59581 TITHIS (Gr)

59590 ARGO PIONEER Gr/Gr (Argo) 1976; C; 1600; 79.99 × 5.34 (262.43 × 17.52); M (Alpha-Diesel); 13.5
Sisters (Gr flag):
59591 ARGO CHALLENGE
59592 ARGO FAITH
59593 ARGO GLORY
59594 ARGO HOPE
59595 ARGO SPIRIT
59596 ARGO VALOUR

● ★ **59600 POTIRNA** Ys/Pd (Gdanska) 1967; C; 1500; 87.58 × 4.81 (287.34 × 15.78); M (Atlas-MaK); 12; ex *Normannsund*; ex *Gdynia* 1976; Lengthened 1970 (Gdanska); **'B-459'** type
Sisters:
★ **59601 PERNA** (Ys) ex *Normannbay*; ex *Caroline* 1975; ex *Germa Lord* 1973
★ **59602 POPLAT** (Ys) ex *Normannvaag*; ex *Josefine* 1976; ex *Geisha* 1975
59603 EVANGELIA (Cy) ex *Jade* 1981; ex *Fondal* 1974; ex *Gdansk* 1973
Similar (not lengthened):
59604 BERKBORG (Ne) ex *Carebeka VI* 1982; ex *Lionel*

● **59610 SOMMY** Pa/Pd (Gdanska) 1972; C; 2000; 93.73 × 5.57 (307.51 × 18.27); M (KHD); 13; ex *Eggli* 1982; ex *Rommy* 1983; ex *Enid* 1977; **'B-431'** type
Sisters:
59611 HILDEGARD (Pa) ex *Mildred* 1977
59612 SUNRISE (Gr) ex *Cupid* 1982
59613 PLOCE (Pa) ex *Drid* 1984; ex *Eldrid* 1983
59614 GUDRID (No)
59615 NICOLAS (Pa) ex *Sigrid* 1982

● **59620 BREEHORN** Ne/No (Batservice) 1971; C; 1600; 80.02 × 5.32 (262.53 × 17.45); M (Polar); 13; ex *Lyshav* 1975
Sister:
59621 ANTHOULA II (Cy) ex *Breehelle* 1983; ex *Angelika Lehmann* 1973
Similar:
59622 PUERTO PLATA (Do) ex *Argo Spray* 1983; ex *Gallic Minch* 1981; ex *Tornes* 1974
59623 MONAC (Pa) ex *Monach* 1983; ex *Mornes* 1974
59624 BREEHOEK (Ne) ex *Blankenburg* 1976
59625 DELTA (FRG)
59626 NIAGA XLII (Ia) ex *Zuidwal* 1982; ex *Kalmarvind*
59627 STAVRAKIS II (Gr) ex *Karin Lehmann* 1980
59628 MAIK PRIMO (It) ex *Rudolf Kurz* 1981
59629 PINGO (Fi) ex *Pingvin* 1979

59630 LAURA Gr/Ne (Zaanlandsche) 1965; C; 1600; 81.79 × 4.97 (268.34 × 11.31); M (Werkspoor); 13.5; ex *Breevecht*; ex *Karen Winther* 1971

59640 MOKHA Si/DDR ('Neptun') 1967; C; 2600/4000; 112.1 × 7.17 (367.78 × 23.52); M (Werkspoor); 13.5; ex *Eurabia Spring* 1978; ex *Clari* 1975; ex *Karlsburg* 1970; ex *Claudia Maria* 1967
Sister:
59641 LE ROVE (Fr) ex *Scol Independent* 1975; ex *Germanica* 1975; ex *Wilri* 1975; ex *Germanic* 1974; ex *Wilri* 1974; ex *Atlanta* 1973
Similar:
59642 TRITON (Gr) ex *Irenes Sun* 1980; ex *Blockland* 1977; ex *Jiri* 1969; ex *Hoegh Jiri* 1968; ex *Jiri* 1966
59643 ORION (Gr) ex *Irenes Sea* 1981; ex *Werderland* 1977; ex *Wilri* 1969; ex *Hoegh Wilri* 1969; ex *Wilri* 1967
59644 CAPTAIN COSMAS M (Pa) ex *Conti Almania* 1982; ex *Grimsnis* 1975; ex *Hein Jenevelt* 1970; ex *Bari* 1968
59645 SANAA (Si) ex *Eurabia Progress*; ex *Claudia Maria* 1975
59646 BILSTEIN (FRG) ex *Duburg* 1980; ex *Bilstein* 1978; ex *Conti Syria* 1978; ex *Antony* 1977; ex *Bilstein* 1975; ex *Hoegh Susann* 1968; Launched as *Susan Von Bargen*
59647 LIDES (Pa) ex *Cavally* 1983; ex *Rinkenis* 1975; ex *Dirk von Minden* 1970; ex *Mari* 1968; ex *Hoegh Mari* 1968; ex *Mari* 1967

★ **59650 KLOSTERFELDE** DDR/DDR ('Neptun') 1972; C; 3100; 104.91 × 6.39 (344.19 × 20.97); M (Dieselmotorenwerk Rostock); 14.5
Sisters (DDR flag):
★ **59651 NEUHAUSEN**
★ **59652 RADEBERG**

59660 BLUE SPIRIT Cy/DDR ('Neptun') 1964; C; 2800; 97.57 × 6.63 (320 × 21.75); M (MAN); 13; ex *Egon Wesch* 1973; ex *Jiri* 1965

59670 EDY 1 Le/FRG (Brand) 1965; C; 500/1000; 68.59 × 4.02/5.13 (225.03 × 13.19/16.83); M (KHD); 12; ex *Bierum*; ex *Hilda Eckhardt* 1971
Probable sister:
59671 MUKALLA (Ye) ex *Renate S* 1974; ex *Golzwardersand* 1972

59680 ALAMAK Ne/Ne (Jonker) 1978; C; 3400; 83.52 × 8.2 (274.02 × 26.9); M (MWM); 12.5

★ **59690 ZULAWY** Pd/Pd (Gdanska) 1974; FC; 8100; 151.31 × 7.4 (496.42 × 24.28); M (Sulzer); 19; **'B 68'** type
Sisters:
★ **59691 KASZUBY II** (Pd)
★ **59692 WINETA** (Pd)
★ **59693 MAZURY** (Pd)

59710 MOSEL FRG/FRG (Howaldts DW) 1978; C/Con/HL; 7800/13100; 163.02 × 8.11/9.62 (535 × 26.6/31.56); M (MAN); 16.5
Sister:
59711 ELBE (FRG)

59720 AUVERGNE FRG/FRG (Howaldts DW) 1978; C/Con; 9300; 151.03 × 8.13 (495.51 × 26.67); M (Atlas-MaK); 17; ex *Carolina* 1983; ex *Tielbank* 1981; ex *Carolina*; Modified **'CL 10'** type
Sister:
59721 CHARLOTTA (FRG) ex *Testbank* 1981; ex *Charlotta*

59730 KOWIE Pa/Ja (Yamanishi) 1978; C; 6400; 129.32 × 7.83 (424.3 × 25.7); M (B&W); 15; ex *Esteblick* 1982; ex *Ville du Ponant*; ex *Esteblick* 1980; ex *B M I Exporter* 1978
Similar:
59731 MARIPASOULA (Fr) ex *Atalanta II* 1982; ex *Atalanta*
59732 KAIROS (Pa) ex *Germanic* 1980
59733 IMPALA (Pa)
Probably similar:
59734 PHAROS (Pa) ex *Adria 1* 1980; ex *Naxos I* 1979; ex *Renate Wunsche* 1978; ex *Nordwelle* 1977
59735 MARE SARINA (Sg) ex *Hilda Wesch* 1983; Launched as *Blue Sovereign*

59740 FLORENZ FRG/FRG (Bremer V) 1977; C; 10000; 142.07 × 9.06 (466.11 × 29.72); M (MAN); 14.5; **'Modified German Liberty'** type
Sisters (FRG flag):
59741 WILLIAM SHAKESPEARE
59742 TOLEDO

● **59750 LINERA** Cy/FRG (Flensburger) 1971; C; 6700/9500; 139.76 × 8.23/9.18 (458.53 × 27/30.12); M (MAN); 16; ex *Lina Fisser* 1983; ex *Sunlina* 1980; Launched as *Lina Fisser*; **'German Liberty'** type
Similar:
59752 FLEUR (Cy) ex *Sunvreeland* 1981; Launched as *Carl Fisser*
59753 HEIDE LEONHARDT (FRG) ex *Finn Heide* 1970
59754 KLAUS LEONHARDT (FRG)
59755 CASON (Pa) ex *Finn Leonhardt* 1980; ex *Wolfgang Russ* 1978; ex *Finn Leonhardt* 1978
59756 MARITA LEONHARDT (FRG) ex *Altenfels* 1970; Launched as *Marita Leonhardt*
59757 ALPAMAYO (Pe) ex *Martha Fisser* 1980; ex *Sunbaden* 1978; ex *Martha Fisser* 1974; ex *Sunbaden* 1973
59758 ALFA (Gr) ex *Petradi* 1983; ex *Pitria* 1980

● **59770 EDITA** Pa/FRG (O&K) 1972; C; 5000/8300; 143.8 × 7.07/8.33 (471.78 × 23.19/27.33); M (Pielstick); 18; ex *Edith Howaldt Russ* 1980; ex *Cambridge* 1976; ex *Edith Howaldt Russ* 1975; Launched as *Edith Howaldt*
Sisters:
59771 ALBION STAR (FRG) ex *Rheingold* 1982; ex *Columbus California* 1979; ex *Rheingold* 1973
59772 DEVON (FRG) ex *Walkure* 1982; ex *Bavaria Trieste* 1980; ex *Columbus Canada* 1980; Launched as *Walkure*

59780 SARI BUDI Ia/Ja (Hakodate) 1961; C; 4200; 108.82 × 6.52 (357.02 × 21.39); M (MAN); —; ex *Gunung Guntur* 1978
Sisters:
59781 SEATRA EXPRESS (Pa) ex *Vivi* 1982; ex *Mira Permata* 1981; ex *Gunung Kerintji* 1978
59782 PENTA ACE (Sg) ex *Rantih Gumala* 1978; ex *Gunung Tambora* 1978

59790 **PRVIC** Ys/No (Lothe) 1972; C; 4200; 112.83 × 6.89 (370.18 × 22.6); M (Stork-Werkspoor); 13.75; ex *Lindo* 1981

59800 **MILAS** Tu/FRG (Lindenau) 1970; C; 4000; 117 × 6.61 (383.86 × 21.69); M (Atlas-MaK); 15; ex *John M* 1983; ex *John M Rehder*
Similar:
59802 **ADELAIDE** (Cy) ex *Leo Schroder* 1983
59803 **LUTZ SCHRODER** (FRG)

59810 **BERGE DUKE** No/Ja (Mitsui) 1973; Tk; 139800; 342.91 × 21.78 (1125.03 × 71.8); M (B&W); 15.5
Sisters (No flag):
59811 **BERGE SEPTIMUS**
59812 **BERGE LORD**

59815 **MONT VENTOUX** Fr/Fr (Havre) 1980; RoC/HL; 3600; 109.63 × 5.75 (360 × 18.86); M (Pielstick); 14; Stern door

---

59820 **GROOTSAND** Cy/FRG (Buesumer) 1978; R; 1600; 78.11 × 5.75 (256.27 × 18.86); M (MaK); 14
Sisters (Cy flag):
59821 **WITTSAND**
59822 **REEFER KNIGHT** ex *Yorksand* 1980
59823 **KNIEPSAND**
 (Sd flag):
59824 **BASILEA**
59825 **TURICIA**

59830 **CYCLOPUS** Gr/Fr (L'Atlantique) 1957; C; 9100; 138.33 × 8.89 (453.84 × 29.17); M (Sulzer); 14; ex *Maestrale* 1980; ex *Lily M* 1978; ex *Louis L.D.* 1970

59840 **MOUNT ELLEROS** Gr/Sp (U N de Levante) 1958; C; 6400; 138.41 × 9.49 (454.1 × 31.14); M (Fiat); 14; ex *Mariannina* 1981; ex *La Selva* 1967

59850 **ESSO BONN** FRG/FRG (A G 'Weser') 1974; Tk; 126200; 347.81 × 20.05 (1141 × 65.78); T (GEC); 15.5; Launched as *Esso Bilbao*
Similar:
59851 **ESSO SABA** (Na)

59865 **SRIWIJAYA** Ia/FRG (Schlichting) 1981; C/Con; 13400; 158.38 × 9.50 (520 × 31.17); M (MAN); 17
Sister:
59866 **MATARAM** (Ia)

59870 **LEONCE VIELJEUX** Fr/Fr (La Ciotat) 1970; C; 7900/12500; 171 × 7.7/9.7 (561 × 25.6/32); M (Sulzer); 19
Sisters:
59871 **SANTA RITA** (Pe) ex *Christian Vieljeux* 1981
59872 **GEORGES VIELJEUX** (Fr)
59873 **PIERRE VIELJEUX** (Fr)
59874 **THORON** (Fr) ex *Eric Vieljeux*
Possibly similar:
59875 **CUZCO II** (Pe) ex *Patrick Vieljeux* 1981
59876 **LIMA II** (Pe) ex *Stephane Vieljeux* 1981; ex *Taj* 1979; ex *Stephane Vieljeux* 1978

★ 59880 **BORIS CHILIKIN** Ru/Ru (Baltic) 1971; Rmt; 23400 Dspl; 162 × 8.6 (532 × 28.1); M (Sulzer); 16.5
Similar (Ru flag):
★ 59881 **DNESTR**
★ 59882 **GENRIK GASANOV**
★ 59883 **IVAN BUBNOV**
★ 59884 **VLADIMIR KOLECHITSKY**

★ 59890 **VELIKIY OKTYABR** Ru/Ru (Baltic) 1967; Tk; 11000; 162.31 × 8.93 (532.51 × 29.3); M (B&W); 16.25
Sisters (Ru flag):
★ 59891 **POBYEDA OKTYABRYA**
★ 59892 **TSEZAR KUNIKOV**
★ 59893 **NIKOLAY SIPYAGIN**
★ 59894 **KERCH**
★ 59895 **EYZHENS BERGS**
★ 59896 **KONSTANTIN TSIOLKOVSKIY**
★ 59897 **GENERAL BAGRATION**
★ 59898 **ZAKHARIY PALIASHVILI**
★ 59899 **FRIDRIKH TSANDER**
★ 59900 **VASILIY KIKVIDZE**
 (Bu flag):
★ 59901 **MARITZA**
★ 59902 **REZVAYA**
★ 59903 **VELEKA**
 (Cu flag):
★ 59904 **9 DE ABRIL**
★ 59905 **7 DE NOVIEMBRE**
 (In flag):
59906 **BHAGAT SINGH**
59907 **SAROJINI NAIDU**
59908 **VISVESVARAYA**

59910 **AMOCO SEAFARER** Li/Ja (Mitsui) 1974; Tk; 127000; 331.53 × 20.6 (1087.7 × 67.59); M (B&W); 16; ex *Polybritannia* 1979

59920 **ESSO CARIBBEAN** Li/Ja (IHI) 1976; Tk; 177300; 378.39 × 22.27 (1241.44 × 73.06); T (IHI);

15.25; ex *Andros Petros* 1977
Sisters:
59921 **BURMAH ENDEAVOUR** (Br) (builder China SB)
59922 **BURMAH ENTERPRISE** (Br) (builder China SB)
59923 **ESSO MEDITERRANEAN** (Li) ex *Homeric* 1977
Similar:
59924 **ANDROS CHRYSSI** (Li)
59925 **ETHNIC** (Li)
59926 **SUNSHINE LEADER** (Li)
59927 **AKAMA MARU** (Ja)
59928 **ISE MARU** (Ja)
59929 **SETAGAWA MARU** (Ja)
59929/1 **SHUHO MARU** (Ja)

59930 **MUNETAMA MARU** Ja/Ja (Sasebo) 1973; Tk; 128800; 341.11 × 20.04 (1119.13 × 65.75); T (Mitsubishi); 15.25

59940 **OGDEN NELSON** Li/Ja (Hitachi) 1972; Tk; 124400; 331 × 22.02 (1085.96 × 72.24); T (Kawasaki); 15.5
Sisters (Li flag):
59941 **COALINGA** ex *Ioannis Chandris* 1976
Similar (Li flag):
59942 **WORLD CROWN**
59943 **WESTERN LION**
59944 **SOUTHERN LION**
59945 **NORTHERN LION**
59946 **EASTERN LION**

59950 **OLYMPIC BOND** Li/Ja (Hitachi) 1972; Tk; 126000; 331 × 22.02 (1085.96 × 72.24); T (Kawasaki); 15.5

59960 **MEITAI MARU** Ja/Ja (Mitsui) 1974; Tk; 123900; 324.01 × 19.51 (1063.03 × 64.01); M (B&W); 16

● 59970 **NORMAN PACIFIC** Sg/Ys ('Split') 1971; OBO; 42200; 252.36 × 14.78 (827.95 × 48.49); M (MAN); 16; ex *Capetan Carras*

59980 **TRADE ENDEAVOR** Li/Ja (IHI) 1970; Tk; 63400; 274.02 × 17.03 (899.02 × 55.87); M (Sulzer); 15.25; ex *Venture Britain* 1983; ex *Ocean Champion* 1981; ex *Seiko Maru* 1976

59990 **ESSO FUJI** Pa/Ja (Hitachi) 1972; LGC; 55900; 246.01 × 13.08 (807.12 × 42.91); M (B&W); 15.5

59995 **YUHO MARU** Ja/Ja (Hitachi) 1980; Tk; 51700; 233 × 12.77 (764 × 42.00); M (Sulzer); 15.75

59997 **COLUMBIA LIBERTY** Li/Ja (Sasebo) 1980; Tk; 43600; 243.01 × 12.73 (797 × 41.77); M (MAN); 14.5
Possible sister:
59998 **DIANA** (Ja)

60000 **PETRO SEA** Th/Ja (Mitsubishi N) 1962; LGC; 17800; 183.72 × 10.54 (602.76 × 34.58); M (MAN); 18.5 ex *Sea Petro* 1983; ex *Petron Gasul* 1982; ex *Contank Bridgestone* 1980; ex *Bridgestone Multina* 1978; ex *Bridgestone Maru* 1971

60010 **GAS GLORIA** Ko/FRG (A G 'Weser') 1968; LGC; 19700; 173.84 × 10.26 (570.34 × 33.66); M (Sulzer); 17.5; ex *Antilla Cape* 1983

60020 **WAITAKI** NZ/Ja (Tohoku) 1972; C; 3200; 85.83 × 7.44 (281.6 × 24.41); M (Hanshin); 12.5; ex *Union Australia* 1977; 'Camit' type
Sisters:
60021 **DUNEDIN** (NZ) ex *Union New Zealand* 1978
60022 **ARNON** (Is) ex *Union Trans Tasman* 1977

● 60030 **OCEAN SKY** Ko/Ja (Shikoku) 1975; C; 3700; 131.48 × 6.99 (431.36 × 22.93); M (Mitsubishi); 17.75; ex *Summer Birdie* 1979; ex *Rose Daphne* 1978
Sisters:
60031 **ROSE MALLOW** (Pa)
60032 **WHITE JASMIN** (Pa) ex *Rose Acacia* 1978
60033 **OSAKA REEFER** (Ja) ex *Aden Maru* 1978

60035 **NIPPON REEFER** Ja/Ja (Kyokuyo) 1982; R; 8000; 142.40 × 8.62 (467 × 28.28); M (Pielstick); 17.25
Sister:
60036 **NEW ZEALAND REEFER** (Ja)

60040 **EITOKU MARU** Ja/Ja (Nishii) 1977; R; 3500; 127.41 × 7.07 (418.01 × 23.2); M (Mitsubishi); 20.5
Similar:
60041 **NITTOKU MARU** (Ja)

60050 **MASBON** Li/Ja (Asakawa) 1975; C; 4800; 102.16 × 6.02 (335.17 × 19.75); TSM (Akasaka); 12
Sisters (Li flag):
60051 **MINAROSA**
60052 **MINADOR**
60053 **MASLUCK**

60060 **UNITY** Li/Ja (Imabari) 1973; C; 3700; 108.01 × 7.7 (354.36 × 25.26); M (Hanshin); 12.25

● 60070 **'FREEDOM'** type. —/Ja (IHI) & Sg (Jurong Spyd) 1968 onwards C; 8000 approx; 142.3 × 9.06 (466.86 × 29.72); M (Pielstick); 14.5; Some ships under K3MF, Some later ships have HL derrick
Sisters (Gr flag):
60071 **ACRITAS**
60073 **AEOLOS**
60074 **AGAPI**
60076 **AGENOR**
60077 **AMYNTAS**
60077/1 **ANATOLI** ex *Pomposa* 1983; ex *Unilion*; ex *Lija*
60078 **ANNOULA**
60079 **ANTHEMIOS**
60080 **AQUAMARINE**
60082 **ARGOS**
60083 **ARIS**
60084 **ARISTARCHOS**
60085 **ARISTEUS**
60086 **ASSOMATOS** ex *Prosperity*
60087 **ATHOS**
60089 **COMET**
60090 **CAPE KENNEDY**
60091 **CAPE MONTEREY** ex *Kastraki*
60091/1 **CAPE SUPERIOR** ex *Telfair Challenger* 1981; ex *Estina* 1980
60092 **DELOS** ex *Acropolis* 1978
60093 **DIMOS HALCOUSSIS**
60094 **EFTHITIS**
60095 **ELPIS**
60096 **EPIMELIA**
60097 **EPOS**
60098 **EVNIA**
60100 **FRINTON**
60101 **FRONISIS**
60104 **LACON** ex *Sparta*
60105 **LARA S** ex *Sharpeville* 1980
60106 **LIPS** ex *Star of Kuwait*
60108 **MARABOU**
60109 **MARIGO**
60110 **MELITON**
60110/1 **MELOI** ex *Emerald* 1982
60111 **NATA**
60112 **NAXOS** ex *Athens*
60113 **OCEANIS**
60114 **PATMOS** ex *Pacqueen* 1979
60115 **PELLEAS**
60116 **POUNENTES** ex *Shamaly*
60117 **PROSPATHIA**
60118 **RELIANT**
60120 **SANTO PIONEER**
60124 **SEA TIDE**
60125 **SILVER ATHENS**
60126 **SITHONIA**
60128 **TETI N**
60129 **TINTOS** ex *Delphi*
60130 **TITIKA HALCOUSSI**
60130/1 **TOPROTO** ex *Sea Bird* 1983
60131 **UNITY**
60132 **YANNIS HALCOUSSIS**
Probable sisters: (Gr Flag)
60140 **AKRATA**
60142 **SEA STAR**
60143 **THASSOS ISLAND**
Sisters (Li flag):
60150 **AL RAKEEB**
60151 **AL RASHED**
60152 **AL RAZAK**
60153 **ALEA** ex *Neptune Sakura* 1974
60154 **ARKANDROS**
60155 **CONSTANCE**
60157 **ENDURANCE EXPRESS**
60158 **ENDURANCE FRIENDSHIP**
60158/1 **GEORGIOS M** ex *Georgios Matsas* 1983
60159 **LUCKY WAVE**
60160 **MESIS** ex *Kuwait Horizon*
60161 **MICHALIS**
60162 **MILOS ISLAND**
60163 **NEGO MAY** ex *Volta Friendship*
60163/1 **PACIFIC FAIRWIND** ex *Union Expansion* 1983
60166 **POLA**
60169 **POZEGA**
60169/1 **RAJAAN** ex *Aramis* 1981
60169/2 **SEA CONDOR** ex *Saturnia* 1983; ex *Pomposa* 1975
60170 **SOROKOS** ex *Dawn of Kuwait*
60171 **SOUTHERN FRIENDSHIP** ex *Bounteous*
60172 **TELFAIR LEADER** ex *Hermina* 1980
Probable sisters: (Li Flag)
60175 **AL RAHIM** ex *Concordia Glory* 1980; ex *Al Rahim*
60176 **AL RAHMAN**
60178 **AL REDHA**
60179 **TELFAIR PIONEER**
Sisters (Pa flag):
60180 **GALLANTRY** ex *Santo Fortune*
60181 **JOHN A** ex *Barahona* 1981; ex *Marigo*

Yemelos 1980
60185 **LONG BEACH**
60186 **OAKLAND**
60186/1 **PIONEER** ex *Lydia*
60186/2 **PRINCE SHAUL** ex *Pacprince* 1982
60186/3 **PRINCESS MIRI** ex *Pacprincess* 1982
60187 **REGINA S.**
60187/1 **STAVR** ex *Ios* 1983; ex *Georgios Paravalos* 1980
Probable sisters: (Pa Flag)
60188 **DUTEOUS**
60189 **SPACIOUS**
Sisters (Sg flag):
60190 **IKAN TAMBAN** ex *Potenza* 1983; ex *Nego Harmony* 1974
60200 **HIGHSEA PRIDE** ex *Wistaria Marble* 1979
60201 **NEPTUNE CYPRINE**
60202 **NEPTUNE IOLITE**
60203 **NEPTUNE IRIS**
60204 **NEPTUNE KIKU**
60205 **NEPTUNE PERIDOT**
60206 **NEPTUNE RUBY**
60207 **NEPTUNE SARDONYX**
60208 **NEPTUNE SPINEL**
60209 **NEPTUNE TOURMALINE**
60210 **NEPTUNE TURQUOISE**
60211 **WISTARIA CORAL**
60212 **WISTARIA PEARL**
(Ta flag)
★60215 **RUVU** ex *Sea Horse*
(Cy flag):
60220 **ADVENTURE** ex *Carnival Venture* 1980
(In flag):
60230 **INDIAN FAITH**
60231 **INDIAN FAME** ex *Pericles Halcoussis*
60232 **INDIAN FORTUNE** ex *Leonis Halcoussis*
60234 **INDIAN FRATERNITY**
60235 **INDIAN FREEDOM**
(RC flag):
★60236 **GUI JIANG** ex *Sea Falcon* 1980
★60240 **JIA LING JIANG'** ex *Aran*
★60241 **LAN CANG JIANG** ex *Zografnia Y* 1977
★60242 **QUI JIANG** ex *Sea Swan* 1980
★60243 **SONG HUA JIANG** ex *Evie*
★60244 **XUAN CHENG** ex *Theodoros A S*
★60245 **WU JIANG** ex *Sea Eagle* 1980
Similar—Taiwan built (China SB) & flag:
60250 **AMEX** ex *Glorious Trader* 1982
60251 **SINOEX** ex *Sincere Trader* 1982
Similar (shorter third kingpost and superstructure differs—see inset):
60252 **LUCKY WAVE** (Gr)
60253 **LEONIS HALCOUSSIS** (Gr)
60254 **FREE WAVE** (Gr)
60255 **AL RAZIQ** (Li)

60260 **FATHER PANOS** Gr/Br (Doxford & S) 1968; C; 6200/9300; 140.87 × —/8.58 (462.17 × —/28.15); M (Doxford); 14.25; ex *Sheaf Crest* 1974

60270 **M CEYHAN** Tu/Ja (Mitsui) 1971; Tk; 112700; 324.21 × 19.65 (1063.68 × 64.47); T (Westinghouse); 16; ex *Tish Pion* 1981; ex *British Pioneer* 1981
Possibly similar (may be K₂MF):
60272 **SHOUSH** (Ir) ex *British Surveyor* 1976

60280 **YUKONG LEADER** Pa/Ja (NKK) 1974; Tk; 128100; 338.13 × 20.90 (1109 × 68.54); T (Mitsubishi); 15; ex *Jarabella* 1982
Sisters:
60281 **YUKONG PIONEER** (Ko) ex *Jastella* 1982
Similar:
60282 **VIOLANDA** (Gr) ex *Violando N Goulandris* 1978

60300 **AMOCO CAIRO** Li/Ja (Mitsubishi HI) 1975; Tk; 76500; 280.02 × 15.24 (918.7 × 50); M (Sulzer); 15.25
Sisters:
60301 **AMOCO WHITING** (Li) ex *Amoco Tehran* 1980
60302 **AMOCO TRINIDAD** (Li)

60310 **CELTIC LINK** Br/Ja (Mitsubishi HI) 1976; Tk; 84600; 280.42 × 15.24 (920.01 × 50) M (Sulzer); 15.25; ex *Grey Warrior* 1981

●60320 **GRADIENT ENERGY** Li/Ja (Mitsubishi HI) 1967; Tk; 39000; 243.85 × 13.24 (800 × 44.03); M (Sulzer); 16; ex *Mosduke* 1978

60340 **SEA VICTORY** Li/Ja (IHI) 1969; OBO; 43500; 254.52 × 14.01 (835.04 × 45.96); M (Sulzer); 15.5; ex *Mozart* 1983

60350 **AGHIA MARINA** Li/Ja (Kure) 1969; OBO; 43400; 254.52 × 14.02 (835.04 × 46); M (Sulzer); 14.75; ex *Balbina* 1983

★60360 **BELCHATOW** Pd/Ja (Mitsubishi HI) 1976; B; 39300; 232.37× 13.85 (762 × 45.44); M (Sulzer); 14.5
Sister:

★60361 **TUROSZOW** (Pd)

60370 **DELTAGAS** FRG/FRG (Meyer) 1975; LGC; 4300; 106.41 × 7.44 (349.11 × 24.41); M (KHD); 16.5
Possible sister:
60372 **CORAL ISIS** (NA)

60380 **THALASSINI EFHI** Gr/Ja (Mitsui) 1976; B; 42300; 239.05 × 14 (784.28 × 45.93); M (B&W 15.2; ex·*Ikan Bawal* 1980; ex *Thorsdrake* 1979

60390 **CHIEFTAIN BULKER** Li/Ja (Hitachi) 1977; B; 19500; 182.23 × 11.28 (597.87 × 37.01); M (B&W); 14.75
Sisters (Li flag):
60391 **CAVALIER BULKER**
60393 **CONQUEROR BULKER**
(Tw flag):
60394 **CHARIOT BULKER** ex *Centurion Bulker* 1982

60400 **MENELAOS** Gr/Br (Doxford & S) 1969; B; 12700; 160.03 × 9.15 (525.03 × 30.02); M (Sulzer); 15.5; ex *Federal Lakes* 1980
Sisters:
60401 **MICHALIS** (Gr) ex *Federal Seaway* 1980; ex *Simsmetal* 1972

60410 **ELAFINA** Gr/Ja (Shin Yamamoto) 1973; B; 15000; 154.11 × 10.52 (505.61 × 34.51); M (Sulzer); 15.5; ex *Trans Ruby* 1973

60415 **BENEDICT** Br/Bz (Emaq) 1979; C; 3600; 115.65 × 6.50 (379 × 21.33); M (MAN); 15
Sister:
60416 **BONIFACE** (Br)

60420 **OCEAN DYNAMIC** Pa/Ja (Kishimoto) 1975; R; 3600; 124.08 × 6.92 (407.08 × 22.7); M (B&W); 17.5;
Sister:
60421 **OCEAN FRESH** (Pa)

60430 **OLDENBURG** FRG/FRG (Norderwerft) 1971; C; 2900; 97.24 × 6.44 (319 × 21.13); M (Atlas-MaK); 15

60440 **JULES VERNE** Fr/Fr (La Seine) 1965; LGC; 22300; 201.02 × 7.53 (659.51 × 24.7); T (Parsons); 17

60450 **WEST JINORIWON** Pa/Ja (Sumitomo) 1972; B; 24600; 194.91 × 11.44 (636.52 × 37.53); M (Sulzer); 14.75; ex *Inveralmond* 1980

60460 **ASHLEY** Gr/Ja (Sumitomo) 1970; B; 13400; 163.51 × 9.63 (536.45 ×31.59); M (Sulzer);16.5; ex *Seafox* 1981

★60470 **ZHONG TIAO SHAN** RC/FRG (Bremer V) 1970; C; 6600/9300; 139.58 × —/9.19 (457.94 × —/30.15); M (MAN); 16; ex *Atlantis* 1978; 'German Liberty' type
Sisters:
★60471 **HAN YIN** (RC) ex *Okeanis* 1974
★60472 **XIN AN JIANG** (RC) ex *Octavia* 1977
★60473 **FENG HUANG SHAN** (RC) ex *Ia* 1978; ex *Niriis* 1974
60474 **ALTAVIA** (Sg)
60475 **NOVIA** (Sg)
60476 **LONTUE** (Li) ex *Megalopolis* 1976

60480 **ARGOLIKOS** Gr/FRG (A G 'Weser') 1977; C; 7200/10000; 149.82 × 8.18/9.26 (491.53 × 26.84/30.38); M (MAN); 16.5; '36-L' type
Probable sisters:
60481 **ARISTAGELOS** (Li)
60482 **ARISTANAX** (Gr)

★60484 **XIANG JIANG** RC/FRG (A G 'Weser') 1978; C/Con; 7100/10000; 149.79 × 8.17/9.26 (491 × 26.8/30.38); M (MAN); 16.5; '36-L' type
Sisters:
★60485 **MIN JIANG** (RC)
★60486 **YONG JIANG** (RC)
★60487 **YONG XING** (RC)
★60488 **LEOPOLD STAFF** (Pd)

60490 **PELEUS** Gr/FRG (Rickmers) 1970; C; 9200; 139.58 × 9.02 (457.94 × 29.59); M (MAN); 15; ex *Aegis Spirit* 1983; 'German Liberty' type
Sisters:
60491 **AEGIS FAITH** (Gr)
60492 **AEGIS PIONEER** (Gr)
60493 **AEGIS PRIDE** (Gr)
Possibly similar:
60495 **GOLDEN CAMEROON** (Pa) ex *Minerva* 1979

★60500 **GIUSEPPE VERDI** Ru/It (Ansaldo) 1964; Tk; 30300; 227.9 × 12.14 (747.7 × 39.83); M (Ansaldo); 16; Launched as *Maria Adelaide*; May be spelt **DZHUZEPPE VERDI**
Sisters (Ru flag):
★60501 **GALILEO GALILEI** (Ru)
★60502 **RAPHAEL** (Ru) may be spelt **RAFAEL**

60510 **SHABELLE** Gr/Ys ('Ivan Cetenic') 1964/65 LS; 2900; 109.18 × 6.04 (358.2 × 19.82); M (B&W) 15; ex *Dona Clausen* 1980; Launched as Ys 1964 Lengthened & completed FRG 1965 (Nobiskrug)
Sister:
60511 **KOTA TERNAK** (Sg) ex *Al-Kuwait* 1982 Launched as *Dagmar Clausen*

60514 **AZALEA** Ja/Ja (Murushima) 1976; C HL; 7200; 131.81×8.30 (432×27.23); M (MAN); 14
Similar (goalpost mast from bridge):
60515 **CORCEL** (Pa) ex *Yucaly* 1982
Probably similar (Ja flag):
60516 **ASUNARO**
60517 **HAMANASU**
60518 **ACACIA**

60520 **YU KONG** Ko/No (Moss V) 1961;Tk; 8300; 146.31×8.37 (480.02×27.46); M(B&W); 14.5; ex *Husvik* 1969

●60530 **ARMONIKOS** Gr/Sw (Kockums) 1963; Tk; 36800; 236.33 × 12.63 (775.36 × 41.44); M (MAN); 17.25; ex *Vestalis* 1975

60540 **ZOE CHRISTINA** Gr/Sw (Kockums) 1965; Tk; 34500; 236.25 × 12.66 (775.1 × 41.54); M (MAN); 17; ex *Hari* 1983; ex *Zacharia T* 1983; ex *Zacharia Tsirlis* 1979; ex *Patriotic Colocotronis* 1976; ex *Tank Countess* 1969

●60550 **KONG HAAKON VII** No/No (Stord) 1969; Tk; 109400; 327.72 × 20.42 (1075.2 × 66.99); T (GEC); 16
Sister (No flag):
60552 **HADRIAN**

60560 **GLOBE NOVA** Li/No (Fredriksstad) 1964; Tk/LGC; 13500; 169.78 × 9.6 (557.02 × 31.5); M (Gotaverken); 15.75; ex *Granheim* 1978

60565 **ESSO PALM BEACH** Pa/Ja (Kawasaki) 1978; Tk; 27400; 196.53 × 11.28 (644.78 × 37.01); M (MAN); 16.25
Sisters (Li flag):
60566 **ESSO BAYWAY**
60567 **ESSO PORTLAND**

60570 **ESSO PORT JEROME** Fr/Ja (Hitachi) 1972; Tk; 12800; 161.02 × 9.76 (528.28 × 32.02); M (B&W); 15; ex *Esso Kumamoto* 1980; '22' type. Some others in this class may have this sequence

60580 **JUPITER** Li/Sw (Eriksbergs) 1975; Tk; 18300; 170.77 × 11.35 (560.27 × 37.24); M (B&W); 16
Sisters:
60581 **MERCURY** (Li)
60582 **NEZLA** (Ag) ex *Scaptrust* 1976
60583 **HAOUD L'HAMRA** (Ag) ex *Scapmariner* 1976

60590 **ATHENIAN HARMONY** Cy/Ja (IHI) 1970; Tk; 17500; 170.82 × 11.01 (560.43 × 36.12); M (Sulzer); 16; ex *Messiniaki Avra* 1982; ex *Stakara* 1981
Sisters (Gr flag):
60591 **MATHRAKI** ex *Messiniaki Anatoli* 1982; ex *Stabenko* 1981
60592 **MESSINIAKI AVGI** ex *Stamenis* 1981
60593 **ASTIPALEA** ex *Messiniaki Akti* 1982; ex *Stawanda* 1981
60594 **LIMNOS** ex *Messiniaki Aigli* 1982
60596 **MESSINIAKI ANAGENNISIS**
60597 **MESSINIAKI DOXA** ex *Messiniaki Bergen* 1981
60598 **MESSINIAKI GI**
60599 **MESSINIAKI IDEA**
60600 **OTHONI** ex *Messiniaki Dris* 1982; ex *Messiniaki Minde* 1981
60601 **PAROS** ex *Messiniaki Ormi* 1982
60602 **KITHNOS** ex *Messiniaki Paradis* 1982
60605 **MESSINIAKI THEA**
(Li flag):
60606 **MESSINIAKI LAMPSIS**
60607 **WAYUSUT** ex *Messiniaki Timi* 1983
(Cy flag):
60608 **DONA LOULA** ex *Messiniaki Areti* 1983
60609 **DONA MYRTO** ex *Messiniaki Chara* 1983
60609/1 **DONA CHRISTINA** ex *Messiniaki Pnoi* 1983

60610 **BUNGA KESUMBA** My/Ja (Mitsubishi HI) 1975; Ch; 19000; 170.01 × 11.15 (557.78 × 36.58); M (Sulzer); 15.25
Sisters (My flag):
60611 **BUNGA SELASIH**
60612 **BUNGA SEPANG**

★60620 **DAUGAVPILS** Ru/Ys ('Split') 1965; Tk; 15100; 186.21 × 9.84 (610.93 × 32.28); M (B&W); 17
Sisters (Ru flag):
★60621 **GRIGORIY ACHKANOV**

★60622 SPLIT
★60623 GORI
★60624 VASILIY PORIK
★60625 GENERAL ZHDANOV
★60626 MARSHAL BIRYUZOV
★60627 OLEKO DUNDICH
★60628 PETR ALEKSEYEV
★60629 BORZHOMI
★60630 GENERAL KARBYSHEV
★60631 DMITRIY ZHLOBA
★60632 NIKOLOZ BARATASHVILI
★60633 ERIFAN KOVITYUKH
★60634 MITROFAN SEDIN
★60635 MOS SHOVGENOV
★60636 STEPAN VOSTRETSOV
★60637 PYATIDYESYATILYETIYE SOVETSKOY GRUZII also known as 50 LETIYE SOVETSKOY GRUZII
★60638 PAVEL DYBENKO
★60639 REZEKNE
★60640 RIJEKA
★60641 GENERAL BOCHAROV
★60642 GENERAL KRAVTSOV
★60643 GENERAL SHKODUNOVICH
★60644 NIKOLAY PODVOSKIY
(Ag flag)
60645 SKIKDA ex Kutaisi 1974
60646 ARZEW ex Batumi 1974

★60660 LUGANSK Ru/Ja (Mitsubishi Z) 1962; Tk 22100; 207.02 × 11.08 (679.2 × 36.35); M (Sulzer); 16.5
Sisters (Ru flag):
★60661 LEBEDIN
★60662 LIKHOSLAVL
★60663 LUBNY
★60664 LENINO
★60665 LYUBLINO
★60666 LYUBERTSY
★60667 LUKHOVITSY (may be spelt LUHOVITSY)

★60670 LISICHANSK Ru/Ru (IHI) 1962; Tk; 23100; 207.04 × 11.11 (679.27 × 36.45); M (Sulzer); 16.5
Sisters (Ru flag):
★60671 LENKORAN
★60672 LYUBOTIN

★60680 INTERNATSIONAL Ru/Pd (Gdynska) 1968; Tk; 13800; 177.27 × 9.37 (581.59 × 30.74); M (Sulzer); 16; 'B-72' type
Sisters (Ru flag):
★60681 DRUZHBA
★60682 NARODOV
★60683 ISKRA
★60684 LENINSKOE ZNAMYA
★60685 NAKHODKA
★60686 PROLETARSKAYA POBEDA
★60687 PAMYAT LENINA
★60688 PETR STUCHKA
★60689 ZAVYETY ILYICHA

60700 WIGAN Br/Ja (Mitsubishi HI) 1964; Tk; 36100; 237.80 × 12.70 (780.2 × 41.67); T (Mitsubishi); 16; ex Aristides 1983; ex Agios Nikolas 1983; ex Venture Oklahoma 1982; ex Turbina 1978; ex Andking 1978; ex Mosking 1976

60710 LORD MOUNT STEPHEN Br/Ja (Mitsubishi HI) 1966; Tk; 41500; 231.02 × 13.13 (757.94 × 43.08); M (Sulzer); 16.25
Sister:
60711 LORD STRATHCONA (Br)

★60720 TAI HU RC/Sw (Gotav) 1965; Tk; 41000; 239.28 × 12.74 (785.04 × 41.8); M (Gotaverken); 16; ex Beauregard 1974
Sisters:
60721 BASHAYER 1 (Pa) ex Katherine Alexandra 1981; ex Beaufort 1978
★60722 GAO HU (RC) ex Beaumont 1974
Similar:
★60724 DA QING NO 252 (RC) ex Zhen Hu 1978; ex Anna Knudsen 1975
★60725 STRUMA (Bu) ex Thelma 1972
60726 FOTINI (Gr) ex Jane Stove 1973; ex Tank Regina 1970

60770 HASSAN B Pa/Sw (Uddevalla) 1964; Tk; 35400; 236.13 × 12.82 (774.71 × 42.06); M (B&W); 16; ex Athelking 1977
Sister:
60771 KIMOLOS (Gr) ex Will Adams 1980; ex Athelregent 1977

60790 STELIOS Pa/Ja (Mitsubishi HI) 1968; Tk; 103200; 324.44 × 18.70 (1064 × 61.35); M (B&W); 15.5; ex Berge Commander 1981

★60805 LAS GUASIMAS Cu/Ja (Niigata) 1976; RT; 3600; 106.99 × 6.99 (351 × 22.93); M (Niigata); 12.75; Operated by State Fishing Fleet

60810 PASS OF BRANDER Br/Br (Dunston) 1975; Ch; 2500; 97.52 × 6.2 (329.95 × 20.35); M (Mirrlees

Blackstone); 15
Similar:
60811 PASS OF BALMAHA (Br)

60820 AL KHLOOD Si/FRG (Kroegerw) 1973; Ch; 4500; 113.14 × 7.41 (371.19 × 24.31); M (Mirrlees Blackstone); 14; ex Silverpelerin 1980

60830 UM EL FAROUD Ly/Br (Smith's D) 1969; Ch; 3100; 109.56 × 6.41 (359.45 × 21.03); M (Smit & Bolnes); 14; ex Seafalcon 1973
Sister:
60831 RED IBIS (Li) ex Storna 1982; ex Seatern 1975
60832 LUHUAN (Pa) ex F. Wiborg Fekete 1973

60840 PERMINA 109 Ia/It (Adriatico) 1973; Tk; 7700; 140.21 × 7.9 (460.01 × 25.92); M (Stork-Werkspoor); 15; ex Donna Gabriella 1974
Sister:
60841 ELISA d'ALESIO (It) ex Donna Mariella

60850 PRESIDENT DELCOURT Fr/It (Pietra Ligure) 1972; Ch; 6000; 125.46 × 7.75 (411.61 × 25.43); M (Fiat); 17

60860 INGE MAERSK De/No (Moss V) 1972; LGC/Ch; 9200; 138.74 × 9.21 (455.18 × 30.22); M (Sulzer); 17
Sister:
60861 FERNWAVE (Li)
Similar (smaller) (No flag):
60862 HARDANGER
60863 BOW ELM
Similar (later built):
60866 HESPERUS (No) ex Fernbrook 1978

60870 BERNARDO HOUSSAY Ar/Fr (La Ciotat) 1969; LGC; 6900; 126.22 × 7.32 (414.11 × 24.02); M (Sulzer); 16; ex Barfonn 1979

60880 SARRAT Pi/Fr (France-Gironde) 1963/65; LGC; 8000; 145.01 × 8.38 (475.75 × 27.49); M (B&W); 15; ex Ang Pangarap 1980; ex Rye Gas; ex Crystal 1977; ex Cap Martin 1975; ex Savoie 1965; Converted from ore carrier 1965

60890 GAZ PROGRESS Pa/No (Moss V) 1966; LGC; 2700; 90.56 × 6.03 (297.11 × 19.78); M (Sulzer); 12.25; ex Coral Obelia 1979; ex Arctic Propane 1971

★60900 GEORGIY LEONIDZE Ru/Pd (Szczecinska) 1974; B; 20300; 202.34 × 10.64 (663.85 × 34.91); M (Sulzer); 15; 'B 447' type
Sister:
★60901 GENERAL LESELIDZE (Ru)

60910 CYPRESS Li/Sp (AESA) 1974; B; 30300; 206.76 × 13.28 (678.35 × 43.57); M (Sulzer); 15.25; ex King Charles 1983
Similar:
60911 NACIONAL BRAGANCA (Po) ex Garthnewydd 1981

60920 UNITY Ma/Br (Doxford & S) 1968; B; 28900; 218.35 × 12.56 (716.37 × 41.21); M (Doxford); 15.5; ex Leda 1982; ex Ripon Grange 1980; ex Orotava 1979; ex Orotava Bridge 1974; ex Orotava 1969

60940 SOUTH COUNTY Li/Ko (Dae Sun) 1976; B; 6800; 125 × 7.56 (410.1 × 24.8); M (Mitsubishi); 14.25; ex Roebuck 1982
Sisters:
60941 SOUTH FAITH (Li) ex Ravenswood 1982
60942 FALKON (Sw) ex Riverina 1982

60950 GHADAMES Ag/Ja (Fukuoka) 1977; C; 8600; 136.38 × 8.33 (447.44 × 27.33); M (Mitsubishi); 18; ex Jenny Porr 1977
Sisters:
60952 KASSANTINA (Ly)
60953 CAPE GATA (Cy) ex Henriette Schulte 1983
60954 WILHELM SCHULTE (Cy) ex Lloyd Virginia 1981; ex Wilhelm Schulte 1980; ex Concordia Hawk 1980; ex Wilhelm Schulte 1979
60955 RENATE SCHULTE (FRG) ex Ville de Saint Pierre 1981; ex Renate Schulte 1981
Similar:
60956 REGINA (Sd)

60960 AKBAR In/De (Helsingor) 1971; P/C; 8300; 149.51 × 7.71 (490.52 × 25.29); M (B&W); 18.5

60970 TAISEI MARU No.98 Ja/Ja (Shin Yamamoto) 1977; FC; 9700; 155 × 8.22 (508.53 × 26.97); M (Mitsubishi); 19

60980 URANUS 1 FRG/FRG (Schuerenstedt) 1977; C/Con; 3600/6700; 131.71 × 6.35/8.03 (432.12 × 20.83/26.35); M (Atlas-MaK); 15.25; ex Diplomat 1978; ex Uranus 1977

60990 JOHNNY Gr/Ja (Imai Z) 1976; B; 9900; 143.39 × 9.39 (470 × 30.81); M (Mitsubishi); 15.5; ex Wistaria Alamo 1980; ex Blue Neptune 1979
Sister:

60991 ROYAL SAPPHIRE (Pa)
Possible sisters:
60992 APJ PRITI (In)
60993 FYLYPPA (Pa) ex Nisshin Maru 1981
★60994 QI LIAN SHAN (RC) ex Canadian Express 1980; Launched as Duck Yang Rose

61000 ROSANA Gr/Ja (Hitachi) 1978; B; 11300; 156.24 × 9.5 (512.6 × 31.17); M (B&W); 15.5
Possibly similar:
61001 THALASSINI IDEA (Li) ex Young Statesman 1982
61002 PROVIDENCE (Ja)

61005 HELMUT HERMANN Cy/Ja (Hashihama) 1977; C; 6500/10700; 148.39 × 7.56/9.12 (487 × 24.80/29.92); M (Sulzer); 14.5; ex Nicolaos Angelakis 1978

●61010 SANAGA Sg/Ja (Hitachi) 1971; B; 12100; 156.17 × 9.29 (512.37 × 30.48); M (B&W); 15; ex Woermann Sanaga 1976
Sisters:
61011 HUDSON DEEP (Sg) ex Woermann Sassandra
61012 THEANO (Gr) ex Woermann Ubangi 1980
61013 ARIZONA SUN (Sg) ex Sankuru 1981; ex Woermann Sankuru 1976
61014 SWAKOP (Pa) ex Maritime Courier 1978; ex Swakop 1976
61015 ZAMBESI (Pa) ex Maritime Transporter 1978; ex Woermann Sambesi 1976
61016 SAN PEDRO (Pa) launched as Woermann San Pedro
Similar:
61017 BO AH (Ko) ex Maritime Victor 1980
61018 TRANSOCEAN RAM (Pi) ex Van Warrior 1980
61019 ANGEATLANTIC (Gr) ex Van Hawk
61020 KALYN (Cy) ex Calypso N 1983; ex Mariner 1978; ex Eastern Cherry 1980
61021 STEPHANOS (Gr) ex Merlin 1980; ex Eastern Mary
61022 CANAL ACE (Pa) ex World Hercules 1981
61023 ZINI (Gr)
61024 GEORTINA (Gr)
Possibly similar:
61025 ISLAND SKY (Li)
61026 ANGEARCTIC (Gr) ex World Champion
61027 NIKOLETA K (Gr) ex United Pride 1982; ex World Pride 1981
61028 HAN SONG (Ko) ex Golden Explorer 1982
61029 KRONOS (Gr) ex Golden Pioneer 1982
Similar (Ko built):
61030 PAN KOREA (Ko)
Possibly similar (Ko built-Korea SB):
61031 KOREAN PRIDE (Li)
61032 KOREAN FIR (Li)
61033 CATHERINE ANN (Li) ex Glory River 1980
61034 ARGUS (Li) ex Rebecca Elyse 1983; ex Great River 1980
61035 AKTION (Gr)
61036 ALKAIOS (Gr)

●61040 ARCHIMEDES Gr/Ja (Osaka) 1970; B; 10500; 154.34 × 9.18 (506.36 × 30.12); M (B&W); 15; ex Hae Duck No 3 1980; ex Federal Yodo 1979
Sister:
61041 ALMAR (Gr) ex Federal Mackenzie
Similar:
61042 IRAN NAMJOO (Ir) ex Asia Momo 1983
Probably similar:
61043 ASIA RINDO (Li)
61044 MANILA ENTERPRISE (Pi) ex Asia Botan
61044/1 ORION STAR (Ko) ex Agelos Seraphim 1981; ex Silver Light 1980; ex Ganges Maru 1971

●61045 GLORY OCEAN Ja/Ja (Yamanishi) 1977; C/TC; 10700; 146.08 × 9.31 (479.27 × 30.54); M (Akasaka); 14
Sister:
61045/1 SWEET SULTAN (Pa)
Similar:
61046 COBALT ISLANDS (Li) ex Pacific Charger 1981
61047 BALDER HOPE (Pa)

●61050 MAR TRANSPORTER Tu/Ja (Mitsui) 1969; B; 10300; 154.05 × 9.19 (505.41 × 30.15); M (B&W); 14.75; ex Irenes Ecstacy 1982; ex Midas Arrow; ex Nagato Maru 1971
Sister:
61051 NIKOS N (Gr) ex Dona Juana 1979; ex Retladawn 1979; ex Overseas Navigator 1975; ex Haiko Maru 1973
Similar:
61052 ANGEKRITI (Pa) ex Nikolaos A 1982; ex Midas Prince; ex Oriental Prince 1971; ex Yamato Maru 1970
61053 MIDAS RHEIN (Li) ex Rhein Maru 1972
61054 MONTROSE (Li)
61054/1 ALBORADA (Ch) ex Montigny 1983

61055 YUE RIVER Ja/Ja (Kochiken) 1975; C/TC; 129.88 × 7.75 (426.4 × 25.43); M (Mitsubishi); 13.25; ex *Kong Hoi* 1976
Sisters:
61056 YUE MAN (Pa)
61057 BRIGHT MELBOURNE (Pa)
Possible sisters:
61058 AGATHA (Gr) ex *Pearl Lotus* 1979
61059 EXTRACO 1 (Pi) ex *Pearl River* 1979
61059/1 EXTRACO II (Pi) ex *Ocean Explotar* 1978
61059/2 GREAT HONOR (Pa) ex *Great Success* 1976
61059/3 SALVIA STAR (Pi) ex *Caribbean Hope* 1982; ex *Ruby Lotus* 1979
61059/4 SEIBUN MARU (Ja) ex *Ho Chung* 1981
61059/5 MARIA MARIOS H (Gr) ex *Sunny Sydney* 1979
61059/6 SUN ALKES (Ja) ex *Matsufukujin Maru*
61059/7 BETTY No 2 (Ia) ex *Timber Leader* 1981
61059/8 TYCHE (Pa)
61059/9 HIRA-1 (Tu) ex *Virgo* 1982; ex *Sun Antares* 1979
61059/10 WONJIN (Ko) ex *Namyang Crown* 1980; ex *Nanpo Maru* 1976

61060 GOMASA Gr/Ja (Onomichi) 1971; C; 4700; 114.2 × 7.04 (374.67 × 23.1); M (Kobe); 13; ex *Kisshu Maru* 1975
Possible sisters:
61061 PRINCESS SEIKO (Pa) ex *Petrelo* 1983; ex *Tofuku Maru* 1977
61062 YPAPANTI (Pa) ex *Ziria* 1983; ex *Toju Maru* 1975

● **61065 LINGAL TRADER** Pa/Ja (Hashihama) 1969; C; 6100; 127.62 × 7.53 (419 × 24.70); M (Kobe); 13.5; ex *Irenes Nostalgia* 1982; ex *Kintai Maru* 1979
Probable sisters:
61066 KRATINOS (Gr) ex *Prairie* 1979; ex *Shotai Maru* 1976
61067 KALYPSO (Pa) ex *Shintai* 1975; ex *Shintai Maru* 1973
61068 NEGEV ARAD (Sg) ex *Bangkok Venture* 1981; ex *Ocean Trader* 1977; ex *Bruce Bay* 1976; ex *Yutai Maru* 1975

● **61070 ORIENT FISHER** Pa/Ja (Ujina) 1974; Cem; 6600; 127.77 × 8.25 (419.19 × 27.07); M (Ito Tekkosho); 13.25; ex *Union Amsterdam* 1980; ex *Oriental Victory* 1977
Sisters:
★ **61071 QINLING** (RC) ex *Myoken Maru* 1975
61072 HAND LOONG (Pa)
61073 HAND FORTUNE (Pa)
61073/1 GARDENIA (Sg) ex *Dixy Porr* 1981; ex *Golden Valley* 1976
Possible sisters:
61074 CHERRYFIELD (Li)
61075 KNIGHT (Pa) ex *Seven Daffodil* 1980; ex *Georgia Merry* 1978; ex *Sun Deneb* 1977
61076 JELAU (Pa) ex *Akitana Maru* 1978
61077 EVANGELOS D (Pa) ex *Sun Sirius;* ex *Koryu Maru* 1975
61078 GOLDEN DRAGON (Pa)
61079 EASTERN NEPTUNE (Pa) ex *Shuwa Maru* 1983
61080 HAUDA BEAUTY (Cy) ex *Yancey*
61081 SUN ORION (Pa)
61082 KOREA STAR (Sg) ex *Jayne H B* 1982; ex *Hilary B* 1981; ex *Blue Jupiter* 1977
61083 NATIONAL LEADER (Pi) ex *National Steel Four* 1983; ex *Yu-Lin* 1978
61084 SWEE LEAN (Ja) ex *Lusty* 1979
61085 GOLDEN STAR (Pa)
61086 REGENT (Pa)

★ **61090 KOPALNIA MOSZCZENICA** Pd/De (Nakskov) 1968; B; 8400; 141.71 × 8.2 (464.93 × 26.9); M (B&W); 15.25
Sisters (Pd flag):
★ **61091 KOPALNIA KLEOFAS** (Pd)
★ **61092 KOPALNIA MARCEL**
★ **61093 KOPALNIA SOSNICA**
★ **61094 KOPALNIA SZCZYGLOWICE**
★ **61096 KOPALNIA WIREK**
★ **61096 GLIWICE II**

★ **61100 RIZHSKIY ZALIV** Ru/Fr (Dubigeon-Normandie) 1969; FC; 12900; 164.62 × 7.01 (540.09 × 23); M (Pielstick); 17.5
Sisters (Ru flag):
★ **61101 AMURSKIY ZALIV**
★ **61102 BOTNICHESKIY ZALIV**
★ **61103 DVINSKIY ZALIV**
★ **61104 FINSKIY ZALIV**
★ **61105 KANDALAKSHSKIY ZALIV**
★ **61106 NARVSKIY ZALIV**
★ **61107 ONEZHSKIY ZALIV**
★ **61108 TAGANROGSKIY ZALIV**
★ **61109 USSURIYSKIY ZALIV**

● **61120 KASTORIA** Cy/Ys ('Split') 1967; C; 5400; 128.96 × 7.42 (423.1 × 24.34); M (Sulzer); —; ex *Diamond* 1983; ex *Tamar* 1971
Sister:
61121 FALANI (Gr) ex *Rimon* 1983; ex *Opal* 1973; ex *Rimon* 1970

61130 NADIA S Pa/FRG (Rhein Nordseew) 1963; B; 12300; 165.51 × 10.01 (543.01 × 32.84); M (MAN) —; ex *Agnic II* 1983; ex *Skylark* 1978; ex *Riviera* 1969

61140 OLIVIA CUATRO Pa/It (Riuniti) 1964; B; 10600; 160.1 × 9.6 (525.26 × 31.5); M (B&W); 16; ex *Eolia* 1981
Probably similar:
61141 SPIRIT (Gr) ex *Ilice* 1981
61142 HECTOR (Ma) ex *Saudi Spirit* 1984; ex *Orfeo* 1984

61150 ELEFTHERIOS Gr/Ja (Hitachi) 1966; B; 11300; 156.01 × 9.48 (511.8 × 31.1); M (B&W); 15; ex *Hudson Bay;* ex *Transocean Transport* 1977; 'Hitachi Standard 19' type
Sisters:
61151 FIFTH AVENUE (Gr)
61152 CORONIA (Gr)
61153 ALKYONIA (Gr)
61154 DENISH (Pa) ex *Andromachi* 1981; ex *Wilshire Boulevard* 1976
61155 ORESTIA (Gr)
61156 SEA PIONEER (Li)
61157 ANTIOCHA (Gr)
61158 OLYNTHIA (Gr)

● **61160 GOLDEN TENNYO** Gr/Ja (NKK) 1977; B; 14500; 172.27 × 9.78 (565.19 × 32.09); M (Sulzer); 15
Sisters (Gr flag):
61161 GOLDEN CHASE
61162 GOLDEN HORIZON
61163 GOLDEN PANAGIA
61164 GOLDEN SHIMIZU
61165 MYRINA ex *Polytropos* 1980
Similar: (Gr Flag):
61166 GOLDEN CHARIOT
61167 GOLDEN CROWN
61168 GOLDEN SPEAR
61169 GOLDEN SWORD

61170 OCEAN STEELHEAD Pa/Ja (NKK) 1982; B; 16400; 175.01 × 10.45 (574 × 34.28); M (Pielstick); 14.5

61180 FEDERAL FRASER Li/Ja (Sanoyasu) 1977; B; 22400; 183.67 × 12 (602.59 × 39.37); M (Sulzer); 15.5
Sister:
61181 PALMSTAR SUMIDA (Sg) ex *Federal Sumida* 1983
Similar:
61182 SEINE MARU (Ja)
61183 THAMES MARU (Ja)
61184 NEW STAR (Ko) ex *Royal Fornax* 1983; ex *Rhein Maru* 1980
Possibly similar:
61185 SUIKO MARU (Ja)

61190 TOXOTIS Gr/Ja (Kanasashi) 1974; B; 19200; 182.2 × 10.92 (597.77 × 35.83); M (B&W); 16
Sisters:
61191 DIDYMI (Gr)
61192 HYDROMOS (Gr)
61193 ZYGOS (Gr)
Similar:
★ **61194 NOVA GORICA** (Ys)
61195 BUFFALO (Ko) ex *Coral Arcadia* 1978; ex *Cascade Maru* 1973
Possibly similar:
61196 MAMMOTH FIR (Li)
61197 MAMMOTH PINE (Li)
61198 CISSUS (Li) ex *Zinnia* 1975
61199 STADION (Li)
61200 TROPHY (Li)

● **61205 ASIA BEAUTY** Li/Ja (Kanda) 1974; B; 15000; 175.85 × 9.62 (577 × 31.56); M (Sulzer); 14.5
Sisters:
61206 ASIA BRAVERY (Li)
61207 ASIA HONESTY (Li)

★ **61210 WAN LING** RC/Ja (Kanasashi) 1977; B; 15400; 175.8 × 9.6 (576.77 × 31.5); M (MAN); 14.5; ex *Lucent Star* 1983
Sisters:
61211 SEA LANTERN (Li) ex *Brilliant Star* 1984
★ **61212 YUN LING** (RC) ex *Radiant Star* 1982
61213 SHINING STAR (Li)
61214 WORLD CANDOUR (Li)
61215 WORLD PROBITY (Li)
Probable sisters—may have cranes:
61216 MORNING GLORY (Li)
61217 RED ARROW (Li)

61220 IRAN ENGHELAB Ir/Ja (Onomichi) 1979; B; 19300; 179.91 × 11.26 (590.26 × 36.94); M (B&W); 15; ex *Oinoussian Destiny* 1981
Sisters:

61221 IRAN AZADI (Ir) ex *Oinoussian Friendship* 1981
61222 IRAN JOMHOURI (Ir) ex *Oinoussian Leadership* 1981
61223 IRAN ENTEKHAB (Ir) ex *Oinoussian Prestige* 1981
61224 IRAN ESTEGHLAL (Ir) ex *Oinoussian Virtue* 1981

61230 SEA FURY Pa/Br (Lithgows) 1962; B; 10000; 152.56 × 8.94 (500.52 × 29.33); M (B&W); 14; ex *Caribbean Dreams* 1982; ex *Marcos M F* 1980; ex *Brunes* 1969

61250 SAN JOHN Gr/Ja (Sanoyasu) 1967; B; 10300; 147.53 × 9.07 (484.02 × 29.76); M (Sulzer); 15; ex *Grand Justice* 1980

61260 PRABHU SATRAM In/Br (Scotts' SB) 1969; B; 12300; 158.5 × 9.26 (520.01 × 30.38); M (Sulzer); 14.75; ex *Erisort* 1977; ex *World President* 1974
Sisters:
61261 ANADRIA (Br) ex *Eriboll* 1977; ex *World Hong Kong* 1973
61262 ARGONAVI (Li) ex *Siganto A S* 1980; ex *Eriskay* 1978

★ **61270 PRIBOY** Ru/Sw (Gotav) 1964; FC; 10900; 156.93 × 7.4 (514.86 × 24.28); M (Gotaverken); 18.25
Sisters (Ru flag):
★ **61271 KARL LINNE**
★ **61272 KHIBINSKIE GORY**
★ **61273 KRYMSKIE GORY**
★ **61274 LENINSKIYE GORY**
★ **61275 URALJSKIE GORY**

● **61280 CONSTANCIA** Pa/FRG (B+V) 1961; C; 8500/11200; 151.21 × 9.06/9.9 (496.1 × 29.72/32.48); 15.5; ex *Constantia*

● **61290 TIARET** Ag/Fr (Nantes) 1963; B; 11400; 155.4 × 9.28 (509.84 × 30.45); M (Sulzer); 14.75; ex *Arthur Stove* 1972
Sisters:
61291 CAPE KAMARI (Gr) ex *Kostos M* 1978; ex *Johs Stove* 1973; ex *Brissac* 1969
61292 ALKOR (Gr) ex *Timur Endurance* 1980; ex *Lita* 1974; ex *Sneland* 1972

★ **61310 JING HAI** RC/Br (Lithgows) 1968; B; 12400; 159.06 × 9.47 (521.85 × 31.07); M (B&W); 14.75; ex *Baynes* 1973
Sisters:
61311 KAPTAN YUSUF KALKAVAN (Tu) ex *Albaforth* 1982; ex *Silverforth* 1978; ex *Bellnes* 1974
61312 MARIA LEMOS (Gr) ex *Captain Pandelis S Lyras* 1975; ex *Birknes* 1973
61313 SATYA PADAM (In) ex *Borgnes* 1973

61320 GENERAL CAPINPIN Pi/Ja (NKK) 1972; B; 13000; 155.53 × 9.84 (510.27 × 32.28); M (Pielstick); 15.5; ex *Swiftnes* 1982
Sisters:
61321 EUROPA POINT (Br) ex *Beagle* 1983; ex *Saltnes* 1980
61322 AL-KARAMEH (Jo) ex *Sealnes* 1983
61323 MONTARIK (Br) ex *Spraynes* 1983
61324 HITTEEN (Jo) ex *Sharpnes* 1983
61325 MED TRANSPORTER (Tu) ex *Surenes* 1981

61330 SOUNION Gr/Br (Lithgows) 1968; B; 13900; 167.65 × 9.58 (550.03 × 31.43); M (B&W); 15.5; ex *Sugar Crystal*
Sister:
61331 CAPE AVANTI DUE (Gr) ex *Sugar Producer*
Similar (centre line kingposts):
61332 SEA TRANSPORTER (Gr) ex *Kefalonia Wind* 1984; ex *Sugar Transporter*
61333 KEFALONIA STAR (Gr) ex *Sugar Refiner*

61340 SALAMIS Gr/Ne (Verolme SH) 1963; B; 9600; 153.7 × 8.94 (504.27 × 29.33); M (MAN); 15; ex *Canadian Farmer* 1980; ex *Salamis* 1976; ex *Irish Plane* 1976
Sister:
61341 ASPYR (Pa) ex *Paralos* 1983; ex *Irish Cedar* 1976

61350 SPERANZA Pa/Sw (Oresunds) 1963; B; 12800; 167.65 × 10.02 (550.03 × 32.87); M (Gotaverken); 15; ex *Esperanza* 1982; ex *Scottish Wasa* 1978; ex *Scandic Wasa* 1977; ex *Eva Brodin* 1971

61360 SAN GEORGE Cy/Br (A&P) 1968; B; 11100; 154.67 × 9.02 (507.48 × 29.6); M (Doxford); 14; ex *Brembo* 1983; ex *Lugano* 1982; ex *Tamworth* 1978

61380 EKTON Gr/Br (A&P) 1962; B; 11400; 159.11 × 9.55 (522.01 × 31.33); M (Gotaverken); 15; ex *Bridgepool* 1975

61390 TRANSCOLUMBIA US/US (Kaiser Co) 1945; C/HL; 12400; 158.5 × 9.88 (520.01 × 32.42); T (Hendy); 17; ex *Marine Lynx* 1967; Converted

passenger/troopship (Newport News)
Sister:
61391 **TRANSCOLORADO** (US) ex *Marine Adder* 1967

●61400 **DOUCE FRANCE III** Fr/DDR ('Neptun') 1977; C; 6600/9800; 150.17 × 7.7/9.07 (492.68 × 25.26/29.76); M (MAN); 17; ex *Barbarella*; ex *Hoegh Apapa*; ex *Claudia Maria*; 'Neptun' type
Similar:
61401 **CAM BUBINGA** (Cn) launched as *Ivory Uranus*
61402 **CAM DOUSSIE** (Cn)
61403 **IRON BARON** (Au)
61404 **IVORY TELLUS** (Sg)
61405 **ALLGAEU** (Cy) ex *Vestland* 1982
61407 **RAYA HAPPINESS** (Pa) ex *Xin Hua Men* 1983; ex *Sol Tulla* 1982
61408 **THESEE** (Fr)
61409 **GALATEE** (Fr) ex *Soldrott* 1982
61409/1 **GANDA PERKASA** (Ia) ex *Sagaland* 1982; ex *Ellora* 1979; ex *Sagaland* 1978
61409/2 **EGIZIA** (It) ex *Merkur Sea* 1981
61409/3 **MERKUR RIVER** (Li) ex *Lloyd Hudson* 1982; ex *Merkur River* 1981
61409/4 **MERKUR BAY** (Li)
61409/5 **BANGLAR ROBI** (Bh) ex *Merkur Island* 1983; ex *Hoegh Apapa* 1982; ex *Merkur Island* 1982
61409/6 **MERKUR LAKE** (Li)
61409/7 **PACIFIC DRAGON** (Pa)
61409/8 **SAINTE ALEXANDRINE** (Pi)
★61409/9 **FLIEGERSKOSMONAUT DER DDR SIGMUND JAHN** (DDR)
★61409/10 **PRITZWALK** (DDR)
★61409/11 **PASEWALK** (DDR)
★61409/12 **GLACHAU** (DDR)
★61409/13 **CRIMMITSCHAU** (DDR)
61409/14 **NEPTUN** (Li)
61409/15 **BIMANTARA DUA** (Ia) ex *Merkur Beach* 1982
61409/16 **BIMANTARA SATU** (Ia) ex *Merkur Delta* 1982

61410 **AMBIKA** Pa/Ja (Fukuoka) 1977; C; 8100; 144 × 8.22 (472.44 × 26.97); M (IHI); 16.5; ex *Oslofjord* 1981
Sister:
61411 **ARIMBI** (Pa) ex *Bergensfjord* 1981
Possibly similar:
61412 **AMBALIKA** (Ia) ex *Tanafjord* 1981

61420 **CAMPHOR** Ja/Ja (Kochi) 1977; B; 9600; 141.97 × 9.1 (465.78 × 29.86); M (Mitsubishi); 14
Similar:
61421 **DE BURGO** (Cy) ex *Sea Zephyr* 1983; ex *Seizan Maru* 1977

61430 **SEA LINDEN** Pa/Ja (Usuki) 1971; B; 9500; 147.2 × 9.09 (482.94 × 29.82); M (Sulzer); 14.5; ex *Skyline* 1973

61440 **SITI NOVA** My/Ja (Hashihama) 1974; C; 9100; 138.41 × 9.01 (454.1 × 29.56); M (Pielstick); 14.25; ex *Sea Nova* 1983; ex *Seishin Maru* 1979
Possibly similar:
61443 **AGIA THALASSINI** (Pa) ex *Sea Triumph* 1983; ex *Seiten Maru* 1977
61444 **GRAND FELICITY** (Pa)

61450 **QUEEN VASSILIKI II** Pa/Ja (Setoda) 1970; C; 3900; 111 × 6.7 (364.17 × 21.98); M (B&W); 13; ex *Dona Amalia* 1983
Sister:
61451 **ATTICA** (Cy) ex *Don Ambrosia* 1983

●61460 **ARCADIAN SUN** Gr/Ja (Imabari) 1971; C; 5000; 124.31 × 7.52 (407.84 × 24.67); M (Mitsubishi); 13.75; ex *Pamela* 1981; ex *Hosho Maru* 1980
Similar:
61461 **MILANGO** (Pa) ex *Marugame Maru* 1980
61462 **RHODIAN HELMSMAN** (Gr) ex *Sea Dynamics* 1982; ex *Seaward*; ex *Rejoice* 1976; ex *Seiwa Maru* 1976
Probably similar:
61463 **MINOLA** (Cy) ex *Higashikawa Maru* 1983
61464 **MARY K** (Gr) ex *Koyo Maru* 1979
61465 **CHRISTOS K** (Gr) ex *Cereza* 1980; ex *Chokei Maru* 1976
61466 **SUMMER LIGHT** (Gr) ex *Irenes Harmony* 1981; ex *Sumiho Maru* 1977
61467 **VANGUARD 8** (Pa) ex *Somaria* 1978; ex *Kyowa Maru No 8* 1978

★61470 **JIN GANG LIN** RC/Ja (Kurinoura) 1974; C; 4200; 109.05 × 7.01 (357.78 × 23); M (Makita); 14.5; ex *Qin Fen 22* 1980; ex *Gulf President* 1978
Probable sisters:
★61471 **NAN GUAN LING** (RC) ex *Qin Fen 21* 1980
61472 **ASIA REGULUS** (Pa) ex *Tres Mar* 1981
61473 **GARZA OCEAN** (Pa)
61474 **MARIGOLD** (Pa) ex *Abs* 1980; ex *Bungalow* 1978; ex *Emprise* 1976; ex *Senko Maru* 1976
61475 **BERDIKARI** (Ia) ex *May Breeze*

61476 **KAPUAS** (Pa) ex *Sun Salvia* 1977
61477 **ORIENTAL BEAR** (Ko) ex *Tong Myung No.5* 1981; ex *Sea Bloom* 1979; ex *Ocean Star No 1* 1975
61478 **ANGELITA** (Pa) ex *Kyonan Maru* 1976
61479 **CHUN UNG** (Pa) ex *Sanryo Maru* 1976
61480 **HOYU MARU** (Ja) ex *Sanyo Maru* 1975

61490 **SITI ANITA** Pa/Ja (Hashihama) 1973; C; 6600; 129.06 × 7.98 (423.43 × 26.18); M (Mitsubishi); 13.5; ex *Canis Major* 1983; ex *Luxuriant*
Possibly similar:
61491 **LADY 1** (Pa) ex *Boe Oak* 1983; ex *Green Lime* 1983; ex *Shinpo Maru* 1979

61510 **LEAH** Pa/Ja (Shinhama) 1975; C; 3400; 106.46 × 6.6 (349.28 × 21.65); M (Mitsubishi); 12.5; ex *Srikandi* 1982; ex *Musashi* 1980

●61520 **NEW CONCORD** Pa/Ja (Hayashikane) 1970; C; 4000; 110.98 × 6.66 (364.11 × 21.85); M (B&W); 12.5; ex *Taiho* 1983
Similar:
61521 **CAMERO M** (Pa) ex *Agios Nicolaos* 1983; ex *Sincere No 2* 1976
61522 **JACKSON OCEAN** (Tw) ex *Sincere No 1* 1982
61523 **EVA** (Li) ex *Lally* 1983; ex *Dawn Ray* 1980
61524 **HARRY D** (Gr) ex *Atlantis Strength* 1981; ex *Eurco Strength*; ex *Tsen Hsing* 1977

61530 **CENTRAL CRUISER** Tw/Ja (Hayashikane) 1970; C; 3000; 97.39 × 6.38 (319.52 × 20.93); M (Kobe); 12.5

61540 **RYUSEI MARU** Pa/Ja (Fukuoka) 1972; C; 3300; 100.87 × 6.71 (330.94 × 22.01); M (Kobe); 12.5; ex *Nan A* 1981

61550 **POONSRI MARINE** Th/Ja (Kurushima) 1969; C; 3000; 97.21 × 6.38 (318.93 × 20.93); M (Akasaka); 13; ex *Chang Chun* 1979
Possibly similar:
61551 **CHUN JIN** (Pa) ex *Shinnan Maru* 1973
61552 **HUNG MING** (Tw) ex *Ta Ho* 1978; ex *Ichizan Unzen* 1971
61553 **TARAKAN MARU** (Ja) ex *Hashihama Maru* 1972

61560 **OLYMPIC 88** Pa/Ja (Geibi) 1977; C; 4200; 107.85 × 6.75 (353.84 × 22.15); M (Hanshin); 12; ex *Virginia Rhea* 1982; ex *Kasuga* 1980
Sisters (Pa flag):
61561 **BELA KOSMO**
61562 **BELA ROZO**
Possible sisters:
61563 **ANDHIKA ADIRAJA** (Pa)
61564 **ADHIGUNA DHARMA** (Ia)

61570 **CACABAN** Ia/Ja (Onomichi) 1965; C; 3700; 109.94 × 6.66 (360.7 × 21.85); M (Akasaka); 13; ex *Yung Lee* 1982; ex *Shinsei Maru No 7* 1973

61580 **RAINBOW STAR** Pa/Ja (Nishi Z) 1975; C; 4400; 109.99 × 6.91 (360.86 × 22.67); M (Mitsubishi); 13.5; ex *Sun Crocus* 1980
Probable sisters:
61581 **ROSEBAY** (Pa) ex *Sun Begonia* 1980
61582 **EVERGRAND** (Pa)

61590 **KALIMANTAN SATU** My/Ja (Shikoku) 1970; C; 4100; 110.5 × 6.86 (362.53 × 22.51); M (Kobe); 12.75; ex *Sunglow* 1982; ex *Lucid* 1978; ex *Ursa No 1* 1973; ex *Ryusei Maru* 1973

61600 **AUSTRAL** Gr/Ja (Koyo) 1967; C; 3000; 101.96 × 6.63 (334.51 × 21.75); M (Mitsubishi); 14.5; ex *Aikaterine K* 1983; ex *Wakatomi* 1977; ex *Bing Maru* 1974

●61610 **TAKASAGO MARU No 12** Ja/Ja (Kurushima) 1971; C; 3000; 101.12 × 6.81 (331.76 × 22.34); M (Kobe); 12.5
Possible sisters:
61611 **EASTERN DRAGON** (Ko) ex *Toryu Maru* 1976
61612 **GOLD STATE** (Pa) ex *Pacific Echo* 1976; ex *Toshin Maru* 1975
61613 **BUNGA MERAH** (Pa) ex *Oasis Emperor* 1982; ex *Papiliona* 1980; ex *Toko Maru* 1976
61614 **ALA KALA** (Pa) ex *Ala Wai* 1982; ex *Happy Rex* 1980; ex *Asian Park* 1976; ex *Tokei Maru No 2* 1974
61615 **MOGES AGATHIS** (Ia) ex *Umiyama Maru* 1975
61616 **MELION** (Pa) ex *Yamato Maru* 1983
61617 **SUN ISLAND 1** (Pa) ex *Sun Island* 1983; ex *Umeshima Maru* 1977
61618 **SANVASS** (Pa) ex *Taiyo Maru* 1978
61619 **SHINKO MARU** (Ja)
61620 **CRESTA VII** (Pi) ex *Asian Palm* 1981; ex *Shingen Maru* 1976
61621 **NANSHIN MARU** (Ja)
61622 **MOUNT ORO** (Pa) ex *Seizan Maru* 1980
61623 **ORIENTAL PRINCE** (Ko) ex *Dong San* 1982; ex *Maya Maru* 1980

61624 **ROBIN** (Pa) ex *Runna* 1980; ex *Masaharu Maru* 1974
61625 **GOLD MARINE** (Pa) ex *Green Ray* 1977; ex *Kuwana Maru* 1975
61626 **EKOWATI** (Pa) ex *Alexandra* 1981; ex *Kuching* 1976
61627 **TEMA** (Ko) ex *Geppo Maru* 1973
61628 **KEN JOHN** (Pa) ex *Fountain Azalea* 1983; ex *Kodai Maru* 1974
61629 **FORTUNE MARINER** (Pa) ex *Kinriki Maru No 21* 1978
61630 **VOLTERA** (Pa) ex *Chrisanthema* 1983; ex *Tini P* 1981; ex *Kairyu Maru* 1976
61631 **FAR EAST VANGUARD** (Pa) ex *Hoso Maru* 1980
61632 **BRIGHT SKY** (Gr) ex *Koyo Maru* 1976
61633 **DON PABLO** (Pi) ex *Bonanza* 1980; ex *Ocean Betelguese* 1978; ex *Doun Maru* 1976
61634 **DONG AH** (Ko) ex *Oshima Maru* 1973
61635 **PRONAOS** (Pa) ex *Rambut* 1978; ex *Eimei Maru* 1977
61636 **DAE YANG** (Ko) ex *Shoyo Maru* 1973
61637 **ROUBINI II** (Cy) ex *Roubini* 1983; ex *Nagos* 1982; ex *Amagi Maru* 1979
61638 **VARDE** (Pa) ex *Hengshan* 1983; ex *Shinko Maru* 1979

●61640 **BO CHURN** Ko/Ja (Hashihama) 1970; C; 3200; 101.05 × 6.61 (331.53 × 21.69); M (Kobe); 12.75; ex *Calamus* 1978; ex *Gulf Gallant* 1977; ex *Kobe Maru No 7* 1975
Possible sisters:
61641 **KAISEI MARU** (Ja)
61642 **ASIAN NEPTUNE** (Pa) ex *Akihiro Maru* 1981
61643 **WAHYUNI** (Ia) ex *Kamellia* 1977; ex *Akiyoshi Maru* 1974
61644 **GOLDEN HARVEST** (Pa) ex *Kokai Maru* 1977; Launched as *Kenyo Maru*
61645 **SANKO MARU** (Ja)
61646 **HELIOS MARU** (Ja) ex *Shinwa Maru* 1975
61647 **ASIA SPICA** (Pa) ex *Shoshin Maru* 1980
61649 **SDR VICTORY** (Ia) ex *Yaett 1* 1981; ex *Shinyo Maru* 1973
61650 **YUWA MARU** (Ja) ex *Oriental Antelope* 1982; ex *Zuiryu Maru* 1974
61651 **DAYAKA TIGA** (Ia) ex *Kobne Maru* 1974
61653 **RIMBA DUA** (Ia) ex *Handseng* 1977; ex *Shunyo Maru* 1971
61654 **RAINBOW** (Ja) ex *Horyu Maru* 1975
61655 **SEATRAN SILVIA** (My) ex *Chamnarn Samut* 1981; ex *Hoei Maru* 1976
61656 **FLAMINGO** (Pa) ex *Kowa Maru* 1979
61657 **PAKALONG SERAYA** (Ia) ex *Oriental Lion* 1974; ex *Ultramar* 1973; ex *Rokko Maru* 1972
61658 **LILAC ACE** (Pa) ex *Reiyo Maru* 1978
61659 **MOUNT BOLIVAR** (Pa) ex *Mount Palma* 1982; ex *Palma* 1980; ex *Knight* 1976; ex *Shuho Maru* 1975
61660 **HONAM** (Pa) ex *Basca* 1982; ex *Kokai Maru* 1976
Possibly similar:
61661 **EXPLORER** (Gr) ex *Good Explorer* 1983; ex *Maroriente* 1976; ex *Sundakan Maru* 1974
61662 **GREAT GUIDE** (Pa) ex *Anabel Glory* 1974; ex *Kinyo Maru* 1973
61663 **NISSHO MARU** (Ja)
61664 **SAM ICK** (Ko) ex *White Oak* 1975; ex *Asian Envoy* 1974; ex *Eisho Maru* 1971
61665 **SEO RA BUL** (Ko) ex *Namyang Ace* 1980; ex *Lucent* 1974; ex *Hoyo Maru* 1972; ex *Nippi Maru* 1972
61666 **TAIYO MARU** (Ja)
61667 **TOW TRADER** (Sg) ex *Shuyo Maru* 1973
★61668 **TRUONG VINH** (Vn) ex *Kyotoku Maru* 1973; ex *Shoyo Maru* 1970
61669 **NEO** (Cy) ex *Eihaku Maru* 1979

61670 **WOOSTER KING** Pa/Ja (Shinhama) 1974; C; 3500; 106.28 × 6.58 (348.69 × 21.59); M (Kobe); 12.5

★61675 **LIN SHAN** RC/Ja (Shikoku) 1970; C/HL; 3100; 99.47 × 6.35 (326 × 20.83); M (Hanshin); 12.5; ex *Don Rufino* 1974
Sister:
★61676 **SHEN SHAN** (RC) ex *Dona Marcelina* 1974

61680 **HAPPY STAR** Ko/Ja (Kurushima) 1975; C/HL; 3800; 106.46 × 7.11 (349.28 × 23.33); M (Sulzer); 16; ex *Boswick* 1981
Sister:
61681 **ALDRICH** (Li)

61690 **CAP BAITAR** FRG/Ja (Ujina) 1977; C; 4600; 118.01 × 6.96 (387.17 × 22.84); M (MAN); 14.5; ex *Max Bastian* 1977
Sister:
61691 **CAP BIZERTA** (FRG) ex *Inga Bastian* 1977

61700 **MEHMET KEFELI** Tu/DDR ('Neptun') 1973; C; 5900; 121.75 × 7.73 (399.44 × 25.36); M (MAN); 15.5; ex *Belle Isle* 1982; ex *Bellea* 1981; ex *Split*

1978; ex *Jobella* 1977
Sisters:
61701 **BRUNLA** (Sg)
61702 **BRUNHORN** (Sg)
61703 **CLYMENE** (Br) ex *Barbizon*; ex *Oyapok* 1978; ex *Jocare* 1977
61704 **ARC MINOS** (Gr) ex *Bougival*; ex *Bochica* 1978; Launched as *Jodew*
61705 **CHARLOTTE BASTIAN** (Pa) ex *Joada* 1978
61706 **PIRKKOLA** (Fi) ex *Savonia* 1980; ex *Hetland Ranger* 1978; ex *Hansa* 1974
61707 **MOUTSAINA** (Gr)
★61708 **HETTSTEDT** (DDR) ex *Jobebe* 1977
★61709 **BURG** (DDR) ex *Joboy* 1977
★61710 **AKEN** (DDR)
★61711 **FREITAL** (DDR)
★61712 **KOTHEN** (DDR)
Probable sisters:
61713 **BAUNTON** (Pa)
61714 **MANOLIS L** (Gr)
61715 **TRAUN** (As)
61716 **WELLWOOD** (Cy)
61717 **GAVIOTA** (FRG) ex *Gaviota II* 1983

61720 **MOKHA** Si/DDR ('Neptun') 1967; C; 2600/4000; 112.1 × 7.17 (367.78 × 23.52); M (Werkspoor); 13.5; ex *Eurabia Spring* 1978; ex *Clari* 1975; ex *Karlsburg* 1970; ex *Claudia Maria* 1967
Sister:
61721 **LE ROVE** (Fr) ex *Scol Independent* 1975; ex *Germanica* 1975; ex *Wilri* 1975; ex *Germanic* 1974; ex *Wilri* 1974; ex *Atlanta* 1973
Similar:
61722 **TRITON** (Gr) ex *Irenes Sun* 1980; ex *Blockland* 1977; ex *Jiri* 1969; ex *Hoegh Jiri* 1968; ex *Jiri* 1966
61723 **ORION** (Gr) ex *Irenes Sea* 1981; ex *Werderland* 1977; ex *Wilri* 1969; ex *Hoegh Wilri* 1969; ex *Wilri* 1967
61724 **CAPTAIN COSMAS M** (Pa) ex *Conti Almania* 1982; ex *Grimsnis* 1975; ex *Hein Jenevelt* 1970; ex *Bari* 1968
61725 **SANAA** (Si) ex *Eurabia Progress*; ex *Claudia Maria* 1975
61726 **BILSTEIN** (FRG) ex *Duburg* 1980; ex *Bilstein* 1978; ex *Conti Syria* 1978; ex *Antony* 1977; ex *Bilstein* 1975; ex *Hoegh Susann* 1968; Launched as *Susan Von Bargen*
61727 **LIDES** (Pa) ex *Cavally* 1983; ex *Rinkenis* 1975; ex *Dirk von Minden* 1970; ex *Mari* 1968; ex *Hoegh Mari* 1968; ex *Mari* 1967

61730 **PATROKLOS 1** Pa/Ja (Mitsubishi HI) 1957; C; 10300; 154.84 × 9.36 (508.01 × 30.71); T (Mitsubishi); —; ex *Alhaja Mama Bakare* 1982; ex *Tharros* 1977
Similar:
61731 **DUPE BAKARE** (Pa) ex *Rythme* 1977

61740 **DJATIPURA** Ia/Ja (Hakodate) 1961; C; 9900; 157.03 × 9.02 (515.19 × 29.59); M (MAN); 15; ex *South Breeze* 1976

61750 **KALENTZI** Gr/Fr (Nantes) 1964/71; C; 4600/7600; 159.19. × 6.68/7.92 (522 × 22.0/30.01); M (Pielstick); —; ex *Giant Pilot* 1981; ex *Gold Pilot* 1978; ex *Hadar* 1977; Lengthened 1971

●61760 **LEDRA** Ma/Br (Bartram) 1959; B; 10100; 158.05 × 9.68 (518.54 × 31.76); M (Doxford); 14.25; ex *Sea Ranger* 1984; ex *Wandby* 1972

●61761 **ARCHIMEDES** Gr/Ja (Osaka) 1966; B; 16100; 171.33 × 10.23 (562.11 × 33.56); M (B&W); 15; 'Algonquin II' type
Sisters (Gr flag):
61771 **APOLLONIUS**
61772 **CAPETAN PSARROS**
61773 **CAPETAN RAHIOTIS** ex *Capetan Yemelos* 1975

★61780 **BANIJA** Ys/Ys ('Split') 1966; B; 16900; 187.03 × 10.74 (613.62 × 35.24); M (Fiat); 16
Sister:
★61781 **BOSANKA** (Ys)

61800 **SEMIRA** Gr/Sw (Uddevalla) 1965; B; 11900; 165.06 × 10.05 (541.54 × 32.97); M (B&W); 17; ex *Cesira* 1980; ex *Norse Carrier* 1976
Similar (taller funnel):
61801 **REGAL SCOUT** (Pa) ex *Mary Stove* 1974

61810 **STAR CARRIER** Ko/Ja (Hakodate) 1967; B; 16200; 178.52 × 10.39 (585.7 × 34.09); M (MAN); 15.5; ex *Valiant Racer* 1978; ex *Hoegh Musketeer* 1974
Similar:
61811 **PAN PACIFIC** (Ko) ex *Hoegh Marlin* 1974
61812 **AVON** (Gr) ex *Hoegh Merchant* 1974
61813 **BARRY** (Gr) ex *Hoegh Merit* 1974
★61814 **YANG ZONG HAI** (RC) ex *Southern Ruby* 1978; ex *Hoegh Mallard* 1974

61820 **GLYFADA MIMI** Gr/No (Tangen) 1965; B;

12900; 164.9 × 10.18 (541.01 × 33.4); M (B&W); 15; ex *Belmar* 1978; ex *Hoegh Belmar* 1971; ex *Belmar* 1970

★61840 **YAKHROMA** Ru/No (Tangen) 1967; B; 13000; 166.45 × 10.17 (546.1 × 33.37); M; (B&W); 15.5; ex *Farmand* 1973
Sister:
61841 **UNION PRIDE** (Gr) ex *Blanca* 1972

61860 **ERGINA 1** Pa/De (B&W) 1961; B; 10300; 152.43 × 9.36 (500.1 × 30.71); M (B&W); 13.5; ex *Byzantion* 1978; ex *Paraskevi Yemelos* 1973; ex *Mogen* 1971; ex *Stove Transport* 1969
Similar:
61861 **NESTOR** (Pa) ex *Tetien* 1983; ex *Robert Kabelac* 1972

61870 **AETOS** Gr/No (Bergens) 1965; B; 18500; 185.63 × 11.18 (609.02 × 36.68); M (B&W); 15.5; ex *Basil III* 1982
Sister:
61871 **TRITON C** (Gr) ex *Aegean Triton* 1980

●61880 **GRECIAN FLAME** Gr/Fr (L'Atlantique) 1962; B; 15400; 178.24 × 10.02 (584.78 × 32.87); M (B&W); 15
Sisters:
61881 **KING NESTOR** (Gr)
61882 **URANIA C** (Gr)
61883 **PETROS V** (Gr) ex *Marine Grande*; ex *Cape Marina* 1969; ex *Marina Grande* 1966
★61884 **ZHEN HAI** (RC) ex *Timor Sea* 1974; ex *Destrehan* 1972
★61885 **ZHU HAI** (RC) ex *Ceram Sea* 1973; ex *Victoria 1* 1972; ex *Victoria* 1968

61890 **ANTONIA** Gr/Ja (Hitachi) 1963; B; 13900; 176.87 × 10.42 (580.28 × 34.19); M (B&W); 15.5; ex *Kyriakoula* 1980; ex *Delphic Sky* 1980

●61900 **MARINA** It/Br (Fairfield SB) 1964; B; 17800; 194.7 × 10.4 (638.78 × 34.12); M (Sulzer); 15; ex *Chikuma* 1976; ex *Wilkawa* 1974; ex *Australian City* 1969
Sister:
61901 **CHIYODA** (Gr) ex *Eastern City* 1970

61910 **PEGASOS** Gr/Ja (Namura) 1966; B; 12400; 155 × 9.17 (508.53 × 30.09); M (B&W); 14.5; ex *Galissa* 1980; ex *Syra* 1976; ex *Dona Corazon* 1972; May be spelt PEGASUS

61920 **SATYA KAMAL** In/Ja (Fujinagata) 1967; B; 16500; 173.67 × 10.94 (569.78 × 35.89); M (Sulzer); 15.5; ex *World Union* 1973

61940 **MARATHA ENVOY** Br/Ja (Mitsubishi HI) 1968; B; 16500; 176.79 × 10.5 (580.02 × 34.45); M (Sulzer); 17

★61950 **CONG HUA** RC/Sw (Oskarshamns) 1962; C; 6700/9000; 148.62 × 8.54/9.32 (487.6 × 28.02/30.58); M (Stork); 15.75; ex *Vaasa Leader* 1973

★61960 **LONG HAI** RC/Be (Boelwerf) 1968; B; 25000; 203.77 × 11.48 (668.54 × 37.66); M (MAN); —; ex *Agioi Victores* 1974
Sister:
★61961 **PING HAI** (RC) ex *Ioannis N Pateras* 1974

61970 **AGIOS CONSTANTINOS** Gr/Ja (Sanoyasu) 1965; B; 14300; 179.1 × 10.14 (587.6 × 33.27); M (Sulzer); —; ex *Megalohari II* 1981

61980 **SETIF** Ag/Sw (Gotav) 1963; B; 12100; 157.99 × 9.71 (518.38 × 31.86); M (Gotaverken); 14.5; ex *Evina* 1971; ex *Saga Sailor* 1968; ex *Farland* 1967

61990 **EKTOR** Gr/Be (Boelwerf) 1970; B; 16300; 190.02 × 10.81 (623.43 × 35.47); M (MAN); 15
Sisters:
61991 **ERMIS** (Gr)
61992 **GAREFOWL** (Br) ex *Rossetti* 1978
61993 **REYNOLDS** (Br)

62000 **GOOD WIND** Pa/Sp (AESA) 1970; C; 11300; 147.02 × 9.87 (482.34 × 32.4); M (MAN); 16; ex *Good Helmsman* 1978; ex *David, Marquess of Milford Haven* 1973; 'Santa-Fe' type
Sister:
62001 **PAPHOS** (Cy) ex *Panagia Myrtidiotissa* 1984; ex *Jocelyne* 1980

62010 **MARATHON LAKE** Gr/No (Kaldnes) 1962; B; 8900; 152.48 × 8.99 (500.26 × 29.49); M (MAN); 13.5; ex *Ptolemais* 1979; ex *Jeanine* 1972; ex *Beltana* 1968
Sister:
62011 **AGORAS** (Ma) ex *Mathios* 1982; ex *Polyfyton* 1978; ex *Marita* 1972

62020 **POLLY** Li/Tw (Taiwan SB) 1977; B; 17900; 181.31 × 10.28 (594.85 × 33.73); M (Sulzer); 15

62021 **ROSSANA** (Li) ex *Juliana* 1980
Similar:
62022 **CAMERONA** (Li)
62023 **FRANCES** (Li) ex *Irene* 1981
★62024 **BUDVA** (Ys) launched as *Pacific Endeavour*
Possibly similar:
62025 **ALLY** (Tw)
62026 **DIANNA** (Pa) ex *Anita* 1981
62027 **ZORINA** (Pa) ex *Christina* 1982
62028 **EVER RELIANCE** (Tw)
62029 **GINGER** (Pa) ex *Harriet* 1982
62030 **FLORENCE** (Li) ex *Jeannie* 1981
62031 **MING BELLE** (Tw)
62032 **TAI SHING** (Tw)
62033 **VIRTUOUS** (Tw)
62034 **LUCINA** (Li)
62035 **SILVER CLIPPER** (Li)
62036 **TAUROS** (Gr)
62037 **HARMONY SEA** (Pa) ex *Justina* 1980
62038 **SALCANTAY** (Pe) ex *Righteous* 1973

★62060 **PIRAN** Ys/Ja (Hakodate) 1959; C; 8000/10600; 158.25 × —/9.70 (519.19 × —/31.82); M (Sulzer); 14

62070 **LORD BYRON** Gr/Sp ('Astano') 1964; C; 4200/6500; 127.23 × 6.96/8.34 (417.42 × 22.83/27.36); M (Gotaverken); —; ex *North Star* 1973; ex *Alex* 1973

●62075 **BAMENDA PALM** Br/Ko (Hyundai) 1979; C/Con; 6900/11200; 149.82 × —/9.64 (492 × —/31.63); M (MAN); 17

62080 **GOLDEN BENIN** Pa/Ja (Osaka) 1968; C; 6200/9900; 145.7 × 7.92/9.27 (478.02 × 25.98/30.41); M (B&W); 15.5; ex *Protoklitos* 1982; ex *Silja Dan* 1975; ex *Sylvia Cord* 1973; 'Mitsui Concord' type
Sister:
★62081 **FU PING** (RC) ex *Margaret Cord* 1977

62085 **FLORENCE SCHRODER** FRG/FRG (Rickmers) 1976; C/Con; 6700; 139.33 × 7.82 (457 × 25.66); M (MaK); 14.5
Sister:
62086 **FRANK SCHRODER** (FRG)

★62100 **HUA YIN** RC/FRG (Bremer V) 1969; C; 6700/9400; 139.45 × —/9.2 (457.51 × —/30.18); M (MAN); 15.5; ex *Jens Jost* 1974; 'German Liberty' type
Similar:
62101 **AMATHUS** (Cy) ex *Sunfrancis* 1981; Launched as *Franciska Fisser*
62102 **FRANZ XAVER KOGEL** (Pa) ex *Olga Jacob* 1976
62103 **ELISABETH ROTH** (FRG)
62104 **BERTHA FISSER** (FRG) ex *Suncapri* 1973; Launched as *Bertha Fisser*
★62105 **PING DING SHAN** (RC) ex *Klaus Schoke* 1981; ex *Nyanga*; ex *Klaus Schoke*; ex *Verena Wiards* 1972
62106 **CAWA** (Pa) ex *Fjord Master* 1981
62107 **RIZCUN HONG KONG** (Br) ex *Pitria Star* 1980
62108 **ROBERTO** (Pa) ex *Paula Howaldt Russ* 1979; ex *Paula Howaldt* 1974

62110 **LEIDENSCHAFT** Li/Ja (Hitachi) 1972; C; 6900/10000; 145.01 × —/9.08 (475.75 × —/29.79); M (B&W); 14.5; 'UT-15' type
Sister:
62111 **LIECHTENSTEIN** (Li)

62120 **SPLENDID HOPE** Pa/Ja (Shin Yamamoto) 1974; B; 16800; 181.52 × 10.06 (592.26 × 34.74); M (Sulzer); 15; ex *Seiho Maru* 1978

62130 **FRANK DELMAS** Fr/Ja (Onomichi) 1975; B; 16700; 167.16 × 13.08 (548.43 × 42.91); M (Sulzer); 17.5

●62140 **ELEFTHERIOS** —/Ja (Fujinagata) 1965; B; 15400; 178.19 × 9.83 (584.61 × 32.25); M (Sulzer); 15; ex *Andros* 1983
Sisters:
62141 **ANTIGUA** (Gr)
62142 **POSEIDON L** (Pa) ex *Phaedra* 1982
62143 **TOKYO OLYMPICS** (Gr)

62150 **VASILAKIS** Gr/Ja (Uraga HI) 1968; B; 14800; 159.01 × 10.65 (521.69 × 34.94); M (Sulzer); 15.5; ex *Marcalan* 1983; ex *Verdala* 1978; ex *Shropshire* 1977; ex *Verdala* 1975

62160 **MUO** Pa/FRG (Flensburger) 1963; B; 9500; 153.98 × 9.13 (505.18 × 29.95); M (MAN); 13.5; ex *Bijela* 1983; ex *Rigel* 1977; ex *Splendid Breeze* 1977; ex *Executive Trader* 1974; ex *Bernhard* 1973; After kingpost may be removed

62170 **ARCADIAN SKY** Gr/Ja (Hakodate) 1965; B; 12200; 157.54 × 9.62 (516.86 × 31.56); M (Sulzer); 14.5; ex *Eastern Kiku*

Sister:
62171 **ARCADIAN FAITH** (Gr) ex *World Harmony*

★62180 **KOPER** Ys/Be (Boel) 1967; B; 9100; 149.41 × 8.59 (490.19 × 28.18); M (B&W); 12
Sister:
★62181 **KRPAN** (Ys)

★62190 **DACHENG** RC/Ja (Hitachi) 1973; C/HL; 6900/10700; 154.95 × —/9.08 (508.37 × —/29.79); M (B&W); 16.25
Sister:
★62191 **DATIAN** (RC)

62200 **OKPO PEARL** Ko/Ja (Mitsubishi HI) 1969; B; 10100; 146.01 × 9.35 (479.04 × 30.68); M (Sulzer); 14.5; ex *Cresta IV* 1980; ex *Kusunoki Maru* 1977

62210 **CENK** Tu/Ja (Sanoyasu) 1971; B; 9400; 147.53 × 9.27 (484 × 30.41); M (MAN); 14.75; ex *Eastern Mariner* 1983; '16 BC 5' type

●62220 **PACIFIC FAIR** Li/Ja (Sanoyasu) 1969; B; 10000; 143.54 × 9.16 (470.93 × 30.05); M (Sulzer); 15; ex *Union Wisdom* 1983
Sisters:
62221 **TIARA** (Gr) ex *Captain Lemos* 1982; ex *Union Friendship* 1976
62222 **KING GEORGE** (Pa) ex *Ever Faith* 1983
62223 **RENACIMIENTO** (Pa) ex *Cosmos Eltanin* 1977
Possible sisters:
62224 **ROYAN** (Pa) ex *Lombardy* 1981; ex *Petersberg* 1981; ex *Victoria* 1980; ex *Georgiana* 1979
62225 **KOSTAR** (Ko) ex *Katrina* 1978
62226 **MYUNG JIN** (Ko) ex *Pearl Venture* 1978

●62230 **ATAIR** Sg/Ja (Fukuoka) 1976; C; 7400; 127.79 × 8.05 (419.26 × 26.41); M (Mitsubishi); 13.25; ex *Merzario Asia* 1981; ex *Zepsea* 1980; ex *Gulf Unity* 1978; ex *Zepsea* 1977
Sisters:
62231 **CHARLOTTE** (Li) ex *Lily Venture* 1981
62232 **OCEAN ACE** (Ja)
62233 **RIGEL** (Sg) ex *Singapore Merchant* 1983; ex *Ace America* 1979; ex *Zephawk* 1978
Sister:
62234 **PACIFIC LEISURE** (Tw) ex *Ocean Express* 1982; ex *Bright Star* 1979
Possible sister:
62235 **SANTORIN** (Sg) ex *Kitty Porr*

62240 **ANITA 1** Cy/Ja (Watanabe) 1976; C; 5000; 117.61 × 7.3 (385.8 × 23.9); M (Mitsubishi) 16; ex *Anita* 1981
Sisters:
62241 **KAREN** (Gr)
62242 **HELEN SCHULTE** (Cy)
62243 **JOHANNA SCHULTE** (Cy)
62244 **NORDHEIM** (Sg)
62245 **NORDFELS** (Sg)
62246 **NORDHOLM** (Sg)
62247 **NORDMARK** (Sg)
62248 **RAUTE** (Cy) ex *Singapura* 1983; ex *Raute* 1979
62249 **RHOMBUS** (As) ex *Wachau* 1984; ex *Bayu* 1983; ex *Rhombus* 1979
62250 **TOROS ALIZE** (Tu) ex *Rio Explorer* 1983
62251 **KIRSTEN WESCH** (Sg)
62252 **CORAL VOLANS** (Li)
62253 **RAINBOW VOLANS** (Li)
62254 **NEPTUNE VOLANS** (Pa)

●62270 **HSIEH YUNG** Tw/Ja (Hayashikane) 1969; C; 5000; 117.05 × 7.43 (384.02 × 24.38); M (Kobe); 13; ex *Hsieh Ho* 1983; ex *Hsieh Yung* 1982
Possible sisters:
62271 **LUNG YUNG** (Tw)
62272 **OSMAN KURT** (Tu) ex *Mui Kim* 1983

62280 **CAPIRA** Pa/Ja (Shimoda) 1976; C; 5700; 116.06 × 7.62 (380.77 × 24.99); M (Ito Tekkosho); 12.5; ex *Koyo Maru* 1980; ex *Happusan Maru*

62290 **AGIOS LOUKAS** Pa/Ja (Kurushima) 1968; C; 4700; 117.46 × 6.91 (385.37 × 22.67); M (Sulzer); 13; ex *John P* 1982; ex *Kwong Fung* 1980; ex *Wah Fei* 1974; ex *Shinpo Maru* 1971

62300 **BONA** Pa/Ja (Kurushima) 1973; C; 6100; 126.04 × 7.85 (413.52 × 25.75); M (Kobe); 14; ex *Jesamine* 1981; ex *Jasmine* 1978
Possibly similar:
62301 **KATSURA MARU** (Ja)

62310 **ASIAN FALCON** Pa/Ja (Kanasashi) 1970; C/HL; 5600; 122.05 × 7.7 (400.43 × 25.26); M (Pielstick); 13.5; ex *Kamo Maru* 1981
Sister:
62311 **CENPAC 2** (NA) ex *Bright Moon* 1982; ex *Kyokyu Maru* 1978
Possible sister:
62312 **ALPHA PACIFIC** (Pa) ex *Kitano Maru* 1983

●62320 **SEALOGGER** Ma/Ja (Nipponkai) 1965; C; 6700; 130.1 × 7.99 (426.83 × 26.2); M (MAN); 13; ex *Eurologger* 1981; ex *Theoris* 1974; ex *Koyo Maru* 1972

62340 **MARKINA** Ve/Sp (Euskalduna) 1965; C; 3700; 111.69 × 6.09 (366.44 × 20); M (MAN); 12.75; ex *Maurine K* 1980; ex *Hannah Blumenthal* 1975; ex *Pinto* 1969

●62350 **ATLANTIC SKY** Gr/Bz (Ish do Brasil) 1962; C; 3900/5400; 115.3 × —/6.32 (378.28 × —/20.73); M (Sulzer); 12; ex *Volta Redonda* 1978
Sisters:
62351 **SUNNY MED** (Li) ex *Cidade De Belem* 1970
62352 **LONDRINA** (Bz)
62353 **MARILIA** (Bz)

★62360 **PRVIC** Ys/No (Lothe) 1972; C; 4200; 112.83 × 6.89 (370.18 × 22.6); M (Stork-Werkspoor); 13.75; ex *Lindo* 1981

62370 **EBN JUBAIR** Ly/Ja (Asakawa) 1976; C; 3500/6200; 105.7 × 7.5/7.62 (346.78 × 24.61/25); M (B&W); 13
Sister:
62371 **EBN BATUTA** (Ly)

62380 **UNITY** Ma/Br (Doxford & S) 1968; B; 28900; 218.35 × 12.56 (716.37 × 41.21); M (Doxford); 14.5; ex *Leda* 1982; ex *Ripon Grange* 1980; ex *Orotava* 1978; ex *Orotava Bridge* 1974; ex *Orotava* 1969

62390 **GAMBADA** Br/Br (Cammell Laird) 1973; LGC; 21360; 177.86×10.02 (583.5×32.9); M(B&W); 16.25;
Sister:
62391 **GAZANA** (Br)

62400 **MEITAI MARU** Ja/Ja (Mitsui) 1974; Tk; 123900; 324.01 × 19.51 (1063.03 × 64.01); M (B&W); 16

62405 **EUROCARRIER** Gr/Ja (Shin Yamamoto) 1973; RoVC/C; 16100; 153.24 × 10.52 (503 × 34.51); M (Mitsubishi); 13.75; ex *Tokusho Maru* 1976
Sister:
62406 **EASTERN GRACE** (Sg) ex *Shinyo Maru* 1979

●62410 **SKYRIAN ROVER** Gr/Sw (Uddevalla) 1958; 8600; 148.7 × 8.81 (487.86 × 28.9); M (Gotaverken); 15.25; ex *Skyrian Spirit* 1980; ex *Lefteris* 1980; ex *Sunriver* 1974

●62420 **JOULE** Br/No (Moss V) 1965; LGC; 8700; 141.33 × 9.52 (463.68 × 31.23); M (MAN); 16; ex *Havgas* 1974
Sister:
62421 **GAZ CHANNEL** (Pa) ex *Ocean Frost* 1982; ex *Havfrost* 1981

●62430 **BROTHER STAR** Ko/Br (Lithgows) 1970; B; 12900; 158.60 × 9.54 (520 × 31.3); M (Pielstick); 14.75; ex *Efthalia* 1980; ex *Manos Save* 1979; ex *Janet¦C* 1978; ex *Brisknes* 1974; ex *Aquila* 1971
Sisters:
62431 **BULKNES** (Br)
62432 **WESTBON** (Ko) ex *Baugnes* 1980
62433 **KAMPOS** (Gr) ex *Blidnes* 1980
62434 **LAPIS** (Pa) ex *Topaz* 1982; ex *Chios Pilot* 1980; ex *Argo Clyde*; ex *Silverclyde* 1979; ex *Baknes* 1974
62435 **DENNIS CARRIER** (Pa) ex *Chios Captain* 1982; ex *Argo Tweed*; ex *Silvertweed* 1979; ex *Binsnes* 1974

62440 **GOLDEN BENIN** Pa/Ja (Osaka) 1968; C; 6200/9900; 145.7 × 7.92/9.27 (478.02 × 25.98/30.41); M (B&W); ex *Protoklitos* 1982; ex *Silja Dan* 1975; ex *Sylvia Cord* 1973; 'Mitsui Concord' type
Sister:
★62441 **FU PING** (RC) ex *Margaret Cord* 1977

★62450 **DACHENG** RC/Ja (Hitachi) 1973; C/HL; 6900/10700; 154.95 × —/9.08 (508.37 × —/29.79); M (B&W); 16.25
Sister:
★62451 **DATIAN** (RC)

★62460 **ZVENIGOROD** Ru/Pd (Gdynska) 1967; B; 16000; 187.15 × 9.54 (614 × 31.29); M (Sulzer); 15.5; 'B 470' type
Sisters (Ru flag):
★62461 **ZAPOROZHY**
62462 **ZAKARPATYE**
★62463 **ZADONSK**
★62464 **ZARECHENSK**
★62465 **ZLATOUST**
★62466 **ZORINSK**
(Pd flag):
★62467 **ZIEMIA KRAKOWSKA**
★62468 **ZIEMIA LUBELSKA**
★62469 **ZAGLEBIE MIEDZIOWE**

★62480 **HAU GIANG** Vn/De (B&W) 1977; RoC; 9700; 132.92 × 9.4 (436.09 × 30.84); M (Alpha-Diesel); 15; Launched as *Hamlet Alice*: 'Hamlet Multiflex' type
Sisters:
62481 **PILBARA** (Au) ex *Hamlet Arabia* 1981
62482 **KOOLINDA** (Au) ex *Hamlet Saudia* 1981
★62483 **NEN JIANG** (RC) ex *Nópal Audrey* 1978
★62484 **IZVESTIYA** (Ru)
62485 **KIMBERLEY** (Au)
★62486 **KNUD JESPERSEN** (Ru) ex *Aleksey Stakhanov*

62490 **SIVAND** Ir/Ja (Mitsubishi HI) 1971; Tk; 108700; 326.02 × 19.01 (1070 × 62.37); T (Mitsubishi); 15.5; ex *British Navigator* 1976

62495 **LIBERTY BELL VENTURE** Li/Ja (Oshima Z) 1981; Tk; 31800; 225.03 × 12.52 (738 × 41.08); M (Sulzer); 15
Sisters:
62496 **EASTERN RANGER** (Li)
62497 **NORSE VENTURE** (Li)
62498 **OCEAN THISTLE** (Br) launched as *Asian Thistle*

62500 **AL ANDALUS** Ku/Sp ('Astano') 1975; Tk; 191000; 362.57 × 26.09 (1189.5 × 85.6); TST (Kawasaki); 14.5
Probable sister:
62501 **SANTA MARIA** (Sp) launched as *La Santa Maria*

62505 **PROSPECTOR II** Pa/Ja (Hitachi) 1982; B/Tk; 29000; 209.02 × 11.00 (686 × 36.09); M (B&W); 14.75; Launched as *Prospector*

62510 **MONTESA** Sp/Sp (Cadiz) 1969; Tk; 58800; 269.35 × 14.17 (884 × 46.14); M (Sulzer); —
Similar:
62511 **MUNATONES** (Sp)
Similar (converted to storage vessel 1982):
62512 **AFRAN ZENITH** (Li) ex *La Nina* 1979

62520 **AN ANNE** Li/Br (Lithgows) 1962; B; 9900; 152.56 × 8.66 (500.52 × 28.41); M (B&W); 14.75; ex *Kian An* 1982; ex *Bernes* 1972
Sister:
62521 **APILIOTIS** (Li) ex *Brimnes* 1970
Similar:
62522 **ELPIDA** (Gr) ex *Granton* 1978; ex *Binsnes* 1970

●62530 **GRANIKOS** Gr/FRG (Kieler H) 1961; B; 9400; 151.19 × 9.21 (496.03 × 30.22); M (Kieler H); 14.75; ex *Captain Pappis* 1980; ex *Ogooue* 1976; ex *Dracula* 1973; ex *Ringulv* 1969
Sister:
62531 **SILVERCORN** (Li) ex *Jagona* 1973

●62540 **MARTIN S** Pa/Br (Short Bros) 1961; C; 11900; 161.63 × 9.64 (530.28 × 31.63); M (B&W); 13.5; ex *Martis* 1982; ex *Arc* 1980; ex *Marco Botzaris* 1976; ex *Virana* 1967

●62550 **ELENI** Gr/FRG (Rhein Nordseew) 1960; C/V; 14600; 174.56 × 10.11 (572.7 × 33.17); M (Fiat); 14.75; ex *Evangelos Lemos* 1983; ex *Carl Trautwein* 1975; Lengthened & deepened 1966

★62570 **LUGANSK** Ru/Ja (Mitsubishi Z) 1962; Tk; 22100; 207.02 × 11.08 (679.2 × 36.35); M (Sulzer); 16.5
Sisters (Ru flag):
★62571 **LEBEDIN**
★62572 **LIKHOSLAVL**
★62573 **LUBNY**
★62574 **LENINO**
★62575 **LYUBLINO**
★62576 **LYUBERTSY**
★62577 **LUKHOVITSY** (may be spelt **LUHOVITSY**)

★62580 **DAUGAVPILS** Ru/Ys ('Split') 1965; Tk; 15100; 186.21 × 9.84 (610.93 × 32.28); M (B&W); 17
Sisters (Ru flag):
★62581 **GRIGORIY ACHKANOV**
★62582 **SPLIT**
★62583 **GORI**
★62584 **VASILIY PORIK**
★62585 **GENERAL ZHDANOV**
★62586 **MARSHAL BIRYUZOV**
★62587 **OLEKO DUNDICH**
★62588 **PETR ALEKSEYEV**
★62589 **BORZHOMI**
★62590 **GENERAL KARBYSHEV**
★62591 **DMITRIY ZHLOBA**
★62592 **NIKOLOZ BARATASHVILI**
★62593 **EPIFAN KOVTYUKH**
★62594 **MITROFAN SEDIN**
★62595 **MOS SHOVGENOV**
★62596 **STEPAN VOSTRETSOV**
★62597 **PYATIDYESYATILYETIYE SOVETSKOY GRUZII** (also known as **50 LETIYE SOVETSKOY GRUZII**)
★62598 **PAVEL DYBENKO**

★62599 **REZEKNE**
★62600 **RIJEKA**
★62601 **GENERAL BOCHAROV**
★62602 **GENERAL KRAVTSOV**
★62603 **GENERAL SHKODUNOVICH**
★62604 **NIKOLAY PODVOYSKIY**
(Ag flag)
62605 **SKIDA** ex *Kutaisi* 1974
62606 **ARZEW** ex *Batumi* 1974

★62610 **JING HAI** RC/Br (Lithgows) 1968; B; 12400; 159.06 × 9.47 (521.85 × 31.07); M (B&W); 14.75; ex *Baynes* 1973
Sisters:
62611 **KAPTAN YUSUF KALKAVAN** (Tu) ex *Albaforth* 1982; ex *Silverforth* 1978; ex *Bellnes* 1974
62612 **MARIA LEMOS** (Gr) ex *Captain Pandelis S Lemos* 1975; ex *Birknes* 1973
62613 **SATYA PADAM** (In) ex *Borgnes* 1973

●62630 **NEDLLOYD NIGER** Ne/FRG (Rickmers) 1971; C; 6500; 139.55 × 9.19 (457.84 × 30.15); M (MAN); 15.5; 'German Liberty' type

62640 **GOGO RANGER** Li/Sw (Lindholmens) 1958; Tk; 12500; 170.57 × 9.58 (559.61 × 31.43); M (Gotaverken); 15; ex *Post Ranger* 1977; ex *Anco Stripe* 1971; ex *Anco Bergljot* 1969; ex *Bergljot* 1964

62650 **SELAS** Gr/Ne (Nederlandsche) 1963; C; 8300/10900; 154.13 × 8.59/9.91 (505.68 × 28.18/32.51); M (Gotaverken); 15; ex *Jag Asha* 1976; ex *Dageid* 1967

62660 **ELENI** Gr/De (B&W) 1963; C; 10900; 158.25 × 9.51 (519.19 × 31.2); M (B&W); 16.25; ex *Novo Redondo* 1983; ex *Ferncape* 1970

62670 **PAPACAROLOS** Gr/Ja (Mitsubishi N) 1959; 0; 10200; 156.11 × 8.54 (512.17 × 28.02); M (MAN); 12; ex *Tomiura Maru* 1975

★62680 **KARL LIEBKNECHT** Ru/DDR (Mathias-Thesen) 1970; FC; 11900; 155 × 7.79 (508.53 × 25.58); M (MAN); 17.25; 'Polar' type
Similar (Ru flag):
★62681 **ERNST THALMANN**
★62682 **OTTO GROTEVOHL**
★62683 **WILHELM PIECK**
★62684 **ROSA LUXEMBURG**
★62685 **FRITZ HECKERT**
★62686 **MATHIAS THESEN**
★62687 **ANTANAS SNECHKUS** launched as *Ignalina*
★62688 **DIMANT**
★62689 **LAZURNYY BEREG**
★62690 **SOLNECHNYY BEREG**
★62691 **YANTARNIY BEREG**
★62692 **IZUMRUDNYY BEREG**
★62693 **GRANITNYY BEREG**
★62694 **SKALISTYY BEREG**
★62695 **ZHEMCHUYNYY BEREG**
(Rm flag):
★62696 **POLAR III**
★62697 **POLAR IV**
★62698 **POLAR V**
★62699 **POLAR VI**
Possibly similar (DDR flag):
★62700 **LICHTENHAGEN**

62710 **LUMUMBA** Zr/FRG (Bremer V) 1974; C; 6600/9400; 139.55 × —/9.17 (457.84 × —/30.09); M (MAN); 16; 'German Liberty' type
Sisters (Zr flag):
62711 **BANDUNDU**
62712 **BUKAVU**
62713 **KISANGANI**
62714 **MBANDAKA**
62715 **MBUJI-MAYI**

62720 **THASSOS** Gr/Sw (Gotav) 1958; Tk; 12400; 169.7 × 9.57 (556.75 × 31.4); M (Gotaverken); 14.75; ex *Pacifica* 1978; ex *Stolt Pacific* 1975; ex *Stolt Sildra* 1972; ex *Sildra* 1964; ex *Signe Ingelsson* 1964

★62730 **DUBNA** Ru/Fi (Rauma-Repola) 1974; RT; 6000; 130 × 7.19 (426.51 × 23.59); M (B&W); 16
Sisters (Ru flag):
★62731 **IRKUT**
★62732 **PECHENGA**
★62733 **SVENTA**

62740 **SISAL TRADER** Gr/Br (Cammell Laird) 1964; C; 5400/7600; 139.25 × 7.62/7.74 (456.86 × 25/25.39); M (Sulzer); 16.5; ex *Merchant*; ex *Scythia* 1969
Sisters:
62741 **STEEL TRADER** (Gr) ex *Scholar*; ex *Samaria* 1970

62750 **LUMUMBA** Zr/FRG (Bremer V) 1974; C; 6600/9400; 139.55 × —/9.17 (457.84 × —/30.09); M (MAN); 16; 'German Liberty' type
Sisters (Zr flag):
62751 **BANDUNDU**

62752 **BUKAVU**
62753 **KISANGANI**
62754 **MBANDAKA**
62755 **MBUJI-MAYI**

62760 **CIUDAD DE POPAYAN** Co/Pd (Gdanska) 1976; C; 11700/16100; 180.7 × 8.7/9.67 (592.85 × 28.54/31.73); M (Sulzer); 21; 'B-464' type
Sisters (Co flag):
62761 **CIUDAD DE NENA**
62762 **CIUDAD DE SANTA MARTA**
Similar (B-469 type):
62764 **CIUDAD DE PASTO** (Co)

62770 **SHUNKO MARU** Ja/Ja (Hitachi) 1974; Tk; 120500; 324.01 × 19.43 (1063.02 × 63.73); T (Kawasaki); 15.75
Similar:
62771 **HOKO MARU** (Ja)

62780 **JAPIN LUPINUS** Ja/Ja (Hitachi) 1972; Tk; 120500; 324.01 × 19.47 (1063.02 × 63.88); T (Kawasaki); 15.75
Sister:
62781 **JAPAN CARNATION** (Ja)
Similar:
62782 **WORLD ADMIRAL** (Li)
62783 **WORLD AMBASSADOR** (Li)
62784 **KHARK** (Ir)

●62790 **MELPO LEMOS** Li/FRG (A G 'Weser') 1971; Tk; 113800; 347.81 × 19.96 (1141.1 × 65.55); T (GEC); 16
Sisters:
62791 **CHRYSANTHY M LEMOS** (Li)
62792 **IRENE LEMOS** (Li)
62793 **MICHAEL C LEMOS** (Gr)

62820 **LORETO II** Pe/Fr (La Ciotat) 1976; Tk; 44500; 250.53 × 14.25 (820.96 × 46.75); M (CCM); 16; ex *St Vincent* 1983
Sisters:
62821 **PLAKOURA** (Li) ex *St Marcos* 1983; ex *Dominant* 1977
62822 **TOURAINE** (Fr) ex *Changi Star* 1980; ex *St Raphael* 1977; ex *Adamant* 1977

62830 **LEPTON** Li/Ne (Verolme Dok) 1975; Tk; 155300; 352.61 × 22.35 (1156.86 × 73.33); T (GEC)
—
Similar:
62831 **ANNIE** (Fi) ex *Lembulus* 1981

62840 **ESSO NORMANDIE** Fr/Fr (L'Atlantique) 1974; Tk; 137600; 343.04 × 21.06 (1125.46 × 69.09); T (Stal-Laval); 16
Sisters:
62841 **ESSO PICARDIE** (Fr)
62842 **ESSO AFRICA** (Bs)

62850 **AGIP SICILIA** It/It (Italcantieri) 1972; Tk; 126100; 348.32 × 20.02 (1142.78 × 65.68); M (Fiat); 16
Sisters:
62851 **AGIP SARDEGNA** (It)
62852 **HENRIETTE II** (Gr) ex *Paraggi* 1981; ex *Sant' Ambrogio* 1978
62853 **NIRVANA** (It) ex *Oceania* 1977
Possible sisters (It flag):
62854 **AGIP ABRUZZO**
62855 **AGIP CAMPANIA**
62856 **AGIP LAZIO**
62857 **AGIP MARCHE**
62858 **NAI MARIO PERRONE**
62859 **NAI DI STEFANO**
62860 **NAI MATTEINI**
62861 **NAI ROCCO PIAGGIO**
62864 **VOLERE**

62870 **THEOMITOR** Gr/Ja (Mitsui) 1970; Tk; 99200; 324.29 × 19.28 (1064 × 63.25); T (IHI); 16; ex *Perch* 1983; ex *Paula* 1980; ex *Ardvar* 1979

62875 **FAIRFIELD VENTURE** Li/Ja (Koyo) 1981; Tk; 29800; 228.73 × 11.92 (750 × 39.11); M (B&W); 14.25
Probable sister:
62876 **BUENA VENTURA** (Gr)

62880 **LUNA** Cy/Ja (Hitachi) 1969; Tk; 93500; 305.7 × 16.99 (1002.95 × 55.75); M (B&W); 15.75; ex *Platres* 1983; ex *Golden Mariner* 1982; ex *Nikko Maru* 1980

62890 **MOBIL KESTREL** Li/Ja (Mitsui) 1970; Tk; 104400; 324.01 × 19 (1063.02 × 62.34); M (B&W); 15.75; ex *Mitsuminesan Maru* 1977

●62900 **TANTALUS** Br/Ja (NKK) 1972; 00; 120800; 327.82 × 19.1 (1075.53 × 62.66); T (Mitsubishi); 15.5
Similar:
62901 **ALSTER ORE** (Pa) ex *Tsurumi* 1982; ex *Tsurumi Maru* 1982
62902 **DONAU ORE** (Li) ex *World Era* 1981; ex *Jarl*

Malmros 1979
62903 **WORLD LADY** (Li) ex *Tartar* 1978
Similar (larger):
62904 **DOCECANYON** (Li)

62910 **OLYMPIC ASPIRATION** Li/Fr (L'Atlantique) 1972; Tk; 106100; 329.85 × 19.41 (1082 × 63.71); T (Stal-Laval); 15.75
Sister:
62911 **OLYMPIC AVENGER** (Li)

62940 **PROSPERITY** Li/Ko (Hyundai) 1974; Tk; 124700; 344.43 × 20.77 (1130.02 × 68.14); T (Stal-Laval); 16; ex *Atlantic Baron* 1977
Sister:
62941 **KOREA SUN** (Ko) launched as *Atlantic Baroness*
Possible sisters:
62942 **KOREA STAR** (Ko)
62493 **KOREA BANNER** (Ko)
62944 **CATTLEYA** (Li)

62950 **MAASBREE** Ne/Ja (IHI) 1973; Tk; 135400; 337.07 × 21.05 (1105.87 × 69.06); T (IHI); 16; ex *Sinde* 1973

62960 **ASIATIC** Gr/Ja (IHI) 1971; OBO; 70500; 290.99 × 17.03 (953 × 55.87); T (IHI); 16.5
Sisters (Gr flag):
62961 **SYMPHONIC**
62962 **CLASSIC**
62963 **AUTHENTIC**

62970 **WORLD DUKE** Pa/Ja (Mitsui) 1975; Tk; 111400; 324.01 × 20.03 (1063.03 × 65.68); T (Stal-Laval); 16.5

62980 **JAPAN VIOLET** Ja/Ja (Kawasaki) 1974; Tk; 116300; 319.95 × 19.66 (1049.7 × 64.5); T (Kawasaki); 16.25; Launched as *World Consul*
Similar:
62981 **ENERGY GROWTH** (Li)

62990 **PAUL L FAHRNEY** Li/Ja (Mitsubishi HI) 1971; Tk; 118860; 337.5 × 20.49 (1107.3 × 67.2); T (Nagasaki); 15.5
Sister:
62991 **J R GREY** (Li)

63000 **ELENI P** Pa/Ja (Mitsubishi HI) 1972; 00; 95000; 295.03 × 17.5 (967.95 × 57.42); T (Mitsubishi); 16; ex *Cypress King* 1981: Launched as *Taiko Maru*

●63020 **OGDEN SUNGARI** Li/Ja (Sumitomo) 1975; Tk; 124100; 338.87 × 21.01 (1111.78 × 68.93); T (Toyo); 16
Similar:
63021 **MOSCLIFF** (No)

63030 **SAUDI GLORY** Li/Ja (Sumitomo) 1974; Tk; 122300; 340.8 × 21.07 (1118.11 × 69.13); T (Stal-Laval); 16.25; ex *Mobil Mariner* 1974
Sisters:
63031 **AL HARAMAIN** (Li) launched as *Mobil Supplier*
63032 **ATHOS** (Fr)
63033 **D'ARTAGNAN** (Fr)
63034 **MOBIL FALCON** (Li)

63050 **USA MARU** Ja/Ja (IHI) 1972; 00; 142200; 337.02 × 21.02 (1105.71 × 68.96); T (IHI); 16

63060 **VENTURE AMERICA** Li/Ja (IHI) 1973; Tk; 119700; 337.12 × 21.01 (1106.04 × 68.93); T (IHI); 16; ex *Conoco America* 1978
Possibly similar:
63061 **VENTURE INDEPENDENCE** (Li) ex *Conoco Independence* 1978

63070 **KYPROS** Cy/Ja (Sumitomo) 1974; Tk; 122900; 340.8 × 21.07 (1118.11 × 69.13); T (Stal-Laval); 15.5; ex *Saint Marcet* 1983
Sisters (Li flag):
63071 **PRIMROSE**
63072 **VENTURE EUROPE** ex *Conoco Europe*
Probable sisters (Li Flag):
63073 **VENTURE CANADA** ex *Conoco Canada*
63074 **WORLD CANADA**

63080 **WORLD BERMUDA** Li/Ja (IHI) 1974; Tk; 117800; 336.99 × 21.05 (1105.61 × 69.06); T (IHI); 16; Launched as *World Monarch*

63090 **LAUREL WREATH** Li/Ja (IHI) 1975; BO; 27300; 286.65 × 22 (940.45 × 72.18); M (Sulzer); 15.5

63100 **AMAZON MARU** Ja/Ja (Hitachi) 1973; 00; 89500; 300.01 × 16.99 (984.28 × 55.74); M (B&W); 16; ex *Sanko Robin* 1980
Sister:
63101 **TRIPHAROS** (Li)
Similar:
63102 **WAKAZURA MARU** (Ja)
63103 **COBALT TRANSPORTER** (Tw) ex *Miranda*

Seaventure 1983; ex *Yamazuru Maru* 1983
63104 ZUIHO MARU (Ja)
63105 LARINA (Li)

63110 GOLDEN CLOVER Li/Ja (Mitsubishi HI) 1971; OBO; 89100; 295.03 × 17.45 (967.95 × 57.25); T (Mitsubishi); 16
Sisters (Li flag):
63111 GOLDEN TULIP
63112 WORLD SPLENDOUR
Possibly similar:
63113 EASTERN SPIRIT (Li)

63120 KAIMON MARU Ja/Ja (Mitsubishi HI) 1968; Tk; 95600; 300.24 × 18.01 (985.04 × 59.09); T (Mitsubishi); 15.75

● **63130 CARTHAGO-NOVA** Sp/Sp ('Astano') 1976 Tk; 136400; 344.33 × 20.1 (1129.69 × 65.94); T (Kawasaki); 15.5
Similar:
63131 BISHAH (Si) ex *Texaco London* 1983
63132 TEXACO SOUTH AMERICA (Pa)
63133 CANARIA (Gr) ex *Monica Maria* 1983
63134 MUNDACA (Sp)
63135 MUNGUIA (Sp)

63160 ARAGON Sp/Sp (AESA) 1976; Tk; 122600; 321.55 × 20.35 (1054.95 × 66.77); M (B&W); 15.25
Sister:
63161 GIBRALTAR (Sp)

63170 BARCELONA Sp/Sp (AESA) 1973; Tk; 122800; 334.02 × 19.81 (1095.87 × 64.99); M (B&W) 16.5
Similar (Li flag):
63171 AMOCO EUROPA
63172 AMOCO MILFORD HAVEN
63173 BON BATEAU ex *Amoco Singapore* 1983

63180 PILIO Gr/FRG (Howaldts DW) 1971; Tk; 109700; 325.99 × 20.65 (1069.52 × 67.75); T (Allgemeine); 15.5; ex *Sagitta* 1981

63190 WORLD SCHOLAR Li/Br (Lithgows) 1979; Tk; 126200; 344.43 × 20.68 (1130 × 68.10); M (B&W); 14
Sister:
63191 WORLD SCORE (Li); Aft section launched as *Cartsdyke Glen*

● **63220 LATONA** Fr/Fr (L'Atlantique) 1973; Tk; 138500; 343.04 × 21.36 (1125.46 × 70.08); T (Stal-Laval); 15.5
Sisters (Fr flag):
63221 LEDA
63222 LUCINA
63222/1 AUTAN ex *Labiosa* 1981
(Br flag):
63223 LATIRUS
63224 LATIA

63230 URANIA Gr/Fr (L'Atlantique) 1967; Tk; 105300; 324.72 × 18.99 (1065 × 62.30); T (Stal-Laval); 16; ex *Miralda* 1981

63240 SAPHIR Fr/Fr (L'Atlantique) 1973; Tk; 138200; 343.04 × 21.36 (1125.46 × 70.08); T (Stal-Laval); 16
Sisters:
63241 ISEULT (Fr)
63242 OPALE (Fr)

● **63260 GOKTURK** Tu/Fi (Valmet) 1977; Tk; 75000; 285.02 × 15.5 (935.1 × 50.85); M (B&W) 16.5; ex *Tornado* 1983; ex *Sommerstad* 1983
Sisters:
63261 ALTANO (Fi) ex *Sangstad* 1983
63262 CALDERETA (Fi) ex *Siljestad* 1983
63263 BUYUK HUN (Tu) ex *Solstad* 1983

63270 YPERMACHOS Pa/Ja (Mitsui) 1972; OO; 96700; 311.82 × 18.04 (1023.03 × 59.19); M (B&W); 15.25; ex *Arafura Maru* 1982
Sister:
63271 EMERALD TRANSPORTER (Tw) ex *Adria Maru* 1982

● **63280 AL RAFIDAIN** Iq/FRG (Bremer V) 1975; Tk; 16200; 351.44 × 22.38 (1153.02 × 73.43); T (Stal-Laval); 15.75; ex *Belfri* 1976
Sister:
63281 AMICA (No)

63300 GREGORIO DEL PILAR Pi/Ja (Hitachi) 1969; Tk; 105500; 324.93 × 18.97 (1066 × 62.24); T (Mitsubishi); 16; ex *Mytilus* 1981

63310 NOTOS Gr/Ja (Sasebo) 1964; Tk; 49100; 244.51 × 14.45 (802.2 × 47.41); M (MAN); 15.5; ex *Biyo Maru* 1984

63320 GARYVILLE Li/Ja (IHI) 1972; Tk; 65600; 274.94 × 17.32 (902.03 × 56.82); M (Sulzer); 15.75; ex *Fairfield* 1977
Sister:

63321 ORIENTAL PHOENIX (Li)

63325 SANKO HERON Pa/Ja (Onomichi) 1982; Tk; 34000; 235.80 × 12.23 (774 × 40.12); M (B&W); 14.5
Sister:
63326 KOYO MARU (Ja)

63330 GLOBTIK TOKYO Br/Ja (IHI) 1973; Tk; 238230; 378.88 × 28.2 (1243 × 92.5); T (IHI); 15
Sisters:
63331 GLOBTIK LONDON (Br)
63332 NISSEI MARU (Ja)
Similar:
63333 NISSEKI MARU (Ja)

63340 CAIRU Bz/Ja (IHI) 1974; Tk; 129400; 337.09 × 21.62 (1105.94 × 70.93); T (IHI); 15.75
Sister:
63341 VIDAL DE NEGREIROS (Bz)

63350 GRESHAM Li/Ja (IHI) 1975; Tk; 104400; 317 × 20.79 (1040.03 × 68.21); T (IHI); 16
Probable sister:
63351 LOMBARD (Li)

63360 AZARPAD Ir/Ja (IHI) 1975; Tk; 122000; 317 × 20.78 (1040.68 × 68.18); T (IHI); 16
Similar:
63361 GEKKO MARU (Ja) ex *Golden Daffodil* 1980
63362 EISHO MARU (Ja)
63363 WORLD DIPLOMAT (Li)

63370 KIRSTEN MAERSK De/De (Odense) 1975; Tk; 167200; 370.47 × 22.46 (1215.45 × 73.69); T (Stal-Laval); 15.75
Similar (De flag):
63372 KAREN MAERSK
63373 KAROLINE MAERSK
63374 KATE MAERSK
63375 KATRINE MAERSK
63376 KRISTINE MAERSK

● **63390 AMURIYAH** Iq/Sw (Gotav) 1977; Tk; 81200; 285.02 × 17.15 (935.11 × 56.27); M (B&W); 16.25
Sisters:
63391 ALMUSTANSIRIYAH (Iq)
63392 ALQADISIAH (Iq)
63393 PERSEUS (Li)
63394 ZENIT AURORA (Li) ex *Messiniaki Fisis* 1983
63395 ZENIT BELLONA (Li) ex *Messiniaki Frontis* 1983
63396 ELFWAIHAT (Ly)
63397 ELGURDABIA (Ly)
63398 BRALANTA (No)
63399 SIR JOHN (Gr) ex *Johaki* 1981; ex *Esthel* 1980
63400 MARGAUX (Gr) ex *Limousin* 1981
63401 THALASSINI DOXA (Gr)
63402 WILNORA (No) ex *Thalassini Niki* 1979

63410 AMERICA SUN US/US (Sun SB) 1969; Tk; 37300; 249.33 × 13.29 (818.01 × 43.6); T (GEC); 16.5
Sister:
63411 GLACIER BAY (US) ex *Joseph D. Potts* 1977
Probable sisters:
63412 SOHIO INTREPID (US)
63413 SOHIO RESOLUTE (US)
Similar (larger):
63414 MOBIL ARCTIC (US)

● **63420 POGEEZ** Li/FRG (Howaldts DW) 1974; Tk; 110000; 326.02 × 20.65 (1070 × 67.75); T (Allgemeine); 15.25; ex *St Benedict* 1983; ex *Minerva* 1982
Sisters:
63421 GOOD NEWS (Li) ex *Egmond* 1982
63422 SANKO STRESA (Li)
63423 ENERGY RENOWN (Li) ex *Schleswig-Holstein* 1983
63424 NINEMIA (Gr) ex *Niedersachsen* 1983
63425 VIRGINIA (Pa) ex *Victoria* 1983
63426 SANKO CREST (Li)
63427 HAVDROTT (No)

63440 WORLD RECOVERY Li/FRG (Howaldts DW) 1973; OO; 126000; 327.74 × 20.5 (1075.26 × 67.26); T (A G 'Weser'); 15.5; ex *Havkong* 1976
Sister:
63441 KONKAR DINOS (Gr) ex *Falkefjell* 1976

63450 SAUDA It/Sw (Gotav) 1974; OBO; 61500; 256.85 × 17.07 (842.68 × 56); M (B&W); 15.25
Sisters:
63451 OSLO (It)
63452 OBO PRINCESS (No) ex *Britannia Team* 1981; ex *Angelic Blessing* 1978
63453 FERNTEAM (No) ex *Gothia Team* 1981; ex *Angelic Harmony* 1978
63454 MOHAWK (Li) ex *Nordic Sky* 1980; ex *Angelic Sky* 1977
63455 FJORDAAS (No) ex *Bjorgholm* 1981
63456 HAVPRINS (No)
63457 JAG LAXMI (In)

63458 JAG LEELA (In)
63459 MAHARISHI DAYANAND (In)
63460 MAHARISHI KARVE (In)

63470 GOLDEN ARROW Gr/Fr (L'Atlantique) 1967; OBO; 51600; 250.86 × 14.54 (823.03 × 47.7); M (B&W); 15; ex *Amalia II* 1984; ex *Jacques Cartier* 1978

63480 MARINICKI Cy/Br (Sunderland) 1973; OBO; 86100; 291.85 × 18.22 (975.51 × 59.78); M (B&W); 15.5; ex *Cast Fulmar* 1983; ex *Nordic Crusader* 1980; ex *Naess Crusader* 1974
Similar:
63481 HELM (Br) ex *Cast Heron* 1983; ex *Nordic Chieftain* 1980

63490 WORLD PATHFINDER Li/Br (Swan Hunter) 1971; OBO; 77300; 294.19 × 18.44 (965.19 × 60.5); M (B&W); 15.5; ex *Marcona Pathfinder* 1983; ex *Lake Arrowhead* 1982; ex *Furness Bridge* 1977
Sister:
63491 IRON TRANSPORTER (Tw) ex *Tyne Bridge* 1983
Similar:
63492 SIR ALEXANDER GLEN (Br)
63493 KONA (Br) ex *Cast Kittiwake* 1983; ex *Nordic Challenger*; ex *Sir John Hunter*
63494 CRYSTAL TRANSPORTER (Tw) ex *Mercurio* 1983; ex *Sunshine* 1980; ex *English Bridge* 1979

63500 OBO ZIHNI Tu/Ja (Kawasaki) 1970; OBO; 57500; 250.05 × 15.52 (820.37 × 50.92); M (MAN); 15.5; ex *Hoegh Rainbow* 1982
Sisters:
63501 DAEYANG CHARITY (Ko) ex *Hoegh Rover* 1982
63502 TREADWIND (Br) ex *Vega Seal* 1982; ex *Hoegh Robin* 1978
Similar:
63503 DAEYANG BOUNTY (Ko) ex *Hoegh Rider* 1982

63510 BELOBO No/FRG (Bremer V) 1974; OBO; 42800; 253.63 × 14.24 (832.12 × 46.72); M (MAN); 15
Sisters:
63511 SKYE TRADER (Br) ex *Tai Cheung* 1983; ex *Obo Duke* 1980
63512 SIBOSIX (No) ex *Jarmina* 1980; (Being used as storage vessel at Singapore)
Possible sister:
63513 SOUTH PEARL (Li) ex *Arica* 1983

63520 DELAWARE Li/FRG (Bremer V) 1973; OBO; 42400; 253.68 × 14.23 (832.28 × 46.69); M (MAN); 15.25; ex *Saxonia* 1984; ex *Mercedes*

63530 FINA NORVEGE Be/Be (Boel) 1965/67; Tk; 39500; 249.26 × 12.54 (817.78 × 41.14); M (B&W); 17; Aft section 1965, forward and cargo sections 1967 (Cockerill)

63540 ARCHONTISSA KATINGO Gr/Ys ('Split') 1972; BO; 42300; 252.38 × 14.82 (828.02 × 48.62); M (MAN); 15
Sister:
63541 SIBOTEM (Li) ex *Transud III*; ex *Diamantis Pateras* 1979
Possibly similar:
63542 NORMAN ATLANTIC (Sg) ex *Annitsa Carras*

● **63550 LAKE MENDOCINO** Li/Ja (Sumitomo) 1971; OBO; 71600; 266.02 × 18.1 (872.77 × 59.38); M (Sulzer); 15.5; ex *Avon Bridge* 1976
Sisters (Br flag):
63551 BISE ex *Cast Petrel* 1983; ex *Eden Bridge*
63552 OAK STAR ex *Cast Gull* 1983; ex *Silver Bridge*
63553 CHILI ex *Cast Puffin* 1983; ex *Enterprise Transporter*; ex *Australian Bridge* 1978

63560 MOTILAL NEHRU In/Ys ('Split') 1973; OBO; 62900; 254.52 × 16.87 (835.04 × 55.35); M (MAN); 16
Sister (In flag):
63561 ABUL KALAN AZAD
Similar (In flag):
63562 VALLABHBHAI PATEL
63563 VALLATHOL

63565 HOEGH FALCON No/FRG (Howaldts DW) 1981; OBO; 45800; 246.95 × 14.95 (810 × 49.05); M (B&W); 15
Sister (satellite aerial on radar mast):
63566 HOEGH FAVOUR (No)

★ **63570 BORIS BUTOMA** Ru/Ru (Okean) 1978; BO; 63200; 258.22 × 15.65 (847.17 × 51.34); M (B&W); 15; ex *Oktyabrsk*
Sisters (Ru flag):
★ **63571 AKADEMIK KRYLOV**
★ **63572 AKADEMIK PAVLOV**
★ **63573 AKADEMIK SECHENOV**
★ **63574 NIKOLAY ZHUKOVSKIY**

63580 TRADE INDEPENDENCE Gr/Ja (Kawasaki D) 1967; Tk; 72400; 265.01 × 15.98 (869 × 52.43); M (MAN); 15.75; ex *Kinokawa Maru* 1976

63590 NICOS I VARDINOYANNIS Gr/Br (Lithgows) 1971; Tk; 65300; 274.4 × 16.96 (900.26 × 55.64); M (B&W); 16; ex *Gold Star* 1973

63610 YUSHO Li/Ja (Hitachi) 1971; LGC; 47800; 227.03 × 11.51 (744.85 × 37.76); M (B&W); 15.75; ex *Yusho Maru* 1978

63620 PALACE TOKYO Ja/Ja (Hitachi) 1974; LGC; 64400; 246.11 × 12.7 (807.45 × 41.67); M (B&W); 16.5

63630 NORMAN LADY Br/No (Moss R) 1973; LGC; 76400; 249.51 × 10.62 (818.6 × 34.84); T (GEC); 19

★**63640 YURMALA** Ru/FRG (Meyer) 1976; LGC; 9100; 139.71 × 8.22 (458.37 × 26.97); M (B&W); 16.25
Sisters (Ru flag):
★**63641 BOLDURI**
★**63642 DUBULTY**
★**63643 DZINTARI**
★**63644 LIELUPE**
★**63645 MAYORI**

63650 CHEMTRANS WEGA FRG/FRG (Kroegerw) 1977; LGC; 7000; 112.76 × 7.5 (369.59 × 24.61); M (Atlas-MaK); 15; ex *Bavaria Multina* 1978

63655 PAUL FRG/FRG (Kroegerw) 1980; Ch/Tk; 1600; 89.21 × 5.66 (293 × 18.57); M (MWM); —
Sisters:
63656 GERHARD (FRG)
63657 RICHARD (FRG)
Similar (see inset):
63658 EBERHARD (FRG)

63660 AFRICAN HYACINTH Li/FRG (Elsflether) 1970; Tk; 1300; 81.59 × 5.2 (267.68 × 17.06); M (KHD); 12.5; ex *Oliver* 1982
Sister (lengthened 1976):
63661 ERIK (FRG)

63670 DENIZATI Tu/Tu (Marmara) 1978; C; 1600; 87.7 × 6 (287.73 × 19.69); M (Mirrlees Blackstone); 15

63680 ALEDREESI Iq/FRG (Buesumer) 1976; C; 1600; 81.62 × 6.1 (267.78 × 20.1); M (Atlas-MaK); 12.5
Sisters (Iq flag):
63681 ALZAWRAA
63682 ALKHANSAA
63683 ZANOOBIA
Similar:
63684 FLAMEL (Be) ex *Rosa Dania* 1983
★**63686 LIAN JIANG** (RC) ex *Calabar* 1979; ex *Annett Bentsen* 1978
★**63687 HUAN JIANG** (RC) ex *Susann Bentsen* 1978
63688 PEP ATLANTIC (De) ex *Alice Steen* 1980; ex *Baltic Sea*; ex *Alice Steen* 1979; ex *Baltic Sea* 1977
63689 EGE MELTEMI (Tu) ex *Mercandian Sea* 1976
63690 PEP ANTARES (De) ex *Mercandian Sky* 1981

63700 GULF DUCHESS Ne/FRG (Buesumer) 1977; C; 1600; 93.3 × 6.04 (306.1 × 19.82); M (Alpha-Diesel); 12.5; ex *Mercandian Moon* 1982
Sister:
63701 GULF EMPRESS (Ne) ex *Mercandian Star* 1982

63710 ABIRIBA Li/FRG (Buesumer) 1973; C; 1600; 89.34 × 5.86 (293 × 19.23); M (Alpha-Diesel); 13; ex *Birgitte B* 1980; ex *Birgitte Bentsen* 1978; ex *Wivi Bewa* 1977; Lengthened 1977
Similar:
63711 HANNATU (Li) ex *Gerda B* 1980; ex *Gerda Bentsen* 1978; ex *Conny Bewa* 1977
63712 ARWAD (Sy) ex *Viggo Scan* 1975
★**63713 STON** (Ys) ex *Heavy Scan* 1983
★**63714 KUTINA**

●**63720 BRAGA** No/No (Ulstein) 1970; RoC/C 1500; 87.03 × 6.15 (285.53 × 20.18); M (Werkspoor); 14.75; Side doors
Sister:
63721 BISMILLAH (No)

★**63730 GAN QUAN** RC/Fr (La Rochelle) 1970; R; 2000; 100.44 × 6.2 (329.53 × 20.34); M (KHD); —; ex *Sirara* 1980
Sister:
63731 ALMIRANTE (Ho) ex *Ea* 1979

63740 MINOGAZ 1 Gr/Ne ('De Gideon') 1955/64; LGC; 1000; 63.23 × 3.77 (207.45 × 12.37); M (British Polar); 12.25; ex *Cryomar* 1980; ex *Capo Cervo* 1972; ex *Abbas* 1968; ex *Broughty* 1963; Converted from general cargo 1964 (Hawthorn, L)

63750 MUNDIAL CAR Le/FRG (Sietas) 1965; C; 1000; 81.84 × 5.1 (268.5 × 16.7); M (KHD); 11; ex

---

Passat 1982

63760 NIKI AGUSTINA Pa/Ja (Miho) 1969; RoC; 2200; 95.41 × 6 (313.02 × 19.69); M (Pielstick); 14; ex *Shinju Maru* 1983; Stern doors

63770 NEWTON Br/Br (Scott Lithgow) 1976; A/Trials; 3900 Dspl; 98.6 × 5.7 (324 × 18.5); D-E (Mirrlees Blackstone); 15; Also serves as cable layer

63780 FORT FRASER Br/Ja (Mitsui) 1967; B 42400; 251.49 × 13.6 (825.09 × 44.61); M (B&W), 16; ex *Alcyone* 1980; ex *Fernie* 1979

63790 EEKLO Be/Be (Boelwerf) 1978; B; 38500; 242.02 × 13.83 (794. × 45.37); M (MAN); 16

63800 ATLANTIC EMPEROR Li/De (Odense) 1974; Tk; 128400; 347.23 × 22.32 (1139.21 × 73.23); T (Stal-Laval); 15.5

63820 RIMULA Br/Sw (Gotav) 1974; OO; 117200; 332.77 × 20.51 (1091.76 × 67.29); T (Stal-Laval); 16; ex *Ambrosiana* 1980; ex *Rinda* 1974
Sisters:
63821 RAPANA (Br) ex *San Giusto* 1980; ex *Runa* 1973
Similar:
63822 RUHR ORE (Li) ex *Sysla*

63830 M. CEYHAN Tu/Ja (Mitsui) 1971; Tk; 112700; 324.21 × 19.65 (1063.68 × 64.47); T (Westinghouse); 16; ex *Tish Pion* 1981; ex *British Pioneer* 1981
Possible sister:
63831 SHOUSH (Ir) ex *British Surveyor* 1978

63840 AVIN OIL TRADER Gr/Sw (Eriksbergs) 1968; Tk; 51100; 277.05 × 14.72 (908.95 × 48.29); M (B&W); 16; ex *Alexandros M* 1979; ex *Fruen* 1975; ex *Solstad* 1973

63850 HONAM RUBY Li/Ja (Kawasaki) 1970; Tk; 99000; 327.01 × 19.61 (1027.87 × 64.34); T (Kawasaki); 16.5; ex *Golar Nichu* 1980
Sister:
63851 GOLAR ROBIN (Li)
Similar:
63852 GOLAR KANTO (Li)
63853 GOLAR KANSAI (Li)
Possibly similar:
63855 HONAM TOPAZ (Li) ex *Fernmount* 1978

63860 YANBU PRIDE Si/Ja (Sasebo) 1971; Tk; 107600; 326.02 × 19.33 (1069.62 × 63.42); T (IHI) 16.75; ex *Mobil Pride* 1981
Sisters:
63862 YANBU PROGRESS (Si) ex *Mobil Progress* 1981
63863 MOBIL PETROLEUM (Li) ex *Al Bilad* 1983; ex *Mobil Petroleum* 1980

63870 HOEGH HOOD No/Ja (Kawasaki) 1973; OO; 129000; 326.04 × 20.49 (1069.68 × 67.22); T (Kawasaki); 15.5
Sisters:
63871 HOEGH HILL (No)
63872 WORLD TRUTH (Li) ex *La Loma* 1978

63880 SPYROS A LEMOS Gr/Ja (IHI) 1972; Tk; 103300; 322.99 × 19.73 (1059.6 × 64.73); T (IHI) 16.25; ex *Gondwana*

63890 ESSO DEUTSCHLAND FRG/Ja (Kawasaki) 1976; Tk; 203900; 378.01 × 22.98 (1240.19 × 75.39); T (Kawasaki); 15.75
Probable sister:
63891 HILDA KNUDSEN (No)
Possibly similar:
63892 CORRAGIO (It)
63893 ROBINSON (Li) ex *Golar Patricia*

●**63900 KOKKO MARU** Ja/Ja (Mitsubishi HI) 1973; Tk; 117600; 321.83 × 19.89 (1056 × 64.99); T (Mitsubishi) 15.75
63901 AMUR MARU (Ja)
63902 JAPAN ADONIS (Ja)
63903 JAPAN ASTER (Ja)
63904 HOEN MARU (Ja)
63905 TOKIWA MARU (Ja)
63906 TOTTORI MARU (Ja)

63910 GEORGE M KELLER Li/Ja (Mitsubishi HI) 1972; Tk; 118300; 337.5 × 20.52 (1107.28 × 67.32); T (Mitsubishi); 15.75
Sister:
63911 HOWARD W BELL (Li)

63930 SOUTH ANGELA Li/Bz (Verolme E R do Brazil) 1977; Tk; 65100; 271.66 × 15.01 (891.27 × 49.24); M (B&W); —; ex *Bocaina*
Sisters:
63931 SOUTH VIVIEN (Li) ex *Beberibe*
63932 BAURU (Bz) ex *Braganca* 1982

63940 GOLDEN SUNRAY Sg/Ja (Sumitomo) 1974;

Tk; 48900; 241.51 × 14.14 (792.35 × 46.39); M (Sulzer); 16.5
Probable sister:
63941 CANADIAN OWL (Sg)

63960 AL ANDALUS Ku/Sp ('Astano') 1975; Tk; 191000; 362.57 × 26.09 (1189.5 × 85.6); TST (Kawasaki); 14.5
Probable sister:
63961 SANTA MARIA (Sp) launched as *La Santa Maria*
Similar:
63962 DALMA (Li) launched as *Afran Odyssey*

63970 PATRIOT US/US (Todd) 1975; Tk; 21600; 216.8 × 10.52 (711.29 × 34.51); M (Pielstick); 16 ex *Zapata Patriot* 1981
Sisters (US flag):
63971 COURIER ex *Zapata Courier* 1981
63972 RANGER ex *Zapata Ranger* 1981
63973 ROVER ex *Zapata Rover* 1981

★**63980 KRYM** Ru/Ru (Zaliv) 1975; Tk; 88700; 295.05 × 17 (968.01 × 55.77); T (Kirov); 17
Sister (Ru flag):
★**63981 KUBAN**

63990 OLYMPIC SPLENDOUR Gr/Br (Swan Hunter) 1976; Tk; 66300; 260.33 × 15.18 (854.1 × 49.8); M (Sulzer); 16; ex *Geroi Sevastopolya*; Launched as *Kyra Lynn*
Sisters:
63991 ARTEMIS GAROFALIDIS (Gr) ex *Geroi Novorossiyska*; Launched as *Interoceanic I*
63992 AFRAN EQUATOR (Li) ex *Geroi Kerchi*; ex *Interoceanic II*; Launched as *Robcap VI*
Similar:
63993 YORKSHIRE (Br)

64000 TIGRE No/No (Stord) 1974; Tk; 140300; 347.84 × 22.14 (1141.2 × 72.63); T (Stal-Laval); 15.5

●**64010 KAIA KNUDSEN** No/Sw (Uddevalla) 1974; Tk; 114000; 325.0 × 20.44 (1066 × 67.06); T (GEC); 15.75; ex *Norse Queen* 1983
Sisters:
64011 PHILLIPS ENTERPRISE (Li) ex *Kollbjorg*
64012 SYLVANIA (Li) ex *Marga*; ex *Margaret Onstad* 1978
64013 ADNA (No)
64014 THORSHAVET (No) ex *Norseman* 1983
64015 POLYVICTORIA (No)
64016 MARGARON (Sw) ex *Regina* 1984

●**64020 NORBEGA** No/Sw (Gotav) 1971; Tk; 113500; 332.24 × 20.65 (1090 × 67.74); T (Stal-Laval); 16; ex *Synia* 1977

64030 MANNA Gr/FRG (Howaldts DW) 1970; Tk; 73000; 285.53 × 17.07 (936.78 × 56); T (Allgemeine); 16; ex *Sea Antwerp* 1982; ex *Claviger* 1980; ex *Clavigo* 1979

64050 NANNY Sw/Sw (Uddevalla) 1978; Tk; 245100; 364.02 × 25.07 (1194.29 × 82.25); TST (GEC); 16

●**64060 ANNA I ANGELICOUSSI** Gr/It (Italcantieri) 1971; Tk; 115900; 329.73 × 19.91 (1082 × 65.28); T (Stal-Laval); 16; ex *Santa Rosalia* 1980

64070 ULTRASEA US/US (National Steel) 1973; OBO; 39800; 272.04 × 13.97 (892.51 × 45.83); M (GEC); 16.5
Sister:
64071 ULTRAMAR (US)

64080 TATIANA Gr/FRG (Howaldts DW) 1970; OBO; 73500; 280.07 × 16.61 (918.86 × 54.49); T (A G 'Weser'); 15.75; ex *Polarbris* 1978
Similar:
64081 IRFON (Br)
Possibly similar:
64082 ALEXANDRA DIO (Pa) ex *Al Qasim* 1981; ex *John Augustus Essberger* 1978

64090 PANDITA NATNA SAGHARA Pa/FRG (Howaldts DW) 1975; Tk; 70700; 283.85 × 15.72 (931 × 15.72); T (Allgemeine); 15.5; ex *Giewont II* 1983
Sisters:
64091 ANASTASIS II (Gr) ex *Rysy II* 1983
64092 BADEN (FRG)
64093 BAYERN (FRG)
64094 ARIZONA (Pa) ex *Dona Margaro* 1982; ex *Heinrich Essberger* 1979
Similar (converted to storage vessel):
64095 SEREPCA 1 (Cm) ex *Kasprowy Wierch* 1983

64100 TANGA Li/Ja (Hitachi) 1967; OO; 55800; 252.1 × 14.45 (827.1 × 47.41); M (B&W); 15.75; ex *Banglar Noor* 1982; ex *Vestan* 1977
Sister:
64101 MUSCAT CEMENT (Li) ex *Skyros* 1981; ex *Apache* 1979; ex *Ivory Sun* †1978; ex *Fernstar* 1973

64110 SHIN OSAKA MARU Pa/Ja (Hitachi) 1966;

Tk; 51400; 258.53 × 15.01 (848.19 × 49.24); M (B&W); 15.5; ex *Daichi Maru* 1982; ex *Yanbu* 1982; ex *Mobil Arrow* 1978; ex *Shin Osaka Maru* 1977

64120 SAINT ANDREW Pa/Ja (Kurushima) 1973; Tk; 44800; 245.98 × 13.27 (807.02 × 43.53); M (MAN); 15.5; ex *Kurushima Maru* 1982
Sisters (Sg flag):
64121 VIRGINIA LILY
64122 VIRGINIA STAR

64130 HAMILTON LOPES Bz/De (Odense) 1969; Tk; 62600; 271.66 × 15 (891.27 × 49.21); M (B&W); 16
Sister:
64131 HORTA BARBOSA (Bz)

64140 POLYTRADER No/Sw (Uddevalla) 1978; Tk (offshore loading); 65200; 263.71 × 16.77 (865.19 × 55.02); M (B&W); 16
Sister:
64141 POLYTRAVELLER (No)
Similar:
64142 HERVANG (No)
64143 GEORGIA (No)
64144 WANGLI (No)
64145 WANGSKOG (No)
64146 WANGKOLL (No)
64147 BURMAH LEGACY (Li) ex *Fagerjell* 1979
64148 CREDO (No) ex *Ronacastle* 1979
64150 SOLVA (Li) ex *Afran Wave* 1982; ex *Wind Endeavour* 1977
64151 GERINA (No)

64160 ALABAMA GETTY Li/Sw (Uddevalla) 1971; Tk; 63200; 284.13 × 16.7 (932.18 × 54.79); M (B&W); 16; ex *Curro* 1976
Sister:
64161 IRINI (Gr) ex *Juanita* 1983

⬤**64180 TRANSUD IV** Li/Fr (L'Atlantique) 1969; Tk; 51700; 275.01 × 15.06 (902 × 49.41); M (B&W); 15.5; ex *Saintonge* 1980

64190 DIALA FRG/FRG (Deutsche Werft) 1966; Tk; 39400; 243.77 × 13.08 (799.77 × 42.91); T (Stal-Laval); 15.5

64200 VOO SHEE Tw/Ja (IHI) 1969; Tk; 52400; 253.04 × 15.57 (830.18 × 51.08); M (Sulzer); 16.5
Sisters (some Tw built-Taiwan SB):
64201 HSIEN YUAN (Tw)
64202 SHEN NON (Tw)
64203 YU TSAO (Tw)
64204 FORTUNE (Li)
64205 GLORY (Li)
64206 AFRAN ENERGY (Li)

64220 NARICA FRG/Br (Swan Hunter) 1967; Tk; 59900; 264.9 × 14.91 (869.09 × 48.91); M (Sulzer); 14.5
Sister:
64221 NACELLA (FRG)
Similar:
64222 NEVERITA (FRG)

64230 DONAX Br/Br (H&W); 1966; Tk; 41400; 243.85 × 13.12 (800.03 × 43.04); M (B&W); 15.5

64240 ARCO JUNEAU US/US (Bethlehem Steel) 1974; Tk; 57700; 269.15 × 15.77 (883.03 × 51.73); T (GEC); 16.75
Sisters (US flag):
64241 ARCO ANCHORAGE
64242 ARCO FAIRBANKS
64243 OVERSEAS JUNEAU

64250 ARCO PRUDHOE BAY US/US (Bethlehem Steel) 1971; Tk; 35600; 246.9 × 13.18 (810.04 × 43.24); T (GEC); 15.5
Sister:
64251 ARCO SAG RIVER (US)
Probable sister:
64252 SANSINENA II (US)
Similar (US flag):
64253 CHEVRON CALIFORNIA
64254 CHEVRON HAWAII
64255 CHEVRON MISSISSIPPI
64255/1 ARCO TEXAS ex *Chevron Hawaii* 1981
Probably similar (US flag):
64256 OVERSEAS ALASKA
64257 OVERSEAS ARCTIC

64270 PANAMAX STAR Pa/Ja (Kawasaki) 1966; OBO; 42100; 242.5 × 13.69 (795.6 × 44.91); M (MAN); 15.5; ex *Hoegh Ranger* 1982
Sister:
64271 BYZANTION (Gr) ex *Vega Stingray*; ex *Hoegh Ray* 1978

64290 SAFINA SAHARA Si/Sw (Kockums) 1974; Tk; 178500; 362.75 × 22.32 (1190.1 × 73.22); T (Stal-Laval); 15.5; ex *Sea Saint* 1981
64291 SEA SAGA

64293 SEA SCAPE
64294 SEA SONG
(Li flag)
64295 WORLD SYMPHONY ex *Sea Symphony*
64296 LONDON TRADER ex *Sea Stratus* 1978
(Gr flag)
64297 TINA
64298 STAVROS G L
(No flag)
64299 VANJA
64300 VELA
64301 WIND EAGLE
64302 WIND ENTERPRISE
64303 WIND ESCORT

⬤**64310 JAARLI** Fi/Sw (Kockums) 1972; Tk; 125400; 340.52 × 20.07 (1117.1 × 65.8); T (Stal-Laval); 16; ex *Sea Soldier*
Similar:
64311 SEA SCOUT (Sw)
64312 SAFINA SWIFT (Si) ex *Sea Swift* 1980
64313 JURMO (Fi) ex *Sea Splendour*
64314 MT CABRITE (Li) ex *Sea Serpent*
64315 SAINT LUCIA (Li) ex *Sea Swan*
64316 ATHENE (No)
64317 ANDRES BONIFACIO (Pi) ex *World Joy* 1980; ex *Bolette* 1980; ex *Daghild*
64318 ATLANTICOS (Li) ex *Atlantic Sun* 1981
64319 WORLD SUN (Li) ex *Pacific Sun*
64320 ESSO DALRIADA (Br)
64321 ESSO DEMETIA (Br)

⬤**64322 ALEXANDER** Li/FRG (Bremer V) 1981; OBO; 37900; 240.72 × 14.34 (790 × 47.05); M (MAN); 15
Sisters:
64323 AUGUST THYSSEN (Li)
64324 VIATOR (No)
64325 SIBOSEVEN (No)
Sister (shorter funnel):
64326 KASZONY (Li)
Possible sisters:
64327 ARIEL (No)
64328 BELOCEAN (FRG)
64329 KONKAR HYPHESTOS (Gr)
64329/1 PHAROS (FRG)

⬤**64330 MOBIL ALADDIN** Li/Sw (Gotav) 1974; Tk; 74100; 270.09 × 17.06 (886.12 × 55.97); M (B&W); 16; ex *Aramis* 1982; ex *Hoegh Lance* 1979; ex *Sydhav* 1980
Sisters:
64332 JAGRANDA (No) ex *Pellos* 1979
64333 JARITA (No) ex *Aino* 1979
64334 IN-SAFRA (Ag) ex *Emma Fernstrom* 1976
64335 IN-AMENAS (Ag) ex *Teakwood* 1975
64336 INTISAR (Ly) launched as *Mistral*
Similar (larger):
64337 LIBERATOR (Gr) ex *Archontas* 1982
64338 ZENIT DIANA (Li) ex *Messiniaki Filia* 1983
64339 ZENIT FORTUNA (Li) ex *Messiniaki Floga* 1983
Similar (shortened by 25.5 metres and other conversion work, may be considerably altered in appearance):
64340 INTERMAR ATLANTIC (Li) ex *Jaricha* 1981

64345 CALIFORNIA GETTY Bs/Sw (Gotav) 1979; OBO; 71200; 250.02 × 16.11 (820 × 52.85); M (B&W); 15.25; ex *Norrland* 1982

64346 PERMEKE Be/Be (Boelwerf) 1982; OBO; 70800; 249.10 × 16.80 (817 × 55.12); M (MAN); 13.5
Sisters:
64347 ENSOR (Be)
64348 VESALIUS (Be)

64350 WESTIN Ko/Fr (France-Gironde) 1974; OBO; 76400; 299.25 × 17.6 (981.79 × 57.74); M (Sulzer); 16; ex *Recife* 1982
Sister:
64351 GULF BEAUFORT (Ca) ex *Yemanja* 1983

64360 AL-AIN Li/Sw (Eriksbergs) 1974; Tk; 68400; 280.07 × 16.71 (918.86 × 54.82); M (B&W); 16; ex *Orator* 1977
Sisters:
64361 NOGA (Li) ex *Ibnu* 1977
64362 HOUSTON GETTY (Li)
64363 EVITA (No)
64365 MARIANNA VII (Gr) ex *Kollskeg* 1981
64366 JOHS STOVE (No) ex *Gorm* 1977
64367 SEA BREEZE (No)
64368 JEROM (Li) ex *Gina* 1978
64369 CHAMAL (Fr) ex *Jonny* 1983
64370 CAMARGUE (Fr)
64371 RABIGH BAY 3 (Gr) ex *Erika*
64372 POITOU (Fr)
64373 SOLOGNE (Fr)

⬤**64375 CERRO COLORADO** Sp/Sp (AESA) 1978; Tk; 64300; 279.51 × 16.90 (917 × 55.45); M (B&W); 15.25
Sisters:

64376 ELVIRA C (Sp) ex *Beatriz Maria*
64377 CORTA ATALAYA (Sp)
64378 IRANZU (Sp)
64379 ROSARIO DEL MAR (Sp)
64380 STRATUS (Li) ex *Astrapesa Uno* 1980
64381 TAVIRA (Sp)
64382 VITORIA (Sp) ex *Julia Wilson* 1982; ex *Ondiz* 1980

64385 TULSA GETTY Li/Sw (Eriksbergs) 1971; Tk; 69200; 280.07 × 16.17 (918.86 × 53.05); M (B&W); 15.5; ex *Markland* 1977
Sister:
64386 NORTHIA (Br) ex *Oceanic Renown* 1980; ex *Kronoland* 1979; (Converted for use as offshore loading tanker)

64390 MARAO Po/Sw (Eriksbergs)- Po (Lisnave) 1972/73; Tk; 69300; 280.09 × 16.7 (918.9 × 54.8); M (B&W); 15.5; Forward section built Portugal 1972; aft section built Sweden 1973
Sisters (Po flag):
64391 MAROFA
64392 MONTEMURO

64400 PERA Gr/Sw (Eriksbergs) 1967; Tk; 57800; 277.02 × 14.72 (908.86 × 48.29); M (B&W); 16; ex *Kungaland* 1976

64410 FRIESLAND FRG/FRG (Rhein Nordseew) 1974; Tk; 65200; 272.27 × 16.51 (893.27 × 54.17); M (Sulzer); 17; Launched as *Titurel*
Probable sister:
64411 ESSO ORIENT (Pa) ex *Svea Marina* 1978

64420 SILVER TRANSPORTER Tw/It (Italcantieri) 1968; OO; 48500; 260.1 × 15.2 (853.34 × 49.86); M (Fiat); 16; ex *Marcona Transporter* 1982; ex *Ross Sound* 1973; ex *Rivalta* 1971
Probable sister:
64421 ASTAKOS (Li) ex *Hastings* 1977; ex *Ross Point* 1975; ex *Vittorio Valletta* 1971

64430 BELLARY In/Ys ('Uljanik') 1970; OO; 45800; 256.62 × 14.98 (841.93 × 49.15); M (MAN); —
Sisters (In flag):
64431 BAILADILA
64432 BARAUNI

64440 MOSEL ORE Li/Sw (Gotav) 1969; OO; 58800; 253.02 × 15.13 (830.12 × 49.64); M (Gotaverken); 15; ex *Baron Venture* 1980; ex *Pajala* 1978
Sister:
64441 SAAR ORE (Li) ex *United Venture*; ex *Porjus* 1978; ex *Flowergate* 1974

64450 NEWFOREST Br/Sw (Eriksbergs) 1972; OBO; 80000; 291.7 × 16.3 (957.02 × 53.47); M (B&W); 16; ex *Lake Tahoe* 1983; ex *Koll* 1976

64460 BRISTOL LAKE Li/Ja (Hitachi) 1968; OBO; 48600; 261.53 × 13.32 (858.03 × 43.7); M (B&W); 16; ex *Lafumina* 1983; ex *Teheran*

64470 SALVIA Ko/Sw (Eriksbergs) 1970; OBO; 83000; 302.98 × 16.94 (994.02 × 55.57); M (B&W); 16.5; ex *Atlantic Splendour* 1982; ex *Muirfield* 1978; ex *Tibetan* 1972
Sisters:
64471 TIFFANY (Li) ex *Dashwood* 1981; ex *Resolute*; ex *Turcoman* 1978

64480 KILDARE Br/Sw (Eriksbergs) 1972; OBO; 83700; 291.65 × 17.01 (956.85 × 55.8); M (B&W); 16.25
Sisters:
64481 GULF PHOENIX (Li) ex *Pacific Jasmin* 1983; ex *Cast Cormorant* 1983; ex *Nordic Clipper* 1981; ex *Nordic Clipper* 1980; ex *Naess Viking* 1974
64482 JEDFOREST (Br)

64490 NAVIOS. COMMODORE Li/Sw (Gotav) 1971; OBO; 55600; 256.55 × 15.11 (841.7 × 49.57); M (Gotaverken); 16; ex *Atlantic Bounty* 1982; ex *Dalsland* 1980; ex *Eric K Fernstrom* 1978
Sister:
64491 NAVIOS COLLIER (Li) ex *Atlantic Endeavour* 1982; ex *Fujisan* 1978
Similar (larger KP amidships):
64492 SILVERLAND (Sw) ex *A K Fernstrom* 1977

64500 NAVIOS CRUSADER Li/Sw (Oresunds) 1972; OBO; 54800; 256.52 × 15.11 (841.6 × 49.57); M (Gotaverken); 15.75; ex *Dagfred* 1977
Similar (No flag):
64501 VARVARA
64502 VISCAYA

64510 PALOMA DEL MAR Sp/Sp ('Bazan') 1972; OBO; 65100; 263.99 × 16.68 (866.1 × 54.72); M (Sulzer); 16
Sisters:
64511 ELISABETH (Li) ex *Eulalia Del Mar* 1981
64512 FILATRA LEGACY (Gr) launched as *Spirit of Phoenix*

64513 OBO KING (No) ex *Victoria Venture* 1981; ex *Snestad* 1978

64520 WESER ORE Li/Yş ('Uljanik') 1973; OO; 141800; 335.03 × 21.99 (1099.17 × 72.14); TSM (B&W); 16.5; ex *Brazilian Wealth* 1981; ex *Tarfala* 1978
Sister:
64521 RHINE ORE (Pa) ex *Torne* 1979
Similar:
64522 MARY R KOCH (Li)

64530 WORLD GALA Li/Sw (Eriksbergs) 1973; OO; 152000; 338.16 × 21.69 (1109.44 × 71.16); M (B&W); 15.25; ex *Svealand* 1978

64540 PANAMAX GEMINI Pa/Sw (Gotav) 1968; OBO; 44300; 258.66 × 13.73 (848.62 × 45.04); M (Gotaverken); 15.75; ex *Siboen* 1982
Sisters:
64541 SIBOTO (Li)
64542 SIBOTRE (No)

64550 BERGEBONDE No/Sw (Eriksbergs)-Po (Lisnave) 1973; OBO; 84200; 291.68 × 17.01 (956.96 × 55.77); M (B&W); 16.5; ex *Atland* 1976; Aft section built Sweden; forward section built Portugal
Sister:
64551 BERGE ODEL (No) ex *Lappland* 1976

64560 MIGHTIOUS Pa/Sw (Gotav) 1972; OBO; 56300; 256.04 × 15.08 (840.03 × 49.48); M (B&W); 15.75; ex *Cast Shearwater* 1983; ex *Cast Osprey* 1981; ex *Anglia Team*
Sisters:
64561 OSWAYA (Pa) ex *Cast Skua* 1982; ex *Norvegia Team*
64562 OSTIA (Pa) ex *Cast Gannet* 1982; ex *Suecia Team*
64563 LONDON TEAM (Br)
64564 SCANDIA TEAM (Br)
64565 BOUKADOURA (Li) ex *Navios Conqueror* 1983; ex *Sevonia Team* 1981
64566 WALCHAND(In)

64568 RABIGH BAY-2 Gr/Sw (Uddevalla) 1979; OBO; 32000; 206.86 × 12.65 (679 × 41.50); M (B&W); 16.75; ex *Sibofir* 1980
Sisters:
64569 THORHILD (No)
64570 THORGULL (No)
64571 VIKING HEAD (Sg)
64572 VIKING CAPE (Sg)
64573 GERANTA (No)
64574 VARDAAS (No)
64575 PHILIPPINE OBO 2 (Pi)
64576 PHILIPPINE OBO 3 (Pi)
Probable sisters:
64577 KOLLBJORG (No)
64578 UGLAND OBO-ONE (No)

64580 GALINI Gr/No 1973; OO; 71300; 282 × 17 (925.19 × 55.77); M; 16; ex *Ancora* 1983
Sisters (No flag):
64581 ACINA
64582 SANDEFJORD

64590 AMANDA MILLER Au/Au (Whyalla) 1971; Tk; 39100; 239.28 × 13.17 (785.04 × 43.21); M (Sulzer); 16.5

64600 CAPO EMMA It/It (Italcantieri) 1967; Tk; 48500; 243.85 × 14.21 (800.03 × 46.62); M (B&W); —; ex *Mare Aegeum* 1978; ex *Petrolsade* 1973

64610 DONA OURANIA Gr/Fr (Howaldts DW) 1971; Tk; 17800; 170.69 × 10.82 (560.01 × 35.5); M (MAN); 15.5; ex *St. Jacobi* 1979
Sisters:
64611 DELFINI (Pa) ex *Sentosa Bay* 1982; ex *Eberhart Essberger*
64612 RODOSEA (Pa) ex *Raffles Bay* 1982; ex *Roland Essberger* 1979
64613 DONA EVGENIA (Cy) ex *St. Katharinen* 1978

64620 LUCERNA Li/Ca (Davie SB) 1977; Tk; 24100; 182.81 × 11.42 (599.77 × 37.47); M (Sulzer); 15.5; ex *Baraka* 1983; ex *Alrai* 1982; ex *Athelmonarch*
Sister:
64621 ALTANIN (Br) ex *Athelqueen*

64630 SEALIFT ANTARCTIC US/US (Bath) 1975; Tk; 17200; 178.92 × 10.54 (587 × 34.58); M (De Laval); 16; Operated commercially for the US Military Sealift Command
Sisters (US flag):
64631 SEALIFT ARABIAN SEA
64632 SEALIFT ARCTIC
64633 SEALIFT ATLANTIC
64634 SEALIFT CARIBBEAN
64635 SEALIFT CHINA SEA
64636 SEALIFT INDIAN OCEAN
64637 SEALIFT MEDITERRANEAN
64638 SEALIFT PACIFIC

64640 MELTEMI Gr/FRG (A G 'Weser') 1976; Tk; 24700; 193.02 × 11.65 (633.26 × 38.22); M (MAN); 16; ex *Taifun* 1978 'Key 40' type

64650 TEAM BORGA No/No (Horten) 1973; Ch; 18700; 170.62 × 11.37 (559.78 × 37.3); M (Sulzer); 16; ex *Borga* 1981; ex *Team Vesta*
Similar:
64651 CIELO DI NAPOLI (It) ex *Team Astwi* 1979; launched as *Astwi*
64652 TEAM HADA (No) ex *Hada* 1982; ex *Team Castor*
64653 TEAM SOLVIKEN (No) ex *Solviken* 1982; ex *Team Pollux*
64654 MYKONOS (Li) ex *Team Augwi* 1979
64655 MYRTEA (Li) ex *Team Hilwi* 1979

64660 MARINE EAGLE US/US (Sun SB) 1944/69; LGC; 15900; 187.38 × 10.08 (516.33 × 33.07); T-E (Westinghouse); 14.5; ex *Parkersburg* 1968; ex *Esso Parkersburg* 1956; ex *Fort Cornwallis* 1946; converted from 'T2' tanker and lengthened 1969 (Newport News)

64670 MOBIL ENGINEER Li/No (Haugesund) 1973; Tk; 18800; 170.69 × 11.33 (560 × 37.17); M (Sulzer); 15.75
Sister:
64671 MOBIL NAVIGATOR (Li)

64675 SIOUX FRG/FRG (Lindenau) 1981; Tk; 3500; 115.02 × 7.30 (377 × 23.95); M (Krupp-MaK); 14
Sisters:
54676 INDIO (FRG)
64677 UNKAS (FRG)

64680 ARCADIA Pa/FRG (Meyer) 1972; LGC; 4300; 106.41 × 7.26 (349.11 × 23.8); M (KHD); 15.5; ex *Gammagas* 1983
Possibly similar:
64683 CORAL ISIS (NA)

64690 GAS FUEGUINO Ar/FRG (Meyer) 1971; LGC; 4300; 106.41 × 7.27 (349.11 × 23.85); M (Smit & Bolnes); 16; ex *Fritz Haber* 1982; ex *Irene* 1974

64700 OSWEGO STAR Li/Ne (Zaanlandsche) 1972; Ch; 4000; 96.88 × 7.49 (317.84 × 24.57); M (Werkspoor); 13; ex *Silver Eirik* 1977; Now has two long tanks (30m) on deck and some alteration to superstructure

64720 AMERICANA It/It (Italcantieri) 1974; Con/V; 22200; 208 × 10.3 (683. × 34.1); T (GEC); 23.5; Side door on port side
Sister:
64721 ITALICA (It)

64730 DWEJRA II Ma/Ne ('De Biesbosch') 1969; C; 1000; 84.26 × 5.11 (276.44 × 16.77); M (MWM); —; ex *ASD Iris* 1976; ex *Iris* 1973

64740 ANNELIESE OLTMANN FRG/No (Aukra) 1972; C; 1000; 77.09 × 5.1 (252.92 × 16.73); M (Atlas-MaK); 14
Sister (Pa flag):
64742 ESTETAL

64750 MARHAVA Va/FRG (Sietas) 1964; C; 955/1590; 83.72 × 4.52/5.89 (274.67 × 14.82/19.32); M (MAN); 14; ex *Italian Express* 1981; ex *Thesee* 1977

64760 FADEL Le/FRG (Norderwerft) 1953; C; 1300; 83.37 × 5.25 (273.52 × 17.22); M (MaK); 12; ex *Temaya* 1978; ex *Ammerland* 1972; ex *Caldas* 1967; ex *Falkenburg* 1962; ex *Sankt Marien* 1962

64770 PANCHRATNA In/FRG (Atlas MaK) 1969; Con; 1600; 99.22 × 5.36 (325.5 × 17.58); M (Atlas-MaK); 14.5; ex *Mondo* 1981; ex *Fondo* 1981; ex *Mondo* 1981; ex *Maersk Mondo* 1980; ex *Mondo* 1975; ex *Beavermondo* 1971; Launched as *Mondo*
Sister:
64771 PANCHABHA (In) ex *Rando* 1981; ex *Maersk Rando* 1980; ex *Rando* 1975; ex *Beaverrando* 1971; Launched as *Rando*

★**64780 QU JIANG** RC/FRG (Meyer) 1970; C; 1500/3300; 103.38 × 4.78/6.37 (339.17 × 15.68/20.89); M (KHD); 15.5; ex *Blue Marlin* 1983; ex *Hartford Express* 1982; ex *Conti Holanda* 1982; ex *Hartford Express* 1982; Launched as *Peter Wehr*

64790 RECOMONE It/Br (Cochrane) 1970; C; 1600; 86.34 × 5.03 (283.27 × 16.5); M (English Electric); 12; ex *Stirlingbrook* 1983
Sister:
64791 STAVROS H (Cy) ex *Solentbrook* 1982
64792 FIRMUS (Cy) ex *Somersetbrook* 1983
64793 ROMANA (Do) ex *Surreybrook* 1982
64794 IERANTO (It) *Sussexbrook* 1982

64800 PELOR Gr/Br (H Robb) 1968; C; 1500; 94.24 × 5.01 (309.19 × 16.44); M (Mirrlees); 13; ex *Fenchurch* 1983; ex *City of Istanbul* 1978; ex *Mediterranian* 1974

★**64810 MAN CHENG** RC/FRG (Husumer) 1975; C; 1600; 91.47 × 6.12 (300 × 20); M (KHD); 15; ex *Lindinger Light* 1979
Sisters (RC flag):
★**64811 XIONG ER SHAN** ex *Lindinger Karat* 1978
★**64812 KUAN CHENG** ex *Lindinger Ivory* 1978
★**64813 TIAN LI SHAN** ex *Lindinger Jade* 1978
★**64814 A CHENG** ex *Ya Cheng* 1983; ex *Lindinger Nimbus* 1978
★**64815 HAI CHENG** ex *Lindinger Moonstone* 1978
★**64816 LI CHENG** ex *Lindinger Silver* 1978
(De flag):
64817 LEIF STAERKE ex *Lindinger Topaz* 1979
64817/1 GERT STAERKE
64817/2 THOR STAERKE ex *Lindinger Unique* 1979
Possible sisters (RC flag):
★**64818 HE LAN SHAN** ex *Lindinger Opal* 1978
★**64819 SHI ZUI SHAN** ex *Lindinger Quetzal* 1978

64830 EIDER FRG/FRG (Husumer) 1978; C; 1600; 91.47 × 6.2 (300.1 × 20.34); M (KHD); 13
Sister:
64831 HEVER (FRG)

64840 CELAL CESUR Tu/De (Aalborg) 1977; C; 1700/3300; 96.53 × —/6.8 (316.69 × —/22.3); M (Alpha-Diesel); 14; ex *Mercandian Atlantic* 1982
Sister:
64841 MERCANDIAN PACIFIC (De)

64850 NIAGA XLI Ia/Ne (Van Diepen) 1974; C; 800; 76 × 4.45 (249.34 × 14.6); M (Atlas-MaK); 11; ex *Mira* 1982; ex *Amigo Express* 1975
Similar:
64851 KASPAR SIF (De)
64852 TARUNA ABADI (Ia) ex *Jette Sif* 1982
64853 ANN SANDVED (De)
64854 APOLLONIA X (Cy) ex *Chris Isa* 1983; ex *Balton* 1975
64855 MELINA (Cy) ex *Rikke Isa* 1983
64856 HERMAN SIF (De) ex *Gerda Lonborg* 1977
64859 AMIGO FORTUNA
64860 SWIFT (Ne)
64863 NIELSE DANIELSEN (Ne) ex *Amigo Defender* 1978:
64864 ERIK SIF (De)
64865 GRETA SIF (De)
64866 NIAGA XLV (Ia) ex *Pia Sandved*
64867 RUNATINDUR(Fa) ex *Lotte Scheel* 1976

64890 KAREN WINTHER De/De (Frederikshavn) 1977; C; 1600; 96.53 × 5.64 (316.69 × 18.5); M (Atlas-MaK); 12.5

64900 NAJA ITTUK De/De (Nystads) 1973; C; 3300; 93.93 × 7.36 (308.16 × 24.14); M (Pielstick); 14.75; ex *Linda Dan* 1983
Sister:
64901 NUNGU ITTUK (De) ex *Gronland* 1983

64910 HELEN Pa/Sg (Singapore Slip) 1975; C; 1600; 69.07 × 4.23 (226.6 × 13.87); TSM (MWM); 9; ex *Ocean Pioneer* 1983; ex *Asean Pioneer* 1981
Sisters (Pa flag):
64911 ANGELA ex *Ocean Prosperity* 1983; ex *Asean Prosperity* 1981
64914 OCEAN PROGRESS ex *Asean Progress* 1980
64915 YVONNE C ex *Ocean Promoter* 1983; ex *Asean Promoter* 1980

64920 ZUHAL K Tu/FRG (Nobiskrug) 1972; C; 3000/5200; 125 × 6.61/7.64 (410.1 × 21.69/25.07); M (MAN); 17.25; ex *Triumph Orient* 1983; ex *Emma Jebsen*
Sister:
64921 ZIGANA (Tu) ex *Signal* 1982; ex *Heinrich Jessen*

64930 TEMARA Cy/FRG (Schlichting) 1969; C; 2800/4800; 116.8 × 6.52/7.53 (383.2 × 21.39/24.7); M (Atlas-MaK); 15.5; ex *Mejean III* 1980; ex *Nordwelle* 1977; 'Trampco' type
Sisters:
64931 DIAMOND MOON (Gr) ex *Nordkap* 1981
64932 DIAMOND SUN (Gr) ex *Nordwoge* 1980
64933 NORDSTRAND (FRG)
64934 PERLA (Gr) ex *Drucilla U* 1983; ex *Carlo Porr* 1976
64935 ILLERBERG (Cy) ex *Hamburger Senator* 1978
64936 HEKTOR (Cy) ex *Parzival* 1972
64937 CAROLINE SCHULTE (Cy) ex *Achill* 1984; ex *Lohengrin* 1974
64938 CAP BRETON (FRG) launched as *Sonnholm*
64939 ISAR (FRG) ex *Cap Vincent* 1972; Launched as *Isar*
64940 ANTJE SCHULTE (Pa)
64941 JUDITH SCHULTE (Br)
64942 GEORG KURZ (Pa) ex *Eastern Lake* 1977; ex *Hamburger Fleet* 1975
64943 TECONA (Cy) ex *Prominent 1*; ex *Scol Promi-*

nent 1977; ex *Eastern Bridge* 1974; ex *Cape Henry* 1974; ex *Hinrich Witt* 1972

64944 MARIANNE ROTH (Cy) ex *Cape Ray* 1978; ex *Hamburger Dom* 1974

64945 RIDGE (SA)

64946 RANGE (SA) ex *Verge* 1981

Similar (Stulcken derricks):

64947 TERENGA (Cy) ex *Bachue* 1981; ex *Dorothea Bolten* 1978

64948 PAMPERO (FRG) ex *Nopal Pampero* 1977; ex *Schirokko* 1975

64949 TAIFUN (FRG)

64950 STINNES ZEPHIR (Sg) ex *Zephir* 1972

64960 IBN ROCHD Ag/FRG (Schlichting) 1973; C; 2800/4800; 116.69 × 6.51/7.52 (328.84 × 21.36/24.67); M (Atlas-MaK); 15.75; 'Trampco' type
Sisters (Ag flag):
64961 IBN BADIS
64962 IBN BATOUTA
64963 IBN SIRAJ
64964 AURES
64965 DJORF
64966 DJURDJURA
64967 EDOUGH
64968 OUARSENIS
Sisters (with Stulcken derrick) (Ag Flag):
64969 IBN KHALDOUN
64970 IBN SINA II
(Note: some of these vessels are 10m longer than the name ship)

64980 FLENSAU FRG/FRG (O&K) 1978; C; 5000; 116.64 × 7.52 (382.68 × 24.67); M (Atlas-MaK); 15.25
Sister:
64981 KRUSAU (FRG)

64990 NIVI ITTUK De/De (Aalborg) 1973; R; 5000; 135.11 × 7.62 (443.3 × 25); M (B&W); 17; ex *Bamsa Dan* 1983

65000 IBN JUBAIR Eg/Sp (Duro Felguera) 1970; C; 650/1200; 72.7 × 5.19 (238.5 × 16.96); M (Deutz); —; ex *Atlan Esmeralda* 1974
Sister:
65001 IBN KORRA (Eg) ex *Atlan Rubi* 1975
Possibly similar:
65002 LUR-TXORI (Sp) ex *Jade* 1975; ex *Lian* 1974
65003 UR-TXORI (Sp) ex *Topacio* 1976; ex *Lian Dos* 1973

65010 ADRIATIC Ne/Fr (Havre) 1968; R; 500/1200; 75.55 × 4.02/5.11 (247.86 × 13.18/16.76); M (Atlas-MaK); 15; ex *Jofrigo* 1975
Sisters:
65011 REEFER GIULIA (It) ex *Atlantide*; ex *Joquita* 1975
65012 GRIPO (Fi) ex *Evofrio* 1976; ex *Jo-Rivka* 1974
65013 TEMEHANI II (NZ) ex *Toa Moana* 1981; ex *Jogela* 1974

65030 ALPRO Sp/Sp (Corcho) 1957; C; 700; 61.07 × 3.9 (200.36 × 12.79); M (Werkspoor); 12; ex *Mirenchu* 1968

65040 AGIP TRIESTE It/It (Adriatico) 1964; Tk; 30400; 228.61 × 12.14 (750.03 × 39.83); M (Adriatico); 17

65050 ZANTE Gr/Ja (Hitachi) 1969; Tk; 54300; 263.51 × 14.73 (864.53 × 48.32); M (B&W); —; ex *Vivita* 1983; ex *Bergevik* 1978

65060 ADONIS US/FRG (A G 'Weser') 1966; Tk; 38700; 250.55 × 12.87 (822 × 42.22); M (B&W); 15.5; ex *Aikaterini* 1982; ex *Atlantic Conqueror* 1980; ex *Courageous Colocotronis* 1977; ex *St. Petri* 1972

65065 KARRAS Pa/Sw (Lindholmens) 1962; B; 10800; 152.56 × 9.16 (501 × 30.05); M (Lindholmens); 14.25; ex *Kimoliaki Aigli* 1983; ex *Oinoussian Captain* 1981; ex *Falster* 1972

65070 HEMINA No/No (Moss R) 1977; LGC; 2000; 75.72 × 5.5 (248.42 × 18.04); M (Wichmann); 13
Sister:
65071 HESTIA (No)

65090 ENAK Ne/Ne ('De Waal') 1979; HL/C; 1600; 81.45 × 4.9 (267.22 × 16.08); M (Bolnes); 12.75; Kingpost in well has six legs and is on a travelling gantry
Sisters (Ne flag):
65091 ELGER (Travelling KP may not be fitted)
65092 ELDIR

65100 GIBEAGLE Br/Fi (Crichton-Vulcan) 1961; Cem; 1600; 90.84 × 4.95 (298.03 × 16.24); M (Sulzer); 12.5; ex *Granvik* 1982

65110 CEMBULK No/FRG (Sietas) 1973; Cem; 2200; 84.89 × 5.8 (278.51 × 19.03); M (Normo); 14

65140 ELEFTHEROS Gr/It (Adriatico) 1966; Tk; 48700; 253.6 × 13.29 (832.02 × 43.6); M (Fiat); —; ex *Santa Cristina Prima* 1981
Sisters:
65141 POLYMICHANOS (Gr) ex *Santa Anna Prima* 1982
65142 DYNAMIKOS (Gr) ex *Santa Augusta* 1982

●**65150 GUNGNIR 1** Cy/It (Adriatico) 1966; Tk; 48500; 253.6 × 13.32 (832.02 × 43.7); M (Fiat) 16.25; ex *Nai Giuseppina*; ex *Giuseppina Lolli Ghetti* 1974; ex *Ross Lake* 1972; ex *Fort St. Catherine* 1971
Sister:
65151 ROBERTA 1 (Pa) ex *Elizabeth II* 1981; ex *Margaret Simone* 1980; ex *Petra* 1973; ex *Warwick Fort* 1971
Similar:
65152 DRASTIRIOS (Gr) ex *Sarissola* 1981; ex *Claudio R* 1979
65153 FILIKOS (Gr) ex *Ombrina* 1981; ex *Monica R* 1979
65154 IRINIKOS (Gr) ex *Scrivia* 1981; ex *Andrea Leopoldo*
Similar (Bulk/Oil):
65156 SHINWA (In) ex *Daya Parvati*; ex *Ross Head* 1977

65160 LUNNI Fi/FRG (Nobiskrug) 1976; Tk/IB; 11000; 162.01 × 9.5 (531.52 × 31.16); M (Atlas-MaK); 14.5
Sisters (Fi flag):
65161 SOTKA
65162 TIIRA
65163 UIKKU

65170 IBN ROCHD Mo/Ne ('De Hoop') 1977; Ch; 13500; 172.29 × 10.5 (565.26 × 34.45); M (Pielstick); 17
Sister (Mo flag):
65171 IBN ALBANNA
Sisters (Norwegian built-Sarpsborg):
65172 IBN OTMAN (Mo)
65173 IBN SINA (Mo)

65180 SANGATTA/PERMINA 1015 Ia/No (Sarpsborg) 1975; Tk/Ch; 9500; 152.3 × 8.97 (499.67 × 29.43); M (Pielstick); 16.5
Sister:
65181 KLAMONO/PERMINA 1016 (Ia)

65190 BERGE BRIONI No/Ys ('Uljanik') 1973; OO; 117000; 314 × 20.42 (1030.18 × 66.99); TSM (B&W); 16
Sister:
65191 BERGE ADRIA (No)

65200 SINMAR No/No (Stord) 1971; Tk; 109500; 327.72 × 20.35 (1075.2 × 66.77); T (Stal-Laval); 16; ex *Norbird* 1982; ex *Raila* 1977
Possibly similar:
65202 BERGE BOSS (No) ex *Berge Beaumaris* 1982; ex *Beaumaris* 1981

65220 INAYAMA No/Ja (Hitachi) 1964; OO; 48100; 249.99 × 13.74 (820.18 × 45.08); M (B&W); 16
Similar (Li flag):
65221 SHIGEO NAGANO
65222 MARSHALL CLARK

65270 CALATRAVA Sp/Sp (Cadiz) 1965; Tk; 29200; 224.64 × 12.48 (737 × 40.94); M (B&W); 17

★**65290 DA QING 250** RC/Sw (Oresunds) 1964; Tk; 29000; 220.78 × 11.93 (724.34 × 39.14); M (Gotaverken); 16; ex *Wuhu* 1976; ex *Anmaj* 1975; ex *Belmaj* 1971

65300 JEVERLAND FRG/Ja (Hitachi) 1967; Tk; 49200; 263.51 × 14.63 (864.53 × 47.99); M (B&W); 16; ex *Mobil Weser* 1983; ex *Al Bilad*; ex *Berge Sigval* 1975
Similar:
65301 CIS BROVIG (Li)
65302 ZANTE (Gr) ex *Vivita* 1983; ex *Bergevik* 1978

●**65310 AGIP ANCONA** It/It (Riuniti) 1963; Tk; 31300; 229.17 × 12.3 (751.87 × 40.35); M (Riuniti); 16.5
Sister:
65311 AMETHYST (Cy) ex *Agip Genova* 1983

65330 OPALIA Br/Br (Cammell Laird) 1963; Tk; 31700; 228.02 × 12.24 (748.08 × 40.16); T (Cammell Laird); —

65340 DANA JOY Pa/No (Tangen) 1965; Tk; 31600; 236.2 × 12.33 (774.93 × 40.45); M (B&W); 16.25; ex *Fadi B* 1981; ex *Gimle* 1976

65350 EPTANISSOS Gr/Ne (Rotterdamsche) 1963; Tk; 31100; 231.5 × 11.83 (759.51 × 38.81); T (Rotterdamsche); 16.5; ex *Doelwijk* 1978

65360 SOUTHWAY Br/Sw (Kockums) 1965; Tk; 39000; 243.85 × 13.16 (800.03 × 43.17); M (MAN); —; ex *Panteleimon* 1983; ex *Saint Spyridon* 1982; ex *Historic Colocotronis* 1978; ex *Hoegh Lance* 1969

65380 FARMER Pa/Sw (Kockums) 1963; Tk; 36900; 236.28 × 12.64 (775.2 × 41.47); T (Stal-Laval); —; ex *Polarvik* 1978

65390 KYRNICOS E Li/Sw (Kockums) 1963; Tk; 25300; 213.21 × 11.67 (699.21 × 38.28); M (MAN); 16; ex *Barcola* 1982; ex *Oktania* 1973

65400 SINOIA Li/Br (Swan Hunter & WR) 1966; Tk; 51200; 259.47 × 14.88 (851.28 × 48.82); T (GEC); 17; ex *Clementina* 1977; ex *Clementine Churchill* 1973
Similar:
★**65401 ON SUNG** (RK) ex *Gallant Seahorse*; ex *Valentinian* 1972
65402 VENTURE (Gr) ex *Thistle Venture* 1983; ex *Jarita* 1977; ex *Gratian* 1972

65410 GARGI In/Ja (Mitsubishi Z) 1964; Tk; 34700; 229.95 × 12.03 (754.43 × 39.47); M (Sulzer); 16.5; ex *Vikram Jayanti* 1974

65420 GIULIANA 1 Pa/Sp (AESA) 1968; Tk; 15100; 184 × 10.1 (606 × 33); M (Sulzer); 15; ex *Sunniao*; ex *Stolt Heron* 1974; ex *Tunaco* 1970

65430 VITREA Ne/Ne (Wilton-Fije) 1962; Tk; 21900; 202.75 × 10.56 (665.19 × 34.64); T (Wilton-Fije); 15

65440 ESTRELLA PATAGONICA Ar/Br (Furness) 1962; Tk; 24400; 202.65 × 11.24 (664.86 × 36.88); T (AEI); —; ex *Voluta* 1970

●**65450 EASTWAY** Br/Ja (Kawasaki D) 1963; Tk; 29700; 228.51 × 12.01 (750 × 39.40); T (Kawasaki); 16.5; ex *Taxiarhis* 1983; ex *Ralph O Rhoades* 1981

●**65460 ALECOS M** Gr/Ja (Kure) 1965; Tk; 40000; 237.01 × 12.71 (778. × 41.70); T (IHI); 16; ex *Vasiliki* 1980; ex *Thomas A Pappas* 1970

65470 BEGONIA 1 Pa /Ja (Kure) 1964; Tk; 31800; 236.18 × 12.69 (774.87 × 41.63); M (Sulzer); 15; ex *Santa Marina* 1983
Similar:
65472 SPIROS (Gr) ex *Trysbej* 1969; ex *Carib Trader* 1968

65480 LEONIDAS Li/Sp ('Bazan') 1966; Tk; 29300; 227.77 × 12.35 (747.28 × 40.52); T (Parsons); —; ex *Sardinero* 1974

65490 CORALI Li/Ja (IHI) 1964; Tk; 37300; 242.98 × 11.99 (797.12 × 39.34); M (Sulzer); 15.25; ex *Fairfield Archer* 1981; ex *Fairfield Copa* 1979; ex *Asia Maru No2* 1973

●**65500 CAPRICORN** US/US (Alabama) 1943/61; Tk; 14100; 184.41 × 9.92 (605 × 32.55); T-E (GEC); 15; ex *Bunker* 1977; ex *Hess Bunker* 1977; ex *Powder River* 1955; Lengthened widened & deepened 1961 (Bethlehem Steel)
Sister:
65501 PISCES (US) ex *Hess Refiner* 1976; ex *Esso Worcester* 1961; ex *Multnomah* 1947

★**65540 DA QING 256** RC/Sw (Oresunds) 1965; Tk; 28900; 221.14 × 12.05 (725.52 × 39.53); M (Gotaverken); 15; ex *Chang Hu* 1983; ex *Anne* 1975; ex *Acina* 1971
Sister:
65541 ALMALAZ (Li) ex *Serra Trader* 1978; ex *Osco Surf* 1975; ex *Saga Surf* 1975; ex *Birgitta Fernstrom* 1972

65550 DOLPHIN II Gr/Sw (Gotav) 1959; Tk; 12700; 169.81 × 9.57 (557.11 × 31.38); M (Gotaverken); 15; ex *Vibeke* 1978
Similar:
★**65551 DA QING No41** (RC) ex *Anella* 1972; ex *Oscar Gorthon* 1971; ex *Vinstra*
Similar (Asphalt tanker):
65552 VIBIT (No)

65570 NINFEA It/Sw (Gotav) 1958; Tk; 19500; 198.15 × 10.85 (650.1 × 35.6); M (Gotaverken); 15.25; ex *Inger Knudsen* 1970

65580 NEW FORTUNE V Pa/No (Akers) 1961; Tk; 13000; 169.7 × 9.67 (556.76 × 31.73); M (B&W); 15; ex *Katya* 1983; ex *Lake Katya* 1980; ex *Iver Swift* 1978; ex *Anco Swift* 1976; ex *Skogaas* 1964

●**65590 VIKING** Gr/Br (Swan Hunter & WR) 1962; Tk; 13300; 172.27 × 10.11 (565.19 × 33.17); M (Doxford); 14.5; ex *Stolt Viking* 1982; ex *Stolt Tiger* 1974; ex *Stolt Abadesa* 1973; ex *Abadesa* 1969

65610 ESSO MILFORD HAVEN Br/Sw (Lindholmens) 1968; Tk; 10900; 162.67 × 8.54 (533.69 × 28.02); M (Pielstick); 16.75
Sister (Br flag):
65611 ESSO FAWLEY

65620 ESSO MERSEY Br/Br (Cammell Laird) 1972; Tk; 12300; 166.5 × 9.21 (546.26 × 30.22); M (Pielstick); 15.5
Sisters (Br flag):

65621 ESSO CLYDE
65622 ESSO SEVERN

65630 PETROMAR BAHIA BLANCA II Bz/Ja (Hitachi) 1974; Tk; 12800; 161.02 × 9.81 (528.28 × 32.19); M (B&W); 15; ex *Esso Mukaishima* 1978
Sisters:
65631 PETROMAR CAMPANA II (Bz) ex *Esso Bayway* 1978
65632 STENA ADRIATICA (Li) ex *Esso Nagoya* 1983
65633 ESSO GENOVA (It) ex *Esso Brisbane* 1981
65634 ESSO PARENTIS (Fr) ex *Esso Guam* 1982
65635 ESSO ALBANY (Li)
65636 ESSO CALLUNDA (De)
65637 ESSO HAFNIA (De)
Similar (also under K₃MF):
65638 ESSO PORT JEROME (Fr) ex *Esso Kumamoto* 1980

● **65650 ESSO BANGKOK** Pa/Ja (IHI) 1968; Tk; 13000; 170.08 × 9.40 (558 × 30.87); M (Sulzer); 14.5
Sisters:
65651 ESSO BOMBAY (Pa)
65652 ALEXIA V (Pa) ex *Esso Interamerica* 1982
65653 TESUBU II (Pa) ex *Esso Kure* 1982
65654 TESUBU III (Pa) ex *Esso Karachi* 1983
65655 TESUBU IV (Pa) ex *Esso Nagasaki* 1983
65656 ESSO PORT DICKSON (Sg)
65657 ESSO YOKOHAMA (Sg)
65658 ESSO HUMBER (Br) ex *Esso Penang* 1978
65659 ESSO TEES (Br) ex *Esso Bataan* 1983
65660 ESSO TYNE (Br) ex *Esso Kobe* 1982
65661 LACONIA II (Cy) ex *Esso Malacca* 1983
65662 ESSO VENEZIA (It) ex *Esso Chittagong* 1981
65663 ESRAM (Tu) ex *Tesubu* 1983; ex *Esso Goa* 1982

● **65670 BRUSSELS** Gr/Ne ('De Schelde') 1968; Tk; 14900; 180.22 × 10.33 (591.27 × 33.89); T (GEC); 18; ex *Texaco Brussels* 1983
Sisters:
65671 TEXACO GHENT (Br)
65672 MYRTIA (Gr) ex *Texaco Rotterdam* 1982

65680 ENDURANCE Li/Ca (Saint John SB) 1973; Tk; 18800; 187.76 × 10.42 (616 × 34.19); M (B&W); 15; ex *Esso Halifax* 1983
Sisters (Li flag):
65681 AMAZON PIONEER ex *Esso Montreal* 1983
65682 AMAZON PROSPERITY ex *Esso Saint John* 1982

65690 ESSO EVERETT Li/Ca (Saint John SB) 1975; Tk; 21600; 191.57 × 11.25 (628.51 × 36.91); M (Sulzer); 15.5
Sisters:
65691 PETROMAR SAN SEBASTIAN (Ar) ex *Esso Providence* 1983
65692 ESSO SAINT PETERSBURG (Li)
65693 PETROMAR SANTA CRUZ (Ar) ex *Esso Toronto* 1981
Possible sisters (Ca flag):
65694 IRVING ARCTIC
65695 IRVING ESKIMO
65696 IRVING OCEAN

65700 CAMPEADOR Sp/Sp (AESA) 1969; Tk; 20500; 209.02 × 10.73 (685.76 × 35.2); M (B&W); 16.5
Sister:
65701 CAMPOMAYOR (Sp)

65710 OKTURUS Sw/Ne (Wilton-Fije) 1973; Tk; 17900; 188.2 × 10.36 (617.45 × 33.99); M (Gotaverken); 15
Sister:
65711 OKTAVIUS (Sw)

● **65720 GOGO REGAL** Li/No (Horten) 1972; Tk/Ch; 16000; 165.08 × 9.94 (541.6 × 32.61); M (Sulzer); 15.5; ex *Anco Challenger* 1983; ex *Post Challenger* 1979
Sisters:
65721 IVER CHAMPION (Li) ex *Anco Champion* 1983; ex *Post Champion* 1979
65722 ANCO CHARGER (Br) ex *Post Charger* 1979
65724 ANCO ENDEAVOUR (Br) ex *Post Endeavour* 1977
65725 DUA-MAR (Sg) ex *Anco Enterprise* 1983; ex *Post Enterprise* 1978
65726 ANCO ENTENTE (Fr) ex *Post Entente* 1978
65727 STOLT ENERGIE (Fr) ex *Anco Energie* 1983; ex *Post Energie* 1978

65730 TEXACO BERGEN No/No (Horten) 1977; Tk; 18400; 168.79 × 11.16 (553.77 × 36.61); M (Sulzer); 16
Sisters (No flag):
65731 TEXACO BALTIC
65732 TEXACO STOCKHOLM

65735 MAKNASSY Tn/FRG (O&K) 1982; Ch; 11200; 158.00 × 9.22 (518 × 30.25); M (MaK); 16

65740 PAMINA Fi/No (Horten) 1975; Tk; 19100; 168.76 × 10.9 (553.67 × 35.76); M (Sulzer); 16; ex *Pandora C* 1983; ex *Ardmay*
Sister:
65741 IDA HELENE (Li) ex *Ardmore* 1983

65750 MOBIL MARKETER Li/Fi (Rauma-Repola) 1974; Tk; 18300; 170.49 × 11.06 (559.35 × 36.29); M (Sulzer); 15; Kingpost abreast funnel on port side
Sisters:
65751 MOBIL PRODUCER (Li)
65752 MOBIL REFINER (SA)
65753 PAOLA (Fi)

65760 OCEAN PIONEER Li/FRG (Rhein Nordseew) 1972; Tk; 17600; 172.04 × 10.68 (564.43 × 35.04); M (Fiat); 15.5; ex *Nordpartner* 1983; ex *Thor Asgard* 1983; ex *Globe Comet* 1981; ex *Thor Asgard*
Sisters (Li flag):
65761 SALLY I ex *Amisia* 1973; launched as *PCI*
65762 SALLY II

65780 PROCYON Gr/Ne (Giessen-De Noord) 1975; Tk; 32600; 210.32 × 12.41 (690.01 × 40.71); M (B&W); 16.75; ex *Cyclops* 1983
Sister:
65781 CLYTONEUS (Br)
Probable sister:
65782 RAIKO MARU (Ja) ex *Sanko Trust* 1979; launched as *Hellespont Argosy*

65790 CAMPONAVIA Sp/Sp (Juliana) 1973; Tk; 4200; 123.68 × 6.03 (405.77 × 19.78); M (B&W); 13
Sister:
65791 CAMPAMINO (Sp)

65800 VENTURE Li/Sw (Gotav) 1967; OBO; 39700; 258.66 × 13.27 (848.62 × 43.55); M (Gotaverken); 16; ex *Venture Italia* 1982; ex *Conoco Italia* 1978; ex *Rinda* 1972
Sister:
65801 CHANDOS (Li) ex *Delaware* 1982; ex *Ranger* 1973; ex *Runa* 1972

65810 MEGA BAY Li/Sw (Gotav) 1967; OBO; 44500; 258.66 × 13.47 (848.62 × 44.19); M (Gotaverken); 16.5; ex *Falcon Bay* 1982; ex *Mospoint* 1979; ex *Vitoria* 1976

● **65820 M EFES** Tu/Sw (Uddevalla) 1967; OBO; 42500; 243.85 × 13.93 (800 × 45.70); M (B&W); 16; ex *Bantry* 1978; ex *Havtor* 1975
Similar (converted to bulk/container. May be altered in appearance):
65821 ASEAN KNOWLEDGE (Pi) ex *Bjorgfjell*
65822 ASEAN LIBERTY (Pi) ex *Brali* 1978 ex *Havmoy* 1975
65823 MONARCH (Pi) ex *Asean Mission* 1983; ex *Bjorghav* 1979

65830 RIO SUN Li/Ja (Hitachi) 1967; OBO; 42500; 250.96 × 13.98 (823.36 × 45.87); M (B&W); 16; ex *Tokyo* 1977
Sister:
65831 GARBIS (Li) ex *Canto* 1975; ex *Vestfold* 1971

● **65840 CETRA CENTAURUS** Fr/Fr (France-Gironde) 1972; OO; 88100; 299.27 × 18.31 (981.86 × 60.07); M (B&W); 15

★ **65850 FELIKS DZIERZYNSKI** Pd/Pd (Szczecinska) 1978; B; 20300; 198.18 × 11 (650.2 × 36.09); M (Sulzer); 15.2; 'B-517' type
Sisters (Pd flag):
★ **65851 WALKA MLODYCH**
★ **65852 UNIWERSYTET SLASKI**
★ **65853 POWSTANIEC WARSZAWSKI**
★ **65854 JANUSZ KUSOCINSKI**

65860 AGUA GRANDE Bz/De (B&W) 1961; Tk; 8000; approx 154.11 × 7.17 (505.61 × 23.52); M (B&W); 13; Lengthened 1972. Note: drawing shows vessel before lengthening
Sisters (Bz flag):
65862 CANDEIAS
65863 ITAPARICA
65864 POJUCA
65865 TAQUIPE

65870 MARAJO Bz/Ja (Ish do Brazil) 1968; FA/Tk; 6600; 134.4 × 7.3 (440.7 × 24); M (Sulzer); 13.5

65880 LE CHENE NO 1 Ca/Ca (Marine Indust) 1961/78; Tk; 5100; 125.71 × 6.85 (412.43 × 22.47); M (B&W); 12; ex *Edouard Simard* 1982; ex *J. Edouard Simard* 1967; New forward section added 1978 (Marine Indust)

65890 TEXACO BOGOTA No/Sw (Eriksbergs) 1960; Tk; 13600; 181.67 × 9.57 (596.03 × 31.38); M (B&W); 14.5; Lengthened and converted 1968 (Eriksbergs)

65900 ALASKAN US/US (Sun SB) 1944/69; Tk; 15200; 202.7 × 10.43 (665.02 × 34.21); T (GEC); 17; ex *Clendenin* 1969; ex *Haven* 1945; ex *Marine Hawk*;

Forward and aft sections built 1944; Cargo section built 1969; Converted from hospital ship 1969; Lengthened 1969 (Sun SB)

65910 PETROGAS 1 Si/Sw (Kockums) 1964; LGC; 18000; 180.58 × 10.61 (592.45 × 34.8); M (MAN); 16; ex *Cassie Hill* 1979; ex *Norfolk Multina* 1978; ex *Paul Endacott* 1973

65920 PETERSBURG Li/US (Bethlehem Steel) 1963; Tk; 27500; 224.44 × 12.13 (735.69 × 39.79); T (Bethlehem Steel); 16.5; ex *Sinclair Texas* 1981

65930 GEORGE Z Cy/De (Odense) 1966; Tk; 52700; 263.48 × 14 (864.43 × 45.93); T (Kockums); 17; ex *Loreto* 1983; ex *Strofades* 1981; ex *A P Moller* 1980
Similar (Br flag):
65931 MAERSK BUCHAN ex *Elisabeth Maersk*
65932 MAERSK ANGUS ex *Evelyn Maersk*

65950 ADONIS US/FRG (A G 'Weser') 1966; Tk; 38700; 250.55 × 12.87 (822 × 42.22); M (B&W); 15.5; ex *Aikaterini* 1982; ex *Atlantic Conqueror* 1980; ex *Courageous Colocotronis* 1977; ex *St Petri* 1972

65960 THARALEOS Gr/Sp ('Astano') 1969; Tk; 51800; 267.62 × 13.94 (878 × 45.73); M (B&W); 16; ex *Santander* 1983

65970 HAWAIIAN SEA Li/Sp (AESA) 1970; Tk; 48500; 265.69 × 13.94 (871.70 × 45.73); M (Sulzer); 16; ex *Hagensee* 1977; ex *Bamberg* 1973
Similar:
65971 BLUE OCEAN (Li) ex *Cervara* 1983; ex *Jole Fassio* 1977; ex *Loyola* 1971;
65972 ALENDALE (Li) ex *Maritime Lawyer* 1979; ex *Oldenfield* 1976; ex *Arnsberg* 1973; Launched as *Petro Zulia*;
65973 OCEAN IDEAL (Li) ex *Ocean Victory* 1983; ex *Dora* 1976;
Similar (larger):
65974 ORDUNA (Sp)
65975 MARIA DE LOS DOLORES (Sp)
65976 EUGENIA 1 (Pa) ex *Vanesa* 1981; ex *Irache* 1978

● **66020 FANARI** Li/De (Odense) 1967; Tk; 52700; 265.74 × 13.95 (773.43 × 45.76); M (B&W); 16.25; ex *Nordhav* 1975
Similar:
66021 YPAPANTI (Li) ex *Afran Coast* 1980; ex *Stavik* 1976; ex *Permina III* 1976; ex *Permina I* 1972; ex *Stavik* 1972

66030 NEWTON PRINCESS Li/Sw (Eriksbergs) 1967; Tk; 48700; 265.13 × 14.66 (869.85 × 48.1); M (B&W); 16.5; ex *Lily H.* 1983; ex *Mobil Radiant*; ex *Cerno* 1976; ex *Stiklestad* 1973

66040 MYTILENE Li/FRG (Kieler H) 1967; Tk; 44700; 253.12 × 12.27 (830.45 × 40.26); M (MAN); 16.5; ex *Helga Essberger* 1979

66050 MARIA Gr/FRG (Kieler H) 1965; Tk; 42100; 249.11 × 13.77 (817.29 × 45.18); T (Kieler H); 17; ex *Genral Colocotronis* 1977; ex *Barbro* 1969
Similar:
66051 ERAWAN (Pa) ex *Trade Resolve* 1980; ex *Katingo Colocotronis* 1979; ex *Hoegh Laurel* 1973

66060 NEDI Gr/Br (J L Thompson) 1965; Tk; 35300; 243.72 × 13.23 (799.61 × 43.41); M (Doxford); —; ex *Aeolus* 1977; ex *North Sands* 1970
Similar:
66061 MENA (Th) ex *Donacilla* 1976
66062 PALAIMA (Ve) ex *Catalunya* 1981; ex *Philippine Star* 1980; ex *Daphnella* 1976

66070 STROFADES II Gr/Ne (Nederlandsche) 1967; Tk; 39100; 243.85 × 13.37 (800.03 × 43.86); M (Stork); —; ex *Dione* 1981
Sisters:
66071 YEROTSAKOS (Gr) ex *Dosina* 1981
66072 DIADEMA (NA)
66073 TAKIS E (Gr) ex *Diloma* 1981
Similar:
66074 DONOVANIA (Br)
66075 SIAM (Th) ex *Dorcasia* 1977
Possible sisters:
66076 DALLIA (NA)
66077 DAPHNE (NA)

66090 ESSO ZURICH Pa/Ja (Mitsui) 1965; Tk; 37300; 243.85 × 12.75 (800.03 × 41.83); M (B&W); 15.5
Sisters (Pa flag):
66092 EXXON HOUSTON ex *Esso Houston* 1973
66093 EXXON NEW ORLEANS ex *Esso New Orleans* 1973

66100 ESSO FORTH Br/No (Akers) 1967; Tk; 42100; 246.59 × 12.7 (809.02 × 41.67); M (B&W); 17; ex *Esso Antwerp* 1983
Sister:
66101 ESSO CASTELLON (Pa)

66110 **CLERK-MAXWELL** Br/Br (Hawthorn, L) 1966; LGC; 8300; 140.67 × 8.25 (461.52 × 27.07); M (Sulzer); 17
Similar:
66111 **MARIANO ESCOBEDO** (Me)

66120 **PALUDINA** Br/Ne (Verolme Dok) 1968; TB/Tk; 15400; 157.17 × 10.11 (574.7 × 33.17); M (MAN); 15.25; ex *Urshalim* 1973
Similar:
66121 **POMELLA** (Br) ex *Horama* 1974; Launched as *Nordvard*

66130 **CAMPONUBLA** Sp/Sp (AESA) 1979; Tk; 14900; 166 × 9.25 (544.62 × 30.35); M (Sulzer); 14.87; May be named **CAMPONUBIA**
Sister:
66131 **CAMPEON** (Sp)

66140 **AQUARIUS** Br/Br (Swan Hunter) 1972; Tk; 19900; 192.01 × 10.38 (629.95 × 34.05); M (Sulzer); 16; ex *Newburn* 1980; ex *Afghanistan;* ex *Joseph R Smallwood* 1975
Sisters:
66141 **AURA ADVENTURE** (Li) ex *Strait of Canso* 1982
66142 **AURA BRAVERY** (Li) ex *Simonburn* 1982; ex *Kurdistan;* ex *Frank D Moores* 1976
Probable sister:
66143 **AMOKURA** (NZ) ex *Hindustan* 1978

66150 **STOLT VENTURE** Li/No (Ankerlokken) 1976; Tk/Ch; 18600; 170.31 × 9.91 (558.76 × 32.51); M (B&W); 15.25; ex *Stolt Sagona* 1983; ex *Osco Sagona* 1983; ex *Sagona* 1980
Possibly similar (No flag):
66151 **VINCITA**
66152 **VENTURA**

66160 **CHAC** Me/No (Ankerlokken) 1976; Ch; 17600; 170.72 × 10 (560.1 × 32.8); M (B&W); 15.5; ex *Fossanger* 1977
Sister:
66161 **BACAB** (Me) ex *Bow Clipper* 1977

66180 **GUDRUN MAERSK** De/No (Kaldnes) 1973; Tk; 19900; 170.54 × 11.75 (559.51 × 38.55); M (B&W); 15.5
Sisters:
66181 **GJERTRUD MAERSK** (De)
66182 **CASTOR** (Bs) ex *Grete Maersk* 1981
66183 **POLLUX** (Li) ex *Titipor* 1983; ex *Gunvor Maersk* 1980

66190 **PREMUDA ROSA** It/It (Italcantieri) 1974/76; Tk; 18000; 170.69 × 10.95 (560 × 35.95); M (GMT); 16.5; Launched 1974. Completed 1976.
Sisters:
66191 **PREMUDA BIANCA** (It)
66192 **BUFFALO** (SA)
(Ar flag—some have fenders on deck):
66193 **CAMPO DURAN**
66194 **CANADON SECO**
66195 **MEDANITO**
66196 **PUERTO ROSALES**
Possibly similar (It flag):
66197 **AGIP GELA**
66198 **AGIP RAVENNA**
66199 **CIELO DI ROMA**
66200 **CIELO DI SALERNO**

66210 **CONASTOGA** Li/It (Italcantieri) 1972; Tk; 17500; 171.61 × 10.93 (563.02 × 35.86); M (Fiat) 16
Sisters:
66211 **CORSICANA** (It)
66212 **SACHEM** (Br)
66213 **SATUCKET** (Br)
Possible sisters:
66214 **INDEPENDENCIA 1** (Ve) launched as *Independencia*
66215 **INDEPENDENCIA II** (Ve)

66220 **NITSA** Gr/Sw (Oresunds) 1971; Tk; 16400; 170.97 × 10.21 (560.93 × 33.5); M (Gotaverken); 15.25
Sisters (Gr flag):
66221 **CEPHEUS**
66222 **CYGNUS**
66223 **LIBRA**

66230 **SOUTHERN CROSS** Bs/Sw (Gotav) 1977; Tk; 18500; 170.97 × 11.36 (560.93 × 37.27); M (B&W); 15; ex *Osco Tampimex Eagle* 1984; ex *Tampimex Eagle* 1980; ex *Nordic Aurora*
Sister:
66231 **LADY EMA** (Gr) ex *Bera* 1981; ex *Nordic Breeze*

⬤66250 **HOPECLIPPER** Br/Ja (Kure) 1967; B; 35300; 223.96 × 13.7 (734.78 × 44.95); M (Sulzer); 15.5; ex *Captain W D Cargill* 1977; Kingposts on travelling gantry

66260 **ACHILLEUS** Gr/Ja (Mitsui) 1965; B; 21500; 195.84 × 10.62 (642.51 × 34.84); M (B&W); 15;

Kingposts on travelling gantry
Sister:
66261 **EPHESTOS** (Gr)

66270 **LORENZO HALCOUSSI** Li/Ja (IHI) 1968; OBO; 39600; 257.79 × 12.91 (846 × 42.36); M (Sulzer); 16; ex *Arctic* 1971

66280 **ABU AMIRA** Si/Ja (IHI) 1964; B; 29400; 227.03 × 12.2 (744.85 × 40.03); T (GEC); 16; ex *Liryc* 1982; Kingposts on travelling gantry

66300 **ATHENIC** Gr/Ja (Kure) 1967; OO; 36700 ORE/48700 OIL; 254.26 × 13.31 (834.18 × 43.67); M (Sulzer); —
Sisters (Gr flag):
66301 **GLORIC**
66302 **PLATONIC**
Similar (tankers):
66304 **HARMONIC** (Gr)
66305 **IONIC** (Gr)
66306 **TROPIC** (Gr)
66307 **DORIC** (Gr)

66310 **PACIFIC** Gr/Ja (IHI) 1965; Tk; 38100; 248.42 × 12.19 (815 × 39.99); M (Sulzer); —

66320 **RAFFAELE CAFIERO** It/It ('Navalmeccanica') 1962; Tk; 24400; 210.52 × 11.55 (690.68 × 37.9); M (Fiat); 17.5

66340 **COLUMBIA** US/US (Ingalls SB) 1971; Tk; 20800; 204.93 × 11.04 (672.34 × 36.22); M (Pielstick); 16.25; ex *Falcon Lady* 1976; Chartered to Military Sealift Command
Sisters (US flag):
66341 **HUDSON** ex *Falcon Princess* 1976
66342 **NECHES** ex *Falcon Duchess* 1976
66343 **SUSQUEHANNA** ex *Falcon Countess* 1976

66350 **PERMINA XXII** Ia/Ja (Hitachi) 1971; Tk; 9200; 141.26 × 9 (463.45 × 29.53); M (B&W); 14.5; ex *Bruce Bali* 1981; ex *Golar Bali* 1978
Sisters (Ia flag):
66351 **PERMINA XXVII** (Ia) ex *Bruce Bawgan* 1981; ex *Golar Bawgan* 1978
66352 **PERMINA XXIV** (Ia) ex *Bruce Bintan* 1981; ex *Golar Bintan* 1978
66353 **PERMINA XXIII** (Ia) ex *Bruce Buatan* 1981; ex *Golar Buatan* 1978
66354 **PERMINA XXVI** (Ia) ex *Bruce Surabaya* 1981; ex *Golar Surabaya* 1978
66355 **PERMINA XXVII** (Ia) ex *Bruce Sabang* 1978; ex *Golar Sabang* 1978
66356 **PERMINA XXX** (Ia) ex *Bruce Sigli* 1980; ex *Golar Sigli* 1978
66357 **PERMINA XXXI** (Ia) ex *Bruce Padang* 1980; ex *Indotank* 1978

66360 **AL BACHIR** Pa/Sw (Gotav) 1960; Tk; 12800; 169.81 × 9.61 (557.12 × 31.53); M (Gotaverken); 15; ex *Babaneft One* 1983; ex *Olivia* 1979; ex *Dolphin Olivia* 1979; ex *Braconda* 1978

663870 **ASTRASOL** Ar/Sw (Lindholmens) 1960; Tk; 15400; 186.09 × 10.33 (610.53 × 33.89); M (Gotaverken); 15.5; ex *Epiros* 1982; ex *Thomas B Kimball* 1972

★66380 **KALININGRADNEFT** Ru/Fi (Rauma-Repola) 1978; RT/Tk; 4500; 115.53 × 6.5 (379.04 × 21.33); M (B&W); 16
Sisters (Ru flag):
★66381 **OKHANEFT**
★66382 **GALVYE**
★66383 **KALININGRADSKIY-NEFTYANIK**
★66384 **MYS SARYCH**
★66386 **UST-KARSK**
★66387 **UST-KUT**
★66388 **VESYEGONSK**
★66389 **VIDNOYE**
★66390 **LINKUVA**
★66391 **DELEGAT**
★66392 **KROPOTKIN**
★66393 **MYS KHRUSTALNYY**
★66394 **UST-ILIMSK**
★66395 **UST-KAN**
★66396 **MYS KODOSH**
★66397 **LUKOMORYE**

66400 **THEODOSIA** Pa/Fi (Valmet) 1960; Tk; 2700; 92.11 × 6.27 (302.2 × 20.57); M (B&W); 13.5; ex *Reem B* 1981; ex *Esso Fennia* 1976

66410 **BATU** Tu/Br (Hall, Russell) 1970; Ch/Tk; 4600; 106.99 × 7.34 (351.02 × 24.08); M (Mirrlees Blackstone); 14; ex *Kyrgo* 1981; ex *Silverharrier* 1980

66430 **ONCU** Tu/Tu (Denizcilik) 1969; Tk; 3300; 111.56 × 5.88 (366.01 × 19.29); M (Sulzer); —; Lengthened 1971

66440 **ESSO TENBY** Br/Br (Appledore) 1970; Tk; 2200; 91.42 × 5.9 (299.93 × 19.36); M (English Electric); —

66450 **PORT TUDY** Fr/Br (Robb Caledon) 1969; Tk; 3100; 101.73 × 6.57 (333.76 × 21.56); M (English Electric); 14

66460 **MARK VII** Gr/Ne (Arnhemsche) 1958; Tk; 1700; 83.57 × 5.24 (274.18 × 17.19); M (Werkspoor); 12; ex *Airismaa* 1977

66470 **ALLURITY** Br/Ne (Nieuwe Noord) 1969; Tk; 700; 73.97 × 3.96 (242.68 × 12.99); M (KHD); 12
Sister:
66471 **ACTIVITY** (Br)

66480 **GIMONE** Fr/Fr (La Rochelle) 1969; Tk; 3400; 100.03 × 5.61 (328.18 × 18.41); TSM (Werkspoor); 11.75

★66482 **DA QING 18** RC/RC (Hu Tung) 1965; Tk; 2400; 96 × 5.65 (315 × 18.54); M (Hudong); 11.5; ex *Chien She 18*
Sisters (RC flag:
★66483 **DA QING 19**
★66484 **DA QING 20**
★66485 **DA QING 21**
★66486 **DA QING 22**
★66487 **DA QING 23**

66490 **BALTIC PROSPERITY** Pa/Sw (Lodose) 1965; Tk; 2250; 86.75 × 5.79 (284.6 × 19); M (MWM); 12; ex *Rathowen* 1983; ex *Bellona* 1974; ex *Luna* 1974
Similar (One less deck on superstructure):
66491 **WENA** (Ma) ex *Lena* 1977
Similar:
66493 **SIDON** (Gr) ex *Bellona* 1978; ex *Lisa* 1975
Possibly similar:
66494 **BELLONA** (Sw) ex *Stella Atlantic* 1978

66497 **LINGNAN** Pa/FRG (Luerssen) 1968; Tk; 2800; 100.72 × 6.29 (330 × 20.64); M (KHD); 12.5; ex *Delbros Mt Arayat* 1973

66500 **MELROSE** Br/FRG (Brand) 1971; LGC; 2000; 86.95 × 6.12 (285.27 × 20.08); M (MWM); 14

66510 **HUMBOLDT** Br/Fr (La Ciotat) 1968; LGC; 5200; 116.9 × 6.5 (383.53 × 21.32); M (MAN); 15
Similar:
66511 **BERGA** (Ag) ex *Pascal* 1970
66512 **LAVOISIER** (Ar)

66520 **KYOSEKI MARU No 3** Ja/Ja (Naikai) 1977; LGC; 1000; 65.28 × 4.56 (214.17 × 14.96); M (Hanshin); 12.5

66530 **SANKYO ETHYLENE MARU** Ja/Ja (Naikai) 1974; LGC; 1600; 65.54 × 4.12 (215.03 × 13.52); M (Daihatsu); 11.25

66540 **KEPLERO** It/FRG (Meyer) 1968; LGC; 1600; 77.78 × 4.65 (255.18 × 15.26); M (KHD); 14; ex *Johann Kepler* 1979; ex *Kap Roland* 1974

66550 **NESTEGAS** Fi/No (Moss R) 1973; LGC; 4400; 105.01 × 7.06 (344.52 × 23.16); M (Wartsila); 14.75

66560 **NESTEFOX** Fi/No (Moss R) 1977; LGC; 6800; 116.54 × 7.81 (382.35 × 25.62); M (Lindholmens) 15.25

⬤66570 **ALCHEMIST BREMEN** Li/No (Langvik) 1973; Ch; 4800; 129.85 × 7 (426.01 × 22.97); M (GMT); 16; ex *Thoralbe* 1983
Sisters (Pa flag):
66571 **THORHEIDE**
66572 **CORDILLERAS** ex *Thordrache* 1983
66573 **THORODLAND**
Possible similar:
66574 **CHEMTANK HAMBURG** (Li) ex *Alchemist Hamburg* 1983; ex *Thorhamer* 1983
66575 **THORHAVEN** (Pa)

66577 **CABLEMAN** Br/Br (Appledore) 1980; Tk; 4900; 116.52 × 7.2 (382.28 × 23.62); M (Ruston); 13
Sister:
66578 **ECHOMAN** (Br)
Similar (larger):
66579 **TANKERMAN** (Br)

66580 **AL GHASSANI** Mo/No (Kleven) 1977; LGC; 4100; 102.06 × 7.4 (334.84 × 24.27); M (Atlas-MaK); 14.75

66590 **ANNA BROERE** Ne/FRG (Brand) 1976; Ch; 1600; 82.5 × 5.74 (270.66 × 18.83); M (Atlas-MaK); 13.5

66600 **DUTCH GLORY** Ne/Ne (Nieuwe Noord) 1975; Ch; 1400; 80.24 × 5.42 (263.25 × 17.78); M (KHD); 13.5
Sister:
66601 **DUTCH MASTER** (Ne)
Similar (superstructure more open):
66602 **CORRIE BROERE** (Ne)

66610 **BENVENUE** Br/Ne (Nieuwe Noord) 1974; Ch;

1600; 80.78 × 5.38 (265.02 × 17.65); M (Smit & Bolnes); 12.75
Sisters (Br flag):
66611 BENCLEUCH
66612 BENMACDHUI

66620 ISMARA Ag/FRG (Schlichting) 1978; Tk/WT; 2000; 87.76 × 5.72 (287.93 × 18.77); M (Atlas-MaK); 13.5
Sisters (Ag flag):
66621 DAHRA
66622 ZACCAR

66630 MOBIL LUBCHEM Br/Sp (Cantabrico) 1973; Tk/Ch; 2100; 93.33 × 5.36 (306.2 × 17.59); M (Deutz); 12.75

66635 SILVERHAWK Br/Br (Cammell Laird) 1969; Tk/Ch; 6800; 130.21 × 7.53 (427.2 × 24.7); M (Pielstick); 14.5

66640 PICCOLA Cy/Br (Cammell Laird) 1970; Ch; 4100; 108.08 × 7.32 (354.59 × 24.02); M (Lister Blackstone Mirrlees); 13.75; ex Yau Fook 1983; ex Silvereagle 1981
Similar (lengthened & may be altered):
66641 IRAN PASDAR (Ir) ex Crazy Horse 1984; ex Kyrgo 1983; ex Silverosprey 1981

66650 GUN Li/No (Karmsund) 1973; Ch; 1600; 82.76 × 6.06 (271.52 × 19.88); M (MWM); 13; ex Stella Nova 1980; ex Joy Saphir 1978; ex Bow Saphir 1978
Sister:
66651 LIVIA (Pa) ex Bimbo 1981; ex Alecto; ex Bow Alecto 1978
Possibly similar:
66652 JO SAILOR (Li) ex Joy Sailor 1980; ex Bow Sailor 1978

66660 PETROSTAR V Si/FRG (Lindenau) 1969; Tk 2000; 93.91 × 5.68 (308.1 × 18.64); M (MAN); 12.5; ex Solheim 1976
Sister:
66661 PETROSTAR VI (Si) ex Solstreif 1976

66670 BRAENNAREN Sw/FRG (Kremer) 1965; Tk; 660; 61.63 × 3.58 (202.21 × 11.75); M (MaK); 11; ex Indio 1972; Swedish Navy

66680 THORAIIA Si/No (Vaagen) 1965; Tk; 500/900; 71.05 × 5.16 (233.1 × 16.93); M (KHD); 12; ex Andine 1979; ex Modena 1978; ex Thuntank 1

66690 VINGASJO Sw/FRG (Luehring) 1972; Tk; 2000; 96.12 × 5.96 (315.35 × 19.55); M (Atlas-MaK); 12; ex Tarnsjo 1980

66700 PYTHEAS Fr/It (INMA) 1972; Tk; 3300; 108.51 × 4.7 (356 × 15.42) TSM (KHD); 11.5
Sister:
66701 EUTHYMENES (Fr)

66710 SENKAKU MARU Ja/Ja (Ishikawajima S&C) 1971; LGC; 800; 57 × 3.51 (187 × 11.52); M (Daihatsu); 10.75
Possible Sisters (Ja flag):
66711 SHOKAKU MARU
66712 TONEN ETHYLENE MARU

66720 KINGSABBEY Br/Br (Burntisland) 1966; LGC; 700; 56.7 × 3.43 (186.02 × 11.25); M (Davey, Paxman); 11.5; ex Rudi M 1980; ex Teviot

66730 HAPPY FALCON Pa/No (Kleven) 1965; LGC; 1400; 71.18 × 5.51 (233.53 × 18.08); M (MaK); 12.5; ex Sunny Baby 1981; ex Kings Star 1970; Converted cargo ship 1971
Sister:
66731 HAPPY FELLOW (Pa) ex Sunny Boy 1981; ex Teresa 1970

66740 NIELS HENRIK ABEL No/Ne (Pattje) 1973; LGC; 1600; 79.48 × 6.04 (260.76 × 19.82); M (Atlas-MaK); 13.5; Launched as Anita
Sister:
66741 SIGURD JORSALFAR (No)

66750 FORT POINT Br/Ne ('De Hoop') 1968; C; 4400; 110.42 × 6.85 (362.27 × 22.47); M (MAN); 12.5; ex Dunvegan Head 1977
Sister:
66751 BEACON POINT (Br) ex Duncansby Head 1977

66760 SCANCARRIER Pa/De (Sonderborg) 1971; C; 500; 70.67 × 3.6 (231.86 × 11.81); M (Alpha-Diesel); 12; ex Spes 1 1984; ex Spes 1982; ex Mette Bravo 1980; ex Kirsten Bech 1975; ex Captain Magellan 1975; ex Kirsten Bech 1973

66770 RECOMONE It/Br (Cochrane) 1970; C; 1600; 86.34 × 5.03 (283.27 × 16.5); M (English Electric); 12; ex Stirlingbrook 1983
Sisters:
66771 STAVROS H (Cy) ex Solentbrook 1982
66772 FIRMUS (Cy) ex Somersetbrook 1983

66773 ROMANO (Do) ex Surreybrook 1982
66774 IERANTO (It) ex Sussexbrook 1982

66790 ANTARES Ne/FRG (Schuerenstedt) 1966; C; 1300; 73.61 × 5.28 (241.5 × 17.32); M (MaK); 12.5; ex Danesea 1973; ex Antares 1 1971; ex Tantzen 1967

66800 ARUNTO No/DDR ('Neptun') 1966; C; 1200; 78.59 × 5.06 (257.84 × 16.6); M (MaK); 11.5; ex Brunto 1970
Similar:
66801 EASTERN LADY (Li) ex Avant 1981; ex Blue Lady 1974; ex Brunette 1971
66802 JAOUHAR (Cy) ex Anglo 1982; ex Janja 1974; ex Recto 1971
66803 CAREBECA (It) ex Carebeka 1 1982; ex Hanseatic 1970
66804 NORDON (Sw) ex Blue Moon 1973; ex Brunita 1972
66806 LE GOELO (Fr) ex Janne 1974; ex Jobella 1970
66807 ANTONIO M (It) ex Rethymnon 1978; ex Jocefa 1969
66808 PALMAVERA (It) ex Rubicone 1983; ex Bente Sleire 1977; ex Fagertind 1976; ex Stokktind 1973
66810 MAYA (It) ex Domenico Palumbo 1981; ex Douce France 1978; ex Hanseat 1970
66811 IOLE C (It) ex Maik 1983; ex Altair 1976; ex Fro 1974
66812 ELVIRA (It) ex Heemskerk 1978; ex Hansa 1970
66813 JONIKA (It) ex Teresa Scotto 1982; ex Saronis 1978; ex Jonika 1969

66830 NIAGA XXIV Ia/FRG (M Jansen) 1969; C; 700/1500; 75.49 × 4.22/6 (247.6 × 13.84/19.68); M (KHD); 14; ex Bilbao; ex Inger 1973; ex Truro 1971; Launched as Bele
Sister:
66831 ELDVIK (Ic) ex Heidi 1975; ex Tasso 1971

66840 DONA PETRA M R Pa/Ne ('Hoogezand' JB) 1966; C; 500/1100; 73.06 × 3.84/4.27 (239.7 × 12.6/14); M (Appingedammer Brons); 12.5; ex Jan 1982
Sisters (Hu built—Angyalfold):
66841 DIEGO DE BLASIO (It) ex Amari; ex Joerka 1975
66842 PELTI (Gr) ex Gabrielle 1980; ex Rodon 1979; ex Jodonna 1976

66850 GAVILAN Pa/De (Aalborg) 1965; C; 1700/2400; 95.61 × 5.59/6.58 (313.68 × 18.34/21.59); M (B&W); 14; ex Reykjafoss 1980
Sister:
66851 LEFKAS (Cy) ex Skogafoss 1980

66860 STRAITS VENTURE Sg/FRG (Sietas) 1970; C; 1000; 90.81 × 4.77 (297.93 × 15.65); M (Atlas-MaK); 14; ex Gothia 1981; Launched as Taurus

66870 COLOMBO MARU Pa/FRG (Sietas) 1970; C; 1700/3300; 100.56 × 5.47/6.76 (329.92 × 17.94/22.17); M (KHD); 15.25; ex Colombo Venture 1982; ex Ashdod
Sister:
66871 APUS (Is)

66880 AL HODEIDAH Si/FRG (Sietas) 1970; C; 1900/3900; 113.77 × 6.48 (373.26 × 21.26); M (Atlas-MaK); 15; ex Victrix 1983; ex Al Hodeidah 1982; ex Carolina 1978; Lengthened 1973
Similar (Lengthened):
66881 DEXENA (Cy) ex Niugini Chief 1981; ex Forum Niugini 1980; ex Arosia 1980
Similar (Unlengthened):
66882 BURDIGALA (Fr) ex Arcasea 1980; ex Isabella 1976
★**66883 WAH YEE** (RC) ex Madeira 1983; ex Amanda 1 1982; ex Anny 1977; ex Amanda 1 1976; ex Amanda 1972; Launched as Suderfehn
66884 AL BATTANI (Eg) ex Birta Andrea 1977; ex Andrea 1977; Launched as Birta Andrea
66885 RIGGI 1 (Pa) ex Rigi 1982; ex Anita-Adele 1980; ex Cheshire Resolve 1978; ex Anita 1976; Launched as Anita-Adele
66886 HOESHENG (Sg) ex Heinrich Wesch 1982; ex Mascareignes; ex Weser Dispatcher

66890 FAITH Cy/Ne (Sander) 1971; C; 1600/3000; 103.5 × 5.14/6.52 (339.51 × 16.86/21.39); M (Atlas-MaK); 14; ex Cheshire Faith 1979; ex Osterfehn 1978
Sister:
66891 GANVIE (Bi) ex Faros 1978; Launched as Westerfehn

66900 ILHA DE SAO MIGUEL Po/FRG (Roland-werft) 1970; Con; 2900; 102.42 × 6.24 (336.02 × 20.47); M (Atlas-MaK); 11; ex Anja 1980; ex Cheshire Challenge; ex Anja 1974; Launched as Norderfehn
Sister:
66901 AL MANSOURA (Qt) ex Pacific 1980

66905 NORDFJORD Pa/No (Aukra) 1970/78; C; 1500; 89.11 × 4.73 (292 × 15.52); M (Atlas-MaK); 13.5; Lengthened 1978
Sisters (probably with centre-line kingposts foreward):
66906 SUDFJORD (Pa)
66907 WESTFJORD (Pa)

66910 HIRMA No/No (Aukra) 1978; C; 800/1600; 79.46 × 5.35 (260.7 × 17.55); M (Alco); 14

66920 NORTHRIDGE Br/FRG (M Jansen) 1973; C/HL; 1600; 96.45 × 5.19 (316.44 × 17.03); M (KHD); 14.5; ex Cairngorm 1977; Converted from general cargo (M Jansen)

66930 ZEIDA Mo/Sp (Construcciones SA) 1971; C; 700/1600; 84.82 × —/5.67 (278.28 × —/18.6); M (Deutz); 11; ex Vilya 1975
Sisters:
66931 ZERHOUN (Mo) ex Nenya 1975
66932 PELLA (Gr) ex Celtic Venture 1982; ex Monkchester 1978; ex Waynegate 1976
Similar (Ne built-E J Smit):
66933 MARIA MONICA (It) ex Monica 1976

66940 AMALI Si/Ne ('Vooruitgang') 1961; C/HL; 600/1200; 80.7 × —/4.76 (264.76 × —/15.61); M (Werkspoor); —; ex Amal 1980; ex Bellatrix 1 1977; ex Bellatrix 1974; Launched as Marijke Irene; Lengthened & widened 1970

★**66950 BOSUT** Ys/FRG (Luerssen) 1967; C; 2800; 95.81 × 6.36 (314.34 × 20.87); M (Bergens); 12.25; ex Raknes 1977
Sisters (Ys flag):
★**66952 CIKOLO** ex Tinnes 1978
★**66953 ROGOZNICA** ex Vigsnes 1978
(It flag):
66954 MARIA DORMIO ex Telnes 1979
66955 PIETRO ex Altnes 1978
66956 BEATRICE ex Korsnes 1977
66957 VISPY ex Garnes 1978
66958 ALBERTO DORMIO ex Isnes 1983; ex Frines 1977; ex Fritre 1973

66970 BREEKANT Ne/No (Sterkoder) 1972; C; 1600; 79.91 × 5.28 (262.17 × 17.32); M (Polar); 14; ex Keizersgracht 1979; ex Mini Sun 1973
Sisters:
66971 BREEKADE (Ne) ex Mini Cloud 1978
66972 CEBO MOON (Gr) ex Mini Moon 1979
66973 NABEEL (Pa) ex Eerbeek 1981; ex Mini Sky 1974;
66974 MACORIX (Do) ex Strombeek 1981; ex Mini Star 1973

★**66980 JAROSLAW** Pd/Pd (Gdanska) 1979; C; 1600; 84 × 5.65 (275.59 × 18.54); M (GMT); 14; 'B 431' type

66990 MARIANN Pa/Ma (Malta DD) 1972; C; 1600; 91.37 × 5.12 (299.77 × 16.8); M (Atlas-MaK); 14
Sister:
66991 THERESE (Cy)

67000 AMIR My/FRG (Brand) 1970; C; 1000/2000; 92.31 × 4.65/6.10 (303 × 15.26/20.01); M (KHD); 15; ex Bostonsand 1981
Sisters:
67001 AUDAX (Pa) ex Burhaversand 1981
67002 DANIELLE 2 (Pa) ex Parouth 1983; ex Stollhammersand 1981
67003 ANDY'S PRIDE (Sg) ex Leo Pride 1980; ex Marocsand 1977
★**67004 GRADINA** (Ys) ex Seefeldersand 1983

★**67010 ANTON GUBARYEV** Ru/Rm (Turnu-Severin) 1974; C; 1200/2100; 88.75 × 4.15/5.2 (291.17 × 13.62/17.06); M (Sulzer); 13
Sisters (Ru flag):
★**67011 DZHEMS BANKOVICH**
★**67012 GRISHA PODOBEDOV**
★**67013 KHENDRIK KUYVAS**
★**67014 LIDA DEMESH**
★**67015 MALDIS SKREYA**
★**67016 MARAT KOZLOV**
★**67017 NADE RIBAKOVAYTE**
★**67018 NYURA KIZHEVATOVA**
★**67019 PECHORA**
★**67020 PETYA KOVALYENKO**
★**67021 PETYA SHITIKOV**
★**67022 PINEGA**
★**67023 RICHARDAS BUKAUSKAS**
★**67024 TANYA KARPINSKAYA**
★**67025 TURGAY**
★**67026 VALYA KURAKINA**
★**67027 VANYA KOVALYEV**
★**67028 YASHA GORDIYENKO**
★**67029 VASYA STABROVSKIY**
★**67030 VASYA KURKA**
★**67031 VITYA NOVITSKIY**
★**67032 YUNYY PARTIZAN**

67040 TEQUILA SUNRISE FRG/FRG (Sietas) 1970;

C; 1000; 87.61 × 5.29 (287.43 × 17.35); M (KHD); 14.5; ex *Svealand* 1981; ex *Conti Syria* 1980; ex *Svealand* 1980; ex *Helga Russ* 1979; ex *Svealand* 1977; ex *Royal Enterprise* 1975; Launched as *Svea land*

★67050 **RUCIANE** Pd/Pd (Wisla) 1972; C; 800; 59.82 × 4.2 (196.26 × 13.78); M (Sulzer); 11.5; '**B457**' type; Kingpost amidships may now be re-moved—see '**BARLINEK**'

67060 **CARICOM EXPRESS** Bb/Ne (Groot & VV) 1976; C; 1600; 84.31 × 6.32 (276.6 × 20.73); M (Smit & Bolnes); 13; ex *Kirsten Smits* 1983
Probable sister:
67061 **CARICOM VENTURE** (Bb) ex *Marinus Smits* 1983

67070 **FRISIAN TRADER** Ne/Ne ('Harlingen') 1976; C; 1600; 79.81 × 5.44 (261.84 × 17.85); M (Alpha-Diesel); 13

67080 **HOOP** Ne/Ne (Bodewes Bergum) 1978; C; 1500; 78.67 × 5.04 (258.1 × 16.54); M (Appinge-dammer Brons); 12

67090 **LA BAHIA** Br/No (Ankerlokken) 1972; Ch; 1600; 100.72 × 5.89 (330.45 × 19.32); M (Nydqvist & Holm); 16; ex *Wavemark* 1974
Sister:
67091 **LA FALDA** (Br) ex *Sunmark* 1974

67100 **ZOR** Qt/De (Odense) 1965; Tk; 3900; 112.68 × 6.1 (369.68 × 20.01); M (B&W); 13.5; ex *Dangulf Maersk* 1982
Sister:
67101 **PETRO PYLA** (Fr) ex *Svengulf Maersk* 1982

67110 **MANITOU** FRG/FRG (Lindenau) 1968; Tk; 1000; 76.92 × 4.67 (252.36 × 15.32); M (Atlas-MaK); 12
Sisters (FRG flag):
67111 **WINNETOU**
67112 **YUMA**

67120 **THUNTANK 1** Sw/Sw (Falkenbergs) 1973; Ch; 3700; 107.19 × 6.7 (351.67 × 21.98); M (Polar); 12

●67130 **CORNELIA** No/Ne (Pattje) 1968; Tk; 500; 72.98 × 3.57 (239.44 × 11.71); M (Atlas-MaK); 12; ex *Tora* 1982

67140 **CAMPOTEJAR** Sp/Sp (Cadagua) 1967; Tk; 1800; 76.91 × 5.13 (261.18 × 16.83); M (Stork-Werkspoor); 14
Sisters (Sp flag):
67141 **CAMPOSALINAS**
67142 **CAMPOLONGO**

67150 **BOREA** Pa/Sw (Kalmar) 1971; Tk; 1600; 86.42 × 5.26 (283 × 17.26); M (Alpha-Diesel); 12

67160 **HECHT V** FRG/Sw (Solvesborgs) 1970; Tk; 1100; 75.29 × 3.51 (247.01 × 11.52); M (Alpha-Diesel); 12.5; ex *Transtank* 1972; ex *Contank Lubeck* 1972
Similar:
67161 **THUNTANK 10** (Sw) ex *Credo* 1974

67165 **PROOF GALLANT** Li/Ne (Groot & VV) 1980; Ch/WT; 1600; 89.52 × 6.16 (294 × 20.21); M (Atlas-MaK); —

67170 **ESSI BALTIC** No/No (Aukra) 1977; TB/Ch; 1500; 69.73 × 5.4 (228.77 × 17.72); M (Liebknecht); 11.5; ex *Johot* 1979
Sister:
67171 **ELAND** (Pa) ex *Essi Coral* 1982; ex *Johero* 1979

●67180 **OCEAN GIRL** Li/Sw (Gotav) 1968; B; 22700; 200.24 × 11.17 (656.96 × 36.65); M (Gotaverken); 15.5; ex *Greta Thulin*

67190 **FLAMINGO** Sg/Br (Vickers Ltd) 1965; Con; 6800; 141.94 × 8.09 (465.68 × 26.54); M (Sulzer); 15; ex *New Penguin* 1981; ex *Atalanta* 1980; ex *Zim Atalanta* 1980; ex *Atalanta*; ex *C P Ambassador* 1974; ex *Beavercove* 1970; Converted from general cargo 1969 and lengthened 1970 (Boele's Sch)

67200 **TERRA NORDICA** Ca/Ca (Port Weller) 1964; R; 2000; 77.12 × 5.12 (253.02 × 16.78); M (Werkspoor); 13.5; ex *Chesley A Crosbie* 1982; Helicopter deck aft
Sister:
67201 **TERRA NOVA** (Ca) ex *Sir John Crosbie* 1980

67210 **STARMAN AUSTRALIA** FRG/FRG (Luerssen) 1977; RoC/HL; 3500; 91.5 × 5.17 (300.2 × 16.96); TSM (MWM) 13.5; ex *Stahleck* 1981
Similar (US flag) (US built-Peterson):
67211 **JOHN HENRY**
67212 **PAUL BUNYAN**

67220 **KOWIE** Pa/Ja (Yamanishi) 1978; C; 6400; 129.32 × 7.83 (424.3 × 25.7); M (B&W); 15; ex

Esteblick 1982; ex *Ville du Ponant*; ex *Esteblick* 1980; ex *BMI Exporter* 1978
Similar:
67221 **MARIPASOULA** (Fr) ex *Atalanta II* 1982; ex *Atalanta*
67222 **KAIROS** (Pa) ex *Germanic* 1980
67223 **IMPALA** (Pa)
Probably similar:
67224 **PHAROS** (Pa) ex *Adria 1* 1980; ex *Naxos 1* 1979; ex *Renate Wunsche* 1978; ex *Nordwelle* 1977
67225 **MARE SARINA** (Sg) ex *Hilda Wesch* 1983; Launched as *Blue Sovereign*

★67230 **FU SHUN CHENG** RC/FRG (Elsflether) 1969; C; 3400/5400; 117.35 × 6.68/7.06 (385.01 × 21.92/23.16); M₁(B+V) 17; ex *Jorg Kruger* 1981; ex *Caparnauti* 1975; ex *Jorg Kruger* 1974
Sister:
★67231 **PING XIANG CHENG** (RC) ex *Britta Kruger* 1977

67240 **SLOMAN NEREUS** FRG/FRG (Howaldts DW) 1977; C; 4400/7400; 129.52 × 6.81/8.06 (424.93 × 22.34/26.44); M (Atlas-MaK); 16.75; ex *Tabuco* 1980; ex *Sloman Nereus* 1980; ex *Carol Nereus* 1980; ex *Sloman Nereus* 1978; '**CL-10**' type
Sisters (FRG flag):
67241 **SLOMAN NAJADE**
67242 **STUBBENHUK**
67243 **STEINHOFT** ex *ELMA Seis* 1982; ex *Stein-hoft* 1981; ex *Gongola Hope* 1979; ex *Steinhoft* 1978

67250 **KRANTOR** Gr/Ne (Amsterdamsche D) 1964; C; 1400/2300; 87.89 × —/6.31 (288.35 × —/20.7); M (Werkspoor); 13; ex *Astra* 1980; ex *Rahel* 1978
Sister:
67251 **BRANT POINT** (Br) ex *Oran* 1978; ex *Devora* 1978

67260 **THOROLD** Ca/Br (Hall, Russell) 1962; B; 5700; 125.05 × 7.58 (410.27 × 24.87); M (Sulzer); —; ex *Gosforth* 1972

67270 **MAISENI** Gh/Ja (IHI) 1965; C; 3200; 100.89 × 6.35 (331. × 20.83); M (Sulzer); 12; ex *Esco* 1981; ex *Olateju* 1981; ex *Davies 1* 1977; ex *Dayaka Dua* 1977; ex *Miura Maru* 1972

67280 **GOLDEN VENTURE** Li/Ja (Hayashikane) 1971; B; 10100; 148.42 × 8.99 (486.94 × 29.49); M (IHI); 14.75
Possibly similar (some may have deck cranes):
67281 **GRAND WISE** (Li) ex *Fides* 1982
67282 **SAE BA DA** (Ko) ex *Hsing May* 1981; ex *Nationa* 1980
67283 **BETTY** (Gr) ex *Sammi No 1* 1981
67284 **ALEXANDRAKI** (Cy) ex *Sincere No 3* 1983
67285 **CAPE SOUNION** (Gr) ex *Epidavros Gulf* 1983; ex *Indah Jumbo* 1980; ex *Harngjin* 1980; ex *Daishowa Venture* 1978

67290 **JALATARANG** In/Br (Hamiliton) 1963; C; 8800/12100; 164.57 × 8.48/9.51 (539.93 × 27.82/31.2); M(B&W);¡ex *Bente Brovig* 1969

67310 **NICOLAOS CH** Gr/Fr (Mediterranee) 1960; C; 6900/9400; 141.18 × 8.4/9.56 (463.19 × 27.56/31.36); M (Gotaverken); —; ex *Apostolos M III* 1980; ex *Kavo Grossos* 1979; ex *Triaena* 1974; ex *Lambros M Fatsis* 1972; ex *La Hortensia* 1968; may be spelt **NIKOLAOS CH**
Similar:
★67311 **GEORGI BENKOVSKI** (Bu) ex *La Estancia* 1963
Similar (with goalposts):
67312 **KYRARINI** (Gr) ex *Dirphys* 1982; ex *Armonia* 1980

67320 **THEOTOKOS** Gr/Fr (Mediterranee) 1961; C; 7000/9400; 141.18 × —/9.56 (463.19 × —/31.36); M (Sulzer); 14; ex *Star Flower*; ex *Dahlia* 1978
Sister:
67321 **DESPINA** (Gr) ex *Star Fish*; ex *Nurith* 1978

67335 **SARAMACCA** Sn/Ne (Amels/'Friesland') 1980; C/Con; 4100; 114.05 × 6.65 (374 × 21.82); M (Stork-Werkspoor); 15

★67340 **BATALLA DE STA. CLARA** Cu/Fi (Nystads) 1975; R; 500/1300; 74.12 × —/4.71 (243.18 × —/15.45); M (Bofors); 14
Sister:
★67341 **BATALLA DE YAGUAJAY** (Cu)

★67350 **ROSTOK** Ru/DDR ('Neptun') 1973; C; 2900/4500; 117.79 × 5.8/6.92 (386.45 × 19.03/22.7); M (MAN); 16.5; '**POSEIDON**' class
Sisters (Ru flag):
★67351 **CHITA**
★67352 **KHASAN**
★67353 **NOVOCHERKASSK**
★67354 **RYSHKANY**
★67355 **RUSHANY**
★67356 **RUDNYY**
★67357 **ROMNY**

★67358 **RUBEZHNOYE**
★67359 **RZHEV**
★67360 **RAKHOV**
★67361 **REUTOV**
★67362 **RATNO**
★67363 **RADOMYSHI**
★67364 **RYAZAN**
★67365 **ROSLAVL**
★67366 **RYBINSK**
★67367 **MAGO**

67380 **TROPICANA** Gr/Sp (Cadagua) 1969; R; 1800; 84 × 5 (275.59 × 16.4); M (Cadiz); —; ex *Horus* 1981

67390 **SHELL CRAFTSMAN** Br/Br (Hall, Russell) 1968; Tk; 1500; 75.95 × 4.67 (249.18 × 15.32); M (Nydqvist & Holm); 14.5; ex *Ardrossan* 1979

67400 **KANCHENJUNGA** In/Ys ('Uljanik') 1975; Tk; 140000; 332.39 × 21.79 (1090.52 × 71.49); TSM (B&W); 17
Sister:
67401 **KOYALI** (In)
Probable sister:
67402 **OLOIBIRI** (Ng)

67410 **SINMAR** No/No (Stord) 1971; Tk; 109500; 327.72 × 20.35 (1075.2 × 66.77); T (Stal-Laval); 16; ex *Norbird* 1982; ex *Raila* 1977
Possibly similar:
67412 **BERGE BOSS** (No) ex *Berge Beaumaris* 1982; ex *Beaumaris* 1981

67420 **FINNY** Fi/No (Stord) 1967; Tk; 52900; 258.53 × 15.29 (848.19 × 50.16); M (B&W); 16; ex *Symra* 1975
Sister:
67421 **FANNY** (Fi) ex *Ruth* 1975

67430 **SEAPRIDE** Cy/Br (Doxford & S) 1969; Tk; 14800; 169.78 × 9.75 (557.02 × 31.99); M (Doxford); 15.5; ex *Saucon* 1983; ex *Laurelwood* 1975
Sisters:
67431 **SEAVENTURE** (Cy) ex *Shabonee* 1983; ex *Sea Griffin* 1974
67432 **NAND KAVITA** (In) ex *Captain X Kyriakou* 1980; ex *Dafni C* 1978; ex *Hollywood* 1977

67440 **BALDER LONDON** Br/Br (Cammell Laird) 1975; Tk; 19000; 170.69 × 11.83 (560 × 38.81); M (Pielstick); 16.25; ex *Hudson Progress*; '**STAT 32**' type

67450 **LUIGI CASALE** It/Fr (La Ciotat) 1966; LGC; 10900; 150.48 × 8.86 (493.7 × 29.06); M (Sulzer); 16; ex *Capella* 1973; ex *Franklin* 1967; ex *Capella* 1967; Launched as *Benjamin Franklin*
Sister:
67451 **PYTHAGORE** (Pa) ex *Arquimedes* 1975

●67460 **BRAS** No/No (Fosen) 1976; Ch; 2000; 92.79 × 6.8 (304.43 × 22.31); M (Atlas-MaK); 13
Sister:
67461 **AL SABAH 1** ex *Bravur* 1982
Similar:
67462 **BRAGD** (No)

67470 **DANISH ARROW** De/De 1976; LGC; 500; 66.5 × 3.27 (218.17 × 10.71); M; 12.5
Sister:
67471 **DANISH DART** (De)

67480 **SCANCARRIER** Pa/De (Sonderborg) 1971; C; 499; 70.82 × 3.60 (232 × 11.81); M (Alpha-Diesel); 12; ex *Spes 1* 1984; ex *Spes* 1982; ex *Kannik* 1980; ex *Mette Bravo* 1980; ex *Kirsten Bech* 1975; ex *Captain Magellan* 1975; ex *Kirsten Bech* 1973
Sister:
67481 **EMY** (It) ex *Inge Bech* 1980

67490 **MORESBY CHIEF** Pp/FRG (Husumer) 1972; C; 900/1600; 81.01 × 4.4/5.49 (265.78 × 14.43/18.01); M (Alpha-Diesel); 13; ex *Petra*; ex *Lindinger Brilliant* 1978
Sisters:
67491 **ANCHANA** (Sg) ex *Lindinger Emerald* 1977
67492 **MINDELO** (CV) ex *Atlantisch* 1982; ex *Lindinger Facet* 1978
67493 **ZARKA** (Qt) ex *Mercandian Caix* 1980; ex *Lindinger Coral* 1978
67494 **MOR** (Br) ex *Lindinger Amber* 1978
67495 **SANTO ANTAO** (CV) ex *Lindinger Diamond* 1977
Possible sisters:
67496 **ILHA DE KOMO** (CV) ex *Lindinger Hyacinth* 1978
67497 **PRACETIA** (Ia) ex *Nautilus* 1981; ex *Lindinger Gold* 1978

67510 **MOUNT ELLEROS** Gr/Sp (U N de Levante) 1958; C; 6400; 138.41 × 9.49 (454.1 × 31.14); M (Fiat); 14; ex *Mariannina* 1981; ex *La Selva* 1967

67530 **AGIP SICILIA** It/It (Italcantieri) 1972; Tk; 126100; 348.32 × 20.02 (1142.78 × 65.68); M (Fiat);

16
Sisters:
67531 **AGIP SARDEGNA** (It)
67532 **HENRIETTE II** (Gr) ex *Paraggi* 1981; ex *Sant' Ambrogio* 1978
67533 **NIRVANA** (It) ex *Oceania* 1979
Possible sisters (It Flag):
67534 **AGIP ABRUZZO**
67535 **AGIP CAMPANIA**
67536 **AGIP LAZIO**
67537 **AGIP MARCHE**
67538 **NAI MARIO PERRONE**
67539 **NAI DI STEFANO**
67540 **NAI MATTEINI**
67541 **NAI ROCCO PIAGGIO**
67544 **VOLERE**

●67550 **MELPO LEMOS** Li/FRG (A G 'Weser') 1971; Tk; 113800; 347.81 × 19.96 (1141.1 × 65.55); T (GEC); 16
Sisters:
67551 **CHRYSANTHY M LEMOS** (Li)
67552 **IRENE LEMOS** (Li)
67553 **MICHAEL C LEMOS** (Gr)

67560 **WORLD SCHOLAR** Li/Br (Lithgows) 1979; Tk; 126200; 344.43 × 20.68 (1130 × 68.10); M (B&W); 14
Sister:
67561 **WORLD SCORE** (Li) Aft section launched as *Cartsdyke Glen*

67570 **LORETO II** Pe/Fr (La Ciotat) 1976; Tk; 44500; 250.53 × 14.25 (820.96 × 46.75); M (Sulzer); 16; ex *St Vincent* 1983
Sisters:
67571 **PLAKOURA** (Li) ex *St Marcos* 1983; ex *Dominant* 1977
67572 **TOURAINE** (Fr) ex *Changi Star* 1980; ex *St Raphael* 1977; ex *Adamant* 1977

67580 **YUSHO** Li/Ja (Hitachi) 1971; LGC; 47800; 227.03 × 11.51 (744.85 × 37.76); M (B&W); 15.75; ex *Yusho Maru* 1978

67590 **TIGRE** No/No (Stord) 1974; Tk; 140300; 347.84 × 22.14 (1141.2 × 72.63); T (Stal-Laval); 15.5

67600 **HOEGH HOOD** No/Ja (Kawasaki) 1973; OO; 129000; 326.04 × 20.49 (1069.68 × 67.22); T (Kawasaki); 15.5
Sisters:
67601 **HOEGH HILL** (No)
67602 **WORLD TRUTH** (Li) ex *La Loma* 1978

67610 **AVIN OIL TRADER** Gr/Sw (Eriksbergs) 1968; Tk; 51100; 277.05 × 14.72 (908.95 × 48.24); M (B&W); 16; ex *Alexandros M* 1979; ex *Fruen* 1975; ex *Solstad* 1973

●67620 **NORBEGA** No/Sw (Gotav) 1971; Tk; 113500; 332.24 × 20.65 (1090 × 67.74); T (Stal-Laval); 16; ex *Synia* 1977

67630 **AMANDA MILLER** Au/Au (Whyalla) 1971; Tk; 39100; 239.28 × 13.17 (785.04 × 43.21); M (Sulzer); 16.5

67632 **VALENCIA** Sp/Sp ('Bazan') 1977; Tk; 77600; 287.66 × 18.62 (944 × 61.09); M (MAN); 14.25
Sister:
67633 **GERONA** (Sp)
Probable sisters (Sp flag):
67634 **ALMIRANTE ROTAECHE**
67635 **LERIDA**
67636 **PUERTOLLANO**
Similar (originally sisters but now rebuilt):
67637 **CASTILLO DE LORCA** (Sp)
67638 **CASTILLO DE MONTEARAGON** (Sp)

67640 **BENHOPE** Br/Br (Sunderland) 1978; B; 39100; 228.12 × 14.02 (748.42 × 45.99); M (Doxford); 15

★67650 **VELIKIY OKTYABR** Ru/Ru (Baltic) 1967; Tk; 11000; 162.31 × 8.93 (532.51 × 29.3); M (B&W); 16.25
Sisters (Ru flag):
★67651 **POBYEDA OKTYABRYA**
★67652 **TSEZAR KUNIKOV**
★67653 **NIKOLAY SIPYAGIN**
★67654 **KERCH**
★67655 **EYZHEN BERG**
★67656 **KONSTANTIN TSIOLKOVSKIY**
★67657 **GENERAL BAGRATION**
★67658 **ZAKHARIY PALIASHVILI**
★67659 **FRIDRIKH TSANDER**
★67660 **VASILIY KIKVIDZE**
(Bu flag):
★67661 **MARITZA**
★67662 **REZVAYA**
★67663 **VELEKA**
(Cu flag):
★67664 **9 DE ABRIL**

★67665 **7 DE NOVIEMBRE**
(In flag):
67666 **BHAGAT SINGH**
67667 **SAROJINI NAIDU**
67668 **VISVESVARAYA**

★67670 **ASHKHABAD** Ru/Ys ('Split') 1978; Tk; 15600; 183.01 × 10.00 (601 × 32.81); M (B&W) 16.75
Sisters:
★67671 **TUAPSE** (Ru)
★67672 **LIPETSK** (Ru)

●★67680 **KOMANDARM FEDKO** Ru/Ru (Kherson) 1976; Tk; 18500; 178.49 × 10.4 (585.6 × 34.12); M (B&W); 15.25; Some sisters may be K₂MFK—see 'ALEKSANDR TSULUKIDZE'
Sisters (Ru flag):
★67681 **GENERAL MERKVILADZE**
★67682 **KHERSON**
★67683 **VSEVELOD KOCHETOV**
★67684 **ALEKSANDR KORNEYCHUK**
★67685 **DMITRIY MEDVEDEV**
★67686 **GRIGORIY NIKOLAYEV**
★67687 **JAN SUDRABKALN**
★67688 **NATA VACHNADZE**
★67689 **VLADIMIR GAVRILOV**
Probable sisters:
67689/1 **ATHENIAN OLYMPICS** (Cy) ex *Moscow Olympics* 1981
67689/2 **ATHENIAN VICTORY** (Cy)
67689/3 **ATHENIAN XENOPHON** (Cy)
67689/4 **CAPTAIN X KYRIAKOU** (Cy)
67689/5 **ATHENIAN THEODORE** (Cy)

★67690 **FELIKS DZIERZYNSKI** Pd/Pd (Szczecinska) 1978; B; 20300; 198.18 × 11 (650.2 × 36.09); M (Sulzer); 15.2; 'B-517' type
Sisters (Pd flag):
★67691 **WALKA MLODYCH**
★67692 **UNIWERSYTET SLASKI**
★67693 **POWSTANIEC WARSZAWSKI**
★67694 **JANUSZ KUSOCINSKI**

67700 **POSEIDON** Gr/Ne (Wilton-Fije) 1973; Tk; 17900; 188.2 × 10.36 (617.45 × 33.99); M (Gotaverken); 15; ex *Okturus* 1982
Sister:
67701 **MONSUN** (Fi) ex *Oktavius* 1982

67710 **OCEAN PIONEER** Li/FRG (Rhein Nordseew) 1972; Tk; 17600; 172.04 × 10.68 (564.43 × 35.04); M (Fiat); 15.5; ex *Nordpartner* 1983; ex *Thor Asgard* 1983; ex *Globe Comet* 1981; ex *Thor Asgard*
Sisters (Li flag):
67711 **SALLY I** ex *Amisia* 1973; Launched as *P C 1*
67712 **SALLY II**

67720 **NEWTON PRINCESS** Li/Sw (Eriksbergs) 1967; Tk; 48700; 265.13 × 14.66 (869.85 × 48.1); M (B&W); 16.5; ex *Lily H* 1983; ex *Mobil Radiant*; ex *Cerno* 1976; ex *Stiklestad* 1973

67725 **ST MICHAELIS** FRG/FRG (A G 'Weser') 1981; Tk; 26900; 182.96 × 12.09 (600 × 39.67); M (MAN); 14.5
Sisters (FRG flag):
67726 **ST NIKOLAI**
67727 **ST PETRI**

67730 **GUDRUN MAERSK** De/No (Kaldnes) 1973; Tk; 19900; 170.54 × 11.75 (559.51 × 38.55); M (B&W); 15.5
Sisters:
67731 **GJERTRUD MAERSK** (De)
67732 **CASTOR** (Bs) ex *Grete Maersk* 1981
67733 **POLLUX** (Li) ex *Titipor* 1983; ex *Gunvor Maersk* 1980

67734 **RAGNHILD BROVIG** No/No (Horten) 1981; Tk; 30700; 207.42 × 12.60 (681 × 41.34); M (Sulzer); 15.5
Sisters:
67735 **BARBARA BROVIG** (No)
67736 **RANDI BROVIG** (No)
Sisters (with satellite aerial on radar mast):
67737 **TAURUS HORTEN** (No)
67738 **TORO HORTEN** (No)

⚓67740 **AI AHOOD** Si/Sp (AESA) 1972; Tk; 58300; 279.31 × 15.26 (916 × 50.06); M (Sulzer); 16; ex *Venture Britannia* 1980; ex *Conoco Britannia* 1978

67770 **JAWAHARLAL NEHRU** In/Ys ('Split') 1969; Tk; 48400; 256.85 × 14.05 (842.68 × 46.09); M (MAN); 15.5; Has small twin 'funnels' near after kingposts
Sister (used as offshore loading tanker):
67771 **LAL BAHADUR SHASTRI** (In)

67780 **ESSO CARIBBEAN** Li/Ja (IHI) 1976; Tk; 177300; 378.39 × 22.27 (1241.44 × 73.06); T (IHI); 15.25; ex *Andros Petros* 1977
Sisters:
67781 **BURMAH ENDEAVOUR** (Br) (builder-China SB)
67782 **BURMAH ENTERPRISE** (Br) (builder-China SB)
67783 **ESSO MEDITERRANEAN** (Li) ex *Homeric* 1977
Similar:
67784 **ANDROS CHRYSSI** (Li)
67785 **ETHNIC** (Li)
67786 **SUNSHINE LEADER** (Li)
67787 **ISE MARU** (Ja)

67800 **GAZIANTEP** Tu/Ja (IHI) 1974; Tk; 79800; 286.52 × 16.84 (940.03 × 55.25); M (Sulzer) 15.5

67805 **SAIRYU MARU No 2** Ja/Ja (Kasado) 1982; Tk; 43100; 229.06 × 11.64 (752 × 38.19); M (Mitsubishi); 14.5

67810 **NIPPON MARU No 3** Ja/Ja (IHI) 1971; OO; 89500; 305.01 × 17.47 (1000.69 × 57.32); T (IHI); 16.25

67820 **BERGE KING** No/Ja (Mitsui) 1970; Tk; 140000; 342.91 × 21.78 (1125.03 × 71.46); M (B&W); 15
Sisters: (No flag):
67821 **BERGE QUEEN**
67822 **BERGE PRINCE**
67823 **BERGE PRINCESS**

●67830 **FABIAN** No/No (Stord) 1972; Tk; 140500; 347.84 × 22.14 (1141.21 × 72.64); T (Kvaerner); 15.5
Sisters:
67831 **BERGE BORG** (No) ex *Julian* 1982;
67832 **OCEAN TRADER** (No) ex *Vespasian* 1982
Possibly similar (no short uprights on deck):
67833 **BERGE CHIEF** (No) ex *Berge Beaumont* 1982; ex *Beaumont* 1981|
67834 **BERGE PILOT** (No) ex *Berge Beaurivage* 1982; ex *Beaurivage* 1981
Similar:
67835 **BERGE BIG** (No) ex *Cyprian* 1982
67836 **SIR CHARLES HAMBRO** (No)
67837 **SEABORN** (Cy) ex *Norborn* 1983; ex *Songa* 1971
67838 **COUGAR** (Cy) ex *Norbright* 1983; ex *Radny* 1977

67840 **WAKO MARU** Ja/Ja (Kawasaki) 1975; Tk; 116400; 319.92 × 19.66 (1049.61 × 64.5); T (Kawasaki); 16.5

67850 **FUJIKAWA MARU** Ja/Ja (Kawasaki) 1975; Tk; 116800; 319.95 × 19.66 (1049.7 × 64.5); T (Kawasaki); 16.75

67860 **TOKUYAMA MARU** Ja/Ja (IHI) 1975; Tk; 136100; 337.07 × 19.94 (1105.87 × 65.42); T (IHI); 16.25

67870 **ANDES MARU** Ja/Ja (IHI) 1974; Tk; 135600; 337.02 × 21.03 (1105.7 × 68.1); T (IHI); 16

67880 **VALPARAISO** Ch/Ja (Mitsubishi HI) 1971; OBO; 58200; 261.5 × 17.61 (857.94 × 57.78); M (Sulzer); 15.5; ex *Chu Fujino*

67890 **LAUREL WREATH** Li/Ja (IHI) 1975; BO; 72300; 286.65 × 22 (940.45 × 72.18); M (Sulzer); 15.5

67900 **USA MARU** Ja/Ja (IHI) 1972; OO; 142200; 337.02 × 21.02 (1105.71 × 68.96); T (IHI); 16

●67910 **OGDEN SUNGARI** Li/Ja (Sumitomo) 1975; Tk; 124100; 338.87 × 21.01 (1111.78 × 68.93); T (Toyo); 16
Similar:
67911 **MOSCLIFF** (No)
67912 **KYPROS** (Cy) ex *Saint Marcet* 1983

67920 **IKUYO MARU** Ja/Ja (Sasebo) 1972; Tk; 128700; 341.13 × 20.04 (1119.19 × 65.75); T (IHI); 15.5

67930 **OGDEN NELSON** Li/Ja (Hitachi) 1972; Tk; 12400; 331 × 22.02 (1085.96 × 72.24); T (Kawasaki); 15.5
Sister:
67931 **COALINGA** (Li) ex *Ioannis Chandris* 1976
Similar (Li flag):
67932 **WORLD CROWN**
67933 **WESTERN LION**
67934 **SOUTHERN LION**
67935 **NORTHERN LION**
67936 **EASTERN LION**

67940 **CONCORDIA C** Pa/Ja (Hitachi) 1976; Tk; 61100; 265.62 × 16.78 (871.46 × 55.05); M (B&W); 15.5; ex *Concordia* 1981
Sisters:
67941 **ANIA** (Li)
67943 **RUTH M** (Pa) ex *Ruth* 1980
67944 **SHIRLEY** (Li)
Similar:
67945 **MESOLOGI** (Gr)

67946 **MONEMVASIA** (Gr)
67947 **AFRAN STREAM** (Li) ex *Mantinia* 1977

67950 **OAK RIVER** Li/Ja (Koyo) 1981; Tk; 30700;
228.63 × 11.92 (750 × 39.11); M (B&W); 14.5;
Launched as *Salena*

67990 **NICHIO MARU** Ja/Ja (Hitachi) 1972; Tk;
120300; 324.01 × 19.36 (1063.02 × 63.52); T (Hitachi); 15.5
Similar:
67991 **EIKO MARU** (Ja)

68020 **KINKO MARU** Ja/Ja (NKK) 1971; Tk;
129200; 331.53 × 20.53 (1087.7 × 67.36); T (IHI);
15.75

68030 **YOKO MARU** Ja/Ja (Mitsui) 1975; Tk;
135100; 331.5 × 20.55 (1087.6 × 67.42); T (Stal-
Laval); 16.25; ex *Barbara T Shaheen* 1976
Similar:
68031 **JAPAN COSMOS** (Ja)
68032 **MOBIL SWIFT** (Li) ex *Takakurasan Maru*
1978

68040 **HONAM PEARL** Li/Ja (Hitachi) 1974; Tk;
83800; 314.99 × 18.91 (1033.43 × 62.04); M (B&W);
15.5
Possible sister:
68041 **HONAM JADE** (Li)

68050 **JAPAN ORCHID** Ja/Ja (Kawasaki) 1971; Tk;
116100; 318.83 × 19.51 (1046.03 × 64.01); T (Kawasaki); 16.25
Similar (Li flag):
68051 **HARMONY VENTURE**
68052 **TIVOLI**
68054 **WORLD SAGA** ex *Ujigawa Maru* 1977

68080 **LEPTON** Li/Ne (Verolme Dok) 1975; Tk;
155300; 352.61 × 22.35 (1156.86 × 73.33); T (GEC);
—
Similar:
68081 **ANNIE** (Fi) ex *Lembulus* 1981

68090 **RAJENDRA PRASAD** In/Ys ('Split') 1975;
Tk; 63500; 248.39 × 16.51 (814.93 × 54.17); M
(MAN); 15
Probable sister:
68091 **ZAKIR HUSSAIN** (In)

68100 **CHAMPAGNE** Fr/Ja (Mitsubishi HI) 1975;
OO; 93900; 295.03 × 17.9 (967.95 × 58.72); M
(Sulzer); 16.5
Similar:
68101 **CETRA VELA** (Fr)
68102 **BUNGA MAWAR** (My)
68103 **GARDEN GREEN** (Li) launched as *Henry J.
Kaiser*
68104 **COSMIC JUPITER** (Li)

68110 **WORLD HAPPINESS** Li/Ja (Mitsui) 1971;
Tk; 102326; 324.19 × 19.62 (1063.62 × 64.37); T
(IHI); 17

68120 **OPAL TRANSPORTER** Tw/Ja (Mitsui)
1970; OO; 95400; 307.83 × 17.37 (1009.94 ×
56.99); M (B&W); 16.5; ex *Polysaga* 1983

68130 **WORLD CHALLENGER** Li/Ja (Hitachi)
1973; OO; 85700; 313.93 × 17.00 (1030 × 55.77); M
(B&W); 16

68140 **AMAZON MARU** Ja/Ja (Hitachi) 1973; OO;
89500; 300.01 × 16.99 (984.28 × 55.74); M (B&W);
16; ex *Sanko Robin* 1980
Sister:
68141 **TRIPHAROS** (Li)
Similar:
68142 **WAKAZURA MARU** (Ja)
68143 **COBALT TRANSPORTER** (Tw) ex *Miranda
Seaventure* 1983; ex *Yamazuru Maru* 1983
68144 **ZUIHO MARU** (Ja)
68145 **LARINA** (Li)

68150 **GOONZARAN** Ko/Ja (NKK) 1968; OO;
55500; 251.75 × 15.04 (826 × 49.34); M (Sulzer);
12.5; ex *Fukuyama Maru* 1981; Adapted for ore
cargoes only

68160 **SLURRY EXPRESS** Li/Ja (Hitachi) 1978; B
(Sand); 48500; 240.52 × 17.04 (821.92 × 55.91); M
(Sulzer); 14.25

● 68170 **TANTALUS** Br/Ja (NKK) 1972; OO; 120800;
327.82 × 19.1 (1075.53 × 62.66); T (Mitsubishi);
15.5
Similar:
68171 **ALSTER ORE** (Pa) ex *Tsurumi* 1982; ex
Tsurumi Maru 1982
68172 **DONAU ORE** (Li) ex *World Era* 1981; ex *Jarl
Malmros* 1979
68173 **WORLD LADY** (Li) ex *Tartar* 1978
Similar (larger):
68174 **DOCECANYON** (Li)

68200 **DOCEPOLO** Bz/Bz (Ish do Brazil) 1975; OO;

72400; 273.52 × 16.12 (897.37 × 52.89); M (Sulzer);
16
Probable sisters (Bz flag):
68202 **DOCECORAL**
68203 **JAPURA**
68204 **JACUI** ex *Jari* 1983
68205 **JOINVILLE**
68206 **JURUA**
68207 **JURUPEMA**

68220 **OBO ZIHNI** Tu/Ja (Kawasaki) 1970; OBO;
57500; 250.05 × 15.52 (820.37 × 50.92); M (MAN);
15.5; ex *Hoegh Rainbow* 1982
Sisters:
68221 **DAEYANG CHARITY** (Ko) ex *Hoegh Rover*
1982
68222 **TREADWIND** (Br) ex *Vega Seal* 1982; ex
Hoegh Robin 1978
Similar:
68223 **DAEYANG BOUNTY** (Ko) ex *Hoegh Rider*
1982

68230 **ANDROS ANTARES** Li/Ja (IHI) 1973; OO;
Ore 57900/Oil 115100; 323.63 × 20.49 (1061.78 ×
67.22); T (IHI); 15
Sisters:
68231 **ANDROS ARIES** (Gr)
68232 **ANDROS ATLAS** (Gr)
Similar (tanker):
68234 **ANDROS TITAN** (Gr)

68240 **GARYVILLE** Li/Ja (IHI) 1972; Tk; 65600;
274.94 × 17.32 (902.03 × 56.82); M (Sulzer); 15.75;
ex *Fairfield* 1977
Sister:
68241 **ORIENTAL PHOENIX** (Li)

★ 68250 **MARSHAL BUDYONNYY** Ru/Pd (Gdanska) 1975; BO; 59600; 245.52 × 16 (805.51 × 52.49);
M (Sulzer); 16; '**B-524**' type
Sisters (Ru flag):
★ 68251 **MARSHALL KONYEV**
★ 68252 **MARSHAL ROKOSSOVSKIY**
★ 68253 **MARSHAL ZHUKOV**

● 68260 **LAKE MENDOCINO** Li/Ja (Sumitomo)
1971; OBO; 71600; 266.02 × 18.1 (872.77 × 59.38);
M (Sulzer); 15.5; ex *Avon Bridge* 1976
Sisters:
68261 **BISE** (Br) ex *Cast Petrel* 1983; ex *Eden Bridge*
68262 **OAK STAR** (Br) ex *Cast Gull* 1983; ex *Silver
Bridge*
68263 **CHILI** (Br) ex *Cast Puffin* 1983; ex *Enterprise
Transporter*; ex *Australian Bridge* 1978

68270 **DELAWARE** Li/FRG (Bremer V) 1973; OBO;
42400; 253.68 × 14.23 (832.28 × 46.69); M (MAN);
15.25; ex *Saxonia* 1984; ex *Mercedes*

68280 **BELOBO** No/FRG (Bremer V) 1974; OBO;
42800; 253.63 × 14.24 (832.12 × 46.72); M (MAN)
15
Sisters:
68281 **SKYE TRADER** (Br) ex *Tai Cheung* 1983; ex
Obo Duke 1983
68282 **SIBOSIX** (No) ex *Jarmina* 1980; (Being used
as storage vessel at Singapore)
Possible sister:
68283 **SOUTH PEARL** (Li) ex *Arica* 1983

● 68290 **BROCKMAN** Li/Ja (Mitsui) 1974; O; 33900;
259.39 × 16.13 (851.02 × 52.92); M (B&W); 15
Sisters (Li flag):
68291 **MARRA MAMBA**
68292 **SEVEN TEAM** ex *Sevenseas Conqueror* 1979

● 68310 **NORMAN PACIFIC** Sg/Ys ('Split') 1971;
OBO; 42200; 252.36 × 14.78 (827.95 × 48.49); M
(MAN); 16; ex *Capetan Carras*

● 68320 **SENECA** Li/Ys ('Split') 1975; OBO; 42000;
252.86 × 14.81 (829.59 × 48.59); M (MAN); 14.5; ex
Excomm Merchant 1980
Sister:
68321 **SEQUOIA** (Li) ex *Excomm Mariner* 1980
Possible sister:
68322 **ATARI** (Br) ex *Setoda* 1982; ex *Carlantic* 1981
Similar:
68323 **CARBAY** (Li)
Similar (radar mast from bridge):
68324 **CARCAPE** (Li)
68325 **AVENGER** (Li) ex *Cape Clear* 1982; ex *Carisle*
1981

68330 **NICOS I. VARDINOYANNIS** Gr/Br (Lithgows) 1971; Tk; 65300; 274.4 × 16.96 (900.26 ×
55.64); M (B&W); 16; ex *Gold Star* 1973

68340 **JOYAMA MARU** Ja/Ja (IHI) 1965; LGC;
29500; 198.03 × 11.02 (649.7 × 36.15); M (Sulzer);
15.75

68350 **SANDRINA** Pa/Fr (CNIM) 1973; LGC;
34300; 216.47 × 11.02 (710.1 × 36.15); M (Sulzer);
17.5; ex *Atlante* 1980; ex *Providence Multina*; ex

Dorsetown 1973
Sisters:
68351 **STENA OCEANICA** (Br) ex *Mandrill* 1980; ex
Malmros Multina 1979; ex *Dovertown* 1974
68352 **ANTILLA BAY** (NA)
Similar:
68353 **REYNOSA** (Me)
68354 **MONTERREY** (Me)

● 68360 **OCEAN SKY** Ko/Ja (Shikoku) 1975; R; 3700;
131.48 × 6.99 (431.36 × 22.93); M (Mitsubishi);
17.75; ex *Summer Birdie* 1979; ex *Rose Daphne*
1978
Sisters:
68361 **ROSE MALLOW** (Pa)
68362 **WHITE JASMIN** (Pa) ex *Rose Acacia* 1978
68363 **OSAKA REEFER** (Ja) ex *Aden Maru* 1978

68370 **UNION EVERGREEN** Tw/Tw (Taiwan SB)
1968; C; 3600; 106.99 × 7.12 (351.02 × 23.36); M
(MAN); 14.5

68390 **JULIANA** Pa/Be (Boelwerf) 1971; B; 36800;
234.75 × 13.2 (770.18 × 43.31); M (MAN); 15; ex *E R
Brabantia* 1983
Sisters:
68391 **ASEAN GREATNESS** (Pi) ex *E R Antverpia*
68392 **JAGAT SAMRAT** (In)

● 68400 **KAIA KNUDSEN** No/Sw (Uddevalla) 1974;
Tk; 114000; 325.0 × 20.44 (1066 × 67.06); T (GEC);
15.75; ex *Norse Queen* 1983
Sisters:
68401 **PHILLIPS ENTERPRISE** (Li) ex *Kollbjorg*
68402 **SYLVANIA** (Li) ex *Marga*; ex *Margaret Onstad* 1978
68403 **ADNA** (No)
68404 **THORSHAVET** (No) ex *Norseman* 1983
68405 **POLYVICTORIA** (No)
68406 **MARGARON** (Sw) ex *Regina* 1983

68420 **YUKONG LEADER** Pa/Ja (NKK) 1974; Tk;
128100; 338.13 × 20.90 (1109 × 68.54); T (Mitsubishi); 15; ex *Jarabella* 1982
Sister:
68421 **YUKONG PIONEER** (Ko) ex *Jastella* 1982
Similar:
68422 **VIOLANDO** (Gr) ex *Violando N Goulandris*
1978

68430 **FABIAN** No/No (Stord) 1972; Tk; 140500;
347.84 × 22.14 (1141.21 × 72.64); T (Kvaerner);
15.5
Sisters (No flag):
68431 **BERGE BORG** ex *Julian* 1982
● 68432 **OCEAN TRADER** ex *Vespasian* 1982
Possibly similar (no short uprights on deck):
68433 **BERGE CHIEF** ex *Berge Beaumont* 1982; ex
Beaumont 1981
68434 **BERGE PILOT** ex *Berge Beaurivage* 1982; ex
Beaurivage 1981
Similar:
68435 **BERGE BIG** (No) ex *Cyprian* 1982
68436 **SIR CHARLES HAMBRO** (No)
68437 **SEABORN** (Cy) ex *Norborn* 1983; ex *Songa*
1971
68438 **COUGAR** (Cy) ex *Norbright* 1983; ex *Radny*
1977

68450 **LICORNE OCEANE** Li/No (Stord) 1975; Tk;
137900; 347. × 22.01 (1138.45 × 72.21); T (Stal-
Laval); 15.5

68460 **SPYROS A. LEMOS** Gr/Ja (IHI) 1972; Tk;
103300; 322.99 × 19.73 (1059.6 × 64.73); T (IHI);
16.25; ex *Gondwana*

68470 **WESER ORE** Li/Ys ('Uljanik') 1973; OO;
141800; 335.03 × 21.99 (1099.17 × 72.14); TSM
(B&W); 16.5; ex *Brazilian Wealth* 1981; ex *Tarfala*
1978
Sister:
68471 **RHINE ORE** (Pa) ex *Torne* 1979
Similar:
68472 **MARY R. KOCH** (Li)

68480 **ALABAMA GETTY** Li/Sw (Uddevalla) 1971;
Tk; 63200; 284.13 × 16.7 (932.18 × 54.74); M
(B&W); 16; ex *Curro* 1976
Sister:
68481 **IRINI** (Gr) ex *Juanita* 1983

68490 **AGHIA MARINA** Li/Ja (Kure) 1967; OBO;
43400; 254.52 × 14.02 (835.04 × 46); M (Sulzer);
14.75; ex *Balbina* 1983

68500 **SEA VICTORY** Li/Ja (IHI) 1969; OBO; 43500;
254.52 × 14.01 (835.04 × 45.96); M (Sulzer); 15.5;
ex *Mozart* 1983

68520 **AMOCO CAIRO** Li/Ja (Mitsubishi HI) 1975;
Tk; 76500; 280.02 × 15.24 (918.7 × 50); M (Sulzer);
15.25
Sisters:
68521 **AMOCO WHITING** (Li) ex *Amoco Tehran*
1980

68522 **AMOCO TRINIDAD** (Li)

68525 **SUNNY HOPE** Li/Ja (Tsuneishi) 1981; Tk; 30800; 225.51 × 12.22 (740 × 40.09); M (B&W); 14.75

● 68530 **DONAU MARU** Ja/Ja (Mitsubishi HI) 1969; OO; 45200; 239.02 × 13.34 (784 × 43.77); M (Mitsubishi); 15.5
Sisters:
68531 **BRIOLETTE** (Li) ex *Volga Maru* 1981
68532 **CASPIAN TRADER** (Li) ex *Caspi Maru* 1971
68533 **MOSTUN** (No) ex *Mostun Sanko* 1980
68534 **REGENT PIMPERNEL** (Li) ex *Kiev Maru* 1972
68535 **SPRING ODESSA** (Pa) ex *Odessa Maru* 1972
Similar:
68536 **CAUCASUS MARU** (Ja)
68537 **EASTERN HAZEL** (Li)

● 68551 **NIGMA** Pa/Ja (Hashihama) 1976; Tk; 47300; 242.98 × 14.5 (797.18 × 47.57); M (Sulzer); 16; ex *Cumberlandia* 1980
Similar (↓ some! Sg built-Jurong Spyd):
68552 **MOORFIELDS MONARCH** (Sg)
68553 **MAMMOTH MONARCH** (Li) ex *Euroasia Monarch* 1978
68554 **NEPTUNE LEO** (Sg)
68555 **MINT PROSPERITY** (Li) ex *Northern Victory* 1983
68556 **OLYMPIC RAINBOW** (Gr) ex *Oceanic Erin* 1980
68557 **SANKO HONOUR** (Sg)
68558 **TATINA** (Gr) ex *Noga* 1980
68559 **PAGEANTRY** (Li)
68559/1 **PALMSTAR CHERRY** (Sg)
68559/2 **PALMSTAR ORCHID** (Sg)
68559/3 **BRILLIANCY** (Sg)
68559/4 **GYOKO MARU** (Ja) ex *Bruce Ruthi II* 1978
68559/5 **CONTINENTAL MONARCH** (Li)
68559/6 **ASIA MARU No 2** (Ja) ex *Oceanic Kristin* 1979

★ 68560 **MESTA** Bu/Ja (Kasado) 1974; Tk; 46800; 237.01 × 12.92 (777.59 × 42.39); M (Sulzer); 16.5
Sister:
★ 68561 **OSAM** (Bu)

68570 **PETROSHIP A** Si/Ys ('3 Maj') 1975; Tk; 25000; 197.64 × 11.7 (648.43 × 38.39); M (Sulzer); 16.5
Sister:
68571 **PETROSHIP B** (Si)

68580 **NAVIOS COMMODORE** Li/Sw (Gotav) 1971; OBO; 55600; 256.55 × 15.11 (841.7 × 49.57); M (Gotaverken); 16; ex *Atlantic Bounty* 1982; ex *Dalsland* 1980; ex *Eric K Fernstrom* 1978
Sister:
68581 **NAVIOS COLLIER** (Li) ex *Atlantic Endeavour* 1982; ex *Fujisan* 1978
Similar (larger KP amidships):
68582 **SILVERLAND** (Sw) ex *A K Fernstrom* 1977

68590 **HOEGH RANGER** No/Ja (Kawasaki D) 1966; OBO; 42100; 242.5 × 13.69 (795.6 × 44.91); M (MAN); 15.5
Sister:
68591 **BYZANTION** (Gr) ex *Vega Stingray*; ex *Hoegh Ray*

68600 **SAINT ANDREW** Pa/Ja (Kurushima) 1973; Tk; 44800; 245.98 × 13.27 (807.02 × 45.53); M (MAN); 15.5; ex *Kurushima Maru* 1982
Sisters (Sg flag):
68601 **VIRGINIA LILY**
68602 **VIRGINIA STAR**

68610 **MARAO** Po/Sw (Eriksbergs)-Po (Lisnave) 1972/73; Tk; 69300; 280.09 × 16.7 (918.9 × 54.8); M (B&W); 15.5; Foreward section built Portugal 1972—aft section built Sweden 1973
Sisters (Po flag):
68611 **MAROFA**
68612 **MONTEMURO**

● 68620 **PENTELI** Gr/Ja (Mitsubishi HI) 1972; OBO; 57800; 261.02 × 15.85 (856.36 × 52); M (Sulzer); 16; ex *Aegean Island* 1980
Sister:
68621 **NEMEA** (Li) ex *Aegean Wave* 1980
Probable sister:
68622 **AEGEAN SEA** (Li)

68640 **THYELLA** Li/Ja (IHI) 1966; OO; 19400 (Ore) 40900 (Oil); 242.02 × 13.68 (794.03 × 44.88); M (Sulzer); 16
Sister:
68641 **TORNADO** (Gr)

68650 **VOO SHEE** Tw/Ja (IHI) 1969; Tk; 52400; 253.04 × 15.57 (830.18 × 51.08); M (Sulzer); 16.5
Sisters (some Tw built-Taiwan SB):
68651 **HSIEN YUAN** (Tw)

68652 **SHEN NON** (Tw)
68653 **YU TSAO** (Tw)
68654 **FORTUNE** (Li)
68655 **GLORY** (Li)
68656 **AFRAN ENERGY** (Li)

68660 **BONNY** Fi/Sw (Uddevalla) 1969; Tk; 51500; 255.25 × 14.38 (837.43 × 47.18); M (B&W); 16
Sister:
68661 **PEGGY** (Fi) ex *Pegny* 1984

68670 **SERIFOS** Gr/Sw (Uddevalla) 1972; Tk; 50400; 255.25 × 14.38 (837.46 × 47.18); M (B&W); 16.5; ex *Afran Leeward* 1983; ex *Evita Dan* 1978; ex *Evina* 1976
Possible sister:
68671 **TITAN** (Gr) ex *Sea Rover* 1983; ex *Rona River* 1978

● 68680 **CLEARWATER BAY** Br/Sw (Gotav) 1973; OO; 120700; 332.57 × 20.65 (1091.11 × 67.75); T (Stal-Laval); 16; ex *Alva Bay* 1983
Sister:
68681 **ALVA SEA** (Br)—motor ship (MAN)

68690 **AGUILA AZTECA** Me/Sw (Gotav) 1969; Tk; 113500; 332.24 × 20.68 (1090.03 × 67.85); T (Stal-Laval); 16; ex *Brali* 1982; ex *Veni* 1980
Sisters:
68692 **ATIA C** (Gr) ex *Ile de La Cite* 1981
68693 **BUENA SUERTE** (Gr) ex *Brita Onstad* 1979

68700 **ENERGY PROSPERITY** Li/Sw (Gotav) 1971; Tk; 104200; 332.32 × 20.66 (1090 × 67.78); T (Stal-Laval); 16; ex *Halcyon the Great* 1974; Now used as storage tanker
Similar:
68701 **DOLCE** (Cy) ex *Trajan* 1982; ex *Corona*

68710 **LANTAU** Sg/Sw (Eriksbergs) 1969; Tk; 60200; 256.22 × 16.7 (840.62 × 54.79); M (Pielstick); 16; ex *Oceanus* 1982; Shortened 1978; Drawing shows vessel under original length

68720 **TASSIA** Gr/Sw (Gotav) 1969; Tk; 64000; 272.24 × 16.28 (893.18 × 53.41); M (Gotaverken); 16; ex *New Star*

68730 **DORIOS** Li/Sw (Gotav) 1967; Tk; 43200; 258.02 × 13.5 (846.52 × 44.29); M (Gotaverken) 16; ex *Pappas Thessaloniki* 1970
Sisters:
68731 **ANTARES** (Gr) ex *Megas* 1983; ex *Bessie A. Pappas* 1970
68732 **ANDROMEDA** (Li) ex *Zoe* 1983; ex *Katherine A. Pappas* 1970
Similar:
68733 **MARILIA** (Li) ex *Beauval* 1978

68740 **CATHAY SEATRADE** Li/Sw (Oresunds) 1973; B; 35500; 224.06 × 13.1 (735.1 × 42.98); M Gotaverken); 16; ex *Lili Billner* 1978

68750 **THEONYMPHOS** Gr/Sw (Eriksbergs) 1968; Tk; 44900; 255.33 × 14.38 (837.7 × 47.18); M (B&W); 16; ex *Wangstar* 1979; ex *Foldstar* 1978; ex *Wangstar* 1976; ex *Artemis* 1974

68755 **COLUMBIA NEPTUNE** Li/Ja (Tsuneishi) 1981; Tk; 30600; 225.51 × 12.22 (740 × 40.09); M (B&W); 14.75
Similar:
68756 **HOUSTON ACCORD** (Li)

★ 68760 **JADRAN** Ys/Br (Sunderland) 1976; B; 38500; 228.12 × 14.03 (748.43 × 46.03); M (Doxford); 15
Sisters (Ys flag):
★ 68761 **KORDUN**
★ 68762 **KOSMAJ**
★ 68763 **ORJEN**
★ 68764 **SUTJESKA**

68770 **THETIS** Gr/Br (Sunderland) 1974; B; 35500; 228.05 × 14.03 (748.2 × 46.03); M (Doxford); 15
Sisters (Gr flag):
68771 **MELETE**
68772 **NAIAD**

68780 **RHETORIC** Li/Ja (NKK) 1971; OBO; 77000; 303.51 × 18.25 (995.76 × 59.88); T (Mitsubishi); 15.75
Sister:
68781 **ROMANTIC** (Li)

68790 **AMOCO VOYAGER** Li/Ja (Hitachi) 1973; Tk; 35500; 239.3 × 13.24 (785.1 × 43.44); M (Sulzer); 16; ex *Navarchos Miaoulis* 1977

★ 68800 **MARSHAL BUDYONNYY** Ru/Pd (Gdynska) 1975; OBO; 59600; 245.52 × 16 (805.51 × 52.49); M (Sulzer); 16; 'B524' type
Sisters (Ru flag):
★ 68801 **MARSHAL KONYEV**
★ 68802 **MARSHAL ROKOSSOVSKIY**
★ 68803 **MARSHAL ZHUKOV**

68810 **POINT CLEAR** Li/Ja (NKK) 1972; OBO; 57100; 264.35 × 14.63 (867.29 × 48); M (Sulzer); 16; Helicopter deck aft
Similar:
68811 **NAVIOS COURIER** (Li) ex *Ross Isle*
68812 **VERGO** (Gr)

● 68830 **COAL TRANSPORTER** Li/Sw (Gotav) 1972; OBO; 51400; 256.55 × 15.11 (841.7 × 49.57); M (Gotaverken); 16; ex *Lake Berryessa* 1982; ex *Ariadne* 1976
Sister:
68831 **JAG LAADKI** (In) ex *Athel Laadki* 1977; ex *Jag Laadki* 1974

● 68840 **VARENNA** No/Sw (Oresunds) 1970; OBO; 55000; 256.52 × 15.11 (841.6 × 49.57); M (Gotaverken); 15.5
Similar:
68841 **IVORY** (Li) ex *Cast Razorbill* 1983; ex *Cast Tern* 1981; ex *Thistle Star*; ex *Spyros A. Lemos* 1978; ex *Vianna* 1976
68842 **VANESSA** (No)

● 68850 **PLATINUM TRANSPORTER** Li/Sw (Oresunds) 1973; OBO; 54800; 256.47 × 15.11 (841.44 × 49.57); M (Gotaverken); 16; ex *Lake Shasta* 1982; ex *Aphrodite* 1976
Similar:
68851 **OBO QUEEN** (No)
68852 **MIHALIS** (Gr) ex *Kongshav* 1978

● 68870 **TAL** Pa/Ja (Mitsubishi HI) 1968; Tk; 47000; 256.01 × 13.33 (839.93 × 43.73); M (Mitsubishi); 16; ex *Heinersdorf* 1981; ex *Atlantic Marchioness* 1974
Sister:
68871 **ATLANTIC MARQUESS** (Li)

68900 **FULTON II** Sg/Ja (Kawasaki) 1969; Tk; 38500; 329.73 × 19.5 (1081.79 × 63.98); T (Kawasaki); 16.75; ex *World Chief* 1981

68910 **ELOUNDA** Li/Ja (Mitsui) 1969; Tk; 41500; 257.49 × 13.37 (844.78 × 43.86); M (B&W); 17; ex *World Kindness* 1982
Sister:
68911 **KRITI** (Li) ex *World Knowledge* 1982

● ★ 68920 **ZAWRAT** Pd/Ja (Mitsubishi HI) 1975; Tk; 81200; 293 × 15.29 (961.29 × 50.16); M (Sulzer); 16.25
Sisters (Pd flag):
★ 68921 **CZANTORIA**
★ 68922 **SOKOLICA**

68930 **PETROSTAR XV** Si/Ja (Sasebo) 1966; Tk; 48200; 271.03 × 14.19 (889.21 × 46.56); M (Sulzer); 16.25; ex *World Standard* 1980

68940 **SHIN-EN MARU** Ja/Ja (NKK) 1971; Tk; 133700; 338.11 × 20.58 (1109.28 × 67.52); M (B&W); ex *T.G Shaugnessy* 1982
Sister:
68941 **PORT HAWKESBURY** (Br)
Similar:
68942 **I D SINCLAIR** (Br)

68970 **LYRA** It/FRG (A G'Weser') 1970; OBO; 84200; 293.2 × 17.44 (961.94 × 57.22); M (B&W); 16; ex *Nai Marcus* 1980; ex *Marcus Lolli-Ghetti* 1974; ex *Tarim* 1972

69010 **CIUDAD DE BARRANCABERMEJA** Co/Ca (Davie SB) 1975; Tk; 23700; 182.89 × 11.42 (600.03 × 37.47); M (Sulzer); 15; ex *Lucellum* 1978
Sister:
69011 **LUCERNA** (Br)
Possibly similar (Li flag):
69012 **OGDEN OTTAWA**
69013 **OGDEN SAGUENAY**

★ 69020 **RADE KONCAR** Ys/Ja (IHI) 1967; Tk; 36300; 226.52 × 12.79 (743.18 × 41.96); M (Sulzer); 16.5
Sisters (Ys flag):
★ 69021 **JORDAN NIKOLOV**
★ 69022 **MILOS MATIJEVIC**
★ 69023 **SLAVISA VAJNER**

69030 **ALAMO** Li/Ja (Kawasaki) 1978; Tk; 33100; 238.01 × 12.16 (780.87 × 39.9); M (MAN); 15

69040 **AMANDA MILLER** Au/Au (Whyalla) 1971; Tk; 39100; 239.28 × 13.17 (785.04 × 43.21); M (Sulzer); 16.5

69050 **BRAZILIAN FRIENDSHIP** Li/Tw (Taiwan SB) 1971; OO; 48900; 253.02 × 15.15 (830.12 × 49.7); M (Sulzer); 15.5

69060 **SITIA GLORY** Pa/Ja (Hitachi) 1970; O; 43600; 250.02 × 13.31 (820.28 × 43.67); M (B&W); 15.25; ex *Kakogawa Maru* 1982

69070 **PRINKIPOS** Li/Ja (Mitsubishi HI) 1964; Tk; 27400; 213.01 × 14.3 (698.85 × 46.92); M (Sulzer); 16; ex *Conoco Libya* 1976; ex *Continental C.* 1978

9080 ESPERANZA II Pa/Ja (NKK) 1964; Tk; 2700; 225 × 12.38 (738.19 × 40.62); M (B&W); 16; x Buena Esperanza 1983; ex Jarelsa

9090 OCEANIC ENERGY Li/Sw (Oresunds) 1967; Tk; 47000; 253.47 × 13.06 (831.59 × 42.85); M (Gotaverken); 16.5; ex H M Wrangell 1978

9100 GEORGIA P Li/FRG (Howaldts) 1966; Tk; 45900; 230.31 × 11.61 (755.61 × 38.09); T (Howaldts); 16.75; ex Shinyon 1982; ex Tula 1981; ex Fortuna 1978
Sister:
9101 TULUM (Me) ex Union 1978

69110 IN-NAHALA Ag/Ja (NKK) 1975; Tk; 71900; 266. × 16.99 (872.7 × 55.74); M (Sulzer); 15.75; ex Polartank 1976
Possibly similar:
69111 HALUL (Qt) launched as North Monarch
69112 JANE STOVE (No)
69113 UMM SHAIF (UAE) launched as Vincenzia

69120 METAL TRANSPORTER Tw/Ja (Kure) 1967; OO; 56300; 253.02 × 14.48 (830.12 × 47.51); M (Sulzer); 15.25; ex Catharina 1981; ex Japan Wisteria 1981
Sister:
69121 ORE TRANSPORTER (Tw) ex Mineral Transporter 1983; ex Tasmanian 1983; ex Mineral Transporter 1983; ex White Rose 1980; ex Japan Lilac 1977
Similar:
69122 OCEAN VENTURE (Li) ex Oriental Titan 1973; ex Daiko Maru 1971
69123 ELMINA (Gr) ex Japan Magnolia
69124 JIZAN CEMENT (Si) ex Tsugaru Maru 1979
Possibly similar:
69126 ACACIA (Ko) ex Tsurusaki Maru 1981
69127 DR. D K SAMY (Li) ex Kaiko Maru 1972 (now converted to tanker)

69140 KRITI STAR Gr/Ca (Davie SB) 1973; Tk; 42500; 239.25 × 13 (784.94 × 43.77); M (Sulzer); 16
Sisters (Gr flag):
69141 KRITI LAND
69142 KRITI WAVE

69150 FREESIA Ko/Ja (Kawasaki) 1972; OO; 87100; 289.01 × 17.96 (948.2 × 58.92); M (MAN); 15.5; ex Ohtsukawa Maru 1982

69190 JAWAHARLAL NEHRU In/Ys ('Split') 1969; Tk; 48400; 256.85 × 14.05 (842.68 × 46.09); M (MAN); 15.5; Has small twin 'funnels' near after kingposts
Sister (used as offshore loading tanker):
69191 LAL BAHADUR SHASTRI (In)

69200 SPEY BRIDGE Br/Ja (Sumitomo) 1969; OBO; 66100; 259.01 × 15.89 (849.77 × 52.13); M (Sulzer); 16
Sister:
69201 OCEANIC VICTORY (Li) ex Ocean **Bridge** 1978

69210 GALINI Gr/No (Fredriksstad) 1973; OO; 71300; 282 × 17 (925.19 × 55.77); M (Sulzer); 16; ex Ancora 1983
Sisters (No flag):
69211 ACINA
69212 SANDEFJORD

69220 CALIOPE E Li/Sw (Oresunds) 1969; Tk; 44000; 257.67 × 13.5 (845.37 × 44.29); M (Gotaverken); 16.5; ex Atlantic Trader 1981; ex Tide Crown; Launched as Butanga

69230 EIRAMA Br/Ja (Mitsui) 1968; Tk; 54500; 271.28 × 14.26 (890 × 46.78); M (B&W); 14.5; ex Thorshovdi 1978

69250 SEABORNE Li/Ja (Namura) 1973; Tk; 15000; 171.02 × 10.71 (561.09 × 35.14); M (Sulzer); 15
Sisters (Li flag):
69251 SEASERVICE
69252 SEASTAR
Possibly similar:
69253 CYS INTEGRITY (Li)
69254 KOREA SUNNYHILL (Ko) ex Cys Hope 1980

69260 PANAMAX APOLLO Pa/Ja (NKK) 1966; OBO; 39600; 248.42 × 12.56 (815.03 × 41.21); M (B&W); 15.5; ex Marcona Trader 1982; ex San Juan Trader 1973

69280 JULES VERNE Fr/Fr (La Seine) 1965; LGC; 22300; 201.02 × 7.53 (659.51 × 24.7); T (Parsons); 17

69290 KIMITSU MARU Ja/Ja (Nipponkai) 1971; O; 8000; 136.18 × 8.28 (446.78 × 27.17); M (IHI); 13; Limestone carrier
Sister:
69291 KIMITETSU MARU (Ja)

69300 LIKE ONE Pa/Fr (Provence) 1959; O; 10300; 164.42 × 9.86 (539.44 × 32.35); M (Doxford); 14.5; ex Ville De Mexico 1975; ex Jacques D'Anglejan U.N 1 1969

69310 YONA B. Sg/Ru (Vyborg) 1977; C; 6500; 136.81 × 7.49 (448.85 × 24.57); M (B&W); —; ex Nopal Yona 1978; 'Universal' type
Sisters (Sg flag):
69311 CAMILLE B ex Camille 1978; ex Nopal Camille 1978;
(Ru flag):
★**69312 NIKOLAY ZHUKHOV**
★**69313 NIKOLAY MOROZOV**
★**69314 GRIGORIY KOVALCHUK**
★**69315 KONSTANTIN ZANKOV**
★**69316 VASILIY BYELOKONYENKO**
★**69317 VITALIY KRUCHINA**
★**69318 IVAN KOROTEYEV**
★**69319 MIKHAIL STENKO**
★**69320 NIKOLAY SHCHUKIN**
★**69321 PETR STAROSTIN**
★**69322 ANDRIAN GONCHAROV**
★**69323 INZHENIER YAMBURENKO**

★**69330 ZHONG SHAN** RC/Be (Boelwerf) 1969; C; 13000; 160.03 × 9.88 (525.03 × 32.41); M (MAN); 15.5; ex Marina Del Cantone 1982; ex Zelzate
Sisters:
69331 TEMA (Li) ex Charleroi 1980
69332 ANTOFAGASTA (Pa) ex Chertal 1981
69333 BRAINPOWER (Pa) ex Belval 1978

69340 DAITOKU MARU No 31 Ja/Ja (Kishimoto) 1974; C/R; 3000; 120.53 × 6.96 (395.44 × 22.83); M (B&W); 17.5

69350 OCEAN DYNAMIC Pa/Ja (Kishimoto) 1975; R; 3600; 124.08 × 6.92 (407.08 × 22.7); M (B&W); 17.5
Sister:
69351 OCEAN FRESH (Pa)

69360 ELAFINA Gr/Ja (Shin Yamamoto) 1973; B; 15000; 154.11 × 10.52 (505.61 × 34.51); M (Sulzer); 15.5; ex Trans Ruby 1973

69370 LENTSKY —/FRG (A.G. 'Weser') 1961; C; 9300/11800; 159.44 × 9.83/10.22 (523.1 × 32.25/33.53); M (B&W); 15.25; ex Levante C 1983; ex Tina Lentoudis 1980; ex Wienertor 1976

●**69380 CHERRY NES** Sg/Sw (Eriksbergs) 1960; Tk; 28200; 217.81 × 12.27 (714.6 × 40.26); M (B&W); 16.25; ex Katarina 1978

69390 NYALA Gr/Br (Smith's D) 1962; Tk; 12400; 170.47 × 9.44 (559.28 × 30.97); M (Doxford); 15; ex Anatoli 1981; ex Lucigen 1975

69410 ANDESGAS Ch/FRG (Howaldts DW) 1968; LGC; 13100; 166.15 × 9.22 (545.11 × 30.25); M (MAN); 16.5; ex Nopal Tellus 1983; ex Katrisa 1982; ex Trina Multina 1977; ex Roland 1974

●**69420 TA TUNG No 2** Tw/Ja (Nishi Z) 1969; C; 2100; 91.9 × 5.82 (301.51 × 19.09); M (Ito Tekkosho); 13; ex Seng Kong No 1 1982; ex Marukichi **Maru No 3** 1976
Possible sisters:
69421 REIKO (Pa) ex Philippine Pine 1982; ex Horned Owl 1980; ex Meisho Maru 1976
69422 KYOHO MARU (Ja)
69423 RIAMA (Pa) ex Phoenix 1983; ex Lim Glory 1983; ex Shorei Maru

69430 DANUBE Cy/Br (Laing) 1960; O; 12600; 160.03 × 9.01 (525.03 × 29.56); M (Doxford); 12; ex Puerto Madryn 1977; ex Silvershore 1975; ex Aldersgate 1969
Sister:
69431 CAPITANO FRANCO V (It) ex Nicolas C 1976; ex Beechwood 1975; ex Bishopsgate 1969
Similar (smaller):
69432 STENIES (Gr) ex Tornado 1977; ex Sheaf Field 1969

●**69450 EVA** Gr/Br (Swan Hunter & WR) 1959; O; 11900; 156.11 × 9.01 (512.17 × 29.56); M (Doxford); 12; ex Bamburgh Castle 1976
Similar:
69451 DAPO TRADER (Sg) ex Cheviot 1977
★**69452 BONG SAN** (RK) ex Cosmos Traders 1980; ex Lindisfarne 1975
69453 PARNASSOS (Gr) ex Longstone 1975

69460 AVEDAT Is/It ('Navalmeccanica') 1964; B; 23500; 195.99 × 10.67 (643.01 × 35.01); M (Fiat); 16

●**69470 ORION** Gr/Sw (Kockums) 1963; B; 14600; 175.88 × 10.83 (577.03 × 35.53); M (MAN); 14.5

●**69480 KONG HAAKON VII** No/No (Stord) 1969; Tk; 109400; 327.72 × 20.42 (1075.2 × 66.99); T (GEC); 16
Sister (No flag):

69482 HADRIAN

69490 RIO SUN Li/Ja (Hitachi) 1967; OBO; 42500; 250.96 × 13.98 (823.36 × 45.87); M (B&W); 16; ex Tokyo 1977
Sister:
69491 GARBIS (Li) ex Canto 1975; ex Vestfold 1971

69500 MARIZINA Gr/Sw (Uddevalla) 1967; Tk; 40100; 244.89 × 13.69 (803.44 × 44.91); M (B&W); 16.75; ex Norse Mountain 1973

69510 EFYRA Li/Ja (Uraga HI) 1965; Tk; 35400; 238.03 × 12.77 (780.94 × 41.9): M (Sulzer); 15.5
Sister:
69511 EVDORI (Li)

69520 RAS TANURA Si/Br (Lithgows) 1965; Tk; 37700; 237.68 × 12.83 (779.79 × 42.09); T (Westinghouse); 16; ex Yannis V 1976; ex Pyrros V 1976; ex Spectra J 1975; ex Pyrros V 1971; ex Laristan 1970

69570 BABA GURGUR Iq/Sp (AESA) 1973; Tk; 21400; 201.02 × 10.96 (659.51 × 35.96); M (Sulzer); 16
Sisters (Iq flag):
69571 AIN ZALAH
69572 BUZURGAN
69573 JAMBUR ex Mina Abdullah 1982; ex Jambur 1981
69574 KHANAQUIN
69575 KIRKUK
69576 RUMAILA

69590 TEXACO MELBOURNE Br/US (Kaiser Co)-Ja 1945/67; Tk; 39900; 172.4 × 10 (565.62 × 32.81); T-E (GEC); 13.25; ex Caltex Melbourne 1967; ex Victory Loan 1951; Lengthened & converted from 'T-2' tanker 1967 (Hitachi)

●**69610 ENERGY MOBILITY** Li/Ja (Sasebo) 1972; Tk; 103200; 327.01 × 20.05 (1073 × 65.78); T (IHI);
Sister:
69611 ENERGY PRODUCTION (Li)

69630 HALKI Gr/Ja (Mitsui) 1966; Tk; 41100; 240.57 × 12.73 (789.27 × 41.65); M (B&W); 16.5; ex Kinna Dan 1977

★**69640 LING HU** RC/Sw (Sorviks) 1965; Tk; 33100; 236.1 × 12.68 (774.61 × 41.6); M (B&W); 16; ex Kismet II 1975; ex Minoru 1972

69650 OCTONIA SUN Li/Sw (Eriksbergs) 1964; Tk; 26200; 216.36 × 12.16 (709.84 × 39.9); M (B&W); 16.5; ex La Fleche 1981; ex Tartar 1969

69660 LUNAMAR Pe/Sw (Eriksbergs) 1965; Tk; 32200; 236.8 × 12.83 (775 × 42.09); M (B&W); 16.5; ex Atlas Explorer 1980; ex Kristina 1976; ex Turcoman 1968
Similar (tall pipe from funnel):
69661 THANASSIS A (Gr) ex Dynamic Colocotronis 1979; ex Bjorgholm 1968

69670 HASSAN B Pa/Sw (Uddevalla) 1964; Tk; 35400; 236.13 × 12.82 (774.71 × 42.06); M (B&W); 16; ex Athelking 1977
Sister:
69671 KIMOLOS (Gr) ex Will Adams 1980; ex Athelregent 1977

69690 TRIDENT Gr/Ja (Mitsui) 1965; Tk; 41200; 237.73 × 12.78 (779.95 × 41.93); M (B&W); 16; ex Langeais 1982; ex Thorsheimer 1971
Similar:
69691 TRISTAR (Gr) ex Susan 1982; ex Tamarit 1977; ex Thorstar 1972

69710 AFTHOROS Gr/Ja (IHI) 1965; Tk; 38600; 246.82 × 12.76 (809.78 × 41.96); M (Sulzer); 16.75; ex Olympic Garland 1981
Sister:
69712 ANTONIOS (Gr) ex Olympic Goal 1981

★**69720 GRIMMEN** DDR/Sw (Eriksbergs) 1966; Tk; 28700; 217.81 × 12.16 (714.6 × 39.9); M (B&W); 16.5; ex Sea Breeze 1974

★**69725 ISKAR** Bu/Ja (Osaka) 1966; Tk; 15900; 174.00 × 10.06 (571 × 33.01); M (B&W); 13.5
Sister:
★**69726 OGOSTA** (Bu)

●**69730 STOW PRINCESS** Li/Ja (Mitsui) 1965; Tk; 37100; 239.28 × 12.66 (785.04 × 41.53); M (B&W); 15.5; ex Aphrodite B 1983; ex Illustrious Colocotronis 1979; ex Moster 1972

69740 THANASSIS M. Gr/Ja (Mitsubishi HI) 1965; OO; 37400; 243.21 × 12 (797.93 × 39.37); M (MAN); ex Mistral 1981; ex Rautas 1977

●**69760 YANXILAS** Gr/Sw (Eriksbergs) 1965; Tk; 28900; 217.81 × 12.16 (714.6 × 39.9); M (B&W); 16; ex Polycommander 1970

69770 **PASADENA** Gr/Ja (Mitsui) 1967; Tk; 45100; 258.17 × 14.05 (847.01 × 46.1); M (B&W); 16; ex *Skyron* 1979; ex *Carpo* 1975; ex *Polymonarch* 1972

69780 **MEGA PILOT** Li/Ja (Mitsui) 1967; Tk; 37900; 243.85 × 13.3 (800.03 × 43.64); M (B&W); 16; ex *Levant* 1982; ex *Gimlevang* 1978

69790 **SINOIA** Li/Br (Swan Hunter & WR) 1966; Tk; 51200; 259.47 × 14.88 (851.28 × 48.82); T (GEC); 17; ex *Clementina* 1977; ex *Clementine Churchill* 1973
Similar:
★69791 **ON SUNG** (RK) ex *Gallant Seahorse*; ex *Valentinian* 1972
69792 **VENTURE** (Gr) ex *Thistle Venture* 1983; ex *Jarita* 1977; ex *Gratian* 1972

69800 **CAMPEADOR** Sp/Sp (AESA) 1969; Tk; 20500; 209.02 × 10.73 (685.76 × 35.2); M (B&W); 16.5
Sister:
69801 **CAMPOMAYOR** (Sp)

69810 **LAJPAT RAI** In/Ja (Hitachi) 1965; Tk; 28800; 217.51 × 11.16 (713.62 × 36.61); M (B&W); —

69820 **AMOCO BRISBANE** Li/Ja (Mitsui) 1968; Tk; 35500; 240.55 × 12.76 (789.21 × 41.86); M (B&W); 16
Sisters (Li flag):
69821 **AMOCO BALTIMORE**
69822 **AMOCO CREMONA**
69823 **AMOCO YORKTOWN**

69840 **WIGAN** Br/Ja (Mitsubishi HI) 1964; Tk; 36100; 237.80 × 12.70 (780 × 41.67); T (Mitsubishi); 16; ex *Aristides* 1983; ex *Agios Nikolas* 1983; ex *Venture Oklahoma* 1982; ex *Turbina* 1978; ex *Andking* 1978; ex *Mosking* 1976

69850 **RIGEL** Fr/Fr (L'Atlantique) 1960; Tk; 30800; 224.64 × 11.6 (737.76 × 38.06); M (B&W); 16.25

69870 **HUGO** Fi/No (Rosenberg) 1965; Tk; 52100; 264.78 × 14.73 (869 × 48.33); M (B&W); 15.5; ex *Bergeland* 1975

69880 **INAYAMA** No/Ja (Hitachi) 1964; OO; 48100; 249.99 × 13.74 (820.18 × 45.08); M (B&W); 16
Similar (Li flag):
69881 **SHIGEO NAGANO**
69882 **MARSHALL CLARK**

69900 **LORENZO HALCOUSSI** Li/Ja (IHI) 1968; OBO; 39600; 257.79 × 12.91 (846 × 42.36); M (Sulzer); 16; ex *Arctic* 1971

69910 **GIANNIS N.** Gr/Ja (Mitsui) 1965; B; 21400; 204.71 × 10.62 (671.62 × 34.84); M (B&W); 15.75; ex *Pentas*; Kingposts on travelling gantry

● 69920 **HOPECLIPPER** Br/Ja (Kure) 1967; B; 35300; 223.96 × 13.7 (734.78 × 44.95); M (Sulzer); 15.5; ex *Captain W.D. Cargill* 1977; Kingpost on travelling gantry

● 69930 **CORINTHIAN** Li/Ja (Mitsui) 1967; Tk; 43100; 246.9 × 13.55 (810.04 × 44.46); M (B&W); 16; ex *Blankenberg* 1973

69940 **PELOPIDAS** Gr/Ja (Mitsubishi HI) 1965; Tk; 34400; 238.51 × 12.19 (782.51 × 39.99); M (Mitsubishi); 15.75; ex *Galva* 1976; ex *Heiwa Maru* 1972

● 69950 **M EFES** Tu/Sw (Uddevalla) 1967; OBO; 42500; 243.85 × 13.93 (800 × 45.70); M (B&W); 16; ex *Bantry* 1978; ex *Havtor* 1975
Similar (converted to bulk/container. May be altered in appearance):
69951 **ASEAN KNOWLEDGE** (Pi) ex *Bjorgfjell*
69952 **ASEAN LIBERTY** (Pi) ex *Brali* 1978; ex *Havmoy* 1975
69953 **MONARCH** (Pi) ex *Asean Mission* 1983; ex *Bjorghav* 1979

69960 **ATHENIAN HARMONY** Cy/Ja (IHI) 1970; Tk; 17500; 170.82 × 11.01 (560.43 × 36.12); M (Sulzer); 16; ex *Messiniaki Avra* 1982; ex *Stakara* 1981
Sisters (Gr flag):
69961 **MATHRAKI** ex *Messiniaki Anatoli* 1982; ex *Stabenko* 1981
69962 **MESSINIAKI AVGI** ex *Stamenis* 1981
69963 **ASTIPALEA** ex *Messiniaki Akti* 1982; ex *Stawanda* 1981
69964 **LIMNOS** ex *Messiniaki Aigli* 1982
69966 **MESSINIAKI ANAGENNISIS**
69967 **MESSINIAKI DOXA** ex *Messiniaki Bergen* 1981
69968 **MESSINIAKI GI**
69969 **MESSINIAKI IDEA**
69970 **OTHONI** ex *Messiniaki Dris* 1982; ex *Messiniaki Minde* 1981
69971 **PAROS** ex *Messiniaki Ormi* 1982
69972 **KITHNOS** ex *Messiniaki Paradis* 1982
69975 **MESSINIAKI THEA**

69976 **MESSINIAKI LAMPSIS**
69977 **WAYUSUT** ex *Messiniaki Timi* 1983
(Cy flag):
69978 **DONA LOULA** ex *Messiniaki Areti* 1983
69979 **DONA MYRTO** ex *Messiniaki Chara* 1983
69980 **DONA CHRISTINA** ex *Messiniaki Pnoi* 1983

69990 **BENITO JUAREZ** Me/Ja (IHI) 1968; Tk; 12800; 170.75 × 9.47 (560.2 × 31.07); M (Sulzer); 15.5
Sisters (Me flag):
69991 **ALVARO OBREGON**
69992 **FRANCISCO I MADERO**
69993 **MELCHOR OCAMPO**
69994 **PLAN DE AYALA**
69995 **PLAN DE AYUTLA**
69996 **JOSE MARIA MORELOS**
69997 **PLAN DE GUADELUPE**
Possibly similar:
69998 **PLAN DE SAN LUIS** (Me)

70000 **PETROMAR BAHIA BLANCA II** Bz/Ja (Hitachi) 1974; Tk; 12800; 161.02 × 9.81 (528.28 × 32.19); M (B&W); 15; ex *Esso Mukaishima* 1978
Sisters:
70001 **PETROMAR CAMPANA II** (Bz) ex *Esso Bayway* 1978
(Li flag):
70002 **STENA ADRIATICA** ex *Esso Nagoya* 1983
70005 **ESSO ALBANY**
(De flag):
70006 **ESSO CALLUNDA**
70007 **ESSO HAFNIA**
(It flag):
70007/1 **ESSO GENOVA** ex *Esso Brisbane* 1981
(Fr flag):
70007/2 **ESSO PARENTIS** ex *Esso Guam* 1982
Similar (also under K₃MF):
70008 **ESSO PORT JEROME** (Fr) ex *Esso Kumamoto* 1980

70010 **MATSUKAZE** Ja/Ja (Mie) 1981; Tk/Ch; 10600; 149.61 × 8.65 (491 × 28.38); M (Mitsubishi); 13.5

★70020 **SAMOTLOR** Ru/Fi (Rauma-Repola) 1975; Tk/IB; 12200; 160 × 9.17 (524.93 × 30.09); M (B&W); 16.25
Sisters (Ru flag):
★70021 **URENGOY**
★70022 **BEREZOVO**
★70023 **GORNOPRAVDINSK**
★70024 **NADYM**
★70025 **NIZHNEVARTOVSK**
★70026 **SAMBURG**
★70027 **USINSK**
★70028 **BAM**
★70029 **VILYUYSK**
★70030 **LENINSK-KUZNETSKIY**
★70031 **KAMENSK-URALSKIY**
★70032 **YENISEYSK**
★70033 **IGRIM**

70040 **MANUEL AVILA COMACHO** Me/Ne ('De Hoop') 1973; Tk; 14700; 170.69 × 9.48 (560.01 × 31.1); M (Sulzer); —
Sisters (Me flag):
70041 **INDEPENDENCIA**
70042 **REFORMA**
70043 **REVOLUCION**
70044 **MARIANO MOCTEZUMA**
70045 **FRANCISCO J MUGICA**

70050 **MAGIC MERCURY** Li/Ko (Korea SB) 1974; Tk; 14300; 171.05 × 9.99 (561.19 × 32.78); M (GMT); 15.5; ex *Belgulf Mercury* 1981; ex *Afran Mercury* 1977
Sisters (Li flag):
70051 **MYRICA** ex *Globe Venus* 1981; ex *Afran Venus* 1978
70052 **GOGO RAMBLER** ex *Globe Constellation* 1981; ex *Afran Constellation* 1978
70053 **GOGO RAHN** ex *Afran Galaxy* 1981; ex *Globe Galaxy*; ex *Korea Galaxy* 1978
Probably similar (larger) (Li Flag):
70054 **AFRAN JUPITER**
70055 **AFRAN NEPTUNE**
70056 **GOLDEN CANARY** ex *Golden Crane* 1978
70057 **GOLDEN CAPE** launched as *Sweet Briar*
Similar (lower boat deck etc):
70058 **PRIMA** (Li)

70060 **BEJAIA** Ag/Sw (Oskarshamns) 1977; Tk; 18000; 170.7 × 10.97 (560.1 × 39.99); M (Sulzer); 13.5; Launched as *Messiniaki Proodos*
Sister:
70061 **BETHIOUA** (Ag) launched as *Messiniaki Doxa*
Similar:
70062 **SONJA** (Sw)
70063 **RABIGH BAY 1** (Gr) ex *Susanne* 1980
★70064 **TATRY** (Pd)

★70066 **PIENINY II** (Pd)
70067 **ATHENIAN VENTURE** (Cy) ex *Karkonosze* 1983

70070 **BUNGA KESUMBA** My/Ja (Mitsubishi) 1975; Tk 19000; 170.01 × 11.15 (557.78 × 36.58); M (Sulzer); 15.25
Sisters:
70071 **BUNGA SELASIH** (My)
70072 **BUNGA SEPANG** (My)

70080 **POMELLA** Br/Ne (Verolme Dok) 1967; Tk; 15800; 175.17 × 10.11 (574.7 × 33.17); M (MAN); 15; ex *Horama* 1974; Launched as *Nordvard*
Sister (may be K₂MF, which see):
70081 **PALUDINA** (Br) ex *Urshalim* 1973

70090 **GLOBE EMPRESS** Li/Sw (Uddevalla) 1971; Tk; 15400; 169.7 × 9.69 (556.76 × 31.79); M (B&W); 16; ex *Anco Empress* 1983
Sisters:
70091 **JAMAC** (Li) ex *Molaventure* 1982; ex *Anco Princess* 1981
70092 **STOLT SCEPTRE** (Br) ex *Anco Sceptre* 1983
70093 **IVER SOVEREIGN** (Li) ex *Anco Sovereign* 1982
70094 **STOLT STANE** (Br) ex *Anco Stane* 1983
70095 **STOLT TEMPLAR** (Br) ex *Anco Templar* 1983

70100 **TAURUS ERRE** It/Sw (Uddevalla) 1968; Tk; 11100; 160.13 × 9.15 (525.36 × 30.02); M (B&W); 16; ex *Tarn* 1983; ex *Anco Duchess* 1978; ex *Athelduchess* 1969
Sisters:
70101 **SATU MAR** (Sg) ex *Lake Anette* 1982; ex *Anco Duke* 1980; ex *Athelduke* 1970
70102 **JAG JYOTI** (In) ex *Anco Jyoti* 1977; ex *Jag Jyoti* 1974; ex *Anco Knight* 1972; ex *Athelknight* 1970

70110 **ENDURANCE** Li/Ca (Saint John SB) 1973; Tk; 18800; 187.76 × 10.42 (616 × 34.19); M (B&W); 15; ex *Esso Halifax* 1983
Sisters (Li flag):
70111 **AMAZON PIONEER** ex *Esso Montreal* 1983
70112 **AMAZON PROSPERITY** ex *Esso Saint John* 1982

70120 **ESSO EVERETT** Li/Ca (Saint John SB) 1975; Tk; 21600; 191.57 × 11.25 (628.51 × 36.91); M (Sulzer); 15.5
Sisters:
70121 **PETROMAR SAN SEBASTIAN** (Ar) ex *Esso Providence* 1983
70122 **ESSO SAINT PETERSBURG** (Li)
70123 **PETROMAR SANTA CRUZ** (Ar) ex *Esso Toronto* 1981
Possible sisters (Ca flag):
70124 **IRVING ARCTIC**
70125 **IRVING ESKIMO**
70126 **IRVING OCEAN**

70130 **MAASKADE** Be/Be (Boelwerf) 1975; Tk/Ch; 18300; 170.69 × 11.41 (560 × 37.43); M (B&W); 15.75
Sisters (Be flag):
70131 **MAASKANT**
70132 **MAASKERK**
70133 **MAASKROON**
Possibly similar:
70134 **MANDO V** (Gr)
70135 **MARIANNA** (Gr)
70136 **ERIKOUSSA** (Li) ex *Esso Bahamas* 1982; ex *Tethys* 1972
70137 **POLARIS** (Li) ex *Esso Nassau* 1982

70150 **G A WALKER** Br/Ne (Giessen-De Noord) 1973; Tk; 18700; 170.69 × 11 (560.01 × 36.09); M (B&W); 15
Sisters (Br flag):
70151 **R A EMERSON**
70152 **W A MATHER**
70153 **FORT COULOGNE**
70154 **FORT EDMONTON**
70155 **FORT KIPP**
70156 **FORT MACLEOD**
70157 **FORT STEELE**

70160 **VALIANT PORPOISE** Li/Gr (Hellenic) 1974; Tk; 18300; 170.62 × 11.02 (559.78 × 36.15); M (Sulzer); 15; ex *World Promise* 1981
Sisters:
70161 **WORLD PROTECTOR** (Gr) launched as *World Prospector*
70162 **RIO PANUCO** (Me) ex *World Provider* 1981
70163 **OLYMPIC DREAM** (Gr) ex *World Prospect* 1975
70164 **BRASSIE** (Pa) ex *Failaka* 1981; ex *Team Sinmar*; ex *Team Gerwi* 1976

★70165 **URZHUM** Ru/Gr (Hellenic) 1983; Tk; 18300; 170.69 × 10.76 (560 × 35.30); M (B&W); 16
Sisters:
★70166 **DZERZHINSK** (Ru)
★70167 **NOVOROSSIYSK** (Ru) launched as *World*

roduct
70168 STAVROPOL (Ru)
70169 ULYANOVSK (Ru)
0169/1 WORLD PROCESS (Gr)

0170 THEBEN Li/Sw (Eriksbergs) 1977; Tk/Ch;
8200; 170.72 × 11.33 (560.1 × 37.17); M (B&W);
6; ex Crown Inland 1983; ex Inland 1982
sters:
0171 CROWN BROLAND (Br) ex Broland 1982
0172 CROWN ATLAND (Sw) ex Atland 1982

0180 PANAMA De/De (Nakskov) 1977; Tk; 20900;
70.69 × 11.59 (560 × 38.02); M (B&W); 15.25
sters (De flag):
0181 PARANAGUA
0182 PATTAYA

0190 OCEAN TRADER Sg/De (Nakskov) 1974; Tk;
400; 170.69 × 10.42 (560.01 × 34.19); M (B&W);
; ex Neptune Aries 1983
ster:
191 NEPTUNE ORION (Sg)

200 PROCYON Gr/Ne (Giessen-De Noord) 1975;
; 32600; 210.32 × 12.41 (690.01 × 40.71); M
&W); 16.75; ex Cyclops 1983
ster:
201 CLYTONEUS (Br)
obable sister:
202 RAIKO MARU (Ja) ex Sanko Trust 1979;
unched as Hellespont Argosy

210 ESSO SLAGEN No/Sw (Lindholmens) 1968;
; 11000; 162.67 × 8.87 (533.69 × 29.1); M (Piel-
ck); 16.25

0230 AUE DDR/Sw (Kockums) 1959; OO; 15800;
1.62 × 9.99 (595.87 × 32.78); M (MAN); 14.5; ex
tala 1969

240 GLOBE NOVA Li/No (Fredriksstad) 1964;
/LGC; 13500; 169.78 × 9.6 (557.02 × 31.5); M
otaverken); 15.75; ex Granheim 1978

250 PIONEER II Pa/No (Haugesund) 1961; Tk;
OO; 155.02 × 8.8 (508.6 × 28.87); M (Gotaverken);
; ex Chelsea Pioneer 1983; ex Acron C 1980; ex
genpuma 1979; ex Post Runner 1977; ex Saga
te 1970; ex Anco State 1967; ex Berean 1964

270 DONATELLO Pa/Sw (Oresunds) 1962; Tk;
800; 170.62 × 9.7 (559.78 × 31.82); M (Gotaverk-
); 15.5; ex Lake Aniara 1982; ex Aniara 1977; ex
a Gorthon 1971

280 ESTRELLA ANTARTICA Ar/No (Akers)
62; Tk; 13000; 169.7 × 9.68 (556.76 × 31.76); M
W); 14.5; ex Fleettrader 1979; ex Herstein 1978;
Landvard 1969
nilar:
281 LAKE ANJA (No) ex Gimlekollen 1977; ex
rd 1963
282 PRETTY (Cy) ex Gunda Brovig 1981; ex Olymp
68
283 ANTONIO D'ALESSIO (It) ex Ergina 1 1977;
Anna Odland 1975

0290 DA QING No 38 RC/No (Moss V) 1962; Tk;
00; 152.41 × 8.46 (500.03 × 27.76); M (B&W); 14;
Dansborg 1970; ex Kindvik 1969

800 CHEMICAL SOL Li/No (Akers) 1967; Tk/Ch;
00; 149.41 × 9.02 (490.19 × 29.59); M (B&W); 16;
Canso Transport 1981; ex Lonn

810 MONTELEON Sp/Sp (UN de Levante) 1969;
5200; 123.37 × 7.32 (404.76 × 24.02); M (B&W);

20 UNGAVA TRANSPORT Ca/No (Sarpsborg)
9/71; Tk; 4700; 122.97 × 7.11 (403.44 × 23.33);
B&W); 12; ex Tommy Wiborg 1974; ex Varangnes
0; Converted from ore/oil 1971

30 RAAD AL-BAKRY VIII Si/No (Fredriksstad)
0; Ch; 13300; 176.18 × 9.59 (578.02 × 31.46); M
taverken); 14.5; ex Maya Farber 1983; ex Bjor-
im 1978; ex Lysefjell 1972; Converted from tank-
970

40 STELLA AZZURRA It/Br (Doxford) 1961; Tk;
00; 170.47 × 9.48 (559 × 31.1); M (Doxford); —
5; ex Stolta 1977; ex Stolt Tudor 1975; ex Tudor
ce 1971

55 ELEFTHERIA M. Li/Ja (IHI) 1965; Tk; 38300;
01 × 12.78 (797 × 41.93); M (Sulzer); 15.75; ex
el 1982; ex Splendid Arrow 1977; ex Benedict
3

60 ATHENA Li/Ja (IHI) 1964; OO; 30700 (oil)
00 (ore); 224.29 × 12.08 (735.86 × 39.63); T (IHI);
ex Santa Fe Pioneer 1968
er:
61 DAPHNE (Li) ex Santa Fe Explorer 1968

70 ARHON Li/Ja (Mitsui) 1966; Tk; 30600;

236.23 × 12.48 (775.03 × 40.94); M (B&W); 17; ex
Moorgate Queen 1977; ex Vassos Georgiadis 1976;
ex Kongsholm 1973

70440 DOLORES Ch/No (Marinens) 1967; Tk;
14500; 169.02 × 9.53 (554.53 × 31.27); M (Sulzer);
16.5; ex Iver Stream; ex Saga Stream 1977; ex Anco
Stream 1973

●70460 LETO Gr/Ja (Mitsubishi HI) 1967; Tk; 44600;
250.12 × 14.05 (821 × 46.1); M (Sulzer); —; ex M J
Carras 1978
Similar:
70461 DIONE (Li) ex Ioannis Carras 1978
70462 WILLIAM DAMPIER (Au) ex Iolcos; ex Fotini
Carras 1978

70470 CALEDONIA Li/Ja (Uraga HI) 1967; OO;
34500; 228.51 × 12.68 (749.7 × 41.6); M (Sulzer);
16.25
Sister:
70471 MAKEDONIA STAR (Ch) ex Obo Makedonia
Star 1982; ex Makedonia Star 1981; ex Makedonia
1981

70490 KATINA Gr/Ja (Hitachi) 1966; Tk; 38900;
238.59 × 11.99 (782.78 × 39.34); M (B&W); 15.5; ex
Yuyo Maru No 2 1981

70500 PETROLA 31 Gr/Ja (IHI) 1966; Tk; 43400;
246.49 × 13.83 (808.69 × 45.37); M (Sulzer); 16; ex
Petrola XXXI 1976; ex Hellas 1975; ex Henrietta Latsi
1973

★70540 SYN PULKU Pd/Pd (Szczecinska) 1974; B;
20600; 199.17 × 10.63 (653.44 × 34.88); M (Sulzer);
15.25; 'B 447' type
Sisters (Pd flag):
★70541 CEDYNIA
★70542 MIROSLAWIEC
★70543 NARWIK II
★70544 POWSTANIEC WIELKOPOLSKI
★70545 STUDZIANKI

70550 SEABORNE Li/Ja (Namura) 1973; Tk;
15000; 171.02 × 10.71 (561.09 × 35.14); M (Sulzer);
15
Sisters:
70551 SEASERVICE (Li)
70552 SEASTAR (Li)
Possibly similar:
70553 CYS INTEGRITY (Li)
70554 KOREA SUNNYHILL (Ko) ex Cys Hope 1980

70560 IRATI Bz/Ys ('3 Maj') 1970; Tk; 9700; 142.53
X 7.32 (467.62 X 14.02); M (Sulzer); 13.5
Sisters (Bz flag):
70561 IPANEMA
70562 ITORORO

70570 PERMINA XXIX Ia/Sw (Finnboda) 1971; Tk;
9400; 139.3 × 9.2 (457.02 × 30.18); M (B&W); 15.5;
ex Bruce Soverino 1980
Sister:
70571 PERMINA XXV (Ia) ex Bruce Torres 1981

★70572 MAYKOP Ru/Br (Swan Hunter) 1975; Tk;
19600; 171.00 × 11.30 (561 × 37.07); M (Sulzer); 15;
Launched as Helena K
Sisters:
★70573 APSHERON (Ru) launched as Robkap II
★70574 GROZNY (Ru) launched as Robkap 1
★70575 GUDERMES (Ru) launched as Robkap IV
★70576 MAKHACHKALA (Ru) launched as
Robkap III
70577 LAGOVEN QUIRIQUIRE (Ve)
70578 LAGOVEN SANTA RITA (Ve)
Similar:
70579 OSCO INGRAM OSPREY (Br) launched as
Ingram Osprey

70580 AQUARIUS Br/Br (Swan Hunter) 1972; Tk;
19900; 192.01 × 10.38 (629.95 × 34.05); M (Sulzer);
16; ex Newburn 1980; ex Afghanistan; ex Joseph R
Smallwood 1975
Sisters:
70581 AURA ADVENTURE (Li) ex Strait of Canso
1982
70582 AURA BRAVERY (Li) ex Simonburn 1982; ex
Kurdistan; ex Frank D Moores 1976
Probable sister:
70583 AMOKURA (NZ) ex Hindustan 1978

●★70590 MATE ZALKA Ru/Ys ('3 Maj') 1976; Tk;
27700; 195 × 12.2 (639.76 × 40.03); M (Sulzer); 17
Sisters (Ru flag-some have taller funnel):
★70591 ANTONIO GRAMSCI
★70592 PABLO NERUDA
★70593 DAVID SIQUEIROS
★70594 VIKTORIO CODOVILLA
★70595 JACQUES DUCLOS
★70596 JOHN REED
★70597 JOSE MARTI
★70598 PAUL ROBESON
★70599 KLEMENT GOTTWALD

★70600 SUKHE BATOR

★70610 KUTAISI Ru/Ys ('Split') 1976; Tk; 15700;
182.99 × 10 (600.36 × 32.81); M (MAN); 17
Sister (Ru flag):
★70611 SUKHUMI

●70620 KYNOSSOURA Gr/Sw (Kockums) 1964; Tk;
30600; 236.23 × 12.42 (775.03 × 40.75); M (Kockums); 15.5; ex Oriental Discoverer 1981; ex Defiant
Colocotronis 1977; ex Bruse Jarl 1969

70630 STERLING Li/Ja (Uraga HI) 1966; Tk; 30700;
234.02 × 11.86 (767.78 × 38.91); M (Sulzer); 15.75

70640 UBARANA Gr/Ja (Uraga HI) 1965; Tk;
24000; 222.51 × 11.96 (730.02 × 39.24); M (Uraga);
—; ex Michael 1982; ex Michael J Goulandris 1978

70650 WILLIAM R GRACE Li/Ne (Verolme Dok)
1964; LGC; 10000; 156.47 × 7.51 (513.35 × 24.64);
M (MAN); 17
Sister:
70651 JOSEPH . GRACE (Li)

70660 CITADEL HILL Va/Br (Furness) 1967; B;
29300; 213.39 × 12.68 (700.1 × 41.6); M (B&W); 15;
ex Canadian Highlander 1983; ex Cape Breton Highlander 1980; ex Thorsdrake 1975

●70670 IRENES RHAPSODY Cy/Br (Barclay, Curle)
1967; B; 29300; 213.37 × 12.75 (700.03 × 41.83); M
(B&W); 15.75; ex Mediolanum; ex Hamlet 1972

70680 EVANGELIA C Gr/Br (Furness) 1967; B;
29400; 213.37 × 12.75 (700.32 × 41.83); M (B&W);
15; ex Polyfreedom 1978
Sister:
70681 PAN WESTERN (Gr) ex Norseman 1975

70690 ADOLF LEONHARDT Li/FRG (Flensburger)
1964; B; 18600; 201.66 × 11.53 (661.6 × 37.83); M
(MAN); 15

★70695 JENA DDR/DDR (Mathias-Thesen) 1978;
B/Con; 16000; 176.69 × 10.11 (580 × 33.17); M
(MAN); 16
Sisters:
★70696 MEISSEN (DDR)
★70697 WEIMAR (DDR)

70700 GLAFKI Li/Fr (L'Atlantique) 1964; B; 15200;
178.24 × 9.46 (584.78 × 31.04); M (B&W); —

70720 FUTURE Pa/Br (A&P) 1968; B; 14000;
177.71 × 9.85 (583.04 × 32.32); M (Gotaverken);
14.5; ex New Future 1982; ex Vancouver Trader; ex
Essex Trader 1971

70730 DOAN TRANSPORT Ca/Br (Robb Caledon)
1972; Tk; 6800; 131.37 × 8.39 (431 × 27.53); M
(Pielstick); 15; ex Jon Ramsoy 1975

★70740 KAPITAN SHVETSOV Ru/Bu (G Dimitrov)
1973; Tk; 4200; 116.08 × 6.69 (381 × 21.95); M
(B&W); 14
Sisters (Ru flag):
★70741 DROGOBYCH
★70742 KAPITAN IZOTOV
★70743 INZHEHIER AGEYEV
★70744 KAPITAN GRIBIN
★70745 KAPITAN MAKATSARIYA
★70746 FORE MOSULISHVILI
★70747 KAPITAN DYACHUK
★70748 KAPITAN DOTSYENKO
★70749 KAPITAN KOBETS
★70750 KAPITAN NEVEZHKIN
(Ia flag):
70751 BEKASAP/PERMINA 54 ex Slora 1982
70752 BESITANG/PERMINA 53 ex Slagen 1982
Similar (larger) (Ia flag):
70753 BEKAPAI/PERMINA 56 ex Sletta 1982
70754 BETUNG/PERMINA 55 ex Slitan 1982
70755 BENAKAT/PERMINA 57 ex Slensvik 1982

★70760 ALTAY Ru/Fi (Rauma-Repola) 1967; Tk;
3500; 106.15 × 6.74 (348.26 × 22.11); M (B&W);
13.25
Sisters (Some have bipod masts foreward—Ru flag):
★70761 AKTAU
★70762 AKTYUBINSK
★70763 AMGUN
★70764 ADYGENI
★70765 ANAKLIYA
★70766 AYKHAL
★70767 AKHALTSIKHE
★70768 ARARAT
★70769 AUTSE
★70770 AYNAZHI
★70771 AYON
★70772 ANTARES
★70773 AUSEKLIS
★70774 ABAVA
★70775 ANUYU
★70776 ASPINDZA
★70777 KOLA

★70778 **KHERSONES**
★70779 **RAUMA**
★70780 **YELNYA**
★70781 **BIRYUZA**
★70782 **OMSK**
★70783 **YEGORLIK**
★70784 **YUGANSK**
★70785 **ZHALGIRIS**
★70786 **ZUGDIDI**
★70787 **SURGUTNEFT**
★70788 **ILIM**
★70789 **NEFTEGORSK**
★70790 **TARKHANKUT**
★70791 **DEBRECEN**
★70792 **NEFTEKAMSK**
★70793 **RUMBALA**
★70794 **SAKHALINNEFT**
★70795 **SIBIRNEFT**

★70810 **PRUT** Ru/Fi (Rauma-Repola) 1971; RT; 3700; 106.08 × 6.5 (348.03 × 21.33); M (B&W); 14; Converted from oil tanker
Sister:
★70811 **IZHORA** (Ru); May be others of the ALTAY class similarly converted

70820 **PRIMA JEMIMA** Br/Br (Furness) 1967; Tk; 2800; 98.61 × 5.87 (323.52 × 19.26); M (English Electric); 12; ex *Esso Purfleet* 1983

★70825 **LONG HU** RC/Ja (Ujina) 1973; Tk; 9800; 153.70 × 9.37 (504 × 30.74); M (Mitsubishi); 15; ex *Akitsushima Maru* 1975
Probable sister:
70826 **GEMINI IV** (Pa) ex *Hiroshima Maru* 1981

70830 **BUTATRES** Sp/Sp (Euskalduna) 1965; LGC; 1500; 80.8 × 4.93 (265.09 × 16.17); M (Gotaverken); —
Sister:
70831 **BUTACUATRO** (Sp)

70840 **AL KHLOOD** Si/FRG (Kroegerw) 1973; Ch; 4500; 113.14 × 7.41 (371.19 × 24.31); M (Mirrlees Blackstone); 14; ex *Silverpelerin* 1980

70850 **MASSA** Mo/Ja (Naikai) 1978; Tk; 4500; 114.8 × 6.6 (376.64 × 21.65); M (Daihatsu); 13

70860 **ELENI V** Gr/No (Drammen) 1964; Tk; 1900; 86.24 × 5.67 (282.94 × 18.6); M (Sulzer); 12.25; ex *Libra*; ex *Panglobal Unity* 1977; ex *Seadrake* 1972; ex *Solglimt* 1970

70870 **PETROSTAR III** Si/Br (Smith's D) 1968; Tk; 0000 86.21 × 5.67 (282.84 × 18.6); M (Smit & McInes); 12; ex *Nette Theresa* 1974; ex *Preciosa* 1972

70880 **B P JOUSTER** Br/Br (Appledore) 1972; Tk; 1600; 78.95 × 4.74 (259.02 × 15.55); M (Alpha-Diesel); 12; ex *Swansea* 1976
Sister:
70881 **SHELL EXPLORER** (Br) ex *Dundee* 1979
Similar:
70882 **SHELL DIRECTOR** (Br) ex *Caernarvon* 1979
70883 **SHELL SUPPLIER** (Br) ex *Plymouth* 1979

70890 **ALADEWE** Ng/Br (Burntisland) 1966; Tk; 3700; 111.74 × 7.32 (366.6 × 24.02); M (B&W); 16; ex *Naesborg* 1983; ex *Sea Transport* 1977; ex *Olau Mark* 1971
Sister:
★70891 **WAN TAI** (RC) ex *Bailu*; ex *Olau Leif* 1972

70900 **INGE MAERSK** De/No (Moss V) 1972; LGC/Ch; 9200; 138.74 × 9.21 (455.18 × 30.22); M (Sulzer); 17
Sister:
70901 **FERNWAVE** (No)
Similar (smaller):
70902 **HARDANGER** (No)
70903 **BOW ELM** (No)
Similar (later built):
70906 **HESPERUS** (No) ex *Fernbrook* 1978

70910 **BERNARDO HOUSSAY** Ar/Fr (La Ciotat) 1969; LGC; 6900; 126.22 × 7.32 (414.11 × 24.02); M (Sulzer); 16; ex *Barfonn* 1980

70920 **SENKO MARU** Ja/Ja (Tokushima Z S) 1971; Ch; 1000; 68.03 × 4.01 (223.2 × 13.16); M (Makita); 12
Probable sister:
70921 **OGISHIMA MARU** (Ja)
Possibly similar (LGC):
70922 **KOSHIN MARU No 3** (Ja)

70930 **SANKYO ETHYLENE MARU** Ja/Ja (Naikai) 1974; LGC; 1600; 65.54 × 4.12 (215.03 × 13.52); M (Daihatsu); 11.25

70940 **SARRAT** Pi/Fr (France-Gironde) 1963/65; LGC; 8000; 145.01 × 8.38 (475.75 × 27.49); M (B&W); 15; ex *Ang Pangarap* 1980; ex *Rye Gas*; ex *Crystal* 1977; ex *Cap Martin* 1975; ex *Savoie* 1965;

Converted from ore carrier 1965

70950 **JAVELIN** Li/Ja (Uraga HI) 1968; B/Con; 17100; 167.01 × 10.67 (547.93 × 35.01); M (Sulzer); 15.5; ex *Hickory* 1982; ex *Star Mostangen* 1978; ex *Mostangen* 1975; Converted from bulk carrier 1969
Sisters:
70951 **GREAT COSMOS** (Pa) ex *Georges Chr Lemos* 1980; ex *Mosengen* 1975
70952 **BERJAYA** (Sg) ex *Mosbay* 1978
70953 **SENTOSA** (Sg) ex *Mosgulf* 1979

70960 **NADIA** Ng/Sp (Euskalduna) 1964/72; Tk; 3500; 102.49 × 6.29 (336.25 × 20.64); M (MAN); 12.5; ex *Ashurst* 1983; ex *Finse* 1972; Converted from cargo 1972 (Smith's D)

●70970 **ETHEL EVERARD** Br/Br (Clelands) 1966; C; 1600; 85.1 × 5.1 (279.1 × 16.73); M (Mirrlees Blackstone); 11

70980 **ZEIDA** Mo/Sp (Construcciones SA) 1971; C; 700/1600; 84.82 × —/5.67 (278.28 × —/18.6); M (Deutz); 11; ex *Vilya* 1975
Sisters:
70981 **ZERHOUN** (Mo) ex *Nenya* 1975
70982 **PELLA** (Gr) ex *Celtic Venture* 1982; ex *Monkchester* 1978; ex *Waynegate* 1976
Similar. Ne built-E J Smit:
70983 **MARIA MONICA** (It) ex *Monica* 1976

★70990 **BOSUT** Ys/FRG (Luerssen) 1967; C; 2800; 95.81 × 6.36 (314.34 × 20.87); M (Bergens); 12.25 ex *Raknes* 1977
Sisters (Ys flag):
★70992 **CIKOLO** ex *Tinnes* 1978
★70993 **ROGOZNICA** ex *Vigsnes* 1978
(It flag):
★70994 **MARIA DORMIO** ex *Telnes* 1979
70995 **PIETRO** ex *Altnes* 1978
70996 **BEATRICE** ex *Korsnes* 1977
70997 **VISPY** ex *Garnes* 1978:
70998 **ALBERTO DORMIO** ex *Isnes* 1983; ex *Frines* 1977; ex *Fritre* 1973

★71000 **SHU HE** RC/Ja (Kagoshima) 1978; C; 5300; 116.97 × 7.29 (384 × 23.92); M (Mitsubishi); 14.5; ex *Leo Tornado* 1983

★71010 **KORCULA** Ys/Ys ('Jozo Lozovina-Mosor') 1968; C; 2100; 102.14 × 5.67 (335.1 × 18.6); M (B&W); 14.5

★71020 **KRAPANJ** Ys/Br (Caledon) 1967; C; 4900; 123.81 × 7.1 (406.2 × 23.29); M (British Polar); 14; ex *Lyminge* 1975

71030 **LEO SHARPY** Pa/Rm (Galatz) 1975; C; 5000; 105.97 × 8.24 (347.67 × 27.03); M (MWM); 15.5; ex *Brest* 1980; ex *Cypress*; ex *Bow Ek*
Sisters:
71031 **BEBEDOURO** (Li) ex *Oak* 1979; ex *Bow Oak* 1978
71032 **FOMALHAUT** (Li) ex *Fellowship* 1981; Launched as *Frendo-Fellowship*
71033 **SHAULA** (Li) ex *Membership* 1981; ex *Frendo-Membership* 1976
71034 **MARIA ELENA** (Ve) ex *Partnership* 1981; ex *Frendo Partnership* 1977; ex *Partnership* 1975; Launched as *Frendo-Partnership*

●★71040 **PIONER MOSKVY** Ru/Ru (Vyborg) 1973; C/Con; 4800; 130.31 × 7.36 (428. × 24.15); M (B&W); 15.5
Sisters (Ru flag):
★71041 **PIONER ARKHANGELSKA**
★71042 **PIONER SAKHALINA**
★71043 **PIONER YUZHNO SAKHALINSKA**
★71044 **PIONER CHUKOTKI**
★71045 **PIONER KHOLMSKA**
★71046 **PIONER ONEGI**
★71047 **PIONER ESTONII**
★71048 **PIONER KAMCHATKI**
★71049 **PIONER ROSSI**
★71050 **PIONER BURYATII**
★71051 **PIONER LITVY**
★71052 **PIONER SEVERODVINSKA**
★71053 **PIONER SLAVYANKI**
★71054 **PIONER AYKUTI**
★71055 **PIONER BELORUSSII**
★71056 **PIONER KARELII**
★71057 **PIONER KAZAKHSTANA**
★71058 **PIONER KIRGIZII**
★71059 **PIONER MOLDAVII**
★71060 **PIONER UZBEKISTANA**
Possible sister:
★71061 **JUGO NAVIGATOR** (Ys)

71090 **VISHVA PREM** In/Ys ('3 Maj') 1966; B; 9700; 146.01 × 8.94 (479 × 29.33); M (Sulzer); 13.5; ex *Vishva Tilak* 1973
Sisters (In flag):
71091 **VISHVA VIJAY**
71093 **LOK SEVAK**

71100 **DON ALEJO** Co/No (Framnaes) 1966; C; 3900; 111.36 × 6.33 (365 × 20.77); M (Sulzer); 13; ex *Fossum* 1977

71110 **ELAZIG** Tu/No (Drammen) 1960; C; 4800; 116.29 × 6.45/7.93 (381.53 × 21.16/26.02); M (Sulzer); —; ex *Marosa* 1960

71120 **ISORA** Sp/Sp ('Astano') 1967; C; 1600; 96.68 × 5.67 (317.19 × 18.6); M (B&W); —; ex *Lago San Mauricio* 1975

●71130 **PACIFIC FAIR** Li/Ja (Sanoyasu) 1969; B; 10000; 143.54 × 9.16 (470.93 × 30.05); M (Sulzer); 15; ex *Union Wisdom* 1983
Sisters:
71131 **TIARA** (Gr) ex *Captain Lemos* 1982; ex *Union Friendship* 1976
71132 **KING GEORGE** (Pa) ex *Ever Faith* 1983
71133 **RENACIMIENTO** (Ch) ex *Cosmos Eltanin* 1977
Possible sisters:
71134 **ROYAN** (Pa) ex *Lombardy* 1981; ex *Petersberg* 1981; ex *Victoria* 1980; ex *Georgiana* 1979
71135 **KOMARINE 7** (Ko) ex *Kostar* 1982; ex *Katrina* 1978
71136 **MYUNG JIN** (Ko) ex *Pearl Venture* 1978

71140 **MARKOS N** Gr/Ja (Maizuru) 1969; B; 11400; 156.17 × 9.54 (512.37 × 31.3); M (B&W); 15; ex *United Brightness* 1981; ex *Asia Brightness* 1980
Sister:
71141 **BALTIC TRANSPORTER** (Tu) ex *Pacific Mariner* 1983; ex *United Grace* 1981; ex *Asia Grace* 1981; ex *United Grace* 1980; ex *Asia Grace* 1980

●71150 **PACIFIC QUEEN** Ja/Ja (Onomichi) 1968; B; 10700; 154.18 × 8.76 (505.84 × 28.74); M (B&W); 14.75; ex *Pacific Ares* 1975; ex *Tajima Maru* 1974; ex *Shoku Maru* 1968
Similar:
71151 **IRAN ETEGHAD** (Ir) ex *Goldenrod* 1983; ex *Oriental Light* 1973; ex *Shinko Maru* 1971
Similar (centre line KP instead of Goalposts):
71152 **MIRA** (Pa) ex *Evergreen* 1982; ex *Koho Maru* 1972
71153 **AUGUST MOON** (Pa) ex *Wakaosan Maru* 1972
Possibly similar:
71154 **CITY OF CAMELOT** (Cy) ex *Midas Seine* 1983; ex *Seine Maru* 1972
71155 **REIHO MARU** (Ja)
71156 **COURAGEOUS** (Li) ex *Van Union* 1981
★71157 **KOCEVJE** (Ys) ex *Pioneer Merchant* 1975; ex *Tanba Maru* 1973
71158 **LUMBER STATE** (Pa) ex *Kenan Maru* 1982
71159 **KOH EUN** (Ko) ex *New Zealanders* 1977; ex *Kosho Maru* 1973

●71170 **SANAGA** Sg/Ja (Hitachi) 1971; B; 12100; 156.17 × 9.29 (512.37 × 30.48); M (B&W); 15; ex *Woermann Sanaga* 1976
Sisters:
71171 **HUDSON DEEP** (Sg) ex *Woermann Sassandra*
71172 **THEANO** (Gr) ex *Woermann Ubangi* 1980
71173 **ARIZONA SUN** (Sg) ex *Sankuru* 1981; ex *Woermann Sankuru* 1976
71174 **SWAKOP** (Pa) ex *Maritime Courier* 1978; ex *Swakop* 1976
71175 **ZAMBESI** (Pa) ex *Maritime Transporter* 1978; ex *Woermann Sambesi* 1976
71176 **SAN PEDRO** (Pa) launched as *Woermann San Pedro*
Similar:
71177 **BO AH** (Ko) ex *Maritime Victor* 1980
71178 **TRANSOCEAN RAM** (Pi) ex *Van Warrior* 1980
71179 **ANGEATLANTIC** (Gr) ex *Van Hawk*
71180 **KALYN** (Cy) ex *Calypso N* 1983; ex *Mariner* 1978; ex *Eastern Cherry* 1980
71181 **STEPHANOS** (Gr) ex *Merlin* 1980; ex *Eastern Mary*
71182 **CANAL ACE** (Pa) ex *World Hercules* 1981
71183 **ZINI** (Gr)
71184 **GEORTINA** (Gr)
Possibly similar:
71185 **ISLAND SKY** (Li)
71186 **ANGEARCTIC** (Gr) ex *World Champion*
71187 **NIKOLETA K** (Gr) ex *United Pride* 1982; ex *World Pride* 1981
71188 **HAN SONG** (Ko) ex *Golden Explorer* 1982
71189 **KRONOS** (Gr) ex *Golden Pioneer* 1982
Similar (Ko built—Korea SB):
71190 **PAN KOREA** (Ko)
Possibly similar (Ko built—Korea SB):
71191 **KOREAN PRIDE** (Li)
71192 **KOREAN FIR** (Li)
71193 **CATHERINE ANN** (Li) ex *Glory River* 1980
71194 **ARGUS** (Li) ex *Rebecca Elyse* 1983; ex *Great River* 1980
71195 **AKTION** (Gr)

1196 **ALKAIOS** (Gr)

1200 **DALMAR** Sg/Ja (IHI) 1966; B; 9400; 147.02
8.71 (482.35 × 28.58); M (Sulzer); 14.5; ex *Woer-
ann Nyanga* 1974; ex *Meridian* 1969

71205 **LOGATEC** Ys/Ja (Kanasashi) 1968; C;
300; 148.04 × 8.68 (486 × 28.48); M (B&W); 14; ex
anetoshi Maru 1971
ossible sisters:
206 **ALEON** (Pa) ex *Kaneoka Maru* 1983
207 **IVORY GLORY** (Pa) ex *Daikei Maru* 1983

220 **PROIKONISOS** Cy/Ja (IHI) 1969; B; 9800;
5.65 × 9.11 (477.85 × 29.89); M (Sulzer); 16.5; ex
stern Ace* 1982
ters:
221 **EVER SPLENDOR** (Tw) ex *Ever Success*
73
222 **MAREL** (Cy) ex *Cape Mustang* 1983; ex
ustang*; ex *World Pelagic* 1978
milar:
223 **SAM CHOONG** (Pa) ex *Kinyo Maru* 1978
224 **DONA ROSSANA** (Li)

230 **KYOSEI MARU** Ja/Ja (Mitsubishi HI) 1971;
8500; 141.28 × 8.81 (464 × 29.00); M (Kobe); 14.5

240 **AMGIS KATASYRTA** Gr/Ja (Tsuneishi)
71; C; 5900; 127.97 × 7.54 (419.85 × 24.74); M
itsubishi); 13.5; ex *Ssang Yong No 333* 1976; ex
o Yong*; ex *Tensa Maru* 1974

250 **ATAIR** Sg/Ja (Fukuoka) 1976; C; 7400;
7.79 × 8.05 (419.26 × 26.41); M (Mitsubishi);
25; ex *Merzario Asia* 1981; ex *Zepsea* 1980; ex
lf Unity* 1978; ex *Zepsea* 1977
ters:
251 **CHARLOTTE** (li) ex *Lily Venture* 1981
252 **OCEAN ACE** (Ja)
252/1 **PACIFIC LEISURE** (Tw) ex *Ocean Express*
32; ex *Bright Star* 1979
253 **RIGEL** (Sg) ex *Singapore Merchant* 1983; ex
e America* 1979; ex *Zephawk* 1978
sible sister:
254 **SANTORIN** (Sg) ex *Kitty Porr*

260 **ORIENT FISHER** Pa/Ja (Ujina) 1974; Cem;
00; 127.77 × 8.25 (419.19 × 27.07); M (Ito Tek-
ho); 13.25; ex *Union Amsterdam* 1980; ex *Orien-
Victory* 1977
ters:
261 **QINLING** (RC) ex *Myoken Maru* 1975
62 **HAND LOONG** (Pa)
63 **HAND FORTUNE** (B&V)
63/1 **GARDENIA** (Sg) ex *Dixy Porr* 1981; ex
den Valley* 1976
sible sisters:
64 **CHERRYFIELD** (Li)
65 **KNIGHT** (Pa) ex *Seven Daffodil* 1980; ex
rgia Merry* 1978; ex *Sun Deneb* 1977
66 **JELAU** (Pa) ex *Akitaka Maru* 1978
67 **EVANGELOS D** (Pa) ex *Sun Sirius*; ex *Koryu
u* 1975
68 **GOLDEN DRAGON** (Pa)
69 **EASTERN NEPTUNE** (Pa) ex *Shuwa Maru*
3
70 **HAUDA BEAUTY** (Cy) ex *Yancey*
71 **SUN ORION** (Pa)
72 **KOREA STAR** (Sg) ex *Jayne H B* 1982; ex
ry B* 1981; ex *Blue Jupiter* 1977
73 **NATIONAL LEADER** (Pi) ex *National Steel*
1983; ex *Yu Lin* 1978
74 **SWEE LEAN** (Ja) ex *Lusty* 1979
75 **GOLDEN STAR** (Pa)
76 **REGENT** (Pa)

285 **MOSOR** Ys/Ja (Setoda) 1967; C;
0/5800; 120.30 × —/7.88 (395 × —/25.85); M
W); 13; ex *Tropical Plywood* 1975
er:
286 **PRVI SPLITSKI ODRED** (Ys) ex *Tropical
eer* 1975

90 **URANUS 1** FRG/FRG (Schuerenstedt) 1977;
on; 3600/6700; 131.71 × 6.35/ 8.03); (432.12
0.83/26.35); M (Atlas-MaK); 15.25; ex *Diplomat
8; ex *Uranus* 1977

00 **HODO** Tg/FRG (Flensburger) 1978; C; 7600;
81 × 8.25 (439.01 × 27.07); M (Atlas-MaK) 15
ers:
01 **PIC D'AGOU** (Tg)
02 **MAW-LA-MYAING** (Bm)
03 **SIT-TWAY** (Bm)

310 **OSTROV RUSSKIY** Ru/Sw (Lindholmens)
9; FC; 9800; 150.55 × 7.47 (494 × 24.51); M
stick); 18.25
ers (Ru flag):
311 **OSTROV ATLASOVA**
312 **OSTROV BERINGA**
313 **OSTROV KARAKINSKIY**
314 **OSTROV KOTLIN**
315 **OSTROV LISYANSKOGO**

★ 71316 **OSTROV LITKE**
★ 71317 **OSTROV MEDNYY**
★ 71318 **OSTROV SHMIDTA**
★ 71319 **OSTROV SHOKALSKOGO**
★ 71320 **OSTROV SIBIRYAKOVA**
★ 71321 **OSTROV USHAKOVA**

★ 71330 **BAEK DU SAN** RK/Ne (Verolme Scheeps)
1965; FC; 7200; 130.33 × — (427.59 × —); M (MAN);
May also be known as **TOP VAN WITTE BERG**

★ 71340 **BATALLA DE STA. CLARA** Cu/Fi (Nystads)
1975; R; 500/1300; 74.12 × —/4.71 (243.18 × —
/15.45); M (Bofors); 14
Sister:
★ 71341 **BATALLA DE YAGUAJAY** (Cu)

71350 **KORFOS 1** Cy/Fr (La Seine) 1960; O; 6000;
132.52 × 7.56 (434.78 × 24.8); M (B&W); 16.5; ex
Omega Rhodos 1983; ex *Penchateau* 1980; ex *Aequator* 1980; ex *Queen of Ampelos* 1978; ex *Penchateau* 1974

★ 71360 **ROSTOK** Ru/DDR ('Neptun') 1973; C;
2900/4500; 117.79 × 5.8/6.92 (386.45 ×
19.03/22.7); M (MAN); 16.5; 'POSEIDON' class
Sisters (Ru flag):
★ 71361 **CHITA**
★ 71362 **KHASAN**
★ 71363 **MAGO**
★ 71364 **NOVOCHERKASSK**
★ 71365 **RYSHKANY**
★ 71366 **RUSHANY**
★ 71367 **RUDNYY**
★ 71368 **ROMNY**
★ 71369 **RUBEZHNOYE**
★ 71370 **RZHEV**
★ 71371 **RAKHOV**
★ 71372 **REUTOV**
★ 71373 **RATNO**
★ 71374 **RADOMSYSHI**
★ 71375 **RYAZAN**
★ 71376 **ROSLAVL**
★ 71377 **RYBINSK**

71380 **NIPPONHAM MARU No 1** Ja/Ja (Shikoku)
1972; R; 2900; 109.02 × 6.73 (357.68 × 22.08); M
(Kobe); 16.5
Probably similar:
71381 **DAIRYO MARU** (Ja)

71400 **SEAPRIDE** Cy/Br (Doxford & S) 1969; Tk;
14800; 169.78 × 9.75 (557.02 × 31.99); M (Doxford);
15.5; ex *Saucon* 1983; ex *Laurelwood* 1975
Sisters:
71401 **SEAVENTURE** (Cy) ex *Shabonee* 1983; ex
Sea Griffin 1974
71402 **NAND KAVITA** (In) ex *Captain X. Kyriakou*
1980; ex *Dafni C* 1978; ex *Hollywood* 1977

71410 **DIRK JACOB** FRG/Ne (Verolme Scheeps)
1976; Tk; 19500; 170.69 × 11.85 (560.06 × 38.88);
M (Sulzer); 16
Sisters (FRG flag):
71411 **GERTRUD JACOB**
71412 **ERIKA JACOB** launched as *Protan Maas*

71420 **ORIENTAL STAR** Pa/Fr (Loire-Normandie)
1957; C; 9200; 128.39 × 9.49 (454.05 × 31.14); M
(Sulzer); 14

71430 **BENHOPE** Br/Br (Sunderland) 1978; B;
39100; 228.12 × 14.02 (748.42 × 45.99); M (Doxford); 15

★ 71433 **ALEKSANDR TSULUKIDZE** Ru/Ru (Kherson) 1978; Tk; 18500; 178.49 × 10.40 (586 × 34.12);
M (B&W); 15.25; May be others in this class with this
appearance—see No 67680; Kingpost abaft funnel is
on port side and the crane on the starboard side

71435 **GOHO MARU** Ja/Ja (Kawasaki) 1979; Tk;
35600; 208.01 × 11.95 (682 × 39.21); M (MAN); 15

71440 **WORLD CHALLENGER** Li/Ja (Hitachi)
1973; OO; 85700; 313.93 × 17.00 (1030 × 55.77); M
(B&W); 16

71450 **BRAZILIAN VITORIA** Li/Ja (Kawasaki)
1977; OO; 69300; 273.24 × 16.39 (896.46 × 53.77);
M (MAN); 15.25
Probable sister:
71451 **BRAZILIAN TRADER** (Li)

71460 **IN-NAHALA** Ag/Ja (NKK) 1975; Tk; 71900;
266 × 16.99 (872.7 × 55.74); M (Sulzer); 15.75; ex
Polartank 1976
Possibly similar:
71461 **HALUL** (Qt) launched as *North Monarch*
71462 **JANE STOVE** (No)
71463 **UMM SHAIF** (Ag) launched as *Vincenzia*

71470 **PRODROMOS** Pa/Sw (Gotav) 1968; OBO;
48800; 256.52 × 14.44 (841.6 × 47.38); M (Gotaverken); 15.25; ex *Thalassini Tyhi* 1982; ex *Obo
Prince* 1978

Similar:
71471 **TREBIZOND** (Pa) ex *Navios Challenger* 1983;
ex *Thorfrid* 1978

● 71490 **GOOD CHAMPION** Cy/Sw (Kockums) 1967;
OBO; 38500; 243.85 × 13.81 (800.03 × 45.31); M
(MAN); 16.5; ex *Saint Chris*; ex *Bjorn Ragne* 1978
Sister:
71491 **GOOD HARVEST** (Pa) ex *La Libertad* 1981;
ex *Balder Alvar*; ex *Aimee* 1977

● 71500 **KRITI GERANI** Gr/Sw (Eriksbergs) 1968; Tk;
14900; 169.63 × 9.55 (556.53 × 31.33); M (Pielstick); 14.75; ex *Al Hofuf* 1984; ex *Lustrous* 1977
Sisters:
71501 **KRITI EPISKOPI** (Gr) ex *Al Khafji* 1984; ex
Luminous 1977
71502 **AL DAMMAM 1** (Si) ex *Lumen* 1977
71503 **LUMIERE** (Br)
71504 **LUMINETTA** (Br)

● 71505 **MELODY** Cy/Ja (Tohoku) 1969; C/TC; 6100;
127.41 × 7.25 (418 × 23.79); M (B&W); 12.75; ex
Irenes Melody 1983; ex *Eastern Beauty* 1978
Similar (superstructure varies):
71506 **GOLDEN ENTERPRISE 1** (Li) ex *Allied Enterprise* 1983
Possibly similar:
71507 **ELONA** (Gr) ex *Salute* 1975; ex *Mokusei Maru*
1974
71508 **SILVERDOLPHIN** (Li) ex *Kosei Maru* 1970
71509 **SUMMER DAY** (Gr) ex *Irenes Trust* 1980; ex
Diadem 1975; ex *Rinsei Maru* 1973
71509/1 **SUMMER SKY** (Gr) ex *Crystal Camellia*
1979

● 71510 **VENUS** Ma/No (Porsgrunds) 1962; C; 5000;
116.29 × 8.1 (381.53 × 26.57); M (MAN); 13; ex
Alithia 1981; ex *Diakan Truth* 1977; ex *Dianet* 1974

★ 71530 **MAGNITOGORSK** Ru/Fi (Valmet) 1975;
RoC; 15300; 205.8 × 9.7 (675.2 × 31.82); M (B&W);
22; Stern door and angled ramp
Sister:
★ 71531 **KOMSOMOLSK** (Ru)
Similar:
★ 71532 **ANATOLIY VASILYEV** (Ru)
★ 71533 **SMOLENSK** (Ru)

71540 **AMOCO SINGAPORE** Li/Sp (AESA) 1973;
Tk; 109700; 334.02 × 19.94 (1095.87 × 65.42); M
(B&W); 15.25
Sisters:
71541 **AMOCO EUROPA** (Li)
71542 **AMOCO MILFORD HAVEN** (Li)
Similar:
71544 **BARCELONA** (Sp)

71550 **ALCAZAR** Sp/Sp (AESA) 1971; Tk; 80800;
288.04 × 17.20 (945 × 56.43); M (B&W); 16
Sister:
71551 **GORGONA** (Li) ex *Ocean Lion* 1981

71560 **SIVAND** Ir/Ja (Mitsubishi HI) 1971; Tk;
108700; 326.02 × 19.01 (1070 × 62.37); T (Mitsubishi); 15.5; ex *British Navigator* 1976

71565 **ORCHID B** Br/Ja (Onomichi) 1982; Tk;
22100; 183.22 × 10.97 (601 × 35.99); M (B&W);
14.5; Launched as *Orchid*
Sister:
71566 **JASMINE B** (Br)
71567 **BLUE EXCELSIOR** (Li)
71568 **WHITE EXCELSIOR** (Li)

71580 **BANGLAR NOOR** Bh/Ja (Hitachi) 1967; OO;
55800; 252.1 × 14.45 (827.1 × 47.41); M (B&W);
15.75; ex *Vestan* 1977
Sister:
71581 **MUSCAT CEMENT** (Li) ex *Skyros* 1981; ex
Apache 1979; ex *Ivory Sun* 1978; ex *Fernstar* 1973

71590 **GOLDEN SUNRAY** Sg/Ja (Sumitomo) 1974;
Tk; 48900; 241.51 × 14.14 (792.35 × 46.39); M
(Sulzer); 16.5
Probable sister:
71591 **CANADIAN OWL** (Sg)

71595 **SENTINEL II** Li/Ja (Hitachi) 1982; B; 29000;
209.00 × 11.00 (686 × 36.09); M (B&W); —; Caustic
Soda carrier

71600 **LIBERTADOR SAN MARTIN** Ar/Ar (Alianza) 1979; Tk; 10000; 153 × 8.24 (501.97 × 27.03); M
(Sulzer); 15
Sisters (Ar flag):
71601 **INGENIERO VILLA**
71602 **MINISTRO EXCURRA** (also reported as
MINISTRO EZCURRA)

★ 71610 **HONG HU** RC/Sw (Gotav) 1965; Tk; 29000;
223.45 × 12.64 (733.1 × 41.47); M (Gotaverken);
16.5; ex *Bralinda* 1974

71630 **KOLANDIA** In/Ys ('Jozo Lozovina-Mosor')
1976; Tk; 15000; 159.75 × 10.79 (524.11 × 35.4); M

(Sulzer); 15
Sisters (In flag):
71631 **AUROBINDO**
71632 **DADABHAI NAOROJI**
71633 **JAINARAYAN VYAS**
71634 **RAFI AHMED KIDWAI**

71640 **VISHVA KAUSHAL** In/Ys ('3 Maj') 1966; B; 9700; 146.01 × 8.66 (479.04 × 28.41); M (Sulzer); 13.5
Sisters (In flag):
71641 **VISHVA PREM** ex Vishva Tilak 1973
71642 **VISHVA VIJAY**
71643 **LOK SEVAK**

71650 **STARMAN AMERICA** Na/Br (Brooke) 1974; RoC/HL; 1600/2500; 93.63 × 4.13/— (307.19 × 13.55/—); TSM (W H Allen); 12; ex Starman 1977

71660 **AMCO 1** Pa/Fr (Havre) 1965; LGC; 1800; 80.88 × 3.61 (265.35 × 11.84); M (MAN); 14.25; ex Sorine Tholstrup 1980; ex Niels Henrik Abel 1970

★71670 **LENINSKIY LUCH** Ru/Ja (Hitachi) 1964; FF; 5000; 115.02 × 5.6 (377 × 18.37); M (B&W); 14
Sisters (Ru flag):
★71671 **KRASNYY LUCH**
★71672 **SOLNECHNYY LUCH**
★71673 **VARKIY LUCH**
★71674 **SVETLYY LUCH**

★71680 **PRIGNITZ** DDR/Ne ('De Merwede') 1967; C; 4200/6100; 135.79 × 6.67/7.61 (446 × 21.88/24.97); M (Stork) 17
Sisters (DDR flag):
★71681 **FLAMING**
★71682 **EICHSFELD**

71690 **DIANA** Bz/Bz (Ish do Brazil) 1968; C; 6900; 145.52 × 8.75 (477.43 × 28.71); M (Sulzer); 17; ex Bage 1968
Probable sister:
71691 **CORINA** (Bz) ex Curvelo 1968

71710 **ANNITA** Gr/Br (Denny/Stephen) 1964; C; 11100; 159.49 × 9.9 (523.26 × 32.48); M (Sulzer); 16; ex Exmoor 1978; ex Melbrook 1972

71720 **KASSIAN GLORY** Gr/Fi (Valmet) 1959; C; 2700/4600; 121.52 × 6.1/7.67 (398.69 × 20.01/25.16); M (—); 15; ex Altmark 1981; ex Inge Toft 1964

71730 **ARETHUSA** Gr/Ja (Mitsubishi HI) 1963; B; 9800; 153.52 × 9.18 (503.67 × 30.12); M (Sulzer); 14.5; ex Maritime Star 1978; ex Dona Viviana 1969

71740 **FERNANDOEVERETT** Li/Fi (Crichton-Vulcan) 1964/69; C/Con; 8700; 152 × 8.6 (500 × 28.7); M (Sulzer); 16; ex Finnhawk; ex Maltesholm 1976; Converted from cargo and lengthened 1969 (Wartsila)
Sisters:
71741 **CORDILLERA** (Ch) ex Finnarrow; ex Vasaholm 1976
71742 **CORRAL** (Pa) ex Mah 1980; ex Finn-Enso 1979
71743 **CONDOR** (Ch) ex Palladia 1980; ex Finnmaid 1979
★71744 **FENG NING** (RC) ex Hue Lu 1983; ex Poyang 1981; ex Asian Exporter 1975; ex Finnboston 1973; ex Finnenso 1964

71750 **RASSEM** Le/Sw (Ekensbergs) 1960; C; 2700/4300; 114.33 × —/7.19 (375 × —/23.59); M (B&W); 14.5; ex Bindal 1964

71760 **CELIA** Pa/Ja (Mitsui) 1962; C; 9300; 152.43 × 8.12 (500.1 × 26.64); M (B&W); 17.5; ex Anette Maersk 1980
Possibly similar:
71761 **EMILIA UNO** (Pa) ex Henriette Maersk 1980
Similar (De built-Helsingor):
71762 **VILLIA** (Pa) ex Torben Maersk 1981

71770 **GAZ PROGRESS** Pa/No (Moss V) 1966; LGC; 2700; 90.56 × 6.03 (297.11 × 19.78); M (Sulzer); 12.25; ex Coral Obelia 1979; ex Arctic Propane 1971

★71780 **LONG CHUAN JIANG** RC/Ja (Mitsui) 1971; C; 6600/10200; 145.7 × 8.02/9.1 (478 × 26.31/29.8); M (B&W); 17; ex Heelsum 1978; 'Mitsui-Concord 15' type
Sister:
★71781 **JIN CHENG JIANG** (RC) ex Leersum 1977

71790 **NILE MARU** Ja/Ja (Hitachi) 1970; C/HL; 10100; 148.52 × 8.99 (487.27 × 29.49); M (B&W); 15

★71800 **KAI PING** RC/Ja (lino) 1961; C; 8300/10700; 156.19 × —/9.48 (512.43 × —/31.1); M (Sulzer); 15; ex Oceanic 1973
Similar:
71802 **TROVATORE** (Br) ex Athina B 1977; ex Fay 1976; ex Leonidas Voyazides 1976; ex World Japoni-

ca 1965

★71805 **CHENG DE** RC/It (Pellegrino) 1959; C; 3600/5300; 126.52 × 6.73/7.72 (415 × 22.08/25.33); M (Fiat); —; ex Feiyueh 1976; ex Marivia 1972; ex Para 1968
Sister:
★71806 **JIAO JIANG** (RC) ex Feichi 1981; ex Flavia 1972

★71810 **JOZEF CONRAD KORZENIOWSKI** Pd/Pd (Szczecinska) 1978; C/Con; 17600; 190.28 × 9.55 (624.28 × 31.33); M (Pielstick); 25; 'B-467' type
Sisters (Pd flag):
71811 **ADAM MICKIEWICZ**
71812 **GENERAL KLEEBERG**

★71820 **50 LET SSSR** Ru/Ru ('61 Kommunar') 1973; FC; 13100; 172.12 × 8.1 (564.7 × 26.57); M (B&W); 19; also known as **PYATIDYESYATILYETIYE S S S R**
Sisters (Ru flag):
★71821 **BERINGOV PROLIV**
★71822 **IRBENSKIY PROLIV**
★71823 **PROLIV LAPERUZA**
★71824 **PROLIV SANNIKOVO**
★71825 **PROLIV VILKITSKOGO**
★71826 **XXV SYEZD KPSS**

71840 **LUISE BORNHOFEN** FRG/FRG (A G 'Weser') 1976; C; 6800/9800; 149.82 × 8.18/9.28 (491.54 × 26.84/30.45); M (MAN); 16.5; '36-L' type
Similar (some have 5-deck superstructure):
71841 **CAROLINE OLDENDORFF** (Pa) ex Breda 1973; ex Caroline Oldendorff 1972
71842 **HUGO OLDENDORFF** (Pa)
71843 **GERDT OLDENDORFF** (Pa) ex Bennekom 1974; ex Gerdt Oldendorff 1972
71844 **ELISABETH OLDENDORFF** (Pa) ex Baarn 1974; ex Elisabeth Oldendorff 1972
71845 **GRETKE OLDENDORFF** (Pa)
71846 **MARIA OLDENDORFF** (Pa) ex Barneveld 1975; ex Maria Oldendorff 1972
71847 **ALMUT BORNHOFEN** (FRG)
71848 **KARIN BORNHOFEN** (FRG)
★71849 **QIAN SHAN** (RC) ex Charlotte Kogel 1982
71851 **PASSAT** (Pa) ex Susanne Vinnen 1982; ex Concordia Moon 1980; ex Susanne Vinnen 1979; ex Elise Schulte 1978
71852 **ALIKI I P** (Gr)
★71853 **DA SHA PING** (RC) ex Tarpon Seaway 1978
★71854 **DA SHI ZHAI** (RC) ex Tarpon Sands 1978
★71855 **JIN JIANG** (RC) ex Aquitania 1981; ex Ilse Schulte 1977
★71856 **MU DAN JIANG** (RC) ex Cape Magdalena 1977; ex Hedi Wiards 1972
★71856/1 **NEI JIANG** (RC) ex Andalusia 1981; ex Elisabeth Schulte 1977
★71857 **BI SHENG** (RC) ex Boleslaw Prus 1982
★71858 **LEOPOLD STAFF** (Pd)
The following may be similar (190 ton derrick):
71859 **SARONIKOS** (Gr)

71870 **HELENE ROTH** Cy/FRG (Unterweser) 1969; C; 3300/5600; 124.49 × 6.4/8 (408.4 × 21/26.2); M (KHD); 17
Sisters:
71871 **ERIKA NABER** (FRG) ex Erika Schulte 1978
71872 **BANGKOK** (Th) ex Carbet 1982; ex Gunther Schulte 1976; ex Wameru 1976; ex Gunther Schulte 1975
71873 **EL GRECO** (Gr) ex Carimare 1983; ex Wangoni 1976; ex Auguste Schulte 1975

71880 **LIONELLO L** It/Sw (Gotav) 1957; Tk; 12600; 169.81 × 9.58 (557.12 × 31.43); M (Gotaverken); 15.25; ex Chemical Marketer 1978; ex Vincita 1973; ex Seven Skies 1965; ex Harry R Trapp 1959

71890 **ESSO MILFORD HAVEN** Br/Sw (Lindholmens) 1968; Tk; 10900; 162.67 × 8.54 (533.69 × 28.02); M (Pielstick); 16.75
Sister:
71891 **ESSO FAWLEY** (Br)

71900 **HAUGO** No/Pd (Gdanska) 1973; C; 1600; 84.18 × 5.3 (276.18 × 17.39); M (Fiat); 13.75; 'B-431' type; ex Sig 1982
Sisters (No flag):
719 **EIR**
71904 **GEILO** ex Fro 1982
71906 **LYSPOL**
71907 **SOKNATUN**
(It flag):
71913 **CANOVA** ex Log 1978
71914 **SINNI** ex Ran 1978; ex Pan 1975
71914/1 **KARUNIA** ex West Cliff 1982; ex Germa Gloria
71914/2 **PELIKAN** ex Hop 1982
71914/3 **POSITANO** ex West Reef 1982; ex Germa Star
71914/4 **REGINA** ex Eva 1982
71914/5 **TONY SECONDO** ex Stavsund 1983; Launched as Lionel

71914/6 **TINUAS** ex West End 1982; ex Germa Gracia
71914/7 **WEST BAY 1** ex West Bay 1982; ex Germa Girl
(DDR flag):
★71915 **ARTERN** ex Grong 1973
★71916 **COSWIG** ex Garli 1973

●71920 **SOMMY** Pa/Pd (Gdanska) 1972; C; 2000; 93.73 × 5.57 (307.51 × 18.27); M (KHD); 13; ex Eggli 1983; ex Rommy 1983; ex Enid 1977; 'B-431' type
Sisters:
71921 **HILDEGARD** (Pa) ex Mildred 1977
71922 **SUNRISE** (Gr) ex Cupid 1982
71923 **PLOCE** (Pa) ex Drid 1984; ex Eldrid 1983
71924 **GUDRID** (No)
71925 **NICOLAS** (Pa) ex Sigrid 1982

●★71930 **POTIRNA** Ys/Pd (Gdanska) 1967; C; 1500; 87.58 × 4.81 (287.34 × 15.78); M (Atlas-MaK); 12; ex Normannsund; ex Gdynia 1976; Lengthened 1970 (Gdanska); 'B-459' type
Sisters:
★71931 **PERNA** (Ys) ex Normannbay; ex Caroline 1975; ex Germa Lord 1973
★71932 **POPLAT** (Ys) ex Normannvaag; ex Josefine 1976; ex Geisha 1975
71933 **EVANGELIA** (Cy) ex Jade 1981; ex Fondal 1974; ex Gdansk 1973
Similar (not lengthened):
71934 **BERKBORG** (Ne) ex Carebeka VI 1982; ex Lionel

71940 **NIAGA XXVI** Ia/De (Orskovs) 1972; C; 500/1400; 71.48 × 3.76/5.67 (235 × 12.34/18.60); M (Alpha-Diesel); 12; ex Pep Ocean 1979; ex Chris Lion 1974
Sister:
71941 **FARIDA** (Eg) ex Phoenix Trader 1981; ex Phoenix 1979; ex Kis Bewa 1976
Similar (lengthened):
71942 **WAKENITZ** (FRG) ex Mette Christensen 1976

71945 **ASKO** Fi/Fi (Rauma-Repola) 1979; R; 500/1200; 74.61 × 4.70 (245 × 15.42); M (Polar); 14
Sisters (Fi flag):
71946 **FINNO**
71947 **TERSO**

●71950 **SCILLA** FRG/FRG (Schuerenstedt) 1977; C/Con; 3600/6700; 131.6 × 6.36/8.03 (431.76 × 20.87/26.35); M (Atlas-MaK); 16; ex ELMA Nueve 1982; ex Scilla 1980

71960 **OUTOKUMPU** Fi/Fi (Valmet) 1958; O; 3800; 110.19 × 6.4 (361.52 × 21); M (B&W); 13

●71970 **OCEAN SKY** Ko/Ja (Shikoku) 1975; R; 3700; 131.48 × 6.99 (431.36 × 22.93); M (Mitsubishi); 17.75; ex Summer Birdie 1979; ex Rose Daphne 1978
Sisters:
71971 **ROSE MALLOW** (Pa)
71972 **WHITE JASMINE** (Pa) ex Rose Acacia 1978
71973 **OSAKA REEFER** (Ja) ex Aden Maru 1978

71980 **LUISE BORNHOFEN** FRG/FRG (A G 'Weser') 1976; C; 6800/9800; 149.82 × 8.18/9.28 (491.54 × 26.84/30.45); M (MAN); 16.5; '36-L' type
Similar:
★71981 **MU DAN JIANG** (RC) ex Cape Magdalena 1977; ex Hedi Wiards 1972; May be others of this type with this sequence

★71990 **JUN LIANG CHENG** RC/FRG (A G 'Weser') 1970; C; 7100/1000; 150.15 × 8.31/9.27 (492.62 × 27.26/30.41); M (MAN); 16; ex Arabonne 1977; '36-L' type
Sisters:
71991 **SEA FALCON 1** (Pa) ex Aragrace 1982
71994 **SEA OSPREY** (Li) ex Josefa 1982; ex Trajan 1976
★71995 **ARBERIA** (Al) ex Arapride 1978

●72000 **CAPE RION** Gr/FRG (A G 'Weser') 1977; C; 9800; 149.82 × 9.25 (491.54 × 30.35); M (MAN); 16.5; ex Hildesheim 1983; '36-L' type
Sisters:
72001 **STARLET** (Gr) ex Rudesheim 1983
72002 **CORONET** (Gr) ex Ingelheim 1983
72003 **CAPE CORFU** (Gr) ex Hapag Lloyd Kiel 1983; ex Russelsheim 1982
72004 **SUNSET** (Gr) ex Heidenheim 1983
72005 **PLANET** (Gr) ex Unterturkheim 1983

72010 **VESTRI** No/No (Moss V) 1971; LGC; 9000; 138.72 × 9.23 (455.12 × 30.28); M (Sulzer); 17

72020 **GUAYANA** Ve/Sp (Euskalduna) 1963; C; 3500; 111.61 × 6.1 (366.17 × 20); M (MAN); 12; ex Argo 1963

72030 **CENTRAL CRUISER** Tw/Ja (Hayashikane) 1970; C; 3000; 97.39 × 6.38 (319.52 × 20.93); M (Kobe); 12.5

72040 **POONSRI MARINE** Th/Ja (Kurushima) 1969; C; 3000; 97.21 × 6.38 (318.93 × 20.93); M (Akasaka); 13; ex *Chang Chun* 1979
Possibly similar:
72041 **CHUN JIN** (Pa) ex *Shinnan Maru* 1973
72042 **HUNG MING** (Tw) ex *Ta Ho* 1978; ex *Ichizan Unzen* 1971
72043 **TARAKAN MARU** (Ja) ex *Hashihama Maru* 1972

● 72050 **GRIMSBY** Pa/Ja (Ujina) 1966; C; 2800; 94.8 × 6.15 (311.02 × 20.18); M (Hanshin); 12; ex *Carrie* 1981; ex *Lion* 1980; ex *Aspa* 1980; ex *Steely Carrier* 1974; ex *Kyonan Maru* 1971
Similar:
72051 **GIORGOS K** (Gr) ex *Blue Bill* 1979; ex *May Plum* 1977; ex *Northern Star* 1976; ex *Kyokei Maru* 1972
Probably similar:
72052 **RIMBA DUA** (Ia) ex *Handseng* 1977; ex *Shunyo Maru* 1971

72060 **EKMAN** Pa/Ja (Hashihama) 1970; C; 4000; 110.7 × 6.66 (363.19 × 21.85); M (Kobe); 12; ex *Lilia* 1978
Sister:
72061 **SIGMA** (Li) ex *Laguna* 1978
Possibly similar:
72062 **SARUNTA 1** (Pa) ex *Yushin Maru* 1972
72063 **YUNAM No 9** (Pa) ex *Bineka No 4* 1980; ex *Yufuku Maru* 1976

72075 **FENG TENG** Pa/Fr (La Seine) 1962; B; 14300; 182.28 × 10.10 (598 × 33.14); M (Sulzer); —; ex *Naseem* 1982; ex *Artemis* 1980; ex *Stylehurst* 1966

72080 **MAYUMBA GLORY** Pa/Ja (Hitachi) 1968; B; 13300; 172.02 × 9.63 (564.37 × 31.59); M (B&W); 14.25; ex *Eastern Fortune* 1982; ex *Japan Azalea* 1973
Similar:
72081 **DEKKA CONCORD** (Gr) ex *Mipo* 1980; ex *Wayway* 1978
72082 **ALEXANDRA DYO** (Gr) ex *Magenta* 1980; ex *Halo* 1979

72100 **GOOD HERALD 1** Pa/Ne (Rotterdamsche) 1960; C; 7200; 162.85 × 8.21 (534.28 × 26.94); M (Stork); 17; ex *Good Herald* 1982; ex *Gaasterdyk* 1978
Similar:
72101 **HELLENIC SKY** (Gr) ex *Grebbedyk* 1974
72102 **HELLENIC GRACE** (Gr) ex *Gorredyk* 1974
72103 **H CAPELO** (Po) ex *Moerdyk* 1973

★ 72110 **JUN LIANG CHENG** RC/FRG (A G 'Weser') 1970; C; 7100/10000; 150.15 × 8.31/9.27 (492.62 × 27.26/30.41); M (MAN); 16; ex *Arabonne* 1977; '36-L' type
Sisters:
72111 **SEA FALCON 1** (Pa) ex *Aragrace* 1982
72114 **SEA OSPREY** (Li) ex *Josefa* 1982; ex *Trajan* 1976
★ 72115 **ARBERIA** (Al) ex *Arapride* 1978

72117 **GOLF** FRG/FRG (Cassens) 1981; Pal; 1000; 95.71 × 4.40 (314 × 14.44); M (Krupp-MaK); 11; Sea/river type. Side door. Paper carrier

72120 **ERIKA BOJEN** FRG/FRG (M Jansen) 1978; C(sea/river); 500; 81.62 × 3.28 (267.78 × 10.76); M (MWM); 11; Hinged masts
Sister (FRG flag):
72121 **KONIGSEE**

72125 **LUCKY STAR** FRG/FRG (Koetter) 1981; C; 300; 75.01 × 2.91 (246 × 9.55); M (KHD); 10; Sea/river type. Lifeboat on starboard side (see inset)
Sisters:
72126 **GERHARD PRAHM** (FRG)
72127 **WARFLETH** (FRG) (builder—Hegemann)

72130 **CONDOR** FRG/FRG (Sietas) 1978; C(sea/river); 500; 73.11 × 3.4 (239.86 × 11.15); M (KHD); 11; Masts hinge
Sister:
72131 **ANGELA JURGENS** (FRG)

● 72140 **BIELEFELD** FRG/Ne (Kramer & Booy) 1973; C (sea/river); 900; 80.02 × 3.18 (262.53 × 10.43); M (Liebknecht); 10; Masts & bridge can be lowered
Sisters (FRG flag):
72141 **MARIA** (Ne) ex *Pia* 1982; ex *Cargo-Liner II* 1981
72142 **FARNESE** (Br) ex *Amy* 1983; ex *Cargo-Liner III* 1982
72143 **MANJA** (Ne) ex *Uelzen* 1982; ex *Cargo-Liner IV*
72144 **INEZ V** (Pa) ex *Cargo-Liner V* 1981
72145 **TERSCHELLING** (Ne) ex *Cargo-Liner VI* 1981

72150 **MALLECO** Ch/Ja (Mitsui) 1967; C; 8800/12500; 168.26 × 9.08/10.18 (552.03 × 29.79/33.4); M (B&W); 21.5; ex *New Dawn* 1980; ex *Talabot* 1979; Side doors
Sisters:
72151 **TAIKO** (No)
72152 **SOUTHERN DIAMOND** (Li) ex *Taimyr* 1981
72153 **MAULE** (Ch) ex *New Sun* 1980; ex *Tamano* 1979; ex *Trinidad* 1978

72160 **HALLDOR** Pa/Ja (Sasebo) 1968; C; 5500/8300; 138.06 × 7.72/8.42 (452.95 × 25.33/27.62); M (Pielstick); 16.25; ex *Tyr* 1980
Sister:
72161 **HALLVARD** (Pa) ex *Toro* 1980

72170 **LAODIKI** Gr/Pd (Szczecinska) 1964; C/B; 10300; 159.59 × 8.14/8.85 (523.59 × 26.71/29.04); M (Sulzer); ex *Cape Blanco* 1978; ex *Republika* 1973; 'B-512' type
Sisters (some may have cranes removed):
72171 **ULYSSUS** (Le) ex *Brno* 1981
★ 72172 **ZEUNG SAN** (RK) ex *Kolejarz* 1980
72173 **ELEISTRIA 1** (Gr) ex *Stoczniowiec*

● 72180 **NEDLLOYD WISSEKERK** Ne/Ne (P Smit) 1967; C; 7400/10700; 166.6 × 7.8/9.6 (546 × 25.6/31.6); M (Stork); 20; ex *Wissekerk* 1977
Sisters (Ne flag):
72181 **WAALEKERK** ex *Nedlloyd Waalekerk* 1984; ex *Waalekerk* 1977
72182 **NEDLLOYD WESTERKERK** ex *Westerkerk* 1977
72183 **NEDLLOYD WILLEMSKERK** ex *Willemskerk* 1977

72190 **IRON MONARCH** Au/Au (Whyalla) 1973; RoC; 10600; 179.33 × 8.87 (588.35 × 29.1); GT (GEC); 20.5; Stern and side doors
Sister:
72191 **IRON DUKE** (Au)

72200 **LNG AQUARIUS** US/US (General Dynamics) 1977; LGC; 83100; 285.3 × 11.51 (936.02 × 37.76); T (GEC); 20.5
Sisters (US flag):
72201 **LNG ARIES**
72202 **LNG CAPRICORN**
72203 **LNG GEMINI**
72204 **LNG LEO**
72205 **LNG LIBRA**
72206 **LNG TAURUS**
72207 **LNG VIRGO**
72208 **LAKE CHARLES**
72209 **LOUISIANA**

72210 **HOEGH GANDRIA** No/FRG (Howaldts DW) 1977; LGC; 95700; 287.54 × 11.52 (943.37 × 37.8); T (A G 'Weser'); 20
Sister:
72211 **GOLAR FREEZE** (No)

72220 **NORMAN LADY** Br/No (Moss R) 1973; LGC; 76400; 249.51 × 10.62 (818.6 × 34.84); T (GEC); 19
Similar:
72221 **POLLENGER** (Br) ex *LNG Challenger* 1979

72230 **FORUM PRIDE** Gr/Sp (AESA) 1970; B; 11800; 144.96 × 9.6 (475.59 × 31.5); M (Sulzer); 14; ex *Asturias* 1981
Sister:
72231 **JOVELLANOS** (Sp)

72240 **NACIONAL AVEIRO** Po/Sp (AESA) 1971; B; 12900; 148.72 × 10.34 (487.93 × 33.92); M (Sulzer); 13.75; ex *Llaranes* 1981
Similar (taller funnel):
72241 **TRASONA** (Sp)

72250 **BERNHARD OLDENDORFF** Pa/FRG (Bremer V) 1967; B; 30500; 213.88 × 12.18 (701.71 × 39.96); M (Bremer V); 15.5
Sister:
72251 **OLDEN** (Pa) ex *Harmen Oldendorff* 1983

72260 **M ISTANBUL K.** Tu/Ne (Verolme Dok) 1967; B; 28500; 205.49 × 11.99 (674.18 × 39.34); M (Sulzer); 15; ex *London Bridge* 1977
Sister:
72261 **ALKEOS C** (Gr) ex *Yauza* 1980; ex *Forth Bridge* 1978

72270 **TIMUR LIGHT** Sg/Ja (Mitsubishi HI) 1973; B; 69900; 261.02 × 17.58 (856.36 × 57.68); M (Mitsubishi); 15.5; ex *Meynell* 1983; ex *Eyne* 1983; ex *Meynell*
Sister:
72271 **THEOKEETOR** (Gr) ex *Nordic Patriot* 1984; ex *Naess Patriot* 1974

● 72280 **GOOD LEADER** Gr/Ja (Mitsubishi HI) 1973; B; 59200; 261.02 × 17.62 (856.36 × 57.81); M (Sulzer); 14.75; ex *Elwood Mead* 1974
Sister:
72281 **TRENTWOOD** (Sg)

72290 **D C COLEMAN** Br/Ja (NKK) 1974; B; 69900; 260 × 16.79 (853.02 × 55.09); M (B&W); 15
Sisters (Br flag):

72291 **E W BEATTY**
72292 **W M NEAL**
73393 **OCEANIC CREST**

72300 **KATORI MARU** Ja/Ja (Sumitomo) 1973; B; 65300; 257.03 × 16.93 (843.27 × 55.54); M (Sulzer); 15.5

72310 **KOHSHO MARU** Ja/Ja (NKK) 1972; O; 87400; 295 × 17.01 (967.85 × 55.81); M (Sulzer); 15.25
Probable sister:
72311 **KOHJUSAN MARU** (Ja)

72320 **BONTRADER** Br/Br (H&W) 1970; B; 35900; 224.04 × 12.52 (735.04 × 41.08); M (B&W); 15.25; ex *Amorgos* 1980; ex *Sydney Bridge* 1978

72330 **MAERSK NEPTUN** Li/De (B&W) 1975; B; 35700; 219.56 × 12.5 (720.34 × 41.01); M (B&W); 15.75; ex *Caledonia*
Sisters:
72331 **MAERSK TRITON** (Li) ex *Calabria*
72332 **BESOR** (Li) ex *Bonnieway* 1982
72333 **DAGAN** (Li) ex *Causeway* 1983
72334 **BENLEDI** (Br) ex *Ros Castle* 1980; Launched as *Sheaf Crest*
72335 **ELENI II** (Gr) ex *Specialist* 1983
72336 **BARNWORTH** (Br) ex *Strategist* 1983
72337 **PORT QUEBEC** (Br)
72338 **PORT VANCOUVER** (Br)
72339 **BENALBANACH** (Br) ex *Eredine* 1981
72340 **ATLANTIS** (Gr) ex *Hamlet Beatrice*
72341 **MALACCA** (De)
72342 **MORELIA** (De)

● 72345 **BERGE MASTER** Sg/Ja (Mitsubishi HI) 1982; B; 66400; 270.00 × 17.33 (886. × 56.86); M (Sulzer); 15

72350 **ZEEBRUGGE** Be/Be (Cockerill) 1974; B; 37700; 224.01 × 13.09 (734.94 × 42.95); M (Sulzer); 15.5
Sisters (Be flag):
72351 **MARTHA**
72352 **KYOTO**
72353 **YAFFA**
72354 **RUTH**
Similar (In flag):
72355 **MARATHA MARINER**
72356 **MARATHA MELODY**
Possibly similar (larger):
72357 **VICTORIA PEAK** (Br) ex *Argosy Pacific* 1983
72358 **LEON & PIERRE C** (Be)

72370 **MISTRAL** Li/FRG (Flender) 1974; B; 44700; 260.79 × 14.2 (855.61 × 46.59); M (B&W); 16.5; ex *Golden Cameo* 1982; ex *Malmland* 1978
Sister:
★ 72371 **MIAN ZHU HAI** (RC) ex *Thalassini Avra* 1980; ex *Ferroland* 1978

72375 **HITACHI VENTURE** Li/Ja (Hitachi) 1982; O; 70200; 324.10 × 20.47 (1063 × 67.16); M (B&W); 14.3

72380 **HERITAGE** Gr/Ih (Verolme Cork) 1977; B; 39400; 225.61 × 14.09 (740.19 × 46.23); M (B&W); 16; ex *Irena Dan* 1983
Sister:
72381 **IRISH SPRUCE** (Ih)

● 72383 **DANELOCK** Li/De (B&W) 1981; B; 33500; 225 × 13.1 (738.19 × 42.98); M (B&W); 15
Sisters (Li flag):
72384 **HYDROLOCK**
72385 **BAUMARE**
72386 **SUSAN B**
72387 **SEA SCOUT** ex *Karen T* 1982
(Br flag):
72388 **MARILOCK**
72389 **FORT DUFFERIN**
72389/1 **FORT FRONTENAC**
(RC flag):
★ 72389/2 **TAI ZHOU HAI**
★ 72389/3 **LEI ZHOU HAI**
★ 72389/4 **WEN ZHOU HAI**
★ 72389/5 **QUAN ZOU HAI**
Probable sister:
72389/6 **BRIDGEWORTH** (Br)

72390 **NIIHATA MARU** Ja/Ja (Hitachi) 1970; O; 62200; 261.02 × 15.71 (856.36 × 51.54); M (B&W); 14.75

72400 **KASHIMA MARU** Ja/Ja (Sumitomo) 1970; B; 65300; 256.01 × 16.92 (839.93 × 55.51); M (Sulzer); 15.25

72410 **AUSTRALIAN PIONEER** Au/Sw (Gotav) 1976; B; 64900; 267.6 × 16.45 (877.95 × 53.97); M (B&W); 15.75
Sister:
72411 **AUSTRALIAN PURPOSE** (Au)
Similar (lower superstructure):

667

72412 MONTCALM (Fr)
72413 PENCHATEAU (Fr)
72414 TARCOOLA (No)
72415 TONGALA (No)

72420 MERAKLIS Gr/FRG (Rhein Nordseew) 1975; B; 28100; 227.24 × 12.57 (745.54 × 41.24); M (Sulzer); 16
Sisters (Gr flag):
72421 MARQUISE
72422 MINOS
72423 MISTER MICHAEL

● **72430 SCHERPENDRECHT** NA/Ja (NKK) 1974; B; 38600; 223.98 × 13.59 (734.84 × 44.59); M (Sulzer); 14.75
Sister:
72431 ASTYANAX (Gr) ex Sliedrecht 1981
Possibly similar:
72432 ROLLON (Gr) ex Zwijndrecht 1981
Similar:
72433 AMAK (Li) ex Hampton Bay 1977
72434 OGDEN AMAZON (Li)
72435 PANAMAX UNIVERSE (Pa) ex Roberts Bank 1982

72440 GOLDEN FLAG FRG/FRG (LF-W) 1973; B; 43500; 255.91 × 14.2 (839.6 × 46.59); M (MAN); 16; ex Proserpina 1981
Sister:
72441 MADDALENA D'AMATO (It) ex Propontis 1982

72450 EMMA OLDENDORFF FRG/FRG (Bremer V) 1969; B; 37600; 251.01 × 12.52 (823.52 × 41.08); M (MAN) 15.5
Sister:
72451 ECKERT OLDENDORFF (FRG)

72460 SANTAGATA It/It (Italcantieri) 1967; B; 39700; 243.85 × 13.01 (800.03 × 42.68); M (Fiat); —

72485 CANADA EXPRESS FRG/FRG (Thyssen) 1980; Con; 17500; 164.01 × 10.32 (538 × 33.86); M (MAN); 18; ex Balandra 1983; ex Nedlloyd van Diemen 1983; Launched as Balandra
Sister:
72486 BARBAROSSA (FRG) ex Ibn Al-Akfani 1983; Launched as Barbarossa

● **72490 ANIARA** Br/Sw (Lodose) 1963; RoC; 500/1700; 75.57 × 3.40/5.1 (248 × 11.15/16.77); M (MWM); 12; ex Ciudad de Leon 1980; ex Leon 1975; ex Roro New Brunswick 1975; ex Apollo New Brunswick 1972; ex Aniara 1971; Bow door
Sisters:
72491 SINNO M E (Le) ex Jeanne R E 1979; ex Oberon 1972
72492 AEGEAN POLYVOS (Gr) ex Alpha Carrier 1980; ex Nopal Sea 1975; ex Sergel 1973; ex Elektra 1972

72500 LARA DIANA Ho/Be (SABARN) 1950; C; 840/1400; 75.29 × 4.6/4.7 (247.01 × 15.09/15.42); M (Atlas-MaK); 12.5; ex Alexandra K II 1981; ex Owenbawn 1976; ex Lady Sanchia 1968; ex Alfonso 1966

★ **72510 NER** Pd/Pd (Gdanska) 1958; C; 474; 59.85 × 3.41 (196.36 × 11.19); M (Crossley); 9; 'B-51' type. May now be MMF (see INA)
Sister:
★ **72511 SOLA** (Pd)

72520 FERRUCCIO It/Fr (Havre) 1973; RoC; 500; 78.87 × 4.22 (258.76 × 13.85); M (Crepelle); 15; ex Antinea 1983; Stern door
Similar (larger):
72521 ANAHITA (Fr)

72530 SOLVENT EXPLORER Br/FRG (Hitzler) 1974; Ch; 1500; 77.12 × 4.78 (253.02 × 15.68); M (Atlas-MaK); 12; ex Essberger Pilot 1977
Sister:
72531 ELLEN ESSBERGER (FRG) ex Solvent Venturer 1981; ex Essberger Pioneer 1977

● **72535 RODENBEK** FRG/FRG (Buesumer) 1981; Ch; 1600; 91.72 × 6.22 (301 × 20.41); M (MaK); 12.5
Sisters:
72536 FLOTTBEK (FRG)
72537 REINBEK (FRG)
72538 LAUENBURG (FRG)
72539 CAPE ISLAND (Fa)
72540 CREST ISLAND (Fa)

● **72550 OT-MARINA** Sw/Sw (Oskarshamns) 1972; Tk/Ch; 5800; 126.12 × 7.2 (413.78 × 23.6); M (Ruston Paxman); 14.25; ex Marina 1982
Sister:
72551 CARIA (Br) ex Maria 1981

72570 TONI SAFI Le/FRG (S&B) 1973; RoC; 800; 92.56 × 3.87 (303.67 × 12.7); M (KHD); 14; ex Ramsgate 1984; Stern and side doors

72580 ANTARES FRG/FRG (Schlichting) 1967; RoC; 500; 76.43 × 4.22 (250.75 × 13.85); M (MAN); 14.5; Stern door
Sisters:
72581 ANGELIKI IV (Cy) ex Arneb 1981
72582 ARCTURUS (FRG)

● **72590 MONTE D'ORO** Fr/FRG (S&B) 1970; RoC; 500; 77.98 × 3.86 (255.84 × 12.66); M (MAN); 14

72600 ANTARA Sg/Ja (Setoda) 1964; RoC; 2800; 88.55 × 4.5 (290.52 × 14.76); M (Ito Tekkosho); 13; ex Prince Maru No 2 1981

72610 TOCHO MARU Ja/Ja (Hashihama) 1962; V; 1400; 68.1 × 3.1 (223.43 × 10.17); M (Nippon Hatsudoki); 10.75

72620 ROCKY GIANT Ne/No (Ulstein)-Ne 1972/78; Self-discharging stone carrier; 2600; 91.37 × — (299.77 × —); M (Atlas-MaK); —; ex Grete Nielsen 1978; Converted from cargo ship & widened 1978 ('De Schelde'); Bow & stern thrust propellors. Has now been jumboised and fitted with a frame for handling a diving bell. Drawing shows vessel before these latter modifications

72630 GENEVE Li/Ja (Tohoku) 1971; C/B; 3000; 85.83 × 7.45 (281.59 × 24.44); M (Hanshin); 11; 'Camit' type
Sisters:
72631 STANLEY BAY (Br) ex Sulu 1983; ex Amsterdam 1981
72632 HAMBURG (Li)
72633 GHENT (Li)
72634 MAWAN (Br) ex Bohol 1983; ex Saint Nazaire 1981
72635 TARAGONA (Li)
72636 EARLY BIRD (NA) ex Sete 1973

72650 PAOLINO Ho/Br (Hill) 1954/69; C/Con; 1000; 78.03 × 4.26 (256 × 13.98); M (G Clark); 12; ex Lancashire Coast 1980; ex Trojan Prince 1969; ex Lancashire Coast 1968; Converted from General Cargo 1969 (H&W)

72660 LEMMEN Fi/FRG (Luerssen) 1958/70; Con; 3900; 98.46 × 7.25 (323.03 × 23.79); M (B&W); 13.5; ex Katrina 1982; ex Neva 1969; ex Fenja Dan 1967; Converted from cargo 1970

72670 ECO DOURO Po/FRG (Schuerenstedt) 1968; Con; 500; 73.51 × 3.66 (241.17 × 12.01); M (Atlas-MaK); 13.25; ex Craigavad 1973

● **72680 BARKENKOPPEL** FRG/Ja (Hashimoto) 1976; C/Con; 1000; Approx. 74 × 4.77 (242.78 × 15.65); M (Yanmar); 12; ex Nordholm 1979
Sisters (FRG flag):
72681 SIGGEN
72682 SANDERSKOPPEL
72683 OELAND II ex Oeland 1983
72684 LANGELAND II ex Langeland 1983
72685 ALAND II ex Aland
72686 ALSTERBERG
72687 BOBERG
72688 MESSBERG
72689 SYBILLE
72690 LIBRA

72700 PACIFIC FISHER Br/DDR ('Neptun') 1970; C; 3600; 103 × 5.8 (337.93 × 19.03); M (Atlas-MaK); 13; ex Jopulp 1975; Carries Nuclear Waste; Converted from General Cargo 1978 (Hall, Russell)

72710 KILKENNY Ih/Ih (Verolme Cork) 1973; Con; 1500; 99.6 × 4.43 (326.77 × 14.53); M (MAN); 15
Sister:
72711 WICKLOW (Ih)

72720 THE LADY PATRICIA Br/Br (Hill) 1962/74; C/WT; 1300; 64.93 × 4.59 (213.02 × 15.06); M (British Polar); 11; Modernised 1974 (Hill)

72730 BALTIC OSPREY Br/Ne (Jadewerft) 1972; Con; 1000; 88.3 × 4.35 (289.7 × 14.27); M (MWM); 14; ex Atlantic Viscount 1977; ex Nad Prince 1975; ex Kalkgrund 1974
Similar (probably with shorter funnel):
72731 STOLLER GRUND (FRG)

72740 FAST TRADER Pa/Sp (Luzuriaga) 1972; Con; 700; 74.71 × 4.24 (245.11 × 13.91); M (Stork-Werkspoor); 12.5; ex Scan Venture 1983; ex Biscayne Sea 1981; ex Kerry 1978; ex Astiluzu 201 1972

● **72750 MINIFOREST** Fi/FRG (H. Peters) 1972; C/Con; 500; 78.14 × 4.13 (256.36 × 13.55); M (Atlas-MaK); 13; ex Ilse Wulff 1979
Similar (FRG flag):
72751 ARA launched as Schwarzenberg
72752 ARNIS
72753 HELLA ex Gazelle 1982
72755 EURO SAILOR ex Jenny Graebe 1983; ex Heidberg 1978; ex Skeppsbron 1972; Launched as Heidberg

72756 EURO TRAMPER ex Jorn Graebe 1983; ex Falkenberg 1978; ex Velazquez 1973; Launched as Falkenberg
72757 EURO CARRIER ex Gerda Graebe 1983; ex Slottsbron 1975; Launched as Rieksbron
72758 EURO FREIGHTER ex Maria Graebe 1983; ex Kungsbron 1973; Launched as Maria Graebe
72759 MIGNON (Sw) ex Anne Catharina 1982
72760 EURO PARTNER ex Helene Graebe 1983; ex Seeberg 1978; ex Strombron 1973; Launched as Seeberg
72761 GABRIELLA
72762 EURO BROKER ex Jan Graebe 1983; ex Munkbron 1973; Launched as Jan Graebe
72763 KIEFERNBERG
72764 EURO LINER ex Caroline Graebe 1983; ex Fuchsberg 1980; ex Caribou 1972; Launched as Fuchsberg

72770 HENRY STAHL FRG/FRG (S&B) 1973; RoC; 700; 79.41 × 4.24 (260.53 × 13.91); M (KHD); 12.5; Lengthened 1975; Stern door

72780 ATLANTIC SAGA Sw/Sw (Oresunds) 1967; RoC/Con; 15000; 222.84 × 9.33 (731.1 × 30.61); M (Gotaverken); 19; Lengthened 1976 (Gotav); Side and stern doors

72790 ATLANTIC SPAN Sw/FRG (Rhein Nordseew) 1967; RoC/Con; 15100; 222.79 × 9.28 (730.94 × 30.45); M B&W) 21.5; Lengthened & widened 1976; Stern door

72800 ATLANTIC SONG Sw/Fr (France-Gironde) 1967; RoC/Con; 14900; 223.02 × 9.15 (731.69 × 30.02); M (MAN); 21.5; Lengthened 1976; Stern door
Sister:
72801 ATLANTIC STAR (Br)

72810 LYSAGHT ENTERPRISE Au/Au (NSW Govt) 1973; RoC; 7600; 168.05 × 7.7 (551.34 × 25.26); M (MAN); 18; Lengthened 1977. Drawing before lengthening. Stern door
Sister:
72811 LYSAGHT ENDEAVOUR (Au)

72820 KAPRIFOL Sw/Sw (Lodose) 1977; RoC/Con; 5500; 162.11 × 6.6 (531.86 × 21.65); M (Sulzer); 17.25; Stern door/ramp
Sisters:
72821 MATINA (Be) ex Vallmo 1983
72822 LINNE (Sw) (funnel variations)

● **72830 CORA** Ma/Sw (Lodose) 1972; RoC; 3400; 130.71 × 6.74 (428.84 × 22.11); M (Ruston Paxman); 14.75; ex Rosso 1982; ex Valerie 1979; Stern & side doors
Sisters:
72831 TRANSCON (Li) ex Vallann
72832 SAINT SERVAN (Fr) ex Alpha Mariner 1978; ex Saint Servan 1977; ex Vallmo 1975

72840 TUULIA Fi/FRG (Lindenau) 1974; RoC; 1600; 99.7 × 4.98 (327.1 × 16.34); M (Atlas-MaK); 15; ex Iggesund 1981; Stern door/ramps
Sister:
72841 IVAN GORTHON (Sw) ex Bravik 1981
Similar (larger):
72842 MODO GORTHON (Sw)
72843 KALMARSUND (Sw) ex Merzario Olimpia 1981; ex Kalmarsund 1977

72850 TRANSCONTAINER 1 Fr/Fr (CNIM) 1968; RoC/P/Con; 2800; 104.02 × 4.7 (341.27 × 15.42); TSM (MWM); 16

72860 FREDENHAGEN FRG/Ne (Vuyk) 1977; RoC; 1000; 89.34 × 4.23 (293.11 × 13.88); M (Atlas-MaK); 13.75; Bow door/ramp. Stern door/ramp. Side door/ramp

72870 MARY HOLYMAN Br/Ne (Boele's Sch.) 1971; RoC; 2600; 101.2 × 5.18 (332.02 × 16.99); M (B&W); 15; Stern door

72880 RAAD Si/Fr (Havre) 1969; RoC; 2100; 99.68 × 4.5 (327.03 × 14.76); TSM (Ruston & Hornsby); 15.5; ex Monte Cinto 1980; Stern door

72890 FRIGO MURAT Tu/No (Bergens) 1968; C; 200; 81.44 × 3.8/5.02 (267.19 × 12.47/16.47); M (Bergens); 16; ex Basto 1982; ex Frio Trader 1973
Sister:
72891 BORGO (Fi) ex Frio Carrier 1973

★ **72900 GAN QUAN** RC/Fr (La Rochelle) 1970; R; 2000; 100.44 × 6.2 (329.53 × 20.34); M (KHD); —; ex Sirara 1980
Sister:
72901 ALMIRANTE (Ho) ex Ea 1979

72910 ATLANTIC Pa/Fr (La Rochelle) 1968; R; 1800; 97.01 × 6.22 (318.27 × 20.41); M (KHD); —; ex Good Islander 1 1983; ex Good Islander 1982; ex Selena 1980; ex Reeferjo 1978; ex Barrad Foam 1975

72930 REEFER CHAMP Br/FRG (Schlichting) 1966; R; 500/1200; 75.57 × 3.81/5.02 (247.93 × 12.5/16.47); M (MaK); 15; ex *Visko Reefer* 1983; ex *Keppo* 1975

72940 ATSUMI Ja/Ja (Sasebo) 1972; A/LST; 1500 Dspl; 89 × 2.6 (292.8 × 5); TSM (—); 14; Japanese Defence Force
Sisters (Ja flag):
72941 MOTOBU
72942 NEMURO

72950 MAGAR In/Br (—) —; LC; 5000 Dspl; 106 × 3.4 (348 × 11.2); TSR (—); 13; ex *H.M.S. Avenger*; Indian Navy

72960 FRUCUBA Cu/Fr (Rhin) 1956; R; 900; 64.62 × 4.51 (212.01 × 14.8) M (MaK); 12.5; ex *Ice Bird* 1957
Sisters:
72961 AGNES (Gr) ex *Agios Georgios* 1981; ex *Sea Challenge* 1973; ex *Ice Flower* 1968; ex *Atlantic Flower* 1966; ex *Ice Flower* 1965
72962 SOL REEFER (Br) ex *Ice Pearl* 1966; ex *Atlantic Princess* 1966; ex *Ice Pearl* 1965

● **72970 OREA KETI** Pa/Be (Beliard, Crichton) 1957; C; 1100; 70.72 × 4.85 (232.02 × 15.91); M (KHD); 13; ex *Nice Kathrine* 1982; ex *Lone Wolf* 1980; ex *Jason* 1976

● **72980 ANIARA** Br/Sw (Lodose) 1963; RoC; 500/1700; 75.57 × 3.40/5.11 (248 × 11.15/16.77); M (MWM); 12; ex *Ciudad de Leon* 1980; ex *Leon* 1975; ex *Roro New Brunswick* 1975; ex *Apollo New Brunswick* 1972; ex *Aniara* 1971; Bow door
Sisters:
72981 SINNO M.E. (Le) ex *Jeanne R E* 1979; ex *Oberon* 1972
72982 AEGEAN POLYVOS (Gr) ex *Alpha Carrier* 1980; ex *Nopal Sea* 1975; ex *Sergel* 1973; ex *Elektra* 1972

72990 OLAF Br/FRG (Hagelstein) 1957; C; 1000; 80.22 × 5 (263.19 × 16.4); M (KHD); 11.5; ex *Brise II* 1983; ex *Dora Reith* 1968; ex *Dinklage* 1964; Lengthened & deepened 1968
Sister:
72991 LARYMNA (Gr) ex *Gotland* 1975; ex *Nordlander* 1968; ex *Anne Reith* 1968; ex *Assen* 1964
Similar (unlengthened):
72992 SEELAND (Cy) ex *Grethe Reith* 1969; ex *Berolina* 1964

73000 MINERAL MARCHIENNE Be/Be (Cockerill) 1973; B; 35900; 234.8 × 13.27 (770.34 × 43.54); M (Sulzer); 16
Sister:
73001 MINERAL ALEGRIA (Be)
Possible sister:
73002 TRADE UNITY (Li) ex *Belgium* 1983; ex *Mineral Belgium*

73010 HELEN Be/Be (Cockerill) 1978; B/Con; 24100; 199.02 × 11.05 (652.95 × 36.25); M (Sulzer); 16
Sister:
73011 DELORIS (Be)

73020 MEISTERSINGER FRG/FRG (Flensburger) 1973; B; 28300; 215.53 × 12.55 (707.12 × 41.17); M (MAN); 15
Sisters:
73021 ADRIANO (FRG)
73022 HANSE (Pa) ex *Hans Sachs* 1982
73023 PARNASSOS (Pa) ex *Tannhauser* 1982; ex *Parnassos* 1980; ex *Tannhauser* 1975
73024 WIEN (FRG) ex *Hapag Lloyd Wien* 1983; ex *Wien* 1982 (now converted to bulk/container)
73025 FJORD WIND (FRG) ex *Wera Jacob* 1982

73030 ERMINIA PRIMA It/It (Italcantieri) 1973; OO; 72700; 297.29 × 16.48 (975.36 × 54.07); T (Ansaldo); 16.5
Probable sister:
73031 WISTERIA (Li) ex *Eraclide*; ex *Igara* 1974

73040 IRON SIRIUS Br/Ja (IHI) 1967; B; 57300; 250.07 × 14.94 (820.44 × 49.02); M (Sulzer); 14.75; ex *Chelsea Bridge* 1973; ex *Sigsilver* 1971

73050 REBECCA R Pa/Ja (Sasebo) 1967; B; 37600; 224.01 × 13.95 (734.94 × 45.77); M (Gotaverken); 16; ex *Rebecca* 1982; ex *Berge Sigwaldo* 1972; ex *Sigwaldo* 1970

73060 THEOMANA Gr/Ja (Mitsui) 1965; B; 40500; 250.02 × 13.73 (820.28 × 45.05); M (B&W); 18; ex *Susanne Schulte* 1976; ex *Sigtina* 1970

73070 NACIONAL MONCHIQUE Pa/FRG (Rhein Nordseew) 1967; B; 31000; 229.09 × 12.56 (751.61 × 41.21); M (MAN); 15.25; ex *Brussels* 1980; ex *Brussel* 1978

73080 DAMADAR GENERAL T J PARK In/FRG (Rhein Nordseew) 1974; B; 31300; 229.12 × 12.57 (751.71 × 41.24); M (MAN); 15.25
Sister:
73081 JALVALLABH (In)

● **73090 DANIELLE** Gr/De (Odense) 1966; B; 27100; 212.22 × 11.82 (896.26 × 38.78); M (B&W); 15.75; ex *Gaucho Moreira* 1982; ex *Laura* 1978; ex *Laura Maersk* 1978
Similar:
73091 ANTARTICO (Ar) ex *Olkas* 1980; ex *St Asimi* 1978; ex *Laust Maersk* 1976

73100 FJORDSHELL No/No (Haugesund) 1973; Tk; 18600; 170.69 × 11.37 (560 × 37.3); M (Sulzer); 16

73110 ALEXANDER STAR Pa/FRG (Kieler H) 1967; B; 23700; 202.11 × 10.82 (663.09 × 35.5); M (Gotaverken); 16; ex *Steendorp* 1978; ex *Sognefjell* 1975
Sister:
73111 OCEAN JADE (Sg) ex *Omega* 1978; ex *Irongate* 1978; ex *Holtefjell* 1975
Similar (converted to container ship):
73112 CAST SEAL (Gr) ex *Cast Otter* 1982; ex *Dovrefjell* 1977

73120 IRENE PATERAS Gr/FRG (Kieler H) 1966; B; 23700; 202.11 × 10.82 (663.09 × 35.5); M (Gotaverken); 16; ex *Norefjell* 1977
Similar:
73121 RIO NANEZ (Gr) ex *Rio Nunez* 1982; ex *Filefjell* 1976

73130 CASTILLO DE LA MOTA Sp/Sp ('Bazan') 1971; B; 29600; 212.78 × 12.28 (698.1 × 40.29); M (Sulzer); 17; KP abreast funnel

★ **73140 ZIEMIA KIELECKA** Pd/It (Italcantieri) 1969; B; 15700; 195.97 × 10.59 (642.95 × 34.74); M (Fiat); 15
Sister:
★ **73141 ZIEMIA KOSZALINSKA** (Pd)

73150 AEOLOS C Gr/Br (Cammell Laird) 1966; B; 40800; 249.94 × — (820.01 × —); M (Sulzer); 15; ex *Yalta*; ex *Berge Siglion* 1973; ex *Siglion* 1971

73160 AEGIR FRG/FRG (Rhein Nordseew); 1968; B; 45800; 254.9 × 13.75 (836.29 × 45.11); M (MAN); 16
Sister:
73161 BRAGE (FRG)

73170 KOWLOON PEAK Br/Br (Doxford & S) 1969; B; 31400; 220.99 × 12.62 (725.03 × 41.4); M (Doxford); 15; ex *Amber Pacific* 1983
Sister:
73171 GOLDEAN ENTERPRISE (Li) ex *August Pacific*

73180 CAPE AGRILOS Gr/Ja (IHI) 1966; B; 24000; 193.4 × 10.59 (634.51 × 34.74); M (Sulzer); 15; ex *Cabo Engano* 1983; ex *Shozen Maru* 1982

73181 BRILLIANT VENTURE Br/Ja (Koyo) 1981; B; 34300; 222.99 × 12.35 (732 × 40.52); M (B&W); 16.75
Sisters:
73182 COSTAS KONIALIDIS (Gr) ex *Eva Venture* 1981
73183 FA FA VENTURE (Li)
73184 CRUSADER VENTURE (Br)
73185 SLANEY VENTURE (Li)
73186 ANITA VENTURE (Li)
Probable sisters:
73187 YAMANAKA MARU (Ja) ex *Sansan Venture* 1982
73188 NICHIGO MARU (Ja) ex *Pioneer Spirit* 1982
73189 WORLD ACCLAIM (Pa)
73189/1 FRANCOIS VENTURE (Li)

73190 EEKLO Be/Be (Boelwerf) 1978; B; 38500; 242.02 × 13.83 (794.03 × 45.37); M (MAN); 16

73200 THEMIS No/FRG (Rhein Nordseew) 1976; B; 64100; 272.32 × 16.08 (893.44 × 52.76); M (Sulzer); 16; ex *You're My Sunshine* 1983; ex *Fernsea* 1981
Sisters:
73201 FARLAND (Br) ex *Nawala* 1980; ex *Nawada*; ex *Fernbay*
73202 JOSTELLE (Br) ex *Estelle J* 1983; ex *Fernhill* 1981
73203 ENDEAVOR (Li) ex *Sealane*; ex *Fernlane* 1978
73204 PAN YARD (Ko) ex *Pan Young* 1982; ex *Sealeaf* 1980; ex *Fernleaf* 1978

73210 EARL OF SKYE Br/Br (H&W) 1966; Tk; 37800; 248.65 × 12.90 (816 × 42.32); M (B&W); 15.5; ex *British Centaur* 1983
Sister:
73211 HALCYON MED (Gr) ex *British Captain* 1976

● **73220 GOOD HORIZON** Pa/De (Odense) 1967; B; 38600; 255.63 × 14.03 (838.68 × 46.03); M (Sulzer); 16.75; ex *Navios Patriot* 1981; ex *Leise Maersk* 1976
Sister:

73221 GOOD TARGET (Pa) ex *Navios Pioneer* 1981; ex *Louis Maersk* 1976

73230 ATLANTICO It/Sp (AESA) 1975; B; 43700; 256.22 × 14.42 (840.62 × 47.31); M (B&W); 15.75; ex *King George* 1982
Sister:
73231 PANAMAX SUN (Tw) ex *King William* 1982

73240 DOCEDELTA Bz/Bz (Verolme E R do Brazil) 1974; B; 24600; 205.49 × 12.42 (674.18 × 40.75); M (Sulzer); 15.5

73250 PANAMAX GEMINI Pa/Sw (Gotav) 1968; OBO; 44300; 258.66 × 13.73 (848.62 × 45.04); M (Gotaverken); 15.75; ex *Siboen* 1982
Sisters:
73251 SIBOTO (Li)
73252 SIBOTRE (No)

73260 WIDAR FRG/FRG (B+V) 1971; B; 79000; 303.16 × 16.53 (994.62 × 54.23); M (MAN); 16.25

73270 DURHAM Br/Br (Furness) 1968; B; 35400; 246.59 × 14.47 (809.02 × 47.47); M (B&W); 16; ex *Yamato* 1982; ex *Har Addir* 1975
Sisters (Li flag):
73272 GOSFORTH ex *Mikasa* 1983; ex *Mount Katherina* 1974
73273 MOUNT EDEN

73280 LENA Sr/Pd (Gdynska) 1970; B; 32800; 218.42 × 12.4 (716.6 × 40.68); M (Sulzer); 15.25; ex *Manifest Lipcowy* 1983; 'B-521' type

★ **73290 ZOYA KOSMODEMYANSKAYA** Ru/Ru (Okean) 1973; B; 30100; 215.37 × 11.73 (706.59 × 38.48); M (B&W); 15.7
Sisters (Ru flag):
★ **73291 ALEKSANDR MATROSOV**
★ **73292 ION SOLTYS** (small crane amidships others may also have this)
★ **73293 IZGUTTY AYTYKOV**
★ **73294 PARFENTIY GRECHANYY**
★ **73295 UNAN AVETISYAN**
Similar (Bu flag):
★ **73296 BULGARIA**
★ **73297 RODINA**

73310 PACIFIC JASMIN Li/Ja (Sumitomo) 1976; B; 74400; 266.99 × 16.54 (875.95 × 54.27); M (Sulzer); 16

73320 STOVE TRADER Sw/Fi (Navire) 1976; B; 60000; 265.6 × 15.39 (871.39 × 50.49); M (Sulzer); 14.5; ex *Horn Crusader*

73330 POLYCRUSADER No/Sw (Uddevalla) 1977; B; 63100; 253.65 × 15.91 (832.19 × 52.2); M (B&W); 16
Sister:
73331 ABBEY (Br) ex *Andwi* 1979

73335 WORLD DULCE Pa/Ja (Hitachi) 1981; B; 63100; 270.9 × 16.35 (888.78 × 53.64); M (B&W); —

73340 AFRICA MARU Ja/Ja (Sumitomo) 1977; O; 74900; 267.01 × 16.6 (876.02 × 54.46); M (Sulzer); 14.75
Possible sister:
73341 OCEANIA MARU (Ja)

73345 SHOGO MARU Ja/Ja (NKK) 1982; B; 48800; 241.10 × 14.00 (791 × 45.93); M (Pielstick); 14; Drawing is approximate

73350 SITIA GLORY Pa/Ja (Hitachi) 1970; O; 43600; 250.0 × 13.31 (820.28 × 46.67); M (B&W); 15.25; ex *Kakogawa Maru* 1982

73355 HELLESPONT MONARCH Gr/Ja (Sumitomo) 1979; B; 36200; 230.21 × 13.02 (755 × 42.72); M (Sulzer); 15; ex *Navios Monarch* 1983
Similar:
73356 HELLESPONT MARINER (Gr) ex *Navios Mariner* 1983
73357 HELLESPONT MERCHANT (Gr) ex *Navios Merchant* 1983
73358 HELLESPONT MINER (Gr) ex *Navios Miner* 1983
73359 CERRO BOLIVAR (Ve)

● **73360 IKAN BILIS** Sg/Ja (Hitachi) 1977; B; 36200; 224.54 × 12.45 (736.68 × 40.85); M (Sulzer); 15.25; ex *Adriatic Wasa* 1978
Sisters:
73361 EASTERN RIVER (Li) ex *Pearl Castle* 1978
73362 RAVENNA (Li) ex *Salvatore d'Amico* 1983; ex *Pacific Crown*; ex *Pearl Crown* 1978
73363 TEMPLE BAY (Li) ex *South Sky* 1982; ex *English Wasa* 1978
73364 SHOMEI MARU (Ja) ex *Ariake* 1982; Launched as *Pearl Citadel*
73365 CO-OP GRAIN (Li) launched as *Sonette*
73366 NYON (Sd) ex *Itel Polaris*; ex *Pearl Corona* 1978

Possible sister:

73367 ANGLE BAY (Li) ex *South Rainbow* 1982
Similar:

73368 CO-OP GRAIN II (Li) ex *Argo Explorer*

73369 YAMAHIRO MARU (Ja) ex *Argo Enterprise*

73370 MOUNT PENTELI Gr/Ja (Hitachi) 1980; B; 32200; 224.52 × 12.46 (737 × 40.88); M (Sulzer); 14.5; Kingpost alongside funnel
Sisters:

73371 MOUNT PARNIS (Gr)

73372 MOUNT TAYGETOS (Gr)

73375 MARITIME BARON Pa/Ja (Hitachi) 1982; B; 33400; 224.52 × 12.96 (737 × 42.52); M (B&W); 15
Similar:

73376 ASCONA (Gr)

73377 IKAN BAWAL Br/Ja (Hitachi) 1982; B; 30900; 224.52 × 12.96 (737 × 42.52); M (Sulzer); 14.75

73378 ITTERSUM Ne/Ja (Namura) 1982; B; 35600; 225.03 × 12.40 (738 × 40.68); M (Sulzer); 14.75
Sister:

73379 HILVERSUM (Ne)

● **73380 ITALMARE** It/It (Italcantieri) 1974; B; 43800; 259.01 × 14.05 (849.77 × 46.1); M (GMT); 16
Sisters (It flag):

73381 MARE LIGURE

73382 MARE TIRRENO

73383 URSA MAJOR

73384 CAPRICORNUS

73385 DRACO

73386 DELPHINUS

73387 PERSEUS
(Pa flag)

73388 AMUNDSEN SEA ex *Sextum* 1979
Probable sister:

73389 LUPUS (It)

73400 CARIBIA EXPRESS FRG/Pd (Gdanska) 1976; Con; 27900; 203.99 × 10 (669.26 × 32.81); M (Sulzer); 22; 'B-463' type
Sisters:

73401 SIERRA EXPRESS (FRG) ex *Cordillera Express* 1983

73402 ALLEMANIA EXPRESS (FRG)

73403 AMERICA EXPRESS (FRG)

73404 ASIA WINDS (Br) ex *Adviser* 1982

73406 CARAIBE (Fr)

73407 NEDLLOYD HOLLANDIA (Ne) ex *Hollandia* 1982

73408 AUTHOR (Br) ex *Benarmin;* ex *Author* 1981
Similar (built up forward and aft, extra lifeboats etc—operated by RFA as helicopter support ship):

73409 RELIANT (Br) ex *Astronomer* 1983

73410 ADDIRIYAH Si/Ko (Hyundai) 1979; Con; 20700; 183.24 × 10.02 (601 × 32.87); M (B&W); 17.75
Sisters:

73411 AL WATTYAH (Ku)

73412 BAR'ZAN (Qt)

73413 JEBEL ALI (Ku)

73420 BALTIMORE US/US (Sun SB/Kaiser Co) 1944/45/67/70; Con; 10900; 151.59 × 9.17 (497.34 × 30.09); T-E (Westinghouse); —; Aft section ex *Roanoke* 1970; ex *Esso Roanoke* 1956; Forward section ex *Baltimore* 1970; ex *Marine Cardinal* 1965; Converted from 'C4' type cargo & 'T-2' type tanker

73430 ACADIA It/FRG (LF-W) 1971; Con; 13100; 174.86 × 9.9 (573.69 × 32.48); M (MAN); 20; ex *Atlantica Genova* 1976; ex *Gruenfels* 1971; Lengthened 1974 (A. G. 'Weser')
Sister:

73431 RUHR EXPRESS (Pa) ex *Geyerfels* 1980; ex *Seatrain Bremen;* ex *Seatrain Valley Forge* 1979; ex *Atlantic Livorno* 1977; Launched as *Geyerfels*

73433 HANJIN BUSAN Ko/Ko (Hyundai) 1979; Con; 200.62 × 8.34 (658 × 27.36); M (Sulzer); 18.75
Sisters:

73434 HANJIN INCHEON (Pa)

73435 HANJIN POHANG (Ko)

73436 HANJIN SEOUL (Pa)

73437 KOREAN JACEWON Ko/Ko (Hyundai) 1979; Con; 26500; 207.50 × 10.86 (681 × 35.63); T (Kawasaki); 23.75
Sister:

73438 KOREAN JACEJIN (Ko)
Possible sister:

73439 KOREAN WONIS SEVEN (Ko)

73440 KOREAN WONIS SUN Ko/Fr (CNIM) 1975; Con; 25700; 208.19 × 9.27 (683.04 × 30.4); M 23.5; ex *Korean Jupiter* 1980; ex *Oriental Financier* 1978
Sister:

73444 CHEVALIER VALBELLE (Fr)

Similar: (Lengthened):

73445 CHEVALIER ROZE (Fr)

73446 CHEVALIER PAUL (Fr)

73447 MERCATOR (Be)

73448 ORIENTAL EXECUTIVE (Li)

73449 ORIENTAL EDUCATOR (Br) ex *Seapac Lexington* 1983; ex *Oriental Researcher* 1981; Launched as *Oriental Chevalier*

73450 ORIENTAL EXPLORER (Tw) ex *Seapac Princeton* 1984; ex *Oriental Statesman* 1981

73460 SEA-LAND PATRIOT US/Ja (Mitsubishi HI) 1980; Con; 24900; 226.96 × 10 (744.62 × 32.81); M (Sulzer); 22
Sisters (US flag):

73461 SEA-LAND DEFENDER

73462 SEA-LAND DEVELOPER

73463 SEA-LAND EXPLORER

73464 SEA-LAND INDEPENDENCE

73465 SEA-LAND LIBERATOR

73466 SEA-LAND EXPRESS

73467 SEA-LAND VOYAGER

73468 SEA-LAND FREEDOM

73469 SEA LAND MARINER

73470 SEA-LAND ENDURANCE

73471 SEA-LAND INNOVATOR

73480 OCEAN LEGEND Li/Fr (CNIM) 1971; Con; 22600; 234.5 × 9.68 (769.36 × 31.76) M (Sulzer); 22.25; ex *Oriental Leader* 1982; Lengthened 1976
Similar:

73481 OMEX PIONEER (Sg) ex *Oriental Scholar* 1981; ex *Oriental Educator* 1981; ex *Atlantic Phoenix* 1975; Launched as *Oriental Educator*

73482 OCEAN COMMANDER (Li) ex *Oriental Commander* 1982; ex *Pacific Phoenix* 1975; Launched as *Oriental Commander*

73483 KOREAN WONIS ONE (Ko) ex *Korean Leader* 1980; ex *Oriental Chevalier* 1975

73490 INCOTRANS PROMISE FRG/Ne (Giessen-De Noord) 1972; Con; 13300; 172.52 × 7.2 (566 × 23.62); M (MAN); 21; ex *Pluvius* 1983; ex *Hellenic Prince* 1983; ex *Pluvius* 1982; ex *Seatrain Princeton* 1981; ex *Pluvius* 1977
Sister:

73491 KOREAN LOADER (Pa) ex *Seatrain Lexington* 1980; ex *Plutos* 1977

73500 OCEAN CONTAINER Pa/Br (Smith's D) 1968; Con; 12000; 161.47 × 8.26 (529.76 × 27.1); M (Pielstick); 19.5; ex *Manchester Challenge* 1979
Sisters:

73501 PACIFIC CONTAINER (Pa) ex *Manchester Courag 1979*

73504 RATIH (Ia) ex *Manchester Renown* 1982; ex *Asian Renown* 1979; ex *Manchester Renown* 1974

73505 R R RATNA (Tw) ex *Manchester Reward* 1982; ex *Asian Reward* 1979; ex *Manchester Reward*

73510 CHARLOTTE LYKES US/FRG (Bremer V) 1968; Con; 17100; 201.12 × — (659.84 × —); M (MAN); 20; ex *Weser Express* 1984; Lengthened 1973
Sister:

73511 ADABELLE LYKES (US) ex *Mosel Express* 1984
Similar (taller funnels):

73512 SHELDON LYKES (US) ex *Alster Express* 1984

73513 MARGARET LYKES (US) ex *Elbe Express* 1984
Similar (unlengthened):

73514 NGAN CHAU (Pa) ex *Main Express* 1981; ex *Oriental Importer* 1976 ex *Main Express* 1973

73515 GREEN ISLAND (Pa) ex *Rhein Express* 1981; ex *Oriental Exporter* 1976; ex *Rhein Express* 1973

73520 COLUMBUS VICTORIA FRG/FRG (A.G 'Weser') 1976; Con; 14200; 161.02 × 9.42 (528.28 × 30.91); M (MAN); 19
Sisters (FRG flag):

73521 COLUMBUS VIRGINIA

73522 COLUMBUS WELLINGTON

73530 COLUMBUS AUSTRALIA FRG/FRG (Howaldts DW) 1971; Con; 19100; 193.94 × 10.85 (636.29 × 35.6); T (A.G. 'Weser'); 22
Sisters (FRG flag):

73531 COLUMBUS AMERICA

73532 COLUMBUS NEW ZEALAND

73535 ALMUDENA Sp/Sp (AESA) 1982; Con; 18200; 184.00 × 9.52 (604 × 31.23); M (B&W); 20.25
Sister:

73536 PILAR (Sp)

73537 PLANTIN Be/Be (Boelwerf) 1981; Con; 20800; 186.01 × 10.82 (610 × 35.50); M (B&W); 20

73540 LAMARA Sg/Gr (Salamis) 1977; Con; 2000; 102.16 × 5.01 (394 × 16.44); M (KHD); 16; ex *Meteor*

// 1982
Sister:

73541 METEOR 1 (Sg)

★ **73550 TARNOBRZEG** Pd/Sw (Lodose/Oskarshamns) 1973; Ch; 7000; 146.11 × 7.61 (479.36 × 24.97); M (Ruston, Paxman); 14.5
Sisters (Pd flag):

★ **73551 PROFESOR K BOHDANOWICZ**

★ **73552 SIARKOPOL**

★ **73553 ZAGLEBIE SIARKOWE**

73560 GARRISON POINT Br/Br (Robb Caledon) 1977; C; 8000; 127.44 × 8.12 (418.11 × 26.64); M (Pielstick); 13

73570 ZIM MANILA II Pa/Ne (Giessen-De Noord) 1969; Con; 2900; 95.61 × 4.85 (313.68 × 15.91); M (Atlas-MaK); 15; ex *Dror II* 1983; ex *Deror II;* ex *Ville D'Orient;* ex *Hope* 1977; ex *Hope Isle* 1974
Sister:

73571 ZIM NAPOLI II (Pa) ex *Hehaluz II* 1983; ex *Sally;* ex *Sally Isle* 1974

73580 RODRIGUES CABRILHO Po/FRG (Schuerenstedt) 1969; Con; 2800; 95.59 × — (313.62 × —); M (Atlas-MaK); 15; ex *Eagle* 1972; ex *Seetrans* 1972; ex *Ellen Isle* 1972
Similar:

73581 MAURICIO DE OLIVEIRA (Po) ex *Contrans* 1972; ex *Weser Isle* 1972

73590 MARGARITA II Pa/FRG (Schuerenstedt) 1969; Con; —; 82.1 × 3.82 (269.36 × 12.53); M (Atlas-MaK); 15; ex *Kormoran 1* 1982; ex *Kormoran* 1977; ex *Kormoran Isle* 1972

73600 EKENIS FRG/FRG (Schlichting) 1968; C/Con; 1000; 86.75 × 4.55 (284.61 × 14.93); M (Atlas-MaK); 14.5; ex *Theano;* ex *Barbel Bolten* 1973
Sister:

73601 HERMIA (FRG) ex *Marietta Bolten* 1974

73610 COMMODORE ENTERPRISE Br/Br (Appledore) 1977; C/Con; 1200; 95.18 × 4.87 (312.27 × 15.98); M (Mirrlees Blackstone); 13

73620 EL GUAIQUERI Pa/Ne 1971; C/Con; 700; 76.82 × 4 (252.03 × 13.12); M (Atlas-MaK); 13.5; ex *Biscayne Surf* 1983; ex *Rubin* 1980; ex *Craigaboy* 1979; ex *Rubin* 1972

73630 DOLPHIN POINT Br/Br (Blyth) 1965; C; 4800; 112.76 × 7.32 (369.95 × 24.02); M (British Polar); 12; ex *Corchester* 1977

73640 ISABEL Ne/Ne ('Voorwaarts') 1972; C/Con; 1400; 71.28 × 4.97 (233.86 × 16.31); M (Appingedammer Brons); 12
Probable sister:

73642 LUTHER (Ne) ex *Irina* 1981

★ **73650 SKRZAT** Pd/Pd (Gdynska) 1961; Con; 500/1000; 65.84 × 3.7/— (216.01 × 12.14/—); M (Alpha-Diesel); 11.5; Converted from 'B-57' type cargo ship
Sister:

★ **73651 SYRENKA** (Pd)
Similar (lengthened):

★ **73652 WILA** (Pa)

★ **73653 WROZKA** (Pd)
   May be others of this class similarly lengthened — see **KRASNAL** etc

● **73660 FRAT 1** Pa/FRG (Husumer) 1976; C/Con; 1000; 83.52 × 4.96 (274.02 × 16.27); M (Atlas-MaK); 14; ex *Voline* 1982
Sister:

73661 BALTIC HERON (FRG) ex *Theodor Storm* 1978

73670 LADY ULRIKA FRG/FRG (Husumer) 1976; C/Con; 1000; 84.26 × 4.96 (276.44 × 16.27); M (KHD); 14; ex *Hejo* 1983
Sister:

73671 BOKELNBURG (FRG) ex *Isle of Man* 1982; ex *Bokelnburg* 1981; ex *Bourgogne* 1978; ex *Bokelnburg* 1975
Similar (smaller):

73672 HUSUM (FRG)

73680 SPECIALITY Br/Br (Goole) 1977; C; 1600; 89.67 × 6.04 (294.19 × 19.82); M (Alpha-Diesel); 12.5
Possible sisters (may be geared like **SINGULARITY** — see **MCMF**) (Br flag):

73681 STABILITY

73682 JACK WHARTON

73690 PIONEER CONTAINER Pa/FRG (M. Jansen) 1971; C/Con; 1500; 94.01 × 5.6 (308.43 × 8.37); M (KHD); 15; ex *Lyndaret* 1981; ex *Marecloud* 1980; ex *Scantrain;* Launched as *Ino J*

73700 FAST TRADER Pa/Sp (Luzuriaga) 1972; Con; 700; 74.71 × 4.24 (245.11 × 13.91); M (Stork-

Werkspoor); 12.5; ex *Scan Venture* 1983; ex *Biscayne Sea* 1981; ex *Kerry* 1978; ex *Astiluzu 201* 1972

73710 HENRY STAHL FRG/FRG (S&B) 1973; RoC; 700; 79.41 × 4.24 (260.53 × 13.91); M (KHD); 12.5; Lengthened 1975. Stern door

● **73720 REGINE** FRG/FRG (Sietas) 1976; Con; 1600; 93.53 × 6.08 (306.86 × 19.88); M (KHD); 14.5
Sisters:
73721 JAN (FRG)
73722 NORDIC 1 (Pa) ex *Zim Northland* 1983; ex *Nordic* 1980
73723 WIELAND (FRG) ex *Strathspey* 1980; ex *Wieland* 1978
73724 LUCY BORCHARD (FRG) ex *Triton 1* 1980; ex *Contship Three* 1979; ex *Triton* 1977
Similar (mast from bridge):
73725 DIANA (FRG)

● **73730 BONAVENTURE II** Ca/As 1972; C/Con; 1000; 90.4 × 4.64 (296.59 × 15.22); M (MWM); 14.5; ex *Atlantic King* 1981; ex *Shaikah Al Quraichi* 1979; ex *Atlantic King* 1978; ex *Nad King* 1975; ex *Korneuburg* 1972
Sisters:
73731 ATLANTIC EARL (Pa) ex *Monarch* 1975; ex *Hainburg* 1972
73732 GARGOYLE EXPRESS (Pa) ex *Atlantic Count* 1982; ex *Salzburg* 1974
73733 UNICORN EXPRESS (Pa) ex *Atlantic Baron* 1982; ex *Katharina* 1974
73734 ILE DE BATZ (FRG) ex *Ile de France* 1982; ex *Roswitha* 1978
73735 NEDLLOYD PRIDE (Pa) ex *Mare Pride* 1982; ex *Atlantic Duke* 1982; ex *Stuart Prince* 1979; ex *Atlantic Duke* 1977; ex *Joachim* 1975

● **73740 VERNIA** Sw/Ne (Zaanlandsche) 1970; Con; 1100; 81.64 × 5.03 (267.85 × 16.5); M (Werkspoor); —; ex *Rane* 1980
Sisters:
73741 ATLANTIC NAVIGATOR (Cy) ex *Dania* 1983; ex *Ring* (Spanish built— Cadagua)
73742 NOVIA (Sw) ex *Mercia* 1981; ex *Brage* 1979

● **73743 NATHANIEL** Is/Sg (Singapore SB) 1979; Con; 1600/4700; 120.53 × 4.51/6.50 (395 × 14.80/21.33); M (Mitsubishi); 13.5; ex *Navalis* 1984; ex *Eurobridge Cross* 1980; ex *Navalis* 1979; ex *Tauria* 1979
Sisters:
73744 NORDWELLE (Sg)
73745 NORDWIND (Sg)
73746 NORDHEIDE (Sg)
73747 NORDBAY (Sg)
73748 GLORIA EXPRESS (Sg)
73749 CITY OF SALERNO (Sg) ex *Nordstar* 1983
Probable sister:
73749/1 NORDSUND (Sg) ex *Eastmead King* 1982; ex *Nordsund* 1981
Possibly similar:
737749/2 PEGASIA (Pa)
73749/3 VILLE DU MISTRAL (Pa) ex *Este* 1984

● **73750 LADY M A CROSBIE** Ca/Br (Doxford & S) 1966/77; Con; 4000; 118.73 × 6.5 (389.53 × 21.33); M (MAN); 14.75; ex *Cortes* 1978; ex *Baltic Vanguard* 1977; Converted from cargo & lengthened 1977 (Middle Docks)

73760 LLOYD BERMUDA Cy/Fi (Reposaaren) 1972; Con; 800; 78.01 × 4.16 (256 × 13.65); M (Atlas-MaK); 15; ex *Nedlloyd Bermuda* 1983; ex *Craigwood* 1982

● **73770 BELL ROVER** Ih/Ja (Kagoshima) 1976; Con/C; 500/1600; 80.02 × 3.32/3.77 (262.53 × 10.89/12.37); M (Atlas-MaK); 13.75
Sisters (Ih flag):
73771 BELL RACER
73772 BELL RAIDER
73773 BELL RANGER
73774 BELL REBEL
73775 BELL RULER
73776 BELL RENOWN
73777 BELL RELIANT
73778 BELL RESOLVE
(FRG Flag):
73779 MARETAINER ex *Bell Rival* 1982

● **73790 NORDWIND** FRG/FRG (H Peters) 1976; C/Con; 900; 87 × 4.73 (285.43 × 15.52); M (Atlas-MaK); 13.25
Sisters (FRG flag):
73791 BRIGITTE GRAEBE
73792 LUBECA
Similar (FRG Flag):
73793 SPAROS ex *Inka* 1979
73794 ALITA
73795 BARBARA-BRITT
73797 HISPANIA ex *Lindaunis* 1983; ex *Isle of Man* 1981; ex *Lindaunis* 1980
73798 CHRISTEL
73799 ISNIS
73800 CHRISTOPHER MEEDER
73801 BARBARA-CHRIS
73802 MARGRET CATHARINA ex *Thiassi* 1976; ex *Margret Catharina* 1975
73803 FRAUKE CATHARINA

73810 CARINE Cy/Ne (Groot & VV) 1969; C/Con; 1000; 70.57 × 3.52 (231.53 × 11.55); M ('Bolnes'); 12.5; ex *Bart* 1983; ex *Garza*; ex *Geestduin* 1976
Sister:
73811 CARAVELLE (Pa) ex *Geestroom* 1976

73815 NAVIGATOR FRG/FRG (Luehring) 1981; C/Con; 1000; 78.59 × 4.60 (258 × 15.09); M (Krupp-MaK); 10.25; Sea/river type

73820 PIETER WINSEMIUS Ne/Ne (Groot & VV) 1959; HL/C; 700; 73.87 × 3.72 (242.36 × 12.2); M (MWM); 11.5; Lengthened 1961. Widened & converted from cargo 1968 (Groot & VV)
Sister:
73821 DON MANOLO (Ve) ex *Cargo* 1981; ex *Ank Winsemius* 1981

● **73830 BASALT** FRG/Hu (Angyalfold) 1970; C; 1500; 76.41 × 5.31 (250.69 × 17.42); M (MWM); 11.5; Lengthened 1975
Sisters:
73831 ORCHID SEA (Sg) ex *Diorit* 1983
73832 ORCHID WAVE (Sg) ex *Diabas* 1983
73833 ORCHID MOON (Sg) ex *Gabbro* 1983
73834 ORCHID SUN (Sg) ex *Granit* 1983
Similar (fitted with satellite communication aerial):
73835 ORCHID STAR (Sg) ex *Dolomit* 1983

★ **73840 ANDRZWJ BOROWY** Pd/Pd (Gdynska) 1963; Con; 1200; 69.04 × 4.45 (226.51 × 14.6); M (Nydqvist & Holm); 11.5; 'B-458' type. Converted from cargo. May be others of this type similarly converted

73850 ANTXON MARI Sp/Sp (Luzuriaga) 1976; C; 700; 63.91 × 3.96 (209.68 × 12.99); M (Duvant); 12

73860 MALARVIK Sw/Fi (Crichton-Vulcan) 1965; Cem; 2200; 90.33 × 5.77 (296.36 × 18.93); M (Nydqvist & Holm); —
Sister:
73861 VASTANVIK (Sw)

★ **73865 CAPITAN SAN LUIS** Cu/Sw (Gotav Solvesborg) 1975; Cem; 4300; 107.12 × 6.01 (351 × 19.72); M (Pielstick); —

73866 ELIZA HEEREN FRG/FRG (Brand) 1981; C/Con; 1000; 79.71 × 5.07 (262 × 16.63); M (Krupp-MaK); 12
Sister:
73867 NORA HEEREN (FRG)

73870 ATLANTIC SWAN Sg/Ne (van der Werf) 1969; Con; 1400; 121.54 × 3.8 (398.75 × 12.47); M (MWM); 14.5; ex *ASD Black Swan* 1978; ex *Atlantic Swan* 1976; Lengthened 1976

● **73880 ECO MONDEGO** Pa/Ne (Vuyk) 1969; Con; 1600; 85.32 × 4.71 (279.92 × 15.45); M (Werkspoor); 16; ex *City of Milan* 1980; ex *Minho* 1974; 'HUSTLER' class
Sisters:
73881 CAPE HUSTLER (Br) ex *City of Lisbon* 1980; ex *Tagus* 1974
73882 ECO GUADIANA (Pa) ex *City of Oporto* 1980; ex *Tormes* 1974
73883 HUSTLER FAL (Br) ex *City of Florence* 1982; ex *Tua* 1974
73884 BERMUDIANA (Br) ex *Hustler Ebro* 1983; ex *City of Genoa* 1982; ex *Tamega* 1974
73885 HYBUR CLIPPER (Br) ex *Atlantic Clipper* 1983; ex *Tiber* 1979; ex *City of Naples* 1979; ex *Tiber* 1974
73886 HUSTLER INDUS (Br) ex *Atlantic Resolute* 1982; ex *City of Venice* 1980; ex *Mondego* 1974
73887 ZIM MANILA (Li) ex *Hustler Cheyenne* 1981; ex *Isbrit* 1976; ex *England* 1974
73888 HYBUR INTREPID (Br) ex *Atlantic Intrepid* 1983; ex *Tronto* 1980; ex *City of La Spezia*; ex *Tronto* 1974

73900 SAGITTA 1 Pa/FRG (Sietas) 1973; C/Con; 1000; 93.2 × 4.88 (305.77 × 16.01); M (Atlas-MaK); 15; ex *Sagitta* 1982
Sisters (FRG flag):
73901 WIKING
73902 ELBE
73903 WESER
73903/1 JANNE WEHR ex *Roxane Kersten* 1983; ex *Janne Wehr* 1981; ex *Roxane Kersten* 1980; ex *Janne Wehr* 1980
Similar:
73904 MANCHESTER FAITH ex *Francop* 1978; ex *Manchester Faith* 1977; ex *Francop* 1976

73910 THUNAR FRG/FRG (Norderwerft/Sietas) 1979; Con; 1000; 88.65 × 4.88 (290.85 × 16.01); M (KHD); 'Sietas type 81'
Sisters (FRG flag):
73911 WOTAN
73912 NORDSEE
73913 ATLANTIS

73920 OUEZZANE Mo/FRG (Sietas) 1976; C/Con; 1600; 93.38 × 5.56 (307.02 × 18.24); M (Atlas-MaK); 14.5
Sisters (Mo flag):
73921 OUARZAZATE
73922 OUIRGANE
73923 OUALIDIA
73924 OULMES

73930 NEWFOUNDLAND CONTAINER Ca/Br (Ardrossan) 1962/72; Con; 1500; 78.64 × 5.04 (258.01 × 16.54); M (British Polar); 13; ex *Roe Deer* 1977; ex *Norbrae* 1974; ex *Buffalo* 1972; Converted from cargo 1972
Sister:
73931 FLAMINGO (Sn) ex *Norbank* 1980; ex *Bison* 1971

● **73940 VANTAGE** FRG/FRG (Sietas) 1974; C/Con; 1000; 81.41 × 4.91 (267.09 × 16.11); M (Atlas-MaK); 13.5; ex *Bell Vantage* 1978
Similar (FRG flag):
73941 OSTECLIPPER ex *Nic Clipper* 1979; ex *Osteclipper* 1978
73942 CANOPUS
73943 ECO LIZ ex *Odin* 1981
73944 ACHAT ex *Osteland* 1981; ex *Nic Trader*; ex *Osteland* 1979; ex *Thunar* 1976; ex *Osteland* 1974
73945 NAVIGIA (Sg) ex *Donar* 1979
73946 PATRIA ex *American Comanche* 1978
73947 NAUTILUS ex *American Cherokee* 1979; Launched as *Nautilus*
73948 BRITTA I ex *American Cheyenne* 1979; ex *Britt* 1977
73949 BOURGOGNE ex *Komet I* 1978; ex *Saracen Prince* 1976; Launched as *Komet*
73950 YANKEE CLIPPER ex *Lappland* 1980; ex *Manchester Falcon* 1976; Launched as *Lappland*
73950/1 INA LEHMANN
73950/2 SIEGFRIED LEHMANN
73950/3 CORVETTE ex *Eco Dao* 1983; ex *Corvette* 1981; ex *Else Beth* 1978; Launched as *Corvette*
73950/4 SUDERELV
73950/5 HORNBELT ex *Hornbaltic* 1980
73951 ANNA BECKER ex *Killarney* 1980; ex *Anna Becker* 1977; ex *Scol Enterprise* 1977; Launched as *Anna Becker*
73952 CRANZ ex *Aros Olympic* 1981; ex *Ute Wulff* 1980; ex *Galway* 1980; ex *Ute Wulff* 1977; ex *American Apache* 1977; Launched as *Ute Wulff*
73953 OSTERHEIDE
73954 JAN KAHRS
73955 FALKENSTEIN
73956 PASSAT
73957 SEEVETAL ex *Eco Mira* 1983; ex *Seevetal* 1982
73958 ORION
73959 JULIANE ex *Niedermehnen* 1983; ex *Ibesca Portugal* 1982; Launched as *Niedermehnen*
73960 PARNASS
73961 MELTON CHALLENGER (Br)
Similar (large funnel):
73962 MAJGARD (Fi) ex *Tajani* 1983; ex *Rie Bres* 1980
73963 DORI BRES (De)
73964 NINA BRES (De)
73965 HEIDE-CATRIN (FRG)

73970 KATHE JOHANNA FRG/FRG (Husumer) 1976; C/Con; 1600; 100.28 × 5.56 (329 × 18.24); M (Atlas-MaK); 14; ex *Manchester Trader* 1979; ex *Kathe Johanna* 1978; Probably spelt **KAETHE JOHANNA**

73980 SERTAN Ne/Ne ('Friesland') 1978; Con/C; 1300; 81.84 × 5.65 (268.5 × 18.54); M ('Bolnes'); 12.75
Sister:
73981 MIDSLAND (Ne)

73990 CHRISTIANE SCHULTE Cy/Ne (Vuyk) 1972; C; 3900; 96.68 × 7.11 (317.19 × 23.33); M (Atlas-MaK); 13
Similar (some may have travelling crane—see **VILLIERS**):
73991 PHILEMON (Cy) ex *Carlota Bolten* 1973
73992 ANGELICA SCHULTE (Cy) ex *Esther Bolten* 1974
73993 ARTEMIS 1 (Cy) ex *Artemis* 1982; ex *Susan Miller*
73994 VENTUS (Cy) ex *Erika Fisser*
73995 DANAE (Sg) ex *Negah* 1980; ex *Otto Porr* 1978
73996 ESTHER (Cy) ex *Esther Bolten* 1974

★73997 **SIBIRSKIY 2101** Ru/Fi (Valmet) 1979; C (Riv); 3200; 127.50 × 3.00 (418 × 9.84); M (Russkiy); 11
Sisters (Ru flag):
★73998 **SIBIRSKIY 2102**
★73999 **SIBIRSKIY 2108**
★73999/1 **SIBIRSKIY 2109**
★73999/2 **SIBIRSKIY 2123**
★73999/3 **SIBIRSKIY 2124**
★73999/4 **SIBIRSKIY 2125**
★73999/5 **SIBIRSKIY 2126**
★73999/6 **SIBIRSKIY 2127**
★73999/7 **SIBIRSKIY 2128**

● 74000 **GERMA KARMA** No/Sg (Singapore Slip) 1979; C/B/Con; 1600/3300; 81.01 × 5.75/7.21 (266 × 18.86/23.65); M (Atlas-MaK); 13.5; May be other vessels with this sequence which are currently under KCMF—see 'GERMA TARA' etc
Sisters:
74001 **GERMA FONDAL** (No)
74002 **GARDENIA** (Cy) ex *Germa Dolphin* 1983; ex *Germa Team* 1981

● 74005 **VELA** FRG/FRG (M. Jansen) 1981; C/Con; 1000; 95.61 × 4.29 (314 × 14.07); M (Krupp-MaK); 12.5

74010 **DELTA** FRG/FRG (M. Jansen) 1978; Con; 1000; 82.02 × 4.9 (269.09 × 16.08); M (Atlas-MaK);—

74015 **YMIR** FRG/FRG (Nobiskrug) 1980; C/Con; 1600; 99.95 × 5.09 (327.92 × 16.7); M (KHD); 12.25
Sisters (FRG flag):
74016 **NJORD**
74017 **KINI KERSTEN** ex *Hermann Behrens* 1983

74020 **DONAR** FRG/FRG (Nobiskrug) 1979; Con; 1000; 89 × 4.95 (292 × 16.24); M (KHD); 13 (max)
Sisters (FRG flag):
74021 **THIASSI**
74022 **ALGERIA** ex *Haldem* 1980
74023 **ESPANA** ex *Stemwede* 1980
Possible sister (may have deck crane):
74024 **LUSITANIA** (FRG) ex *Westerfelde* 1980

74030 **ANNIKA** FRG/Ne ('Hoogezand' JB) 1974; C; 1000; 87.89 × 4.85 (288.35 × 15.91); M (KHD); 14; May be fitted with two deck-cranes

● 74040 **ALFA** Gr/Ne (Ijsselwerf) 1971; Con; 1600; 85.93 × 4.9 (281.92 × 16.08); M (Stork-Werkspoor); 16; ex *Soldier Prince*; ex *Sailor Prince* 1977; ex *Pennine Prince* 1972

74050 **ARISTEOS** Gr/Br (Robb Caledon) 1971; RoC; 3700; 117.48 × 6.32 (385.43 × 20.73); TSM (Pielstick); ex *Caribbean Progress*; ex *Iranian Progress* 1976; ex *Caribbean Progress* 1975; May be spelt **ARISTAIOS**; Stern door
Sisters (FRG built- Sietas):
74051 **SUCRE** (Ve) ex *Aristefs* 1981; ex *Caribbean Endeavour*

● 74060 **ATLANTIC PREMIER** Sw/Fi (Wartsila) 1972; RoC/Con; 11000; 162.36 × 7.22 (532.68 × 23.69); TSM (Pielstick); 17; ex *Mont Royal* 1978; Stern door/ramp; Lengthened and converted 1978 (Nobiskrug)
Sister:
74061 **ATLANTIC PRELUDE** (Sw) ex *Montmorency* 1978

● 74070 **MONT LOUIS** Fr/Fi (Wartsila) 1972; RoC; 4200; 135.01 × 6.65 (442.95 × 21.82); TSM (Pielstick); 17.5; ex *Bore Moon* 1981; ex *Mont Louis* 1979; Stern door/ramp

● 74090 **MANAURE VI** Ve/Ne (van der Werf) 1972; RoC; 3400; 127.26 × 6.4 (417.52 × 21); TSM (Deutz); 17.5; ex *Merzario Saudia* 1978; ex *Iranian Prosperity* 1976; ex *Nike* 1975; Launched as *Cora*; Stern and side doors
Sister:
74091 **MANAURE V** (Ve) ex *Kratos* 1978

74110 **NADA D.** Le/Fi (Rauma-Repola) 1956; C; 2000; 97.85 × 5.82 (321.03 × 19.09); M (MAN); 13; ex *Parthenon* 1982; ex *Red Sky* 1977; ex *Finnkraft* 1973

● 74120 **MONOSANDALOS** Pa/Ne (M Jansen) 1960; C; 500; 70.36 × 3.71 (230.84 × 12.17); M (Werkspoor); 11.5; ex *Good Sailor* 1981; ex *Stray Dog* 1979; ex *Royksund* 1977; ex *Karmsund* 1972; ex *Kong Sigurd* 1969; ex *Bore IX* 1965; ex *Kuurtanes* 1962

★74140 **NALECZOW** Pd/Rm (Turnu-Severin) 1970; C; 1200/2000 85.88 × 4.5/5.1 (281.76 × 14.76/73); M (Sulzer); 14; Others of this class may be similarly modified — See **BUSKO ZDROJ**
Sisters (Pd flag):
★74141 **SWINOUJSIE**
★74142 **SWIERADOW ZDROJ**

Possible sister (container ship):
★74143 **POLCZYN ZDROJ** (Pd)

74150 **ISVANIA** Pa/De (Aalborg) 1938; C; 1000; 65.94 × 4.38 (216.3 × 14.37); M (Atlas-Diesel); 10; ex *Svano* 1971; ex *Fryken* 1961

74160 **SOCRATES** Pa/FRG (A Normand) 1954; LGC; 1100; 73.11 × 4.17 (239.86 × 13.68); M (Pielstick); 10; ex *Marcelin Berthelot* 1968; ex *Cantenac* 1961; Converted from cargo 1961

● 74170 **FRATERNIA** Pa/No (Hatlo) 1966; C; 500; 75.75 × 3.76 (248.52 × 12.34); M (Atlas-MaK); 13.5; ex *Fratern* 1981; ex *Mercur* 1980; ex *Fraternia* 1971; Side doors; Kingpost may be replaced by crane—same could apply to sisters
Sisters:
74172 **PEZZATA ROSA** (It) ex *Pirholm* 1979; ex *Nerlandia* 1976
Similar:
74173 **IRIS** (No) ex *Helenia* 1969

74180 **AGIP TRIESTE** It/It (Adriatico) 1964; Tk; 30400; 228.61 × 12.14 (750.03 × 39.83); M (Adriatico); 17

74210 **TESSA** Pa/Br (J S White) 1965; C; 1000; 67.32 × 3.82 (220.87 × 12.53); M (Blackstone); 12; ex *Cresset* 1982; ex *Crescence* 1981

★74220 **PEI CHING No.1** RC/Fr (Rhin) 1957; R; 1200; 74.2 × 4.6 (243.44 × 15.09); M (MaK); —; ex *Ice Princess* 1961
Sister:
74221 **FRIGORA** (Br)

74230 **LITORAL SANTAFECINO** Ar/US (Ingalls SB) 1948; C; 1100; 66.51 × — (218.21 × —); TSM (Enterprise Eng); —; ex *941* 1969; ex *M.O.P. 941* 1958
Probable sister:
74231 **KARINA RIO GRANDE** (Ar) ex *Karina* 1971; ex *942* 1968; ex *M.O.P. 942* 1958

★74240 **TEUTA** Al/It (Apuania) 1960; C; 1100; 72.42 × 4.77 (237.6 × 15.65); M (Fiat); 11.75

74250 **JESICA** Ho/Be (Beliard, Crichton) 1953; C; 900; 67.11 × 4.47 (220.18 × 14.67); M (KHD); 12; ex *Orgeo* 1982; ex *Ardenne* 1975; ex *Marie-Flore* 1974

74260 **ANABELA** Gr/Sp ('Elcano') 1956; C; 700; 67.85 × 3.86 (22.6 × 12.66); M (Polar); 13; ex *Balkan Unity* 1978; ex *Bayren* 1977; ex *Amelia De Aspe* 1968; ex *Astene Primero* 1962
Sister:
74261 **MAGALI** (Cy) ex *Paula De Aspe* 1965; ex *Astene Segundo* 1962

74280 **VROUWE ALIDA** Ne/Ne (Bijlholt) 1976; C; 1500; 78.67 × 5.03 (258.1 × 16.5); M (Appingedammer Brons); 11.5

74290 **MARITTA JOHANNA** Ne/Ne (Peter's Schpsbw) 1978; C; 1600; 73 (bp) × 5.45 (239.5 (bp) × 17.88); M (Brons); 12.5

74300 **LIFT-ON** Li/No (Batservice); 1977; C/HL; 1600; 97.06 × 5.91 (318.44 × 19.39); M; (Atlas-MaK); 14.5; ex *Lifton* 1980

74310 **NADIA 1** Le/Br (Cammell Laird) 1962; C; 900; 61.96 × 4.3 (203.28 × 14.11); M (Sulzer); 12.5; ex *Portmarnock* 1980; ex *Shevrell* 1973; ex *Wirral Coast* 1972

74320 **OROSI** CR/Sp (AESA) 1965; C/R; 800; 56.24 × 4.2 (184.5 × 13.78); M (MWM); 11; ex *Sierra Espuna* 1977
Sisters:
74322 **AL DHAID STAR** (Sh) ex *Sierra Estrella* 1980

74330 **NIKA** Gr/FRG (Hagelstein) 1958; C; 1000; 71.73 × 4.68 (235.33 × 15.35); M (KHD); 10; ex *Leon* 1980; ex *Sunray* 1979; ex *Eldvik* 1975; ex *Grjoety* 1970; ex *Susanna* 1967; ex *Susanne Reith*

74345 **FERRING** Br/Br (Hall, Russell) 1969; C; 1600; 86.87 × 5.30 (285 × 17.39); M (Mirrlees Blackstone); 12.5
Sister:
74346 **MALLING** (Br)

74350 **HELEEN-C** Br/Br (Clelands) 1967; C; 700; 68.23 × 3.72 (223.85 × 12.2); M (Mirlees Blackstone)—; ex *Apricity* 1982
Sister:
74351 **GRETA-C** (Br) ex *Hughina* 1983; ex *Actuality* 1982

74360 **ZILLERTAL** As/Hu (Angyalfold) 1964; C; 1600; 84.44 × 4.93 (277.03 × 16.17); M (Liebknecht); 12.5; ex *Bulk Trader* 1983; ex *Primrose* 1980; ex *Gyram* 1974; ex *Pauline* 1973; ex *Patricia X* 1972; ex *Sagafjell* 1971; May be others of this class with similar appearance—see MMF

74370 **GRACE BONNY II** Cy/Hu (Angyalfold) 1968; C; 1200; 74.81 × 4.99 (245.44 × 16.37); M (MWM) 11.75; ex *De Gele Tulp* 1978; ex *Petro Aquamarine* 1973; ex *Petro Coco* 1971
Sisters:
74371 **DE RODE TULP** (NA) ex *Petro Ruby* 1973; ex *Petro Prince* 1971
74372 **DE WITTE TULP** (NA) ex *Giovanni Tricoli* 1978; ex *Soknavik* 1977; ex *Petro Duke* 1972

74380 **DART BRITAIN** Br/Ja (Namura) 1979; Con; 15700; 177.03 × 10.13 (583.96 × 33.23); M (Sulzer); 19; ex *Seapac Oriskany* 1981; ex *Seatrain Oriskany* 1981
Sisters:
74381 **TFL FRANKLIN** (FRG) ex *Seatrain Bennington* 1981
74382 **DART ATLANTICA** (Br) ex *Seapac Chesapeake* 1981; ex *Seatrain Chesapeake* 1981
74383 **DART CONTINENT** (Be) ex *Seatrain Yorktown* 1981; ex *Seatrain Yorktown* 1981
74384 **DART AMERICANA** (Br) ex *Seapac Independence* 1981; ex *Seatrain Independence* 1981
74385 **TFL JEFFERSON** (Sg) ex *Seatrain Saratoga* 1980

74390 **EVER VALIANT** Pa/Ja (Hayashikane) 1977; Con; 14400; 186.75 × 10.02 (612.7 × 32.87); M (Sulzer); 22
Similar (Pa flag):
74391 **HANJIN KWANG YANG** ex *Ever Victory* 1983
74392 **HANJIN CHEJU** ex *Ever Voyager* 1983
74393 **EVER VIGOR**
74394 **EVER VITAL**
Possibly similar (Pa Flag):
74395 **EVER VALOR**
74396 **EVER VALUE**

74410 **SYDNEY EXPRESS** FRG/FRG (B+V) 1970; Con; 27400; 226.47 × 11.56 (743 × 37.93); T (Stal-Laval); 21.5
Sister (Ne built—Giessen-De Noord):
74411 **NEDLLOYD TASMAN** (Ne) ex *Mounts Bay* 1982; ex *Nedlloyd Tasman* 1981; ex *Abel Tasman* 1977
Similar (It built—Muggiano):
74412 **LLOYDIANA** (It)

● 74420 **IVOR** Cy/Ne (Giessen-De Noord) 1971; Con; 6700; 144.94 × 7.62 (475.52 × 25); M (MAN); 22; ex *Atlantic Prowess* 1983; ex *Cathy* 1982; ex *New England Hunter* 1981; ex *Fiery Cross Isle* 1973
Sister:
74421 **GRAND HAVEN** (Li) ex *New England Trapper* 1980;

74430 **VISURGIS** As/FRG (Elsflether) 1971; Con; 6000; 128.43 × 8.07 (421.36 × 26.48); M (Atlas-MaK); 18; ex *Atlantic Prospect* 1982; ex *Visurgis* 1981

74431 **NEW ZEALAND TRADER** NZ/Tw (China SB) 1980; Con; 6200; 118.01 × 8.00 (387 × 26.25); M (MAN); 15.75; ex *Atlantic* 1983
Sisters:
74432 **ALTONIC** (Pa) ex *Gold Africa* 1982; Launched as *Altonic*
74433 **HANSEATIC** (Pa) ex *Zim Osaka* 1983; ex *Hanseatic* 1983; ex *Gold Asia* 1982; ex *Hanseatic* 1981
74434 **HOLSATIC** (Pa) ex *Zim Busan* 1983; ex *Holsatic* 1983
74434/1 **CARMEL** (Pa) ex *Zim Carmel* 1983; ex *Carmel* 1983; ex *Zim Carmel* 1983; ex *Maersk Pinto 1* 1982; ex *Maersk Pinto* 1981; Launched as *Arctic*

● 74435 **AMBROSIA** FRG/FRG (Flensburger) 1980; Con; 15000; 170.21 × 9.65 (558.43 × 31.66); M (MAN); 19; ex *TFL Washington* 1983; Launched as *Ambrosia*
Sister (FRG flag):
74436 **TFL ADAMS**

74437 **ZIM KAOHSIUNG** FRG/FRG (O&K) 1982; C/Con; 10600; 153.63 × 8.25 (504 × 27.07); M (Krupp-MaK); 16.5; ex *Arktic* 1982

★74440 **HRELJIN** Ys/FRG (Sietas) 1977; Con; 8100; 153.88 × 8.59 (504.86 × 28.18); M (Pielstick); 18.5
Sister:
★74441 **SUSAK** (Ys)

74450 **ZIM MONTREAL** Li/FRG (Bremer V) 1973; Con; 23100; 218.6 × 11.51 (717.19 × 37.76); T (Stal-Laval); 23.5
Sister:
74451 **ZIM HONG KONG** (Is)

74460 **HERMES ACE** Ja/FRG (O&K) 1976; Con; 9100; 159.01 × 8.26 (521.69 × 27.1); M (Pielstick); 17.5; ex *Seatrain Italy* 1981; ex *Sovereign Express* 1977
Sister:

74461 SOVEREIGN ACCORD (Ja)

74470 BORINQUEN US/US (Kaiser Co.) 1945/66; Con; 17200; 208.77 × 9.19 (684.94 × 30.15); T (Hendy); 17; ex *Trenton* 1975; ex *Marine Falcon* 1966; Converted from 'C-4' type general cargo; Lengthened and deepened 1966 (Ingalls SB)
Similar (some lengthened—US flag):
74471 **LONG BEACH** ex *Marine Flasher* 1966
74472 **OAKLAND** ex *Marine Tiger* 1966
74473 **PANAMA** ex *Marine Jumper* 1966
74474 **SAN JUAN** ex *Chicago* 1975; ex *General C H Muir* 1969
74475 **PHILADELPHIA** ex *General A W Brewster* 1968
74478 **CHARLESTON** ex *Marine Shark* 1968

74490 MELBOURNE EXPRESS FRG/FRG (Bremer V) 1970; Con; 25600; 217.91 × 11.51 (714.93 × 37.76); T (Stal-Laval); 21.5

74500 ACT 1 Br/FRG (Bremer V) 1969; Con; 24800; 217.25 × 10.83 (712.76 × 35.53); T (Stal-Laval); 22
Sisters (Br flag):
74501 **LOS ANGELES** ex *ACT 2* 1983
74502 **AUSTRALIAN ENDEAVOUR** Launched as ACT 3
Similar:
74503 **ACT 6** (Br)

★ **74510 BANJA LUKA** Ys/It (Adriatico) 1968; B; 16000; 190.48 × 10.59 (624.93 × 34.74); M (Fiat); 15.5
Sister:
★ **74511 BARANJA** (Ys)

74520 CANADIAN EXPLORER Br/FRG (Bremer V) 1978; Con; 26700; 218.6 × 11.77 (717.19 × 38.62); M (MAN) 23; ex *Dart Canada* 1981

74530 KANGOUROU Fr/Fr (La Ciotat) 1970; Con; 26500; 227.95 × 10.69 (747.87 × 35.07); T (Stal-Laval); 21.5

★ **74540 FILIPP MAKHARADZE** Ru/Pd (Szczecinska) 1972; B; 20300; 198.71 × 10.68 (651.93 × 35.03); M (Sulzer); 15; **B-447** type
Sisters (Ru flag):
★ **74541 NIKO NIKOLADZE**
★ **74542 MIKHA TSKHAKAYA**
(Pd flag):
★ **74544 OBRONCY POCZTY**
★ **74545 POWSTANIEC SLASKI**
★ **74546 SIEKIERKI**
★ **74547 TOBRUK**
(Cy flag):
74548 **AGAPI** ex *Czwartacy AI* 1983

● **74560 ORIENT VENTURE** Li/FRG (Rhein Nordseew) 1965; B; 26500; 227.11 × 10.53 (745.11 × 34.55); M (MAN); 14.5; ex *Eschersheim* 1980; Lengthened 1968
Sister:
74561 **WALTER LEONHARDT** (Cy) ex *Bornheim* 1982

74570 ONESSILUS Pa/FRG (B+V) 1963; B; 24700; 214.66 × 10.47 (704.27 × 34.35); M|(B+V) 15; ex *Strassburg*

74590 ANASTASIA L Gr/Fr (L'Atlantique) 1967; B; 53400; 264.24 × 13.72 (866.93 × 45.01); M (B&W); 14.5; ex *Cetra Columba* 1978

74600 YIANNIS Pa/Sw (Gotav) 1964; O; 24800; 199.88 × 11.37 (655.77 × 37.3); M (Gotaverken); 15.75; ex *Yasnaya Polyana* 1980; ex *Laidaure* 1978
Sister:
74601 **SILVER MOON** (Pa) ex *Ela Mana Mou* 1982; ex *Yakutsk* 1980; ex *Laponia* 1978

74610 POLYXENI Gr/Sw (Gotav) 1962; O; 18000; 178.09 × 10.9 (584.28 × 35.76); M (Gotaverken); 14.25; ex *Luossa* 1977

74620 NAUTIC PIONEER Li/FRG (Flensburger) 1967; B; 22400; 201.66 × 11.53 (661.61 × 37.83); M (MAN); 16; ex *Tete Oldendorff* 1983
Sister:
74621 **NOBLE SUPPORTER** (Li) ex *Rixta Oldendorff* 1983
Similar:
74622 **SAVOY DEAN** (Li) ex *Buntentor* 1980

74630 CURTIS CAPRICORN Br/Au (Whyalla) 1972; B; 48900; 255.43 × 15.14 (838.02 × 49.67); T (GEC); —; ex *Clutha Capricorn* 1977

74640 PROTEKTOR FRG/FRG (LF-W) 1967; B; 43200; 253.02 × 13.67 (830.12 × 44.85); M (GMT); 15; ex *Ursula Schulte* 1978

74650 TRUE ENDEAVOUR Li/FRG (LF-W) 1965; B; 19300; 200.13 × 11.5 (656.59 × 37.73); M (MAN); 15.25; ex *Helena Oldendorff* 1983
Sister:

74651 BOLD CHALLENGER (Li) ex *Regina Oldendorff* 1983

★ **74655 KOPALNIA GOTTWALD** Pd/Br (Swan Hunter) 1980; B; 11000; 158.73 × 8.38 (521 × 27.49); M (B&W); 14.75
Sisters:
★ **74656 KOPALNIA MIECHOWICE** (Pd) (builder—Smith's D)
★ **74657 KOPALNIA SIERSZA** (Pd) (builder—Govan)

★ **74660 ZIEMIA BYDGOSKA** Pd/Br (Smith's D) 1967; B; 15700; 179.51 × 9.91 (588.94 × 32.51); M (Sulzer); 15
Sister:
★ **74661 ZIEMIA MAZOWIECKA** (Pd)

74670 ARCADIAN SEA Gr/FRG (Rhein Nordseew) 1965; B; 21000; 191.27 × 11.32 (627.53 × 37.14); M (B&W); 15.25; ex *Astramarina* 1980; ex *Torm Helvig* 1975; ex *Helvig* 1974
Sisters:
74671 **VERA** (Gr); ex *Astradiego* 1981; ex *Torm Herdis* 1975; ex *Herdis* 1974
74672 **TRADE MASTER** (Gr); ex *Ocean Master* 1977
74673 **ODYSSEUS** (Pa) ex *Tyrol* 1978; ex *Fernglen* 1975

● **74680 ALFIE 1** Pa/Sw (Uddevalla) 1957; B; 10900; 162.97 × 9.32 (534.68 × 30.58); T (GEC); 17; ex *Louise* 1982

74720 WESTERN GLORY Li/FRG (Flensburger) 1965; B; 19400; 201.73 × 11.53 (661.84 × 37.83); M (MAN); 15.25; ex *Dietrich Oldendorff* 1983

74730 MENITES Gr/Ja (NKK) 1959; B; 12300; 169.17 × 9.53 (555 × 31.27); M (MAN); 14.75; ex *Saas Fee* 1977; ex *Butterfly* 1972

● **74740 PALLADE** It/It ('Navalmeccanica') 1959; B; 12600; 174.71 × 9.88 (573.2 × 32.41); M (Fiat); 15

74750 MEDCEMENT CARRIER Gr/Br (Short Bros) 1962; B/Cem; 11900; 170.9 × 10.12 (560.7 × 33.2); M (Sulzer); 14.25; ex *Atlantic Carrier* 1977; ex *World Explorer* 1972; Converted from bulk 1972

74760 ARCTIC OCEAN Cy/It (Breda) 1962; B; 17300; 192.03 × 10.61 (630.02 × 34.81); M (Fiat); 16; ex *Polinnia* 1981
Sisters:
74761 **MINORIES PROGRESS** (Pa) ex *Massimo Primo* 1981
74762 **TRADE WIND** (Gr) ex *Umberto d'Amato* 1980; ex *Peppino D'Amato* 1978; ex *Donatella* 1978

74770 EMS ORE Li/Sw (Gotav) 1966; O; 44000; 243.85 × 12.26 (800.03 × 40.22); M (Gotaverken); 16.25; ex *Nimba* 1981; ex *Nuolja* 1974;
Sister:
74771 **ALIANZA** (Ar) ex *Nikkala* 1978

74780 VENTURE Li/Sw (Gotav) 1967; OBO; 39700; 258.36 × 13.27 (848.62 × 43.54); M (Gotaverken); 16; ex *Venture Italia* 1982; ex *Conoco Italia* 1978; ex *Rinda* 1972
Sister:
74781 **CHANDOS** (Li) ex *Delaware* 1982; ex *Ranger* 1973; ex *Runa* 1972

74790 MEGA BAY Li/Sw (Gotav) 1967; OBO; 44500; 258.66 × 13.47 (848.62 × 44.19); M (Gotaverken); 16.5; ex *Falcon Bay* 1982; ex *Mospoint* 1978; ex *Vitoria* 1976

74800 FORT ST. LOUIS Ca/Ca (Davie SB) 1963; C; 5900; 142.14 × 7.21 (466.34 × 23.65); M (Canadian Locomotive); —

74810 OCEAN LADY Pa/FRG (Kieler H) 1963; B; 25400; 215.91 × 11.13 (708.37 × 36.52); M (Gotaverken); 14.5; ex *Kimpo* 1981; ex *Bandak* 1973

★ **74820 THALE** DDR/FRG (Kieler H) 1960; B; 14500; 171.79 × 10.28 (563.62 × 33.73); M (MAN); 14.75; ex *H L Lorentzen* 1964

74830 CASTLE POINT Br/Br (Readhead) 1965; C; 5600; 112.68 × 9.09 (369.69 × 29.82); M (Doxford); 13.5; ex *Hudson Light* 1976

74840 ISLAND CONTAINER Pa/Au (NSW Govt.) 1964; Con; 5700; 126.17 × 7.62 (413.94 × 25); M (Sulzer); 16; ex *Kooringa*; May have two travelling gantries.

74850 DELTA FLAG Gr/No (Kaldnes) 1958; O; 10600; 153.93 × 9.19 (505.02 × 30.15); M (Doxford); 11.75; ex *Malessina* 1981; ex *Good Trainer* 1975; ex *Nordland* 1972

74860 FRANKFURT EXPRESS Pa/FRG (Howaldts) 1956/69; Con; 6600; 137.45 × 6.54 (450.95 × 21.46); M (MAN); 14; ex *Hong Kong Express* 1982; ex *Lilac* 1980; ex *Karin-Elise* 1973; ex *Hother Isle* 1973;

ex *Christiane* 1968; Converted from cargo 1969 (Bremer V)

★ **74870 HUAI HAI** RC/FRG (Kieler H) 1962; B; 14800; 179.38 × 10.92 (588.52 × 35.83); M (MAN); 14; ex *Georgios A Georgilis* 1974; ex *Benedicte* 1969
Similar:
★ **74871 HUANG HAI** (RC) ex *Amundsen Sea* 1975; ex *Antonis P Lemos* 1974; ex *Beatrice* 1969

74880 ALIKI Gr/FRG (Kieler H) 1959; B; 13000; 171.79 × 10.55 (563.62 × 34.61); M (MAN); 14; ex *Jarilla* 1977

74890 ROSYTH Sg/FRG (Kieler H) 1961; O; 17400; 184.41 × 9.77 (605.02 × 32.05); M (MAN); 13.75; ex *Norita* 1977; ex *Filefjell* 1967

74900 RAUTARUUKKI FI/FRG (Schuerenstedt) 1976; B; 7400; 143.31 × 7.57 (470.18 × 24.84); M (Atlas-MaK); 15.25
Sister:
74901 MADZY (Sw) ex *Kuurtanes* 1981
Possibly similar:
74902 **STORON** (Sw) ex *Mini Orbit* 1983

74910 BERGON Sw/No (Ulstein H) 1978; C; 1600/3400; 100.84 × —/5.05 (330.84 × —/16.57); M (Atlas-Mak); ex *Mini Star* 1983; Deck is strengthened to allow a gantry crane to be fitted

74920 ALBRIGHT PIONEER Br/Br (Vickers Ltd) 1968; Ch; 6800; 125.81 × 8.88 (412.76 × 29.13); M; 14.5
Similar:
74921 **ALBRIGHT EXPLORER** (Br)

74930 CAPE RACE Br/No (Kaldnes) 1971; B; 14900; 165.21 × 10.22 (542.03 × 33.53); M (Sulzer); 15
Sister:
74931 **BARON BELHAVEN** (Br)

74940 PAXO Pa/Br (H&W) 1957; O; 8600; 160.28 × 8.76 (525.85 × 28.74); M (B&W); 11.5; ex *Levantino* 1982; ex *Afghanistan* 1972
Similar:
74941 **ASPIDOFOROS** (Fr) ex *Iron Horse* 1970
74942 **JEANNIE** (Gr) ex *Scottish Wasa* 1977; ex *Iron Crown* 1971
74943 **MAHINDA** (Sg) ex *Iron Barque* 1970
74944 **HERAKLIA** (Pa) ex *Onorato* 1981; ex *Nino* 1969; ex *Iron Age* 1968
74945 **SKYROS** (Pa) ex *Siroco* 1981; ex *Iron Ore* 1969
74946 **MERCURY** (Sg) ex *Lovinda* 1981; ex *Daghestan* 1975

74950 GRAND ENCOUNTER Pa/Ca (Port Weller) 1972; RoC; 16400; 208.19 × 9.3 (683.04 × 30.51); TSM (Pielstick); 19; ex *Laurentian Forest* 1980
Sister:
74951 **AVON FOREST** (Br)

74960 RIO VERDE Bz/Bz (Emaq) 1977; B; 21700; 193.86 × 10.9 (636.02 × 35.76); M (Sulzer); 16
Sister:
74961 **RIO NEGRO** (Bz)
Sisters (superstructure extended aft):
74962 **RIO BRANCO** (Bz)
74963 **RIO GRANDE** (Bz)

74980 ORIENT HARMONY Li/Br (Doxford & S) 1967; B; 29500; 215.96 × 12.43 (708.53 × 40.78); M (Doxford); 16.75; ex *Gaucho Guemes*; ex *Mardulce II*; ex *Fernspring*
Probable sister:
74981 **WELFARE** (Gr) ex *Pilio* 1980; ex *Fernriver* 1978

● **74990 BREEZE** Pa/FRG (Kieler H) 1964; OO; 35100; 235.64 × 12.52 (773.1 × 41.08); M (Gotaverken); 15; ex *Howard Smith* 1979; ex *Hoegh Helm* 1969

75000 DRUPA Br/FRG (Deutsche Werft) 1966; Tk; 39800; 243.8 × 13.25 (799.87 × 43.47); T (Stal-Laval); 15; Fenders on upper deck are on port side

75010 LYRA Gr/Fr (France-Gironde) 1967; B; 41900; 254.52 × 13.49 (835.04 × 44.26); M (Sulzer); 16; ex *Cetra Lyra*
Sister:
75011 **CARINA** (Gr) ex *Cetra Carina*

75020 RUDDERMAN Br/Br (Cochrane) 1968; Tk; 1600; 83.52 × 5.15 (274.02 × 16.9); M (Brons); 12

75030 VINGAVAG Sw/Fi (Valmet) 1973; Tk; 3800; 107.32 × 6.62 (352.1 × 21.72); M (Stork-Werkspoor); 14; ex *Tarnvag* 1980; ex *Vuosaari* 1978
Probably similar:
75031 **TEBOSTAR** (Fi)

75040 SAVE Fr/Sw (Ekensbergs) 1962; Tk; 4500; 118.78 × 6.86 (389.7 × 22.5); M (Uddevalla); 14; ex *Alor Star* 1972; ex *Rogn* 1968

75050 ALBAY HAKKI BURAK Tu/Tu (—) 1964; FA/Tk; 3800 Dspl; 83.7 × 5.5 (275 × 18); D-E (General Motors); 16

75060 BILLESBORG De/De (Frederikshavn) 1970; Tk/Ch; 1400; 107.32 × 5.21 (352.1 × 17.09); M (KHD); 12; Lengthened 1974
Sister:
75061 BRATTINGSBORG (De)

75070 ASPERITY Br/Ne (Nieuwe Noord) 1967; Tk/Ch; 700; 71.86 × 3.84 (235.76 × 12.6); M (KHD); 12
Similar (smaller):
75071 AUTHORITY (Br)

75080 ROCHE'S POINT Br/FRG (Nobiskrug) 1968; Tk/Ch; 1600; 94.32 × 5.3 (309.45 × 17.39); M (MAN); 15; ex Samos Fortune 1980; ex Thorhagen 1973

75085 ESSO PLYMOUTH Br/Br (Cochrane) 1980; Tk; 1400; 70.82 × 4.71 (232.35 × 15.45); M (APE Allen); 11.75

75090 ESSO INVERNESS Br/Br (Appledore) 1971; Tk; 2200; 91.42 × 5.9 (299.93 × 19.36); M (English Electric); 13
Sister:
75091 ESSO PENZANCE (Br)

75100 SAND SAPPHIRE Br/Br (Laing) 1963/75; D; 900; 61.88 × 3.83 (203.02 × 12.57); M (Nydqvist & Holm); 11; ex Cy-Threesome 1974; ex Pass of Glenogle 1973; Converted from tanker 1975

75110 DEVON CURLEW Br/Sp (Ruiz) 1969; Ch; 800; 68.18 × 3.96 (223.69 × 12.99); M (Stork-Werkspoor); 12.5; ex Fenol
Sisters:
75111 HIAWATHA (Pa) ex Dorset Fulmar 1982; ex Formol 1979
75112 THITA STAINLESS (Gr) ex Metanol 1974

75130 BENVENUE Br/Ne (Nieuwe Noord) 1974; Ch; 1600; 80.78 × 5.38 (265.02 × 17.65); M (Smit & Bolnes); 12.75
Sisters (Br flag):
75131 BENCLEUCH
75132 BENMACHDHUI

75140 UNICORN DANIEL Li/FRG (Kroegerw) 1968; Tk; 600; 69.5 × 4.32 (228.02 × 14.17); M (MWM); 12.5; ex Bobodi 1977
Similar (smaller and with lower superstructure etc):
75141 UNICORN MICHAEL (Br) ex Onabi 1977

75150 DUTCH GLORY Ne/Ne (Nieuwe Noord) 1975; Ch; 1400; 80.24 × 5.42 (263.25 × 17.78); M (KHD); 13.5
Sister:
75151 DUTCH MASTER (Ne)
Similar (superstructure more open):
75152 CORRIE BROERE (Ne)

75160 ANNA BROERE Ne/FRG (Brand) 1976; Ch; 1600; 82.5 × 5.74 (270.66 × 18.83); M (Atlas-MaK); 13.5

★**75170 BUNA** DDR/Ne (Vuyk) 1979; Ch; 1800; 73.46 × 4.91 (241.01 × 16.11); M (Atlas-MaK); 13
Sister:
★**75171 SCHKOPAU** (DDR) (may be spelt **ZSCHOPAU**)

75172 MULTITANK ADRIA FRG/FRG (Sietas) 1981; Ch; 1600; 93.07 × 5.45 (305 × 17.88); M (B&W); 13.5
Sisters:
75173 MULTITANK ARCADIA (FRG)
75174 MULTITANK ARMENIA (FRG)
75175 MULTITANK ASCANIA (FRG)

75177 HANNE LUPE De/FRG (Nobiskrug) 1981; AT; 1600; 86.01 × 5.04 (282 × 16.54); M (KHD); 11.75

75180 CENTAURMAN Br/Br (Hall, Russell) 1976; Ch; 2500; 89.18 × 5.9 (292.59 × 19.36); M (Mirrlees Blackstone); 13.5; ex Essex Trophy 1983; ex Centaurman 1983
Sister:
75181 VEGAMAN (Br) ex Essex Triumph 1983; ex Vegaman 1983

75190 STELLAMAN Br/Br (Cochrane) 1976; Ch; 1500; 79.51 × 5.27 (260.26 × 17.29); M (W H Allen); 13.75
Sister:
75191 MARSMAN (Br)

75200 OMANIAH Ku/FRG (Kroegerw) 1971; Ch; 2900; 106.03 × 6.43 (347.87 × 21.1); M (Alpha-Diesel); 14.5; ex Opobo 1980; ex Terkol 1972

75210 LA COLINA Br/No (Batservice) 1976; Ch; 1600; 96.02 × 5.47 (315.03 × 17.95); M (KHD); 13.75
Sisters:

75211 LA PRADERA (Br)
75212 POLISAN 1 (Tu) ex Stainless Patriot 1982

75220 KIISLA Fi/Fi (Valmet) 1974/79; Tk/Ch; 4700; 130.33 × 6.28 (428 × 20.60); M (Stork-Werkspoor); 14; Lengthened 1979

75221 SHELL MARKETER Br/Br (Clelands) 1981; Tk; 1600; 79.25 × 5.03 (260 × 16.50); M (Mirrlees Blackstone); 12
Sisters (Br flag):
75222 SHELL SEAFARER
75223 SHELL TECHNICIAN

75224 ABILITY Br/Br (Goole) 1979; Tk; 1400; 79.25 × 4.97 (260 × 16.31); M (Ruston); 13
Sisters:
75225 AMENITY (Br)
75226 AUTHENTICITY (Br)

75230 CHEMICAL LAUSANNE Li/FRG (O&K) 1974; Ch; 3900; 109 × 8.54 (357.61 × 28.02); M (Atlas-MaK); 14.5; ex Alchimist Lausanne 1980
Sisters:
75231 CHEMIST LUTETIA (Li)
75232 QUIMICO LISBOA (Pa)
75233 QUIMICO LEIXOES (Po)
75234 CHIMISTE SAYID (Mo)

75236 ANTIGUA FRG/FRG (Menzer) 1981; Ch; 2800; 99.12 × 6.01 (325 × 19.72); M (Mitsubishi); 14
Sister:
75237 BONAIRE (FRG)

75240 PROOF SPIRIT Li/Ne (Groot & VV) 1975; Ch; 1500; 73.46 × 6.15 (241.01 × 20.18); M ('Bolnes'); 12.5
Sister:
75241 PROOF TRADER (Li)

●**75250 CYMBELINE** Br/Br (Bartram) 1966; C; 5600; 112.78 × 7.64 (370.01 × 25.66); M (Sulzer); —; ex Dalewood 1974
Similar:
75251 OSWESTRY GRANGE (Br); ex Chelwood 1974

75253 ALDRINGTON Br/Br (Swan Hunter) 1978; B; 4300; 103.61 × 7.03 (340 × 23.06); M (Mirrlees Blackstone); 14.75
Sister (Builder Clelands):
75254 ASHINGTON (Br)

75260 ANEMOS Gr/FRG (O&K) 1976; Con; 8400; 143.82 × 8.32 (471.85 × 27.3); M (Pielstick); 18.25; The towers are crane bases and cranes are probably fitted now
Sister:
75261 PELAGOS (Gr)
Similar (probably has no 'towers' on deck):
75262 MONTE RUBY (Pa) ex Hermes 1 1983

75270 ESLA Sp/Sp (Atlantico) 1977; C/Con; 3300; 99.73 × 6.9 (327.2 × 22.64); M (MAN); 14; ex Gabriela De Perez 1980; ex Zim Atlantic 1978; Launched as Gabriela De Perez
Sister:
75271 TAJO (Sp) ex Maria De Las Angustias 1980; ex Zim Iberia 1979; ex Maria De Las Angustias 1976
Possibly similar (may have deck cranes);
75272 AVE (Sp)
75273 TERMANCIA (Sp)
75274 GALIA (Sp); ex Chief Abule; Launched as Galia

★**75280 PIONIR** Ys/FRG (Schuerenstedt) 1973; Con; 4000; 118.88 × 6.4 (390.03 × 21); M (MAN); 15.5; ex Eurobridge Pionir; ex Pionir 1978; ex Maritime Champ 1974
Sister:
75281 SUN FLOWER (Ko) ex Maritime Ace 1973

●**75290 EVE** Pa/FRG (Sietas) 1971; C/Con; 1000; 88.5 × 5.28 (290.35 × 17.32); M (Atlas-MaK); 14; ex Heino 1983; ex Scol Venture 1976; ex Baltic Unit; ex Heino 1971
Similar (some may have deck cranes):
75291 SABINE D (FRG) ex Twiehausen 1983; ex Ibesca Algeria 1980; ex Ibesca Espana 1978; ex Twiehausen 1977
75294 FRAUDEN (Fi) ex Frauke 1982; ex Comar II 1974; ex Frauke 1972
75295 MARGRET (FRG) ex Margret Knuppel 1976; ex Pinto 1973; ex Hannes Knuppel 1973
75296 DEICHLAND (Pa) ex Bomberg 1983; ex Roxane Kersten 1980; ex Bomberg
75297 NAUTIC (Fi)
75298 WIDUKIND (FRG) ex Zim Constantza 1982; ex Widukind 1981

75310 THAI PAILIN Th/FRG (Unterweser) 1969; C/Con; 2200; 94.98 × 5.72 (311.61 × 18.77); M (KHD); —; ex Bluhm 1; ex Ida Blumenthal 1979; ex Ida Isle 1972; Launched as Ida Blumenthal
Sister:

75311 THAI TUBTIM (Th) ex Pacific Convoy 1981; ex Johann Blumenthal 1979; ex Gretchen Isle 1972; ex Johann Isle 1969; Launched as Johann Blumenthal

75315 ROMA FRG/FRG (Werftunion) 1981; C/Con; 1000; 80.80 × 4.66 (265 × 15.29) M (Krupp); 11.5

★**75320 BOLTENHAGEN** DDR/DDR (Elbewerften) 1970; C/Con; 300; 57.79 × 3.68 (189.6 × 12.07); M (Liebknecht); 12
Sisters (DDR flag):
★**75321 DIERHAGEN**
★**75322 NIENHAGEN**
★**75323 TRINWILLERSHAGEN**
(Ru flag):
★**75324 FRITSIS GAYLIS** (also known as **F GAYLIS**) ex Jocon; Launched as Nienhagen
★**75325 V KUCHER** ex Jobox

★**75327 HAJNOWKA** Pd/Pd (Wisla) 1971; C/Con; 800; 59.82 × 4.20 (196 × 13.78); M (Sulzer); 11.5; **'B457'** type
Sister:
★**75328 BARLINEK** (Pd)

★**75330 FRITSIS ROSIN** Ru/DDR (Elbewerften) 1971; C/Con; 500; 71.07 × 3.68 (233.17 × 12.07); M (Liebknecht); 12
Sisters (Ru flag):
★**75331 GLEB SEDIN**
(DDR flag):
★**75332 WARIN**
★**75333 BANSIN**
★**75334 TESSIN**
★**75335 KROPELIN**
★**75336 RECHLIN**

★**75350 'BALTIYSKIY'** type. Ru/Ru ('Krasnoye S') 1962 onwards; C (sea/river); 1900; 95.61 × 3.26 (313.68 × 10.7); TSM (Liebknecht); 10; Most of this class of over 70 ships have the sequence KMFK—which see; Funnel heights vary;
Among vessels known to be KMF (Ru flag):
★**75351 KILIYA**
★**75352 VLAS CHUBAR**
★**75353 GOROKHOVETS**

★**75360 'LADOGA'** type. Ru/Fi (Laiva) 1972 onwards; C (sea/river); 1600; 81.01 × 4.01 (265.78 × 13.16); TSM (Liebknecht); 12 approx
Sisters (Ru flag—funnels vary in shape and height):
★**75361 LADOGA 1**
★**75362 LADOGA 2**
★**75363 LADOGA 3**
★**75364 LADOGA 4**
★**75365 LADOGA 5**
★**75366 LADOGA 6**
★**75367 LADOGA 7**
★**75368 LADOGA 9**
★**75369 LADOGA 8** ex Norppa 1981; ex Ladoga 8 1974

★**75380 BALTIYSKIY 101** Ru/Fi (Laiva) 1978; C/Con (sea/river); 2000; 95 × 4 (311.68 × 13.12); TSM (Liebknecht); 11.5; Hinged masts
Sisters (Ru flag):
★**75381 BALTIYSKIY 102**
★**75382 BALTIYSKIY 103**
★**75383 VASILIY MALOV** ex Baltiyskiy 104 1981
★**75384 BALTIYSKIY 105**
★**75385 BALTIYSKIY 106**
★**75386 BALTIYSKIY 107**
★**75387 BALTIYSKIY 108**
★**75388 BALTIYSKIY 109**
★**75389 BALTIYSKIY 110**
★**75390 BALTIYSKIY 111**

★**75400 SAYMENSKIY KANAL** Ru/Fi (Rauma-Repola) 1978; C (sea/river); 1600; 81.01 × 4 (265.78 × 13.12); TSM (Liebknecht); 12; ex Ladoga 10 1980
Sisters (Ru flag):
★**75401 LADOGA 11**
★**75402 LADOGA 12**
★**75403 LADOGA 13**
★**75404 LADOGA 14**
★**75405 LADOGA 15**
★**75406 LADOGA 16**
★**75407 LADOGA 17**
★**75408 LADOGA 18**
★**75409 LADOGA 19**
★**75410 LADOGA 20**

★**75412 MIELEC** Pd/Br (Govan) 1980; B; 3000; 95.00 × 6.05 (312 × 19.85); M (Sulzer); 13.5
Sisters:
★**75413 WARKA** (Pd) (builder—Scotstoun)
★**75414 MALBORK II** (Pd)
★**75415 GOLENIOW** (Pd) (builder-Ailsa)

75420 STERN Fi/Fr (Havre) 1967; Ch; 2000; 87 × 5.97 (285.43 × 19.59); M (Werkspoor); 13.75; ex Tyysterniemi 1983

75430 ORAN Pa/Ne ('De Hoop') 1960; C/Con;

500/1100; 79.08 × 3.68/4.9 (259.45 × 12.07/16.08); M (Werkspoor); 14.5; ex *Brigitte* 1979; ex *Freia* 1976; ex *Hagno*

75440 **EMINENCE** Br/Br (Goole) 1969; C; 1000; 67.67 × 4.22 (222.01 × 13.85); M (Mirrlees Blackstone); 10.5
Similar (lower poop, pole masts):
75441 **SENTENCE** (Br)

● 75450 **FRED EVERARD** Br/Br (Goole) 1972; C; 1600; 91.14 × 5.14 (299.02 × 16.86); M (British Polar); 12.75
Sisters (Br flag):
75451 **SAGACITY**
75452 **SERENITY**
75453 **SUMMITY**
75454 **SUPERIORITY**
75455 **SUAVITY**
Similar (As flag):
75456 **RAUTZ** ex *Eildon* 1982
75457 **STUBEN** ex *Ettrick* 1982
Similar (extended poop & forecastle):
75458 **MARTINDYKE** (Br)
75459 **MAIRI EVERARD** (Br)

75470 **SECURITY** Br/Br (Dunston) 1971; C; 1600; 85.02×5..07 (278.94×16.63); M (British Polar); 13;
Sister:
75471 **SINCERITY** (Br)

75480 **FAIRMEAD** Br/Ne (E.J. Smit) 1974; C; 1600; 83.5 × 5.13 (273.95 × 16.83); M (Atlas-MaK); 12; ex *Hyde Park* 1982; ex *Syon Park* 1974
Sister:
75481 **MISHNISH** (Br)
Possibly similar:
75482 **BALLYKERN** (Br) ex *Baxtergate* 1980
75483 **COTINGA** (Br)
75484 **ATLANTIC SUN** (Ne) ex *Okko Bosma* 1978
75485 **WHITEHALL** (Br) ex *Bloempoort* 1983; ex *Flowergate* 1982

75490 **STEVEN K.** Cy/Ne (Coops) 1978; C; 1000; 71.38 × 4.53 (234.19 × 14.86); M (Atlas-MaK); —; ex *Star Venus* 1984

75500 **PAULINA BRINKMAN** Ne/Ne ('Voorwaarts') 1975; C; 1000; 65.82 × 4.3 (215.94 × 14.11); M (Appingedammer Brons); —
Sisters (Ne flag):
75501 **ALLIANCE**
75502 **CALYPSO**
75503 **DOGGERSBANK**
75504 **KWINTEBANK** ex *Els Teekman* 1984
75505 **POLARIS** ex *Emmaplein* 1981
75506 **HUGO BRINKMAN**
75507 **PLATO** ex *Flevo* 1981
75508 **KARIN**
75509 **MARJAN**
75510 **PAVONIS**

75520 **GEZIENA** Ne/Ne (Gruno) 1976; C; 1400; 76.41 × 4.83 (250.69 × 15.85); M (Appingedammer Brons); 13; ex *Merak* 1980

75530 **IJSSELMEER** Ne/Ne ('Harlingen') 1977; C; 1600; 80.22 × 5.55 (263.19 × 18.21); M (MWM); 13.25; ex *Norrbotten* 1982; Launched as *Mallarsee*
Sisters:
75531 **REGULUS** (Ne) ex *Bottenvikken* 1983; Launched as *Deltasee*
75532 **KARLSVIK** (Ne) ex *Eriesee* 1977

75533 **ARKLOW CASTLE** Ih/Ne (Bijlsma) 1981; C; 1100; 70.59 × 4.24 (231 × 13.91); M (Brons); 11
Sister (builder—Ferus Smit):
75534 **ARKLOW ABBEY** (Ih)
Similar:
75535 **SHEVRELL** (Ih) (builder Niestern-S)
75536 **DARELL** (Ih) (builder—Bijholt)
75537 **SHAMROCK ENDEAVOUR** (Br) (builder—Coops)
75538 **SHAMROCK ENTERPRISE** (Br) (builder—Gruno)
75539 **ANGELIQUE V** (Br) (builder—'Volharding')

75540 **SYLVIA ALPHA** Ne/Ne (Tille) 1977; C; 1600; 81.72 × 5.5 (268.11 × 18.04); M (Brons); 12.5
Sisters (Ne flag):
75541 **SYLVIA BETA**
75542 **SYLVIA DELTA**
75543 **SYLVIA EPSILON**
75544 **SYLVIA GAMMA**
75545 **SYLVIA OMEGA**

75550 **MATHILDE** Ne/Ne ('Voorwaarts') 1977; C; 1600; 75.11 × 5.37 (246.42 × 17.62); M (Brons); 12
Probable sister:
75551 **MENNA** (Ne)
Similar:
75552 **LIGATO** (Ne)

75560 **ALTAPPEN** Ne/Ne (Pattje) 1978; C; 1600; 80.68 × 5.12 (264.7 × 16.8); M (MWM); 12
Sisters (Ne flag):
75561 **HELGEZEE** ex *Silvia* 1983
75562 **GARDAZEE** ex *Susanna* 1983

75565 **PEACOCK VENTURE** Br/Br (J W Cook) 1982; C; 999; 67.42 × 4.11 (221.2 × 13.48); M (Ruston); 10; Salt carrier

75570 **LESLIE GAULT** Br/Br (Appledore) 1977; C; 1600; 91.52 × 5.16 (300.26 × 16.93); M (Mirrlees Blackstone); 12.5; May have deck cranes as indicated
Sisters (Br flag):
75571 **CERINTHUS**
75572 **GALLIC FJORD**
75573 **MARKINCH**

75580 **CITY OF PLYMOUTH** Br/Br (Appledore) 1978; Con; 1600; 104.17 × 5.56 (341.77 × 18.24); M (Doxford); 14.5; 'AS-300' type
Sisters (Br flag):
75581 **CITY OF PERTH**
75582 **CITY OF HARTLEPOOL**
75583 **CITY OF IPSWICH** ex *Manchester Fulmar* 1983; ex *City of Ipswich* 1981
75584 **BAKKAFOSS** (Bs) ex *City of Oxford* 1983

75587 **MANCHESTER CROWN** Br/Br (Swan Hunter) 1979; Con; 1600; 104.20 × 5.69 (342 × 18.67); M (Doxford); 15; ex *Crown Prince* 1983
Sister:
75588 **CITY OF OPORTO** (Br) ex *Royal Prince*

🖢 75600 **BREEZAND** Ne/FRG (M Jansen) 1975; C; 1600; 79.51 × 5.55 (260.86 × 18.21); M (Atlas-MaK); 12.5
Sisters:
75601 **TEQUILA SUNSET** (Pa) ex *Cairncarrier* 1982
75602 **TJONGERWAL** (Ne) ex *Cairnfreighter* 1982
75603 **LINDEWAL** (Ne) ex *Cairnleader* 1982

75610 **SELNES** Ic/Br (Appledore) 1975; C/B; 3600; 102.01 × 6.83 (334.68 × 22.41); M (Pielstick); 14; ex *Risnes*
Sisters (Br flag):
75611 **RINGNES**
75612 **ROCKNES**
75613 **ROLLNES**
Similar (centre-line kingpost foreward):
75615 **RAFNES** (No)
75616 **RADNES** (No)
75617 **REKSNES** (No)
75618 **ROGNES** (No)
75619 **RONNES** (No)
75619/1 **SAINT JAMES** (Fr) ex *Ramnes* 1983
75619/2 **SAINT BREVIN** (Fr) ex *Refsnes* 1983
75619/3 **SAINT JEAN** (Fr) ex *Riknes* 1983
75619/4 **SAINT BRICE** (Fr) ex *Rossnes* 1982

75620 **SUDWIND** FRG/FRG (Nobiskrug) 1978; C/Con; 500; 79.23 × 3.5 (259.94 × 11.48); M (Atlas-Mak); 12.5
Sisters (FRG flag):
75621 **DETLEF SCHMIDT**
75622 **EIDER**
75623 **MAJA-M**
75624 **ST. ANTONIUS**

75630 **ROF BEAVER** Br/FRG (Kremer) 1971; RoC; 1000; 80.7 × 4.14 (264.76 × 13.58); M (Alpha-Diesel); 14; ex *Helga 1* 1975; ex *Bibiana* 1973; ex *Monarch Fame* 1972; ex *Irish Fame* 1971; ex *Bibiana* 1971; Stern door

★ 75640 **KESSULAID** Ru/Tu (Beykoz) 1972; RoC; 1000; 80.22 × 4.15 (263.19 × 13.62); M (Alpha-Diesel); 13 ex *Wotan* 1975; Stern door
Similar (Ru flag):
★ 75641 **MANILAID** ex *Thunar* 1975
★ 75642 **SUURLAID** ex *Donar* 1975
Similar (FRG built (Suerken)-Ru flag):
★ 75643 **HEINLAID** ex *Ymir* 1974; ex *Frej* 1972; Launched as *Ymir*
★ 75644 **VIIRELAID** ex *Thiassi* 1974; ex *Irish Trader* 1972; Launched as *Thiassi*

75650 **DELLYS** Ag/Sp (Construcciones SA) 1974; RoC; 1600; 107 × 4.85 (351.05 × 15.91); TSM (Deutz); 18
Sisters (Ag flag):
75651 **COLLO**
75652 **TENES**

75660 **GOGO REGAL** Li/No (Horten) 1972; Tk/Ch; 16000; 165.08 × 9.94 (541.6 × 32.61); M (Sulzer); 15.5; ex *Anco Challenger* 1983; ex *Post Challenger* 1979
Sisters:
75661 **IVER CHAMPION** (Li) ex *Anco Champion* 1983; ex *Post Champion* 1979
75662 **ANCO CHARGER** (Br) ex *Post Charger* 1979
75664 **ANCO ENDEAVOUR** (Br) ex *Post Endeavour* 1977

75665 **DUA-MAR** (Sg) ex *Anco Enterprise* 1984; ex *Post Enterprise* 1978;
(Fr flag):
75666 **STOLT ENTENTE** ex *Anco Entente* 1983; ex *Post Entente* 1978
75667 **STOLT ENERGIE** ex *Anco Energie* 1983; ex *Post Energie* 1978

75680 **CARIBGAS 20** Pa/FRG (Meyer) 1967; LGC; 1200; 67.67 × 5.03 (222.01 × 16.5); M (KHD); 12; ex *Claude* 1982
Similar (Pa flag):
75681 **BRIGITTA** ex *Ligur* 1973
75682 **HAPPY BIRD** ex *Sunny Fellow* 1982; ex *Libra* 1973

75690 **ESSO FLAME** Fi/Fi (Valmet) 1966; LGC/Tk; 1000; 74.53 × 4.08 (244.52 × 13.39); M (KHD); 12

75700 **GABY** Pa/Sp (Cadiz) 1969; Cem; 5300; 120.12 × 7.03 (394.09 × 23.06); TSM (Sulzer); —; ex *Anahuac II* 1981

75710 **CHIKUMA MARU** Ja/Ja (Setoda) 1970; Cem; 6400; 131.5 × 7.82 (431.43 × 25.66); M (B&W); 12.75

★ 75720 **VITKOVICE** Cz/Br (Barclay, Curle) 1966; B; 24300; 209.91 × 11.56 (688 × 37.93); M (Sulzer); —

★ 75730 **ZAGLEBIE DABROWSKIE** Pd/Pd (Szczecinska) 1967; B; 11000; 156.37 × 9.51 (513.02 × 31.2); M (Sulzer); 15.5; 'B-520' type
Sisters (Pd flag):
★ 75731 **DOLNY SLASK**
★ 75732 **GORNY SLASK**
★ 75733 **PODHALE**
★ 75734 **KUJARWY**
★ 75735 **BIESZCZADY**

75740 **FIDES** It/It (Adriatico) 1964; B; 16100; 193.63 × 10.35 (635.27 × 33.96); M (Fiat); 16

75750 **SUNNY** Pa/No (Moss V) 1959; O; 6900; 130.16 × 7.86 (427.03 × 25.79); M (B&W); 11.5; ex *Sunny Prince* 1977; ex *Arabella* 1974

75760 **LUIGI GARDELLA** It/No (Kristiansands) 1959; O; 6500; 130.16 × 7.88 (427.03 × 25.85); M (Mirrlees, Bickerton & Day); —; ex *Gerore* 1971

★ 75770 **TARNOW** Pd/Pd (Gdanska) 1970; O; 3800; 108.77 × 6.86 (356.86 × 22.51); M (Sulzer); 14; 'B-522' type
Sisters:
★ 75771 **KEDZIERZYN** (Pd)
★ 75772 **NOWY SACZ** (Pd)
★ 75773 **EUGENIE COTTON** (Pd)

75780 **GYPSUM KING** Br/Ca (Collingwood) 1975; B; 12800; 150.81 × 9.25 (494.78 × 30.35); T (GEC); 15
Sister:
75781 **GYPSUM BARON** (Br)

★ 75790 **VERILA** Bu/Bu (G Dimitrov) 1969; B; 7800; 134.02 × 7.48 (439.7 × 24.54); M (B&W); 13
Sisters:
★ 75791 **VESLETS** (Bu)
★ 75792 **VIDEN** (Bu)
75793 **FLAG TRADER** (Gr) ex *Eira* 1981

75800 **FORT POINT** Br/Ne ('De Hoop') 1968; C; 4400; 110.42 × 6.85 (362.27 × 22.47); 12.5; ex *Dunvegan Head* 1977
Sister:
75801 **BEACON POINT** (Br) ex *Duncansby Head* 1976

75810 **WILMINGTON** Br/Br (Hall, Russell) 1969; B; 5700; 124.96 × 7.71 (410.01 × 25.3); M (B&W); 13

★ 75820 **SUTOMORE** Ys/Fr (Loire-Normandie) 1958; O; 6100; 130.16 × 7.67 (427 × 25.16); M (KHD); 13; ex *La Colina* 1974

75830 **VALANI** Cy/Br (Grangemouth) 1968; Con; 1600; 98.48 × 4.85 (323.1 × 15.91); M (MAN); 16; ex *Cervantes;* Converted from cargo & lengthened 1970
Sister:
75831 **CONTMAR** (Pa) ex *Churruca*

● 75840 **LADY M A CROSBIE** Ca/Br (Doxford & S) 1966; Con; 4000; 118.73 × 6.5 (389.53 × 21.33); M (MAN); 14.75; ex *Cortes* 1978; ex *Baltic Vanguard* 1977; Converted from cargo 1977 (Middle Docks)

75850 **THE LADY PATRICIA** Br/Br (Hill) 1962; C/Tk; 1300; 64.93 × 4.59 (213.02 × 15.06); M (British Polar); 11; Modernised 1974 (Hill)

75860 **LLOYD BERMUDA** Cy/Fi (Reposaaren) 1972; Con; 800; 78.01 × 4.16 (256 × 13.65); M (Atlas-Mak); 15; ex *Nedlloyd Bermuda* 1983; ex *Craigwood* 1982

● 75870 **STEYR** As/Ne (Bijlholt) 1974; B; 2200; 63.61

× 6.54 (208.7 × 21.46); M (Normo); 11; ex *Monitor* 1982; ex *Caroline Weston* 1982; ex *Frendo Grace* 1976; May now be lengthened
Sisters (may be lengthened):
75871 MUR (As) ex *Agate Prosperity* 1982; ex *Atlantic Prosperity* 1982; ex *Frendo Danship* 1977
75872 MAROI (As) ex *Agate Pioneer* 1982; ex *Atlantic Pioneer* 1982; ex *Danboat* 1978
75873 MATTUN (As) ex *Gretchen* 1982; ex *Gretchen Weston* 1982; ex *Frendo Star*
75874 PATZIEL (As) ex *Louise* 1982; ex *Louise Weston* 1982; ex *Frendo Faith* 1976
Similar (some Gr built—United SY):
75875 ANNA DRENT (Ne)
75876 CHANTENAY (Fr)
75877 AGIOS SPYRIDONAS (Cy) ex *Agios Spyridon* 1982; Launched as *Frendo Venture*
Similar (lengthened):
75878 CARIB (Cy) ex *Frendo Carib* 1977; ex *Frendo United* 1976
75879 NORNED THOR (Ne) ex *Holberg* 1979; ex *Atlantic Progress* 1977
75880 LITZEN (As) ex *Wendy M* 1983; ex *Wendy Weston* 1982; ex *Frendo Spirit* 1976
75881 MONZABON (As) ex *Agate Progress* 1982; ex *Panstar* 1982; ex *Danstar*
75882 RENDL (As) ex *Barbara M* 1983; ex *Barbara Weston* 1982; ex *Frendo Pride* 1976
75883 SALZACH (As) ex *Hilary M* 1983; ex *Hilary Weston* 1982; ex *Frendo Hope* 1976

75890 KATHLEEN Li/Sp ('Corbasa') 1970; Con; 3200; 99.73 × 6.37 (327.2 × 20.9); M (Deutz); 14.5; ex *Fortuna* 1975; ex *Manchester Merit* 1972; ex *Manchester Merito* 1970; Launched as *Catalina Del Mar*
Similar:
75891 BOX TRADER (Gr) ex *Frontier*
75892 ST. ANN'S BAY (Li) ex *Progress* 1981; ex *Ville D'Orient* 1980; ex *Progress* 1979; ex *Cheshire Progress*; ex *Stadt Elsfleth* 1976; Launched as *Magdalena Del Mar*

75900 SEA HAWK Sg/Br (Appledore) 1973; Con; 2500/5300; 112.1 × 5.74/6.38 (367.78 × 18.8/20.93); M (Pielstick); 15.5; ex *Manchester Zeal* 1981; ex *Cargo Zeal* 1976; ex *Manchester Zeal* 1975
Sister:
75901 VILLE D'ORIENT (Fr) ex *Manchester Vigour* 1980; ex *Cargo Vigour* 1976; ex *Manchester Vigour* 1975

75910 LONDONBROOK Br/Ne (Kramer & Booy) 1975; C; 1600; 93.6 × 5.64 (307.09 × 18.5); M (Smit & Bolnes); 13; ex *Towerstream* 1979; ex *Londonbrook* 1977
Sister (Br flag):
75911 LANCASTERBROOK ex *Chelseastream* 1979; ex *Lancasterbrook* 1977
Similar:
75913 MARIE (Sw) ex *Junior Lotte* 1983; (fitted with small travelling crane)
75915 NOVA (Sw) ex *Junior Lotte* 1983; (small travelling crane)

75920 BIRLING Br/Br (Clelands) 1977; C; 1600; 91.22 × 5.45 (299 × 17.88); M (Mirrlees Blackstone); 14
Sister:
75921 EMERALD (Br)
75922 HARTING (Br)
75923 STEYNING (Br)

75930 HELENA FRG/Ne (Van Diepen) 1972; C; 1600; 87.46 × 5.45 (286.94 × 17.88); M (Atlas-MaK); 12; ex *Whitegate* 1982
Sisters:
75931 MOIDART (Br)
75932 MINGARY (Br)
75933 BIRTA (FRG) ex *Regent's Park* 1983
Possible sisters:
75934 MARIA (FRG) ex *Highgate* 1982
75935 BONA FE (Fi) ex *Norrstal* 1977

75940 WESTSTREAM Br/Ne ('Volharding') 1971; C; 1000; 71.43 × 4.49 (234.35 × 14.73); M (Atlas-MaK); 12; ex *Osteturm* 1983

★**75950 COMANDANTE VILO ACUNA** Cu/Sp (Musel) 1977; Cem; 1800; 81.46 × 5.11 (267.26 × 16.77); M (Deutz); 12

★**75960 JUAN DE DIOS FRAGA MORENA** Cu/De (Frederikshavn) 1970; Tk/AT; 500; 70.67 × 3.39 (231.86 × 11.12); M (KHD); 12; ex *Charlottenborg* 1974
Sister:
★**75961 ELPEDIO BEROVIDES** (Cu) ex *Christiansborg* 1976
Similar:
75962 ISLAND KING (Pa) ex *Aggersborg*

75970 URRIDAFOSS Ic/De (Frederikshavn) 1971;

C; 500; 76.61 × 3.47 (251.35 × 11.38); M (Alpha-Diesel); 12; ex *Merc Europa* 1974; Travelling cranes. Starboard side of superstructure differs—see inset
Sisters:
75971 ASMAA (Mo) ex *Merc Phoenecia* 1977
75972 MERIEM (Mo) ex *Eco Sado* 1981; ex *Merc Asia* 1973
75973 ECO TEJO (Po) ex *Merc Continental* 1973
75974 GRUNDARFOSS (Ic) ex *Merc Australia* 1974
75975 NEXUS (Pa) ex *Albert S* 1978; ex *Nordsee* 1977; ex *Merc Groenlandia* 1974

75990 VANDA Ne/Ne (Gruno) 1974; C; 1500; 78.77 × 5.02 (258.43 × 16.47); M (Appingedammer Brons); 12
Sister:
75991 VICTORY (Ne)
Similar:
75992 VANESSA (Ne)

76000 TUVINA Br/Ne ('Hoogezand' JB) 1972; C; 1400; 78.01 × 4.92 (255.94 × 16.14); M (Smit & Bolnes); —; ex *Tuvana* 1983

76010 KORTINA Br/Pd (Gdanska) 1968; C; 1500; 82.17 × 4.89 (269.59 × 16.04); M (Atlas-MaK); —; ex *Kortenaer* 1984; ex *Hovin* 1971; **'B-459'** type; Lengthened 1973

76020 VISCOUNT Ne/Ne (Gruno) 1976; C; 1000; 65.84 × 4.29 (216.01 × 14.07); M (Appingedammer Brons); 13
Sister:
76021 VELOX (Ne)

76030 CARMEN DEL MAR Sp/Sp (Construcciones SA) 1970; Con; 2800; 88.22 × 5 (289.44 × 16.4); M (Stork-Werkspoor); 12; ex *Isla Del Mediterraneo* 1974
Sisters:
76031 LUISA DEL CARIBE (Pa) ex *Isla del Atlantico* 1982
76032 RATANA BHUM (Th) ex *Ming Chun* 1981; ex *Echuca* 1976; Launched as *Ardan*

76040 MINA COTO Sp/Sp (Juliana) 1972; C; 3800; 108.21 × 6.62 (355.02 × 21.72); M (Stork-Werkspoor); 13.25
Sister:
76041 DYSTOS (Gr) ex *Mina Entrego* 1981

76050 PROCYON Ne/Ne (Gruno) 1977; C; 1400; 66.53 × 5.2 (218.27 × 17.06); M (MWM); 11

76060 MIN LIE Tw/FRG (Schlichting) 1968; Con; 1500; 78.06 × 3.62 (256.1 × 11.88); M (Atlas-MaK); —; ex *Pacific Despatcher* 1982; ex *Kildare* 1974

76070 EXTRAMAR NORTE Sp/Sp (Celaya) 1976; C; 1200; 77.02 × 4.52 (252.69 × 14.83); M (Atlas-MaK); 11
Sister (Sp flag):
76071 EXTRAMAR ESTE
Similar (Sp Flag):
76072 EXTRAMAR OESTE
76073 EXTRAMAR SUR
Possible sisters (Sp Flag):
76074 CATALINA DEL MAR
76075 MARIONA DEL MAR

76080 MYRIAM DEL TORO Sp/Sp (Celaya) 1972; C/Con; 800; 61.65 × — (202.26 × —); M (MAN); 11.5
Sisters (Sp flag):
76081 BEGONA DEL MAR
76082 JOSE ESQUIVEL
76083 SANTURIO
76084 LOLA DEL MAR
76085 PILAR DEL MAR
76086 SOMIO
76087 JUAN CARLOS TORO (Sp)
76088 NORTHUMBRIA ROSE (Br) ex *Kielder Stag* 1978; ex *Begona De Astobiza* 1975
Similar (smaller):
76089 ASTONDO (Sp)
76090 MOUNTCREST (Br) ex *Anzoras* 1976
76091 CAPECREST (Br) ex *Akorda* 1976

76100 ESTHER DEL MAR Sp/Sp (Musel) 1971; Con; 2000; 79.94 × 5.65 (262.27 × 18.54); M (Deutz); 13; ex *Manchester Rapido* 1977; Launched as *Esther Del Mar*
Sisters:
76101 DIEGO NABOU (Sp) ex *Mercedes del Mar* 1982
76102 BEATRIZ DEL MAR (Sp)
76103 NAVY PROGRESS (Gr) ex *Folita* 1982; ex *Manchester Mercurio* 1980

76110 CAREBEKA VIII Ne/Ne ('Friesland') 1976; C; 1600; 81.01 × 5.38 (265.78 × 17.65); M (Polar); 12.5
Sister:
76111 ELSBORG (Ne) ex *Carebeka IX* 1983

76120 FLORIDA STAR Pa/Sp (Cadagua) 1976; C; 1600; 82.1 × 5.44 (269.36 × 17.85); M (Deutz); 11.5 ex *Fer Baltico* 1981

Sister:
76121 FER BALEAR (Sp)

76130 BEEDING Br/Sw (Falkenbergs) 1971; C 1600; 87.03 × 4.96 (285.53 × 16.27); M (Appingedammer Brons); 12

76140 LUMINENCE Br/Br (Clelands) 1977; C; 1600; 91.24 × 5.15 (299.34 × 16.9); M (British Polar); 13
Sister:
76141 KINDRENCE (Br)

76150 DAUNT ROCK Ih/Br (Hancocks) 1976; C; 800; 64.01 × 3.8 (210.01 × 12.47); M (Mirrlees Blackstone); 11
Sisters (Ih flag):
76151 SKELLIG ROCK
76152 FASTNET ROCK
Possible similar (Ih Flag):
76153 TUSKAR ROCK

76160 HAJE NAIME Cy/Ne (van der Werf) 1971; Con; 2100/3600; 105.92 × 5.49/6.36 (347.51 × 18.01/20.87); M (KHD); 14.5; ex *Violette* 1983; ex *Haje Naime* 1983; ex *Brathay Fisher*; ex *Calderon* 1979; ex *Brathay Fisher* 1976

76170 FORMOSA CONTAINER Pa/Sp (Construcciones SA) 1973; Con; 3100; 104.53 × 4.73 (342.95 × 15.52); M (MAN); 16.75; ex *American Islander* 1979; ex *American Ming* 1977
Sisters:
76171 MARINE CONTAINER (Pa) ex *American Comanche* 1980; ex *American Mist* 1978
76172 STRAIT CONTAINER (Li) ex *American Main* 1978

●**76180 NAUTILUS** Ne/Ne ('Voorwaarts') 1975; C; 1600; 81.67 × 5.38 (267.95 × 17.65); M (Smit & Bolnes); 12.5; ex *Antiklea* 1982; ex *Alstertal* 1981; ex *Tell* 1977
Similar (Ne flag):
76181 BARENDSZ
76182 VEERHAVEN

76190 FENJA Ne/Ne (Stroobos) 1977; C; 1600; 81.01 × 5.38 (265.78 × 17.65); M (Alpha-Diesel); 12.5; ex *Tina Howerda* 1977

76191 SELENA FRG/FRG (Hegemann) 1982; C (sea/river); 1000; 80.29 × 4.25 (263 × 13.94); M (KHD); 11
Sisters:
76192 LENA-S (FRG)
76193 SIMONE (FRG)

●**76195 JOHANNA V** Br/Ne ('Voorwaarts') 1980; C; 970; 65.72 × 4.32 (215.62 × 14.17); M (Atlas-MaK); 11.25
Similar (with lifeboats):
76196 SARAH WESTON (Br)
76197 ALANNAH WESTON (Br)

●**76200 ALICIA** FRG/FRG (Sietas) 1970; C; 1000; 73.84 × 5.04 (242.26 × 16.54); M (KHD); 12.5; ex *Alicia D* 1975; ex *Alicia* 1972

76210 TAKARI 1 Ia/FRG (O & K) 1966; C; 2300; 94.9 × 5.26 (311.35 × 17.26); M (MAN); 12.5
Sisters (Ia flag):
76211 TAKARI II
76212 TAKARI III
76213 TAKARI IV
76214 TAKARI V
76215 TAKARI VI
76216 TAKARI VII
76217 TAKARI VIII

★**76220 STAROGARD GDANSKI** Pd/Sp (Construcciones SA) 1971; RoC; 1000; 79.33 × 4.7 (260.27 × 15.42); M (Stork-Werkspoor); 14; ex *Cometa* 1973; Stern door **'Porter'** type
Sister:
76221 CHERCHELL (Ag) ex *Ardan* 1974

76230 ODET Fr/FRG (Buesumer) 1975; WT/Ch; 1600; 90.1 × 5.72 (295.6 × 18.77); M (Atlas-MaK); 13.5
Sister:
76231 RHONE (Sd)

76240 ISMARA Ag/FRG (Schlichting) 1978; Tk/WT; 2000; 87.76 × 5.72 (287.93 × 18.77); M (Atlas-MaK); 13.5
Sisters (Ag flag):
76241 DAHRA
76242 ZACCAR

★**76250 DA QING No 216** RC/Ma (Malta DD) 1978; Tk; 3900; 106.28 × 6.88 (348.69 × 22.57); M (B&W); 13
Sisters:
★**76251 DA QING No 217** (RC)
★**76252 DA QING No 218** (RC)

76260 **CLERVILLE** Fr/Fr (La Rochelle) 1975; Tk/WT; 1600; 91.01 × 5.39 (298.6 × 17.68); M (Atlas-MaK); 14.5

76270 **LEMAN** Sd/FRG (Brand) 1965; Tk/WT; 1600; 79.51 × 5.99 (260.86 × 19.65); M (KHD); 13.5; ex *Stainless Anne*; ex *Danelake*; ex *Nordenhamersand* 1972; Converted from cargo 1974

76280 **RIVER SHANNON** Br/Br (Cochrane) 1970; Tk; 1600; 83.52 × 5.13 (274.02 × 16.83); M (Appingedammer Brons); 12; ex *Steersman* 1976

76290 **POINTSMAN** Br/Br (Goole) 1970; Tk; 2900; 99.29 × 6.17 (325.75 × 20.24); M (English Electric); 12

76300 **PHILIP BROERE** Ne/Ne (Groot & VV) 1971; Tk/Ch; 1300; 81.11 × 4.97 (266.11 × 16.31); M ('De Industrie'); 13

★76310 **ALTAIR** Ru/It (Solimano) 1970; Tk/WT; 1200; 68.92 × 4.6 (226.12 × 15.09); M (MWM); 12
Sister:
★76311 **ARKTUR** (Ru)

76320 **LADY MARIANNA** It/FRG (Elsflether) 1964; Tk; 1000; 64.57 × 5.19 (211.84 × 17.03); M (KHD); 12.25; ex *Heinrich Essberger* 1975

76340 **MARE LIBERUM** Ne/Ne (Nieuwe Noord) 1964; Tk/Ch; 800; 76.08 × 4.19 (249.61 × 13.75); M (Smit & Bolnes); 11; Lengthened and deepened 1971
Sisters:
76341 **VASILIOS V** (Gr) ex *Mare Iratum* 1983
76342 **MARE SILENTUM** (Ne)

76350 **NERVA** Sp/Sp (Cantabrico) 1976; Ch; 700; 62.21 × 4.23 (204.1 × 13.88); M (Deutz); 11.5
Sister:
76351 **NIEBLA** (Sp)

76360 **AUDACITY** Br/Br (Goole) 1968; Tk; 700; 72.6 × 4.4 (238.19 × 14.44); M (KHD); —

76370 **KINGSABBEY** Br/Br (Burntisland) 1966; LGC; 700; 56.7 × 3.43 (186.02 × 11.25); M (Davey, Paxman); 11.5; ex *Rudi M* 1980; ex *Teviot*

76380 **CARIBGAS V** Pa/Fr (Duchesne & B) 1963; LGC; 1200; 62.03 × 4.27 (203.51 × 14.01); M (MAN); 12; ex *Celia* 1979; ex *Celsius* 1976

76390 **PASS OF DRUMOCHTER** Br/Ne (Ysselwerf) 1974; Ch; 1600; 80.75 × 5.56 (264.93 × 18.24); M (Mirrlees Blackstone); 13.5
Sister:
76391 **PASS OF DIRRIEMORE** (Br)

76400 **THUNTANK 7** Sw/Sw (Falkenbergs) 1967; LGC; 1200; 72.95 × 5.17 (239.34 × 16.96); M (KHD); 12.5; ex *Thungas* 1975; ex *Thungas 1* 1974; ex *Porsgrunn* 1974

76410 **MARE NOVUM** Ne/No (Karmsund) 1977; Ch; 1600; 83.01 × 5.91 (272.34 × 19.4); M (Smit & Bolnes); 13
Sisters (Ne flag):
76411 **MARE BONUM**
76412 **MARE MAGNUM**

76415 **HAI** FRG/FRG (Sieghold) 1981; Tk; 1600; 86.70 × 5.76 (284 × 18.90); M (Krupp); 12.5
Sisters (FRG flag):
76416 **LACHS**
76417 **STINT**
76418 **WELS**

76420 **ALCHIMIST ROTTERDAM** Cy/Sw (Kalmar) 1973; Ch; 1600; 85.86 × 5.4 (281.69 × 17.72); M (Alpha-Diesel); 13.5; ex *Chemaphrodite* 1980; ex *Alchimist Marathon* 1979; ex *Alchimist Rotterdam* 1978; ex *Chimiste Nantes* 1977
Sisters:
76421 **MULTITANK FRISIA** (Sg) ex *Ofrisia* 1974; ex *Frisia* 1973; ex *Monsun* 1972
76422 **MULTITANK HOLSATIA** (Sg) ex *Holsatia* 1974
Possibly similar:
76423 **POINTE DU ROC** (Fr)
76424 **POINTE DU VAN** (Fr) ex *Pointe De Penharn*

76430 **ALCHIMIST LUBECK** Cy/FRG (Menzer) 1970; Ch; 1600; 87.03 × 5.1 (285.53 × 16.73); M (Atlas-MaK); 12.5
Possible sister:
76431 **ALCHIMIST FLENSBURG** (Cy) ex *Chemathene* 1980; ex *Alchimist Flensburg* 1979

76440 **PIC ST LOUP** Fr/FRG (Menzer) 1974; WT; 1600; 89.24 × 5.26 (192.78 × 17.26); M (Atlas-MaK);

—

76450 **ASTRAMAN** Br/Br (Cochrane) 1973; Ch; 1600; 87.41 × 5.5 (286.74 × 18.04); M (Ruston Paxman); 14
Sister:

76451 **POLARISMAN** (Br)

76460 **ERIKA BOJEN** FRG/FRG (M. Jansen) 1978; C (sea/river); 500; 81.62 × 3.28 (267.78 × 10.76); M (MWM); 11; Hinged masts
Sister (FRG flag):
76461 **KONIGSEE**

76470 **CONDOR** FRG/FRG (Sietas) 1978; C (sea/river) 900; 73.11 × 3.4 (239.86 × 11.15); M (KHD); 11; Hinged masts
Sister:
76471 **ANGELA JURGENS** (FRG)

76472 **DEIKE** FRG/FRG (Sietas) 1981; C (sea/river); 1000; 87.97 × 4.67 (289 × 15.32); M (KHD); 11.5; Type 110
Sisters (FRG flag):
76473 **CAROLA**
76474 **HELGA**
76475 **MARGARETHA**
76476 **JULE**
76477 **CATHARINA**
76478 **SVENJA**
76479 **NIEDERELBE**
76479/1 **TINI**
76479/2 **COMET**
76479/3 **ILKA**
76479/4 **KATJA**
76479/5 **SEA WESER**
76479/6 **SEA ESTE** ex *Esteburg* 1983

●76480 **BIELEFELD** FRG/Ne (Kramer & Booy) 1973; C (sea/river); 900; 80.02 × 3.18 (262.53 × 10.43); M (Liebknecht); 10; ex *Cargo Liner I* 1981
Sister:
76481 **MARIA** (Ne) ex *Pia* 1982; ex *Cargo-Liner II* 1981
Possible sisters:
76482 **FARNESE** (Br) ex *Amy* 1983; ex *Cargo-Liner III* 1982
76483 **MANJA** (Ne) ex *Uelzen* 1982; ex *Cargo-Liner IV*
76484 **INEZ V** (Pa) ex *Cargo-Liner V* 1981
76485 **TERSCHELLING** (Ne) ex *Cargo-Liner VI* 1981

★76490 **IVAN AIVAZOVSKIY** Ru/Ru ('61 Kommunar') 1963; FC; 6100; 130 × 7.17 (426.51 × 23.52); D-E (—); 16.5
Sisters (Ru flag):
★76491 **ALEKSEY VENETSIANOV**
★76492 **VIKTOR VASTNETSOV**
★76493 **ALEKSANDR IVANOV**
★76494 **VASILIY PEROV**
★76495 **ILYA REPIN**
★76496 **VASILIY POLENOV**
★76497 **MOLODAYA GVARDIYA**
★76498 **IMENI 61 KOMMUNARA**
★76499 **PIONER MURMANA**
★76500 **HANS POGELMANN**
★76501 **SEVERNYY VETER**
★76503 **DEMYAN KOROTCHENKO**
★76504 **MARSHALL ROKOSSOVSKIY**
★76505 **GORETS**
★76506 **ALMAZNYY**
★76507 **SIBIR**
★76508 **KONSTANTIN OLSHANSKIY**
★76509 **ARKHIP KUINDZHI**
★76510 **VIKTOR LYAGIN**
★76511 **IVAN SHISHKIN**
★76512 **VASILIY SURIKOV**
★76513 **ZOLOTOY ROG**
★76514 **KHUDOZHNIK S. GERASIMOV**
★76515 **PIONER VOLKOV**
★76516 **KAZIS PREYKSHAS**
★76517 **ULAN-UDE**
★76518 **POLYARNYE ZORI**
★76519 **KHUDOZHNIK DEYNEKA**
★76520 **KHUDOZHNIK VRUBEL**
★76521 **GRANITNYY**
★76522 **VASILIY VERESCHCHAGIN**
★76523 **IVAN KRAMSKOY**
★76524 **VALENTIN SEROV**
★76525 **KOSMONAUT GAGARIN**
★76526 **OBUKHOVSKAYA OBORONA**
★76527 **MARSHAL MALINOVSKIY**
★76528 **POLYARNYY KRUG**
(Bu flag):
★76529 **SLANCHEV BRIAG**
★76530 **ZLANTNI PIASATZI**
★76531 **LAZUREN BRIAG**
★76532 **ALBENA**
★76533 **KITEN**
(DDR flag):
★76534 **EVERSHAGEN**
★76535 **LUTTENKLEIN**
(Rm flag):
★76536 **POLAR I**
★76537 **POLAR II**

76560 **GIANNIS DIMAKIS III** Gr/FRG (Norderwerft) 1956; C; 1000; 67.09 × 5.15 (220.11 × 16.9);

M (KHD); 11; ex *Pollendam* 1977; ex *Victor* 1971; ex *Vormann Rass* 1966

★76570 **COMBATE DE PALMAMOCHA** Cu/Sw (Solvesborgs) 1957; C; 487; 65.94 × 3.77 (216.34 × 12.37); M (Alpha-Diesel); 12; ex *Cora* 1964

★76580 **ABRAM ARKHIPOV** Ru/Fi (Nystads) 1973; C/TC; 3200; 97.31 × 6.7 (319.26 × 21.98); M (B&W); 14
Sisters (Ru flag):
★76581 **VLADIMIR FAVORSKIY**
★76582 **MITROFAN GREKOV**
★76583 **VASILIY POLENOV**
★76584 **NIKOLAY YAROSHENKO**
★76585 **NIKOLAY KASATKIN**
★76586 **KONSTANTIN YUON**
★76587 **IGOR GRABAR**
★76588 **IVAN SHADR**
★76589 **MIKHAIL CHEREMNYKH**
★76590 **VERA MUKINA**
★76591 **YEKATERINA BELASHOVA**

76600 **GEVISA** It/FRG (Rolandwerft) 1966; C; 500; 69.96 × 5.46 (229.53 × 17.91); M (MaK); 12; ex *Kotibe* 1977; ex *Edda Buur* 1974; ex *Elba* 1971
Sisters:
76601 **CEDROS** (Po) ex *Ibiza* 1972
76602 **GORGULHO** (Po) ex *Mallorca* 1972
76603 **LIMA** (Po) ex *Korsika* 1972
76604 **SINNO M.E. V** (Le) ex *Dina R E* 1981; ex *Malta* 1971
76605 **RENEE R E** (Fr) ex *Kreta* 1971

76610 **ISELTAL** As/Hu (Angyalfold) 1964; C; 1600; 84.44 × 4.93 (277.03 × 16.17); M (Lang Gepgyar); 11.5; ex *Bulk Merchant* 1983; ex *Fleur* 1980; ex *Mariam* 1974; ex *Fofo*; ex *George X* 1972; ex *Sagaland* 1971; Lengthened 1976
Sisters:
76611 **OETZTAL** (As) ex *Bulk Pioneer* 1983; ex *Ixia* 1980; ex *Garorm* 1974; ex *Irene* 1973; ex *Nicholas X* 1972; ex *Sagahorn* 1971
76612 **ZILLERTAL** (As) ex *Bulk Trader* 1983; ex *Primrose* 1980; ex *Gyram* 1974; ex *Pauline* 1973; ex *Patricia X* 1972; ex *Sagafjell* 1971

●76630 **CHEMIK** Pd/Pd (Szczecinska) 1965; C/B; 7500/10600; 156.67 × 8.11/8.86 (514.01 × 26.61/29.07); M (Sulzer); 14.25; 'B512' type
Probable sister:
76631 **KARUNA** (Sr) ex *Energetyk* 1983

★76640 **RUCIANE** Pd/Pd (Wisla) 1972; C; 800; 59.62 × 4.20 (195.6 × 13.78); M (Sulzer); 11.5; 'B457' type; Probably altered now—like 'BARLIN-EK'—which see

76650 **PIAVE** It/It (Odero) 1973; A/Wa; 5000 Dspl

76660 **NADIA 2** Pa/Br (Laing) 1963; Tk; 1400; 74.73 × 4.67 (245.18 × 15.32); M (Nydqvist & Holm); 11.5; ex *Pass of Glenclunie* 1983

76680 **DUTCH SAILOR** Ne/Ne (Groot & VV) 1966; Tk/Ch; 600; 65.38 × 3.74 (214.5 × 12.27); M (KHD);-; Lengthened 1971
Sister:
76681 **DUTCH MATE** (Ne)

76700 **PACIFIQUE** Fr/Br (Upper Clyde) 1970; D; 7300; 131.68 × 7.49 (432.02 × 24.57); TSM (Smit & Bolnes); 13

76710 **SAINT MITRE** Fr/It (Pellegrino) 1965; Tk; 2700; 99.57 × 6.07 (326.67 × 19.91); M (Fiat); —; Launched as *Sisina Pellegrino*

76720 **UNYO MARU** Ja/Ja (Uraga Dock) 1959; Cem; 5700; 127.06 × 7.42 (416.86 × 24.34); M (Sulzer); 11.5
Possibly similar:
76721 **ZUIYO MARU** (Ja)
76722 **GULFCEM** (Pa) ex *Kyuyo Maru* 1975

76730 **FRECCIA BLU** It/It (Breda) 1970; RoC; 5700; 163.96 × 5.98 (537.93 × 19.62); TSM (Fiat); 21; Stern doors; Lengthened 1977
Sister:
76731 **FRECCIA ROSSA** (It) (extra superstructure on foredeck)

76740 **GRIEG** Fr/Ne (Boele's Sch.) 1972; RoC; 4000; 138.26 × 7.01 (453.61 × 23); M (Stork-Werkspoor); 18.5; Stern door
Sister:
76741 **SIBELIUS** (Fr)

76745 **ARCTURUS** Fi/Fi (Rauma-Repola) 1982; RoC/Con; 8400; 155.02 × 8.46 (509 × 27.76); M (Pielstick); 18.5; stern door/ramp
Similar (Fi flag):
76746 **FINNMERCHANT**
76747 **OIHONNA**

76750 **NAVARCO** Fr/Fr (Havre) 1972; RoC; 500;

100.51 X 3.99 (329.76 × 13.09); TSM (MAN); 17.5; ex *Montlhery;* Stern door
Sisters:
76751 **ION** (Pa) ex *Monaco* 1983
76752 **KALIDORA** (Pa) ex *Monza* 1983

76755 **CASTORP** FRG/FRG (Flender) 1982; RoVC; 1000; 89.52 × 4.26 (294 × 13.98); M (MaK); 13.5; Side door/ramp; stern door/ramp

● 76760 **ELK** Br/Ko (Hyundai) 1977; RoC; 5500; 151.01 × 7.32 (495.44 × 24.02); M (Pielstick); 18.5; Bow door/ramp; Stern door/ramp
Sisters:
76761 **CONSTELLATION ENTERPRISE** (Gr) ex *Merzario Ionia* 1981; ex *Stena Shipper* 1980; ex *Norsky* 1980
76764 **MERZARIO HISPANIA** (Ma) ex *Atlantic Project* 1981
76765 **STENA IONIA** (Ma) ex *Merzario Ionia* 1982; ex *Stena Ionia* 1981; ex *Atlantic Prosper* 1981
76766 **STENA GRECIA** (Br) ex *Merzario Grecia;* ex *Tor Felicia* 1978
76767 **STENA FREIGHTER** (Br) ex *Jolly Turchese* 1983; ex *Jolly Giallo* 1982; ex *Stena Freighter* 1982; ex *Merzario Ausonia* 1980
76768 **STENA CARRIER** (Br) ex *Jolly Smeraldo* 1983; ex *Jolly Bruno* 1982; ex *Stena Carrier* 1982; ex *Imparca Miami* 1981; ex *Stena Carrier* 1980; ex *Imparca Express I* 1980

76785 **BALTIC FERRY** Br/Ko (Hyundai) 1978; RoC; 6500; 151.01 × 7.32 (495 × 24.02); TSM (Pielstick); 17; ex *Stena Transporter* 1980; ex *Finnrose* 1980; *Stena Transporter* 1979; Stern door; Rebuilt 1980
Sister:
76786 **NORDIC FERRY** (Br) ex *Merzario Hispania* 1979; ex *Merzario Espana* 1978
Similar (lengthened):
76787 **HELLAS** (Cy) ex *Alpha Progress* 1979; ex *Stena Runner* 1977
76788 **STENA TRANSPORTER** (Cy) ex *Syria* 1983; ex *Alpha Enterprise* 1979

76790 **ROF BEAVER** Br/FRG (Kremer) 1971; RoC; 1000; 80.7 × 4.14 (264.76 × 13.58); M (Alpha-Diesel); 14; ex *Helga I* 1975; ex *Bibiana* 1973; ex *Monarch Fame* 1972; ex *Irish Fame* 1971; ex *Bibiana* 1971; Stern ramp

76800 **CALA GALDANA** Sp/Sp (Duro Felguera) 1974; RoC; 684; 75.01 × 4.27 (246.1 × 14.01); M (MWM); 14; ex *Rivamahon* 1982
Sister:
76801 **CALA PORTALS** (Sp) ex *Rivanervion* 1982

76810 **LYRA** US/FRG (Howaldts DW) 1977; RoC; 14200; 193.33 × 8.61 (634.28 × 28.25); M (MAN); 19; ex *Reichenfels* 1981; Slewing stern ramp; Stern door
Sister:
76811 **RADBOD** (FRG) ex *Norefjord* 1982; ex *Rheinfels* 1981
Similar (Ja built-Sasebo):
76812 **CYGNUS** (US) ex *Rabenfels* 1981
76813 **KONGSFJORD** (FRG) ex *Essen* 1981; ex *Rauenfels* 1980

76820 **ATLANTIC SONG** Sw/Fr (France-Gironde) 1967; RoC/Con; 14900; 223.02 × 915 (731.69 × 30.02); M (MAN); 21.5; Lengthened 1976; Stern door
Sister:
76821 **ATLANTIC STAR** (Br)

76830 **LYSAGHT ENTERPRISE** Au/Au (NSW Govt) 1973; RoC; 7600; 168.05 × 7.7 (551.34 × 25.26); M (MAN); 18; Lengthened 1977 (Note—drawing shows vessel before lengthening); Stern door
Sister:
76831 **LYSAGHT ENDEAVOUR** (Au)

76840 **NORDIC WASA** Sw/FRG (Lindenau) 1977; RoC; 5100; 144.48 × 6.7 (474.02 × 21.98); TSM (Atlas-MaK); 18.5; ex *Tana* 1983; ex *Project Wasa* 1981; ex *Merzario Gallia* 1981; Stern door

76850 **VILLE DE DUNKERQUE** Fr/Fr (Dunkerque-Normandie) 1978; RoC; 8700; 169.25 × 7.74 (555.2 × 25.3); M (Sulzer); 18.5; ex *Foss Dunkerque* 1981; ex *Ville De Dunkerque* 1979; Stern door/ramp; Side doors
Sister:
76851 **VILLE DU HAVRE** (Fr) ex *Foss Havre* 1981; ex *Ville Du Havre* 1979
Similar:
76852 **RO-RO MANHATTAN** (Fr)
76853 **RO-RO GENOVA** (Fr) ex *Qatar Express;* ex *Ro-Ro Genova*

76860 **CAP BENAT** Fr/Fr (Havre) 1977; RoC; 1600; 109.71×5.21 (359.94×17.09); TSM(Atlas-MaK); 16; Stern door/ramp
Sisters:
76861 **AL HOCEIMA** (Mo) ex *Cap Camarat* 1981

76862 **GYPTIS** (Fr) ex *Cap Lardier* 1983
76863 **ANWAL** (Mo) ex *Cap Taillat* 1981

76870 **BALDER HAREN** NA/Ne (Pattje) 1979; RoC; 1200; 93.9 × 3.53 (308.07 × 11.58); TSM (Polar); 15; ex *Balder Maracai* 1981; ex *Balder Haren* 1979; Stern door/ramp
Sister:
76871 **BALDER EMS** (NA)

76880 **RAAD** Si/Fr (Havre) 1969; RoC; 2100; 99.68 × 4.5 (327.03 × 14.76); TSM (Ruston & Hornsby); 15.5; ex *Monte Cinto* 1980; Stern door

★ 76890 **ALIOT** Ru/Fi (Rauma-Repola) 1970; WT/Ch; 3100; 93.88 × 6.5 (308.01 × 21.33); M (B&W); 14
Sisters (Ru flag):
★ 76891 **POLLUKS**
★ 76892 **PROTSION**

76895 **CORAL ESSBERGER** FRG/FRG (Buesumer) 1981; Ch; 1600; 81.31 × 5.34 (267 × 17.52); M (Krupp-MaK); 12.5
Sisters (FRG flag):
76896 **HELGA ESSBERGER**
76897 **LIESEL ESSBERGER**

★ 76900 **STAROGARD GDANSKI** Pd/Sp (Construcciones SA) 1971; RoC; 1000; 79.33 × 4.7 (260.27×15.42); M (Stork-Werkspoor); 14; ex *Cometa;* Stern door; 'Porter' type
Sister:
76901 **CHERCHELL** (Ag) ex *Ardan* 1974

76910 **BALTIC OSPREY** Br/FRG (Jadewerft) 1972; Con; 1000; 88.3 × 4.35 (289.7 × 14.27); M (MWM); 14; ex *Atlantic Viscount* 1977; ex *Nad Prince* 1975; ex *Kalkgrund* 1974
Similar (probably with shorter funnel):
76911 **STOLLER GRUND** (FRG)

76940 **FRIGO MURAT** Tu/No (Kleven) 1968; R; 1200; 81.44 × 3.8/5.02 (267.19 × 12.47/16.47); M (Bergens); 16; ex *Basto* 1982; ex *Frio Trader* 1973
Sister:
76941 **BORGO** (Fi) ex *Frio Carrier* 1973

76950 **DART EUROPE** Be/Be (Cockerill) 1970; Con; 31000; 231.55 × 10.08 (759.68× 33.07); M (Sulzer); 21
Sisters (Br flag):
76951 **C P AMBASSADOR** ex *Dart Atlantic* 1981
76952 **MANCHESTER CHALLENGE** ex *Dart America* 1981

76960 **ATLANTIC SONG** Sw/Fr (France-Gironde) 1967; RoC/Con; 14900; 223.02 × 9.15 (731.69 × 30.02) M (MAN); 21.5; Lengthened 1976; Stern door
Sister:
76961 **ATLANTIC STAR** (Br)

● 76970 **MADOURI** Cy/FRG (Meyer) 1966; RoC; 2260; 99.22×5.83 (325.52× 19.13); M (KHD); 13; ex *Moundra* 1977; ex *Salome* 1973; Lengthened 1969; Side doors; Stern door/ramp
Sisters:
76971 **FAST CARRIER** (Le) ex *Manara* 1982; ex *Al-Karim* 1982; ex *Cedre* 1981; ex *Alpha Conveyor* 1981; ex *Bellman* 1975; ex *Aida* 1972
★ 76973 **INSELSBERG** (DDR) ex *Berwald* 1974; ex *Otello* 1972; (deck house forward of bridge)

76980 **MINERAL MARCHIENNE** Be/Be (Cockerill) 1973; B; 35900; 234.8 13.27 (770.34 × 43.54); M (Sulzer); 16
Sister:
76981 **MINERAL ALEGRIA** (Be)
Possible sister:
76982 **TRADE UNITY** (Li) ex *Belgium* 1983; ex *Mineral Belgium*

★ 76984 **HUTA LENINA** Pd/Ja (Mitsubishi HI) 1976; B; 36200; 223.98 × 13.35 (735 × 43.80); M (Sulzer); 14.5; ex *Varamis* 1976
Sisters:
★ 76985 **HUTA KATOWICE** (Pd) Launched as *Vigan*
★ 76986 **HUA TONG HAI** (RC) ex *Vinstra* 1980
★ 76987 **KAN SU HAI** (RC) ex *Vesteroy* 1980

76990 **THEMIS** No/FRG (Rhein Nordseew) 1976; B; 64100; 272.32 × 16.08 (893.44 × 52.76); M (Sulzer); 16; ex *You're My Sunshine* 1983; ex *Fernsea* 1981
Sisters:
76991 **FARLAND** (Br) ex *Nawala* 1980; ex *Nawada;* ex *Fernbay*
76992 **JOSTELLE** (Br) ex *Estelle J* 1983; ex *Fernhill* 1981
76993 **ENDEAVOR** (Li) ex *Sealane;* ex *Fernlane* 1978
76994 **PAN YARD** (Ko) ex *Pan Young* 1982; ex *Sealeaf* 1980; ex *Fernleaf* 1978

76996 **LA PAMPA** Br/Br (Sunderland) 1982; B; 41900; 230.00 × 14.87 (755 × 48.79); M (B&W); 14

Sister:
76997 **LA CHACRA** (Br)

77000 **SEARADIANCE** Br/Br (Sunderland) 1977; B; 39200; 228.12 × 14.05 (748.43 × 46.1); M (Doxford); 15; ex *Orient City* 1978
Sister:
77001 **GALENE** (Gr) ex *Welsh City* 1983

● 77010 **BASALT** FRG/Hu (Angyalfold) 1970; C; 1500; 76.41 × 5.31 (250.69 × 17.42); M (MWM); 11.5; Lengthened 1975
Sisters:
77011 **ORCHID SEA** (Sg) ex *Diorit* 1983
77012 **ORCHID WAVE** (Sg) ex *Diabas* 1983
77013 **ORCHID MOON** (Sg) ex *Gabbro* 1983
77014 **ORCHID SUN** (Sg) ex *Granit* 1983
Similar (fitted with satellite communication aerial):
77015 **ORCHID STAR** (Sg) ex *Dolomit* 1983

77020 **ARISTEOS** Gr/Br (Robb Caledon) 1971; RoC; 3700; 117.48 × 6.32 (385.43 × 20.73); TSM (Pielstick); 17.5; ex *Caribbean Progress;* ex *Iranian Progress* 1976; ex *Caribbean Progress* 1975; May be spelt **ARISTAIOS;** Stern door
Sisters (FRG built):
77021 **SUCRE** (Ve) ex *Aristefs* 1981; ex *Caribbean Endeavour*

77030 **LEVERKUSEN EXPRESS** FRG/FRG (Howaldts DW)-FRG 1970/78; Con; 16700; 176.49 × 10.59 (579 × 34.74); M (MAN); —; ex *Leverkusen* 1978; Converted from general cargo, lengthened and widened 1978 (Bremer V)
Sisters (FRG flag):
77031 **ERLANGEN EXPRESS** ex *Incotrans Progress* 1982; ex *Erlangen Express* 1981; ex *Erlangen* 1979
77032 **HOECHST EXPRESS** ex *Incotrans Promise* 1982; ex *Hoechst Express* 1981; ex *Hoechst* 1978
77033 **LUDWIGSHAFEN EXPRESS** ex *Ludwigshafen* 1979

77040 **AL AHMADIAH** Ku/Ru (Nosenko)-Sp 1969/80; Con; 14400; 194.33 X 9.5 (637.57 × 31.17); M (B&W); 18.5; Converted from cargo ship of 'Feodosiya' type (AESA)
Sisters (Ku flag):
77041 **AL RUMAITHIAH**
77042 **AL SHAMIAH**

77043 **TFL ENTERPRISE** Sg/Ja (Hitachi) 1979; Con; 13900; 157.05× 9.19 (515 × 30.15); M (Sulzer); 18; ex *Alltrans Enterprise* 1982; ex *Incotrans Enterprise* 1982; ex *TFL Enterprise* 1981; ex *Alltrans Enterprise* 1980
Sisters (Sg flag):
77044 **TFL DEMOCRACY**
77045 **TFL EXPRESS** ex *Altrans Express* 1980
77046 **TFL FREEDOM**
77047 **TFL INDEPENDENCE**
77048 **TFL LIBERTY**

77050 **ENCOUNTER BAY** Br/FRG (Howaldts DW) 1969; Con; 26800; 227.31× 10.69 (745.77× 35.07); M (B&W); 18
Sisters (Br flag):
77051 **BOTANY BAY**
77052 **DISCOVERY BAY**
77053 **FLINDERS BAY**
77055 **MORETON BAY**

★ 77060 **ALEKSANDR FADEYEV** Ru/Ru (Kherson) 1973; Con; 6500; 130.21 × 7.5 (427 × 24.61); M (B&W); 17
Sisters (Ru flag):
★ 77061 **ALEKSANDR PROKOFYEV**
★ 77062 **ALEKSANDR TVARDOVSKIY**
★ 77063 **MIKHAIL PRISHVIN**
★ 77064 **MIKHAIL SVETLOV**

● 77067 **AMBROSIANA** FRG/FRG (Flensburger) 1980; Con; 15000; 170.21 × 9.65 (558.43× 31.66); M (MAN); 19; ex *TFL Washington;* Launched as *Ambrosia*
Sister (FRG flag):
77068 **TFL ADAMS**

★ 77080 **KHUDOZHNIK FEDOROVSKIY** Ru/Bu (G. Dimitrov) 1978; B; 15600; 185.22 × 10.1 (607.68 × 33.14); M (Sulzer); 15.25; This vessel may be fitted with 4 deck cranes. This could also apply to the sisterships
Sisters (Ru flag):
★ 77081 **KHUDOZHNIK A GERASIMOV**
★ 77082 **KHUDOZHNIK GABASHVILI**
★ 77083 **KHUDOZHNIK KASIYAN**
★ 77084 **KHUDOZHNIK KUSTODIYEV**
★ 77085 **KHUDOZHNIK TOIDZE**
★ 77086 **KHUDOZHNIK VLADIMIR SEROV**
★ 77087 **SOVIETSKIY KHUDOZHNIK**
(Bu flag):
★ 77088 **CHIPKA** (or **SHIPKA**)
★ 77089 **RILA**

★ 77089/1 **RODOPI**
★ 77089/2 **VITOCHA**
★ 77089/3 **MILIN KAMAK**
★ 77089/4 **SLAVIANKA**

77090 **GERRINGONG** Au/Au (Whyalla) 1965; O; 14500; 177.43 × 9.99 (582.02 × 32.78); M (Sulzer); 15; ex *Iron Gerringong* 1979; ex *Gerringong* 1977

77100 **RIO VERDE** Bz/Bz (Emaq) 1977; B; 21700; 193.86 × 10.9 (636.02 × 35.76); M (Sulzer); 16
Sister:
77101 **RIO NEGRO** (Bz)
Sisters (superstructure extended aft):
77102 **RIO BRANCO** (Bz)
77103 **RIO GRANDE** (Bz)

77110 **FIDES** It/It (Adriatico) 1964; B; 16100; 193.63 × 10.35 (635.27 × 33.96); M (Fiat); 16

77120 **JOLLY GRIGIO** Sg/Ja (Kawasaki) 1977; RoC/Tk/B; 9500; 143.85 × 7.8 (471.95 × 25.59); M (MAN); 14.75; ex *Bellman* 1981; **'Boro'** type
Sister:
77121 **JOLLY AMARANTO** (Sg) ex *Taube* 1981

77125 **TERTRE ROUGE** Fr/Fr (Graville) 1976; RoC; 1600; 100.52 × 4.15 (330 × 13.62); M (MaK); 15; Stern door
Similar:
77126 **HUNAUDIERES** (Fr)

77130 **GOLDEN FLAG** FRG/FRG (LF-W) 1972; B; 43500; 255.91 × 14.2 (839.6 × 46.59); M (MAN); 16; ex *Proserpina* 1981
Sister:
77131 **MADDALENA D'AMATO** (It) ex *Propontis* 1982
Similar (heavier Kingposts aft):
77132 **FJORD BULKER** (Pa) ex *Wiking Bulker* 1983; ex *Johann Schulte* 1978

● 77140 **LUTZ JACOB** FRG/Ih (Verolme Cork) 1973; B; 28100; 205.49 × 12.33 (674.18 × 40.52); M (MAN); 15.5
Sisters:
77141 **FJORD BRIDGE** (Pa) ex *Babette Jacob* 1982
77142 **FJORD MARINER** (Pa) ex *Margot Jacob* 1983
77143 **ROLF JACOB** (FRG)

77150 **ZEEBRUGGE** Be/Be (Cockerill) 1974; B; 37700; 224.01 × 13.09 (734.94 × 42.95); M (Sulzer); 15.5
Sisters (Be flag):
77151 **MARTHA**
77152 **KYOTO**
77153 **YAFFA**
77154 **RUTH**
Similar (In flag):
77155 **MARATHA MARINER**
77156 **MARATHA MELODY**
Possibly similar (larger):
77157 **VICTORIA PEAK** (Br) ex *Argosy Pacific* 1983
77158 **LEON & PIERRE C** (Be)

77160 **D C COLEMAN** Br/Ja (NKK) 1974; B; 69900; 260 × 16.79 (853.02 × 55.09); M (B&W); 15
Sisters (Br flag):
77161 **E W BEATTY**
77162 **W M NEAL**
77163 **OCEANIC CREST**

77170 **TIMUR LIGHT** Sg/Ja (Mitsubishi HI) 1973; B; 69900; 261.02 × 17.58 (856.36 × 57.68); M (Mitsubishi); 15.5; ex *Meynell* 1983; ex *Eyne* 1983; ex *Meynell*
Sister:
77171 **THEOKEETOR** (Gr) ex *Nordic Patriot* 1984; ex *Naess Patriot* 1974

● 77180 **GOOD LEADER** Gr/Ja (Mitsubishi HI) 1973; B; 59200; 261.02 × 17.62 (856.36 × 57.81); M (Sulzer); 14.75 ex *Elwood Mead* 1974
Sister:
77181 **TRENTWOOD** (Sg)

77190 **KATORI MARU** Ja/Ja (Sumitomo) 1973; B; 65300; 257.03 × 16.93 (843.27 × 55.54); M (Sulzer); 15.5

77193 **SAKAIDE MARU** Ja/Ja (Mitsubishi HI) 1982; B; 56500; 257.80 × 12.63 (846 × 41.44); M (MAN); 13.3

77195 **IKAN TONGKOL** Br/Ja (Mitsubishi HI) 1982; B; 76800; 270.01 × 16.72 (886 × 54.86); M (Sulzer); 14.5

77200 **CHIHIROSAN MARU** Ja/Ja (Mitsui) 1973; B; 63200; 259.82 × 15.62 (852.43 × 51.25); M (B&W); 15.25
Sisters (Ja flag):
77201 **CHITA MARU**
77202 **HOSHO MARU**

77203 **IBARAKI MARU**

77210 **JADE TRANSPORTER** Tw/Ja (Mitsubishi HI) 1970; B; 68000; 261.02 × 15.98 (856.36 × 52.43); M (Mitsubishi); 14.75; ex *Chikugo Maru* 1983
Similar (built 1975):
77211 **CHIKUHO MARU** (Ja)

● 77220 **SHINREI MARU** Ja/Ja (Mitsubishi HI) 1973; B; 68200; 260.99 × 16.38 (856.27 × 53.74); M (Mitsubishi); 15.25
Sister:
77221 **SHINZUI MARU** (Ja)
Similar:
77221/1 **JAPAN ACACIA** (Ja)
77222 **JAPAN POPLAR** (Ja)
77223 **GIBRALTAR PANSY** (Li) ex *Riko Maru* 1974
77224 **THEODORE A** (Li) ex *Tweedfield* 1978; ex *Tweed Bridge* 1978
Possibly similar:
77225 **GUAICURI** (Me) ex *Chokai Maru* 1983
77226 **SUPER STAR** (Ko) ex *Kasagisan Maru* 1982

77230 **SAMRAT ASHOK** In/Ja (Mitsubishi HI) 1974; B; 72600; 261.02 × 17.58 (856.36 × 57.68); M (Sulzer); 15.5; ex *Gautama Buddha* 1974

77240 **WEST DAORI** Pa/Ja (Mitsui) 1973; B; 64000; 260.03 × 16.45 (853.12 × 53.97); M (B&W); 16.5; ex *Polyviking* 1981

77250 **MARLIN** Li/Ja (Hitachi) 1977; BO; 9400; 155.15 × 6.86 (509.02 × 22.51); TSM (Polar); 13
Sister:
77251 **TARPON** (Li)

77260 **NACIONAL SINES** Po/Sp ('Astano') 1971; B; 30400; 210.75 × 12.15 (691.44 × 39.86); M (B&W); 15; ex *Manuel Yllera* 1981

77270 **NELSON MARU** Ja /Ja (Hayashikane) 1971; B; 17400; 165.11 × 9.72 (541.7 × 31.89); M (Pielstick); 14.75

77280 **BUNGA TEMBUSU** My/Ja (Sumitomo) 1972; BWC; 32300; 196.02 × 9.7 (643.11 × 31.82); M (Sulzer); 14.75
Sister:
77281 **BUNGA MELAWIS** (My)
Probably similar:
77282 **EASTERN WORLD** (Li)
77283 **VALENTINA** (Li)

77300 **SHINRYU MARU** Ja/Ja (IHI) 1971; O; 88800; 292.44 × 17.91 (959.45 × 58.76); M (Sulzer); 15.75
Possibly similar (may be H1):
77301 **SHIN-YU MARU** (Ja)

77310 **SHINYO MARU** Ja/Ja (Mitsui) 1973; O; 63100; 259.37 × 16.16 (850.95 × 53.02); M (B&W); 15

● 77320 **BROCKMAN** Li/Ja (Mitsui) 1974; O; 33900; 259.39 × 16.13 (851.02 × 52.92); M (B&W); 15
Sisters (Li flag):
77321 **MARRA MAMBA**
77322 **SEVEN TEAM** ex *Sevenseas Conqueror* 1979

77330 **NIIZURU MARU** Ja/Ja (Hitachi) 1971; O; 92100; 313.62 × 16.99 (1028.94 × 55.74); M (B&W); 15.75

77333 **RIVER ACE** Ja/Ja (Hitachi) 1982; B; 75500; 270 × 16.30 (886 × 53.48); M (B&W); 13.3

77335 **NEW VENTURE** Li/Ja (Mitsui) 1982; B; 59400; 263.02 × 16.48 (863 × 54.07); M (B&W); 14.5
Sisters:
77336 **KEPWAVE** (Sg)
77337 **CATHERINE VENTURE** (Li)
77338 **COAL STAR** (Li) ex *Coal Venture* 1983

★ 77340 **KHUDOZHNIK SARYAN** Ru/DDR (Warnow) 1975; Con; 17800; 169.63 × 9.2 (556.52 × 30.18); M (Sulzer); 20; **'Mercur'** type
Sisters (Ru flag):
★ 77341 **KHUDOZHNIK IOGANSON**
★ 77342 **KHUDOZHNIK PAKHOMOV**
★ 77343 **KHUDOZHNIK PROROKOV**
★ 77344 **KHUDOZHNIK REPIN**
★ 77345 **KHUDOZHNIK ROMAS**
★ 77346 **KHUDOZHNIK ZHUKOV**
★ 77347 **NADEZHDA OBUKHOVA**
★ 77348 **NIKOLAY GOLOVANOV**
★ 77349 **MAKSIM MIKHAYLOV**

77360 **HYOGO MARU** Ja/Ja (Kawasaki) 1973; RoC/Con; 9100; 181.74 × 8.98 (596.26 × 29.46); M (MAN); 21; Stern door
Similar (Au flag):
77361 **AUSTRALIAN SEAROADER**
Similar (lengthened by 29 metres):
77362 **AUSTRALIAN ENTERPRISE** (Au)
77363 **AUSTRALIAN EXPLORER** (Au) ex *Matthew Flinders* 1975

77370 **SAND SHORE** No/Sw (Finnboda) 1970; RoC; 2800; 112.71 × 6.82 (369.78 × 22.38); M (Atlas-MaK); 16; ex *Nopal Shore* 1977; ex *Mignon* 1974; Stern door

77380 **JOLLY ROSSO** It/Sw (Lodose) 1968; RoC; 2300; 100.72 × 6.59 (330.45 × 21.62); M (MWM); 15.25; ex *Claude Debussy* 1973; ex *Neva* 1971; ex *Arabella* 1969

77390 **GENEVE** Li/Ja (Tohoku) 1971; C/B; 3000; 85.83 × 7.45 (281.59 × 24.44); M (Hanshin); 11; **'Camit'** type
Sisters (Li flag):
77392 **HAMBURG**
77393 **GHENT**
77395 **TARRAGONA**
(NA flag):
77396 **EARLY BIRD** ex *Sete* 1973;
(Br flag):
77397 **MAWAN** ex *Bohol* 1983; ex *Saint Nazaire* 1981
77398 **STANLEY BAY** ex *Sulu* 1983; ex *Amsterdam* 1981

77400 **JULIANA** Pa/Be (Boelwerf) 1971; B; 36800; 234.75 × 13.2 (770.18 × 43.31); M (MAN); 15; ex *E R Brabantia* 1983
Sisters:
77401 **E R ANTVERPIA** (Be)
77402 **JAGAT SAMRAT** (In)

77420 **AEOLOS C** Pa/Br (Cammell Laird) 1966; B; 40800; 249.94 × — (820.01 × —); M (Sulzer); 15; ex *Yalta*; ex *Berge Siglion* 1973; ex *Siglion* 1971

77430 **CATHAY SEATRADE** Li/Sw (Oresunds) 1973; B; 35500; 224.06 × 13.1 (735.1 × 42.98); M (Gotaverken); 16; ex *Lili Billner* 1978

● 77440 **NEWAYS** Pa/Ys ('3 Maj') 1972; B; 40600; 243.75 × 12.91 (799.7 × 42.36); M (Sulzer); 15.5; ex *Maris Huntsman* 1981; ex *Ragna Gorthon* 1978
Sisters:
77441 **ROUNTON GRANGE** (Br) ex *Pacific Wasa* 1980
77442 **CASSIOPEIA** (Sw)
Similar (see inset):
77443 **OCEAN TRAVELLER** (Sg) ex *Birte Oldendorff* 1981
77444 **DORA OLDENDORFF** (Sg)
77445 **UNITED VENTURE** (Sg) ex *Helga Oldendorff* 1981
77446 **LUDOLF OLDENDORFF** (Sg)
Similar:
★ 77447 **SHI TANG HAI** (RC) ex *Dimitris A Lemos* 1980
Possibly similar:
77448 **CETRA NORMA** (Fr)

77460 **JESSIE STOVE** No/No (Fredriksstad) 1972; B; 60400; 265.62 × 15.78 (871.46 × 51.77); M (Sulzer); 15
Sisters:
77461 **GOOD ENDEAVOUR** (Li) ex *Ariel* 1982
77462 **NEGO VICTORIA** (No) ex *Olav Ringdal* 1978
Possibly similar:
77463 **BELCARGO** (No)
77464 **VIVA** (No) ex *Columbia* 1979

77470 **PORT LATTA MARU** Ja /Ja (Uraga HI) 1968; O; 50800; 249 × 14.15 (816.93 × 46.42); M (Sulzer); 15.25

★ 77480 **WEN DENG HAI** RC/Br (H&W) 1968; B; 41100; 251.47 × 14.26 (825.03 × 46.78); M (B&W); 16.5; ex *Essi Kristine* 1978
Sisters (RC flag):
★ 77481 **DEN LONG HAI** ex *Fjordaas* 1979
★ 77482 **LUO SHAN HAI** ex *Thara* 1978

77490 **PERINTHOS** Gr/Ja (IHI) 1968; B; 44800; 246.9 × 14.53 (810.04 × 47.67); M (Sulzer); 16; ex *Dorsetshire* 1983; ex *Atlantic Bridge* 1977
Sister:
77491 **PETINGO** (Gr) ex *Pacific Bridge* 1974

77500 **PANAMAX NOVA** Tw/Ja (Mitsui) 1967; B; 36900; 230 × 12.87 (754.59 × 42.22); M (B&W); 15.5; ex *Mikunisan Maru* 1983
Similar (Ja flag):
77501 **ROKKOHSAN MARU**
Similar (smaller) (Ja Flag):
77502 **MITSUI MARU**
77503 **TETSUZUI MARU**
77504 **MITSUI MARU No 2**

77510 **SEAGLOSS** Cy/Ja (NKK) 1968; B; 28400; 226.42 × 12.9 (742.85 × 42.32); M (Sulzer); 16.25; ex *Gungnir X* 1983; ex *Grischuna* 1980
Sister:
77511 **EASTERN GRACE** (Li) ex *Pampero* 1978

★77520 **BAO QING HAI** RC/Ja (Mitsubishi HI) 1971; O; 45800; 239.07 × 14.36 (784.35 × 47.11); M (Sulzer); 15.5; ex *Moslane* 1978
Sister:
77521 **MOSBROOK** (No)

77530 **SANTO DOMINGO** Do/FRG (Stuelcken) 1959; B; 9400; 150.96 × 9.2 (495.28 × 30.18); M (KHD); — ;ex *Pacsea* 1978; ex *Stad Gent* 1971; Launched as *Hans Berckmeyer*

77540 **AUSTRALIAN PROSPECTOR** Au/FRG (B+V) 1976; B; 74500; 282.07 × 16.43 (925.43 × 53.9); M (B&W); 15
Sister:
77541 **AUSTRALIAN PROGRESS** (Au)

77550 **MARQUES DE BOLARQUE** Sp/Sp (AESA) 1972; B; 44700; 256.22 × 14.44 (840.62 × 47.38); M (B&W); 15; May have deck cranes

77560 **MARE NORDICO** It/Pd (Gdynska) 1972; B; 33000; 220 × 12.43 (721.78 × 40.78); M (Sulzer); 15.75; ex *Viking* 1981; ex *Pearl Sea* 1976; ex *Hampton Bridge* 1974; 'B-521' type
Sister:
77561 **GLOBAL E SUN** (Ko) ex *Politechnika Szczecinska*; ex *Politechnika Gliwicka* 1974
Possible sisters (some may be like drawing no. 77840 which see):
77562 **SERRAI** (Gr) ex *Industry Trader*; ex *Jotunfjell* 1977
77563 **GENERAL GUISAN** (Sd) launched as *Londrina*
77565 **SOUTH PACIFIC** (Pa) ex *Konitsa* 1983; ex *Engiadina*; ex *Gunnar Carlsson* 1978
77567 **JANA PRIYA** (In)
Sisters (Rm built—Constantza and Galatz):
★77568 **BEIUS** (Rm)
★77569 **BICAZ** (Rm)
★77570 **BIRLAD** (Rm)
★77571 **BOCSA** (Rm)
★77572 **BORSEC** (Rm)
★77573 **BORZESTI** (Rm)
★77574 **BOTOSANI** (Rm)
★77575 **BREADZA** (Rm)
★77576 **BUHUSI** (Rm)
★77577 **CALLATIS** (Rm)
★77578 **TOMIS** (Rm)
★77578/1 **BLAJ** (Rm)
★77578/2 **BUZIAS** (Rm)
77579 **DANUBE SEA** (Pa)
77579/1 **ILONA** (Pa)
77579/2 **LEANDROS** (Gr)
77579/3 **TOMIS SEA** (Pa)
Similar:
77579/4 **MASOVIA** (Li)

77580 **TENOCH** Me/Pd (Gdynska) 1977; B; 39600; 251.16 × 12.35 (824.02 × 40.52); M (Sulzer); 15.25; ex *Knut Mark* 1981; 'B 526' type
Similar (Rm built—Constantza):
77581 **STAVROULA** (Pa)

77590 **TAKACHIHO** Br/Ja (Mitsubishi HI) 1968; B; 36100; 224.01 × 12.24 (735 × 40.16); M (Sulzer); 15; ex *Tolga* 1983; ex *Tonga* 1969
Similar:
77591 **TAKASAGO** (Br) ex *Tambo River* 1979; ex *Takasago* 1975
77592 **DERBY** (Gr) ex *Caloric* 1981
Similar (small crane aft):
77593 **TACHIBANA** (No)
77594 **TAKAMINE** (No)
77595 **MOUNT PARNASSOS** (Gr) ex *Takachiho* 1978

77600 **FUERTE VENTURA** FRG/FRG (A.G. 'Weser') 1970; B; 74600; 282.23 × 16.42 (925.95 × 53.87); M (MAN); 15; ex *Stadt Bremen* 1979

77610 **THALATTA** No/Ja (Mitsubishi HI) 1973; B; 65900; 261.02 × 16.5 (856.36 × 54.13); M (Sulzer); 15; ex *Yu Sing* 1983; ex *Erskine Bridge* 1982
Sister:
77611 **POHANG** (Ko) ex *Lake Almanor* 1983; ex *Severn Bridge* 1976
Similar:
77612 **TAGELUS** (Ne) ex *Stirling Bridge* 1979

77620 **PANAMAX SOLAR** Tw/Br (Furness) 1966; B; 40800; 249.94 × 13.36 (820.01 × 43.83); M (Sulzer); 15.5; ex *Panamax Uranus* 1984; ex *Nordic Trader* 1978; ex *Iron Parkgate* 1975; ex *Naess Parkgate* 1974

77630 **MAJESTY** Li/Ja (Kawasaki) 1972; B; 31900; 228.61 × 12.93 (750.03 × 42.42); M (MAN); 15

77640 **KONKAR INDOMITABLE** Gr/Ja (Mitsui) 1972; B; 39200; 259.52 × 13.61 (851.44 × 44.65); M (B&W); 16
Sister:
77641 **KONKAR VICTORY** (Gr)

77642 **KONKAR INTREPID** (Gr)

77650 **JHANSI KI RANI** In/Br (Lithgows) 1975; B; 42100; 245.37 × 13.83 (805.02 × 45.37); M (B&W); 15.25
Sisters (In flag):
77651 **JALAVIHAR**
77652 **KASTURBA**

77660 **AEGIR** FRG/FRG (Rhein Nordseew) 1968; B; 45800; 254.9 × 13.75 (836.29 × 45.11); M (MAN); 16
Sister:
77661 **BRAGE** (FRG)

77670 **GRAIGFFION** Br/Br (H&W) 1968; B; 57200; 260.61 × 14.8 (855.02 × 48.56); M (B&W); 15.25; ex *Energy Pioneer* 1983; ex *Mount Pelion* 1983; ex *Skaufast* 1978
Similar:
77671 **MEGA STAR** (Sr) ex *Aino* 1983
77672 **WEST JUNORI** (Ko) ex *Barbro* 1980
77673 **BELINDA** (Li)
77674 **GRAIGLAS** (Br) ex *Benwyvis* 1983; ex *Alnwick Castle* 1981
77675 **GLOBAL HOPE** (Ko) ex *Global Ambition* 1982; ex *Dunstanburgh Castle* 1981
77676 **SOUTH VICTOR** (Li) ex *Mount Newman* 1982
77677 **TECTUS** (Br) ex *Canadian Bridge* 1978

77680 **ESSI CAMILLA** No/Br (H&W) 1975; B; 63500; 261.53 × 16.2 (858.04 × 53.15); M (B&W); 15.5
Similar:
77681 **LACKENBY** (Br) ex *Otterpool* 1977
77681/1 **RAVENSCRAIG** (Br)
Possibly similar:
77682 **APPLEBY** (Br)

●77690 **GOOD HORIZON** Gr/De (Odense) 1967; B; 38600; 255.63 × 14.03 (838.68 × 46.03); M (Sulzer); 16.75; ex *Navios Patriot* 1981; ex *Leise Maersk* 1976
Sister:
77691 **GOOD TARGET** (Gr) ex *Navios Pioneer* 1981; ex *Louis Maersk* 1976

77700 **AKRON** Li/Sw (Uddevalla) 1972; B; 53100; 263.66 × 15.89 (865.03 × 52.13); M (B&W); 15.5; ex *Norse Lion* 1978
Sisters:
77701 **HORNCHURCH** (Br) ex *Delwind* 1982; ex *Constance* 1980
77702 **LOUSSIOS** (Gr) ex *Ronastar*
Similar:
77703 **ENTERPRISE** (Li) ex *Varangfjell*

77710 **ARGONAUT** Gr/Br (Doxford & S) 1968; B; 24900; 211.44 × 12.22 (693.7 × 40.09); M (Doxford); 15.75
Sister:
77711 **NEPHELE** (Gr) ex *G M Livanos* 1978

77720 **KOWLOON PEAK** Br/Br (Doxford & S) 1969; B; 31400; 220.99 × 12.62 (735.03 × 41.4); M (Doxford); 15; ex *Amber Pacific* 1983
Sister:
77721 **GOLDEAN ENTERPRISE** (Li) ex *August Pacific*

★77730 **LUO FU SHAN** RC/Sw (Eriksbergs) 1968; B; 29400; 217.58 × 12.82 (713.85 × 42.06); M (B&W); 14.75; ex *King Alfred* 1982; ex *Hemsefjell*
Similar:
77731 **LUCIANA DELLA GATTA** (It) ex *Eastern Charm* 1980; ex *Polyhymnia* 1979
Probably similar:
77732 **MARITSA** (Gr) ex *Orunda*

77740 **SUNDA CAREER** Pa/Ja (IHI) 1964; B; 24600; 191.01 × 10.9 (626.67 × 35.76); M (Sulzer); 14.5; ex *Fugo Maru* 1978

◗77750 **UNIMAR** Gr/Fr (La Seine) 1961; O; 10700; 165.92 × 9.58 (544.36 × 31.43); M (MAN); 14.5; ex *Laodice* 1972; ex *Pentellina* 1972

77770 **DURHAM** Br/Br (Furness) 1968; B; 35400; 246.59 × 14.47 (809.02 × 47.47); M (B&W); 16; ex *Yamato* 1982; ex *Har Addir* 1975
Sisters (Li flag):
77772 **GOSFORTH** ex *Mikasa* 1983; ex *Mount Katherina* 1974
77773 **MOUNT EDEN**

77780 **ALEXANDER STAR** Pa/FRG (Kieler H) 1967; B; 23700; 202.11 × 10.82 (663.09 × 35.5); M (Gotaverken); 16; ex *Steendorp* 1978; ex *Sognefjell* 1975
Sister:
77781 **OCEAN JADE** (Sg) ex *Omega* 1978; ex *Irongate* 1978; ex *Holtefjell* 1975
Similar (converted to container ship):
77782 **CAST SEAL** (Gr) ex *Cast Otter* 1982; ex *Dovrefjell* 1977

77790 **DAMODAR GENERAL T J PARK** In/FRG (Rhein Nordseew) 1974; B; 31300; 229.12 × 12.57 (751.71 × 41.24); M (MAN); 15.25
Sister:
77791 **JALVALLABH** (In)

77800 **AMELIA TOPIC** Li/Ja (IHI) 1972; B; 30100; 223.02 × 12.82 (731.69 × 42.06); M (Sulzer); 14.75
Probable sisters:
77801 **JADE GLORIOUS** (Pa) ex *Galaxia* 1980; ex *Polestar* 1980; ex *Kyriaki* 1979
77802 **OLGA TOPIC** (Li)
Possible sisters:
77803 **ANDROS MELTEMI** (Gr)
77804 **GARDEN MOON** (Li)
77805 **CASSIOPEIA MARU** (Ja) ex *Ocean Harmony* 1981
77807 **KUROTAKISAN MARU** Ja/Ja (Tsuneishi) 1982; B; 42200; 228 × 12.53 (748 × 41.11); M (MAN); 14.5

77810 **ZORA** Cy/Ja (Mitsui) 1968; B; 35000; 228.58 × 12.42 (749.93 × 40.75); M (B&W); 15.25; ex *Chiekawa Maru* 1982
Sister:
77811 **SEA QUEEN** (Cy) ex *Yakumokawa Maru* 1983

77820 **SUGAR ISLANDER** US/US (Lockheed) 1972; B; 15500; 195.38 × 10.21 (641.01 × 33.5); M (Fairbanks, Morse); 15

77830 **AEGEAN LION** Gr/Ja (Mitsubishi HI) 1977; B; 38500; 232.75 × 13.85 (736.62 × 45.44); M (Sulzer); 15.5
Probable sister:
77831 **ANTHONY III** (Li)

77840 **AMSTELMEER** Ne/Pd (Gdynska) 1975; B; 34000; 221.47 × 12.4 (726.61 × 40.68); M (Sulzer); 16.5; Launched as *Politechnika Gdanska*; 'B-521' type
Sister:
77841 **BALTIC SEA** (Pa) ex *Politechnika Slaska* 1980; ex *Politechnika Gliwicka* 1974
77842 **SEABULK** (Cy) ex *Molista* 1983; ex *Anastasia*; Launched as *Politechnika Gdanska*

77850 **AMSTELMOLEN** Ne/Pd (Gdynska) 1976; B; 34000; 221.47 × 12.4 (726.61 × 40.68); M (Sulzer); 15.75; 'B-521' type

77860 **SHORYU MARU** Ja/Ja (Sasebo) 1971; O; 20400; 188.02 × 9.15 (616.86 × 30.12); M (Sulzer); 14.5

●77870 **GOLDEN LAUREL** Li/Ja (Hitachi) 1977; B; 29700; 225.03 × 12.4 (738.29 × 40.68); M (Sulzer); 14.75
Similar (may vary in details—particularly aft Kingposts):
77871 **OGDEN THAMES** (Li)
77872 **OGDEN DANUBE** (Li)
77873 **SUNOSAKI MARU** (Ja) ex *Oslo Venture* 1982
77874 **ARCHANGELOS** (Li)
77875 **WORLD MEDAL** (Li)
77876 **MINERVA** (Li) ex *Sapphire* 1983
77877 **PRIAMOS** (Li) ex *Showa Venture* 1975
77878 **CONTINENTAL FRIENDSHIP** (Li)
77879 **CONTINENTAL TRADER** (Li)
77880 **EVNIKI** (Li)
77881 **CARYANDA** (Gr)
77882 **MOUNT PINDOS** (Gr)
77883 **HOAN MARU** (Ja)
Possibly similar (may have kingposts between hatches):
77884 **KYUKO MARU** (Ja)
77885 **MARITIME KING** (Pa)
77886 **PANAMAX MARS** (Li)
77887 **ZANNIS MICHALOS** (Gr)

77900 **OTTO LEONHARDT** FRG/FRG (Kieler H) 1967; B; 23400; 202.34 × 11.27 (663.85 × 36.98); M (MAN); 16

77910 **OWARI MARU** Ja/Ja (Mitsui) 1969; O; 58800; 259.01 × 14.17 (849.77 × 47.24); M (B&W); 15

77920 **NEPTUNIA** Li/Ja (NKK) 1965; B; 28000; 226.4 × 12.27 (742.78 × 40.26); M (Sulzer); —; ex *Theodore* 1975
Sister:
77921 **OCEANICA** (Li) ex *Dimitri* 1968

77930 **IMA** Li/Ja (NKK) 1968; B; 28000; 226.42 × 12.4 (742.85 × 40.68); M (Sulzer); 16
Similar:
77931 **ZINA** (Li) ex *Virginia* 1982

77940 **CHI SONG** Li/Ja (NKK) 1966; B; 36600; 248.47 × 11.89 (815.19 × 39.01); M (Sulzer); 15.25; ex *Shobu Maru* 1977

77950 **GINI** Pa/Ja (NKK) 1965; B; 33800; 226.4 × 11.61 (741.7 × 38.16); M (Sulzer); 15; ex *Chi Ching*

1983; ex *Shozan Maru* 1976

77960 **AFRICA MARU** Ja/Ja (Sumitomo) 1977; O; 74900; 267.01 × 16.6 (876.02 × 54.46); M (Sulzer); 14.75
Possible sister:
77961 **OCEANIA MARU** (Ja)

77970 **LOUISIANE** Br/Br (Cammell Laird) 1970; Con; 15700; 167.09 × 9.17 (548.2 × 30.9); M (B&W); 19; ex *Andes Voyageur* 1984; ex *CP Voyageur* 1983; ex *Andes Voyageur* 1982; ex *C P Voyageur* 1982
Sisters (Br flag):
77971 **CP DISCOVERER** ex *Andes Discoverer* 1982; ex *CP Discoverer* 1982
77972 **CP TRADER** ex *Andes Trader* 1982; ex *CP Trader* 1982

★ 77980 **LYULIN** Bu/Ja (Hakodate) 1965; B; 6100; 126.02 × 7.6 (413.45 × 24.93); M (B&W); 13
Sisters (Bu flag):
★ 77981 **PLANA**
★ 77982 **BELASITZA**
★ 77983 **HEMUS**
★ 77984 **OGRAJDAN**
★ 77985 **OSOGOVO**

77990 **SUDESTADA** Ar/Ja (Hitachi) 1967; O; 18000; 219.36 × 11.61 (719.69 × 38.09); M (B&W); 15; ex *Azar 1* 1983; ex *Shinzan Maru*

78000 **HELLENIC ADVENTURER** Gr/Fr (Dubigeon-Normandie) 1973; Con; 13100; 163.91 × 7.8 (537.76 × 25.59); M (Pielstick); 19; ex *Seatrain Le Havre* 1980; ex *Medorfea* 1969
Sisters:
78001 **HELLENIC FRIENDSHIP** (Gr) ex *Seatrain Bunker Hill* 1980; ex *Atlantic Iberia* 1977; ex *Mediariana* 1975
78002 **HELLENIC CONCORD** (Gr) ex *Seatrain Concord* 1980; ex *Medelena* 1977
Similar (lengthened):
78003 **HELLENIC SPIRIT** (Fr) ex *Chevalier de Blois* 1982; ex *Seatrain Ticonderoga* 1980; ex *American Arrow* 1979; ex *Atlantic Marseille*

★ 78010 **KAPITAN PANFILOV** Ru/Ru (Kherson) 1975; B; 10100; 146.21 × 9.43 (479.69 × 30.94); M (B&W); 14
Sisters (Ru flag):
★ 78011 **KAPITAN KHROMTSOV**
★ 78012 **KAPITAN DUBININ**
★ 78013 **KAPITAN IZHMYAKOV**
★ 78014 **KAPITAN MESHCHRYAKOV**
★ 78015 **KAPITAN REUTOV**
★ 78016 **KAPITAN GUDIN**
★ 78017 **KAPITAN STULOV**
★ 78018 **KAPITAN VAVILOV**
★ 78019 **IVAN NESTEROV**

78030 **OCEAN CONTAINER** Pa/Br (Smith's D) 1968; Con; 12000; 161.47 × 8.26 (529.76 × 27.1); M (Pielstick); 19.5; ex *Manchester Challenge* 1979
Sisters:
78031 **PACIFIC CONTAINER** (Br) ex *Manchester Courage* 1979
78034 **RATIH** (Ia) ex *Manchester Renown* 1982; ex *Asian Renown* 1979; ex *Manchester Renown* 1974
78035 **R R RATNA** (Tw) ex *Manchester Reward* 1982; ex *Asian Reward* 1979; ex *Manchester Reward*

★ 78041 **SIBIRSKIY 2113** Ru/Fi (Hollming) 1980; C (sea/river); 3800; 129.00 × 2.50 (423 × 8.20); TSM (Russkiy); 10
Sisters (Ru flag):
★ 78042 **SIBIRSKIY 2114**
★ 78043 **SIBIRSKIY 2116**
★ 78044 **SIBIRSKIY 2117**
★ 78045 **SIBIRSKIY 2118**
★ 78046 **SIBIRSKIY 2119**
★ 78047 **SIBIRSKIY 2130**
★ 78048 **SIBIRSKIY 2131**

78050 **NOPAL DANA** Pa/Fi (Wartsila) 1972; RoC; 4800; 162.36 × 7.72 (532.68 × 23.69) TSM (Pielstick); 17.5; ex *Leena Dan* 1979; ex *Union Sydney* 1977; ex *Leena Dan* 1974; ex *Mont Laurier* 1973; Lengthened 1978 (Wartsila); Stern door/ramp

78055 **FOREST LINK** Sw/Sp (Construcciones SA) 1973; RoC; 3400; 127.26 × 6.40 (418 × 21.00); TSM (Deutz); 17.5; ex *Stellaria* 1980; Side door (starboard). Stern door. Lengthened 1977
Sister:
78056 **OCEAN LINK** (Fi) ex *Fragaria* 1980

★ 78060 **IVAN SKURIDIN** Ru/Ru ('Zhdanov') 1975; RoC/Con; 4000; 139.6 × 6.62 (458 × 21.72); M (B&W); 17; Bow door; 'Neva' type
Sisters (some have bow & stern doors—Ru flag):
★ 78061 **GAVRILL KIRDISHCHEV**
★ 78062 **YURIY SMIRNOV**
★ 78063 **NIKOLAY VILKOV**
★ 78064 **IVAN DERBENEV**

★ 78065 **ZNAMYA OKTYABRYA**
★ 78066 **KATYA ZELENKO**
★ 78067 **ALEKSANDR OSIPOV**
★ 78068 **TIMUR FRUNZE**
★ 78069 **BORIS BUVIN**
★ 78069/1 **VIKTOR TALALIKHIN**
★ 78069/2 **VERA KHORUZHKAYA**

78070 **SIGAL** Is/Is (Israel Spyds) 1977; Con; 6100; 129.85 × 8.07 (426.02 × 26.48); M (Sulzer); 17
Sisters (Is flag):
78071 **PALMAH II** ex *Zim Sydney* 1983; ex *Palmah II* 1979
78072 **VERED** ex *Zim Melbourne* 1980; ex *Vered* 1978
78073 **RAQEFET**

78075 **HOLSTENCRUISER** Pa/FRG (A G 'Weser') 1980; C/Con; 8800; 145.01 × 8.21 (476 × 26.94); M (MaK); 17.75; May have deck cranes; 'Key 12' type

● 78090 **ARCHANGELOS III** Gr/FRG (Rhein Nordseew) 1963; B; 22800; 217.99 × 11.59 (715.19 × 38.02); M (B&W); 15; ex *Naess Liberty* 1974
Sister:
78091 **PYTHEUS** (Gr) ex *Rubycorn* 1980; ex *Frigga* 1973
Similar:
78092 **TRADE LIGHT** (Gr) ex *Baldur* 1978

78100 **ALBANY** Li/Pd (Szczecinska) 1971; B; 19300; 202.34 × 10.71 (663.85 × 35.14); M (Sulzer); 15; ex *Abercorn* 1983; ex *Saint Pierre* 1981; ex *Glyntawe* 1975; 'B-447' type
Sister:
78101 **RIO CUANZA** (Po)
Similar (centre-line KP forward with crows nest—Po flag):
78102 **CASSINGA**
78103 **RIO ZAMBEZE**

78110 **EVANGELIA C** Gr/Br (Furness) 1967; B; 29400; 213.37 × 12.75 (700.32 × 41.83); M (B&W); 15; ex *Polyfreedom* 1978
Sister:
78111 **PAN WESTERN** (Gr) ex *Norseman* 1975

78120 **CURTIS CAPRICORN** Au/Au (Whyalla) 1972; B; 48900; 255.43 × 15.14 (938.02 × 49.67); T (GEC); —; ex *Clutha Capricorn* 1977

78123 **RIVER BOYNE** Au/Ja (Mitsubishi HI) 1982; B; 52000; 255 × 12.82 (837 × 42.06); T (Mitsubishi); 16; Coal-fired
Sister:
78124 **RIVER EMBLEY** (Au)

★ 78140 **ZIEMIA BYDGOSKA** Pd/Br (Smith's D) 1967; B; 15700; 179.51 × 9.91 (588.94 × 32.51); M (Sulzer); 15
Sister:
★ 78141 **ZIEMIA MAZOWIECKA** (Pd)

● 78150 **DOMINIC** Li/FRG (LF-W) 1962; B; 17800; 200.01 × 9.81 (656.2 × 32.19); M (MAN); 16; ex *Christoffer Oldendorff* 1983
Sister:
78151 **CREATOR** (Li) ex *Henning Oldendorff* 1983
Similar:
78152 **LABRADOR CURRENT** (Li) ex *Vulkan* 1972

78160 **ALEXANDROS A** Gr/FRG (LF-W) 1962; B; 19800; 199.98 × 9.81 (656.1 × 32.19); M (MAN); 14.5; ex *Jorge S* 1982; ex *Stad Ghent* 1976; ex *Stadt Emden* 1974

78180 **CHENNAI MUYARCHI** In/Sp (AESA) 1973; B; 29300; 206.86 × 13.27 (678.67 × 43.54); M (B&W); 16.5; ex *Seneca* 1974
Sisters:
78181 **CASTILLO MANZANARES** (Sp)
78182 **NICHOLAS G. PAPALIOS** (Gr)
Similar (pole mast):
78183 **ERMUA** (Sp)

78210 **DIOGENES** Gr/FRG (LF-W) 1959; B; 13400; 176.79 × 9.89 (580.02 × 32.45); M (Krupp); 13.5; ex *Arkadia* 1982; ex *Slesvig* 1974

78240 **DELFI** Gr/Br (Connell) 1965; B; 19000; 192.03 × 11.11 (630.02 × 36.45); M (Sulzer); 15.2; ex *Drepanon* 1977; ex *Romandie* 1974

78250 **CINTA** Pa/Fr (La Ciotat) 1962; O; 16500; 188.02 × 10.02 (616.86 × 32.87); M (Gotaverken); 16.25; ex *Francois L D* 1983

● 78270 **EPIMITHEFS** Gr/Ne (Wilton-Fije) 1959; B; 11800; 164.78 × 9.86 (540.62 × 32.35); M (MAN); 14.25; ex *Meerdrecht* 1977
Sister:
78272 **SUCCESSOR** (Gr) ex *Huandoy* 1976; ex *Zwijndrecht* 1970

★ 78280 **HONG QI 302** RC/Br (Lithgows) 1961; B;

13500; 173.54 × 10.26 (569.4 × 33.66); M (Sulzer); 15; ex *Beaufort Sea* 1980; ex *Sunprince* 1974; ex *Sunmalka* 1970; ex *Mylla* 1965

★ 78290 **HUTA ZGODA** Pd/FRG (Schlichting) 1974; B; 9300; 145.65 × 8.35 (477.85 × 27.4); M (B&W); 15
Sisters (Pd flag):
★ 78291 **HUTA ZYGMUNT**
★ 78292 **BUDOWLANY**
★ 78293 **ROLNIK**
★ 78294 **KOPALNIA SOSNOWIEC**
★ 78295 **KOPALNIA WALBRZYCH**
★ 78296 **KOPALNIA ZOFIOWKA**

78310 **SAUDI CHALLENGER** Si/Ne (Giessen-De Noord) 1966; B; 23200; 205.32 × 10.83 (673.62 × 35.53); M (Sulzer); 18; ex *Amstelwal* 1983; ex *Walcheren* 1978

78330 **VASSILIOS BACOLITSAS** Ma/FRG (LF-W) 1964; B; 30500; 231.25 × 11.2 (758.69 × 36.75); M (Borsig); 15; ex *Heinrich Schulte* 1978

78340 **LAKE BIWA** Br/Fr (La Ciotat) 1963; B; 16600; 188.14 × 10.03 (617.26 × 32.91); M (Sulzer); 15.25; ex *La Chacra* 1981

78350 **BRAVERY** Br/Br (H&W) 1966; B; 28000; 219.46 × 12.34 (720 × 40.49); M (H&W); 15; ex *La Sierra* 1980
Sister:
78351 **EMMANUEL COMMINOS** (Gr) ex *La Estancia* 1978

78360 **NOBLE SUPPORTER** Li/FRG (Flensburger) 1967; B; 22100; 201.66 × 11.53 (661.61 × 37.83); M (MAN); —; ex *Rixta Oldendorff* 1983

● 78370 **OLIVIA** Tw/No (Bergens) 1963; B; 16300; 186.29 × 11.2 (611.19 × 36.75); M (Gotaverken); 14.5; ex *Eleanor* 1982; ex *Antartico* 1981; ex *Wilmara* 1977
Sister:
78371 **SUNWAVE** (Br) ex *Mar Terso* 1978; ex *Wilyama* 1978

78380 **ARCADIAN SEA** Gr/FRG (Rhein Nordseew) 1965; B; 21000; 191.27 × 11.32 (627.53 × 37.14); M (B&W); 15.25; ex *Astramarina* 1980; ex *Torm Helvig* 1975; ex *Helvig* 1974
Sisters:
78381 **VERA** (Gr) ex *Astradiego* 1981; ex *Torm Herdis* 1975; ex *Herdis* 1974
78382 **TRADE MASTER** (Gr) ex *Ocean Master*
78383 **ODYSSEUS** (Ar) ex *Tyrol* 1978; ex *Fernglen* 1975

● 78390 **NAROTTAM MORARJEE** In/FRG (Rhein Nordseew) 1967; B; 30000; 222.51 × 12.92 (730.02 × 42.39); M (B&W); 15; ex *Orm Jarl* 1969
Sisters:
78391 **STEPHANITOR** (FRG) ex *Golden Master* 1969
78392 **RALU** (Li) ex *Unas* 1978; ex *Mosborg* 1977; ex *Leiv Eriksson* 1970

78400 **MARION** Gr/Ja (NKK) 1967; B; 33600; 226.5 × 12.41 (743.11 × 40.72); M (Sulzer); 16.5; ex *Jaraconda* 1977
Sister:
78401 **ORIENT ROSE** (Li) ex *Fort Erie* 1981; ex *Nemesis* 1980; ex *Jasaka* 1978
Similar:
78402 **ASSIMINA** (Li) ex *Texada* 1971

78410 **SEAGLOSS** Cy/Ja (NKK) 1968; B; 24800; 226.42 × 12.9 (742.85 × 42.32); M (Sulzer); 16.25; ex *Gungnir X* 1983; ex *Grischuna* 1980
Sister:
78411 **EASTERN GRACE** (Li) ex *El Pampero* 1978

● 78420 **PAN UNION** Ko/Ja (Hakodate) 1973; B; 36100; 219.01 × 13.62 (718.54 × 44.69); M (Sulzer); 15; ex *Skeppsbron* 1980; ex *Voywi* 1975
Possible sisters:
78421 **MOSDUKE** (No) ex *Norse Duke* 1983
78422 **SPERANZA** (Pa) ex *Esperanza* 1982; ex *Catherine* 1977; ex *Ingwi* 1977
78423 **TIROL** (As) ex *South Beauty* 1982; ex *Gard* 1978
78424 **MARO** (Gr)
Similar:
78425 **FAVORITA** (No) ex *Moldanger* 1977
78426 **JARILLA** (No) ex *Berganger* 1977

● 78430 **ST PAUL** Li/Ja (Uraga HI) 1967; B; 30700; 219.01 × 12.5 (718.54 × 41.01); M (Sulzer); 16.5
Probable sister:
78431 **LUIGI GRIMALDI** (It) ex *Oceanic First* 1973
Similar:
78432 **RIRUCCIA** (Li)

78450 **ANASTASIA L** Gr/Fr (L'Atlantique) 1967; B; 53400; 264.24 × 13.72 (866.93 × 45.01); M (B&W); 14.5; ex *Cetra Columba* 1978

78460 **LUIGI ORLANDO** It/It (Adriatico) 1964; B; 15600; 196.63×10.35 (645.11×33.96); M (Fiat); —

78470 **FIESTA 1** Pa/It (Adriatico) 1962; B; 16000; 193.66 × 10.39 (635.37 × 34.09); M (Fiat); —; ex *Fenice* 1977

78480 **ELISA F** It/It (Tirreno) 1967; B; 28200; 215.5 × 11.65 (707.02 × 38.22); M (B&W); —
Probable sister:
78481 **DESIDERIA F** (It)
Sisters: (CL kingpost on focsle):
78482 **BENEDETTA F** (It)
78483 **FRANCESCO F** (It)

78490 **GOLDEN DAY** Pa/Br (Fairfield SB) **1965**; B; 21500; 201.78×11.18 (662.01×36.68); **M (Sulzer)**; 15; ex *Suzanne H* 1983; ex *Suzanne* **1980**; ex *Garthnewydd* 1972; ex *Cluden* 1972

●78500 **ORION** Gr/Sw (Kockums) 1963; B; 14600; 175.88 × 10.83 (577.03 × 35.53); M (MAN); 17.5

●78510 **OREMAR** Li/Ja (Hakodate) 1968; B; 35700; 261.58 × 13.58 (858.2 × 44.55); M (Sulzer); 16.25; ex *Marka L* 1974

★78520 **SOVFRACHT** Ru/Ys ('3 Maj') 1967; B; 26000; 211.41 × 11.79 (693.6 × 38.68); M (Sulzer); 16; ex *Magdi* 1973; ex *Saara Aarnio* 1973
Sister:
78521 **SUSAN TRIDENT** (Fr) ex *Kriti*; ex *Joh. Gorthon* 1977
Similar (inset):
★78522 **SOVINFLOT** (Ru) ex *Olga* 1973; ex*Annukka Arnio* 1973

★78530 **KOTOR** Ys/Ja (Kure) 1965; B; 23100; 199.52 × 11.48 (654.59 × 37.66); M (Sulzer); 15;
Sisters (Ys flag):
★78531 **ZOZARA**
★78532 **KRUSEVAC**
★78533 **KUMANOVO**

★78540 **ZARECHENSK** Ru/Pd (Gdynska) 1967; B; 16000; 187.12 × 9.54 (614.17 × 31.3); M (Sulzer); 15.5; **'B-470'** type
Sisters (Ru flag):
★78541 **ZVENIGOROD**
★78542 **ZAPOROZHYE**
★78543 **ZAKARPATYE**
★78544 **ZADONSK**
★78545 **ZLATOUST**
★78546 **ZORINSK**
Similar (Pd flag):
★78547 **ZIEMIA KRAKOWSKA**
★78548 **ZIEMIA LUBELSKA**
★78549 **ZAGLEBIE MIEDZIOWE**

78560 **KONKAR RESOLUTE** Gr/Ja (Mitsui) 1970; B; 25100; 203 × 12.49 (666 × 40.98); M (B&W); 16

78570 **HALKIS EXPRESS** Gr/Br (A&P) 1963; B; 19500; 187.46 × — (615.03 × —); M (Gotaverken); 13; ex *Victore* 1979

★78580 **BUCEGI** Rm/Ja (Hitachi) 1966; B; 16600; 181.13 × 9.5 (594.26 × 31.17); M (B&W); 16
Sisters (Rm flag):
★78581 **RESITA**
★78582 **HUNEDOARA**
★78583 **LUPENI**
★78584 **CARPATI**
★78585 **DUNAREA**
★78586 **MARAMURES**
★78587 **OLTUL**

78610 **MARGARITA** Gr/Be (Boel) 1960/66; B; 10800; 172.22 × 9.70 (565×31.82); M (MAN); 14; ex *Georgios C* 1980; ex *Tielrode* 1974; ex *Tamise* 1966; Lengthened 1966 (Cockerill)
Sister:
78611 **TAIHANG** (Pa) ex *Tonje* 1982; ex*Calbe* 1981; ex *Marly 1* 1965

78620 **SUNRISE** Li/FRG (Bremer V) 1963; B; 23000; 214.18×11.66 (702.69×38.26); M (MAN); 15; ex *Skyline* 1980; ex *Leros* 1978; ex *Splendid Honour* 1977; ex *Delphina* 1974
Sister:
★78621 **TIAN SHUI HAI** (RC) ex *Dorado* 1979

78630 **ALINE** Gr/No (Akers) 1963; B; 9400; 148.39 × 9.35 (487 × 30.68); M (B&W); 14; ex *Rosedale* 1984; ex *Rosita* 1977; ex *Rose* 1975; ex *Sunrose* 1969

★78640 **SKRADIN** Ys/Sw (Gotav) 1963; B; 12200; 157.92×9.7 (518.11×31.82); M (Gotaverken); 14.5; ex*Baltic Wasa* 1975; ex *Argo* 1971

78650 **UNGAVA TRANSPORT** Ca/No (Sarpsborg) 1959/71; Tk; 4700; 122.97×7.11 (403.44×23.33); M (B&W); 13; ex*Tommy Wiborg* 1974; ex *Varangnes* 1970; Converted from ore/oil 1971

78660 **BRITSUM** Ne/Ja (Kure) 1967; B; 25500; 207.37 × 11.72 (680.35 × 38.45); M (MAN); 14.5
Sister:
78661 **FARMSUM** (Ne)

78670 **KYRAKATINGO** Gr/FRG (Kieler H) 1967; B; 26500; 281.52 × 12.02 (716.93 × 39.44); M (B&W); 15.5; ex *Britta* 1973
-Sister:
78671 **HOWARD STAR** (Pa) ex *Bettina* 1978

78680 **ASYA 1** Tu/De (B&W) 1970; B; 30000; 218.85 × 12.1 (718 × 39.7); M (B&W); 16; ex *Olga Maersk* 1981
Sisters:
78681 **GLOBAL SUNSHINE** (Ko) ex *Olivia Maersk* 1980
78682 **DANIELLE** (Li) ex *Danita* 1978
78683 **MIRANDA** (Li) ex *Lisita* 1978
78684 **REGAL SEA** (Gr) ex *Cast Beaver* 1983; ex *Holthav* 1977
78685 **TRAMCO GLORY** (Br) ex*Cast Dolphin* 1982; ex *Berit* 1978
★78686 **UNIWERSYTET JAGIELLONSKI** (Pd)
78687 **MICHELE D'AMATO** (It) ex *Uniwersytet Torunski* 1982

●78690 **BANDAR DEMAK** Ia/Fr (France-Gironde) 1966; B; 24700; 200.51 × 11.87 (657.84×38.94); M (Fiat); 14.5; ex *Deltadrecht* 1981
Sisters:
78691 **BANDAR DEMTA** (Ia) ex*Duivendrecht* 1981
78692 **IRENE S. LEMOS** (Gr) ex*Heering Mille* 1977; ex *Ville De Metz* 1972
78693 **BANDAR DENPASAR** (Ia) ex *Dordrecht* 1981

78700 **VERA** Li/Br (Furness) 1965; B; 24300; 205.75 × 12.11 (675.03 × 39.73); M (B&W); 15.5; ex *Atlantico* 1982; ex *Argo Castor* 1977; ex *Buccleuch* 1973
Sister:
78701 **KALAVRIA** (Gr) ex *Pacifico* 1982; ex *Argo Pollux* 1977; ex *Cotswold* 1973

78710 **LUCY L.** Pa/Br (Doxford & S) 1967; B; 27500; 218.45 × 12.56 (716.7 × 41.21); M (Gotaverken); 16; ex *Lucy* 1981; ex *Roslagen* 1973

78720 **OCEANUS** Gr/Br (Doxford) 1967; B; 28000; 218.29 × 12.55 (716.17 × 41.17); M (Doxford); 15.75; ex *Mylla* 1968

★78730 **GORLITZ** DDR/Ru (Baltic) 1974; B; 22800; 201.38 X 11.21 (660.7 × 36.78); M (B&W); 15.75; 'Baltika' type
Sister:
★78731 **GRODITZ** (DDR)
Similar:
★78732 **NIKOLAY VOZNESENSKIY** (Ru)
Similar (with crane aft):
★78733 **COLDITZ** (DDR)

78740 **RIVIERA** Li/Sp (AESA) 1974; B; 18500; 196.02 × 11.15 (643.11 × 36.58); M (Sulzer); 15.25; ex *Fadura*
Similar (Sp flag):
78741 **MARCOAZUL**
78742 **MARCOVERDE**

78750 **JANA VIJAY** In/Br (Fairfield SB) 1966; B; 25400; 205.75 × 12.14 (675.03 × 39.83); M (B&W); 15.5; ex *Duhallow* 1966

78760 **STONEPOOL** Li/Br (Connell) 1966; B; 27000; 218.85 × 11.87 (718×38.94); M (Sulzer); 16

78770 **MATILDE R.** Pa/Ja (Maizuru) 1966; B; 26600; 209.4 × 12.56 (687.01 × 41.21); M (Sulzer); 15; ex *Matilde* 1983
Sisters (Lighter pole mast forward) (Li flag):
78772 **NEBO** ex*Portofino* 1983; ex*Har Meron* 1974
78773 **RIMINI** ex *Har Castel* 1975

78780 **FALSTRIA** De/De (Nakskov) 1971; Con; 20200; 201.86 × 9.48 (662.27 × 31.1); M (B&W); 21.5
Sister:
78781 **MEONIA** (De)

78800 **ACHILLEUS** Gr/Ja (Mitsubishi Z) 1961; B; 16500; 198.08 × 10.53 (649.87 × 34.55); M (Sulzer); —; ex *Gaucho Pampa* 1978; ex *Skauborg* 1973; Lengthened 1965
Sisters:
78801 **GRIGOROUSA** (Li) ex *Gaucho Laguna* 1980; ex *Golar Coal* 1970; ex *Skauholt* 1966
78802 **ST. LAWRENCE** (Ca) ex *Gaucho Taura* 1976; ex *Skaustrand* 1973
78803 **GAUCHO CRUZ** (Ar) ex *Golar Grain* 1970; ex *Skauvaag* 1966

78830 **LUIS PEREDA** Sp/Sp (AESA) 1965; B; 15300; 180.02 × 10.62 (590.62 × 34.84); M (Sulzer); 14

★78841 **PIONIERUL** Rm/Rm (Galatz) 1976; B; 10300; 145.12 × 10.14 (476× 33.27); M (Sulzer); 15
Sisters (Rm flag):
★78842 **TIRGU BUJOR**
★78843 **TIRGU LAPUS**
★78844 **TIRGU FRUMOS**
★78845 **TIRGU NEAMT**
★78846 **TIRGU OCNA**
★78847 **TIRGU SECUIESC**
★78848 **TIRGU TROTUS**

★78850 **MUSALA** Bu/Ja (Hitachi) 1967; B; 9100; 139.83 × 9.26 (458.76 × 30.38); M (B&W); 14
Sisters (Bu flag):
★78851 **RUEN**
★78852 **VEJEN**

★78860 **VITABULK** Gr/Fr (Provence) 1963/71; B; 9300; 165.41 × 8.28 (542.68 × 27.14); M (Doxford); 15.5; ex *Meltemi II* 1980; ex *Christine* 1974; Lengthened 1971 (Dubigeon-Normandie)

78880 **TONY** Gr/FRG (A.G.'Weser') 1962; B; 6200; 121.34 × 8.51 (398.1 × 27.92); M (MAN); 13; ex *Atlas* 1979; ex *Eckenheim* 1974
Sister:
78881 **ATLANTIS** (Gr) ex *Langelsheim* 1974

★78890 **PODGORICA** Ys/Br (Gray) 1954; O; 6900; 130.16 × 8.1 (427.03 × 26.57); M (Polar); 11.5; ex *Mariluck* 1974; ex*Oreosa Star* 1973; ex *Oreosa* 1971

★78891 **VLADIMIR LENORSKIY** Ru/Ru (Navashinskiy) 1970; O; 4200; 123.53 × 4.80 (405 × 15.75); TSM (Russkiy); 11.25; ex*Volnogorsk;* Hot ore carrier
Sisters (Ru flag):
★78892 **ARSHINTSEVO**
★78893 **AZOVSTAL**
★78894 **MAKAR MAZAY**
★78895 **NIKITOVKA**
★78896 **STEPAN MARKYELOV**
★78897 **YENAKIYEVO**

78900 **ALPHA** Gr/FRG (Kieler H) 1962; OO/Ch; 4800; 109.81 × 7.43 (360.27 × 24.38); M (MAN); 13; ex *Salem* 1979; ex *Singo* 1978

78910 **DALLINGTON** Br/Ne (Verolme SH) 1975; B; 7700; 137.6 × 7.93 (451.44 × 26.02); M (Stork-Werkspoor); 14
Sisters:
78911 **DONNINGTON** (Br)
78912 **DURRINGTON** (Br)
78913 **STORRINGTON** (Br)

78914 **WASHINGTON** Br/Ja (Kagoshima) 1977; B; 6200; 127.01 × 7.58 (417 X 24.87); M (Pielstick); 14

78915 **SUMBURGH HEAD** Br/Ja (Hashihama) 1977; B; 4700; 110.55 × 7.02 (363 × 23.03); M (Mitsubishi); 15
Sisters:
78916 **BARRA HEAD** (Br)
78917 **RORA HEAD** (Br)

★78920 **HUAI HAI** RC/FRG (Kieler H) 1962; B; 14800; 179.38 × 10.92 (588.52 × 35.83); M (MAN); 14; ex*Georgios A Georgilis* 1974; ex*Benedicte* 1969
Similar:
★78921 **HUANG HAI** (RC) ex*Amundsen Sea* 1975; ex *Antonis P Lemos* 1974; ex *Beatrice* 1969

78930 **CARIBBEAN CARRIER** Gr/Ys ('Split') 1962; B; 16000; 180.68 × 6.82 (592.78 × 22.38); M (Fiat); 14.5; ex *Cadimare* 1973; ex *Split* 1970
Similar:
78931 **MEDITERRANEAN CARRIER** (Gr) ex*Arcola* 1973; ex *E H Bird* 1970

★78940 **KOSICE** Cz/Ja (Hitachi) 1963; O; 16800; 181.21 × 9.91 (594.52 × 32.51) M (B&W); 16

●78960 **PACIFIC** Pa/Br (Lithgows) 1966; B; 21900; 200.34×11.22 (657.28×36.81); M (B&W); 14.5; ex *Anna Ch* 1983; ex *Oinoussian Mother* 1981; ex *Jersey Bridge* 1972

★78970 **DESSAU** DDR/Ru (Admiralteiskiy) 1958/68; O; 7600; 145.5×8.42 (477.36×27.62); M (Skoda); 12; ex*Leuna II* 1968; Converted from tanker 1968

★78980 **GENERAL SWIERCZEWSKI** Pd/Bu (G Dimitrov) 1973; B; 23300; 201.17 × 11.2 (660.01 × 36.75); M (B&W); 17
Sisters (Pd flag):
★78981 **GENERAL BEM**
★78982 **GENERAL JASINSKI**
★78983 **GENERAL MADALINSKI**
★78984 **GENERAL PRADZYNSKI** (Bu flag)
★78985 **JORDANKA NIKOLOVA**
★78986 **PETIMATA OT RMS**
★78987 **ADALBERT ANTONOV MALCHIKA** (may now be called **ADALBERT ANTONOV**)

Probable sister (may have four deck cranes):

★ 78988 **MEKHANIK P KILIMENCHUK** (Ru) ex *Kamar* 1983

79000 **EMS ORE** Li/Sw (Gotav) 1966; O; 44000; 243.85 × 12.26 (800.03 × 40.22); M (Gotaverken); 16.25; ex *Nimba* 1981; ex *Nuolja* 1974
Sister:
79001 **ALIANZA** (Ar) ex *Nikkala* 1978

79020 **MARALUNGA** It/It (Ansaldo) 1962; B; 26400; 229.74 × 11.7 (753.74 × 38.39); M (Fiat); 16; ex *Maria Amelia Lolli-Ghetti* 1966; Lengthened 1968

79040 **SAN VINCENZO** Pa/It (Ansaldo) 1965; B; 14600; 185.25 × 10.45 (597.93 × 34.28); M (Fiat); 16.25; ex *Garden Gemini* 1979; ex *Portoria* 1975

79050 **NAI MEY** It/It (Breda) 1967; B; 27100; 207.02 × 12.99 (679.2 × 42.62); M (Fiat); —; ex *Mey Lolli-Ghetti* 1974
Sister:
79051 **NAI ALBERTO** (It) ex *Alberto Lolli-Ghetti* 1974

79060 **GLADIATOR** Ar/De (B&W) 1965; B; 20200; 193.83 × 11.05 (635.93 × 36.25); M (B&W); 15.5; ex *Bulk Venture* 1975

79070 **FORUM GRACE** Gr/Sw (Eriksbergs) 1963; B; 15600; 181.85 × 10.57 (596.62 × 34.68); M (B&W); 15.5; ex *Cape Pacific*; ex *Uppland* 1976

79080 **UNITY** Ma/Br (Doxford & S) 1968; B; 28900; 218.35 × 12.56 (716.57 × 41.21); M (Doxford); 15.5; ex *Leda* 1982; ex *Ripon Grange* 1980; ex *Orotava* 1979; ex *Orotava Bridge* 1974; ex *Orotava* 1969

79090 **FORTITUDE** Pa/Sw (Eriksbergs) 1965; B; 27200; 215.86 × 12.11 (708.2 × 39.73); M (B&W); 16.25; ex *Achipelagos* 1980; ex *F.S.B.02* 1976; ex *Norland* 1975

79100 **SAC MALAGA** Sp/Sp (AESA) 1976; B; 17400; 190.66 × 10.69 (625.52 × 35.07); M (Sulzer); 15
Sister:
79101 **CASTELLBLANCH** (Sp) launched as *Ponte Sampayo*
Probable sisters:
79102 **DRY SACK** (Sp) lauched as *Ponte Pasaje*
79103 **BANDA AZUL** (Sp) launched as *Ponte Pedrido*

79110 **BEER SHEVA** Li/De (B&W) 1973; B; 29700; 218.85 × 12.09 (718.01 × 39.66); M (B&W); 15.5; ex *Thorunn* 1983
Similar:
79111 **CARLOVA** (Gr)
79112 **MARIJEANNIE** (Gr) ex *Tramco Asia* 1983; ex *Cast Orca* 1982; ex *Hector* 1979
★ 79113 **UNIWERSYTET WARSZAWSKI** (Pd)
★ 79115 **UNIWERSYTET WROCLAWSKI** (Pd)
79116 **SAMJOHN MARINER** (Li)
79117 **JACARA** (No) ex *Heering Christel* 1977

79130 **LENA** Li/Ja (IHI) 1968; B; 23300; 194.52 × 12.1 (638.19 × 39.7); M (Sulzer); 14.5; ex *World Neighbour* 1982
Sisters (Li flag):
79131 **WORLD NAUTILUS** launched as *World Happiness*
79132 **WORLD NATURE**
Similar:
79133 **NORTHERN NAIAD**

79140 **PLOTUS** It/FRG (B+V) 1965; B; 35000; 236.53 × 11.91 (776.02 × 39.07); M (MAN); 15.75; ex *Fritz Thyssen* 1983
Sister:
79141 **MILVUS** (It) ex *Odin* 1982

79150 **ACUMEN** Pa/Br (A&P) 1967; B; 27400; 217.23 × 12.37 (712.7 × 40.58); M (B&W); 15.5; ex *Norman Merchant* 1980; ex *Pilot Merchant*; ex *Happy Dragon* 1978

79170 **ANDROS CASTLE** Li/Ja (IHI) 1968; B; 21400; 190 × 11.36 (623.36 X 37.27); M (Sulzer); 16
Sisters (Li flag):
79171 **ANDROS CITY**
79172 **ANDROS HILLS**
79173 **ANDROS ISLAND**
79174 **ANDROS MARINER**

79180 **LEONIDAS D** Li/Ja (IHI) 1967; B; 28600; 216.06 × 12.08 (708.86 × 39.63); M (Sulzer); —
Sister:
79181 **EKATERINI M GOULANDRIS** (Gr)

79190 **HAHNENTOR** FRG/FRG (A.G. 'Weser') 1965; B; 23200; 212 × 10.18 (695.54 × 33.4); M (B&W); 15

79200 **PANAMAX MOON** Pa/De (B&W) 1967; B; 42700; 249.21 × 14.33 (817.62 × 47.01); M (B&W);

15.75; ex *King Richard* 1982; ex *Elbe Ore* 1974
Similar (shorter funnel):
79201 **MAIN ORE** (Li)

79210 **ORIENT HARMONY** Li/Br (Doxford & S) 1967; B; 29500; 215.96 × 12.43 (708.53 × 40.78); M (Doxford); 16.75; ex *Gaucho Guemes* 1981; ex *Mardulce II*; ex *Fernspring*
Probable sister:
79211 **WELFARE** (Gr) ex *Pilio* 1980; ex *Fernriver* 1978

● 79220 **GOOD MOTHER** Gr/Be (Boel) 1966; B; 36400; 266.73 × 13.11 (875.1 × 43.01); M (MAN); 16.25; ex *Anastasia Super* 1980; ex *San Moritz*; ex *Temse* 1973

★ 79230 **GEORGIY LEONIDZE** Ru/Pd (Szczecinska) 1974; B; 20300; 202.34 × 10.64 (663.85 × 34.91); M (Sulzer); 15; '**B-447**' type
Sister (Ru flag):
★ 79231 **GENERAL LESELIDZE**
Similar (Cz flag):
★ 79232 **BRATISLAVA**
★ 79233 **PRAHA**
★ 79234 **TRINEC**

★ 79240 **JU HAI** RC/Sw (Uddevalla) 1966; B; 26500; 215.7 × 12.09 (707.68 × 39.67); M (B&W); 16; ex *Drake Sea* 1976; ex *Vardaas* 1974

79250 **IMA** Li/Ja (NKK) 1968; B; 28000; 226.42 × 12.4 (742.85 × 40.68); M (Sulzer); 16
Similar:
79251 **ZINA** (Li) ex *Virginia* 1982

79260 **GOLD BOND CONVEYOR** Li/Ja (Sasebo) 1974; O; 14900; 177.98 × 10.02 (583.92 × 32.87); M (Sulzer); 15.25; ex *Colon Brown* 1975; Side doors; New mid body 1976
Sister:
79261 **GOLD BOND TRAILBLAZER** (Li) rebuilt from part of *Gold Bond Conveyor*

★ 79270 **LAN HAI** RC/Sw (Oskarshamns) 1960; B; 12100; 161.19 × 9.9 (528.84 × 32.48); M (Gotaverken); 13; ex *Mary Xilas* 1974; ex *Sea Master* 1970

79280 **MENITES** Gr/Ja (NKK) 1959; B; 12300; 169.17 × 9.53 (555 × 31.27); M (MAN); 14.75; ex *Saas Fee* 1977; ex *Butterfly* 1972

79290 **PANAMA** US/US (Kaiser Co) 1945/66; Con; 17200; 208.77 × 9.18 (684.94 × 30.12); T (Hendy); 16; ex *Marine Jumper* 1966; Converted from '**C-4**' type cargo ship 1966 (Ingalls SB)

● 79300 **WERRA EXPRESS** Sg/Ja (Mitsui)-Sg 1974/78; Con; 14200; 169.46 × — (555.97 × —); M (B&W); 18; ex *Freudenfels* 1980; ex *Drachenfels* 1976; ex *Aristotelis* 1975; Converted from '**Mitsui-Concord**' type cargo ship 1978 (Jurong Spyd). May now be fitted with three deck cranes. Same applies to sisters (see '**ISAR EXPRESS**')
Sisters (Sg flag):
79301 **NECKAR EXPRESS** ex *Freienfels* 1980; ex *Aristarchos* 1975
79302 **FULDA EXPRESS** ex *Frankenfels* 1980; ex *Aristandros* 1974

79310 **HERMES ACE** Ja/FRG (O&K) 1976; Con; 9100; 159.01 × 8.26 (521.69 × 27.1); M (Pielstick); 17.25; ex *Seatrain Italy* 1981; ex *Sovereign Express* 1977
Sister:
79311 **SOVEREIGN ACCORD** (Ja)

● 79320 **BREEZAND** Ne/FRG (M Jansen) 1975; C; 1600; 79.51 × 5.55 (260.86 × 18.21); M (Atlas-MaK); 12.5
Sisters:
79321 **TEQUILA SUNSET** (Pa) ex *Cairncarrier* 1982
79322 **TJONGERWAL** (Ne) ex *Cairnfreighter* 1982
79323 **LINDEWAL** (Ne) ex *Cairnleader* 1982

★ 79340 '**SORMOVSKIY**' type. Ru/Ru ('Krasnoye S'/Volodarskiy etc) 1967/79; C (Sea/river); 2500; 114.2 × 3.42 (374.67 × 11.22); TSM (Liebknecht); 10.5
Sisters (Ru flag):
★ 79341 **SORMOVSKIY 2**
★ 79342 **ALEKSANDR PASHKOV** ex *Sormovskiy-4*
★ 79343 **SORMOVSKIY 5**
★ 79344 **SORMOVSKIY 6**
★ 79345 **SORMOVSKIY 7**
★ 79346 **SORMOVSKIY 9**
★ 79347 **NIKOLAY LEBEDYEV** ex *Sormovskiy-11*
★ 79348 **SORMOVSKIY 12**
★ 79349 **SAVVA LOSHKIN** ex *Sormovskiy-13*
★ 79350 **SORMOVSKIY 14**
★ 79351 **SORMOVSKIY 17**
★ 79352 **SORMOVSKIY 18**
★ 79353 **SORMOVSKIY 19**
★ 79354 **SORMOVSKIY 22**
★ 79355 **SORMOVSKIY 27**

★ 79356 **SORMOVSKIY 28**
★ 79357 **SORMOVSKIY 29**
★ 79358 **SORMOVSKIY 30**
★ 79359 **SORMOVSKIY 31**
★ 79360 **SORMOVSKIY 33**
★ 79361 **SORMOVSKIY 34**
★ 79362 **SORMOVSKIY 40**
★ 79362/1 **SORMOVSKIY 41**
★ 79362/2 **SORMOVSKIY 118**
★ 79362/3 **SORMOVSKIY 3001**
★ 79362/4 **SORMOVSKIY 3002**
★ 79363 **SORMOVSKIY 42**
★ 79364 **SORMOVSKIY 109**
★ 79365 **SORMOVSKIY 110**
★ 79366 **SORMOVSKIY 112**
★ 79367 **SORMOVSKIY 117**
★ 79368 **SO LET SOVIETSKOY VLASTI**
★ 79369 **BUREVESTNIK REVOLYUTSKIY**
★ 79370 **ALEKSANDR VERMISHEV**
★ 79371 **LENINSKAYA SMENA**
★ 79372 **VELIKIY POCHIN**
★ 79373 **VOZNESENSK**
★ 79374 **ALEKSANDR TSYURUPA**
★ 79375 **DMITRY MANUILSKIY**
★ 79376 **SHUSHENSKOYE**
★ 79377 **STANISLAV KOSIOR**
★ 79378 **ALEKSANDR PROKOFYEV**
★ 79379 **GEROY MEKHTI**
★ 79380 **PARIZHSKAYA KOMMUNA**
★ 79381 **GEROY MEKHTI** ex *Vishnevets*
★ 79382 **ANATOLIY VANEYEV**
★ 79384 **PETR BOGDANOV**
★ 79385 **STRANA SOVIETOV**
★ 79386 **50 LET S S S R**
★ 79387 **NIKOLAY BAUMAN**
★ 79388 **PETR ZAPOROZHETS**
★ 79389 **IVAN KOLYSHKIN**
★ 79390 **POET SABIR**
★ 79400 **ALEKSANDR PASHKOV**
★ 79401 **DESYATAYA PYATILETKA**
★ 79402 **POET VIDADI**
★ 79403 **DZHAMBUL DZHABAYEV**
★ 79404 **GRIGORIY PETROVSKIY**
★ 79405 **50 LET VLKSM**
★ 79406 **VISHNEVOGORSK**
★ 79407 **GORKY LENINSKOYE**
★ 79408 **PETR ZALOMOV**
★ 79409 **XVI SYEZD VLKSM**
★ 79410 **DEVYATAYA PYATILETKA**
★ 79411 **NIZHEGORODSKIY KOMSOMOLETS**
★ 79412 **750—LETIYE GORODA GORKOGO**
★ 79413 **XXIV SYEZD KPSS**
★ 79414 **50 LET PIONERII**
★ 79415 **KEMINE**
★ 79416 **SOVIETSKIY SEVER**
★ 79417 **VLADIMIR ZATONSKIY**
★ 79418 **NASIMI**
★ 79419 **PETR LIDOV**
★ 79420 **XVII SYEZD VLKSM** ex *Sormovskiy-32*
★ 79421 **9 MAYA 1945 GODA**
★ 79422 **SEMYON MOROZOV**
★ 79423 **VITALIY PRIMAKOV**
★ 79424 **ALEKSEY VIKHORYEV**
★ 79425 **FEDOR PODTELKOV**
★ 79426 **PROFESSOR I.I. KRAKOVSKIY**
★ 79427 **ALIYA MOLDAGULOV**
★ 79428 **XVII SYEZD VLKSM**
★ 79429 **GAZLI**
★ 79430 **IVAN LESOVIKOV**
★ 79431 **IVAN KUDRIYA**
★ 79432 **LENINGRADSKIY KOMSOMOLETS**
★ 79433 **MARSHAL VOROBYEV**
★ 79434 **MIKHAIL KRIVOSHLIKOV**
★ 79435 **MUKHTAR ASHRAFI**
★ 79436 **PAVEL GRABOVSKIY**
★ 79437 **PAVEL MOCHALOV**
★ 79438 **PROFESSOR KERICHYEV**
★ 79439 **60 LET VELIKOGO OKTYABR**
★ 79440 **60 LET VLKSM**
★ 79441 **TAVRIYA**
★ 79442 **UZEIR GADZHIBEKOV**
★ 79443 **YURIY KOTSYUBINSKY**
★ 79444 **VERA VOLOSHINA**

★ 79450 '**NEFTERUDOVOZ**' type. Ru/Ru (Kama) 1972/77; OO (sea/river); 2700; 118.93 × 3.42 (390.19 × 11.22); TSM (Liebknecht); 11
Sisters (Ru flag):
from
NEFTERUDOVOZ 8M to **NEFTERUDOVOZ 33N** inclusive

★ 79500 '**BALTIYSKIY**' type. Ru/Ru ('Krasnoye S') 1962/68; C (sea/river); 1900; 96.02 × 3.26 (315.03 × 10.7); TSM (Liebknecht); 10; Vessel illustrated is *Baltiyskiy 32;* Some have lower funnels; Aftermast omitted on some vessels
Sisters (Ru flag):
from
BALTIYSKIY 1 to **BALTIYSKIY 73** inclusive

★79550 **PIONER NAKHODKI** Ru/Ru (Vyborg 1972; Con; 4800; 130.31 × 6.93 (427.53 × 22.74); M (Sulzer); 15
Sisters (Ru flag):
★79551 **SESTRORETSK**
★79552 **PIONER ODESSY**
★79553 **PIONER VLADIVOSTOKA**
★79554 **PIONER PRIMORYA**
★79555 **PIONER VYBORGA**

79560 **TUDELA** Sp/Sp (Cantabrico) 1977; Tk/Ch; 3900; 111.92 × 6.73 (367.19 × 22.08); M (Stork); 15

79570 **PERTUSOLA** It/It (Benetti) 1975; Tk; 4000; 117.66 × 7.32 (386.02 × 24.02); M (GMT); 15.5
Sister:
79571 **PUGLIOLA** (It)

79580 **COMMANDANT HENRY** Fr/Fr (La Rochelle) 1975; WT/Ch; 1600; 90.99 × 5.52 (298.52 × 18.11); M (Atlas-MaK); 14.5
Sister:
79581 **POINTE DE LESVEN** (Fr)

79590 **BP JOUSTER** Br/Br (Appledore) 1972; Tk; 1600; 78.95 × 4.74 (259.02 × 15.55); M (Alpha—Diesel); 12; ex Swansea 1976
Sister (Br flag):
79591 **SHELL EXPLORER** ex Dundee 1979
Similar:
79592 **SHELL DIRECTOR** ex Caernarvon 1979
79593 **SHELL SUPPLIER** ex Plymouth 1979

79600 **SENKO MARU** Ja/Ja (Tokushima ZS) 1971; Ch; 1000; 68.03 × 4.01 (223.2 × 13.16); M (Makita); 12
Probable sister:
79601 **OGISHIMA MARU** (Ja)
Possibly similar (LGC):
79602 **KOSHIN MARU No 3** (Ja)

79610 **GREEN SEA** Li/Ja (Tokushima ZS) 1974; LGC; 1500; 73.18 × 4.62 (240.09 × 15.16); M (Akasaka); 12

79620 **KOKUSHU MARU No 2** Ja/Ja (Naikai) 1976; LGC; 1600; 75.16 × 5.17 (246.6 × 16.96); M (Yanmar); 12

79630 **BUTAUNO** Sp/Sp (AESA) 1965; LGC; 1500; 79.56 × 4.93 (261.02 × 16.17); M (Gotaverken); —
Sister:
79631 **BUTADOS** (Sp)

●79640 **SOPHIA C** Gr/Bu (G Dimitrov) 1971; B; 15700; 185.2 × 9.86 (607.61 × 32.35); M (Sulzer); 15.25; ex Vikhren
Sisters (Bu flag):
★79641 **BELMEKEN**
★79642 **GENERAL VLADIMIR ZAIMOV**
★79643 **BALKAN**
(Pd flag):
★79644 **ZIEMIA BIALOSTOCKA**
★79645 **ZIEMIA OLSZTYNSKA**
★79646 **ZIEMIA OPOLSKI**

79650 **KAITY** Gr/Ja (Kure) 1965; B; 23000; 191.17 × 11.72 (627.2 × 38.45); M (Sulzer); —
Similar:
79651 **ERO** (Gr)

79660 **MARINE PRINCESS** US/Br (Doxford & S) 1967; B; 29000; 215.96 × 12.63 (708.53 × 41.44); M (Sulzer); 15.5; ex Kuniang 1983; ex Elounda; ex Sheaf Tyne 1978

79670 **KEN VICTORY** Pa/Ja (Sasebo) 1966; B; 35700; 254.16 × 12.92 (833.86 × 42.39); M (Sulzer); 16; ex Minories Hope 1980; ex Cretan Bay; ex World Soya 1975

79680 **GYPSUM KING** Br/Ca (Collingwood) 1975; B; 12800; 150.81 × 9.25 (494.78 × 30.35); T (GEC); 15
Sister:
79681 **GYPSUM BARON** (Br)

79690 **GENERAL M MAKLEFF** Is/Br (Laing) 1965; B; 22200; 196.76 × 11.65 (645.54 × 38.22); M (B&W); 16.5; ex Ocean Valour 1980; ex St Providence 1976; ex Sneholt 1973; ex Tower Bridge 1970; Launched as Silverhow ; May be spelt **GEN. M. MAKLEFF**

79700 **AL TAHIR** Sg/Br (J L Thompson) 1965; B; 22200; 196.76 × 11.71 (645.54 × 38.42); M (Sulzer); —; ex Kirriemoor 1978

●79710 **DRYS** Gr/Br (Laing) 1965; B; 20200; 196.7 × 11.65 (645.34 × 38.22); M (B&W); 15; ex Oakwood 1971

79720 **FUTURE** Pa/Br (A&P) 1968; B; 14000; 177.71 × 9.85 (583.04 × 32.32); M (Gotaverken); 14.5; ex New Future 1982; ex Vancouver Trader; ex Essex Trader 1971

★79730 **LUBBENAU** DDR/DDR (Warnow) 1961; O; 8200; 151.59 × 8.31 (497.34 × 27.26); M (Dieselmotorenwerk Rostock); 15
Sisters (DDR flag):
★79731 **MANSFELD**
★79732 **ESPENHAIN**
★79733 **SENFTENBERG**
★79734 **TRATTENDORF**
★79735 **VOCKERODE**

●79740 **EGLANTINE** Fr/Fr (France-Gironde) 1968; B; 18700; 196.58 × — (644.95 × —); M (B&W); 17
Sister:
79741 **HERMINE** (Fr)

79750 **DISCOVERY BAY** Pa/Be (Boel) 1963; B; 23300; 218.75 × 11.67 (717.68 × 38.29); M (MAN); 16; ex Good Carrier 1979; ex Eeklo 1973

●79760 **RIO LINDO** Gr/Ih (Verolme Cork) 1964; B; 20000; 183.91 × 11.17 (603.35 × 36.65); M (MAN); 14; ex Amstelhof 1979; May now be fitted with cranes
Probable sister:
79761 **CANADIAN BULKER** (Pa) ex Synetos 1981; ex Rijn 1975

79770 **QUEBEC** Li/Ja (Uraga HI) 1965; B; 29200; 210.01 × 11.31 (718.85 × 37.11); M (Sulzer); 15.25; ex Baron Holberg 1967

79780 **GEORGIOS T KOROPOULIS** Gr/Ys ('3 Maj') 1964; B; 17500; 195.99 × 11.02 (643.01 × 36.15); M (MAN); 17; ex Myron
Sisters (Li flag):
79781 **DROMON**
79782 **SKIRON**

79790 **FOUR FLAGS II** Gr/FRG (Flensburger) 1958; B; 10300; 157.82 × 9.45 (517.78 × 31); M (MAN); 14; ex Stavfjord 1980; ex Magdalena Oldendorff 1971

79810 **PATVIN** Pa/Ys ('3 Maj') 1962; B; 13800; 170.36 × 9.56 (599 × 31.36); M (Sulzer); 14.5; ex Calvin 1980; ex St. Cergue 1978; ex Bariloche 1966

79820 **KAPETAN GEORGIS** Li/Br (Scotts' SB) 1963; C; 16900; 186.09 × 10.85 (610.53 × 35.6); M (Sulzer); 14

★79830 **XI QIAO SHAN** RC/Br (Scotts' SB) 1965; B; 16900; 186.09 × 10.78 (610.53 × 35.37); M (Sulzer); 15.5; ex Golden Sun 1984; ex Karaiskaki 1982; ex British Monarch 1973
Sister:
★79831 **LU HAI** (RC) ex Ocean Mariner 1976; ex Vennachar 1973

★79840 **HONG QI 301** RC/FRG (B+V) 1958; B; 10400; 165 × 9.59 (541.34 × 31.46); M (MAN); 16; ex Salton Sea 1980; ex Asmidiske 1973

★79850 **WU ZHI SHAN** RC/FRG (B+V) 1958; B; 10400; 165 × 9.59 (541 × 31.46); M (MAN); 15; ex Chukchi Sea 1978; ex Asterope 1973; Name may be spelt **WUZHISHAN**

★79860 **ASANO** Pa/Sw (Oresunds) 1960; B; 9900; 157.26 × 9.13 (515.94 × 29.95); M (Gotaverken); —; ex Cape Palmas 1978; ex Anna Brodin 1969

★79870 **SUWALKI** Pd/Bu (G Dimitrov) 1969; C; 2400; 95.89 × 5.66 (314.6 × 18.57); M (Sulzer); 13
Sisters (Pd flag):
★79871 **KUTNO II**
★79872 **PIOTRKOW TRYBUNALSKI**
★79873 **WADOWICE**
★79874 **CIECHANOW**
★79875 **STARACHOWICE**
★79876 **PRZEMYSL**

79880 **ZABAT DOS** Sp/Sp (Cadagua) 1977; C; 5900; 119.64 × 7.99 (392.52 × 26.21); M (MAN); 14;
Sister:
79881 **ZABAT UNO** (Sp)

★79890 **INHARRIME** Mb/Sp (Duro Felguera) 1974; C; 1600; 81.82 × 5.6 (268.44 × 18.37); M (Deutz) 13.5; ex Allul 1983
Sister:
★79891 **LUGELA** (Mb) ex Alfer 1983

79900 **FLORIDA STAR** Pa/Sp (Cadagua) 1976; C; 1600; 82.1 × 5.44 (269.36 × 17.85); M (Deutz); 11.5; ex Fer Baltico 1981
Sister:
79901 **FER BALEAR** (Sp)

79910 **BEEDING** Br/Sw (Falkenbergs) 1971; C; 1600; 87.03 × 4.96 (285.53 × 16.27); M (Appingedammer Brons); 12

79920 **MIRAMAR** Sw/Sw (Falkenbergs) 1971; C; 1600; 87.03 × 4.96 (285.53 × 16.27); M (Appingedammer Brons); 12; ex Anders 1983; The small deck cranes may be removed
Sister:

79921 **FALKENBERG** (FRG) ex Pontos 1976; ex Falkenberg 1973; Launched as Isotat

★79930 **ABRAM ARKHIPOV** Ru/Fi (Nystads) 1973; C/TC; 3200; 97.31 × 6.7 (319.26 × 21.98); M (B&W); 14
Sisters (Ru flag):
★79931 **VLADIMIR FAVORSKIY**
★79932 **MITROFAN GREKOV**
★79933 **VASILIY POLENOV**
★79934 **NIKOLAY YAROSHENKO**
★79935 **NIKOLAY KASATKIN**
★79936 **KONSTANTIN YUON**
★79937 **IGOR GRABAR**
★79938 **IVAN SHADR**
★79939 **MIKHAIL CHEREMNYKH**
★79940 **VERA MUKINA**
★79941 **YEKATERINA BELASHOVA**

79950 **ANADOLU BIR** Tu/Ja (Mitsubishi HI) 1967; B; 32500; 235.52 × 13.74 (772.7 × 45.08); M (Sulzer); 17; ex Aegean Monarch 1982
Sister:
79951 **AEGEAN NEPTUNE** (Gr)

79960 **NYMPH C** Gr/Ja (Mitsubishi HI) 1966; B; 22300; 193.55 × 11.84 (635.01 × 38.85); M (Sulzer); —; ex Aegean Nymph 1980
Sister:
79961 **NUEVA ESPERANZA** (Gr) ex Aegean Sky 1982

79963 **PENGALL** Fr/Ja (Kawasaki) 1982; B; 74500; 280.02 × 16.15 (919 × 52.99); M (MAN); 14
Sisters:
79964 **CETRA CORONA** (Fr)
79965 **GALION** (Fr) ex Gallant Lion 1982
Similar:
79966 **NIELS ONSTAD** (No)
79967 **ONSTAD TRADER** (No)

79970 **SEARADIANCE** Br/Br (Sunderland) 1977; B; 39200; 228.12 × 14.05 (748.43 × 46.1); M (Doxford); 15; ex Orient City 1978
Sister:
79971 **GALENE** (Gr) ex Welsh City 1983

79980 **PAN JOURNEY** Ko/Ja (Mitsubishi HI) 1975; B; 35800; 224.01 × 13.32 (734.94 × 43.7); M (Sulzer); 14.5; ex Pan Justice 1982; ex Halla Grieg 1981

★79990 **KAPITAN PANFILOV** Ru/Ru (Kherson) 1975; B; 10100; 146.21 × 9.43 (479.69 × 30.94); M (B&W); 14
Sisters (Ru flag):
★79991 **KAPITAN KHROMTSOV**
★79992 **KAPITAN DUBININ**
★79993 **KAPITAN IZHMYAKOV**
★79994 **KAPITAN MESHCHRYAKOV**
★79995 **KAPITAN REUTOV**
★79996 **KAPITAN GUDIN**
★79997 **KAPITAN STULOV**
★79998 **KAPITAN VANILOV**
★79999 **IVAN NESTEROV**

★80000 **KHUDOZHNIK FEDOROVSKIY** Ru/Bu (G Dimitrov) 1978; B; 15600; 185.22 × 10.1 (607.68 × 33.14); M (Sulzer); 15.25; This vessel may be fitted with 4 deck cranes; This could also apply to the sistership
Sisters (Ru flag):
★80001 **KHUDOZHNIK A GERASIMOV**
★80002 **KHUDOZHNIK GABASHVILI**
★80003 **KHUDOZHNIK KASIYAN**
★80004 **KHUDOZHNIK KUSTODIYEV**
★80005 **KHUDOZHNIK TOIDZE**
★80006 **KHUDOZHNIK VLADIMIR SEROV**
★80007 **SOVIETSKIY KHUDOZHNIK**
(Bu flag):
★80008 **CHIPKA** (or **SHIPKA**)
★80009 **RILA**
★80009/1 **RODOPI**
★80009/2 **VITOCHA**
★80009/3 **MILIN KAMAK**
★80009/4 **SLAVIANKA**

80010 **BELGRANO** Li/Pd (Gdynska) 1976; BC; 33000; 224.42 × 12.37 (736.29 × 40.58); M (Sulzer); 15.75; ex Juthlandia 1982; 'B-521' type; Side doors

★80020 **HUTA ZGODA** Pd/FRG (Schlichting) 1974; B; 9300; 145.65 × 8.35 (477.85 × 27.4); M (B&W); 15
Sisters (Pd flag):
★80021 **HUTA ZYGMUNT**
★80022 **BUDOWLANY**
★80023 **ROLNIK**
★80024 **KOPALNIA SOSNOWIEC**
★80025 **KOPALNIA WALBRZYCH**
★80026 **KOPALNIA ZOFIOWKA**

80030 **JOLLY GRIGIO** Sg/Ja (Kawasaki) 1977; RoC/Tk/B; 9500; 143.85 × 7.8 (471.95 × 25.59); M (MAN); 14.75; ex Bellman 1981; 'Boro' type
Sister:

80031 JOLLY AMARANTO (Sg) ex *Taube* 1981

80040 T AKASAKA Br/Ja (NKK) 1969; B; 33300; 226.88 × 12.3 (744.36 × 40.35); M (B&W); 15.5; Sister:
80041 W C VAN HORNE (Br)

★**80052 SIMON BOLIVAR** Ru/Bu (G Dimitrov) 1981; Con; 8700; 148.67 × 7.65 (488× 25.10); M (B&W); 18
Sisters:
★**80053 PYER PUYYAD** (Ru)
★**80054 GENERAL GORBATOV** (Ru)
★**80055 ROSTOV NA DONU** (Ru)
★**80056 STANKO STAIKOV** (Bu)
Probable sister:
★**80057 MIKHAIL ISAKOVSKIY** (Ru)

★**80060 KAPITAN TOMSON** Ru/Ja (Kurushima) 1977; RoC/Con; 4600; 113.49 × 6.87 (372.34 × 22.54); M (Mitsubishi); —; ex *R S Ixion* 1978; Launched as *R S One*
Sister:
★**80061 KAPITAN YAKOVLEV** (Ru) ex *R S Jason* 1978

80070 GRAND ENCOUNTER Pa/Ca (Port Weller) 1972; RoC; 16400; 208.19 × 9.3 (683.04 × 30.51); TSM (Pielstick); 19; ex *Laurentian Forest*
Sister:
80071 AVON FOREST (Br)

●**80080 HELLENIC VALOR** Gr/Ja (Sasebo) 1978; RoC; 17200; 190.53 × 11.9 (625.1 × 39.04); TSM (MAN); 17; Stern door/ramp
Sisters (Gr flag):
80081 HELLENIC EXPLORER
80082 HELLENIC INNOVATOR

★**80090 INZHENER MACHULSKIY** Ru/Fi (Hollming) 1975; RoC/Con; 4000; 124.21 × 6.6 (407.51 × 21.65); M (Pielstick); 16.75; Stern quarter ramp
Sisters (Ru flag):
★**80091 INZHENER BASHKIROV**
★**80092 INZHENER SUKHORUKOV**
★**80093 INZHENER KREYLIS**
★**80094 MEKHANIK KONOVALOV**
Similar (stern ramp and no extension before bridgefront) (Ru flag):
★**80095 INZHENER NECHIPORENKO**
★**80097 MEKHANIK FEDOROV**
★**80098 MEKHANIK YEVGRAFOV**
★**80099 MEKHANIK GERASIMOV**

80110 SVENDBORG GRACE Pa/Ne (Boot) 1963; C; 500; 72.67 × 3.82 (238.42 × 12.53); M ('De Industrie'); 13; ex *Kittiwake* 1974; Launched as *Breewijd*
Sister:
80111 AQABA (Jo) ex *Imber* 1976

80120 ROSELAND Pa/Br (Clelands) 1961; B; 1100; 69.5 × 4.59 (228.02 × 15.06); M (Mirrlees, Bickerton & Day); 11; ex *Barney Mac* 1982; ex *Estland* 1982; ex *Turquoise*; ex *Kylebank* 1975

★**80130 ZARECHENSK** Ru/Pd (Gdynska) 1967; B; 16000; 187.12 × 9.54 (614.17 × 31.3); M (Sulzer); 15.5; 'B-470' type
Sisters (Ru flag):
★**80131 ZVENIGOROD**
★**80132 ZAPOROZHYE**
★**80133 ZAKARPATYE**
★**80134 ZADONSK**
★**80135 ZLATOUST**
★**80136 ZORINSK**
Similar (Pd flag):
★**80137 ZIEMIA KRAKOWSKA**
★**80138 ZIEMIA LUBELSKA**
★**80139 ZAGLEBIE MIEDZIOWE**

80150 STEPHEN BROWN Au/Br (Hall, Russell) 1954; C; 1500; 77.27 × 4.43 (253.51 × 14.53); M (British Polar); —

★**80160 PIONIR** Ys/FRG (Schuerenstedt) 1973; Con; 4000; 118.88 × 6.4 (390.03 × 21); M (MAN); 15.5; ex *Pionir* 1978; ex *Maritime Champ* 1974
Sister:
80161 SUN FLOWER (Ko) ex *Maritime Ace* 1973

80170 STERN Fi/Fr (Havre) 1967; Ch; 2000; 87 × 5.97 (285.43 × 19.59); M (Werkspoor); 13.75; ex *Tyysterniemi* 1983

★**80171 DMITRIY DONSKOY** Ru/DDR (Warnow) 1977; B/Con; 13600; 162.11 × 9.88 (532 × 32.41); M (MAN); 15.25; 'UL-ESC' type
Sisters (Ru flag):
★**80172 DMITRIY POZHARSKIY**
★**80173 ALEKSANDR NEVSKIY**
★**80174 ALEKSANDR SUVOROV**
★**80175 MIKHAIL KUTUZOV**
★**80176 ADMIRAL USHAKOV**
★**80177 KUZMA MININ**

★**80178 PETR VELIKIY**
★**80179 STEPAN RAZIN**
★**80179/1 YEMELYAN PUGACHEV**

★**80180 KAPITAN SMIRNOV** Ru/Ru ('Chernomorskiy') 1979; RoC/Con; 14300; 227.3 × 9.87 (745.74 × 32.38); TS GT/M (—); 25; Stern quarter ramp
Sisters (Ru flag):
★**80181 KAPITAN MEZENTSEV** (different design of ramp)
★**80182 INZHENER YERMOSHKIN**

80190 ABUJA EXPRESS Fi/Sw (Oskarshamns) 1978; RoC; 9100; 183.5 × 8.44 (602.03 × 27.69); M (Sulzer); 18; ex *Emirates Express* 1981; Stern doors-/ramps

★**80200 MAGNITOGORSK** Ru/Fi (Valmet) 1975; RoC; 15700; 205.8 × 9.7 (675.2 × 31.82); M (B&W); 22; Stern door/quarter ramp
Sisters (Ru flag):
★**80201 KOMSOMOLSK**
★**80202 ANATOLIY VASILYEV**
★**80203 SMOLENSK**

80210 LALANDIA De/Sw (Eriksbergs) 1974; RoC; 13900/24000; 207.4 × 9.58 (680.45 × 31.43); M (Pielstick); 22.75; Stern door
Similar (superstructure varies):
80211 BARRANDUNA (Sw)
80212 TARAGO (No)
80213 TOMBARRA (No)
80214 TRICOLOR (No)
Similar (Fr built and Fr flag):
80215 RODIN
80216 ROSTAND
80217 ROUSSEAU

80220 KAPRIFOL Sw/Sw (Lodose) 1977; RoC/Con; 5500; 162.11 × 6.6 (531.86 × 21.65); M (Sulzer); 17.25; Stern door/ramp
Sisters:
80221 MATINA (Be) ex *Vallmo* 1983
80222 LINNE (Sw) (funnel variation)

●**80230 HELLENIC VALOR** Gr/Ja (Sasebo) 1978; RoC; 17200; 190.53 × 11.9 (625.1 × 39.04); TSM (MAN); 17; Stern door/ramp
Sisters (Gr flag):
80231 HELLENIC EXPLORER
★**80232 HELLENIC INNOVATOR**

80240 MARY HOLYMAN Br/Ne (Boele's Sch.) —; 2600; 101.2 × 5.18 (332.02 × 16.99); 15; Stern door

★**80250 AKADEMIK ARTSIMOVICH** Ru/Fr (CNIM) 1975; RoC; 3200; 119.03 × 5.77 (390.52 × 18.93); M (Pielstick); 17; Stern door
Sisters (Ru flag):
★**80251 AKADEMIK GUBER**
★**80252 AKADEMIK KUPREVICH**
★**80253 AKADEMIK MILLIONSCHIKOV**
★**80254 AKADEMIK STECHKIN**
★**80255 AKADEMIK TUPOLEV**

●**80260 SKULPTOR KONENKOV** Ru/Pd (Gdanska) 1975; RoC/Con; 18500; 181.41 × 9.64 (595.18 × 31.63); M (Sulzer); 20.5; Stern door/quarter ramp 'B-481' type
Sisters (Ru flag):
★**80261 SKULPTOR VUCHETICH**
★**80262 SKULPTOR GOLUBKINA**
★**80263 SKULPTOR ZALKALNS**
★**80264 NIKOLAY CHERKASOV**
★**80265 AGOSTINHO NETO** ex *Boris Limanov*
★**80266 PETR MASHEROV**

80267 NEDLLOYD ROUEN Ne/Ja (NKK) 1978; RoC/Con; 21500; 212.10 × 10.72 (696 × 35.17); M (Sulzer); 19; Quarter ramp (starboard)
Sister:
80268 NEDLLOYD ROSARIO (Ne)

●**80270 ELK** Br/Ko (Hyundai) 1977; RoC; 5500; 151.01 × 7.32 (495.44 × 24.02); M (Pielstick); 18.5; Bow door/ramp; Stern door/ramp
Sisters:
80271 CONSTELLATION ENTERPRISE (Gr) ex *Merzario Ionia* 1981; ex *Stena Shipper* 1980; ex *Norsky* 1980
80274 MERZARIO HISPANIA (Ma) ex *Atlantic Project* 1981
80275 STENA IONIA (Ma) ex *Merzario Ionia* 1982; ex *Stena Ionia* 1981; ex *Atlantic Prosper* 1981
80276 STENA GRECIA (Br) ex *Merzario Grecia*; ex *Tor Felicia* 1982
80277 STENA FREIGHTER (Br) ex *Jolly Turchese* 1983; ex *Jolly Giallo* 1982; ex *Stena Freighter* 1982; ex *Merzario Ausonia* 1980
80278 STENA CARRIER (Br) ex *Jolly Smeraldo* 1982; ex *Jolly Bruno* 1982; ex *Stena Carrier* 1982; ex *Imparca Miami* 1981; ex *Stena Carrier* 1980; ex *Imparca Express I* 1980

80280 SAUDI ABHA Si/Sw (Kockums) 1982; RoC-/Con 25000; 248.72 × 10.80 (816 × 35.43); M (B&W); 18.5; Stern quarter ramp (starboard)
Sisters (Si flag):
80281 SAUDI DIRIYAH
80282 SAUDI HOFUF
80283 SAUDI TABUK

80290 BOOGABILLA Sw/Ja (Mitsubishi HI) 1978; RoC/Con; 22300; 228.51 × 9.05 (749.7 × 29.69); M (Sulzer); 22; Angled stern door/ramp
Sisters:
80291 ELGAREN (Sw)
80292 TOURCOING (No)
80293 KOLSNAREN (Sw) ex *Merzario Asia* 1979; ex *Kolsnaren* 1979

●**80294 BULLAREN** Sw/Sw (Gotav) 1979; RoC; 18300; 187.60 × 7.20 (615 × 23.62); M; 18; ex *Tarifa* 1983; ex *Vindafjord* 1981; ex *Bullaren* 1981; Quarter ramp (starboard)

80296 ANDREA MERZARIO It/It (Italcantieri) 1980; RoC/Con; 21300; 194.37 × 10.8 (637.7 × 35.43); M (GMT); 19.15; Quarter ramp on starboard side; Lengthened 1983 by 31m (Riuniti); Drawing shows vessel prior to this
Sister:
80297 COMANDANTE REVELLO (It)

80300 KUSHIRO MARU Ja/Ja (Shimoda) 1974; RoC; 4700; 130 × 6.02 (426.51 × 19.75); M (Pielstick); 17

80320 GOLD CLOUD Pa/Sp ('Astano') 1964; C; 1800/2800; 92.39 × —/7.13 (303.12 × —/23.39); M (MAN); 12.5; ex *Janca* 1975; ex *Carmen* 1970

80330 SOFIA Le/Ne (Terneuzensche) 1958; C; 3400; 99.65 × 5.74/7.15 (326.94 × 18.83/23.46); M (MAN); 12; ex *Saale* 1980; ex *Olivia Winther* 1963

●**80340 TRANSEAST** Pa/FRG (Unterweser) 1967; C; 1800; 88.45 × 5.22 (290.19 × 17.13); M (KHD); 14; ex *Charm* 1981; ex *Ayan 1* 1980; ex *Himno 1* 1980; ex *Cap Hero* 1977; ex *Scomber* 1977; ex *Hippo Sailor* 1976; ex *Marie Reith* 1975
Sisters:
80341 NANO K (Gr) ex *Hippo Lady* 1977; ex *Perca* 1977; ex *Hippo Lady* 1976; ex *Susanne Reith* 1974
80342 GLOBAL (Pa) ex *Emilia K* 1983; ex *Luzon* 1982; ex *Eme* 1981; ex *Emil P* 1978; ex *Emil Reith* 1978
Possible sister:
80343 REST (Pa) ex *Crestena* 1983; ex *Raja* 1977; ex *Hippo Carrier* 1976; ex *Elisabeth Reith* 1975

80350 PREVEZE Tu/Tu (Denizcilik) 1973; C; 1300; 80.02 × 5.51 (262.53 × 18.08); M (Atlas-MaK); —
Sister (Tu flag):
80351 NIGBOLU
Probable sisters (Tu Flag):
80352 AGRI
80353 ANTAKYA
80354 ARTVIN
80355 ANTALYA
80356 CALDIRAN
80357 MOHAC

80370 KOREAN WONIS-SUN Ko/Fr (CNIM) 1975; Con; 21300; 208.19 × 9.27 (683.04 × 30.4); T (GEC); 23.5; ex *Korean Jupiter* 1981; ex *Oriental Financier* 1978
Sisters:
80374 CHEVALIER VALBELLE (Fr)
Similar (lengthened):
80375 CHEVALIER ROZE (Fr)
80376 CHEVALIER PAUL (Fr)
80377 MERCATOR (Be)
80378 ORIENTAL EXECUTIVE (Li)
80379 ORIENTAL EDUCATOR (Br) ex *Seapac Lexington* 1983; ex *Oriental Researcher* 1981
80380 ORIENTAL EXPLORER (Tw) ex *Seapac Princeton* 1984; ex *Oriental Statesman* 1981

80385 PACIFIC PROMINENCE Br/Ja (Hitachi) 1982; B; 35600; 224.52 × 12.95 (737 × 42.49); M (B&W); —
Sister:
80386 PACIFIC PRESTIGE (Br)

80390 GOLD CLOUD Pa/Sp ('Astano') 1964; C; 1800/2800; 92.39 × —/7.13 (303.12 × —/23.39); M (MAN); 12.5; ex *Janca* 1975; ex *Carmen* 1970

80400 MONTONE It/FRG (Nobiskrug) 1963; C; 3000; 105.92 × 6 (347.51 × 19.69); M (MAN); 14.5; ex *Jobst Oldendorff* 1980
Sisters:
80401 KATERINE (Pa) ex *Christine Oldendorff*
80402 RIMA G (Le) ex *Erna Oldendorff* 1980
80403 LAMONE (It) ex *Hans Oldendorff* 1980

80410 CIRO TERZO It/FRG (Ottensener) 1958; C; 2700; 96.7 × 6.1 (317.26 × 20.21); M (MWM); 13.75;

ex *Angeliki H* 1980; ex *Persia Lydia* 1973; ex *Coudebec U N 2* 1968; ex *Caudebec* 1960

80420 PLAYA Pa/FRG (Meyer) 1958; C; 1000/1800; 80.7 × 4.32/5.96 (264.76 × 14.17/19.55); M (KHD); 12.5; ex *Merket* 1979; ex *Moura* 1978; ex *Marita* 1975; ex *Akko* 1969
Sister:
80421 MELITA (Ma) ex *Dusk* 1983; ex *Dusan* 1978; ex *Runo* 1975; ex *Ashdod* 1969
Possibly similar:
80422 DADO (Is) ex *Kesarya* 1978; ex *Jasper* 1975; ex *Kesarya* 1970

80430 MARE AMICO It/FRG (Ottensener) 1953; 1600; 87.74 × 4.85 (287.86 × 15.91); M (Ottensener); 12.5; ex *Francesca Seconda* 1977; ex *Gretke Oldendorff* 1971; ex *Mary Robert Muller* 1961

80460 CONDE DEL CADAGUA Sp/Sp (AESA) 1959; C; 3900; 113.11 × 6.36 (371.1 × 20.87); M (B&W); 13.5

80490 MASTROGIORGIS Gr/FRG (Hanseatische) 1958; C; 3000; 95 × 6.9 (311.68 × 22.64); M (MAN) 14; ex *Palmah* 1978; ex *Atid* 1960

80500 QUICKTHORN Br/Br (Ailsa) 1967; C; 1600; 85.35 × 4.93 (280.02 × 16.17); M (British Polar); 13; ex *Tanmerack* 1973

★**80520 KORNAT** Ys/FRG (Ottensener) 1957; C; 1200/1800; 83.98 × —/6.10 (276 × —/20.01); M (MAN); 12; ex *Fidas* 1967; ex *Sunny Boy* 1965; ex *Monterey* 1964; ex *Norfarer* 1957
Sister:
80521 MARIANNA DORMIO (It) ex *Anna Nielsen* 1970; ex *Siweka* 1961

80530 ANTHOULA 1 Cy/No (Kristiansands) 1965; C; 500/1200; 71.73 × 3.77/5.31 (235.33 × 12.37/17.42); M (MaK); 12.5; ex *Calandplein*; ex *Marmara* 1974; ex *Marmorfjell* 1970
Probable sister:
80531 SEA CROWN (No) ex *Marmorhav* 1973; ex *Marmorian* 1968; ex *Marmorhav* 1967

80540 VANGELI Pa/Sp (Euskalduna) 1964; C; 2800; 93.68 × 6.13 (307.35 × 20.11); M (MAN); —; ex *Evangelia* 1983; ex *Argo* 1974; ex *Mango* 1969; Launched as *Malkenes*

80550 RAMSLI No/FRG (Hagelstein) 1957; C; 1000; 71.38 × 4.7 (234.19 × 15.42); M (KHD); 12; ex *Austvik* 1980; ex *Maria Althoff* 1967

80570 CHARTA Me/FRG (Hagelstein) 1958; C; 1000; 71.4 × 4.68 (234.25 × 15.35); M (KHD); 12; ex *Neuwarsersand* 1971; ex *Hamme* 1965

80590 LAGO FORTUNE Ho/FRG (Schlichting) 1959; C; 2000; 86.06 × 5.64 (282.35 × 18.5); M (KHD); 14; ex *Lago Atitlan* 1982; ex *Rotersand* 1973

80600 VATSY Mg/No (Drammen) 1957; C; 1400; 72.55 × 4.74 (238.02 × 15.55); M (Nydqvist & Holm); 12; ex *Le Scandinave* 1959

80610 CATALAN BAY Br/Br (Hayes) 1957; C; 1000; 65.41 × 4.07 (214.6 × 13.35); M (British Polar); 12; ex *Myrtidiotissa II* 1981; ex *Kirtondyke* 1975

80620 HTAN TAW YWA Bm/FRG (Lindenau) 1961; C; 2700; 91.5 × 6.03 (300.2 × 1978); M (MAN); —; ex *Lindo* 1968;
Similar (lengthened):
80621 DONGA (Pa) ex *Georgios P P* 1980; ex *Olympios Athina* 1980; ex *Eirin Maru* 1979; ex *Habernis* 1974; ex *Bongo* 1969

80630 FRIDAY Pa/It (Adriatico) 1965; B; 15900; 190.48 × 9.93 (624.93 × 32.98); M (B&W); —; ex *Ida Teresa* 1983
Sisters:
80631 LIA (Pa) ex *Eleonora F* 1983
80632 ALEXANDER K (Pa) ex *Alessandra F* 1983
80632/1 MONTE OLIVETO (It) ex *Carlotta F* 1983
(Pd flag—some have taller funnels):
★**80633 ZIEMIA GDANSKA**
★**80635 ZIEMIA SZCZECINSKA**
★**80636 ZIEMIA WIELKOPOLSKA**
(Cy flag):
80636/1 ANKA D ex *Ziemia Lubuska* 1983

80640 ANNA BIBOLINI It/It (Italcantieri) 1967; B; 27600; 213.32 × 12.51 (699.87 × 41.04); M (Fiat); 17.25

80650 BANGLAR JOY Bh/Br (Burntisland) 1961; C; 4900/7200; 137.17 × 7.65/8.57 (450.03 × 25.1/18.12); M (Doxford); 15; ex *Mardulce* 1976; ex *Gilsland* 1968

80660 MINFU Pa/FRG (Rickmers) 1965; C; 2700/4300; 116.74 × 6.36/7.54 (383.01 × 20.87/24.74); M (Borsig); 15; ex *Martin Schroder*
Sister:

80661 SHOU SHAN (Pa) ex *Monique Schroder*

●**80670 LOS CARIBES** Pa/Br (Burntisland) 1969; C; 3200/5100; 121.62 × 6.63/7.91 (399 × 21.75/25.95); M (Fiat); 16; ex *Caribe VI* 1977; ex *Christiane Bolten* 1977
Sister:
80671 LINHAVEN (Cy) ex *Nausica* 1981; ex *Lydia*; ex *Helen Miller*; ex *Ana Renata* 1973; ex *Helen Miller* 1972

80680 GOOD YEAR Th/FRG (Renck) 1953; C; 600; 63.71 × 5.06 (209.02 × 16.6); M (Mirrlees); 12; ex *Holmni*; ex *Holmpark* 1974; ex *Command* 1966; ex *Commandant Milliasseau* 1965

80690 GALLOWAY EXPRESS Li/Ne (Giessen) 1960/77; LS; —; 119.49 × 5.68/6.41 (392.03 × 18.64/21.03); M (Stork); 16; ex *European Express* 1977; ex *Cap Ivi* 1976; ex *European Express* 1976; ex *Ladon* 1974; Converted from general cargo 1977 (Meyer)

80700 NERA Br/Ne (Boele's Sch) 1961; C; 800; 77.17 × 4.02 (253.18 × 13.19); M (Werkspoor); 11.25; ex *Asuncion* 1981; ex *Adara* 1973
Sisters:
80701 YOKAMU (Br) ex *Villarrica* 1981; ex *Situla* 1973
80702 FEDROS (Br) ex *Talita* 1977
80704 RITSA M (Gr) ex *Solon*; ex *Nashira* 1977

80705 MIYAJIMA MARU Ja/Ja (Koyo) 1982; B; 34000; 222.13 × 13.02 (729× 42.72); M (B&W); 14.75
Possible sisters:
80706 GORGEOUS (Tw) ex *World Carmen Romano* 1982
80707 YOUNG SHINKO (Ja)

80710 JHANSI KI RANI In/Br (Lithgows) 1975; B; 42100; 245.37 × 13.83 (805.02 × 45.37); M (B&W); 15.25
Sisters (In Flag):
80711 JALAVIHAR
80712 KASTURBA

80720 PANAMAX CENTAURUS Tw/Br (Lithgows) 1966; B; 40800; 249.94 × 13.36 (820 × 43.83); M (Sulzer); 15; ex *Baltic Neptune* 1983; ex *Panamax Jupiter* 1980; ex *Nordic Talisman* 1977; ex *Naess Talisman* 1974

80730 SATYA KAILASH In/Br (Lithgows) 1967; B; 42200; 245.37 × 13.84 (805.02 × 45.41); M (B&W); 15; ex *Gallic Bridge* 1974
Sister:
80731 PROTEUS (Gr) ex *Westminster Bridge* 1973

★**80750 LEONID TELIGA** Pd/FRG (Lindenau) 1969; C; 2800/5700; 125.18 × 6.45/7.64 (410.7 × 21.16/25.07); M (MAN); 12; ex *Scol Eminent* 1976; ex *Cape Canaveral* 1974; ex *Cape Race* 1972; ex *Kathe Wiards* 1970
Sisters:
80751 INA (Pa) ex *Ina B* 1983; ex *Trimar Sky* 1982; ex *Inalotte Blumenthal* 1980; ex *Inre* 1979; ex *Inalotte Blumenthal* 1978; ex *Adelheid Wiards* 1972
80752 EBN MAGID (Ly) ex *Cape Sear* 1975; ex *Adel Weert Wiards* 1973

80760 GEODRILL Br/Ne (E J Smit) 1962; RS; 1500; 80.6 × 4.77 (264.44 × 15.65); M (Werkspoor); —; ex *Briarthorn* 1981; ex *Anne* 1973; ex *Anne Bogelund* 1969; Converted from cargo

80770 CENTAURO It/It (Ansaldo) 1962; B; 26400; 229.75 × 11.73 (753.77 × 38.4S); M (Fiat); 15; Lengthened 1967
Sister (It flag):
80771 POSEIDON
Possibly similar (It Flag):
80773 GALASSIA

80780 SAN VINCENZO Pa/It (Ansaldo) 1965; B; 14600; 185.25 × 10.45 (597.93 × 34.28); M (Fiat); 16.25; ex *Garden Gemini* 1979; ex *Portoria* 1975

80810 KUSHIRO MARU Ja/Ja (Shimoda) 1974; RoC; 4700; 130 × 6.02 (426.51 × 19.75); M (Pielstick); 17

80820 EIRIK RAUDE No/FRG (A G 'Weser') 1967; LGC; 6100; 116.31 × 7.77 (381.59 × 25.49); M (MAN); 15; ex *Mundogas Bermuda* 1976

80830 TALETE It/Fr (Havre) 1967; LGC; 1600; 80.98 × 4.62 (265.68 × 15.16); M (MAN); 13; ex *Thales* 1972

80840 FARADAY Br/Br (Swan Hunter) 1971; LGC; 19800; 186.85 × 9.75 (613.02× 31.99); M (Doxford); 15.75
Sister:
80841 LINCOLNSHIRE (Br)

80850 INDIAN VALOUR In/FRG (A G 'Weser') 1971; C; 7000/9600; 144.91 × 9.42 (475.43 × 30.91); M (MAN); 16; '36-L' type
Sister:
80851 INDIAN VENTURE (In)

80860 GAMA GETAH Pa/Fi (Wartsila) 1967/75; C; 8200/12100; 182.61 × 8.05/9.4 (599.11 × 26.41/30.84); M (Sulzer); 17; ex *Hoegh Opal* 1982; Lengthened 1975 (Kawasaki)
80861 GAMA KASIA (Pa) ex *Hoegh Orchid* 1982
80862 GAMA PALA (Pa) ex *Hoegh Orris* 1982
Similar (taller funnel etc.):
80863 GAMA ROBUSTA (Pa) ex *Hoegh Pilot* 1982

80870 RIA MAR 1 Le/Sw (Oresunds) 1954; C; 3700; 112.27 × 6.34 (368.34 × 20.8); M (Gotaverken); 12; ex *Milos V* 1982; ex *Arabert*; Lengthened 1965
Sister:
80871 HIND G (Le) ex *Arabritt* 1979

★**80890 ADAM ASNYK** Pd/FRG (A G 'Weser') 1974; C; 7000/9600; 145.04 × 8.23/9.43 (475.85 × 27/30.94); M (MAN) 16; '36-L' type
Sisters (RC flag):
★**80891 CHANGXING**
★**80892 DEXING**

★**80900 PETKO R SLAVEJNOV** Bu/Ys ('Uljanik') 1968; C; 9100; 143.64 × 8.87 (471.26 × 29.1); M (B&W); 15; Launched as *Atria*
★**80901 IVAN VAZOV** (Bu) launched as *Almak*
Similar (heavier radar mast):
80902 OMDURMAN (Su)

80910 TRADER Cy/Br (Clelands) 1970; Tk; 3300; 98.3 × 6.55 (322.51 × 21.49); M (English Electric); 12.75; ex *Texaco Warrior* 1984; ex *Anteriority* 1975; ex *Thuntank 6* 1972
Sister:
80911 EKFJORD (Sw) ex *Amity* 1977; ex *Pointe De Toulinquet* 1976; ex *Amity* 1975; ex *Thuntank 5* 1972
Similar:
80912 UNICORN JONI (Li) ex *Rathmore* 1982; ex *Alk* 1977

★**80920 LI IICHANSK** Ru/Ru(IHI) 1962; Tk; 23100; 207.04×11.11 (679.27×36.45); M(Sulzer); 16.5
Sisters (Ru flag):
★**80921 LENKORAN**
★**80922 LYUBOTIN**

80930 DOBROTA Ma/Ja (Nagoya) 1960; B; 11100; 161.96 × 9.21 (531.4 × 30.21); M (B&W); 14.75; ex *Rosina Topic*
Sister:
80931 LJUTA (Ma) ex *Serafin Topic* 1979

80940 IRENE Pi/Ja (Hayashikane) 1966; C; 7100; 131.93 × 7.6 (432.8 × 24.9); M (Hitachi); 15

80970 FREO ZUTA Gh/FRG (Schlichting) 1969; R; 2000; 93.71 × 5.51 (307.45 × 18.08); M (KHD); 17.5; ex *Nyanaw* 1982; ex *Cooler Scan* 1974

80980 FREEZER LEVA Cy/FRG (Buesumer) 1968; R; 500/1200; 75.6 × 3.81/5 (248.03 × 12.5/16.4); M (Atlas-MaK); 14.75; ex *Freezer Finn* 1982; ex *Freezer Scan* 1973
Sisters:
80981 REEFER TRADER (Cy) ex *Ice Flower* 1977; ex *Frigo Scan* 1973
80982 JOKULFJELL (Ic) ex *Bymos* 1975
Probable sister:
80983 PAULA LEE (Cy) ex *Dana Frio* 1982; ex *Zalagh* 1976; ex *Ahmos* 1972

80990 ABOITIZ CONCARRIER IX Pi/FRG (Schlichting) 1961; C; 900/1500; 81.82 × —/5.27 (268.44 × —/17.29); M (KHD); 14.5; ex *Mindanao Transport* 1982; ex *Piso* 1974; ex *Vinland Saga* 1969

★**81000 NOVY BUG** Ru/Rm (Galatz) 1963; C; 3300; 100.59 × 6.55 (330.02 × 21.49); M (Sulzer); 12.5
Sisters (Ru flag):
★**81001 NOVY DONBASS**
★**81002 NOVAYA KAKHOVKA**
★**81003 NOVORZHEV**
★**81004 NOVOSHAKHTINSK**

★**81010 DA LONG TIAN** RC/Ja (A G 'Weser') 1966; C/HL; 7010/9450; 152.25 × 8.31/9.48 (499.5 × 27.2/31.1); M (MAN); 19; ex *Crostafels* 1978
Sisters:
★**81011 DA HONG QIAO** (RC) ex *Kybfels* 1979
★**81012 WU YI SHAN** (RC) ex *Birkenfels* 1978
★**81013 DA QING SHAN** (RC) ex *Schonfels*
81014 AIAS (Gr) ex *Falkenfels* 1980
81015 HOHENBELS (Gr) ex *Hohenfels*

81020 MATINA Gr/FRG (Lindenau) 1963; C; 2900;

94.16 ×6.77 (308.92 × 22.21); M (MAN); —; ex *Bulwark*; ex *Nahoon* 1971; ex *Tronstad* 1967

81030 MUMTAZ Sh/FRG (Stuelcken) 1952; C; 1200/1900; 78.67 × —/6.24 (258.1 × —/20.47); M (MaK); ex *Astron* 1981; ex *Lebanese Wind* 1970; ex *Sulaphat* 1967; ex *Leamitra* 1963; ex *Leada*

81040 MARIA K Le/FRG (O&K) 1962; C; 1800; 88.52 × 5.26 (290.42 × 17.26); M (KHD); 15.5; ex *La Molinera* 1980; ex *Stephan Reith* 1972

81050 HAJ ABDUL RAHMAN Cy/FRG (Nobiskrug) 1966; C; 2100; 90.05 × 5.67 (295.44 × 18.6); M (MAN); 13.75; ex *Isabelle* 1978; ex *Botany Bay* 1973
Sisters:
81051 ANNA (Gr) ex *Rona* 1981; ex *Cap Falcon* 1980; ex *Stern Sirius* 1973; ex *Sirius* 1972;
81052 ABDUL LATIF (Cy) ex *Stern Saturn*; ex *Saturn* 1974

81060 WILCON III Pi/FRG (Nobiskrug) 1966; CP; 2100; 90.05 × 5.67 (295.44 × 18.6); M (MAN); 13.5; ex *Zamboanga* 1979; ex *Zamboanga City* 1979; ex *Luzon Transport* 1975; ex *Leinster Bay* 1973

★**81070 KRUSEVO** Ys/Sp (AESA) 1967; C; 1700/2700; 95.54 × —/6.7 (313.45 × —/21.98); M (MAN); 14; ex *Idrissi* 1969
Sister:
81071 MAGHREB (In) ex *Miljet* 1974; ex *Tariq* 1969

81080 MUSING So/FRG (Atlas-Werke) 1957; C; 3900/5400; 130.41 × 6.89/7.77 (427.85 × 22.6/25.49); M (MAN); 15.5; ex *Rendsburg* 1972; ex *Tove Lilian* 1965

81090 HIMALAYA Gr/FRG (Howaldts) 1962; C; 8200/11000; 158.5 × 8/9.2 (520 × 26.25/30.18); M (MAN); 15; ex *Olympian* 1983; ex *Maratha Endeavour* 1971

81100 BODRUM Tu/FRG (A G 'Weser') 1961; C; 3100/4400; 115.73 × —/7.16 (379.69 × —/23.49); M (MAN); —
Sisters (Tu flag):
81101 MARMARIS 1
81102 MUGLA
Similar (Tu Flag):
81103 FETHIYE

81110 GOLDEN WAVE Pa/FRG (Nobiskrug) 1969; C; 2800/5000; 124.97 × 6.53/7.67 (410 × 21.42/25.16); M (Atlas-MaK); 16.5; ex *Juno* 1983
Sister:
81111 JUPITER II (Pa) ex *Jupiter* 1980

81120 PETROLA 30 Gr/FRG (Atlas-Werke) 1956; C; 2800; 101 × 6.25 (331.36 × 20.5); M (MaK); 12.5; ex *Petrola XXX* 1976; ex *Yellow Star 1* 1975; ex *Arras* 1974; ex *Julius Hugo Stinnes* 1971; ex *Mylady* 1966;
Sister:
81121 ISSA 1 (Le) ex *Valeriana* 1980; ex *Scalmike* 1976; ex *Holnis* 1974; ex *Hugo Oldendorff* 1969; ex *Nora Hugo Stinnes* 1964

81130 LEEGAS Pa/No (Moss V) 1967; LGC; 2900; 90.56 × 6.1 (297.11 × 20.01); M (Sulzer); 12.5; ex *Silversky* 1983; ex *Marco Polo*; ex *Gazania* 1970
Sisters:
81131 BARGAS (Pa) ex *Silversea* 1983; ex *Columbus*; ex *Janegaz* 1970
81132 CAP AKRITAS (Gr) ex *Byzantine Energy* 1981; ex *Fridtjof Nansen* 1978
Similar:
81133 GAZ PROGRESS (Pa) ex *Coral Obelia* 1979; ex *Arctic Propane* 1971

81140 AVLIS EXPRESS Gr/FRG (Atlas-Werke) 1960/70; C; 3500; 110.75 × 6.14 (360.93 × 19.72); M (MaK); 12.5; ex *Maria* 1981; ex *Vamos* 1979; ex *Bellatrix 1* 1977; ex *Koholyt* 1971; ex *Koholyt Hugo Stinnes* 1971; ex *Koholyt* 1962; Lengthened 1970
Sisters:
81141 ANDROMEDA (Gr) ex *Aggela* 1982; ex *Elounda* 1981; ex *Aquila 1* 1977; ex *Achgelis* 1971; ex *Achgelis Hugo Stinnes*
81142 MARIASSIMI (Br) ex *Marisa* 1982; ex *Marisa Kar* 1981; ex *Therissos* 1980; ex *Velerofontis* 1975; ex *Columba* 1975; ex *Mak* 1971; ex *Mak Hugo Stinnes* 1971

81150 NEAPOLI Pa/Sw (Oskarshamns) 1952; C; 1500; 87.03 × 4.62 (285.53 × 15.16); M (Nydqvist & Holm); 11.25; ex *Neapolis* 1982; ex *Sunnanhav* 1975; ex *Gapern* 1967; ex *Storfors* 1961

81160 PERMINA VIII Ia/Ne ('De Biesbosch') 1954; Tk; 2400; 88.25 × 5.44 (289.53 × 17.85); M (Nydqvist & Holm); 11.5; ex *Elizabeth Broere* 1966; ex *Elizabeth B* 1960

81170 BETINA THOLSTRUP De/No (Moss V) 1969; LGC; 3000; 101.94 × 5.72 (334.45 × 18.77); M (Sulzer); 13; ex *Thor* 1981; ex *Thor Heyerdahl* 1979

81180 MATADI PALM Br/Br (Swan Hunter) 1970; Tk; 8900; 147.83 × 8.55 (485 × 28.05); M (Doxford); 15

81190 LUANA Pa/FRG (Nobiskrug) 1965; C; 3200; 106.63 × 6.99 (349.84 × 22.93); M (MAN); 13.5; ex *Maxi Porr* 1980

★**81195 TATARSTAN** Ru/Ru (Zelenodolskiy) 1977; FC; 2400; 95.28 × 5.48 (313 × 17.98); M (Praha); 14.5
Sisters:
★**81196 TURKMENISTAN** (Ru)
★**81197 UZBEKISTAN** (Ru)

●**81200 SITI MIDAH** Pa/Ja (Kurushima) 1971; C/HL; 7000; 131.81 × 8.23 (262.5 × 27); M (Kobe); 14; ex *Sri Hamida* 1983; ex *Sun Eternal* 1983; ex *Seiyo Maru* 1982
Sisters:
81201 IPPOLITOS (Gr) ex *Sakura Maru* 1980
81202 FORUM STAR (Gr) ex *Tachibana Maru*

81220 BUNGA VANDA Pa/Ja (Kawasaki D) 1959; C/HL; 5000; 122.81 × 7.39 (409.92 × 24.25); M (MAN); 13.5; ex *Bomi* 1982; ex *Caribbean Star No. 1* 1980; ex *Kumano Maru* 1975

●**81230 DESPINA V** Pa/Ne ('Ijssel') 1971; C; 3000; 91.45 × 7.18 (300.03 × 23.56); M (MAN); 13.5; ex *Belemar* 1983; ex *Reem 1* 1982; ex *Raha* 1980; ex *Nelly Maersk* 1976
Sister:
81231 MARIANNA (Gr) ex *Atlas River* 1980; ex *Niels Maersk* 1976

81240 LAGADA BAY Gr/FRG (Rickmers) 1968; C; 4400; 110.75 × 7.29 (363.35 × 23.92); M (KHD); —; ex *Inge* 1978; ex *Ursula C* 1977; ex *Alexandra Botelho* 1974

81250 NAVI STAR Le/FRG (Kroegerw) 1959; R; 1500; 91.01 × 4.85 (298.59 × 15.91); M (MAN); 14; ex *Baltic Jet*

81260 DIMACHK Sy/No (Sarpsborg) 1963; C; 2700; 91.52 × 6.03 (300.26 × 19.78); (MAN); 12.25; ex *Anneliese Porr* 1975

81270 MARANAR Cy/FRG (Hagelstein) 1961; C; 800/1200; 76.1 × —/5.03 (249.67 × —/16.5); M (KHD); 12; ex *Lauter* 1973; ex *Siegfried* 1965; ex *Karl-Heinz Parchmann* 1962

81280 STORM Pa/FRG (Renck) 1953; C; 2000; 73.43 × 6.48 (240.91 × 21.26); M (MaK); 12; ex *Wren* 1983; ex *Minoa* 1981; ex *El Mina* 1972; ex *Johanna* 1965

81290 NICOS A Pa/FRG (Stuelcken) 1956; C; 1200/2200; 78.67 × 4.98/6.57 (258.1 × 16.34/21.56); M (MAN); —; ex *Rampart I* 1977; ex *Rampart* 1976; ex *Leabeth* 1966
Sister:
81291 ALASSIA (Pa) ex *Platana* 1981; ex *Ilios* 1972; ex *Sertan* 1971; ex *Lebanese Wave* 1970; ex *Sheliak* 1967; ex *Leanna* 1963

81300 LESLIE Gr/FRG (Lindenau) 1965; C; 2400; 92.06 × 5.6 (302.03 × 18.37); M (Sulzer); 13; ex *Anna Rehder* 1973
Sister:
★**81301 KRKA** (Ys) ex *Matthias Rehder* 1974

★**81310 CAMAGUEY** Cu/Ja (Niigata) 1959; C; 2300; 93.22 × 5.77 (305.84 × 18.93); M (Niigata); —

81320 ARIEL 1 Pa/FRG (Rolandwerft) 1967; C; 800/1400; 79.23 × 4.22/5.51 (259.9 × 13.85/18.08); M (Atlas-MaK); 13.75; ex *Saumaty* 1982; ex *Asser Rig* 1973; ex *Vela* 1969; ex *Asser Rig* 1968

81330 CARIGULF PIONEER Br/Ne ('Ijssel') 1962; C; 1100/1700; 81.84 × 4.02/5.50 (269 × 13.19/18.04); M (Smit-Bolnes); 12.5; ex *Etai* 1981; ex *Ytai* 1977; ex *Carmela* 1976; ex *Barok* 1974; ex *Raila Dan* 1969

81340 TACAMAR VII Pa/Fi (Valmet) 1965; C; 3200/4800; 118.01 × —/7.13 (387.17 × —/23.39); M (B&W); —; ex *Tamanaco* 1980; ex *Citta Di Viareggio* 1974; ex *Concordia Finn* 1971; ex *Finnmill* 1970; ex *Concordia Finn* 1969; ex *Finnmill* 1968; ex *Finnbrod* 1967

★**81350 ZULAWY** Pd/Pd (Gdanska) 1974; FC; 8100; 151.31 × 7.4 (496.42 × 24.28); M (Sulzer); 19; **'B 68'** type
Sisters (Pd flag):
★**81351 KASZUBY II**
★**81352 WINETA**
★**81353 MAZURY**

81370 UNION BALTIMORE Pa/Ja (Mitsui) 1958; C; 8700; 147.33 × 8.6 (483.37 × 28.22); M (B&W); 14; ex *Kibi Maru* 1978

★**81380 YONG CHENG** RC/Br (Burntisland) 1968; C; 3200/5000; 121.62 × 6.61/7.89 (399 × 21.69/25.89); M (B&W); 16.5; ex *Paul Schroder* 1981
Sister:
★**81381 FANG CHENG** (RC) ex *Peter Schroder* 1981

●**81390 ASTRID SCHULTE** Cy/FRG (Lindenau) 1967; C; 2200/3600; 107.85 × 6.31/7.42 (353.84 × 20.7/24.34); M (MAN); 15.5; ex *Cap Maleas* 1978; ex *Astrid Schulte* 1976;
Sister:
81391 MORITZ SCHULTE (Cy)

★**81400 ALIOT** Ru/Fi (Rauma-Repola) 1970; WT/Ch; 3100; 93.88 × 6.5 (308.01 × 21.33); M (B&W); 14
Sisters (Ru flag):
★**81401 POLLUKS**
★**81402 PROTSION**

81410 FERNANDOEVERETT Li/Fi (Crichton-Vulcan) 1964/69; C/Con; 8700; 152 × 8.6 (500 × 28.7); M (Sulzer); 16; ex *Finnhawk*; ex *Maltesholm* 1976; Converted from cargo and lengthened 1969 (Wartsila)
Sisters:
81411 CORDILLERA (Ch) ex *Finnarrow*; ex *Vasaholm* 1976;
81412 CORRAL (Pa) ex *Mah* 1980; ex *Finn-Enso*
81413 CONDOR (Ch) ex *Palladia*; ex *Finnmaid* 1979
★**81414 FENG NING** (RC) ex *Hue Lu* 1983; ex *Poyang* 1981; ex *Asian Exporter* 1975; ex *Finnboston* 1973; ex *Finnenso* 1964

81420 EBN JUBAIR Ly/Ja (Asakawa) 1976; C; 3500/6200; 105.7 × 7.5/7.62 (346.78 × 24.61/25); M (B&W); 13
Sister:
81421 EBN BATUTA (Ly)

81430 AL REAFA 1 Pa/FRG (A G 'Weser') 1959; C; 1600/2300; 88.85 × 5.08/6.27 (291.5 × 16.67/20.57); M (Krupp); 13; ex *Circle Pioneer* 1982; ex *Sta Maria* 1975; ex *Mieke Legenhausen*.1969

81440 RASSEM Le/Sw (Ekensbergs) 1960; C; 2700/4300; 114.33 × —/7.19 (375 × —/23.59); M (B&W); 14.5; ex *Rhon* 1982; ex *Bindal* 1964

★**81450 LEONID TELIGA** Pd/FRG (Lindenau) 1969; C; 2800/5700; 125.18 × 6.45/7.64 (410.7 × 21.16/25.07); M (MAN); 12; ex *Scol Eminent* 1976; ex *Cape Canaveral* 1974; ex *Cape Race* 1972; ex *Kathe Wiards* 1970
Sisters:
81451 INA (Pa) ex *Ina B* 1983; ex *Trimar Sky* 1982; ex *Inalotte Blumenthal* 1980; ex *Inre* 1979; ex *Inalotte Blumenthal* 1978; ex *Adelheid Wiards* 1972
81452 EBN MAGID (Ly) ex *Cape Sear* 1975; ex *Adel Weert Wiards* 1973
Similar:
81453 CARIBE MAR (Br) ex *Fairsky F* 1983; ex *Fairsky* 1980; ex *Stephan Reith* 1979

81460 PERMINA 109 Ia/It (Adriatico) 1973; Tk; 7700; 140.21 × 7.9 (460.01 × 25.92); M (Stork-Werkspoor); 15; ex *Donna Gabriella* 1974
Sister:
81461 ELISA d'ALESIO (It) ex *Donna Mariella*

81470 ELISABETTA MONTANARI It/No (Kristiansands) 1969; LGC; 3300; 101.94 × 6.06 (334.45 × 19.88); M (Sulzer); 13.75; ex *Caty Multina* 1978; ex *Cabo Tres Montes* 1971
Sisters:
81471 CRISTINA MONTANARI (It) ex *Hoegh Scout* 1974; Launched as *Rita*
81472 TROIKA (No)
Similar:
81473 BETINA THOLSTRUP (De) ex *Thor* 1981; ex *Thor Heyerdahl* 1979

●**81480 OLIVIA CUATRO** Pa/It (Riuniti) 1964; B; 10600; 160.1 × 9.6 (525.26 × 31.5); M (B&W); 16; ex *Eolia* 1981
Probably similar:
81481 SPIRIT (Gr) ex *Ilice* 1981
81482 ORFEO (It)

★**81490 PRIBOY** Ru/Sw (Gotav) 1964; FC; 10900; 156.93 × 7.4 (514.86 × 24.28); M (Gotaverken); 18.25
Sisters (Ru flag):
★**81491 KARL LINNE**
★**81492 KHIBINSKIE GORY**
★**81493 KRYMSKIE GORY**
★**81494 LENINSKIE GORY**
★**81495 URALJSKIE GORY**

81500 YACU WASI Pe/Ja (IHI) 1962; C/HL; 7400; 133.66 × 8 (438.52 × 26.25); M (Sulzer); 14; ex *Goliath* 1980; ex *Korean Diamond* 1980; ex *Wakasa Maru* 1978

81510 MICHALIS K Gr/FRG (A G 'Weser') 1957; C; 3200; 95.89 × 7.39 (314.6 × 24.25); M (KHD); 13.25; ex *Michalis* 1981; ex *Michalis K* 1981; ex *Johnny K* 1980; ex *Kekenis* 1973; ex *Phonizien* 1971

81520 SKIPPER Pa/FRG (A G 'Weser') 1957; C; 2000/3100; 95.94 × 6.08/7.39 (314.76 × 19.95/24.25); M (KHD); 13; ex *Conti Med* 1974; ex *Clipper Argonaut* 1974; ex *Sovereign Crystal* 1974; ex *Erika* 1970

81530 AEGEAN SEA Pa/Fr (Mediterranee) 1962; C; 7500/11100; 160.2 × 8.1/10 (525.9 × 26.57/32.8); M (Gotaverken); —; ex *Silverbeach* 1972; ex *Totem Star* 1964; ex *Norse Coral* 1963; Launched as *Totem Star*
Sister:
81531 NEW CORAL SEA (Pa) ex *Coral Sea* 1977; ex *Silversea* 1972; ex *Totem Queen* 1964; Launched as *Norse Reef*

81540 PATROKLOS 1 Pa/Ja (Mitsubishi HI) 1957; C; 10300; 154.84 × 9.36 (508.01 × 30.71); T (Mitsubishi); —; ex *Alhaja Mama Bakare* 1982; ex *Tharros* 1977
Similar:
81541 DUPE BAKARE (Pa) ex *Rythme* 1977

● **81550 IOTA** Gr/Ih (Verolme Cork) 1962; C; 7700/10160; 152.25 × 8.61/9.38 (499.51 × 28.25/30.77); M (Doxford); 14.5; ex *Pantavra* 1982; ex *Avra* 1978; ex *Irish Rowan* 1973
Sister:
81551 MALDIVE NOBLE (Mv) ex *Eliane* 1980; ex *Maria* 1978; ex *Irish Sycamore* 1973

★ **81555 SLATINA** Rm/Rm (Galatz) 1973; C; 2500/3500; 106.20 × 5.64/7.06 (348 × 18.50/23.16); M (Sulzer); 14
Sisters:
★ **81556 SLOBOZIA** (Rm)
81557 KOTA ANGKASA (Sg) ex *Pitria Sky* 1980; ex *Highland Prince* 1978; ex *Pitria Sky* 1977;
81558 KOTA BERKAT (Sg) ex *Pitria Sun* 1980; ex *Aries* 1977; ex *Pitria Sun* 1975
81559 KOTA BERLIAN (Sg) ex *Pitria Galaxy* 1980
81560 KOTA PELANGI (Sg) ex *Pitria Rainbow* 1980
81561 QUEEN (Ne) ex *Agona* 1983; ex *Annabel* 1983; ex *Pitria Spirit* 1980; ex *Evros 1* 1973
81562 AVRA (Gr) ex *Pitria Sea* 1980; ex *Ardas* 1973

81580 BRADEVERETT Li/FRG (Rhein Nordseew) 1963/68; C; 6600/9000; 152.33 × 7.11/8.58 (499.77 × 23.33/28.15); M (B&W); 16; ex *Finnforest* 1979; Converted from general cargo and lengthened 1968 (Rhein Nordseew)
Sisters (Li flag):
81581 ROSSEVERETT ex *Finneagle* 1979; ex *Trolleholm* 1976; ex *Finneagle* 1971
81582 LEONOREVERETT ex *Finnclipper* 1979

81590 SELAS Gr/Ne (Nederlandsche) 1963; C; 8300/10900; 154.13 × 8.59/9.91 (505.68 × 28.18/32.51); M (Gotaverken); ex *Jag Asha* 1976; ex *Dageid* 1967

81600 SHENG LI Br/Fr (La Seine) 1963; C; 4700/7300; 151.62 × —/7.87 (497.74 × —/25.82); M (Sulzer); 16; ex *Copihue* 1981; ex *Hoegh Beaver* 1978; ex *Moose Jaw* 1968; ex *N O Rogenaes* 1964; Lengthened 1969

81610 GULF TRADER Pa/No (Trondhjems) 1959; C; 4000; 111.77 × 7.83 (366.7 × 25.69); M (MAN); —; ex *Bravotrader* 1980; ex *Laurie U* 1976; ex *Elgy* 1973; ex *Arlesiana* 1972; ex *Elg* 1970; ex *Elg Viking* 1968; ex *Sunbear* 1965

81620 BAHARI Ia/Ne (Duijvendijk's) 1952; C/HL; 1100/1300; 84.51 × 4.15/4.74 (277.26 × 13.62/15.55); M (Werkspoor); 12; ex *Marijke Irene* 1974; ex *Erasmus* 1965; ex *Rampart* 1960; Lengthened 1965

81630 SEMELI Gr/Fr (La Seine) 1964; C; 6700/10100; 154.82 × 8.04/9.42 (507.94 × 26.38/30.91); M (MAN); 17.5; ex *Ariadni* 1982; ex *Ville D'Anvers* 1976

★ **81640 ZAKOPANE** Pd/Pd (Szczecinska) 1968; C; 4200/6600; 135.41 × 6.78/7.67 (444.26 × 22.24/25.16); M (Sulzer); 17; **'B446'** type
Sisters (Pd Flag):
★ **81641 ZAMOSC**
★ **81642 ZAMBRZE**
★ **81643 ZAMBROW**
★ **81644 ZAWICHOST**
★ **81645 ZAWIERCIE**
Similar (see inset):
★ **81646 FENG CHENG** (RC)
★ **81647 YAN CHENG** (RC)

81660 BAILUNDO Po/Pd (Szczecinska) 1969; C; 7700/11600; 158.4 × 8.41/10.03 (519.69 × 27.59/32.91); M (Sulzer); 14; Launched as *Artemonis*; **'B441'** type
Sister:
81661 CUNENE (Po)

81670 WIHAR 1 Pa/FRG (A.G. 'Weser') 1956; C; 1600; 78.64 × 5.62 (258 × 18.44); M (KHD); 12.5; ex *Selatan Maju* 1981; ex *Woodchuck* 1974; ex *Bat Golan* 1974; ex *Sheldrake* 1968; ex *Manchester Vanguard* 1963

81680 MINOGAZ 1 Gr/Ne ('De Gideon') 1955/64; LGC; 1000; 63.23 × 3.77 (207.45 × 12.37); M (British Polar); 12.25; ex *Cryomar* 1980; ex *Capo Cervo* 1972; ex *Abbas* 1968; ex *Broughty* 1963; Converted from general cargo 1964 (Hawthorn, L)

81690 ALBAFRIGO Gr/Ne (Gusto) 1962; R; 1500; 83.57 × 4.82 (274.18 × 15.81); M (KHD); 14; ex *Calanca* 1977
Sister:
81690/1 CASTANEDA (Br) ex *Albacore* 1980; ex *Castaneda* 1977
Possible sisters:
81691 RISA PAULA (Br) ex *Aztec* 1979; ex *Risa Paula* 1977
81692 WINDFROST (Cy) ex *Inca* 1977

81700 FREEZER LEVA Cy/FRG (Buesumer) 1968; R; 500/1200; 75.6 × 3.81/5 (248.03 × 12.5/16.4); M (Atlas-MaK); 14.75; ex *Freezer Finn* 1982; ex *Freezer Scan* 1973
Sisters:
81701 REEFER TRADER (Cy) ex *Ice Flower* 1977; ex *Frigo Scan* 1973
81702 JOKULFELL (Ic) ex *Bymos* 1975
Probable sister:
81703 PAULA LEE (Cy) ex *Dana Frio* 1982; ex *Zalagh* 1976; ex *Ahmos* 1972

81710 AGIOS ELEFTHERIOS Cy/FRG (Howaldts) 1950; C; 1500; 75.44 × 4.85 (247.51 × 15.91); M (Henschel); 10.5; ex *Chinta* 1980; ex *Ralph Von Bargen* 1975; ex *Irmgard Jacob* 1967; ex *Annemarie* 1963
Sister:
81711 STELLA A (Cy) ex *Stella* 1974; ex *Calypso* 1971; ex *Elfriede* 1962

81720 DWEJRA II Ma/Ne ('De Biesbosch') 1969; C; 1000; 84.26 × 5.11 (276.44 × 16.77); M (MWM); —; ex *ASD Iris* 1976; ex *Iris* 1973

81730 P KROL Ho/Ne (Boele's Sch) 1965; C; 500; 69.35 × 3.72 (227.53 × 12.2); M (KHD); 11.5; ex *Sarah Elizabeth* 1981

81740 NORMAND EXPRESS Ne/Be (SABARN) 1959; LS; 1000; 82.3 × 4.83 (270.01 × 15.85); M (KHD); 13.5; ex *Liveox* 1975; ex *Sinjoor* 1973; ex *Maria* 1967; Converted from general cargo

81750 JARASH Jo/Ne (Kramer & Booy) 1966; C; 500/1500; 80.29 × 3.52/4.5 (263.42 × 11.55/14.76); M (KHD); 13; ex *Ghada* 1983; ex *Sela* 1980; ex *Grecian* 1974; ex *Andromeda* 1969
Similar:
81751 LOTUS (Eg) ex *Brandaris* 1980

81760 FRANCISKA SCHULTE Cy/FRG (Lindenau) 1964; C; 2900; 94.29 × 8.61 (309.35 × 28.25); M (MAN); 14.5; ex *Friederike Ten Doornkat* 1973

81770 ANNELIESE OLTMANN FRG/No (Aukra) 1972; C; 1000; 77.09 × 5.1 (252.92 × 16.73); M (Atlas-MaK); 14
Sister (Pa flag):
81771 ESTETAL

81780 RASHIDAH Qt/Br (Clelands) 1970; C; 1500; 86.87 × 5.07 (285 × 16.63); M (English Electric); 13.5; ex *Qatar 1* 1979; ex *Cheviot Prince* 1978; ex *Mendip Prince* 1974
Sisters:
81781 FRIENDSHIP (Pa) ex *Chiltern Prince* 1981
81782 VICTORY 1 (Pa) ex *Malvern Prince* 1981
81783 FIJIAN (Fj) ex *Onehunga*; ex *Fijian* 1981; ex *Cotswold Prince* 1979

81790 LAVINIA COPPOLA It/FRG (Ottensener) 1957; C; 1800; 83.47 × 6.04 (273.95 × 19.85); M (MAN); 12; ex *Medov Grecia* 1973; ex *Sigurd Rinde* 1967

★ **81800 LISKI** Ys/No (Drammen) 1959; C; 1100/1800; 78.06 × 4.44/5.65 (256.1 × 14.57/18.54); M (Sulzer); 13; ex *Bestum* 1974; ex *Sjofna* 1962

81810 MAMBDOUN Cy/FRG (A Pahl) 1954; C; 780/1000; 68.89 × 4.27/— (226.35 × 14.01/—); M (KHD); 10; ex *Chrisoula H* 1981; ex *Diamondsea* 1975; ex *Beyrouth* 1973; ex *Naiade* 1969; ex *Najade* 1958

81820 ADI VITI Fj/FRG (Husumer) 1970; C; 1000/2000; 83.8 × 5.05/6.33 (274.93 × 16.57/20.77); M (Werkspoor); 13.5; ex *Lautoka* 1981; ex *Anna von Bargen* 1981
Sisters:
81821 FRANKA (FRG) ex *Frieda Graebe* 1983; ex *Gitta Von Bargen* 1974
81822 FAST CARRIER (Pa) ex *Susann von Bargen* 1982
81823 SORRO (Pa) ex *Movensteert* 1983
81824 BOKE (Pa) ex *Westgate Token* 1982; ex *Dukegat* 1982
Similar (lengthened—Pa flag):
81825 GROENLAND II ex *Vela* 1980

● **81830 SUN EAGLE 1** Pa/Ne (Van Diepen) 1968; C; 500/1100; 72.95× /5.21 (239.34× /17.09); M (Werkspoor); —; ex *Alnar* 1982; ex *Pulpca* 1973

81840 PACIFIC VIOLET Pa/In (Mazagon) 1978; C; 1600; 91.19 × 5.58 (299.18 × 18.31); M (Alpha-Diesel); 14.5; ex *Mechi Venture* 1981; ex *Gomba Venture* 1979
Sisters:
81841 OUED SEBOU (In)
81842 PACIFIC LILY (Pa) ex *Gomba Nile* 1980; ex *Balakram*; Launched as *Gomba Endeavour*
81843 PACIFIC TULIP (Pa) ex *Gomba Endurance* 1981; ex *Santo Vastiram*; ex *Vastiram* 1978
81844 PACIFIC FREESIA (Pa) ex *Gomba Victoria* 1981; ex *Santo Alakhram* 1978; ex *Alakhram* 1978
81845 PACIFIC ROSE (Li) ex *Gomba Endeavour* 1981

★ **81850 DIKA** Ys/Sw (Ekensbergs) 1965; RoC; 800/2200; 80.85 × 3.77/6.53 (256.26 × 12.37/21.42); M (MWM); 12; ex *Don Juan* 1972; Bow door
Sister:
81851 ARACELY (Ni) ex *Carla* 1980; ex *Nopal Sand* 1977; ex *Don Carlos* 1973

★ **81860 IWONICZ ZDROJ** Pd/Rm (Turnu-Severin) 1970; C; 1200/2000; 85.91 × 4.5/5.1 (281.86 × 14.76/16.73); M (Sulzer); 13
Sisters (Superstructure varies—Pd flag):
★ **81861 BUSKO ZDROJ**
★ **81862 CIECHOCINEK**
★ **81863 DUSZNIKI ZDROJ**
★ **81865 CIEPLICE ZDROJ**
★ **81866 KARPACZ**
★ **81868 RABKA ZDROJ**

81880 GABRIELE It/FRG Unterweser 1956; C; 2200; 90×5.7 (295.28×18.7); M (MaK); 13; ex *Hille Oldendorff* 1971

81900 CEMBULK No/FRG (Sietas) 1973; Cem; 2200; 84.89 × 5.8 (278.51 × 19.03); M (Normo); 4

81910 MALDEA Br/Br (Bolson) 1960; Tk; 500; 52.02 × 3.54 (170.67 × 11.61); M (Mirrlees, Bickerton & Day); 9.5; ex *Celtic Lee* 1982; ex *Esso Tynemouth* 1978

81920 POLAR GAS Pa/De (Svendborg) 1957; LGC; 400; 59.62 × 3 (195.6 × 9.84); M (Alpha-Diesel); 11.5; ex *Signe Tholstrup* 1981
Sister:
81921 KARIN GRENIUS (De) ex *Susanne Tholstrup* 1981

81930 ARMENISTIS 1 Gr/Ne (Van Diepen) 1958; C; 1000; 71.51 × 4.27 (234.6 × 14.01); M (L Smit); 11; ex *Georgios D* 1983; ex *Nusakan* 1979

81940 ARANUI Pa/FRG (Sietas) 1967; C; 1000/1500; 76.66 × 4.59/5.81 (261.35 × 15.06/19.06); M (MAN); 13.5; ex *Cadiz* 1981
Sister:
81942 NIAGA XXIX (Ia) ex *Sevilla* 1980

81950 TRIOS Pa/Sp (Juliana) 1963; C; 1200; 74.91 × 4.93 (245.77 × 16.17); M (MAN); ex *Kai Kavoos* 1979; ex *Eco Sol* 1975; Launched as *Skagatind*
Similar:
81951 PUERTO DE HANGA ROA (Ch) ex *Puerto de Amberes* 1983
81952 DIONISSIOS K (Cy) ex *Monte Balerdi* 1982; Launched as *Monte Cuarto*
81954 HELLINORA (Cy) ex *Patricio* 1977; ex *Monte Cinco* 1977
81956 VIOLA (Pa) ex *Kai Ghobad* 1980; ex *Eco Gabriela* 1975
81957 AGAETE (Pa) ex *Kai Khosrow* 1980; ex *Eco Luisa* 1975; Launched as *Monte Uno*

81970 HTAN TAW YWA Bm/FRG (Lindenau) 1961; C; 2700; 91.5×6.03 (300.2 × 19.78); M (MAN); —; ex *Lindo* 1968
Similar (lengthened):
81971 DONGA (Pa) ex *Georgios P P* 1980; ex *Olympios Athina* 1980; ex *Eirin Maru* 1979; ex *Bongo* 1969

81980 IRO Gr/FRG (Schichau) 1956; C; 1600; 77.5

× 5.72 (254.27 × 18.77); M (KHD); 12; ex *Euterpe* 1982; ex *Margaretha Bischoff* 1962

● 81990 **SKIATHOS** Gr/FRG (Meyer) 1953; C; 1900; 77.7 × 5.97 (254.92 × 19.59); M (KHD); 12; ex *Gunther Schulte* 1970; ex *Kurt Arlt* 1963

82000 **SADAROZA** Pa/FRG (A. Pahl) 1957; C; 1100/1800; 78.75 × 4.32/5.84 (258.37 × 14.17/19.16); M (KHD); 14; ex *Aetos* 1981; ex *Sunlink* 1977; ex *Laxfoss* 1976; ex *Vatnajokull* 1969; ex *Hvitanes* 1964; ex *Steendiek* 1963
Probable sister:
82001 **EL CINCO** (Pa) ex *Tasman Dertien* 1977; ex *Capitaine Tasman* 1976; ex *Nemours* 1971; ex *Marita* 1960; Launched as *Steendiek*

82010 **MARA** Pa/FRG (A Pahl) 1955; C; 900; 72.7 × 5.39 (238.52 × 17.68); M (KHD); 13; ex *Caribbean Mara* 1976; ex *Vigilante* 1968; ex *Montrose* 1958

82020 **CAPAL** Cy/FRG (Meyer) 1955; C; 1600; 81.78 × 5.7 (268.31 × 18.7); M (KHD); 12; ex *Georgios* 1977; ex *Patricia* 1973; ex *Korbach* 1970

82030 **FAITH** Cy/Ne (Sander) 1971; C; 1600/3000; 103.51 × 5.14/6.52 (339.51 × 16.86/21.39 M (Atlas-MaK); 15; ex *Cheshire Faith* 1979; ex *Osterfehn* 1978
Sister:
82031 **GANVIE** (Bi) ex *Faros* 1978; Launched as *Westerfehn*

82040 **WESER BROKER** FRG/FRG (Sietas) 1970; C; 1600/3300; 100.56 × 5.24/6.77 (329.92 × 17.19/22.21); M (KHD); 15.5

82050 **VICTORIA** Gr/FRG (M Jansen) 1970; C/Con; 1200/2800; 99.04 × 4.24/6.3 (324.93 × 13.91/20.67); M (MWM); 14; ex *Rabat* 1980; ex *Ino A* 1974; ex *Boston Express* 1971; Launched as *Ino*
Similar:
82051 **CURRENT TRADER** (Br) ex *Merchant Clipper* 1980; ex *Dwejra* 1976; ex *Ino F* 1975
82052 **CURRENT EXPRESS** (Br) ex *Mercandian Express* 1980; ex *Caribic* 1975; ex *Kathe Bos* 1973
82053 **TINHINAN** (Ag) ex *Holmia* 1975; ex *Johannes Bos* 1973
82054 **HODNA** (Ag) ex *Annette Bos* 1972

82060 **TRIANTAFILOS M.** Cy/Ne (Pattje) 1970; C; 800/1600; 79.69×4.56/5.89 (261.45×14.96 19.32); M (MWM); 13.5; ex *Saba* 1983; ex *Shipmair V* 1978; ex *Gaelicc* 1974; ex *Hendrik Bros* 1972
Sister:
82061 **ALIANORA** (It) ex *Shipmair VI* 1980; ex *Gerd* 1974; ex *Gerd Bos* 1973;
Probable Sister:
82062 **TIBESTI** (Gr) ex *Safi*; ex *Irmgard Bos* 1976

82070 **ADI VITI** Fj/FRG (Husumer) 1970; C; 1000/2000; 83.8 × 5.05/6.33 (274.93 × 16.57/20.77); M (Werkspoor); 13.5; ex *Lautoka* 1981; ex *Anna von Bargen* 1981
Similar:
82071 **FRANKA** (FRG) ex *Frieda Graebe* 1983; ex *Gitta von Bargen* 1974
82072 **FAST CARRIER** (Pa) ex *Susann von Bargen* 1982
82073 **SORRO** (Pa) ex *Movensteert* 1983
82074 **BOKE** (Pa) ex *Westgate Token* 1982; ex *Dukegat* 1982
Similar (lengthened—Pa flag):
82075 **GROENLAND II** ex *Vela* 1980

82080 **GIANT** Li/Fr (Havre) 1969; C/HL; 500/1400; 90.23×/—; (296.03 × /—); M (Werkspoor) 15.5; ex *La Gavotte* 1975; Converted from general cargo

82100 **ALTA MAR** Sw/Sw (Falkenbergs) 1966; C; 1300; 73.77 × 5.6 (242.03 × 18.37); M (Scania); 12; ex *Ostanhav* 1982; ex *Tento* 1974

★ 82110 **BRAD** Rm/Rm (Galatz) 1971; C; 2500/3500; 106.2 × —/7.06 (348.43 × —/23.16); M (Sulzer); 14
Sisters (Rm flag):
★ 82111 **AZUGA**
★ 82112 **TIRGU JIU**
★ 82113 **CODLEA**
★ 82114 **SULINA**
★ 82115 **TIRNAVENI**
★ 82116 **RIMNICU VILCEA**
★ 82117 **PLOPENI**
★ 82120 **FALTICENI**
★ 82121 **SACELE**
★ 82122 **DUMBRAVENI**
★ 82123 **CALARASI**
★ 82124 **GHEORGHIENI**
★ 82125 **SADU**
★ 82126 **SADOVA**
★ 82127 **SNAGOV**
★ 82128 **TOPOLOVENI**
★ 82129 **SOVEJA**

★ 82130 **SOVATA**
★ 82131 **SEGARCEA**
★ 82132 **SAVINESTI**
★ 82133 **SAVENI**
★ 82134 **SUCEVITA**
★ 82135 **SOUSA**
★ 82136 **SALISTE**
★ 82136/1 **SABARENI**
★ 82136/2 **SCAIENI**
★ 82136/3 **SARMISEGETURA**
★ 83136/4 **SLANIC**
★ 82137 **SEBES**
(Bu flag):
★ 82138 **LOVECH**
(Ir flag):
82140 **IRAN SHAHEED** ex *Arya Marmar* 1980
82141 **IRAN TOWHEED** ex *Arya Noosh* 1980

82150 **CEMENTIA** Pa/FRG (Deutsche Werft) 1967; Cem; 3400; 106.61 × 6.74 (349.77 × 22.11); M (KHD); 14.75
Sister:
82151 **DALIA** (Pa)

82155 **MARYLANDER** Ih/Ne (E J Smit) 1976; C; 1600; 83.52 × 5.19 (274 × 17.03); M (MaK); 12.5; ex *Argo Island* 1982; ex *Mary Anderson* 1982
Sister:
82156 **ALL STATE** (Ih) ex *Gallic Wave* 1983

82160 **MENELAOS TH** Gr/Sp (AESA) 1968; C; 1300/2200; 93.02 × —/5.37 (305.18 × —/17.62); M (B&W); 15; ex *Anamilena* 1975
Sister:
82161 **COSTIA PEFANIS** (Gr) ex *Adriana* 1965

82170 **FRISIAN TRADER** Ne/Ne ('Harlingen') 1976; C; 1600; 79.81 × 5.44 (261.84 × 17.85); M (Alpha-Diesel); 13

82180 **CORAL MAEANDRA** NA/Ne ('De Waal') 1969; LGC; 3400; 103.21 × 6.35 (338.61 × 20.83); M (Smit & Bolnes); 15.75

82190 **GLARIOS** Pa/It (Adriatico) 1947; Sal; 500; 61.68 × 4.1 (202.36 × 13.45); M (MAN); 11; ex *Naxos*; ex *Cleo* 1978; ex *Guttorm Jarl*; Converted from general cargo 1970

82200 **GOGO RANGER** Li/Sw (Lindholmens) 1958; Tk; 12500; 170.57 × 9.58 (559.61 × 31.43); M (Gotaverken); 15; ex *Post Ranger* 1977; ex *Anco Stripe* 1971; ex *Anco Bergljot* 1969; ex *Bergljot* 1964

82210 **FRED H BILLUPS** Li/Ne ('Ijssel') 1960; LGC; 2900; 99.32 × 5.12 (325.85 × 16.8); M (Werkspoor); 13

★ 82220 **URICANI** Rm/Rm (Galatz) 1971; B; 9600; 148.72 × 7.93 (487.93 × 26.02); M (Sulzer); 12.5
Sisters (some have cranes and some have goalpost forward) (Rm flag):
★ 82221 **PETROSANI**
★ 82222 **ANINA**
★ 82223 **CUGIR**
★ 82224 **ROVINARI**
★ 82225 **VULCAN**
★ 82226 **MUSCEL**
★ 82227 **CIMPULUNG**
★ 82228 **AGNITA**
★ 82229 **CALAN**

82240 **FISKO** Fi/Fi (Nystads) 1974; R; 500/1300; 74.12 × 3.62/4.8 (243.18 × 11.88/15.75); M (Polar); 14
Sister:
82241 **LINDO** (Fi)

82250 **GIANNIS DIMAKIS III** Gr/FRG (Norderwerft) 1956; C; 1000; 67.09 × 5.15 (220.11 × 16.9); M (KHD); 11; ex *Pollendam* 1977; ex *Victor* 1971; ex *Vormann Rass* 1966

●★ 82260 **WARNA** Pd/Bu (G Dimitrov) 1968; C; 2500; 95.89 × 5.64 (314.6 × 18.5); M (Sulzer); 13
Sisters (some have heavier radar mast and some have cowl round funnel top) (Pd flag):
★ 82261 **JELENIA GORA**
★ 82262 **PLOCK**
★ 82263 **KOLOBRZEG II**
★ 82264 **ZYWIEC**
★ 82265 **OSWIECIM**
★ 82266 **CHRZANOW**
★ 82267 **RYBNIK**
★ 82268 **JELCZ II**

82280 **CEMENT KING** NZ/No (Ankerlokken) 1973; Cem; 2900; 98.66 × 5.51 (323.69 × 18.08); M (Nydqvist & Holm); 14

82300 **ACQUAVIVA** It/FRG (Schlichting) 1957; C;

1300; 74.17 × 4.55 (243.34 × 14.93); M (KHD); 12.5; ex *Komtur* 1974; ex *Vogelsand* 1968

82310 **DEEPA JUWITA** Ia/Ne ('Harlingen') 1967; C; 1200; 69.19 × 3.37 (227 × 12.24); M (MWM); 11; ex *Westmeep* 1977; ex *Mildstedt* 1975; ex *Westmeep* 1970

82320 **NYMIT** Li/Ja (Miho) 1970; RoC; 4500; 87.31 × — (286.45 × —); TSM (Daihatsu); 11.5; ex *Cosmos Bellatrix* 1977 ex *Cosmos No2* 1975

82330 **NIKKO MARU No 53** Ja/Ja (Imai S) 1976; C/Con; 1900; 76.76 × 5.18 (251.84 × 17); TSM (Akasaka); 9.5; ex *Tungho No1* 1980
Probable sisters:
82331 **TUNGHO No2** (Pa)
82332 **WILCON V** (Pi) ex *Tungho No3*

◆ 82340 **GEBE OLDENDORFF** Sg/FRG (O&K) 1971; C; 1800/4800; 116.72 × 6.53/7.53 (382.94 × 21.42/24.7); M (Atlas-MaK); 15; ex *Terespolis* 1973; ex *Gebe Oldendorff* 1971

★ 82350 **TU MEN JIANG** RC/Fr (La Seine) 1964; C; 9100; 155.2 × 9.15 (509.19 × 30.02); M (B&W); 19.5; ex *Ville De Bordeaux* 1977
Sisters:
★ 82351 **HEI LONG JIANG** (RC) ex *Ville De Lyon* 1977
82353 **MARIKA** (Gr) ex *Aliakmon Light* 1981; ex *Ville De Brest* 1977

82360 **HIND 1** Le/Ne (Van Diepen) 1971; C; 1600; 87.61 × 5.37 (287.43 × 17.62); M (Atlas-MaK); 12; ex *Mohannad* 1982; ex *Troup Head* 1981
Sister:
82361 **NAZIR** (Pa) ex *Tod Head* 1981

82370 **STELLAPRIMA** NA/FRG (S&B) 1975; C/HL; 4000; 105.42 × 6.3 (345.87 × 20.67); M (Atlas-MaK); 14; ex *Internavis 1* 1981; Launched as *Mammoth Scan*

82380 **SHOHO MARU** Ja/Ja (Kurushima) 1966; C; 3000; 98.35 × 6.25 (322.67 × 20.51); M (Akasaka); 13

★ 82390 **BRAD** Rm/Rm (Galatz) 1971; C; 2500/3500; 106.2 × —/7.06 (348.43 × —/23.16); M (Sulzer); 14
Sisters (Rm flag):
★ 82391 **AZUGA**
★ 82392 **TIRGU JIU**
★ 82393 **CODLEA**
★ 82394 **SULINA**
★ 82395 **TIRNAVENI**
★ 82396 **RIMNICU VILCEA**
★ 82397 **PLOPENI**
★ 82400 **FALTICENI**
★ 82401 **SACELE**
★ 82402 **DUMBRAVENI**
★ 82403 **CALARASI**
★ 82404 **GHEORGHIENI**
★ 82405 **SADU**
★ 82406 **SADOVA**
★ 82407 **SNAGOV**
★ 82408 **TOPOLOVENI**
★ 82409 **SOVEJA**
★ 82410 **SOVATA**
★ 82411 **SEGARCEA**
★ 82412 **SAVINESTI**
★ 82413 **SAVENI**
★ 82414 **SUCEVITA**
★ 82415 **SOUSA**
★ 82415/1 **SABARENI**
★ 82415/2 **SCAIENI**
★ 82415/3 **SARMISEGETURA**
★ 82415/4 **SLANIC**
★ 82416 **SALISTE**
★ 82417 **SEBES**
(Bu flag):
★ 82418 **LOVECH**
(Ir Flag):
82420 **IRAN SHAHEED** ex *Arya Marmar* 1980
82421 **IRAN TOWHEED** ex *Arya Noosh* 1980

82430 **KYOSEI MARU** Ja/Ja (Mitsubishi HI) 1971; C; 8500; 141.28 × 8.81 (464 × 29.00); M (Kobe); 14.5

★ 82435 **VRHNIKA** Ys/Ja (Namura) 1968; B; 11200; 149.92 × 9.14 (492 × 29.99); M (Sulzer); 15.25; ex *Saloma* 1975; ex *Sobrino* 1975; ex *Shokai Maru* 1975

82440 **DAYAKA** Ia/Ja (Mitsubishi HI) 1966; C; 3700; 106.69 × 6.57 (350.03 × 21.56); M (MAN); 12.5; ex *Dayaka Satu* 1982; ex *Izu Maru* 1971

● 82450 **STEVE GLORY** Pa/Ja (Osaka) 1962; C; 3900; 108.92 × 6.83 (357.35 × 22.41); M (Kobe); 12; ex *Mightiness* 1982; ex *Pender* 1980; ex *Mingren Enterprise* 1980; ex *Bung Joop* 1974; ex *Toyo Maru No2* 1971
Possible sisters:

82452 NITYA NANAK (In) ex Noda Wood Maru 1967

82454 MARIA N K (Pa) ex New Spirit 1982; ex Zenovia D 1980; ex Shinyubari Maru 1976

★82460 OSTROV RUSSKIY Ru/Sw (Lindholmens) 1969; FC; 9800; 150.55 × 7.47 (494 × 24.51); M (Pielstick); 18.25
Sisters (Ru flag):
★82461 OSTROV ATLASOVA
★82462 OSTROV BERINGA
★82462/1 OSTROV KARAKINSKIY
★82463 OSTROV KOTLIN
★82464 OSTROV LISYANSKOGO
★82465 OSTROV LITKE
★82466 OSTROV MEDNYY
★82467 OSTROV SHMIDTA
★82468 OSTROV SHOKALSKOGO
★82469 OSTROV SIBIRYAKOVA
★82470 OSTROV USHAKOVA

82480 NAM SAN Ko/Ko (Dae Sun) 1972; C; 1500; 82.66 × 5.26 (271.19 × 17.26); M (Akasaka); 11

82490 INDIAN VALOUR In/FRG (A G 'Weser') 1971; C; 7000/9600; 144.91 × 9.42 (475.43 × 30.91); M (MAN); 16; '36L' type
Sister:
82491 INDIAN VENTURE (In)

82510 ASTRA IV Ar/No (Framnaes) 1969; LGC; 6800; 112.89 × 8.79 (403.18 × 28.84); M (B&W); 16; ex Mundogas Atlantic

82530 TORM AMERICA Sg/FRG (LF-W) 1970; C/HL; 7500/10500; 153.27 × 9.01/10.01 (502.85 × 29.56/32.84); M (MAN); 20; ex Goldenfels 1980; ex Atlantica Montreal 1976; ex Goldenfels 1972; Converted container ship

82540 CRUSADER Gr/FRG (Abeking) 1958; C; 1600; 79.2 × 5.24 (259.84 × 17.19); M (MaK); 12; ex Marie Louise 1978; ex Inga Bastian 1974; Lengthened 1959

★82550 PAN SHAN RC/FRG (Meyer) 1967; C; 2500/4200; 110.5 × —/7.57 (362.53 × —/24.84); M (Fiat); 16.25; ex Inge Kruger 1977; ex Cap Doukato 1977; ex Inge Kruger 1975; ex Thessalia 1970; ex Inge Kruger 1967

82560 NAM IL Ko/Ja (Sanoyasu) 1958; C; 3400; 102.39 × 6.46 (335.93 × 21.19); M (Sulzer); 12; ex Sansei Maru 1966
Sister:
82561 CHUN SUNG (Ko) ex Mizuki Maru 1968; ex Suisei Maru 1966

82570 SRI PHEN SINN Th/Ja (Usuki) 1959; C; 2700; 92 × 5.77 (301.84 × 18.93); M (Kobe); 11; ex Ikuta 1974; ex Seikai Maru 1971

82580 TAI LAI Tw/Ja (Setoda) 1962; C; 1000; 69.73 × 4.59 (228.77 × 15.06); M (Hanshin); 11; ex Yamatsune Maru 1969

82590 KING LEAR Pa/FRG (Atlas-Werke) 1965; C; 500; 73.44 × 3.65 (240.94 × 11.98); M (MaK); 11.5; ex Pamir 1 1979; ex Haslach Bewa 1975; ex Haslach 1971

82600 ALTA MAR Sw/Sw (Falkenbergs) 1966; C; 1300; 73.77 × 5.6 (242.03 × 18.37); M (Scania); 12; ex Ostanhav 1982; ex Tento 1974

82610 BARENTS SEA Pa/FRG (Kieler H) 1960; C; 6200/8800; 151.42 × 8.21/9.27 (496.78 × 26.94/30.41); M (Kieler H); 13.5; ex Saab 1972; ex Jarita 1968

★82620 TU MEN JIANG RC/Fr (La Seine) 1964; C; 9100; 155.2 × 9.15 (509.19 × 30.02); M (B&W); 19.5; ex Ville De Bordeaux 1977
Sisters:
★82621 HEI LONG JIANG (RC); ex Ville De Lyon 1977
82623 MARIKA (Gr) ex Aliakmon Light 1981; ex Ville De Brest 1977

82630 SAUDI TAJ Si/Ne (Verolme Scheeps) 1963; C; 12300; 163.07 × 9.86 (535 × 32.35); M (Sulzer); 13.5; ex Amstelveen 1982

82640 MAR TRANSPORTER Tu/Ja (Mitsui) 1969; B; 10300; 154.05 × 9.19 (505.41 × 30.15); M (B&W); 14.75; ex Irenes Ecstacy 1982; ex Midas Arrow; ex Nagato Maru 1971
Sister:
82641 NIKOS N (Gr) ex Dona Juana 1979; ex Retladawn 1979; ex Overseas Navigator 1975; ex Haiko Maru 1973
Similar:
82642 ANGEKRITI (Pa) ex Nikolaos A 1982; ex Midas Prince; ex Oriental Prince 1971; ex Yamato Maru 1970
82643 MIDAS RHEIN (Li) ex Rhein Maru 1972
82644 ROZITA (Li) ex Montrose 1983

82645 ALBORADA (Ch) ex Montigny 1983

●82650 VILLE DE MAHEBOURG Ms/Fr (La Seine) 1962; C; 6400; 130 × 7.49 (426.51 × 24.57); M (B&W); 15; ex Kimon 1973; ex Ville De Djibouti 1972; ex Saint Francois 1970

82660 BAILUNDO Po/Pd (Szczecinska) 1969; C; 7700/11600; 158.4 × 8.41/10.03 (519.69 × 27.59/32.91); M (Sulzer); 14; launched as Artemonas; 'B441' type
Sister:
82661 CUNENE (Po)

82670 THEOGENNITOR Gr/Ja (IHI) 1968; B; 35500; 223.91 × 12.19 (734.61 × 39.99); M (Sulzer); 15.5; ex Agamemnon

82680 MODENA Pa/FRG (Rickmers) 1972; B/V; 8900; 141.61 × 7.27 (464.6 × 23.85); M (MAN); 16; ex Weyroc 1982; Side doors and ramps

82690 KOTKA LILY Fi/Fi (Rauma-Repola) 1972; RoC; 4300; 137.52 × 6.64 (451.18 × 21.78); TSM (Stork-Werkspoor); 18; ex Nedlloyd Rockanje 1983; ex Rheinfels 1977; ex Antares 1975; Stern doors
Sisters:
82691 ORION (Fi)
82692 SIRIUS (Fi)
82693 LIPA (Pa) ex Baltic Enterprise 1983
82694 BALTIC PROGRESS (Br)

82706 JAVA WINDS Ne/Ne (Giessen-De Noord) 1980; Con; 28400; M (Sulzer); —; ex Nedlloyd Zeelandia 1983; ex Benattow 1982; ex Zeelandia 1980

82710 CARIBIA EXPRESS FRG/Pd (Gdanska) 1976; Con; 27900; 203.99 × 10 (669.26 × 32.81); M (Sulzer); 22; 'B-463' type
Sisters:
82711 SIERRA EXPRESS (FRG) ex Cordillera Express 1983
82712 ALLEMANIA EXPRESS (FRG)
82713 AMERICA EXPRESS (FRG)
82714 ASIA WINDS (Br) ex Adviser 1982
82716 CARAIBE (Fr)
82717 NEDLLOYD HOLLANDIA (Ne) ex Hollandia 1982
82718 AUTHOR (Br) ex Benarmin; ex Author 1981
Similar (built up foreward and aft, extra lifeboats etc—operated by RFA as helicopter support ship):
82719 RELIANT (Br) ex Astronomer 1983

82720 LANKA ATHULA FRG/FRG (Howaldts DW) 1977; Con; 10900; 145.01 × 9.02 (475.75 × 29.59); M (MAN); 19; ex Urundi 1982; ex Gulf Ranger 1978; ex Urundi 1977; Launched as Brabant
Sisters (FRG flag):
82721 ULANGA ex Gulf Clipper 1978; Launched as Ulanga
82722 LANKA ABHAYA ex Usambara 1982; ex Gulf Lancer 1978; ex Usambara 1977; Launched as Eschenbach

82730 STAR YORK Br/FRG (Kieler H) 1959; B; 13200; 171.81 × 10.24 (563.68 × 33.6); M (B&W); 13.5; ex Star Supreme 1981; ex Star Ballarat 1976

82740 JOLLY ARANCIONE It/FRG (Adler) 1957/74; RoC; 2700; 126.4 × 5.43 (414.7 × 17.81); M (Borsig); 15.25; ex Else Reith 1974; ex Aquila 1972; Converted from general cargo 1974

82750 KOTA SAHABAT Sg/Ja (Miho) 1977; Con; 6200; 118.12 × 7.42 (387.53 × 24.34); M (B&W); —; ex Ranger 1981; ex Hodeidah Crown 1981; ex Ranger 1979; ex Strathkeith 1979
Sister:
82751 CHENGTU (Sg) ex Jeddah Crown 1981; ex Timber Bay 1979; ex Strathkirn 1979

82760 SIBONEY II Li/Ne (Vuyk) 1971; RoC/Con; 1000/1600; 85.32 × 4.71 (279.92 × 15.45); M (Werkspoor); 15; ex Captain Paddon 1982; ex Britis 1974; ex Atlantic Jamaican 1973; Stern ramp; 'Tarros' type
Sisters (Some Spanish built—Atlantico):
82761 NATAL HUSTLER (Br) ex Tarros Alder 1983; ex Zim Alexandria 1982; ex Tarros Alder 1982; ex Merzario Etruria 1980; ex Vento Di Scirocco 1976
82762 DORLI (Li)
82764 TARROS FIR (Br) ex Cheshire Endeavour 1977; ex Laula 1973
82765 TARROS GAGE (Br) ex Lahneck 1978; ex Bergen Juno 1977
82766 TARROS CEDAR (Br) ex Merzario Liguria 1979; ex Vento Di Maestrale 1976
82767 TARROS PAXICON (Br) ex Tarros Hazel 1978; ex Union South Pacific 1978
82768 TARROS ILEX (Br) ex Zim Manila 1982; ex Tarros Ilex; ex Marisud Prima 1978; ex Tarros Ilex 1977; ex Cheshire Venture 1977
82769 DADIANGAS (Pi) ex Tarros Juniper 1980; ex Zim Bangkok 1980; ex Tarros Juniper 1979; ex Mer-

zario Sicilia 1979; ex Swift Arrow 1976

82790 PANAY (Pi) ex Tarros Elm; ex Zim Manila; ex Tarros Elm; ex Voorloper 1978; Launched as Vento Di Libeccio

82800 KLAREDON Br/DDR ('Neptun') 1969; C; 3000; 102.98 × 5.85 (338 × 19.19); M (Atlas-MaK); 13.5; ex Laredo 1979; ex Hansa Nord 1979
Similar:
82801 RIO BRAVO (Br) ex Hansa Trade 1980
82802 NAZIE BEAUTY (UAE) ex Hanseat 1980
82803 ANATOLIA (Pa) ex Larch 1980; ex Jowood 1979
82804 HVALVIK (Ic) ex Mambo 1975; ex Samba 1972
82805 ELISABETH (Cy) ex Eskdalegate 1977; ex Fredericksgate 1974; ex Bruni 1974

82810 MONTE ROSA FRG/FRG (A G 'Weser') 1981; Con; 21900; 184.89 × 10.02 (607 × 32.87); M (Sulzer); 17.5
Sisters (FRG flag):
82811 MONTE CERVANTES
82812 COLUMBUS QUEENSLAND
Similar (shorter) (FRG flag):
82813 COLUMBUS LOUISIANA
82814 MONTE SARMIENTO ex Columbus Canterbury 1983

★82820 LEDENICE Ys/Ys ('3 Maj') 1979; RoC-/Con/C; 5600; 144.4 × 6.5 (473.75 × 21.33); M (Pielstick); 17.9; Travelling gantry (with slewing deck crane); Stern slewing ramp
Probable sister:
★82821 BRIBIR (Ys)

82830 THEOLIPTOS Gr/FRG (Deutsche Werft) 1965; B; 41900; 250.02 × 13.8 (820.28 × 45.28); M (B&W); 15.5; ex Mathilde Schulte 1976; ex Sighansa 1969

82840 BERG SA/SA (Dorman Long) 1977; Con; 8200; 137.78 × 7.5 (452.03 × 24.61); M (Atlas-MaK); 17
Sister:
82841 BREEDE (SA)

82845 PACIFIC TEAL Br/Br (Swan Hunter) 1982; C; 4700; 103.92 × 6.02 (341 × 19.75); TSM (A P E Allen); 13; Spent nuclear fuel carrier
Probable Sister (builder—Appledore):
82846 PACIFIC SANDPIPER (Br)

82850 PAPUAN CHIEF Br/Ja (Miho) 1977/81; C/Con; 7400; 132.11 × — (433 × —); M (B&W); 15; Lengthened 1981 (Miho); Drawing shows vessel before lengthening
Sisters:
82851 CORAL CHIEF (Br)
82852 NIMOS (Br)

82860 RICHMOND HILL Li/Ja (Mitsubishi HI) 1969; B; 36500; 259.52 × 13.23 (851.44 × 43.41); M (MAN); 15.5; ex Phosphore Conveyor 1983

82870 AEGEAN LIGHT Gr/No (Bergens) 1961; B; 13200; 170.85 × 10.46 (560.53 × 34.32); M (Gotaverken); 15; ex Star Light 1982; ex Star Bay 1977; ex Songa 1965

82880 STAR YORK Br/FRG 1959; B; 13200; 171.81 × 10.24 (563.68 × 33.6); ex Star Supreme 1981; ex Star Ballarat 1976

82890 ANNA C Gr/FRG (Deutsche Werft) 1962; B; 11500; 149.97 × 9.49 (492 × 31.14); M (Sulzer); 15; ex Banak 1978
Sisters:
82891 ANASTASIOS C (Gr) ex Hariwa 1978; ex Bardu 1975
82892 AEOLIAN SUN (Gr) ex Bavang 1974

●82900 STAR PRIDE Gr/No (Bergens) 1962; B; 15600; 170.85 × 10.45 (560.53 × 34.28); M (Gotaverken); 15.5; ex Star Fjellanger 1977; ex Fjellanger 1972; ex Silja 1965

82910 CONVEYOR Li/Ja (Kure) 1968; B; 39500; 143.59 × 14.55 (799.18 × 47.74); T (GEC); 15.5; ex Universe Conveyor 1980

●82920 STRIDER AUSTRALIA Li/Ja (Shinhama) 1975; RoC/Con; 3400; 119.61 × 7.47 (392.42 × 24.51); M (MAN); 16.75; ex Merzario Ionia 1978; ex Maersk Tempo 1976; Quarter ramp; 'Strider' type
Sisters:
82921 STRIDER CRYSTAL (Br) ex Nedlloyd Crystal 1982; ex Strider Crystal 1980; ex Aqaba Crown
82922 STRIDER BROADSWORD (Li) ex Jeddah Crown; ex Strider Broadsword 1978
82923 INDIAN COURIER (In) ex Strider Diamond 1981; ex Saudi Crown 1980
Similar (some have larger funnels):
82924 JADE BOUNTY (Br) ex Strider Gallant 1978
82925 STRIDER EXETER (Li) ex CCNI Antartico

1983; ex *Opal Bounty* 1982
82926 SAPPHIRE BOUNTY (Br) ex *Nedlloyd Bounty* 1981; ex *Sapphire Bounty* 1980; Launched as *Strider Hero* 1978
82927 STRIDER FEARLESS (Li) ex *CCNI Andino* 1983; ex *Turquoise Bounty* 1982

82940 INGER US/US (Sun SB)-FRG 1945/62; B; 114200; 190.81 × 9.26 (626.02 × 30.38); T-E(Westinghouse); 14; ex *Transnorthern* 1962; ex *Wang Hunter* 1960; ex *Atlantic Exporter*; ex *Fort Caspar* 1946; Converted from 'T-2' type tanker 1962 (Schlieker)

82950 MALAHAT Br/Fi (Wartsila) 1971; B/TC/V; 23600; 184.21 × 10.78 (604.36 × 35.37); M (Pielstick); 16.5; ex *Pacific Lumberman* 1981; ex *Pacific*
Sister:
82951 KEMANO (Br) ex *Pacific Forester* 1981; ex *Suecia*

82960 DARWIN TRADER Au/Au (NSW Govt) 1970; B/Con; 10800; 139.6 × 9.15 (458 × 30.02); M (Pielstick); 15

82970 SEA-LAND LEADER US/FRG (Schlieker)-Ja (Mitsubishi HI) 1962/78; Con; 17400; 201.84× 8.28 (662.2 × 27.17); M (Sulzer); 18.5; ex *Elizabethport* 1978
Sisters (US flag):
82971 SEA-LAND ADVENTURER ex *San Francisco* 1978
82972 SEA-LAND PACER ex *San Juan* 1978
82973 SEA-LAND PIONEER ex *Los Angeles* 1978

82980 BORG No/Be (Cockerill) 1972; B/Ch; 19600; 172.52 × 10.52 (566 × 34.51); M (B&W); 15.25

82990 FALCON Gr/Ja (IHI) 1978; B; 14100; 164.34 × 9.4 (539.11 × 30.84); M (Pielstick); 15; **'Friendship'** type
Sisters:
82991 ANANGEL MIGHT (Gr)
82992 ANANGEL SPIRIT (Gr)
82993 PRESTIGIOUS (Br) launched as *Efdim Junior*
82994 ACE AUSTRALIA (—)
82995 GEORGE (Gr)
82996 ANANGEL ENDEAVOUR (Gr)
82997 ANANGEL FIDELITY (Gr)
82998 THEREAN MARINER (Gr)
82999 AMETHYST (Gr)

83010 ISLAND CONTAINER Pa/Au (NSW Govt) 1964; Con; 5700; 126.17 × 7.62 (413.94 × 25); M (Sulzer); 16; ex *Kooringa*

83020 ANGELIC GLORY Gr/Ja (Mitsubishi HI) 1967; B; 24800; 206.03 × 10.9 (675.95 × 35.76); M (Sulzer); 15.25; ex *Nelson C White* 1970

83030 STAR LANAO Pi/Sw (Kockums) 1969; B/Con; 16500; 171.91 × 10.41 (564 × 34.15); M (MAN); —; ex *Star Clipper* 1981
Similar (some have different gantries):
83031 STAR VISAYAS (Pi) ex *Star Perseus* 1981; ex *Star East* 1980; ex *Star Heranger* 1978; ex *Heranger* 1972
83032 STAR LUZON (Pi) ex *Star Orpheus* 1981; ex *Star Najd* 1980; ex *Star Taranger* 1978; ex *Taranger* 1972
83033 STAR MINDANAO (Pi) ex *Star Theseus* 1981; ex *Star Oasis* 1980; ex *Star Malmanger* 1978; ex *Malmanger* 1972
83034 STAR DELTA (Gr) ex *Star Olympian* 1979; ex *Star Columba* 1977
83035 STAR INDONESIA (Pi) ex *Star Ionian* 1980; ex *Star Atlantic* 1979; ex *Star Abadan* 1979; ex *Star Atlantic* 1977
83036 STAR THAILAND (Pi) ex *Star Laconian* 1981; ex *Astoria* 1979; ex *Star Astoria* 1978; ex *Star Assyria* 1975
83037 STAR MALAYSIA (Pi) ex *Star Rhodian* 1980; ex *Star Shahpour* 1979; ex *Star Asahi* 1977; ex *Star Acadia* 1975
83038 STAR PHILIPPINES (Pi) ex *Star Dorian* 1980; ex *Star Amalfi* 1978; ex *Irish Stardust* 1976
83039 STAR GAZER (Gr) ex *Star Athenian* 1979; ex *Star Cariboo* 1978
83040 STAR SUNG (Br) ex *Star Bulford* 1982; ex *Star Pinewood* 1974
83042 STAR SINGAPORE (Pi) ex *Star Delphian* 1980; ex *Irish Star* 1978
83043 AEOLIAN CARRIER (Gr) ex *Star Proteus* 1980; ex *Star Sea* 1980; ex *Star Davanger* 1978; ex *Davanger* 1972
83044 STAR SULU (Pi) ex *Star Ching* 1983; ex *Star Boxford* 1982

83050 STAR MAGNATE Br/Ja (Mitsui) 1978; B/Con; 26900; 182.91 × 12.03 (600.1 × 39.47); M (B&W); 15
Sisters (Br flag):
83051 STAR HONG KONG

83052 STAR WORLD
Similar (No flag):
83053 STAR DIEPPE ex *Star Shiraz* 1979; ex *Star Dieppe* 1977
83054 STAR DOVER ex *Star Esfahan* 1979; ex *Star Dover* 1977

83060 EAGLE ARROW Br/Br (H&W) 1970; B; 17200; 167.57 × 10.37 (549.77 × 34.02); M (B&W); 15; ex *Bulk Eagle* 1974
Sisters:
83061 POLYDEFKIS (Gr) ex *La Pampa*
Similar:
83062 ANTAR (Gr) ex *Heina*
83063 ALTAIR (Gr) ex *Lista*
Similar (built in Norway—Bergens):
83064 FJORD THISTLE (Br) ex *Ogna* 1982

83070 BOXY Sw/Sw (Kalmar) 1978; B/TC; 6200; 121 × 7.62 (396.98 × 25); M (B&W); 14.6; Travelling cranes; Jibs are normally stowed athwartships as shown in drawing
Sister:
83071 DONNY (Sw) ex *Dania* 1983

★ **83080 DAI HAI** RC/Ja (Mitsui) 1967; B; 19900; 176 × 10.7 (577.43 × 35.1); M (B&W); 14.25; ex *Chuetsusan Maru* 1978

83090 STAR ENTERPRISE Li/Ja (Kawasaki) 1978; B/Con; 25100; 183 × 12.05 (600.39 × 30.53); M (MAN); 14.6
Sister:
83091 STAR CARRIER (Li)

83100 HOEGH MALLARD No/Ja (Kawasaki) 1977; B; 29200; 200.51 × 11.51 (657.84 × 37.62); M (MAN); 15.25
Sisters (No flag):
83101 HOEGH MASCOT
83102 HOEGH MARLIN
Possibly similar:
83103 HOEGH MERCHANT
83104 HOEGH MERIT
83105 HOEGH MINERVA
83106 HOEGH MUSKETEER
83107 HOEGH MIRANDA

83110 STAR LANAO Pi/Sw (Kockums) 1969; B/Con; 16500; 171.91 × 10.41 (564 × 34.15); M (MAN); —; ex *Star Clipper* 1981
Similar (some have different gantries):
83111 STAR VISAYAS (Pi) ex *Star Perseus* 1981; ex *Star East* 1980; ex *Star Heranger* 1978; ex *Heranger* 1972
83112 STAR LUZON (Pi) ex *Star Orpheus* 1981; ex *Star Najd* 1980; ex *Star Taranger* 1978; ex *Taranger* 1972
83113 STAR MINDANAO (Pi) ex *Star Theseus* 1981; ex *Star Oasis* 1980; ex *Star Malmanger* 1978; ex *Malmanger* 1972
83114 STAR DELTA (Gr) ex *Star Olympian* 1979; ex *Star Columba* 1977
83115 STAR INDONESIA (Pi) ex *Star Ionian* 1980; ex *Star Atlantic* 1979; ex *Star Abadan* 1979; ex *Star Atlantic* 1977
83116 STAR THAILAND (Pi) ex *Star Laconian* 1981; ex *Astoria* 1979; ex *Star Astoria* 1978; ex *Star Assyria* 1975
83117 STAR MALAYSIA (Pi) ex *Star Rhodian* 1980; ex *Star Shahpour* 1979; ex *Star Asahi* 1977; ex *Star Acadia* 1975
83118 STAR PHILIPPINES (Pi) ex *Star Dorian* 1980; ex *Star Amalfi* 1978; ex *Irish Stardust* 1976
83119 STAR GAZER (Gr) ex *Star Athenian* 1979; ex *Star Cariboo* 1978
83120 STAR SUNG (Br) ex *Star Bulford* 1982; ex *Star Pinewood* 1974
83122 STAR SINGAPORE (Pi) ex *Star Delphian*; ex *Irish Star* 1978
83123 AEOLIAN CARRIER (Gr) ex *Star Proteus* 1980; ex *Star Sea* 1980; ex *Star Davanger* 1978; ex *Davanger* 1972
83124 STAR SULU (Pi) ex *Star Ching* 1983; ex *Star Boxford* 1982

83130 FALCON ARROW Br/Ja (Mitsui) 1977; B; 25300; 182.00 × 11.55 (597 × 37.89); M (B&W); 14.5
Sister:
83131 SWAN ARROW (No)
Similar:
83132 BORRENMILL (Br) ex *La Ensenada* 1981
83133 LA PRIMAVERA (Br)
83134 LA ENSENADA (Br)
83135 LARKFIELD (Br) ex *Alain L-D* 1983
83136 NANDU ARROW (Br)
83137 RAVEN ARROW (Br)
83138 RICHFIELD (Br)
83139 SUN SUMA (Br)
83140 EGDA (Br)
83141 FOLGA (No)

83142 GRENA (No)
83143 HORDA (No)
83144 MOLDA (No)
83145 KIWI ARROW (No)
83146 TOKI ARROW (No)
83147 TSURU ARROW (No)
83148 GERARD L-D (Fr)
83149 JEAN L-D (Fr)
83150 SUN ROKKO (Sr)

83160 EAGLE ARROW Br/Br (H&W) 1970; B; 17200; 167.57 × 10.37 (549.77 × 34.02); M (B&W); 15; ex *Bulk Eagle* 1974
Sister:
83161 POLYDEFKIS (Gr) ex *La Pampa*
Similar:
83162 ANTAR (Gr) ex *Heina*
83163 ALTAIR (Gr) ex *Lista*
Similar (built in Norway-Bergens):
83164 FJORD THISTLE (Br) ex *Ogna* 1982

83170 ERINIO Gr/Ja (Fujinagata) 1965; B; 16400; 178.01 × 9.49 (584 × 31.14); M (Sulzer); 15; ex *Sugela* 1982; ex *S A Sugela* 1977; Launched as *Sugela;* Gantries may have been removed

83180 SEAPRINCESS Cy/Ja (Fujinagata) 1965; B; 16200; 178.64 × 10.19 (586.09 × 33.43); M (Sulzer); 15.5; ex *Pacific Reliance* 1983; ex *Tropwood*

83190 MUNKSUND Sw/Sw (Lindholmens) 1968; B; 9400; 153.4 × 8.4 (503.28 × 27.56); M (Pielstick); 16.5
Sisters (Sw flag):
83191 HOLMSUND
83192 TUNADAL

83200 AIFANOURIOS Gr/Ja (Mitsubishi HI) 1965; B; 8600; 128.71 × 9.64 (422.28× 31.63); M (Mitsubishi); 14.25; ex *Sitka Maru* 1975

83210 TRAMONTANE Pa/Ja (Uraga HI) 1967; B; 29100; 223.02 × 12.05 (731.69× 39.53); M (Sulzer); 15.75; ex *Pacific Lady* 1984; ex *Fedra* 1983; ex *Tlaloc* 1981; ex *Strathearn*

83220 WEST SUNORI Pa/Ja (Mitsubishi HI) 1968; B; 21400; 181.01 × 19.47 (593.86 × 34.35); M (Sulzer); 14.75; ex *J V Clyne*
Sisters:
83221 GRAND RELIANCE (Pa) ex *H R MacMillan* 1978
83222 TEXISTEPEC (Me) ex *West Jinori*; ex *N R Crump* 1979

83230 SAINT BERNARD Fr/Sw (Uddevalla) 1967/71; C/Con; 9000/12000; 172.19 × 8.41/9.38 (564.93 × 27.59/30.77); M (Pielstick); 19.5; ex *Telendos* 1980; ex *Tamerlane* 1978; Converted from general cargo & lengthened 1971
Sister:
83231 SAINT BERTRAND (Fr) ex *Tilos* 1980; ex *Tirranna* 1978

83240 YAGUARI Ur/Sw (Uddevalla) 1967/71; C/Con; 8900/12400; 174.11 × 8.47/9.39 (573.2 × 27.79/30.81); M (B&W); 19.5; ex *Torre-S* 1983; ex *Torrens* 1983; Converted from general cargo & lengthened 1971
Sister:
83241 SEA MOON (Pa) ex *Taronga* 1983

83260 ON YEUNG Pa/Ru (Baltic) 1972; B; 23200; 199.9 × 11.23 (655.84 × 36.84); M (B&W); 16; ex *Figaro* 1978; 'Baltika' type
Sister:
83261 BEDFORD (Li) ex *Saint Etienne* 1982; ex *Ravenna*; ex *Nopal Ravenna* 1976; ex *Star Ravenna* 1975
Similar:
83262 ON LEE (Pa) ex *Madame Butterfly* 1978
83263 AKBAR (Br) ex *Traviata* 1977
83264 WILLIAM (Sg) ex *August Bolten* 1977; Launched as *Renate*
Possibly similar:
83265 LUIS BANCHERO (Pe)
83266 COCKROW (Pa) ex *Ostria II* 1980; ex *Gerlin* 1975
83267 TRAMOUNTANA (Li) ex *Gerlena* 1975

★ **83280 SONG HUONG** Vn/Sw (Lindholmens) 1965; C; 4600/6700; 134.17× 7.99/8.99 (440.19× 26.21/29.49); M (Pielstick); 17.5; ex *Andros* 1974
Sister:
★ **83281 DONG NAI** (Vn) ex *Lemnos* 1975
Similar:
★ **83282 HAI PHONG** (Vn) ex *Milos* 1975

83300 SUNNINGDALE Sg/No (Fredrikstad) 1969; B; 11300; 165.67 × 9.31 (543.53 × 30.54); M (Gotaverken) 15; ex *Stove Tradition*
Similar:
83301 ELJIANNI (Gr) ex *Melsomvik* 1973
83302 NEGEV ORON (Li) ex *Agioi Victores* 1981; ex

Expectation 1976
83303 **MARIA X** (Gr) ex *Stove Ocean* 1977; ex *Belocean* 1975
83304 **UNION AUCKLAND** (Br) ex *Columbia*
83306 **GEORGIOS F** (Gr) ex *Frixos D* 1980; ex *James Stove* 1973
83307 **CAROLINE** (Pa) ex *Eastwind* 1980; ex *Stove Scotia* 1973
83308 **TELFAIR TRADER** (Li) ex *Santa Pola* 1981; ex *Ringvard* 1973
★83309 **AN JI HAI** (RC) ex *Stove Friend* 1977

83320 **ATHOLL FOREST** Gr/Sw (Oresunds) 1967; B; 17400; 175.22 × 9.88 (574.86 × 32.41); M (Gotaverken); 15.5; ex *Columbialand* 1976
Sister:
83321 **OCEAN VENUS** (Pa) ex *Karamu Forest* 1981; ex *Victoria* 1977
Similar:
83322 **KANUKA FOREST** (Sg) ex *Gimleland* 1977
83323 **ASIAN FOREST** (Gr) ex *Caledonian Forest* 1978; ex *Virginia* 1976; ex *Gimleskog* 1972

83330 **JAVARA** (Li) /De (B&W) 1970; B; 25200; 192.06 × 10.12 (630.12 × 33.2); M (B&W); 15.5; ex *Skogstad* 1976
Sisters:
83331 **TROLL VIKING** (Li) ex *Mannheim* 1981; ex *Roland Bremen* 1974
83332 **TROLL MAPLE** (Li) ex *Kelkheim* 1981; ex *Roland Kelkheim* 1971; Launched as *Kelkheim*
Similar:
83333 **JANEGA** (Li)

●83340 **CEBU** Sg/Ru (Baltic) 1972; B; 22700; 199.83 × 11.24 (655.61 × 36.88); M (B&W); 15.75; ex *Care* 1980; ex *Carola P* 1978; ex *Carola Reith* 1978; 'Baltika' type; Cranes are paired
Probable sister:
83341 **LABO** (Sg) ex *Mare* 1980; ex *Magdalena* 1979; ex *Magdalena Reith* 1978
Possibly similar:
83342 **CRESCO** (No)
83343 **ALCOR** (Li) ex *Ataman* 1984; ex *Tento* 1979

83360 **SUNRISE** Li/Fi (Crichton-Vulcan) 1960; C; 1500/2700; 101.12 × 5.17/6.13 (331.76 × 16.96/20.11); M (Sulzer); 13; ex *Arcturus* 1981; Lengthened 1968
Sisters:
83363 **SUNSHINE** (Le) ex *Corona* 1981
83364 **EASTERN GLORY** (My) ex *Pacific Carrier* 1982; ex *Hektos* 1981
83367 **EBE** (Pa) ex *Hebe* 1982

83380 **ALHALEMI** Eg/Sp (Juliana) 1971; C; 1200; 87 × 4.87 (285.43 × 15.97); M (Stork-Werkspoor); 13.5; ex *Benimusa* 1980
Sisters:
83381 **INTER IV** (Pa) ex *Benimamet* 1981
83382 **NIAGA XXXVI** (Ia) ex *Benisalem* 1981
83383 **ALHAKEM** (Eg) ex *Beniajan*
83384 **NIAGA XXXV** (Ia) ex *Benifaraig* 1981
Similar (shorter):
83385 **MARIA ZAKELINA S** (Gr) ex *Benimar* 1977
83386 **ALHAMBRA** (Eg) ex *Benisa* 1978
83387 **BENIALI** (Sp)

●83400 **NEDLLOYD WISSEKERK** Ne/Ne (P Smit) 1967; C; 7400/10700; 166.6 ×7.8/9.6 (546 × 25.6/31.6); M (Stork); 20; ex *Wissekerk* 1977
Sisters (Ne flag):
83401 **WAALEKERK** ex *Nedlloyd Waalekerk* 1984; ex *Waalekerk* 1977
83402 **NEDLLOYD WESTERKERK** ex *Westerkerk* 1977
83403 **NEDLLOYD WILLEMSKERK** ex *Willemskerk* 1977

83410 **PING CHAU** Pa/Sw (Oresunds) 1968; B/Con; 17400; 172.22 × 9.9 (565.03 × 32.48); M (Gotaverken); 16; ex *Asia Pacific* 1984; ex *Andros* 1983; ex *Fermland* 1975; Converted from bulk carrier 1975

●83420 **PANDORA** Gr/Sw (Oresunds) 1961; B; 10900; 157.97 × 9.4 (518.27 × 30.84); M (Gotaverken); 15; ex *Floridaland* 1970; ex *Aralizz* 1966

★83430 **DEBALTSEVO** Ru/DDR (Warnow) 1960; O; 6800; 139.5 × 8 (457.68 × 26.25); M (MAN); 14.25
Sisters (some may have 3 cranes) (Ru flag):
★83431 **DOBRUSH**
★83432 **DUBNO**
★83433 **DUBOSSARY**
★83435 **DIMITROVO**
★83436 **DOBROPOLYE**
★83438 **DUDINKA**
★83439 **DAGESTAN**
★83440 **DASHAVA**
★83441 **DNEPRODZERZHINSK**
★83442 **DONSKOY**
★83443 **DEDOVSK**

●83450 **SUNRISE** Li/Fi (Crichton-Vulcan) 1960; C; 1500/2700; 101.12 × 5.17/6.13 (331.76 × 16.96/20.11); M (Sulzer); 13; ex *Arcturus* 1981; Lengthened 1968
Sisters:
83453 **SUNSHINE** (Le) ex *Corona* 1981
83454 **EASTERN GLORY** (My) ex *Pacific Carrier* 1982; ex *Hektos* 1981
83457 **EBE** (Pa) ex *Hebe* 1980

83470 **PHA SHWE GYAW YWA** Bm/De (Aarhus) 1964; C; 800; 77.35 × 4.01 (253.77 × 13.16); M (B&W); 13.5; ex *Bergenhus* 1968

83480 **CARIBIC** Ne/No (Ulstein) 1967; R; 500/1400; 75.77 × 3.7/6.02 (248.59 × 12.14/19.75); M (Atlas-MaK); 15; ex *Caribia* 1979

83490 **CANADIA** Sw/Fi (Hollming) 1970; C; 3000/5600; 114.31 × 5.79/8.08 (375 × 18.99/28.47); M (B&W); 15; ex *Maria Gorthon* 1981; Lengthened 1975
Sisters:
83491 **TEVERA** (Cy) ex *Ada Gorthon* 1983
83492 **CARL GORTHON** (Sw)
83493 **AGIOS MATTHEOS** (Gr) ex *Ivan Gorthon* 1981

83510 **DETTIFOSS** Ic/De (Aalborg) 1970; C; 2000/3000; 95.56 × 6.09/7.17 (313.52 × 19.98/23.52); M (B&W); 14
Sisters (Ic flag):
83511 **GODAFOSS**
83512 **MANAFOSS**

83520 **PINGUINO** Li/Sp (Juliana) 1970; R; 1000/1700; 88.8 × 15.25 (291.34 × —/17.22); M (MAN); 14

83530 **DIANA** Li/Ja (Kanasashi) 1969; B; 19300; 154.31 × 9.17 (506.27 × 30.09); M (B&W); 14.25; ex *Daian Maru* 1979

83540 **PLAYA DEL MEDANO** Sp/Sp (AESA) 1967; R; 1600; 91.01 × 5.56 (298.59 × 18.24); M (B&W); 16

83550 **HADJANNA** Gr/FRG (Bremer V) 1965; B; 18000; 196.63 × 11.04 (645.11 × 36.22); M (MAN); —; ex *Amica* 1974
Similar (RC flag):
★83551 **GUANG HAI** ex *Angelic Protector* 1975; ex *Aino* 1968
★83552 **QIONG HAI** ex *Arica* 1974

83570 **RISHI ATRI** In/De (Nakskov) 1966; C; 7700/11000; 164.65 × 8.64 (540.19 × 28.35); M (B&W); 20.75; ex *Aranya*
Sisters:
83571 **RISHI AGASTI** (In) ex *Arosia*
83572 **AZUMA** (Gr)

★83575 **DING HAI** RC/Sw (Lindholmens) 1963; B; 11470; 152.53 × 9.10 (500 × 29.86); M (Gotaverken) 13.5; ex *Successor* 1974; ex *Matumba* 1969

●83580 **KOTA MAKMUR** Sg/Sw (Eriksbergs) 1960; C; 9600; 155.58 × 8.46 (510 × 27.76); M (B&W); 19.5; ex *Belalcazar* 1980; ex *Troja* 1979; ex *Tricolor* 1971
Sisters:
83581 **DEFIANT** (Li) ex *Ocean Defiant* 1981; ex *Terepaima* 1980; ex *Tonsberg* 1977
83582 **NEW DOLPHIN** (Sg) ex *Toledo* 1979

83590 **ATHANASIOS-S** Cy/Ne (Arnhemsche) 1962; C; 800; 79.18 × 4.1 (259 × 13.45); M (Werkspoor); 12.5; ex *Texelstroom* 1976

83600 **AFEDULA M** Cy/DDR (Peene) 1960; C; 539; 59.47 × 3.60 (195 × 11.81); M (Liebknecht); 10; ex *My Destiny* 1983; ex *Avon* 1981; ex *Atair* 1980
Sisters (some may be MCMF):
★83601 **MALCHIN** (DDR)
★83602 **NORDSTERN** (DDR)
83603 **ATHLOS 1** (Cy) ex *Eurabia Lake* 1978; ex *Markab* 1977
83604 **MY CHARM** (Cy) ex *Severn* 1981; ex *Denebola* 1979
★83605 **DOC LAP** (Vn) ex *Algenib*
★83606 **SONG BA** (Vn) ex *Poel* 1981
★83607 **THON NHUIT** (Vn) ex *Schedir*
83608 **ARI** (Pa) ex *Insel Reims* 1981
83609 **FREDERIQUE LEONIE** (Pa) ex *Vilm* 1980
83610 **HYE MENG 1** (Pa) ex *Mersey* 1982; ex *Deneb*
83611 **KERMIT** (Ho) ex *Uckermunde* 1982
83613 **PETER** (Ho) ex *Stavenhagen*
83614 **QUEEN VASSILIKI** (Ho) ex *Zinnowitz* 1981
83615 **STAVROS V** (Ho) ex *Athlos II* 1983; ex *Eurabia Bay* 1978; ex *Aldebaran* 1977
83616 **MANAL S** (Le) ex *Venus Glory* 1981; ex *Arcturus* 1977
83617 **ARCHON** (Gr) ex *Aurora* 1980; ex *Putbus* 1979
83618 **ALEXANDROS G** (Gr) ex *Palma* 1981; ex

Humber 1979; ex *Sirrah* 1979
83619 **NORMA** (Sy) ex *Rerik* 1981

83630 **MADELEINE** Co/De (Aarhus) 1959; C; 730; 77.35 × 4 (253.77 × 13.12); M (B&W); 13.5; ex *C T M A* 1975; ex *Koldinghus* 1969

83640 **SIGURD JARL** No/FRG (Luerssen) 1962; C; 1600; 83.83 × 5.91 (275.03 × 19.39); M (Sulzer); 13; Lengthened 1973
Sister:
83641 **SOTE JARL** (No)

83660 **DON NICKY** Pa/FRG (Travewerft) 1958; C; 2000; 82 × 5.52 (269.03 × 18.11); M (KHD); 12; ex *Stavfoss* 1974; ex *Bantry* 1971; ex *Stavmoy* 1968; ex *Mosjoen* 1965

●83670 **CARIB DAWN** Br/De (Sonderborg) 1975; C; 1400; 78.77 × 5.06 (258.43 × 16.6); M (Alpha-Diesel); 12.5; ex *Esther Silvana* 1981; ex *Esther Bech* 1978; Travelling cranes
Sisters:
83671 **CARIB EVE** (Br) ex *Louise Bravo* 1981
Similar (converted to research—may be altered in appearance):
83672 **SOFIE BRAVO** (De) ex *Leila Bech*
83673 **OLGA BRAVO** (Sg) ex *Anna Marie Bech* 1978

★83680 **CHEREPOVETS** Ru/Rm (Constantza) 1970; C; 1500; 80.27 × 4.9 (263.35 × 16.08); M (Sulzer); 12
Sisters (Ru flag):
★83681 **SOSNOVETS**
★83682 **SARATA**
★83683 **SOSNOVKA**
★83684 **SUVOROVO**
★83685 **SERNOVODSK**
★83686 **SNEZHNOGORSK**
★83687 **SUDAK**
★83688 **SLAUTNOYE**
★83689 **SOFIYSK**
★83690 **SURGUT**
(Rm flag):
★83691 **NAZARCEA**
★83692 **PALAS**
★83693 **POIANA**
★83694 **NOVACI**

83700 **LUCKY LADY** Cy/DDR (Elbewerft) 1956; C; 430; 50.07 × 3.2 (164.27 × 10.5); M (Liebknecht); —; ex *Elena Demet* 1977; ex *Sandra Demet* 1976; ex *Bibia Demet* 1975; ex *Evangelia*; ex *Zing* 1975; ex *Zingst* 1973
Sister (Cy Flag):
83710/1 **ENTERPRISE II** (Gr Flag): ex *Foreman* 1982 ex *Maria Demet* 1981; ex *Sea Wave* 1974; ex *Ero* 1973; ex *Prerow* 1973;
(Gr Flag):
83711 **AGIOS DIONISSIOS** ex *Poros* 1976; ex *Sea Calm* 1975; ex *Bar* 1974; ex *Barhoft* 1973
83713 **MYROVLITIS** ex *Giannis* 1974; ex *Grei* 1973; ex *Greifswald* 1973
(No flag):
83714 **ARGOVIND** ex *Avald* 1973; ex *Deang* 1972; ex *Koserow* 1971
83715 **FEANG** ex *Heringsdorf* 1972

★83720 **BATAK** Bu/Bu (Ivan Dimitrov) 1966; C; 1300/1800; 80.65 × 4.35/5.29 (264.6 × 14.27/17.36); M (Sulzer); 12
Sisters (some are reported to have a 3rd crane on foc'sle. Some may be converted to container ships similar to **ELENA**—which see) (Bu flag):
★83721 **SOPOT**
★83722 **KALOFER**
★83724 **PERUSTICA**
★83725 **KOTEL**
★83726 **TROJAN**
★83727 **KOPRIVSTICA**
★83728 **ZERAVNA**
★83729 **KLISURA**
★83730 **SAMOKOV**
★83731 **ZLATOGRAD**
(RC flag):
★83732 **HONG QI 191** ex *Melnik* 1969
★83733 **HONG QI 192** ex *Razlog* 1969
(Gr flag):
83734 **LEMONIA** ex *Bracigovo* 1981

83740 **EVITA II** Cy/FRG (Jadewerft) 1965; C; 1400; 72.8 × 5.31 (238.85 × 17.42); M (MAN); 13; ex *La Bonita* 1981

83750 **CABO FRIO** Cy/No (Langesunds) 1960; R; 1600; 74.71 × 5.8 (245.11 × 19.03); M (Sulzer); 14.75

83760 **TANAMBI** Co/FRG (Norderwerft) 1959; C; 1600; 100.84 × 4.64 (330.84 × 15.22); M (MAN); 12.5; ex *Veloz* 1973; ex *Valiente* 1969; ex *Spenser* 1961; Lengthened 1966
Similar (bi-pod masts):
83762 **PIGOANZA** (Co) ex *Viajero* 1973
83763 **BAHIA** (Eg) ex *Rima Star* 1983; ex *Holcor 1*

1978; ex *Veewave* 1978; ex *Falcon 1* 1978; ex *Atahualpa* 1976; ex *Velos* 1967

★ 83780 **UGLEURALSK** Ru/DDR (Warnow) 1958; O; 5200; 133.69 × 7.42 (438.62 × 24.34); M (MAN); 15.5;
Sisters (some may have 4 cranes—see No 83430) (Ru flag):
★ 83781 **URITSK**
★ 83782 **URGENTCH**
★ 83783 **URYUPINSK**
★ 83784 **URZHUM**
★ 83785 **USOLJE**
★ 83786 **USTYUZHNA**
★ 83787 **USTILUG**

83800 **SANJEEVANI** In/US (Kaiser Co)—Ja 1945/69; B; 10300; 159.57 × 9.2 (523.52 × 30.18); T-E (GEC); —; ex *Nissei Maru* 1964; ex *Kings Canyon* 1951; Converted from 'T2' type tanker

83820 **SEA WIND 1** Pa/Sw (Eriksbergs) 1961; C; 5700/8200; 144.23 × 7.74/8.97 (473.2 × 25.39/29.43); M (B&W); 15; ex *Santos* 1982; ex *Canadia* 1973; ex *Silverland* 1969
Sister:
83821 **NESTOR SPIRIT** (Gr) ex *Irene M* 1980; ex *Finland* 1973; ex *Marieholm* 1967

83830 **KALLSO** Fi/Fi (Nystads) 1960; R; 500; 71.81 × 3.62 (235.6 × 11.88); M (KHD); 14

83850 **BP SPRINGER** Br/Br (Hall, Russell) 1969; Tk; 1100; 65.46 × 4.45 (214.76 × 14.6); M (B&W); 11.5; ex *Dublin* 1976
Sisters (Br flag):
83851 **BP BATTLER** ex *Inverness* 1976
83852 **BP WARRIOR** ex *Grangemouth* 1976

83860 **JENNIE W** Br/Br (Grangemouth) 1965; Tk; 1000; 61.45 × 4.22 (201.61 × 13.85); M (British Polar); 11; ex *Shell Mariner* 1982; ex *Falmouth* 1979
Sister:
83862 **NIGERIAN STAR** (Ho) ex *BP Scorcher* 1983; ex *Killingholme* 1976
Probable sister:
83863 **METRO SUN** (Ca) ex *Shell Scientist* 1981; ex *Partington* 1979
83864 **SHELL TRADER** (Br) ex *Teesport* 1979
Similar (lower superstructure, taller funnel):
83865 **SHELL ENGINEER** (Br) ex *Dingle Bank* 1979

83880 **JOSE MARIA RAMON** Sp/Sp (Cadagua) 1973; C/R; 1700; 108.39 × 4.16 (355.61 × 13.65); M (MAN); 18
Sister:
83881 **PEDRO RAMIREZ** (Sp)

83890 **ATREVIDA** Gr/De (Nakskov) 1968; C/Con; 8900; 167.06 × 8.55 (548.1 × 28.05); M (B&W); 21.5; Cranes are on travelling gantries

83900 **EVANTHIA I** Cy/Sw (Kalmar) 1962; C; 500; 61.3 × 3.77 (201.12 × 12.37); M (Alpha - Diesel); 11.5; ex *Agioi Anargyroi* 1983; ex *Friendship* 1981; ex *Manos* 1977; ex *Radiant Victor* 1976; ex *Vestholm* 1974; ex *Kalmarsund I* 1970

83910 **IOANNIS K** Cy/De (Aarhus) 1957; C; 1100; 77.65 × 4.19 (254.76 × 13.75); M (B&W); 12.5; ex *Ntama* 1984; ex *Tonna* 1975; Lengthened 1964

83920 **SELA** Ic/No (Trondhjems) 1970; RoC/C; 1500; 87 × 6.13 (285.43 × 20.11); M (Werkspoor); 15; ex *Bomma* 1980; Stern door/ramp. Side doors.
Sisters:
83921 **RANGA** (Ic) ex *Barok* 1983
83922 **BERBY** (No)
83923 **SKAFTA** (Ic) ex *Borre* 1981
★ 83924 **PLATAK** (Ys) ex *Bard* 1975
★ 83925 **SNJEZNIK** (Ys) ex *Bolt* 1975

★ 83930 **BELLATRIX** DDR/DDR (Peene) 1961; C; 500; 59.47 × 3.66 (195.11 × 12.01); M (Liebknecht); 10; (See 'Avon' MC₂MF for others of this class which may have this sequence)

83940 **MINI LADY** Gr/Ja (Hakodate) 1969; C/B; 1600; 65.51 × 4.95 (214.93 × 16.24); TSM (Daihatsu); 10.25;
Similar (some vessels have tandem cranes and some later ones have taller superstructure and funnel) (Gr flag):
83941 **MINI LABOR**
83942 **MINI LACE** (has been experimentally fitted with a large sail foreward which may now be removed)
83943 **MINI LAD**
83944 **MINI LAGOON**
83946 **MINI LANCE**
83947 **MINI LANE**
83948 **MINI LANTERN**
83949 **MINI LAP**
83950 **MINI LARK**
83951 **MINI LASS**
83952 **MINI LATRIA**
83953 **MINI LAUD**
83954 **MINI LAW**
83955 **MINI LEAD**
83956 **MINI LEAF**
83957 **MINI LEAGUE**
83958 **MINI LEE**
83959 **MINI LEGEND**
83960 **MINI LENS**
83961 **MINI LIBRA**
83962 **MINI LID**
83963 **MINI LIDO**
83964 **MINI LIFT**
83965 **MINI LIGHT**
83966 **MINI LINER**
83967 **MINI LINK**
83969 **MINI LIONESS**
83970 **MINI LIZARD**
83971 **MINI LOAF**
83972 **MINI LOOM**
83973 **MINI LORY**
83974 **MINI LOT**
83975 **MINI LOTUS**
83976 **MINI LUCK**
83977 **MINI LUX**
83978 **MINI LYMPH**
83979 **MINI LAMA** ex *American Minx* 1971; Launched as *Mini Lama*
83980 **MINI LOGIC** ex *American Mini* 1971
83981 **MINI LUNAR** ex *American Ming* 1973; Launched as *Mini Lunar*
83982 **MINI LILAC**
83983 **MINI LADY**
(Ko flag):
83984 **AMERICAN MARK** ex *American Mace* 1974; Launched as *Mini Lyra*
83985 **MORNING SUN** ex *Mini Limit* 1975
83986 **KOREAN SHIPPER** ex *Mini Life* 1972
83987 **GLOBAL CHALLENGER** ex *Mini Look* 1974; ex *American Main* 1973; Launched as *Mini Look*
(Si flag):
83988 **DALIA 1** ex *Mini Lake* 1980; ex *American Muse* 1971; ex *Mini Lake* 1970
83989 **DALIA II** ex *Mini Leo* 1980; ex *American Mark* 1971; ex *Mini Leo* 1970
(Pa flag):
83990 **KIAEN** ex *Global Trader* 1979;
(Me flag):
83990/1 **DEL CHAP** ex *Mini Lamp* 1981;
(larger cranes—Ko flag):
82991 **KOREAN FLOWER**
83991 **KOREAN LIFTER**

● 84000 **CHIOS FROST** Gr/Ne ('Friesland') 1962; R; 1800; 91.55 × 4.5 (300.36 × 14.76); M (MAN); 16; ex *Gogo Reefer* 1982; ex *Gogofrio* 1980; ex *Poolster* 1974

84010 **AMULET** De/De (Svendborg) 1975; C; 1600; 94.39 × 5.77 (309.67 × 18.93); M (Alpha-Diesel); 13; travelling crane
Sisters:
84011 **TALISMAN** (De)
84012 **KEFLAVIK** (Ic) ex *Charm* 1982
84013 **FETISH** (De)
84014 **MEDALLION** (De)

84020 **SAMSON SCAN** De/FRG (M. Jansen) 1976; C/HL; 3900; 94.49 × 7.9 (310 × 25.92); M (Alpha-Diesel); —; Travelling cranes
Sister:
84021 **HERMES SCAN**

84030 **CELTIC CRUSADER** Br/Ne (Nieuwe Noord) 1970; C; 700; 80.73 × 4.14 (264.48 × 13.58); M (British Polar); 13.5; ex *Supremity*

84040 **SEVEN** It/Ne ('Friesland') 1969; C; 600/1500; 77.65 × 4.14/5.83 (254.75 × 13.58/19.12); M (Atlas-MaK); 12; ex *Mangen* 1982
Sister:
84041 **WADDENZEE** (Ne) ex *Unden*

84050 **MARINE PACKER** Ca/No (Soviknes) 1965; C; 1100; 70.8 × 3.62 (232.28 × 11.88); M (KHD); 12.5; ex *Blikur* 1974; Lengthened 1971

● 84060 **PEP REGULUS** De/De (Frederikshavn) 1977; C; 1600; 96.53 × 5.64 (316.69 × 18.51); M (Atlas-MaK); 12.25; ex *Mercandian Prince* 1981; 'COMMANDER' class
Sisters:
84061 **POLYDORUS** (Ne) ex *Mercandian Admiral*
84062 **CASABLANCA** (FRG) ex *Mercandian Ambassador* 1980
84063 **SEVILLA** (FRG) ex *Mercandian Commander* 1980
84064 **PEP RIGEL** (De) ex *Mercandian Queen* 1981

● 84070 **ARNAFELL** Ic/De (Frederikshavn) 1974; C; 700/1600; 78.52 × 4/5.67 (257.61 × 13.12/18.6) M (Alpha-Diesel); 13; ex *Mercandian Exporter* 1979
Sisters (Ic flag):

84074 **HELGAFELL** ex *Mercandian Shipper* 1979
84075 **FJALLFOSS** ex *Mercandian Transporter* 1977
(Tu flag):
84076 **SELIN** ex *Shipmair VII* 1977; ex *Mercandian Supplier* 1974
(Ag flag):
84077 **CHELIA** ex *Mercandian Agent* 1975
(Cy flag):
84078 **RIO TEJO** ex *Lagarfoss* 1982; ex *Mercandian Importer* 1977
(Pa flag):
84079 **URSULA** ex *Laxfoss* 1983; ex *Mercandian Carrier* 1977
(Sw flag):
84080 **NOGI** ex *Haifoss* 1982; ex *Mercandian Supplier* 1977

84090 **SINGULARITY** Br/Br (Swan Hunter) 1977; C; 1600; 89.72 × 6.04 (294.36 × 19.82); M (Alpha-Diesel); 12.5

84100 **NAWAF** Si/It (Felszegi) 1966; RoC; 1200; 94.19 × 3.73 (390.02 × 12.24); M (Atlas-MaK); 14; ex *Suffolk*; ex *Nopal Spray* 1976; ex *Suffolk* 1974; Launched as *Forenede*; Stern door: Lengthened 1969 (Boele's Sch)
Sister:
84101 **SATTAM** (Si) ex *Sussex*; ex *Nopal Surf* 1975; ex *Sussex* 1974; Launched as *United*

84110 **LUN SHAN** Pa/Fi (Crichton-Vulcan) 1964; C; 1600/2600; 91.57 × 5.42/6.67 (300.43 × 17.78/21.88); M (Sulzer); 14.5; ex *Finnfighter* 1975
Sisters (Pa flag):
84111 **DU SHAN** ex *Finnstrip* 1975; ex *Rekola* 1974
84112 **KUN SHAN** ex *Finnseal* 1975
84113 **PING SHAN** ex *Finntube* 1975; ex *Lotila* 1974

84120 **MARINA** Ma/FRG (A. Pahl) 1959; C; 2600/4000; 105.75 × 6.72/7.6 (346.95 × 22.05/24.93); M (B&W); 14; ex *Antama* 1982; ex *Holstenkamp* 1981; ex *Mikes Kasmas* 1974; ex *Brusnis* 1974; ex *Cap Delgado* 1971; ex *Fusan* 1960

84130 **NIAGA XXVIII** Ia/Ne ('Vooruitgang') 1970; C; 1500; 78.75 × 5.84 (258.37 × 19.16); M (Werkspoor); 12; ex *Peter H* 1980; ex *Holland*; ex *Heerengracht* 1979; ex *Hilvarenbeek* 1973
Sister:
84131 **NIAGA XXXII** (Ia) ex *Noordwal* 1980; ex *Noorbeek* 1979; ex *Timca* 1973

84140 **DON NICKY** Pa/FRG (Travewerft) 1958; C; 2000; 82 × 5.52 (269.03 × 18.11); M (KHD); 12; ex *Stavfoss* 1974; ex *Bantry* 1971; ex *Stavmoy* 1968; ex *Mosjoen* 1965

★ 84150 **BALKHASH** Ru/Ru (Krasnoyarsk) 1969; C; 1100; 72.12 × 4.63 (236.61 × 15.19); M (Russkiy) 11
Sisters (Ru flag):
★ 84151 **BAKHCHISARAY**
★ 84152 **BELOMORYE**

84160 **LIBEXCEL** Pa/Ja (Sumitomo) 1969; O; 17900; 175.04 × 11 (574.28 × 36.09); M (Sulzer); 14.25; ex *Nikkei Maru No 3* 1983

84170 **LUN SHAN** Pa/Fi (Crichton-Vulcan) 1964; C; 1600/2600; 91.57 × 5.42/6.67 (300.43 × 17.78/21.88); M (Sulzer); 14.5; ex *Finnfighter* 1975
Sisters (Pa flag):
84171 **DU SHAN** ex *Finnstrip* 1975; ex *Rekola* 1974
84172 **KUN SHAN** ex *Finnseal* 1975
84173 **PING SHAN** ex *Finntube* 1975; ex *Lotila* 1974

84180 **FOLGOET** Fr/Sw (Eriksbergs) 1968; Tk; 15100; 169.63 × 9.55 (556.52 × 31.33); M (B&W); 16; ex *British Liberty* 1981
Similar:
84181 **PETER KIRK** (Pa) ex *Hala* 1981; ex *British Loyalty* 1981
84182 **BRITISH SECURITY** (Br)
84183 **BRITISH TENACITY** (Br)
84184 **SEBASTIANO** (Pa) ex *British Unity* 1981
84185 **BRITISH FIDELITY** (Br)

● 84190 **MARIVERDA IV** Pa/Br (Lithgows) 1961; Tk; 13300; 174.35 × 9.91 (572 × 32.5); M (B&W); 14; ex *Border Shepherd* 1981
Sisters:
84191 **FIVE BROOKS** (Pa) ex *Border Castle* 1981
84192 **GARDENIA B** (Br) ex *Border Falcon* 1982
84193 **FIVE STREAMS** (Pa) ex *Border Pele* 1981
84194 **ACHILLET** (Gr) ex *Border Chieftain* 1979

84200 **IVORY** Pa/Fr (France - Gironde) 1969; Ch; 1400; 79.53 × 5.11 (260.93 × 16.77); M (Atlas-MaK); 13.75; ex *Casimir Le Quellec* 1981

★ 84210 **GALATA** Bu/Bu (Ivan Dimitrov) 1960; C; 300; 49.31 × 3.09 (161.78 × 10.14); M (Liebknecht); 9; ex *Kamtchia* 1981

Sisters (Bu flag):
★ 84211 KITEN
★ 84212 KOM
★ 84213 PAPIA

84220 CARIB SUN Br/FRG (O&K) 1969; V; 1000; 77.12 × 5.08 (253.02 × 16.63); M (Atlas-MaK); 13.25; ex Overbeck 1982

● 84230 MERENGUE EXPRESS Br/It (Cassaro) 1973; RoC/P; 3300; 115.12×5.97 (377.69×19.59); TSM (Stork-Werkspoor); 20.5; ex Seaspeed Challenger 1980; ex Gisella 1974; ex Monica Russoti 1974; Stern door/ramp
Sister (lengthened by 80 feet):
84231 ADELAIDE (Pa) ex Tambu Express 1982; ex Seaspeed Master 1980; ex Laura Russotti 1976

84240 BAT SHEVA Is/Ne 1967; Transport; 900; 95 × 8 (311 × 26.9); M; 10; Israeli Navy

84250 IFFCO 1 UAE/Ne 1960; R; 700/1200; 72.32 × —/4.48 (237.27 × —/14.7); M; 14; ex Frigo King 1981; ex Megrez 1976; ex Gerda 1973; ex Silver Star 1969; ex Silver Comet 1968

84260 CHAMPLAIN Fr/Fr (DCAN) 1974; Transport; 1400 Dspl; 80 × 2.4 (260 × 7.9); TSM (SACM); 16; 'BATRAL' type; Helicopter platform
Sisters:
84261 FRANCIS GARNIER (Fr)
84262 ABOU ABDALLAH EL AYACHI (Mo)
84263 AHMED ES SAKAH (Mo)
84264 DAOUD BEN AICHA (Mo)

84270 OCEAN SERVANT 1 Ne/Ja (Sumitomo) 1976; RoC/HL; 7700; 108× — (354 × —); M (—); —; Submersible—broken line shows line of maximum immersion
Sister:
84271 OCEAN SERVANT II (Ne)

84280 ATLANTIC FREEZE Pa/FRG (Schlichting) 1958; R; 1000; 66.30× 4.34 (218×14.24); M (KHD); 11; ex Sea Sorceress 1977; ex Waldtraut Horn 1969

84290 MARIA ROSA 1 Pa/FRG (A G 'Weser') 1952; C. 500; 57 × 3.51 (187.01 × 11.52); M (MaK); 10; ex Ben Sufian 1983; ex Atlantique 1983; ex Brunneck 1967; ex Acaste 1955
Sister:
84291 TAT LEE No 2 (My) ex Getah Kinabalu 1980; ex Baltique 1974; ex Bagheera; ex Ville De Bastia 1970; ex Marie Therese Le Borgne 1960

84300 BARAO DE TEFFE Bz/De 1957; RS; 2200; 75.14 × 6.29 (246.52 × 20.64); M; 12; ex Thala Dan 1982; Operated by Brazilian Navy as a survey ship. Helicopter pad aft. Pendant no H.42

84310 ARCTIC GAEL Br/De (Aalborg) 1952; RS; 1200; 64.9 × 6 (212.93 × 19.69); M (B&W); 11.5; ex Benjamin Bowring 1983; ex Martin Karlsen; ex Kista Dan 1967; Converted from general cargo 1968
Similar (passenger cargo—extra superstructure deck):
84311 BOUVET (Pa) ex Calulo 1981; ex Sao Nicolau; ex Magga Dan 1970

84320 MERINO EXPRESS Li/Ne (Vuyk) 1960; LS; 2400/3400; 119.49 × 5.68/6.41 (392.03 × 18.64/21.03); M (Stork); 16; ex Cap Farina 1976; ex Caribbean Express 1974; ex Kreon 1973; Converted from cargo 1976 (Meyer)

★ 84330 ZVAYGZNE Ru/De (B&W) 1953; FC; 1600; 70.01 × 4.31 (229.69 × 14.14); M (B&W); 10.75; ex Refrigerator No 7
Similar (Ru flag):
★ 84331 REFRIGERATOR No 4
★ 84332 REFRIGERATOR No 5
★ 84333 REFRIGERATOR No 6
★ 84334 REFRIGERATOR No 8
★ 84335 REFRIGERATOR No 12
★ 84336 REFRIGERATOR No 13
★ 84337 GELENDZHIK
★ 84338 GORNOZAVODSK
★ 84339 KRASNOGORSK
★ 84340 SAMARKAND
★ 84341 UGLEGORSK
★ 84342 PROVORNY ex Refrigerator No 11
★ 84343 TRUDOLYUBIVYY ex Refrigerator No 9

★ 84350 DONETS Ru/Sw (Lidingoverken) 1951; C; 900; 61.52 × 4.29 (201.84 × 14.07); M (Nydqvist & Holm); 13
Similar (Ru flag):
★ 84351 YENISEY
★ 84352 MEDVEDITSA

★ 84360 BOLON Ru/DDR (Stralsund) 1961; FC; 2300; 82.4 × 5.15 (270.34× 16.9); M (Goerlitzer) 11
Similar (Ru flag):
★ 84361 EVORON
★ 84362 KHANKA

★ 84363 KIZI
★ 84364 OREL
★ 84365 BASKUNCHAK
★ 84366 ELTON
★ 84367 KHASAN
★ 84368 MIKHAYLO LOMONOSOV

84380 RYUJIN MARU Ja/Br (H Robb) 1954; Cem; 1600; 74.81 × 4.28 (245.44 × 14.04); TSM (British Polar); 10.5; ex Golden Bay 1976

● 84390 PANORMITIS Gr/Ne ('Westerbroek') 1956; C; 1100; 70.11 × 4.74 (230.02× 15.55); M (Werkspoor); 12; ex Melissa M 1977

84400 SEA MEDWAY Pa/Ja (Kanrei) 1977; C; 1100; 69.02 × 3.62 (226.44 × 11.88); M (Niigata); 10.5
Sisters:
84401 SEA HUMBER (Pa)
84402 SEA AVON (Pa)
84403 SEA RHINE (Bs)

84410 PALMAIOLA It/FRG (Kremer) 1954; Tk; 1000; 60.3 × 4.89 (197.83 × 16.04); M (MaK); 10; ex Lucy 1977; ex Michael M 1970

84420 ALKYON Gr/Fr (Crichton-Vulcan) 1950; Tk; 900; 63.56 × 4.4 (208.53 × 14.44); M (ABO); 11; ex Isla Finlandia 1972; ex Esso Finlandia 1971

84430 NORRIS CASTLE Br/Br (Thornycroft) 1968; RoC/F; 900; 67.42 × — (221.19 × —); TSM (Crossley); 14; Lengthened 1976 (Boele's Sch)

84440 MARIA ROSA 1 Pa/FRG (A.G. 'Weser') 1952; C; 500; 57 × 3.51 (187.01 × 11.52); M (MaK); 10; ex Ben Sufian 1983; ex Atlantique 1983; ex Brunneck 1967; ex Acaste 1955
Sister:
84441 TAT LEE No 2 (My) ex Getah Kinabalu 1980; ex Baltique 1974; ex Bagheera 1972; ex Ville De Bastia 1970; ex Marie Therese Le Borgne 1960

84450 TANJA Pa/Fi (Crichton-Vulcan) 1961; C; 6300; 134.65 × 8.61 (441.77 × 28.25); M (Gotaverken); 16; ex Tatrina 1980; ex Thebeland 1976
Sisters:
★ 84451 RUI CHANG ex Tyrusland 1977
84452 BRIGHTNESS (Pa) ex Trojaland 1978

★ 84460 IRTISH Ru/Sw (Norrkopings) 1951; Tk; 1100; 68.48 × 3.72 (224.67 × 12.2); M (Nydqvist & Holm); 9
Similar (Ru flag):
★ 84461 KARADAG
★ 84462 SUNGARI
★ 84463 UKHTA
★ 84464 KARTALY

84480 NERA Br/Ne (Boele's Sch.) 1961; C; 800; 77.17 × 4.02 (253.18 × 13.19); M (Werkspoor); 11.25; ex Asuncion 1981; ex Adara 1973
Sisters:
84481 YOKAMU (Br) ex Villarrica 1981; ex Situla 1973
84482 FEDROS (Br) ex Talita 1977
84484 RITSA M (Gr) ex Solon; ex Nashira 1977

84490 GALLOWAY EXPRESS Li/Ne (Giessen) 1960/77; LS; 3400; 119.49 × 5.68/6.41 (392.03 × 18.64/21.03); M (Stork); 16; ex European Express 1977; ex Cap Ivi 1976; ex European Express 1976; ex Ladon 1974; Lengthened 1967; Converted from general cargo 1977 (Meyer)

84500 DONG SOO No 501 Ko/Ja (Mitsubishi Z) 1954; R; 1900; 79.89× 5 (262.11× 16.4); M (Mitsubishi); 13; ex Kum Yong No 501; ex Kuroshio Maru No 21 1976

★ 84510 PALEKH Ru/DDR (Stralsund) 1959; FC; 2300; 82.4× 5.15 (270.34× 16.9); M (Goerlitzer); 11; ex Bratsk; This vessel is reported to have been converted to a research vessel

84520 RABUNION VI Le/Ne (E J Smit) 1958; C; 900; 64.85 × 4.56 (212.76× 14.96); M (Werkspoor); 10.75; ex Phoebus 1975; ex Leonidas 1974
Similar (Le flag):
84521 RABUNION V ex Croesus 1975; ex Berta 1973; ex Libertas 1972
84522 RABUNION XIII ex Arcas 1978
84523 RABUNION XIV ex Calchas 1978
84524 RABUNION XV ex Taras
84525 RABUNION XVI ex Boreas 1978
84527 AL SALAM 1 ex La Perla 1 1978; ex Pallas 1978; ex Spalla 1973; ex Pallas 1972
84527/1 HOSS M ex Dimitrios 1982;
(Gr flag):
84528 GIANNIS DIMAKIS II ex Smithra 1973; ex Mithras 1972
84529 GIANNIS MALLIS ex Dimitris 1982; ex Prodromos II 1980

84530 STAVROS G ex Alexis K 1981; ex Maria S; ex Amyntas 1972
84532 AMIN (Sy) ex Apollon 1980; ex Philetas 1972
84533 MUSHRIF (Db) ex Geena 1980; ex Abota 1973; ex Labotas 1972
84534 SAID 1 (Le) ex Ilias 1978
84536 MARE 1 (Pa) ex Etas 1976; ex Alcetas 1972
84537 SORAYA (Cy) ex Maga 1983; ex Magas 1973

★ 84540 LOVRAN Ys/Br (Grangemouth) 1954; C; 900; 66.78 × 4.54 (219.09 × 14.9); M (British Polar); 10; ex Woodwren 1969; ex Eddystone 1956

84550 ABIDIN DAVER Tu/Tu (Denizcilik) 1955/60; C; 4400; 106.89 × 7.46 (350.69×24.48); M (Fiat); —

★ 84560 AN HUA RC/Sw (Eriksbergs) 1960; C; 6300/8500; 143.9 × 7.74/8.97 (472.11 × 25.39/29.43); M (B&W); 15; ex Buku 1974; ex Sydland 1972

● 84580 RIO BRAVO Gr/Br (H&W) 1960; B; 12000; 169.88 × 9.68 (557.35 × 31.76); M (B&W); 14.5; ex Cuyo 1978; ex Drymos 1975; ex St Mary 1974; ex Tresfonn 1973
Sister:
34581 LEROS ISLAND (Gr) ex Sarandi 1981; ex San Francesco 1974; ex Krossfonn 1972

84590 NORTH EMPEROR Li/Ja (Mitsubishi HI) 1967; B; 25800; 206.03 × 12.2 (675.95 × 40.03); M (Sulzer); 16.5
Sister:
84591 NORTH KING (Li)

★ 84610 YANG MING SHAN RC/Ja (Hitachi) 1965; B; 25100; 206.03 × 12.32 (675.95 × 40.42); M (B&W); 15; ex Goldean Alliance 1982; ex Atherstone 1978

84630 KARRAS Pa/Sw (Lindholmens) 1962; B; 10800; 152.56 × 9.16 (500.52 × 30.05); M (Lindholmens); 14.25; ex Kimoliaki Aigli 1983; ex Oinoussian Captain 1981; ex Falster 1972

84650 IRAN HOJJAT Ir/Sw (Gotav) 1964; C; 8200/11000; 154.84 × 8.59/9.48 (508.01 × 28.18/31.1); M (Gotaverken); 14.5; ex Arya Far 1980; ex Arya Pey 1973; ex Vinstra 1969

84660 JAGAT MOHINI In/FRG (Rhein Nordseew) 1958; B; 12200; 160.97 × 9.39 (528.12 × 30.8); M (MAN); 13; ex Rheinstahl 1969
Sister:
84661 JAGAT SWAMINI (In) ex Otto Springorum 1971

★ 84690 HONG QI 113 RC/FRG (Flensburger) 1958; O; 10600; 159.34 × 9.42 (522.97 × 30.91); M (MAN); 13.5; ex Caspian Sea 1976; ex August Leonhardt 1972
Sister (may have aft KP removed):
84691 MARIE LEONHARDT (Li)

★ 84700 FOUR FLAGS II Gr/FRG (Flensburger) 1958; B; 10300; 157.82 × 9.45 (517.78 × 31); M (MAN); 14; ex Stavfjord 1980; ex Magdalena Oldendorff 1971

★ 84710 BOTEVGRAD Bu/No (Kristiansands) 1962; C; 2300; 102.77 × 6.01 (337.17 × 19.72); M (B&W); 14; ex Germa 1969

84720 NEW SULU SEA Pa/No (Fredriksstad) 1961; C; 12200; 166.48 × 10.21 (546 × 33.50); M (Gotaverken); 15; ex Sulu Sea 1976; ex Gjendefjell 1972; ex Angeline 1968

84730 CEYLAN WAVE Sr/Br (Lithgows) 1961; B; 12200; 159.87 × 8.38 (524.5 × 27.49); M (B&W) 11.5; ex Evpo Wave 1982; ex Dapo Wave 1978; ex Cape Nelson 1976

84740 HERIOT Br/FRG (Brand) 1972; LGC; 1600; 78.11 × 6.22 (256.27 × 20.41); M (MWM); 14.5
Sisters:
84741 ANNA SCHULTE (FRG)
84742 TARQUIN ROVER (Pa) ex Pentland Glen 1981; ex Abbotsford 1976
Probable sisters:
84743 LEIBNIZ (Cy) ex Alexander Schulte 1980
Similar:
84744 SOPHIE SCHULTE (FRG)
84745 LISSY SCHULTE (FRG) ex Elisabeth 1980; ex Lissy Schulte 1977

84750 TALETE It/Fr 1967; LGC: 1600; 80.98×4.62 (265.68 × 15.16); M; 13; ex Thales 1972

84760 CARIBGAS 7 Pa/Sp (U N de Levante) 1965; LGC; 1500; 75.72 × 5.25 (248.43 × 17.22); M (Werkspoor); 12.5; ex Tamames 1982
Similar:
84761 ISLA DE MARNAY (Sp)

84770 TINE THOLSTRUP De/FRG (Meyer) 1967; LGC; 1400; 71.2 × 4.52 (233.6 × 14.83); M (KHD); 12

84780 HALLDIS No/Hong Kong (Taikoo) 1960; C; 4000/6000; 130.89 × 6.97/7.89 (429.43 × 22.87/25.89); M (Gotaverken); 15; ex *Bragernes* 1973; ex *Halldis* 1969

84790 SPICE ISLAND GIRL Pa/Br (Goole) 1958; C; 1500; 73.72 × 4.33 (241.86 × 14.21); M (Ruston & Hornsby); —; ex *Spice Island* 1979; ex *Isle of Ely* 1978

★ **84810 LIVNY** Ru/Ja (IHI) 1963; Tk; 22500; 207.04 × 11.11 (679.27 × 36.45); M (Sulzer); 17.25
Sisters (Ru flag):
★ **84811 LOZOVAYA**
★ **84812 LENINAKAN**
★ **84813 LYUDINOVO**
Probable sister (Ru Flag):
★ **84814 NOVOROSSISKIY PARTIZAN** ex *Liski* 1976
Similar (Ru Flag):
★ **84815 LENKORAN**
★ **84816 LISICHANSK**
★ **84817 LYUBOTIN**

84820 EVELINE Gr/Sw (Eriksbergs) 1963; B; 11900; 163.23 × 9.38 (535.53 × 30.77); M (B&W); 15.5; ex *Ocean Triton* 1981; ex *Troja* 1970

84830 RODANTHI A Pa/No (Stord) 1962; B; 12000; 159.65 × 9.95 (523.79 × 32.64); M (B&W); 15; ex *Maureen B* 1982; ex *Glyfada Spirit* 1980; ex *Gudvang* 1974; ex *Norbega* 1969

84840 HADIOTIS Gr/Br (Gray) 1960; O; 7900; 156.65 × 8.80 (514 × 28.87); M (Doxford); 12.5; ex *St Margaret* 1978; ex *Joya McCance* 1966

84850 DAVID SALMAN Fi/Sw (Uddevalla) 1962; C; 7100; 129.29 × 7.94 (424.18 × 26.05); M (Gotaverken); 16; ex *Grim* 1976; ex *David Salman* 1975

84860 AL KAHERAH Eg/Sw (Uddevalla) 1961; C; 4100/5900; 126.93 × 6.81/8.14 (416.44 × 22.34/26.71); M (Gotaverken); 16.25; ex *Concordia Seahorse* 1975; ex *Seahorse* 1972; ex *Sunseahorse* 1972; ex *Seahorse* 1963

★ **84870 LENINABAD** Ru/Ja (IHI) 1964; Tk; 23100; 207.04 × 11.11 (679.27 × 36.45); M (Sulzer); 16.5;
Sister:
★ **84871 LUTSK** (Ru)

★ **84880 CAPITAN OLO PANTOJA** Cu/No (Trosvik) 1965; Ch; 500; 63.71 × 3.89 (209.02 × 12.76); M (MWM); 11; ex *Rier* 1975; ex *Stainless Carrier* 1974
Sister:
★ **84881 CAPITAN MARTINEZ TAMAYO** (Cu) ex *Stain* 1975; ex *Stainless Tanker* 1974

84900 STUDLAFOSS Ic/Br (Grangemouth) 1964; R; 2400; 89.46 × 5.35 (293.5 × 17.55); M (KHD); —; ex *Hofsjokull* 1977

● **84910 OTELIA** Sw/Sw (Lodose) 1969; Tk; 2700; 98.94 × 6.43 (324.61 × 21.11); M (MWM); 12
Similar:
84911 OTTAWA (Sw)
84912 KHALIJIAH (Ku) ex *Otello* 1978
84913 OTARU (Sw)
84914 WOTONI (Ma) ex *Otoni* 1977

84920 CANAIMA Ve/Br (Inglis) 1955; C; 1400; 76.82 × 3.98 (252 × 13.06); M (Sulzer); 12; ex *Tacamar III* 1982; ex *Alftan* 1976; ex *Vasilia* 1972; ex *Kelvin* 1968; ex *Ulster Premier* 1963
Similar:
84921 HONG SHEN (My) ex *Woodbine* 1975; ex *Bat Snapir* 1973; ex *Talisker* 1968; ex *Ulster Pioneer* 1963

84930 ZINGARA It/DDR ('Neptun') 1963; C; 900/1600; 82.4 × 4.26/5.75 (270.34 × 13.98/18.86); M (Halberstadt); 12; ex *Adamastos* 1980; ex *Kormoran* 1976
Sisters (DDR flag):
★ **84931 BUSSARD**
★ **84932 CONDOR**
★ **84933 FALKE**
★ **84934 FLAMINGO**
★ **84935 PINGUIN**

★ **84940 OELSA** DDR/DDR ('Neptun') 1967; C; 2500; 92.82 × 5.92 (304.53 × 19.42); M (Dieselmotoren-werk Rostock); 12.75
Sisters (DDR flag):
★ **84941 EISENBERG**
★ **84942 HELLERAU**
★ **84943 THEMAR**
★ **84944 ZEULENRODA**

84950 HERIOT Br/FRG (Brand) 1972; LGC; 1600; 78.11 × 6.22 (256.27 × 20.41); M (MWM); 14.5
Sisters:
84951 ANNA SCHULTE (FRG)
84952 TARQUIN ROVER (Pa) ex *Pentland Glen* 1981; ex *Abbotsford* 1976
Similar:

84953 LEIBNIZ (Cy) ex *Alexander Schulte* 1980
84954 SOPHIE SCHULTE (FRG)
84955 LISSY SCHULTE (FRG) ex *Elisabeth* 1980; ex *Lissy Schulte* 1977

84960 SULFURICO Sp/Sp (Ruiz) 1969; Ch; 1200; 77.32 × 4.76 (253.67 × 15.62); M (Stork-Werkspoor); 12
Sisters:
84961 FOSFORICO (Sp)
★ **84962 CAPITAN ALBERTO FERNANDEZ** (Cu)
84963 LITRIX (It) ex *Nitrico*

84970 SILVERMERLIN Br/Sw (Lodose) 1968; Tk/Ch; 1300; 77.32 × 4.8 (253.67 × 15.75); M (MWM) 12;
Similar:
84971 SILVERFALCON (Br)

● **84980 PASS OF CAIRNWELL** Br/Br (Appledore) 1970; Tk/Ch; 900; 70.16 × 4.19 (230.18 × 13.75); M (English Electric); 11; ex *Cordale* 1975; Lengthened 1972
Sister:
84981 DANAE (Gr) ex *Pass of Chisholm* 1984; ex *Cordene* 1975

84990 CAP FALCONE It/Fr (Dubigeon) 1962; LGC; 1600; 74.68 × 4.99 (245 × 16.37); M (Werkspoor); 12; ex *Yuki Multina* 1972; ex *Cap Griz-Nez* 1971
Similar:
84991 CAP PHAISTOS (Gr) ex *Cap Frehel* 1969

85000 KIRSTEN THOLSTRUP De/FRG (Meyer) 1961; LGC; 1000; 67.39 × 3.65 (221 × 11.98); M (MWM); 12.5
Sisters:
85001 BIRTHE THOLSTRUP (De)
85002 ULLA THOLSTRUP (De

85010 CHIQUITA Ec/No (Trondhjems) 1963; Tk/Ch; 2700; 101.45 × 5.81 (332.84 × 19.06); M (Werkspoor); 12.25; ex *Michelle F* 1978; ex *St Panteleimon* 1975; ex *Ek* 1974
Sister:
85011 TRADE WIND (Pa) ex *Oak* 1974

85030 PALMEA Gr/No (Fredriksstad) 1960; B; 10800; 166.48 × 10.22 (546.19 × 33.53); M (Gotaverken); 14; ex *Almea* 1981; ex *Fiona 1* 1978; ex *St Fotini* 1977; ex *Bjorgheim* 1969

85050 PATROKLOS 1 Pa/Ja (Mitsubishi HI) 1957; C; 10300; 154.84 × 9.36 (508.01 × 30.71); T (Mitsubishi); —; ex *Alhaja Mama Bakare* 1982; ex *Tharros* 1977
Similar:
85051 DUPE BAKARE (Pa) ex *Rythme* 1977

85060 FENG SHENG Pa/Fr (Mediterranee) 1963; B; 15700; 177.27 × 10.56 (581.59 × 34.65); M (Sulzer); —; ex *King Leonidas* 1982

85070 UM EL FAROUD Ly/Br (Smith's D) 1969; Ch; 3100; 109.56 × 6.41 (359.45 × 21.03); (Smit & Bolnes); 14; ex *Seafalcon* 1973
Sisters:
85071 RED IBIS (Li) ex *Storna* 1982; ex *Seatern* 1975
85072 LUHUAN (Pa) ex *F Wiborg Fekete* 1973

85080 KHADER WALI Sg/Ja (Hitachi) 1962; C; 3800/5700; 126.45 × 6.67/7.88 (414.86 × 21.88/25.85); M (B&W); 15.5; ex *14 July* 1982
Sister:
85081 14 RAMADAN (Iq) ex *Kassim* 1963

85100 SETE CIDADES Po/Sw (Falkenbergs) 1961; C; 1100; 74.5 × 3.67 (244.42 × 12.04); M (MWM); —; ex *Bruse* 1972; ex *Nordpol* 1964
Sister:
85101 LAGOA (Po) ex *Bure* 1972 ex *Vaasa* 1964

85110 VILI To/Sw (Falkenbergs) 1967; C; 500/1300; 73.41 × 3.63/5.72 (240.85 × 11.88/18.77); M (MWM); 13; ex *Nogi* 1979; ex *Marin* 1974

85130 LONE TERKOL De/FRG (Kroegerw) 1972; Tk; 1300; 81.01 × 5.27 (265.78 × 17.29); M (MWM); 12

85150 SELAT MAKASSAR Ia/Ja (Shikoku) 1962; C; 1100; 64.98 × 4 (213.19 × 13.12); M (MAN); 12
Sister:
85151 SELAT KARIMATA (Ia)

★ **85170 BOTEVGRAD** Bu/No (Kristiansands) 1962; C; 2300; 102.77 × 6.01 (337.17 × 19.72); M (B&W); 14; ex *Germa* 1969
Similar (without large vents in well):
85171 NOUR D (Le) ex *Karyatis* 1983; ex *Tarva* 1972; ex *Germont* 1962

85180 SETE CIDADES Po/Sw (Falkenbergs) 1961; C; 1100; 74.5 × 3.67 (244.42 × 12.04); M (MWM); —; ex *Bruse* 1972; ex *Nordpol* 1964

Sister:
85181 LAGOA (Po) ex *Bure* 1972; ex *Vaasa* 1964

85190 FIVE FLOWERS Pa/De (Aarhus) 1958; C; 1000/1500; 78.52 × 4.42/5.65 (257.61 × 14.5/18.54); M (B&W); —; ex *Bakkafoss* 1974; ex *Mille Heering* 1963
Similar:
85191 INGRID JUDITH (Co) ex *Cataima* 1973; ex *Christel Heering* 1962

85200 JVONNE Pa/Sw (Falkenbergs) 1966; C; 1300; 73.41 × 3.62 (240.85 × 11.88); M (MWM); —; ex *Divona* 1979; Launched as *Sunnanhav*

85210 JUMBO JOIST Pa/Ne ('Vooruitgang') 1955; C/HL; 800/1200; 80.5 × 5.11/— (264.11 × 16.77/—); M (Werkspoor); 10.5; ex *Singapore Jati* 1983; ex *Bernard John* 1974; Gear amidships consists of quadpod and sheerlegs

85220 ALEXANDER Gr/No (Stord) 1957; C; 2700/4400; 114.28 × 6.22/7.19 (374.93 × 20.41/23.59); M (Stork); 15; ex *Minerva* 1981; ex *Helios* 1978; ex *Kongsholm* 1963
Sister:
85221 SKOPELOS STAR (Gr) ex *Martina* 1981; ex *Wanja* 1973; ex *Jeanette* 1966

85230 IBN JUBAIR Eg/Sp (Duro Felguera) 1970; C; 660/1180; 72.7 × 5.19 (238.5 × 16.96); M (Deutz); —; ex *Atlan Esmeralda* 1974
Sister:
85231 IBN KORRA (Eg) ex *Atlan Rubi* 1975
Possibly similar:
85232 LUR TXORI (Eg) ex *Jade* 1975; ex *Lian* 1974
85233 UR-TXORI (Eg) ex *Topacio* 1976; ex *Lian Dos* 1973

85240 SALEH 2 Si/Ne (Duijvendijk's) 1958; C; 1600; 78.64 × 4.47 (258 × 14.67); M (Werkspoor); 12; ex *Anna* 1981; ex *Charente* 1970
Sister:
85241 MAYA (Cy) ex *Myrto* 1976; ex *Biscaya* 1970

85250 IOANNIS Gr/Sw (Norrkopings) 1958; C; 2000/3100; 102.14 × 5.79/6.57 (335.1 × 21.56); M (Nydqvist & Holm); 13.5; ex *Oder* 1980; ex *Cecilia Falkland* 1982

85260 SUGAR TRADER Pa/Sw (Ekensbergs) 1959; C; 2700/4300; 114.33 × 6.2/7.19 (375.1 × 20.34/23.59); M (B&W); 14.5; ex *Orla* 1981; ex *Artensis* 1968

● **85270 NISSAKI** Ma/Sw (Ekensbergs) 1958; C; 4500; 114.33 × 7.21 (375 × 23.65); M (B&W); 14; ex *Agios Nikolaos* 1984; ex *Zanet* 1980; ex *Beaverash* 1969; ex *Mimer* 1963; May be broken up

85280 PARDI Pa/Ne (Duijvendijk's) 1959; C; 1400; 88.09 × 5.26 (289 × 17.26); M (Werkspoor); 13; ex *Mudistar* 1979; ex *Stalheim* 1972
Sister:
85281 BONAWIND 1 (Sg) ex *Daliastar* 1980; ex *Stanford* 1972

85290 CORANTIJN Sn/Ne (Amels) 1968; C; 2700; 101.99 × 6.17 (334.61 × 20.24); M (KHD); 15

85310 ESPERANZA No 2 Pa/Ne ('De Gideon') 1956/70; C; 1100; 70.85 × 4.4 (232.45 × 14.47); M (KHD); 11.25; ex *Atlantico 1* 1978; ex *Fibrook* 1973; ex *Warwickbrook* 1972; Lengthened 1970

★ **85320 TAVRIYA** Ru/Ru (Nosenko) 1960; FC; 3000; 99.35 × 5.65 (325.95 × 18.54); D-E (—); 13
Sisters (some vary—taller funnels etc) (Ru flag): ★
★ **85321 DALNEVOSTOCHNY**
★ **85322 VOLZHSK**
★ **85324 ANDREY EVDANOV**
★ **85325 SOVIETSKAYA LATVIYA**
★ **85326 SOVIETSKAYA RODINA**
★ **85327 VITALIY BONIVUR**
★ **85328 BUREVSTNIK**
★ **85329 DMITRY CHASOVITIN**
★ **85330 KAZIS GEDRIS**
★ **85331 RUDNYY**
★ **85332 ALTAIR**
★ **85333 MIKHAIL YANKO**
★ **85334 NEVELSKIY**
★ **85335 OKTYABRSK**
★ **85336 SEREBRYANSK**
★ **85337 SVETLYY**
★ **85338 IRBIT**
★ **85339 ISHIM**
★ **85340 ISKONA**
★ **85341 PRANAS ZIBERTAS**
★ **85342 SALNA**
★ **85343 SARMA**
★ **85344 PARSLA**
★ **85345 SAYANI**
★ **85346 SUKHINICHI**
★ **85347 GUTSUL**
★ **85348 MONGOL**

★ 85349 **NANAYETS**
★ 85350 **PFUSUNG**
★ 85351 **AUGUST KORK**
★ 85352 **BOEVOY**
★ 85353 **LEDUS**
★ 85354 **KOSMONAUT**
★ 85355 **MOLODYOZNYY**
★ 85356 **MOREKHOD**
★ 85357 **VETERAN**
★ 85358 **DON**
★ 85359 **KREUTSWALD**
★ 85360 **NAMANGAN**
★ 85361 **VIKTORAS YATSENYAVICHUS**
(Bu flag):
★ 85362 **KHAN OMTURAG** ex *Betelgeuse*
(DDR flag):
★ 85363 **BREITLING**
(Gh flag):
85364 **AGYASI MANKO**

85380 **DIANA** Ho/Br (Lamont) 1965; C; 1100; 67.98 × 4.33 (223 × 14.21) M (British Polar); 11; ex*Angelina S* 1982; ex *Mariyos Hope* 1980; ex *Balmerino* 1977; ex *Ardgarvel* 1975

●85390 **ORESTIS** Gr/Ne (Bodewes NV) 1958; C; 1100; 73.94 × 4.4 (242.59 × 14.44); M (KHD); 11.25; ex *Houtman* 1974; ex *Erasmus* 1970; ex *Argonaut* 1968; Lengthened 1971

85400 **CRETE** Gr/Ne (Bodewes NV) 1956; C; 1000; 66.45 × 4.42 (218. × 14.5); M (KHD); 11.25; ex*Mahi* 1978; ex *Wallona* 1971; ex *Windsor Queen* 1969; ex *Mortlake* 1966; ex*Lockwood* 1965; ex*Nordgas* 1964; ex *Windsorbrook* 1963

85420 **BREDAL** Br/FRG (A Pahl) 1953; C; 1300; 80.52 × 4.43 (264.17 × 14.53); M (KHD), 10.5; ex *Bredo* 1972; ex *Joruna* 1968; ex *Margaret C Ertel* 1963; Lengthened 1957

85430 **ANN M** Br/Br (Burntisland) 1961; C; 1200; 70.11 × 4.47 (230.02 × 14.67); M (Lister Blackstone); 11.5

85440 **IOANNA V** Gr/Sw (Eriksbergs) 1961; Tk; 22100; 208.03 × 11.56 (682.51 × 37.93); M (B&W); 16; ex *Alba* 1977; ex *Hemland* 1972

★ 85450 **DUNAV** Bu/Br (Laing) 1961; Tk; 13600; 170.47 × 9.48 (559.28 × 31.1); M (Doxford); 15; ex *Montana* 1963

85460 **RESILIENCE** Br/Ne ('Voorwarts') 1969; Starch carrier; 1000; 66.3 × 4.1 (217.52 × 13.45); M (Lister Blackstone Mirrlees); 12.5

85470 **CEDERBORG** Ne/No (Aukra) 1972; C; 1200; 77.17 × 4.76 (253 × 15.61); M (Atlas-Mak); 13; ex *Carebeka VII* 1982; ex *Nortrio* 1974
Sisters:
85471 **NIAGA XXXIII** (Ia) ex *Maasplein* 1981; ex *Norcato* 1974
85472 **ATLANTIC RIVER** (Ne) ex *Munte* 1981; ex *Norimo* 1974

85480 **MAYA** Cy/FRG (Meyer) 1966; C; 800/1500; 74.81×4.02/5.75 (245.44×13.19/18.86); M (KHD) 13.5; ex *Eridan* 1980; ex *Austrian Sailor* 1978; ex *Wien* 1977; ex *Seeadler* 1972

★ 85500 **KOM** Ys/FRG (Meyer) 1956; C; 1400; 74.48 × 5.22 (244.36 × 17.13); M (KHD); 12; ex*Hum* 1980; ex*Urania* 1974; ex*Dorothea G* 1974; ex*Urania* 1968

★ 85510 **PUPNAT** Ys/FRG (Travewerft) 1959; C; 2200; 92.72 × 5.85 (304.2 × 19.19); M (KHD); 12.5; ex *Victor* 1973; ex *IG Nichelson* 1972

85530 **NICOLAOS M** Cy/FRG (Brand) 1954; C; 800; 65.69 × 3.80 (215.5 × 12.47); M (MaK); 11.5; ex *Homer* 1973; ex *Katerina K* 1972; ex *Kurt Bastian* 1970

85540 **MERCATOR** Pa/FRG (Unterweser) 1952; C; 1100; 72.04 × 4.61 (236.35 × 15.12); M (MaK); 11; ex *Katie* 1978; ex *Hammonia* 1965; ex *Anni Ahrens* 1957

85550 **MANUEL** Pa/Br (Ardrossan) 1955; C; 900; 68.43 × 5.6 (224.51 × 18.37); M (Sulzer); —; ex *Proodos* 1980; ex*Michalis* 1976; ex*Evdelos* 1972; ex *Mountstewart* 1969; ex *Essex Coast* 1957

85570 **RAMSLAND** No/FRG (Kremer) 1956; C; 900; 64.95 × 4.31 (213.09 × 14.14); M (MaK); 11; ex *Simon* 1975; ex *Ortrud Muller* 1965

85580 **PETROLA 40** Gr/FRG (Travewerft) 1958; C; 1800; 82 × 5.73 (269.03 × 18.8); M (KHD); 12.5; ex *Petrola XL* 1976; ex *Varodd* 1975; ex *Estremadurian* 1970; ex *Varodd* 1968

85600 **TABALO** Sy/Fi (Valmet) 1961; C; 1800; 85.81 × 5.39 (281.53 × 17.68); M (KHD); 13; ex*Gaist* 1977; ex *Else Reith* 1969; ex *Pulptrader* 1966

★ 85610 **BIRA** Ru/Ru (—) —; —; 2100 (displacement); 75× — (246× —); M (—); 12; Probably used as a naval transport or landing craft
Sister:
★ 85611 **BUREYA** (Ru)

85620 **ARUBA BAY** NA/Sw (Solvesborgs) 1964; R; 500/1300; 72.8 × 3.72/5.00 (238.85 × 12.2/16.47); M (Polar); 14.5; ex *Polar Viking* 1974
Similar:
85621 **GMC-3-WALEED** (Db) ex *Caracas Bay* 1983; ex *Hastings* 1973

★ 85630 **NAPALSAN** RK/De (van der Werf) 1961; R; 1900; 78.03 bp × 5.02 (256 bp × 5.02); M (KHD); 13; ex *Mag 2* 1968; ex *Drangajokull* 1968
Probably used as a fish carrier; May be spelt **NA PAL SAN**
Sister:
★ 85631 **POONGDESAN** (RK) ex *Mag 1* 1968; ex *Langjokul* 1968; May be spelt **POONG DE SAN**

85640 **LAKESHELL** Ca/Ca (Marine Indust) 1969; Tk; 5700; 121.93 × 7.1 (400 × 23.29); M (Ruston & Hornsby); 13

85650 **GAZ ATLANTIC** Gr/Fr (Dubigeon-Normandie) 1965; LGC; 3000; 99.29 × 5.46 (325.75 × 17.91); M (MAN); 13.75; ex*Amedeo Avogadro* 1980; ex *Uranus* 1971

85660 **GIMONE** Fr/Fr (La Rochelle) 1969; Tk; 3400; 100.03 × 5.61 (328.18 × 18.41); TSM (Werkspoor); 11.75

85665 **BASTIAAN BROERE** Ne/Ne (Nieuwe Noord) 1968; Tk/Ch; 1300; 82.30 × 5.00 (270 × 16.40); M ('De Industrie'); 12.5;
Sister:
85666 **JACOBUS BROERE** (Ne)

85680 **MELROSE** Br/FRG (Brand) 1971; LGC; 2000; 86.95 × 6.12 (285.27 × 20.08); M (MWM); 14

85690 **CAPO NOLI** It/Ne (Wilton-Fije) 1969; Tk/Ch; 1500; 80.52 × 5.2 (264.17 × 17.06); M (English Electric); 13.5; ex *La Quinta* 1981
Sister:
85691 **LA HACIENDA** (Br)

●85700 **PASS OF CAIRNWELL** Br/Br (Appledore) 1970; Tk/Ch; 900; 70.16 × 4.19 (230.18 × 13.75); M (English Electric); 11; ex *Cordale* 1975; Lengthened 1972 (Appledore)
Sister:
85701 **DANAE** (Gr) ex *Pass of Chisholm* 1984; ex *Cordene* 1975

85710 **PASS OF DRUMOCHTER** Br/Ne (Ijsselwerf) 1974; Ch; 1600; 80.75 × 5.56 (264.93 × 18.24); M (Mirrlees Blackstone); 13.5
Sister:
85711 **PASS OF DIRRIEMORE** (Br)

85720 **JOHN WILSON** NZ/Br (H Robb) 1961; Cem; 1600; 81.49 × 4.92 (267.36 × 16.14); D-E (Belliss & Morcom); 11.5

85730 **PETROSTAR XIV** Si/FRG (Bayerische) 1961; Tk; 1600; 87 × 5.26 (285.43 × 17.26); M (MAN); —; ex *Maria II* 1980; ex *Gertrude Wiener* 1977

85740 **DALAVIK** Sw/Sw (Karlstads) 1966; Tk; 1000; 78.09 × 4.64 (256.2 × 15.22); M (KHD); —; Lengthened and deepened 1972

85750 **HALLIBURTON 602** Pa/No (Langesunds) 1960; Cem; 900; 63.89 × 4.21 (209.61 × 13.81); M (Bergens); 12; ex *Cementine* 1978

85760 **REDO** Sw/FRG (Kremer) 1963; TB; 1400; 72.95 × 4.64 (239.34 × 15.22); M (KHD); 11; ex *Nynas* 1976

85770 **AL BACHIR** Pa/Sw (Gotav) 1960; Tk; 12800; 169.81 × 9.61 (557.12 × 31.53); M (Gotaverken); 15; ex *Babaneft One* 1983; ex *Olivia* 1979; ex *Dolphin Olivia* 1979; ex *Braconda* 1978

85780 **DOLPHIN II** Gr/Sw (Gotav) 1959; Tk; 12700; 169.81 × 9.57 (557.11 × 31.38); M (Gotaverken); 15; ex *Vibeke* 1978
Similar:
★ 85781 **DA QING No 41** (RC) ex *Anella* 1972; ex *Oscar Gorthon* 1971; ex *Vinstra*
Similar (asphalt tanker):
85782 **VIBIT** (No)

85790 **ORYX** Gr/Ne (Verolme Scheeps) 1959; Tk; 12900; 170.59 × 9.37 (560 × 30.74); M (MAN); 14; ex *Aegeon* 1980; ex*Hope Sky* 1979; ex*Kef Eagle* 1975; ex *Pedro* 1973; ex*Benwell* 1968; ex *Belmar* 1962
Similar:
85791 **ROAN** (Gr) ex *Mpenitses* 1980; ex *Tamara* 1975

85810 **RIO GRANDE** Gr/Sw (Eriksbergs) 1957; Tk;

12800; 170.67 × 9.63 (560 × 31.62); M (B&W); 14.5; ex *Sunares* 1979; ex *Benares* 1974; ex *Angelus* 1966; ex*Lysefjell* 1959

85820 **CARIBE No 1** Pa/De (Aarhus) 1961; LGC; 800; 65.33 × 3.56 (214.34 × 11.68); M (MaK); 13; ex *Lili Tholstrup* 1971

85840 **HARZ** FRG/FRG (Norderwerft) 1953; RT; 2600; 92.4 × 6.6 (303 × 21.7); M (—); 12; ex *Claere Jung* 1963. In German naval service

85850 **IVO DORMIO** It/FRG (Kremer) 1964; Ch; 800; 63.51 × 4.22 (208.37 × 13.85); M (MAN); 11.5; ex *Chemicoaster* 1972

85860 **BETTY THERESA** De/De (Helsingborgs) 1964; Tk/Ch; 79.66 × 5.21 (261.35 × 17.09); M (MAN); 12; ex *Irla Lupe* 1982; ex *Irland* 1979

85870 **JENNIE W** Br/Br (Grangemouth) 1965; Tk; 1000; 61.45 × 4.22 (201.61 × 13.85); M (British Polar); 11; ex*Shell Mariner* 1982; ex*Falmouth* 1979
Sisters:
85872 **NIGERIAN STAR** (Ho) ex*BP Scorcher* 1983; ex *Killingholme* 1976
85873 **SHELL TRADER** (Br) ex *Teesport* 1979
85874 **METRO SUN** (Ca) ex*Shell Scientist* 1981; ex *Partington* 1979
Similar (lower superstructure—taller funnel):
85875 **SHELL ENGINEER** (Br) ex*Dingle Bank* 1979

★ 85880 **KLYAZMA** Ru/Fi (Crichton-Vulcan) 1952; Tk; 1100; 63.51 × 4.48 (208.37 × 14.7); M (Nydqvist & Holm); 10
Sisters (Ru flag):
★ 85881 **NERCHA**
★ 85882 **ORSK**
★ 85883 **CHARDZHOV**
★ 85884 **URZHUM**
★ 85885 **AZNEFT**
★ 85886 **NOVINSK**
★ 85887 **GROSNEFT**
★ 85888 **ELBAN**
★ 85889 **KREKING**
★ 85890 **BASHKIRNEFT**

85900 **ROCAS** Po/Po (Viana) 1965; Tk; 1400; 76.51 × 4.73 (251 × 15.52); TSM (MWM); 12

85910 **VASILIOS VII** Gr/FRG (Hitzler) 1959; Tk; 1500; 85.55 × 4.67 (280.68 × 15.32); M (KHD); 11.5; ex *Scharhorn* 1977; ex *Josef Joham* 1967; Lengthened 1968

85920 **VASILIOS 1** Gr/FRG (Hitzler) 1958; Tk; 1400; 76.51 × 4.65 (251 × 15.26); M (KHD); 11.5; ex*Eole* 1974; ex *Ellen Essberger* 1958
Similar (lengthened):
★ 85921 **HERMANAS GIRALT** (Cu) ex*Borkum* 1970

85930 **BALTIC PROSPERITY** Pa/Sw (Lodose) 1965; Tk; 2250; 86.75 × 5.79 (284.6 × 19); M (MWM); 12; ex*Rathowen* 1983; ex*Bellona* 1974; ex *Luna* 1974
Similar (one less deck on superstructure):
85931 **WENA** (Ma) ex *Lena* 1977
Possibly similar:
85936 **BELLONA** (Sw) ex *Stella Atlantic* 1978

85940 **ESMERALDAS** Ec/Br (Hill) 1960; Tk; 3600; 106.08 × 4.87 (348.03 × 15.98); TSM (British Polar); 9.5; ex*Anglo* 1976

85950 **ESSO CAERNARVON** Br/Br (J L Thompson) 1962; Tk; 1100; 70.52 × 4.36 (231.36 × 14.3); M (English Electric); 10
Similar:
85951 **MALDIVE VALOUR** (Mv) ex *Esso Ipswich* 1981

85960 **VALENTINE K** Gr/FRG (Rolandwerft) 1959; Tk; 1000; 65.99 × 4.35 (216.5 × 14.27); M (Nydqvist & Holm); 11; ex*Alfa Ena* 1984; ex*Fotoula* 1983; ex *Rathgar* 1983; ex*Pass of Kildrummy* 1970

★ 85970 **KRIPTON** Ru/Ru (Zaliv) 1964; Tk; 1800; 83.67 × 4.6 (274.51 × 15.09); M (Skoda); 12.5
Sisters (some have taller funnels—Ru flag):
★ 85971 **UKHTA**
★ 85972 **GROZNYY**
★ 85973 **ABAKAN**
★ 85974 **AKADEMIK MAMEDALIEV**
★ 85975 **EKIMCHAN**
★ 85976 **LASPI**
★ 85977 **EVENSK**
★ 85978 **TEMRYUK**
★ 85979 **KEKUR**
★ 85980 **NARVA**
★ 85981 **NIVA**
★ 85982 **NEFTEGORSK**
★ 85983 **NERCHINSK**
★ 85984 **SOVIETSKIY POGRANICHNIK**
★ 85985 **IMANT SUDMALIS**
★ 85986 **NIKOPOL**

★85987 NOGINSK
★85988 SEVAN
★85989 FIORD
★85991 NOVIK
★85992 KHRUSTALNYY
★85993 SAMTREDIA
★85994 SILVET
★85995 BERDSK
★85996 SOLNECHNYY
★85997 STEPANOKERT
★85998 BALADZHARY
★85999 BELOYARSK
★86000 BORISOGLEBSK
★86001 KARAKUMNEFT
★86002 KARELI
★86003 NARYMNEFT
★86004 BEREZOVNEFT
★86005 ICHA
★86006 ELTIGEN
★86007 KUMBYSH
★86008 NADEZHDA KURCHYENKO
★86009 KERCHENSKIY KOMMUNIST
(Bu flag):
★86010 CHAYA ex Benetnash 1970
★86012 VACHA ex Bellatrix 1970

★86020 AKTIAN Cu/Br (Hall, Russell) 1960/66; C; 2100/3200; 108.29 × 5.40/— (355 × 17.72/-); M (British Polar); 12.5; ex Andrew C Crosbie 1977; ex Colina 1967; Lengthened 1966(Barclay, Curle). Has probably been renamed

86030 NISYROS ERA Gr/Br (H Robb) 1958; C; 5300; 126.24 × 6.92 (414.17 × 22.7); M (Sulzer); —; ex Sherwood 1974; ex Thackeray 1968; Lengthened 1966

86040 AIKATERINI Gr/Sp (Cadiz) 1964; C; 3800/5900; 127.67 × /8.43 (418.86 × —/27.66); M (Sulzer) 15; ex Azalea 1981; ex Cross River 1977; ex Stamatios 1973; ex Iran Sepah 1973; ex Stamatios 1972; ex Sundale 1970; ex Ima Sam 1964

★86045 JADRO Ys/No (Sarpsborg) 1957; C; 2800; 112.78 × 6.24 (370 × 20.47); M (B&W); 14; ex Tautra 1967; ex Glomeggen 1960

●★86050 UVERO Cu/Fr (Mediterranee) 1960; C/HL; 9500; 141.13 × 9.3 (463 × 30.51); M (Sulzer);13.5; ex Bridgedale 1964; ex Southwick 1964
Similar (larger funnel):
86051 ARETI S (Gr) ex Grantleyhall 1976; ex Skycrest 1968

86060 TIZI M'LIL Mo/Sw (Solvesborgs) 1970; R; 2000; 98.81 × 5.92 (324.18 × 19.42); M (Pielstick); 17.5
Sisters (Mo flag):
86061 TIZI N'TEST
86062 TIZI N'TICHKA

★86070 'KORSAKOV' type. Ru/Hu ('Gheorghiu Dej'/Angyalfold) 1949/61; C; 1300; 65.97 × 3.8 (216.44 × 12.47); TSM (Liebknecht/Ganz); 9.5; The existence of some of the following is doubtful and some have been reported as passenger/cargo; For similar vessels see BLAGOVESHCHENSK
Sisters (Ru flag):
★86071 KURILSK
★86072 OKHA
★86073 TYUMEN
★86074 NALCHIK
★86075 AKOP
★86076 AKOPYAN
★86077 TIKHORETSK
★86078 TRUSKAVETS
★86079 KALEV
★86081 SHEMAKHA
★86082 VILSANDI
★86083 EDUARD WILDE
★86084 KAGUL
★86085 KREMENETS
★86086 NARYN
★86087 SAAREMAA
★86088 SULEV
★86089 ZAYARSK
★86090 AKHTUBA
★86091 JAN KREUKS
★86092 KANIN
★86093 PESHT
★86094 TAKELI
★86095 BELBECK
(RC flag):
★86096 FU CHOU No 651
★86097 CHE HAI No 103
★86098 LIEN YUN No 28

86110 IRAN SEDAGHAT Ir/Bu (G Dimitrov) 1971; C; 4500; 114.26 × 6.55 (374.87 × 21.49); M (MAN); 13.75; ex Arya Rad 1980; ex Slevik 1975
Sisters:
86111 IRAN SHAFAAT (Ir) ex Arya Dad 1980; ex Wyvern 1975

86112 REMADA (Tn) ex Ontario 1974; ex Sariba 1973
86113 KOHENG (Pa) ex Tauloto II; ex Safia 1973
★86114 YANG ZI JIANG 4 (RC) ex Woolga 1983; ex Woolgar 1982
★86115 TAI SHAN (RC) ex Tai An 1983
★86116 TAI NING (RC)
★86117 TAI SHUN (RC)
★86118 BUDAPEST(Hu)
★86119 HUNGARIA (Hu)

86130 WEASEL Pa/Ja (Shikoku) 1964; C; 1900; 85.58 × 5.44 (280.77 × 17.85); M (Ito Tekkosho); 12; ex Hie 1982; ex Ichiyo Maru 1972
Possible sisters:
86131 HAEGUI (Ko) ex Nam Jung No 3 1982; ex Empire 1980; ex Houzan 1974; ex Houzan Maru 1972
86132 TA HANG (Pa) ex Seiryu; ex Seiryu Maru 1972; ex Kensho Maru 1969
86133 HWAPYUNG JINJU (Ko) ex Ace 1980; ex Eastern Ace 1972; ex Tsushima Maru 1971; ex Kinyo Maru 1967

86140 HONG HWA Sg/Ja (Shioyama) 1960; C; 1600; 80.75 × 5.2 (264.93 × 17.06); M (Ito Tekkosho); 11.5; ex Selat Baru 1977; ex Golden Fish 1976; ex Gay Phoenix 1972; ex Red Dragon 1970; ex Mui Kim 1967

86150 HWAPYUNG BUSAN Ko/Ja (Taiyo) 1962; C; 1900; 86.24 × 5.64 (283. × 18.50); M (Mitsubishi); 12; ex Hwapyung Pusan 1980; ex Shoho Maru 1973

86160 YAMAUME No2 Ko/Ja (Hitachi) 1962; C; 1900; 86.98 × 5.46 (285.37 × 17.91); M (Hanshin); 11; ex Yamaume Maru No 2 1981; ex Futuba Maru No 3 1970

86170 BLAGOVESHCHENSK Ru/Hu ('Gheorghiu Dej') 1953; C; 1200; 69.98 × 3.8 (229.6 × 12.47); TSM (Ganz); 9.5; The existence of some of the following is doubtful and some are reported as cargo/passenger; See similar vessels 'Korsakov' type
Sisters (Ru flag):
★86171 IVAN ZEMNUKHOV
★86172 SERGEY TYULENIN
★86173 BORODIN
★86174 LUGA
★86175 OM
★86176 TURA
★86177 ARALSK
★86178 GOMEL
★86179 OLENSK
★86180 TSELINOGRAD
★86181 YUZHNO-SAKHALINSK
★86182 BEZHETSK
★86183 GDOV
★86184 OSTROV
★86185 PAVLIK MOROZOV ex Porkhov
★86186 ABAY KUNANBAYEV ex Nerchinsk
★86187 DANILO NECHAY
★86188 KOLA
★86189 IVAN BOGUN
★86200 BELOGORSK
★86201 SCHOLLAR
★86202 SHONGAR
★86203 TELMANSK
★86204 TEMIR
★86205 ALEKSANDR OBUKHOV ex Meganom;
(Ia Flag):
86206 TULUK WEDA ex Bhima Karya 1973; ex Teluk Weda 1963; ex Barnaul
86207 PAINAN ex Teluk Bintuni 1962; ex Bolcherek 1958
(Sg flag):
86208 SILVILAI ex Lagoligo 1975; ex Teluk Tomini 1975; ex Taimyr 1958
Similar (Rm built-Rm flag):
★86209 BUZAU
★86210 ARAD
★86211 PITESTI
★86212 ROMAN

★86220 ANANYEV Ru/Hu ('Gheorghiu Dej') 1960; C; 1200; 78.49 × 4.1 (257.51 × 13.45); M (Lang Gepzyar); 10.75; Some of the following have taller funnels and other smaller differences; For later ships in this class see KEKHRA —M2F
Sisters (Ru flag):
★86221 HAAPSALU
★86222 KOTOVSK
★86223 PILTUN
★86224 TARTU
★86225 TERMEZ
★86226 VILKOVO
★86227 BELTSY
★86228 KONOSHA
★86229 NYANDOMA
★86230 SERGEY KIROV
★86231 SHKOTOVO
★86232 TAMSALU

★86233 PALDISKI
★86234 PINEGA
★86235 UST-BOLSHERETSK
★86236 ZEYA
★86238 GLUKHOV
★86239 KIHELKONA
★86240 UST-TIGIL
★86241 VILYANDY
★86242 ENGURE
(Vn flag):
★86243 SONG LO ex Ust-Kamchatsk
★86244 SONG KAU ex Elva 1977
★86245 SONG THAO ex Tymlat 1975
The following Ru vessels are reported sold to Angola:
★86246 HIYUMAA
★86247 KEYLA

86260 PENGUINS Pa/FRG (Meyer) 1952; C; 1300; 71.63 × 5 (235.01 × 16.4); M (Werkspoor); 11; ex Lugano Penguins 1982; ex Dimos 1980; ex Sparti 1980; ex Eyal 1974; ex Wulp 1961; ex Blockland 1956

86270 ALBORADA Do/De (Svendborg) 1953; C; 500; 63.51 × 3.63 (208.37 × 11.91); M (B&W); 11; ex Despina S; ex Tello 1974

86290 ST HELENA Br/Ca (Burrard DD) 1963; PC; 3200; 100.28 × 5.51 (329 × 18.08); M (Stork); —; ex Northland Prince 1977

86320 HABIB Z Le/Fr (Rhin) 1962; R; 1300; 79.48 × 4.8 (261.94 × 15.75); M (KHD); 14; ex Laura 1982; ex Laura Christina
Sisters:
86321 NORTH POLE (NA) ex Frio Express 1977; ex Coral Acropora 1974
86322 JANICE ANN (Br) ex South Pole 1981; ex Iglo Express 1977; ex Coral Actinia 1974
86323 MAYA (Br) ex Maya V 1977; ex Maya 1976

86330 PANAGIA Pa/Ne (L Smit) 1957; C; 1000; 82.12 × 4.64 (269.42 × 15.22); M (Werkspoor); 14.5; ex Olympios Hermes 1977; ex Ovambo 1976; ex Marc Laurent V 1968

86340 ESPERANZA II Pa/Ja (NKK) 1964; Tk; 32700; 225 × 12.38 (738.19 × 40.62); M (B&W); 16; ex Buena Esperanza 1983; ex Jarelsa 1973

86350 NIAGA XXXVII Ia/Ne ('Friesland') 1971; C; 1500; 94.52 × 5.4 (310.1 × 17.72); M (MWM); 14; ex Karlsburg 1981
Similar:
86351 AMANDA (It) ex Moresby Express 1978; ex Perm 1972
★86352 BREZA (Bu) ex Pamela 1983; ex Lae Express 1978; ex Trias 1972

●86370 ETHEL EVARARD Br/Br (Clelands) 1966; C; 1600; 85.1 × 5.1 (279.2 × 16.73); M (Mirrlees Blackstone); 11

86410 ESSI FLORA No/FRG (Rhein Nordseew) 1959/64; Ch; 12000; 157.69 × 9.34 (517.36 × 30.64); M (MAN); 13.75; ex Essi Flora 1963; Converted from bulk 1964 (Akers)

★86420 EISENHUTTENSTADT DDR/Sw (Gotav) 1960; OO; 23400; 199.65 × 11.38 (655 × 37.34); M (Gotaverken); 14.5; ex Mertainen 1970
Similar (converted to tanker):
86421 FFM MATARENGI (Sw) ex Matarengi 1971

86430 TEXACO MELBOURNE Br/US (Kaiser Co)- Ja 1945/67; Tk; 13900; 172.4 × 10 (565.62 × 32.81); T-E (GEC); 13.25; ex Caltex Melbourne 1967; ex Victory Loan 1951; Lengthened & converted from 'T-2' tanker 1967 (Hitachi)

86450 ALLURITY Br/Ne (Nieuwe Noord) 1969; Tk; 700; 73.97 × 3.96 (242.68 × 12.99); M (KHD); 12; Sister:
86451 ACTIVITY (Br)

86460 ALICIA 1 Pa/Ne ('De Waal') 1970; LGC; 2100; 80.98 × 6.21 (265.68 × 20.37); M (KHD); 14; ex Alphagas 1980
Sister:
86461 AMELIA (Pa) ex Betagas 1980

★86470 KEGUMS Ru/Ja (Mitsubishi HI) 1965; LGC; 3500; 96.53 × 5.02 (316.7 × 16.47); M (Sulzer); 13.75
Sister:
★86471 KRASLAVA (Ru)

86480 BENITO JUAREZ Me/Ja (IHI) 1968; Tk; 12800; 170.75 × 9.47 (560.2 × 31.07); M (Sulzer); 15.5
Sisters (Me flag):
86481 ALVARO OBREGON
86482 FRANCISCO I MADERO
86483 MECHOR OCAMPO
86484 PLAN DE AYALA

86485 **PLAN DE AYUTLA**
86486 **JOSE MARIA MORELOS**
86487 **PLAN DE GUADELUPE**
Possibly similar:
86488 **PLAN DE SAN LUIS** (Me)

86500 **PETROSTAR XVI** Si/FRG (Rhein Nordseew); 1963; Tk; 13700; 170.49 × 9.37 (559.35 × 30.74); M (MAN); 14.5; ex *Overseas Adventurer* 1981; ex *Cherryleaf*; ex *Overseas Adventurer* 1973

86510 **PETROSTAR III** Si/Br (Smith's D) 1968; Tk; 1900; 86.21 × 5.67 (282.84 × 18.6); M (Smit & Bolnes); 12; ex *Nette Theresa* 1974; ex *Preciosa* 1972

★ 86520 **POMORAVLJE** Ys/Ys ('Jozo Lozovina-Mosor') 1967; Tk; 2800; 98.53 × 6.23 (323.26 × 20.44); M (B&W); 14.25
Sister (Ys flag):
★ 86521 **PODUNAVLJE**
Similar (larger) (Ys flag):
★ 86522 **PODRAVINA**
★ 86523 **POSAVINA**

86530 **TSIMISARAKA** Mg/It (INMA) 1966; Ch; 1600; 84.49 × 4.78 (277.2 × 15.68); TSM (KHD); 12

★ 86540 **OZERNOYE** Ru/Pd (Gdynska) 1962; Tk; 1300; 75.62 × 4.74 (248.1 × 15.55); M (Sulzer); 12.5; **'B-74'** type
Sisters:
★ 86541 **DIVNOGORSK** (Ru)
★ 86542 **PLAYA DUABA** (Cu) ex *Ogre* 1974
86543 **BULA** (Ia) ex *Opala*
86544 **TARAKAN** (Ia) ex *Ozersk*

86550 **IONIAN PRINCESS** Pa/Br (Gray) 1961; C; 9000; 145.88 × 9.28 (478.6 × 30.45); M (Doxford); 15; ex *Eugenia M* 1982; ex *Blanchland* 1968

86560 **ISORA** Sp/Sp ('Astano') 1967; R; 1600; 96.68 × 5.67 (317.19 × 18.6); M (B&W); —; ex *Lago San Mauricio* 1975

86570 **KORFOS 1** Cy/Fr (La Seine) 1960; O; 6000; 132.52 × 7.56 (434.78 × 24.8); M (B&W); 16.5; ex *Omega Rhodos* 1983; ex *Penchateau* 1980; ex *Aequator* 1980; ex *Queen of Ampelos* 1978; ex *Penchateau* 1974

86590 **ESSO CAERNARVON** Br/Br (J L Thompson) 1962; Tk; 1100; 70.52 × 4.36 (231.36 × 14.3); M (English Electric); 10
Similar:
86591 **MALDIVE VALOUR** (Mv) ex *Esso Ipswich* 1981

86600 **DOUGGA** Tn/Fr (Loire-Normandie) 1963; C/WT; 2100; 86.9 × 5.57 (285.1 × 18.27); M (MWM); 14
Sister:
86601 **ZARZIS** (Tn)

86610 **O DAE YANG No 106** Ko/Ja (Shikoku) 1968; R; 2700; 104.5 × 5.84 (342.85 × 19.16); M (IHI); 15; ex *Bela Nickerie* 1979; ex *Tonichi Maru* 1977
Sisters:
86611 **MISHIMA MARU** (Ja)
86612 **FRIO POSEIDON** (Pa) ex *Sakurashima Maru* 1975; ex *Susukasan Maru* 1971; ex *Nipponham Maru No 2* 1969

86620 **HAI MING** Tw/Ja (Kanasashi) 1966; C; 2000; 90.48 × 5.59 (296.85 × 18.34); M (Ito Tekkosho); 12; ex *Eitoku Maru* 1972

86630 **NIPPONHAM MARU No 1** Ja/Ja (Shikoku) 1972; R; 2900; 109.02 × 6.73 (357.68 × 22.08); M (Kobe); 16.5
Probably similar:
86631 **DAIRYO MARU** (Ja)

★ 86640 **LU DING** RC/Fi (Valmet) 1959; C; 2700/4800; 121.54 × 6.15/7.67 (398.75 × 20.18/25.16); M (B&W); 15; ex *Chingsing* 1976; ex *Flensburg* 1971; ex *Amazonas* 1962

86650 **RIO GRANDE** Gr/Sw (Eriksbergs) 1957; Tk; 12800; 170.67 × 9.63 (560 × 31.62); M (B&W); 14.5; ex *Sunares*; ex *Benares* 1974; ex *Angelus* 1966; ex *Lysefjell* 1959

86660 **ORYX** Gr/Ne (Verolme Scheeps) 1959; Tk; 12900; 170.59 × 9.37 (560 × 30.74); M (MAN); 14; ex *Aegeon* 1980; ex *Hope Sky* 1979; ex *Kef Eagle* 1975; ex *Pedro* 1973; ex *Benwell* 1968; ex *Belmar* 1962
Similar:
86661 **ROAN** (Gr) ex *Mpenitses* 1980; ex *Tamara* 1975

86670 **MONT-ALBAN** Fr/Ne (Verolme SH) 1959; Tk; 12900; 170.64 × 9.37 (559.84 × 30.74); M (MAN); 14.5; ex *Presto* 1968

★ 86690 **BOLIVAR** Cu/De (Helsingor) 1976; C; 9700; 154.11 × 9.51 (506 × 31.2); M (B&W); 18
Sisters (Cu flag):

86691 **JUAREZ**
86692 **O'HIGGINS**
86693 **SAN MARTIN**
86694 **SANDINO**

86700 **BENNY SKOU** De/De (Helsingor) 1969; C; 6600/9600; 156.37 × 8.09/9.52 (513 × 26.54/31.23); M (B&W); ex *Ditte Skou* 1982
Sisters:
86701 **JUTHA PHANSIRI** (Th) ex *Dinna Skou* 1983
86702 **JYTTE SKOU** (De) ex *Ditte Skou* 1982
Similar:
86703 **DAGMAR SKOU** (De)
86704 **JUTHA MALEE** (Th) ex *Diana Skou* 1983
86705 **DOLLY SKOU** (De)
86706 **DORIT SKOU** (De)
86707 **PEARL BAY** (Gr) ex *Dagny Skou*

86720 **TIARET** Ag/Fr (Nantes) 1963; B; 11400; 155.4 × 9.28 (509.84 × 30.45); M (Sulzer); 14.75; ex *Arthur Stove* 1972
Sisters:
86721 **CAPE KAMARI** (Gr) ex *Kostos M* 1978; ex *Johs Stove* 1973; ex *Brissac* 1969
86722 **ALKOR** (Gr) ex *Timur Endurance* 1980; ex *Lita* 1974; ex *Sneland* 1972

86750 **RAMSLAND** No/FRG (Kremer) 1956; C; 900; 64.95 × 4.31 (213.09 × 14.14); M (MaK); 11; ex *Simon* 1975; ex *Ortrud Muller* 1965

86760 **GALINI** Gr/Br (Smith's D) 1960; C; 10200; 149.92 × 9.52 (491.86 × 31.23); M (Pielstick); —; ex *Rembrandt* 1967

86770 **HELLENIC LEADER** Gr/Ja (Kure) 1962; C; 8900; 144.18 × 8.99 (473.03 × 29.49); M (Mitsubishi); 18

86780 **DJATIPURA** Ia/Ja (Hakodate) 1961; C; 9900; 157.03 × 9.02 (515.19 × 29.59); M (MAN); 15; ex *South Breeze* 1976

86800 **WESTERENCE** Br/Br (J W Cook) 1977; C; 400; 45.55 × 3.25 (149.44 × 10.66); M (Mirrlees Blackstone); 9.5; ex *Gainsborough Miller* 1980
Sister:
86801 **XANTHENCE** (Br) ex *Hull Miller* 1981

86810 **MAELIFELL** Ic/No (Aukra) 1964; C; 1900; 88.85 × 5.09 (291.5 × 16.7); M (KHD); 13

86820 **THYELLA** Gr/FRG (Kremer) 1959; C; 700; 59.44 × 4.24 (195 × 13.91); M (KHD); 10; ex *Hermes G* 1977; ex *Vega* 1977; ex *Laxa* 1974

★ 86824 **INA** Pd/Pd (Gdanska) 1958; C; 500; 59.85 × 3.41 (196 × 11.18); M (Crossley); 9; **'B51'** type. Others of this type may have this appearance—see no 72510
Sister:
★ 86825 **KRUTYNIA** (Pd)

86830 **UNION** Bs/FRG (Nobiskrug) 1952; C; 900; 61.93 × 4.41 (203.18 × 14.47); M (MaK); 11; ex *Georgia P* 1980; ex *Skaanang*; ex *Julin* 1965

86850 **CAYMAN** Br/Ne (Groot & VV) 1956; C; 900; 63.58 × 4.12 (208.6 × 13.52); M ('De Industrie') 10.5; ex *Brinda*; Lengthened & deepened 1969

86860 **REGINA VALERIA** Pa/FRG (Abeking) 1953; C; 800; 62.01 × 4.83 (203.44 × 15.85); M (KHD); 11; ex *Azuero Uno* 1980; ex *Taifun* 1976; ex *Neuwied* 1967

86870 **CONDOR II** Pa/FRG (A G 'Weser') 1952; C; 800; 57 × 4.66 (187 × 15.29); M (MWM); 10.5; ex *Apollo II* 1981; ex *Diamant* 1971

86880 **GRUNNVAAG** No/Br (Appledore) 1972; Con; 500; 76.66 × 3.7 (251.51 × 12.14); M (Lister Blackstone Mirrlees); 13.75; ex *Fallow Deer* 1981; ex *Federal Bermuda* 1977; ex *Fallow Deer* 1976

86882 **STAR SKANDIA** Fa/No (Gravdal) 1978; Pal; 500; 63.28 × 3.80 (208 × 12.47); M (Caterpillar); 11.5; ex *Coaster Conny* 1981; Lengthened 1978 (Eides). Side door (starboard) and stern door
Sisters (No flag):
86883 **BREMER NORDEN** ex *Coaster Emmy* 1982
86884 **COAST BODO** ex *Coaster Anny* 1982
86885 **COAST HARSTAD** ex *Coaster Florry* 1981
86886 **COAST NARVIK** ex *Coaster Betty* 1981
86887 **COAST TROMSO** ex *Coaster Debby* 1981

86890 **GOOD LUCK** Ho/No (Trondhjems) 1962; C; 1900/3100; 99.22 × 6.52/— (325.52 × 21.39/—); M (MAN); 12.5; ex *Captain Leo* 1983; ex *Frol* 1972

86900 **BUSALEH** UAE/FRG (Atlas-Werke) 1953; C; 1300; 71.1 × 5.02 (233.27 × 16.47); M (MAN); 12; ex *Italo* 1983; ex *Lello* 1976; ex *Soneck* 1962

86910 **CARIBBEAN TIUNA** Bs/FRG (S&B) 1952; C; 700; 68.59 × 3.94 (225.03 × 12.93); M (KHD); 10.5; ex *Auguste Schulte* 1968; ex *Veria* 1961; ex *Auguste*

Schulte 1960
Sisters:
86911 **MERCURIO** (Pe) ex *Maria Schulte* 1964
86912 **KYPROS** (Gr) ex *Berni Nubel* 1968

★ 86920 **GALCOAST** Cy/Ne (Pattje) 1961; C; 500/1000; 66.81 × 3.66/— (219.19 × 12.01/—); M ('De Industrie'); 12; ex *Agios Nikolaos* 1980; ex *Gavina* 1974; ex *Heenvliet* 1973

★ 86930 **PALE** Ys/Ne ('Hoogezand' JB) 1960; C; 500; 68.81 × 4.02 (225.75 × 13.19); M (MaK); 10.5; ex *Nordanhav* 1974; ex *Dagny* 1965; ex *Inger Hojsgaard* 1963; Lengthened 1969

86950 **HONG JOO** My/FRG (Kremer) 1953; C; 800; 66.5 × 5.4 (218.18 × 17.72); M (Waggon); 11.5; ex *Silver River* 1979; ex *Isabel Mitchell* 1978; ex *Mathios* 1973; ex *Viking* 1970; ex *Nerissa* 1967
Similar:
86951 **BISLIG TRANSPORT** (Pi) ex *San Miguel Malster* 1973; ex *Pickhuben* 1967
86953 **FREEDOM 1** (Pa) ex *Loucy* 1982; ex *Stavros K* 1980; ex *Indiza* 1979; ex *Dornbusch* 1963
86954 **NARDEN** (Ho) ex *Castle Spirit* 1983; ex *Indola* 1980; ex *Kajen* 1963

86960 **DHOFAR** Om/It (Pellegrino) 1958; C/TS; 550; 66.71 × 3.71 (218.86 × 12.17); M (MaK); 10.5; ex *Resurgence* 1971; ex *Signorita* 1962; ex *Bermudiana* 1961; ex *Signorita* 1958; Oman Navy

86970 **PELKA** Gr/As (Erste Donau) 1957; C; 500/1000; 66.3 × 3.61/4.65 (217.52 × 11.84/15.26); M (KHD); 11.25; ex *Perseus* 1972
Sister:
86971 **PROTEUS** (Pa)

86980 **MR AL** Pa/Ne (Van Diepen) 1968; C; 500/1500; 77.42 × 4.06/5.94 (254 × 13.32/19.49); M (Werkspoor); 11.5; ex *Karin* 1984; ex *Westerbeek* 1977

86990 **BLAVET** Fr/Fr (La Rochelle) 1968; R; 1500; 86.67 × 6.21 (284.35 × 20.37); M (KHD); —; ex *Barrad Wave* 1977

★ 87000 **PERVOMAYSK** Ru/De (B&W) 1959; FC; 3300; 94.8 × 4.37 (311.02 × 14.34); M (B&W); 13
Sisters (Ru flag):
★ 87001 **NEVA**
★ 87002 **PRIMORSK**
★ 87003 **YULYUS YANONIS**

87010 **WINSTON** Pa/Br (A Hall) 1955; LS; 900; 74.38 × 4.29 (244.03 × 14.07); M (Sulzer); 13; ex *St. Rognvald* 1978

87020 **ULTRA FREEZE** Pa/FRG (Sietas) 1959; R; 500/900; 63.18 × 3.33/3.76 (207.28 × 10.93/12.34); M (KHD); 11.5; ex *Mary B* 1970; ex *Herbert Horn* 1968
Similar:
87022 **CASUARINA** (Cy) ex *Lupita Castro* 1980; ex *Dora Horn* 1968
87023 **WATER LILY** (Cy) ex *Maria Castro* 1980; ex *Stadt Schleswig* 1968
87024 **EVANGELISTRIA IV** (Gr) ex *Judith R* 1976; ex *Therese* 1971; ex *Therese Horn* 1965

87040 **FREO ZUTA** Gh/FRG (Schlichting) 1969; R; 2000; 93.71 × —/5.51 (307.45 × —/18.08); M (KHD); 17.5; ex *Nyanaw* 1982; ex *Cooler Scan* 1974

87050 **ALBAFRIGO** Gr/Ne (Gusto) 1962; R; 1500; 83.57 × 4.82 (274.18 × 15.82); M (KHD); 14; ex *Calanca* 1977
Sister:
87050/1 **CASTANEDA** (Br) ex *Albacore* 1980; ex *Castaneda* 1977
Possible similar:
87051 **AZTEC** (Li) ex *Risa Paula* 1977
87052 **WINDFROST** (Cy) ex *Inca* 1977

87060 **AGIOS NEKTARIOS** Pa/FRG (Mutzelfeldt) 1961; R; 900; 75.19 × 3.82 (246.69 × 12.53); M (KHD); 14; ex *Olympos* 1979; ex *Cedar Freeze* 1975; ex *Drame Oumar* 1973; ex *Neve* 1966; Launched as *Optimum*

87070 **BLUE MOON** Cy/Pd (Polnocna) 1962; C/LS; 500; 59.85 × 3.42 (196.36 × 11.22); M (Crossley); 11; ex *Evon* 1978; ex *Boruta !973*; **'B-475'** type
Sister:
87071 **BLUE STAR** (Sg) ex *Robita* 1978; ex *Rokita* 1973

87080 **PAMPILLA** Pe/No (Trosvik) 1970; Ch; 1400; 87.74 × 5.51 (287.86 × 18.08); M (Sulzer); 12.5; ex *Chemie Carrier* 1983; ex *Hoegh Vedette* 1972

87090 **LONG ISLAND EXPRESS 1** Bs/Ne ('Ijssel') 1956; LGC; 1900; 87.1 × 4.61 (285.76 × 15.12); M (Werkspoor); 13; ex *Marian P Billups* 1983

87100 **STARMAN ASIA** NA/FRG (Luehring) 1977;

RoC/HL; 1600; 80.37× 4.15 (263.68× 13.62); TSM (Liebknecht); 11.5; ex *Gloria Virentium* 1982; Stern ramp. Total lifting capacity 800 tons

87110 SLETTER No/No (Storviks) 1976; C; 300; 68.51× 3.38 (224.77× 11.09); M (Alpha-Diesel); 12

87120 AUTO COURIER Gr/Fi (Laiva) 1972; RoC; 1300; 75.85× 5.18 (248.85× 16.99); TSM (Wartsila); 12; ex *Auto Gulf* 1981; ex *Aegean Mark* 1978; ex *Rah* 1977; ex *Ra* 1974; Launched as *Navirus*; Stern & side doors. Reported to be fitted with a 60 ton crane

◆**87130 CORA** Ma/Sw (Lodose) 1972; RoC; 3400; 130.71× 6.74 (428.84× 22.11); M (Ruston Paxman); 14.75; ex *Rosso* 1982; ex *Valerie* 1979; Stern & side doors
Sisters:
87131 TRANSCON (Li) ex *Vallann*
87132 SAINT SERVAN (Fr) ex *Alpha Mariner* 1978; ex *Saint Servan* 1977; ex *Vallmo* 1975

◆**87140 MERENGUE EXPRESS** Br/It (Cassaro) 1973; RoC/P; 3300; 115.12× 5.97 (377.69× 19.59); TSM (Stork-Werkspoor); 20.5; ex *Seaspeed Challenger* 1980; ex *Gisella* 1974; Stern door/ramp
Sister (lengthened by 80 feet):
87141 ADELAIDE (Pa) ex *Tambu Express* 1982; ex *Seaspeed Master* 1980; ex *Laura Russotti* 1976

★**87160 FRUCUBA** Cu/Fr (Rhin) 1956; R; 900; 64.62× 4.51 (212.01× 14.8); M (MaK); 12.5; ex *Ice Bird* 1957
Sisters:
87161 AGNES (Gr) ex *Agios Georgios* 1981; ex *Sea Challenge* 1973; ex *Ice Flower* 1968; ex *Atlantic Flower* 1966; ex *Ice Flower* 1965
87162 SOL REEFER (Br) ex *Ice Pearl* 1966; ex *Atlantic Princess* 1966; ex *Ice Pearl* 1965

87170 MUSKETIER II NA/Ne (Boot) 1967; C; 500/1400; 79.61 × 3.98/5.77 (261.19 × 13.06/18.93); M ('De Industrie'); 12.5; ex *Brouwersgracht* 1977
Sister:
87171 FUZLAAN (Pa) ex *Algenib 1* 1982; ex *Schippersgracht* 1977

87180 BUKHARA Ho/FRG (Ottensener) 1957; C; 500/900; 66.02× 3.66/4.8 (216.6× 12.01/15.75); M (KHD); 11; ex *Ghina 1*-1983; ex *Thule II* 1975; ex *Karin K* 1965

87190 PATRIA It/FRG (Abeking) 1955; C; 900; 66.1 × 5.11 (216.86 × 16.77); M (MaK); 12; ex *Racisce* 1970; ex *Stellaprima* 1965

●**87200 KLASSEN** Ca/FRG (Sietas) 1961; C; 600; 68 × 3.71 (223.1× 12.17); M (KHD); 12; ex *Sigrid* 1972; ex *Sigrid K* 1969
Sister:
87201 RACHAD (Le) ex *Rudan* 1981; ex *Ingrid K* 1973

87220 RAAFAT Le/Ne ('Vooruitgang') 1956; C; 700; 74.83× 3.87 (245.5× 12.7); M (Werkspoor); 12; ex *Anne Christine*

87250 UNA Fi/Sw (Solvesborgs) 1959; C/WT; 1100; 74.07× 4.12 (243× 13.52); M (Alpha-Diesel); 12; ex *Vingard* 1980; ex *Vinia* 1979; Lengthened 1963

●**87260 ECO MONDEGO** Pa/Ne (Vuyk) 1969; Con; 1600; 85.32× 4.71 (279.92× 15.45); M (Werkspoor); 16; ex *City of Milan* 1979; ex *Minho* 1974; 'Hustler' class
Sisters:
87261 CAPE HUSTLER (Br) ex *City of Lisbon* 1980; ex *Tagus* 1974
87262 ECO GUADIANA (Pa) ex *City of Oporto* 1980; ex *Tormes* 1974
87263 HUSTLER FAL (Br) ex *City of Florence* 1982; ex *Tua* 1974
87264 BERMUDIANA (Br) ex *Hustler Ebro* 1983; ex *City of Genoa* 1982; ex *Tamega* 1974
87265 HYBUR CLIPPER (Br) ex *Atlantic Clipper* 1983; ex *Tiber* 1979; ex *City of Naples* 1979; ex *Tiber* 1974
87266 HUSTLER INDUS (Br) ex *Atlantic Resolute* 1982; ex *City of Venice* 1980; ex *Mondego* 1974
87267 ZIM MANILA (Li) ex *Hustler Cheyenne* 1981; ex *Isbrit* 1976; ex *England* 1974
87268 HYBUR INTREPID (Br) ex *Atlantic Intrepid* 1983; ex *Tronto* 1980; ex *City of La Spezia*; ex *Tronto* 1974

87280 EL MALEK KHALED Eg/FRG (Buesumer) 1969; RoC/C; 500; 76.41× 4.18 (251× 13.71); M (MAN); 14.5; ex *Cogolin* 1977; Stern & side doors
Sisters:
87281 RAS EL KHAIMA (Eg) ex *King Khaled* 1978; ex *Cotignac* 1977; ex *Cassis* 1973; ex *Cotignac* 1971
87282 AUSTRI (No) ex *Carnoules* 1974

87290 WIS Br/Br (Yorkshire DD) 1977; C; 500; 45.93 × 3.88 (150.69× 12.73); TSM (Caterpillar); 9.75
Sister:
87291 WILKS (Br)

87310 OWENGLAS Pa/Ne ('Hoogezand' JB) 1970; C/Con 800; 78.47× 4.03 (257.45× 13.22); M (Atlas-MaK); 12.5; ex *Irish Coast* 1976; ex *Owenglas* 1971
Sister:
87311 COMMODORE CLIPPER (Ih) ex *Mayo* 1974; ex *Hibernian Enterprise* 1971

87320 CONTAINER ENTERPRISE Pa/Br (Ailsa) 1958; C; 1000; 80.09 × 4.08 (262.76 × 13.39); M (British Polar); 10
Sister:
87321 CONTAINER VENTURER (Br)

87330 LINDE FRG/FRG (Sietas) 1967; C/Con; 500; 74.66 × 3.56 (244.95× 11.7); M (Atlas-MaK); 13; ex *Bell Venture* 1977; Launched as *Anke*
Sister:
87331 FALLWIND (FRG) ex *Bell Vanguard* 1977

87340 SPECIALITY Br/Br (Goole) 1977; C; 1600; 89.67 × 6.04 (294.19 × 19.82); M (Alpha-Diesel); 12.5
Possible sisters (may be geared like **SINGU-LARITY**—see MCMF) (Br flag):
87341 STABILITY
87342 JACK WHARTON

87350 MIRAMAR Cy/Ne (van der Werf) 1968; Con; 500; 74.86 × 3.7 (244.62 × 12.14); M (MWM) 13.5; ex *Seadoll III* 1983; ex *Virginia Express* 1983; ex *Senta* 1981; ex *Kydor Pioneer* 1975; ex *Stadt Aschendorf* 1973
Similar:
87351 CANTACLARO II (Ve) ex *Eline* 1983; ex *Nieuwland*
87352 GUIDO BALDO (It) ex *Relay* 1982
87353 JENWEL (Sg) ex *Mare Jada* 1981; ex *ASD Plainsman* 1978; ex *Plainsman* 1973

87360 SEA FREIGHTLINER 1 Br/Br (Readhead) 1968; Con; 4000; 118.42 × 4.42 (388.52 × 14.5); TSM (Mirrlees); 13.5
Sister:
87361 SEA FREIGHTLINER II (Br)

87370 KUWAIT Eg/Ne ('De Noord') 1961; C; 3100; 96.96 × 6.64 (318.11 × 21.78); M (B&W); 13.5; ex *Kakawi* 1975; ex *Ritva Dan* 1974
Sister:
87371 KOSTAS K (Gr) ex *Saima Dan* 1975

87380 SIN HOCK CHEW My/FRG (Luerssen) 1959; C; 2200/3300; 99.7 × —/6.74 (327.1 × —/22.1); M (B&W); 13.5; ex *Pacific Sky* 1982; ex *Nassiouka* 1980; ex *Neni* 1978; ex *Finnriver* 1973; ex *Taina* 1971; ex *Manja Dan* 1968

87390 PANTANASSA Pa/Sp (Construcciones SA) 1964; C; 1300; 86.57 × 4.81 (284.02 × 15.78); M (B&W); 12; ex *Panarab One* 1983; ex *Avior* 1981; ex *La Laja* 1977
Sister:
87391 ASSOS ENA (Cy) ex *Arco* 1984; ex *La Cinta* 1977; ex *La Rabida* 1967

87400 FRIO DOLPHIN Gr/It (Esercizio) 1969; C; 1600; 82.81 × 4.81 (271.69 × 15.78); M (MAN); —; ex *Gelesiae* 1982

87410 ANGSA MAS Pa/FRG (Gleue) 1954; C; 2000; 75.44 × 6.64 (248 × 21.78); M (MAN); 12; ex *Adelaide* 1981; ex *Pearl Nile* 1981; ex *Nikos M* 1980; ex *Rosa T* 1977; ex *Malabar* 1972; ex *Erika Schulte* 1970; ex *Ilse E Gleue* 1954

●**87420 AMAZON TRADER** Br/Ne (Boele's Sch.) 1965; C; 500; 69.35× 3.72 (227.53× 12.2); M (KHD); 11.5; ex *Southern Sky* 1983; ex *Atlantic Sky* 1982
Sisters:
87421 HAIFFA AL KULAID (Ku) ex *Atlantic Comet* 1981
87422 ITALIAN SUN (Br) ex *Atlantic Sun* 1983
87424 DABEMA (Pa) ex *Alban* 1975; ex *Atlantic Star* 1973
87425 REGULUS (Br) ex *Mereghan* 1982; ex *Atlantic Intrepid* 1977
Similar (lengthened):
87426 CHOUNGUI (Cm) ex *Bilinga* 1983; ex *Atlantic Merchant I* 1975; ex *Atlantic Merchant* 1969

87450 NAGINA Sh/It (Cassaro) 1953; C; 1000; 82.5 × 4.57 (270.67× 14.99); M (MAN); 12; ex *Jetpur City* 1982; ex *Mariner* 1980; ex *Rainbow* 1980; ex *Speedy* 1976; ex *Lionello C* 1973; ex *Vega* 1973

★**87470 ZHAN DOU 59** RC/RC (Hu Tung) 1959; C; 2800; 99.36× 5.49 (326× 18); M (—); 12; ex *Ho Ping 59*
Sisters (RC flag):
★**87471 ZHAN DOU 67** ex *Ho Ping No 67*

87480 M A ULUSOY Tu/Sp ('Astano') 1965; R; 1600; 81.69× 5 (267.88 × 16.4); M (MWM); 15; ex *Glaciar Rojo* 1980
Sisters:
87483 A O ULUSOY (Tu) ex *Glaciar Negro* 1981;
87485 MAR (Ic) ex *Edda* 1983; ex *Glaciar Blanco* 1977

87500 FRIGO ISABEL Sp/Sp ('Astano') 1965; C; 1200; 75.14× — (246.52× —); M (Werkspoor); 13.5; ex *Guayadegue* 1975; ex *Cotos* 1970; ex *San Cyr* 1966; May have been converted to passenger cargo

★**87505 LAS MERCEDES** Cu/Sp (Palma) 1966; R; 700/1200; 72.75 × 4.47/— (239 × 14.67/—); M (Werkspoor); 14

87510 CAMARGO Sp/Sp (Barreras) 1959; C; 1500; 76.66× 5.91 (251.51× 19.39); M (Werkspoor); 11; ex *Isabel Flores* 1970

87520 ALEJANDRA G Pa/No (Liaaen) 1964; C; 1700; 80.04× 4.41 (262.6× 14.47); M (MaK); 13; ex *Repulse Bay* 1981; ex *Skanderborg* 1973

87530 OCEAN FREEZE Pa/FRG (F Schichau) 1962; C; 1900; 83.29×4.37 (273.26×20.41) M; (KHD); 13; ex *Holstenau* 1977;

87540 ZENITH It/No (Drammen) 1956; C; 1600; 78.09×5.49 (256.2×18.01); M; (Sulzer); 13; ex *Blood* 1967; ex *Eika* 1963.

●**87550 MALIANO** Sp/Sp (Euskalduna) 1958; C; 1600; 76.36× 5.72 (250.5× 18.77); M (Polar); —; ex *Trovador* 1979; ex *Lago Enol* 1976
Sister (Sp flag):
87551 AZUERO DOS ex *Labrador* 1976; ex *Lago Isoba* 1976
Possibly similar (Sp Flag):
87552 LAGO COMO
87553 LAGO GARDA

87560 AGROTAI Sp/Sp ('Elcano') 1960; C; 700; 72.6 × 3.91 (238.19 × 12.83); M (Smit & Bolnes); 12.5

87570 PUERTO DE CHACABUCO Ch/Sp ('Elcano') 1960; C; 700; 72.6 × 3.91 (238.19 × 12.83); M (Polar); 12.25; ex *Puerto De Alicante* 1983
Sisters:
87571 SIERRA URBION (Sp) launched as *Lukus Primero*
87572 LINA (Si) ex *Titi B* 1980; ex *Virgen De Los Reyes* 1978; ex *Astene Veintinueve* 1960

87580 MARIMAR Sp/Sp ('Elcano') 1958; C; 700; 72.6 × 3.91 (238.19 × 12.83); M (Sulzer); 11.25

87590 BATIK Ia/FRG (Schlichting) 1957; C; 900; 66.55 × 4.91 (218.34 × 16.11); M (KHD); 15; ex *Tropic Venture* 1975; ex *Arne Vik* 1974; ex *Normannvik* 1973; ex *Sirabuen* 1970; ex *Blink* 1969

87600 PELIKI Gr/FRG (Nobiskrug) 1957; C; 800/1300; 71.33 × 4.12/5.47 (234.02 × 13.5/17.95); M (KHD); 12; ex *Apollo* 1972

●**87610 AGIOS NIKOLAOS** Gr/FRG (Nobiskrug) 1955; C; 1200; 71.25 × 5.16 (233.76 × 16.93); M (KHD); 12; ex *Pelias* 1982; ex *Franz Doerenkamp* 1968
Sister:
87611 PELOR (Gr) ex *Klosterfrau* 1968

★**87620 FUNDADOR** Cu/FRG (O&K) 1955; R; 700/1000; 66.27× 3.67 (217.42× 12.04); M (Alpha-Diesel); 11.5; ex *Frigus* 1957

87630 SELE It/FRG (Rolandwerft) 1959; C; 1000; 70.92× 5.07 (232.68× 16.63); (KHD); 12; ex *Parsifal* 1971; ex *Helmut Parchmann* 1962; Lengthened 1965

★**87640 BEGA** Rm/Rm (Turnu-Severin) 1972; C; 1900; 85.88 × 5.1 (281.76 × 16.73); M (Sulzer); 13.25
Sisters (Rm Flag):
★**87641 MEDIAS**
★**87642 TIMIS**
★**87643 DROBETA 1850**

87650 CIVRA Pa/FRG (Kroegerw) 1957; C; 1300/2000; 91.6× —/5.72 (300.52× —/18.77); M (MWM); 14; ex *Star Trek* 1982; ex *Tristar* 1982; ex *Sun* 1977; ex *Gulf Express* 1976; ex *Zeptrader* 1974; ex *Seeteufel* 1972; ex *Carpathia* 1968

87660 PLAYA DE MASPALOMAS Sp/Sp (AESA) 1965; R; 1600; 82.68 × 4.81 (271.26 × 15.78); M (Sulzer); 15.75
Sister:
87661 PLAYA DE LAS CANTERAS (Sp)

87670 URSULA Fr/FRG (Sietas) 1959; R; 800/1300; 75.09 × 3.86/4.5 (246.36 ×

12.66/14.76); M (KHD); 13.5; ex *Donibane* 1982; ex *Atlantic* 1972; ex *Ursula Horn* 1969; ex *Ursula H* 1960; ex *Ursula Horn* 1960
Sisters:
87671 SEAFROST (Cy) ex *Radiant Bella* 1976; ex *Victor* 1975; ex *Jal Exporter* 1973; ex *Auckland Exporter* 1970; ex *Caroline Horn* 1968
87672 TANGAROA (NZ) (converted to research ship) ex *Wellington Exporter* 1973; ex *Harald Horn* 1968
87673 NOVI T (Le) ex *Abid* 1980; ex *Jal Importer* 1974; ex *Ingga Dan* 1973; ex *Jal Importer* 1973; ex *Polo Sur* 1973; ex *Reefer Basse* 1969; ex *Ornefjell* 1964; ex *Fjell Reefer* 1960
87674 MUDI (Le) ex *Jamil* 1979; ex *Heinz Horn* 1969

87680 JACARANDA Cy/FRG (Sietas) 1959; R; 1100; 70.16 × 3.58/3.8 (230.18 × 11.75/12.47); M (KHD); 13; ex *Tinito Castro* 1980; ex *Hilde Horn* 1969

87690 FIVE RIVERS Pa/Ne (Van Diepen) 1957; C; 500/900; 68.89 × 3.96/5.01 (226.02 × 12.99/16.44); M (Werkspoor); 10; ex *Sister Amalia* 1973; ex *Rijsbergen* 1968
Sisters:
87691 MATTERA MIMMO (It) ex *Zevenbergen* 1967
87693 NITA II (Gr) ex *Kostas* 1983; ex *Costas* 1980; ex *Katerina El*; ex *Hella Schaa* 1976; ex *Ubbergen* 1968
87694 GALSTREAM (Gr) ex *Spithead* 1978; ex *Aerdenhout* 1970

● **87700 SCHILDMEER** Ne/Ne (Van Diepen) 1966; C; 500/1100; 73 × 3.82/5.02 (239.5 × 12.53/16.47); M (Werkspoor); —; ex *Looiersgracht* 1975
Similar (some have mast from funnel):
87701 WENDY (Ne) ex *Raamgracht* 1973; ex *Aukes* 1969
87702 MARINER (Ne) ex *Armada Mariner* 1983; ex *Dicky* 1980; ex *Kraftca* 1975
87703 ALNILAM (Pa) ex *Esbeek* 1973; ex *Bontekoning* 1969
87704 ANKO (Cy) ex *Mount Zeria* 1978; ex *Silver Cloud* 1977; ex *Schoonebeek* 1974
87705 AL AHRAM 2 (Eg) ex *Al Kaid* 1983; ex *Lijnbaansgracht* 1973

87710 SOUTH SEA 1 Pa/FRG (Mutzelfeldt) 1958; R; 1300; 75.19 × 4.13 (246.69 × 13.55); M (KHD); 13; ex *South Sea* 1980; ex *Sea Enterprise* 1979; ex *Carnelian* 1973; ex *Lakhish* 1970
Sister:
87711 CARIB FREEZE (Pa) ex *Armic* 1974; ex *Tsefat* 1970

87720 MENTON Pa/FRG (Brand) 1967; LGC; 500; 62.31 × 3.5 (204.43 × 11.48); M (Atlas-MaK); 12; ex *Ida Hoyer* 1982

★ **87740 KRASNAL** Pd/Pd (Gdynska) 1959; C; 500/900; 66.2 × 3.68/— (217.19 × 12.07/—); M (Alpha-Diesel); 11.5; '**B-57**' type
Similar (some may be converted to cargo/container—see SKRZAT) ('Pd flag):
★ **87741 GOPLANA**
★ **87742 CHOCHLIK**
★ **87743 NIMFA**
★ **87744 RUSALKA**
★ **87745 SWIETLIK**

★ **87750 KAPITAN KANSKI** Pd/Pd (Gdynska) 1963; C; 1200; 69.02 × 4.45 (226.44 × 14.6); M (Nydqvist & Holm); 12.5; '**B-458**' type
Sisters (Pd flag) (some may be converted to cargo/container):
★ **87752 KAPITAN ZIOLKOWSKI**
★ **87753 MARYNARZ MIGALA**
(Gr Flag):
87754 SIMONA ex *Kapitan M. Stankiewicz* 1983

87770 TINA Gr/Pd (Gdynska) 1964; C; 500; 60.66 × 3.45 (199 × 11.32); M (Alpha-Diesel); 11.5; ex *Boginka* 1981; '**B 476**' type
Sisters:
87771 SONIA (Gr) ex *Dziwozona* 1981
87772 LINA (Gr) ex *Nereida* 1982

87780 EMILIA DEL MAR Sp/Sp ('Astano') 1960; C; 1400; 71.1 × 5.42 (233.27 × 17.78); M (B&W); 12; ex *Eco Mercedes* 1973; ex *La Pared* 1964; Converted to container ship; (Drawing shows vessel before conversion)
Sister:
87781 BLANCA DEL MAR (Sp) ex *Eco Maria* 1973; ex *Herada* 1964

87790 ARQUITECTO GAUDI Sp/Sp (Ruiz) 1965; Cem; 900; 64.78 × 4.85 (212.53 × 15.91); M (Werkspoor); 11; ex *Cementos Rezola Tres* 1975
Sister:
87791 CARIBBEAN CEMENT (Pa) ex *Terra* 1981; ex *Cementos Rezola Galicia* 1977

87800 RIO GUAYAS Ec/Br (Hall, Russell) 1959; Tk;

1000; 66.91 × 4.27 (219.52 × 14.01); M (Crossley); —; ex *Point Fortin* 1978
Sister:
87801 REY MAR (Pa) ex *United Star* 1982; ex *Halcyon Star* 1976; ex *Ortoire* 1974

87810 NORTH ARMAC Li/FRG (Buesumer) 1971; C/HL; 500; 71.4 × 3.98 (234.25 × 13.06); M (B&W); 14; ex *Atlantic Sprinter* 1982; ex *Atlas Scan* 1979
Sister:
★ **87811 XUE FENG SHAN** (RC) ex *Biscayne Sun* 1983; ex *Biscayne Navco* 1983
★ **87812 BEI FENG SHAN** (RC) ex *Biscayne Navco* 1983; ex *Hercules Scan* 1979

87830 FAIR JENNIFER Pa/Ne ('De Gideon') 1961; C; 1100; 66.12 × 4.48 (216.93 × 14.7); M (KHD); 11; ex *Westminsterbrook* 1974; Lengthened 1970

87840 PARHAM Ho/Ne (Nieuwe Noord) 1966; C; 1100; 66.12 × 4.52 (217.52 × 14.47); M (KHD); 11; ex *Derwent Fisher* 1979
Similar:
87841 PELASGOS (Gr) ex *Lune Fisher* 1978

87850 BLACKTHORN Br/Ne ('Foxhol') 1965; C; 1200; 72.27 × 4.53 (237.11 × 14.86); M (KHD); —; ex *Eden Fisher* 1979

87860 CELTIC ROSE Br/Br (Goole) 1963; C; 700; 60.05 × 3.65 (197.01 × 11.98); M (Lister Blackstone); —; ex *Mariyos 1* 1982; ex *Foxtongate* 1974

87870 NADIA Si/FRG (Norderwerft) 1954; Tk; 2500; 96.12 × 5.69 (315.35 × 18.67); M (MAN); 12.5; ex *Magid* 1980; ex *Britt* 1976; ex *Fleurtje* 1973; ex *Johann Haltermann* 1971; Lengthened 1960

87880 CAMILLA It/Ne (van der Werf) 1957; C; 1100; 67.06 × 4.48 (220 × 14.67); M (MaK); 12; ex *Tita* 1971; ex *Salling* 1967

87890 QUIJOTE Ur/Ne (van der Werf) 1957; C; 1100; 67.06 × 4.48 (220 × 14.70); M (MaK); 11.75; ex *Murell* 1973; ex *Terrier* 1972; ex *Stege* 1963; ex *Ebba Robbert* 1959

● **87900 SIGMA 1** Pa/Ne (van Diepen) 1964; C; 1000; 66.12 × 4.52 (216.93 × 14.83); M (KHD); 11.5; ex *Velet* 1982; ex *Havelet* 1981
Sister:
87901 HIKMAT (Le) ex *Abdullah* 1981; ex *Portelet* 1979

87910 NICOS S Gr/FRG (Abeking) 1956; C; 1000; 68.48 × 4.88 (224.67 × 16.01); M (MaK); 11.5; ex *Velos* 1978; ex *Katina* 1973; ex *Fursund Eftychia* 1969; ex *Fursund* 1966

87920 MAIA Po/Fr (A Normand) 1954; C; 1000; 73.23 × 4.05 (240.26 × 13.29); GT (SIGMA/Alsthom); 12; ex *Corvo* 1974; ex *Meringnac* 1958; Lengthened 1955

87930 DE HOOP Ne/Ne (Pot) 1964; Hospital-/Church Ship; 1100; 63.4 × 5.1 (208 × 16.73); M ('Bolnes'); 12

★ **87940 'KORSAKOV'** class Ru/Hu Passenger/cargo conversions of class; See MKMF 'Korsakov' type & 'Blagoveshchensk'

★ **87950 ZVAYGZNE** Ru/De (B&W) 1953; FC; 1700; 70.01 × 4.31 (229.69 × 14.14); M (B&W); 10.75; ex *Refrigerator No 7*

87960 MANIA Cy/Br (Ailsa) 1952; C; 1600; 83.72 × 4.46 (274.67 × 14.63); M (British Polar); 10.5; ex *Cameo* 1976; ex *Gem* 1960; Lengthened 1960

87980 FYLRIX Br/Ne ('Appingedam') 1962; C; 600; 61.91 × 3.54 (203.12 × 11.61); M (Appingedammer Brons); 10.5; Lengthened 1967

87990 PARHAM Ho/Ne (Nieuwe Noord) 1966. C; 1100; 66.12 × 4.52 (217.52 × 14.47); M (KHD); 11; ex *Derwent Fisher* 1979
Similar:
87991 PELASGOS (Gr) ex *Lune Fisher* 1978

● **88000 BRENDONIA** Br/Br (Goole) 1966; C; 600; 54.03 × 3.61 (177.26 × 11.84); M (Blackstone); —;
Similar (Br flag):
88001 ECCTONIA
88002 GLADONIA
88003 TRENTONIA

88010 DENTON VENTURE Ho/Br (Ardrossan) 1959; Con; 800/1200; 67.09 × 4.4/4.43 (220.11 × 14.43/14.53); M (Sulzer); 11.5; ex *El Hussein* 1981; ex *Dorset Coast* 1979; Converted from general cargo

88020 CHIOS AEINAFTIS Gr/Br (A&P) 1962; C; 2200; 86.87 × 5.57 (285.01 × 18.27); M (Polar); 14.5; ex *Greenland*

88030 NIKE It/FRG (Abeking) 1954; C; 1000; 66.71 × 6.2 (218.86 × 20.34); M (MAN); 11; ex *Armelia*

1970; ex *Seeclipper* 1967
Sister:
88031 SILVIA ONORATO (It) ex *Seetramper* 1965

88040 ORPENA SV/Ne ('De Gideon') 1963; C; 900; 62.46 × — (204.92 × —); M (English Electric); 12; ex *Claudia P* 1983; ex *Saint Colman* 1982

88050 SAINT AIDAN Br/Br (Connell) 1962; C; 1000; 66.45 × 4.18 (218 × 13.71); M (English Electric); 12

● **88080 SULTANA 1** Ho/Br (Scott & Sons) 1967; C; 800; 62.24 × 3.9 (204.2 × 12.8); M (Pielstick); 12; *Saint William* 1984

88090 IVOR Cy/Ne (Giessen-De Noord) 1971; Con; 6700; 144.94 × 7.62 (475.52 × 25); M (MAN); 22; ex *Atlantic Prowess* 1983; ex *Cathy* 1982; ex *New England Hunter* 1981; ex *Fiery Cross Isle* 1973
Sisters:
88091 PHOENIX VENTURE (Li) ex *Grand Haven* 1984; ex *New England Trapper* 1980; ex *Lord of the Isle* 1973

● **88100 EVE** Pa/FRG (Sietas) 1971; C/Con; 1000; 88.5 × 5.28 (290.35 × 17.32); M (Atlas-MaK); 14; ex *Heino* 1983; ex *Scol Venture* 1976; ex *Baltic Unit* 1973; ex *Heino* 1971
Similar (some may have deck cranes)
88101 SABINE D (FRG) ex *Twiehausen* 1983; ex *Ibesca Algeria* 1980; ex *Ibesca Espana* 1978; ex *Twiehausen* 1977
88105 MARGRET (FRG) ex *Margret Knuppel* 1976; ex *Pinto* 1973; ex *Hannes Knuppel* 1973
88106 DEICHLAND (Pa) ex *Bomberg* 1983; ex *Roxane Kersten* 1980; ex *Bomberg*
88107 WIDUKIND (FRG) ex *Zim Costantza* 1982; ex *Widukind* 1981
88108 FRAUDEN (Fi) ex *Frauke* 1982; ex *Comar II* 1974; ex *Frauke* 1972
88109 NAUTIC (Fi)

88110 JENNY Na/Ne (Groot & VV) 1966; C; 600; 65.46 × 3.84 (214.76 × 12.6); M (MWM); 11; ex *Jenny Smits* 1982; ex *Kala Priva* 1971; Lengthened 1973
Sisters:
88111 ANNA HEIDA (Ne) ex *Gerda Smits* 1981; ex *Norstrand Partner* 1969; ex *Norstrand Priva* 1968
88112 HEGA (NA) ex *Hega Smits* 1982; ex *Hega Priva* 1971
88113 WILLY (NA) ex *Willy Smits* 1982; ex *Gerda Priva* 1971
88113/1 INGA (NA) ex *Inger Smits* 1982; ex *Surveyor* 1975
Similar (unlengthened):
88114 ORCA (Ne) ex *Anna Verena* 1983; ex *Lady Anne* 1980; ex *Pedro* 1976; ex *Pauline Lonborg* 1973; ex *Pedro Smits* 1971
88115 GALLANT (Ne) ex *Atlanta* 1983; ex *Lady Carina* 1980; ex *Micky* 1975; ex *Stacia* 1972; ex *Stacia Smits* 1971

88120 KARIN It/FRG (Sterkrade) 1954; Ch; 1300; 66.12 × 5.54 (216.93 × 18.18); M (KHD); 11; ex *Karin Cords* 1968; Converted from general cargo 1969; (Drawing shows vessel before conversion)

★ **88130 YAKAN** Ru/Fi (Hollming) 1952; C; 900; 59.47 × 4.57 (195.11 × 14.99); M (Russkiy); 10

88140 GRAN RIO Sn/Ne ('Ijssel) 1957; C; 1000; 68.61 × 4.07 (225.1 × 12.35); M (Werkspoor); —

88150 KARTALA Mg/Ne (Duijvendijk's) 1954; C; 1500; 78.67 × 4.69 (258 × 15.39); M (Werkspoor); 13; ex *Kelibia* 1962

★ **88160 PEI CHING No 1** RC/Fr (Rhin) 1957; R; 1200; 74.2 × 4.6 (243.44 × 15.09); M (MaK); —; ex *Ice Princess* 1961
Sister:
88161 FRIGORA (Br)

88170 HYBUR STAR Br/Ne (Noord) 1962; R; 500/1100; 74.12 × 3.76/4.73 (243.18 × 12.34/15.52); M (KHD); 13; ex *Arctic* 1977

88180 TRITON Gr/FRG (Buschmann/Steinwerder) 1952/54; Tk; 600; 61.18 × 3.43 (200.72 × 11.25); M (KHD); 10; ex *Konstantinos* 1971; ex *Delta* 1969; ex *Brodick* 1969; ex *Charles Eckelmann* 1961; Aft section built 1952; Forward section built 1954

88200 JANE-SEA Br/Ne ('Westerbroek') 1960; C; 700; 57.76 × 3.9 (189.5 × 12.8); M (Crossley); 11; ex *Rudyard* 1980; ex *Blackthorn* 1976

88210 KOTA PAHLAWAN Sg/Br (Ardrossan) 1958; C; 1300; 67.32 × 5.02 (220.87 × 16.47); M (British Polar); —; ex *Chantala Fortune* 1977; ex *Moanui* 1975; ex *Bay Fisher* 1970

88220 NIKOS Pa/FRG (Meyer) 1961; C; 1500; 82.4

× 4.71 (270.34 × 15.45); M (KHD); 15.5; ex *Mana* 1981; ex *Cypress Point* 1981; ex *Hoylake* 1979; ex *Warstade* 1974; ex *Jenny Porr* 1969; ex *Brosund* 1962; Lengthened 1969

★88230 **NAN HAI 136** RC/Pd (Gdynska) 1955; C; 600; 57.64 × 4.25 (189.11 × 13.94); M (MaK); 10.5; ex *Orlowo* 1956; 'B-53' type; 'MELITOPOL' class
Sisters (Pd flag):
★88231 **REDA**
★88232 **KARTUZY**
★88233 **BRANIEWO**
★88234 **RUMIA**
★88235 **SOPOT**
(Ru flag):
★88236 **MINGECHAUR**
★88237 **MONCHEGORSK**
★88238 **NIKYEL**
★88239 **OSIPENKO**
★88240 **URALSK**
★88243 **GVARDEYSK**
★88244 **KHOLMSK**
★88245 **SIND**
(Gr flag):
88246 **SPYROS K** ex *Annoula* 1983; ex *Jastarnia* 1976
88247 **DIMITRAKIS** ex *Nogat* 1976
Similar (Ru flag):
★88248 **MELITOPOL**
★88249 **VORMSI**

88260 **CHATA TWO** Br/Br (Mitchison) 1956; C; 500; 58.02 × 3.6 (190.35 × 11.81); M (Caterpillar); 10; ex *Hancock Clipper* 1980; ex *Sol Eclipse* 1978; ex *Sandy Point No 1* 1976; ex *Blue Trader* 1971; ex *Eskwater* 1958

◗88270 **LISA HEEREN** FRG/FRG (Brand) 1977; C; 1000; 72.8 × 4.5 (238.85 × 14.76); M (Atlas-MaK); 12

88280 **UDO** Ne/Ne (Ton) 1978; C; 1000; 65.84 × 4.3 (216.01 × 14.11); M (Bofors); 12; ex *Pechudo* 1983

88290 **SAMSUN EXPRESS** Ne/Ne (Stroobos) 1978; C; 1600; 81.01 × 5.21 (265.78 × 17.09); M (Alpha-Diesel); 12.5; ex *Sundsviken* 1980; ex *Gerda Holwerda* 1978

88300 **ELISABETH HOLWERDA** Ne/Ne (Barkmeijer) 1975; C; 900; 65.82 × 4.27 (215.94 × 14.01); M (Caterpillar); 11
Sisters:
88301 **TANJA HOLWERDA** (Ne) ex *Roelof Holwerda* 1981
88302 **EENDRACHT** (Ne)
88303 **EXPANSA II** (Ne)
Possibly similar:
88304 **WILHELMINA V** (Ne)

88310 **MARITTA JOHANNA** Ne/Ne (Peter's Schpsbw) 1978; C; 1600; 73(bp) × 5.45 (239.5 (bp) × 17.88); M (Brons); 12.5

★88320 **YANG MING SHAN** RC/Ja (Hitachi) 1965; B; 25100; 206.03 × 12.32 (675.95 × 40.42); M (B&W); 15; ex *Goldean Alliance* 1982; ex *Atherstone* 1978

88330 **DELTA FLAG** Gr/No (Kaldnes) 1958; O; 10600; 153.93 × 9.19 (505.02 × 30.15); M (Doxford); 11.75; ex *Malessina* 1981; ex *Good Trader* 1975; ex *Nordland* 1972

88350 **AUBADE** Pa/Ne (Verolme Scheeps.) 1961; B; 14900; 180.35 × 10.85 (591.7 × 35.6); M (MAN); —

★88380 **ZAGLEBIE DABROWSKIE** Pd/Pd (Szczecinska) 1967; B; 11000; 156.37 × 9.51 (513.02 × 31.2); M (Sulzer); 15.5; 'B 520' type
Sisters (Pd flag):
★88381 **DOLNY SLASK**
★88382 **GORNY SLASK**
★88383 **PODHALE**
★88384 **KUJAWY**
★88385 **BIESZCZADY**

88390 **FORWARDER** Pa/Ne ('De Noord') 1949; Con; 1000; 85.58 × 4.33 (280.77 × 14.21); M (Werkspoor); 13.5; ex *Domburgh* 1975; Converted from general cargo; Lengthened 1962

88400 **CRAIGMORE** Br/Br (Dunston) 1966; C; 1400; 73.03 × 5.04 (239.6 × 16.54); M (British Polar); 11

88420 **EMINENCE** Br/Br (Goole) 1969; C; 1000; 67.67 × 4.22 (222.01 × 13.85); M (Mirrlees Blackstone); 10.5
Similar (lower poop, pole masts):
88421 **SENTENCE** (Br)

88430 **CAMILLA WESTON** Br/Ne (Boele's Sch) 1966; C; 500; 55.94 × 3.34 (183.53 × 10.96); M (Blackstone); 10.5; ex *Crouch* 1971

Sister:
88431 **BEN AIN** (Br) ex *Gretchen Weston* 1976; ex *Deben* 1971

88440 **SEA STAR** UAE/Ne ('Vooruitgang') 1971; C; 1400; 82.1 × 4.53 (269.36 × 14.86); M (MWM); 13; ex *Haiffa Al Kulaib* 1983; ex *Atlantic Comet* 1981; ex *Cornelia Bosma* 1978; Lengthened 1977

◗88450 **SAN PEDRO** De/De (Aarhus) 1971; Cem; 2800; 98.25 × 6.27 (322.34 × 20.57); M (B&W); 13.5; ex *Cimbria* 1982

★88460 **TURQUINO** Cu/Sw (Helsingborgs) 1962; Cem; 1100; 72.37 × 3.86 (237.43 × 12.66); M (KHD); 13; ex *Rapido* 1972; ex *Rapid* 1972

88470 **LEADSMAN** Br/Br (Drypool) 1968; Tk; 800; 62.49 × 4.19 (205 × 13.75); M (Brons); 11

88475 **OILMAN** Br/Br (Dunston) 1982; Tk; 1000; 65.51 × 4.08 (215 × 13.39); M (Ruston); 11; May now be experimentally fitted with auxiliary sails

88480 **GULF GATINEAU** Ca/Ca (Marine Indust) 1976; Tk; 5900; 131.93 × 6.84 (432.84 × 22.44); M (MAN); 13.5
Sisters (Ca flag):
88421 **GULF MACKENZIE**
88482 **ARSENE SIMARD**
88483 **LE CEDRE No 1** ex *Arthur Simard* 1982
88484 **L'ORME No 1** ex *Leon Simard* 1982
Similar (Cu flag):
★88485 **5 DE SEPTIEMBRE**
★88486 **PRIMERO DE MAYO**

88520 **RATHDOWN** Ih/FRG (Nobiskrug) 1965; Tk/Ch; 1400; 77.09 × 5.6 (252.92 × 18.37); M (MAN); —; ex *Thorheide* 1971; ex *Mikhal* 1967
Similar:
88521 **ETRUSCO** (It) ex *Gea Prima* 1982; ex *Refola* 1975; ex *Thoralbe* 1970

88530 **CARIBGAS 20** Pa/FRG (Meyer) 1967; LGC; 1200; 67.67 × 5.03 (222.01 × 16.5); M (KHD); 12; ex *Claude* 1982
Similar:
88531 **BRIGITTA MONTANARI** (It) ex *Ligur* 1973
88532 **HAPPY BIRD** (Pa) ex *Sunny Fellow* 1982; ex *Libra* 1973

◗88550 **TOURLAVILLE** Fr/Ne (Vuyk) 1969; RoC; 800; 74.99 × 4.19 (246.03 × 13.75); M (MWM); 15; ex *Duke of Holland* 1982; Stern door
Sister:
88551 **DUKE OF NORFOLK** (Ne)

88560 **PULBOROUGH** Br/Br (Blyth) 1965; C; 5000; 112.76 × 7.39 (369.95 × 24.25); M (British Polar); —
Sister:
88561 **ROGATE** (Br)

88570 **BRIAN BOROIME** Br/Ih (Verolme Cork) 1970; Con; 4100; 107.14 × 4.44 (351.51 × 14.57); TSM (Mirrlees Blackstone); 14
Sister:
88571 **RHODRI MAWR** (Br)

88580 **GLORIANA** Le/Br (Goole) 1959; Con; 1900; 90 × 4.43 (295.87 × 14.53); M (Ruston & Hornsby); 13; ex *Taurus II* 1979; ex *Colchester* 1975; Converted from cargo and lengthened 1969 (Ailsa)

88590 **VENTURA** Ne/Ne (Gruno) 1972; C; 1300; 76.43 × 4.64 (250.75 × 15.22); M (Appingedammer Brons); 11.5

★88600 **ELENA** Bu/Bu (Ivan Dimitrov) 1970; Con; 1300/1800; 80.73 × 4.34/5.31 (264.86 × 14.27/17.42); M (Sulzer); —; Converted from general cargo. Others of this class may be similarly converted

88610 **ROCQUAINE** Br/Br (J W Cook) 1977; C; 1000; 66.91 × 4.12 (219.52 × 13.52); M (Mirrlees Blackstone); 11; Modified 'Colne' type
Sisters (Br flag):
88611 **BELGRAVE**
88612 **PERELLE**

88620 **CARMEN DEL MAR** Sp/Sp (Construcciones SA) 1970; Con; 2800; 88.22 × 5 (289.44 × 16.4); M (Stork-Werkspoor); 12; ex *Isla Del Mediterraneo* 1974
Sisters:
88621 **LUISA DEL CARIBE** (Pa) ex *Isla del Atlantico* 1982
88622 **RATANA BHUM** (Th) ex *Ming Chun* 1981; ex *Echuca* 1976; Launched as *Ardan*

88640 **SOLWAY FISHER** Br/Ne (van der Werf) 1968; Con; 1400; 90.12 × 4.64 (295.67 × 15.22); M (KHD); 14.5
Sister:
88641 **ORWELL FISHER** (Br)

88650 **LIGAR BAY** NZ/Br (H Robb) 1964; Cem; 1300; 69.07 × 4.28 (226.61 × 14.04); TS D-E (English Electric); 11

88660 **HAWTHORN** Br/FRG (Kremer) 1967; C; 1000; 75.24 × 4.42 (246.85 × 14.5); M (KHD); 12.75; ex *Francinaplein* 1977; ex *Hunnau* 1973; ex *Ortrud Muller* 1969

88670 **IONION** Gr/FRG (Nobiskrug) 1964; AT; 1000; 73.72 × 4.8 (241.86 × 15.75); M (MaK); 11; ex *Spiekeroog* 1972
Sister:
88671 **CHRISTINE FIRST** (Pa) ex *Donna Licia* 1974; ex *Asphaltjo* 1973; ex *Wangeroog* 1972

88680 **SILVERMERLIN** Br/Sw (Lodose) 1968; Tk/Ch; 1300; 77.32 × 4.8 (253.67 × 15.75); M (MWM); 12
Similar:
88681 **SILVERFALCON** (Br)

88690 **PETROSTAR XIV** Pa/FRG (Bayerische) 1961; Tk; 1600; 87 × 5.26 (285.43 × 17.26); M (MAN); —; ex *Maria II* 1980; ex *Gertrude Wiener* 1977

88700 **QUARTERMAN** Br/Br (Dunston) 1973; Tk; 1200; 72.85 × 4.92 (239 × 16.14); M (Ruston Paxman); 11.5

88730 **LADY RAFFAELLA** It/FRG (Elsflether) 1964; Tk; 1000; 64.57 × 5.19 (211.84 × 17.03); M (KHD); 12.25; ex *Heinrich Essberger* 1975

88740 **SAINT BRANDAN** Br/Br (J W Cook) 1976; C/RoC; 900; 63.81 × 4.12 (209.35 × 13.52); M (Ruston Paxman); 12; Bow ramp

88750 **COCCINELLA** It/No (Stord) 1954; Tk; 3000; 105.11 × 6.16 (345 × 20.21); M (B&W); 12; ex *Suroit* 1972; ex *Vibran* 1965

88760 **QUITO** Ec/Br (Hill) 1953; Tk; 1400; 77.27 × 4.12 (253.51 × 13.52); TSM (British Polar); 9.5; Kingposts abreast mainmast

88770 **VALLOMBROSA** It/No (Haugesund) 1957; Tk; 2500; 100.77 × 5.84 (331 × 19.16); M (B&W); ex *Haforninn* 1971; ex *Lonn* 1966; Drawing is approximate

88780 **CAPUTERRA** It/Sw (Ekensbergs) 1948; Tk; 1200; 71.2 × 4.57 (233.6 × 14.99); M (Atlas-Diesel); 11; ex *Louis Frederic Dewulf* 1963; ex *Jean Guiton* 1953; ex *Runn* 1953; ex *Bie* 1951; ex *Lovo* 1950
Sister:
88781 **STELLA DI LIPARI** (It) ex *Zitmar* 1982; ex *Zit* 1957; ex *Lind* 1949
Similar:
88782 **AMAZONIA** (Bz) ex *Lind* 1959

88800 **TEXACO COLON** Pa/No (Fredrikstad) 1966; Tk/LGC; 3600; 103.66 × 5.93 (340.09 × 19.46); TSM (Sulzer); —; ex *Texaco Puerto Rico* 1971

88810 **SAVE** Fr/Sw (Ekensbergs) 1962; Tk; 4500; 118.78 × 6.86 (389.7 × 22.51); M (Uddevalla); 14; ex *Alor Star* 1972; ex *Rogn* 1968

88820 **JET V** Gr/Ys ('Jozo Lozovina-Mosor') 1962; Tk; 1800; 84.89 × 5.23 (278.51 × 17.19); M (Sulzer); 12; ex *Olib* 1981
Sister:
88821 **AGIOS GEORGIOS** (Gr) ex *Vinjerac* 1981

88830 **AMALIA** Gr/Br (G Brown) 1958; Tk; 1100; 70.72 × 4.2 (232.02 × 13.78); M (British Polar); 11; ex *Kingennie* 1972

88840 **MAYAYCU** Ec/Br (Grangemouth) 1957; Tk; 2000; 87.58 × 4.94 (287.34 × 16.21); M (British Polar); 11; ex *Filicudi* 1982; ex *Redrose* 1969; ex *Chailey* 1969

88850 **BARBAROSSA** Gr/Br (Clelands) 1958; Tk; 1000; 71.25 × 4.19 (233.76 × 13.75); M (British Polar); —; ex *Eftyhia* 1980; ex *Petworth* 1978

88860 **WHEELSMAN** Br/Br (Clelands) 1967; Tk; 2900; 98.3 × 6.08 (322.51 × 19.95); M (Ruston & Hornsby); 12.75

88870 **THITA TRIENA** Gr/Br (Goole) 1961; Tk; 1600; 81.16 × 4.83 (266.27 × 15.85); M (Mirrlees Blackstone); 10; ex *Annuity* 1983

88880 **INGA THOLSTRUP** De/De (Aalborg) 1965; LGC; 2000; 83.32 × 5.51 (273.36 × 18.08); M (KHD); 13

88890 **THIRLMERE** Br/Ne (Pattje) 1955; Tk; 800; 60.3 × 4.03 (197.83 × 13.22); M (Crossley); 10.5; ex *Kyndill* 1974

88900 **BP SPRINGER** Br/Br (Hall, Russell) 1969; Tk; 1100; 65.46 × 4.45 (214.76 × 14.6); M (B&W); 11.5; ex *Dublin* 1976
Sisters (Br flag):
88901 **BP BATTLER** ex *Inverness* 1976
88902 **BP WARRIOR** ex *Grangemouth* 1976

88910 **CASTELLO** It/It (Felszegi) 1964; Tk; 1200;

79.2 × 3.86 (259.84 × 12.66); M (MWM); 11.5; ex *Antonella Montanari* 1967; Lengthened 1971

88930 MARK VI Gr/Br (Scarr) 1957; Tk; 1000; 68.08 × 4 (223.36 × 13.12); M (British Polar); 10.5; ex *Rathmines* 1976; ex *Stansted* 1972

88940 ESMERALDA It/FRG (Bayerische) 1954; Tk; 1300; 77.09 × 4.48 (252.92 × 14.7); M (MAN); 12; ex *Marie Boettger* 1967

88950 GHAZI-B Si/Br (British Polar) 1959; Tk; 1000; 65.33 × 4.48 (214.34 × 14.7); M (British Polar); 11; ex *Maldive Enterprise* 1977; ex *agility* 1976

88960 VALENTINE K Gr/FRG (Rolandwerft) 1959; Tk; 1000; 65.99 × 4.35 (216.5 × 14.27); M (Nydqvist & Holm); 11; ex *Alfa Ena* 1984; ex *Fotoula* 1983; ex *Rathgar* 1983; ex *Pass of Kildrummy* 1970

88970 VASILIKI III Gr/Br (Drypool) 1962; Tk. 800; 61.88 × 3.91 (203 × 12.83); M (Brons); 10.75; ex *Anchorman* 1983

88980 KALI LIMENES Gr/Br (Grangemouth) 1944; Tk; 900; 67.37 × 3.89 (221.03 × 12.76); R (Aitchison, Blair); 8; ex *Passamare* 1965; ex *Pass of Kintail* 1963; ex *Christine* 1956; ex *Medea* 1951; ex *Empire Mull* 1946

89000 HAJ ANWAR Le/Fr (Dubigeon) 1959; WT; 3000; 104.86 × 5.97 (344.03 × 19.59); M (Fiat); 13.5; ex *Atar* 1981; ex *Dahra* 1978

★ **89010 NAN HAI 138** RC/No (Langesunds) 1961; Tk; 900; 65.92 × 4.24 (216.27 × 13.91); M (MWM); —; ex *Timur Star* 1970; ex *Slamet Timur* 1969; ex *Rübistar* 1968; ex *Rush* 1965; Lengthened 1965

89020 VASILIKI II Gr/Br (Blyth) 1961; Tk; 1500; 79.25 × 4.42 (260 × 14.5); M (Nydqvist & Holm); 10.25; ex *Maplehurst* 1981; Lengthened 1971
Sisters (Br flag):
89021 DAVAK ex *Fernhurst* 1983
89022 MIDHURST

89030 HUMBERGATE Br/Br (Dunston) 1969; Tk; 1600; 84.66 × 4.9 (277.76 × 16.08); M (Ruston & Hornsby); —

89040 IVORY Pa/Fr (France-Gironde) 1969; Ch; 1400; 79.53 × 5.11 (260.93 × 16.77); M (Atlas-MaK); 13.75; ex *Casimir Le Quellec* 1981

89050 DUTCH SAILOR Ne/Ne (Groot & VV) 1966; Tk/Ch; 600; 65.38 × 3.74 (214.5 × 12.27); M (KHD); —; Lengthened 1971
Sister:
89051 DUTCH MATE (Ne)

89060 ANGLEZARKE Br/FRG (Schlichting) 1956; Tk; 600; 62.82 × 3.25 (206.1 × 10.66); M (KHD); 10.5; ex *Mabuli* 1975; ex *Otto Terkol* 1971; ex *Otto* 1968; ex *Nessland* 1967

89080 NIKE Pa/Fr (Provence) 1958; C; 4200; 116.69 × 6.4 (382.84 × 21); M (Doxford); 12.5; ex *Paros Trader* 1978; ex *Kyrarini* 1976; ex *Rhea* 1972; ex *Jacqueline* 1971

89090 CEYLION Sr/FRG (Luerssen) 1959; C; 3200; 100.16 × 6.87 (328.61 × 22.54); M (MAN); —; ex *Naweza* 1982; ex *Uniparagon* 1974; ex *Hoegh Binny*; ex *Binny*

89100 WELL RAINBOW Pa/Ne ('De Hoop') 1963; C/R; 3100/4000; 109.43 × 6.17/7.37 (359.02 × 20.24/24.18); M (MAN); —;
Sister:
89101 FAIR RAINBOW (Pa) ex *Sifnos* 1979

89110 MAYA Ma/Br (A&P) 1958; C; 2800; 102.42 × 5.5 (336.02 × 18.04); M (Sulzer); 12; ex *Astarte* 1983; ex *Pambola* 1981; ex *Greathope* 1976; ex *Queensland* 1964

89120 TARA Cy/Br (Hall, Russell) 1957; C; 5000; 120.71 × 6.88 (396.03 × 22.57); M (Sulzer); 13; ex *Nicolas P* 1980; ex *Galaxy Faith* 1976; ex *Insco Producer* 1971; ex *Sugar Producer* 1966
Sister:
89121 MOLLY (Pa) ex *Sailor II* 1979; ex *Navisailor* 1978; ex *Elarkadia* 1978; ex *Irenes Faith* 1974; ex *Arkadia* 1972; ex *Sugar Refiner* 1967

★ **89130 CUNSKI** Ys/Br (Gray) 1956; C; 4000; 116.31 × 6.62 (381.59 × 21.72); M (British Polar); 11.5; ex *Samantha M* 1975; ex *Lottinge* 1974

89140 OCEAN GLORY No 6 Pa/Br (H. Robb) 1958; C; 1400; 90.51 × 4.54 (296.95 × 14.9); M (Sulzer); —; ex *Ocean Glory* 1977; ex *Catanian* 1972

★ **89150 FRIMARO** Cu/Sp (UN de Levante) 1966; R; 1700; 87 × 5.77 (285.43 × 18.93); M (B&W); —; ex *Frimar* 1972

89160 MAS Le/FRG (Holst) 1956; C; 1400; 70.99 ×

5.97 (232.91 × 19.59); M (KHD); 11; ex *Aida* 1981; ex *Blue Stone* 1975; ex *Hilda Wesch* 1972

89170 CHELLI Pa/FRG (S&B) 1958; C; 1800; 80.17 × 6.55 (263.02 × 21.49); M (Werkspoor); —; ex *Munsur* 1982; ex *Incem Arsem* 1981; ex *Ocean Blue* 1978; ex *Geertje Buisman* 1970

89180 ALPHA MICHEL Pa/FRG (S&B) 1956; C; 1200/1900; 78.97 × 4.75/6.07 (259.09 × 15.58/19.91); M (MWM); 12; ex *Corrado* 1981; ex *Nordina* 1974; ex *Ingrid* 1972; ex *Nordheim* 1969; ex *Anni Nubel* 1967
Sisters:
89181 EAGLE (Gr) ex *Byzantine Eagle* 1981; ex *Tehonga* 1977; ex *Maria Anna Schulte* 1970
89182 VONNY (Sg) ex *Unison II* 1980; ex *Orchid Flower* 1974; ex *Elise Schulte* 1972

89190 FAYROUZ Gr/Br (G Brown) 1959; C; 1500; 100.49 × 4.64 (329.69 × 15.22); M(MAN); 12.5; ex *Kydonia* 1976; ex *Veras* 1973; ex *Siddons* 1962; Lengthened 1966

★ **89200 KEKHRA** Ru/Hu (Angyalfold) 1966; C; 1200; 74.55 × 4.67 (244.59 × 15.32); M (Lang Gepgyar); 11.5
Sisters (Some of the Russian vessels have a large house ahead of bridge and may be naval auxiliaries):
(Ru Flag):
★ **89201 KUNDA**
★ **89202 OTEPYA**
★ **89203 ARTSIZ**
★ **89204 KUYVASTU**
★ **89206 MASSANDRA**
★ **89207 TIRASPOL**
★ **89208 VYANDRA**
★ **89209 KALMIUS**
★ **89210 SOLOMBALA**
★ **89211 VIRTSU**
★ **89212 BEREZINA**
★ **89213 OSMUSSAAR**
★ **89214 TAKHKUNA**
★ **89215 KARL KRUSHTEYN**
(Hu flag):
★ **89216 DEBRECEN**
★ **89217 HEVIZ**
★ **89218 HAJDUSZOBOSZLO**
★ **89219 HEREND**
★ **89220 SOMOGY**
★ **89221 TATA**
(Bh flag):
89222 CHATTAGRAM ex *Rapla* 1973
89223 DACCA ex *Ambla* 1973
89224 KHULNA ex *Imatra* 1972
(Cy flag):
89227 OLYMPIA II ex *Olympia* 1975; ex *Helena* 1973; ex *Petro Hauge* 1968; ex *Sagatun* 1966
(Gr flag):
89227/1 GEORGIOS T ex *Mycenae* 1982; ex *Nerina* 1973; ex *Petro Stranda* 1968; ex *Sagastrand* 1966
(Ia flag):
89228 KARIMATA
89229 NARVA
89230 SAWU
89231 SELAYAR
89232 ARU ex *Lovatj* 1964
89233 PELITA JAYA ex *Misool* 1981; ex *Palana* 1964
The following vessels are now converted to wine/vegetable tankers (Ru flag):
★ **89234 SEVERNYY DONETS**
★ **89235 TARAKLIYA**
★ **89236 YARGORA**

★ **89250 SPARTAK** Ru/Hu (Angyalfold) 1967; C; 1500; 77.81 × 4.73 (255.28 × 15.52) M (Sulzer); 12.5;
Sisters (Ru flag):
★ **89251 IVAN BOLOTNIKOV**
★ **89252 KONDRATIY BULAVIN**
★ **89253 NIKOLAY BAUMAN**
★ **89254 PETR KAKHOVSKIY**
★ **89255 SALAVAT YULAYEV**
★ **89256 AEGNA**
★ **89257 ANGYALFOLD**
★ **89258 AUGUST KULBERG**
★ **89259 ANABAR**
★ **89260 MOKHNI**
★ **89261 ARAKS**
★ **89262 KABONA**
★ **89263 VITIM**
★ **89264 SEMYON ROSHAL**
★ **89265 TERIBERKA**
★ **89266 AMBLA**
★ **89267 RAPLA**
(Ye flag):
89268 ADEN ex *Mate Zalka* 1974
(So flag):
89269 BOLIMOG ex *Anabar* 1974

89280 CAPITAN CARLO It/Sp (Construcciones SA)

1964; C; 2800; 103.43 × 5.68 (339.34 × 18.64); M (MWM); 12.5; ex *Juan Nespral* 1981; Lengthened 1970

89290 CASTLE FAITH Ma/Fr (Bretagne) 1956; C; 2300; 84.87 × 5.95 (278.45 × 19.52); M (MAN); 11.5; ex *Agios Nicolaos* 1983; ex *Calamos* 1981; ex *Titsa* 1976; ex *Alexia* 1976; ex *Phebe* 1970
Similar (Cement carrier):
89291 PHOENICIAN FLAG (Pa) ex *Nicolaos K Hadjikyriakos* 1983; ex *Aristee* 1963

89300 GEVISA It/FRG (Rolandwerft) 1966; C; 500; 69.96 × 5.46 (229.53 × 17.91); M (MaK); 12; ex *Kotibe* 1977; ex *Edda Buur* 1974; ex *Elba* 1971
Sisters:
89301 CEDROS (Po) ex *Ibiza* 1972
89302 GORGULHO (Po) ex *Mallorca* 1972
89303 LIMA (Po) ex *Korsika* 1972
89304 SINNO M E V (Le) ex *Dina R E* 1981; ex *Malta* 1971
89305 RENEE R E (Fr) ex *Kreta* 1971

89310 SOUTH SEA 1 Pa/FRG (Mutzelfeldt) 1958; C; 1300; 75.19 × 4.13 (246.69 × 13.55); M (KHD); 13; ex *South Sea* 1980; ex *Sea Enterprise* 1979; ex *Carnelian* 1973; ex *Lakhish* 1970
Sister:
89311 CARIB FREEZE (Pa) ex *Armic* 1974; ex *Tsefat* 1970

89320 AGIA MARINA Cy/FRG (Nobiskrug) 1956; C; 1400; 71.51 × 5.79 (234.61 × 19); M (MAN); 12.5; ex *Rasajes* 1982; ex *Pasajes* 1973

89330 ARMENISTIS 1 Gr/Ne (Van Diepen) 1958; C; 1000; 71.51 × 4.27 (234.6 × 14.01); M (L Smit); 11; ex *Georgios D* 1983; ex| *Nusakan*\1979

89340 CHINDE Mb/Po (Uniao) 1958; C; 1700; 81.67 × 4.01 (267.95 × 13.16); M (KHD); 11.5

89350 AXIOS Pa/Fr (La Pallice) 1957; C; 2300; 90.23 × 6.04 (296.03 × 19.82); M (KHD); 12; ex *Border* 1975; ex *Casamance* 1965

89370 RAYES 1 Le/Ne (Arnhemsche) 1960; C; 1200; 81.29 × 4.73 (266.7 × 15.52); M (MAN); 12; ex *Levensau*; ex *City of Cork* 1971

89380 ILO It/Ne (Arnhemsche) 1954; C; 1300; 73.72 × 5.54 (241.86 × 18.18); M (Werkspoor); 12; ex *Ilias* 1970; ex *Ballygally Head* 1968

89400 LANGA Ic/FRG (Kremer) 1965; C; 800/1300; 74.73 × 4.2/5.4 (245.18 × 13.78/17.72); M (KHD); 11.5

89410 CAPT SALAH Si/FRG (Adler) 1957; C; 700/1000; 69.04 × 3.70/5.41 (227 × 12.14/17.75); M (Henschel); 12; ex *Reem* 1983; ex *Star* 1982; ex *Sea Star* 1981; ex *Smaro* 1979; ex *Albatros* 1971

89420 ARANUI Pa/FRG (Sietas) 1967; C; 1000/1500; 79.66 × 4.59/5.81 (261.35 × 15.06/19.06); M (MAN); 13.5; ex *Cadiz* 1981
Sister:
89422 NIAGA XXIX (Ia) ex *Sevilla* 1980

89430 CHERRY BAGUS Sg/Br (Inglis) 1959; C; 1700; 74.48 × 4.95 (244.36 × 16.24); M (Ruston & Hornsby); 12; ex *York* 1969

89440 MAWAR Sg/Ne (Jan Smit) 1952; C; 1300; 75.29 × 4.87 (247.01 × 15.98); M (Werkspoor); 11; ex *Ministar* 1974; ex *Vesta* 1974

89450 APOLLONIA VII Cy/Br (Ailsa) 1966; C; 1300; 69.45 × 4.74 (227.85 × 15.55); M (KHD); 11; ex *Sapphire* 1981

★ **89460 LOKSA** Ru/Ru (—) 1957; Tk; 800; 63.96 × 3.71 (209.84 × 12.17); TSM (Russkiy); 12.5
Sisters (Ru flag):
★ **89461 CHAIKA**
★ **89462 SUNGARY**
★ **89463 TITAN**
★ **89464 KOKCHETAV**
★ **89465 SAMBOR**
★ **89466 SULA**
★ **89467 BAYMAK**
★ **89468 BUGURUSLAN**
★ **89469 KANIN**
★ **89470 ALEKSANDR LEYNER**
★ **89471 ALITUS**
★ **89472 SIGULDA**
★ **89473 VYRU**
★ **89474 KANDAGACH**
★ **89475 YURYUZAN** ex *Barguzin* 1966
★ **89476 METAN**

89490 ARAGONITE Br/Br (Ardrossan) 1958; C; 700; 53.19 × 3.66 (174.51 × 12.01); M (British Polar); —; ex *Lady Roslin* 1982

★ **89500 YURILSK** Ru/Ru (—) 1961; FC; 500; 51.9 ×

2.94 (170.28 × 9.65); M (Russkiy); 9
Sisters (Ru flag):
★ 89501 **AMGUN**
★ 89502 **ARAKS**
★ 89503 **ALDAN**
★ 89504 **AYSBERG**
★ 89505 **GRODEKOVO**
★ 89506 **ANGARSK**
★ 89507 **KAPITAN SCHUKIN**
★ 89508 **KORIAKI**
★ 89509 **ALPERIN**
★ 89510 **KAPITAN KARTASHOV**
★ 89511 **KIPARISOVO**
★ 89512 **YELIZOVO**
Similar (Ru Flag):
★ 89513 **AMUR**

89520 **YUZBASI TOLUNAY** Tu/Tu (Taskizak) 1951;
FA/Tk; 3500 Dspl; 79 × 5.9 (260 × 19.5); TSM (Polar);
14; Turkish Navy

89530 **CARIBGAS DOS** Pa/It (INMA) 1967; LGC;
1100; 71.51 × 4.37 (234.61 × 14.34); M (MWM); ex
Birgit Hoyer 1975; ex *Alette Stove* 1972

89550 **UCANCA** Pa/Br (Drypool) 1967; Tk; 800;
61.88 × 3.91 (203.02 × 12.83); M (Brons); 10; ex
River Lee 1983; ex *Chartsman* 1976

89560 **BLUE MOON** Cy/Pd (Polnocna) 1962; C/LS;
500; 59.85 × 3.42 (196.36 × 11.22); M (Crossley); 11;
ex *Evon* 1978; ex *Boruta* 1973; 'B 475' type
Sister:
89561 **BLUE STAR** (Sg) ex *Robita* 1978; ex *Rokita*
1973

89570 **NORTHERN** De/Ne ('Ijssel') 1962/68; Cbl;
1700; 82 × 5.5 (269.03 × 18.04); M (Smit & Bolnes);
12; ex *Sirpa Dan* 1967; Converted from general cargo
1968

89580 **SAINT MITRE** Fr/It (Pellegrino) 1965; Tk;
2700; 99.57 × 6.07 (326.67 × 19.91); M (Fiat); —;
Launched as *Sisina Pellegrino*

89590 **FAIRLANE** NA/Ne (Groot & VV) 1977; C/HL;
1600/3800; 98.02 × 5.15/6 (321.59 × 16.9/19.69);
TSM (Atlas-MaK); 13
Sister:
89591 **MIRABELLA** (NA)

89600 **GABRIELLA** NA/Ne (Van Diepen) 1974;
C/HL; 1300; 88.22 × 5.51 (289.44 × 18.08); M
(Atlas-MaK); 13.5
Sister:
89601 **FAIRLOAD** (NA)
Similar (built 1978):
89602 **VALKENIER** (Ne)

89610 **DANIELLA** NA/Ne (Zaanlandsche) 1969;
C/HL; 1600; 77.65 × 5.5 (254.76 × 18.04); M (Atlas-
MaK) 12.5

89620 **FAIRLIFT** NA/Ne (Zaanlandsche) 1969;
C/HL; 900/1600; 78.72 × —/5.5 (258.27 × —
/18.04); M (Atlas-MaK); 12.5

★ 89630 **MOLUNAT** Ys/De (Sonderborg) 1970;
C/HL/RoC; 400; 66.1 × 3.44 (216.86 × 11.29); M
(Atlas-MaK); 11.5; ex *Biscayne Star* 1982; ex *Titan
Scan*; Bow door

89650 **TROPIC STAR** Sg/Sw (Oresunds) 1972; C;
1600; 93.22 × 5.13 (305.84 × 16.83); M (Atlas-MaK);
15; ex *Jota*

★ 89660 **IVAN AIVAZOVSKIY** Ru/Ru ('61 Kommunar') 1963; FC; 6100; 130 × 7.17 (426.51 × 23.52) D-E
(—); 16.5; For list of sisters see No 76490

89670 **CHIKUMA MARU** Ja/Ja (Setoda) 1970;
Cem; 6400; 131.5 × 7.82 (431.43 × 25.66); M (B&W);
12.75

★ 89680 **SEVERODVINSKIY** Ru/Br (Stephen) 1966;
D; 2000; 82.05 × 4.13 (269.19 × 13.55); TS D-E
(Mirrlees); 11.5
Sisters (Ru flag):
★ 89681 **ARABATSKIY**
★ 89682 **ONEGSKIY**

89684 **DYVI SWAN** No/No (Kaldnes) 1981; HL/Tk;
19200; 180.96 × 9.46 (594 × 31.04); M (B&W); 16;
Semi-submersible
Sister:
89685 **DYVI SWIFT** (No) (builder—Samsung)
Similar (tripod radar mast and satcom aerial on
superstructure):
89686 **DYVI TEAL** (No) (builder—Samsung)
89687 **DYVI TERN** (No)

89690 **GRIEG** Fr/Ne (Boele's Sch) 1972; RoC; 4000;
138.26 × 7.01 (453.61 × 23); M (Stork-Werkspoor);
18.5; Stern door
Sister:
89691 **SIBELIUS** (Fr)

89700 **BRIAN BOROIME** Br/Ih (Verolme Cork)
1970; Con; 4100; 107.14 × 4.44 (351.51 × 14.57);
TSM (Mirrlees Blackstone); 14
Sister:
89701 **RHODRI MAWR** (Br)

89710 **MARITZA ARLETTE** Pa/FRG (Norderwerft)
1952/66; RoC; 1100; 90.91 × 4.06 (298.26 × 13.32);
M (MaK); 11.5; ex *Ghibli* 1981; ex *Anna Catharina*
1965; Converted from tanker 1966 (Giessen-De
Noord)

89720 **ATLAS** Fr/Fr (La Rochelle) 1972; C/HL/RoC;
2600; 100.06 × 6.35 (328.28 × 20.83); M (Werkspo-
or); 14; Stern door
Sisters (Ag flag):
89721 **GARA DJEBILET**
89722 **TINDOUF**

89730 **ISABELLA** Ch/FRG (Sietas) 1952; C; 1300;
70.41 × 5.28 (231 × 17.32); M (MaK); 10.5; ex *Hans
Brohan* 1960

89740 **ZULA** Pa/FRG (Nobiskrug) 1952; C; 1800;
84.28 × 5.51 (276.51 × 18.08); M (MaK); ex *Dominic*
1980; ex *Wren* 1975; ex *Duino Bay* 1973; ex *Mira*
1970; ex *Tarragona* 1963; ex *Irmgard Pleuger* 1959

89750 **KENGARAGS** Ru/Ru (—) 1973; FC; 600; 55
× 4.18 (180.45 × 13.71); M (Liebknecht); 11.5
Probable sisters (Ru flag):
★ 89751 **BASTION**
★ 89752 **PECHORSK**
★ 89753 **KRISTALNYY**
★ 89754 **MALAKHITOVYY**
★ 89755 **RECHITSA**
★ 89756 **REDUT**
★ 89757 **KORALLOVYY**
★ 89758 **AZURITOVYY**
★ 89759 **RADUZHNYY**
★ 89760 **KVARTSEVYY**
★ 89761 **KORUNDOVYY**
★ 89762 **VSEVOLOD TIMONOV**
★ 89764 **MANGALI**
★ 89765 **BAZALTOVYY**

◣89780 **TRANS LINK** Cy/FRG (Meyer) 1966; RoC;
2260; 99.22 × 5.83 (325.52 × 19.13); M (KHD); 13; ex
Madouri 1980; ex *Moundra* 1977; ex *Salome* 1973;
Lengthened 1969; Side doors; Stern door/ramp
Sisters:
89781 **FAST CARRIER** (Le) ex *Manara* 1983; ex *Al-
Karim* 1982; ex *Cedre* 1981; ex *Alpha Conveyor*
1981; ex *Bellman* 1975; ex *Aida* 1972
★ 89783 **INSELSBERG** (DDR) ex *Berwald* 1974; ex
Otello 1972; (deck house forward of bridge)

89790 **CHERRY BUNGA** Sg/Br (Smith's D)
1967/71; Con; 11200; 153.02 × 8.73 (502.03 ×
28.64); M (Crossley); 17.5; ex *Manchester Concept*
1980; ex *Manchester Progress* 1972; Converted from
general cargo 1971

89800 **HALADI 1** Pa/FRG (A G 'Weser') 1955; C;
1300; 70.69 × 5.03 (231.92 × 16.5); M (KHD); 12; ex
Murten; ex *Linora* 1966; ex *Klaus* 1959

89810 **STARMAN ASIA** Pa/FRG (Luehring) 1977;
RoC/HL; 1600; 80.37 × 4.15 (263.68 × 13.62); TSM
(Liebknecht); 11.5; ex *Gloria Virentium* 1982; Stern
ramp; Total lifting capacity 800 tons

★ 89820 **LUO FU SHAN** RC/Sw (Eriksbergs) 1968; B;
29400; 217.58 × 12.82 (713.85 × 42.06); M (B&W);
14.75; ex *King Alfred* 1982; ex *Hemsefjell*
Similar:
89821 **LUCIANA DELLA GATTA** (It) ex *Eastern
Charm* 1980; ex *Polyhymnia* 1979
Probably similar:
89822 **MARITSA** (Gr) ex *Orunda*

89825 **JUMBO STELLATWO** NA/Fr (Dubigeon-
Normandie) 1978; HL/Con; 5000; 99.80 × 5.40 (327
× 17.72); TSM (Pielstick); 14.5; ex *Internavis II* 1982;
2 × 220 ton capacity derricks. Has a travelling crane
on the foredeck which can be removed

◣89840 **GILLIAN EVERARD** Br/Br (Clelands) 1963;
C; 1600; 81.23 × 5.16 (266.5 × 16.93); M (British
Polar); —
Sisters (Br flag):
89841 **PENELOPE EVERARD**
89842 **ROSEMARY EVERARD**
89844 **JULIA** (Pa) ex *Steyning* 1981; ex *Glanton*
1971
89845 **JUPITER** (Cy) ex *Clarebrook* 1976
89846 **ALMA** (Gr) ex *Katja* 1980; ex *Chesterbrook*
1976
89847 **LAKONIKOS** (Gr) ex *Neapolis II* 1981; ex
Corkbrook 1976
89848 **STAR** (Gr) ex *Meridian Sky* 1980; ex *Caernar-
vonbrook* 1976

89860 **LOKMA 1** Cy/Br (Lamont) 1958; C; 1000;
67.59 × 4.36 (221.75 × 14.3); M (KHD); 10.5; ex *Mary*

M 1977; ex *Yewforest* 1974
Sister:
89861 **SILVERTHORN** (Br) ex *Yewhill* 1974

89870 **NORTH SKY** To/Au (Walkers Ltd) 1957; C;
1600; 80.37 × 4.9 (263.68 × 16.08); M (Polar); 10; ex
North Esk

89890 **ABUELO GIORGIO** Li/FRG (Rhein Nordseew) 1961; B; 16700; 189.01 × 10.31 (620.11 ×
33.83); M (MAN); 14.75; ex *Puerto Acevado* 1981; ex
Pearlstone 1975; ex *Twinone* 1973; ex *Anneliese*
1972
Sister:
89891 **FLAG WILLIAMS** (Gr) ex *Puerto Rocca* 1980;
ex *Twintwo* 1973; ex *Inge* 1972

★ 89900 **HONG QI 113** RC/FRG (Flensburger) 1958;
O; 10600; 159.34 × 9.42 (522.97 × 30.91); M (MAN);
13.5; ex *Caspian Sea* 1976; ex *August Leonhardt*
1972
Sister (may have after KP removed):
89901 **MARIE LEONHARDT** (Li)

89905 **REAL** Ho/Sw (Gotav) 1955; B; 10800; 149.36
× 9.6 (490.03 × 31.5); M (Gotaverken); 14.5; ex
Fisons Realf 1982; ex *Abisko* 1964

★ 89910 **YASNOGORSK** Ru/Sw (Gotav) 1958; B;
10600; 149.36 × 9.61 (490 × 31.5); M (Gotaverken);
14.5; ex *Arvidsjaur* 1976
Sister:
★ 89911 **YARTSYEVO** (Ru) ex |Adak |1976
Similar:
89912 **PRINCESS JADE** (Pa) ex *Acandi* 1979; ex
Pluton 1974; ex *Kookaburra* 1968

89920 **DIOGENES** Gr/FRG 1959; B; 13400; 176.79
× 9.89 (580.02 × 32.45); M (Krupp); 13.5; ex *Arkadia*
1982; ex *Slesvig* 1974; Lengthened 1964

89930 **MELVIN H BAKER** Li/FRG (A G 'Weser')
1956; O; 10200; 159.95 × 9.46 (524.77 × 31.04); M
(Nydqvist & Holm); 15

◣89940 **ARCHANGELOS III** Gr/FRG (Rhein Nordseew) 1963; B; 22800; 217.99 × 11.59 (715.19 ×
38.02); M (B&W); 15; ex *Naess Liberty* 1974
Sister:
89941 **PYTHEUS** (Gr) ex *Rubycorn* 1980; ex *Frigga*
1973
Similar:
89942 **TRADE LIGHT** (Gr) ex *Baldur* 1978

◣89950 **RIO BRAVO** Gr/Br (H&W) 1960; B; 12000;
169.88 × 9.68 (557.35 × 31.76); M (B&W); 14.5; ex
Cuyo 1978; ex *Drymos* 1975; ex *St. Mary* 1974; ex
Tresfonn 1973
Sister:
89951 **LEROS ISLAND** (Gr) ex *Sarandi* 1981; ex *San
Francesco* 1974; ex *Krossfonn* 1972

89960 **ACHILLEUS** Gr/Ja (Misubishi Z) 1961; B;
16500; 198.08 × 10.53 (649.87 × 34.55); M (Sulzer);
—; ex *Gaucho Pampa* 1978; ex *Skauborg* 1973;
Lengthened 1965 (Gotav)
Sisters:
89961 **GRIGOROUSA** (Li) ex *Gaucho Laguna* 1980;
ex *Golar Coal* 1970; ex *Skauholt* 1966
89962 **ST LAWRENCE** (Ca) ex *Gaucho Taura* 1976;
ex *Skaustrand* 1973
89963 **GAUCHO CRUZ** (Ar) ex *Golar Grain* 1970; ex
Skauvaag 1966

★ 89980 **GORLITZ** DDR/Ru (Baltic) 1974; B; 22800;
201.38 × 11.21 (660.7 × 36.78); M (B&W); 15.5;
'Baltika' type
Sister:
★ 89981 **GRODITZ** (Ru)
Similar:
★ 89982 **NIKOLAY VOZNESENSKIY** (Ru)
Similar (crane aft):
★ 89983 **COLDITZ** (DDR)

89990 **FORUM GRACE** Gr/Sw (Eriksbergs) 1963;
B; 15600; 181.85 × 10.57 (596.62 × 34.68); M
(B&W); 15.5; ex *Cape Pacific*; ex *Uppland* 1976

◣90000 **ELISA** Gr/Sw (Eriksbergs) 1958; B; 12000;
177.65 × 9.13 (582.84 × 29.95); M (B&W); 14; ex
Trollegen 1977; ex *Aktion* 1972; ex *Altamira* 1969; ex
Cerro Altamira 1968

90010 **MERINGA** Pa/Br (Hall, Russell) 1958; C;
5500; 125.43 × 7.22 (411.52 × 23.69); M (Doxford);
12.5

90020 **NORTH EMPEROR** Li/Ja (Mitsubishi HI)
1967; B; 25800; 206.03 × 12.2 (675.95 × 40.03); M
(Sulzer); 16.5
Sister:
90021 **NORTH KING** (Li)

★ 90030 **'BALTIYSKIY'** type. Ru/Ru ('Krasnoye S')
1962/68; C (sea/river); 1900; 96.02 × 3.26 (315.03
× 10.7); TSM (Liebknecht); 10; Vessel illustrated is

BALTIYSKIY 32; Some have lower funnels; After-mast omitted on some vessels
Sisters (Ru flag): from **BALTIYSKIY 1** to **BALTIYSK-IY 73** inclusive

90060 CECILE ERICKSON Pa/Ja (Osaka) 1957; C; 3300; 113.54 × 6.24 (372.51 × 20.47); TrSM (Caterpillar); 12

90070 ROCQUAINE Br/Br (J W Cook) 1977; C; 1000; 66.91 × 4.12 (219.52 × 13.52); M (Mirrlees Blackstone); 11; Modified **'Colne'** type
Sisters (Br flag):
90071 BELGRAVE
90072 PERELLE

90080 BRIDGEMAN Br/Br (Hall, Russell) 1972; Tk; 3700; 103.64 × 6.99 (340.03 × 22.93); M (Ruston Paxman); 13
Similar:
90081 HELMSMAN (Br)

90090 VASILIKI V Gr/Br (Goole) 1964; Tk; 1200; 71.48 × 4.47 (234.51 × 14.67); M (Mirrlees Blackstone); —; ex Assiduity 1983

90100 KOSMOS Gr/Be (Flandre) 1959; C; 2700; 103.66 × 6.41 (340.09 × 21.03); M (Fiat); 14; ex Panagiotis A 1980; ex Galaxy 1976; ex Angara 1970

90110 M SYCOUTRIS Ma/Br (Burntisland) 1960; B; 6600; 126.19 × 8.57 (414 × 28.12); M (Doxford); 13; ex Avance 1983; ex Arthur Albright 1968

90120 JOHN M Br/Br (Burntisland) 1963; Tk; 1300; 70.11 × 4.83 (230 × 15.85); M (Lister Blackstone); —

90130 FRANK M Br/Br (Burntisland) 1965; Tk; 1300; 70.72 × 4.83 (232 × 15.85); M (Blackstone); —
Sister:
90131 NICHOLAS M (Br)

90140 ALACRITY Br/Br (Goole) 1966; Tk/Ch; 900; 65.99 × 4.36 (216.5 × 14.3); M (Mirrlees Blackstone); —

★ **90150 KUSTANAY** Ru/Sw (Oskarshamns) 1955; FF; 1800; 79.25 × 6.12 (260 × 20.08); M (MAN); 11.5
Sisters (Ru flag):
★ **90151 MAGADAN**
★ **90152 POLESSK**
★ **90153 SARANSK**
★ **90154 ZELENOGRAD**

90160 MT APO Pi/Ja (Nipponkai) 1966; Tk; 2600; 92.79 × 6.3 (304.43 × 20.67); M (Nippon Hatsudoki); 11.75; ex Delbros Mt Apo II 1982; ex Nichiyo Maru 1970
Possibly similar:
90161 NISSHIN MARU (Ja)

90170 KEMAL KOLOTOGLU Tu/Tu (Gaye) 1978; C; 1600; 79.84 × — (261.94 × —); M (Atlas-MaK); 12
Probable sister:
90171 HACI ARIF KAPTAN (Tu)

★ **90175 SONG DO HO** RK/Ja (Koyo) 1964; C; 1000; 67.82 × 4.73 (223 × 15.52); M (Nippon Hatsudoki); 12.25; ex Shoto Maru

90180 MULTI SERVICE 125 Pa/Ne (Groot & VV) 1957; C/HL; 1500; 77.5 × 4.7 (254.27 × 15.42); M (Werkspoor); 10.5; ex Gloria Carib 1983; ex Gloria Maris 1983

★ **90190 YANA** Ru/Ne (IHC Holland) 1974; D; —; 72 × — (236.22 × —); M; —
Sister:
★ **90191 URENGOI** (Ru)

90200 AUTOSTRADA Br/No (Langvik) 1971; RoVC; 600; 92.36 × 3.89 (303 × 12.76); M (Bergens); 14.25; Stern door/ramp
Sister:
90201 AUTOLLOYD (Bz) ex Autoroute 1976

90210 REAL Ho/Sw (Gotav) 1955; B; 10800; 149.36 × 9.6 (490.03 × 31.5); M (Gotaverken); 14.5; ex Fisons Realf 1982; ex Abisko 1964

★ **90220 YASNOGORSK** Ru/Sw (Gotav) 1958; B; 10600; 149.36 × 9.61 (490 × 31.5); M (Gotaverken) 14.5; ex Arvidsjaur 1976
Sister:
★ **90221 YARTSYEVO** (Ru) ex Adak 1976
Similar:
90222 PRINCESS JADE (Pa) ex Acandi 1979; ex Pluton 1974; ex Kookaburra 1968

90230 KATERINA Gr/De (Svendborg) 1956; C; 1000; 66.60 × 4.66 (218.5 × 15.29); M (Alpha-Diesel); 11.5; ex Frej 1969; ex Ingga Dan 1962
Sister:
90231 LEDA (Gr) ex Karna Dan 1963

90260 TRANS CORAL Pa/FRG (Kroegerw) 1957; C; 1100/1800; 78.47 × —/4.9 (257.45 × —/16.08); M

(KHD); 13; ex Blue Trader 1983; ex Nikopolis 1981; ex Sea Horse 1 1979; ex Sea Horse 1978; ex Northman 1978; ex Inyula 1977; ex Erna Witt 1963

90280 SAMAR Le/FRG (Elsflether) 1961; C; 1600; 77.81 × 5.4 (255.28 × 17.72); M (MaK); 12; ex Fotis 1983; ex Nolese 1975; ex Else Retzlaff 1971

● **90290 CHRYS** Ma/Br (H Robb) 1957; C; **3900**; 108.69 × 6.65 (356.59 × 21.82); M (Sulzer); 11; ex Gianna A 1983; ex Arlington 1980; ex Ashington 1978; ex Tennyson 1968

90300 ABDUL RAZZAK Le/FRG (Sietas) 1956; C; 900/1400; 74.48 × 3.82/5.12 (244.36 × 12.53/16.8); M (KHD); 13; ex Atlanta 1974; ex Bonita 1968

90310 HANOOVER Pa/Ne (Zaanlandsche) 1962; C; 1500; 79.15 × 4.9 (259.68 × 16.08); M (Werkspoor); 12; ex Regina Express 1982; ex Windle Sky 1975; ex Cap Falcon 1973; ex Lis Frellsen 1967
Sister:
90311 DORTEA (It) ex Dorthea 1972; ex Thea Danielsen 1969

90320 OMAR EXPRESS Pa/Ne (Arnhemsche) 1962; C; 700/1400; 73.54 × 3.96/4.96 (241.27 × 12.99/16.27); M (Werkspoor); 12.5; ex Birooni 1971; ex Nico P W 1969

90330 SUTAS Pa/Br (Ailsa) 1962; C; 1600; 81.62 × 5.21 (267.78 × 17.09); M (KHD); 13; ex Topaz 1982
Sister:
90331 PROBA (Br) ex Tourmaline 1982

90340 KYDONIA Gr/Is (Israel Spyds) 1965; C; 1300/2000; 84.31 × —/6.27 (276.61 × —/20.57); M (Werkspoor); —; ex Hanna 1976
Sisters:
90341 MASSALIA (Gr) ex Lea 1974
90342 KOTA BANTENG (Sg) ex Eastern Luck 1974; ex Sara 1974
90343 KOTAH GAJAH (Sg) ex Eastern Prosperous 1974; ex Miryam 1974
90345 GREAT POINT (Pa) ex Rivka 1979

90350 AUBADE Pa/Ne (Verolme Scheeps) 1961; B; 14900; 180.35 × 10.85 (591.7 × 35.6); M (MAN); —

90360 MARINER Ho/Br (Hall, Russell) 1960; C; 5800; 131.53 × 7.84 (431.53 × 25.71); M (Sulzer); 15.5; ex Omega Leros 1983; ex Elminer 1980; ex Vallila 1976; ex Sugar Carrier 1969

90380 HIN ANN Pa/De (Frederikshavn) 1957; C; 4500; 116.59 × 7.41 (383 × 24.31); M (B&W); 13; ex Marijke 1980; ex Helene Maersk 1978; ex Ras Maersk 1972

★ **90390 PINAR DEL RIO** Cu/Br (Atlantic SB) 19t; C; 3100; 101.94 × 6.29 (334.45 × 20.64); M (Davey, Paxman); —
Sisters (Cu flag):
★ **90391 HABANA**
★ **90392 LAS VILLAS**
★ **90393 MATANZAS**

90400 MILAS I Tu/Sp ('Astano') 1964; C; 2600/4600; 107.12 × 6.45/7.53 (351.44 × 21.16/24.7); M (Gotaverken); 14.5; ex Victor 1978; ex Stubbenhuk 1973; ex Alar 1966

90410 EL EXPORTADOR Ve/Ne (van der Werf) 1962; C; 1400; 73.54 × 4.96 (241.27 × 16.27) ; M (Werkspoor); 12.5; ex Jose Express 1983; ex Any H 1971; ex Eny Hojsgaard 1970

★ **90420 'VOLGONEFT'** type. Ru/Ru-Bu (Volgograd G Dimitrov) 1969/72; Tk; 3600; 135.01×3.5 (442.95×11.48); TSM (Liebknecht); 10.5; This drawing represents the later vessels of this type. For earlier ships see 'VOLGONEFT' under M4F. Names have the prefix 'VOLGONEFT' and a number. There are approx. 27 in the whole group

90450 MARATHON Ec/Ne (Vuyk) 1960; C; 2000/2900; 119.49 × 5.68/6.41 (392 × 18.64/21.03); M (Stork); 16; ex Niki 1977; ex San Salvador 1977; ex Marathon 1973; Lengthened 1967
Sisters:
90451 KANIKA (Pa) ex Panormos 1983; ex Eurabia Moon 1979; ex Parthenon 1974
90452 EFIE (Gr) ex Eurabia Sky 1980; ex Sinon 1974
90453 ARTURO MICHELINA (Ve) ex Ammon 1972
90454 NELA ALTOMARE (Ve) ex Arabian Express 1976; ex Chiron 1974

90470 KOTA BAHAGIA My/Ne (Giessen) 1954; C; 2900; 98.28 × 6.27 (322 × 20.57); M (Stork); 13; ex Adonis 1972
Sisters:
90471 KOTA HARAPAN (My) ex Artemis 1972
90472 KOTA INDAH (My) ex Themis 1972

90480 KETTY It/Ne (E J Smit) 1963; C; 1300; 80.68

× — (264.7 × —); M (Werkspoor); 13; ex Ketty Danielsen 1970

90490 ARISTOTELIS Gr/Ne (E J Smit) 1965; C; 1400; 80.68 × 5 (264.7 × 16.4); M (MaK); —; ex Breevoort 1977; ex Flynderborg 1970
Sister:
90491 SIBYLLA (Gr) ex Leena 1981; ex Breevliet 1975; ex Frederiksborg 1970

90500 ALPINA Sd/FRG (Flensburger) 1970; C; 6900/9600; 139.76 × 8.22/9.19 (458.53 × 26.97/30.15); M (Bremer V); 16; **'German Liberty'** type
Possible sister:
90501 ASCONA (Sd)

★ **90510 DA LONG TIAN** RC/FRG (A G 'Weser') 1966; C/HL; 7010/9450; 152.25×8.31/9.48 (499.5 × 27.2/31.1); M (MAN); 19; ex Crostafels 1978
Sisters:
★ **90511 DA HONG QIAO** (RC) ex Kybfels 1979
★ **90512 WU YI SHAN** (RC) ex Birkenfels 1978
★ **90513 DA QING SHAN** (RC) ex Schonfels
90514 AIAS (Gr) ex Falkenfels 1980
90515 HOHENBELS (Gr) ex Hohenfels

90520 MOTHI Pa/No (Pusnaes) 1959; C; 2400; 83.83 × 6.05 (275.03 × 19.85); M (B&W); 12.5; ex Baie James 1981; ex Percy M. Crosbie 1981; ex Perla Dan 1971

● **90530 ZSA ZSA** Pa/Ne ('Westerbroek') 1961; C; 1200; 73.51 × 4.57 (241.17 × 14.99); M (KHD); 12; ex Dornach 1983; ex Elfy North 1969
Similar:
90531 ZUNA (Le) ex Zephir 1 1981; ex Maria Mare 1977; ex Malchow 1975; ex Perseverance Bay 1966
90532 BEN MAJED (Le) ex Mamaya 1980; ex Kiakow 1973; ex Fortuna Bay 1965
90533 BOA NOVA (Cy) ex Spyros 1983; ex Limpopo 1977; ex Berea 1975; ex Kongsholm 1968
90534 MONTANA (It) ex Aziza 1983; ex Coral 1974; ex Birthe Scan 1969; ex Knudsholm 1968
90535 EMEBORG (Cy) ex Saeborg 1977; ex Passat 1973; ex Stavholm 1969; ex Kyholm 1965
90536 CARIGULF FREEDOM (St. Lucia) ex Hourico 1982; ex Jovo 1979; ex Vilsund 1969; ex Skals 1968; ex Klausholm 1968

90550 GOLDEN WAVE Pa/FRG (Nobiskrug) 1969; C; 2800/5000; 124.97 × 6.53/7.67 (410 × 21.42/25.16); M (Atlas-MaK); 16.5; ex Juno 1983
Sister:
90551 JUPITER II (FRG) ex Jupiter 1980

★ **90560 MEZENLES** Ru/Ru (Baltic) 1961; C; 4600; 121.77 × 7.16 (399.51 × 23.49); GT (SIGMA/Alsthom); 14.25
Sisters (Ru flag):
★ **90561 UMBALES**
★ **90562 PECHORALES**
★ **90563 TEODOR NETTE**
★ **90564 JOHANN MAHMASTAL** (also spelt IOHANN MAMASTAL)

90570 AL JAMAL Le/FRG (Kroegerw) 1961; C/WT; 1100; 75.65 × 4.27 (248.2 × 14.01); M (MAN); —; ex Jean Dark 1981; ex Jean d'Arc; ex Nazih 1979; ex Barakat 1979; ex Palacio 1977

★ **90580 LIDIA DOCE** Cu/No (Langesunds) 1957; C; 2100; 91.27 × 5.82 (299.44 × 19.09); M (MAN); —; ex Maria Teresa 1964

90590 CARIGULF PIONEER Br/Ne ('Ijssel') 1962; C; 1100/1700; 81.84 × 4.02/5.50 (269 × 13.19/18.04); M (Smit & Bolnes); 12.5; ex Etai 1981; ex Ytai 1977; ex Carmela 1976; ex Barok 1974; ex Raila Dan 1969

★ **90600 OELSA** DDR/DDR ('Neptun') 1967; C; 2500; 92.82 × 5.92 (304.53 × 19.42); M (Dieselmotorenwerk Rostock); 12.75
Sisters (DDR flag):
★ **90601 EISENBERG**
★ **90602 HELLERAU**
★ **90603 THEMAR**
★ **90604 ZEULENRODA**

● **90610 SEAJAY** Cy/Sp (Ruiz) 1966; C; 1000/1600; 82.5 × —/6 (270.67 × —/19.69); M (Stork-Werkspoor); —; ex Alexandra 1 1982; ex Athina 1981; ex Proton 1980; ex Marichu 1976
Sisters:
90611 NIKOLAS (Gr) ex Andros 1981; ex Zebras Fortune 1980; ex Maria Dolores Tartiere 1977
90613 SAMOS SPIRIT (Gr) ex Maria de Aranzazu 1982
90614 SAMOS HARMONY (Gr) ex Maria de Covadonga 1981

90620 GUARDIAN Pa/Br (H Robb) 1962; C; 4800; 115.6 × 6.73 (379.27 × 22.08); M (Sulzer); 15; ex

Good Guardian 1982; ex *Hebe* 1979
Sister:
90621 **CHERRY LANKA** (Sg) ex *Bacchus* 1981

90630 **ANASTASIA Y** Pa/FRG (O&K) 1959; C;
2200/3300; 103.33 × 5.86/— (339 × 19.23/—); M
(MAN); 14; ex *Ulysses 1* 1982; ex *Yarden* 1979; ex
Gasos 1978; ex *Yarden* 1977
Sister:
90631 **KRANAOS** (Pa) ex *Anthoula* 1980; ex *Kineret*
1978; ex *Agate* 1975; ex *Fabio* 1970; ex *Kineret* 1970

90640 **ASTRID SCHULTE** Cy/FRG (Lindenau)
1967; C; 2200/3600; 107.85 × 6.31/7.42 (353.84 ×
20.7/24.34); M (MAN); 15.5; ex *Cap Maleas* 1978; ex
Astrid Schulte 1976
Sister:
★ 90641 **HUA AN** (RC) ex *Moritz Schulte* 1983

90650 **ALTAIR 1** Pa/Sp (Euskalduna) 1968; C; 4300;
117.96 × 6.71 (387.01 × 22.01); M (MAN); 14; ex
Acmi 1983; ex *Sierra Jara*; ex *Mirenchu* 1972
Sister:
90651 **KALYON** (Tu) ex *Arianne Laura* 1982; ex
Kallidromos 1980; ex *Spartan Bay* 1976; ex *Arcadia
Wien* 1973; ex *Marta* 1971

● 90654 **CAPE VALS** Cy/Sp (Juliana) 1972; C; 5200;
118.12 × 7.35 (388 × 24.11); M (B&W); 14; ex
Auguste S 1982; ex *Miraflores* 1979
Sisters:
90655 **LUCIE S** (Cy) ex *Jupiter* 1979
90656 **JOHN K** (Pa) ex *Chiqui* 1980; Launched as
Monte Albertia
90657 **MONTE ABRIL** (Sp) (sold Ys 1984)
90658 **KUTLU ISIK** (Tu) ex *Marianne S* 1982; ex
Monte Ayala 1980

90680 **AMPARO** Br/FRG (A G 'Weser') 1967; C/HL;
8200/11400; 155.53 × —/9.44 (510.27 × —
/30.97); M (B&W); 16.5; ex *Star Alcyone* 1974; ex
Heering Lotte 1971
Sister:
90681 **JALAPA** (Me) ex *Samia* 1981; ex *Elena*; ex
Star Procyon 1974; ex *Heering Susan* 1969

● 90690 **MAYFAIR** Pa/Ja (IHI) 1961; C; 10900;
154.03 × 9.49 (505.35 × 31.14); M (Sulzer); —; ex
Atrotos 1983; ex *Apollonia* 1981
Similar:
90691 **STILIANOS S** (Gr) ex *Lindos* 1981

90700 **MARKINA** Ve/Sp (Euskalduna) 1965; C;
3700; 111.69 × 6.09 (366.44 × 20); M (MAN); 12.75;
ex *Maurine K* 1980; ex *Hannah Blumenthal* 1975; ex
Pinto 1969

90710 **PATRAIKOS** Gr/Fr (L'Atlantique) 1962; C;
8800/11800; 162.64 × 8.69/10.05 (533.6 ×
28.51/32.97); M (B&W); 16; ex *Delphian* 1978; ex
Thorunn 1971

★ 90720 **INTERNATSIONAL** Ru/Pd (Gdynska)
1968; Tk; 14200; 177.27 × 9.37 (581.59 × 30.74); M
(Sulzer); 16; '**B-72**' type
Sisters (Ru Flag):
★ 90721 **DRUZHBA NARADOV**
★ 90722 **ISKRA**
★ 90723 **LENINSKOE ZNAMYA**
★ 90724 **NAKHODKA**
★ 90725 **PROLETARSKAYA POBEDA**
★ 90726 **PAMYAT LENINA**
★ 90727 **PETR STUCHKA**
★ 90728 **ZAVYETY ILYICHA**

90740 **NORTHWIND** Li/Sp (Euskalduna) 1970; B;
11300; 147.02 × 9.93 (482.35 × 32.58); M (MAN);
16; '**Santa Fe**' type
Sisters (Li flag):
90741 **SOUTHWIND**
90742 **WESTWIND**

90750 **DIES** It/FRG (Meyer) 1956; C; 900; 71.38 ×
4.27 (234.19 × 14.01); M (KHD); 13; ex *Northumbrian
Queen* 1972; ex *Chevychase* 1972

90770 **KERKYRA** Cy/FRG (Kroegerw.) 1965; C;
1600; 78.47 × 5.5 (257.45 × 18.04); M (KHD); 12.5;
ex *Haroula* 1976; ex *Scheersburg A* 1970; ex *Scheersburg* 1968

● 90790 **MONOMER VENTURE** Pa/US (Todd)-FRG
1945/62; LGC; 4600; 116.52 × 7.2 (382.28 ×
23.62); M (Nordberg); 11; ex *Esso Centro America*
1969; ex *Esso Venezuela* 1962; ex *Montebello* 1947;
ex *Tarauca* 1945; Converted from '**T-1**' type tanker
and lengthened 1962 (A.G. 'Weser')

90800 **NORSUN** Ma/De (Helsingor) 1962; C;
3100/4600; 119.54 × 6.07/7.01 (392.19 ×
19.91/23); M (B&W) 15; ex *Manaure IV* 1980; ex
Lucy Borchard 1978; ex *Heering Rose* 1969

● 90810 **REEFER MERCHANT** Cy/FRG (Schlichting)
1967; R; 900/1700; 88.7 × 4.13/5.21 (291.01 ×
13.55/17.09); M (Atlas-MaK); —; ex *Fahrmannsand*

1974
Sisters:
90811 **LUHESAND** (Cy)
★ 90812 **HARMATTAN** (Pd) ex *Pagensand* 1972

90820 **GOOD LUCK** Ho/No (Trondhjems) 1962; C;
1900/3100; 99.22 × 6.52/— (325.52 × 21.39/—);
M (MAN); 12.5; ex *Captain Leo* 1983; ex *Frol* 1972

90830 **IRAKLIS** Pa/No (Trondhjems) 1957; C; 2000;
96.12 × 5.75 (315.35 × 18.8); M (MAN); 12; ex *Ios*
1983; ex *Lia G* 1979; ex *Dekatria* 1976; ex *Forra* 1972
Similar:
90831 **AL AHRAM** (Eg) ex *Helen Pappas* 1982; ex
Marabou 1980; ex *Skauma* 1971

90840 **RIO ASON** Sp/Sp (AESA) 1965; R; 1500;
83.55 × 5.7 (274.11 × 18.7); M (Werkspoor); 15; ex
Punta Ureka 1967

90850 **RANNO** Fi/Fi (Nystads) 1966; R; 500/1100;
73.82 × 3.49/4.71 (242.19 × 11.45/15.45); M
(KHD); 13.5
Sister:
90851 **REEFER INSEL** (Cy) ex *Saggo* 1982

90860 **ATLANTIC ISLE** Gr/Sp (Duro Felguera)
1971; C; 800/1400; 77.4 × 4.07/5.32 (253.94 ×
13.35/17.45); M (Deutz); —; ex *Wickenburgh* 1979;
ex *Atlan Turquesa* 1975
Sisters (Eg flag):
90861 **AL BIRUNI** ex *Atlan Zafiro*
90862 **AL IDRISI** ex *Atlan Diamante* 1975

90870 **TUKWILA CHIEF** Pa/FRG (Meyer) 1961; C;
2900; 94.01 × 6.77 (308.43 × 22.21); M (MAN); 13.5;
ex *Esther Charlotte Schulte* 1980
Sisters:
90871 **JOHANN CHRISTIAN SCHULTE** (Cy)
90872 **NADA G** (Le) ex *Donata Schulte* 1980; ex *Jan
Ten Doornkaat* 1973

★ 90880 **SECIL BRASIL** An/FRG (Meyer) 1966;
C/HL; 2000/3100; 98.84 × 5.72/6.80 (324.28 ×
18.77/22.31); M (MAN); 15; ex *Papenburg* 1974

★ 90890 **KURILA** Ys/FRG (Lindenau) 1958; C; 2000;
79.13 × 5.9 (259.61 × 19.36); M (MAN); 12; ex *Ragni*
1974
Sisters:
90891 **UMA** (In) ex *Jameela* 1983; ex *Himing* 1964
90893 **CRUZ DEL SUR** (Br) ex *Caribbean Tamanaco*
1980; ex *Eva* 1969; ex *Tronstad* 1962
90894 **HONG MING** (My) ex *Crazy Harry* 1981; ex
Sofia B 1980; ex *Navarino* 1975; ex *Malka* 1968; ex
Negus 1963; ex *Sunny Girl* 1962
90895 **TOUFIC** (Le) ex *Mammy Yoko* 1978; ex *Cape
Cod* 1975; ex *Hamburger Tor* 1972; ex *Angelica
Schulte* 1970
90896 **HOE ONN** (Sg) ex *Naimbana* 1978; ex *Hamburger Michel* 1973; ex *Heinrich Udo Schulte* 1970

90910 **KATERINA** Gr/Sp (Euskalduna) 1963; C;
1000; 74.78 × 4.89 (245.34 × 16.04); M (MaK); 13;
ex *Nicholas* 1982; ex *Aries* 1979; ex *Anavissos* 1976;
ex *Sounion* 1975; ex *Tequila* 1971; ex *Linglee* 1971;
ex *Linglea* 1967

90930 **SALLY ANN** Pa/Sp ('Corbasa') 1963; C;
900/1600; 82.53 × 4.67/5.98 (270.77 ×
15.32/19.62); M (Werkspoor); 13; ex *Sierra Andia*
1980

● 90940 **OCEANIA** De/De (Svendborg) 1972; C; 500;
75.42 × 3.47 (247.44 × 11.38); M (Atlas-Mak); 12; ex
Moss Maroc 1978; ex *Oceania* 1972
Sisters (De flag):
90941 **ANNE METTE**
90942 **ANNETTE S**
90943 **ELIN S**
90944 **SIGRID S**

90950 **JUMBO JOIST** Pa/Ne ('Vooruitgang') 1955;
C/HL; 800/1200; 80.5 × 5.11/— (264.11 × 16.77/—
); M (Werkspoor); 10.5; ex *Singapore Jati* 1983; ex
Bernard John 1974; Gear amidships consists of
quadpod & sheelegs

90960 **VALKENBURG** Ne/Ne ('Friesland') 1966;
C/HL; 500/1300; 75.42 × 3.99/5.01 (247.44 ×
13.09/16.44); M (Werkspoor); 10

90970 **PIA DANIELSEN** De/Ne (Bodewes B V)
1976; C; 1000; 79.48 × 4.83 (260.76 × 15.85); M
(Atlas-Mak); 12.5
Similar:
90971 **KALOUM** (De) ex *Gudrun Danielsen* 1982
90971/1 **JYTTE DANIELSEN** (De)
90971/2 **GRETE DANIELSEN** (De)
90972 **HERMAN BODEWES** (Ne)
Similar (sloping uprights to goalpost):
90973 **FRELLSEN HILLE** (De) ex *Hille Frellsen* 1980

90980 **MINNESOTA** It/FRG (Brand) 1968; C;
1000/1600; 80.09 × 5.11/6.05 (262.76 ×

16.77/19.85); M (KHD); 13; ex *Eckwardersand* 1981
Sisters:
90981 **MINNEAPOLIS** (It) ex *Boitwardersand* 1980
90982 **BELL COMET** (Gr) ex *Lemwardersand* 1981

90990 **DIBI HAMID** Cy/FRG (Elsflether) 1964; C;
1000; 68.00 × 5.01 (223 × 16.4); M (KHD); 11.25; ex
Nordwik 1981; ex *Pep Sea* 1974; ex *Seehausersand*
1972
Sisters:
90991 **EASTHOLM** (Sw) ex *Anne Sobye* 1983; ex
Lankenauersand 1972
90992 **BANDAR-E-DEYLAN** (Ir) ex *Kolstrup* 1977;
ex *Warfleethersand* 1972

91000 **LADY SYLVIA** Cy/FRG (Elsflether) 1965; C;
1000; 70.03 × 4.97 (229.76 × 16.31); M (KHD); 11.5;
ex *Lienersand* 1972

91010 **ANTARCTIC** Ne/Ne (Nieuwe Noord) 1967; R;
500/1400; 80.96 × 4.12/4.92 (265.62 ×
13.52/16.14); M (KHD); 15
Similar:
91011 **SANTA LUCIA** (Ne) ex *Coolhaven* 1975; ex
Frost Scan 1974; ex *Spitsbergen* 1972

91020 **PACIFIC COUNTESS** Ne/De (Frederikshavn) 1978; R; 1600; 74.5 × 5.01 (244.42 × 16.44);
M (Alpha-Diesel); 13; ex *Gomba Reefer I* 1980; '**613-
B**' type
Sister:
91021 **PACIFIC EMPRESS** (Ne) ex *Gomba Reefer II*
1979

91030 **NIAGA XLI** Ia/Ne (Van Diepen) 1974; C; 800;
76 × 4.45 (249.34 × 14.6); M (Atlas-MaK); 11; ex
Mira 1982; ex *Amigo Express* 1975
Similar (De flag):
91031 **KASPAR SIF**
91033 **ANN SANDVED**
91036 **HERMAN SIF** ex *Gerda Lonborg* 1977
91039 **AMIGO FORTUNA**
(Ne flag):
91040 **SWIFT**
91041 **NIELSE DANIELSEN** ex *Amigo Defender*
1978
91044 **ERIK SIF** (De)
91045 **GRETE SIF** (De)
(Fa flag):
91047 **RUNATINDUR** ex *Lotte Scheel* 1976
(Ia flag):
91048 **NIAGA XLV** ex *Pia Sandved* 1982
91049 **TARUNA ABADI** ex *Jette Sif* 1982
(Cy flag):
91050 **APOLLONIA X** ex *Chris Isa* 1983
91051 **MELINA** ex *Rikke Isa* 1983

● 91070 **ZSA ZSA** Pa/Ne ('Westerbroek') 1961; C;
1200; 73.51 × 4.57 (241.17 × 14.99); M (KHD); 12; ex
Dornach 1983; ex *Elfy North* 1969
Similar:
91071 **ZUNA** (Le) ex *Zephir 1* 1981; ex *Maria Mare*
1977; ex *Malchow* 1975; ex *Perseverance Bay* 1966
91072 **BEN MAJED** (Le) ex *Mamaya* 1980; ex *Krakow* 1973; ex *Fortuna Bay* 1965
91073 **BOA NOVA** (Cy) ex *Spyros* 1983; ex *Limpopo*
1977; ex *Berea* 1975; ex *Kongsholm* 1968
91074 **MONTANA** (It) ex *Aziza* 1983; ex *Coral* 1974;
ex *Birthe Scan* 1969; ex *Knudsholm* 1968
91075 **EMEBORG** (Cy) ex *Saeborg* 1977; ex *Passat*
1973; ex *Stavholm* 1969; ex *Kyholm* 1965
91076 **CARIGULF FREEDOM** (St Lucia) ex *Hourico*
1982; ex *Jovo* 1979; ex *Vilsund* 1969; ex *Skals* 1968;
ex *Klausholm* 1968

91090 **MARIA IRENE** Po/Ne (Zaanlandsche) 1967;
C; 500/1200; 76.94 × 3.76/5.28 (252 ×
12.34/17.32); M (Werkspoor); 13.5; ex *Leonard Bohmer* 1981

★ 91100 **VELA LUKA** Ys/FRG (Luerssen) 1955; C;
300/600; 55.99 × 2.72/3.81 (183.69 × 8.92/12.5);
M (KHD); 9.5; ex *Pirol* 1969; ex *Ipswich Pioneer* 1968;
ex *Meise* 1960
Sisters:
91101 **ALPHA** (FRG) ex *Star* 1968
91102 **INGI** (Pa) ex *Pewsum* 1973; ex *Uppland* 1971;
ex *Schwalbe* 1962; Some of these vessels may have
the bipods removed, making the sequence KMF

91110 **VIJAYA JIWAN** In/FRG (Atlas-Werke) 1958;
C; 3900; 114.31 × 6.12 (375 × 20.08); M (MaK); 15.5;
ex *Vishva Anand* 1980; ex *Sturmfels* 1968; ex *Nortropic* 1958
Sister:
91111 **VIJAYA VAIBHAV** (In) ex *Vishva Pratibha*
1981; ex *Stolzenfels* 1968; Launched as *Norcastle*

91120 **MARGO** Gr/FRG (Luerssen) 1958; C;
1900/3000; 97.57 × —/6.69 (320.11 × —/21.95);
M (MAN); 11.5; ex *Malvina* 1980; ex *Range* 1972; ex
Seadrake 1967

91130 **KUWAIT** Eg/Ne ('De Noord') 1961; C; 3100;

96.96 × 6.64 (318.11 × 21.78); M (B&W); 13.5; ex
Kakawi 1975; ex Ritva Dan 1974
Sister:
91131 **KOSTAS K** (Gr) ex Saima Dan 1975

91140 **ASHRAF AL AWAL** Si/Fi (Nystads) 1961; R;
500; 71.81 × 3.62 (235.6 × 11.88); M (KHD); 14; ex
Jarso 1980
Similar:
91141 **TINGO** (Fi)
91142 **HERRO** (Fi)
91143 **NORRO** (Fi) ex Evocrystal 1981; ex Crystal
Green 1975; ex Crystal Scan 1975; Launched as
Arctic Scan
91144 **POLAR** (Cy) ex Polar Scan 1974
91145 **REEFER CARRIER** (Cy) ex Evopearl 1978; ex
Ice Pearl 1975; ex Reefer Scan 1973

91150 **RIO ASON** Sp/Sp (AESA) 1965; R; 1500;
83.55 × 5.7 (274.11 × 18.7); M (Werkspoor); 15; ex
Punta Ureka 1967

91160 **RANNO** Fi/Fi (Nystads) 1966; R; 500/1100;
73.82 × 3.49/4.71 (242.19 × 11.45/15.45); M
(KHD); 13.5
Sister:
91161 **REEFER INSEL** (Cy) ex Saggo 1982

91170 **RIBUAN JAYA** Sg/Ne (Zaanlandsche) 1968;
C/HL; 500/1500; 70.9 × 3.84/5.5 (232.61 ×
12.6/18.04); M (Atlas-MaK); 13; ex Stellanova 1983

91180 **CLOUD** Cy/No (Aukra) 1963; C; 1200; 77.27
× 5.18 (253.51 × 16.99); M (MaK); 12; ex Gulf Africa
1977; ex Gracia 1974
Sister:
91181 **PINGUIN** (It) ex Dominique 1978; ex Sokna
1974; ex Gloria 1971

91190 **RAMON** It/FRG (Unterweser) 1958; C; 1500;
76.59 × 5.32 (251.28 × 17.45); M (MaK); 12; ex
Mabica 1982; ex Emma Retzlaff 1972; ex Seefahrer
1960

91200 **SATWAH** Db/Br (Hall, Russell) 1962; C; 900;
59.44 × 4.28 (195 × 14.04); M (Mirrlees Bickerton &
Day); 11.25; ex Yasin 1980; ex Spray 1973

91210 **THEODOROS DEMET** Gr/Br (A&P) 1957; C;
1900; 80.78 × 5.11 (265.03 × 16.77); M (British
Polar); 11; ex Safra Prima 1982; ex Paluma 1978; ex
Medina 1972; ex Marchon Trader 1969

● 91220 **CARIGULF EXPRESS** Pa/Br (Lamont) 1960;
C; 1200; 70.03 × 4.59 (229.76 × 15.06); M (Mirrlees,
Bickerton & Day); 11.5; ex Mary D 1978; ex Toward
1976; ex Yewglen 1974; ex Tolsta 1971
Similar:
91222 **RANA 1** (Le) ex Rosethorn 1980; ex Yewkyle
1974; ex Laksa 1971
91223 **ADHAM 1** (Sy) ex Sabina 1980; ex Katerina
Pa; ex Bell Crusader 1976; ex Ajax 1971; ex Fidra
1969

91230 **NEDA** Cy/FRG (Sieghold) 1961; C; 1500;
74.68 × 5.65 (245.01 × 18.54); M (KHD); 12.5; ex
Max Sieghold 1973

91240 **PSATHI** Gr/De (B&W) 1954; C; 1600; 93.1 ×
5.35 (305.45 × 17.55); M (B&W); 13.5; ex Casciotis
1981; ex Fjallfoss 1977

91250 **STRAITS PRIDE** Sg/Sp (Cadagua) 1971; C;
1500/3000; 104.25 × —/6.53 (342 × —/21.42); M
(Deutz); 15; ex Dollart 1981; ex Ambrose 1976; ex
Dollart 1974
Probable sister:
91251 **RAJAH BROOKE** (Sg) ex Nahoon 1980; ex
Amasis 1974

★ 91260 **PAVLIN VINOGRADOV** Ru/Ru (Baltic)
1960; C; 4600; 121.77 × 7.06 (399.51 × 23.16); GT
(SIGMA/Alsthom); 14; See also **MEZENLES**—
M₂KMF

● 91270 **SOROLLA** Sp/Sp (UN de Levante) 1967; C;
5200; 124.21 × 6.66 (407.51 × 21.85); M (B&W); 13
Sister:
91271 **RIBERA** (Sp)
Similar:
91272 **PINAZO** (Sp)

91280 **GEM** Br/Ne (Nieuwe Noord) 1969; C; 1600;
92.72 × 5.19 (304.2 × 17.03); M (KHD); 12

91290 **ROSEMOUNT** Br/Br (Goole) 1967; C; 1600;
92 × 5.2 (301.84 × 17.06); M (Mirrlees); 11.5; ex
Pearl 1983; ex Somersbydyke 1979

91300 **SUND** Pa/FRG (Elsflether) 1967; C; 1600;
86.01 × 5.14 (282.19 × 16.86) M (KHD); 12.75; ex
Ostesund 1980; ex Bremersand 1973
Sisters:
91301 **SIGRID** (Pa) ex Wesersand
91302 **SARINE** (Li) ex Nordseesand 1977

● 91310 **ILEIGH** Mo/De (Frederikshavn) 1972; C; 500;
76.61 × 3.47 (251.35 × 11.38); M (Alpha-Diesel); 12;
ex Merc Caribia 1981; Starboard side superstructure
differs—see inset
Sisters:
91311 **DAKHLA** (Mo) ex Anglian Merchant 1981; ex
Merc Nordia 1977
91312 **LADY CONTINENTALE** (It) ex Merc Continental 1981
91313 **NIAGA XXI** (Ia) ex Merc Polaris 1979
91314 **NIAGA XXII** (Ia) ex Merc Aequator 1979
91315 **ORIENT** (De) ex Pep Orient 1982; ex Merc
Orientalis 1976
91316 **SLOT SCANDINAVIA** (No) ex Merc Scandinavia 1980
91318 **UDAFOSS** (Ic) ex Merc Africa 1974
Similar:
91319 **A.E.S.** (De)
91320 **ADRIATIC** (Cy) ex Peder Most 1980
91321 **BRITANNIA** (De)
91322 **CHARLOTTE S** (De)
91323 **MOGENS S** (De)
91324 **PATRICIA S** (De)

91330 **CHERRY MANIS** Sg/FRG (Brand) 1957; C;
1000; 69.47 × 4.22 (227.92 × 13.85); M (KHD); 12; ex
Singapore Meranti 1979; ex Arina Holwerda 1974; ex
Haseldorf 1970

91340 **RAMSLI** No/FRG (Hagelstein) 1957; C; 1000;
71.38 × 4.7 (234.19 × 15.42); M (KHD); 12; ex
Austvik 1980; ex Maria Althoff 1967

91350 **PILION** Cy/FRG (H. Peters) 1964; C; 1000;
71.63 × 4.93 (235 × 16.17); M (KHD); 11.25; ex
Christian Matthiesen 1978

91360 **BOUSTANY 1** Le/FRG (Lindenau) 1953; C;
1600; 78.64 × 4.66 (258 × 15.29); M (MAN); 11.5; ex
Kanielle 1 1982; ex Danielle 1980; ex Archangelos
1980; ex Brakersand 1972; ex Fossum 1961

91380 **SIERRA** Pa/FRG (Brand) 1959; C; 1000;
72.47 × 4.32 (237.76 × 14.17); M (MaK); 11; ex Lia
1979; ex Rotesand 1975

91390 **ANGELA** It/FRG (Elsflether) 1957; C; 1000;
70.52 × 4.73 (231.36 × 15.52); M (MaK); 12; ex
Contentia 1970
Sisters:
91391 **COSTAS G** (Cy) ex Kali 1980; ex Inanda 1972;
ex Bernhard Althoff 1959; ex Prudentia 1957
91392 **THEOSKEPASTI** (Gr) ex Regnitz 1971; ex
Fidentia 1965

91400 **ANNE OPEM** No/DDR ('Neptun') 1963; C;
500/1100; 75.24 × 3.6/5.19 (246.85 ×
11.81/17.03); M (KHD); 11.5; ex Siralyn 1975; ex
Havlyn 1973; ex Bari IV 1964
Sister:
91401 **MERIAM** (Eg) ex Sirapil 1981; ex Havpil 1973;
ex Bari II 1964

91410 **KEHDINGEN** FRG/FRG (Sietas) 1967; C;
500/1300; 75.34 × 3.71/5.55 (247.18 ×
12.17/18.21); M (KHD); 13
Similar:
91411 **STEFAN E** (Pa) ex Helga Wehr 1983
91412 **SUSAN** (Pa) ex Wilken 1981
91413 **STRILVANG** (No) ex Kreyvang 1981; ex Ann-
Carina 1980; ex Kunsten 1979; ex Cecilia 1972

91420 **PELIAS** Gr/De (Aarhus) 1967; C; 500/1200;
70.44 × 3.77/5.31 (231.1 × 12.37/17.42); M (Atlas-
MaK); 12.5; ex Disarfjell 1984; ex Lene Nielsen 1973

91430 **NIAGA XXV** Ia/De (Aarhus) 1969; C;
500/1200; 70.44 × 5.3/5.54 (231.1 ×
17.39/18.18); M (Atlas-MaK); 12.5; ex Dorthe Ty; ex
Balco 1975; ex Lotte Nielsen 1973

91440 **TRIANTAFILOS M** Cy/Ne (Pattje) 1970; C;
800/1600; 79.69 × 4.56/5.89 (261.45 ×
14.96/19.32); M (MWM); 13.5; ex Saba 1983; ex
Shipmair V 1978; ex Gaelic 1974; ex Hendrik Bos
1972
Sister:
91441 **ALIANORA** (It) ex Shipmair VI 1980; ex Gerd
1974; ex Gerd Bos 1973
Probable sister:
91442 **TIBESTI** (Gr) ex Safi; ex Irmgard Bos 1976

91450 **VICTORIA** Gr/FRG (M Jansen) 1970; C/Con;
1200/2800; 99.04 × 4.2/6.3 (324.93 ×
13.91/20.67); M (MWM); 14; ex Rabat 1980; ex Ino A
1974; ex Boston Express 1971; Launched as Ino
Similar:
91451 **CURRENT TRADER** (Br) ex Mercandian
Clipper 1980; ex Dwejra 1976; ex Ino F 1975
91452 **CURRENT EXPRESS** (Br) ex Mercandian
Express 1980; ex Caribic 1975; ex Kathe Bos 1973
91453 **TINHINAN** (Ag) ex Holmia 1975; ex Johannes
Bos 1973
91454 **HODNA** (Ag) ex Annetta 1973; ex Annette

Bos 1972

91460 **COLOMBO MARU** Pa/FRG (Sietas) 1970; C;
1700/3300; 100.56 × 5.47/6.76 (329.42 ×
17.94/22.17); M (KHD); 15.25; ex Colombo Venture
1982; ex Ashdod
Sister:
91461 **APUS** (Is)

91470 **ILHA DE SAO MIGUEL** Po/FRG (Rolandwerft) 1970; Con; 2900; 102.42 × 6.24 (336.02 ×
20.47); M (Atlas-MaK); —; ex Anja 1980; ex Cheshire
Challenge; ex Anja 1974; Launched as Norderfehn
Sister:
91471 **AL MANSOURA** (Qt) ex Pacific 1980

91480 **EDITH NIELSEN** De/De (Aalborg) 1967; C;
1600/2700; 94.11 × 5.08/6.62 (308.76 ×
16.67/21.72); M (B&W); 14.5

91490 **NIAGA XXIV** Ia/FRG (M Jansen) 1969; C;
700/1500; 75.49 × 4.22/6 (247.6 × 13.84/19.68);
M (KHD); 14; ex Bilbao; ex Inger 1973; ex Truro 1971;
Launched as Bele
Sister:
91491 **ELDVIK** (Ic) ex Heidi 1975; ex Tasso 1971

● 91500 **DRIANOVO** Bu/Sp (Euskalduna) 1962; C;
500/1100; 74.91 × 3.56/4.93 (245.77 ×
11.68/16.17); M(MAN); 12; ex Amethyst 1970; ex
Slitan 1966
Similar:
91501 **PUERTO DE HANGA ROA** (Ch) ex Puerto de
Amberes 1983
91502 **DIONISSIOS K** (Cy) ex Monte Balerdi 1982;
Launched as Monte Cuarto
91504 **HELLINORA** (Cy) ex Patricio 1977; ex Monte
Cinco 1977
91505 **TRIOS** (Pa) ex Kai Kavoos 1975; ex Eco Sol
1975; Launched as Skagatind
91506 **VIOLA** (Pa) ex Kai Ghobad 1980; ex Eco
Gabriela 1975
91507 **AGAETE** (Pa) ex Kai Khosrow 1980; ex Eco
Luisa 1975; Launched as Monte Uno

91510 **NAVI STAR** Le/FRG (Kroegerw.) 1959; C;
1500; 91.01 × 4.85 (298.59 × 15.91); M (MAN); 14;
ex Baltic Jet

★ 91520 **SUSAK** Ys/Br (Grangemouth) 1963; C;
1100/1700; 74.73 × 4.31/5.77 (245.18 ×
14.14/18.93); M (Mirrlees); 13.5; ex Palomares 1973
Sister:
91521 **PISANG PERAK** (Ia) ex Bonapart 1972; ex
Pelayo 1971
Similar:
★ 91522 **SRAKANE** (Ys) ex Pacheco 1972

91530 **CEDERBORG** Ne/No (Aukra) 1972; C; 1200;
77.17 × 4.76 (253.18 × 15.62); M (Atlas-MaK); 13; ex
Carebeka VII 1982; ex Nortrio 1974
Sister:
91531 **ATLANTIC RIVER** (Ne) ex Munte 1981; ex
Norimo 1974
Similar:
91532 **NIAGA XXXIII** (Ia) ex Maasplein 1981; ex
Norcato 1974

91540 **ASTOR** Pa/FRG (Brand) 1969; C;
1000/2000; 92.33 × 4.65/6.1 (302.92 ×
15.26/20.01); M (KHD); 15; ex Tegelersand 1981

91550 **BREEKANT** Ne/No (Sterkoder) 1972; C;
1600; 79.91 × 5.28 (262.17 × 17.32); ex Keizersgracht 1979; ex Mini Sun 1973
Sisters:
91551 **BREEKADE** (Ne) ex Mini Cloud 1978
91552 **CEBO MOON** (Gr) ex Mini Moon 1979
91553 **NABEEL** (Pa) ex Eerbeek 1981; ex Mini Sky
1974
91554 **MACORIX** (Do) ex Strombeek 1981; ex Mini
Star 1973

91560 **KRIS** Gr/FRG (Sieghold) 1957; C; 1000;
65.31 × 4.29 (214.27 × 14.07); M (MaK); 12; ex
Gardiki 1983; ex Titika D 1981; ex Star Lion 1980; ex
Skylab 1975; ex Yewarch 1974; ex Hinrich Sieghold
1960

★ 91570 **MIKULIC OREB** Ys/FRG (Elsflether) 1970;
C; 2000; 95.28 × 5.53 (312.6 × 18.14); M (Atlas-
MaK); 14.5; ex Baltrumersand
Sister:
★ 91571 **MARKO TASILO** (Ys) ex Borkumersand
1980
91572 **KALOS 1** (Pa) ex Mellumersand 1981

91580 **FAITH** Pa/Br (Ailsa) 1958; C; 1600; 78.64 ×
5.21 (258 × 17.09); M (KHD); 12; ex Amethyst 1980

91600 **TEXACO BOGOTA** No/Sw (Eriksbergs)
1960; Tk; 13600; 181.67 × 9.57 (596.03 × 31.38); M
(B&W); 14.5; Lengthened and converted 1968 (Eriksbergs)

91610 **STELLA PROCYON** Ne/Ne (Tille) 1978; TB;

706

2700; 83.62 × 6.61 (274.34 × 21.69); M (KHD); 11.75

91630 FIRETHORN Br/Ne (Pattje) 1967; C; 1000; 67.21 × 4.59 (220.51 × 15.06); M (Werkspoor); 12

91640 LILIAN S Pa/No (Stord) 1962; Tk; 3800; 114.28 × 6.54 (374.93 × 21.46); M (B&W); 13.25; ex *Wadhurst* 1982; ex *Saphir* 1970
Similar:
91641 BINTANG UTARA (Pa) ex *Caltex Sydney* 1975; ex *Widan* 1968

★**91650 FU SHUN CHENG** RC/FRG (Elsflether) 1969; C; 3400/5400; 117.35 × 6.68/7.06 (385.01 × 21.92/23.16); M(B+V); 17; ex *Jorg Kruger* 1981; ex *Caparnauti* 1975; ex *Jorg Kruger* 1974
Sister:
★**91651 PING XIANG CHENG** (RC) ex *Britta Kruger* 1977

91660 THOROLD Ca/Br (Hall, Russell) 1962; C; 5700; 125.05 × 7.58 (410.27 × 24.87); M (Sulzer); —; ex *Gosforth* 1972

91670 KRANTOR Gr/Ne (Amsterdamsche D) 1964; C; 1400/2300; 87.89 × —/6.31 (288.35 × —/20.7); M (Werkspoor); 13; ex *Astra* 1980; ex *Rahel* 1978
Sister:
91671 BRANT POINT (Br) ex *Oran* 1978; ex *Devora* 1978

★**91680 FRIMARO** Cu/Sp (U.N. de Levante) 1966; R; 1700; 87 × 5.77 (285.43 × 18.93); M (B&W); —; ex *Frimar* 1975

91690 OCEAN GLORY No 6 Pa/Br (H. Robb) 1958; C; 1400; 90.51 × 4.54 (296.95 × 14.9); M (Sulzer); —; ex *Ocean Glory* 1977; ex *Catanian* 1972

★**91700 SOFIA** Bu/Bu (G. Dimitrov) 1963; C; 2900/4400; 114.18 × 6.32/7.54 (374.61 × 20.73/24.74); M (MAN); 14
Sisters (Bu flag):
★**91701 PRESLAV**
★**91702 VELIKO TIRNOVO**

91710 IRAN SEDAGHAT Ir/Bu (G Dimitrov) 1971; C; 4500; 114.26 × 6.55 (374.37 × 21.49); M (MAN); 13.75; ex *Arya Rad* 1980; ex *Slevik* 1975
Sisters:
91711 IRAN SHAFAAT (Ir) ex *Arya Dad* 1980; ex *Wyvern* 1975
91712 REMADA (Tn) ex *Ontatio* 1974; ex *Sariba* 1973
91713 KOHENG (Pa) ex *Tauloto II*; ex *Safia* 1973
★**91714 YANG ZI JIANG 4** (RC) ex *Woolga* 1983; ex *Woolgar* 1982
★**91715 TAI SHAN** (RC) ex *Tai An* 1983
★**91716 TAI NING** (RC)
★**91717 TAI SHUN** (RC)
★**91718 BUDAPEST** (Hu)
★**91719 HUNGARIA** (Hu)

91730 TARABLOS Le/No (Langesunds) 1958; C; 2300/3700; 106.46 × 5.94/6.99 (349.28 × 19.49/22.93); M (B&W); 14.5; ex *Georgios A* 1982; ex *Kefallonia* 1981; ex *Havel*; ex *Ceara* 1964

91740 FALCON REEFER Pa/Fr (Rhin) 1961; R; 900/1400; 7.04 × 3.87/4.92 (252.76 × 12.7/16.14); M (Sulzer); 13; ex *Daniela* 1967

91750 STARMAN AUSTRALIA FRG/FRG (Luerssen) 1977; RoC/HL; 3500; 91.5 × 5.17 (300.2 × 16.96); TSM (MWM); 13.5; ex *Stahleck* 1981
Similar (US flag -US built (Peterson)):
91751 JOHN HENRY
91752 PAUL BUNYAN

91760 DEBORAH I Pa/Br (Cook, W & G) 1953; C/R; 1000; 65.11 × 3.98 (213.62 × 13.06); M (British Polar); 11; ex *Argyro*; ex *Avra* 1970; ex *Tern* 1964

★**91765 JAHORINA** Ys/FRG (Schlichting) 1969; C/HL; 1000; 78.52 × 4.98 (258 × 16.34); M (Atlas-MaK); 11; ex *Thor Scan* 1980; ex *Tipperary* 1974; Converted from cargo/container

●**91770 REEFER MERCHANT** Cy/FRG (Schlichting) 1967; R; 900/1700; 88.7 × 4.13/5.21 (291.01 × 13.55/17.09); M (Atlas-MaK); 16; ex *Fahrmannsand* 1974
Sisters:
91771 LUHESAND (Cy)
★**91772 HARMATTAN** (Pd) ex *Pagensand* 1972

91780 ATLANTIC ISLE Gr/Sp (Duro Felguera) 1971; C; 800/1400; 77.4 × 4.07/5.32 (259.94 ×13.35/17.45); M(Deutz); —; ex *Wickenburgh* 1979; ex *Atlan Turquesa* 1975
Sisters (Sp flag):
91781 AL BIRUNI ex *Atlan Zafiro*
91782 AL IDRISI ex *Atlan Diamante* 1975

★**91790 PRESIDENTE MACIAS NGUEMA** Gn/Ja (Shikoku) 1973; PC; 3300; 100.51 × 5.68 (329.76 ×

18.64); M (B&W); 14; ex *Hai Ou*

91800 NYMIT Li/Ja (Miho) 1970; RoC; 4500; 87.31 × — (286.45 × —); TSM (Daihatsu); 11.5; ex *Cosmos Bellatrix* 1977; ex *Cosmos No 2* 1975

91810 PALLAS FRG/FRG (Nobiskrug) 1971; C; 2800/5000; 125.02 × 6.52/7.62 (410.17 × 21.39/25); M (Atlas-MaK); 16.5
Possible sister:
91811 NEPTUN (FRG)

●**91820 CARIGULF EXPRESS** Pa/Br (Lamont) 1960; C; 1200; 71.03 × 4.59 (229.76 × 15.06); M (Mirrlees, Bickerton & Day); 11.5; ex *Mary D* 1978; ex *Toward* 1976; ex *Yewglen* 1974; ex *Tolsta* 1971
Similar:
91822 RANA 1(Le) ex *Rosethorn* 1980; ex *Yewkyle* 1974; ex *Laksa* 1971
91823 ADHAM 1 (Sy) ex *Sabina* 1980; ex *Katerina Pa* 1979; ex *Bell Crusader* 1976; ex *Ajax* 1971; ex *Fidra* 1969

●**91830 MUHIEDDINE** Le/Ne (E J Smit) 1968; C; 700/1500; 77.55 × 4.31/5.74 (254.43 × 4.14/18.83); M (Atlas-MaK); 12; ex *Adine* 1981; ex *Nina Lonborg* 1976; ex *Trongate* 1973; ex *Holland Park* 1971
Sisters:
91831 GHADAMES (Gr) ex *Eric*; ex *Passaat Santos* 1977; ex *Shipmair III* 1976; ex *Cairnventure* 1974
91832 PELLINI (Gr) ex *Harco* 1980; ex *Corato* 1978;
91834 ALEXANDRA 1 (Cy) ex *Aruba* 1983; ex *Passaat Santos* 1980; ex *Passaat Bonaire* 1978; ex *Shipmair IV* 1976; ex *Vida* 1974; ex *Voreda* 1973
91835 CELTIC ENDEAVOUR (Br) ex *Embassage* 1978
91836 OUADAN (Gr) ex *Calandria*
91837 NIKOLAOS M II (Cy) ex *Virgilia* 1983; ex *Camarina* 1981
91839 LA PALMA (Le) ex *Phoenicia* 1982; ex *Sudri* 1977; ex *Isborg* 1975; ex *Philip Lonborg* 1974; ex *Hyde Park* 1973
91840 LADY NINA (Cy) ex *Lustar* 1982; ex *Saltersgate* 1977
Similar:
91841 BORMLA (Ma) ex *Tudor Prince* 1975; ex *Lise Nielsen* 1974
91842 NIAGA XXXIV (Ia) ex *Multon* 1980; ex *Balton* 1978; ex *Gudrun Danielsen* 1975
91843 VAGERO (It) ex *White Crest*; ex *British Prince* 1973; ex *White Crest* 1972
91844 LADY SARAH (Pa) ex *Bretwalda*; ex *Nordic Prince* 1978; ex *Bretwalda* 1976
91845 ADARA (Ne) ex *Saxon Prince* 1976; ex *Cairntrader* 1976; ex *Saxon Prince* 1975; Launched as *Cairntrader*
91846 ASUNCION (Py) ex *Situla* 1981; ex *Jytte Danielsen* 1976
Similar (larger):
91847 CAIRNROVER (Br)
91848 BENEDETTO SCOTTO (It) ex *Mountpark* 1983; ex *Cairnranger* 1976
91849 DOMENICO SCOTTO (It) ex *Aiden* 1981; ex *Jackie Silvana* 1980; ex *Thea Danielsen* 1978
Similar (Sp built - Construcciones SA):
91850 LADY SERENA (Pa) ex *Narya* 1978

91860 SPYROS G II Cy/Ne (E J Smit) 1966; C; 600/1400; 83.5 × 3.65/4.3 (273.95 × 11.98/14.12); M (Werkspoor); 14.25; ex *Armada Medliner* 1981; ex *Spyros G II*; ex *Oostereems* 1979; ex *Ionian* 1977; ex *Oostereems* 1972; ex *Ionian* 1971

91870 DON ALEJO Co/No (Framnaes) 1966; C; 3900; 111.36 × 6.33 (365 × 20.77); M (Sulzer); 13; ex *Fossum* 1977

91880 GUIA Pa/FRG (Bremer V) 1960; C; 8400; 138.08 × 8.85 (453.02 × 29.04); M (MAN); 14.5; ex *Baie Comeau* 1978

91890 APICO Gr/Ja (Mitsubishi N) 1964; C; 9700; 149.61 × 9.55 (490.85 × 31.33); M (MAN); 15; ex *Loulwa Al Khalifa*; ex *Pavlina* 1970; ex *Araneta Ma—Ao* 1974

★**91910 KAMCHATSKIE GORY** Ru/Sw (Lindholmens) 1964; FC; 9700; 153.5 × 7.47 (503.61 × 24.51); M (Gotaverken); 17
Sisters (Ru flag):
★**91911 SAYANSKIE GORY**
★**91912 SAKHALINSKIE GORY**

91920 MEGHNA In/Ja (Ujina) 1969; C; 2000; 89.62 × 5.72 (294 × 18.77); M (Akasaka); 12.25; ex *Megna* 1978; ex *Nikkai Maru* 1976
Possible sister:
91921 KWANG TA No 2 (Tw) ex *Tung Fau* 1981
Probable sisters:
91922 SEVEN LOG MASTER (Pi) ex *Asia Pacific* 1976; ex *Shinkyo Maru* 1973
91924 WILCON II (Pi) ex *General Santos City* 1979; ex *Kyofuku Maru* 1978

★**91927 SOO GEUN HO** RK/Ja (Shin Naniwa) 1970; C; 2000; 88.02 × 5.59 (289 × 18.34); M (Akasaka); 13; ex *Yamafuji Maru* 1976
Possible sister:
91928 HWAPYUNG ACE (Ko) ex *Suehirozan Maru* 1974

●**91970 SHANNON** Cy/FRG (Hitzler) 1966; C; 1000; 71.61 × 4.98 (234.94 × 16.34); M (Atlas-MaK); 11.5; ex *Bulk Navigator* 1983; ex *Stockhorn* 1981; ex *Uthoern* 1976; ex *Uthorn* 1972

91980 PIA DANIELSEN De/Ne (Bodewes B V) 1976; C; 1000; 79.48 × 4.83 (260.76 × 15.85); M (Atlas-MaK); 12.25
Similar:
91981 HERMAN BODEWES (Ne)
91982 KALOUM (De) ex *Gudrun Danielsen* 1982
91983 JYTTE DANIELSEN (De)
91984 GRETE DANIELSEN (De)

91990 AL JAMAL Le/FRG (Lindenau) 1961; C/WT; 1100; 75.65 × 4.27 (248.2 × 14.01); M (MAN); —; ex *Jean Dark* 1981; ex *Jean d'Arc*; ex *Nazih* 1979; ex *Barakat* 1979; ex *Palacio* 1977

92000 MARIA PIA ESSE It/FRG (Lindenau) 1959; C; 2700; 91.52 × 6.03 (300.26 × 19.78); M (MAN); 12; ex *Irenes Luck* 1979; ex *Piraeus E* 1971; ex *Ioannina* 1970; ex *Theodoros Kyriakos* 1968; ex *President Pierre Angot* 1968; ex *Stella Orion* 1962

92010 BUILDER III Sg/FRG (Lindenau) 1960; C; 2000; 84.69 × 5.6 (277.85 × 18.37); M (MAN); 12; ex *Johnson Hale* 1979; ex *Siragard* 1974; ex *Amron* 1973; ex *Fossheim* 1966

★**92020 BAHIA DE NIPE** Cu/US (Consolidated Steel) 1945; C; 3000; 98.73 × 7.14 (323.92 × 23.43); M (Nordberg); 10.5; ex *Coastal Challenger* 1948; 'C1—M—AV3' type
Sister:
★**92021 BAHIA DE MARIEL** (Cu) ex *Half Hitch* 1948

★**92030 'VOLGONEFT'** type Ru/Ru-Bu (G Dimitrov-/Volgograd) 1966-69; Tk; 3500; 128.59 × 3.58 (435 × 11.75); TSM (Liebknecht); 10.5; This drawing represents the earlier vessels of this type. For later vessels with prefix 'VOLGONEFT' under M_2KFK. Names have the prefix 'VOLGONEFT' and a number. Approx. 27 in the whole group

92080 MULTI SERVICE 300 Pa/Ne (Groot & VV) 1956-69; C/HL/Catamaran; 1000; 56.65 × 3.65 (185.86 × 11.98); TSM ('De Industrie'); —; ex *Gloria Siderum* 1983; Formed by joining two coasters 1969 (Groot & VV); Port Hull ex *Hada II*; Starboard Hull ex *Hermes*

92090 KLAREDON Br/DDR ('Neptun') 1969; C; 3000; 88.02 × 5.85 (338 × 19.19); M (Atlas-MaK); 13.5; ex *Laredo* 1979; ex *Hansa Nord* 1979
Similar:
92091 RIO BRAVO (Br) ex *Hansa Trade* 1980
92092 NAZIE BEAUTY (UAE) ex *Hanseat* 1980
92093 ANATOLIA (Pa) ex *Larch* 1980; ex *Jowood* 1979
92094 HVALVIK (Ic) ex *Mambo* 1975; ex *Samba* 1972
92095 ELISABETH (Cy) ex *Eskdalegate* 1977; ex *Fredericksgate* 1974; ex *Bruni* 1974

92110 RIO CARIBE Li/No (Kaldnes) 1963; B; 7400; 139.96 × 7.75 (459.19 × 25.43); M (Stork); 15; ex *Bessegen* 1983
Sister:
92111 RIO CHICO (Li) ex *Rondeggen* 1983

★**92150 VOSTOCK** Ru/Ru (Admiralteiskiy) 1971; FF; 26400; 224.57 × 10.02 (736.78 × 32.87); TST (Kirov); 19

★**92160 EMBA** Ru/Fi (Wartsila) 1980; Cbl; 1900; 75.9 × 3 (249 × 9.84); TSD-E (Wartsila); approx 11
Sisters:
★**92161 NEPRYADVA** (Ru)
★**92162 SETUN** (Ru)

92170 DEL MUNDO US/US (Ingalls SB) 1968; C; 7100/10400; 159.11 × —/9.47 (522.01 × —/31.07); T (GEC); 18.5; ex *Delta Argentina* 1980
Sisters (US flag):
92171 DEL CAMPO ex *Delta Paraguay* 1980
92172 DEL MONTE ex *Delta Brasil* 1980
92173 DEL VIENTO ex *Delta Mexico* 1980
92174 DEL VALLE ex *Delta Uruguay* 1980

92180 HAPPY MAMMOTH Ne/Ne ('De Merwede') 1967/74/78; Dk/Bg/HL; 3800; 129.78 × 5.95 (428.8 × 19.51); TrSM (Atlas-MaK); 12.5; ex *Docklift 2* 1981; ex *Lady Jane* 1974; Rebuilt from Ro/Ro ship 1974; Lengthened 1978 (Boele's Sch); Stern ramp

92190 TREUENBELS Gr/FRG (Stuelcken) 1960; C/HL; 6800/9300; 139.48 × 8.57/9.19 (457.61 ×

28.12/30.15); M (MAN); 14.5; ex *Treuenfels* 1981

★ **92200 DADE** RC/FRG (A G 'Weser') 1962; C/HL; 6900/9600; 152.25 × 8.29/9.35 (499.51 × 27.2/30.68); M (MAN); 18.5; ex *Werdenfels* 1973; Cranes move along main deck
Sisters (RC flag):
★ **92201 DA NING** ex *Wachtfels* 1972
★ **92202 DA SHI QIAO** ex *Wallenfels* 1978
★ **92203 DA JIN CHUAN** ex *Wildenfels* 1978
★ **92204 DA CHANG ZHEN** ex *Wasserfels* 1978

92210 H W BATES Pa/De (B&W) 1948/67; DS; 18400; 194.8 × 10.61 (639.1 × 34.8); TSM (B&W); —; ex *Sonda 2* 1972; ex *Drillship* 1970; ex *Star I* 1970; ex *Drillship* 1969; ex *Thorshovdi* 1967; Converted from whale factory 1967 (Nylands)

92220 PRESIDENT Pa/Ja (Hitachi) 1977; V; 9200; 180.02 × 7.5 (590.62 × 24.61); M (B&W); 18; Side doors
Sister:
92221 NISSAN SILVIA (Pa)
Similar (goalpost radar mast):
92222 YOUNG SPLENDOR (Li)

★ **92230 DATONG** RC/FRG (Stuelcken) 1959; C/HL; 6800/9200; 145 × 8.57/9 (475.7 × 28.1/29.5); M (MAN); 14.5; ex *Tannenfels* 1971
Sisters (RC flag):
★ **92231 DAAN** ex *Spitzfels* 1972
★ **92232 DAPU** ex *North Sea* 1971; ex *Trautenfels* 1971
★ **92233 DAMING** ex *Schwarzenfels* 1971

★ **92240 DADE** RC/FRG (A G 'Weser') 1962; C/HL; 6900/9600; 152.25 × 8.29/9.35 (499.51 × 27.2/30.68); M (MAN); 18.5; ex *Werdenfels* 1973; Cranes move along main deck
Sisters (RC flag):
★ **92241 DA NING** ex *Wachtfels* 1972
★ **92242 DA SHI QIAO** ex *Wallenfels* 1978
★ **92243 DA JIN CHUAN** ex *Wildenfels* 1978
★ **92244 DA CHANG ZHEN** ex *Wasserfels* 1978

92247 CHIJIN MARU Ja/Ja (Tsuneishi) 1982; RoVC; 11900; 176.00 × 8.22 (577 × 26.97); M (B&W); 18.5; 2 side door/ramps (1 port, 1 starboard); Stern quarter ramp (starboard)
Sister:
92248 SHOJIN MARU (Ja)
Possible sister:
92249 ORCHID ACE (Ja)

92260 KILDARE Li/Hong Kong (Elling) 1973; Sply-/Con; 1200; 58.5 × 3.96 (191.9 × 12.9); TSM (Yanmar); —

92270 CONDOCK 1 FRG/FRG (Nobiskrug) 1979; Dk/Con/RoC; 1000; 92.4 × 4.58 (303.15 × 15.03); TSM (Atlas-MaK); 12
Sister:
92271 CONDOCK II (FRG)

92280 DANWOOD ICE De/Fr (Ch. de France) 1959/74; DS; 13700; 172.5 × 10.05 (565.9 × 32.9); M (Doxford); 16.25; ex *Jean Schneider*; Converted from ore carrier 1974 (Hapag-Lloyd)

● **92290 SLOMAN RANGER** FRG/FRG (Howaldts DW) 1979; RoC/Con; 1000; 92.07 × 3.65 (302 × 11.98); TSM (KHD); 12.5; Stern ramp
Sisters (FRG flag):
92291 SLOMAN RECORD
92292 SLOMAN RIDER
92293 SLOMAN ROVER
92294 TILIA ex *Sloman Royal* 1982; Launched as *Tilia*
92295 SLOMAN RUNNER
92295/1 SLOMAN REGENT
Similar:
92296 ADELE J (FRG)
92297 BANGUI (Cy)
92298 HEINRICH S (FRG) ex *Paoua* 1979
92299 HEINRICH HUSMANN (FRG)
92300 PETRA SCHEU
92301 VILLE DE SYRTE (FRG) ex *Obotrita* 1981
92302 SLOMAN ROYAL (FRG)
Similar (lower superstructure-Bz built (CCN)):
92303 AMARAGY (Bz)

● **92305 NORLANDIA** FRG/FRG (Rickmers) 1983; RoC/Con; 1300; 105.50 × 4.56 (346 × 14.96); M (Wichmann); —; 'RW 29' type
Sister:
92306 HANS BEHRENS (FRG)

92310 NEDDRILL 1 Ne/Ne (Giessen-De Noord) 1963/76; DS; 12400; 160.1 × 9.2 (525.2 × 30.18); M (Stork); 14.5; ex *Goeree* 1976; Converted Ore Carrier 1976 (Mitsubishi HI)
Sister:
92311 NEDDRILL 2 (Ne) ex *Schouwen* 1977

92320 GLOMAR EXPLORER US/US (Sun SB)

1973; DS/Sal/M; 27500; 188.58 × 11.63 (618.7 × 38.15); TSD-E (Nordberg); 12; ex *Hughes Glomar Explorer* 1978

92330 PORSOY No/No (Fosen) 1977; Pal/Con; 500; 69.6 × 4.6 (228.3 × 14.7); M (Normo); 14; Side doors
Similar:
92331 FJELL (FRG)
92332 FJORD (No)

92350 SASSARI 1 It/No (Eides) 1970; RoC/Con; 400; 67.95 × 3.01 (222.9 × 9.87); M (Atlas-MaK); 10; ex *Floriana* 1974; ex *Channelbridge I* 1974; ex *Malta Cross* 1972; Stern door/ramp. Bow door

● **92360 SLOMAN RANGER** FRG/FRG (Howaldts DW) 1979; RoC/Con; 1000; 92.07 × 3.65 (302 × 11.98); TSM (KHD); 12.5; Stern ramp
Sisters (FRG flag):
92361 SLOMAN RECORD
92362 SLOMAN RIDER
92363 SLOMAN ROVER
92364 TILIA ex *Sloman Royal* 1982; Launched as *Tilia*
92365 SLOMAN RUNNER
92366 SLOMAN REGENT
Similar (lower superstructure-Bz built (CCN)):
92367 AMARAGY (Bz)

● ★ **92380 VLADIVOSTOK** Ru/FRG (Kieler H) 1962; FF/WF; 17100; 181.9 × 8.89 (596.7 × 29.16); M(B&W); 14
Sister:
★ **92381 DALNIY VOSTOK** (Ru)

92400 IRIS Is/Rm (Galatz) 1973; RoC; 8200; 128.33 × 6.58 (421 × 21.5); TSM (Pielstick); —; Stern door
Sister:
92401 NARCIS (Is)

92410 INAGUA LIGHT Pa/US (Levingston) 1970; RoC/LC; 800; 81.51 × 3.49 (267.4 × 11.45); TrS M (Caterpillar); 12; Bow doors
Sisters (Pa flag):
92411 INAGUA BEACH
92412 INAGUA SOUND
92412/1 INAGUA TRADER II
Possible sisters:
92413 INAGUA BAY
92414 INAGUA SURF

92420 SASSARI 1 It/No (Eides) 1970; RoC/Con; 400; 67.95 × 3.01 (222.9 × 9.87); M (Atlas-MaK); 10; ex *Floriana* 1974; ex *Channelbridge I* 1974; ex *Malta Cross* 1972; Stern door/ramp. Bow door

92430 KILDARE Li/Hong Kong (Elling) 1973; Sply-/Con; 1200; 58.5 × 3.96 (191.9 × 12.9); TSM (Yanmar); —

★ **92435 KOSMONAUT YURIY GAGARIN** Ru/Ru (Baltic) 1971; MTV; 32300; 231.71 × 10.00 (760 × 32.81); T (Kirov); 17.75

92440 CONDOCK I FRG/FRG (Nobiskrug) 1979; Dk/Con/RoC; 1000; 92.4 × 4.58 (303.15 × 15.03); TSM (Atlas-MaK); 12
Sister:
92441 CONDOCK II (FRG)

92450 DANWOOD ICE De/Fr (Ch. de France) 1959/74; DS; 13700; 172.5 × 10.05 (565.9 × 32.9); M (Doxford); 16.25; ex *Jean Schneider*; Converted from Ore Carrier 1974 (Hapag-Lloyd)

92455 SUPER SERVANT 3 Ne/Ja (Oshima Z) 1982; RoC/HL; 10100; 139.91 × 6.26 (459 × 20.54); TSM (Stork-Werkspoor); 13; Semi-submersible—broken line indicates maximum extent of immersion
Sister (builder—Sumitomo):
92456 SUPER SERVANT 4 (Ne)

92460 DANSBORG Sg/No (Bergens) 1962/76; LS; 8600; 169.73 × 6.97 (556.8 × 31.7); M (B&W); 15.5; ex *Team Dansborg* 1975; ex *Team Vega* 1973; ex *Vega* 1970; Converted tanker 1976 (Keppel Shipyard)

92470 UNION ROTORUA NZ/Au (Whyalla) 1976; RoC; 13000/24000; 203.21 × 8.04/9.53 (666.6 × 26.3/31.2); TSGT (GEC); 19; Bow ramp/Stern door
Sister:
92471 UNION ROTOITI (NZ)

92490 VESTA FRG/FRG (Sterkrade) 1979; Incinerator ship; 1000; 71.8 × 4.3 (235.56 × 14.11); M (MWM); 11

92500 RIGOLETTO Sw/Ja (Hitachi) 1977; RoVC; 17500; 190.02 × 8.5 (623.4 × 27.8); M (Sulzer); 18.25;
Sister:
92501 TRAVIATA (Sw)

92510 DANSBORG Sg/No (Bergens) 1962/76; LS; 8600; 169.73 × 6.97 (556.8 × 31.7); M (B&W); 15.5; ex *Team Dansborg* 1975; ex *Team Vega* 1973; ex

---

Vega 1970; Converted tanker 1976 (Keppel Shipyard)

92520 PIA ANGELA Pi/Ja (Hakodate) 1961; ST; 1500; 79.46 × 5.61 (260.6 × 18.4); M (Mitsubishi); 12.5; ex *Akebono Maru No 51* 1977
Similar:
92522 AKEBONO MARU No 50 (Ja)
92523 AKEBONO MARU No 53 (Ja)

92530 UNION ROTORUA NZ/Au (Whyalla) 1976; RoC; 13000/24000; 203.21 × 8.04/9.53 (666.6 × 26.3/31.2); TSGT (GEC); 19; Bow ramp/Stern door
Sister:
92531 UNION ROTOITI (NZ)

92540 GAE CHEOG Ko/Ne (Wilton-Fije) 1955/67; FF; 23800; 206.51 × 10.73 (677.5 × 35.2); TSM (MAN); 14.5; *Gae Cheog Ho No 2*; ex *Yu Shin* 1979; ex *Willem Barendsz* 1973; Converted from whale-oil factory ship 1967

92550 PELTO SEAHORSE US/US (Halter) 1968; Con; 400; 50.3 × 3.07 (165 × 10.07); M (Stork); 11.5; ex *Rio Haina* 1980; May now be converted to an ORSV

92560 HAMANA Ja/Ja (Uraga HI) 1962; RT/FA; 7600; Dspl; 128.1 × 6.3 (420 × 20.5); M(—); 16

92570 PRINCE MARU No 7 Ja/Ja (Mitsubishi HI) 1973; RoVC; 8500; 169.12 × 7.21 (554.8 × 23.6); M (MAN); 17

92590 PETER RICKMERS Sg/FRG (Rickmers) 1962; C/HL; 9600; 159.7 × 9.37 (523.9 × 30.74); M (MAN); 17

92600 WICHITA US/US (General Dynamics) 1969; RT/FA; 37400 Dspl; 206.9 × 10.2 (659 × 33.3); TST (GEC); 20; Helicopter deck & two helicopters
Sisters (US flag):
92601 KALAMAZOO
92602 KANSAS CITY
92603 MILWAUKEE
92604 ROANOKE
92605 SAVANNAH
92606 WABASH

92620 KOYO MARU No 2 Ja/Ja (Fujinagata) 1967; ST; 2900; 95.51 × 6 (313.3 × 19.6); M (B&W); 13.5
Sister (Ja flag):
92621 TAKACHIHO MARU
Similar (Ja Flag):
92622 ASO MARU
92623 KIRISHIMA MARU

92630 CHALLWA V Pe/Ja (Kawasaki D) 1961; FF; 8000; 153.02 × 8.29 (502.03 × 27.19); M (MAN); 14; ex *Meisei Maru* 1980

★ **92640 LIAO YING** RC/Ja (NKK) 1960; C; 8000; 147.53 × 7.93 (484.02 × 26.01); M (B&W); 14.25; ex *Hai Ying 8001* 1983; ex *Ohtsu Maru* 1978

92645 TOYOFUJI No 7 Ja/Ja (Naikai) 1981; RoVC; 13800; 190.08 × 8.02 (624 × 26.31); M (B&W); 18; 1 side ramp (port); 1 stern door/ramp (port)

● **92650 DYVI SKAGERAK** No/Ne (P. Smit) 1973; RoVC; 7300; 187.51×8.01 (615.19×26.27); M(Sulzer); 18; ex *Hual Skagerak* 1983; ex *Dyvi Skagerak*; Side doors
Sisters (No flag):
92651 DYVI KATTEGAT
92652 TARGET ex *Hoegh Target* 1982; ex *Dyvi Adriatic* 1975
92653 HOEGH TRIGGER
Similar (tall pipes from funnel):
92654 NOPAL SEL (No)

92660 PVT. LEONARD C. BROSTROM US/US (—) 1943; C/FA; 13900 dwt; 158.5 × 10.1 (520 × 33); T (—); 15.8; ex *Marine Eagle*; Modified 'C-4' type

92690 TRUCK TRADER Gr/No (Trosvik) 1971; RoC; 1600; 106 × 4.94 (347.76 × 16.2); TSM (Normo); 17; ex *Anderida* 1981; Bow, stern and side doors

● **92700 STARMAN AFRICA** FRG/FRG (M. Jansen) 1977; RoC/HL; 2800; 93.53 × 64.65 (306.85 × 15.25); TSM (KHD); 12; Stern and side ramp
Sister:
92701 STARMAN ANGLIA (Br)

92710 BEAGLE Ch/US (Cargill) 1944; Tk/FA; 4200 Dspl; 94.8 × 4.9 (310 × 16); TSD-E (—); 14; ex *USS Genesee*; 'PATAPSCO' class
Sisters:
92711 TUMACO (Co) ex *USS Chewaucan*
92712 ARETHOUSA (Gr) ex *USS Natchaug*
92713 ARIADNI (Gr) ex *USS Tombigbee*
92714 CHANG PEI (Tw) ex *USS Pecatonica*
92715 LUNG CHUAN (Tw) ex *HMNZ Endeavour*; ex *USS Namakagon*
92716 HSIN LUNG (Tw) ex *USS Elkhorn*

92730 DON CARLOS Sw/Fi (Wartsila) 1976; V;

14500; 202.62 × 8.48 (664.76 × 27.82); M (Sulzer); 19; Side doors
Sister:
92731 DON JUAN (Sw)

92740 MARI-LIFT Pa/Ne (Duijvendijk's) 1969/75; RoC/HL; 700; 92 × 2.86 (301.83 × 9.38); TSM (Caterpillar); 13; ex *Mariaeck* 1981; Bow & stern doors; Lengthened 1975

92750 DONG BANG No 71 Ko/Ja (Niigata) 1972; ST; 1500; 80.75 × 5.2 (264.92 × 17.06); M (Niigata); 14

★ **92780 CHIL BO SAN** RK/Ne (Verolme SH) 1969; FF; 10200; 138 × 6.81 (452.7 × 22.34); M (MAN); 15
Sister:
★ **92781 KEUM GANG SAN** (RK)

★ **92782 MAR OCEANO** Cu/Sp (Construcciones SA) 1968; SS; 2400; 106.00 × 5.50 (348 × 18.04); M (Deutz); 15.5; ex *Pescafria Cuarto* 1970; 'ACSA 95' type
Sisters (some built by Barreras):
★ **92783 MAR CARIBE** (Cu); Launched as *Arcos*
92784 ARACENA (Ar)
92785 ARCOS (Ar)
92786 MATACO (Ar) ex *Gelmirez* 1978
92787 PATAGON (Ar) ex *Gondoma* 1978
92788 RAS EL BAR (Eg)
92789 BALTIM (Eg)
Similar (superstructure differs):
92789/1 MAR DE VIGO (Sp); Launched as *Mar de Espana*

92790 GOLIATH Pa/Br (Lamont) 1964/70/73; RoC/HL; 1600; 89.74 × 4.5 (294.42 × 14.76); TSM ('Bolnes'); —; ex *Paclog Goliath* 1982; ex *Happy Pioneer* 1982; ex *Harbo* 1973; ex *Sir Joseph Rawlinson* 1970; Converted sludge—carrier 1970; Converted cargo 1973

92800 HAPPY RIDER Ne/Ne (Arnhemsche/Stami) 1976; RoC/HL; 1600; 81.82 × 5.55 (268.43 × 18.2); TSM (Stork-Werkspoor); 12; Stern door
Sister:
92801 DOCK EXPRESS TEXAS (Ne) ex *Happy Runner* 1983

92810 ACADIA FOREST Li/Ja (Sumitomo) 1969; Bg/Con; 37000; 261.42 × 12.12 (857.67 × 39.76); M (Sulzer); 19; 'LASH' type
Sister:
92811 ATLANTIC FOREST (Li)

92820 OCEAN BUILDER 1 Li/Br (Fairfield SB) —Ne; 1957/75; PLC/CS; 11900; 194.95 × 10.95 (639.59 × 35.92); M (Stork-Werkspoor); —; ex *Santos* 1975; ex *Cuyahoga* 1972; Converted from Ore/Oil & widened 1975 (Boele's Sch.)

92830 ORCA Pa/Sw (Kockums) —Ne 1954/72; PLC/CS; 9500; 181.62 × 10.03 (595.86 × 32.9); M (Stork-Werkspoor); 15; ex *Soya-Atlantic* 1972; Converted from Ore/Oil and widened 1972 (Boele's Sch)

92840 SEDCO 445 Li/Ja (Mitsui) 1971; DS; 6700; 136.05 × 7.61 (446.35 × 24.96); TSD-E; 14
Similar (Li flag):
92841 SEDCO 471
92842 SEDCO 472

92850 DEL MUNDO US/US (Ingalls SB) 1968; C; 7100/10400; 159.11 × —/9.47 (522.01 × —/31.07) T (GEC); 18.5; ex *Delta Argentina* 1980
Sisters (US flag):
92851 DEL CAMPO ex *Delta Paraguay* 1980
92852 DEL MONTE ex *Delta Brasil* 1980
92853 DEL VIENTO ex *Delta Mexico* 1980
92854 DEL VALLE ex *Delta Uruguay* 1980

92860 DEL ORO US/US (Avondale) 1961; C; 7100/9800; 154.31 × —/9.48 (506.26 × —/31.1); T (Westinghouse); 18
Sisters (US flag):
92861 DEL RIO
92862 DEL SOL

92870 HAIDA BRAVE Ca/Ca (Yarrows Ltd) 1979; Log carrier; 10000 dwt; 121.5 × 5.82 (398.5 × 19.1); TSM (General Motors); 14

92880 BEN OCEAN LANCER Br/Br (Scotts SB) 1977; DS; 10800; 153.68 × 8 (504.19 × 26.2); TSD-E (SACM); 13
Similar:
92881 CANMAR EXPLORER III (Ca) ex *Havdrill* 1976
92882 PELERIN (No)
92883 PETREL (Be)
92884 PELICAN (Fr)
92885 POLLY BRISTOL (Br)
★ **92886 VALENTIN SHASKIN** (Ru)
★ **92887 VIKTOR MURAVLENKO** (Ru)
★ **92888 MIKHAIL MIRCHINK** (Ru)

92890 NOPAL VERDE Li/Pd (Gdanska) 1972/75; RoVC; 14200; 190.58 × 9.93 (625.26 × 32.57); M (Sulzer); 19.5; ex *Joana* 1973; Lengthened 1975; Converted general cargo 1975 ('3 Maj'); Side doors-/ramps
Sister:
92891 NOPAL BRANCO (No) ex *Amalia* 1973

92900 MERCED II FRG/FRG (Schlichting) 1978; C/Con/RoC; 7100; 124 × 8.2 (406.8 × 26.9); TSM (Atlas-MaK); 16.35; ex *Neugraben* 1982; ex *Merzario Emilio*; ex *Neugraben*; Stern ramp; Funnel on port side only
Sister:
92901 CAMINO II (FRG) ex *Uta-Sabine* 1982; ex *Merzario Lombardia*; ex *Uta-Sabine*

92910 FINNROSE Fi/Sw (Oskarshamns) 1980; RoC/Con; 13400; 194.11 × 8.4 (636.84 × 27.56); TSM (Sulzer); 19.2; stern ramps
Sister:
92911 FINNHAWK (Fi)

92920 ASPEN Sw/Ne (van der Werf) 1975; C; 3000; 88.02 × 6.67 (288.77 × 21.88); M (Normo); 12; Wood pulp carrier

92930 EMERALD Sh/Br (Atlantic SB) 1956; C; 2200; 79 × 5.04 (269.18 × 16.53); TSM (Blackstone); 8.5; ex *Lachinedoc* 1975

92932 AMERICAN EAGLE US/Sw (Kockums) 1981; RoC; 15600; 194.01 × 9.22 (637 × 30.25); TSM (Sulzer); 19.75; ex *Zenit Eagle* 1983; ex *Finneagle* 1983; 2 stern door/ramps
Sisters:
92933 ZENIT CLIPPER (Sw) ex *Finnclipper* 1983
92934 ZENIT EXPRESS (Sw) ex *Kuwait Express* 1983

92936 RAGNA GORTHON Sw/Sw (Finnboda/ Marstrands) 1979; RoC/C; 4100; 119.89 × 5.97 (393 × 19.59); M (MaK); 14.5; Stern door/ramp; Fwd section built by Marstrands, aft section built by Finnboda
Sisters:
92937 LOVISA GORTHON (Sw)
92938 STIG GORTHON (Sw)

92940 SAIPEM DUE It/It (Italcantieri) 1972; DS; 8500; 131.58 × 6.99 (431.69 × 22.93); TSD-E (Pielstick); 13.25

● **92950 ARABELLA** Li/Hong Kong (Highfield) 1975; C/Con; 1600; 76.23 × 3.83 (250.09 × 12.56); TSM (KHD); 11; ex *Deckship Arabella* 1978; Stern ramp; 'Deckship' type
Sisters:
92951 CARINIA (Sg) ex *Unicon* 1982; ex *Ghazi* 1980; ex *Carinia*
92952 SAN JUAN (Li) ex *Beulah* 1981; ex *Lissette* 1980; ex *Tarek* 1978; ex *Khorramshahr* 1976; ex *Deckship Brigida* 1976
92953 DELICIA (Li) ex *Malaysian Exporter* 1983; ex *Delicia* 1982
92954 PEGASUS PEACE (Ko)
Similar (stern ramp & new design of crane):
92955 FRANCESCA (Li)
92956 ELEANORA (Li) ex *Santa Cruz* 1981; ex *Finnorient* 1981; ex *Eleanora*
92957 MAERSK ASTRO (Li) ex *Gisela* 1980

92970 LILLIAN XXII Bn/No (Blalids) 1971; C; 150; 33 × 3.20 (108.26 × 10.5); TSM (Scania); 10; ex *Nanna Buur* 1974
Sisters:
92971 LILLIAN XXIII (Bn) ex *Tina Buur* 1974
92972 LILLIAN XXIV (Bn) ex *Fenja Buur* 1974
92973 LILLIAN XXI (Bn) ex *Frigga Buur* 1974
92974 CHIARA (It) ex *Merc Contractor* 1977; ex *Tora Buur* 1975

92980 HIRYU Pa/Sg (Far East-Levingston) 1977; OSS; 2900; 77.91 × 4.61 (255.61 × 15.12); TSM (Wichmann); 11; ex *Northern Installer* 1980
Sister:
92981 PACIFIC INSTALLER (Sg)

92990 PACIFIC HIGHWAY Ja/Ja (Kawasaki) 1977; V; 13500; 192.08 × 8.03 (630.18 × 26.34); M (MAN); 20.5
Sister:
92991 ATLANTIC HIGHWAY (Li)

93000 KARMSUND No/No (Lothe) 1979; Pal/Con; 500; 70.8 × 4.57 (232.28 × 14.99); M (Wichmann); 14; Side door (port)
Sister:
93001 ROYKSUND (No)
Probable Sister:
93002 ROGALAND (No)

93010 NORDKYN No/No (Fosen) 1979; Pal/Con; 700; 77.5 × 4.52 (254.27 × 14.83); M (Wartsila); 14; Side door (port)

Sisters (Fa flag):
93011 BLIKUR
93012 LOMUR

93030 BACO-LINER 1 FRG/FRG (Thyssen) 1979; Bg/Con; 204.1 × 6.67 (669.62 × 21.88); M (B&W); 15; Bow doors; Barges float on and off; Crane is shown in stowed position—dotted lines represent it swung fore-and-aft
Sister:
93031 BACO-LINER 2 (FRG)
Similar:
93032 BACO-LINER 3 (FRG)

93040 SCHELDE II Be/Be (Beliard-Murdoch) 1979; D; 4000; 98.5 × 7 (323.16 × 22.97); M (MWM); 11; Trailing suction type

93050 CIUDAD DE BARRANQUILLA Co/US (Gulfport) 1949; D; 3700; 68.89 × — (226.01 × —); TSR (Unaflow); —

★ **93060 TRAPEZITZA** Bu/Sw (Kockums) 1979; RoC; 8500; 166 × 7.9 (544.62 × 25.92); TSM (Sulzer); 18; ex *Soca* 1982; ex *Ariadne* 1980; Twin stern ramps (slewing)
Sister:
★ **93061 TZAREVETZ** (Bu) ex *Scandinavia* 1982

93070 FINNJET Fi/Fi (Wartsila) 1977; RoPCF; 24600; 212.81 × 7.2 (698.2 × 23.62); TSGT (Pratt & Whitney)/D-E (Wartsila); 30.5/18.5

93075 SONG OF AMERICA No/Fi (Wartsila) 1982; P; 37600; 214.51 × 6.50 (704 × 21.33); TSM (Sulzer); 20.5

93077 SEA GODDESS 1 No/Fi (Wartsila) 1984; P; 4300; 105.00 × 3.99 (344 × 13.09); TSM (Wartsila); 17.5
Sister:
93078 SEA GODDESS II (No)

93080 IRIS Is/Rm (Galatz) 1973; RoC; 8200; 128.33 × 6.58 (421 × 21.5); TSM (Pielstick); —; Stern door
Sister:
93081 NARCIS (Is)

93090 MASHALA Br/FRG (Rickmers) 1977; RoC; 1600; 116.01 × 5.38 (380.61 × 17.65); TSM (MaK); 16
Sisters:
93091 SALAHALA (Br)
93094 EMADALA (Br)

● **93100 STENA SEATRADER** Cy/Ne (Vuyk) 1973/75; RoC; 3900; 142.22 × approx. 5.94 (467 × approx 19.49); TSM (Werkspoor); 18; ex *Stena Sailer* 1976; Lengthened 1975; Bow and stern doors
Sister:
93101 STENA SEARIDER (Cy) ex *Bahjah* 1982; ex *Seatrader* 1976; Launched as *Stena Seatrader*

93110 CARRIER PRINCESS Ca/Ca (Burrard DD) 1973; RoC/F; 4400; 115.83 × 4.88 (380.01 × 16.01); TSM (General Motors); 18

93130 POINT MANATEE US/US ((Kaiser Co) 1944/70; Con; 13500; 192.92 × 8.93 (633 × 29.30); T (Westinghouse); 16; ex *Carolina* 1982; ex *Transidaho* 1975; ex *General W.F. Hase* 1969; Converted from 'C-4' type passenger/troopship in 1970 (Wiley)
Sisters:
93131 AMCO TRADER (US) ex *Mayaguez* 1982; ex *Transoregon* 1975; ex *General W G Haan* 1969
93132 AMCO VOYAGER (US) ex *Aguadilla* 1982; ex *Transhawaii* 1975; ex *General J H McRae* 1969

93140 BAYARD No/No (Ankerlokken) 1975; RoC; 4000; 136.91 × 6.21 (449.17 × 20.37); TSM (Pielstick); 18.5; Stern door and ramp
Sisters (No flag):
93141 BOHEMUND
93142 BALDUIN

93150 ARGO FRG/FRG (Kroegerw) 1976; RoC; 3900; 127.03 × 5.41/6.55 (416. × 17.74/21.48); TSM (KHD); —; ex *Argo-Hellas* 1980; ex *Brabant* 1978; ex *Argo* 1977; Stern door/ramp

93160 COUTANCES Fr/Fr (Havre) 1978; RoC; 2600; 110 × 4.5 (360.89 × 14.7); M (Atlas-MaK); 17.5; Stern door; Bow door
Sister:
93161 PURBECK (Fr)

93170 ATLAS IV Cy/No (Trondhjems) 1975; RoC/F; 2400; 109.71 × 5.2 (359.94 × 17.06); TSM (Nydqvist & Holm); 19; ex *Tarek B* 1983; ex *Falster* 1980; ex *Prince De Bretagne* 1975; ex *Falster* 1975; Bow door/ramp; Side door/ramp; Two stern doors/ramps; Lengthened 1977

93180 INCAN SUPERIOR Ca/Ca (Burrard DD) 1974; RoC/F; 3800; 116.44 × 4.88 (382.02 × 16.01); TSM (General Motors); 14

Possible sister:
93181 **INCAN ST. LAURENT** (Ca)

● 93190 **DYVI SKAGERAK** No/Ne (P Smit) 1973; V;
7300; 187.51 × 8.01 (615.19 × 26.27); M (Sulzer);
18; ex *Hual Skagerak* 1983; ex *Dyvi Skagerak*; Side
doors
Sisters (No flag):
93191 **DYVI KATTEGAT**
93192 **TARGET** ex *Hoegh Target* 1982; ex *Dyvi
Adriatic* 1975;
93193 **HOEGH TRIGGER**
Similar (tall pipes from funnel):
93194 **NOPAL SEL** (No)

93200 **ARCTIC SALVOR** US/US (Equitable) 1970;
RoC/Con; 500; 63.4 × 3.65 (208 × 11.97); TSM
(Caterpillar); —; ex *Manati* 1980; Stern door

93210 **KIRK CHALLENGER** Br/De (Helsingor)
1979; RoC; 1600; 105.62 × 4.95 (347 × 16.24); M
(MaK); —; ex *Dana Minerva* 1983; ex *Nopal Minerva*
1983; ex *Dana Minerva* 1979; Stern door/ramp; Side
door/ramp (Starboard)

93240 **USURBIL** Sp/Sp (Lorenzo) 1968; ST; 1300;
74.71 × 4.7 (245.11 × 15.4); M (Deutz); 12.5
Sister:
93241 **URQUIL** (Sp)

● 93250 **TOR CALEDONIA** Br/No (Fredriksstad)
1977; RoC; 5100; 162.77 × 6.2 (534.02 × 20.34);
TSM (Pielstick); 18.5; Stern door
Similar (both lengthened) (Sw flag):
93251 **BALTIC WASA** ex *Tor Finlandia* 1984
93252 **TOR DANIA** ex *Bandar Abbas Express* 1979

93255 **NORDIC LINK** Sw/Sw (Finnboda) 1981;
RoC; 5000; 120.20 × 6.22 (394 × 20. 41); M (Pielstick); 14.5; 2 side doors (starboard); Stern door/ramp
Sister (Finnish built—Rauma-Repola):
93256 **BALTIC LINK** (Br)
Probable sister:
93257 **SOLANO** (Fi)

93260 **SAINT REMY** Fr/Ja (Ishikawajima S &C)
1977; RoC; 2600; 122.94 × 4.77 (403.35 × 15,65);
TSM (Pielstick); 16.5; ex *Admiral Caribe* 1982; ex
Admiral Nigeria; ex *Admiral Caribe* 1977; Stern door-
/ramp
Sisters:
93261 **ADMIRAL ATLANTIC** (No)
93262 **SAINT CLAIR** (Fr) ex *Admiral Pacific* 1982

93265 **BORE QUEEN** Fi/Fi (Rauma-Repola) 1980;
RoC; 6900; 142.09 × 7.62 (466 × 25.00); TSM (MaK);
17.5; Stern door/ramp
Sister:
93266 **BORE KING** (Fi)

93270 **UNION DUNEDIN** Br/Ja (Minami) 1978;
RoC; 5800; 140.85 × 7.65 (462.1 × 25); TSM (Sulzer);
14; ex *TFL Progress* 1983; ex *Merzario Emilia* 1983;
ex *TFL Progress* 1981; Foreward ramp (starboard) and
stern slewing ramp
Sister:
93271 **UNION SYDNEY** (Br) ex *TFL Prosperity* 1983
ex *Merzario Lombardia* 1983; ex *TFL Prosperity* 1981

93272 **MERCANDIAN PRESIDENT** De/De (Frederikshavn) 1982; RoC/Con; 3000; 131.71 × 6.16
(432 × 20.21); M (Krupp MaK); 15.5; Quarter ramp
(starboard) and stern ramp
Sisters (De flag):
93273 **MERCANDIAN ADMIRAL II**
93274 **MERCANDIAN AMBASSADOR II**
93275 **MERCANDIAN DIPLOMAT**
93276 **MERCANDIAN GOVERNOR**
93277 **MERCANDIAN PRINCE II**
93278 **MERCANDIAN QUEEN II**
93279 **MERCANDIAN SENATOR**
93279/1 **MERCANDIAN DUKE**

93280 **BACAT I** In/De (Frederikshavn) 1974; Bg;
1400; 103.51 × 5.42 (337.92 × 17.78); TSM (Alpha-
Diesel); 11; Catamaran hull

93290 **CALA MARSAL** Sp/Sp (Mallorca) 1971; RoC;
900; 88.91 × 4.18 (291.69 × 13.71); M (B&W); 17;
Sister:
93291 **CALA LLONGA** (Sp)

● 93300 **LARIMAR** Do/No (Mandal) 1979; RoC/Con;
1500; 103.8 × 5.15 (340.55 × 16.9); M (Wichmann);
16; ex *Seatrain Leonor* 1981; Stern quarter ramp
(starboard)
Sister:
93301 **AMBAR** (Do) ex *Seatrain Libertad* 1981

★ 93310 **NAN KOU** RC/Ja (Kawasaki) 1978; RoC;
3700; 136.19 × 6.81 (446.81 × 22.34); M (MAN);
17.7; ex *Ocean Transporter* 1978
Sisters (RC flag):
★ 93311 **BAI HEI KOU**
★ 93312 **HUA YUAN KOU**
★ 93313 **ZHI JIANG KOU**

★ 93314 **TAI PING KOU**
★ 93315 **XIAO SHI KOU**

93330 **ARGUS CARRIER** Li/Ru (Nosenko)- It
1970/73; RoVC; 7500; 169.63 × 8.31 (556.52 ×
27.26); M (B&W); 18; ex *Nopal Argus* 1983; Converted from general cargo 1973 (INMA); side doors

93340 **THEBELAND** Sw/Ja (Mitsui) 1978; RoC-
/Con; 9400; 165 × 8 (541.34 × 26.25); TSM (B&W);
19.5; Stern quarter ramp/door
Sisters:
93341 **HEKTOS** (Fi) ex *Timmerland* 1983
93342 **TYRUSLAND** (Sw)
93345 **VEGALAND** (Sw) ex *Tarn* 1983; ex *Vegaland*
1982
Sisters (larger crane further aft):
93346 **VIKINGLAND** (Sw)
93347 **HESPERUS** (Fi) ex *Vasaland* 1983

93360 **DANA AMERICA** Li/Ja (NKK) 1979; RoC-
/Con/HL; 145.3 × 6.68 (442.91 × 21.92); M (B&W);
15.3; Stern ramp; 120 ton derrick
Sisters (Li flag):
93361 **DANA AFRICA**
93362 **DANA ARABIA**
93363 **DANA CARIBIA**

93370 **SCANDINAVIAN HIGHWAY** Ja/Ja (Kawasaki) 1978; RoVC; 20400; 197 × 9.52 (646.33 ×
31.23); M (MAN); approx 18.8; Stern ramp; 2 side
doors (1 port, 1 starboard)

★ 93380 **VLADIMIR ILYCH** Ru/DDR (Elbewerften)
1976; Riv/P; 4900; 128.02 × —; (420 × —); —; —;
Possible sisters (Ru flag):
★ 93381 **MARIYA ULYANOVA**
★ 93382 **SOVETSKAYA ROSSIYA**
★ 93383 **60 LET OKTYABRYA**
★ 93384 **ALEKSANDR ULYANOV**
★ 93385 **YEVGENIY VUCHETICH**

93390 **POINT MANATEE** US/US (Kaiser Co)
1944/70; Con; 13500; 192.92 × 8.93 (633 × 29.30);
T (Westinghouse); 16; ex *Carolina* 1982; ex *Transida-
ho* 1975; ex *General W.F. Hase* 1969; Converted from
'C-4' type passenger/ troopship in 1970 (Wiley)
Sisters:
93391 **AMCO TRADER** (US) ex *Mayaguez* 1982; ex
Transoregon 1975; ex *General W G Haan* 1969
93392 **AMCO VOYAGER** (US) ex *Aguadilla* 1982; ex
Transhawaii 1975; ex *General J H McRae* 1969

93400 **TAIYO MARU No 71** Ja/Ja (Hayashikane)
1962; ST; 1500; 75.52 × 5.51 (247.76 × 18.07); M
(Hayashikane); 12.25
Sister:
93401 **CHALLWA No 2** (Pe) ex *Taiyo Maru No 73*
1976

93410 **TAIYO MARU No 65** Ja/Ja (Hayashikane)
1960; ST; 1300; 75.6 × 5.57 (248.03 × 18.27); M
(Hayashikane); 14.5;
Sister (Ja flag):
93411 **TAIYO MARU No 66**
Similar (Ja flag):
93412 **BANSHU MARU No 5** ex *Taiyo Maru No 75*
93413 **BANSHU MARU No 6** ex *Taiyo Maru No 76*

93420 **UNION DUNEDIN** Br/Ja (Minami) 1978;
RoC; 5800; 140.85 × 7.65 (462.1 × 25); TSM (Sulzer);
14; ex *TFL Progress* 1983; ex *Merzario Emilia* 1983;
ex *TFL Progress* 1981; Foreward quarter ramp (starboard) and stern slewing ramp
Sister:
93421 **UNION SYDNEY** (Br) ex *TFL Prosperity* 1983;
ex *Merzario Lombardia* 1983; ex *T F L Prosperity* 1981

93430 **SWELLMASTER** Ca/Ca (Canadian Vickers)
1950; D; 1900; 76.21 × 4.57 (250.03 × 14.99); TSD-
E(General Motors); —; ex *Sandpiper*

93440 **SHINSEI MARU** Ja/Ja (Mitsui) 1978; RoC;
3100; 112.53 × 6.01 (369.2 × 19.72); M (Mitsui); 17;
Stern ramp

93450 **KAZUSHIMA MARU** Ja/Ja (NKK) 1962; C;
3700; 105.01 × 6.22 (344.52 × 20.4); M (B&W);
12.75

93460 **ESSAYONS** US/US (Sun SB) 1950; D; —;
160.05 × 8.22 (525.1 × 27); TST-E (Westinghouse);
15.5

93470 **SACRAMENTO** US/US (Puget Sound ND)
1964; Spt/FA; 53600 dspl; 241.7 × 12 (793 × 29.3);
TST (GEC); 26; Helicopter deck and two helicopters
Sisters (US flag):
93471 **CAMDEN**
93472 **DETROIT**
93473 **SEATTLE**

93480 **TOPIRA** Br/Br (Burntisland) 1954; Tk; 6900;
134.75 × 6.1 (442.09 × 20.01); R (Rankin & Blackmore); 10; ex *Sunbrayton* 1979

93490 **SAN ANTONIO DO TRIUNFO** Bz/Fi (Valmet) 1960; C; 4000/6400; 126.8 × 6.78/— (416.01
× 22.24/—); M (B&W); —; ex *Todos Os Santos* 1980
Sisters (Bz flag):
93491 **ALBERTO MONTEIRO** ex *Guanabara* 1980
93492 **VITORIA DA CONQUISTA** ex *Turiacu* 1980

93500 **NISSHIN MARU No 2** Ja/FRG (Deutsche S
und M) 1937; FF; 27100; 193.45 × 12.19 (634.67 ×
39.99); TSM (Hayashikane); 14.75; ex *Abraham Lars-
en* 1957; ex *Empire Victory* 1950; ex *Unitas* 1945;
Converted from whale factory 1967

93510 **AUTO TRADER** Gr/No (Kristiansands) 1970;
RoC; 1600; 105.9 × 4.95 (347.44 × 16.24); TSM
(Normo); 17; ex *Ulidia* 1981; ex *Stena Carrier* 1974;
Bow, stern and side doors
Sister:
93511 **STENA TRADER** (Fi) ex *Viking Trader* 1981;
ex *Stena Trader* 1980; ex *Dalriada* 1980; ex *Stena
Trailer* 1971
Similar:
93512 **TRUCK TRADER** (Gr) ex *Anderida* 1981

93520 **MANUKAI** US/US (Bethlehem Steel) 1970;
Con; 23800; 219.62 × 10.4 (720.53 × 34.12); T (Stal-
Laval); 23; ex *Hawaiian Enterprise*
Sister (US flag):
93521 **MANULANI** ex *Hawaiian Progress*
Similar (bridge superstructure one deck lower) (US
Flag):
93522 **SEA-LAND ECONOMY** ex *SL 818* 1973; ex
H P Baldwin
93523 **SEA-LAND VENTURE** ex *SL 180* 1973; ex *S
T Alexander*
93524 **SEA-LAND CONSUMER** ex *Australia Bear*
1973
93525 **SEA-LAND PRODUCER** ex *New Zealand
Bear*
Similar (bridge further foreward and one deck higher) (US Flag):
93526 **MAUI**
93527 **KAUAI**

93540 **NISSHIN MARU No 3** Ja/Sw (Gotav) 1947;
FF; 22800; 194.62 × 10.71 (638.51 × 35.13); M
(Gotaverken); 12.5; ex *Kosmos III* 1961

93550 **L'INTERPECHE** Br/Br (Furness) 1948/66;
FF; 18900; 204.6 × — (671.25 × —); TSM (Doxford);
10.5; ex *Suiderkruis* 1971; ex *Kosmos V* 1967; Converted from whale factory 1966 (Globe)

93560 **ARAUCA** Ve/No (Kristiansands) 1954; C;
2500; 94.65 × 6.01 (311 × 19.72); M (MAN); 12.5; ex
Tacamar II 1983; ex *Gelting* 1974; ex *Aun* 1968; ex
Gerstad 1964; ex *Ferm* 1964

93570 **HILLAH** Iq/Ne (Smit K) 1969; D; 6300; 120 ×
6.72 (393.7 × 22.04); TSR (Uniflow); 14

93580 **SILVER HOPE** Pa/Ja (Ube Dock) 1976;
RoVC; 4700; 120.1 × 8.93 (394.02 × 29.29); M
(Pielstick); 17; ex *Emily Moon* 1984; ex *Blue Andro-
meda* 1977; Side doors

93590 **KYOKUSEI MARU** Ko/FRG (Deutsche Werft
Reihers) 1937/51; WF; 13900; 183.06 × 8.89
(600.59 × 29.16); TSM (MAN); 12; ex *Kosmos IV*
1971; ex *Walter Rau* 1946; Lengthened 1951

93610 **WICHITA** US/US (General Dynamics) 1969;
RT/FA; 37400 Dspl; 206.9 × 10.2 (659 × 33.3); TST
(GEC); 20; Helicopter deck & two helicopters
Sisters (US flag):
93611 **KALAMAZOO**
93612 **KANSAS CITY**
93613 **MILWAUKEE**
93614 **ROANOKE**
93615 **SAVANNAH**
93616 **WABASH**

★ 93630 **SOVIETSKAYA ROSSIYA** Ru/Ru (Nosenko) 1961; WF; 33200; 217.51 × 10.85 (713.61 ×
35.59); TSM (B&W); 16

93640 **MARAMA** NZ/Br (Robb Caledon) 1969; RoC;
4500; 130.99 × 6.62 (430 × 21.71); TSM (Pielstick);
18; Stern door

93650 **AKORA** Gh/Ja (Fujinagata) 1965; ST; 2000;
79.5 × 4.97 (260.82 × 16.3); M (B&W); 14.5
Sisters (Gh flag):
93651 **ASEBU**
93652 **BANKO**
93653 **SUBIN**

★ 93660 **VOSTOCK** Ru/Ru (Admiralteiskiy) 1971;
FF; 26400; 224.57 × 10.02 (736.78 × 32.87); TST
(Kirov); 19

★ 93670 **GEROITE NA SEVASTOPOL** Bu/No
(Framnaes) 1978; RoC/TF; 9600; 185.45 × 7.42
(608.43 × 24.34); TSM (B&W); 19; Stern door
Sister:
★ 93671 **GEROITE NA ODESSA** (Bu)

Similar(Ys built—'Uljanik'):
★ 93672 **GEROI PLEVNY** (Ru)
★ 93673 **GEROI SHIPKI** (Ru)

★ 93680 **ANDREY ZAKHAROV** Ru/Ru (Admiral-teiskiy) 1960; FF; 12700; 162.16 × 7.02 (532.02 × 23.03); TSM (Skoda); 12.5
Sisters (Ru flag):
★ 93681 **PAVEL CHEBOTNYAGIN**
★ 93682 **ALEKSANDR OBUKHOV**
★ 93683 **EVGENIY NIKISHIN**
★ 93684 **KONSTANTIN SUKHANOV**
★ 93685 **VASILIY BLUKHER**
★ 93686 **MIKHAIL TUKACHEVSKIY**
★ 93687 **PAVEL POSTYSHEV**
★ 93688 **SERGEY LAZO**
★ 93689 **VASILIY PUTINTSEV**
★ 93690 **ALEKSANDR KOSAREV**
★ 93691 **KRONID KORENOV**
★ 93692 **IERONIM UBOREVICH**

★ 93720 **RIGOLETTO** Sw/Ja (Hitachi) 1977; RoVC; 17500; 190.02 × 8.5 (623.4 × 27.8); M (Sulzer); 18.25
Sister:
93721 **TRAVIATA** (Sw)

★ 93730 **PROFESSOR BARANOV** Ru/Pd (Gdanska) 1967; FF; 13600; 164.02 × 8.08 (538.09 × 26.5); M (B&W); 15.25; 'B-69' type
Similar (Ru flag):
★ 93731 **FELIKS KON**
★ 93732 **NAKHICHEVAN**
★ 93733 **ROBERT EYKHE**
★ 93734 **YULIAN MARKHLEVSKIY**
★ 93735 **KALININGRADSKIY KOMSOMOLETS**
★ 93736 **SEVERNYY POLYUS**
★ 93737 **SOVIETSKIY ZAPOLYARYE**
★ 93738 **TOMSK**
★ 93739 **LENINSKAYA ISKRA**
★ 93740 **MARSHAL MERETSKOV**
★ 93741 **NOVAYA KAKHOVKA**
★ 93742 **NOVAYA LADOGA**
★ 93743 **ARKTIKA**
★ 93744 **OROCHON**
★ 93745 **PALANGA**
★ 93746 **SOVIETSKOYE PRIMORYE**
★ 93747 **AVACHA**
★ 93748 **RYBAK BALTIKA**
★ 93749 **ANTARKTIKA**
★ 93750 **LENINSKIY PUT**
★ 93751 **SOVIETSKAYA SIBIR**
★ 93752 **YUZHINO-SAKJALINSK**
★ 93753 **PRIBALTIKA**
★ 93754 **RIZHSKOYE VZMORYE**
★ 93755 **50 LET OKTYABRYA** (or **PYATIDYESY-ATILYETIYE OKTYABRYA**)
★ 93756 **VINTSAS MITSKYAVICHUS-KAPSUKAS** ex Vintsas Mitskyavichus 1973; ex Zapryba 1971
★ 93757 **SOVIETSKAYA BURYATYA**
★ 93758 **ALEKSANDROVSK SAKHALINSKIY**
★ 93759 **KOMSOMOLETS MAGADANA**
★ 93760 **KOMSOMOLSK NA AMURE**
★ 93761 **MARSHAL SOKOLOVSKIY**
★ 93762 **RYBAK LATVII**
★ 93763 **ZEMLYA KOLSKAYA**
★ 93764 **POGRANICHNIK LEONOV**

★ 93770 **NISSHIN MARU** RC/Ja (Kawasaki D) 1951; WF; 20800; 189.54 × 10.8 (621.85 × 35.43); M (MAN); 13

★ 93780 **VILIS LACIS** Ru/FRG (Kieler H) 1966; FF; 16500; 167.24 × 7.49 (548.68 × 24.57); M (MAN); 14; ex Morskaya Slava 1966
Sisters (Ru flag):
★ 93781 **BOEVAYA SLAVA**
★ 93782 **RYBATSKAYA SLAVA**
★ 93783 **TRUDOVAYA SLAVA**
★ 93784 **BALTIYSKAYA SLAVA**
★ 93785 **CHERNOMORSKAYA SLAVA**
★ 93786 **KRONSHTADTSKAYA SLAVA**
★ 93787 **LENINGRADSKAYA SLAVA**

★ 93800 **SEVEROURALSK** Ru/Ja (Mitsubishi HI) 1966; FF; 174.33 × 7.32 (571.94 × 24.01); M (MAN); 14.5
Sisters (Ru flag):
★ 93802 **SHALVA NADIBAIDZE**
★ 93803 **SLAVYANSK**
★ 93804 **SPASSK**
★ 93805 **SUKHONA**
★ 93806 **SULAK**
★ 93807 **SUZDAL**

★ 93820 **POGRANICHNIK LEONOV** Ru/Pd (Gdanska) 1972; FF; 13100; 164.01 × 8.08 (538.09 × 26.5); M (B&W); 15.25; 'B-69' type
Similar (Ru flag):
★ 93821 **FELIKS KON**
★ 93822 **NAKHICHEVAN**
★ 93823 **ROBERT EYKHE**
★ 93824 **YULIAN MARKHLEVSKIY**

★ 93825 **KALININGRADSKIY KOMSOMOLETS**
★ 93826 **SEVERNYY POLYUS**
★ 93827 **SOVIETSKIY ZAPOLYARYE**
★ 93828 **TOMSK**
★ 93829 **LENINSKAYA ISKRA**
★ 93830 **MARSHAL MERETSKOV**
★ 93831 **NOVAYA KAKHOVKA**
★ 93832 **NOVAYA LADOGA**
★ 93833 **ARKTIKA**
★ 93834 **OROCHON**
★ 93835 **PALANGA**
★ 93836 **SOVIETSKOYE PRIMORYE**
★ 93837 **AVACHA**
★ 93838 **RYBAK BALTIKA**
★ 93839 **ANTARKTIKA**
★ 93840 **LENINSKIY PUT**
★ 93841 **SOVIETSKAYA SIBIR**
★ 93842 **YUZHINO-SAKHALINSK**
★ 93843 **PRIBALTIKA**
★ 93844 **RIZHSKOYE VZMORYE**
★ 93845 **50 LET OKTYABRYA** (or **PYATIDYESY-ATILYETIYE OKTYABRYA**)
★ 93846 **VINTSAS MITSKYAVICHUS-KAPSUKAS** ex Vintsas Mitskyavichus 1973; ex Zapryba 1971
★ 93847 **SOVIETSKAYA BURYATYA**
★ 93848 **ALEKSANDROVSK SAKHALINSKIY**
★ 93849 **KOMSOMOLETS MAGADANA**
★ 93850 **KOMSOMOLSK NA AMURE**
★ 93851 **MARSHAL SOKOLOVSKIY**
★ 93852 **RYBAK LATVII**
★ 93854 **PROFESSOR BARANOV**

★ 93860 **SOVIETSKAYA UKRAINA** Ru/Ru (Nosenko) 1959; WF; 32000; 217.51 × 10.85 (713.61 × 35.59); TSM (B&W); 16

★ 93870 **PIONERSK** Ru/Pd (Gdanska) 1963; FF; 13600; 165.46 × 8.1 (542.84 × 26.57); M (B&W); 14.25; 'B-64' type
Sisters (Ru flag):
★ 93871 **DAURIYA**
★ 93872 **MATOCHKIN SHAR**
★ 93873 **RYBNYY MURMAN**
★ 93874 **FRYDERYK CHOPIN**
★ 93875 **POLYARNAYA ZVEZDA**
★ 93876 **SEVRYBA**
★ 93877 **ALEKSEY KHLOBYSTOV**
★ 93878 **ALEKSEY POZDNYAKOV**
★ 93879 **GRIGORIY LYSENKO**
★ 93880 **NIKOLAY DANILOV**
★ 93881 **SERGEY VASILISIN**
Similar: 'B-67' type (Pd flag):
★ 93882 **POMORZE**
★ 93883 **GRYF POMORSKY**

93885 **UCHI** Ar/Sp (Luzuriaga) 1968; ST: 700; 53.8 × 4.7 (176.51 × 15.42); M (Werkspoor); —; ex Bueno Gonzalez 1975

93890 **SIR CARADOC** Br/No (Trosvik) 1973; RoC; 1900; 124.19 × 4.98 (407.45 × 16.34); TSM (Normo); 16; ex Grey Master 1983; Chartered to the Royal Fleet Auxiliary; Bow, side and stern doors
Similar:
93891 **LEON** (Gr) ex Leo 1976
93892 **NORMANDIA** (Fr) ex Juno

93900 **BEGONIA** NA/No (Kristiansands) 1974; RoC; 1900; 124.59 × 4.98 (408.76 × 16.34); TSM (Normo); 17; ex Fernhill

93910 **GEORGIA** US/US (Sun SB) 1951/62; RoC; 9700; 169.88 × 8.25 (557.35 × 27.07); T (GEC); 16; ex Seatrain Georgia; Lengthened 1962; May have 2 cranes
Sister:
93911 **LOUISIANA** (US) ex Seatrain Louisiana

93920 **AUTO TRADER** Gr/No (Kristiansands) 1970; RoC; 1600; 105.9 × 4.95 (347.44 × 16.24); TSM (Normo); 17; ex Ulidia 1981; ex Stena Carrier 1974; Bow, stern and side doors
Sister:
93921 **STENA TRADER** (Fi) ex Viking Trader 1981; ex Stena Trader 1980; ex Dalriada 1980; ex Stena Trailer 1971
Similar:
93922 **TRUCK TRADER** (Gr) ex Anderida 1981

93930 **PEVERIL** Br/No (Kristiansands) 1971; RoC; 2000; 106.28 × 4.97 (348.69 × 16.31); STSM (Pielstick) 19; ex Jaguar 1982; ex Penda 1980; ex Asd Meteor 1975; ex Holmia 1973; Bow door, stern ramp
Similar (larger):
93931 **GUNILLA** (Fi)
93932 **ARONA** (Fi)
93933 **GRANO** (Fi)
93934 **COASTAL TRADER** (NZ) ex Silvia 1973
93935 **DERNA** (Ly)
93936 **GHAT** (Ly)

93950 **MARINE EVANGELINE** Br/No (Kristiansands) 1974; RoC; 2800; 110.14 × 5.75 (361.35 ×

18.86); TSM (Normo); 18.5; ex Duke of Yorkshire 1978; Bow, side and stern doors

93960 **CARRIER PRINCESS** Ca/Ca (Burrard DD) 1973; RoC/F; 4400; 115.83 × 4.88 (380.01 × 16.01); TSM (General motors); 18

93970 **CIUDAD DE CEUTA** Sp/Sp (Juliana) 1975; RoPCF; 2800; 101.66 × 5.67 (333.53 × 18.6); TSM (Pielstick); 16; Stern door/ramp; ex Monte Contes 1978
Sister:
93971 **CIUDAD DE ZARAGOZA** (Sp) ex Monte Corona 1978

93975 **MANX VIKING** Br/Sp (Juliana) 1976; RoPCF; 3600; 101.66 × 4.81 (334 × 15.78); TSM (Pielstick); 17; ex Monte Castillo 1978; Launched as Monte Cruceta; Bow door/ramp; stern door/ramp

93980 **AICHI MARU** Ja/Ja (Onomichi) 1967; RoC; 2600; 96.7 × 4.8 (317.26 × 15.75); M (B&W); 13.5

● 93990 **KIRSTEN BRAVO** De/FRG (M Jansen) 1974; RS/C; 500; 57.92 × 3.99 (190.03 × 13.09); M (Alpha-Diesel); 8.5
Possible sister:
93991 **ANNE BRAVO** (Pa)

94000 **HERTHA** De/Sw (Kalmar) 1966; RoC/Pal; 300; 49.20 × 3.20 (161.42 × 10.50); M (KHD); 12; ex Camilla Henriksen 1980; ex Nordbornholm 1969; Stern and side doors

94010 **AETOS** Gr/Fi (Rauma-Repola) 1972; RoC; 3100; 113.52 × 6.25 (372.44 × 20.51); M (Atlas-MaK); 16; ex Bore VII; Stern door
Similar:
★ 94011 **ASCHBERG** (DDR) ex Bore IX 1977
★ 94012 **BEERBERG** (DDR) ex Bore X
94013 **BORE XI** (Sw) (may be renamed **BORE XI AV STOCKHOLM**)

● 94020 **BUENAVISTA** Ne/No (Ulstein) 1971/74; RoC/TF; 3300; 106.43 × 6.25 (349.18 × 20.51); TSM (Stork-Werkspoor); 19; Stern and side doors; Lengthened 1974; Drawing shows vessel prior to lengthening
Sister:
94021 **BENCHIJIGUA** (Sp) ex Bonanza 1980; (may not be lengthened)

94030 **AL ZAHER II** Si/No (Hatlo) 1972; RoC; 500; 91.04 × 4.42 (298.69 × 14.5); TSM (Alpha-Diesel); 16; ex Capitaine Le Goff 1981; ex Admiral Carrier I; Stern door
Sister:
94031 **LA GOULETTE** (Tn) ex Olau Vig 1974; ex Admiral Carrier 1974

94040 **BHARAT SEEMA** In/No (Moss V) 1973; RoPCF; 1600; 86.54 × 4.92 (283.92 × 16.14); TSM (Wichmann); —; ex Basto V 1982; ex Hanstholm; ex Basto V 1980; Bow, stern and side doors
Sister:
94041 **SUILVEN** (Br)

94050 **RHONE** Fr/FRG (O&K) 1970; RoC; 2500; 104.02 × 5.03 (341.27 × 16.5); TSM (Atlas-MaK); 17.5; ex Rhonetal; ex Norcape 1974; ex Rhonetal
Similar:
94051 **MAR CARIBE** (Br)

94060 **AQUILA** Fr/FRG (Kroegerw) 1973/76; RoC; 4100; 149.23 × 6.41 (489.6 × 21.03); M (Werkspoor); 18; ex Nahost Pioneer; ex Ehrenfels 1977; ex Ipswich Pioneer II 1976; ex Aquila; Lengthened 1976

94070 **RAILSHIP 1** FRG/FRG (Rickmers)-FRG 1975/80; RoC/TF; 6500; —; 177.22 × 6.32 (581.43 × 20.73); TSM (Atlas-MaK); approx 20; Stern door-/ramp; Lengthened 1979 (A G 'Weser')

94080 **LAURITA** No/FRG (B+V) 1969; V; 6500; 180.02 × 6.8 (590.62 × 22.31); M (Pielstick); 21; Side doors; Lengthened 1976 (Mitsubishi HI)
Sisters:
94081 **SAVONITA** (Pi)
94082 **HUAL TORINITA** (No) ex Torinita 1982

94090 **AMBASSADOR** US/FRG (Meyer) 1980; RoC; 13400; 168.8 × 6.45 (553.8 × 21.16); M (Stork-Werkspoor); 17; Stern ramp
Sister (extra housing above the bridge, adjoining foremast):
94091 **SENATOR** (US) ex Diplomat 1982

94100 **JOLLY VERDE** It/Br (Grangemouth) 1967; RoC; 1600; 88.55 × 4.34 (290.52 × 14.24); M (Mirrlees); 14; ex Carway 1973

94110 **SAUDI MAKKAH** Si/Ja (Kawasaki) 1977; RoC; 14500; 197.52 × 10.03 (648.03 × 32.91); M (MAN); 14; ex Seaspeed Asia 1981; Stern door and side door
Sisters:

94111 SEASPEED AMERICA (Gr)
94112 SAUDI RIYADH (Si) ex *Seaspeed Arabia* 1981

94120 CHARLES SCHIAFFINO Fr/Sp (Cadagua) 1977; RoC; 2000; 110.6 × 5.61 (362.86 × 18.41); M (—); 15.5; ex *Cala d'Or* 1977; Lengthened 1977

94130 ANZERE Sd/Ne (Vuyk) 1978; RoC; 5000; 151 × 6.2 (495.41 × 20.34); M (Sulzer); 18

94140 VIKING TRADER Br/As (Osterreichische) 1977; RoC; 3800; 144.07 × 5.7 (472.67 × 18.7); TSM (KHD); 18; ex *Oyster Bay* 1983; ex *Manaure VII* 1983; ex *Caribbean Sky* 1982; ex *Federal Nova* 1981; ex *Goya*; ex *Stena Tender* 1977; Bow door and stern ramp; Completed in Romania and lengthened in West Germany 1977 (Nobiskrug)

94150 LORETO Me/As (Osterreichische) 1977; RoC; 2500; 114.38 × 5.7 (375.26 × 18.7); TSM (KHD); 18; ex *Stena Timer* 1981; ex *Jaguar* 1979; ex *Stena Timer* 1977

94160 MASHALA Br/FRG (Rickmers) 1977; RoC; 1600; 116.01 × 5.38 (380.61 × 17.65); TSM (MaK); 16
Sisters:
94161 SALAHALA (Br)
94164 EMADALA (Br)

94170 BORE SONG Fi/Fi (Rauma-Repola) 1977; RoC; 3800; 128.91 × 6.3 (422.93 × 20.67); M (Atlas-MaK); 17.25; ex *Abha* 1979
Sister:
94171 BORE SEA (Fi) ex *Buraidah* 1979

● **94180 BRITTA ODEN** Sw/Sw (Gotav) 1978; RoC; 4500; 143.26 × 5.2 (470 × 17.06); TSM (Alpha-Diesel); 15.25; Stern door/ramp
Sisters (Sw flag):
94181 ANNA ODEN
94182 EVA ODEN

94190 CORAL GABLES Br/FRG (Schichau-U) 1977; RoC; 1500; 109 × — (357 × —); TSM (Polar); 15; ex *Miriam* 1981

94200 BACAT I In/De (Frederikshavn) 1974; Bg; 1400; 103.51 × 5.42 (337.92 × 17.78); TSM (Alpha-Diesel); 11; Catamaran Hull

94210 IVA Pa/Ja (Teraoka) 1978; RoC; 900; 93.81 (bp) × 3.52 (307.78 (bp) × 11.55); TSM (Niigata); 13; Stern door/ramp
Sister:
94211 ANI (Pa)

94220 SEADRAKE No/Sw (Marstrands) 1977; RoC; 1100; 93.27 × 3.50 (306 × 11.48); M (MWM); 14; ex *Nopal Sea* 1979

94230 SOL GEORGIOS Cy/No (Trondhjems) 1972; RoC; 600; 91.9 × 3.16 (301.51 × 10.37); TSM (Normo); 15; ex *Transit* 1980; ex *Michel* 1979; ex *Vechtstroom*; ex *Ostend Express* 1973; Side door

94240 VOLCAN DE YAIZA Sp/It (Felszegi) 1967; RoC; 300; 51.08 × 3.3 (167.59 × 10.83); M (Atlas-MaK); 11.5; ex *Firlingen* 1973
Sister:
94243 FLORNES (No) ex *Trillingen* 1971

94250 TUI CAKAU III Fj/Fi (Navire) 1975; RoC; 2500/7200; 129.85 × 5.33/6.4 (458.83 × 17.49/21); TSM (Bergens); 15; ex *Merzario Nubia* 1983; ex *Bia* 1982; ex *Merzario Nubia* 1979; ex *Bia* 1976; Stern door/ramp; 'KATATRAN' type; Semi-catamaran hull

94260 MAUNALEI US/US (Sun SB) 1944/65; Con/V; 17500; 198.74 × 10.03 (606.23 × 32.91); T (GEC); 17; ex *Hawaiian Queen* 1978; ex *Marine Devil* 1965; Lengthened and deepened 1965; Converted from 'C-4' type cargo ship 1965 (Alabama)
Sister:
94261 MAUNAWILL (US) ex *Hawaiian Monarch* 1978; ex *Marine Dragon* 1965

94270 C.V. LIGHTNING US/US (Bath) 1969; Con; 17900; 185.93 × 9.63 (610.01 × 31.59); T (GEC); 21
Sisters (US flag):
94271 C.V. STAGHOUND
94273 EXPORT FREEDOM
94274 EXPORT LEADER
94275 EXPORT PATRIOT
94276 ARGONAUT
94277 AMERICAN RESOLUTE ex *Resolute* 1982

★ **94280 KOSMONAUT VLADIMIR KOMAROV** Ru/Ru (Kherson) 1966; MTV; 13900; 155.8 × 8.5 (511 × 27.89); M (B&W); 17.5; Launched as *Genichesk*; Converted from 'Poltava' class cargo ship

94290 MATHILDA Fr/Fr (La Rochelle) 1977; RoC; 1100; 90.71 × — (297.57 × —); M (Crepelle); 14
Sisters (Fr flag):

94291 L'AUDE
94292 L'ARDECHE
94293 CAP FERRAT ex *Aurelia* 1982
94294 ANTHENOR
94295 LUBERON

94310 MANUKAI US/US (Bethlehem Steel) 1970; Con; 23800; 219.62 × 10.4 (720.53 × 34.12); T (Stal-Laval); 23; ex *Hawaiian Enterprise*
Sister (US flag):
94311 MANULANI ex *Hawaiian Progress*
Similar (bridge superstructure one deck lower) (US Flag):
94312 SEA-LAND ECONOMY ex *SL 181* 1973; ex *H P. Baldwin*
94313 SEA-LAND VENTURE ex *SL 180* 1973; ex *S T. Alexander*
94314 SEA-LAND CONSUMER ex *Australia Bear* 1973
94315 SEA-LAND PRODUCER ex *New Zealand Bear*
Similar (bridge further foreward and one deck higher) (US flag):
94316 MAUI
94317 KAUAI

94330 CAST SALMON Sg/Ne (van der Werf) 1970; Con; 1600; 114.51 × 4.15 (375.69 × 13.62); TSM (MWM); 14.5; ex *Flying Scot* 1983; ex *Greyhound* 1972

94340 DESAFIO Sp/Sp (Lorenzo) 1979; Con; 2000; 103.45 × 6.43 (339.4 × 21.1); M (Deutz); 15

94350 KAIRYU MARU Ja/Ja (Mitsubishi N) 1961; D; 2900; 88.97 × 5.61 (291.9 × 18.41); TSD-E (MAN)

94360 BALI Ia/FRG (O&K) 1957; D; 1400; 73.03 × 4.18 (239.6 × 13.71); TSR (Christiansen & Meyer); 10

94370 NORSEA Br/Ja (Mitsui) 1979; RoC; 6300; 150 × 5.12 (492 × 16.8); TSM (Mitsui); 19; ex *Ibex* 1981; Stern door/ramp
Sister:
94371 TIPPERARY (Br) ex *Puma* 1979

94380 ROLON NORTE Sp/Sp (Cadagua) 1977; RoC; 1800; 111.03 × 4.6 (364.27 × 15.09); M (Sulzer); 14
Sister:
94381 ROLON SUR (Sp)

94390 ROLON PLATA Sp/Sp (Construcciones SA) 1970; RoC; 800; 76.51 × 3.76 (251.02 × 12.34); M (MWM); 15
Sister:
94391 ROLON ORO (Sp)

94400 DUNGENESS Ch/Ne (Duijvendijk's) 1970; RoC; 500; 84 × 3.62 (275.59 × 11.88); M (MWM); 15; ex *ASD Astor* 1980; ex *Astor* 1973; ex *Libyaville* 1971
Similar:
94401 ZAIN (Si) ex *Lamara* 1981; ex *Orientville* 1976

● **94420 GYPSUM EMPRESS** Br/FRG (Deutsche Werft) 1956; B; 8200; 134.45 × 7.72 (440.78 × 25.33); T (GEC); 13; May have unloading gear
Sister:
94421 GYPSUM DUCHESS (Br)

94430 TOPIRA Br/Br (Burntisland) 1954; OO; 6900; 134.75 × 6.1 (442.09 × 20.01); R (Rankin & Blackmore); 10; ex *Sunbrayton* 1979

94440 BULK QUEEN Pa/US (Federal SB & DD) 1947; B; 8000; 132.9 × 7.57 (436.02 × 24.84); T (GEC); 12.25; ex *Gypsum Queen* 1978

94470 MIZAN Ia/FRG (Schlichting) 1963; BT; 1700; 77.98 × — (255.84 × —); R (Christiansen & Meyer); 14
Sister:
94471 MAJANG (Ia)

94490 MELBOURNE TRADER Au/No (Framnaes) 1975; RoC; 4500; 139.91 × 7.16 (459.02 × 23.49); M (Pielstick); 20; Stern door/ramp
Similar:
★ **94491 FICHTELBERG** (DDR) ex *Tor Caledonia*

94500 TOR GOTHIA Sw/No (Framnaes) 1971/77; RoC; 5200; 152.8 × 7.17 (501.31 × 23.52); TSM (Pielstick); 18.5; Stern door; Lengthened 1977
Sisters (Pa flag):
94501 JOLLY ORO ex *Nerlandia* 1980; ex *Tor Nerlandia* 1979
94502 JOLLY ARGENTO ex *Belgia* 1980; ex *Tor Belgia* 1979

94510 ATLAS IV Cy/No (Trondhjems) 1975; RoC/F; 2400; 109.71 × 5.2 (359.94 × 17.06); TSM (Nydqvist & Holm); 19; ex *Tarek B* 1983; ex *Falster* 1980; ex *Prince de Bretagne* 1975; ex *Falster* 1975; Bow door/ramp; Side door/ramp; Two stern doors/ramps; Lengthened 1977

94520 STENA MARINER Sw/No (Trosvik) 1976; RoC; 3500; 132.52 × 6.58 (434.78 × 21.59); M (Sulzer); 18.5; ex *Mariner* 1983; ex *Dana* 1983; ex *Seaspeed Dana* 1981; Funnel is on port side only (not twin funnels)
Sisters:
94521 AMIRA (Fr) ex *Dima* 1983; ex *Seaspeed Dima* 1980
94522 MARCEL C (Be) ex *Inger Express* 1981; ex *Seaspeed Dora* 1978

94525 CATHERINE SCHIAFFINO Fr/Ja (Tokushima ZS) 1978; RoC; 1600; 108.64 × 4.98 (356 × 16.34); M (Pielstick); 15.75; Stern door/ramp

94530 DON CARLOS Sw/Fi (Wartsila) 1976; V; 14500; 202.62 × 8.48 (664.76 × 27.82); M (Sulzer); 19; Side doors
Sister:
94531 DON JUAN (Sw)

94535 GLORIOUS ACE Ja/Ja (Hitachi) 1981; RoVC; 16900; 190.00 × 8.92 (623 × 29.27); M (B&W); 19; 2 side ramps (1 port, 1 starboard); 1 stern door/ramp (starboard)
Similar (2 side ramps and 2 quarter ramps):
94536 KYUSHU MARU (Ja)
94537 ZAMA MARU (Ja)

94540 ARGO FRG/FRG (Kroegerw) 1976; RoC; 3900; 127.03 × 5.41/6.55 (416 × 17.74/21.48); TSM (KHD); —; ex *Argo-Hellas* 1980; ex *Brabant* 1978; ex *Argo* 1977; Stern door/ramp

94550 BALTIC EAGLE Br/Fi (Rauma-Repola) 1979; RoC; 6400; 137.12 × 8.21 (449.87 × 26.94); TSM (Stork-Werkspoor); 18; Two stern doors/ramps
Sister:
★ **94551 INOWROCLAW** (Pd)

94560 BORE SKY Fi/No (Fredriksstad) 1977; RoC; 4700; 142.22 × 7 (466.6 × 22.97); TSM (MWM); 18
Sisters (Fi flag):
94561 BORE SUN
94562 CANOPUS ex *Finnforest* 1982; ex *Rolita* 1979

94570 DORA BALTEA It/It (Apuania) 1975; RoC; 3500; 135.52 × 6 (444.62 × 19.67); TSM (Fiat); 18.5; Stern door/ramp; Side doors/ramps
Sister:
94571 PO (It)
Similar (larger):
94572 DORA RIPARIA (It)

94580 ATLAS III Cy/No (Trondhjems) 1974; RoPCF; 2200; 109.61 × 4.92 (359.61 × 16.14); TSM (Polar); 19; ex *Raed B* 1983; ex *Scandinavia* 1980; Bow, side & stern doors; Lengthened 1976

94590 TRANSGERMANIA FRG/FRG (Sietas) 1976; RoC; 5600; 135.45 × 6.05 (444.39 × 19.85); TSM (MAN); 19; Stern ramp

94600 BUFFALO Br/FRG (Sietas) 1975; RoC; 3500; 125 × 3.79 (410.1 × 12.43); TSM (KHD); 18; Stern door

94605 DARNIA Br/As (Osterreichische) 1977/82; RoC; 2800; 114.38 × 4.58 (375 × 15.03); TSM (KHD); 18; Launched as *Stena Topper*; Bow door/ramp; Stern door/ramp; Rebuilt 1982

94610 PUMA Br/FRG (Sietas) 1975; RoC; 4000; 141.81 × 5.81 (465.26 × 19.06); TSM (KHD); 18; ex *Union Melbourne* 1980; Lengthened 1975; Stern door/ramp
Similar (gap in top superstructure deck):
94611 BISON (Br)

94613 ROLL GALICIA Sp/Sp (Lorenzo) 1982; RoC; 2800; 122.80 × 6.38 (403 × 20.93); TSM (MAN); 17.5; Stern door/ramp
Sister (Sp flag):
94614 ROLL VIGO
Similar (slightly smaller) (Sp flag):
94615 CIUDAD DE ALICANTE ex *Rollman* 1981
94616 CIUDAD DE CADIZ ex *Roll-Al* 1981

94620 ANZERE Sd/Ne (Vuyk) 1978; RoC; 5000; 151 × 6.2 (495.41 × 20.34); M (Sulzer); 18

94630 CORAL GABLES Br/FRG (Schichau-U) 1977; RoC; 1500; 109 × — (357 × —); TSM (Polar); 15, ex *Miriam* 1981

94640 UCHI Ar/Sp (Luzuriaga) 1968; ST; 700; 53.8 × 4.7 (176.51 × 15.42); M (Werkspoor); —; ex *Bueno Gonzalez* 1975

● **94650 MERCANDIAN TRANSPORTER II** De/De (Frederikshavn) 1978; RoC; 1600; 105.62 × 4.97 (346.52 × 16.31); M (MaK); 15; Stern door and side door (starboard); 'Merc Multiflex' type
Sisters:
94651 MERCANDIAN CARRIER II (De)

94652 **ALAFOSS** (Ic) ex *Dana Atlas* 1980
94653 **EYRARFOSS** (Ic) ex *Mercandian Importer II* 1980
Similar (with quarter ramp):
94654 **MERCANDIAN IMPORTER III** (De) ex *Medorient Challenger* 1983; ex *Mercandian Importer III* 1982
94655 **MERCANDIAN EXPORTER II** (De)
94656 **MERCANDIAN MERCHANT II** (De)
94657 **MERCANDIAN SUPPLIER II** (De
94658 **MERCANDIAN TRADER II** (De)

94660 **HONG LEE** My/Hong Kong (Hong Kong & W) 1958; C; 400; 51.08 × 3.11 (187.27 × 10.2); M (National Gas & O); 10; ex *Giang Lee* 1976
Sister:
94661 **HONG SOON** (My) ex *Giang Ann* 1976

94670 **AL ZAHER IV** Si/Sp (Construcciones SA) 1972; RoC; 2200; 99.17 × 5.81 (325.36 × 19.06); TSM (Deutz); 16; ex *La Durance* 1983; ex *Kerisnel* 1974; ex *Lilac* 1972; Stern door
Sister:
94671 **GUAYCURA** (Me) ex *Jasmine*

94680 **ANTONIO SUARDIAZ** Sp/Sp (Lorenzo) 1976; RoC; 2000; 106.36 × 6.2 (348.95 × 20.34); M (—); 16

94690 **ROSE SCHIAFFINO** Fr/Ne ('De Biesbosch-Dordrecht') 1972; RoC; 1500; 98 × 3.85 (321.52 × 12.63); TSM (MWM); 15; ex *Ador* 1980; ex *Saint Christophe* 1975; ex *Ador;* Bow and stern doors
Sister:
94691 **EVANGELISTAS** (Ch) ex *Condor* 1980

★94700 **MIKOLAJ KOPERNIK** Pd/No (Trosvik) 1974; RoC/TF; 2900; 125.61 × 4.5 (412.11 × 14.76); TSM (Sulzer); 16.5
Similar:
★94701 **JAN HEWELIUSZ** (Pd)

94710 **DYVI OCEANIC** Sg/No (Tangen) 1968; V; 5400; 175.8 × 6.86 (576.77 × 22.51); M (B&W); 18.5; Side doors
Sister:
94711 **DYVI PACIFIC** (Sg)

94720 **ATLANTIC** Pi/No (Drammen) 1965; RoVC; 1900; 148.6 × 5.27 (487.53 × 17.29); M (Sulzer); 17; ex *Dyvi Atlantic* 1983; Side doors

94725 **FRENGENFJORD** No/No (Trosvik) 1971; RoC/TF; 2000; 124.67 × 4.95 (409 × 16.24); TSM (Normo); 13; ex *Stubbenkammer* 1983; Stern door

94730 **AL-SHUWAIKH** Ku/Ja (Mitsubishi HI)-FRG 1967/80; LS; 34400; 195 × — (639.8 × —); M (Sulzer); approx 16; ex *Erviken* 1980; Converted from tanker and shortened 1980 (Meyer)

94740 **CALIFORNIA** US/US (Kaiser Co) 1946/54/60; C/Con; 13600; 193 × 10.5 (633.2 × 32.97); T (Hendy); 16.75; ex *Californian* 1980; ex *Mount Greylock* 1951; Converted from 'C-4' type cargo ship & lengthened 1954; Converted from Ore-/Oil 1960

94750 **GYPSUM COUNTESS** Br/Fr (La Seine) 1960; B; 8200; 135.9 × 7.72 (445.87 × 25.33); T (GEC); 12

94760 **UNION HOBART** Br/No (Framnaes) 1976; RoC; 4400; 135.79 × 7.17 (445.5 × 23.52); TSM (Pielstick); 18.5; Stern door
Sister:
94761 **UNION LYTTELTON** (Br)

94770 **AUTOBAHN** No/No (Batservice) 1972 RoVC; 500; 92.46 × 3.88 (303.35 × 12.73); TSM (Bergens); 14; Stern door

94780 **OLIVE ACE** Pa/Ja (Mitsui) 1977; RoVC; 12300; 176.26 × 9.03 (578.28 × 29.63); M (B&W); 19
Sister:
94781 **SUZUKASAN MARU** (Ja)
Probable sister:
94782 **ORANGE ACE** (Pa)

94790 **SUPER SERVANT 1** Ne/Ja (Oshima Z) 1979; RoC/HL; 10200; 139 × 6.18 (456 × 20.28); TSM (Stork-Werkspoor); 13; Submersible; Broken line shows maximum extent of immersion

94800 **SPEEDLINK VANGUARD** Br/Ne (Vuyk 1973/77; RoC/TF; 3200; 142.27 × 5.92 (466.77 × 19.42); TSM (Werkspoor); 18; ex *Stena Shipper;* ex *Alpha Express;* ex *Union Wellington* 1977; Launched as *Stena Shipper;* Stern door; Lengthened 1977

●94810 **NESTOR** FRG/FRG (Meyer) 1980; RoC/Con 5100; 168.8 × 6.45 (553.8 × 21.16); M (Stork-Werkspoor); 19

94812 **HUAL TRACER** Li/Ja (Kanasashi) 1981; RoVC; 12800; 180.02 × 8.82 (591 × 28.94); M

(B&W); 18.5; Side door/ramp (starboard): Stern quarter door/ramp (starboard)
Sister:
94813 **HUAL TRAPPER** (Li)

94815 **MADAME BUTTERFLY** Sw/Sw (Kockums) 1981; RoVC; 18700; 199.70 × 11.61 (655 × 38.22); M (Gotaverken); 18.25; Side door/ramp (starboard); Quarter ramp (starboard)
Sisters (Sw flag):
94816 **CARMEN**
94817 **FIGARO**
94818 **MEDEA**

●94820 **NOPAL MASCOT** No/Ja (Mitsui) 1978; RoVC; 17600; 194.52 × 8.2 (638.19 × 26.9); M (B&W); 19.5; Side door/ramp; Stern door/ramp

94824 **HUAL ANGELITA** No/Ja (Tsuneishi) 1981; RoVC; 14200; 180.02 × 8.52 (591 × 27.95); M (B&W); 17.75; ex *Angelita* 1982; Side door/ramp (starboard); Stern quarter door/ramp (starboard)
Sisters:
94825 **HUAL INGRITA** (Pi) ex *Ingrita* 1982
94826 **HUAL LISITA** (No) ex *Lisita* 1982
94827 **HUAL ROLITA** (Pi) ex *Rolita* 1982

94830 **NORDIC STREAM** Sw/Sw (Oskarshamns) 1979; RoC/Con; 8800; 183.14 × 8.47 (600.85 × 27.79); M (Sulzer); 14; ex *Qatar Express* 1982; ex *Finneagle* 1981; Two stern ramps (slewing)
Sister:
94831 **ATLANTIC STREAM** (Fi) ex *Gulf Express* 1981; ex *Finnclipper* 1981; ex *Gulf Express* 1979
Similar:
94832 **JOLLY AVORIO** (Sw) ex *Saudi Express* 1983; ex *Bandar Abbas Express* 1980

★94850 **HONG HE KOU** RC/Ja (Sumitomo) 1978; Bg/Dk; 1900; 134.5 × 4.8 (441.27 × 15.75); TSM (Pielstick); 10.25; ex *Oak* 1983; ex *Mammoth Oak* 1978; 'L-19' type; Barges float on and off through stern; The openings in the hull will not be apparent when barges are stowed
Sister:
★94851 **SHA HE KOU** (RC) ex *Willow* 1983; ex *Mammoth Willow* 1978

94860 **DAISHIN MARU No 11** Ja/Ja (Hayashikane) 1962; ST; 1500; 75 × 5.53 (246.06 × 18.14); M (Niigata); 13

94870 **KAI YANG** Ko/Ja (Hayashikane) 1970; ST; 3000; 95.61 × 6.71 (313.68 × 22.01); M (Kobe); 14.5; May be spelt '**GAE YANG**'
Sisters (Ko flag):
94871 **CHEOG YANG** (may be spelt **CHEOG YANG HO**)
94872 **SEO YANG**
94873 **POONG YANG**

94880 **CHIKUBU MARU** Ja/Ja (Usuki) 1971; FT; 5500; 110.72 × 6.7 (363.25 × 21.98); M (Mitsubishi) 14

94890 **ROSBORG** Sg/De (B&W) 1958/76; LS; 13100; 170.69 × 9.76 (560 × 32.02); M (B&W); 15; ex *Haukanger* 1976; Converted from tanker 1976 (Keppel Shipyard)

94900 **TAIYO MARU No 83** Ja/Ja (Hayashikane) 1965; ST; 1500; 73.79 × 5 (242.09 × 16.4); M (Kobe); 12.5
Similar (larger—Ja flag):
94901 **SHOYO MARU**
94902 **ZUIYO MARU No 2**

94910 **DAISHIN MARU No 12** Ja/Ja (Mitsubishi N) 1963; ST; 2800; 94.52 × 6.01 (310.1 × 19.72); M (Niigata); 13.25
Similar:
94911 **DAISHIN MARU No 22** (Ja) ex *Shika Maru* 1969

94920 **SHIRANE MARU** Ja/Ja (Shikoku) 1966; ST; 2500; 83.93 × 5.16 (275.36 × 19.63); M (B&W); 13.5
Sister (builder - Mitsui):
94921 **ZAO MARU** (Ja)

94930 **KISO MARU** Ja/Ja (Mitsui) 1963; ST; 2000; 84.97 × 5.31 (278.77 × 17.42); M (B&W); 12.5

94940 **TOYOTA MARU No 10** Ja/Ja (Kawasaki) 1970; RoVC; 12500; 160 × 7.52 (524.93 × 24.67); M (MAN); 18
Sisters (Ja flag):
94941 **TOYOTA MARU No 11**
94942 **TOYOTA MARU No 12**

94950 **PACIFIC HIGHWAY** Ja/Ja (Kawasaki) 1977; RoVC; 13500; 192.08 × 8.03 (630.18 × 26.34); M (MAN); 20.5
Sister:
94951 **ATLANTIC HIGHWAY** (Li)

94960 **EUROPEAN HIGHWAY** Ja/Ja (Kurushima)

1973; RoVC; 13500; 197.14 × 8.99 (646.78 × 29.49); M (MAN); 20
Similar:
94961 **TOYOTA MARU No 15** (Ja)
94962 **TOYOTA MARU No 18** (Ja)
94963 **OBERON** (Sg) ex *Univenture No 1* 1983
94964 **SOUTHERN CROSS** (Sg) ex *Nopal Lane* 1980

94970 **PERLIS** Sg/Br (Caledon) 1954; C; 1400; 64.34 × 3.37 (211.09 × 11.06); M (Ruston & Hornsby); 14
94971 **PERAK** (Sg)
Similar:
94972 **PETALING** (Sg)

94980 **AUBY** My/Br (H Robb) 1954; C; 1700; 69.73 × 3.59 (228.77 × 11.78); TSM (Ruston & Hornsby); 10.5

94990 **AKORA** Gh/Ja (Fujinagata) 1965; ST; 2000; 79.5 × 4.97 (260.82 × 16.3); M (B&W); 14.5
Sisters (Gh flag):
94991 **ASEBU**
94992 **BANKO**
94993 **SUBIN**

95000 **GOLDEN DRAGON No 1** Tw/Ja (Miho) 1967; ST; 1900; 78.49 × 5.79 (257.51 × 19); M (MAN); 14

95010 **WEYMOUTH** Br/No (Trondhjems) 1973; RoC; 1300; 105.39 × 3.52 (345.77 × 11.55); TSM (Normo); 15; ex *Leon R E* 1983; ex *Stena Transporter* 1975; ex *Jarl Transporter* 1975; Bow & stern doors
Sister:
95011 **CARIBBEAN TRAILER** (Br) ex *Kirk Trailer* 1980; ex *Stena Trailer;* ex *Nopal Sky* 1977; ex *Stena Trailer* 1974

95020 **PROJECT AMERICAS** FRG/FRG (M Jansen) 1979; RoC/HL; 9800; 138.95 × 8.5 (455.87 × 27.89); M (Atlas-MaK); 16; Can carry containers; Stern ramp
Sisters:
95021 **PROJECT ORIENT** (NA)
95022 **PROJECT ARABIA** (FRG)

★95025 **YUAN WANG 1** RC/RC (Jiangnan) c 1979; MTV; 17100; (displacement); 190.00 × 7.5 (623 × 24.61); —; 20; Helicopter platform aft
Sister:
★95026 **YUAN WANG 2** (RC)

95030 **MERMAID ACE** Li/Ja (Hashihama) 1972; RoVC; 3300; 130.59 × 6.32 (428.44 × 20.73); M (Sulzer); 17; ex *Daishin Maru* 1982

95040 **RIGOLETTO** Sw/Ja (Hitachi) 1977; RoVC; 17500; 190.02 × 8.5 (623.4 × 27.8); M (Sulzer); 18.25
Sister:
95041 **TRAVIATA** (Sw)

95045 **ASTRO COACH** Ja/Ja (Tsuneishi) 1980; RoVC; 16600; 186.01 × 9.00 (610 × 29.53); M (B&W); 18.5; 2 side doors (1 port, 1 starboard); 1 stern door/ramp
Similar:
95046 **PARAMOUNT ACE** (Pa)

95050 **DAISHIN MARU No 23** Ja/Ja (Usuki) 1966; ST; 2400; 91.29 × 5.51 (299.51 × 18.08); M (MAN); 15.25; ex *Yutaka Maru* 1971

95060 **DAISHIN MARU No 16** Ja/Ja (Osaka) 1965; ST; 1500; 77.81 × 5.53 (255.28 × 18.16); M (Niigata); 12.5

95070 **TAIYO MARU No 83** Ja/Ja (Hayashikane) 1965; ST; 1300; 73.79 × 5 (242.09 × 16.4); M (Kobe); 12.5
Similar (Ja flag):
95071 **SHOYO MARU**
95072 **ZUIYO MARU No 2**

95080 **FUJI** Ch/Ja (Mitsui) 1968; FT; 3900; 102.27 × 5.97 (335.53 × 19.59); M (B&W); 13.75; ex *Fuji Maru* 1979
Sisters (Ja flag):
95081 **HARUNA MARU**
95082 **KASUGA MARU**
95083 **KONGO MARU**
95084 **NIITAKA MARU**
95085 **ROKKO MARU**

95100 **TSUDA MARU** Ja/Ja (Usuki) 1972; FT; 4300; 110.7 × 6.78 (363.19 × 22.24); M (Kobe); 14

95110 **YAMATO MARU** Ja/Ja (Hitachi) 1970; FT; 4000; 108.95 × 6.2 (357.45 × 20.34); M (B&W); 14.25
Sister:
95111 **RIKUZEN MARU** (Ja)

95120 **SILVER GLORY** Gr/FRG (A G 'Weser') 1956;

C/V; 4900/6700; 141.41 × 7.10/8.03 (464 × 23.29/26.35); M (MAN); 16; ex *Ockenfels* 1978

95125 **EUROPEAN VENTURE** Li/Ja (Sumitomo) 1981; RoVC; 15600; 190.00 × 8.92 (623 × 29.27); M (Sulzer); 19.5; 2 side door/ramps (1 port, 1 starboard)

95126 **YOKOHAMA MARU** Ja/Ja (Sumitomo) 1981; RoVC; 17400; 190.00 × 8.92 (623 × 29.27); M (Sulzer); 19; 2 side door/ramps (1 port, 1 starboard); 2 quarter doors (1 port, 1 starboard)
Sister:
95127 **OPPAMA MARU** (Ja)

95130 **LEVANTE EXPRESS** It/Ja (Kanda) 1978; RoC/Con; 5700; 133.94 × 6.51 (439.44 × 21.36); M (MAN); 17.75; 'Boxer' type; Stern ramp
Sisters:
95131 **FENICIA EXPRESS** (It)
95132 **BOXER CAPTAIN COOK** (Br) (no stern ramp)

95140 **MAUNA KEA** US/US (Bethlehem Steel) 1967; Con; 3900; 103.1 × 5.57 (338.25 × 18.27); TSM (Caterpillar); 10; ex *Hawaiian Princess* 1979

95150 **BILDERDYK** Ne/Be (Cockerill) 1972; Bg/Con; 37000; 261.42 × 11.27 (857.68 × 36.98); M (Sulzer); 18; 'Lash' type
Similar (Li flag):
95151 **ACADIA FOREST**
95152 **ATLANTIC FOREST**

● 95160 **ARABELLA** Li/Hong Kong (Highfield) 1975; C/Con; 1600; 76.23 × 3.83 (250.09 × 12.56); TSM (KHD); 11; ex *Nedlloyd Sprinter* 1982; ex *Arabella* 1981; ex *Stefi* 1978; ex *Deckship Arabella* 1978; Stern ramp 'Deckship' type
Sisters:
95161 **CARINIA** (Sg) ex *Unicon* 1982; ex *Ghazi* 1980; ex *Carinia*
95162 **SAN JUAN** (Li) ex *Beulah* 1981; ex *Lissette* 1980; ex *Tarek* 1978; ex *Khorramshahr* 1976; ex *Deckship Brigida* 1976
95163 **DELICIA** (Li) ex *Malaysian Exporter* 1983; ex *Delicia* 1982
95164 **PEGASUS PEACE** (Ko)
Similar (stern ramp & different design of crane):
95165 **FRANCESCA** (Li)
95166 **ELEANORA** (Li) ex *Santa Cruz* 1981; ex *Finnorient* 1981; ex *Eleanora*
95167 **MAERSK ASTRO** (Li) ex *Gisela* 1980

95180 **DANA FUTURA** De/De (Helsingor) 1975; RoVC; 6000; 144 × 7.08 (472.44 × 23.23); TSM (B&W); 22.5; ex *Drosselfels* 1977; ex *Dammam Express* 1976; ex *Dana Futura* 1976; Bow & stern doors
Sister:
95181 **DANA HAFNIA** (De) ex *Drachenfels* 1977; ex *Dana Gloria* 1976

95190 **DANA MAXIMA** De/Ja (Hitachi) 1978; RoC-/Con; 4900; 141.51 × 6.56 (464.27 × 21.52); TSM (Pielstick); 18.2; Stern doors/ramps

95200 **BACO-LINER 1** FRG/FRG (Thyssen) 1979; Bg/Con; 23300; 204.1 × 6.67 (669.6 × 21.88); M (B&W); 15; Bow doors. Barges float on and off. Crane is shown in stowed position—dotted lines represent it swung fore-and-aft
Sister:
95201 **BACO-LINER 2** (FRG)
Similar:
95202 **BACO-LINER 3** (FRG)

95210 **CIUDAD DE CEUTA** Sp/Sp (Juliana) 1975; RoPCF; 2800; 101.66 × 5.67 (333.53 × 18.6); TSM (Pielstick); 18; Stern door/ramp; ex *Monte Contes* 1978
Sister:
95211 **CIUDAD DE ZARAGOZA** (Sp) ex *Monte Corona* 1978

95220 **MONTE BANDERAS** Sp/Sp (Juliana) 1976; RoC; 2000; 101.66 × 5.66 (333.53 × 18.57); TSM (Pielstick) 18; Stern door
Probable sisters (Sp flag):
95221 **MONTE BUITRE**
95222 **MONTE BUSTELO**

95230 **HAPPY MAMMOTH** Ne/Ne ('De Merwede') 1967/74/78; Dk/Bg/HL; 3800; 129.78 × 5.95 (428.8 × 19.51); TrS M (Atlas-MaK); 12.5; ex *Docklift 2* 1981; ex *Lady Jane* 1974; Rebuilt from Ro/Ro ship 1974; Lengthened 1978 (Boele's Sch.); Stern ramp

95240 **HAPPY MARINER** Ne/Ne (Verolme U) 1972; Dk/HL/Bg; 2400; 105.7 × 4.97 (346.78 × 16.31); TSM (Caterpillar); 12.75; ex *Docklift 1* 1982; Stern ramp

★ 95250 **BROCKEN** DDR/Ne ('Holland') 1976; RoC/HL; 1200; 81.01 × 3.95 (265.78 × 12.96); TSM (Liebkecht); 11.75; Bow door

Addenda

The amendments are listed in strict numerical order and are seperated into entries by short lines. The entry number is given in every case whether the ship name has been included or not.

00010
00019   AUSTRAL MOON→AMERICAN VETERAN (US) 1984

00380
00381   AGHIOS NICOLAOS broken up

00560   SHABAAN→ANNOOR II (Br) 1984

00740   BLITAR broken up

00930   MARGARITA III amend name to TIGER'S TAIL; Amend flag to Pa; Amend ex names as follows: ex Takis H 1983; ex Maximus 1982; ex Kassiopi 1970; ex Tennessee 1968
00931   AGILITY→MARGARITA III (Gr) 1981

01050
01053   BUTTON GWINNETT→GREEN VALLEY (US) 1984

01080   EKA DAYA SAMUDERA broken up

01360
01361   SAINT PAUL→CAPITAINE COOK III (Fr) 1984

01470   MONTJOLLY II→GLORIA L (Ch) 1984

01510   KOTA BALI broken up

01520   J.C. CRANE broken up

01630   ARAMEDIA→ANJALENA (Pa) 1984

01760   GALILEO GALILEI→GALILEI (Pa) 1984
01761   GUGLIELMO MARCONI→COSTA RIVIERA (—) 1984

01800   BOREA delete entire entry; appearance altered

01930
*01931 JI MEI→NAN HU (RC) 1983

02210   SAUDI ARABIAN→SAUDI MOON 1 (Si) 1984

02290   COOLHAVEN→HAVEN (Ma) 1984. Now broken up

*02320 FENG BAO→FENG HANG (RC) 1984

02350
*02351 BUKOVINA has been modernised, may be like OSETIYA in appearance (see no. 32915)

02390   GENTILE DA FABRIANO→ATTIKA (Gr) 1983

02480   AUSTRAL MOON→AMERICAN VETERAN (US) 1984

02600   SNOW FLAKE→SOUTH VIEW (Br) 1984
02601   MALAYAN QUEEN→SOUTH JOY (Pa) 1984
02603   SNOW DRIFT→SOUTH CATHAY (Br) 1984
02605   MALAYAN KING→SOUTH FOUNTAIN (Pa) 1984

02630   SNOW FLAKE→SOUTH VIEW (Br) 1984
02631   MALAYAN QUEEN→SOUTH JOY (Pa) 1984
02633   SNOW DRIFT→SOUTH CATHAY (Br) 1984
02635   MALAYAN KING→SOUTH FOUNTAIN (Pa) 1984

02720   BRA amend date of build to 1960/68. Now broken up
02722   SANTOS III broken up

02724   Add further sisters (Ru flag):
*02728/8 ANADYR
*02728/9 NIKEL

02750   SAUDI AL JUBAIL broken up

02760
02762   TZELEPI broken up

02790
02794   DIMITRIS→ALDIMA (Cy) 1984

02840   Add further sisters (Ys built—'Split'):
*02843 RACISCE (Ys)
02843/1 MEDITERAN FRIGO (Pa)

02850   Add further sister:
02854   TINEKE (Ne) (one further sister on order)

02995   Add sister:
02996   CALIFORNIA MARU (Ja)

03080
03091   COPACABANA→COPA (Bz) 1984

03100   Probable sisters 03101/2/3 have all been lengthened

03160   NEDLLOYD AMSTERDAM broken up
03161   NEDLLOYD ADELAIDE broken up
03163   VICTORIA 1→ARROW QUEEN (Pa) 1984
03165   NEDLLOYD ALBANY→ARROW KING (Pa) 1983

03290   HELLENIC PATRIOT→TENON (Br) 1984. Now broken up

03320   RAJAB 1 broken up

03380   REA B→GILLWATER (Br) 1984

03480   ROYAL SEA→NISSOS DELOS (Ma) 1984

03490
03497   JUNIPER→ARIETTA (Li) 1984

03500   VEGESACK broken up

03520
03521   ANTIPOLIS broken up

03580
03587   JUNIPER→ARIETTA (Li) 1984

03670   CORABANK→UNICOSTA (Pe) 1984

03730   CORABANK→UNICOSTA (Pe) 1984

03760   MANISTEE→FLEET WAVE (Br) 1984
03761   MAGDALENA→BLUESTREAM (Br) 1984
03762   MANZANARES→BARRYDALE (Br) 1984
03763   MAZATEC→SKY CLIPPER (Br) 1984

03900   SPARTAN REEFER broken up

04050   REA B→GILLWATER (Br) 1984

04090   VEGESACK broken up

04310   TUI CAKAU II→CAPITAINE SCOTT (Fr) 1984

04380
04381   RAJAB 1 broken up

04590   ANDRICO PROGRESS→NORWALK (Pa) 1984
04591   ANDRICO UNITY→BRIDGEPORT (Pa) 1984

04660
*04665 HEIDELBERG→SU FENG (RC) 1984

04690
04691   S.A. ALPHEN→KOTA AGUNG (Sr) 1984

04710
04713   HELLENIC STAR→C. STAR (Li) 1984

04720   BEACON GRANGE→MERCHANT PIONEER (Br) 1984

04780
04785   GRIGORIOS C IV→TIMIOS STAVROS (Pa) 1984
04786   BELLE amend name to SAINTE MARTHE (Pi)
04787   BELLE ROSE→BELLE (Pa) 1983

04880
04883   HELLENIC STAR→C. STAR (Li) 1984

04940   BEACON GRANGE→MERCHANT PIONEER (Br) 1984

04975
04977   C.C. RED SEA broken up

05070
05071   SELMA broken up

05250   GULF BANKER transferred to US Reserve Fleet
05254   GULF TRADER transferred to US Reserve Fleet

05270   AL BARAT→SEA EAGLE (Li) 1984

05310
*05329 GRAND FAITH→AN YANG JIANG (RC) 1984

05430
05431   NASIPIT BAY→SAINT GERASIMOS (Gr) 1984

05450
05452   AUBRAC→NESTOR SKY (Gr) 1984
        Take in further sister
05459/1 RUKWA (Ta) ex Jitegemee 1983; ex Lord Rajpar 1981; ex Jitegemee 1980; ex Soldrott 1978

05460
05461   WHITE BILLOW→FREEZER PRINCE (Br) 1984
05462   WHITE CASCADE→FREEZER QUEEN (Br) 1984

05710
05713   MANDAMA broken up

05760
05764   UNION KINGSTON→HENNA (Si) 1983→SAADALLAH (Si) 1984

05820
05825   JALAMANGALA→BELIEF (Pa) 1984

05900   SOLANGE P. broken up

05950   KARA CAREER broken up

715

05980
05981 **SMINARCHOS FRANGISTAS** broken up

06010
06012 **JALAMANGALA**→**BELIEF** (Pa) 1984

06190 **KHALIJ EXPRESS** broken up

06290 **FRIO AEGEAN** broken up
06291 **GAFREDO** broken up

06310
06311 **CHAITEN** broken up
06318 **PECAN**→**HISPANIOLA** (Pa) 1984
06322 **ARIANE 1** delete from entry; rebuilt

06410
06414 **AGIOS CONSTANTINOS**→**POLINA MARINA** (Ma) 1984. Now
broken up

06460
06504 **GOOD DOLPHIN**→**PRINCESS** (Pa) 1984
06505 **GOOD SUN**→**WAVE CREST** (Pa) 1984
06524 **SKLERION** add: ex Texel Light 1983; ex Sklerion 1982
06535 **KAPTA MICHALIS**→**EURCO BANNER** (Gr) 1984
06564 **SERRA BRANCA**→**SERRA** (Pi) 1983
06565 **SERRA DOURADA**→**UNIMAR** (Pe) 1983
06589 **TIBATI**→**TOPEGA** (Pa) 1984
06636 **HONESTY II**→**URANIA** (Gr) 1984
06637 **LORI R**→**SAFIR** (Pa) 1984
06639/7 **UNITY 1**→**NAYA** (Cy) 1984
06639/9 **CAPTAIN GEORGE L**→**EVELYN** (Pa) 1984

06690 **PAOLA C**→**PAOLA** (Ma) 1984. Now broken up
06691 **FRANCA** broken up

06750 **CABO SANTA LUCIA**→**KOTA ABADI** (Sg) 1984

06760 **IOANNIS** broken up

06820 **THAMESHAVEN**→**LANIN** (Pa) 1984

06950 **FAMILY ANGEL**→**DOMAN** (Pa) 1984

07030
07032 **GOOD SPIRIT**→**DISCOVERY** (Pa) 1984

07090 **SABINE** broken up

07180
07181 **LEMINA** broken up

07230
07232 **SEA RELIANCE** broken up

07280 **TRANS VASSILIKI**→**DEBRALINAS JOY** (Pa) 1984

07340
07341 **GOLDEN NIGERIA** broken up

07400
07401 **SMINARCHOS FRANGISTAS** broken up

07430
07432 **SEA RELIANCE** broken up

07650 **BALINTAWAK**→**BELINDA**(Ma) 1984

07660 **CANDELARIA** broken up

07680
07681 **SAUDI MOHAMED REZA** broken up

07770
07773 **PACIFIC AMBER** broken up

07820 **CER ALSIRAT** broken up

07830
07832 **SAUDI MOHAMED REZA** broken up

07950
07951 **ROGET** broken up

07990
07991 **OTI RIVER** broken up

08070 **NEDLLOYD FUKUOKA** broken up

08130
08132 **CAPITAINE COOK** broken up
08134 **CAPITAINE LA PEROUSE** broken up

08220 **NEPTUNO** broken up

08370
08373 **TOKIO EXPRESS**→**SCANDUTCH EDO** (FRG) 1984

08670 **ANDERS MAERSK**→**ANNA MAERSK** (De) 1984
08674 **ARTHUR MAERSK**→**ANDERS MAERSK** (De) 1984
08675 **AXEL MAERSK** converted to motor ship

09000 **ANDERS MAERSK**→**ANNA MAERSK** (De) 1984
09004 **ARTHUR MAERSK**→**ANDERS MAERSK** (De) 1984
09005 **AXEL MAERSK** converted to motor ship

09380
09387 **ZAPOLYARNYY** confirmed as a sister

09480 **YAOHUA** amend engine design to Sulzer

09830
09831/1 **KAWANA**→**ACE CONCORD** (—) 1984
Take in similar (shorter; builder IHI):

09837/5 **S.A. VAAL** (SA)

09839/2 **NEPTUNE GARNET**→**PRESIDENT EISENHOWER** (US) 1984
09839/3 **NEPTUNE JADE**→**PRESIDENT F.D. ROOSEVELT** (US) 1984

09910
09912 **FLORIANA** broken up

09940
09941 **ALPAC AFRICA** broken up

09950
09951 **MALDIVE PROMOTER**→**DYNASTY HILALI** (Mv) 1984. Now broken up

10050 **AUSONIA** delete entire entry; rebuilt

10290
10291 **VISHVA MAHIMA** broken up

10310 **KOROTAN** broken up
10311 **GORANKA** broken up
10313 **SAMUDRA JYOTI** total loss

10360 **ANNA A** broken up

10410 **ARABIAN MERCHANT**→**LEMONIA** (Ho) 1984

10620
10624 **SINGAPORE FORTUNE**→**GOLDEN HAVEN** (Pa) 1984

10670
10671 **MUNSTERLANDES** broken up

10700 **MECIS FLAG**→**JEHMAR LIFE** (Le) 1984. Note: now has large pipe
from funnel
10701 **MECIS PIONEER** total loss

10850 **d'IBERVILLE**→**PHILLIP O'HARA** (Br) 1983

10910 **MINOTAURUS** broken up

10930 **LINK LOVE**→**COMET** (Ma) 1984

10940 **ABU MISHARI AL KULAIB** broken up

11130
11131 **IRENE D** broken up

11190 **INTRA TRANSPORTER** broken up

11240 **CITY OF HYDRA** delete entire entry; now rebuilt

11530
11532 **SING TAO** broken up

11540 **MALDIVE PEARL** broken up

12230
12252 **KAIRA** amend to **KAYRA**

12700 **GOLDEN PRINCESS** broken up

12910 **EURCO R.** broken up
12911 **DAPHNEMAR** broken up

12940 **NATALIA** broken up

13050 **CITY OF CREMORNE** broken up

13150 **AURELIA DI MAIO** broken up

13440 **GOOD SKIPPER** broken up

13510
13514 **MUNSTERLANDES** broken up

13520
13521 **SAUDI AMBASSADOR** broken up

13580 **GOLDEN SAUDI**→**SHEIKH SAMEER** (Si) 1984

13590 **MILDA A.** broken up
13591 **DAMENHAN** broken up

13751 Later '**Super Atlantik**' type
Take in further sisters (Ru flag):
★13766/2 **PROSTOR**
★13768/1 **ALEKSEY GRACHYEV**

13780 **MALDIVE PRIVILEGE**→**DYNASTY HURA** (Mv) 1984

13930 **MALDIVE UNITY**→**DYNASTY MALE** (Mv) 1984

14020 **FELICITY**→**VARVARA TWO** (Gr) 1984. Now broken up

14040 **RIEDERSTEIN** broken up

14110 **SAUDI CLOUD** broken up

14170
14175 **CHERRY**→**CAYMAN** (Pi) 1984

★14260 **SAKURA**→**ZHILUO LAN** (RC) 1984

14290 **BIG ORANGE** broken up
14291 **MICHALIS** broken up

14300
14305 **GRAZKA** broken up

14530 **SEA CARRIER** broken up

14570
14571 **SARIA** broken up

14580
14585 **LUDWIK SOLSKI** broken up

14780	**MALDIVE PRIVILEGE**→**DYNASTY HURA** (Mv) 1984
14860	**DEVON EXPRESS** broken up
14870	**THEODOROS** broken up
15080	
15087	**WARSZAWA** broken up
15220	
15222	**RIVER ETHIOPE**→**NIC** (Cy) 1984
15270	
15271	**NAKWA RIVER** broken up
15273	**SAKUMO LAGOON** broken up
15276	**OTI RIVER** broken up
15280	**HANKA SAWICKA** broken up
15330	**NAFEESA** broken up
15370	
15374	**SINGAPORE FORTUNE**→**GOLDEN HAVEN** (Pa) 1984
15380	**JOHANNES LATUHARHARY** broken up
15390	**LADY JOSEPHINE** broken up
15630	
15631	**WESERLAND**→**KOTA TIMUR** (Sg) 1984
15830	**NEDLLOYD WISSEKERK**→**WISSEKERK** (Ne) 1984
15831	**NEDLLOYD WAALEKERK**→**WAALEKERK** (Ne) 1984
15832	**NEDLLOYD WILLEMSKERK**→**WILLEMSKERK** (Ne) 1984
15833	**NEDLLOYD WESTERKERK**→**WESTERKERK** (Ne) 1984
15930	**HADI** broken up
15990	**BRUARFOSS**→**HORIZON** (Pa) 1984
16460	
16462	**STENA NORDICA**→**ROI BAUDOUIN** (Be) 1983; add: ex Stena Danica 1981; launched as Stena Nordica; widened & deepened 1977
17343	Take in similar (different design of crane etc):
17344	**SEACOM** (Fr)
17580	**EDDA**→**ROGALIN** (Pd) 1984
18190	
18192	**ANASTASIA** broken up
18370	**ISLAND KOS** broken up
18480	**ALKMINI A.** broken up
18990	**QUEEN OF ALBERNI** Note: to be heightened by addition of new deck, c. 1984. Drawing shows vessel before this modification
19010	**HALSINBORG** amend spelling to **HALSINGBORG**
19210	**WILHEMSHAVEN** amend spelling to **WILHELMSHAVEN**
19290	
19291	**VIKING EXPRESS** amend to **WASA EXPRESS**. Renamed **KHALID 1** (Fi) 1984
19600	**MARINE CRUISER**→**MAJORCA ROSE** (Ma) 1984→**EQUATOR** (Ma) 1984
19740	**VOLENDAM**→**ISLAND SUN** (Pa) 1984
19741	**VEENDAM**→**BERMUDA STAR** (Pa) 1984
20875	Add further sister (Ru flag):
★20879	**KAPITAN MECAIK**
	Add probable sister (Ru flag):
★208791/1	**AVRAAMIY ZAVENYAGIN**
	Delete reference to ships on order
21110	**TUI CAKAU II**→**CAPITAINE SCOTT** (Fr) 1984
21180	**NISSOS RHODOS** broken up
21200	
21201	**ISLAND KOS** broken up
21360	**CHOAPA** broken up
21480	**HEBE 1** broken up
21510	**VARAZDIN** broken up
21512	**ZEMUN** broken up
22060	
22061	**ALA** delete from entry—altered in appearance
22790	Mod. **LEVANT** type. Delete entire entry; sequence is now CMFM
22793	
22830	
22833	**LEBLON** broken up
22840	
22847	**DAUGAVA** broken up
23040	**SEALOGS**→**SAHAR** (Pa) 1983
23140	**MIGHTY SPIRIT**→**NIRAU** (Ma) 1984. Now broken up
23144	**ISLAND OF MARMARA** broken up
23250	**BAHIA AGUIRRE** broken up
23251	**BAHIA BUEN SUCESO** broken up
23700	
23701	**VIKING EXPRESS** amend to **WASA EXPRESS**. Now renamed **KHALID 1** (Fi) 1984

23860	Add further sisters (Ru flag):
★23869	**BRIZ**
★23869/1	**GALS**
★23869/2	**MANGYSHLAK**
★23869/3	**MARSHAL GELOVANI**
★23869/4	**NIKOLAY MATUSEVICH**
★23869/5	**VIZIR**
★23869/6	**STVOR**
★23869/7	**GORIZONT**
23910	**FALCON** broken up
24030	
24082	**PRIDYATLES** amend spelling to **PRIPYATLES**
24270	
24272	**LAMTONG CHAU** broken up
24290	
24291	**FAWZIA** broken up
24292	**WAHEED** broken up
24540	**MASTER TONY K** broken up
24541	**DELFINI V** broken up
24570	**CALIOPE**→**LUCKY** (Pa) 1984
25240	**MEI ABETO** broken up
25300	**SEAWIND** broken up
★25650	**PEIKIANG**→**YU XIN** (RC) 1984
25700	
25704	**GOOD WARRIOR**→**CHIEFTAIN** (Pa) 1984
25880	**LEFKADIAN SKY** broken up
25881	**CEYOCEAN** broken up
26020	
26029	**BLUE WAVE**→**MINOAS** (Ma) 1984
26040	**GEMAR** broken up
26100	**IONIAN VICTORY** broken up
26110	**IONIAN SEA** broken up
26113	**AIS GIORGIS** broken up
26440	**SPAN** broken up
26570	**MAYSUN II** broken up
26571	**MIGHTY BREEZE**→**CAPITOL** (Pa) 1984. Now broken up
26680	**SANTA CLAUS** broken up
26700	**ALKMINI A.** broken up
26720	**TACAMAR VI**→**TAKAFA** (Pa) 1984
26770	**BARAO DE JACEGUAY**→**ANNA JO** (Gr) 1984
★26800	**GUANG PING**→**HONG QI 104**(RC) 1983
26840	
26841	**AIS GIORGIS** broken up
26890	**MOFARRIJ 1** broken up
26980	
26981	**IRINI**→**SPIRIT** (Ma) 1984
26990	**PACIFICO** broken up
28210	**TURBO P.** broken up
28220	**HONG MING** total loss
28260	**ARION** broken up
28280	**CEYLAN SAILOR** broken up
28340	**MIGHTY SPIRIT**→**NIRAU** (Ma) 1984. Now broken up
28344	**ISLAND OF MARMARA** broken up
28450	**CROESUS** broken up
28600	
28612	**ANGELIKI** broken up
28630	**MALDIVE PRIZE**→**DYNASTY UTHEEM** (Mv) 1984
28650	**UNILUCK** broken up
28720	**MOFARRIJ B.** broken up
28820	**GLAROS**→**ASTRAPI** (Ma) 1984
28880	**TAMBA** amend engine design to Sulzer
29270	**LEON PROM**→**ST. CERGUE** (Pa) 1984
29330	**SAUDI SUNRISE** broken up
29360	
29362	**TANIA** broken up
29380	**HELLENIC DESTINY**→**TINI** (Ma) 1984→**LISBOA** (Ma) 1984
29381	**HELLENIC LAUREL** broken up
29382	**HELLENIC SPLENDOUR** broken up
29410	**DIAMANTIS** broken up
29420	**TEGAL** broken up
★29520	**CHANG HUA**→**HUA DU** (RC) 1983

29690   **KALLISTO** broken up

29700
★29701   **WEILI→GUANG PING** (RC) 1976

29830   **CHERRY LAJU** total loss

29950
29952   **SHAHZAD→AYESHA** (Ho) 1984

30190
30191   **FORTUNE STAR** broken up
30192   **BLUE WAVE→MINOAS** (Ma) 1984

30425
30427   **C.C. RED SEA** broken up

30520   **EASTERN PEARL** broken up
30521   **EASTERN LEADER** broken up

30550   **DJATILUHUR** broken up

30580   **TANIA** broken up

30640   **TEGAL** broken up

30720
30721   **SAMUDRA DAYA** broken up

30730   **PACIFIC RIDE** broken up

31070   **HOLLAND** broken up

31220   **MOUNT CARIBBEAN** broken up

31270   **EASTERN PEARL** broken up

31700   **LADY KATINA** broken up

31730   **BRAZILIA** broken up

31750   **DESPINA→SEAIR** (Ma) 1984

31920   **HONG MING** total loss

31930   Add sister:
31931   **MARINA A.** (Gr) ex Paean 1984

32000   **ISLAND OF MARMARA** broken up

32020   **MIGHTY WIND→VASSILAS** (Pa) 1984

32070   **PAN ANTILLES→FREEPORT EXPRESS** (Pa) 1983

32230   **HANKYU No. 16→FERRY PUKWAN** (Ko) 1983

32300   **POLAR EXPRESS→AL FARIS 3** (Si) 1984

32840   **LINDBLAD EXPLORER→WORLD EXPLORER** (—) 1984

32915   **OSETIYA** add note: **BUKOVINA** (see nos. 02351 and 35370) has also been modified and may be a sister of **OSETIYA**

33200
33201   **CARIARI→EXXTOR-1** (Pa) 1983

33260   Add similar:
33262   **JACQUELINE** (Bz)

33810   **CHION TRADER→BANQUISE** (Pa) 1983

34050   **CAGAYAN DE ORO CITY** add: mast against bridgefront is a goalpost. Superstructure is now extended aft

34180   **MALDIVE FAITH→NORTHERN STAR** (Mv) 1984

34200
34204   **FRIGOANTARTICO→CAP FERRATO** (Pa) 1984
34206   **NORDLAND V.→ARAWAK** (Pi) 1984

34260
34261   **CER AMITY** broken up

34300   **LABRADOR REX→AZALEA** (Pa) 1984

34310   **HEBE 1** broken up

34370
34371   **KOSZALIN→BADR** (Eg) 1983

34470
34477   **DAUGAVA** broken up

34700   **BAHIA AGUIRRE** broken up
34701   **BAHIA BUEN SUCESO** broken up

34870   **GOLDEN HORSE** broken up

34872
34879   **DMITRIY POKROVICH** may be called **DMITRIY POKRAMOVICH**
  Add further sister (Ru flag):
★34879/1   **PAVEL STRELTSOV**

34890
34895   **ASTEROID→ASTERO** (Cy) 1984

34920
34921   **MALDIVE TOPAZ** broken up

35040   **SAKUMO LAGOON** broken up
35042   **NAKWA RIVER** broken up

35130
35138   **AUSTRAL MOON→AMERICAN VETERAN** (US) 1984

35370
35371   **BUKOVINA** has been rebuilt now and may have same appearance as **OSETIYA**—see no. 32915

35480
35482   **CEGLED→AGRIA** (Pa) 1984

35690   **PETROLA 33** broken up
35691   **PETROLA 34** broken up

35800   **LAKE PALOURDE** broken up

35820   **CORTEMAGGIORE→MELORIA** (It) 1984

35910   **EGMONT** broken up
35911   **DEVONSHIRE** broken up

35970   **MORVEN** broken up

36210   **TAXIARCHIS** amend flag to Ma. Now broken up

36410   **TAXIARCHIS** amend flag to Ma. Now broken up

36650
36654   **OVERSEAS JOYCE** broken up

36680
36683   **FIVE LAKES** broken up

36740
★36741   **CHUN HU→DA QING 52** (RC)

36790   **TZINA M** broken up

37000   **MIR** broken up

37100   **PETROLA 33** broken up
37101   **PETROLA 34** broken up

37260
37262   **SAROULA** broken up

37510   **ACAVUS** broken up
37510/1   **ACHATINA** broken up (appears as 37510)

37700
37701   **HENNING MAERSK→AGAPI** (Pa)1984

37790
37796   **SAN MARCOS** broken up

37830   **MARIE MAERSK→GIORGIONE** (Br) 1984

38130   **VIGIL** broken up

38140   **NICOLE SEA** broken up

38200   **RALLYTIME III** broken up

38330
38341   **PENHORS→FAL XII** (UAE) 1984

38630   **SICILMOTOR→SICILMO** (Br) 1984

38660   **HONESTAS→PIBIQUATTRO** (It) 1984

38730
38732   **WOLFEN→TAUNUS** (Pa) 1984**→NIAGARA** (It) 1984

38790
38791   **DEVONSHIRE** broken up
38792   **EGMONT** broken up

38940   **ASAHAN** broken up

★39000   **SAKURA→ZHILUO LAN** (RC) 1984

39010   **CLEOPATRA II** broken up

39050   **IONIAN SEA** broken up

39090   **ASAHAN** broken up

39260
39261   **SAPHO→ALECOS N. AGOUDIMOS** (Ma) 1984

40090   **BLUE SKY 1→SKY ONE** (Pa) 1984

40200
40202   **CRANIA** broken up

40250   **GELIGA** broken up

40750
40751   **PETROLA 11** broken up 1984
40753   **KYLIX** broken up

40840   **AL-BAKRY** broken up

41230   **DYNAMIC SAILOR** broken up

41310
★41322   **HONG QI 150→HONG QI 160** (RC)

41480
41481   **PETROLA 11** broken up
41483   **KYLIX** broken up

41760
41761   **ARGYRO M.→PANAGIA M.** (Pa) 1983

42030
42033   **DANE→ANVIL CROSS** (Pa) 1984

42390   **ALKMINI** amend country of build to Ge

42410   **MINOS** broken up

42460
42461   **SIMONE→SIMON** (Pa) 1984

42770	JOYCE CLARE broken up
43320	OSHEA EXPRESS amend type to RoVC
43860	GEORGIOS MII broken up

42770 JOYCE CLARE broken up

43320 OSHEA EXPRESS amend type to RoVC

43860 GEORGIOS MII broken up

44080 MALDIVE NATION broken up
44081 NIKY→MILENA A. (Ma) 1984

44200 SHOMAR HANAN→ROUA (Si) 1983

44250
44251 HENNING MAERSK→AGAPI (Pa) 1984

44270 LEFKAS→BELLINI (Pa) 1984

44390 MALDIVE NATION broken up
44391 NIKY→MILENA A. (Ma) 1984

44410 DRUZHBA broken up

44420 MARIE MAERSK→GIORGIONE (Br) 1984

44490 STRONG SKIPPER→LAMBOUSA (Ma) 1984

44570
44574 RED RIVER broken up

44690
44701 PENHORS→FAL XII (UAE) 1984

44720 GEORGIOS broken up

44870
44871 WOLFEN→TAUNUS (Pa) 1984→NIAGARA(It) 1984

44970 TOLMIROS→VOYAGER(Ma) 1984

45090 STAGAN broken up

45350
45383 AL SALEHIAH→BARU LUCK (Gr) 1984
45402 PAYIME→NEW FAME (Cy) 1984

45460 MIRAMAR PRIMA→ANTIGUA (It) 1983

45550
45551 ST. PAUL amend to SAINT PAUL. Now renamed CAPITAINE
       COOK III (Fr) 1984

45730 Add sisters (Ru flag):
*45732 DAUGAVA
*45733 VETLUGA

45770
45771 HELLENIC SEAMAN→PANAMA STAR (Pa) 1984

45790 WOOLLAHRA→OCEAN LYNX (Pa) 1984
45791 SAINT LUC→CABO SANTA INES (Pa) 1984

*45850 BUDAPEST→GOTHA (DDR) 1984

45860
45861 THEODOROS GIAVRIDIS→PROGRESSIVE (Pa) 1984

45930
45936 IRAN TEYFOURI amend to IRAN TIFORI

46020
46021 THEODOROS GIAVRIDIS→PROGRESSIVE (Pa) 1984

46040
46041 SATYA SOHAN→ARUN THAI (Th) 1984

46212
46213 IRENE GREENWOOD has been given a new 80 foot bow section
       which adds 20 feet to the overall length

46240
46245 SCOL RESIDENT→CINDERELLA 1984→FANNY (Br) 1984

46250
*46252 WEI HE amend to WEI HEI

46255
46256 CITY OF LIVERPOOL→CAMPANIA (FRG) 1984

46280
46283 PARTEM→NEW HAIHUA (Pa) 1984

46310 NEW ZEALAND ALLIANCE→GENERAL TINIO (Pi) 1984
46312 BRAVENES→MANILA BRAVE (Pi) 1984
46314 BELLNES→MANILA HOPE (Pi) 1984

46430
46431 PORT ALBERNI CITY→NORTHERN VALLEY (Sg) 1984

46480 ASIA HUNTER→IRAN TORAB (Ir) 1984

46520 SUNNINGDALE→PAGSANJAN (Pi) 1984

46560 NEW ZEALAND ALLIANCE→GENERAL TINIO (Pi) 1984
46562 BRAVENES→MANILA BRAVE (Pi) 1984
46564 BELLNES→MANILA HOPE (Pi) 1984

46660 Amend nos. 46663—46664 from probably similar to similar
46664 ROSELINE→DOMINIQUE L-D (Fr) 1983

46690 Add further similar (Gr flag):
46696 JANICE L
46697 JULIA L
46698 GEORGE L
46699 MARKA L
46699/1 PANTAZIS L
46699/2 TATIANA L

46710 CAPE STROVILI→STROVILI (Ma) 1984. Now broken up
46712 MYLOI→KALIM (Br) 1983

46900
46905 LABO→GAMBIA RIVER (—) 1984

46951 WORLD FRATERNITY→IRAN ADL (Ir) 1984 (possibly IRAN ADI)

47000
47003 TOCHIGI MARU→VLAHERNA (Cy) 1984

47020 COSMOTOR ACE→FLAMINGO (Cy) 1984

47030
47031 HODEIDAH CROWN→E.R. BRUSSEL (Be) 1984

47195 Add further sister:
47199/1 CANDIA (FRG)

47200 Amend all sisters to similar.
       Add further similar:
47212 MAGIC SKY (Li)

47213 WAARDRECHT→WILLINE TOKYO(Ne) 1984

47300
47301 TATAI SEA→SISSY H (Cy) 1984

47375 MANUELA PRIMA→MICHELE (Pa) 1984

47440
47446 IRAN TEYFOURI amend to IRAN TIFORI

47447 OVE SKOU→LLOYD EUROPA (—) 1984

47540
*47568 GIURGU amend to GIURGIU
       Add further sisters (Rm flag):
*47571/1 GIURGENI
*47571/2 GRADISTEA
*47571/3 HOREZU

47610
47612 CHEMIK broken up

47620 SHAYMA THREE broken up

47635
47637 MANILA→NEDLLOYD MANILA (Ne) 1984

47654 Add further similar:
47659/3 BENTHEIM (Pa)

47710
47711 MAGDALENA DEL MAR Add note: may now have one deck
       crane only

47730
47732 PIONEER No. 3→UNION GRAIN (Pa) 1984

47750 KEFALONIA SUN→SEA CROWN (Cy) 1984

47780 ADVARA→CALETA LEONES (Ar) 1984

47810 PEGASUS TIMBER→PEGASUS (Pi) 1984
47811 LIONS ROCK→FAT CHOY (Li) 1984
47813 ORKNEY→TORRES STRAIT (Sg) 1984

47920
47921 ASIAN ANVIL→BLUE DIAMOND (Cy) 1984

47930 Delete the following:
47933 DESERT PRINCE
47934 DESERT QUEEN

48072 Add word "sisters" before no. 48073.
       Add further sister:
48077/1 ALNAVE(Bz)

48079/1 CAPE TRAFALGAR→PORT ROYAL (Br) 1984

48150 ARIETTA GREGOS→ARIETTA (Cy) 1984
       Add further similar:
*48157/1 SVILEN RUSSEV (Bu)
48157/2 VARI (Gr)
*48157/3 GENERAL DABROWSKI (Pd)
*48157/4 LILIANA DIMITROVA (Bu)

48180 Add possible sisters:
48198 LOK VIKAS (In)
48199 LOK VINAY (In)
48199/1 LOK VIVEK (In)

48280 JAMAICAN STARS amend engine design to B&W

48390 SEKI ROKAKO→EASTERN UNICORN (Pa) 1984
48391 SEKI ROKEL→EASTERN PHOENIX (Pa) 1984

48410
48411 HELLENIC SEAMAN→PANAMA STAR (Pa) 1984

48420
48422 HOEGH STAR→CONCORDIA STAR (No) 1984
48423 HOEGH SUN→CONCORDIA SUN (No) 1984

48430 Add further sister:
48460/1 ATHENIAN ZOE (Cy) ex Athenian Anna 1984
48465 ACDIR II→JUGOAGENT (Ys) 1984

48580 Add similar (kingpost on forecastle and first crane aft of
       forecastle):
48581 LUIS CALVO (Sp)

48630	
48631	BLUE MASTER→NAHODA BIRU (Sg) 1984
48720	MIRAMAR PRIMA→ANTIGUA (It) 1983
48730	SLOMAN MERCUR→WOERMANN MERCUR (FRG) 1984
48731	SLOMAN MIRA→WOERMANN MIRA (FRG) 1984
49180	SHARK BAY→BEAUFORT ISLAND (Pa) 1984
49220	
49223	IOANNIS→IOANNIS DYO (Cy) 1984
49280	
49284	WAH LOK→HUA LI (RC) 1984
49342	Add further sisters (Ru flag):
★49347/1	IVAN BOGUN
★49347/2	IVAN SUSANIN
★49347/3	IVAN MAKARIN
49460	
49462	HOEGH STAR→CONCORDIA STAR (No) 1984
★49463	HOEGH SUN→CONCORDIA SUN (No) 1984
49470	
★49501	ACDIR II→JUGOAGENT (Ys) 1984
	Add further sister:
49503/1	ATHENIAN ZOE (Cy) ex Athenian Anna 1984
49510	
49512	HOEGH STAR→CONCORDIA STAR (No) 1984
49513	HOEGH SUN→CONCORDIA SUN (No) 1984
49640	TRISTAN→CALA MEDITERRANEA (Pa) 1984
49641	RIENZI→CALA ATLANTICA (Pa) 1984
49650	ELISABETH broken up
49660	
49662	LLOYD MARABA→FROTAMARABA (Bz) 1984 (may be FROTA MARABA)
49690	SANTA MONICA 1→SANTA ERINA (Pa) 1984
49740	
★49772	ACDIR II→JUGOAGENT (Ys) 1984
	Add further sister:
49774/1	ATHENIAN ZOE (Cy) ex Athenian Anna 1984
49850	
49851	TRANSAFE STAR→SEA ELITE (Pa) 1983
49865	ISLAND→TANGER (FRG) 1984
49866	CAPE→CADIZ (FRG) 1984
49875	Add sisters (with free-fall lifeboat system aft):
49879	INKA DEDE (FRG)
49879/1	AKAK SUCCESS (FRG) ex Robert 1984
49880	AROS ATHENE→ELBSTROM (FRG) 1984
49892	Add further sisters (De flag):
49899/2	SIGGA SIF
49899/3	OCEAN SIF
49899/4	FINN SIF
49900	ESTEBOGEN→VESTURLAND (Ic) 1984
50090	
50091	TRANSAFE STAR→SEA ELITE (Pa) 1983
50111	Add further similar:
50114/1	FLAMENGO (Bz) delete reference to ship on order
50130	MATTHIAS CLAUDIUS→LAKMUTHU 1983→MATTHIAS CLAUDIUS 1984→LHOTSE (FRG) 1984
50130/1	KALKARA→HEINRICH HEINE (FRG) 1984
50131	Add further similar:
50133/1	KARTAGENA (FRG) ex Concorde Tide 1984; launched as Birte Ritscher
50134	AHLERS BREEZE→RUTH BORCHARD (Be) 1983
50135	AHLERS BRIDGE→BUYO (Be) 1984
50137	KAHIRA→KALKARA (FRG) 1984.
	Add probably similar:
50138	KAHIRA (FRG)
50139	SCOL TRADER (FRG) ex Iceland 1984; ex Karthago 1984
50145	
50150	ALEXANDER SCHRODER→MAERSK BRAVO (FRG) 1984
50155	VILLE DE GABES→MARIS (FRG) 1984
50243	Delete the following:
50244	CAROLA SMITS
	Add further sister:
50246	CHRISTINA SMITS (Ne) delete reference to 3 more on order
50263	
50265	TAURIA→LOUISIANE 1984→MERZARIO SAUDIA (FRG) 1984
50310	
50312	PEP SPICA→RICKY LIFT (It) 1984
50330	
50333	OLGA BRAVO→ANVIL MOUNTIE (Pa) 1984
50340	ESTEBOGEN→VESTURLAND (Ic) 1984
50490	
50491	SOUTHERN STAR→UGUR YILDIZI (Tu) 1984

50575	
50577	USAMBARA→VICTORIA BAY (FRG) 1984
50585	
50586	SCANDUTCH CORONA→ATLANTIC CORONA (FRG) 1984
50660	
50663	PHILIPPINE JASMINE→AVRO VENTURE (1983)→JACK (Ma) 1984
50664	PHILIPPINE ROSAL→AVRO ENTERPRISE (1983)→JOHN (Ma) 1984
50930	
50932	LLOYD MARABA→FROTAMARABA (Bz) 1984 (may be spelt FROTA MARABA)
50980	
50981	TAGAMA→MARINGA (Pa) 1984
51030	
51036	SANTA MONICA→TAMAITAI SAMOA (Western Samoa) 1984
51310	LAGENA broken up
51540	
51543	MAHONIA→ELIZA (Va) 1984
51620	Add further sister:
51622	VAERMLAND II (FRG) ex Vaermland 1984
51740	
51743	SEVILLA→HOLLY 1 (Pa) 1984
51780	
51782	GERMA FOREST→FRANCOIS VILLON (Fr) 1984
51870	
51872	ZEPPACIFIC→CONCORD PACIFIC (Sg) 1984
51900	
51901	CARIA→PRINCE SCYNTHIUS (Pa) 1984
52200	ROBERTA 1→OBERTA (Br) 1984. Now broken up
52440	
52441	OLYMPIC STAR. Confirmed as a sister ship
52450	
52451	NORDIC TEXAS broken up
52720	Add further sister:
52720/2	ARKLOW RIVER (Ih) ex Bay Fisher 1984; ex Atlantic Coast 1979
52760	
52761	KATERINA M→HIBA (Ma) 1983
52863	
52865	SARGODHA→IRAN TAKHTI (Ir) 1984
52920	
52924	STRATHETTRICK→CHRYSOVALANDOU GRACE (Pa) 1984
53070	
53075	LYRIA→LOUISIANA (Bs) 1984
53135	Add sister (builder—Drammen):
53138	HAVLYN (No)
53210	
53211	NORDIC TEXAS broken up
53320	
53323	LATIRUS broken up
53390	
53393	REST→PUNTA CARENA (It) 1984
53480	CONSTANCIA→SPINOZACAG (Pa) 1984
53650	BEN FRANKLIN broken up
53660	ITALMARE→NELLION (It) 1984
53700	ARCHANGELOS III→ANGEL 1 (Pa) 1984
53710	
53711	DOMINIC→DENVER (—) 1984
53712	CREATOR→ALAMO 1 (Li) 1984
53740	BEN FRANKLIN broken up
53840	DRYS→DRYAS (Ma) 1984
54190	BARBER MENELAUS→MENELAUS (Br) 1984
54191	BARBER MEMNON→MEMNON (Br) 1984→LLOYD SAO FRANCISCO (Br) 1984
54192	MENESTHEUS→LLOYD PARANA (Br) 1984
54270	DORITAL→ORITA (Pa) 1984. Now broken up
54340	BARBER MENELAUS→MENELAUS (Br) 1984
54341	BARBER MEMNON→MEMNON (Br) 1984→LLOYD SAO FRANCISCO (Br) 1984
54342	MENESTHEUS→LLOYD PARANA (Br) 1984
54390	RESOLUTE→OPPORTUNITY (Li) 1983. Now broken up
54540	
54542	JAPAN ADONIS broken up
54660	
54662	SAUDI GIZAN→FREEDOM (Ma) 1984
54850	
54852	TAKAOKA MARU broken up

55050	HAR CARMEL→NORA (Pa) 1984
55100	ALBION→PYLOS (Gr) 1984
55170	IAPETOS broken up
55250	KOREAN CEMENT II broken up
55380	SIRENA amend tonnage to 10900
55500	OGDEN SUNGARI→SUNGARI (—) 1984
55590	STAFFORDSHIRE amend flag to Br. Amend tonnage to 45300
55630	ESSO BREGA→SNAM PALMARIA (It) 1984

55894 Add sisters (Fr built—L'Atlantique):
55896 CAM BILINGA (Cn)
55897 CAM EBENE (Cn)

56090 SLOMAN MERCUR→WOERMANN MERCUR (FRG) 1984
56091 SLOMAN MIRA→WOERMANN MIRA (FRG) 1984

56120
56121 ALBION STAR→RHEINGOLD (FRG) 1984
56122 DEVON→WALKURE (FRG) 1984

56370
56372 TAKOAKA MARU amend to TAKAOKA MARU. Now broken up

56410 FABIAN broken up
56412 OCEAN TRADER→MIRAFIORI (Li) 1984

56430 TOKUHO MARU→RAINBOW GAS (Pa) 1984

56580
56581 OROPESA→MERCHANT PRINCIPAL (Br) 1984

56630 PHILIPPINE QUIRINO→PHILIPPINE OCEAN (Pi) 1984

56639
56641 LAGOS PALM→LLOYD RIO (Br) 1984
56645 LAREDO (now confirmed as a sister)→LANKA ASITHA (Li) 1984
56646 EURO SEA→MANILA BAY (Pi) 1984→LLOYD SAO PAULO (Pi) 1984

56649 SANDVIKEN→TURK (Th) 1984

56700 HIRA II may be spelt HIRA 2

56900 MOFARRIJ C. broken up

56920 FLORES→FAI HONG (Li) 1984

56950 JILL CORD→ORION (Li) 1984

57100 LEFTHERO broken up

57150 GLYFADA BREEZE→VIRGINIA (Bs) 1984. Amend ex names as follows: ex Glyfada Breeze 1984; ex Oriental Merchant; ex Emilia Rosello 1977

57340
57341 MARITIME PIONEER→FORTUNE FALCON (Mv) 1984

57350
57351 YERUPAJA→ATLANTIC PROSPERITY (Pa) 1984

57360 AMETHYSTOS→HIGH TIDE 1 (Pa) 1984

57420 TEL-AVIV→LAVI (Ma) 1984

57590 ALBION→PYLOS (Gr) 1984

57620 PHILIPPINE QUIRINO→PHILIPPINE OCEAN (Pi) 1984

57625
57625/1 SWEET SULTAN→MIKOLADY (Pa) 1984
57627 BALDER HOPE→WOOD STAR (Pa) 1984

57730 HIRA II may be spelt HIRA 2

57840 AVIN OIL LEADER broken up

58420 OGDEN CHARGER→OMI CHARGER (—) 1984
58425 OGDEN CHAMPION→OMI CHAMPION (—) 1984
58426 OGDEN WABASH→OMI WABASH (—) 1984
58427 OGDEN WILLAMETTE→OMI WILLAMETTE (—) 1984

58490
58491 OTTAWA→JESSICA (Sw) 1984

58560 Add similar (improved version with satellite aerial from radar mast etc):
58587 ARITA (Li)

58600
58604 PETRADI→ALPHA (1983)→ALPHA III (Pa) 1983

58630 SHANNON→LAVANTTAL (As) 1984

58700 SKYRIAN ROVER broken up

58750 ARMONIKOS→VERITAS (Ma) 1984

58810
58811 MEGA TRAVELLER broken up

58840
58843 TESUBU II total loss

58870
58871 ANANGEL PRUDENCE broken up

58880 ERNE broken up

59260 GRANIKOS broken up

59300 LEDRA broken up

59320
59321 CEYLAN SKIPPER→ATAMAS (Ma) 1984

59410 MALDIVE PLEDGE→SOUTHERN QUEEN (Mv) 1984

59520
59521 IPPOLITOS→ELLIOT (Pa) 1984
59522 FORUM STAR→SITIA BEAUTY (Ho) 1984

59540 DESPINA V→TABATHA G (Br) 1984

59560 DIANA→ROMANA (Le) 1984

59600
59604 BERKBORG→CHIARETTE (It) 1984

59610
59611 HILDEGARD→ILDE (Pa) 1984
59614 GUDRID→GUDRIDE (Pa) 1982

59620 BREEHORN→PORTHOS (Gr) 1984.
        Add further sister:
59621/1 ATHOS (Gr) ex Breehees 1984; ex Vaddas 1975

59750
59757 ALPAMAYO→GOLDEN AMMAN (Pa) 1984
59758 ALFA amend to ALPHA. Now renamed ALPHA III (Pa) 1983

59770
59771 ALBION STAR→RHEINGOLD (FRG) 1984
59772 DEVON→WALKURE (FRG) 1984

59970 NORMAN PACIFIC→SINGA PACIFIC (Sg) 1984

60030
60031 ROSE MALLOW→FRIO CARIBIC (Pa) 1984

60070
60181 JOHN A. broken up

60320 GRADIENT ENERGY→ARMONIKOS (Li) 1984

60530 ARMONIKOS→VERITAS (Ma) 1984

60550 KONG HAAKON VII broken up

61010
61011 HUDSON DEEP→SUNDA SEA (Pa) 1984
61013 ARIZONA SUN→BANAWE (Pi) 1984
61033 CATHERINE ANN→KOREAN TRADER (Li) 1983

61040 ARCHIMEDES amend to ARCHIMIDIS. Now renamed MERCUR I(Pa) 1984
61044 MANILA ENTERPRISE→IRAN EMDAD (Ir) 1984

61045
61045/1 SWEET SULTAN→MIKOLADY (Pa) 1984
61047 BALDER HOPE→WOOD STAR (Pa) 1984

61050
61054 MONTROSE→ROZITA (Li) 1983

61065
61066 KRATINOS→LAS ROSAS (Cy) 1984
61067 KALYPSO→TUXPAN (Pa) 1984

61070
61073 HAND FORTUNE→KRITONAS (Gr) 1983

61120
61121 FALANI→KOZANI (Cy) 1984

61160
61165 MYRINA→BRAVE MOTHER (Cy) 1984

61205 ASIA BEAUTY→SEA JADE (Li) 1984
61206 ASIA BRAVERY→SEA DIAMOND (Pa) 1984
61207 ASIA HONESTY→SEA FORTUNE (Li) 1984

61280 CONSTANCIA→SPINOZACAG (Pa) 1984

61290 TIARET→CLARET (Ma) 1984

61400
61409/7 PACIFIC DRAGON→HUEY AN (Tw) 1984
        Add further sisters:
61409/17 BANGLAR MONI (Bh) ex Antje 1983
61409/18 L'ABANGA (Ga)
61409/19 LA MPASSA (Ga)
61409/20 MERKUR BEACH (Li)
61409/21 MERKUR DELTA (Li)
61409/22 SAXONIA (Li)

61460
61461 MILANGO→BINTAN (Pa) 1983
61462 RHODIAN HELMSMAN→WESTFLOW (Pa) 1984

61520
61524 HARRY D→ANGETIMOR (Pa) 1983

61610
61622 MOUNT ORO→TELSTAR (Tw) 1984

61640
61646 HELIOS MARU amend to HELIOS. Now renamed SANG THAI POWER (Th) 1984
61659 MOUNT BOLIVAR→NEW STAR (Pa) 1984
61660 HONAM→TROPICAL RAINBOW (Pa) 1983
61667 TOW TRADER→NEW GENSTAR (Sg) 1984

61760 LEDRA broken up

61770	
61772	CAPETAN PSARROS→ALEXIA (Gr) 1984
61880	
61881	KING NESTOR→LINA S. (Pa) 1984
61900	MARINA→MIRANDA (Pa) 1984
62075	BAMENDA PALM→LLOYD TEXAS (Br) 1984
62140	
62141	ANTIGUA→FIDELITE (Pa) 1984
62220	
62221	TIARA→KALLIPOLIS (Cy) 1984
62224	ROYAN→SAINTE MAXIMILIEN (Pi) 1983
62230	
62232	OCEAN ACE→LEO TORNADO (Pa) 1984
62234	PACIFIC LEISURE amend from sister to similar. Add similar (builder—Minami):
62236	YUE HOPE (Pa)
62237	EMERALD STAR (Pa) ex Yue Flower 1984
62270	
62271	LUNG YUNG→PALEMBANG (Pa) 1982
62320	SEALOGGER broken up
62350	
62351	SUNNY MED broken up
62410	SKYRIAN ROVER broken up
62420	JOULE broken up
62430	
62434	LAPIS→INDUSTRIAL TRADER (Pa) 1984
62530	GRANIKOS broken up
62540	MARTIN S. broken up
62550	ELENI broken up
62630	NEDLLOYD NIGER→NIGER (Ne) 1984. Add sister:
62631	NILE (Ne) ex Nedlloyd Nile 1984
62790	
62793	MICHAEL C. LEMOS broken up
62900	TANTALUS→TANTRA (Cy) 1984
63020	OGDEN SUNGARI→SUNGARI (—) 1984
63130	
63134	MUNDACA→YUCATAN VALLEY (Li) 1984
63220	
63223	LATIRUS broken up
63260	
63262	CALDERETA→BUYUK TIMUR (Tu) 1984
63280	AL RAFIDAIN→VULCAN (Cy) 1984
63390	
63393	PERSEUS→TRISEA (Gr) 1984
63420	POGEEZ→CARIBBEAN BREEZE (Li) 1984
63550	LAKE MENDOCINO→DIAMOND GLORIOUS (Li) 1984
63720	BRAGA→OSOR (Pa) 1984
63900	
63902	JAPAN ADONIS broken up
64010	
64012	SYLVANIA broken up
64020	NORBEGA broken up
64050	NANNY→KING ALEXANDER (Gr) 1984
64180	TRANSUD IV→MYSTRAS (Gr) 1984
64310	
64320	ESSO DALRIADA→SEAL ISLAND (Li) 1984
64322	
64324	VIATOR→MOSTOLES (Pa) 1984
64330	
64332	JAGRANDA→MOSBORG (No) 1984
64375	
64376	ELVIRA C→STENA PACIFICA (Li) 1984
64660	MARINE EAGLE broken up
65150	GUNGNIR 1 broken up
65151	ROBERTA 1→OBERTA (Br) 1984. Now broken up
65310	AGIP ANCONA→SPLENDOR (Cy) 1984
65450	EASTWAY broken up
65460	ALECOS M broken up
65500	CAPRICORN broken up
65590	VIKING→TRITON (—) 1984
65650	
65653	TESUBU II total loss

65670	
65671	TEXACO GHENT→ASTERIAS (Cy) 1984
65720	
65726	ANCO ENTENTE→STOLT ENTENTE (Fr) 1983
65820	
65822	ASEAN LIBERTY broken up
65823	MONARCH broken up
65840	CETRA CENTAURUS→SKRIM (Li) 1984
66020	
66021	YPAPANTI→ERSI (1984). Now broken up
66250	HOPECLIPPER→STANDARD ARDOUR (Gr) 1984
66570	
66571	THORHEIDE→POINTE DE CORSEN (Fr) 1984
66573	THORODLAND→ST. MONICA (Li) 1984
66574	CHEMTANK HAMBURG→CHEMICAL CONTENDER (Li) 1984
67130	CORNELIA→MARIAN (Ne) 1984
67180	OCEAN GIRL→CAROLINE (Li) 1984
67460	BRAS→OLIVER (FRG) 1984
67550	
67553	MICHAEL C. LEMOS broken up
67620	NORBEGA broken up
67680	Add further probable sisters:
67689/6	ATHENIAN FIDELITY (Cy)
67689/7	ATHENIAN BEAUTY (Cy)
67689/8	ATHENIAN CHARM (Cy)
67740	
67741	AL AHOOD broken up
67830	FABIAN broken up
67832	OCEAN TRADER→MIRAFIORI (Li) 1984
67910	OGDEN SUNGARI→SUNGARI (—) 1984
68170	TANTALUS→TANTRA (Cy) 1984
68260	LAKE MENDOCINO→DIAMOND GLORIOUS (Li) 1984
68290	
68292	SEVEN TEAM amend to SEVENSEAS CONQUEROR. Now renamed SHIN-KOBE MARU (Ja). Amend ex name to: ex Sevenseas Conqueror 1984
68310	NORMAN PACIFIC→SINGA PACIFIC (Sg) 1984
68320	
68323	CARBAY→SOUTH BAY (Br) 1984
68324	CARCAPE→SUNSET PEAK (Br) 1984
68325	AVENGER→LANTAU PEAK (Br) 1984
68360	
68361	ROSE MALLOW→FRIO CARIBIC (Pa) 1984
68400	
68402	SYLVANIA broken up
68430	FABIAN broken up
68432	OCEAN TRADER→MIRAFIORI (Li) 1984
68530	
68533	MOSTUN→MAGNUS (No) 1984
68551	NIGMA→ENDEAVOUR (Pa) 1984
68620	
68621	NEMEA→ELEFTHERIA (Pa) 1984
68680	CLEARWATER BAY broken up
68830	COAL TRANSPORTER→TRANSPORTER (Li) 1984
68840	VARENNA→OBO BARON (No) 1984
68850	PLATINUM TRANSPORTER→VOYAGER (Li) 1984
68870	TAL broken up
68920	
*68922	SOKOLICA→ARGOSY (Cy) 1983→SOKOLICA II (Pd) 1984
69100	GEORGIA P. broken up
69120	METAL TRANSPORTER broken up
69121	ORE TRANSPORTER→CRETAN SKY (Pa) 1984
69300	LIKE ONE broken up
69380	CHERRY NES→ROVER STAR (Pa) 1984
69420	
69421	REIKO→JAMAL SHAH (Ms) 1984
69450	EVA broken up
69470	ORION broken up
69480	KONG HAAKON VII broken up
69610	
69611	ENERGY PRODUCTION broken up
69730	STOW PRINCESS broken up
69760	YANXILAS broken up

69920	HOPECLIPPER→STANDARD ARDOUR (Gr) 1984
69930	CORINTHIAN broken up
69950	
69952	ASEAN LIBERTY broken up
69953	MONARCH broken up
70250	PIONEER II→LARA (Pa) 1984
70360	ATHENA→ELOTA (Gr) 1984
70460	LETO→ALKYON (Gr) 1984. Now broken up
70590	
70593	DAVID SIQUEIROS could be spelt DAVID SIKEYROS
70620	KYNOSSOURA broken up
70670	IRENES RHAPSODY broken up
70970	ETHEL EVERARD→ANGIE (Ma) 1984
71040	Add further sister (Ru flag):
★71060/1	PIONER KOLY
	Add sisters (DDR flag):
★71060/2	HEIDENAU
★71060/3	RABENAU
71130	
71131	TIARA→KALLIPOLIS (Cy) 1984
71134	ROYAN→SAINTE MAXIMILIEN (Pi) 1983
71150	PACIFIC QUEEN→SWALLOW (Cy) 1984
71170	
71171	HUDSON DEEP→SUNDA SEA (Pa) 1984
71173	ARIZONA SUN→BANAWE (Pi) 1984
71193	CATHERINE ANN→KOREAN TRADER (Li) 1983
71220	PROIKONISOS→KYZIKOS (Cy) 1984
71250	
71252	OCEAN ACE→LEO TORNADO (Pa) 1984
71252/1	PACIFIC LEISURE amend from sister to similar
	Add similar (builder Minami):
71255	EMERALD STAR (Pa) ex Yue Flower 1984
71256	YUE HOPE (Pa)
71260	
71263	HAND FORTUNE→KRITONAS (Gr) 1983
71490	GOOD CHAMPION→JASMINE II (Pa) 1984
71500	
71502	AL DAMMAM 1→KRITI SAMARIA (Gr) 1984
71505	
71507	ELONA→PLONA (Cy) 1984
71510	VENUS→CASTOR (—) 1984
71920	
71921	HILDEGARD→ILDE (Pa) 1984
71924	GUDRID→GUDRIDE (Pa) 1982
71930	
71934	BERKBORG→CHIARETTE (It) 1984
71950	SCILLA→JENLINK (Sg) 1984
71970	
71971	ROSE MALLOW→FRIO CARIBIC (Pa) 1984
★72000	CAPE RION→PING GUE (RC) 1984
72050	GRIMSBY→ROSEHILL (Pa) 1984
72051	GIORGOS K→AFRICAN (Pa) 1983
72140	
72144	INEZ V→ARGO (Ne) 1983
72180	NEDLLOYD WISSEKERK→WISSEKERK (Ne) 1984
72182	NEDLLOYD WESTERKERK→WESTERKERK (Ne) 1984
72183	NEDLLOYD WILLEMSKERK→WILLEMSKERK (Ne) 1984
72280	GOOD LEADER→PRESIDENT 1 (Pa) 1984
72345	Add sister:
72346	TOKUMARU (Li) ex Berge Captain 1984
72383	
72384	HYDROLOCK amend flag to Br.
	Add sister (Pa flag):
72387/1	BALTIC MERMAID
72430	
72435	PANAMAX UNIVERSE→STAR OF MIRANDA (Pa) 1984
72490	
72492	AEGEAN POLYVOS→OLYMPOS (Gr) 1983
72535	Add further sister:
72541	SOUTHERN ISLAND (Fa)
72550	
72551	CARIA→PRINCE SCYNTHIUS (Pa) 1984
72590	MONTE D'ORO→MOUNIVET (Ho) 1984
72680	
72687	BOBERG→COBURG (FRG) 1984
72750	
72759	MIGNON→KATARINA (Sw) 1984

72830	
72831	TRANSCON→CATHY G (Li) 1984
72970	OREA KETI→PAOLA O (Pa) 1984
72980	
72982	AEGEAN POLYVOS→OLYMPOS (Gr) 1983
73090	DANIELLE broken up
73220	
73221	GOOD TARGET→PELLA (Pa) 1984
73360	IKAN BILIS→OSTRIA (Li) 1984
73361	EASTERN RIVER→KARMILA (1980)→ESPEROS (Gr) 1984
73380	ITALMARE→NELLION (It) 1984
73660	FRAT 1→AROS FREIGHTER (Pa) 1983
	Add sister:
73661	THEODOR STORM (FRG) ex Baltic Heron 1983; ex Theodor Storm 1978
73720	
73724	LUCY BORCHARD→DISARFELL (Ic) 1984
73730	
73735	NEDLLOYD PRIDE→MARE PRIDE (Pa) 1983
73740	VERNIA→SEAFIELD (Br) 1984
73743	
73749/3	VILLE DU MISTRAL→ESTE (Pa) 1984
73750	LADY M.A. CROSBIE→DAUPHINE (Cy) 1984
73770	The following have been lengthened by 13 m but sequence remains KMF:
73771	BELL RACER
73775	BELL RULER
73790	
73797	HISPANIA→LINDAUNIS (FRG) 1984
73830	
73835	ORCHID STAR→LADY DOROTHY (Cy) 1984
73880	
73887	ZIM MANILA→HARVESTER (Sg) 1983
73940	
73959	JULIANE→AKAK VICTORY (FRG) 1984
74000	GERMA KARMA→KEPWEALTH (Sg) 1984
74005	Add similar:
74006	MAGNOLIA (FRG)
	Add probably similar (shorter):
74007	VANERNSEE (FRG)
74040	ALFA→PHAEDRA (Cy) 1984
74060	ATLANTIC PREMIER→INCOTRANS PREMIER (Sw) 1984
74061	ATLANTIC PRELUDE→INCOTRANS PRELUDE (Sw) 1983
74070	MONT LOUIS total loss
74090	
74091	MANAURE V→RIO CAPAYA (Ve) 1984
74120	MONOSANDALOS→ATTAVIROS (—) 1984
74170	FRATERNIA→LERNIA (Sw) 1984
74420	
74421	GRAND HAVEN→PHOENIX VENTURE (Li) 1984
74435	
74436	TFL ADAMS→ARTIMON (1984)→WESER EXPRESS (FRG) 1984.
	Add similar:
★74436/1	QUI HE (RC)
74560	ORIENT VENTURE broken up
74680	ALFIE 1 broken up
74740	PALLADE broken up
74990	BREEZE→AKTI (Br) 1984
75250	CYMBELINE→GREEN ROCK (Br) 1984
75290	
75295	MARGRET→SKANDEN (Fi) 1984
75450	
75455	SUAVITY→SPEED BULK (No) 1984
75600	BREEZAND→ARAMIS (Gr) 1984
75840	LADY M.A. CROSBIE→DAUPHINE (Cy) 1984
75870	
75876	CHANTENAY→SEFROU (Mo) 1984
76080	
76090	MOUNTCREST→WAVECREST (Pa) 1984
76100	
76101	DIEGO NABOU→MERCEDES DEL MAR (Sp) 1984
76180	
76181	BARENDSZ→KYRA ARGYRO (Cy) 1984
76195	
76197	ALANNAH WESTON→CELTIC VOYAGER (Br) 1984

76200	Add sisters (FRG flag):
76201	**ANGLIA**
76202	**AROSETTE**
76203	**AROSITA** ex John Wulff
76204	**EURO CLIPPER** ex Destel 1980; ex Owen Kersten 1977; ex Destel 1973
76205	**EURO TRADER** ex Kini Kersten 1981; ex Relay 1974; ex Osterland 1973
76206	**EUROTAINER** ex Ragna 1982 (poop differs)
76208	**RHEIN**
	Add similar (funnel smaller etc.) (FRG flag):
76209	**ALBERT K** ex Albert F 1983; ex Albert Friesecke 1978
76209/1	**ANNETTE** ex Osteriff 1982
76209/2	**AROS**
76209/3	**BISMARCKSTEIN** ex Stephanie; ex Bismarckstein; ex Elbestrom; ex Eland
76209/4	**CORVUS** ex Impala; launched as Obotrita
76209/5	**ELKE KAHRS** ex Baltic Concord 1974; launched as Elke Kahrs
76209/6	**FRANK** ex Frank Friesecke; ex Rosita Maria; ex Zaanstroom
76209/7	**FRANK NIBBE** ex Ostetern; ex Owen Kersten 1973
76209/8	**KLINTE** (Sw) ex Larus 1984; ex Bergvik 1977; ex Larus 1976; ex Actuaria 1976; ex City of Dublin 1971
76209/9	**MARIANNA** ex Heike Lehmann
76209/10	**SIMONE** ex Tina 1976
76480	
76484	**INEZ V**→**ARGO** (Ne) 1983
76630	**CHEMIK** broken up
76760	
76764	**MERZARIO HISPANIA**→**STENA HISPANIA** (Ma) 1983
76970	**MADOURI**→**TRANSLINK** (1984)→**FREIGHTLINE ONE** (Cy) 1984
77010	
77015	**ORCHID STAR**→**LADY DOROTHY** (Cy) 1984
77067	
77068	**TFL ADAMS**→**ARTIMON** 1984→**WESER EXPRESS** (FRG) 1984. Add similar:
★77069	**QIU HE** (RC)
77140	**LUTZ JACOB**→**FJORD LAND** (FRG) 1984
77180	**GOOD LEADER**→**PRESIDENT 1** (Pa) 1984
77220	Add further similar:
77224/1	**ORCO TRADER** (Li)
77224/2	**MERMAID JUPITER** (Li)
	Add further possibly similar:
77227	**AMANDA** (Li)
77228	**TAHAROA VENTURER** (Li)
77320	
77322	**SEVEN TEAM** amend name to **SEVENSEAS CONQUEROR**. Renamed **SHIN-KOBE MARU** (Ja) 1984. Amend ex name to: ex Sevenseas Conqueror 1984
77440	
77441	**ROUNTON GRANGE**→**CHINA MARQUIS** (Tw) 1984
77690	
77691	**GOOD TARGET**→**PELLA** (Pa) 1984
77750	**UNIMAR**→**UNIMAR K** (Br) 1984
77870	
77871	**OGDEN THAMES**→**THAMES** (Li) 1984
78060	Add sister (Ys flag):
★78069/3	**MARJAN**
78090	**ARCHANGELOS III**→**ANGEL 1** (Pa) 1984
78150	**DOMINIC**→**DENVER** (Li) 1984
78151	**CREATOR**→**ALAMO 1** (Li) 1984
78270	**EPIMITHEFS** broken up
78272	**SUCCESSOR**→**SUCCESSORS** (Gr) 1984. Now broken up
78370	
78371	**SUNWAVE**→**EMBARCADERO** (Pa) 1984
78390	**NAROTTAM MORARJEE**→**CONTINENTAL LOTUS** (—) 1984
78420	
78426	**JARILLA**→**CAPTAIN GEORGE** (Li) 1984. Add note: (bulk/vehicle)
78430	
78431	**LUIGI GRIMALDI**→**RIVIERA SKY** (Pa) 1984
78500	**ORION** broken up
78510	**OREMAR**→**POLITO** (Gr) 1984
78690	**BANDAR DEMAK**→**ECHO STAR** (Pa) 1984
78691	**BANDAR DEMTA**→**UNIFORM STAR** (Pa) 1984
78693	**BANDAR DENPASAR**→**OSCAR STAR** (Pa) 1984
78960	**PACIFIC** broken up
79220	**GOOD MOTHER**→**MOTHER** (Cy) 1984
79300	**WERRA EXPRESS**→**WERRA** (Sg) 1984
79320	**BREEZAND**→**ARAMIS** (Gr) 1984
79640	**SOPHIA C**→**PORTO ALLEGRE** (Ma) 1984
79710	**DRYS**→**DRYAS** (Ma) 1984

79740	
79741	**HERMINE**→**OSRAM** (Li) 1984
79760	**RIO LINDO** broken up 1984
80080	
80082	**HELLENIC INNOVATOR**→**C. INNOVATOR** (Li) 1984
80230	
80232	**HELLENIC INNOVATOR**→**C. INNOVATOR** (Li) 1984
80260	
80266	**PETR MASHEROV** also spelt **PYOTR MASHEROV**
	Add further sister (Ru flag):
★80266/1	**GEORGIY PYASETSKIY**
80270	
80274	**MERZARIO HISPANIA**→**STENA HISPANIA** (Ma) 1983
80294	**BULLAREN**→**SAINT ROLAND** (Fr) 1984
80340	
80343	**REST**→**PUNTA CARENA** (It) 1984
80670	**LOS CARIBES** total loss
81200	
81201	**IPPOLITOS**→**ELLIOT** (Pa) 1984
81202	**FORUM STAR**→**SITIA BEAUTY** (Ho) 1984
81230	**DESPINA V**→**TABATHA G** (Br) 1984
81390	
★81391	**MORITZ SCHULTE**→**HUA AN** (RC) 1983
81480	
81482	**ORFEO**→**SAUDI SPIRIT** (1984)→**HECTOR** (Ma) 1984
81550	**IOTA**→**EURCO ATHINA** (Ma) 1984
81551	**MALDIVE NOBLE** broken up
81830	Add similar:
81831	**TRES MARIE** (Cy) ex El Greco 1983; ex May-Lis 1976; ex Trica 1973
81990	**SKIATHOS**→**SKYROS** (1984)→**ZUBAIDA** (Ma) 1984
82260	**WARNA**→**VARNA** (Pa) 1984
82340	**GEBE OLDENDORFF**→**ALYBELLA** (Sg) 1984
82450	**STEVE GLORY**→**HALAL SEJATI 1** (Pa) 1984
82650	**VILLE DE MAHEBOURG**→**BETSIBOKA** (Mg) 1984
82900	**STAR PRIDE**→**STATHIS** (Ma) 1984
82920	
82926	**SAPPHIRE BOUNTY**→**ADELAIDE EXPRESS** (Br) 1984
82960	**DARWIN TRADER**. Delete entry. Rebuilt as container ship; gantries removed
83030	
83034	**STAR DELTA**→**MARINA BREEZE** (Pa) 1984
83040	**STAR SUNG**→**SLEEPING BEAUTY** (Br) 1984
83110	
83114	**STAR DELTA**→**MARINA BREEZE** (Pa) 1984
83120	**STAR SUNG**→**SLEEPING BEAUTY** (Br) 1984
83130	
83149	**JEAN L-D**→**PRINCEFIELD** (Br) 1984
83200	**AIFANOURIOS** broken up
83230	**SAINT BERNARD**→**BERN** (Br) 1984
83231	**SAINT BERTRAND**→**HERMION** (Pa) 1984
83240	
83241	**SEA MOON**→**PUNTA ANCIA** (Ar) 1984
83250	**SAINT BERNARD**→**BERN** (Br) 1984
83251	**SAINT BERTRAND**→**HERMION** (Pa) 1984
83300	**SUNNINGDALE**→**PAGSANJAN** (Pi) 1984
83340	
83341	**LABO**→**GAMBIA RIVER** (—) 1984
83400	**NEDLLOYD WISSEKERK**→**WISSEKERK** (Ne) 1984
83402	**NEDLLOYD WESTERKERK**→**WESTERKERK** (Ne) 1984
83403	**NEDLLOYD WILLEMSKERK**→**WILLEMSKERK** (Ne) 1984
83420	**PANDORA**→**LION** (Ma) 1984
83580	
83582	**NEW DOLPHIN** broken up
83670	
83673	**OLGA BRAVO**→**ANVIL MOUNTIE** (Pa) 1984
83780	
83783	**URYUPINSK**. Delete from entry. Probably has three deck-cranes
84000	**CHIOS FROST**→**ATLANTIC REEFER** (Pa) 1984
84060	
84063	**SEVILLA**→**HOLLY 1** (Pa) 1984
84070	
84075	**FJALLFOSS**→**SANDRA K** (Pa) 1983→**PICO DO FUNCHAL** (Pa)
84190	**MARIVERDA IV**→**AL NABILA II** (Eg) 1983
84230	
84231	**ADELAIDE**→**ROADA** (Sw) 1984

84390	PANORMITIS→MARIOS M (Ho) 1984
84580	RIO BRAVO total loss
84581	LEROS ISLAND broken up
84910	
84911	OTTAWA→JESSICA (Sw) 1984
84980	PASS OF CAIRNWELL→POWER HEAD (—) 1984
85270	NISSAKI broken up
85390	ORESTIS→SALAMEE (1984)→EKTOR (—) 1984
85700	PASS OF CAIRNWELL→POWER HEAD (—) 1984
86050	
86051	ARETI S.→EURCO WIZARD (Br) 1984
86370	ETHEL EVERARD→ANGIE (Ma) 1984
87130	
87131	TRANSCON→CATHY G. (Li) 1984
87140	
87141	ADELAIDE→ROADA (Sw) 1984
87200	
87201	RACHAD→NEJEM (Le) 1983
87260	
87267	ZIM MANILA→HARVESTER (Sg) 1983
87420	
87424	DABEMA→LAILA 1 (Pa) 1984
87550	
87551	AZUERO DOS→ATLANTIS III (1978)→ATLANTIS V (1979)→SIR SCOTT (Pa) 1980
87610	AGIOS NIKOLAOS→GEORGIOS 1 (Ho) 1984
87700	Add further similar:
87706	ATANER (Pa) ex Rena Z 1984; ex Hermann Bodewes 1976
87900	SIGMA 1→EBRO (Pa) 1984
88000	
88003	TRENTONIA→TRENTON (Br) 1984
88080	SULTANA 1→SUZIMAR (Ho) 1984
88100	
88105	MARGRET→SKANDEN (Fi) 1984
88270	LISA HEEREN→FJALLFOSS (Ic) 1984
88450	SAN PEDRO→CIMBRIA (De) 1984
85550	Add similar (builder—'Friesland'):
88552	DUCHESS OF HOLLAND (Ne)
89200	
89227	OLYMPIA→OLYMPIA II NINOS (1980)→DEMETRIOS TH (Cy) 1983
89350	AXIOS broken up
89490	ARAGONITE→SILVER SEA (Pa) 1984
89780	TRANS LINK→FREIGHTLINE ONE (Cy) 1984
89840	
89841	PENELOPE EVERARD→PANAYIOTIS G (Ma) 1984
89842	ROSEMARY EVERARD→THEODOROS G (Ma) 1984
89845	JUPITER→LEFKAS STAR (Cy). Now a total loss
89940	ARCHANGELOS III→ANGEL 1 (Pa) 1984
89950	RIO BRAVO total loss
89951	LEROS ISLAND broken up
90000	ELISA total loss
90290	CHRYS broken up
90530	
90532	BEN MAJED→MANSOUR 1 (Le) 1984
90610	SEAJAY→SAMOS FAITH (Cy) 1984
90654	
90655	LUCIE S.→CAPE KILA (Cy) 1984
90690	
90691	STILIANOS S.→MALDIVE PROMOTION (1983)→OCEAN SEER (Mv) 1984
90790	MONOMER VENTURE→GAS VENTURE (Pa) 1984

90810	
90811	LUHESAND→REEFER STAR (Cy) 1984
90940	
90941	ANNÉ METTE→SILVANA (It) 1984
91070	
91072	BEN MAJED→MANSOUR 1 (Le) 1984
91220	
91223	ADHAM 1→NEGWAN (Sy) 1982
91270	SOROLLA→EVANGELOS (Cy) 1984
91271	RIBERA→GLAFKOS (Cy) 1984
91272	PINAZO→PACOS (Pa) 1984
91310	
91316	SLOT SCANDINAVIA→FRAKT (No) 1984
91318	UDAFOSS→BRAVA PRIMA (It) 1984
91500	DRIANOVO total loss
91770	
91771	LUHESAND→REEFER STAR (Cy) 1984
91820	
91823	ADHAM 1→NEGWAN (Sy) 1982
91830	
91844	LADY SARAH total loss
91847	CAIRNROVER→GIANNIS (1978)→ANASTASSIA (Gr) 1984
91970	SHANNON→LAVANTTAL (As) 1984
92290	
92301	VILLE DE SYRTE→OBOTRITA (FRG)
	Add further similar (Bz built):
92304	APODY (Bz)
92305	Add further sister:
92307	JOHANNA (FRG)
92360	Add further similar (Bz built):
92368	APODY (Bz)
92380	VLADIVOSTOK. Delete from entry—rebuilt
92650	
92653	HOEGH TRIGGER→TRIGGER (Li) 1984
92700	
★92701	STAR ANGLIA→LAPAD (Ys) 1984
92950	
92953	DELICIA transferred to Sri Lankan Navy
92955	FRANCESCA transferred to Sri Lankan Navy
93100	
93101	STENA SEARIDER→TRUCKER (Cy) 1984
93190	
93193	HOEGH TRIGGER→TRIGGER (Li) 1984
93250	TOR CALEDONIA→GOTHIC WASA (Br) 1984
93300	LARIMAR→BOLIVAR (Ec) 1984
93301	AMBAR→COLON (Ec) 1984
93340	
93342	TYRUSLAND→JOLLY OCRA (Sw) 1984
93990	KIRSTEN BRAVO→ANVIL SCOUT (Pa) 1984
94020	BUENAVISTA→BISMILLAH (Mo) 1984
94180	
94182	EVA ODEN Now has a large housing between superstructure and funnel. Other ships in class may also have this feature
94420	GYPSUM EMPRESS broken up
94650	MERCANDIAN TRANSPORTER II→TRANSPORTER II (De) 1984
94657	MERCANDIAN SUPPLIER II. Add: ex Lider 1984; ex Mercandian Supplier II 1983
94810	NESTOR→NESTOR 1 (Pa) 1984
94820	NOPAL MASCOT→NOSAC MASCOT (No) 1984
94940	TOYOTA MARU No. 10→SACRAMENTO HIGHWAY (Ja) 1984
94941	TOYOTA MARU No. 11→COLUMBIA HIGHWAY (Ja) 1984
94942	TOYOTA MARU No. 12→UNICORN (Pi) 1984
95160	
95163	DELICIA transferred to Sri Lankan Navy
95165	FRANCESCA transferred to Sri Lankan Navy

Alphabets

The English letters following the symbols are transliterations. Other sources, eg Lloyds Register, may use different equivalents.

GREEK				CYRILLIC (USSR AND BULGARIA)	
A	α	alpha	a	А а	a
B	β	beta	v	Б б	b
Γ	γ	gamma	j	В в	v
Δ	δ	delta	th	Г г	g
E	ε	epsilon	e	Д д	d
Z	ζ	zeta	z	Е е	e
H	η	eta	e	Ё ё	e
Θ	θ	theta	th	Ж ж	zh
I	ι	iota	e	З з	z
K	κ	kappa	k	И и	i
Λ	λ	lambda	l	Й й	y
M	μ	mu	m	К к	k
N	ν	nu	n	Л л	l
Ξ	ξ	xi	x	М м	m
O	o	omicron	o	Н н	n
Π	π	pi	p	О о	o
P	ρ	rho	r	П п	p
Σ ς	σ ς	sigma	s	Р р	r
T	τ	tau	t	С с	s
Y	υ	upsilon	e or v	Т т	t
Φ	φ	phi	f	У у	u
X	χ	chi	kh	Ф ф	f
Ψ	ψ	psi	ps	Х х	kh
Ω	ω	omega	o	Ц ц	ts
				Ч ч	ch
				Ш ш	sh
				Щ щ	shch
				Ъ ъ	*hard sign*
				Ы ы	i
				Ь ь	*soft sign*
				Э э	e
				Ю ю	yu
				Я я	ya

Indexes

Initials and abbreviations. Initials are regarded as words in their own right. For example, a name such as D C COLEMAN appears at the beginning of the D section. There are instances, however, where what appear to be initials appear as a word, eg BP, CP and TFL. Abbreviations of titles, such as DR for DOCTOR or ST for SAINT, are inserted under their abbreviated form.

Transliterations. Transliterated names, such as those from Russian or Chinese, can vary according to the source of the transliteration. A typical example is a Russian name such as YAROSLAVL, which could be spelt JAROSLAVL. With Chinese names there is doubt sometimes as to whether the name is one word or separated into syllables. For example, the name LIULINHAI may appear as LIU LIN HAI in some sources. Crosschecking may be necessary with these types of names.

Numbers suffixed with a disc(●). This indicates that the name is new and appears in the addenda as a change of name, an amended spelling or an entirely new vessel added to the entry.

Named Ships

A

Name	No.	Name	No.	Name	No.	Name	No.
A C CROSBIE	50530	ACADIA FOREST	92810	ADELAIDE	59802	AEGEAN REEFER	03525
A CHENG	64814	ACADIA FOREST	95151	ADELAIDE	84231	AEGEAN SEA	68622
A.E.S.	91319	ACAVUS	37510	ADELAIDE	87141	AEGEAN SEA	81530
A G FANOURIOS	55967	ACCIAIERE	35590	ADELAIDE EXPRESS	82926●	AEGEAN SKY	24511
A G FANOURIOS	56727	ACCIAIERE	36490	ADELE J	92296	AEGEAN SPIRIT	21244
A.O. ULUSOY	87483	ACDIR II	48465	ADELFOTIS	05340	AEGEAN WAVE	06361
ABAGUR	36910	ACDIR II	49501	ADELIA	56160	AEGEON	20070
ABAGUR	43810	ACDIR II	49772	ADELIA	59190	AEGEON	46913
ABAGURLES	24031	ACE AUSTRALIA	82994	ADEN	89268	AEGIR	73160
ABAKAN	36918	ACE CONCORD	09831/1●	ADHAM 1	91223	AEGIR	77660
ABAKAN	43818	ACHAT	73944	ADHAM 1	91823	AEGIS ATHENIC	48181
ABAKAN	85973	ACHATINA	37510	ADHEMAR	15172	AEGIS ATOMIC	48182
ABAKANLES	24032	ACHATINA	44215	ADHIGUNA DHARMA	61564	AEGIS BALTIC	48183
ABAVA	70774	ACHILLE LAURO	01790	ADI VITI	81820	AEGIS BANNER	06481
ABAY KUNANBAYEV	86186	ACHILLES	37601	ADI VITI	82070	AEGIS BLAZE	49702
ABBEY	73331	ACHILLES	44311	ADIB	47997	AEGIS BLAZE	52862
ABBY	45900	ACHILLES	46580	ADINA	42250	AEGIS BRAVERY	57231
ABDUL LATIF	81052	ACHILLET	84194	ADITYA KIRAN	46912	AEGIS BRITANNIC	48184
ABDUL RAZZAK	90300	ACHILLEUS	05457	ADM WM M CALLAGHAN	05160	AEGIS COSMIC	48185
ABEER DELTA	42710	ACHILLEUS	09390	ADMIRAL ARCISZEWSKI	22351	AEGIS DORIC	48186
ABEL SANTAMARIA	53316	ACHILLEUS	66260	ADMIRAL ATLANTIC	93261	AEGIS DYNAMIC	48187
ABEL SANTAMARIA	57781	ACHILLEUS	78800	ADMIRAL GOLOVKO	00140	AEGIS FAITH	06491
ABERTHAW FISHER	23990	ACHILLEUS	89960	ADMIRAL KOLYSHKIN	00141	AEGIS FAME	06480
ABHA ZAHABIA	31441	ACILA	37011	ADMIRAL LUNIN	01967	AEGIS FREEDOM	06511
ABHA ZAHABIA	31611	ACINA	64581	ADMIRAL MAKAROV	20871	AEGIS HARMONIC	48188
ABIDA	37010	ACINA	69211	ADMIRAL NAKHIMOV	09220	AEGIS HARVEST	49703
ABIDIN DAVER	84550	ACMAEA	37012	ADMIRAL PURISIC	48448	AEGIS HARVEST	52863
ABILITY	39600	ACONCAGUA	03164	ADMIRAL PURISIC	49488	AEGIS HELLENIC	48188/1
ABILITY	75224	ACONCAGUA	05912	ADMIRAL PURISIC	49758	AEGIS HISPANIC	48189
ABIRIBA	63710	ACORES	30331	ADMIRAL SARYCHEV	17921	AEGIS IONIC	48190
ABKHAZIYA	06825	ACQUAVIVA	82300	ADMIRAL USHAKOV	80176	AEGIS LOGIC	48191
ABOABO	27210	ACRE	43310	ADMIRAL VLADIMIRSKIY	04240	AEGIS LYRIC	48192
ABOITIZ CONCARRIER III.	37930	ACRITAS	60071	ADNA	64013	AEGIS MAGIC	48193
ABOITIZ CONCARRIER IX	80990	ACROPOLIS	58141	ADNA	68403	AEGIS MAJESTIC	48180
ABOU ABDALLAH EL AYACHI	84262	ACT 1	74500	ADOLF LEONHARDT	70690	AEGIS MYSTIC	48194
ABRAM ARKHIPOV	76580	ACT 3	51940	ADOLF VINNEN	21730	AEGIS PIONEER	60492
ABRAM ARKHIPOV	79930	ACT 3	52430	ADONIS	65060	AEGIS PRACTIC	48195
ABRANTSEVO	12231	ACT 4	51941	ADONIS	65950	AEGIS PRIDE	60493
ABRAU-DYURSO	01960	ACT 4	52431	ADONIS T	58121	AEGIS PROGRESS	57232
ABRENE	36895	ACT 5	51942	ADRIAN MAERSK	08671	AEGIS SONIC	48196
ABRENE	43795	ACT 5	52432	ADRIAN MAERSK	09001	AEGIS STOIC	49704
ABU AMIRA	66280	ACT 6	74503	ADRIANA	29050	AEGIS STOIC	52864
ABU BASMA	50413	ACT 7	08441	ADRIANA	52721	AEGIS TOPIC	48197
ABU BASMA	50823	ACTEON	37014	ADRIANA	58640	AEGIS TRADE	06482
ABU EL KASSEM	21061	ACTIVITY	66471	ADRIANO	73021	AEGIS WISDOM	49705
ABU MISHARI AL KULAIB	10940	ACTIVITY	86451	ADRIASTAR	00450	AEGIS WISDOM	52865
ABU SALAMA	54657	ACUMEN	79150	ADRIATIC	65010	AEGNA	89256
ABU SALAMA	55077	ADA	27212	ADRIATIC JI.	91320	AELLO	43840
ABU SIMBEL	40100	ADA	47341	ADRIATIC FREEZER	03482	AENEAS	48052
ABUEGILA	49352	ADABELLE LYKES	00080	ADRIATIKI	38780	AEOLIAN CARRIER	83043
ABUELO GIORGIO	89890	ADABELLE LYKES	00230	ADVARA	47780	AEOLIAN CARRIER	83123
ABUJA EXPRESS	80190	ADABELLE LYKES	73511	ADVENTURE 1	43570	AEOLIAN SUN	82892
ABUL KALAN AZAD	63561	ADALBERT ANTONOV MALCHIKA	78987	ADVENTURER	15701	AEOLOS	60073
ABULFEDA	00854	ADAM ASNYK	80890	ADY	45369	AEOLOS C	73150
ABULWAFA	00853	ADAM MICKIEWICZ	54971	ADYGENI	70764	AEOLOS C	77420
ABUQIR	49680	ADAM MICKIEWICZ	71811	ADZHARIYA	02150	AESAREA	20510
ABURDEES	49353	ADAM MITSKEVICH	10431	ADZHARIYA	06826	AETHALIA	20770
ABUSABAA 1	13802	ADAMANTIOS	05050	AEGEAN LIGHT	82870	AETOPETRA	27691
ABUZENIMA	49354	ADAMANTIOS S	31802	AEGEAN LION	77830	AETOS	61870
ACACIA	60518	ADARA	91845	AEGEAN NEPTUNE	79951	AETOS	94010
ACACIA	69126	ADAYKHOKH	13751/1	AEGEAN POLYVOS	72492	AFALA	23440
ACADIA	73430	ADDIRIYAH	73410	AEGEAN POLYVOS	72982	AFANASAY NIKITIN	12382
ACADIA FOREST	35100	ADELAIDE	56112	AEGEAN PRIDE	06364	AFANASIY BOGATYREV	50731

Name	No.
AFANASIY NIKITIN	22221
AFEDULA M	83600
AFGHANISTAN	02359
AFGHANISTAN	35378
AFOVOS	52141
AFOVOS	52532
AFRAN ENERGY	64206
AFRAN ENERGY	68656
AFRAN EQUATOR	58342
AFRAN EQUATOR	63992
AFRAN JUPITER	70054
AFRAN NEPTUNE	70055
AFRAN OCEAN	54520
AFRAN OCEAN	55440
AFRAN OCEAN	55730
AFRAN STREAM	67947
AFRAN ZENITH	58772
AFRAN ZENITH	62512
AFRIC STAR	02560
AFRIC STAR	02660
AFRICA	08808
AFRICA	09140
AFRICA	10710
AFRICA FREEZER	06360
AFRICA MARU	73340
AFRICA MARU	77960
AFRICA PALM	05450
AFRICAN	72051●
AFRICAN AZALEA	50709
AFRICAN BEGONIA	50709/1
AFRICAN CAMELLIA	50705
AFRICAN DAHLIA	50706
AFRICAN EVERGREEN	50707
AFRICAN EXPRESS	05074
AFRICAN EXPRESS	05326
AFRICAN FERN	50708
AFRICAN GARDENIA	50704
AFRICAN HYACINTH	63660
AFRICAN MARINER	08050
AFRIQUIA	27840
AFROESSA	37410
AFROS	48771
AFTHOROS	69710
AGADIR	19260
AGAETE	81957
AGAETE	91507
AGAMEL	36830
AGAMEL	37990
AGAMEMNON	58557
AGAPI	59228
AGAPI	60074
AGAPI	74548
AGAPI	37701●
AGAPI	
AGAT	12383
AGATE	06626
AGATE ISLANDS	29930
AGATHA	57617
AGATHA	61058
AGATOVYY	11916
AGDAM	50772
AGELIKI II	45440
AGELOS MICHAEL	57750
AGENOR	45500
AGENOR	49790
AGENOR	60076
AGENT	15703
AGHIA MARINA	40421
AGHIA MARINA	42331
AGHIA MARINA	42591
AGHIA MARINA	60350
AGHIA MARINA	68490
AGHIOS GEORGIOS III	07260
AGHIOS NICOLAOS	00381
AGIA ERINI II	56980
AGIA MARINA	89320
AGIA SKEPI	06537
AGIA THALASSINI	61443
AGIA VARVARA	26880
AGILITY	00931
AGINOR	30322
AGIOI ANARGYROI III	42210
AGIOS CONSTANTINOS	06414
AGIOS CONSTANTINOS	61970
AGIOS DIONISSIOS	83711
AGIOS ELEFTHERIOS	81710
AGIOS FANOURIOS VI	28931
AGIOS GEORGIOS	19610
AGIOS GEORGIOS	43030
AGIOS GEORGIOS	88821
AGIOS LOUKAS	62290
AGIOS MATTHEOS	48823
AGIOS MATTHEOS	83493
AGIOS NECTARIOS	15110
AGIOS NECTARIOS	23200
AGIOS NEKTARIOS	87060
AGIOS NIKOLAOS	52773
AGIOS NIKOLAOS	87610
AGIOS NIKOLAOS III	57001
AGIOS NIKOLAOS THALASSOPOROS	58233
AGIOS NIKOLAOS	52410
AGIOS SPYRIDONAS	75877
AGIP ABRUZZO	62854
AGIP ABRUZZO	67534
AGIP ANCONA	65310
AGIP CAMPANIA	62855
AGIP CAMPANIA	67535
AGIP GELA	66197
AGIP LAZIO	62856
AGIP LAZIO	67536
AGIP MARCHE	62857
AGIP MARCHE	67537
AGIP RAVENNA	66198
AGIP SARDEGNA	62851
AGIP SARDEGNA	67531
AGIP SICILIA	62850
AGIP SICILIA	67530
AGIP TRIESTE	65040
AGIP TRIESTE	74180
AGNES	72961
AGNES	87161
AGNES PRIDE	42760
AGNITA	82228
AGONISTIS	59546
AGORAS	62011
AGOSTINHO NETO	80265
AGOSTINO LAURO	18890
AGRI	80352
AGRIA	35482●
AGRILIA	26801
AGROTAI	87560
AGUA GRANDE	65860
AGUILA AZTECA	68690
AGUILA II	42551
AGYASI MANKO	85364
AGYIMFRA	27211
AHLERS BREEZE	50134
AHLERS BRIDGE	50135
AHMAD AL-FATEH	49403
AHMAD AL-FATEH	50963
AHMED AL-BAKRY II	36960
AHMED AL-BAKRY II	43900
AHMED AL-BAKRY II	44600
AHMED ES SAKAH	84263
AHMOS	01416
AHMOS	01676
AIAS	58614
AIAS	81014
AIAS	90514
AICHI MARU	93980
AIDE	15702
AIFANOURIOS	83200
AIGEORGIS	55090
AIHUA	13240
AIKATERINI	86040
AIKO MARU	54490
AIKO MARU	54920
AIKO MARU	55720
AILSA PRINCESS	32791
AIMEE LYKES	00081
AIMEE LYKES	00231
AIMIN	13241
AIN ZALAH	69571
AINOS	19410
AIS GIORGIS	26113
AIS GIORGIS	26840
AISHAH	11111
AISHAH	34142
AJANTA	56781
AJAX	46581
AJDABYA	51313
AKAD	49060
AKADEMIK ALEKSANDR NESMEYANOV	14906
AKADEMIK ARTOBOLEVSKIY	10752
AKADEMIK ARTSIMOVICH	80250
AKADEMIK BERG	12573
AKADEMIK EVGENIY PATON	02671
AKADEMIK FILATOV	02526
AKADEMIK GUBER	80251
AKADEMIK IOSIF ORBELI	02527
AKADEMIK KHOKHLOV	10753
AKADEMIK KNIPOVICH	12570
AKADEMIK KOROLYOV	12000
AKADEMIK KRYLOV	02460
AKADEMIK KRYLOV	63571
AKADEMIK KUPREVICH	80252
AKADEMIK KURCHATOV	07620
AKADEMIK MAMEDALIEV	85974
AKADEMIK MILLIONSCHIKOV	80253
AKADEMIK MSTISLAV KELDYSH	14955
AKADEMIK MSTISLAV KELDYSH	15095
AKADEMIK PAVLOV	63572
AKADEMIK RYKACHEV	02528
AKADEMIK SECHENOV	63573
AKADEMIK SERGEY KOROLOV	08115
AKADEMIK SHIMANSKIY	01561
AKADEMIK SHIRSHOV	12001
AKADEMIK SHOKALSKIY	04254
AKADEMIK SHUKHOV	02529
AKADEMIK SHULEYKIN	04253
AKADEMIK STECHKIN	80254
AKADEMIK TUPOLEV	80255
AKADEMIK VERNADSKIY	07621
AKADEMIK YANGEL	03968
AKADEMIK YURYEV	02530
AKADEMOS	58171
AKAK SUCCESS	49879/1●
AKAK VICTORY	73959●
AKAMA MARU	56405
AKAMA MARU	59927
AKARNANIA	06534
AKBAR	46093
AKBAR	60960
AKBAR	83263
AKDENIZ	01580
AKEBONO MARU No 50	92522
AKEBONO MARU No 53	92523
AKEBONO REEFER	05193
AKEN	61710
AKHALTSIKHE	70767
AKHILLEON	13652
AKHILLES	11802
AKHMETA	13751/2
AKHTARSKIY LIMAN	33621
AKHTUBA	11803
AKHTUBA	35315
AKHTUBA	36861
AKHTUBA	86090
AKHUN	11804
AKIS S	28150
AKIS S	31910
AKMOLINSK	11805
AKOP	86075
AKOPYAN	86076
AKORA	93650
AKORA	94990
AKRA RION	53170
AKRA TENARON	53171
AKRANES	59460
AKRATA	60140
AKRITAS	58142
AKRON	77700
AKSAY	36894
AKSAY	43794
AKSTAFA	50773
AKTASH	36893
AKTASH	43793
AKTAU	70761
AKTEA	47371
AKTI	74990●
AKTIAN	86020
AKTINJA	23441
AKTION	61035
AKTION	71195
AKTYUBINSK	45210
AKTYUBINSK	70762
AKUSTIK	11806
AKVAMARIN	23549
AL AHMADIAH	09010
AL AHMADIAH	77040
Al AHOOD	67740
AL AHRAM 2	87705
AL AHRAM	90831
AL AHWAR	23470
AL AKBER	42220
AL AKBER	42740
AL AMIRAH	51171
AL ANDALUS	58311
AL ANDALUS	62500
AL ANDALUS	63960
AL ANOUD	19630
AL BACHIR	66360
AL BACHIR	85770
AL BASEER	07011
AL BATTANI	66884
AL BERRY	54197
AL BIDA	54198
AL BIRUNI	90861
AL BIRUNI	91781
AL DAMMAM 1	71502
AL DHAID STAR	74322
AL ESRAA	03251
AL ESRAA	03630
AL FAHD	11112
AL FARIS 3	32300●
AL FARY	26330
AL FUJAIRAH	49400
AL FUJAIRAH	50960
AL GHASSANI	66580
AL HAIDER	07821
AL HAMRAA	03252
AL HAMRAA	03631
AL HARAMAIN	63031
AL HASAN	26830
AL HOCEIMA	76861
AL HODEIDAH	66880
AL HUSSEIN B	37740
AL IDRISI	90862
AL IDRISI	91782
AL JAMAL	90570
AL JAMAL	91990
AL KAHERAH	57580
AL KAHERAH	84860
AL KAHLA	23471
AL KARIM	59348
AL KHAIRAT	01310
AL KHLOOD	60820
AL KHLOOD	70840
AL KULSUM	10368
AL MANSOURA	66901
AL MANSOURA	91471
AL MAREEKH	06365
AL MEDINA	24571
AL MORGAN	38141
AL MUBARAKIAH	49398
AL MUBARAKIAH	50958
AL MUHARRAQ	49401
AL MUHARRAQ	50961
AL NABILA II	84190●
AL OSMAN	52370
AL QASEEM	26200
AL RAFIDAIN	63280
AL RAHIM	60175
AL RAHMAN	60176
AL RAKEEB	60150
AL RASHED	60151
AL RAWDATAIN	53642
AL RAYYAN	49402
AL RAYYAN	50962
AL RAZAK	60152
AL RAZAZA	23472
AL RAZIQ	60255
AL REAFA 1	81430
AL REDHA	60178
AL REKKAH	54492
AL REKKAH	54922
AL REKKAH	55722
AL RIYADH	16740
AL RUBAYIA	35760
AL RUMAITHIAH	09011
AL RUMAITHIAH	77041
AL SABAH 1	67461
AL SABAH IV	38190
AL SABAH IV	38740
AL SADIQ	58172
AL SALAAM	58173
AL SALAM 1	49993
AL SALAM II	84527
AL SALAMA	02860
AL SALAMA	03001
AL SALEHIAH	45383
AL SALIMIAH	49397
AL SALIMIAH	50957
AL SAMAD	58174
AL SAMIE	58175
AL SHAMIAH	09012
AL SHAMIAH	77042
AL SHEHABIA	13350
AL SHIDADIAH	45381
AL SOLAIBIAH	45382
AL SUDAN	18390
AL SULTANA	52050
AL TAHIR	79700
AL TAHSEEN	59341
AL TAIF	22390
AL TAJDAR	46060
AL TAMMAR	47480
AL TAMMAR	47980
AL TAWFIQ	59340
AL WATTYAH	73411
AL YAMAMAH	49399
AL YAMAMAH	50959
AL YARMOUK	03249
AL YARMOUK	03633
AL ZAHER II	94030
AL ZAHER IV	94670
AL ZAHRA	02861
AL ZAHRA	03000
ALA	22061
ALA KALA	61614
ALABAMA GETTY	64160
ALABAMA GETTY	68480
ALACRITY	90140
ALADEWE	70890
ALADIN	49283
ALAFOSS	94652
ALAGIR	36905
ALAGIR	43805
AL-AIN	64360
ALALMA	59576
ALAMAK	59680
ALAMAR	35991
ALAMO	69030
ALAMO 1	53712●
ALAMO 1	78151●
ALAND II	72685
ALANFUSHI	50701
ALANNAH WESTON	76197
ALAPAYEVSK	00341
ALAPAYEVSK	01021
ALAPAYEVSKLES	24033
ALASKA I	34201
ALASKA MARU	09850
ALASKAN	65900
ALASSIA	81291
ALATYR	40013
ALATYRLES	24034
ALBA	11939
ALBA IULIA	06142
ALBACORA FRIGO	03411
ALBACORA FRIGO	15971
ALBAFRIGO	81690
ALBAFRIGO	87050
ALBAKORA	22331
AL-BAKRY	40840
ALBANY	45389
ALBANY	78100
ALBATROS	12311
ALBAY HAKKI BURAK	75050
ALBENA	76532
ALBERT J MEYER	22741
ALBERT K	76209●
ALBERT MAERSK	08672
ALBERT MAERSK	09002
ALBERTO DORMIO	66958
ALBERTO DORMIO	70998
ALBERTO MONTEIRO	39531
ALBERTO MONTEIRO	93491
ALBIN KOBIS	06384
ALBIN KOBIS	15413
ALBION	55100
ALBION	57590
ALBION 1	59350
ALBION STAR	56121
ALBION STAR	59771
ALBIREO	32581
ALBORADA	61054/1
ALBORADA	82645
ALBORADA	86720
ALBRIGHT EXPLORER	74921
ALBRIGHT PIONEER	74920
ALCA	47520
ALCA	48215
ALCAEUS	32770
ALCAZAR	71550
ALCHATBY 15-1-91	50702
ALCHEMIST BREMEN	66570
ALCHEVSK	25552
ALCHIMIST FLENSBURG	59051
ALCHIMIST FLENSBURG	76431
ALCHIMIST LUBECK	59050
ALCHIMIST LUBECK	76430
ALCHIMIST ROTTERDAM	59070
ALCHIMIST ROTTERDAM	76420
ALCOR	46904/1
ALCOR	83343
ALCOUTIM	07970
ALCYON	48074

Name	No.	Name	No.
ALDABI	04350	ALEXANDER STAR	77780
ALDABI	52820	ALEXANDER THE GREAT	54391
ALDAN	06795/1	ALEXANDER'S POWER	02941
ALDAN	89503	ALEXANDRA	28513
ALDANLES	24035	ALEXANDRA 1	91834
ALDEBARAN	40420	ALEXANDRA DIO	64082
ALDEBARAN	42330	ALEXANDRA DYO	72082
ALDEBARAN	42590	ALEXANDRA N	46610
ALDEBARAN	50551	ALEXANDRA N	52780
ALDEN W. CLAUSEN	53059	ALEXANDRA T	56051
ALDERAMIN	12232	ALEXANDRAKI	67284
ALDERAMINE	35810	ALEXANDRIA	03972
ALDERAMINE	41580	ALEXANDRIA	46927
ALDIMA	02794●	ALEXANDROS	09391
ALDO CECCONI	43410	ALEXANDROS	10367
ALDONZA MANRIQUE	19190	ALEXANDROS	35713
ALDRICH	61681	ALEXANDROS	41423
ALDRINGTON	75253	ALEXANDROS A	78160
ALE	23670	ALEXANDROS G	83618
ALEA	60153	ALEXANDROS G. TSAVLIRIS	49110
ALECOS M	65460	ALEXANDROS K	24961
ALECOS N. AGOUDIMOS	39261●	ALEXIA	44626
ALEDREESI	63680	ALEXIA	61772●
ALEGRIA DE PIO	48214	ALEXIA V	58842
ALEJANDRA G	87520	ALEXIA V	65652
ALEKSANDER ZAWADSKI	10572	ALEXION HOPE	06508
ALEKSANDER ZAWADSKI	15342	ALEXSANDR ULYNOV	03657
ALEKSANDR BARANOV	17922	ALEYSK	36906
ALEKSANDR BLOK	14371	ALEYSK	43806
ALEKSANDR BOGOLYUBOV	23518	ALEYSK	51989
ALEKSANDR BORISOV	34873	ALFA	59758
ALEKSANDR DOVZHENKO	15120	ALFA	74040
ALEKSANDR FADEYEV	77060	AL-FALAH	55705
ALEKSANDR GERTSEN	14372	ALFEUS	23442
ALEKSANDR GRIAZNOV	34873/1	ALFIE 1	74680
ALEKSANDR GRIN	14373	ALFITO	35901
ALEKSANDR IVANOV	76493	ALFITO	41591
ALEKSANDR IVANOVICH VOEYKOV	23770	ALFONSAS CHEPONIS	12384
ALEKSANDR KORNEYCHUK	67684	ALGARMI	59575
ALEKSANDR KOSAREV	93690	ALGAZAYER	33760
ALEKSANDR LEYNER	89470	ALGERIA	74022
ALEKSANDR MAKSUTOV	12385	ALGILANI	26071
ALEKSANDR MATROSOV	73291	ALHAKEM	47323
ALEKSANDR MIROSHNIKOV	50295	ALHAKEM	83383
ALEKSANDR NEVSKII	17501	ALHALEME	47320
ALEKSANDR NEVSKIY	80173	ALHALEMI	83380
ALEKSANDR OBUKHOV	86205	ALHAMBRA	07320
ALEKSANDR OBUKHOV	93682	ALHAMBRA	47326
ALEKSANDR OSIPOV	78067	ALHAMBRA	83386
ALEKSANDR PANKRATOV	50282	ALHANA	14570
ALEKSANDR PASHKOV	79342	ALHENA	04351
ALEKSANDR PASHKOV	79400	ALHENA	52821
ALEKSANDR POKALCHUK	49241	ALI AMIROV	52745
ALEKSANDR POKALCHUK	49241	ALIAKMON	57185
ALEKSANDR POPOV	17923	ALIANORA	91441
ALEKSANDR PROKOFYEV	77061	ALIANZA	74771
ALEKSANDR PROKOFYEV	79378	ALIANZA	79001
ALEKSANDR PUSHKIN	01750	ALIBRAHIMIYA	55080
ALEKSANDR SERAFIMOVIC	14374	ALICAMPOS	57340
ALEKSANDR SUVOROV	80174	ALICAMPOS	46583
ALEKSANDR TEREKHIN	17924	ALICIA	76200
ALEKSANDR TORTSYEV	00142	ALICIA 1	86460
ALEKSANDR TSULUKIDZE	61433	ALIDA SMITS	52043
ALEKSANDR TSYURUPA	03962	ALIDADE	20910
ALEKSANDR TSYURUPA	79374	ALIKI	74880
ALEKSANDR TVARDOVSKIY	77062	ALIKI I P	71852
ALEKSANDR TYURIN	11334/1	ALINA P	39820
ALEKSANDR ULYANOV	03065	ALINE	78630
ALEKSANDR ULYANOV	93384	ALIOSHA POPOVICH	17502
ALEKSANDR VERMISHEV	14375	ALIOT	12233
ALEKSANDR VERMISHEV	79370	ALIOT	76890
ALEKSANDR VINOKUROV	03771	ALIOT	81400
ALEKSANDR VINOKUROV	04011	ALISHER NAVOI	14376
ALEKSANDRA ARTYUKHINA	03772	ALITA	73794
ALEKSANDRA ARTYUKHINA	04012	ALITUS	89471
ALEKSANDRA KOLLONTAY	10721	ALIYA MOLDAGULOV	79427
ALEKSANDRIT	23528	ALKA	11807
ALEKSANDROVSK	00330	ALKA	11956
ALEKSANDROVSK	11808	ALKA	33450
ALEKSANDROVSK SAKHALINSKIY	93758	ALKAIOS	05238
ALEKSANDROVSK SAKHALINSKIY	93848	ALKAIOS	61036
ALEKSEY BORDUNOV	11809	ALKAIOS	71196
ALEKSEY CHIRIKOV	10432	AL-KARAMEH	61322
ALEKSEY CHIRIKOV	22181	ALKEOS C	72261
ALEKSEY GENERALOV	00147	AL-KHALEEJ	33040
ALEKSEY GMYREV	12386	AL-KHALEEJ	33340
ALEKSEY GRACHYEV	13768/1●	AL-KHAMES	45832
ALEKSEY KHLOBYSTOV	93877	AL-KHAMES 2	45833
ALEKSEY KRYLOV	41150	ALKHANSAA	63682
ALEKSEY KRYLOV	44950	ALKISMA ALARABIA	58291
ALEKSEY MAKHALIN	12387	ALKMAN	47954
ALEKSEY POZDNYAKOV	93878	ALKMINI	42390
ALEKSEY STAKHANOV	11334/2	ALKMINI	58571
ALEKSEY TOLSTOY	07919	ALKMINI A.	18480
ALEKSEY VENETSIANOV	76491	ALKMINI A	26700
ALEKSEY VIKHORYEV	79424	ALKOR	61292
ALEKSEYEVKA	36902	ALKOR	86722
ALEKSEYEVKA	43802	ALKYON	23610
ALEKSEYEVSK	36903	ALKYON	47860
ALEKSEYEVSK	43803	ALKYON	84420
ALEKSIN	36907	ALKYON	70460●
ALEKSIN	43807	ALKYONIA	61153
ALENDALE	65972	ALKYONIS	47660
ALEON	71206	ALKYONIS	58143
ALEPPO	46001	ALL STATE	82156
ALESSANDRA	02729/4	ALLA TARASOVA	02341
ALEUTIAN DEVELOPER	32071	ALLEMAGNA EXPRESS	18002
ALEV	46451	ALLEMANIA EXPRESS	73402
ALEXA II	45408	ALLEMANIA EXPRESS	82712
ALEXANDER	64322	ALLGAEU	61405
ALEXANDER	85220	ALLIANCE	75501
ALEXANDER K	43730	ALLIGATOR III	45720
ALEXANDER K	80632	ALLISON LYKES	00082
ALEXANDER SCHRODER	50150	ALLISON LYKES	00232
ALEXANDER STAR	73110		

Name	No.	Name	No.
ALLUNGA	52631	ALUSHTA	01963
ALLURITY	66470	ALUSHTA	12236
ALLURITY	86450	ALVA MAERSK	08677
ALLY	62025	ALVA MAERSK	09007
ALMA	11810	ALVA SEA	68681
ALMA	89846	ALVARO OBREGON	69991
ALMA M	21471	ALVARO OBREGON	86481
ALMA-ATA	44103	ALVERI HOPE	57240
ALMAK	12234	ALVORADA	59478
ALMALAZ	65541	ALYBELLA	82340●
ALMANDARAH	49681	ALYOLEX	59577
ALMAR	61041	ALZAHRAA	20140
ALMARIS	48075	ALZAWRAA	63681
ALMAZ	12388	AMADO	45921
ALMAZNYY	76506	AMAK	72433
ALMEA	57020	AMALI	66940
ALMEDA STAR	02561	AMALIA	04637
ALMEDA STAR	02661	AMALIA	88830
ALMERIA LYKES	08860	AMALINDA	12861
ALMERIA STAR	02564	AMALTHEA	12211
ALMERIA STAR	02664	AMAMI MARU	22630
ALMETYEVSK	00342	AMANDA	86351
ALMETYEVSK	01022	AMANDA	77227●
ALMI SKY	46926	AMANDA MILLER	64590
ALMIRANTE	63731	AMANDA MILLER	67630
ALMIRANTE	72901	AMANDA MILLER	69040
ALMIRANTE ANICETO	47659	AMANDA SMITS	52046
ALMIRANTE GRACA ARANHA	55881	AMAR	26673
ALMIRANTE GRACA ARANHA	56551	AMAR	31735
ALMIRANTE GRACA ARNHA	55011	AMAR 1	07130
ALMIRANTE IRIZAR	22210	AMARAGY	92303
ALMIRANTE IRIZAR	23650	AMARAGY	92367
ALMIRANTE LUIS BIRON	19184	AMARANTA	50146
ALMIRANTE ROTAECHE	67634	AMARANTE	07971
ALMIRANTE STORNI	06672/1	AMARANTOS	58583
ALMONA	24260	AMAREL	23449
ALMOUNTAZAH 1	49682	AMARYLLIS	11270
ALMUDENA	73535	AMARYLLIS	58556
ALMUSTANSIRIYAH	63391	AMASTRA	37511
ALMUT BORNHOFEN	71847	AMASTRA	44210
ALNASL	33301	AMATHUS	62101
ALNASL	34991	AMAZON	58572
ALNATI	04352	AMAZON MARU	56695
ALNATI	52822	AMAZON MARU	63100
ALNAVE	48077/1●	AMAZON MARU	68140
ALNEGMA ALKHADRA	51830	AMAZON PIONEER	65681
ALNILAM	87703	AMAZON PIONEER	70111
ALPAC AFRICA	09941	AMAZON PROSPERITY	65682
ALPAC ASIA	09940	AMAZON PROSPERITY	70112
ALPAMAYO	59757	AMAZON TRADER	87420
ALPASHA	23790	AMAZONA	38600
ALPERIN	89509	AMAZONIA	51542
ALPHA	78900	AMAZONIA	88782
ALPHA	91101	AMBALIKA	61412
ALPHA BAY	03980	AMBAR	93301
ALPHA BAY	35520	AMBARCHIK	11302
ALPHA III	58604●	AMBASADOR	32090
ALPHA III	59758●	AMBASADOR	33081
ALPHA MICHEL	89180	AMBASSADOR	15700
ALPHA PACIFIC	62312	AMBASSADOR	94090
ALPHACCA	04353	AMBER	35010
ALPHACCA	52823	AMBER ISLANDS	30622
ALPINA	57480	AMBERES	22490
ALPINA	90500	AMBIKA	61410
ALPINE ROSE	48949/1	AMBLA	89266
ALPRO	65030	AMBROSE SHEA	19540
ALRIYAD	16740	AMBROSIA	74435
ALQADISIAH	63392	AMBROSIANA	77067
AL-QAMAR AL-SAUDI II	01900	AMBURAN	43520
ALSACE	57830	AMCO 1	53930
ALSAD ALAALY	36970	AMCO 1	71660
ALSAD ALAALY	37480	AMCO TRADER	93131
AL-SALMA	13030	AMCO TRADER	93391
ALSAMA ALARABIA	53071	AMCO VOYAGER	93132
AL-SAYESTHA	52670	AMCO VOYAGER	93392
AL-SHUWAIKH	94730	AMDERMA	02728/5
ALSTER ORE	62901	AMDERMA	11812
ALSTER ORE	68171	AMDERMA	25551
ALSTERBERG	72686	AMELIA	86461
ALSU	11811	AMELIA TOPIC	77800
ALSYTA SMITS	52044	AMENITY	75225
ALTA	58000	AMER	30330
ALTA MAR	82100	AMERICA	49600
ALTA MAR	82600	AMERICA EXPRESS	73403
AL-TAHA	57350	AMERICA EXPRESS	82713
ALTAI	17503	AMERICA FREEZER	34222
ALTAI MARU	51210	AMERICA MARU	08745
ALTAIF	22390	AMERICA SUN	63410
ALTAIR	50370	AMERICAN ACCORD	09724
ALTAIR	76310	AMERICAN ACE	09720
ALTAIR	83063	AMERICAN ALLIANCE	09721
ALTAIR	83163	AMERICAN ALTAIR	04560
ALTAIR	85332	AMERICAN APOLLO	09716
ALTAIR 1	90650	AMERICAN AQUARIUS	09717
ALTAJ	58123	AMERICAN ARCHER	09723
ALTANIN	64621	AMERICAN ARGO	04562
ALTANO	63261	AMERICAN ARGOSY	09722
ALTAPPEN	75560	AMERICAN ASTRONAUT	09715
ALTAVIA	58594	AMERICAN CHALLENGER	05670
ALTAVIA	60476	AMERICAN CHAMPION	05671
ALTAY	11301	AMERICAN CHARGER	05672
ALTAY	70760	AMERICAN CHIEFTAIN	05673
ALTAYLES	24048	AMERICAN CORSAIR	05674
ALTCAR	03522	AMERICAN DRACO	04561
ALTE LIEBE	02030	AMERICAN EAGLE	92932
ALTENBELS	52923	AMERICAN ENTENTE	11341
ALTENBURG	03870	AMERICAN ENVOY	11340
ALTENBURG	04423	AMERICAN EXPLORER	36800
ALTHEA	47370	AMERICAN LANCER	09710
ALTIS	58567	AMERICAN LARK	09713
ALTNES	50120	AMERICAN LEADER	09725
ALTONIC	74432	AMERICAN LEGACY	09726
ALUKSNE	36891	AMERICAN LEGEND	09727
ALUKSNE	43791	AMERICAN LEGION	09711●
ALUPKA	12235	AMERICAN LIBERTY	09712

Name	No.	Name	No.	Name	No.	Name	No.
AMERICAN LYNX	09714	AN JI HAI	83309	ANDROMEDA	12237	ANNA MAERSK	08673
AMERICAN MARK	83984	AN YANG JIANG	05329●	ANDROMEDA	68732	ANNA MAERSK	09003
AMERICAN MARKETER	11350	ANA LUISA	02729/3	ANDROMEDA	81141	ANNA MAERSK	08670●
AMERICAN MERCHANT	11352	ANABAR	89259	ANDROMEDA STAR	56115	ANNA MARIA LAURO	22530
AMERICAN MONARCH	05094	ANABELA	74260	ANDROS ANTARES	68230	ANNA ODEN	94181
AMERICAN PIONEER	11342	ANADOLU BIR	79950	ANDROS ARIES	68231	ANNA SCHULTE	84741
AMERICAN PURITAN	11343	ANADOLU GUNEY	47397	ANDROS ATLAS	68232	ANNA SCHULTE	84951
AMERICAN RACER	05930	ANADOLU GUNEY	47967	ANDROS CASTLE	79170	ANNA ULYANOVA	03064
AMERICAN RANGER	05931	ANADRIA	61261	ANDROS CHRYSSI	56404	ANNA ULYANOVA	03656
AMERICAN RELIANCE	05932	ANADYR	10430	ANDROS CHRYSSI	59924	ANNAMINA	57009
AMERICAN RESERVIST	04564	ANADYR	35335	ANDROS CHRYSSI	67784	ANNAPURNA	45778
AMERICAN RESOLUTE	94277	ANADYR	02728/8●	ANDROS CITY	79171	ANNAPURNA	50152
AMERICAN RIGEL	04563	ANADYRLES	24036	ANDROS HILLS	79172	ANNE BRAVO	93991
AMERICAN SAGA	08000	ANAHITA	72521	ANDROS ISLAND	79173	ANNE METTE	90941
AMERICAN SEA	08002	ANAKENA	06654	ANDROS MARINER	79174	ANNE OPEM	91400
AMERICAN SPITFIRE	05090	ANAKLIYA	70765	ANDROS MELTEMI	77803	ANNE SIF	49893
AMERICAN TIDE	08003	ANANGEL ARES	58561	ANDROS MENTOR	58152	ANNELIESE OLTMANN	64740
AMERICAN TITAN	05091	ANANGEL CHAMPION	06539	ANDROS OCEANIA	47207	ANNELIESE OLTMANN	81770
AMERICAN TROJAN	05093	ANANGEL ENDEAVOUR	82996	ANDROS TITAN	68234	ANNETTE	76209/1●
AMERICAN VEGA	04565	ANANGEL FIDELITY	82997	ANDROS TRANSPORT	58176	ANNETTE S	90942
AMERICAN VETERAN	00019●	ANANGEL FORTUNE	58165	ANDRUS YOKHANI	12575	ANNIE	62831
AMERICAN VETERAN	02480●	ANANGEL FRIENDSHIP	58870	ANDRZEJ STRUG	15300	ANNIE	68081
AMERICAN VETERAN	35138●	ANANGEL GLORY	58145	ANDRZWJ BOROWY	73840	ANNIE JOHNSON	04103
AMERICANA	06170	ANANGEL HAPPINESS	58166	ANDY'S PRIDE	67003	ANNIKA	74030
AMERICANA	64720	ANANGEL HARMONY	54100	ANEMOS	39673	ANNIKA N	46831
AMERIKANIS	08270	ANANGEL HARMONY	54600	ANEMOS	50180	ANNITA	71710
AMETHYST	65311	ANANGEL HONOUR	58146	ANEMOS	75260	ANNITSA L	49280
AMETHYST	82999	ANANGEL HOPE	58147	ANESTO D	45402/1	ANNOOR II	00560●
AMETHYSTOS	57360	ANANGEL LIBERTY	58148	ANG PANGULO	09290	ANNOULA	60078
AMETIST	12389	ANANGEL MIGHT	82991	ANGAMOS	19110	ANNOULA K	17800
AMEX	60250	ANANGEL PEACE	58167	ANGARA	17811	ANNOULA TSIRIS	34750
AMGA	11813	ANANGEL PROSPERITY	58149	ANGARLES	24051	ANONA	06317
AMGA	45730	ANANGEL PRUDENCE	58871	ANGARSK	28070	ANTACUS	46470
AMGIS KATASYRTA	71240	ANANGEL SKY	58580	ANGARSK	34540	ANTAIOS	57191
AMGUEMA	21610	ANANGEL SPIRIT	82992	ANGARSK	89506	ANTAKYA	80353
AMGUEMA	34100	ANANGEL TRIUMPH	58150	ANGARSKLES	24038	ANTALYA	80355
AMGUN	70763	ANANGEL WISDOM	58151	ANGEARCTIC	61026	ANTANAS SNECHKUS	62687
AMGUN	89501	ANANYEV	86220	ANGEARCTIC	71186	ANTAR	83062
AMICA	63281	ANAPA	36908	ANGEATLANTIC	61019	ANTAR	83162
AMIGO FORTUNA	64859	ANAPA	43808	ANGEATLANTIC	71179	ANTARA	72600
AMIGO FORTUNA	91039	ANAPKA	36899	ANGEBALTIC	45571	ANTARCTIC	34202
AMILLA	58144	ANAPKA	43799	ANGEKRITI	61052	ANTARCTIC	91010
AMIN	47998	ANASTASIA	18192	ANGEKRITI	82642	ANTARES	10543
AMIN	84532	ANASTASIA L	74590	ANGEL 1	53700●	ANTARES	12238
AMINUL BAHR	36150	ANASTASIA L	78450	ANGEL 1	78090●	ANTARES	39460
AMIR	67000	ANASTASIA Y	56941	ANGEL 1	89940●	ANTARES	50550
AMIRA	94521	ANASTASIA Y	90630	ANGELA	51861	ANTARES	66790
AMIRAL S ALTINCAN	30811	ANASTASIOS	12373	ANGELA	64911	ANTARES	68731
AMIRAL S OKAN	30810	ANASTASIOS	46448	ANGELA	91390	ANTARES	70772
AMIS	47999	ANASTASIOS C	82891	ANGELA JURGENS	72131	ANTARES	72580
AMOCO BALTIMORE	69821	ANASTASIS	04130	ANGELA JURGENS	76471	ANTARKTIKA	93749
AMOCO BRISBANE	69820	ANASTASIS II	64091	ANGELA SMITS	52047	ANTARKTIKA	93839
AMOCO CAIRO	60300	ANASTASSIA	56792	ANGELIC GLORY	83020	ANTARTICO	73091
AMOCO CAIRO	68520	ANASTASSIA	91847●	ANGELICA SCHULTE	73992	ANTCHAR	12392
AMOCO CREMONA	69822	ANATOLI	60077/1	ANGELIKI	01112	ANTHEMIOS	60079
AMOCO EUROPA	63171	ANATOLIA	82803	ANGELIKI	28612	ANTHENOR	94294
AMOCO EUROPA	71541	ANATOLIA	92093	ANGELIKI	56611	ANTHI L	22440
AMOCO MILFORD HAVEN	63172	ANATOLIY BREDOV	11625	ANGELIKI H	47460	ANTHIA	31440
AMOCO MILFORD HAVEN	71542	ANATOLIY KHALIN	04521	ANGELIKI IV	72581	ANTHIA	31610
AMOCO SEAFARER	59910	ANATOLIY LUNACHARSKIY	03063	ANGELIKI S	10600	ANTHIPPE L	47872
AMOCO SINGAPORE	71540	ANATOLIY LUNACHARSKIY	03654	ANGELIQUE V	75539	ANTHONY III	77831
AMOCO TRINIDAD	60302	ANATOLIY VANEYEV	79382	ANGELITA	61478	ANTHOS	58568
AMOCO TRINIDAD	68522	ANATOLIY VASILYEV	71532	ANGETIMOR	61524●	ANTHOULA 1	80530
AMOCO VOYAGER	68790	ANATOLIY VASILYEV	80202	ANGIE	70970●	ANTHOULA II	59621
AMOCO WHITING	60301	ANBOTO	46700	ANGIE	86370●	ANTIGONE	46929/1
AMOCO WHITING	68521	ANCAP SEXTO	40850	ANGIE BABY	28920	ANTIGUA	62141
AMOCO YORKTOWN	69823	ANCAP SEXTO	41060	ANGLE BAY	73367	ANTIGUA	75236
AMOKURA	66143	ANCHAN	02760	ANGLEZARKE	89060	ANTIGUA	45460●
AMOKURA	70583	ANCHANA	67491	ANGLIA	76201●	ANTIGUA	48720●
AMOUN	01414	ANCO CHARGER	65722	ANGLIA EXPRESS	18001	ANTILLA	12850
AMOUN	01674	ANCO CHARGER	75662	ANGOL	06653	ANTILLA BAY	56442
AMPARO	90680	ANCO ENDEAVOUR	65724	ANGSA MAS	87410	ANTILLA BAY	68352
AMPERE	18640	ANCO ENDEAVOUR	75664	ANGYALFOLD	89257	ANTILLIA	49602
AMPHION	05239	ANCO ENTENTE	65726	ANI	94211	ANTING	05370
AMPHIOPEA	36370	ANDALUCIA STAR	02562	ANIA	67941	ANTIOCHA	61157
AMPHIOPEA	37390	ANDALUCIA STAR	02662	ANIARA	72490	ANTIOPI	58565
AMPOL SAREL	53065	ANDAMAN SEA	45810	ANIARA	72980	ANTIPOLIS	03521
AMPURIA	51747	ANDERS MAERSK	08670	ANIELLO	59433	ANTIPOLO	07651
AMSTELDIEP	46860	ANDERS MAERSK	09000	ANINA	82222	ANTJE SCHULTE	53410
AMSTELDREEF	46361	ANDERS MAERSK	08674●	ANINGA	36290	ANTJE SCHULTE	64940
AMSTELLAAN	47752	ANDERS MAERSK	09004●	ANINGA	37870	ANTLIA	11650
AMSTELMEER	77840	ANDERSO	50554	ANINGA	43080	ANTOFAGASTA	69332
AMSTELMOLEN	77850	ANDES MARU	51561	ANINGA	44460	ANTON BUYUKLY	06797
AMSTELPARK	47751	ANDES MARU	67870	ANISIMOVKA	12391	ANTON CHEKOV	14377
AMSTELVAART	48153	ANDESGAS	69410	ANITA	24190	ANTON DOHRN	24170
AMSTELVLIET	48152	ANDHIKA ADIRAJA	61563	ANITA 1	57600	ANTON GUBARYEV	67010
AMSTELVOORN	48154	ANDINO	24380	ANITA 1	62240	ANTON IVANOV	40580
AMU-DARYA	35316	ANDIZHAN	22840	ANITA DAN	46114	ANTON LOPATIN	11629
AMULET	51350	ANDIZHAN	34470	ANITA SMITS	52048	ANTON MAKARENKO	07925
AMULET	52700	ANDOMALES	24037	ANITA VENTURE	73186	ANTON SAEFKOW	06380
AMULET	84010	ANDRE DELMAS	48260	ANIVA	36904	ANTON SAEFKOW	15410
AMUNDSEN SEA	53668	ANDREA MANTEGNA	44280	ANIVA	43804	ANTON STJEPOV	55910
AMUNDSEN SEA	73388	ANDREA MERZARIO	80296	ANJALENA	01630●	ANTON TAMMSAARE	12393
AMUNDSEN SEA	73388	ANDREA SMITS	52045	ANJOU	49530	ANTONELLO	43160
AMUR	89513	ANDREAS A	42230	ANKA D	80636/1	ANTONELLO DA MESSINA	01340
AMUR MARU	54541	ANDREAS A	42750	ANKARA	20359	ANTONELLOESSE	43280
AMUR MARU	63901	ANDREAS LEMOS	57009/1	ANKO	87704	ANTONI GARNUSZEWSKI	07860
AMURIYAH	63390	ANDRES BONIFACIO	64317	AN-LI	00950	ANTONIA	61890
AMURSK	12390	ANDREY ANDREYEV	03773	ANN M	85430	ANTONIA JOHNSON	04101
AMURSK	36896	ANDREY ANDREYEV	04013	ANN SANDVED	64853	ANTONINA NEZHDANOVA	01935
AMURSK	43796	ANDREY ANDREYEV	11318	ANN SANDVED	91033	ANTONIO D'ALESSIO	70283
AMURSKIY ZALIV	61101	ANDREY EVDANOV	85324	ANNA	81051	ANTONIO GRAMSCI	70591
AMURSKLES	24050	ANDREY IVANOV	50286	ANNA A	10360	ANTONIO M	66807
AMYNTAS	60077	ANDREY KIZHEVATOV	50746	ANNA BAKKE	59430	ANTONIO MACEO	48387
AN ANNE	59250	ANDREY LAVROV	03963	ANNA BECKER	73951	ANTONIO SUARDIAZ	94680
AN ANNE	62520	ANDREY MARKIN	11780	ANNA BIBOLINI	80640	ANTONIOS	69712
AN CHI	29040	ANDREY VILKITSKIY	22182	ANNA BROERE	66590	ANTONIOS G	55470
AN DA HAI	46446	ANDREY ZAKHAROV	93680	ANNA BROERE	75160	ANTONIOS G	56340
AN DONG JIANG	05324	ANDRIAN GONCHAROV	69322	ANNA C	82890	ANTONIS	06067
AN FU JIANG	05325	ANDRICO PROGRESS	04590	ANNA DRACOPOULOS	06484	ANTONIS P LEMOS	46911
AN HAI	46006	ANDRICO UNITY	04591	ANNA DRENT	75875	ANTRIM PRINCESS	32790
AN HING	24382	ANDRIOTIS	46671	ANNA HEIDA	88111	ANTS LAYKMAA	12394
AN HUA	84560	ANDROMEDA	03370	ANNA I ANGELICOUSSI	64060	ANTXON MARI	73850
AN JI HAI	46529	ANDROMEDA	11640	ANNA JO	26770●	ANTZELA	31303

Name	No.	Name	No.	Name	No.	Name	No.
ANUPAMA	45777	ARAKS	89502	ARGONAUT	94276	ARSENEYEV	12397
ANUYU	70775	ARALAR	52500	ARGONAVI	61262	ARSENIA K.	25450
ANVIL CROSS	42033●	ARALSK	12395	ARGOS	42550	ARSENIY MOSKVIN	50283
ANVIL MOUNTIE	50333●	ARALSK	86177	ARGOS	60082	ARSENYEV	45113
ANVIL MOUNTIE	83673●	ARAMEDIA	01630	ARGOSY	68922●	ARSHINTSEVO	78892
ANVIL SCOUT	93990●	ARAMIL	23170	ARGOVIND	83714	ARTEK	11818
ANWAL	76863	ARAMIS	75600●	ARGUN	11816	ARTEMIDA	11941
ANWAR	36190	ARAMIS	79320●	ARGUN	24049	ARTEMIS	46925
ANWAR	48383	ARAMOKO	17730	ARGUS	12576	ARTEMIS 1	73993
ANWAR M	41850	ARAN	58573	ARGUS	61034	ARTEMIS GAROFALIDIS	58341
ANYI	05420	ARANUI	19960	ARGUS	71194	ARTERN	71915
ANYI	06120	ARANUI	81940	ARGUS	93330	ARTHUR	54661
ANZERE	94130	ARANUI	89420	ARGUS CARRIER	41761	ARTHUR BECKER	23412
ANZERE	94620	ARARAT	70768	ARGYRO M	70370	ARTHUR MAERSK	08674
AOI MARU	08570	ARAS	07881	ARHON	83608	ARTHUR MAERSK	09004
AOTEA	09870	ARAS	15644	ARI	47819	ARTHUR PHILLIP	53540
APAPA PALM	55872	ARATIKA	19950	ARIA	19130	ARTIMON	74436●
APAPA PALM	56602	ARAUCA	93560	ARIADNE	47820	ARTIMON	77068●
APE	36892	ARAUCANO	37980	ARIADNE	92713	ARTIS	52091
APE	43792	ARAUCO	47052	ARIADNI	08770	ARTLENBURG	33923
APETIT	09384	ARAWA BAY	57558	ARIAKE	05192	ARTOIS	49531
APHRODITE	01830	ARAWAK	34206●	ARIAKE REEFER	20970	ARTSIZ	89203
APHRODITE	46110	ARAXOS	26761	ARIANE	06322	ARTUR GROTTGER	49656
APICO	91890	ARBELA	46928	ARIANE I	48632	ARTURO MICHELINA	90453
APILIOTIS	59251	ARBERIA	71995	ARICA	45910	ARTVIN	80354
APILIOTIS	62521	ARBERIA	72115	ARIEL	64327	ARTYOM	36251
APJ ANJLI	46305	ARC AEOLOS	48512	ARIEL	81320	ARTYOM	42801
APJ PRITI	60992	ARC MINOS	61704	ARIEL 1	11652	ARU	89232
APJ PRIYA	15232	ARC ODYSSEUS	48510	ARIES	28121	ARUBA BAY	85620
APJ SUSHMA	46306	ARCADIA	54413	ARIES	28640	ARUN THAI	46041●
APLI CHAU	24270	ARCADIA	57873	ARIES	56522	ARUNACHAL PRADESH	47046
APODY	92304●	ARCADIAN FAITH	64680	ARIETTA	03497●	ARVEPRINS KNUD	18930
APODY	92368●	ARCADIAN SEA	62171	ARIETTA	03587●	ARWAD	63712
APOGEY	13654	ARCADIAN SEA	74670	ARIETTA	48150●	ARZAMAS	11819
APOLLO 1	08221	ARCADIAN SKY	78380	ARIETTA GREGOS	48150	ARZAMAS	31830
APOLLO III	16580	ARCADIAN STAR	62170	ARILD MAERSK	08676	ARZEW	60646
APOLLON	56863	ARCADIAN SUN	29071	ARILD MAERSK	09006	ARZEW	62606
APOLLONIA	18070	ARCHANA	61460	ARIMBI	61411	ASAHAN	38940
APOLLONIA VII	89450	ARCHANGELOS	45779	ARION	28260	ASAHAN	39090
APOLLONIA X	64854	ARCHANGELOS G	77874	ARION	46471	ASAKAZE MARU	03560
APOLLONIA X	91050	ARCHANGELOS III	32010	ARION	58168	ASANO	79860
APOLLONIUS	61771	ARCHANGELOS III	53700	ARIS	25080	ASA-THOR	21960
APOSTOLOS M IV	39060	ARCHANGELOS III	78090	ARIS	25320	ASCHBERG	94011
APPIA	20600	ARCHIMEDES	89940	ARIS	60083	ASCONA	57481
APPLE BLOSSOM	33890	ARCHIMEDES	31132	ARIS EPTA	45651	ASCONA	73376
APPLEBY	77682	ARCHIMEDES	61040	ARIS V	39744	ASCONA	90501
APSHERON	11461	ARCHIMIDIS	61770	ARISTAGELOS	60481	ASCONIA	73376
APSHERON	70583	ARCHON	61040●	ARISTAIOS	74050	ASD HEKTOR	51850
APSHERONSK	36897	ARCHONTISSA KATINGO	83617	ARISTAIOS	77020	ASEAN GREATNESS	68391
APSHERONSK	43797	ARCO ANCHORAGE	63540	ARISTANAX	60482	ASEAN KNOWLEDGE	65821
APTMARINER	46650	ARCO FAIRBANKS	64241	ARISTARCHOS	60084	ASEAN KNOWLEDGE	69951
APUS	11656	ARCO JUNEAU	64242	ARISTARKH BELOPOLSKIY	10741	ASEAN LIBERTY	65822
APUS	11665	ARCO PRUDHOE BAY	64240	ARISTEOS	74050	ASEAN LIBERTY	69952
APUS	66871	ARCO SAG RIVER	64250	ARISTEOS	77020	ASEBU	93651
APUS	91461	ARCO TEXAS	64251	ARISTEUS	60085	ASEBU	94991
AQABA	80111	ARCOS	64255/1	ARISTO	25140	ASHINGTON	75254
AQABA CROWN	50151	ARCTIC	92785	ARISTON	35660	ASHKHABAD	12341
AQUA STAR	21000	ARCTIC	22141	ARISTOTELIS	90490	ASHKHABAD	39973
AQUABELLE	48175	ARCTIC	48020	ARISTOTLE S ONASSIS	54418	ASHKHABAD	67670
AQUACHARM	48170	ARCTIC FREEBOOTER	52696	ARISTOTLE S ONASSIS	57878	ASHLEY	60460
AQUAFAITH	48171	ARCTIC GAEL	17700	ARITA	58587●	ASHLEY LYKES	00060
AQUAGEM	48177	ARCTIC OCEAN	84310	ARIZONA	64094	ASHRAF AL AWAL	91140
AQUAGLORY	48172	ARCTIC OCEAN	06330	ARIZONA SUN	61013	ASHTABULA	35960
AQUAGRACE	48173	ARCTIC OCEAN	08081	ARIZONA SUN	71173	ASHUG ALEKSER	50760
AQUAJOY	48174	ARCTIC OCEAN	54700	ARK	57543	ASIA ANVIL	47921
AQUAMARINE	09491	ARCTIC SALVOR	74760	ARKADIY CHERNYSHEV	13755/6	ASIA BEAUTY	61205
AQUAMARINE	60080	ARCTIC STAR	93200	ARKADIY KAMANIN	15511	ASIA FALCON	47162
AQUARAMA	02505	ARCTIC TOKYO	38410	ARKADY GAYDAR	14378	ASIA FREEZER	06363
AQUARIUS	11339	ARCTIC TRAWLER	53871	ARKANDROS	60154	ASIA HERON	48995
AQUARIUS	32650	ARCTIC TROLL	24150	ARKAS	32580	ASIA HONESTY	61207
AQUARIUS	35460	ARCTIC VIKING	48970	ARKHANGELSK	02728/4	ASIA HUNTER	46480
AQUARIUS	66140	ARCTURUS	51510	ARKHANGELSK	17935	ASIA INDUSTRY	48996
AQUARIUS	70580	ARCTURUS	10544	ARKHANGELSKLES	24039	ASIA MARU	04701
AQUILA	11337	ARDATOV	72582	ARKHIMED	34881	ASIA MARU	05011
AQUILA	94060	ARDATOV	76745	ARKHIP KUINDZHI	76509	ASIA MARU	10020
AQUITAINE	57831	ARDATOV	11815	ARKLOW ABBEY	75534	ASIA MARU No 2	68559/6
ARA	72751	AREF	36911	ARKLOW CASTLE	75533	ASIA PALHO	25706
ARAB DABBOR	02611	ARENDSEE	43811	ARKLOW RIVER	52720/2●	ASIA REGULUS	61472
ARAB DABBOR	04331	ARENDSEE	42720	ARKOVO	12396	ASIA RINDO	61043
ARAB MAZIN	07510	ARETHOUSA	46379	ARKTIKA	93743	ASIA SPICA	61647
ARABAT	13655	ARETHOUSA II	47079	ARKTIKA	93833	ASIA SWALLOW	47922
ARABATSKIY	89681	ARETHOUSA II	92712	ARKTUR	76311	ASIA WINDS	73404
ARABELLA	58555	ARETHUSA	54654	ARLBERG	47222	ASIA WINDS	82714
ARABELLA	92950	ARETHUSA	55075	ARMAN	25841	ASIA-AFRIKA	30740
ARABELLA	95160	ARETHUSA	56060	ARMAVIR	25553	ASIAN EAGLE	50269/6
ARABI	20850	ARETI	71730	ARMENISTIS 1	81930	ASIAN FALCON	62310
ARABIAN KARIMAN	34893	ARETI S	58153	ARMENISTIS 1	89330	ASIAN FOREST	46643
ARABIAN LULUAH	50030	ARETUSA	86051	ARMENIYA	11817	ASIAN FOREST	83323
ARABIAN MERCHANT	10410	ARGIRO	51638	ARMERIA	58184/1	ASIAN NEPTUNE	61642
ARABIAN SEA	53070	ARGIRO	07230	ARMONIA	45400	ASIAN REEFER	05112
ARABIAN VICTORY	27930	ARGIRO	07430	ARMONIKOS	58750	ASIATIC	62960
ARACELIO IGLESIAS	07755	ARGO	48490	ARMONIKOS	60530	ASIR	55709
ARACELIO IGLESIAS	07898	ARGO	12239	ARMONIKOS	60320●	ASIR	58279
ARACELY	81851	ARGO	17310	ARMORIQUE	32210	ASKANIYA	11303
ARACENA	92784	ARGO	33290	ARNAFELL	84070	ASKO	71945
ARACRUZ VENTURE	49305	ARGO	94540	ARNAGE	52306	ASKOLD	12398
ARAD	57421	ARGO	93150	ARNIS	72752	ASMAA	03253
ARAD	86210	ARGO	72144●	ARNOLD MAERSK	08678	ASMAA	03632
ARADHANA	45779/1	ARGO	76484●	ARNOLD MAERSK	09008	ASMAA	50201
ARAFAT	49404	ARGO CHALLENGE	59591	ARNOLD ZWEIG	13769	ASMAA	75971
ARAFAT	50964	ARGO FAITH	59592	ARNON	60022	ASO MARU	92622
ARAFURA	09880	ARGO GLORY	59593	ARONA	31201	ASPA QUARTO	23851
ARAFURA SEA	06587	ARGO HOPE	59594	ARONA	93932	ASPASIA M	38930
ARAGON	63160	ARGO PIONEER	59590	AROS	76209/2●	ASPEN	92920
ARAGONIT	11917	ARGO SPIRIT	59595	AROS ATHENE	49880	ASPERITY	75070
ARAGONITE	89490	ARGO VALOUR	59596	AROS FREIGHTER	73660●	ASPHERON	11814
ARAGUA	04372	ARGOLIKOS	60480	AROSETTE	76202●	ASPIA	59471
ARAGUA	04432	ARGON	36890	AROSITA	76203●	ASPIDOFOROS	74941
ARAGVI	21220	ARGON	43790	ARPAD	46900	ASPINDZA	70776
ARAHANGA	19970	ARGONAFTIS	05235	ARQUITECTO GAUDI	87790	ASPROPYRGOS	43020
ARAHANGA	23340	ARGONAFTIS	16610	ARRAN	20860	ASPYR	61341
ARAKS	36898	ARGONAUT	16610	ARROW KING	03165●	ASSIA	47340
ARAKS	43798	ARGONAUT	23443	ARROW QUEEN	03163●	ASSIMINA	78402
ARAKS	89261	ARGONAUT	77710	ARSENE SIMARD	88482	ASSOMATOS	60086

Name	No.
ASSOS ENA	87391
ASTAKOS	51651
ASTAKOS	64421
ASTAN KESAYEV	13754/8
ASTARA	50777
ASTARTE	48602
ASTERI	16220
ASTERIAS	65671●
ASTERION	58154
ASTERO	34895●
ASTEROID	11940
ASTEROID	34895
ASTILLERO	00640
ASTIPALEA	60593
ASTIPALEA	69963
ASTIR	58155
ASTONDO	76089
ASTOR	16925
ASTOR	91540
ASTRA	12399
ASTRA IV	82510
ASTRA PEAK	46050
ASTRAL	56971
ASTRAMAN	59060
ASTRAMAN	76450
ASTRAPI	28820●
ASTRASOL	663870
ASTREA	50553
ASTREA	52600
ASTRID SCHULTE	81390
ASTRID SCHULTE	90640
ASTRO	40540
ASTRO COACH	95045
ASTRONAFTIS	27430
ASTRONOM	11820
ASTYANAX	72431
ASUBONE	27213
ASUKA REEFER	56467
ASUNARO	60516
ASUNCION	91846
ASYA 1	78680
ATACAMA	47051
ATAIR	62230
ATAIR	71250
ATAKOY	32162
ATALANTA	54110
ATALANTA	54580
ATALANTE	33180
ATALANTI	05476
ATALANTI	16221
ATALAYA	50552
ATAMAS	59321●
ATANER	87706●
ATARI	68322
ATHANASIOS K	52801
ATHANASIOS-S	83590
ATHANASSIA	06487
ATHENA	10921
ATHENA	70360
ATHENE	64316
ATHENIAN BEAUTY	67689/7●
ATHENIAN CHARM	67689/8●
ATHENIAN FIDELITY	67689/6●
ATHENIAN HARMONY	60590
ATHENIAN HARMONY	69960
ATHENIAN OLYMPICS	67689/1
ATHENIAN REEFER	06221
ATHENIAN REEFER	07451
ATHENIAN SPIRIT	56638/5
ATHENIAN THEODORE	67689/5
ATHENIAN VENTURE	55314
ATHENIAN VENTURE	70067
ATHENIAN VICTORY	67689/2
ATHENIAN XENOPHON	67689/3
ATHENIAN ZOE	48460/1●
ATHENIAN ZOE	49503/1●
ATHENIAN ZOE	49774/1●
ATHENIC	53150
ATHENIC	66300
ATHENS EXPRESS	20530
ATHENS SEA	25901
ATHENS STAR	38992
ATHERAS	06539/1
ATHINA K	48461
ATHINA K	49504
ATHINA K	49775
ATHINA ZAFIRAKIS	57188
ATHINAI	01522
ATHINAI	25010
ATHINAI	45610
ATHLON	58569
ATHLOS 1	83603
ATHLOS IV	50221
ATHOL	58193
ATHOLL FOREST	46640
ATHOLL FOREST	83320
ATHOS	60087
ATHOS	63032
ATHOS	59621/1●
ATHOS 1	03524
ATIA C	68692
ATIGUN PASS	58030
ATILOLA	42090
ATILOLA	42300
ATKARSK	00331
ATLANT	12574
ATLANTA	45760
ATLANTIC	52171
ATLANTIC	72910
ATLANTIC	94720
ATLANTIC CAUSEWAY	08350
ATLANTIC CHAMPAGNE	08354
ATLANTIC CHARITY	45570
ATLANTIC CINDERELLA	08352
ATLANTIC COGNAC	08353
ATLANTIC CORONA	50586●
ATLANTIC CROWN	08355
ATLANTIC CURRENT	58600
ATLANTIC EARL	73731
ATLANTIC EMPEROR	55750
ATLANTIC EMPEROR	63800
ATLANTIC EXPRESS	46180
ATLANTIC EXPRESS	49300
ATLANTIC FISHER	50490
ATLANTIC FOREST	35101
ATLANTIC FOREST	92811
ATLANTIC FOREST	95152
ATLANTIC FREEZE	84280
ATLANTIC HAWK	57181
ATLANTIC HELMSMAN	57182
ATLANTIC HERITAGE	57183
ATLANTIC HERO	57180
ATLANTIC HIGHWAY	92991
ATLANTIC HIGHWAY	94951
ATLANTIC HORIZON	57184
ATLANTIC ISLE	90860
ATLANTIC ISLE	91780
ATLANTIC JOY	59481
ATLANTIC MARINER	45862
ATLANTIC MARINER	46022
ATLANTIC MARQUESS	68871
ATLANTIC NAVIGATOR	73741
ATLANTIC OCEAN	14711
ATLANTIC PRELUDE	74061
ATLANTIC PREMIER	74060
ATLANTIC PROSPERITY	57351●
ATLANTIC REEFER	84000●
ATLANTIC RIVER	85472
ATLANTIC RIVER	91531
ATLANTIC SAGA	72780
ATLANTIC SEA	49840
ATLANTIC SKY	62350
ATLANTIC SONG	72800
ATLANTIC SONG	76820
ATLANTIC SONG	76960
ATLANTIC SPAN	72790
ATLANTIC STAR	72801
ATLANTIC STAR	76821
ATLANTIC STAR	76961
ATLANTIC STREAM	94831
ATLANTIC SUN	75484
ATLANTIC SWAN	73870
ATLANTICO	14350
ATLANTICO	73230
ATLANTICOS	64318
ATLANTIK	18721
ATLANTIS	33140
ATLANTIS	33830
ATLANTIS	55421
ATLANTIS	72340
ATLANTIS	73913
ATLANTIS	78881
ATLANTIS 1	40880
ATLANTIS EXPRESS	48290
ATLANTIS III	87551●
ATLANTIS V	87551●
ATLAS	01860
ATLAS	52981
ATLAS	89720
ATLAS 1	23330
ATLAS 1	53360
ATLAS CHALLENGER	56750
ATLAS COUNSELLOR	57210
ATLAS II	23331
ATLAS III	94580
ATLAS IV	93170
ATLAS IV	94510
ATLAS MARU	51560
ATLE	33000
ATOLL	11821
ATRA	15170
ATREUS	58164/2
ATREUS	58155/1
ATREVIDA	83890
ATROPOS	06630
ATSUMI	72940
ATTAVIROS	74120●
ATTICA	61451
ATTICA REEFER	06220
ATTICA REEFER	07450
ATTIKA	02390●
ATTIKA HOPE	58606
ATTIKI	45170
AUBADE	88350
AUBADE	90350
AUBRAC	05452
AUBY	94980
AUCTORITAS	35594
AUCTORITAS	36494
AUDACIA	18380
AUDACIA	33931
AUDACITY	76360
AUDAX	67001
AUE	70230
AUGUST ALLE	12400
AUGUST JAKOBSON	45122
AUGUST KORK	85351
AUGUST KULBERG	89258
AUGUST MOON	71153
AUGUST THYSSEN	64323
AUGUSTO MONTENEGRO	08330
AUKSHAYTIKA	13653
AULICA	37512
AULICA	44214
AURA ADVENTURE	66141
AURA ADVENTURE	70581
AURA BRAVERY	66142
AURA BRAVERY	70582
AURELIA	33474
AURELIA	58891
AURELIA DI MAIO	13150
AURES	64964
AURIGA	11653
AURIGA	35462
AURITA	58471
AUROBINDO	71631
AURORA	45761
AURORA	70773
AUSEKLIS	10050
AUSONIA	53296
AUSTANGER	02331
AUSTRAL	61600
AUSTRAL	00013
AUSTRAL LIGHTNING	02483
AUSTRAL LIGHTNING	35133
AUSTRAL LIGHTNING	00019
AUSTRAL MOON	02484
AUSTRAL MOON	35138
AUSTRAL MOON	34223
AUSTRALIA FREEZER	04700
AUSTRALIA MARU	05010
AUSTRALIA MARU	02870
AUSTRALIA STAR	50263
AUSTRALIAN EAGLE	09800
AUSTRALIAN EMBLEM	10040
AUSTRALIAN EMBLEM	74502
AUSTRALIAN ENDEAVOUR	09552
AUSTRALIAN ENTERPRISE	33310
AUSTRALIAN ENTERPRISE	77362
AUSTRALIAN ENTERPRISE	09801
AUSTRALIAN ESCORT	57351●
AUSTRALIAN ESCORT	84000●
AUSTRALIAN EXPLORER	09553
AUSTRALIAN EXPLORER	33311
AUSTRALIAN EXPLORER	77363
AUSTRALIAN EXPORTER	51943
AUSTRALIAN EXPORTER	52433
AUSTRALIAN GRAIN	58176/1
AUSTRALIAN PIONEER	72410
AUSTRALIAN PROGRESS	77541
AUSTRALIAN PROSPECTOR	77540
AUSTRALIAN PURPOSE	72411
AUSTRALIAN SEAROADER	09551
AUSTRALIAN SEAROADER	33312
AUSTRALIAN SEAROADER	77361
AUSTRALIAN VENTURE	08440
AUSTRI	87282
AUTAN	53325
AUTAN	63222/1
AUTHENTIC	62963
AUTHENTICITY	75226
AUTHOR	73408
AUTHOR	82718
AUTHORITY	75071
AUTO COURIER	87120
AUTO TRADER	93510
AUTO TRADER	93920
AUTOBAHN	94770
AUTOLLOYD	90201
AUTOROUTE	12810
AUTOROUTE	15690
AUTOSTRADA	90200
AUTSE	70769
AUVERGNE	53560
AUVERGNE	59720
AVA	13270
AVACHA	93747
AVACHA	93837
AVALO	41990
AVARE	22420
AVAX	28614
AVE	75272
AVEDAT	53830
AVEDAT	69460
AVELONA STAR	02563
AVELONA STAR	02663
AVENGER	68325
AVETIK ISAAKYAN	50742
AVIAN WREN	15560
AVIATOR	11822
AVIN OIL LEADER	57840
AVIN OIL TRADER	63840
AVIN OIL TRADER	67610
AVLIS	58570
AVLIS EXPRESS	81140
AVON	48623
AVON	61812
AVON FOREST	74951
AVON FOREST	80071
AVONDALE	27870
AVONDALE	34420
AVRA	81562
AVRAAMIY ZAVENYAGIN	20879/1●
AVRAFROST	33822
AVRO ENTERPRISE	50664●
AVRO VENTURE	50663●
AXEL JOHNSON	04102
AXEL MAERSK	08675
AXEL MAERSK	09005
AXIOS	48560
AXIOS	89350
AY PETRI	44108
AYAN	06795/2
AYESHA	29952●
AYKHAL	70766
AYNAZHI	70770
AYON	70771
AY-PETRI	01964
AY-PETRI	11823
AYSBERG	89504
AYTODOR	46582
AYUBIA	56576
AYU-DAG	11801
AYVALIK	15810
AYVAZOVSKIY	20650

B

Name	No.
BA SHAN	13393
BAABDA	17781
BABA GURGUR	69570
BABAYEVSK	11334/3
BABOR	48906
BABUSHKIN	45356
BABYKINO	11335
BABYLON	45385
BACAB	54681
BACAB	66161
BACAT I	93280
BACAT I	94200
BACAU	41318
BACCARAT	39381
BACO-LINER 1	93030
BACO-LINER 1	95200
BACO-LINER 2	93031
BACO-LINER 2	95201
BACO-LINER 3	93032
BACO-LINER 3	95202
BADEN	64092
BADGER	19561
BADJAO	14812
BADR	34371●
BADRE	45405
BAEK DU SAN	71330
BAFFIN	22130
BAGANOVO	11335/1
BAGAREVO	11335/2
BAGAS	42200
BAGHDAD	45384
BAGH-E-DACCA	15251
BAGH-E-KARACHI	15250
BAGRATION	17504
BAGRATIONOVSK	13659
BAHAGIA VI	25340
BAHAMASTARS	46970
BAHARI	81620
BAHIA	83763
BAHIA AGUIRRE	23250
BAHIA AGUIRRE	34700
BAHIA BLANCA	03910
BAHIA BUEN SUCESO	23251
BAHIA BUEN SUCESO	34701
BAHIA DE COCHINOS	31012
BAHIA DE MARIEL	92021
BAHIA DE NIPE	92020
BAHIA MAGDALENA	46711
BAHIA PORTETE	50680
BAHIA SANTIAGO DE CUBA	33711
BAHLUI	13770
BAI HEI KOU	93311
BAI YIN SHAN	05070
BAI YUN HAI	46336
BAI YUN HAI	55930
BAI YUN SHAN	15021
BAIA DE SAO BRAS	50211
BAIA MARE	39660
BAILADILA	53222
BAILADILA	64431
BAILUNDO	81660
BAILUNDO	82660
BAIMA	30840
BAIPAO	30841
BAIRE	12790
BAJKA	50683
BAKAR	05650
BAKAR	50684
BAKAYEVO	12401
BAKHCHISARAY	11942
BAKHCHISARAY	52021
BAKHCHISARAY	84151
BAKKAFOSS	75584
BAKLAN	12556
BAKLANOVO	11334
BAKU	50770
BAKURIANI	45357
BALABAC	45080
BALADZHARY	85998
BALAKHNA	11333
BALAKHNALES	24052
BALAKLAVA	12240
BALAKLAVA	38611
BALAO	50685
BALASHIKHA	45363
BALASHOV	28063
BALDBUTTE	37261
BALDER B	52090
BALDER CHUANCHOW	07761
BALDER CHUANCHOW	07811
BALDER EMS	76871
BALDER HAREN	76870
BALDER HOPE	57627
BALDER HOPE	61047
BALDER JIANGCHOW	15672
BALDER LONDON	67440
BALDER ZEA DAWN	07812
BALDER ZEA DAWN	07760
BALDER ZEA STAR	07816
BALDER ZEA STAR	38612
BALDONE	93142
BALDUIN	94360
BALI	07650
BALINTAWAK	79643
BALKAN	05113
BALKAN REEFER	

Name	No.
BALKANIJA	19180
BALKHASH	20791
BALKHASH	33991
BALKHASH	52020
BALKHASH	84150
BALLENITA	18440
BALLYKERN	75482
BALLYRUSH	42471
BALMORAL	18900
BALTA	11825
BALTA	36252
BALTA	42802
BALTCHIK	29000
BALTIC	52172
BALTIC EAGLE	33280
BALTIC EAGLE	94550
BALTIC FERRY	76785
BALTIC HERON	73661
BALTIC LINK	93256
BALTIC MERMAID	72387/1●
BALTIC OSPREY	72730
BALTIC OSPREY	76910
BALTIC PROGRESS	15784
BALTIC PROGRESS	82694
BALTIC PROSPERITY	66490
BALTIC PROSPERITY	85930
BALTIC SEA	77841
BALTIC STAR	02440
BALTIC TRANSPORTER	71141
BALTIC WASA	93251
BALTICA	49903
BALTICA	50343
BALTIKA	18010
BALTIM	92789
BALTIMORE	73420
BALTIMORE TRADER	35650
BALTISKAYA KOSA	13751/3
BALTIYSK	21601
BALTIYSKAYA SLAVA	93784
BALTIYSKIY 101	75380
BALTIYSKIY 102	75381
BALTIYSKIY 103	75382
BALTIYSKIY 105	75384
BALTIYSKIY 106	75385
BALTIYSKIY 107	75386
BALTIYSKIY 108	75387
BALTIYSKIY 109	75388
BALTIYSKIY 110	75389
BALTIYSKIY 111	75390
BALTIYSKIY 1 to BALTIYSKIY 73	79500
BALTIYSKIY 1 to BALTIYSKIY 73	90030
BALVY	38613
BAM	70028
BAMENDA PALM	62075
BAMMEN	51610
BANANA CARRIER	33861
BANANA EXPRESS	31642
BANANA TRADER	33863
BANANERA	31640
BANANG	42110
BANAT	15320
BANAT	55780
BANAT	56480
BANAWE	61013●
BANAWE	71173●
BANDA AZUL	79103
BANDA SEA	03850
BANDAK	56040
BANDAR DEMAK	78690
BANDAR DEMTA	78691
BANDAR DENPASAR	78693
BANDAR-E-DEYLAN	90992
BANDERAS	48070
BANDUNDU	62711
BANDUNDU	62751
BANGKOK	58552
BANGKOK	71872
BANGLAR ALO	35740
BANGLAR ASHA	09072
BANGLAR BAANI	06642
BANGLAR DOOT	25785
BANGLAR JOY	80650
BANGLAR KHEYA	35940
BANGLAR MAAN	49711
BANGLAR MAITRI	29921
BANGLAR MITA	49710
BANGLAR MONI	61409/17●
BANGLAR NOOR	71580
BANGLAR PROGOTI	15131
BANGLAR ROBI	61409/5
BANGLAR SAMPAD	25777
BANGLAR SWAPNA	15130
BANGLAR TARANI	30270
BANGLAR UPOHAR	09071
BANGUI	92297
BANIJA	61780
BANJA LUKA	74510
BANJAMAS	02761
BANKO	40470
BANKO 1	41760
BANKO	93652
BANKO	94992
BANNER	35603
BANQUISE	33810●
BANSHU MARU No 5	93412
BANSHU MARU No 6	93413
BANSIN	75333
BANTA	50686
BAO AN	52735
BAO QING HAI	53800
BAO QING HAI	77520
BAO SHAN	10590
BAO SHAN	13391
BAO XING	44514
BAOTING	04860
BAR	13960
BAR PROTECTOR	01354
BARABASH	12403
BARABINSK	12404
BARABINSK	22841
BARABINSK	34471
BARADA	03250
BARADA	03634
BARAKATALLAH	29364
BARAKUDA	22332
BARANJA	74511
BARAO DE JACEGUAY	26770
BARAO DE TEFFE	84300
BARAO DO RIO BRANCO	26771
BARAUNI	53221
BARAUNI	64432
BARBA	22810
BARBARA BROVIG	67735
BARBARA LEONHARDT	46282
BARBARA-BRITT	73795
BARBARA-CHRIS	73801
BARBAROSSA	72486
BARBAROSSA	88850
BARBARY	56752
BARBATA	22333
BARBER MEMNON	54191
BARBER MEMNON	54341
BARBER MENELAUS	54190
BARBER MENELAUS	54340
BARBER NARA	52642
BARBER PERSEUS	52644
BARBER PRIAM	52643
BARBER TAIF	52641
BARBER TOBA	52645
BARBER TONSBERG	52640
BARCELONA	71544
BARDALAND	57559
BARDU	50021
BARENBELS	52980
BARENDSZ	76181
BARENTS SEA	82610
BARENTSEE	18722
BARENTZGRACHT	49827
BARGAS	81131
BARGUZIN	15461
BARIT	11918
BARKENKOPPEL	72680
BARLINEK	75328
BARNAUL	24056
BARNWORTH	72336
BAROGRAF	07471
BAROJA	51890
BARON BELHAVEN	74931
BARON KINNAIRD	48079/2
BARON MINTO	47944
BARRA HEAD	78916
BARRANCA	35121
BARRANDUNA	80211
BARRIER	41810
BARRIOS	02991
BARRIOS	03031
BARRISTER	46255
BARRUETA	49308
BARRY	50022
BARRY	61813
BARRYDALE	03762●
BARS	22161
BARTOLOME MOSA	06615
BARU	42890
BARU LUCK	45383●
BARU SPIRIT	06761
BARU TRUST	06068
BARWA	50688
BARWENA	22334
BAR'ZAN	73412
BASALT	73830
BASALT	77010
BASARGIN	12405
BASHAYER 1	60721
BASHKIR	45121
BASHKIRIYA	02140
BASHKIRIYA	06827
BASHKIRNEFT	85890
BASILEA	59514
BASILEA	59824
BASKA	15240
BASKUNCHAK	11460
BASKUNCHAK	84365
BASRAH	45386
BASSEIN	13271
BASTIAAN BROERE	85665
BASTION	57041
BASTION	89751
BASTO III	19030
BAT SHEVA	84240
BATAAFGRACHT	49829/2
BATAK	83720
BATALLA DE STA. CLARA	67340
BATALLA DE STA. CLARA	71340
BATALLA DE YAGUAJAY	67341
BATALLA DE YAGUAJAY	71341
BATANGHARI	21570
BATAYSK	23760
BATIK	87590
BATILLUS	52950
BATILLUS	55480
BATILMAN	13657
BATROUN	28200
BATU	66410
BATUMI	11826
BATUMI	44140
BAUCHI	50023
BAUCIS	51811
BAUMARE	72385
BAUNTON	61713
BAURU	63932
BAUSKA	38610
BAVANG	50024
BAVARIA	04641
BAY	35600
BAYAMON	08341
BAYANO	35120
BAYARD	93140
BAYERN	64093
BAYEVO	11335/3
BAYKAL	02120
BAYKAL	12402
BAYKAL	17812
BAYKAL	20792
BAYKAL	33990
BAYKALLES	04181
BAYKONUR	24059
BAYMAK	45364
BAYMAK	89467
BAYNUNAH	15142
BAZALT	11827
BAZALTOVYY	89765
BEACHWAY	37366
BEACON GRANGE	04720
BEACON GRANGE	04940
BEACON HILL	05710
BEACON POINT	66751
BEACON POINT	75801
BEAGLE	92710
BEATRICE	55382
BEATRICE	66956
BEATRICE	70996
BEATRIZ DEL MAR	76102
BEATRIZ MONTEIRO	04890
BEATRIZ MONTEIRO	57520
BEAUFORT ISLAND	49180●
BEAUJOLAIS	36850
BEAUTY ROSE	21900
BEBEDOURO	71031
BECENA	13460
BEDFORD	46091
BEDFORD	83261
BEDOUIN BIRKNES	46315
BEDOUIN BIRKNES	46565
BEEDING	76130
BEEDING	79910
BEER SHEVA	79110
BEERBERG	94012
BEGA	87640
BEGONA DEL MAR	76081
BEGONIA	93900
BEGONIA 1	65470
BEI AN	51295
BEI FENG SHAN	87812
BEI HAI	56880
BEI SHAN	02770
BEISHU MARU	04702
BEISHU MARU	05012
BEISHU MARU	09892
BEITEDDINE	28350
BEITO	58734
BEIUS	77568
BEJAIA	55316
BEJAIA	70060
BEKAPAI/PERMINA 56	70753
BEKAS	11957
BEKASAR/PERMINA 54	70751
BEKENGRACHT	49826
BELA KHUN	05634
BELA KHUN	14463
BELA KOSMO	61561
BELA ROZO	61562
BELASITZA	77982
BELBECK	86095
BELCARGO	77463
BELCHATOW	60360
BELEN	03221
BELEN	03891
BELGIAN REEFER	06281
BELGICA	51750
BELGOROD DNESTROVSKIY	45365
BELGRAD	36862
BELGRANO	80010
BELGRAVE	88611
BELGRAVE	90071
BELI	28540
BELIEF	05825●
BELIEF	06012●
BELINDA	77673
BELINDA	07650●
BELINSKIY	12361
BELINSKIY	20790
BELITSK	01071
BELL COMET	90982
BELL RACER	73771
BELL RAIDER	73772
BELL RANGER	73773
BELL REBEL	73774
BELL RELIANT	73777
BELL RENOWN	73776
BELL RESOLVE	73778
BELL ROVER	73770
BELL RULER	73775
BELLAMYA	52951
BELLAMYA	55481
BELLARY	53220
BELLARY	64430
BELLATRIX	83930
BELLE	04786
BELLE	04887●
BELLE P	24899
BELLE ROSE	04787
BELLINI	44270●
BELLNES	46314
BELLNES	46564
BELLO	03390
BELLONA	66494
BELLONA	85936
BELMEKEN	79641
BELNOR	45990
BELOBO	68280
BELOCEAN	64328
BELOGORSK	12299
BELOGORSK	86200
BELOMORSKLES	24047
BELOMORY	11304
BELOMORYE	52022
BELOMORYE	84152
BELONA	22330
BELORETSK	01070
BELORUSSIYA	10433
BELOVODSK	01072
BELOYARSK	85999
BELOZERSKLES	24057
BELSTAR	46000
BELTSY	86227
BELVAUX	12690
BEN AIN	88431
BEN FRANKLIN	53650
BEN FRANKLIN	53740
BEN MAJED	90532
BEN MAJED	91072
BEN OCEAN LANCER	92880
BENADIR	21240
BENAKAT/PERMINA 57	70755
BENALBANACH	72339
BENALDER	08410
BENAVON	08411
BENCHIJIGUA	94021
BENCLEUCH	66611
BENCLEUCH	75131
BENEDETTA F	78482
BENEDETTO SCOTTO	91848
BENEDICT	60415
BENGAL PRIDE	31600
BENGAL PROGRESS	56116
BENGAL STAR	07010
BENGAL TOWER	31410
BENGAWAN	21571
BENGHAZI	58480
BENGUELA CURRENT	26751
BENHOPE	67640
BENHOPE	71430
BENIALI	47327
BENIALI	83387
BENIGNITY	58185
BENITO JUAREZ	19371
BENITO JUAREZ	69990
BENITO JUAREZ	86480
BENJAMIN HARRISON	01056
BENLEDI	72334
BENMACDHUI	66612
BENMACHDHUI	75132
BEN-MY-CHREE	20501
BENNY SKOU	86700
BENODET	19290
BENODET	23700
BENTHEIM	47659/3●
BENVENUE	66610
BENVENUE	75130
BENYA RIVER	15270
BENYA RIVER	35041
BEOGRAD	48065
BERBERA II	32984
BERBY	83922
BERDIKARI	61475
BERDSK	85995
BERDY KERBABAYEV	50743
BERDYANSK	00332
BERESFORD	39380
BEREZEN	11828
BEREZINA	89212
BEREZINALES	24058
BEREZNIK	06770
'BEREZNIK'	07550
BEREZNIKI	01074
BEREZNIKI	11314
BEREZOVKA	45366
BEREZOVNEFT	86004
BEREZOVO	70022
BERG	82840
BERGA	59161
BERGA	66511
BERGE ADRIA	65191
BERGE ARROW	56455
BERGE BIG	56415
BERGE BIG	67835
BERGE BIG	68435
BERGE BORG	56411
BERGE BORG	67831
BERGE BORG	68431
BERGE BOSS	65202
BERGE BOSS	67412
BERGE BRIONI	65190
BERGE CHIEF 7-5-91	56413
BERGE CHIEF	67833
BERGE CHIEF	68433
BERGE DUKE	58010
BERGE DUKE	59810
BERGE EAGLE	56456
BERGE EMPEROR	56380
BERGE EMPRESS	56381
BERGE FISTER	53554
BERGE KING	67820
BERGE LORD 7-5-9	58012
BERGE LORD	59812

BERGE MASTER	72345	BIMA	43198	BOKA	57234	BOW ELM	60863
BERGE ODEL	64551	BIMANTARA DUA	61409/15	BOKE	81824	BOW ELM	70903
BERGE PILOT	56414	BIMANTARA SATU	61409/16	BOKE	82074	BOW FAGUS	54552
BERGE PILOT	67834	BIN HAI	46750	BOKELNBURG	73671	BOW FIGHTER	53001
BERGE PRINCE	67822	BIN HAI 504	08501	BOKSIT	11919	BOW FIGHTER	53291
BERGE PRINCESS	67823	BIN HAI 511	14960	BOLAN	52863	BOW FLOWER	54553
BERGE QUEEN	67821	BIN HAI 512	14961	BOLD CHALLENGER	74651	BOW FORTUNE	54130
BERGE SAGA	55643	BINTAN	61461●	BOLD KNIGHT	36340	BOW FORTUNE	54250
BERGE SAGA	55843	BINTANG BOLONG	52100	BOLERO	1,6941	BOW HUNTER	53295
BERGE SEPTIMUS	58011	BINTANG SAMUDRA III	37320	BOLESLAW CHOBRY	14920	BOW PIONEER	53294
BERGE SEPTIMUS	59811	BINTANG SAMUDRA IV	45070	BOLESLAW CHOBRY	15730	BOW SEA	54131
BERGE SISAR	55642	BINTANG UTARA	91641	BOLESLAW KRZYWOUSTY	14922	BOW SEA	54251
BERGE SISAR	55842	BIOSFERA	13660	BOLESLAW KRZYWOUSTY	15732	BOW SKY	54132
BERGE SISU	55641	BIRA	85610	BOLESLAW RUMINSKI	49657	BOW SKY	54232
BERGE SISU	55841	BIRD OF PARADISE	22080	BOLESLAW SMIALY	14921	BOW SPRING	54133
BERGE STRAND	55643/1	BIRLAD	77570	BOLESLAW SMIALY	15731	BOW SPRING	54253
BERGE STRAND	55843/1	BIRLING	75920	BOLESLAWIEC	50460	BOW STAR	54134
BERGE SUND	55643/2	BIRSHTONAS	12409	BOLGRAD	57541	BOW STAR	54254
BERGE SUND	55843/2	BIRTA	75933	BOLIMOG	89269	BOW SUN	54135
BERGEBONDE	64550	BIRTHE THOLSTRUP	85001	BOLIVAR	34210	BOW SUN	54255
BERGLJOT	50689	BIRYUSINSK	11742	BOLIVAR	86690	BOX TRADER	75891
BERGO	50025	BIRYUSINSK	34632	BOLIVAR	93300●	BOXER CAPTAIN COOK	95132
BERGON	74910	BIRYUZA	12410	BOLIVIA	04640	BOXY	50480
BERILL	12406	BIRYUZA	15462	BOLON	84360	BOXY	83070
BERING SEA	47831	BIRYUZA	70781	BOLSHEVIK	11623	BP ACHIEVER	58058
BERING TRADER	43260	BISCHOFSTOR	47205	BOLSHEVIK KARAYEV	44100	BP BATTLER	83851
BERINGOV PROLIV	58511	BISE	68261	BOLSHEVIK SUKHANOV	13011	BP BATTLER	88901
BERINGOV PROLIV	71821	BISLIG TRANSPORT	86951	BOLSHEVO	12241	BP JOUSTER	70880
BERISLAV	45358	BISMARCKSTEIN	76209/3●	BOLTENHAGEN	75320	BP JOUSTER	79590
BERJAYA	25371	BISMILLAH	94020●	BONA	62300	BP SPRINGER	83850
BERJAYA	34771	BISON	11598	BONA FE	75935	BP SPRINGER	88900
BERJAYA	70952	BISON	94611	BONA TIDE	39741	BP WARRIOR	83852
BERKBORG	59604	BISTRITA	13732	BONAHOPE	42940	BP WARRIOR	88902
BERKBORG	71934	BIYSK	01075	BONAIRE	75237	BRA	02720
BERKUT	13658	BIZERTE	51290	BONANZA	56989	BRAD	82110
BERLIN	58362	BLACK PRINCE	16351	BONAVENTURE II	73730	BRAD	82390
BERLIN-HAUPSTADT	04924	BLACK WATCH	16350	BONAVISTA	22010	BRADEVERETT	14521
BERMUDA STAR	19741●	BLACKPOOL	36170	BONAWIND 1	85281	BRADEVERETT	81580
BERMUDIANA	73884	BLACKPOOL	41900	BONG SAN	69452	BRADFORD	36171
BERMUDIANA	87264	BLACKTHORN	87850	BONITA	34200	BRADFORD	41901
BERN	83230●	BLACKWELL POINT	36070	BONITO	23450	BRADING	20930
BERN	83250●	BLACKWELL POINT	41790	BONN	58360	BRAENNAREN	66670
BERNARDINO CORREA	05364	BLAGOVESHCHENSK	07552	BONNY	68660	BRAGD	67462
BERNARDINO CORREA	15664	BLAGOVESHCHENSK	86170	BONTEGRACHT	49829	BRAGE	73161
BERNARDO HOUSSAY	60870	BLAJ	77578/1	BONTRADER	72320	BRAGE	77661
BERNARDO HOUSSAY	70910	BLANCA DEL MAR	87781	BOOGABILLA	80290	BRAHMAN EXPRESS	41980
BERNBURG	03871	BLANIK	15093	BOONKRONG II	31480	BRAILA	39672
BERNBURG	04424	BLANKENBURG	03872	BORA	18271	BRAINPOWER	69333
BERNHARD BASTLEIN	06385	BLANKENBURG	04424/1	BORE KING	93266	BRANDAL	22370
BERNHARD BASTLEIN	15414	BLANKENSEE	46380	BORE QUEEN	93265	BRANIEWO	88233
BERNHARD KELLERMANN	10251	BLANKENSEE	47080	BORE SEA	94171	BRANSFIELD	16240
BERNHARD KELLERMANN	12631	BLAVET	86990	BORE SKY	94560	BRANT POINT	67251
BERNHARD OLDENDORFF	72250	BLIKUR	93011	BORE SONG	94170	BRANT POINT	91671
BERNHARD S	50260	BLITAR	00740	BORE SUN	94561	BRANTAS	21573
BERRY	37330	BLIX	50690	BORE XI	94013	BRAS	67460
BERTHA FISSER	62104	BLOUDAN	40101	BOREA	01800	BRASILIA	51637
BERTOLT BRECHT	12620	BLUE BAY	09591	BOREA	67150	BRASLAV	12411
BERTRAM RICKMERS	52810	BLUE CRYSTAL	40092	BORG	82980	BRASLAVLES	24061
BERYTE	17782	BLUE DIAMOND	47921●	BORGESTAD	46260	BRASOV	41313
BESITANG/PERMINA 53	70752	BLUE EXCELSIOR	71567	BORGO	72891	BRASSIE	70164
BESOR	72332	BLUE MASTER	48631	BORGO	76941	BRATISLAVA	36863
BETACRUX	59142	BLUE MOON	87070	BORINQUEN	74470	BRATISLAVA	79232
BETH	50020	BLUE MOON	89560	BORIS ALEKSEYEV	13754/10	BRATSK	02728/2
BETHIOUA	55317	BLUE NILE	49351	BORIS BUVIN	78069	BRATSKLES	24054
BETHIOUA	70061	BLUE OCEAN	55580	BORIS CHILIKIN	59880	BRATSTVO	01562
BETINA THOLSTRUP	81170	BLUE OCEAN	56460	BORIS DAVIDOV	22183	BRATTINGSBORG	75061
BETINA THOLSTRUP	81473	BLUE OCEAN	65971	BORIS GORBATOV	07920	BRAVA PRIMA	91318●
BETSIBOKA	82650●	BLUE PEARL	27010	BORIS LAVRENEV	07926	BRAVE MOTHER	61165●
BETTY	67283	BLUE SEA 1	40090	BORIS NIKOLAICHUK	06797/2	BRAVE THEMIS	57475
BETTY No 2	57619/7	BLUE SHINE	57540	BORIS TSINDELIS	13751/4	BRAVENES	46312
BETTY No 2	61059/7	BLUE SHINYO	52590	BORIS ZHEMCHUZIN	03652	BRAVENES	46562
BETTY THERESA	85860	BLUE SKY	40091	BORIS ZHEMCHUZIN	03072	BRAVERY	78350
BETULA	19080	BLUE SKY	44480	BORISLAV	57542	BRAVO ARES	34890
BETULA	58470	BLUE SPIRIT	59660	BORISOGLEBSK	86000	BRAVO CERES	34894
BETUNG/PERMINA 55	70754	BLUE SPIRIT	58720	BORISPOL	11734	BRAVO GEORGE	55015
BEURSGRACHT	49828	BLUE STAR	52361	BORISPOL	34624	BRAVO GEORGE	55885
BEXLEY	40320	BLUE STAR	87071	BORIYA TSARIKOV	15512	BRAVO GEORGE	56555
BEYKOZ	16730	BLUE STAR	89561	BORMLA	91841	BRAVO KATERINA	34900
BEZHETSK	86182	BLUE WAVE	30192	BORODIN	86173	BRAVO LUIS	26104
BHAGAT SINGH	59906	BLUEBIRD	48310	BORODINO	36881	BRAVO MARIA	13400
BHAGAT SINGH	67666	BLUENOSE	16460	BORODINSKOYE POLYE	13755/8	BRAVO SIF	49898
BHAGIRATHI	39400	BLUESTREAM	03761●	BOROVICHI	11380	BRAZIL VENTURE	49306
BHANURANGSI	34970	BLUMENTHAL	48485	BORRENMILL	83132	BRAZILIA	31730
BHARAT SEEMA	94040	BO AH	61017	BORSEC	77572	BRAZILIAN EXPRESS	05078
BHARATA	56840	BO AH	71177	BORUSSIA	04642	BRAZILIAN EXPRESS	06130
BHASKARA	55220	BO BENGTSSON	54890	BORZESTI	77573	BRAZILIAN EXPRESS	07840
BHASKARA	57250	BO CHURN	61640	BORZHOMI	60629	BRAZILIAN FRIENDSHIP	69050
BHOJA MARINER	27960	BOA ESPERANCA	51050	BORZHOMI	62589	BRAZILIAN HOPE	58363
BI SHENG	71857	BOA NOVA	90533	BOSANKA	61781	BRAZILIAN REEFER	06280
BIA RIVER	07990	BOA NOVA	91073	BOSFOR	12413	BRAZILIAN SKY	48949/2
BIA RIVER	15275	BOA VISTA 1	52280	BOSHNYAKOVO	17925	BRAZILIAN TRADER	71451
BIAKH	50410	BOBERG	72687	BOSNA	15285	BRAZILIAN VITORIA	71450
BIAKH	50820	BOBRUYSKLES	24060	BOSUT	66950	BREADZA	77575
BIANCA	31650	BOCCACCIO	32552	BOSUT	70990	BREDAL	85420
BIBAN	48907	BOCHNIA	03231	BOTANY BAY	77051	BREEDE	82841
BICAZ	77569	BOCHNIA	03621	BOTEVGRAD	84710	BREEHOEK	59624
BICKERSGRACHT	49829/1	BOCSA	77571	BOTEVGRAD	85170	BREEHORN	59620
BIELEFELD	72140	BODAYBO	24062	BOTNIA EXPRESS	19294	BREEKADE	66971
BIELEFELD	76480	BODE THOMAS	18650	BOTNIA EXPRESS	23705	BREEKADE	91551
BIESZCZADY	75735	BODO UHSE	17980	BOTNICHESKIY ZALIV	61102	BREEKANT	66970
BIESZCZADY	88385	BODRUM	81100	BOTOGAN	48841	BREEKANT	91550
BIG ORANGE	14290	BOEVAYA SLAVA	93781	BOTOSANI	77574	BREEZAND	75600
BIHOR	47550	BOEVOY	85352	BOTSMAN MOSHKOV	54730	BREEZAND	79320
BIKIN	12407	BOGDAN	39130	BOTSMAN MOSHKOV	55300	BREEZE	40390
BIKIN	22842	BOGDAN KHMELNITSKY	28750	BOTSMAN ZOTOV	22843	BREEZE	74990
BIKIN	34472	BOGOWONTO	21572	BOTSMAN ZOTOV	34473	BREITLING	85363
BILBARAKAH	45650	BOHEME	08250	BOUJNIBA	48384	BREIZH-IZEL	33220
BILDERDYK	35102	BOHEME	17050	BOUKADOURA	58407	BREMEN	26082
BILDERDYK	95150	BOHEMUND	93141	BOUKADOURA	64565	BREMEN EXPRESS	08370
BILLESBORG	75060	BOIN	51090	BOUNTY	31160	BREMER HORST BISCHOFF	47330
BILSTEIN	58716	BOIN	51480	BOUNTY III	03750	BREMER NORDEN	86883
BILSTEIN	59646	BOIZENBURG	03873	BOURGOGNE	73949	BREMERHAVEN	48486
BILSTEIN	61726	BOIZENBURG	04424/2	BOUSTANY 1	91360	BRENDONIA	88000
		BOJNICE	35480	BOUVET	84311	BRESTSKAYA KREPOST	33901

(handwritten note: 4-10-90 near BRAD)

734

Name	No.
BREZA	86352
BRIAN BOROIME	88570
BRIAN BOROIME	89700
BRIBIR	04121
BRIBIR	15791
BRIBIR	52321
BRIBIR	82821
BRIDGEMAN	90080
BRIDGEPORT	04591●
BRIDGESTONE MARU V	54460
BRIDGESTONE MARU V	54910
BRIDGEWORTH	72389/6
BRIGHT FRUIT	21150
BRIGHT MELBOURNE	57616
BRIGHT MELBOURNE	61057
BRIGHT SKY	61632
BRIGHTNESS	24242
BRIGHTNESS	84452
BRIGITTA	75681
BRIGITTA MONTANARI	88531
BRIGITTE GRAEBE	73791
BRILLIANCY	68559/3
BRILLIANT	12412
BRILLIANT VENTURE	73181
BRIMANGER	54136
BRIMANGER	54256
BRINTON LYKES	00061
BRIOLETTE	53681
BRIOLETTE	53811
BRIOLETTE	68531
BRIONI	01680
BRISBANE TRADER	33061
BRISSAC	57980
BRISTOL LAKE	64460
BRITANIA	47270
BRITANIS	09150
BRITANNIA	91321
BRITISH AVON	53341
BRITISH BEECH	53121
BRITISH DART	53340
BRITISH ENTERPRISE FOUR	04246
BRITISH ENTERPRISE THREE	04245
BRITISH ESK	53342
BRITISH FIDELITY	51975
BRITISH FIDELITY	84185
BRITISH FORTH	53343
BRITISH HUMBER	53344
BRITISH KENNET	53345
BRITISH NORNESS (struck through; handwritten "7-5-91")	57941
BRITISH PROGRESS	58330
BRITISH PURPOSE	58331
BRITISH RANGER	57942
BRITISH RELIANCE	57943
BRITISH RENOWN	57940
BRITISH RESOLUTION	57944
BRITISH RESOURCE	57945
BRITISH RESPECT	58320
BRITISH SECURITY	51972
BRITISH SECURITY	84182
BRITISH SKILL	58055
BRITISH SPEY	53346
BRITISH SPIRIT	58057
BRITISH SUCCESS	58056
BRITISH TAMAR	53347
BRITISH TAY	53348
BRITISH TENACITY	51973
BRITISH TEST	53349
BRITISH TRENT	53350
BRITISH TRIDENT	57946
BRITISH TWEED	53351
BRITISH VOYAGER	11990
BRITISH WYE	53352
BRITSUM	78660
BRITTA I	73948
BRITTA ODEN	94180
BRIZ	23869●
BROCKEN	95250
BROCKMAN	68290
BROCKMAN	77320
BRONISLAW LACHOWICZ	14482
BROOKNES	46316
BROOKNES	46566
BROTHER STAR	62430
BROTHERS UNION	03861
BRUARFOSS	15990
BRUAS	40391
BRUNHORN	61702
BRUNLA	61701
BRUNO TESCH	23413
BRUSSELS	65670
BRYANSKIY MASHINOSTROITEL	01386
BRYANSKIY MASHINOSTROITEL	01646
BRYANSKIY RABOCHIY	45362
BUARQUE	55014
BUARQUE	55884
BUARQUE	56554
BUCANERO	02250
BUCEGI	78580
BUCHAREST	36841
BUCURESTI	15420
BUDAPEST	36842
BUDAPEST	45850
BUDAPEST	86118
BUDAPEST	91718
BUDI	45572
BUDOWLANY	78292
BUDOWLANY	80022
BUDVA	62024
BUENA FORTUNA	41080
BUENA FORTUNA	47937
BUENA SUERTE	68693
BUENAVISTA	94020
BUENO	40451
BUFFALO	32370
BUFFALO	61195
BUFFALO	66192
BUFFALO	94600
BUGURUSLAN	39990
BUGURUSLAN	89468
BUHUSI	77576
BUILDER	35601
BUILDER	35643
BUILDER	41303
BUILDER II	42077
BUILDER III	92010
BUKAVU	62712
BUKAVU	62752
BUKHARA	24055
BUKHARA	87180
BUKHTARMA	15463
BUKOVINA	02351
BUKOVINA	35371
BULA	86543
BULGARIA	73296
BULK QUEEN	94440
BULKNES	62431
BULLAREN	80294
BULUNKHAN	50744
BUNA	52070
BUNA	75170
BUNGA ANGSANA	09750
BUNGA ARANDA	14790
BUNGA BINDANG	48932
BUNGA CHEMPAKA	54653
BUNGA CHEMPAKA	55074
BUNGA DAHLIA	50351
BUNGA GELANG	48933
BUNGA KESUMBA	60610
BUNGA KESUMBA	70070
BUNGA MAS	48931
BUNGA MAWAR	68102
BUNGA MELATI	09752
BUNGA MELAWIS	77281
BUNGA MERAH	61613
BUNGA ORKID	03200
BUNGA ORKID	03600
BUNGA PENAGA	50350
BUNGA PERMAI	08470
BUNGA PERMAI	09560
BUNGA SELASIH	60611
BUNGA SELASIH	70071
BUNGA SEPANG	60612
BUNGA SEPANG	70072
BUNGA SEROJA	09753
BUNGA SETAWAR	48930
BUNGA SRIPAGI	46929/2
BUNGA SURIA	08471
BUNGA SURIA	09561
BUNGA TANJONG	03201
BUNGA TANJONG	03601
BUNGA TEMBUSU	77280
BUNGA TERATAI	09751
BUNGA VANDA	81220
BUNKEROVSCHCHIK-3	36250
BUNKO MARU	51020
BUNKO MARU	52880
BURAN	10260
BURAN	10760
BURAN	22222
BURAN	23512
BURDIGALA	66882
BUREVESTNIK	11829
BUREVESTNIK	12312
BUREVESTNIK REVOLYUTSKIY	79369
BUREYA	85328
BUREYALES	85611
BURG	24053
BURGAS	61709
BURGAS	28991
BURITACA	36874
BURITACA	35580
BURMAH ENDEAVOUR	36430
BURMAH ENDEAVOUR	56401
BURMAH ENDEAVOUR	59921
BURMAH ENTERPRISE	67781
BURMAH ENTERPRISE	56402
BURMAH ENTERPRISE	59922
BURMAH LEGACY	67782
BUSALEH	64147
BUSKO ZDROJ	86900
BUSSARD	81861
BUSSOL	84931
BUSTENI	09375
BUTACUATRO	47547
BUTADOS	70831
BUTATRES	79631
BUTAUNO	70830
BUTTON GWINNETT	79630
BUYER	01053
BUYO	35602
BUYUK TIMUR	50135●
BUZAU	63262●
BUZET	86209
BUZIAS	57491
BUZLUDJA	77578/2
BUZOVNY	49160
BUZURGAN	44115
BYELKINO	69572
BYELOKAMENKA	12414
BYELOMORSK	17953
BYELOMORSK	11722
BYELORUSSIYA	34612
BYELOVO	20370
BYEREZINA	11830
BYKOVO	17954
BYKOVO	11721
BYRON 1	34611
	07340
BYTOM	50466
BYZANTINE MONARCH	26600
BYZANTION	64271
BYZANTION	68591

C

Name	No.
C C ORIENT	04976
C.C. ORIENT	30426
C C RED SEA	04977
C.C. RED SEA	30427
C. INNOVATOR	80082●
C. INNOVATOR	80232●
C K APOLLO	57270
C P AMBASSADOR	76951
C S IRIS	02411
C.S. IRIS	32941
C S MONARCH	02410
C.S. MONARCH	32940
C. STAR	04713●
C. STAR	04883●
C.V. LIGHTNING	94270
C.V. STAGHOUND	94271
C.W. KITTO	55708
C W KITTO	58278
CABLE ENTERPRISE	23400
CABLE RESTORER	08920
CABLEMAN	66577
CABO BOJADOR	14531
CABO BOLINAO	21400
CABO CORRIENTES 1	38191
CABO DE LA VELA	07370
CABO DE LA VELA	15175
CABO FRIO	83750
CABO GUARDIAN	37680
CABO GUARDIAN	44261
CABO SANTA ANA	14150
CABO SANTA INES	45791●
CABO SANTA LUCIA	06750
CABO VERDE	14532
CACABAN	61570
CACICA ISABEL	17171
CACICA ISABEL	32321
CACIULATA	47561
CADIZ	49866●
CADMUS	28451
CAGAYAN DE ORO	21030
CAGAYAN DE ORO CITY	34050
CAICARA	04636
CAIRNROVER	91847
CAIRU	55540
CAIRU	63340
CALA ATLANTICA	49641●
CALA GALDANA	76800
CALA LLONGA	23741
CALA LLONGA	93291
CALA MARSAL	23740
CALA MARSAL	93290
CALA MEDITERRANEA	49640●
CALA PORTALS	76801
CALABRIA	01720
CALAFIA	58541
CALAN	82229
CALANDA	50421
CALANDRINI	14492
CALARASI	82123
CALARASI	82403
CALATRAVA	65270
CALDERETA	63262
CALDIRAN	80356
CALEDONIA	32280
CALEDONIA	70470
CALETA-LEONES	47780●
CALIFORNIA	05232
CALIFORNIA	43440
CALIFORNIA	94740
CALIFORNIA	08005
CALIFORNIA GETTY	64345
CALIFORNIA MARU	02996●
CALIFORNIA STAR	08880
CALIMANESTI	47544
CALIOPE	24570
CALIOPE E	69220
CALIXTO GARCIA	06614
CALLATIS	77577
CALOOSAHATCHEE	35961
CALY	06631
CALYPSO	75502
CAM BILINGA	55896●
CAM BUBINGA	61401
CAM DOUSSIE	61402
CAM EBENE	55897●
CAM ILOMBA	55894
CAM IROKO	55895
CAMAGUEY	81310
CAMARGO	87510
CAMARGUE	64370
CAMBRIDGE FERRY	33090
CAMDEN	93471
CAMELIA	26101
CAMERO M	61521
CAMERONA	62022
CAMILLA	87880
CAMILLA WESTON	88430
CAMILLE B	69311
CAMINO II	92901
CAMPAMINO	65791
CAMPANAR	38521
CAMPANIA	46256●
CAMPANIA SECONDA	16725
CAMPAZAS	38522
CAMPEADOR	65700
CAMPEADOR	69800
CAMPECHE	24990
CAMPEON	66131
CAMPHOR	61420
CAMPO DURAN	66193
CAMPOAZUR	38673
CAMPOAZUR	44843
CAMPOCERRADO	38672
CAMPOCERRADO	44842
CAMPOCERRADO	44882
CAMPODARRO	40921
CAMPOGENIL	40922
CAMPOGRIS	44760
CAMPOGULES	38671
CAMPOGULES	44841
CAMPOLLANO	37050
CAMPOLONGO	67142
CAMPOMAYOR	65701
CAMPOMAYOR	69801
CAMPONALON	40920
CAMPONAVIA	65790
CAMPONEGRO	44761
CAMPONUBLA	66130
CAMPOO	42990
CAMPORRASO	44880
CAMPORROJO	38670
CAMPORROJO	44840
CAMPORRUBIO	38674
CAMPORRUBIO	44844
CAMPORRUBIO	44881
CAMPOSALINAS	67141
CAMPOTEJAR	67140
CAMPOVERDE	38900
CAMPROVIN	42991
CAMSELL	09920
CANABAL	39420
CANADA EXPRESS	72485
CANADIA	48820
CANADIA	83490
CANADIAN ACE	39180
CANADIAN ACE	45230
CANADIAN BULKER	79761
CANADIAN EXPLORER	74520
CANADIAN OWL	63941
CANADIAN OWL	71591
CANADIAN PROGRESS	52150
CANADIAN REEFER	05110
CANADON SECO	66194
CANAIMA	84920
CANAL ACE	61022
CANAL ACE	71182
CANALGRANDE	39743
CANARIA	63133
CANBERRA	36130
CANBERRA MARU	08620
CANBERRA MARU	09820
CANDEIAS	65862
CANDELARIA	07660
CANDIA	32910
CANDIA	47199/1●
CANG SHAN	25101
CANGURO FULVO	22383
CANGURO GRIGIO	22381
CANISTEO	35962
CANMAR EXPLORER III	92881
CANMAR KIGORIAK	09060
CANMAR KIGORIAK	17330
CANOPUS	22280
CANOPUS	73942
CANOPUS	94562
CANOPY	47165
CANOVA	71913
CANTACLARO II	87351
CANTAL	51071
CAP AKRITAS	81132
CAP ANAMUR	59545
CAP BAITAR	61690
CAP BENAT	76860
CAP BIZERTA	61691
CAP BRETON	53408
CAP BRETON	64938
CAP FALCONE	84990
CAP FERRAT	94293
CAP FERRATO	34204●
CAP FRIO	34205
CAP PHAISTOS	84991
CAP SAN MARCO	02292
CAPAL	82020
CAPE	14557
CAPE	49866
CAPE AGRILOS	73180
CAPE ALAVA	05960
CAPE ALEXANDER	05962
CAPE ANN	05963
CAPE ANTIBES	47396
CAPE ANTIBES	47966
CAPE ARCHWAY	05964
CAPE ARNHEM	48078
CAPE AVANTI DUE	59291
CAPE AVANTI DUE	61331
CAPE AVINOF	05965
CAPE CORFU	72003
CAPE DON	02090
CAPE FINISTERRE	48079
CAPE GATA	60953
CAPE GRENVILLE	47394
CAPE GRENVILLE	47964
CAPE HAWK	47392
CAPE HAWK	47962
CAPE HENLOPEN	02500
CAPE HUSTLER	73881
CAPE HUSTLER	87261
CAPE ISLAND	72539

Name	No.	Name	No.
CAPE ITEA	45452	CARIBBEAN UNIVERSAL	07453
CAPE ITEA	48712	CARIBE	49800
CAPE KAMARI	61291	CARIBE MAR	81453
CAPE KAMARI	86721	CARIBE MARINER	51870
CAPE KENNEDY	60090	CARIBE No 1	85820
CAPE KILA	90655●	CARIBGAS DOS	89530
CAPE MONTEREY	60091	CARIBGAS V	54170
CAPE MORETON	02091	CARIBGAS 7	76380
CAPE PILAR	02092	CARIBGAS 20	84760
CAPE RACE	74930	CARIBGAS 20	75680
CAPE RION	72000	CARIBI	88530
CAPE RODNEY	47871	CARIBI	35641
CAPE SOUNION	67285	CARIBIA EXPRESS	41301
CAPE STROVILI	46710	CARIBIA EXPRESS	73400
CAPE SUPERIOR	60091/1	CARIBIC	82710
CAPE TRAFALGAR	48079/1	CARICOM EXPRESS	83480
CAPE VALS	90654	CARICOM EXPRESS	52110
CAPE YORK	22640	CARICOM VENTURE	67060
CAPECREST	76091	CARICOM VENTURE	52111
CAPELLA	08522	CARICOM VENTURER	67061
CAPELLA	24860	CARIDDI	50194
CAPETAN COSTIS 1	56986	CARIGULF EXPRESS	17430
CAPETAN COSTIS 1	05711	CARIGULF EXPRESS	91220
CAPETAN LEONIDAS	00170	CARIGULF FREEDOM	91820
CAPETAN NICOLAS	61772	CARIGULF FREEDOM	90536
CAPETAN PSARROS	61773	CARIGULF PIONEER	91076
CAPETAN RAHIOTIS	56791	CARIGULF PIONEER	81330
CAPETAN TASSOS	62280	CARINA	90590
CAPIRA	08132	CARINA	11695
CAPITAINE COOK	01361●	CARINE	75011
CAPITAINE COOK III	45551●	CARINIA	73810
CAPITAINE COOK III	08134	CARINIA	92951
CAPITAINE LA PEROUSE	04310●	CARINTHIA	95161
CAPITAINE SCOTT	21110●	CARL GORTHON	14173
CAPITAINE SCOTT	30900	CARLA A HILLS	83492
CAPITAINE TASMAN	30901	CARLA C	53058
CAPITAINE WALLIS	55430	CARLA II	01230
CAPITAN ALBERTO	84962	CARLEVERETT	40980
CAPITAN ALBERTO FERNANDEZ	89280	CARLO M	21420
CAPITAN CARLO	84881	CARLO SCHONHAAR	47206
CAPITAN MARTINEZ TAMAYO	84880	CARLOS BORGES	23414
CAPITAN OLO PANTOJA	73865	CARLOS MANUEL DE CESPEDES	57523
CAPITAN SAN LUIS	69431	CARLOVA	06612
CAPITANO FRANCO V	26571●	CARLOW HILL	79111
CAPITOL	32350	CARMANIA	06462
CAPO BIANCO	64600	CARMEL	14174
CAPO EMMA	33050	CARMEN	74434/1
CAPO FALCONARA	40260	CARMEN DEL MAR	94816
CAPO MADRE	41490	CARMEN DEL MAR	76030
CAPO MADRE	36320	CARNIVALE	88620
CAPO MANNU	50400	CAROLA	06204
CAPO MELE	50830	CAROLA	19361
CAPO MELE	85690	CAROLA SMITS	76473
CAPO NOLI	65500	CAROLINA	50244
CAPRICORN	53664	CAROLINE	50381
CAPRICORNUS	73384	CAROLINE	46527
CAPRICORNUS	03991	CAROLINE OLDENDORFF	83307
CAPRIOLO	59080	CAROLINE P	71841
CAPT F GAIGNEROT	89410	CAROLINE SCHULTE	58177
CAPT SALAH	31930	CAROLINE SCHULTE	53407
CAPTAIN ANDREADIS	58714	CARPATI	64937
CAPTAIN COSMAS M	59644	CARRIER PRINCESS	78584
CAPTAIN COSMAS M	61724	CARRIER PRINCESS	93110
CAPTAIN COSMAS M	78426●	CARSTEN RUSS	93960
CAPTAIN GEORGE	06639/9	CARTHAGONOVA	54940
CAPTAIN GEORGE L	49281	CARUAO	63130
CAPTAIN GEORGE L	39880	CARVALHO ARAUJO	51683
CAPTAIN GREGOS	30843	CARYANDA	03097
CAPTAIN JOHN	35501	CASABLANCA	77881
CAPTAIN JOHN L	06980	CASABLANCA	51742
CAPTAIN NASOS	48140	CASABLANCA	58542
CAPTAIN NICOLAS	56820	CASAMANCE EXPRESS	84062
CAPTAIN VENIAMIS	67689/4	CASAMICCIOLA EXPRESS	19200
CAPTAIN X KYRIAKOU	35907	CASON	16724
CAPTAIN YANNIS	41597	CASPIAN SEA	59755
CAPTAIN YANNIS	88780	CASPIAN TRADER	47832
CAPUTERRA	55963	CASSINGA	68532
CAR STAR	56723	CASSIO	78102
CAR STAR	03142	CASSIOPEIA	18711
CARACAS	73406	CASSIOPEIA MARU	77442
CARAIBE	82716	CASSJOPEJA	77805
CARAIBE	38520	CAST SALMON	11338
CARAIBI	11706	CAST SEAL (SCRAPED)	94330
CARAIMAN	19181	CAST SEAL	73112
CARAVAGGIO	73811	CASTALIA	77782
CARAVELLE	68323	CASTANEDA	32640
CARBAY	68324	CASTANEDA	81690/1
CARCAPE	22491	CASTANEDA	87050/1
CARDIFF	08401	CASTELLBLANCH	79101
CARDIGAN BAY	32553	CASTELLO	88910
CARDUCCI	66803	CASTILLO DE LA MOTA	73130
CAREBECA	76110	CASTILLO DE LORCA	67637
CAREBEKA VIII	47593	CASTILLO DE MONTEARAGON	67638
CARELIA	50523	CASTILLO MANZANARES	78181
CARELIA	51901	CASTLE DIGNITY	09961
CARIA	72551	CASTLE FAITH	89290
CARIA	33201	CASTLE POINT	74830
CARIARI	75878	CASTLE SPIRIT	09960
CARIB DAWN	50330	CASTOR	43181
CARIB DAWN	83670	CASTOR	47198
CARIB EVE	50331	CASTOR	47592
CARIB EVE	83671	CASTOR	50522
CARIB FREEZE	87711	CASTOR	58290
CARIB FREEZE	89311	CASTOR	66182
CARIB SUN	84220	CASTOR	67732
CARIBBEAN ARROW	21470	CASTOR	71510●
CARIBBEAN BREEZE	63420●	CASTORP	76755
CARIBBEAN CARRIER	78930	CASUARINA	87022
CARIBBEAN CEMENT	87791	CATALAN BAY	80610
CARIBBEAN MARU	02995	CATALINA	09090
CARIBBEAN STARS	48282	CATALINA DEL MAR	76074
CARIBBEAN TIUNA	86910	CATAMARCA II	53101
CARIBBEAN TRAILER	95011	CATAMARCA II	53331
CARIBBEAN UNIVERSAL	06222	CATEPAN	07980

Name	No.	Name	No.
CATHARINA	76477	CHAC	66160
CATHAY SEATRADE	68740	CHACO	48371
CATHAY SEATRADE	77430	CHAI TRADER	08120
CATHERINE ANN	61033	CHAIKA	89461
CATHERINE ANN	71193	CHAITEN	06311
CATHERINE L	46691	CHALLENGER 1	45740
CATHERINE SCHIAFFINO	94525	CHALLWA No 2	22771
CATHERINE VENTURE	77337	CHALLWA No 2	93401
CATHERINE Y	38650	CHALLWA V	92630
CATHY G	72881●	CHALMEVERETT	21440
CATHY G	87131●	CHAMAL	64369
CATTLEYA	55564	CHAMBORD	57947
CATTLEYA	62944	CHAMPAGNE	68100
CAUCASUS MARU	53686	CHAMPLAIN	84260
CAUCASUS MARU	53816	CHAMWINO	06063
CAUCASUS MARU	68536	CHANAKYA	55221
CAVACO	39220	CHANAKYA	57251
CAVALIER BULKER	60391	CHANDA	48141
CAVALLO	33261	CHANDOS	65801
CAVENDISH	54901	CHANDOS	74781
CAVO AZURO	19230	CHANG AN	41321
CAVO SIDERO	23240	CHANG HAI	55950
CAVOURELLA	46493	CHANG HAI	57080
CAWA	62106	CHANG HUA	29280
CAYAMBE	05612	CHANG HUA	29520
CAYENNE	03496	CHANG JIN	20319/2
CAYENNE	03586	CHANG KEN	20319/3
CAYMAN	86850	CHANG LI	20317
CAYMAN	14175●	CHANG PEI	92714
CAYUGA	51671	CHANG SHAN	20319
CEAHLEAUL	11707	CHANG SHEN	20319/4
CEBO MOON	66972	CHANG XIU	20318
CEBO MOON	91552	CHANG ZHENG	30930
CEBU	46901	CHANGDE	30423
CEBU	83340	CHANGDU	10366
CEBU CITY	33460	CHANGMING	15349
CECILE ERICKSON	90060	CHANGNING	01170
CECILIA SMITS	50245	CHANGSHU	05371
CEDERBORG	85470	CHANGTING	80891
CEDERBORG	91530	CHANGXING	75876
CEDROS	76601	CHANTENAY	20020
CEDROS	89301	CHANTILLY	15215
CEDYNIA	70541	CHAO YANG	45972
CEFALLONIAN AMBITION	15173	CHAOHU CAREER	33914
CEFALLONIAN CHARIS	07371	CHAPAEV	37571
CEFALLONIAN CHARIS	15174	CHAPARAL II	38320
CEFALLONIAN PROSPERITY	07372	CHAPARAL II	44670
CEFALLONIAN SKY	10923	CHAPARAL II	12140
CEFALLONIAN SUN	27690	CHAPAYEVSK	24290
CEFALLONIAN WAVES	04460	CHAR KWEI	56988
CEGLED	35482	CHARALAMBOS F	85883
CELAL CESUR	64840	CHARDZHOV	60394
CELEBES	55660	CHARIOT BULKER	46611
CELEBES	55860	CHARISMA N	52781
CELERINA	46940	CHARISMA N	53124
CELERINA	47100	CHARITAS	52621
CELESTINO	04891	CHARLES LYKES	55703
CELESTINO	35080	CHARLES PIGOTT	58273
CELESTINO	57521	CHARLES PIGOTT	94120
CELIA	71760	CHARLES SCHIAFFINO	74478
CELINA TORREALBA	04814	CHARLESTON	53561
CELJE	57443	CHARLOTTA	59721
CELLANA	51980	CHARLOTTA	62231
CELTIC	52170	CHARLOTTE	71251
CELTIC CRUSADER	84030	CHARLOTTE	61705
CELTIC ENDEAVOUR	91835	CHARLOTTE BASTIAN	00083
CELTIC LINK	60310	CHARLOTTE LYKES	00233
CELTIC ROSE	87860	CHARLOTTE LYKES	73510
CELTIC SKY	46950	CHARLOTTE LYKES	91322
CELTIC VOYAGER	76197●	CHARLOTTE S	04420
CELYA	48905	CHARLOTTENBORG	13310
CEMBULK	65110	CHARMYL	34830
CEMBULK	81900	CHARMYL	23600
CEMENT KING	82280	CHARRUA	80570
CEMENTIA	82150	CHARTA	19910
CEMENTO PUERTO RICO	39650	CHARTRES	88260
CEMENTO PUERTO RICO	40070	CHATA TWO	89222
CENK	56650	CHATTAGRAM	11943
CENK	62210	CHATYR-DAG	57948
CENPAC 2	62311	CHAUMONT	86010
CENTAUR	03180	CHAYA	07551
CENTAURMAN	59000	CHAZHMA	39110
CENTAURMAN	75180	CHAZHMA	33680
CENTAURO	54010	CHE HAI No 1	33681
CENTAURO	80770	CHE HAI No 2	86097
CENTAURUS	11663	CHE HAI No 103	39987
CENTRAL CRUISER	61530	CHEBOKSARY	27214
CENTRAL CRUISER	72030	CHECHEKU	56660
CENTURY	55820	CHEER MAY	12342
CENTURY	56621	CHEKHOV	84077
CEPHEUS	66221	CHELIA	89170
CER AGILITY	34262	CHELLI	03232
CER ALACTRITY	34260	CHELM	03622
CER ALSIRAT	07820	CHELM	22844
CER AMITY	34261	CHELYABINSK	34474
CERAM SEA	14210	CHELYABINSK	66574●
CERINTHUS	48751	CHEMICAL CONTENDER	56250
CERINTHUS	75571	CHEMICAL LAUSANNE	75230
CERNA	13734	CHEMICAL LAUSANNE	55330
CERRO BOLIVAR	73359	CHEMICAL SOL	70300
CERRO COLORADO	64375	CHEMICAL SOL	47612
CERRO PELADO	12791	CHEMIK	76630
CERVO	03992	CHEMIK	56251
CETRA CENTAURUS	65840	CHEMIST LUTETIA	75231
CETRA CORONA	79964	CHEMIST LUTETIA	66574
CETRA NORMA	77448	CHEMTANK HAMBURG	58976
CETRA VELA	68101	CHEMTRANS SIRIUS	63650
CETUS	11664	CHEMTRANS WEGA	15252
CEYLAN SAILOR	28280	CHENAB	71805
CEYLAN SKIPPER	59321	CHENG DE	82751
CEYLAN WAVE	84730	CHENGTU	45960
CEYLION	89090	CHENNAI JAYAM	78180
CEYOCEAN	25881	CHENNAI MUYARCHI	45961
CHAC	54680	CHENNAI OOKKAM	

Name	No.	Name	No.	Name	No.	Name	No.
CHENNAI PERUMAI	45962	CHIPKA	77088	CITY OF SALERNO	73749	COLOMBO MARU	66870
CHENNAI SADHANAI	45963	CHIPKA	80008	CITY OF TEMA	51150	COLOMBO MARU	91460
CHENNAI SELVAM	45964	CHIQUITA	85010	CITY OF YORK	48513	COLON	93301●
CHENONCEAUX	57949	CHITA	67351	CITY OF ZUG	07180	COLORADO	05236
CHEOG YANG	94871	CHITA	71361	CIUDAD DE ALICANTE	94615	COLOSSUS	06621
CHERCHELL	76221	CHITA MARU	77201	CIUDAD DE BADAJOZ	16532	COLTAIR	36100
CHERCHELL	76901	CHITRAL	52864	CIUDAD DE BADAJOZ	17592	COLUMBA	08196
CHERCHESK	13755/5	CHIYODA	61901	CIUDAD DE BARCELONA	33400	COLUMBA	11660
CHEREMKHOVO	10434	CHKALOV	17505	CIUDAD DE BARRANCABERMEJA	69010	COLUMBIA	16370
CHEREPOVETS	83680	CHKALOV	39983	CIUDAD DE BARRANQUILLA	93050	COLUMBIA	66340
CHERNIGOV	06797/3	CHLOE	46585	CIUDAD DE BOGOTA	04850	COLUMBIA HIGHWAY	94941●
CHERNISHEVSKIY	20793	CHOAPA	21360	CIUDAD DE BUCARAMANGA	04851	COLUMBIA LIBERTY	59997
CHERNOGORSK	12142	CHOCANO	07941	CIUDAD DE BUENAVENTURA	04852	COLUMBIA NEPTUNE	68755
CHERNOMORSKAYA SLAVA	93785	CHOCHLIK	87742	CIUDAD DE CACERES	08182	COLUMBIA STAR	08881
CHERNYAKHOVSK	01023	CHOHU CAREER	02551	CIUDAD DE CACERES	09442	COLUMBIALAND	46411
CHERNYAKHOVSK	00343	CHOKO MARU	54570	CIUDAD DE CACERES	16534	COLUMBUS AMERICA	73531
CHERNYAKHOVSK	21602	CHOKO MARU	54950	CIUDAD DE CACERES	17594	COLUMBUS AUSTRALIA	73530
CHERNYSHEVSKIY	12362	CHOLGUAN	06324	CIUDAD DE CADIZ	94616	COLUMBUS C	09240
CHERRY	14175	CHON JIN	25000	CIUDAD DE CEUTA	93970	COLUMBUS LOUISIANA	82813
CHERRY	58170	CHORZOW	50461	CIUDAD DE CEUTA	95210	COLUMBUS NEW ZEALAND	73532
CHERRY BAGUS	89430	CHOUNGUI	87426	CIUDAD DE COLONIA	17630	COLUMBUS QUEENSLAND	82812
CHERRY BUNGA	89790	CHRISTA THIELEMANN	51760	CIUDAD DE COMPOSTELA	01291	COLUMBUS VICTORIA	73520
CHERRY CHEPAT	40120	CHRISTEL	73798	CIUDAD DE CUCUTA	04853	COLUMBUS VIRGINIA	73521
CHERRY CRYSTAL	02811	CHRISTIAN IV	19150	CIUDAD DE GRANADA	33402	COLUMBUS WELLINGTON	73522
CHERRY JET	44910	CHRISTIAN WESCH	49426	CIUDAD DE IBAGUE	08082	COMANDANTE REVELLO	80297
CHERRY LAJU	29830	CHRISTIANE SCHULTE	73990	CIUDAD DE LA LAGUNA	19280	COMANDANTE VILO ACUNA	75950
CHERRY LANKA	90621	CHRISTIANSBORG	04421	CIUDAD DE MANIZALES	04440	COMBATE DE PALMAMOCHA	76570
CHERRY MANIS	91330	CHRISTINA	02851	CIUDAD DE MANTA	08080	COMBI TRADER	52720
CHERRY NES	69380	CHRISTINA	15332	CIUDAD DE MAR DEL PLATA II	17451	COMET	60089
CHERRY ORIENT	02810	CHRISTINA C	47935	CIUDAD DE MEDELLIN	04441	COMET	76479/2
CHERRYFIELD	61074	CHRISTINA SMITS	50246●	CIUDAD DE NEIVA	53371	COMET	10930●
CHERRYFIELD	71264	CHRISTINE FIRST	88671	CIUDAD DE NENA	62761	COMFORT	21243
CHERSO	53130	CHRISTO BOTEV	48431	CIUDAD DE PALMA	16531	COMMANDANT HENRY	79580
CHERVONOGRAD	12143	CHRISTO BOTEV	49471	CIUDAD DE PALMA	17591	COMMANDANTE CAMILO CIENFUEGOS	10276
CHEVALIER DARBY	14600	CHRISTO BOTEV	49741	CIUDAD DE PASTO	53374	COMMANDANTE CAMILO CIENFUEGOS	15186
CHEVALIER PAUL	73446	CHRISTOFOROS	36072	CIUDAD DE PASTO	62764	COMMODORE CLIPPER	87311
CHEVALIER PAUL	80376	CHRISTOFOROS	41792	CIUDAD DE POPAYAN	53370	COMMODORE ENTERPRISE	73610
CHEVALIER ROZE	73445	CHRISTOPHER LYKES	00084	CIUDAD DE POPAYAN	62760	CONASTOGA	66210
CHEVALIER ROZE	80375	CHRISTOPHER LYKES	00234	CIUDAD DE SALAMANCA	08181	CONCEPCION MARINO	17170
CHEVALIER VALBELLE	73444	CHRISTOPHER MEEDER	73800	CIUDAD DE SALAMANCA	09441	CONCEPCION MARINO	32320
CHEVALIER VALBELLE	80374	CHRISTOS K	30230	CIUDAD DE SALAMANCA	16535	CONCORD PACIFIC	51872●
CHEVRON ARIZONA	53274	CHRISTOS K	61465	CIUDAD DE SALAMANCA	17595	CONCORDIA C	67940
CHEVRON ARIZONA	58434	CHRISTOS M	27961	CIUDAD DE SANTA CRUZ LA PALMA	16530	CONCORDIA I	06632
CHEVRON BRUSSELS	58240	CHRYS	90290	CIUDAD DE SANTA CRUZ LA PALMA	17590	CONCORDIA STAR	48422●
CHEVRON CALIFORNIA	64253	CHRYSANTHY H	39340	CIUDAD DE SANTA MARTA	53372	CONCORDIA STAR	49462●
CHEVRON COLORADO	53271	CHRYSANTHY M LEMOS	62791	CIUDAD DE SANTA MARTA	62762	CONCORDIA STAR	49512●
CHEVRON COLORADO	58431	CHRYSANTHY M LEMOS	67551	CIUDAD DE SEVILLA	08180	CONCORDIA SUN	48423●
CHEVRON COPENHAGEN	55704	CHRYSOVALANDOU GRACE	52924●	CIUDAD DE SEVILLA	09440	CONCORDIA SUN	49463●
CHEVRON COPENHAGEN	58274	CHRYSSI V	39020	CIUDAD DE SEVILLA	16533	CONCORDIA SUN	49513●
CHEVRON EDINBURGH	58275	CHRYSSI V	44930	CIUDAD DE SEVILLA	17593	CONDATA	06315
CHEVRON FELUY	55702	CHRZANOW	82266	CIUDAD DE TARIFA	17210	CONDE DEL CADAGUA	80460
CHEVRON FELUY	58272	CHUBUT	48379	CIUDAD DE ZARAGOZA	93971	CONDOCK I	92270
CHEVRON HAWAII	64254	CHUGUYEV	12144	CIUDAD DE ZARAGOZA	95211	CONDOCK I	92440
CHEVRON LONDON	58241	CHUKOTKA	22721	CIVRA	87650	CONDOCK II	92271
CHEVRON LOUISIANA	53272	CHUKOTKO	25842	CLABUCET	11679	CONDOCK II	92441
CHEVRON LOUISIANA	58432	CHULYMLES	11430	CLAIRE A TSAVLIRIS	49111	CONDOR	14284
CHEVRON MISSISSIPPI	64255	CHUMIKAN	39111	CLAN MACBOYD	07770	CONDOR	71743
CHEVRON NAGASAKI	55700	CHUN HU	36741	CLAN ROSE	52760	CONDOR	72130
CHEVRON NAGASAKI	58270	CHUN JIN	61551	CLANSMAN	18160	CONDOR	76470
CHEVRON NORTH AMERICA	54494	CHUN JIN	72041	CLARA CLAUSEN	50880	CONDOR	81413
CHEVRON NORTH AMERICA	54924	CHUN SUNG	82561	CLARET	61290●	CONDOR	84932
CHEVRON NORTH AMERICA	55724	CHUN UNG	61479	CLASSIC	62962	CONDOR II	86870
CHEVRON OREGON	53272	CHUNG SHING	48630	CLAUDIA KOGEL	06622	CONDORA	06314
CHEVRON OREGON	58433	CHUNGLIN	06031	CLAUDIA SMITS	50243	CONFEDERATION	19020
CHEVRON PACIFIC	53062	CHURKIN	45115	CLAYMORE	22360	CONFIDENCE	25100
CHEVRON PERTH	55701	CICERO	33260	CLEARWATER BAY	68680	CONG HUA	61950
CHEVRON PERTH	58271	CIDADE DE ALCANTARA	22837	CLEMENTINE	06317	CONGO	10672
CHEVRON SOUTH AMERICA	54493	CIDADE DE IMPERATRIZ	22831	CLEO 1	45250	CONGO	13511
CHEVRON SOUTH AMERICA	54923	CIECHANOW	79874	CLEOPATRA	18251	CONNACHT	16490
CHEVRON SOUTH AMERICA	55723	CIECHOCINEK	81862	CLEOPATRA II	39010	CONQUEROR BULKER	60393
CHEVRON WASHINGTON	53270	CIELO DI GENOVA	48973	CLERK-MAXWELL	54740	CONRADO BENITEZ	27070
CHEVRON WASHINGTON	58430	CIELO DI LIVORNO	57557	CLERK-MAXWELL	66110	CONSCIENCE	46257
CHEYENNE	44561	CIELO DI NAPOLI	55790	CLERVAUX	12691	CONSORTIUM 1	22691
CHEYENNE	51670	CIELO DI NAPOLI	64651	CLERVILLE	76260	CONSTANCE	60155
CHI CHENG	10274	CIELO DI ROMA	66199	CLIO	47491	CONSTANCIA	53480
CHI CHENG	15184	CIELO DI SALERNO	66200	CLODIA	33471	CONSTANCIA	61280
CHI SONG	77940	CIELO DI TRIESTE	57553	CLOUD	91180	CONSTANTA	17661
CHI STAR	46334	CIELO ROSSO	44850	CLUJ	39661	CONSTANTIA	46452
CHIARA	92974	CIEPLICE ZDROJ	81865	CLYDE	43340	CONSTANTINOS MALTEZOS	15256
CHIARA S.	47910	CIKAT	26320	CLYDEBANK	03671	CONSTELLATION	09160
CHIARETTE	59604●	CIKOLO	66952	CLYDEBANK	03731	CONSTELLATION	09431
CHIARETTE	71934●	CIKOLO	70992	CLYMENE	61703	CONSTELLATION ENTERPRISE	76761
CHIDAMBARAM	06800	CIMBRIA	88450●	CLYTONEUS	65781	CONSTELLATION ENTERPRISE	80271
CHIEFTAIN	25704●	CIMPULUNG	82227	CLYTONEUS	70201	CONSTELLATION FAROS	04668
CHIEFTAIN BULKER	60390	CINDERELLA	46245●	COAL STAR	77338	CONSTELLATION GALAXY	04669
CHIEH HSING	29760	CINDRELUL	13735	COAL TRANSPORTER	68830	CONSTITUTION	09190
CHIEH SHENG	28090	CINTA	78250	COALINGA	59941	CONTAINER ENTERPRISE	87320
CHIGIRIN	12145	CINULIA	40201	COALINGA	67931	CONTAINER VENTURER	87321
CHIHIROSAN MARU	77200	CIRO SECONDO	39250	COAST BODO	86884	CONTENDER ARGENT	35140
CHIJIN MARU	92247	CIRO SECONDO	39271	COAST HARSTAD	86885	CONTENDER BEZANT	35141
CHIKUBU MARU	94880	CIRO TERZO	80410	COAST NARVIK	86886	CONTI BELGICA	48680
CHIKUHO MARU	77211	CIROLANA	22300	COAST TROMSO	86887	CONTINENTAL CARRIER	46886
CHIKUMA MARU	75710	CIRON	58940	COASTAL TRADER	93934	CONTINENTAL FRIENDSHIP	77878
CHIKUMA MARU	89670	CIS BROVIG	58911	COBALT ISLANDS	57626	CONTINENTAL LOTUS	78390●
CHIL BO SAN	92780	CIS BROVIG	65301	COBALT ISLANDS	61046	CONTINENTAL MONARCH	68559/5
CHILI	63553	CISSUS	61198	COBALT MARU	32470	CONTINENTAL TRADER	77879
CHILI	68263	CITADEL HILL	70660	COBALT TRANSPORTER	63103	CONTMAR	75831
CHILLAN	06321	CITTA DI META	22710	COBALT TRANSPORTER	68143	CONTSHIP EUROPE	50269/4
CHIMISTE SAYID	56254	CITTA DI NAPOLI	01270	COBAN	41361	CONUS	52288
CHIMISTE SAYID	75234	CITTA DI NUORO	01271	COBAN	41531	CONVEYOR	82910
CHIMO	58199	CITY OF CAMELOT	71154	COBETAS	48058	COOLHAVEN	02290
CHINA CONTAINER	09830	CITY OF CREMORNE	13050	COBRES	39421	CO-OP EXPRESS 1	47185
CHINA MARQUIS	77441●	CITY OF DURBAN	08421	COBURG	72687●	CO-OP EXPRESS II	47186
CHINA WINDS	04111	CITY OF EDINBURGH	08412	COCCINELLA	88750	CO-OP GRAIN	73365
CHINDE	89340	CITY OF HARTLEPOOL	75582	COCKROW	83266	CO-OP GRAIN II	73368
CHINON	57950	CITY OF HYDRA	11240	CODLEA	82113	CO-OP GRAIN II	73368
CHINTA	12760	CITY OF IPSWICH	75583	CODLEA	82393	COPA	03091●
CHION TRADER	33810	CITY OF LIVERPOOL	46256	COENTROEVERETT	11173	COPACABANA	03091
CHIOS AEINAFTIS	88020	CITY OF MIDLAND	19560	COFFEE TRADER	02940	COPACABANA	50114
CHIOS CLIPPER	34225	CITY OF OPORTO	75588	COHO	17230	COPIAPO	05911
CHIOS FAITH	09260	CITY OF PERTH	75581	COLD EXPRESS	51346	COPPER TRADER	07170
CHIOS FROST	84000	CITY OF PIRAEUS	22060	COLDITZ	78733	CORA	72830
CHIOS PRIDE	34208	CITY OF PLYMOUTH	75580	COLDITZ	89983		
CHIOS SPIRIT	09263	CITY OF RHODOS	16431	COLLO	75651		

Name	No.
CORA	87130
CORABANK	03670
CORABANK	03730
CORAGGIO	54512
CORAIN I	04666
CORAIN II	04667
CORAJE	59371
CORAL	27201
CORAL	46160
CORAL CHIEF	82851
CORAL ESSBERGER	76895
CORAL GABLES	94190
CORAL GABLES	94630
CORAL ISIS	64683
CORAL MAEANDRA	82180
CORAL PRINCESS	09490
CORAL REEFER	33930
CORAL VOLANS	62252
CORALI	65490
CORANTIJN	85290
CORCEL	60515
CORDIALITY	48100
CORDILLERA	14281
CORDILLERA	71741
CORDILLERA	81411
CORDILLERAS	66572
CORINA	55001
CORINA	71691
CORINTHIAN	69930
CORIOLANUS	18710
CORNELIA	67130
CORNER BROOK	51701
CORNER BROOK	52291
CORNOUILLES	33210
COROMUEL	19295
COROMUEL	23703
CORONA	48740
CORONA AUSTRALE	35461
CORONA BOREALE	35591
CORONA BOREALE	36491
CORONET	72002
CORONIA	61152
CORRAGIO	63892
CORRAL	14282
CORRAL	71742
CORRAL	81412
CORREZE	51072
CORRIE BROERE	66602
CORRIE BROERE	75152
CORRIENTES II	48370
CORSICA MARINA	19191
CORSICA NOVA	19141
CORSICA SERENA II	17030
CORSICA VIVA	32721
CORSICANA	66211
CORTA ATALAYA	64377
CORTEMAGGIORE	35820
CORTINA	03280
CORTINA	53006
CORVETTE	73950/3
CORVUS	76209/4●
COSMIC JUPITER	68104
COSMOS	34896
COSMOTOR ACE	47020
COSTA ARABICA	51235
COSTA LIGURE	51236
COSTA RICA	56595
COSTA RIVIERA	01761●
COSTAS G	91391
COSTAS KONIALIDIS	73182
COSTIA PEFANIS	82161
COSWIG	71916
COTES DU NORD	51071
COTINGA	75483
COTNARI	06069/11
COTOPAXI	05613
COTTBUS	04921
COTTON TRADER	07173
COTTY	25141
COUGAR	56418
COUGAR	67838
COUGAR	68438
COURAGE	13803
COURAGEOUS	71156
COURIER	05675
COURIER	35604
COURIER	58441
COURIER	63971
COURSON	14926
COURSON	15737
COUTANCES	17300
COUTANCES	93160
COVADONGA	12990
COVADONGA	52300
COVE LEADER	38820
COVE MARINER	38541
COVE MARINER	44811
COVE NAVIGATOR	44800
COVE SAILOR	38030
COVE SPIRIT	44560
COVE TRADE	36655
CP DISCOVERER	77971
CP TRADER	77972
CRACKER STATE MARINER	07850
CRAIGMORE	88400
CRAIOVA	41311
CRANACH	46258
CRANIA	40202
CRANZ	73952
CRATER	11661
CREATOR	53712
CREATOR	78151
CREDO	64148
CRESCENT	09890

Name	No.
CRESCO	46904
CRESCO	83342
CREST HILL	01370
CREST ISLAND	72540
CRESTA VII	61620
CRESTBANK	04770
CRETAN SKY	69121●
CRETE	85400
CREUSE	51070
CRIKVENICA	07894
CRIMMITSCHAU	61409/13
CRISANA	55781
CRISANA	56481
CRISPI	14404
CRISTINA MONTANARI	81471
CRISUL ALB	13771
CROESUS	28450
CROWN ATLAND	70172
CROWN BROLAND	70171
CROWN PEAK	03523
CRUSADER	82540
CRUSADER VENTURE	73184
CRUZ DEL SUR	90893
CRYSOULA P	39710
CRYSTAL ISLAND	40425
CRYSTAL ISLAND	42335
CRYSTAL ISLAND	42595
CRYSTAL TRANSPORTER	63494
CSOKONAI	14928
CSOKONAI	15738
CUBA	36921
CUBA	43821
CUGIR	82223
CUMULUS	34070
CUNARD COUNTESS	16860
CUNARD PRINCESS	16861
CUNENE	81661
CUNENE	82661
CUNEWALDE	46371
CUNEWALDE	47071
CUNSKI	89130
CURACAO MARU	04411
CURITIBA	06700
CURRENT EXPRESS	82052
CURRENT EXPRESS	91452
CURRENT TRADER	82051
CURRENT TRADER	91451
CURTEA DE ARGES	06143
CURTIS CAPRICORN	74630
CURTIS CAPRICORN	78120
CUU LONG I	35920
CUU LONG II	35921
CUZCO II	05125
CUZCO II	59875
CVIJETA ZUZORIC	48063
CYCLOPUS	59830
CYGNUS	11662
CYGNUS	66222
CYGNUS	76812
CYMBELINE	75250
CYNTHIA G	04919
CYPRESS	60910
CYPRIOT MARINER	57362
CYPRUS TRADER	15550
CYRNOS	20670
CYRUS	49831
CYS INTEGRITY	69253
CYS INTEGRITY	70553
CZANTORIA	68921
CZESTOCHOWA	15081

D

Name	No.
D C COLEMAN	72290
D C COLEMAN	77160
DA CHANG ZHEN	92204
DA CHANG ZHEN	92244
DA HONG QIAO	58611
DA HONG QIAO	81011
DA HONG QIAO	90511
DA JIN CHUAN	92203
DA JIN CHUAN	92243
DA LONG TIAN	58610
DA LONG TIAN	81010
DA LONG TIAN	90510
DA MOSTO	03461
DA NING	92201
DA NING	92241
DA QING 9	43070
DA QING 10	40662
DA QING 11	40663
DA QING 12	43071
DA QING 13	41050
DA QING 14	40810
DA QING 15	40060
DA QING 15	42980
DA QING 15	40560
DA QING 17	38614
DA QING 18	66482
DA QING 19	66483
DA QING 20	66484
DA QING 21	66485
DA QING 22	66486
DA QING 23	66487
DA QING 29	38361
DA QING 30	38362
DA QING 34	40670
DA QING 35	36950
DA QING 36	35720
DA QING 37	36700
DA QING 38	70290

Name	No.
DA QING 39	40820
DA QING 41	65551
DA QING 41	85781
DA QING 42	38407
DA QING 44	38408
DA QING 45	37254
DA QING 46	37254/1
DA QING 47	37255
DA QING 48	37255/1
DA QING 49	37256
DA QING 50	37256/1
DA QING 52	36741
DA QING 52	37257●
DA QING 53	37257/1
DA QING 136	38331
DA QING 136	44691
DA QING 212	38365
DA QING 213	38366
DA QING 214	38367
DA QING 215	38368
DA QING 216	76250
DA QING 217	76251
DA QING 218	76252
DA QING 230	38620
DA QING 231	37253/1
DA QING 232	37253
DA QING 233	37258
DA QING 234	37259
DA QING 235	38330
DA QING 235	44690
DA QING 240	38405
DA QING 241	38406
DA QING 250	65290
DA QING 251	38700
DA QING 252	60724
DA QING 253	38690
DA QING 256	65540
DA QING 410	39930
DA QING 410	40570
DA QING 412	38369
DA QING 413	38370
DA QING 414	38371
DA QING 415	38372
DA QING 416	38373
DA QING 417	38374
DA QING SHAN	58613
DA QING SHAN	81013
DA QING SHAN	90513
DA SHA PING	71853
DA SHI QIAO	92202
DA SHI QIAO	92242
DA SHI ZHAI	71854
DAAN	92231
DABEMA	87424
DACCA	40760
DACCA	89223
DACEBANK	04670
DACHENG	62190
DACHENG	62450
DACIA	55782
DACIA	56482
DADABHAI NAOROJI	71632
DADE	92200
DADE	92240
DADES	54265
DADIANGAS	82769
DADO	80422
DAE WON	54266
DAE YANG	61636
DAEYANG BOUNTY	63503
DAEYANG BOUNTY	68223
DAEYANG CHARITY	63501
DAEYANG CHARITY	68221
DAGAN	72333
DAGESTAN	83439
DAGMAR SKOU	86703
DAGONYS	57200
DAHRA	66621
DAHRA	76241
DAI HAI	83080
DAI YUN SHAN	15020
DAIHO MARU	48949/3
DAIKOH MARU	58200
DAIRYO MARU	71381
DAIRYO MARU	86631
DAISETSU	32571
DAISHIN MARU No 11	94860
DAISHIN MARU No 12	94910
DAISHIN MARU No 16	95060
DAISHIN MARU No 22	94911
DAISHIN MARU No 23	95050
DAITOKU MARU No 31	69340
DAKHLA	91311
DAKLA	85740
DALAVIK	03460
D'ALBERTIS	82151
DALIA	29110
DALIA A	83988
DALIA 1	83989
DALIA II	53146
DALLIA	66076
DALLIA	78910
DALLINGTON	58310
DALMA	63962
DALMA	71200
DALMAR	12615
DALMOR	15464
DALNEGORSK	22845
DALNERECHENSK	34475
DALNERECHENSK	85321
DALNEVOSTOCHNY	22846
DALNIY	34476
DALNIY	92381
DALNIY VOSTOK	39413
DALNIYE ZELYENTSK	

Name	No.
DALSLAND	51620
DAMENHAN	13591
DAMING	92233
DAMMAM	23090
DAMODAR GANGA	54586
DAMADAR GENERAL T J PARK	73080
DAMADAR GENERAL T J PARK	77790
DAMODAR TANABE	47700
DAMODAR TASAKA	47701
DAMODOR GANGA	54116
DANA	02260
DANA AFRICA	93361
DANA AMERICA	93360
DANA ANGLIA	17080
DANA ARABIA	93362
DANA CARIBIA	93363
DANA CORONA	01905
DANA FUTURA	35110
DANA FUTURA	95180
DANA HAFNIA	95181
DANA JOY	65340
DANA MAXIMA	95190
DANA REGINA	32200
DANA SCARLETT	19360
DANAE	01711
DANAE	16391
DANAE	73995
DANAE	84981
DANAE	85701
DANAH	49405
DANAH	50965
DANAI	25870
DANBJORN	23940
DANE	42033
DANELOCK	72383
DANIA HAFNIA	35111
DANIELLA	06633
DANIELLA	89610
DANIELLE	73090
DANIELLE	78682
DANIELLE 2	67002
DANILO NECHAY	86187
DANILOVGRAD	48066
DANISH ARROW	67470
DANISH DART	67471
DANJIANG	26520
DANKO	12415
DANMARK	20090
DANNEBROG	18620
DANSBORG	92460
DANSBORG	92510
DANUBE	69430
DANUBE SEA	77579
DANWOOD ICE	92280
DANWOOD ICE	92450
DAOUD BEN AICHA	84264
DAPHNE	01710
DAPHNE	16390
DAPHNE	42000
DAPHNE	46107
DAPHNE	53147
DAPHNE	66077
DAPHNE	70361
DAPHNEMAR	12911
DAPO TRADER	69451
DAPU	92232
DARASUN	24063
DARELL	75536
DARFUR	51427
DARIEN	12994
DARNIA	94605
DARNITZA	36912
DARNITZA	43812
DART AMERICANA	08874
DART AMERICANA	74384
DART ATLANTICA	08872
DART ATLANTICA	74382
DART BRITAIN	08870
DART BRITAIN	74380
DART CONTINENT	08873
DART CONTINENT	74383
DART EUROPE	76950
D'ARTAGNAN	63033
DARVIN	13751/5
DARVISH VANANCA	42320
DARWIN TRADER	82960
DARYA KAMAL	46655
DARYA MA	46656
DARYAL	11831
DARYAL	15400
DASHAKI	48640
DASHAKI	49010
DASHAVA	83440
DATIAN	62191
DATIAN	62451
DATONG	92230
DAUGAVA	22847
DAUGAVA	34477
DAUGAVA	45732●
DAUGAVPILS	60620
DAUGAVPILS	62580
DAUNT ROCK	76150
DAUNTLESS	14000
DAUPHINE	73750●
DAUPHINE	75840●
DAURIYA	11462
DAURIYA	93871
DAVAK	89021
DAVAO	33880
DAVAO CITY	26170
DAVAO GULF	33922
DAVID GAS	55350
DAVID P REYNOLDS	52550
DAVID PACKARD	54495

Name	No.
DAVID PACKARD	54925
DAVID PACKARD	55725
DAVID SALMAN	84850
DAVID SIKEYROS	70593●
DAVID SIQUEIROS	70593
DAVOS	29880
DAVYDOV	09381
DAWN	05961
DAWN	49867
DAYAKA	82440
DAYAKA TIGA	61651
DAYNAVA	23547
DAYSPRING	57141
D'AZEGLIO	14405
DE BURGO	61421
DE DU	04610
DE HOOP	87930
DE HUA	29553
DE RODE TULP	74371
DE WITTE TULP	74372
DE YIN	14051
DE YIN	14231
DEA BROVIG	37550
DEBALTSEVO	83430
DEBORAH I	91760
DEBRALINA 1	04471
DEBRALINA 1	10991
DEBRALINA 1	34151
DEBRALINAS JOY	07280●
DEBRECEN	70791
DEBRECEN	89216
DEDOVSK	83443
DEEPA JUWITA	82310
DEEPA RAYA	22930
DEEPA SAKTI	42075
DEEPSEA MINER II	36530
DEFIANCE	17710
DEFIANT	83581
DEICHLAND	75296
DEICHLAND	88106
DEIKE	76472
DEIMOS	04086
DEKA FRATERNITY	57271
DEKA NAVIGATOR	45830
DEKABRIST	03704
DEKKA CONCORD	72081
DEL CAMPO	92171
DEL CAMPO	92851
DEL CHAP	83990/1
DEL MONTE	92172
DEL MONTE	92852
DEL MUNDO	92170
DEL MUNDO	92850
DEL ORO	92860
DEL RIO	92861
DEL SOL	92862
DEL VALLE	92174
DEL VALLE	92854
DEL VIENTO	92173
DEL VIENTO	92853
DELAWARE	63520
DELAWARE	68270
DELEDDA	32550
DELEDDA	33370
DELEGAT	66391
DELFBORG	50240
DELFI	78240
DELFIN	23451
DELFIN ADRIATICO	27711
DELFIN DE SALAZAR	27710
DELFIN DEL CANTABRICO	27712
DELFINI	32057
DELFINI	64611
DELFINI V	24541
DELICIA	92953
DELICIA	95163
DELIMA	30150
DELJES	54663
DELLYS	75650
DELMA QUEEN	48590
DELMAR 4	34380
DELORIS	73011
DELOS	60092
DELPHIC REEFER	15071
DELPHINUS	53666
DELPHINUS	73386
DELTA	59625
DELTA	74010
DELTA CARIBE	00018
DELTA CARIBE	02488
DELTA CARIBE	35137
DELTA DUNARII	10535
DELTA FLAG	74850
DELTA FLAG	88330
DELTA MAR	00015
DELTA MAR	02485
DELTA MAR	35134
DELTA NORTE	00017
DELTA NORTE	02487
DELTA NORTE	35136
DELTA SUD	00016
DELTA SUD	02486
DELTA SUD	35135
DELTAGAS	60370
DEMETRIOS	46190
DEMETRIOS TH	89227●
DEMON	01530
DEMOSTHENES V	44360
DEMYAN BEDNYY	14379
DEMYAN KOROTCHENKO	76503
DEN LONG HAI	77481
DENA 1	49961
DENA 1	51821
DENEB	12242
DENEB	51276
DENEBOLA	11672
DENIS	42040
DENIS M	34891
DENISH	61154
DENIZATI	63670
DENIZLI	34590
DENNIS CARRIER	62435
DENTON VENTURE	88010
DENVER	53711●
DENVER	78150●
DEPPY	07014
DEPUTAT LUTSKIY	13012
DERBY	77592
DERNA	93935
DESAFIO	33150
DESAFIO	94340
DESCARTES	53860
DESDEMONA	18250
DESERT FALCON	47938
DESERT PRINCE	47933
DESERT QUEEN	47934
DESERT WIND	46501
DESIDERIA F	78481
DESNA	38950
DESNA	39112
DESPINA	06491
DESPINA	31750
DESPINA	67321
DESPINA G K	57594
DESPINA GIAVRIDIS	45860
DESPINA GIAVRIDIS	46020
DESPINA V	59540
DESPINA V	81230
DESPINA Z	56973
DESSAU	78970
DETLEF SCHMIDT	75621
DETROIT	93472
DETTIFOSS	83510
DEUSTO	48059
DEUTSCHLAND	32510
DEVA	41314
DEVARAYA	56841
DEVI	06080
DEVON	56122
DEVON	59772
DEVON CURLEW	59030
DEVON CURLEW	75110
DEVON EXPRESS	14860
DEVONIUN	06160
DEVONSHIRE	38791
DEVONSHIRE	55601
DEVOTION	47223
DEVYATAYA PYATILETKA	79401
DEVYATAYA PYATILETKA	79410
DEXENA	66881
DEXING	80892
DHARINI	11410
DHAULAGIRI	50149
DHOFAR	86960
DIADEMA	53142
DIADEMA	66072
DIAKLIS	29554
DIALA	64190
DIAMANTIS	29410
DIAMOND GLORIOUS	63550●
DIAMOND GLORIOUS	68260●
DIAMOND MOON	53401
DIAMOND MOON	64931
DIAMOND SUN	53402
DIAMOND SUN	64932
DIANA	55000
DIANA	59560
DIANA	59998
DIANA	71690
DIANA	73725
DIANA	83530
DIANA	85380
DIANA II	20360
DIANE	53074
DIANNA	62026
DIAS	57192
d'IBERVILLE	10850
DIBI HAMID	90990
DICLE	07882
DICLE	15645
DICTO	48341
DIDO	04840
DIDYMI	61191
DIEGO	30902
DIEGO DE BLASIO	66841
DIEGO NABOU	76101
DIEGO SUAREZ	39791
DIERHAGEN	75321
DIES	90750
DIJEY	50990
DIJEY	51460
DIKA	81850
DIKSON	11321
DIKSON	11463
DIKSON	11497
DIKSON	34741
DILIGENCE	01355
DILKARA	52632
DIMACHK	81260
DIMANT	62688
DIMBOVITA	13772
DIMITAR BLAGOEV	20735
DIMITRAKIS	13280
DIMITRAKIS	14660
DIMITRAKIS	88247
DIMITRIOS	29101
DIMITRIOS A	42280
DIMITRIOS P PAPASTRATIS	10230
DIMITRIS	02794
DIMITRIS	23931
DIMITRIS	28831
DIMITRIS P	49282
DIMITRIY ULYANOV	03658
DIMITROVO	83435
DIMMER	31170
DIMMER	33520
DIMOS HALCOUSSIS	60093
DINARA	48062
DING HAI	83575
DING HU	01770
DIOGENES	78210
DIOGENES	89920
DIOMID	12416
DIONE	70461
DIONIS	11920
DIONISSIOS K	81952
DIONISSIOS K	91502
DIPLOT	07472
DIRK JACOB	71410
DISARFELL	73724●
DISCARIA	54471
DISCOVERY	16230
DISCOVERY	07032●
DISCOVERY BAY	77052
DISCOVERY BAY	79750
DISKO	32830
DIVNOGORSK	14700
DIVNOGORSK	86541
DJAKARTA	05850
DJATILUHUR	30550
DJATIPURA	61740
DJATIPURA	86780
DJERUK	42074
DJORF	64965
DJURDJURA	64966
DJURSLAND	16471
DJURSLAND	32801
DMITRI DONSKOI	17507
DMITRI POZHARSKII	17506
DMITRIY DONSKOY	80171
DMITRIY FURMANOV	07921
DMITRIY GULIA	14380
DMITRIY KANTEMIR	50747
DMITRIY MEDVEDEV	67685
DMITRIY MENDELEYEV	07622
DMITRIY POKRAMOVICH	34879●
DMITRIY POKROVICH	34879
DMITRIY POZHARSKIY	80172
DMITRIY SHOSTAKOVICH	20354
DMITRIY ULYANOV	03066
DMITRIY ZHLOBA	60631
DMITRIY ZHLOBA	62591
DMITRY CHASOVITIN	85329
DMITRY FURMANOV	12417
DMITRY LAPTEV	35421
DMITRY MANUILSKIY	79375
DMITRY OVTSYN	35420
DMITRY POLUYAN	05635
DMITRY POLUYAN	14464
DMITRY STERLEGOV	35422
DNEPRODZERZHINSK	11832
DNEPRODZERZHINSK	83441
DNEPROVSKIY LIMAN	21250
DNESTR	25554
DNESTR	59881
DNESTROVSKIY LIMAN	21251
DOAN TRANSPORT	70730
DOBRA	07890
DOBRINYA NIKITICH	22220
DOBROGEA	15421
DOBROPOLYE	83436
DOBROTA	56930
DOBROTA	80930
DOBROVOLSK	12243
DOBRUSH	83431
DOBRINYA NIKITCH	22220
DOBRYNA NIKITCH	17508
DOC LAP	83605
DOCECANYON	62904
DOCECANYON	68174
DOCECORAL	68202
DOCEDELTA	73240
DOCEPOLO	68200
DOCK EXPRESS 10	12670
DOCK EXPRESS 11	12671
DOCK EXPRESS 12	12672
DOCK EXPRESS 20	12673
DOCK EXPRESS TEXAS	92801
DOCTOR LYKES	08861
DODONE	39850
DOGGERSBANK	75503
DOLCE	68701
DOLFIN	26322
DOLINSK	00335
DOLJ	47560
DOLLART	50840
DOLLY II	45407
DOLLY SKOU	86705
DOLLY TURMAN	14421
DOLLY TURMAN	14891
DOLMABAHCE	32151
DOLMATOVO	50900
DOLNY SLASK	75731
DOLNY SLASK	88381
DOLOMIT	11921
DOLORES	70440
DOLPHIN II	65550
DOLPHIN II	85780
DOLPHIN IV	10770
DOLPHIN POINT	73630
DOMAN	06950●
DOMENICO SCOTTO	91849
DOMINIC	53711
DOMINIC	78150
DOMINIQUE L-D	46664●
DOMIZIANA	33470
DOMODYEDOVO	11735
DOMODYEDOVO	36245
DON	85358
DON ALEJO	53500
DON ALEJO	71100
DON ALEJO	91870
DON AMANDO	25440
DON CAMILO	23220
DON CARLOS	92730
DON CARLOS	94530
DON CLAUDIO	14980
DON EUSEBIO	10790
DON JOLLY	21020
DON JUAN	92731
DON JUAN	94531
DON JULIO	08240
DON JULIO	32120
DON MANOLO	73821
DON NICKY	83660
DON NICKY	84140
DON PABLO	61633
DON SALVADOR III	46463
DON VICENTE	14970
DONA ANGELINA	43123
DONA ANITA	21091
DONA CHRISTINA	60609/1
DONA CHRISTINA	69980
DONA CONCHITA	19530
DONA EVGENIA	64613
DONA GLORIA	18500
DONA HELENA	43120
DONA HORTENCIA II	46462
DONA JULIETA	23221
DONA LILY	40912
DONA LILY	45152
DONA LOLITA	27540
DONA LOULA	60608
DONA LOULA	69978
DONA MAGDALENA	46461
DONA MARILYN	33780
DONA MYRTO	60609
DONA MYRTO	69979
DONA OURANIA	64610
DONA PAMELA	21810
DONA PAZ II	46460
DONA PETRA M R	66840
DONA RITA	43122
DONA ROSSANA	71224
DONA SOPHIA	46600
DONAR	74020
DONATELLO	70270
DONATO MARMOL	06616
DONAU MARU	53680
DONAU MARU	53810
DONAU MARU	68530
DONAU ORE	62902
DONAU ORE	68172
DONAX	64230
DONBASS	11464
DONETS	02281
DONETS	25555
DONETS	35181
DONETSK	84350
DONETSK	25556
DONETSKIY KHIMIK	01382
DONETSKIY KHIMIK	01642
DONETSKIY KOMSOMOLETS	01381
DONETSKIY KOMSOMOLETS	01641
DONETSKIY METALLURG	01383
DONETSKIY METALLURG	01643
DONETSKIY SHAKHTER	01384
DONETSKIY SHAKHTER	01644
DONG AH	61634
DONG AN	52736
DONG BANG No 71	92750
DONG HAI	57390
DONG MYUNG	26080
DONG NAI	83281
DONG SOO No 501	84500
DONG YANG EXPRESS FERRY NO 2	19510
DONGA	80621
DONGA	81971
DONGMING	13100
DONGOLA	51425
DONGPING	30842
DONGSHAN	04450
DONISAR	13751/6
DONNINGTON	78911
DONNY	50481
DONNY	83071
DONOVANIA	53144
DONOVANIA	66074
DONSKOY	83442
DONUZAV	54630
DONUZLAV	55060
DORA BALTEA	33270
DORA BALTEA	94570
DORA OLDENDORFF	77444
DORA PAPALIOS	06492
DORA RIPARIA	33271
DORA RIPARIA	94572
DORADA	22335
DORI BRES	73963
DORIC	53154
DORIC	66307
DORIC CARRIER	50401
DORIC CARRIER	50831
DORIOS	68730
DORIS	47521
DORIS	47616

Name	No.
DORIS	50262
DORIT SKOU	86706
DORITAL	54270
DORLI	82762
DORNA	13736
DORNBUSCH	45710
DOROTHEA SCHULTE	58484
DORTEA	90311
DORTHE OLDENDORFF	06582
DORYFOROS	57004
DOSTOYEVSKIY	12321
DOUCE FRANCE III	61400
DOUGGA	86600
DOULOS	16310
DOUMEN	06069/1
DOVATOR	17500
DR ATILIO MALVAGNI	06677
DR D K SAMY	69127
DR FRIDTJOF NANSEN	17360
DRACO	53665
DRACO	73385
DRAGASANI	06069/12
DRAGON	32500
DRAGOR MAERSK	05020
DRAGOR MAERSK	08760
DRAKE SEA	56830
DRASTIRIOS	52202
DRASTIRIOS	65152
DRAVA	55992
DRESDEN	04911
DRESDEN	36867
DRESDEN	45842
DRIANOVO	91500
DROBETA 1850	87643
DROGOBYCH	70741
DROMON	79781
DRONNING INGRID	16031
DRONNING INGRID	19991
DROTTEN	16980
DRUPA 2-1-91	51960
DRUPA	75000
DRUSKININKAY	12418
DRUZHBA	12591
DRUZHBA	44410
DRUZHBA	60681
DRUZHBA NARADOV	90721
DRUZHBA SSSR-DDR	36140
DRUZHBA SSSR-GDR	11833
DRY SACK	79102
DRYAS	53840●
DRYAS	79710●
DRYS	53840
DRYS	79710
DRZIC	40230
DU SHAN	84111
DU SHAN	84171
DUA-MAR	65725
DUA-MAR	75665
DUBNA	56270
DUBNA	62730
DUBNO	83432
DUBOSSARY	83433
DUBROVNIK	14381
DUBROVNIK	47710
DUBULTY	63642
DUCHESS OF HOLLAND	88552●
DUDINKA	83438
DUKE OF HOLLAND II	36345
DUKE OF NORFOLK	88551
DUKUH	42072
DUMAS PERDANA	18151
DUMBRAVENI	82122
DUMBRAVENI	82402
DUNA	27520
DUNAREA	78585
DUNAV	85450
DUNEDIN	02890
DUNEDIN	60021
DUNGENESS	94400
DUNGHUA	29361
DUNGHUA	30582
DUNHUANG	05660
DUPE BAKARE	61731
DUPE BAKARE	81541
DUPE BAKARE	85051
DUREN	42073
DURHAM	73270
DURHAM	77770
DURIAN	02541
DURR	20272
DURRESI	17934
DURRINGTON	78912
DUSHANBE	12343
DUSSELDORF EXPRESS	08780
DUSZNIKI ZDROJ	81863
DUTCH GLORY	66600
DUTCH GLORY	75150
DUTCH MASTER	66601
DUTCH MASTER	75151
DUTCH MATE	76681
DUTCH MATE	89051
DUTCH SAILOR	76680
DUTCH SAILOR	89050
DUTEOUS	60188
DVINOLES	24041
DVINSKIY ZALIV	61103
DWEJRA II	64730
DWEJRA II	81720
DYNAMIC SAILOR	41230
DYNAMIKOS	52212
DYNAMIKOS	65142
DYNASTY	15221
DYNASTY HILALI	09951●
DYNASTY HURA	13780●
DYNASTY HURA	14780●
DYNASTY MALE	13930●
DYNASTY UTHEEM	28630●
DYSTOS	76041
DYVI KATTEGAT	92651
DYVI KATTEGAT	93191
DYVI OCEANIC	94710
DYVI PACIFIC	94711
DYVI SKAGERAK	92650
DYVI SKAGERAK	93190
DYVI SWAN	89684
DYVI SWIFT	89685
DYVI TEAL	89686
DYVI TERN	89687
DZERZHINSK	70166
DZHAFER DZHABARLY	50761
DZHAMBUL DZHABAYEV	79403
DZHEBRAIL	44106
DZHEMS BANKOVICH	67011
DZHORAT	44116
DZHORDANO BRUNO	38580
DZHURMA	24064
DZHUZEPPE GARIBALDI	36940
DZHUZEPPE VERDI	60500
DZIECI POLSKIE	07460
DZIECI POLSKIE	10758
DZINTARI	63643
DZINTARYURA	12419
DZINTARZEME	23548
DZINTERKRASTS	23524
DZUKIYA	23523

E

Name	No.
E.L.M.A. CINCO	50264
E R ANTVERPIA	77401
E R BRUGGE	47030
E R BRUSSEL	47031●
E W BEATTY	72291
E W BEATTY	77161
EAGLE	89181
EAGLE ARROW	83060
EAGLE ARROW	83160
EARL GODWIN	19420
EARL GRANVILLE	19292
EARL GRANVILLE	23706
EARL OF SKYE	51660
EARL OF SKYE	73210
EARL WILLIAM	19432
EARLY BIRD	72636
EAST RAINBOW	49620
EASTER BAY	51305
EASTERN BRIDE	46840
EASTERN DRAGON	61611
EASTERN ENTERPRISE	58041
EASTERN GLORY	83364
EASTERN GLORY	83454
EASTERN GOLD	49862
EASTERN GRACE	62406
EASTERN GRACE	77511
EASTERN GRACE	78411
EASTERN HAZEL	53687
EASTERN HAZEL	53817
EASTERN HAZEL	68537
EASTERN HIGHWAY	36570
EASTERN HUNTER	13581
EASTERN JUPITER	14610
EASTERN LADY	66801
EASTERN LAUREL	54036
EASTERN LEADER	30521
EASTERN LILAC	54639
EASTERN LILAC	55069
EASTERN LION	31280
EASTERN LION	59946
EASTERN LION	67936
EASTERN MARINER	35712
EASTERN MARINER	41422
EASTERN MARINER I	05690
EASTERN NAV	26670
EASTERN NEPTUNE	61009
EASTERN NEPTUNE	71269
EASTERN PEARL	30520
EASTERN PEARL	31270
EASTERN PHOENIX	48391●
EASTERN POWER	31140
EASTERN RANGER	62496
EASTERN REEFER	02981
EASTERN RIVER	73361
EASTERN SATURN	30381
EASTERN SPIRIT	63113
EASTERN SPLENDOR	48160
EASTERN STAR	27490
EASTERN UNICORN	48390●
EASTERN VALLEY	46870
EASTERN WISEMAN	56540
EASTERN WORLD	77282
EASTHOLM	90991
EASTPORT	57160
EASTWAY	65450
EBALINA	52313
EBE	83367
EBE	83457
EBERHARD	63658
EBN BATUTA	62371
EBN BATUTA	81421
EBN JUBAIR	62370
EBN JUBAIR	81420
EBN MAGID	80752
EBN MAGID	81452
EBO	06644
EBRO	87900●
EBURNA	52310
ECCTONIA	88001
ECHO STAR	78690●
ECHOMAN	66578
ECKERO	19090
ECKERT OLDENDORFF	72451
ECLAIR	56030
ECO DOURO	72670
ECO GUADIANA	73882
ECO GUADIANA	87262
ECO LIZ	73943
ECO MONDEGO	73880
ECO MONDEGO	87260
ECO TEJO	50203
ECO TEJO	75973
ECUADORIAN REEFER	05111
EDDA	17580
EDDAR EL BEIDA	46243
EDEL SIF	49899
EDGAR ANDRE	04231
EDINBURGH UNIVERSAL	06223
EDINBURGH UNIVERSAL	07452
EDITA	56120
EDITA	59770
EDITH NIELSEN	91480
EDOUGH	64967
EDRA	11260
EDUARD CLAUDIUS	13768/1
EDUARD SYRMUS	12420
EDUARD TOLL	35423
EDUARD VEYDENBAUM	12421
EDUARD WILDE	86083
EDWARD RUTLEDGE	01057
EDY 1	59670
EEKLO	63790
EEKLO	73190
EENDRACHT	88302
EFDIM HOPE	58574
EFDIM JUNIOR	58575
EFIE	90452
EFSTATHIA	00880
EFTHITIS	60094
EFTICHIA	41140
EFTICHIA	42580
EFTYHIA	45392
EFYRA	69510
EGDA	83140
EGE	01590
EGE MELTEMI	63689
EGE YILDIZI	49660
EGE YILDIZI	50930
EGEON	21140
EGERSHELD	45114
EGIZIA	61409/2
EGLANTINE	79740
EGMONT	38792
EGNATIA	20260
EGORYEVSK	44621
EGTON	06940
EGVEKINOT	06795/3
EHIME MARU	48950
EICHSFELD	71682
EICHWALDE	46377
EICHWALDE	47077
EIDER	64830
EIDER	75622
EIFEL	37290
EIFFEL	49550
EIGAMOIYA	16260
EIGIGU	57552
EIHAB 1	15880
EIKO MARU	67991
EILENBURG	03874
EILENBURG	04425
EIR	71902
EIRA	46172
EIRAMA	69230
EIRIK RAUDE	80820
EISENBERG	84941
EISENBERG	90601
EISENHUTTENSTADT	86420
EISHO MARU	63362
EITOKU MARU	60040
EKA DAYA SAMUDERA	01080
EKATERINI M GOULANDRIS	79181
EKENIS	73600
EKFJORD	56191
EKFJORD	80911
EKHOLOT	09376
EKIMCHAN	85975
EKMAN	72060
EKOWATI	61626
EKTON	61380
EKTOR	61990
EKTOR	85390●
EKVATOR	12577
EL ARISH	32620
EL CARRIER	48385/1
EL CHAMPION	48054
EL CINCO	82001
EL COMMODORE	48385/2
EL CRUSADER	48385/3
EL DJAZAIR	34090
EL EXPORTADOR	90410
EL GAUCHO	18200
EL GRECO	08210
EL GRECO	58553
EL GRECO	71873
EL GUAIQUERI	73620
EL HADJ ABOUL AZZIZ SY	56230
EL HASSAN	21060
EL JEM	47061
EL JIGUE	12792
EL MALEK KHALED	87280
EL MEXICANO	55012
EL MEXICANO	55882
EL MEXICANO	56552
EL OBEID	51423
EL PASO CONSOLIDATED	53641
EL PASO PAUL KAYSER	53640
EL TOR	32621
EL ZANJON	31520
ELAFI	56521
ELAFINA	60410
ELAFINA	69360
ELAMIR FAHD	15881
ELAND	67171
ELAZIG	06730
ELAZIG	31190
ELAZIG	71110
ELBAN	85888
ELBE	59711
ELBE	73902
ELBE MARU	08390
ELBIA	59470
ELBJORN	23830
ELBRUS	11305
ELBRUS	39993
ELBSTROM	49880●
ELCANO	22650
ELDE	31960
ELDIR	65092
ELDVIK	66831
ELDVIK	91491
ELEANORA	92956
ELEANORA	95166
ELEFTHERIA	00120
ELEFTHERIA	36050
ELEFTHERIA	68621●
ELEFTHERIA M	70355
ELEFTHERIOS	61150
ELEFTHERIOS	62140
ELEFTHEROS	52210
ELEFTHEROS	65140
ELEISTRIA	47602
ELEISTRIA 1	72173
ELEISTRIA IV	39630
ELEISTRIA V	27570
ELEISTRIA VIII	41280
ELEISTRIA VIII	44990
ELEKRENAY	12422
ELEKTROSTAL	24066
ELENA	02553
ELENA	45971
ELENA	88600
ELENA P	16630
ELENA ZETA	41030
ELENI	62550
ELENI	62660
ELENI II	72335
ELENI M	46512
ELENI P	63000
ELENI V	70860
ELETS	17931
ELEUROPA	48283
ELFO	15991
ELFWAIHAT	63396
ELGAREN	80291
ELGAVA	44370
ELGER	65091
ELGURDABIA	63397
ELIMAM MALEK	27940
ELIN S	90943
ELIOS	51636
ELISA	90000
ELISA d'ALESIO	60841
ELISA d'ALESIO	81461
ELISA F	78480
ELISABETH	49650
ELISABETH	64511
ELISABETH	82805
ELISABETH	92095
ELISABETH HOLWERDA	88300
ELISABETH MAERSK	48920
ELISABETH OLDENDORFF	71844
ELISABETH ROTH	62103
ELISABETTA MONTANARI	81470
ELIZA	56050
ELIZA	51543●
ELIZA HEEREN	73866
ELIZABETH BAKKE	59431
ELIZABETH LYKES	05580
ELIZABETH LYKES	14420
ELIZABETH LYKES	14890
ELIZABETH MAERSK	56320
ELJIANNI	46521
ELJIANNI	83301
ELK	76760
ELK	80270
ELKA	47754
ELKE KAHRS	76209/5●
ELLEN ESSBERGER	55681
ELLEN ESSBERGER	72531
ELLI	26630
ELLI	42780
ELLINIS	09180
ELLIOT	59521●
ELLIOT	80201●
ELLITSA	24350
ELLY	05233
ELMINA	69123
ELNIL DELTA	21700
ELOCEAN	45800
ELONA	71507
ELOTA	70360●
ELOUNDA	68910
ELPEDIO BEROVIDES	75961
ELPIDA	59252

Name	No.
ELPIDA	62522
ELPIDOFOROS	46450
ELPIS	29461
ELPIS	60095
ELSBORG	76111
ELTIGEN	86006
ELTON	84366
ELVA	13754/9
ELVINA	35570
ELVIRA	66812
ELVIRA C	64376
ELVIRA EISENSCHNEIDER	23415
EMADALA	93094
EMADALA	94164
EMANUEL	11160
EMBA	44122
EMBA	92160
EMBARCADERO	78371●
EMDEN	51987
EMEBORG	90535
EMEBORG	91075
EMEKSIZ	32169
EMERALD	75921
EMERALD	92930
EMERALD ISLANDS	06634
EMERALD SEAS	17390
EMERALD STAR	62237●
EMERALD STAR	71255●
EMERALD TRANSPORTER	63271
EMETSK	22848
EMETSK	34478
EMILIA	33473
EMILIA DEL MAR	87780
EMILIA PLATER	14580
EMILIA S	51031
EMILIA UNO	71761
EMINENCE	75440
EMINENCE	88420
EMIRATES EXPRESS	25863
EMMA JOHANNA	45841
EMMA OLDENDORFF	72450
EMMANUEL COMNINOS	78351
EMOULI	43870
EMPIRE STATE	12220
EMPRESS OF AUSTRALIA	16410
EMPROS	05328
EMS ORE	74770
EMS ORE	79000
EMSLAND	19480
EMY	67481
ENAK	65090
ENATON	55101
ENATON	57591
ENAYATALLAH	36330
ENCOUNTER BAY	77050
ENDEAVOR	73203
ENDEAVOR	76993
ENDEAVOUR	68551●
ENDURANCE	29210
ENDURANCE	65680
ENDURANCE	70110
ENDURANCE EXPRESS	60157
ENDURANCE FRIENDSHIP	60158
ENERGY GROWTH	54371
ENERGY GROWTH	54820
ENERGY GROWTH	62981
ENERGY MOBILITY	69610
ENERGY PRODUCTION	69611
ENERGY PROSPERITY	68700
ENERGY RENOWN	63423
ENGLAND	01920
ENGURE	86242
ENIM	41962
ENRICO C	12740
ENRIQUETA	07667
ENSOR	64347
ENTERPRISE	77703
ENTERPRISE II	83710/1
ENTRE RIOS II	48372
EOLOS	32310
EPHESTOS	66261
EPIFAN KOVTYUKH	62593
EPIMELIA	60096
EPIMENIDIS	06501
EPIMITHEFS	78270
EPOMEO PRIMO	16650
EPOS	60097
EPTANISSOS	65350
EQUATOR	19600●
ERAWAN	66051
ERDEMIR	57237
EREBUS	36913
EREBUS	43813
ERFURT	04923
ERGINA 1	61860
ERICH STEINFURTH	23416
ERIDAN	12244
ERIFAN KOVITYUKH	60633
ERIK	63661
ERIK SIF	64864
ERIK SIF	91044
ERIK WEINERT	12621
ERIKA BOJEN	72120
ERIKA BOJEN	76460
ERIKA BOLTEN	49950
ERIKA BOLTEN	58500
ERIKA JACOB	71412
ERIKA NABER	58551
ERIKA NABER	71871
ERIKOUSSA	70136
ERINIO	83170
ERITHIANI	56520
ERLANGEN EXPRESS	08831
ERLANGEN EXPRESS	09031
ERLANGEN EXPRESS	77031
ERMA	44127
ERMINIA PRIMA	73030
ERMIONE	56760
ERMIONI	14406
ERMIS	61991
ERMUA	78183
ERNE	58880
ERNST HAECKEL	17670
ERNST KRENKEL	02271
ERNST MORITZ ARNDT	34215
ERNST SCHNELLER	04232
ERNST TELMAN	17509
ERNST THALMANN	05623
ERNST THALMANN	14453
ERNST THALMANN	62681
ERO	79651
EROS	08281
ERSI	66021●
ERVILIA	52311
ERZURUM	57236
ESLA	75270
ESMERALDA	88940
ESMERALDAS	85940
ESPANA	74023
ESPENHAIN	79732
ESPERANZA II	69080
ESPERANZA II	86340
ESPERANZA No 2	85310
ESPEROS	73361●
ESPRESSO CORINTO	02170
ESPRESSO EGITTO	17270
ESPRESSO GRECIA	17271
ESPRESSO LIGURIA	32980
ESPRESSO RAVENNA	17273
ESPRESSO VENEZIA	17272
ESQUILINO	24341
ESRAM	58853
ESRAM	65663
ESSAYONS	93460
ESSI BALTIC	67170
ESSI CAMILLA	77680
ESSI FLORA	86410
ESSO ABERDEEN	54620
ESSO AFRICA	62842
ESSO ALBANY	65635
ESSO ALBANY	70005
ESSO BANGKOK	58840
ESSO BANGKOK	65650
ESSO BAYWAY	60566
ESSO BILBAO	54531
ESSO BILBAO	54791
ESSO BOMBAY	58841
ESSO BOMBAY	65651
ESSO BONN	57820
ESSO BONN	59850
ESSO BREGA	55630
ESSO CAERNARVON	85950
ESSO CAERNARVON	86590
ESSO CALLUNDA	70006
ESSO CALLUNDA	65636
ESSO CARIBBEAN	56400
ESSO CARIBBEAN	59920
ESSO CARIBBEAN	67780
ESSO CASTELLON	66101
ESSO CLYDE	58821
ESSO CLYDE	65621
ESSO DALRIADA	64320
ESSO DEMETIA	64321
ESSO DEUTSCHLAND	54510
ESSO DEUTSCHLAND	63890
ESSO EVERETT	65690
ESSO EVERETT	70120
ESSO FAWLEY	65611
ESSO FAWLEY	71891
ESSO FINLANDIA	52074
ESSO FLAME	75690
ESSO FORTH	66100
ESSO FUJI	59990
ESSO GENOVA	65633
ESSO GENOVA	70007/1
ESSO HAFNIA	65637
ESSO HAFNIA	70007
ESSO HONOLULU	54530
ESSO HONOLULU	54790
ESSO HUMBER	58848
ESSO HUMBER	65658
ESSO INVERNESS	75090
ESSO LIGURIA	65631
ESSO MEDITERRANEAN	56403
ESSO MEDITERRANEAN	59923
ESSO MEDITERRANEAN	67783
ESSO MERSEY	58820
ESSO MERSEY	65620
ESSO MILFORD HAVEN	65610
ESSO MILFORD HAVEN	71890
ESSO NORMANDIE	62840
ESSO ORIENT	64411
ESSO OSAKA	54532
ESSO OSAKA	54792
ESSO PALM BEACH	60565
ESSO PARENTIS	65634
ESSO PARENTIS	70007/2
ESSO PENZANCE	75091
ESSO PICARDIE	62841
ESSO PLYMOUTH	75085
ESSO PORT DICKSON	58846
ESSO PORT DICKSON	65656
ESSO PORT JEROME	58830
ESSO PORT JEROME	60570
ESSO PORT JEROME	65638
ESSO PORT JEROME	70008
ESSO PORTLAND	60567
ESSO PORTOVENERE	55632
ESSO SABA	57801
ESSO SABA	59851
ESSO SAINT PETERSBURG	65692
ESSO SAINT PETERSBURG	70122
ESSO SEVERN	58822
ESSO SEVERN	65622
ESSO SLAGEN	70210
ESSO TEES	58849
ESSO TEES	65659
ESSO TENBY	66440
ESSO TYNE	58850
ESSO TYNE	65660
ESSO VENEZIA	58852
ESSO VENEZIA	65662
ESSO WARWICKSHIRE	38070
ESSO WESTERNPORT	54210
ESSO YOKOHAMA	58847
ESSO YOKOHAMA	65657
ESSO ZURICH	66090
ESTADO DA GUANABARA	37890
ESTAFETA OKTYABRYA	12423
ESTE	73749/3●
ESTEBAN S	21500
ESTEBOGEN	49900
ESTEBOGEN	50340
ESTETAL	64742
ESTETAL	81771
ESTHER	73996
ESTHER DEL MAR	76100
ESTONIYA	02160
ESTRELLA	40040
ESTRELLA	44961
ESTRELLA ANTARTICA	70280
ESTRELLA DEL MAR	15840
ESTRELLA FUEGUINA	43630
ESTRELLA FUEGUINA	44780
ESTRELLA PATAGONICA	65440
ETAIWI 1	16020
ETAIWI 2	30590
ETHA RICKMERS	07750
ETHEL EVARARD	86370
ETHEL EVERARD	70970
ETHNIC	59925
ETHNIC	67785
ETRUSCO	88521
ETTORE	52460
EUCLIDE	54760
EUGEN SCHONHAAR	23417
EUGENIA 1	65976
EUGENIE C	47936
EUGENIE COTTON	75773
EUGENIO C	01240
EUGENIO C	35230
EUGENIUSZ KWIATKOWSKI	14483
EUPLECTA	52312
EURCO ATHINA	81550●
EURCO BANNER	06535●
EURCO R	12910
EURCO WIZARD	86051●
EURO BROKER	72762
EURO CARRIER	72757
EURO CLIPPER	76204●
EURO FREIGHTER	72758
EURO LINER	72764
EURO PARTNER	72760
EURO SAILOR	72755
EURO SEA	56646
EURO STAR	56647
EURO SUN	56648
EURO TRADER	76205●
EURO TRAMPER	72756
EUROASIA CONCORDE	46875
EUROCARRIER	62405
EUROFREEDOM	48281
EUROPA	08809
EUROPA	16875
EUROPA FREEZER	34209
EUROPA POINT	61321
EUROPAFARJAN	20290
EUROPAFARJAN IV	23821
EUROPE	14081
EUROPE II	14080
EUROPEAN CLEARWAY	14976
EUROPEAN EAGLE	50269
EUROPEAN ENTERPRISE	14978
EUROPEAN EXPRESS	05327
EUROPEAN HIGHWAY	94960
EUROPEAN MARCHIONESS	26530
EUROPEAN MASTER	49191
EUROPEAN MASTER	52791
EUROPEAN TRADER	14977
EUROPEAN VENTURE	95125
EUROPIC FERRY	23310
EUROSEA	46914
EUROTAINER	76206●
EUROUNITY	46915
EUSTATHIA	39810
EUTHALIA	54572
EUTHALIA	54952
EUTHYMENES	66701
EVA	61523
EVA	69450
EVA ODEN	94182
EVA P	37681
EVA P	44260
EVAGELIA S	07210
EVALD TAMMLAAN	12424
EVALI	25270
EVANGELIA	59603
EVANGELIA	71933
EVANGELIA C	70680
EVANGELIA C	78110
EVANGELISTAS	94691
EVANGELISTRIA	20820
EVANGELISTRIA	22110
EVANGELISTRIA	57130
EVANGELISTRIA IV	87024
EVANGELOS	91270●
EVANGELOS D	61077
EVANGELOS D	71267
EVANGELOS L	47873
EVANTHIA 1	83900
EVDORI	69511
EVDOXIA K	43330
EVE	75290
EVE	88100
EVELINE	57260
EVELINE	84820
EVELYN	54560
EVELYN	54960
EVELYN	06639/9●
EVENSK	36909
EVENSK	85977
EVER	39700
EVER GRACE	31820
EVER HONOR	46883
EVER LAUREL	08701
EVER LEVEL	08700
EVER LINKING	08704
EVER LIVING	08702
EVER LOADING	08705
EVER LYRIC	08703
EVER RELIANCE	62028
EVER SHINE	10000
EVER SPLENDOR	71221
EVER SPRING	10001
EVER SUMMIT	10002
EVER SUPERB	10003
EVER VALIANT	08890
EVER VALIANT	74390
EVER VALOR	08895
EVER VALOR	74395
EVER VALUE	08896
EVER VALUE	74396
EVER VIGOR	08893
EVER VIGOR	74393
EVER VITAL	08894
EVER VITAL	74394
EVEREST	18340
EVEREST	33840
EVERGRAND	61582
EVERGREEN STATE	18980
EVERSHAGEN	76534
EVGENIY NIKISHIN	93683
EVGENIY NIKONOV	50284
EVGENIY ONUFRIEV	50287
EVIA	26491
EVIA LUCK	48466
EVIA LUCK	49502
EVIA LUCK	49773
EVIMERIA	58158
EVITA	64363
EVITA II	83740
EVLALIA	06960
EVNIA	60098
EVNIKI	77880
EVOICOS GULF	07270
EVORON	84361
EVPO KETTY	07765
EVPO KETTY	07815
EVRIKA	11944
EVRIPOS EXPRESS	25360
EVY L	46694
EWALDEVERETT	21411
EXCELSIOR REEFER	06300
EXPANSA II	88303
EXPLORER	61661
EXPORT CHALLENGER	35605
EXPORT CHAMPION	35606
EXPORT COMMERCE	35607
EXPORT FREEDOM	94273
EXPORT LEADER	94274
EXPORT PATRIOT	94275
EXPRESS CARRIER	31801
EXTRACO 1	57618
EXTRACO 1	61059
EXTRACO II	57619
EXTRACO II	61059/1
EXTRAMAR ESTE	76071
EXTRAMAR NORTE	76070
EXTRAMAR OESTE	76072
EXTRAMAR SUR	76073
EXXON BALTIMORE	38011
EXXON BALTIMORE	38881
EXXON BANGOR	37794
EXXON BATON ROUGE	53551
EXXON BATON ROUGE	55571
EXXON BOSTON	38010
EXXON BOSTON	38880
EXXON CHESTER	37791
EXXON GETTYSBURG	38570
EXXON HOUSTON	66092
EXXON HUNTINGTON	37792
EXXON JAMESTOWN	38571
EXXON LEXINGTON	38572
EXXON NEW ORLEANS	66093
EXXON NEWARK	37793
EXXON PHILADELPHIA	53552
EXXON PHILADELPHIA	55572
EXXON SAN FRANCISCO	53550
EXXON SAN FRANCISCO	55570
EXXON WASHINGTON	38573
EXXTOR 1	33201●
EYRARFOSS	94653
EYSK	22849
EYSK	34479
EYZHEN BERG	67655
EYZHENS BERGS	59895

(handwritten margin note: 19-2-91)

F

Name	No.	Name	No.	Name	No.	Name	No.
F FREILIGRATH	33870	FEAX	05477	FIJIAN	81783	FLORIDA	05230
F J GARAYGORDOBIL	48580	FEAX	07960	FILATRA LEGACY	64512	FLORIDA STAR	76120
FA FA VENTURE	73183	FEDERAL FRASER	61180	FILIA WAVE	46929/3	FLORIDA STAR	79900
FABIAN	67830	FEDERAL MAPLE	23620	FILIASI	47552	FLORISSANT	59343
FABIAN	68430	FEDERAL PIONEER	48822	FILIDARA	47543	FLORNES	94243
FABIO SAVERIO	36075	FEDOR BREDIKHIN	10742	FILIKOS	65153	FLOTTBEK	72536
FABIO SAVERIO	41795	FEDOR GADKOV	07927	FILIO AVGERIS	00382	FOBOS	04085
FABIOLAVILLE	16190	FEDOR GLADKOV	11835	FILIPINAS	34250	FOCSANI	06069/13
FADEL	64760	FEDOR KRAYNOV	12425	FILIPP MAKHARADZE	59220	FODELE II	41370
FADEL G	45883	FEDOR LITKE	22184	FILIPP MAKHARADZE	74540	FOKA	10811
FADY	41070	FEDOR LITKE	22224	FILIPPOS	42150	FOLGA	83141
FAETHON	05478	FEDOR MATISEN	39173	FILON	56638/4	FOLGOET	84180
FAETHON	07961	FEDOR PETROV	03774	FINA AMERICA	58040	FOMALHAUT	71032
FAGARAS	47546	FEDOR PETROV	04014	FINA NORVEGE	63530	FONTANKA	35317
FAGET	47541	FEDOR PODTELKOV	79425	FINIX	05472	FOOCHOW	24650
FAHAD	40160	FEDOR POLETAEV	38581	FINLANDIA	16895	FOOCHOW	26250
FAI HONG	56920●	FEDOR SHALYAPIN	06201	FINN SIF	49899/4●	FORE MOSULISHVILI	70746
FAIR JENNIFER	87830	FEDORA	06538	FINNARCTIS	47294	FOREL	11788/3
FAIR LADY	19300	FEDROS	80702	FINNBEAVER	47992	FOREL	34674
FAIR MARINE	24885	FEDROS	84482	FINNFELLOW	08521	FOREST LINK	78055
FAIR RAINBOW	89101	FEDYA GUBANOV	44101	FINNFIGHTER	47291	FORMOSA	48373
FAIR REEFER	21340	FEICUIHAI	46680	FINNFURY	47993	FORMOSA CONTAINER	76170
FAIR SPIRIT	06583	FEICUIHAI	47110	FINNHAWK	92911	FOROS	13664
FAIR WIND	47670	FELICIA	47945	FINNJET	93070	FORT AUSTIN	00051
FAIRFIELD VENTURE	62875	FELICIDADE FERRAZ	48077	FINNMARKEN	02380	FORT CALGARY	46801
FAIRFIELD VISCOUNT	24010	FELICITY	10120	FINNMARKEN	35350	FORT CARLETON	47011
FAIRLANE	89590	FELICITY	14020	FINNMERCHANT	76746	FORT COULOGNE	70153
FAIRLIFT	89620	FELIKS DZIERZYNSKI	65850	FINNO	71946	FORT DUFFERIN	72389
FAIRLOAD	89601	FELIKS DZIERZYNSKI	67690	FINNOAK	47490	FORT EDMONTON	70154
FAIRMEAD	75480	FELIKS DZERZHINSKIY	02162A	FINNOCEANIS	47292	FORT FLEUR d'EPEE	08791
FAIRMEAD	75480	FELIKS KON	93731	FINNPINE	47590	FORT FRASER	63780
FAIRNESS	47209	FELIKS KON	93821	FINNPOLARIS	47297	FORT FRONTENAC	72389/1
FAIRSEA	01221	FELIPE II	27245	FINNROSE	92910	FORT GRANGE	00050
FAIRSTAR	01210	FELIX	47559	FINNTIMBER	47816	FORT HAMILTON	47010
FAIRWIND	01220	FELIX S	04480	FINNY	67420	FORT KAMLOOPS	46791
FAITH	66890	FELIX S	12650	FINSKIY ZALIV	61104	FORT KIPP	70155
FAITH	82030	FELLOWSHIP L	56471	FINWAL	10816	FORT MACLEOD	70156
FAITH	91580	FENBANK	04771	FIOLENT	11945	FORT NANAIMO	46802
FAIZI	30130	FENERBAHCE	32150	FIORD	85989	FORT NELSON	46800
FAJAR	58126	FENG BAO	02320	FIORITA	34080	FORT POINT	66750
FAL XI	38339	FENG CAI	14631	FIRAT	07883	FORT POINT	75800
FAL XI	44699	FENG CHENG	81646	FIRAT	15646	FORT ROYAL	08790
FAL XII	38341●	FENG GE	14632	FIRETHORN	91630	FORT ST LOUIS	74800
FAL XII	44701●	FENG GUANG	02322	FIRIZA	47549	FORT STEELE	70157
FALANI	61121	FENG HANG	02320●	FIRMUS	64792	FORT VICTORIA	46792
FALCON	04373	FENG HUANG SHAN	58593	FIRMUS	66772	FORT WALSH	47012
FALCON	00443	FENG HUANG SHAN	60473	FIRST JAY	06648	FORT YALE	46790
FALCON	23910	FENG LANG	02321	FIRYUZA	21563	FORTALEZA	08342
FALCON	82990	FENG MAO	02325	FISKO	82240	FORTHBANK	03672
FALCON ARROW	83130	FENG MING	02326	FIVE BROOKS	84191	FORTHBANK	03732
FALCON EXPRESS	08511	FENG NING	14280	FIVE FLOWERS	85190	FORTITUDE	79090
FALCON REEFER	91740	FENG NING	71744	FIVE ISLANDS	47154	FORTUNA 1	48601
FALCON SEA	48155	FENG NING	81414	FIVE LAKES	36683	'FORTUNE'	58140
FALESHTY	21560	FENG QING	14630	FIVE RIVERS	87690	FORTUNE	64204
FALKE	84933	FENG SHENG	85060	FIVE STAR	57410	FORTUNE	68654
FALKENBERG	79921	FENG TENG	72075	FIVE STREAMS	84193	FORTUNE FALCON	57341●
FALKENSTEIN	73955	FENG YUN	02324	FIZALIA	23444	FORTUNE LEADER	58178
FALKON	59442	FENGLEI	14633	FIZIK KURCHATOV	01579	FORTUNE MARINER	61629
FALKON	60942	FENGTAI	14634	FIZIK LEBEDYEV	31051	FORTUNE STAR	30191
FALLWIND	87331	FENGTAO	14635	FIZIK VAVILOV	31052	FORTUNE VICTORY	25750
FALSTRIA	78780	FENGXIANG	14636	FJALLFOSS	84075	FORTUNESHIP L	56470
FALTICENI	82120	FENGYAN	14637	FJALLFOSS	88270●	FORUM EAGLE	05360
FALTICENI	82400	FENGYANG	14638	FJELL	92331	FORUM EAGLE	15660
FAMILY ANGEL	06950	FENGYI	14639	FJORD	92332	FORUM GRACE	79070
FAMILY ANTHONY	48463	FENGYING	146391	FJORD BRIDGE	77141	FORUM GRACE	89990
FAMILY ARROW	05072	FENGYUN	02327	FJORD BULKER	77132	FORUM HOPE	05363
FAMILY DELTA	05700	FENGZHAN	02328	FJORD LAND	77140●	FORUM HOPE	15663
FAMILY FOTINI	48462	FENICIA EXPRESS	95131	FJORD THISTLE	83064	FORUM PRIDE	72230
FANARI	66020	FENIKS	11654	FJORD THISTLE	83164	FORUM PROGRESS	05365
FANEOS	56638/3	FENIX	12313	FJORD WIND	73025	FORUM PROGRESS	15665
FANG CHENG	81381	FENJA	76190	FJORDAAS	63455	FORUM STAR	59522
FANG XING	44512	FENNIA	19250	FJORDSHELL	73100	FORUM STAR	81202
FANNY	67421	FEODOR OKK	23534	FLAG FORTUNE	56972	FORUM SUN	56751
FANNY	46245●	FEODOSIYA	12245	FLAG SUPPLIER	36280	FORWARDER'	88390
FANNYAN	57331	FEOSO AMBASSADOR	38270	FLAG SUPPLIER	36480	FOSFORICO	84961
FANOMA	27215	FEOSO STAR	37420	FLAG TRADER	75793	FOSHAN	26470
FAR EAST VANGUARD	61631	FER BALEAR	76121	FLAG WILLIAMS	89891	FOSO	56981
FAR STAR	39150	FER BALEAR	79901	FLAMEL	63684	FOTINI	46108
FARAB	21561	FERAX	27580	FLAMENGO	03092	FOTINI	60726
FARADAY	80840	FERDINAND FREILIGRATH	33870	FLAMENGO	50114/1●	FOUR FLAGS II	79790
FARAH 1	32730	FERIAL	13171	FLAMING	71681	FOUR FLAGS II	84700
FARID M	11480	FERIAL	34801	FLAMINGO	11958	FOURKERO II	29100
FARIDA	71941	FERMITA	47631	FLAMINGO	12300	FRAKT	91316●
FARIDPUR	27330	FERNANDO ESCANO	33020	FLAMINGO	27521	FRAMNAS	58460
FARISI	47942	FERNANDOEVERETT	14283	FLAMINGO	61656	FRANCA	06691
FARLAND	73201	FERNANDOEVERETT	71740	FLAMINGO	67190	FRANCE I	20900
FARLAND	76991	FERNANDOEVERETT	81410	FLAMINGO	73931	FRANCE II	20901
FARMER	65380	FERNTEAM	63453	FLAMINGO	84934	FRANCES	62023
FARMSUM	78661	FERNWAVE	60861	FLAMINGO	47020●	FRANCESCA	92955
FARNESE	72142	FERNWAVE	70901	FLAMINGO II	33970	FRANCESCA	95165
FARNESE	76482	FERO CADIZ	48831	FLAMINIA	33476	FRANCESCO F	78483
FAST CARRIER	76971	FERRING	74345	FLAVIAN	09310	FRANCESCO NULLO	10570
FAST CARRIER	81822	FERRUCCIO	72520	FLEESENSEE	46381	FRANCESCO NULLO	15340
FAST CARRIER	82072	FERRY FUKUE	20400	FLEESENSEE	47081	FRANCIS GARNIER	84261
FAST CARRIER	89781	FERRY GOLD	32450	FLEET WAVE	03760●	FRANCISCO DE MIRANDA	09351
FAST TRADER	72740	FERRY HANKYU	19710	FLENSAU	64980	FRANCISCO DE MIRANDA	33421
FAST TRADER	73700	FERRY KANPU	19711	FLEUR	59752	FRANCISCO I MADERO	69992
FASTNET ROCK	76152	FERRY KOGANE MARU	33300	FLEVOLAND	05454	FRANCISCO I MADERO	86482
FASTOV	17830	FERRY KOGANE MARU	34990	FLIEGERSKOSMONAUT DER DDR SIGMUND JAHN	61409/9	FRANCISCO J MUGICA	70045
FAT CHOY	47811●	FERRY PEARL	32451	FLINDERS BAY	77053	FRANCISKA SCHULTE	81760
FATEZH	17831	FERRY PUKWAN	32230●	FLORA	39560	FRANCISZEK ZUBRZYCKI	14480
FATHER PANOS	60260	FESTIVALE	16780	FLORA C	47930	FRANCO PIERACCINI	45180
FAUNA	48600	FESTOS	20160	FLORA II	21441	FRANCOIS VENTURE	73189/1
FAUREI	47545	FETHIYE	81103	FLORENCE	37790	FRANCOIS VILLON	51782●
FAVORITA	58133	FETISH	84013	FLORENCE	62030	FRANK	76209/6●
FAVORITA	78425	FFM MATARENGI	86421	FLORENCE SCHRODER	62085	FRANK DELMAS	62130
FAWZIA	24291	FICHTELBERG	94491	FLORENTIA	29010	FRANK M	90130
FAYROUZ	89190	FIDES	75740	FLORENZ	59740	FRANK NIBBE	76209/7●
FAYZABAD	21562	FIDES	77110	FLORES	47941	FRANK PAIS	57782
FEANG	83715	FIENI	47562	FLORES	56920	FRANK SCHRODER	62086
FEATHER	41020	FIERBINTI	47542	FLORESHTY	17832	FRANKA	81821
		FIESTA 1	78470	FLORIA	59472	FRANKA	82071
		FIFTH AVENUE	61151	FLORIAN	39590	FRANKFURT EXPRESS	08455
		FIGARO	94817	FLORIANA	09912	FRANKFURT EXPRESS	74860

Name	No.
FRANKFURT/ODER	04922
FRANTS BOGUSH	05639
FRANTS BOGUSH	14468
FRANZ STENZER	15100
FRANZ XAVER KOGEL	62102
FRASINET	47558
FRAT 1	73660
FRATERNIA	74170
FRATERNITY	06751
FRAUDEN	75294
FRAUDEN	88108
FRAUKE CATHARINA	73803
FRECCIA BLU	76730
FRECCIA DEL NORD	08901
FRECCIA DEL NORD	17291
FRECCIA DELL'OUEST	08900
FRECCIA DELL'OUEST	17290
FRECCIA ROSSA	76731
FRED EVERARD	75450
FRED H BILLUPS	82210
FREDENHAGEN	72860
FREDERIC JOLIOT CURIE	34961
FREDERICK CARTER	32930
FREDERICK LYKES	05581
FREDERICK LYKES	14422
FREDERICK LYKES	14892
FREDERIK ZHOLIO-KYURI	01563
FREDERIQUE LEONIE	83609
FREE ENTERPRISE III	20230
FREE ENTERPRISE IV	20190
FREE ENTERPRISE V	20191
FREE ENTERPRISE VI	20192
FREE ENTERPRISE VII	20200
FREE ENTERPRISE VIII	20201
FREE WAVE	60254
FREEDOM	54662●
FREEDOM 1	86953
FREEDOM A S	06539/2
FREEPORT EXPRESS	32070●
FREESIA	69150
FREEZER ACE	05468
FREEZER KING	05460
FREEZER LEVA	80980
FREEZER LEVA	81700
FREEZER PRINCE	05461●
FREEZER QUEEN	05462●
FREGATA	12557
FREIGHTLINE ONE	76970●
FREIGHTLINE ONE	89780●
FREITAL	61711
FREJ	33001
FRELLSEN HILLE	90973
FRENGENFJORD	94725
FREO ZUTA	80970
FREO ZUTA	87040
FREYBURG	03875
FREYBURG	04425/1
FRIDAY	80630
FRIDRICH ENGELS	17510
FRIDRIKH TSANDER	59899
FRIDRIKH TSANDER	67659
FRIEDRICH ENGELS	03151
FRIEDRICH ENGELS	05637
FRIEDRICH ENGELS	14466
FRIEDRICH WOLF	12632
FRIENDSHIP	49220
FRIENDSHIP	81781
FRIENDSHIP L	56472
FRIESENSTEIN	04545
FRIESLAND	64410
FRIGO AFRICA	49022
FRIGO AMERICA	49021
FRIGO ASIA	49023
FRIGO ESPANA	49024
FRIGO EUROPA	49025
FRIGO H	42060
FRIGO ISABEL	87500
FRIGO LAS PALMAS	49027
FRIGO MURAT	72890
FRIGO MURAT	76940
FRIGO OCEANIA	49026
FRIGO TENERIFE	49028
FRIGOANTARTICO	34204
FRIGORA	74221
FRIGORA	88161
FRIJSENBORG	47131
FRIMARO	89150
FRIMARO	91680
FRINTON	60100
FRIO AEGEAN	06290
FRIO CARIBIC	60031●
FRIO CARIBIC	68361●
FRIO CARIBIC	71971●
FRIO DOLPHIN	87400
FRIO POSEIDON	86612
FRISIAN EXPRESS	40361
FRISIAN TRADER	67070
FRISIAN TRADER	82170
FRITHJOF	34060
FRITSIS GAYLIS	75324
FRITSIS GAYLIS	75324
FRITSIS ROSIN	75330
FRITZ HECKERT	33330
FRITZ HECKERT	62685
FRITZ REUTER	34331
FROLOVO	17833
FRONISIS	60101
FROSSO K	06493
FROTA MARABA	49662●
FROTA MARABA	50932●
FROTABRASIL	47655
FROTACHILE	47656
FROTADURBAN	04810
FROTAKOBE	04812
FROTAMANILA	04813
FROTAMARABA	49662●
FROTAMARABA	50932●
FROTAMERICA	47654
FROTARGENTINA	47657
FROTARIO	03093
FROTASANTOS	03094
FROTASINGAPORE	04811
FROTAURUGUAY	47658
FRUCUBA	72960
FRUCUBA	87160
FRUITION	47224
FRUNZANESTI	47557
FRUNZE	39980
FRYANOVO	21564
FRYAZINO	17834
FRYCZ MODRZEWSKI	04862
FRYDERYK CHOPIN	93874
FU CHOU No 651	86096
FU CHUNG JIANG	15023
FU JIN HAI	56881
FU PING	62081
FU PING	62441
FU SHUN CHENG	67230
FU SHUN CHENG	91650
FUERTE VENTURA	77600
FUJI	16210
FUJI	35090
FUJI	95080
FUJI REEFER	05190
FUJIKAWA MARU	67850
FULDA EXPRESS	79302
FULDATAL	33200
FULTON II	68900
FUNCHAL	09470
FUNDADOR	87620
FUNDULEA	47567
FURAMA	06992
FURSTENWALDE	46376
FURSTENWALDE	47076
FUSHIMI MARU	04570
FUSO MARU	04571
FUTAMI MARU	04540
FUTURE	70720
FUTURE	79720
FUTURE HOPE	06604
FUZLAAN	87171
FYLRIX	87980
FYLYPPA	60993
FYN	17461
FYODOR YEROZIDI	13754/12

G

Name	No.
G A WALKER	70150
GABBIANO	18460
GABRIEL DA FONSECA	38450
GABRIELE	81880
GABRIELLA	72761
GABRIELLA	89600
GABRIELLA C	43560
GABROVO	29012
GABY	51950
GABY	75700
GADA	46244
GADILA	53581
GADILA	53731
GADINIA	53580
GADINIA	53730
GAE CHEOG	92540
'GAE YANG'	94870
GAELIC FERRY	23332
GAFREDO	06291
GAIETY	02610
GAIETY	04330
GALASSIA	54013
GALASSIA	80773
GALATA	84210
GALATEE	61409
GALATI	17660
GALATI	39670
GALATIA	27050
GALAXIAS	16600
GALAXY II	31800
GALCOAST	86920
GALDOR	13751/7
GALEA	47990
GALENE	77001
GALENE	79971
GALEONA	03222
GALEONA	03892
GALERIE	58020
GALIA	75274
GALIFAN BATARSHIN	12428
GALILA	46290
GALILA	48700
GALILEO	01760●
GALILEO GALILEI	01760
GALILEO GALILEI	06501
GALINI	64580
GALINI	69210
GALINI	86760
GALIOLA	18530
GALION	79965
GALLANT	88115
GALLANTRY	60180
GALLEON CORAL	14811
GALLIC FJORD	48752
GALLIC FJORD	75572
GALLOWAY EXPRESS	80690
GALLOWAY EXPRESS	84490
GALLOWAY PRINCESS	19466
GALLURA	32180
GALPARA	58077
GALS	23869/1●
GALSTREAM	87694
GALVYE	66382
GALYA KOMLEVA	15513
GAMA GETAH	14140
GAMA GETAH	80860
GAMA KASIA	14141
GAMA KASIA	80861
GAMA PALA	14142
GAMA PALA	80862
GAMA ROBUSTA	14143
GAMA ROBUSTA	80863
GAMBADA	58070
GAMBADA	62390
GAMBELA	00420
GAMBHIRA	53280
GAMBIA RIVER	46905●
GAMBIA RIVER	83341●
GAMBOMA	42880
GAMID SULTANOV	20324
GAMZAT TSADASA	09995
GAN JIANG	51551
GAN QUAN	63730
GAN QUAN	72900
GANDA PERKASA	61409/1
GANGUT	11773
GANGUT	34664
GANN	18100
GANVIE	66891
GANVIE	82031
GAO HU	60722
GAO SHAN	15950
GAOPENG	04980
GARA DJEBILET	89721
GARALA	58078
GARBETA	53105
GARBIS	65831
GARBIS	69491
GARCILASO	07940
GARDAZEE	75562
GARDEN GREEN	68103
GARDEN MOON	77804
GARDENIA	61073/1
GARDENIA	71263/1
GARDENIA	74002
GARDENIA B	84192
GAREFOWL	61992
GARGI	58800
GARGI	65410
GARGOYLE EXPRESS	73732
GARI	53582
GARI	53732
GARIFALIA C	02730
GARINDA	58075
GARNATA	16951
GARNELA	23452
GARNES	50121
GARNET	01090
GAROUFALIA	46540
GARPUNER ZARVA	13751/12
GARPUNNER PROKOPYENKO	13670
GARRISON POINT	73560
GARWOLIN	03233
GARWOLIN	03623
GARYOUNIS	32590
GARYVILLE	63320
GARYVILLE	68240
GARZA OCEAN	61473
GARZAN	35741
GAS AL-AHMADI	54042
GAS AL-BURGAN	54043
GAS AL-KUWAIT	54044
GAS AL-MINAGISH	54045
GAS DIANA	53951
GAS DIANA	54001
GAS ENTERPRISE	54041
GAS FOUNTAIN	54900
GAS FUEGUINO	64690
GAS GEMINI	53952
GAS GEMINI	54002
GAS GLORIA	56450
GAS GLORIA	60010
GAS PILOT	57680
GAS RISING SUN	55640
GAS RISING SUN	55840
GAS VENTURE	90790●
GASTOR	53890
GASTRANA	53583
GASTRANA	53733
GATTAN	11788/2
GATTAN	34675
GAUCHO CRUZ	78803
GAUCHO CRUZ	89963
GAUGUIN	48404
GAVANA	18270
GAVESHANI	39100
GAVILAN	66850
GAVIOTA	61717
GAVRIIL DERZHAVIN	14382
GAVRIL SARITCHEV	22189
GAVRILL KIRDISHCHEV	78061
GAY FIDELITY	26650
GAY FORTUNE	15360
GAZ ATLANTIC	85650
GAZ CHANNEL	62421
GAZ MED	56172
GAZ NORDSEE	58486
GAZ PACIFIC	58487
GAZ PIONEER	56170
GAZ PROGRESS	60890
GAZ PROGRESS	71770
GAZ PROGRESS	81133
GAZ UNITY	56171
GAZANA	58071
GAZANA	62391
GAZGAN	13755/7
GAZI OSMAN PASA	34580
GAZIANTEP	67800
GAZLI	79429
GAZZELLA	03990
GDANSK	36868
GDOV	23520
GDOV	86183
GDYNIA	36864
GDYNIA II	15082
GDYNSKI KOSYNIER	07461
GDYNSKI KOSYNIER	10757
GEBE OLDENDORFF	82340
GEDAREF	51424
GEDIZ	07884
GEDIZ	15647
GEDSER	17280
GEESTBAY	03545
GEESTLAND	03262
GEESTPORT	03546
GEESTSTAR	03263
GEFEST	13669
GEHAN AL SADAT	59485
GEHAN AL SADAT II	59486
GEIZER	09361
GEKKO MARU	63361
GELA	00090
GELENDZHIK	40009
GELENDZHIK	84337
GELIGA	40250
GELIOGRAF	11836
GELTING	19140
GELTING SYD	20380
GEM	91280
GEM CARRIERS	31141
GEM TRANSPORTER	56280
GEMA	21490
GEMA	34320
GEMAR	26040
GEMINI	11674
GEMINI	31570
GEMINI IV	70826
GEMLIK	15811
GEN M MAKLEFF	53850
GEN. M. MAKLEFF	79690
GENCLIK	30660
GENERAL A F CEBESOY	05641
GENERAL A F CEBESOY	14470
GENERAL AGUINALDO	47665
GENERAL ASLANOV	53161
GENERAL BABAYAN	53162
GENERAL BAGRATION	59897
GENERAL BAGRATION	67657
GENERAL BEM	78981
GENERAL BOCHAROV	60641
GENERAL BOCHAROV	62601
GENERAL CAPINPIN	61320
GENERAL CHERNIAKOVSKI	17512
GENERAL CHERNYAKHOVSKIY	13744
GENERAL DABROWSKI	48157/3●
GENERAL DE MIRANDA	03137
GENERAL DE MIRANDA	03347
GENERAL FR KLEEBERG	54972
GENERAL GORBATOV	80054
GENERAL GUISAN	77563
GENERAL JASINSKI	78982
GENERAL K ORBAY	05642
GENERAL K ORBAY	14471
GENERAL KARBYSHEV	60630
GENERAL KARBYSHEV	62590
GENERAL KLEEBERG	71812
GENERAL KRAVTSOV	60642
GENERAL KRAVTSOV	62602
GENERAL LESELIDZE	60901
GENERAL LESELIDZE	79231
GENERAL LIM	59461
GENERAL LUNA	59451
GENERAL M MAKLEFF	53850
GENERAL M MAKLEFF	79690
GENERAL MADALINSKI	78983
GENERAL MALVAR	59450
GENERAL MANUEL BELGRANO	06678
GENERAL MASCARDO	46317
GENERAL MASCARDO	46567
GENERAL MERKVILADZE	67681
GENERAL OSTRYAKOV	13671
GENERAL PAEZ	26000
GENERAL PRADZYNSKI	78984
GENERAL R GUMUSBALA	05643
GENERAL R GUMUSBALA	14472
GENERAL RACHIMOW	11649
GENERAL RODIMTSYEV	00148
GENERAL SHKODUNOVICH	60643
GENERAL SHKODUNOVICH	62603
GENERAL STANISLAW POPLAWSKI	14487
GENERAL SWIERCZEWSKI	78980
GENERAL TINIO	46310●
GENERAL TINIO	46560●
GENERAL VLADIMIR ZAIMOV	03958
GENERAL VLADIMIR ZAIMOV	79642
GENERAL Z DOGAN	05644
GENERAL Z DOGAN	14473
GENERAL ZHDANOV	60625
GENERAL ZHDANOV	62585
GENEVE	25930
GENEVE	72630
GENEVE	77390
GENEVIEVE LYKES	05582
GENEVIEVE LYKES	14423
GENEVIEVE LYKES	14893
GENIE	07050
GENNARGENTU	16570

Name	No.	Name	No.	Name	No.	Name	No.
GENOVA	22492	GEROITE NA SEVASTOPOL	93670	GLOBTIK TOKYO	57970	GOLDEN SEA	06353
GENRIK GASANOV	59882	GERONA	67633	GLOBTIK TOKYO	63330	GOLDEN SEASON	24861
GENTILE DA FABRIANO	02390	GEROY MEKHTI	79379	GLOBUS	13746	GOLDEN SHIMIZU	61164
GEODRILL	80760	GEROY MEKHTI	79381	GLOGOW	31181	GOLDEN SOURCE	44041
GEOKCHAY	50774	GEROYEVKA	13751/11	GLOMAR EXPLORER	92320	GOLDEN SPEAR	61168
GEOPOTES 12	37363	GERRINGONG	77090	GLORIA ELENA	52303	GOLDEN STAR	27760
GEOPOTES VI	41550	GERT STAERKE	64817/1	GLORIA L	01470●	GOLDEN STAR	61085
GEOPOTES VII	43590	GERTRUD JACOB	71411	GLORIA PEAK	46051	GOLDEN STAR	71275
GEOPOTES IX	41820	GEVISA	76600	GLORIANA	88580	GOLDEN STATE	52360
GEORG BUCHNER	00650	GEVISA	89300	GLORIC	53151	GOLDEN SUNRAY	63940
GEORG HANDKE	15674	GEYA	13751/9	GLORIC	66301	GOLDEN SUNRAY	71590
GEORG KURZ	53412	GEZIENA	75520	GLORIOUS ACE	94535	GOLDEN SWORD	61169
GEORG KURZ	64942	GHADAMES	60950	GLORY	64205	GOLDEN TAIF	15255
GEORG OTS	20353	GHADAMES	91831	GLORY	68655	GOLDEN TENNYO	61160
GEORG SCHUMANN	06388	GHAT	93936	GLORY OCEAN	57625	GOLDEN TRADER	47951
GEORG SCHUMANN	15417	GHAWDEX	19380	GLORY OCEAN	61045	GOLDEN TULIP	63111
GEORG WEERTH	33871	GHAZI-B	88950	GLORY STAR	52363	GOLDEN VENTURE	67280
GEORGE	82995	GHENT	72633	GLUKHOV	86238	GOLDEN VERGINA	32430
GEORGE F	28510	GHENT	77393	GLYFADA	55966	GOLDEN WAVE	81110
GEORGE F	30320	GHEORGHIENI 9-10-90	82124	GLYFADA	56726	GOLDEN WAVE	90550
GEORGE GEORGIU-DEZH	36872	GHEORGHIENI	82404	GLYFADA BREEZE	57150	GOLDEN WONDER	39720
GEORGE H WEYERHAUSER	53060	GHIKAS	58576	GLYFADA FAITH	46333	GOLDEN YENBO	31443
GEORGE L	46698●	GIAMAICA	51520	GLYFADA MIMI	61820	GOLDEN YENBO	31612
GEORGE M KELLER	63910	GIANNAKIS	40960	GLYFADA SUN	48120	GOLEMI	05210
GEORGE S EMBIRICOS	57002	GIANNIS DIMAKIS II	84528	GMC-3-WALEED	85621	GOLENIOW	75415
GEORGE WYTHE	01054	GIANNIS DIMAKIS III	76560	GNEVNYY	13755/10	GOLF	72117
GEORGE Z	65930	GIANNIS DIMAKIS III	82250	GNIEZNO II	50464	GOLFO DE BATABANO	06303
GEORGES VIELJEUX	05123	GIANNIS M	06590	GODAFOSS	83511	GOLFO DE GUACANAYBO	06304
GEORGES VIELJEUX	59872	GIANNIS MALLIS	84529	GOGO RAHN	41201	GOLFO DE GUANAHACABIBES	06305
GEORGI BENKOVSKI	67311	GIANNIS N	69910	GOGO RAHN	70053	GOLFO DI PALERMO	54090
GEORGI DIMITROV	01980	GIANNIS XILAS	06490	GOGO RAMBLER	70052	GOLFO PARADISO	15060
GEORGI KIRKOV	20736	GIANT	82080	GOGO RANGER	62640	GOLFSTRIM	11306
GEORGIA	64143	GIANT KIM	50600	GOGO RANGER	82200	GOLIATH	52060
GEORGIA	93910	GIANT KIM	52350	GOGO REGAL	65720	GOLIATH	92790
GEORGIA F	24870	GIANT TREASURE	45882	GOGO REGAL	75660	GOMASA	61060
GEORGIA P	69100	GIBEAGLE	65100	GOGOL	17513	GOMEL	86178
GEORGIAN GLORY	49190	GIBRALTAR	63161	GOHO MARU	71435	GONCALO	57524
GEORGIAN GLORY	52790	GIBRALTAR PANSY	77223	GOKTURK	63260	GONCHAROV	12592
GEORGIOS	29180	GIDROLOG	23861	GOLAR FREEZE	54081	GONG NONG BING 3	23370
GEORGIOS	38230	GIL EANES	23920	GOLAR FREEZE	72211	GONG NONG BING No 10	18110
GEORGIOS	44720	GILBERT J FOWLER	22690	GOLAR FROST	55644	GONG NONG BING No 11	18111
GEORGIOS	58530	GILLIAN EVERARD	89840	GOLAR FROST	55844	GONG NONG BING No 14	18120
GEORGIOS 1	87610●	GILLWATER	03380●	GOLAR KANSAI	63853	GONG NONG BING No 15	18121
GEORGIOS A	21870	GILLWATER	04050●	GOLAR KANTO	63852	GONG NONG BING No 16	18122
GEORGIOS A	41380	GIMI	53882	GOLAR ROBIN	63851	GONG NONG BING 17	23870
GEORGIOS B	20030	GIMONE	66480	GOLD ALISA	51270	GONG NONG BONG 18	20690
GEORGIOS EXPRESS	20050	GIMONE	85660	GOLD BEETLE	07282	GONG NONG BONG 19	20691
GEORGIOS F	46526	GINA	24271	GOLD BOND CONVEYOR	79260	GONZALEZ LINES	10275
GEORGIOS F	83306	GINA JULIANO	46030	GOLD BOND TRAILBLAZER	79261	GONZALEZ LINES	15185
GEORGIOS G II	39611	GINGER	62029	GOLD CLOUD	80320	GOOD BREEZE	07016
GEORGIOS M	25271	GINI	77950	GOLD CLOUD	80390	GOOD CHAMPION	71490
GEORGIOS M	60158/1	GIOACCHINO LAURO	59432	GOLD HILLA	51271	GOOD DOLPHIN	06504
GEORGIOS M II	43860	GIORDANO BRUNO	38580	GOLD MARINE	61625	GOOD ENDEAVOUR	77461
GEORGIOS S	39900	GIORGIONE	37830●	GOLD MOUNTAIN	13301	GOOD FAITH	06605
GEORGIOS S	40220	GIORGIONE	44420●	GOLD ORLI	51272	GOOD FRIEND	58120
GEORGIOS T	89227/1	GIORGIS	06533	GOLD STATE	61612	GOOD HARVEST	71491
GEORGIOS T KOROPOULIS	79780	GIORGOS K	72051	GOLD STREAM	13300	GOOD HERALD 1	08020
GEORGIOS TSAKIROGLOU	56872	GIOTTO	19381	GOLD VARDA	51273	GOOD HERALD 1	72100
GEORGIOS V	37570	GIOVANNI C	43530	GOLDEAN ENTERPRISE	73171	GOOD HORIZON	73220
GEORGIOS VERGOTTIS	38440	GISELLE	56260	GOLDEAN ENTERPRISE	77721	GOOD HORIZON	77690
GEORGIOS XYLAS	46670	GISSAR	13755/9	GOLDEN ABIDJAN	51550	GOOD LEADER	72280
GEORGIOS Z	49920	GIULIANA 1	65420	GOLDEN AMMAN	59757●	GOOD LEADER	77180
GEORGIOS Z	50620	GIURGENI	47571/1●	GOLDEN ARROW	63470	GOOD LION	07015
GEORGIS A GEORGILIS	46910	GIURGIU	47568●	GOLDEN BEAR	01151	GOOD LORD	06506
GEORGIS GERONTAS	46601	GIURGU	47568	GOLDEN BENIN	62080	GOOD LUCK	86890
GEORGIS PROIS	57008	GIUSEPPE DI VITTORIO	05624	GOLDEN BENIN	62440	GOOD LUCK	90820
GEORGIY CHICHERIN	05621	GIUSEPPE DI VITTORIO	14454	GOLDEN CAMEROON	58605	GOOD MASTER	31530
GEORGIY CHICHERIN	14451	GIUSEPPE GARIBALDI	36940	GOLDEN CAMEROON	60495	GOOD MOTHER	79220
GEORGIY DIMITROV	05622	GIUSEPPE VERDI	60500	GOLDEN CANARY	70056	GOOD NEWS	63421
GEORGIY DMITROV	14452	GIZHIGA	12578	GOLDEN CAPE	70057	GOOD OCEAN	47350
GEORGIY LEONIDZE	60900	GIZHIGA	21612	GOLDEN CHALLENGER	47952	GOOD PATRIOT	06507
GEORGIY LEONIDZE	79230	GIZHIGA	34101	GOLDEN CHARIOT	61166	GOOD SKIPPER	13440
GEORGIY MAKSIMOV	39174	GJERTRUD MAERSK	66181	GOLDEN CHASE	61161	GOOD SPIRIT	07032
GEORGIY PYASETSKIY	80266/1●	GJERTRUD MAERSK	67731	GOLDEN CITY	07671	GOOD SUN	06505
GEORGIY SEDOV	22241	GLACHAU	61409/12	GOLDEN CLOVER	63110	GOOD TARGET	73221
GEORGIY USHAKOV	02272	GLACIAR AMEGHINO	02844	GOLDEN CROWN	61167	GOOD TARGET	77691
GEORGIY VASILIEV	15121	GLACIAR PERITO MORENO	02845	GOLDEN DAISY	54650	GOOD WARRIOR	25704
GEORGY	06910	GLACIAR VIEDMA	02846	GOLDEN DAISY	55071	GOOD WIND	57510
GEORTINA	61024	GLACIER BAY	63411	GOLDEN DAY	53980	GOOD WIND	62000
GEORTINA	71184	GLADIATOR	79060	GOLDEN DAY	78490	GOOD YEAR	80680
GERAKL	11946	GLADONIA	88002	GOLDEN DOLPHIN	01120	GOOILAND	34940
GERANTA	64573	GLAFKI	70700	GOLDEN DRAGON	31591	GOONZARAN	68150
GERARD L-D	83148	GLAFKOS	57187	GOLDEN DRAGON	61078	GOPLANA	87741
GERD MAERSK	51681	GLAFKOS	91271●	GOLDEN DRAGON	71268	GORAN KOVACIC	05655
GERDT OLDENDORFF	71843	GLARIOS	82190	GOLDEN DRAGON No 1	95000	GORANKA	10311
GERHARD	63656	GLAROS	28820	GOLDEN EASTERN	44040	GORECHJE	12246
GERHARD PRAHM	72126	GLARUS	11959	GOLDEN ENTERPRISE 1	71506	GORETS	76505
GERHART HAUPTMANN	34214	GLASGOW	06649	GOLDEN FALCON	37411	GORGEOUS	80706
GERINA	65151	GLEB KRZHIZHANOVSKIY	03775	GOLDEN FLAG	72440	GORGO	26850
GERINGSWALDE	46374	GLEB KRZHIZHANOVSKIY	04015	GOLDEN FLAG	77130	GORGONA	71551
GERINGSWALDE	47074	GLEB SEDIN	75331	GOLDEN GATE	08510	GORGULHO	76602
GERMA FONDAL	51781	GLEB USPENSKIY	12363	GOLDEN GATE BRIDGE	08730	GORGULHO	89302
GERMA FONDAL	74001	GLENCOE	42660	GOLDEN GHANA	58602	GORI	60623
GERMA FOREST	51782	GLETCHER	09362	GOLDEN GLOBE	25480	GORI	62583
GERMA FRAM	51783	GLIWICE II	61096	GOLDEN GLORY	01121	GORIZONT	34711
GERMA KARMA	74000	GLOBAL	53392	GOLDEN GRAMPUS	48949/4	GORIZONT	23869/7●
GERMA LIONEL	51785	GLOBAL	80342	GOLDEN HARVEST	61644	GORJ	47556
GERMA TARA	51780	GLOBAL CHALLENGER	83987	GOLDEN HAVEN	10624●	GORKOVSKAYA KOMSOMOLIYA	49242
GERMIK	38721	GLOBAL E SUN	77561	GOLDEN HAVEN	15374●	GORKOVSKAYA KOMSOMOLIYA	49242
GEROI ADZHIMUSHKAYA	07473	GLOBAL HOPE	77675	GOLDEN HILL	46140	GORKY	35318
GEROI ADZHIMUSHKAYA	11837	GLOBAL MED	26010	GOLDEN HORIZON	61162	GORKY LENINSKOYE	79407
GEROI BRESTA	36875	GLOBAL PEACE	54562	GOLDEN HORSE	34870	GORLICE	31182
GEROI PANFILOVTSY	48441	GLOBAL PEACE	54962	GOLDEN LAUREL	77870	GORLITZ	78730
GEROI PANFILOVTSY	49481	GLOBAL STAR	46353	GOLDEN LOTUS	47152	GORLITZ	89980
GEROI PANFILOVTSY	49751	GLOBAL STAR	46923	GOLDEN MED	59480	GORNO-ALTAYSK	15465
GEROI PLEVNY	31152	GLOBAL SUN	55201	GOLDEN NIGERIA	07341	GORNOPRAVDINSK	70023
GEROI PLEVNY	93672	GLOBAL SUNSHINE	78681	GOLDEN ODYSSEY	16520	GORNOZAVODSK	84338
GEROI SHIPKI	31153	GLOBE EMPRESS	70090	GOLDEN ODYSSEY	17610	GORNY SLASK	75732
GEROI SHIPKI	93673	GLOBE NOVA	60560	GOLDEN ORCHID	47153	GORNY SLASK	88382
GEROI ZAPOLYARYA	11741	GLOBE NOVA	70240	GOLDEN PANAGIA	61163	GORNYAK	49246
GEROI ZAPOLYARYA	34631	GLOBE TRADER	06606	GOLDEN POLYDINAMOS	47953	GORNYAK	49246
GEROITE NA ODESSA	31151	GLOBTIK BRITAIN	56475	GOLDEN PRINCESS	12700	GORODETSKIY	17927
GEROITE NA ODESSA	93671	GLOBTIK LONDON	57971	GOLDEN RIO	47659/2	GOROKHOVETS	75353
GEROITE NA SEVASTOPOL	31150	GLOBTIK LONDON	63331	GOLDEN SAUDIA	13580	GORTYS	55786

Name	No.
HORTA BARBOSA	64131
HORYU MARU	36600
HOSHO MARU	77202
HOSS M	84527/1
HOUNSLOW	40321
HOUSTON ACCORD	68756
HOUSTON GETTY	64362
HOVE	49881
HOWARD STAR	78671
HOWARD W BELL	63911
HOWELL LYKES	05583
HOWELL LYKES	14424
HOWELL LYKES	14894
HOYU MARU	61480
HRELJIN	74440
HRVATSKA	15286
HSIEH YUNG	62270
HSIEN YUAN	64201
HSIEN YUAN	68651
HSIN LUNG	92716
HTAN TAW YWA	80620
HTAN TAW YWA	81970
HU JIU LAO 5	30333
HU PO HAI	46007
HUA AN	90641
HUA AN	81391●
HUA DU	29520●
HUA HAI	56850
HUA HONG	35905
HUA HONG	41595
HUA LI	49284●
HUA SHAN	00290
HUA SHENG	46360
HUA TAI	35903
HUA TAI	41593
HUA TONG HAI	76986
HUA XING	44511
HUA YANG	35904
HUA YANG	41594
HUA YIN	62100
HUA YING	46280
HUA YUAN KOU	93312
HUAI AN	41326
HUAI HAI	74870
HUAI HAI	78920
HUAI YIN	13120
HUAL ANGELITA	94824
HUAL INGRITA	94825
HUAL LISITA	94826
HUAL ROLITA	94827
HUAL TORINITA	94082
HUAL TRACER	94812
HUAL TRAPPER	94813
HUAN JIANG	63687
HUANG HAI	74871
HUANG HAI	78921
HUANG JIN SHAN	12900
HUANG LONG SHAN	04661
HUANG PU JIANG	15022
HUATING	05372
HUDAIBAH	11370
HUDSON	02190
HUDSON	66341
HUDSON DEEP	61011
HUDSON DEEP	71171
HUEY AN	61409/7●
HUGHEVERETT	04752
HUGO	69870
HUGO BRINKMAN	75506
HUGO OLDENDORFF	71842
HUI JIU 101	34401
HUI QUAN	02570
HUI YANG	14639/2
HULIN	06030
HUMANIST	47771
HUMANITAS	53120
HUMBAK	23455
HUMBER ARM	51700
HUMBER ARM	52290
HUMBER RIVER	04281
HUMBERGATE	89030
HUMBOLDT	59160
HUMBOLDT	66510
HUMBOLDT REX	04741
HUMBOLT	52461
HUNAUDIERES	52308
HUNAUDIERES	77126
HUNEDOARA	78582
HUNG MING	61552
HUNG MING	72042
HUNGARI	91719
HUNGARIA	86119
HUNJIANG	05319
HUSI	47570
HUSTLER FAL	73883
HUSTLER FAL	87263
HUSTLER INDUS	73886
HUSTLER INDUS	87266
HUSUM	73672
HUTA KATOWICE	76985
HUTA LENINA	76984
HUTA ZGODA	78290
HUTA ZGODA	80020
HUTA ZYGMUNT	80021
HUTA ZYGMUNT	78291
HVALVIK	82804
HVALVIK	92094
HVASSAFELL	50800
HVASSAFELL	52610
HWA GEK	07120
HWAPYUNG ACE	91928
HWAPYUNG BUSAN	86150
HWAPYUNG JINJU	86133
HYANG SAN	25705
HYBUR CLIPPER	73885
HYBUR CLIPPER	87265
HYBUR INTREPID	73888
HYBUR INTREPID	87268
HYBUR STAR	88170
HYDERABAD	52866
HYDROLOCK	72384
HYDROMOS	61192
HYE MENG 1	83610
HYOGO MARU	09550
HYOGO MARU	33313
HYOGO MARU	77360
HYOK SIN	07100

I

Name	No.
I D SINCLAIR	68942
IALOMITA	11973
IAPETOS	55170
IASI	41315
IASON	05473
IBARAKI MARU	77203
IBERIA	51040
IBERIA	52890
IBN ABDOUN	46770
IBN AL-ATHEER	49381
IBN AL-ATHEER	50941
IBN ALBANNA	58971
IBN ALBANNA	65171
IBN ALBEITAR	49384
IBN ALBEITAR	50944
IBN AL-MOATAZ	49383
IBN AL-MOATHAZ	50943
IBN AL-NAFEES	49414
IBN AL-NAFEES	50974
IBN ASAKIR	49385
IBN ASAKIR	50945
IBN BADIS	64961
IBN BAJJAH	46772
IBN BASSAM	49386
IBN BASSAM	50946
IBN BATOUTA	64962
IBN BATTOTAH	49387
IBN BATTOTAH	50947
IBN DURAID	49388
IBN DURAID	50948
IBN HAYYAN	49389
IBN HAYYAN	50949
IBN HAZM	46773
IBN JUBAIR	65000
IBN JUBAIR	85230
IBN JUBAYR	46776
IBN KHALDOON	33591
IBN KHALDOON	49390
IBN KHALDOON	50950
IBN KHALDOUN	64969
IBN KHALLIKAN	49391
IBN KHALLIKAN	50951
IBN KORRA	65001
IBN KORRA	85231
IBN MALIK	49392
IBN MALIK	50952
IBN OTMAN	58972
IBN OTMAN	65172
IBN QUTAIBAH	49393
IBN QUTAIBAH	50953
IBN ROCHD	58970
IBN ROCHD	64960
IBN ROCHD	65170
IBN RUSHD	49394
IBN RUSHD	50954
IBN SHUHAID	49380
IBN SHUHAID	50940
IBN SINA	46774
IBN SINA	58973
IBN SINA	65173
IBN SINA II	64970
IBN SIRAJ	46963
IBN TUFAIL	49395
IBN TUFAIL	50955
IBN YOUNUS	49396
IBN YOUNUS	50956
IBN ZUHR	46775
ICE EXPRESS	51345
ICE STAR	49980
ICELAND	34207
ICELANDIC	52695
ICHA	18310
ICHA	21401
ICHA	86005
IDA 1	47342
IDA HELENE	58861
IDA HELENE	65741
IDEAL	03360
IERANTO	66774
IERANTO	64794
IERONIM UBOREVICH	93692
IEZER	11677
IFFCO 1	84250
IFNI	34217
IGARKA	02728/1
IGARKALES	45682
IGLOO FINN	53135
IGLOO NORSE	53136
IGLOO POLAR	53137
IGNACIO AGRAMONTE	06613
IGNATIY SERGEYEV	05620
IGNATIY SERGEYEV	14450
IGOR GRABAR	76587
IGOR GRABAR	79937
IGRIM	70033
IJSSELMEER	75530●
IJZER	23360
IKAGURI	58682
IKAN	12761
IKAN BAWAL	73377
IKAN BILIS	73360
IKAN TAMBAN	60190
IKAN TONGKOL	77195
IKARIA	31370
IKARIAN REEFER	18301
IKAROS	19580
IKHNATON	01417
IKHNATON	01677
IKHTIANDR	12586
IKTINOS	05474
IKUYO MARU	56390
IKUYO MARU	67920
ILDE	59611●
ILDE	71921●
ILE DE BATZ	73734
ILE DE LA MARTINIQUE	28881
ILE DE LA REUNION	48400
ILE MAURICE	48401
ILEIGH	91310
ILHA DE KOMO	67496
ILHA DE SAO MIGUEL	66900
ILHA DE SAO MIGUEL	91470
ILIA	41327
ILICHOVO	07554
ILIM	70788
ILIRIJA	32290
ILITCH	17514
ILKA	76479/3
ILLERBERG	53405
ILLERBERG	64935
ILLIRIA	09680
ILMATAR	20300
ILMEN	11838
ILMENLES	45687
ILO	52660
ILO	89380
ILOLUTA	58685
ILONA	77579/1
ILOSANGI	58684
ILSE WULFF	49875
ILYA KATUNIN	11582
ILYA KULIK	02672
ILYA KULIN	13751/8
ILYA METCHNIKOV	10751
ILYA METCHNIKOV	34240
ILYA MUROMETS	17515
ILYA MUROMETS	22226
ILYA REPIN	76495
ILYA SELVINSKIY	50754
ILYA ULYANOV	03659
ILYA ULYANOV	03067
ILYA VOLYNKIN	11781
ILYICH	17490
ILYICHYOVSK	11839
ILYINSK	07553
IMA	77930
IMA	79250
IMAD S	39790
IMAN	36916
IMAN	43816
IMANDRA	25557
IMANT SUDMALIS	12433
IMANT SUDMALIS	85985
IMENI 61 KOMMUNARA	76498
IMERITI	11840
IMILCHIL	34218
IMMANUEL KANT	53107
IMME OLDENDORFF	06586
IMOUZZER	34219
IMPALA	59733
IMPALA	67223
IMPERIAL	05910
IMPERIAL SARNIA	43220
IMPERIAL SKEENA	45580
IMPERIAL STAR	34923
INA	80751
INA	81451
INA	86824
INA LEHMANN	73950/1
INABUKWA	58681
INAGUA BAY	92413
INAGUA BEACH	92411
INAGUA LIGHT	92410
INAGUA SOUND	92412
INAGUA SURF	92414
INAGUA TRADER II	92412/1
IN-AMENAS	64335
INARAN	58680
INAU	11681
INAYAMA	65220
INAYAMA	69880
INCA	58543
INCAN ST LAURENT	39391
INCAN ST LAURENT	93181
INCAN SUPERIOR	39390
INCAN SUPERIOR	93180
INCONFIDENTE	00510
INCOTRANS PRELUDE	74061●
INCOTRANS PREMIER	74060●
INCOTRANS PROMISE	73490
INCOTRANS SPIRIT	04110
INDEPENDENCE	09191
INDEPENDENCIA	70041
INDEPENDENCIA 1	66214
INDEPENDENCIA II	66215
INDIAN COURIER	82923
INDIAN FAITH	60230
INDIAN FAME	60231
INDIAN FORTUNE	60232
INDIAN FRATERNITY	60234
INDIAN FREEDOM	60235
INDIAN GLORY	54117
INDIAN GLORY	54587
INDIAN GRACE	54118
INDIAN GRACE	54588
INDIAN HIGHSEA SPLENDOUR	56546
INDIAN HIGHSEA SUCCESS	56545
INDIAN OCEAN	06331
INDIAN PRESTIGE	57460
INDIAN PROGRESS	57461
INDIAN PROSPERITY	57462
INDIAN SECURITY	13563
INDIAN TRIBUNE	07772
INDIAN TRIUMPH	13561
INDIAN TRUST	13562
INDIAN VALOUR	80850
INDIAN VALOUR	82490
INDIAN VENTURE	80851
INDIAN VENTURE	82491
INDIANA	05234
INDIANIC	52697
INDIANO	36690
INDIANO	41390
INDIGA	11490
INDIGIRKA	17810
INDIGIRKA	21581
INDIGIRKA	35319
INDIO	54676
INDUS	10545
INDUSTRIAL TRADER	62434●
INESSA ARMAND	05628
INESSA ARMAND	14457
INEY	21190
INEZ V	72144
INEZ V	76484
INGA	88113/1
INGA THOLSTRUP	88880
INGAPIRCA	59240
INGE MAERSK	60860
INGE MAERSK	70900
INGEBORG II	49904
INGEBORG II	50343/1
INGENIERO VILLA	52651
INGENIERO VILLA	71601
INGER	82940
INGER WONSILD	54151
INGI	91102
INGRID JUDITH	85191
INGUL	02110
INGUL	12146
INGUL	22163
INGUL	23060
INGUL	35170
INGUR	21221
INGURI	04210
INGURI	35190
INHARRIME	79890
INICIATIVA	57040
INIOCHOS EXPRESS II	33320
INKA DEDE	49879●
INKERMAN	36914
INKERMAN	43814
INKILAP	32165
INKURLES	45683
IN-NAHALA	69110
IN-NAHALA	71460
INNAREN	29923
INNISFALLEN	32720
INOWROCLAW	33281
INOWROCLAW	94551
IN-SAFRA	64334
INSELSBERG	76973
INSELSBERG	89783
INSELSEE	46385
INSELSEE	47085
INSTALLER 1	51440
INTAN	43060
INTANIN	45482
INTANIN	49432
INTER II	09962
INTER IV	47321
INTER IV	83381
INTERAMICITY	27150
INTERDOS	09962
INTERMAR ATLANTIC	64340
INTERNATSIONAL	60680
INTERNATSIONAL	90720
INTISAR	64336
INTRA TRANSPORTER	11190
INZHEHIER AGEYEV	70743
INZHENER BASHKIROV	80091
INZHENER KREYLIS	80093
INZHENER MACHULSKIY	80090
INZHENER NECHIPORENKO	80095
INZHENER SUKHORUKOV	80092
INZHENER YERMOSHKIN	12682
INZHENER YERMOSHKIN	80182
INZHENER YUDINTSEV	13756
INZHENIER BELOV	50771
INZHENIER PARKHONTUK	48653
INZHENIER YAMBURENKO	69323
IO	06503
IOANNA 1	41840
IOANNA V	85440
IOANNIS	06760
IOANNIS	40424
IOANNIS	42334
IOANNIS	42594
IOANNIS	49223
IOANNIS	85250
IOANNIS DYO	49223●
IOANNIS III	22836
IOANNIS K	42270

Name	No.	Name	No.	Name	No.	Name	No.
IOANNIS K	83910	IRAN TEYFOURI	45936	ISKONA	85340	IVAN LESOVIKOV	79430
IOANNIS ZAFIRAKIS	57190	IRAN TEYFOURI	47446	ISKRA	60683	IVAN MAKARIN	49347/3●
IOHANN MAMASHAL	90564	IRAN TIFORI	45936●	ISKRA	90722	IVAN MOSKALENKO	48440
IOHANNES LAURISTIN	03779	IRAN TIFORI	47446●	ISLA BALTRA	14489	IVAN MOSKALENKO	49750
IOHANNES LAURISTIN	04019	IRAN TORAB	46480●	ISLA DE COCHE	19321	IVAN MOSKVIN	28491
IOKHAN KYOLER	12434	IRAN TOWHEED	82141	ISLA DE CUBAGUA	19320	IVAN MOSKVITIN	22227
IOKHANNES SEMPER	23535	IRAN TOWHEED	82421	ISLA DE LA JUVENTUD	18691	IVAN MUSKALENKO	49480
IOLE C	66811	IRAN VOJDAN	49035	ISLA DE LA JUVENTUD	34025	IVAN NESTEROV	78019
ION	05475	IRANZU	64378	ISLA DE MARNAY	84761	IVAN NESTEROV	79999
ION	76751	IRATI	70560	ISLA DE MENORA	16690	IVAN PANOV	12440
ION SOLTYS	73292	IRBENSKIY PROLIV	58512	ISLA FERNANDINA	58512	IVAN PAVLOV	34241
IONA YAKIR	05629	IRBENSKIY PROLIV	71822	ISLA FERNANDINA	06812	IVAN POKROVSKIY	03778
IONA YAKIR	14458	IRBIT	85338	ISLA GENOVESA	05482	IVAN POKROVSKIY	04018
IONAS BILYUNAS	12435	IRBITLES	45684	ISLA GENOVESA	06813	IVAN POLZUNOV	10748
IONIAN CAPE	31660	IRENE	57570	ISLA LEONES	43010	IVAN SECHENOV	34242
IONIAN CARRIER	48055	IRENE	80940	ISLA PINTA	05480	IVAN SHADR	76588
IONIAN DESTINY	31662	IRENE D	11131	ISLA PINTA	06810	IVAN SHADR	79938
IONIAN GLORY	19670	IRENE GREENWOOD	46213	ISLA PINZON	57562	IVAN SHEPETKOV	48439
IONIAN GLORY	26280	IRENE LEMOS	62792	ISLA VERDE	33950	IVAN SHEPETKOV	49479
IONIAN GRACE	31661	IRENE LEMOS	67552	ISLAND	49865	IVAN SHEPETKOV	49749
IONIAN MARINER	36021	IRENE PATERAS	73120	ISLAND CONTAINER	74840	IVAN SHISHKIN	76511
IONIAN MOON	25860	IRENE S LEMOS	78692	ISLAND CONTAINER	83010	IVAN SIVKO	00143
IONIAN PRINCESS	86550	IRENES EMERALD	57470	ISLAND JESTER	59020	IVAN SKURIDIN	78060
IONIAN REEFER	03520	IRENES FANTASY	56970	ISLAND KING	75962	IVAN STEPANOV	45214
IONIAN SEA	26110	IRENES GALAXY	55961	ISLAND KOS	18370	IVAN STROD	50734
IONIAN SEA	39050	IRENES GALAXY	56721	ISLAND KOS	21201	IVAN SUSANIN	49347/2●
IONIAN SKY	26750	IRENES LOGIC	05421	ISLAND LADY	56690	IVAN SYRYKH	54711
IONIAN SPIRIT	11530	IRENES LOGIC	06121	ISLAND MARINER	46892	IVAN SYRYKH	55281
IONIAN STAR	19331	IRENES MAGIC	05550	ISLAND OF MARMARA	23144	IVAN VAZOV	80901
IONIAN STAR	23710	IRENES ODYSSEY	55960	ISLAND OF MARMARA	28344	IVAN ZAGUBANSKI	48430
IONIAN VICTORY	26100	IRENES ODYSSEY	56720	ISLAND OF MARMARA	32000	IVAN ZAGUBANSKI	49470
IONIAN WIND	26410	IRENES RHAPSODY	70670	ISLAND PRINCESS	16831	IVAN ZAGUBANSKI	49740
IONIC	53156	IRENES SAPPHIRE	57471	ISLAND SKY	61025	IVAN ZEMNUKHOV	41152
IONIC	66305	IRENES SUCCESS	46337	ISLAND SKY	71185	IVAN ZEMNUKHOV	44952
IONIO	44190	IRENES ZEAL	55968	ISLAND SUN	19740●	IVAN ZEMNUKHOV	86171
IONIO	57230	IRENES ZEAL	56728	ISLAND SUPPLIER	41880	IVAN ZIMAKOV	34873/3
IONION	88670	IRENES ZEST	55965	ISLAS GALAPAGOS	04140	IVANOVO	39985
IOS 1	03430	IRENES ZEST	56725	ISMAILIYA	03969	IVER CHAMPION	65721
IOSIF DUBROVINSKIY	03776	IRFON	64081	ISMARA	66620	IVER CHAMPION	75661
IOSIF DUBROVINSKIY	04016	IRIMAWA	58686	ISMARA	76240	IVER HERON	53000
IOSIF LAPUSHKIN	13673	IRINI	26981	ISMENE	53570	IVER HERON	53290
IOTA	81550	IRINI	64161	ISNIS	73799	IVER SOVEREIGN	70093
IOZAS VITAS	12436	IRINI	68481	ISONZO	24351	IVER SWAN	57664
IPANEMA	70561	IRINI G F	07030	ISORA	06740	IVI	39674
IPPOLITOS	59521	IRINI II	06513	ISORA	31200	IVO DORMIO	85850
IPPOLITOS	81201	IRINIKOS	52204	ISORA	71120	IVO VOJNOVIC	58130
IRAKLIS	90830	IRINIKOS	65154	ISORA	86560	IVOR	74420
IRAN ABAD	51162	IRIS	74173	ISPARTA	46890	IVOR	88090
IRAN ABAD	51531	IRIS	92400	ISSA 1	81121	IVORY	68841
IRAN ADI	46951●	IRIS	93080	ISSLEDOVATEL	39415	IVORY	84200
IRAN ADL	46951●	IRISEVERETT	11170	ISTRA	45690	IVORY	89040
IRAN AFZAL	46952	IRISH CEDAR	46810	ISVANIA	74150	IVORY GLORY	71207
IRAN AZADI	61221	IRISH MAPLE	46443	ISYK KOL	20794	IVORY MARU	32471
IRAN BAYAN	49037	IRISH ROWAN	46811	ITABERA	05361	IVORY TELLUS	61404
IRAN BESAT	05143	IRISH SPRUCE	72381	ITABERA	15661	IVYBANK	03673
IRAN BORHAN	49033	IRKUT	56271	ITAGIBA	03085	IVYBANK	03733
IRAN DAHR	48040	IRKUT	62731	ITAIMBE	03080	IWERI	58687
IRAN EHSAN	49034	IRKUTSK	02520	ITAITE	03185	IWONICZ ZDROJ	81860
IRAN EJTEHAD	03322	IRKUTSK	45116	ITALIA	01450	IYO MARU	32480
IRAN EJTEHAD	04380	IRKUTSKLES	45681	ITALIA	35260	IYUN KORAN	11782
IRAN EKRAM	14923	IRMA DELMAS	48881	ITALIAN SUN	87422	IZGUTTY AYTYKOV	73293
IRAN EKRAM	15734	IRO	81980	ITALICA	06171	IZHEVSK	00851
IRAN ELHAM	14924	IRON BARON	61403	ITALICA	64721	IZHEVSK	12344
IRAN ELHAM	15733	IRON CAPRICORN	46318	ITALMARE	53660	IZHEVSKLES	45686
IRAN EMAMAT	56301	IRON CAPRICORN	46568	ITALMARE	73380	IZHMA	22851
IRAN EMDAD	61044●	IRON CARPENTARIA	51250	ITANAGE	03186	IZHMA	34481
IRAN ENGHELAB	61220	IRON CARPENTARIA	53620	ITAPAGE	03188	IZHMALES	45680
IRAN ENTEKHAB	61223	IRON CUMBERLAND	46115	ITAPARICA	65863	IZHORA	02521
IRAN ERSHAD	51163	IRON CURTIS	51251	ITAPE	03187	IZHORA	70811
IRAN ERSHAD	51533	IRON CURTIS	53621	ITAPUCA	03087	IZHORALES	45689
IRAN ESTEGHLAL	61224	IRON DUKE	72191	ITAPUI	03083	IZMAIL	02522
IRAN ETEGHAD	71151	IRON KESTREL	47885	ITAPURA	03089	IZMAIL	11841
IRAN GHEYAM	14925	IRON KIRBY	47880/1	ITAQUATIA	03189	IZMIR	01591
IRAN GHEYAM	15735	IRON MONARCH	72190	ITAQUICE	03084	IZU MARU No 3	23720
IRAN GHEYAMAT	56300	IRON SIRIUS	73040	ITASSUCE	03090	IZU MARU No 3	32240
IRAN HEJRAT	05140	IRON TRANSPORTER	63491	ITATINGA	05362	IZU MARU No 11	23721
IRAN HEMMET	07661	IRSHALES	45685	ITATINGA	15662	IZU MARU No 11	32241
IRAN HOJJAT	55033	IRTISH	84460	ITELMAN	12437	IZUMISAN MARU	54220
IRAN HOJJAT	84650	IRTYSHLES	45688	ITORORO	70562	IZUMRUD	12441
IRAN JAHAD	51164	IRVING ARCTIC	65694	ITTERSUM	73378	IZUMRUD	35390
IRAN JAHAD	51534	IRVING ARCTIC	70124	IVA	94210	IZUMRUDNYY	11922
IRAN JOMHOURI	61222	IRVING ESKIMO	65695	IVAN AIVAZOVSKIY	76490	IZUMRUDNYY BEREG	62692
IRAN KALAM	07444	IRVING ESKIMO	70125	IVAN AIVAZOVSKIY	89660	IZVESTIYA	62484
IRAN KALAM	15311	IRVING FOREST	47591	IVAN BABUSHKIN	28980	IZVESTIYA	57764
IRAN KEYHAN	56302	IRVING FOREST	50521	IVAN BOCHKOV	34872		
IRAN MEEAD	51160	IRVING OCEAN	65696	IVAN BOGUN	86189		
IRAN MEEAD	51530	IRVING OCEAN	70126	IVAN BOGUN	49347/1●		
IRAN MEELAD	51161	IRVINGWOOD	35620	IVAN BOLOTNIKOV	89251	**J**	
IRAN MEELAD	51532	ISABEL	73640	IVAN BORZOV	24314		
IRAN MEEZAN	49030	ISABELA	58683	IVAN BORZOV	39456		
IRAN MOTHARAI	48101	ISABELLA	89730	IVAN BUBNOV	59883	J C CRANE	01520
IRAN NAHAD	51230	ISADORE HECHT	18381	IVAN BYELOSTOTSKIY	03777	J R GREY	62991
IRAN NAMJOO	61042	ISADORE HECHT	33932	IVAN BYELOSTOTSKIY	04017	J R GREY	57901
IRAN NASR	48041	ISAKOGORKA	11432	IVAN CHERNOPYATKO	12439	JAAN KOORT	12442
IRAN NEHZAT	05141	ISAR	53409	IVAN CHERNYKH	11433	JAARLI	64310
IRAN OKHUVAT	07662	ISAR	64939	IVAN DERBENEV	78064	JACARA	79117
IRAN PASDAR	66641	ISAR EXPRESS	49050	IVAN DVORSKIY	12438	JACARANDA	87680
IRAN RESHADAT	04552	ISAVENA	56420	IVAN FEDEROV	25843	JACEK MALCZEWSKI	49655
IRAN SABR	48043	ISBJORN	23941	IVAN FRANKO	01751	JACK	50663●
IRAN SALAM	07443	ISCHIA	32130	IVAN GOLUBETS	12251	JACK WHARTON	73682
IRAN SALAM	15312	ISCHIA EXPRESS	21080	IVAN GONCHAROV	07922	JACK WHARTON	87342
IRAN SEDAGHAT	86110	ISE MARU	56406	IVAN GORTHON	72841	JACKSON OCEAN	61522
IRAN SEDAGHAT	91710	ISE MARU	59928	IVAN GREN	23513	JACOB BECKER	49882
IRAN SEEYAM	07440	ISE MARU	67787	IVAN KIREYEV	39175	JACOB RUSS	54941
IRAN SEEYAM	15310	ISELTAL	76610	IVAN KOLYSHKIN	79389	JACOBUS BROERE	85666
IRAN SEPEHR	56303	ISEULT	63241	IVAN KOROBTSOV	03957	JACQUELINE	33262●
IRAN SHAD	05142	ISHIKARI	32570	IVAN KOROTEYEV	69318	JACQUES DUCLOS	70595
IRAN SHAFAAT	86111	ISHIKARI MARU	23732	IVAN KORZUNOV	13752/1	JACUI	68204
IRAN SHAFAAT	91711	ISHIM	85339	IVAN KOTLYAREVSKIY	09996	JADE	14240
IRAN SHAHAB	56304	ISIDOR BARAKHOV	50753	IVAN KRAMSKOY	76523	JADE BAY	06495
IRAN SHAHEED	82140	ISIS	01413	IVAN KRUZENSHTERN	22228	JADE BOUNTY	82924
IRAN SHAHEED	82420	ISIS	01673	IVAN KRUZHENSTERN	04241	JADE GLORIOUS	77801
IRAN SOKAN	49032	ISKAR	69725	IVAN KUDRIYA	79431	JADE II	05330
IRAN TAKHTI	52865●	ISKATEL	39414	IVAN KULIBIN	10749	JADE III	05331
						JADE STAR	57280

Name	No.	Name	No.	Name	No.	Name	No.
JADE TRANSPORTER	77210	JANALES	11491	JIAN HUA	16120	JOLLY AMARANTO	80031
JADRAN	68760	JANE MAERSK	53191	JIANDE	24896	JOLLY ARANCIONE	82740
JADRO	86045	JANE STOVE	69112	JIANG AN	52737	JOLLY ARGENTO	94502
JAG DEESH	54111	JANE STOVE	71462	JIANG CHENG	14927	JOLLY AVORIO	94832
JAG DEESH	54581	JANEGA	46993	JIANG CHENG	15736	JOLLY BIANCO	32410
JAG DHARMA	54112	JANEGA	83333	JIANG CHUAN	05100	JOLLY GRIGIO	77120
JAG DHARMA	54582	JANEK KRASICKI	14583	JIANG LOONG	31803	JOLLY GRIGIO	80030
JAG DHIR	54113	JANE SEA	88200	JIANG MEN	08034	JOLLY OCRA	93342●
JAG DHIR	54583	JANI	13230	JIANGCHANG	03170	JOLLY ORO	94501
JAG DOOT	54114	JANICE ANN	86322	JIANGDU	30422	JOLLY ROSSO	77380
JAG DOOT	54584	JANICE L	46696●	JIANGMIN	06064	JOLLY VERDE	94100
JAG JYOTI	70102	JANNE WEHR	73903/1	JIANGTING	05373	JOLO	46284
JAG LAADKI	68831	JANUS	53588	JIANGYIN	30250	JONIKA	66813
JAG LAXMI	63457	JANUSZ KUSOCINSKI	67694	JIANGYIN	31080	JONNI	56523
JAG LEELA	63458	JANUSZ KUSOCINSKI	65854	JIANSHUI	01533	JONNY WESCH	49427
JAG PARI	53336	JAN WILLEM	58540	JIAO JIANG	71806	JOO HENG	07530
JAG PREETI	53337	JAOUHAR	66802	JIAO ZHOU HAI	47666	JORDAN	35664
JAG RAKSHAK	51082	JAPAN ACACIA	77221/1	JIAXING	15581	JORDAN NIKOLOV	69021
JAG RATNA	51083	JAPAN ADONIS	54542	JIBACOA	16761	JORK	49906
JAG SHAKTI	48050	JAPAN ADONIS	63902	JIEYANG	146393	JORK	50344
JAG SHANTI	48051	JAPAN AMBROSE	08640	JIJIA	13773	JOSE ANTONIO ECHEVARRIA	26450
JAGAT MOHINI	55400	JAPAN ASTER	54543	JILFAR	49408	JOSE ANTONIO ECHEVARRIA	48453
JAGAT MOHINI	84660	JAPAN ASTER	63903	JILFAR	50968	JOSE ANTONIO ECHEVARRIA	49493
JAGAT NETA	53820	JAPAN CANELA	03741	JILL	50661	JOSE ANTONIO ECHEVARRIA	49763
JAGAT PRIYA	54115	JAPAN CANELA	51121	JILL CORD	56950	JOSE DIAS	06786
JAGAT PRIYA	54585	JAPAN CARNATION	55460	JIN CHENG JIANG	57451	JOSE DIAS	07587
JAGAT SAMRAT	68392	JAPAN CARNATION	62781	JIN CHENG JIANG	71781	JOSE ESQUIVEL	76082
JAGAT SAMRAT	77402	JAPAN COSMOS	54801	JIN GANG LIN	61470	JOSE MARIA MORELOS	69996
JAGAT SWAMINI	55401	JAPAN COSMOS	68031	JIN HAI	46008	JOSE MARIA MORELOS	86486
JAGAT SWAMINI	84661	JAPAN LUPINUS	62780	JIN HU QUAN	04620	JOSE MARIA RAMON	83880
JAGAT VIJETA	53821	JAPAN ORCHID	56350	JIN HU QUAN	05080	JOSE MARTI	33590
JAGRANDA	64332	JAPAN ORCHID	68050	JIN HU QUAN	30400	JOSE MARTI	70597
JAGUAR	53587	JAPAN POPLAR	77222	JIN JIANG	71855	JOSEF ROTH	06623
JAHORINA	91765	JAPAN TUNA No 2	50890	JIN PING	30830	JOSEPH DUHAMEL	33491
JAINARAYAN VYAS	71633	JAPAN VIOLET	54370	JIN RUN	51540	JOSEPH GRACE	70651
JAKHONT	12443	JAPAN VIOLET	62980	JIN XIAN QUAN	29161	JOSEPH LYKES	00065
JAKOB MAERSK	53190	JAPURA	68203	JIN YANG No 1	22771/1	JOSTELLE	73202
JAKOV ALKSNIS	10730	JARASH	81750	JIN YANG No 2	22770	JOSTELLE	76992
JAKOV KUNDER	50288	JARILLA	78426	JIN YANG No 13	31340	JOULE	62420
JAKOV SMUSHKEVICH	12444	JARITA	64333	JIN YANG No 17	31390	JOVELLANOS	72231
JALABALA	47042	JAROSLAW	66980	JIN ZHOU HAI	56861	JOWAKI	57551
JALADURGA	25770	JASLO	16270	JINCHANG	03171	JOWISZ	11646
JALAGIRIJA	25730	JASMINE B	71566	JING HAI	61310	JOY 18	12640
JALAJAYA	04250	JASMINE II	71490●	JING HAI	62610	JOYAMA MARU	68340
JALAJYOTI	15230	JASNOMORSK	22853	JING JIANG	06841	JOYCE CLARE	42770
JALAKALA	30750	JASNOMORSK	34483	JINING	10581	JOZEF CHELMONSKI	49658
JALAKANTA	30751	JASON	20460	JINING	15351	JOZEF CONRAD KORZENIOWSKI	54970
JALAKENDRA	30752	JASTARNIA-BOR	04341	JINKO MARU	54491	JOZEF CONRAD KORZENIOWSKI	71810
JALAMANGALA	05825	JASTARNIA-BOR	04401	JINKO MARU	54921	JOZEF WYBICKI	10575
JALAMANGALA	06012	JAURSINGHWALA	28730	JINKO MARU	55721	JOZEF WYBICKI	15345
JALAMATSYA	05826	JAVA WINDS	51895	JINSHA	05661	JU HAI	79240
JALAMATSYA	06014	JAVA WINDS	82706	JINYU MARU	37880	JUAN CARLOS TORO	76087
JALAMAYOR	06017	JAVARA	46990	JINYU MARU	38850	JUAN DE DIOS FRAGA MORENA	75960
JALAMAYUR	05824	JAVARA	83330	JIUJIANG	35031	JUAN MARCH	01290
JALAMOHAN	05823	JAVELIN	70950	JIUL	11974	JUAREZ	86691
JALAMOHAN	06015	JAWAHARLAL NEHRU	67770	JIZAN CEMENT	69124	JUBA	31643
JALAMOKAMBI	05820	JAWAHARLAL NEHRU	69190	JO BIRK	48876	JUDITH P	10640
JALAMOKAMBI	06010	JAY BHAVANI	55964	JO CLIPPER	53028	JUDITH SCHULTE	53411
JALAMOTI	05827	JAY BHAVANI	56724	JO LIND	58472	JUDITH SCHULTE	64941
JALAMOTI	06016	JAY DURGA	56991	JO LONN	48875	JUGO NAVIGATOR	71061
JALAMUDRA	04935	JAYA PUTRA II	42310	JO OAK	48877	JUGOAGENT	48465●
JALAMURUGAN	04934	JAYAKARTA	50117	JO SAILOR	66652	JUGOAGENT	49501●
JALANIDHI	09660	JEAN CHARCOT	02510	JOAKIM VACIETIS	13675	JUGOAGENT	49772●
JALAPA	90681	JEAN L-D	83149	JOANA	04638	JUHAN SIUTISTE	12449
JALAPUTRA	06641	JEAN LYKES	00063	JOANA	56940	JUJUY II	06671
JALARAJAN	05170	JEANNE LABOURBE	05630	JOANNA	46109	JULE	76476
JALARAJAN	14321	JEANNE LABOURBE	14459	JOHAN NORDENANKAR	33095	JULES VERNE	60440
JALARASHMI	05172	JEANNIE	74942	JOHAN PETERSEN	49971	JULES VERNE	69280
JALARASHMI	14320	JEDFOREST	64482	JOHANN CHRISTIAN SCHULTE	90871	JULIA	89844
JALARATNA	05171	JEFF DAVIS	02300	JOHANN MAHMASTAL	90564	JULIA L	46697●
JALARATNA	14322	JEHMAR LIFE	10700●	JOHANNA	92307●	JULIANA	68390
JALATARANG	67290	JELAU	61076	JOHANNA SCHULTE	62243	JULIANA	77400
JALAVIHAR	77651	JELAU	71266	JOHANNA SCHULTE	57609	JULIANE	73959
JALAVIHAR	80711	JELCZ II	82268	JOHANNA V	76195	JULIE A	02772
JALAYAMINI	15681	JELENIA GORA	82261	JOHANNES LATUHARHARY	15380	JULIETTA	01111
JALAYAMUNA	15680	JELSA	16065	JOHANNES R BECKER	12623	JULIO ANTONIO MELLA	48454
JALVALLABH	73081	JENA	70695	JOHANNES RUVEN	12448	JULIO ANTONIO MELLA	49494
JALVALLABH	77791	JENLINK	71950●	JOHANNES VARES	25844	JULIO ANTONIO MELLA	49764
JAMAC	70091	JENNIE W	83860	JOHN	48865	JULIUS FUCIK	00240
JAMAICA FAREWELL	48360	JENNIE W	85870	JOHN	50664●	JULIUS FUCIK	14975
JAMAICA FAREWELL	50870	JENNY	59141	JOHN A	60181	JUMBO JOIST	85210
JAMAICAN STARS	48280	JENNY	88110	JOHN A MACDONALD	10860	JUMBO JOIST	90050
JAMAL B	49992	JENS KOFOED	20351	JOHN BISCOE	23680	JUMBO STELLATWO	89825
JAMAL SHAH	69421●	JENSON II	41750	JOHN BRINCKMAN	34330	JUMPA	45480
JAMBI	59280	JENWEL	87353	JOHN C	47931	JUMPA	49430
JAMBUR	69573	JEPPESEN MAERSK	53193	JOHN CABOT	02200	JUN LIANG CHENG	71990
JAMES ENSOR	52285	JERKO TOMASIC	35510	JOHN HAMILTON GRAY	19450	JUN LIANG CHENG	72110
JAMES LYKES	00062	JEROM	64368	JOHN HENRY	67211	JUN SHAN	15920
JAMES ROWAN	42450	JERRYEVERETT	21410	JOHN HENRY	91751	JUNGE GARDE	24160
JAMHURI	20990	JERVIS BAY	17200	JOHN K	90656	JUNGE WELT	24161
JAMI 2	04550	JESBON	51110	JOHN LYKES	00064	JUNIOR K	13351
JAMIL	27770	JESBON	51490	JOHN M	90120	JUNIOR LILIAN	50270
JAN	73721	JESENICE	15290	JOHN MICHALOS	06496	JUNIPER	03497
JAN ANVELT	10435	JESICA	74250	JOHN P	05920	JUNIPER	03587
JAN BERZIN	12445	JESPER MAERSK	53194	JOHN P	27230	JUNO	33110
JAN FABRITSIUS	12446	JESSICA	58491●	JOHN PERO	03133	JUNO	47211
JAN FOUR	14302	JESSICA	84911●	JOHN PERO	03343	JUOZAS GREYFENBERGIS	12451
JAN HEWELIUSZ	09251	JESSIE STOVE	77460	JOHN REED	70596	JUOZAS VAREYKIS	12450
JAN HEWELIUSZ	33381	JESUS MENENDEZ	07756	JOHN ROSS	22170	JUPITER	12610
JAN HEWELIUSZ	94701	JESUS MENENDEZ	07899	JOHN SCHEHR	06387	JUPITER	16350
JAN KAHRS	73954	JET V	88820	JOHN SCHEHR	15416	JUPITER	16540
JAN KREUKS	86091	JETPUR VICTORY	25070	JOHN W MACKAY	23280	JUPITER	33111
JAN MATEJKO	14582	JEVERLAND	58910	JOHN WILSON	85720	JUPITER	52623
JAN MAYEN	18724	JEVERLAND	65300	JOHNEVERETT	04751	JUPITER	60580
JAN RAINBERG	13674	JHANSI KI RANI	77650	JOHNNY	60990	JUPITER	89845
JAN RUDZUTAK	12447	JHANSI KI RANI	80710	JOHNSON CHEMSPAN	53003	JUPITER II	81111
JAN SUDRABKALN	67687	JHUFEL	08540	JOHNSON CHEMSTAR	52265	JUPITER II	90551
JAN WILHELM	50841	JI HAI 10	50415	JOHNSON CHEMSUN	52266	JURANDY	22600
JANA	02111	JI HAI 10	50825	JOHS STOVE	64366	JURANDY	23350
JANA	21580	JI MEI	01931	JOINVILLE	68205	JURATA	04342
JANA	35171	JI MEI	20560	JOKULFELL	81702	JURATA	04402
JANA	06795/4	JIA HAI	46339	JOKULFJELL	80982	JURINA	48211
JANA PRIYA	77567	JIA LING JIANG	60240	JOLLITY	58187	JURMO	64313
JANA VIJAY	78750	JIA YU HAI	56942	JOLLY AMARANTO	77121	JURUA	68206

Name	No.	Name	No.	Name	No.	Name	No.
JURUPEMA	68207	KAMCHATKA	15470	KAPITAN KRUTOV	22205	KAREN	57610
JUTHA MALEE	86704	KAMCHATSKIE GORY	91910	KAPITAN KUDLAY	49348	KAREN MAERSK	54452
JUTHA PHANSIRI	86701	KAMCHATSKIY	07568	KAPITAN KUSHNARENKO	02800	KAREN MAERSK	63372
JUTHA RAJATA	13388	KAMCHATSKLES	04183	KAPITAN LEDOCHOWSKI	07861	KAREN WINTHER	64890
JUTHAH KARNCHANA	13387	KAMELA	37340	KAPITAN LEONTIY BORISENKO	02803	KARHU	23981
JUTLANDIA	08491	KAMELA	45200	KAPITAN LEV SOLOVYEV	02804	KARIMATA	89228
JUVENA	26660	KAMENOGORSK	45215	KAPITAN LUKHMANOV	03961	KARIN	32055
JUVENITA	48385/8	KAMENSKOYE	11947	KAPITAN LYUBCHENKO	54733	KARIN	47615
JUVENTIA	52614	KAMENSK-URALSKIY	70031	KAPITAN LYUBCHENKO	55303	KARIN	50261
JUVENTUS	06526	KAMIROS	17090	KAPITAN M IZMAYLOV	02080	KARIN	75508
JUYO MARU	09991	KAMNIK	5744	KAPITAN M IZMAYLOV	22250	KARIN	88120
JUYO MARU	34410	KAMPOS	62433	KAPITAN MAKATSARIYA	70745	KARIN BORNHOFEN	71848
JVONNE	85200	KAN SU HAI	76987	KAPITAN MAKLAKOV	00149	KARIN GRENIUS	81921
JYLLAND	22030	KANANGA	16191	KAPITAN MARKOV	21616	KARIN VATIS	48151
JYTTE DANIELSEN	90971/1	KANARIS	09392	KAPITAN MARKOV	34103	KARINA RIO GRANDE	74231
JYTTE DANIELSEN	91983	KANARYJKA	18742	KAPITAN MECAIK	20879●	KARIPANDE	57500
JYTTE SKOU	86702	KANCHENJUNGA	67400	KAPITAN MEDVEDEV	48861	KARL KRUSHTEYN	89215
		KANDAGACH	89474	KAPITAN MELEKHOV	23971	KARL LIEBKNECHT	05631

K

Name	No.	Name	No.	Name	No.	Name	No.
		KANDALAKSHA	02728/6	KAPITAN MESHCHRYAKOV	78014	KARL LIEBKNECHT	14460
		KANDALAKSHA	23553	KAPITAN MESHCHRYAKOV	79994	KARL LIEBKNECHT	17516
		KANDALAKSHALES	24069	KAPITAN MEZENTSEV	12681	KARL LIEBKNECHT	62680
		KANDALAKSHSKIY ZALIV	61105	KAPITAN MEZENTSEV	80181	KARL LINNE	61271
K CHALLENGER	54563	KANDAVA	03261	KAPITAN MILOVZOROV	54721	KARL LINNE	81491
K CHALLENGER	54963	KANEV	03042	KAPITAN MILOVZOROV	55291	KARL MARX	03150
K K S MUTHOO	40940	KANEV	50912	KAPITAN MOCHALOV	54714	KARL MARX	17517
KAAREL LIYMAND	12452	KANG DING	30120	KAPITAN MOCHALOV	55284	KARL MARX STADT	04914
KABONA	89262	KANG DING	31030	KAPITAN MODEST IVANOV	02805	KARL WOLF	23425
KABRYL	18741	KANG DONG	07025	KAPITAN MYSHEVSKIY	21617	KARLIS ZIEDINS	10724
KADAS 1	45750	KANG HAI	59330	KAPITAN MYSHEVSKIY	34106	KARLSVIK	75532
KADIEVKA	10459	KANGOUROU	74530	KAPITAN NEVEZHKIN	70750	KARMILA	73361●
KAETHE JOHANNA	73970	KANGUK	51140	KAPITAN NIKOLAYEV	02061	KARMSUND	93000
KAFUR MAMEDOV	53163	KANIKA	90451	KAPITAN NIKOLAYEV	02231	KAROLINE MAERSK	54453
KAGHAN	56577	KANIN	86092	KAPITAN PANFILOV	78010	KAROLINE MAERSK	63373
KAGUL	86084	KANIN	89469	KAPITAN PANFILOV	79990	KAROLIS POZHELA	12454
KAHAGIA IV	18154	KANISHKA	56842	KAPITAN PETKO VOIVODA	48434	KAROSSA	18153
KAHIRA	50137	KANLIKA	32166	KAPITAN PETKO VOIVODA	49474	KARPACZ	81866
KAHIRA	50138●	KANNIKAR	45481	KAPITAN PETKO VOIVODA	49744	KARPATY	11313
KAI HUA	01160	KANNIKAR	49431	KAPITAN PLAHIN	22202	KARPOGORY	11326
KAI HUA	45490	KANOPUS	12254	KAPITAN PLAUSHEVSKIY	03955	KARRAS	54690
KAI PING	57720	KANSAS CITY	92602	KAPITAN PURGIN	13768	KARRAS	65065
KAI PING	71800	KANSAS CITY	93612	KAPITAN REDKOKASHA	11335/4	KARRAS	84630
KAI YANG	94870	KANTAR	18743	KAPITAN REUTOV	78015	KARSKOYE MORE	55130
KAIA KNUDSEN	64010	KANUKA FOREST	46642	KAPITAN REUTOV	79995	KARTAGENA	50133/1●
KAIA KNUDSEN	68400	KANUKA FOREST	83322	KAPITAN SAMOYLENKO	54722	KARTALA	88150
KAIMON MARU	63120	KAO JIANG	47241	KAPITAN SAMOYLENKO	55292	KARTALY	84464
KAIRA	12252	KAPETAN ANDREAS	39240	KAPITAN SCHUKIN	89507	KARTHAGO	50136
KAIROS	59732	KAPETAN GEORGIS	79820	KAPITAN SHANTSBERG	03964	KARTLI	12255
KAIROUAN	51291	KAPETAN MARKOS N L	37620	KAPITAN SHEVCHENKO	54732	KARTUZY	88232
KAIRYU MARU	94350	KAPITAN A POLKOVSKIY	47167	KAPITAN SHEVCHENKO	55302	KARUNA	47613
KAISEI MARU	61641	KAPITAN A RADZHABOV	02081	KAPITAN SHVETSOV	70740	KARUNA	76631
KAITY	79650	KAPITAN A RADZHABOV	22251	KAPITAN SKORNYAKOV	09363	KARUNIA	71914/1
KAKHETI	11842	KAPITAN ABAKUMOV	24081	KAPITAN SLIPKO	02806	KARYATEIN	50131
KALAMAZOO	92601	KAPITAN ALEKSEYEV	02795	KAPITAN SMIRNOV	12680	KARYATIS	47155
KALAMAZOO	93611	KAPITAN ANDREI TARAN	12453	KAPITAN SMIRNOV	80180	KARYSA	38830
KALAR	02285	KAPITAN ANDREYEV	34876/2	KAPITAN SOROKIN	02060	KASHIMA MARU	72400
KALAR	23551	KAPITAN ANISTRATYENKO	02801	KAPITAN SOROKIN	02230	KASHINO	06773
KALAVRIA	78701	KAPITAN BABICHEV	20876	KAPITAN STULOV	78017	KASHINO	07583
KALENTZI	05490	KAPITAN BAKANOV	54715	KAPITAN STULOV	79997	KASHIRA	51989/1
KALENTZI	07950	KAPITAN BAKANOV	55285	KAPITAN SVIRIDOV	49345	KASHIRSKOYE	07947/1
KALENTZI	61750	KAPITAN BELOSHAPKIN	24042	KAPITAN TELOV	00144	KASIMOV	03040
KALEV	86079	KAPITAN BELOUSOV	23970	KAPITAN TOMSON	80060	KASIMOV	50910
KALI LIMENES	88980	KAPITAN BOCHEK	49343	KAPITAN TRUBKIN	46427	KASIMPASA	19041
KALIA	27310	KAPITAN BONDARENKO	21613	KAPITAN V TSIRUL	49346	KASKAD	12455
KALIDORA	76752	KAPITAN BONDARENKO	34102	KAPITAN VAKULA	49349	KASPAR SIF	64851
KALIM	46712●	KAPITAN BORODKIN	20878	KAPITAN VANILOV	79998	KASPAR SIF	91031
KALIMANTAN SATU	61590	KAPITAN BUKAYEV	22204	KAPITAN VASILYEVSKIY	54727	KASPIJSK	03045
KALININABAD	03041	KAPITAN BURMAKIN	54725	KAPITAN VASILYEVSKIY	55297	KASPIJSK	50914
KALININABAD	50911	KAPITAN BURMAKIN	55295	KAPITAN VAVILOV	78018	KASPIY	35310
'KALININGRAD'	01380	KAPITAN CHADAYEV	22201	KAPITAN VISLOBOKOV	45360	KASPIY	50780
'KALININGRAD'	01640	KAPITAN CHECHKIN	22200	KAPITAN VODENKO	49347	KASSAMBA	57501
KALININGRAD	06775	KAPITAN CHIRKOV	02796	KAPITAN VORONIN	23972	KASSANDRA	48340
KALININGRAD	07577	KAPITAN CHUDINOV	20877	KAPITAN YAKOVLEV	80061	KASSANTINA	60952
KALININGRAD	45110	KAPITAN CHUKHCHIN	49344	KAPITAN YEVDOKIMOV	20875	KASSIA	46436
KALININGRADNEFT	66380	KAPITAN DEMIDOV	11613	KAPITAN ZAMYATIN	54728	KASSIAN GLORY	56140
KALININGRADSKIY KOMSOMOLETS	93735	KAPITAN DOTSYENKO	70748	KAPITAN ZAMYATIN	55298	KASSIAN GLORY	71720
KALININGRADSKIY KOMSOMOLETS	93825	KAPITAN DRANITSYN	02062	KAPITAN ZARUBIN	22203	KASSIOPEYA	12256
KALININGRADSKIY-NEFTYANIK	66383	KAPITAN DRANITSYN	02232	KAPITAN ZIOLKOWSKI	87752	KASSOS	21200
KALINOVO	11923	KAPITAN DUBININ	78012	KAPRELA	23445	KASSOS	27290
KALITVA	23552	KAPITAN DUBININ	79992	KAPRIFOL	72820	KASSOS	45951
KALJMAR	12253	KAPITAN DUBLITSKIY	54720	KAPRIFOL	80220	KASTAMONU	50133
KALKARA	50130/1	KAPITAN DUBLITSKIY	55290	KAPSUKAS	06772	KASTAV	05653
KALKARA	50137●	KAPITAN DYACHUK	70747	KAPSUKAS	07592	KASTOR	12611
KALKAVANLAR	40427	KAPITAN DZHURASHEVICH	02797	KAPTAI	52681	KASTORIA	61120
KALKAVANLAR	42337	KAPITAN EVDOKIMV	20875	KAPTAMICHALIS	06535	KASTRO K	26950
KALKAVANLAR	42597	KAPITAN EVSEYEV	35321	KAPTAN NECDET OR	32991	KASTURBA	77652
KALLIOPI L	46882	KAPITAN GASTELLO	06776	KAPTAN SAIT OZEGE	32990	KASTURBA	80712
KALLIPOLIS	62221●	KAPITAN GASTELLO	07585	KAPTAN YUSUF KALKAVAN	61311	KASUGA MARU	51280
KALLIPOLIS	71131●	KAPITAN GEORGIY BAGLAY	02802	KAPTAN YUSUF KALKAVAN	62611	KASUGA MARU	52690
KALLISTO	12301	KAPITAN GLAZACHYEV	54726	KAPUAS	61476	KASUGA MARU	95082
KALLISTO	29690	KAPITAN GLAZACHYEV	55296	KARA	06774	KASUGAI MARU	48942
KALLSO	83830	KAPITAN GOTSKIY	21614	KARA	07580	KASZALOT	10812
KALMAR	23456	KAPITAN GOTSKIY	34104	KARA CAREER	05950	KASZONY	64326
KALMAR	30160	KAPITAN GRIBIN	70744	KARA SEA	29243	KASZUBY II	59691
KALMARSUND	72843	KAPITAN GRITSUK	17928	KARA UNICORN	07211	KASZUBY II	81351
KALMIUS	89209	KAPITAN GUDIN	78016	KARACHAJEVO-CHERKESSIJA	03043	KATANGLI	06798
KALOFER	83722	KAPITAN GUDIN	79996	KARACHAJEVO-CHERKESSIJA	50913	KATARINA	72759●
KALOMIRA V	02793	KAPITAN IZHMYAKOV	78013	KARA-DAG	11948	KATAWA	51788
KALOS 1	53442	KAPITAN IZHMYAKOV	79993	KARADAG	84461	KATE MAERSK	54454
KALOS 1	91572	KAPITAN IZOTOV	70742	KARADENIZ	01581	KATE MAERSK	63374
KALOUM	90971	KAPITAN KADETSKIY	02798	KARAGA	06797/5	KATENDRECHT	47421
KALOUM	91982	KAPITAN KAMINSKIY	02799	KARAGACH	11925	KATERINA	56990
KALPER	13752	KAPITAN KANSKI	87750	KARAGANDA	02523	KATERINA	90230
KALTAN	11924	KAPITAN KARTASHOV	89510	KARAGAT	23536	KATERINA	90910
KALYMNOS	21940	KAPITAN KHROMTSOV	78011	KARAKUM KANAL	44119	KATERINA A	35661
KALYN	61020	KAPITAN KHROMTSOV	79991	KARAKUMNEFT	86001	KATERINA DRACOPOULOS	06540
KALYN	71180	KAPITAN KIRIY	54716	KARAKUMY	11316	KATERINA E	47398
KALYON	90651	KAPITAN KIRIY	55286	KARAMA MAERSK	54451	KATERINA E	47968
KALYPSO	61067	KAPITAN KLEBNIKOV	02063	KARAMAN	50142	KATERINA K	41340
KAMA	35320	KAPITAN KLEBNIKOV	02233	KARANA DELAPAN	13260	KATERINA M	52761
KAMAKURA MARU	33600	KAPITAN KOBETS	70749	KARANA ENAM	31810	KATERINA V	43480
KAMALES	11503	KAPITAN KONDRATYEV	21615	KARE	49861	KATERINA V	43510
KAMBUNA	02347	KAPITAN KONDRATYEV	34105	KARELI	86002	KATERINE	80401
KAMCHADAL	06793	KAPITAN KOSOLAPOV	04184	KARELYALES	62241	KATHE JOHANNA	73970
KAMCHADAL	07555	KAPITAN KOSOLAPOV	02082	KAREN	57330	KATHLEEN	75890

Name	No.
KATHRINE SIF	49892
KATIA K	18230
KATIE	10365
KATINA	70490
KATINA C	45171
KATIPUNAN	18800
KATJA	76479/4
KATJANA	50119
KATORI MARU	51281
KATORI MARU	52691
KATORI MARU	72300
KATORI MARU	77190
KATRINAMAR	06990
KATRINE MAERSK	54455
KATRINE MAERSK	63375
KATSURA MARU	62301
KATTEGAT	18725
KATUNJ	02280
KATUNJ	35180
KATYA ZELENKO	78066
KATYN	02280
KATYN	35180
KAUAI	93527
KAUAI	94317
KAUGURI	13754/17
KAVALEROVO	06798/1
KAVKAZ	24145
KAVO ALKYON	28610
KAVO DELFINI	28611
KAVO GROSSOS	07021
KAVO MATAPAS	48200
KAVO PEIRATIS	48201
KAVO YOSSONAS	07022
KAVRAY	11926
KAVRAZ	17518
KAWANA	09830/1
KAWISHIWI	45053
KAWKAB 1	06362
KAYRA	12252●
KAZAKHSTAN	12456
KAZAKHSTAN	20374
KAZALINSK	23539
KAZAN	34874/2
KAZANTIP	11843
KAZATIN	06798/2
KAZATIN	23542
KAZBEK	39975
KAZIMIERZ PULASKI	12686
KAZIS GEDRIS	85330
KAZIS PREYKSHAS	76516
KAZUKAWA MARU	08720
KAZUKAWA MARU	09700
KAZUSHIMA MARU	93450
KDD MARU	02430
KDD MARU	35450
KEBAN	07880
KEBAN	15648
KEBON AGUNG	18152
KEDAYNYAY	06777
KEDAYNYAY	07591
KEDZIERZYN	75771
KEFAL	11789
KEFAL	34676
KEFALONIA HOPE	46453
KEFALONIA LIGHT	57380
KEFALONIA SPIRIT	09070
KEFALONIA STAR	61333
KEFALONIA STAR	59293
KEFALONIA SUN	47750
KEFLAVIK	51352
KEFLAVIK	52702
KEFLAVIK	84012
KEGOSTROV	11381
KEGUMS	86470
KEHDINGEN	91410
KEIY KOKEB	51131
KEIY KOKEB	51501
KEKHRA	89200
KEKUR	85979
KELEKAR	41963
KELLYEVERETT	21421
KEM	06795/5
KEMAL II	45450
KEMAL II	48710
KEMAL KOLOTOGLU	90170
KEMANO	82951
KEMEROVO	02728/7
KEMEROVO	10437
KEMINE	79415
KEN JOHN	61628
KEN VICTORY	79670
KENGARAGS	89750
KENNETH T DERR	53061
KENTAVROS	16620
KENTUCKY HOME	46587
KEPLERO	66540
KEPWAVE	77336
KEPWEALTH	74000●
KERASOUS II	29510
KERCH	12230
KERCH	39976
KERCH	59894
KERCH	67654
KERCHENSKIY	12302
KERCHENSKIY KOMMUNIST	86009
KEREN	16385
KERINCI	02346
KERKYRA	90770
KERMIT	83611
KERO	00110
KERO	36040
KESSULAID	75640
KETA LAGOON	04834
KETTY	90480
KEUM GANG SAN	92781
KEYLA	86247
KEYSTONE CANYON	58032
KEYSTONE MARINER	07710
KEYSTONER	38170
KHABAROVSK	02123
KHABAROVSK	12345
KHADER WALI	85080
KHADIJAAN	29920
KHALID 1	16551
KHALID 1	19291●
KHALID 1	23701●
KHALIJ COOLER	05467
KHALIJ CRYSTAL	03901
KHALIJ EXPRESS	03720
KHALIJ EXPRESS	06190
KHALIJ FREEZER	05465
KHALIJ FROST	05466
KHALIJ REEFER	05463
KHALIJ SKY	00352
KHALIJ SKY	26210
KHALIJIAH	58492
KHALIJIAH	84912
KHALIL III	35682
KHAN ASPARUKH	52440
KHAN OMTURAG	85362
KHANAQUIN	69574
KHANKA	84362
KHANNUR	53880
KHARITON LAPTEV	22190
KHARK	55463
KHARK	62784
KHARKU	13755/1
KHARLOV	07565
KHARLOVKA	17975
KHAROVSK	11757
KHAROVSK	34648
'KHASAN'	25550
KHASAN	67352
KHASAN	71362
KHASAN	84367
KHASAVYURT	50788
KHATANGA	24071
KHATANGALES	11492
KHATIJAH	11114
KHAYRYUZOVO	23554
KHENDRIK KUYVAS	67013
KHENGIS	21472
KHERMAN ARBON	12457
KHERSON	67682
KHERSONES	70778
KHIAN CAPTAIN	58091
KHIAN ENGINEER	58092
KHIAN HILL	58093
KHIAN ISLAND	58094
KHIAN SAILOR	58095
KHIAN SEA	58096
KHIAN STAR	58097
KHIAN SUN	58098
KHIAN WAVE	58099
KHIAN ZEPHYR	58100
KHIBINSKIE GORY	61272
KHIBINSKIE GORY	81492
KHIBINY	11320
KHIMIK ZEUNSKIY	01579/1
KHIRURG VISHNEVSKIY	01564
KHOLMOGORY	11307
KHOLMOGORY	22852
KHOLMOGORY	34482
KHOLMSK	24072
KHOLMSK	88244
KHRONOMETR	11949
KHRUSTAL	12459
KHRUSTALNYY	11927
KHRUSTALNYY	85992
KHUDOZHNIK A GERASIMOV	77081
KHUDOZHNIK A GERASIMOV	80001
KHUDOZHNIK DEYNEKA	76519
KHUDOZHNIK FEDOROVSKIY	77080
KHUDOZHNIK FEDOROVSKIY	80000
KHUDOZHNIK GABASHVILI	77082
KHUDOZHNIK GABASHVILI	80002
KHUDOZHNIK IOGANSON	77341
KHUDOZHNIK KASIYAN	77083
KHUDOZHNIK KASIYAN	80003
KHUDOZHNIK KUINDZHA	50737
KHUDOZHNIK KUSTODIYEV	77084
KHUDOZHNIK KUSTODIYEV	80004
KHUDOZHNIK PAKHOMOV	77342
KHUDOZHNIK PLASTOV	50748
KHUDOZHNIK PROROKOV *11-10-90*	77343
KHUDOZHNIK REPIN	77344
KHUDOZHNIK ROMAS	77345
KHUDOZHNIK S GERASIMOV	76514
KHUDOZHNIK SARYAN	77340
KHUDOZHNIK TOIDZE	77085
KHUDOZHNIK TOIDZE	80005
KHUDOZHNIK V KRAYNEV	10438
KHUDOZHNIK VLADIMIR SEROV	77086
KHUDOZHNIK VLADIMIR SEROV	80006
KHUDOZHNIK VRUBEL	76520
KHUDOZHNIK ZHUKOV	77346
KHULIO ANTONIO MELYA	36876
KHULNA	89224
KHUMBU 1	33811
KIAEN	83990
KIDRIC B	55993
KIEFERNBERG	72763
KIEL	49440
KIELDRECHT	47420
KIEV	02071
KIFANGONDO	05312
KIGILYAKH	50745
KIHELKONA	86239
KII MARU	20390
KIISLA	75220
KIKCHIK	06792
KIKHCHIK	07584
KILDARE	64480
KILDARE	92260
KILDARE	92430
KILDIN	11434
KILDIN	11583
KILDRUMMY	47461
KILIYA	06798/3
KILKENNY	72710
KILLIN	47395
KILLIN	47965
KILMUN	47870
KILWICK	09511
KIM ANN	17760
KIMBERLEY	62485
KIMBERLEY	57765
KIMITETSU MARU	69291
KIMITSU MARU	69290
KIMOLOS	33951
KIMOLOS	40970
KIMOLOS	60771
KIMOLOS	69671
KIMOVSK	03046
KIMOVSK	50915
KIMRY	07590
KINDRENCE	76141
KING ALEXANDER	64050●
KING GEORGE	62222
KING GEORGE	71132
KING HORSE	27910
KING HORSE	34440
KING LEAR	82590
KING LION	41955
KING NESTOR	61881
KING STAR	27920
KING TOWER	27911
KING TOWER	34441
KINGAN	12458
KINGFORD	25173
KINGISEPP	06778
KINGISEPP	07572
KINGSABBEY	66720
KINGSABBEY	76370
KINGSNORTH FISHER	23991
KINI KERSTEN	74017
KINKO MARU	56330
KINKO MARU	68020
KIPARISOVO	89511
KIRENSK	06798/4
KIRGHIZSTAN	02352
KIRGHIZSTAN	35372
KIRIR	23555
KIRISHIMA MARU	92623
KIRK CHALLENGER	93210
KIRK EXPRESS	17260
KIRKELLA	31130
KIRKUK	69575
KIROVABAD	44121
KIROVOGRAD	11844
KIROVSK	00850
KIROVSK	11602
KIROVSKLES	04180
KIRSTEN BRAVO	93990
KIRSTEN MAERSK	54450
KIRSTEN MAERSK	63370
KIRSTEN SKOU	31302
KIRSTEN THOLSTRUP	85000
KIRSTEN WESCH	62251
KIRSTEN WESCH	57607
KISANGANI	62713
KISANGANI	62753
KISHINEV	49240
KISHINEV	49240
KISLOVODSK	00333
KISO MARU	09810
KISO MARU	10180
KISO MARU	94930
KITA	27912
KITANO MARU	33601
KITEN	76533
KITEN	84211
KITHAIRONAS	48385/4
KITHNOS	52930
KITHNOS	60602
KITHNOS	69972
KIVACH	11308
KIWI ARROW	83145
KIZI	84363
KIZKULESI	19040
KLAHOWYA	18981
KLAIPEDA	39960
KLAMONO/PERMINA 1016	65181
KLARA ZETKIN	10725
KLAREDON	82800
KLAREDON	92090
KLASSEN	87200
KLAUS LEONHARDT	59754
KLAVDIYA YELANSKAYA	01937
KLELIA	58361
KLEMENT GOTTWALD	70599
KLIM VOROSHILOV	03965
KLIMOVO	11929
KLIN	03930
KLINTE	76209/8●
KLIO	29910
KLISURA	83729
KLORTE LAGOON	07993
KLORTE LAGOON	15278
KLOSTERFELDE	59650
KLYAZMA	12257
KLYAZMA	85880
KLYUCHEYSKOY	23556
KNIAZIK	18744
KNIEPSAND	59513
KNIEPSAND	59823
KNIGHT	61075
KNIGHT	71265
KNUD JESPERSEN	62486
KNUD JESPERSEN	57766
KNUDSHOVED	18940
KOBULETI	11845
KOCEVJE	71157
KOCHANOWSKI	06890
KODINO	11494
KOH EUN	71159
KOHENG	86113
KOHENG	91713
KOHJUSAN MARU	72311
KOHSHO MARU	72310
KOITELI	47492
KOKAN SEWAK	33440
KOKAN SEWAK	33610
KOKAND	36258
KOKAND	42808
KOKCHETAV	89464
KOKHTLA	15471
KOKKO MARU	54540
KOKKO MARU	63900
KOKUSHU MARU No 2	79620
KOLA	02728/3
KOLA	70777
KOLA	86188
KOLANDIA	71630
KOLASIN	58131
KOLEN	18745
KOLGUYEV	11498
KOLIAS	23461
KOLKHIDA	02350
KOLKHIDA	12258
KOLKHIDA	35370
KOLLBJORG	64577
KOLN EXPRESS	08781
KOLOBRZEG II	82263
'KOLOMNA'	28060
KOLPINSEE	46384
KOLPINSEE	47084
KOLSKIY	11585
KOLSNAREN	80293
KOLTSOV	12365
KOLYA MYGATIN	15514
KOLYMA	35323
KOLYMALES	04185
KOM	84212
KOM	85500
KOMANDARM FEDKO	67680
KOMANDARM GAY	50752
KOMANDARM MATVEYEV	03966
KOMARINE 7	71135
KOMARINE NO 9	09600
KOMERING	18155
KOMETA	11580
KOMILES	24043
KOMISSAR POLUKHIN	45126
KOMMUNAR	13678
KOMMUNARSK	03937
KOMMUNIST	05632
KOMMUNIST	12460
KOMMUNIST	14461
KOMMUNIST UKRAINY	12461
KOMMUNISTICHESKOYE ZNAMYA	05633
KOMMUNISTICHESKOYE-ZNAMYA	14462
KOMPAS	09385
KOMSOMOL	23543
KOMSOMOL	40007
KOMSOMOL UKRAINI	12462
KOMSOMOLETS	01385
KOMSOMOLETS	01645
KOMSOMOLETS	07569
KOMSOMOLETS	12303
KOMSOMOLETS ADZHARII	01399
KOMSOMOLETS ADZHARII	01659
KOMSOMOLETS ARMENII	01389
KOMSOMOLETS ARMENII	01649
KOMSOMOLETS AZERBAYDZHANA	01390
KOMSOMOLETS AZERBAYDZHANA	01650
KOMSOMOLETS BYELORUSSII	01400
KOMSOMOLETS BYELORUSSII	01660
KOMSOMOLETS ESTONII	03931
KOMSOMOLETS GRUZII	01391
KOMSOMOLETS GRUZII	01651
KOMSOMOLETS KAZAKHSTANA	01398
KOMSOMOLETS KAZAKHSTANA	01658
KOMSOMOLETS KIRGIZII	03932
KOMSOMOLETS KUBANI	36873
KOMSOMOLETS LATVII	03933
KOMSOMOLETS LENINGRADA	36879
KOMSOMOLETS LITVY	03934
KOMSOMOLETS MAGADANA	93759
KOMSOMOLETS MAGADANA	93849
KOMSOMOLETS MOLDAVII	01392
KOMSOMOLETS MOLDAVII	01652
KOMSOMOLETS PRAVDA	01402
KOMSOMOLETS PRAVDA	01662
KOMSOMOLETS ROSSII	01397
KOMSOMOLETS ROSSII	01657
KOMSOMOLETS SPASSKA	01394
KOMSOMOLETS SPASSKA	01654
KOMSOMOLETS TADZHIKISTANA	03935
KOMSOMOLETS TURKMENII	01401
KOMSOMOLETS TURKMENII	01661
KOMSOMOLETS UKRAINY	39994
KOMSOMOLETS USSURIYSKA	01395
KOMSOMOLETS USSURIYSKA	01655
KOMSOMOLETS UZBEKISTANA	03936
KOMSOMOLETS VLADIVOSTOKA	01656

KOMSOMOLETS VLADIVOSTOKA	01396	KOREAN FIR	61032	KOTA TIMUR	15631●
KOMSOMOLSK	71531	KOREAN FIR	71192	KOTA WANGSA	12713
KOMSOMOLSK	80201	KOREAN FLOWER	82991	KOTA WIJAYA	12712
KOMSOMOLSK NA AMURE	93760	KOREAN JACEJIN	73438	KOTA WIRAWAN	12711
KOMSOMOLSK NA AMURE	93850	KOREAN JACEWON	73437	KOTA WISATA	08072
KOMSOMOLSKAYA SLAVA	02681	KOREAN LIFTER	83992	KOTAH GAJAH	90343
KONA	63493	KOREAN LOADER	73491	KOTAYKA	23557
KONDA	21582	KOREAN PEARL	48270	KOTEL	83725
KONDOPOGA	06795/6	KOREAN PRIDE	61031	KOTELNICH	11324
KONDOR	09386	KOREAN PRIDE	71191	KOTHEN	'61712
KONDOR	11960	KOREAN SHIPPER	83986	KOTKA LILY	15780
KONDRATIY BULAVIN	89252	KOREAN TRADER	61033●	KOTKA LILY	82690
KONG FREDERIK IX	19590	KOREAN TRADER	71193●	KOTKANIEMI	47790
KONG HAAKON VII	60550	KOREAN WONIS JIN	08800	KOTLAS	28064
KONG HAAKON VII	69480	KOREAN WONIS ONE	73483	KOTLASLES	04186
KONG OLAV	01940	KOREAN WONIS SEVEN	73439	KOTOR	78530
KONG OLAV V	01910	KOREAN WONIS SUN	73440	KOTOVSK	86222
KONG SVERRE	33430	KOREAN WONIS-SUN	80370	KOTOVSKIY	20796
KONGER	22337	KOREIZ	06798/5	KOTOVSKIY	33910
KONGO MARU	35092	KOREIZ	12260	KOTUKU	53111
KONGO MARU	95083	KORENGA	23558	KOTUKU	53181
KONGSFJORD	76813	KORFOS 1	71350	KOUKOUNARIES K	25710
KONIGSEE	72121	KORFOS 1	86570	KOURION	41250
KONIGSEE	76461	KORIAKI	89508	KOVDA	24073
KONIN	05645	KORINTHIA	43620	KOVDALES	04189
KONIN	14474	KORLE LAGOON	15272	KOVDOR	15472
KONINGIN FABIOLA	20060	KORLE LAGOON	35043	KOVEL	22855
KONINGIN JULIANA	20470	KORNAT	80520	KOVEL	34485
KONKAN SHAKTI	33441	KOROLENKO	12366	KOVROV	03047
KONKAN SHAKTI	33611	KOROLENKO	20795	KOVROV	50916
KONKAR DINOS	63441	KOROTAN	10310	KOWIE	59730
KONKAR DORIS	48853	KORRIGAN	09690	KOWIE	67220
KONKAR HYPHESTOS	64329	KORSAKOV	06796	KOWLOON BAY	08402
KONKAR INDOMITABLE	77640	'KORSAKOV'	86070	KOWLOON PEAK	73170
KONKAR INTREPID	77642	'KORSAKOV'	87940	KOWLOON PEAK	77720
KONKAR NEREUS	48854	KORSNES	50122	KOYALI	67401
KONKAR POSEIDON	48855	KORTINA	76010	KOYO MARU	34390
KONKAR RESOLUTE	78560	KORUND	11846	KOYO MARU	38980
KONKAR THETIS	48851	KORUNDOVYY	89761	KOYO MARU	63326
KONKAR TRIAINA	48852	KORWIN	18746	KOYO MARU No 2	92620
KONKAR TRITON	48856	KOSCIERZYNA	50468	KOZANI	61121●
KONKAR VICTORY	77641	KOSHIN MARU No 3	70922	KOZELSK	50736
KONOSHA	86228	KOSHIN MARU No 3	79602	KOZEROG	12304
KONSTANTIN ALEKSEYEV	13752/2	KOSICE	78940	KOZYREVSK	07559
KONSTANTIN DUSHENOV	00149/1	KOSMAJ	68762	KR AVINASH	25172
KONSTANTIN FOMTSHENKO	34876/1	KOSMAS K	24670	KRAGUJEVAC	40241
KONSTANTIN KORSHUNOV	50289	KOSMONAUT	01073	KRAIGHER B	55994
KONSTANTIN OLSHANSKIY	76508	KOSMONAUT	85354	KRAKOW	15080
KONSTANTIN PAULOVSKIY	09997	KOSMONAUT GAGARIN	76525	KRALJEVICA	05651
KONSTANTIN PETROVSKIY	54717	KOSMONAUT GEORGIY	00251	KRAMATORSK	45218
KONSTANTIN PETROVSKIY	55287	DOBROVOLSKIY		KRANAOS	90631
KONSTANTIN SAVELYEV	50285	KOSMONAUT KOMAROV	45127	KRANJ	57442
KONSTANTIN SHESTAKOV	50281	KOSMONAUT PAVEL BELYAEU	00250	KRANJCEVIC	05654
KONSTANTIN SIMONOV	20356	KOSMONAUT VIKTOR PATSAYEV	00252	KRANSK	24070
KONSTANTIN SUKHANOV	93684	KOSMONAUT VLADIMIR KOMAROV	94280	KRANTOR	21920
KONSTANTIN TSIOLKOVSKIY	59896	KOSMONAUT VLADISLAV VOLKOV	00253	KRANTOR	67250
KONSTANTIN TSIOLKOVSKIY	67656	KOSMONAUT YURIY GAGARIN	92435	KRANTOR	91670
KONSTANTIN YUON	76586	KOSMOS	11584	KRAPANJ	71020
KONSTANTIN YUON	79936	KOSMOS	90100	KRAS	55270
KONSTANTIN ZANKOV	69315	KOSTA KHETAGUROV	50762	KRASICA	04915
KONSTANTIN ZASLONOV	50735	KOSTAKIS	43121	KRASIN	20872
KONSTANTINOVKA	12147	KOSTAR	62225	KRASKINO	24067
KONSTANTIS YEMELOS	06498	KOSTAS K	87371	KRASLAVA	86471
KONSTITUTSIYA SSSR	45270	KOSTAS K	91131	KRASNAL	87740
KONTULA	47190	KOSTINO	06781	KRASNAYA GORKA	11436
KOOLINDA	62482	KOSTINO	07579	KRASNAYA PRESNYA	01565
KOOLINDA	57762	KOSTIS	14304	KRASNOARMEYSK	06798/6
KOPALNIA GOTTWALD	74655	KOSTRENA	15291	KRASNOBORSK	06780
KOPALNIA GRZYBOW	48660	KOSTROMA	40003	KRASNOBORSK	07553
KOPALNIA JASTRZEBIE	48835	KOSTROMALES	11493	KRASNODAR	12259
KOPALNIA JEZIORKO	49211	KOSZALIN	34371	KRASNODON	03940
KOPALNIA KLEOFAS	61091	KOTA ABADI	10363	KRASNOE SELO	03944
KOPALNIA MACHOW	48661	KOTA ABADI	06750●	KRASNOE ZNAMYA	01566
KOPALNIA MARCEL	61092	KOTA AGUNG	04691●	KRASNOGORSK	84339
KOPALNIA MIECHOWICE	74656	KOTA ANGKASA	81557	KRASNOGORSKLES	04187
KOPALNIA MOSZCZENICA	61090	KOTA BAHAGIA	90470	KRASNOGRAD	03049
KOPALNIA MYSLOWICE	48836	KOTA BALI	01510	KRASNOGRAD	50918
KOPALNIA PIASECZNO	49210	KOTA BANTENG	90342	KRASNOGVARDEYETS	23559
KOPALNIA SIEMIANOWICE	48837	KOTA BERJAYA	07250	KRASNOGVARDEYSK	03938
KOPALNIA SIERSZA	74657	KOTA BERKAT	81558	KRASNOKAMSK	03939
KOPALNIA SOSNICA	61093	KOTA BERLIAN	81559	KRASNOPOLYE	06798/7
KOPALNIA SOSNOWIEC	78294	KOTA CAHAYA	05801	KRASNOPUTILOVETS	11614
KOPALNIA SOSNOWIEC	80024	KOTA CANTIK	05800	KRASNOTURINSK	06798/8
KOPALNIA SZCZYGLOWICE	61094	KOTA CEMPAKA	08131	KRASNOUFIMSK	03048
KOPALNIA SZOMBIERKI	48838	KOTA DJAJA	42160	KRASNOUFIMSK	03941
KOPALNIA WALBRZYCH	78295	KOTA HARAPAN	90471	KRASNOUFIMSK	50917
KOPALNIA WALBRZYCH	80025	KOTA INDAH	90472	KRASNOURALSK	03942
KOPALNIA WIREK	61096	KOTA JADE	48493	KRASNOYARSK	07566
KOPALNIA ZOFIOWKA	78296	KOTA JAYA	13092	KRASNOYARSKI KOMSOMOLETS	01388
KOPALNIA ZOFIOWKA	80026	KOTA MAKMUR	83580	KRASNOYARSKI KOMSOMOLETS	01648
KOPER	62180	KOTA MAS	00900	KRASNOZAVODSK	03943
KOPET-DAG	11300	KOTA MEWAH	07231	KRASNYY LUCH	71671
KOPORYE	06779	KOTA MEWAH	07431	KRASNYY-OKTYABAR	01567
KOPORYE	07582	KOTA MULIA	51081	KRASZEWSKI	15580
KOPRIVSTICA	83727	KOTA MURNI	15610	KRATILAOS	31490
KORALL	12463	KOTA MUTIARA	51080	KRATINOS	61066
KORALLE	28530	KOTA PAHLAWAN	88210	KRAYEV	12464
KORALLOVYY	89757	KOTA PELANGI	81560	KREKING	85889
KORANA	07892	KOTA PETANI	14730	KREMEN	11928
KORCHAGINETS	23531	KOTA PUSAKA	07680	KREMENCHUG	39997
KORCULA	71010	KOTA RAJA	08122	KREMENETS	86085
KORDUN	68761	KOTA RAKYAT	57522	KREML	01568
KOREA BANNER	55563	KOTA RATNA	17870	KRETAN SPIRIT	28511
KOREA BANNER	62493	KOTA RIA	17871	KRETAN SPIRIT	30321
KOREA EDINBURGH	38160	KOTA RUKUN	17872	KRETINGA	07558
KOREA STAR	55562	KOTA SAHABAT	82750	KREUTSWALD	85359
KOREA STAR	61082	KOTA SALAM	04978	KRIOS	36510
KOREA STAR	62942	KOTA SALAM	30428	KRIPTON	85970
KOREA STAR	71272	KOTA SEGAR	04975	KRIS	91560
KOREA SUN	55561	KOTA SEGAR	30425	KRIS MADURA	49611
KOREA SUN	62941	KOTA SEJATI	15672	KRIS MELELA	49610
KOREA SUNNYHILL	69254	KOTA SILAT XII	43149	KRIS MERUBI	49612
KOREA SUNNYHILL	70554	KOTA SINGAPURA	24440	KRISHYANS VOLDEMARS	12367
KOREAN CEMENT II	55250	KOTA TERNAK	60511	KRISTALL	12465

KRISTALNYY	89753
KRISTINA	52480
KRISTINA BRAHE	20830
KRISTINE MAERSK	54456
KRISTINE MAERSK	63376
KRISTIONAS DONELAYTIS	12466
KRISTYAN RAUD	12467
KRITI	08200
KRITI	68911
KRITI EPISKOPI	71501
KRITI GERANI	71500
KRITI LAND	69141
KRITI SAMARIA	71502●
KRITI STAR	69140
KRITI WAVE	69142
KRITON	41720
KRITONAS	61073●
KRITONAS	71263●
KRIVAN	15090
KRK	04916
KRKA	59571
KRKA	81301
KRONID KORENOV	93691
KRONOS	05341
KRONOS	61029
KRONOS	71189
KRONPRINS FREDERIK	16032
KRONPRINS FREDERIK	19992
KRONPRINS HARALD	16920
KRONPRINSESSAN VICTORIA	16910
KRONSHTADT	11736
KRONSHTADT	34626
KRONSHTADTSKAYA SLAVA	93786
KROPELIN	75335
KROPOTKIN	66392
KRPAN	62181
KRUPSKAYA	17519
KRUSAU	64981
KRUSEVAC	78532
KRUSEVO	81070
KRUSZWICA	14300
KRUTYNIA	86825
KRYLOV	17520
KRYM	24146
KRYM	63980
KRYMSK	06799
KRYMSKIE GORY	61273
KRYMSKIE GORY	81493
KSAR CHELLALA	49451
KSAR EL BOUKHARI	49452
KSAR ETTIR	49450
KUAKA	53110
KUAKA	53180
KUAN CHENG	64812
KUANG HAI	45890
KUBA	12468
KUBA	18280
KUBAN	02141
KUBAN	63981
KUBATLY	50784
KUBBAR	49410
KUBBAR	50970
KUJARWY	75734
KUJAWY	88384
KULBAK	18747
KULBIN	18748
KULDIGA	03260
KULIKOVO	07947/2
KULIKOVO POLYE	13752/3
KULOY	21583
KULUNDA	06799/1
KUMANOVO	78533
KUMBYSH	86007
KUN SHAN	84112
KUN SHAN	84172
KUNATKA	18749
KUNDA	89201
KUNG HEI	47812
KUNGUR	24068
KUNGURLES	04188
KUNMING	13101
KUNTSEVO	06784
KUNTSEVO	07589
KUNUNGUAK	12110
KUPA	47756
KUPISHKIS	06783
KUPISHKIS	07576
KUPRIN	12593
KURA	21222
KURA	35322
KURAMA MARU	33601
KURE	50040
KURE	51880
KURENAI MARU	20710
KURGAN	45211
KURILA	90890
KURILSK	86071
KUROSHIO MARU	02420
KUROSHIO MARU	08990
KUROSHIO MARU	15030
KUROSHIO MARU	35410
KUROSHIO REX	34301
KUROTAKISAN MARU	77807
KURS	09364
KURSHAYA DUGA	13676
KURSK	40008
KURSOGRAF	07474
KURT ILLIES	53109
KUSHIRO MARU	80300
KUSHIRO MARU	80810
KUSHKA	23560
KUSKOV	17933
KUSTANAY	06799/2
KUSTANAY	90150

LENINSKAYA ISKRA	93829
LENINSKAYA SMENA	79371
LENINSKIY	20798
LENINSKIY KOMSOMOL	31050
LENINSKIY LUCH	71670
LENINSKIY PIONER	01569
LENINSKIY PUT	93750
LENINSKIY PUT	93840
LENINSKIYE GORY	61274
LENINSKIYE GORY	81494
LENINSKIYE ISKRY	01647
LENINSKIYE ISKRY	01387
LENINSK-KUZNETSKIY	70030
LENINSKOE ZNAMYA	60684
LENINSKOE ZNAMYA	90723
LENKORAN	57634
LENKORAN	60671
LENKORAN	80921
LENKORAN	84815
LENSOVET	53535
LENTSKY	69370
LEO SHARPY	71030
LEO STAR	25890
LEO TORNADO	62232●
LEO TORNADO	71252●
LEON	56503
LEON	93891
LEON PAEGLE	12471
LEON & PIERRE C	72358
LEON & PIERRE C	77158
LEON POPOV	03780
LEON POPOV	04020
LEON PROM	29270
LEONARDO DA VINCI	38582
LEONCE VIELJEUX	05120
LEONCE VIELJEUX	59870
LEONIA	53198
LEONID BREZHNEV	20373
LEONID ILICH BREZHNEV	02415
LEONID IVANOV	34875/3
LEONID LEONIDOV	28492
LEONID NOVOSPASSKIY	34877/1
LEONID SEVRYUKOV	12262
LEONID SMIRNYKH	06799/4
LEONID SOBINOV	06200
LEONID TELIGA	80750
LEONID TELIGA	81450
LEONID YELKIN	34874/3
LEONIDAS	65480
LEONIDAS D	79180
LEONIS HALCOUSSIS	60253
LEONOREVERETT	04520
LEONOREVERETT	81582
LEOPARD	32501
LEOPARDI	32554
LEOPOLD STAFF	60488
LEOPOLD STAFF	71858
LEPETA	53196
LEPTON	62830
LEPTON	68080
LEPUS	11710
LERIDA	67635
LERNIA	74170●
LEROS ISLAND	34581
LEROS ISLAND	89951
LESKOV	12594
LESKOV	12590
LESLIE	59570
LESLIE	81300
LESLIE GAULT	48750
LESLIE GAULT	75570
LESNOY	12305
LESOGORSK	12472
LESOZAVODSK	13014
LETING	05130
LETITIA LYKES	05584
LETITIA LYKES	14425
LETITIA LYKES	14895
LETO	70460
LEV TITO	39416
LEV TOLSTOY	12369
LEV TOLSTOY	20355
LEVANTE EXPRESS	95130
LEVERKUSEN EXPRESS	08830
LEVERKUSEN EXPRESS	09030
LEVERKUSEN EXPRESS	77030
LEWANT II	31770
LEWANTER	10262
LEWANTER	10762
LEYTE GULF	18190
LEYTE GULF	33920
LHOTSE	50130●
LI CHENG	64816
LI SHAN	26350
LI SHAN	31690
LI SHUI	01531
LIA	80631
LIA PERO	12901
LIAN JIANG	63686
LIAN YUN SHAN	03031
LIAN YUN SHAN	03341
LIAO YANG	14640
LIAO YING	92640
LIAO YUAN	25051
LIAOHAI	57035
LIAOHE	50582
LIAZI	04500
LIBERATOR	64337
LIBERTADOR BOLIVAR	12991
LIBERTADOR GENERAL JOSE DE SAN MARTIN	06673
LIBERTADOR SAN MARTIN	52650
LIBERTADOR SAN MARTIN	71600
LIBERTY BELL VENTURE	62495
LIBEXCEL	52220
LIBEXCEL	84160
LIBRA	11716
LIBRA	66223
LIBRA	72690
LIBURNIJA	32710
LICHIANG	07666
LICHTENHAGEN	62700
LICORNE OCEANE	68450
LICUNGO	29060
LIDA DEMESH	67014
LIDES	61727
LIDES	58717
LIDES	59647
LIDIA DOCE	90580
LIEBENWALDE	46370
LIEBENWALDE	47070
LIECHTENSTEIN	62111
LIELUPE	63644
LIEN YUN No 28	86098
LIEPAYA	44622
LIESEL ESSBERGER	76897
LIESELOTTE HERRMANN	06382
LIESELOTTE HERRMANN	15412
LIFT-ON	74300
LIGAR BAY	88650
LIGATO	75552
LIGOVO	07567
LIJNBAANSGRACHT	49812
LIKA	04470
LIKA	10990
LIKA	34150
LIKE ONE	69300
LIKHOSLAVL	62572
LIKHOSLAVL	60662
LIKODYN	18751
LIKOMUR	18752
LIKOSAR	18753
LIKOWAL	18754
LILAC ACE	61658
LILAC ISLANDS	05336
LILIAN S	91640
LILIANA DIMITROVA	48157/4●
LILIENTHAL	50269/2
LILLIAN	55200
LILLIAN XXI	92973
LILLIAN XXII	92970
LILLIAN XXIII	92971
LILLIAN XXIV	92972
LILY VILLAGE	56502
LIMA	53199
LIMA	76603
LIMA	89303
LIMA II	05126
LIMA II	59876
LIMAN	11849
LIMB	13757
LIMBAZHI	38531
LIMENDA	17956
LIMING	10625
LIMING	15375
LIMNOS	60594
LIMNOS	69964
LIMON	33900
LIMOZA	11961
LIN HAI	46210
LIN SHAN	61675
LINA	87572
LINA	87772
LINA S	61881●
LINARD LAYTSEN	12473
LINCOLN	15760
LINCOLNSHIRE	80841
LINDAUNIS	73797●
LINDBLAD EXPLORER	32840
LINDBLAD POLARIS	20760
LINDE	87330
LINDEN	47878
LINDENBELS	52925
LINDENGRACHT	49813
LINDEWAL	75603
LINDEWAL	79323
LINDO	82241
LINERA	36074
LINERA	41794
LINERA	59750
LING HU	69640
LING JIANG	47240
LING LONG HAI	48010
LING YUNG	05610
LINGAL TRADER	61065
LINGNAN	66497
LINHAVEN	80671
LINK LOVE	10930
LINKUVA	66390
LINNE	72822
LINNE	80222
LINO	42460
L'INTERPECHE	93550
LINTONG	13370
LINYIN	29611
LION	19470
LION	83420●
LION OF CHAERONEA	28069
LION OF ETHIOPIA	04580
LION OF ETHIOPIA	34910
LIONELLO L	71880
LIONS ROCK	47811
LIOTINA	51311
LIPA	15783
LIPA	82693
LIPARI	09270
LIPETSK	67672
LIPS	60106
LIPSK N/BIEBRZA	58731
LIRA	12306
LIRIJA	12152
LISA B	49960
LISA B	51820
LISA HEEREN	88270
LISBOA	29380●
L'ISERE	32100
LISICHANSK	57635
LISICHANSK	60670
LISICHANSK	80920
LISICHANSK	84816
LISKI	81800
LISSY SCHULTE	84745
LISSY SCHULTE	84955
LITA	47994
LITIJA	05215
LITIOPA	57932
LITORAL SANTAFECINO	74230
LITRIX	84963
LITSA	56610
LITTLE NICOS	45020
LITTLE NIKOS	45020
LITVA	02162/2
LITZEN	75880
LIU KIANG	26521
LIULINHAI	46009
LIVADIYA	12263
LIVERPOOL BAY	08400
LIVIA	66651
LIVNY	57630
LIVNY	84810
LIZA CHAYKINA	41154
LIZA CHAYKINA	44956
LJGOV	00340
LJGOV	01020
LJUBLJANA	04871
LJUBLJANA	07801
LJUTA	56931
LJUTA	80931
LJUTOMER	04870
LJUTOMER	07800
LLOYD ALEGRETE	02567
LLOYD ALTAMIRA	49663
LLOYD ALTAMIRA	50933
LLOYD ARGENTINA	03547
LLOYD AUSTRALIA	56642
LLOYD BAGE	03470
LLOYD BAGE	03540
LLOYD BAHIA	02568
LLOYD BERMUDA	73760
LLOYD BERMUDA	75860
LLOYD BRAS	06558
LLOYD CUIABA	49661
LLOYD CUIABA	50931
LLOYD EUROPA	47447●
LLOYD GENOVA	06559
LLOYD HAMBURGO	06555
LLOYD HOUSTON	03549
LLOYD LIVERPOOL	06556
LLOYD MANDU	04800
LLOYD MARABA	49662
LLOYD MARABA	50932
LLOYD MARSELHA	06560
LLOYD MEXICO	03548
LLOYD NEW YORK	47281
LLOYD PARANA	54192●
LLOYD PARANA	54342●
LLOYD RIO	56641●
LLOYD SANTAREM	49664
LLOYD SANTAREM	50934
LLOYD SANTOS	03541
LLOYD SANTOS	03471
LLOYD SAO FRANCISCO	54191●
LLOYD SAO FRANCISCO	54341●
LLOYD SAO PAULO	56646●
LLOYD TEXAS	62075●
LLOYD TUPIARA	04806
LLOYDIANA	74412
LNG AQUARIUS	72200
LNG ARIES	72201
LNG CAPRICORN	72202
LNG GEMINI	72203
LNG LEO	72204
LNG LIBRA	72205
LNG TAURUS	72206
LNG VIRGO	72207
LO SHAN	32661
LOBITO	24720
LOBO D'ALMADA	08332
LODOWIK	18755
LOFOTEN	02370
LOFOTEN	18726
LOFOTEN	35360
LOGATEC	71205
LOGOS	21120
LOK MANYA	45774
LOK NAYAK	45772
LOK PALAK	45773
LOK SAHAYAK	45775
LOK SEVAK	71093
LOK SEVAK	71643
LOK VAIBHAV	30870
LOK VIHAR	45776
LOK VIKAS	48198●
LOK VINAY	48199●
LOK VIVEK	48199/1●
LOKATOR	09377
LOKBATAN	40664
LOKKY	48781
LOKMA 1	89860
LOKSA	22858
LOKSA	34488
LOKSA	89460
LOLA DEL MAR	76084
LOMBARD	55531
LOMBARD	63351
LOMONOSOVO	07560
LOMUR	93012
LOMZA	50469
LONDINON	25180
LONDON ENTERPRISE	55770
LONDON GLORY	55771
LONDON TEAM	58403
LONDON TEAM	64563
LONDON TRADER	64296
LONDONBROOK	75910
LONDRINA	62352
LONE STAR MARINER	07852
LONE TERKOL	85130
LONG BEACH	60185
LONG BEACH	74471
LONG CHARITY	57140
LONG CHAU	37365
LONG CHUAN JIANG	57450
LONG CHUAN JIANG	71780
LONG HAI	61960
LONG HAI	57370
LONG HU	70825
LONG ISLAND EXPRESS 1	87090
LONG LINES	02400
LONG PHOENIX	44580
LONG SHAN	10140
LONGHUA	26730
LONGLIN	06037
LONGMEN	06069/3
LONGTIME	26753
LONGVA	34010
LONGVA	34460
LONIA PRIMA	55850
LONTUE	58596
LONTUE	60476
LOOIESGRACHT	49815
LORD BYRON	62070
LORD CREVECOEUR	18341
LORD CREVECOEUR	33842
LORD DE FRANCE	18342
LORD DE FRANCE	33841
LORD D'ORLEANS	33844
LORD FLEUR D'EPEE	18343
LORD FLEUR D'EPEE	33843
LORD MOUNT STEPHEN	60710
LORD SELKIRK	16770
LORD SINAI	32680
LORD STRATHCONA	60711
LORD TRINITE	15391
LORENZO	45780
LORENZO HALCOUSSI	66270
LORENZO HALCOUSSI	69900
LORETO	25703
LORETO	94150
LORETO II	62820
LORETO II	67570
LORI R	06637
LORIA	52161
L'ORME No 1	88484
LORNA	11962
LOS ANGELES	74501
LOS CARIBES	80670
LOS TEQUES	51190
LOSINJ	07895
LOTILA	47290
LOTTE SCHEEL	49894
LOTTIA	51312
LOTUS	81751
LOTUS ACE	39280
LOTUS ISLANDS	05337
LOUCAS N	58159
LOUDI	06870
LOUIS S ST LAURENT	01840
LOUISE LYKES	05585
LOUISE LYKES	14426
LOUISE LYKES	14896
LOUISIANA	72209
LOUISIANA	93911
LOUISIANA	53075●
LOUISIANE	77970
LOUISIANE	50265●
LOULLIA	28801
LOUSSIOS	77702
LOUTFALLAH	05940
LOVECH	82138
LOVECH	82418
LOVISA GORTHON	92937
LOVOZYERO	11723
LOVOZYERO	34613
LOVRAN	84540
LOYALTY	06483
LOZOVAYA	57631
LOZOVAYA	84811
LSCO CAMRANH	42822
LSCO PIONEER	41620
LU CHENG	14500
LU CHUN	07664
LU DING	86640
LU HAI	79831
LU LIANG SHAN	00722
LUAN HE	46250
LUANA	59500
LUANA	81190
LUBBENAU	79730
LUBECA	73792
LUBEN KARAVELOV	48433
LUBEN KARAVELOV	49473
LUBEN KARAVELOV	49743
LUBERON	94295
LUBLIN	15084
LUBNY	62573

Name	No.
LUBNY	60663
LUC NGAN	06270
LUCENDRO	48178
LUCERNA	64620
LUCERNA	69011
LUCERO DEL MAR	02515
LUCHANA	09900
LUCHEGORSK	23490
LUCHEGORSK	23480
LUCIANA DELLA GATTA	77731
LUCIANA DELLA GATTA	89821
LUCIE	17191
LUCIE	32961
LUCIE DELMAS	48882
LUCIE S	90655
LUCIEN DELMAS	48261
LUCINA	53322
LUCINA	63222
LUCINA	62034
LUCJAN SZENWALD	06091
LUCJAN SZENWALD	14801
LUCKENWALDE	46372
LUCKENWALDE	47072
LUCKY	34211
LUCKY	24570●
LUCKY LADY	83700
LUCKY STAR	72125
LUCKY STAR II	14010
LUCKY TRADER	42610
LUCKY WAVE	60159
LUCKY WAVE	60252
LUCNAM	05315
LUCY	27590
LUCY	46893
LUCY BORCHARD	73724
LUCY L	78710
LUCY MAUD MONTGOMERY	19350
LUDOGORETZ	49162
LUDOLF OLDENDORFF	77446
LUDWIG	59120
LUDWIG RENN	13769/1
LUDWIG TUREK	13740
LUDWIGSHAFEN EXPRESS	08833
LUDWIGSHAFEN EXPRESS	09033
LUDWIGSHAFEN EXPRESS	77033
LUDWIK SOLSKI	14585
LUDZA	22859
LUDZA	34489
LUFENG	05831
LUFENG	06125
LUGA	86174
LUGANSK	62570
LUGANSK	60660
LUGELA	79891
LUHE	50843
LUHESAND	90811
LUHESAND	91771
LUHOVITSY	62577
LUHUAN	60832
LUHUAN	85072
LUIGI CASALE	54780
LUIGI CASALE	67450
LUIGI D'AMICO	30410
LUIGI D'AMICO	34930
LUIGI GARDELLA	75760
LUIGI GRIMALDI	78431
LUIGI ORLANDO	78460
LUIS BANCHERO	46095
LUIS BANCHERO	83265
LUIS CALVO	48581●
LUIS PEREDA	78830
LUISA DEL CARIBE	76031
LUISA DEL CARIBE	88621
LUISE BORNHOFEN	71840
LUISE BORNHOFEN	71980
LUISE LEONHARDT	55110
LUJAN DE CUYO	37720
LUJUA	46120
LUKA BOTIC	06412
LUKHOVITSY	62577
LUKHOVITSY	60667
LUKOMORYE	66397
LUMBER STATE	71158
LUMIERE	71503
LUMINENCE	76140
LUMINETTA	71504
LUMUMBA	62710
LUMUMBA	62750
LUN	35670
LUN SHAN	84110
LUN SHAN	84170
LUNA	62880
LUNAMAR	69660
LUNDOGE	05313
LUNG CHUAN	92715
LUNG TAN	13990
LUNG YUNG	62271
LUNJ	11599
LUNNI	51990
LUNNI	65160
LUNNIK	12595
LUNOKHOD I	23486
LUO DING	28160
LUO FU SHAN	77730
LUO FU SHAN	89820
LUO SHAN HAI	77482
LUOHE	50580
LUPENI	78583
LUPIN	47879
LUPUS	53669
LUPUS	73389
LUR TXORI	85232
LUR TXORI	65002
LUSITANIA	74024
LUSSIN	37850
LUSSIN	44430
LUTHER	73642
LUTJAN	18756
LUTSK	57771
LUTSK	84871
LUTTENKLEIN	76535
LUTZ JACOB	77140
LUTZ SCHRODER	56113
LUTZ SCHRODER	59803
LUZYTANKA	18757
LVOV	11850
LYCAON	48457
LYCAON	49497
LYCAON	49767
LYDI	46170
LYNX	57361
LYONYA GOLIKOV	07610
LYONYA GOLYKOV	15516
LYRA	11713
LYRA	68970
LYRA	75010
LYRA	76810
LYRIA	53075
LYSAGHT ENDEAVOUR	72811
LYSAGHT ENDEAVOUR	76831
LYSAGHT ENTERPRISE	72810
LYSAGHT ENTERPRISE	76830
LYSPOL	71906
LYUBAN	06785
LYUBAN	07571
LYUBERTSY	36900
LYUBERTSY	43800
LYUBERTSY	62576
LYUBERTSY	60666
LYUBLINO	62575
LYUBLINO	60665
LYUBOTIN	57636
LYUBOTIN	60672
LYUBOTIN	80922
LYUBOTIN	84817
LYUBOV ORLOVA	02343
LYUBOV SHEVTSOVA	41153
LYUBOV SHEVTSOVA	44953
LYUDAS GIRA	12474
LYUDINOVO	57633
LYUDINOVO	84813
LYUDMILA PAVLICHENKO	13679
LYUDMILA STAL	03781
LYUDMILA STAL	04021
LYULIN	77980

M

Name	No.
M A ULUSOY	87480
M CEYHAN	60270
M CEYHAN	63830
M EFES	65820
M EFES	69950
M G TSANGARIS	48176
M ISTANBUL K	72260
M P GRACE	58080
M SYCOUTRIS	90110
M URITSKIY	02126
MAASBREE	55490
MAASBREE	62950
MAASKADE	70130
MAASKANT	70131
MAASKERK	70132
MAASKROON	70133
MACAELA DRESCHER	50051
MACAPA	52281
MACCA	29922
MACEDON	25361
MACEDONIAN REEFER	04361
MACHITIS	34120
MACORIX	66974
MACORIX	91554
MADAME BUTTERFLY	94815
MADDALENA D'AMATO	72441
MADDALENA D'AMATO	77131
MADELEINE	83630
MADOURI	76970
MADZY	74901
MAELIFELL	86810
MAERSK ANGUS	65932
MAERSK ASCENSION	53192
MAERSK ASTRO	92957
MAERSK ASTRO	95167
MAERSK BRAVO	50150●
MAERSK BUCHAN	65931
MAERSK NEPTUN	72330
MAERSK SEBAROK	56485
MAERSK SELETAR	56486
MAERSK SEMBAWANG	47672
MAERSK SENTOSA	56484
MAERSK SERANGOON	47671
MAERSK TRITON	72331
MAFFO	12793
MAGADAN	34406
MAGADAN	90151
MAGALI	74261
MAGAR	72950
MAGDALENA	03761
MAGDALENA	58545
MAGDALENA DEL MAR	47711
MAGDALENE WESCH	49428
MAGDALINI K	12880
MAGDEBURG	03876
MAGDEBURG	04425/2
MAGDUS	43940
MAGED	35640
MAGED	41300
MAGHREB	81071
MAGIC MERCURY	70050
MAGIC SKY	47212●
MAGID	55891
MAGID	58691
MAGIDA	39612
MAGNA SPES	13070
MAGNISI	42850
MAGNIT	09374
MAGNITOGORSK	71530
MAGNITOGORSK	80200
MAGNOLIA	74006●
MAGNUS	53683
MAGNUS	53813
MAGNUS	68533●
MAGNUS JENSEN	49970
MAGNUS POSER	23426
MAGO	67367
MAGO	71363
MAH II	25861
MAHA NUWARA	48550
MAHARASHMI	25862
MAHARISHI DAYANAND	63459
MAHARISHI KARVE	63460
MAHAVIJAY	30720
MAHINDA	74943
MAHMOUDY	34372
MAHONIA	51543
MAHTRA	22860
MAHTRA	34490
MAI RICKMERS	28710
MAIA	87920
MAIJIN	24780
MAIK PRIMO	59628
MAIN ORE	79201
MAINE	50383
MAIRANGI BAY	08443
MAIRI EVERARD	75459
MAISENI	67270
MAISTROS	57003
MAJ SANDVED	49899/1
MAJA-M	75623
MAJANG	94471
MAJAPAHIT	50115
MAJESTIC	57310
MAJESTY	77630
MAJGARD	73962
MAJOR SUCHARSKI	07441
MAJOR SUCHARSKI	15313
MAJORCA ROSE	19600●
MAK	47601
MAKAR MAZAY	78894
MAKEDONIA STAR	70471
MAKELIS BUKA	07475
MAKELIS BUKA	11930
MAKHACHKALA	70576
MAKHACKHALA	40001
MAKHTUM-KULI	14383
MAKIRI SMITS	50192
MAKNASSY	65735
MAKRA	06532
MAKRAN	45935
MAKRAN	47445
MAKSIM AMMOSOV	50755
MAKSIM GORKIY	16810
MAKSIM KHOMYAKOV	13755/4
MAKSIM MIKHAYLOV	77349
MAKSIM RYLSKIY	50764
MALACCA	72341
MALACCA MARU	51420
MALAHAT	82950
MALAKAND	52868
MALAKHIT	12475
MALAKHITOVYY	89754
MALAKHOV KURGAN	10880
MALANGE	14750
MALANGEN	18727
MALARVIK	73860
MALASPINA	20130
MALAYA VISHERA	31890
MALAYA ZEMLYA	13683
MALAYAN EMPRESS	02604
MALAYAN EMPRESS	02634
MALAYAN KING	02635
MALAYAN KING	02605
MALAYAN PRINCESS	03513
MALAYAN QUEEN	02601
MALAYAN QUEEN	02631
MALAYAN REEFER	21390
MALBORK II	75414
MALCHIN	83601
MALDEA	81910
MALDIS SKREYA	67015
MALDIVE AMBASSADOR	34924
MALDIVE FAITH	34180
MALDIVE JADE	34920
MALDIVE NATION	44080
MALDIVE NATION	44390
MALDIVE NEIGHBOUR	24920
MALDIVE NOBLE	81551
MALDIVE PEARL	11540
MALDIVE PLEDGE	59410
MALDIVE PRIVILEGE	13780
MALDIVE PRIVILEGE	14780
MALDIVE PRIZE	28630
MALDIVE PROMOTER	09951
MALDIVE PROMOTION	90691●
MALDIVE TOPAZ	34921
MALDIVE UNITY	13930
MALDIVE VALOUR	85951
MALDIVE VALOUR	86591
MALDIVE VISION	30335
MALENE OSTERVOLD	17650
MALIGAYA	52420
MALKI	23562
MALLECO	72150
MALLING	74346
MALLORY LYKES	05586
MALLORY LYKES	14427
MALLORY LYKES	14897
MALLOWEVERETT	11171
MALMROS MONSOON	02581
MALMROS MONSOON	02951
MALOJA	50420
MALOYAROSLAVETS	31891
MALTA EXPRESS	32530
MALUKA	40911
MALUKA	45151
MAMAIA	13850
MAMAYEV KURGAN	13681
MAMBDOUN	81810
MAMIN SIBIRYAK	12476
MAMIN SIBIRYAK	12597
MAMIN SIBIRYAK	20799
MAMMOTH FIR	61196
MAMMOTH MONARCH	68553
MAMMOTH PINE	61197
MAN CHENG	64810
MAN PO	13390
MANAFOSS	83512
MANAL S	83616
MANAURE V	74091
MANAURE VI	74090
MANCHESTER CHALLENGE	76952
MANCHESTER CROWN	75587
MANCHESTER FAITH	73904
MANDAMA	05713
MANDARIN	24660
MANDARIN	26270
MANDO V	70134
MANGALI	89764
MANGANESE	18260
MANGYONGBONG	12770
MANGYSHLAK	44120
MANGYSHLAK	53160
MANGYSHLAK	23869/2●
MANHATTAN	36590
MANIA	59370
MANIA	87960
MANICA	10670
MANICA	13512
MANILA	47637
MANILA	51033
MANILA BAY	56646●
MANILA BRAVE	46312●
MANILA BRAVE	46562●
MANILA CITY	10800
MANILA ENTERPRISE	61044
MANILA HOPE	46314●
MANILA HOPE	46564●
MANILAID	75641
MANISTEE	03760
MANITOU	67110
MANJA	72143
MANJA	76483
MANKOADZE	12559
MANNA	64030
MANOLIS L	61714
MANOLOEVERETT	04750
MANSART	49552
MANSFELD	79731
MANSOOR	28770
MANSOUR	41920
MANSOUR 1	90532●
MANSOUR 1	91072●
MANTA	23462
MANUEL	85550
MANUEL AVILA COMACHO	70040
MANUEL SOTO	16420
MANUELA PRIMA	47375
MANUKAI	93520
MANUKAI	94310
MANULANI	93521
MANULANI	94311
MANX MAID	20500
MANX VIKING	93975
MANYCH	15474
MANYCH	45590
MANZANARES	03762
MANZONI	32555
MAO LIN	06415
MAR	87485
MAR CADIZ	48832
MAR CARIBE	32390
MAR CARIBE	92783
MAR CARIBE	94051
MAR COURRIER	06639/10
MAR DE VIGO	92789/1
MAR GRANDE	00490
MAR OCEANO	92782
MAR PACIFICO	59353
MAR TRANSPORTER	61050
MAR TRANSPORTER	82640
MARA	82010
MARABOU	60108
MARACAIBO	12992
MARACAIBO	15711
MARAJO	65870
MARAKAZ	18840
MARAKI	05237
MARALUNGA	53970
MARALUNGA	79020
MARAM	02391
MARAMA	93640
MARAMURES	78586
MARANAO	14813
MARANAO	30801
MARANAR	81270

Name	No.
MARANO	40841
MARAO	64390
MARAO	68610
MARAT KOZEY	15517
MARAT KOZLOV	67016
MARATHA ENVOY	61940
MARATHA MARINER	72355
MARATHA MARINER	77155
MARATHA MELODY	72356
MARATHA MELODY	77156
MARATHA PROGRESS	55150
MARATHON	90450
MARATHON LAKE	62010
MARATHON REEFER	04360
MARAZUL 1	56754
MARBONITA	58111
MARCEL C	94522
MARCHEN MAERSK	47380
MARCHEN MAERSK	47650
MARCIA	04920
MARCO POLO	52287
MARCOAZUL	78741
MARCONA CONVEYOR	52540
MARCOS SOUZA DANTAS	51060
MARCOVERDE	78742
MARDAKYANY	44117
MARDI GRAS	06830
MARE 1	84536
MARE AMICO	80430
MARE ANTARTICO	33860
MARE AUSTRALE	33862
MARE BONUM	59101
MARE BONUM	76411
MARE CARIBICO	31641
MARE GARANT	51784
MARE ITALICO	47850
MARE LIBERUM	76340
MARE LIGURE	53661
MARE LIGURE	73381
MARE MAGNUM	59102
MARE MAGNUM	76412
MARE NORDICO	77560
MARE NOVUM	59100
MARE NOVUM	76410
MARE PRIDE	73735●
MARE SARINA	59735
MARE SARINA	67225
MARE SILENTUM	76342
MARE TIRRENO	53662
MARE TIRRENO	73382
MAREA NEAGRA	10536
MAREL	71222
MARELIA	35902
MARELIA	41592
MAREN 1	49921
MAREN 1	50621
MARESOL	49224
MARFRIO	01435
MARGARET JOHNSON	04101/1
MARGARET LYKES	73513
MARGARETA	35711
MARGARETA	41421
MARGARETHA	76475
MARGARETHA SMITS	50190
MARGARITA	47680
MARGARITA	54301
MARGARITA	78610
MARGARITA II	73590
MARGARITA III	00930
MARGARITA III	00931●
MARGARITA L	01480
MARGARITE 1	56985
MARGARITIS	38720
MARGARON	64016
MARGARON	68406
MARGAUX	63400
MARGELAN	07902
MARGIO	56530
MARGO	91120
MARGRET	88105
MARGRET	75295
MARGRET CATHARINA	73802
MARGRETHE MAERSK	47381
MARGRETHE MAERSK	47651
MARHABA	14403
MARHAVA	64750
MARI	06488
MARI BOEING	48361
MARI BOEING	50871
MARI CHANDRIS	47681
MARIA	56871
MARIA	66050
MARIA	72141
MARIA	75934
MARIA	76481
MARIA A	40462
MARIA A	44902
MARIA C	43561
MARIA DA PENHA	05367
MARIA DA PENHA	15667
MARIA DE LOS DOLORES	65975
MARIA DORMID	66954
MARIA DORMID	70994
MARIA ELENA	71034
MARIA G L	46880
MARIA GLYPTIS	58119
MARIA GREEN	50193
MARIA IRENE	91090
MARIA K	06499
MARIA K	81040
MARIA LEMOS	61312
MARIA LEMOS	62612
MARIA MARIOS H	57619/4
MARIA MARIOS H	61059/5
MARIA MONICA	66933
MARIA MONICA	70983
MARIA N	58160
MARIA N K	82454
MARIA OLDENDORFF	71846
MARIA PAOLINA G	34040
MARIA PIA ESSE	92000
MARIA ROSA 1	84290
MARIA ROSA 1	84440
MARIA SITINAS	48302
MARIA SOFIA	24470
MARIA TOPIC	47210
MARIA X	46523
MARIA X	83303
MARIA XILAS	55102
MARIA XILAS	57592
MARIA ZAKELINA S	47325
MARIA ZAKELINA S	83385
MARIA-J	50157
MARIAM	09930
MARIAN BUCZEK	07442
MARIAN BUCZEK	15314
MARIANN	66990
MARIANNA	59482
MARIANNA	59541
MARIANNA	70135
MARIANNA	76209/9●
MARIANNA	81231
MARIANNA DORMIO	80521
MARIANNA VI	09420
MARIANNA VII	64365
MARIANNE BOLTEN	55661
MARIANNE BOLTEN	55861
MARIANNE ROTH	53414
MARIANNE ROTH	64944
MARIANNE SCHULTE	56118
MARIANO ESCOBEDO	54741
MARIANO ESCOBEDO	66111
MARIANO MOCTEZUMA	70044
MARIANTHE	02642
MARIANTHI M	53125
MARIAS	45040
MARIASSIMI	81142
MARIB	23290
MARIBOR	57441
MARIE	52041
MARIE	75913
MARIE DELMAS	48883
MARIE LEONHARDT	84691
MARIE LEONHARDT	89901
MARIE MAERSK	37830
MARIE MAERSK	44420
MARIETTA	01110
MARIETTA	42560
MARIFLIP	39745
MARIGO	60109
MARIGOLD	61474
MARIINSK	07903
MARIJEANNIE	79112
MARIJKE	50191
MARIKA	49930
MARIKA	50630
MARIKA	82353
MARIKA	82623
MARILENA	08550
MARILIA	62353
MARILIA	68733
MARI-LIFT	92740
MARILOULA	46400
MARILY	46589/1
MARILYN L	46695
MARIMAR	87580
MARIMO	32582
MARIMO	34980
MARINA	18880
MARINA	35070
MARINA	61900
MARINA	84120
MARINA A	31931●
MARINA BREEZE	83034●
MARINA BREEZE	83114●
MARINA DI ALIMURI	46320
MARINA DI CASSANO	55990
MARINA RASKOVA	10726
MARINA TWO	05400
MARINE ATLANTICA	16990
MARINE BLUENOSE	20240
MARINE CHEMIST	58960
MARINE CONTAINER	76171
MARINE CRUISER	19600
MARINE EAGLE	64660
MARINE EVANGELINE	93950
MARINE NAUTICA	16991
MARINE PACKER	84050
MARINE PRINCESS	79660
MARINE TRANSPORT	42500
MARINER	06646
MARINER	53450
MARINER	87702
MARINER	90360
MARINGA	03095
MARINGA	50981●
MARINICKI	53090
MARINICKI	63480
MARION	78400
MARION DUFRESNE	06180
MARION DUFRESNE	07520
MARIONA DEL MAR	76075
MARIPASOULA	59731
MARIPASOULA	67221
MARIPRIMA	37630
MARIPRIMA	44160
MARIS	50155●
MARIS OTTER	48903
MARIS SPORTSMAN	48904
MARITA LEONHARDT	59756
MARITIME ALLIANCE	49671
MARITIME BARON	73375
MARITIME KING	77885
MARITIME LEADER	47675
MARITIME OPTIMUM	07290
MARITIME PIONEER	55081
MARITIME PIONEER	57341
MARITIME PRIDE	47676
MARITIME QUEEN	47677
MARITIME TRADER	54634
MARITIME TRADER	55064
MARITIME VICTOR	47674
MARITSA	89822
MARITSA	77732
MARITSA P LEMOS	46070
MARITTA JOHANNA	88310
MARITTA JOHANNA	74290
MARITZA	59901
MARITZA ARLETTE	89710
MARIVERDA IV	84190
MARIYA POLIVANOVA	04522
MARIYA SAVINA	02344
MARIYA ULYANOVA	02125
MARIYA ULYANOVA	93381
MARIYA YERMOLOVA	02340
MARIZINA	69500
MARJAN	78069/3●
MARJAN	75509
MARJORIE LYKES	00068
MARK RESHETNIKOV	12477
MARK VI	88930
MARK VII	66460
MARKA L	46699●
MARKINA	62340
MARKINA	90700
MARKINCH	48753
MARKINCH	75573
MARKO MARULIC	06410
MARKO MILAT	35512
MARKO ORESKOVIC	05562
MARKO POLO	21210
MARKO TASILO	53441
MARKO TASILO	91571
MARKOS N	71140
MARLEN	28480
MARLENE S	58650
MARLIN	23463
MARLIN	77250
MARLINDA	58112
MARLOW	50440
MARLOW	52000
MARLY	56570
MARMARIS 1	81101
MARMORICA	17132
MARNEULI	07904
MARO	78424
MAROFA	64391
MAROFA	68611
MAROI	75872
MARON	54194
MARON	54344
MARQUISE	72421
MARRA MAMBA	68291
MARRA MAMBA	77321
MARS-2	23565
MARSA	04300
MARSDIEP	18971
MARSHA	06601
MARSHAL BIRYUZOV	60626
MARSHAL BIRYUZOV	62586
MARSHAL BUDYONNYY	68250
MARSHAL BUDYONNYY	68800
MARSHAL GELOVANI	23869/3●
MARSHAL KONYEV	68801
MARSHAL MALINOVSKIY	76527
MARSHAL MERETSKOV	93740
MARSHAL MERETSKOV	93830
MARSHAL ROKOSSOVSKIY	68252
MARSHAL ROKOSSOVSKIY	68802
MARSHAL ROKOSSOVSKIY	76504
MARSHAL SOKOLOVSKIY	93761
MARSHAL SOKOLC-SKIY	93851
MARSHAL VOROBYEV	79433
MARSHAL YAKUBOVSKIY	00145
MARSHAL ZHUKOV	68253
MARSHAL ZHUKOV	68803
MARSHALL CLARK	65222
MARSHALL CLARK	69882
MARSHALL KONYEV	68251
MARSMAN	58991
MARSMAN	75191
MART SAAR	12478
MARTHA	72351
MARTHA	77151
MARTIN ANDERSEN NEXO	17990
MARTIN S	62540
MARTINDYKE	75458
MARUN	53353
MARY	35872
MARY HOLYMAN	72870
MARY HOLYMAN	80240
MARY K	61464
MARY R KOCH	64522
MARY R KOCH	68472
MARYBETH	03492
MARYBETH	03582
MARYLAND	50384
MARYLANDER	82155
MARYLISA	59351
MARYNARZ MIGALA	87753
MARYUT	49683
MAS	89160
MASBON	60050
MASHALA	93090
MASHALA	94160
MASHITAGI	44118
MASHU MARU	19683
MASHUK	22162
MASIR	06880
MASLUCK	60053
MASON LYKES	05587
MASON LYKES	14428
MASON LYKES	14898
MASOVIA	77579/4
MASSA	70850
MASSALIA	16942
MASSALIA	90341
MASSANDRA	89206
MASTER PETROS	35873
MASTER TONY K	24540
MASTROGIORGIS	80490
MASTURA ZAHABIA	07020
MATACO	92786
MATADI PALM	58950
MATADI PALM	81180
MATANUSKA	32190
MATANZAS	90393
MATARAM	59866
MATCO AVON	37950
MATE 1	44627
MATE ZALKA	70590
MATEMATIK	23481
MATHIAS THESEN	06389
MATHIAS THESEN	15418
MATHIAS THESEN	62686
MATHILDA	45831
MATHILDA	58546
MATHILDA	94290
MATHILDE	35908
MATHILDE	41599
MATHILDE	75550
MATHILDE MAERSK	47383
MATHILDE MAERSK	47653
MATHRAKI	60591
MATHRAKI	69961
MATIJA GUBEC	05561
MATIJA IVANIC	05560
MATILDE R	78770
MATINA	72821
MATINA	80221
MATINA	81020
MATIS PLUDON	12479
MATOCHKIN SHAR	93872
MATROS KOSHKA	10881
MATROSOV	17521
MATSESTA	07901
MATSONIA	08950
MATSUKAZE	70010
MATSUMAE MARU	19684
MATTERA MIMMO	87691
MATTERHORN	31450
MATTERHORN	54431
MATTERHORN	54811
MATTHIAS CLAUDIUS	50130
MATTUN	75873
MATVEY MURANOV	03782
MATVEY MURANOV	04022
MAUI	93526
MAUI	94316
MAULE	72153
MAUMEE	38420
MAUNA KEA	95140
MAUNALEI	94260
MAUNAWILL	94261
MAURANGER	53027
MAURICE THOREZ	36869
MAURICIO DE OLIVEIRA	73581
MAURITIUS	24140
MAVRO VETRANIC	58132
MAWAN	72634
MAWAR	89440
MAW-LA-MYAING	71302
MAX REICHPIETSCH	06386
MAX REICHPIETSCH	15415
MAXHUTTE	36270
MAXHUTTE	43100
MAXIM LITVINOV	03783
MAXIM LITVINOV	04023
MAXIMO GOMEZ	05311
MAYA	58547
MAYA	66810
MAYA	85241
MAYA	85480
MAYA	86323
MAYA	89110
MAYA 1	41360
MAYA 1	41530
MAYAKOVSKIY	12370
MAYAYCU	88840
MAYFAIR	90690
MAYFLOWER	30552
MAYKOP	39970
MAYKOP	39971
MAYKOP	70572
MAYON	03840
MAYORI	63645
MAYSUN II	26570
MAYUMBA GLORY	72080
MAZATEC	03763
MAZATLAN	20440
MAZURY	59693
MAZURY	81353
MAZZINI	14400
MB 15	22151
MB 18	22150
MB 29	23665

Name	No.
MB 32	23665/1
MB 35	23666
MB 36	23666/1
MB 38	23667
MB 61	23667/1
MB 62	23668
MB 64	23669
MB 105	22152
MB 119	22153
MBANDAKA	62714
MBANDAKA	62754
MBUJI-MAYI	62715
MBUJI-MAYI	62755
McKINNEY MAERSK	47382
McKINNEY MAERSK	47652
MEADOWBANK	03674
MEADOWBANK	03734
MECHISLOVAS GEDVILAS	13758
MECHOR OCAMPO	86483
MECIS FLAG	10700
MECIS LEADER	10702
MECIS PIONEER	10701
MED SEA	21971
MED TRADER	27140
MED TRANSPORTER	61325
MEDALLION	51354
MEDALLION	52704
MEDALLION	84014
MEDANITO	66195
MEDCAPE	24480
MEDCEMENT CARRIER	74750
MEDEA	94818
MEDJ SEA	56640
MEDI STAR	56639
MEDIAS	87641
MEDIK	23563
MEDINA	38540
MEDINA	44810
MEDITERAN FRIGO	02843/1●
MEDITERRANEA	08806
MEDITERRANEAN CARRIER	78931
MEDITERRANEAN EAGLE	50269/3
MEDITERRANEAN EXPRESS	41981
MEDITERRANEAN SEA	16800
MEDITERRANEAN SKY	16801
MEDITERRANEAN STAR	10060
MEDITERRANEAN STAR	20862
MEDITERRANEAN SUN	20861
MEDNOGORSK	14701
MEDROCK	31360
MEDUSA	53201
MEDVEDITSA	84352
MEDYN	07906
MEE PYA	22730
MEERDRECHT	47220
MEGA BAY	65810
MEGA BAY	74790
MEGA PILOT	69780
MEGA STAR	77671
MEGA TRADER	58810
MEGA TRAVELLER	58811
MEGAMA	41950
MEGANOM	11852
MEGANOM	47150
MEGHNA	91920
MEHMET KEFELI	61700
MEI ABETO	25240
MEI GUI HAI	46010
MEI JIANG	06652
MEIHOU	49330
MEIKI	13471
MEIRU	13470
MEISHAN	07310
MEISSEN	70696
MEISTERSINGER	73020
MEITAI MARU	59960
MEITAI MARU	62400
MEKHANIK AFANASYEV	36880
MEKHANIK DREN	48862
MEKHANIK FEDOROV	80097
MEKHANIK GERASIMOV	80099
MEKHANIK GORDYENKO	54718
MEKHANIK GORDYENKO	55288
MEKHANIK KALUSHNIKOV	20800
MEKHANIK KONOVALOV	80094
MEKHANIK KULUBIN	20801
MEKHANIK P KILIMENCHUK	48158
MEKHANIK P KILIMENCHUK	78988
MEKHANIK RYBASHUK	24075
MEKHANIK YEVGRAFOV	80098
MELA	48082
MELAMPUS	54193
MELAMPUS	54343
MELANITA	11963
MELBOURNE EXPRESS	74490
MELBOURNE TRADER	94490
MELCHOR OCAMPO	69993
MELETE	53781
MELETE	68771
MELINA	16550
MELINA	41870
MELINA	64855
MELINA	91051
MELION	61616
MELITA	41953
MELITA	80421
MELITON	60110
MELITOPOL	11853
MELITOPOL	88248
MELKKI	51998
MELLINO VI	33550
MELODY	71505
MELOI	60110/1
MELORIA	35820●
MELPO K	45391
MELPO LEMOS	62790
MELPO LEMOS	67550
MELROSE	66500
MELROSE	85680
MELTEMI	64640
MELTEMI II	56770
MELTON CHALLENGER	73961
MELVIN H BAKER	89930
MEMNON	54191●
MEMNON	54341●
MEMPHIS	01678
MEMPHIS	01418
MENA	66061
MENANTIC	54416
MENANTIC	57876
MENDOZA	53100
MENDOZA	53330
MENELAOS	60400
MENELAOS TH	82160
MENELAUS	54190●
MENELAUS	54340●
MENESTHEUS	54192
MENESTHEUS	54342
MENHIR	46701
MENITES	74730
MENITES	79280
MENNA	75551
MENTON	87720
MENTOR	52181
MENTOR	54195
MENTOR	54345
MEONIA	50810
MEONIA	78781
MERAKLIS	72420
MERAPI	52920
MERAWI	51426
MERBABU	52921
MERCANDIAN ADMIRAL II	93273
MERCANDIAN AMBASSADOR II	93274
MERCANDIAN CARRIER II	94651
MERCANDIAN DIPLOMAT	93275
MERCANDIAN DUKE	93279/1
MERCANDIAN EXPORTER II	94655
MERCANDIAN GOVERNOR	93276
MERCANDIAN IMPORTER III	94654
MERCANDIAN MERCHANT II	94656
MERCANDIAN PACIFIC	64841
MERCANDIAN PRESIDENT	93272
MERCANDIAN PRINCE II	93277
MERCANDIAN QUEEN II	93278
MERCANDIAN SENATOR	93279
MERCANDIAN SUPPLIER II	94657
MERCANDIAN TRADER II	94658
MERCANDIAN TRANSPORTER II	94650
MERCATOR	85540
MERCATOR	73447
MERCATOR	80377
MERCED II	92900
MERCEDES DEL MAR	76101●
MERCHANT NAVIGATOR	17190
MERCHANT NAVIGATOR	32960
MERCHANT PIONEER	04720●
MERCHANT PIONEER	04940●
MERCHANT PRINCIPAL	56581●
MERCHANT PROVIDENCE	15670
MERCUR	61040●
MERCURIO	86911
MERCURY	14990
MERCURY	52622
MERCURY	60581
MERCURY	74946
MERCURY LAKE	08133
MERENGUE EXPRESS	84230
MERENGUE EXPRESS	87140
MERGUI	07421
MERIAM	91401
MERIC	07885
MERIC	15649
MERIDIAN	34712
MERIDIAN SKY	58231
MERIEM	50202
MERIEM	75972
MERINGA	90010
MERINO	41110
MERINO EXPRESS	52750
MERINO EXPRESS	53260
MERINO EXPRESS	84320
MERITIA	22835
MERKUR BAY	61409/4
MERKUR BEACH	61409/20●
MERKUR DELTA	61409/21●
MERKUR LAKE	61409/6
MERKUR RIVER	61409/3
MERKURY	11644
MERMAID	18660
MERMAID ACE	95030
MERMAID JUPITER	77224/2●
MERMOZ	08260
MEROWAH	23750
MEROWAH	24180
MERSIN	38090
MERZARIO HISPANIA	76764
MERZARIO HISPANIA	80274
MERZARIO SAUDIA	50265●
MERZARIO SYRIA	32360
MESANGE	45940
MESAWA	41954
MESIS	60160
MESKUPAS ADOMAS	12480
MESOLOGI	67945
MESSBERG	72688
MESSINIA	42050
MESSINIAKI ANAGENNISIS	60596
MESSINIAKI ANAGENNISIS	69966
MESSINIAKI AVGI	60592
MESSINIAKI AVGI	69962
MESSINIAKI DOXA	60597
MESSINIAKI DOXA	69967
MESSINIAKI GI	60598
MESSINIAKI GI	69968
MESSINIAKI IDEA	60599
MESSINIAKI IDEA	69969
MESSINIAKI LAMPSIS	60606
MESSINIAKI LAMPSIS	69976
MESSINIAKI THEA	60605
MESSINIAKI THEA	69975
MESTA	54870
MESTA	68560
METAL TRANSPORTER	69120
METALLURG ANASOV	01560
METALLURG BARDIN	01570
METALLURG BAYKOV	31053
METALLURG KURAKO	01571
METAN	89476
METEOR	34790
METEOR 1	51852
METEOR 1	73541
METEORIT	11854
METEOROLOG	23564
METHANE PRINCESS	55650
METHANE PRINCESS	56290
METHANE PROGRESS	55551
METHANE PROGRESS	56291
METHANIA	54050
METHANIA	54180
METOHIJA	15321
METON	37260
METRO SUN	83863
METRO SUN	85874
METTE SIF	49895
MEXICAN GULF	54571
MEXICAN GULF	54951
MEXICO 1	55873
MEXICO 1	56603
MEYENBURG	03877
MEYENBURG	04426
MEZADA	53720
MEZEN	17974
MEZENLES	90560
MEZHDURECHENSK	07907
MEZHGORYE	07908
MEZOSFERA	13686
MGA	22861
MGA	34491
MGACHI	12481
MIA	46494
MIA	48540
MIAN ZHU HAI	55671
MIAN ZHU HAI	72371
MIAO FENG SHAN	04664
MIAOULIS	09393
MICHAEL	26870
MICHAEL C LEMOS	62793
MICHAEL C LEMOS	67553
MICHALAKIS	35871
MICHALIS	14291
MICHALIS	60161
MICHALIS	60401
MICHALIS K	81510
MICHEL DELMAS	46980
MICHELANGELO	09200
MICHELE	47375●
MICHELE D'AMATO	78687
MICHELE GAROFANO	21921
MICHELLE C	06638
MICHURIN	07909
MIDAS RHEIN	61053
MIDAS RHEIN	82643
MIDHURST	89022
MIDNATSOL NORGE	17770
MIDSLAND	73981
MIECZYSLAW KALINOWSKI	14484
MIELEC	75412
MIESZKO 1	14919
MIESZKO I	15729
MIGHTIOUS	58400
MIGHTIOUS	64560
MIGHTY BREEZE	26571
MIGHTY SEA	00180
MIGHTY SPIRIT	23140
MIGHTY SPIRIT	28340
MIGHTY WIND	28680
MIGHTY WIND	32020
MIGNON	72759
MIHALIS	68852
MIJDRECHT	47221
MIKAIL MUSHFIK	50751
MIKHA TSKHAKAYA	59222
MIKHA TSKHAKAYA	74542
MIKHAIL BARSUKOV	23537
MIKHAIL BORONIN	34875
MIKHAIL CHEREMNYKH	76589
MIKHAIL CHEREMNYKH	79939
MIKHAIL ISAKOVSKIY	80057
MIKHAIL IVCHENKO	11586
MIKHAIL KALININ	02162
MIKHAIL KORNITSKIY	11894
MIKHAIL KRIVOSHLIKOV	79434
MIKHAIL KUTUZOV	17522
MIKHAIL KUTUZOV	80175
MIKHAIL KVASHNIKOV	34874
MIKHAIL LAZAREV	10441
MIKHAIL LERMONTOV	01754
MIKHAIL LOMONOSOV	10743
MIKHAIL LOMONOSOV	18090
MIKHAIL LUKONIN	50765
MIKHAIL MIRCHINK	92888
MIKHAIL OLMINSKIY	03785
MIKHAIL OLMINSKIY	04025
MIKHAIL ORLOV	13687
MIKHAIL PRISHVIN	77063
MIKHAIL SOMOV	21622
MIKHAIL STENKO	69319
MIKHAIL SUSLOV	20357
MIKHAIL SVETLOV	77064
MIKHAIL TUKACHEVSKIY	93686
MIKHAIL VERBITSKIY	34875/4
MIKHAIL VIDOV	11855
MIKHAIL VLADIMIRSKY	04024
MIKHAIL VLADIMIRSKY	03784
MIKHAIL YANKO	85333
MIKHAYLO LOMONOSOV	84368
MIKI	36390
MIKOLADY	57625/1●
MIKOLADY	61045/1●
MIKOLAJ KOPERNIK	09250
MIKOLAJ KOPERNIK	33380
MIKOLAJ KOPERNIK	94700
MIKOLAJ REJ	04861
MIKOLOYUS CHYURLYONIS	12482
MIKULIC OREB	91570
MIKULICA OREB	53440
MILA GOJSALIC	10220
MILANGO	61461
MILAS	56110
MILAS	59800
MILAS I	90400
MILCOV	11975
MILDA A	13590
MILENA	46261
MILENA A	44081●
MILENA A	44391●
MILFORD	28010
MILIN KAMAK	77089/3
MILIN KAMAK	80009/3
MILLEROVO	07910
MILLICOMA	41461
MILLY GREGOS	46112
MILOGRADOVO	11950
MILOS	45770
MILOS	48410
MILOS ISLAND	58577
MILOS ISLAND	60162
MILOS MATIJEVIC	69022
MILTZOW	50442
MILTZOW	52002
MILVUS	79141
MILWAUKEE	92603
MILWAUKEE	93613
MIMAR SINAN	34570
MIMITSU MARU	32610
MIMOSA TRADER	10660
MIN CHU CHI	42111
MIN CHU No 8	18490
MIN CHU No 9	23050
MIN CHU No 13	23120
MIN CHU No 7	42111
MIN JIANG	60485
MIN LIE	76060
MIN YUN HAI	47170
MIN ZHUI	02000
MINA	25660
MINA COTO	76040
MINAB	53354
MINADOR	60052
MINAROSA	60051
MINDANAO	33881
MINDELO	67492
MINDRA	11682
MINERAL ALEGRIA	73001
MINERAL ALEGRIA	76981
MINERAL MARCHIENNE	73000
MINERAL MARCHIENNE	76980
MINERVA	03101
MINERVA	77876
MINFU	80660
MING AUTUMN	47412
MING AUTUMN	48222
MING BELLE	62031
MING COMFORT	09837/1
MING ENERGY	09837/2
MING FORTUNE	09837/3
MING GALAXY	09831
MING GLORY	09832
MING HAI	46338
MING HO	23030
MING HU	57690
MING JOY	46350
MING JOY	46920
MING LEADER	46351
MING LEADER	46921
MING LONGEVITY	09837/4
MING MOON	09833
MING OCEAN	09834
MING PING	22963
MING SHINE	46352
MING SHINE	46922
MING SPRING	47410
MING SPRING	48220
MING STAR	09835
MING SUMMER	47411
MING SUMMER	48221
MING SUN	09836
MING UNITY	26480
MING UNIVERSE	09837
MING WINTER	47413
MING WINTER	48223
MING YOUTH	51330
MING YOUTH	52960
MINGARY	75932
MINGECHAUR	88236

Name	No.	Name	No.	Name	No.	Name	No.
MINGHUA	01820	MITTENWALDE	47075	MONTE CRISTO	02729/1	MOZHAISK	07911
MINI LABOR	83941	MIXORAM	47043	MONTE D'ORO	72590	MOZYR	07916
MINI LACE	83942	MIYAJIMA MARU	24400	MONTE OLIVETO	80632/1	MOZYR	36253
MINI LAD	83943	MIYAJIMA MARU	80705	MONTE PASCOAL	02729/2	MOZYR	42803
MINI LADY	83940	MIZAN	94470	MONTE ROSA	82810	MR AL	86980
MINI LADY	83983	MIZAR	12266	MONTE RUBY	75262	MRAMOR	12484
MINI LAGOON	83944	MIZAR	29170	MONTE RUBY	75262	MRAMORNY	11931
MINI LAMA	83979	MLAWA	50463	MONTE SARMIENTO	82814	MREZNICA	07893
MINI LANCE	83946	MLECHNYY PUT	13759	MONTE ZALAMA	46081	MT APO	90160
MINI LANE	83947	MMP WISDOM	27130	MONTE ZAMBURU	46122	MT CABRITE	64314
MINI LANTERN	83948	MOANA PACIFIC	56117	MONTE ZAPOLA	46121	MTSENSK	07905
MINI LAP	83949	MOBIL AERO	38121	MONTE ZARAYA	46123	MTSKHETSA	12264
MINI LARK	83950	MOBIL ALADDIN	64330	MONTEGO BAY II	02571	MU DAN JIANG	71856
MINI LASS	83951	MOBIL ARCTIC	63414	MONTELEON	70310	MU DAN JIANG	71981
MINI LATRIA	83952	MOBIL ENGINEER	64670	MONTEMURO	64392	MUDI	87674
MINI LAUD	83953	MOBIL FALCON	63034	MONTEMURO	68612	MUDYUG	34405
MINI LAW	83954	MOBIL FUEL	38100	MONTENAKEN	06051	MUGGELSEE	46382
MINI LEAD	83955	MOBIL KESTREL	62890	MONTEREY	06840	MUGGELSEE	47082
MINI LEAF	83956	MOBIL LUBCHEM	66630	MONTERREY	01430	MUGLA	81102
MINI LEAGUE	83957	MOBIL MARKETER	65750	MONTERREY	56444	MUHIEDDINE-	91830
MINI LEE	83958	MOBIL NAVIGATOR	64671	MONTERREY	68354	MUHLHAUSEN	03706
MINI LEGEND	83959	MOBIL PETROLEUM	63863	MONTESA	58770	MUHUTI	51085
MINI LENS	83960	MOBIL PRODUCER	65751	MONTESA	62510	MUKACHEVO	07914
MINI LIBRA	83961	MOBIL REFINER	65752	MONTFORT	06052	MUKAIRISH ALTHALETH	10630
MINI LID	83962	MOBIL SEARCH	14951	MONTJOLLY II	01470	MUKALLA	59671
MINI LIDO	83963	MOBIL SWIFT	54802	MONTLHERY	35535	MUKHTAR ASHRAFI	79435
MINI LIFT	83964	MOBIL SWIFT	68032	MONTONE	80400	MULDE	26064
MINI LIGHT	83965	MOBILOIL	38120	MONTPELIER VICTORY	36650	MULHEIM	47659/1
MINI LILAC	83982	MOBY BLU	20420	MONTROSE	61054	MULSANNE	52305
MINI LINER	83966	MODENA	82680	MONTSALVA	06053	MULTAN	52867
MINI LINK	83967	MODO GORTHON	72842	MONTT	45310	MULTI CARRIER	02550
MINI LIONESS	83969	MOENJODARO	15640	MONZABON	75881	MULTI CARRIER	45970
MINI LIZARD	83970	MOFARRIJ 1	26890	MOOLCHAND	06639	MULTI SERVICE 125	90180
MINI LOAF	83971	MOFARRIJ B	28720	MOORDRECHT	47226	MULTI SERVICE 300	92080
MINI LOGIC	83980	MOFARRIJ C	56900	MOORFIELDS MONARCH	68552	MULTITANK ADRIA	75172
MINI LOOM	83972	MOFARRIJ D	59311	MOR	67494	MULTITANK ARCADIA	75173
MINI LORY	83973	MOFARRIJ G	35906	MORAYBANK	03675	MULTITANK ARMENIA	75174
MINI LOT	83974	MOFARRIJ G	41596	MORAYBANK	03735	MULTITANK ASCANIA	75175
MINI LOTUS	83975	MOGENS S	91323	MOREKHOD	17932	MULTITANK FRISIA	59071
MINI LUCK	83976	MOGES AGATHIS	61615	MOREKHOD	85356	MULTITANK FRISIA	76421
MINI LUNAR	83981	MOGILEV	25559	MORELIA	72342	MULTITANK HAMMONIA	54751
MINI LUX	83977	MOHAC	80357	MORESBY CHIEF	67490	MULTITANK HAMMONIA	56211
MINI LYMPH	83978	MOHAMMED ABBAS	00810	MORETON BAY	77055	MULTITANK HOLSATIA	59072
MINIFOREST	72750	MOHAWK	63454	MORFREEZE	00351	MULTITANK HOLSATIA	76422
MINIMO	27400	MOIDART	75931	MORFREEZE	26211	MULTITANK WESTFALIA	54752
MINISTRO EXCURRA	52652	MOJAIL-5	12840	MORILLO	14170	MULTITANK WESTFALIA	56212
MINISTRO EXCURRA	71602	MOKHA	58710	MORITZ SCHULTE	81391	MUMTAZ	81030
MINISTRO EZCURRA	57625 1●	MOKHA	59640	MORMACDAWN	05933	MUNAKATA MARU	31391
MINNEAPOLIS	90981	MOKHA	61720	MORMACGLEN	14550	MUNATONES	58771
MINNESOTA	90980	MOKHNI	89260	MORMACMOON	05934	MUNATONES	62511
MINO	42190	MOKRAN	53355	MORMACWAVE	08004	MUNAWER	28120
MINOAS	26029●	MOKSTEIN	48790	MORNING GLORY	61216	MUNAWER	28560
MINOAS	30192●	MOLARA	39890	MORNING SUN	83985	MUNDACA	63134
MINOGAZ 1	63740	MOLAT	48636	MORS	23457	MUNDIAL CAR	58210
MINOGAZ 1	81680	MOLDA	83144	MORSHANSK	07913	MUNDIAL CAR	63750
MINOLA	61463	MOLDAVIA	02353	MORSKOY GEOFIZIK	39417	MUNDOGAS AMERICA	55610
MINORIES PRIDE	46130	MOLDAVIA	35373	MORUKA	42140	MUNDOGAS EUROPE	54470
MINORIES PROGRESS	54701	MOLDAVIYA	06828	MORVEN	35970	MUNDOGAS PACIFIC	54472
MINORIES PROGRESS	74761	MOLDOVEANU	11702	MORZHOVETS	11382	MUNDOGAS RIO	55830
MINOS	42410	MOLENGAT	18955	MOS SHOVGENOV	60635	MUNETAMA MARU	57960
MINOS	72422	MOLLENDO	36742	MOS SHOVGENOV	62595	MUNETAMA MARU	59930
MINOTAUR	58364	MOLLY	89121	MOSA PIJADE	05563	MUNGO	51074
MINOTAURUS	10910	MOLOCHANSK	07912	MOSBORG	64332●	MUNGUIA	63135
MINSK	07900	MOLODAYA GVARDIYA	76497	MOSBROOK	53801	MUNKSUND	83190
MINT PROSPERITY	68555	MOLODECHNO	40006	MOSBROOK	77521	MUNSTERLANDES	10671
MINTSUNG	10141	MOLODOGVARDEYSK	07915	MOSCENICE	04917	MUNSTERLANDES	13514
MIR	06069/10	MOLODYOZNYY	85355	MOSCHA D	24892	MUNTENIA	55783
MIR	12596	MOLUCCA SEA	06416	MOSCLIFF	55501	MUNTENIA	56483
MIR	37000	MOLUNAT	89630	MOSCLIFF	67911	MUNZUR	35681
MIRA	46215	MOMOLI	48500	MOSDUKE	78421	MUO	59400
MIRA	71152	MONAC	59623	MOSEL	59710	MUO	62160
MIRABELLA	89591	MONARCH	65823	MOSEL ORE	52380	MUOSTAKH	49248
MIRAFIORI	56412●	MONARCH	69953	MOSEL ORE	64440	MUOSTAKH	49261
MIRAFIORI	67832●	MONA'S QUEEN	20180	MOSELLE	54415	MUR	75871
MIRAFIORI	68432●	MONCADA	06611	MOSELLE	57875	MURASAKI MARU	20711
MIRAMAR	50860	MONCALVO	25211	MOSKALVO	40000	MURASAKI MARU	43290
MIRAMAR	87350	MONCHEGORSK	02726	MOSKOVSKIY KOMSOMOLETS	01403	MURAT M	36120
MIRAMAR	79920	MONCHEGORSK	88237	MOSKOVSKIY KOMSOMOLETS	01663	MURAT M	37900
MIRAMAR PRIMA	45460	MONEMVASIA	67946	MOSKVA	02070	MURES	11976
MIRAMAR PRIMA	48720	MONET	48403	MOSLAVINA	15323	MURGAB	50775
MIRANDA	61900●	MONGE	54040	MOSMAN STAR	49307	MURGASH	49161
MIRANDA	78683	MONGIBELLO	19001	MOSOR	71285	MURMAN	15475
MIRANDA 1	32951	MONGOL	85348	MOSSOVET	53536	MURMANSELD	11767
MIRGOROD	25558	MONGOLIYA	12483	MOSTEFA BEN BOULAID	53651	MURMANSELD	34658
MIRNYY	07562	MONIA	45060	MOSTEFA BEN BOULAID	53741	MURMANSK	02073
MIRONAVE	40430	MONIMBO	51112	MOSTOLES	64324●	MURMANSK	12346
MIRONYCH	24074	MONIMBO	51492	MOSTUN	68533	MURMASH	22862
MIROSLAWIEC	70542	MONISBON	51111	MO'TAH	45406	MURMASHI	34492
MIROW	50443	MONISBON	51491	MOTHER	79220●	MUROM	07917
MIROW	52003	MONOMER VENTURE	90790	MOTHI	90520	MUROMSK	11600
MISA	13754/15	MONOSANDALOS	74120	MOTILAL NEHRU	63560	MURRAYEVERETT	04753
MISAMIS OCCIDENTAL	11210	MONOWAI	04060	MOTOBU	72941	MURREE	56575
MISHA S AMITY	13860	MONS CALPE	17240	MOTOVUN	04918	MURTAJA	23980
MISHIMA MARU	86611	MONSUN	55874	MOUNIVET	72590●	MUSA DZHALIL	14384
MISHNISH	75481	MONSUN	56604	MOUNT ATHOS	47950	MUSALA	55410
MISIONES II	48377	MONSUN	67701	MOUNT BOLIVAR	61659	MUSALA	78850
MISKHOR	12265	MONT BLANC MARU	09770	MOUNT CARIBBEAN	31220	MUSCAT BAY	49642
MISPILLION	38920	MONT LOUIS	74070	MOUNT EDEN	77773	MUSCAT CEMENT	64101
MISS MARIETTA	35870	MONT VENTOUX	59815	MOUNT ELLEROS	59840	MUSCAT CEMENT	71581
MISSISSINEWA	45051	MONTAIGLE	06050	MOUNT ELLEROS	67510	MUSCEL	82226
MISTER MICHAEL	72423	MONT-ALBAN	86670	MOUNT ORO	61622	MUSHRIF	84533
MISTI	45820	MONTANA	46944	MOUNT OTHRYS	56860	MUSI	18157
MISTRAL	20750	MONTANA	47104	MOUNT PARNASSOS	77595	MUSING	81080
MISTRAL	55670	MONTANA	90534	MOUNT PARNIS	73371	MUSKETIER II	87170
MISTRAL	72370	MONTANA	91074	MOUNT PENTELI	73370	MUSSON	02270
MITHAT PASA	34581	MONTARIK	61323	MOUNT PINDOS	77882	MUSSON	18272
MITRIDAT	11856	MONTCALM	08850	MOUNT TAYGETOS	73372	MUSTYARV	13682
MITROFAN GREKOV	76582	MONTCALM	72412	MOUNT VERNON VICTORY	36653	MUTAN CAREER	58·25
MITROFAN GREKOV	79932	MONTE ABRIL	90657	MOUNT WASHINGTON	36652	MUTIARA	01460
MITROFAN SEDIN	60634	MONTE ALTO	02729	MOUNTAIN AZALEA	05321	MUTIARA	08560
MITROFAN SEDIN	62594	MONTE BANDERAS	95220	MOUNTCREST	76090	MUTSU	35400
MITSUI MARU	77502	MONTE BUITRE	95221	MOUTSAINA	61707	MUTSU	35540
MITSUI MARU No 2	77504	MONTE BUSTELO	95222	MOWLAVI	04551	MUXIMA	10673
MITTENWALDE	46375	MONTE CERVANTES	82811	MOZART FESTIVAL	47161	MUXIMA	13513

Name	No.	Name	No.	Name	No.	Name	No.
MY CHARM	83604	NACALA	08010	NANWU	13630	NEDLLOYD BAHRAIN	49420
MY KATERINA	07767	NACELLA	64221	NANXIANG	29360	NEDLLOYD BALTIMORE	49421
MY KATERINA	07813	NACIONAL AVEIRO	72240	NANXIANG	30583	NEDLLOYD BANGKOK	49422
MYASSAR	43490	NACIONAL BRAGANCA	60911	NAPAL SAN	85630	NEDLLOYD BARCELONA	49423
MYKONOS	03190	NACIONAL MONCHIQUE	73070	NAPALSAN	85630	NEDLLOYD DEJIMA	08374
MYKONOS	03590	NACIONAL SAGRES	06639/11	NAPOLEON	20660	NEDLLOYD DELFT	08375
MYKONOS	55793	NACIONAL SETUBAL	06639/1	NARA	48420	NEDLLOYD EVEREST	55210
MYKONOS	64654	NACIONAL SINES	77260	NARA	49460	NEDLLOYD FUKUOKA	08070
MYLOI	46712	NADA D.	74110	NARA	49510	NEDLLOYD GOOILAND	05540
MYOMA YWA	52671	NADA G	90872	NARCIS	92401	NEDLLOYD HOLLANDIA	73407
MYRIAM DEL TORO	76080	NADAZ	49853	NARCIS	93081	NEDLLOYD HOLLANDIA	82717
MYRICA	70051	NADAZ	50093	NARDEN	86954	NEDLLOYD HOORN	08431
MYRINA	61165	NADE PIBAKOVAYTE	67017	NARICA	64220	NEDLLOYD HOUTMAN	08430
MYRMIDON	54196	NADEZHDA	11857	NARISSA	58126/2	NEDLLOYD KATWIJK	04394
MYRMIDON	54346	NADEZHDA KRUPSKAYA	03705	NAROCH	11732	NEDLLOYD KATWIJK	52904
MYROVLITIS	83713	NADEZHDA KURCHYENKO	86008	NAROCH	34622	NEDLLOYD KEMBLA	04390
MYRTEA	55794	NADEZHDA OBUKHOVA	77347	NARODNYY OPOLCHENETS	13752/4	NEDLLOYD KEMBLA	52900
MYRTEA	64655	NADEZHDINSK	12485	NARODOV	60682	NEDLLOYD KIMBERLEY	04391
MYRTIA	65672	NADIA	46902	NAROTTAM MORARJEE	78390	NEDLLOYD KIMBERLEY	52901
MYRTIDIOTISSA	28670	NADIA	70960	NARVA	85980	NEDLLOYD KINGSTON	04392
MYS ARKTICHESKIY	11737	NADIA	87870	NARVA	89229	NEDLLOYD KINGSTON	52902
MYS ARKTICHESKIY	34627	NADIA 1	74310	NARVAL	03494	NEDLLOYD KYOTO	04393
MYS BABUSHKIN	11786	NADIA 2	76660	NARVAL	03584	NEDLLOYD KYOTO	52903
MYS BABUSKIN	34671	NADIA S	61130	NARVSKAYA ZASTAVA	11632	NEDLLOYD LEUVE	03300
MYS BARANOVA	23496	NADIR	12267	NARVSKAYA ZASTAVA	50290	NEDLLOYD LINGE	03302
MYS BELKINA	23489	NADIR	24970	NARVSKIY ZALIV	61106	NEDLLOYD LOIRE	03301
MYS BOBROVA	23491	NADYM	70024	NARWAL	10813	NEDLLOYD MADRAS	47636
MYS BUDYONNOGO	11748	NAECO	38102	NARWIK II	70543	NEDLLOYD MANILA	47637●
MYS BUDYONNOGO	34638	NAFEESA	15330	NARYAN—MAR	24077	NEDLLOYD MARSEILLE	47635
MYS CHAKO	13684	NAFTILOS	05342	NARYMNEFT	86003	NEDLLOYD NAGASAKI	02710
MYS CHASOVOY	11763	NAFTILOS	57186	NARYN	86086	NEDLLOYD NAGASAKI	47640
MYS CHASOVOY	34654	NAGAEVO	22863	NASAUD	01410	NEDLLOYD NAGOYA	92711
MYS CHAYKOVSKOGO	11764	NAGAEVO	34493	NASAUD	01670	NEDLLOYD NAGOYA	47641
MYS CHAYKOVSKOGO	34655	NAGAN	31300	NASIMI	79418	NEDLLOYD NAPIER	02712
MYS CHELYUSKIN	11749	NAGARA	02582	NASIPIT BAY	05431	NEDLLOYD NAPIER	47642
MYS CHELYUSKIN	34639	NAGARA	02952	NATA	60111	NEDLLOYD NASSAU	02713
MYS DALNIY	11778	NAGARAT	23031	NATA VACHNADZE	67688	NEDLLOYD NASSAU	47643
MYS DALNIY	34669	NAGINA	87450	NATAL HUSTLER	82761	NEDLLOYD NIGER	62630
MYS FRUNZE	11750	NAGINA TRADER	27361	NATALIA	12940	NEDLLOYD ORANJESTAD	03141
MYS FRUNZE	34640	NAHODA BIRU	48631●	NATALIE BOLTEN	49951	NEDLLOYD PRIDE	73735
MYS GAMOVA	23492	NAI ALBERTO	79051	NATALIE BOLTEN	58501	NEDLLOYD ROSARIO	80268
MYS GRINA	23497	NAI DI STEFANO	62859	NATALIYA KOVSHOVA	04520	NEDLLOYD ROUEN	80267
MYS GROTOVYY	11724	NAI DI STEFANO	67539	NATHALIE	35675	NEDLLOYD TASMAN	74411
MYS GROTOVYY	34614	NAI LUISA	51590	NATHALIE	48902	NEDLLOYD WAALEKERK	15831
MYS GROZNYY	11765	NAI LUISA	52340	NATHALIE D	21751	NEDLLOYD WESTERKERK	15833
MYS GROZNYY	34656	NAI MARIA AMELIA	51635	NATHALIE DELMAS	47216	NEDLLOYD WESTERKERK	72182
MYS ILMOVYY	11760	NAI MARIO PERRONE	62858	NATHANIEL	73743	NEDLLOYD WESTERKERK	83402
MYS ILMOVYY	34651	NAI MARIO PERRONE	67538	NATICINA	52970	NEDLLOYD WILLEMSKERK	15832
MYS KHRUSTALNYY	66393	NAI MATTEINI	62860	NATIONAL LEADER	61083	NEDLLOYD WILLEMSKERK	72183
MYS KODOSH	66396	NAI MATTEINI	67540	NATIONAL LEADER	71273	NEDLLOYD WILLEMSKERK	83403
MYS KRONOTSKIY	11751	NAI MEY	79050	NATIONAL STEEL TWO	30651	NEDLLOYD WILLEMSTAD	03140
MYS KRONOTSKIY	34641	NAI ROCCO PIAGGIO	62861	NATKO NODILO	06411	NEDLLOYD WISSEKERK	15830
MYS KRYLOVA	23493	NAI ROCCO PIAGGIO	67541	NAUKA	12307	NEDLLOYD WISSEKERK	72180
MYS KURILSKIY	11725	NAIAD	53782	NAULI	42683	NEDLLOYD WISSEKERK	83400
MYS KURILSKIY	34615	NAIAD	68772	NAUMBURG	03878	NEDROMA	46930
MYS KUZNETSOVA	11761	NAIAS II	32431	NAUMBURG	04426/1	NEFELI	37181
MYS KUZNETSOVA	34652	NAIEF	20720	NAUSHON	16710	NEFELI	44010
MYS LAZAREVA	23494	NAIRA	42680	NAUSICAA	48421	NEFELI	57142
MYS LOPATKA	11726	NAJA ITTUK	64900	NAUSICAA	49461	NEFERTITI	01412
MYS LOPATKA	34616	NAJAT	05075	NAUSICAA	49511	NEFERTITI	01672
MYS MALTSYEVA	23498	NAJD	20080	NAUTIC	75297	NEFTECHALA	44104
MYS NADEZHDY	23499	NAJRAAN ZAHABIA	05520	NAUTIC	88109	NEFTEGORSK	70789
MYS OBRUCHYEVA	23495	NAKHICHEVAN	44123	NAUTIC PIONEER	74620	NEFTEGORSK	85982
MYS OREKHOVA	23500	NAKHICHEVAN	93732	NAUTILUS	73947	NEFTEKAMSK	70792
MYS OSIPOVA	23501	NAKHICHEVAN	93822	NAUTILUS	76180	NEFTERUDOVOZ to NEFTERUDOVOZ 33M	79450
MYS OSTROVSKOGO	11787	NAKHODA VANANCA	28110	NAVARCO	76750		
MYS OSTROVSKOGO	34672	NAKHODKA	12486	NAVARIN	21618	NEGEV ARAD	61068
MYS OTRADNYY	11752	NAKHODKA	60685	NAVARIN	34107	NEGEV ORON	46522
MYS OTRADNYY	34642	NAKHODKA	90724	NAVASHINO	50785	NEGEV ORON	83302
MYS PROKOFYEVA	11727	NAKORNTHON	14160	NAVASOTA	38921	NEGEV TAMAR	57220
MYS PROKOFYEVA	34617	NAKWA RIVER	15271	NAVI STAR	81250	NEGO MAY	60163
MYS RATMANOVA	11728	NAKWA RIVER	35042	NAVI STAR	91510	NEGO VICTORIA	77462
MYS RATMANOVA	34618	NALANDA	56782	NAVIGATOR	09365	NEGOIU	11703
MYS SARYCH	66384	NALCHIK	86074	NAVIGATOR	73815	NEGWAN	91223●
MYS SHELIKHOVA	23538	NALECZOW	74140	NAVIGIA	73945	NEGWAN	91823●
MYS SILINA	11762	NALO EXPRESS	55211	NAVIKAPOL	26300	NEI JIANG	71856/1
MYS SILINA	34653	NAM IL	82560	NAVIKAPOL	29490	NEJEM	87201●
MYS SINYAVINA	23482	NAM SAN	82480	NAVIOS COLLIER	64491	NELA	04690
MYS SKALISTYY	11766	NAM SHAN	32662	NAVIOS COLLIER	68581	NELA ALTOMARE	90454
MYS SKALISTYY	34657	NAMANGAN	22864	NAVIOS COMMODORE	64490	NELE MAERSK	53021
MYS SVOBODNYY	11770	NAMANGAN	34494	NAVIOS COMMODORE	68580	NELE MAERSK	53051
MYS SVOBODNYY	34661	NAMANGAN	85360	NAVIOS COURIER	68811	NELIA	25790
MYS TAYMYR	11729	NAN FUNG	47995	NAVIOS CRUSADER	64500	NELLA DAN	22620
MYS TAYMYR	34619	NAN GUAN LING	61471	NAVY PROGRESS	76103	NELLION	53660●
MYS TIKHIY	11777	NAN HAI 136	88230	NAWAF	84100	NELLION	73380●
MYS TIKHIY	34668	NAN HAI 138	89010	NAXOS	60112	NELLY MAERSK	53022
MYS VAYGACH	11730	NAN HAI 145	00160	NAXOS ISLAND	58584	NELLY MAERSK	53052
MYS VAYGACH	34620	NAN HAI 158	12158	NAYA	06639/7●	NELSON	26675
MYS VODOPADNYY	11753	NAN HAI 169	39461	NAZ K	28514	NELSON	31734
MYS VODOPADNYY	34643	NAN HAI 502	04220	NAZ K	30324	NELSON MARU	77270
MYS VORONINA	11731	NAN HAI 502	04260	NAZARCEA	83691	NELY P	44960
MYS VORONINA	34621	NAN HU	01931●	NAZIE BEAUTY	82802	NEMAN	21584
MYS YEGOROVA	23483	NAN JIANG	06652/1	NAZIE BEAUTY	92092	NEMEA	58578
MYS YELAGINA	23484	NAN KOU	93310	NAZIM KHIKMET	14385	NEMEA	68621
MYS YERMAK	23502	NAN KUN	46281	NAZIR	53491	NEMEMCHA	46931
MYS YUDINA	23503	NAN SHANG	02771	NAZIR	82361	NEMESIS	50660
MYS YUNONY	11788	NAN TA	46720	NAZLI	57120	NEMURO	72942
MYS YUNONY	34673	NANAYETS	85349	NAZLI K	46454	NEN JIANG	57763
MYS ZOLOTOY	11336	NANCHENG	13493	NEAJLOV	11977	NEN JIANG	62483
MYSTRAS	64180●	NANCY LYKES	00066	NEAPOLI	81150	NEO	61669
MYTILENE	66040	NAND KAVITA	67432	NEBIT DAG	44109	NEOSHO	45050
MYTISHCHI	07918	NAND KAVITA	71402	NEBO	78772	NEOTIS	06512
MYUNG JIN	62226	NANDU ARROW	83136	NECHES	44590	NEPHELE	77711
MYUNG JIN	71136	NANGKA	42071	NECHES	66342	NEPRYADVA	92161
		NANHUA	13490	NECKAR EXPRESS	79301	NEPTUN	07862
		NANHUEI	13130	NECTARINE	06319	NEPTUN	12579
N		NANJIANG	43731	NEDA	91230	NEPTUN	12612
		NANKUO	13492	NEDDRILL I	92310	NEPTUN	61409/14
'n.f. PANTHER'	32781	NANNY	64050	NEDDRILL 2	92311	NEPTUN	91811
'n.f. TIGER'	32780	NANO K	53391	NEDI	66060	NEPTUNE	20700
NABEEL	66973	NANO K	80341	NEDLLOYD ADELAIDE	03161	NEPTUNE	22740
NABEEL	91553	NANPING	31460	NEDLLOYD ALBANY	03165	NEPTUNE	57556
NABIL	16050	NANSHIN MARU	61621	NEDLLOYD AMSTERDAM	03160	NEPTUNE AMBER	09838
NACALA	06020	NANTAO	13491	NEDLLOYD AUCKLAND	03162	NEPTUNE CORAL	09830/4

759

Name	No	Name	No	Name	No	Name	No
NEPTUNE CRYSTAL	09839	NEW ZEALAND ALLIANCE	46310	NIKE	89080	NIKYEL	11626
NEPTUNE CYPRINE	60201	NEW ZEALAND ALLIANCE	46560	NIKEA	46943	NIKYEL	88238
NEPTUNE DIAMOND	09839/1	NEW ZEALAND CARIBBEAN	02820	NIKEA	47103	NILE	04410
NEPTUNE DOLPHIN	46555	NEW ZEALAND PACIFIC	08444	NIKEL	02728/9●	NILE	62631●
NEPTUNE DOLPHIN	49056	NEW ZEALAND REEFER	60036	NIKI AGUSTINA	63760	NILE CARRIER	51470
NEPTUNE GARNET	09839/2	NEW ZEALAND STAR	02871	NIKI R	34899	NILE MARU	71790
NEPTUNE IOLITE	60202	NEW ZEALAND TRADER	74431	NIKIFOR PAVLOV	13689	NILS HOLGERSSON	17071
NEPTUNE IRIS	60203	NEWAYS	77440	NIKIFOR ROGOV	53164	NIMAS 1	39800
NEPTUNE JADE	09839/3	NEWCASTLE	53129	NIKITA MITCHENKO	48437	NIMERTIS	39910
NEPTUNE KIKU	60204	NEWFOREST	64450	NIKITA MITCHENKO	49477	NIMERTIS	40830
NEPTUNE LEO	68554	NEWFOUNDLAND CONTAINER	73930	NIKITA MITCHENKO	49747	NIMFA	87743
NEPTUNE MARLIN	50132	NEWHAM	40322	NIKITAS	37170	NIMOS	82852
NEPTUNE ORION	70191	NEWHAVEN	38335	NIKITAS	43960	NIN	58196
NEPTUNE PEARL	09830/3	NEWTON	63770	NIKITAS F	07013	NINA BRES	73964
NEPTUNE PERIDOT	60205	NEWTON PRINCESS	66030	NIKITOVKA	78895	NINA KUKOVEROVA	15518
NEPTUNE RUBY	60206	NEWTON PRINCESS	67720	NIKKO MARU No 53	82330	NINEMIA	63424
NEPTUNE SARDONYX	60207	NEXUS	50205	NIKO NIKOLADZE	59221	NINETA	06752
NEPTUNE SPINEL	60208	NEXUS	75975	NIKO NIKOLADZE	74541	NINFEA	65570
NEPTUNE STAR	57281	NEZHIN	28061	NIKOLA TESLA	11100	NING HUA	25950
NEPTUNE TOURMALINE	60209	NEZLA	60582	NIKOLAI ZUBOV	22180	NINGDU	30132
NEPTUNE TURQUOISE	60210	NGAHERE	45881	NIKOLAOS M II	91837	NIOBE	57381
NEPTUNE VOLANS	57613	NGAN CHAU	73514	NIKOLAS	90611	NIPPON MARU	09161
NEPTUNE VOLANS	62254	NGAPARA	45880	NIKOLAY AFANASYEV	13755/3	NIPPON MARU	09430
NEPTUNIA	20110	N'GOLA	10674	NIKOLAY ANANYEV	48443	NIPPON MARU No 3	67810
NEPTUNIA	77920	N'GOLA	13510	NIKOLAY ANANYEV	49483	NIPPON REEFER	60035
NEPTUNO	08220	NIAGA XLI	64850	NIKOLAY ANANYEV	49753	NIPPONHAM MARU No 1	71380
NER	72510	NIAGA XLI	91030	NIKOLAY BAUMAN	79387	NIPPONHAM MARU No 1	86630
NERA	80700	NIAGA XLII	59626	NIKOLAY BAUMAN	89253	NIPPONICA	08807
NERA	84480	NIAGA XLV	91048	NIKOLAY BERAZIN	13688	NIPPOU MARU	49331
NERCHA	85881	NIAGA XX	52093	NIKOLAY BOSHNYAK	17929	NIRAU	23140●
NERCHINSK	85983	NIAGA XXI	91313	NIKOLAY BROVTSYEV	11858	NIRAU	28340●
NEREUS	19390	NIAGA XXII	91314	NIKOLAY BURDYENKO	34243	NIREUS	28230
NERVA	76350	NIAGA XXIV	66830	NIKOLAY CHERKASOV	80264	NIRVANA	62853
NESTEFOX	66560	NIAGA XXIV	91490	NIKOLAY CHERNYSHEVSKIY	28981	NIRVANA	67533
NESTEGAS	66550	NIAGA XXV	91430	NIKOLAY DANILOV	93880	NISHNIJ TAGIL	11438
NESTOR	53891	NIAGA XXVI	71940	NIKOLAY DUBROLYUBOV	14386	NISSAKI	85270
NESTOR	56510	NIAGA XXVIII	52190	NIKOLAY EMELYANOV	50296	NISSAN MARU	47000
NESTOR	61861	NIAGA XXVIII	84130	NIKOLAY GOGOL	14387	NISSAN SILVIA	92221
NESTOR	94810	NIAGA XXIX	81942	NIKOLAY GOLOVANOV	77348	NISSEI MARU	57972
NESTOR 1	94810●	NIAGA XXIX	89422	NIKOLAY GRIBANOV	13752/5	NISSEI MARU	63332
NESTOR SKY	05452●	NIAGA XXXII	52191	NIKOLAY ISAYENKO	43301	NISSEKI MARU	57973
NESTOR SPIRIT	83821	NIAGA XXXII	84131	NIKOLAY KARAMZIM	14388	NISSEKI MARU	63333
NESTOS	35909	NIAGA XXXIII	85471	NIKOLAY KASATKIN	76585	NISSHIN MARU	90161
NESTOS	41598	NIAGA XXXIII	91532	NIKOLAY KASATKIN	79935	NISSHIN MARU	93770
NETUNO	03103	NIAGA XXXIV	91842	NIKOLAY KOLOMEYTSYEV	35425	NISSHIN MARU No 2	93500
NEUBOKOW	50444	NIAGA XXXV	47324	NIKOLAY KONONOV	11607	NISSHIN MARU No 3	93540
NEUBOKOW	52004	NIAGA XXXV	83384	NIKOLAY KOPERNIK	10740	NISSHO MARU	61663
NEUBRANDENBURG	03883	NIAGA XXXVI	47322	NIKOLAY KREMLYANSKIY	05636	NISSOS CHIOS	32750
NEUBRANDENBURG	04428/1	NIAGA XXXVI	83382	NIKOLAY KREMLYANSKIY	14465	NISSOS DELOS	03480●
NEUHAUSEN	59651	NIAGA XXXVII	86350	NIKOLAY KRYLENKO	03068	NISSOS KYTHERA	03483
NEUQUEN II	06675	NIAGA XXXVIII	52160	NIKOLAY KRYLENKO	03660	NISSOS MYKONOS	14060
NEU-ULM	51275	NIAGA XXXIX	52162	NIKOLAY LEBEDYEV	79347	NISSOS RHODOS	21180
NEVA	87001	NIAGARA	38732●	NIKOLAY MAKSIMOV	48444	NISSOS SERIFOS	15820
NEVALES 25-10-90	11495	NIAGARA	44871●	NIKOLAY MAKSIMOV	49484	NISSOS SPETSES	15821
NEVEL	11383	NIARCHOS	27246	NIKOLAY MAKSIMOV	49754	NISYROS ERA	86030
NEVELSKIY	85334	NIC	15222●	NIKOLAY MATUSEVICH	23869/4●	NITA II	87693
NEVELSKOY	22195	NICHIGO MARU	73188	NIKOLAY MIRONOV	24078	NITSA	66220
NEVER	15476	NICHIGOH MARU	09895	NIKOLAY MOROZOV	69313	NITTOKU MARU	60041
NEVERITA	64222	NICHIO MARU	67990	NIKOLAY NEKRASOV	07923	NITYA NANAK	82452
NEVEZHIS	35311	NICHOLAS G. PAPALIOS	78182	NIKOLAY NOVIKOV	54710	NIVA	85981
NEVKA	35312	NICHOLAS M	90131	NIKOLAY NOVIKOV	55280	NIVI ITTUK	58620
NEVSKAYA DUBROVSKA	13754/14	NICIA	04815	NIKOLAY OGARYEV	14389	NIVI ITTUK	64990
NEVYANSK	11733	NICOLA VAPTZAROV	07863	NIKOLAY OSTROVSKIY	12347	NIZAMI	50757
NEVYANSK	34623	NICOLAI MAERSK	53023	NIKOLAY OSTROVSKIY	12487	NIZHEGORODSKIY KOMSOMOLETS	79411
NEW APOLLO	47661	NICOLAI MAERSK	53053	NIKOLAY OSTROVSKIY	28982	NIZHNEUDINSK	15477
NEW BEAR	12710	NICOLAKIS	35673	NIKOLAY PAPIVIN	23567	NIZHNEVARTOVSK	70025
NEW CONCORD	61520	NICOLAOS CH	67310	NIKOLAY PIROGOV	34244	NIZHNEYANSK	02725
NEW CORAL SEA	81531	NICOLAOS M	85530	NIKOLAY PODVOSKIY	60644	NJEGOS	16723
NEW DALIA	47740	NICOLAOS RIGAS	23890	NIKOLAY PODVOYSKIY	62604	NJORD	23663
NEW DALIA	49310	NICOLAOS S. EMBIRICOS	57005	NIKOLAY POGODIN	03069	NJORD	74016
NEW DOLPHIN	83582	NICOLAS	59615	NIKOLAY POGODIN	03661	NOAH VI	38338
NEW DOVE	14091	NICOLAS	71925	NIKOLAY PUSTOVOYTENKO	113754/16	NOAH VI	44698
NEW DRAGON	12870	NICOLAS MIHANOVICH	19770	NIKOLAY SEMASHKA	03786	NOBLE EVELYN	46702
NEW EAGLE	07665	NICOLAS P.	18331	NIKOLAY SEMASHKO	04026	NOBLE SUPPORTER	74621
NEW FAITH	45402/2	NICOLAS P	33650	NIKOLAY SHCHETININ	49243	NOBLE SUPPORTER	78360
NEW FAME	45402●	NICOLAS V	40080	NIKOLAY SHCHETININ	49243	NODAWAY	42825
NEW FORMULA II	24962	NICOLE	51761	NIKOLAY SHCHORS	33911	NOGA	09460
NEW FORTUNE	53122	NICOLE SEA	38140	NIKOLAY SHCHUKIN	69320	NOGA	15050
NEW FORTUNE V	65580	NICOLINE MAERSK	53024	NIKOLAY SHVERNIK	03787	NOGA	64361
NEW GALACTICA	47310	NICOLINE MAERSK	53054	NIKOLAY SHVERNIK	04027	NOGI	84080
NEW GALACTICA	48760	NICOS A	81290	NIKOLAY SIPYAGIN	59893	NOGINSK	85987
NEW GENSTAR	61667●	NICOS I VARDINOYANNIS	63590	NIKOLAY SIPYAGIN	67653	NOJIMA MARU	46546
NEW HAIHUA	46283●	NICOS I. VARDINOYANNIS	68330	NIKOLAY TSYGANOV	13690	NOKUYEV	11315
NEW HAIHUNG	31301	NICOS S	87910	NIKOLAY VILKOV	78063	NOMADA	58126/3
NEW HAILEE	31250	NICOS V	39840	NIKOLAY VOZNESENSKIY	78732	NOMENTANA	33472
NEW HAINING	10490	NIDA	23566	NIKOLAY VOZNESENSKIY	89982	NOOR JEHAN	10100
NEW HAINING	15261	NIDO OIL	36710	NIKOLAY YAROSHENKO	76584	NOORD NEDERLAND	19070
NEW HERO	21651	NIEBLA	76351	NIKOLAY YAROSHENKO	79934	NOORDLAND	52030
NEW HERO	27561	NIEDERELBE	76479	NIKOLAY YEVGENOV	35424	NOPAL BRANCO	92891
NEW HOPE	36310	NIELS HENRIK ABEL	59210	NIKOLAY ZAKORKIN	34873 2	NOPAL DANA	78050
NEW HOPE	43090	NIELS HENRIK ABEL	66740	NIKOLAY ZAZOLOTSKIY	50756	NOPAL MASCOT	94820
NEW HORSE	08071	NIELS MAERSK	53025	NIKOLAY ZHUKHOV	69312	NOPAL SEL	92654
NEW HYDE	21650	NIELS MAERSK	53055	NIKOLAY ZHUKOVSKIY	63574	NOPAL SEL	93194
NEW HYDE	27560	NIELS ONSTAD	79966	NIKOLAY ZYSTSTAR	45123	NOPAL VERDE	92890
NEW HYSAN	30161	NIELSE DANIELSEN	64861	NIKOLAYEV	11859	NORA	55050●
NEW INDEPENDENCE	48944	NIELSE DANIELSEN	91041	NIKOLAYEV	45353	NORA HEEREN	73867
NEW JERSEY MARU	08650	NIENBURG	03879	NIKOLAYEVSK	02127	NORA MAERSK	53020
NEW PANDA	06629	NIENBURG	04426 2	NIKOLAYEVSKIY KOMSOMOLETS	23532	NORA MAERSK	53050
NEW PANTHER	05000	NIENHAGEN	75322	NIKOLAYEVSKIY KORABEL	11779	NORASIA CARTHAGO	47199
NEW PEACOCK	29160	NIEWIADOW	58730	NIKOLAYEVSKIY KORABEL	34670	NORASIA DAGMAR	46217
NEW STALLION	07782	NIGBOLU	80351	NIKOLETA K	61027	NORASIA GABRIELE	47196
NEW STAR	61184	NIGER	62630●	NIKOLETA K	71187	NORASIA KARSTEN	47197
NEW STAR	61659●	NIGERIA VENTURE	57623	NIKOLOZ BARATASHVILI	60632	NORASIA REBECCA	47195
NEW SULU SEA	55920	NIGERIAN STAR	83862	NIKOLOZ BARATASHVILI	62592	NORB	38941
NEW SULU SEA	84720	NIGERIAN STAR	85872	NIKOLSK	12269	NORB	39091
NEW SWAN	14090	NIGMA	68551	NIKOPOL	85986	NORBEGA	64020
NEW UNITED	05200	NIHON	08440	NIKOS	15671	NORBEGA	67620
NEW VENTURE	55900	NIHON	09570	NIKOS	39620	NORBRIT FAITH	50485
NEW VENTURE	57060	NIIHATA MARU	72390	NIKOS	88220	NORBRIT HOPE	50486
NEW VENTURE	77335	NIITAKA MARU	35093	NIKOS 1	07540	NORCAN	50110
NEW WHALE	06590	NIITAKA MARU	95084	NIKOS N	61051	NORDANGER	54137
NEW YELLOW SEA	10130	NIIZURU MARU	77330	NIKOS N	82641	NORDANGER	54257
NEW YELLOW SEA	10320	NIKA	74330	NIKY	44081	NORDBAY	73747
NEW YORK MARU	09860	NIKE	88030	NIKY	44391	NORDFELS	57602

Name	No.	Name	No.	Name	No.	Name	No.
NORDFELS	62245	NOSIRA SHARON	46653	NYMPH C	79960	OCEANO PACIFICO	04142
NORDFJORD	66905	NOSTOS	43740	NYON	73366	OCEANOS	08282
NORDHAUSEN	03707	NOTOS	63310	NYURA KIZHEVATOVA	67018	OCEANUS	78720
NORDHEIDE	73746	NOUR D	85171			OCTONIA SUN	69650
NORDHEIM	57601	NOVA	52040			ODELIA	35610
NORDHEIM	62244	NOVA	75915	**O**		ODEN	23950
NORDHOLM	57603	NOVA GORICA	61194			ODESSA	16960
NORDHOLM	62246	NOVACI	83694			ODET	56200
NORDHVAL	49174	NOVASBEST	13753	O DAE YANG No 106	86610	ODET	59090
NORDIC 1	73722	NOVAYA ERA	12488	OAK RIVER	67950	ODET	76230
NORDIC FERRY	76786	NOVAYA KAKHOVKA	81002	OAK STAR	63552	ODIN	45600
NORDIC LINK	93255	NOVAYA KAKHOVKA	93741	OAK STAR	68262	ODISSEJ	12585
NORDIC LOUISIANA	52450	NOVAYA KAKHOVKA	93831	OAK SUN	45845	ODISSEY	12585
NORDIC LOUISIANA	53210	NOVAYA LADOGA	11439	OAKLAND	60186	ODORHEI	47554
NORDIC PRINCE	16871	NOVAYA LADOGA	93742	OAKLAND	74472	ODYSEFS	05150
NORDIC STREAM	94830	NOVAYA LADOGA	93832	OAKWOOD	01190	ODYSSEAS ELYTIS	17581
NORDIC TEXAS	52451	NOVAYA ZEMLYA	10443	OASIS	36730	ODYSSEUS	33924
NORDIC TEXAS	53211	NOVAYA ZEMLYA	11440	OB	35325	ODYSSEUS	74673
NORDIC WASA	76840	NOVGOROD	02690	OBA	26180	ODYSSEUS	78383
NORDKAP	49170	NOVGOROD	03110	OBERNAI	53361	ODYSSEY 10	46881
NORDKYN	49173	NOVI T	87673	OBERON	94963	OELAND II	72683
NORDKYN	93010	NOVI VINODOLSKI	15243	OBERTA	52200●	OELSA	84940
NORDLAND	46941	NOVIA	58595	OBERTA	65151●	OELSA	90600
NORDLAND	47101	NOVIA	60475	OBO BARON	68840●	OETZTAL	76611
NORDLAND V	34206	NOVIA	73742	OBO KING	65413	OFELIA	19401
NORDLYS	01300	NOVIGRAD	58197	OBO PRINCESS	63452	OFELIA	23446
NORDMARK	57604	NOVIK	85991	OBO QUEEN	68851	OFFSHORE PROVIDER	29241
NORDMARK	62247	NOVIKOV PRIBOY	09998	OBO ZIHNI	63500	OGAN	18158
NORDMEER	18728	NOVIKOV PRIBOY	12324	OBO ZIHNI	68220	OGDEN AMAZON	72434
NORDNORGE	01950	NOVINSK	85886	OBORISHTE	49163	OGDEN BRIDGESTONE	54215
NORDON	66804	NOVO MESTO	47159	OBOTRITA	92301●	OGDEN CHAMPION	58425
NORDPOL	49171	NOVOALTAISK	02697	OBRONCY POCZTY	59224	OGDEN CHARGER	58420
NORDSCHAU	19650	NOVOALTAISK	03117	OBRONCY POCZTY	74544	OGDEN **DANUBE**	77872
NORDSEE	18720	NOVOANGARSK	13752/6	OBRONCY POCZTY	74544	OGDEN **EXPORTER**	59360
NORDSEE	36080	NOVOARKHANGELSK	13752/7	OBSERVER	44540	OGDEN **IMPORTER**	59361
NORDSEE	73912	NOVOBATAYSK	13753/1	OBUKHOVSKAYA OBORONA	76526	OGDEN LEADER	58421
NORDSEE I	20780	NOVOBIRYUSINSKIY	13753/2	OCEAN ACE	46777	OGDEN NELSON	59940
NORDSTERN	83602	NOVOBOBRUYSK	13753/3	OCEAN ACE	62232	OGDEN NELSON	67930
NORDSTJERNEN	01301	NOVOCHEBOKSARSK	13775	OCEAN ACE	71252	OGDEN OTTAWA	69012
NORDSTRAND	53403	NOVOCHERKASSK	67353	OCEAN ADVENTURE	03740	OGDEN SAGUENAY	69013
NORDSTRAND	64933	NOVOCHERKASSK	71364	OCEAN ADVENTURE	51120	OGDEN SUNGARI	55500
NORDSUND	73749/1	NOVODRUTSK	13753/4	OCEAN BEAUTY	46778	OGDEN SUNGARI	63020
NORDTRAMP	49172	NOVODRUZHESK	02700	OCEAN BUILDER I	92820	OGDEN SUNGARI	67910
NORDVIK	24076	NOVODRUZHESK	03120	OCEAN CHALLENGE	50531	OGDEN THAMES	77871
NORDWELLE	73744	NOVOGRUDOK	02703	OCEAN COMMANDER	73482	OGDEN WABASH	58426
NORDWIND	26081	NOVOGRUDOK	03123	OCEAN CONTAINER	73500	OGDEN WILLAMETTE	58427
NORDWIND	73745	NOVOKACHALINSK	13753/5	OCEAN CONTAINER	78030	OGISHIMA MARU	70921
NORDWIND	73790	NOVOKAZALINSK	13753/6	OCEAN CROWN	46779	OGISHIMA MARU	79601
NORGE	22000	NOVOKIYEVKA	13753/7	OCEAN DUKE	46780	OGLASA	17133
NORILSK	02724	NOVOKOTORSK	13753/8	OCEAN DYNAMIC	60420	OGNYAN NAYDOV	50759
NORILSK	23880	NOVOKUIBYSHEVSK	02693	OCEAN DYNAMIC	69350	OGOSTA	69726
NORITA	47360	NOVOKUIBYSHEVSK	03113	OCEAN ENDURANCE	03550	OGRAJDAN	77984
NORITA	47890	NOVOKUIBYSHEVSK	11616	OCEAN ENVOY	06650	O'HIGGINS	86692
NORLAND	17060	NOVOKUZNETSK	02692	OCEAN FREEZE	87530	OHIO	30171
NORLAND	32600	NOVOKUZNETSK	03112	OCEAN FREEZER	34216	OHIO	50385
NORLANDIA	92305	NOVOLADOZHSKIY	13753/9	OCEAN FRESH	60421	OHRMAZD	14880
NORMA	83619	NOVOLVOVSK	02701	OCEAN FRESH	69351	OHSHIMA MARU	57910
NORMAN ATLANTIC	63542	NOVOLVOVSK	03121	OCEAN GIRL	67180	OHTORI	58181
NORMAN LADY	63630	NOVOLYANOVSK	13777	OCEAN GLORY	27370	OIHONNA	76747
NORMAN LADY	72220	NOVOMALTINSK	13753/10	OCEAN GLORY No 6	89140	OIL ENDEAVOUR	09040
NORMAN PACIFIC	59970	NOVOMIRGOROD	02698	OCEAN GLORY No 6	91690	OILMAN	88475
NORMAN PACIFIC	68310	NOVOMIRGOROD	03118	OCEAN IDEAL	65973	OINOUSSAI	57142
NORMAND EXPRESS	81740	NOVOMOSKOVSK	02694	OCEAN JADE	73111	OJCOW	15451
NORMANDIA	93892	NOVOMOSKOVSK	03114	OCEAN JADE	77781	OJI MARU No 1	48948
NORNED THOR	75879	NOVONIKOLSK	13753/11	OCEAN LADY	74810	OKA	11441
NORRIS CASTLE	84430	NOVOORENBURG	13753/13	OCEAN LEGEND	73480	OKA	35313
NORRLAND	51840	NOVOORSK	13753/12	OCEAN LEO	46220	OKAH	10780
NORRO	91143	NOVOPOLOTSK	02699	OCEAN LEO	46760	OKEAN	02273
NORRONA	16512	NOVOPOLOTSK	03119	OCEAN LINK	78056	OKEANIS	59580
NORSE	42031	NOVOPSKOV	13753/14	OCEAN LYNX	45790●	OKHA	02727
NORSE MARSHAL	46438	NOVOROSSISKIY PARTIZAN	84814	OCEAN MERCURY	12750	OKHA	86072
NORSE TRANSPORTER	55120	NOVOROSSIYSK	70167	OCEAN PEGASUS	47760	OKHANEFT	66381
NORSE VENTURE	62497	NOVOROSSIYSKIY RABOCHIY	13755	OCEAN PIONEER	65760	OKHOTSK	03271
NORSEA	94370	NOVORZHEV	81003	OCEAN PIONEER	67710	OKHOTSK	49721
NORSK BARDE	51985	NOVOSHAKHTINSK	81004	OCEAN PROGRESS	51864	OKHOTSKOYE MORE	55131
NORSTAR	17061	NOVOSIBIRSK	02691	OCEAN PROGRESS	64914	OKINA	57740
NORSTAR	32601	NOVOSIBIRSK	03111	OCEAN SEAGULL	48385/5	OKINAWA MARU	34450
NORSUN	90800	NOVOSOKOLNIKI	13753/15	OCEAN SEER	90691●	OKINOSHIMA MARU	54440
NORTH ARMAC	87810	NOVOTROITSK	02695	OCEAN SERVANT 1	84270	OKPO PEARL	62200
NORTH EMPEROR	84590	NOVOTROITSK	03115	OCEAN SERVANT II	84271	OKTANT	11860
NORTH EMPEROR	90020	NOVOUKRAINA	13776	OCEAN SIF	49899/3●	OKTAVIUS	65711
NORTH KING	84591	NOVOURALSK	11336/2	OCEAN SKY	60030	OKTURUS	65710
NORTH KING	90021	NOVOVOLYNSK	02704	OCEAN SKY	68360	OKTYABRSK	85335
NORTH POLE	86321	NOVOVOLYNSK	03124	OCEAN SKY	71970	OKTYABRSKAYA	45367
NORTH SEA	23000	NOVOVORONEZH	15501	OCEAN STEELHEAD	61170	OKTYABRSKOYE	11861
NORTH SKY	89870	NOVOVYATSK	02696	OCEAN THISTLE	62498	OLA	01541
NORTH WAVE	26980	NOVOVYATSK	03116	OCEAN TRADER	56412	OLA	45630
NORTHERN	89570	NOVOYELNYA	13753/16	OCEAN TRADER	67832	OLAF	72990
NORTHERN CHERRY	56501	NOVOYENISEYSK	13753/17	OCEAN TRADER	68432	OLANCHO	06313
NORTHERN CRUISER	20480	NOVOZLATOPOL	13754	OCEAN TRADER	70190	OLANESTI	47551
NORTHERN HORIZON	31133	NOVOZYBKOV	03122	OCEAN TRAVELLER	77443	OLAU BRITANNIA	16956
NORTHERN LIGHT	14551	NOVY BUG	81000	OCEAN VENTURE	69122	OLAU HOLLANDIA	16955
NORTHERN LION	59945	NOVY DONBASS	81001	OCEAN VENUS	46641	OLD DOMINION STATE	07851
NORTHERN LION	67935	NOVYY MIR	11744	OCEAN VENUS	83321	OLDEN	72251
NORTHERN NAIAD	79133	NOVYY MIR	34634	OCEANHAVEN	04721	OLDENBURG	01990
NORTHERN STAR	34180●	NOVZYBKOV	02702	OCEANHAVEN	04941	OLDENBURG	60430
NORTHERN VALLEY	48431●	NOWOWIEJSKI	44513	OCEANIA	28613	OLEKMA	39120
NORTHIA	64386	NOWY SACZ	75772	OCEANIA	90940	OLEKO DUNDICH	60027
NORTHLAND	05220	N'TCHENGUE	55773	OCEANIA MARU	73341	OLEKO DUNDICH	62587
NORTHRIDGE	66920	NUEVA ESPARTA	31192	OCEANIA MARU	77961	OLENEGORSK	11587
NORTHUMBRIA ROSE	76088	NUEVA ESPERANZA	79961	OCEANIC	01250	OLENEGORSK	15478
NORTHWIND	53380	NUNGU ITTUK	64901	OCEANIC	22140	OLENSK	86179
NORTHWIND	90740	NUNKI	43760	OCEANIC	35220	OLENTUY	11603
NORTREFF	33010	NURAGE	42681	OCEANIC CREST	73393	OLGA ANDROVSKAYA	01938
NORWALK	04590●	NUREK	44110	OCEANIC CREST	77163	OLGA ANDROVSKAYA	02345
NORWAVE	17120	NURNBERG EXPRESS	08782	OCEANIC ENERGY	69090	OLGA BRAVO	50333
NORWAVE	32440	NWAKUSO	21941	OCEANIC VICTORY	69201	OLGA BRAVO	83673
NORWAY	09165	NYALA	69390	OCEANIS	77921	OLGA SADOVSKAYA	01936
NORWEGIAN SEA	47830	NYANDOMA	86229	OCEANIS	60113	OLGA TOPIC	77802
NORWIND	17121	NYHAMMER	54047	OCEANO ANTARTICO	21280	OLGA ULYANOVA	03070
NORWIND	32441	NYHOLT	54550	OCEANO ARTICO	06307	OLGA ULYANOVA	03662
NOSAC MASCOT	94820●	NYHORN	54551	OLGA VARENTSOVA	03788
NOSIRA LIN	46652	NYMIT	82320	OCEANO ATLANTICO	06306	OLGA VARENTSOVA	04028
NOSIRA MADELEINE	46654	NYMIT	91800	OCEANO INDIO	04143	OLINDA	03096

Name	No.	Name	No.	Name	No.	Name	No.
PALANGA	02901	PANTAI	42682	PAUL BUNYAN	67212	PENDIK	32167
PALANGA	93745	PANTANASSA	17881	PAUL BUNYAN	91752	PENELOPE EVERARD	89841
PALANGA	93835	PANTANASSA	87390	PAUL L FAHRNEY	57900	PENELOPE II	12981
PALAS	83692	PANTAZIS L	46699/1●	PAUL L FAHRNEY	62990	PENGALL	79963
PALATINO	24340	PANTELEYMON LEPESHINSKIY	03790	PAUL ROBESON	70598	PENGUINS	86260
PALAWAN	05430	PANTELEYMON LEPESHINSKIY	04030	PAULA LEE	80983	PENHORS	38341
PALDISKI	86233	PANTHER	02994	PAULA LEE	81703	PENHORS	44701
PALE	86930	PANTHER	32781	PAULINA BRINKMAN	75500	PENMARCH	46663
PALEKH	03691	PAOLA	65753	PAVAN DOOT	55320	PENMEN	48061
PALEKH	84510	PAOLA	06690●	PAVEL CHEBOTNYAGIN	93681	PENN AR BED	32250
PALEMBANG	48910	PAOLA C	06690	PAVEL DAUGE	03799	PENNSYLVANIA SUN	38040
PALEMBANG	62271●	PAOLA O	72970●	PAVEL DAUGE	04039	PENTA ACE	59782
PALIAT	43145	PAOLINO	72650	PAVEL DYBENKO	60638	PENTA WORLD	00020
PALIZZI	29231	PAPACAROLOS	55160	PAVEL DYBENKO	62598	PENTA WORLD	35470
PALLADA	12273	PAPACAROLOS	62670	PAVEL GRABOVSKIY	79436	PENTA-Y	09950
PALLADE	74740	PAPACOSTAS	31710	PAVEL KAYKOV	34874/1	PENTELI	68620
PALLAS	45912	PAPADO	43143	PAVEL MOCHALOV	79437	PENZHINA	21611
PALLAS	91810	PAPHOS	57511	PAVEL PANIN	34878	PENZHINA	34108
PALM BEACH	51141	PAPHOS	62001	PAVEL PARENAGO	10744	PEP ANTARES	63690
PALM TRADER	56560	PAPIA	84213	PAVEL PONOMARYEV	21619	PEP ATLANTIC	63688
PALMA	07942	PAPUA	46230	PAVEL PONOMARYEV	34111	PEP REGULUS	51740
PALMA MOCHA	48213	PAPUAN CHIEF	82850	PAVEL POSTYSHEV	93687	PEP REGULUS	84060
PALMA SORIANO	16760	PAQUISHA	07501/1	PAVEL RYBIN	50671	PEP RIGEL	51744
PALMAH II	78071	PARADISE	53072	PAVEL SHTERNBERG	10745	PEP RIGEL	84064
PALMAIOLA	84410	PARALLA	52630	PAVEL STRELTSOV	34879/1●	PEPE LE MOKO	47925
PALMAVERA	66808	PARALLAKS	11601	PAVLIK LARISHKIN	15520	PEPITO TEY	05880
PALMEA	85030	PARAMOUNT ACE	95046	PAVLIK MOROZOV	86185	PERA	64400
PALMIRA ZETA	43880	PARAMUSHIR	02903	PAVLIN VINOGRADOV	91260	PERAK	94971
PALMIRO TOGLIATTI	36871	PARANA	43311	PAVLODAR	93692	PERAST	08320
PALMIS	00380	PARANA STAR	06647	PAVLOGRAD	03693	PEREDOVIK	11865
PALMSTAR CHERRY	68559/1	PARANAGUA	70181	PAVLOS V	38210	PEREDOVIK	43040
PALMSTAR ORCHID	68559/2	PARDI	85280	PAVLOS V	38760	PEREIRA d'ECA	03100
PALMSTAR SUMIDA	61181	PARFENTIY GRECHANYY	73294	PAVLOVO	02906	PEREKAT	12496
PALOMA DEL MAR	64510	PARGA	32040	PAVLOVO	09368	PEREKOP	45351
PALUDINA	66120	PARGOLOVO	02905	PAVLOVSK	45354	PERELIK	36391
PALUDINA	70081	PARHAM	87840	PAVONIS	75510	PERELLE	88612
PALVA	36091	PARHAM	87990	PAWCATUCK	38922	PERELLE	90072
PALVA	36221	PARIATA	51684	PAXI	48492	PEREMYSHLJ	09370
PAMINA	58860	PARING	13774/2	PAXO	74940	PERENNIAL ACE	36550
PAMINA	65740	PARITA	51995	PAYAS	43741	PERESLAVL-ZALESSIK	15480
PAMIR	02902	PARIZHSKAYA KOMMUNA	01572	PAYDE	15479	PERESVET	22230
PAMIR	11309	PARIZHSKAYA KOMMUNA	79380	PAYIME	45402	PERICLES	34901
PAMIR	22163	PARKHOMENKO	33912	PAZ	25690	PERIGEY	13696
PAMIT C	04788	PARMA	23458	PAZIN	05652	PERINTHOS	77490
PAMPERO	47996	PARMENION	49340	PEACE	42650	PERKUN	20880
PAMPERO	53418	PARNASS	73960	PEACOCK VENTURE	75565	PERLA	53404
PAMPERO	64948	PARNASSOS	69453	PEARL BAY	86707	PERLA	64934
PAMPILLA	87080	PARNASSOS	73023	PEARL CITY	26572	PERLAMUTR	11590
PAMYAT 26 KOMISSAROV	44102	PARNASSUS	28660	PEARLEAF	38490	PERLIS	94970
PAMYAT LENINA	60687	PAROMAY	02904	PEBANE	45394	PERM	02900
PAMYAT LENINA	90726	PAROS	60601	PECAN	06318	PERMEKE	64346
PAN ANTILLES	32070	PAROS	69971	PECHENGA	02907	PERMINA 109	60840
PAN BLESS	57593	PARSLA	85344	PECHENGA	12495	PERMINA 109	81460
PAN DYNASTY	46002	PARTEM	46283	PECHENGA	25845	PERMINA IX	43270
PAN EXPRESS	47203	PARTIZAN BONNIVUR	13015	PECHENGA	56272	PERMINA SAMUDRA V	37020
PAN JOURNEY	79980	PARTIZANI	12153	PECHENGA	62732	PERMINA SAMUDRA V	43850
PAN KOREA	61030	PARTIZANSKAYA ISKRA	45359	PECHEUR BRETON	59490	PERMINA VIII	81160
PAN KOREA	71190	PARTIZANSKAYA SLAVA	45361	PECHORA	67019	PERMINA XXII	66350
PAN LONG	27401	PARVATI	56844	PECHORALES	90562	PERMINA XXIII	66353
PAN PACIFIC	61811	PASABAHCE	32152	PECHORSK	89752	PERMINA XXIV	66352
PAN QUEEN	47204	PASADENA	69770	PECONIC	54414	PERMINA XXIX	70570
PAN SHAN	82550	PASCOLI	32556	PECONIC	57874	PERMINA XXV	70571
PAN UNION	78420	PASEWALK	61409/11	PEDRO RAMIREZ	83881	PERMINA XXVI	66354
PAN VIGOR	39200	PASIGI	43144	PEDRO TEIXEIRA	51052	PERMINA XXVII	66351
PAN WESTERN	70681	PASIONARIYA	12494	PEGAS	12308	PERMINA XXVII	66355
PAN WESTERN	78111	PASOSO	43147	PEGAS	23862	PERMINA XXX	66356
PAN YARD	73204	PASS OF BALMAHA	57700	PEGASIA	737749/2	PERMINA XXXI	66357
PAN YARD	76994	PASS OF BALMAHA	60811	PEGASOS	61910	PERMLES	45691
PAN ZENITH	54561	PASS OF BRANDER	57701	PEGASUS	61910	PERNA	59601
PAN ZENITH	54961	PASS OF BRANDER	60810	PEGASUS	09590	PERNA	71931
PANAGHIA LOURION	12101	PASS OF CAIRNWELL	84980	PEGASUS	14190	PERNAMBUCO	43312
PANAGHIA LOURION	13891	PASS OF CAIRNWELL	85700	PEGASUS	47810●	PERNAT	43162
PANAGHIA P	05551	PASS OF DIRRIEMORE	76391	PEGASUS PEACE	92954	PERSEUS	11673
PANAGHIA TINOU	17150	PASS OF DIRRIEMORE	85711	PEGASUS PEACE	95164	PERSEUS	53667
PANAGHIS VERGOTTIS	06514	PASS OF DRUMOCHTER	76390	PEGASUS TIMBER	47810	PERSEUS	63393
PANAGIA	43580	PASS OF DRUMOCHTER	85710	PEGGY	68661	PERSEUS	73387
PANAGIA	86330	PASSAT	02274	PEI CHING No.1	74220	PERSEVERANZA	24890
PANAGIA ELEOUSSA	06981	PASSAT	18273	PEI CHING No 1	88160	PERSEY	12274
PANAGIA M	41761●	PASSAT-2	23568	PEIKIANG	25650	PERSEY	23863
PANAGIOTIS A L	08060	PASSAT	71851	PEKIN	10271	PERSEY III	12571
PANAGIOTIS G	89841●	PASSAT	73956	PEKIN	15181	PERSIA	08930
PANAGIOTIS S	46080	PASSUMPSIC	38924	PEKIN	36840	PERTOMINSK	02908
PANAGIS K	37920	PASVALIS	34884	PELAGIAL	13754/13	PERTUSOLA	53990
PANAMA	70180	PATAGON	92787	PELAGOS	46150	PERTUSOLA	79570
PANAMA	74473	PATMOS	60114	PELAGOS	50181	PERUSTICA	83724
PANAMA	79290	PATRAI	27720	PELAGOS	75261	PERUVIAN REEFER	06332
PANAMA STAR	45771●	PATRAIKOS	90710	PELASGOS	87841	PERVOMAJSK	87000
PANAMA STAR	48411●	PATRIA	46391	PELASGOS	87991	PERVOMAYSK	03701
PANAMAX APOLLO	69260	PATRIA	73946	PELEGO DUVO	23100	PERVOURALSK	11499
PANAMAX CENTAURUS	80720	PATRIA	87190	PELENGATOR	09369	PESHT	86093
PANAMAX GEMINI	64540	PATRICIA	33155	PELERIN	92882	PESQUERA	25171
PANAMAX GEMINI	73250	PATRICIA	46171	PELEUS	60490	PESTOVO	03694
PANAMAX MARS	77886	PATRICIA	49905	PELIAS	91420	PETALING	94972
PANAMAX MOON	79200	PATRICIA	50343/2	PELICAN	92884	PETALUMA	42826
PANAMAX NOVA	77500	PATRICIA 1	21040	PELIKAN	12314	PETAR BARON	24630
PANAMAX SOLAR	77620	PATRICIA DELMAS	47217	PELIKAN	71914/2	PETER	83613
PANAMAX STAR	64270	PATRICIA L	46693	PELIKI	87600	PETER GORING	23427
PANAMAX SUN	73231	PATRICIA S	91324	PELITA DELI	42070	PETER KAST	10252
PANAMAX UNIVERSE	72435	PATRIOT	13760	PELITA JAYA	89233	PETER KAST	12633
PANAY	82790	PATRIOT	58440	PELKA	86970	PETER KIRK	51971
PANAY GULF	33921	PATRIOT	63970	PELLA	58579	PETER KIRK	84181
PANAYIOTIS XILAS	25800	PATRIS	34190	PELLA	66932	PETER L	35500
PANCALDO	03462	PATRIZIA	08531	PELLA	70982	PETER NELL	10253
PANCHABHA	64771	PATROCLOS	30380	PELLA	73221●	PETER NELL	12634
PANCHDEEP	10510	PATROKL	13694	PELLA	77691●	PETER PAN	17070
PANCHRATNA	64770	PATROKLOS 1	61730	PELLEAS	60115	PETER RICKMERS	92590
PANDELIS	01810	PATROKLOS 1	85050	PELLINI	91832	PETER SIF	49897
PANDITA NATNA SAGHARA	64090	PATROKLOS 1	81540	PELOPIDAS	69940	PETERSBURG	65920
PANDORA	83420	PATTAYA	70182	PELOR	64800	PETIMATA OT RMS	78986
PANEHAN	43142	PATVIN	79810	PELOR	87611	PETINGO	77491
PANKY	11520	PATZIEL	75874	PELTI	66842	PETKO R SLAVEJNOV	80900
PANORMITIS	84390	PAUDZHA	23533	PELTO SEAHORSE	92550	PETOFI	45370
PANORMOS	29900	PAUL	14341	PEMBA	01140	PETR ALEKSEYEV	60628
PANORMOS HORIZON	03751	PAUL	63655	PENCHATEAU	72413	PETR ALEKSEYEV	62588

Name	No.	Name	No.
PETR BOGDANOV	79384	PHENIAN	10272
PETR DUTOV	48438	PHENIAN	15182
PETR DUTOV	49478	PHENIAN	36843
PETR DUTOV	49748	PHILADELPHIA	74475
PETR GUTCHENKO	49244	PHILEMON	73991
PETR GUTCHENKO	49244	PHILIP BROERE	76300
PETR KAKHOVSKIY	89254	PHILIPP MULLER	23428
PETR KRASIKOV	03791	PHILIPPE L.D.	48083
PETR KRASIKOV	04031	PHILIPPINE BATAAN	14814
PETR LEBEDEV	17560	PHILIPPINE BATAAN	30800
PETR LIDOV	79419	PHILIPPINE JASMINE	50663
PETR LIZYUKOV	11866	PHILIPPINE OBO 2	64575
PETR MASHEROV	80266	PHILIPPINE OBO 3	64576
PETR PAKHTUSOV	22242	PHILIPPINE OCEAN	56630●
PETR SGIBNEV	00146	PHILIPPINE QUIRINO	56630
PETR SMIDOVICH	54723	PHILIPPINE QUIRINO	57620
PETR SMIDOVICH	55293	PHILIPPINE ROSAL	50664
PETR STAROSTIN	69321	PHILIPPINES	06230
PETR STRELKOV	54734	PHILIPPINES FRUIT	05571
PETR STRELKOV	55304	PHILIPPOS	40110
PETR STUCHKA	12497	PHILLIP O'HARA	10850●
PETR STUCHKA	60688	PHILLIPS ENTERPRISE	64011
PETR STUCHKA	90727	PHILLIPS ENTERPRISE	68401
PETR VELIKIY	80178	PHOENICIAN FLAG	89291
PETR YEMTSOV	48445	PHOENIX	27730
PETR YEMTSOV	49485	PHOENIX VENTURE	88091
PETR YEMTSOV	49755	PHOENIX VENTURE	74421●
PETR ZALOMOV	79408	PHOLAS	10005
PETR ZAPOROZHETS	79388	PIA ANGELA	92520
PETRA	34370	PIA DANIELSEN	90970
PETRA	42630	PIA DANIELSEN	91980
PETRA	46929	PIAVE	76650
PETRA SCHEU	92300	PIBIDUE	35821
PETRADI	58604	PIBIQUATTRO	38660●
PETRARCA	32557	PIC D'AGOU	71301
PETREL	92883	PIC ST LOUP	76440
PETRO BOUSCAT	42631	PICCOLA	66640
PETRO PYLA	67101	PICHINCHA	12993
PETRO SEA	54880	PICHIT SAMUT	49730
PETRO SEA	60000	PICO DO FUNCHAL	84075●
PETRO SOULAC	59150	PICT	42034
PETRODVORETS	03695	PIENINY II	55315
PETRODVORETS	12498	PIENINY II	70066
PETROGAS 1	65910	PIERO DELLA FRANCESCA	17131
PETROGRADSKAYA STORONA	13699	PIERRA DELLA FRANCESCA	17131
PETROKREPOST	02909	PIERRE VIELJEUX	05124
PETROKREPOST	23540	PIERRE VIELJEUX	59873
PETROLA 1	43000	PIETER WINSEMIUS	73820
PETROLA 11	40751	PIETRO	66955
PETROLA 11	41481	PIETRO	70995
PETROLA 13	36230	PIETRO NOVELLI	17130
PETROLA 17	40752	PIGOANZA	83762
PETROLA 17	41482	PIKEBANK	04671
PETROLA 20	42860	PILAR	73536
PETROLA 30	81120	PILAR DEL MAR	76085
PETROLA 31	70500	PILARMAST	06639/2
PETROLA 32	43660	PILBARA	57761
PETROLA 33	35690	PILBARA	62481
PETROLA 33	37100	PILIO	63180
PETROLA 34	35691	PILION	91350
PETROLA 34	37101	PILOS	58164/1
PETROLA 36	37810	PILOTA ALSINA	17450
PETROLA 40	85580	PILOTO PARDO	01740
PETROLAGAS-2	55581	PILTUN	86223
PETROLAGAS-2	56461	PINAGORIY	11617
PETROLINA VI	53128	PINAR DEL RIO	90390
PETROMAR BAHIA BLANCA II	65630	PINAZO	91272
PETROMAR BAHIA BLANCA II	70000	PINDAROS	10620
PETROMAR CAMPANA	37797	PINDAROS	15370
PETROMAR CAMPANA II	65631	PINEGA	67022
PETROMAR CAMPANA II	70001	PINEGA	86234
PETROMAR MENDOZA	43720	PINELOPI	24761
PETROMAR ROSARIO	37450	PINELOPI	29542
PETROMAR ROSARIO	44220	PINELOPI	30771
PETROMAR SAN SEBASTIAN	65691	PING CHAU	48030
PETROMAR SAN SEBASTIAN	70121	PING CHAU	83410
PETROMAR SANTA CRUZ	65693	PING DING SHAN	62105
PETROMAR SANTA CRUZ	70123	PING GUE	72000●
PETROPAVLOVSK	02128	PING HAI	57371
PETROPAVLOVSK-KAMCHATSKIY	10444	PING HAI	61961
PETROPOLIS	46490	PING JIANG	05320
PETROS V	61883	PING SHAN	84113
PETROS Z	47300	PING SHAN	84173
PETROSANI	82221	PING XIANG CHENG	67231
PETROSHIP A	68570	PING XIANG CHENG	91651
PETROSHIP B	68571	PING YIN	30000
PETROSTAR III	70870	PING YIN	30981
PETROSTAR III	86510	PINGO	59629
PETROSTAR IV	44180	PINGUIN	84935
PETROSTAR V	66660	PINGUIN	91181
PETROSTAR VI	66661	PINGUINO	83520
PETROSTAR XIV	85730	PINGVIN	11965
PETROSTAR XIV	88690	PINO DEL AGUA	48210
PETROSTAR XV	68930	PINSK	25560
PETROSTAR XVI	86500	PINTO	49270
PETROSTAR XVII	53123	PINYA	07420
PETROVSKIY	02910	PIONEER	60186/1
PETROZAVODSK	02911	PIONEER COMMANDER	05676
PETROZAVODSK	23530	PIONEER CONTAINER	73690
PETYA KOVALYENKO	67031	PIONEER CONTENDER	05677
PETYA SHITIKOV	67032	PIONEER CONTRACTOR	05678
PEVEK	11310	PIONEER CRUSADER	05679
PEVEK	42800	PIONEER II	70250
PEVERIL	93930	PIONEER LOUISE	53950
PEYPSI	13697	PIONEER LOUISE	54000
PEZZATA ROSA	51930	PIONEER MOON	05680
PEZZATA ROSA	74172	PIONEER No 3	47732
PFUSUNG	85350	PIONER	15521
PHA SHWE GYAW YWA	83470	PIONER ARKHANGELSKA	71041
PHAEDRA	74040●	PIONER AYKUTII	71054
PHAISTOS	42400	PIONER BELORUSSII	71055
PHAROS	59734	PIONER BURYATII	71050
PHAROS	64329/1	PIONER CHUKOTKI	71044
PHAROS	67224	PIONER ESTONII	71047

Name	No.	Name	No.
PIONER KAMACHATKI	71408	PLYAVINYAS	38530
PIONER KARELII	71056	PNOC AMIHAN	42820
PIONER KAZAKHSTANA	71057	PNOC CANTHO	42821
PIONER KHOLMSKA	71045	PNOC PETROPARCEL	42823
PIONER KIRGIZII	71058	PNOC TAWI-TAWI	36440
PIONER KOLY	71060/1●	PNOC TAWI-TAWI	43420
PIONER LITVY	71051	PNOC TRANSASIA	42830
PIONER MOLDAVII	71059	PO	94571
PIONER MOSKVY	71040	POBYEDA OKTYABRYA	59891
PIONER MURMANA	76499	POBYEDA OKTYABRYA	67651
PIONER NAKHODKI	79550	POBYEDINO	24084
PIONER ODESSY	79552	POCAHONTAS	02841
PIONER ONEGI	71046	POCANTICO	02840
PIONER PRIMORYA	79554	PODGORA	29102
PIONER ROSSI	71049	PODGORICA	78890
PIONER SAKHALINA	71042	PODHALE	75733
PIONER SEVERODVINSKA	71052	PODHALE	88383
PIONER SLAVYANKI	71053	PODMOSKOVYE	11311
PIONER UKRAINY	12499	PODRAVINA	86522
PIONER UZBEKISTANA	71060	PODUNAVLJE	86521
PIONER VLADIVOSTOKA	79553	POEL	39300
PIONER VOLKOV	76515	POET	11881
PIONER VYBORGA	79555	POET SABIR	79390
PIONER YUZHNO SAKHALINSKA	71043	POET VIDADI	79402
PIONER ZAPOLYARYA	12500	POGEEZ	63420
PIONERSK	93870	POGRANICHNIK LEONOV	93764
PIONERSKAYA PRAVDA	15522	POGRANICHNIK LEONOV	93820
PIONERSKAYA ZORKA	15523	POHANG	54931
PIONIERUL	78841	POHANG	77611
PIONIR	75280	POIANA	83693
PIONIR	80160	POINT CLEAR	68810
PIOTR DUNIN	10576	POINT MANATEE	93130
PIOTR DUNIN	15346	POINT MANATEE	93390
PIOTRKOW TRYBUNALSKI	79872	POINTE DE CORSEN	66571●
PIRAN	62060	POINTE DE LESVEN	79581
PIREAS	49931	POINTE DU ROC	59073
PIREAS	50631	POINTE DU ROC	76423
PIRIN	49040	POINTE DU VAN	59074
PIRIT	11932	POINTE DU VAN	76424
PIRKKOLA	61706	POINTE LA ROSE	02621
PIROT	21511	POINTE MADAME	02622
PIRYATIN	36254	POINTE SANS SOUCI	02620
PIRYATIN	42804	POINTER	32953
PISANG	02540	POINTSMAN	76290
PISANG PERAK	91521	POITOU	64372
PISANG RAJA	41000	POJUCA	65864
PISATEL	11867	POKKINEN	47296
PISCES	65501	POLA	60166
PISHCHEVAYA INDUSTRIYA	45274	POLAR	91144
PISOLO	43390	POLAR ALASKA	53870
PISTIS	29460	POLAR BRASIL	09261
PISTIS	58161	POLAR COLOMBIA	09262
PITESTI	86211	POLAR EXPRESS	32300
PITSUNDA	11868	POLAR GAS	81920
PIURA	29440	POLAR I	76536
PIURA	30610	POLAR II	76537
PIVA	05322	POLAR III	62696
PKHEN HOA	28992	POLAR IV	62697
PLAKOURA	62821	POLAR V	62698
PLAKOURA	67571	POLAR VI	62699
PLAN DE AYALA	69994	POLAR PARAGUAY	09264
PLAN DE AYALA	86484	POLAR SEA	01781
PLAN DE AYUTLA	69995	POLAR STAR	01780
PLAN DE AYUTLA	86485	POLAR URUGUAY	09265
PLAN DE GUADELUPE	69997	POLARIS	70137
PLAN DE GUADELUPE	86487	POLARIS	75505
PLAN DE SAN LUIS	69998	POLARISMAN	59061
PLAN DE SAN LUIS	86488	POLARISMAN	76451
PLANA	77981	POLARLYS	01302
PLANERIST	11869	POLARSTERN	01351
PLANET	72005	POLCZYN ZDROJ	74143
PLANETA	11588	POLESSK	03696
PLANTA DE MAMONAL	49801	POLESSK	90152
PLANTIN	73537	POLESYE	11312
PLATAK	83924	POLEVOD	11871
PLATINUM TRANSPORTER	68850	POLFJORD	05459
PLATO	75507	POLIAIGOS	28930
PLATON OYUNSKIY	50758	POLIKOS	16640
PLATONIC	53152	POLINA MARINA	06414●
PLATONIC	66302	POLINA OSIPENKO	10728
PLAYA	80420	POLISAN 1	75212
PLAYA COLORADO	11968	POLITO	78510●
PLAYA DE EZARO	49991	POLLENGER	54070
PLAYA DE EZARO	50640	POLLENGER	72221
PLAYA DE LAS CANTERAS	87661	POLLUKS	11791
PLAYA DE MASPALOMAS	87660	POLLUKS	76891
PLAYA DEL MEDANO	83540	POLLUKS	81401
PLAYA DUABA	11969	POLLUX	46390
PLAYA DUABA	86542	POLLUX	66183
PLAYA GIRON	11970	POLLUX	67733
PLAYA HIRON	18274	POLLY	62020
PLAYA LARGA	31011	POLLY BRISTOL	92885
PLAYA VARADERO	11972	POLNORD	05453
PLAYITAS	11971	POLOTSK	11611
PLESETSK	02912	POLOTSK	45352
PLETWAL	10818	POLSTAR	57554
PLISKA	37310	POLSUND	05458
PLITVICE	40240	POLTAVA	11872
PLOCE	59613	POLTAVA	45350
PLOCE	71923	POLWIND	57550
PLOCK	82262	POLYARNAYA ZVEZDA	93875
PLOD	21310	POLYARNOYE SIYANIE	11608
PLONA	71507●	POLYARNYE ZORI	76518
PLOPENI	82117	POLYARNYY	11591
PLOPENI	82397	POLYARNYY	22865
PLOTINOS	10621	POLYARNYY	34495
PLOTINOS	15371	POLYARNYY KRUG	76528
PLOTUS	79140	POLYCRUSADER	73330
PLOVDIV	37300	POLYDEFKIS	83061
PLUG	22231	POLYDEFKIS	83161
PLUMLEAF	38500	POLYDORUS	51741
PLUNGE	34882	POLYDORUS	84061
PLUTON	11870	POLYKLIS	36400
PLUTON	23860	POLYMICHANOS	52211
PLUTONIY	11589		

Name	No.
POLYMICHANOS	65141
POLYS	57991
POLYTIMI ANDREADIS	35890
POLYTIMI ANDREADIS	41670
POLYTRADER	64140
POLYTRAVELLER	64141
POLYUS	33980
POLYVICTORIA	64015
POLYVICTORIA	68405
POLYXENI	45393
POLYXENI	74610
POMALAA	38932
POMELLA	66121
POMELLA	70080
POMERANIA	08170
POMONA	06639/3
POMORAVLJE	86520
POMORYE	02913
POMORZE	93882
PONCE	08340
PONCHATOULA	45055
PONOY	02914
PONTA DELGADA	08230
PONTA GARCIA	33530
PONTALVA	14810
PONTENEGRO	47299
POOLSTER	35250
POOLTA	03450
POONG YANG	94873
POONGDESAN	85631
POONSRI MARINE	61550
POONSRI MARINE	72040
POPI	16180
POPLAT	59602
POPLAT	71932
PORECHIE	12275
PORKHOV	11442
PORONIN	24080
POROZINA	08321
PORSANGER	54138
PORSANGER	54258
PORSOY	92330
PORT ALBERNI CITY	46431
PORT HAWKESBURY	68941
PORT ILYICH	44124
PORT LATTA MARU	77470
PORT QUEBEC	72337
PORT ROYAL	48079/1●
PORT SAID	03970
PORT SAID	27841
PORT TUDY	66450
PORT VANCOUVER	72338
PORTFIELD	36341
PORTHOS	59620●
PORTO	14751
PORTO ALLEGRE	79640●
PORTO SANTO	02330
POSAVINA	86523
POSEIDON	19220
POSEIDON	32700
POSEIDON	48110
POSEIDON	50662
POSEIDON	54011
POSEIDON	67700
POSEIDON	80771
POSEIDON 8	36283
POSEIDON 8	36483
POSEIDON C	24610
POSEIDON C	26370
POSEIDON	62142
POSEIDONIA	11470
POSEYDON	12580
POSITANO	71914/3
POSSIDONIA	36010
POSTIRA	08322
POSYET	12501
POSYET	22866
POSYET	34496
POTI	12276
POTI	39977
POTIRNA	59600
POTIRNA	71930
POTOMAC	02842
POTSDAM	04926
POUNENTES	60116
POVL ANKER	20350
POVOLZHYE	11325
POVONETS	15502
POWER HEAD	84980●
POWER HEAD	85700●
POWSTANIEC SLASKI	59225
POWSTANIEC SLASKI	74545
POWSTANIEC WARSZAWSKI	65853
POWSTANIEC WARSZAWSKI	67693
POWSTANIEC WIELKOPOLSKI	70544
POYANG CAREER	58126/4
POZEGA	60169
PRABHU SATRAM	61260
PRACETIA	67497
PRACTICIAN	47770
PRAG	45851
PRAGA	36844
PRAHA	79233
PRAHOVA	41630
PRAIRIAL	52953
PRAIRIAL	55483
PRANAS EYDUKYAVICHUS	12504
PRANAS ZIBERTAS	85341
PRASHANTI	27950
PRAVDA	07561
PRAVDINSK	03697
PRAVOVYED	11873
PREDEAL	48480
PREMUDA BIANCA	66191
PREMUDA ROSA	66190
PRESERVER	40170
PRESIDENT	92220
PRESIDENT 1	72280●
PRESIDENT 1	77180●
PRESIDENT ADAMS	31120
PRESIDENT CLEVELAND	31121
PRESIDENT DELCOURT	56180
PRESIDENT DELCOURT	58980
PRESIDENT DELCOURT	60850
PRESIDENT EISENHOWER	09839/2●
PRESIDENT F.D. ROOSEVELT	09839/3●
PRESIDENT FILLMORE	10532
PRESIDENT FILLMORE	11552
PRESIDENT GARCIA	05951
PRESIDENT HARRISON	15200
PRESIDENT JACKSON	31122
PRESIDENT JEFFERSON	11352
PRESIDENT JOHNSON	11355
PRESIDENT KENNEDY	11361
PRESIDENT LINCOLN	00260
PRESIDENT MACAPAGAL	59310
PRESIDENT MAGSAYSAY	49260
PRESIDENT McKINLEY	10533
PRESIDENT MCKINLEY	11553
PRESIDENT MONROE	00261
PRESIDENT MONROE	15201
PRESIDENT PIERCE	11354
PRESIDENT PIK	13695
PRESIDENT POLK	15202
PRESIDENT QUEZON	53900
PRESIDENT QUIRINO	31580
PRESIDENT ROXAS	47800
PRESIDENT TAFT	10530
PRESIDENT TAFT	11550
PRESIDENT TAYLOR	31124
PRESIDENT TRUMAN	11363
PRESIDENT VAN BUREN	10531
PRESIDENT VAN BUREN	11551
PRESIDENT WASHINGTON	00262
PRESIDENT WILSON	31123
PRESIDENTE ALLENDE	46589
PRESIDENTE CASTILLO	00520
PRESIDENTE DEODORO	37910
PRESIDENTE DEODORO	38860
PRESIDENTE DIAZ ORDAZ	32260
PRESIDENTE FLORIANO	37911
PRESIDENTE FLORIANO	38861
PRESIDENTE GONZALEZ VIDELA	56638/2
PRESIDENTE IBANEZ	56638/1
PRESIDENTE KENNEDY	55010
PRESIDENTE KENNEDY	55880
PRESIDENTE KENNEDY	56550
PRESIDENTE MACIAS NGUEMA	35000
PRESIDENTE MACIAS NGUEMA	91790
PRESIDENTE RAMON CASTILLO	06674
PRESLAV	91701
PRESTIGIOUS	82993
PRETORIANO	05366
PRETORIANO	15666
PRETTY	70282
PREVEZE	80350
PREYLI	38532
PREZHEVALSK	02916
PRIAMOS	26970
PRIAMOS	77877
PRIAMURYE	02162
PRIAMURYE	09210
PRIAMURYE	12502
PRIBALTIKA	93753
PRIBALTIKA	93843
PRIBOY	02275
PRIBOY	61270
PRIBOY	81490
PRIDE	14555
PRIDE OF FREE ENTERPRISE	20212
PRIDNEPROVSK	45355
PRIDYATLES	24082
PRIGNITZ	71680
PRIKARPATYE	11322
PRIKUMSK	25561
PRILIV	02276
PRILIV	11874
PRILUKI	09371
PRIMA	70058
PRIMA DONNA	38460
PRIMA JEMIMA	70820
PRIMERA PEAK	46052
PRIMERO	36630
PRIMERO DE JUNIO	26940
PRIMERO DE MAYO	88486
PRIMORJE	12040
PRIMORLES	24044
PRIMORSK	03698
PRIMORSK	10445
PRIMORSK	87002
PRIMORYE	11995
PRIMROSE	54381
PRIMROSE	63071
PRINCE GEORGE	20430
PRINCE LAURENT	19931
PRINCE MARU No 7	92570
PRINCE NOVA	17220
PRINCE OF BRITTANY	16450
PRINCE OF TOKYO	48951
PRINCE SCYNTHIUS	51901●
PRINCE SCYNTHIUS	72551●
PRINCE SHAUL	60186/2
PRINCEFIELD	83149●
PRINCESS	06504●
PRINCESS JADE	89912
PRINCESS JADE	90222
PRINCESS MAHSURI	16945
PRINCESS MARGUERITE	17420
PRINCESS MIRI	60186/3
PRINCESS OF ACADIA	18810
PRINCESS OF NEGROS	22040
PRINCESS OF VANCOUVER	19720
PRINCESS PATRICIA	17421
PRINCESS SEIKO	61061
PRINCESSE MARGARETHE	01911
PRINCESSE MARIE CHRISTINE	19940
PRINKIPOS	·69070
PRINS ALBERT	19942
PRINS JOACHIM	16030
PRINS JOACHIM	19990
PRINS PHILIPPE	19930
PRINSES BEATRIX	18961
PRINSES BEATRIX	32760
PRINSES CHRISTINA	18950
PRINSES IRENE	18962
PRINSES MARGRIET	18960
PRINSES MARGRIET	22050
PRINSES MARIA ESMERALDA	19941
PRINSES PAOLA	20040
PRINSESSAN	17091
PRINSESSE ANNE-MARIE	19570
PRINSESSE BENEDIKTE	19591
PRINSESSE ELISABETH	20610
PRINSESSE RAGNHILD	16915
PRINZ HAMLET	16511
PRINZ OBERON	16510
PRIONEZHYE	11327
PRIOZERSK	12503
PRIPYATLES	24082●
PRITZWALK	61409/10
PRIVOLZHSK	45219
PRIZVANIE	13745
PROBA	90331
PROCYON	65780
PROCYON	70200
PROCYON	76050
PRODROMOS	71470
PROFESOR K BOHDANOWICZ	73551
PROFESOR MIERZEJEWSKI	56634
PROFESOR RYLKE	56635
PROFESOR SIEDLECKI	11690
PROFESOR SZAFER	56633
PROFESSOR	11951
PROFESSOR ANICHKOV	09082
PROFESSOR BARANOV	93730
PROFESSOR BARANOV	93854
PROFESSOR BAYKONOVSKIY	04258
PROFESSOR BOGOROV	39170
PROFESSOR BOGUCKI	23467
PROFESSOR BUZNIK	03967
PROFESSOR DERYUGIN	12573
PROFESSOR I I KRAKOVSKIY	79426
PROFESSOR KERICHYEV	79438
PROFESSOR KHROMOV	04255
PROFESSOR KLENOVA	13747
PROFESSOR KLYUSTIN	09085
PROFESSOR KOLESNIKOV	01965
PROFESSOR KOSTIUKOV	48651
PROFESSOR KOZHIN	13748
PROFESSOR KUDREVICH	09081
PROFESSOR KURENTSOV	39171
PROFESSOR MESYATSYEV	11952
PROFESSOR MINYAYEV	09088
PROFESSOR MULTANOVSKIY	04256
PROFESSOR NESTOR SMYERNOV	17969
PROFESSOR NIKOLSKIY	13749
PROFESSOR PAVEL MOLCHANOV	04257
PROFESSOR PAVLENKO	09083
PROFESSOR POPOV	10750
PROFESSOR RYBALTOVSKIY	09084
PROFESSOR SERGEY DOROFEYEV	17968
PROFESSOR SHCHYOGOLEV	09080
PROFESSOR UKHOV	09087
PROFESSOR VISE	12002
PROFESSOR VODYANITSKIY	39172
PROFESSOR VOYEVODIN	13750
PROFESSOR YUSHENKO	09086
PROFESSOR ZUBOV	12003
PROFITIS ELIAS	26522
PROGRESS	11606
PROGRESS	23571
PROGRESSIST	47772
PROGRESSIVE	45861●
PROGRESSIVE	46021●
PROIKONISOS	71220
PROJECT AMERICAS	95020
PROJECT ARABIA	95022
PROJECT ORIENT	95021
PROKOPIY GALUSHIN	06796/3
PROKOPYEVSK	02915
PROKOPYEVSK	09372
PROLETARSK	12148
PROLETARSKAYA POBEDA	60686
PROLETARSKAYA POBEDA	90725
PROLIV	11875
PROLIV LAPERUZA	58513
PROLIV LAPERUZA	71823
PROLIV SANNIKOVO	58514
PROLIV SANNIKOVO	71824
PROLIV VILKITSKOGO	58515
PROLIV VILKITSKOGO	71825
PROMETEY	13742
PROMETHEUS	26674
PROMETHEUS	31733
PROMETHEUS V	28512
PROMETHEUS V	30323
PROMINA	05564
PROMYSLOVIK	11876
PRONAOS	61635
PROOF GALLANT	67165
PROOF SPIRIT	75240
PROOF TRADER	56261
PROOF TRADER	75241
PROPAGANDIST	11877
PROSPATHIA	60117
PROSPECTOR II	62505
PROSPERITAS	45404
PROSPERITY	55560
PROSPERITY	62940
PROSPERITY SEA	48156
PROSTOR	13766/2●
PROSVETITEL	11878
PROTECTEUR	40171
PROTECTOR	47876
PROTEKTOR	74640
PROTEUS	48111
PROTEUS	86971
PROTEUS	80731
PROTSION	76892
PROTSION	81402
PROVENCE	16440
PROVENCE	32520
PROVIDENCE	61002
PROVIDENCE BAY	08486
PROVIDER	38960
PROVORNY	84342
PRUT	70810
PRUZANIY	34883
PRVI SPLITSKI ODRED	71286
PRVIC	59790
PRVIC	62360
PRZEMYSL	79876
PSARA REEFER	06351
PSATHI	91240
PSILI	55940
PSKOV	03699
PSKOV	23527
PSKOVITYANKA	35326
PU JIANG	04663
PUBLIKIST	11879
PUEBLA	55013
PUEBLA	55883
PUEBLA	56553
PUERTO CADIZ	48830
PUERTO DE CHACABUCO	87570
PUERTO DE HANGA ROA	91501
PUERTO DE HANGA ROA	81951
PUERTO DE VITA	25200
PUERTO PLATA	59622
PUERTO PRINCESA	03841
PUERTO RICO	08344
PUERTO RICO	50380
PUERTO ROSALES	66196
PUERTO VALLARTA	19296
PUERTO VALLARTA	23704
PUERTOLLANO	67636
PUGIOLA	53991
PUGLIOLA	79571
PUHOS	48084
PULA	10924
PULA	14370
PULBOROUGH	88560
PULKOVO	02917
PULKOVO	12505
PULKOVSKIY MERIDIAN	11336/1
PULKOWNIK DABEK	15361
PUMA	02993
PUMA	94610
PUNAT	08323
PUNTA ANCIA	83241●
PUNTA ANGELES	36740
PUNTA ARENAS	50320
PUNTA ARENAS	50850
PUNTA ATALAYA	14672
PUNTA BIANCA	02833
PUNTA BIANCA	03420
PUNTA BRAVA	51076
PUNTA CARENA	53393●
PUNTA CARENA	80343●
PUNTA DELGADA	45140
PUNTA MALVINAS	51075
PUNTA MEDANOS	45100
PUNTA STELLA	02830
PUNTA VERDE	02831
PUPNAT	85510
PURBECK	17301
PURBECK	93161
PUSHLAKHTA	02918
PUSSUR	06400
PUSTOZERSK	02919
PUTIVL	03700
PUTIVL	12506
PUTNA	13738
PUTYATIN	24083
PVT. LEONARD C. BROSTROM	92660
PYARNU	15500
PYATIDYESYATILETIYE KOMSOMOLA	01100
PYATIDYESYATILETIYE KOMSOMOLA	01180
PYATIDYESYATILYETIYE OKTYABRYA	36878
PYATIDYESYATILYETIYE OKTYABRYA	93755
PYATIDYESYATILYETIYE OKTYABRYA	93845
PYATIDYESYATILYETIYE SOVETSKOY GRUZII	60637
PYATIDYESYATILYETIYE SOVETSKOY GRUZII	62597
PYATIDYESYATILYETIYE SSSR	45290
PYATIDYESYATILYETIYE SSSR	58510
PYATIDYESYATILYETIYE S.S.S.R.	71820
PYATIGORSK	11880
PYATIGORSK	25562
PYER PUYYAD	80053

Name	No.
PYLOS	55100●
PYLOS	57590●
PYONG HWA	28993
PYOTR MASHEROV	80266●
PYOTR OVCHINNIKOV	12507
PYOTR PAKHTUSOV	22242
PYOTR SGIBNEV	00146
PYOTR SMORODIN	46313
PYOTR SMORODIN	46563
PYRAMIDS	07766
PYRAMIDS	07814
PYRROS V	36780
PYTHAGORE	54781
PYTHAGORE	67451
PYTHEAS	66700
PYTHEUS	53701
PYTHEUS	78091
PYTHEUS	89941

Q

Name	No.
QAROUH	49409
QAROUH	50969
QI LI HAI	36350
QI LIAN SHAN	60994
QI LIN HU	36720
QIAN SHAN	71849
QIAN TANG JIANG	50991
QIAN TANG JIANG	51461
QIANJIN	10560
QIMEN	06069
QIN HUAI	14670
QING HE CHENG	05041
QING SHAN	04600
QINGHAI	45980
QINGHE	50112
QINGSHUI	15960
QINLING	61071
QINLING	71261
QIONG HAI	49152
QIONG HAI	83552
QIU HE	77069●
QORMI	08500
QU JIANG	64780
QUAN ZOU HAI	72389/5
QUARTERMAN	88700
QUARTZ	06627
QUE LIN	38990
QUEBEC	79770
QUEDLINBURG	03881
QUEDLINBURG	04427/1
QUEEN	81561
QUEEN ELIZABETH 2	01700
QUEEN OF ALBERNI	18990
QUEEN OF BURNABY	17164
QUEEN OF COQUITLAM	18920
QUEEN OF COWICHAN	18921
QUEEN OF ESQUIMALT	17163
QUEEN OF NANAIMO	17165
QUEEN OF NEW WESTMINSTER	17166
QUEEN OF PRINCE RUPERT	19440
QUEEN OF SAANICH	17162
QUEEN OF SHEEBA	04581
QUEEN OF SHEEBA	34911
QUEEN OF SIDNEY	16680
QUEEN OF THE ISLANDS	19060
QUEEN OF THE NORTH	16500
QUEEN OF TSAWWASSEN	19780
QUEEN OF VANCOUVER	17161
QUEEN OF VANCOUVER	32271
QUEEN OF VICTORIA	17160
QUEEN OF VICTORIA	32270
QUEEN OPAL	39281
QUEEN VASSILIKI	83614
QUEEN VASSILIKI II	61450
QUELIMANE	29560
QUELLIN	48891
QUELLIN	49321
QUI HE	74436/1●
QUI JIANG	60242
QUIBERON	17040
QUICKTHORN	80500
QUIJOTE	87890
QUIMICO LEIXOES	56253
QUIMICO LEIXOES	75233
QUIMICO LISBOA	56252
QUIMICO LISBOA	75232
QUINTANA ROO	33130
QUIRINALE	24342
QUITAUNA	52250
QUITO	88760
QUIXADA	52251

R

Name	No.
R A EMERSON	70151
R R RATNA	73505
R R RATNA	78035
R.S.A.	31950
RAAD	72880
RAAD	76880
RAAD AL-BAKRY VIII	70330
RAAFAT	87220
RAAMGRACHT	49816
RAB	07897
RABA	27460
RABAC	18571
RABENAU	71060/3●
RABIGH BAY 1	55312
RABIGH BAY 1	70063
RABIGH BAY-2	64568
RABIGH BAY 3	64371
RABKA ZDROJ	81868
RABOCHAYA SMENA	01406
RABOCHAYA SMENA	01666
RABUNION IV	40370
RABUNION V	84521
RABUNION VI	84520
RABUNION XIII	84522
RABUNION XIV	84523
RABUNION XV	84524
RABUNION XVI	84525
RACHAD	87201
RACISCE	02843●
RAD	35671
RADAUTI	47540
RADBOD	76811
RADE KONCAR	69020
RADEBERG	59652
RADHOST	15091
RADIANT VENTURE	47200
RADIOSA	20730
RADISHEV	12371
RADISHEV	20803
RADIY	36917
RADIY	43817
RADNES	75616
RADNOTI	14929
RADNOTI	5739
RADOM	15085
RADOMYSHI	71374
RADOMYSHI	67363
RADUGA	12309
RADUZHNYY	89759
RADVILISKIS	35328
RADZIONKOW	03620
RADZIONKOW	03230
RAFAEL	60502
RAFAELA	52910
RAFFAELE CAFIERO	66320
RAFFAELLO	09201
RAFI AHMED KIDWAI	71634
RAFNES	75615
RAGNA GORTHON	92936
RAGNHILD BROVIG	67734
RAGNI BERG	07500
RAGNVALD JARL	02381
RAGNVALD JARL	35351
RAHIM	56638/7
RAIKO MARU	65782
RAIKO MARU	70202
RAILSHIP 1	94070
RAIMOL	47431
RAIMOL	47901
RAINBOW	61654
RAINBOW 1	49370
RAINBOW FREEZER	05841
RAINBOW GAS	56430●
RAINBOW HOPE	49601
RAINBOW REEFER	05840
RAINBOW STAR	61580
RAINBOW VOLANS	62253
RAINBOW VOLANS	57614
RAINFROST	27190
RAJAAN	60169/1
RAJAB 1	03320
RAJAB 1	04381
RAJAH BROOKE	91251
RAJAH MAS	00040
RAJAH SARAWAK	42690
RAJENDRA PRASAD	68090
RAKHOV	67360
RAKHOV	71371
RAKOW	50445
RAKOW	52006
RAKVERE	22867
RAKVERE	34497
RALEN	17771
RALIDA	11966
RALLYTIME III	38200
RALU	78392
RAMADA	22338
RAMBUTAN	42076
RAMON	91190
RAMON ABOITIZ	33770
RAMONA	40423
RAMONA	42333
RAMONA	42593
RAMONEVERETT	30170
RAMSES II	01411
RAMSES II	01671
RAMSLAND	85570
RAMSLAND	86750
RAMSLI	80550
RAMSLI	91340
RANA 1	91222
RANA I	91822
RAND-1	35336
RAND-2	35337
RAND-3	35338
RAND-4	35339
RANDI BROVIG	67736
RANGA	83921
RANGAMATI	15641
RANGATIRA	20000
RANGE	53416
RANGE	64946
RANGELOCK	47180
RANGER	63972
RANGER	58442
RANIA B	43161
RANKKI	51999
RANNO	90850
RANNO	91160
RAPANA	63821
RAPHAEL	60502
RAPID	01492
RAPLA	89267
RAPOCA	15061
RAPOLAS CHARNAS	12508
RAQEFET	78073
RAS DEDGEN	10221
RAS EL BAR	92788
RAS EL KHAIMA	87281
RAS MAERSK	54430
RAS MAERSK	54810
RAS TANURA	69520
RASA	28541
RASELTIN	50700
RASHIDAH	81780
RASLAN	16010
RASLAN	16850
RASSEM	71750
RASSEM	81440
RATAN	06982
RATANA BHUM	76032
RATANA BHUM	88622
RATHDOWN	88520
RATIH	78034
RATIH	73504
RATNA KIRTI	49701
RATNA KIRTI	52861
RATNA MANORAMA	49700
RATNA MANORAMA	52860
RATNA VANDANA	47883
RATNO	67362
RATNO	71373
RAUMA	70779
RAUTARUUKKI	74900
RAUTE	62248
RAUTE	57609/1
RAUTZ	75456
RAVA RUSSKAYA	44890
RAVEN ARROW	83137
RAVENNA	73362
RAVENSCRAIG	77681/1
RAVENSTVO	01573
RAVNI KOTARI	58198
RAW LINES 1	25960
RAWAS	41960
RAYA HAPPINESS	61407
RAYCHIKHINSK	24093
RAYES 1	89370
RAZDOLNOYE	22868
RAZDOLNOYE	34498
RAZDOLNOYE	51989/2
RAZELM	11708
RAZLIV	22870
RAZLIV	34500
RAZLIV	35327
RAZZAN 1	21530
REA	06515
REA	16060
REA	21290
REA B	03380
REA B	04050
REA SILVIA	59484
READY	18670
REAL	89905
REAL	90210
REALENGRACHT	49817
REBECCA R	73050
RECALADA LIGHT	06639/4
RECHITSA	89755
RECHLIN	75336
RECOMONE	64790
RECOMONE	66770
RECONQUISTA	13250
RECORDER	11570
RED ARROW	61217
RED IBIS	60831
RED IBIS	85071
RED STONE	47231
RED STONE	47511
REDA	88231
REDESTOS	05350
REDO	85760
REDUT	89756
REEFER CARRIER	91145
REEFER CHAMP	58220
REEFER CHAMP	72930
REEFER CIKU	34213/1
REEFER DUKU	34213
REEFER GIULIA	65011
REEFER INSEL	90851
REEFER INSEL	91161
REEFER KNIGHT	59512
REEFER KNIGHT	59822
REEFER MANGGIS	11150
REEFER MERCHANT	90810
REEFER MERCHANT	91770
REEFER NANGKA	11151
REEFER PENGUIN	56468
REEFER QUEEN	24510
REEFER STAR	90811●
REEFER STAR	91771●
REEFER TRADER	80981
REEFER TRADER	81701
REFORMA	70042
REFRIGERATOR No 4	84331
REFRIGERATOR No 5	84332
REFRIGERATOR No 6	84333
REFRIGERATOR No 8	84334
REFRIGERATOR No 12	84335
REFRIGERATOR No 13	84336
REGAL SCOUT	
REGAL SEA	78684
REGAL SKY	55390
REGENCY	17640
REGENT	41740
REGENT	61086
REGENT	71276
REGENT PALM	47877
REGENT PIMPERNEL	53684
REGENT PIMPERNEL	53814
REGENT PIMPERNEL	68534
REGGIO	19750
REGINA	60956
REGINA	71914/4
REGINA CELI	06561
REGINA FERRAZ	48072
REGINA S	24273
REGINA S.	60187
REGINA VALERIA	86860
REGINE	73720
REGULA	19081
REGULIERSGRACHT	49818
REGULUS	10540
REGULUS	50143
REGULUS	75531
REGULUS	87425
REIHO MARU	71155
REIKO	69421
REINA DEL FRIO	21070
REINBEK	72537
REINE ASTRID	16992
REIYO MARU	09990
REIYO MARU	34600
REKIN	23459
REKSNES	75617
RELIANT	60118
RELIANT	73409
RELIANT	82719
RELUME	51920
REMADA	86112
REMADA	91712
REMCO	13170
REMCO	34800
REMUERA BAY	08360
RENA	47391
RENA	47961
RENACIMIENTO	62223
RENACIMIENTO	71133
RENATA B	13811
RENATE SCHULTE	60955
RENATO GUITART	28731
RENDL	75882
RENEE DELMAS	47218
RENEE R E	76605
RENEE R E	89305
RENEE RICKMERS	52811
RENI	22871
RENI	34501
RENOIR	48402
REPINO	12277
REPINO	22872
REPINO	34501
REPUBLICA DEL ECUADOR	04856
RESILIENCE	85460
RESITA	78581
RESOLUTE	54390
RESOLUTION BAY	08442
RESOURCE	41741
REST	53393
REST	80343
RETAVAS	13700
RETEZATUL	11700
RETHIMNON	32911
RETRIEVER	23401
REUNION	07390
REUTOV	67361
REUTOV	71372
REVDA	22869
REVDA	34499
REVOLUCION	70043
REVOLYUTSIYA	11592
REVOLYUTSIYA	45368
REWI	48603
REY MAR	87801
REYNOLDS	61993
REYNOSA	56443
REYNOSA	68353
REZEKI	51151
REZEKNE	62599
REZEKNE	60639
REZVAYA	59902
REZVAYA	67662
RHAPSODY	09320
RHEA	45911
RHEIN	76208●
RHEINGOLD	56121●
RHEINGOLD	59771●
RHETORIC	68780
RHIN	59081
RHINE MARU	33603
RHINE ORE	64521
RHINE ORE	68471
RHINO	44790
RHINSEE	46386
RHINSEE	47086
RHODIAN HELMSMAN	61462
RHODRI MAWR	88571
RHODRI MAWR	89701
RHOMBUS	62249
RHOMBUS	57606
RHONE	56201
RHONE	59091
RHONE	76231
RHONE	94050
RIA LUNA	58191

Name	No.	Name	No.	Name	No.	Name	No.
RIA MAR 1	80870	RIO NAJASA	15637	ROCKY GIANT	72620	ROSEMARY	06316
RIAMA	69423	RIO NANEZ	73121	ROCQUAINE	88610	ROSEMARY EVERARD	89842
RIBEIRA GRANDE	17840	RIO NEGRO	74961	ROCQUAINE	90070	ROSEMOUNT	91290
RIBERA	91271	RIO NEGRO	77101	RODANO	49901	ROSINA TOPIC	47201
RIBUAN JAYA	91170	RIO NEGRO II	48374	RODANO	50341	ROSLAVL	12278
RICE TRADER	56561	RIO NEUQUEN	05535	RODANTHI A	84830	ROSLAVL	67365
RICHARD	63657	RIO NEVERI	50431	RODENBEK	72535	ROSLAVL	71376
RICHARD BORDO	21840	RIO PANUCO	70162	RODIN	80215	ROSS CAREER	05763
RICHARD SORGE	36877	RIO PARANA	14363	RODINA	17524	ROSS KELETCHEKIS	43125
RICHARDAS BUKAUSKAS	67023	RIO PLATA	47920	RODINA	24310	ROSS SEA	29230
RICHFIELD	83138	RIO SAGUA	15637/1	RODINA	39450	ROSSANA	62021
RICHMOND HILL	82860	RIO SALADO	15638	RODINA	73297	ROSSEVERETT	14522
RICKY LIFT	50312●	RIO SALADO	30531	RODNA	13774/3	ROSSEVERETT	81581
RIDGE	53415	RIO SAMO	23300	RODONAS	13800	ROSSIYA	16040
RIDGE	64945	RIO SAN JUAN	26430	RODONIT	07476	ROSTAND	80216
RIEDERSTEIN	14040	RIO SIXAOLA	07464	RODOPI	11933	ROSTOCK	03882
RIEMS	39302	RIO SIXAOLA	10754	RODOPI	77089/1	ROSTOCK	04428
RIENZI	49641	RIO SULACO	07465	RODOS	80009/1	ROSTOCK	19985
RIGA	25846	RIO SULACO	10756	RODOSEA	08190	ROSTOK	67350
RIGA	38533	RIO SUN	65830	RODOSI	64612	ROSTOK	71360
RIGEL	62233	RIO SUN	69490	RODOSTO	57009/2	ROSTOV NA DONU	80055
RIGEL	69850	RIO TEJO	84078	RODOSTO	35950	ROSYTH	74890
RIGEL	71253	RIO TOA	15638/1	RODRIGUES CABRILHO	38750	ROTALIA	23447
RIGGI 1	66885	RIO VERDE	74960	ROELOF HOLWERDA	73580	ROTTERDAM	12030
RIGHTEOUS	56504	RIO VERDE	77100	ROF BEAVER	51712	ROUA	44200●
RIGOLETTO	92500	RIO YATERAS	15639	ROF BEAVER	75630	ROUBINI II	61637
RIGOLETTO	93720	RIO ZAMBEZE	78103	ROG	76790	ROUNTON GRANGE	77441
RIGOLETTO	95040	RIO ZAZA	15639/1	ROGALAND	48102	ROUSSEAU	80217
RIHENG	28910	RIRUCCIA	78432	ROGALIN	93002	ROVER	01490
RIJEKA	62600	RISA PAULA	81691	ROGATE	17580●	ROVER	63973
RIJEKA	60640	RISAN	04931	ROGET	88561	ROVER	58443
RIJEKA EXPRESS	56643	RISANGER	54139	ROGET	05491	ROVER STAR	69380●
RIJNBORG	45430	RISANGER	54259	ROGNES	07951	ROVINARI	82224
RIJPGRACHT	49819	RISHI AGASTI	15871	ROGOZNICA	75618	ROVNO	39998
RIKHARD MIRRING	23569	RISHI AGASTI	83571	ROGOZNICA	66953	ROYAL LILY	05615
RIKUZEN MARU	95111	RISHI ATRI	15870	ROI BAUDOUIN	70993	ROYAL SAPPHIRE	60991
RIMA G	80402	RISHI ATRI	83570	ROJEN	16462●	ROYAL SEA	03480
RIMAC	52661	RISNJAK	48770	ROKISHKIS	48385	ROYAL SEA	24151
RIMBA DUA	61653	RISTNA	15494	ROKKO MARU	35329	ROYAL STAR	21247
RIMBA DUA	72052	RITA MARIA	27740	ROKKOHSAN MARU	95085	ROYAL VIKING SEA	16821
RIMBA MERANTI	46960	RITSA M	80704	ROLAND VON BREMEN	77501	ROYAL VIKING SKY	16822
RIMBA RAMIN	46961	RITSA M	84484	ROLF JACOB	08290	ROYAL VIKING STAR	16820
RIMINI	78773	RIVA	10623	ROLL GALICIA	77143	ROYAL ZULU	11250
RIMNICU VILCEA	82116	RIVA	15373	ROLL VIGO	94613	ROYALE	08160
RIMNICU VILCEA	82396	RIVER	15220	ROLLNES	94614	ROYALE	09100
RIMULA	63820	RIVER ABOINE	04821	ROLLON	75613	ROYAN	62224
RINCON	42824	RIVER ACE	77333	ROLNIK	72432	ROYAN	71134
RINGGRACHT	49820	RIVER ADADA	04730	ROLNIK	78293	ROYKSUND	93001
RINGNES	75611	RIVER ANDONI	04826	ROLON NORTE	80023	ROZENGRACHT	49821
RINI	35900	RIVER ASAB	04822	ROLON ORO	94380	ROZITA	82644
RINI	41590	RIVER BOYNE	78123	ROLON PLATA	94391	ROZITA	61054●
RINJANI	02348	RIVER EMBLEY	78124	ROLON SUR	94390	ROZMARY	42120
RIO	06539	RIVER ETHIOPE	15222	ROMA	94381	RUBENS	04722
RIO ABAUCAN	05530	RIVER GUMA	04827	ROMAN	75315	RUBENS	04942
RIO AMAZONAS	04141	RIVER GURARA	04734	ROMAN	42032	RUBENS	46630
RIO ASON	90840	RIVER HADEJIA	55875	ROMAN PAZINSKI	86212	RUBEZHNOYE	67358
RIO ASON	91150	RIVER HADEJIA	56605	ROMAN REEFER	14485	RUBEZHNOYE	71369
RIO BABAHOYA	07504	RIVER IKPAN	04830	ROMAN ROLLAN	06333	RUBIN	12510
RIO BESAYA	50210	RIVER JIMINI	04820	ROMANA	07928	RUBINOVYY	11934
RIO BRANCO	74962	RIVER KERAWA	04828	ROMANA	64793	RUBTSOVSK	24086
RIO BRANCO	77102	RIVER MADA	04825	ROMANA	59560●	RUBY ISLANDS	06639/5
RIO BRAVO	82801	RIVER MAJE	04737	ROMANDIE	46942	RUCIANE	67050
RIO BRAVO	84580	RIVER MAJIDUN	04732	ROMANDIE	47102	RUCIANE	76640
RIO BRAVO	89950	RIVER NGADA	04829	ROMANO	66773	RUDDERMAN	75020
RIO BRAVO	92091	RIVER OGBESE	04736	ROMANTIC	68781	RUDER BOSKOVIC	48064
RIO CALCHAQUI	14360	RIVER OJI	04731	ROMANZA	01730	RUDI ARNT	23429
RIO CALINGASTA	05533	RIVER OLI	04733	ROMER	10280	RUDNYY	67356
RIO CANIMAR	15633	RIVER OSHUN	04735	ROMNEY	04673	RUDNYY	71367
RIO CAONAO	15633/1	RIVER OSSE	04823	ROMNY	67357	RUDNYY	85331
RIO CAPAYA	74091●	RIVER RIMA	04824	ROMNY	71368	RUDO	48637
RIO CARCARANA	24281	RIVER SHANNON	76280	ROMO MAERSK	54432	RUDOLF BLAUMANIS	12511
RIO CARIBE	92110	RIVER SIDE	29140	ROMO MAERSK	54812	RUDOLF BREITSCHEID	15413
RIO CAUCA	04854	RIVIERA	10070	RONCESVALLES	03220	RUDOLF BREITSCHIED	06383
RIO CAUTO	15633/2	RIVIERA	47991	RONCESVALLES	03890	RUDOLF DIESEL	46378
RIO CHICO	92111	RIVIERA	78740	RONG CHENG	47041	RUDOLF DIESEL	47078
RIO CHONE	07502	RIVIERA SKY	78431●	RONG HUA SHAN	56631	RUDOLF LEONHARD	10254
RIO CONTRAMAESTRE	15633/3	RIZCUN HONG KONG	62107	RONG HUA SHAN	57621	RUDOLF LEONHARD	12635
RIO CORRIENTES	24280	RIZHSKIY ZALIV	61100	RONG JIANG	05310	RUDOLF SAMOYLOVICH	39418
RIO CUANZA	78101	RIZHSKOYE VZMORYE	93754	RONHILL	10241	RUDOLF SCHWARZ	23430
RIO CUYAGUATEJE	15633/4	RIZHSKOYE VZMORYE	93844	RONNEBURG	03884	RUDOLF SIRGE	23504
RIO CUYAMEL	07463	RJECINA	07891	RONNEBURG	04429	RUDOLF VAKMAN	23505
RIO CUYAMEL	10755	ROACHBANK	04672	RONNES	75619	RUEN	55411
RIO DAMUJI	15633/5	ROADA	84231●	RONSON	10240	RUEN	78851
RIO DE JANEIRO	16170	ROADA	87141●	RORA HEAD	78917	RUGEN	32890
RIO DULCE	30530	ROALD ADMUNDSEN	59191	RO-RO GENOVA	08963	RUHR EXPRESS	73431
RIO ESMERALDAS	07503	ROALD AMUNDSEN	56161	RO-RO GENOVA	76853	RUHR ORE	63822
RIO FRIO	02853	ROAN	85791	RO-RO MANHATTAN	08962	RUI CHANG	24241
RIO GRANDE	03410	ROAN	86661	RO-RO MANHATTAN	76852	RUI CHANG	84451
RIO GRANDE	15970	ROANA	18860	RORO TRADER	32970	RUKHULLA AKHUNDOV	53165
RIO GRANDE	74963	ROANOKE	92604	ROSA	40350	RUKWA	05459/1●
RIO GRANDE	77103	ROANOKE	93614	ROSA LUXEMBURG	05638	RUMAILA	69576
RIO GRANDE	85810	ROBERT E. LEE	01051	ROSA LUXEMBURG	14467	RUMBALA	70793
RIO GRANDE	86650	ROBERT EYDEMAN	12509	ROSA LUXEMBURG	62684	RUMIA	88234
RIO GRANDE DO NORTE	43313	ROBERT EYKHE	93733	ROSA ROTH	50161	RUMIJA	06651
RIO GRANDE DO SUL	43314	ROBERT EYKHE	93823	ROSA ROTH	50711	RUNATINDUR	91047
RIO GUALEGUAY	14364	ROBERT KOCH	22550	ROSA S	45409	RUPEA	47563
RIO GUAYAS	87800	ROBERT KOCH	40422	ROSANA	61000	RUPIT	41961
RIO HANABANA	15634	ROBERT KOCH	42332	ROSARIO	06517	RUSALKA	87744
RIO IGUAZU	14362	ROBERT KOCH	42592	ROSARIO DEL MAR	64379	RUSHANY	67355
RIO JATIBONICO	15634/1	ROBERT M	41090	ROSARIO DOS	25700	RUSHANY	71366
RIO JIBACOA	15634/2	ROBERT MILLER	53205	ROSARITA	45461	RUSHDI	15931
RIO JOBABO	00270	ROBERTA 1	52200	ROSARITA	48721	RUSLAN	12279
RIO JOBABO	15634/3	ROBERTA 1	65151	ROSARITO	43250	RUSNE	23485
RIO JUBONES	02832	ROBERTO	62108	ROSBORG	94890	RUSSE	37211
RIO LA PALMA	15634/4	ROBIN	61624	ROSE	51710	RUSSOYE POLYE	13761
RIO LAS CASAS	15634/5	ROBINSON	54513	ROSE MALLOW	60031	RUSTAVI	12280
RIO LINDO	79760	ROBINSON	63893	ROSE MALLOW	68361	RUTH	72354
RIO LOS PALACIOS	15635	ROC SEA	48157	ROSE MALLOW	71971	RUTH	77154
RIO LOS SAUCES	05531	ROCADAS	02790	ROSE SCHIAFFINO	94690	RUTH BORCHARD	51034●
RIO MAGDALENA	04855	ROCAS	85900	ROSEBAY	61581	RUTH LYKES	05588
RIO MARAPA	05534	ROCHE'S POINT	75080	ROSEHILL	72050●	RUTH LYKES	14429
RIO MAYABEQUE	15635/1	ROCHFORD	00500	ROSELAND	80120	RUTH LYKES	14899
RIO MAYARI	15636	ROCK	02723	ROSELINE	46664	RUTH M	67943
RIO MOA	15636/1	ROCKNES	75612	ROSELLA	20341	RUTHENSAND	50066

Name	No.	Name	No.	Name	No.	Name	No.
RUVU	60215	SAINT BERNARD	83230	SAM ICK	61664	SANKO HERON	63325
RUZA	12281	SAINT BERTRAND	83231	SAM SOO	57383	SANKO HONOUR	68557
RUZA	14085	SAINT BRANDAN	88740	SAM WON No 27	22772	SANKO MARU	61645
RYAZAN	67364	SAINT BREVIN	75619/2	SAMAINA	23810	SANKO STRESA	63422
RYAZAN	71375	SAINT BRICE	75619/4	SAMAR	90280	SANKYO ETHYLENE MARU	66530
RYAZHSK	25563	SAINT CLAIR	93262	SAMAR SEA	07511	SANKYO ETHYLENE MARU	70930
RYBACHIY	11593	SAINT COLUM-1	16451	SAMARA	23541	SANOK	34362
RYBACHKA	23411	SAINT ELOI	32560	SAMARGA	12513	SANSINENA II	64252
RYBAK	23410	SAINT FRANCOIS	01360	SAMARIA	04631	SANT ANDREA	01721
RYBAK BALTIKA	93748	SAINT FRANCOIS	45550	SAMARIA	04761	SANT JORDI	54160
RYBAK BALTIKA	93838	SAINT GERASIMOS	05431●	SAMARKAND	40011	SANTA	43180
RYBAK CHUKOTKI	45273	SAINT GERMAIN	19660	SAMARKAND	84340	SANTA ADELA	05601
RYBAK KAMCHATSKIY	45271	SAINT JAMES	75619/1	SAMBOR	89465	SANTA ANNA	08001
RYBAK LATVII	93762	SAINT JEAN	75619/3	SAMBOW CHAMPION	25707	SANTA CLARA	15333
RYBAK LATVII	93852	SAINT LUC	45791	SAMBURG	70026	SANTA CLAUS	26680
RYBAK MORSKI	22350	SAINT LUCIA	64315	SAMIRA	24293	SANTA CRUZ	51450
RYBAK PRIMORIYA	45272	SAINT MITRE	76710	SAMJOHN GOVERNOR	52411	SANTA CRUZ DE TENERIFFE	01293
RYBAK VLADIVOSTOKA	45275	SAINT MITRE	89580	SAMJOHN MARINER	79116	SANTA CRUZ II	48375
RYBATSKAYA SLAVA	93782	SAINT NEKTARIOS	45981	SAMJOHN PIONEER	52412	SANTA ERINA	49690●
RYBINSK	67366	SAINT PATRICK II	20630	SAMOA	45930	SANTA FE	04531
RYBINSK	71377	SAINT PAUL	01361	SAMOA	47440	SANTA FE	06150
RYBNIK	82267	SAINT PAUL	45551●	SAMOAN REEFER	05180	SANTA FE II	48378
RYBNYY MURMAN	93873	SAINT PAULIA	32630	SAMOAN REEFER	06334	SANTA JUANA	05600
RYLYEV	17525	SAINT REMY	93260	SAMOKOV	83730	SANTA KATERINA	27311
RYSHKANY	67354	SAINT ROLAND	80294●	SAMOS	54280	SANTA LUCIA	91011
RYSHKANY	71365	SAINT SERVAN	72832	SAMOS FAITH	90610●	SANTA MAGDALENA	15800
RYTTERHOLM	26140	SAINT SERVAN	87132	SAMOS HARMONY	90614	SANTA MARGARITA DOS	17140
RYUJIN MARU	84380	SAINTE ALEXANDRINE	61409/8	SAMOS LUCK	42470	SANTA MARIA	15801
RYUSEI MARU	61540	SAINTE MARTHE	04786●	SAMOS SEA	21460	SANTA MARIA	62501
RZESZOW	15086	SAINTE MAXIMILIEN	62224●	SAMOS SPIRIT	90613	SANTA MARIA	63961
RZHEV	11319	SAINTE MAXIMILIEN	71134●	SAMOS STORM	21461	SANTA MARIA	58312
RZHEV	67359	SAIPEM DUE	92940	SAMOS SUN	15890	SANTA MARIA DE LA CARIDAD	09926
RZHEV	71370	SAIRYU MARU	58050	SAMOTLOR	70020	SANTA MARIA DE LA PAZ	09925
		SAIRYU MARU No 2	67805	SAMPO	23982	SANTA MARIA III	40140
		SAKAIDE MARU	77193	SAMRAT ASHOK	77230	SANTA MARIANA	15802
		SAKARTVELO	11883	SAMSHIT	23506	SANTA MAVRA	03860

S

ST STEPHEN   76370

Name	No.	Name	No.	Name	No.	Name	No.
S A AGULHAS	04070	SAKHALIN	12512	SAMSON SCAN	84020	SANTA MERCEDES	15803
S A ALPHEN	04691	SAKHALIN	22722	SAMSUN CARRIER	51715	SANTA MONICA	51036
S A CONSTANTIA	04680	SAKHALIN-1	20310	SAMSUN DAWN	52120	SANTA MONICA 1	49690
S A MORGENSTER	04681	SAKHALIN-2	20311	SAMSUN EXPRESS	88290	SANTA PAULA	11360
S A SKUKUZA	46590	SAKHALIN-3	20312	SAMTREDIA	85993	SANTA RITA	05121
S.A. VAAL	09837/5●	SAKHALIN-4	20313	SAMUDRA	18681	SANTA RITA	59871
S A VERGELEGEN	04682	SAKHALIN-5	20314	SAMUDRA DAYA	30721	SANTA ROSA	10080
S.B.S. III	42835	SAKHALIN-6	20315	SAMUDRA JYOTI	10313	SANTA URSULA	34922
SAADALLAH	05764●	SAKHALIN-7	20316	SAMUDRAGUPTA	56845	SANTAGATA	72460
SAADI	48042	SAKHALINLES	24087	SAMUIL MARSHAK	07924	SANTIAGO	53520
SAADYARV	13705	SAKHALINNEFT	70794	SAN ANTONIO	02293	SANTIAGO DE CUBA	02525
SAAR ORE	52381	SAKHALINSKIE GORY	91912	SAN ANTONIO	56681	SANTISIMA TRINIDAD	37860
SAAR ORE	64441	SAKINA	34141	SAN ANTONIO DO TRIUNFO	93490	SANTISTA	48850
SAAREMAA	86087	SAKINA	15273	SAN BENITO	03512	SANTO AMARO	33741
SAATLY	50786	SAKUMO LAGOON	35040	SAN BERNARDINO	21330	SANTO ANDRE	33740
SABANG	43148	SAKUMO LAGOON	14260	SAN BLAS	03510	SANTO ANTAO	67495
SABARENI	82136/1	SAKURA	39000	SAN BRUNO	03511	SANTO ANTONIO DO TRIUNFO	39530
SABARENI	82415/1	SAKURA	05191	SAN DENIS	41500	SANTO DOMINGO	77530
SABIE	46588	SAKURA REEFER	49411	SAN DIEGO	02291	SANTO PIONEER	60120
SABINE	07090	SALAH ALDEEN	50971	SAN EDUARDO	56680	SANTORIN	62235
SABINE D	75291	SALAH ALDEEN	93091	SAN FRANCESCO DI PAOLA	19760	SANTORINI	71254
SABINE D	88101	SALAHALA	94161	SAN FRANCISCO	04100	SANTORINI	58162
SABIRABAD	50782	SALAHALA	01409	SAN GEORGE	06518	SANTOS	24301
SABLE	43770	SALAJ	01669	SAN GEORGE	61360	SANTOS III	02722
SABOGAL	07943	SALAJ	15457	SAN JOHN	51300	SANTURIO	76083
SABUNCHI	44113	SALAJAR	33670	SAN JOHN	61250	SANVASS	61618
SAC MALAGA	79100	SALAMAH 1	13200	SAN JOSE	27200	SAO GABRIEL	44550
SACELE	82121	SALAMAH 4	30350	SAN JUAN	53103	SAO GABRIEL	45280
SACELE	82401	SALAMAH-5	40930	SAN JUAN	53333	SAO JOSE	23601
SACHEM	66212	SALAMINA	47815	SAN JUAN	74474	SAONA	12210
SACRAMENTO	93470	SALAMIS	61340	SAN JUAN	92952	SAOS	33120
SACRAMENTO HIGHWAY	94940●	SALAMIS	13701	SAN JUAN	95162	SAPELE	56592
SADAROZA	82000	SALANTI	40600	SAN LUIS	53104	SAPEN 1	54267
SADKO	11882	SALAT	10611	SAN LUIS	53334	SAPFIR	12514
SADKO	22232	SALAVAT	89255	SAN MARCO	38790	SAPHIR	63240
SADOVA	82126	SALAVAT YULAYEV	62038	SAN MARCOS	37796	SAPHO	39261
SADOVA	82406	SALCANTAY	11500	SAN MARTIN	86693	SAPLA	26661
SADRIDDIN AYNI	50766	SALDUS	85240	SAN MING	28222	SAPPHIRE BOUNTY	82926
SADU	82125	SALEH 2	23572	SAN MING	31921	SAPPHO	01890
SADU	82405	SALEKHARD	24091	SAN PEDRO	61016	SAPUDI	15455
SAE BA DA	67282	SALEKHARD	07981	SAN PEDRO	71176	SAPUN GORA	11885
SAFETY UNION	49852	SALEM A	12162	SAN PEDRO	88450	SAQR AL DAMMAM	54659
SAFETY UNION	50092	SALEM B	07982	SAN TOMAS SECONDO	37380	SAQR AL DAMMAM	55079
SAFINA NAJD	33640	SALEM N	07983	SAN VINCENZO	79040	SAQR JEDDAH	54659/2
SAFINA RIYADH	33641	SALEM S	10010	SAN VINCENZO	80780	SAQR JEDDAH	55079/1
SAFINA SAHARA	64290	SALERNUM	12282	SANAA	61725	SAQR JIZAN	54659/3
SAFINA SWIFT	64312	SALGIR	24960	SANAA	58715	SAQR JIZAN	55079/2
SAFINA SWIFT	58353	SALI	49802	SANAA	59645	SAQR JUBAIL	54659/4
SAFINA-E-ARAB	14070	SALINA DE MANAURE	34221	SANAGA	61010	SAQR JUBAIL	55079/3
SAFINA-E-BARKAT	06650/1	SALINAS	82136	SANAGA	71170	SAQR YANBU	54659/5
SAFINA-E-HAIDER	07330	SALISTE	82416	SANANDAJ	57860	SAQR YANBU	55079/4
SAFINA-E-ISMAIL	00600	SALISTE	11884	SANCHI	56780	SARAH	18240
SAFINA-E-REHMAT	24898	SALKHINO	47293	SAND SAPPHIRE	75100	SARAH WESTON	76196
SAFIR	06637●	SALLA	05455	SAND SHORE	77370	SARAMACCA	67335
SAGACITY	75451	SALLAND	90930	SANDEFJORD	64582	SARANSK	22874
SAGAFJORD	08140	SALLY ANN	52800	SANDEFJORD	69212	SARANSK	34504
SAGAMI MARU	39031	SALLY D	65761	SANDERSKOPPEL	72682	SARANSK	90153
SAGAMI MARU	43372	SALLY I	67711	SANDERUS	43360	SARATA	83682
SAGAR	16200	SALLY I	65762	SANDINO	86694	SARATOV	10449
SAGAR	18680	SALLY II	67712	SANDOMIERZ	34361	SARATOVSK	07948
SAGAR KANYA	09130	SALLY II	40030	SANDRA K	84075●	SARDINIA NOVA	19120
SAGARDEEP	02470	SALMIAH COAST	85342	SANDRA MARIA	18550	SAREYAH	28030
SAGITA	23448	SALNA	22873	SANDRA S	13982	SARFARAZ RAFIQI	39230
SAGITTA	10542	SALSK	34501	SANDRA WESCH	49425	SARGODHA	45931
SAGITTA 1	73900	SALSK	06600	SANDRINA	56440	SARGODHA	47441
SAHAR	23040●	SALTA	12325	SANDRINA	68350	SARGODHA	52865
SAI JONG	25951	SALTIKOV SHCHEDRIN	03702	SANDVIKEN	56649	SARI BUDI	59780
SAIBURI	23190	SALVADOR ALLENDE	64470	SANESTO	42240	SARIA	14571
SAID 1	84534	SALVIA	61059/3	SANG THAI POWER	61646	SARINE	91302
SAID II	58660	SALVIA STAR	57619/2	SANG THAI STEEL	18400	SARMA	85343
SAIKYO MARU	14740	SALVIA STAR	33070	SANG THAI STEEL	22950	SARMISEGETURA	82136/3
SAILFLIP	05760	SALVISCOUNT	50778	SANGARLES	11443	SARMISEGETURA	82415/3
SAILFLIP	30670	SALYANY	11631	SANGATTA/PERMINA 1015	65180	SARNY	02676
SAINT AIDAN	88050	SALYUT	75883	SANGERHAUSEN	03708	SAROJINI NAIDU	59907
SAINT ANDREW	64120	SALZACH	71223	SANGIHE	15456	SAROJINI NAIDU	67667
SAINT ANDREW	68600	SAM CHOONG	39760	SANJEEVANI	83800	SAROMA	32591
		SAM G	01052	SANJOHN BAY	05231	SARONIC	59483
		SAM HOUSTON		SANKO CREST	63426	SARONIC REEFER	18300

SARONICOS GULF	39051	SCANDUTCH EDO	08373●	SEABORN	56417	SEEVETAL	73957
SARONIKOS	71859	SCANDUTCH ORIENT	49896	SEABORN	67837	SEFROU	75876●
SARONIS	48530	SCANIA	19620	SEABORN	68437	SEGARCEA	82131
SAROS	49230	SCANSILVA	48947	SEABORNE	69250	SEGARCEA	82411
SAROULA	37262	SCANSPRUCE	48949	SEABORNE	70550	SEGEZHA	15481
SARRAT	60880	SCAPLAKE	27440	SEABULK	77842	SEGEZHALES	24090
SARRAT	70940	SCAPMOUNT	38730	SEACALF	56740	SEIBUN MARU	61059/4
SARUNTA 1	72062	SCAPMOUNT	44870	SEACOM	17344●	SEIBUN MARU	57619/3
SASHA BORODULIN	15524	SCAPWIND	06521	SEADRAKE	94220	SEINE	21565
SASHA KONDRATYEV	15525	SCARLET IBIS	22081	SEADRIFT	43050	SEINE MARU	61182
SASHA KOTOV	15526	SCHELDE II	93040	SEAFIELD	73740●	SEISELLA	22780
SASHA KOVALYOV	15527	SCHELDEBORG	45431	SEAFORTH CLANSMAN	09050	SEIUN MARU	22120
SASSA	02591	SCHERPENDRECHT	72430	SEAFORTH EMPEROR	08842	SEIYEI MARU	48250
SASSA	46421	SCHIAFFINO	32950	SEAFORTH MONARCH	08843	SEJWAL	10810
SASSARI I	92350	SCHILDMEER	87700	SEAFROST	01436	SEKI REX	05616
SASSARI I	92420	SCHILUTE	13703	SEAFROST	87671	SEKI ROKAKO	48390
SASSNITZ	23690	SCHIPPERSGRACHT	49822	SEAGAIR	09065	SEKI ROKEL	48391
SASSTOWN	35840	SCHKOPAU	52071	SEAGLOSS	77510	SEKONDI	56591
SATOW	50446	SCHKOPAU	75171	SEAGLOSS	78410	SEKSTAN	13761/1
SATOW	52007	SCHOLLAR	86201	SEAGULL	02640	SELA	83920
SATSUMA	06323	SCHONWALDE	46373	SEAHAIL	07763	SELAMAT	22510
SATTAM	84101	SCHONWALDE	47073	SEAHAIL	07810	SELANDIA	08490
SATU MAR	70101	SCHOUWENBANK	52163	SEAIR	31750●	SELAS	62650
SATU MARE	47553	SCHUYLER OTIS BLAND	29970	SEAJAY	90610	SELAS	81590
SATUCKET	66213	SCHUYLKILL	41463	SEAKITTIE	56500	SELAT KARIMATA	85151
SATURN	11712	SCHWABENSTEIN	04547	SEAL ISLAND	64320●	SELAT MAKASSAR	85150
SATURN	12283	SCHWARZA	02310	SEA-LAND ADVENTURER	82971	SELAYAR	89231
SATURN	33100	SCHWARZBURG	03885	SEA-LAND CONSUMER	93524	SELCE	26321
SATWAH	91200	SCHWARZBURG	04429/1	SEA-LAND CONSUMER	94314	SELE	87630
SATYA KAILASH	80730	SCHWIELOSEE	46387	SEA-LAND DEFENDER	08681	SELEMDZHA	15482
SATYA KAMAL	61920	SCHWIELOSEE	47087	SEA-LAND DEFENDER	73461	SELENA	13754/1
SATYA PADAM	61313	SCILLA	71950	SEA-LAND DEVELOPER	08683	SELENA	76191
SATYA PADAM	62613	SCILLONIAN III	04160	SEA-LAND DEVELOPER	73462	SELENGA	06796/4
SATYA SOHAN	46041	SCOL RESIDENT	46245	SEA-LAND ECONOMY	93522	SELENGALES	· 24094
SAUDA	63450	SCOL TRADER	50139●	SEA-LAND ECONOMY	94312	SELIGER	11612
SAUDI ABHA	80280	SCOMBRUS	07480	SEA-LAND ENDURANCE	08689	SELIN	84076
SAUDI AL GHASIM	10681	SCORPIO	28180	SEA-LAND ENDURANCE	73470	SELINTI	40601
SAUDI AL JUBAIL	02750	SCORPION 1	45160	SEA-LAND EXPLORER	08682	SELMA	05071
SAUDI AL MEDINA	13520	SCOTIA PRIDE	16463	SEA-LAND EXPLORER	73463	SELMA	59130
SAUDI AL TAIF	34820	SCYTHIA	04632	SEA-LAND EXPRESS	08684	SELNES	75610
SAUDI AMBASSADOR	13521	SCYTHIA	04762	SEA-LAND EXPRESS	73466	SEMELI	57030
SAUDI ARABIAN	02210	SDR VICTORY	61649	SEA-LAND FREEDOM	08685	SEMELI	81630
SAUDI CHALLENGER	78310	SEA ARCHITECT	47035	SEA-LAND FREEDOM	73468	SEMEN CHELYUSKIN	22234
SAUDI CLOUD	14110	SEA AVON	84402	SEA-LAND INDEPENDENCE	08686	SEMENIC	11678
SAUDI CROWN	14510	SEA BREEZE	64367	SEA-LAND INDEPENDENCE	73464	SEMIPALATINSK	10612
SAUDI DIRIYAH	80281	SEA CARRIER	14530	SEA-LAND INNOVATOR	08690	SEMIRA	61800
SAUDI EAGLE	13430	SEA CONDOR	60169/2	SEA-LAND INNOVATOR	73471	SEMIRAMIS	06562
SAUDI ENTERPRISE	08130	SEA CONQUEROR	57011	SEA-LAND LEADER	82970	SEMLOW	50447
SAUDI FALCON	13431	SEA CROWN	47750●	SEA-LAND LIBERATOR	73465	SEMLOW	52008
SAUDI GIZAN	54662	SEA CROWN	80531	SEA-LAND MARINER	08687	SEMYON CHELYUSKIN	22185
SAUDI GLORY	63030	SEA DIAMOND	61206●	SEA-LAND MARINER	73469	SEMYON DEZHNEV	12515
SAUDI GOLDEN ARROW	19640	SEA EAGLE	05270●	SEA-LAND PACER	82972	SEMYON DEZHNEV	22186
SAUDI GOLDEN STAR	20511	SEA ELITE	49851●	SEA-LAND PATRIOT	08680	SEMYON DEZHNEV	22233
SAUDI HOFUF	80282	SEA ELITE	50091●	SEA-LAND PATRIOT	73460	SEMYON EMELYANOV	12284
SAUDI JAMAL	04646	SEA ESTE	76479/6	SEA-LAND PIONEER	82973	SEMYON LAPSHENKOV	34875/1
SAUDI JEDDAH	07682	SEA FALCON 1	71991	SEA-LAND PRODUCER	93525	SEMYON MOROZOV	79422
SAUDI KAWTHER	03321	SEA FALCON 1	72111	SEA-LAND PRODUCER	94315	SEMYON ROSHAL	89264
SAUDI KAWTHER	04382	SEA FORTUNE	61207●	SEA-LAND VENTURE	93523	SENATOR	94091
SAUDI LUCK	29331	SEA FREIGHTLINER 1	87360	SEA-LAND VENTURE	94313	SENDAI	48943
SAUDI MAKKAH	94110	SEA FREIGHTLINER II	87361	SEA-LAND VOYAGER	08688	SENECA	68320
SAUDI MOHAMED REZA	07681	SEA FURY	61230	SEA-LAND VOYAGER	73467	SENEZH	23864
SAUDI MOON 1	02210●	SEA GLORY	00383	SEALIFT ANTARCTIC	64630	SENFTENBERG	79733
SAUDI PALM	13981	SEA GODDESS 1	93077	SEALIFT ARABIAN SEA	64631	SENIOR K	31510
SAUDI RIYADH	94112	SEA GODDESS II	93078	SEALIFT ARCTIC	64632	SENIOR SPYROS V	47720
SAUDI ROSE	13980	SEA GULL III	24590	SEALIFT ATLANTIC	64633	SENKAKU MARU	66710
SAUDI SUNRISE	29330	SEA HAWK	15111	SEALIFT CARIBBEAN	64634	SENKO MARU	70920
SAUDI TABUK	80283	SEA HAWK	75900	SEALIFT CHINA SEA	64635	SENKO MARU	79600
SAUDI TAJ	82630	SEA HERON	02792	SEALIFT INDIAN OCEAN	64636	SENLAC	19902
SAUDI VENTURE	13410	SEA HORSE	28800	SEALIFT MEDITERRANEAN	64637	SENTENCE	75441
SAUDI YENBO	10680	SEA HUMBER	84401	SEALIFT PACIFIC	64638	SENTENCE	88421
SAUDI ZAMZAH	03323	SEA JADE	61205●	SEALIONET	46330	SENTINEL II	71595
SAUDI ZAMZAH	04383	SEA KING	04900	SEALOCK	47181	SENTOSA	49850
SAUGATUCK	41462	SEA LANTERN	61211	SEALOGGER	62320	SENTOSA	50090
SAUNIERE	52560	SEA LINDEN	61430	SEALOGS	23040	SENTOSA	70953
SAVA	47757	SEA LORD	02641	SEAPRIDE	67430	SEO RA BUL	61665
SAVANNAH	49058	SEA LORD	10922	SEAPRIDE	71400	SEO YANG	94872
SAVANNAH	92605	SEA MASTER	47730	SEAPRINCESS	83180	SEQUOIA	36291
SAVANNAH	93615	SEA MEDWAY	84400	SEARADIANCE	77000	SEQUOIA	37871
SAVARONA	17540	SEA MOON	06463	SEARADIANCE	79970	SEQUOIA	43081
SAVE	75040	SEA MOON	83241	SEARANGER	56870	SEQUOIA	44461
SAVE	88810	SEA OSPREY	71994	SEASERVICE	69251	SEQUOIA	68321
SAVENI	82133	SEA PIONEER	61156	SEASERVICE	70551	SERAFIM II	35680
SAVENI	82413	SEA PRINCESS	14940	SEASONG	46513	SERAFIMOVICH	12326
SAVILCO	22470	SEA QUEEN	77811	SEASPEED AMERICA	94111	SERANTES	46124
SAVINESTI	82132	SEA RELIANCE	07232	SEASPRITE	01202	SERDOLIK	07477
SAVINESTI	82412	SEA RELIANCE	07432	SEASTAR	69252	SERDOLIK	11938
SAVONITA	94081	SEA RELIANCE 1	12863	SEASTAR	70552	SEREBRYANKA	17952
SAVOY DEAN	74622	SEA RENOWN	27410	SEATRA EXPRESS	59781	SEREBRYANSK	02673
SAVVA LOSHKIN	79349	SEA RHINE	84403	SEATRAN SILVIA	61655	SEREBRYANSK	85336
SAWA	23473	SEA ROSE	07160	SEATTLE	93473	SERENISSIMA EXPRESS	18000
SAWU	15458	SEA SAGA	64291	SEAVENTURE	67431	SERENITY	75452
SAWU	89230	SEA SCAPE	64293	SEAVENTURE	71401	SEREPCA 1	64095
SAXON STAR	48624	SEA SCOUT	64311	SEAWAY CONDOR	17345	SERGEI LAZO	33913
SAXONIA	04630	SEA SCOUT	58352	SEAWAY FALCON	12780	SERGEI TSENSKAY	20804
SAXONIA	04760	SEA SCOUT	72387	SEAWAY PRINCE	51910	SERGEI VAVILOV	17561
SAXONIA	61409/22●	SEA SONG	64294	SEAWAY PRINCESS	51911	SERGEY BOTKIN	34245
SAYANI	85345	SEA STAR	47731	SEAWIND	25300	SERGEY BURYACHEK	49249
SAYANLES	24089	SEA STAR	60142	SEAWISE GIANT	54205	SERGEY BURYACHEK	49249
SAYANSKIE GORY	91911	SEA STAR	88440	SEBAROK	39740	SERGEY EYZENSHTEYN	15122
SAYMENSKIY KANAL	75400	SEA STRUGGLER	45520	SEBASTIANO	51974	SERGEY GRITSEVETS	50749
SCAIENI	82136/2	SEA TIDE	60124	SEBASTIANO	84184	SERGEY GUSEV	03792
SCAIENI	82415/2	SEA TIGER	58163	SEBES	82137	SERGEY GUSEV	04032
SCAMPER UNIVERSAL	02651	SEA TRADER	06522	SEBES	82417	SERGEY KANDACHIK	11886
SCAN	14556	SEA TRANSPORT	46889	SECHELT QUEEN	16670	SERGEY KIROV	86230
SCANCARRIER	66760	SEA TRANSPORTER	61332	SECIL BRASIL	90880	SERGEY KRAVKOV	35440
SCANCARRIER	67480	SEA TRANSPORTER	59292	SECONDO ASPROMONTE	19000	SERGEY LAZO	93688
SCANDIA TEAM	58404	SEA VICTORY	60340	SECURITY	75470	SERGEY LYULIN	13702
SCANDIA TEAM	64564	SEA VICTORY	68500	SEDA	11935	SERGEY MAKAREVICH	34877
SCANDINAVIA	08520	SEA WALRUS	46741	SEDCO 445	92840	SERGEY SMIRNOV	50767
SCANDINAVIA	16885	SEA WESER	76479/5	SEDCO 471	92841	SERGEY TYULENIN	41155
SCANDINAVIAN HIGHWAY	93370	SEA WIND	47840	SEDCO 472	92842	SERGEY TYULENIN	44954
SCANDINAVIAN SUN	16970	SEA WIND 1	83820	SEEFALKE	33075	SERGEY TYULENIN	86172
SCANDUTCH CONCORDIA	50585	SEABEX ONE	17343	SEELAND	72992	SERGEY VASILIEV	15123
SCANDUTCH CORONA	50586	SEABLUE	48311	SEEMOWE II	19310	SERGEY VASILISIN	93881

Name	No.	Name	No.	Name	No.	Name	No.
SERGEY YESENIN	12516	SHELL MARKETER	75221	SIBIRKIJ	04083	SILVERMERLIN	88680
SERGEY YESENIN	14391	SHELL SEAFARER	75222	SIBIRLES	06796/5	SILVERTHORN	89861
SERIFOS	03191	SHELL SUPPLIER	70883	SIBIRNEFT	70795	SILVET	85994
SERIFOS	03591	SHELL SUPPLIER	79593	SIBIRSKIY 2101	73997	SILVIA ONORATO	88031
SERIFOS	39580	SHELL TECHNICIAN	75223	SIBIRSKIY 2102	73998	SILVIA REGINA	16896
SERIFOS	68670	SHELL TRADER	83864	SIBIRSKIY 2108	73999	SILVICULTURE	50601
SERIUS	52770	SHELL TRADER	85873	SIBIRSKIY 2109	73999/1	SILVICULTURE	52351
SERNOVODSK	83685	SHELLTRANS	51997	SIBIRSKIY 2113	78041	SILVILAI	86208
SEROGLAZKA	12517	SHEMAKHA	86081	SIBIRSKIY 2114	78042	SIMALI 1.	23930
SEROV	02677	SHEN NON	64202	SIBIRSKIY 2116	78043	SIMALI 1	28830
SERPA PINTO	02791	SHEN NON	68652	SIBIRSKIY 2117	78044	SIMEIZ	12286
SERPUKOV	25174	SHEN SHAN	61676	SIBIRSKIY 2118	78045	SIMERIA	47555
SERRA	06564●	SHENANDOAH	46586	SIBIRSKIY 2119	78046	SIMFEROPOL	10610
SERRA AZUL	06563	SHENG LI	81600	SIBIRSKIY 2123	73999/2	SIMFEROPOL	45112
SERRA BRANCA	06564	SHENKURSK	22875	SIBIRSKIY 2124	73999/3	SIMON	42461●
SERRA DOURADA	06565	SHENKURSK	34505	SIBIRSKIY 2125	73999/4	SIMON BOLIVAR	80052
SERRA VERDE	06566	SHEPETOVKA	13763	SIBIRSKIY 2126	73999/5	SIMONA	87754
SERRAI	77562	SHEREMTYEVO	11740	SIBIRSKIY 2127	73999/6	SIMONA 1	46300
SERTAN	73980	SHEREMTYEVO	34630	SIBIRSKIY 2128	73999/7	SIMONE	42461
SERVIA	04633	SHERRY	55871	SIBIRSKIY 2130	78047	SIMONE	76193
SERVIA	04763	SHERRY	56601	SIBIRSKIY 2131	78048	SIMONE	76209/10●
SESTRORETSK	79551	SHETLAND	50371	SIBIRTSYEVO	06796/6	SIMYAVINO	23487
SETAGAWA MARU	56407	SHEVRELL	75535	SIBIRYAK	12523	SIN HOCK CHEW	87380
SETAGAWA MARU	59929	SHI JING SHAN	58603	SIBIU	41317	SINALOA	45934
SETANTA	22750	SHI TANG HAI	77447	SIBONEY	51191	SINALOA	47444
SETE CIDADES	85100	SHI ZUI SHAN	64819	SIBONEY II	82760	SINAR SURYA	27900
SETE CIDADES	85180	SHIELDHALL	39490	SIBOSEVEN	64325	SINCERE ORIENT	40900
SETIF	61980	SHIGEO NAGANO	65221	SIBOSIX	63512	SINCERITY	75471
SETUN	92162	SHIGEO NAGANO	69881	SIBOSIX	68282	SIND	88245
SEVAN	02674	SHIJIAN	12035	SIBOTEM	63541	SINDBAD	45387
SEVAN	11465	SHIKISHIMA MARU	36000	SIBOTO	64541	SINDIBAD	20273
SEVAN	20805	SHILKA	15484	SIBOTO	73251	SINEGORSK	15460
SEVAN	85988	SHIN OSAKA MARU	64110	SIBOTRE	64542	SINEGORSK	22879
SEVASTOPOL	45111	SHIN-EN MARU	68940	SIBOTRE	73252	SINEGORSK	34509
SEVEN	5173C	SHINIAS	07012	SIBUYAN CAREER	07780	SINEGORSK	36901
SEVEN	84040	SHINING STAR	61213	SIBYLLA	90491	SINEGORSK	43801
SEVEN LOG MASTER	91922	SHIN-KASHU MARU	09775	SICILIA	01722	SING TAO	11532
SEVEN SEAS BRIDGE	04951	SHINKAWA MARU	51113	SICILMO	38630●	SINGA PACIFIC	59970●
SEVEN SEAS BRIDGE	08612	SHINKAWA MARU	51493	SICILMOTOR	38630	SINGA PACIFIC	68310●
SEVEN TEAM	68292	SHINKO MARU	61619	SIDERIS	46584	SINGAPORE CAR	56810
SEVEN TEAM	77322	SHIN-KOBE MARU	68292●	SIDON	66493	SINGAPORE EAGLE	50267
SEVENSEAS	68292●	SHIN-KOBE MARU	77322●	SIDOR KOVPAK	03951	SINGAPORE FORTUNE	10624
SEVENSEAS CONQUEROR	77322●	SHINREI MARU	77220	SIEGFRIED LEHMANN	73950/2	SINGAPORE FORTUNE	15374
SEVER	22325	SHINRYO ETHYLENE MARU	57710	SIEKIERKI	59226	SINGELGRACHT	49823
SEVERLES	24045	SHINRYU MARU	77300	SIEKIERKI	74546	SINGULARITY	84090
SEVERNAYA PALMIRA	12518	SHINSEI MARU	93440	SIEMIATYCZE	02338	SINKAI	14220
SEVERNOYE SIYANIE	12348	SHINTOKU MARU	11230	SIEMIATYCZE	03628	SINMAR	65200
SEVERNYY DONETS	89234	SHINWA	52206	SIENKIEWICZ	24560	SINMAR	67410
SEVERNYY POLYUS	93736	SHINWA	65156	SIERADZ	50465	SINNI	71914
SEVERNYY POLYUS	93826	SHINYO MARU	77310	SIERRA	91380	SINNO M E	72491
SEVERNYY VETER	76501	SHIN-YU MARU	77301	SIERRA EXPRESS	73401	SINNO M.E.	72981
SEVERODONETSK	02678	SHINZUI MARU	77221	SIERRA EXPRESS	82711	SINNO M.E. IV	51600
SEVERODVINSK	25840	SHIRAHAMA MARU	46545	SIERRA GRANA	50611	SINNO M.E. V	76604
SEVERODVINSKIY	89680	SHIRANE MARU	94920	SIERRA GRANERA	50612	SINNO M E V	89304
SEVEROMORSK	10451	SHIRDEL VANANCA	42321	SIERRA GREDOS	50610	SINOE	11704
SEVEROURALSK	93800	SHIRLEY	67944	SIERRA GUADELUPE	50613	SINOEX	60251
SEVERYANIN	11624	SHIROGANE	46262	SIERRA GUADARRAMA	50614	SINOIA	65400
SEVILLA	51743	SHIRVANNEFT	44114	SIERRA LUCENA	49910	SINOIA	69790
SEVILLA	84063	SHKIPER GIEK	17920	SIERRA LUNA	49911	SIOUX	64675
SEVORODVINSK	15483	SHKODRA	24881	SIERRA MAESTRA	35272	SIR ALEXANDER GLEN	63492
SEVRYBA	93876	SHKOTOVO	86231	SIERRA NEVADA	34212	SIR BEDIVERE	50390
SEXTUM	09020	SHKVAL	21450	SIERRA URBION	87571	SIR CARADOC	93890
SHA HE KOU	94851	SHKVAL	34290	SIFNOS	49713	SIR CHARLES HAMBRO	56416
SHABAAN	00560	SHOGO MARU	73345	SIGAL	78070	SIR CHARLES HAMBRO	67836
SHABELLE	60510	SHOGUN	15223	SIGANTO A S	46449	SIR CHARLES HAMBRO	68436
SHABNAM	14662	SHOHO MARU	82380	SIGGA SIF	49899/2●	SIR FRED PARKES	17720
SHABOOT	11789/1	SHOJIN MARU	92248	SIGGEN	72681	SIR GERAINT	50303
SHABOOT	34677	SHOJU MARU	38470	SIGI SIGI	51084	SIR JOHN	63399
SHADRINSK	24088	SHOKAKU MARU	66711	SIGMA	72061	SIR JOSEPH BAZALGETTE	40323
SHAHE	50581	SHOKAWA MARU	08750	SIGMA 1	87900	SIR LAMORAK	17192
SHAHEED SALAMUDDIN	20960	SHOMAR HANAN	44200	SIGRID	91301	SIR LAMORAK	32962
SHAHJEHAN	56846	SHOMAR SHAIMA	42840	SIGRID S	90944	SIR LANCELOT	50391
SHAHZAD	29952	SHOMEI MARU	73364	SIGULDA	22877	SIR PERCIVAL	50394
SHAKHTERSK	12149	SHONGA	55870	SIGULDA	34507	SIR ROBERT BOND	11560
SHAKHTY	10452	SHONGA	56600	SIGULDA	89472	SIR SCOTT	87551●
SHAKOPOVO	13762/1	SHONGAR	86202	SIGURD JARL	83640	SIR TRISTRAM	50395
SHALAMAR	15141	SHORTHORN EXPRESS	40360	SIGURD JORSALFAR	59211	SIREN	32087
SHALVA NADIBAIDZE	93802	SHORYU MARU	77860	SIGURD JORSALFAR	66741	SIRENA	55380
SHAMA	27216	SHOSHONE	38421	SIGYN	14979	SIRET	11978
SHAMKHOR	50776	SHOTA RUSTAVELI	01752	SIJILMASSA	34224	SIRICHAL BULAKUL	34898
SHAMROCK ENDEAVOUR	75537	SHOTA RUSTAVELI'	12285	SIKU	42035	SIRIUS	00030
SHAMROCK ENTERPRISE	75538	SHOU SHAN	80661	SILAGA	06628	SIRIUS	11675
SHAMS	31630	SHOUSH	63831	SILESIA	08171	SIRIUS	12287
SHAN YIN	30001	SHOUSH	60272	SILJA STAR	20640	SIRIUS	15782
SHAN YIN	30980	SHOYO MARU	94901	SILVANA	90941●	SIRIUS	16340
SHANGHAI	25230	SHOYO MARU	95071	SILVAPLANA	56983	SIRIUS	22281
SHANNON	58630	SHTURMAN YELAGIN	12521	SILVER ATHENS	60125	SIRIUS	50118
SHANNON	91970	SHU HE	71000	SILVER CITY	12100	SIRIUS	82692
SHANTA ROHAN	48520	SHU YU QUAN	10491	SILVER CITY	13890	SIRT	51787
SHANTA SHIBANI	57233	SHU YU QUAN	15260	SILVER CLIPPER	62035	SISAK	49020
SHANTAR	11953	SHUHO MARU	56408	SILVER CLOUD	06523	SISAL TRADER	62740
SHAO YAO	16330	SHUHO MARU	59929/1	SILVER DRAGON	31590	SISSILI RIVER	04833
SHAPOSHNIKOVO	13762	SHUI HSIEN	17620	SILVER EAGLE	31320	SISSY H	47301●
SHARK BAY	49180	SHUN OH	58182	SILVER EXPRESS	47001	SISU	33003
SHATURA	24092	SHUN YI	05323	SILVER GLORY	95120	SITHONIA	60126
SHAULA	71033	SHUNKO MARU	62770	SILVER HOPE	93580	SITI ANITA	61490
SHAYMA THREE	47620	SHUNKO MARU	57790	SILVER MED	59479	SITI MIDAH	59520
SHEARWATER BAY	45620	SHURA BURLACHENKO	49245	SILVER MOON	74601	SITI MIDAH	81200
SHEARWATER CAPE	17380	SHURA KOBER	15510	SILVER PIT	18730	SITI NOVA	61440
SHEDAR	12310	SHUSHENSKOYE	07593	SILVER SEA	89490●	SITIA BEAUTY	59522●
SHEIKH ALI	12862	SHUSHENSKOYE	79376	SILVER SHELTON	57311	SITIA BEAUTY	81202●
SHEIKH IBRAHIM	30680	SHVENTOY	11887	SILVER TRANSPORTER	51650	SITIA GLORY	69060
SHEIKH SAMEER	13580●	SHYAULYAY	12522	SILVER TRANSPORTER	64420	SITIA GLORY	73350
SHEKSNALES	11501	SIAM	53145	SILVER ZEPHYR	46884	SITIA VENTURE	54660
SHELDON GAS	55360	SIAM	66075	SILVERCORN	62531	SITNO	15092
SHELDON LYKES	00085	SIAM VENTURE	48350	SILVERCORN	59261	SIT-TWAY	71303
SHELDON LYKES	73512	SIARKOPOL	73552	SILVERDOLPHIN	71508	SIULI	27360
SHELL CRAFTSMAN	67390	SIBA EDOLO	10170	SILVERFALCON	84971	SIVAND	62490
SHELL DIRECTOR	70882	SIBELIUS	76741	SILVERFALCON	88681	SIVAND	71560
SHELL DIRECTOR	79592	SIBELIUS	89691	SILVERHAWK	56185	SIVASH	11888
SHELL ENGINEER	83865	SIBENIK	05565	SILVERHAWK	66635	SIYANIE	11605
SHELL ENGINEER	85875	SIBIR	02416	SILVERLAND	64492	SJAELLAND	17460
SHELL EXPLORER	70881	SIBIR	22723	SILVERLAND	68582	SKADARLIJA	57235
SHELL EXPLORER	79591	SIBIR	76507	SILVERMERLIN	84970	SKAFTA	83923

Name	No.
SKAFTAFELL	50801
SKAFTAFELL	52611
SKAGERN	51611
SKAGERRAK	18733
SKALISTYY	11889
SKALISTYY BEREG	62694
SKANDEN	75295●
SKANDEN	88105●
SKANDI ALFA	04312
SKANDI BETA	08845
SKANE	19240
SKAROS	10622
SKAROS	15372
SKAUBORD	35530
SKAUGRAN	36110
SKAUGRAN	36560
SKAZOCHNIK ANDERSEN	09366
SKEENA	36111
SKEENA	36561
SKELLIG ROCK	76151
SKENDERBEG	28990
SKIATHOS	81990
SKIKDA	62605
SKIKDA	60645
SKIPPER	81520
SKIRON	79782
SKLERION	06524
SKOCZOW	03237
SKOCZOW	03627
SKOPELOS	19370
SKOPELOS STAR	85221
SKOPJE	33580
SKORPIOS	42271
SKRADIN	78640
SKRIM	65840●
SKRYPLEV	09380
SKRZAT	73650
SKULE	18540
SKULPTOR GOLUBKINA	80262
SKULPTOR KONENKOV	80260
SKULPTOR VUCHETICH	80261
SKULPTOR ZALKALNS	80263
SKY CLIPPER	03763●
SKY HAWK	47926
SKY ONE	40090●
SKYE TRADER	63511
SKYE TRADER	68281
SKYPTRON	46003
SKYRIAN ROVER	62410
SKYRIAN ROVER	58700
SKYROS	74945
SKYWARD	01871
SLANEY VENTURE	73185
SLANIC	83136/4
SLANIC	82415/4
SLATINA	81555
SLAUTNOYE	83688
SLAVA SEVASTOPOLYA	10882
SLAVGOROD	11620
SLAVGOROD	39986
SLAVIANKA	77089/4
SLAVIANKA	80009/4
SLAVIJA 1	19170
SLAVISA VAJNER	69023
SLAVONIJA	04472
SLAVONIJA	10992
SLAVONIJA	34152
SLAVSK	10613
SLAVSK	12288
SLAVYANKA	25564
SLAVYANSK	02679
SLAVYANSK	93803
SLAVYANSKIY	11336/3
SLEEPING BEAUTY	83040●
SLEEPING BEAUTY	83120●
SLETTER	87110
SLIVEN	29011
SLOBODA	21720
SLOBOZIA	81556
SLOMAN MERCUR	48730
SLOMAN MERCUR	56090
SLOMAN MIRA	48731
SLOMAN MIRA	56091
SLOMAN NAJADE	45531
SLOMAN NAJADE	67241
SLOMAN NEREUS	45530
SLOMAN NEREUS	67240
SLOMAN RANGER	92290
SLOMAN RANGER	92360
SLOMAN RECORD	92291
SLOMAN RECORD	92361
SLOMAN REGENT	92295/1
SLOMAN REGENT	92366
SLOMAN RIDER	92292
SLOMAN RIDER	92362
SLOMAN ROVER	92293
SLOMAN ROVER	92363
SLOMAN ROYAL	92302
SLOMAN RUNNER	92295
SLOMAN RUNNER	92365
SLOT SCANDINAVIA	91316
SLOVENIJA	04928
SLUPSK	34363
SLURRY EXPRESS	68160
SLUSKEN	22610
SLUTSK	10614
SMARA	34203
SMELA	28062
SMENA	01407
SMENA	01667
SMINARCHOS FRANGISTAS	05981
SMOLENSK	71533
SMOLENSK	80203
SMOLNY	10577
SMOLNYY	11610
SMYRIL	19182
SNABZHENETS PERVYY	12524
SNAGOV	82127
SNAGOV	82407
SNAM PALMARIA	55630●
SNEZHNOGORSK	83686
SNIADECKI	15191
SNJEZNIK	83925
SNOLNY	15347
SNOW CRYSTAL	02602
SNOW CRYSTAL	02632
SNOW DRIFT	02603
SNOW DRIFT	02633
SNOW FLAKE	02600
SNOW FLAKE	02630
SNOW HILL	02607
SNOW HILL	02637
SNOW STORM	02606
SNOW STORM	02636
SNOWFROST	26070
SOBOLEVO	22876
SOBOLEVO	34506
SOCHI	02682
SOCRATES	13820
SOCRATES	54610
SOCRATES	74160
SOFIA	80330
SOFIA	91700
SOFIA A	43581
SOFIA PEROVSKAYA	06789
SOFIE	55310
SOFIE BRAVO	50332
SOFIE BRAVO	83672
SOFIYA	36860
SOFIYA PEROVSKAYA	07586
SOFIYSK	83689
SOGNEFJORD	09510
SOHIO INTREPID	63412
SOHIO RESOLUTE	63413
SOKNATUN	71907
SOKOL	03952
SOKOLICA	68922
SOKOLICA II	68922●
SOKOLINOYE	11890
SOKOTO	56590
SOKRAT	13754/2
SOL EXPRESS	19860
SOL GEORGIOS	94230
SOL OLYMPIA	32881
SOL PHRYNE	32900
SOL REEFER	72962
SOL REEFER	87162
SOLA	72511
SOLANGE P	05900
SOLANO	93257
SOLIDOR	32820
SOLNECHNOGORSK	13016
SOLNECHNYY	85996
SOLNECHNYY BEREG	62690
SOLNECHNYY LUCH	71672
SOLNTSEDAR	11891
SOLOGNE	64373
SOLOMBALA	89210
SOLON TURMAN	00067
SOLOVIETSKIY	11739
SOLOVIETSKIY	34629
SOLVA	64150
SOLVENT EXPLORER	55680
SOLVENT EXPLORER	72530
SOLWAY FISHER	88640
SOMALI NAVIGATOR	05076
SOMES	11979
SOMIO	76086
SOMMY	59610
SOMMY	71920
SOMOGY	89220
SOMSUK	17900
SONDERHAUSEN	03709
SONG BA	83606
SONG DO HO	90175
SONG DUONG	05317
SONG GIANH	10520
SONG HUA JIANG	60243
SONG HUONG	83280
SONG KAU	86244
SONG KHAN	22884
SONG KHAN	34514
SONG LIM	40660
SONG LO	86243
SONG NHUE	31330
SONG OF AMERICA	93075
SONG OF NORWAY	16870
SONG THAO	86245
SONG TRA LY	22960
SONGDA	22883
SONGDA	34513
SONGKHLA	47450
SONGKHLA	48320
SONGLIN	06032
SONIA	87771
SONIA M	45483
SONIA M	49433
SONID	46830
SONJA	55311
SONJA	70062
SONORA	25640
SOO GEUN HO	91927
SOPHIA C	79640
SOPHIE	27650
SOPHIE C	47932
SOPHIE RICKMERS	07751
SOPHIE SCHULTE	84744
SOPHIE SCHULTE	84954
SOPKA GEROYEV	11892
SOPOT	34360
SOPOT	83721
SOPOT	88235
SORACHI MARU	19701
SORACHI MARU	23734
SORAYA	84537
SOREN TOUBRO	47875
SORMOVSKIY 2	79341
SORMOVSKIY 5	79343
SORMOVSKIY 6	79344
SORMOVSKIY 7	79345
SORMOVSKIY 9	79346
SORMOVSKIY 12	79348
SORMOVSKIY 14	79350
SORMOVSKIY 17	79351
SORMOVSKIY 18	79352
SORMOVSKIY 19	79353
SORMOVSKIY 22	79354
SORMOVSKIY 27	79355
SORMOVSKIY 28	79356
SORMOVSKIY 29	79357
SORMOVSKIY 30	79358
SORMOVSKIY 31	79359
SORMOVSKIY 33	79360
SORMOVSKIY 34	79361
SORMOVSKIY 40	79362
SORMOVSKIY 41	79362/1
SORMOVSKIY 42	79363
SORMOVSKIY 109	79364
SORMOVSKIY 110	79365
SORMOVSKIY 112	79366
SORMOVSKIY 117	79367
SORMOVSKIY 118	79362/2
SORMOVSKIY 3001	79362/3
SORMOVSKIY 3002	79362/4
SOROKOS	60170
SOROLLA	91270
SORONG	44440
SORRO	81823
SORRO	82073
SOSNOGORSK	03950
SOSNOVETS	83681
SOSNOVKA	83683
SOTE JARL	83641
SOTKA	51991
SOTKA	65161
SOUFFLOT	49553
SOUND OF ISLAY	17250
SOUNION	61330
SOUNION	59290
SOUSA	82135
SOUSA	82415
SOUTH ANGELA	63930
SOUTH BAY	68323●
SOUTH CATHAY	02603●
SOUTH CATHAY	02633●
SOUTH COUNTY	60940
SOUTH COUNTY	59440
SOUTH FAITH	60941
SOUTH FAITH	59441
SOUTH FOUNTAIN	02605●
SOUTH FOUNTAIN	02635●
SOUTH ISLANDER	47120
SOUTH ISLANDER	49360
SOUTH JOY	02601●
SOUTH JOY	02631●
SOUTH PACIFIC	34925
SOUTH PACIFIC	77565
SOUTH PEARL	63513
SOUTH PEARL	68283
SOUTH SEA 1	87710
SOUTH SEA 1	89310
SOUTH VICTOR	77676
SOUTH VIEW	02600●
SOUTH VIEW	02630●
SOUTH VIVIEN	63931
SOUTH WIND	56987
SOUTHDENE	09640
SOUTHERN CONQUEST	37650
SOUTHERN CROSS	14552
SOUTHERN CROSS	66230
SOUTHERN CROSS	94964
SOUTHERN DIAMOND	72152
SOUTHERN FIGHTER	31134
SOUTHERN FRIENDSHIP	60171
SOUTHERN GLORY	33190
SOUTHERN ISLAND	72541●
SOUTHERN LADY	05470
SOUTHERN LION	59944
SOUTHERN LION	67934
SOUTHERN QUEEN	59410●
SOUTHERN RANGER	17680
SOUTHERN STAR	50491
SOUTHLAND STAR	04115
SOUTHSEA	20931
SOUTHWARD	17000
SOUTHWAY	65360
SOUTHWEST CAPE	37602
SOUTHWEST CAPE	44312
SOUTHWIND	53381
SOUTHWIND	90741
SOVATA	82130
SOVATA	82410
SOVEJA	82129
SOVEJA	82409
SOVEREIGN ACCORD	74461
SOVEREIGN ACCORD	79311
SOVEREIGN VENTURE	47202
SOVETSKAYA ROSSIYA	93382
SOVETSKIY POGRANICHNIK	50294
SOVFRACHT	78520
SOVGANSKIY KOMSOMOLETS	11772
SOVGANSKIY KOMSOMOLETS	34663
SOVGAVAN	12525
SOVIETSK	09382
SOVIETSK	10615
SOVIETSKAYA ARKTIKA	26220
SOVIETSKAYA ARKTIKA	31680
SOVIETSKAYA BURYATYA	93757
SOVIETSKAYA BURYATYA	93847
SOVIETSKAYA KAMCHATKA	25847
SOVIETSKAYA LATVIYA	85325
SOVIETSKAYA LITVA	25849
SOVIETSKAYA RODINA	85326
SOVIETSKAYA ROSSIYA	93630
SOVIETSKAYA SAKHALIN	25848
SOVIETSKAYA SIBIR	93751
SOVIETSKAYA SIBIR	93841
SOVIETSKAYA UKRAINA	93860
SOVIETSKAYA YAKUTIYA	50730
SOVIETSKIE PROFSOYUZY	12526
SOVIETSKIY AZERBAIDZHAN	20320
SOVIETSKIY KAZAKHSTAN	20322
SOVIETSKIY KHUDOZHNIK	77087
SOVIETSKIY KHUDOZHNIK	80007
SOVIETSKIY MORYAK	50297
SOVIETSKIY POGRANICHNIK	85984
SOVIETSKIY SEVER	79416
SOVIETSKIY SOYUZ	12010
SOVIETSKIY TURKMENISTAN	20321
SOVIETSKIY UZBEKISTAN	20323
SOVIETSKIY VOIN	50280
SOVIETSKIY ZAPOLYARYE	93737
SOVIETSKIY ZAPOLYARYE	93827
SOVIETSKIYE PROFSOYUZY	48447
SOVIETSKIYE PROFSOYUZY	49487
SOVIETSKIYE PROFSOYUZY	49757
SOVIETSKOYE PRIMORYE	93746
SOVIETSKOYE PRIMORYE	93836
SOVINFLOT	78522
SOYUZ	11893
SOZER BIRADERLAR	11400
SPACIOUS	60189
SPAN	26440
SPAROS	73793
SPARTAK	89250
SPARTAN	19562
SPARTAN REEFER	03900
SPARTO	55785
SPASSK	22720
SPASSK	93804
SPASSK-DALNIY	15485
SPECIALITY	73680
SPECIALITY	87340
SPEED BULK	75455●
SPEEDLINK VANGUARD	94800
SPERANZA	61350
SPERANZA 7	78422
SPERO	48342
SPERUS	22670
SPEY BRIDGE	69200
SPHINX	07764
SPHINX	07817
SPICA	00032
SPICE ISLAND GIRL	84790
SPIEGELGRACHT	49824
SPIJKENISSE	01203
SPINANGER	54140
SPINANGER	54260
SPINOZACAG	53480●
SPINOZACAG	61280●
SPIRIT	61141
SPIRIT	26981●
SPIRIT	81481
SPIRIT OF FREE ENTERPRISE	20210
SPIROS	65472
SPLENDID FORTUNE	06581
SPLENDID HOPE	62120
SPLENDID HOPE	56960
SPLENDOR	65310●
SPLIT	62582
SPLIT	60622
SPOKANE	18910
SPRAVEDLIVYY	04081
SPRING ODESSA	53685
SPRING ODESSA	53815
SPRING ODESSA	68535
SPROGO	18941
SPRUT	09120
SPRUT	17350
SPRUT	34880
SPRY CARRIER	52501
SPUTNIK	12599
SPYROS	18520
SPYROS A LEMOS	63880
SPYROS A. LEMOS	68460
SPYROS G	25720
SPYROS G II	91860
SPYROS K	88246
SRAKANE	91252
SREDNA GORA	49041
SRETENSK	00034
SRI CHOL	22970
SRI PHEN SINN	82570
SRI THAMARACH	25470
SRIWIJAYA	59865
ST ANN'S BAY	75892
ST ANSELM	19460
ST ANTONIUS	75624
ST CERGUE	29270●
ST CHRISTOPHER	19461
ST CLAIR	23820
ST COLUMBA	19890
ST DAVID	19465
ST EMILION	36640
ST EMILION	43680
ST GEORGE	16380

Name	No.	Name	No.	Name	No.	Name	No.
ST HELENA	86290	STARMAN AMERICA	53530	STEPHEN BROWN	80150	SU FENG	04665●
ST JASON	17740	STARMAN AMERICA	71650	STERLING	70630	SU LONG	16290
ST JASPER	17741	STARMAN ANGLIA	92701	STERN	75420	SUADIYE	32140
ST JEROME	17742	STARMAN ASIA	87100	STERN	80170	SUAVITY	75455
ST LAWRENCE	78802	STARMAN ASIA	89810	STEVE GLORY	82450	SUBICEVAC	06413
ST LAWRENCE	89962	STARMAN AUSTRALIA	67210	STEVEN K.	75490	SUBIN	93653
ST MAGNUS	32952	STARMAN AUSTRALIA	91750	STEYNING	75923	SUBIN	94993
ST MARGARETS	09280	STAROGARD GDANSKI	76220	STEYR	75870	SUBIN RIVER	07992
ST MICHAELIS	67725	STAROGARD GDANSKI	76900	STIG GORTHON	92938	SUBIN RIVER	15277
ST MONICA	66573●	STARWARD	01870	STILIANOS S	90691	SUBSEA MARAUDER	08090
ST NICHOLAS	16911	STARYY BOLSHEVIK	01408	STINNES ZEPHIR	53420	SUCCESS	13560
ST NIKOLAI	67726	STARYY BOLSHEVIK	01668	STINNES ZEPHIR	64950	SUCCESSOR	78272
ST OLA	32870	STASIA	46430	STINT	76417	SUCCESSOR III	48081
ST PAUL	45551	STASZIC	15192	STIRLING UNIVERSAL	02652	SUCCESSORS	78272●
ST PAUL	78430	STATE OF HIMACHAL PRADESH	05456	STO NINO	39320	SUCEAVA	39671
ST PETRI	67727	STATE OF MADHYA PRADESH	30753	STOLETIYE PARIZHOSKOY	03956	SUCEVITA	82134
ST TOBIAS	58350	STATE OF MAHARASHTRA	26803	KOMMUNY		SUCEVITA	82414
STABILITY	73681	STATE OF MYSORE	30754	STOLIV	59320	SUCRE	74051
STABILITY	87341	STATE OF PUNJAB	25784	STOLLBERG	34962	SUCRE	77021
STADION	61199	STATE OF RAJASTHAN	25621	STOLLER GRUND	72731	SUDAK	83687
STADIONGRACHT	49825	STATE OF TRAVANCORE-COCHIN	29500	STOLLER GRUND	76911	SUDERELV	73950/4
STADT ESSEN	54750	STATE OF UTTAR PRADESH	25622	STOLT BOEL	52261	SUDESTADA	77990
STADT ESSEN	56210	STATE OF WEST BENGAL	30755	STOLT BOEL	53601	SUDFJORD	66906
STAFFETTA ADRIATICA	22380	STATHEROS	38180	STOLT CASTLE	52132	SUDURLAND	48780
STAFFETTA TIRRENICA	22382	STATHIS	82900●	STOLT CASTLE	52512	SUDURLAND	49902
STAFFORD	34780	STAUPER	21010	STOLT CONDOR	53914	SUDURLAND	50342
STAFFORDSHIRE	54060	STAVERN	50691	STOLT CROWN	52131	SUDUVA	23507
STAFFORDSHIRE	55590	STAVR	60187/1	STOLT CROWN	52511	SUDWIND	75620
STAGAN	45090	STAVRAKIS II	59627	STOLT EAGLE	53915	SUERTE	23142
STAKHANOVETS	04082	STAVROPOL	70168	STOLT ENERGIE	65727	SUERTE	28342
STAKHANOVETS KOTOV	35150	STAVROS G	84530	STOLT ENERGIE	75667	SUERTE	32001
STAKHANOVETS PETRASH	35151	STAVROS G L	64298	STOLT ENTENTE	65726●	SUEZ	03971
STAKHANOVETS YERMOLENKO	35152	STAVROS H	64791	STOLT EXCELLENCE	52526	SUGAN	13754/3
STALO 2	46335	STAVROS H	66771	STOLT EXCELLENCE	53596	SUGAR ISLANDER	77820
STAMATA II	41100	STAVROS V	83615	STOLT FALCON	53910	SUGAR TRADER	85260
STAMATIOS G EMBIRICOS	24800	STAVROULA	77581	STOLT HAWK	53912	SUHADIWARNO PANANG	48908
STAMY	54565	STAVROULA K	09620	STOLT HERON	53913	SUHL	04913
STAMY	54965	STEEL TRADER	62741	STOLT INTEGRITY	52523	SUI JIU 201	34400
STANDARD ARDOUR	66250●	STEFAN BATORY	02180	STOLT INTEGRITY	53593	SUIKO MARU	61185
STANDARD ARDOUR	69920●	STEFAN CZARNIECKI	10350	STOLT LLANDAFF	52262	SUILVEN	94041
STANISLAV KOSIOR	79377	STEFAN E	91411	STOLT LLANDAFF	53602	SUKHE BATOR	70600
STANISLAVSKIY	28490	STEFAN KARADJA	47572	STOLT LOYALTY	51525	SUKHINICHI	85346
STANISLAW DUBOIS	10578	STEFAN STARZYNSKI	12687	STOLT LOYALTY	53595	SUKHONA	35330
STANISLAW DUBOIS	15348	STEFANIA A.	58790	STOLT OSPREY	53911	SUKHONA	93805
STANKO STAIKOV	80056	STEINHOFT	45533	STOLT PRIDE	52520	SUKHONALES	31892
STANLEY BAY	72631	STEINHOFT	67243	STOLT PRIDE	53590	SUKHUMI	70611
STANLEY BAY	77398	STELIOS	60790	STOLT SCEPTRE	70092	SULA	89466
STANYUKOVICH	12527	STELITSA	25740	STOLT SEA	57660	SULAK	93806
STAPAFELL	51800	STELLA	32086	STOLT SHEAF	52260	SULEV	86088
STAPAFELL	52080	STELLA	56490	STOLT SHEAF	53600	SULEYMAN STALSKIY	14392
STAR	12528	STELLA A	81711	STOLT SINCERITY	52522	SULFURICO	84960
STAR	41570	STELLA AZZURRA	70340	STOLT SINCERITY	53592	SULINA	82114
STAR	89848	STELLA DI LIPARI	88781	STOLT SPAN	57661	SULINA	82394
STAR I	06624	STELLA LYKES	05589	STOLT SPIRIT	52521	SULOY	11628
STAR I	42272	STELLA LYKES	14430	STOLT SPIRIT	53591	SULTANA	40910
STAR 1	24580	STELLA LYKES	14900	STOLT SPUR	57662	SULTANA	45150
STAR ALCYONE	47047	STELLA MARIS II.	32420	STOLT STANE	70094	SULTANA 1	88080
STAR CAPELLA	47880	STELLA OCEANIS	20590	STOLT SURF	57663	SULU BAY	07512
STAR CARRIER	61810	STELLA PROCYON	91610	STOLT SYDNESS	52133	SUMADIJA	15322
STAR CARRIER	83091	STELLA SOLARIS	09410	STOLT SYDNESS	52513	SUMBAWA	47451
STAR CASTOR	47881	STELLA SOLARIS	17600	STOLT TEMPLAR	70095	SUMBAWA	48231
STAR CLIPPER	54573	STELLAMAN	58990	STOLT TENACITY	52524	SUMBURGH HEAD	78915
STAR CLIPPER	54953	STELLAMAN	75190	STOLT TENACITY	53594	SUMIRE MARU	32472
STAR DELTA	83034	STELLAPRIMA	82370	STOLT VENTURE	66150	SUMMER BREEZE	12166
STAR DELTA	83114	STELVIO	21062	STON	63713	SUMMER DAY	71509
STAR DIEPPE	83053	STENA ADRIATICA	65632	STONEPOOL	78760	SUMMER LIGHT	61466
STAR DOVER	83054	STENA CARRIER	76768	STONEWALL JACKSON	01050	SUMMER SKY	71509/1
STAR ENTERPRISE	83090	STENA CARRIER	80278	STORK	47156	SUMMITY	75453
STAR GAZER	83039	STENA CONSTRUCTOR	01352	STORM	81280	SUMY	11895
STAR GAZER	83119	STENA DANICA	16913	STORON	74902	SUMY	39999
STAR HERCULES	08840	STENA FREIGHTER	76767	STORRINGTON	78913	SUN ALKES	61059/6
STAR HONG KONG	83051	STENA FREIGHTER	80277	STOVE CAMPBELL	46004	SUN ALKES	57619/6
STAR INDONESIA	83035	STENA GRECIA	76766	STOVE TRADER	73320	SUN BOAT	19430
STAR INDONESIA	83115	STENA GRECIA	80276	STOVE TRANSPORT	46005	SUN CHON	37861
STAR LANAO	83030	STENA HISPANIA	76764●	STOW PRINCESS	69730	SUN EAGLE 1	81830
STAR LANAO	83110	STENA HISPANIA	80274●	STRADJA	49043	SUN FLOWER	16400
STAR LUZON	83032	STENA IONIA	76765	STRAIT CONTAINER	76172	SUN FLOWER	75281
STAR LUZON	83112	STENA IONIA	80275	STRAITS PRIDE	91250	SUN FLOWER	80161
STAR MAGNATE	83050	STENA JUTLANDICA	16914	STRAITS STAR	25752	SUN FLOWER 2	16401
STAR MALAYSIA	83037	STENA MARINER	94520	STRAITS VENTURE	66860	SUN FLOWER 5	16402
STAR MALAYSIA	83117	STENA NORDICA	16462	STRALSUNDSKIY KORABEL	13754/4	SUN FLOWER 8	16403
STAR MINDANAO	83033	STENA NORDICA	32810	STRANA SOVIETOV	79385	SUN FLOWER 11	17400
STAR MINDANAO	83113	STENA NORMANDICA	16993	STRATHETTRICK	52924	SUN ISLAND 1	61617
STAR OF ASSUAN	21050	STENA OCEANICA	56441	STRATHFIFE	56636	SUN ORION	61081
STAR OF MEDINA	41860	STENA OCEANICA	68351	STRATHFYNE	56637	SUN ORION	71271
STAR OF MIRANDA	72435●	STENA PACIFICA	64376●	STRATOSFERA	13706	SUN PRINCESS	17020
STAR ORIENT	46953	STENA SAILER	32340	STRATUS	64380	SUN RIVER	53940
STAR PHILIPPINES	83038	STENA SCANDINAVICA	20330	STREAM BOLLARD	48991	SUN ROKKO	83150
STAR PHILIPPINES	83118	STENA SEARIDER	93101	STREAM DOLPHIN	48992	SUN SUMA	83139
STAR PRIDE	82900	STENA SEASPREAD	01353	STREAM HAWSER	48993	SUN VIKING	16872
STAR PROTOMACHOS	46873	STENA SEASPREAD	01356	STREAM RUDDER	48994	SUNARAWAK	58582
STAR SHIP	30300	STENA SEATRADER	93100	STRELETS	12289	SUND	18731
STAR SINGAPORE	83042	STENA TRADER	93511	STRELETS	23865	SUND	91300
STAR SINGAPORE	83122	STENA TRADER	93921	STRIDER AUSTRALIA	82920	SUNDA CAREER	77740
STAR SKANDIA	86882	STENA TRANSPORTER	76788	STRIDER BROADSWORD	82922	SUNDA SEA	61011●
STAR SULU	83044	STENHOLM	51762	STRIDER CRYSTAL	82921	SUNDA SEA	71171●
STAR SULU	83124	STENIES	69432	STRIDER EXETER	82925	SUNDANCE	57290
STAR SUNG	83040	STENTOR	52182	STRIDER FEARLESS	82927	SUNDANCER	20641
STAR SUNG	83120	STEPAN ARTEMENKO	48860	STRILVANG	91413	SUNDERBANS	15642
STAR THAILAND	83036	STEPAN KHALTURIN	15486	STROFADES II.	53140	SUNDERLAND VENTURE	05338
STAR THAILAND	83116	STEPAN KRASHENINIKOV	10453	STROFADES II	66070	SUNFLOWER	45640
STAR UNITED	47882	STEPAN MALYGIN	35426	STROMBOLI	51400	SUNFLOWER	51580
STAR VISAYAS	83031	STEPAN MARKYELOV	78896	STROMNESS	00031	SUNGARI	24095
STAR VISAYAS	83111	STEPAN RAZIN	80179	STRONG SKIPPER	44490	SUNGARI	55500●
STAR WORLD	83052	STEPAN SAVUSHKIN	06799	STROPTIVYY	04080	SUNGARI	63020●
STAR YORK	82730	STEPAN VOSTRETSOV	62596	STROVILI	46710●	SUNGARI	67910●
STAR YORK	82880	STEPAN VOSTRETSOV	60636	STRUMA	60725	SUNGARI	84462
STARA PLANINA	49042	STEPANOKERT	85997	STUBBENHUK	45532	SUNGARY	89462
STARACHOWICE	79875	STEPHAN JANTZEN	22240	STUBBENHUK	67242	SUNGUAJIRA	58587
STARFORD	30280	STEPHANITOR	78391	STUBEN	75457	SUNLUCK	45470
STARITSA	39290	STEPHAN-J	50156	STUDLAFOSS	84900	SUNNINGDALE	46520
STARLET	72001	STEPHANOS	61021	STUDZIANKI	70545	SUNNINGDALE	83300
STARLIGHT	00680	STEPHANOS	71181	STUTTGART EXPRESS	08783	SUNNY	37513
STARMAN AFRICA	92700	STEPHANOS VERGOTTIS	06525	STVOR	23869/6●	SUNNY	44216

SUNNY	75750
SUNNY CHRISTINA	51746
SUNNY HOPE	68525
SUNNY L	35642
SUNNY L	41302
SUNNY MED	62351
SUNNY STATE	48946
SUNOSAKI MARU	77873
SUNRISE	54290
SUNRISE	59612
SUNRISE	71922
SUNRISE	78620
SUNRISE	83360
SUNRISE	83450
SUNRIVER	57021
SUNSET	72004
SUNSET PEAK	68324●
SUNSHINE	83363
SUNSHINE	83453
SUNSHINE ISLAND	39370
SUNSHINE LEADER	59926
SUNSHINE LEADER	67786
SUNTAIRONA	58585
SUNWARD II	16840
SUNWARD II	55962
SUNWARD II	56722
SUNWAVE	78371
SUPER SERVANT 1	01010
SUPER SERVANT 1	94790
SUPER SERVANT 3	92455
SUPER SERVANT 4	92456
SUPER STAR	77226
SUPERIORITY	75454
SUPPLY	45320
SURABAYA	29470
SURAJ	22660
SURAKARTA	28390
SURAKHANY	44111
SUREN SPANDARYAN	03793
SUREN SPANDARYAN	04033
SURGUT	83690
SURGUTNEFT	70787
SURREY	15740
SURUGA MARU	39032
SURUGA MARU	43371
SUSAK	74441
SUSAK	91520
SUSAN	91412
SUSAN B	72386
SUSAN TRIDENT	78521
SUSANGIRD	57850
SUSANNA	55892
SUSANNA	58692
SUSQUEHANNA	66343
SUTAS	90330
SUTJESKA	68764
SUTOMORE	75820
SUURLAID	75642
SUVALKIYA	13743
SUVARNABHUMI	51390
SUVOROVETS	04084
SUVOROVO	83684
SUWALKI	79870
SUZANNE	44570
SUZANNE DELMAS	47219
SUZDAL	03953
SUZDAL	93807
SUZIMAR	88080●
SUZUKASAN MARU	94781
SUZURAN	56466
SVANETIYA	02680
SVEA CORONA	20643
SVEALAND	33250
SVEALAND AV MALMO	19981
SVENDBORG GRACE	80110
SVENJA	76478
SVENTA	56273
SVENTA	62733
SVERDLOVSK	12349
SVERDLOVSK	40002
SVETI STEFAN	20250
SVETLOGORSK	02670
SVETLOGORSK	21604
SVETLYY	85337
SVETLYY LUCH	71674
SVIATOGOR	25850
SVILEN RUSSEV	48157/1●
SVINOY	18732
SVIR	35331
SVIRSK	15487
SVOBODA	01574
SVORTSOV-STEPANOV	03800
SVORTSOV—STEPANOV	04040
SWAKOP	61014
SWAKOP	71174
SWALLOW	71150●
SWAN	33960
SWAN ARROW	83131
SWAN LAKE	38212
SWAN LAKE	38762
SWANSEA BAY	43380
SWEE LEAN	61084
SWEE LEAN	71274
SWEET RORO	32452
SWEET ROSE	21090
SWEET SULTAN	61045/1
SWEET SULTAN	57625/1
SWELLMASTER	93430
SWIERADOW ZDROJ	74142
SWIETLIK	87745
SWIFT	64860
SWIFT	91040
SWINOUJSIE	74141
SYBILLE	72689
SYDNEY EXPRESS	74410
SYDNEY TRADER	33060
SYKTYVKAR	15488
SYLVANIA	64012
SYLVANIA	68402
SYLVIA ALPHA	75540
SYLVIA BETA	75541
SYLVIA DELTA	75542
SYLVIA EPSILON	75543
SYLVIA GAMMA	75544
SYLVIA OMEGA	75545
SYLVO	47817
SYMPHONIC	62961
SYN PULKU	70540
SYRENKA	73651
SYRIA	33761
SYROS	33642
SYROS REEFER	06352
SYRVE	22878
SYRVE	34508
SYZRAN	02675
SZEKESFEHERVAR	35483
SZYEZDA CHERNOMORYA	13767

T

T AKASAKA	80040
TA HANG	86132
TA TUNG No 2	69420
TABALO	85600
TABATHA G	59540●
TABATHA G	81230●
TABLA	51812
TABORA	50980
TABUK	49413
TABUK	50973
TACAMAR VI	26720
TACAMAR VII	81340
TACHIBANA	77593
TACHIRA	04370
TACHIRA	04430
TACKLER ARABIA	15750
TACKLER DOSINIA	15751
TACLOBAN CITY	33800
TACNA	29441
TACNA	30611
TACOMA CITY	46435
TACTIC	54034
TADEUSZ KOSCIUSKO	12685
TADEUSZ OCIOSZYNSKI	14486
TADZHIKISTAN	02355
TADZHIKISTAN	35374
TADZHIKISTAN	12529
TAE YANG No 11	00001
TAFELBERG	45010
TAGAMA	50981
TAGANROG	11896
TAGANROG	51989/3
TAGANROGSKIY ZALIV	61108
TAGELUS	54932
TAGELUS	77612
TAGIL	45591
TAHAROA VENTURER	77228●
TAHASIN	30940
TAI HANG SHAN	04662
TAI HU	60720
TAI LAI	59550
TAI LAI	82580
TAI LIENG	57400
TAI NING	04990
TAI NING	86116
TAI NING	91716
TAI PING KOU	93314
TAI SHAN	32660
TAI SHAN	86115
TAI SHAN	91715
TAI SHING	62032
TAI SHUN	86117
TAI SHUN	91717
TAI SUN	04991
TAI TUNG	55230
TAI WU SHAN	35662
TAI YANG SHAN	35663
TAI YUAN	21160
TAI YUNG	28040
TAI ZHOU HAI	72389/2
TAIBAH	00470
TAIBAH III	12980
TAIBAH IV	14407
TAIFUN	53419
TAIFUN	64949
TAIHANG	54300
TAIHANG	78611
TAIHO	49672
TAIKAI MARU	48941
TAIKO	72151
TAINARON	35280
TAISEI MARU	11221
TAISEI MARU	11420
TAISEI MARU No.98	60970
TAISETU MARU	19681
TAISHAN	26710
TAIWO	49670
TAIXING	13110
TAIYO MARU	61666
TAIYO MARU No 65	93410
TAIYO MARU No 66	93411
TAIYO MARU No 67	22774
TAIYO MARU No 67	34021
TAIYO MARU No 68	22775
TAIYO MARU No 68	34020
TAIYO MARU No 71	22776
TAIYO MARU No 71	34022
TAIYO MARU No 71	93400
TAIYO MARU No 72	22777
TAIYO MARU No 72	34023
TAIYO MARU No 73	34024
TAIYO MARU No 83	94900
TAIYO MARU No 83	95070
TAJIN	15752
TAJO	75271
TAKA	36282
TAKA	36482
TAKACHIHO	77590
TAKACHIHO MARU	32611
TAKACHIHO MARU	92621
TAKAFA	26720●
TAKAMINE	77594
TAKAMIYA MARU	54441
TAKAOKA MARU	54852
TAKAOKA MARU	56372●
TAKARI 1	76210
TAKARI I	52240
TAKARI II	52241
TAKARI II	76211
TAKARI III	52242
TAKARI III	76212
TAKARI IV	52243
TAKARI IV	76213
TAKARI V	52244
TAKARI V	76214
TAKARI VI	52245
TAKARI VI	76215
TAKARI VII	52246
TAKARI VII	76216
TAKARI VIII	52247
TAKARI VIII	76217
TAKASAGO	77591
TAKASAGO MARU No 12	61610
TAKASAKA MARU	55520
TAKASE MARU	54850
TAKASE MARU	56370
TAKELI	86094
TAKHKUNA	89214
TAKIS E	53143
TAKIS E	66073
TAKIS H	24700
TAKOAKA MARU	56372
TAL	68870
TALAVERA	14710
TALETE	80830
TALETE	84750
TALISMAN	51351
TALISMAN	52701
TALISMAN	84011
TALLINN	02356
TALLINN	35375
TALLULAH	41460
TALNIKI	07948/1
TALSY	38535
TALUGA	45041
TAMA MARU	39030
TAMA MARU	43370
TAMAITAI SAMOA	51036●
TAMAN	11466
TAMAN	12531
TAMAN	35332
TAMARA	02950
TAMARA	02580
TAMARITA	47630
TAMATAVE	32056
TAMBA	28880
TAMIM II	43481
TAMIM II	43511
TAMMANNA	38211
TAMMANNA	38761
TAMMO	53240
TAMMO	53430
TAMPERE	07592
TAMPOMAS	18040
TAMSALU	86232
TAMULA	13717
TANAMBI	83760
TANG YIN	31620
TANGA	64100
TANGAROA	87672
TANGER	49865●
TANGHE	50113
TANGSHAN	25952
TANIA	29362
TANIA	30580
TANIT	52462
TANJA	24240
TANJA	84450
TANJA HOLWERDA	88301
TANJUNG OISINA	27800
TANJUNG PANDAN	17410
TANKERMAN	66579
TANNENBELS	52922
TANO RIVER	04831
TANTAL	11783
TANTALUS	62900
TANTALUS	68170
TANTRA	62900●
TANTRA	68170●
TANYA KARPINSKAYA	67024
TAO YUAN	47414
TAO YUAN	48224
TAOLIN	06036
TAPUZ	05811
TAQUIPE	65865
TAQUY	48076
TARA	89120
TARABLOS	91730
TARAGO	80212
TARAKAN	86544
TARAKAN MARU	61553
TARAKAN MARU	72043
TARAKLIYA	89235
TARAS SHEVCHENKO	01753
TARAS SHEVCHENKO	12520
TARAS SHEVCHENKO	17526
TARASCO	45933
TARASCO	47443
TARASOVSK	07948/2
TARBELA	52680
TARCOOLA	72414
TARGET	92652
TARGET	93192
TARKHANKUT	47151
TARKHANKUT	70790
TARKHANSK	07947
TARMO	23661
TARNOBRZEG	73550
TARNOW	75770
TARPOL	22339
TARPON	77251
TARPON SEALANE	46111
TARPON SENTINEL	57382
TARPON STAR	48385/6
TARPON SUN	48385/7
TARQUIN ROVER	84742
TARQUIN ROVER	84952
TARRAGONA	72635
TARRAGONA	77395
TARROS CEDAR	82766
TARROS FIR	82764
TARROS GAGE	82765
TARROS ILEX	82768
TARROS PAXICON	82767
TARRY	36060
TARRY	41800
TARTOUS STAR	43124
TARTU	86224
TARUNA ABADI	64852
TARUNA ABADI	91049
TARUSA	11720
TARUSA	34610
TASERGAL	22340
TASMAN REX	04740
TASMAN SEA	49090
TASMANIA	47814
TASSIA	57320
TASSIA	68720
TASSILI	19500
TAT LEE No 2	84291
TAT LEE No 2	84441
TAT LEE No 3	40020
TATA	89221
TATAI SEA	47301
TATARIYA	02357
TATARIYA	35376
TATARSTAN	81195
TATIANA	64080
TATIANA L	46699/2●
TATINA	68558
TATRY	55313
TATRY	70064
TAUFAU	48464
TAUFAU	49503
TAUFAU	49774
TAURAGE	13714
TAURIA	50265
TAUROS	62036
TAURUS	11714
TAURUS	51680
TAURUS ERRE	70100
TAURUS HORTEN	67737
TAUYSK	00350
TAVDA	02284
TAVERNER	02100
TAVIRA	64381
TAVRIDA	11897
TAVRIYA	79441
TAVRIYA	85320
TAXIARCHIS	36210
TAXIARCHIS	36410
TAXIARCHIS	42360
TAXILA	15643
TAYBOLA	17961
TAYGA	23866
TAYGA	24100
TAYGETUS	11110
TAYGETUS	34143
TAYGONOS	24097
TAYLAN KALKAVAN	42970
TAYMYR	11445
TAYSHEN	24101
TAYSHET	12530
TAZAR	23468
TBILISI	12290
TCHAIKA	12315
TEAKWOOD	01191
TEAM BORGA	58450
TEAM BORGA	64650
TEAM FROSTA	53134
TEAM HADA	55791
TEAM HADA	64652
TEAM SOLVIKEN	55792
TEAM SOLVIKEN	64653
TEAM TROMA	53133
TEBO OLYMPIA	51996
TEBOSTAR	75031
TECONA	53413
TECONA	64943
TECTUS	77677
TEGAL	29420
TEGAL	30640
TEGMEN ALI IHSAN KALMAZ	32161

Name	No.	Name	No.	Name	No.	Name	No.
TEIDE	39950	TEXACO TEXAS	41183	THONG NHAT	20550	TIRASPOL	23516
TEISTIN	19183	TEXACO VERAGUAS	54420	THONON	05122	TIRASPOL	89207
TEL-AVIV	57420	TEXACO VERAGUAS	57880	THONON	59874	TIRGOVISTE	41319
TELEMACHUS	56010	TEXAS	04776	THOR STAERKE	64817/2	TIRGU BUJOR	78842
TELEORMAN	47548	TEXAS SUN	38041	THOR VIKING	16660	TIRGU FRUMOS	78844
TELFAIR LEADER	60172	TEXELSTROOM	18970	THORAIIA	66680	TIRGU JIU	82112
TELFAIR PIONEER	60179	TEXISTEPEC	83222	THORGULL	64570	TIRGU JIU	82392
TELFAIR TRADER	46528	TFL ADAMS	74436	THORHAVEN	66575	TIRGU LAPUS	78843
TELFAIR TRADER	83308	TFL ADAMS	77068	THORHEIDE	66571	TIRGU MURES	41320
TELINDA	46241	TFL DEMOCRACY	77044	THORHILD	64569	TIRGU NEAMT	78845
TELLHOLM	36281	TFL ENTERPRISE	77043	THORLINA	52730	TIRGU OCNA	78846
TELLHOLM	36481	TFL EXPRESS	77045	THORODLAND	66573	TIRGU SECUIESC	78847
TELLO	07944	TFL FRANKLIN	08871	THOROLD	67260	TIRGU TROTUS	78848
TELMANSK	86203	TFL FRANKLIN	74381	THOROLD	91660	TIRNAVA	13739
TELSHYAY	13763/1	TFL FREEDOM	77046	THORSAGA	54351	TIRNAVENI	82115
TELSTAR	61622●	TFL INDEPENDENCE	77047	THORSAGA	54771	TIRNAVENI	82395
TEMA	61627	TFL JEFFERSON	08875	THORSHAVET	64014	TIROL	78423
TEMA	69331	TFL JEFFERSON	74385	THORSHAVET	68404	TIRTA KARYA	41970
TEMARA	53400	TFL LIBERTY	77048	THORSHOLM 11-10-90-	54350	TIRTA MULIA	18150
TEMARA	64930	THAI PAILIN	75310	THORSHOLM	54770	TITAN	68671
TEMEHANI II	65013	THAI RAINBOW	28320	THREE OCEAN	26102	TITAN	89463
TEMIR	86204	THAI TUBTIM	75311	THULE	22270	TITANIYA	45212
TEMPESTA	40890	THAI-BINH	05314	THULELAND	46410	TITHIS	59581
TEMPLE BAY	73363	THALASSA	22320	THUNAR	73910	TITIKA	36076
TEMPO	52678	THALASSINI DOXA	63401	THUNDERFROST	33821	TITIKA	41796
TEMRYUCHANIN	13713	THALASSINI EFHI	58380	THUNTANK 1	59110	TITIKA HALCOUSSI	60130
TEMRYUK	85978	THALASSINI EFHI	60380	THUNTANK 1	67120	TITOGRAD	33581
TEMURA	46242	THALASSINI IDEA	61001	THUNTANK 7	56220	TITOVKA	17970
TENACITY	24572	THALASSINI KYRA	49561	THUNTANK 7	76400	TITOVSK	07949/1
TENCHBANK	04674	THALASSINI KYRA	49581	THUNTANK 10	67161	TIVAT	04930
TENDRA	39982	THALASSINI MANA	49560	THURINGA	04655	TIVOLI	56352
TENES	75652	THALASSINI MANA	49580	THUTMOSE	01415	TIVOLI	68052
TENO	03290●	THALASSOPOROS	49140	THUTMOSE	01675	TIZI M'LIL	86060
TENOCH	77580	THALATTA	54930	THYELLA	68640	TIZI N'TEST	86061
TEODOR NETTE	12532	THALATTA	77610	THYELLA	86820	TIZI N'TICHKA	86062
TEODOR NETTE	90563	THALE	74820	TIAN HU	19143	TIZIANO	32670
TEPIC	12800	THAMES	77871●	TIAN LI SHAN	64813	TJONGERWAL	75602
TEQUILA SUNRISE	52230	THAMES MARU	61183	TIAN SHAN	50100	TJONGERWAL	79322
TEQUILA SUNRISE	67040	THAMESFIELD	45843	TIAN SHUI HAI	54291	TOBAGO	09540
TEQUILA SUNSET	75601	THAMESHAVEN	06820	TIAN SHUI HAI	78621	TOBELO	16251
TEQUILA SUNSET	79321	THANASSIS A	69661	TIANHAI	47985	TOBOL	07556
TERAAKA	09350	THANASSIS K	21750	TIANLIN	06033	TOBOLLES	24096
TERAAKA	33420	THANASSIS M.	69740	TIANMEN	06069/4	TOBRUK	59227
TEREKHOVSK	07948/3	THANIC	56000	TIANSHUI	15961	TOBRUK	74547
TERENGA	53417	THARALEOS	65960	TIARA	62221	TOCHIGI MARU	47003
TERENGA	64947	THASSOS	62720	TIARA	71131	TOCHO MARU	72610
TERIBERKA	89265	THASSOS ISLAND	60143	TIARET	61290	TOGARAN	16252
TERJE VIGEN	19431	THE LADY PATRICIA	72720	TIARET	86720	TOHBEI MARU	08630
TERMANCIA	75273	THE LADY PATRICIA	75850	TIBATI	06589	TOHBEI MARU	09740
TERMEZ	86225	THE LADY SCOTIA	40990	TIBESTI	91442	TOHGO MARU	08590
TERNEY	06796/7	THE VICTORIA	09530	TIBOR SZAMUELY	00241	TOHGO MARU	09730
TERNEY	12533	THE VIKING	16470	TIBOR SZAMUELY	14975/1	TOHOKU MARU	48940
TERNOVSK	07948/4	THE VIKING	32800	TIBURTINA	33475	TOHOKU MARU	48940
TERRA NORDICA	67200	THEANO	61012	TIDESPRING	45311	TOKACHI MARU	23735
TERRA NOVA	67201	THEANO	71172	TIEN GIANG	54268	TOKALA	16253
TERSCHELLING	72145	THEBELAND	93340	TIEPOLO	20270	TOKARYEVSK	07949/2
TERSCHELLING	76485	THEBEN	70170	TIERIBERKA	17967	TOKI ARROW	83146
TERSO	71947	THEEKAR	49412	TIERRA DEL FUEGO II	48376	TOKIO EXPRESS	08373
TERTRE ROUGE	52307	THEEKAR	50972	TIFFANY	64471	TOKIWA MARU	54545
TERTRE ROUGE	77125	THEMAR	84943	TIGER	32780	TOKIWA MARU	63905
TERUTOKU MARU	54263	THEMAR	90603	TIGER'S TAIL	00930●	TOKUHO MARU	56430
TERVI	36090	THEMIS	73200	TIGIL	23529	TOKUMARU	72346●
TERVI	36220	THEMIS	76990	TIGRE	03993	TOKUYAMA MARU	54840
TESABA	46240	THEOCHARIS	58601	TIGRE	64000	TOKUYAMA MARU	67860
TESEY	11936	THEODOR FONTANE	11141	TIGRE	67590	TOKYO BAY	08404
TESINA	51541	THEODOR HEUSS	19550	TIHA	27750	TOKYO MARU	24220
TESSA	74210	THEODOR KORNER	34220	TIIRA	51992	TOKYO OLYMPICS	62143
TESSIN	75334	THEODOR STORM	11140	TIIRA	65162	TOKYO REEFER	05194
TESUBU II	58843	THEODOR STORM	73661●	TIISKERI	36121	TOLAGA BAY	08420
TESUBU II	65653	THEODORE A	77224	TIISKERI	37901	TOLAGA BAY	08980
TESUBU III	58844	THEODOROS	14870	TIKHOOKEANSKIY	11758	TOLANDO	16254
TESUBU III	65654	THEODOROS DEMET	91210	TIKHOOKEANSKIY	34649	TOLBACHIK	23545
TESUBU IV	58845	THEODOROS G	89842●	TIKHORETSK	11898	TOLEDO	56644
TESUBU IV	65655	THEODOROS GIAVRIDIS	45861	TIKHORETSK	86077	TOLEDO	59742
TETI N	60128	THEODOROS GIAVRIDIS	46021	TIKHVIN	12534	TOLETELA	16950
TETSUZUI MARU	77503	THEODOROS II	22830	TIKSI	02728	TO-LICH	05316
TEUTA	74240	THEODOSIA	66400	TILEMACHOS	29620	TOLMIROS	44970
TEVERA	48821	THEOGENNITOR	52142	TILIA	92294	TOLUCA	01431
TEVERA	83491	THEOGENNITOR	52531	TILIA	92364	TOLYA KOMAR	15528
TEVIOTBAN	07017	THEOGENNITOR	82670	TILLIE LYKES	08862	TOLYA SHUMOV	15529
TEXACO ALASKA	44000	THEOKEETOR	72271	TILLIKUM	18982	TOM	12150
TEXACO BALTIC	65731	THEOKEETOR	77171	TILLY	14340	TOM	13090
TEXACO BERGEN	65730	THEOLIPTOS	82830	TIMBO	35841	TOMAKO	16255
TEXACO BOGOTA	65890	THEOMANA	73060	TIMIOS STAVROS	04785●	TOMBARRA	80213
TEXACO BOGOTA	91600	THEOMITOR	62870	TIMIRYAZEV	17527	TOMBATU	16256
TEXACO BRASIL	54437	THEONYMPHOS	68750	TIMIS	87642	TOMIS	77578
TEXACO BRASIL	54817	THEOSKEPASTI	31540	TIMISOARA	41312	TOMIS SEA	77579/3
TEXACO CARIBBEAN	54419	THEOSKEPASTI	36213	TIMOFEY GORNOV	11899	TOMSK	93738
TEXACO CARIBBEAN	57879	THEOSKEPASTI	36413	TIMOFEY KHRYUKIN	11627	TOMSK	93828
TEXACO COLON	88800	THEOSKEPASTI	91392	TIMOFEYEVSK	07949	TONEN ETHYLENE MARU	66712
TEXACO GEORGIA	36670	THEOTOKOS	44710	TIMOR CAREER	25430	TONG AN	24441
TEXACO GHENT	65671	THEOTOKOS	67320	TIMUR FRUNZE	78068	TONG BAI SHAN	51451
TEXACO IRELAND	54435	THEOUPOLIS	40290	TIMUR LIGHT	72270	TONG CHENG	47045
TEXACO IRELAND	54815	THEREAN MARINER	82998	TIMUR LIGHT	77170	TONG CHUAN	05103
TEXACO JAPAN	55710	THERESE	66991	TINA	64297	TONGGON AE GUK HO	57628
TEXACO JAPAN	58280	THERMIDOR	58232	TINA	87770	TONG HUA	29350
TEXACO KENTUCKY	41180	THERMOPYLAI	37970	TINDALO	30650	TONG HUA	30570
TEXACO MAINE	36770	THERMOPYLAI	40550	TINDOUF	89722	TONG JIANG	04660
TEXACO MARYLAND	36671	THESEE	61408	TINE THOLSTRUP	84770	TONGALA	72415
TEXACO MASSACHUSETTS	36672	THETIS	53780	TINEKE	02854●	TONGGON AE GUK	57628
TEXACO MELBOURNE	69590	THETIS	68770	TINGO	91141	TONI SAFI	72570
TEXACO MELBOURNE	86430	THIASSI	74021	TINHINAN	82053	TONY	55420
TEXACO MONTANA	36673	THIRLMERE	88890	TINHINAN	91453	TONY	78880
TEXACO NEDERLAND	54436	THITA OLIVA	40860	TINI	76479/1	TONY SECONDO	71914/5
TEXACO NEDERLAND	54816	THITA STAINLESS	59032	TINI	29380●	TONYA BONDARCHUK	15530
TEXACO NORGE	36681	THITA STAINLESS	75112	TINOS	28550	TOPAZ	12535
TEXACO OHIO	41181	THITA TRIENA	88870	TINTORETTO	32690	TOPAZ	53510
TEXACO OSLO	36682	THJELVAR	19142	TINTOS	60129	TOPAZ	54566
TEXACO OSLO	36990	THOMAS NELSON	30460	TINUAS	71914/6	TOPAZ	54966
TEXACO PENNSYLVANIA	41182	THOMAS ROTH	06625	TIORA	24311	TOPAZ EXPRESS	49200
TEXACO RHODE ISLAND	36674	THOMASEVERETT	04754	TIORA	39451	TOPAZ ISLANDS	30620
TEXACO SKANDINAVIA	36680	THOMPSON LYKES	00069	TIPAZA	32633	TOPEGA	06589●
TEXACO SOUTH AMERICA	63132	THOMPSON PASS	58033	TIPPERARY	94371	TOPEKA	00210
TEXACO STOCKHOLM	65732	THON NHUIT	83607	TIRANA	15160	TOPIRA	93480

Name	No.
TOPIRA	94430
TOPOLOVENI	82128
TOPOLOVENI	82408
TOPROTO	60130/1
TOP VAN WITTE BERG	71330
TOR	23660
TOR BAY	08485
TOR BRITANNIA	16890
TOR CALEDONIA	93250
TOR DANIA	93252
TOR GOTHIA	94500
TOR SCANDINAVIA	16891
TORGELOW	50448
TORGELOW	52009
TORILL KNUDSEN	55471
TORILL KNUDSEN	56341
TORM AMERICA	51035
TORM AMERICA	82530
TORM HERDIS	48650
TORM HILDE	48652
TORNADO	68641
TORO HORTEN	67738
TOROS	11630
TOROS ALIZE	62250
TOROS ALIZE	57615
TOROS BAY	06639/6
TORRES STRAIT	47813●
TORVANGER	54141
TORVANGER	54261
TORZHOK	11738
TORZHOK	34628
TOSA MARU	32481
TOTTORI MARU	54546
TOTTORI MARU	63906
TOUFIC	90895
TOULA	11290
TOULON	01062
TOUNDYA	36820
TOURAINE	62822
TOURAINE	67572
TOURCOING	80292
TOURLAVILLE	88550
TOW TRADER	61667
TOWADA MARU	19686
TOWNSVILLE TRADER	33062
TOWUTI	16250
TOXOTIS	06528
TOXOTIS	44290
TOXOTIS	61190
TOYA	00901
TOYAMA	08970
TOYAMA	10030
TOYOFUJI No 2	47062
TOYOFUJI No 7	92645
TOYOTA MARU No 10	94940
TOYOTA MARU No 11	94941
TOYOTA MARU No 12	94942
TOYOTA MARU No 15	94961
TOYOTA MARU No 16	52870
TOYOTA MARU No 18	94962
TOYOTA MARU No 19	46514
TOYVO ANTIKAYNEN	05640
TOYVO ANTIKAYNEN	14469
TOZEUR	47060
TRADE CONTAINER	33030
TRADE ENDEAVOR	59980
TRADE INDEPENDENCE	63580
TRADE LIGHT	53702
TRADE LIGHT	78092
TRADE LIGHT	89942
TRADE MASTER	74672
TRADE MASTER	78382
TRADE UNITY	73002
TRADE UNITY	76982
TRADE VISION	47158
TRADE WIND	54702
TRADE WIND	74762
TRADE WIND	85011
TRADER	56190
TRADER	80910
TRAKAY	23508
TRAKYA 1	55951
TRAKYA 1	57081
TRALFLOT	11594
TRAMCO AMITY	46730
TRAMCO GLORY	46731
TRAMCO GLORY	78685
TRAMONTANE	83210
TRAMOUNTANA	83267
TRANS COMMERCE	42701
TRANS CORAL	90260
TRANS KOSTAS	02552
TRANS KOSTAS	45973
TRANS LINK	89780
TRANS ST LAURENT	19050
TRANS VASSILIKI	07280
TRANSAFE STAR	49851
TRANSAFE STAR	50091
TRANSAFRICAN I	23110
TRANSBALT	01575
TRANSCOLORADO	61391
TRANSCOLUMBIA	61390
TRANSCON	72831
TRANSCON	87131
TRANSCONTAINER 1	72850
TRANSEAST	53390
TRANSEAST	80340
TRANSFINLANDIA	33285
TRANSGERMANIA	00970
TRANSGERMANIA	94590
TRANSLINK	76970●
TRANSMUNDUM 1	37364
TRANSOCEAN PEARL	47399
TRANSOCEAN PEARL	47969
TRANSOCEAN RAM	61018
TRANSOCEAN RAM	71178
TRANSOCEAN REEFER	02740
TRANSOCEAN REEFER	48380
TRANSOCEAN TRANSPORT II	58188
TRANSOCEANICA MARIO	51630
TRANSONDO EXPRESS	47260
TRANSONDO EXPRESS	50060
TRANSPORTER	68830●
TRANSPORTER II	94650●
TRANSPORTOWIEC	47610
TRANSUD II	37610
TRANSUD IV	64180
TRANSVAAL	08450
TRAPEZITZA	93060
TRASONA	72241
TRATTENDORF	79734
TRAUN	61715
TRAUTENBELS	57463
TRAVIATA	92501
TRAVIATA	93721
TRAVIATA	95041
TREADWIND	63502
TREADWIND	68222
TREASURY ALPHA	15331
TREBIZOND	71471
TRELLEBORG	16905
TRENNTSEE	46388
TRENNTSEE	47088
TRENTON	88003●
TRENTONIA	88003
TRENTWOOD	72281
TRENTWOOD	77181
TREPCA	04473
TREPCA	10993
TREPCA	34153
TRES MARIE	81831●
TRETYAKOVO	12536
TREUENBELS	92190
TREVINCA	50212
TRIAENA 1	17780
TRIANTAFILOS M	91440
TRIBELS	52840
TRICOLOR	80214
TRIDENT	69690
TRIDTSATILETIYE POBEDY	01665
TRIGGER	92653●
TRIGGER	93193●
TRINEC	79234
TRINITE	38731
TRINITE	44872
TRINWILLERSHAGEN	75323
TRIOS	81950
TRIOS	91505
TRIPHAROS	63101
TRIPHAROS	68141
TRIPOSFERA	13710
TRISEA	63393●
TRISTAN	49640
TRISTAR	69691
TRITON	13711
TRITON	55030
TRITON	61722
TRITON	58712
TRITON	59642
TRITON	88180
TRITON	65590●
TRITON C	61871
TRIVIA	52720/1
TROCHUS	24312
TROCHUS	39455
TROIKA	81472
TROJAN	83726
TROLL LAKE	48971
TROLL MAPLE	46992
TROLL MAPLE	83332
TROLL PARK	48972
TROLL VIKING	46991
TROLL VIKING	83331
TRONDELAG	18590
TROPHY	61200
TROPIC	53157
TROPIC	66306
TROPIC DAWN	47251
TROPIC STAR	89650
TROPICAL GOLD	33941
TROPICAL LAND	14172
TROPICAL LION	58230
TROPICAL MOON	33850
TROPICAL QUEEN	21242
TROPICAL RAINBOW	61660●
TROPICAL SEA	33940
TROPICAL SUN	21241
TROPICALE	16865
TROPICANA	67380
TROPIK	12316
TROTUS	11980
TROUBRIDGE	32490
TROUTBANK	04675
TROVADOR	87550
TROVATORE	57722
TROVATORE	71802
TRUCK TRADER	92690
TRUCK TRADER	93512
TRUCK TRADER	93922
TRUCKEE	45054
TRUCKER	93101●
TRUD	37780
TRUDOLYUBIVYY	84343
TRUDOVAYA SLAVA	93783
TRUDOVYE RESERVY	12537
TRUE ENDEAVOUR	74650
TRUJILLO	04371
TRUJILLO	04431
TRUNOVSK	07949/3
TRUONG VINH	61668
TRUSEVIK MORYA	13712
TRUSKAVETS	23526
TRUSKAVETS	86078
TRUVA	20410
TRYDAKNA	24319
TRYDAKNA	39459
TRYM	50692
TSEFEY	12291
TSELINOGRAD	45213
TSELINOGRAD	86180
TSEMESSKAYA BUKHTA	13716
TSENTAUR	12292
TSESIS	38536
TSEZAR KUNIKOV	59892
TSEZAR KUNIKOV	67652
TSIGLOMEN	06790
TSIGLOMEN	07575
TSIKLON	18320
TSIKLON	21248
TSIMENTAVROS II	42920
TSIMENTIAS	42910
TSIMISARAKA	86530
TSIMLYANSK	11774
TSIMLYANSK	34665
TSIN YUEN	25380
TSING YI ISLAND	01150
TSKHALTUBO	11900
TSNA	35182
TSUDA MARU	35094
TSUDA MARU	95100
TSUGARU	39330
TSUGARU MARU	02040
TSUGARU MARU	19685
TSURU ARROW	83147
TSURUMI MARU	39033
TSURUMI MARU	43373
TSVETKOVO	13755/2
TU MEN JIANG	82350
TU MEN JIANG	82620
TUAN CHIEH	33745
TUAN JIE	33745
TUAPSE	67671
TUAREG	58164
TUCANA	11709
TUCUMAN	06672
TUDELA	79560
TUGELA	47250
TUI CAKAU II	04310
TUI CAKAU II	21110
TUI CAKAU III	94250
TUIRA	47493
TUKUMS	44371
TUKWILA CHIEF	90870
TULA	02524
TULEN KABILOV	11901
TULOMA	21585
TULOMA	24098
TULSA GETTY	64385
TULSK	07949/4
TULUK WEDA	86206
TULUM	12167
TULUM	69101
TUMACO	92711
TUMAN-2	23546
TUMILCO	50148
TUNADAL	83192
TUNEK	23469
TUNG PAO	25372
TUNGHO No2	82331
TUNGUSKA	15489
TUNISIAN REEFER	05181
TUNISIAN REEFER	06335
TUO HE	46251
TURA	86176
TURAN	32168
TURAYDA	13715
TURBO P.	28210
TURELLA	20340
TURGAY	67025
TURGENEV	12538
TURGUT GUNERI	47940
TURICIA	59515
TURICIA	59825
TURK	56649●
TURKIA	25012
TURKIYE	49131
TURKMENISTAN	81196
TURKMENIYA	02162
TURKU	06787
TURKU	07570
TURKUL	23509
TURMALIN	12539
TUROSZOW	60361
TURPIAL	52130
TURPIAL	52510
TURQUINO	88460
TURQUOISE	01091
TURTLE	33953
TURTLE BAY	04530
TURTLE BAY	06151
TURUKHANSK	22880
TURUKHANSK	34510
TUSHINO	06799/6
TUSKAR ROCK	76153
TUSTUMENA	24230
TUULIA	72840
TUVINA	76000
TUXPAN	50147
TUXPAN	61067●
TUYUTI	03136
TUYUTI	03346
TWILIGHT	34530
TWILLINGATE	41881
TYCHE	61059/8
TYCHE	57619/8
TYCHO BRAHE	53106
TYLER	15761
TYMLAT	23510
TYMOVSK	06799/7
TYNDA	11759
TYNDA	34650
TYRO	45510
TYRSUS	20450
TYRUSLAND	93342
TYSON LYKES	52620
TYUMEN	24099
TYUMEN	86073
TYUMENNEFT	36919
TYUMENNEFT	43819
TZAREVETZ	93061
TZELEPI	02762
TZINA M	36790

U

Name	No.
UBARANA	70640
UBENA	50576
UCANCA	89550
UCHI	93885
UCHI	94640
UCO XVII	50416
UCO XVII	50826
UDAFOSS	91318
UDO	88280
UDZHARY	44107
UELEN	57476
UGANDA	08300
UGLAND OBO-ONE	64578
UGLEGORSK	84341
UGLEN	04320
UGLEURALSK	83780
UGO M	42480
UGOLNYY	11902
UGUR YILDIZI	50491●
UHENBELS	39500
UIKKU	51993
UIKKU	65163
UJE	37514
UJE	44211
UJPEST	35484
UKHTA	84463
UKHTA	85971
UKRAINA	16140
UKRAINE	12151
UKRAINY	05626
ULAN-BATOR	36846
ULANGA	82721
ULANUDE	24102
ULAN-UDE	76517
ULCINJ	09910
ULISSE I	27721
ULLA THOLSTRUP	85002
ULTRA FREEZE	87020
ULTRAGAS	53750
ULTRAMAR	64071
ULTRASEA	64070
ULYANA GROMOVA	41156
ULYANA GROMOVA	44955
ULYANOVSK	10454
ULYANOVSK	12350
ULYANOVSK	70169
ULYSSUS	72171
UM EL FAROUD	60830
UM EL FAROUD	85070
UMA	90891
UMANJ	21586
UMBALES	90561
UMM SHAIF	69113
UMM SHAIF	71463
UNA	87250
UNAMUNO	51891
UNAN AVETISYAN	73295
UNGAVA TRANSPORT	70320
UNGAVA TRANSPORT	78650
UNIBAKSH	22560
UNICORN	94942●
UNICORN DANIEL	75140
UNICORN EXPRESS	73733
UNICORN JONI	56192
UNICORN JONI	80912
UNICORN MICHAEL	75141
UNICOSTA	03670●
UNICOSTA	03730●
UNIDO	45920
UNIFORM STAR	78691●
UNILUCK	28650
UNILUCK	58180
UNIMAR	77750
UNIMAR	06565●
UNIMAR K	77750●
UNION	86830
UNION AUCKLAND	46524
UNION AUCKLAND	83304
UNION BALTIMORE	81370
UNION DUNEDIN	93270
UNION DUNEDIN	93420
UNION EVERGREEN	68370
UNION GRAIN	47732●
UNION HOBART	94760
UNION KINGSTON	05764
UNION LYTTELTON	94761
UNION NELSON	51745
UNION PRIDE	61841

[handwritten note near TURKU entry: 30-10-70]

Name	Number
UNION ROTOITI	92471
UNION ROTOITI	92531
UNION ROTORUA	92470
UNION ROTORUA	92530
UNION SYDNEY	93271
UNION SYDNEY	93421
UNIQUE FORTUNE	58183
UNISON	47225
UNISON 1	39610
UNISON II	26760
UNIT I	06639/7
UNIT LINK	51786
UNITED DRIVE	05323
UNITED EFFORT	05333
UNITED ENTERPRISE	05334
UNITED REEFER	33630
UNITED SPIRIT	05335
UNITED SPIRIT	39282
UNITED STATES	09170
UNITED VENTURE	77445
UNITY	60920
UNITY	62380
UNITY	60060
UNITY	60131
UNITY	79080
UNITY III	51720
UNITY III	52710
UNITY REEFER	06302
UNIVERSAL TAIO	48962
UNIVERSE	06250
UNIVERSE BURMAH	54411
UNIVERSE BURMAH	57871
UNIVERSE EXPLORER	54412
UNIVERSE EXPLORER	57872
UNIWERSYTET JAGIELLONSKI	78686
UNIWERSYTET SLASKI	65852
UNIWERSYTET SLASKI	67692
UNIWERSYTET WARSZAWSKI	79113
UNIWERSYTET WROCLAWSKI	79115
UNKAS	64677
UNYO MARU	76720
UNZHA	06795
URAGAN	18321
URAGAN	21249
URAL	17528
URAL	52270
URALJSKIE GORY	61275
URALJSKIE GORY	81495
URALLES	24103
URALSK	88240
URAN	12614
URANIA	53080
URANIA	63230
URANIA	06636●
URANIA C	61882
URANIYA	13754/5
URANOS	50063
URANUS 1	60980
URANUS 1	71290
URENGOI	90191
URENGOY	70021
URFA	46891
URGAL	11754
URGAL	34644
URGENTCH	83782
URHO	33002
URICANI	82220
URITSK	83781
URQUIL	93241
URRIDAFOSS	50200
URRIDAFOSS	75970
URSA	24940
URSA MAJOR	53663
URSA MAJOR	73383
URSULA	19082
URSULA	84079
URSULA	87670
URSUS	06040
URSUS	14770
UR-TXORI	65003
UR-TXORI	85233
URYUPINSK	83783
URZHUM	70165
URZHUM	83784
URZHUM	85884
USA MARU	63050
USA MARU	67900
USAMBARA	50577
USARAMO	50575
USHUAIA	03412
USHUAIA	15972
USINSK	70027
USKOK	13950
USOLJE	83785
USSURI	15490
USSURIYSKIY ZALIV	61109
UST-BOLSHERETSK	86235
UST-ILIMSK	66394
USTILUG	83787
UST-KAN	66395
UST-KARSK	66386
UST-KUT	66387
USTRINE	48620
UST-TIGIL	86240
USTYUZHNA	83786
USURBIL	93240
UTILA PRINCESS	13172
UTILA PRINCESS	34802
UTILITAS	53127
UTRILLO	48405
UVAROVSK	24313
UVAROVSK	39452
UVERO	86050
UZBEKISTAN	02358

Name	Number
UZBEKISTAN	35377
UZBEKISTAN	81197
UZEIR GADZHIBEKOV	79442
UZGORSK	24315
UZGORSK	39453

V

Name	Number
V KUCHER	75325
VACHA	86012
VAERMLAND II	51622●
VAGA	07564
VAGERO	91843
VAGIF	50740
VAGULA	13720
VALANI	75830
VALDAY	11330
VALDAYLES	24108
VAL-DE-CAES	22834
VALENCAY	20281
VALENCIA	67632
VALENTIN KHUTORSKOY	03960
VALENTIN KOTELNIKOV	12540
VALENTIN SEROV	76524
VALENTIN SHASKIN	92886
VALENTINA	77283
VALENTINA FRIAS	09981
VALENTINA TERESHKOVA	01576
VALENTINE K	85960
VALENTINE K	88960
VALERIA	51030
VALERIAN ALBANOV	35427
VALERIAN KUIBYSHEV	03061
VALERIAN KUIBYSHEV	03651
VALERIAN URYVAYEV	39411
VALERIY BYKOVSKIY	12541
VALERIY MEZHLAUK	03959
VALERIY VOLKOV	15532
VALHALL	55952
VALHALL	57082
VALI PERO	07031
VALIANT PORPOISE	70160
VALKA	23525
VALKENBURG	90960
VALKENIER	89602
VALLABHBHAI PATEL	63562
VALLATHOL	63563
VALLEJO	07945
VALLOMBROSA	88770
VALMIERA	38534
VALOR	58189
VALPARAISO	67880
VALVANUZ	03223
VALVANUZ	03893
VALYA KOTIK	15531
VALYA KURAKINA	67026
VAMPO	24891
VAN DYCK	48890
VAN DYCK	49320
VAN ENTERPRISE	51101
VANDA	75990
VANDARATANA	40426
VANDARATANA	42336
VANDARATANA	42596
VANERNSEE	74007●
VANESSA	68842
VANESSA	75992
VANGELI	80540
VANGUARD	46511
VANGUARD 8	61467
VANINO	22881
VANINO	34511
VANJA	64299
VANKAREM	21620
VANKAREM	34109
VANTAGE	73940
VANYA KOVALYEV	67027
VARAZDIN	21510
VARDAAS	64574
VARDE	61638
VARDIANI	06539
VARENNA	68840
VARI	48157/2●
VARJAKKA	47295
VARKIY LUCH	71673
VARMA	23662
VARNA	82260●
VARNA	36866
VARSHAVA	36845
VARSHUGA	17966
VARUNA ADHAR	26812
VARUNA KACHHAPI	06640
VARUNA YAMINI	40460
VARUNA YAMINI	44900
VARUNA YAN	40461
VARUNA YAN	44901
VARVARA	64501
VARVARA TWO	14020●
VASIL KOLAROV	01971
VASIL KOLAROV	01981
VASIL LEVSKY	48435
VASIL LEVSKY	49475
VASIL LEVSKY	49745
VASILAKIS	62150
VASILIKI II	89020
VASILIKI III	88970
VASILIKI V	90090
VASILIOS 1	85920
VASILIOS V	76341
VASILIOS VII	85910
VASILIS IV	36062
VASILIS IV	41802

Name	Number
VASILIY BLUKHER	93685
VASILIY BYELOKONYENKO	69316
VASILIY CHERNYSHYEV	45291
VASILIY DOKUCHAEV	28983
VASILIY FEDOSEYEV	21621
VASILIY FEDOSEYEV	34110
VASILIY FESENKOV	10746
VASILIY FOMIN	13721
VASILIY GOLOVNIN	10455
VASILIY GOLOVNIN	22188
VASILIY GRECHISNIKOV	13764
VASILIY KIKVIDZE	59900
VASILIY KIKVIDZE	67660
VASILIY KOSENKHOV	11618
VASILIY MALOV	75383
VASILIY MUSINSKIY	54724
VASILIY MUSINSKIY	55294
VASILIY PEROV	76494
VASILIY POLENOV	76496
VASILIY POLENOV	76583
VASILIY POLENOV	79933
VASILIY PORIK	62584
VASILIY PORIK	60624
VASILIY POYARKHOV	22235
VASILIY PRONCHISHCHEV	22236
VASILIY PUTINTSEV	93689
VASILIY REVYAKIN	13723
VASILIY SHUKSHIN	50763
VASILIY STRUVE	10747
VASILIY SURIKOV	76512
VASILIY YAN	50741
VASILY GOLOVKIN	11903
VASILY KLOCHKOV	48442
VASILY KLOCHKOV	49482
VASILY KLOCHKOV	49752
VASILY SHELGUNOV	03796
VASILY SHELGUNOV	04036
VASILY VERESCHCHAGIN	76522
VASILY VINEVITIN	12542
VASSILAS	32020●
VASSILIOS BACOLITSAS	78330
VASSILOS	41329
VASTANVIK	73861
VASYA ALEKSEEV	11446
VASYA KOROBKO	15533
VASYA KURKA	67030
VASYA SHISHKOVSKIY	15534
VASYA STABROVSKIY	67029
VATSLAV VOROVSKIY	02130
VATSY	80600
VATUTINO	08032
VAYGACH	11619
VEENDAM	19741
VEER VARUNA	54119
VEER VARUNA	54589
VEERHAVEN	76182
VEGA	11670
VEGA	12293
VEGA	14553
VEGA	46216
VEGA	51682
VEGALAND	93345
VEGAMAN	59001
VEGAMAN	75181
VEGESACK	03500
VEGESACK	04090
VEJEN	55412
VEJEN	78852
VELA	19490
VELA	54564
VELA	54964
VELA	64300
VELA	74005
VELA LUKA	91100
VELEKA	59903
VELEKA	67663
VELENJE	57440
VELIKIY OKTYABR	59890
VELIKIY OKTYABR	67650
VELIKIY POCHIN	79372
VELIKIY USTYUG	07574
VELIKIYE LUKI	06060
VELIKIYE USTYUG	06791
VELIKO TIRNOVO	91702
VELIZH	06062
VELMA LYKES	05590
VELMA LYKES	14431
VELMA LYKES	14901
VELOX	76021
VELSK	17930
VENATOR	55821
VENATOR	56620
VENDEE	52470
VENERA IV	11904
VENEZIA	39601
VENEZUELA	03143
VENI II	48080
VENICE	12080
VENTSPILS	36255
VENTSPILS	42805
VENTSPILS	51988
VENTURA	66152
VENTURA	88590
VENTURE	65402
VENTURE	65800
VENTURE	69792
VENTURE	74780
VENTURE AMERICA	63060
VENTURE AMERICA	57890
VENTURE CANADA	54383
VENTURE CANADA	63073
VENTURE EUROPE	54382
VENTURE EUROPE	63072
VENTURE INDEPENDENCE	63061

Name	Number
VENTURE INDEPENDENCE	**57891**
VENTURIA	**53202**
VENTUS	**73994**
VENUS	16351
VENUS	32920
VENUS	71510
VENUS DEL MAR	01521
VENUS DEL MAR	45611
VENUS II	22580
VENUS II	23210
VENUTA	22792
VERA	74671
VERA	78381
VERA	78700
VERACRUZ PRIMERO	09340
VERA KHORUZHKAYA	78069/2
VERA LEBEDYEVA	03794
VERA LEBEDYEVA	04034
VERA MUKINA	76590
VERA MUKINA	79940
VERA VOLOSHINA	79444
VERACRUZ I	09340
VERDI	37700
VERDI	44250
VERED	78072
VEREYA	06061
VERGA	32551
VERGA	33371
VERGINA	23800
VERGO	68812
VERILA	75790
VERITAS	58750●
VERITAS	60530●
VERKHOVINA	11769
VERKHOVINA	34660
VERKHOYANSKLES	06796/8
VERKHOYANY	11328
VERNIA	73740
VERRAZANO BRIDGE	04950
VERRAZANO BRIDGE	08610
VESALIUS	64348
VESLETS	75791
VESTA	19491
VESTA	92490
VESTRI	59170
VESTRI	72010
VESTURLAND	49900●
VESTURLAND	50340●
VESUVIO	51401
VESYEGONSK	66388
VETERAN	85357
VETLUGA	45733●
VETLUGALES	24104
VIATOR	64324
VIBIT	65552
VIBIT	85782
VICTOR BUGAEV	02277
VICTORIA	08310
VICTORIA	39662
VICTORIA	82050
VICTORIA	91450
VICTORIA 1	03163
VICTORIA BAY	50577●
VICTORIA DE GIRON	31010
VICTORIA PEAK	72357
VICTORIA PEAK	77157
VICTORIA U	25810
VICTORIA U	30960
VICTORY	75991
VICTORY 1	81782
VICTORY STAR	52362
VIDA	55381
VIDAL DE NEGREIROS	55541
VIDAL DE NEGREIROS	63341
VIDEN	75792
VIDNOYE	66389
VIET BAO	21680
VIETNAM HEROICO	16111
VIETNAM THUONG TIN 1.	24910
VIGIL	38130
VIGNES	50123
VIIRELAID	75644
VIJAYA DARSHANA	39780
VIJAYA JIWAN	91110
VIJAYA VAIBHAV	91111
VIJAYA VASANT	27951
VIKING	65590
VIKING 2	16480
VIKING 2	32802
VIKING 3	19293
VIKING 3	23702
VIKING CAPE	64572
VIKING EXPRESS	19291
VIKING EXPRESS	23701
VIKING HEAD	64571
VIKING SAGA	17010
VIKING SALLY	16880
VIKING SALLY	20680
VIKING SONG	17011
VIKING TRADER	94140
VIKING VALIANT	20221
VIKING VENTURER	20220
VIKING VISCOUNT	20222
VIKING VOYAGER	20223
VIKINGLAND	93346
VIKLA	51986
VIKTOR KHARA	50768
VIKTOR KHUDYAKOV	23488
VIKTOR KURNATOVSKIY	03795
VIKTOR KURNATOVSKIY	04035
VIKTOR LYAGIN	76510
VIKTOR MURAVLENKO	92887
VIKTOR STRELTSOV	34875/2
VIKTOR TALALIKHIN	78069/1

Name	No.
VIKTOR TKACHYOV	49342
VIKTOR VASTNETSOV	76492
VIKTORAS YATSENYAVICHUS	85361
VIKTORIO CODOVILLA	70594
VILI	85110
VILIS LACIS	93780
VILKOVO	86226
VILLA DE AGAETE	19270
VILLABLANCA	49590
VILLABLANCA	49630
VILLAFRANCA	49591
VILLAFRANCA	49631
VILLAFRIA	49592
VILLAFRIA	49632
VILLANDRY	20280
VILLAVERDE	49593
VILLAVERDE	49633
VILLE DE DUNKERQUE	08960
VILLE DE DUNKERQUE	76850
VILLE DE GABES	50155
VILLE DE GENES	49441
VILLE DE MAHEBOURG	82650
VILLE DE MARSEILLE	51000
VILLE DE MARSEILLE	51180
VILLE DE NANTES	51001
VILLE DE NANTES	51181
VILLE DE ROUEN	49532
VILLE DE STRASBOURG	51002
VILLE DE STRASBOURG	51182
VILLE DE SYRTE	92301
VILLE D'ORIENT	75901
VILLE DU HAVRE	08961
VILLE DU HAVRE	76851
VILLE DU MISTRAL	73749/3
VILLE DU PONANT	49878
VILLIA	71762
VILLIERS	51810
VILSANDI	86082
VILYANDY	86241
VILYANY	15491
VILYUY	22793
VILYUYLES	24106
VILYUYSK	36256
VILYUYSK	42806
VILYUYSK	70029
VIMINALE	24343
VINCITA	66151
VINGAREN	01551
VINGASJO	66690
VINGAVAG	75030
VINNITSA	39988
VINTSAS MITSKYAVICHUS-KAPSUKAS	93846
VINTSAS MITSKYAVICHUS-KAPSUKAS	93756
VIOLA	81956
VIOLA	91506
VIOLANDA	60282
VIOLANDO	68422
VIOLETTA	56800
VIRGEN DE AFRICA	08311
VIRGEN DEL CAMINO	18690
VIRGINIA	57150●
VIRGINIA	04775
VIRGINIA	63425
VIRGINIA LILY	64121
VIRGINIA LILY	68601
VIRGINIA STAR	64122
VIRGINIA STAR	68602
VIRGO	11655
VIRPAZAR	27350
VIRTSU	89211
VIRTUOUS	62033
VISAYAS	21590
VISBY	16900
VISCAYA	64502
VISCOUNT	76020
VISHNEVOGORSK	79406
VISHVA ABHA	45398
VISHVA ASHA	45397
VISHVA BANDHAN	15593
VISHVA BHAKTI	25771
VISHVA BINDU	14911
VISHVA BINDU	15720
VISHVA CHETANA	14910
VISHVA CHETANA	15721
VISHVA DHARMA	25775
VISHVA JYOTI	25780
VISHVA KALYAN	10292
VISHVA KARUNA	15590
VISHVA KAUMUDI	04937
VISHVA KAUSHAL	71640
VISHVA MADHURI	15591
VISHVA MAHIMA	10291
VISHVA MAMTA	15592
VISHVA MANGAL	25782
VISHVA MAYA	25783
VISHVA MOHINI	04932
VISHVA NANDINI	04933
VISHVA NAYAK	25778
VISHVA NIDHI	25620
VISHVA PALLAV	48363
VISHVA PANKAJ	48362
VISHVA PARAG	48366
VISHVA PARIJAT	48365
VISHVA PARIMAL	48364
VISHVA PRAFULLA	48367
VISHVA PRAYAS	04936
VISHVA PREM	71090
VISHVA PREM	71641
VISHVA RAKSHA	10293
VISHVA SANDESH	14912
VISHVA SANDESH	15722
VISHVA SEVA	30756
VISHVA SHAKTI	25773
VISHVA SHOBHA	25772
VISHVA SIDDHI	25774
VISHVA SUDHA	40251
VISHVA TARANG	45396
VISHVA TIRTH	30757
VISHVA UMANG	45395
VISHVA VIBHUTI	10290
VISHVA VIJAY	71091
VISHVA VIJAY	71642
VISHVA VIKAS	14913
VISHVA VIKAS	15723
VISHVA VIKRAM	25776
VISHVA VIVEK	12070
VISHVA YASH	15594
VISPY	66957
VISPY	70997
VISSANI	46200
VISSARION BELINSKIY	14393
VISTAFJORD	08150
VISTAFJORD	09330
VISTEN	50250
VISURGIS	74430
VISVESVARAYA	59908
VISVESVARAYA	67668
VITABULK	78860
VITALITY	47999/2
VITALIY BONIVUR	12543
VITALIY BONIVUR	85327
VITALIY KRUCHINA	69317
VITALIY PRIMAKOV	79423
VITASEA	26731
VITAUTAS MONTVILA	12544
VITAUTAS PUTNA	12545
VITIM	89263
VITINA	45950
VITKOVICE	75720
VITOCHA	77089/2
VITOCHA	80009/2
VITORIA	64382
VITORIA DA CONQUISTA	39532
VITORIA DA CONQUISTA	93492
VITREA	65430
VITTORE CARPACCIO	01330
VITTORIO GARDELLA	39360
VITTORIO GARDELLA	42430
VITUS BERING	09383
VITYA CHALENKO	15535
VITYA KHONENKO	15536
VITYA NOVITSKIY	67031
VITYA SITNITSA	15537
VITYAZ	14905
VIVA	77464
VIYTNA	13754/6
VIZIR	23869/5●
VLADAS REKASHYUS	12546
VLADIMIR	40010
VLADIMIR ATLASOV	12547
VLADIMIR FAVORSKIY	76581
VLADIMIR FAVORSKIY	79931
VLADIMIR GAVRILOV	46311
VLADIMIR GAVRILOV	46561
VLADIMIR GAVRILOV	67689
VLADIMIR ILYCH	03071
VLADIMIR ILYCH	03663
VLADIMIR ILYCH	93380
VLADIMIR KAVRAYSKIY	23640
VLADIMIR KOLECHITSKY	59884
VLADIMIR KOROLENKO	14394
VLADIMIR LENORSKIY	78891
VLADIMIR MAYAKOVSKIY	14395
VLADIMIR MORDVINOV	54712
VLADIMIR MORDVINOV	55282
VLADIMIR NAZOR	16720
VLADIMIR RUSANOV	22237
VLADIMIR SUKHOTSKIY	35428
VLADIMIR TIMOFEYEV	54713
VLADIMIR TIMOFEYEV	55283
VLADIMIR ZATONSKIY	79417
VLADIVOSTOK	02074
VLADIVOSTOK	92380
VLAHERNA	47003●
VLAS CHUBAR	75352
VLAS NICHKOV	54719
VLAS NICHKOV	55289
VLORA	24880
VNUKOVO	11743
VNUKOVO	34633
VOCE	21430
VOCKERODE	79735
VOIMA	02240
VOIMA	22260
VOJVODINA	04929
VOLCAN DE YAIZA	94240
VOLCHANSK	05410
VOLCHANSK	45124
VOLDEMAR AZIN	23511
VOLENDAM	19740
VOLERE	62864
VOLERE	67544
VOLFRAM	36915
VOLFRAM	43815
VOLGA	24109
VOLGOBALT	11317
VOLGODON	39972
VOLGOLES	2403Q
VOLGONEFTGAROZ	44125
VOLKERFREUNDSCHAFT	10090
VOLKHOV	40014
VOLKHOVSTROY	11905
VOLNA	02278
VOLNOMER	11906
VOLNOVAKHA	42960
VOLNYY VETER	13765
VOLOCHAYEVSK	45217
VOLODYA SCHERBATSEVICH	15538
VOLOGDA	45125
VOLOGDALES	04190
VOLTA RIVER	04832
VOLTERA	61630
VOLUNTAS	35710
VOLUNTAS	41420
VOLVOX FRISIA	37367
VOLVOX ZELANDIA	37368
VOLZHANIN	23573
VOLZHSK	08033
VOLZHSK	85322
VOMAR	57189
VONNY	89182
VOO SHEE	64200
VOO SHEE	68650
VORKUTA	10457
VORKUTA	24110
VORMSI	88249
VORONEZH	06788
VORONEZH	07588
VOROSHILOVGRAD	13722
VOROSMARTY	48460
VOROSMARTY	49500
VOROSMARTY	49770
VORRAS	30310
VORRAS	36882
VORTIGERN	19920
VOSGES	52471
VOSKHOD	11447
VOSKHOD	11595
VOSKHOD	12548
VOSKRESENSK	24107
VOSTOCK	92150
VOSTOCK	93660
VOSTOK 2	11448
VOSTOK 5	11449
VOSTOK 6	11450
VOYAGER	44970●
VOYAGER	68850●
VOZNESENSK	79373
VOZROZHDENIYE	13754/7
VRANCEA	25786
VRHNIKA	82435
VROUWE ALIDA	74280
VSEVOLOD KOCHETOV	67683
VSEVOLOD BERYEZKIN	39410
VSEVOLOD PUDOVKIN	15124
VSEVOLOD TIMONOV	89762
VSPOLOKH	11596
VUK KARADZIC	16721
VULCAN	63280●
VULCAN	82225
VULKAN	23517
VULKANLOG	39419
VYACHESLAV DENISOV	50298
VYACHESLAV SHISHKOV	10458
VYANDRA	89208
VYATKALES	06796/9
VYAZMA	08032
VYBORG	08030
VYBORGSKAYA STORONA	11621
VYBORGSKAYA STORONA	50291
VYCHEGDA	35333
VYCHEGDALES	24105
VYMPEL	11622
VYOVSK	34666
VYRU	15492
VYRU	89473
VYSHINSKII	17529
VYSHOGOROD	11776
VYSHOGOROD	34667
VYSOVSK	11775
VYTEGRA	11451
VYUGA	22239
VZMORYE	06797
VZMORYE	11907

W

Name	No.
W A MATHER	70152
W C VAN HORNE	80041
W M NEAL	72292
W M NEAL	77162
WAALEKERK	72181
WAALEKERK	83401
WAALEKERK	15831●
WAARDRECHT	47213
WABASH	92606
WABASH	93616
WACCAMAW	38923
WADDENZEE	51731
WADDENZEE	84041
WADEEVERETT	21412
WADOWICE	79873
WAH FAI	23232
WAH LOK	49284
WAH PANG	48000
WAH YEE	66883
WAHEED	24292
WAHEHE	56638
WAHRAN	23230
WAHRAN	58365
WAHYUNI	61643
WAIAL	55890
WAIAL	58690
WAITAKI	60020
WAJABULA	18210
WAKAGIKU MARU	51012
WAKAKUSA MARU	56632
WAKAKUSA MARU	57622
WAKAMIZU MARU	51011
WAKANAMI MARU	51010
WAKATAKE MARU	51013
WAKAUME MARU	51220
WAKAZURA MARU	63102
WAKAZURA MARU	68142
WAKENITZ	71942
WAKO MARU	54200
WAKO MARU	67840
WAKOLO	24131
WALCHAND	58406
WALCHAND	64566
WALEN	23460
WALKA MLODYCH	65851
WALKA MLODYCH	67691
WALKURE	56122●
WALKURE	59772●
WALLA-WALLA	18911
WALTER BARTH	23431
WALTER DEHMEL	10250
WALTER DEHMEL	12630
WALTER LEONHARDT	74561
WALTER ULBRICHT	03703
WAN LING	61210
WAN PING	12751
WAN TAI	70891
WANDA	55980
WANDAJEAN	42530
WANDEBORI	24132
WANDERER	46661
WANG No. 1	27480
WANGKOLL	64146
WANGLI	64144
WANGSKOG	64145
WANGTING	05374
WAPPEN VON HAMBURG	02020
WARENDORP	36346
WARFLETH	72127
WARISANO	24133
WARKA	75413
WARNA	82260
WARNEMUNDE	03690
WARNEMUNDE	17480
WARRIOR	46662
WARSAK	52682
WARSCHAU	45840
WARSZAWA	15087
WASA EXPRESS	23701●
WASA STAR	16901
WASHINGTON	78914
WASHINGTON TRADER	37600
WASHINGTON TRADER	44310
WATAMPONE	24130
WATER LILY	87023
WATERGEUS	46212
WATUDAMBO	24134
WAVE	41200
WAVE CREST	06505●
WAVE CREST	76090●
WAVERLEY	17440
WAWEL	19330
WAWEL	23711
WAYBRIDGE	48491
WAYFARER	46660
WAYFUL	25751
WAYUSUT	60607
WAYUSUT	69977
WEASEL	86130
WEDELLSBORG	47130
WEI HAI	48001
WEI HE	46252
WEI HEI	46252●
WEIKUO	29700
WEIKUO	30831
WEILI	29701
WEIMAR	70697
WEJADIA	50266
WEJHEROWO	51262
WELFARE	74981
WELFARE	79211
WELL RAINBOW	89100
WELL RUNNER	56753
WELL VOY No 1	25210
WELLINGTON STAR	04116
WELLPARK	48300
WELLWOOD	61716
WELS	76418
WELSH JAY	06639/8
WEN DENG HAI	77480
WEN HE	51871
WEN ZHOU HAI	72389/4
WENA	66491
WENA	85931
WENDY	87701
WENJIANG	38337
WENJIANG	44697
WENSHUI	01534
WERBELLINSEE	46383
WERBELLINSEE	47083
WERNER KUBE	23432
WERNER SEELENBINDER	04233
WERRA	79300●
WERRA EXPRESS	79300
WESER	73903
WESER BROKER	82040
WESER EXPRESS	74436●
WESER EXPRESS	77068●
WESER ORE	64520
WESER ORE	68470
WESERTAL	33202
WEST BAY 1	71914/7
WEST DAORI	77240
WEST JINORIWON	58520
WEST JINORIWON	60450

WEST JUNORI	77672	WINSTON	59352
WEST POINT	24381	WINSTON	87010
WEST SUNORI	83220	WINSTON CHURCHILL	20570
WEST WONORI	51639	WINSTON CHURCHILL	32085
WESTBON	62432	WINTER MOON	02931
WESTERENCE	86800	WINTER SEA	02932
WESTERKERK	15833●	WINTER STAR	02933
WESTERKERK	72182●	WINTER SUN	02934
WESTERKERK	83402●	WINTER WATER	02930
WESTERLAND	50145	WINTER WAVE	02935
WESTERMOOR	49870	WIS	87290
WESTERN ARCTIC	23850	WISHFORD	30281
WESTERN CITY	54501	WISLICA	14306
WESTERN GLORY	74720	WISMAR	34960
WESTERN LION	59943	WISSEKERK	15830●
WESTERN LION	67933	WISSEKERK	72180●
WESTERN REEFER	02980	WISSEKERK	83400●
WESTERN SUN	38542	WISTARIA CORAL	60211
WESTERN SUN	44812	WISTARIA PEARL	60212
WESTERN VALLEY	46871	WISTERIA	73031
WESTERPLATTE	10352	WITTENBERG	34963
WESTFJORD	66907	WITTSAND	59511
WESTFLOW	61462●	WITTSAND	59821
WESTGATE	22990	WLADYSLAW BRONIEWSKI	15301
WESTGATE	45390	WLADYSLAW JAGIELLO	14914
WESTIN	64350	WLADYSLAW JAGIELLO	15724
WESTIN	58370	WLADYSLAW LOKIETEK	15725
WESTRIDGE	41830	WLADYSLAW LOKIETEK	14915
WESTSTREAM	75940	WLADYSLAW ORKAN	14800
WESTWARD HO	20920	WLADYSLAW SIKORSKI	12688
WESTWARD VENTURE	08345	WLADYSLAWOWO	04343
WESTWIND	53382	WLADYSLAWOWO	04404
WESTWIND	90742	WLAYDYSLAW ORKAN	06090
WEYMOUTH	95010	WLOCZNIK	11790
WHEELSMAN	88860	WOENSDRECHT	47215
WHITE BEACH	37500	WOERMANN MERCUR	48730●
WHITE BEACH	44340	WOERMANN MERCUR	56090●
WHITE BILLOW	05461	WOERMANN MIRA	48731●
WHITE CASCADE	05462	WOERMANN MIRA	56091●
WHITE EXCELSIOR	71568	WOERMANN WADAI	56638/6
WHITE JASMIN	60032	WOLFE	08851
WHITE JASMIN	68362	WOLFEN	38732
WHITE JASMINE	71972	WOLFEN	44871
WHITE NILE	49350	WOLRAAD WOLTEMADE	22171
WHITE ROSE	24530	WOLWOL	51130
WHITE ROSE	31290	WOLWOL	51500
WHITE SHARK	24950	WONJIN	61059/10
WHITEHALL	75485	WONJIN	57619/11
WHITEHEAD	51340	WOOD STAR	57627●
WICHITA	92600	WOOD STAR	61047●
WICHITA	93610	WOOLLAHRA	45790
WICKLOW	72711	WOOSTER KING	61670
WID	01930	WORLD ACCLAIM	73189
WIDAR	73260	WORLD ACHILLES II	46116
WIDUKIND	75298	WORLD ADMIRAL	55461
WIDUKIND	88107	WORLD ADMIRAL	62782
WIELAND	73723	WORLD AEGEUS	46117
WIELDRECHT	47214	WORLD AGAMEMNON	46104
WIELICZKA	03236	WORLD AJAX	46103
WIELICZKA	03629	WORLD AMBASSADOR	55462
WIELUN	50470	WORLD AMBASSADOR	62783
WIEN	73024	WORLD AMITY	46954
WIGAN	60700	WORLD AMPHION	46113
WIGAN	69840	WORLD APOLLO	46101
WIHAR 1	81670	WORLD ARES	46102
WIKING	73901	WORLD ARETUS	46105
WILA	73652	WORLD ARGUS	46100
WILCON 1	50560	WORLD ASPIRATION	46955
WILCON II	91925	WORLD AZALEA	54031
WILCON III	81060	WORLD BERMUDA	54400
WILCON V	82332	WORLD BERMUDA	63080
WILDRAKE	17340	WORLD BRIDGESTONE	54216
WILHELM FLORIN	04230	WORLD BRIGADIER	54030
WILHELM PIECK	62683	WORLD CANADA	54384
WILHELM SCHULTE	60954	WORLD CANADA	63074
WILHELMINA V	88304	WORLD CANDOUR	61214
WILHELMSHAVEN	19210●	WORLD CHALLENGER	68130
WILKS	87291	WORLD CHALLENGER	71440
WILLEMSKERK	15832●	WORLD CHEER	46425
WILLEMSKERK	72183●	WORLD COMET	54032
WILLEMSKERK	83403●	WORLD CONCORD	53941
WILLI BREDEL	17981	WORLD CREATION	53942
WILLIAM	46094	WORLD CROWN	59942
WILLIAM	83264	WORLD CROWN	67932
WILLIAM DAMPIER	70462	WORLD DIPLOMAT	63363
WILLIAM FOSTER	03062	WORLD DISCOVERER	32850
WILLIAM FOSTER	03653	WORLD DUKE	54360
WILLIAM HOOPER	01055	WORLD DUKE	62970
WILLIAM R ADAMS	46820	WORLD DULCE	73335
WILLIAM R GRACE	70650	WORLD EXPLORER	32840●
WILLIAM SHAKESPEARE	59741	WORLD FINANCE	48990
WILLINE TARO	48980	WORLD FRATERNITY	46951
WILLINE TOKYO	47213●	WORLD GALA	64530
WILLINE TOYO	49181	WORLD GLEN	46426
WILLOWBANK	02880	WORLD HAPPINESS	68110
WILLY	16051	WORLD HARVEST	46956
WILLY	88113	WORLD LADY	62903
WILMINGTON	75810	WORLD LADY	68173
WILNORA	63402	WORLD MARINE	46106
WILTSHIRE	55340	WORLD MEDAL	77875
WILTSHIRE	57670	WORLD MITSUBISHI	54851
WIND EAGLE	64301	WORLD MITSUBISHI	56371
WIND ENTERPRISE	64302	WORLD NATURE	79132
WIND ESCORT	64303	WORLD NAUTILUS	79131
WINDFROST	81692	WORLD NAVIGATOR	54980
WINDFROST	87052	WORLD NAVIGATOR	55140
WINDRAIDER	47230	WORLD NEGOTIATOR	54981
WINDRAIDER	47510	WORLD NEGOTIATOR	55141
WINDRATI	36240	WORLD NEWS	54982
WINEDROP	54637	WORLD NEWS	55142
WINEDROP	55067	WORLD NOBILITY	54983
WINETA	59692	WORLD NOBILITY	55143
WINETA	81352	WORLD NOMAD	54984
WINNETOU	67111	WORLD NOMAD	55144

WORLD OAK	46957	YACU CASPI	34897
WORLD OCEANIC	06635	YACU RUNA	27401
WORLD PATHFINDER	63490	YACU TAITO	25871
WORLD PRIZE	46424	YACU WASI	81500
WORLD PROBITY	61215	YACU WAYO	14192
WORLD PROCESS	70169/1	YAEL	48671
WORLD PROGRESS	54500	YAEL	48811
WORLD PROTECTOR	70161	YAFFA	72353
WORLD RECOVERY	63440	YAFFA	77153
WORLD RENAISSANCE	23380	YAGOTIN	49101
WORLD RUBY	54652	YAGUAR	22160
WORLD RUBY	55073	YAGUARI	83240
WORLD SAGA	56354	YAKAN	88130
WORLD SAGA	68054	YAKHROMA	61840
WORLD SCHOLAR	63190	YAKOV BONDARENKO	48446
WORLD SCHOLAR	67560	YAKOV BONDARENKO	49486
WORLD SCORE	63191	YAKOV BONDARENKO	49756
WORLD SCORE	67561	YAKOV GAKKEL	39412
WORLD SHELTER	15430	YAKOV REZNICHENKO	50299
WORLD SOVEREIGN	54037	YAKOV SVERDLOV	28984
WORLD SPLENDOUR	63112	YAKUB KOLAS	50733
WORLD SUN	64319	YAKUTSKLES	06797/1
WORLD SYMPHONY	64295	YALTA	12295
WORLD TRUTH	63872	YAMAHIRO MARU	73369
WORLD TRUTH	67602	YAMAL	11452
WORLD VIGOUR	53943	YAMANAKA MARU	73187
WORLD WOOD	48960	YAMAOKI MARU	46235
WOTAN	45601	YAMASHIN MARU	08591
WOTAN	73911	YAMASHIN MARU	09731
WOTONI	58494	YAMATO MARU	95110
WOTONI	84914	YAMAUME No2	86160
WROZKA	73653	YAN CHENG	81647
WU CHANG	03173	YAN HU	57695
WU JIANG	60245	YAN SHAN	52830
WU SHENG HAI	46071	YAN SHAN	52940
WU TAI SHAN	03132	YANA	90190
WU TAI SHAN	03342	YANBU PRIDE	63860
WU XING	45030	YANBU PROGRESS	63862
WU YI SHAN	58612	YANG CHENG	05040
WU YI SHAN	81012	YANG CHUN	56310
WU YI SHAN	90512	YANG MING SHAN	84610
WU ZHI SHAN	79850	YANG MING SHAN	88320
WUMEN	06069/5	YANG QUAN	02572
WUPPERTAL	23580	YANG ZI JIANG 3	01204
WUPPERTAL	33203	YANG ZI JIANG 4	86114
WUXI	33660	YANG ZI JIANG 4	91714
WYSPIANSKI	06891	YANG ZONG HAI	61814
WYSZKOW	50462	YANGI-YUL	50779
WYUNA	20890	YANGLIN — 4-10-90	06034
		YANGTING	05375
X		YANIS LENTSMANIS	10729
		YANIS RAYNIS	10720
		YANKA KUPALA	50738
XANADU	20740	YANKEE CLIPPER	73950
XANTHENCE	86801	YANMEN	06069/7
XI FESTIVAL	48456	YANNIS	31230
XI FESTIVAL	49496	YANNIS	51091
XI FESTIVAL	49766	YANNIS	51481
XI QIAO SHAN	79830	YANNIS HALCOUSSIS	60132
XIAMEN	06069/6	YANTAR	12549
XIANG CHENG	47040	YANTARNIY BEREG	62691
XIANG JIANG	60484	YANTARNYY	07557
XIANG YANG	15216	YANTARNYY	45120
XIANG YANG HONG 9	04196	YANXILAS	69760
XIANG YIN	29950	YAOHUA	09480
XIAO SHI KOU	93315	YAQUI	46432
XIII CONGRESO	58194	YARA	14130
XIN AN	41328	YARACUY	13813
XIN AN JIANG	58592	YARGORA	89236
XIN AN JIANG	60472	YARONIMAS UBORYAVICHUS	12550
XIN HUA	18020	YAROSLAVL	12327
XIN LE	24542	YAROSLAVL	45220
XIN LE	31305	YARTSYEVO	89911
XINDU	46246	YARTSYEVO	90221
XINFENG	05832	YASENYEVO	49100
XINFENG	06126	YASHA GORDIYENKO	67028
XING CHENG	04910	YASHIMA MARU	08631
XING HAI	46517	YASHIMA MARU	09741
XING HU	32330	YASHMA	12551
XING HUA	29551	YASNOGORSK	89910
XING KONG	13550	YASNOGORSK	90220
XING MING	28250	YASNOYE	46620
XINGHANG	30420	YASTREBOVO	13764/1
XINGNING	10582	YAT LEE	24640
XINGNING	15352	YAT SHING	24641
XINYANG	14639/4	YDRA	49540
XIONG ER SHAN	64811	YE LAN	47415
XIONG YUE CHENG	05483	YE LAN	48225
XIUSHAN	10591	YEGORLIK	70783
XUAN CHENG	13392	YEH YUNG	05611
XUAN HUA	60244	YEKATERINA BELASHOVA	76591
XUAN HUA	30060	YEKATERINA BELASHOVA	79941
XUCHANG	31020	YELENE STASOVA	04038
XUE CHENG	00852	YELIZOVO	89512
XUE CHENG	41610	YELNYA	44623
XUE FENG SHAN	45031	YELNYA	70780
XV SYEZD PROFSOYUZOV	87811	YELSK	44620
XV SYEZD PROFSOYUZOV	23522	YEMELYAN PUGACHEV	80179/1
XVI SYEZD VLKSM	11784	YEMELYAN YAROSLAVSKIY	03801
XVII SYEZD VLKSM	79409	YEMELYAN YAROSLAVSKIY	04041
XVII SYEZD VLKSM	79420	YENAKIYEVO	78897
XVIII SYEZD VLKSM	79428	YENISEY	84351
XX ANIVERSARIO	11785	YENISEYSK	25565
XXIV SYEZD KPSS	16110	YENISEYSK	70032
XXV SYEZD KPSS	79413	YEOFIM KRIVOSEYEV	34876
XXV SYEZD KPSS	58516	YEREWA	18601
	71826	YEREWA	22540
		YERMAK	20870
Y		YEROFEY KHABAROV	22223
		YEROTSAKOS	53141
		YEROTSAKOS	66071
		YERUPAJA	57351
YAAN ANVELT	03797	YESILADA	19160
YAAN ANVELT	04037	YESSENTUKI	44624

Name	No.
YEVGENIY CHAPLANOV	06799/8
YEVGENIY LEBEDYEV	45292
YEVGENIY POLYAKOV	13766/1
YEVGENIY PREOBRAZENSKIY	24318
YEVGENIY PREOBRAZENSKIY	39458
YEVGENIY VUCHETICH	93385
YEVPATORIYE	12296
YEYSK	11834
YEYSKIY LIMAN	33620
YI CHI	28850
YI NING HAI	56691
YIANNIS	74600
YICHANG	03172
YICHUN	12721
YIDU	30421
YIMEN	06069/8
YIN CHUAN	05102
YIN HU	37640
YIN SHAN HAI	46722
YING GE HAI	49130
YING SHAN	13383
YMER	33001/1
YMIR	74015
YOKAMU	80701
YOKAMU	84481
YOKO MARU	54800
YOKO MARU	68030
YOKOHAMA MARU	95126
YONA B.	69310
YONAVA	13726
YONG CHENG	81380
YONG CHUN	12720
YONG DING	29552
YONG FENG HAI	57006
YONG JIANG	60486
YONG JIN	05730
YONG KANG	26060
YONG MING	28221
YONG MING	31922
YONG XING	60487
YONGCHANG	03174
YONGMEN	06069/9
YONGNING	10583
YONGNING	15353
YORKSHIRE	63993
YORKSHIRE	58343
YORKTOWN	58586
YOTEI MARU	19680
YOU YI	25830
YOUHAO	38840
YOUNG AMERICA	01493
YOUNG SHINKO	80707
YOUNG SPLENDOR	92222
YOUNG SPORTSMAN	51100
YPAPANTI	61062
YPAPANTI	66021
YPERMACHOS	63270
YU CAI	14191
YU CHENG	41611
YU CHUN	14540
YU HONG	30429
YU HU	58890
YU HUA	16150
YU JIANG	45941
YU KONG	60520
YU M SHOKALSKIY	23771
YU QING	15102
YU QUAN SHAN	00720
YU TSAO	64203
YU TSAO	68653
YU XIN	25650●
YU YING	15101
YUAN WANG 1	95025
YUAN WANG 2	95026
YUANJIANG	05318
YUBILEY OKTYABRYA	12551
YUCATAN VALLEY	63134●
YUE HOPE	62236●
YUE HOPE	71256●
YUE MAN	61056
YUE MAN	57615
YUE RIVER	61055
YUE RIVER	57614
YUE YANG	14639/5
YUG	23392
YUG	23867
YUGANSK	70784
YUGLA	36920
YUGLA	43820
YUHAI	26062
YUHENG 2	31760
YUHO MARU	59995
YUKHAN SMUUL	11908
YUKON	38422
YUKONG LEADER	60280
YUKONG LEADER	68420
YUKONG PIONEER	60281
YUKONG PIONEER	68421
YULIAN MARKHLEVSKIY	93734
YULIAN MARKHLEVSKIY	93824
YULIMISTE	11909
YULIN	06035
YULIUS FUCHIK	00240
YULIUS FUCHIK	14975
YULIYA ZHEMAYTE	10436
YULSAN POSEIDON	58184
YULYUS YANONIS	87003
YUM	20271
YUMA	67112
YUMEN	06065
YUN CHENG	47044
YUN HAI	57010
YUN LING	61212
YUNAM No 9	72063
YUNOST	12552
YUNYY LENINETS	01577
YUNYY PARTIZAN	67032
YUOZAS GARYALIS	12553
YUOZAS VAREYKIS	12554
YURBARKAS	13725
YURILSK	89500
YURIY GAGARIN	01578
YURIY KOSTIKOV	11636
YURIY KOTSYUBINSKY	79443
YURIY KRINOV	50769
YURIY LISYANSKIY	22238
YURIY MALAKHOV	11910
YURIY SAVINOV	54729
YURIY SAVINOV	55299
YURIY SMIRNOV	78062
YURMALA	13724
YURMALA	63640
YURYUZAN	89475
YUSHAN	10592
YUSHO	63610
YUSHO	67580
YUSUF ZIYA ONIS	33240
YUTA BONDAROVSKAYA	15539
YUTING	05376
YUTNIEKS	11911
YUWA MARU	61650
YUZBASI TOLUNAY	89520
YUZHNO-SAKHALINSK	93842
YUZHNO-SAKJALINSK	93752
YUZHNOMORSK	11912
YUZHNO-SAKHALINSK	86181
YUZHNYY KREST	12297
YVONNE C	51865
YVONNE C	64915
YZONA	26740

Z

Name	No.
ZABAT DOS	79880
ZABAT UNO	79881
ZABAYKALSK	24111
ZABAYKALYE	09211
ZABAYKALYE	12588
ZABAYKALYE	45128
ZACCAR	66622
ZACCAR	76242
ZACHARIAS Z	17880
ZADAR	10925
ZADONSK	78544
ZADORIE	17971
ZAGLEBIE DABROWSKIE	75730
ZAGLEBIE MIEDZIOWE	78549
ZAGLEBIE SIARKOWE	73553
ZAGORIANA	17957
ZAGORSKIY	17972
ZAHARI STOIANOV	47573
ZAHI	15452
ZAIN	94401
ZAIN AL-QAWS	07501
ZAISAN	34512
ZAK	26490
ZAKARPATYE	12587
ZAKARPATYE	78543
ZAKAVKAZYE	11323
ZAKHARIY PALIASHVILI	67658
ZAKHAROVO	17963
ZAKIR HUSSAIN	68091
ZALAU	48452
ZALAU	49492
ZALAU	49762
ZALESOVO	17955
ZAMA MARU	94537
ZAMBESI	71175
ZAMBEZE	01060
ZAMBOANGA	51034
ZAMZAM	22410
ZANET	14401
ZANGELAN	50787
ZANNIS MICHALOS	77887
ZANTE	65050
ZANTE	65302
ZAO MARU	94921
ZAPADNAYA DVINA	25566
ZAPOLYARNYY	09387
ZAPOLYARNYY	15493
ZAPOROZHYE	12589
ZAPOROZHYE	78542
ZARAYSK	12298
ZARECHENSK	78540
ZARKA	67493
ZARNITSA	11597
ZARNITSA	23391
ZARNITZA	17320
ZASLONOVO	17958
ZAVOLZHSK	12351
ZAVOLZHYE	11329
ZAVYETY ILYICHA	90728
ZAWRAT	68920
ZEEBRUGGE	01061
ZEEBRUGGE	72350
ZEEBRUGGE	77150
ZEELAND	16452
ZEENA	26811
ZEFIR	13729
ZEIDA	66930
ZEIDA	70980
ZELENETS	11635
ZELENOBORSK	09373
ZELENOGORSK	21600
ZELEZNOGORSK	11745
ZELEZNOGORSK	34635
ZEMLYA KOLSKAYA	93763
ZEMLYANSK	24316
ZEMLYANSK	39457
ZEMUN	21512
ZENA	27771
ZENIT	34710
ZENIT CLIPPER	92933
ZENIT EXPRESS	92934
ZENITH	87540
ZENO	46924
ZENTA OZOLA	10731
ZEPPACIFIC	51872
ZERALDA	32631
ZERHOUN	66931
ZERHOUN	70981
ZEROMSKI	24561
ZETA	04474
ZETA	10994
ZETA	34154
ZETAGAS	53108
ZEULENRODA	90604
ZEUNG SAN	72172
ZEUS	03102
ZEUS	16450
ZEUS	40130
ZEYA	02283
ZEYALES	11502
ZEYNEP K	46455
ZGORZELEC	50467
ZHALGIRIS	70785
ZHAN DOU 14	33700
ZHAN DOU 16	33690
ZHAN DOU 27	—
ZHAN DOU 28	—
ZHAN DOU 29	01030
ZHAN DOU 30	00460
ZHAN DOU 41	01031
ZHAN DOU 44	28065
ZHAN DOU 45	28066
ZHAN DOU 47	01040
ZHAN DOU 49	25540
ZHAN DOU 50	01032
ZHAN DOU 51	00960
ZHAN DOU 52	01033
ZHAN DOU 55	00700
ZHAN DOU 65	25541
ZHAN DOU 66	25542
ZHAN DOU 71	25040
ZHAN DOU 72	25050
ZHAN DOU 77	25520
ZHAN DOU 79	00963
ZHAN DOU 155	28067
ZHAN DOU 155	31831
ZHAN DOU 156	28068
ZHAN DOU 156	31832
ZHAO YANG HAI	46073
ZHDANOV	39961
ZHDANOVSKIY KOMSOMOLETS	01404
ZHDANOVSKIY KOMSOMOLETS	01664
ZHEMAYTIYA	11914
ZHEN RONG HAI	46340
ZHEN XING	10273
ZHEN XING	15183
ZHEN ZHU QUAN	01200
ZHENJIANG	35030
ZHI JIANG KOU	93313
ZHIGANSK	44126
ZHIGULEVSK	12353
ZHILUO LAN	14260●
ZHILUO LAN	39000●
ZHITOMIR	39989
ZHONG SHAN	69330
ZHUKOVSKIY	12372
ZIEMIA BIALOSTOCKA	79644
ZIEMIA BIALOSTOCKA	79644
ZIEMIA BYDGOSKA	74660
ZIEMIA BYDGOSKA	78140
ZIEMIA KIELECKA	73140
ZIEMIA KOSZALINSKA	73141
ZIEMIA KRAKOWSKA	78547
ZIEMIA LUBELSKA	78548
ZIEMIA MAZOWIECKA	74661
ZIEMIA MAZOWIECKA	76141
ZIEMIA OLSZTYNSKA	79645
ZIEMIA OLSZTYNSKA	79645
ZIEMIA OPOLSKI	79646
ZIGANA	64921
ZIGMAS ANGARETIS	12555
ZIKONIYA	11967
ZILLERTAL	74360
ZILLERTAL	76612
ZIM BARCELONA	08777
ZIM CALIFORNIA	08801
ZIM GENOVA	08802
ZIM HAIFA	08803
ZIM HONG KONG	74451
ZIM KAOHSIUNG	74437
ZIM KEELUNG	08775
ZIM MANILA	73887
ZIM MANILA II	73570
ZIM MONTREAL	74450
ZIM NAPOLI II	73571
ZIM NEW YORK	08804
ZIM SAVANNAH	08776
ZIM TOKYO	08805
ZINA	77931
ZINA	79251
ZINA PORTNOVA	15540
ZINC TRADER	05073
ZINI	71183
ZIWAY HAIQ	41621
ZIYA KALKAVAN II	26050
ZLATNI PIASATZI	76530
ZLARIN	01471
ZLATOUST	12352
ZLATOUST	78545
ZNA	02282
ZNAMYA KERCHIL	13728
ZNAMYA OKTYABRYA	78065
ZNAMYA I OBEDY	11746
ZNAMYA POBEDY	34636
ZODCHIY	11633
ZODIAC	23868
ZOE II	23900
ZOLOTITZA	11453
ZOLOTOY KOLOS	11915
ZOLOTOY ROG	36257
ZOLOTOY ROG	42807
ZOLOTOY ROG	76513
ZOR	67100
ZORA	77810
ZORINSK	78546
ZOYA KOSMODEMYANSKAYA	73290
ZOZARA	78531
ZSA ZSA	90530
ZSA ZSA	91070
ZUBAIDA	81990●
ZUBARYEVO	17973
ZUBOVO	17965
ZUGDIDI	70786
ZUHAL K	64920
ZUIDER SEA	29240
ZUIDERKRUIS	35240
ZUIHO MARU	68144
ZUIKO MARU	54035
ZUIYO MARU	76721
ZUIYO MARU No 2	94902
ZUIYO MARU No 2	95072
ZUNA	90531
ZUNA	91071
ZUND	11954
ZUNHUA	29550
ZUROW	50449
ZUROW	52010
ZUSSOW	50450
ZUSSOW	52011
ZVAYGZNE	87950
ZVENIGOROD	78541
ZVEZDA	13727
ZVEZDA	23390
ZVEZDA KRIMA	11955
ZVYAGIHO	17960
ZVYEROBOY	17950
ZVYERYEVO	17964
ZVYEZDA ASOVA	13766
ZVYEZDA SEVASTOPOLYA	13767/1
ZWICKAU	36300
ZWICKAU	36460
ZWICKAU	43110
ZYEMCHUSNYY	11937
ZYGMUNT AUGUST	14916
ZYGMUNT AUGUST	15726
ZYGMUNT III WAZA	14918
ZYGMUNT III WAZA	15728
ZYGMUNT STARY	14917
ZYGMUNT STARY	15727
ZYKOVO	17959
ZYRARDOW	07462
ZYRARDOW	10759

Numerical Section

Ship Classes and Types

16 BC 5 — 62210
22 TYPE — 58830
26 BC 5 — 46350
46351
46352
46353
46920
46921
46922
46923
36L — 53100
53101
53102
53103
53104
53105
53330
53331
53332
53333
53334
60480
60481
60482
60484
60485
60486
60487
60488
71840
71841
71842
71843
71844
71845
71846
71847
71848
71849
71851
71852
71853
71854
71855
71856
71856/1
71857
71858
71859
71980
71981
71990
71991
71994
71995
72000
72001
72002
72003
72004
72005
72110
72111
72114
72115
80850
80851
80890
80891
80892
82490
82491
613B — 91020
91021
ACSA 95 — 92782
92783
92784
92785
92786
92787
92788
92789
92789/1
AFRIKA — 34960
34961
34962
34963
ALGONQUIN II — 61770
61771
61772
61773
ALTAY — 70810
70811
AMUR — 50570
AS300 — 75580
75581
75582
75583
75584
ATLANTIK — 07470
07471
07472
07473
07474
07475
07476
07477
11800
11801
11802
11803
11804
11805

ATLANTIK (contd.) — 11806
11807
11808
11809
11810
11811
11812
11813
11814
11815
11816
11817
11818
11819
11820
11821
11822
11823
11824
11825
11826
11827
11828
11829
11830
11831
11832
11833
11834
11835
11836
11837
11838
11839
11840
11841
11842
11843
11844
11845
11846
11847
11848
11849
11850
11851
11852
11853
11854
11855
11856
11857
11858
11859
11860
11861
11862
11863
11864
11865
11866
11867
11868
11869
11870
11871
11872
11873
11874
11875
11876
11877
11878
11879
11880
11881
11882
11883
11884
11885
11886
11887
11888
11889
11890
11891
11892
11893
11895
11896
11897
11898
11899
11900
11901
11902
11903
11904
11905
11906
11907
11908
11909
11910
11911
11912
11914
11915
11916
11917
11918
11919
11920

ATLANTIK (contd.) — 11921
11922
11923
11924
11925
11926
11927
11928
11929
11930
11931
11932
11933
11934
11935
11936
11937
11938
11939
11940
11941
11942
11943
11944
11945
11946
11947
11948
11949
11950
11951
11952
11953
11954
11955
11957
11958
11959
11960
11961
11962
11963
11964
11965
11966
11967
11968
11969
11970
11971
11972
11973
11974
11975
11976
11977
11978
11979
11980
B15 — 11640
11644
11646
11649
11650
11652
11653
11654
11655
11656
11660
11661
11662
11663
11664
11665
12590
12591
12592
12593
12594
12595
12596
12597
12598
12599
12610
12611
12612
12614
12615
B18 — 10810
10811
10812
10813
10814
10815
10816
10817
10818
B22 — 10535
10536
11695
11700
11702
11703
11704
11706
11707
11708
11709
11710
11711
11713

B22 (contd.) — 11714
11716
B23 — 22330
22331
22332
22333
22334
22335
22336
22337
22338
22339
22340
B25 — 57350
57351
B26 — 11580
11581
11582
11583
11584
11585
11586
11587
11588
11589
11590
11591
11592
11593
11594
11595
11596
11597
11598
11599
11600
11601
11602
11603
11604
11605
11606
11607
11608
11610
11611
11612
11613
11614
11615
11616
11617
11618
11619
11620
11621
11622
11623
11624
11625
11626
11627
11628
11629
11630
11631
11632
11633
11634
11635
11636
45950
45951
47690
47691
47692
47693
56500
56501
56502
56503
56504
B29 — 18740
18741
18742
18743
18744
18745
18746
18747
18748
18749
18750
18751
18752
18753
18754
18755
18756
18757
B31 — 10430
10431
10432
10433
10434
10435
10436
10437
10438
10439
10441
10443
10444

B31 (contd.) — 10445
10449
10451
10452
10453
10454
10455
10457
10458
10459
10460
10461
10462
10463
10464
10465
17920
17921
17922
17923
17924
17925
17926
17927
17928
17929
17930
17931
17932
17933
17934
17935
17940
22720
22721
22722
22723
22830
22831
22832
22833
22834
22835
22836
22837
B32 — 10640
12140
12142
12143
12144
12145
12146
12147
12148
12149
12150
12151
12152
12153
12154
12155
12156
12157
12158
12159
12161
12162
12166
12167
B40/B401 KOMMUNIST — 05620
05621
05622
05623
05624
05625
05626
05627
05628
05629
05630
05631
05632
05633
05634
05635
05636
05637
05638
05639
05640
14450
14451
14452
14453
14454
14455
14456
14457
14458
14459
14460
14461
14462
14463
14464
14465
14466
14467
14468
14469
B41 — 10570
10571

B444 (contd.) — 15666, 15667

B445 — 14910, 14911, 14912, 14913, 14914, 14915, 14916, 14917, 14918, 14919, 14920, 14921, 14922, 14923, 14924, 14925, 14926, 14927, 15720, 15721, 15722, 15724, 15725, 15726, 15727, 15728, 15729, 15730, 15731, 15732, 15733, 15734, 15735, 15736, 15737

B446 — 81640, 81641, 81642, 81643, 81644, 81645, 81646, 81647

B447 — 59220, 59221, 59222, 59224, 59225, 59226, 59227, 59228, 60900, 60901, 70540, 70541, 70542, 70543, 70544, 70545, 74540, 74541, 74542, 74544, 74545, 74546, 74547, 74548, 78100, 78101, 78102, 78103, 79230, 79231, 79232, 79233, 79234

B450 — 16250, 16251, 16252, 16253, 16254, 16255, 16256

B454 — 10560

B455 — 15080, 15081, 15082, 15084, 15085, 15086, 15087, 15090, 15091, 15092, 15093

B457 — 67050, 75327, 75328

B458 — 73840, 87750, 87752, 87753

B459 — 59600, 59601, 59602, 59603, 59604, 71930, 71931, 71932, 71933, 71934, 76010

B463 — 73400, 73401, 73402, 73403, 73404, 73406, 73407, 73408, 73409, 82710, 82711, 82712, 82713, 82714, 82716, 82717, 82718, 82719

B463 (contd.) — 82720, 82721, 82722

B464 — 53370, 53371, 53372, 53374, 62760, 62761, 62762

B466 — 52920, 52921, 52922, 52923, 52924, 52925

B467 — 54970, 54971, 54972

B469 — 62764

B470 — 62460, 62461, 62462, 62463, 62464, 62465, 62466, 62467, 62468, 62469, 78540, 78541, 78542, 78543, 78544, 78546, 78547, 78548, 78549, 80130, 80131, 80132, 80133, 80134, 80135, 80136, 80137, 80138, 80139

B471 — 42070, 42071, 42072, 42073, 42074, 42075, 42076, 42077

B472 — 51260, 51261, 51262

B474 — 14928, 14929, 15738, 15739

B475 — 87070, 87071, 89560, 89561

B476 — 87770, 87771, 87772

B478 — 06142, 06143

B481 — 80260, 80261, 80262, 80263, 80264, 80265, 80266

B490 — 08170, 08171

B492 — 20354, 20355, 20356, 20357

B493 — 20353

B512 — 47600, 47601, 47602, 47610, 47612, 47613, 72170, 72171, 72172, 72173, 76630, 76631

B513 — 34370, 34371, 34372

B514 — 24030, 24031, 24032, 24033, 24034, 24035, 24036, 24037, 24038, 24039, 24041, 24042, 24043, 24044, 24045

B515 — 50020, 50021, 50022, 50023, 50024, 50025

B516 — 10280, 10281, 15190, 15191, 15192

B517 — 65850, 65851, 65852, 65853, 65854

B517 (contd.) — 65860, 65862, 65863, 65864, 65865, 67690, 67691, 67692, 67693, 67693, 67694

B520 — 75730, 75731, 75732, 75733, 75734, 75735, 88380, 88381, 88382, 88383, 88384, 88385

B521 — 73280, 77560, 77561, 77562, 77563, 77565, 77567, 77568, 77569, 77570, 77571, 77572, 77573, 77574, 77575, 77576, 77577, 77578, 77578/1, 77578/2, 77579, 77579/1, 77579/2, 77579/3, 77579/4, 77840, 77841, 77842, 77850, 80010

B522 — 75770, 75771, 75773

B523 — 50680, 50681, 50682, 50683, 50684, 50685, 50686, 50688, 50689, 50690, 50691, 50692, 50693

B524 — 68250, 68251, 68252, 68253, 68800, 68801, 68802, 68803

B526 — 77580, 77581

B550 — 55580, 55581, 55582, 56460, 56461, 56462

B551 — 56455, 56456

B670 — 45270, 45271, 45272, 45273, 45274, 45275

BALTIKA — 46090, 46091, 46092, 46093, 46094, 46095, 46900, 46901, 46902, 46903, 46904, 46904/1, 46905, 78730, 78731, 78732, 78733, 78740, 78741, 78742, 83260, 83261, 83262, 83263, 83264, 83265, 83266, 83267, 83340, 83341, 83342, 83343, 89980, 89981, 89982, 89983

BALTIYSKIY — 75350, 75351, 75352, 75353

BALTIYSKIY (contd.) — 75380, 75381, 75382, 75383, 75384, 75385, 75386, 75387, 75388, 75389, 75390, 79500, 90030

BATRAL — 84260, 84261, 84262, 84263, 84264

BEREZNIK — 07550, 07551, 07552, 07553, 07554, 07555, 07556, 07557, 07558, 07559, 07560, 07561, 07562, 07563, 07564, 07565, 07566, 07567, 07568, 07569, 07570, 07571, 07572, 07573, 07574, 07575, 07576, 07577, 07578, 07579, 07580, 07581, 07582, 07583, 07584, 07585, 07586, 07587, 07588, 07589, 07590, 07591, 07592, 07592, 07593, 07600

BOIZENBURG — 50440, 50441, 50442, 50443, 50444, 50445, 50446, 50447, 50448, 50449, 50450, 52000, 52001, 52002, 52003, 52004, 52006, 52007, 52008, 52009, 52010, 52011

BORO — 77120, 77121, 80030, 80031

BOXER — 95130, 95131, 95132

BREMEN PROGRESS — 48510, 48512, 48513

BREMEN PROGRESS B — 56130

C1 — 26140

C1 M AV3 — 92020, 92021

C3 — 07730

C4 — 43440, 92660

C5 S AXI — 39560

C6 — 11360, 11361, 11363

CAMIT — 60020, 60021, 60022, 72630, 72631, 72632, 72633, 72634, 72635, 72636, 77390, 77392, 77393, 77395, 77396, 77397, 77398

CARDIFF — 46430, 46431, 46432, 46433, 46434, 46435, 46436, 46437, 46438

CARDIFF (contd.) — 46443, 46446, 46448, 46449, 46450, 46451, 46452, 46453, 46454, 46455, 46460, 46461, 46462, 46463, 47870, 47871, 47872, 47873

CAROLINER — 48920, 56230

CARTAGO — 48210, 48211, 48212, 48213, 48214, 48215

CASPIAN-VOLGO-BALT — 50770, 50771, 50772, 50773, 50774, 50775, 50776, 50777, 50778, 50779, 50780, 50781, 50782, 50783, 50784, 50785, 50786, 50787, 50788

CIMARRON/T3 — 45040, 45041

CL10 — 45530, 45531, 45532, 45533, 53560, 53561, 59720, 59721

CLYDE — 51270, 51271, 51272, 51273, 52410, 52411, 52412

COLNE (Modified) — 88610, 88610/1, 88611, 88612, 88620, 88621, 88622, 90070, 90071, 90072

COLUMBUS 44 — 47220, 47221, 47222, 47223, 47224, 47225, 47226

COMMANDER — 51740, 51741, 51742, 51743, 51744

D9 — 08680, 08681, 08682, 08683, 08684, 08685, 08686, 08687, 08688, 08689, 08690

DECKSHIP — 92950, 92951, 92952, 92953, 92954, 92955, 92956, 92957, 95160, 95161, 95162, 95163, 95164, 95165, 95166, 95167

DNEPR — 48430, 48431, 48432, 48433, 48434, 48435, 48436, 48437, 48438, 48439, 48440, 48441, 48442, 48443, 48444, 48445, 48446, 48447, 48448, 48449, 48450

KALININGRAD ___ 01674
(contd.) 01675
01676
01677
01678
KATATRAN ___ 94250
KAZBEK ___ 38950
39960
39961
39970
39971
39972
39973
39975
39976
39977
39980
39981
39982
39983
39985
39986
39987
39988
39989
39990
39993
39994
39997
39998
39999
40000
40001
40002
40003
40006
40007
40008
40009
40010
40011
40013
40014
44890
KEY 12 ___ 46555
46556
57490
57491
57492
KEY 17 ___ 56545
56546
KEY 26 ___ 47900
47901
KEY 40 ___ 64640
KHASAN ___ 25550
25551
25552
25553
25554
25555
25556
25557
25558
25559
25560
25561
25562
25563
25564
25565
25566
25567
25568
25569
25570
25571
25572
KLASMA ___ 02110
02111
02280
02281
02282
02283
02284
02285
04210
35170
35171
35180
35181
35182
35190
KOLOMNA ___ 28060
28061
28062
28063
28064
28065
28066
28067
28068
28069
28070
KORSAKOV ___ 86070
86071
86072
86073
86074
86075
86076
86077
86078
86079
86081
86082
86083
86084
86085
86086
86087
86088
86089
86090
86091
86092
86093
86094
86095
86096
86097
86098
86170
86171

KORSAKOV (contd.) ___ 86172
86173
86174
86175
86176
86177
86178
86179
86180
86181
86182
86183
86184
86185
86186
86187
86188
86189
86200
86201
86202
86203
86204
86205
86206
86207
86208
86209
86210
86211
86212
87940
KUWAIT ___ 46770
46772
46773
46774
46775
46776
46777
46778
46779
46780
49380
49381
49383
49384
49385
49386
49387
49388
49389
49390
49391
49392
49393
49394
49395
49396
49397
49398
49399
49400
49401
49402
49403
49404
49405
49406
49407
49408
49409
49410
49411
49412
49413
49414
50940
50941
50943
50944
50945
50946
50947
50948
50949
50950
50951
50952
50953
50954
50955
50956
50957
50958
50959
50960
50961
50962
50963
50964
50965
50966
50967
50968
50969
50970
50971
50972
50973
50974
L19 ___ 94850
94851
LADOGA ___ 75360
75361
75362
75363
75364
75365
75366
75367
75368
75369
75400
75401
75402
75403
75404
75405
75406
75407
75408
75409
75410

LASH ___ 00010
00011
00012
00013
00015
00016
00017
00018
00019
01050
01051
01052
01053
01054
01055
01056
01057
02480
02481
02482
02483
02484
02485
02486
02487
02488
35100
35101
35102
35130
35131
35132
35133
35134
35135
35136
35137
35138
92810
92811
95150
95151
95152
LEVANT/KOVEL ___ 22790
22791
22792
22793
22840
22841
22842
22843
22844
22845
22846
22847
22848
22849
22850
22851
22852
22853
22855
22856
22857
22858
22859
22860
22861
22862
22863
22864
22865
22866
22867
22868
22869
22870
22871
22872
22873
22874
22875
22876
22877
22878
22879
22880
22881
22882
22883
22884
22885
34470
34471
34472
34473
34474
34475
34476
34477
34478
34479
34480
34481
34482
34483
34485
34486
34487
34488
34489
34490
34491
34492
34493
34494
34495
34496
34497
34498
34499
34500
34501
34501
34504
34505
34506
34507
34508
34509
34510
34511

LEVANT/KOVEL ___ 34512
(contd.) 34513
34514
34515
LUCHEGORSK ___ 23480
23481
23482
23483
23484
23485
23486
23487
23488
23489
23490
23491
23492
23493
23494
23495
23496
23497
23498
23499
23500
23501
23502
23503
23504
23505
23506
23507
23508
23509
23510
23511
23512
23513
23514
23515
23516
23517
23518
23519
23520
23522
23523
23524
23525
23526
23527
23528
23529
23530
23531
23532
23533
23534
23535
23536
23537
23538
23539
23540
23541
23542
23543
23544
23545
23546
23547
23548
23549
23550
23551
23552
23553
23554
23555
23556
23557
23558
23559
23560
23561
23562
23563
23564
23565
23566
23567
23568
23569
23571
23572
23573
MARINDUS ___ 48900
48901
48902
48903
48904
48905
48906
48907
48908
48909
48910
51070
51071
51072
51073
51074
51075
51076
MARINER ___ 07710
07850
07851
07852
07853
MAYAKOVSKIY ___ 12360
12361
12362
12363
12364
12365
12366
12367
12369
12370
12371
12372
12373
12570

MAYAKOVSKIY ___ 12571
(contd.) 12573
12573
12574
12575
12576
12577
12578
12579
12580
12587
12588
12589
23770
23771
MBC ___ 46212
46213
46214
46215
46216
46217
MERC MULTIFLEX ___ 94650
94651
94652
94653
94654
94655
94656
94657
94658
94660
94661
MERCATOR ___ 03690
03691
03692
03693
03694
03695
03696
03697
03698
03699
03700
03701
03702
03703
03704
03705
03706
03707
03708
03709
MERCUR ___ 77340
77341
77342
77343
77344
77345
77346
77347
77348
77349
MERIDIAN ___ 04910
04911
04912
04913
04914
04915
04916
04917
04918
04919
04920
04921
04922
04923
04924
04925
04926
04927
04928
04929
04930
04931
04932
04933
04934
04935
04936
04937
MITSUI CONCORD ___ 52840
52850
52851
53040
53041
62080
62081
62440
62441
71780
71781
79300
79301
79302
MITSUI-CONCORD 18 ___ 47040
47041
47042
47043
47044
47045
47046
47047
57440
57441
57442
57443
57444
57460
57461
57462
57463
MM14 ___ 51430
MODIFIED
MAYAKOVSKIY ___ 12380
12382
12383
12384
12385
12386
12387
12388
12389
12390

Printed in Great Britain by

Butler & Tanner Ltd, Frome and London